The Law of Companies

Third Edition

THOMAS B COURTNEY
BA, LLB, LLD, Solicitor
Partner, Arthur Cox

with contributions from

G BRIAN HUTCHINSON
BCL, LLM, DAL, BL
Senior Lecturer, School of Law
University College Dublin

and

DÁIBHÍ O'LEARY
B Comm (French), M Acc, Solicitor
Associate, Arthur Cox

Bloomsbury Professional

Published by
Bloomsbury Professional
Maxwelton House
41–43 Boltro Road
Haywards Heath
West Sussex
RH16 1BJ

Bloomsbury Professional
The Fitzwilliam Business Centre
26 Upper Pembroke Street
Dublin 2

ISBN: 978 184766 9513

Bloomsbury Professional, an imprint of Bloomsbury Publishing Plc

British Library Cataloguing-in-Publication Data
A catalogue record for this book is available from the British Library

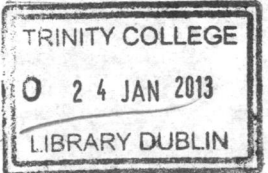

Typeset by Marlex Editorial Services Ltd, Dublin, Ireland
Printed and bound in Great Britain by
CPI Group (UK) Ltd, Croydon, CR0 4YY

Foreword to the First Edition

It has often been pointed out that our company law has its roots in mid-nineteenth century English legislation which is of limited relevance only to contemporary Ireland. In particular, the fact that the Victorian legislators had as their object the regulation of joint stock companies seeking funds from the public has resulted in a statutory framework which fails to reflect the reality of Irish commercial life, ie that the private company is the standard form of business organization.

Naturally, Irish textbooks, in common with their English counterparts, have sought to provide students and practitioners alike with a comprehensive guide to the complex structures of modern company law. Mr Courtney has, however, adopted a bold and imaginative new approach in confining his new study to the private company. The result is a valuable addition to the growing library of Irish commercial law.

Judges have frequently lamented the ever growing complexity of the regulatory structure they are called upon to interpret. There is a growing anxiety that legislation tends to provide elaborate machinery for the prevention of various evils, particularly the abuse of limited liability, without any accompanying effort by the executive to ensure that there are sufficient resources to ensure that breaches of the law are effectively policed.

Mr Courtney as the editor of the Commercial Law Practitioner is well aware of these problems and keeps a vigilant eye on the constant flow of judicial decisions and new laws and regulations, emerging from the courts, the Oireachtas, government departments and the Commission of the European Union. His book brings together all these divers elements as they effect the private company with great skill. His task is not made easier by the vast number of unreported judgments with which he has to cope, to say nothing of the avalanche of decisions from across the Irish sea which, while of persuasive authority only, must also form part of the Irish lawyer's armoury. Mr Courtney's remarkable industry will make the task of practitioners in particular much easier in ensuring that all relevant materials are before them as they come to advise their clients on the more abstruse aspects of law which affect private companies.

I have had experience of Mr Courtney's energy and learning for some time. He has told me of the considerable assistance he received from Mr Brian Hutchinson, of whose abilities I had also personal experience when he worked as a researcher in the Law Reform Commission. The result is this remarkable and encyclopaedic work on the law of Irish private companies which will prove of incalculable benefit to generations of practitioners and students – not the mention judges – to come.

Ronan Keane,
The High Court,
Four Courts,
Dublin 7.
23 November 1994.

Foreword to the First Edition

Preface

There have been many developments in company law since the second edition of this book was published in 2002. No less than six Companies Acts and in excess of 20 statutory instruments have been enacted and the courts have never been busier in handing down significant decisions on important aspects of company law.

Yet all of these developments will be put in the shadows by the proposed new Companies Bill which is scheduled to be initiated in the Houses of the Oireachtas in the coming months. Drafted on the basis of the recommendations of the Company Law Review Group, the Bill proposes to repeal all 16 Companies Acts and many statutory instruments as well as consolidating many common law and equitable company law rules. Estimated to be over 1,400 sections long, it will be the largest single piece of legislation in the history of the State. Unless all political parties agree to confine debate to its new and reforming provisions while expediting those provisions which effectively consolidate existing law, its passage is likely to be long and tortuous. It would be brave to suggest a date for when the new Companies Bill will be enacted and commenced, but it is hoped that the new edition of this book will serve practitioners and students in the intervening years.

There are a number of changes in the structure of this edition. In the first place, its name has been changed to reflect the fact that its scope extends to all companies and not just private companies. Private companies are, of course, its primary focus because they are still the most popular type of company formed and registered in Ireland. This edition loosely follows the structure of the new Companies Bill. Its first 28 chapters concern the private company limited by shares (as it is proposed will the first 16 Parts of the Companies Bill) before then considering the law applicable to every other type of company by reference to how it differs from that applicable to the private company limited by shares (as is proposed for the remaining Parts of the Companies Bill). In this way, it is hoped that this edition will go some way towards bridging the gap between the existing company law regime and the new regime proposed by the Companies Bill.

Once again, I have had invaluable assistance from my good friend Brian Hutchinson who has contributed six chapters to this edition. It is hard to believe that it is nearly 20 years since Brian first agreed to contribute to the first edition of the book. I am very much obliged to Brian for finding the time in his busy schedule to continue the journey we set out on together in 1993. I would also like to thank my friend and associate in Arthur Cox, Dáibhí O'Leary who has contributed chapter 17 on *Financial Statements, Audit and Annual Return* and the paragraphs dealing with financial statements in chapters 29 to 31 and 34. A chartered accountant who re-qualified as solicitor, Dáibhí has completely restructured this chapter to reflect the proposed structure of Part 6 of the new Companies Bill in its treatment of accounts, audit and annual returns.

There are a number of others whose help I want to acknowledge. My friend of many years' standing and now my partner in Arthur Cox, William Johnston, read and commented on the security and banking related chapters; I continue to appreciate his guidance and encouragement. Many of my other partners and associates in Arthur Cox also helped me in my understanding of company law, whether or not they realise it, through the breadth and depth of their knowledge of the subject which they demonstrate on a daily basis. I would especially like to thank my own practice group, Company Compliance & Governance, where my team, led by James Heary and Jacqui McGowan-Smyth, keep me constantly challenged!

Sandra Mulvey, Publishing Manager and Martin Casmir, Managing Director of Bloomsbury Professional have been very supportive of me in this edition and I am very grateful to them for their constant encouragement.

Last but not least, I would like to thank my wife Aileen for her love and support in life as well as in writing. My daughters, Ally and Sophie, not only encouraged but actively assisted me in this book by checking certain cross-referencing. I would also like to thank my mother Susan Courtney and my close friends, who know who they are, for their encouragement in this and other endeavours.

I have taken every care to state the law applicable as at 30 September 2012. No legal responsibility or liability is accepted, warranted or implied by the writers or publisher in respect of any errors, omissions or misstatements.

Dr Thomas B Courtney

Blackrock

Co Dublin

30 September 2012

Contents Overview

Chapter 1: The Private Company in Context 1
Chapter 2: Incorporation by Registration 71
Chapter 3: Constitutional Documentation 91
Chapter 4: Incorporation and its Consequences 157
Chapter 5: Disregarding Separate Legal Personality 211
Chapter 6: Corporate Civil Litigation 267
Chapter 7: Corporate Contracts, Capacity and Authority 335
Chapter 8: Shares and Membership 415
Chapter 9: Share Transfer 477
Chapter 10: The Maintenance of Capital 551
Chapter 11: Shareholders' Remedies 617
Chapter 12: Groups of Companies 697
Chapter 13: Corporate Governance: Management by the Directors 725
Chapter 14: Corporate Governance: Meetings 799
Chapter 15: Duties of Directors and Other Officers 865
Chapter 16: Statutory Regulation of Directors' Transactions 965
Chapter 17: Financial Statements, Audit and Annual Return 1029
Chapter 18: Corporate Borrowing: Debentures and Security 1165
Chapter 19: Corporate Borrowing: Registration of Charges 1233
Chapter 20: Corporate Borrowing: Receivers 1293
Chapter 21: Schemes of Arrangement and Reconstructions 1345
Chapter 22: Examinerships 1379
Chapter 23: Winding Up Companies 1461
Chapter 24: Liquidators 1539
Chapter 25: Realisation and Distribution of Assets in a Winding Up 1573
Chapter 26: Strike-Off and Restoration 1677
Chapter 27: Investigations and Inspectors 1709
Chapter 28: Compliance and Enforcement 1755
Chapter 29: Public Limited Companies and SEs 1875
Chapter 30: Guarantee Companies 1949
Chapter 31: Unlimited Companies 1979
Chapter 32: Prospectus, Market Abuse and Transparency Law 1995
Chapter 33: Conversion by Re-registration 2053
Chapter 34: External Companies and Branches 2063

Contents

Foreword to the First Edition v
Preface vii
Contents Overview ix
Contents xi
Table of Cases liii
Table of Legislation cxxxiii

Chapter 1 The Private Company in Context

(Thomas B Courtney)

Introduction 1
[A] Legal Forms of Business Organisation 2
Sole traders 2
(a) Restrictions on acting as a sole trader 3
(b) The Registration of Business Names Act 1963 3
(c) Advantages and disadvantages of being a sole trader 6
Partnerships 7
(a) Partnership defined and described 7
(b) Partners' dealings with outsiders and inter se 9
(c) Dissolution of partnerships 10
(d) Limited partnerships 10
(e) Advantages and disadvantages of partnerships 11
Industrial and provident societies 11
Building societies 13
(a) Formation 15
(b) Powers of building societies 16
(c) Membership 17
(d) Central Bank supervision 17
(e) Management, meetings and accounts 18
(f) Conversion of building societies to companies 18
(g) Amalgamations and transfer of engagements 19
Credit unions 19
Unincorporated associations 20
Friendly societies 21
Unregistered companies 22
[B] An Historical Outline of Registered Companies 22
Private companies, registered companies, and corporate status 22
The concession theory of corporations 24
(a) Corporations created by royal charter 26
(b) Corporations created by statute 27
(c) Corporations created by registration under the Companies Acts 28
Developments in the law of business corporations since the 1700s 29
(a) Joint stock companies 29
(b) The Bubble Act 1720 30

(c) Deed of settlement companies 32
(d) The repeal of the Bubble Act 32
(e) The Joint Stock Companies Act 1844 33
(f) The Limited Liability Act 1855 33
(g) The Joint Stock Companies Act 1856 34
(h) The Companies Act 1862 35
(i) The Companies Act 1907 35
(j) The Companies (Consolidation) Act 1908 35

[C] An Overview of Irish Company Law 36

Irish company law statutes from independence to 1963 36

The Companies Acts 37
(a) The Companies Act 1963 37
(b) The Companies (Amendment) Act 1977 37
(c) The Companies (Amendment) Act 1982 37
(d) The Companies (Amendment) Act 1983 38
(e) The Companies (Amendment) Act 1986 38
(f) The Companies (Amendment) Act 1990 38
(g) The Companies Act 1990 39
(h) The Companies (Amendment) Act 1999 40
(i) The Companies (Amendment) (No 2) Act 1999 40
(j) The Company Law Enforcement Act 2001 40
(k) The Companies (Auditing and Accounting) Act 2003 41
(l) The Investment Funds, Companies and Miscellaneous Provisions Act 2005 41
(m) The Investment Funds, Companies and Miscellaneous Provisions Act 2006 42
(n) The Companies (Amendment) Act 2009 42
(o) The Companies (Miscellaneous Provisions) Act 2009 42
(p) The Companies (Amendment) Act 2012 43

The European Community dimension to the development of Irish company law 43
(a) First Directive – disclosure, validity and nullity 43
(b) Second Directive – capital requirements of PLCs 44
(c) Third Directive – national mergers of PLCs 44
(d) Fourth Directive – annual corporate accounts 44
(e) Sixth Directive – division of PLCs 45
(f) Seventh Directive – corporate consolidated accounts 45
(g) Eighth Directive – corporate auditors 45
(h) Eleventh Directive – disclosure by branches 45
(i) Twelfth Directive – single member private companies 46
(j) Directive 2004/25/EC – takeover bids 46
(k) Directive 2005/56/EC – cross-border mergers 46
(l) Directive 2007/36/EC – shareholders' rights 46
(m) Council Regulation (EEC) 2137/85 – European economic interest groupings 47
(n) Council Regulation (EC) 2157/2001 – statute for a European company (SE) 47
(o) The EU Insolvency Regulations 47

[D] The Private Company ... 48
Private companies and public companies ... 48
Concessions to the private company ... 49
The private company defined ... 49
(a) The single-member private limited company ... 52
(b) Family owned private companies ... 56
(c) Closely-held private companies ... 57
(d) Quasi-partnership private companies ... 58
(e) Private companies with unconnected membership ... 60
[E] The Meaning of 'Company' and of the 'Companies Acts' ... 60
[F] Modern Company Law Reform ... 63
The Company Law Review Group ... 63
The CLRG's first report ... 64
Other reports ... 65
The draft Companies Bill ... 65
(a) Part 1 – preliminary and general ... 67
(b) Part 2 – incorporation and registration ... 67
(c) Part 3 – share capital, shares and certain other instruments ... 67
(d) Part 4 – corporate governance ... 67
(e) Part 5 – duties of directors and other officers ... 67
(f) Part 6 – financial statements, annual return and audit ... 68
(g) Part 7 – charges and debentures ... 68
(h) Part 8 – receivers ... 68
(i) Part 9 – reorganisations, acquisitions, mergers and divisions ... 68
(j) Part 10 – examinerships ... 69
(k) Part 11 – winding up ... 69
(l) Part 12 – strike off and restoration ... 69
(m) Part 13 – investigations ... 69
(n) Part 14 – compliance and enforcement ... 69
(o) Part 15 – functions of registrar and of regulatory and advisory bodies ... 70

Chapter 2 Incorporation by Registration

(Thomas B Courtney)

Why incorporate? ... 71
Incorporating an existing business ... 72
Incorporation of private companies ... 75
(a) Private companies limited by shares ... 75
(b) Private companies limited by guarantee ... 76
(c) Private unlimited companies with a share capital ... 76
(d) Single-member private limited companies ... 77
Methods of incorporation ... 78
(a) The ordinary list ... 78
(b) The Company Incorporation Scheme ... 78
(c) The CRODisk Scheme ... 80
(d) Shelf companies ... 80
The steps in forming a private company ... 80

The requirement that a company carries on an 'activity' in the State 82
Registration by the registrar of companies 83
Delivery of particulars to the Revenue Commissioners 84
Statutory obligations incidental to registration 85
(a) Registered office 85
(b) Directors and secretary 86
(c) Display of certain information 87
(d) Publication of notices 88
(e) Use of a business name 89
Irish registered non-resident companies 89

Chapter 3 Constitutional Documentation

(Thomas B Courtney)

Introduction 91
[A] The Memorandum of Association 92
The memorandum of association 92
(a) The name clause 93
(b) The objects clause 95
(c) The liability clause 96
(d) The capital clause 96
(e) The association or subscription clause 98
Non-compulsory clauses 98
Alteration of the memorandum of association 99
(a) Alteration of the name clause 99
(b) Alteration of the objects clause 100
(c) Alteration of the liability clause 102
(d) Alteration of the capital clause 102
Alteration of the non-compulsory clauses 106
[B] The Articles of Association 107
The nature of the articles 107
The model articles of private companies 108
Usual amendments to the model articles 109
(a) Shares 110
(b) Members' meetings 111
(c) Directors 111
(d) Voting rights 112
Alteration of the articles 114
(a) Where contrary to law 115
(b) Where an additional liability is imposed on members 115
(c) Where class rights are altered 118
(d) Alterations not bona fide and in the interests of the company as a whole 120
Informal alteration of the articles of association by shareholders' agreement 131
The relationship between the memorandum and the articles 133
The construction of the memorandum and articles of association 133

[C] The Statutory Contract in s 25 of the CA 1963 ... 135
Section 25 creates a 'statutory contract' ... 135
The distinctive features of the s 25 contract ... 137
(a) Section 25 binds the members and the company ... 137
(b) Section 25 binds members to members ... 138
(c) Only rights and obligations qua member ... 140
The 'statutory contract' distinguished from 'special contracts' ... 142
[D] Shareholders' Agreements ... 144
The articles of association contrasted ... 145
The circumstances in which shareholders' agreements must be filed in the CRO ... 146
The uses of shareholders' agreements ... 147
Types of shareholders' agreements ... 149
The enforcement of shareholders' agreements ... 150
(a) Injunctions to enforce shareholders' agreements ... 151
(b) Directors fettering their fiduciary powers ... 152
(c) Binding companies through shareholders' agreements ... 153

Chapter 4 Incorporation and its Consequences

(G Brian Hutchinson)

[A] The Acquisition of Corporate Status ... 157
Registration, and issue of the certificate of incorporation ... 157
Failure or refusal by the registrar of companies ... 158
Effect of the certificate of incorporation ... 158
Rationale for the conclusive effect of the certificate of incorporation ... 159
The First EU Companies Directive's nullity provisions ... 160
Effect of the First EU Companies Directive's nullity provisions in Ireland ... 161
Impeachment of incorporation ... 162
(a) Trade unions registered as companies ... 162
(b) Judicial review of the registrar's decision to issue a certificate of incorporation ... 163
(c) Constitutionality of the conclusive effect of the certificate of incorporation ... 165
Cesser of corporate status ... 166
[B] The Consequences of Incorporation ... 167
Separate legal personality ... 167
(a) Artificial or fictional personality ... 168
(b) *Salomon's* case ... 168
(c) Corporate property ... 171
(d) Suing and being sued ... 176
(e) Privileges and obligations ... 202
Limited liability ... 204
Transferability of interests ... 206
Perpetual succession ... 207
Common seal ... 207
Floating charges ... 207
Formation of large associations ... 209

Taxation 209
Other consequences of incorporation 209

Chapter 5 Disregarding Separate Legal Personality

(G Brian Hutchinson)

Introduction 211
The manner in which separate legal personality may be disregarded 215
With whom will the company be identified? 216
The circumstances in which separate legal personality may be disregarded 217
[A] Contract, Tort, Agency and Trusts 217
Contracts 218
(a) Personal guarantees 219
(b) Indemnities 221
(c) Comfort letters 221
Torts 222
Agency 224
(a) Implied agency 225
(b) Undisclosed agency 228
Trusts 228
[B] Misuse of the Corporate Form...229
Concealment of impropriety 229
Mismanagement 231
Evasion of existing legal obligations 232
Avoidance of future legal obligations 237
[C] The Single Economic Entity...238
[D] Injunctions and Orders..248
[E] Characterisation 251
Residence 251
Culpability and *mens rea* *254*
Character for licensing purposes 254
[F] Statute...255
The Companies Acts 255
(a) Reduction of number of members below the legal minimum 256
(b) Failure to state correctly the company's name 257
(c) Breach of restriction or disqualification order 259
(d) Failure to meet capital requirements 260
(e) Failure to keep proper records 261
(f) Unreasonably inaccurate declaration of solvency 261
(g) Liquidation of related companies 262
(h) Fraudulent or reckless trading 262
Other legislation 262

Chapter 6 Corporate Civil Litigation

(Thomas B Courtney)

[A] The Proper Plaintiff where a Company is Wronged ... 267
[B] Authority to Institute Proceedings by a Company ... 270
[C] Service of Proceedings ... 272
[D] Security for Costs ... 274
The jurisdiction to order security for costs against non-residents ... 275
The justification for treating limited companies differently to individuals ... 276
Constitutionality and human rights ... 277
The test for an order for security for costs under s 390 of the CA 1963 ... 278
(a) Section 390 may be invoked in any 'action or other legal proceedings' ... 280
(b) The plaintiff company must have limited liability ... 281
(c) The plaintiff company can be a 'plaintiff', an 'appellant' or a 'counter-claiming defendant' ... 284
(d) The defendant includes a notice party ... 285
(e) The defendant's onus to adduce credible testimony of the plaintiff's inability to pay costs ... 286
(f) The defendant's onus to establish a prima facie defence ... 289
(g) Judicial discretion and 'special circumstances' ... 292
(h) The amount required as security ... 304
[E] Discovery and Interrogatories against Companies ... 307
[F] Appearance in Court ... 311
[G] Enforcing Judgments and Orders Against a Company. ... 314
(a) Enforcing money judgments against companies ... 314
(b) Enforcing court orders and judgments ... 317

Chapter 7 Corporate Contracts, Capacity and Authority

(Thomas B Courtney)

[A] Corporate Contracts: Form and Formalities ... 335
Oral contracts ... 336
Written contracts ... 337
Deeds and contracts required to be under seal ... 341
The requirement to have a seal ... 344
Attestation of the common seal ... 346
(a) Regulation 115 of Table A of the First Schedule to the CA 1963 ... 346
(b) Regulation 76 of Table A of the First Schedule to the Companies (Consolidation) Act 1908 ... 348
Delivery of deed by a company ... 350
Execution by power of attorney ... 350
[B] Pre-Incorporation Contracts ... 353
The old quagmire ... 353
Section 37 of the CA 1963 ... 354
Liability of corporate agents ... 356
Limitations on the application of s 37 of the CA 1963 ... 357

[C] Contractual Capacity and *Ultra Vires* 358
The objects clause and *ultra vires* 358
Restraining *ultra vires* activities 359
Contractual capacity 360
(a) Judicial construction of the objects clause 360
(b) Classifying corporate capacity 363
(c) The significance of conditions on the exercise of powers 366
(f) Implied ancillary powers 373
(g) Gratuitous dispositions of company property 374
(h) Section 8 of the CA 1963 381
(i) Regulation 6 of the EC(C)R 1973 385
(j) Corporate enforcement of *ultra vires* contracts 386
(k) Recovery of money given by a company *ultra vires* 386
(l) Reform of the doctrine of *ultra vires* 390
[D] The Authority of Corporate Agents 391
Actual and implied authority of corporate agents 392
Ostensible authority of corporate agents 393
(a) Corporate representations 395
(b) The actual authority of the representor 398
(c) Relying on the representation 398
(d) The contract was within the permitted capacity and authority of the company 398
The usual and ostensible authority of particular corporate organs 399
(a) The board of directors 399
(b) The managing director 400
(c) The chairman of the board 401
(d) Directors 402
(e) The company secretary 402
(f) The sole member of a single-member private company 402
Constructive notice of public documents 402
The indoor management rule 404
The scope of the rule in *Turquand's* case 407
(a) Where the irregularity is of public record 409
(b) The outsider must act in good faith 409
European intervention: the EC(C)R 1973 410
(a) Regulation 10 of the EC(C)R 1973 410
(b) Regulation 6 of the EC(C)R 1973 411

Chapter 8 Shares and Membership

(G Brian Hutchinson)

Introduction 415
[A] Membership 416
What constitutes membership? 416
(a) Definition of member 416
(b) Membership agreements 417
(c) Estoppel 417

Persons who may become members 418
(a) Natural members 418
(b) Corporate members 419
The register of members 422
(a) Form and location of the register 422
(b) Inspection of the register 423
(c) Particulars to be registered 424
(d) Legal significance of the particulars registered 425
(e) Registration of changes in particulars 425
(f) Rectification of the register 425
(g) Beneficial interests 427
(h) Cesser of membership 431
[B] Shares 432
The legal nature of shares 432
(a) A share confers no interest in the company's assets 433
(b) A share is an interest in the nature of personalty 433
(c) A share is a chose in action 434
(d) A share confers contractual rights and obligations 434
(e) A share confers an interest in the company itself 435
(f) A share confers statutory rights and obligations 436
(g) A share confers interests and rights protected by the Constitution 436
Formal requirements relating to shares 437
(a) Nominal value of shares 437
(b) Numbering of shares 438
(c) Share certificates 438
Allotment of shares 440
(a) Directors' authority to allot shares 440
(b) The mechanics of allotment 442
(c) Statutory pre-emption rights on the allotment of shares 442
(d) Consideration for shares on allotment 444
(d) The court's power to rectify a defective allotment 447
Shareholders' rights and duties 449
(a) Dividend 450
(b) Attendance and voting at meetings 454
(c) Participation in a winding up 456
(d) Shareholders' statutory rights 456
(e) Shareholders' 'personal' rights 457
(f) Shareholders' duties 459
Classes of shares 461
(a) Preliminary presumptions 461
(b) Power to create different classes of shares 462
(c) Particular categories of shares 463
Conversion of shares 469
(a) Consolidation 470
(b) Conversion of shares into stock, and vice versa 470
(c) Subdivision 470
Conversion into redeemable shares 470

Liens on shares 471
Forfeiture and surrender of shares 471
(a) Forfeiture 471
(b) Surrender 472
Disclosure of interests in shares 472
(a) Scope of disclosure order 473
(b) Powers of the court in relation to disclosure orders 474
(c) Consequences of contravention of a disclosure order 475

Chapter 9 Share Transfer

(Thomas B Courtney)

Introduction 477
[A] The Mechanics of Share Transfer....................478
The requirement for a 'proper instrument of transfer' 478
Execution of the instrument of transfer 481
The transferee's obligations on transfer 481
[B] Transferability and Restrictions....................482
Shares are transferable but subject to restrictions 482
The rationale for restrictions in private companies 484
Registration by the directors 485
Transferees' position pending registration 485
[C] Transmission of Shares by Operation of Law 487
The transmission of shares on death 487
Transmission of shares on bankruptcy 490
Transmission on a merger 490
[D] Security Over Shares....................492
Legal mortgage of shares 492
Equitable mortgage of shares 493
Protection for mortgagees – stop notices 494
[E] Directors' Powers to Refuse Registration....................497
The model reg 3 restriction 497
The transferee's status 500
The transferee's qualities 501
The bona fides of the directors 502
The lapsing of the directors' powers 507
Relief under s 205 of the CA 1963 509
The consequences of declining registration 510
The procedure for challenging a refusal to register 511
[F] Pre-Emption Rights on Share Transfer....................513
The need for pre-emption rights in private companies....................516
The judicial construction of pre-emption clauses 519
Application to beneficial interests in shares 520
The enforceability of pre-emption rights 523
[G] Compulsory Transfers of Shares....................525
Compulsory transfer under the articles 525
Compulsory transfer under s 204 of the CA 1963 526
(a) The mandatory statutory requirements 527
(b) The court's discretion 529

[H] Share Purchase Agreements 538
The relative merits of the share purchase versus the asset purchase 539
The nature of a share purchase agreement 539
(a) Disclosure letters 539
(b) Warranties on share sales 540
(c) Indemnities on share sales 541
[I] The Valuation of Shares in Private Companies 541
The principles of share valuation 541
(a) Determination of a company's total worth 542
(b) The assessment of the value of the shareholding 543
(c) Discounting share value for a minority holding 544
Establishing fair value 546
The appropriate valuation date 547

Chapter 10 The Maintenance of Capital

(Thomas B Courtney)

Introduction 551
The rationale behind share capital maintenance rules 551
Private companies and capital maintenance rules 552
Overview of capital maintenance rules 555
[A] Acquisition by a Company of its Own Shares 555
The common law prohibition on the purchase of own shares 555
The statutory prohibition on acquiring own shares 556
Exceptions to prohibition on acquiring own shares 558
(a) The acquisition of fully paid shares for no consideration 559
(b) The redemption of shares pursuant to s 65 of the CA 1963 559
(c) Acquisition pursuant to a s 72 of the CA 1963 reduction of capital 559
(d) Purchase of shares on foot of remedial court orders 559
(e) Forfeiture of shares 560
Acquisition of own shares pursuant to Part XI of the CA 1990 560
(a) Own-share purchase under s 211 of the CA 1990 560
(b) Funding can only come from distributable profits 562
(c) Authorised by articles of association 562
(d) The requirement for a special resolution 562
(e) Contingent purchase contracts 565
(f) Statutory safeguards 565
(g) Repudiation by company and the effect of winding up 565
(h) Ministerial regulations 566
[B] Acquisition of Shares in Holding Company 566
[C] Redemption of Shares 570
[D] Assisting the Purchase of Own Shares 573
Section 60 of the CA 1963 and private companies 573
The consequences of contravening s 60(1) of the CA 1963 574
(a) Criminal consequences 574
(b) Civil consequences – voidability 574

(c) The meaning of 'any transaction' 575
(d) The meaning of 'notice' 577
The meaning of 'financial assistance' 581
(a) The express forms of 'financial assistance' 582
(b) The breadth of the prohibition: 'otherwise' and 'in connection with' 583
(c) Warranties and covenants that constitute financial assistance 584
(d) Actual versus potential financial assistance 586
The validation procedure: resolution and declaration 587
(a) The validation procedure in practice 587
(b) Not all companies can utilise the validation procedure 591
(c) The directors' statutory declaration 591
(d) The shareholders' special resolution 593
(e) The importance of strict compliance in Ireland 593
(f) The validation procedure cannot be utilised retrospectively 594
(g) Shareholder protection 595
Dividends and lawful liabilities: s 60(12) of the CA 1963 596
Miscellaneous exceptions: s 60(13) of the CA 1963 599
[E] Court Ordered Capital Reduction 599
Section 10(6A) of the CA 1963 600
Section 205(3) of the CA 1963 600
Section 15 of the C(A)A 1983 600
[F] Distributions and the Payment of Dividends 601
(a) The meaning of distribution 601
(b) The meaning of 'profits available for distribution' 602
(c) Determining whether profits are available for distribution 606
(d) To be a distribution, it must be made to a 'member', qua member 608
(e) Disguised distributions 608
(f) Liability of directors for unlawful distributions 612
(g) Liability of members for unlawful distributions 612
[G] Miscellaneous Capital Maintenance Rules 613
Forfeiture of unpaid or partly paid shares 613
Issuing shares at a discount 614
Liens on shares 614
Shares issued at a premium 614

Chapter 11 Shareholders' Remedies

(Thomas B Courtney)

Introduction to shareholders' remedies 617
(a) Petitioning to wind up on just and equitable grounds 617
(b) Miscellaneous statutory remedies in particular situations 617
(c) Shareholders' personal rights 618
[A] Oppression and Disregard of Interests 618
The nature of the remedy 619
Oppression 620
(a) The test for oppression 620
(b) Oppression need not be qua member 623

(c) Isolated acts of oppression 624
(d) Fraudulent and unlawful transactions 625
(e) Oppressive management 626
(f) Exclusion from management 629
(g) Non-consultation with shareholders 630
(h) Technical oppression 631
Disregarding members' interests 632
'Affairs of the company' and 'powers of directors' 633
Quasi-partnership companies and 'legitimate expectations' 634
The *locus standi* to petition 638
(a) Members of the company 639
(b) Personal representatives of deceased members 642
Abuse of process and inordinate delay in prosecuting petitions 643
The position of the company 646
In camera applications 647
Remedies: restraining the removal of a shareholding director 650
Remedies: ending the matters complained of 653
(a) Section 205(3) of CA 1963 does not permit a general award of compensatory damages 654
(b) Section 205(3) does not justify orders to desist from litigation 656
(c) Futile orders will not be made 657
(d) Permissible orders under s 205(3)'to end the matters complained of' 657
Costs of the petition 660
The unfairly prejudicial remedy contrasted 662
Contracting out of s 205 663
[B] The Rule in *Foss v Harbottle* 663
The principles behind the rule 664
The rule in *Foss v Harbottle* 664
The rule summarised 666
Corporate rights distinguished from members' personal rights 667
Personal rights and personal actions for reflective loss distinguished 669
[C] Derivative Actions and Exceptions to *Foss v Harbottle* 673
Preliminary considerations 673
The derivative action 673
(a) The nature of a derivative action 674
(b) The twin test to bring a derivative action 675
(d) The indemnity for costs 680
The exceptions to the rule in *Foss v Harbottle* 683
(a) *Ultra vires* and illegal acts 683
(b) Transactions unratifiable by a bare majority 686
(c) Actions for infringement of personal rights 686
(d) Fraud on a minority by those in control 686
(e) Where justice requires a derivative action to be brought 694

Chapter 12 Groups of Companies

(Thomas B Courtney)

Significance of the holding–subsidiary relationship in company law 697
The definition of holding company in company law 699
The definition of subsidiary in company law 699
(a) The 'golden share': a member controlling the composition of the board of directors 700
(b) Holding more than half in nominal value of the equity share capital or of the shares carrying voting rights 703
(c) Shares held and powers exercisable in a fiduciary capacity, as nominee or pursuant to a debenture or trust 704
(d) A subsidiary of a subsidiary 708
(e) Wholly-owned subsidiaries 709
Definitions of undertakings, parent undertakings and subsidiary undertakings for group accounting purposes 709
(a) Controlling the composition of the board of directors 710
(b) Shares held/powers exercisable by 'nominees' 711
(c) Circumstances in which voting rights shall be discounted 711
(d) The meaning of 'dominant influence' 712
(e) The meaning of 'participating influence' 713
(f) The meaning of 'associated undertaking' 714
Capital maintenance definitions of parent public company and public company subsidiary 714
Taxation definitions of holding and subsidiary companies 715
(a) Corporation tax 715
(b) Stamp duty 717
Select issues in the holding-subsidiary relationship 718
(a) The sanctity of the separate legal personality of group companies 718
(b) Holding company's liability for subsidiary's negligence 721
(c) Group companies' directors' and holding companies' duties 722

Chapter 13 Corporate Governance: Management by the Directors

(Thomas B Courtney)

Introduction 725
[A] Officers 726
Who are officers? 726
The consequences of being an officer 727
[B] The Directors 729
Two directors, one EEA-resident, and all natural persons 730
(a) Two directors 730
(b) At least one EEA-resident director 730
(c) Only natural persons can become directors 733
Persons disqualified from and restricted in becoming directors 734
(a) Persons debarred from being directors 734
(b) Qualification shares 734

(c) Persons restricted in their directorships ... 734
(d) Disqualification of directors and others ... 735
The number of directorships that can be held by one person ... 735
The formal appointment of directors ... 737
(a) Consent to act as a director ... 738
(b) Appointment as a first director ... 739
(c) Appointments to an existing company ... 739
Types of formally appointed directors ... 741
(a) Managing directors ... 741
(b) Chairmen ... 742
(c) Executive directors ... 743
(d) Non-executive directors ... 743
(e) Nominee directors ... 744
(f) Caretaker directors ... 744
(g) Alternate directors ... 745
(h) Assignee directors ... 745
(i) Associate directors ... 745
De facto directors ... 746
(a) The English authorities on the test for *de facto* directorship ... 748
(b) The Irish authorities on the test for *de facto* directorship ... 749
Shadow directors ... 754
(a) The professional advice exception ... 755
(b) The proofs required to establish a person is a shadow director ... 755
(c) 'Directed or instructed' ... 758
(d) 'Acted in accordance with such directions or instructions' ... 761
(e) 'Were accustomed so to act' ... 761
(f) Can bodies corporate be shadow directors? ... 762
The remuneration of directors ... 765
Ceasing to be a director ... 766
(a) Resignation ... 766
(b) Retirement by rotation ... 767
(c) The removal of directors ... 767
(d) Notification to CRO of cessation of a directorship ... 771
(e) Compensation on loss of office ... 772
Disclosures concerning directors and secretaries ... 775
(a) Register of directors and secretary ... 776
(b) Disclosure and registration of directors' and secretaries' interests in shares and debentures ... 777
[C] The Secretary ... 785
The requirement to have a secretary ... 785
Appointment and cessation ... 785
Status and remuneration ... 786
Functions and duties ... 786
Disclosure requirements for secretaries ... 787
[D] Delegating Managerial Power to the Directors ... 788
Root authority begins with the members ... 788
Delegation of powers of management to the directors ... 788

The express reservations of power to members in reg 80 of Table A 790
(a) Subject to the Companies Acts 790
(b) Subject to other regulations in the articles of association 791
(c) Subject to directions given by the members 791
The resurgence of members' powers 795
(a) Where there are no directors capable of acting 795
(b) Where the directors exceed their delegated authority 796
(c) Where directors act in breach of their duties 797

Chapter 14 Corporate Governance: Meetings

(Thomas B Courtney)

[A] Members' Meetings 800
The annual general meeting 801
(a) The purpose of the AGM 801
(b) AGMs must generally be held within the State 802
(c) Ministerial direction to call an AGM 802
(d) Possible consequences where AGM not held 803
(e) AGMs in single-member private limited companies 805
Extraordinary general meetings 806
(a) EGMs convened by the directors 806
(b) EGMs convened on the requisition of qualified members 807
(c) EGMs convened by order of the court 810
(d) EGMs convened on the requisition of retiring auditor 815
Notice of members' meetings 816
(a) The requirements of a notice 817
(b) Those who should receive notice 817
(b) Notice periods for AGMs and EGMs 819
(c) Extended notice 822
(d) Accidental omission to give notice 823
(e) Summary of notice provisions 824
Notice of business to be conducted at a meeting 825
(a) Notice of special business 825
(b) Notice of special resolutions 825
(c) Other matters 826
The quorum 827
Postponing and adjourning meetings 828
Voting at members' meetings 830
(a) 'One member one vote' or one vote per share 830
(b) Voting on a poll 832
(c) Voting by representatives 835
(d) Voting by proxy 837
Minutes of members' meetings 838
Resolutions 839
(a) Ordinary resolutions 840
(b) Special resolutions 840
(c) Decisions by sole members of single-member private companies 843
(d) The written resolution procedure 844

(e) The 'Buchanan principle': unanimous consent of members to a course of action ... 845
(f) Filing of resolutions ... 850
[B] Directors' Meetings ... 851
Regulation of directors' meetings ... 851
Convening and notice of a directors' meeting ... 852
Holding directors' meetings ... 853
The business transacted ... 856
The quorum ... 856
The chairman ... 857
Adjourned meetings ... 857
Minutes of directors' meetings ... 857
Committees ... 859
Resolutions and voting ... 860
(a) Formal resolutions at board meetings ... 860
(b) Written resolutions without a board meeting ... 861
(c) Unanimous acts of the directors ... 863

Chapter 15 Duties of Directors and Other Officers

(Thomas B Courtney)

Introduction ... 865
[A] The Subject of Directors' and Other Officers' Duties ... 866
The general rule: duties are owed to the company ... 866
The expansion of directors' duties ... 868
(a) Duties to creditors ... 868
(b) Duties to employees and members ... 874
(c) Duties to shareholders ... 874
[B] Duties of Directors at Common Law ... 879
The nature and source of directors' common law duties ... 879
The exercise of directors' powers ... 880
(a) Acting in the interests of the company as a whole ... 880
(b) Good faith ... 881
(c) The exercise of independent discretion and fettering discretion ... 884
(d) The duties of executive and non-executive directors ... 889
(e) The duties of nominee directors ... 892
(f) 'Token directors' in family companies and 'sexually transmitted debt' ... 895
(g) The delegation of directors' powers ... 898
(h) The consequences of abuse of directors' powers ... 900
Fiduciary duties: conflicts of interests ... 900
(a) The general rule: no profit ... 902
(b) Rejected business opportunities ... 904
(c) The remedies available where directors wrongly profit from their office ... 908
Directors' duties: competition with the company ... 910
Directors' duties of care, skill and diligence ... 912
(a) General principles ... 912
(b) Qualifications: their presence or absence ... 914

(c) The need for diligence 916
(d) Reliance on others for advice 917
(e) Tortious liability to third parties 918
Judicial relief for directors and indemnities 919
(a) Judicial relief for directors and other officers 919
(b) Indemnities for directors and other officers 921
(c) Directors' and officers' liability insurance 922
[C] Directors' Statutory Duties Arising on Insolvency 923
Reckless trading 923
(a) The meaning of 'knowingly' and 'reckless' 924
(b) Deemed reckless trading 928
(c) The requirement that the company is insolvent 930
(d) The meaning of 'a party' and 'business' 930
(e) The requirement to be an applicant 931
(f) Potential respondents 932
(g) Defences to reckless trading 933
(h) The scope of the court's order 934
(i) The date of the conduct complained of 935
(j) Reckless trading proceedings in an examinership 935
Civil fraudulent trading 936
(a) The intention to defraud 937
(b) Proving fraudulent trading 938
(c) The beneficiary of an award 940
Criminal fraudulent trading 942
Personal liability for failure to keep proper books of account 943
(a) The power to declare officers personally liable where proper books of account not kept 944
(b) The imposition of personal liability is discretionary 945
(c) The proofs required for an order under s 204 946
Section 251 of the CA 1990: invocation of statutory remedies where a company is not being wound up 950
(a) Those with *locus standi* to apply under s 251 951
(b) The orders that can be made under s 251 951
(c) The insufficiency of assets as a precondition to jurisdiction 953
(d) The operation of the section 953
Misfeasance 954
[D] Secretaries' Duties 957
The subject of secretaries' duties 957
Secretaries' common law duties 957
Secretaries' statutory duties 958
[E] Promoters' Duties 960
Corporate promoters 960
Fiduciary duties of promoters 961
Breach of the promoter's fiduciary duty 962
Promoters' transactions with a company 964

Chapter 16 Statutory Regulation of Directors' Transactions

(Thomas B Courtney)

[A] Directors and Persons Connected with Directors 966
Directors of the company and of its holding company 966
Natural persons that are connected persons 967
Bodies corporate that are connected persons 968
(a) The meaning of 'control' 969
(b) 'Interested in' one-half or more of the equity share capital 970
(c) Body corporate controlled by body corporate controlled by a director 973
(d) A subsidiary can be a body corporate controlled by a director 973
Summary 973
[B] Substantial Property Transactions 974
The regulation of substantial property transactions 976
The meaning of 'non-cash asset' 976
The meaning of 'requisite value' 978
Exceptions 982
(a) Inter-group arrangements 982
(b) Arrangements in insolvent windings up 983
(c) Acquisitions by members acting 'qua member' 985
Compliance by approving resolution 986
The consequences of breaching s 29(1) 988
Liability of directors and others for breach 990
[C] Loans, Quasi-loans, Credit Transactions, Guarantees and the Provision of Security in favour of Directors and other Relevant People 995
Section 31 prevents companies from making or entering into transactions or arrangements 997
Anti-avoidance by preventing indirect activity 998
The five prohibited transactions and arrangements 998
(a) Loans 999
(b) Quasi-loans 999
(c) Credit transactions 1000
(d) Guarantees in connection with loans, quasi-loans or credit transactions 1001
(e) Providing security in connection with loans, quasi-loans or credit transactions 1001
The meaning of 'for' a director or other relevant person 1001
The application of s 31 to directors and other relevant people 1002
The five exceptions to the s 31 prohibition 1003
(a) Applicability of exceptions to prohibited transactions and arrangements 1003
(b) Section 32: the *de minimis* exception 1003
(c) Section 34: the validation procedure for guarantees and security 1005
(d) Section 35: the group exception 1010
(e) Section 36: directors' expenses 1011

(f) Section 37: business transactions 1012
(g) The repealed exception 1013
Civil consequences of contravention: voidability 1013
(a) *Restitutio in integrum* is impossible 1014
(b) The indemnity 1014
(c) *Bona fide* and without actual notice 1015
Civil consequences of contravention: account and indemnity 1018
Civil consequences of contravention: personal liability 1020
Criminal consequences of contravention 1021
[D] Disclosure of Interests in Contracts with Companies 1022
The scope of s 194: to whom does it apply? 1023
The meaning of 'directly or indirectly, interested in a contract' 1023
(a) Contracts are deemed to include transactions which are not contracts 1023
(b) Transactions and arrangements with connected persons are deemed to be contracts with directors 1024
Making disclosure 1024
The register of directors' interests and its inspection 1026
The civil consequences of its breach 1026
The criminal consequences of breach 1027

Chapter 17 Financial Statements, Audit and Annual Return

(Dáibhí O'Leary)

Preliminary 1029
[A] The Books of Account 1030
Introduction 1030
Contents of the books of account 1030
Location of the books of account 1031
Form of the books of account 1032
Inspection of the books of account 1032
Liability for failure to keep proper books of account 1034
(a) Criminal liability 1034
(b) Civil liability 1035
Concealment, destruction and falsification of books of account 1036
[B] Financial Year 1037
[C] The Annual Accounts 1038
Introduction 1038
Accounting frameworks 1041
Companies Act individual accounts 1043
(a) 'True and fair view' 1043
(b) Statutory accounting principles 1044
The balance sheet in Companies Act individual accounts 1045
(a) The balance sheet formats 1045
(b) Statutory valuation rules 1049
The profit and loss account in Companies Act individual accounts 1055

Notes to Companies Act individual accounts 1060
(a) Notes relating to the balance sheet 1060
(b) Notes relating to the profit and loss account 1068
(c) Other notes forming part of Companies Act individual accounts 1072
IFRS individual accounts 1082
(a) Directors' remuneration 1082
(b) Transactions with directors and connected persons 1082
(c) Interests of director or secretary in the company's shares and debentures 1082
(d) Details on group undertakings 1083
(e) Details of share capital and debentures 1083
(f) Restriction on the distributability of profits 1083
(g) Guarantees and other financial commitments 1083
(h) Financial assistance for the purchase of own shares 1083
(i) Details of staff numbers and remuneration 1083
(j) Shares and debentures held by subsidiary undertakings 1083
(k) Off balance sheet items 1083
(l) Remuneration of auditors 1083
[D] Group Accounts 1084
Introduction 1084
The obligation to prepare group accounts 1086
Exemptions from preparing group accounts 1087
(a) Exemptions related to size of group 1088
(b) Exemptions for parent undertakings that are fully or 90% owned subsidiary undertakings of EEA undertakings 1089
(c) Exemptions for other parent undertakings that are subsidiary undertakings of EEA undertakings 1090
(d) Exemptions for other parent undertakings that are subsidiary undertakings of non-EEA undertakings 1090
Companies Act group accounts 1092
(a) Form of Companies Act group accounts 1092
(b) Format of Companies Act group accounts 1095
(c) Contents of Companies Act group accounts 1095
(d) Notes to Companies Act group accounts 1097
(d) Acquisition and merger accounting 1101
(e) Joint ventures 1104
(f) Associated undertakings 1105
IFRS group accounts 1106
(a) Directors' remuneration 1107
(b) Transactions with directors 1107
(c) Interests in shares and debentures 1107
(d) Details of group undertakings 1107
(e) Details of staff numbers and remuneration 1107
(f) Details of share capital and debentures 1108
(g) Restriction on distributability of profits 1108
(h) Guarantees and other financial commitments 1108
(i) Financial assistance for the purchase of own shares 1108

(j) Shares and debentures held by subsidiary undertakings 1108
(k) Off-balance sheet arrangements 1108
[E] Approval Of Accounts 1109
Signature and circulation of the balance sheet and profit and loss account 1109
[F] Directors' Report 1110
General obligation 1110
Additional obligations in respect of Companies Act group accounts 1112
Additional obligations in respect of IFRS individual and group accounts 1112
Additional obligation in respect of companies listed on a regulated market 1113
Approval and signing of directors' report 1115
Offences and penalties 1115
[G] Audit Requirement for Statutory Accounts 1115
Requirement to appoint an auditor 1115
Requirement for the auditor to report on the accounts 1116
[H] Auditor's Report 1116
Requirement for auditors to report on the accounts 1116
Contents of the auditor's report 1116
(a) Form of the auditor's opinion 1118
(b) Signature and dating of the auditor's report 1121
Auditor's report to be read at the AGM 1121
[I] Publication Of Accounts 1121
Obligation to circulate accounts and reports 1121
Right to demand copies of accounts and reports 1122
Requirements in relation to publication of accounts 1122
Accounts and reports to be laid before the company in general meeting 1123
[J] Annual Return 1123
Time for filing of the annual return 1124
Consequences of failure to file annual return on time 1125
Contents and form of the annual return 1126
(a) Contents 1126
(b) Form 1128
Documents to be annexed to the annual return 1128
Exemptions from annexing documents to annual return 1129
[K] Exclusions, Exemptions and Special Arrangements with Regard to Filing Obligation 1129
'Medium-sized' companies 1129
(a) Definition of 'medium-sized' company 1129
(b) Requirement to file 'abridged' accounts 1130
'Small' companies 1134
(a) Definition of 'small' company 1134
(b) Requirement to file 'abridged' accounts 1135
Exemption for subsidiary of EU parent undertaking 1138
[L] Audit Exemption 1139
Exemption from the requirement to have accounts audited 1139

[M] Appointment of Statutory Auditors ... 1140
The requirement to appoint an auditor ... 1140
Qualification for appointment as auditor ... 1141
Approval as statutory auditor ... 1142
(a) Member of a recognised accountancy body ... 1142
(b) Member State auditor ... 1143
(c) Third country auditor ... 1143
Approval as statutory audit firm ... 1143
Persons who may not act as auditor ... 1146
Remuneration and expenses of auditors ... 1147
[N] Rights, Obligations and Duties of Auditors ... 1148
The rights and powers of auditors ... 1148
Status and duties of auditors ... 1150
(a) Status ... 1150
(b) Statutory duties ... 1151
(c) Common law duties ... 1154
Civil liability of auditors ... 1156
(a) Liability to the company ... 1156
(b) Liability to others ... 1156
(c) Excluding liability ... 1159
[O] Removal and Resignation of Auditors ... 1160
Removal and replacement of auditors ... 1160
Resignation of auditor ... 1162
[P] Notification to Supervisory Authority of Certain Matters ... 1163

Chapter 18 Corporate Borrowing: Debentures and Security

(Thomas B Courtney)

Borrowing as a source of capital ... 1165
[A] Corporate Capacity and Authority to Borrow ... 1166
The capacity to borrow, guarantee and secure ... 1166
(a) The capacity to borrow ... 1166
(b) The capacity to guarantee ... 1166
(c) The capacity to secure ... 1167
The authority to borrow, guarantee and secure ... 1167
(a) The authority to borrow and secure ... 1167
(b) Authority to guarantee ... 1168
[B] Debentures and Security ... 1168
The mechanics of secured borrowing ... 1168
Facility letters ... 1170
The debenture defined ... 1171
Debentures as debt securities ... 1172
Transfer of debentures ... 1173
Secured debentures: the four kinds of consensual security ... 1174
(a) Pledge ... 1175
(b) Liens ... 1175
(c) Equitable charge ... 1176
(d) Mortgages: legal and equitable ... 1177

Mortgages and charges, defined and distinguished 1177
All sums due debentures 1182
Fixed charges on book debts 1183
(a) Judicial acceptance of the validity of fixed charges on book debts 1184
(b) The importance of restrictions on the chargor's use of the debts 1185
(c) The chargee must exercise control as of legal right 1191
(d) Hybrid charges on book debts 1192
(e) Legislative curtailment of the priority of fixed charges on book debts 1196
Fixed charges on deposit accounts 1199
Floating charges 1201
(a) The nature and characteristics of a floating charge 1201
(b) The chargor's ability to deal with the charged property 1205
(c) Fixed or floating? – the Cosslett (Contractors) Ltd saga 1207
(d) Floating charges are peculiar to companies 1210
Negative pledge clauses 1210
(a) Priority of floating charges accompanied by negative pledge clauses 1211
(b) Negative pledge clauses and competition law 1214
Events which affect assets subject to floating charges 1215
(a) Subsequent mortgages and charges 1215
(b) Set-off 1216
(c) Liens 1216
(d) Execution of judgment 1216
Crystallisation of floating charges 1217
The causes of crystallisation 1221
(a) The appointment of a receiver 1222
(b) The winding up of the chargor company 1222
(c) Ceasing to carry on business 1222
(d) Express and automatic crystallisation clauses 1226
De-cystallisation of floating charges 1232

Chapter 19 Corporate Borrowing: Registration of Charges

(Thomas B Courtney)

Introduction 1233
The register of charges 1233
(a) The rationale for the register of charges 1234
(b) Notice of the register of charges 1235
The consequences of non-registration 1235
The conclusiveness of the certificate of registration 1238
(a) The significance of mistakes in the Form C1 1239
(b) The limits to the decision in the *Amurec* case 1242
Non-registrable security interests 1244
(a) Charges which are not created by companies 1244
(b) Charges over proceeds of sale 1245

(c) Liens 1246
(d) Pledges 1251
(e) Trusts 1251
(f) Otherwise registrable charges provided as part of a financial collateral arrangement 1251
Registrable charges 1255
(a) Charges for the purpose of securing the issue of debentures 1256
(b) Charges on uncalled share capital of the company 1256
(c) Charges created or evidenced by an instrument which, if executed by an individual, would require registration as a bill of sale 1256
(d) Charges on land 1260
(e) Charges on book debts of the company 1263
(f) Floating charges 1268
(g) Charges on calls of shares made but not paid 1268
(h) Charges on – or any share in – a ship or aircraft 1268
(i) Charges on goodwill and other intellectual property 1269
Disguised registrable charges: retention of title clauses 1269
(a) Simple retention of title clause 1270
(b) An aggregation retention of title clause 1272
(c) Proceeds of sale clause 1273
(d) Current account clause 1277
Judgment mortgages 1278
Charges over property outside of the State 1278
Late registration of registrable charges 1280
(a) The discretionary nature of s 106 of the CA 1963 1280
(b) Distinguishing a complete failure to register from a mere misstatement or omission 1281
(c) The *Joplin* proviso 1284
(d) Application for late registration where company being wound up 1286
(e) Agreement to late registered charge taking priority over prior registered charge 1288
Registration 1289
Particulars required to be registered 1289
Satisfaction of charges 1290
The chargor company's obligations 1291

Chapter 20 Corporate Borrowing: Receivers

(Thomas B Courtney)

Introduction 1293
Receiver defined 1293
Considerations on the appointment of a receiver under a debenture 1294
(a) Default: the basis for the appointment of a receiver 1295
(b) Appointment following default in repaying money repayable on demand 1297
(c) No additional duty of care over and above contract 1299
Qualifications of receivers 1300

Appointment of a receiver 1301
(a) Appointment on foot of a debenture 1301
(b) Appointment on foot of a court order 1304
(c) Appointment to income under the Land and Conveyancing Law Reform Act 2009 1304
(d) Statutory receivers 1305
(e) Notice of appointment 1306
The effect of the appointment of a receiver 1307
(a) Effect on management 1307
(b) Effect on employees 1309
The status of a receiver 1311
(a) Receivers appointed by the court 1311
(b) Receivers appointed by a debenture holder 1311
(c) The receiver as agent of the company 1311
The remuneration of a receiver 1316
Duties of receivers 1317
(a) The duty to provide information to the company 1317
(b) Duties of receiver-managers 1320
(c) Duties arising on the disposal of assets 1322
(d) Duties to guarantors 1330
(e) Duties in applying the proceeds of sale of assets 1331
(f) Duties to supply information to the registrar of companies and the Director of Corporate Enforcement 1335
Liabilities of receivers 1336
Powers of receivers 1338
Applications for directions 1341
Multiple receivers to the same company 1342
Resignation and removal of receivers 1342
(a) Resignation 1342
(b) Removal by the court 1343
(c) Removal of receiver at the instigation of a liquidator 1343
(d) Removal of receiver at the instigation of an examiner 1343

Chapter 21 Schemes of Arrangement and Reconstructions

(Thomas B Courtney)

Introduction 1345
[A] Schemes of Arrangement 1345
Key criteria in a s 201 application 1346
(a) Compromise or arrangement must be proposed by a 'company' 1347
(b) Meaning of members 1347
(c) Creditors: ordinary, secured and preferential 1347
(d) The meaning of 'arrangement', 'compromise' and 'between' 1348
Limitations to schemes of arrangement 1351
(a) The applicant must have *locus standi* 1351
(b) The company must support the application 1351
(c) Schemes must not be contrary to law or ultra vires 1352
(d) Where capital is reduced the normal rules apply 1352

(e) Where relevant, there must be compliance with the rules of the Irish Takeover Panel 1353
Initiating a scheme of arrangement: meetings of members and creditors 1353
(a) The responsibility for constituting proper classes 1354
(b) Constituting proper classes 1356
(c) Classes of members: shareholders' rights and interests 1359
(d) Providing information to members and creditors 1362
(e) Voting at meetings 1364
(f) Repeat applications under s 201 where first scheme proposed unacceptable 1366
Staying proceedings where application made under s 201(1) 1366
Court sanction of scheme of arrangement 1367
(a) Sufficient steps to identify and notify all interested parties 1368
(b) Compliance with statute and court directions 1368
(b) Class fairly represented and majority act bona fide 1369
(c) A man of business would reasonable approve 1369
Solvent schemes of arrangement 1371
Judicial powers to assist schemes in contemplation of reconstruction 1372
Setting aside a scheme for fraud 1373
[B] Reconstructions 1374
The s 260 machinery 1375
(a) Only available in a voluntary winding up 1375
(b) The proposal 1375
(c) The requirement for sanction by special resolution of members 1376
(d) Distribution of shares, policies or other interests 1377

Chapter 22 Examinerships

(Thomas B Courtney)

Introduction 1379
(a) The background to the Companies (Amendment) Act 1990 1379
(b) The Gallagher Company Law Review Group 1380
(c) The Companies (Amendment) (No 2) Act 1999 1380
The purpose of the legislation 1381
[A] The Appointment of an Examiner: Presenting the Petition 1382
The jurisdiction to appoint an examiner: presenting the petition 1382
Locus standi to petition the court and be heard on the petition 1383
The grounds for appointing an examiner 1386
(a) The test for the appointment of an examiner 1386
(b) The need to show a 'reasonable prospect of survival of the company' 1387
(c) The need to show a 'reasonable prospect of survival of the whole or any part of its undertaking as a going concern' 1392
(d) Companies with obligations to NAMA 1393
The petition and grounding affidavit 1393
The petition must be made in the utmost of good faith 1395
The pre-petition report from an independent accountant 1396

Interim protection pending the submission of a pre-petition report ... 1398
Presentation of the petition ... 1400
The hearing of the petition ... 1401
Related companies ... 1403
Formalities in the appointment of an examiner ... 1405
The commencement of protection ... 1406
[B] The Effects of Court Protection ... 1406
[C] The Position of Creditors ... 1409
Ordinary and preferential creditors ... 1410
Provisional liquidators ... 1410
Receivers ... 1411
Secured creditors: general ... 1412
Negative pledge clauses in debentures ... 1413
De-crystallisation of floating charges ... 1414
Sureties and guarantors ... 1416
Priority of secured creditors and liquidators' costs, charges and expenses ... 1419
(a) Secured creditors ... 1419
(b) Liquidators' costs, charges and expenses ... 1420
[D] The Powers of Examiners ... 1421
To seek a transfer of the directors' powers ... 1421
To obtain information ... 1423
To seek directions from the court ... 1424
To discharge pre-petition debts ... 1424
To borrow ... 1425
To deal with charged property ... 1426
(a) Floating charges ... 1426
(b) Fixed charges and mortgages, etc ... 1427
To certify expenses ... 1428
To regularise improper transactions ... 1431
[E] The Examiner's Report and Schemes of Arrangement ... 1431
Examiners' duties ... 1431
Hearing regarding irregularities ... 1432
The formulation of proposals ... 1433
Restriction on compromise of leasing claims ... 1436
Meetings of creditors and members to consider the proposals ... 1439
The examiner's report under s 18 of the C(A)A 1990 ... 1441
Hearing the proposals: court confirmation or rejection ... 1443
(a) Substantive objections to court confirmation ... 1445
(b) Other substantive grounds for not confirming a scheme ... 1450
(c) Procedural and other objections to court confirmation ... 1451
(d) Unfairly prejudicial proposals ... 1452
Evidence of wrongdoing ... 1456
Matters arising after court confirmation of the proposals ... 1456
[F] The Examiner's Remuneration, Costs and Expenses ... 1457
Examiner's remuneration ... 1457
Examiner's costs ... 1459
Examiner's expenses ... 1459

Chapter 23 Winding Up Companies

(Thomas B Courtney)

Introduction 1461
[A] Members' Voluntary Winding Up 1461
Declaration of solvency 1462
The report of an independent person 1464
Personal liability of the directors 1465
The resolution to wind up 1466
Commencement of a members' voluntary winding up 1467
Termination of a members' voluntary liquidation 1467
[B] Creditors' Voluntary Winding Up 1468
Statement of the position of the company's affairs 1468
The members' general meeting 1469
The creditors' meeting 1470
The committee of inspection 1476
Termination of a creditors' voluntary liquidation 1476
[C] Compulsory Court Winding Up 1477
Jurisdiction to compulsorily wind up companies 1477
Locus standi to petition the court 1479
(a) The company 1479
(b) Creditors 1480
(c) Contributories and members 1483
(d) The Director of Corporate Enforcement 1484
(e) The registrar of companies 1485
(f) Trustees of investment companies 1485
Procedural issues in compulsory windings up 1485
(a) The petition 1485
(b) Advertisement of the petition 1486
(c) Options for a respondent company 1486
(d) Substitution of petitioner 1488
(e) Hearing the petition 1489
Grounds for ordering a company to be wound up 1492
(a) The company has resolved by special resolution to wind up the company 1494
(b) The company does not commence its business within a year from its incorporation or suspends its business for a whole year 1494
(c) The number of members is reduced, in the case of a private company, below two, or, in the case of any other company, below seven 1494
(d) The company is unable to pay its debts 1494
(e) The court is of the opinion that it is just and equitable that the company should be wound up 1510
(f) Oppression 1522
[D] Conversion of Windings Up 1523
Converting a members' winding up to a creditors' winding up 1523
Converting a voluntary winding up to a compulsory winding up 1524

[E] The Winding-up Order ... 1530
Annulling a members' winding up ... 1531
Rescission of a compulsory winding-up order ... 1532
Voiding dissolution following the making of a winding-up order ... 1532
[F] Winding Up Licensed Banks and Other Authorised Credit Institutions ... 1536
Rights enjoyed by the Central Bank ... 1537
Rules applicable to liquidators of authorised credit institutions ... 1537
The liquidation committee ... 1538

Chapter 24 Liquidators

(Thomas B Courtney)

Introduction ... 1539
The four types of liquidator ... 1539
(a) Voluntary liquidators appointed by members and creditors ... 1539
(b) Official liquidators ... 1540
(c) Provisional liquidators ... 1540
Liquidators' qualifications ... 1540
The appointment and removal of liquidators ... 1541
(a) Members' voluntary liquidators ... 1541
(b) Creditors' voluntary liquidators ... 1542
(c) Official liquidators ... 1542
(d) Provisional liquidators ... 1545
Liquidators' duties ... 1547
(a) Fiduciary duties ... 1547
(b) Statutory duties to members ... 1547
(c) Statutory duties to creditors ... 1547
(d) The statutory duty to report to the Director of Corporate Enforcement ... 1548
Liquidators' powers ... 1549
(a) Powers of official liquidators ... 1549
(b) Powers of provisional liquidators ... 1556
(c) Powers of voluntary liquidators ... 1557
(d) Restrictions on the exercise of powers by members' voluntary liquidators and other restrictions ... 1559
(e) Seeking directions from court ... 1561
Remuneration of liquidators ... 1561
Foreign liquidators and the EU Council Regulation on Insolvency Proceedings ... 1563
(a) Assistance to foreign liquidators in Ireland ... 1563
(b) The European Council Regulation on Insolvency Proceedings ... 1565
(c) Assistance to Irish liquidators abroad ... 1570
The Director of Corporate Enforcement's power to supervise liquidators ... 1570

[D] Non-Registration Offences 1783
Indictable offences 1783
Failure to keep and maintain registers and records 1788
Miscellaneous offences 1788
[E] Restriction of Directors 1790
The purpose of restriction orders 1791
(a) Persons who have been directors on or within 12 months of the winding up 1798
(b) Directors: *de jure*, *de facto* and shadow 1798
(c) Non-resident directors 1802
The duties of liquidators of insolvent companies and the Director's role 1802
The *locus standi* of liquidators, receivers, creditors and the Director 1806
Procedural aspects of restriction applications 1808
The costs of the application for a restriction order 1809
(a) The costs of a successful application 1809
(b) The costs of an unsuccessful application 1810
The defence of acting 'honestly and responsibly' 1811
(a) Acting honestly in relation to the affairs of the company 1812
(b) Acting responsibly in relation to the conduct of the affairs of the company 1813
(c) Acting responsibly – the factors which the courts consider relevant 1814
(d) Otherwise just or equitable to make restriction order 1830
The defence of being a nominee 1831
The defence of delay and estoppel 1832
Post-order relief on just and equitable grounds 1834
The enforcement of restriction orders 1839
(a) Breach of a s 150 order by restricted directors – criminal sanction 1839
(b) Breach of a s 150 order by restricted directors – civil sanctions 1839
(c) Criminal sanctions for officers of companies who act in accordance with the directions or instructions of restricted directors 1839
(d) Civil sanctions for officers of companies with which restricted directors become involved which fail to comply with the requirements in s 150(3) 1840
[F] Disqualification of Directors and Other Officers 1840
Deemed disqualification following conviction for fraud or dishonesty 1841
Discretionary disqualification: the persons who may be disqualified and the meaning of 'company' 1843
The *locus standi* to apply for a disqualification order and the role of the Director of Corporate Enforcement 1844
Notice to persons where application is to be made to disqualify 1846
The grounds for discretionary disqualification 1847
(a) Preliminary issues 1848
(b) Guilty of any fraud: s 160(2)(a) 1854
(c) Guilty of breach of duty: s 160(2)(b) 1854

(d) Proof of a declaration of liability for fraudulent trading: s 160(2)(c) 1854
(e) Unfit to be concerned in the management of a company: s 160(2)(d) 1854
(f) Unfitness appearing from an inspector's report: s 160(2)(e) 1860
(g) Persistently in default in relation to 'relevant requirements': s 160(2)(f) 1862
(h) Guilty of two or more offences for failing to keep proper books of account: s 160(2)(g) 1864
(i) Directorship of a company that has been struck off: s 160(2)(h) 1864
(j) The subject of a disqualification order made in a foreign state: s 160(2)(i) 1866

The nature of the disqualification order and the period of disqualification 1866
Relief for the disqualified 1869
The enforcement of disqualification orders 1870
(a) Breach of disqualification order – criminal sanction 1870
(b) Breach of disqualification order – civil sanctions 1871
(c) Criminal sanctions for officers of companies who act in accordance with the directions or instructions of disqualified directors 1871
(d) Civil sanctions for officers of companies with which disqualified directors become involved 1871

[G] Injunctions to Compel Compliance with the Companies Acts 1872

Chapter 29 Public Limited Companies and SEs

(G Brian Hutchinson)

[A] Public Limited Companies 1875
Public companies generally 1875
Public limited companies defined 1876
Approach adopted to treatment of the law of PLCs 1877
Formation and registration 1878
(a) Formation of PLCs 1878
(b) Registration of PLCs and commencement of business 1878
(c) Converting from a private company to a PLC 1882
(d) Migration of PLCs 1885
Constitutional documentation 1885
(a) Memorandum of association 1885
(b) Articles of association 1886
(c) Alteration of constitutional documentation 1886
Incorporation and its consequences 1886
Corporate contracts: capacity and authority 1887
(a) Securities seal 1887
(b) Uncertificated securities 1887
(c) Validity of trading or borrowing carried out without an authorisation 1887

Shares and membership 1888
(a) Membership of PLCs 1888
(b) Legal nature of shares in PLCs and the formalities which apply to them 1889
(c) Allotment of shares in PLCs, and consideration therefor 1890
(d) Disclosure of interests in shares in PLCs 1894
(e) Disclosure of stabilising activity during a stabilisation period 1895
Share transfer 1896
(a) Certificated and uncertificated securities 1896
The maintenance of capital 1899
(a) Acquisition by PLCs of their own shares 1899
(b) Treatment of own shares acquired by PLCs 1901
(c) Financial assistance by PLCs in the purchase of their own shares 1902
(d) Distributions and the payment of dividends in PLCs 1903
(e) Restrictions on reduction of capital by PLCs 1903
(f) Power of creditors to object to a reduction of capital 1904
Corporate governance: management by the directors 1904
(a) Differences for PLCs 1904
(b) Board committees 1905
(c) Corporate governance regulation 1907
(d) Failed intervention by the Companies Acts 1908
(e) The UK Corporate Governance Code 1908
(f) Main principles of the Code 1909
(g) The Irish Corporate Governance Annex 1911
(h) Other corporate governance codes 1911
Corporate governance: meetings 1911
(a) Notice requirements generally 1912
(b) Additional rights conferred under the Shareholders' Rights Directive 1913
(c) The requirements of the UK Corporate Governance Code as regards meetings 1919
Financial statements, audit and annual return 1921
Corporate borrowing 1923
Strike off and restoration 1924
Investigations and inspectors 1924
Compliance and enforcement 1926
Investment companies 1926
(a) Formation and registration 1928
(b) Constitutional documentation 1929
(c) Incorporation and its consequences 1930
(d) Corporate contracts: capacity and authority 1931
(e) Shares and membership 1931
(f) The maintenance of capital 1932
(g) Financial Statements, audit and annual return 1933
(h) Winding up 1933
[B] Societas Europaea 1934
Introduction and overview 1934

Sources of the law applicable to SEs 1936
Particular aspects of the law relating to SEs 1937
(a) Formation and registration of SEs 1937
(b) Constitutional documentation in SEs 1941
(c) Governance structures of SEs 1942
(d) Requirements for employee involvement in SEs 1943
(e) Meetings in SEs 1945
(f) Financial reporting, audit and annual returns in SEs 1946
(g) Transfer of an SE's registered office between Member States 1946
(h) Conversion of SE to PLC 1948
(i) Winding up SEs 1948

Chapter 30 Guarantee Companies

(Thomas B Courtney)

The guarantee company in context 1949
The primary uses of the guarantee company 1949
(a) Charities 1950
(b) Management companies 1951
(c) Sports or social clubs 1952
The key features of the guarantee company 1952
(a) Guarantee companies have no shares 1952
(b) Guarantee companies are public companies 1952
(c) Guarantee companies are limited by their members' guarantee 1952
Formation and constitutional documentation of guarantee companies 1953
(a) Formation of guarantee companies 1953
(c) Memorandum of association: name clause 1953
(d) Memorandum of association: objects clause 1955
Disregarding separate legal personality 1962
Membership 1962
The maintenance of capital 1964
Corporate governance: management by the directors 1965
Corporate governance: meetings 1966
(a) Voting: one vote for each unit and fair and equitable voting rights 1967
(b) Meetings to consider annual report 1968
(c) Service charge must be considered in general meeting and can be disapproved 1970
(d) Service charges cannot include costs that are developers' responsibility unless approved of in general meeting 1971
(e) House rules must be considered and approved by general meeting 1971
Financial statements, audit and annual return 1972
(a) Books of account 1972
(b) Accounts of guarantee companies 1972
(c) Annual return of guarantee companies 1974
(d) Exemptions in relation to preparation, audit and disclosure of accounts 1975

Winding up guarantee companies and realisation and distribution of assets 1976
Strike-off and restoration 1976
Compliance and enforcement 1977

Chapter 31 Unlimited Companies

(Thomas B Courtney)

The unlimited company in context 1979
Formation and constitutional documentation of unlimited companies 1980
(a) Formation of unlimited companies 1980
(b) The memorandum of association of an unlimited company 1980
(c) The articles of association of an unlimited company 1981
(d) Restrictions on the commencement of business 1981
Incorporation and its consequences 1982
Disregarding separate legal personality 1983
Corporate civil litigation 1983
Corporate contracts, capacity and authority 1985
Shares and membership 1985
Share transfers in unlimited companies 1985
The maintenance of capital 1985
Financial statements, audit and annual returns 1987
(a) Annual return 1987
(b) Financial statements 1988
(c) Exemptions in relation to preparation, audit and disclosure of accounts 1990
Winding up, liquidators and realisation and distribution of assets 1991

Chapter 32 Prospectus, Market Abuse and Transparency Law

(G Brian Hutchinson)

Introduction 1995
'Regulated market' defined 1997
[A] Prospectuses 1997
Introduction 1997
Sources of law on prospectuses 1998
Key features of the EU prospectus regime 2000
Scope of the Prospectus Directive 2000
Public offer of securities 2002
Offerings exempt from prospectus requirements 2003
(a) Offers to qualified investors 2004
(b) Offers of exempted securities 2005
Admission to trading on a regulated market 2006
Format and content of the prospectus 2007
Requirement for prospectus to contain a summary 2008
Approval and publication of a prospectus 2009
Passporting of prospectuses 2010
Languages used in prospectuses 2010

Supplements to prospectuses 2011
Liability and sanctions for misstatements in prospectuses 2011
(a) Civil sanctions for false particulars 2011
(b) Criminal liability relating to prospectuses 2015
(c) Administrative sanctions 2017
[B] Market Abuse 2017
Application of the market abuse measures 2020
Financial instruments to which the Market Abuse Directive applies 2021
Central Bank as competent authority in Ireland 2022
The elements of market abuse 2022
(a) Insider dealing 2022
(b) Market manipulation 2038
(c) Notification obligations under the Market Abuse Directive 2040
(d) Criminal liability for breaches of the Market Abuse Directive 2042
(e) Administrative sanctions for breaches of the Market Abuse Directive 2043
(f) Civil liability for breaches of the Market Abuse Directive 2043
[C] Transparency 2044
Scope of the Transparency Directive 2045
(a) Periodic financial reports required by the Transparency Directive 2046
(b) Civil liability for false or misleading information in the periodic reports 2048
(c) On-going information requirements 2050
(d) Continuing obligations and access to information 2051
(e) General obligations with regard to the dissemination of regulated information 2052

Chapter 33 Conversion by Re-registration

(Thomas B Courtney)

Unlimited to limited 2053
(a) Unlimited company to private limited company 2053
(b) Unlimited company to PLC 2056
Limited to unlimited 2057
Converting from PLC to private 2059
Converting from private to PLC 2060
Multi-member private company to single-member private company 2060
Single-Member Private Company to Multi-Member Private Company 2061

Chapter 34 External Companies and Branches

(Thomas B Courtney)

[A] External Companies 2063
Companies to which Part XI of the CA 1963 applies 2064
Establishing a place of business 2064
(a) The external company must conduct a business 2065
(b) Indicia in determining whether a place of business has been established 2066

(c) Business carried on may be incidental to a company's main business 2067
(d) Places of business and branches distinguished 2068
The obligation to register 2068
The ongoing obligation to file documents 2069
Other obligations of external companies 2070
Charges created by external companies 2070
(a) External companies 2071
(b) Unregistered external companies: the Slavenburg file 2071
(c) Established place of business in the context of creating charges 2073
Service of documents 2074
Offences for breach of the requirements under Part XI of the CA 1963 2075
[B] Branches 2075
Companies to which the EC(BD)R 1993 apply 2075
The meaning of 'branch' 2076
Establishing a branch 2076
EU companies: the obligation to register and deliver documents 2078
Non-EU companies: the obligation to register and deliver documents 2079
Requirements in relation to letterheads 2080
Accounting documents to be delivered to the registrar of companies 2081
Miscellaneous obligations 2082
Service of process or notice 2082
Duty to secure compliance with Regulations 2082
Offences for breach of Regulations 2083

Appendix 2085

Index 2087

Table of Cases

A

A&BC Chewing Gum Ltd, Re [1975] 1 All ER 1017 .... 23.101
A&J Fabrications (Batley) Ltd v Grant Thornton [1998] 2 BCLC 227, [1999] BCC 807 .... 24.021
Aaron's Reefs v Twiss [1895] 2 IR 207 (CA), [1896] AC 273 .... 32.047
Aas v Benham [1891] 2 Ch 244 .... 15.065
Abbey Films Ltd v Attorney General [1981] IR 158 .... 4.018, 4.068, 6.066
Abbey Trinity Retail Ltd, Re [2010] IEHC 5 .... 23.078
Aberdeen Railway Co v Blaikie Bros (1854) 1 Macq 461 .... 15.056, 15.069
ABM Construction v Habbingley Ltd [2012] IEHC 61 .... 6.025, 31.015–31.016
Abraham v Thompson [1997] 4 All ER 362 .... 24.036
Abrahams & Sons, Re [1902] 1 Ch 695 .... 19.090, 19.097
Acatos & Hutcheson plc v Watson [1995] 1 BCLC 218 .... 10.016
ACC Bank plc v Kelly & Kelly [2011] IEHC 7 .... 20.019
ACC Bank plc v McCann & Griffin [2012] IEHC 236 .... 7.121, 7.123, 8.049
ACT General Cleaning Pty Ltd v Naoum (1996) 67 FCR 361 .... 6.067
Adair v Old Bushmills Distillery [1908] WN 24 .... 8.104
Adam Eyton Ltd, Re; ex p Charlesworth (1887) 36 Ch D 299 .... 24.015
Adams v Cape Industries [1990] Ch 433 .... 5.005, 5.049, 5.051, 12.049
Addlestone Linoleum Co, Re (1887) 37 Ch D 191 .... 32.048
Adlards Motor Group Holding Ltd, Re [1990] BCLC 68 .... 25.030
ADT Ltd v BDO Binder Hamlyn [1996] BCC 808 .... 17.335
Advanced Technology College Ltd, Re [1997] IEHC 51 .... 22.042, 22.055, 22.089
Advantage Healthcare (T10) Ltd, Re [2000] BCC 985 .... 19.016, 19.019–19.020
Aerospares Ltd v Thompson [1999] IEHC 76 .... 15.068
Afric Sive Ltd v Gas and Exploration Ltd [1989] IEHC 35 .... 15.033
AGA Estate Agencies Ltd, Re [1986] BCC 99 .... 26.037
Agnew v Commissioner on Inland Revenue [2001] 2 AC 710 .... 18.109
Agra Bank Ltd v Barry (1874) LR 7 HL 135 .... 16.107
AH Masser Ltd v Revenue Commissioners [1978–1987] III ITR 706 .... 18.044
AI Levy (Holdings) Ltd, Re [1963] 2 All ER 556 .... 25.080
AI Levy (Holdings) Ltd, Re [1963] 2 All ER 85 .... 25.077
AIB Finance Ltd v Bank of Scotland [1995] 1 BCLC 185 .... 18.080
Air Ecossee Ltd v Civil Aviation Authority [1987] 3 BCC 492 .... 22.061
Air France Aircraft Leasing v Registrar of Companies (30 April 2007, unreported) HC 8.055
Aircool Installations v British Telecommunications (1995) Current Law Week 19 May 1995 .... 19.075, 19.078
Airlines Airspace Ltd v Handley Page Ltd [1970] 1 All ER 29 .... 20.075
Aktieselskabet Dansk Skibsfinansiering v Brothers [2001] 2 BCLC 324 .... 15.130
Alabama, New Orleans, Texas and Pacific Junction Railway Co, Re [1891] 1 Ch 213 .... 21.014, 21.050, 21.055

Alba Radio Ltd v Haltone (Cork) Ltd [1995] 2 IR 170, [1995] 2 ILRM 466 .... 15.146–15.148, 25.029
Albion Enterprises Ltd, Re [2012] IEHC 115 .... 23.062
Alchemea Ltd, Re [1998] BCC 964 .... 11.014
Alder v Dobie and Gallop (8 April 1999) SC (BC) 15.037
Alexander v Automatic Telephone Co [1900] 2 Ch 56 .... 8.005, 8.095
Alice Springs Abattoirs Pty Ltd v Northern Territory of Australia (1996) 134 FLR 440 .... 6.067
Alipour v UOC Corp [2002] 2 BCLC 770 .... 8.024
Allen v Gold Reefs of West Africa Ltd [1900] 1 Ch 656 .... 3.057 .... 3.067–3.069, 3.102, 3.127, 10.110
Allen v Hyatt (1914) 30 TLR 444 (PC) 8.091, 15.020
Allied Arab Bank Ltd v Hajjar [1987] 3 All ER 39 .... 25.041
Allied Business and Financial Consultants Ltd, Re [2009] BCC 517 .... 15.065
Allied Domecq plc, Re [2000] 1 BCLC 134 .... 21.022
Allied Irish Bank plc v Diamond [2011] IEHC 505 .... 15.058
Allied Irish Banks Ltd v Ardmore Studios International (1972) Ltd (30 May 1973, unreported) HC 7.122
Allied Irish Banks Ltd v Glynn [1973] IR 188 .... 18.071
Allied Irish Coal Supplies Ltd v Powell Duffryn International Fuels Ltd (19 June 1996, unreported) HC 12.049
Allied Irish Coal Supplies Ltd v Powell Duffryn International Fuels Ltd [1998] 2 IR 519 .... 4.033, 5.005–5.006, 5.009, 5.046 .... 5.051, 5.062, 12.049
Allied Metropole Hotel Ltd, Re (19 December 1988, unreported) HC 8.032, 11.046, 26.036
Allied Pharmaceutical Distributions Ltd v Walsh [1991] IR 8 .... 7.104
Alma Spinning Co, Re (Bottomley's case) (1880) 16 Cr D 681 .... 14.113
Alpha Co Ltd, Re [1913] 1 Ch 203 .... 11.118
Alton Corporation, Re [1985] BCLC 27 .... 9.036, 34.021
Aluminium Fabricators Ltd, Re [1984] ILRM 399 .... 15.120, 25.031, 25.035
Aluminium Industrie Vaasen BV v Romalpa Aluminium Ltd [1976] 2 All ER 552 .... 19.072
Alvona Developments Ltd v The Manhattan Loft Corporation (AC) Ltd [2006] BCC 119 .... 14.031
Amadeus Trading Ltd, Re [1997] TLR 184 .... 23.078
Amalgamated Investment and Property Co Ltd, Re [1984] 3 All ER 272, ... 25.179
Amalgamated Syndicates Ltd [1901] 2 Ch 181 .... 24.052
Amantiss Enterprises Ltd, Re; Framus Ltd v CRH plc [1999] IEHC 74, [2000] 2 ILRM 177 .... 23.130, 26.056, 26.059–26.060
Amaron Ltd, Re [1998] BCC 264 .... 28.203
American Cyanamid Co v Ethicon Ltd [1975] 1 All ER 504 .... 25.047
American Express International Banking Corp v Hurley [1985] 3 All ER 564 .... 20.063
American Express International Banking Corp v Hurley [1986] BCLC 52 .... 20.053, 20.062
American Pioneer Leather Co, Re [1918] 1 Ch 556 .... 23.101

AMS IT Consultants Ltd, Re; Keane v Kalsi and Kalsi [2006] IEHC 12 .... 28.113
Analog Devices BV v Zurich Insurance [2005] 1 IR 274 .... 18.109
Anderson (WB) & Sons v Rhodes [1967] 2 All ER 850 .... 15.086
Anderson Kershaw Ltd and Anderson Conforming Ltd, Re; Director of Corporate Enforcement v Collins and O'Connell [2008] IEHC 456 .... 28.196
Andrabell Ltd, Re [1984] 3 All ER 407 .... 19.076
Andrew, Re [1937] Ch 122 .... 25.054
Andrew, Re, ex p Official Receiver [1937] Ch 122 .... 6.074
Andrews v Gas Meter Co [1897] 1 Ch 361 .... 8.099
Angelis v Algemene Bank Nederland (Ireland) Ltd (4 July 1974, unreported) HC 14.026, 20.020
Anglesea Colliery Co, Re [1866] 1 Ch App 555 .... 23.045
Anglo French Co-Operative Society, Re; ex p Pelly [1882] 21 Ch D 492 .... 25.154
Anglo Irish Bank Corporation plc v Edward Kavanagh Maynooth Ltd [2003] IEHC 113 .... 18.032, 19.023
Anglo Maltese Hydraulic Dock Co Ltd, Re [1885] 33 WR 652 .... 17.309
Anglo-Continental Produce Ltd, Re [1939] All ER 99 .... 23.102
Anglo-Continental Supply Co Ltd, Re [1922] 2 Ch 723 .... 21.050
Anglo-Oriental Carpet Manufacturing Co, Re [1903] 1 Ch 914 .... 19.098
Anglo-Overseas Agencies Ltd v Green [1961] 1 QB 1, [1960] All ER 244 .... 7.051
Angostura Bitters (Dr JGB Siegert & Sons) Ltd v Kerr [1933] AC 550 .... 3.088
Anns v Merton London Borough Council [1978] AC 728 .... 17.334
Ansbacher (Cayman) Ltd, Re [2002] 2 IR 517 .... 27.053
Ansbacher (Cayman) Ltd, Re [2004] IEHC 222 .... 27.056
Ansbacher (Cayman) Ltd, Re; Director of Corporate Enforcement v Collery [2007] 1 IR 580 .... 28.167, 28.188, 28.200
Anthony v Seger (1879) 1 Haag Cas Con 9 .... 8.083
Antigen Holdings Ltd, Re (8 November 2001, unreported) HC 22.154
ANZ Nominees Ltd v Allied Resources Corporation Ltd (1984) 2 ACLC 783 .... 14.073
Apollo Cleaning Services Ltd, Re; Richards v Lundy [1999] BCC 786 .... 1.151, 11.025, 11.035, 11.038
Applied Database Ltd, Re (17 February 1995, unreported) HC (Eng) 23.111
Aquila Design v Cornhill Insurance [1988] BCLC 134 .... 6.047
Arbuthnot Leasing Ltd v Havelet Leasing Ltd [1990] BCLC 802 .... 6.067
Ardmore Studios (Ireland) Ltd v Lynch [1965] IR 1 .... 20.041, 20.076
Arenson v Arenson [1972] 2 All ER 939 .... 9.126
Armagas Ltd v Mundagas SA [1985] 3 All ER 795 .... 7.104
Armagh Shoes Ltd, Re [1984] BCLC 405 .... 18.044
Armour Hick Northern Ltd v Armour Trust Ltd [1980] 3 All ER 833 .... 10.082
Armour v Thyssen Edelstahlwerke AG [1990] 3 WLR 810 .... 19.084
Armstrong Whitworth Securities Co Ltd, Re [1947] 1 Ch 673 .... 25.174
Arnold (RM) & Co Ltd, Re [1984] BCLC 535 .... 19.090, 19.098
Arrow Nominees Inc v Blackledge [2000] 1 BCLC 709 .... 11.055
Article 26 and the Employment Equality Bill 1996, Re [1997] IR 321 .... 4.058
Artistic Colour Printing Co, Re (1880) 14 Ch D 502 .... 6.074

Arulchelvan v Wright (7 February 1996, unreported) HC 14.025, 14.036, 14.056
ARV Aviation Ltd, Re [1989] BCLC 664 ....22.102
As Fresh As It Gets Ltd, Re [2011] IEHC 195 ....23.078
Ashbury Railway Carriage and Iron Co v Riche (1875) LR 7 HL 256 ....13.140
Ashbury Railway Carriage and Iron Co v Riche (1875) LR 7 HL 653
.... 7.045, 7.088, 7.094, 11.122
Ashclad Ltd, Re; Forrest v Harrington and Culleton [2000] IEHC 174
....15.028, 15.138, 28.114
Ashcoin Ltd v Moriarty Holdings Ltd [2012] IEHC 365 ....18.041
Ashley Guarantee plc v Zacaria [1993] 1 All ER 254 ....20.060
Ashmark Ltd (No 1), Re [1990] ILRM 330 ....25.075
Ashmark Ltd (No 2), Re [1990] ILRM 455 ....16.095, 25.068
Ashmark Ltd, Re; Ashmark Ltd v Allied Irish Bank plc [1994] 1 ILRM 223
....25.074
Ashpurton Estates Ltd, Re [1983] Ch 110 ....19.098
Ashpurton Estates Ltd, Re [1983] Ch 54 ....19.098
Ashtiani v Kashi [1986] 2 All ER 970 ....25.047
ASIC v Healey [2011] FCA 717 ....15.080
ASIC v Rich [2009] NSWSC 1229 ....15.080
ASIC v Vines [2003] NSWSC 1095 ....15.080
ASRS Establishment Ltd, Re [2000] 2 BCLC 631 ....18.055
Assignees of Taylor v Thompson (1869–70) IRCL 129 ....25.094
Associated Alloys Pty Ltd v Metropolitan Engineering & Fabrication Ltd
[1998] NSWSC 442, [2000] HCA 25 .... 19.034, 19.078, 19.081–19.082
Astec (BSR) plc, Re [1999] BCC 59 .... 1.151, 11.035, 11.038
Aston Colour Print Ltd, Re [1997] IEHC 33 .... 6.006, 14.003, 4.109
....14.125, 22.013
Astor Chemicals v Synthetic Technology [1990] BCLC 1 ....20.077
At Hand Cleaning Services Ltd, Re; ODCE v Hutton (8 March 2004,
unreported) HC 28.073
Atherton v Anderson 99 F 2nd 883 ....15.053
Atkins & Co v Wardle (1889) 61 LT 23 ....5.081
Atlantic & General Investment Trust Ltd v Richbell Information
Services Inc [2000] BCC 111 ....23.036
Atlantic Computers Ltd (in liq), Re;National Australia Bank Ltd v Soden
[1995] BCC 696 ....5.017
Atlantic Magnetics Ltd, Re [1993] 2 IR 561 .... 20.004, 22.004–22.005
.... 22.020, 22.084, 22.102
Atlas Development Co Ltd v Calof and Gold (1963) 31 WWR 575 ....3.126
Attorney General for Ceylon v Silva [1953] AC 461 .... 7.104
Attorney General for England and Wales v Brandon Books Publishers Ltd
[1986] IR 579 ....4.073
Attorney General for Ireland v Jameson [1904] 2 IR 644
....3.098, 4.032, 8.036, 8.039, 9.019, 9.120
Attorney General for Tuvalu v Philatelic Distribution Corp Ltd
[1990] 2 All ER 216 ....6.086, 6.098
Attorney General v Great Eastern Railway (1880) 5 App Cas 473 ....7.068, 18.005

Attorney General v Paperlink Ltd [1984] ILRM 373 ....4.068, 4.071, 4.073
Attorney General v Southern Industiral Trust Ltd (1957) 94 ILTR 161
.... 4.069–4.070
Attorney General v Walthamstow UDC [1895] 11 TLR 533 .... 6.080
Attorney General v Wheatley & Co Ltd (1903) 48 Sol Jo 116 .... 6.087
Attorney General's Reference (No 2 of 1982) [1984] QB 624 .... 4.035
Attorney General's Reference (No 2 of 1999), Re [2000] QB 796 .... 4.065, 4.066
August Investments Pty Ltd v Poiseidon Ltd and Samin Ltd
[1971] 2 SASR 71 .... 10.016
Austin Securities v Northgate [1969] 1 WLR 529 .... 25.174
Australia Securities Commission v Multiple Sclerosis Society of Tasmania
[1993] 10 ACSR 489 .... 3.090
Australian Consolidated Press Ltd v Morgan (1965) 112 CLR 483 .... 6.101
Australian Securities Commission v AS Nominees Ltd (1995) 133 ALR 1,
(1995) 13 ACLC 1822 .... 13.063–13.065
Autodata v Gibbons (13 July 2000, unreported), SC (NSW) 9.066
Automatic Bottle Makers Ltd, Re [1926] Ch 412 .... 18.089
Automatic Self-Cleansing Filter Syndicate Co Ltd v Cunningham
[1906] 2 Ch 34 .... 13.0133, 13.135
Automobile Association (Canterbury) Inc v Australasian Secured
Deposits Ltd [1973] 1 NZLR 417 .... 19.044
AV Sorge & Co Ltd, Re [1986] BCLC 490 .... 25.167
Aveling Barford Ltd v Perion Ltd [1989] BCLC 626, (1989) 5 BCC 677
.... 7.076, 10.098, 10.101
Avoca Capital Holdings, Re [2005] IEHC 302 .... 11.071, 13.082
AWA Ltd v Daniels (1992) 10 ACLC 933 .... 13.036
AWA Ltd v Daniels [1995] 16 ACSR 607 .... 15.087
Ayerst v C & K (Construction) Ltd [1974] 1 All ER 676 .... 15.013
Ayre v Skesley's Adamant Cement Co Ltd (1904) 20 TLR 587 .... 4.005

B

B v DPP [1997] 2 ILRM 118 .... 28.038
Babanaft International Co SA v Bassatne [1989] WLR 232 .... 25.047
Badgerhill Properties Ltd v Cottrell [1991] BCLC 805 ....7.011–7.012, 7.041
Bahaia and San Francisco Railway Co, Re (1868) LR 3 QB 584 .... 8.024, 8.048
Bailey and Leetham's Case (1869) LR 8 Eq 94 .... 25.169
Bailey Hay, Re [1971] WLR 1352 .... 10.074
Bailey v New South Wales Medical Defence Union Ltd (1996) 18 ACSR 521
.... 3.093, 3.100–3.102
Baillie v Oriental Telephone and Electric Co Ltd [1915] 1 Ch 503,
[1914–15] All ER Rep 1420 .... 11.143, 14.052
Bain v Fothergill (1874) LR 7 HL 158 .... 8.037
Bairstow v Queens Moat Houses plc [2001] EWCA Civ 712,
[2001] 2 BCLC 531 .... 10.103–10.104, 15.089
Baker v Jones [1916] 2 AC 15 .... 1.051
Balbradagh, Re [2009] 1 IR 597 .... 23.059
Balgooley Distillery Co, Re (1886) 17 LR Ir 239 .... 7.088, 11.122

Balkanbank v Taher (19 January 1995, unreported) SC 11.098
....11.119, 11.137
Balkis Consolidated Co v Tomkinson [1893] AC 396 ....8.048
Ball v Metal Industries Ltd [1957] SLT 124 ....14.022
Ballymitty Supplies Stores Ltd, Re [2011] IEHC 471 ....25.061
Baltic Real Estate Ltd (No 1), Re [1993] BCLC 498 ....11.046–11.049
Bamford v Bamford [1969] 2 WLR 1107 ....8.052
Bamford v Bamford [1970] 1 Ch 212 ....13.141, 14.108
Banco Exterior Internaçional v Mann [1995] 1 All ER 936 ....5.015
Banfi Ltd v Moran [2006] IEHC 257 .... 8.024, 9.044, 9.053, 11.044
Bank of Baroda v Panessar [1986] 3 All ER 751 ....20.009, 20.018
Bank of Credit and Commerce International SA (No 2)
[1992] BCLC 579 ....24.016
Bank of Credit and Commerce International SA (No 5), Re
[1994] 1 BCLC 429 ....23.040
Bank of Credit and Commerce International SA (No 8), Re
[1997] 4 All ER 568 ....25.150–25.153
Bank of Credit and Commerce International SA, Re [1992] BCC 83 ....24.017
Bank of Credit and Commerce International SA, Re [1993] BCC 787 ....24.069
Bank of Cyprus (London) Ltd v Gill [1980] 2 Lloyds' Rep 51 ....20.057
Bank of Hindustan, China and Japan, Re; Higg's Case
(1865) 2 H & M 657 ....21.071
Bank of Ireland Finance Ltd v DJ Daly Ltd [1978] IR 79 ....19.029
Bank of Ireland Finance Ltd v Rockfield Ltd [1979] IR 21 ....7.036, 7.082
.... 10.053–10.054, 10.057, 10.080, 16.107
Bank of Ireland v McCabe (19 December 1994) SC 5.015
Bank of Ireland v North City Providers Ltd (1953–1954) Ir Jur Rep 16 ....6.011
Bank of Ireland v Smyth [1993] 2 IR 102 ....5.015
Bank of Syria, Re (1901) 1 Ch 115 ....14.113
Banner Lane Realisations v Berisford [1997] 1 BCLC 380 ....18.038
Banque Brussels Lambert SA v Australian National Industries Ltd
(1989) 21 NSWLR 502 ....5.017
Banque de I'Indochine et de Suez SA v Euroseas Group Finance Co Ltd
[1981] 3 All ER 198 ....5.081, 7.012
Barakot Ltd v Epiette Ltd [1997] 1 BCLC 303 ....6.005
Barber & Nicholls Ltd v R & G Associates (London) Ltd (1981) 132
NLJ 1076 ....5.081
Barber v Burke [1980] ILRM 186 ....19.069
Barclays Bank v O'Brien [1993] 4 All ER 417 ....5.015
Barclays Bank Ltd v TOSG Trust Fund Ltd [1984] BCLC 1 ....25.141
Barclays Bank plc v British & Commonwealth Holdings plc
[1996] 1 BCLC 1 .... 7.073, 7.076, 10.014, 10.064–10.065
Barclays Bank plc v British & Commonwealth Holdings plc
[1996] 1 WLR 1, [1995] BCC 1059 ....21.021
Barclays Bank plc v Homan [1993] BCLC 680 ....22.010
Barclays Bank plc v Stuart Landon Ltd [2001] 2 BCLC 316 ....19.099

Barclays Mercantile Business Finance Ltd v Sibec Development Ltd [1993] BCLC 1077 .... 22.059
Barings plc (No 5), Re; Secretary of State for Trade and Industry v Baker (No 5) [1999] 1 BCLC 433 .... 15.043, 15.053 .... 15.079, 28.115, 28.118–28.120
Barings plc, Re; Secretary of State for Trade and Industry v Baker [1999] BCC 960 .... 28.203
Barker (George) (Transport) Ltd v Enyon [1974] 1 WLR 462 .... 19.025
Barker (SM) Ltd, Re [1950] IR 123 .... 7.078, 15.150
Barlow Clowes International Ltd v Vaughan [1992] BCLC 1910 .... 25.149
Barnard, Re [1932] 1 Ch 272 .... 1.026
Barned's Banking Co, Re (1867) LR 3 Ch 105 .... 8.010
Barnett v Hyndman (1840) 3 Ir LR 109 .... 5.016
Barnett, Hoares & Co v South London Tramways Co (1887) 18 QBD 815 .... 13.123, 15.152
Barrett Apartments Ltd, Re (15 July 1983, unreported) HC 19.030
Barrett v Duckett [1995] 1 BCLC 243 .... 11.115
Barron v Potter [1914] 1 Ch 895 .... 14.109
Barrowland Ltd, Re [2004] 3 IR 27 .... 26.055
Barry v The Medical Defence Union Ltd [2005] IESC 41 .... 3.090, 3.105
Barton v London and Northwestern Railway (1888) 38 ChD 144 .... 8.024
Barton v Taylor [1886] 11 App Cas 197 .... 14.112
Basic Inc v Levinson 485 US 224 (US SCt) 32.078
Bass Brewers Ltd v Appleby [1997] 2 BCLC 700 .... 1.015
Bath Glass Ltd, Re [1988] BCLC 329 .... 28.169
Battle v Irish Art Promotion Centre Ltd [1968] IR 252 .... 6.066, 23.066
Bay Marine Pty Ltd v Clayton Country Properties Pty Ltd (1986) 8 NSWLR 104 .... 6.067
Bayer AG v Winter [1986] 1 All ER 733 .... 25.041
Bayoil SA, Re [1991] 1 WLR 147 .... 23.080
Bayoil SA, Re [1999] 1 All ER 374 .... 23.079
Bayswater Trading Co Ltd, Re [1970] 1 WLR 343 .... 26.036
Bayworld v McMahon O'Brien Downes [2004] IR 199 .... 4.034, 5.029
BCCI (No 8), Re [1997] 4 All ER 568 .... 18.065
BCON Communications Ltd, Re [2012] IEHC 362 .... 23.077
BDG Roof-Bond Ltd v Douglas [2000] BCC 770 .... 10.074
BDG Roof-Bond Ltd v Douglas [2000] 1 BCLC 401 .... 14.098
Beam Tube Products Ltd, Re [2006] BCC 615 .... 18.049
Beauforte (Jon) (London) Ltd, Re [1953] 1 All ER 634 .... 7.080, 7.119
Beauross Ltd v Kennedy (18 October 1995, unreported) HC 6.039, 6.049, 6.055
Beddoe, Re, Downes v Cottam [1893] 1 Ch 547 .... 11.118
Bede Steam Shipping Co Ltd, Re [1917] 1 Ch 123 .... 9.047, 9.051
Beesly v Hallwood Estates Ltd [1961] Ch 105 .... 7.029
Beeton & Co Ltd, Re [1913] 2 Ch 279 .... 25.187
Belfast Empire Theatre of Varieties Ltd, Re [1963] IR 41 .... 8.074–8.075, 24.004, 25.193
Belfast Tailors' Co-Partnership Ltd, Re [1909] 1 IR 49 .... 23.043, 23.122

Bell Brothers Ltd, Re 7 TLR 689 .... 9.045
Bell Houses Ltd v City Wall Properties Ltd (1966) 1 QB 207, [1966] 2 All ER 674 .... 7.053, 7.094
Bell Lines Ltd, Re [2010] IESC 15 .... 25.188
Bell v Burton (1993) 12 ACSR 325 .... 14.110
Bell v Lever Brothers Ltd [1932] AC 161 .... 4.048, 15.070
Bellerby v Rowland & Marwood's SS Co [1902] 2 Ch 14 .... 8.126
Belmont Finance Corporation Ltd v Williams Furniture Ltd [1980] 1 All ER 393 .... 7.092
Belton v Carlow County Council [1997] 1 IR 172 .... 4.040, 6.004
Benfield Greig Group plc, Re [2000] 2 BCLC 488 .... 9.026, 9.126
Bennets v Board of Fire Commissioners of New South Wales (1967) 87 WN (NSW) 307 .... 15.046
Bentley-Stevens v Jones [1974] 1 WLR 638 .... 11.068, 13.082
Berkley Administration Inc v McClelland [1990] 1 All ER 959 .... 6.014
Berkley v Third Avenue Railway (1926) 50 ALR 599 .... 5.002
Berlai Hestia (NZ) Ltd v Fernyhough [1980] 2 NZLR 150 .... 15.047
Best illustrated by Cane v Jones [1980] 1 WLR 1451 .... 10.074
Bestseller Retail Ltd, Re [2010] IEHC 155 .... 22.128
Betts & Co Ltd v Mcnaghten [1910] Ch 430 .... 14.051
Bhullar v Bhullar [2003] 2 BCLC 241 .... 15.057
Biala PTY v Mallina Holdings Ltd [1993] ACFR 785 .... 11.143
Biba Ltd v Stratford Investments Ltd [1972] 3 All ER 1041 .... 6.080, 6.087, 6.096–6.097
Biosource Technologies Inc v Axis Genetics plc (in administration) [1999] TLR 814 .... 22.061
Birch v Cropper, Re, Bridgewater Navigation Co (1899) 14 App Cas 525 .... 8.098, 8.102, 8.107
Birch v Sullivan [1957] 1 WLR 1247 .... 8.009
Birch v Sullivan [1958] 1 All ER 56 .... 11.133
Birchwell Developments Ltd, Re [2010] IEHC 319 .... 23.006, 23.115, 23.128
Bird Moyer & Co (Ireland) Ltd, Re 98 ILTR 202 .... 6.013
Bird Precision Bellows Ltd, Re [1986] 2 WLR 158, [1984] Ch 409 .... 9.123
Bisgood v Henderson's Transvaal Estate Ltd [1908] 1 Ch 743 .... 3.062
Bishopsgate Investment Management Ltd v Maxwell (No 2) [1993] BCLC 1282 .... 15.053
Bishopsgatc v Maxwell [1992] 2 All ER 856 .... 27.045
Black v Homersham (1878) 4 Ex D 24 .... 8.074
Blake v Attorney General [1982] IR 117 .... 4.070
Blascaod Mór Teoranta v Commissioners of Public Works in Ireland and Minister for the Arts Culture and the Gaéltacht (27 February 1998, unreported) HC 4.070
Blenheim Leisure (Restaurants) Ltd, Re [1999] TLR 603 .... 26.041
Blenheim Leisure (Restaurants) Ltd (No 2), Re [2000] BCC 821 .... 26.042
BLM Group Ltd v Harman (1994) Times, 8 April (CA) 14.055
Bloomberg Developments Ltd, Re; Good v Philips Electrical (Ireland) Ltd [2002] 2 IR 613 .... 26.043

Blue Arrow plc, Re (1987) 3 BCC 618 .... 1.151, 11.035
Blue Metal Industries Ltd v Dilley [1970] AC 827 .... 9.103
Blue Note Enterprises Ltd, Re [2001] 2 BCLC 427 .... 26.042
Bluebird Investments Pty Ltd v Graf (1994) 12 ACLC 724 .... 12.014
Blum v OCP Repartition SA [1988] BCLC 170 .... 5.081
Bluston and Bramley Ltd v Leigh [1950] 2 KB 548 .... 25.056
Bluzwed Metals Ltd v Transworld Metals SA [2001] IEHC 89 .... 23.098
BML Group Ltd v Harman (1994) Times, 8 April 14.030
BNY Corporate Trustee Services Ltd v Eurosail-UK 2007 3BL plc [2011] EWCA 227 .... 23.040
Boarman v Phipps [1966] 3 All ER 721 .... 15.057
Bolands Ltd (in receivership) v Ward [1988] ILRM 382 .... 20.033
Bolton (HL) (Engineering) Ltd v TJ Graham & Sons Ltd [1957] 1 QB 159 .... 4.065
Bolton (HL) (Engineering) Ltd v TJ Graham & Sons Ltd [1972] AC 153 .... 4.065
Bolton, Re [1920] 2 IR 324 .... 24.057
Bond v Barrow Haematite Steel Co [1902] 1 Ch 353 .... 8.074
Bond Worth Ltd, Re [1979] 3 All ER 919 .... 19.074
Bonelli's Telegraph Co, Re; Collie's Claim (1871) LR 12 EQ 246 .... 14.110
Bonsor v Musician's Union [1956] AC 101 .... 4.014
Borden (UK) Ltd v Scottish Timber Products Ltd [1979] 3 All ER 961 .... 19.077
Borden (UK) Ltd v Scottish Timber Products Ltd [1981] Ch 35 .... 19.067, 19.081
Borland's Trustee v Steel Brothers & Co Ltd [1901] 1 Ch 279 .... 8.039, 9.019, 9.088
Borough Commercial and Building Society, Re [1893] 2 Ch 242 .... 31.022
Boulting v Association of Cinematography, Television and Allied Technicians [1963] 2 QB 606 .... 15.037–15.038
Bovale Developments Ltd, Re; Director of Corporate Enforcement v Bailey and Bailey [2008] 2 ILRM 13 .... 28.171
Bovey Hotel Ventures Ltd, Re (31 July 1980, unreported) HC (Eng & Wales) 11.089
Bowes v Hope Life Insurance and Guarantee Co (1865) 11 HL 389 .... 23.073
Bowlby v Bell (1846) 3 CB 284 .... 9.006
Bowman v Secular Society Ltd [1917] AC 406 ......3.013, 4.005, 4.015–4.017, 23.106
Boxco Ltd, Re [1970] Ch 442 .... 26.058
Boyd, Re [1885–1886] 15 LR Ir 521 .... 25.094
Boyle and Boyle v McGilloway [2006] IEHC 37 .... 6.015
BPB Industries and British Gypsum (Case T- 65/89) [1993] ECR II-442 .... 5.064
Bradbury v Morgan (1862) 1 H & C 249 .... 5.015
Bradford Banking Co v Briggs (1886) 12 App Cas 29 .... 3.095, 8.122
Bradford Investments (No 2), Re [1991] BCC 379 .... 29.055
Bradford Old Bank v Sutcliffe [1918] 2 KB 833 .... 5.015
Bradman v Trinity Estates plc [1989] BCLC 757 .... 14.048
Brady v Brady (1988) BCC 390 .... 10.065
Brady v Brady [1988] BCLC 20 .... 7.073, 7.076
Braemar Investments Ltd, Re [1988] BCLC 556 .... 19.098

Braemar Investments Ltd, Re [1989] Ch 54 ....19.090, 19.099
Bramblevale Ltd, Re [1970] Ch 128 ....6.083
Brandao v Barnett (1846) 12 Cl & Fin 787 ....19.027
Brasserie du Pecheur SA v Germany (Factortame) (C46/93)
[1996] 1 CMLR 889 ....4.010, 4.014
Bratton Seymour Service Co Ltd v Oxborough [1992] BCLC 693 ....3.090, 3.093
Bray Travel and Bray Travel (Holdings) Ltd, Re (13 July 1981,
unreported) SC 5.051, 5.054, 12.049
Bray v Ford [1896] AC 44, [1895–9] All ER Rep 1009 ....15.056
Brazilian Rubber Plantations & Estates Ltd, Re [1911] 1 Ch 425 ....15.053, 15.078
Breckenridge Speedway Ltd 64 DLR 488 ....7.094
Breckland Group Holdings Ltd v London and Suffolk Properties Ltd
[1989] BCLC 100 ....13.0133
Bredin (Gerry) Hardware Ltd, Re [2011] IEHC 442 ....25.084
Brenes & Co v Downie (1914) SC 97 ....15.083
Brenfield Squash Racquets Club Ltd [1996] 2 BCLC 184 ....11.082
Brett v Niall Collins Ltd (in receivership) and Oyster
Investments Ltd [1995] ELR 69 ....20.034
Brian (JD) Ltd, Re [2011] IEHC 113, [2011] IEHC 383 ....18.056, 18.068
.... 18.070, 18.094, 18.095–18.096
.... 18.105–18.109, 19.041, 25.114
Briggs v James Hardie & Co Pty Ltd [1989] 16 NSWLR 549 ....5.004
Briggs v Spaulding 141 US 132 ....15.053
Brightlife Ltd, Re [1986] BCLC 418 ....18.044, 18.065, 18.106
Brightlife Ltd, Re [1986] 3 All ER 673 ....19.065
Brightlife Ltd, Re [1987] Ch 200 ....18.096, 18.107
Brightwater v Allen & Robert Walters Ltd [2005] IEHC 155 ....6.083
Brighty v Norton (1862) 122 ER 116 ....20.009
Brinsmead (Thomas Edward) & Sons Ltd, Re [1897] 1 Ch 45 ....23.106
Bristol and West Building Society v Mothew [1996] 4 All ER 698 ....15.021, 15.031
British Airways Board v Parish [1979] 2 Lloyd's Rep 361 ....5.081–5.082
British America Nickel Corporation Ltd v MJ O'Brien Ltd [1927] AC 369 ....21.054
British and Commonwealth Holdings plc (No 3), Re [1992] BCLC 322 ....22.154
British and Commonwealth Holdings plc v Barclays Bank plc
[1986] BCLC 1 ....10.061
British and Commonwealth Holdings plc v Spicer & Oppenheim
[1993] BCLC 168 ....22.094
British Association of Glass Bottle Manufacturers (Ltd) v
Nettlefold (1911) TLR 527 ....4.013
British Bank of the Middle East v Sun Life Assurance Co of
Canada [1985] BCLC 78 ....7.107
British Eagle International Airlines Ltd v Compagnie Nationale Air France
[1975] 2 All ER 390 ....25.151, 25.157
British India Steam Navigation Co v IRC (1881) 7 QBD 165 ....7.018, 18.018
....................18.019
British Midland Tool Ltd v Midland International Tooling
[2003] 2 BCLC 523 ....15.061

British Murac Syndicate Ltd v Alperton Rubber Co Ltd [1915] 2 Ch 186 .... 3.057
British Racing Drivers' Club Ltd v Hextall Erskine & Co (a firm)
[1996] 3 All ER 667 ....16.023, 16.042, 16.048, 16.054, 20.059
British Thomson-Houston Co v Sterling Accessories Ltd [1924] 2 Ch 33 .... 4.049
British Union for the Abolition of Vivisection, Re [1995] 2 BCLC 1 .... 14.027
Broadnet Ireland Ltd v Office of the Director of Telecommunications
Regulation and Eircom plc [2000] 3 IR 281 .... 6.032, 6.052
Broderip v Salomon [1895] 2 Ch 323 .... 4.027
Brook's Wharf and Bull Ltd v Goodman Brothers [1937] 1 KB 534 .... 5.082
Brook's Wharf Ltd v Goodman Brothers [1937] 1 KB 534 .... 5.079
Brosnan v Sommerville [2006] IEHC 329 .... 28.212
Brosnan v Sommerville [2007] 4 IR 135 .... 17.006–17.010
Brown & Grogory Ltd, Re [1904] 1 Ch 827 .... 18.023
Brown Bayley's Steel Works Ltd, Re [1904–05] 21 TLR 374 .... 26.062
Brown v British Abrasive Wheel Co [1919] 1 Ch 290 .... 3.081, 3.084
Browne v La Trinidad (1877) 37 Ch D 1 .... 3.095, 3.099
Brumark Investments Ltd, Re; Commissioner of Inland Revenue
v Agnew [2000] 1 BCLC 354 .... 18.053
Brumark Investments Ltd, Re; Commissioner of Inland Revenue
v Agnew [2001] 2 BCLC 188, [2001] UKPC 28 .... 18.045, 18.053–18.055
Brunninghausen v Glavanics (1999) 32 ACSR 294 .... 15.005, 15.019, 15.023
Bryanston Finance Ltd v De Vries (No 2) [1976] 1 Ch 63 .... 23.084
BTR plc, Re [1999] 2 BCLC 675 .... 21.036, 21.050
Buchan v Secretary of State for Employment [1997] BCC 145 .... 4.077
Buchanan Ltd v McVey [1954] IR 89 .... 3.085, 7.077, 11.122
.... 11.125, 14.093, 14.096
Buckingham v Francis [1986] 2 All ER 738 .... 9.119
Bucks Constabulary Widows' and Orphans' Fund Friendly
Society (No 2), Re [1979] 1 WLR 936 .... 1.051
Bugle Press Ltd, Re [1960] 3 All ER 791, [1961] 1 Ch 270 .... 5.034, 9.099–9.103
Bula Ltd v Crowley [1997] IEHC 72 .... 20.042
Bula Ltd v Crowley [2002] IEHC 4 .... 16.040, 20.040
Bula Ltd v Crowley (No 3) [2003] 1 IR 396 .... 20.042
Bula Ltd v Crowley [2009] IESC 35 .... 20.042
Bula Ltd v Tara Mines Ltd [1987] IR 494 .... 6.016, 6.034, 6.039, 6.047, 6.054
Bula Ltd v Tara Mines Ltd [1987] IR 85 .... 4.071
Bula Ltd v Tara Mines Ltd (26 March 1998, unreported) SC
.... 6.030, 6.035, 6.050
Bula Ltd, Re [1990] 1 IR 440 .... 23.044, 23.063, 23.072, 23.073, 23.078
Bula Ltd, Re (20 June 2002, unreported) HC 20.002, 20.050–20.051, 20.057
Bula Ltd, Re [2003] 2 IR 431 .... 20.051
Bumper Development Corporation v Commissioner of the Metropolis
[1991] 4 All ER 638 .... 4.025
Bunbury Foods Pty Ltd v National Bank of Australasia Ltd
(1984) 51 ALR 609 .... 20.009
Burgess (Thomas), Re [1988] 23 LR Ir 5 .... 25.181
Burgess v Auger; Burgess v Vansstock Ltd [1998] 2 BCLC 478 .... 20.064

Burgess v Purchase & Sons (Farms) Ltd [1983] 1 Ch 216 ....9.126–9.128
Burke Clancy & Co Ltd, Re (23 May 1974, unreported) HC 7.113, 13.140, 15.056
Burkinshaw v Nicholls (1878) 3 App Cas 1004 ....8.048
Burland v Earle [1902] AC 83 .... 8.073, 11.093, 11.129, 11.137, 11.141
Burlinson v Hall (1884) 12 QBD 347 ....18.032
Burn v New London & South Wales Coal Co [1908] WN 209 ....17.010
Burren Springs Ltd, Re [2011] IEHC 480 ....23.043, 23.065
Burrough v Cranston (1840) 2 Ir Eq R 203 ....18.033
Burton v Deakin [1977] 1 All ER 631 ....23.125
Burton v Palmer [1980] 2 NSWLR 878 ....10.064
Bushell v Faith [1970] AC 1099, [1969] 1 All ER 1002 ....3.053, 3.114
....3.127, 11.093, 12.013, 13.079, 14.062, 14.082
Business City Express Ltd, Re [1997] BCC 826 ....22.158, 24.069
Business Communications Ltd v Baxter and Parsons (21 July 1995,
unreported) HC 28.006, 28.062–28.067, 28.082
.... 28.097, 28.105, 28.111, 28.138
.... 28.165, 28.168, 28.173–28.177
Butcher v Stead (1875) LR 7 HL 839 ....25.089
Butler v Broadhead [1974] 2 All ER 401 ....25.177
Butlers Engineering Ltd, Re (1 March 1996, unreported) HC, ...22.065
Byblos Bank SAL v Al–Khudhairy [1987] BCLC 232 ....20.006, 20.013
Byrne v Allied Irish Banks Ltd [1978] IR 446 ....19.061
Byrne v Byrne [2005] IEHC 55 ....3.125
Byrne v Ireland [1972] IR 241 ....1.061, 4.017
Byrne v Judge Scally and Dublin Corporation [2000] IEHC 72 ....4.075
Byrne v Shelbourne FC Ltd [1984] IEHC 11 ....15.012

C

Cade (JE) & Son Ltd, Re [1992] BCLC 213 ....11.014
Cafolla v Ireland [1986] ILRM 177 ....4.071
Cahill v Grimes [2002] IESC 12 ....13.052
Cahill v Sutton [1980] IR 269 ....4.071–4.072
Caldwell v Mahon [2007] 3 IR 542 ....4.068
Caldwell v Sumpters [1972] Ch 478 ....19.029
Callao Bis Co, Re (1889) 42 Ch D 169 ....21.068
Calmex Ltd, Re; Calmex Ltd v C Lila Ltd [1989] 1 All ER 485 ....19.093
Cambridge Group plc, Re (1998) Irish Times, 10 February 14.026
Camburn Petroleum Products Ltd, Re [1979] 3 All ER 297 ....23.043
Camburn Products Ltd, Re [1980] 1 WLR 86 ....23.073
Campbell Seafoods Ltd v Brodene Gram A/S (21 July 1994,
unreported) HC 6.034, 6.047
Campbell v Edwards [1976] 1 WLR 403 ....9.126
Campbell v Paddington Corporation [1911] 1 KB 869 ....4.051
Campbell v Rofe [1933] AC 91 ....8.099
Campus Oil Ltd v Minister for Industry and Energy (No 2)
[1983] IR 88 .... 23.084, 25.047, 25.051
Canadian Aero Services Ltd v O'Malley [1973] 40 DLR 371 ....15.064, 15.068

Canadian Aero Services Ltd v O'Malley [1974] SCR 592 .... 15.063
Canadian Dredge & Dock Co Ltd v R (1985) 19 DLR (4d) 314 .... 4.065, 4.065
Canadian Land Reclaiming and Colonizing Co, Re (1880) 14 Ch D 660 .... 13.046
Candler v Crane Christmas [1951] 1 All ER 426 .... 17.329
Cane v Jones [1981] 1 All ER 533 .... 3.085, 3.110, 14.094
Cannon v Trask (1875) 20 Eq 669 .... 14.061
Caparo Industries plc v Dickman [1990] 1 All ER 568 .... 17.329–17.333
Cape Breton Co, Re [1885] 29 Ch D 795 .... 15.164, 15.165
Capital Auto Group Ltd, Re; Foster v Swords and Chambers [2005] IEHC 434 .... 28.112
Capital Cameras Ltd v Harold Lines Ltd [1991] BCLC 884 .... 22.063
Capital Finance Co Ltd v Stokes [1968] 1 All ER 573, [1968] 3 All ER 625 .... 19.057
Capital Fire Insurance Association, Re (1883) 24 Ch D 408 .... 8.017, 17.309
Capital Prime Properties plc v Worthgate Ltd [2000] BCC 525 .... 25.062
Capper's case (1868) LR 3 458 .... 8.009
Car Replacements Ltd, Re (11 May 1992, unreported) HC 25.179
Car Replacements Ltd, Re (15 December 1999, unreported) HC 24.053
Caratal (New) Mines Ltd, Re [1902] 2 Ch 498 .... 14.086
Caratti Holding Co Party Ltd v Zampatti [1975] WAR 183 .... 25.132
Cardiff Savings Bank (the Marquis of Bute's case), Re [1892] 2 Ch 100 .... 15.081
Cardile v LED Builders Pty Ltd (1999) 162 ALR 294 .... 25.049
Careca Investments Ltd; Ferris v Farrell and Coady [2005] IEHC 62 .... 28.116
Caribbean Co, Re (1875) 10 Ch App 614 .... 8.049
Caribbean Producers (Yam Importers) Ltd [1966] Ch 331 .... 25.054
Carlen v Drury (1812) 1 V & B 154 .... 11.101
Carr v British International Helicopters Ltd [1994] 2 BCLC 47 .... 22.061
Carrigaline Community TV v Minister for Transport Energy and Communications (10 November 1995, unreported) HC 4.069
Carroll Group Distributors Ltd v G&JF Bourke Ltd [1990] ILRM 285 .... 19.009, 19.012, 19.080, 19.082
Carroll Industries plc v Ó Cualacháin [1988] IR 705 .... 17.037
Carruth v ICI Ltd [1937] AC 707 .... 8.040
Carter's Case 31 Ch D 496 .... 13.004
Carvill v Irish Industrial Bank Ltd [1968] IR 325 .... 13.080
Carway v The Attorney General (3 July 1996, unreported) HC 28.072
CAS (Nominees) Ltd v Nottingham Forest plc [2001] 1 All ER 954 .... 6.063–6.064
Casali v Crisp (3 October 2001) SC (NSW) 860 .... 26.028
Casey v Bentley [1902] 1 IR 376 .... 8.032, 9.019, 9.065
Casey v Irish Intercontinental Bank Ltd [1979] IR 364 .... 20.050, 20.052
Casey, Re (21 July 1986, unreported) HC 25.153
Casson Beckman & Partners v Papi [1991] BCLC 299 .... 20.048
Castell and Brown Ltd, Re [1898] 1 Ch 315 .... 18.080
Castle Brand Ltd (In liq), Re (25 March 1985, unreported) HC 20.034
Castle Brand Ltd, Re [1990] ILRM 97 .... 25.171
Castleburn Ltd, Re [1991] BCLC 89 .... 9.090, 9.130

Castlemahon Poultry Products Ltd, Re [1987] ILRM 222 ....25.185
Caudron v Air Zaire [1986] ILRM 10 ....25.047, 25.049
Cavan Crystal Glass Ltd, Re [1998] 3 IR 570 ....22.012–22.015
....22.047–22.050, 22.067
Cavan Crystal Group Ltd, Re (26 April 1996, unreported) HC
....28.066, 28.075, 28.088, 28.093, 28.108, 28.131
Cavendish-Bentinck v Fenn [1887] 12 AC 652 ....15.149
Cawley & Co, Re [1888] 42 Ch 209 ....14.112
CB Readymix Ltd, Re; Cahill v Grimes [2001] IEHC 226 ....28.182–28.184
CB Readymix Ltd, Re; Cahill v Grimes [2002] 1 IR 372
....28.155, 28.166, 28.170, 28.180, 28.184, 28.198, 28.202
Cedarlease Ltd, Re [2005] IEHC 67 ....24.067
Cedarwood Productions Ltd, Re [2001] TLR 450 ....28.151
CEM Connections Ltd, Re [2000] BCC 917 ....13.027, 28.078, 28.155
Central Dublin Development Association v The Attorney General
(1969) 109 ILTR 69 ....8.042
Central Trust Investment Society, Re (1982) Irish Times, 31 August 25.046
Centrebind Ltd, Re [1966] 3 All ER 889 ....23.028, 24.046
Centros (Case C-208/00) [1999] ECR I-1459 ....29.152
Centrum Products Ltd, Re [2009] IEHC 592 ....23.029, 23.030
Century Communications Ltd, Re (1996) Irish Times, 12 October 28.093
CH (Ireland) Inc (in liq) v Credit Suisse Canada [1999] 4 IR 542
....10.051, 10.057–10.059
CHA Ltd, Re [1999] 1 IR 437 ....25.166, 25.169, 25.178
Chaigley Farms Ltd v Crawford, Kaye & Greyshire Ltd [1996] BCC 957 ....19.075
Chalk v Kahn [2000] 2 BCLC 361 ....18.053
Champion Publications Ltd, Re (4 June 1991, unreported) HC 9.024, 9.085
Chan v Zacharia (1984) 154 CLR 178 ....15.067
Chancery plc, Re [1991] BCLC 712 ....22.048
Chandler v Cape plc [2011] EWHC 951 ....12.051
Chandler v Cape plc [2012] EWCA Civ 525 ....12.051
Chantery Martin & Co v Martin [1953] 2 All ER 691, [1953] 2 QB 286 ....20.048
Chantry House Developments plc, Re [1990] BCLC 813 ....19.090, 19.099
Charge Card Services Ltd, Re [1986] 3 All ER 289 ....18.032, 18.066
Charge Card Services Ltd, Re [1987] BCLC 17 ....25.153
Charitable Corporation v Sutton (1742) 2 Atk 400 ....15.075
Charles (LH) & Co Ltd, Re [1935] WN 15 ....19.098–19.099
Charnley Davies Ltd, Re [1988] BCLC 243 ....22.092
Charnley Davies Ltd (No 2), Re [1990] BCLC 760 ....20.051
Charterbridge Corp Ltd v Lloyds Bank Ltd [1969] 2 All ER 1185,
[1970] Ch 407 ....7.065, 7.074, 15.016, 16.085
Charterhouse Investment Trust Ltd v Tempest Diesels Ltd
[1986] BCLC 1 ....10.059, 10.064, 10.080
Chartmore Ltd, Re [1990] BCLC 673 ....28.182, 28.202
Chelsea Man plc v Chelsea Girl Ltd [1988] FSR 217 ....6.083
Chemco Leasing SPA v Rediffusion [1987] FTLR 201 ....5.017
Chemical Bank v McCormack [1983] ILRM 350 ....28.081

Chequepoint SARL v McClelland [1997] 1 BCLC 117 .... 6.028
Chesterfield Catering Co Ltd, Re [1976] 3 All ER 294 .... 23.045
Chestvale Properties Ltd v Glackin [1993] 3 IR 35 .... 4.069, 27.003
.... 27.020, 27.028–27.030, 27.038–27.041
Chestvale Properties Ltd, Re [1992] ILRM 221 .... 25.122
Chez Nico (Restaurants) Ltd, Re [1992] BCLC 192 .... 15.019, 15.021
Chida Mines Ltd v Anderson (1905) 22 TLR 27 .... 8.021
Chief Commissioner of Stamp Duties v Buckle (1998) 151 ALR 1 .... 20.070
Child v Hudson's Bay Co (1723) 2 P Wms 207 .... 8.036
Chipboard Products Ltd, Re (27 February 1997, unreported) HC 25.005, 25.163
Chisholm (Ian) Textiles Ltd v Griffiths [1994] BCC 96 .... 19.078
Choppington Collieries v Johnson [1944] 1 All ER 762 .... 14.051
Church of England Building Society v Piskor [1954] 1 Ch 553,
[1954] 2 All ER 85 .... 19.057
Church, Re [2010] IEHC 113 .... 26.020
Churchill Hotel (Plymouth) Ltd, Re [1988] BCLC 341 .... 28.162, 28.182
CIBC Mortgages v Pitt [1993] 4 All ER 433 .... 5.015
Cimex Tissues Ltd, Re [1995] 1 BCLC 409 .... 18.037, 18.068
Ciro Citterio Menswear plc, Re [2002] EWHC 293 (Ch),
[2002] 2 All ER 717 .... 16.111
Cisti Gugan Barra Teoranta, Re [2008] IEHC 251 .... 22.147, 22.156
Citco Banking Corp NV v Pusser's Ltd [2007] BCC 205 .... 3.067, 3.075, 3.079
Citizens' Theatre Ltd, Re (1948) SC 14 .... 14.065
City & Suburban Pty Ltd v Smith [1998] Federal Court of Australia,
9 July 1998 .... 24.015, 24.024
City Car Sales Ltd, Re [1995] ILRM 221 .... 20.044
City Equitable Fire Insurance Co Ltd, Re [1925] Ch 407
.... 15.001, 15.053, 15.076, 17.327, 28.116
City of Edinburge Council [2010] CSOH 20 .... 26.042
City of Westminister Assurance Company Ltd v Registrar of Companies
(28 June 1996, unreported) HC, Eng 26.037
City View Press v An Comhairle Oiliúna [1980] IR 381 .... 27.007
Citywide Leisure Ltd v IBRC Ltd [2012] IEHC 220 .... 6.048
Civica Investments Ltd, Re [1983] BCLC 456 .... 28.200
Civil Service Co-Operative Society Ltd v Chapman (1914) TLR 376 .... 5.081
CL Nye Ltd, Re [1970] 3 All ER 1061 .... 19.013
Cladrose Ltd, Re [1990] BCLC 204 .... 28.179, 28.182–28.183
Clandown Ltd v Davis [1994] 2 ILRM 536 .... 23.081
Clare Textiles Ltd, Re (1 February 1993, unreported) HC 18.032
Clare Textiles Ltd, Re [1993] 2 IR 213 .... 22.026, 22.116, 22.134, 22.166
Clarete Ltd, Re; Spain v McCann [1978] ILRM 215
.... 19.006, 19.008, 19.092, 19.094
Clark v Cutland [2003] 4 All ER 733 .... 7.122
Clark v Workman [1920] 1 IR 107 .... 3.093, 8.039, 9.045, 13.134
.... 14.125, 15.030, 15.036–15.037
Clarke (John) & Co Ltd, Re [1912] IR 24 .... 21.024
Clarkes of Ranelagh Ltd and Parmer Products Ltd, Re [2004] IEHC 320 .... 26.018

Clasper Group Services Ltd, Re [1989] BCLC 143 ....25.102–25.104
Clawhammer Ltd, Re; Director of Corporate Enforcement v McDonnell and Endicott [2005] 1 IR 503 ....28.195
Clemens v Clemens Brothers Ltd [1976] 2 All ER 268 ....3.081, 8.052
Cleve v Financial Corporation (1873) LR 16 Eq 363 ....21.070
Cleveland Trust plc, Re [1991] BCLC 424 ....8.024
Clough Mill Ltd v Martin [1984] 3 All ER 982 ....19.083
Club Tivoli Ltd, Re; Foster v Davis and May [2005] IEHC 468 ....28.122
Clubman Shirts Ltd, Re [1983] ILRM 323, [1991] ILRM 43 ....9.118–9.120, 9.132, 11.019–11.021, 11.027, 11.080, 17.010
CMC (Ireland) Ltd, Re; Carolan and Cosgrave v Fennell [2005] IEHC 340 ....28.139, 28.140
CMC (Ireland) Ltd, Re; Fennell v Carolan [2005] IEHC 59 ....28.102, 28.130
CMC Medical Operations Ltd v VHI [2012] IEHC 232 ....6.048
CMS Dolphin Ltd v Simonet [2001] 2 BCLC 704 ....15.067
CMS Dolphin Ltd v Simonet [2002] BCC 600 ....15.065
Coalport Building Company Ltd v Castle Contracts (Ireland) Ltd [2004] IEHC 6 ....23.088
Coalport China Co, Re [1895] 2 Ch 404 ....9.057
Coates v Lewes (1808) 1 Camp 444 ....5.028
Cockburn v Newbridge Sanitary Steam Laundry Co [1915] 1 IR 237 ....11.125
Cognotec Ltd, Re [2010] IEHC 309 ....10.056, 10.073, 20.032
Cohen v Selby [2001] 1 BCLC 176 ....15.077
Coleman Taymar Ltd v Oakes [2001] 2 BCLC 749 ....15.088–15.090
Coleman v Myers [1977] 2 NZLR 225 ....8.091, 15.019–15.022
Coles v Trecothick (1804) 9 VES 234 ....7.011
Colgan v Colgan & Colgan (22 July 1993, unreported) HC 9.118, 9.122, 9.132, 11.006, 11.028, 11.080
Collier v Mason (1858) 25 Beav 200 ....9.126
Colman v Myers [1977] 2 NZRL 225 ....15.019
Colonia Reinsurance (Ireland) Ltd, Re [2005] IEHC 115 ....21.055, 21.058
Colonial Bank v Whinney (1886) 11 App Cas 426 ....8.038
Colonial Trusts Corp, Re (1879) 15 Ch D 465 ....18.099
Colthurst and Tenips Ltd v La Touche Colthurst and Colthurst [2000] IEHC 14 ....6.008, 14.039
Coltman, Re [1881] 19 Ch D 64 ....7.094
Columbian Fireproofing Co Ltd, Re [1910] 2 Ch 120 ....25.117
Comet Food Machinery Company Ltd, Re [1999] 1 IR 485 ....25.028
Comhlucht Páipear Ríomhaireachta Teo v Údarás na Gaeltachta [1990] ILRM 266 ....6.034, 6.037–6.038
Comhlucht Páipear Ríomhaireachta Teo v Údarás na Gaeltachta [1991] IR 320 ....25.169
Commercial and Industrial Insulations Ltd, Re [1986] BCLC 191 ....23.112
Commercial Buildings Co of Dublin, Re [1938] IR 477 ....1.063
Commercial Solvents Joined Cases 6 and 7/73 [1974] ECR 254 ....5.064
Commissioner of Taxation v Linter Textiles Australia Ltd [2003] FCAFC 63 (14 April 2003) 15.013, 25.015

Commissioners of Inland Revenue v Adam & Partners Ltd
[2001] 1 BCLC 222 .... 21.014
Compania de Electricidad de la Provencia de Buenos Aires Ltd, Re
[1980] Ch 146 .... 8.075–8.076
Compania Merabello San Nicolas SA, Re [1972] 3 All ER 448,
[1973] Ch 75 .... 23.036
Company (No 0012209 of 1991), Re [1992] BCLC 865 .... 23.081
Company (No 001448 of 1989), Re [1989] BCLC 715 .... 23.081
Company (No 001992 of 1988), Re [1989] BCLC 9 .... 22.059
Company (No 002015 of 1995), Re [1997] 2 BCLC 1 .... 11.037
Company (No 002015 of 1996), Re [1997] 2 BCLC 1 .... 11.041
Company (No 002180 of 1996), Re [1996] 2 BCLC 409 .... 24.016
Company (No 002567 of 1982), Re [1983] 1 WLR 927 .... 9.132
Company (No 003160 of 1986), Re [1986] BCLC 391 .... 8.006, 11.046
Company (No 0032314) of 1992, Re; Duckwari plc v
Offerventure Ltd [1995] BCC 89 .... 16.028, 16.048, 16.050
Company (No 00359 of 1987), Re [1987] Ch 210 .... 23.036
Company (No 00477 of 1986), Re [1986] BCLC 376 .... 11.089
Company (No 005009 of 1987), Re 15.110
Company (No 006341 of 1992), Re [1994] 1 BCLC 225 .... 24.027
Company (No 006798 of 1995), Re [1996] 1 WLR 491 .... 23.089
Company (No 00709 of 1992), Re [1999] 2 BCLC 739 .... 11.039
Company (No 007356 of 1998) (ITC Infotech Ltd), Re [2000] BCC 214 .... 23.089
Company (No 00789 of 1987), Re, ex p Shooter [1990] BCLC 384 .... 11.021
Company (No 008725 of 1991), Re [1992] BCLC 633 .... 23.081
Company (No 00962 of 1991), Re, ex p Electrical Engineering Contracts
(London) Ltd [1992] BCLC 248 .... 23.081
Company, Re (1985) [1985] BCLC 333 .... 5.004
Company, Re , (1997) Irish Times, 18 November 14.029
Company, Re [1980] Ch 138 .... 13.007
Company, Re [1983] 1 WLR 927 .... 11.054
Company, Re [1983] 2 All ER 36 .... 11.052
Company, Re [1985] BCLC 333 .... 5.005, 5.067
Company, Re [1985] BCLC 37 .... 23.076
Company, Re [1986] BCLC 127 .... 23.081
Company, Re [1986] BCLC 362 .... 11.054
Company, Re [1986] BCLC 391 .... 8.032
Company, Re [1987] BCLC 562 .... 11.053
Company, Re [1987] BCLC 563 .... 11.054
Company, Re [1987] BCLC 80 .... 11.054
Company, Re [1987] BCLC 94 .... 11.054
Company, Re [1989] BCLC 365 .... 11.054
Company, Re [1991] BCLC 561 .... 23.077
Company, Re [1995] 1 BCLC 459 .... 23.029–23.030
Company, Re [1996] 2 BCLC 192 .... 11.054
Company, Re, ex p F Ltd [1991] BCLC 567 .... 6.067
Company, Re; ex p Holden [1991] BCLC 597 .... 11.053–11.054

Company, Re; ex p Kremer [1989] BCLC 365 ....11.053
Compaq Computers Ltd v Abercorn Group Ltd [1991] BCC 484 ....19.076
Compaq Computers Ltd v Abercorn Group Ltd [1993] BCLC 602 ....19.080
Competition Authority and the Licensed Vintners Association [2009] IEHC 439 ....6.080, 6.083, 6.087
Components Tube Co v Naylor [1900] 2 IR 1 ....8.024, 32.047
Compustore Ltd, Re [2006] IEHC 52 ....25.167
Conachey v Little Chic Knitwear (1985) UD342/85 ....15.073
Conegrade Ltd v Clarke and Clarke [2002] EWHC 2411 (Ch) 16.044
Con-Mech Ltd v Amalgamated Union of Engineering Workers [1973] ICR 620 ....6.101
Connaughton Road Construction Ltd v Laing O'Rourke Ireland Ltd [2009] IEHC 7 ....6.048
Connolly Bros (No 2), Re [1912] 2 Ch 25 ....19.057
Connolly v Seskin Properties Ltd [2012] IEHC 332 ....11.110, 11.117, 11.129
Conrad Hall & Co Ltd [1916] WN 275 ....26.043
Conroy v Corneill and Corneill (7 October 2003, unreported) HC 15.135
Conservative and Unionist Central Office v Burrell [1982] 1 WLR 522 ....1.050
Consolidated Gold Fields of New Zealand Ltd, Re [1953] All ER 791 ....25.193
Consolidated Nickel Mines Ltd, Re [1914] 1 Ch 883 .... 13.074, 14.012, 14.013
Consolidated South Rand Mines Deep Ltd, Re [1909] 1 Ch 491 ....21.068
Continental Assurance Co of London plc, Re; Secretary of State for Industry v Burrows [1997] 1 BCLC 48 ....28.107
Continental Tyre & Rubber Co (GB) Ltd v Daimler & Co [1915] 1 KB 893 ....7.001, 7.099
Contiv Uebersee Bank AG, Re (1998) The Times Scots Law Report, 12 October 26.028
Contract Corporation, Re [1871] LR 5 Ch App 112 ....25.181
Contract Packaging Ltd, Re (16 January 1992, unreported) HC 15.083, 15.150
Contract Packaging Ltd, Re (1992) Irish Times, 16, 17 & 18 January 5.035
Cook v Deeks [1916] 1 AC 554 ....11.139
Cooke v Cooke & Cooke [1919] 1 IR 227 ....6.083, 6.095
Cooke v Cooke [1997] 2 BCLC 28 ....11.111
Cooke v Walsh [1984] IR 710 ....27.007
Cooke's Events Co Ltd, Re; Kavanagh v Cooke and Byrne [2006] 1 ILRM 191 ....28.122
Coolfadda Developers Ltd, Re [2009] IEHC 263, [2009] IESC 54 ....23.063, 24.019
Coombe Importers Ltd (22 June 1995, unreported) SC 22.166
Coombe Importers Ltd, Re [1999] 1 IR 492 ....25.160
Cooper (Gerard) Chemicals Ltd, Re [1978] 2 All ER 49 ....15.107
Cooper, Cooper & Johnson Ltd, Re [1902] WN 119 ....21.022
Coöperatieve Rabobank Vecht en Plassengebied BA v Minderhoud (receiver in bankruptcy of Mediasafe BV) [1998] 2 BCLC 507 ....7.135
Co-operative Ltd v An Bord Bainne Co-operative Ltd [1991] ILRM 851 ....1.032
Cope (Benjamin) & Sons Ltd, Re [1914] 1 Ch 800 ....18.089

Cope v Destination Education Pty Ltd [1999] (12 January 1999, unreported) SC (NSW) 24.016
Copeland & Craddock Ltd, Re [1997] BCC 294 .... 23.091
Copp, ex p, Re a Company (No 005009 of 1987) [1989] BCLC 12 .... 13.066, 15.110
Corbenstoke Ltd (No 2), Re [1990] BCLC 60 .... 24.014
Corbenstoke Ltd, Re [1989] BCLC 496 .... 23.054
Corbett v Corbett [1998] BCC 93 .... 11.072
Corfield v Stenvwaus Garage Ltd (1985) RTR 109 .... 15.107
Cork and Bandon Railway v Cazenove (1847) 10 QB 935 .... 8.040, 8.094
Cork Communications Ltd and Kerr v Dennehy (4 October 1993, unreported) HC 4.069
Cork County Council v CB Readymix Ltd and Cronin (15 June 1999, unreported) HC 6.098
Cork County Council v CB Readymix Ltd (12 December 1997, unreported) SC 24.030
Cork County Council v O'Regan [2009] 3 IR 39 .... 5.066
Cork Electric Supply Co Ltd v Concannon [1932] IR 314 .... 8.071, 8.109, 25.195
Cornhill Insurance plc v Cornhill Financial Services Ltd [1993] BCLC 914 .... 22.034
Cornwall Mining Co v Bennett (1860) H & N 423 .... 8.095
Coronation Syndicate Ltd v Lilkienfield (1903) TS 489 .... 15.036
Corporate Affairs Commission v Drysdale (1978) 141 CLR 236 .... 13.046
Corran Construction Company v Bank of Ireland Finance Ltd [1976–7] ILRM 175 .... 25.091, 25.096
Cosslett (Contractors) Ltd, Re [1996] 4 All ER 46, [1996] 1 BCLC 407, [1996] BCC 515 .... 18.075
Cosslett (Contractors) Ltd, Re [1997] BCC 724 .... 18.075
Cosslett (Contractors) Ltd, Re [1997] 4 All ER 115 .... 18.025, 18.027, 18.074
Cosslett (Contractors) Ltd, Re [2000] BCC 1155 .... 18.075
Cosslett (Contractors) Ltd, Re [2000] 1 BCLC 775 .... 19.007
Cosslett (Contractors) Ltd, Re; Smith (Administrator of Cosslett (Contractors) Ltd v Bridgend County Borough Council [2001] UKHL 58, [2002] 1 All ER 292 .... 18.032
Costello Doors Ltd, Re (21 July 1995, unreported) HC 28.111
Cotman v Brougham [1918] AC 514, [1918–19] All ER 265 .... 4.005, 7.049–7.055
Cotronic (UK) Ltd v Dezonie [1991] BCLC 721 .... 7.044
Cotter v National Union of Seamen [1929] 2 Ch 58 .... 11.143
Cotton Box Design Group Ltd v Earls Construction Co Ltd [2009] IEHC 312 .... 23.078
Cotton Plantation Company of Natal, Re [1868] WN 79 .... 25.044
Coubrough v James Panton & Co Ltd [1965] IR 272 .... 13.077
Coulson Sanderson & Ward v Ward [1986] BCLC 99 .... 23.084
Countrywide Banking Corporation Ltd v Dean [1998] 2 WLR 441 .... 25.078
County Monaghan Anti-Pylon Ltd v Eirgrid plc [2012] IEHC 103 .... 6.053

County of Gloucester Bank v Rudry Merthyr Steam and House Coal Colliery Co [1895] 1 Ch 629 ....7.122
Countyglen plc v Carway [1995] 1 IR 208 ....25.047, 27.058
Countyglen plc v Carway [1998] 2 IR 514 ....27.059
Countyglen plc, Re [1995] 1 IR 220 ....24.040, 27.021
Coutts & Co v Stock [2000] 1 BCLC 183 ....25.070, 25.072
Cox v Dublin City Distillery Co (No 2) [1915] IR 345 ....7.125, 7.132
Cox v Hickman (1860) 8 HL Cas 268 ....1.015
Craven Textile Engineers Ltd v Batley Football Club Ltd [2001] BCC 679 ....16.134
Craven-Ellis v Cannons Ltd [1936] 2 KB 403 ....13.070
Crawley's case (1869) LR 4 Ch 322 ....8.008
Creasey v Breachwood Motors Ltd [1993] BCLC 480 ....5.043
Creatanor Maritime Co Ltd v Irish Marine Management Ltd [1978] 3 All ER 164 ....20.078
Creation Printing Co Ltd, Re; Crowley v Northern Bank Finance Co [1981] IR 353 ....20.006, 25.111
Creative Handbook Ltd, Re [1985] BCLC 1 ....23.058
Credit Finance Bank plc, Re (9 June 1989) HC 8.083
Crichton's Oil Co, Re [1902] 2 Ch 86 ....8.105
Criminal Assets Bureau v MacAviation Ltd [2010] IEHC 121 ....11.060
Crindle Investments v Wymes [1995] 2 IR 175 ....11.076
Crindle Investments v Wymes [1998] 2 ILRM 275, [1998] 4 IR 567 ....1.151, 11.013, 11.036, 11.065, 11.077 ....11.112, 11.140–11.144, 15.019, 15.022
Crofter Properties Ltd v Genport Ltd (No 3) [2002] IEHC 26 ....6.002
Crompton & Co Ltd, Re [1914] 1 Ch 954 ....18.099, 18.100
Cronje No v Stone (1985) (3) SA 597 (T) 15.049, 15.106, 15.111
Crowe (W&L) Ltd v Electricity Supply Board (9 May 1984, unreported) HC 20.037, 20.074
Crowley v Flynn (13 May 1983, unreported) HC 7.131
Crowther (John) Group plc v International plc [1990] BCLC 460 ....15.037
CU Fittings Ltd, Re [1989] BCLC 556 ....28.179, 28.182
Cuckmere Brick Co Ltd v Mutual Finance Ltd [1971] Ch 949 ....20.050, 20.051, 20.057
Cuff Knox (deceased), Re [1963] IR 263 ....8.038, 18.030
Cuff v London and County Land and Building Co Ltd [1912] 1 Ch 440 ....17.310
Cuff v London and County Land and Building Co Ltd [1958] 1 WLR 822 ....17.312
Cumann Luthchlas Gael Teo v Windle (1993, unreported) SC 28.027
Cummings v Stewart [1911] 1 IR 236 ....5.039
Cummins (MJ) Ltd, Re; Barton v Bank of Ireland [1939] IR 60 ....7.063, 7.065, 7.119
Currencies Direct Ltd v Ellis [2001] TLR 654 ....16.065
Currie v Cowdenbeath Football Club Ltd [1992] BCLC 1029 ....13.077
Curtis v JJ Curtis & Co Ltd [1986] BCLC 86 ....3.046
Curtiss (DH), Re [1978] 1 Ch 162 ....25.153

Customs and Excise Commissioners v Hedon Alfa Ltd [1981] 1 QB 81 .... 15.088
Cuthbertson & Richards Pty Ltd v Thomas [1999] Federal Court of Australia of 30 March 1999 .... 25.111
CVC/Opportunity Equity Partners Ltd v Almeida [2002] UK PC 16 .... 23.045
Cyclists' Touring Club, Re (1907) 1 Ch 269 .... 3.026–3.027

D

D and F Partnership Ltd v Horan Keogan Ryan Ltd [2011] IEHC 333 .... 23.084
D&L Caterers and Jackson v D'Ajou [1945] KB 364 .... 4.049
D'Jan of London Ltd, Re [1993] BCC 646 .... 13.142, 14.108, 15.089
D'Jan of London Ltd, Re, Copp v D'jan [1994] BCLC 561 .... 15.053
Dafen Tinplate Co Ltd v Llanelly Steel Co (1907) Ltd [1920] 2 Ch 124 .... 3.073
Daimler Co Ltd v Continental Tyre and Rubber Co (Great Britain) Ltd [1916] 2 AC 307 .... 4.044, 4.071, 5.007, 5.072
Dallhold Estates (UK) Pty Ltd [1992] BCLC 621 .... 22.010
Dallhold Estates (UK) Pty Ltd, Re [1992] BCC 394 .... 24.069
Dallinger v Halcha Holdings Pty Ltd (1995) 134 ALR 178 .... 24.015
Daly & Co, Re [1887–8] 19 LR Ir 83 .... 25.094
Daly v The Revenue Commissioners [1995] 3 IR 1 .... 4.070
Daniels v Anderson (1995) 16 ACSR 607 .... 15.053, 15.079
Daniels v Daniels [1978] 2 All ER 89, [1978] Ch 406 .... 11.138–11.141 .... 15.028, 15.077, 16.001
Darby, Re; ex p Brougham [1911] 1 KB 95 .... 5.033
Dashwood v Dashwood [1927] WN 276 .... 10.030
Davey & Co v Williamson & Sons Ltd [1898] 2 QB 194 .... 18.100
David Ireland & Co Ltd, Re [1905] IR 133 .... 15.151
Davidson & Begg Antiques Ltd v Davidson [1997] BCC 77 .... 14.126
Davies v Gas Light and Coke Co [1909] 1 Ch 248, aff'd [1909] 1 Ch 708 .... 8.018
Davies v Jenkins [1900] 1 QB 133 .... 4.089
Davis & Co Ltd, Re [1945] Ch 402 .... 24.031
Davis Investments (East Ham) Ltd, Re [1961] 3 All ER 926 .... 23.101
Davis v Bank of England [1824] 2 Bing 393 .... 8.024
Dawnfleet Ltd t/a TES Technology v Shorte and McGowan (1991) Irish Times, 6 September 15.072
Dawson International plc v Coats Paton plc [1989] BCLC 233 .... 15.005–15.007, 15.020
Dawson Print Group Ltd, Re [1987] BCLC 601 .... 28.179
DBP Construction Ltd, Hennerty & Hennerty v ICC Bank plc (21 May 1998, unreported) SC 6.002, 6.068
DCS Ltd; Henley and Henley [2006] IEHC 179 .... 28.125
De Bary (H Albert) & Co NV v TF O'Mullane (2 June 1992, unreported) HC 5.054
De Beers Consolidated Mines Ltd v Howe [1906] AC 455 .... 5.070, 6.029
De Bry v Fitzgerald [1990] 1 All ER 561 .... 6.014
de Jong & Co Ltd, Re [1946] Ch 211 .... 8.104–8.105
De Tastet v Carroll (1813) 1 Stark 88 .... 25.081
Deakin v Faulding [2001] EWHC (Ch) 7 .... 14.095

Dean v Dean [1987] 1 FLR 55 .... 6.083
Dean v Prince [1954] Ch 409, [1954] WLR 538, [1954] 1 All ER 749 .... 3.097, 9.069, 9.127
Deangrove Pty Ltd (Rec & Mgrs Aptd) v Commonwealth Bank of Australia [2001] FCA 173, 6 March 2001 .... 20.031
Deangrove Pty Ltd v Commonwealth Bank of Australia (2001) 108 FCR 77, [2002] FCA 1545, 11 December 2002 .... 20.031
Deauville Communications Worldwide Ltd, Re [2002] 2 IR 32 .... 26.038–26.039, 26.053
Debtor (No 340 of 1992), Re [1994] 2 BCLC 171 .... 23.075
Debtor v Goacher [1979] 1 All ER 870 .... 23.041
Debtor, Re [1956] 3 All ER 225 .... 25.153
Debtor's Summons, Re [1929] IR 136 .... 7.018
Deering v Hyndman (1886) LR (Ir) 18 QBD 323 .... 25.150
Defries N and Co Ltd, Re [1904] 1 Ch 366 .... 19.018
Deloitte & Touche AG v Johnson [1999] BCC 992 .... 24.014
Demaglass Holdings Ltd, Re [2001] 2 BCLC 633 .... 23.063–23.065
Demite Ltd v Protec Health Ltd [1998] BCC 638 .... 14.098, 16.039, 16.048, 20.059
Demite Ltd v Protec Health Ltd (No 2) (24 June 1999) CA (Eng) 16.039
Dempsey v Bank of Ireland (6 December 1985, unreported) SC 25.153, 25.156
Denham & Co, Re (1884) 25 Ch D 752 .... 15.078
Dennis & Sons Ltd v West Norfolk Farmers' Manure and Chemical Co-Op Co Ltd [1948] 2 All ER 94 .... 6.063, 11.059
Denver United Breweries Ltd, Re (1890) 63 LT 96 .... 6.011
Depfa Bank plc, Re [2007] IEHC 463 .... 21.037, 21.044, 21.053, 21.058–21.059
Deputy Commissioner of Taxation v Austin (27 August 1998) FCA 13.045
Derbar Developments Ltd, Re; McGuinness v Dobbin and Lavelle [2012] IEHC 144 .... 28.128
Derby v Weldon [1989] WLR 276 .... 25.047
Derek Randall Enterprises Ltd v Randall [1991] BCLC 379 .... 15.150
Derry v Peek (1889) 14 App Cas 337 .... 32.049
Derverall v Grant Advertising Inc [1954] 3 All ER 389 .... 34.009
Desmond v Glackin (No 2) [1993] 3 IR 67 .... 27.019, 27.023–27.025 .... 27.047, 27.050
Deutsche Bank Aktiengesellschaft v Murtagh & Murtagh [1995] 2 IR 122 .... 25.047
Dev Oil and Gas Ltd, Re; Jackson v Devlin [2008] IEHC 252 .... 15.139
Deverges v Sandeman, Clark & Co [1902] 1 Ch 579 .... 9.036
Devey Enterprises Ltd, Re; Stafford v Devey and Devey [2011] IEHC 340 .... 25.105, 25.108
Devona Ltd; Pyne v Vandeventer [2012] IEHC 263 .... 13.059, 13.065
DHN Food Distributors Ltd v Tower Hamlet London Borough Council [1976] 3 All ER 462 .... 5.052, 12.049
Digital Channel Partners Ltd, Re [2004] 2 ILRM 35 .... 28.128
Digital Rights Ireland Ltd v Minister for Communications [2010] 3 IR 251 .... 4.068, 4.074
Dimbleby & Sons v National Union of Journalists [1984] 1 WLR 427 .... 5.096

Ding v Sylvania Waterways Ltd [1999] NSWSC 58 ....3.029, 3.061, 30.044
Director General of Fair Trading v Buckland [1990] 1 All ER 545 .... 6.097
Director General of Fair Trading v Smiths Concrete Ltd
[1991] 4 All ER 150 .... 6.085
Director of Corporate Enforcement v Boner [2008] IEHC 151 .... 13.008
Director of Corporate Enforcement v D'Arcy [2006] 2 IR 163 .... 13.007
Director of Corporate Enforcement v DCC plc [2009] 1 IR 464
....27.002, 27.014, 27.016
Discoverers Finance Corporation Ltd, Re, Lindlar's case
[1910] 1 Ch 312 .... 9.058
DKG Contracting Ltd (1990) (UK) 15.109
DMK Building Materials Pty Ltd v CB Baker Timbers Pty Ltd
(1985) 10 ACLR 16 .... 23.058
Document Imaging Systems Ltd, Re [2005] 3 IR 103 .... 28.089, 28.140
Doherty (G&S) v Doherty (4 April 1968 & 19 June 1968) HC,
(19 December 1969) SC 3.072, 8.052, 8.122, 15.027, 15.033
Doherty Advertising Ltd, Re [2006] IEHC 198 .... 24.014
Doherty Advertising Ltd, Re; Stafford v Beggs [2006] IEHC 258 .... 28.096
Dolan v AB Co Ltd [1969] IR 247 .... 17.027
Dollar Land Holdings plc, Re [1994] 1 BCLC 404 .... 23.041
Don Bluth Entertainment Ltd (No 1), Re (27 August 1992, unreported) HC 22.012
Don Bluth Entertainment Ltd (No 2), Re [1994] 3 IR 141
....22.012, 22.104–22.106, 22.166
Don Bluth Entertainment Ltd (No 2), Re [1994] 3 IR 155 .... 22.099
Don King Productions Inc v Warren [2000] 1 BCLC 607 .... 15.067
Donahue v Rodd Electrotype Co of New England, Inc (1975) 367
Mass 578, 328 NE 2d 505 .... 1.150
Donoghue v Stevenson [1932] AC 562 ....4.050, 15.024, 15.075
Donovan v Landys Ltd [1963] IR 441 .... 15.101
Donovan v North German Lloyd Steamship Co [1933] IR 33 .... 34.006
Dorchester Finance Co Ltd v Stebbing [1989] BCLC 498 .... 15.083
Dorman Long and Co Ltd, Re [1934] 1 Ch 635 .... 21.055
Double S Printers Ltd, Re [1999] BCC 303 .... 18.050
Dougherty (Charles) Ltd, Re [1984] ILRM 437 .... 19.078
Dovey v Corey [1901] AC 477 .... 10.103, 15.053, 17.027
Dowley & Dowley v O'Brien [2009] IEHC 566 .... 25.047
Downes v Grazebrook (1817) 3 Mer 200 .... 4.078
Downs (George) & Co Ltd, Re [1943] IR 420 .... 23.043
Downs Wine Bar Ltd [1990] BCLC 839 .... 14.019
Downside Nominees Ltd v First City Corporation Ltd [1993] BCC 46,
[1993] AC 295 ....20.049, 20.057, 20.063
DPP v Corrigan [1986] IR 190 .... 4.068
DPP v Kent and Sussex Contractors Ltd [1944] 1 KB 146 ....4.065, 4.067
DPP v Roberts [1987] IR 268 .... 4.064
DPP v Roseberry Construction Ltd [2003] 4 IR 338 .... 4.060
DR Chemicals Ltd, Re (1989) 5 BCC 39 .... 9.131

Dr Developments (Youghal) Ltd, Re [2011] IEHC 307 ....24.002–24.004
.... 24.021, 24.033, 24.054
Drax Holdings Ltd, Re [2003] EWHC 2743 ....21.007
Dredd Scott v Sandford 60 US 393 ....4.025
Drimmie v Davies [1899] 1 IR 176 ....7.018
Drogheda Steampacket Co Ltd, Re [1903] IR 512 ....8.074
DSC Ltd, Re, Fitzpatrick v Henley [2006] IEHC 179 ....15.015
DSG Retail Ltd v PC World Ltd [1998] IEHC 3 ....1.011
DSQ Properties v Lotus Cars [1987] 1 WLR 127 ....6.026
DTC (CNC) Ltd v Gary Sargent [1996] 2 All ER 369 ....8.017
Dublin and Eastern Regional Tourism Organisation Ltd, Re
[1990] 1 IR 579 ....23.101
Dublin City Distillery (Great Brunswick Street, Dublin) Ltd v Doherty
[1914] AC 823 ....18.026, 19.051
Dublin County Council v Elton Homes Ltd [1984] ILRM 297 ....5.037, 5.065
Dublin County Council v O'Riordan [1986] ILRM 104 ....5.038
Dublin Heating Co Ltd v Hefferon (14 January 1993,
unreported) HC 15.100–15.101
Dublin International Arena Ltd v Campus & Stadium Ireland Development Ltd
(26 May 2004, unreported) HC 6.023
Dublin International Arena Ltd v Campus & Stadium Ireland
Development Ltd [2008] 1 ILRM 496 ....6.042–6.044
Dublin North City Milling Co Ltd, Re [1909] 1 IR 179
.... 9.045, 9.057, 15.030
Dublin Sports Cafe Ltd, Re [2008] IESC 66 ....13.039, 15.043
Dublin Sports Cafe Ltd, Re; Fennell v Long and Wright
[2005] IEHC 458 ....15.042, 28.118
Duck v The Tower Galvanising Co Ltd [1901] 2 KB 314 ....7.122
Duckwari plc (No 2), Re [1997] 2 WLR 48 .... 16.001, 16.046–16.048
....16.050–16.053
Duckwari plc v Offerventure (No 2) [1999] BCC 11 (CA)
....................15.088, 16.026, 16.048, 16.050–16.053, 16.110
Duggan v Bourke (30 May 1986, unreported) HC 11.105
Duggan v The Governor and Company of the Bank of Ireland
[1998] IEHC 124 ....14.067–14.071
Duncan Gilmore and Co Ltd The Company v Inman [1952] 2 All ER 871 ....3.088
Dundalk AFC Interim Co Ltd v The FAI National League
[2001] 1 IR 434 ....7.011
Dunlaoghaire Corporation v Park Hill Developments [1989] IR 447 ....5.038
Dunleckney Ltd, Re [1999] IEHC 109 ....26.057, 28.074
Dunlop Pneumatic Tyre Co Ltd v Selfridge & Co Ltd [1915] AC 847 ....4.043
Dunlop, Re (1882) 21 Ch D 583 ....8.121
Dunn v MBS Distribution Ltd (1990) EAT/132/89, 12 June 1990 (UK) 7.108
Dunnes Stores Ireland Company v Houlihan (9 May 2003) HC 27.074
Dunnes Stores Ireland Company v Maloney [1999] 3 IR 542 ....27.072–27.073
Dunnes Stores Ireland Company v Ryan [2002] 2 IR 60
.... 27.002, 27.007, 27.019, 27.069–27.074

Duomatic Ltd, Re [1969] 2 Ch 365, [1969] 1 All ER 161 .... 10.029
....10.073–10.074, 13.093, 14.093
Durham Fancy Goods Ltd v Michael Jackson (Fancy Goods) Ltd
[1968] 2 QB 839 .... 5.081
Dyason v JC Hutton Pty Ltd (1935) Argus LR 419 .... 10.016

E

E Host Europe Ltd; Coyle v O'Brien [2003] 2 IR 627 .... 28.132
EAEL, Re, (1998) Irish Times, 12 February 24.016
East Cork Foods v O'Dwyer Steel [1978] IR 103 .... 7.093
East Donegal Co-Operative Livestock Mart Ltd v Attorney General
[1970] IR 317 .... 4.069
East Norfolk Tramways Co, Re, Barber's Case (1877) 5 Ch D 963 .... 14.124
East Pant Du United Lead Mining Co v Merryweather (1864) 2
Hem & M 254 .... 11.111
Eastern Metropolitan Regional Council v Four Seasons
Construction Pty Ltd (13 July 2000, unreported) SC (WA) 6.067
Ebeed (t/a Egyptian International Foreign Trading Co) v Soplex
Wholesale Supplies Ltd (The Raffaella) [1985] BCLC 404 .... 7.104, 7.106
Ebrahimi v Westbourne Galleries Ltd [1972] 2 All ER 492,
[1973] AC 360 .... 1.151, 3.028, 3.081, 13.081, 23.091–23.094
Eccles Hall Ltd v Bank of Nova Scotia (3 February 1995,
unreported) HC 10.078–10.080
Eddystone Marine Insurance Co, Re [1893] 3 Ch 9 .... 8.062
Eden Quay Investments Ltd, Re (1994) Irish Times, 12 April 26.033
Edenfell Holdings Ltd, Re [1999] 1 IR 443 (HC) 20.051, 20.054
Edennote Ltd (No 2), Re [1997] 2 BCLC 89 .... 24.036
Edenpark Construction Ltd, Re [1994] 3 IR 126 ....22.026, 22.053, 22.085, 22.089,
22.103– 22.107, 22.163, 22.168
Edinburgh and District Aerated Water Manufacturers Defence Association
v James Jenkinson & Co (1903) 5 SC 1159 .... 4.013
Edington v Fitzmaurice (1885) 29 ChD 459 .... 32.050
Edmonds v Blaina Co [1887] 36 Ch D 215 .... 18.018
Educational Co of Ireland Ltd v Fitzpatrick [1961] IR 323 .... 4.068
Educational Co of Ireland Ltd v Fitzpatrick (No 2) [1961] IR 345 .... 4.069, 4.075
Edwards v Halliwell [1950] 2 All ER 1064 .... 8.087–8.089, 11.098
....11.102, 11.127, 11.143
Egan Electric Co Ltd, Re [1987] IR 398 .... 25.180
Egyptian Delta Land & Investment Co Ltd v Todd [1929] AC 1 .... 5.073
Ehrmann Bros Ltd, Re [1906] 2 Ch 697 .... 19.096
EIC Services Ltd v Phipps [2003] BCC 931 .... 7.132
Eircom Ltd, Re [2012] IEHC 158 .... 22.023, 22.042
Eisc Teoranta, Re [1991] ILRM 760 .... 19.097, 20.068
El Ajou v Dollar Land Holdings plc [1994] 2 All ER 685 .... 4.052
El Sombrero, Re [1958] 3 All ER 1, [1958] Ch 900 .... 14.025
Elder v Elder (1952) SC 49 .... 11.014
Electro Services Ltd v Issa Nicholas (Grenada) Ltd [1998] 1 WLR 202 .... 6.030

Eley v Positive Government Security Life Assurance Co Ltd (1876) 1 Ex D 20 ....3.095, 30.028
Eley v Positive Government Security Life Assurance Co Ltd (1876) 1 Ex D 88 .... 3.099, 3.113, 12.037
Elgindata Ltd, Re [1991] BCLC 959 ....11.025
Elite Logistics Ltd v McNamara [2012] IEHC 246 ....25.086
Elkington v Vockbay Pty Ltd 10 ACSR 785 ....9.099
Elliott (James) Construction Ltd v Irish Asphalt Ltd [2010] IEHC 234 ....6.049
Ellis & Co's Trustees v Dixon–Johnson [1925] AC 489 ....9.035
Ellis Pharmaceuticals Ltd, Re (1988) Irish Times, 13 August 25.040–25.041
Ellis Sons & Vidler Ltd, Re [1994] BCC 532 ....25.149
Ellis v Nolan [1983] IEHC 38 ....5.038
Eloc Electro-Optiek and Communicatie BV, Re [1981] 2 All ER 111, [1982] Ch 43 ....23.036
Elve v Boylton [1891] 1 Ch 501 ....1.063
Embassy Art Products Ltd, Re [1988] BCLC 1 ....25.027–25.028
Emerald Group Holdings Ltd & Banfi Ltd v Moran [009] IEHC 440 ....11.012, 11.050
Emerald Portable Building Systems Ltd, Re [2005] IEHC 301 ....23.080
Emmadart Ltd, Re [1979] 1 All ER 599 ....23.039
Emo Oil Ltd v Sun Alliance and London Insurance plc [2009] IESC 2 ....23.125
Employers' Liability Assurance Corporation v Sedgwick, Collins & Co [1927] AC 95 ....34.024
English and Scottish Mercantile Investment Co Ltd v Bruton [1892] 2 QB 700 ....18.080, 18.089
English Colonial Produce Co Ltd, Re [1906] 2 Ch 435 ....7.036
English, Scottish and Australian Chartered Bank, Re [1893] 3 Ch 385 ....21.050, 21.055
Enviroco v Farstad Supply A/S [2010] 2 All ER 1013 ....12.010, 12.027
Environmental Protection Agency v Neiphin Trading Ltd [2011] IEHC 67 ....5.066, 13.123
Equitable Life Assurance Society, Re [2002] BCC 319 ....21.044
Equiticorp International plc, Re [1989] BCLC 597 ....22.012
Erlanger v New Sombrero Phosphate Co [1878] 3 AC 1218 ....15.163, 15.170
Ernest v Nicholls (1857) 6 HL Cas 401 ....7.119
Erris Investments Ltd, Re [1991] ILRM 377 ....25.064
Esal (Commodities) Ltd v Punjab National Bank, Re [1997] 1 BCLC 705 ....15.124
Esberger & Son Ltd v Capital and Counties Bank [1913] 2 Ch 366 ....19.003 ....19.018, 28.044
ESG Reinsurance Ireland Ltd, Re [2010] IEHC 365 ....22.167
ESS-Food Eksportlagtiernes Sallgsforening v Crown Shipping (Ireland) Ltd [1991] ILRM 97 ....7.104
Esso Standard (Inter-America) Inc v JW Enterprises (1963) 37 DLR 598 ....9.100, 9.103
Estmanco (Kilner House) Ltd v Greater London Council [1982] 1 All ER 437 ....11.121, 11.138

Euro Travel Ltd, Re; Dempsey v The Governor and Company of the Bank of Ireland (28 May 1984, unreported) HC, [1963–93] Irish Company Law Reports 207 .... 18.067
Eurochick (Ireland) Ltd, Re [1988] IEHC 51 .... 23.124
Eurocopy plc v Teesdale [1992] BCLC 1067 .... 9.115
Eurofinance Group Ltd, Re (16 June 2000, unreported) HC (Eng) 11.025
Eurofood IFSC Ltd, Re [2004] 4 IR 370 (HC), [2006] IESC 41 (SC), [2006] Ch 508 ECJ (Case C-341/04) 24.062
Euroking Miracle (Ireland) Ltd Re; Fennell v Frost [2003] 3 IR 80 ...... 28.081, 28.091
European Home Products plc, Re (1988) 4 BCC 779 .... 14.053
Evan's case, Re London, Hamburg and Continental Exchange Bank (1867) 2 Ch App 427 .... 8.005
Evans v Grey (1882) 9 LR Ir 539 .... 7.029
Evans v Rival Granite Quarries Ltd [1910] 2 KB 979 .... 18.070, 18.098, 18.100–18.102
Evertite Locknuts Ltd, Re [1945] 1 Ch 220 .... 9.096, 9.097
Exchange Travel (Holdings) Ltd [1993] BCLC 887 .... 22.056
Exchange Trust Ltd, Re, Larkworthy's Case [1903] 1 Ch 711 .... 8.125
Exeter City Association Football Club Ltd v Football Conference Ltd [2004] All ER 1179 .... 11.091
Exeter Trust Ltd v Screenways Ltd [1991] BCLC 888 .... 19.093, 19.098
Expanded Plugs Ltd, Re [1966] 1 All ER 877, [1966] 1 WLR 514 .... 23.045
Expo International Proprietary Ltd v Torma [1985] 3 NSWLR 225 .... 25.102
Express Engineering Works Ltd, Re [1920] 1 Ch 466 .... 14.093
Eylewood Ltd, Re [2010] IEHC 57 .... 22.081–22.082, 22.122
Eyre v McDowell (1861) 9 HL Cas 619 .... 6.075, 18.034, 19.054

F

Fablehill Ltd, Re [1991] BCLC 830 .... 19.095
Faccenda Chicken Ltd v Fowler [1986] 1 All ER 617 .... 15.073
Fagin's Bookshop plc, Re [1992] BCLC 118 .... 8.024
FAI Finance Corporation Ltd, Re; O'Riordan and Granger v Harvey [2010] IEHC 225 .... 28.201
Fairbrother v Stiefel Laboratories (Ireland) Ltd (1985) UD665/1985 .... 15.073
Fairclough & Sons v Manchester Ship Canal Co (No 2) [1897] WN 7 .... 6.080
Fairline Shipping Corporation v Adamson [1975] 1 QB 180 .... 5.018, 15.087
Falcon RJ Development Ltd, Re [1987] BCLC 437 .... 23.122, 23.124
Fallon v An Bord Pleanála [1992] 2 IR 380 .... 6.052
Fallon v An Bord Pleanála and Burke [1991] ILRM 779 .... 6.057
Fanning v Murtagh [2008] IEHC 277 .... 11.111, 11.115, 11.116 .... 11.120, 11.143–11.145
Fares v Wiley [1994] 2 IR 379 .... 6.038
Farm Fresh Frozen Foods Ltd, Re [1980] ILRM 131 .... 19.027, 19.091
Farnell Electronic Components Pty Ltd, Re (1997) 25 ACSR 345 .... 8.070
Farrar v Farrars Ltd (1888) 40 Ch D 395 .... 4.038, 4.078
Farrell v Balzarini and Balzarini [2007] IEHC 424 .... 28.093
Fate Park Ltd, Re [2009] IEHC 375 .... 22.090

Favon Investments Co Ltd, Re [1993] 1 IR 87 ....23.008, 23.115
Fay v Tegral Pipes Ltd and ors [2005] IESC 34 ....23.011
Federal Capital Press of Australia Pty Ltd, Re [1995] ACTAAT 102 (1 February 1995) 12.014
Federal Deposit Insurance Corp v Bierman 2 Fed Rep (3rd series) 1424 ....15.053
Feighery v Feighery [1999] IR 321 ....11.069, 13.082
Fell v Derby Leather Co Ltd [1931] 2 Ch 252 ....3.055
Felton v Callis [1968] 3 All ER 673 ....25.041, 25.044
Fencore Services Ltd, Re [2010] IEHC 358 ....23.119
Fenton, Re [1931] 1 Ch 85 ....25.153
Ferguson v Wallbridge [1935] 3 DLR 66 (PC) 11.130
Ferngara Associates Ltd, Re; Robinson v Forrest (11 February 1999, unreported) HC 28.136
Ferngara Associates Ltd, Re; Robinson v Forrest [1999] IEHC 103 .....28.137–28.138
Ferris v Ward; Ward's Wholesale Meats Ltd v Ferris [1998] 2 IR 194 ....20.009
FG (Films) Ltd, Re [1953] 1 All ER 615 ....5.026
FH Lloyd Holdings Ltd, Re [1985] BCLC 293 ....29.126
Fildes Bros Ltd, Re [1970] 1 All ER 923 ....23.095
Financial Services Compensation Scheme v Larnell (Insurances) Ltd [2006] QB 808 ....25.174
Fine Industrial Commodities Ltd, Re [1956] Ch 256 ....25.181
Finzel, Berry & Co v Eastcheap Dried Fruit Co [1962] 1 Lloyd's Rep 370 ....5.028
Fireproof Doors Ltd, Re [1916] 2 Ch 142 .... 14.077, 14.116, 14.122
Firestone Tyre and Public Co v Llwellin [1957] 1 All ER 561 ....5.026
First City Corporation Ltd v Downsview Nominees Ltd (1990) 5 NZCLC 66, [1990] 3 NZLR 265 ....19.020
First Class Toy Traders Ltd, Re; Gray v McLoughlin [2004] IEHC 289 ....13.053, 28.077
First Class Toy Traders Ltd, Re; Gray v McLoughlin, McLoughlin & Tuohy [2004] IEHC 421 ....13.053
First Energy (UK) Ltd v Hungarian International Bank Ltd [1993] BCLC 1409 ....7.104
Firth v Staines [1897] 2 QB 70 ....7.036
Fisher v St John Opera House Co [1937] 4 DLR 337 ....11.133
Fitness Centre (South East) Ltd, Re [1986] BCLC 518 ....23.041–23.043
Fitzpatrick v Criminal Assets Bureau [2000] 1 ILRM 299 ....19.079
Fitzwilton plc, Rc; Duggan v Stoneworth Investment Ltd [2000] 2 ILRM 263 ....9.091, 9.099–9.102, 9.103–9.104
Five Minute Car Wash Service Ltd, Re [1966] 1 All ER 242 ....11.020
FLE Holdings Ltd, Re [1967] 1 WLR 1409 ....25.092
Fleming v Ranks [1983] ILRM 541 ....25.047
Fletcher Hunt (Bristol) Ltd, Re [1989] BCLC 109 ....14.094
Fletcher v Royal Automobile Club Ltd [2000] 1 BCLC 331 ....21.063
Flint v Barnard (1888) 22 QBD 90 ....18.038
Flitcroft's Case, Re Exchange Banking Co (1882) LR 21 Ch D 519 ....4.025, 10.103
Floor Fourteen Ltd, Re; Lewis v Inland Revenue Commissioners [2001] 2 BCLC 392 .... 25.012, 25.139, 25.170

Foakes v Beer (1888) 9 App Cas 605 .... 23.072, 23.084
Focus Insurance Co Ltd, Re [1996] BCC 659 .... 24.069
Foley v Irish Land Commission [1952] IR 118 .... 4.015
Fomento (Sterling Area) Ltd v Selsdon Fountain Co [1958] 1 All ER 11 .... 17.326
Ford & Carter Ltd v Midland Bank Ltd (1979) 129 New L J 543 .... 5.012
Forest Mill Investments Ltd, Re; MacAvin v Fleming (14 July 1998, unreported) SC 11.079
Forrest Lennon Business Support Services Ltd, Re [2011] IEHC 523 .... 23.073
Forte's Manufacturing Ltd, Re [1994] BCC 84 .... 26.041
Foss v Harbottle (1843) 2 Hare 461 .... 3.094–3.096, 6.002
.... 8.042, 11.092–11.096
.... 15.005, 27.056, 27.063
Foster (John) & Sons v IRC [1894] 1 QB 516 .... 4.038
Foster Bryant Surveying Ltd v Bryant [2007] BCC 804 .... 15.065
Foster v Foster [1916] 1 Ch 532 .... 14.116
Foster Yates & Thom Ltd v HW Edgehill Equipment Ltd (1978) 122 SJ 60 .... 23.131
Fourie v Le Roux and others [2007] 1 All ER 1087 .... 25.047, 25.049
Fowler v Commercial Timber Co Ltd [1930] 2 KB 1 .... 4.077
Fowler v Gruber [2010] 1 BCLC 563 .... 9.125
Framlington Group plc v Anderson [1995] 1 BCLC 475 .... 15.060
Framus Ltd v CRH plc [2004] 2 IR 20 .... 6.017
Francovich v Italian Republic [1993] 2 CMLR 66 .... 4.010, 4.014
Fraser v Buckle [1996] 2 ILRM 34 .... 24.036
Frederick Inns Ltd, Re [1991] ILRM 582 (HC), [1994] 1 ILRM 387 (SC)
.... 4.031, 6.004, 7.066, 7.074, 7.083, 7.087
.... 10.083, 11.107, 12.048, 15.008–15.018, 23.018
.... 23.084, 24.024, 25.015, 25.048, 28.116
Freeman & Lockyer v Buckhurst Park Properties (Mangal) Ltd [1964] 2 QB 480 .... 1.022, 7.100, 7.102–7.103
French's (Wine Bar) Ltd, Re [1987] BCLC 499 .... 25.066
Frigioscandia (Contracting) Ltd v Continental Irish Meat Ltd [1982] ILRM 396 .... 19.073–19.074, 19.080
Fry v Tapson (1884) 28 Ch D 268 .... 15.085
Fry, Re, Chase National Executors & Trustees Corp v Fry [1946] Ch 312 .... 9.024
F2G Realisations Ltd, Re; Gray v GTP Group Ltd [2011] 1 BCLC 313 .... 18.049, 19.039
Fulham Football Club (1987) Ltd v Rochards [2011] EWCA Civ 855, [2012] 1 BCLC 335 .... 11.091
Fulham Football Club Ltd v Cabra Estates plc [1994] 1 BCLC 363
.... 3.126, 15.036, 15.039–15.040, 15.111
Fullerton v Provincial Bank of Ireland [1903] 1 IR 483 .... 19.052
Fyffes plc v DCC plc [2005] IEHC 477 .... 13.062–13.067, 32.070
Fyffes plc v DCC plc [2009] 2 IR 417 .... 4.066, 5.006, 5.063
.... 32.076, 32.080, 32.098

G

Gabbett v Lawder (1883) 11 LR Ir 295 ....3.126, 9.030
Gaiman v National Association for Mental Health [1971] Ch 317 ....4.005
Galden Properties Ltd, Re [1988] IR 213 ....19.028
Galler v Galler 32 Ill 2d 16, 203 NE 2d 577 (1965) 1.150
Gallium Ltd, Re [2009] IESC 8 ....22.022–22.023
Galloway v Halle Concerts Society Ltd [1915] 2 Ch 233 ....8.095
Galoo Ltd v Bright Grahame Murray Ltd [1995] 1 All ER 16 ....17.335
Galvanised Tank Manufacturers' Association's Agreement, Re [1965] 2 All ER 1003 ....6.089, 6.098
Galway & Salthill Tramways Co, Re [1918] 1 IR 62 ....22.012, 23.039
Gambotto v WCP Ltd (1995) 13 ACLC 342 .... 3.067–3.068, 3.083
Gamlestaden Fastigheter AB v Baltic Partners Ltd [2007] 4 All ER 164 ....11.014
Garage Equipment Associations' Agreement, Re (1964) LP 4 RP 491 ....6.089
Garden Gully United Quartz Mining Co v McLister (1875) 1 App Cas 39 ....8.095
Garrard v Hardey (1843) 5 M & G 471 ....1.077
Garrard v James [1925] Ch 616 ....5.015, 5.016
Gartner v Ernst & Young [2003] FCA 152 ....20.031
Garton (Western) Ltd, Re [1989] BCLC 304 ....23.081
Gartside v Silkstone (1882) 21 Ch D 762 ....7.029
Garvey v Metafile Ltd, Re [2006] IEHC 407 ....23.102–23.104
Gasco Ltd, Re [2001] IEHC 20 .... 13.046, 28.075–28.077 ....28.101, 28.111
Gee and Co (Woolich) Ltd, Re [1975] Ch 52 ....10.074
Gencor ACP Ltd v Dalby [2000] 2 BCLC 734 ....15.063
General Accident Assurance Corporation Ltd, Re [1904] 1 Ch 147 ....26.020
General Rolling Stock Co Ltd, Re [1872] LR 7 Ch App 646 ....25.174
Genport Ltd, Re [1996] IEHC 34 ....23.072
Genport Ltd (No 2), Re [2001] IEHC 156 ....23.072
German Date Coffee Co Ltd, Re [1882] 20 Ch 169, [1881–85] All ER 372 ....7.051, 23.102
Gerrard (Thomas) & Son Ltd, Re [1967] 2 All ER 525 ....17.327
Gertzenstein Ltd, Re [1936] 3 All ER 341, [1937] Ch 115 ....24.002, 24.021
Ghyll Beck Driving Range Ltd, Re [1993] BCLC 1126 ....11.025
Gibson v Barton (1875) QB 329 ....14.006
GIGA Invcstments Pty Ltd (in admin) v Ferguson [1995] 13 ACLC 1050 ....14.110
Giles v Rhind [2001] TLR 497 ....11.106
Gilford Motor Co Ltd v Horne [1933] Ch 939 .... 5.008–5.009, 5.042
Gill All Weather Bodies Ltd v All Weather Motor Bodies Ltd 77 Law Journal 123 ....6.047
Gilligan and Bowen v O'Grady [1999] 1 ILRM 303 ....11.070
Gilligan and Bowen v O'Grady [1999] 1 IR 346 ....11.067–11.069
Gilt Construction Ltd, Re (3 June 1994, unreported) HC 23.122–23.124
Glackin v Trustee Savings Bank [1993] 3 IR 55 ....27.039
Glennon v Comr of Taxation (1972) 127 CLR 503 ....10.064
Glover v BLN Ltd [1973] IR 388 .... 13.003, 13.007, 13.080, 28.178

Glow Heating v Eastern Health Board [1988] IR 110 .... 25.157
Gluckstein v Barnes [1900] AC 240 .... 15.163, 15.170
Glynn and McCabe v Owen [2007] IEHC 328, [2012] IESC 15
.... 11.097, 11.115, 11.135, 11.142–11.145
Glynn v McCabe (No 2) [2007] IEHC 452 .... 11.120
GMT Engineering Services Ltd, Re; Luby v McMahon [2003] 4 IR 133 .... 28.094
Gold Co, Re (1879) 11 Ch D 701 .... 23.120
Goldcorp Exchange Ltd, Re [1994] 2 All ER 806 .... 25.149
Goldsmith (Sicklesmere) Ltd v Baxter [1969] 3 All ER 733 .... 7.011
Goldsmith (Sicklesmere) Ltd v Baxter [1970] Ch 85 .... 5.082
Gomba Holdings Ltd v Minories Finance Ltd [1988] 1 WLR 1231 .... 20.042
Gomba Holdings UK Ltd v Minorities Finance Ltd
[1989] BCLC 115 .... 20.040, 20.041, 20.048
Gomba Holdings v Homan [1986] BCLC 331 .... 20.041
Goodbody Ltd (J and LS) v The Clyde Shipping Co Ltd (9 May 1967,
unreported) SC 6.061
Goode Concrete v CRH plc [2012] IEHC 116 .... 5.063, 6.025, 31.016
Goodman International v Hamilton [1992] 2 IR 542 .... 4.015
Goodman International, Re (20 December 1991, unreported) HC 22.149
Goodman International, Re (28 January 1991, unreported) HC 22.148
Goodwill Merchant Financial Services Ltd, Re [2001] 1 BCLC 259 .... 24.042
Gormanstown Equestrian Centre Ltd v Anglo Irish Bank Corporation plc
(14 July 1994, unreported) CC 4.049
Gough's Garages Ltd v Pugsley [1930] 1 KB 615 .... 20.081
Government Stock v Manila Ry Co [1901] 1 Ch 326 .... 18.102
Governments Stock and Other Securities Investment Co Ltd v
Manila Railway Co [1897] AC 81 .... 18.070, 18.100
Goy & Co Ltd, Re [1900] 2 Ch 149 .... 18.023
Gradwell Property Ltd v Rostra [1959] 4 SA 419 .... 10.080
Graham's Morocco Co, Re [1932] SC 269 .... 14.086
Gramophone and Typewriter Ltd v Stanley [1980] 2 KB 89,
[1908–10] All ER Rep 833 .... 13.134
Grange Holdings Ltd v Citibank NA [1991] 4 All ER 1 .... 20.031
Grant v United Kingdom Switchback Railways Co
(1888) 40 Ch D 135 .... 13.140
Gray (Tony) & Sons Ltd, Re [2009] IEHC 557 .... 22.157
Gray's Inn Construction Co Ltd, Re [1980] 1 All ER 814 .... 25.069–25.071, 25.078
Grayan Building Services Ltd [1995] 2 WLR 1 .... 28.067
Great Eastern Electric Co Ltd, Re [1941] 1 All ER 409 .... 24.031
Greenacre Publishing Group v The Manson Group [2000] BCC 11 .... 23.079
Greendale Developments Ltd, Re (20 February 1997,
unreported) SC, [1998] 1 IR 8 .... 7.072, 7.077–7.078, 14.093, 25.138, 25.154
Greendale Developments Ltd, Re [1997] 3 IR 540 .... 6.009, 24.030, 24.040, 25.001
Greene, Re [1949] 1 All ER 167 .... 9.028
Greenhalgh v Arderne Cinemas Ltd [1946] 1 All ER 512 .... 8.119
Greenhalgh v Arderne Cinemas Ltd [1950] 2 All ER 1120, [1951] 1 Ch 286 ..... 3.071
.... 3.074, 3.075, 3.080, 11.130, 15.027

Greenhalgh v Mallard [1943] 2 All ER 234 .... 9.086
Greenham v Gray (1855) 4 ICLR 501 .... 1.015
Greenhaven Motors Ltd, Re [1997] BCC 547 .... 24.030
Greenmount Holdings Ltd, Re; Stafford v O'Connor [2007] IEHC 246 .... 28.114
Greenore Trading Co Ltd, Re [1980] ILRM 94 .... 3.083, 11.011, 11.016
.... 11.076, 11.080, 14.093
Greenwell v Porter [1902] 1 Ch 530 .... 3.114
Greers Gross plc, Re [1987] 1 WLR 1649 .... 27.087
Gresham Industries Ltd v Cannon (2 July 1980, unreported) HC 5.058
Grierson, Oldham & Adams Ltd [1968] 1 Ch 17 .... 9.097
Griffin Hotel Co Ltd, Re [1941] Ch 129 .... 18.096
Griffiths v Secretary of State for Social Services [1974] QB 468 .... 20.033
Griffiths v Studebakers Ltd [1924] 1 KB 102 .... 4.064
Griffiths v Yorkshire Bank [1994] 1 WLR 1427 .... 18.089
Grosvenor and West End Railway Terminus Hotel Co Ltd, Re (1897) 76 LT 337 .... 27.029
Grovewood Holdings plc v James Capel & Co Ltd [1994] 4 All ER 417 .... 24.036
Growth Management and Hillside Apex Fund Ltd v Mutavchiev & Minev [2007] 1 BCLC 645 .... 29.020
Guardian Assurance Co, Re [1917] 1 Ch 431 .... 21.013, 21.015
Guardian Builders Ltd v Sleecon Ltd and Berville Ltd (18 August 1988, unreported), HC 9.006
Guidezone Ltd, Re [2000] 2 CLC 321 .... 23.091
Guilford Borough Council v Smith (1993) The Times, 18 May 6.081
Guinness plc v Saunders [1988] 2 All ER 940 .... 16.128
Guinness plc v Saunders [1990] 1 All ER 652 .... 15.056
Guinness v Land Corporation of Ireland (1882) 22 Ch D 349 .... 3.088, 10.003, 10.012, 29.067
Gutta Percha Corpn, Re [1900] 2 Ch 665 .... 23.120
Guy v Churchill (1888) 40 Ch D 481 .... 24.036
Gwembe Valley Development Co Ltd v Koshy [1998] 2 BCLC 613 .... 15.028
GWI Ltd, Re (16 November 1987, unreported) HC 25.169
Gwyer (Colin) & Associates Ltd v London Wharf (Limehouse) Ltd [2002] EWHC 2748, [2003] 2 BCLC 152 .... 15.011
Gye v McIntyre (1990–1991) 171 CLR 609 .... 25.151

H

(H) (Restraint Order, Re; Realisable Property) [1996] 2 All ER 391 .... 5.036
Hackney Pavilion Ltd, Re [1924] 1 Ch 276 .... 9.026, 9.059
Hadleigh Castle Gold Mines Ltd, Re [1900] 2 Ch 419 .... 14.063
Hafner, Olhausen v Powderly, Re [1943] IR 426 .... 9.018, 9.045, 9.054
.... 9.056, 9.083, 9.107, 15.030
Halesowen Presswork and Assemblies Ltd v Westminster Bank Ltd [1971] 1 QB 1 .... 25.074
Halifax Building Society v Meridian Housing Association Ltd [1994] 1 BCLC 540 .... 7.068

Halifax plc v Halifax Repossessions Ltd [2004] TLR 87 .... 3.024
Hall (WJ) & Co Ltd, Re [1909] 1 Ch 521 .... 8.106
Hallett v Dowdall (1852) 21 LJ QB 98 .... 1.082
Hallett's Estate, Re; Knatchbull v Hallett (1880) 13 Ch D 696 .... 19.082
Halpin v Cremin [1954] IR 19 .... 18.098, 18.101
Halt Garage, Re (1964) Ltd [1982] 3 All ER 1016 .... 15.016
Haltone (Cork) Ltd, Re (7 February 1995, unreported) HC 26.046
Hamlet International plc (in administration), Re [1998] 2 BCLC 164 .... 18.027, 19.032
Harben v Phillips (1883) 23 Ch D 14 .... 14.074–14.075
Hardie v Hanson (1960) 105 CLR 451 (Australia) 15.117
Hardoon v Belilios [1901] AC 118 .... 11.118
Hardwick, Re (1886) 17 QBD 690 .... 18.026, 19.033
Harlequin Property (SVG) Ltd v O'Halloran and O'Halloran [2012] IEHC 13 .... 6.026–6.027, 6.060
Harlowe's Nominees Pty Ltd v Woodside (Lakes Entrance) Oil Co NL (1968) 121 CLR 483 .... 8.052
Harman v BLM Group Ltd [1994] 2 BCLC 674 .... 3.121
Harmony Care Homes Ltd, Re [2010] BCC 358 .... 18.049
Harold v Plenty [1901] 2 Ch 314 .... 9.036
Harrington v JVC (UK) Ltd (16 March 1995, unreported) HC 1.158, 6.016, 6.026, 6.049
Harris Simons Construction Ltd, Re [1989] BCLC 202 .... 22.026
Harrison (Properties) Ltd v Harrison [2001] EWCA Civ 1467, [2002] 1 BCLC 162 .... 15.024, 15.067–15.069
Harrison (Properties) Ltd v Harrison [2001] 1 BCLC 158 .... 15.059, 15.069
Harrison (Saul D) & Sons plc, Re [1994] BCC 475 .... 11.038
Harrison v Heathorn (1843) 6 M & G 81 .... 1.077
Harrisson v Pryse (1740) Barn Ch 324 .... 8.036
Hartlebury Printers Ltd (in liq), Re [1993] BCLC 902 .... 22.113
Hartley Baird Ltd, Re [1954] Ch 143 .... 14.055
Harvard Securities Ltd, Re [1997] 2 BCLC 369 .... 8.028
Harvest Lane Motor Bodies Ltd, Re [1969] 1 Ch 457 .... 26.038
Haughey, Re [1971] IR 217 .... 27.028, 27.030, 27.047, 28.072
Hawk Insurance Co Ltd, Re [2001] BCC 57 .... 21.026
Hawk Insurance Co Ltd, Re [2002] BCC 300 .... 21.026, 21.028
Hawke v E Hulton & Co [1909] 2 KB 93 .... 4.062
Hawkesbury Development Co Ltd v Landmark Finance Pty Ltd (1969) 92 WN (NSW) 199 .... 20.030
Hawks v McArthur [1951] 1 All ER 22 .... 9.024, 9.065, 9.074, 9.081, 9.107
Hayes Homes Ltd, Re [2004] IEHC 124 .... 23.024
Hayes Homes Ltd, Re [2004] IEHC 253 .... 23.119
Haynes (Fergus) (Developments) Ltd, Re [2008] IEHC 327 .... 22.026
HBM Abels v Administrative Board of Bedrijfsvereniging Voor De Metaal – Industrie en de Electrotechnische Industrie 2 ELC 434, [1987] 2 CMLR 406 .... 20.034
Head (Henry) & Co Ltd v Ropner Holdings Ltd [1952] Ch 124 .... 8.067, 10.112

Headstart Global Fund Ltd v Citico Bank Nederland NC, Re [2011] IEHC 5 .... 16.108
Heald v O'Connor [1971] 2 All ER 1105 .... 5.015, 5.016
Health Service Executive v PJ Carroll & Co Ltd [2012] IEHC 147 .... 10.061
Healy v Healy Homes Ltd [1973] IR 209 .... 17.009
Hearts of Oak Assurance Co Ltd v AG [1932] AC 392 .... 27.029, 27.042
Heatons Transport (St Helens) Ltd v Transport and General Workers' Union [1972] 3 All ER 101 .... 6.080, 6.085
Hedley Byrne & Co Ltd v Heller & Partners Ltd [1963] 2 All ER 575, [1964] AC 465 .... 4.050, 15.086, 17.331, 32.050
Hefferon Kearns Ltd (No 1), Re [1992] ILRM 51 .... 15.114, 25.122
Hefferon Kearns Ltd (No 2), Re [1993] 3 IR 191 .... 15.103, 15.104, 15.109 .... 15.112–15.114, 28.067
Heidelstone Co Ltd, Re [2006] IEHC 408 .... 26.021
Hellenic and General Trust Ltd, Re [1975] 3 All ER 382, [1976] 1 WLR 123 .... 8.099, 21.004, 21.027, 21.035
Helmore v Smith (1886) 35 Ch D 436 .... 1.024
Hely-Hutchinson v Brayhead Ltd [1968] 1 QB 549 .... 7.114, 7.125, 16.132
Henderson v Astwood [1894] AC 150 .... 4.078
Henderson v Bank of Australasia (1890) 45 Ch D 330 .... 14.052
Henderson's Transvaal Estates Ltd [1908] 1 Ch 743 .... 21.071
Hendon v Adelman (1973) 117 JJ 631 .... 5.081
Hendy Lennox Ltd v Grahame Puttick Ltd [1984] 1 WLR 485 .... 19.076
Henley Forklift (Ireland) Ltd v Lansing Bagnall & Co Ltd [1979] ILRM 257 .... 7.007
Hennessy v National Agricultural and Industrial Development Association [1947] IR 159 .... 3.059, 11.122–11.124, 30.043
Henry Head v Ropner Holdings Ltd [1952] Ch 124 .... 17.194
Heron International Ltd v Lord Grade [1983] BCLC 244 .... 11.106, 15.021
Hersom v Bernett [1955] 1 QB 98 .... 5.028
Heyford Co, Re, Pell's Case (1869) 5 Ch App 11 .... 8.062
Heything v Dupont [1964] 1 WLR 843 .... 11.143
Hibernia National Review, Re [1976] IR 388 .... 4.062
Hibernian Transport Co Ltd, Re [1984] ILRM 583 .... 25.168
Hibernian Transport Co Ltd, Re [1990] ILRM 42 .... 25.141
Hibernian Transport Co Ltd, Re [1994] 1 ILRM 48 .... 25.181, 26.033
Hickey (WJ) Ltd, Re [1988] IR 126 .... 19.079, 19.082, 25.149
Hickman v Kent or Romney Marsh Sheepbreeders' Association [1915] 1 Ch 881 .... 3.095, 3.099
Hidden Ireland Heritage Holidays Ltd v Indigo Service Ltd [2005] 2 IR 115, [2005] 2 ILRM 498 .... 6.038, 6.055
Hi–Fi Equipment (Cabinets) Ltd, Re [1988] BCLC 65 .... 18.037
Highland Finance (Ireland) Ltd v Sacred Heart College of Agriculture Ltd [1993] ILRM 260 .... 19.029
Highland Finance (Ireland) Ltd v Sacred Heart College, McEllin and Bank of Ireland [1997] 2 ILRM 87 .... 19.029, 19.033
Highway Foods Ltd, Re (1994) Times, 1 November 19.075

Hiley v Peoples Prudential Assurance Co Ltd (1938) 60 CLR 468 .... 25.153
Hilger Analytical Ltd v Rank Precision Industries Ltd [1984] BCLC 301 .... 18.023
Hillman v Crystal Bowl Amusement Ltd [1973] 1 WLR 162 .... 14.073
Hillman v Crystal Bowl Amusements Ltd [1973] 1 All ER 379 .... 8.080
Hilton (Dennis) Ltd, Re [2001] TLR 431 .... 28.174
Hindcastle Ltd v Barbara Attenborough Associates Ltd [1996] 2 BCLC 234 .... 25.062
Hirschler v Birch [1987] RTR 13 .... 5.095
HKN Invest OY v Incotrade PVT Ltd [1993] 3 IR 152 .... 7.039–7.040, 15.166
Hoare and Co Ltd, Re (1933) 150 LT 374 .... 9.097
Hockerill Athletic Club Ltd, Re [1990] BCLC 921 .... 23.013
Hocroft Developments Ltd, Re [2009] IEHC 580 .... 13.050, 13.055
.... 13.059, 13.062–13.065, 28.080
Hogan v The President of the Circuit Court (21 June 1994,
unreported) SC 28.038
Hogg v Cramphorn Ltd [1966] 3 All ER 420, [1966] 3 WLR 254 .... 8.052, 15.034
Hoicrest Ltd, Re [1998] 2 BCLC 175 .... 9.068
Hoicrest Ltd, Re, Keane v Martin [2000] 1 BCLC 194 .... 8.024
Holbern Investments Ltd, Re (1991) Irish Times, 9 October 25.049
Holborne Investments Trust Ltd, Re (1991) Irish Times, 9 October 6.061
Hold Southy v Catnic Components Ltd [1978] 2 All ER 276 .... 23.042
Holidair (No 2), Re (6 May 1994, unreported) HC 22.154
Holidair Ltd, Re [1994] 1 ILRM 481 .... 18.043, 18.047, 18.084
.... 18.110, 19.059, 22.005, 22.071
.... 22.074, 22.077, 22.086
Holidair Ltd, Re [1994] 1 IR 416 .... 22.098
Holland v Dickson (1888) 37 Ch D 669 .... 8.018
Holland v McGill (16 March 1990, unreported) HC 14.106
Hollicourt (Contracts) Ltd v Bank of Ireland [2001] 1 BCLC 233
.... 25.065, 25.070, 25.071
Holmes (Eric) (Property) Ltd, Re [1965] Ch 1052 .... 19.012
Holmes v Keyes [1958] 2 All ER 129 .... 3.089
Holmes v Keyes [1959] 1 Ch 199 .... 14.060
Holohan v Friends Provident and Century Life Office [1966] IR 1 ...... 20.050, 20.052
Home Treat Ltd, Re [1991] BCLC 705 .... 22.090
Homer District Consolidated Gold Mines, Re; ex p Smith (1888) 39 Ch 546
.... 14.106
Hone v Page [1980] FSR 500 .... 6.086
Hong Kong and Shanghai Banking Corp v Kloecker & Co AG
[1989] BCLC 776 .... 18.090
Honniball v Cunningham and BPI Property Co Ltd [2006] IEHC 326 .... 9.040
Hood (John) & Co Ltd v Magee [1918] 2 IR 34 .... 5.071
Hood Sailmakers Ltd v Axford [1996] 4 All ER 830 .... 14.107, 14.126
Hoole v Great Western Railway Co (1867) LR 3 Ch App 262
.... 8.079, 11.122–11.123
Hopkins (JJ) & Co Ltd, Re [1959] 93 ILTR 32 .... 17.309
Hopkins v Shannon Transport Systems Ltd (10 January 1972,
unreported) HC 15.169, 16.128

Hoplins v Worcester and Birmingham Canal Proprietors (1868) LR 6 Eq 437 ....20.002
Horbury Bridge Co, Re (1879) 11 Ch D 109 ....8.082
Horgan (John) Livestock Ltd, Re; O'Mahony v Horgan [1995] 2 IR 411 ....25.047, 25.050
Horgan v Murray [1997] 3 IR 23 ....27.016
Horgan v Murray and Milton [1999] IEHC 65 ....11.036
Horsley & Weight Ltd, Re [1982] 3 All ER 1045, [1982] 1 Ch 442 ....7.056, 7.073, 14.094, ...15.016
Hot Radio Co Ltd v IRTC and NP [2000] IESC 55 ....6.034, 6.052, 6.057
Houghton & Co v Nothard Lowe & Wills Ltd [1927] 1 KB 246, [1927] All ER 97 ....7.126
Houldsworth v City of Glasgow Bank (1880) 5 App Cas 317 ....3.093, 32.048
House of Spring Gardens Ltd v Waite [1985] 11 FSR 173 ....25.042
House Property and Investment Co Ltd, Re [1953] 2 All ER 1525 ....25.178
Household Fire Insurance Co v Grant (1879) 4 Ex D 216 ....8.054
Howard Smith Ltd v Ampol Petroleum Ltd [1974] AC 821 ....13.126
Howard v Mechtle (16 March 1999) SC (NSW) 14.023
Howard v Patent Ivory Manufacturing Co [1883] 3 Ch D 156 ....7.125, 7.132
Howard's Case (1866) 1 Ch 561 ....14.122
HR Harmer Ltd, Re [1958] 3 All ER 689 ....11.022, 11.086
HSS, Re [2011] IEHC 497 ....20.086
Hubbard Association of Scientologists International v Anderson & Just [1972] VR 340 ....6.067
Hubbuck v Helms (1887) 56 LJ Ch 536 ....18.100
Huckerby v Elliott [1970] 1 All ER 189 ....5.094–5.095
Hughes v Hitachi Koki Imaging Solutions Europe [2006] IEHC 233 ....15.014, 25.047–25.048
Huis v Ellis [1995] BCC 462 ....20.057
Humber Ironworks and Shipbuilders Co, Re [1869] 41 Ch App 643 ....25.181
Hunter Kane Ltd v Watkins [2003] EWHC 186 ....15.065
Hunter v Hunter [1936] AC 222 ....9.078, 9.083
Hunting Lodges Ltd, Re [1985] ILRM 75 ....15.049, 15.083, 15.106–15.107 ....15.121–15.126
Huntington Poultry Ltd, Re [1969] 1 WLR 204 ....26.062
Hurley's Estate, Re [1894] 1 IR 488 ....18.034
Hussain v Hussain [1986] 1 All ER 961 ....6.087
Hussain v Wycombe Islamic Mission and Mosque Trust Ltd [2011] EWHC 971 (Ch) 14.029
Hussey (Sean), A Bankrupt, Re (23 September 1987, unreported) HC 7.027
Hussey v Palmer [1972] 3 All ER 744, [1972] 1 WLR 1286 ....7.040, 15.166
Hutton v West Cork Railway Co Ltd (1883) 23 Ch D 654 ....7.072, 7.074, 11.123, 13.070
Hydro Klenze Ltd, Re; Trehy v Rutherford [2007] IEHC 456 ....15.160, 16.046
Hydrodam (Corby) Ltd, Re [1994] 2 BCLC 180, [1994] BCC 161 ....13.046, 13.058
Hydrosan Ltd, Re [1991] BCLC 418 ....6.063–6.065, 11.059
Hyland v Ireland [1998] IESC 28 ....7.122

I

Iarnród Éireann v Ireland [1986] 3 IR 370 .... 4.070
Iarnród Eireann v Ireland [1996] 3 IR 321 .... 4.070
IBB Internet Services Ltd v Motorola [2011] IEHC 504 .... 12.049
IC Johnson & Co Ltd, Re [1902] 2 Ch 101 .... 19.097
Igote Ltd v Badley Ltd [2004] 4 IR 511 .... 10.092
igroup Ltd v Ocwen [2003] 4 All ER 1063 .... 19.093
Illingworth v Houldsworth [1903] 2 Ch 284 .... 18.072
Illingworth v Houldsworth [1904] AC 355 .... 18.035, 18.069
Imperial Bank of China, India and Japan v Bank of Hindustan, China
and Japan (1868) LR 6 Eq 91 .... 21.070
Imperial Hotel (Cork) Ltd, Re [1950] IR 115 .... 8.077, 8.106
Imperial Hydropathic Hotel Co, Blackpool v Hampson 23 Ch D 1 .... 3.095
Imperial Land Company of Marseilles, Re (LR 10 Eq 298) 13.004
Imperial Land Company of Marseilles, Re [1871] LR 11 Eq 478 .... 25.181
Imperial Mercantile Credit Company, Re (1867) LR 5 Eq 264 .... 25.044
Indian Zoedone Co, Re (1884) 26 Ch D 70 .... 14.077, 14.116
Industrial Development Authority v Moran [1978] IR 159 ....7.026, 7.031, 20.038
Industrial Development Consultants v Cooley [1972] 2 All ER 162 .... 15.064
Industrial Equity (Pacific) Ltd, Re [1991] 2 HKLR 614 .... 21.036
Industrial Services Company (Dublin) Ltd, Re [2001] 2 IR 118 .... 25.071–25.073
Industrial Services Company (Dublin) Ltd (No 2), Re
[2002] IEHC 57 .... 25.023, 25.079
Industrial Yarns Ltd v Greene [1984] ILRM 15 .... 13.080
Inland Revenue Commissioners v Goldblatt [1972] 2 All ER 202 .... 20.070
Inland Revenue Commissioners v Hoogstraten [1984] 3 All ER 25 .... 6.101
Innovare Displays plc v Corporate Broking Services Ltd (1991) BCC 726 .... 6.057
Innovate Displays plc v Corporate Broking Services Ltd [1991] BCC 174 .... 6.058
Inquiry under the Company Securities (Insider Dealing) Act 1985, Re
[1988] AC 660 .... 27.039
Inside Sports Ltd, Re [2000] BCC 40 .... 23.124
Inspire Art Case C-411/03 [2003] ECR I-10155 .... 29.152
Instrumentation Electrical Services Ltd, Re [1988] BCLC 550 .... 22.012, 23.045
Inter Finance Group Ltd v KPMG Peat Marwick [1998] IEHC 217 .... 6.019, 6.038
.... 6.040–6.044, 6.047
International Contract Co (Hankey's Case), Re (1872) 26 LT 358,
20 WR 506 .... 21.018
International Credit and Investment Co (Overseas) Ltd v Adham
[1994] 1 BCLC 66 .... 8.024
International Credit and Investment Co (Overseas) Ltd v Adham
[1998] BCC 134 .... 5.067
International Retail Ltd, Re (1963–1993) Irish Company Law Reports 199
.... 19.003, 19.098
International Sales and Agencies Ltd v Marcus [1982] 3 All ER 551 ..... 7.131, 16.109
International Westminster Bank plc v Okeanos Maritime Corp
[1987] BCLC 450, [1987] 2 All ER 137 .... 23.035–23.036
Interview Ltd, Re [1975] IR 382 .... 18.070, 18.093, 19.064

Interview Ltd, Re [1984] ILRM 437 ....19.073
Introductions Ltd, Re [1968] 2 All ER 1221, [1969] 1 All ER 887 ....7.057, 7.060, 7.062, 18.006
Inverdeck Ltd, Re [1998] 2 BCLC 242 ....8.024, 9.060
Investment Options and Solutions Ltd, Re; Bank of Scotland (Ireland) Ltd v Investment Options and Solutions Ltd [2010] IEHC 107 ....19.012, 19.092
Investors Compensation Scheme v West Bromwich Building Society [1998] 1 WLR 896 ....18.109
Ipourgos Ikonomikon and Proistamenos DOY Amfissas v Charilaos Georgakis (Case C-391/04) [2007] CMLR 4 ....32.084
Ipourgos Ikonomikon v Georgakis (Case C-391/04) [2007] ECR I-3741 ....32.075
IRC v Blott [1920] 2 KB 657 ....8.077
IRC v Burrell [1924] 2 KB 52 ....8.077
IRC v Crossman [1937] AC 26 ....8.040
IRC v Duple Motor Bodies Ltd [1961] 1 WLR 739 ....17.027
Ireland (David) & Co Ltd, Re [1905] 1 IR 133 .... 4.035, 16.116, 25.033
Ireland v Hart [1902] 1 Ch 522 .... 8.025, 8.038, 9.024, 9.037
Irish Car Rentals Ltd, Re [2010] IEHC 235 ....22.159
Irish Civil Service Building Society v Registrar of Friendly Societies [1985] IR 167 ....1.037
Irish Club Ltd, Re (1906) WN 127 ....2.011, 30.024
Irish Commercial Society Ltd v Plunkett [1985] IR 1 ....6.038
Irish Commercial Society Ltd v Plunkett [1986] ILRM 624 ....25.035
Irish Commercial Society Ltd v Plunkett [1987] ILRM 504 ....25.025
Irish Conservation and Cleaning Ltd v International Cleaners Ltd (19 July 2001, unreported) SC 6.049
Irish Grain (Trading Board) Ltd, Re (26 November 1984, unreported) HC 7.122
Irish ISPAT Ltd, Re [2004] IEHC 604 ....25.185
Irish ISPAT Ltd, Re; Minister for Environment v Irish ISPAT Ltd [2005] 2 IR 338 ....5.066, 25.060
Irish Life and Permanent Group Holdings PLC and the Credit Institutions Stabilization Act 2010, Re [2012] IEHC 89 .... 8.004, 8.032, 11.047
Irish Life and Permanent plc, Re [2009] IEHC 567 ....10.095
Irish Microforms Ltd v Browne (3 April 1987, unreported) HC 14.120
Irish Oil and Cake Mills (Manufacturing) Ltd v Donnelly (27 March 1984, unreported) HC 20.017, 20.037–20.040, 20.041–20.042, 20.046, 20.050
Irish Penal Reform Trust Ltd v Governor of Mountjoy Prison [2005] IEHC 305 ....4.071
Irish People's Assurance Society v Dublin City Assurance Co [1929] IR 25 ....4.049
Irish Permanent Building Society v Registrar of Building Societies [1981] ILRM 242 ....1.037, 4.015
Irish Press plc v EM Warburg Pincus & Company International Ltd [1997] IEHC 49 .... 6.034–6.037, 6.041
Irish Press plc v Ingersoll Irish Publications Ltd (13 May 1994, unreported) HC 9.118–9.120, 11.023

Irish Press plc v Ingersoll Irish Publications Ltd (15 December 1993, unreported) HC ....1.153–1.154, 9.118, 9.133, 11.006 .... 11.023, 11.035, 11.049, 11.074, 11.082, 15.047
Irish Press plc v Ingersoll Irish Publications Ltd [1993] ILRM 747 .... 11.060–11.062, 22.048
Irish Press plc v Ingersoll Irish Publications Ltd [1995] 2 IR 175 ....9.125, 11.053, 11.073–11.076
Irish Provident Assurance Co Ltd, Re [1913] IR 352 .... 10.014, 15.149
Irish Shell Ltd v Ballylynch Motors Ltd and Morris Oil Co Ltd (5 March 1997, unreported) SC 6.080–6.082, 6.105
Irish Shipping, Re [1986] ILRM 518 .... 25.151
Irish Times Ltd v Ireland [1998] 1 IR 359 .... 4.075
Irish Tourist Promotions Ltd, Re (1963–1993) ICLR 383 .... 23.045
Irish Tourist Promotions Ltd, Re (22 April 1974, unreported) HC 23.098, 23.101
Irish Visiting Motorists' Bureau Ltd, Re (7 February 1972, unreported) HC 11.012, 11.084
Irish Woollen Co v Tyson [1900] 26 .... 17.324–17.327
Irvine v Irvine [2006] 4 All ER 102 .... 9.125
Irvine v Union Bank of Australia (1877) 2 App Cas 366 .... 7.124, 13.140
Isle of Thanet Electricity Supply Co Ltd, Re [1950] Ch 161 .... 8.107–8.109
It's a Wrap (UK) Ltd v Gula [2006] EWCA 544 .... 10.104

J

Jaber v Science and Information Technology Ltd [1992] BCLC 764 .... 11.046
Jackson v Munster Bank (1884–85) 13 LR 118 .... 14.051
Jackson v Munster Bank Ltd (1885) 15 LR Ir 356 ....15.052, 15.082
Jacob (Walter L) & Co Ltd, Re [1989] BCLC 345 .... 27.057
Jacobus Marler Estates Ltd v Marler [1916–17] All ER Rep 291 .... 15.168
Jarvis Motors (Harrow) Ltd v Carabott [1964] 1 WLR 1101 ....4.020, 9.048
Jarvis plc v PricewaterhouseCoopers [2001] BCC 670 .... 14.032
Jaymar Management Ltd, Re [1990] BCLC 617 .... 28.162
JEB Fasteners v Mark Bloom & Co [1981] 3 All ER 289 .... 17.331–17.332
Jer Ryan Electrical Contractors Ltd, Re [2011] IEHC 424 .... 23.059
Jermyn Street Turkish Baths Ltd, Re [1971] 3 All ER 184, [1971] 1 WLR 1042 ....8.052, 9.123, 11.052, 15.033
Jetmara Teo, Re [1992] 1 IR 147 .... 22.154
Jewish Colonial Trust, Re (1908) 2 Ch 287 .... 3.027
Johannesburg Hotel Co, Re, ex p Zoutpansberg Prospecting Co [1891] 1 Ch 119 .... 8.062
John v Price Waterhouse [2001] TLR 533 .... 15.092
Johnson & Co (Builders) Ltd, Re [1955] 2 All ER 775, [1955] 1 Ch 634 .... 15.074, 15.150, ...20.041, 20.049, 20.057, 20.075
Johnson v Church of Scientology, Mission of Dublin Ltd [2001] IESC 25 .... 6.061
Johnson v Gore Wood & Co [2001] 2 WLR 72 .... 11.106
Johnson v Lyttle's Iron Agency (1877) 5 Ch D 687 .... 8.123
Johnston v Chestergate Hat Manufacturing Co Ltd [1915] 2 Ch 338 .... 9.126
Johnstown Ltd v Thiennez Ltd [2001] IEHC 44 ....6.039, 6.049

Joint Receivers and Managers of Niltan Carson Ltd v Hawthorne [1988] BCLC 298 .... 16.023, 16.030, 16.034, 16.046
Joint Stock Discount Co, Re [1869] LR 5 Ch App 86 .... 25.181
Jones and Tarleton v Gunn [1997] 2 ILRM 245 .... 15.010, 15.016, 15.147
Jones v Lipman [1962] 1 All ER 442 .... 5.008, 5.041
Joplin Brewery Co Ltd, Re [1902] 1 Ch 79 .... 19.090, 19.094
Joshua Stubbs Ltd, Re [1891] 1 Ch 475 .... 20.093
Jowett (Angus) & Co v Taylors and Garment Workers Union [1985] IRLR 326 .... 20.034
Jubilee Cotton Mills v Lewis [1924] AC 958 .... 4.005
Jury v Stoker & Jackson (1882) 9 LR Ir 385 .... 32.049

K

Kansen v Rialto (West End) Ltd [1944] Ch 346 .... 14.012
Kanwell Developments Ltd and Salthill Properties Ltd, Re [2008] IEHC 3 .... 23.063
Kavanagh & Cantwell, Re (23 November 1984, unreported) HC 26.020, 26.064
Kavanagh v Delaney [2004] IEHC 283 .... 28.115
Kavanagh v Riedler, Re [2004] 3 IR 498 .... 28.118
Kay Hian & Co (Pte) v Jon Phua Ooi Yong [1989] 1 MLJ 284 .... 18.082
Kaye v Croydon Tramways Co [1898] 1 Ch 358 .... 13.093
Kaytech International plc, Re [1999] BCC 390 .... 13.053, 13.054, 28.155
Kaytech International plc, Re [1999] 2 BCLC 351 .... 13.046
Keane v An Bord Pleanála [1977] 1 IR 184 .... 1.067
Keary Developments Ltd v Tarmac Construction Ltd [1995] 2 BCLC 400 .... 6.058
Keech v Sandford (1726) Sel Cas Ch 61 .... 15.058
Keenan Bros Ltd, Re [1985] IR 401, [1985] BCLC 302 (HC), [1986] BCLC 242 (SC) 18.043–18.045, 18.047, 18.078, 18.108
Keenan Brothers Ltd, Re [1985] IR 401 .... 19.059
Keene v Martin [2000] BCC 904, [2000] TLR 777 .... 9.068
Kehoe v The Waterford and Limerick Railway Co (1888) LR 21 (Ire) Ch 221 .... 10.089
Kellar v Stanley Williams (Turks and Caicos Islands) [2000] 2 BCLC 390 .... 3.019
Kelleher v Continental Irish Meat Ltd (9 May 1978, unreported) HC 25.091
Kelly (Charles) Ltd, Re; Kelly v Kelly (No 2) [2011] IEHC 349 .... 11.011 11.013, 11.033, 11.083
Kelly (Charles) Ltd, Re; Kelly v Kelly [2010] IEHC 38 .... 9.006, 11.048
Kelly (Charles) Ltd, Re; Kelly v Kelly and Charles Kelly Ltd [2012] IEHC 335 .... 11.057
Kelly Technical Services (Ireland) Ltd, Re; Kavanagh v Kelly [2005] IEHC 421 .... 13.050–13.053, 28.078
Kelly v Haughey Boland & Co [1989] ILRM 373 .... 17.327–17.331, 17.334
Kelly v Kelly [1986] SLT 101 .... 15.154
Kelly v Scales [1994] 1 IR 42 .... 25.013
Kelly's Carpetdrome Ltd, Re (1 July 1983, unreported) HC 15.120, 28.148
Kelner v Baxter (1866) LR 2 CP 174 .... 7.042

Kendall v Hamilton (1879) 4 App Cas 504 .... 5.028
Kenford Securities Ltd; Director of Corporate Enforcement v McCann [2010] IESE 59 .... 28.166, 28.180
Kenneally (Christy) Communications Ltd, Re (July 1992, unreported) HC 11.086, 28.177
Kenny v Browne (1796) 3 Ridg PC 462 .... 24.036
Kenoughty Ltd, Re, (1995) Irish Times, 16 October 14.026
Kent Adhesive Products Co t/a KAPCO v Ryan (5 November 1993, unreported) HC 1.010
Kent and Sussex Contractors, Re [1944] 1 KB 146 .... 4.065
Kent Coalfields Syndicate, Re [1898] 1 QB 754 .... 8.018
Kent v Sussex Sawmills Ltd [1946] All ER 638 .... 19.062
Kenyon (Donald) Ltd, Re [1956] 1 WLR 1397 .... 26.063
Kerr v Conduit Enterprises Ltd [2010] IEHC 300 .... 14.096–14.097, 16.022, 16.030–16.033, 16.044
Kerr v John Mottram Ltd [1940] 1 Ch 657 .... 14.077, 14.116
Kerry Co-operative Creamery Ltd v An Bord Bainne Co-Op Ltd [1983] IR 339 .... 8.042
Kerry Co-operative Ltd v An Bord Bainne Co-operative Ltd [1990] ILRM 664 (HC), [1991] ILRM 851 (SC) 1.034, 3.092, 8.036, 8.040
Kerry Tree Ltd v Sun Alliance and London Insurance plc [2001] IEHC 144 .... 6.038
Kett v Shannon & English [1987] ILRM 364 .... 1.022, 7.100–7.103
Keypak Homecare Ltd, Re [1987] BCLC 409 .... 20.091
Keypak Homecare Ltd, Re [1990] BCLC 440 .... 28.182
Kilgobbin Mink and Stud Farms Ltd v National Credit Co Ltd [1980] IR 175 .... 7.107, 7.115
Kill Inn Motel Ltd, Re [1978–1987] Vol 3 ITR 706 (16 September 1987, unreported) HC 25.109
Kimberley North Block Diamond Co, Re, ex p Wernher (1888) 59 LT 579 .... 9.068
King (Cottingham) v Justices of County Cork [1906] 2 IR 415 .... 4.062, 5.008, 5.075
Kingscroft Insurance Co Ltd, Re [1994] 2 BCLC 80 .... 24.018
Kingston Cotton Mill Co, Re [1896] 1 Ch 6 .... 13.004
Kingston Cotton Mills Co (No 2), Re [1896] 2 Ch 279 .... 17.325
Kinsella v Alliance and Dublin Consumers Gas Co (5 October 1982, unreported) HC 9.022–9.023, 14.061
Kinsella v Russell Kinsella Property Ltd [1986] 4 NSWLR 722 .... 15.010, 23.084
Kinsella v Somers (22 November 1999, unreported) HC 20.047–20.049, 20.057, 20.086
Kirby's Coaches Ltd, Re [1991] BCLC 414 .... 15.149
Kitson & Co Ltd, Re [1946] 1 All ER 435 .... 23.103–23.105
KL Tractors Ltd, Re (1961) 106 CLR 318 .... 7.094
Kleinwort Benson Ltd v Malaysia Mining Corporation Berhad [1989] 1 All ER 785 .... 5.017
Knight v Frost [1999] 1 BCLC 364 .... 15.038
Knightsbridge Estates Trust v Byrne [1940] AC 613 .... 18.018

Knocklofty House Hotel Ltd, Re; Kelly v O'Keeffe and O'Keeffe [2005] 4 IR 497 .... 28.134
Knowles v Scott [1891] 1 Ch 717 .... 24.021
Kodak Ltd v Clark [1902] 2 KB 450 .... 5.026
Kolotex Hoisely (Australia) Pty Ltd v Federal Commission of Taxation (1973) 130 CLR 64 .... 12.013
Kosmopolous v Constitution Insurance Co of Canada (1984) 149 DLR (3d) 77 .... 4.039
Kranks Korner Ltd, Re; McCarthy v Gibbons and Gibbons [2008] IEHC 423 .... 28.096
Kris Cruisers Ltd, Re [1949] Ch 138 .... 19.091
Kruger v Gerth, 16 NY 2d 802 .... 1.150
Kruppstahl AG v Quitmann Products Ltd [1982] ILRM 551 .... 19.022, 19.078
Kum Tong Restaurant (Dublin) Ltd, Re; Byrne v AIB Ltd [1978] IR 446 .... 19.023, 19.059, 19.063
Kushler (M) Ltd, Re [1943] 2 All ER 22 .... 25.098
Kushler (M) Ltd, Re [1990] ILRM 341 .... 25.101
Kuwait Asia Bank EC v National Mutual Life Nominees Ltd [1990] 3 All ER 404, [1990] BCLC 868 .... 15.111
Kuwait Asia Bank EC v National Mutual Life Nominees Ltd [1991] 1 AC 187 .... 15.047

L

La Compagnie de Mayville v Whitley [1896] 1 Ch 788 .... 14.106
La Moselle Clothing Ltd and Rosegem Ltd v Soualhi [1998] 2 ILRM 345 .... 28.062
.... 28.082, 28.098, 28.105–28.107
.... 28.123, 28.129, 28.166, 28.180
La Plagne Ltd, Re [2011] IEHC 91 .... 23.042, 23.045, 23.073
Lac Minerals Ltd v Chevron Mineral [1995] 1 ILRM 161 .... 5.063
Ladenburg & Co v Goodwin Ferreira Co Ltd & Garnett [1912] KB 275 .... 19.065
Lady Gwendolen [1965] 2 WLR 91 .... 4.053
Ladywell Mining Co v Brookes [1887] 35 Ch D 400 .... 15.164
Lafayette Ltd, Re [1950] IR 100 .... 8.077, 8.103
Laing (H) Demolition Building Contractors Ltd, Re [1998] BCC 561 .... 28.155
Lake Communications Ltd, Re [2011] IEHC 455 .... 8.070
Lakeglen Construction Co Ltd, Re [1980] IR 347 .... 18.072, 25.116–25.117
Lambert Jones Estates Ltd v Donnelly [1982] IEHC 25 .... 20.053
Lancefort Ltd v An Bord Pleanála (23 January 1997, unreported) HC 6.024
Lancefort Ltd v An Bord Pleanála [1998] 2 ILRM 401 .... 6.046, 6.052
Lancefort Ltd v An Bord Pleanala, Ireland and the Attorney General and Treasury Holdings Ltd (Notice Party) [1998] IEHC 199 .... 4.070, 4.072
Lancefort Ltd v An Bord Pleanála, Ireland, Attorney General and Treasury Holdings Ltd (Notice Party) (6 June 1997, unreported) HC 4.070
Land and Property Trust Co (No 3), Re [1991] BCLC 856 .... 22.049
Land Credit Co of Ireland v Lord Fermoy (1870) LR 5 Ch App 763 .... 15.084
Landall Holdings Ltd v Caratti [1979] WAR 97 .... 18.071

Lander v Premier Pict Petroleum Ltd [1998] BCC 248 ....13.091, 16.028–16.030
Langton v Waite (1868) LR 6 Eq 165 .... 9.035
Laois County Council v Scully [2006] 2 IR 292 .... 5.066
Larkin Partnership Ltd, Re [2010] IEHC 163 .... 23.124
Larkins v NUM [1985] IR 671 ....6.100, 25.047
Larocque v Beauchemin [1897] AC 358 .... 8.062
Lascomme Ltd v UDT Bank [1993] 3 IR 412 .... 20.041
Lascomme Ltd v United Dominions Trust (Ireland) Ltd and James Gilligan [1994] 1 ILRM 227 ....20.031–20.032
Latec Investments Ltd v Hotel Terrigal Pty Ltd (1965) 113 CLR 265 .... 18.071
Lathia v Dronsfield Bros Ltd [1987] BCLC 321 ....20.065, 20.075
Latreefers Inc, Re [1999] TLR 37 .... 23.079
Lawlor v Gray (10 July 1979, unreported) CA (Eng) 10.065
Lawrence's case, Re, Cachar Co (1867) LR 2 Ch 412 .... 8.008
LB Holliday & Co Ltd, Re [1986] BCLC 227 .... 25.193
Le Chatelaine Thudichum Ltd v Conway [2008] IEHC 349 ....25.097, 25.104–25.108
Lee & Co (Dublin) Ltd v Egan (Wholesale) Ltd (18 October 1979, unreported) HC 4.032, 8.037
Lee & Co (Dublin) Ltd v Egan (Wholesale) Ltd (27 April 1978, unreported) HC 3.046, 3.098, 9.013, 9.024
............9.065, 9.082–9.084, 9.107
Lee Behrens & Co, Re [1932] All ER 889, [1932] 2 Ch 46 ....7.069, 7.078, 18.005
Lee v Chou Wen Hsien [1985] BCLC 45 .... 13.076
Lee v Lee's Air Farming Ltd [1961] AC 12 ....4.077, 25.187
Leeds and Hanley Theatres of Varieties Ltd, Re [1902] 2 Ch 809 .... 15.163–15.167
Leeds Estate Building and Investment Co v Shepherd (1887) 36 Ch D 787 .... 15.035
Leeds United Holdings plc, Re [1996] 2 BCLC 545 .... 11.034
Legal Costs Negotiators Ltd, Re [1999] BCC 547 ....1.151, 11.035
Leinster Contract Corporation, Re [1902] 1 IR 349 ....8.062–8.063
Leitch Bros (William C) Ltd, Re [1932] All ER 892 ....15.117, 15.126
Lennard's Carrying Co v Asiatic Petroleum Co [1915] AC 705 .... 4.052
Lennon v Ganley & Fitzgerald [1981] ILRM 84 .... 25.042
Lett v Lett [1906] IR 618 ....25.047
Levin v Clark [1962] NSWR 686 .... 15.047
Levitt (Jeffrey S) Ltd, Re [1992] 2 All ER 509 .... 25.035
Levy v Abercorris Co [1887] 33 Ch D 260 .... 18.018
Lewis Merthyr Consolidated Collieries Ltd, Re [1929] 1 Ch 498 .... 18.096, 20.067
Lewis v Bland [1985] RTR 171 .... 5.095
Lewis v Haas (1970) SLT 67 .... 23.095
Lewis v Pontypridd Caerphilly and Newport Railway Co 1 ITLR 203 .... 6.081
LHF Woods Ltd, Re [1970] Ch 27 .... 23.079
Liberator Permanent Benefit Building Society, Re (71 LT (NS) 406) 13.004
Lillyman and Pinkerton (23 December 1982) Federal Court of Australia 28.033
Linden Ltd v Glenon [2007] IEHC 59 .... 13.029
Lindgen v L & P Estates Ltd [1968] 1 Ch 572 .... 15.025
Lindholst & Co A/S v Fowler [1988] BCLC 166 .... 5.081

Lindsay Bowman Ltd, Re [1969] 1 WLR 1443 ....26.024, 26.062
Linen Supplies of Ireland Ltd, Re [2010] IEHC 28 ....22.129
Linen Supply of Ireland Ltd, Re (10 December 2009,
ex tempore) SC 22.126, 22.139
Lines Bros Ltd (No 4), Re [1982] 2 All ER 183 ....25.179
Lines Bros Ltd, Re [1983] Ch 1 ....25.140
Lines Bros Ltd, Re [1984] BCLC 215 ....25.181
Linz v Electric Wire Co of Palestine [1948] AC 371 ....8.008
Lion Mutual Marine Insurance Association Ltd v Tucker
(1883) 12 QBD 176 ....3.062
Lismore Homes Ltd v Bank of Ireland Finance Ltd [1992] ILRM 798 ....6.055
Lismore Homes Ltd v Bank of Ireland Finance Ltd [1992] 2 IR 57 ....6.017
Lismore Homes Ltd v Bank of Ireland Finance Ltd [1999] 1 IR 501 ....6.031
....6.038–6.039, 6.041, 6.049, 6.050–6.051
Lismore Homes Ltd v Bank of Ireland Finance Ltd [2000] IEHC 35 ....6.057
Lismore Homes v Bank of Ireland (No 3) [2001] IESC 79, [2001] 3 IR 536 ....6.058
Lister (RE) Ltd v Dunlop Canada Ltd [1982] 1 SCR 726 ....20.009
Lister v Romford Ice and Cold Storage Co Ltd [1957] AC 555 ....4.052
Little Olympian Each Ways Ltd, Re [1994] 4 All ER 561 ....2.046, 6.029, 31.017
Liverpool and District Hospital for Diseases of the Heart v Attorney General
[1981] 1 All ER 994 ....8.085
Llewellyn v Kasintoe Rubber Estates [1914] 2 Ch 670 ....21.071
Lloyd Cheyham & Co Ltd v Littlejohn & Co [1987] BCLC 303 ....17.027
Lloyds Bank plc v Lampert [1999] BCC 507 ....20.009
Lloyds Bank v Bullock [1896] 2 Ch 192 ....7.029
Lloyds Bank v Bundy [1975] QB 326 ....5.015
Lloyds v Harper (1880) 16 Ch D 290 ....5.015
Logicrose Ltd v Southend United Football Club Ltd (1988) Times, 5 March 11.055
Lo-Line Electric Motors Ltd, Re (1988) 4 BCC 415 ....13.046
Lo-Line Electric Motors Ltd, Re [1988] BCLC 698, [1988] 2 All ER 692 ....13.046
....28.105, 28.155, 28.166
....28.169, 28.180, 28.182
Lo-Line Ltd, Re [1988] Ch 477 ....28.180
Lombard & Ulster Banking Ireland Ltd v Amurec Ltd
[1976–7] ILRM 222 ....4.015, 19.012
Lombard & Ulster Banking Ltd v Bank of Ireland (2 June 1987,
unreported) HC 10.049, 10.055, 10.068, 10.074
London & Birmingham Railway v Grand Junction Canal Co
(1835) 1 Ry CA 224 ....6.087
London & South–Western Railway Co v Gomm 20 Ch D 562 ....9.019
London and Birmingham Railway Co v Grand Junction Canal Co
(1835) 1 Ry & Can Cas 224 ....6.087
London and General Bank, Re [1895] 2 Ch 166 ....13.004
London and Mashonaland Exploration Co v New Mashonaland Exploration Co
[1891] WN 165 ....15.070
London and Midland Bank v Mitchell [1899] 2 Ch 161 ....9.036
London and Provincial Pure Ice Manufacturing Co, Re (1904) WN 136 ....23.055

London Cheshire Co v Laplagrene Co [1971] Ch 499 .... 19.029
London County and Westminster Bank Ltd [1918] 1 KB 515 .... 18.032
London County Council v Vitamins Ltd [1955] 2 All ER 229 .... 7.011
London Flats Ltd, Re [1969] 1 WLR 711 ....14.025, 14.055–14.056
London General Bank, Re [1895] 2 Ch 166 ....17.312
London India Rubber Co, Re (1868) LR 5 Eq 519 .... 8.085
London School of Electronics Ltd, Re [1983] 3 WLR 474 .... 9.131
Londonderry Equitable Co-Operative Society, Re [1910] 1 IR 69 .... 1.034
Lonrho plc v Secretary of State for Trade and Industry
[1989] 2 All ER 609 .... 27.054
Lonrho v Shell Petroleum Ltd [1980] 1 WLR 627 .... 15.016
Lough Neagh Exploration Ltd v Morrice [1997] IEHC 224 .... 6.014
....6.027–6.028, 6.038, 6.050
Lovell Construction Ltd v Independent Estates plc [1994] 1 BCLC 31 .... 19.022
Lowe v Burns and Burns [2012] IEHC 162 ....20.042, 20.049
Lowerstoft Traffic Services Ltd, Re [1986] BCLC 81 ....23.120–23.122
Lowry (Inspector of Taxes) v Consolidated African Selection
Trust Ltd [1940] 2 All ER 545 .... 10.111
Lubin, Rosen & Associates Ltd, Re [1975] 1 WLR 122 .... 27.057
Lummus Agricultural Services Ltd, Re [1999] BCC 953 .... 23.072
Lumsden v Long [1998] 1304 Federal Court of Australia
(16 October 1998) 20.070
Lundie Brothers Ltd, Re [1965] 2 All ER 692, [1965] 1 WLR 1051 .... 11.014, 23.095
Lycatel (Ireland) Ltd, Re [2009] IEHC 264 .... 23.058
Lyle & Scott Ltd v Scott's Trustees [1959] 2 All ER 661 ....3.046, 9.078–9.080
Lynch (J&B) (Builders) Ltd, Re [1988] BCLC 376 .... 28.182
Lynch v Ardmore Studios (Ireland) Ltd [1966] IR 133 ....18.090–18.093, 25.158
Lynch v Darlington Properties [2011] IEHC 273 .... 18.092
Lynch, Monaghan & O'Brien Ltd, Re (9 June 1989, unreported) HC 25.075
Lynrowan Enterprises Ltd, Re [2002] IEHC 90 ....13.046, 13.049, 13.055, 15.049
Lyons, Keleghan and Murphy v Curran [1993] ILRM 375 ......27.025–27.026, 27.051

M

M Ltd v T (1991) Irish Times, 19 September 6.095
M Wheeler & Co Ltd v Warren [1928] Ch 840 .... 20.081
M'Leod (Neil) & Sons [1967] SLT 46 .... 9.030
Macauley v Minister for Posts and Telegraphs [1966] IR 345 .... 4.071
Macaura v Northern Assurance Co Ltd [1925] AC 619 .... 4.039
MacDougall v Gardiner (1875) 1 Ch D 13 ....3.095, 11.100–11.101
Mace Builders (Glasgow) Ltd v Lunn [1987] Ch 191, [1987] BCLC 55 .... 25.113
Macfarlane's Claim (1880) 17 Ch D 337 ....25.177
MacIntyre v Connell 1 Sim NS 225 .... 9.040
Macken v Revenue Commissioners [1962] IR 302 .... 1.015
MacKenzie & Co Ltd, Re [1916] 2 Ch 450 .... 8.080
MacKereth v Wigan Coal and Iron Co Ltd [1916] 2 Ch 293 .... 8.029
Mackley's case (1875) 1 Ch D 247 .... 8.005

Maclaine Watson & Co Ltd v Department of Trade and Industry [1990] BCLC 102 ....4.044, 4.084
Maclaine Watson & Co Ltd v International Tin Council [1987] BCLC 653 ....20.020
MacPherson v European Strategic Bureau Ltd [1999] TLR 144 ....10.102
MacPherson v European Strategic Bureau Ltd [2002] BCC 39 ....10.092, 10.102
Madden (Michael) Quality Meats Ltd, Re; Ballon Meats Ltd v Leahy [2012] IEHC 122 ....23.024
Madden v Anglo Irish Bank plc [1998] IESC 6 ....20.018
Madison v Alderson (1883) 8 App Cas 467 ....5.015
Magadi Soda Co Ltd, Re (1925) 41 TLR 297 ....20.042
Magna Crete Ltd v Douglas-Hill (1988) 48 SASR 565 ....14.110
Magnus Consultants Ltd, Re [1995] 1 BCLC 203 ....23.124
Maher v Attorney General [1973] IR 140 .... 4.019, 27.047, 28.072
Mahomed v Morris [2000] 2 BCLC 536 ....24.039
Mahony v East Holyford Mining Co (1875) LR 7 HL 869, [1874–80] All ER 427 .... 7.107–7.112, 13.139
Mahony v East Holyford Mining Co (1875) 7 HL 869 ....7.119
Maidstone Buildings Provisions Ltd [1971] 3 All ER 363 ....15.106
Majestic Recording Studios Ltd, Re [1989] BCLC 1 ....28.183, 28.202
Mal Bower's Macquarie Electrical Centre Pty Ltd, Re [1974] 1 NSWLR 245 ....25.070–25.071
Malayan Plant (PT) Ltd v Moscow Narodny Bank Ltd (1980) MLJ 53 ....23.079
Malleson v National Insurance and Guarantee Corporation [1894] 1 Ch 200 ....3.057
Maloe Construction Ltd v Chadwick Lovegrove and Beo [1986] 3 NZCLC 99 ....15.131, 15.137
Manchester and Milford Railway Co, Re (1880) 14 Ch D 645 ....20.003
Manchester Trust v Furness [1895] 2 QB 539 ....10.053
Manchester, Sheffield and Lincolnshire Railway Co v North Central Wagon Co (1888) 13 App Cas 554 ....19.046
Manlon Trading Ltd, Re [1995] 4 All ER 14 ....28.133
Mann v Goldstein [1968] 2 All ER 769 .... 23.078, 23.081, 23.083
Manners v St David's Gold and Copper Mines Ltd [1904] 2 Ch 593 ....3.062
Manning Furniture Ltd (in receivership), Re [1996] 1 ILRM 13 .... 19.094–19.097, 20.068
Manurcwa Transport Ltd, Re [1971] NZLR 909 ....18.106
Marble and Granite Tiles Ltd, Re [2009] IEHC 455 ....23.066
Marchday Group plc, Re [1998] BCC 800 ....11.055
Marcon Developments, Re [2010] IEHC 373 ....23.117, 23.119
Mares Associates Ltd, Re [2006] IEHC 73 ....23.078
Mareva Compania Naviera SA v International Bulk Carriers [1980] 1 All ER 213 ....25.047
Maria Anna & Steinbank Coal and Coke Co Ltd, Re, Maxwell's Case (1874) 20 Eq 585 ....3.062
Maria Anna & Steinbank Coal and Coke Co Ltd, Re, McKewan's Case (1877) 6 Ch D 447 ....3.062

Marino Ltd, Re [2010] IEHC 394 .... 22.167
Marleasing SA v La Comercial Internacional de Alimentacion SA [1992] 1 CMLR 305 .... 4.011
Marshall v Southampton and South West Hampshire Area Health Authority (No 1) [1986] 1 CMLR 688 .... 4.010
Martialone Ltd, Re; Hennessy v Griffin [2009] IEHC 570 .... 11.056
Martin v Colfer [2006] IEHC 124 .... 19.028
Martin v Webb 110 US 7 .... 15.053
Maskelyne British Typewriter Ltd, Re [1898] 1 Ch 133 .... 20.092
Mason v Harris (1879) 11 Ch D 97 .... 11.111
Massey v Sladen (1868) LR 4 Exch 13 .... 20.009
Mastertrade (Exports) Ltd v Phelan [2001] IEHC 172 .... 5.040
Matchnet plc v William Blair & Co LLC [2003] 2 BCLC 195 .... 34.008
Mattimoe v Uniprop Ltd (15 March 2010), HC 13.032
Maunsell v Midland Great Eastern (Ireland) Rly Co (1863) 1 Hem & M 130 .... 11.122
Mauri Development Corporation Ltd v Power Beat International Ltd [1995] 2 NZLR 568 .... 14.073–14.074
Mawcon Ltd, Re [1969] 1 WLR 78 .... 24.027
Maxwell Communication Corporation, Re [1992] BCLC 465 .... 22.012
Maxwell v Department of Trade & Industry [1974] QB 523, [1974] 2 All ER 122 .... 27.029, 27.032
MB Group plc, Re [1989] BCLC 672 .... 21.042
MC Bacon Ltd (No 2), Re [1990] BCLC 607 .... 25.139, 25.170
MCA Records Inc v Charly Records Ltd [2003] 2 BCLC 93 .... 6.094
McAleenan v AIG (Europe) Ltd [2010] IEHC 128 .... 1.015
McArdle v Irish Iodine Co (1864) 15 ICLR 146 .... 7.029
McAteer v Lismore [2000] NI 477 .... 6.014
McAuliffe v Lithographic Group Ltd (2 November 1993, unreported) SC 3.120, 9.077
McBirney and Co Ltd, Re (2 July 1992, unreported) HC 25.076
McCairns (PMPA) plc, Re [1989] ILRM 19, [1989] ILRM 501 .... 25.141–25.144, 25.180
McCartaigh v Daly [1986] ILRM 116 .... 1.026
McClelland v Hyde [1942] NI 1 .... 10.095
McCormick v Cameo Investments Ltd [1978] ILRM 191 .... 9.096–9.097, 10.049, 11.021
McCourt v Tiernan [2005] IEHC 268 .... 25.047
McCoy v Greene [1984] IEHC 70 .... 8.062
McDonald v Bord na gCon (No 2) [1965] IR 217 .... 4.015, 24.040, 27.042
McDonald v Twiname Ltd [1953] 2 All ER 589 .... 7.011
McDonald's Restaurants Ltd v Urbandivide Co Ltd [1994] 1 BCLC 306 .... 23.078
McDonnell v Reid [1987] IR 51 .... 4.076
McEllistrim v Ballymacelligott Co-operative and Dairy Society Ltd [1919] AC 549 .... 3.013, 23.106
McEnaney Construction Ltd [2008] IEHC 43 .... 22.147
McEnery v Sheahan [2012] IEHC 331 .... 20.013

McGee v Attorney General [1974] IR 284 ....4.068
McGill v Bogue (11 July 2000, unreported) SC 10.065
McGilligan & Bowen v O'Grady [1998] IESC 38, [1999] 1 IR 347 ....7.047, 13.082
McGilligan v O'Grady [1999] 1 ILRM 303 ....1.151
McGowan v Gannon [1983] ILRM 516 .... 20.046, 20.050, 20.057, 20.061
McGrattan v McGrattan [1985] NI 28 ....8.029, 14.064
McGuinness v Bremmer plc [1988] BCLC 673 ....14.023
McInerney Homes Ltd, Re [2010] IEHC 340 ....22.025, 22.151
McInerney Homes Ltd (No 2), Re [2011] IEHC 4 ....22.151
McInerney Homes Ltd (No 3), Re [2011] IEHC 25 ....22.151
McInerney Homes Ltd (No 4), Re [2011] IEHC 61 ....22.151
McInerney Homes Ltd (No 5), Re [2011] IEHC 63 ....22.151
McKinnon v Armstrong (1877) 2 App Cas 531 ....25.151
McLaughlin and Co Ltd, Re (1996) Irish Times, 9 July 23.084
McLoughlin (Michael) (Pharmacy) Ltd, Re [2011] IEHC 28 ....22.123
McMahon v Murtagh [1982] ILRM 342 ....4.064
McMahon v Murtagh Properties Ltd (20 October 1981, unreported) HC 5.075
McMillan Graham Printers v RR (UK) Ltd [1993] TLR 152 ....6.104
McNeill v McNeill's Sheepfarming Co Ltd [1955] NZLR 15 ....3.039
McNulty's Interchange Ltd, Re [1989] BCLC 709 ....28.179
MCR Personnel Ltd, Re [2011] IEHC 319 ....23.057
McSweeney Dispensers 1 Ltd, Re [2011] IEHC 494 ....22.157
McSweeney v Bourke (24 November 1980, unreported) HC 4.050
MDN Rochford Construction Ltd, Re; Fennell v Rochford and Rochford [2009] IEHC 397 ....28.141
Meagher v Meagher [1962] IR 96 ....10.095
Mechanisations (Eaglecliffe) Ltd, Re [1964] 3 All ER 840 ....19.014
Medforth v Blake [1999] BCC 771 ....20.049, 20.081
Mehigan v Duignan [1997] 1 IR 340, [1997] 1 ILRM 171 ..... 15.132–15.138, 28.066, 28.114
Melbase Corporation Pty Ltd v Segenhoe Ltd (1995) 17 ACSR 187 ....25.111
Melhado v Porto Alegre Ry Co LR 9 CP 503 ....3.095
Menier v Hooper's Telegraph Works Ltd (1874) 9 Ch App 350 .... 11.111, 11.132, 11.137
Mercantile Credit Company of Ireland and Highland Finance (Ireland) Ltd v Heelan [1994] ILRM 406 ....6.061
Mercantile Investment and General Trust Co v International Co of Mexico [1893] 1 Ch 484 ....21.012
Mercer v Heart of Midlothian plc (2001) SLT 945 ....13.089–13.093
Merchandise Transport Ltd v British Transport Commission [1962] 2 QB 173 ....5.047
Merchant Banking Ltd, Re [1987] ILRM 163 ....24.053
Merchant Navy Supply Association Ltd, Re (1947) 177 LT 386 ....8.085
Meridian Communications Ltd v Eircell Ltd [2001] IESC 42 ....23.085
Meridian Global Funds Management Asia Ltd v Securities Commission [1995] 2 AC 500 ....4.066
Mersey Steel & Iron Co Ltd v Naylor, Benzon & Co (1884) 9 App Cas 434 .....25.070

Meskell v CIÉ [1973] IR 121 .... 4.075
Metafile Ltd, Re;Garvey v Metafile Ltd [2006] IEHC 407 .... 3.028, 23.102–23.104
Metcalfe v Brian (1810) 12 East 400 .... 1.077
Metropolitan Coal Consumers' Association, Re, ex p Wainwright [1890] WN 3 .... 8.024
MHMH Ltd v Carwood Barker Holdings Ltd [2006] 1 BCLC 279 .... 23.064, 24.019
Michaels v Harley House (Marylebone) Ltd [1997] 2 BCLC 166, [1999] 1 BCLC 670 .... 12.023–12.024, 12.033
Michaels v Harley House (Marylebone) Ltd [1999] 1 All ER 356 .... 9.075
Micro Leisure Ltd v Country Properties & Developments Ltd [2000] BCC 872 .... 16.034
Micro Leisure Ltd v County Properties & Developments Ltd (No 1) (19 January 1999, unreported) Scottish Court of Sessions 16.028, 16.034
Mid East Trading Ltd, Re; Lehman Bros Inc v Phillips [1997] 3 All ER 481 .... 23.129
Midland Coal, Coke and Iron Co, Re [1895] 1 Ch 267 .... 21.009
MIG Trust Ltd, Re [1933] Ch 542 .... 19.098
Miles Aircraft Ltd (No 2), Re [1948] WN 178 .... 27.014
Milgate Developments Ltd, Re [1993] BCLC 291 .... 11.057
Millhouse Taverns Ltd, Re [2000] IEHC 55 .... 23.078
Mills v Mills (1938) 60 CLR 150 .... 8.052, 15.032
Millstream Recycling Ltd v Tierney [2010] IEHC 55 .... 6.044, 6.049, 6.053
Millstream Recycling Ltd, Re [2009] IEHC 571 .... 21.009, 21.026, 21.028 .... 21.030, 21.038, 21.047 21.049
Millstream Recycling Ltd, Re [2010] IEHC 106 .... 21.024
Milroy v Lord (1862) 4 De GF & J 264 .... 9.024
Minister Assets plc, Re [1985] BCLC 200 .... 21.042
Minister for Enterprise, Trade and Employment v The Muckross Park Hotel Ltd (20 February 2001) DC 28.033
Minister for Justice v Siúicre Éireann, Greencore [1992] 2 IR 215 .... 27.023–27.024, 27.056, 27.061–27.063
Minrealm Ltd, Re [2008] 2 BCLC 141 .... 23.063
Mirror Group Newspapers, Re (1992) Irish Times, 30 January 25.035
Missford Ltd t/a Residence Members Club, Re [2010] IEHC 11 .... 22.023, 22.038
Missford Ltd, Re [2010] IEHC 240 .... 22.167
Mister Broadloom Corp (1968) Ltd v Bank of Montreal (1979) 25 OR (2d) 198 (HC) 20.009
Mitek Ltd, Re; Grace v Kachkar [2005] IEHC 63, [2010] IESC 31 .... 28.116, 28.117, 28.121
Mixhurst Ltd, Re [1994] 2 BCLC 19 .... 26.061
MMDS Television Ltd and Suir Nore Relays Ltd v South East Community Deflector Association Ltd and Kirwan [1997] IEHC 60 .... 4.069
Modelboard Ltd v Outer Box Ltd [1993] BCLC 623 .... 19.080
Molnar Engineering Pty Ltd v Burns (1984) 3 FCR 68 .... 6.067
Money Markets International Stock Brokers Ltd v Fanning [2000] IEHC 15, [2000] 3 IR 215 .... 6.061
Money Markets International Stockbrokers Ltd (No 1) [1999] 4 IR 267 .... 25.149

Money Markets International Stockbrokers Ltd (No 3), Re
[2001] 2 IR 17 ....25.149
Money Markets International Stockbrokers Ltd v Fanning
[2000] 3 IR 437 ....25.138, 25.152
Money Markets International Stockbrokers Ltd, Re
[2006] IEHC 350 ....25.149, 28.122
Money Markets International Stockbrokers, Re [2012] IEHC 214 ....25.174
Mono Food Equipment Ltd, Re (21 May 1986, unreported) HC 19.055
Monolithic Building Co, Re [1915] 1 Ch 643 ....19.006–19.008
Montgomery v Wanda Modes Ltd [2002] 1 BCLC 289 ....23.079
Moodie v W&J Shepherd (Bookbinders) Ltd [1949] 2 All ER 1044 ....9.030, 9.059
Moone v Attorney General (No 2) [1929] IR 544 ....6.052
Mooney, in b [1938] IR 354 ....6.054
Moore v I Bresler Ltd [1944] 2 All ER 515 ....4.065
Moore v M'Glynn [1894] 1 IR 74 ....15.070
Moore v NW Bank [1891] 2 Ch 599 ....9.024
Mooreview Developments Ltd v William Fanagan Ltd (9 June 2004,
unreported) SC 6.059
Moorgate Mercantile Holdings Ltd, Re [1980] 1 All ER 40 ....14.052–14.054
Moorgate Metals Ltd, Re [1995] 1 BCLC 503 ....28.155
Moorview Developments Ltd et al v First Active plc [2010] IEHC 35 ....20.043
Moran v Moranco Enterprises Pty Ltd (1996) 22 ACSR 65 ....8.070
Morgan v Gray [1953] Ch 83 ....8.009
Morgan v Morgan Insurance Brokers Ltd [1993] BCLC 676 ....8.023
Morphites v Bernasconi [2001] 2 BCLC 1 ....15.119
Morris v Banque Arabe et Internationale d'Investissment SA (No 2)
[2000] TLR 749 ....15.107, 15.116
Morris v Harris [1927] AC 252 ....23.130–23.133, 26.062
Morris v Kanssen [1946] AC 459 ....7.125, 13.046, 13.048, 22.088
Morrissey and Morrissey, Re [1961] IR 442 ....9.039
Morrisson v Barking Chemicals Ltd [1919] 2 Ch 325 ....5.015
Mortgage Insurance Corporation, Re [1896] WN 4 ....21.026
Moschi v Lep Air Services [1973] AC 331 ....5.015, 5.016
Mosely v Koffyfontein Mines Ltd [1911] 1 Ch 73 ....11.127
Mosley v Koffyfontein Mines Ltd [1904] 2 Ch 108 ....8.063
Motherwell v Schoof [1949] 2 WWR 529, [1949] 4 DLR 812 ....3.126, 15.037
Motor Racing Circuits Ltd, Re (31 January 1997, unreported) SC 6.068
....................7.026, 7.121, 9.006, 18.039
....................20.016, 20.026, 25.053, 25.067
Mount Capital Fund Ltd (in liq), Re [2012] IEHC 97 ....24.057
Mount Edon Gold Mines (Aust) Ltd v Burmine Ltd (1994) 12 ACLC 185 ....12.014
Mousell v London & North Western Railway Co [1917] 2 KB 836 ....4.064
Movites Ltd v Bulfield [1988] BCLC 104 ....15.069
Moylan v Irish Whiting Manufacturers Ltd (14 April 1980,
unreported) HC 11.143, 13.029
Moylist Construction Ltd v Doheny et al [2010] IEHC 162 ....20.075–20.077
Moypool Ltd, Re; Gannon v O'Hora and O'Hora [2007] 3 IR 563 ....28.094

Mozley v Alston (1847) 1 Ph 790 .... 11.100–11.101
MS Fashions Ltd v Bank of Credit and Commerce International (1993) Independent, 6 January 25.151
MS Fashions v BCCI SA [1993] BCC 360 .... 25.150, 25.153
Muckross Park Hotel Ltd, Re (21 February 2001) DC, (2001) Irish Times, 22 February 14.011
Mulchrone v Feeney (1983) UD1023/1982 .... 15.073
Muller v Shell E&P Ireland Ltd [2010] IEHC 238 .... 6.083
Multinational Gas & Petrochemical Co v Multinational Gas & Petrochemical Services Ltd [1983] Ch 258 .... 13.142
Multinational Gas & Petrochemical Co v Multinational Gas & Petrochemical Services Ltd [1983] 3 WLR 492 .... 15.016
Municipal Mutual Insurance Ltd v Harrop [1998] 2 BCLC 540 .... 14.124, 14.128
Munster and Leinster Bank, Re [1930] 1 IR 237 .... 3.027
Munster Bank, Re; Dillon's Claim (1886–87) 17 LR Ir 341 .... 8.032
Munton Bros Ltd v Secretary of State [1983] NI 369 .... 5.025, 5.058
Murnane (Jim) Ltd, Re [2009] IEHC 412 .... 23.029
Murph's Restaurants Ltd, Re [1979] ILRM 141 .... 1.151–1.154, 3.028
.... 11.015, 11.025, 11.035, 11.041, 11.050, 11.057
.... 11.078, 13.081, 23.091–23.094, 23.112
Murphy (Daniel) Ltd, Re [1964] IR 1 .... 25.117
Murphy (James) & Sons Sales (Dundalk) Ltd, Re; Stafford v Murphy and Murphy [2010] IEHC 115 .... 28.066, 28.127
Murphy (Russell) [1976] IR 15 .... 25.158
Murphy v Kirwan (9 April 1992, unreported) HC 16.095
Murphy v Sawyer-Hoare [1994] 2 BCLC 59 .... 25.062
Murray Browne Mulcahy Ltd v Companies Acts [2010] IEHC 112 ..... 17.009, 28.211
Murray Consultants Ltd and Nocrumb Ltd, Re; Horgan v Murray and Milton [1997] 3 IR 23 (HC) and 29 (SC) 11.009, 11.053–11.054
Murray Consultants Ltd and Nocrumb Ltd, Re; Horgan v Murray and Milton (9 October 1998, unreported) HC 6.062
Murray Consultants Ltd and Nocrumb Ltd, Re; Horgan v Murray and Milton (No 2) [1999] 1 ILRM 257 .... 11.058
Murray Consultants and Nocrumb Ltd, Re; Horgan v Murray and Milton (9 July 1999, unreported) SC 23.091
Murray v Attorney General [1985] IR 532 .... 4.018, 4.068
Murray v Wilken and Wilken (31 July 2003, unreported) HC 18.032, 19.023
Musselwhite v CH Musselwhite & Son Ltd [1962] 1 All ER 210, [1962] Ch 964 .... 9.065, 9.073–9.074, 12.024
Mutual Life and Citizens' Assurance Co Ltd v Evatt [1971] 1 All ER 150, [1971] AC 793 .... 10.064, 15.086
Mutual Life Insurance Co of New York v The Rank Organisation Ltd [1985] BCLC 11 .... 15.033
Mutual Life Stock Financial and Agency Co Ltd, Re (1886) 12 VLR 777 .... 24.015
Mutual Reinsurance Co Ltd v Peat Marwick Mitchell & Co [1996] BCC 1010 .... 13.004
Mythen v The Employment Appeals Tribunal [1989] ILRM 844 .... 20.034

N

Naiad Ltd, Re (13 February 1995, unreported) HC 23.123
Nalto Construction Ltd, Re [2011] IEHC 251 .... 26.038, 26.053
Nanwa Gold Mines Ltd, Ballantyne v Nanwa Gold Mines Ltd, Re [1955] 3 All ER 219 .... 29.056
Nash v Halifax Building Society [1979] Ch 584 .... 1.038
Nash v Lancegaye Safety Glass (Ireland) Ltd (1958) 92 ILTR 11 .... 7.115, 8.052, 13.134, 15.033
Nash v Lynde [1929] AC 158 .... 32.017
Nassau Steam Press v Tyler (1894) 70 LT 376 .... 5.081
National Australia Bank Ltd v Market Holdings Pty Ltd (26 October 2000) SC (NSW) 21.009
National Australia Bank Ltd v Soden, Re [1995] BCC 696 .... 21.009
National Bank Ltd, Re [1966] 1 All ER 1006, [1966] 1 WLR 819 .... 21.004, 21.040, 21.050
National Building and Land Co, Re (1885–86) 15 LR Ir 47 .... 25.170
National Gas Engine Co Ltd v Estate Engineering Co Ltd [1913] 2 IR 474 .... 6.011
National Irish Bank Ltd (No 1), Re [1993] 3 IR 145 .... 27.031, 27.044, 27.069
National Irish Bank Ltd (No 2), Re [1999] 3 IR 190 .... 27.032, 27.065
National Irish Bank Ltd (No 3), Re [2004] 4 IR 186 .... 27.052–27.056
National Irish Bank Ltd (No 4), Re [2005] 3 IR 90 .... 27.056, 27.061
National Irish Bank Ltd (No 6), Re [2007] 4 IR 451 .... 27.056
National Irish Bank Ltd and National Irish Bank Financial Services; ODCE v D'Arcy [2006] 2 IR 163 .... 28.170, 28.178, 28.186–28.187, 28.200
National Irish Bank Ltd v Graham [1994] 1 IR 215 .... 6.083
National Irish Bank Ltd, Re; Director of Corporate Enforcement v Byrne [2009] 2 ILRM 328 .... 28.188
National Irish Bank Ltd, Re; Director of Corporate Enforcement v Seymour [2006] IEHC 369 .... 28.171
National Irish Bank, Re; Director of Corporate Enforcement v Boner [2008] IEHC 151 .... 28.188
National Provincial & Union Bank v Charnley [1924] 1 KB 431 .... 19.014
National Provincial Bank [1924] 1 KB 431 .... 34.020
National Telephone Co Ltd v The Constables of St Peter Port [1900] AC 317 .... 4.049
National Trustees Co of Australia v General Finance Co of Australia [1905] AC 373 .... 15.089
Nationwide Building Society v Lewis & Williams [1997] 3 All ER 498 .... 1.022
Nationwide Transport Ltd, Re; Forrest v Whelan [2006] IEHC 87 .... 28.181
Natural Nectar Products Canada Ltd v Michael Theodor (6 June 1990) CA (BC) 26.060
NBH Ltd v Hoare [2006] EWHC 73 (Ch), [2006] 2 BCLC 649 .... 14.096 .... 16.044, 16.052
Neath Rugby Ltd, Re [2010] BCC 597 .... 15.045, 15.047
Nelson (Edward) & Co Ltd v Faber & Co [1903] 2 KB 367 .... 18.098, 18.100
Nelson Car Hire Ltd, Re (1973) 107 ILTR 97 .... 26.038, 26.053

Neptune (Vehicle Washing Equipment) Ltd v Fitzgerald
[1995] 1 BCLC 352 .... 14.115
Neville v Krikorian [2006] EWCA Civ 943, [2006] BCC 937] 16.112
Neville v Wilson [1996] 3 All ER 171 .... 3.117
New Ad Advertising Co Ltd [1997] IEHC 219,
(26 March 1998, unreported) SC 6.003, 9.120, 11.009, 11.058, 11.081
New Ad Advertising Ltd, Re [2006] IEHC 19 .... 26.047
New British Iron Co, Re [1989] 1 Ch 324 .... 13.070
New Bullas Trading Ltd, Re [1994] 1 BCLC 485 .... 18.052
New Cedos Engineering Co Ltd, Re [1994] 1 BCLC 797
.... 8.024, 9.060, 9.079, 14.095
New London and Brazilian Bank v Brocklebank (1882) 21 Ch D 302 .... 8.122
New Millenium Experience Co Ltd, Re [2004] 1 BCLC 19 .... 8.024
New Orleans, Texas and Pacific Junction Railway Co [1981] 1 Ch 213 .... 21.010
New Timbiqui Gold Mines, Re [1961] Ch 319 .... 26.037
Newborne v Sensolid (Great Britain) Ltd [1954] 1 QB 45 .... 7.042
Newbridge Sanitary Steam Laundry Ltd, Re [1917] 1 IR 237 .... 23.091
Newbridge Sanitary Steam Laundry Ltd, Re [1917] 1 IR 67 .... 11.125
Newcastle Timber Ltd, Re [2001] 4 IR 586 .... 28.128, 28.169
Newell v Hemmingway (1888) 60 LT 544 .... 5.030
Newhart Developments Ltd v Cooperative Commercial Bank Ltd
[1978] 2 All ER 896 .... 20.031
Newman (George) & Co, Re [1895] 1 Ch 674 .... 10.100
Newport County Association Football Club Ltd, Re [1987] BCLC 582 .... 22.112
Newton v Birmingham Small Arms Co [1906] 2 Ch 378 .... 17.314
NFU Development Trust, Re [1972] 1 WLR 1548 .... 21.014, 21.045
Nicholas v Soundcraft Electronics Ltd [1993] BCLC 360 .... 11.011
Nicholson v Permakraft (NZ) Ltd [1985] 1 NZLR 242 .... 15.016
Nicol's case (1885) 29 Ch D 421 .... 8.004–8.006
Nicoll v Cutts [1985] BCLC 322 .... 20.033
Niedersachsen, The [1984] 1 All ER 398 .... 25.047
Niltan Carson Ltd v Nelson [1988] BCLC 298 .... 16.033
Nisbet v Shepherd [1994] 1 BCLC 300 .... 3.016, 5.080, 9.006
NL Electrical Ltd, Ghosh v 3i, Re [1994] 1 BCLC 22 .... 10.056, 10.073
No 9 Bomore Road, Re [1906] 1 Ch 359 .... 26.020
Nordic Bank plc v International Harvester Australia Ltd [1983] 2 VR 298 .... 21.027
Norditrack (UK) Ltd, Re [1999] TLR 782 .... 23.014
Norman Holding Co Ltd, Re [1990] 3 All ER 757 .... 25.152
Norman Holding Co Ltd, Re [1991] BCLC 1 .... 15.053
Normandy Marketing Ltd, Re [1993] BCC 879 .... 23.109
North Bucks Furniture Depositories Ltd, Re [1939] 2 All ER 549–551 .... 21.009
North Holdings Ltd v Southern Tropics Ltd; Re a Company No
004837 of 1998 [1999] BCC 746 .... 11.054
North West Holdings plc, Re; Secretary of State for Trade and Industry v
Blackhouse [2001] BCLC 468 .... 23.109
North Western Railway v M'Michael (1851) 5 Exch 114 .... 8.040

Northern Bank Finance Co Ltd v Quinn and Achates Investment Co [1979] ILRM 221 .... 7.045, 7.069, 7.086, 18.082, 31.018
Northern Bank Finance v Charlton (26 May 1977, unreported) HC 6.061
Northern Bank Ltd v Laverty [2001] NI 315 ....9.037
Northern Bank Ltd v Ross [1990] BCC 883 ....18.065
Northern Bank Ltd v Ross [1991] BCLC 504 ....19.059
Northern Counties Securities Ltd v Jackson & Steeple Ltd [1974] 2 All ER 625 ....6.084, 6.090–6.092, 15.036
Northside Motor Co Ltd, Re; Eddison v Allied Irish Banks (24 July 1985, unreported) HC 10.060, 10.075, 10.080
Northumberland and Durham District Banking Co, Re (1858) 2 De G & J 357 ....23.120
Nowmost Co Ltd, Re [1996] 2 BCLC 492 ....23.057
Noyek & Sons Ltd, Re; Burns v Hearne [1989] ILRM 155 (SC), [1987] ILRM 508 (HC) 25.168
NO2GM Ltd v Environmental Protection Agency [2012] IEHC 369 ....6.066
NR & Gardiner & Sons Pty Ltd v Osborne Cold Stores (WA) Pty Ltd (1988) 7 SR (WA) 62 ....6.067
NS Distribution Ltd, Re [1990] BCLC 169 ....22.112
NV Slavenburg's Bank v Intercontinental Natural Resources Ltd [1980] 1 All ER 955 ....1.040, 18.078, 34.018–34.021
NW Robbie & Co v Witney Warehouse Co [1963] 3 All ER 316 ....18.098
Nymph Products Ltd v Heating Centre Pty Ltd (1992) 7 ACSR 365 ....18.082

O

O'Brien's Sandwich Bars Ltd, Re [2009] IEHC 465 ....22.126
O'Connor's Nenagh Shopping Centre Ltd, Re; Fitzpatrick v O'Connor [2011] IEHC 508 ....25.092, 25.097
O'Donnell v Shanahan [2009] BCC 822 ....15.065
O'Dowd (1989) DULJ 120 ....15.169
O'Dwyer (Alfred) & Co Ltd, Re (11 November 1988, unreported) HC 25.181
O'Gorman v Kelleher (19 July 1999, unreported) HC 9.075, 9.084, 13.082
O'Keeffe and O'Keeffe v Scales [1998] 1 IR 290 ....24.036–24.038
O'Keeffe v Ferris [1993] 3 IR 165 ....5.008
O'Keeffe v Ferris [1994] 1 ILRM 425 ....15.118
O'Keeffe v Ferris [1997] 3 IR 463 ....15.118, 15.127
O'Keeffe v O'Flynn Exhams and Partners and Allied Irish Banks (31 July 1992, unreported) HC 18.028, 18.034
O'Mahony v Bennet Enterprises Inc [1999] 2 IR 221 ....25.047
O'Mahony v Shields (22 February 1988, unreported) HC 4.068
O'Neill (Colm) Engineering Services Ltd, Re (13 February 2004, ex tempore) HC 28.105, 28.122
O'Neill (Colm) Engineering Services Ltd, Re [2004] IEHC 83 ....28.065
O'Neill (Thomas), a bankrupt, Re [1989] IR 544 ....16.109
O'Neill and Chiswick Ltd v O'Keeffe (19 February 2002, unreported) HC 25.041–25.042
O'Neill v Phillips [1999] BCC 600 .... 11.026, 11.038, 11.040

O'Neill v Ryan [1993] ILRM 557
....4.040, 6.002, 11.093, 11.104–11.105
....11.109, 11.143–11.144, 15.008
O'Shea v DPP (30 November 2000, unreported) HC 6.012
O'Sheas (Dublin) Ltd, Re (1984) Irish Times, 6 July and (1987)
Irish Times, 5 May 25.046
O'Toole (Jack) Ltd v MacEoin Kelly Associates [1986] IR 277 .... 6.034, 6.043, 6.049
Oak Pits Colliery Co, Re [1882] 21 Ch D 322 .... 25.169
Oakdale (Richmond) Ltd v National Westminster Bank plc
[1997] 1 BCLC 63 .... 18.046, 18.085
Oakes v Lynch (27 November 1953, unreported) SC 6.055
Oakes v Turquand (1867) LR 2 HL 325 ....4.006, 8.008, 8.024, 25.141, 32.047
Oakthorpe Holdings Ltd, Re [1988] ILRM 62 .... 23.118, 23.128
Oasis Merchandising Services Ltd, Re [1997] 1 BCLC 689 ....24.036, 25.139, 25.170
OBA Enterprises Ltd v TMC Trading International Ltd
[1998] IEHC 169 .... 20.082, 25.051
OC (Transport) Services Ltd, Re [1984] BCLC 251 .... 9.132, 11.080
Ocean Coal Co Ltd v The Powell Duffryn Steam Coal Co Ltd
[1932] 1 Ch 654 .... 9.078
Oceanic Steam Navigation Co Ltd, Re [1939] Ch 41 .... 21.020
Ochre Ridge Ltd v Cork Bonded Warehouses Ltd and Port of Cork Co Ltd
[2000] IEHC 107 .... 6.036, 6.043
Odessa Tramways v Mendel (1878) 8 Ch D 235 .... 8.095
Odhams Press Ltd, Re [1924] WN 10 .... 21.015
Official Assignee of Madras v Mercantile Bank of India Ltd
[1935] AC 53 .... 18.026
Official Receiver as Liquidator of Celtic Extraction Ltd & Bluestone
Chemicals Ltd v Environment Agency [2000] BCC 487 .... 25.012
Official Receiver v B Ltd [1994] 2 BCLC 1 .... 28.157
Official Receiver v Nixon (1992) Financial Times Law Reports,
6 March (CA) 28.154
Official Receiver v Vass [1999] BCC 516 .... 13.022, 28.199
Olde Court Holiday Hostel Ltd, Re; Trehy v Murtagh [2006] IEHC 424
.... 8.024, 9.067
Oldham Tradesmens' Insurance Co Ltd, Re (19 December 1980) HC (UK)
.... 25.181
Online Catering Ltd v Acton [2010] EWCA 58 .... 19.046
Onslow Salt Pty Ltd, Re (2003) 45 ACSR 322 .... 8.070
Ooregram Gold Mining Co of India v Roper [1892] AC 92 .... 10.108
Opera Phonographic Ltd, Re [1989] BCLC 763 .... 14.025
Opera Photographic Ltd, Re (1989) 5 BCC 601 .... 14.031
Ord v Belhaven Pubs Ltd [1998] 2 BCLC 447 .... 5.005, 5.043–5.045
Oriel Ltd, Re [1985] 3 All ER 216, [1985] BCLC 343 ....34.009, 34.021–34.023
Oriental Credit Ltd, Re [1988] 1 All ER 892 .... 25.040
Oriental Gas Co Ltd, Re [2000] 1 BCLC 209 .... 11.055
Oriental Inland Steam Co, Re (1874) 9 Ch App 557 ....15.013, 15.017, 25.015
Orion Media Marketing Ltd v Media Brook Ltd [2002] 1 BCLC 184 .... 23.079

Orion Pictures Corporation v Hickey (18 January 1991, unreported) HC 6.083
Orisis Insurance Ltd, Re [1999] 1 BCLC 182 .... 21.034, 21.045, 21.050–21.058
Orr (Michael) (Kilternan) Ltd, Re [1986] IR 273 .... 25.144, 25.181
Oshkosh B'Gosh Inc v Dan Marbel Inc Ltd [1989] BCLC 507 .... 5.082, 7.044
Othery Construction Ltd, Re [1966] 1 All ER 145 .... 23.045
Outdoor Advertising Services Ltd, Re (28 January 1997, unreported) HC 28.075, 28.099, 28.123
Overseas Aviation Engineering (GB) Ltd, Re [1963] 1 Ch 24 .... 25.055
Oxford Legal Group Ltd v Sibbasbridge Services plc [2008] 2 BCLC 381 .... 17.010
Oxted Motor Co, Re [1921] 3 KB 32 .... 14.094

P

P&O Case (1991) 93 Cr App R 72 .... 4.065
Pacific and General Insurance Co Ltd v Hazell [1997] BCC 400 .... 24.016
Pageboy Couriers Ltd, Re [1983] ILRM 510 .... 23.078, 23.081
Palmer Marine Surveys Ltd, Re [1986] 1 WLR 573, [1986] BCLC 106 .... 23.120–23.122
Palmer's Decoration and Furnishing Co, Re [1904] 2 Ch 743 .... 18.023
Pamstock Ltd, Re [1994] 1 BCLC 716 .... 28.200
Pan Foods Company Importers & Distributors Pty Ltd v Australia and New Zealand Banking Group Ltd [2000] HCA 20 .... 20.008
Panabridge Co Ltd, Re (12 October 2007) HC 28.157, 28.172
Panama, New Zealand and Australian Royal Mail Co, Re (1870) 10 Ch D 530 .... 18.098
Panama, New Zealand, and Australian Royal Mail Co, Re [1870] 5 Ch App 318 .... 25.111
Panorama Developments (Guilford) Ltd v Fidelis Furnishing Fabrics Ltd [1971] 3 All ER 16, [1971] 2 QB 711 .... 7.117, 15.152
Pantmaenog Timber Co Ltd, Re [2003] 4 ALL ER 18 .... 25.029
Paradise Motor Co Ltd, Re [1968] 2 All ER 625 .... 9.006
Paragon Finance plc v DB Thakerar & [1999] 1 All ER 400 .... 15.067
Paramount Airways Ltd, Re [1990] BCC 130 .... 22.061
Paramount Airways Ltd, Re [1993] Ch 233 .... 28.081
Paringa Mining and Exploration Co PLC v North Flinders Mines Ltd (1989) 7 ACLC 153 .... 13.041
Park Gate Waggon Works Co, Re (1881) 17 Ch D 234 .... 24.036–24.038
Parke v Daily News Ltd [1962] Ch 927, [1962] 2 All ER 929 .... 7.071, 7.074, 7.078
Parker and Cooper Ltd v Reading [1926] 1 Ch 975 .... 14.093–14.094
Parkes & Sons Ltd v Hong Kong and Shanghai Banking Corp [1990] ILRM 341 .... 7.066, 15.010, 15.012, 15.015 .... 16.038, 25.081, 25.095, 25.099, 25.101
Parkinson (Sir Lindsay) & Co Ltd v Triplan Ltd [1973] 2 All ER 273 .... 6.041, 6.045
Parlett v Guppys (Bridport) Ltd [1996] 2 BCLC 34, [1996] BCC 299 .... 10.065
Parnell GAA Club Ltd, Re [1984] ILRM 246 .... 1.056, 5.030
Parolen Ltd v Doherty and Lindat Ltd [2010] IEHC 71 .... 15.063
Parsons v Sovereign Bank of Canada [1913] AC 160 .... 20.036

Partizan Ltd v OJ Kilkenny & Co Ltd [1998] BCC 912 .... 23.090
Patenwood Keg Syndicate Ltd v Pearse [1906] WN 164 .... 14.019
Patrick and Lyon Ltd, Re [1933] Ch 786 .... 15.117, 25.111
Paul & Frank Ltd v Discount Bank (Overseas) Ltd [1966] 2 All ER 922 .... 19.059–19.060
Paul (H & R) & Son Ltd, Re (1974) 118 Sol Jo 166 .... 14.025
Paulger v Butland Industries Ltd [1989] 3 NZLR 549 .... 5.017
Pavlides v Jensen [1956] Ch 565 .... 11.129
Pavlides v Jensen [1956] 2 All ER 518 .... 11.133, 11.139
Payne (David) & Co Ltd, Re, Young v David Payne & Co Ltd [1904] 2 Ch 608 .... 7.057, 7.064
Payne v Cork Co Ltd [1900] 1 Ch 308 .... 21.071
PDC (Moate) Ltd AIB plc [2008] IEHC 281 .... 6.022
Peachdart Ltd [1984] 1 Ch 131, [1983] All ER 204 .... 19.078
Peacock v Peacock (1809) 16 Ves Jr 49 .... 1.020
Peak (RW) (Kings Lynn) Ltd [1998] BCC 597 .... 10.027
Pearce Duff & Co Ltd, Re [1960] 3 All ER 693, [1960] 1 WLR 1014 .... 3.123, 14.085
Pearks, Dunston & Tee Ltd v Ward [1902] 2 KB 1 .... 4.062, 4.064
Pearl Maintenance Services Ltd, Re; Pearl Building Contracts Ltd [1995] BCC 657, [1995] 1 BCLC 449 .... 18.042, 20.070
Pearlberg v O'Brien [1982] Crim LR 829 .... 4.035
Pearson & Son Ltd v Dublin Corporation [1907] 2 IR 27 .... 4.052
Pearson v Naydler [1977] 3 All ER 531 .... 6.016
Peat v Gresham Trust Ltd [1934] AC 252 .... 25.092, 25.098
Pectel Ltd, Re [1998] BCC 405 .... 11.038–11.039
Peel's Case, Re Barned's Banking Co (1867) LR 2 Ch App 674 .... 4.006
Pegler v Craven [1952] 2 QB 69 .... 4.041
Peleton Ltd, Re [2011] IEHC 479 .... 19.008–19.010, 19.094
Pelling v Families Need Fathers Ltd [2001] EWCA Civ 1280 .... 8.018
Pelzan v Boaron Diamonds Ltd (December 1996) Supreme Court of Israel 3.062
Pender v Lushington (1877) 6 Ch D 70 .... 3.068, 3.095, 8.090, 11.102
Peninsular Co Ltd v Fleming (1872) 27 LT (NS) 93 .... 3.062
Pennell v Venida Investments Ltd (25 July 1974, unreported) HC (Eng) 3.120
Penny, ex p LR 8 Ch 446 .... 9.051
Penrose v Martyr (1858) EB & E 499 .... 5.081
People (Attorney General) v O'Brien [1965] IR 142 .... 4.068
People (DPP) v Mark A Synnott (7 May 1996) CC 15.129
People v Murray [1977] IR 360 .... 15.099
People v Roddy [1977] IR 177 .... 4.056
Peppard & Co Ltd v Bogoff [1962] IR 180 .... 6.041, 6.047, 6.054
Percival v Wright [1902] 2 Ch 421 .... 8.091, 12.052, 15.006, 15.019, 15.023
Perfectair Holdings Ltd, Re [1990] BCLC 423 .... 23.102, 23.105
Performing Rights Society Ltd, Re [1978] 2 All ER 712 .... 8.019, 8.100
Pergamon Press Ltd, Re [1970] 3 All ER 589 .... 27.029
Permanent Formwork Systems Ltd, Re [2007] IEHC 268 .... 23.121
Permanent Houses (Holdings) Ltd, Re [1988] BCLC 563 .... 18.065, 18.096, 18.106

Perrins v State Bank of Victoria (1991) 1 VR 749 ....18.065
Personal Service Laundry Ltd v National Bank Ltd [1964] IR 49 ....6.041, 6.047
Peskin v Anderson [2000] 2 BCLC 1 .... 15.019, 15.021–15.022
Peso Silver Mines Ltd v Cropper (1966) 58 DLR 1 ....15.062
Peter's American Delicacy Co Ltd v Heath (1938–39) 61 CLR 457 ....3.057, 3.080
Pfeifer Weinkellerei v Arbuthnot Factors Ltd [1988] 1 WLR 150 ....19.076
Phelan v Goodman [2001] IEHC 142 ....9.080
Phelan v Master Meats Ltd an application reported in (1989) Irish Times, 1 August 25.047
Phoenix Shannon plc v Purkey [1998] 4 IR 597 .... 13.028, 13.074, 14.013
Phonogram Ltd v Lane [1981] 3 All ER 182 ....7.041
Phonographic Performances Ltd v Amusement Caterers (Peckham) Ltd [1963] 3 All ER 493 ....6.104
Picadilly Radio plc, Re [1989] BCLC 683 ....8.024
Pickles (William) plc, Re [1996] 1 BCLC 681 ....24.051
Pierce v The Dublin Cemeteries Committee [2006] IEHC 182 ....1.067
Pierce v Wexford House Co [1915] 2 IR 310 ....6.074
Piercy v S Mills and Co Ltd [1920] 1 Ch 77 ....8.052
Pierson (Brian D) (Contractors) Ltd, Re [1998] BCC 26 ....15.089
Pigot's Case (Winchcombe v Pigot (1614) 2 Bulst 246 ....9.037
Pilmer v Duke Group Ltd [2001] 2 BCLC 773 ....8.063
Pineroad Distribution Ltd, Re; Stafford v Fleming and Fleming [2007] IEHC 55 ....28.128
Pinnel's Case (1605) 5 Co Rep 117a 23.072
Piper v Piper [1876] WN 202 ....6.095
Pitner Lighting Co of Ireland v Geddis and Pickering [1912] 2 IR 163 ....4.046
Pitt v Bolger [1996] 1 ILRM 68 ....6.014, 6.028
Plain Ltd v Kenley [1931] 1 DLR 468 ....7.078
Planet Organic Ltd, Re [2000] 1 BCLC 366 ....11.035
Platt v Platt [1999] 2 BCLC 745 ....15.019, 15.021
Plus Group Ltd v Pyke [2002] 2 BCLC 201 ....15.066
PMPA Garage (Longmile) Ltd (No 1), Re [1992] ILRM 337 ....7.058, 7.067, 12.052, 14.120, 18.007
PMPA Garage (Longmile) Ltd (No 2), Re [1992] ILRM 349 .... 7.067, 7.089, 7.092–7.095
PMPS Insurance Co Ltd and Moore v Attorney General [1984] ILRM 88 ....3.068
Polly Peck International plc (In Administration) (No 4), Re [1996] 2 All ER 433 .... 5.005, 5.006, 5.061
Polly Peck International plc (in administration), Re [1996] 2 All ER 433 ....12.049
Polly Peck International plc v Nadir (No 2) [1992] 4 All ER 769 ....25.051
Polly Peck International plc, Re [1992] BCLC 1025 ....22.094
Pongakawa Sawmill Ltd v New Zealand Forest Products Ltd [1992] 3 NZLR 304 ....19.075
Poole v Middleton (1861) 29 Beav 646 ....8.040
Poole, Jackson and Whyte's case (1879) 9 Ch D 322 ....8.096
Popely v Planarrive Ltd [1997] 1 BCLC 8 ....9.055, 9.061
Port of Cork Co v The Commissioner of Valuation [2003] IESC 47 ....4.091

Port Supermarket Ltd, Re [1978] NZLR 330 .... 25.114
Portman Provincial Cinemas Ltd, Re (1964) 108 Sol J 581 .... 23.079
Portrafram Ltd, Re [1986] BCLC 533 .... 26.041
Portuguese Consolidated Copper Mines Ltd, Re [1889] 42 Ch 160 .... 14.106
Porzelac KG v Porzclac (UK) Ltd [1987] 1 WLR 420 .... 6.039
Potters Oils Ltd (No 2), Re [1986] BCLC 98 .... 20.010, 20.093
Pound (Henry) Son and Hutchins, Re (1889) 42 Ch D 402 .... 20.081
POW Services Ltd v Clare [1995] 2 BCLC 435 .... 13.032, 13.073
.... 14.061, 28.047
Powell Cotton's Settlement, Re, Henniker Major v Powell Cotton
[1957] Ch 159 .... 8.099
Powell v London and Provincial Bank [1893] 2 Ch 555 .... 9.006, 9.022, 9.037
Power (John) & Son Ltd, Re [1934] IR 412 .... 21.041, 21.050, 21.055, 22.142
Power Supermarkets Ltd v Crumlin Investments Ltd and Dunnes Stores
(Crumlin) Ltd (22 June 1981, unreported) HC
.... 5.008, 5.044, 5.051, 5.053, 5.062, 5.090, 12.049
Power v Hoey (1871) 19 WR 916 .... 7.025
Powerscourt Estates v Gallagher [1984] ILRM 123 .... 25.047
Powertech Logistics Ltd, Re; Airscape Ltd v Powertech Logistics Ltd,
O'Reilly and McKee [2007] IEHC 43 .... 28.213–28.214
Powis (Philip) Ltd, Re [1997] 2 BCLC 481 .... 23.132, 26.061
Pramatha Nath Mullick v Pradyumna Kumar Mullick (1925) LR
52 Ind App 245 .... 4.025
Pratt v Inman (1889) 43 Ch D 175 .... 6.100
Precision Dippings Ltd v Precision Dippings Marketing Ltd
[1985] 3 WLR 812, [1986] Ch 447 .... 10.104, 14.098
Prendergast & Prendergast (third parties) [1997] 2 ILRM 405 .... 6.004
Presswell Ltd, Re (4 November 1991, unreported) HC 22.080, 22.153
Priceland Ltd, Re [1997] 1 BCLC 467 .... 26.042
Pricelans Ltd, Re [1997] 1 BCLC 467 .... 26.062
Prichard's case LR 8 Ch 965 .... 3.095
Primlaks (UK) Ltd, Re [1989] BCLC 734 .... 22.026
Primor plc v Stokes Kennedy Crowley [1996] 2 IR 459 .... 28.133
Princess of Reuss v Bos (1871) LR 5 HL 176 .... 4.015, 8.009
Prior v Johnston 27 ILTR 108 .... 28.213
Private Motorist's Provident Society Ltd & Moore v Attorney General
[1984] ILRM 988 .... 8.040
Private Motorists Provident Society Ltd, Re; Horgan v Minister for Justice
(23 June 1995, unreported) HC 25.005, 25.008–25.011, 25.161–25.162
Private Motorists' Provident Society Ltd v Attorney General
[1983] IR 339 .... 1.061, 4.069–4.070, 11.107
Probets v Glackin [1993] 3 IR 134 .... 27.019, 27.043
Production Association Minsk Tractor Works and Belarus Equipment
(Ireland) Ltd v Saenko (25 February 1998, unreported) HC 25.050
Profinance Trust SA v Gladstone [2000] 2 BCLC 516 .... 9.122, 9.131
Profinance Trust SA v Gladstone [2002] 1 BCLC 141 .... 9.132

Progress Property Co Ltd v Moorgarth Group Ltd [2011] 2 All ER 432
.... 7.079, 10.100, 10.101
Provincial Bank of Ireland Ltd v O'Connor (23 July 1973) HC 8.039
Prudential Assurance Co Ltd v Newman Industries Ltd (No 2)
[1982] 1 All ER 354, [1982] 1 Ch 204 ....4.040, 6.002, 11.093, 11.098–11.099
.....................................11.104, 11.112–11.114, 11.121, 11.133, 11.141–11.144
Prudential Assurance Co Ltd v Newman Industries Ltd [1981] 1 Ch 229 ....11.113
Prudential Assurance Co v Chatterly Whitfield Collieries Co Ltd
[1949] AC 462 ....8.109
PSK Construction Ltd, Re; Kavanagh v Killeen and Higgins
[2009] IEHC 538 ....15.102, 15.103, 15.123–15.127, 15.140, 28.180
Public Prosecutor v Allen Ng Poh Meng [1990] 1 MLJ (Singapore) 32.078
Public Prosecutor v Chua Seng Huat [1999] 3 MLJ 305 (Malaysia) 32.078
Puddephatt v Leith [1916] 1 Ch 200 ....3.123–3.126
Pugh and Sharman's case (1872) LR 13 566 ....8.009
Pulse Group Ltd v O'Reilly [2006] IEHC 50 ....15.073
Pulsford v Devenish [1903] 2 Ch 625 ....25.174
Punt v Symons & Co Ltd [1903] 2 Ch 506 ....3.057, 8.052
Pye (Ireland) Ltd, Re [1985] IEHC 62 ....21.027, 21.030
.... 21.033–21.035, 21.042
Pye (Ireland) Ltd, Re; Hogan [1984] IEHC 23 ....21.011, 21.048
Pyle Works, Re (1890) 44 Ch D 534, 59 LJ Ch 489, CA 30.024

Q

Queensland Mines Ltd v Hudson (1978) 18 ALR 1 ....15.062
Queenstown Dry Dock Ship Building Co, Re [1918] 1 IR 356 ....26.020
Quickdome Ltd, Re [1988] BCLC 370 ....8.032, 11.046
Quin & Axtons v Salmon [1909] 1 Ch 311 ....8.089
Quinlan v Essex Hinge Co Ltd [1996] 2 BCLC 417 ....11.037
Quinn v Irish Bank Resolution Corporation Ltd [2012] IEHC 36 ....10.050
....32.098, 32.117
Quinn's Supermarket Ltd v Attorney General [1972] IR 1 ....4.068

R

R (Cottingham) v The Justices of Cork [1906] 2 IR 415 ....4.076
R (IUDWC) v Rathmines UDC [1928] IR 260 ....4.014
R (on the application of Mercury Tax Group Ltd) v HMRC & Co
[2008] EWHC 2721 ....7.013
R Ltd, Re [1988] ILRM 126 ....22.048, 25.032, 27.042
R Ltd, Re [1989] ILRM 757 ....3.066, 11.060, 11.062
R v Associated Octel Co Ltd [1996] 1 WLR 1543 ....4.063
R v Bennett [1985] 2 NZCLC 96-034 ....15.131
R v Birmingham and Gloucester Railway Co (1841) 2 QB 47 ....4.064
R v Board of Trade ex parte St Martins Preserving Co Ltd
[1965] 1 QB 603 ....27.021
R v British Steel plc [1995] 1 WLR 1356 ....4.063
R v Brockley [1994] 1 BCLC 606 ....13.018

R v Cauldwell [1982] AC 341 .... 15.099
R v Chester (1843) 1 Ad & El 342 .... 8.083
R v Consolidated Churchill Copper Corp Ltd [1978] WLR 652 .... 18.106
R v Cory Brothers & Co [1927] 1 KB 810 .... 4.064
R v Cunningham [1957] 2 All ER 412 .... 15.099
R v Dickson [1991] Crim LR 854, [1991] BCC 719 .... 5.094
R v Gateway Foodmarkets Ltd [1997] 2 Cr App R 40 .... 4.063
R v Goodwin (1980) 71 Cr App R 97 .... 5.033
R v Grantham [1984] 3 All ER 166 .... 15.130
R v Great North of England Railway Co (1846) 9 QB 315, (1846) 2 Cox CC 70 .... 4.064
R v Harris [1970] 3 All ER 746 .... 27.045
R v ICR Haulage Ltd [1944] KB 551 .... 4.064–4.065
R v Irish [2001] EWCA Crim 1393 .... 32.056
R v Kite and OLL Ltd (8 December 1994) Winchester Crown Court (1994) The Independent, 9 December 4.065
R v Lambeth County Court Judge and Jonas (1887) 36 WR 475 .... 6.095
R v LCC, ex p London and Provincial Electric Theatres Ltd [1915] 2 KB 466 .... 5.075
R v Mc Donnell [1966] 1 QB 233 .... 4.067
R v McCredie [2000] BCC 617 .... 25.006, 25.012
R v McCredie and Re v French [1999] TLR 671 .... 28.033
R v McMillan Aviation (4 June 1981) Crown Court, Kingston upon Thames 5.095
R v P&O European Ferries (Dover) Ltd (1991) 93 Cr App R 72 .... 4.064
R v Registrar of Companies, ex p Bowen [1914] 3 KB 1161 .... 4.003
R v Registrar of Companies, ex p Central Bank of India [1985] BCLC 465 .... 19.019
R v Registrar of Companies, ex p Central Bank of India [1986] 1 All ER 105, [1986] QB 1114 .... 4.015, 19.098
R v Registrar of Companies, ex p Esal (Commodities) Ltd [1985] BCLC 84 .... 19.019
R v Registrar of Companies, ex p Her Majesty's Attorney General [1991] BCLC 476 .... 4.003, 4.017
R v Registrar of Joint Stock Companies [1931] 2 KB 197 .... 3.013, 4.003, 23.106
R v Secretary of State for Trade, ex p Perestrello [1981] QB 19 .... 27.019
R v Shacter (1960) 44 Cr App R 42 .... 17.312
R v Shacter [1960] 2 QB 252 .... 13.003–13.004, 17.012
R v Smith [1996] 2 BCLC 109 .... 15.108
R v Thames Magistrates' Court 28.038
R v The Daily Mirror Newspapers Ltd (1922) 16 Cr App R 131 .... 4.062
R v Westminster CC, ex p Mayfair Residents [1991] COD 182, QBD 6.025
R v Wilson [1997] 1 All ER 119 .... 5.093
R v Wiltshire and Berkshire Canal Navigation (1835) 3 Ad & El 477 .... 8.018
R v Wimbledon Local Board (1882) 8 QBD 459 .... 8.083
R&H Electrical Ltd v Haden Bill Electrical Ltd [1995] 2 BCLC 280 .... 11.014–11.015
Rackham v Peel Foods Ltd [1990] BCLC 895 .... 15.037

Radivojevic v LR Industries Ltd (22 November 1984, unreported) CA (Eng) 23.090
Rafidain Bank, Re (2000) LTL 23/3/2000 ....23.063
Rafsanjan Pistachio Producers v Reiss [1990] BCLC 352 ....5.081
Railway and General Light Improvement Col Marzetti's Case, Re (1880) 42 LT 206 ....15.035
Railway Timetables Publishing Co, Re (1889) 42 Ch D 98 ....8.008
Rainham Chemical Works Ltd (in liq) v Belvedere Fish Guano Co Ltd [1921] 2 AC 465 ....4.049, 4.053, 5.018, 5.021
Rakusens Ltd v Baser Ambalaj Plastik Sanayi Ticaret Asi [2002] 1 BCLC 104 ....34.006
Rama Corporation Ltd v Proved Tin & General Investments Ltd [1952] 1 All ER 554 ....7.123
Rankin v Cooper 149 F 1010 ....15.053
Ranks Ireland Ltd, Re [1988] ILRM 751 ....25.063
Rantzen v Rothchild (1865) 14 WR 96 ....6.085
Ravenshaw Ltd, Re [2012] IEHC 37 ....10.052
Rayfield v Hands [1960] 1 Ch 1, [1958] 2 WLR 851 ....3.096–3.097, 8.089
Rayhill Property Co Ltd, Re; Conroy v Corneill and Corneill (7 October 2003, unreported) HC 15.131, 15.135
Read v Astoria Garage (Streatham) Ltd [1952] Ch 637 ....13.080
Readymix plc, Re [2012] IEHC 170 ....21.022, 21.052, 21.060
Real Estate Development Co [1991] BCLC 210 ....23.036
Real Meat Co Ltd, Re [1996] BCC 254 ....18.100
Rearden v Provincial Bank of Ireland [1896] 1 IR 532 ....8.025, 8.029, 8.122, 9.039
Red Label Fashions Ltd, Re [1999] BCC 308 ....13.054, 28.155
Red Sail Frozen Foods Ltd, Re [2006] IEHC 328 ....20.044, 20.067
Redbreast Preserving Co (Ireland) Ltd, Re [1958] IR 234, 91 ILTR 12 ....25.032 ....25.167, 27.042
Redfern Ltd v O'Mahony and McFeely, Caroll, Tafica Ltd and Aifca Ltd [2010] IEHC 253 ....4.033, 5.027
Regal (Hastings) Ltd v Gulliver [1942] 1 All ER 378 ....15.058–15.059 ....15.063, 16.133
Regal (Hastings) Ltd v Gulliver [1967] 2 AC 134 ....13.142
Regentcrest plc v Cohen [2001] 2 BCLC 80 ....15.031
Regina Fur Co Ltd v Bossom [1958] 2 Lloyd's Rep 466 ....4.048
Regional Airports Ltd, Re [1999] 2 BCLC 30 ....9.131
Reid v Explosives Co Ltd [1887] 19 QBD 264 ....20.033
Reitzman v Grahame-Chapman and Derustit Ltd (1950) 68 RPC 25 ....5.018
Republic of Haiti v Duvalier [1989] 1 All ER 456 ....25.047, 25.051
Resinoid & Mica Products Ltd, Re [1983] Ch 132 ....19.090, 19.098
Resinoid and Victoria Housing Estates, Re [1983] Ch 132 ....19.098
Response Engineering Ltd v Caherconlish Treatment Plant Ltd [2011] IEHC 345, [2012] 2 ILRM 67 ....18.041, 19.059–19.061
Revenue and Customs Commissioners v Egleton [2007] 1 All ER 606 ....25.049

Revenue and Customs Commissioners v Holland [2010] UKSC 51, [2011] 1 All ER 430, [2010] 1 WLR 2793 ....13.046, 13.051–13.052
Revenue Commissioners v Bank of Ireland [1925] 2 IR 90 .... 4.084
Revenue Commissioners v Donnelly [1983] ILRM 329 .... 25.168
Revenue Commissioners v O'Flynn Construction Ltd [2011] IESC 47 .... 3.019
Rex Pet Foods Ltd and Murphy v Lamb Brothers (Dublin) Ltd [1982] IEHC 33 .... 20.082
Rex Pet Foods Ltd and Murphy v Lamb Brothers (Dublin) Ltd (No 2) [1985] IEHC 65 .... 5.056, 5.062, 12.049
Reynard v Secretary of State for Trade and Industry, Re [2001] TLR 441 .... 28.172
Rhondda Waste Disposal Co Ltd (in administration), Re [1999] TLR 605 .... 22.061
Rica Gold Washing Co, Re (1879) 11 CH D 36 .... 23.045
Ricardo Group PLC (No 3), Re [1989] BCLC 771 .... 29.127
Richard Mills & Co (Brierly Hill), Re [1905] WN 36 .... 26.020
Richardson, Re, ex p Governors of St Thomas's Hospital [1911] 2 KB 705 ..... 11.118
Richbell Information Services Inc, Re [1999] TLR 49 .... 23.079
Richborough Furniture Ltd, Re [1996] 1 BCLC 507, [1996] BCC 155 .... 13.048, 28.155
Richmond Building Products Ltd v Soundgables Ltd, Re [2005] 3 IR 321 .... 26.062
Richmond Gate Property Co Ltd, Re [1964] 2 All ER 936 .... 13.070
Ridge Securities Ltd v IRC [1964] 1 All ER 275 .... 7.079, 10.099
Rights & Issues Investment Trust Ltd v Stylo Shoes Ltd [1965] 1 Ch 250 .... 3.076
Ring v Kennedy [1999] 3 IR 316, (1997) ITLR 6 October 1997 .... 19.028
Ringuet v Bergeron (1960) 24 DLR (2d) 449 .... 15.038
Ringinfo Ltd [2002] 1 BCLC 210 .... 23.078
Ringway Roadmarking v Adbruf Ltd [1998] 2 BCLC 625 .... 12.050
Riviera Leisure Ltd, Re [2009] IEHC 183 .... 23.077
RMCA Reinsurance Ltd, Re [1994] BCC 378 .... 21.026
Roache v Newsgroup Newspapers Ltd (1992) CAT 1120 .... 11.087
Robb v Green [1895] 2 QB 315 .... 15.155
Roberts v Coventry Corporation [1947] 1 All ER 308 .... 4.040
Robinson Printing Co Ltd v Chic Ltd [1905] 2 Ch 123 .... 20.037
Robson v Smith [1895] 2 Ch 118 .... 18.100
Roburn Construction Ltd v William Irwin (Sough) & Co Ltd [1991] BCC 726 .... 6.058
Rodencroft Ltd, Re [2004] 1 WLR 1566 .... 23.073
Rolland v La Caisse d'Economie Notre-Dame de Quebec (1895) 24 SCR 405 .... 7.094
Rolled Steel Products (Holdings) Ltd v British Steel Corp [1985] 3 All ER 52, [1986] 1 Ch 246 ....7.055–7.058, 7.061–7.065, 7.069 .... 15.054, 18.006–18.007
Rolls Royce Ltd, Re [1974] 1 WLR 1584 .... 25.181
Rome v Punjab National Bank (No 2) [1989] BCLC 328 .... 34.007–34.010
Romilly v Romilly [1963] 3 All ER 607 .... 6.100
Ronan (John) and Sons v Clean Build Ltd (in liq) [2011] IEHC 350 .... 5.066
Ronbow Management Company Ltd v Sorohan Builders Ltd [2010] IEHC 60 ....6.020, 6.033, 6.038, 6.055

Ronson Products Ltd v Ronson Furniture Ltd [1966] 2 All ER 381 ....6.080, 6.096
Roper v Ward [1981] ILRM 408 ....3.088, 3.092, 7.074, 7.078, 24.051
Rose v McGivern [1998] 2 BCLC 593 ....14.021–14.021
Rose, Re [1949] Ch 78 ....9.024
Ross v Telford [1997] BCC 945 ....14.031
Ross v Telford [1998] 1 BCLC 82 ....14.029, 14.105
Rother Iron Works Ltd v Canterbury Precision Engineers Ltd [1974] QB 1 ....18.090
Rottenberg v Monjack [1993] BCLC 374 ....20.041
Roundabout Ltd v Beirne [1959] IR 423 ....4.079, 5.050
Roundwood Colliery Co, Re [1897] 1 Ch 371 ....18.098
Routestone Ltd v Minorities Finance Ltd [1997] BCC 180 ....20.057
Rover International Ltd v Cannon Film Sales Ltd [1987] BCLC 540 ....1.158, 7.043
Rowe v Wood (1795) 2 J & W 553 ....1.020
Royal Bank of Canada v W Got & Associates Electric Ltd
(15 October 1999) SC (Can) 20.009
Royal British Bank v Turquand (1856) 6 E & B 327,
[1843–60] All ER Rep 435 .... 7.026, 7.063, 7.121
Royal Marine Hotel Company Kingstown Ltd, Re [1895] 1 IR 368 ....19.046
Royal Trust Bank v Buchler [1989] BCLC 130 ....22.060
Royal Trust Bank v National Westminster Bank plc [1996] 2 BCLC 682 ....18.045
Rubber and Produce Investment Trust, Re [1915] 1 Ch 382 ....24.014
Ruben v Great Fingall Consolidated [1906] AC 439 ....7.123
Ruben v Great Fingall Consolidated Co (1875) 10 Ch App 614 ....8.049
Ruby Property Co Ltd v Kilty and Superquinn [1999] IEHC 50 ....16.105
.... 20.051, 20.053, 20.056
Ruby Property Co v Kilty and Superquinn (31 January 2003,
unreported) HC 20.063–20.065
Rugby Auto Electric Services Ltd, Re (14 December 1959,
unreported) HC 26.062
Runciman v Walter Runciman plc [1992] BCLC 1084 ....14.128
Rushden Heel Company Ltd v Keane [1946] 2 All ER 141 ....10.095
Russel v Russel (1783) 1 Bro CC 269 ....18.034
Russell Murphy (Russell), Re [1976] IR 15 ....18.090
Russell v Northern Bank Development Corp Ltd [1992] 3 All ER 161
..........3.032, 3.115, 3.123, 3.127
Russell v Wakefield Waterworks Co (1875) LR 20 Eq 474
.... 11.124, 11.133–11.135, 11.143
Russell, ex p [1882] 19 Ch D 588 ....25.111
Russell-Cooke Trust Co Ltd v Elliott [2007] 2 BCLC 637 ....18.049
Ruth (Pat) Ltd, Re [1981] ILRM 51 .... 25.070, 25.071, 25.078
RW Peak (Kings Lynn) Ltd, Re [1998] BCC 596 ....10.014, 10.029
..........10.073, 14.098
Ryan v Attorney General [1965] IR 294 ....4.068
Ryanair Ltd v Aer Lingus Group plc [2011] IEHC 170 ....13.135
Ryhope Coal Co Ltd v Foyer (1881) 7 QBD 485 ....4.038

S

Safeera Ltd v Wallis & O'Regan (12 July 1994, unreported) HC 7.024, 7.028, 14.090
Safeguard Industrial Investments Ltd v National Westminster Bank Ltd [1982] 1 All ER 449 ....3.046, 9.078
Sage Holdings Ltd v The Unisec Group Ltd (1982) 1 SA 337 ....27.014
Sainsbury plc v O'Connor (Inspector of Taxes) [1990] STC 516 ....9.080
Salih v General Accident [1987] IR 628 ....6.017
Sallyview Estates Ltd, Re; Farrell v Balzarini and Balzarini [2007] IEHC 424 ....28.093
Salmon v Quin & Axtens Ltd [1909] AC 442, [1909] 1 Ch 311 ....11.127, 13.0133
Salomon v A Salomon & Co Ltd [1897] AC 22 ....1.057, 1.144, 4.026
........4.029, 4.033, 5.001–5.003, 5.046, 5.062, 5.096
6.002–6.003, 7.074, 7.099, 8.036, 10.016, 11.081
........12.048, 18.020, 25.119, 27.024, 31.013
Salomons v Laing (1850) 12 Beav 377 ....11.122
Salters Hall School Ltd, Re; Merrygold v Horton [1998] 1 BCLC 401 ....24.055
Salthill Properties Ltd, Re [2004] IEHC 145 ....18.080–18.083, 19.005
Salthill Properties Ltd, Re [2006] IESC 35 ....18.080–18.083
Salthill Properties Ltd and Cunningham v Royal Bank of Scotland plc [2010] IEHC 31 ....6.052–6.054
Salton v New Boston Cycle Co [1900] 1 Ch 43 ....20.015
Sammel v President Brand Gold Mining Co Ltd (1963) 37 DLR (2d) 9.103
Sanders v Europieces (Case C–399/96) (12 November 1998) 20.034
Sarflax Ltd, Re [1979] 1 All ER 529 ....15.107, 15.117
Saunders (GL) Ltd, Re [1986] BCLC 40, [1986] WLR 215 ....20.067
Saunders v United Kingdom [1997] BCC 872 (Case 43/1994/490/572) 27.045
Savage River Pty Ltd v Fordcorp Industries Pty Ltd (14 August 1998, unreported) SC (Vict) 7.025
Saver Ltd, Re [1999] BCC 221 ....28.199
Savory (EW) Ltd, Re [1951] 2 All ER 1036 ....8.105
Savoy Hotel Ltd, Re [1981] 1 Ch 351, [1981] 3 All ER 646 ....21.014–21.018
Scandinavian Group plc, Re [1987] 2 WLR 752 ....8.044
Schagen v The Queen (1993) 8 WAR 410 ....6.067
Schofield v Schoflield [2011] EWCA Civ 154, [2011] 2 BCLC 319 ....14.094
Scott v Brown, Douring McNab and Co (1892) 2 QB 724 ....5.040
Scott v Scott [1943] 1 All ER 582 ....8.078, 13.126, 13.0133–13.135
Scottish Co-operative Wholesale Society Ltd v Meyer [1959] AC 324
........3.083, 9.132, 11.011, 11.023–11.024
........11.076, 12.052, 15.047
Scottish Insurance Corporation v Wilsons and Clyde Coal Co [1949] AC 462
........8.071, 8.109
Scottish Petroleum Co, Re (1882) 23 Ch D 413 ....8.008, 14.113
Scotto v Petch [2000] 2 BCLC 211, [2000] TLR 107 ....9.070, 9.080
Seagull Manufacturing Co Ltd (No 2), Re [1994] 1 BCLC 273 ....28.154
Second Consolidated Trust Ltd v Ceylon Amalgamated Tea & Rubber Estates Ltd [1943] 2 Ch 567 ....14.068

Secretary of State for Employment v Spence [1986] IRLR 248 ....20.034
Secretary of State for Trade and Industry v Aurum Marketing Ltd [2000] TLR 615 ....25.166
Secretary of State for Trade and Industry v Bottrill [2000] 1 All ER 915 ....4.077
Secretary of State for Trade and Industry v Deverell [2000] BCC 1057 .... 13.058, 13.060, 13.064, 28.155
Secretary of State for Trade and Industry v Jones [1999] BCC 336 ......13.054, 28.155
Secretary of State for Trade and Industry v Langridge [1991] 3 All ER 591 ......28.162
Secretary of State for Trade and Industry v North West Holdings plc [1998] BCC 997 ....23.111
Secretary of State for Trade and Industry v Tjolle [1998] BCC 282 ......13.044, 13.048 .... 13.053–13.054, 28.155
Secretary of State for Trade v Markus [1976] AC 35 ....5.095
Securities Trust Ltd v Associated Properties Ltd (19 November 1980, unreported) HC 9.096, 9.099, 15.021
Securities Trust Ltd v Hugh Moore & Alexander Ltd [1964] IR 417 ....3.039, 4.050, 32.050
Sedgefield Steeplechase Co, Re (1927) Ltd 9.070
SEE Co Ltd v Public Lighting Services Ltd [1987] ILRM 255 ....4.071, 6.031, 6.034, 6.041, 6.047, 6.055
Seear v Lawson (1880) 15 Ch D 426 ....24.036
Selectmove Ltd, Re [1995] 2 All ER 531 ....23.072
Selukwe, Re (20 December 1991, unreported) HC 22.034, 22.080, 22.148, 22.159
Senator Hanseatische Verwaltungsgessellschaft mbh, Re [1996] 2 BCLC 562 ....23.109
Sevenoaks Stationers (Retail) Ltd, Re [1991] 3 All ER 578, [1991] BCLC 325, [1990] 3 WLR 1165 ....28.182, 28.199
Sevic Systems [2005] ECR I-10805 ....29.152
Sewell's case, Re, New Zealand Banking Corporation 8.008
SH & Co (Realisations) 1990 Ltd, Re [1993] BCLC 1309 ....10.073–10.074
Shalfoon v Chedar Valley Co-operative Dairy Co Ltd [1924] NZLR 561 ....3.062, 3.093, 3.113
Shamji v Johnson Matthey Bankers Ltd [1986] BCLC 278 ....20.010, 20.062
Shanahans Stamp Auctions Ltd, Re [1962] IR 38 ....25.149
Shannonside Holdings Ltd, Re (20 May 1993, unreported) HC ....3.051, 3.086, 7.113, 7.120, 10.074 ....13.140, 14.094, 19.014, 19.092, 23.018, 28.116
Shapland Inc, Re [2000] BCC 106 ....25.093
Sharman (RW) Ltd, Re [1957] 1 All ER 737 ....23.043
Sharmane Ltd, Re [2009] IEHC 377 .... 22.087, 22.164–22.167
Sharp v Dawes [1876] 2 QBD 26 ....14.056
Sharp v Woolwich Building Society [1998] BCC 115 ....18.087
Sharpe, Re; Masonic and General Life Assurance Co v Sharpe [1892] Ch 154 ....10.103
Shaw (John) & Sons (Salford) Ltd v Shaw [1935] 2 KB 113, [1935] All ER 456 ....13.0133, 13.137
Shaw v Sloan [1982] NI 393 ....6.004

Shawinigan v Vokins [1961] 1 WLR 1206 .... 15.101
Shearer (Inspector of Taxes) v Bercain Ltd [1980] 3 All ER 295
.... 8.067, 10.111, 17.194
Sheffield and Sough Yorkshire Permanent Building Society, Re
[1889] 22 QBD 470 .... 1.063
Shell E&P Ireland Ltd v McGrath [2006] IEHC 108, [2007] 1 IR 671
.... 6.095, 6.099
Sheppard & Cooper Ltd v TSB Bank plc [1996] 2 All ER 654 .... 20.009
Shinkwin v Quin-Con Ltd and Quinlan [2001] 1 IR 514 .... 5.013, 5.018
Shirlaw v Southern Foundries (1926) Ltd [1939] 2 All ER 113 .... 13.034
Short v Spackman (1831) 2 B & Ad 962 .... 5.028
Short v Treasury Commissioners [1948] AC 534 .... 4.032, 9.120
Short v Treasury Commissioners [1948] 1 KB 116 .... 8.036
Shortt v Ireland [1996] 2 IR 195 .... 6.039
Shrinkpak Ltd, Re (20 December 1989, unreported) HC 5.035, 14.120
.... 23.041–23.042, 23.107
Shrinkwin v Quinn-Con Ltd [2001] 1 IR 514 .... 15.087
Shusella Ltd, Re [1983] BCLC 505 .... 23.057
Shuttleworth v Cox Brothers & Co (Maidenhead) Ltd [1927] 2 KB 9 .... 3.074–3.077
Shuttleworth v Secretary of State for Trade and Industry; Re Dawes
and Henderson (Agencies) Ltd [2000] BCC 204 .... 28.203
Shwernell v Combined Incandescent Mantles Syndicate [1907] WN 110 .... 32.017
SIAC Construction Ltd, Re; Feighery v Feighery [1998] IEHC 31,
[1999] 1 IR 321 .... 11.068
Sichel v Raphael (1861) 4 LT 114 .... 25.044
Sidebottom v Kershaw Leese & Co Ltd [1920] 1 Ch 154
.... 3.071, 3.076–3.078, 3.084, 11.130
Siebe Gorman & Co Ltd v Barclays Bank Ltd [1979] 2 Lloyds
Rep 142 .... 18.042, 19.004, 19.059, 19.062
Silken Construction Ltd; Kavanagh v O'Donoghue [2003] 4 IR 443 .... 28.091
Silverhold Ltd, Re [2010] IEHC 111 .... 23.078, 23.080, 23.083
Simpson and Miller v British Industries Trust Ltd (1923) 39 TLR 286 .... 11.118
Simpson v Westminster Palace Hotel (1860) 8 HLC 712 .... 8.089, 11.122–11.123
Sinclair v Brougham [1914] AC 398 .... 7.091
Siney v Dublin Corporation [1980] IR 400 .... 17.334
Singer Manufacturing Co v Robinow (1971) SC 11 .... 21.015
Sisk (John) & Son v Flinn (18 July 1984, unreported) HC 17.337
Siskina, The [1977] 3 All ER 803 .... 25.047, 25.049
Skinner v City of London Marine Insurance Corp
(1885) 14 QBD 882 .... 9.013, 9.022, 9.064
Skinner, Re [1958] 3 All ER 273 .... 21.020
Skipton Building Society v Bratley [2000] TLR 15 .... 20.062
Skytours Travel Ltd, Re; Doyle v Bergin [2011] IEHC 517
.... 9.123–9.125, 9.132–9.134, 11.087
Skytours Travel Ltd, Re; Doyle v Bergin (No 2) [2011] IEHC 518 .... 11.087
Sligo Corporation v Cartron Bay Construction Ltd, Maguire and Maguire
[2001] IEHC 94 .... 6.081

'Slogger' Automatic Feeder Co Ltd, Re [1915] 1 Ch 478 ....20.020, 20.092
Sloman v Bank of England [1845] 14 Sim 475 ....8.024
Slyne Properties Ltd, Re [2010] IEHC 37 ....22.022
Smallman (J) Ltd v O'Moore & Newman [1959] IR 220 ....4.048
SMC Electronics Ltd v Akhter Computers Ltd [2001] 1 BCLC 433 ....7.100
Smedley v Registrar of Joint Stock Companies [1919] 1 KB 97 ....14.011
Smith & Fawcett Ltd, Re [1942] 1 All ER 542 ....15.029–15.031
Smith (Administrator of Cosslett (Contractors) Ltd) v Bridgend County
Borough Council [2001] UKHL 58, [2002] 1 All ER 292 ....18.071
.... 18.074–18.077, 19.007
Smith (Howard) Ltd v Ampol Petroleum Ltd [1974] AC 821 ....8.052, 15.032
Smith and Fawcett Ltd, Re [1942] 1 Ch 304 .... 9.021, 9.044, 9.052–9.054
Smith v Butler [2011] EWHC 2301 (Ch), [2012] 1 BCLC 444 ....14.029
Smith v Croft (No 2) [1987] 3 All ER 909, [1988] Ch 114 .... 8.089, 9.075, 12.025
Smith v Croft (No 3) [1987] BCLC 355 .... 11.114, 11.122–11.129
....................11.133, 11.144
Smith v Henniker-Major & Co [2002] BCC 544 ....7.130–7.131
Smith v Paringa Mines Ltd [1906] 2 Ch 193 ....14.058, 14.109
Smith v Peters (1875) LR 20 Eq 511 ....25.041
Smith v White Knight Laundry Ltd [2001] EWCA Civ 660,
[2001] 3 All ER 862 ....23.132
Smith, Knight & Co, Re (1868) LR 4 Ch App 20 ....9.018
Smith, Stone & Knight Ltd v Birmingham Corporation [1939] 4
All ER 116 ....5.009, 5.024
Smith's case [1994] 4 All ER 150 ....6.085
Smiths Ltd v Middleton [1979] 3 All ER 842 ....20.046
Smurfit Paribas Bank Ltd v AAB Export Finance Ltd (No 2)
[1991] 2 IR 19 ....25.117
Smyth v Darley (1849) 2 HL Cas 789 ....8.080
Snead v Valley Gold Ltd [1893] 1 Ch 477 ....21.012
Société Generale de Paris v Walker (1885) 11 App Cas 20 ....8.028, 9.024
Society for the Protection of Unborn Children (Ireland) Ltd v Coogan
[1989] IR 734 ....4.071–4.072
Society for the Protection of Unborn Children (Ireland) Ltd v Grogan
[1992] ILRM 461 ....6.034, 6.038
Soden v British and Commonwealth Holdings plc [1997] 4 All ER 353 ....25.193
Somafer SA v Saar-Ferngas AG Case 33/78 [1978] ECR 2183 ....34.030
Somers v Allen [1984] ILRM 437 .... 19.022, 19.046, 19.050
South Hetton Coal Co v North Eastern News Association [1894] 1 QB 133 ....4.049
South India Shipping Corp Ltd v Export-Import Bank of Korea
[1985] 2 All ER 219, [1985] BCLC 163 ....34.010
South London Greyhound Racecourses Ltd v Wake [1931] 1 Ch 496 ....8.049
South of England Natural Gas and Petroleum Co Ltd, Re
[1911] 1 Ch 573 ....32.017
Southard & Co Ltd, Re [1979] 1 WLR 1198 ....25.119
Southard & Co Ltd, Re [1979] 1 WLR 546 ....23.119
Southend Borough Council v White (1992) 156 JP 463 ....5.095

Southern Counties Fresh Foods Ltd, Cobden Investments Ltd v RWM Langport Ltd, Re [2008] EWHC 2810 .... 15.048
Southern Cross Interiors Pty Ltd v Deputy Commissioner of Taxation [2001] NSWSC 621 .... 15.049–15.050
Southern Foundries (1926) Ltd v Shirlaw [1940] AC 701 .... 3.057
Southern Resources, Re (1989) 15 ACLR 770 .... 14.110
Southern v Watson [1940] 3 All ER 439 .... 5.021
Sovereign Life Assurance Co v Dodd (1892) 2 QB 573 .... 21.029–21.034
Spackman v Evans [1868] LR 3 HL 171 .... 17.312
Spackman, ex p (1849) 1 Mac & G 170–174 .... 23.091
Spain v McCann [1978] ILRM 215 .... 19.100
Spanish Prospecting Co Ltd, Re [1911] 1 Ch 92 .... 8.106, 10.095
Spector Photo Group NV v Commisie voor het Bank, Financie en Assurantiewezen [2010] 2 CMLR 30 .... 32.076, 32.081
Spectrum Plus Ltd, Re [2005] 2 BCLC 269 .... 18.043–18.044 .... 18.048–18.049, 18.056
SPH Ltd, Re [2005] IEHC 152 .... 28.128
Spiral Globe Co Ltd, Re [1902] 1 Ch 396 .... 19.096
Spokes v Grosvenor Hotel Co Ltd [1897] 2 QB 124 .... 11.118, 11.122
Spring Grove Services (Ireland) Ltd v O'Callaghan [2000] IEHC 62 .... 15.071
Springline, Re [1999] 1 IR 467, [1999] 1 ILRM 15, [1998] 1 ILRM 301 .... 22.087, 25.165
Squash (Ireland) Ltd, Re [2001] 3 IR 35 .... 28.107–28.108, 28.122 .... 28.136, 28.166, 28.180
Squires v AIG Europe (UK) Ltd [2006] BCC 233 .... 19.034
SRA Properties Ltd, Re [1967] 2 All ER 615 .... 27.029
Sri Lanka Omnibus Co Ltd v Perera [1952] AC 76 .... 8.024
St George's Estate, Re (1887) 19 LR Ir 556 .... 20.091
St James' Court Estate Ltd, Re [1944] Ch 6 .... 21.022
Stacey v Hill [1901] 1 KB 660 .... 25.062
Stainless Pipeline Supplies (IRL) Ltd, Re; Tyner v Lafferty [2010] IEHC 318 .... 7.025, 23.024
Stancomb v Trowbridge UDC [1910] 2 Ch 190 .... 6.080, 6.084, 6.085
Standard Chartered Bank Ltd v Walker [1982] 3 All ER 938 .... 20.050, 20.062–20.063
Standard Chartered Bank of Australia Ltd v Antico (1995) 13 ACLC 1381 .... 13.066
Standard Manufacturing Co, Re [1891] 1 Ch 627 .... 4.089, 19.046
Stanford Services Ltd, Re [1987] BCLC 607 .... 28.182
Stanley, Re [1906] 1 Ch 131 .... 1.058
Stanton (F&E) Ltd, Re [1929] 1 Ch 180 .... 25.117
State (Batchelor & Co Ireland Ltd) v O'Leannain [1957] IR 1 .... 6.070
State (Commins) v McRann [1977] IR 78 .... 6.095
State (Crowley) v Irish Land Commission [1951] IR 250 .... 4.015
State (Ennis) v Farrell [1966] IR 107 .... 28.027
State (Finglas Industrial Estate Ltd) v Dublin County Council [1983] IESC 8 .... 7.037
State (Hennessy and Chariot Inns Ltd) v Commons [1976] IR 238 .... 5.075

State (Lynch) v Cooney [1982] IR 337 ....27.019
State (McEldowney) v Kelleher [1983] IR 289 ....28.072
State (McInerney & Co Ltd) v Dublin County Council (12 December 1984, unreported) HC 5.057
State (Shannon Atlantic Fisheries Ltd) v McPolin [1976] IR 93 ....27.030
State v District Justice Donnelly (1977) Irish Times, 5 November 5.048
State v Goertz (1980) (1) SA 269 ....15.099
Station Motors Ltd v Allied Irish Banks Ltd, Re [1985] IR 756 ....25.092–25.094, 25.097–25.098
Steadman v Steadman [1976] AC 536 ....5.015
Steamline Ltd, Re [1998] IEHC 102 ....28.089, 28.108
Steel Company of Canada Ltd v Ramsay [1931] AC 270 ....8.107
Stein v Blake [1995] 2 All ER 961 ....25.150
Stein v Blake [1998] 1 All ER 724 ....11.106
Stein v Saywell (1969) 121 CLR 529 ....18.096, 20.070
Steinberg v Scala (Leeds) Ltd [1923] 2 Ch 452 ....8.040
Sterileair Pty Ltd v George Ralph Papallo [1998] 1446 Federal Court of Australia (16 November 1998) 10.063
Stevenson [1902] 1 IR 23 and [1903] 1 IR 403 ....19.018
Stevenson v Wilson (1907) SC 445 ....9.065, 9.074
Stewart v Engel [2000] BCC 741, [1999] TLR 804 ....24.003
Stewart's Case (1886) 1 Ch App 574 ....8.024
Stewarts Supermarkets Ltd v Secretary of State [1982] NI 286 ....4.040
Sticky Fingers Restaurant Ltd, Re [1992] BCLC 84 ....14.024, 14.105
Stillwell Trucks Party Ltd v Nectar Brook Investments Party Ltd [1993] 10 ACSR 615 ....3.089
Stocznia Gdanska SA v Latreefers Inc (No 2) [2000] TLR 182 ....23.036
Stokes & McKiernan, Re [1978] ILRM 240 ....19.074, 19.083
Stone & Rolls Ltd (in liq) v Moore Steven [2009] AC 1391 ....4.054
Stonegate Securities Ltd v Gregory [1980] 1 All ER 241 .... 23.078, 23.081–23.083
Stoneleigh Finance Ltd v Phillips [1965] 1 All ER 513 ....19.048
Stothers v William Steward (Holdings) Ltd [1994] 2 BCLC 266 ....9.028–9.029 ....9.058
Strahan v Wilcock [2006] 2 BCLC 555 ....9.125
Strathblaine Estates Ltd, Re [1948] Ch 228 ....4.038, 25.197
Straume (UK) Ltd v Bradlor Developments Ltd [1999] TLR 478 ....22.061
Stubbs v Slater [1910] 1 Ch 632 ....9.036
Sugar Distributors Ltd v Monaghan Cash & Carry Ltd [1982] ILRM 399 ....19.079
Sugar Distributors Ltd, Re [1995] 2 IR 194 ....8.069
Sullivan, Re [1984] Crim LR 405 ....4.035
Sun Tai Cheung Credits Ltd v AG of Hong Kong [1987] 1 WLR 948 (PC) 19.019
Sunday Tribune Ltd, Re [1985] ILRM 698 ....25.187
Sunlink International Ltd v Wong Shu Wing [2010] 5 HKLRD 653 ....3.079
Sunrise Radio, Re [2010] 1 BCLC 367 ....9.132
Super John Pty v Marsford Investments Pty Ltd (18 April 1997) FCA 9.099
Superwood Holdings plc v Sun Alliance and London Plc Assurance plc (27 June 1995, unreported) SC 4.052

Superwood Holdings plc v Sun Alliance and London plc [1995] 3 IR 303 .... 6.031
Superwood Holdings plc v Sun Alliance and London Insurance plc [2002] IESC 22 .... 6.014
Superwood Holdings plc v Sun Alliance and London Insurance plc [2005] 3 IR 398 .... 6.017–6.018
Superwood Holdings plc v Sun Alliance and London Insurance plc [2006] IEHC 123 .... 6.018
Supply of Ready Mixed Concrete, Re; Director General of Fair Trading v Pioneer Concrete (UK) Ltd [1994] ICR 57 .... 6.085
Supply of Ready Mixed Concrete (No 2), Re; Director General of Fair Trading v Pioneer Concrete (UK) Ltd [1995] 1 All ER 135, [1995] 1 AC 456 .... 4.066, 6.085, 6.089
Supreme Oil Co Ltd, Re; Hughes v Duffy & Hanratty [2005] 1 IR 571 .... 28.134
Surchin v Approved Business Machine Co 286 NYS 2d 580 .... 1.150
Sutton's Hospital case (1612) 10 Co Rep 1 .... 1.063
Swabey v Port Darwin Gold Mining Co (1889) 1 Meg 385 .... 13.070
Swain (JD) Ltd, Re [1965] 2 All ER 761, [1965] 1 WLR 909 .... 23.043 .... 23.119, 23.120–23.122
Swaledale Cleaners Ltd, Re [1968] 3 All ER 619, [1968] 1 WLR 1710 .... 9.060 .... 9.080, 9.086
Swanpool Ltd, Re; McLoughlin v Lannen [2006] 2 ILRM 217 .... 28.116
Swedex Windows & Doors Ltd, Re [2010] IEHC 237 .... 23.125, 24.008
Swedish Central Railway v Thompson [1925] AC 495 .... 5.073
Sweeney v Duggan [1991] 2 IR 274 .... 5.013
Swift v Dairywise Farms Ltd [2000] BCC 642 .... 25.012
Swiss Bank Corporation v Lloyds Bank Ltd [1980] 2 All ER 419 .... 18.036
Sykes (Butchers) Ltd, Re; Secretary of State v Richardson [1998] 1 BCLC 110 .... 13.054, 28.155
Sykes' case (1872) LR 13 Eq 255 .... 8.096
Synnott (Mark) (Life and Pensions) Brokers Ltd, Re (1991) Irish Times, 15 June 25.049
Synnott (Mark) (Life and Pensions) Brokers Ltd, Re (1991) Irish Times, 2 July 24.016
Synnott (Mark) (Life and Pensions) Brokers Ltd, Re (1991) Irish Times, 3 July 25.041
Synnott (Mark) (Life and Pensions) Brokers Ltd, Re (1991) Irish Times, 8 November 25.035
Synnott (Mark) (Life and Pensions) Brokers Ltd, Re and Re Bishopsgate Investment Management (1991) Irish Times, 10 December 25.046

T

Tai Hing Cotton Mill Ltd v Liu Chong Hing Bank Ltd [1985] 2 All ER 947 .... 20.010
Tailteann Freight Services Ltd, Re [1975] IR 376 .... 24.003
Tain Construction Ltd, Re; Rose v ABI Group (UK) plc [2003] 2 BCLC 374 .... 25.077

Tait Consibee (Oxford) Ltd v Tait [1997] 2 BCLC 349 ....16.065
Tangney v The Clarance Hotels Co Ltd [1933] IR 51 ....9.022, 9.050
Tansoft Ltd, Re [1991] BCLC 339 ....28.182
Targe Towing Ltd v The Owners and all Persons Claiming an interest in the Vessel 'Von Rocks' [1998] 1 ILRM 481 ....19.069
Target Holdings v Redferns [1995] 3 All ER 785 ....10.103
Tasbian Ltd (No 3), Re [1991] BCLC 792 ....15.111
Tate, ex p (1876) 35 LT 531 ....25.089
Tatiangela, The [1980] 2 Lloyd's Reports 193 ....25.047
Taupo Totara Timber Co Ltd v Rowe [1977] 3 All ER 123, [1978] AC 537 ....13.091
Tay Bok Choon v Tahanson Sdn Bhd [1987] BCLC 472 ....11.014, 23.097
Taylor v Smith [1991] IR 142 ....4.052, 4.067
Taylor's Industrial Flooring Ltd v M&H Plant Hire (Manchester) Ltd [1990] BCLC 216 ....23.075, 23.083
TCB Ltd v Gray [1986] 1 All ER 587 .... 7.026, 7.131–7.133, 16.109
TDG plc, Re [2009] 1 BCLC 445 ....21.004
TDK Tape Distributor (UK) Ltd v Videochoice Ltd [1985] 3 All ER 345 ....6.086
Tea Corporation, Re [1904] 1 Ch 12 ....21.026
Teck Corporation Ltd v Millar (1972) 3 DLR (3d) 288 ....8.052, 15.034
Tedman Holdings, Re [1967] QR 561 ....4.086
Teele & Bishop , Re (1901) 70 LJ 409 ....14.054
Telenor Invest AS v IIU Nominees Ltd and Esat Telecom Holdings Ltd [1999] IEHC 188 ....3.125
Telewest Communications plc (No 1), Re [2004] EWHC 924 (Ch) 21.037
Telford Motors Ltd, Re (27 January 1978, unreported) HC 19.096, 19.098
Telomatic Ltd, Re [1994] 1 BCLC 90 ....19.091
Tempany v Hynes [1976] IR 101 ....18.093
Tempany v Royal Liver Trustees Ltd [1984] ILRM 273 .... 5.015, 25.062, 25.064
Tennant v City of Glasgow Bank (1880) 5 App Cas 317 ....8.024
Termascan Ltd v Norman [2011] BCC 535 ....15.065
Tesco Stores Ltd v Brent London Borough Council [1993] 2 All ER 718 ....4.064
Tesco Supermarkets Ltd v Natrass [1971] 2 All ER 127, [1972] 2 AC 153 ....4.064, 6.085
Tett v Phoenix Property and Investment Co Ltd [1986] BCLC 149 ....9.024, 9.086
TGM v Al Babtain Trading [1982] ILRM 349 ....3.117, 3.124
Thake v Soares [1957] IR 152 ....6.057
Thames Magistrates' Court; ex p Hogan [1997] TLR 633 ....28.038
The 19th Ltd, Re [1989] ILRM 652 ....24.032
Theakston v London Trust plc [1984] BCLC 390 ....9.081
Third v North East Ice & Cold Storage Co Ltd [1998] BCC 242 .... 1.151, 11.035, 11.038
Thompson v Douglas Amateur Football Club Social Club [1999] Scot SC (27 June 1999) 1.051
Thorby v Goldberg (1964) 112 CLR 597 .... 3.126, 15.036, 15.040
3V Multimedia Group, Re (20 August 1992, ex temp) HC 22.0141

360Atlantic (Ireland) Ltd, Re; O'Ferral v Coughlan
[2004] 4 IR 266 ...., 28.103, 28.117
Thundercrest Ltd, Re [1995] 1 BCLC 117 ....3.042, 8.024
Tierney v Midserve Ltd, t/a Sachs Hotel and Genport Ltd
[2002] IEHC 12 ....1.010, 2.044
Tipperary Fresh Foods Ltd, Re [2005] IEHC 96 ....28.093
Tipperary Self-Drive Ltd, Re (1992) Irish Times, 21 January 25.020
Tipperary Self-Drive Ltd, Re (1992) Irish Times, 4 February 25.041, 25.049
Titan Transport Logistics Ltd, Re (19 February 2003, unreported) HC 23.029
Tivoli Freeholds Ltd, Re [1972] VR 445 ....1.154
Tivway Ltd, Re [2010] IESC 11 ....22.024, 22.150
TLL Realisations Ltd, Re [2000] BCC 998 ....28.203
Tolstoy Miloslavsk v United Kingdom (1995) 20 EHRR 432 ....6.018
Tomkins (HJ) & Son Ltd, Re [1990] BCLC 76 ....23.120
Tommy Hilfiger Europe Inc v Derek McGarry t/a 'Lifejacket'
[2005] IEHC 66 ....6.094
Top Creative Ltd v St Albans District Council [1999] BCC 999 ....26.056
Torbett v Faulkner [1952] 2 TLR 659 ....4.038
Torkington v Magee [1902] 2 KB 427 ....18.030
Tottenham Hotspur plc, Re [1994] 1 BCLC 655 ....11.025
Towers v African Tug Co [1904] 1 Ch 558 ....11.124
Townreach Ltd, Re [1995] Ch 8 ....26.060
TR Technology Investment PLC, Re [1988] BCLC 256 ....29.125
Tracey v Bowen [2005] IEHC 138 ....25.047
Tracy v Mandalay Party Ltd (1952) 88 CLR 215 ....15.167
Trade Practices Commission v Australian Iron & Steel Pty Ltd
(1990) 22 FCR 305, 92 ALR 395 ....10.016
Traffic Group Ltd, Re [2008] 3 IR 253 ....22.128, 22.157, 22.159
Tralee Beef & Lamb Ltd, Re [2008] IESC 1 ....13.039, 15.043, 15.053
Tralee Beef & Lamb Ltd, Re; Kavanagh v Delaney [2008] 3 IR 347 ... 28.115, 28.119
Tramway Building and Construction Co Ltd, Re [1987] BCLC 632 ....25.077
Transplanters (Holding Co) Ltd, Re [1958] 1 WLR 822 ....17.312
Trebanog Working Men's Club v MacDonald [1940] 1 KB 576 ....5.030
Trench Tubeless Tyre Co, Re [1900] 1 Ch 408 ....14.054
Trevor v Whitworth (1887) 12 App Cas 409 ....3.033, 7.074, 8.023
....9.020, 10.009–10.014, 31.022
Trident International Freight Services v Manchester Ship Canal
Company [1990] BCLC 263 ....6.039
Triffit Nurseries v Salads Etcetera Ltd [2000] BCC 98 ....20.029
Trinity Products Ltd, Re (2005) Irish Times, of 26 April 24.015
Trocko v Renlita Products Pty Ltd (1973) 5 SASR 207 ....21.009
Troon Developments Ltd v Harrahill [2009] IEHC 590 ....23.087
Truck and Machinery Sales Ltd v Marubeni Komatsu Ltd
[1996] 1 IR 12 ....23.042, 23.072, 23.082, 23.086
Trustee Savings Bank Dublin v Maughan [1992] 1 IR 488 ....25.179
Trustor AB v Smallbone (No 2) [2001] 3 All ER 987 ....5.005, 5.036
TSB Private Bank International SA v Chabra [1992] 2 All ER 245 .... 5.067, 25.049

TSC Industries Inc v Northway Inc 426 US 438 (US SCt) 32.078
Tucker (Brian) Ltd, Re; Farrell v Equity Bank Ltd [1990] 2 IR 549
 .... 18.041, 19.059–19.061
Tudor Grange Holdings Ltd v Citibank NA [1992] Ch 53 ....20.031
Tugwell v Hooper (1847) 10 Beav 348 ....6.063, 11.059
Tullow Engineering (Holdings) Ltd, Re [1990] 1 IR 452 ....18.070
Tulsesence Ltd; Rolfe v Rolfe [2010] EWHC 244, [2010] 2 BCLC 525 ....14.094
Tumacacori Mining Co, Re (1874) LR 17 Eq 534 ....25.052, 25.132
Tunstall v Steigman [1961] AC 12 ....4.041
Turner (P) (Wilsden) Ltd, Re [1987] BCLC 149 ....24.014, 25.128
Turquand v Marshall (1869) LR 4 Ch App 376 ....15.075
Tuskar Resources plc, Re [2001] 1 IR 668 .... 1.158, 22.010, 22.021, 22.027
 ....22.031–22.034, 22.036, 22.051–22.052
Tutt v Mercer (1725) 2 Bro PC 563 ....9.035
Tweeds Garage Ltd in Patrick Butterly and Sons Ltd v Top Security Ltd, Re
 (27 September 1995, unreported) HC 23.083
Tweeds Garage Ltd, Re [1962] 1 All ER 121 ....23.083
Twycross v Grant (1877) CPD 469 ....15.161
TXU Europe Group plc (in administration), Re [2004] 1 BCLC 519 ....18.028
Tyman's Ltd v Craven [1952] 1 All ER 613, [1952] 2 QB 100 ....26.056
 ....26.060, 26.062

U

UBAF Ltd v European American Banking Corporation [1984] QB 713 ....4.048
Überseering Case C-167/01 [2002] ECR I-9919 ....29.152
Ulster Factors Ltd v Entonglen Ltd and Maloney [1994] 1 ILRM 387 ....7.092
Ulster Factors Ltd v Entonglen Ltd and Maloney [1997] IEHC 34 ....7.083
 .... 7.092, 7.103–7.106
Ulster Investment Bank Ltd v Euro Estates Ltd and Drumkill Ltd
 [1982] ILRM 57 ....7.026, 7.122
Ulster Land, Building and Investment Co Ltd, Re (1887) 17 LR Ir 591 ....25.045
Ultraframe (UK) Ltd v Fielding [2005] EWHC 1638, [2006] FSR 17 ....16.033
Underwood (AL) Ltd v Bank of Liverpool & Martins [1924] All ER 230,
 [1924] 1 KB 775 ....4.036, 7.126
Underwood, Re (1903) 51 WR 335 ....25.044
Unidare plc, Re [2012] IEHC 114 ....25.173
Union Accident Insurance Co Ltd, Re [1972] 1 All ER 1105 ....23.126, 24.041
Unisoft Group Ltd (No 2) [1993] BCLC 532 ....6.058
Unisoft Group Ltd, Re [1994] BCC 766 ....13.060
Unisoft Group Ltd, Re [1994] BCC 11 ....6.021
Unit Construction Co Ltd v Bullock [1959] 3 All ER 831,
 [1960] AC 351 ....5.073, 6.029
United Bank of Kuwait Ltd v Hammond [1988] 1 WLR 1051 ....7.104
United Bars Ltd v Revenue Commissioners [1991] 1 IR 396 ....20.067
United English and Scottish Life Insurance Co, Re (1868) Lr 5 Eq 300 ....25.052
United Provident Assurance Co Ltd, Re [1910] 2 Ch 477 ....21.027
United Service Co, Re (1868) LR 7 Eq 76 ....23.120

United Stock Exchange Ltd, Re; ex p Philip & Kidd (1884) 28 CD D 183 .... 23.058
Universalebau v Ensor Gunsbethrieba Simmering (1999) ECJ C470 .... 6.023
UOC Corporation, Re; Alipour v Ary [1997] BCC 377 .... 23.047
UOC Corporation, Re; Alipour v UOC Corporation [1998] BCC 191 .... 24.053
UPM v BWG [1999] IEHC 178 .... 18.109
USIT Ireland Ltd, Re [2003] 2 IR 635 .... 28.075, 28.084
USIT World plc [2005] IEHC 285 .... 28.100
Usk and District Residents Association Ltd v The Environmental Protection
Agency [2006] 1 ILRM 363 .... 6.020, 6.025, 6.032
Utilicorp Nz Inc v Powerer New Zealand Ltd (1997) 8 NZCLC 261 .... 13.041

V

Vale Sewing Machines v Robb [1997] SCLR 797 .... 19.075
Valley Ice Cream (Ireland) Ltd, Re [1998] IEHC 119 .... 18.036, 19.015
.... 19.052, 19.092
Van Hool McArdle Ltd, Re [1982] ILRM 340 .... 25.168
Vantive Holdings, Re [2009] IESC 68 .... 22.022–22.023, 22.035
.... 22.037, 22.151
Vantive Holdings (No 2) Ltd, Re [2009] IEHC 409 .... 22.025
Vectone Entertainment Holding Ltd v South Entertainment Ltd
[2005] BCC 123 .... 14.030
Vehicle Buildings and Insulations Ltd, Re [1986] ILRM 239 .... 23.098–23.100
Vehicle Imports Ltd, Re (23 November 2000, unreported) HC 13.046, 13.057
.... 15.053, 15.053, 15.134, 28.077
.... 28.111–28.112, 28.118–28.120
Vendor and Purchaser Act 1874, Re; Crowley v Flynn (13 May 1983,
unreported) HC 16.109
Verderame v Commercial Union Assurance Co plc [1992] BCLC 793 .... 4.039, 4.050
Verit Hotel and Leisure (Ireland) Ltd, Re [2001] IESC 74 .... 28.065
Verit Hotel and Leisure (Ireland) Ltd, Re; Duignan v Carway [2002] IEHC 1
.... 28.068, 28.085, 28.090, 28.124, 28.128, 28.133–28.135
VGM Holdings, Re [1942] Ch 235 .... 8.038
Via Net Works Ireland Ltd, Re [2002] 2 IR 47 .... 8.032, 11.044
Victoria Housing Estates Ltd v Ashpurton Estates Ltd [1982] 3 All ER 665
.... 19.091, 19.098
Victoria Steamboats Ltd, Re [1897] 1 Ch 228 .... 18.100
Village Cay Marine Ltd v Acland (Barclays Bank Plc third party)
[1998] 2 BCLC 327 .... 9.029, 9.047, 9.054
Village Cay Marine Ltd v Acland et al [1998] BCC 417 .... 20.030
Village Residents Association Ltd v An Bord Pleanála (No 2)
[2004] 4 IR 321, [2001] 2 ILRM 22 .... 6.021
Village Residents Association Ltd v An Bord Pleanála and McDonalds
Restaurants of Ireland Ltd [2000] IEHC 34 .... 6.046, 6.052, 6.056
Virdi v Abbey Leisure [1990] BCLC 342 .... 11.054
Vision Express (UK) Ltd v Wilson [1998] BCC 173 .... 10.030, 10.065
Visual Impact and Display Ltd, Re; Murphy v Murphy
[2003] IEHC 91 .... 28.095

Vitara Foods Ltd, Re [1999] BCC 315 ....11.055
Vocam Europe Ltd, Re [1998] BCC 396 ....3.121
Von Sandau v Moore (1825) 1 Russ 441 ....1.078

W

Wagner v International Health Promotions [1994] 12 ACLC 986 ....14.110
Wah Tat Bank Ltd v Chan Cheng Kum [1975] AC 507 ....5.018
Waitomo Wools (NZ) Ltd v Nelsons (NZ) Ltd [1974] 1 NZLR 484 .....19.031, 19.049
Waldcourt Investment Co Pty Ltd, Re (1986) 11 ACLR 12 ....26.028
Walkden Sheet Metal Co Ltd, Re [1960] Ch 170 ....25.056
Walker v London Tramways Co (1879) 12 Ch D 705 ....3.057
Wallace v Evershed [1899] Ch 891 ....18.070
Wallersteiner v Moir [1974] 3 All ER 217 ....10.062, 10.064
Wallersteiner v Moir (No 2) [1975] 1 QB 373 .... 11.111, 11.115, 11.118
Wallis & Simmonds (Builders) Ltd, Re [1974] 1 All ER 561 ....19.031
Walls Properties Ltd, Re; Walls v PJ Walls Holdings Ltd
[2007] IESC 41 .... 3.088, 3.098, 9.097, 9.106
Walsh Maguire & O'Shea Ltd, Re [2011] IEHC 457 ....23.131–23.135
Walsh v Butler [1997] IEHC 9 ....1.051
Walsh Western Holdings Ltd, Re; Meehan v Walsh Western Holdings Ltd
and Enright [2009] IEHC 505 ....11.056
Ward (Alexander) & Co Ltd v Samyang Navigation Co Ltd
(1973) SLT 80 ....14.012
Ward (Alexander) & Co Ltd v Samyang Navigation Co Ltd
[1975] 2 All ER 424, [1975] 1 WLR 673 .... 13.0133, 13.139–13.140
Ward and Henry's case (1867) 2 Ch App 431 ....9.074
Ward v Dublin North City Milling Co Ltd [1919] 1 IR 5 ....8.076
Waterford Foods plc, Re (1992) Irish Times, 12 May 14.048
Waters v Kelly [2009] IEHC 222 ....4.044
Watson v Duff Morgan and Vermont (Holdings) Ltd [1974] 1 All ER 794,
[1974] 1 WLR 450 ....19.094
Watson v Parapara Coal Co Ltd (1915) 17 GLR 791 ....18.065
Weatherall v Satellite Receiving Systems (Australia) Pty Ltd
[1999] Federal Court of Appeal 218 (12 March 1999) 11.034
Webb v Earle (1875) LR 20 Eq 556 ....8.104
Weddel (NZ) Ltd, Re (1996) 5 NZBLC 104 ....19.075
Wedgewood Coal and Iron Co (Andersons Case), Re 7 Ch D 75 ....3.088
Wedgewood Coal and Iron Co, Re (1877) 6 Ch D 627 ....21.054
Welch v Bank of England [1955] Ch 508 ....8.024
Welch v Bowmaker (Ireland) Ltd [1980] IR 251 ....18.035, 18.069
.... 18.073, 18.081, 18.089, 19.005
Welding Plant Ltd, Re; Cooney v Dargan, Re (27 June 1984,
unreported) HC 25.083, 25.092
Weldtech Ltd, Re [1991] BCC 16 ....19.076
Weller (Sam) & Sons, Re [1990] BCLC 80 ....11.030
Wellingford Construction Ltd, Re; Joyce v Wellingford
Construction Ltd [2005] IEHC 392 ....25.080

Welsh Brick Industries Ltd, Re [1946] 2 All ER 197 .... 23.075
Welsh Highland Railway Light Railway Co, Re [1993] BCLC 338 .... 23.035
Welsh Irish Ferries Ltd, Re [1985] BCLC 327 .... 19.062
Welton v Saffery [1897] AC 299 .... 3.095, 3.127
Wenborn & Co, Re (1905) 1 Ch 413 .... 25.169
West Cumberland Iron and Steel Co, Re (1889) 40 Ch D 361 .... 23.014
West Donegal Land League Ltd v Údarás na Gaeltachta
[2007] 1 ILRM 1 .... 6.042–6.044
West Mercia Safetywear Ltd v Dodd [1988] BCLC 250 .... 15.012, 15.016
Westbourne Galleries Ltd, Re [1970] 3 All ER 374, [1970] 1 WLR 1378 .... 11.016
Westbourne Galleries Ltd, Re [1971] 2 WLR 618 .... 11.014
Westbourne Galleries Ltd, Re [1973] AC 360 .... 11.026, 11.040, 11.068
Western Counties Construction Ltd v Whitney Town Football and
Social Club (1993) Times, 19 November 23.035
Western Counties Steam Bakeries and Milling Co, Re
[1897] 1 Ch 617 .... 13.004, 17.312
Westmaze (1998), Re (15 May 1998, unreported) HC (Eng) 18.045
Westmid Packing Services Ltd, Re [1998] 2 BCLC 646 .... 15.053
Westminister Property Management Ltd (No 3), Re; Boyden v Stern
[2004] BCC 599 .... 16.101
Westminster Bank Ltd v Hilton (1926) 136 LT 315 .... 25.070
Westminster Property Group plc, Re [1985] 1 WLR 676 .... 27.087
Westminster Property Management Ltd, Re [2000] TLR 28 .... 28.160
Westwinds Holding Co Ltd, Re (21 May 1974, unreported) HC
.... 2.007, 11.016–11.017, 11.049, 11.080, 11.084
Wexford Rope and Twine Co Ltd v Gaynor and Modler
[2000] IEHC 23 .... 6.038, 6.040–6.043, 6.049
Whaley Bridge Calico Printing Co v Green & Smith (1879) 5 QBD 109 .... 15.162
Wheatcroft's case (1873) 29 LT 324 .... 8.021
Wheatley v Silkstone and Haigh Moor Coal Co [1885] 29 Ch D 715 .... 18.089
Wheeler v Ross [2011] EWHC 2527 (Ch) 14.029
White & Osmond (Parkinstone) Ltd, Re (30 June 1960,
unreported) HC (Eng) 15.117
Whitehouse v Carlton Hotel Party Ltd [1976] 2 All ER 268 .... 8.052, 15.033
Whiting Inc v Prudential Bache Securities Australia Ltd [1998] VSC 86
(18 September 1998) 9.036
Whitworth Street Estates Ltd, Re [1980] AC 583 .... 18.046
Wicklow County Council v Fenton [2002] 4 IR 44 .... 5.066
Wicklow County Council v O'Reilly [2006] IEHC 265, [2007] IEHC 71 .... 5.066
Wicklow Textiles Ltd, Re (1953) 87 ILTR 72 .... 23.120
Wigan Coal and Iron Co Ltd v Inland Revenue Commissioners
[1945] 1 All ER 392 .... 25.198
Wilkes (John) Footwear Ltd v Lee International Footwear Ltd
[1985] BCLC 444 .... 5.082
Will v United Lankat Plantations Co [1914] AC 11 .... 8.107–8.109
Willaire Systems plc, Re [1987] BCLC 67 .... 14.052
Willcocks (WR) & Co Ltd, Re [1973] 3 WLR 669 .... 23.045

William (H) (Tallaght) Ltd, Re [1976] IR 314 ....25.187
William (H) (Tallaght) Ltd, Re [1996] 3 IR 531 ....25.184–25.185
William Dixon Ltd, Re (1948) SLT 423 ....14.082
William Gaskell Group Ltd et al v Highley (Nos 1, 2, 3) [1994] 1 BCLC 197 ....18.044
Williams (H)(Tallaght) Ltd (in receivership and liquidation) [1996] 3 IR 531 ....20.069
Williams Group Tullamore Ltd, Re [1985] IR 613 ....3.071, 3.079, 3.082, 11.016, 11.031, 11.084
Williams v Natural Life Health Foods Ltd [1998] BCC 428 ....4.053, 15.087
Williams v Natural Life Health Foods Ltd [1998] 2 All ER 577 ....5.019
Williams v Quebrada Railway Land and Copper Co Ltd [1895] 2 Ch 751 ....16.095
Williamson (Thomas) Ltd v Bailieborough Co-Operative Agricultural Society Ltd (31 July 1986, unreported) HC 7.060–7.062, 7.100
Willis v Jermin (1590) Cro Eliz 167 ....7.029
Wilson (Inspector of Taxes) v Dunnes Stores (Cork) Ltd (22 January 1976, unreported) HC 8.077, 8.105, 10.095, 25.193
Wilson Smithett & Cape Sugar v Bangladesh Sugar and Food Industries [1986] 1 Lloyds' Rep 378 ....5.017
Wilson v Jones (1866) LR 1 Exch 193 ....4.039
Wilson v Kelland [1910] 2 Ch 306 ....18.080, 18.089
Wilson Vehicle Distribution Ltd v Colt Car Co Ltd [1984] BCLC 93 ....6.026
Wiltshire Iron Co, Re (1868) 3 Ch App 443 ....25.065
Wily v George Partnership Banking Ltd [1999] Federal Court of Appeal (29 January 1999) 18.071
Wimbush, Re [1940] Ch 92 ....8.074
Windmaster Developments Ltd v Airoglen Ltd and Kelly [2000] IEHC 59 ....1.158, 6.026, ...6.035, 6.057
Windward Islands (Enterprises) UK Ltd, Re [1983] BCLC 293 ....14.023
Winkworth v Edward Baron Developments Ltd [1987] 1 All ER 114 ....15.016
Winthrop Engineering and Contracting Ltd v CED Construction Ltd, Re [2011] IEHC 420 ....23.024
Wise Finance Co Ltd v O'Regan [1998] IEHC 105 ....20.011, 20.026
Wise v Landsell [1921] 1 Ch 420 ....9.073
Witherdale, Re [2006] BCC 412 ....26.037
Witt v Banner (1887) 20 QBD 794 ....4.089
WLD Worldwide Leather Distribution Ltd v Revenue Commissioners (27 July 1994, unreported) HC 2.046
WMG (Toughening) Ltd, Re [2001] IEHC 65, [2001] 3 IR 113 ....23.073 ....23.076, 23.079
WMG (Toughening) Ltd, Re (No 2) [2003] 1 IR 389 ....23.078
Wogan's (Drogheda) Ltd, Re [1994] 1 ILRM 481 ....18.047
Wogan's (Drogheda) Ltd (No 2), Re (7 May 1992, unreported) HC 22.034, 22.143–22.144, 22.159
Wogan's (Drogheda) Ltd (No 3), Re [1993] 1 IR 157 ....18.046, 18.104, 19.059, 22.031, 22.113, 22.168
Wolf v Sumners (1811) 2 Camp 631 ....19.025

Wolfe v Wolfe [2006] IEHC 106 .... 11.056
Wondoflex Textiles Pty Ltd, Re [1951] VLR 458 .... 23.095–23.096
Wood Products (Longford) Ltd, Re [2005] IEHC 41 .... 28.192
Wood Products (Longford) Ltd, Re; Director of Corporate Enforcement v McGowan and McGowan [2008] 4 IR 598 .... 28.167
Woodhouse & Co (1914) 30 TLR 559 .... 6.063
Woodroffes (Musical Instruments) Ltd, Re [1985] BCLC 227, [1986] Ch 366 .... 18.071, 18.100–18.102
Woolfson v Strathclyde Regional Council (1978) SC 90 .... 5.059
Woonda Nominees Pty Ltd v Chng (19 October 2000) SC (WA) 13.041
Workvale Ltd, Re [1991] BCLC 528 .... 26.041
Worldport Ireland Ltd, Re [2005] IEHC 189 .... 25.065, 25.073
Worldport Ireland Ltd, Re [2005] IEHC 467 .... 13.067
Worldport Ireland Ltd, Re [2008] IESC 68 .... 13.055, 13.068
Worldport Ireland Ltd, Re; Hughes v Worldport Communications Inc [2009] 1 IR 398 .... 28.079
Woven Rugs Ltd, Re [2002] 1 BCLC 324 .... 14.029
Wragg Ltd, Re [1897] 1 Ch 796 .... 8.062–8.063
Wright (David) & Co Ltd, Re (1905) 39 ILT 204 .... 7.025
Wright v Horton [1887] 12 AC 371 .... 19.006
Wright v Wright (7 February 1996, unreported) HC 9.030
Wymes v Crowley (27 February 1987, unreported) HC 20.031

X

Xnet Information Systems Ltd, Re; Higgins v Stafford [2006] IEHC 289 .... 28.139
XYZ Ltd (1986) 2 BCC 520 .... 9.126

Y

Yenidje Tobacco Co Ltd, Re [1916] 2 Ch 426, [1916–1917] All ER Rep 1050 .... 23.095, 23.098
Yeoman Credit v Latter [1961] 2 All ER 294 .... 5.015, 5.016
Yolland v Husson & Birkett Ltd [1908] Ch 152 .... 19.018
Yorkshire Woolcombers' Association Ltd, Re [1903] 2 Ch 284 .... 18.047
.... 18.069, 18.076
Yorkshire Woolcombers' Association Ltd, Re [1904] AC 355 .... 18.100
Young v Matthew Hall Mechanical and Electrical Engineers Pty Ltd (1988) 13 ACLR 399 .... 18.027
Young v Sough African and Australian Exploration and Development Syndicate [1896] 2 Ch 275 .... 14.063
Ystalyfera Gas Co, Re [1887] WN 30 .... 8.024
Yukong Line Ltd of Korea v Rendsburg Investments Corp of Liberia (No 2) [1998] 4 All ER 82 .... 15.011

Z

Zinotty Properties Ltd, Re [1984] 3 All ER 754, [1984] 1 WLR 1249 .. 14.012, 23.097
Zirceram Ltd, Re; Brodie & So v Zirceram Ltd [2000] BCC 1048 .... 23.124
Zota Manufacturing Ltd, Re, Application of Topping, Re [2010] IEHC 114 ..... 26.048

Table of Legislation

Ireland

Agricultural Credit Act 1978 ......18.069, 19.050
s 36(1) 4.089
Air Navigation and Transport Act 1936 ......1.066
s 68 ......1.066
Aliens Act 1935 ......1.006
Anglo Irish Bank Corporation Act 2009 ......23.137
s 4 ......9.006
5 (2) 9.006
21(1) 13.046
14(4)(a) 9.006
Auditor General and Committees of the Houses of the Oireachtas (Special Provisions) Act 1998 ......27.032
Bank of Ireland Act 1781/2 ......1.055
Bankrupt and Insolvent Act 1857 ......25.141
Bankruptcy Act 1988 ......2.005, 4.089, 25.057, 25.087, 25.141
s 3 ......25.143
44(1) 9.031
51 ......25.057
(1) 25.055
57 ......25.081, 25.087
124 ......25.042
129 ......5.033
136(1) 25.143
(2) 25.143, 25.189
Sch 1 para 17(1) 25.145
para 24(1) 25.150, 25.152, 25.158
para 24(4)(a) 25.145
Betting Act 1931
s 4(1) 4.076
Bills of Exchange Act 1882
s 3(1) 25.068
73 ......25.068
Bills of Sale (Ireland) Act 1879 ......19.046, 19.050, 19.073
s 4 ......4.089, 19.048–19.051
Bills of Sale (Ireland) Act 1879 (Amendment) Act 1883 ......19.046
s 4 ......19.050

Bills of Sale (Ireland) Act 1879 (Amendment) Act 1883 (contd)
9 .... 4.089
17 .... 4.089, 19.046
Bills of Sale (Ireland) Acts 1879–1883 .... 1.013, 4.089, 19.003, 19.033, 19.046
Broadcasting Authority Act 1960 .... 1.066
Bubble Act 1720 .... 1.071–1.077
Building Societies Act 1976 .... 4.016
Building Societies Act 1989 .... 1.036, 1.068
s 9 .... 1.039
10 .... 1.037
11 (1) 1.037
12 (1) 1.038
16 (1) 1.041
17 .... 1.037
(1) 1.039
(8) 1.039
18 .... 1.039
(1A) 1.041
20–23 .... 1.039
24–28 .... 1.039
29 .... 1.039
30 .... 1.039
31–35 .... 1.039
36 .... 1.039
37 .... 1.042
39 .... 1.042
40 (2) 23.139
40–47 .... 1.042
47 .... 1.043
48 .... 1.043
50 .... 1.043
51 .... 1.043
53–59 .... 1.043
64 .... 1.037
69 (3A) 1.041
95 .... 1.047
96 .... 1.047
101(2) 1.046
111 .... 1.045
112 .... 1.045
Pt IV 1.042
Pt VI 1.044
Pt VII 1.045
Pt X 1.047
Pt XI 1.046
Sch 2 .... 1.037

Building Societies (Amendment) Act 2006 .... 1.036
Capital Gains Tax Act 1975 .... 5.092, 25.185
s 31 .... 16.014
Capital Acquisitions Tax Consolidation Act 2003 .... 5.092
Central Bank Reform Act 2010 .... 32.057
Central Bank and Credit Institutions (Resolution) Act 2011 .... 1.048, 23.138
.... 23.142, 24.024
s 76 .... 23.138
77 .... 23.139
78 (1) 23.139
(2)–(4) 23.140
79 (1) 23.141
80 .... 23.141
(1)–(3) 23.141
83(1) 23.142
84(3) 23.142
85 .... 23.142
86 .... 23.142
87 .... 23.142
89 .... 23.138
90 .... 23.138
Pt 7 .... 23.138
Central Bank and Financial Services Authority of Ireland Act 2004
s 10 .... 32.057
Central Bank Act 1942 .... 1.066
s 33AK 17.214
33AQ 32.057
33AR 32.057
Central Bank Act 1971
s 9 .... 13.024, 22.016, 23.138
Central Bank Act 1972
s 9 .... 27.049
Central Bank Acts 1942–1998 .... 27.080
Charities Act 1961
s 46 .... 8.131, 13.112, 16.014
Charities Act 2009
s 2 (1) 30.068
3 (1) 30.020
(11) 30.020
52 .... 30.068
Pt 2 .... 30.062
Pt 6 .... 30.062

Civil Liability Act 1961
s 61 .... 25.153
Civil Partnership and Certain Rights and Obligations of Cohabitants Act 2010 .... 16.006–16.008, 25.086
97(1) 16.006
Pt 3 .... 16.006
Committees of the Houses of the Oireachtas (Compellability, Privileges and Immunities of Witnesses) Act 1997
s 3 .... 27.080
14 .... 27.080
16 .... 27.080
Common Law Procedure Act 1853 .... 9.040
132 .... 9.038
Companies Clauses Consolidation Act 1845 .... 13.045
Companies Clauses Act 1845 .... 19.046
90 .... 23.039
Companies Clauses Act 1862 .... 19.046
Companies Act 1862 .... 1.071, 1.084, 1.144, 1.160, 3.062
.... 4.026, 23.035, 27.003, 31.022
s 6 .... 4.006
8 .... 31.022
12 .... 31.022
30 .... 8.029
35 .... 9.068
38 .... 3.062
56 .... 27.003
69 .... 6.016
95 .... 24.036
118 .... 25.044
165 .... 13.046
Companies Act 1880
s 7 (5) 26.062
Companies Act 1907 .... 1.071, 1.132, 4.030
s 37 .... 1.086
(1) 1.002, 1.085, 1.134
Companies (Amendment) Act 1907
s 10(1)(d) 19.056
Companies (Consolidation) Act 1908 .... 1.071, 1.086, 1.160, 5.039
.... 14.090, 19.029, 23.035, 27.003
s 22 .... 9.018
93 (1) 19.056
121(1) 1.086

Companies (Consolidation) Act 1908 (contd)
209 .... 18.096
223 .... 23.130
109–111 .... 27.003
Table A model reg
71 .... 13.0134
76 .... 7.027
Companies Act 1959
8 .... 9.104
Companies Act 1963 .... 1.091
s 2 .... 1.156–1.159, 3.004, 6.012, 6.015, 6.020
.... 6.026, 6.096, 7.027, 9.091, 11.116, 12.007
.... 12.030, 13.007, 13.012, 13.066, 16.010, 16.024, 16.061
.... 19.087, 21.007, 21.069, 22.010, 23.035, 23.109
(1) 1.058, 1.162, 13.003, 13.009, 13.045, 13.049
.... 15.008, 16.089, 17.012, 17.016, 17.024, 17.154
.... 17.225, 17.292–17.296, 18.018, 23.138
.... 26.037, 27.012, 28.074–28.076, 29.116
(2) 16.010
(3) 12.007
3 (4) 4.013
5 .... 1.147, 3.003, 29.012, 29.029, 29.135
(1) 3.092, 4.002, 31.008
(2)(a) 4.083
(b) 4.083
(c) 2.013
6 .... 30.013, 31.005
(1) 31.006
(a) 3.006, 30.031
(b) 7.045, 30.015
(c) 3.012, 30.031, 31.005
(2) 30.024, 30.031
(3) 30.024, 30.031
(4) 8.043
(a) 3.017
7 .... 3.004
8 .... 1.038, 6.012, 7.046, 7.048, 7.075, 7.081, 7.083, 7.120, 7.135
(1) 7.080–7.087, 7.092, 10.083, 31.018
(2) 7.047, 11.122–11.123, 21.021, 28.029
9 .... 3.021–3.022, 30.031
(3) 3.087
10 .... 3.026, 3.085, 7.045, 10.017–10.021, 14.087, 31.007
(1) 3.026, 10.086
(3) 3.026, 28.011
(4) 3.026
(5) 3.026

Companies Act 1963 (contd)

(6) 3.027
(6A) 10.021, 10.086
(8) 3.026
(9) 28.049
11 .... 2.028, 3.039, 30.035
12 (1) 3.039, 31.010
(2) 2.028, 3.039, 30.036
(3) 2.028, 28.049, 30.036, 30.067, 31.010
13A(1) 30.035
(2) 30.035
13 (2) 3.039
14 .... 3.039
(1) 3.039
(8) 10.029
(d) 3.092
15 .... 3.056–3.059, 3.069, 3.085, 8.078, 14.087
(1) 3.059
16 .... 2.024–2.028, 3.004
17 .... 2.032, 3.001
18 .... 1.057, 28.006
(1) 4.002
(2) 2.033, 4.021, 4.087, 7.022, 13.126
19 .... 1.113, 4.004
20 .... 4.002, 33.003
21 .... 3.006, 31.006
(4)(a) 23.077
22 .... 2.044
(1) 3.011
(2) 3.008
23 .... 3.023, 14.087, 30.017, 31.007
(2) 3.024, 28.061
(3) 3.023, 4.002
(4) 3.025
(6) 23.055
24 .... 2.041, 3.009, 3.023, 29.028, 30.012–30.015, 30.071
(1) 30.016
(a) 30.023–30.025
(b), (c) 30.017
(2) 30.017
(3) 30.016
(4) 3.059, 30.017
(5) 30.017
(6) 3.025, 30.017
(7) 30.017
(8) 28.061, 30.017

Companies Act 1963 (contd)
25 .... 3.002, 3.062–3.063, 3.092–3.096, 3.100–3.104
.... 3.107, 8.039, 8.075, 8.089, 9.107, 11.100, 25.193
(1) 3.092
(2) 8.094
26 .... 30.028
(1) 30.028
(2) 30.029
27 .... 3.029, 3.062, 30.033, 33.009
(1) 3.060–3.061, 3.091, 30.044
(2) 3.029, 3.063
28 .... 14.087, 30.033, 31.007
(1) 3.037, 30.032
(2) 30.033
(3) 3.021, 3.037, 13.077, 30.034
29 .... 8.086
(1) 3.039, 28.061
30 (1) 3.022
(2) 28.061
31 .... 8.004, 9.030, 11.047, 11.116, 12.010, 14.035
.... 14.057–14.061, 26.036, 30.040
(1) 8.04
(2) 8.004–8.006, 30.041
32 .... 8.010, 8.014, 10.036
(1) 8.012, 10.016, 10.036–10.037
(2) 8.013, 10.036
(3) 8.013, 10.036
(4) 10.016, 10.036
(5) 8.013, 10.036, 10.040
(6) 8.013, 10.036
(7) 8.012, 10.036
(8) 8.013, 10.036
(9) 8.012, 10.036
33 .... 1.002, 1.085, 1.136–1.138, 2.008, 9.018, 15.156
.... 18.021, 19.102, 29.002, 29.007, 29.039, 31.024
(1) 1.133–1.145, 1.149, 2.010–2.013, 3.041, 4.085
.... 4.090, 8.001, 9.020, 19.044, 27.012, 30.010, 33.014
(a) 1.135, 9.001, 9.010
(c) 1.136
(2) 1.134
(3) 1.134
(5) 3.041
(6) 1.138
(7) 1.136
34 .... 1.139
35 .... 28.058, 28.061
(2) 28.061

Companies Act 1963 (contd)

36 .... 1.139, 1.145, 3.016, 5.078–5.080, 29.012, 30.039
37 .... 1.158, 7.035–7.037, 7.042–7.044
(1) 7.037
(2) 7.041–7.042
(3) 7.043
38 .... 7.003–7.007, 7.100
(1) 7.014, 7.098
(a) 7.014–7.018, 7.021, 7.031, 9.011
(b) 7.007, 7.010, 7.131
(c) 7.005
(3) 7.014
40 (1) 7.030–7.031
(2) 7.030
41 .... 7.022
(1)–(5) 7.023
42 .... 7.018
43 (1) 14.100
44 .... 28.061
(3) 32.007
45 (2) 25.033
46 .... 28.061
47 (1) 28.049
49 (1) 32.045
53 .... 28.061
(1) 28.049
(2) 13.105
(4) 29.046
54 .... 28.061
(5) 28.058
56 .... 28.061
57 .... 28.061, 29.056
(2) 29.056
(3) 29.056
58 (1)(a) 8.055
(b) 8.062
(3) 8.062
(4) 8.062
59 (1) 28.049
60 .... 8.115, 9.098, 10.010, 10.037, 10.046–10.050
.... 10.056–10.060, 10.064, 10.080, 11.011, 13.131
.... 14.087, 14.092, 16.080–16.081, 16.087–16.088
17.085, 20.018, 25.033, 25.136, 25.147, 28.070, 29.076–29.077
(1) 10.046–10.048, 10.053, 10.054, 10.057–10.058, 10.062
.... 10.065, 10.071, 10.075–10.078, 10.081–10.083, 16.107
(2) 10.038, 10.055–10.056, 10.065–10.068
.... 10.069–10.071, 10.074, 11.083, 16.087, 29.077

Companies Act 1963 (contd)
(a) 10.067, 10.071, 10.072
(b) 10.067–10.068, 10.071
(2)–(11) 10.066
(2)–(5) 10.068
(3) 10.067, 10.071
(4) 10.067
(a), (d) 10.071
(5) 10.071, 28.061
(6) 10.068, 10.072, 14.092
(7) 10.067
(8)–(11) 10.077
(12) 10.046, 10.078, 10.081–10.083, 29.078
(13) 10.046, 10.084
(a) 29.078
(b) 8.115, 29.078
(c) 8.115
(14) 10.049–10.054, 10.057, 16.107
(15) 10.048, 28.058
(15A) 10.069, 29.077
62 .... 8.066, 10.112
(1) 10.025, 10.041, 10.111, 17.194
(2) 10.112
64 .... 8.111
65 .... 10.017–10.019, 10.090
66 .... 3.018
67 .... 3.017
68 .... 3.032, 3.127–3.128, 8.116
69 .... 3.032, 8.116
(1) 28.049
(2) 8.116
70 .... 3.032
(1) 28.049
71 .... 3.032
72 .... 3.065, 10.017, 14.087, 21.022, 29.075, 29.082, 29.146, 31.023
(1) 3.034, 10.015, 22.147, 31.022
(2) 3.034, 10.020
72–77 .... 3.033
73 .... 3.034, 21.022, 29.075, 29.082
(2) 3.035
(a) 29.082
(3) 3.035
74 .... 3.035
75 .... 3.036
76 .... 3.036
(1) 3.036
(3) 3.036

Companies Act 1963 (contd)

77 .... 3.036, 28.061
78 .... 3.066
(5) 28.049
79 .... 8.037, 9.017–9.018
80 .... 8.043–8.046
81 .... 9.006, 18.022
(1) 9.006, 9.068
(2) 9.025, 9.033
84 .... 9.060
(1) 9.061
85 .... 9.015
86 .... 8.043–8.047, 28.061
(1) 9.008
(3) 8.047
87 .... 8.047, 9.027
(1) 29.064
88 .... 29.042
89 .... 8.068
(1) 8.068
90 .... 28.058
91 .... 2.037, 28.060
92 .... 28.061
98 .... 18.096, 20.066–20.069, 20.074, 22.072, 25.184
(1) 20.067
99 .... 18.026, 18.063, 19.004, 19.009–19.017, 19.021
.... 19.023–19.033, 19.057, 19.060, 19.064–19.067
.... 19.084, 22.073, 34.021
(1) 10.068, 18.014, 18.036, 18.070, 19.006
.... 19.012, 19.022, 19.031, 19.035, 19.041
.... 19.050, 19.071–19.073, 19.078, 19.080
.... 19.089, 25.096, 25.147
(2) 19.002, 19.022, 19.035, 19.042, 19.056, 19.067, 19.074, 34.019
(c) 19.046–19.050, 19.073
(d) 19.023, 19.052, 19.066
(e) 19.023, 19.059–19.065
(f) 19.066–19.067
(g) 19.068
(h) 19.069
(i) 19.070
(2A) 19.043
(2B) 19.043
(3) 19.086–19.087
(4) 19.086–19.088
(5) 19.086–19.089, 19.104
(6) 19.065
(7) 19.058

Companies Act 1963 (contd)

(8) 19.044
(10)(a) 19.042, 19.049
100 .... 19.089
(1) 19.101, 28.049
(3), (4) 19.101
101(1) 19.057, 28.049
(2) 19.057
102(1) 6.075, 19.085, 28.049
(2) 19.085
103 .... 19.002
104 .... 4.015, 19.011, 19.014, 19.019
105 .... 19.105
106 .... 19.091–19.092, 19.094–19.097, 19.099, 20.068
(1) 19.090, 19.106
107(1) 20.026, 20.071, 28.050
(2) 20.026, 28.050
(3) 20.026
108 .... 19.056
109 .... 2.037, 19.107
110 .... 28.061
(1) 19.107
(f) 28.040
(2) 19.107, 28.040
(3) 19.107
111 .... 19.087, 19.107, 34.009, 34.019
112(1) 28.049
113 .... 2.036, 28.061
(2) 2.036
(3) 2.036, 28.049
114 .... 2.042, 3.010, 7.012, 28.061
(1)(a) 2.042, 3.010
(b) 2.042, 3.010, 7.022
(c) 2.042, 3.010
(2) 2.042, 3.010
(3) 3.010
(4) 3.010, 5.081, 7.011
(5) 5.081
115 .... 28.061, 29.011, 31.012
(1) 31.011
(2) 31.003–31.011
(3) 31.011
(4) 31.011
(6) 31.011
(7)(a) 31.011
(d) 31.012

Companies Act 1963 (contd)

116 .... 8.017, 8.019, 28.060
(1)(a) 8.046
(2) 8.019
(5) 2.037, 8.017
(6) 8.017
(7) 8.017, 28.049, 29.011, 29.135
(9) 8.005, 8.017
116–124 .... 28.033
117(1) 28.060
118 .... 28.058
119 .... 8.018, 8.086, 28.061, 29.145
(1) 8.018
(3) 8.018
(4) 8.018
121 .... 9.018, 29.065
(1) 8.018
(2) 8.018
122 .... 8.024, 9.054
(1) 9.066–9.068
(2) 9.066–9.068
(3) 8.023, 9.068
(4) 9.066
(5) 8.022, 9.066
123 .... 8.025–8.029, 9.035, 9.039
124 .... 8.020
125 .... 17.250, 17.257–17.259, 26.001–26.06, 26.045, 28.046, 28.049, 28.192
(1) 17.252, 30.066, 31.024
(2) 17.320
126 .... 26.001–26.006, 26.045, 28.046
127 .... 17.252, 28.046, 28.049
(1) 15.156
(2) 17.252
(4) 28.049
(5) 17.252
(6) 17.252
(8) 17.253
(9) 17.253
(10) 17.016, 17.253
(12) 17.255, 17.320
(13) 17.255
128 .... 1.139, 30.066, 31.024
(1) 28.049, 30.066
(a) 15.156
(4) 1.139, 17.251
(a) 31.024
(c) 30.062

Companies Act 1963 (contd)
(5) 30.062
(6B) 30.066
(6C) 30.066
129 .... 15.156
131 .... 5.038, 14.013–14.014, 28.033, 28.061, 30.055
(1) 14.006, 17.016
(2) 14.006
(3) 14.011, 14.013
(3)–(5) 14.011
(5) 28.049
(6) 14.011, 28.033
132 .... 14.019, 14.045, 14.053
132A 29.107
132(1) 14.019
(2) 14.019
(3) 14.023
(4) 14.023
(6) 14.023
133 .... 3.065, 14.040, 29.100
(1) 14.040, 23.020
(a) 29.098, 29.102
(b) 29.098
(2) 14.040, 14.042, 14.049
(b) 23.020
(3) 14.041, 14.049
133A 29.101
133B 13.136
(1) 29.103
(2) 29.103
(3) 29.102
(4) 29.102
134 .... 3.065, 14.019, 14.035, 14.039
(5) 14.023
(a) 8.080, 14.035
(c) 14.055
(d) 14.080
(e) 8.083, 14.062
134A 29.104
(5) 29.104
(6) 29.104
134B 29.105
(2)(a) 29.105
(c) 29.105
134C(1) 29.106
(2) 29.106

Companies Act 1963 (contd)
135 ... 3.121, 14.025–14.028, 14.056, 14.105
(1) ... 14.024
(2) ... 14.024
136 ... 8.084, 28.061, 29.108
(1) ... 14.074
(1A) ... 29.109
(b) ... 29.108
(1B) ... 29.109
(2) ... 14.074
(2A) ... 29.109
(3)–(5) ... 14.074
137 ... 8.083, 10.028
(1) ... 14.068
(b) ... 14.068
(2) ... 14.069
138 ... 14.069, 29.110
(3) ... 29.110
139 ... 8.080, 23.024, 23.029, 29.149
(1)(a) ... 14.073
(2) ... 14.073
140 ... 14.010
(1) ... 14.010
(2)(b) ... 3.061
141 ... 3.047, 9.030, 14.040
(1) ... 14.042, 14.049–14.052, 14.084
(2) ... 14.042, 14.049
(3) ... 14.086
(4) ... 14.086
(5) ... 14.052
(8) ... 3.048, 3.056, 3.086, 3.110, 6.008, 10.068, 10.072
... 13.078, 14.004, 14.041, 14.091, 16.043, 16.044
... 16.082–16.083, 21.070, 23.013, 30.057
(a) ... 14.088–14.092
(b) ... 14.091
(c) ... 13.078, 14.092
142 ... 14.045–14.049
(1) ... 14.044–14.046
(2) ... 14.042, 14.046
(4)(a) ... 3.110
143 ... 3.110, 14.093, 28.061, 29.070
(1) ... 3.109, 14.091, 14.100
(2) ... 14.101, 28.049
(3) ... 8.086, 14.101
(4) ... 14.100
(a) ... 7.124
(c) ... 3.109
(5) ... 14.100

Companies Act 1963 (contd)
144 ....14.060, 14.117, 21.046, 22.131
145 ....14.077, 16.130, 28.050
(1) 14.078, 14.118, 28.060
(2) 7.115, 14.077, 14.116–14.119
(3) 14.077, 14.119
(3A) 14.078, 14.118
(4) 14.078, 14.118
145A 29.111
146 ....28.061
(1) 2.037, 14.079
(2) 8.086, 14.079
(3) 14.079
(4) 14.079
147 ....7.074, 12.048, 17.005
(3) 2.037
148 ....5.038, 10.095, 10.097, 14.014, 16.029, 16.077, 17.016, 31.027
(1) 17.016, 17.030, 17.059, 17.253
(2) 17.024
(b) 17.131
(3) 17.024, 30.062
(4) 17.024
(5) 17.024
(7) 17.016, 17.249
(11) 17.018
149 ....10.097, 17.021–17.024
(1) 17.030, 17.059
(a) 17.017
(b) 17.017
(2) 17.021–17.024, 31.030, 30.062
(3)(a) 17.024
(e) 30.062, 31.029
(5) 10.112, 17.194
149A 17.024, 17.131, 17.152, 29.147
(1)(a) 17.027
(2) 17.280
150 ....12.029, 17.152, 17.266, 28.061
(1) 17.017, 17.144
(2)(a) 17.144, 17.201
(3) 17.149
(4) 30.064
(5) 12.029, 16.037
(8) 31.036
(9) 17.017, 17.249
(10)(a) 17.247
150–154 ....12.049

Companies Act 1963 (contd)
150A 17.149
(1) 17.165
(2) 17.166, 31.030, 30.062
150B 17.201
(2)(a) 17.202
(k) 17.201
151 .... 17.144
152 .... 31.029
(1) 10.062
153(1) 17.155
(2) 17.253
(2) 17.155
154 .... 8.086, 17.144, 28.061
155 .... 1.156, 10.036, 10.068, 12.003, 12.016–12.019
.... 12.030–12.042, 12.046, 16.005, 16.013, 16.020
.... 16.037, 16.090, 16.099, 17.127, 20.006, 25.120–25.121
(1) 10.037, 12.008, 12.012, 12.022
(a) 12.016
(i) 12.009–12.013
(ii) 12.017–12.019
(iii) 12.020
(b) 10.037, 12.028
(2) 12.012
(3) 12.022
(a) 12.022
(b) (i) 10.068
(c) 12.026
(d) 9.035, 12.026
(4) 12.006
(5) 1.162, 12.007, 16.089, 22.052
156 .... 10.097, 17.028
(1) 17.019, 17.213
(3) 17.019, 17.213
(4) 17.019, 17.213
157 .... 17.244, 17.249, 28.061
(1) 17.019, 17.213
(2) 17.019, 17.213
158 .... 17.017, 17.223, 28.061, 30.063, 31.033
(1) 17.214
(2) 17.213, 17.221
(3) 17.214
(4) 17.217
(6) 17.217
(6A) 17.214
(6B) 17.214
(6C) 17.218

Companies Act 1963 (contd)
(6D) 17.218
(6E) 17.219
(6F) 17.213, 17.219
(6G) 17.219
(6I) 17.218
(6J) 17.218
(7) 17.223
159 ..... 8.086, 14.014, 28.061
(1) 17.019, 17.243, 28.058
(3) 17.019, 17.245
(4) 17.019, 17.246
(5) 17.019, 17.245
160 ..... 13.021, 13.078, 14.004, 14.092
(1) 13.004, 17.292
(2)(b) 3.087, 14.088, 17.295, 17.338
(c) 17.237, 17.343
(2)–(3) 17.293
(4) 17.294
(5A)(a) (i) 17.294, 28.049
(ii) 28.049
(b) 17.294
(5) 3.087, 14.088, 17.338
(6) 17.295
(a) 17.338
(7) 17.295
(8) 17.308
161A 17.342, 17.346–17.348
161(1) 17.338
(a) 14.044
(b) 14.044
(1)–(2) 17.295
(2) 17.338
(2A) 14.037, 17.341
(3) 17.340, 17.347
(4) 17.340
161B 17.342, 17.346–17.348
161C(1) 17.338
(2) 17.338
161D 17.122, 17.143, 30.062, 31.029
162 ..... 14.047, 28.061
(5) 13.018
163 ..... 10.097
165–166 ..... 27.003
165–173 ..... 11.043, 27.003
168(3) 27.047
170 ..... 11.043
(3) 11.043, 23.048

Companies Act 1963 (contd)
174 .... 1.143, 2.038, 13.011, 13.128, 28.047
175 .... 2.038, 13.011, 13.119
176 .... 4.076, 13.066–13.068, 28.079, 29.083
(1) 13.016, 13.067, 13.119, 28.079
177 .... 7.025, 13.011
178 .... 13.046, 22.088, 29.040
179 .... 13.025
(1) 28.049, 29.040, 29.084
(b) 29.040
(4) 29.040
(5) 29.040
180 .... 13.019, 28.061, 29.040
181 .... 13.029
182 .... 8.078, 11.067–11.068, 13.078–13.082, 14.004, 14.047, 14.092
(1) 3.053, 13.077–13.080, 13.138, 14.044
(2) 14.044
(3) 14.037
(5) 13.029
(7) 13.080
183 .... 13.018, 28.058
183A 28.160
184 .... 28.148
185 .... 13.094
186 .... 13.086, 13.092
187 .... 13.094
189(3) 13.086–13.092
190 .... 8.086, 15.156, 28.061
191 .... 17.112, 17.0132, 17.181, 17.202, 17.319, 30.062, 31.029
(5) 17.112
(8) 17.231, 17.319
193 .... 28.061
(1) 15.156
194 .... 15.132, 15.137, 16.001–16.004, 16.121–16.128, 16.135, 17.113, 28.061
(1) 16.121–16.133
(2) 16.127
(3) 16.126–16.130
(4) 16.128
(5) 28.051, 28.060
(a) 2.037, 16.131, 16.135
(b) 16.135
(5A) 16.135
(6) 16.135
(7) 16.132
195 .... 2.038, 8.086, 13.096, 15.156, 26.013, 28.047–28.049, 28.059–28.060
(1) 2.037
(2) 13.098

Companies Act 1963 (contd)
(3) 13.098
(4) 13.099, 13.119, 13.125
(5)(b) 16.131
(6) 13.083, 13.096
(a) 13.032
(7) 13.026, 13.096
(8) 13.083, 13.096, 28.153
(10) 13.097
(11) 13.097, 15.156
(11A) 13.083, 13.120, 26.013
(11B) 13.084, 26.013
(11C) 13.083
(11D) 13.084
(11E) 13.084
(12) 13.097
(a) 13.055
(15) 13.098
196 ..... 2.039–2.041, 28.061
(1) 34.017
(3)(a) 34.017
(4) 2.039
(5) 2.039
(6) 2.040
197 ..... 15.132, 15.137, 25.131, 28.061
(2) 15.156
198 ..... 14.087
199 ..... 13.043, 16.133
200 ..... 15.092, 17.336
(1) 15.091
201 ..... 10.095, 21.001–21.013, 21.022, 21.046, 21.052, 21.057, 22.119, 28.061
(1) 21.006, 21.017, 21.024–21.026, 21.028–21.030, 21.045–21.048, 28.049
(2) 21.002, 21.049
(3) 21.030, 21.043–21.047, 21.050, 21.058
(4) 21.046
(5) 21.050
(6A) 21.023
(6B) 21.023
(7) 21.007–21.012
201–203 ..... 21.002–21.012, 21.016, 21.023
202 ..... 28.061
(1) 21.039–21.042
(2)–(6) 21.039
203 ..... 21.057, 21.061
(1) 21.061
(2) 21.062
(3) 28.049

Companies Act 1963 (contd)

204 .... 1.122, 3.088, 3.098, 8.033, 9.087–9.092
.... 9.096–9.097, 9.101, 9.106, 9.107
.... 15.021, 21.004, 21.057
(1) 5.034, 9.091–9.093, 9.098, 9.103
(2) 9.094, 9.102–9.104
(3) 9.094–9.094
(4) 9.093
205 .... 1.142, 3.066, 3.079, 3.082–3.083, 3.097, 3.101, 6.003
.... 8.073, 8.078, 8.086, 9.004, 9.042, 9.054, 9.062
.... 9.066, 9.076, 9.088, 9.117–9.119, 9.123–9.125
.... 9.129–9.133, 10.017–10.021, 11.001–11.008
.... 11.012–11.016, 11.018–11.023, 11.028–11.033
.... 11.042–11.046, 11.051–11.053, 11.056–11.057
.... 11.067–11.069, 11.077, 11.085–11.093, 11.105
.... 11.108, 11.140, 13.081, 14.025, 14.031, 15.048
.... 22.059, 23.094, 23.104, 23.112, 25.080, 26.011
.... 27.013, 30.033
(1) 9.023, 11.007, 11.014, 11.026, 11.032
(2) 11.043
(3) 8.033, 9.087, 9.133, 10.021, 10.087, 11.011
.... 11.023, 11.026, 11.073–11.078, 11.083
(4) 11.085
(5) 28.049
(6) 9.023, 9.062, 11.052, 26.036
(7) 11.060, 11.061, 25.032
206(2) 21.045
207 .... 8.001, 8.111, 10.003, 17.021, 25.130, 25.133, 31.038
(1) 2.013, 4.083, 25.130, 31.039
(a) 4.083, 30.070, 31.039
(b) 30.070, 31.039
(c) 30.070, 31.039
(d) 25.131
(e) 4.083, 25.131, 30.070
(g) 8.077, 8.106, 25.193
(2) 25.131
208 .... 23.045, 23.117, 25.006, 25.130, 31.038
209 .... 25.134
(1) 25.130, 31.040
(2) 25.130, 31.040
210 .... 14.087, 21.024, 25.134
(1) 25.130, 31.040
211 .... 25.134
(a) 25.130, 31.040
212 .... 23.035
213 .... 1.139–1.142, 3.097, 8.086, 14.087, 15.145, 23.052
.... 23.067, 23.072, 23.081, 23.085–23.091, 23.104
.... 23.118, 24.013, 27.013

Companies Act 1963 (contd)
(a), (g) 23.045
(b) 23.067
(c), (f) 23.038–23.040
(d) 1.139, 1.145, 1.147, 23.038–23.040, 23.045, 23.070
(e) 23.071, 23.074, 24.067
(f) 1.154, 3.028, 11.002, 11.015, 11.028, 13.081, 29.148
(fa) 23.050, 29.148
(ii) 29.148
(g) 11.015
(h) 23.049
(i) 23.049
214 .... 15.105, 20.006, 22.018, 23.062, 23.073–23.074
.... 23.077, 23.078, 23.087, 24.067, 28.072–28.074
(a) 23.075, 23.077–23.078
(c) 23.041
215 .... 1.139, 23.037–23.040, 23.048
(a) 23.046
(i) 1.139, 1.145, 1.147, 23.046, 23.070
(c) 23.042
(d) 23.048
(g) 23.050
216(1) 23.057, 23.061
(2) 23.061
(3) 23.061
217 .... 6.074
218 .... 25.023, 25.065, 25.067–25.070, 25.071–25.072
.... 25.074–25.076, 25.079, 25.132
219 .... 10.045, 25.052
220 .... 13.124, 18.094, 25.080, 25.153
(2) 23.125, 25.065
221 .... 23.126
(1) 28.049
222 .... 20.016, 23.125, 24.041, 25.053
223 .... 13.124, 24.024
224 .... 23.126, 24.041, 25.020, 28.061
(1) 15.156, 25.022
(2) 15.156, 25.021
(3)–(8) 25.020
225 .... 24.013, 24.020, 25.005
226(1) 24.016
(2) 24.041
227 .... 28.061
(1) 24.013
(2) 24.013
227A 24.064
227B 24.064

Companies Act 1963 (contd)
228 .... 10.045
(a) 24.013
(b) 24.004
(c) 24.014
(d) 24.053
(e) 24.013
(f) 24.013
229(1) 24.017, 25.008, 25.012
(2) 24.016, 25.008
230 .... 25.011, 25.161
231 .... 6.009, 23.063, 24.028
(1) 6.009, 24.029
(a) 24.030–24.032, 24.040, 24.045, 25.137
(b) 23.063, 24.031, 24.045
(c) 24.045
(d)–(f) 24.044
(1A) 24.035–24.035
(b) 24.035
(2) 24.033–24.034, 24.040
(a) 24.033, 24.045
(b)–(h) 24.045
(i) 7.039, 24.045, 25.010
(3) 6.009, 24.039, 24.051
(4) 24.032
232 .... 23.142
(2) 24.024
233(2), (9) 23.032
234 .... 23.128
(1) 23.127
(1A) 24.070
(2) 23.127
(4) 28.049
235 .... 15.017, 25.005
(1) 8.024, 25.008, 25.194
(2) 25.194
236 .... 19.007, 25.023, 25.134
237 .... 25.134
(1)–(3) 25.155
238 .... 25.133, 31.041
239(1) 25.009
241 .... 25.173
242 .... 15.137, 25.181, 25.194
243 .... 15.143, 24.070
(1) 24.070
244 .... 24.055, 25.166, 25.169–25.170
244A 25.013

Companies Act 1963 (contd)

245 .... 15.143–15.146
.... 15.148, 24.041, 24.057, 25.028
.... 25.031–25.036, 25.039, 25.040, 28.019
(1) 25.024–25.029
(2) 25.024
(3) 25.024, 25.033
(4) 25.024, 25.033
(5) 25.033
(6) 25.035
(7) 25.025, 25.034
(8) 25.039
245A 15.143, 25.037, 25.036, 28.019
(1) 25.036
(4) 25.037
(5) 25.037
(6) 25.036, 25.037
246 .... 25.024
247 .... 15.143, 24.041, 25.043–25.044, 28.019
249 .... 4.020
(2) 28.050
250 .... 24.061
(1) 24.056–24.057
(2)–(4) 24.056
251 .... 14.087
(1) 14.100, 23.002
(c) 23.002, 23.017–23.020
(4)(a) 15.109, 15.125
252 .... 28.061
(1) 23.013
(2) 23.013, 23.020
253 .... 23.014, 23.020, 25.153
(1) 25.065
254 .... 23.020
255 .... 25.132, 25.198
256 .... 5.089, 23.004, 23.007
(1) 23.004
(2) 23.005
(b) 25.022
(3) 23.007
(1) 23.008–23.009
(5) 23.114
(6) 28.050
(7) 23.114
(8) 5.089, 23.010
(9) 5.089
(10) 5.089
(11) 23.006

Companies Act 1963 (contd)
258(1) 24.009, 24.020, 24.052, 25.010
(2) 24.027
259(1) 24.009
260 .... 8.033, 21.001, 21.066–21.070, 24.048
(1) 21.067–21.069
(2) 21.071, 24.048
(3) 21.071
(4) 21.071
(6) 21.071
261 .... 23.115, 24.022, 28.059
(1) 23.115
262(1) 23.015, 28.059
(2) 23.015
263 .... 4.020, 28.061
(1) 23.016
(2) 23.016
(3) 23.016, 28.050
(4) 23.016
(5) 23.016
(6) 23.016, 28.052
(7) 23.016
266 .... 23.006, 23.008, 23.115, 23.123, 28.061
(1) 23.023, 24.047
(2) 23.023, 24.047
(3)(a) 23.019, 23.025, 25.022
(5) 23.022
267 .... 23.024
(1) 23.021, 24.020, 25.010
(2) 23.021, 23.029–23.030
(3) 23.028–23.029, 23.123
267A 24.069
268(1) 23.031, 24.023
(2) 23.031
269(1) 23.032, 24.052
(3) 23.032, 24.027
270 .... 24.012
271 .... 21.068, 24.048
272(1) 28.059
273 .... 4.020, 28.061
(1) 23.033
(2) 23.033
(3) 28.050
(4) 23.033
(5) 23.033
(6) 28.052
274 .... 24.009, 25.195

Companies Act 1963 (contd)

275 .... 8.085, 25.157, 25.193
(1) 25.065, 25.183
(a) 25.183
(b) 25.195, 30.071
(2) 25.183
275–282 .... 25.195
276 .... 24.046
(1) 24.043
(b) 24.045, 25.010
(c)–(e) 24.045
(2) 25.194
(3) 24.043
276A(1) 24.009, 24.013
277(1) 24.009
(2) 24.009
278(3) 28.050
279(1) 24.049
(2) 24.049
280 .... 6.022, 18.094, 23.006, 23.008, 23.059, 23.117
.... 23.122, 23.142, 24.046
(1) 24.051, 25.022, 25.028, 25.036, 25.039, 25.043
(3) 23.128, 28.049, 28.050
281 .... 24.055, 25.167–25.168
282 .... 23.117, 23.128
282A 28.019
(1) 24.070
282B 25.028–25.029, 28.019
(1) 25.039
(8) 25.039
282C 25.036, 28.019
282D 25.043, 28.019
283(1) 25.172
284 .... 25.181
(1) 25.141–25.143, 25.150
(2) 23.018, 23.044, 25.055
285 .... 18.094, 20.068–20.069, 22.0133, 25.184
(2) 18.106, 25.159, 25.183–25.184
(a) (i) 25.185
(ii) 25.185
(6) 25.188
(7) 18.094–18.096
(a) 25.186
(b) 18.094, 25.110, 25.189
(14) 25.185
286 .... 5.012, 22.110, 25.081, 25.090, 25.100–25.104, 29.149
(1) 25.081, 25.085, 25.092

Companies Act 1963 (contd)
(2) 25.088
(3) 25.086, 25.093
(4) 25.089
(5) 25.086
287(1) 25.090
(b) 25.087
(2) 25.090
288 .... 18.040, 18.106
(1) 25.110–25.117
(3) 25.112
289(1) 25.118
290 .... 5.015, 25.058–25.063
(1) 25.059
(3) 25.062
(7) 25.064
291 .... 6.074, 25.054, 25.055
(1) 25.054
(5) 6.074, 25.054
292 .... 6.073, 25.056
(1) 6.073
(3) 25.056
293 .... 17.015, 25.006
(1) 25.006, 25.022, 28.058
(c) 25.006
(2) 17.015, 25.006
294 .... 28.058
295 .... 15.143, 28.058
(2) 25.185
(7) 18.096
297 .... 13.046, 13.059, 15.083, 15.122, 15.128, 15.143, 15.143, 22.036, 25.035
(1) 15.118
(2) 15.128
(b) 28.057
(3) 15.118
297A 5.091, 13.059, 15.096, 15.109, 15.115, 15.125
.... 15.140, 15.143, 15.144–15.147, 17.013, 22.036
.... 22.109, 28.137, 28.155, 28.163, 28.176, 28.180
(1) 15.116
(a) 15.102, 15.106, 15.110
(b) 5.008, 15.116–15.117, 15.123
(2) 15.102–15.103
(a) 15.102
(b) 15.104, 15.109, 15.112
(3)(a) 15.105
(b) 15.108
(4) 15.109

Companies Act 1963 (contd)

(5) ... 15.109
(6) ... 15.104, 15.112
(7)(a) ... 15.113
(b) ... 15.109, 15.113, 15.125, 15.142
(10) ... 15.097, 15.110, 15.116
298 ... 4.035, 15.074, 15.083, 15.143, 15.147–15.150, 25.138
(1) ... 15.149
(2) ... 15.149, 28.023
299 ... 28.024
300 ... 4.076, 24.006, 24.008, 28.061
300A ... 24.007, 28.059–28.061
(1)(c) ... 24.008
(4)–(5) ... 24.007
301 ... 28.061
301A ... 24.011, 28.061
(4) ... 24.007, 24.011
(5) ... 24.007, 24.011
(6) ... 24.011
303 ... 23.126, 28.061
305 ... 28.061
306 ... 28.059
(1) ... 28.045, 28.050
309(1) ... 23.072
(2) ... 23.072
310 ... 4.020, 23.130–23.132
(1) ... 23.130, 23.133–23.135, 26.061
(2) ... 23.130, 28.052
311 ... 4.020, 26.004, 26.005, 26.07, 26.0014, 29.123, 30.072
(1) ... 26.009–26.014
(2) ... 26.009–26.012, 26.051
(3) ... 26.012
(5) ... 29.015
(6) ... 26.015
(7) ... 26.024
(8) ... 23.134, 26.024, 26.029–26.038, 26.046
... 26.051–26.054, 26.057–26.057, 30.072
(9) ... 26.012
311A ... 23.130, 26.029
(1) ... 26.031–26.032, 30.072
(2) ... 26.031
(3) ... 26.031
312 ... 23.024
314 ... 4.076, 20.011, 28.061
315 ... 20.011, 28.059
(2) ... 20.011
(5) ... 20.011

Companies Act 1963 (contd)

316 .... 19.097, 20.047, 20.055, 20.086
(1) 20.054, 20.085–20.087
(1A) 20.085
(1B) 20.086
(2) 20.074
(3) 20.074
316A 20.054–20.056
(1) 16.040, 20.052, 20.054, 20.059, 20.064
(2) 20.051
(3) 16.040, 20.059
(a), (b) 20.058
317 .... 20.028, 28.061
(2) 20.028
319 .... 15.156, 20.027, 20.046, 28.061
(1) 28.050
(2) 20.071, 28.045, 28.050, 28.059
(2A) 20.072, 28.015, 28.050
(7) 20.026
320 .... 20.027, 28.061
(2) 15.156
320A 28.058, 28.059
321(1) 28.045, 28.059
322A 20.091
(1) 20.090
(2) 20.090
322B 20.093
322C 20.088
323A 28.015
(1)–(4) 20.073
324 .... 7.028, 23.035
(1) 1.159, 7.028
325 .... 23.035
(1) 1.160
326 .... 1.160
326A 20.051
327 .... 1.160
328(1) 1.161
336 .... 4.002
340(2) 1.161
(3) 1.161
344 .... 23.035
345 .... 23.035, 24.058
(1) 23.036
(3) 23.036
(4) 23.036
(5) 23.036
(7) 23.036, 24.058–24.060

Companies Act 1963 (contd)
351 ....28.074, 28.081, 34.005
352 ....23.131, , 34.020
(1) 34.013, 34.020, 34.025
(a) 34.012
(b) 34.012
(2) 34.012–34.013
353 ....34.014
354(1) 34.015
(4) 34.015
355 ....34.017
356(1) 34.024
(2) 34.024
(b) 34.025
357 ....34.016
358 ....28.049, 34.026
360 ....34.006, 34.013
361 ....28.058
364 ....28.058
365 ....28.058
368(1) 28.007, 28.043
(2) 28.007
(4) 28.007
370(1)(a) 28.044
(b) 28.044
371 ....3.111, 17.009, 28.023, 28.028, 28.191–28.192, 28.210–28.213
(1) 28.213
(2) 28.215
(4) 28.212
376 ....1.017, 4.090
377 ....7.042, 14.070
(1) 1.054, 1.160, 16.061
(2) 1.054
(4) 1.064
(6) 28.049
378 ....28.060
(1) 8.017
(2) 8.017
379 ....6.012, 6.082, 23.077
(1) 6.011, 23.076–23.077
(2) 6.013
381 ....3.008, 26.022, 28.058
(1) 3.008
(2) 3.008, 26.022
(3) 26.022
382 ....6.066, 6.070
(2) 6.070

Companies Act 1963 (contd)

383 .... 17.012, 28.033
(1) 16.118
(3) 13.124, 15.003, 15.095, 15.156
390 .... 6.014, 6.017, 6.020–6.026, 6.030, 6.036
.... 6.041–6.042, 6.046, 6.049, 6.057, 31.015–31.017
391 .... 10.103, 15.075, 15.088–15.089, 15.092, 15.104, 16.053, 17.312, 17.336
(1) 16.053
395 .... 18.071
(3) 17.255
Pt IV 4.018, 19.002, 34.021
Pt X 1.055, 1.157, 23.035, 28.156
Pt XI 1.120, 34.003–34.007, 34.011–34.015, 34.022, 34.026, 34.030
Sch 1 .... 3.004
Table A Pt I 1.133
model reg
2 .... 3.053, 8.071, 8.099
3 .... 3.043–3.046, 9.032, 9.042–9.045, 9.053, 9.074
5 .... 8.051, 14.055
6 .... 9.056, 10.067, 13.078
7 .... 8.026–8.029
8 .... 3.040
11 .... 8.121, 10.110
12 .... 8.122, 10.110
13 .... 8.122
15 .... 8.095
15–21 .... 8.095
18 .... 8.095
19 .... 8.093
20 .... 8.095
21 .... 8.096
22 .... 3.043, 9.012, 29.062, 31.021
23 .... 9.006, 9.012
24 .... 3.040, 3.046
29 .... 9.027, 9.030
30 .... 9.029, 9.031
31 .... 8.007, 9.028–9.031
32 .... 9.030
33 .... 10.106
33–39 .... 8.123, 10.106
34 .... 10.106
35 .... 10.106
36 .... 10.106
37 .... 8.125, 10.106
38 .... 8.124, 10.106
40– 45 .... 8.116

Companies Act 1963 (contd)
model reg
42 .... 8.118
44 .... 3.032, 3.128
47 .... 3.086, 14.010
48 .... 14.006
50 .... 14.016–14.019
51 .... 3.040, 14.034, 14.040, 14.051
53 .... 14.009, 14.015, 14.051
55 .... 14.055
56 .... 14.037, 14.080
57 .... 14.080
58 .... 14.059
59 .... 8.082–8.083, 14.062–14.068
60 .... 14.069
61 .... 14.062
62 .... 8.083, 14.069
63 .... 8.082–8.083, 14.062
64 .... 14.066
66 .... 14.066
67 .... 14.066
68 .... 14.074
69 .... 14.075
70 .... 14.074
71 .... 14.075
72 .... 14.069
73 .... 14.076
74 .... 14.073
75 .... 13.028, 14.072
76 .... 3.043, 13.070
77 .... 3.043, 13.019, 13.031, 29.040
79 .... 3.051, 3.086, 7.112, 7.119, 13.132, 13.141
80 .... 3.052, 7.011, 7.031, 7.038, 7.107
.... 7.112–7.114, 7.118, 11.033, 11.110, 13.054
.... 13.124–13.140, 15.005, 15.024, 16.022
.... 18.012, 22.089, 23.039, 30.047
81 .... 7.031, 20.013
82 .... 7.023
89 .... 14.077
91 .... 13.038, 13.073
92 .... 13.028, 13.074, 14.012, 14.013
93 .... 13.028
93–100 .... 13.074
94 .... 13.028
96 .... 3.043, 13.029
97 .... 3.043, 13.011
98 .... 3.043, 13.030, 14.013
99 .... 3.050

Companies Act 1963 (contd)

model reg

100 .... 3.043

101 .... 13.128, 14.104, 14.107–14.111
.... 14.116, 14.120, 14.126, 15.157

102 .... 3.043, 14.113, 14.126

103 .... 14.013, 14.113

104 .... 7.115, 13.036

105 .... 14.123

106 .... 14.107, 14.122

107 .... 14.122

109 .... 3.043, 3.052, 14.126

110 .... 13.034

111 .... 13.034

112 .... 7.114, 7.119, 13.034

113 .... 13.120

115 .... 7.019, 7.025, 7.116, 7.131, 15.157

116 .... 8.078, 13.136

117 .... 8.078, 13.136

123 .... 8.079

130A 8.114

133 .... 14.048

136 .... 9.030, 14.036, 14.041

137 .... 25.197

138 .... 15.075, 15.092

Pt II 2.025, 3.039–3.040

model reg

1 .... 3.040

2 .... 1.135, 3.041

3 .... 1.135, 3.040, 3.046, 9.042–9.043, 9.048, 9.073, 13.136

4 .... 3.040, 14.040

5 .... 3.040

6 .... 3.041, 3.048, 14.004, 14.090, 16.043, 16.109

7 .... 3.040, 14.114

8 .... 3.040

9 .... 3.041–3.043

10 .... 3.040

101 .... 14.105

104 .... 14.116

133 .... 14.048

133–136 .... 14.028

Table C 30.013, 30.035

model reg

2 .... 30.036

35 .... 30.047

Table D 3.039

Companies Act 1963 (contd)

Table E 2.029, 3.039

Pt II 31.009

model reg 1 .... 31.010

Pt III 31.009

model reg 1 .... 31.010

model reg 2 .... 31.010

model reg 3 .... 31.023

Sch 3 .... 32.007, 32.047

Sch 6 .... 10.096, 17.021, 30.062, 31.029–31.032

Pt III 10.097

Sch 8 .... 17.255

Sch 9 .... 1.160, 14.070, 16.061

Companies (Amendment) Act 1977 .... 1.092, 1.163

s 3 .... 7.022, 29.035

4(1) 8.017

5(5) 3.041

11(2) 1.163

Companies (Amendment) Act 1982 .... 1.093

s 2 .... 3.039

3 .... 2.030, 13.014

(1) 13.028

(b) 13.120

(3) 13.026–13.028, 13.120

(5) 13.028, 13.032

3A 28.153

4(1) 2.036

6 .... 13.018

7 .... 27.047

10 .... 25.185

11 .... 26.004

12 .... 4.020, 17.256, 26.004, 26.007–26.009, 28.015, 28.194, 30.072

(1) 26.006

(2) 26.006

(3) 26.006, 26.035, 26.044

(6) 26.024, 26.059–26.060

12A 2.034, 26.007, 26.009

(1) 26.007

(2) 26.007

(3) 26.07, 26.027, 26.035, 26.044

12B 26.034, 26.039, 26.047–26.048, 30.072

(1) 26.015

(2) 26.024

(3) 26.021, 26.029–26.037, 26.048–26.050, 26.055, 26.057–26.057

(4) 26.049

(5) 26.045

(a) 26.048

Companies (Amendment) Act 1982 (contd)
(6) 26.045–26.046
(7) 26.029–26.031, 26.050, 26.055, 26.057
(9)–(11) 26.039
12C 23.130
(1) 26.027–26.031, 26.040
(2) 26.027
(3) 26.027, 26.062
12D 26.008
13 .... 1.017, 4.090
15 .... 19.057, 19.085, 19.101, 20.011
20 .... 8.017
Sch 1 .... 2.039, 8.116

Companies (Amendment) Act 1983 .... 1.094, 13.024, 23.067, 29.002, 29.010, 31.006
1 (3) 29.004
2 .... 28.069, 29.002–29.005, 29.139
(1) 8.115, 29.004, 29.028
(2) 8.050, 8.054, 8.062, 29.047
(3)(a) 8.061
4 (1) 29.028
5 .... 7.050
(1) 2.032, 29.012, 29.135
(2) 29.011
(3) 4.002
(4) 1.113, 4.004
(a) 29.020
(b) 29.020
6 .... , 29.014, 29.037, 29.123, 29.135
(1) 29.011, 29.121
(2) 29.011–29.014
(3) 29.014
(b) 10.004
(5) 29.014
(6) 29.014
(7) 29.014
(8) 29.014, 29.037
7 .... 29.004, 30.029
8 .... 29.123
(2) 26.004
(3) 26.004, 29.123
9 .... 4.002, 14.087, 29.019, 29.022, 33.015
(1) 29.020
(3) 29.021
(e) 29.021
(4) 29.021
(5) 29.022
(6) 29.023

Companies (Amendment) Act 1983 (contd)
(7) 29.023
(9) 4.004, 29.023
(10) 29.024
10 .... 29.019, 29.025, 33.015
(1) 29.020–29.025
11 .... 14.087, 33.008
12(3)(a) 14.100
(9) 23.067
14 .... 4.002, 14.087, 33.014
(5) 4.004
15 .... 10.017–10.021, 10.048, 10.088, 29.081, 33.014
(5) 28.049
(7) 10.021
17 .... 29.081
(3) 21.022
(4) 29.081
(5) 29.081
19 .... 4.002, 10.004, 29.011, 29.135, 33.015
(2) 29.011
20 .... 3.065, 8.051, 29.043
(3) 8.051
21 .... 8.053,
22 .... 29.045
(2) 29.046
(3) 29.046
23 .... 8.056–8.058, 8.086, 8.115
(2) 29.050
(4) 8.058
(6) 8.058
(7) 8.056
(9) 8.057
(10) 8.057–8.058
(13) 8.058
23–25 .... 29.044, 29.145
24 .... 8.057, 14.087
(2) 8.058
26 .... 8.062, 29.055
24(6) 28.058
26(4) 28.069, 29.049
27 .... 8.048
(1) 10.109
28 (1) 10.004, 29.011, 29.047, 29.135
(2) 29.048
(4) 29.047
(5) 29.049
29 .... 29.050, 29.055

Companies (Amendment) Act 1983 (contd)
30 .... 29.017, 29.022, 29.050, 29.055
(6) 29.053
(d) 29.051
(8) 29.054
(d) 29.051
(14)(c) 29.052
31 .... 29.022
(1) 29.052
(2) 29.053
(3) 28.058, 29.052
32 .... 29.017–29.018, 29.055
(1) 29.017
(2)(b) 29.017
(3) 29.017
(c) 29.017
(d) 29.017
(5) 29.017
(7)(a) 29.018
(b) 29.018
(8) 29.018
32–36 .... 28.070
33 (1) 29.017
(2) 28.049
(b) 29.017
34 .... 29.055
(2) 29.055
(3) 29.055
(4)(a) 29.055
(6) 29.018, 29.055
35 .... 29.013
36 .... 28.059
38 .... 3.064–3.065, 14.087
(2) 3.064–3.065
(3) 3.065
(a) 3.065
(4) 3.065
(5) 3.065
(6) 3.065
(7)–(11) 3.065
39 (1) 28.049
(3) 28.049
(4) 28.049
40 .... 10.012, 14.004, 14.017
(1) 14.017, 17.229, 28.058
(2) 14.018

Companies (Amendment) Act 1983 (contd)

41 .... 29.074, 31.023
(1) 10.015–10.018, 31.022
(2) 8.126, 10.017–10.022
(4) 29.074
(a) 10.017
(b) 10.017
(c) 10.017
(d) 10.017, 10.107
42 .... 17.336
(2) 10.038
43 .... 10.018, 10.039, , 29.074, 29.117
(1)(c) 29.117
(d) 29.117
(3) 10.039, 14.100, 29.075–29.076
(5) 29.075
(7) 29.075
(8) 29.075
43A 10.037
44 .... 10.110, 29.117
(1) 29.122
45 .... 7.076, 7.078, 10.005, 10.096, 10.099, 29.079, 30.042, 31.023
(1) 10.089–10.093, 10.098, 10.104
(2) 10.093
(4) 10.094
46 .... 29.079, 29.146
(2) 29.080
(4) 29.080
47 .... , 29.146
(5) 29.146
49 (1) 10.094, 10.096
(2) 10.096
(3) 10.097
(4) 10.097
(5) 10.097
(7) 10.097
(8) 10.097
(9) 10.096–10.097
(10) 10.097
50 .... 10.104
51 .... 10.090
52 .... 3.030, 4.002, 14.087, 33.009
(1) 33.009–33.011
(2) 33.010
(a) 33.010
(3) 33.011
(5) 4.004

Companies (Amendment) Act 1983 (contd)
(6) 33.012
(7) 33.013
53 .... 3.030, 4.002, 14.087, 33.003
(1) 33.003
(2) 33.003
(3) 33.003
(5) 4.004, 33.005
(7) 33.006
(a) 33.006
(b) 33.006
(8) 33.005
54 .... 33.003
55 .... 29.016
(1)(e) 29.017
(3) 29.016
56 .... 3.023, 29.028
57 .... 28.061
58 .... 29.028
Sch 1 .... 3.006
para 10 .... 29.077
para 11 .... 10.111
para 13 .... 5.081
para 24 .... 8.114
Sch 2 .... 29.012, 29.028
Pt II 2.038
Sch 3 .... 23.067
Companies (Amendment) Act 1986 .... 1.095, 2.014, 10.096, 17.270
.... 30.062, 31.025–31.030
1(1) 1.140, 17.024, 31.024
2(1) 30.062, 30.064
3 .... 30.062, 31.030
(1) 17.025
(a) 17.025
(b) 17.023, 17.026, 17.032, 17.037, 17.061
(c) 17.026
(d) 17.026, 17.029
(e) 17.026
4 .... 17.033, 17.062, 17.171
(1) 17.025, 17.031, 17.037, 17.061
(3) 17.032, 17.061
(4) 17.032, 17.061
(5) 17.033, 17.062
(6) 17.033, 17.062
(7) 17.033
(8) 17.033, 17.062
(9)–(13) 17.033, 17.062

Companies (Amendment) Act 1986 (contd)
(14) 17.068
(15) 17.110
5 ....17.025, 17.028, 17.174
(c) 17.028
(e) 17.028, 17.038
6 ....17.029, 17.174
7 ....17.251
(1) 17.262, 31.024
(a) 15.156
(1A) 17.152, 17.266
(1B) 17.152
(1C) 17.253
(2) 17.262
8(1) 17.123
(2) 17.277
(3) 17.267
(4) 17.268
(6) 17.268
(8) 17.269
(9) 17.268
(13) 17.158
9 ....17.269
10 (1) 17.279, 17.282
(2)(b) 17.279
11 (1) 17.270, 17.273
(2)(a) 17.272
(b) 17.270, 17.271
(3)(b) 17.273
12 (1)(a) 17.280
(b) 17.280
(2)(b) 17.273
13 ....17.215, 17.222, 30.063, 31.033
(1) 17.215
14 ....17.215, 17.222, 29.117, 30.063, 31.033
15 ....17.232
16 ....17.127, 17.135, 17.217
(1) 15.156, 17.127
(2) 17.127
(3)(a) 15.156, 17.129
(b) 15.156, 17.129
(5) 17.128, 17.217
16A 17.135
17 ....17.285
(1)(b) 12.048
18 (2) 17.275, 17.281
(3) 15.156

Companies (Amendment) Act 1986 (contd)
(5) 15.156, 17.276, 17.283
(3)–(4) 17.276, 17.283
19(1A) 17.248
(3A) 17.248
(1) 17.248
(2) 17.248
22 .... 28.058, 28.061
(1) 17.263
(2) 17.222
(3) 17.263
Sch 17.025, 17.171–17.174, 29.078
Pt I 17.031, 17.035–17.037, 17.061, 17.068, 17.089, 17.102, 17.273
Pt II 17.037
Pt III 17.037
Pt IIIA 17.037
Pt III 17.042, 17.055
Pt IIIA 17.182
para 1 .... 17.070, 17.098
(3) 17.076
para 5 .... 17.040
para 6 .... 17.040
para 7 .... 17.102–17.104
(1) 17.040, 17.183
(2) 17.040
(3) 17.040
para 8 .... 17.040
(2) 17.082, 17.280
para 9 .... 17.040, 17.083
para 10 .... 17.051
para 11 .... 17.051
para 12 .... 17.053, 17.086
para 13 .... 17.040, 17.052
para 14 .... 17.051
(1) 17.040
(2) 17.040
(3) 17.040, 17.074
(4) 17.051
para 15
(1) 17.052
(3) 17.052, 17.074
(4) 17.052
(5) 17.052
(6) 17.040
para 16 .... 17.041, 17.054
para 19 .... 17.042, 17.055

Companies (Amendment) Act 1986 (contd)
para 20
(1) 17.044
(3) 17.044, 17.103
para 21
(2) 17.043
(3) 17.043
(4) 17.076
para 22 ....17.045
(5) 17.091
para 22A 17.046
para 22B 17.047
para 22C 17.048
para 22CA 17.049
para 24 ....17.099, 17.280
(3) 17.071
para 26 ....17.092
para 26–27 ....17.280
para 26–28 ....17.136, 17.207
para 27 ....17.092
para 28 ....17.092
para 29 ....17.073
para 30 ....17.077
para 31A 17.078
para 31B 17.079
para 31B–31C 17.280
para 31C 17.080
para 31D 17.081
para 31 ....17.084
para 32 ....17.094
para 32A 17.095, 17.137, 17.208
para 33 ....17.090, 17.280
para 34 ....17.087, 17.280
(1) 17.179
para 35 ....17.088
para 36 ....17.138, 17.209
(1) 17.097, 17.125
(2) 17.097, 17.125
(3) 17.097, 17.125
(4) 17.097, 17.125
(5) 17.097
(6) 17.097
para 36A 17.126, 17.142
para 37
(1) 17.075
(2) 17.085, 17.139, 17.210
(3) 17.096

para 39 .... 17.106
(3) 17.105
(4) 17.105
(5) 17.122, 17.201
(6) 17.105, 17.112, 17.0132
para 40 .... 17.107
para 41 .... 17.100, 17.273
para 42 .... 17.101, 17.140, 17.180
(4) 17.101
para 43 .... 17.105–17.108
para 44 .... 17.280
para 45 .... 17.072
para 45A 17.097
para 46A 17.130
(1) 17.109
para 46 .... 17.141, 17.211
(1) 17.093
(2) 17.093
para 55 .... 17.155
para 60 .... 17.039, 17.050
para 66 .... 17.105
para 67 .... 17.106
para 70 .... 16.029
para 71 .... 17.040
para 72 .... 17.028
para 74 .... 17.101
para 75 .... 17.068, 17.268

Companies (Amendment) Act 1990 .... 1.096, 15.096–15.097, 15.114–15.116
.... 18.110, 20.004–20.006, 21.001, 22.002, 22.064
1A 22.158
2 .... 22.017, 22.023–22.026, 22.037–22.039, 22.049, 22.059, 22.150
(1) 22.004, 22.018
(2) 22.005, 22.019–22.021, 22.024–22.026
(3) 22.018
(4) 22.018
(5) 22.028
(6) 22.028
3 .... 22.011
(1)(a) 22.011
(b) 22.012
(c) 22.014
(d) 22.015
(2) 22.115, 22.131, 22.0141, 22.162
(a) 22.016, 22.115, 22.134, 22.162
(b) 22.016, 22.134
(c) 22.016, 22.037

Companies (Amendment) Act 1990 (contd)

(3) 22.004, 22.036
(a) 22.030
(b) 22.033
(c) 22.032
(3A) 22.036
(3B) 22.036
(4)(a) 22.030
(b) 22.029
(5) 22.014, 22.115
(6) 20.094, 22.045–22.047, 22.070, 22.115
(7) 22.015–22.017, 22.042, 22.048
(9) 22.009
3A 22.039, 22.046, 22.066
(1) 22.039, 22.108
(2) 22.040
(3) 22.039, 22.046
(4) 22.041
(5) 22.041
(6) 22.039
(7) 22.039
(8) 22.040–22.042, 22.108
3B(1) 22.017
(2) 22.017
(g) 22.023
3C(1) 22.037
(2) 22.037
(3) 22.037
(4) ....
4 .... 22.010, 22.027, 22.052
(1) 22.051
(2) 22.051
(3) 22.054
(5) 22.010, 22.052
(6) 22.010, 22.052
(7) 22.052
4A 22.034
5 .... 22.006, 22.060, 22.064, 22.104, 22.136
(1) 22.059
(2) 22.059
(a) 22.066
(b) 20.014, 22.070, 22.077
(d) 19.031, 22.059, 22.073–22.074, 22.077
(f) 22.079–22.081
(h) 22.059, 22.068
(3) 22.061
(4) 11.051, 22.060

Companies (Amendment) Act 1990 (contd)
5A(1) ... 22.066, 22.097
(2) ... 22.097
6 ... 22.059
(1) ... 22.071
(2) ... 22.069
(c) ... 22.069
(3) ... 22.069–22.071
(4) ... 22.069–22.071
(5) ... 22.069
6A(1)(a) ... 22.072
(b) ... 22.072
(2) ... 22.072
7 ... 18.084
(1) ... 22.093
(2) ... 22.091
(3) ... 22.091
(4) ... 22.091
(5) ... 22.075
(6) ... 22.096
(5A) ... 22.075
(5A)–(5C) ... 18.084
(5B) ... 22.075
8 (1) ... 22.094
(2) ... 22.094
(3) ... 22.094
(4) ... 22.095
(5) ... 22.095
(5A) ... 22.095
9 ... 18.084, 22.063, 22.076, 22.089–22.092, 22.098, 22.167
(1) ... 22.090
(2) ... 22.090
(3) ... 22.090
(4) ... 22.090
10 ... 22.076, 22.085, 22.099, 22.107
(1) ... 22.104
(2) ... 22.040, 22.108
11 ... 22.100
(1) ... 22.101–22.102
(2) ... 22.101–22.102
(3) ... 22.101
(4) ... 22.102
(7) ... 28.050
(8) ... 22.059
12 (1) ... 22.055, 22.134
(2) ... 22.055, 22.134
(3) ... 22.055

Companies (Amendment) Act 1990 (contd)
(4) 22.064, 28.059
(5) 22.055, 28.045, 28.049–28.052, 28.059
13 (1)–(3) 22.056
(4) 22.057
(5) 22.088
(6) 22.092, 22.123
(7) 22.096
13A 22.114, 22.115
14 .... 22.004
(3) 28.059
15 .... 22.004, 22.134
16 .... 22.004
17 .... 22.004
18 .... 22.111, 22.116, 22.137
(1) 22.116
(2) 22.130
(3) 22.112, 22.136
(4) 22.136
(5) 22.134
(6) 22.134
(7) 22.135
(8) 22.135–22.137
(9) 22.117, 22.137
19 .... 22.0133
20 .... 22.102–22.103, 22.147
(1) 22.126–22.128, 22.139–22.140
(2) 22.129, 22.140
(3) 22.128
(4) 22.139
(5) 22.139
21 .... 22.056
22 (1) 22.118–22.120
(2) 22.120
(3) 22.120
(5) 22.129, 22.154
(6) 22.118
23 .... 22.152
(1) 22.131
(2) 22.132
(4) 22.131
(4A) 22.131
(5) 22.131
(8) 22.131
24 .... 22.114, 22.136–22.142, 28.050
(1) 22.137
(2) 22.0141–22.143

Companies (Amendment) Act 1990 (contd)
(3) ... 22.137, 22.143, 22.148
(4) ... 22.142–22.143, 22.148
(a) ... 22.143
(c) ... 22.148
(4A) ... 22.142
(5) ... 22.138, 22.147
(6) ... 22.138
(7) ... 22.147
(8) ... 22.122, 22.147
(9) ... 22.083
(11) ... 22.137
(12) ... 22.142
25 ... 22.083, 22.142, 22.148
(1) ... 22.152, 22.155
(c) ... 22.152
(d) ... 22.080, 22.153
(2) ... 22.155
(3) ... 22.155
25A ... 22.081
(1) ... 22.081
(a) ... 22.081
(b) ... 22.081
(c) ... 22.083
(d) ... 22.082–22.083
(2)(a) ... 22.081
25B ... 22.126
(1) ... 22.139
(a) ... 22.124
(2) ... 22.125
(3) ... 22.124
(4) ... 22.125
26 (1), (2) ... 22.160
27 ... 22.114, 22.161
(1) ... 22.161
(2) ... 22.162
28 ... 4.076
(2) ... 28.059
29 ... 22.092, 22.103–22.105, 22.163–22.168
(1) ... 22.164
(2) ... 22.163
(3) ... 18.047, 22.085–22.086, 22.099, 25.165
(3A) ... 22.004, 22.076, 22.085, 22.099
(3B) ... 22.087, 25.165
30 (1) ... 22.114
(2) ... 28.050
31 ... 22.048

Companies (Amendment) Act 1990 (contd)
33 .... 13.059, 15.096, 15.100, 15.115, 28.067
(1) 15.101, 15.108
(a) 15.101
(2) 15.103
(4) 15.109
34 .... 13.059
36 (1) 22.010
(2) 22.010
(3) 22.010

Companies Act 1990 .... 1.098
2 .... 28.187
3 .... 1.157
(1) 27.014, 27.022
4(2) 13.102, 13.107
5(2)(d) 18.047
6 .... 11.043
(1) 20.094, 23.048
7 .... 27.008, 27.012, 27.050, 27.061, 27.066, 28.185
(1) 27.012
(2) 27.014
(3) 27.014
(4) 27.021, 27.065
8 .... 27.008, 27.012–27.014, 27.050, 27.063, 28.185
(1) 27.014–27.015
(a) 27.016
(b) 27.016
(c) 27.016
(2)(a) 27.012
(b) 27.016
9 .... 27.023–27.027, 27.051, 28.185
10 .... 27.034, 27.044, 27.049
(1) 27.035, 27.038–27.040, 27.050
(2) 27.037–27.040, 27.050
(3) 27.050
(5) 27.046–27.048
(6) 27.046–27.048
(7) 27.035
11 .... 23.109, 27.056
(1) 27.051
(2) 27.051
(3) 27.052–27.054
(4) 27.053
12 .... 11.043, 23.048, 23.109, 27.056
(1) 27.056
(b) 27.056
(2) 23.109, 27.057

Companies Act 1990 (contd)
13 .... 27.063
(1) 27.061–27.062
(a) 27.063
(2) 27.062–27.063
(3) 27.051
14 .... 27.004, 27.008, 27.017, 27.024, 27.027, 27.050–27.054
.... 27.064–27.066, 27.074, 27.085
(1) 27.024–27.026
(2) 27.054
(4) 27.024
(5) 27.026
(b) 27.054
15 .... 27.008, 27.067, 27.083–27.085, 28.058
(1) 27.083
(2) 27.084
16 .... 27.085, 28.058, 29.127
(2) 27.085
(3)–(4) 27.085
(5) 27.087
(6) 27.087
(7) 27.088
(8) 27.088
(9) 27.088
(10) 27.088
(11) 27.088
(12) 27.088
(14) 27.086
(17) 27.085
(18) 27.085
17 .... 27.015, 27.023–27.024, 27.063
18 .... 27.044
19 .... 27.008, 27.019, 27.072–27.074, 27.080, 27.082, 28.058
(1) 27.068
(2) 27.070
(3) 27.071
(4) 27.071
(5) 27.076
(6) 27.069, 27.077
(7) 27.076
(8) 27.076
(9) 27.078
(10)–(12) 27.082
19–20 .... 27.067
19A 27.078
20 .... 20.059, 27.079–27.080
(4) 27.079

Companies Act 1990 (contd)
21 .... 28.058
(1) 27.080–27.081
(a) 27.081
(2) 27.081
22 .... 27.016, 27.058–27.060
23 .... 27.044
(1) 27.038, 27.075
(2) 27.075
(3) 27.055
23A 27.002
24 .... 27.007
25 .... 16.032, 16.068, 28.131
(1) 5.016, 16.069
(2)(a) 16.066, 16.071
(b) 16.066
(3) 16.067
(4) 16.076
(5) 16.035
(6) 16.071, 16.106
(7) 16.024, 16.062
(8) 16.024
26 .... 1.147, 12.016, 16.027, 16.091, 16.123
.... 16.129, , 20.058, 24.035, 27.049
(1) 16.006–16.008
(2) 12.005, 16.010, 16.015, 16.020, 16.037
(3) 16.011–16.014, 16.018–16.019
(4)(a) 16.013
(b) 16.012, 16.018–16.019
(5) 16.018
(6) 16.009, 18.008
27 .... 13.055–13.058, 13.060, 13.065–13.066, 28.079
(1) 13.059, 13.068, 16.004
(3) 16.121, 16.123, 16.130
28 .... 13.071, 16.001, 28.058
(4) 13.071
(5) 13.071
(7) 13.071
29 .... 12.016, 13.131, 14.016, 14.096–14.098, 15.088, 16.001–16.006
.... 16.010, 16.019–16.027, 16.032, 16.040, 16.044–16.045
.... 16.048, 16.121, 20.058–20.059, 24.035, 25.033, 25.136
(1) 14.096, 16.024–16.026, 16.029, 16.037–16.038
.... 16.040–16.049, 16.053–16.054, 16.060, 16.076
.... 16.104, 16.110
(a) 16.049, 25.197
(b) 16.031, 16.049
(2) 16.029, 16.077

Companies Act 1990 (contd)
(3) ... 16.039, 16.046
(a) ... 16.047
(b) ... 16.047
(c) ... 16.048
(4) ... 16.049–16.052, 16.110
(b) ... 16.047
(5) ... 16.053, 16.104, 16.110
(6) ... 12.029
(7) ... 20.059
(a) ... 12.029, 16.037
(b) ... 16.038
(8) ... 16.041, 25.197
(9) ... 16.029
(a) ... 16.028
(b) ... 16.028
30 ... 13.118, 27.018
31 ... 1.162, 7.059, 7.078, 10.047, 10.068, 10.084, 12.002
... 12.016, 13.055, 16.001–16.006, 16.010, 16.019
... 16.055–16.065, 16.069–16.078, 16.092–16.105
... 16.110–16.118, 16.123, 17.113, 17.117, 17.231
... 18.008, 25.033, 25.136, 25.147, 28.058, 28.070
(1) ... 16.058, 16.062–16.064, 16.072
(a) ... 16.065
(b) ... 16.071
(c) ... 16.063, 16.071, 16.105
(2) ... 16.062
(3) ... 16.063
32 ... 16.073–16.079, 16.114, 17.117, 28.070
(1) ... 16.075–16.077
(2)(b) ... 16.077
32–37 ... 16.120
33 ... 15.115, 16.078
(1)(c) ... 18.002, 18.021
(2) ... 16.078
(3) ... 16.078
(5) ... 18.002, 18.021
34 ... 7.059, 12.016, 14.087, 16.073, 16.080, 16.088, 16.098–16.099
(1) ... 16.081
(2) ... 16.084
(3) ... 16.084
(e) ... 7.059
(4) ... 16.087
(5) ... 16.088
(6) ... 16.082
(7)–(11) ... 16.083
35 ... 1.162, 10.068, 12.002, 12.016, 16.073, 16.089–16.092

Companies Act 1990 (contd)

36 .... 16.073, 16.093, 28.058
37 .... 16.073, 16.095–16.097, 28.070
38 .... 18.008
(1) 16.047, 16.101
(a) 16.103
(b) 16.105–16.108
(2) 16.071, 16.110
(a) 16.104, 16.111
(b) 16.104
(3) 16.104, 16.110
39 .... 16.115
(1) 16.071, 16.113–16.114
40 .... 16.093, 16.118
(1) 28.058
(b) 28.034
(2) 28.058
41 .... 16.001, 17.113, 17.117, 30.062, 31.029
(1) 17.113
(c) 17.113, 17.117
(2) 17.113
(c) 17.113, 17.117
(3) 17.114
(5) 17.113, 17.117
(7) 17.116
(8) 17.113
(11) 17.115
41–43 .... 17.185
41–45 .... 17.133, 17.203
42 .... 17.114
43 (1) 17.118
(2) 17.118
(3) 17.118
44 .... 28.058, 28.060
45 (1) 17.117
(2) 17.117
46 .... 17.231
47 (1) 16.123, 17.113
(2) 16.126
50 .... 28.060
51 .... 15.156
52 .... 15.018
(1) 15.008
53 .... 8.127, 13.110, 13.113–13.117, 15.156, 27.018, 28.058, 32.131
(1) 13.101, 15.156
(2) 13.103
(7) 13.114

Companies Act 1990 (contd)

(8) 13.110–13.113
(9) 13.100, 13.110–13.113
(10) 13.101
54 .... 13.110, 16.014, 16.019
(1) 13.111, 16.017
(2) 13.108, 13.111, 16.015–16.017
(3) 13.109, 16.016–16.017
(4) 16.017
(a) 13.109, 16.017
(b) 13.109, 13.112, 16.017
(5) 16.018
(a) 13.109
(b) 13.109, 16.018
(6) 13.109, 16.018
(7) 13.109, 16.017
(a) 13.109
(b) 13.109
(8) 13.109, 16.017
(9) 13.109, 16.017
(10) 16.018, 13.109
(11) 13.109, 16.018
(12) 13.109, 16.018
(13) 13.104, 16.017
55 .... 13.110, 16.014
(1) 13.112
(2) 13.112
56 (1) 13.102
(2) 13.107
56–58 .... 13.112, 16.014
57 (1) 13.105
(2) 13.105
(3) 13.106
(4) 13.106
58 .... 28.058
(1) 13.113
(2) 13.113
(3) 13.115
(5) 13.106, 13.115
(6) 13.115
(7) 13.113
59 .... 2.037
(1) 13.116
(2) 13.116
(3) 13.116
(4) 13.116
60 .... 13.116, 28.060

Companies Act 1990 (contd)

61 .... 13.116
62 .... 13.116, 28.059
63 .... 17.134, 17.204, 17.214, 30.062, 31.029
(1) 15.156, 17.121
64 .... 13.117, 28.058
(1) 13.110
(2) 13.110
(3) 13.111, 13.118, 15.156
(3)–(5) 27.018
(4)–(6) 13.111
(7) 13.110
65 .... 28.058
(1) 13.117
(2) 13.117
(3) 13.117
66 .... 13.118, 27.004, 27.008, 27.018
67 .... 17.218, 29.058
(2) 29.125
72 .... 8.130, 29.058
73 .... 29.058, 29.126
74 .... 29.058
77 .... 8.130, 29.059
(2) 8.130
(4)(b) 8.130
78 .... 29.059
(1) 8.131
(3) 8.131
(4) 8.131
79 .... 28.058
80 .... 28.060
80 .... 29.057
81 .... 29.125–29.126
(1) 29.125
83 .... 29.128
84 .... 28.059, 29.129
85 .... 28.058
(4) 29.127
(5) 29.127
91 .... 17.218
98(5) 8.132
98–104 .... 29.125
99 .... 8.128
100(1) 8.129
(3) 8.130
101(3) 8.132
(4) 8.132
(5) 8.132

Companies Act 1990 (contd)

102 .... 8.133
103(1) 8.133
104 .... 8.134
107 .... 32.093–32.094
108 .... 4.066, 32.097
(6) 5.063
109 .... 5.063, 32.095
110 .... 32.093
111 .... 32.096
114 .... 32.096
115 .... 32.096
116 .... 32.096
122 .... 19.042, 19.069
123 .... 23.075
124 .... 24.035
125 .... 25.013
126 .... 15.143, 25.024, 25.039
127 .... 15.143, 25.036
128 .... 5.089, 23.004, 23.007
129 .... 23.115
130 .... 25.105
131 .... 23.006, 23.025–23.028, 24.046, 28.058
(2) 23.116, 24.046
(3) 23.116, 24.046
(4) 23.116, 24.046
(5) 23.006, 23.115, 24.047
(6) 24.047
(7) 24.047
132 .... 25.183, 25.195
133 .... 24.009
135 .... 25.081, 25.087
136 .... 25.110
137 .... 13.059, 15.143
138 .... 5.091, 13.059, 15.096, 15.115–15.116, 15.143
139 .... 15.143, 22.110, 25.028, 25.097, 25.103–25.107
(1)(b) 25.107
(2) 22.110
(3) 22.110, 25.107
140 .... 5.090, 15.143, 25.119–25.121
(2) 25.123
(3) 25.124
(5) 25.086, 25.120, 25.127, 27.022
141 .... 5.008, 5.090, 23.108, 25.125
(2) 25.126
(3) 25.128
(c), (d) 25.129
(5) 25.127

Companies Act 1990 (contd)
142 ... 15.143, 15.149
145 ... 28.045
146 ... 24.007
147 ... 24.011
149 ... 15.143, 28.074
(1) ... 28.074
(b) ... 28.072
(2) ... 28.074, 28.084
(4) ... 28.074
(5) ... 13.055, 28.074
149–158 ... 28.050
150 ... 5.083–5.086, 10.069, 13.020, 13.046, 13.049, 13.057–13.059
... 13.067–13.069, 15.042, 15.049, 15.053, 15.134–15.136
... 15.160, 24.015, 24.025, 25.029, 26.057, 28.023
... 28.062–28.067, 28.074–28.079, 28.083–28.085
... 28.089, 28.093, 28.097, 28.111, 28.117, 28.118–28.122
... 28.134, 28.138, 28.169, 29.084
(1) ... 28.064, 28.068–28.069, 28.082, 28.088, 28.091, 28.123, 28.129
... 28.131–28.133, 28.137, 28.159, 28.165, 28.182
(2) ... 28.064–28.066, 28.131–28.131, 28.136
(a) ... 28.097–28.098, 28.103
(c) ... 28.131
(3) ... 10.006, 13.020, 28.069, 28.079, 28.139–28.146, 29.084
(a) ... 28.069
(ii) ... 13.020
(4) ... 28.071
(4A) ... 28.084, 28.089, 28.140
(4B) ... 28.093
(5) ... 13.020, 28.131
150–152 ... 10.037
151 ... 28.045, 28.050
(1) ... 28.086
(2) ... 28.086
(3) ... 28.086
152 ... 28.066, 28.137–28.138, 28.140–28.141
(1) ... 28.136
(2) ... 10.062, 28.136
(3) ... 28.136–28.137
(4) ... 28.136, 28.140
153 ... 28.071, 28.139
154 ... 28.075, 28.086–28.088
155 ... 25.120, 28.070, 28.139
(2) ... 10.069, 28.070
(3) ... 28.070, 28.146
(4) ... 28.070
(5) ... 5.086, 28.070, 28.146

Companies Act 1990 (contd)

156 .... 13.020, 28.069
(1) 28.069
(2) 15.156, 28.069
(3) 28.069
(6) 28.069
157 .... 13.020
(1) 28.070
(2) 28.070
158 .... 13.020, 28.069
159 .... 13.007, 13.055, 28.148, 28.154–28.156
.... 28.163, 28.178, 28.190
160 .... 5.083, 13.007, 13.059, 25.029, 27.080, 28.023, 28.067
.... 28.157, 28.166, 28.180
(1) 13.018, 28.151, 28.174
(a) 17.307
(1A) 28.153, 28.197
(2) 28.089, 28.157, 28.162–28.165, 28.167, 28.170
(a) 28.154, 28.174
(b) 28.175
(c) 28.155, 28.176
(d) 28.163, 28.177–28.178, 28.180, 28.201
(e) 13.008, 28.185, 28.201
(f) 28.182, 28.190
(g) 28.193
(h) 28.196
(3)(a) 28.182, 28.191
(b) 28.191
(3A) 28.194
(3B) 28.197
(4) 28.089, 28.157
(b) 28.089
(7) 28.162
(8) 28.202
(9) 28.173
(9A) 28.172
(9B) 28.161
161 .... 28.058, 28.061
(1) 28.143, 28.202–28.205
(2) 28.143, 28.205
(3) 28.202–28.205
(5) 28.087
(6) 28.087
163(2) 28.144–28.146, 28.206
(3) 5.084–5.086, 28.144–28.146
(4) 5.086, 28.146
(5) 5.086, 28.144–28.146, 28.206

Companies Act 1990 (contd)

164 .... 28.058, 28.208
(1) 5.085, 28.145, 28.207
(2) 28.145, 28.207
165 .... 5.085, 28.147, 28.209
(1) 5.085, 28.208
(2) 5.085, 28.147, 28.208
166 .... 28.058, 28.152
167 .... 28.152
169 .... 13.018
170 .... 20.011
172 .... 20.051, 20.053
175 .... 20.090
176(3) 20.093
178 .... 25.103
180 .... 22.002
(2) .... , 25.103
(3) 15.115
181 .... 22.002
(1)(c) 22.068
185 .... 14.032, 17.237, 17.343–17.347, 28.045, 28.051, 28.058
(1) 17.343
(2) 17.344
(3) 17.344
(4) 17.344
(5) 17.344
186 .... 28.045, 28.049, 28.051, 28.058
(1) 14.032, 14.038, 17.345
(2) 14.032, 17.345
(3) 14.032, 17.345
(4) 14.032, 17.345
(5) 14.038, 17.345
(6) 17.345
187(12) 28.015
187–192 .... 29.051
191 .... 17.300
(3) 17.300
192(6) 28.015
193 .... 14.039–14.041, 17.276, 17.283, 30.066
(1) 17.017, 17.226, 17.314
(2) 17.017, 17.242, 17.249
(3) 17.010, 17.310
(4) 17.230
(4A) 17.229–17.233
(4B) 17.229
(4C) 17.228
(4D) 17.228–17.233

Companies Act 1990 (contd)
(4G) ... 17.241
(5) ... 14.038, 17.311
(6) ... 17.225, 17.315
194 ... 17.317, 17.329, 28.045, 28.051, 28.058
(1) ... 17.316–17.318
(3A) ... 17.317, 28.015
(4) ... 17.317
(5) ... 17.320, 28.015
(5A) ... 16.131
(6) ... 17.321, 28.015
195 ... 17.307, 28.058
196 ... 28.058
(1) ... 17.310
(3) ... 17.310
197 ... 28.058
(1)–(2) ... 17.310
(4) ... 17.310
199 ... 28.045, 28.051, 28.058
200 ... 28.045, 28.051, 28.058
202 ... 5.087, 15.134–15.140, 17.005, 17.010, 28.033
... 28.058, 28.060, 28.193, 28.212
(1) ... 15.131, 17.005, 17.008
(2) ... 17.005
(3)–(5) ... 17.006
(6) ... 17.007
(7) ... 17.008
(8) ... 17.009, 28.211
(9) ... 17.008
(10) ... 17.011
203 ... 15.143, 17.012, 28.058, 28.060
(1) ... 17.012–17.014
(2) ... 17.012
204 ... 5.087, 15.132–15.137, 15.140, 15.143, 17.013, 28.114
(1) ... 15.132, 15.137, 17.310, 17.318
(2) ... 15.132
(3) ... 15.133
(4) ... 15.134
(5) ... 15.133, 17.013
205 ... 17.010
205B ... 13.038, 29.088
205E ... 29.088
207 ... 10.018, 10.041
(1) ... 10.041
(2) ... 10.025–10.026, 10.111
(a) ... 10.025, 10.041
(b) ... 10.041

Companies Act 1990 (contd)
(c) 10.041
(d) (i) 10.026, 10.041
(ii) 10.041
(e) 10.041
(f) 10.041
208 .... 10.018, 10.026, 10.041
209 .... 10.026, 14.087
(1) 10.018
(2) 10.039, 29.076
(a) 10.043
(3) 10.043
(4) 10.018, 10.044
(6) 10.044
(7) 10.044
210 .... 8.120, 10.041
211 .... 10.018–10.023, 10.029, 31.023
(2) 10.025–10.026
(3) 10.025
212 .... 8.015, 10.024
(1)(b) 29.069
(1A) 29.069
(2) 10.024, 29.069
212–217 .... 10.037
213 .... 8.015, 10.024, 14.087, 29.070
(2) 8.015, 10.028, 10.031
(3) 10.028
(4) 10.028
(5) 8.015
(5) 10.028
(6) 10.028
(7) 10.028
214(1) 10.031
215 .... 29.070
(1) 8.015, 29.071
(4) 29.071
216 .... 29.068–29.072
(1) 29.072
(2) 29.072
217 .... 10.028
218 .... 10.045
(1) 10.026
(2) 10.026
219(2) 10.033
(4) 10.034
(6) 10.034
220 .... 8.066, 10.090, 10.112

Companies Act 1990 (contd)
221 .... 29.068
222 .... 10.032, 28.058
(2) 29.073
224 .... 8.010, 8.014, 10.037–10.038, 14.087, 17.095
(1) 8.015, 10.036
(2) 8.015, 10.037, 10.038
(b) 8.016, 17.095
(3) 8.015, 10.037–10.039, 29.076
(4) 8.015, 10.037
(5) 10.037
(6) 10.037
225 .... 8.015
226 .... 10.032, 28.045, 28.049
227 .... 8.068
228 .... 28.058
(1) 10.035, 10.044
(2) 10.035
(3) 10.035
229 .... 28.058
231(1) 10.111
232 .... 10.090
(a) 10.017
233(2)(b) 17.034
234 .... 28.058
236 .... 29.084
237 .... 24.007
239(3) 8.047
240 .... 8.005, 16.119, 26.022, 28.003, 28.034, 28.143, 28.205
240 .... 29.040
(1) 13.114, 17.011, 17.115, 17.124
.... 17.222, 17.0263, 17.310, 17.318, 17.344–17.345, 28.034
(2) 17.310, 28.034
(3) 28.020
(5)(a) 28.038
(c) 28.038
(5A) 28.038
(7) 28.034
(8) 28.034, 28.056
240A 28.039
242(1) 28.057
(2) 28.057
243 .... 17.014, 28.058
(1) 14.121
244A 17.309
247(4) 28.049

Companies Act 1990 (contd)

248 ....17.255, 28.054
(2) 28.053
(3)–(5) 28.054
(8) 28.053
249(2) 28.053–28.054
(5)–(7) 28.054
249A 28.054
(1) 17.255, 28.054
(2) 17.255, 28.054
(3) 28.054
250 ....1.160
251 ....15.095, 15.109, 15.125, 15.141, 15.145–15.149
....20.072, 25.029, 28.023
(1) 15.141
(2) 15.143
(b) 15.144
(2A) 15.142, 28.073
(4)(a) 15.142
(b) 15.142
253 ....29.139
(1) 29.139, 29.144
(2) 29.132, 29.140–29.144
(4) 29.140
254 ....29.146
255 ....29.146
(2) 29.146
256 ....29.132
(1) 29.136
(3) 29.135
(8) 29.136
256A 29.142
256E 29.143
(6) 29.142
(8) 29.149
(9) 29.149
256F 29.026, 29.037, 29.137–29.138
(9) 29.137
257(4)(c) 23.050, 23.067, 29.148
259 ....29.132
260 ....29.145–29.146
(1) 8.018, 10.069
(2) 29.145
(3) 29.135
(4) 29.147
260A 17.024
(1) 29.147
(4) 29.147

Companies Act 1990 (contd)
Pt II 27.001, 27.005, 27.010, 27.080, 28.017
Pt III 1.043, 5.016, 16.001–16.003, 16.011, 16.021
.... 16.032, 16.057, 16.072, 16.091
Pt IV 8.128, 13.100, 29.057, 32.131
Pt V 5.063, 13.059, 32.003, 32.062, 32.070, 32.076–32.079, 32.093
Pt VII 5.083, 28.062, 28.081, 28.088, 28.148, 28.156
Pt XI 10.017, 10.023, 10.032, 10.037, 10.040, 10.090, 12.042
Pt XII 17.024
Pt XIII 23.067, 29.132–29.144, 29.148
Companies (Amendment) Act 1999 .... 1.100
3 .... 29.061
(2) 29.061
46 .... 4.020
Companies (Amendment) (No 2) Act 1999 .... 1.089, 1.101–1.105
.... 2.038, 17.341, 22.003, 22.022, 22.036, 22.068, 22.073
.... 22.076, 22.097, 22.142, 23.134, 26.002–26.004
.... 26.014, 26.039, 26.046, 26.049
4(5) 1.158
5 .... 22.018
(b) 22.004–22.005, 22.019
7 .... 22.036
9 .... 22.039, 22.046
10 .... 22.017
12 .... 22.051
13 .... 22.034
14(a) 22.059
(b) 19.031
(i) 22.059, 22.073
(ii) 22.059, 22.068
15 .... 22.097
16 .... 22.069–22.071
18 .... 18.084, 22.075
20(1) 22.134
(4) 22.064
22 .... 22.123
(a) 22.116
(b) 22.130
(d) 22.117
22 .... 22.123
23 .... 22.131
24 (a) 22.0141
(b) 22.142
25 .... 22.081
26 .... 22.124
27 (a) 22.161
(b) 22.162

Companies (Amendment) (No 2) Act 1999 (contd)
28 .... 22.076, 22.085, 25.165
32 .... 17.287
(1)(b) 17.287
(2) 17.284
(3) 17.287
32A 17.287
32B 17.288
33 (1) 17.288
(2) 17.288
(4) 17.289
(5) 17.289
34 .... 17.290
(5) 17.341
35 .... 17.291
41 .... 28.003, 28.038
42 .... 2.017, 2.024, 2.032
(1) 2.030
(2) 2.030
(3) 2.030
(4) 2.030
(7) 2.030
43 .... 2.038, 13.012, 13.015, 26.014, 26.054
(1) 13.012, 26.014
(2)–(8) 13.012, 26.014
(9) 13.014, 13.083, 28.049
(10) 13.014
(11) 13.014
(13) 13.012
(14) 13.012
(15) 13.012, 26.014, 26.051
(b) 26.054
(16) 13.012
44 .... 2.038
(1)–(7) 13.015
(7) 13.015
(8) 13.013
(a)(ii) 13.013
(9) 13.013
(10) 13.013
45 .... 29.084
(1) 13.023
(2) 13.023
(3) 13.024, 29.084
(4) 13.024
(5) 13.024
(7) 13.024
(8)–(13) 13.023

Companies (Amendment) (No 2) Act 1999 (contd)
46 .... 26.06
47 .... 13.083
48 .... 26.013
52(1) 28.007
53 .... 27.080
Pt III 17.226
Sch 2 .... 13.024, 22.016

Companies (Auditing and Accounting) Act 2003 .... 1.103, 1.164, 15.094
s 46 .... 17.252

Companies (Amendment) Act 2009 .... 1.108
s 2 .... 17.024
(b) ....
7 .... 16.118
10(1) 13.012

Companies (Miscellaneous Provisions) Act 2009 .... 1.109
s 1 .... 17.024, 29.118
2 .... 29.119
3 .... 27.001
(b) 27.014
(d)(i) 29.069
(j) 29.137

Companies (Amendment) Act 2012 .... 1.110
s 2 .... 29.118

Company Law Enforcement Act 2001 .... 1.102, 3.009, 16.012, 25.002
.... 26.022, 27.005, 27.064, 27.075, 28.001, 28.025–28.030
.... 28.063, 28.082, 28.148, 30.015
s 7 (1)–(3) 28.010
8 (1), (3) 28.011
10 (1), (2) 28.011
11 .... 28.010
(2), (3) 28.010
12 (1) 28.013
(a) 28.018–28.023
(b) 28.016
(c) 28.018
(d) 28.018–28.021
(e) 28.015
(2) 28.013
(3) 28.012
(5) 28.011
14 .... 23.048, 27.017, 28.020
16 .... 28.011
17 .... 28.011
(4) 28.058

Company Law Enforcement Act 2001 (contd)
18 .... 28.018
21 .... 27.015
22 .... 27.023
23 .... 27.035, 27.046
24 .... 27.052
25 .... 27.061
26 .... 27.017
29 .... 27.068
31 .... 27.080
37 .... 32.096
40 .... 28.160
41 .... 28.069
(1) 28.067–28.069
(b) 13.020
(c) 28.089
(2) 28.069
(a) 29.084
(c) 28.093
42 .... 28.153, 28.163, 28.171, 28.194, 28.197
(b)(ii) 28.163
(d) 28.157
(e) 28.157
43 .... 24.070
44 (a) 25.024
(b) 25.035
45 .... 25.036
(c) 25.037
46 .... 25.043
47 .... 23.028–23.029, 23.123
49 .... 24.070, 25.039, 25.043, 28.019
51 .... 28.024
52 .... 28.015
(2) 28.007
53 .... 28.015
(a) 28.050
54 .... 28.073
(b) 15.142
55 .... 20.084, 25.048–25.051, 28.023
(b) 20.084
56 .... 24.025, 28.082–28.083, 28.085, 28.091
(1) 24.026, 28.096, 28.159
(2) 28.075, 28.084, 28.091, 28.132
(3) 28.058, 28.132
57 .... 28.015
(1)–(3) 24.070
(4) 24.070, 28.058

Company Law Enforcement Act 2001 (contd)
58 .... 24.071, 28.015, 28.058
(1) 28.049
59 .... 28.046, 28.049
60 .... 28.046, 28.049
66 .... 28.041, 28.054
(1) 17.255, 28.041
(2) 17.255
(c) 28.041
67–71 .... 1.166
68 .... 1.166
72 .... 28.015
73 .... 28.015
74 .... 28.015, 28.051, 28.058
75 .... 16.068
76 (b) 16.011
(c) 16.009
77 .... 16.078
78 .... 7.059, 14.087, 16.073, 16.080, 16.098
79 .... 16.089
80 .... 3.004–3.005, 3.039
(1) 2.021, 3.005
(2) 2.021, 3.005
(3) 2.021, 3.005
(4) 2.021, 3.005
81 .... 3.004
82 .... 3.039
85 .... 3.026
86 .... 3.006
87 .... 3.023
88 .... 3.009, 30.015
(1) 3.059, 30.015
(2) 3.009, 30.015
88 (2) 30.015
89 .... 10.072
(1) 10.067
(a) 10.067–10.068
(b) 10.068, 14.092
91 .... 28.153
92 .... 21.023
93 .... 23.067
94 (c) 23.050
96 .... 28.028, 28.210
(c) 28.212
98 .... 3.008, 28.058
100 .... 15.095, 28.033
101 .... 28.153

Company Law Enforcement Act 2001 (contd)
104 .... 28.056, 29.040
(a) 28.020, 28.034
(b), (c) 28.034
105 .... 28.039
107 .... 28.054
109(1) 28.042
(2) 28.042
110(1) 28.040
Pt 3 .... 27.001
Pt 9 .... 16.057
Competition Act 2002
s 26(6) 5.093
Consumer Credit Act 1995 .... 16.095
Pt III 7.008
Conveyances (Ireland) Act 1634 .... 25.109
Conveyancing Act 1881 .... 20.023, 20.080
s 19 .... 20.013
24(6) 20.044
Corporate Manslaughter and Corporate Homicide Act 2007 .... 4.059
s 1 (1) 4.059
(2) 4.059
18 .... 4.060
Corporation Tax Act 1976 .... 25.185
Courts (Maritime Conventions) Act 1989
s 13(2) 19.069
Courts and Enforcement of Judgments (European Communities) Act 1988 .... 5.069
Courts Act 1971
s 15 .... 28.039
Courts of Justice Act 1936
s 65 .... 25.161
68 .... 23.024
Credit Institutions (Stabilisation) Act 2010 .... 1.036, 1.046, 8.032, 15.008
s 4(f) 15.008
11(1) 11.047
48(1) 15.008
49 .... 13.046
71 .... 1.046
Pt 4 .... 23.137
Sch 1 Pt 1 .... 1.046
Credit Institutions (Stabilisation) Act 2012
s 11(1) 8.04

Credit Union Act 1997 .... 1.048, 1.068
s 6 (1) 1.049
(2) 1.049
(3) 1.049
13 .... 1.049
46(1) 1.049
47 .... 1.049
87 .... 23.139
Criminal Justice Act 1984 .... 28.035
s 4 .... 15.128, 16.119, 17.011, 28.022, 28.056
Criminal Law Act 1997
s 4 .... 28.022
Customs Consolidation Act 1876 .... 5.093
s 191 .... 5.093
259 .... 5.093
Data Protection Act 1988
s 8 .... 18.023
Debtors (Ireland) Act 1840 .... 9.040
s 23 .... 9.038, 9.040
24 .... 9.038–9.040
27 .... 6.075
28 .... 6.075
Debtors (Ireland) Act 1872
s 7 .... 25.041, 25.044
Dentists Act 1985
s 52 .... 4.076
Dáil Éireann (Privilege and Procedure) Act 1970
s 3(4) 27.047
Economic and Monetary Union Act 1998
s 6 .... 28.034, 29.011
Electoral Act 1997
s 26 .... 17.214, 17.258
Electronic Commerce Act 2000 .... 7.003, 28.053
s 2 (1) 7.009, 7.019
10 .... 7.009
(1) 7.010
(a)(ii) 7.010
(b) 7.010, 7.020
(2)(c) 7.010
12 .... 7.010
(1) 7.009, 7.019

Electronic Commerce Act 2000 (contd)
13 (1) 7.009
(2)(a) 7.009
16 .... 7.019
18 .... 8.017
19 .... 7.009
(1) 7.010
23 .... 7.010
Annex I 7.019
Annex II 7.019
European Communities Act 1972 .... 27.080
s 3 .... 32.051
9(2) 7.041
European Parliament Elections Act 1997
Sch 2 Pt XIII 28.011
Exchange Control Acts 1954–1986 .... 27.080
Finance Act 1972 .... 25.185
Finance Act 1977
s 34 .... 16.014
Finance Act 1983
s 46 .... 25.168
56 .... 25.168
Finance Act 1986
s 115 .... 18.057
Finance Act 1995
s 174 .... 18.058
Finance Act 1996
s 112 .... 3.004, 3.039, 3.092
Finance Act 1999 .... 26.07
s 82 .... 2.034, 26.07
(1) 2.045
(2) 2.045, 5.069
(3) 2.045
83 .... 2.034, 26.07
(1) 2.045
(2) 2.034, 26.07
Finance Act 2003
s 136 .... 12.046
Finance Act 2007
s 120 .... 18.059, 18.063

Fines Act 2010 .... 1.185, 17.011, 28.020, 28.032, 28.034, 32.096
s 3 .... 17.011–17.015, 17.019, 17.115, 17.124, 17.0263
.... 17.310, 17.318, 17.344–17.345, 28.036
4 .... 28.037
4–8 .... 28.037
5 .... 28.037
6 .... 15.128, 16.119, 17.015, 19.085, 20.011, 28.034–28.037
(2) 28.034, 28.037, 34.041
(3) 1.009–1.011, 8.017–8.018, 28.037, 34.026
7 .... 28.037
(3) 1.010
8 .... 20.011, 28.037
9 .... 15.128, 16.119, 20.011, 28.034–28.035
12 .... 28.034
14 .... 28.034
Pt 1 .... 28.034
Pt 2 .... 28.034–28.037

Fire Services Act 1981 .... 4.056

Fraudulent Conveyances Act 1634 .... 16.109

Friendly Societies Act 1896
Sch 1 .... 1.053

Friendly Societies Acts 1896–1977 .... 28.156

Gas Regulation Act 1982 .... 1.068

Hotel Proprietors Act 1963
s 8 .... 19.025

Housing (Miscellaneous Provisions) Act 1992 .... 1.036

Income Tax Act 1967 .... 25.185
s 96 .... 16.014
Ch IV 17.036

Industrial and Provident Societies Act 1893 .... 1.048, 7.058
s 4(a) 1.035
5(1) 1.033
10 .... 1.034
21 .... 1.032
40 .... 7.067
51 .... 1.035
52 .... 1.035
53 .... 1.035
54 (1) 1.035

Industrial and Provident Societies (Amendment) Act 1913
s 1 .... 1.033

Industrial and Provident Societies Act 1971 .... 1.035

Industrial and Provident Societies (Amendment) Act 1978
Pt III 1.048
Industrial and Provident Societies Acts 1893–1978 .... 28.148, 28.151
Insurance (No 2) Act 1983 .... 22.167, 25.076
Insurance Act 1990
s 9(1) 10.037
Insurance Acts 1909–1990 .... 27.080
Interpretation Act 1937 .... 13.068
s 11 (c) 13.068–13.069, 28.079
(d) 13.067
20 (1) 11.043
Interpretation Act 1978
s 12(1) 25.006
Interpretation Act 2005 .... 1.163, 3.055, 11.043
s 5 .... 16.044
6 .... 9.040
18(c) 4.076, 13.067, 28.079
21 .... 14.006
(2) 1.163
23 .... 25.006
26(2)(f) 11.043
27(1)(a) 20.013
Investment Funds, Companies and Miscellaneous Provisions Act 2005
.... 1.106, 29.131, 32.062, 32.076
s 25 .... 29.142
31 .... 29.060, 32.062
32 .... 28.057, 32.113
33 .... 32.115
34 .... 32.066
38 .... 32.052
(1) 32.025, 32.051
(3) 32.052
38A 32.052
40 .... 32.008
41 .... 32.045–32.046
42 (3)–(4) 32.046
43 .... 32.046
47 .... 32.052
48 .... 32.055
(5) 32.055
49 .... 32.013, 32.045
56(1) 29.078
59 .... 2.026, 3.007
(4) 3.007

Investment Funds, Companies and Miscellaneous Provisions Act 2005 (contd)
60 .... 2.026, 3.007
72 .... 22.055, 23.013, 23.020, 23.115, 24.013, 26.006–26.009
.... 26.014, 26.027–26.031, 29.016, 29.017, 29.123
Pt 3 .... 1.106
Pt 4 .... 1.106, 13.059
Pt 5 .... 1.106
Pt 6 .... 1.106
Investment Funds, Companies and Miscellaneous Provisions Act 2006
.... 1.107, 1.134, 17.218, 32.118
s 1 .... 1.163
(2) 1.164
7 .... 1.002, 1.085, 1.134, 3.041, 29.039
8 .... 8.053
11(1) 28.093
15(a) 32.052
22 .... 32.120
Pt 3 .... 1.107
Investment Limited Partnerships Act 1994 .... 29.131
Irish Bankrupt and Insolvent Act 1857
s 311 .... 25.057
313 .... 4.089
Irish Takeover Panel Act 1997 .... 1.122, 21.057, 32.083
s 8 .... 21.023
Irish Anonymous Partnership Act 1781 .... 1.081
Joint Stock Companies Act 1844 .... 1.071, 1.080–1.082, 18.078, 28.006
Joint Stock Companies Act 1856 .... 1.071, 1.083–1.084, 3.062
Judgment Mortgage (Ireland) Act 1850 .... 6.075
s 6 .... 6.075, 25.055
7 .... 25.055
Judgment Mortgage (Ireland) Act 1858 .... 6.075
Jurisdiction of the Courts (Enforcement of Judgments) Act 1988 .... 6.014
Land Purchase Act 1925 .... 7.028
Land Registry under the Registration of Title Act 1964 .... 19.055
Land and Conveyancing Law Reform Act 2009 .... 19.053, 20.023, 20.044
s 5 .... 20.044
8 .... 20.013
62 (1) 7.016
63 .... 7.017
64 (1) 7.014
(b) 7.015

Land and Conveyancing Law Reform Act 2009 (contd)
(2) 7.015
(b) 7.029
(i) 7.015, 7.030
(ii) 7.016, 7.027
65 (1) 7.029
(2) 7.029
68 (2)(b)(ii) 7.024
89 (1) 18.033, 19.053
(2) 18.033
(6) 18.034
96 ..... 20.019
97 ..... 20.019
100(2) 20.023
108(1) 20.021
(7) 20.044
109(1) 20.021
116 ..... 25.055
117 ..... 25.055
Pt 10 ..... 18.033
Ch 3 ..... 20.019
Landlord and Tenant Law Amendment (Ireland) Act 1860 (Deasy's Act) 25.064
s 7 ..... 25.064
Landlord and Tenant (Amendment) Act 1980
s 5(3) 4.041
Limitation Act 1939 ..... 17.312
Limited Liability Partnership Act 2000 ..... 1.028
Limited Liability Act 1855 ..... 1.071, 1.082, 11.095
Limited Partnership Act 1907 ..... 1.026, 28.007
s 4(2) 1.026
5 ..... 1.026
6(1) 1.026
Local Government (Planning and Development) Act 1976
s 14(8) 4.072
27 ..... 5.037, 5.065
Local Government Act 1941 ..... 27.080
Malicious Injuries Act 1981 ..... 4.040, 6.004
Medical Practitioners Act 1978
s 59 ..... 4.076
Mercantile Marine Act 1955 ..... 4.089, 23.119
Merchandise Marks Act 1877
s 2(2) 5.093

Merchant Shipping Act 1894
s 31 ... 7.018
502 ... 4.053
503 ... 4.053
Mines and Quarries Act 1965 ... 5.013
Minimum Notice (Terms of Employment) Act 1973 ... 20.033, 25.185
Multi-Unit Developments Act 2011 ... 30.006, 30.038, 30.048–30.050
s 1 (1) ... 30.006, 30.052
(3) ... 30.006
2 ... 30.006
(4) ... 30.052
8 (1) ... 30.041
(2) ... 30.041
14 ... 30.014, 30.018
(1) ... 30.051
(2) ... 30.051
(4) ... 30.018
(5) ... 30.052
15 ... 30.054
16 ... 30.048
17 ... 30.055
(1)(a) ... 30.055
(2) ... 30.055
(3) ... 30.056
(4) ... 30.056
(5) ... 30.057
(6) ... 30.055
18 ... 30.058, 30.059
23 ... 30.060
24 ... 30.054, 30.074
30 ... 30.072
National Standards Authority Ireland Act 1996
s 26 ... 3.006
National Asset Management Agency Act 2009 ... 1.036, 1.066, 20.022
s 15 (3) ... 13.046
49 ... 20.024
142(7) ... 20.051
147(1) ... 20.022
147–151 ... 20.022
148(1) ... 20.023
(3) ... 20.023
(4) ... 20.023
150(1) ... 20.025
(2) ... 20.025
218(1) ... 10.049

National Asset Management Agency Act 2009 (contd)
228 .... 1.041–1.043
233 .... 23.061
234 .... 22.028, 22.052
Sch 1 Pt 1 .... 1.043, 20.023
Sch 2 Pt 1 .... 1.041
Sch 3 Pt 4 .... 22.028
Office Premises Act 1958
s 31(4) 5.093
Partnership Act 1890 .... 1.016
s 1 .... 1.015, 3.116
(1) 1.056, 16.006–16.008
(2)(a) 1.056, 1.151, 11.036
4 .... 1.018, 4.084
5 .... 1.022
9 .... 1.021
17 .... 4.085
20 .... 1.019
22 .... 1.025
23 .... 1.025
24 .... 1.023–1.025
(7) 4.085
28 30 .... 1.024
31(1) 4.085
(2) 4.085
45 .... 1.015
Planning and Development Act 2000
s 160 .... 5.065
Postal and Telecommunications Services Act 1983 .... 1.066
Powers of Attorney Act 1996 .... 7.023, 20.039
s 15 (2) 7.030–7.031, 20.013
(3) 7.030–7.031, 20.013
17 .... 7.032
(1) 7.032, 7.033
18 .... 7.034
20 .... 20.015
(1) 7.034, 9.037, 20.039
(2) 20.039
(3) 20.039
Proceeds of Crime Act 1996 .... 24.050
s 13 (1) 24.050
(2) 24.050
Prohibition of Incitement to Hatred Act 1989
s 6 .... 28.037

Prosecution of Offences Act 1974 .... 28.024
Protection of Employees (Employers' Insolvency) Act 1984 .... 20.034
Protection of Employment Act 1977
s 21(3) 5.093
Provident Societies Act 1893 .... 1.032
Public Health (Tobacco) Act 2002
s 36 .... 10.061
Redundancy Payments Act 1966
s 52 .... 5.093
Redundancy Payments Acts 1967–1979 .... 25.185
Registration of Business Names Act 1963 .... 1.005, 2.044, 3.011, 28.007
s 3 (1)(a) 1.018
(b) 1.007
(c) 1.007
4 .... 1.008, 1.009
5 (1) 1.009
6 (1) 1.009
8 .... 1.009
9 .... 1.008
10 .... 1.008
11 .... 1.008
12 (1) 1.009
(3)–(5) 1.009
13 .... 1.007
14 .... 1.011
15 .... 1.007
17 .... 1.007
18 (1) 1.010
(2) 1.010
20 (1) 1.008
Registration of Deeds and Title Act 2006 .... 19.054
s 38 .... 19.054
73 .... 18.034, 19.055
Registration of Title Act 1964
s 62 .... 19.055
Revenue Act 1862 .... 5.048
s 15 .... 5.048
Road Traffic Act 1968
s 44(2) 4.019
Safety, Health and Welfare at Work Act 1989
s 6 (1) 4.063

Safety, Health and Welfare at Work Act 2005 .... 17.214
s 12(6) 17.214
80 .... 5.093
Sale of Goods Act 1893 .... 8.038
s 17 .... 19.072–19.073
62 .... 8.038
Social Welfare (Consolidation) Act 1981
s 120 .... 25.160
Social Welfare (Consolidation) Act 1993
s 16(2) 25.160
Social Welfare (Consolidation) Act 2005
s 19 .... 25.159, 25.160
Solicitors Act 1954
s 64 .... 4.076
Solicitors Act 1974
s 73 .... 11.118
Stamp Duties Consolidation Act 1999
s 30(5) 25.198
79 .... 12.046
129(1) 9.007
Stamp Act 1891
s 13 .... 5.093
State Property Act 1954 .... 26.016
s 28 .... 26.016, 26.018, 26.064
(1) 26.016
(2) 26.016
(a) 26.019
(b) 26.019
30 .... 26.064
Statute of Frauds (Ireland) 1695
s 2 .... 5.015, 7.008
6 .... 29.036, 29.063
Statute of Limitations 1957 .... 20.042
s 11(1)(a) 25.174
13 .... 18.102
18(1) 20.041
33 .... 20.041
38 .... 20.041
56 .... 8.076
Stock Exchange Act 1995
s 17(2) 10.040

Stock Transfer Act 1963 .... 31.021
s 2 .... 9.009–9.012
(1) 9.009–9.011
(2) 9.012
(3) 9.009
(4) 31.021
Succession Act 1965 .... 25.141
s 13 .... 8.131
51(1) 16.109
Supreme Court of Judicature (Ireland) Act 1877
s 28 .... 7.008, 7.018
(6) 29.036, 29.063
(8) 20.020, 25.041, 25.042
Taxes Consolidation Act 1997 .... 5.092, 12.045, 13.013, 27.080
s 9 .... 12.044
(2) 12.043
(3) 12.043
(4) 12.044
21 .... 4.091
23A 2.034, 26.07
(1)(a) 2.045
83(2) 26.07
430 .... 5.092
571 .... 25.168
819(3) 13.013
882 .... 13.014, 26.07, 26.045
(1) 2.034, 26.07
(2) 2.034, 2.045
(3) 26.07
1001 .... 18.059, 18.060
(1) 18.060
(3)(a) 18.061
(b) 18.062
(c) 18.063
(4) 18.064
1078 .... 13.014
(1) 27.080
Trade Descriptions Act 1968 .... 5.095
Trade Disputes Act 1906 .... 4.079
Trade Union Act 1871
s 5 .... 4.013–4.014
Trade Union Acts 1871–1982 .... 4.013
Tribunals of Inquiry (Evidence) Acts 1921–1998 .... 27.080

Trustee Act 1893 .... 26.064
s 25 .... 26.020
26 .... 26.020
Unfair Dismissals Act 1977
s 12 .... 25.185
Unfair Dismissals (Amendment) Act 1993
s 15 .... 20.034
Unit Trusts Act 1972
3 .... 16.014
Unit Trusts Act 1990 .... 29.131
Value Added Tax Act 1972 .... 25.185
Veterinary Surgeons Act 1931
s 47 .... 4.076
Waste Management Act 1996 .... 6.078, 25.060

Bunreacht na hÉireann 1937

art 15 .... 27.007
art 15.5 .... 15.114
art 28.2 .... 1.061, 1.064
art 34.1 .... 4.019, 11.061, 11.066, 24.040. 25.032
art 37 .... 4.019
art 40 .... 4.071
art 40.1 .... 4.070
art 40.3 .... 4.018, 4.070, 8.042
art 40.5 .... 4.068
art 40.3.1° 4.071
art 40.3.2° 4.070
art 40.3.3° 4.071
art 40.4.2° 4.068
art 40.6 .... 1.061
art 40.6.1°i 4.073
art 40.6.1°iii 4.075
art 43 .... 4.070
art 44 .... 30.062, 30.066
art 49.1.2° 1.061, 1.064
art 50.1 .... 7.121

United Kingdom

Bills of Sale Act 1878 .... 19.046
Building Societies Act 1986
s 9B(1) 1.040
Cinematograph Films Act 1938 .... 5.026

Companies Act 1929
s 264(4)(b) 18.096
Companies Act 1948 .... 14.022, 17.312, 21.040
s 56 .... 10.112
95 .... 19.029, 19.081
132 .... 14.022
141(2) 14.085
165(a)(1) 27.021
176 .... 1.149
184 .... 3.053, 23.096
(1) 3.053
199 .... 16.133
206 .... 21.015–21.018, 21.027
209 .... 9.101
(1) 5.034
210 .... 11.011, 11.088
223(a) 23.076
325 .... 25.055
353(6) 26.060
437(1) 23.076
441 .... 13.007
447 .... 6.016
455 .... 13.007
Sch 8 Pt 3 ....
Companies Act 1980
s 48(2) 16.030
75 .... 9.123
Companies Act 1981
s 37 .... 10.112
Companies Act 1985 .... 1.158, 9.066, 10.073, 14.098
s 1 (3) 1.133
13(5) 13.032
14 .... 8.075
(1) 25.193
35 .... 7.097
35A 7.130–7.132
36(4) 7.043
123 .... 23.077
125(2) 23.091
131–134 .... 8.067
131–135 .... 17.194
143 .... 10.029
(1) 10.016
151 .... 10.064–10.065
(1) 10.062, 10.065

Companies Act 1985 (contd)
156 .... 10.073
164(2) 10.029
(5) 10.029
183 .... 9.068
210 .... 11.011, 11.014, 11.020
210–459 .... 11.014
263(1) 10.102
282 .... 1.148
283 .... 1.149
300 .... 13.046
312 .... 13.089
320 .... 14.096–14.098, 16.023, 16.030, 16.034, 16.039
.... 16.046, 16.050–16.051, 16.054, 20.059
(2) 16.034
321(2)(b) 16.039
322 .... 16.051
(3) 16.110
(b) 15.088, 16.053
(5) 16.053
(6) 16.053
330 .... 16.056, 16.065, 16.101, 16.111
341(2)(a) 16.111
(b) 16.112
371 .... 3.121, 14.029, 14.031, 14.105
381A 10.029
386 .... 14.023
395 .... 18.075, 19.032
425 .... 21.063
(1) 21.037
(2) 21.044
432 .... 27.016
459 .... 6.021, 11.030, 11.039, 11.046, 11.057, 14.031, 23.091
(1) 11.030
459–461 .... 27.016
464 .... 18.080
478(6) 22.078
651 .... 23.132, 26.061
703A 34.020
703N 34.020
705 .... 19.016
706 .... 19.016
725 .... 23.077
726 .... 6.026, 6.028
(1) 6.021
727 .... 15.088
(1) 15.088, 16.053

Companies Act 1985 (contd)
731(2) 28.038
736 .... 9.075, 12.024–12.025
736A 12.024
(5) 12.024
(6) 12.027
(7) 12.027
736(1) 12.010, 12.027
739(2) 16.028
Sch 15 .... 34.020

Companies Act 1989 .... 23.109
s 108 .... 7.097
Sch 19 para 9 .... 14.023

Companies Act 2006 .... 8.018, 10.100, 34.020
s 116–119 .... 8.018
190 .... 16.023, 16.030
197 .... 16.056, 16.061
306 .... 14.024
611–613 .... 17.194
994(1) 11.088
(2) 11.089
1159 .... 12.027
Sch 6 para 7 .... 12.027

Company Directors Disqualification Act 1986
s 16(1) 28.162
17 .... 28.203

Company Securities (Insider Dealing) Act 1985 .... 27.039

Criminal Justice Act 1988
s 77 .... 5.036

Disqualification of Directors Act 1986 .... 25.029
s 6 .... 28.067

Employment Rights Act 1996 .... 4.077

Enemy Act 1914 .... 5.072

Finance (No 2) Act 1940 .... 4.065

Financial Collateral Arrangements (No 2) Regulations 2003 (SI 2003/3226) 19.039

Foreign Companies (Execution of Documents) Regulations 1994 (SI 1994/950) 7.043

Housing Grants, Construction and Regeneration Act 1986 .... 22.061

Insolvency Rules 1986
r 490 .... 25.153
r 4.31 .... 24.053
r 7.47 .... 23.129

Insolvency Act 1986 .... 18.071, 22.010, 22.026, 22.048
.... 22.056, 22.061, 22.112, 23.035
s 11(3)(d) 22.061
40 .... 20.070
74(2)(f) 25.193
115 .... 25.170
120 .... 25.070
124A 23.109
208(1) 25.006, 28.033
214 .... 15.109, 15.112
(3) 15.112
234 .... 19.007
239(6) 25.093
251 .... 18.094, 25.114
426 .... 22.158, 24.069
Landlord and Tenant Act 1987 .... 12.025
s 4 .... 12.024
Limitations Act 1980 .... 15.069
Restrictive Practices Act 1976 .... 4.066
s 35(1) 6.085
Rules of the Supreme Court 1965 .... 6.080
Ord 23 r 1(1)(a) 6.029
Ord 45 r 7 .... 6.082
Trade Descriptions Act 1978 .... 4.065

European Legislation

Directives

First EU Directive on Company Law (68/151/EEC) 1.113, 4.008, 7.127
Section III 4.008
art 9 .... 7.135
art 12 .... 4.011
art 11.2 .... 4.008
art 12.2 .... 4.008
art 12.3 .... 4.008
Second EU Directive on Company Law (77/91/EEC) 1.114
Third EU Directive on Company Law (78/855/EEC) 1.115
Fourth EU Directive on Company Law (78/660/EEC) 1.116
Sixth EU Directive on Company Law (82/891/EEC) 1.117
Eighth EU Directive on Company Law (84/253/EEC) 1.119
Eleventh Company Law Directive 1.120, 34.027
Seventh EU Directive on Company Law (83/349/EEC) 1.118
Twelfth EU Directive on Company Law (89/667/EEC) 1.121, 1.146

Commission Directive 2003/124/EC
art 1(1) 32.071, 32.074, 32.076
Commission Directive 2010/43/EC 29.131
Commission Directive 2010/44/EC 29.131
Council Directive 68/151/EEC
art 1 .... 34.028
Council Directive 77/187/EEC 20.034
Council Directive 78/660/EEC 1.119
Council Directive 78/855/EEC 29.158, 29.164
art 3 .... 29.159
art 7 .... 29.169, 29.192
Council Directive 83/349/EEC 1.119, 17.146, 17.163, 17.285
art 37 .... 17.285
Council Directive 86/635/EEC 17.163
Council Directive 89/592/EEC 32.059
Council Directive 89/666/EEC 34.027
art 1 .... 34.027
art 1.4 .... 34.027
art 5a 34.027
Council Directive 91/674/EEC 17.163
art 2(1) 29.086
Council Directive 93/22/EC 32.011
Council Directive 93/22/EEC 32.004
art 1(13) 32.004
Council Directive 2000/12/EC
art 1 .... 29.086
Council Directive 2001/34/EC 32.008
Council Directive 2001/86/EC 29.160, 29.185
art 2 .... 29.180
art 3(6) 29.178
art 4 .... 29.178
art 5 .... 29.178
Annex Pt 3(a) 29.181
Council Directive 2002/47/EC 19.035, 19.037, 19.041
Council Directive 2003/6/EC 32.004, 32.058, 32.059–32.063
.... 32.071, 32.076, 32.079
art 1.3 .... 32.061, 32.065
art 2 .... 32.081
art 3 .... 32.083
art 6.5 .... 32.092

Council Directive 2003/6/EC (contd)
art 7 .... 32.064
art 9 .... 32.063
art 14 .... 32.081
Council Directive 2003/58/EC 1.113
Council Directive 2003/71/EC 29.060, 32.008, 32.028, 32.062, 32.105
art 1.2 .... 32.012
art 1.3 .... 32.014
art 2.1 .... 32.004
(d) 32.016
(m) 32.009, 32.040
(n) 32.009
art 3 .... 32.010
art 3.1 .... 32.010
art 3.2 .... 32.018
art 3.3 .... 32.010, 32.025
art 4 .... 32.019
art 4.1 .... 32.023
art 4.2 .... 32.026
art 5.1 .... 32.007, 32.035
art 5.2 .... 32.034
art 5.3 .... 32.029
art 5.4 .... 32.029
art 6 .... 32.045
art 7 .... 32.035
art 9 .... 32.030
art 10 .... 32.039
art 13 .... 32.036
art 14 .... 32.037
art 15 .... 32.038
art 16 .... 32.042
Ch IV 32.040
Ch V 32.041
Council Directive 2004/25/EC 1.122
Council Directive 2004/39/EC 32.004, 32.020
art 4 .... 32.004
art 4.1 .... 17.218, 29.086
art 4.18 .... 32.121
art 24 .... 32.021
art 69 .... 32.004
Annexe I 32.020
Annexe II 32.022
Council Directive 2004/72/EC 32.059
Council Directive 2004/109/EC 1.107, 32.118, 32.122, 32.136
art 1 .... 32.121

Council Directive 2004/109/EC (contd)
art 1.2 ..... 32.121
art 2.1 ..... 32.121
art 4 ..... 32.123
art 4.2 ..... 32.123
art 4.3 ..... 32.123
art 4.4 ..... 32.123
art 5 ..... 32.124
art 5.2 ..... 32.124
art 5.4 ..... 32.124
art 5.5 ..... 32.124
art 6 ..... 32.125
art 6.1 ..... 32.125
art 6.2 ..... 32.125
art 7 ..... 32.127
art 8 ..... 32.126
art 16–18 ..... 32.134
art 19 ..... 32.135
art 34 ..... 32.119
art 20.1 ..... 32.137
art 20.6 ..... 32.137

Council Directive 2005/56/EC 1.115, 1.123, 9.033, 29.026

Council Directive 2006/43/EC 1.119

Council Directive 2006/68/EC 1.114

Council Directive 2007/36/EC 1.124
art 5.1 ..... 29.100
art 7.1 ..... 29.104
art 10.3(b) 29.108

Council Directive 2008/98/EC 5.066

Council Directive 2009/65/EC 29.131

Council Directive 2009/101/EC 1.113

Council Directive 2010/73/EU 32.008, 32.022, 32.118
art 2.2 ..... 32.126
art 2.4 ..... 32.137

Council Directive 2012/17/EU 34.003, 34.027

Regulations

Commission Delegated Regulation 486/2012/EU 32.008, 32.033
Recital 7 ..... 32.031
Annex 32.033

Commission Regulation (EC) 1725/2003 ..... 17.048

Commission Regulation (EC) 2273/2003 ..... 32.059

Commission Regulation (EC) 809/2001 ..... 32.028

Commission Regulation (EC) 809/2004 ..... 32.008

Council Regulation (EEC) 3037/90 .... 2.030

Council Regulation (EC) 1103/97 .... 28.034, 29.011

Council Regulation (EC) 974/98 .... 28.034, 29.011

Council Regulation (EC) 2866/98 .... 28.034, 29.011

Council Regulation (EC) 1346/2000 .... 1.127, 22.158, 24.059

art 3 (1) 24.060–24.063

(2) 24.060, 24.063

(3) 24.060

art 4 (1) 24.060

(2) 24.060

art 5 .... 24.063

art 5–15 .... 24.060

art 7 .... 24.063

art 16(1) 24.061, 24.064

art 18 .... 24.063

art 19 .... 24.064

art 21 .... 24.064

art 22 .... 24.064

art 25 .... 24.064–24.066

art 26 .... 24.064

art 27–38 .... 24.065

art 29 .... 24.065

art 31 .... 24.065

Council Regulation (EC) 44/2001 .... 24.066

art 38–58 .... 24.066

art 53 .... 24.066

Council Regulation (EC) 2157/2001 .... 1.126, 29.001, 29.150, 29.153

art 2 .... 29.157

art 2.1 .... 29.157

art 2.2 .... 29.157

art 2.3 .... 29.157

art 2.4 .... 29.157

art 2.5 .... 29.157

art 3.2 .... 29.166

art 8 .... 4.002, 29.187, 29.194

art 8.2 .... 29.187

art 8.3 .... 29.187

art 8.4 .... 29.187

art 8.6 .... 29.187

art 8.7 .... 29.187

art 8.9 .... 29.190

art 8.10 .... 29.190

art 8.11 .... 29.190

art 8.14 .... 29.188

art 8.15 .... 29.187

Council Regulation (EC) 2157/2001 (contd)
art 8.16 .... 29.191
art 9 .... 29.171
art 11.1 .... 29.171
art 12 .... 29.154, 29.170
art 12.2 .... 29.178
art 13 .... 29.170
art 14 .... 29.111, 29.170
art 17 .... 29.158
art 17.2 .... 29.159
art 19 .... 29.162
art 20 .... 29.164
art 29 .... 29.163
art 32.1 .... 29.164
art 32.2 .... 29.164–29.165
art 32.3 .... 29.164
art 32.6 .... 29.164
arts 32–34 .... 29.164
art 33.3 .... 29.165
art 33.4 .... 29.164
art 36 .... 29.166
art 37 .... 29.167
art 37.2 .... 29.167
art 37.7 .... 29.169
art 37.8 .... 29.169
art 38 .... 29.174
art 39–42 .... 29.175
art 43–45 .... 29.176
art 46–51 .... 29.177
art 49 .... 29.177
art 50 .... 29.185
art 51 .... 29.177
art 52–60 .... 29.182
art 53 .... 29.182
art 57 .... 29.184
art 58 .... 29.184
art 59 .... 29.172
art 60 .... 29.184
art 61 .... 29.186
art 62 .... 29.186
art 63 .... 29.193
art 66 .... 29.192
art 59.1 .... 29.172
art 59.2 .... 29.172
Annex II 29.157
Council Regulation (EC) 1606/2002 .... 17.024, 17.048, 17.148, 32.123
art 6 .... 32.124

International Treaties and Conventions

Brussels Convention
art 5(5) 34.030
EC Treaty
art 54(3)(g) 29.158
art 85 .... 18.046, 18.085
art 86 .... 18.046, 18.085
European Convention on Human Rights 6.018, 27.058
art 6 .... 6.014
art 6.1 .... 11.055, 27.045
Treaty of Rome
art 189 .... 4.011
Treaty on the Functioning of the European Union
art 293(2) 32.060

Other Jurisdictions

Companies Act 1955 (NZ)
s 143 .... 14.073
266 .... 25.078
Companies Act 1973 (RSA)
s 103 .... 9.103
424(1) 15.099
Companies Act 1961 (Aust)
s 67 .... 10.064
196 .... 18.096
292(4) 18.096
Companies Act (Grenada)
584 .... 6.030
Corporations Law (Australia)
s 140(2)(b) 3.061
Corporations Act 2001 (Aust)
s 189(1) 15.080
Spanish Code
s 1261 .... 4.011
1275 .... 4.011
Worker's Compensation Act 1922 (NZ) 4.077

Statutory Instruments

Business Names Regulations 1964 (SI 47/1964) 1.007
Business Names Regulations 1976 (SI 63/1976) 1.007
Business Names Regulations 1980 (SI 399/1980) 1.007
Business Names Regulations 1983 (SI 260/1983) 1.007
Business Names Regulations 1987 (SI 100/1987) 1.007
Business Names Regulations 1993 (SI 138/1993) 1.007
Business Names Regulations 1997 (SI 357/1997) 1.007
Companies (Forms) Order 1994 (SI 100/1994) 1.120
Companies (Forms) Order 2001 (SI 466/2001) 19.103
Companies (Forms) Order 1964 (SI 45/1964) 19.103
Companies (Forms) Order 2000 (SI 62/2000) 2.030
Companies (Forms) Order 2011 (SI 94/2011)
art 4 .... 17.250, 17.257–17.260
Sch 17.258–17.259
Companies (Recognition of Countries) Order 1964 (SI 42/1964) 24.056
Companies (Stock Exchange) Regulations 1990 (SI 337/1990) 8.131
Companies (Stock Exchange) Regulations 1995 (SI 310/1995) 32.003
Companies Act 1990 (Commencement) (No 2) Order 1991 (SI 117/1991) 13.101
Companies Act 1990 (Form and Content of Documents Delivered to the Registrar) Regulations 2002 (SI 39/2002) 17.260
Companies Act 1963 (Ninth Schedule) Regulations 1999 (SI 63/1999) 1.055
Companies Act 1990 (Parts IV and VII) Regulations 1991 (SI 209/1991) 28.152
Companies Act 1963 (Section 24) Regulations 2001 (SI 571/2001)
Sch 30.016
Companies Act 1990 (Section 34) Regulations 2001 (SI 439/2001) 16.087
Companies Act 1963 (Section 377(1)) Order 1999 (SI 64/1999) 1.055
Companies Act 1990 (Uncertificated Securities) Regulations 1996 (SI 68/1996) 8.019, 8.047, 9.010, 29.063
reg 4 .... 29.063
(3) 29.063, 29.132
(9) 29.132
reg 5 .... 29.036, 29.063
reg 7(1) 29.064
reg 8(1) 29.064
(2) 9.010
(3) 29.064
reg 10(1) 29.065
reg 13 .... 29.065
reg 14 .... 29.104
reg 16(1) 29.066

Companies Act 1990 (Uncertificated Securities) Regulations 1996 (contd)
reg 18 ....29.066
reg 19 ....29.064
Companies (Amendment) (No 2) Act 1999 (Commencement) Order 1999 (SI 406/1999) 22.004
Companies (Amendment) (No 2) Act 1999 (Section 32) Order 2012 (SI 308/2012) 17.287
Companies (Amendment) (No 2) Act, 1999 (Commencement) Order 2000 (SI 61/2000) 13.012, 13.023
Companies (Amendment) Act 1983 (Commencement) Order 1983 (SI 288/1983) 29.004
Companies (Amendment) Act, 1982 (Section 13(2)) Order 1988 (SI 54/1988) 1.017
Company Law Enforcement Act 2001 (Section 56) Regulations 2002 (SI 324/2002) 24.026
Company Law Enforcement Act, 2001 (Commencement)(No. 2) Order 2001 (SI 438/2001) 23.028
District Court Rules 1948 (SI 431/1947)
Ord 47 r 2 (a) 6.012
Ord 136 ....6.073
District Court Rules (No 1) 1962 (SI 7/1962)
Ord 5 ....6.012
European Communities (Branch Disclosures) Regulations 1993 (SI 395/1992) 34.027–34.029
reg 3 ....34.028
reg 4(1) 34.032, 34.038
(2) 34.038
reg 5(1) 34.034
(2) 34.034
reg 6 ....34.028
reg 7(1) 34.038
(2) 34.033, 34.038
reg 8(1) 34.035
(2) 34.035
reg 11(1) 34.036
(2) 34.036
(3) 34.036
(4) 34.037
(5) 34.037
reg 12 ....34.036
reg 14(1) 34.005, 34.011, 34.030
(2) 34.031
(3) 34.011
(4)(a) 34.031

European Communities (Branch Disclosures) Regulations 1993 (contd)
reg 15(1) 34.038
(2) 34.038
(3) 34.038
reg 16(1) 34.012
(2) 34.012
reg 17 .... 34.039
(2) 34.039
reg 18 .... 34.040
reg 19(1) 34.041
(3) 34.041
(4) 34.041
(5) 34.041

European Communities (Branch Disclosures) Regulations 1993
(SI 395/1993) 1.120, 1.157

European Communities (Commercial Agents) Regulations 1994
(SI 33/1994) 7.100
reg 5 .... 7.100

European Communities (Companies) Regulations 1973 (SI 163/1973)
.... 1.113, 2.041–2.043, 4.009, 6.012
.... 7.026, 7.099, 7.127–7.130, 7.135, 18.013
reg 3 .... 7.134, 31.018
reg 4 .... 7.128
(1) 2.043, 7.128
(2) 2.043, 7.128
reg 6 .... 7.026, 7.048, 7.060, 7.087, 7.129–7.133, 31.018
(2) 7.129
reg 9 .... 2.041
reg 10 .... 7.128, 7.129

European Communities (Companies) Regulations 2004 (SI 839/2004)
reg 5 .... 7.128

European Communities (Companies) (Amendment) Regulations 2007 (SI 49/2007)
reg 3(c) 2.041

European Communities (Companies: Group Accounts) Regulations 1992
(SI 201/1992) 1.118, 12.003, 12.030–12.035, 12.042, 17.146–17.154
.... 17.156, 17.164–17.168, 17.190–17.191, 17.194–17.198
.... 17.201, 30.062–30.064, 31.028–31.032
reg 3 .... 17.017, 17.266
(1) 12.030, 17.154
(3) 12.033
reg 4 .... 12.031, 12.041, 17.017, 17.130, 17.186, 17.266
(1) 12.031, 17.154
(b) 12.031, 12.036
(i) 12.037
(ii) 12.036
(c) 12.031, 12.039

European Communities (Companies: Group Accounts) Regulations 1992 (contd)
(4) 12.034
(5) 12.035–12.040
(6) 12.038
(7) 12.040
reg 5(1) 17.155
(3) 17.164, 31.024
(a) 17.154
(b) 17.154
(4) 17.164
reg 6 .... 17.158, 17.164
reg 7 .... 31.036
(1) 17.157
(2) 17.157, 17.212
(4) 17.157
(5) 17.157
(7) 17.157
(8) 17.158
(10) 17.157
reg 8 .... 31.036
(1) 17.159
(b) 17.159
(2) 17.159
(3) 17.160
(4) 17.159
reg 9 .... 17.162, 31.036
(1) 17.161, 31.025
(2) 17.161
(3) 17.161
reg 9A 17.162, 31.036
(3) 17.163
(4) 17.163
(5) 17.162
(6) 17.163
reg 10 .... 17.167
reg 11 .... 17.167
reg 12 .... 17.168
reg 13 .... 17.165
reg 14 .... 30.062, 31.030
(1) 17.166
(2) 17.169
(3) 17.169
(4) 17.169
reg 15 .... 17.170
reg 16 .... 17.165
reg 17(1) 17.190
reg 18 .... 17.190

European Communities (Companies: Group Accounts) Regulations 1992 (contd)
reg 19 .... 17.191
reg 20 .... 17.191
reg 21 .... 17.297
(1) 17.190
(2) 17.190
reg 22 .... 17.192
reg 23 .... 17.190
reg 24 .... 17.175
reg 25 .... 17.172
reg 26(1) 17.155
(2) 17.155
reg 27 .... 17.173
reg 28 .... 17.174
reg 29 .... 17.174
(3) 17.174
reg 30 .... 17.174
reg 31 .... 17.174
reg 32 .... 12.041
(1) 17.196
reg 33 .... 17.197
reg 34 .... 17.199
reg 35 .... 12.041
(1) 12.039, 17.199
(2) 12.039, 17.199
(3) 12.039–12.041
(4)–(6) 12.039
reg 36 .... 17.205
reg 37(1) 17.216
(2) 17.216
reg 39 .... 17.224, 31.024
reg 40(1) 17.248
(2) 17.248
(3) 17.248
reg 41(1) 17.224
Sch para 8 .... 17.171
para 9 .... 17.171
para 10 .... 17.171
para 12 .... 17.194
para 13 .... 17.178
para 14 .... 17.179
para 15 .... 17.180, 17.206
para 16 .... 17.181, 17.202
para 16A 17.182
para 16B 17.182
para 16C 17.183
para 16D 17.184

European Communities (Companies: Group Accounts) Regulations 1992 (contd)
para 17 .... 17.185, 17.203
para 18–22 .... 17.205
para 19 .... 17.187
para 20 .... 17.187, 17.200
para 21 .... 17.187–17.188, 17.196
para 22 .... 17.187–17.188
European Communities (Corporate Insolvency) Regulations 2002 (SI 333/2002) 22.158, 24.059
reg 3(8) 24.064
(c) 24.064
(d) 24.056
(e) 24.069
reg 6 .... 24.066
reg 9(1) 24.066
European Communities (Credit Institutions: Accounts) Regulations 1992 (SI 294/1992) 17.201
European Communities (Cross-Border Mergers) Regulations 2008 (SI 157/2008) 1.123, 9.032, 21.005, 29.026
reg 14(1) 9.033
reg 19 .... 9.032
European Communities (Directive 2006/46/EC) Regulations 2009 (SI 450/2009) 17.125
reg 7(1) 17.212
European Communities (European Public Limited Company) (Forms) Regulations 2007 (SI 22/2007) 29.170
European Communities (European Public Limited Liability Company) (Employee Involvement) Regulations 2006 (SI 623/2006) 29.154, 29.179
Sch 1.126, 29.180
European Communities (European Public Limited Liability Company) Regulations 2007 (SI 21/2007) 1.126, 29.153
reg 5(5) 29.076
reg 6 .... 29.157
reg 11 .... 29.187
reg 12 .... 29.189
(1) 29.065
reg 14 .... 29.188
reg 16 .... 29.162
reg 17 .... 29.175
reg 19 .... 29.176
reg 20 .... 29.183
reg 21 .... 29.164
reg 24 .... 29.173

European Communities (European Public Limited Liability Company) (Forms) Regulations 2007 (SI 22/2007) 1.126
European Communities (Financial Collateral Arrangements) Regulations 2010 (SI 626/2010) 19.035–19.037, 19.041
reg 2(1) 19.037
reg 3(1) 19.037–19.040
reg 4(1) 19.036
(2) 19.036–19.038
(3) 19.036
European Communities (Financial Collateral Arrangements) Regulations 2004 (SI 1/2004) 19.035
European Communities (Insurance Undertakings: Accounts) Regulations 1996 (SI23/1996) 17.201
European Communities (International Financial Reporting Standards and Miscellaneous Amendments) Regulations 2005 (SI 116/2005) 10.097, 17.023–17.024, 17.148, 29.146
reg 4 .... 17.024
reg 6(i) 17.168
European Communities (Mergers and Division of Companies) Regulations 1987 (SI 137/1987) 29.164
reg 13.2 .... 29.169
European Communities (Mergers and Divisions of Companies) (Amendment) Regulations 2008 (SI 572/2008) 1.115
European Communities (Public Limited Companies – Directive 2006/68/EC) Regulations 2008 (SI 89/ 2008) 1.114
European Communities (Public Limited Companies Subsidiaries) Regulations 1997 (SI 67/1997) 10.040, 12.042
reg 2(a) 10.038
reg 4(1) 10.037, 12.042
(3) 10.037
(4) 10.037
reg 5 .... 10.038
(1) 10.038
(2) 10.038
(c) 10.039, 10.070
(3) 10.038
(5) 10.039, 29.076
(6) 10.040
(7) 10.040
reg 8 .... 10.040
regs 11–14 .... 10.110
European Communities (Public Limited Company) Regulations 2008
reg 3(b) 29.082

European Communities (Safeguarding of Employees' Rights on Transfer of Undertakings) Regulations 1980 (SI 306/1980) 4.080
reg 4 .... 20.034, 20.076
European Communities (Single-Member Private Limited Companies) (Forms) Regulations 1994 (SI 306/1994) 2.027
Pt I 33.016
Pt II 33.017
reg 5(2) 33.016
European Communities (Single-Member Private Limited Companies) Regulations 1994 (SI 275/1994) .... 1.121, 1.141–1.147, 2.008, 2.015 .... 3.002–3.003, 3.016, 3.049, 3.056, 3.087, 5.078 .... 7.006, 7.118, 8.025, 10.004–10.008, 14.088, 14.115 .... 16.009, 31.008, 33.016
reg 1 .... 1.147
reg 2 .... 1.147
reg 3 .... 1.147
(1) 1.141, 2.015
(2) 2.016
reg 4 .... 1.147, 2.016, 3.020, 3.092
reg 5 .... 1.147
(1) 33.016
(3) 33.016
reg 6 .... 1.147
(1) 16.109, 33.017
(2) 33.017
(3) 33.017
reg 7 .... 1.147
(1) 1.145, 3.016, 5.078
(2) 3.016, 5.078
reg 8 .... 1.147, 17.020
(1) 14.014
(3) 14.014, 17.311
(4) 14.014
(5) 14.014
(7) 17.020
(9) 14.014, 17.020
reg 9 .... 1.147, 3.056, 6.008, 13.078, 14.004, 14.088
(1) 3.023, 14.088
(2) 3.087, 13.078, 14.088
(3) 3.087, 14.088
(4)–(7) 14.089
(8) 3.087, 14.089
reg 10 .... 1.147, 3.049, 14.056
reg 11 .... 1.147, 23.038–23.040, 23.045–23.046, 23.067–23.070
reg 12 .... 1.147, 16.009
reg 13 .... 1.147
(1)–(5) 7.006

European Communities (Single-Member Private Limited Companies) Regulations 1994 (contd)
reg 14 .... 1.147
reg 29 .... 14.057
reg 32 .... 14.057
European Communities (Single-Member Private Limited Companies) Regulations 1994 (Amendment) Regulations 2001 (SI 437/2001)
reg 3 .... 1.147, 16.009
European Communities (Statutory Audits) (Directive 2006/43/EC) Regulations 2010 (SI 83/2010) 1.119
European Communities (Statutory Audits) (Directive 2006/43/EC) Regulations 2010 (SI 220/2010) 1.119, 13.038, 17.201
.... 17.225, 17.296, 17.306, 29.088, 29.174
reg 2 .... 17.241, 17.346
reg 3 .... 13.038
(1) 17.296–17.301, 29.086
reg 4 .... 17.301
(1)(b) 17.292
(3) 17.201
reg 9 .... 13.042
reg 10 .... 17.300
reg 20 .... 17.296
reg 21 .... 17.298
reg 22 .... 17.297
reg 23(1) 17.298
(2) 17.298
reg 24 .... 17.0299–17.302
reg 26 .... 17.300
reg 27 .... 17.303
reg 28 .... 17.304
reg 30 .... 17.301
reg 57 .... 17.241
reg 62 .... 17.338–17.342, 17.346–17.347
reg 63 .... 17.305
reg 64 .... 17.305
reg 66 .... 17.305
reg 67 .... 17.305
reg 70 .... 17.306
reg 71 .... 17.306
reg 91 .... 29.086
(3) 13.038, 29.086
(4)–(9) 29.086
reg 112 .... 17.302
reg 120 .... 17.122, 17.201
Sch para 1–4 .... 17.305

European Communities (Takeover Bids (Directive 2004/25/EC) Regulations 2006 (SI 255/2006) 1.122, 17.218

European Communities (Undertakings for Collective Investment in Transferable Securities) Regulations 2011 (SI 352/2011) 29.131–29.135

reg 4 ....29.132

(6) 29.131

reg 18(2)(b) 29.141

reg 39 ....29.132, 29.145

reg 40 ....29.132, 29.145

(7) 29.135

(a) 29.135

European Communities (Undertakings for Collective Investment in Transferable Securities) Regulations 1989 (SI 78/1989) 16.014, 23.067

European Communities (Accounts) Regulations 1993 (SI 396/1993) 2.014, 31.025

Pt III 31.025

reg 6 ....17.021, 17.122, 17.145, 31.029–31.033

(1) 31.025–31.026

(2) 31.026

reg 7(1) 17.021, 31.025

European Communities (Adjustment of Non-Comparable Amounts in Accounts and Distributions by Certain Investment Companies) Regulations 2005 (SI 840/2005)

reg 8 ....29.146

European Community (European Economic Interest Grouping) Regulations 1989 (SI 191/1989) 1.125

European Community (Mergers and Divisions of Companies) Regulations 1987 (SI 137/1987) 1.115–1.117

European Union (Accounts) Regulations 2012 (SI 304/2012) 17.277

Fines Act 2010 (Commencement) Order 2010 (SI 662/2010) 28.034

Investment Funds, Companies and Miscellaneous Provisions Act 2005 (Commencement) Order 2005 (SI 323/2005) 32.093

reg 5 ....29.060

reg 6 ....32.062

Land Registration Rules 1972 (SI 230/1972)

rr 131–145 ....19.055

Market Abuse (Directive 2003/6/EC) Regulations 2005 (SI 342/2005) 1.106, 32.059

reg 2 ....32.074, 32.099

(1) 32.067

(a) 32.100, 32.103

reg 4(2)(b) 32.063

(3) 32.064

reg 5 ....32.113

(1) 32.068

Market Abuse (Directive 2003/6/EC) Regulations 2005 (contd)
(2) 32.068
(3) 32.069
(c) 32.069
(4) 32.080
(5) 32.083
reg 6 .... 32.113
reg 8(4) 32.083
reg 9 .... 32.083
reg 10 .... 32.085
(8) 32.086
(9) 32.087
(11) 32.088
reg 11 .... 32.089
(5) 32.089
(6) 32.089
reg 12 .... 32.105–32.106, 32.131
(4) 32.105
(6) 32.107
reg 13(1) 32.108
(6) 32.112
reg 14(2) 32.112
reg 16 .... 32.092
reg 18 .... 32.092
reg 26 .... 32.092
reg 33 .... 32.066
reg 41 .... 32.114
reg 49 .... 32.113
reg 52 .... 32.113
Pt 3 .... 32.092
Pt 4 .... 32.114
Sch 32.083
Sch 1 .... 32.083, 32.103
Sch 2 .... 32.101
Sch 3 .... 32.102
Sch 4 .... 32.089
Sch 5 .... 32.083
Prospectus (Directive 2003/71) Regulations 2005 (SI 324/2005)
.... 1.106, 1.136, 32.008, 32.028
reg 2(1) 32.016, 32.018
(6) 32.016
reg 8(1)(h) 32.013
reg 9(1) 32.018
reg 10 .... 32.023
reg 11 .... 32.026
reg 13 .... 32.025
reg 14 .... 32.052

Prospectus (Directive 2003/71) Regulations 2005 (contd)
reg 15 .... 32.052
reg 21(4) 32.029
reg 22(1) 32.029
reg 24 .... 32.033
reg 83 .... 32.057
reg 85 .... 32.057
reg 86 .... 32.057
reg 91 .... 32.057
reg 107(1) 32.053
(2) 32.054
(3) 32.053
Pt 2 .... 32.012
Pt 7 .... 32.057
Pt 9 .... 32.040
Pt 12 .... 32.038
Sch 2 .... 32.038
Annexes IX and XIII 32.027

Prospectus (Directive 2003/71/EC) (Amendment) Regulations 2012
(SI 317/2012) 32.008, 32.020, 32.032

Registration Rules 1986 (SI 310/1986)
r 4 .... 19.055

Registration of Business Names Act 1963 (Commencement) Order 1964
(SI 46/1964) 1.007

Rules of the Circuit Court (SI 510/2001)
Ord 33 .... 6.073

Rules of the Superior Courts 1986 (SI 15/1986) 23.052, 28.081
Ord 6 .... 6.012
Ord 9 r 2 .... 28.091
Ord 15
r 13 .... 28.089
r 38 .... 11.116, 11.117, 11.120
Ord 24 rr 24–28 .... 25.020
Ord 28 r 12 .... 22.015
Ord 29 .... 6.015, 6.027–6.028, 6.038, 6.057, 6.060, 31.016–31.017
r 1 .... 6.024–6.027
r 4 .... 6.029
r 6 .... 6.057
Ord 31 .... 6.061
r 2 .... 25.138
r 5 .... 6.061
r 29 .... 6.062
Ord 36 r 22 .... 6.105
Ord 40 r 21 .... 25.041

Rules of the Superior Courts 1986 (contd)
Ord 42 r 6 .... 6.100
r 7 .... 6.072, 6.080
r 32 .... 6.078–6.080, 6.087, 6.095, 6.103, 28.213
rr 13–25 .... 6.073
Ord 43 r 2 .... 6.100–6.102
r 3 .... 6.100
Ord 44 .... 8.134
r 1 .... 6.095
r 2 .... 6.095
r 3 .... 6.095
r 4 .... 6.095, 6.105
r 5 .... 6.105
r 7 .... 6.095
Ord 45 r 5 .... 6.097, 6.098
Ord 46 .... 8.031, 9.038
r 1 .... 9.040
r 10 .... 9.039
r 12 .... 8.031
r 13 .... 8.031
rr 5–11 .... 8.031
rr 5–13 .... 9.038
Ord 50 r 4 .... 25.051
r 6 .... 25.041
(1) 20.020
Ord 58 r 17 .... 6.014, 6.030
Ord 74 .... 23.024
r 10 .... 23.055
r 11 .... 23.054
r 14(1) 24.016
(2) 24.017
r 15 .... 23.056
r 17 .... 23.056
r 18 .... 23.058
r 19 .... 24.041
r 24(2) 25.021
r 38 .... 24.054
r 44 .... 24.033
r 62 .... 23.028
r 66 .... 23.026
r 68 .... 23.027
r 69 .... 23.027
r 70 .... 23.027
r 71 .... 23.029–23.030
r 74 .... 23.024
r 74–83 .... 23.029
r 75 .... 7.025, 23.024

Rules of the Superior Courts 1986 (contd)
r 76 .... 23.023
r 77 .... 23.023
r 81(1) 23.024
r 82(1) 23.024, 23.029
(3) 23.024
rr 86–89 .... 25.130, 30.070, 31.038
rr 92–94 .... 25.133, 31.041
r 95 .... 25.173
r 96 .... 25.173
r 97 .... 25.174
r 98 .... 25.174
r 99 .... 25.175
r 101 .... 25.174
r 102 .... 25.175
r 103 .... 25.175
r 104 .... 25.175
r 105 .... 25.176
r 106 .... 25.178
r 107 .... 25.179
r 108 .... 25.177
r 117 .... 24.033
r 128 .... 25.166–25.168
(1) 24.055, 25.165–25.166, 25.170
r 129(1) 25.167
(2) 25.171
r 135(2) 25.043
r 138 .... 23.059
Ord 75A r 3 .... 22.029
r 16 .... 22.112
r 17 .... 22.134
r 18 .... 22.130
r 22 .... 22.167
r 4(4) 22.043
r 5(1) 22.043
r 5(2) 22.042
r 5(4) 22.044
Ord 75B r 3(a) 27.014
Ord 83 .... 9.076
Ord 84 .... 3.120
r 22 .... 6.032
Ord 99 .... 23.057
r 1 .... 28.093–28.096
r 1A 11.087
r 1(1) 22.168
Ord 122 r 7 .... 21.024
App F 6.073

Rules of the Superior Courts (Derivative Actions) 2010
(SI 503/2010) 11.116
Rules of the Superior Courts (No 3) 1991 (SI 147/1991)
Ord 75A, r 2 .... 22.009
Shareholders' Rights (Directive 2007/36/EC) Regulations 2009
(SI 316/2009) 1.124, 14.020, 29.099–29.110
reg 8 .... 29.106
reg 9 .... 29.108
Stock Transfer (Forms) Regulations 1996 (SI 263/1996) 9.011
Supreme Court and High Court (Fees) Order 2012 (SI 110/2012)
Sch 1 Pt 3 .... 25.161
Transparency (Directive 2004/109/EC) Regulations 2007
(SI 277/2007) 1.107, 32.118, 32.124, 32.130–32.131
reg 4 .... 32.123
reg 5 .... 32.123
reg 6(3) 32.124
reg 8 .... 32.124
reg 12 .... 32.127
(6) 32.128
(7) 32.128
(8) 32.128
(9) 32.127
reg 14–17 .... 32.130
reg 15 .... 32.130
reg 17 .... 32.130
reg 18 .... 32.131
reg 19 .... 32.133
reg 20 .... 32.133
reg 21 .... 32.132
reg 22 .... 32.132
reg 25(2)(a) 32.135
reg 25–29 .... 32.134
reg 30 .... 32.030
reg 31 .... 32.136
reg 32 .... 32.137
(6) 32.137
reg 36 .... 32.119
reg 37 .... 32.119
Pts 9–10 .... 32.119
Transparency (Directive 2004/109/EC) (Amendment) Regulations 2010
(SI 102/1010) 32.118
Transparency (Directive 2004/109/EC) (Amendment) Regulations 2012
(SI 316/2012)
reg 2 .... 32.137
Transparency (Directive 2004/109/EC) (Amendment) Regulations 2012
(SI 328/2012) 32.118

Chapter 1

The Private Company in Context

Introduction

[1.001] The private company has a place of particular prominence in Irish business. The *Companies Registration Office Report, 2010*[1] records that of the 185,608 companies registered with the registrar of companies in the Companies Registration Office ('CRO') at year's end 2011, 86.15% were private companies limited by shares[2]. Although no breakdown is given for the other two types of private company (the private company limited by guarantee and the private unlimited company) it can reasonably be assumed that the total percentage of private companies is in the region of 90%. A private company is one in which the membership is confined to 99 members, the public are not invited to join and in which the transfer of shares is restricted.

[1.002] As shall be considered later, the private company is defined by s 33 of the Companies Act 1963[3] ('CA 1963') not as being the norm, but as being a particular manifestation of the standard type of 'company' referred to in the Companies Acts[4]. Although almost nine in ten of all companies on the Irish register are private companies, since its creation the private company has been a legislative afterthought. Section 37(1) of the Companies Act 1907 – the Act that gave birth to the private company – located the provisions on this most commonly utilised type of company under the heading '*Miscellaneous*'. This notion was perpetuated in the CA 1963 in, for example, Table A which sets out model *articles of association*, the internal rules by which a company is governed. So, although most companies limited by shares are private companies, the articles for public companies limited by shares are set out in Part I of Table A and Part II then *applies* a modified Part I of Table A to private companies. In its first report in 2001, the Company Law Review Group (CLRG) recommended that Irish company law should be re-written from the perspective of the private company limited by shares[5], a recommendation that has been accepted by government. The effect of the CLRG's proposed change will mean that the *private company limited by shares* will cease to be a legislative after-thought and will be moved to centre stage. So, it is proposed that the first group of parts of the pending Companies Bill will deal exclusively with the private company limited by shares (in a manner similar to the way this book since its first

1 See the CRO's website: http://www.cro.ie/ena/downloads-corporate.aspx.

2 Of the remaining 13.85%, 0.97% are public limited companies, 2.23% are unlimited companies, 8.45% are guarantee companies and 2.19% are external companies as at 31 December 2011.

3 As substituted by s 7 of the IFCMPA 2006, with effect from 1 July 2005.

4 See para **[1.156]**.

5 *Company Law Review Group – First Report, 2001* (Government Publications).

edition treated the private company) and each other company type – the PLC, guarantee company, unlimited company, etc – will be provided for separately, each in their own part[6].

[1.003] Before considering the nature of the Irish private company this chapter first overviews other legal structures available for the organisation of business in Ireland and then examines the origins of the private company's generic form: the *registered company.* Next, the history and sources of Irish company law are examined, the nature and attributes of the Irish private company and the meaning of 'company' and, finally, we consider company law reform and the draft Companies Bill. This chapter is structured under the following sections:

- [A] Legal Forms of Business Organisation.
- [B] An Historical Outline of Registered Companies.
- [C] An Overview of Irish Company Law.
- [D] The Private Company.
- [E] The Meaning of 'Company' and of the 'Companies Acts'.
- [F] Modern Company Law Reform.

[A] LEGAL FORMS OF BUSINESS ORGANISATION

[1.004] There are a number of legal forms of business organisation from which Irish entrepreneurs can choose in establishing themselves in business. Some of the available forms of business organisation do not involve the creation of an independent legal status for the organisation (eg, sole traders, partnerships, friendly societies and unincorporated associations); others do involve the creation of a separate legal person (eg, registered companies, industrial and provident societies, building societies and credit unions). Each particular entity has its own advantages and disadvantages. Each of the following legal forms of business organisation is considered next:

1. Sole traders.
2. Partnerships.
3. Industrial and provident societies.
4. Building societies.
5. Credit unions.
6. Unincorporated associations.
7. Friendly societies.
8. Unregistered companies.

Sole traders

[1.005] The most basic form of business organisation is where a person chooses to engage in business as a sole or single trader[7]. A sole trader may be defined as a natural person who is engaged in a trade, profession or business on his or her own account. Traditionally, farmers, tradesmen, small retail outlets (eg, newsagents, grocers, etc) and

6 See para **[1.171]** *et seq*.

7 See, generally, Forde, *Commercial Law* (2nd edn, 1997) at p 10 and O'Malley, *Business Law* (1982) at p 14.

professionals (eg, solicitors, doctors, dentists, accountants, barristers, etc) working on their own account have conducted business as sole traders. Nowadays, where permitted by law[8], such people commonly elect to incorporate a private limited company, the spectre of unlimited liability for a failed business's debts – and possible bankruptcy – being the primary motivating force. The following issues are now considered:

(a) Restrictions on acting as a sole trader.
(b) The Registration of Business Names Act 1963.
(c) Advantages and disadvantages of being a sole trader.

(a) Restrictions on acting as a sole trader

[1.006] There are very few restrictions imposed upon persons who seek to conduct business as sole traders for we live in a society which, in principle, recognises (and occasionally vindicates) private enterprise. Of course all sole traders engaged in business for profit must comply with revenue law and register with their local inspector of taxes. Actual *restrictions* on acting as a sole trader may be categorised as either relating to the *person* or relating to the *business activity.*

Restrictions on the *person* are few and far between. Generally, anybody can become a sole trader in business, including convicted criminals. Exceptions to this general rule are aliens, ie, non-Irish or non-EU citizens who may be subject to restrictions under the Aliens Act 1935, and minors. In the case of the latter, whilst there are no restrictions *per se* on minors acting as sole traders, the law of contract may make it difficult if not impossible for minors to effectively conduct business due to the legal restrictions on enforcing certain contracts against minors.

Restrictions relating to engaging in particular *business activities* do exist. On grounds of public policy a person cannot establish himself in business as a solicitor, barrister, auditor, doctor, etc without first having obtained the appropriate qualifications and membership of a recognised professional body. Other business activities such as selling insurance, lending money to consumers, operating a public house or dance hall, acting as an auctioneer or taxi-driver, etc are subject to regulation in the form of registration and/or licensing. The general rationale for restrictions relating to business activity is the protection of the public and if so there must be a lot of concern for the public as regulation is being continuously increased.

(b) The Registration of Business Names Act 1963

[1.007] The purpose of the Registration of Business Names Act 1963[9] ('RBNA 1963') is to make public the identities of individuals, partnerships and companies that carry on business under a business name which is different from his, their or its own name[10]. To

[8] Certain professions are not permitted to incorporate, for example, solicitors, barristers, vets, etc.

[9] See MacCann & Courtney, *Companies Acts 1963–2009* (3rd edn, Bloomsbury Professional, 2010) at pp 3–12. The RBNA 1963 was commenced by the Registration of Business Names Act, 1963 (Commencement) Order 1964, SI 46/1964. See also the Business Names Regulations: SI 47/1964, SI 63/1976, SI 399/1980, SI 260/1983, SI 100/1987, SI 138/1993 and SI 357/1997, made pursuant to s 17 of the RBNA 1963.

[10] As at 31 December 2011, 407,151 business names had been registered pursuant to the RBNA 1963: *Companies Registration Office Report, 2011* at p 32.

that end the registrar of companies, who is also registrar for the purposes of the RBNA 1963[11], keeps an index of business names registered under the RBNA 1963[12]. Consequently, where a sole trader (or partnership[13] or body corporate[14]) carries on business under any name other than his own he is required to furnish certain particulars to the registrar of companies. Section 3(1)(b) of the RBNA 1963 provides that subject to the provisions of that Act:

> 'every individual having a place of business in the State and carrying on business under a business name which does not consist of his true surname without any addition other than his true Christian names or the initials thereof;
>
> ... shall be registered in the manner directed by this Act.'

Moreover, the requirement to register also arises where an individual has changed his name (except in the case of a woman in consequence of marriage)[15].

[1.008] Section 4(1) of the RBNA 1963 specifies the particulars which a person must furnish to the registrar of companies. In the case of a sole trader these are: (a) the business name, including in the case of the proprietor of a newspaper, the title of the newspaper; (b) the general nature of the business; (c) the principal place of the business; (e) the present Christian name and surname, any former Christian name or surname, the nationality, if not Irish, the usual residence, and the other business occupation (if any) of such individual; and (g) the date of the adoption of the business name by that person. Where a business is carried on under two or more business names each of those business names must be stated[16]. Under s 9(1) of the RBNA 1963, the Minister for Jobs, Enterprise and Innovation may require any person to furnish to the Minister within such time as the Minister may require, a statement of such particulars as may appear necessary to the Minister for the purpose of ascertaining whether or not the person should be registered under the RBNA 1963 whether or not an alteration should be made in the registered particulars. In appropriate cases the Minister may subsequently require that the person furnishes the required particulars to the registrar of companies: s 9(2) of the RBNA 1963[17].

[1.009] The statement required for the purpose of registration must be signed by the sole trader[18]. The particulars required to be furnished under s 4 of the RBNA 1963 must be

---

11 Section 15 of the RBNA 1963.

12 Section 13 of the RBNA 1963.

13 See para **[1.014]**.

14 See Ch 2, *Incorporation by Registration*, at para **[2.044]**.

15 Section 3(c) of the RBNA 1963.

16 Section 4(2) of the RBNA 1963.

17 A failure to furnish such a statement or particulars or of change 'without reasonable excuse in so doing' is punishable, on summary conviction, by a Class C fine: s 10 of the RBNA 1963. It is also an offence to furnish a statement which contains any matter which is false in any material particular to the knowledge of any person signing it and punishable, on summary conviction, by imprisonment for a term not exceeding six months or to a Class C fine or to both: s 11 of the RBNA 1963. Generally, the RBNA 1963 provides that summary proceedings in relation to any offence under the Act may be brought and prosecuted by the Minister for Jobs, Enterprise and Innovation: s 20(1) of the RBNA 1963.

18 Section 5(1) of the RBNA 1963.

furnished within one month after the adoption of the business name[19]. Details of any changes in the particulars registered must be delivered to the registrar of companies within one month after the change; this is referred to as a 'section 7 statement'. Section 8(1) of the RBNA 1963 provides that upon receiving a statement pursuant to either s 4 or 7 the registrar of companies shall issue a certificate of the registration of the business name to the person applying for registration. A certificate of registration must 'be kept exhibited in a conspicuous position at' the sole trader's principal place of business and every branch office or place where business is normally carried on; on summary conviction, default attracts a class C fine[20]. Section 12(1) of the RBNA 1963 obliges a person (or, if deceased, his personal representatives) who has registered a business name, but who ceases to carry on business under that name, to send a statement in the prescribed form to that effect to the registrar of companies within three months. The registrar is also given powers to remove a business name from the register in specified circumstances[21].

[1.010] One of the few consequences of the registration of a business name by a sole trader is that s 18(1) of the RBNA 1963 provides that in all business letters, circulars and catalogues on or in which the business name appears and which are sent by that person, he shall state in legible characters his present Christian name or the initials thereof, and present surname, any former Christian names and surnames, and his nationality if not Irish. Default in compliance with this provision will render the sole trader liable on summary conviction for each offence to a class D fine: s 18(2) of the RBNA 1963[22]. In *Kent Adhesive Products Company trading as KAPCO and another v Ryan et al*[23], the defendant company registered a business name under the RBNA 1963 but Costello J found that it did not comply with s 18(1) because it had failed to put the name of the company on the business letters of the company. The plaintiffs sought injunctive relief for, *inter alia*, passing off. Costello J required, *inter alia*, an undertaking from the defendant to comply with the provisions of the Companies Acts and the RBNA 1963 and to refrain from using the company's then existing letterheads and to print further letterheads in accordance with the Acts. It was held in *Tierney v Midserve Ltd, trading as Sachs Hotel and Genport Ltd*[24] that where a company acquired a business name from another company but did not register that business name, a plaintiff who claimed to have suffered personal injuries would not be statute barred where the plaintiff did not join the correct defendant within the limitation period because the failure to comply with the RBNA 1963 operated to conceal the right of action as against the correct defendant.

[1.011] Section 14 of the RBNA 1963 provides that the Minister for Jobs, Enterprise and Innovation may refuse to permit the registration of any name which in his opinion is undesirable; however, an appeal may be made to the High Court against such refusal.

---

19 Section 6(1) of the RBNA 1963.

20 Section 8 of the RBNA 1963, as required to be construed by s 6(3) of the Fines Act 2010 ('FA 2010').

21 Section 12(3)–(5) of the RBNA 1963.

22 As required to be construed by s 7(3) of the FA 2010.

23 *Kent Adhesive Products Company trading as KAPCO and another v Ryan et al* (5 November 1993, unreported) HC, Costello J.

24 *Tierney v Midserve Ltd, trading as Sachs Hotel and Genport Ltd* (23 January 2002, unreported) HC, Kinlen J.

The use of a business name, the registration of which has been refused by the Minister, is an offence which on summary conviction attracts a class C fine: s 14(2) of the RBNA 1963[25]. It is especially important to note that the mere registration of a business name does not make the person who uses it immune from civil action by an aggrieved third party. Section 14(3) of the RBNA 1963 states:

> 'The registration of a business name under this Act shall not be construed as authorising the use of that name if apart from such registration the use thereof could be prohibited.'

It is, accordingly, no defence to an action for passing off or for infringement of a trademark to claim that registration of a particular business name was effected under the RBNA 1963[26]. In this respect the effect of registration of a business name under the RBNA 1963 is no different to the registration of a company name under the CA 1963[27].

(c) Advantages and disadvantages of being a sole trader

[1.012] The *advantages* of carrying on a business as a sole trader may be categorised under the headings of formation, compliance and management. The most significant advantage is the relative ease with which a person can commence business as a sole trader. For an Irish citizen, subject to registration for taxation purposes, there are minimal registration requirements for a sole trader and a minimum of legal expense. After formation, compliance for the sole trader is at a minimum; no annual return is required to be filed and the business cannot be 'struck off' any register[28]. As regards management, the advantages enjoyed by a sole trader are that he has complete control over the business and can make lawful decisions without having regard to any other person. Furthermore, where the business makes a profit, the net profit belongs alone to the sole trader. Finally, details of a sole trader's finances and accounts can be kept confidential as there is no requirement for the public disclosure of accounts, etc.

[1.013] The *disadvantages* to conducting business as a sole trader will for many be found to by far outweigh the advantages. The principal disadvantages are as follows.

First, the sole trader has unlimited liability for the debts of his business, so just as profits belong alone to him, so too do debts; where a sole trader's debts exceed his assets (personal as well as business) the sole trader may be declared a bankrupt and his assets divided amongst his creditors[29].

Second, it can be relatively more difficult to dispose of a sole trader's business – whether on death or *inter vivos* – than, say, a business owned by a private company.

---

25 As required to be construed by s 6(3) of the FA 2010.

26 In *DSG Retail Ltd v PC World Ltd et al* [1998] IEHC 3, Laffoy J, the plaintiff, which operated a chain of computer superstores in the United Kingdom, Northern Ireland and Ireland under the title of PC World, sought an injunction to prevent a passing off by the first defendant. In the evidence it was heard that there were a number of other parties using the name 'PC World' in Ireland and that one of those parties had registered the name as a business name under the CA 1963. It was noted that this did not prevent the plaintiff from commencing injunction proceedings against that party also.

27 See Ch 2, *Incorporation by Registration*, at para **[2.044]**.

28 *Cf* companies incorporated under the Companies Acts which can be struck off the register and cease to exist as separate legal entities: see Ch 26, *Strike-Off and Restoration*.

29 On bankruptcy, see generally, Sanfey & Holohan, *Bankruptcy Law and Practice in Ireland* (2nd edn, Round Hall, 2012).

Apart from the possible legal uncertainty in transferring chattels and goodwill, the transfer of any real property may incur substantial stamp duty; by contrast the owner of the shares in a company which owns a business can sell the shares, and thus the business, more tax efficiently[30]. Partial disposal (where, say, a sole proprietor wishes to reward a deserving employee by giving him a share in the business) is not possible for a sole trader as the effect of creating an additional proprietary interest is to create a partnership (even if the partners' entitlements are unequal).

Third, a sole trader may be restricted in obtaining finance because of the inability to create floating charges over his chattels and other property and also because of the difficulties in creating fixed charges over chattels by reason of the Bills of Sale (Ireland) Acts 1879–1883[31]. This may prove a particular problem to a sole trader where a considerable amount of his assets are in the nature of personalty or are otherwise of a nature which is more amenable to being secured by a floating rather than a fixed charge, eg, a publican. It may be noted, however, that a sole trader who is engaged in farming will not encounter the same difficulties when creating fixed or floating charges over 'agricultural stock'.

Fourth, for many businesses the tax code applicable to sole traders is less favourable than that applicable to companies.

Partnerships

[1.014] It is beyond the scope and purpose of this book to consider the law of partnerships in any detail and the reader is referred to the many excellent specialised works on that topic[32]. What follows here is a short analysis, by way of comparison, which seeks to place partnerships in context *vis-à-vis* the private company. Partnerships are considered now under the following headings:

(a) Partnership defined and described.
(b) Partners' dealings with outsiders and *inter se*.
(c) Dissolution of partnerships.
(d) Limited partnerships.
(e) Advantages and disadvantages of partnerships.

(a) Partnership defined and described

[1.015] Partnership is defined by s 1 of the Partnership Act 1890 ('PA 1890') as 'the relation which subsists between persons carrying on business in common with a view to profit'. Whether or not a partnership exists is a question of fact, not law[33]. In order to be

---

30 See generally, Ch 9, *Share Transfer*.

31 See Ch 19, *Corporate Borrowing: Registration of Charges*, at para **[19.046]** and also Maguire, 'The Bill of Sale: The Forgotten Relation?' (1997) 4 CLP 3.

32 See Twomey, *Partnership Law* (2000, Butterworths); Ivamy, *Underhill's Principles of the Law of Partnership* (12th edn, 1986); and L'Anson Banks, *Lindley and Banks on the Law of Partnership* (16th edn, 1990). For a succinct overview of Irish partnership law see O'Malley, *Business Law* (1982) at pp 17–26.

33 The question as to whether or not a partnership existed has been considered by the courts in a number of cases, eg, *McAleenan v AIG (Europe) Ltd* [2010] IEHC 128; *Macken v Revenue Commissioners* [1962] IR 302; *Greenham v Gray* (1855) 4 ICLR 501 and *Cox v Hickman* (1860) 8 HL Cas 268 to mention but four. See also *Bass Brewers Ltd v Appleby et al* [1997] 2 BCLC 700.

valid, a general (as opposed to a limited) partnership does not need to be registered anywhere and the intentions of the partners are generally irrelevant; all that is required is that (a) two or more persons (b) carry on a 'business'[34] (c) with a view to making profit. A partnership can be composed of natural persons, bodies corporate or a combination of both. Critical to understanding the nature of a partnership is recognition of the fact that a partnership is *not* a separate legal entity and does not have an existence, independent to that of its partners.

[1.016] The law of partnership evolved as part of the common law and equity. The PA 1890 merely codified the existing common law of partnership. The legal basis for a partnership is rooted in the laws of contract and agency. In the first place the basis for every partnership is a contract, whether express or implied, between the partners. The law of agency is important as otherwise one partner could not bind his fellow partners to contracts entered into between him and outsiders; by virtue of the law of agency each partner makes his fellow partners his agents with full power to bind him. The PA 1890 will only govern the relations between partners *inter se* to the extent to which a partnership agreement does not otherwise provide.

[1.017] The minimum number of persons required to constitute a valid partnership is two; one person acting alone in business is a sole trader. By law the maximum number of partners which a partnership can have is 20[35]. There are, however, a number of exceptions in respect of which the upper limit does not apply: first, banking partnerships[36]; second, partnerships of solicitors and partnerships of accountants[37]; and third, partnerships formed for the purpose of carrying on the business of thoroughbred horse breeding[38].

[1.018] A partnership which adopts a firm name[39] other than the true names of the partners must register that name as a business name under the RBNA 1963. In this respect s 3(1)(a) of the RBNA 1963 requires registration in relation to:

> 'every firm having a place of business in the State and carrying on business under a business name which does not consist of the true surnames of all partners who are individuals and the corporate names of all partners which are bodies corporate without any addition other than the true Christian names of individual partners or initials of such Christian names.'

The RBNA 1963 has been considered above[40] in the context of sole traders and its provisions apply *mutatis mutandis* to partnerships.

[1.019] Property (real or personal) used by a partnership may either be owned by all of the partners collectively, in which case it is 'partnership property', or it may be owned

34 Defined by s 45 of the PA 1890 to include 'every trade, occupation or profession'.

35 Section 376 of the CA 1963.

36 Section 376 of the CA 1963.

37 Section 13 of the C(A) A 1982.

38 SI 54/1988.

39 Section 4 of the PA 1890 provides that partners are collectively called a firm and that the name under which they carry on business is called the firm name.

40 See para **[1.007]**.

by an individual partner personally. Any property bought with partnership money is deemed, by s 20 of the PA 1890, to be *prima facie* 'partnership property'.

[1.020] In the absence of agreement to the contrary each and every partner is entitled to participate in the management of the partnership[41]. This general rule can, however, be varied by the agreement of the partners.

(b) Partners' dealings with outsiders and inter se

(i) Dealings with outsiders

[1.021] In the absence of an agreement to the contrary all partners are *jointly and severally* liable on the partnership's contracts and debts and for the partnership's torts[42]. Each and every partner is liable to the full extent of his personal assets for the debts of the partnership[43].

[1.022] The partners in a partnership may, by agreement, limit the actual authority of individual partners. Notwithstanding any such internal agreement, each partner will be bound by the acts of a fellow partner by reason of s 5 of the PA 1890 which provides:

> 'Every partner is an agent of the firm and his other partners for the purpose of the business of the partnership; and the acts of every partner who does any act for carrying on in the usual way business of the kind carried on by the firm of which he is a member bind the firm and his partners, unless the partner so acting has in fact no authority to act for the firm in the particular matter, and the person with whom he is dealing either knows that he has no authority, or does not know or believe him to be a partner.'

This section makes clear the application of the doctrine of ostensible or apparent authority to partners' dealings with outsiders[44]. The leading Irish case in point is that of *Kett v Shannon & English*[45] where the Supreme Court applied the doctrine of ostensible authority as set out in the leading English decision in *Freeman & Lockyer v Buckhurst Park Properties (Mangal) Ltd*[46].

(ii) Dealings inter se

[1.023] Section 24 of the PA 1890 provides that, in the absence of agreement to the contrary, (a) every partner may participate in the management of the partnership; (b) the consent of all of the partners is required to vary the partnership agreement; and (c) every partner is entitled to share equally in the profits and obliged to share equally in the losses of the partnership.

[1.024] Partners are in a fiduciary position *vis-à-vis* each other[47]. Indeed today, it may be said, the very term 'partnership' as used in the context of certain private 'quasi-

---

41 *Peacock v Peacock* (1809) 16 Ves Jr 49; *Rowe v Wood* (1795) 2 J & W 553.

42 Section 9 of the PA 1890.

43 *Cf* the liability of limited partners considered at para **[1.026]**.

44 *Nationwide Building Society v Lewis & Williams* [1997] 3 All ER 498.

45 *Kett v Shannon & English* [1987] ILRM 364. See Ch 7, *Corporate Contracts: Capacity and Authority*, at para **[7.101]**.

46 *Freeman & Lockyer v Buckhurst Park Properties (Mangal) Ltd* [1964] 2 QB 480.

47 *Helmore v Smith* (1886) 35 Ch D 436.

partnership' companies[48] *implies* notions of mutuality, good faith and trust between the participants. Partners are each entitled to full disclosure from the other partners as to the affairs of the partnership. A partner is obliged to account to the other partners for any personal gain from the use of partnership property and, like a company director or other fiduciary, is liable for any gain made through undisclosed competition with the partnership[49].

(c) Dissolution of partnerships

[1.025] A partnership may be dissolved after a specific date or event; it can be dissolved by a partner giving notice of his intention to dissolve the partnership; it will dissolve on the death or bankruptcy of a partner; it may be dissolved by order of the court on a petition grounded on, *inter alia*, insanity, incapacity, misconduct or where such is just and equitable[50].

(d) Limited partnerships

[1.026] The Limited Partnership Act 1907 ('LPA 1907') facilitates the creation of a partnership in which some of the members may have limited liability for the debts of the partnership[51]. A limited partnership is not, however, a separate legal entity[52]. The LPA 1907 requires that there must be at least one 'general partner' whose liability is unlimited and there must be at least one 'limited partner' whose liability is limited to the amount of capital contributed by him to the partnership[53]. A further restriction is that the limited partner must be excluded from the management of the firm and cannot have any authority to bind the other partners. The sanction for contravention of this is that the limited partner will automatically have unlimited liability for the debts and liabilities of the firm incurred during the period when he participated in its management[54]. Moreover, every limited partnership must be registered with the registrar of companies; the sanction for non-compliance is that a limited partner cannot claim limited liability[55]. As at 31 December 2011 there were 901 limited partnerships registered with the registrar of companies[56].

[1.027] In 1991 the US state of Texas was the first jurisdiction to create the limited liability partnership or 'LLP' in order to protect professionals such as accountants and lawyers exposed to liability claims for negligence or the wrongful acts of their partners. The original model provided a shield from liability for a partner from the negligence or wrongful act of another partner but many US states later extended this to cover ordinary contractual debts too. A key feature of the US model of LLP is that while innocent partners will have no personal liability for the negligent acts of other partners, the partnership itself is liable, as is the negligent partner.

---

48 See para **[1.151]**.

49 Sections 28–30 of the PA 1890.

50 See ss 22, 23 and 24 of the PA 1890.

51 See Twomey, 'The Limited Partnership Act 1907' (1996) 3 CLP 211.

52 *Re Barnard* [1932] 1 Ch 272.

53 Section 4(2) of the LPA 1907.

54 Section 6(1) of the LPA 1907.

55 Section 5 of the LPA 1907. See *McCartaigh v Daly* [1986] ILRM 116.

56 See *Companies Registration Office Report 2011* at p 31.

[1.028] In the United Kingdom, the Limited Liability Partnership Act 2000, which applies in England, Wales and Scotland, facilitates the establishment of an LLP with a legal personality separate from those of its members. The LLP is liable for the wrongful acts or omissions of a member but the members are not jointly and severally liable for the acts or omissions of another member. The LLP is also 'tax transparent' for tax purposes and whilst the separate legal entity that is the LLP pays no tax, the fully liability falls on the partners as it would in a general partnership.

[1.029] In Ireland the Company Law Review Group ('CLRG') first considered the introduction of LLPs as part of its 2007 work programme. In its report on that work programme the CLRG concluded that before making a final decision on whether LLPs should be introduced in Ireland public consultation should be conducted to establish the demand and need for LLPs. In the CLRG's 2008–2009 work programme, it was ultimately recommended that because it appeared that the main proponent of the LLP in Ireland was the solicitors' profession, the issue could best be progressed by an inter-departmental committee comprised of representatives from the Department of Justice and the Courts Service which share responsibility for the regulation of solicitors.

(e) Advantages and disadvantages of partnerships

[1.030] The primary *advantages* of organising a business as a partnership include the following. First, the formation of a partnership and the partners' on-going compliance with partnership law involves minimal effort; there is no requirement that a partnership be registered[57] or even that there be a written contract, although it is, in practice, often advisable for the partnership agreement to be reduced to writing to avoid ambiguity. Second, because the law of contract is the essential basis of a partnership it is relatively easy to tailor a particular partnership to meet the needs of the partners. Third, the confidentiality of the relationship between the partners *inter se* (and particularly of their finances) can be maintained. Fourth, each and every partner is entitled to participate in the management of the partnership.

[1.031] The primary *disadvantages* of organising business as a partnership include the following. First, the general rule[58] is that each and every partner in a partnership is jointly and severally liable for all of the debts of the partnership which can be satisfied from their personal assets up to and including making them bankrupt. The absence of limited liability is probably the greatest disadvantage. Second, the continuity of a partnership is affected by the death or insanity or bankruptcy of any one partner and the consequence will be its dissolution. Third, shares in a partnership cannot be as easily transferred as can the shares in a company. Fourth, for many partnerships, there are limits on the numbers of persons who can be partners in a partnership.

Industrial and provident societies

[1.032] Industrial and provident societies – commonly referred to as co-operatives or co-operative societies – may be registered under the Industrial and Provident Societies Acts

[57] *Cf* a limited partnership. Note also the possible application of the RBNA 1963.

[58] *Cf* a limited partnership.

1893–1978 ('IPS Acts')[59]. An industrial and provident society is defined by s 4 of the Industrial and Provident Societies Act 1893 ('IPSA 1893') as:

> 'a society for carrying on any industries, businesses, or trades specified in or authorised by its rules, whether wholesale or retail and including dealings of any description with land.'

In Ireland, traditionally, the co-operative movement was particularly strong in the area of agricultural food produce. In recent times, however, a number of the larger co-operatives have converted to public limited companies (PLCs). When registered, a co-operative becomes a body corporate with limited liability. Section 21 of the IPSA 1893 Act provides:

> 'The registration of a society shall render it a body corporate by the name described in the acknowledgement of registry, by which it may sue and be sued, with perpetual succession and a common seal, and with limited liability ...'

This is the main difference between an industrial and provident society and a friendly society; a friendly society is *not* a body corporate with a separate legal personality[60]. Although co-operatives have much in common with registered companies, they have a fundamentally different nature to that of many forms of registered companies. In *Kerry Co-operative Ltd et al v An Bord Bainne Co-operative Ltd et al*[61], McCarthy J said a co-operative may be contrasted:

> ...with a company of limited liability in that its shareholders invest their efforts in the betterment of activity in co-operation with each other being persons of a like interest, rather than their seeking a return on investment capital, which is the role of the investor in a company of limited liability; the latter is indifferent to the operation of the company so long as he is assured of an adequate return on his investment.

Whilst this is undoubtedly true when comparing a co-operative society to a public limited company, it is thought that this comparison does not hold up as well when comparing a co-operative society with a private company.

[1.033] Co-operatives are registered on the register of friendly societies. This is located, like the register of companies, within the Department of Jobs, Enterprise and Innovation which is responsible for the administration of the IPSA Acts. A co-operative society must have at least seven members[62] and registration is effected by completing the appropriate form, which must be signed by the seven members and the intended secretary, and sending it, together with two copies of the rules (also signed by the eight persons), and the appropriate fee to the registrar of friendly societies. Unlike the members of registered companies, the members of co-operatives have just one vote each.

---

59 See Baden-Fuller, *Friendly Societies and Industrial and Provident Societies* (4th edn, 1926); O'Malley, *Business Law* (1982) at pp 36–39; Ussher & O'Connor, *Doing Business in Ireland* (1997) at 3.04[2]; Forde, *Commercial Law* (2nd edn, 1997) at p 19 and at p 464; Schmitthoff, *Palmer's Company Law* (24th edn, 1987) at p 1691.

60 See para **[1.052]**.

61 *Co-operative Ltd et al v An Bord Bainne Co-operative Ltd et al* [1991] ILRM 851 at 863.

62 Section 5(1) of the 1893 Act. Note that a society consisting solely of two or more registered societies may be formed: s 1 of the Industrial and Provident Societies (Amendment) Act 1913.

[1.034] All co-operative societies must have rules which are similar to a registered company's articles of association[63]. The rules of a co-operative society bind the members and the company[64]. In many respects, however, there are differences between the rules of a co-operative and those of a registered company. In the first place, the rules of a co-operative must be approved by the registrar of friendly societies. In the second place, the second schedule to the IPSA 1893 specifies certain matters which *must* be covered by the rules. In the third place, amendments to the rules have no validity until such time as they are actually registered under s 10 of the IPSA 1893[65].

[1.035] Industrial and provident societies are subject to certain rules and regulations although they are not as regulated as registered companies since the IPSA 1893 has not been amended to keep it up to date with changes in company law such as the regulation and disclosure of transactions and arrangements involving directors. Under the IPSA 1893 a special resolution is required for a change of name (s 52); to approve the amalgamation with another co-operative (s 53(1)); to transfer engagements to another co-operative (s 53(2)); and to convert into a company or amalgamate or transfer engagements to a company (s 54(1)). 'Special resolution' has a different meaning here than it has in company law and s 51(a) and (b) of the IPSA 1893 provide that a special resolution is one that is passed by a majority of not less than 75% of the co-operative's members for the time being entitled to vote under the rules and that is *subsequently confirmed* by a majority of such members at a subsequent general meeting held not less than 14 days nor more than one month after the passing of the first resolution. In the case of the amalgamation of two or more co-operatives each of which has amongst its objects and is engaged in the manufacture of butter, cream or other dairy product, the 75% requirement in s 51(1) of the IPSA 1893 was changed to a simple majority by the Industrial and Provident Societies Act 1971. It may also be noted that s 4(a) of the IPSA 1893 restricts the number of shares that can be held by a member (other than another co-operative) in a co-operative. This restriction varies, however, depending upon the type of co-operative and a member of an agricultural and fisheries co-operative can hold shares to a value of no more than €126,973.81.

Building societies

[1.036] Building societies have a long and distinguished history in facilitating the provision of houses for their members[66]. The law of building societies is found in the Building Societies Act 1989 ('BSA 1989')[67] which introduced reforms and consolidated

---

63 As to which see generally, Ch 3, *Constitutional Documents*.

64 See *Kerry Co-operative Ltd et al v An Bord Bainne Co-operative Ltd et al* [1990] ILRM 664 (HC) and [1991] ILRM 851 (SC).

65 *Re Londonderry Equitable Co-Operative Society* [1910] 1 IR 69.

66 See Forde, *Commercial Law* (2nd edn, 1997) at p 462. For a short analysis see Murdoch, *Building Society Law in Ireland* (1989, Topaz Publications) at pp 1–6. For analysis of the English law on building societies, see Wurtzburg & Mills, *Building Society Law* (Sweet & Maxwell).

67 The BSA 1989 was materially amended by the Housing (Miscellaneous Provisions) Act 1992, the Building Societies (Amendment) Act 2006, the National Asset Management Agency Act 2009 and the Credit Institutions (Stabilisation) Act 2010.

the then existing legislation[68]. Building societies originated in the late eighteenth century as small associations of private individuals who banded together to assist each other in obtaining housing. Typically, a small number of people made contributions towards the cost of site acquisition and then the cost of building houses, one by one, for the group until all members were housed whereupon the group was dissolved. In later years such societies began to have members who made contributions to the common pool to earn interest on their savings as opposed to using their savings to build houses.

Following the conversion of two of Ireland's leading building societies – Irish Permanent Building Society and First National Building Society – into public limited companies, three building societies remained: namely, EBS Building Society ('EBS'), Irish Nationwide Building Society ('INBS') and ICS Building Society ('ICS'). In more recent years, EBS and INBS became involved in commercial lending and, following significant balance sheet losses due to the property crash, were obliged to have resort to the National Asset Management Agency ('NAMA'). Even this could not save them and ultimately the Minister for Finance had to recapitalise them and in so doing became the holder of special investment shares issued in both building societies, the effect of which was to take them into effective State control. After acquiring the special investment shares in both EBS and INBS the Minister for Finance was also obliged to take a majority stake in AIB Bank plc; following the nationalisation of Anglo Irish Bank Corporation Limited (now, Irish Bank Resolution Company Limited or 'IBRC') the Minister had become its sole shareholder. To stabilise the Irish banking system, the Minister made orders under the Credit Institutions (Stabilisation) Act 2010 ('CISA 2010') as a result of which EBS was acquired by AIB and INBS by IRBC. EBS was converted to a private limited company but is it understood that INBS continues to be a building society.

Accordingly, ICS is the sole remaining building society that is not in State ownership, although the State does hold a significant investment in its parent, the Governor and Company of the Bank of Ireland. ICS was always a peculiar building society in that up to the mid 1980s it had investment shares quoted on the stock exchange and when the entire of its investment shares were acquired by the Governor and Company of the Bank of Ireland, it became its subsidiary.

It is beyond the scope and purpose of this work to comprehensively treat the law relating to building societies; what follows is a brief analysis of the following issues:

(a) Formation.

(b) Powers of building societies.

(c) Membership

(d) Central Bank supervision.

(e) Management, meetings and accounts.

(f) Conversion of building societies to PLCs.

(g) Amalgamations and transfers of engagements.

---

68 See Johnston, O'Connor & Henry, *Arthur Cox Banking Law Handbook* (2007, Tottel Publishing).

(a) Formation

[1.037] Upon incorporation, a building society becomes 'a body corporate ... having perpetual succession and a seal and the power to hold land'[69]. Section 10(2) of the BSA 1989 provides that a building society may be formed by ten or more persons acting in the following way[70]: (a) agreeing on the objects of the society and on the extent of its powers in a memorandum[71]; (b) agreeing in its rules[72] for the regulation of the society[73]; and (c) delivering to the Central Bank three copies of the memorandum and rules[74], each signed by the ten persons and the society's intended secretary. The authority to incorporate a building society rests with the Central Bank which took over the regulation and supervision of building societies from the registrar of friendly societies pursuant to the BSA 1989. The Central Bank's discretion to register a building society and issue it with a certificate of incorporation will be exercised where it is satisfied[75] that:

(a) its memorandum and rules are in conformity with the BSA 1989 and any regulations made thereunder and that the name of the proposed society is not undesirable;

(b) there is no reason to believe that the society will not be authorised to raise funds in accordance with s 17 of the BSA 1989; and

(c) registration would not be prejudicial to the orderly and proper regulation of building societies generally.

A refusal by the Central Bank to register a building society may be appealed to the High Court by all ten of the persons seeking to form the society[76]. Where registration is effected and a certificate of incorporation is issued, the certificate shall be 'sufficient evidence until the contrary is shown that all the requirements of this Act in respect of registration and of matters precedent and incidental thereto have been complied with and that the society is a society duly registered and incorporated under this Act'[77]. There have been no new building societies registered since the enactment of the BSA 1989 and it is likely that the age of the Irish building society is over.

---

69 Section 10(6) of the BSA 1989.

70 Who are not disqualified under s 64 of the BSA 1989.

71 The provisions of the memorandum must comply with Part I of the Second Schedule to the BSA 1989.

72 In *Irish Civil Service Building Society v Registrar of Friendly Societies* [1985] IR 167, it was held that the building society legislation only provided a framework for making rules and that individual building societies could make such rules as they thought fit for their administration and management.

73 The provisions of the rules must comply with Part II of the Second Schedule to the BSA 1989.

74 When registered the memorandum and rules are binding upon the society, every member and officer thereof and all persons claiming on account of a member or under the rules and all such members, officers and persons are taken to have notice of those provisions: s 11(1) of the BSA 1989.

75 Section 10(3) of the BSA 1989.

76 Section 10(4) of the BSA 1989.

77 Section 10(7) of the BSA 1989. A mistake made in the incorporation of a building society has been held not to render its incorporation void: *Irish Permanent Building Society v Registrar of Building Societies* [1981] ILRM 242.

(b) Powers of building societies

[1.038] The doctrine of *ultra vires* applies to building societies as it applies to registered companies[78]. A measure of protection is afforded to outsiders by s 12(1) of the BSA 1989, which provides:

> 'Any act or thing done by a building society, which if the society had been empowered to do the same would have been lawfully and effectively done, shall, subject to *section 11(1)*, be effective in favour of any person relying on such act or thing who dealt with the society in good faith notwithstanding that the society had no power to do such act or thing.'

Section 12(1) of the BSA 1989 is based on s 8 of the CA 1963 and case law on the latter section would influence, if not bind, the interpretation of s 12(1) of the BSA 1989[79]. In England, it has been held that even where a building society acts outside its legislative framework, such action will not necessarily be unenforceable[80].

[1.039] Subject to certain exceptions, a building society may not raise funds or advertise for or otherwise solicit deposits or subscriptions for shares unless there is in force an authorisation granted by the Central Bank: s 17(1) of the BSA 1989. A breach of this provision entitles the Central Bank to petition to have a building society wound-up[81]. Building societies may have as their objects the undertaking of any of the activities permitted by or under the BSA 1989 and shall have as one of their objects 'the raising of funds for making housing loans'[82]. Building societies have the powers conferred by the BSA 1989 and any incidental powers necessary for the achievement of their objects subject to (a) compliance with any requirement that, for a power to be exercisable, it must be adopted by a building society and (b) the exercise by the Central Bank of its functions under the BSA 1989 and the Currency and Central Bank Acts or regulations made thereunder[83]. Building societies have power to raise funds and borrow money subject the restrictions contained in s 18 of the BSA 1989. Other powers enjoyed by building societies include: the acquisition and provision of premises; the holding and developing of land; the making of housing loans and other loans[84]. The charging of tiered interest rates, the assessment of security for loans, the sale or retention of mortgaged property, the discharge of mortgages, the investment in and support of bodies corporate, the provision of conveyancing services, auctioneering services and other services relating to land, the exercise of powers outside the State, the hedging of interest rates and the linking of services are all regulated by the BSA 1989[85]. The power to provide financial services and to give bonds and sureties were, in 1989, new powers for

---

78 See Ch 7, *Corporate Contracts: Capacity and Authority*, at para **[7.045]** *et seq*.

79 See Ch 7, *Corporate Contracts: Capacity and Authority*, at para **[7.080]** *et seq*.

80 In *Nash v Halifax Building Society* [1979] Ch 584, it was held that where a building society took as security a 'second' mortgage (ie, ranking after a mortgage in favour of another lending institution) that security was still enforceable although it contravened the English legislation.

81 Section 17(8) of the BSA 1989.

82 Section 9(1) of the BSA 1989.

83 Section 9(2) of the BSA 1989.

84 Sections 20–23 of the BSA 1989.

85 Sections 24–28 and 31–35 of the BSA 1989, respectively.

building societies[86]. Section 36 regulates the exercise, by a building society, of its powers.

[1.040] There are some major differences between the Irish law of building societies and that pertaining in England. An example of this is a building society's ability to create a floating charge. An English building society is prohibited from creating a floating charge[87]. There is no such prohibition on Irish building societies. Moreover, the obstacle to an individual creating a floating charge – the Bills of Sale Acts – does not apply to corporations[88] or other bodies corporate such as building societies.

(c) Membership

[1.041] Section 16(1) of the BSA 1989 provides that every person holding one or more shares in a building society shall be a member of the society. Membership is the prerequisite to having rights in a building society. The general rule in building societies was one member one vote on a special resolution or conversion resolution although it was possible for a member to have more than one vote per share on a vote on an ordinary resolution. When EBS and INBS required emergency recapitalisation from the State, the BSA 1989 was amended[89] by the insertion of s 18(1A) into the BSA 1989 which permitted the issue of special investment shares to the Minister for Finance and, reflective of the risk to the holder of the shares, permitted the Minister to have the majority voting rights as provided for in s 69(3A) of the BSA 1989[90].

(d) Central Bank supervision

[1.042] Building societies are supervised by the Central Bank which is given wide-ranging powers under the BSA 1989. Part IV of the BSA 1989 specifically concerns the control and supervision of building societies. Section 37(1) imposes a duty on the Central Bank to supervise and regulate building societies with a view to the protection by each society of the funds of its shareholders and depositors and the maintenance of the financial stability and wellbeing of societies generally. Specifically, building societies are required to meet certain asset and liability ratios[91]. The Central Bank's powers include the power to revoke a building society's authorisation; it can also authorise inspection, require information, control advertising by building societies, apply to court to prohibit certain contraventions of the BSA 1989, require the disclosure of information and appoint inspectors to a building society[92]. In all respects the supervision of building societies by the Central Bank is on a par with its supervision of banks.

---

86 Sections 29 and 30 of the BSA 1989.

87 Section 9B(1) of the English Building Societies Act 1986.

88 In *NV Slavenburg's Bank v Intercontinental Natural Resources Ltd et al* [1980] 1 All ER 955 at 975, Lloyd J said that 'the Bills of Sale Acts apply to individuals only and not to corporations at all'.

89 Section 18(1A) was inserted by s 228 of the National Asset Management Agency Act 2009 and Part 1 of Schedule 2, Item 5.

90 Section 69(3A) was inserted by s 228 of the National Asset Management Agency Act 2009 and Part 1 of Schedule 2, Item 11.

91 Section 39 of the BSA 1989.

92 Sections 40–47 of the BSA 1989.

(e) Management, meetings and accounts

[1.043] Every building society must have at least three directors, one of whom must be the chairman of the board of directors; the chairman may not, however, also be the chief executive (or managing director) unless the Central Bank consents to this[93]. A building society is required to have a chief executive and a secretary who again, and save with the Central Bank's consent, may not be one and the same person[94]. The appointment and retirement of directors are regulated by ss 50 and 51 of the BSA 1989 and Central Bank approval is required to the appointment of directors or secretaries of building societies. Changes were made to the BSA 1989 to give effective control of the board of a building society in which special investment shares have been issued to the Minister for Finance[95]. Many of the provisions contained in Part III of the Companies Act 1990 had fore-runners in the BSA 1989[96]. These include: the disclosure by directors of interests in contracts; directors' contracts of employment; the inspection of directors' service contracts; substantial property transactions involving directors and connected persons; and restrictions on loans, quasi-loans, credit transactions, guarantees and the provision of security to directors[97].

[1.044] Meetings of members of building societies and resolutions at such meetings are regulated by Part VI of the BSA 1989. In practice, however, a society's rules (which must be in conformity with the provisions of the BSA 1989) will regulate the convening and holding of meetings and the passing of resolutions thereat. Particular care needs to be taken to distinguish the law applicable to building societies in the context of the meaning of, say, a special resolution or conversion resolution from the law applicable to companies registered under the Companies Acts.

[1.045] Accounts and audit of building societies are regulated by Part VII of the BSA 1989. The failure by a building society to keep proper accounting records and to establish and maintain systems of control of their businesses would entitle the Central Bank to revoke or suspend authorisation. Section 112 of the BSA 1989 makes provision for the imposition of personal liability on the officers of a building society where proper accounting records are not kept[98].

(f) Conversion of building societies to companies

[1.046] Part XI of the BSA 1989 originally only facilitated the conversion of a building society to a public limited company (PLC) but this was amended by the CISA 2010 and now a building society can be converted into a private company limited by shares[99]. EBS

93 Section 47(1), (3) and (4) of the BSA 1989. Subsection (2) provides that a society shall not have a body corporate as a director.

94 Section 48 of the BSA 1989.

95 Subsections (18) to (20) of s 50 of the BSA 1989 were inserted by s 228 of the National Asset Management Agency Act 2009 and Part 1 of Schedule 2, Item 8.

96 As to Part III of the CA 1990, see, generally, Ch 16, *Statutory Regulation of Directors' Transactions*.

97 Sections 53–59 of the BSA 1989.

98 Section 111 of the BSA 1989 also makes such officers liable to criminal sanction.

99 Section 71 of the CISA 2010 effected the amendments to the BSA 1989 provided for in Part 1 of Schedule 1 of the CISA 2010.

used this procedure to convert to a private limited company. Section 101(2) of the BSA 1989 details the conditions which a building society must fulfil in order to convert to a limited company. This provides that a building society must pass a conversion resolution approving of a conversion scheme, obtain the Central Bank's confirmation to the conversion scheme and have itself registered as a company under the Companies Acts in accordance with the provisions in Part XI and regulations made thereunder.

(g) Amalgamations and transfer of engagements

[1.047] Part X of the BSA 1989 facilitates the amalgamation of two or more building societies by forming a new building society (s 95) and the transfer by one building society of its engagements to another society which undertakes to fulfil those engagements (s 96).

Credit unions[100]

[1.048] Credit unions were originally formed under and regulated by the IPSA 1893; credit unions were simply financial co-operatives. As they grew in popularity and number it became apparent that separate, specialist legislation was required and in 1966 the Credit Union Act was passed. This legislation was later supplemented by Part III of the Industrial and Provident Societies (Amendment) Act 1978. Both the 1966 Act and Part III of the 1978 Act were repealed and replaced by the current legislation, the Credit Union Act 1997 ('CUA 1997')[101]. The CUA 1997 was necessitated by the fact that many credit unions had evolved from being small, unsophisticated, local saving-societies to becoming large organisations offering a wide range of financial services to their members. The supervision of credit unions continues to vest in the registrar of friendly societies, whose powers of supervision have been bolstered by the CUA 1997. Credit unions were not, however, immune to the financial crisis as loans made went bad. Although originally included in CISA 2010, no orders were made under that Act against credit unions. They have also been included in the Central Bank and Credit Institutions (Resolution) Act 2011 ('CBCIRA 2011'), which provides a 'steady-state' resolution regime for banks and other regulated bodies such as credit unions, and an order, appointing a special manager, was made in respect of Newbridge Credit Union Limited under the CBCIRA 2011 on 13 January 2012.

[1.049] Section 6(1) of the CUA 1997 facilitates the formation of a credit union. It provides that a society may be registered as a credit union if the central bank is satisfied as to certain matters. First, it must be formed for the objects detailed in s 6(2)(a)–(c) and no other objects save those in (d)–(g)[102]. Those objects are:

(a) the promotion of thrift among its members by the accumulation of their savings;

(b) the creation of sources of credit for the mutual benefit of its members at a fair and reasonable rate of interest;

---

100 Quinn, *Credit Unions in Ireland* (2nd edn, Oak Tree Press, 1999); McKillop, Goth and Hyndman, *Credit Unions in Ireland* (2006, Institute of Chartered Accountants in Ireland).

101 See generally Bird's annotations on the CUA 1997 in *Irish Current Law, 1997* (Round Hall Sweet & Maxwell) at 1997 No 15.

102 Section 6(1)(a) of the CUA 1997.

(c) the use and control of members' savings for their mutual benefit;
(d) the training and education of its members in the wise use of money;
(e) the education of its members in their economic, social and cultural wellbeing as members of the community;
(f) the improvement of the wellbeing and spirit of the members' community; and
(g) subject to section 48, the provision to its members of such additional services as are for their mutual benefit[103].

Second, admission to membership of the society must be restricted to persons each of whom has, in relation to all of the other members, at least one of the following common bonds[104]:

(a) following a particular occupation;
(b) residing or being employed in a particular locality;
(c) being employed by a particular employer or having retired from employment with a particular employer;
(d) being a member of a *bona fide* organisation or being otherwise associated with other members of a society for a purpose other than that of forming a society to be registered as a credit union;
(e) any other common bond approved by the Central Bank[105].

A credit union must have at least 15 members who are of full age[106], its rules must comply with s 13 of the CUA 1997[107] and its registered office must be within the State[108]. A condition of registration is that a credit union must participate in a savings protection scheme approved under s 46(1) of the CUA 1997[109] and a credit union must have in force on registration a policy of insurance of the kind required by s 47 of the CUA 1997[110].

Unincorporated associations

[1.050] Unincorporated associations can refer to a wide variety of organisations, eg, clubs, political parties, campaign groups, residents' associations, etc[111]. The meaning of

---

103 As detailed in s 6(2) of the CUA 1997.

104 Section 6(1)(b) of the CUA 1997.

105 As detailed in s 6(3) of the CUA 1997. In ascertaining whether a common bond exists between the members of a society, the registrar of friendly societies is required, by s 6(4), (a) to have regard to the qualifications which are stated in the rules to be required for admission to membership of the society, and (b) may, if he considers it proper in the circumstances of the case, treat the fact that admission to membership is restricted as mentioned in sub-s (1)(b) as sufficient evidence of the existence of a common bond.

106 Section 6(1)(c) of the CUA 1997.

107 Section 6(1)(d) of the CUA 1997.

108 Section 6(1)(e) of the CUA 1997.

109 Section 6(1)(f) of the CUA 1997.

110 Section 6(1)(g) of the CUA 1997.

111 See generally, Warburton, *Unincorporated Associations* (2nd edn, Sweet & Maxwell, 1992); McNamara, *A Legal Guide for Clubs and Associations* (2005, First Law); and Reed and Ambrose, 'Unincorporated Associations: Getting to Grips with the Basics' (2007) PLC 47.

'unincorporated association' was defined by Lawton LJ in *Conservative and Unionist Central Office v Burrell*[112] in the following terms:

> '… two or more persons bound together for one or more common purposes, not being business purposes, by mutual undertakings each having mutual duties and obligations, in an organisation which has rules which identify in whom control of it and its funds rests and on what terms and which can be joined or left at will.'

[1.051] An unincorporated association has no separate legal personality – such legal personality as it has is the sum of the legal personalities of its members. The legal basis of an unincorporated association is the law of contract – the rights and duties of the members of an unincorporated association are governed exclusively by contract[113]. The formation of an unincorporated association is a *de facto* process – when two or more come together with a non-business common purpose with the intention of forming an unincorporated association, an unincorporated association may be said to come into existence. Large unincorporated associations will make rules to govern the relations between the members *inter se* and will elect a committee, officers and trustees. Because of the lack of separate legal personality, any property 'owned' by a club or other unincorporated association will have to be held in the names of trustees in trust for the members in accordance with the rules of the club. An unincorporated association cannot be liable in tort, again for the reason that it has no separate existence; individual members of an unincorporated association will only be liable for their personal breaches of duty and will not ordinarily be vicariously liable for the torts of other members[114]. Similarly, an unincorporated association cannot make or be sued on a contract. Where an unincorporated association purports to make a contract, the individual members who actually make it may be personally liable or, if the rules authorised them to act as agent, the principal in such agency – all of the members – will be personally liable.

Friendly societies[115]

[1.052] Friendly societies can be registered under the Friendly Societies Acts 1896–1977 however a critical distinction between a friendly society and an industrial and provident society is that a friendly society does not have a separate legal personality. In much the same way as a club or other unincorporated association, friendly societies must hold property through trustees. Friendly societies are less popular now than in the past and can be established for different purposes such as to provide small life assurance benefits, sick benefits and death benefits to members, to provide benefits to non-members or to promote particular activities or interests.

---

112 *Conservative and Unionist Central Office v Burrell* [1982] 1 WLR 522 at 525.

113 See *Walsh v Butler* [1997] IEHC 9, Morris J where it was said of a particular association that the 'relationship as between members must be regarded as a contractual relationship based upon the rules of the Club'. See also *Re Bucks Constabulary Widows' and Orphans' Fund Friendly Society (No 2)* [1979] 1 WLR 936.

114 *Baker v Jones* [1916] 2 AC 15. See also *Thompson and another v Douglas Amateur Football Club Social Club and another* [1999] Scot SC (27 June 1999), (www.bailii.org).

115 Fuller, *The Law Relating to Friendly Societies and Industrial and Provident Societies* (4th edn, Stevens and Sons, 1926).

[1.053] In order to register a friendly society, at least seven people must draw up a set of rules governing its operation. A society may be registered as a friendly society, benevolent society, a working-men's club or a specially authorised society. The rules must contain at a minimum the matters required to be provided for by the First Schedule of the Friendly Societies Act 1896. The rules, together with the prescribed application form and fee, are submitted to the registrar of companies for registration following examination for compliance with the 1896 Act.

Unregistered companies

[1.054] Section 377(1) of the CA 1963 applies the provisions of the Companies Acts that are listed in the Ninth Schedule to the CA 1963 to all bodies corporate incorporated in and having a place of business in the State, save those mentioned in s 377(2), 'as if they were companies registered under this Act and subject to such adaptations and modifications (if any) as may be prescribed'. The carve-out in s 377(2) is extensive. It disapplies the application of the Companies Acts to (a) any body corporate incorporated by or registered under any public general statute; (b) any body corporate not formed for the purpose of carrying on business which has for its object the acquisition of gain by the body or by the individual members thereof; (c) any body corporate which is prohibited by statute or otherwise from making any distribution of its income or property among its members while it is a going concern or when it is in liquidation; and (d) any body corporate for the time being exempted by the Minister for Jobs, Enterprise and Innovation.

[1.055] The combined effect of these provisions is that there would seem to be only one entity that in practice falls to be classified as an 'unregistered company' to which the provisions listed in the Ninth Schedule to the CA 1963 apply. This is the Governor and Company of the Bank of Ireland, a chartered corporation, the existence of which derives from the Bank of Ireland Act 1781/2[116] and a charter granted by George III in 1783. As a perusal of the Ninth Schedule will show, not all of the provisions of the Companies Acts apply to unregistered companies; however, the list of provisions can be amended by Ministerial order[117].

[B] AN HISTORICAL OUTLINE OF REGISTERED COMPANIES

Private companies, registered companies, and corporate status

[1.056] The modern Irish private company is a species of *registered* company, so described because the company is registered in the Companies Registration Office ('CRO') in accordance with the requirements of the Companies Acts. The registered company is a legal structure which *all* persons – including so-called *fictitious*[118] persons

116 21 & 22 Geo III c 16.

117 See, for example, SI 63/1999, Companies Act, 1963 (Ninth Schedule) Regulations 1999 and SI 64/1999, Companies Act, 1963 (Section 377(1)) Order 1999, which facilitated the application of Part XI of the CA 1990 (which deals with the acquisition of own shares and shares in holding company), the European Communities (Public Limited Companies Subsidiaries) Regulations 1997, etc, to unregistered companies.

118 See generally, Ch 4, *Incorporation and its Consequences*, at para **[4.023]**.

such as the State, government ministers, and even other registered companies – may employ as a means of conducting their affairs[119]. The registered company is principally used in Ireland as a vehicle for conducting business activity, but there is no requirement in the Companies Acts that companies registered under them be formed with a view to the making of a profit[120]. Thus, for example, charities, social clubs[121] and management committees of large shopping centres or apartment complexes are frequently operated through the medium of the registered company.

[1.057] The registered company is a form of *corporation* or *body corporate*, and as such constitutes a legal person with a legal identity separate and distinct from that of its individual members or shareholders[122]. A distinction may be drawn at the outset between *corporations sole* and *corporations aggregate*. A corporation *sole* 'comprises one individual holding an office subject to perpetual succession'[123], the paradigm example of which is a government minister or a clerical bishop[124]. A corporation *aggregate*, on the other hand, may be defined as an association, comprising of a number of individual members, which has a legal existence separate from its members. Until recently all registered companies were corporations aggregate. The advent of the single-member private limited company means that all registered companies cannot be accurately described as being corporations aggregate. It is thought, however, that this goes no deeper than the accuracy of the description and that the significance of there being just one member does not, in fact, cause a registered company to cease, *in law*, to be a corporation aggregate.

It is the separate legal identity, or *corporate personality*, and the consequences which stem from it, which are the principal attraction of the registered company as a means of conducting business. This is because the risk, liability, obligations and duties associated with the business will rest with the company and *not*, generally speaking, with the individual shareholders or members[125]. The registered company acquires this corporate personality through the process of *incorporation by registration*, ie, through registration of the memorandum of association of the company with the registrar of companies in accordance with the Companies Acts. Section 18 of the CA 1963 provides that:

> (1) On the registration of the memorandum of a company the registrar shall certify under his hand that the company is incorporated and, in the case of a limited company, that the company is limited.

---

119 As to registered companies of which the State is a member see para **[1.065]**.

120 By way of contrast, the PA 1890, which is the principal source of the law governing partnerships in this jurisdiction, defines a partnership as 'the relation which subsists between persons carrying *on a business in common with a view to a profit*': s 1(1) of the PA 1890 (italics added). Where, however, such a relation subsists between the members of a registered company it is not a partnership: s (2)(a) of the PA 1890. On partnerships see para **[1.004]** *et seq*.

121 See, for example, *Re Parnell GAA Club Ltd* [1984] ILRM 246.

122 Section 18 of the CA 1963; *Salomon v Salomon & Co* [1897] AC 22. See generally, Ch 4, *Incorporation and its Consequences*.

123 See Wylie, *Irish Land Law* (4th edn, Bloomsbury Professional, 2010) at para [4.028].

124 On the corporation sole, see, Maitland, 'The Corporation Sole' (1900) 16 LQR 335.

125 See Ch 4, *Incorporation and its Consequences*. For exceptions to this principle see Ch 5, *Disregarding Separate Legal Personality*.

> (2) From the date of incorporation mentioned in the certificate of incorporation, the subscribers of the memorandum, together with such other persons as may from time to time become members of the company, shall be a body corporate with the name contained in the memorandum, capable forthwith of exercising all the functions of an incorporated company, and having perpetual succession and a common seal, but with such liability on the part of the members to contribute to the assets of the company in the event of its being wound up as is mentioned in this Act.

Upon registration, then, a metamorphosis occurs and the signatories to a company's memorandum of association become members of a new body corporate which is a registered company. This process and its consequences are described in detail in later chapters[126].

[1.058] It would be inaccurate to equate the incorporation of a company by registration with the *formation* of a company. It may prove useful at this stage to observe that although nowadays we tend to think of a company as a corporation, it has been said 'the word *company* has no strictly legal meaning'[127]. In common parlance the word is used to connote an association of some kind. It is common, and quite legal, for partners, notably solicitors' firms, to carry on their business in the name of, say, 'A, B, C & Company'[128]. The Companies Acts impose no requirements for the formation of a company as such, instead they provide a means of registration through which a company may achieve corporate status, and lay down a number of minimum requirements for companies seeking such corporate status[129]. They also contain a number of provisions regulating the activities of companies which have been registered and have achieved corporate status.

[1.059] An examination of some of the more significant historical developments in the law of business corporations may assist in understanding the basis of the Companies Acts. First, brief reference will be made to a development of paramount significance to all corporations which has shaped the way corporate status may be obtained to this day, namely, the *concession theory* of corporations.

The *concession theory* of corporations[130]

[1.060] The general idea of a corporation as a legal person has been identified in the Code of Hammurabi dating back to 2,000 BC[131], and there are indications that primitive society was regarded by its members as being made up of corporate bodies of groups of

---

126 See Ch 4, *Incorporation and its Consequences*. For exceptions to this principle see Ch 5, *Disregarding Separate Legal Personality.*

127 *Re Stanley* [1906] 1 Ch 131 at 134, *per* Buckley J. Of course when the Companies Acts refer to 'company' the term means 'company' as defined by s 2(1) of the CA 1963: see para **[1.156]** *et seq*.

128 However, where the trading name of a partnership does not consist of the true names of all the partners it must be registered in the Registry of Business Names, maintained by the CRO, pursuant to the RBNA 1963.

129 See Ch 2, *Incorporation by Registration.*

130 For an excellent analysis of the development of legal personality and theories of the corporation, see O'Neill, *The Constitutional Rights of Companies* (2007, Thomson Round Hall) at pp 9–28.

131 See Henn & Alexander, *Laws of Corporations and Other Business Enterprises* (3rd edn, West Publishing Co, 1983).

men united by the reality or the fiction of blood relationship, and that the family, clan and tribe were recognised as distinct entities of society before individuals were so regarded[132]. The importance of the *túath* ('tribe' or 'petty kingdom') and *fine* ('kin group') in early Irish law suggest that our Irish ancestors of the seventh and eighth centuries AD regarded society in a similar light[133]. The concept of the corporation was well known to the ancient Romans, and the writings of Savigny identify corporations of dependent towns, brotherhoods of priests, gods, temples, and brotherhoods of artisans, such as blacksmiths, bakers, and boatmen, in ancient Rome[134]. It seems that in those early days a corporation could be formed through the simple gathering together of persons with a shared interest; thus Blackstone refers to the early Roman maxim '*tres faciunt collegium*'[135]. Corporate personality in those days was simply the legal recognition of group interests which, as a practical matter, already existed.

[1.061] All this was to change, however, with the fostering, late in the Roman Empire, of the *concession theory*[136] of corporations. The central thesis of this theory is the notion that a corporation may be formed only by imperial concession or *fiat*. By Blackstone's time, the theory was firmly rooted in English law and he wrote: 'with us here in England the King's consent is absolutely necessary to the erection of any corporation[137].' Although the Sovereign power in Ireland is no longer vested in the Crown but in the State[138], the concession theory continues to be a feature of the Irish law of corporations, with the consequence that all corporations formed here must be created by, or in accordance with, statutes. Thus, the constitutional right of free association[139] does not "include the right to form bodies with corporate existence ... [t]he latter is a statutory right, given by statute and controlled by statute'[140].

[1.062] Continued adherence to the concession theory of corporations requires the assent of the Sovereign or the State to the incorporation of a body corporate. The Sovereign or State may give this assent to incorporation in any of three ways:

---

132 Sir Henry Maine, *Ancient Law: Its Connection with the Early History of Society and its Relation to Modern Ideas* (12th edn, John Murray, 1930); see Williston, 'History of the Law of Business Corporations Before 1800' (1888) 2 Harv LR 105.

133 See generally Kelly, *A Guide to Early Irish Law* (1988, Dublin Institute for Advanced Studies).

134 Savigny, *System des Heutigen Römischen Rechts*, vol II; see generally Williston, 'History of the Law of Business Corporations Before 1800' (1888) 2 Harv LR 105.

135 Blackstone, *Commentaries on the Laws of England* I:472.

136 There are signs of this theory in Savigny's accounts of corporations in ancient Rome; see Williston, 'History of the Law of Business Corporations Before 1800' (1888) 2 Harv LR 105, at p 107, fn 2. Its chief protagonist was Pope Innocent IV, Sinibald Fieschi, who was made Bishop of Rome in 1243. The spread of the Church's influence can have played no small part in the propagation of the concession theory in Western Europe and the British Isles. See Hessen, *In Defence of the Corporation* (1979, Hoover Institution), Chs 1 & 2; Halliss, *Corporate Personality: A Study in Jurisprudence* (1930, Oxford University Press); Henn & Alexander, *Laws of Corporations and Other Business Enterprises* (3rd edn, West Publishing Co, 1983) at p 145.

137 Blackstone, *Commentaries on the Laws of England,* I:471.

138 *Byrne v Ireland* [1972] IR 241. See Articles 28.2 and 49.1.2° of Bunreacht na hÉireann 1937.

139 See Article 40.6 of Bunreacht na hÉireann 1937.

140 *Private Motorists Provident Society Ltd v Attorney General* [1983] IR 339, *per* Carroll J at 355.

(a) by charter;

(b) by statute;

(c) by registration under the Companies Acts.

(a) Corporations created by royal charter

[1.063] One means of obtaining the assent of the Sovereign or State to the creation of a corporation was to obtain the grant of a royal charter. This method enjoyed some popularity in the past, and a number of corporations created by the grant of a royal charter still exist in Ireland today. The most obvious examples of these are the Law Society of Ireland – the solicitors' professional body – which was founded in 1830 and which was incorporated by royal charter in 1852[141], the Governor and Company of the Bank of Ireland, which obtained its charter in 1783, the Royal College of Surgeons, which obtained its charter in 1785, and Trinity College, Dublin which obtained its latest charter in 1911. It is thought that the oldest functioning chartered company in Ireland is The Goldsmiths' Company in Dublin which obtained its charter in 1637. The granting of a charter had the effect of creating a body corporate which was distinct from its members, enjoyed perpetual succession, could sue and be sued in its own name and had a seal[142]. Until the liability of members was limited by statute, and in the absence of the charter providing to the contrary, the members and officers of chartered corporations had no liability for the debts of the corporation since the debts of the corporation were just that, debts of the corporation and not of its members or officers[143]. The primary motivation for obtaining a charter, however, was not so much the achievement of corporate status. Rather, it was the obtaining of patronage and monopoly rights from the Crown. Thus, the procedure by which such a charter was obtained was often founded in nepotism, since it operated on the basis of representation to the Crown requesting the grant of a charter. Bartholomew Duhigg, describing the events which led to the obtaining by the Honourable Society of King's Inns of a charter in 1792, depicted the events as 'the outcome of efforts by a minority ... to extend the sphere of influence and patronage of the local governing élite in Ireland'[144]. The power of the Crown to grant a charter was subsequently curtailed by Parliament as gradually the House of Commons assumed the entire effective control of the government, and the Crown's authority to grant a charter became referable to parliamentary permission[145].

---

141 See Hogan, *The Legal Profession in Ireland 1789–1922* (1986, Incorporated Law Society of Ireland). Interestingly, the Honourable Society of King's Inns – the barristers' professional body – which was founded in 1539, was denied incorporation by King Henry VIII (in whose honour the society had been named) in 1542. It was finally incorporated by royal charter from King George III in 1792 – only to lose its charter in the following year; see Kenny, *King's Inns and the Kingdom of Ireland* (1992, Irish Academic Press in association with the Irish Legal History Society).

142 *Sutton's Hospital case* (1612) 10 Co Rep 1.

143 *Elve v Boylton* [1891] 1 Ch 501; *Re The Sheffield and Sough Yorkshire Permanent Building Society* [1889] 22 QBD 470.

144 Kenny, *King's Inns and the Kingdom of Ireland* (1992, Irish Academic Press in association with the Irish Legal History Society) at p 240.

145 An example of the procedure involved in obtaining a charter in those days is to be found in *Re Commercial Buildings Co of Dublin* [1938] IR 477 at 480.

[1.064] The foundation of the State in 1922 closed the avenue of incorporation by royal charter, but the prerogative to create corporations by charter was probably succeeded to by the government[146]. Nevertheless, no new chartered corporations have been created in Ireland since 1922.

(b) Corporations created by statute

[1.065] A second means of obtaining the assent of the Sovereign or State to the creation of a corporation is by way of a special statute creating the corporation. A corporation may, of course, be formed by statutes other than the Companies Acts, and such corporations are generically referred to as *statutory corporations*. The principal feature of the statutory corporation is that it may be incorporated without having to observe the requirements of the Companies Acts. The statutory corporation was a popular means of conducting large scale enterprise in the past, particularly in the realm of quasi-state services such as railways and canals[147], although it was also used as a means of enriching those who had enough influence to persuade Parliament to pass an Act. Nowadays, the requirement of special legislation for the creation of a statutory corporation renders it impractical as a means for the conduct of private business; however, it is an ideal means for the conduct of state-controlled public utilities and for bodies with special objects. Statutory corporations fall into one of two categories: State corporations and non-State statutory corporations.

(i) State corporations

[1.066] Many of the statutory corporations created before the foundation of the State have been dissolved and their assets and undertakings transferred to State-controlled corporations. Examples of statutory corporations established since the foundation of the State and controlled by the State[148] include the Central Bank[149], Radio Telefís Éireann[150] and, perhaps the most significant statutory corporation ever created, the National Asset Management Agency or 'NAMA'[151]. However, corporations of this kind should be distinguished from State-controlled companies established by special statutes which authorise them to become incorporated by registration under the Companies Acts. Since the foundation of the State it has not been uncommon for the Oireachtas to pass enabling Acts of this nature, such as the Air Navigation and Transport Act 1936, which authorised the Minister for Finance to apply for the incorporation of a registered company[152]. The result was a company (Aer Rianta Teoranta) incorporated under the Companies Acts 1908–1924, but conceived by an enabling Act of the Oireachtas. Other corporations organised in this way include ACC Bank plc and An Post plc[153]. Although these companies are registered companies, their power to operate is often circumscribed

146 Under Articles 49.1.2° and 28.2 of Bunreacht na hÉireann, 1937. See also s 377(4) of the CA 1963, which recognises the power of the Government to grant charters.

147 See Hessen, *In Defence of the Corporation* (1979, Hoover Institution) at p 28.

148 See Goulding, 'The Juristic Basis of Irish State Enterprise' (1978) 13 Ir Jur (ns) 302.

149 Central Bank Act 1942.

150 Broadcasting Authority Act 1960.

151 National Asset Management Agency Act 2009.

152 Section 68 of the Air Navigation and Transport Act 1936.

153 Postal and Telecommunications Services Act 1983.

by their establishing Acts. While these State-controlled statutory corporations share many of the features of the companies considered in this work, a detailed discussion is outside its scope.

[1.067] The doctrine of *ultra vires* applies to statutory corporations, and the following passage from Halsbury's *Laws of England*[154] was adopted by the Supreme Court in *Keane v An Bord Pleanála*[155] as a correct statement of the law:

> 'The powers of a corporation created by a statute are limited and circumscribed by the statutes which regulate it, and extend no further than is expressly stated therein or is necessarily and properly required for carrying into effect the purposes of incorporation or may be fairly regarded as incidental to or consequential upon those things which the legislature has authorised. What the statute does not expressly or impliedly authorise is to be taken to be prohibited[156].'

(ii) Non-State statutory corporations

[1.068] A second type of statutory corporation is the non-State statutory company incorporated by private persons pursuant to *special statutes* which provide a means for the incorporation of bodies having special objects such as, for example, the supply of gas[157], the operation of a building society[158], or credit union[159], or industrial and provident society[160]. These special statutes bear many resemblances to the Companies Acts, and occasionally may even apply provisions of the Companies Acts to the corporations formed under them; however, detailed discussion of these kinds of corporations also lies outside the scope of this work.

(c) Corporations created by registration under the Companies Acts

[1.069] The third means of obtaining the assent of the Sovereign or State to the creation of a corporation is by way of registration in accordance with the provisions of the Companies Acts. This procedure is discussed in further detail later[161].

[1.070] The facility to incorporate by registration is a convenient mechanism for the formation of corporations. It does away with the difficulties involved in the acquisition of a charter (which due to competition law would not nowadays carry with it the incidental benefits of patronage and monopoly) or in acquiring a special statute. But why should the State provide such a convenient means of incorporation? Indeed, why should the State allow private enterprise to be conducted through the means of a corporation at all? To answer these questions we must consider, albeit briefly, a number of developments in the law of business corporations since the 1700s which have led to the introduction of today's system of incorporation by registration.

---

154 Halsbury, *Laws of England* (4th edn) vol 9, para 133.

155 *Keane v An Bord Pleanála* [1977] 1 IR 184 at 212.

156 See also *Pierce v The Dublin Cemeteries Committee and others* [2006] IEHC 182 (Laffoy J).

157 See the Gas Regulation Act 1982.

158 See the Building Societies Act 1989, considered at para **[1.036]**.

159 See the Credit Union Act 1997, considered at para **[1.048]**.

160 See the Industrial and Provident Societies Acts 1893–1978, considered at para **[1.032]**.

161 See, generally, Ch 2, *Incorporation by Registration*.

Developments in the law of business corporations since the 1700s[162]

[1.071] The history of the developments in the law of companies from the 1700s to the early part of the twentieth century are sketched as follows:

(a) Joint stock companies.
(b) The Bubble Act 1720.
(c) Deed of settlement companies.
(d) The repeal of the Bubble Act.
(e) The Joint Stock Companies Act 1844.
(f) The Limited Liability Act 1855.
(g) The Joint Stock Companies Act 1856.
(h) The Companies Act 1862.
(i) The Companies Act 1907.
(j) The Companies (Consolidation) Act 1908.

(a) Joint stock companies

[1.072] Although the law of business corporations can be traced back through the Middle Ages to Roman times[163], it is convenient for present purposes to skip to the decades immediately preceding 1720[164]. At that time so-called *joint stock companies*, which had their roots in the medieval guilds, were flourishing in the realm of domestic trade. Unlike the medieval guilds, these companies traded on their members' behalf, each member contributing to the *joint stock* or capital of the company, and each member taking a share of the profits proportionate to the amount contributed by him. Also, by that time the members of joint stock companies, unlike the members of the medieval guilds, had, in general, long since ceased to act as traders themselves; instead, they were investors in a business enterprise. Gambling with investment in joint stock companies was endemic during the early decades of the eighteenth century.

[1.073] Where the joint stock company enjoyed corporate status (whether by obtaining a charter or through special Act of Parliament) the members of the corporation were absolutely immune from suit in respect of the company's liabilities. This was because, as a corporation, the company was a separate legal person with rights and obligations distinct from those of its members. However, the advantages of incorporation were not apparent to many members of incorporated joint stock companies. Not all of these joint stock companies enjoyed corporate status – indeed, it appears, incorporation may not even have been high on the list of priorities for many of the rash and unwary investors of that time. However, for those companies wishing to improve their reputation, and hence their marketability, the obtaining of a royal charter was perceived to be an important step in attracting investors rather than as a means of achieving immunity from suit for the

[162] See Gower, *Principles of Modern Company Law* (5th edn, Sweet & Maxwell, 1992), Chs 2 and 3. For an examination of the major economic themes in the development of modern company law see Farrar, Furey & Hannigan, *Farrar's Company Law* (3rd edn, Butterworths, 1991), at pp 7–14.

[163] See para **[1.060]**.

[164] For an interesting account of England's first joint-stock corporation, the Russia Company, see Griffith, 'The Russia Company – 439 Years Not Out!' (1994) 15 Co Law 105.

company's debts. But since obtaining a royal charter was a difficult, lengthy and expensive process[165], the practice began of acquiring 'second hand' charters from defunct companies and carrying on the new business of a joint stock company in the old corporate name. For example, a company which proposed to lend money on the security of land in Ireland, and, later, a banking company, both in turn acquired the charter of the old Sword Blade Company which had been incorporated in 1690 to manufacture hollow or channelled sword blades[166]. Where the obtaining of a charter was impossible because of lack of finance or influence, joint stock companies carried on business as unincorporated associations in a manner not unlike the modern partnership. The many varieties of joint stock company led to confusion among investors, for they could be certain neither of whether the company had corporate status, nor, if it was incorporated, of whether it would pursue the objects set out in its charter. In this confusion, rash speculation and fraudulent deception flourished. One deception involved the invitation to the public to subscribe for shares in a 'company for carrying on an undertaking of great advantage, but nobody to know what it is'. An observer wrote:

> 'The man of genius who essayed this bold and successful inroad upon public credibility, merely stated in his prospectus that the required capital was half a million, in five thousand shares of £100 each, deposit £2 per share. Each subscriber, paying his deposit, would be entitled to £100 per annum per share. How this immense profit was to be obtained, he did not condescend to inform them at that time, but promised, that in a month full particulars should be duly announced, and a call made for the remaining £98 of the subscription. Next morning, at nine o'clock, he found that no less than one thousand shares had been subscribed for, and the deposits paid. He was thus, in five hours, the winner of £2,000. He was philosopher enough to be contented with his venture, and set off the same evening for the Continent. He was never heard of again'[167].

Whether it be the 'dot.com' bubble or the Irish property market bubble, plus ça change, plus c'est la même chose.

(b) The Bubble Act 1720

[1.074] In 1720, a House of Commons Resolution[168] drew attention to the many joint stock companies which were falsely purporting to act as corporate bodies, and the many joint stock companies which had acquired incorporation through the acquisition of second hand charters which were not pursuing the objects stated in the charter. The resolution described these practices as tending 'to the prejudices of the public trade and commerce of the kingdom'. Parliament, responding in no half measure, promptly passed the Bubble Act 1720[169], which prohibited:

> '... all public Undertakings and Attempts tending to the common Grievance, Prejudice or Inconvenience of his Majesty's subjects, or great Numbers of them, in their Trade, Commerce, or other lawful affairs ... and more particularly the acting or presuming to act

---

165 See para **[1.063]**.

166 See Gower, *Principles of Modern Company Law* (5th edn, Sweet & Maxwell, 1992); Pennington, *Company Law* (6th edn, Butterworths, 1990), *Introduction*.

167 MacKay, *Extraordinary Popular Delusions and the Madness of Crowds* (1841). Quotation reproduced courtesy of Litrix Reading Room (www.litrix.com).

168 HC Jour XIX 351.

169 6 Geo 1 c 18.

> as a Corporate Body or Bodies, the raising or pretending to raise transferable Stock or Stocks, the transferring or pretending to transfer or assign any Share or Shares in such Stock or Stocks, without legal Authority, either by Act of Parliament, or by Charter from the Crown ... and all acting or pretending to act under any charter, formerly granted from the Crown, for particular or special Purposes therein expressed, by Persons who do or shall use or endeavour to use the same Charters, for raising a Capital Stock, or for making Transfers or Assignments or pretended Transfers or Assignments of such Stock, not intended by such Charter to be raised or transferred ...'

The result was that many existing incorporated joint stock companies were threatened with the forfeiture of their charters, and unincorporated joint stock companies could no longer pretend to be incorporated.

[1.075] One of the motivations for the passing of the Bubble Act 1720 may have been the protection of a scheme which had been put in motion by the South Sea Company (a trading company founded in 1711 with operations in South America and the Pacific) to take over most of the English national debt, which then exceeded some £31 million[170]. The company's grandiose plan was to entice the holders of government annuities to transfer them to the company in return for shares in the company. The company hoped to use the security of these annuities as a means of raising further investments to expand its trade. The government was heavily involved in the company and hoped that the suppression of other joint stock companies by the Act would result in greater investment in the South Sea Company[171]. The company acquired a monopoly to conduct England's trade with Spanish colonies in the West Indies and South America and it was publicly mooted by the promoters of the company that permission to conduct such trade would be granted by Spain as part of the peace-package for ending the War of the Spanish Succession (1703–1713). Confidence in the stock was staggering and people borrowed to acquire it. Bribery and corruption were widespread. The company actively drove up the price of the stock by artificial means, blocks of stock being given by way of bribes, thereby creating an apparent demand for the stock which induced the public to buy in heavily. Between January and June 1720 the stock rose in price from £128 to £1,050: by December 1720 it had fallen back to £128. Thousands of people were ruined, bankruptcies soared and following a public inquiry many of those whom it could be established had taken bribes were incarcerated in the Tower of London and had their estates confiscated.

[1.076] The Bubble Act 1720 had a disastrous effect on investment in companies. The institution of proceedings for the forfeiture of charters against companies which were carrying on business contrary to the terms of their charters spread a wave of panic amongst investors in all companies, and the South Sea Company ultimately collapsed. The decline and collapse of the South Sea Company is but one illustration of the way in which the Bubble Act 1720 backfired. What was required was an Act which made it easier for joint stock companies to incorporate while at the same time protecting the public and the members from fraud and negligence. Instead, the Act made it more difficult for joint stock companies to assume a corporate form and contained no rules regulating the promotion and management of companies which did obtain corporate

---

170 For an interesting, albeit fictional, account of the fall-out from the South Sea Company, see Robert Goddard, *Sea Change* (2000).

171 See Pennington, *Company Law* (6th edn, Butterworths, 1990).

status[172]. Furthermore, what it did, it did vaguely, so that the confusion which surrounded incorporated joint stock companies in the first two decades of the eighteenth century was replaced by confusion emanating from the rambling Bubble Act.

(c) Deed of settlement companies

[1.077] After the passing of the Bubble Act 1720, and until its subsequent repeal in 1825[173], it was the unincorporated joint stock company which was mainly used as a means of conducting business enterprise. The unincorporated joint stock company was in fact a form of partnership. It was formed by a mutual covenant between the members, contained in a *deed of settlement* (which is analogous to what are now described as the *articles* in modern companies and partnerships), and consequently this species of joint stock company came to be known as the *deed of settlement company.* The more developed deed of settlement companies ingeniously employed the *trust* as a means of settling the mutual assets and undertaking of the company's members on trustees, with whom the members covenanted. The resulting company was an unincorporated association, whose management was controlled by a committee of directors, whose existence was continuous and whose property was held by trustees. The terms of the trust deed commonly provided that the trustees could sue and be sued on behalf of the company – but while the courts of equity seem to have permitted suit by the trustees[174], it was not firmly established until 1843[175] whether the courts of law would allow such action[176]. There were further doubts as to whether the shares and stock of such companies could be transferred without breaching the provisions of the Bubble Act. It was the persistence of these doubts, despite the general acceptance of the deed of settlement company (which was the favoured vehicle for the establishment of insurance companies and friendly societies), that led to the repeal of the Bubble Act 1720, 105 years after its introduction.

(d) The repeal of the Bubble Act

[1.078] The repeal of the Bubble Act in 1825[177], paradoxically, did little to further the cause of the deed of settlement company. Since it was an unincorporated association[178], anyone suing such a company had to worry about tracking down the individual members to make them answerable, which was particularly difficult where the company had numerous members[179]. Clauses in the deed of settlement which allowed the trustees of the company to sue and be sued on behalf of the company were of doubtful effect even then because the repealing statute had provided that undertakings should be dealt with according to common law (as opposed to equity). Nevertheless, a wave of speculation and investment began again in 1834, but a great number of deed of settlement companies were formed at this time to perpetrate frauds on investors by pursuing

172 Holdsworth, *History of English Law* (Methuen, Sweet & Maxwell), vol 8, at pp 219–220.

173 6 Geo 4, c 9, s 1.

174 *Metcalfe v Brian* (1810) 12 East 400.

175 *Garrard v Hardey* (1843) 5 M & G 471; *Harrison v Heathorn* (1843) 6 M & G 81.

176 Because, it seems, considerable use was made of private arbitration rather than litigation: Gower, *Principles of Modern Company Law* (5th edn, Sweet & Maxwell, 1992) at p 30.

177 6 Geo 4 c 91.

178 See para **[1.050]**.

179 See, for example, *Von Sandau v Moore* (1825) 1 Russ 441.

undertakings other than those upon which investment was based. A need for regulation of joint stock companies was quickly perceived; but calls were not answered until 1844.

[1.079] Section 2 of the repealing Act did, however, contain one provision of great significance in the development of company law; it enabled the Crown to declare the extent of the members' liability upon the grant, by charter, of incorporation to a company. This provision meant that the incorporation of a company no longer rendered the members of a corporation absolutely immune from liability for the corporate debts. Indeed, it might be regarded as an early legislative instance of disregarding the separate legal identity of the company and its members. Such liability could be, at the Crown's pleasure, without limit. Limits to the liability of members for corporate debts were not to be imposed by statute for a further thirty years[180].

(e) The Joint Stock Companies Act 1844

[1.080] In 1843, William Gladstone, then president of the Board of Trade, presented the Joint Stock Companies Bill, which was to become law as the Joint Stock Companies Act 1844. The legislation was primarily introduced to provide a system whereby fraud and malpractice would be less likely to occur, and easier to deal with if they did. Thus, it prohibited large unincorporated associations, and provided for simple incorporation by way of registration of the deed of settlement rather than by way of charter or special Act, without any form of prior authorisation from the State. Incorporation by registration under the Act was a two-stage process: first, the company would be registered provisionally, and would be authorised thereupon to conduct only strictly limited activities; and second, the registration would be completed upon the filing of a deed of settlement containing the provisions set out in the Act. Companies were required to incorporate, *inter alia*, in order to reduce the difficulties which persons dealing with them might otherwise encounter in conducting actions against them. However, although no member of the company could be sued for company debts, each member remained personally liable to any of the company's judgment creditors who obtained leave from the courts to levy execution on the private property of the members. This Act also established the office of the Registrar of Companies, which survives to this day.

(f) The Limited Liability Act 1855

[1.081] There had been much debate[181], around the time the Joint Stock Companies Act 1844 was introduced, concerning *limited liability* for the members of joint stock companies. The concept of the limited partnership or *société en commandite* had been popular on the continent for some time, and although legislation permitting such associations had been introduced in Ireland in 178[182], they never really took off in either Ireland or England. In the 1840s it was argued that the introduction of limited liability for the members of joint stock companies would help to revitalise business. A number of companies at this time were seeking incorporation under French and American laws to achieve limited liability for their members. Among the arguments in favour of limited liability were that it would enable small capital to be turned to profitable employment

---

[180] See para **[1.082]**

[181] See Gower, *Principles of Modern Company Law* (5th edn, Sweet & Maxwell, 1992) at pp 41–45 for a detailed account.

[182] Irish Anonymous Partnership Act 1781.

and would encourage work on projects such as railways, canals, and docks; it prevented prudent men from becoming members of unincorporated companies which were still popular among the rash and reckless; and it was in keeping with the idea of free trade which was then in vogue[183]. Despite these arguments, however, a Royal Commission, set up to review the prospects of limited liability, objected to its introduction in 1854[184].

[1.082] The privilege of limited liability for the members of a company incorporated under the Joint Stock Companies Act 1844 was finally granted by the Limited Liability Act 1855. Even if it had not been introduced by statute, the principle would probably have developed as a matter of contract[185]. In *Hallett v Dowdall*[186], the Court of Exchequer upheld the validity of a clause in a deed of settlement which purported to create limited liability for the members of a joint stock company, and held that the clause could be binding on third parties with express notice of it. The widespread use and acceptance of such clauses may have accounted for a change in opinion in favour of limited liability[187]. The Limited Liability Act 1855 provided that the liability of the members of a company would be limited to the amount, if any, unpaid on shares held by them. Limited liability was not lightly granted by Parliament, and certain conditions were imposed upon this legislative gift, such as the requirements that the company should have at least 25 members who between them held at least 75% of the nominal value[188] of the company, each member having paid up at least 20% of the nominal value of his shares; that the word 'limited' be included in the company's name; and that the deed of settlement itself provided that the liability of the members should be limited.

(g) The Joint Stock Companies Act 1856

[1.083] The Joint Stock Companies Act 1844 and the Limited Liability Act 1855 were both repealed and replaced by a single Act, the Joint Stock Companies Act 1856. This new Act did away with the two-stage registration process and required every company registering under the Act to simply present a memorandum and articles of association in the same form as required today. Only seven persons were required to act as signatories to a memorandum of association. Model articles of association were set out in the schedule to the Act. As Gower[189] points out, the provisions of the Act mark the heyday of *laissez faire*, allowing both incorporation and limited liability for the members of joint stock companies, without imposing the restraints contained in the Act of 1855. The only real safeguards were that the word 'limited' be used in the name of the company, and that the directors would incur personal liability if they paid a dividend knowing that the company was insolvent. The Joint Stock Companies Act 1856 is the forerunner of our modern Companies Acts, containing most of the primary concepts which have shaped our company law today.

---

183 See Farrar, Furey & Hannigan, *Farrar's Company Law* (3rd edn, Butterworths, 1991) at p 20.

184 1854 BPP Vol XXVII.

185 Maitland, *Collected Papers* (1911, Fisher (ed)), vol III, 'Trust and Corporation' at p 392. See Farrar, Furey & Hannigan, *Farrar's Company Law* (3rd edn, Butterworths, 1991) at p 21.

186 *Hallett v Dowdall* (1852) 21 LJ QB 98.

187 See Farrar, Furey & Hannigan, *Farrar's Company Law* (3rd edn, Butterworths, 1991) p 82.

188 The total nominal values of the shares which the company was authorised to issue by its deed of settlement.

189 Gower, *Principles of Modern Company Law* (5th edn, Sweet & Maxwell, 1992) at p 46.

(h) The Companies Act 1862

[1.084] Subsequent developments in the history of company law belong to modern company law, and may be dealt with more briefly. The first piece of legislation to carry the principles embodied in the Joint Stock Companies Act 1856 through to our modern companies' legislation was also the first in a long line of 'Companies Acts'; namely the Companies Act 1862. This Act consolidated all previous Joint Stock Companies Acts, giving rise to the 'first great consolidation Act concerning companies [which] was a masterpiece of draughtsmanship and arrangement and, apart therefrom, introduced a number of amendments'[190]. The amendments included the introduction of companies limited by guarantee and unlimited companies, as well as detailed provisions on the winding up of registered companies.

(i) The Companies Act 1907

[1.085] The Companies Act 1907 was the enactment that first introduced the private company[191]. Under the heading of '*Miscellaneous*', s 37(1) of the Companies Act 1907 ('CA 1907') created and defined the private company as follows:

> 'For the purposes of the Act the expression 'private company' means a company which by its articles –
>
> (a) restricts the right to transfer its shares; and
>
> (b) limits the number of its members (exclusive of persons who are in the employment of the company) to fifty; and
>
> (c) prohibits any invitation to the public to subscribe for any shares or debentures of the company.'

The statutory definition of the private company has changed little over the years. The only differences are first, that today, ex-employees are also discounted in determining the number of members in the company; second, the number of permitted members has been increased to 99; third, all private companies must have a share capital (although this was implicit under s 37(1) of the CA 1907); and fourth, today, certain offers or invitations for debentures are expressly excluded from the prohibition, a fact that has permitted private companies to list certain debt instruments[192].

(j) The Companies (Consolidation) Act 1908

[1.086] The Companies (Consolidation) Act 1908 was a consolidating enactment of major significance to Ireland in that it was the last major piece of company legislation which we have had in common with English law. As Keane has observed, this Act formed the bedrock of company law for Irish lawyers for over half a century. The definition afforded to private companies by s 37 of the CA 1907 was reproduced by s 121(1) of the Companies (Consolidation) Act 1908.

---

190 See Schmitthoff (ed), *Palmer's Company Law* (24th edn, Sweet & Maxwell, 1987) at para 2-09.

191 Strongly instrumental in the introduction of private companies was Sir Francis Beaufort Palmer. See generally Ireland, 'The Triumph of the Company Legal Form, 1856-1914', in Adams (ed), *Essays for Clive Schmitthoff* (1983, Professional Books).

192 Section 33 of the CA 1963 was substituted by s 7 of the IFCMPA 2006 with retrospective effect from 1 July 2005.

[1.087] From the foregoing analysis it may be seen that today's registered company is a response to a number of significant developments in the period 1700–1908. In particular, it accorded corporate personality to provide, *inter alia*, a means by which actions against large associations of undertakings may conveniently be pursued. It was also observed that the concept of limited liability was introduced only in the last century[193]; and that it is not necessarily an incident of corporate personality[194]. Furthermore, the registered company is accorded corporate status through the medium of the Companies Acts because corporate personality is a concession which may be granted only by the State[195].

It remains now to examine how the registered company has been treated in Ireland since the foundation of the State in 1922.

[C] AN OVERVIEW OF IRISH COMPANY LAW

Irish company law statutes from independence to 1963[196]

[1.088] The first step towards company law reform taken by the Irish government after independence was the establishment of a committee to investigate the law and procedure relating to bankruptcy and the winding up of companies. This committee reported in 1927 but the government of the day and succeeding governments took no steps to implement its recommendations. In particular, no legislation equivalent to the English 1929 and 1948 Companies Acts was passed in Ireland in this period.

[1.089] The most important committee established during this period was the Cox Committee on Company Law Reform, established in 1951[197]. This committee, chaired by Arthur Cox, reported in 1958. The secretary of the committee was Mr Justice John Kenny whose judicial career and influence on Irish company law has been profound. Some of the issues considered by the Cox Committee were the following:

Company accounts – It was recommended that the essential difference between the public and private company be recognised when implementing any new provisions regarding disclosure of accounts. In particular, the committee recommended, and the CA 1963 later provided, that the exemption from filing accounts in the case of private companies should continue. Any difficulties to creditors were considered to be offset by the enormous inconvenience which would otherwise be caused to small businesses incorporated as private companies[198].

Winding-up provisions – The committee made two recommendations, neither of which was implemented by the legislature. The first concerned the creation of a new office, that of Official Receiver, a position analogous to that of the Official Assignee in Bankruptcy. The second recommendation was that debts owed to the Revenue

---

193 See para **[1.082]**

194 See generally, Ch 4, *Incorporation and its Consequences*.

195 See paras **[1.060]** to **[1.070]**.

196 See Keane, *Company Law* (4th edn, Bloomsbury Professional, 2007), at Ch 2.

197 Report of the Company Law Reform Committee (1958).

198 It is interesting to note that the *Task Force Report on Small Business* which reported in March of 1994 recommended (at pp 133–134) the abolition of the requirement that certain small companies must have their accounts audited. This change was finally introduced into Irish law by the C(A)(No2)A 1999.

Commissioners ought *not* to have priority over debts owed by the company to other unsecured creditors. Again this was not accepted or implemented by the legislature.

Corporate capacity – The committee sought to obviate the effects of the doctrine of *ultra vires*. The doctrine provides that transactions not authorised by a company's objects clause are beyond the capacity of a company and are unenforceable and void, to the obvious detriment of outsiders unaware of the lack of corporate capacity. The committee's suggestion that the effects of the doctrine be curtailed by extending protection to *bona fide* outsiders was in fact accepted by the legislature in the CA 1963[199].

The committee also reported on many other aspects of Irish company law, and although some recommendations were not implemented by the CA 1963, much of what was recommended eventually became law under the subsequent Acts.

The Companies Acts

[1.090] The Companies Acts are the concern of this work. In all, there are at present sixteen Companies Acts. These Acts are now reviewed briefly and the main reasons for their enactment identified.

(a) The Companies Act 1963

[1.091] The Companies Act 1963 ('CA 1963') remains the principal Companies Act in Ireland today, albeit an ever increasingly tattered and piecemeal statement of the law. Since 1977 the CA 1963 has continually been amended and although it contains some 399 sections, the other fifteen Companies Acts, together, contain some 752 sections of legislation. The need for a consolidating Act is now greater than ever in that the fifteen amending Acts of the Oireachtas and numerous statutory instruments have substantially changed the CA 1963 and, following the Company Law Review Group's recommendations,[200] work is underway on the Companies Bill, likely to be published in 2012.

(b) The Companies (Amendment) Act 1977

[1.092] The Companies (Amendment) Act 1977 ('C(A)A 1977') was designed to simplify certain activities connected with stock exchange transactions by companies. This introduced more streamlined procedures in relation to the transfer of shares in public companies.

(c) The Companies (Amendment) Act 1982

[1.093] The Companies (Amendment) Act 1982 ('C(A)A 1982') may best be considered as a work of domestic housekeeping. This Act was concerned with a wide variety of matters: procedural issues in the registration of companies, striking inactive companies off the register of companies, the exception of certain professional partnerships from the numerical constraints on membership imposed by the CA 1963 on partnerships generally and a number of other miscellaneous matters.

---

199 See generally, Ch 7, *Corporate Contracts: Capacity and Authority*, at para **[7.080]** *et seq*.

200 See para **[1.168]**.

(d) The Companies (Amendment) Act 1983[201]

[1.094] The Companies (Amendment) Act 1983 ('C(A)A 1983') owes its introduction not to any particularly conscientious domestic legislative concern, but rather to Ireland's membership of the European Union ('EU'). This Act gave effect to the Second EU Directive on Company Law, the main concern of which was the levels of capitalisation of public companies[202]. Whilst the Act has prominence in this and other texts on Irish company law, many of its provisions are solely applicable to public limited companies. It is the C(A)A 1983 which introduced the term 'public limited company' or 'PLC' and imposed certain basic restrictions on both the formation and continuance of public companies.

(e) The Companies (Amendment) Act 1986

[1.095] Again, the Companies (Amendment) Act 1986 ('C(A)A 1986') owes its existence more to EU harmonisation than it does to national creativity. The C(A)A 1986 gives effect to the Fourth EU Directive on Company Law which concerns annual accounts. One consequence of the 1986 Act was to eschew, on EU insistence, the philosophy of the Cox Committee which considered it too onerous that *all* companies, even small private companies, should publish accounts. This Act provides that both public and private companies must publish accounts. However, private companies were considered a special category and were broken down into three sizes: small, medium and large, each with progressive disclosure requirements. Corporate accounts are considered later in the context of both the private company[203] and the public company[204]. The Fourth EU Directive on Company Law is noted later in this chapter[205].

(f) The Companies (Amendment) Act 1990

[1.096] The Companies (Amendment) Act 1990 ('C(A)A 1990') was most definitely a domestically motivated enactment, albeit prompted by Middle Eastern influences[206], passed by a legislature which feared that were it not brought into law, dire economic consequences would befall Ireland's largest beef company, the Goodman Group. When fear turned to an immediate danger that the group might face liquidation, it was decided to hive off what had been a Part of the Companies Bill 1987[207] and to enact it as the C(A)A 1990.

[1.097] The essence of the C(A)A 1990 is that companies which are in financial difficulties can be given a chance to have their affairs reorganised by an individual, termed an 'examiner', whose principal task is to report to the court on the company's prospects of survival. During the period of the examinership, the company is under the protection of the court and its creditors cannot enforce their claims against the company. Often the examiner's proposals will involve compromising some or all of the creditors'

201 See generally, Forde, 'The Companies (Amendment) Act 1983' (1983) 18 Ir Jur (ns) 289.

202 See para **[1.114]** *et seq*.

203 See Ch 17, *Financial Statements, Audit & Annual Return*.

204 See Ch 29, *Public Limited Companies and SEs*, at para **[29.115]** *et seq*.

205 See para **[1.116]**.

206 See generally, McCormack, *The New Companies Legislation* (1991) at p 185 *et seq*. See also Ch 23, *Examinerships*.

207 This was previously Part IX of the Companies (No 2) Bill 1990.

claims against the company. The C(A)A 1990 gives the court a discretion to confirm such proposals. The desired result is that through the reduction of creditors' claims, the company will be given an opportunity to continue to trade, hopefully back to full financial health.

(g) The Companies Act 1990

[1.098] The Companies Act 1990 ('CA 1990') also owes its existence to domestic concerns that although the CA 1963 had proved to be a successful piece of legislation it needed a radical overhaul. Circumstances and business practices had so changed that it was considered necessary that the Oireachtas should take cognisance of these developments and enact a statute to address such commercial changes.

[1.099] The CA 1990 has 262 sections and is comprised of thirteen Parts[208]. That it is a substantial piece of legislation in its own right is seen in its title since it is the first Act since the CA 1963 not to use the label 'Amendment'. The main provisions of the CA 1990 are as follows:

- Part II replaced the provisions of the CA 1963 which govern the investigation of companies through the appointment of an *inspector*. These provisions have been tested by a number of *cause célèbres* cases, such as the so-called Telecom Affair, considered later[209].
- Part III imposed restrictions on corporate transactions with directors. The measures provided in Part III have proven to be one of the most far reaching series of provisions contained in the Act. Of considerable importance is the application of these provisions to *shadow directors*.
- Part IV imposed certain requirements in respect of the disclosure of certain persons' interests in shares held in companies.
- Part V introduced into Irish company law the concept of *insider dealing*, which had been part of company law in England for many years. In brief terms, Part V criminalises and provides civil redress where certain persons make use of information which they have acquired because of their intimate connection with a public company to make a profit[210].
- Part VI amended some of the provisions of the CA 1963 which concern the winding up of companies. In particular, the statutory declaration as to the solvency of a company in a members' voluntary winding up was substantially bolstered, having the effect of inevitably reducing the number of members' voluntary windings up which occur where the company is in fact *not solvent*[211].
- Part VII concerns the imposition of *restrictions* and *disqualifications* on persons acting as directors of a company, principally where a company becomes insolvent and goes into liquidation. The measures were intended to counteract the so-called *phoenix syndrome* whereby a company which is wound

208 See generally, *McCormack, The New Companies Legislation* (1991).

209 See generally Ch 27, *Investigations and Inspectors*.

210 See Ch 32, *Prospectus, Market Abuse and Transparency Law*, at para **[32.093]**.

211 See Ch 23, *Winding-Up Companies* and Ch 25, *Realisation and Distribution of Assets in a Winding Up*.

up is reincarnated by virtue of the involvement in a later company of persons who were directors or shadow directors of the company wound up[212].

- Part VIII revamped the law on *receivers* and imposed a number of restrictions on both their appointment and their powers[213].
- Part IX amends the Companies (Amendment) Act 1990 relating to the placing of companies under the protection of the court.

(h) The Companies (Amendment) Act 1999

[1.100] The Companies (Amendment) Act 1999 ('C(A)A 1999') is a short, mono-purpose Act of seven sections and one Schedule. It was enacted to permit stabilisation activity in relation to the issue or sale of securities and was considered to be needed in the context of the floatation of what was Bord Telecom, subsequently, Eircom plc.

(i) The Companies (Amendment) (No 2) Act 1999

[1.101] The Companies (Amendment) (No 2) Act 1999 ('C(A)(No2)A 1999') gave effect to certain recommendations that had been made as a result of an initiative by the then Minister for Enterprise and Employment, Mr Ruairí Quinn, who had established a group to review a number of provisions in company law. The group published its report in February 1995 but for many years its recommendations gathered dust[214]. It was not until the passing of the C(A)(No2)A 1999 that effect was eventually given to most of the recommendations under two particular headings – those on examinership and those on an exemption from audit for small companies[215]. In addition, as a result of great political concern over the use of Irish companies by unscrupulous foreign concerns, the C(A)(No2)A 1999 also sounded the death-knell for the so-called *Irish registered non-resident company* or 'IRNR'[216]. The C(A)(No2)A 1999 has 54 sections and two Schedules.

(j) The Company Law Enforcement Act 2001

[1.102] The Company Law Enforcement Act 2001 ('CLEA 2001') is a very substantial piece of legislation, running to 114 sections and one Schedule. The 2001 Act arose directly from the recommendations of the Working Group on Company Law Compliance and Enforcement, chaired by Michael McDowell SC. This working group was established in September 1998 by the Tánaiste and then Minister for Jobs, Enterprise and Innovation, Mary Harney. Its establishment was in response to a growing concern that companies were being abused by the unscrupulous and that compliance with the requirements in the Companies Acts, particularly relating to the filing of documents, was unacceptably low[217]. One of the most significant provisions in the CLEA 2001 is the creation of the Office of the Director of Corporate Enforcement ('ODCE'). Other major changes introduced included: changes to the law relating to

[212] See Ch 13, *Corporate Governance: Management by the Directors*.

[213] See Ch 20, *Corporate Borrowing: Receivers*.

[214] See Courtney, *Company Law Review 1995* (1996, Round Hall Sweet & Maxwell) at pp 1–13.

[215] See further Ch 22, *Examinerships* and Ch 17, *Financial Statements, Audit and Annual Return*, respectively.

[216] See Ch 2, *Incorporation by Registration*, at para **[2.045]**.

[217] See, generally, Ch 28, *Company Law Compliance and Enforcement*.

investigations, changes to the law relating to the restriction and disqualification of directors, changes to the law on winding up, etc.

(k) The Companies (Auditing and Accounting) Act 2003

[1.103] While the primary impetus for the Companies (Auditing and Accounting) Act 2003 ('C(A&A)A 2003') was *The Report of the Review Group on Auditing* ('RGA') published in 2000, its origins can be traced back to the Report of the Comptroller and Auditor General in July 1999 into the administration of deposit interest retention tax (known as 'DIRT') undertaken at the behest of the Dáil's Public Accounts Committee ('PAC'). That report found that the evasion of DIRT by taxpayers was widespread and facilitated by credit institutions to the knowledge of relevant State authorities. Perceived deficiencies in the auditing of credit institutions was identified as facilitating the evasion of tax. The PAC held its own enquiry and heard oral evidence, and in a report concluded that the Department of Jobs, Enterprise and Innovation should establish a review group to identify key issues relating to the regulation and practice of auditing. The Department's response was to establish the RGA chaired by Senator Joe O'Toole which reported in July 2000. The RGA made 80 recommendations dealing with the self-regulation of the accountancy bodies, auditors' independence, the auditing of financial institutions and compliance by auditors and directors with the Companies Acts and other enactments. The legislation enacted to give effect to the RGA's recommendations was the C(A&A)A 2003.

[1.104] One of the most significant effects of the C(A&A)A 2003 was the establishment of the Irish Auditing and Accounting Supervisory Authority ("IAASA") whose principal objects are the supervision of how accountancy bodies regulate and monitor their members, promoting adherence to high professional standards in auditing and accountancy and monitoring whether the accounts of certain classes of companies and other undertakings comply with the Companies Acts.

[1.105] The C(A&A)A 2003 also revised the qualifications for appointment of auditors, increased the thresholds so that more companies could avail of the exemption from audit introduced by the C(A)(No2)A 1999, the disclosure of companies' accounting policies and material departure from applicable standards, disclosure of non-audit remuneration to auditors and many other miscellaneous changes. Two of the provisions (the requirement that certain companies should establish audit committees and that directors of certain companies should be require to provide annual compliance statements which should be reviewed by auditors) were never commenced.

(l) The Investment Funds, Companies and Miscellaneous Provisions Act 2005

[1.106] The main changes to company law[218] introduced by the Investment Funds, Companies and Miscellaneous Provisions Act 2005 ('IFCMPA 2005') were to the law relating to market abuse and prospectuses. It also amends the law relating to investment companies (in Part 3) and makes miscellaneous other changes to company law (in Part 6).

[218] This is the first of two Acts passed in 2005 and 2006 which were not exclusively concerned with company law and Parts 2 and 7 contain non-company law provisions.

Part 4 of the IFCMPA 2005 is an example of the so-called 'Lamfalussy approach' to legislation involving four levels of implementation, and makes the enabling provisions necessary in primary law to facilitate the transposition in secondary legislation[219] of the EU Market Abuse Directive and related directives.

Part 5 of the IFCMPA 2005 approaches the law relating to public offers of securities and prospectuses in a similar manner by amending the CA 1963 to facilitate the transposition of the EU Directive dealing with prospectuses in secondary legislation[220].

(m) The Investment Funds, Companies and Miscellaneous Provisions Act 2006

[1.107] The Investment Funds, Companies and Miscellaneous Provisions Act 2006 Act ('IFCMPA 2006') introduced miscellaneous change to the Companies Acts including changes relating to statutory declarations made under the Companies Acts, the definition of private company, the audit exemption, the restriction of directors, etc. It also followed the IFCMPA 2005 in facilitating the effective transposition of an EU directive, and Part 3 of the IFCMPA 2006 made the enabling provisions necessary in primary law to facilitate the transposition in secondary legislation[221] of the EU Transparency Directive (2004/109/EC) on the harmonisation of requirements to disclose information about issuers whose securities are admitted to trading on a regulated market.

(n) The Companies (Amendment) Act 2009

[1.108] The Companies (Amendment) Act 2009 ('C(A)A 2009') was very much motivated by national concerns. It is essentially compliance and enforcement motivated and is designed to improve the disclosure of loans to directors of licensed banks after it came to light that significant loans had been made to the chairman and former CEO of Anglo Irish Bank Corporation plc (as it was known before it was nationalised) which had not been disclosed in its financial statements because of the existence of certain exemptions for companies holding a banking licence. In addition to amending Part III of the CA 1990, the opportunity was taken also to bolster the ODCE's powers.

(o) The Companies (Miscellaneous Provisions) Act 2009

[1.109] The Companies (Miscellaneous Provisions) Act 2009 ('C(MP)A 2009') made a number of miscellaneous changes to the Companies Acts but its primary purpose was to facilitate Irish holding companies formed by US multinational corporate groups which migrated their headquarters from other locations such as Caymen or Bermuda to use US Generally Accepted Accounting Principles ('GAAP') (instead of Irish GAAP or IFRS) in the preparation of their Companies Acts accounts. This concession is strictly circumscribed with conditions and is designed to facilitate US companies during the period before US companies switch to IFRS.

---

[219] See the Market Abuse (Directive 2003/6/EC) Regulations 2005 (SI 342/2005) and the Central Bank's *Market Abuse Rules* (February 2012).

[220] See the Prospectus (Directive 2003/71/EC) Regulations 2005 (SI 324/2005) and the Central Bank's *Prospectus Rules* (December 2011).

[221] See the Transparency (Directive 2004/109/EC) Regulations 2007 (SI 277/2007) and the Central Bank's *Transparency Rules* (September 2009).

(p) The Companies (Amendment) Act 2012

[1.110] The Companies (Amendment) Act 2012 ('C(A)A 2012') provides for the extension of the use of US GAAP provided for in the C(MP)A 2009 by companies utilising these provisions from financial years ending at the latest on 31 December 2015, until financial years ending at the latest on 31 December 2020. The restriction on the use by a relevant parent undertaking of this facility to four years is also removed.

The European Community dimension to the development of Irish company law

[1.111] Since Ireland's accession to the European Union in 1973, company law in Ireland has been reformed as part of the overall harmonisation of the company law of all Member States. Community law has four major sources:

- The Treaty of Rome;
- Regulations of the Council of Ministers;
- Directives of Council;
- Case law of the European Court of Justice.

[1.112] Harmonisation in general is addressed by Article 100 of the Treaty of Rome, and Article 54(3) is specifically concerned with the harmonisation of company law in Member States[222]. Harmonisation is achieved by *Directives* passed by the European Council which must be implemented by the domestic national law of each Member State. Domestic implementation of EU directives is usually achieved by Ministerial Regulations, in the form of statutory instruments. In addition, the European Council has taken on the task of the harmonisation of company law in EU Member States, through the adoption of certain *Council Regulations*. Council regulations have direct effect in Member States and no not need to be transcribed into domestic law although they are frequently accompanied by a statutory instrument to assist in their interpretation, application or to provide prescribed forms. The result of these directives has been the *ad hoc* and piecemeal reform of Irish company law[223].

(a) First Directive – disclosure, validity and nullity[224]

[1.113] The First EU Directive on Company law, adopted on 9 March 1968, was implemented in Ireland by the European Communities (Companies) Regulations 1973[225] ('EC(C)R 1973'), and is discussed in Chapter 7[226]. The underlying purposes are threefold. The first is the protection of persons who deal with a company which is not properly registered and is consequently a *nullity*. Second is the protection of persons who deal with a company unaware that the company does not have the *capacity* to enter the transaction in question. Third is the protection of persons who enter into transactions

---

[222] See, generally, Looijestijn & O'Keeffe, 'Harmonisation of Company Law in an Expanding European Union' (2002) 9 CLP 9.

[223] For a comprehensive analysis of all directives and conventions of the EC affecting company law, see generally, Myles, *EEC Law Brief* (Locksley Press Ltd) vol 2.

[224] (68/151/EEC) OJ Special Edition 1968(1) pp 41–45.

[225] SI 163/1973.

[226] See Ch 7, *Corporate Contracts: Capacity and Authority.*

with officers who do not have the requisite *authority*. Since by s 5(4) of the C(A)A 1983[227] the certificate of incorporation of a company is conclusive evidence that the requirements of registration have been complied with, it was considered unnecessary to amend the law to address the question of nullity. Accordingly, SI 163/1973 only considered the questions of disclosure, capacity and authority (validity). The First Company Law Directive was amended by Directive 2003/58/EC and those changes were given effect to by SI 49/2007 which amended SI 163/1973[228]. Directive 2009/101/EC of the European Parliament and of the Council of 16 September 2009 codified the First Company Law Directive and the amendments made to it.

(b) Second Directive – capital requirements of PLCs[229]

[1.114] The Second Company Law Directive, adopted on 13 December 1976, was implemented in Ireland by the C(A)A 1983 which created the *public limited company*, or 'PLC' and provided that it must meet certain capital requirements[230]. The changes made to the Second Company Law Directive by Directive 2006/68/EC of the European Parliament of 6 September 2006 were given effect to in Ireland by statutory instrument[231].

(c) Third Directive – national mergers of PLCs[232]

[1.115] The Third Company Law Directive, adopted on 9 October 1978, was implemented in Ireland by the European Community (Mergers and Divisions of Companies) Regulations 1987 ('EC(M&D)R 1987')[233]. The directive is concerned with the merger of PLCs *within* Member States, as opposed to *between* Member States, a topic which is addressed by the Cross-Border Mergers Directive[234]. This directive was amended by Directive 2007/63/EC of the European Parliament and of the Council of 13 November 2007 and the changes to the 1987 Regulations were made by another statutory instrument[235].

(d) Fourth Directive – annual corporate accounts[236]

[1.116] The Fourth Company Law Directive, adopted on 25 July 1978, was implemented in Ireland by the C(A)A 1986[237]. The directive imposes varying disclosure requirements on most companies. Now, in addition to an annual return, accounts must also be filed with the CRO. The classification of a company as being either a PLC or a

---

227 The conclusiveness of the certificate of incorporation was previously provided for in s 19 of the CA 1963. See generally, Ch 4, *Incorporation and its Consequences*, at para **[4.004]** *et seq*.

228 See Ch 2, *Incorporation by Registration*, at para **[2.043]** *et seq*.

229 (77/91/EEC) 20 OJ, L 26, 31 January 1977, pp 1–13.

230 See Ch 29, *Public Limited Companies and SEs*, at para **[29.011]**.

231 See the European Communities (Public Limited Companies – Directive 2006/68/EC) Regulations 2008 (SI 89/2008).

232 (78/855/EEC) 21 OJ, L 295, 20 October 1978, pp 36–43.

233 SI 137/1987.

234 Directive 2005/56/EC. See para **[1.123]**.

235 See the European Communities (Mergers and Divisions of Companies) (Amendment) Regulations 2008 (SI 572/2008).

236 (78/660/EEC) 21 OJ L 22, 14 August 1978, pp 11–31.

237 See Ch 17, *Financial Statements, Audit and Annual Return*.

large, medium or small sized private company, dictates what is required to be delivered to the CRO. It is understood that the Fourth Directive is being revisited with a view to modernisation.

(e) Sixth Directive – division of PLCs[238]

[1.117] The Sixth Company Law Directive, adopted on 17 December 1982, was implemented in Ireland by EC(M&D)R 1987, considered above[239].

(f) Seventh Directive – corporate consolidated accounts[240]

[1.118] The Seventh Company Law Directive, adopted on 13 June 1983, was implemented by the European Communities (Companies: Group Accounts) Regulations 1992 ('EC(C:GA)R 1992')[241]. It is concerned with the availability of information to the public on the finances of companies and the harmonisation of national legislation on the consolidated accounts of company groups. The regulations provide that all companies which have '*subsidiary undertakings*', as defined[242], must prepare group accounts. The format and content of accounts and reports are also set out in the regulations[243]. It is understood that the Seventh Directive is being revisited with a view to modernisation.

(g) Eighth Directive – corporate auditors[244]

[1.119] The Eighth Company Law Directive deals with the professional integrity, independence and qualifications of corporate auditors. The focus is upon the harmonisation of the qualifications of auditors, so that in Member States there will be a basic minimum standard for *approved persons*, who can be auditors. The substance of the original directive was implemented into Irish law by the CA 1990[245]. Directive 2006/43/EC of the European Parliament and of the Council of 17 May 2006 repealed the original Eighth Directive and amended Council Directives 78/660/EEC and 83/349/EEC and has been implemented in Ireland by European Communities (Statutory Audits) (Directive 2006/43/EC) Regulations 2010 ('EC(SA)(D)R 2010')[246].

(h) Eleventh Directive – disclosure by branches[247]

[1.120] The Eleventh Company Law Directive was implemented into Irish law by the European Communities (Branch Disclosures) Regulations 1993 ('EC(BD)R 1993')[248]. Its objective is to facilitate the right to establishment contained in the Treaty of Rome by enabling limited companies to establish branches in other Member States. This directive

---

238 (82/891/EEC) 25 OJ, L 378 31 December 1982, pp 47–54.

239 See para **[1.115]**.

240 (83/349/EEC) 26 OJ, L 193, 18 July 1983, pp 1–17.

241 SI 201/1992.

242 See generally, Ch 12, *Groups of Companies*, at para **[12.031]**.

243 See generally, Ch 17, *Financial Statements, Audit and Annual Return*.

244 (84/253/EEC) 27 OJ, L 126, 12 May 1984, pp 20–26.

245 See, generally, Ch 17, *Financial Statements, Audit and Annual Return*.

246 SI 220/2010.

247 32 OJ 1989, L 395, 30 December 1989.

248 SI 395/1993. See Ch 34, *External Companies and Branches*. SI 100/1994, the Companies (Forms) Order 1994, prescribes the forms to be used for the return of information under Part XI of the CA 1963 and the EC(BD)R 1993.

has limited application to the vast majority of Irish companies which do not operate outside of Ireland, but is very important in practice as many foreign limited companies from outside of the State have opened branches in Ireland[249].

(i) Twelfth Directive – single member private companies[250]

[1.121] The Twelfth Company Law Directive had a significant impact on Irish company law. It was adopted on 21 December 1989 and was implemented by the European Communities (Single-Member Private Limited Companies) Regulations 1994 ('EC(SMPLC)R 1994')[251]. The regulations were signed by the Minister for Jobs, Enterprise and Innovation on 8 September 1994 and took effect from 1 October 1994. The single-member private company is considered below[252]. The Twelfth Directive was codified by Directive 2009/102/EC of the European Parliament and of the Council of 16 September 2009.

(j) Directive 2004/25/EC – takeover bids

[1.122] Directive 2004/25/EC, sometimes referred to as the 'Thirteenth Directive', of the European Parliament and of the Council of 21 April 2004 was transposed into Irish law by statutory instrument in 2006[253] which amended the Takeover Rules made under the Irish Takeover Panel Act 1997 and substitute provisions of s 204 of the CA 1963 in relation to companies admitted to trading on a regulated market.

(k) Directive 2005/56/EC – cross-border mergers

[1.123] Directive 2005/56/EC – cross-border mergers was transposed in Ireland by statutory instrument in 2008[254] and operates to facilitate the merger of limited companies (public and private) located in different Member States. Since its transposition, there have been a steady number of cross-border mergers both into and out of the State utilising this directive.

(l) Directive 2007/36/EC – shareholders' rights

[1.124] Directive 2007/36/EC – shareholders' rights of the European Parliament and of the Council of 11 July 2007 was transposed in Ireland by statutory instrument in 2009[255] which effected a number of significant amendments to the CA 1963 in relation to general meetings of companies that have shares traded on a regulated market[256].

---

249 See Ch 34, *External Companies and Branches*, at para **[34.027]** *et seq*.

250 (89/667/EEC) 32 OJ 1989, L 395/40, 30 December 1989. See generally, MacCann, 'Company Law Reform: One Man Companies' (1990) ILT 166.

251 SI 275/1994.

252 See para **[1.143]** *et seq*.

253 See the European Communities (Takeover Bids (Directive 2004/25/EC) Regulations 2006 (SI 255/2006).

254 See the European Communities (Cross-Border Mergers) Regulations 2008 (SI 157/2008).

255 See the Shareholders' Rights (Directive 2007/36/EC) Regulations 2009 (SI 316/2009).

256 See Ch 29, *Public Limited Companies and SEs*, at para **[29.099]** *et seq*.

(m) Council Regulation (EEC) 2137/85 – European economic interest groupings

[1.125] European economic interest groupings ('EEIGs') are associations in contemplation of commerce which involve an aggregate of sole traders, partnerships or bodies corporate, at least one being from a *different* Member State to the others, with a view to pooling knowledge and resources in areas where they have a common interest[257]. This continental creature appears to have been conceived from the spirited passion of European union. Such is evidenced by the fact that the primary intention of EEIGs is not to generate an economic profit, but rather to enhance the marketing of products and the stimulation of research and development. It should be noted that the making of profit is not prohibited. EEIGs are capable of being formed in Ireland by virtue of the regulation which was facilitated in domestic Irish law by the European Community (European Economic Interest Grouping) Regulations 1989[258]. As at 31 December 2010, 24 EEIGs had been registered in Ireland[259]. Although similar in many respects to our own partnership, unlike a partnership, once formed it becomes a body corporate, possessing many of the usual traits of such entities. The constitution of an EEIG is quite similar to that of a registered company in that its members are bound by its constitutional documentation which takes the form of a contract between the parties who come together.

(n) Council Regulation (EC) 2157/2001 – statute for a European company (SE)

[1.126] Terms for the creation of a European public limited liability company or *Societas Europaea* ('SE') were finally agreed by Member States on 8 October 2001, with the passing of the EU Council Regulation on the Statute for a European Company (SE)[260]. Whilst as a Council Regulation it had direct effect since 8 October 2004, its implementation in Ireland was assisted by a statutory instrument enacted in 2007[261]. There are now a number of SEs registered in Ireland and the law applicable to this type of entity is considered in Ch 29[262].

(o) The EU Insolvency Regulations

[1.127] The draft Convention on Bankruptcy, Winding up, Arrangements, Compositions and Similar Proceedings[263] was superseded by the EU Council Regulation on Insolvency

[257] See Keane, *Company Law* (4th edn, Bloomsbury Professional, 2007) at para 3.23.

[258] SI 191/1989.

[259] *Companies Registration Office Report, 2011* at p 10.

[260] Council Regulation (EC) No 2157/2001 of 8 October 2001 on the Statute for a European company (SE).

[261] See the European Communities (European Public Limited Liability Company) Regulations 2007 (SI 21/2007); the European Communities (European Public Limited Liability Company) (Forms) Regulations 2007 (SI 22/2007); and, in relation to employee participation, the European Communities (European Public Limited Liability Company) (Employee Involvement) Regulations 2007 (SI 623/2006).

[262] See Ch 29, *Public Limited Companies and SEs*, at para **[29.150]** *et seq*.

[263] See Myles, *EEC Law Brief* (Locksley Press Ltd), 'Co Law – Bankruptcy Convention'.

Proceedings[264]. Being a Council Regulation, this applies directly but incidental and optional matters will be implemented into domestic law, most likely by regulation. The primary effect of this regulation is the recognition of other Member States' insolvency proceedings and liquidators across the EU. These regulations are considered further in Ch 24[265].

[D] The Private Company

Private companies and public companies

[1.128] The socio-legal relations underlying many private companies are often vastly different from those that prevail in public companies. Notwithstanding this, it is the one body of law contained in the Companies Acts that governs the legal structure of all companies[266].

[1.129] Although not all public companies will be public limited companies, it is the public limited company (PLC) – and more particularly, the *listed* PLC – that provides the greatest contrast with the private company[267]. The PLC is a company that is, by definition, *public*, in that its membership is largely comprised of the investing public. PLCs are widely rooted companies, in the sense that they will generally have many members who are otherwise unrelated to each other. The association of the members in a listed PLC will usually be the result of their subscription to a prospectus[268]or, alternatively, the result of their purchasing shares on the stock exchange. It usually follows that where the *shareholders* of the company are so widely dispersed they will be divorced from the *management* of the company. So, when the shareholders meet in *general meeting* and elect the directors the election will usually be carried on the basis of the professionalism of those put forward for such positions. The result is a genuine separation of powers between the shareholders and the directors. The shareholders do not usually have a direct say in the day-to-day management of the company, this task being left to the directors, who are accountable to the shareholders for the management of the company. There are surprisingly few PLCs registered in Ireland and no more than 100 PLCs with listed equity share capital.

[1.130] In marked contrast are the many thousands of *private companies* that make up the backbone of Irish commercial life. While it has a number of manifestations[269] the typical private company found in Ireland will not have the features described above. The *shareholders* of a private company will frequently be either the directors of the company

264 Council Regulation (EC) No 1346/2000 of 29 May 2000.

265 See Ch 24, *Liquidations*, at **[24.059]** *et seq*.

266 See para **[1.002]** and Ch 29, *Public Limited Companies and SEs,* where the public company and public limited company are treated and the essential differences between them and the private company are considered.

267 See para **[1.113]** *et seq* and Ch 29, *Public Limited Companies and SEs*.

268 A 'prospectus' is a document which invites the public to subscribe for shares in a new venture so as to give the promoters sufficient capital to launch the company: see Ch 32, *Prospectus, Market Abuse and Transparency Law*, at para **[32.006]**.

269 See para **[1.140]** for the *types* of private company and **[1.142]** *et seq*, for the *forms* which the private company may take.

or personally acquainted with the directors. They will often have decided to join the company because of personal connections. The *separation of powers* in many private companies will be frequently blurred because of the tendency for the shareholders and the directors to be the same persons. As we shall see later, this feature of the private company has given rise to the issue of the 'duality of roles'[270] which arises where the same people are obliged to carry out tasks in different capacities. This difference between private and public limited companies is even more stark when one considers that the single-member private limited company has, by definition, only one member. These features make for a very different model for corporate governance and accountability in private companies.

[1.131] It is important at the outset to distinguish standalone private companies from those which are subsidiaries[271]. Such private companies are controlled by a PLC or foreign holding company which will typically appoint the private company's directors. Often, these private companies are, in effect, puppets that are utilised to permit part of the group operation to be the subject of a more favourable statutory regime. One reason for PLCs to avail of private companies is to avoid full financial disclosure under the C(A)A 1986[272] but the most usual reason is to facilitate the creation of divisions or countrywide operations within a group.

Concessions to the private company

[1.132] Ever since their creation by the Companies Act 1907 the legislature has made certain concessions to private companies. Today's concessions include: only one member is required to form a private company whereas seven are required in the case of public companies; private companies do not need to file a statement *in lieu* of a prospectus; a private company does not need to obtain a trading certificate before commencing business; small and medium sized private companies are not required to file full accounts with the CRO; there is no minimum capitalisation requirement as in the case of public limited companies.

The private company defined

[1.133] Although the vast majority of companies formed and registered under the Companies Acts are *private companies*, the 'company' envisaged by those Acts is the *public company.* Ironically, by according the private company a specific definition, s 33(1) of the CA 1963 presupposes that the typical company will be the public company of which the private company is but a peculiar variation[273].

A company's internal affairs are governed by its articles of association. Part I of Table A of the First Schedule to the CA 1963 sets out the model articles of association for public companies limited by shares. Notwithstanding that the vast majority of companies registered in Ireland are private companies, Part II of Table A *applies* Part I, with a few modifications, to private companies limited by shares[274]. Although there is

---

270 See Ch 13, *Corporate Governance: Management by the Directors*, at para **[13.001]**.

271 See Schmitthoff (ed), *Palmer's Company Law,* (24th edn, 1987) at 4-06.

272 See Ch 17, *Financial Statements, Audit and Annual Return*.

273 Compare the position in the UK by s 1(3) of the Companies Act 1985 (UK).

274 See Ch 3, *Constitutional Documentation*, at para **[3.040]**.

little legal significance attaching to this, such provisions indicate that the private company originated as a legislative afterthought.

[1.134] Section 33(1) of the CA 1963, as substituted by the IFCMPA 2006[275], defines a private company as a company which *has a share capital* and which by its articles of association:

> '(a) restricts the right to transfer its shares, and
>
> (b) limits the number of its members to 99 or fewer persons[276], not including persons who are in the employment of the company and persons who, having been formerly in the employment of the company, were, while in that employment, and have continued after the determination of that employment to be members of the company, and
>
> (c) prohibits any invitation or offer to the public to subscribe for any shares, debentures or other securities of the company.'

To be a private company, a company must have a *share capital*[277]. Where two or more persons hold one or more shares in a company jointly, they shall, for the purposes of s 33, be treated as a 'single member': s 33(3) of the CA 1963.

[1.135] The need for a private company to restrict the right to transfer its shares is typically expressed in articles of association in the form provided for in reg 2(a) and 3 of Part II of Table A. Regulation 2(a) provides that the right to transfer shares is restricted 'in the manner hereinafter prescribed' and reg 3 then provides: 'The directors may, in their absolute discretion, and without assigning any reason therefor, decline to register any transfer of any share, whether or not it is a full paid share.' Section 33(1)(a) of the CA 1963 is sometimes taken as the basis for saying that a private company cannot issue share warrants or bearer shares but with careful drafting it may still be possible to provide for share warrants or bearer shares and still impose restrictions on transfer.

[1.136] Prior to the substitution of s 33, the prohibition in s 33(1)(c) was on any 'invitation to the public to subscribe for any shares or debentures of the company'. The new prohibition was broadened to include 'offers' as well as invitations, and 'securities' as well as shares and debentures. The reason was because the Department of Jobs, Enterprise and Innovation took a policy decision that where the Prospectus Directive did not regulate a particular invitation or offering of shares, debentures or securities then private companies should be able to make such invitations or offerings. The definition of private company was, therefore, amended and aligned to the Prospectus Directive. To avoid the necessity for every private company in the country to have to amend their articles of association, s 33(2) operates as a clever deeming measure, so that an old prohibition on invitations to subscribe for shares or debentures *shall be construed as* a prohibition on any invitation *or offer* to subscribe for any shares, debentures *or other securities*. Words or expressions used in s 33 have the same meaning as they have in the Prospectus Regulations[278].

---

275 Section 7 of the IFCMPA 2006 substituted s 33 with retrospective effect from 1 July 2005.

276 Section 33(2) of the CA 1963.

277 Contrast a private company defined by s 37(1) of the CA 1907 at para **[1.085]**.

278 Section 33(7) of the CA 1963, qualified by sub-s (8) which provides that the Prospectus Regulations (SI 324/2005) shall be construed as if reg 8 was omitted.

[1.137] One of the consequences of the redefinition of the private company is that private companies can now invite or offer the public to subscribe for (and list on the stock exchange) certain debt instruments. Section 33(5) provides that each of the following *offers of debentures* by a company, wheresoever made, shall not be regarded as falling within the prohibition in s 33(1)(c):

(a) an offer of debentures addressed solely to qualified investors,

(b) an offer of debentures addressed to fewer than 100 persons, other than qualified investors,

(c) an offer of debentures addressed to investors where the minimum consideration payable pursuant to the offer is at least €50,000 per investor, for each separate offer,

(d) an offer of debentures whose denomination per unit amounts to at least €50,000,

(e) an offer of debentures where the offer expressly limits the amount of the total consideration for the offer to less than €100,000,

(f) an offer of those classes of instruments which are normally dealt in on the money market (such as treasury bills, certificates of deposit and commercial papers) having a maturity of less than 12 months.

[1.138] In relation to offers of *shares*, s 33(6) provides that an offer by a company of any amount or wheresoever made that is addressed to:

(a) qualified investors, or

(b) 99 or fewer persons, or

(c) both qualified investors and 99 or fewer other persons

is not to be regarded as falling within sub-s (1)(c) or the provision of a company's articles referred to in sub-s (4)(b) of s 33 of the CA 1963.

[1.139] Where a private company's articles of association include the three provisions enumerated in s 33(1)(a)–(c) of the CA 1963 but the company defaults in complying with any of those provisions, s 34 of the CA 1963 provides that it shall cease to be entitled to the privileges and exemptions conferred on private companies under ss 36, 128(4), 213(d) and 215(a)(i) of the CA 1963. Moreover, ss 36, 128, 213 and 215 shall apply as if it were not a private company. Where the failure to comply was accidental or due to inadvertence or to some other sufficient cause or where on other grounds it is just and equitable to grant relief, the court may on the application of the company or any other person interested and on such terms and conditions as seem to the court just and expedient, 'order the company be relieved from the consequences referred to in subsection (1)'[279].

[1.140] The definition accorded a private company by s 33(1) of the CA 1963 permits the creation of three specific *types* of private company. These are:

(a) private companies limited by shares;

(b) private companies limited by guarantee and having a share capital; and

(c) private unlimited companies having a share capital[280].

---

279 Section 34(2) of the CA 1963.

280 It should be noted that for the purposes of the C(A)Act 1986, s 1(1) of the 1986 Act provides that except where the context otherwise requires, 'private company' does *not include an unlimited company.*

Of course the articles of association of all three types of private company must contain the restrictions set out in s 33(1) of the CA 1963. The crucial mark of a private company, apart from the restrictions which it must contain in its articles, is that it must have a *share capital*. Of these three types of private company, the private company limited by shares is by far the most commonly incorporated type.

[1.141] The EC(SMPLC)R 1994[281] permits *single-member* private limited companies. Therefore, not all three types of private company recognised by s 33(1) of the CA 1963 can become single-member companies. A *private unlimited company having a share capital* can neither be formed as, nor convert to being, a single-member company by reason of the fact that all single-member companies must be limited companies. Regulation 3(1) provides:

> 'Notwithstanding any enactment or rule of law to the contrary, a private company limited by shares or by guarantee may be formed by one person, and may have one member (in these regulations referred to as a single-member company), to the extent permitted by the Companies Acts and these regulations[282].'

Accordingly, only private companies limited by shares or by guarantee may be formed as, or convert to, single-member companies[283].

[1.142] Having distinguished the three *types* of private company permissible by s 33(1) of the CA 1963, it is now proposed to distinguish a number of *forms* which the private company may take. Irish private companies may be broken down into a number of related, yet distinct forms, all having in common the basic requirements contained in s 33(1) of the CA 1963. Five forms of private company can be readily identified[284]:

(a) the single-member private limited company;
(b) family owned private companies;
(c) closely-held private companies;
(d) quasi-partnership private companies;
(e) private companies with unconnected membership.

Notwithstanding this fivefold classification, it should be recognised that there will often be cross-over between some of the various forms of private company. Although the single-member company has a clear legal significance, the significance of being one or other of the remaining forms of private company may amount to no more than a factor to be considered when the court exercises its discretion under particular sections of the Companies Acts[285].

(a) The single-member private limited company

[1.143] Until 1 October 1994, the only single-member companies in Ireland were *de facto* single-member companies. Although *de jure* single-member companies have only

281 SI 275/1994.

282 Italics added.

283 See para **[1.045]**.

284 See Courtney, 'Shareholders' Agreements in Irish Private Companies' (1993) Dlí – The Western Law Gazette 69.

285 Eg, under s 205 or 213 of the CA 1963.

been permitted since 1 October 1994, prior to this date, many private companies were in reality owned by only one person. In such companies one person beneficially owned 100% of the shares in the company; that person legally holding 99% of the shares, his spouse or other nominee legally holding the remaining 1%. In this way the former requirement that a private company have two members was satisfied. By virtue of the EC(SMPLC)R 1994[286] it is now legally possible to form a single-member private limited company and to convert an existing private company limited by shares or by guarantee to a single-member company. At the outset it is important to note that notwithstanding that the *ownership* of a private company may vest in one person, it remains the case that the *management* of a private company legally requires the involvement of two persons. This is because s 174 of the CA 1963, which bluntly provides that '[e]very company shall have at least two directors', was not altered by the regulations.

[1.144] The so-called single-member company has long been recognised by the courts as being a *de facto* reality, the legal requirement of the second member being satisfied by a nominee. In the landmark case of *Salomon v Salomon & Co*[287] Lord MacNaghten said:

> 'It has become the fashion to call companies of this class 'one-man companies.' That is a taking nickname, but it does not help one much in the way of argument. If it is intended to convey the meaning that a company which is under the absolute control of one person is not a company legally incorporated, although the requirements of the Act of 1862 may have been complied with, it is inaccurate and misleading: if it merely means that there is a predominant partner possessing an overwhelming influence and entitled practically to the whole of the profits, there is nothing in that I can see contrary to the true intention of the Act of 1862, or against public policy, or detrimental to the interests of the creditors.'

Whilst the legislature decreed that a private company had to have at least two members, it did not attempt to provide that both members must hold equal shares. Moreover, even where one person is the beneficial owner of all of the shares in a company, the principle of separate legal personality will prevail and the company will not, without more, be deemed to be the beneficial owner's agent[288].

[1.145] As has been noted above[289] not all private companies can convert to single-member companies. Unlimited companies, which are private companies by virtue of having a share capital and the restrictions in their articles required by s 33(1) of the CA 1963, *cannot* become single-member companies. Although unlimited private companies cannot achieve *de jure* single-member company status, they may still be *de facto* single-member private companies. Where the membership of an unlimited company falls below two, the corporate existence of the resulting single-member company is not automatically in question[290]. Rather, corporate life continues, although it is possible that a petition may be presented to have the company wound up under s 213(d) of the CA

---

286 SI 275/1994.

287 *Salomon v Salomon & Co* (1898) AC 22 at 53. See further, Ch 4, *Incorporation and its Consequences*.

288 See Ch 5, *Disregarding Separate Legal Personality*, at para **[5.020]** *et seq*.

289 See para **[1.141]**.

290 See Fox & Bowen, *The Law of Private Companies* (1991, Sweet & Maxwell) at p 168.

1963, considered below[291]. The disapplication of s 36 of the CA 1963[292], by reg 7(1), to private companies limited by shares or by guarantee, does not affect unlimited private companies. However s 36 has always been of negligible importance to the members of an unlimited company since their liability for corporate debts is, by definition, unlimited[293].

[1.146] The *objective* of the Twelfth EU Directive on single-member companies is to provide a harmonised legal framework within which a single individual can conduct business as a private limited company. Thus, whilst the label 'single-member private company' is used, it may be equally apt to refer to the objective of this directive as allowing a sole trader to have limited liability. The contents of the Twelfth Directive have been succinctly described by one commentator as follows[294]:

> '... a company may have a sole member, either when it is formed or when all the shares come to be held by a single person (single member company). The Member States may, until such time as their laws relating to groups are co-ordinated, lay down special provisions or sanctions for cases where: (a) a natural person is the sole member of several companies or (b) a single-member company or any other legal person is the sole member of a company. Where a company becomes a single-member company because all its shares come to be held by a single person, that fact, together with the identity of the sole member, must either be recorded in the file or entered in the Register provided for in the First Directive or be entered in a register held by the company and accessible to the public. Decisions taken by the sole member in relation to the powers of the general meeting must be recorded in minutes or drawn up in writing ... A Member State need not allow the formation of single-member companies where its legislation provides that an individual entrepreneur may set up an undertaking the liability of which is limited to a sum devoted to stated activity, on condition that safeguards are laid down for such undertakings which are equivalent to those imposed by the Twelfth Directive or by any other Community provisions applicable to [private companies limited by shares or by guarantee].'

[1.147] The Twelfth Directive was implemented in Ireland by the EC(SMPLC)R 1994[295] with effect from 1 October 1994. Although each regulation is discussed in detail elsewhere in this book as it alters the existing law of private companies, it is convenient to summarise here the fourteen regulations:

- *Citation, commencement and construction* – this provides the proper title of the regulations, the date upon which they become operational, and the fact that they shall be construed as one with the Companies Acts (reg 1).

---

291 Regulation 11 only provides that ss 213(d) and 215(a)(i) are disapplied in the case of private companies limited by shares or by guarantee, and so continue to apply to unlimited private companies. See Ch 23, *Winding Up Companies*.

292 This provides that, in certain circumstances, where the membership of a private company falls below two members, the remaining member may be made personally liable for the company's debts: see Ch 5, *Disregarding Separate Legal Personality*, at para **[5.078]**.

293 But note that the unlimited liability of the members of an unlimited company only arises in the context of a winding up: see Ch 4, *Incorporation and its Consequences*, at para **[4.083]** *et seq* and Ch 31, *Unlimited Companies*, at para **[31.013]**.

294 Myles, *EEC Law Brief* (Locksley Press Ltd) vol 2, Co Law -12, at -03.

295 SI 275/1994.

- *Interpretation* – this contains a number of definitions which are necessary to construe the regulation (reg 2).
- *The operative regulation* – this provides the authority for a single-member company notwithstanding any enactment or rule of law; provides, in much the same way as the English statutory instrument does, that any enactment or rule of law ordinarily applicable to private companies limited by shares or by guarantee shall apply to single-member companies; and applies the provisions of the Companies Acts generally to single-member companies[296] (reg 3).
- *Formation* – this authorises the formation of single-member private companies limited by shares or by guarantee, notwithstanding s 5 of the CA 1963 which required at least two persons to sign the memorandum of association of a private company[297] (reg 4).
- *Conversion* – this authorises the conversion of a private company limited by shares or by guarantee to a single-member company, prescribes the appropriate notification and creates an offence in the event of default in notification[298] (reg 5).
- *Cesser of single-member company status* – this prescribes the conditions applicable where a single-member company becomes a two-member company again; prescribes the notification procedure and again creates an offence in the event of default in notification[299] (reg 6).
- *Disapplication of s 36 of the CA 1963* – this provides that s 36 shall not apply to single-member companies but provides that the regulation is not retrospective in regard to personal liability incurred prior to 1 October 1994[300] (reg 7).
- *Annual general meeting* – this provides, *inter alia*, that the sole member of a single-member company may dispense with the holding of an annual general meeting. There are other detailed provisions and safeguards which are considered below[301] (reg 8).
- *Exercise of powers of sole members* – this provides that instead of passing resolutions, sole members of single-member companies can make a decision recorded in writing. Again, safeguards are included in this regulation[302] (reg 9).
- *Quorum at sole member's meetings* – in a single-member company one person in present or by proxy shall be a quorum[303] (reg 10).
- *Non-application of certain provisions* – ss 213(d) and 215(a)(i) of the CA 1963 are expressed not to apply to single-member private companies limited by shares or by guarantee[304] (reg 11).

---

296 See Ch 2, *Incorporation by Registration*, at para **[2.015]**.
297 See Ch 2, *Incorporation by Registration*, at para **[2.016]**.
298 See Ch 33, *Conversion by Re-registration*, at para **[33.016]**.
299 See Ch 33, *Conversion by Re-registration*, at para **[33.017]**.
300 See Ch 5, *Disregarding Separate Legal Personality*, at para **[5.078]**.
301 See Ch 14, *Corporate Governance: Meetings*, at para **[14.014]**.
302 See Ch 14, *Corporate Governance: Meetings*, at para **[14.088]**.
303 See Ch 14, *Corporate Governance: Meetings*, at para **[14.056]**.
304 See Ch 23, *Winding Up of Companies*, at para **[23.038]**.

- Regulation 12 has been repealed[305].
- *Contracts with sole members* – this provides that contracts entered into by sole members of single-member companies with their companies must be in writing, save where entered into in the ordinary course of business; although a failure to comply with this is an offence, the validity of the contract is not affected[306] (reg 13).
- *Offences* – the final regulation provides that a person guilty of an offence under the regulations shall be liable on summary conviction to a class C fine (reg 14).

Where indicated, each of these new regulations is considered in detail in subsequent chapters.

[1.148] Although it is clear that one person can *own* an Irish private limited company, all Irish companies must still have two directors and a secretary[307]. Even in a single-member company, the 'nominee syndrome' continues as a feature of Irish corporate life, with nominee-directors satisfying the requirement that all companies have two directors.

(b) Family owned private companies

[1.149] Family owned private companies are not a separate statutorily recognised legal category of private company. Yet, since they can be said to be almost intrinsic to Irish business life, they deserve to be recognised here as being a distinct form of private company. Such companies meet the requirements of s 33(1) of the CA 1963 but are peculiar by virtue of the fact that they are exclusively, or predominantly, controlled by the members of the same family, whether of the nuclear or extended variety. Apart from their incestuous membership, there is nothing else especially peculiar about this form of private company. Potentially explosive in such companies is the possibility that there may be a shift in shareholdings, through death, marriage, divorce, sale or otherwise. Such a potential source of dispute may be prospectively catered for by means of strong *pre-emption* rights on the transfer or transmission of shares[308]. Pre-emption rights may be contained in either a company's articles of association or in a shareholders' agreement[309]. Frequently, family owned private companies may also be characterised as being *quasi-partnership* companies, or closely-held companies, the two variants of private company next considered.

---

305 Regulation 12 of SI 275/1994 which deemed a sole member to be a person connected with a director of a company for the purposes of s 26 of the CA 1990 was deleted by reg 3 of SI 437/2001, the European Communities (Single-Member Private Limited Companies) Regulations, 1994 (Amendment) Regulations 2001. See further Ch 16, *Statutory Regulation of Directors' Transactions*, at para **[16.009]**.

306 See Ch 7, *Corporate Contracts: Capacity and Authority*, at para **[7.006]**.

307 Even in England and Wales two persons are required to manage a private limited company because although s 282 of the Companies Act 1985 (UK) (which replaced s 176 of the Companies Act 1948) allows a company to have one director, s 283 provides that a sole director cannot also be the company's secretary.

308 See Ch 9, *Share Transfer*, at para **[9.069]** *et seq*.

309 See Ch 3, *Constitutional Documentation*, at para **[3.106]** *et seq*.

(c) Closely-held private companies

[1.150] A closely-held private company may be described as one where a company's membership is confined to a small number of persons who are known to each other but who are not necessarily family. Descriptions of closely held companies or corporations (to use the terminology of the United States) have varied. One description of a closely-held company is found in *Donahue v Rodd Electrotype Co of New England, Inc*[310] where the Supreme Judicial Court of Massachusetts said:

> 'There is no single, generally accepted definition. Some commentators emphasise an 'integration of ownership and management', in which the stockholders occupy most management positions. Others focus on the number of stockholders and the nature of the market for the stock. In this view, close corporations have few stockholders; there is little market for the corporate stock. The Supreme Court of Illinois adopted this latter view in *Galler v Galler* 32 Ill 2d 16, 203 NE 2d 577 (1965): 'For our purposes, a close corporation is one in which the stock is held in a few hands, or in a few families, and wherein it is not at all, or only rarely, dealt in buying or selling'. We accept aspects of both definitions. We deem a close corporation to be typified by: (1) a small number of stockholders; (2) no ready market for the corporate stock; and (3) substantial majority stockholder participation in the management, direction and operations of the corporation.
>
> As thus defined, the close corporation bears striking resemblance to a partnership. Commentators and courts have noted that the close corporation is often little more than an 'incorporated' or 'chartered' partnership. The stockholders 'clothe' their partnership 'with the benefits peculiar to a corporation, limited liability, perpetuity and the like' ... *Surchin v Approved Business Machine Co* 286 NYS 2d 580 ... In essence, though, the enterprise remains one in which ownership is limited to the original parties or transferees of their stock to whom the other stockholders have agreed, in which ownership and management are in the same hands, and in which the owners are quite dependant on one another for the success of the enterprise. Many close corporations are 'really partnerships, between two or three people who contribute their capital, skills, experience and labor'. *Kruger v Gerth*, 16 NY 2d 802 ...'

Again, the concept of *closely-held company* is not a self-contained category and it is capable of being applied to family companies or quasi-partnership type companies. Moreover, a company may be closely-held even though there is no particular quasi-fiduciary relationship between the members of the company, and so a medium-sized private company can be described as being closely-held where its members are few in number and are all intimately involved in the management of the company. There are no particular consequences in company law for a company being designated a closely-held company[311]. It is only where a closely-held company displays other characteristics, which result in it being properly termed a quasi-partnership, that there are appreciable consequences.

---

[310] *Donahue v Rodd Electrotype Co of New England, Inc* (1975) 367 Mass 578, 328 NE 2d 505.

[311] There may, however, be taxation consequences.

(d) Quasi-partnership private companies[312]

[1.151] Where a relationship of equality, mutuality, trust, and confidence[313], based on a personal relationship[314], subsists between the members of a private company[315] in which the owners (shareholders) and managers (directors) are the same persons, it may be appropriate to describe it as a quasi-partnership company[316]. The closest relationship that the members of a company can have is a *quasi-partnership*; as a matter of law, the members of a registered company cannot be in a legal 'partnership' because s 1(2)(a) of the PA 1890 explicitly provides that their relationship 'is not a partnership within the meaning of this Act'. Murphy J put the matter thus in *Crindle Investments Ltd v Wymes*[317] in a passage cited with approval by Keane J in the Supreme Court:

> 'Whilst I have already indicated that I accept that duties may be imposed or accepted by parties above or beyond those derived from particular offices or status I believe that the presumption must be that parties who elect to have their relationship governed by corporate structures rather than, say, a partnership intend their duties – and where appropriate their rights and remedies – to be governed by the legal provisions relating to such structures and not otherwise. It would require, in my view, reasonably clear evidence to impose obligations on directors or shareholders above and beyond those prescribed by legislation or identified by long established principles[318].'

Although there is a *presumption* that those who chose to incorporate a company have chosen that the legislation governing companies should govern their relationship, that presumption can be rebutted by clear evidence. Indeed, the phenomenon of the quasi-partnership company was clearly recognised by the Supreme Court in *McGilligan v O'Grady*[319] where Keane J said:

---

312 See generally, Fox & Bowen, *The Law of Private Companies* (1991, Sweet & Maxwell) p 178. See also, Twomey, *Partnership Law* (2000, Butterworths) at [8.68] *et seq*.

313 See *Re Murph's Restaurant Ltd* [1979] ILRM 141 at 151.

314 See *Re Astec (BSR) plc* [1999] BCC 59 where Jonathan Parker J found (at 86) that in order to give rise to an equitable constraint based on 'legitimate expectations' 'what is required is a personal relationship or personal dealings of some kind between the party seeking to exercise the legal right and the party seeking to restrain such exercise, such as will affect the conscience of the former'. One of the best examples of a personal relationship is seen in *Re Apollo Cleaning Services Ltd; Richards v Lundy et al* [1999] BCC 786; and see *Re Legal Costs Negotiators Ltd* [1999] BCC 547 where pre-existing partnerships had been converted into a limited company.

315 In England it has been said that there was no room for 'legitimate expectations' in public companies: *Re Blue Arrow plc* (1987) 3 BCC 618 at 623; *Re Astec (BSR) plc* [1999] BCC 59 at 87D. Twomey, *Partnership Law* (2000, Butterworths) at p 177 suggests that once the entity in question is in substance a partnership, 'the court may apply partnership law principles to it'. It is thought to be a matter of evidential proof rather than high principle that gives rise to most quasi-partnership companies being private companies and not public companies.

316 In *Third et al v North East Ice & Cold Storage Co Ltd and another* [1998] BCC 242, it was held that where a company was a quasi-partnership, but circumstances changed rendering it no longer a quasi-partnership, 'legitimate expectations' would be displaced.

317 *Crindle Investments Ltd v Wymes* [1998] 4 IR 567 at 576.

318 [1998] 2 ILRM 275 at 285.

319 *McGilligan v O'Grady* [1999] 1 ILRM 303 at 343, 344.

'It is undoubtedly the case that, if there is a relationship between shareholders in a company indicating a degree of mutual confidence and trust, the court may order the winding up of the company on the just and equitable ground where one or more of the shareholders and/or directors exercise their powers in a manner which is inconsistent with that relationship. Specifically, this may arise where the right of the shareholders to participate in the management of the company is infringed, as for example by the removal of a director. These principles were laid down in *Ebrahimi v Westbourne Galleries* [1973] AC 360 and were adopted in this jurisdiction by Gannon J in *Re Murph's Restaurants Ltd* [1979] ILRM 141 at 144'.

[1.152] The basis for finding the relationship of *quasi-partnership* in a private company is that there are human personalities behind the legal personality which is the separate legal status of the company[320]. In such companies there will be some sort of a relationship which involves '*equality, mutuality, trust and confidence*' between the members of the company. In Ireland, Gannon J recognised in *Re Murph's Restaurant Ltd*[321] that in some private companies the members can be:

'... equal partners in a joint venture, and that the company was no more than a vehicle to secure a limited liability for possible losses and to provide a means of earning and distributing profits to their best advantage with minimum disclosure.'

Clearly this goes beyond the mere fact that persons have associated and subscribed for shares in a company. The relationship between the shareholders must go further and display, to some noticeable extent, characteristics similar to those that tend to prevail in a partnership and they must have acted in a way that is incompatible with the nature of a company. To be a quasi-partnership company, there must be, or have been, a *mutuality of understanding* between the members.

[1.153] It is thought that there is a greater likelihood that a quasi-partnership will be found to exist where the members hold their shares equally[322]. So in *Re Murph's Restaurant Ltd*[323], Gannon J referred to persons being 'equal partners in a joint venture'. Whether there are two, three or more members, it is thought that a court will more readily accept that they had the intention of being treated as partners, where their shares are equal. It is ironic that whilst in real partnerships, partners can and frequently do hold unequal shares, evidentially an inequality of shareholding is anathema to the mutuality that has consistently been found to be a requirement for a quasi-partnership company.

[1.154] What then is the consequence of finding that a company properly falls to be treated as a quasi-partnership? As one writer has observed[324] the 'whole *raison d'être* for the concept of quasi-partnerships is to apply principles of partnership law to non-partnerships'. Finding that a company is a quasi-partnership will, *prima facie*, entitle its quasi-partners to:

---

320 See *Ebrahimi v Westbourne Galleries Ltd* [1972] 2 All ER 492 at 499, 500.

321 *Re Murph's Restaurant Ltd* [1979] ILRM 141 at 150.

322 In *Irish Press plc v Ingersoll Irish Publications Ltd* (15 December 1993, unreported) HC, Barron J referred to 'equal shareholdings in a company'.

323 *Re Murph's Restaurant Ltd* [1979] ILRM 141 at 150.

324 Twomey, *Partnership Law* (2000, Butterworths) at [8.86].

- participate in its management[325];
- expect that their fellow quasi-partner members act in good faith[326];
- object to any fundamental change in the direction of the company's business activities[327].

Breach of any of the foregoing possible entitlements will ground reliance upon the most far-reaching consequence, namely that a petition can be presented to have the company wound-up on the just and equitable ground in s 213(f) of the CA 1963[328].

(e) Private companies with unconnected membership

[1.155] Sight must not be lost of the fact that a great many Irish private companies have an unconnected membership. Their members are not closely related by blood, marriage or friendship. In unconnected private companies, there will be no fiduciary relationship between the members, who will have no connection with each other, save the fact that they are shareholders in the same company. Furthermore, the management of such companies will typically be independent of its ownership and a true separation of powers will exist between the directors and the members. Accordingly, the 'duality of roles' seen so often in the other forms of private companies will not exist here[329]. In unconnected private companies the members will elect the company's directors in general meeting on the basis of their professional expertise to manage the company. The directors may be executive directors, or career-directors, although some of the directors may have a proprietary interest in the company by holding shares. The chief characteristics of such private companies are that their membership is typically larger than other private companies and that there is a discernible *separation of powers* between the members in general meeting and the board of directors.

[E] THE MEANING OF 'COMPANY' AND OF THE 'COMPANIES ACTS'

[1.156] Section 2 of the CA 1963 gives the word '*company*' a very specific meaning. As such, when any provision of the Companies Acts uses the word 'company', only certain bodies corporate are subject to that provision unless there is a local definition which overrides the general definition in s 2[330]. This can be of particular importance in determining the application of restrictive measures in the Companies Acts. The definition assigned to 'company' in the CA 1963 by s 2 is, '*unless the context otherwise requires*':

> '... a company formed and registered under this Act or an existing company.'

This short, but very precise, definition of 'company' shall now be considered.

---

325 *Re Murph's Restaurants Ltd* [1978] ILRM 141.

326 *Irish Press plc v Ingersoll Irish Publications Ltd* (15 December 1993, unreported) HC, Barron J.

327 *Re Tivoli Freeholds Ltd* [1972] VR 445, cited by Twomey, *Partnership Law* (2000, Butterworths) at [8.91].

328 See Ch 23, *Winding Up Companies*, at para **[23.091]**.

329 On the *duality of roles* prevalent in many private companies, see Ch 13, *Corporate Governance: Management by the Directors*, at para **[13.001]**.

330 An example of a local definition is provided by s 155 of the CA 1963 which defines 'holding company' and which provide, in sub-s (5) that 'company' includes any body corporate.

[1.157] The first aspect to the definition of 'company' is that it includes a company which is "formed *and* registered" under the Companies Acts, in so far as they are read as one Act[331]. The word 'and' must be read as a conjunction, so that in order to come within the definition in s 2 of the CA 1963, a company must be both formed *and* registered under the Companies Acts. A company which is registered as a foreign or external company under Part XI of the CA 1963 or as a branch under the EC(BD)R 1993 is not, therefore, a 'company' within the meaning of s 2, as it merely satisfies one limb of the definition, ie, it is 'registered' under the Acts. It follows that unless expressly stated to the contrary, the provisions of the Companies Acts do not apply to foreign companies or any other type of 'company'.

[1.158] Instructive in the definition of company is the case of *Rover International Ltd v Cannon Film Sales Ltd*[332] where a provision in the former English Companies Act 1985 (similar to s 37 of the CA 1963 concerning pre-incorporation contracts) was found to be inapplicable to foreign companies[333]. *Re Tuskar Resources plc*[334] concerned an application to the Irish High Court to appoint an examiner. In refusing to appoint an examiner to Tuskar Resources plc, an Irish company, McCracken J also refused to appoint an examiner to a 'related company' which happened to be a Nigerian company:

> '… in my view the definition of a related company in s 4(5) [of the C(A)(No2)A 1999] does not include a company registered outside this jurisdiction, as it sets out the conditions in which 'a company is related to another company', and the word 'company' as defined in the Companies Act 1963 means a company formed and registered under that Act, or an existing company. In the present case the Nigerian company is not formed or registered under the 1963 Act'[335].

Similarly in *Harrington v JVC (UK) Ltd*[336] O'Hanlon J declined jurisdiction to make an order for security for costs against a Northern Ireland registered company[337]. The making of an order for security for costs against a company that was *allegedly* formed and registered in England and Wales in *Windmaster Developments Ltd v Airoglen Ltd*[338] should not be seen as an exception to the foregoing principles of jurisdiction as in that case it appears only to have been noticed after the making of the order that the company might not, in fact, have been formed and registered in Ireland and in the subsequent hearing no evidence of foreign incorporation was adduced.

[1.159] The second aspect to the definition of 'company' is that it includes an 'existing company'. Section 2 of the CA 1963 provides that an 'existing company' means:

> 'a company formed and registered in a register kept in the State under the Joint Stock Companies Act, the Companies Act 1862, or the Companies (Consolidation) Act 1908.'

---

331 See s 3 of the CA 1990.

332 *Rover International Ltd v Cannon Film Sales Ltd* [1987] BCLC 540.

333 See Ch 7, *Corporate Contracts: Capacity and Authority*, at para **[7.043]**.

334 *Re Tuskar Resources plc* [2001] 1 IR 668.

335 *Re Tuskar Resources plc* [2001] 1 IR 668.

336 *Harrington v JVC (UK) Ltd* (16 March 1995, unreported) HC, O'Hanlon J.

337 See Ch 6, *Corporate Civil Litigation*, at para **[6.026]**.

338 *Windmaster Developments Ltd v Airoglen Ltd* (10 July 2000, unreported) HC, McCracken J.

Although s 2 dictates the automatic application of the Companies Acts to existing companies, Part VIII of the CA 1963 addresses in detail certain companies formed or registered under former Acts. By s 324(1) of the CA 1963, the Companies Acts are deemed to apply to 'existing companies' whether limited or unlimited in the same manner as if they had been formed and registered under the Acts.

[1.160] Section 325(1) of the CA 1963 provides that the Companies Acts apply to every company registered (in a register kept in the State) but *not* formed under the Joint Stock Companies Acts, the Companies Act 1862 or the Companies (Consolidation) Act 1908. Part VIII contains a number of other provisions in relation to other varieties of existing companies[339]. Section 377(1) of the CA 1963, as amended by s 250 of the CA 1990, applies the provisions of the Ninth Schedule to the CA 1963, as replaced by s 250, to all *unregistered companies* incorporated in and having a principal place of business in the State other than those specified in s 377(2). The Ninth Schedule applies many, but not all, of the provisions in the Companies Acts and various companies regulations to such unregistered companies.

[1.161] Where an old company[340] registers under Part IX, by virtue of s 340(2) of the CA 1963:

> 'All provisions contained in any statute or instrument constituting or regulating the company, including, in the case of a company registered as a company limited by guarantee ... shall be deemed to be conditions and regulations of the company, in the same manner and with the same incidents as if so much thereof as would, if the company had been formed under this Act, have been required to be inserted in the memorandum, were contained in a registered memorandum, and the residue thereof were contained in registered articles.'

Section 340(3) further provides that all provisions of the Companies Acts shall apply to the company, its members, contributories and creditors as if it was formed under those Acts, with certain exceptions.

[1.162] The fact that the definition in s 2(1) of the CA 1963 is expressed to be '*unless the context otherwise requires*' means that there will be certain exceptions from the foregoing exposition of the law. In certain cases, where it appears that the legislature did not intend to confine a particular provision to companies formed and registered under the Companies Acts or existing companies, other companies may be included. An example is the exception in s 35 of the CA 1990 to the prohibition in s 31 of the CA 1990 to transactions and arrangements in favour of persons connected with directors[341]. This provides, *inter alia*, that s 31 shall not prohibit a company from making a loan or quasi-loan 'to any *company* which is its holding company, subsidiary or a subsidiary of its holding company'. If s 2(1) of the CA 1963 were applied strictly, this would mean that an Irish company could not rely on the exemption to make a loan to its holding company unless the holding company were itself an Irish company. It is thought that this

---

339 Therefore, s 326 of the CA 1963 applies the Companies Acts to unlimited companies re-registered as limited companies under former Acts, and s 327 addresses old joint stock companies.

340 Ie, a company as defined by s 328(1) of the CA 1963.

341 See MacCann & Courtney, *Companies Acts 1963–2009* (2010, Bloomsbury Professional) at p 1202.

is not the correct construction, however, and that the presence of 'holding company' is sufficient to import the meaning of 'company' as defined by s 155(5) of the CA 1963 in the context of holding companies and subsidiaries as including any body corporate.

[1.163] Following the enactment of the C(A)A 1977, the CA 1963 and it were collectively referred to as the 'Companies Acts 1963 to 1977'[342] and subsequent enactments amending company law continued this collective citation up until the passing of the IFCMPA 2006. That Act departs from that use in the IFCMPA 2005 and previous Companies Acts. Specifically, s 1 of the IFCMPA 2006 *does not* provide that the Companies Acts 1963 to 2005 and Parts 2 and 3 of the IFCMPA 2006 may be cited together as the Companies Acts 1963 to 2006. Rather, s 1(2) merely provides '*The Companies Acts and Parts 2 and 3 shall be read together as one*'. The IFCMPA 2006 is the first company law statute to be passed since the citation of the Companies Acts was amended by the Interpretation Act 2005 (IA 2005). Section 21(2) of the IA 2005 and Part 2 of the Schedule provide that in an enactment which comes into operation after the commencement of the IA 2005, 'Companies Acts' means 'the Companies Acts 1963 to 2001 and every other enactment which is to be read together with any of those Acts'.

[1.164] This definition is not without difficulty since when the IA 2005 was enacted, the then correct collective citation of the Companies Acts was in fact to the Companies Acts 1963 to 2003, not to the Companies Acts 1963 to 2001, this error only being explicable as an oversight occasioned by the passage of time between the publication of the Interpretation Bill and its eventual enactment. There has to be some concern that the term 'Companies Acts' as used in s 1(2) of the IFCMPA 2006 does not include the C(AA)A 2003 since it has never been provided in statute that it is to be 'read together' with the 'Companies Acts'. There is, therefore, no statutory meaning assigned to the collective term, 'Companies Acts 1963 to 2009' and where that term is used in a contract or other private document, it should be defined[343]. It may be noted that the CRO has not dropped the requirement to use the year of the latest statutory provision to be read as one with the Companies Acts and has specified that persons forming companies must use the current citation, eg, 'Companies Acts 1963 to 2012' in all memoranda and articles of association filed with them, despite that formulation of words having no prescribed statutory meaning.

[F] MODERN COMPANY LAW REFORM

The Company Law Review Group

[1.165] One of the recommendations of the McDowell Group's Report was the establishment on a statutory basis of a Company Law Review Group (the 'CLRG'). The

[342] Section 11(2) of the C(A)A 1977.

[343] Using the old convention, 'Companies Acts 1963 to 2012' or 'Companies Acts' could be defined as: 'the Companies Acts 1963 to 2005, Parts 2 and 3 of the Investment Funds, Companies and Miscellaneous Provisions Act 2006, the Companies (Amendment) Act 2009, the Companies (Miscellaneous Provisions) Act 2009 and the Companies (Amendment) Act 2012, all statutory instruments which are to be read as one with, or construed or read together as one with, the Companies Acts and every statutory modification and re-enactment thereof for the time being in force.'

purpose of this was to facilitate considered and comprehensive company law reform: by establishing a statutory group to review company law and charging it with the responsibility for producing a report after every two-year work programme, the State committed itself to achieving a state-of-the-art company law code for Ireland. In anticipation of the 2001 Act the review group was established on an *ad hoc* basis in February 2000.

[1.166] Sections 67 to 71 of the 2001 Act established the CLRG on a statutory basis. Section 68(1) directs that the CLRG shall monitor, review and advise the Minister on matters concerning:

'(a) the implementation of the Companies Acts,

(b) the amendment of the Companies Acts,

(c) the consolidation of the Companies Acts,

(d) the introduction of new legislation relating to the operation of companies and commercial practices in Ireland,

(e) the Rules of the Superior Courts and case law judgments insofar as they relate to the Companies Acts,

(f) the approach to issues arising from the State's membership of the European Union, insofar as they affect the operation of the Companies Acts,

(g) international developments in company law, insofar as they may provide lessons for improved State practice, and

(h) other related matters or issues, including issues submitted by the Minister to the Review Group for consideration.'

Moreover, s 68(2) of the 2001 Act requires that:

> 'In advising the Minister the Review Group shall seek to promote enterprise, facilitate commerce, simplify the operation of the Companies Acts, enhance corporate governance and encourage commercial probity.'

[1.167] Section 69 concerns the membership of the CLRG. The chairperson of the CLRG is appointed by the Minister and is the only person who may not nominate a deputy to attend a meeting of the CLRG if unable to attend a meeting. In such event, the members of the CLRG are required to elect one of their number as chairperson for such meeting. Section 70 deals with the meetings and the business of the CLRG. Every two years, the Minister, in consultation with the CLRG, is required to determine the programme of work to be undertaken over the ensuing specified period. The CLRG is required to hold such and so many meetings as may be necessary for the performance of its functions and is entitled to establish such sub-committees as it thinks appropriate.

The CLRG's first report

[1.168] The CLRG's first report was delivered on 31 December 2001, and published on 28 February 2002. This report recommended the most sweeping changes, in the history of the State, to Irish company law. In tackling the difficult subject of simplification of company law, the CLRG advocated the complete re-focusing of company law so that the private company limited by shares will become *the new model company.*

[1.169] The CLRG conceived that the new legislation would be divided into two groups of parts. The first group would deal exclusively with the 'new model' private company, the private company limited by shares, and the second group would deal with all other types of companies: PLCs, guarantee companies, unlimited companies, external companies, unregistered companies, investment companies and a new type of private company, designated activity companies, which would be private companies limited by shares or by guarantee which have an objects clause. In this vision, the primary company law framework would be contained in the first group dealing with the private company in what the first report referred to as Pillar A and all other company types would be found in what was referred to as Pillar B. It is proposed that the Bill would be structured so that the provisions relating to each type of other company will be contained in their distinct part of Pillar B and that each part will apply or disapply the laws set out in Pillar A to the particular company type in question and each part will also contain additional provisions, only relevant to that company type.

Other reports

[1.170] The CLRG's second report built on the first report and made recommendations in relation to liquidations, Table A articles of association, corporate governance, share capital, debentures and the registration of charges and accounting and audit issues. The third report continued the simplification and consolidation project and the simplification and consolidation project was completed in 2006 and published in 2007[344] with the publication of the three volume report and draft heads of Bill in the nature of the general scheme for the Companies Bill. In 2008 the CLRG produced a report on its 2007 work programme which addressed, among other matters, reform of the law on transactions and arrangements involving directors and connected persons, good-faith reporting of breaches of company law and the preferential status accorded to the Revenue Commissioners on a winding up. In 2010 the CLRG produced a further report in respect of its 2008/2009 work programme and in 2012 a report for the period 2010/2011 was produced. Throughout this time the CLRG also assisted the Department in the preparation of the new Companies Bill.

The draft Companies Bill

[1.171] In May 2011 the Minister for Jobs, Enterprise and Innovation published a draft of the first fifteen parts of the new Companies Bill which focus exclusively on the private company limited by shares – reflecting the CLRG's first recommendation in its First Report (31 December 2001), that 'The private company limited by shares ... should be the primary focus of simplification'. The draft Bill proposes many significant changes to the law of private companies. The main features of the new model private company and the reforms provided for in the draft Bill are:

- It will be limited by shares – private companies limited by guarantee will be permitted but will be subject to the legal regime which will be prescribed for *designated activity companies* (DACs).
- It will have the same contractual capacity as a natural person – private companies will not have an objects clause and so will not be subject to the

[344] In 2005 the CLRG also produced a *Report on Directors' Compliance Statement*. See Courtney, 'Directors' Compliance Statements: Attesting Corporate Governance on a "Comply or Explain" Basis', ch 1 in Keane & O'Neill, *Corporate Governance & Regulation* (2009, Round Hall).

doctrine of *ultra vires*, making it easier to transact with confidence with private companies.

- It may have only one director – in reducing the statutory minimum number of directors to one, accountability in governance will be increased as the need for passive nominee directors to make up the numbers will fall away.
- It may have up to 99 members – whilst many will be single-member companies, private companies can have up to 99 members.
- It will not be permitted to list any securities, whether shares or debts – in so providing the law relating to the model private company can be kept simple; other types of private company such as DACs will continue to be allowed to list debt securities.
- It will have a one-document constitution – the memorandum and articles of association will be replaced by one document.
- The necessity for each company to have detailed specific internal regulations (in the form of articles of association) will be removed as most of the provisions commonly provided for in articles of association on the internal administration and governance of companies will be contained in the Bill and will apply to all private companies (unless their constitution provides otherwise).
- All private companies will be permitted to have 'written' AGMs – where the members consent, the need for an annual physical meeting can be dispensed with.
- Directors' common law fiduciary duties will be codified – the Bill codifies directors' duties as they have been developed by the courts over the last 150 years making the law more transparent and accessible.
- One omnibus validation procedure will apply to regulated activities (eg, transactions with directors, financial assistance, capital reduction and solvent windings up).
- Offences created by the Bill have been categorised on a scale of 1 to 4 (where 1 is the most serious) and the punishment for those found guilty of each category clearly specified – this will facilitate a far greater transparency in the criminal dimension to breaches of company law and facilitate enforcement since a clear and rational regime should be a prerequisite to zero-tolerance.
- The directors of private companies meeting certain thresholds will be required to make compliance statements in line with the proportionate and reasonable regime recommended by the CLRG in its 2005 *Report on Directors' Compliance Statement*.
- Private companies will be permitted to engage in domestic mergers along the lines which are currently only capable of being used in the case of cross-border mergers.

With regard to other types of companies, it is proposed that the law relating to each distinct type of company will be set out in a separate part of the Bill, which are yet to be published. In those parts, appropriate provisions from the law applicable to private companies in Parts 1 to 15 will be applied to each company type as will distinct provisions relevant only to that type of company. So public limited companies, guarantee companies, unlimited companies, designated activity companies, unregistered companies and investment companies will each have their own part.

(a) Part 1 – preliminary and general

[1.172] This part of the draft Bill is largely concerned with house-keeping, defining terms used throughout the Bill, some of which will be very important such as the definitions of 'subsidiary' and 'holding company'.

(b) Part 2 – incorporation and registration

[1.173] Part 2 fundamentally changes the law, establishing the new model private company and providing for the conversion of existing private companies. The new model private company will have a one-document constitution rather than a memorandum and articles of association and will have 'full and unlimited capacity'. If people wish their private company to have a memorandum and articles of association, and objects clause, they will have to use the alternative private company to be known as the designated activity company ('DAC'). Part 2 proposes that certain officers and senior employees authorised to bind the company to facilitate the conclusion of contracts be registered as being so authorised.

(c) Part 3 – share capital, shares and certain other instruments

[1.174] Part 3 consolidates in one place the law relating to shares and share capital. The model private company may not offer securities, whether equity or debt, to the public in any circumstances. Private companies wishing to do this will have to re-register as DACs, having an objects clause. As it cannot make public offerings, the model company can be the subject of a less complicated regime. A central concept in the Bill is that where a company's constitution is silent, its internal regulations default to what is in the Bill, reducing the need for detailed provisions in companies' constitutions. Other significant changes include reforms relating to: the giving of financial assistance; reducing share capital; and own-share acquisition. A form of merger relief is also provided, enabling distributions of amounts that would otherwise stand as share premium following an acquisition.

(d) Part 4 – corporate governance

[1.175] This part sets out in one place the law relating to the appointment and proceedings of officers (directors and secretaries) and members. In addition, it sets out the new summary approval procedure whereby restricted activities can be carried out when validated. Again, Part 4 sets out standard provisions as adopted by most companies in their articles of association, and provides that these shall apply '*save to the extent that the company's constitution provides otherwise*'. Other proposed changes include permitting private companies to have only one director, and permitting majority written resolutions rather than requiring unanimity.

(e) Part 5 – duties of directors and other officers

[1.176] Under the proposed new regime, directors' duties and requirements will apply whether directors are formally appointed or are de facto or shadow directors. The Bill will confirm that it is the duty of directors (and not company secretaries) to ensure compliance with the Companies Act, and codifies fiduciary duties deriving largely from common law and equitable principles:

- to act in good faith in what the director considers to be the company's interests;
- to act honestly and responsibly;
- to act in accordance with the company's constitution and to exercise powers only for lawful purposes;
- not to use company property for own or others' use unless approved by the members or the constitution;
- not to fetter discretion unless permitted by the constitution or entered into in the company's interests;
- to avoid conflicts of interest unless released by members;
- to exercise care, skill and diligence; and to have regard to interests of members.

Directors of private companies meeting certain thresholds will be required to prepare directors' compliance statements, and enforcement measures are also revised and updated. As well as largely retaining restrictions on loans, quasi-loans, credit transactions (and certain guarantees and security), new provisions seek to encourage that any loans between directors and companies be put in writing. A welcome reform provides that de minimis share interests of less than 1% need not be notified which will result in cost-savings for companies by eliminating needless administration.

(f) Part 6 – financial statements, annual return and audit

[1.177] This part consolidates statutory provisions regarding the keeping of accounting records, and the preparation, audit and filing of financial statements. The part clarifies key terms, and gives greater prominence to terms such as 'realised profits' and 'true and fair view'. In addition, the obligation to deliver an annual return is removed while a company is being wound up, or being voluntarily struck off (unless it is then restored to the register). Also, thresholds for a company to qualify as small or medium-sized have been raised. Finally, the part will for the first time allow the preparation, audit and filing of revised financial statements, where a deficiency becomes apparent in a filed set of statutory financial statements.

(g) Part 7 – charges and debentures

[1.178] Part 7 consolidates and reforms the law relating to security. One change relates to the definition of 'charge', in that a charge over cash will not have to be registered. A significant proposed change relating to registration is that there will be two separate procedures, the innovation being the ability to give an early indication of the intention to create a charge. Another significant change is that where the priority of charges is not governed by some other regime (eg, charges over land will be governed by a separate regime), priority will be determined by reference to the date of receipt by the registrar of the prescribed particulars.

(h) Part 8 – receivers

[1.179] The law relating to receivers will also be consolidated and reformed; one proposed change is that the powers of receivers will be enumerated in a non-exhaustive list, without prejudice to powers which may be granted by a debenture.

(i) Part 9 – reorganisations, acquisitions, mergers and divisions

[1.180] In this part, existing means for reorganisations – court-sanctioned schemes of arrangement and compulsory purchase of minority interests – sit alongside two new means: mergers and divisions. For the first time, a statutory mechanism is provided whereby two Irish companies (ie, without the need for a cross-border element) can merge so that the assets and liabilities (and identity) of one are transferred to the other, before the former is dissolved. Moreover, it will be possible for an Irish company to be 'divided' and its undertaking split between two other Irish companies. It is proposed that mergers may be effected through the summary approval procedure, without the need for a High Court order, saving time and money.

(j) Part 10 – examinerships

[1.181] Part 10 follows closely the current regime on examinerships.

(k) Part 11 – winding up

[1.182] Part 11 consolidates and modernises the law on winding up, and reorders it in a more logically coherent way. The Bill seeks to introduce greater consistency between the three different methods of winding up (members' voluntary, creditors' voluntary and official). One objective is to align court-initiated liquidations with creditors' voluntary windings up, to reduce the court's supervisory involvement. Some other proposed reforms include: that the Director of Corporate Enforcement will have the right to petition to wind up a company on the grounds that such is in the public interest; the minimum amount of indebtedness to entitle a creditor to serve a statutory demand will be increased to €10,000; liquidators will be required to be qualified; a provisional liquidator will only have such powers as are provided for by the court order appointing him or her, etc.

(l) Part 12 – strike off and restoration

[1.183] The law relating to strike off will be consolidated and radically overhauled, and for the first time a statutory distinction drawn between voluntary and involuntary strike off. No significant changes are proposed in relation to restoration.

(m) Part 13 – investigations

[1.184] The Bill proposes to substantially re-enact the law relating to the appointment of inspectors.

(n) Part 14 – compliance and enforcement

[1.185] This part gathers together provisions relating to compliance and enforcement, consistent with a stricter and more transparent approach in these areas. The court can order that a company or officer comply with a provision of the Act; that directors not reduce their assets or remove them from the State; and that the beneficial ownership of shares be disclosed. A significant proposed change to restriction of directors is that it will be necessary to satisfy the court that the director has cooperated with the liquidator as far as could reasonably be expected in relation to the conduct of the winding up. The part facilitates the giving and acceptance of restriction and disqualification undertakings from directors, which will facilitate the saving of cost and court time since where directors agree to be restricted or disqualified, it will not be necessary to go to court. One of the most far-reaching reforms provided for in the draft Bill concerns the streamlining of criminal offences under the Companies Acts of which there are currently several hundred. The draft Bill provides for a four-fold categorisation of offences created by the Bill into Categories 1 to 4. Throughout the Bill, offences are, as created, categorised as attracting a particular category of penalty. In Chapter 7 of Part 14, those penalties are set out:

- Category 1 offence – conviction on indictment can result in a term of imprisonment of up to 10 years or a fine of up to €500,000 or both;
- Category 2 offence – conviction on indictment can result in a term of imprisonment of up to five years or a fine of up to €50,000 or both;
- Category 3 offence – a summary offence only, attracting a term of imprisonment of up to six months and a 'Class A fine' (or both); and
- Category 4 offence – also a summary offence only, punishable by the imposition of a Class A fine.

A 'Class A fine' is a fine within the meaning of the Fines Act 2010 (ie, a fine not exceeding €5,000).

(o) Part 15 – functions of registrar and of regulatory and advisory bodies

[1.186] Provisions relating to the registrar, the Irish Auditing and Accounting Supervisory Authority, the Director of Corporate Enforcement and the CLRG are contained in Part 15 of the draft Bill.

Chapter 2

Incorporation by Registration

[2.001] In the previous chapter the private company was placed in its historical context. The modern private company was considered and distinctions were drawn between the various types and forms of private company that are prevalent in Ireland. It now falls to consider how a private company comes to be incorporated through its *formation* and *registration* under the Companies Acts[1]. In this chapter, the following issues in the incorporation by registration of private companies are considered:

1. Why Incorporate?
2. Incorporating an existing business.
3. Formation of private companies.
4. Methods of corporate formation.
5. The steps in forming a private company.
6. The requirement that a company carries on an 'activity' in the State.
7. Registration by the registrar of companies.
8. Delivery of particulars to the Revenue Commissioners.
9. Statutory obligations incidental to registration.
10. Irish registered non-resident companies.

Why incorporate?

[2.002] There is today an almost automatic tendency for entrepreneurs to incorporate before commencing business. The fact is that there are many rational and sensible reasons why an entrepreneur should incorporate his or her business. For the Irish entrepreneur, the following are some of the advantages to be obtained through the incorporation of a private limited company[2]:

- legal certainty for the corporate entity in its operations;
- limited liability for the shareholders;
- tax advantages;
- the ability to raise finance on foot of security unavailable to other business structures;
- the ability to have up to 99 members;
- the ease of transfer of an interest in the business;
- the ability to clearly define the management structure.

---

1 See, generally, the comprehensive review and analysis of the practice and procedure in forming companies in McGowan-Smyth & Daly, *Irish Company Secretary's Handbook* (2011, Bloomsbury Professional) at Ch 5.

2 See Ch 4, *Incorporation and Its Consequences*, at para **[4.021]** *et seq*.

It is important to recognise that the protective veil which limited liability provides to the members of companies is considerably less sacrosanct than it once was, by virtue of statutory inroads, equitable considerations and the realities of commercial practice[3]. Nevertheless, the general rule remains: in a limited liability company the debts and liabilities of the company belong to the separate legal entity that is the company and not to its shareholders, directors or employees.

[2.003] It is perhaps the realities or exigencies of commercial practice which are today the most far reaching claw-back of the statutory advantages of incorporation. More and more frequently the separate legal personality of the private company is being disregarded *by agreement*. An example in point is that where a private company is incorporated, its separate legal personality may be disregarded by agreement between its member-directors and outsiders dealing with the company. This might occur where such a company takes, say, a 35-year lease of its business premises, or is afforded facilities by a lending institution and its controlling member-directors are required to provide personal guarantees for the company's obligations[4]. Notwithstanding this practical dilution of the advantages of incorporation, the entrepreneur behind a business who decides to incorporate still has the advantage that, in other day-to-day transactions involving the company and outsiders, he will not as a general rule personally incur either contractual or tortious liability. This chapter assumes that persons in business have decided that they wish to incorporate, and shows the various options open to them within this form of business association and explains the main steps involved in forming a private company.

Incorporating an existing business

[2.004] Sometimes, it will be the case that the proprietors of an existing business will decide to incorporate their business. They may make this decision for a variety of reasons. Where the existing proprietor is a sole trader, it may be the case that he is contemplating retirement or perhaps inviting one of his children to come into the family business. His concern may be to find a suitable way of achieving this whilst at the same time retaining control of the business and continuing to provide financially for himself and his wife. In such circumstances, it may make good sense to incorporate the existing business. Alternatively, the existing business may be owned by a partnership, whose partners wish to put the management and ownership of the business on a more solid footing and to facilitate the granting of an interest in the business to their industrious employees and worthy children.

[2.005] To understand better why an existing business might be incorporated, we shall look at an example involving the ubiquitous Mr A and Mr B. They have been in partnership together for over ten years, operating a garage business. The partnership holds a 35-year lease to the garage premises from which they sell and repair motor vehicles. Business has been good and they estimate that their gross annual profit is in the region of €80,000. The net worth of the partnership assets is €110,000, which are roughly broken down as follows:

- their leasehold premises is worth €40,000;
- their stock-in-hand is worth €30,000;

[3] See generally, Ch 5, *Disregarding Separate Legal Personality.*

[4] Ch 5, *Disregarding Separate Legal Personality* at para **[5.015]** *et seq.*

- their cash in the bank is €15,000;
- their debtors owe €5,000;
- the goodwill of the business is estimated by the partnership's auditors to be worth €20,000.

Although the business association of the partnership has been advantageous to them, there are a number of reasons why they feel that the time is right for them to incorporate[5].

In the first place, although neither of them intends to retire for some years, they feel that they should at this stage provide for the future and the possible entry of their children into the business. Secondly, one of their longest serving and most valued employees, Mr C, has indicated that unless he is given a share in the business, he may leave their employment and set up in business by himself. Thirdly, Mr A and Mr B are considering whether or not to purchase another garage which has come on the market. To acquire and get this up and running, they will need to borrow €60,000 from a bank. However, because as partners they have unlimited liability, should the new venture fail, they could quite easily lose everything, including their family homes, through judgment being levied against them[6]. How can incorporation help Mr A and Mr B?

[2.006] The three concerns set out above can to a large extent be catered for by the incorporation of a private company limited by shares. A number of possibilities would emerge on the incorporation of a company. In the first place, if Mr A and Mr B wish, they could transfer some of their shares to their respective families and provide that such shares should have no voting rights until a future time, so as to enable Mr A and Mr B to retain control of the business. In the second place, on the incorporation of *A and B Garages Ltd*, shares in the new company could be transferred to Mr C, whether outright or – on the basis of the principle that it's best not to give away the goods too soon – staggered over a period of time based on Mr C's future performance. Thirdly, Mr A and Mr B could arrange for *A and B Garages Ltd* to take a loan in the company's name, secured by the assets which would be transferred to it on its incorporation. By doing this, the bank's security will be confined to the assets of the business[7] and the personal assets of Mr A and Mr B will not be at risk because of the new venture and the vicissitudes of commercial life. Indeed, a bank will be more inclined to lend to a company, particularly as it will be able to take additional security over and above that

---

5 On partnerships see Ch 1, *The Private Company in Context*, at para **[1.014]** *et seq*, and, generally, see Twomey, *Partnership Law* (2000, Butterworths); Ivamy, *Underhill's Principles of the Law of Partnership* (12th edn, 1986) and L'Anson Banks, *Lindley and Banks on the Law of Partnership* (16th edn, 1990).

6 On bankruptcy generally, see Sanfey and Holohan, *Bankruptcy Law and Practice in Ireland* (2012, Round Hall). Bankruptcy should always be borne in mind when one operates business other than through a limited liability company, since for individuals, the Bankruptcy Act 1988 provides an alternative to corporate winding up under the Companies Acts.

7 This assumes that the lending bank does not require personal guarantees from A and B. Even where personal guarantees are required, it may be possible to have these capped at a specific amount.

which Mr A and Mr B as individuals could offer: *A and B Garages Ltd* can create a *floating charge* over its assets[8].

[2.007] The actual mechanics involved in incorporating a private company limited by shares are relatively straightforward although it must be stressed that proper legal, accounting and taxation advice should be obtained to avoid any pitfalls. The steps involved can be summarised as follows:

- *A and B Garages Ltd* is incorporated with a suitable objects clause[9] having an authorised share capital of, for example, €500,000, and an issued share capital of €110,000.
- Mr A and Mr B enter into an agreement and execute all the necessary documents with *A and B Garages Ltd* whereby they exchange their business for 110,000 €1 shares in *A and B Garages Ltd*[10].
- Mr A and Mr B may (and it is submitted, should) enter into a shareholders' agreement which will govern their relations *inter se*, and address issues such as management, the powers of directors and other matters[11]. Problems anticipated and legislated for can be resolved more easily.
- Shares can be allotted to the employee, Mr C, immediately, or a share option agreement entered into whereby Mr C can acquire shares in the new company over a period of time. This may be performance related. It is prudent to provide that if and when shares are allotted to Mr C he will also enter into a shareholders' agreement with Mr A and Mr B so as to ensure that all three are aware of their respective rights and liabilities.
- Mr A and Mr B can bequeath their respective shares to whoever they wish and achieve familial continuity of interest and ownership – if that be desired.

---

8 See Ch 4, *Incorporation and Its Consequences*, at para **[4.088]**, and generally, Ch 18 *Corporate Borrowing: Debentures and Security*, at para **[18.068]** *et seq*.

9 On a company's objects clause, see Ch 3, *Constitutional Documentation*, at para **[3.012]** and Ch 7, *Corporate Contracts: Capacity and Authority*, at para **[7.045]** *et seq*. Upon the incorporation of an existing business it is common to include in the objects clause an express object to acquire the existing business. Such an object may provide that the company has the capacity to, *inter alia*, 'acquire as a going concern the business of sale and repair of motor vehicles now being carried on by A and B currently trading under "A and B's Garage" together with all property, assets and liabilities tangible or intangible of that business and for that purpose, to enter an agreement with A and B and execute all documents required to give effect to the foregoing acquisition'. An example of such an object is to be found in *Re Westwinds Holding Company Ltd* (21 May 1974, unreported) HC, *per* Kenny J, where the company concerned had as its principal object the taking over and carrying on of the business of builders and public works contractors formerly carried on by its promoter.

10 Extreme caution must be exercised from a taxation perspective in carrying out this transaction, in that A and B may be liable for capital gains tax on the disposal of their business, and stamp duty and value added tax may be payable on the assignment of the lease of the business premises to A and B Garages Ltd.

11 For shareholders' agreements generally, see Ch 3, *Constitutional Documentation*, at para **[3.106]** *et seq*.

– As a general rule, Mr A's and Mr B's personal liability is limited to the amount, if any, unpaid on the shares held by them, and so their other personal assets are not at risk.

The primary disadvantage to Mr A and Mr B is that they will open their business to public inspection and will have to comply with the myriad responsibilities and duties imposed – even upon such small enterprises – by the Companies Acts. There are costs involved in pursuing any course of action and in this case the costs may be categorised as the ceding of privacy, additional administrative bureaucracy and being open to the supervision of the Director of Corporate Enforcement.

Incorporation of private companies

[2.008] By far the most common type of company incorporated in Ireland today is the private company limited by shares. Four distinctive types of private company need to be distinguished and considered. Section 33 of the CA 1963 recognises three types of private company: those which are limited by shares, those which are limited by guarantee and have a share capital and those which are unlimited and have a share capital. To these the European Communities (Single-Member Private Limited Companies) Regulations 1994 ('EC(SMPLC)R 1994')[12] has added a fourth, which is a variation on two of the other three types of private company. The formation of the following types of private company is now considered:

(a) Private companies limited by shares.
(b) Private companies limited by guarantee.
(c) Private unlimited companies with a share capital.
(d) Single-member private companies.

It is first proposed to outline the essential features of each type of private company.

(a) Private companies limited by shares

[2.009] The most commonly formed company in Ireland is the private company limited by shares. A private company limited by shares (or indeed, any 'limited' company) does not itself, of course, have limited liability: the company remains, at all times, fully liable for all of its (the company's) debts. Where a company is *limited by shares*, what is meant is that the liability of the company's members to contribute to the assets of the company is limited to the amount, if any, unpaid on the shares for which they have subscribed. Accordingly, if a member holds ten shares of €1 each, once he has paid €10 he will have no further liability for the company's debts. While a company's memorandum of association[13] must state the company's *authorised* share capital and the division of that capital into shares of specific values, the company is not obliged to disclose in its memorandum of association its *issued* share capital, ie the number of shares which have actually been issued, thus disclosing the value of share capital in the company[14].

---

[12] SI 275/1994.

[13] See Ch 3, *Constitutional Documentation*, at para **[3.017]** *et seq*.

[14] See further Ch 10, *The Maintenance of Capital*, at para **[10.004]**. It may be noted, though, that the amount of a company's issued share capital can be ascertained by carrying out a search at the CRO.

Accordingly, one should not be impressed by the fact that a company has an authorised share capital of €1 million – it might have issued just two €1 shares!

(b) Private companies limited by guarantee

[2.010] At the outset it must be recognised that not all companies which are limited by guarantee are private companies. Section 33(1) of the CA 1963 is most specific: only companies limited by guarantee and which *have a share capital* are private companies; a company limited by guarantee which does not have a share capital is a public company. Very few companies that are limited by guarantee have a share capital, and so very few companies limited by guarantee are private companies. Of course, to be a private company, not only must a company limited by guarantee have a share capital, but also its articles of association[15] *must contain the three restrictions* set out in s 33(1) of the CA 1963[16].

[2.011] Where a company is limited by guarantee, this means that the liability of the members is limited to the amount of their guarantee to contribute to the company's assets in a winding up. Accordingly, if the members guarantee to contribute €10 to the company, their liability to the company is limited to €10. It should be noted that a company only can only look to its guarantee fund *when it is being wound up* and cannot rely on the guarantees of its members to secure a loan: *Re Irish Club Ltd*[17].

[2.012] Where a company is limited by its members' guarantees and also has a share capital, the liability of its members on a winding up is limited to pay for the shares for which they have subscribed and to pay the amount that they have guaranteed. Companies limited by guarantee and which *do not* have a share capital are public companies and are most frequently employed as management companies of buildings divided into apartments and in shopping centre developments, where it is necessary that all tenants have an interest in the company and where there may be more than 50 tenants. In such circumstances, a public company limited by guarantee must be used because s 33(1) of the CA 1963 restricts the number in a private company to 99 members. Guarantee companies are considered in Ch 30.

(c) Private unlimited companies with a share capital

[2.013] The third type of private company is a private company which has a share capital and in which the members have unlimited liability. An unlimited company is defined by s 5(2)(c) of the CA 1963 as being:

> 'a company not having any limit on the liability of its members.'

Unlimited companies are not generally used as trading-companies because s 207(1) of the CA 1963 provides that in the event of a company being wound up, past or present members[18]:

---

15 See Ch 3, *Constitutional Documentation*, at para **[3.040]**.

16 See Ch 1, *The Private Company in Context*, at para **[1.134]**.

17 *Re Irish Club Ltd* (1906) WN 127.

18 Ie, contributories: see Ch 25, *The Realisation and Distribution of Assets in a Winding Up*, at para **[25.130]**.

'... shall be liable to contribute to the assets of the company to an amount sufficient for the payment of its debts and liabilities, and the costs, charges and expenses of the winding up, and for the adjustment of the rights of the contributories among themselves ...'

It is possible for an unlimited company to be registered without a share capital, but this is a rare occurrence. Where an unlimited company is incorporated, it will almost always be the case that it will have a share capital and will consequently be a private company where its articles of association comply with s 33(1) of the CA 1963. Public unlimited companies are not, however, unheard of, and a number of Ireland's leading mortgage providers are public unlimited company subsidiaries of their parents, Bank of Ireland and AIB Bank, plc[19].

[2.014] Given the potential for personal financial disaster, why should any promoter[20] cause a company to be registered with unlimited liability for its members? The incorporation of unlimited companies is largely driven by the desire to keep secret financial information concerning the company, particularly if it is a holding company. The use of an unlimited company to avoid the disclosure requirements under the C(A)A 1986 was curtailed by the EC(A)R 1993 which extended the provisions of the 1986 Act to certain types of unlimited companies and partnerships[21]. Previously it was the case that the holding (non-trading) companies of many of the leading companies in Irish commercial life were unlimited, one of the primary reasons being to avoid the provisions of the 1986 Act. As at 31 December 2010, the total number of unlimited companies on the register was 3,927, which represented 2.12% of the total number of companies on the register as at that date[22]. It is not, therefore, apparent that the EC(A)R 1993 have had any appreciable effect on the number of unlimited companies.

(d) Single-member private limited companies

[2.015] By virtue of the EC(SMPLC)R 1994[23] it is now possible to form a single-member private limited company. Regulation 3(1) provides that:

'Notwithstanding any enactment or rule of law to the contrary, a private company limited by shares or by guarantee may be formed by one person, and may have one member (in these regulations referred to as a single-member company), to the extent permitted by the Companies Acts and these regulations.'

Although the regulations do not explicitly state that their application is confined to private companies limited by shares and private companies limited by guarantee *and which have a share capital*, this must be the case by implication since a private company must have a share capital. It should be noted that *not all* types of private companies may convert to single-member companies. By reason of the fact that reg 3(1) specifically

[19] For example, Bank of Ireland Mortgage Bank and AIB Mortgage Bank. On unlimited companies see, generally, Ch 31, *Unlimited Companies*.

[20] For the definition of a promoter, see Ch 15, *Duties of Directors and Other Officers*, at para **[15.161]**.

[21] See SI 396/1993, considered in Ch 31, *Unlimited Companies*, at para **[31.024]**.

[22] Indeed the number of unlimited companies peaked in 1998 when at year's end there were 6,171, which represented 3.5% of companies on the register: *Companies Reports, 1995, 1999 and 2000*.

[23] SI 275/1994.

refers only to private companies 'limited by shares or by guarantee', the regulations do not permit the formation of an unlimited single-member private company[24].

[2.016] A single-member company is formed by one person subscribing his name to the new company's memorandum of association. Accordingly, reg 4 of EC(SMPLC)R 1994 provides:

> 'Notwithstanding s 5(1) of the CA 1963, one person may, for any lawful purpose, by subscribing his or her name to a memorandum of association and otherwise complying with the requirements of the Companies Acts and these regulations relating to registration, form an incorporated company being a private company limited by shares or by guarantee.'

Apart from the fact that only one person will be a subscriber to the memorandum of association of a single-member private limited company, all of the other requirements relating to the registration of a private company will apply to single-member private companies[25]. As at 31 December 2010 the number of single-member private limited companies on the register was 46,429[26].

Methods of incorporation

[2.017] There are three main ways of forming a private company. The first method is by lodging all the forms on the 'ordinary list' in the Companies Registration Office ('the CRO'). The second and shorter way is through membership of the Company Incorporation Scheme, and proceeding on the 'ten day list' or '*Fé Phráinn*' method. The third way is by means of the CRODisk method, whereby incorporation can be achieved within five working days where particulars are lodged with the CRO on floppy disk. In addition, a ready-made 'shelf company', if available, may be purchased from a company formation firm. It should be noted that one effect of s 42 of the C(A)(No2)A 1999, which requires that a company when formed will carry out an activity in the State, has been to make scarce the numbers of 'shelf companies' that are available.

(a) The ordinary list

[2.018] Incorporation of a company by means of the *ordinary list* can, depending on the work-load of the CRO, take up to three weeks from the initial lodging of the application to the issuing of the certificate of incorporation. The documentation which must be lodged to form a company is set out below[27].

(b) The Company Incorporation Scheme

[2.019] The *Fé Phráinn* method of incorporation is referred to by the CRO as the 'Company Incorporation Scheme'[28]. The function of this method of company formation, introduced in 1986, is to provide a scheme whereby participants are guaranteed to have

---

24 See further Ch 1, *Private Companies in Context*, at para **[1.141]**.

25 Regulation 3(2) of SI 275/1994.

26 See *Companies Registration Office Report 2011*, at p 10 and see the *Companies Report 2000*, at p 36.

27 At para **[2.024]**.

28 See, in this regard, and indeed on the topic of company formation generally, CRO, *Company Incorporation*, Information Leaflet No 1, March 2000.

companies incorporated within ten working days of all documentation being lodged in the CRO. Only private companies limited by shares or by guarantee and unlimited companies may be formed by this method. A company can only be formed using this scheme by a participating firm, which is registered with the CRO and which has submitted 'model' memoranda and articles of association. No amendments may be made to the approved text without the express prior approval of the CRO.

[2.020] The CRO has a number of requirements which must be complied with if a firm is to be registered under the Company Incorporation Scheme. These are that:

- the memorandum and articles of association should be *printed* (as opposed to typed or produced by computer) in clear black type on durable paper;
- no alterations may be made to the pre-printed model memorandum and articles save the name, main objects, liability and the share capital;
- only companies required for immediate commercial use are permitted to be registered;
- where the promoter makes an error, and an application has to be resubmitted, it will be treated as a new application;
- the CRO is the final arbitrator as to the interpretation of the scheme's conditions.

The model memorandum and articles of association submitted to the CRO become the standard texts for the constitutional documentation of all companies registered by that participant under the scheme. The speed of the incorporation of a company incorporated under this scheme is achieved through standardisation which allows the CRO to assume safely that the vast majority of the paperwork is in order. Under the ordinary list, every provision of the individual documents submitted should be scrutinised by the staff of the CRO. The model memorandum of association submitted to the CRO under the scheme will only leave the name clause, 'main objects' clause, liability clause, and share capital clause blank. Accordingly, it is only the variations in these clauses which must be scrutinised. It should be borne in mind that this method of incorporation is only available to companies required for immediate use.

[2.021] Section 80(1) of the CLEA 2001 is a variation on the same theme. This provision facilitates swift incorporation through the recognition of reference memoranda and articles of association by providing:

> 'The registrar of companies may accept for registration a document containing standard form text from the objects clause of a memorandum of association or articles of association and shall assign a reference number to each document so registered.'

Company formation firms may lodge reference memoranda and articles of association *that do not relate to a particular company*[29]. Thereafter, they may lodge memoranda and articles of association in relation to specific companies that omit the tracts of text already contained in the 'reference' documents, which are specifically incorporated, by reference, into their memoranda and articles[30]. Where text is referred to in this manner it is 'deemed for all purposes' to be incorporated in the memoranda and articles of

[29] Section 80(2) of the CLEA 2001.

[30] Section 80(3) of the CLEA 2001.

association of companies[31]. A small number of companies have utilised this scheme; however it has generally not proven popular because the resulting memorandum and articles of association are not 'stand-alone' documents and can only be read by reference to the 'reference document' filed. Far from speeding up the process or being efficient, the resulting memorandum and articles of association are a mess, difficult to follow and the initiative is thought to be a failure.

(c) The CRODisk Scheme

[2.022] In 2000 the CRO introduced a new electronic company incorporation scheme whereby incorporation is guaranteed within five working days provided the terms and conditions of the scheme are fulfilled[32]. CRODisk is open to members of the Company Incorporation Scheme and is intended to facilitate presenters who require speedy company incorporation without the inconvenience of manually lodging the documents in the CRO cash office. Instead, company information is presented directly to the new companies' section electronically; however, the usual paper incorporation documents continue to be required, fully completed, in addition to the electronic format. The CRO provides participating presenters with the software necessary to manage data entry, form production and disk creation. In addition to formation, change of principal object, change of name, change of registered office and change of directors can all be lodged using CRODisk[33].

(d) Shelf companies

[2.023] *Shelf companies* are companies that are formed in anticipation of demand by company formation, accountants' and solicitors' firms and which are later sold to persons who require a company immediately. Thus, the company formed will have as its first subscribers and directors the managers of the company formation firm, a nominal share capital and a name. Once a willing buyer is found, the managers of the formation firm will transfer the shares issued in the company to the new owners and, having appointed the new owners or their nominees as directors, they will themselves resign as directors. The share capital, the registered office and the company's name may be subsequently changed at the new owners' leisure. Section 42 of the C(A)(No2)A 1999 has significantly obstructed the formation of shelf companies by reason of the new requirement that, on formation, all companies must carry on an activity in the State and restrictions on the number of directorships a person can hold in private companies.

The steps in forming a private company

[2.024] To incorporate a *private company limited by shares*, the following are usually lodged in the CRO:

- memorandum of association[34];
- articles of association[35];

31 Section 80(4) of the CLEA 2001.

32 See, further, CRO, *Company Incorporation*, Information Leaflet No 1, March 2000.

33 At the time of writing, it is understood that this service is available only in respect of those companies that were incorporated using CRODisk.

34 See Ch 3, *Constitutional Documentation*, at para **[3.003]**.

35 See para **[3.038]**.

- Form No A1[36];
- a statutory declaration that the company will carry on an activity in Ireland[37] (said declaration being incorporated within the A1);
- the appropriate fees[38].

In the case of a private company limited by shares its memorandum of association should be in accordance with the form set out in Table A, or as near thereto as circumstances permit[39]. It is not essential that articles of association are lodged with an application to form a private company limited by shares.

[2.025] Where articles of association are not lodged with an application to form a new company, the unamended model articles set out in Table A Part II of the First Schedule to the CA 1963 will become the articles of the new company by default[40].

[2.026] Before proceeding to lodge the necessary incorporation documentation, it is advisable to check that the proposed name for the company is not similar to the name of a company which has already been incorporated by checking with the registrar of companies. Since 1 September 2009 it has been possible to apply to the CRO to reserve a name for a company that is to be formed at a later date in reliance upon s 59 of the IFCMPA 2005. Where reservation is granted it will last initially for a period not exceeding 28 days although this can be extended before the expiry of the initial period for a further 28 days[41].

(i) Incorporating a single-member private limited company

[2.027] To incorporate a *single-member private limited company* a person must subscribe his or her name to a memorandum of association and comply with the same requirements as apply in the case of a private company limited by shares, considered above. The appropriate form is again a Form No A1. Shortly after it became possible to form a *de jure* single-member private limited company, there were a great many conversions from so-called 'multi-member' private companies. Where a company converts to, or for that matter ceases to be, a single-member company, the appropriate forms for use in the return of this information are prescribed by the European Communities (Single-Member Private Limited Companies) (Forms) Regulations 1994[42].

(ii) Incorporating a private company limited by guarantee having a share capital

[2.028] To incorporate a *private company limited by guarantee and having a share capital*, again, a memorandum and articles of association together with a Form No A1

36 See, McGowan-Smyth & Daly, *Irish Company Secretary's Handbook* (2011, Bloomsbury Professional) at pp 172, 274 for the contents of the Form A1.

37 As required by s 42 of the C(A)(No2)A 1999. See para **[2.030]**.

38 The fees payable to the CRO are listed at www.cro.ie.

39 Section 16 of the CA 1963.

40 See generally, Ch 3, *Constitutional Documentation*, at para **[3.040]** *et seq*.

41 See s 60 of the IFCMPA 2005.

42 SI 306/1994. To change from a multi-member private company to a single-member private company a Form No M1 is used; to convert the other way, from single-member to multi-member, a Form No M2 is used. See Ch 33, *Conversion by Re-registration*, at para **[33.016]**.

must be delivered to the CRO. However, there are some differences in the particulars required. In the first place the memorandum of association will reflect the fact that the company is limited by guarantee. Secondly, unlike a company limited by shares, there *must* be registered with the memorandum of association, articles of association which are signed by the subscribers to the memorandum and which prescribe regulations for the company[43]. In this regard the appropriate form of memorandum is to be found in Part I of Table D of the First Schedule and the appropriate articles of association are to be found in Part III of Table D. Both memorandum and articles of association should be in accordance with the forms set out in Table D, or as near thereto as circumstances admit[44]. Thirdly, the articles must state the number of members with which the company proposes to be registered[45].

(ii) Incorporating a private unlimited company

[2.029] To incorporate an *unlimited private company having a share capital* a memorandum and articles of association and Form No A1 must be lodged with the CRO. As in the case of companies limited by guarantee and having a share capital, again, articles *must* be lodged with the application to form an unlimited company[46]. The form of memorandum for an unlimited private company which has a share capital is set out in Part I of Table E of the First Schedule to the CA 1963. The appropriate articles of association are to be found in Part III of Table E of the First Schedule. Both the memorandum and articles of association of unlimited companies should be in accordance with the forms set out in Table E, or as near thereto as circumstances permit[47].

The requirement that a company carries on an 'activity' in the State

[2.030] In an attempt to combat the perceived abuses of Irish registered non-resident companies (IRNRs)[48], s 42(1) of the C(A)(No2)A 1999 provides that a company 'shall not be formed and registered … unless it appears to the registrar of companies that the company, when registered, will carry on an activity in the State, being an activity that is mentioned in its memorandum'. 'Activity' is widely defined by s 42(7) of the C(A)(No2)A 1999 to mean:

> '… any activity that a company may be lawfully formed to carry on and includes the holding, acquisition or disposal of property of whatsoever kind.'

Section 42(2) provides that the registrar of companies may accept as 'sufficient evidence that a company, when registered, will carry on an activity in the State' a *statutory declaration* in the prescribed form. This additional statutory declaration has been

43 Section 11 of the CA 1963.

44 Section 16 of the CA 1963.

45 Section 12(2) of the CA 1963. Where the numbers of members subsequently increases beyond the registered number, the company must notify the CRO within 15 days after the increase was resolved: s 12(3).

46 Section 11 of the CA 1963.

47 Section 16 of the CA 1963.

48 See para **[2.045]**.

embodied in the Form No A1 used to incorporate all companies[49]. The declaration must include the following particulars:

> '(a) if it appears to the person making the declaration that the activity belongs to a division, group and class appearing in the relevant classification system –
>
> (i) the general nature of the activity, and
>
> (ii) the division, group and class in that system to which the activity belongs,
>
> (b) if it appears to the said person that the activity does not belong to any such division, group and class, a precise description of the activity,
>
> (c) the place or places in the State where it is proposed to carry on the activity,
>
> (d) the place, whether in the State or not, where the central administration of the company will normally be carried on.'

In classifying the particular activity in which the company proposes to engage, the appropriate NACE code classification (which is the common basis for statistical classifications of economic activities within the EU[50]) must be used. If the activity cannot be classified under the NACE code, a precise description of the activity must be given. The NACE code is available on the CRO's website at www.cro.ie. Where the purpose or one or more of the purposes for which the company is being formed is the carrying on of two or more activities, the matters referred to in paras (a) to (c) above shall be those that relate to what the maker of the declaration considers to be the principal activity for which the company is being formed to carry on in the State[51]. Those who are recognised as having the capacity to swear the statutory declaration are: (a) one of the persons named as directors in the statement delivered under s 3 of the C(A)A 1982; (b) the person or persons so named in the s 3 statement as secretary or joint-secretaries; or (c) the solicitor, if any, engaged in the formation of the company[52].

Registration by the registrar of companies

[2.031] Once the requisite documentation has been lodged, it is then for the registrar of companies to decide whether or not to register the company. One of the most common reasons for refusing to register a company is because of a failure on the part of the person who forms the company to complete the Form No A1 properly. A high degree of accuracy is required in completing the Form No A1.

[2.032] The registrar of companies, through her assistants, will scrutinise the documentation, especially the memorandum, to satisfy herself that 'all the requirements of the Companies Acts in respect of registration and of matters precedent and incidental thereto have been complied with'[53]. These requirements include the statutory declaration required by s 42 of the C(A)(No2)A 1999, considered in the preceding paragraph. When a company is registered the memorandum and articles will be retained

---

49 The changes to the Form No A1 were introduced by the Companies (Forms) Order, 2000 (SI 62/2000) which came into operation on 18 April 2000.

50 Set out in the Annex to Council Regulation (EEC) No 3037/90 of 9 October 1990.

51 Section 42(3) of the C(A)(No2)A 1999.

52 Section 42(4).

53 Pursuant to s 5(1) of the C(A)A 1983.

and registered[54] by the registrar of companies and a document analogous to a birth certificate for a human person, a *certificate of incorporation* will issue for the company.

[2.033] The effect of registration is set out in s 18(2) of the CA 1963, which provides that:

> 'From the date of incorporation mentioned in the certificate of incorporation, the subscribers of the memorandum, together with such other persons as may from time to time become members of the company, shall be a body corporate with the name contained in the memorandum, capable forthwith of exercising all the functions of an incorporated company, and having perpetual succession and a common seal, but with such liability on the part of the members to contribute to the assets of the company in the event of its being wound up ...'

And so corporate life begins[55].

Delivery of particulars to the Revenue Commissioners

[2.034] Section 882(1) of the Taxes Consolidation Act 1997 (as inserted by s 83 of the Finance Act 1999) requires every company, incorporated in the State or which commences to carry on a trade, profession or business within the State, to deliver within 30 days of certain stated events[56], a written statement to the Revenue Commissioners[57]. This statement must state:

- (a) the name of the company;
- (b) the company's registered office;
- (c) the address of its principal place of business;
- (d) the name and address of the secretary;
- (e) the date of commencement of the trade, profession or business;
- (f) the nature of such trade, profession or business;
- (g) the date up to which accounts relating to such trade, profession or business will be made up; and
- (h) such other information as the Revenue Commissioners may consider necessary. In addition, in the cases of companies that are incorporated, but not resident in the State, and companies that are neither incorporated nor resident in the State, certain other information is required[58].

This measure, which along with s 23A of the Taxes Consolidation Act 1997 (as inserted by s 82 of the Finance Act 1999) was intended to combat the problem posed by non-

54 Section 17 of the CA 1963.

55 See further Ch 4, *Incorporation and Its Consequences*, at para **[4.004]** *et seq.*

56 The stated events are: (a) the date it commences to carry on a trade, profession or business, wherever carried on; (b) the date at which there is a material change in information previously delivered by the company under that section; and (c) the giving of a notice to the company by an inspector requiring a statement under that section: s 882(2) of the Taxes Consolidation Act 1997.

57 This section applies (a) in the case of companies that are incorporated on or after 11 February 1999, as on and from that date; and (b) in the case of companies that are incorporated before 11 February 1999, as on and from 1 October 1999: s 83(2) of the Finance Act 1999.

58 Section 83(2)(i) and (iii) of the Finance Act 1999.

resident Irish companies[59], is considerably strengthened by the ability to invoke s 12A of the 1982 Act. Section 882(3) of the Taxes Consolidation Act 1997 provides:

> Where a company fails to deliver a statement which it is required to deliver under this section then, notwithstanding any obligations as to secrecy or other restriction upon disclosure of information imposed by or under any statute or otherwise, the Revenue Commissioners may give a notice in writing to the registrar of companies (within the meaning of the Companies Act, 1963) stating that the company has so failed to deliver a statement under this section.

Where the Revenue Commissioners serve such a notice the registrar of companies has power under s 12A of the C(A)A 1982 to strike the company off the register[60]. The cumulative effect of these provisions is to empower the strangulation at birth of non-compliant companies so that corporate life can end as quickly as it has begun where companies fail to deliver the statement required under s 882(1) of the Taxes Consolidation Act 1997.

Statutory obligations incidental to registration

[2.035] Once registration takes place and a company is incorporated, many consequences ensue. The most important of these consequences are considered in Ch 4, *Incorporation and its Consequences*. In addition to these legal consequences, when registered, a company becomes subject to a number of statutory *obligations*. Although the private company is the most popular legal business structure, it is entrammeled by statutory obligations. The more important statutory obligations which arise upon a company's incorporation appertain to:

(a) registered office;
(b) directors and secretary;
(c) display of certain information;
(d) publication of notices;
(e) use of a business name.

It must be stressed that these statutory obligations are far from exhaustive. A comprehensive list of the statutory obligations of companies (and their directors and other officers) is detailed in Chapter 28.

(a) Registered office

[2.036] Every company must have a *registered office* within the State by virtue of s 113 of the CA 1963[61]. The purpose of this requirement is to ensure that every company formed and registered in Ireland has an address to which all communications and other notices may be sent. A company's registered office must be notified to the registrar of companies prior to its incorporation[62]. This is facilitated by the Form No A1 which is lodged with a company's memorandum and articles of association when application is made for registration and incorporation. Where a company changes the location of its

---

59 See para **[2.045]**.

60 For the registrar's power to strike off a company, see Ch 26, *Strike Off and Restoration*, at para **[26.004]**.

61 As amended by s 4(1) of the C(A)A 1982.

62 Section 113(2) of the CA 1963.

registered office, it must notify the registrar of companies within 14 days[63]. The company and every officer who is in default of the foregoing requirements are liable to a class C fine[64].

[2.037] Another feature of a company's registered office is that several provisions of the Companies Acts require that certain documents must be kept and retained at the registered office:

- the register of debenture holders[65];
- copies of instruments which create charges[66];
- the register of members[67];
- the book of minutes of general meetings[68];
- the register of directors' declarations of interest and general notice of interest[69];
- books of account[70];
- the register of directors and secretary[71];
- the register of directors' and secretary's interests in shares[72].

It must be said that although the foregoing are legal requirements, in practice a relaxed approach is taken by some private companies and the requirements of the Companies Acts are all too often an afterthought.

(b) Directors and secretary

[2.038] Sections 174 and 175 of the CA 1963 require that all companies, including single-member private limited companies, have two directors, and a company secretary, who may also be a director[73]. The names of the first two directors must also be delivered to the registrar of companies with the application for registration and their consent to so act, shown by their signatures on the Form No A1[74]. Any change in directors and secretary or in their particulars must be notified to the registrar of companies by the company within 14 days[75]. As a result of the C(A)(No2)A 1999, the general rule is that every Irish company must have at least one director who is resident in the EU or EEA[76].

---

63 Section 113(3) of the CA 1963. Note that it is not sufficient for the company to record the change of the registered office in its annual return for that year.

64 See, generally, Ch 28, *Company Law Compliance and Enforcement*.

65 Section 91 of the CA 1963.

66 Section 109 of the CA 1963.

67 Section 116(5) of the CA 1963.

68 Section 146(1) of the CA 1963.

69 Section 194(5)(a) of CA 1963.

70 Section 147(3) of the CA 1963.

71 Section 195(1) of the CA 1963.

72 Section 59 of the CA 1990.

73 See Ch 13, *Corporate Governance: Management by the Directors*, at para **[13.011]** *et seq*.

74 See s 3 of the C(A)A 1982 as amended by Second Schedule, Part II to the C(A)A 1983.

75 Section 195 of the CA 1963.

76 An alternative to having a director resident in the EU or EEA is to provide a bond pursuant to s 43 or, following incorporation, a certificate pursuant to s 44 of the C(A)(No2)A 1999.

(c) *Display of certain information*

[2.039] When a company has been incorporated, and it commences trading, it will often have headed notepaper printed. Under s 196 of the CA 1963[77], such headed paper, or 'business letters of the company', which contain the company's name and where sent by the company to any person, must state in legible characters in relation to every director the following particulars:

- present Christian name, or initials, and surname;
- any former Christian or surnames;
- his nationality, if not Irish.

The Minister for Jobs, Enterprise, and Innovation may grant an exemption where he is of the opinion that an exemption from this requirement is expedient, subject to such conditions as he may think fit. Where there is default in complying with these provisions, the company and any officers who are in default, will on summary conviction be liable to a fine[78]. Proceedings under this section can only be taken by or with the consent of the Minister for Jobs, Enterprise and Innovation[79].

[2.040] It should be noted that the reference to a 'director' in this section applies to any person in accordance with whose instructions or directions the directors of a company are accustomed to act: s 196(6) of the CA 1963.

[2.041] In addition to s 196 of the CA 1963, reg 9 of the EC(C)R 1973[80] provides that every company shall include the following particulars on its letters, order forms, website and emails:

(a) the name and legal form of the company;

(b) the place of registration of the company and the number with which it is registered;

(c) the address of the registered office of the company;

(d) in the case of a company exempt from the obligation to use the word 'limited' or 'teoranta' as part of its name, the fact that it is a limited company[81];

(e) in the case of a company that is being wound up, the fact that it is being wound up; and

---

77 Which, by sub-s (3) applies to all companies which are registered under the Companies Acts; or registered under the Companies (Consolidation) Act 1908 unless registered before 23 November 1916; or to foreign companies which have an established place of business within the State, unless such was established before 23 November 1916; or which are registered under the Moneylenders Act 1933 (as amended).

78 Section 196(4) of the CA 1963, as amended by First Schedule to the C(A)A 1982.

79 Section 196(5) of the CA 1963.

80 SI 163/1973, as substituted by the European Communities (Companies) (Amendment) Regulations 2007 (SI 49/2007), reg 3(c).

81 It is unlikely that this will have any relevance in practice to private limited companies although such companies could, in theory, qualify under s 24 of the CA 1963, and be relieved from using the word 'limited' in their names since virtually all companies so qualifying are public companies limited by guarantee without a share capital. See Ch 30, *Guarantee Companies*, at para **[30.015]**.

(f) if reference is made to the share capital of the company, the reference shall be to the capital that is subscribed and paid up.

[2.042] Section 114 of the CA 1963 makes further disclosure requirements for a company. These include:

- painting or affixing its name on the outside of every office or place in which its business is carried on, in a conspicuous position, in letters easily legible: s 114(1)(a);
- having its name engraved in legible characters on its seal: s 114(1)(b);
- having its name mentioned in legible characters in all business letters of the company and in all notices and other official publications of the company, and in all bills of exchange, promissory notes, endorsements, cheques and orders for money or goods purporting to be signed by or on behalf of the company and in all invoices, receipts and letters of credit of the company: s 114(1)(c).

Failure to comply will render the company and every officer of the company liable to a fine[82]. Furthermore, in certain circumstances, officers may be made personally liable where the company's name is incorrectly stated[83].

(d) Publication of notices

[2.043] Regulation 4(1) of the EC(C)R 1973[84] obliges a limited liability company[85] to publish in the Companies Registration Office Gazette notice of the delivery to, or the issue by, the registrar of companies, of the following documents and particulars:

- any certificate of incorporation;
- the memorandum and articles of association, or equivalent documents, or documents amending them, together with the amended documents;
- any return relating to the directors or a change in the directors;
- any return relating to the persons, other than the board of directors, who are authorised to enter into transactions binding the company, or notification of a change among such persons ('registered persons');
- its annual returns;
- any notice of its registered office or of a change;
- any copy of a winding-up order;
- any order for the dissolution of the company;
- any return by a liquidator of the final meeting of the company on a winding up.

Regulation 4(2) provides that such notice shall be published within six weeks of the relevant delivery or issue. In practice, the registrar of companies ordinarily obliges companies by causing such notices to be published in the Companies Registration Office Gazette.

---

82 See s 114(2) of the CA 1963.

83 See Ch 5, *Disregarding Separate Legal Personality*, at para **[5.081]** and also see Ch 7, *Corporate Contracts, Capacity and Authority*, at para **[7.011]**.

84 SI 163/1973.

85 Or an unregistered company with limited liability, eg, The Governor and Company of the Bank of Ireland.

(e) Use of a business name

[2.044] The RBNA 1963 has application to companies registered under the Companies Acts. Where a company decides to use a name other than its own corporate name, s 22 of the CA 1963 provides that it shall register that *business name* in the manner directed by law for the registration of business names. The general requirements of the RBNA 1963 have been considered, above[86]. It may be noted that in *Tierney v Midserve Ltd, trading as Sachs Hotel and Genport Ltd*[87] where a company acquired a business name from another company but did not register that business name, a plaintiff who claimed to have suffered personal injuries would not be statute-barred where the plaintiff did not join the correct defendant within the limitation period because the failure to comply with the RBNA 1963 and s 22 of the CA 1963 operated to conceal the right of action as against the correct defendant.

Irish registered non-resident companies

[2.045] Irish registered non-resident (IRNR) companies flourished in the 1990s. Originally, they were primarily formed for tax purposes[88]. With the break-up of the Eastern Block of countries, many nefarious individuals – including, it was reported, members of the Russian mafia and other organised criminals – became acquainted with the utility of IRNR companies. Ireland was one of the few countries that did not have deeming provisions whereby companies formed and registered were deemed to be resident in the jurisdiction for tax purposes. The Department of Foreign Affairs received many complaints from foreign authorities' law and tax enforcement agencies arising from the frequency with which IRNRs were cited as entities involved in international fraud and general malpractice. The result was the taking of steps, the effect of which was to effectively outlaw the IRNR. This was achieved by a number of steps. In the first place, s 82(2) of the Finance Act 1999 provides that subject to certain limited exceptions:

> '… a company which is incorporated in the State shall be regarded for the purposes of the Tax Acts and the Capital Gains Tax Acts as resident in the State.'

The exceptions to this are twofold. First, a company will not be deemed to be resident where it is a 'relevant company' and carries on a trade in the State or is related to a company that carries on a trade in the State: s 82(3) of the Finance Act 1999[89]. Second, a company that is regarded for the purposes of any arrangements as resident in a territory other than the State and not resident in the State shall be treated for the purposes of the Tax Acts and the Capital Gains Tax Acts as not resident in the State. Other steps taken include s 42 of the C(A)(No2)A 1999 (the general requirement that all companies must

86 See Ch 1, *The Private Company in Context*, at para **[1.007]**.

87 *Tierney v Midserve Ltd, trading as Sachs Hotel and Genport Ltd* [2002] IEHC 12, (23 January 2002, unreported) HC, Kinlen J.

88 See Kavanagh, 'Non-Resident Irish Companies' (1994) CLP 141.

89 Relevant company is one, in effect, that is under the control of persons who are resident for tax purposes in the EU or other territory with which the State has made tax arrangements, and not under the control of a person who is not so resident: s 23A(1)(a) of the Taxes Consolidation Act 1997 inserted by s 82(1) of the Finance Act 1999.

carry on an activity in the State)[90], the requirement that all Irish companies have at least one EU or EEA resident director[91] and the requirement that all companies formed and registered must deliver specified particulars to the Revenue Commissioners within 30 days of commencing business[92].

[2.046] By making a company non-resident in Ireland the desired effect was to ensure that it would not be liable, *inter alia*, for Irish corporation tax[93]. The means employed to make a company Irish registered but non-resident was to form and register it in Ireland pursuant to the Companies Acts but to ensure it was prevented, by its constitutional documentation, from being *controlled* from within the State. Although it was not essential to the determination of a company's *residence* that it did not conduct business in Ireland, it was material,[94] and many non-resident companies' constitutional documentation so provided. The IRNR company will be remembered as a short-lived curiosity that had the potential to cause great harm to Ireland's commercial reputation on the international stage.

---

90 See para **[2.030]**.

91 See para **[2.038]**.

92 Section 882(2) of the Taxes Consolidation Act 1997 as inserted by s 83(1) of the Finance Act 1999.

93 Contrast the liability to pay value added tax: *WLD Worldwide Leather Distribution Ltd v Revenue Commissioners* (27 July 1994, unreported) HC, *per* Flood J, noted by Hutchinson, 'Registering For VAT – A Recent Case' (1994) CLP 239.

94 See, for example, *Re Little Olympian Each Ways Ltd* [1994] 4 All ER 561 where Lindsay J held that an English company would not be ordinarily resident there where its central control and the management of the company actually abides and is exercised overseas.

Chapter 3

Constitutional Documentation

Introduction

[3.001] A company's memorandum of association sets out the basic parameters of legitimate corporate existence, finance, capacity and activity. Furthermore, the incorporation of a private company is achieved through the registration of the memorandum of association. The articles of association are the internal rules or regulations of a company and govern relations between the company and its members and between the members *inter se*; the articles define the relationship between members and directors and are the basis of corporate governance. On incorporation, both are normally[1] delivered to the registrar of companies for registration[2]. Together, these two documents form the 'corporate constitution', in that they govern the company's relations with outsiders and insiders and define the company. However, in many private companies there also exists a 'hidden constitution', which arises through the adoption of a shareholders' agreement. Unlike true constitutional documents, shareholders' agreements are only binding on those who are parties to them.

[3.002] The provisions in a company's memorandum and articles of association are of fundamental importance. Although the memorandum of association is the dominant document and its provisions will prevail in any conflict with the articles, the particular articles of association adopted by a company are of great significance in many different company law contexts. The articles of association are the rules by which the members of a company agree to be bound. They are created by the first subscribers and accepted by all future members. As such, the articles underscore the importance of the concept of 'association' to company law. Corporations aggregate are associations, and have always had an internal constitution. Single-member private limited companies[3] will also have articles that will regulate the relationship between the sole shareholder and the company's directors. The fact that both the memorandum and articles are alterable, generally, by the members does not detract from their importance. Unless and until they are altered, they are sacrosanct and the power to alter them must be exercised *bona fide*

---

1 Although it is not necessary to deliver articles of association on an application to incorporate a private company limited by shares and where they are not delivered, Part II of Table A to the First Schedule of the CA 1963 will apply (see para **[3.039]**), it is highly unusual not to deliver tailored articles of association on the incorporation of such a company.

2 Section 17 of the CA 1963. This was amended by s 83 of the CLEA 2001 to facilitate the registration of standard memoranda and articles of association, permitted by s 80 of the CLEA 2001: see Ch 2, *Incorporation by Registration*, at para **[2.021]**.

3 Permitted by the EC(SMPLC)R 1994, SI 275/1994, considered generally in Ch 1, *The Private Company in Context*, at para **[1.143]** *et seq*.

and in the interests of the company[4]. In this chapter the foregoing issues are considered in four separate sections:

[A] The memorandum of association.

[B] The articles of association.

[C] The statutory contract in s 25 of the CA 1963.

[D] Shareholders' agreements.

[A] THE MEMORANDUM OF ASSOCIATION

The memorandum of association

[3.003] A company's memorandum of association is the principal document by which its registration is effected. Section 5 of the CA 1963 facilitates corporate formation by providing:

> '... where the company to be formed will be a private company, any two or more persons, associated for any lawful purpose may, by subscribing their names to a *memorandum of association* and otherwise complying with the requirements of this Act relating to registration, form an incorporated company, with or without limited liability.'

Of course, now a single-member private company can be formed, and reg 4 of the EC(SMPLC)R 1994[5] provides that one person may sign his name to a memorandum of association. Historically, it was perceived that the memorandum contained matters so fundamental to the company that it could not be altered, in contrast with the articles which could always be altered by a special resolution of the members[6]. Today the compulsory clauses in the memorandum of association are also alterable where the alterations are carried out in compliance with the provisions of the Companies Acts.

[3.004] Section 16 of the CA 1963 prescribes that the form of the memorandum of association for private companies shall be in accordance with the forms set out in the First Schedule to the CA 1963 'or as near thereto as circumstances admit':

- Table B – private limited by shares;
- Table D (Part I) – private limited by guarantee; and
- Table E (Part I) – private unlimited.

Furthermore, the memorandum must be printed (in an entire format or in a form pursuant to s 80 of the CLEA 2001[7]), stamped, signed and attested[8]. There are five compulsory clauses, namely:

(a) the name clause;

(b) the objects clause;

(c) the liability clause;

---

4 See para **[3.056]** *et seq post*.

5 SI 275/1994.

6 See Schmithoff (ed), *Palmer's Company Law* (24th edn, 1987) at 6-02.

7 Section 7 of the CA 1963 was amended to so provide by s 81 of the CLEA 2001.

8 Section 7 of the CA 1963 as amended by s 112 of the Finance Act 1996. 'Printed' is defined by s 2 of the CA 1963 to include 'reproduced in any legible and durable form approved by the registrar of companies'.

(d) the capital clause; and

(e) the association or subscription clause.

It is important to note that although the foregoing are compulsory clauses, a company may have additional clauses in its memorandum, such as a clause providing for life directors.

[3.005] Section 80 of the CLEA 2001 facilitates the registration process by allowing persons applying for the registration of a company to lodge only those elements of the memorandum and articles of association that are peculiar to that company. This works in conjunction with a previously lodged 'reference' document for association with the specific elements lodged with the application. Section 80(1) provides that the registrar of companies can accept for registration a document containing standard form text from the objects clause of a memorandum of association or from articles of association and that he shall assign a reference number to each document so registered for identification purposes[9]. Accordingly, a memorandum and articles of association may contain a statement that either or both are to incorporate the text of the reference document previously registered[10]. The effect on a memorandum or articles of such a reference to a previously registered reference articles or memorandum is provided for in s 80(4):

> '… it shall be deemed for all purposes to incorporate within it the text of the relevant document filed with the registrar pursuant to *subsection (1)*, so that it shall form and be read as one entire document, and where such a memorandum or articles of association has been registered by the registrar and is inspected by any person, the registrar shall also make available for inspection the related document filed with him or her pursuant to *subsection (1)*.'

The hope in making this change was to reduce the numbers of memoranda and articles of association that are currently scanned by the CRO; however, it is thought that this initiative was a failure since the resulting memoranda and articles of association are a mess, difficult to follow for practitioners and most probably unintelligible to the users of company law.

(a) The name clause

[3.006] Every company must have a name, for it is this which identifies it from other companies[11]. Choosing a name can often pose a practical problem when forming a company, since delay may be caused where a company is lodged for registration with a name unacceptable to the registrar of companies. Incorporators are well advised to telephone the CRO to ascertain whether or not a proposed name is acceptable. In addition to the registrar objecting to a name which is already on the register, a name can also be refused where it is offensive, misleading or otherwise objectionable[12]. Section 21

[9] Section 80(2) provides that notwithstanding anything in the Companies Acts, a document filed pursuant to sub-s (1) 'need not relate to a particular company or contain the registered number of a company'.

[10] Section 80(3) of the CLEA 2001.

[11] Section 6(1)(a) of the CA 1963, as amended by the First Schedule to the C(A)A 1983.

[12] Certain statutes prohibit the use of certain words in companies' names. So, the National Standards Authority Ireland Act 1996, s 26 provides that a company shall not be registered by a name containing the words 'Irish Standard', 'I.S.' or the Irish language equivalent thereof or by a name so nearly resembling such words or initials as to be likely to deceive.

of the CA 1963 also provides that no name shall be registered which in the opinion of the registrar is undesirable, subject to an appeal to court. This was previously the function of the Minister for Jobs, Enterprise and Innovation but was transferred to the registrar by s 86 of the CLEA 2001, as indeed was the responsibility for administrative decisions, generally, relating to company names.

[3.007] The reservation of an acceptable company name is permitted by s 59 of the IFCMPA 2005[13]. Upon receiving an application to reserve a specified name for a company that is proposed to be formed the registrar of companies may determine that the name shall be reserved[14]. Reservation of a name shall last for a specified period not exceeding 28 days beginning on the making of the notification. Before the expiry of a reservation, application can be made to extend the specified period by up to a further 28 days[15].

[3.008] Furthermore, where a company is limited by shares or by guarantee, the word 'limited' or 'teoranta' must be the last word in the name[16]. Only a company that has limited liability may, however, use the word 'limited' or 'teoranta' in its name. Section 381(1) of the CA 1963 provides:

> 'If any person or persons trade or carry on business under a name or title of which 'limited' or 'teoranta', or any contraction or imitation of either word, is the last word, that person or those persons shall be, unless duly incorporated with limited liability, guilty of an offence[17].'

Where persons who are committing such an offence fail to desist from its continued commission within 14 days of being served notice so to do, the registrar of companies or the Director of Corporate Enforcement is empowered to apply to court for a prohibitory injunction against them[18].

[3.009] Prior to the CLEA 2001 it was the case that Ministerial permission could be sought by a limited company, to dispense with the use of the word 'limited' in its name[19]. It is now the case that any company that satisfies the provisions of s 24 of the CA 1963 (the original wording of which was repealed and substituted by s 88 of the CLEA 2001) will automatically be exempt from having to use the word 'limited' in its name. It is extremely rare for a private limited company to be exempted from having the word 'limited' in its name, and s 24 has most application to not-for-profit guarantee companies[20].

---

13 See, generally, McGowan-Smyth & Daly, *Irish Company Secretary's Handbook* (2011, Bloomsbury Professional) at ch 6, pp 377–383.

14 Section 59(4) of the IFCMPA 2005.

15 Section 60 of the IFCMPA 2005.

16 Section 60 of the IFCMPA 2005. An abbreviation of the words is acceptable, eg, 'Ltd' or 'Teo': s 22(2) of the CA 1963.

17 Section 98 of the CLEA 2001 repealed the old s 381 and substituted a new s 381.

18 Section 381(2) of the CA 1963. The court may order costs against the persons against whom an order is made: sub-s (3).

19 Section 88(2) saves exemptions made by Ministerial direction under the 'old' s 24 of the CA 1963, notwithstanding its repeal by s 88(1).

20 See Ch 30, *Guarantee Companies*, at para **[30.015]**.

[3.010] Where the directors of a company and others use the incorrect name of the company they may, in certain circumstances, incur personal liability[21]. Under s 114 of the CA 1963, every company is by law required to paint or affix its name on the outside of every office or place in which its business is carried on, in a conspicuous position, in letters easily legible[22], have its name on its seal[23] and use its name in legible characters on all business letters of the company and on all notices and other official publications of the company[24]. A failure in any of these respects renders the company liable to a fine[25].

[3.011] It must be stressed that although, subject to the veto of the registrar of companies, a company is free to chose its own name, by using a name similar to that of another company, it may be liable for the tort of passing off. This may occur where its name is so similar to that of another company as to cause a confusion in the minds of the public[26]. Where a company carries on business under a name other than its registered name, it must register that name as a 'business name' with the registrar of companies under the RBNA 1963: s 22(1) of the CA 1963[27].

(b) The objects clause

[3.012] Section 6(1)(c) of the CA 1963 provides that the memorandum of association of every company must state 'the objects of the company'. The objects clause is one of the most important of the compulsory clauses in the memorandum of association, its function being to set out the parameters of permitted corporate activity. As discussed below in the context of *corporate capacity*[28], there is voluminous case law on situations where companies act beyond their capacity, or *ultra vires* their objects clause. For present purposes it is sufficient to say that the objects clauses of practically every company formed today fly in the face of the brevity set out in the model tables to the Companies Acts. Typically, companies are incorporated with a multitude of express objects and powers which are ancillary to the main objects.

[3.013] A company may not have an object that is contrary to the law of the land, and to the extent that it does, that object is void. In *R v Registrar of Joint Stock Companies*[29], the proposed registration of an English company whose objects included the sale of tickets in the Irish Free State Hospitals Sweepstake was objected to by the English registrar of companies because such lotteries were illegal in England. The promoters of the company sought a writ of *mandamus* to compel registration, but failed. In the words

21 See s 114(4) of the CA 1963, which is considered later in Ch 5, *Disregarding Separate Legal Personality*, at para **[5.081]** *et seq*.

22 Section 114(1)(a) of the CA 1963.

23 Section 114(1)(b) of the CA 1963.

24 Section 114(1)(c) of the CA 1963.

25 Section 114(2) and (3) of the CA 1963.

26 See McMahon & Binchy, *The Irish Law of Torts* (3rd edn, Butterworths, 2000), Ch 31.

27 As to the requirements for registration under the RBNA 1963, see Ch 1, *The Private Company in Context*, at para **[1.007]** *et seq.*

28 See Ch 7, *Corporate Contracts, Capacity and Authority*, at para **[7.045]** *et seq.*

29 *R v Registrar of Joint Stock Companies* [1931] 2 KB 197.

of Slesser LJ: '[i]t is clear that a company cannot be formed whose proposed constitution necessarily involves an offence against the general law'[30].

(c) The liability clause

[3.014] The next compulsory clause found in a company's memorandum of association is the liability clause. It is usual for this to state succinctly, 'The liability of the members is limited', or, in the case of an unlimited company, 'The liability of the members is unlimited'.

[3.015] The phrase 'limited liability company', is something of a misnomer in that every company will always have unlimited liability[31]. Rather, what may be limited is the liability *of the members*. Their liability is not non-existent, but 'limited' in the sense that it is limited to the amount, if any, unpaid on their shares or in the case of a company limited by guarantee, to the amount of the guarantee[32]. Typically, private companies will acquire capital in ways other than by share capital, eg, through borrowings. The vast majority of private companies formed are 'one' or 'two' euro companies, because only one or two €1 shares are issued. In view of this, whether they are paid up or not is academic as regards the liability of the members who hold them.

[3.016] Previously, in all cases where the membership of a private company fell below two and the company carried on business for more than six months, the remaining member who knew that it was carrying on business would have unlimited liability for the debts of the company contracted after the period of six months: s 36 of the CA 1963[33]. It is now the case that reg 7(1) of the EC(SMPLC)R 1994[34] provides that s 36 shall not apply to a private company limited by shares or by guarantee[35].

(d) The capital clause

[3.017] Section 6(4)(a) of the CA 1963 provides that the capital clause must set out the total amount of the company's authorised share capital, ie, the amount of share capital with which the company proposes to be registered, and the division thereof into shares of a fixed amount[36]. The amount of the capital can be as large or as small as the

30 *R v Registrar of Joint Stock Companies* [1931] 2 KB 197 at 201. See also *Bowman et al v Secular Society Ltd* [1917] AC 406; and *McEllistrim v Ballymacelligott Co-operative and Dairy Society Ltd* [1919] AC 549. In the latter case, an object which constituted an unreasonable restraint of trade was held to be void.

31 See generally Ch 4, *Incorporation and its Consequences*, at para **[4.081]** *et seq*.

32 In the case of a private company limited by guarantee, that also has a share capital, the liability of the members is double: ie, the amount if any unpaid on their shares *and* the amount of the guarantee. This is unusual, and while only a fraction of companies formed will be limited by guarantee, an even smaller number will be limited by guarantee having a share capital.

33 See *Nisbet v Shepherd* [1994] 1 BCLC 300. See Ch 5, *Disregarding Separate Legal Personality*, at para **[5.080]**.

34 SI 275/1994.

35 However, it should be noted that reg 7(1) is not retrospective: reg 7(2). See further Ch 5, *Disregarding Separate Legal Personality*, at para **[5.078]**.

36 Section 67 of the CA 1963 provides: 'A limited company may by special resolution determine that any portion of its share capital which has not been already called up shall not be capable of being called up except in the event and for the purposes of the company being wound up, and thereupon that portion of its share capital shall not be capable of being called up except in the event and for the purposes aforesaid.'

company's promoters think fit. It is normal for the *authorised* share capital to be a relatively high figure, eg, €1,000,000. Normally, this will be divided into 1,000,000 shares of €1 each. This bears little or no relation to the *issued* share capital, which can be just €1.

[3.018] It is often the case that a company will have not one, but two or more classes of shares with different rights. Rather than set out what these classes are, the capital clause will usually facilitate the division of shares into classes by providing:

> 'The shares in the original or any increased capital may be divided into several classes, and there may be attached thereto respectively any preferential, referred or other special rights, privileges, conditions or restrictions as to dividend, capital, voting or otherwise.'

The company is thereby expressly authorised by its memorandum of association to issue a variety of classes of shares, with different rights attaching thereto as desired. Although the different classes are commonly set out in the capital clause, the *rights* attaching to each class are usually set out in the company's articles of association[37].

[3.019] For regulatory and other reasons[38], sometimes companies will wish to be capitalised to a particular amount other than by loan capital. Previously, one of the disadvantages to capitalising a company by paying into its share capital was that there was 1% capital duty payable on the issued share capital. Although there is now no such capital duty, it was the existence of that duty in the 1990s that prompted the making of 'capital contributions' in lieu of issuing share capital. The legality of these contributions to companies' capital has been accepted, albeit on an informal basis, by the Irish Revenue Commissioners[39]. Capital contributions[40] involve the gifting to a company of capital without having to issue shares. Where made by a company in favour of its holding company (or a sister subsidiary) care must be taken to ensure that the rules of capital maintenance are not infringed: so capital contributions to members of companies (eg, from a subsidiary to its holding company) must be made from distributable profits[41].

In *Kellar v Stanley Williams (Turks and Caicos Islands)*[42], the Privy Council was asked to decide who was entitled to the proceeds of a capital contribution where the company into which it was paid went into liquidation. On the one hand it was argued that the capital contribution was like a loan, repayable to its maker; on the other hand it was contended that after the discharge of the company's debts, the contribution was

---

37 In this regard s 66 of the CA 1963 provides that 'A company, if so authorised by its articles, may do any one or more of the following things—(a) make arrangements on the issue of shares for a difference between the shareholders in the amounts and times of payment of calls on their shares; (b) accept from any member the whole or a part of the amount remaining unpaid on any shares held by him, although no part of that amount has been called up; (c) pay a dividend in proportion to the amount paid up on each share where a larger amount is paid up on some shares than on others'.

38 In Ireland, capitalisation other than by the issue of shares has arisen in the context of companies operating from the IFSC.

39 Reference has been made in passing to the use of capital contributions by the Supreme Court in *Revenue Commissioners v O'Flynn Construction Ltd* [2011] IESC 47.

40 Also referred to as 'equitable contributions', 'equitable capital', 'contributed surplus' and 'contributed capital'

41 See Ch 10, *Maintenance of Capital*, at para **[10.089]**.

42 *Kellar v Stanley Williams (Turks and Caicos Islands)* [2000] 2 BCLC 390.

divisible amongst the company's shareholders in proportion to the nominal amount of shares issued in the company. The facts there were that the applicant was the sole beneficial owner of B Ltd – a company that imported liquor into the Turks and Caicos Islands. A Ltd had been formed to provide a shipping agency that could more economically obtain shipping and trucking services for B Ltd. The respondent was manager of B Ltd and it was agreed that he would hold the majority stake in A Ltd as he was a citizen of the islands. Accordingly, he held 51% of the shares and the applicant held the balance. The applicant capitalised A Ltd through a capital contribution. The Privy Council accepted that on the facts there was no clear indication as to whether the applicant had intended the contribution to be in the nature of a loan or in the nature of a capital contribution and upheld the Court of Appeal's decision that the contribution was distributable amongst the shareholders and not repayable to the applicant. On the propriety of capital contributions, the Privy Council said:

> 'If the shareholders of a company agree to increase its capital without a formal allocation of shares that capital will become like share premium part of the owner's equity and there is nothing in the company law of the Turks and Caicos Islands or in the company law of England on which that law is based to render their agreement ineffective[43].'

In the absence of any evidence to the contrary, in such circumstances the law will lean against presuming the contribution was a loan and in favour of it being divisible amongst the shareholders in proportion to their shareholdings.

(e) The association or subscription clause

[3.020] An *association clause* is required in the memorandum of an ordinary private company. It is not a substantive clause, in that it does not exist for any purpose other than to conform to the requirement that the signatories to the memorandum must bind themselves together. In the case of an ordinary private company it typically provides as follows:

> 'We, the several persons whose names, addresses and descriptions are subscribed, wish to be formed into a company in pursuance of this memorandum of association and we agree to take the number of shares in the capital of the company set opposite our respective names.'

What follows this are the names, addresses and descriptions of the shareholder-members/subscribers and the number of shares taken by each, together with the signature of a witness. In a single-member private company a *subscription clause* will be appropriate whereby the sole member subscribes his name to the memorandum of association[44].

Non-compulsory clauses

[3.021] The vast majority of memoranda of association registered today by private companies do not contain any more than the compulsory clauses. However, on being formed, the members may decide to copper-fasten certain matters by 'enshrining' or 'entrenching' them in the memorandum. One matter which may be enshrined is provision for a life director where the directorship of some person is perceived to be

43 *Kellar v Stanley Williams (Turks and Caicos Islands)* [2000] 2 BCLC 390 at 395.

44 Regulation 4 of the EC(SMPLC)R 1994 (SI 275/1994).

intrinsic to the company. The significance of doing this is that, unlike the obligatory clauses, such clauses can be made unalterable by virtue of s 9 of the CA 1963. This provides that the memorandum of association cannot be altered, save to the extent for which express provision is made by the Companies Acts. As is considered below, s 28(3) of the CA 1963 enables the memorandum itself to provide that certain clauses may be expressed to be unalterable.

Alteration of the memorandum of association

[3.022] Having reviewed the clauses typically found in a memorandum of association, it remains to consider the mechanics of and restrictions on the alteration of the provisions set out in the memorandum. There is no general liberty to amend a memorandum of association; rather, the alteration of each clause of the memorandum is governed by different provisions in the Companies Acts. Indeed, s 9 of the CA 1963 provides:

> 'A company may not alter the provisions contained in its memorandum except in the cases, in the mode and to the extent for which express provision is made in this Act.'

Consequently, each of the compulsory clauses of the memorandum must be considered separately in the light of the authorised means of alteration, and it should be remembered that some clauses can be rendered unalterable. Where an alteration is made to a company's memorandum of association, every copy of the memorandum issued by the company after its alteration must be in accordance with the alteration[45].

(a) Alteration of the name clause

[3.023] A company may change its name by virtue of s 23 of the CA 1963, as amended by s 87 of the CLEA 2001, which transferred the function of the Minister for Jobs, Enterprise and Innovation to the registrar of companies. This provides that the members of a company can change the company's name by passing a *special resolution*[46]. This does not mean that a company can vote in favour of changing its name so as to delete the word 'limited', or its Irish equivalent[47]. Where a company's members vote in favour of changing its name, the consent in writing of the registrar of companies is required. Having obtained the registrar's consent, the company must send the special resolution and two copies of the amended memorandum to the CRO together with the appropriate fee. In due course, the registrar will issue a 'Certificate of Incorporation on Change of Name', which will supersede the original certificate of incorporation[48].

[3.024] A company may be obliged to change its name by order of the registrar. Section 23(2) of the CA 1963 provides:

> 'If, through inadvertence or otherwise, a company on its first registration, or on its registration by a new name, is registered by a name which, in the opinion of the registrar of companics, it too like the name by which a company in existence is already registered,

---

45 Section 30(1) of the CA 1963.

46 In the case of a single-member private company, a written decision of the sole member will suffice instead of a special resolution: reg 9(1) of the EC(SMPLC)R 1994.

47 In a limited liability company, the word 'limited' can only be deleted where consent is obtained under s 24 of the CA 1963. It is an offence for a private company to represent itself as a public limited company or plc when it is not: s 56 of the C(A)A 1983.

48 Section 23(3) of the CA 1963.

> the first mentioned company may change its name with the sanction of the registrar of companies and, if he so directs within 6 months of its being registered by that name, shall change it within a period of 6 weeks from the date of the direction or such longer period as the registrar may think fit to allow.'

It is important to note that the registrar may only direct that a company change its name where the name is, in his opinion, 'too like the name by which a company in existence is already registered', and not because it is, say, offensive, etc. In the United Kingdom it has been held that the registrar cannot be ordered by court to effect a change to a company's name where its directors and shareholders failed to take steps to do so in breach of a prior court order[49].

[3.025] Where a company validly changes its name, such will not affect any rights or obligations of the company or render defective any legal proceedings by or against the company, and any legal proceedings continued or commenced against it by its former name may be continued or commenced against it by its new name[50]. Where a company is wound up within one year of changing its name, its old name as well as its existing name must appear on all notices and advertisements in relation to the winding up[51].

(b) Alteration of the objects clause

[3.026] *Re Cyclists' Touring Club*[52] shows that under former legislation the alteration of a company's objects clause would only be approved of by the court where it did not destroy the *substratum* of the company, ie, where the alteration would make the existing business more efficient rather than to abandon the existing business in favour of another business. Today, however, the objects clause may be altered in any manner by a special resolution of the members. Section 10(1) of the CA 1963 provides that:

> '... a company may, by special resolution, alter the provisions of its memorandum by abandoning, restricting or amending any existing object or by adopting a new object and any alteration so made shall be as valid as if originally contained therein, and be subject to alteration in like manner.'

While principally an enabling section, s 10 embodies certain safeguards. Thus sub-s (2) provides that if an application is made to court, the purported alteration shall not have effect, save where it is confirmed by the court. This procedure safeguards dissident shareholders by affording them the right to apply to the court to overturn any alteration. To seek relief, applicants must be the holders of not less than 15% of the aggregate in nominal value of the company's issued share capital or any class thereof or if the company is not limited by shares, by not less than 15% of the company's members, *or* the holders of not less than 15% of the company's debentures entitling the holders to object to an alteration of its objects[53]. Those who make application to court must not themselves have voted in favour of the special resolution proposing the amendment, or have consented to the alteration[54]. Such application must be made within 21 days after

[49] *Halifax plc et al v Halifax Repossessions Ltd et al* [2004] TLR 87.

[50] Section 23(4) of the CA 1963.

[51] Section 24(6) of the CA 1963.

[52] *Re Cyclists' Touring Club* (1907) 1 Ch 269.

[53] Section 10(3) of the CA 1963.

[54] Section 10(4) of the CA 1963.

the date of the special resolution[55]. Where a limited company that has been authorised to dispense with using the word 'limited' in its name proposes to alter its objects clause, the same notice as is required to be given to the holders of debentures must also be given to the registrar of companies[56].

[3.027] At the hearing of an application by a dissenting minority, s 10(6) of the CA 1963 provides that:

> '... the court may make an order cancelling the alteration or confirming the alteration either wholly or in part and on such terms and conditions as it thinks fit, and may, if it thinks fit, adjourn the proceedings in order that an arrangement may be made to the satisfaction of the court for the purchase of the interests of dissentient members, and may give such directions and make such orders as it may think expedient for facilitating or carrying into effect any such arrangement.'

It can be seen that sub-s (6) specifically provides that the court may order the purchase of dissidents' shares. Regrettably, the subsection is silent as to the factors upon which the court should exercise its jurisdiction. However, it is clear that in order for an objection to be cognisable by the court, it must be made by the members concerned, *qua* member, ie, in their capacity as members and not something else: *Re Munster and Leinster Bank*[57]. In that case, seven solicitors failed to prevent the alteration of a company's objects clause which would enable the company to undertake trusteeship work, as the objections were designed to preserve the solicitors' profits and not the shareholders' interests. The Master of the Rolls said:

> 'If these seven gentlemen had even now come forward and opposed this petition, as shareholders, I should, perhaps, have given more weight to their objections, and to the arguments offered on their behalf; but the learned counsel who nominally appeared for them did not seek to deny, but rather prided himself on the fact, that he represented, not individual shareholders, but the Incorporated Law Society of Ireland and the Southern Law Society ... it is apparent that [the resolutions of the Law Societies] were framed not really in the interests of shareholders but in apprehension of the injury which might result to the solicitor profession from the proposed extension of the objects of the bank[58].'

This passage indicates that although a member's objection must be made *qua* member, the court may not reject a proffered objection merely because the member's objection serves another purpose, divorced from his membership. In *Re Jewish Colonial Trust*[59], it was said that the decisive factor for the court will be the relative 'fairness' or 'unfairness' of the alteration between the shareholders or the classes of shareholders. In *Re Cyclists' Touring Club*[60], it was held that it is incumbent upon the company to alter the objects clause *bona fide* and in the interests of the company as a whole.

[3.028] There may be another alternative, recently recognised by the Irish High Court in *Re Metafile Ltd; Garvey v Metafile Ltd*[61], open to a shareholder who is unhappy with the

55 Section 10(5) of the CA 1963.

56 Section 10(8) of CA 1963, as amended by s 85 of the CLEA 2001.

57 *Re Munster and Leinster Bank* [1930] 1 IR 237.

58 *Re Munster and Leinster Bank* [1930] 1 IR 237 at 247.

59 *Re Jewish Colonial Trust* (1908) 2 Ch 287.

60 *Re Cyclists' Touring Club* (1907) 1 Ch 269.

61 *Re Metafile Ltd; Garvey v Metafile Ltd* [2006] IEHC 407 (20 December 2006), Laffoy J.

alteration of the objects of the company. This is to petition for the winding up of the company on 'just and equitable' grounds, for failure of substratum[62]. *Failure of substratum* can be said to occur where a company, which was formed with a particular purpose in mind, subsequently discontinues that purpose. This recognises that some companies are quasi-partnerships that are formed on the basis of a mutual understanding between the shareholders. Where a company is formed by individuals with a particular purpose in mind, for a majority of them subsequently to divert the aim of the company is perceived to be unfair and in breach of the implicit partnership which subsists[63]. Hence, it is open to a court to hold that an alteration which destroys the substratum justifies the winding up of the company on 'just and equitable' grounds.

(c) Alteration of the liability clause

[3.029] A private company's liability clause can be changed, and the liability of the members *increased*, made *unlimited* or in the case of a company registered as unlimited, made *limited*. In the first place, the liability of the members may be increased. This is regulated by s 27 of the CA 1963, which provides that notwithstanding anything in either the memorandum or articles no member shall be bound by an alteration after he becomes a member that requires him to take or subscribe for more shares than the number held by him at the date on which the alteration is made, or in any way increases his liability as at that date to contribute to the share capital of, or otherwise to pay money to, the company. Clearly, any amendment that gives rise to a liability to subscribe for more shares is prohibited by this provision. As shall be considered below, it has also been held that this section will prohibit *any* forced pecuniary contribution to the company's assets beyond the amount unpaid on shares held[64]. By virtue of s 27(2) members can, however, waive their veto in writing.

[3.030] A limited liability company can change to an unlimited company[65]. This change is facilitated by s 52 of the C(A)A 1983, which details the matters required to achieve such a change in status. Finally, an unlimited company may apply to be re-registered as a limited company by virtue of s 53 of the C(A)A 1983[66].

(d) Alteration of the capital clause

[3.031] The capital clause may also be altered by a company, subject to further built-in safeguards against abuse of this power. However, here a clear distinction must be drawn between an alteration which *increases* and one which *decreases* the capital of the company.

---

62 See s 213(f) of the CA 1963. See generally, Ch 23, *Winding Up Companies*, at para **[23.102]** *et seq*.

63 See *Ebrahimi v Westbourne Galleries Ltd* [1973] AC 360, adopted in Ireland in *Re Murph's Restaurant Ltd* [1979] ILRM 141.

64 See *Ding v Sylvania Waterways* [1999] NSWSC 58 (15 February 1999), Supreme Court of New South Wales. This case is considered in the context of the alteration of the articles of association, at para **[3.061]** *post*.

65 See Ch 33, *Conversion by Re-registration,* at para **[33.009]**.

66 See Ch 33, *Conversion by Re-registration,* at para **[33.002]**.

(i) Increasing share capital

[3.032] Section 68 of the CA 1963 contains a relatively simple procedure whereby the company can *increase* its share capital[67]. Accordingly, provided that the articles of association of that company authorise it[68], on the passing of an ordinary resolution in general meeting, a company may:

(a) increase its share capital by new shares of such amount as it thinks expedient;

(b) consolidate and divide all or any of its share capital into shares of larger amounts than its existing shares;

(c) convert all or any of its paid up shares into stock, and re-convert that stock into paid up shares of any denominations;

(d) subdivide its shares, or any of them, into shares of a smaller amount than is fixed by the memorandum, so however, that in the subdivision, the proportion between the amount paid and the amount, if any, unpaid on each reduced share shall be the same as it was in the case of the share from which the reduced share is derived;

(e) cancel shares which, at the date of the passing of the resolution in that behalf, have not been taken or agreed to be taken by any person, and diminish the amount of its share capital by the amount of the shares so cancelled[69].

Section 70 of the CA 1963 provides that notice of an increase in a company's share capital must be sent to the registrar of companies within 15 days after the passing of the resolution. Notice of any other alteration must, by s 69 of the CA 1963, be given to the registrar within one month. Section 71 of the CA 1963 provides that an unlimited company which re-registers as a limited company can increase its nominal share capital by increasing the nominal amount of each share, provided that the increased capital will only be capable of being called up where the company is being wound up.

Although a company cannot contractually agree not to increase its share capital, the members of a company can contractually agree, *inter se*, not to vote in favour of an alteration of the company's memorandum and articles of association so as to effect an increase in share capital, and such a contract will be enforceable. This is the effect of the finding of the House of Lords in *Russell v Northern Bank Development Corp Ltd et al*[70], a decision considered in the context of shareholders' agreements[71].

(ii) Reducing share capital

[3.033] Where a company decides that it wishes to *reduce* its share capital, the requirements of the Companies Acts are more restrictive. The main reason why the law imposes such restrictions is to protect creditors, a company's share capital being

---

67 The practice of informal increases in share capital through the making of a so-called 'capital contribution' has been noted earlier: see para **[3.019]** *ante*.

68 As will be the case where model reg 44 of Part 1 of Table A, First Schedule to the CA 1963 is adopted.

69 This is not a reduction in share capital because this provision only relates to shares, which have never been issued.

70 *Russell v Northern Bank Development Corp Ltd et al* [1992] 3 All ER 161.

71 See para **[3.127]** *post*.

perceived as a 'creditors' fund': *Trevor v Whitworth*[72]. The rationale for this is based on the fact that where a company has limited liability a creditor can look only to the assets of the company for the payment of his debts. Thus, for creditors it is important that the company's assets remain intact. Where a company reduces its share capital by making repayments to its shareholders, creditors are potentially disadvantaged. It is the same philosophy which motivates the restrictions on a company purchasing its own shares or providing financial assistance for the purchase of its own shares. Accordingly the reduction of a company's share capital is strictly controlled by ss 72–77 of the CA 1963.

[3.034] Section 72(1) of the CA 1963 provides that as a general rule, and save as expressly provided by the Companies Acts, it is not lawful for a private company limited by shares or a private company limited by guarantee and having a share capital, to purchase any of its shares or to reduce its share capital in any way[73]. The purchase by a company of its own shares is dealt with elsewhere[74]. Notwithstanding this general prohibition, a company may reduce its share capital by following the procedure set out in the Companies Acts, namely that:

(a) the company is authorised by its articles of association to reduce its share capital; and
(b) it passes a special resolution approving the reduction; and
(c) the alteration is *confirmed by the court*.

While the reduction of share capital may, subject to the foregoing, be made in any way, s 72(2) of the CA 1963 specifically mentions three methods, namely, where the company decides to:

> '(a) extinguish or reduce the liability on any of its shares in respect of share capital not paid up; or
>
> (b) either with or without extinguishing or reducing liability on any of its shares, cancel any paid up share capital which is lost or unrepresented by available assets; or
>
> (c) either with or without extinguishing or reducing liability on any of its shares, pay off any paid up share capital which is in excess of the wants of the company; and may, if and so far as is necessary, alter its memorandum by reducing the amount of its share capital and of its shares accordingly.'

Accordingly, it is possible to alter the capital clause in the memorandum of association of a company where the effect is to reduce its share capital. It is important to note that, to be effective, court confirmation of the reduction must be obtained[75]. Although s 73 of the CA 1963 says that a company that has passed a special resolution, reducing its share capital, '*may* apply to court for an order confirming the reduction', unless court approval is obtained the reduction is ineffective.

[3.035] In a share capital reduction, the rights of creditors are paramount. Where the proposed reduction involves either the diminution of liability in respect of unpaid share capital, or the payment to any shareholder of any paid up share capital, and in any other

---

72 *Trevor v Whitworth* (1887) 12 App Cas 409. See generally, Ch 10, *The Maintenance of Capital*.

73 See Ch 10, *The Maintenance of Capital*, at para **[10.015]**.

74 See Ch 10, *The Maintenance of Capital*, para **[10.013]** *et seq*.

75 Section 72(2) of the CA 1963.

case if the court so directs, s 73(2) of the CA 1963 provides that the following provisions shall have effect:

> '(a) every creditor of the company who at the date fixed by the court is entitled to any debt or claim which, if that date were the commencement of the winding up of the company, would be admissible in proof against the company, shall be entitled to object to the reduction;
>
> (b) the court shall settle a list of creditors so entitled to object, and for that purpose shall ascertain, as far as possible without requiring an application from any creditor, the names of those creditors and the nature and amount of their debts or claims, and may publish notices fixing a day or days within which creditors not entered on the list are to claim to be so entered or are to be excluded from the right of objecting to the reduction;
>
> (c) where a creditor entered on the list whose debt or claim is not discharged or has not determined does not consent to the reduction, the court may, if it thinks fit, dispense with the consent of that creditor, on the company securing payment of his debt or claim by appropriating, as the court may direct, the following amount:—
>
> (i) if the company admits the full amount of the debt or claim, or, though not admitting it, is willing to provide for it, then the full amount of the debt or claim;
>
> (ii) if the company does not admit and is not willing to provide for the full amount of the debt or claim, or, if the amount is contingent or not ascertained, then an amount fixed by the court after the like inquiry and adjudication as if the company were being wound up by the court.'

This is, however, subject to s 73(3), which provides that where a proposed reduction of share capital involves either the diminution of any liability in respect of unpaid share capital or the payment to any shareholder of any paid up share capital, the court may, if, having regard to any special circumstances of the case, it thinks proper so to do, direct that sub-s (2) shall not apply as regards any class or any classes of creditors.

The important point to note is that it is within the discretion of the court to confirm the reduction or not. Section 74(1) provides:

> 'The court, if satisfied in relation to every creditor of the company who, under section 73, is entitled to object to the reduction, that either his consent to the reduction has been obtained or that his debt or claim has been discharged or has determined, or has been secured, may make an order confirming the reduction on such terms and conditions as it thinks fit.'

By s 74(2) the court may, if it decides to confirm the reduction, direct that the words '*and reduced*', be added to the name of the company, for as long as the court may order.

[3.036] Section 75 of the CA 1963 states that the registrar of companies, when shown the court order, a copy thereof and a 'minute' of the changed capital, must register the order and minute. The consequences for the shareholders of a company that reduces its share capital are detailed in s 76 of the CA 1963. The primary consequence is that 'a member of the company, past or present, shall not be liable in respect of any share to any call or contribution exceeding in amount the difference, if any, between the amount of the share as fixed by the minute and the amount paid, or the reduced amount, if any, which is to be deemed to have been paid, on the share, as the case may be[76]'. This is,

[76] Section 76(1) of the CA 1963.

however, strictly subject to s 76(2), which continues to afford protection to creditors. This provides:

> 'If any creditor entitled in respect of any debt or claim to object to the reduction of the share capital, is, by reason of his ignorance of the proceedings for reduction, or of their nature and effect with respect to his debt or claim, not entered on the list of creditors, and, after the reduction, the company is unable within the meaning of the provisions of this Act relating to winding up by the court, to pay the amount of his debt or claim, then—
>
> (a) every person who was a member of the company at the date of the registration of the order for reduction and minute, shall be liable to contribute for the payment of that debt or claim an amount not exceeding the amount which he would have been liable to contribute if the company had commenced to be wound up on the day before the said date, and
>
> (b) if the company is wound up, the court, on the application of any such creditor and proof of his ignorance as aforesaid, may, if it thinks fit, settle accordingly a list of persons so liable to contribute, and make and enforce calls and orders on the contributories settled on the list, as if they were ordinary contributories in a winding up.'

The provisions of s 76 are, however, without prejudice to the rights of contributories between themselves[77]. It may be noted that although creditors who are ignorant of the reduction have a right to remedial relief, every officer of a company that wilfully conceals the name of any creditor entitled to object to the reduction, or wilfully misrepresents the nature or amount of the debt or claim of any creditor, is guilty of an offence[78].

Alteration of the non-compulsory clauses

[3.037] Unlike the *compulsory* clauses[79], which are contained in the memorandum, the non-compulsory clauses (if any) contained in a memorandum of association are capable of being rendered unalterable where the memorandum itself expressly so provides[80]. Where this is not expressly so provided the non-compulsory clauses can be altered by special resolution, by virtue of s 28(1) of the CA 1963. However, sub-s (4) provides that a dissenting minority of 15% can object to the alteration and may apply to the court for the alteration to be cancelled.

Why would the subscribers of a company provide that certain fundamental matters set out in the memorandum be unalterable? The reason is intrinsically linked to the rationale behind many closely held private companies: while in law they are companies, in reality many are tantamount to partnerships. However, because of the entrenchment of the concept of 'majority rule', the company will be governed by the majority in spite of any real or imagined 'understandings'. Where certain provisions in a company's

77 Section 76(3) of the CA 1963.

78 Section 77 of the CA 1963.

79 See Ussher, *Company Law in Ireland* (1986) at pp 59–60.

80 See s 28(3) of the CA 1963 which provides: 'This section shall not apply where the memorandum itself provides for or prohibits the alteration of all or any of the said provisions, and shall not authorise any variation or abrogation of the special rights of any class of shareholders.' See, further, Ch 30, *Guarantee Companies*, at para **[30.031]** *et seq*.

memorandum of association are made unalterable, this is usually referred to as an 'entrenchment' of rights.

[B] The Articles of Association

The nature of the articles

[3.038] The articles of association are the publicly registered rules of a company which govern its internal regulation[81]. The members of private companies sometimes also adopt a shareholders' agreement, which can supplement the company's statutory constitutional documents. A shareholders' agreement is, however, a private contract to which the company may not be party. Unlike a shareholders' agreement, articles of association both automatically *bind* the company with its members and are also *public documents*.

[3.039] In the case of a private company limited by shares there is no actual requirement that articles be registered with the CRO prior to incorporation[82]. By contrast, the other two types of private company – the private company limited by guarantee which has a share capital[83] and the unlimited private company with a share capital[84] – must both actually register articles of association on incorporation.

Section 12(1) of the CA 1963 provides that in the case of an unlimited private company the articles must state the number of members and the amount of the share capital with which the company proposes to be registered. Any increase in the number of members must be notified to the registrar of companies within 15 days after the increase was resolved or took place[85].

Where private companies limited by shares do not voluntarily register their own articles, the model articles set out in Part II of Table A in the First Schedule to the CA 1963 will automatically be deemed to be the articles of association of the company as if they had been duly registered[86]. In addition, even where such a company does register its own articles, the provisions of Table A of the First Schedule will continue to apply save insofar as they have been excluded or modified[87]. Section 14 of the CA 1963[88] provides

---

81 See, generally, Ramage, *Companies Acts: Model Articles and Table* A (3rd edn, 2009) and Nicholson, *Table A Articles of Association* (1997).

82 See s 11 of the CA 1963, as amended by s 2 of the C(A)A 1982.

83 The form of memorandum and articles for a private company limited by guarantee are set out in Table D, Parts I and III, respectively.

84 The form of memorandum and articles for a private unlimited company are set out in Table E, Parts I and III, respectively.

85 Section 12(2) of the CA 1963.

86 Section 13(2) of the CA 1963 provides: 'In the case of a company limited by shares and registered after the operative date, if articles are not registered or, if articles are registered, in so far as the articles do not exclude or modify the regulations contained in Table A, those regulations shall, so far as applicable, be the regulations of the company in the same manner and to the same extent as if they were contained in duly registered articles.'

87 In *McNeill v McNeill's Sheepfarming Co Ltd* [1955] NZLR 15, it was held that in case of conflict between the model articles and the company's own express articles, the latter would prevail.

88 As amended by s 112 of the Finance Act 1996.

that a company's articles of association must be printed (in an entire format or in a form pursuant to s 80 of the CLEA 2001)[89], divided into paragraphs which are numbered consecutively, bear the same stamp as if they were contained in a deed and be signed by each subscriber of the memorandum of association in the presence of one witness who must attest the signature. Furthermore, by s 29(1) of the CA 1963 a company shall on being so requested by a member, send him a copy of its memorandum and articles on payment of a nominal fee: *Securities Trust Ltd v Hugh Moore & Alexander Ltd*[90].

The model articles of private companies

[3.040] In the case of a private company limited by shares, the relevant model articles are set out in Part II of Table A of the First Schedule to the CA 1963. Regulation 1 of Part II provides that, with certain modifications, the regulations contained in Part I (which apply to public companies limited by shares) shall apply to private companies. The modifications effected by Part II are the disapplication of the following regulations in Part I:

- Reg 8 (entitlements of share transferee);
- Reg 24 (directors' power to decline registration of a share transfer);
- Reg 51 (notice of members' meetings);
- Reg 54 (quorum for members' meetings);
- Reg 84 (directors' voting on contracts in which directors interested);
- Reg 86 (quorum at directors' meetings).

In place of these regulations, Part II applies its own variations in regs 10, 3, 4, 5, 7 and 8.

[3.041] Regulations 2, 6, 9 and 10[91] of Part II are *additional* regulations that are included in the model articles of association of private companies limited by shares. The irony that the articles of association of the most popular type of company registered should be ascertainable by those applicable to companies that are numerically few, has been noted[92].

Regulation 2 is important because it purports to comply with s 33(1) of the CA 1963 which defines a private company by reference to its articles containing certain provisions. Model reg 2 of Part II of Table A is, however, obsolete since s 33(1) of CA 1963 was replaced by s 7 of the IFCMPA 2006 and so it is appropriate for a private company's articles of association to contain the following substitute:

> 'The Company is a private company and accordingly:
>
> (a) the right to transfer shares is restricted in the manner hereinafter prescribed;
>
> (b) the number of members of the Company (exclusive of persons who are in the employment of the Company and of persons who, having been formerly in the employment of the Company, were while in such employment and have continued after the termination of such employment to be members of the Company) is limited to ninety-nine (or such greater number as may be prescribed by the Act as being the maximum permitted number of members in a private

89 Section 14(1) of the CA 1963 was amended to so provide by s 82 of the CLEA 2001.

90 *Securities Trust Ltd v Hugh Moore & Alexander Ltd* [1964] IR 417.

91 Inserted into Part II by s 5(5) of the C(A)A 1977.

92 See Ch 1, *The Private Company in Context*, at para **[1.002]**.

company) so, however, that where two or more persons hold one or more shares in the Company jointly, they shall for the purpose of this article be treated as a single member; and

(c) any invitation or offer to the public to subscribe for any shares, debentures or other securities of the Company is prohibited provided always that the Company may make such offers or invitations to subscribe for debentures as a private company can make in accordance with section 33(5) of the Companies Act 1963 (as amended).'

[3.042] The model articles applicable to a private company limited by shares are sub-divided under the following headings:

– Share capital and variation of rights. – Liens on shares. – Calls on shares. – Transfer, transmission and forfeiture of shares. – Conversion of shares into stock. – Alteration of capital. – General meetings. – Notice of general meetings. – Proceedings at general meetings. – Votes of members. – Bodies Corporate acting by representatives at meetings. – Directors. – Borrowing powers.	– Powers and duties of directors. – Disqualification of directors. – Rotation of directors. – Proceedings of directors. – Managing director. – The secretary. – The company seal. – Dividends and reserves. – Accounts. – Capitalisation of profits. – Audit. – Notices.[93] – Winding-up. – Indemnity.

The fact that a company must have articles does not mean that the legislature is attempting to control the operation of the company. On the contrary, the fact that a company may adopt and adapt the model articles at will indicates that the legislature was merely concerned that doubt and uncertainty should be minimised by ensuring that provision is made for certain basic matters. The draft Companies Bill seeks to take this a step further by providing that the most commonly adopted regulations will apply to companies unless their constitutions provides otherwise.

Usual amendments to the model articles

[3.043] It would be most unusual for any private company limited by shares to adopt *en bloc* the model articles either expressly or by failing to register any articles thereby courting the automatic application of Table A, Part II, without making some modifications or exclusions. Indeed, company formation firms, responsible for the

[93] Note that in *Re Thundercrest Ltd* [1995] 1 BCLC 117 it was held that a provision in a company's articles that deemed members to have received a notice within 24 hours of its positing could be ignored where it was proved that the letter enclosing the notice had been returned undelivered.

incorporation of most Irish companies, invariably amend the model articles[94]. The advisability of modifying the model articles cannot be stressed enough. The model articles provided in the Companies Acts are totally unsuited to many private companies[95]. They do, however, have the advantage of certainty, in that they and their predecessors have been the subject of judicial scrutiny in many courts over the years. In an attempt to make the articles of companies accord more with the needs of their incorporators, practitioners have invariably adopted the articles of private closely-held companies[96].

[3.044] The regulations in Table A that are typically targeted for modification and expansion include those concerning the following:

(a) Shares.
(b) Members' meetings.
(c) Directors.
(d) Voting rights.

It must be stressed that many other amendments are often effected to the model articles. The amendments set out below are simply some selected examples[97].

(a) Shares

[3.045] The first usual amendment of note is the modification of model reg 22 to provide that, in respect of a share transfer, it is sufficient for the transferor alone to execute the instrument of transfer. This simple amendment avoids the otherwise cumbersome practice of both transferor and transferee having to execute a share transfer in order for it to be valid and effective[98].

[3.046] In private companies, model reg 24 of Part I is automatically deleted and replaced by model reg 3 of Part II of the First Schedule to the CA 1963. Model reg 3 provides:

> 'The directors may, in their absolute discretion and without assigning any reason therefor, decline to register any transfer of any share, whether or not it is a fully paid share.'

Model reg 3 will sometimes be bolstered by the inclusion of *pre-emption rights* either in the company's articles of association or in a shareholders' agreement[99]. Although there are many different types of pre-emption rights, the formula which is most used is one

---

94 Thus, some formation firms exclude in private companies articles: 5, 47, 75, 79, 91, 92, 93, 94 and 95 of Table A, Part I, and reg 7 in Part II. Other variations include the deletion of regs 3, 22, 76, 77, 96, 97, 98, 100, 102, 109, and 138 of Table A, Part I, and reg 9 in Part II.

95 See Ussher, *Company Law in Ireland* (1986), pp 62–63 for a short but perceptive commentary on the model articles.

96 See Young, 'Agreements Between Shareholders Relating To The Operation Of A Small Company' (1979) Society of Young Solicitors, Lecture 118.

97 On many of the possible amendments to the model articles, see generally, Stedman & Jones, *Shareholders' Agreements* (3rd edn, 1998), at pp 7–57.

98 See generally, Ch 9, *Share Transfer*, at para **[9.012]**.

99 See Stedman & Jones, *Shareholders' Agreements* (3rd edn, 1998), at p 26 *et seq*. For an old judicially-considered Irish example, see *Attorney General for Ireland v Jameson* [1904] 2 IR 644. See generally, para **[3.106]** *post*.

which provides that where a member desires to sell or otherwise dispose of his shares he must first offer them to the existing members of the company. The offer to the other members will usually entitle them to take up the shares on a *pro rata* basis to the shares which they already hold. Extreme care ought to be exercised in the drafting of such rights because case law shows that they will bc strictly construed, the courts leaning in favour of free alienation of shares[100]. Whether such a policy is justified in the context of private companies, in view of their often quasi-partnership nature, is doubted. A valid pre-emption clause will be upheld by the courts either by injunction[101], or by the court refusing a decree for specific performance[102] for the sale of shares. Pre-emption rights are considered further in Ch 9.

(b) Members' meetings

[3.047] Sometimes the requirement that general meetings are held within the State, provided for by reg 47, is deleted. Furthermore, the notice provisions in respect of company meetings contained in reg 51 are often restricted. Usually the notice provision in s 141 of the CA 1963 is expressly adopted by the articles.

[3.048] It can be important in many companies that model reg 6 of Part II of Table A, First Schedule to CA 1963, be included in the articles of association of private companies. This model article provides the internal authorisation required by s 141(8) of the CA 1963 if a company is to be permitted to utilise the unanimous written resolution procedure[103].

[3.049] An automatic legislative amendment is effected to the articles of association of a single-member private company by reg 10 of EC(SMPLC)R 1994[104]. This provides:

> 'Notwithstanding any provision to the contrary in the articles of a single-member company, one member present in person or by proxy shall be a quorum.'

Meetings in the context of single-member private companies are considered in Ch 14.

(c) Directors

[3.050] Although the directors of a private company are in law officers of the company, bearing all the responsibilities which pertain to that office, in many private companies they may also be the only members of the company. Consequently, provisions providing for the retirement by rotation of the directors (model article 92) are an anomaly in a company where the directors will almost always be the same. In rare cases the articles will provide that the directors of the company will be life directors, and that model reg 99 be deleted, although it should be noted that such can be altered by the passing of a special resolution. Life directors may, however, be provided for in a provision in the memorandum of association, which may be expressed to be unalterable[105].

---

100 See *Safeguard Industrial Investments Ltd v National Westminster Bank Ltd* [1982] 1 All ER 449 and *Lyle & Scott Ltd v Scott's Trustees* [1959] 2 All ER 661.

101 See *Curtis v JJ Curtis & Co Ltd* [1986] BCLC 86, Court of Appeal of New Zealand.

102 *Lee & Co (Dublin) Ltd v Egan (Wholesale) Ltd* (27 April 1978, unreported) HC, *per* Kenny J.

103 See, generally, Ch 14, *Corporate Governance: Meetings*, at para **[14.090]**.

104 SI 275/1994.

105 See para **[3.037]** *ante*.

[3.051] As regards the powers of directors, model reg 79 places a fetter on the power of the directors to borrow, by limiting the maximum amount of borrowings without the authorisation of the members in general meeting to the nominal amount of share capital issued; it is invariably replaced with an unfettered power to borrow[106]. Where a company is of the 'two euro' variety, it would mean that the directors may only borrow up to two euro. Where the company itself does not modify this to give the directors unlimited borrowing powers, the company may be forced to do so on the first occasion it seeks to raise finance by borrowing. In such a situation a lending institution will usually require, as a prerequisite to corporate borrowing, the substitution for model reg 79 of powers unfettered by reference to the company's issued share capital[107].

[3.052] In most private companies it is normal for the provisions of model reg 80 to be adopted unamended, since it gives the directors wide powers as to the management of the business of the company[108]. The proceedings of directors are sometimes modified by the amendment of model reg 109 to provide that unanimous written resolutions of the directors shall be valid where such resolutions are made up of two or more documents. In addition, a recent development, which goes to highlight the latitude allowed to companies as regards the individuality of their articles, is the facilitating of meetings of the board of directors over the telephone where all parties to the meeting can hear the proceedings and be heard.

(d) Voting rights

[3.053] Quite apart from any voting rights which specifically attach to shares of a particular class[109], the members of a company may wish to *load* the voting rights of some or all of the members, either generally, or in respect of a particular vote. This has been considered permissible since the decision of the House of Lords in *Bushell v Faith*[110] which upheld the validity of the following provision inserted in the articles of association of a company:

> 'In the event of a resolution being proposed at any general meeting of the company for the removal from office of any director, any shares held by that director shall on a poll in respect of such resolution carry the right to three votes per share.'

The facts in *Bushell v Faith* may not today seem all that unusual, but the dispute went the whole way to the House of Lords. The company in question had been incorporated by the mother of the parties to the proceedings who had transferred a block of flats to the company in return for an allotment of 300 shares, one being held by her nominee. The

---

106 See *Re Shannonside Holdings Ltd* (20 May 1993, unreported) HC, *per* Costello J, considered *post* at para **[3.086]** where the company's articles of association contained an article in similar terms to model reg 79.

107 Although some companies give directors more elaborate powers to borrow, a simple alternative may provide that: 'The directors may exercise all the powers of the company to borrow money, and to mortgage or charge all or any part of its undertaking, property and uncalled capital, and to issue debentures, debenture stock and other securities whether outright or as security for any debt, liability or obligation of the company or of any third party without any limit.'

108 See Ch 13, *Corporate Governance: Management by the Directors*, at para **[13.127]** for the text of model reg 80.

109 See Ch 8, *Shares and Membership*, at para **[8.098]** *et seq*.

110 *Bushell v Faith* [1970] AC 1099.

shares subsequently came to be held equally by her three children: the plaintiff, her sister and their defendant brother. When a dispute arose as to the defendant's conduct as director, a general meeting was held and the plaintiff and her sister voted in favour of a resolution that their defendant-brother be removed from office as a director. The defendant naturally opposed the resolution. The ensuing dispute centred upon whether the resolution was passed by 200 votes to 100 votes, or defeated by 300 votes to 200 votes. The validity of the article, quoted above, which enabled a director to remain in office, was questioned in the light of s 184(1) of the Companies Act 1948 (UK) which empowered a company to remove a director by ordinary resolution *notwithstanding anything in its articles*[111].

By a four to one majority the House of Lords upheld the validity of the clause. Lord Upjohn began by observing that the *mischief* which the legislature sought to prevent in enacting s 184(1) was to make a director removable by virtue of an ordinary resolution instead of a special resolution, or making it necessary to alter the company's articles of association. After noting that model reg 2 gives companies a completely unfettered right to attach to any share special voting rights on a poll or restrict voting rights, he said:

> 'Parliament has never sought to fetter the right of the company to issue a share with such rights or restrictions as it may think fit. There is no fetter which compels the company to make the voting rights or restrictions of general application and it seems to me clear that such rights or restrictions can be attached to special circumstances and to particular types of resolution[112].'

Lord Upjohn went on to reconcile this with the right contained in s 184 of the Companies Act 1948 UK), saying:

> 'This makes no mockery of s 184; all that Parliament was seeking to do thereby was to make an ordinary resolution sufficient to remove a director. Had Parliament desired to go further and enact that every share entitled to vote should be deprived of its special rights under the articles it should have said so in plain terms by making the vote on a poll one vote one share. Then, what about shares which had no voting rights under the articles? Should not Parliament give them a vote when considering this completely artificial form of ordinary resolution? Suppose there had been some preference shares in the name of Mr Faith's wife, which under the articles had in the circumstances no vote; why in justice should her voice be excluded from consideration in this artificial vote?
>
> I only raise this purely hypothetical case to show the great difficulty of trying to do justice by legislation in a matter which has always been left to the corporators themselves to decide[113].'

Such clauses have now come to be known as '*Bushell v Faith* clauses'.

[3.054] In private companies the ability to provide that certain shares have *weighted* or *loaded* voting rights has an important role to play in copper-fastening the shareholders' understanding of the basis of their relationship. By ousting the right of the majority to prevail in certain votes, minority shareholder-investors are afforded a degree of comfort. Although not yet specifically considered by the Irish courts it is thought that the decision in *Bushell v Faith* should and will be followed. One of the most common

[111] See s 182(1) of the CA 1963.

[112] *Bushell v Faith* [1970] AC 1099 at 1109E.

[113] *Bushell v Faith* [1970] AC 1099 at 1109F–H.

circumstances in which shares are given weighted voting rights is when '*golden shares*' are created; golden shares entitle the holder to control the composition of a company's board of directors and are utilised to create the relationship of holding company and subsidiary[114].

[3.055] The Interpretation Act 2005 will apply to the construction of Table A articles of association and it has been held that it will also apply to 'special' or tailored articles that particular companies adopt[115].

Alteration of the articles

[3.056] Every company may alter its articles of association by passing a special resolution: s 15 of the CA 1963. As shall be considered in Ch 14, special resolution is a resolution passed by at least 75% of the members of the company entitled to vote at a general meeting[116] or a unanimous resolution in writing where permitted by the articles of association[117]. A single-member private limited company's articles may be altered by a decision of the single member drawn up in writing in accordance with reg 9 of the EC(SMPLC)R 1994[118].

[3.057] In addition to a company having a *positive* right to alter its articles of association, it is also the case that a company cannot in law deprive itself of that right[119]. Accordingly, where by agreement a company purports to so deprive itself, the agreement is void to that extent[120]. Where an alteration of the articles has the effect of resulting in the breach of a contract entered into by the company, then the view of the court has been historically that this will not justify the court preventing by injunction the alteration of the company's articles. Where a person has a contract with a company, and becomes aware that the company intends to alter its articles in breach of the contract, he will not get an injunction to restrain the alteration by the company[121]. The rationale is that the outsider affected by the breach has his usual rights in the law of contract. Where, however, a company's shareholders agree not to alter its articles of association as in, say, a shareholders' agreement, that agreement will be enforced by injunction[122].

---

114 See Ch 12, *Groups of Companies*, at para **[12.009]**.

115 *Fell v Derby Leather Company Ltd* [1931] 2 Ch 252.

116 Either an AGM or an EGM.

117 As permitted by s 141(8) of the CA 1963.

118 SI 275/1994. See Ch 14, *Corporate Governance: Meetings*, at para **[14.088]**.

119 *Peter's American Delicacy Co Ltd v Heath* (1938–39) 61 CLR 457; *Walker v London Tramways Company* (1879) 12 Ch D 705.

120 *Allen v Gold Reefs of West Africa Ltd* [1900] 1 Ch 656, considered *post*; and *Malleson v National Insurance and Guarantee Corporation* [1894] 1 Ch 200.

121 *Southern Foundries (1926) Ltd v Shirlaw* [1940] AC 701 at 740 and *Punt v Symons & Co Ltd* [1903] 2 Ch 506. *Cf British Murac Syndicate Ltd v Alperton Rubber Co Ltd* [1915] 2 Ch 186, where an injunction was granted to restrain the alteration of a company's articles, where such would result in the breach of a contract with an outsider.

122 See para **[3.123]** *post*.

[3.058] Notwithstanding the existence of the inalienable power of alteration there are certain restrictions on the members' exercise of the right to alter a company's articles of association by special resolution:

(a) Where contrary to law.
(b) Where an additional liability is imposed on members.
(c) Where class rights are altered.
(d) Where the articles are altered and the members have not acted *bona fide* and in the interests of the company as a whole.

(a) Where contrary to law

[3.059] A company cannot alter its articles where the resulting change would be contrary to the provisions of that company's memorandum of association, the provisions of the Companies Acts or the general law of the land. In *Hennessy & Others v National Agricultural and Industrial Development Association & Others*[123], an alteration of the articles of association of the defendant company, which was limited by guarantee, was declared null and void. This was because the company's memorandum of association provided that the consent of a Minister was required in order to validly alter the company's articles. Since this was not properly obtained, Overend J held:

> 'Now s 13, sub-s 1 of the Companies Act 1908[124] only confers on a company power to alter its articles '*subject to* the provisions of this Act and to the conditions contained in its memorandum of association'. Clause 5 [of the memorandum] imposes such a condition ... and it is clear in my opinion that, until the Minister had given his definite and final approval, the company's power to alter its articles did not come into existence under s 13 [now s 15 of the CA 1963] of the Act. Any amendments purporting to have been made without such previous approval were null and void[125].'

Another example of an invalid alteration is seen in s 24(4) of the CA 1963[126] whereby it is provided that a company that is exempt from the restrictions on the use of the word 'limited' in the company name, shall not alter its articles (or memorandum) so that it ceases to comply with the requirements for exemption in s 24(1) where it does not have the word 'limited'[127] in its name.

(b) Where an additional liability is imposed on members

[3.060] An alteration of the articles of association cannot have the effect of increasing the liability of any member. Section 27(1) of the CA 1963 provides that notwithstanding anything in a company's memorandum and articles of association:

> '... no member of the company shall be bound by an alteration made in the memorandum or articles after the date on which he becomes a member, if and so far as the alteration requires him to take or subscribe for more shares than the number held by him at the date

[123] *Hennessy & Others v National Agricultural and Industrial Development Association & Others* [1947] IR 159.

[124] Now, s 15(1) of the CA 1963.

[125] *Hennessy & Others v National Agricultural and Industrial Development Association & Others* [1947] IR 159 at 191.

[126] As substituted by s 88(1) of the CLEA 2001.

[127] Or 'teoranta'.

> on which the alteration is made, or in any way increases his liability as at that date to contribute to the share capital of, or otherwise to pay money to, the company.'

It is clear that companies may not alter their articles so as to provide that existing members must subscribe for more shares or otherwise increase their liability to contribute to the company's share capital. This rule of company law is a necessary adjunct to the principle of members' limited liability, *viz*, that a member's liability is to pay the unpaid part (if any) of the issue price of the shares, and nothing more. The prohibition on any alteration in the articles or memorandum that increases a member's liability 'or otherwise to pay money to' the company can give rise to real difficulties, particularly for incorporated clubs or schemes of any kind where the members may subsequent to incorporation be required to increase payments to the company.

[3.061] One of the few modern cases to consider this narrow but important point of company law is the decision of the Supreme Court of New South Wales in *Ding et al v Sylvania Waterways Ltd*[128]. There, the net question was whether the articles of a company could be amended to impose on its shareholders a liability to contribute to the recurring or administrative expenses of the company. The essential facts in that case were that the plaintiffs were shareholders in the defendant company. The plaintiffs were residents in a housing estate that abutted a waterway. The company acquired the waterway and most of the adjoining landowners (including the plaintiffs) acquired shares in the company. Each of the plaintiffs paid a fee on joining. In June of 1995 the company in general meeting resolved in favour of altering its articles of association to provide for the payment of an annual levy for the purpose of maintaining the navigability of the waterways and to fund its ongoing expenses. The annual levy was set by ordinary resolution of the members to be $1,275 *per annum* for three years. The plaintiffs sought a declaration that they were not obliged to pay this by reason of s 140(2)(b) of the Australian Corporations Law, which was in all material respects identical to s 27(1) of the CA 1963[129]. Austin J held that the use of the words 'otherwise to pay money' were sufficiently wide as to cover an amendment to oblige members to make payments in respect of recurring administrative and maintenance expenses of the company. The company's claim that those words were to be qualified by some such words as 'in the nature of share capital' was rejected by Austin J on the grounds that 'the word "otherwise" appears to me to be intended to rebut any possible construction *ejusdem generis* with the preceding words of sub-paragraph (b) …'[130].

[3.062] The company claimed that an examination of the legislative history of the provision would show that all that was intended was to make clear that amendments that require payments in the nature of share capital would not be binding on dissenters but that articles could be amended to introduce fees or levies for administration and maintenance. Following a thorough review of the legislative history, and cases that

---

[128] *Ding et al v Sylvania Waterways Ltd* [1999] NSWSC 58 (15 February 1998).

[129] Section 140(2)(b) provided: 'Unless a member of a company agrees in writing to be bound, they are not bound by a modification of the constitution made after the date on which they became a member so far as the modification … increases the member's liability to contribute to the share capital of, or otherwise to pay money to, the company.'

[130] *Ding et al v Sylvania Waterways Ltd* [1999] NSWSC 58 (15 February 1998) at para 20 of the judgment.

tended for (referred to as the *Lion Insurance* group of cases)[131] and against[132] the contention, Austin J rejected the company's submission. Acknowledging the tension between the two groups of authorities, Austin J said:

> 'In my opinion the true explanation for the decisions in the *Lion Insurance* group of cases is that the obligations held to be enforceable against the members, notwithstanding s 38 of the 1862 Act, were found to have been undertaken on the facts as simple contractual obligations. True it is that the obligations arose by virtue of the members becoming members of the company, and their content was defined in the constitution of the company. Nevertheless, the obligations in each of those cases acquired their binding force by virtue of an act of assent which was both assent to membership of the company and assent to the additional contractual obligations known to the assenting members and recorded in the constitution[133].'

In other words, the only circumstances in which members of a company will be required to pay up on foot of an amendment to the company's constitution is where there is found to be a *special contract* between them and the company[134]. Where the only contract is the s 25 *statutory contract*, the courts will not oblige members to make payments in respect of recurring administrative and maintenance expenses of the company[135]. Austin J went on to say:

> 'If, therefore, the constitution of a company contains provisions which impose special pecuniary obligations on members, and those provisions are known to the applicant for membership when the application for membership is made, and the surrounding circumstances point to an intention to make a special contract, the court may well conclude that the pecuniary obligation is enforceable by the company … In this way the law recognises the constitutional provisions of mutual or co-operative companies and

131 Cases that tended to support the contention that under the Joint Stock Companies Act 1856 and the Companies Act 1862, companies could impose a pecuniary liability on shareholders beyond the liability to contribute the amount unpaid on shares included: *Peninsular Company Ltd v Fleming* (1872) 27 LT (NS) 93; *Re Maria Anna & Steinbank Coal and Coke Company Ltd, Maxwells Case* (1874) 20 Eq 585; *Re Maria Anna & Steinbank Coal and Coke Company Ltd, McKewan's Case* (1877) 6 Ch D 447; and *The Lion Mutual Marine Insurance Association Ltd v Tucker* (1883) 12 QBD 176. In the latter case it was held that the original prohibition on increasing members' liability did not limit the contributions that could be payable by a member in his capacity of mutual insurer under the articles, and only applied to liabilities incurred by members in their capacity as such.

132 Cases against the company's contention were: *Shalfoon v Chedar Valley Co-operative Dairy Co Ltd* [1924] NZLR 561; *Manners v St David's Gold and Copper Mines Ltd* [1904] 2 Ch 593 and *Bisgood v Henderson's Transvaal Estate Ltd* [1908] 1 Ch 743.

133 *Ding et al v Sylvania Waterways Ltd* [1999] NSWSC 58 (15 February 1998) at para 43 of the judgment.

134 As to the difference between 'special contracts' and the 'statutory contract' see para **[3.102]** *ante*.

135 *Cf Pelzan v Boaron Diamonds Ltd* (December 1996), Supreme Court of Israel, noted by Berg, [1997] 11 ICCLR C-173. There it seems that the fact that the memorandum and articles of association were a statutory contract coupled with the fact that the legislation permitted them to be altered, was found to be a sufficient basis for the Israeli Supreme Court to uphold an amendment to the articles that was added *after* the plaintiff became a member, which imposed personal liability on members in respect of all business dealings carried out with another member of the company whose members were in the business of a diamond exchange.

> clubs. For example, the obligation of members of an incorporated club to pay an annual membership fee set by its constitution is probably based on this reasoning[136].'

Austin J went on to find that in the instant case there was a 'special contract'. On the facts of the case, however, he held that there was neither an express nor an implied term that authorised the company to introduce a new pecuniary liability in the nature of what it purported to introduce[137]. Accordingly, the plaintiffs were successful in their application for a direction that they were not obliged to pay the annual levy.

[3.063] The ratio of *Ding* is, first, that an article that imposes a pecuniary liability to pay an annual fee or levy is enforceable against members whose membership arises after the article is adopted or who otherwise assent in writing to it as contemplated by s 27(2) of the CA 1963. Second, the statutory limitation on liability does not render such an article invalid because the members expressly or implicitly assent to the obligation when they become members and thereby enter into a special contract in addition to their normal membership contract an envisaged by s 25 of the CA 1963. Third, where, however, such an article is adopted by amendment it cannot bind existing members by reason of the equivalent of s 27(1) of the CA 1963 unless those members have agreed in writing to be bound because that section applies to a modification of the memorandum or articles that increases a member's pecuniary liability to the company in any way. Where it is envisaged that a company will seek to increase annual fees, the advice given by Austin J is instructive:

> '… the only practical solution would appear to be either to draft the original article in such a way as to include within its terms a mechanism for increasing the charge (for example, by authorising the board of directors to determine the charge from time to time), or to ensure that applicants for membership sign a written application form or similar document in which they expressly agree in writing to be bound by subsequent amendments which increase the charge[138].'

In this way, any alteration to increase members' liability will not be thwarted because either (a) no amendment to the articles is needed as the articles delegate the power to fix an increasing charge to the directors *ab initio* or (b) any increase in charge will be in accordance with an express term of a special contract.

(c) Where class rights are altered

[3.064] Where a company's articles of association provide for different class rights, a special resolution will not of itself be sufficient to effect a valid alteration where the effect is to vary class rights. Section 38 of the C(A)A 1983 sets out a series of slightly different scenarios as to how rights arise, what the memorandum and articles say and the nature of the rights being varied. Section 38(2) of the C(A)A 1983 provides:

---

136 *Ding et al v Sylvania Waterways Ltd* [1999] NSWSC 58 (15 February 1998) at para 47 of the judgment.

137 Austin J also said that where there is a special contract, which contains an implied term authorising the amendment which has been made, the effect of a s 27 of the CA 1963 type provision was to 'override the implied term and to declare that non-assenting members are not bound by the amendment even though they have previously entered into a special contract containing an implied term to contrary effect'.

138 *Ding et al v Sylvania Waterways Ltd* [1999] NSWSC 58 (15 February 1998) at para 70 of the judgment.

> 'Where the rights attached to a class of shares in the company otherwise than by the memorandum, and the articles of the company do no contain provisions with respect to the variation of the rights, those rights may be varied if, but only if–
>
> (a) the holders of three-quarters in nominal value of the issued shares of that class consent in writing to the variation; or
>
> (b) a special resolution passed at a separate general meeting of the holders of that class sanctions the variation;
>
> and any requirement (howsoever imposed) in relation to the variation of those rights is complied with to the extent that it is not comprised in paragraphs (a) and (b).'

So, if a company's articles of association provide for class rights for preferential shares and for ordinary shares, even if the holders of the ordinary shares are entitled to pass a special resolution, they cannot amend the articles to vary the rights attaching to the preferential shares unless the holders of 75% of the issued preferential shares consent in writing or the preferential shareholders pass a special resolution sanctioning the variation.

[3.065] Where rights, howsoever arising[139], are attached to a class of shares and the memorandum or articles provide for the variation of those rights and the variation is connected with the giving, variation, revocation or renewal of an authority for the purposes of s 20 of the C(A)A 1983 or with a reduction of the company's share capital under s 72 of the CA 1963, then s 38(3) of the C(A)A 1983 provides that those rights cannot be varied unless the condition mentioned in s 38(2)(a) or (b) is satisfied and any requirement of the memorandum or articles in relation to the variation of rights of that class is complied with. Section 38(4) of the C(A)A 1983 provides that where the rights are attached to a class of shares in the company by the memorandum or otherwise and (a) if they are attached by the memorandum, the articles contain a provision with respect to their variation which has been included in the articles at the time of the company's original incorporation or (b) if they are so attached otherwise, the articles contain such provision (whenever first so included) and in either case the variation of rights is not of a kind mentioned in s 38(3), then those rights may only be varied in accordance with that provision of the articles. Section 38(5) provides that where the rights are attached to a class of shares in the company by the memorandum and it and the articles do not contain a provision with respect to the variation of the rights, those rights may be varied if *all* the members of the company agree to the variation. Section 38(6) provides that the provisions of ss 133 and 134 of the CA 1963 apply to any meetings of classes of shareholders required under s 38, subject to some modifications[140].

[3.066] An alteration of class rights can be made the subject of a court application by the holders of at least 10% of the shares so affected[141]. It should also be noted that under s 205 of the CA 1963 a company may be compelled by the court to alter its articles or memorandum to protect the interests of an oppressed minority of members.

[139] Section 38(3)(a) refers to the rights being 'attached to a class of shares in the company by the memorandum *or otherwise*' so, it seems, it does not matter how the rights arise.

[140] Note also the supplementary and ancillary provisions in s 38(7)–(11).

[141] Section 78 of the CA 1963, and Bourne, 'Variations on the Class Theme' (1988) Accountancy 128.

Furthermore, once so ordered by the court under s 205, the Supreme Court held in *Re R Ltd*[142] that:

> '... subject to the provisions of the order, the company concerned shall not have power without the leave of the court to make any further alteration in or addition to the memorandum or articles inconsistent with the provisions of the order ...'

Alterations made pursuant to a court order have the same effect as if duly made by resolution of the company.

(d) Alterations not bona fide and in the interests of the company as a whole

[3.067] The greatest and most nebulous prohibition on the alteration of the articles of a company is that an alteration will be declared to be null and void where the power to alter the articles is not exercised *bona fide* and in the interests of the company as a whole[143]. At the outset, it should be noted that this, the traditional test for alteration of articles, as promulgated by Lindley MR in *Allen v Gold Reefs of West Africa Ltd*[144] has been rejected as inappropriate by Australia's highest court in *Gambotto and another v WCP Ltd and another*[145] although, more recently, it has been upheld by the Privy Council in *Citco Banking Corp NV v Pusser's Ltd*[146]. The traditional test applied to establish the propriety of alterations of a company's articles of association is considered under the following headings:

(i) The traditional test defined.
(ii) The meaning of 'company as a whole'.
(iii) The appropriate test – who determines what is reasonable?
(iv) Divergent disputes: the traditional test applied.
(v) Alternative approaches: the traditional test discredited.

(i) The traditional test defined

[3.068] The traditional test for determining the validity of an alteration of a company's articles of association is that a resolution altering the articles must be made, *bona fide and in the interests of the company as a whole*. This has its accepted roots in the case of *Allen v Gold Reefs of West Africa Ltd*[147]. Inherent in this test is a conflict between some equally honourable principles, namely, the democratic right of a majority within a company to determine the direction of that company, *and*, the proprietary right of a shareholder to exercise his voting rights as selfishly as he chooses[148], *versus* the right of a minority of the shareholders to have the basis upon which they entered the company

142 *Re R Ltd* [1989] ILRM 757.

143 See *Allen v Gold Reefs of West Africa Ltd* (1900) 1 Ch 656, considered *post*.

144 *Allen v Gold Reefs of West Africa Ltd* [1900] 1 Ch 656.

145 *Gambotto and another v WCP Ltd and another* (1995) 13 ACLC 342. For comment, see Moshinsky and Rosedale, 'A Victory for the Small Shareholder in Australia' [1995] 7 ICCLR 229. See para **[3.083]** *post*.

146 *Citco Banking Corp NV v Pusser's Ltd* [2007] BCC 205.

147 *Allen v Gold Reefs of West Africa Ltd* [1900] 1 Ch 656.

148 See *PMPS Insurance Co Ltd and Moore v Attorney General* [1984] ILRM 88, and *Pender v Lushington* (1877) 6 Ch D 70.

unchanged[149] and, in particular, the right not to have one's shares compulsorily acquired, or expropriated by the majority[150]. Indeed, it is alterations that effect an expropriation of shares where the injustice in allowing a majority to exercise their voting power as they wish, without any restraint, can become most acute.

[3.069] In *Allen v Gold Reefs of West Africa Ltd*, the articles of the company provided that the company had a lien on members' shares for 'all debts, obligations, and liabilities of any member to or towards the company upon all shares (not being fully paid)'. The company purported to alter this regulation by the deletion of the words '(not being fully paid)'. The members were disposed to resolve in favour of this alteration because of the death of the late and unfortunate Zuccani, a member who died insolvent owing the company £6,072 and 10 shillings. Presumably, after the initial mourning for the loss of one of their number, the remaining members decided that it would compound the tragedy were his debt to the company to die with him. So, it was decided to alter the company's articles on the terms outlined, the result being that the company then had a lien over Zuccani's shares – although they were fully paid – thereby entitling the company to take back the shares. When the matter came before the Court of Appeal, Lindley MR held in the often quoted words:

> 'The power thus conferred on companies to alter the regulations contained in their articles is limited only by the provisions contained in the statute and the conditions contained in the company's memorandum of association. Wide, however, as the language of s 50 [now s 15 of the CA 1963] is, the power conferred by it must, like all other powers, be subject to those general principles of law and equity which are applicable to all powers conferred on majorities and enabling them to bind minorities. It must be exercised, not only in the manner required by law, but also *bona fide for the benefit of the company as a whole*, and it must not be exceeded. These conditions are always implied, and are seldom, if ever, expressed[151].'

Lindley MR went on to hold that the alteration in this instance was *valid*. While undoubtedly a generalisation[152], his expression of the restriction on the majority to impose its will on a dissenting minority was, until recently[153], one of the most sacred of shibboleths in company law. While the intention behind the test '*bona fide*' is clear, unfortunately it is characterised by uncertainty in its application. Similarly, the meaning of '*company as a whole*' is far from clear and, as now considered, is open to two interpretations.

(ii) The meaning of 'company as a whole'

[3.070] The phrase, 'company as a whole', can mean either the company as a separate entity, *or* the corporators (members) as a general body. Many of the reported cases interpret the phrase as meaning for the benefit of the company as a separate entity. In the

[149] See Rixon, 'Competing Interests And Conflicting Principles: An Examination Of The Power Of Alteration Of Articles Of Association' (1986) MLR 447, for a detailed and perceptive treatment of the law applicable to the alteration of a company's articles.

[150] *Gambotto and another v WCP Ltd and another* (1995) 13 ACLC 342.

[151] *Allen v Gold Reefs of West Africa Ltd* [1900] 1 Ch 656 at 671 (italics added).

[152] See Rixon, 'Competing Interests and Conflicting Principles: An Examination of the Power of Alteration of Articles of Association' (1986) MLR 447.

[153] *Gambotto and another v WCP Ltd and another* (1995) 13 ACLC 342. See para **[3.083]** *post*.

Allen case itself, the alteration was clearly in the interests of the company as a separate legal entity; it was the direct beneficiary of the alteration and obtained the lien over Zuccani's fully paid shares.

[3.071] In other cases the result is different and the beneficiaries of the alteration will be the very people who vote in favour of the change: the members themselves and the words '*company as a whole*' have also been interpreted as meaning the members or corporators as a general body[154]. Thus in *Greenhalgh v Arderne Cinemas Ltd*[155] the articles of the company in question contained pre-emption rights to the effect that a member could not transfer his shares to a non-member without first offering them to the other members of the company. This pre-emption clause was altered to provide that sales to non-members were permissible where sanctioned by an ordinary resolution without the transferor having to offer them to existing members. The majority shareholder who initiated this alteration had a personal interest in that he wanted to sell his shares to a non-member. However, the plaintiff, Mr Greenhalgh, objected and sought a declaration that the alteration was invalid as not being *bona fide* and in the interests of the company as a whole. It was said by Evershed MR that:

> '... the phrase, "company as a whole", does not (at any rate in such a case as the present) mean the company as a commercial entity as distinct from the corporators. It means the corporators as a general body. That is to say, the case may be taken of an individual hypothetical member and it may be asked whether what is proposed is, in the honest opinion of those who voted in its favour, for that person's benefit[156].'

After distinguishing between the two meanings of 'company as a whole', Evershed MR proposed an alternative test in cases where a company's articles are altered by resolution of the members:

> 'I think the thing can, in practice, be more accurately and precisely stated by looking at the converse and by saying that a special resolution of this kind would be liable to be impeached if the effect of it were to discriminate between the majority shareholders and the minority shareholders so as to give to the former an advantage of which the latter were deprived[157].'

In this case Evershed MR rejected the plaintiff's claim holding that 'when a man comes into a company, he is not entitled to assume that the articles will always remain in a particular form[158]'. He went on to hold that unfair discrimination did not exist and that, accordingly, the resolution to alter the articles was valid.

[3.072] Albeit in another context[159], the Irish High Court, in *G & s Doherty Ltd v Doherty*[160], *per* Henchy J held that '*for the benefit of the company as a whole*' means,

---

154 See *Sidebottom v Kershaw, Leese & Co* [1920] 1 Ch 154 and *Greenhalgh v Arderne Cinemas Ltd* [1951] 1 Ch 286.

155 *Greenhalgh v Arderne Cinemas Ltd* [1950] 2 All ER 1120. See also *Re Williams Group Tullamore Ltd* [1985] IR 613, where Barrington J cited in part the *dictum* of Evershed MR.

156 *Greenhalgh v Arderne Cinemas Ltd* [1950] 2 All ER 1120 at 1126.

157 *Greenhalgh v Arderne Cinemas Ltd* [1950] 2 All ER 1120 at 1126.

158 *Greenhalgh v Arderne Cinemas Ltd* [1950] 2 All ER 1120 at 1127.

159 Namely, that the exercise of the powers of the directors of a company must be exercised, *bona fide* and in the interests of the company as a whole.

160 *G & S Doherty Ltd v Doherty* (19 June 1969, unreported) HC *per* Henchy J, at p 22 of the transcript. See also Mr Justice Henchy's prior judgment of the 4 April 1968, and the later Supreme Court judgment of the 19 December 1969, *per* Ó Dálaigh CJ.

'the shareholders as a whole'. It has been said[161] that in deciding which version of the test is appropriate on an alteration of the articles, it is essential to determine the *context of the alteration*. Thus, alterations which give rise to conflicts between the company and its members must be distinguished from conflicts between the members *inter se*. Depending upon which matter is in issue the phrase 'company as a whole' must, chameleon-like, adapt its colour.

(iii) The appropriate test – who determines what is reasonable?

[3.073] There is, quite rightly, a principled reluctance by the courts to interfere in the internal management of a company[162]. However, the courts are the ultimate *fora* where dissenters can be heard, and are thus faced with the unenviable choice of having to apply a test to the actions of a majority of shareholders. On the one hand the court could apply an *objective test* by which it would look at the action of the majority, and ask could a reasonable shareholder have thought that it was in the interests of the company as a whole. This was the approach taken in *Dafen Tinplate Co Ltd v Llanelly Steel Co (1907) Ltd*[163]where Peterson J said that the question was not whether the shareholders honestly believed that the alteration was for the benefit of the company but whether '*in fact the alteration is genuinely for the benefit of the company*'.

[3.074] On the other hand, the court could apply a *subjective test* and confine its enquiry to whether or not the majority shareholders in the case before it actually believed that what they were doing was in the interests of the company as a whole. It is thought that the better view is that the courts should apply a subjective test, as was done in *Shuttleworth v Cox Brothers & Co (Maidenhead) Ltd*[164]. In this case, the articles of the company provided that five directors should be life directors, unless disqualified by any one of six events. Mr Shuttleworth was thought to be somewhat delinquent in that he had failed to account for company money on no less than 22 occasions within the space of one year. The company reacted by altering its articles to provide that a life director could be disqualified where the other directors resolved that he should resign. The Court of Appeal held that the alteration was valid because it was *bona fide* and in the interests of the company as a whole. Atkin LJ said:

> 'The only question is whether or not the shareholders, in considering whether they shall alter the articles, honestly intend to exercise their powers for the benefit of the company. If they do then, subject to one or two reservations which have been explained, the alteration must stand. It is not a matter of law for the court whether or not a particular alteration is for the benefit of the company; nor is it the business of a judge to review the decision of every company in the country on these questions ... In my view the question is solely for the shareholders acting in good faith[165].'

---

[161] Rixon, 'Competing Interests And Conflicting Principles: An Examination Of The Power Of Alteration Of Articles Of Association' (1986) MLR 447.

[162] See generally, Ch 11, *Shareholders' Remedies*.

[163] See *Dafen Tinplate Co Ltd v Llanelly Steel Co (1907) Ltd* [1920] 2 Ch 124, *per* Peterson J.

[164] *Shuttleworth v Cox Brothers & Co (Maidenhead) Ltd* [1927] 2 KB 9.

[165] *Shuttleworth v Cox Brothers & Co (Maidenhead) Ltd* [1927] 2 KB 9 at 26, 27.

Scrutton LJ said:

> 'Now when persons, honestly endeavouring to decide what will be for the benefit of the company and to act accordingly, decide upon a particular course, then, provided there are grounds on which reasonable men could come to the same decision, it does not matter whether the Court would or would not come to the same decision or a different decision. Or a different decision. It is not the business of the Court to manage the affairs of the company. That is for the shareholders and directors. The absence of any reasonable ground for deciding that a certain course of action is conducive to the benefit of the company may be a ground for finding a lack of good faith or for finding that the shareholders, with the best motives, have not considered the matters which they ought to have considered. On either of these findings their decision might be set aside. But I should be sorry to see the Court go beyond this and take upon itself the management of concerns which others may understand far better than the Court does[166].'

Atkin LJ achieved an honourable balance between the competing tests when he said[167]:

> 'The circumstances may be such as to lead to one conclusion only, that the majority of the shareholders are acting so oppressively that they cannot be acting in good faith; or, to put it another way, it may be that their decision must be one which could be taken by persons acting in good faith with a view to the benefit of the company.'

Thus we see that the primary test is to be seen as being essentially subjective, but having an objective element from an evidential standpoint[168].

[3.075] The decision in *Shuttleworth* received a relatively recent endorsement from the Privy Council. In *Citco Banking Corp NV v Pusser's Ltd*[169], a company had a share capital of $4.4 million divided into 4.4 million class A shares of $1 each of which 1,673,217 shares and 248,000 share warrants had been issued. At an EGM the company passed a special resolution amending its articles of association to create 2,000 class B shares carrying 50 votes and further resolved that 200,000 of the class A shares held by the chairman be converted into class B shares. The resolutions were carried by 1,125,665 votes to 183,000, all 183,000 votes against being cast by Citco which alleged that the resolutions were invalid as they were passed in the interests of the chairman to give him indisputable control and were not *bona fide* and in the best interests of the company. At trial, the judge found that the resolution failed to pass the text for being *bona fide* and for the benefit of the company as a whole. On appeal, the Court of Appeal reversed this decision, finding that the judge should have applied the test in *Shuttleworth v Cox Bros & Co (Maidenhead) Ltd*[170] as to whether reasonable shareholders could have considered that the amendment was for the benefit of the company. The Court of Appeal found the trial judge went wrong in principle 'when he attempted to step into the commercial arena[171]'. It also found that it would have been reasonable for shareholders to have accepted in good faith the arguments put forward by the chairman as to why the

---

166 *Shuttleworth v Cox Brothers & Co (Maidenhead) Ltd* [1927] 2 KB 9 at 23, 24.

167 *Shuttleworth v Cox Brothers & Co (Maidenhead) Ltd* [1927] 2 KB 9 at 27.

168 This seems to have been followed in later cases, eg, *Greenhalgh v Arderne Cinemas Ltd* [1951] 1 Ch 286.

169 *Citco Banking Corp NV v Pusser's Ltd* [2007] BCC 205.

170 *Shuttleworth v Cox Bros & Co (Maidenhead) Ltd* [1927] 2 KB 9.

171 *Citco Banking Corp NV v Pusser's Ltd* [2007] BCC 205 at 212 (para 24).

amendment would be in the best interests of the company as a whole and noted that the only shareholder to give evidence had said he thought that the amendments were in the best interests of the company as a whole. Citco appealed this decision to the Privy Council which upheld the decision of the Court of Appeal and found that the appropriate test was whether reasonable shareholders could have considered that the amendment was for the benefit of the company. The Privy Council went on to endorse the principle that shareholders can vote in their own interests, quoting with approval the following passage from the decision of Evershed MR in *Greenhalgh v Arderne Cinemas Ltd*[172]:

> 'It is ... not necessary to require that persons voting for a special resolution should, so to speak, dissociate themselves altogether from their own prospects ...'

(iv) Divergent disputes: the traditional test applied

[3.076] Where a court does intervene in such a dispute, its primary task will be to establish the *motive* behind the alteration of the articles. The court will ask whether the alteration was motivated by intentions which were *bona fide* and in the interests of the company as a whole, which will mean either the company as a separate entity or all of the shareholders, depending upon the context of the alteration. Sometimes the motive behind the alteration will be obvious, where, for example, the alteration could only affect one member, or one sector of the membership, and such may be evidence of a lack of *bona fides*[173]. On the other hand, the action of the shareholders in altering the articles may clearly show that they have gained nothing personally, thus inclining the court to accept that they acted *bona fide*[174].

Often the motives behind the alteration will be unclear, and the actions of the voting shareholders open to several interpretations. In such cases, the court will have to apply some test. Although several different tests appear in the reported cases, two very different situations must be distinguished. On the one hand, the alteration may result in a conflict between *the company and some of its members*. On the other hand, it may result in a conflict between the members *inter se*.

[3.077] *Company versus members*: where the alteration results in a conflict between the company and its members, it is submitted that the appropriate test is that set out in *Shuttleworth v Cox Brothers & Co (Maidenhead) Ltd*[175] where Bankes LJ said:

> 'So the test is whether the alteration of the articles was in the opinion of the shareholders for the benefit of the company. By what criterion is the court to ascertain opinion of the shareholders upon this question? The alteration may be so oppressive as to cast suspicion on the honesty of the persons responsible for it, or so extravagant that no reasonable men could really consider it for the benefit of the company. In such cases the court is, I think, entitled to treat the conduct of shareholders as it does the verdict of a jury, and to say that the alteration of a company's articles shall not stand if it is such that no reasonable man could consider it for the benefit of the company.'

---

172 *Greenhalgh v Arderne Cinemas Ltd* [1950] 2 All ER 1120, [1951] Ch 286.

173 Eg, *Sidebottom v Kershaw, Leese & Co* [1920] 1 Ch 154, *per* Eve J at 173 *et seq*.

174 See *Rights & Issues Investment Trust Ltd v Stylo Shoes Ltd* [1965] 1 Ch 250, *per* Pennycuick J, who could see no grounds for finding that there was any oppression, at 256D.

175 *Shuttleworth v Cox Brothers & Co (Maidenhead) Ltd* [1927] 1 KB 9.

The essential point is that the test which the court is applying is that the alteration will be invalid where the majority of the shareholders *acting in the interests of the company* pass a special resolution to alter the articles, and such could not be said to be *a reasonable alteration* of the constitution from the viewpoint of the affected minority.

[3.078] In the *Shuttleworth* case, the shareholders were clearly acting reasonably in the interests of the company in that the alteration was directed against a perceived delinquent director. A similar motive was evident in *Sidebottom v Kershaw, Leese & Co*[176]. There, an alteration was made to the articles of association empowering the directors to compel the transfer of the shares (at full value) of any member who competed with the business of the company. In effect the alteration was in the nature of an expropriation of shares, but although such may be evidence of a *mala fide* intention, in this case the expropriation was not motivated by selfish desires of individual shareholders, but rather in the interests of the company. Lord Sterndale MR said:

> 'I think, looking at the alteration broadly, that it is for the benefit of the company that they should not be obliged to have amongst them as members persons who are competing with them in business, and who may get knowledge from their membership which would enable them to compete better[177].'

Again, the test is whether the company's interests are being protected by the use of reasonable measures.

[3.079] *Member versus member:* in *Re Williams Group Tullamore Ltd*,[178] Barrington J said, referring to the dilemma which must be addressed in cases where there is a conflict between members:

> 'There is no doubt that shareholders, voting at a general meeting of the company, are entitled to have regard to their own interests. The problem is the degree to which they are entitled to disregard the interests of other shareholders.'

That shareholders may vote selfishly has received recent support from the Privy Council in *Citco Banking Corp NV v Pusser's Ltd*[179]. The right to vote selfishly was, however, tempered in *Sunlink International Ltd v Wong Shu Wing*[180], a decision of the Hong Kong Companies Court. In that case an injunction was granted to restrain majority shareholders (and the holders of a security interest in those shares) of a listed company

---

176 *Sidebottom v Kershaw, Leese & Co* [1920] 1 Ch 154.

177 *Sidebottom v Kershaw, Leese & Co* [1920] 1 Ch 154 at 166. Lord Sterndale MR went on to say that the fact that it was directed at the wayward Mr Bodden did not, *per se*, render the alteration *mala fides*. That it was directed at Bodden, was, he said, nothing more than the shareholders saying: 'It was the position of Mr Bodden that made us appreciate the detriment that there might be to the company in having members competing with them in their business, and we passed this, and our intention was, if it became necessary, to use it in the case of Mr Bodden; that is what we had in our minds that Mr Bodden is not the only person who might compete, and therefore we passed this general article in order to enable us to apply it in any case where it was for the good of the company that it should be applied.'

178 *Re Williams Group Tullamore Ltd* [1985] IR 613, a case concerning s 205 of the CA 1963, considered in Ch 11, *Shareholders' Remedies*, at para **[11.031]**.

179 *Citco Banking Corp NV v Pusser's Ltd* [2007] BCC 205.

180 *Sunlink International Ltd v Wong Shu Wing* [2010] 5 HKLRD 653. See Wong, 'Can Shareholders vote Irrationally?' (2011) 127 LQR 522.

from voting against resolutions to approve a capital injection and appoint directors and auditors. The injunction was granted on the basis that '... the court will intervene to prevent a shareholder voting in a way which will result in the destruction of the economic value of other shareholders' shares for no rational reason'. It has been suggested that one justification for the departure from the general principle that shareholders can vote selfishly is where the company is insolvent or its solvency is in the balance[181].

[3.080] Where the alteration of the articles leads to a conflict between the members *inter se*, ie, where the alteration is of no tangible benefit to the company, the test should in logic be different. In such cases, it is submitted that the appropriate test is whether or not the majority of the shareholders who vote for the alteration better their interests at the expense of the minority. This is a variation of the test proposed by Evershed MR, and already quoted, in *Greenhalgh v Arderne Cinemas Ltd*[182] where he said that an alteration would be invalid:

> '... if the effect of it were to discriminate between the majority shareholders and the minority shareholders so as to give the former an advantage of which the latter were deprived[183].'

It is suggested that this test should be applied where the majority shareholders try to use their voting power to *unfairly* impose their will on the minority and thereby adversely affect the interests of the minority. Such a situation is totally different to the situation where there is a conflict between the company and its members. There, the members exercise their voting power in the interests of the company, and only indirectly in their own interests. In the present situation, the members exercise their voting power *in their own interests*, and not those of the company.

Here, there is a real conflict between the interests of the minority and the proprietary rights of the majority to exercise their vote as selfishly as they wish. It is suggested that in a member/member conflict in a private company, the proprietary rights of the majority ought not to be allowed to prevail[184]. In such a company the member shareholders will have more in common than simply all having shareholdings in the same company. Rather, they will often be quasi-partners in business and their relations ought to be recognised as such. The test which the courts should apply to such a member/member conflict ought to reflect the sanctity of the relations between the members, and demand an honourable standard from all members in the exercise of their voting rights.

---

181 Wong, 'Can Shareholders vote Irrationally?' (2011) 127 LQR 522.

182 *Greenhalgh v Arderne Cinemas, Ltd* [1950] 2 All ER 1120.

183 See also *Peters' American Delicacy Co v Heath* [1938-9] CLR 512.

184 Here, as in so many other ways, the eternal distinction between the private and public company is evident in that in the case of a public company, the considerations will often be different and it is submitted that in public companies, in the absence of fraud, the members ought to be allowed to vote as they wish, unfettered by consideration for the minority. In a public company the shareholders are in no way related by any bonds or quasi-fiduciary relations and so ought not to be bound to observe the same standards expected of the members of a closely-held private company.

(v) Alternative approaches: the traditional test discredited

[3.081] It is suggested that the so-called traditional test in *Allen* is, at best, merely an attempt to postulate a general principle. Without regard to the nature of the alteration it can, at worst, be interpreted as a misleading generalisation. One alternative approach frees itself of the constraints of the traditional test and is seen in *Clemens v Clemens Brothers Ltd*[185]. There, Foster J said:

> 'I think that one thing which emerges from the cases to which I have referred is that in such a case as the present Miss Clemens is not entitled to exercise her majority vote in whatever way she pleases. The difficulty is in finding a principle, and obviously expressions such as 'bona fide in the interests of the company as a whole', 'fraud on a minority' and 'oppressive' do not assist in formulating a principle. I have come to the conclusion that it would be unwise to try to produce a principle, since the circumstances of each case are infinitely varied. It would not, I think, assist to say more than that in my judgement Miss Clemens is not entitled as of right to exercise her votes as an ordinary shareholder in any way she pleases. To use the phrase of Lord Wilberforce[186], that right is "subject ... to equitable considerations ... which may make it unjust ... to exercise [it] in a particular way".'

In that case the plaintiff owned 45% of the shares in the defendant company and Miss Clemens held the remaining 55% of the shares. It was proposed to make an issue of shares which would, *inter alia*, have the effect of reducing the plaintiff's shareholdings in the company to under 25%. Resolutions were passed to this effect, and the plaintiff sought a declaration that they be set aside as being oppressive. Foster J granted the orders on the grounds as set out above. Although that case was not strictly concerned with the alteration of the articles, it is submitted[187] that in view of the artificialities inherent in the traditional analysis, there is some merit in the 'equitable considerations' approach set out in the *Clemens* case[188].

[3.082] Perhaps it is because of the difficulties associated with the traditional test that more and more members who feel aggrieved by an alteration of a company's articles of association will not seek to rely upon the common law, preferring instead to petition the court under s 205 of the CA 1963[189]. Such is now facilitated by the acceptance that the section has application to isolated incidents of oppression or acts of disregard for the interests of a minority.

---

185 *Clemens v Clemens Brothers Ltd* [1976] 2 All ER 268.

186 In *Ebrahimi v Westbourne Galleries Ltd* [1972] 2 All ER 492 at 500.

187 See also *Brown v British Abrasive Wheel Co* [1919] 1 Ch 291 at 295, where Astbury J said: 'The question therefore is whether the enforcement of the proposed alteration on the minority is within the ordinary principles of justice and whether it is for the benefit of the company as a whole. I find it very difficult to follow how it can be just and equitable that a majority, by failing to purchase the shares of a minority by agreement, can take the power to do so compulsorily.' Clearly, the court took cognisance of the underlying equities of the situation.

188 *Cf* Keane, *Company Law* (4th edn, Bloomsbury Professional, 2007), at 6.20, where he doubts whether as a general principle *Clemens* can be supported.

189 See *Re Williams Group Tullamore Ltd* [1985] IR 613 and generally, Ch 11, *Shareholders' Remedies*, at para **[11.031]** *et seq*.

[3.083] The Australian High Court considered the vexed issue of alteration of articles of association in *Gambotto and another v WCP Ltd and another*[190] and in doing so has lent support in favour of an 'oppression' test. The facts in that case were that the defendant company sought to alter its articles of association to allow any shareholder holding 90% or more of the company's issued share capital to acquire compulsorily all of the remaining shares, in circumstances where the statutory compulsory appropriation provisions were inapplicable[191]. At the relevant time, a corporate group owned 99.7% of the issued share capital in the defendant. The plaintiff minority shareholder objected to the alteration on the basis that the appropriation of his shares was oppressive. In finding for the plaintiff, the Australian High Court departed radically from the traditional test:

> 'In the context of a special resolution altering the articles and giving rise to a conflict of interests and advantages, whether or not it involves an expropriation of shares, we would reject as inappropriate the "*bona fide for the benefit of the company as a whole*" test of Lindley MR in *Allen v Gold Reefs of West Africa Ltd.* The application of the test in such a context has been criticised on grounds which, in our view, are unanswerable. It seems to us that, in such a case not involving an actual or effective expropriation of shares or of valuable proprietary rights attaching to shares, an alteration of the articles by special resolution regularly passed will be valid unless it is *ultra vires*, beyond any purpose contemplated by the articles or oppressive as that expression is understood in the law relating to corporations. Somewhat different considerations apply, however, in a case which as the present where what is involved is an alteration of the articles to allow an expropriation by the majority of the shares, or of valuable proprietary rights attaching to the shares, of a minority. In such a case, the immediate purpose of the resolution is to confer upon the majority shareholder or shareholders power to acquire compulsorily the property of the minority shareholder or shareholders. Of itself, the conferral of such a power does not lie within the 'contemplated objects of the power' to amend the articles'[192].

The distinction was thus made between alterations that involve an expropriation of shares or of valuable property rights from those that do not. Where the alteration does not involve an expropriation of shares, the court was inclined to a test akin to that contained in the Irish s 205 remedy: is the alteration oppressive? In company law, it is established that by oppression is meant 'burdensome, harsh and wrongful'[193]. Apart from not being oppressive, the alteration must also be *intra vires* and not beyond the purpose contemplated by the articles.

[3.084] In relation to alterations that involve the expropriation of shares, the test promulgated in *Gambotto* was stated thus:

> 'The exercise of a power conferred by a company's constitution enabling the majority shareholders to expropriate the minority's shareholding for the purpose of aggrandising

[190] *Gambotto and another v WCP Ltd and another* (1995) 13 ACLC 342. For comment, see Moshinsky & Rosedale, 'A Victory for the Small Shareholder in Australia' [1995] 7 ICCLR 229.

[191] See Ch 9, *Share Transfer*, at para **[9.087]** *et seq*.

[192] *Gambotto and another v WCP Ltd and another* (1995) 13 ACLC 342 at para 25 of the majority judgment.

[193] See *Re Greenore Trading Company Ltd* [1980] ILRM 94 at 100, 101; *Scottish Co-operative Wholesale Society Ltd v Meyer* [1959] AC 324. See, generally, Ch 11, *Shareholders' Remedies*, at para **[11.011]** *et seq*.

the majority *is valid if and only if to the extent that the relevant provisions of the company's constitution so provide*. The inclusion of such a power in a company's constitution at its incorporation is one thing. But it is another thing when a company's constitution is sought to be amended by an alteration of articles of association so as to confer upon the majority power to expropriate the shares of a minority. Such a power could not be taken or exercised simply for the purpose of aggrandising the majority … In our view, such a power can be taken only if

(i) it is exercisable for a proper purpose and

(ii) its exercise will not operate oppressively in relation to minority shareholders.

In other words, an expropriation may be justified where it is reasonably apprehended that the continued shareholding of the minority is detrimental to the company, its undertaking or the conduct of its affairs – resulting in detriment to the interests of the existing shareholders generally – and expropriation is a reasonable means of eliminating or mitigating that detriment[194].'

Examples of justified expropriation that the court gave were: where a shareholder was competing with the company (as in *Sidebottom v Kershaw, Leese and Co*[195]) so long as the *terms* of the expropriation were not oppressive; or where necessary to remove a particular shareholder in order to comply with a regulatory requirement. The test thus formulated by the court seems to only permit expropriation to prevent a negative consequence for the company rather than to positively advance the company's or the majority members' interests. This is further borne out by the court's general comments on alterations to effect expropriations:

'Notwithstanding that a shareholder's membership of a company is subject to alterations of the articles which may affect the rights attaching to the shareholder's shares and the value of those shares, we do not consider that, in the case of an alteration to the articles authorising the expropriation of shares, it is a sufficient justification of an expropriation that the expropriation, being fair, will advance the interests of the company as a legal and commercial entity or those of the majority, albeit the great majority, of corporators. This approach does not attach sufficient weight to the proprietary nature of a share and, to the extent that English authority might appear to support such an approach, we do not agree with it. It is only right that exceptional circumstances should be required to justify an amendment to the articles authorising the compulsory expropriation by the majority of the minority's interests in a company. To allow expropriation where it would advance the interests of the company as a legal and commercial entity or those of the general body or corporators would, in our view, be tantamount to permitting expropriation by the majority for the purpose of some personal gain and thus be made for an improper purpose[196]. It would open the way to circumventing the protection which the Corporations Law gives to minorities who resist compromises, amalgamations and reconstructions, schemes of arrangement and takeover offers[197].'

Clearly, the position of the Australian High Court is that an alteration of the articles to effect an expropriation of shares will only be valid where its purpose is *defensive*, ie, to

194 *Gambotto and another v WCP Ltd and another* (1995) 13 ACLC 342 at para 26 of the majority judgment.

195 *Sidebottom v Kershaw, Leese and Co* [1920] 1 Ch 154. See para **[3.078]** *ante*.

196 Citing *Brown v British Abrasive Wheel Co* (1919) 1 Ch 295, 296.

197 *Gambotto and another v WCP Ltd and another* (1995) 13 ACLC 342 at para 28 of the majority judgment.

prevent *negative* consequences befalling the company and will never be permitted to positively improve or advance the interests of the company or the majority. In those limited circumstances when an expropriation alteration passes this first hurdle, the Australian courts will also require that it be fair. Fairness in this context was held to require the disclosure of all relevant information to the expropriated minority *and* also the payment of market value or above. It was also held that the onus of proof rests with the appropriating majority.

Informal alteration of the articles of association by shareholders' agreement

[3.085] Difficult questions of law arise where the members purport to alter a company's articles of association without formally passing the requisite special resolution referred to in s 15 of the CA 1963. In *Cane v Jones*[198], the articles of association of the company provided that two persons, Percy and Harold Jones, should be its life directors. It was also provided that the directors should elect a chairman of the board of the directors who should have a casting vote at both board and general meetings of the company. However, all of the shareholders entered into an oral shareholders' agreement which provided, *inter alia*, that the chairman should *not* exercise a casting vote and that if an equality of votes occurred, an independent chairman would be appointed. Later, the shareholding in the company changed and a dispute arose concerning, *inter alia*, whether or not the prior unanimous agreement of the shareholders had the effect of altering the articles of association of the company. Michael Wheeler QC held that:

> 'In my judgment, s 10[199] of the Act is merely laying down a procedure whereby some only of the shareholders can validly alter the articles; and, if, as I believe to be the case, it is a basic principle of company law that all the corporators, acting together, can do anything which is *intra vires* the company, then I can see nothing in s 10 to undermine this principle[200].'

It is thought, on the authority of *Buchanan Ltd and another v McVey*[201], that this statement reflects the law in Ireland too.

[3.086] In Ireland, s 141(8) of the CA 1963 may undermine this principle, in that it provides that where a company is so authorised by its articles a special resolution in writing signed by its members is as valid as if it had been passed at a general meeting of the company[202]. The crux of the matter is that for an informal resolution to be validated by statute, it must be in writing. The question is, does s 141(8) of the CA 1963 oust the common law principle that an oral agreement by all the corporators will suffice to alter the articles? There is support for the notion that the Irish courts accept that the common law principle has not been displaced by s 141(8) of the CA 1963. In *Re Shannonside Holdings Ltd*[203], the question before Costello J concerned the existence and validity of a debenture created by the company. After finding that the debenture did on the balance of

198 *Cane v Jones* [1981] 1 All ER 533.

199 Which was similar to s 15 of the CA 1963.

200 *Cane v Jones* [1981] All ER 533 at 539.

201 *Buchanan Ltd and another v McVey* [1954] IR 89.

202 This is considered further in Ch 14, *Corporate Governance: Meetings*, at para **[14.090]**.

203 *Re Shannonside Holdings Ltd* (20 May 1993, unreported) HC *per* Costello J.

probabilities exist, Costello J turned to consider whether it had been validly executed. As in what is now model reg 47, the company's articles of association provided that all members' meetings of the company should be held within the State. Contrary to this, the company's members held a meeting in Chicago, USA for the purpose of resolving that the company's directors could borrow in excess of the issued share capital[204]. It was subsequently claimed that the debenture was invalid because the general meeting was held in Chicago instead of within the State. This was rejected by Costello J who said:

> 'In my opinion, non-compliance with ... Reg [47] does not invalidate any resolutions passed at the meeting. It seems to me that the members of the company can mutually decide to have meetings anywhere they like, even though the articles indicate that they are to be held in the State. Should they decide to hold meetings outside the State, they are entitled to do so provided there is agreement. If there was no formal indication that such agreement was forthcoming, it would be clear that it was to be implied in the circumstances of this case[205].'

The learned Costello J appears to have accepted as a basic principle of Irish company law that the corporators in a company may together do as they wish, and in this regard implicitly proceeded on the same basis as did Michael Wheeler QC in *Cane v Jones*. The alteration of the articles in *Shannonside* may not have been contentious, and it remains to be seen whether the High Court will follow Costello J's decision where, say, the members informally decide to vary a pre-emption clause. Notwithstanding the decision in this case, it would seem prudent, where possible, for all informal resolutions altering articles of association to be in writing, signed by all of the company's members. Informal written and non-written resolutions, generally, are considered in detail in Ch 14[206].

[3.087] Regulation 9(3) of the EC(SMPLC)R 1994[207] provides that:

> 'Subject to paragraph (2)[208], any provision of the Companies Acts which –
>
> (a) enables or requires any matter to be done or to be decided by a company in general meeting, or
>
> (b) requires any matter to be decided by a resolution of the company,
>
> shall be deemed to be satisfied, in the case of a single-member company, by a decision of the member which is drawn up in writing and notified to the company in accordance with this regulation.'

Although reg 9(8) provides that a single member's failure to notify the company of his decision will not invalidate the decision, it is noticeably silent with regard to a failure to draw up the decision *in writing*. In that the operative part of reg 9(3) provides that the

---

204 The company's articles of association contained a fetter on the directors' exercise of their borrowing powers, in terms apparently similar to model reg 79. See generally, para **[3.126]** *post*.

205 *Re Shannonside Holdings Ltd* (20 May 1993, unreported) HC at p 7 of the transcript.

206 See Ch 14, *Corporate Governance: Meetings*, at para **[14.090]** *et seq*.

207 SI 275/1994.

208 Regulation 9(2) provides that a single member company must comply with s 160(2)(b), 160(5) and 160(6) of the CA 1963 and hold a meeting before removing an auditor from office. See further Ch 14, *Corporate Governance: Meetings*, at para **[14.088]** and Ch 17, *Financial Statements, Audit & Annual Return*, at para **[17.338]** *et seq*.

provisions in the Companies Acts, referred to at (a) and (b) above, are *deemed to be satisfied*, it is arguable that if they can be satisfied in the manner found by Costello J in *Shannonside*, an unambiguous oral resolution of a single member may also be valid to alter the company's articles.

The relationship between the memorandum and the articles

[3.088] The accepted rule is that the memorandum of association is the dominant constitutional document which will prevail in a conflict between it and the articles of association. So Carroll J said in *Roper v Ward*[209]:

> 'In construing the articles I am guided by the principle that they are subordinated to and controlled by the memorandum of association which is the dominant document. While the articles cannot alter or control the memorandum or be used to expend the objects of the company, they can be used to explain it generally or to explain an ambiguity in its terms.'

In construing a clause in a company's memorandum of association, the regulations in the articles can only have the role of resolving any anomalies[210]. However, in *Re Walls Properties Ltd and Thornhill Properties Ltd; Walls v PJ Walls Holdings Ltd*[211], the Supreme Court held that the provisions of both a company's memorandum of association and its articles of association were subservient to the provisions of the Companies Acts such that pre-emption rights on share transfer contained in articles of association did not apply where s 204 of the CA 1963 was invoked to compulsorily acquire shares.

The construction of the memorandum and articles of association

[3.089] Where a company's memorandum or articles of association are ambiguous, they will be construed so as to make them workable[212]. In *Roper v Ward*[213], Carroll J held that:

> 'The memorandum and articles of association of a company are commercial documents and should be construed to give them *reasonable business efficacy*[214].'

Where there is an ambiguity which cannot be resolved on a literal interpretation the courts will imply whatever is necessary to make a company's constitutional documents workable.

[3.090] There are very definite limits to the circumstances in which the courts will imply terms into a company's articles of association. Whilst it is accepted that the

---

209 *Roper v Ward* [1981] ILRM 408 at 409.

210 *Duncan Gilmore and Co Ltd The Company v Inman et al* [1952] 2 All ER 871; *Angostura Bitters (Dr JGB Siegert & Sons) Ltd v Kerr* [1933] AC 550; *Guinness v Land Corporation of Ireland* [1885] 22 Ch D 261; *Re Wedgewood Coal and Iron Company (Andersons Case)* 7 Ch D 75.

211 *Re Walls Properties Ltd; Walls v PJ Walls Holdings Ltd* [2007] IESC 41.

212 See *Holmes v Keyes* [1958] 2 All ER 129 at 138, where Jenkins LJ held: '... the articles of association of the company should be regarded as a business document and should be construed so as to give them reasonable business efficacy, where a construction tending to that result is admissible on the language of the articles, in preference to a result which would or might prove unworkable.'

213 *Roper v Ward* [1981] ILRM 408 at 412 (italics added).

214 See also *Stillwell Trucks Party Ltd v Nectar Brook Investments Party Ltd* [1993] 10 ACSR 615.

documents will be construed so as to give them *reasonable business efficacy*, a distinction has been made between a situation where clarification of an express provision in the articles is required, and where it is sought to imply a term into the articles from extrinsic evidence. This distinction was made by the Court of Appeal in *Bratton Seymour Service Co Ltd v Oxborough*[215]. In this case the company was a management company, formed to hold the common areas of a property known as the Bratton House Development. The defendant purchased part of the property, sold off six flats and retained three lots for his own use. In the conveyance of the property to the defendant, he covenanted to contribute to the maintenance of what could be described as the *utility* areas of the development. Later, all of the common parts, including the utility areas, and what can be termed the *amenity areas*, were conveyed to the plaintiff management company.

The defendant was asked to contribute to the maintenance of both the utility and amenity areas of the development. He agreed that he was bound to contribute to the maintenance of the utility areas, but disputed that he was so bound in respect of the amenity areas. The plaintiff company argued that such an obligation was implicit in the company's articles of association, an argument which succeeded at first instance.

The Court of Appeal rejected that such a term could be implied into a company's articles. Steyn LJ held:

> 'Here, the company puts forward an implication to be derived not from the language of the articles of association but purely from extrinsic circumstances. That, in my judgment, is a type of implication which, as a matter of law, can never succeed in the case of articles of association. After all, if it were permitted, it would involve the position that the different implications would notionally be possible between the company and different subscribers. Just as the company or an individual member cannot seek to defeat the statutory contract by reason of special circumstances such as misrepresentation, mistake, undue influence and duress and is furthermore not permitted to seek a rectification, neither the company nor any member can seek to add to or to subtract from the terms of the articles by way of implying a term derived from extrinsic surrounding circumstances. If it were permitted in this case, it would be equally permissible over the spectrum of company law cases. The consequences would be prejudicial to third parties, namely potential shareholders who are entitled to look to and rely on the articles of association as registered[216].'

It is clear that the court will only imply terms into a company's articles of association in exceptional cases[217]. In the Supreme Court in *Barry v The Medical Defence Union Ltd*[218], Geoghegan J noted that in the *Bratton Seymour Service Company* case it was held that it was never permissible to imply into the articles a term not on the basis of a construction or implication derivable purely from the consideration of the language of an instrument but on the basis of extrinsic evidence of surrounding circumstances. In the event, it was not necessary for the Supreme Court to consider whether that was good law in Ireland because, in the case in hand, Geoghegan J held that the term would be in

[215] *Bratton Seymour Service Co Ltd v Oxborough* [1992] BCLC 693.

[216] *Bratton Seymour Service Co Ltd v Oxborough* [1992] BCLC 693 at 698, 699.

[217] See also *Australia Securities Commission v Multiple Sclerosis Society of Tasmania* [1993] 10 ACSR 489.

[218] *Barry v The Medical Defence Union Ltd* [2005] IESC 41.

contradiction of the express terms of the articles and so could not have been implied at any rate[219].

[3.091] Some examples of permitted implications in the case of a company's articles of association are seen in the judgment of Sir Christopher Slade in *Brutton Seymour*. These include surrounding evidence to identify people, places or other subject matter referred to in the articles. The fact that the term which was sought to be implied in this case involved the imposition of a financial burden on the member may be seen as influencing the Court of Appeal's decision. As has been seen, the members of a company may, by passing a special resolution, alter the articles of association, subject to this being *bona fide* and in the interests of the company as a whole. However, the power to alter the articles is subject also to the proviso that where the alteration imposes an additional burden of contribution on a member, that member must agree to its imposition on him[220].

[C] THE STATUTORY CONTRACT IN S 25 OF THE CA 1963

Section 25 creates a 'statutory contract'

[3.092] A company's memorandum and articles of association together comprise a *statutory contract* by virtue of s 25 of the CA 1963. In this section the nature, extent and scope of this unusual contract are examined. When the initial subscribers associate with a view to forming a company it is a prerequisite that they sign the memorandum and articles of association[221]. One of the consequences of this is that by subscribing the members are deemed to have entered into a *statutory contract* by s 25(1) of the CA 1963, which provides:

> 'Subject to the provisions of this Act, the memorandum and articles shall, when registered, bind the company and the members thereof to the same extent as if they respectively had been signed and sealed by each member, and contained covenants by each member to observe all the provisions of the memorandum and of the articles.'

Similarly, when the sole member of a single-member private company signs the memorandum and articles of association, he will enter into a statutory contract with the company[222]. The wording of s 25 can be traced back to the Joint Stock Companies Act 1844, which adopted the old method of forming a company by deed of settlement. The deed of settlement was a contract between the members who sealed it. The effect of s 25 is to bind the members of a company, and the company itself, to observe the provisions of its memorandum and articles of association[223].

---

219 *Barry v The Medical Defence Union Ltd* [2005] IESC 41 at p 6 of the judgment.

220 Section 27(1) of the CA 1963. See para **[3.029]** *et seq ante*.

221 In the case of the memorandum, by virtue of s 5(1) of the CA 1963; in the case of the articles, by virtue of s 14(d) of the CA 1963 as amended by s 112 of the Finance Act 1996.

222 Regulation 4 of the EC(SMPLC)R 1994, SI 275/1994.

223 In *Kerry Co-Operative Ltd & Others v An Bord Bainne Co-Operative Ltd and Others* [1990] ILRM 664, it was said that: '... membership of [a registered company] constitutes a contract between the member and the corporate entity which ... is to be found in its memorandum and articles of association (s 25 of the Companies Act 1963).' (contd.../)

[3.093] In *Clark v Workman*[224], Ross J said, in the context of a company's articles of association, that:

> 'They constitute a contract between every shareholder and all the others, and between the company itself and all the shareholders. It is a contract of the most sacred character, and it is on the faith of it that each shareholder advances his money[225].'

The parties to this contract are the members and the company itself. It is enforceable by the members *inter se*, by the members against the company and by the company against the members. It is, however, an unusual contract, and its interpretation has been the subject of much academic debate[226]. Steyn LJ described the special and distinctive nature of the s 25 contract thus in the Court of Appeal in *Bratton Seymour Service Co Ltd v Oxborough*[227]:

> 'By virtue of [the English equivalent to s 25 of the CA 1963] the articles of association become, upon registration, a contract between a company and members. It is, however, a statutory contract of a special nature with its own distinctive features. It derives its binding force not from a bargain struck between the parties but from the terms of the statute. It is binding only insofar as it affects the rights and obligations between the company and the members acting in their capacity as members. If it contains provisions conferring rights and obligations on outsiders, then those provisions do not bite as part of the contract between the company and the members, even if the outsider is coincidentally a member. Similarly, if the provisions are not truly referable to the rights and obligations of members as such it does not operate as a contract. Moreover, the contract can be altered by a special resolution without the consent of all the contracting parties. It is also, unlike an ordinary contract, not defeasible on the grounds of misrepresentation, common law mistake, mistake in equity, undue influence or duress. Moreover ... it cannot be rectified on the grounds of mistake[228].'

223 (\...contd) In *Roper v Ward* [1981] ILRM 408 at 412, Carroll J said of the memorandum and articles of association, that '[t]hey are in effect a contract between the company and its members. When they are registered they bind the company and its members as is they had been sealed and signed by each member ...'.

224 *Clark v Workman* [1920] 1 IR 107.

225 *Clark v Workman* [1920] 1 IR 107 at 112.

226 See Wedderburn, [1957] Cam LR 194; Goldberg, (1972) MLR 362; Prentice, (1980) Co Law 179; Gregory, (1981) MLR 526 where the English equivalent of the s 25 contract is examined in detail.

227 *Bratton Seymour Service Co Ltd v Oxborough* [1992] BCLC 693.

228 *Bratton Seymour Service Co Ltd v Oxborough* [1992] BCLC 693 at 698. In *Bailey v New South Wales Medical Defence Union Ltd* (1996) 18 ACSR 521, McHugh and Gummow JJ, at para 70 of their judgment, described the unusual features of the statutory contract thus: 'First the members are deemed to have contracted on the basis that, since the articles, and in general the memorandum, can be altered by special resolution of the company, the terms of the contract are variable from time to time without agreement of both parties to that variation. Secondly, there is no jurisdiction in a court of Equity to rectify the articles of association even if they do not accord with the concurrent intention of all the signatories thereof at the moment of signature; the articles may be amended only pursuant to statutory authority. Thirdly, the direct enforcement by a member of rights under such a contract against the company may have to overcome obstacles placed in its path by the rule in *Foss v Harbottle*. (contd.../)

The distinctive features of the *statutory contract* spoken of by Steyn LJ, which arise by virtue of s 25, are considered next.

The distinctive features of the s 25 contract

[3.094] There are three distinctive features of s 25 of the CA 1963:

(a) Section 25 binds the members and the company.
(b) Section 25 binds the members to the members.
(c) Section 25 is only enforceable by and against members acting *qua* member, or in their capacity as members.

The reason why such controversy exists is because of the clash between two principles: the right of a member to see that the existing rules of the company are observed versus the principle of *majority rule* embodied in *Foss v Harbottle*[229], which implies that the majority can alter the rules if they so wish.

(a) Section 25 binds the members and the company

[3.095] The s 25 contract can be enforced by a member against the company and by the company against a member. The rights that can be enforced by a member are solely those *personal rights*, which he has by virtue of his membership[230]. In *Hickman v Kent or Romney Marsh Sheepbreeders' Association*[231], the defendant company was incorporated with the objects of, *inter alia*, encouraging the breeding of Kent or Romney Marsh sheep and the 'establishment and publication of a flock book of recognised and pure-bred sires ... and the annual registration of the pedigrees of such sheep as are proved to the satisfaction of the council to be eligible for entry'[232]. In addition, article 49 of the company's articles of association[233] provided that disputes as to the intent, construction, incidents or consequences of the articles should be referred to arbitration. Alfred J Hickman was a member of the company for just over nine years when the conduct of the company's business became disagreeable to him. Rather than resort to the arbitration provision in the articles, Hickman went to court and, *inter alia*, sought damages from the company for refusing to register his sheep together with a

---

228 (\...contd) Fourthly, as Salmond J pointed out in *Shalfoon v Cheddar Valley Co-operative Dairy Co* (1924) NZLR 561 at 580, whilst a contract binds those who made it and their personal representatives, the articles in a company limited by shares bind the owners thereof for the time being and the obligations imposed by the deemed covenant are appurtenant to the shares and pass with ownership of them. Finally, the view has been taken, not without doubt, that, in the absence of some other statutory provision, the effect of the decision in *Houldsworth v City of Glasgow Bank* (1880) 5 App Cas 317 is to preclude a member of a company limited by shares from suing the company for damages for breach of contract whilst still a member and obtained without seeking recission of the contract whereby the shares were obtained.'

229 *Foss v Harbottle* (1843) 2 Hare 461. On the principle of *majority rule* and the rule in *Foss v Harbottle* generally, see Ch 11, *Shareholders' Remedies*, at para **[11.093]**.

230 See generally Ch 8, *Shares and Membership*, at para **[8.087]** for a discussion of a member's personal rights and Ch 11, *Shareholders' Remedies*, at para **[11.100]** for the distinction between a member's personal rights and the rule in *Foss v Harbottle*.

231 *Hickman v Kent or Romney Marsh Sheepbreeders' Association* [1915] 1 Ch 881.

232 *Hickman v Kent or Romney Marsh Sheepbreeders' Association* [1915] 1 Ch 881 at 882.

233 *Hickman v Kent or Romney Marsh Sheepbreeders' Association* [1915] 1 Ch 881 at 884.

declaration that he was entitled to have his sheep registered. The company was contemporaneously trying to expel Hickman as a member and sought to have his action stayed to force him to abide by the arbitration mechanism contained in the articles. Astbury J held that the company was entitled to have the action stayed, because the articles were binding on the members and so the reference to arbitration was binding on Hickman. In so deciding, Astbury J looked at two streams of *dicta*, one saying that the articles did not constitute a contract[234], the other[235] saying that it did and also that a company is entitled as against its members to enforce and restrain breaches of its articles of association. This latter stream also said that a member could enforce and restrain breaches of his company's regulations[236]. Astbury J eventually said:

> 'It is difficult to reconcile these two classes of decisions and the judicial opinions therein expressed, but I think this much is clear, first, that no article can constitute a contract between the company and a third person; secondly, that no right merely purporting to be given by an article to a person, whether a member or not, in a capacity other than that of a member, as, for instance, as solicitor, promoter, director, can be enforced against the company; and, thirdly, that articles regulating the rights and obligations of the members generally as such do create rights and obligations between them and the company respectively[237].'

It is clear that the memorandum and articles are contractually binding on both the members and the company itself. By initially subscribing to a company's memorandum and articles of association, or by having shares transferred to them, members agree to be contractually bound to abide by the terms of the company's constitutional documentation.

(b) Section 25 binds members to members

[3.096] The s 25 contract is also enforceable as between the members themselves, and in addition to binding members to the company, it binds members to each other[238]. So, a member can sue another member who fails to observe the provisions of the articles or memorandum. In such a case, the member is not bound by the rule in *Foss v Harbottle*[239].

[3.097] Among the cases which establish that the memorandum and articles of association are enforceable by the members *inter se*, is *Rayfield v Hands et al*[240]. In that case, as with many of the cases on this point, the rights which were sought to be

---

234 *Prichard's case* LR 8 Ch 965; *Melhado v Porto Alegre Ry Co* LR 9 CP 503; *Eley v Positive Life Assurance Co* (1876) 1 Ex D 20, 88; *Browne v La Trinidad* (1877) 37 Ch D 1.

235 *MacDougall v Gardiner* (1875) 1 Ch D 13; *Pender v Lushington* (1877) 6 ChD 70; *Imperial Hydropathic Hotel Co, Blackpool v Hampson* 23 Ch D 1.

236 For example see, *Bradford Banking v Briggs* 12 App Cas 29 and *Welton v Saffery* [1897] AC 299.

237 *Hickman v Kent or Romney Marsh Sheepbreeders' Association* [1915] 1 Ch 881 at 900.

238 *Rayfield v Hands et al* [1960] 1 Ch 1, considered *post* at para **[3.097]**.

239 *Foss v Harbottle* (1843) 2 Hare 461. See generally Ch 11, *Shareholders' Remedies*, at para **[11.092]** *et seq*.

240 *Rayfield v Hands et al* [1960] 1 Ch 1, [1958] 2 WLR 851.

enforced were pre-emption rights attaching to shares[241]. The articles of the company provided that:

> Every member who intends to transfer shares shall inform the directors who shall take the said shares equally between them at a fair value ...[242]

The plaintiff, Rayfield, owned 725 fully paid shares of £1 each, and purported to rely on the foregoing article by serving notice on the directors of his intention to transfer his shares to them. The directors refused to buy the shares, contending that the articles did not impose an obligation on them to take shares, but was merely an option which they could exercise. This was rejected by Vaisey J who construed the words '*will take the shares*' as importing an obligation and not an option. Central to that decision was the fact that the contract was enforceable by the plaintiff member against the directors *in their capacity as fellow members*[243]. Vaisey J held that the directors (acting *qua* member) were obliged to buy the shares, saying:

> 'On the whole, if the proper way to construe the articles of association of a company is as a commercial or business document to which the maxim 'validate if possible' applies, I think that the plaintiff in this action ought to succeed. Not one of the judges in the case to which I have already referred, *Dean v Prince*[244], showed any signs of shock or surprise in the assumption there made of a contract between directors being formed by the terms of a company's articles. I am encouraged, not I hope unreasonably, to find in this case a contract similarly formed between a member and member-directors in relation to their holdings of the company's shares in its articles. The conclusion to which I have come may not be of so general an application as to extend to the articles of every company, for it is, I think, material to remember that this private company is one of that class of companies which bears a close analogy to a partnership ...[245]'

The latter sentiment shows that in the case of private companies, the memorandum and articles of association bear a close analogy with a deed of partnership. Where this is the case, it may be seen by the courts that there is a stronger case for giving effect to the contract subsisting between the persons who associate in such circumstances. A breach of such mutually agreed provisions may ground a petition alleging *oppression* under s 205 of the CA 1963[246] or a petition that the company be wound up on *just and equitable* grounds under s 213 of the CA 1963[247].

---

241 Pre-emption rights to shares are the rights enjoyed, usually by a company's members, to buy or otherwise acquire shares which were held by another member before he may dispose of his shares to non-members. Pre-emption rights on share transfer are considered in detail in Ch 9, *Share Transfers*, at para **[9.069]** *et seq*; pre-emption rights on the allotment of shares are considered in Ch 8, *Shares and Membership*, at para **[8.056]** *et seq*.

242 *Rayfield v Hands et al* [1960] Ch 1 at 2.

243 So, Vaisey J said at 6: '[n]ow the question arises at the outset whether the terms of Article 11 relate to the rights of members *inter se* (that being the expression found in so many of the cases), or whether the relationship is between a member as such and directors as such. I may dispose of this point very briefly by saying that, in my judgment, the relationship here is between the plaintiff as a member and the defendants not as directors but as members.'

244 *Dean v Prince* [1954] Ch 409; [1954] WLR 538; [1954] 1 All ER 749.

245 *Rayfield v Hands et al* [1960] Ch 1 at 9.

246 See generally, Ch 11, *Shareholders' Remedies*, at para **[11.006]** *et seq*.

247 See generally, Ch 23, *Winding Up Companies*, at paras **[23.091]** *et seq*.

[3.098] The principle that the memorandum and articles of association bind the members *inter se* has been accepted in Ireland in several cases[248]. An example is *Lee & Co (Dublin) Ltd v Egan (Wholesale) Ltd*[249], where the defendant company's articles contained pre-emption rights. One member contracted to sell his shares to an outsider, without offering the shares to the other members pursuant to the pre-emption rights. When, for his own reasons, he later repudiated the contract with the outsider, an order for specific performance was sought by the would-be purchaser. This action failed, and the court held that it would not succeed until such time as the other members had been given the opportunity to exercise the forgotten (or ignored) pre-emption rights. Where, however, a transfer is effected pursuant to s 204 of CA 1963 it has been held by the Supreme Court that the statutory scheme trumps the articles of association so that pre-emption clauses in the articles will not apply: *Re Walls Properties Ltd and Thornhill Properties Ltd; Walls v PJ Walls Holdings Ltd*[250].

(c) Only rights and obligations qua member

[3.099] The s 25 contract is only enforceable by and against members in their capacity as members, or '*qua* member'. As has been seen in *Hickman's* case, Astbury J made it quite clear that the s 25 contract did not bind, and could not be enforced, by outsiders. Furthermore, he held the s 25 contract was only enforceable by members in their capacity as members and not, for example, in their capacity as directors or solicitors or others, even if they were incidentally shareholders[251]. Therefore, a right conferred on a member by the articles of association to information in respect of the company must be distinguished from a right in the articles of association to be, say, the company's solicitor. In *Eley v Positive Government Security Life Assurance Company Ltd*[252], the articles of a company provided that Eley would be the company's solicitor for life, and that he was only removable for misconduct. Eley acted as company solicitor for some time without a written or oral contract of employment. When the company ceased to engage Eley's services, he sued for breach of contract grounded on the provision in the articles of association. The House of Lords held that the articles did not oblige the company to employ Eley in his capacity of solicitor, and that there was no contract between Eley, the solicitor, and the company. Lord Cairns LC said:

> '... the articles state the arrangement between the members. They are an arrangement *inter socios*, and in that view, if the introductory words are applied ... it becomes a covenant between the parties to it that they will employ the plaintiff. Now, so far as that is concerned, it is *res inter alios acta*, the plaintiff is no party to it. No doubt he thought that

[248] See also *Attorney General for Ireland v Jameson* [1904] 2 IR 644. There too, pre-emption rights were accepted as binding. As Boyd J said at 679: '... the restrictive clauses were as much terms of his contract as his title to the shares. His title was clogged with these clauses, and he accepted the shares which were *allotted* to him ... on the terms and conditions agreed to by him and the other shareholders.' So also Kenny J said (at 670) of the right to share in any surplus of the company's assets on a liquidation that: '[i]n acquiring these rights – that is, in becoming a member of the company – he is deemed to have simultaneously entered into a contract under seal to conform to the regulations contained in the articles of association.'

[249] *Lee & Co (Dublin) Ltd v Egan (Wholesale) Ltd* (27 April 1978, unreported) HC *per* Kenny J.

[250] *Re Walls Properties Ltd; Walls v PJ Walls Holdings Ltd* [2007] IESC 41.

[251] *Hickman v Kent or Romney Marsh Sheepbreeders' Association* [1915] 1 Ch 881 at 900.

[252] *Eley v Positive Government Security Life Assurance Company Ltd* (1876) 1 Ex D 88.

> by inserting it he was making his employment safe as against the company; but his relying on that view of the law does not alter the legal effect of the articles. This article is either a stipulation which would bind the members, or else a mandate to the directors. In either case it is a matter between the directors and the shareholders, and not between them and the plaintiff[253].'

Thus the rule is that the rights conferred on members are only conferred on them *in their capacity* as members and cannot be availed of in any other capacity[254].

[3.100] The corollary to this rule is that obligations imposed upon members in a capacity other than in their capacity as members are not enforceable by s 25 of the CA 1963. Persons who become members should not become bound to do something unrelated to their membership of a company as a consequence of a provision one would not expect to find in the constitution of the company in question. The subject matter of the statutory contract was identified by McHugh and Gummow JJ in *Bailey v New South Wales Medical Defence Union Ltd*[255]:

> '... the broad trend of authority referred to above, particularly since *Hickman*, has been to identify the subject-matter of the 'statutory contract', so far as concerns the relations between the corporation and the members, not as commercial rights but as the government of the corporation and the exercise of the constitutional powers of the corporation. Such matters as inspection of the register, the right to receive a share certificate, to vote, to receive informative notice of meetings, to receive payment of duly declared and payable dividends, and the like, even where not specifically supported by statutory provision, have been treated as inherent in the relationship between the corporation and its members[256].'

In that case, the facts of which are considered below[257], the judges held that the provisions in the articles of association in question – concerning insurance of the company's medical practitioner-members – could not consistently with *Hickman* be described as flowing from the general regulations of the union as applicable alike to all shareholders. It has been contended therefore that the statutory contract does not extend to 'commercial rights' and is confined to the government and exercise of constitutional powers of a company[258].

[3.101] The rule that the s 25 contract is only enforceable *qua* member is not without controversy. The debate has focused on reconciling the apparent anomaly that s 25 cannot be relied upon to enforce the rights or obligations of members enjoyed in an outside capacity. It has been suggested[259] that the Irish courts ought not to feel fettered by the old English authorities and ought not to differentiate between the member

---

253 *Eley v Positive Government Security Life Assurance Company Ltd* (1876) 1 Ex D 88 at 90.

254 See *Browne v La Trinidad* (1877) 37 Ch D 1 where a director could not rely on the articles to secure his tenure as director.

255 *Bailey v New South Wales Medical Defence Union Ltd* (1996) 18 ACSR 521.

256 *Bailey v New South Wales Medical Defence Union Ltd* (1996) 18 ACSR 521 at para 79 of the judgment.

257 See para **[3.102]** *post*.

258 See Lipton & Hertzberg, *Understanding Company Law* (9th edn, 2000) at p 85.

259 See Ussher, *Company Law in Ireland* (1986) at p 165, who suggests that the courts in Ireland should '... eschew the artificialities introduced by *Eley's* case ...', and where 's 25 privity' is found, a member should be able to enforce the contract against the company and the other members.

enforcing his rights as member and a member enforcing outsider-rights which he may have. It is submitted that this is the most sensible way forward, particularly in the case of private closely-held companies[260]. It seems to be self-evident that in a private company there is an unanswerable case that the s 25 contract ought to be enforceable by the parties thereto, *in whatever capacity they may act*.

The 'statutory contract' distinguished from 'special contracts'

[3.102] It is settled law that any rights that a member may have against the company enjoyed in another capacity are not enforceable by virtue of s 25 of the CA 1963. Such rights may, however, be enforceable where a '*special contract*'[261] (as opposed to the *statutory* contract) exists between a member (acting other than as a member) and the company. The position was put thus by the Australian High Court in *Bailey v New South Wales Medical Defence Union Ltd*[262]:

> 'Whilst the articles of association of a company regulate the relations of the members amongst themselves as members and with the company, they do not preclude a member from contracting individually with the company upon terms which may or may not be defined by reference to the articles. Such a contract has been called a special contract to differentiate it from the deemed covenants to which [the Australian equivalent to s 25 of the CA 1963] refers, which regulate the position of a member as a member and not as an individual. Even if the terms of a special contract are to be determined by reference to the articles, an alteration to those articles will not necessarily mean an alteration to the terms of the contract. It will depend upon the intention of the parties to the contract, namely, the member and the company[263].'

In that case Mrs Bailey was the executrix of the late Dr Bailey. Dr Bailey had been sued by a patient for damages for injuries caused during the patient's treatment. The defendant, New South Wales Medical Defence Union Ltd (the Union) had initially conducted Dr Bailey's defence but, subsequent to his death, filed a notice ceasing to act for his estate. The patient obtained judgment against the estate of Dr Bailey and also against the Union. Judgment was also given in favour of Dr Bailey's estate on its cross-claim against the Union and against this the estate and the Union appealed. Both appeals were dismissed but only the Union appealed to the Australian High Court. On this appeal, the issue of relevance was whether the Union was liable to indemnify the estate and that question turned on the construction of the Union's articles of association.

[3.103] The Union's articles provided for an indemnity for members and their personal representatives against liability for damages or costs arising from any claim against a member for professional acts or omissions. The initial articles provided that where a member was expelled, the board of directors of the Union, referred to as the Council, had discretion to refuse an indemnity. The High Court noted that Dr Bailey had never been expelled. The articles of association were amended on several occasions. The most

260 Because s 205 of the CA 1963 has been interpreted as enabling members to petition the court for relief where they are oppressed other than *qua member*, it is arguable that a similar view can be taken of s 25 of the CA 1963.

261 The expression 'special contract' seems to have been coined by Romer LJ in *Allen v Gold Reefs of West Africa Ltd* (1900) 1 Ch 656 at 673, 674.

262 *Bailey v New South Wales Medical Defence Union Ltd* (1996) 18 ACSR 521.

263 From the majority judgment of Brennan CJ, Deane and Dawson JJ at para 14 of the judgment.

significant change was when the articles were amended to provide that the Council had sole and absolute discretion in relation to the assistance (including indemnity) to be given to members and provided that the Council could also terminate an indemnity that had already been given and cease to assist a member, also at its sole and absolute discretion, and without the need to terminate membership. After that change had been made, the Council had resolved in favour of providing assistance to Dr Bailey. Subsequent to Dr Bailey's death, the Council resolved to withdraw assistance. On the facts of the case the Australian High Court held that the relationship between the Union and Dr Bailey was not confined to the statutory contract but extended to a 'special contract'. The majority held:

> 'There can be no doubt that during each of the years in which Mr Crawford suffered injury there was a contract of insurance between the Union and Dr Bailey. Nor, in our view, can there be any real doubt that, notwithstanding that its terms were largely to be found in the company's articles, the contract was made individually with Dr Bailey as an insured and was therefore a special or actual contract which was distinct from the covenants which were deemed to arise from the articles under the relevant companies' legislation[264].'

The High Court held that the terms of the contracts of indemnity were to be found largely, but not wholly, in the company's articles of association and that there was such a contract in place when the patient had been injured. The majority held that it 'cannot have been the intention of the parties that insurance cover already purchased upon terms contained in the articles should be diminished by a subsequent alteration to those articles'[265]. The majority concluded:

> 'Thus, the alteration[s] … to extend the discretion of the Council of the Union to refuse indemnity to a member who had ceased to be a member whether by expulsion or otherwise did not affect the terms of a contract made upon the basis of the articles before the alteration. A fortiori, the amendments … were ineffective to vary the terms of any contract previously made upon the basis of the articles in their unaltered form. Those amendments sought to give the Council sole discretion whether to grant indemnity at all and were entirely inconsistent with the terms of a contract concluded upon the basis of the articles as they stood before the amendments. It follows that the attempt by the Union to vary the terms of such a contract by means of an alteration to its articles giving its Council discretion to terminate any grant of assistance or indemnity to a member who sought assistance from the Union before [a particular date] was ineffective[266].'

[3.104] In the concurring decision of McHugh and Gummow JJ in *Bailey v New South Wales Medical Defence Union Ltd* it was said:

> 'The present case did not involve a 'statutory contract' constituted solely by the articles and unsupplemented by any external facts. The particular rights to indemnity upon which the Estate sues the Union could not, consistently with *Hickman*, be described as flowing from the general regulations of the Union as applicable alike to all shareholders[267].'

---

264 *Bailey v New South Wales Medical Defence Union Ltd* (1996) 18 ACSR 521 at para 21 of the judgment.

265 *Bailey v New South Wales Medical Defence Union Ltd* (1996) 18 ACSR 521 at para 24 of the judgment.

266 *Bailey v New South Wales Medical Defence Union Ltd* (1996) 18 ACSR 521 at para 25 of the judgment.

267 *Bailey v New South Wales Medical Defence Union Ltd* (1996) 18 ACSR 521 at para 81 of the judgment.

Accordingly, where there is a 'special' or 'actual' contract that is based in whole or in part on the company's articles of association, any alteration in the articles will not automatically unilaterally vary that contract. It should be noted, however, that this is a matter of contract as opposed to legal principle and a term in the articles or side-contract might have ousted the decision in *Bailey*. Even if the Irish courts are slow to depart from *Eley* and other authorities that only allow rights enjoyed *qua* member to be enforced under the s 25 contract, rights extraneous to membership might be capable of being enforced in quasi-partnership companies on the basis of a special or actual contract.

[3.105] In the Supreme Court in *Barry v The Medical Defence Union Ltd*[268], Geoghegan J noted that the appellant had sought to rely on the decision in the Australian case of *Bailey* to establish that a collateral contract could conceptually exist independent of the statutory contract. Geoghegan J found that the *Bailey* case offered the appellant no support because the appellant, in that case, had not proved the existence of any collateral contract[269].

[D] SHAREHOLDERS' AGREEMENTS[270]

[3.106] Although rarely[271] referred to or discussed in the standard company law texts, shareholders' agreements are very commonly employed by the members of private companies. A shareholders' agreement may loosely be defined as an agreement between some or all of the shareholders in a company and perhaps the company itself, which is intended to govern the rights and obligations of the parties thereto, whether generally, or in particular circumstances. Frequently, shareholders' agreements will also deal with the management of the company, and in so doing may carefully displace the many inappropriate provisions for private companies which are contained in the Companies Acts. In this regard, a shareholders' agreement may be viewed as supplementing a company's statutory constitutional documentation. Viewed from the position of shareholders' agreements being a compromise between actual shareholder protection and the limitations of a statutory regime, shareholders' agreements are described in one book as:

> '… a device designed to improve the hand dealt to shareholders and to give them more protection than reliance on that compromise would do. It is a legally binding contractual agreement between some or all the shareholders of a limited liability company to which

[268] *Barry v The Medical Defence Union Ltd* [2005] IESC 41.

[269] *Barry v The Medical Defence Union Ltd* [2005] IESC 41 at p 2 of the judgment.

[270] See generally, Cheung, 'Shareholders' Agreements: Shareholders' Contractual Freedom in Company Law' [2012] JBL 504; McGovern, 'Shareholders' Agreements – Their Nature and Effect' (1995) 2 CLP 113; McGovern, 'Shareholders' Agreements – Some Drafting Considerations' (1995) 2 CLP 148; Courtney, 'Shareholders' Agreements in Irish Private Companies' (1993) Dlí 69; Reece Thomas & Ryan, *The Law and Practice of Shareholders' Agreements* (1999, Butterworths); and Stedman & Jones, *Shareholders' Agreements* (3rd edn, Sweet & Maxwell, 1998).

[271] See however, Farrar, Furey & Hannigan, *Farrar's Company Law* (3rd edn, Butterworths, 1991), at pp 138–145 and Hahlo & Farrar, *Hahlo's Cases and Materials on Company Law* (3rd edn, Sweet and Maxwell, 1987) at p 153.

> the company may be a party. The object of the agreement is to specify the way in which the parties' relationship as shareholders will be regulated. Shareholders may lawfully bind themselves by way of an independent shareholders' agreement simply to vote in a specific way on issues regulated by the terms of the agreement or they may enter into a much more detailed and complex agreement, such as where they are parties to a joint venture or a buy-out[272].'

Shareholders' agreements are considered here under the following headings:

1. The articles of association contrasted.
2. The circumstances in which shareholders' agreements must be filed in the CRO.
3. The uses of shareholders' agreements.
4. Types of shareholders' agreement.
5. The enforcement of shareholders' agreements.

The articles of association contrasted

[3.107] The articles of association of any company could easily accommodate most, if not all, of the usual provisions found in shareholders' agreements. Such could be done, *ab initio* on the formation of the company, or subsequently, after the company has been formed, by amending the articles. What then is the difference between a company's articles of association and a shareholders' agreement?

First, while the articles will automatically bind the company to all of its members, all of the members to the company and all of the members *inter se* by virtue of s 25 of the CA 1963, a shareholders' agreement will only bind those parties who are privy to it. By definition it is an agreement between shareholders, although often the company will also be a party. This may easily be achieved where the shareholder-signatories are also directors, or where they have the power to influence the management of the company. However, the general rule is that the predominant influence upon those who are parties to a shareholders' agreement is freedom of contract.

Second, unlike the articles of association, shareholders' agreements are not part of a company's constitutional documentation proper. While often it will be the *hidden constitution* of the company it is not in law a true constitutional document. Consequently, even where adopted, a shareholders' agreement will not be a *public document* in the same way as are articles of association. Where a shareholders' agreement, say, extends or limits directors' authority, outsiders will not have notice of the extent of such authority because the shareholders' agreement is not a public document of which they will have constructive notice.

Third, shareholders' agreements do not enjoy the privilege of being a recognised statutory document, in that they must each be considered on the basis of their own provisions, subject to the ordinary rules of contract law. Consequently, whilst the provisions of shareholders' agreements will no doubt in time, through greater use, become familiar to courts, they do not enjoy the certainty of the articles of association.

---

272 Reece Thomas & Ryan, *The Law and Practice of Shareholders' Agreements* (1999, Butterworths) at para 1.1.

The circumstances in which shareholders' agreements must be filed in the CRO

[3.108] One question which arises in comparing shareholders' agreements with articles of association is when, if ever, will a shareholders' agreement be required to be registered in the CRO? One of the greatest advantages of a shareholders' agreement is that, generally, it will not require to be registered, and, accordingly, its provisions will remain confidential to its parties. The spectre of registration can arise in a number of different ways. In the first place, where the articles of association expressly refer to a shareholders' agreement, it is arguable that the shareholders' agreement is incorporated into the articles (since sense cannot be made of the articles without reference to the shareholders' agreement)[273]. Accordingly, as a matter of good practice, expressly referencing shareholders' agreements in articles of association should be avoided or limited. It may, however, be acceptable and found not to cross the line that requires registration, to acknowledge that a provision in the articles is 'subject to any agreement to the contrary between all the shareholders'.

[3.109] In the second place, s 143(1) of the CA 1963 provides: 'A printed copy of every resolution *or agreement* to which this section applies, shall within 15 days after the passing or making thereof, be forwarded to the registrar of companies and recorded by him'. This expressly includes agreements as well as resolutions, and s 143(4)(c) provides that the section shall apply to two particular types of agreement:

> 'resolutions or *agreements* which have been agreed to by all the members of some class of shareholders but which, if not so agreed, would not have been effective for their purpose unless they had been passed by some particular majority or otherwise in some particular manner, and all resolutions or *agreements* which effectively bind all the members of any class of shareholders though not agreed to by all those members.'

It is far from certain that all shareholders' agreements will meet the conditions of this provision which is somewhat oblique and seems to be directed primarily at written resolutions signed by all shareholders of some class of shares which are signed as an alternative to passing a resolution at a general meeting or class meeting[274]. To come within this provision the matters agreed upon in the shareholders' agreement must have been matters that 'would not have been effective for their purpose unless they had been passed by some particular majority or otherwise in some particular manner'. To the extent that this relates to decisions of the company in general meeting or class meeting it addresses a different kind of matter to that normally addressed in a shareholders' agreement, namely, how shareholders adjust their own rights and interests inter se. The second condition 'agreements which effectively bind all the members of any class of shareholders though not agreed to by all those members' is unlikely to ever arise since a shareholders' agreement can never bind anyone who has not agreed to be so bound.

[3.110] In the third place, where a shareholders' agreement operates to amend the articles of association and where all of the shareholders in the company entitled to

273 See Comben & Wilkinson (eds), *Joint Ventures & Shareholders' Agreements* (2nd edn, Tottel Publishing, 2005) at paras 24.16–24.21.

274 See Comben & Wilkinson (eds), *Joint Ventures & Shareholders' Agreements* (2nd edn, Tottel Publishing, 2005) at para 24.21.

attend and vote on a resolution are parties to that agreement, it could be argued that the shareholders' agreement constitutes a special resolution, passed as a written resolution within the meaning of s 141(8) of the CA 1963 which would require registration under s 142(4)(a) of the CA 1963[275]. It has also been contended that the shareholders' agreement might operate to informally amend the articles of association on the authority of *Cane v Jones*[276]; however, an amendment to the articles of association is not, *per se*, an event contemplated by s 143 of the CA 1963: while a special resolution amending the articles must be filed, where the amendment of the articles is not effected by special resolution, it is not caught by s 143. Perhaps the safest course is to expressly provide in the shareholders' agreement that it does not operate to amend the articles of association.

[3.111] The registration of shareholders' agreements tends not, in practice, to exercise practitioners and this is most likely for a number of reasons. In the first place, even where shareholders' agreements are mentioned in articles of association, the CRO does not in practice query such references. In the second place, comfort is taken from the fact that the only sanction for failing to register is a fine, and the underlying validity of the shareholders' agreement is not affected[277]. In theory, any member, creditor, the registrar of companies or the Director of Corporate Enforcement could make an application under s 371 of the CA 1963[278] to oblige the company or its officers to comply with an alleged breach of s 143 of the CA 1963, but not only is such a course of action unlikely, it is also unclear if any such application would succeed for the reasons set out above.

The uses of shareholders' agreements

[3.112] There are a number of reasons why people choose to govern their relations with shareholders' agreements, notwithstanding that most of their concerns could easily be incorporated into a company's articles of association. Often the predominant reason is to ensure secrecy for those provisions which could be publicly sensitive. Frequently, such agreements are quite explicit as to the remuneration of the directors of the company, and other financially sensitive matters which the parties would not wish to be made known to the public at large. Were such matters dealt with in the articles of association, which are public documents, their contents could easily be discovered by searching the CRO. Accordingly, shareholders' agreements are often the favoured way of regulating relations between shareholders and indeed the internal management of the company. However, there exist other reasons as to why shareholders' agreements are used[279]. These may be summarised as follows:

[3.113] First, shareholders' agreements can be used to give rights and to impose obligations upon shareholders that could not be given or imposed by the articles. Where a shareholders' agreement is employed, a member who was a solicitor may be provided

---

[275] It is not clear that this would be the case since to come within s 141(8), the resolution would have to be *described* as a special resolution which a shareholders' agreement would not do.

[276] *Cane v Jones* [1981] 1 All ER 533; see Comben & Wilkinson (eds), *Joint Ventures & Shareholders' Agreements* (2nd edn, Tottel Publishing, 2005) at para 24.21. See also Ch 14, *Corporate Governance: Meetings*, at para **[14.093]**.

[277] Section 143(5) and (6) of the CA 1963.

[278] See Ch 28, *Compliance and Enforcement*, at para **[28.210]**.

[279] See Stedman & Jones, *Shareholders' Agreements* (3rd edn, 1998), at p 49.

with the security of tenure denied Eley in *Eley v Positive Government Security Life Assurance Co*[280]. In *Eley's* case the company's articles could not be relied upon to enforce a member's rights as an individual, only rights *qua member*[281]. Accordingly, shareholders' agreements can constitute 'special contracts'[282].

[3.114] Second, shareholders' agreements can be used to bolster the rights and powers, especially of veto, of minority shareholders. Particularly in quasi-partnership type private companies where people associate in a joint venture, it is common to give minority investors comfort in the form of loaded or weighted voting rights. The effect of such rights is to oust majority rule which would otherwise prevail[283]. Specific shareholders' agreements, such as *pooling agreements*, may seek to concentrate voting between groups of members[284]. One definition of a pooling agreement is:

> '… an agreement amongst some of the shareholders in a company in which no one shareholder individually has a controlling interest. The shareholder parties to the agreement agree to act as a unit, for example, in managing the company and may agree a right of pre-emption amongst themselves giving each other an option to purchase any shares another party may be selling[285].'

In this way a unified minority of shareholders can contractually agree to combine their interests in furtherance of mutually desirable courses of action.

[3.115] Third, shareholders' agreements are often seen as a way of binding the company or its directors to a certain course of action. It is safer to bind both the company and the directors by making both parties to the agreement, rather than simply the directors. Because directors are fiduciaries who must act *bona fide* and in the best interests of the company[286] there is a potential conflict where they fetter their discretion as to the management of the company, and may be liable for breach of their duty to the company. By making the company a party to the agreement, this danger is lessened. However, even though the company may be joined to the agreement, in law it may be held not to be bound by certain provisions[287]. Moreover, future shareholders will not be bound by a shareholders' agreement automatically, ie, they will not be bound unless they consent[288].

[3.116] Fourth, through the employment of a shareholders' agreement, the members of a private company may mould the form of their chosen legal structure so as to make it accord more with their purposes. Many shareholders' agreements contain terms and conditions commonly found in a partnership agreement, underscoring the similarity between many Irish private companies and a partnership. It is more usual, though, for a

280 *Eley v Positive Government Security Life Assurance Co* (1876) 1 Ex D 88, considered at para **[3.099]** *ante*.

281 See also *Shalfoon v Chedar Valley Cooperative Dairy Co Ltd* [1924] NZLR 561 *per* Salmond J.

282 See para **[3.102]** *ante*.

283 See generally *Bushell v Faith* [1970] AC 1099, which is considered at para **[3.053]**.

284 Kruger, 'Pooling Agreements Under English Company Law' [1978] 94 LQR 557; *Greenwell v Porter* [1902] 1 Ch 530.

285 See Reece Thomas & Ryan, *The Law and Practice of Shareholders' Agreements* (1999, Butterworths), at pp 18–20.

286 See generally, Ch 15, *Duties of Directors and Other Officers*.

287 See para **[3.127]**.

288 *Russell v Northern Bank Development Corp Ltd et al* [1992] 3 All ER 161.

shareholders' agreement to contain a 'no partnership' clause. The purpose of this is to oust the possibility that on proper construction of s 1 of the Partnership Act 1890 the shareholders' agreement would make the parties partners. This could have the unforeseen consequence that one party could incur debts or other liabilities for which the other parties would be liable jointly and severally.

Types of shareholders' agreements

[3.117] Various categorisations of the different types of shareholders' agreements have been put forward[289]. Two broad categories of shareholders' agreements can be distinguished, although it must be stressed that they are not mutually exclusive, and very often an agreement will be a composite of both.

First, there are *formation agreements*. Such can be used by two or more *future shareholders* in a company which is not yet formed, or by existing shareholders, shortly after the incorporation of a company. These will often fall to be categorised as joint venture type agreements. An example of such an agreement can be seen in the case of *TGM v Al Babtain & Others*[290]. The rationale for employing a shareholders' agreement is that the parties recognise that the company about to be formed is in reality a partnership which has the advantage of limited liability, and as such the agreement entered into is tantamount to a deed of partnership. In a private, closely-held, company the pomp and ceremony imported into every company registered under the Companies Acts can be incongruous with the *true* relationship of the parties engaged in business. With careful legal draftsmanship the parties can achieve an agreement that at least strives to reflect the reality of their relationship.

Such agreements will typically detail the shareholdings in the future company and the rights attaching to such shares. Often the first general meeting of the company is planned in advance, and the parties contract that at that meeting, 'the company' will allot a certain number of shares to each member, and go on to provide for the appointment of directors and the secretary. Such agreements are characterised by a forward planning approach of the future shareholders who try to put their 'simple relationship' beyond the complex vicissitudes of the Companies Acts.

Second, there are *limited shareholders' agreements*, which may be entered into by shareholders in respect of matters such as voting at meetings[291], pre-emption rights of members to acquire shares held by members, the appointment of directors, and other miscellaneous matters connected to the management of the company.

[3.118] Shareholders' agreements embody the 'hidden constitution' of many private companies and should be recognised as being incidental to the constitutional

---

289 Farrar Furey & Hannigan, *Farrar's Company Law* (3rd edn, Butterworths, 1991) at 139 distinguish between three types of shareholders' agreements: agreements between the company and the members collateral and supplementary to the articles of association; agreements between all the shareholders *inter se*; and agreements between some of the shareholders. Reece Thomas & Ryan, *The Law and Practice of Shareholders' Agreements* (1999, Butterworths), at p 12–20 suggest six types: joint venture agreements; quasi-partnership company agreements; minority protection agreements; informal and implied agreements; pooling agreements; and express voting trust agreements.

290 *TGM v Al Babtain & Others* [1982] ILRM 349 at 350 *et seq*. See para **[3.124]**.

291 See as an example of an express voting trust agreement *Neville v Wilson* [1996] 3 All ER 171.

documentation of such companies. However it must be stressed that shareholders' agreements are founded on the law of contract, and are only enforceable by the parties thereto *inter se*: they do not concern the separate legal entity which is the company, unless of course the company is also a party to the agreement. Because the parties to a shareholders' agreement are free to contract in respect of whatever they wish, any consideration of 'typical provisions' will necessarily be limited. However, most such agreements will have a number of basic clauses.

[3.119] A typical joint-venture type shareholders' agreement will begin by reciting the parties to the agreement, and go on to define the various phrases referred to in the agreement[292]. From then on, the agreement will address the main concerns of the parties thereto. Normally, the issues to the fore of the minds of the shareholders will be the subscription for shares, defining the business of the company, agreeing contracts of employment, the structure of the company and completion of the contract thus entered into (all in the case of a company to be set-up in the immediate future), the transfer of shares, and in particular pre-emption rights attaching to such shares, the powers of the directors and their remuneration, alteration of capital and dividends payable to the members. It will be noted that there is a considerable overlap between the articles of a company and the provisions in a shareholders' agreement.

The enforcement of shareholders' agreements

[3.120] A shareholders' agreement is quite simply a contract, between the parties thereto. Although not necessarily written contracts, they are generally reduced to writing[293]. As such, ordinary principles of contract law will apply to their interpretation and enforcement[294]. When such agreements come before a court for interpretation, the court will first of all see if there is indeed a contract, then it will ask whether or not the clauses sought to be relied upon have been incorporated into the contract, and finally it will construe the clause in hand. Parties to a shareholders' agreement can avail of Order 83 of the Rules of the Superior Courts 1986 and state a case concerning the interpretation of an agreement to the High Court[295].

[3.121] There is a general willingness on the part of the courts to enforce and respect shareholders' agreements. An example is provided by the Court of Appeal decision in *Harman v BLM Group Ltd*[296], which concerned an application for an order for the convening of a general meeting of a company under s 371 of the UK Companies Act

---

[292] Thus terms such as the 'Board of Directors', 'Equity Share Capital', 'Financial Year', 'Subsidiary', 'Permitted Transferee', 'Shareholder', 'Accountant', and standard references to the 'masculine' including the 'feminine', etc, are defined so as to avoid the possibility of there being an equivocal interpretation of the agreement.

[293] For a type of oral agreement, see *Pennell v Venida Investments Ltd* (25 July 1974, unreported) English HC *per* Templeman J; and Burridge, (1981) 44 MLR 40.

[294] Cheshire, Fifoot & Furmston, *Law of Contract* (12th edn, Butterworths, 1991); see also Clark, *Contract Law in Ireland* (3rd edn, Sweet and Maxwell, 1992).

[295] See *McAuliffe v Litographic Group Ltd* (2 November 1993, unreported) SC, where a pre-emption provision in a shareholders' agreement was the subject of an application under Order 83 of the Rules of the Superior Courts 1986.

[296] *Harman v BLM Group Ltd* [1994] 2 BCLC 674.

1985[297]. To order such a meeting would have resulted in the breach of a shareholders' agreement. The company in question had both 'A' shareholders and 'B' shareholders and the agreement provided that a meeting would only be quorate where one 'B' shareholder was present. The petitioners under s 371 of the 1985 Act were 'A' shareholders who owned in excess of 50% of the shares in the company and were desirous of convening a meeting to dismiss certain directors. The directors whom it was intended to dismiss had the support of the 'B' shareholder who would not attend a meeting of the company's members and so had effectively thwarted the holding of a members' meeting. The Court of Appeal, in reversing the trial judge's decision, held it was inappropriate to make an order under s 371 as to do so would be contrary to what the parties had agreed in the shareholders' agreement and would be in total disregard to the 'B' shareholder's rights which were akin to entrenched voting rights. Parties to a shareholders' agreement cannot, however, pick and choose those provisions that they wish to enforce[298].

[3.122] Some of the issues that can arise in the enforcement of shareholders' agreements are:

(a) Injunctions to enforce shareholders' agreements.
(b) Directors fettering their fiduciary powers.
(c) Binding companies through shareholders' agreements.

(a) Injunctions to enforce shareholders' agreements

[3.123] It is clear that an injunction will be granted[299] where one party to a shareholders' agreement has breached, or is about to breach the agreement[300]. Where there is an anticipated breach of a shareholders' agreement, a party to the agreement may seek relief from the High Court which has discretion to grant an injunction to restrain the breach[301]. An example is provided by *Puddlephatt v Leith*[302] where Sargant J enforced an agreement that the defendant would vote as the plaintiff directed.

[3.124] In *TGM v Al Babtain Trading & Ors*[303], the plaintiffs were the sole distributors and assemblers in Ireland of Datsun (now Nissan) vehicles. The plaintiff and the first defendant formed a company called Datsun Ltd for the purpose of the acquisition of the franchise, and entered into a shareholders' agreement in respect of the venture. Differences arose between the plaintiff and the first defendant over the operations of the company, and in particular, the future role of the chief executive of the company. The

---

297 The similar Irish provision which would empower the court to make such an order is s 135 of the CA 1963.

298 See, for example, *Re Vocam Europe Ltd* [1998] BCC 396.

299 Of course, for an injunction to issue, the court must be satisfied that the requirements for an interlocutory injunction have been fulfilled. See Keane, *Equity and the Law Trusts in the Republic of Ireland* (1988, Butterworth Ireland) at pp 205–243.

300 *Cf Russell v Northern Bank Development Corp Ltd et al* [1992] 3 All ER 161 considered at para **[3.127]**.

301 As with all injunctions, delay or acquiescence may incline the court to refuse relief: *Re Pearce Duff & Co Ltd* [1960] 3 All ER 693.

302 *Puddephatt v Leith* [1916] 1 Ch 200.

303 *TGM v Al Babtain Trading & Ors* [1982] ILRM 349.

first defendant, who owned 375,000 of the 500,000 shares subscribed for in the company, exercised its voting rights to terminate the appointment of the chief executive, managing director and deputy managing director. When the first defendant served notice of a meeting of the company, *inter alia*, dealing with the 'service agreements' of the managing director and deputy managing director, the plaintiff's solicitors wrote to the first defendant, saying that such constituted a breach of the shareholders' agreement. The plaintiff then obtained an injunction restraining the defendants from exercising or procuring the exercise of their voting rights to grant service contracts to persons other than those named in the shareholders' agreement. Keane J continued the injunction on the basis that the shareholders' agreement seemed to prohibit the granting of service contracts, and so the plaintiff had established a *prima facie* case which would be protected by an injunction until the full trial of the case, and the balance of convenience favoured the plaintiff.

[3.125] Shareholders' agreements often provide that disputes between the parties are to be referred to arbitration, and in such cases where the agreement so provides, the decision of the arbitrator will be binding upon the parties[304]. A shareholders' agreement in *Telnor Invest AS v IIU Nominees Ltd and Esat Telecom Holdings Ltd*[305] so provided. In that case, the agreement stated that so long as any party held not less than 10% of the company's equity share capital, that party would be entitled to nominate one person as a director. The second defendant initially held 20% of the equity share capital and on that basis had nominated a director. Subsequently, its shareholding fell to 1% and the plaintiff contended that the second defendant had lost its right to maintain its nominee on the board. This was disputed and it was contended that there was no onus on existing directors to resign. The first defendant sought a stay on the plaintiff's proceedings until the dispute had been determined by arbitration as was provided for in the shareholders' agreement. O'Sullivan J accepted that the dispute was to be referred to arbitration as provided for in the agreement but stated this did not preclude parties from seeking interim relief pending the determination by arbitration. Hence, he stayed the proceedings and also granted an interim injunction restraining the defendants' nominee director from acting until the arbitration had been determined.

(b) Directors fettering their fiduciary powers

[3.126] While a shareholders' agreement will bind the signatory in his capacity *qua* member[306], there are difficulties where a shareholder binds himself in his capacity as a director (*qua* director) since a director is a fiduciary and the office of director carries with it the requirement that a director should only act in the best interests of the company[307]. Thus it has been said[308] that:

---

304 See, for example, *Byrne v Byrne* [2005] IEHC 55.

305 *Telnor Invest AS v IIU Nominees Ltd and Esat Telecom Holdings Ltd* [1999] IEHC 188, O'Sullivan J.

306 It will often be the case that the agreement will dictate that the signatories will exercise their vote in a particular manner: *Puddephatt v Leith* [1916] 1 Ch 200.

307 *Gabbett v Lawder* (1883) 11 LR Ir 295. See also *Motherwell v Schoof* [1949] 4 DLR 812; *Atlas Development Co Ltd v Calof and Gold* (1963) 31 WWR 575; and *Thorby v Goldberg* (1964) 112 CLR 597.

308 *The Encyclopaedia of Forms and Precedents* (5th edn, Butterworths) Vol 9, p 15, para 8.

> 'Unlike a shareholder, whose vote is a right of property he may exercise in furtherance of his own personal interests, a director is a fiduciary in respect of the powers entrusted to him by the company's articles of association, and he is accordingly bound to exercise those powers *bona fide* in the best interests of the company.'

It can sometimes arise in the context of a shareholders' agreement that a director is asked to fetter the future exercise of his fiduciary powers. The fettering of future discretion will not automatically amount to a breach of a director's duty. Directors will not act inconsistently with their fiduciary duties to the company where they fetter their discretion to act in the future in furtherance of a *bona fide* commercial agreement which confers substantial benefit on their company. So in *Fulham Football Club Ltd et al v Cabra Estates plc*[309] it was said:

> 'It is trite law that directors are under a duty to act *bona fide* in the interests of their company. However, it does not follow from that proposition that directors can never make a contract by which they bind themselves to the future exercise of their powers in a particular manner, even though the contract taken as a whole is manifestly for the benefit of the company. Such a rule could well prevent companies from entering into contracts which were commercially beneficial to them[310].'

This matter is considered in detail in Ch 15, *Duties of Directors and Other Officers*[311]where this case and others such as *Thorby v Goldberg* are examined[312]. Suffice it to say here that in entering into a shareholders' agreement, it may be the case that after due deliberation a company's directors can decide *bona fide* that it is in the best interests of the company to agree to act in a particular way in the future. Shareholders' agreements can be of great advantage to a company: by assisting the controlled and orderly management of the company; by underscoring the basis of the participant's relationships; and by serving the company's economic advantage, particularly in a joint venture. Clearly, this general statement cannot be said to be true of all shareholders' agreements and each *fetter* on the directors' discretion will have to be considered individually.

(c) Binding companies through shareholders' agreements

[3.127] Often shareholders' agreements attempt to maintain the *status quo* in a company by preventing any alteration in shareholdings. Moreover, this will sometimes include not only the prohibition of share transfers, but also the prohibition on a company increasing its share capital. The prohibition on a company increasing its share capital may be

[309] *Fulham Football Club Ltd et al v Cabra Estates plc* [1994] 1 BCLC 363.

[310] *Fulham Football Club Ltd et al v Cabra Estates plc* [1994] 1 BCLC 363 at 392a-b. Neill LJ said the 'true rule' was stated by the High Court of Australia in *Thorly v Goldberg* [1964] 112 CLR 597, the headnote of which read: '[i]f, when a contract is negotiated on behalf of a company, the directors *bona fide* think it in the interests of the company as a whole that the transaction should be entered into and carried into effect they may bind themselves by the contract to do whatever is necessary to effectuate it.'

[311] At para **[15.035]** *et seq*. For an interesting international survey of the courts' attitude to fettering directors' discretion in the context of shareholders' agreements, see further Reece Thomas & Ryan, *The Law and Practice of Shareholders' Agreements* (1999, Butterworths), at pp 69–78.

[312] *Thorby v Goldberg* [1964] 112 CLR 597.

unenforceable, as was held in the House of Lords' decision in *Russell v Northern Bank Development Corp Ltd et al*[313]. In that case, four persons entered into a shareholders' agreement to which the company itself was also a party. The agreement provided, *inter alia*, that its terms and conditions would take precedence over the company's articles of association. In particular, it provided that the company would not create or issue any further share capital without the consent in writing of all parties to the agreement. A dispute arose when the directors of the company gave notice to its shareholders of an extraordinary general meeting (EGM), the purpose of which was to increase its share capital. The company was empowered to do this under its articles, the equivalent Irish regulation being model reg 44 of Part I of Table A. The plaintiff, who was a shareholder and a party to the shareholders' agreement, sought an injunction to prevent the other shareholders considering or voting on the proposed resolution at the EGM. At trial the injunction was refused and it was held that the company could not be prevented from increasing its share capital as that was an improper fetter on the statutory power of the company, contained in the UK equivalent to s 68 of the CA 1963. This view was upheld by the Court of Appeal.

In the House of Lords the appeal succeeded in part. It was held that the shareholders' agreement was binding on all parties to it, *except the company.* In so holding the House of Lords made a distinction between private persons who were parties to a 'private agreement'[314] and the company. As for the private persons who were party to the agreement, the *dictum* of Lord Davey in *Welton v Saffeny*[315] was cited by Lord Jauncey:

> 'Of course, individual shareholders may deal with their own interests by contract in such way as they may think fit. But such contracts, whether made by all or some only of the shareholders, would create personal obligations, or an *exceptio personalis* against themselves only, and would not become a Reg of the company, or be binding on the transferees of the parties to it, or upon new or non-assenting shareholders. There is no suggestion here of any such private agreement outside the machinery of the Companies Acts.'

The enforceability of the agreement against the shareholders stands in marked contrast to the position of the company. The House of Lords upheld the old principle in *Allen v Gold Reefs of West Africa Ltd*[316] and *Bushell v Faith*[317] that a company 'cannot by its articles or otherwise deprive itself of the power by special resolution to alter its articles or any of them'. Applied to the present case, Lord Jauncey said:

> '[The company] on the other hand agreed that its capital would not be increased without the consent of each of the shareholders. This was a clear undertaking by [the company] in a formal agreement not to exercise its statutory powers for a period which could, certainly on one view of construction, last for as long as any one of the parties to the agreement remained a shareholder and long after the control of [the company] had passed to shareholders who were not party to the agreement. As such an undertaking it is, in my

313 *Russell v Northern Bank Development Corp Ltd et al* [1992] 3 All ER 161.

314 *Russell v Northern Bank Development Corp Ltd et al* [1992] 3 All ER 161 at 167.

315 *Welton v Saffeny* [1897] AC 299 at 331.

316 *Allen v Gold Reefs of West Africa Ltd* [1900] 1 Ch 656.

317 *Bushell v Faith* [1969] 1 All ER 1002.

> view, obnoxious as if it had been contained in the articles of association and therefore is unenforceable as being contrary to the provisions of [s 68 of the CA 1963][318].'

However, while the company's promise not to increase its share capital was unlawful, it could be severed from the other party-shareholders' promises, which were enforceable against them *inter se*.

[3.128] Where shareholders decide to attempt to maintain the *status quo* by preventing an increase in share capital, it may be possible to join-in the company by ensuring that certain steps are first taken. Although s 68 of the CA 1963 empowers a company to increase its share capital, it does so on the condition that the company has internal power to do this in its articles of association. Thus, by ensuring, *ab initio*, that reg 44 is purged from the company's articles, it is thought that the statutory power contained in s 68 and defended in the *Russell* case would not exist. On the authority of the *Russell* case, a shareholders' agreement can oblige the members, personally, to refrain from voting in favour of altering the company's articles, thereby ensuring that reg 44 cannot be reinstated.

[318] *Russell v Northern Bank Development Corp Ltd et al* [1992] 3 All ER 161 at 167.

Chapter 4

Incorporation and its Consequences

[4.001] As a *corporation*, or *body corporate*, a private company is regarded by the law as having a separate legal personality from its shareholders or members. This chapter examines how the private company achieves corporate status (and how the status may be lost) and the consequences which flow from it. These topics are considered here under the following headings: [A] The Acquisition of Corporate Status; and [B] The Consequences of Incorporation.

[A] The Acquisition of Corporate Status

Registration, and issue of the certificate of incorporation

[4.002] The private company acquires corporate status through the process of *incorporation by registration*, ie, registration of the company in the Companies Registration Office ('CRO') by the registrar of companies in accordance with the procedure detailed in Ch 2[1]. Where the registrar of companies is satisfied that the documents filed are formally in order, and that the purpose for which the incorporators are associated is lawful[2], she must register the company and issue a *certificate of incorporation* certifying that the company is incorporated, and in the case of a limited company, that the company is limited[3]. The certificate serves as a kind of 'birth certificate' evidencing the existence of the company as a corporate body and the date upon which it acquired corporate status.

Continuing the analogy between registration and birth, it may also be said that companies are capable of changing gender by re-registering in a different form, eg, from limited to unlimited, private to public, etc[4]. A certificate of incorporation will, thus, *also* be issued by the registrar where:

(a) an unlimited company is re-registered as a limited company[5];
(b) a public limited company is re-registered as a private company[6];
(c) a limited company is re-registered as an unlimited company[7];

---

§ *This chapter has been contributed by G Brian Hutchinson.*

1 See Ch 2, *Incorporation by Registration*, at para **[2.017]** *et seq*.
2 See s 5(1) of the CA 1963.
3 Section 18(1) of the CA 1963. Where the company is a public limited company, the certificate must also contain a statement to that effect: s 5(3) of the C(A)A 1983.
4 See generally Ch 33, *Conversion by Re-Registration*.
5 Section 20 of the CA 1963; s 53 of the C(A)A 1983.
6 Section 14 of the C(A)A 1983.
7 Section 52 of the C(A)A 1983.

(d) a private company is re-registered as a public limited company[8];

(e) a company incorporated under some other Act becomes registered under the Companies Acts[9];

(f) a *societas europaea* ('SE') from another EU Member State transfers its registered office to Ireland[10];

(g) a company changes its registered name[11].

The principles which govern the original certificate of incorporation are largely applicable to these certificates also.

Failure or refusal by the registrar of companies

[4.003] If the registrar fails or refuses to register the company where all the requirements for registration have been complied with, she may be compelled to do so by order of *mandamus*[12]. The registrar may validly refuse to register where incorporation is sought to perpetrate an unlawful activity. Thus, in *R v Registrar of Joint Stock Companies*[13] the English Court of Appeal refused an application for an order of *mandamus* to compel the registrar to register a company formed for the sale in England, contrary to English law, of Irish Hospital Lottery tickets. It would appear that the registrar might also refuse to register where the business of the company is unlawful on the grounds of being contrary to public policy[14].

Effect of the certificate of incorporation

[4.004] The certificate of incorporation is, by virtue s 5(4) of the C(A)A 1983:

> '*conclusive evidence* that all the requirements of the Companies Acts in respect of registration and of matters precedent and incidental thereto have been complied with, and that the association is a company authorised to be registered under the Companies Act[s][15].'

Similar effect is given to the certificates of incorporation issued upon re-registration in most of the circumstances outlined in para **[4.002]** above[16]. Where a certificate is issued in respect of a change of registered name the Companies Acts do not provide that the new certificate is to constitute conclusive evidence of a valid incorporation. Whether, as one might expect, the courts will give that certificate such an effect by extending the conclusiveness of the original certificate to the new one still remains to be seen. In practice, it is customary to seek the original certificate and any certificates subsequently issued upon change of name as evidence of a valid incorporation. Where a public

8 Section 9 of the C(A)A 1983.

9 Section 19 of the C(A)A 1983; s 336 of the CA 1963.

10 Article 8 of Council Regulation (EC) No 2157/2001 of 8 October 2001 on the Statute for a European Company (SE). See Ch 29, *Public Limited Companies and SEs*, at para **[29.150]**.

11 Section 23(3) of the CA 1963.

12 *R v Registrar of Companies, ex parte Bowen* [1914] 3 KB 1161.

13 *R v Registrar of Joint Stock Companies* [1931] 2 KB 197.

14 *R v Registrar of Companies, ex parte HM's Attorney General* [1991] BCLC 476. See para **[4.017]**.

15 Section 5(4) of the C(A)A 1983 replacing s 19 of the CA 1963 (italics added).

16 See ss 53(5), 14(5), 52(5), 9(9), and 19(6) of the C(A)A 1983 respectively.

limited company is re-registered as a private company the certificate has the additional effect of constituting conclusive evidence that the company so re-registered is a private company[17], even though the company may not meet the requirements[18] for the formation of a private company.

[4.005] The conclusive evidence provision prevents inquiry into matters prior to and contemporaneous with the registration. In *Jubilee Cotton Mills v Lewis*[19], where the date of incorporation as stated in the certificate was patently earlier than the date upon which it was signed by the registrar, the court was obliged to accept the date certified in the certificate as being the true date of incorporation. Consequently a contract entered into by the company on the day following the date certified in the certificate was held to be binding on the company – even though the certificate had not in fact been issued at that time.

A peculiar abstraction of the conclusiveness is its extension to matters concerning the validity of clauses contained in the company's memorandum or articles of association. In *Cotman v Brougham*[20], the conclusiveness of the registrar's certificate was thought to preclude the courts from disputing the validity of an 'independent objects clause' in the company's memorandum of association, since the certificate was conclusive evidence that the memorandum, and the clauses contained therein, were valid and in accordance with the Companies Acts. Despite such conclusiveness, the registrar's certificate does not lend legality to activities contemplated by the company in its memorandum or articles which are patently unlawful or which conflict with the Companies Acts[21].

Rationale for the conclusive effect of the certificate of incorporation

[4.006] The rationale for the conclusiveness of the certificate of incorporation was explained by Lord Cairns in *Peel's Case, Re Barned's Banking Co*[22], as follows:

> 'When once the memorandum is registered and the company is held out to the world as a company undertaking business, willing to receive shareholders and ready to contract engagements, then it would be of the most disastrous consequences, if, after all that has been done, any person was allowed to go back and enter into an examination (it might be years after the company had commenced trade) of the circumstances attending the original registration and the regularity of the execution of the document[23].'

'Were such a thing permissible,' said Palmer[24], 'a company's foundation would be built not on a rock but on sand.' In *Peel's* case, the memorandum of association had, after signature by the requisite number of subscribers, but before registration, been altered

---

17 Section 14(5)(b) of the C(A)A 1983.

18 See Ch 1, *The Private Company in Context*, at para **[1.134]** *et seq*.

19 *Jubilee Cotton Mills v Lewis* [1924] AC 958.

20 *Cotman v Brougham* [1918] AC 514. See further Ch 7, *Corporate Contracts, Capacity and Authority*, at para **[7.049]**.

21 *Bowman v Secular Society Ltd* [1917] AC 406, *per* Sumner LJ at 435. See also *Ayre v Skesley's Adamant Cement Co Ltd* (1904) 20 TLR 587; and *Gaiman v National Association for Mental Health* [1971] Ch 317.

22 *Peel's Case, Re Barned's Banking Co* (1867) LR 2 Ch App 674.

23 *Peel's Case, Re Barned's Banking Co* (1867) LR 2 Ch App 674 at 682.

24 Palmer, *Company Law* (12th edn, Stevens & Sons, 1924), at p 51.

significantly without the privity of the signatories. After registration and the issue of a certificate by the registrar, the question arose as to whether the company had been validly incorporated, since s 6 of the Companies Act 1862 required the memorandum of association to be subscribed 'by seven or more persons' whereas the signatures had been entirely overtaken by events. Lord Cairns held the certificate to be conclusive evidence of the company's incorporation, stating 'once the certificate of incorporation is given, nothing is to be inquired into as to the regularity of the prior proceedings[25]'.

[4.007] By treating the registrar's certificate as conclusive evidence of a valid incorporation, Irish company law is relieved of the difficulties once encountered in continental and US jurisdictions. In such jurisdictions, incorporated companies having traded under the banner of a corporation for some time have, on occasion, had their corporate status rendered null and void, with disastrous consequences for third parties dealing with them[26].

The First EU Companies Directive's nullity provisions

[4.008] The aforementioned hazards were the principal concern of Section III of the First EU Directive on Company Law ('the Directive')[27]. Article 11.2 of the Directive provides:

> "Nullity may be ordered only on the following grounds:
>
> (a) that no instrument of constitution was executed or that the rules of preventative control or the requisite legal formalities were not complied with;
>
> (b) that the objects of the company are unlawful or contrary to public policy;
>
> (c) that the instrument of constitution or the statutes do not state the name of the company, the amount of the individual subscriptions of capital, the total amount of the capital subscribed or the objects of the company;
>
> (d) failure to comply with the provisions of the national law concerning the minimum amount of capital to be paid up;
>
> (e) the incapacity of all the founder members;
>
> (f) that, contrary to the national law governing the company, the number of founder members is less than two.
>
> Apart from the foregoing grounds of nullity a company shall not be subject to any cause of non-existence, nullity absolute, nullity relative or declaration of nullity."

Article 12.2 of the Directive requires Member States to introduce provisions allowing the winding-up of companies whose corporate status has subsequently been found to have been a nullity, and Article 12.3 further requires Member States to provide that 'nullity shall not of itself affect the validity of any commitments entered into by or with the company'.

---

25 *Peel's Case, Re Barned's Banking Co* (1867) 2 Ch App 674 at 681. See also *Oakes v Turquand* (1867) LR 2 HL 325.

26 See Drury, 'Nullity of Companies in English Law' (1985) MLR 644; Van Bodungen, 'The Defective Corporation in American and German Law' (1967) 15 Am J Comp L 313.

27 Council Directive 68/151. See generally Ch 1, *The Private Company in Context*, at para **[1.113]**.

Effect of the First EU Companies Directive's nullity provisions in Ireland

[4.009] So settled was the principle of conclusiveness thought to be in Ireland that the European Communities (Companies) Regulations 1973 ('EC(C)R 1973')[28], which were introduced to implement the provisions of the Directive, do not contain any regulations implementing Section III of the Directive dealing with the nullity of companies.

[4.010] Though not implemented by national law, the Directive's provisions on nullity continue to have some legal effect in Ireland. First, it should be noted that the provisions dealing with nullity are *not* binding on private individuals[29] – because they have not been implemented here by way of statute or statutory instrument. Consequently, private individuals are not prohibited from seeking to have the incorporation of an Irish company declared a nullity on grounds other than those listed in the Directive. Second, the Directive's provisions *are* binding on the State[30], and the State and its agents may not seek to have the incorporation of a company declared a nullity *except* on the grounds listed in the Directive. Third, where private individuals successfully obtain an order declaring the incorporation of a company to be a nullity on grounds other than those listed in the Directive, the State will be liable to compensate the members of the nullified company. Such liability relates to the loss caused to the members by the State's failure to limit the grounds of nullity to those specified in the Directive[31].

[4.011] In addition, when interpreting the provisions of Irish law, the courts will be obliged under European law to have regard to the wording and purpose of the Directive and should choose whichever interpretation best gives effect to it. In *Marleasing SA v La Comercial Internacional de Alimentacion SA*[32], a reference to the European Court of Justice from the Spanish courts, the question to be determined was how should the Spanish courts interpret ss 1261 and 1275 of their Civil Code? Those sections provided for the nullification of contracts made 'without cause'. The Directive had not yet been implemented in Spain, though the date for its implementation there had passed. Marleasing had argued that the incorporation of La Comercial should be declared void under those sections on the basis that the motive for La Comercial's formation was to place the assets of one of its founders beyond the reach of his creditors. The national courts were uncertain of whether they could interpret ss 1261 and 1275 so as to allow a company to be declared void simply because of the motive for which it was formed, particularly since that does not appear as a ground listed in Article 12 of the Directive. Hence the reference to the European Court of Justice.

The European Court held that since the Directive had not yet been implemented in Spain, and since Marleasing was a private company and not an organ of State,

28 SI 163/1973.

29 See *Marshall v Southampton and South West Hampshire Area Health Authority (No 1)* [1986] 1 CMLR 688.

30 *Marshall v Southampton and South West Hampshire Area Health Authority (No 1)* [1986] 1 CMLR 688.

31 *Francovich v Italian Republic* [1993] 2 CMLR 66; *Brasserie du Pecheur SA v Germany (Factortame)* (C46/93) [1996] 1 CMLR 889.

32 *Marleasing SA v La Comercial Internacional de Alimentacion SA* [1992] 1 CMLR 305.

Marleasing was not precluded from seeking to have La Comercial declared void under Spanish national law on grounds other than those listed in the Directive. The court stressed, however, that since Article 189 of the Treaty of Rome obliges Member States to take appropriate measures to implement directives, the Spanish courts, as organs of State, were obliged to interpret the provisions of their existing law in accordance with the wording and purpose of the Directive. This, in effect, meant that the Spanish courts should not interpret ss 1261 and 1275 of the Spanish Code in such a way as to allow nullification of a company simply by reference to the motives for its formation, since that is not a ground listed in the Directive[33].

Impeachment of incorporation

[4.012] Conventional wisdom suggests that the conclusiveness of the certificate of incorporation prevents the reopening of matters prior to and contemporaneous with the registration of the company, and places the corporate existence of the company beyond question[34]. There is at least one (albeit rare) situation in which the certificate certainly will not have that effect – that is in the case of a trade union which is also registered as a company. Furthermore, the full field of challenges which may be made against the certificate has not yet fully been explored. These situations will now be examined under the following headings:

(a) Trade unions registered as companies;

(b) Judicial review of the registrar's decision to issue a certificate of incorporation;

(c) Constitutionality of the conclusive effect of the certificate of incorporation.

(a) Trade unions registered as companies

[4.013] Section 3(4) of the CA 1963 provides that nothing in that Act shall affect 'the provisions of s 5 of the Trade Union Act 1871'. Section 5 of the latter Act provides, in turn, that the Companies Acts 'shall not apply to any trade union, and the registration of any trade union under any of the said Acts shall be void'[35]. The definition of 'trade union' for the purposes of the Trade Union Acts 1871–1982 is very broad, and includes bodies which are not regarded as trade unions in the general sense. For example, employers' associations, associations of self-employed persons, manufacturing associations and trade protection societies may all qualify as trade unions under the Acts[36].

[4.014] Where a trade union is both registered as a company and registered as a trade union under the Trade Union Acts 1871–1982, revocation of its company status and of

---

33 Marleasing's argument that 'objects' in Article 11.2(b) of the Directive could be interpreted as including 'motives' was rejected. The court held that 'objects' refers to the objects of the company as described in the instrument of incorporation.

34 See para **[4.005]**.

35 The analogous English provisions were applied in *British Association of Glass Bottle Manufacturers (Ltd) v Nettlefold* (1911) TLR 527: see Drury, 'Nullity of Companies in English Law' (1985) MLR 644 at pp 649–650; for a Scottish example see *Edinburgh and District Aerated Water Manufacturers Defence Association v James Jenkinson & Co* (1903) 5 SC 1159.

36 See Kerr & Whyte, *Irish Trade Union Law* (1985, Professional Books), at p 39; Hickling, 'Trade Unions in Disguise' (1964) 27 MLR 625; see also generally Kerr, *Trade Union and Industrial Relations Acts* (2001, Round Hall).

its certificate of incorporation will not deprive it of its corporate status, because registered trade unions are themselves bodies corporate[37]. Where, however, the trade union has *not* been registered as a trade union under those Acts, revocation of its certificate of incorporation will deprive it of corporate status, since unregistered trade unions are unincorporated associations similar in legal nature to a social club[38]. Of course where a trade union is initially registered as a company under the Companies Acts it will have slipped through the registrar's net – because the registrar should not have permitted its registration according to s 5 of the Trade Union Act 1871. One may expect such errors never to occur; but, conversely, where a company formed for other purposes subsequently adopts the mantle of a trade union, it will have evaded such scrutiny.

If s 5 of the Trade Union Act 1871 is ever put to use so as to avoid the registration of a company which is not a registered trade union, the State may regret its decision not to implement Section III of the First EU Directive – because anyone suffering loss as a result of the State's failure to implement those provisions (which would have preserved the validity of transactions entered into by the company) may sue the State for compensation[39].

(b) Judicial review of the registrar's decision to issue a certificate of incorporation

[4.015] The conclusive effect of the certificate of incorporation appears to preclude parties from obtaining judicial review of the registrar's decision to register a company and to issue a certificate of incorporation[40].

The registrar's functions may be classed as administrative or quasi-judicial in nature[41]. Ordinarily, administrative functions can be made the subject of judicial review proceedings, since they must be exercised without excess of jurisdiction and in accordance with principles of fundamental procedural fairness[42]. Thus, as was already observed[43], where the registrar, in breach of fair procedures or in excess of jurisdiction, fails or refuses to register a company, she may be compelled to do so by the courts. However, once a certificate has been issued, the courts and the Companies Acts both say that it is the certificate rather than the registrar's actions to which one must look. The

37 *R (IUDWC) v Rathmines UDC* [1928] IR 260.

38 *Bonsor v Musician's Union* [1956] AC 101.

39 *Francovich v Italian Republic* [1993] 2 CMLR 66; *Brasserie du Pecheur SA v Germany (Factortame)* (C46/93) [1996] 1 CMLR 889.

40 *Princess of Reuss v Bos* (1871) LR 5 HL 176. See also *R v Registrar of Companies, ex parte Central Bank of India* [1986] QB 1114 and *Lombard & Ulster Banking (Ireland) Ltd v Amurec* [1976–7] ILRM 222 where the statutory conclusiveness of the registrar's certificate as to the validity of the registration of a company charge (see s 104 of the CA 1963) was held to preclude judicial review of that certificate.

41 *Bowman v Secular Society* [1917] AC 406, *per* Lord Parker of Waddington at pp 439–440. See generally *McDonald v Bord na gCon (No 2)* [1965] IR 217; *Goodman International v Hamilton* [1992] 2 IR 542.

42 See *State (Crowley) v Irish Land Commission* [1951] IR 250; *Foley v Irish Land Commission* [1952] IR 118.

43 See para **[4.003]**.

approach of the courts is clearly evidenced in the case of *Irish Permanent Building Society v Registrar of Building Societies*[44].

[4.016] The *Irish Permanent* case concerned a certificate of incorporation issued *not* by the registrar of companies but by the registrar of building societies under the Building Societies Act 1976. The matter in issue was whether or not the Irish Life Building Society, a society established and controlled by the Irish Life Assurance Co, was registrable under the Building Societies Act 1976. The registrar of building societies had issued a certificate of incorporation under the 1976 Act to the Irish Life Building Society. The plaintiffs, alleging that the wrongful incorporation of a new building society had caused and would cause them loss, sought, *inter alia*, a declaration that the registrar had exceeded the registrar's jurisdiction by registering the society when its internal rules as to voting contravened the provisions of the Act. The plaintiffs also sought a declaration that, consequently, the society had been invalidly registered.

Barrington J found that the rules did indeed contravene the provisions of the Act and that the registrar had mistakenly construed the Act's provisions. But he declined to give any decision as to whether the registrar's mistake amounted to an excess of jurisdiction, because s 11 of the Building Societies Act 1976 provided that the registrar of building societies' certificate is *sufficient* evidence, until the contrary is shown, that the society is authorised to be incorporated. He observed:

> '... it appears to me to be a fair conclusion that the Act contemplates that notwithstanding the vigilance of the Registrar, societies with defective rules will get on to the register and also that societies may be validly incorporated notwithstanding that their rules are in some particular defective ... I would be very surprised if the incorporation of a society could be invalidated by an honest mistake such as was made by the founders and the Registrar in the present case. If the law were otherwise people might in good faith deal with a society for many years only to find that because of some defect in its rules the society did not exist as a corporate body. Such a society, not being a building society incorporated under the Act could not even be wound up in accordance with the provisions of the Act ... To hold that the society was not validly incorporated would clearly cause great damage to many innocent people[45].'

Whereas the certificate in that case was merely 'sufficient evidence until the contrary is shown' of a valid incorporation, the registrar of companies' certificate is 'conclusive evidence' of a valid incorporation. This must, it is submitted, strengthen the proposition that the statutory conclusiveness of the registrar's certificate precludes judicial review of her decision to issue it.

[4.017] The English courts have held the registrar of companies' certificate of incorporation to be amenable to judicial review by way of *certiorari* at the instance of the Attorney General where the objects of the company contemplate the perpetration of a public wrong. In *Bowman v Secular Society*[46], it was held that the Attorney General, as the Crown's servant, could obtain an order of *certiorari* to quash the registration of a company incorporated for unlawful purposes since the provisions of the Companies Acts, while binding on English citizens, are not binding on the Crown. Consequently the

---

44 *Irish Permanent Building Society v Registrar of Building Societies* [1981] ILRM 242.

45 *Irish Permanent Building Society v Registrar of Building Societies* [1981] ILRM 242 at 269–270.

46 *Bowman v Secular Society* [1917] AC 406.

Crown is not bound to treat the registrar's certificate as conclusive evidence of a valid incorporation.

This was taken to extremes in *R v Registrar of Companies, ex parte Her Majesty's Attorney General*[47], where the registration of a company incorporated under the name of 'Lindi St Claire (Personal Services) Ltd' was quashed by the court at the instance of the Attorney General since the company's primary object – 'to carry on the business of prostitution' – was contrary to public policy, though prostitution itself was not a criminal offence.

It is doubtful whether similar proceedings could successfully be brought by the Irish Attorney General in the Irish courts. In *Byrne v Ireland*[48], the Supreme Court held that the State was not heir to a Crown privilege of immunity from the provisions of statutes. Rather, the court held, the wording of a statute would have to be such as to give rise to the implication that the State is not bound by its provisions before the State could ignore them. The wording of the Companies Acts appears to give rise to no such implication; it is probable then that the State must respect the registrar's certificate as being conclusive evidence of a valid incorporation just as private individuals must.

(c) Constitutionality of the conclusive effect of the certificate of incorporation

[4.018] Since the conclusiveness of the certificate of incorporation appears to prevent the courts from questioning the fairness of the registrar's decision to issue a certificate, it might be argued that the statutory conclusiveness leads to a denial of individuals' rights to constitutional justice and to vindication of their constitutional rights[49]. However, if such a challenge were mounted, the courts would have to weigh the rights of the individual challenger against the interests of the common good[50]. In doing so, the court would probably be swayed in favour of upholding the constitutionality of the conclusiveness by the principles explained by Lord Cairns in *Peel's* case, above[51].

Furthermore, it has been suggested that such a challenge might be answered by an assertion that the registrar's actions, whilst impinging upon the constitutional rights of the challengers, do not interfere with them directly[52].

[4.019] The broad question[53] of whether the 'conclusive evidence' provision offends the constitutional prohibition against ousting the jurisdiction of the courts[54] has also not been judicially determined. Again, it would appear that even this avenue of challenge is closed.

---

47 *R v Registrar of Companies, ex parte Her Majesty's Attorney General* [1991] BCLC 476.

48 *Byrne v Ireland* [1972] IR 241.

49 Under Article 40.3 of Bunreacht na hÉireann.

50 *Murray v Ireland* [1985] IR 532.

51 See para **[4.006]**. See also *Abbey Films Ltd v Attorney General* [1981] IR 158.

52 This point is made by Ussher, *Company Law in Ireland* (1986, Sweet & Maxwell) at pp 469–470, in relation to the conclusiveness of the registrar's certificate that the formalities for registration of a company charge – under Part IV of the CA 1963, as amended – have been complied with.

53 The question is raised by Power, *Irish Company Law 1973–1983 – A Guide and Handbook* (1984, Gill & Macmillan) at p 51.

54 Article 34.1 of Bunreacht na hÉireann.

In *Maher v Attorney General*[55], the Supreme Court struck down as unconstitutional s 44(2) of the Road Traffic Act 1968, which provided that an analyst's certificate as to the concentration of alcohol in a blood or urine sample should be 'conclusive evidence' as to the concentration of alcohol in the body of the person from whom the sample was taken. However, that case was concerned only with the administration of *criminal* justice, which the Constitution entrusts *exclusively* to the courts. All that follows from *Maher's* case is that where a company is prosecuted in criminal proceedings, for example, for an illegal activity contemplated by its objects clause, it cannot rely on the registrar's certificate as conclusive evidence of the legality of its activities. Indeed, where a company is prosecuted, it may, following *Maher*, try to challenge the validity of its *own* incorporation so as to evade criminal liability.

But where *civil* proceedings are concerned, it appears that it will be difficult to ignore the conclusiveness of the registrar's certificate. The functions of the registrar, as administrative or quasi-judicial functions[56] rather than judicial functions, may be exercised, under Article 37 of the Constitution, 'in matters other than criminal matters, by any person or body of persons duly authorised to exercise such functions and powers, notwithstanding that such person or body of persons is not a judge or a court appointed or established as such under t[he] Constitution'.' Consequently, in civil cases, the question of whether a company has validly been incorporated in accordance with the Companies Acts is a question which may constitutionally be left to the determination of the registrar, whose decision will be final and binding.

Cesser of corporate status

[4.020] Leaving the aforementioned possibilities aside, a private company validly incorporated in accordance with the Companies Acts continues to exist as a corporation until it is dissolved. Indeed, it continues even though it is in the process of being wound up, or though, in the case of a public company, its membership has fallen below the legal minimum of seven[57]. The Companies Acts provide that a company will be dissolved only when one of the following events occurs[58]:

> '(a) in the case of a winding up by the court, an order is made by the court under s 249 of the CA 1963, dissolving the company; or
>
> (b) in the case of a members' voluntary winding up, the period of three months, or such other time as the court thinks fit, from the registration of the liquidator's final return under s 263 of the CA 1963, has expired; or
>
> (c) in the case of a creditors' voluntary winding up, the period of three months, or such other time as the court thinks fit, from the registration of the liquidator's final return under s 273 of the CA 1963, has expired;
>
> (d) in the case of a company which has been struck off the Companies Register by the Registrar of Companies, for failure to carry on business[59] or for failure to

55 *Maher v Attorney General* [1973] IR 140.

56 See para **[4.015]**.

57 See *Jarvis Motors (Harrow) Ltd v Carabbott* [1964] 1 WLR 1101. See further Ch 5, *Disregarding Separate Legal Personality.*

58 See generally Ch 23, *Winding Up Companies.*

59 Section 311 of the CA 1963, as amended.

> make an annual return[60], the Registrar publishes a notice to that effect in the Companies Registration Office Gazette.'

Any of the above dissolutions may, however, within a period of two years, be declared void by the court upon the application of the liquidator or any interested person[61]. Furthermore, where a company has been struck off the companies' register, the court may, within 20 years, on the application of the company or any member or creditor, restore the company to the register[62]. The effect of the court's order in both cases is that the company is treated as never having been dissolved. These matters are discussed in greater detail in Ch 26, *post*.

[B] The Consequences of Incorporation

[4.021] A company registered under the Companies Acts becomes a body corporate as and from the date mentioned in the certificate of incorporation[63]. Incorporation under the Companies Acts carries with it a number of significant consequences, not all of which are set out in s 18(2) of the CA 1963, which, perhaps vaguely, provides:

> 'From the date of incorporation mentioned in the certificate of incorporation, the subscribers of the memorandum, together with such other persons as may from time to time become members of the company, shall be a body corporate with the name contained in the memorandum, capable forthwith of exercising all the functions of an incorporated company, and having perpetual succession and a common seal, but with such liability on the part of the members to contribute to the assets of the company in the event of its being wound up as is mentioned in this Act.'

[4.022] The courts have elaborated on the consequences of the company becoming, as s 18(2) puts it, a 'body corporate ... capable forthwith of exercising all the functions of an incorporated company'. The consequences are considered in the following paragraphs under these headings:

1. Separate legal personality.
2. Limited liability.
3. Transferability of interests.
4. Perpetual succession.
5. Common seal.
6. Floating charges.
7. Formation of large associations.
8. Taxation.
9. Other consequences of incorporation.

Separate legal personality

[4.023] The separate legal personality of the private company infiltrates almost every aspect of the company's dealings – whether they are between the company and its

---

60 Section 12 of the C(A)A 1982 as inserted by s 46 of the C(A)A 1999.

61 Section 310 of the CA 1963.

62 Section 311 of the CA 1963; and s 12 of the C(A)A 1982 as inserted by s 46 of the C(A)A 1999.

63 Section 18(2) of the CA 1963.

participants or between the company and third parties. Five significant aspects of the concept of separate legal personality are explored here as follows:

(a) Artificial or fictional personality;
(b) *Salomon's* case;
(c) Corporate property;
(d) Suing and being sued;
(e) Privileges and obligations.

(a) Artificial or fictional personality

[4.024] A body corporate, unlike a partnership or other unincorporated association, is more than a mere aggregation of individual units; it constitutes a juristic or legal *person* with a legal identity separate and distinct from that of its individual shareholders or members. It is, of course, a metaphysical person – it has no physical manifestation; it has no body, limbs or brains. Thus, while it maintains a distinct legal existence from other persons such as its members, the corporation suffers from the complication that it is only ultimately capable of acting, thinking and deciding through other persons. Here we encounter one of the fundamental idiosyncrasies of corporate dealings – they may only ever be carried out by human intervention – and it is this aspect of corporate dealing with which much of our company law is concerned[64].

[4.025] Corporations are sometimes described as *artificial* or *fictional* persons, or as a 'mere abstraction of law'[65]. But to describe them so is somewhat of a misnomer, for in the eyes of the law corporations are no more artificial or fictional than natural human persons[66]. As far as the law is concerned, a person is something which is capable of being the subject of rights and duties, regardless of its physical form. For example, in many ancient (and, sadly, not so ancient[67]) societies slaves were not recognised as persons by the law, though they patently had physical existence; while in other societies even religious idols are recognised as persons who may sue and be sued and hold property in their own right[68].

(b) Salomon's case

[4.026] The concept of the registered company as a separate legal person, capable of being the subject of rights and obligations, was firmly established by the House of Lords in *Salomon v A Salomon & Co Ltd*[69].

Aron Salomon had been operating prosperously as a boot manufacturer and leather merchant for some 30 years when, in 1892, bowing to pressure from members of his family who wanted to share in the business, and wishing to expand, he decided to

64 See Ch 7, *Corporate Contracts, Capacity and Authority* and Ch 13, *Corporate Governance: Management by the Directors*.

65 *Flitcroft's Case, In Re Exchange Banking Co* (1882) 21 Ch D 519, *per* Cotton LJ at 536.

66 Except, perhaps, where constitutional rights are concerned; see para **[4.068]** *et seq*.

67 See the American case of *Dredd Scott v Sandford* 60 US 393.

68 See *Pramatha Nath Mullick v Pradyumna Kumar Mullick* (1925) LR 52 Ind App 245; Duff, 'The Personality of an Idol' (1927) 3 Camb LJ 43; also *Bumper Development Corporation v Commissioner of the Metropolis* [1991] 4 All ER 638 and note by Carter, (1991) 62 BYIL 452.

69 *Salomon v A Salomon & Co Ltd* [1897] AC 22.

transfer his operation to a registered company owned and controlled by himself and his family. Of the 20,007 shares issued by the company – Salomon & Co Ltd – Aron Salomon held 20,001, the remaining six being held one-each by six other members of his family[70]. These six shares were, however, held by the family members as *nominees* for Salomon, so the company was *de facto* a 'one-man company'. The contract for the sale of his business to the company provided that the purchase price was to be £38,782 – a price which overvalued the true worth of the business and 'represented the sanguine expectations of a fond owner'[71]. Part of the purchase price was to be satisfied by the issue to Salomon of 20,000 fully paid £1 shares, and the payment to him of £8,872 in cash. The remaining £10,000 was to stand as a debt to Salomon, secured by debentures creating a floating charge over all the company's assets. Therefore, not only was Salomon the principal shareholder of the company but he was also its principal creditor.

When the company subsequently fell upon hard times, Salomon attempted to get the company back on its feet by mortgaging his debentures to obtain funds which he could lend to the company. His efforts to save the company were in vain and the debenture-holder appointed a receiver to the company. The company was subsequently put into liquidation. At that stage, the company's liabilities, including the debt secured in the debentures by the floating charge, exceeded its assets by £7,733, and if the debenture-holder were to be paid, the unsecured trade creditors, who were owed some £11,000, would get nothing.

[4.027] The liquidator took up the torch of the unsecured trade creditors, arguing that the debentures were invalid on the grounds of fraud. Vaughan Williams J, at first instance[72], found in favour of the liquidator, holding that Salomon's sole purpose in transferring his business to the company was to use it as an agent for himself, and therefore Salomon as principal should have to indemnify the company in respect of its debts to the unsecured creditors. He said:

> '... the company was a mere nominee of Mr Salomon's ... and therefore I wish, if I can, to deal with this case exactly on the basis that I should do if the nominee, instead of being a company, had been some servant or agent of Mr Salomon's to whom he had purported to sell his business[73].'

[4.028] On appeal[74], the Court of Appeal, affirming Vaughan Williams J's decision, took a slightly different tack and held that Salomon had abused the privileges of incorporation and limited liability. The court felt such privileges were intended by the Companies Act 1862 only to be conferred on 'independent *bona fide* shareholders, who had a mind and a will of their own, and were not the mere puppets of an individual who, adopting the machinery of the Act, carried on his old business in the same way as before, when he was a sole trader'.'[75] This abuse was sufficient to render Salomon a sort of constructive trustee for the company and thereby liable to indemnify it against its liabilities in full. Lord Lindley explained:

---

70 The Companies Act 1862 required a registered company to have at least seven members.

71 *Salomon v A Salomon & Co Ltd* [1897] AC 22 *per* Lord Macnaghten, at 49.

72 Reported *sub nom Broderip v Salomon* [1895] 2 Ch 323.

73 *Broderip v Salomon* [1895] 2 Ch 323 at p 323.

74 *Broderip v Salomon* [1895] 2 Ch 323.

75 *Broderip v Salomon* [1895] 2 Ch 323 *per* Lopes LJ, at 341.

'... Mr Aron Salomon's liability to indemnify the company in this case is, in my view, the legal consequence of the formation of the company in order to attain a result not permitted by law. The liability does not arise simply from the fact that he holds nearly all the shares of the company ... His liability rests on the purpose for which he formed the company, on the way he formed it, and the use which he made of it[76].'

[4.029] The House of Lords unanimously reversed the rulings of Vaughan Williams J and the Court of Appeal. The Law Lords held that since the Companies Act merely required that there should be seven subscribers to the memorandum – each holding at least one share – and said nothing about whether those subscribers should be independent of the majority shareholder or that they should have a mind and will of their own, the company was validly incorporated and capable of exercising all of the functions of an incorporated company. 'I cannot understand,' said Lord Macnaghten, 'how a body corporate thus made "capable" by statute can lose its individuality by issuing the bulk of its capital to one person.' Furthermore, Salomon had not perpetrated a fraud on the company by wilfully selling his business to it at an overvalue because all the shareholders were made fully aware of these circumstances. As to Vaughan Williams J's hypothesis that the company must be treated as Salomon's agent, Lord Halsbury trenchantly remarked:

'I confess it seems to me that the very learned judge becomes involved by this argument in a very singular contradiction. Either the company was a legal entity or it was not. If it was, the business belonged to it and not to Mr Salomon. If it was not, there was no person and no thing to be an agent at all; and it is impossible to say at the same time that there is a company and there is not[77].'

Lord Macnaghten, in words now regarded as a legal classic, endorsed this view and at the same time put to rest the Court of Appeal's hypothesis that Salomon's use of the company was contrary to the intentions of the Companies Act. He stated unequivocally:

'The company is at law a different person altogether from the subscribers to the Memorandum and, although it may be that after incorporation the business is precisely the same as it was before, and the same persons are managers, and the same hands receive the profits, the company is not at law the agent of the subscribers or a trustee for them. Nor are the subscribers as members liable, in any shape or form, except to the extent and in the manner provided by the Act. That is, I think, the declared intention of the enactment[78].'

Thus, priority was given to Salomon's debentures.

[4.030] The principles enunciated by the House of Lords in *Salomon's* case have a particular significance for the private company. It was that case which first established that the *de facto* one-man company fell within the policy of the Companies Acts; so much so, that the Companies Act 1907 subsequently reduced the minimum number of subscribers required for the incorporation of a private company from seven to two – without adding a requirement that the subscribers should be independent of each other or that one of the subscribers should not be the nominee of the other. Furthermore, the decision shows that the sole trader can limit his liability to the amount which he has invested in the company *and* can protect this investment by subscribing for secured

76 *Broderip v Salomon* [1895] 2 Ch 323 at 338.

77 *Salomon v A Salomon & Co Ltd* [1897] AC 22 at 31.

78 *Salomon v A Salomon & Co Ltd* [1897] AC 22 at 51.

debentures, rather than shares, so as to rank in priority to subsequent debenture-holders, unsecured creditors and other shareholders.

[4.031] The decision has, nevertheless, been the subject of some criticism. A contemporary view of it was one of amazement that a legal person could be created simply through observance of the machinery of the Companies Acts, regardless of the fact that there was *really* only one person involved[79]. Kahn-Freund later described the decision as 'calamitous'; the courts had failed to see through the 'rigidities of the "folklore" of corporate entity in favour of the legitimate interests of the company's creditors'[80]. Interestingly, he suggested that the legislature should mitigate the effects of *Salomon's* case by raising the cost of incorporation; by introducing a minimum capital requirement and minimum subscription on incorporation; by deeming companies under the control of less than ten persons to be the agents of those persons; and by abolishing private companies! Despite such criticism, the courts have applied the principles in *Salomon's* case assiduously[81], though both they and the legislature have established a number of exceptions to the principles so that the separate legal personality of companies may sometimes be disregarded[82]. These exceptions are considered in the next chapter.

(c) Corporate property

[4.032] As a separate legal person, a company that owns property owns and holds it in its own right[83] – not (necessarily) as an agent or trustee for the members. As Lord Halsbury observed in *Salomon's* case, if the company existed (as it did in that case) then 'the business belonged to it and not to Mr Salomon'.' A shareholder then, does not by mere virtue of his shareholding have any proprietary interest in the company's assets[84].

[4.033] This distinction was apparently overlooked by the incorporators of Aifca Ltd in the recent case of *Redfern Ltd v O'Mahony and McFeely, Caroll, Tafica Ltd and Aifca Ltd*[85], where McGovern J found that an agreement made by a partnership to transfer shares in another company was fundamentally flawed in so far as the partnership had no title to the shares which were owned by a separate company, Aifca Ltd. He stated[86]:

> 'The Agreement, as executed, contains some fundamental errors of fact and omits to deal with certain issues that were necessary to carry it into effect. I refer to the recital to the effect that '*the Partnership are the sole beneficial and legal owners of the entire issued share capital of Lowe, free from encumbrances*'. This is incorrect. The share capital was owned by Aifca Ltd, a limited liability company, with a separate legal identity from the

79 See the comment at (1897) 13 LQR 6.

80 Kahn-Freund, 'Some Reflections on Company Law Reform' (1944) 7 MLR 54.

81 See, for example, the citation with approval of *Salomon's* case in the High Court in *Re Frederick Inns Ltd* [1991] ILRM 582, *per* Lardner J at 587.

82 See Ch 5, *Disregarding Separate Legal Personality.*

83 *Short v Treasury Commissioners* [1948] AC 534; *Lee & Co (Dublin) Ltd v Egan (Wholesale) Ltd* (18 October, 1979, unreported) HC, Kenny J.

84 *Attorney General for Ireland v Jameson* [1904] 2 IR 644. On the nature of shareholders' interests generally see Ch 8, *Shares and Membership*.

85 *Redfern Ltd v O'Mahony and McFeely, Caroll, Tafica Ltd and Aifca Ltd* [2010] IEHC 253.

86 *Redfern Ltd v O'Mahony and McFeely, Caroll, Tafica Ltd and Aifca Ltd* at para 87 of the judgment.

> Partnership ... The legal consequences of incorporating a limited liability company are that the company assumes a separate legal identity as distinct from its owners. This is not a fiction. The rule in *Salomon v Salomon & Co* [1897] AC 22 is still the law in this jurisdiction. The Company and its shareholders are separate legal entities. (See *Allied Irish Coal Supplies Ltd v Powell Duffryn International Fuels Ltd* [1998] 2 IR 519.)'

[4.034] There is no objection in principle, of course, to a company being established specifically for the purpose of acting as trustee for its incorporators; but that does not diminish the proposition that it remains a separate legal entity. In *Bayworld v McMahon O'Brien Downes*[87], a company was established to act as bare trustee of lands for the partnership which incorporated it, which included a solicitor who carried out various legal formalities in the name of the company. Smyth J in the High Court held that the fact that the company was a separate person from its members meant that a relationship of solicitor and client could exist between the solicitor and the company, which, in the circumstances, obliged the solicitor to make documentation concerning transactions involving the company available to it. Upholding the decision on appeal in the Supreme Court, McCracken J stated[88]:

> 'The plaintiff was set up solely for the purpose of acting as a bare trustee of lands and it is not in dispute that it never had any beneficial interest in those lands. Both under the terms of the declaration of trust, and indeed on general principles, it was bound to act in accordance with all lawful instructions given by the partnerships, who were beneficially entitled to the various lands. However, that does not mean that as trustee the plaintiff has no rights in relation to the lands, or documentation dealing with the lands, independently of the beneficiaries. It is acknowledged in this case that, as far as the world at large was concerned, the plaintiff was the owner of various properties. It signed contracts to purchase and sell properties, it borrowed money for the purpose of completing sales and it undertook obligations with vendors or purchasers of the properties. As far as third parties dealing with the plaintiff were concerned, obligations were owed to them by the plaintiff and they owed obligations to the plaintiff. For example, the primary obligation to repay monies borrowed from the bank was that of the plaintiff, as was the obligation to discharge stamp duties on the transactions which it carried out. No doubt it was fully indemnified financially by the partnerships, but in many instances it would still retain its primary liability to third parties. In law, the plaintiff, as trustee must be considered as a separate legal entity from the partnerships which were the beneficiaries of the trusts.'

[4.035] The distinction between the members' and the company's property is one which members and persons dealing with companies (in particular *de facto* one-man companies) would do well to remember. It is well established that the controlling shareholders of a company may be convicted of stealing from the company[89]. Likewise, if the directors withdraw assets from the company then they may, in the course of a subsequent winding up, be found liable in misfeasance proceedings under s 298 of the CA 1963, and be compelled to repay or restore any money or property to the company with interest[90]. Indeed, even if the misfeasance proceedings under that section are

---

87 *Bayworld v McMahon O'Brien Downes* [2004] IR 199.

88 *Bayworld v McMahon O'Brien Downes* [2004] IR 199 at 218.

89 *Pearlberg v O'Brien* [1982] Crim LR 829; *Attorney General's Reference (No 2 of 1982)* [1984] QB 624; *Re Sullivan* [1984] Crim LR 405.

90 See Ch 15, *Duties of Directors and Other Officers*, at para **[15.149]**.

unsuccessful, the costs of the application may still be awarded against the directors personally because of any confusion they may have caused[91].

[4.036] Third parties dealing with a company should also be wary of the distinction between the company's property and the members' property. This is illustrated by the case of *A L Underwood Ltd v Bank of Liverpool*[92]. In that case, Mr A L Underwood, who was the controlling shareholder of A L Underwood Ltd, would from time to time indorse cheques which were payable to the company over to himself, and pay them into his private bank account. The bank thought nothing strange of this, failing to appreciate the distinction between the company and Mr Underwood. The bank was punished for its indifference by a successful suit in conversion against it by the company.

[4.037] Some further repercussions of the distinction between the company's property and its members' property are considered here as follows:

(i) Transfer of property;
(ii) Insurable interests;
(iii) Compensation;
(iv) Statutory tenancies.

(i) Transfer of property

[4.038] The transfer of property by the controlling shareholders to the company is a transfer to a distinct body[93]. As Lindley LJ observed in *Farrar v Farrars Ltd*[94]:

> 'A sale by a person to a corporation of which he is a member is not, either in form or in substance, a sale by a person to himself. To hold that it is would be to ignore the principle which lies at the root of the legal idea of a corporate body, and that is that the corporate body is distinct from the members composing it. A sale by a member of a corporation to the corporation itself is in every sense a sale valid in equity as well as at law.'

One important consequence of this is that the transfer of the controllers' assets to the company may be viewed as a conveyance on sale for which *ad valorem* stamp duty may be payable[95]. Conversely, the transfer of assets by the company to the shareholders is a transfer between distinct bodies, and so the requisite formalities of conveyance must be observed. In *Re Strathblaine Estates Ltd*[96], where the shareholders, in a distribution of a company's assets in a voluntary winding up, were given merely the title deeds to freehold estates held by the company, it was held that the shareholders had not been conveyed the legal estate in the properties. However the distinction between the company's property and its controlling shareholder's property worked to the controller's advantage in *Torbett v Faulkner*[97], where a company owned and controlled by a house-owner purported to let the house to an employee. The house-owner was held to be

---

[91] *Re David Ireland & Co Ltd* [1905] 1 IR 133; see Ch 15, *Duties of Directors and Other Officers*, at para **[15.151]**.

[92] *A L Underwood Ltd v Bank of Liverpool* [1924] 1 KB 775.

[93] *Ryhope Coal Co Ltd v Foyer* (1881) 7 QBD 485.

[94] *Farrar v Farrars Ltd* (1888) 40 ChD 395 at 409.

[95] *John Foster & Sons v IRC* [1894] 1 QB 516.

[96] *Re Strathblaine Estates Ltd* [1948] Ch 228.

[97] *Torbett v Faulkner* [1952] 2 TLR 659.

entitled to recover possession of the house on the basis that the company had no title to grant the tenancy in the first place.

It should be noted that all substantial property transactions between a company and its directors must comply with the requirements of the CA 1990, as amended; those are discussed in detail in Ch 16, below.

(ii) Insurable interests

[4.039] The distinction between the company's property and the members' property may occasionally work to deprive the controllers of a right or a remedy which they might have had if they had not transferred their property to a company. This is clearly illustrated in *Macaura v Northern Assurance Co Ltd*[98]. Macaura sold all of the timber from his Co Tyrone estate to The Irish Canadian Saw Mills Ltd for £42,000, which was paid for by the allotment to him of all of that company's 42,000 fully paid £1 shares. When the wood was subsequently destroyed by fire, it was held that Macaura could not recover on an insurance policy taken out in his name. 'No shareholder', Lord Buckmaster explained, 'has any right to any item of property owned by the company, for he has no legal or equitable interest therein.' Since the company owns company property in its own right, a shareholder cannot insure company property, because he has no insurable interest in it[99].

A shareholder can, however, cover himself against loss by the company by insuring his shares (rather than the company's assets) against a drop in their value, for it is the shares, and not the company's assets, in which the shareholder has any legal or equitable interest. This was successfully done in *Wilson v Jones*[100].

(iii) Compensation

[4.040] Where compensation is payable in respect of loss suffered by a company, the shareholders have no right to payment. In *Stewarts Supermarkets Ltd v Secretary of State*[101], a holding company was held not to be entitled to recover compensation under the Northern Ireland criminal injuries compensation scheme for damage to its subsidiary's business in a terrorist attack, since the damage suffered was to the property of the subsidiary – not the holding company, its majority shareholder. In *Roberts v Coventry Corporation*[102], the defendant had compulsorily purchased the plaintiff's freehold which the plaintiff had leased to a company of which she was the majority shareholder. The court refused to allow her claim for compensation in respect of the diminution in the value of her shares resulting from the company's relocation, since the loss was the company's, and not hers. This principle was relied upon by the Irish Supreme Court in *O'Neill v Ryan, Ryan Air Ltd, Aer Lingus plc, Kennedy, GPA Group*

98 *Macaura v Northern Assurance Co Ltd* [1925] AC 619. *Cf* the Canadian case of *Kosmopolous v Constitution Insurance Co of Canada* (1984) 149 DLR (3d) 77, where a sole shareholder was held to have an insurable interest in the company property.

99 See *Verderame v Commercial Union Assurance Co plc* [1992] BCLC 793, discussed in further detail at para **[4.050]**.

100 *Wilson v Jones* (1866) LR 1 Exch 193.

101 *Stewarts Supermarkets Ltd v Secretary of State* [1982] NI 286.

102 *Roberts v Coventry Corporation* [1947] 1 All ER 308.

Ltd and Transport Analysis Inc[103]. In that case, the plaintiff alleged that breaches of competition law by the last four defendants had caused a diminution in the value of his shares in the second defendant, Ryan Air Ltd. The Supreme Court struck out his action for damages on the basis that such actions by the defendants could not cause personal loss to the shareholder. Blayney J quoted from the English Court of Appeal's decision in *Prudential Assurance Co Ltd v Newman Industries Ltd (No 2)*[104] as follows:

> 'What [the shareholder] cannot do is recover damages merely because the company in which he is interested has suffered damage. He cannot recover a sum equal to the diminution in the market value of his shares, or equal to the likely diminution in dividend, because such a loss is merely a reflection of the loss suffered by the company. The shareholder does not suffer any personal loss ... The plaintiff's shares are merely a right of participation in the company on the terms of the articles of association. The shares themselves, his right of participation, are not directly affected by the wrongdoing. The plaintiff still holds all the shares as his own absolutely unencumbered property. The deceit practised upon the plaintiff does not affect the shares; it merely enables the defendant to rob the company[105].'

By way of corollary, however, a determination that a company is not entitled to compensation does not *ipso facto* estop the shareholders from seeking such compensation in their own right. Thus, in *Belton v Carlow County Council*[106]the Supreme Court, in a case stated from the Circuit Court, applied the principle in *Salomon's case* to hold that the applicant shareholder was not estopped from claiming compensation under the Malicious Injuries Act 1981 for damage by fire to his premises, even though the applicant's company had been party to earlier proceedings in which it was determined that the fire was caused by a neighbour.

(iv) Statutory tenancies

[4.041] The distinction between the company's property and the members' property is of particular relevance as far as the rights of tenants to statutory leases are concerned. In *Tunstall v Steigman*[107], a landlord applied to resist the grant of a statutory tenancy to her tenant on the ground that she needed the premises for the expansion of her business which was carried on in an adjoining premises. Her application failed on the basis that the business was not carried on by her, but by a company of which she was the controlling shareholder.

Conversely, in *Pegler v Craven*[108], an application by a tenant to obtain a statutory tenancy was refused because the premises had not been occupied by him but by a company of which he was the majority shareholder. Indeed, the company was held not to be entitled to such a tenancy either, because it was a mere licensee of the tenant and not a tenant itself. The rigours of that decision have been tempered in Ireland by s 5(3) of

103 *O'Neill v Ryan, Ryan Air Ltd, Aer Lingus plc, Kennedy, GPA Group Ltd and Transport Analysis Inc* [1993] ILRM 557.

104 *Prudential Assurance Co Ltd v Newman Industries Ltd (No 2)* [1982] Ch 204 at 222.

105 *O'Neill v Ryan, Ryan Air Ltd, Aer Lingus plc, Kennedy, GPA Group Ltd and Transport Analysis Inc* [1993] ILRM 557 at 569. See further Ch 19, *Shareholders' Remedies*.

106 *Belton v Carlow County Council* [1997] 1 IR 172.

107 *Tunstall v Steigman* [1961] AC 12.

108 *Pegler v Craven* [1952] 2 QB 69.

the Landlord and Tenant (Amendment) Act 1980, which allows a tenant to obtain rights to a statutory tenancy where occupation is by a company which is controlled by him and which occupies the premises under a licence from him.

(d) Suing and being sued

[4.042] Since the company is a separate and distinct legal person, and is not *per se* the agent of its shareholders; it is the company, and not its members, who may be sued for its obligations and who may sue to enforce its rights. Here, the following matters are considered:

(i) Contracts;
(ii) Torts;
(iii) Crimes;
(iv) Constitutional rights and duties;
(v) Legal rights and duties.

Further practical aspects of corporate litigation are considered in Ch 6, below.

(i) Contracts

[4.043] 'Only a person who is a party to a contract can sue on it ... [but] a principal not named in the contract may sue upon it if the promisee really contracted as his agent'.' So held Viscount Haldane LC in *Dunlop Pneumatic Tyre Co Ltd v Selfridge & Co Ltd*[109]. A shareholder cannot sue to enforce a contract made by his company simply by virtue of the fact that he is a shareholder, because he is not a party to the contract. Nor can he claim as a principal not named in the contract, because companies are not *per se* the agents of their shareholders[110].

[4.044] Likewise a shareholder cannot be sued on contracts, including loan contracts, made by the company[111]. It need hardly be said, however, that the loans in question must genuinely have been contracted between the company and the lender and not between the controller and the lender; the courts take a dim view of controllers who attempt to evade their own personal obligations by pretending they were contracting on behalf of the company. In *Waters v Kelly*[112], the defendant sought to deny liability on a loan of approximately £33,500 from a friend in 1999 by claiming, at a late stage in summary judgment proceedings, that the loan was made to a company controlled by him rather than to him personally. Irvine J found no evidence of any intent on either side that the loan was to be anything other than a personal loan between the friends. In a scathing criticism of the defendant's conduct she stated[113]:

> 'Regrettably, the court further concludes that the defendant has sought to defraud one of his personal friends by the manner in which he has attempted to defend these proceedings

---

109 *Dunlop Pneumatic Tyre Co Ltd v Selfridge & Co Ltd* [1915] AC 847.

110 *Per* Macnaghten LJ in *Salomon's* case; see para **[4.029]**.

111 *Daimler Co Ltd v Continental Tyre & Rubber Co (Great Britain) Ltd* [1916] 2 AC 307; *Maclaine Watson & Co Ltd v Department of Trade and Industry* [1990] BCLC 102 – 'Members of a body corporate are not liable for the debts of a body corporate because they are not parties to the corporation's contracts', *per* Templeman LJ, at 108.

112 *Waters v Kelly* [2009] IEHC 222.

113 *Waters v Kelly* [2009] IEHC 222.

> ... What the court finds most distasteful ... is that he has sought to rely on the existence of the corporate veil to absolve himself of any personal liability.'

[4.045] A significant practical consequence of the members not being liable for their company's contractual obligations is that third parties dealing with the company – notably financial institutions – will often require the controlling shareholders, directors (or both) personally to guarantee the performance of the company's obligations[114].

[4.046] Controllers of newly incorporated companies should also be aware that they may continue to be liable for existing obligations to customers who have dealt with them in their capacity as sole traders or partners. In *The Pitner Lighting Co of Ireland v Geddis and Pickering*[115], the defendants had been partners for a few months before incorporation, during which time they contracted to purchase goods from the defendants on account. No monies were paid to the plaintiffs on the account during this period. Upon incorporation, the plaintiffs continued to supply goods to the new company on the same account, and the new company paid some, but not all, of the balance outstanding on the account. The plaintiffs then re-arranged their accounts, appropriating the amount paid by the company as being in respect of goods supplied to the company after incorporation. They then sued the defendants for payment in respect of the goods supplied prior to incorporation. The court found the defendants liable.

[4.047] Contracts by companies are subject to the *ultra vires* doctrine, whereby the contract will be void if not contemplated in the company's objects clause as stated in the memorandum of association. Legislative intervention has done much, however, to temper the rigours of this doctrine, which is discussed in detail in Ch 7.

[4.048] A company cannot, as a separate person, be sued for the contractual obligations of its members, and a misrepresentation or failure to disclose relevant information to a third party by a shareholder does not affect a contract entered into by the third party with the company, since the misrepresentation or non-disclosure must come from the company itself[116]. But the possibility of a company being liable for the contractual activities of its members through agency principles should not be forgotten. This is also discussed in further detail in Ch 7. Attention should be paid to the intentions of the contracting parties. Persons who negotiate contracts with controlling shareholders may intend to contract with them in their personal capacity – particularly if they have dealt with them before as sole traders or partners – while the shareholder may intend to act on the company's behalf. In such cases no contract will be formed because the parties will not be *ad idem*[117].

---

114 See Ch 5, *Disregarding Separate Legal Personality*, at para **[5.015]** *et seq.*

115 *The Pitner Lighting Co of Ireland v Geddis and Pickering* [1912] 2 IR 163.

116 *Bell v Lever Brothers Ltd* [1932] AC 161. Where a question of knowledge or intention arises in relation to whether the misrepresentation was fraudulent, negligent or innocent, the company's knowledge or ignorance must be found in the minds of its agents: *Regina Fur Co Ltd v Bossom* [1958] 2 Lloyd's Rep 466; *UBAF Ltd v European American Banking Corporation* [1984] QB 713.

117 *J Smallman Ltd v O'Moore & Newman* [1959] IR 220.

(ii) Torts

[4.049] A corporation has the same capacity as an individual to sue for torts committed against it[118]. Since the company is a separate legal person, it is the company, not its shareholders, who may sue in respect of torts committed against it[119].

It appears settled that a company may sue even though the tort occurred in connection with an activity which was *ultra vires* the company[120]. Naturally, some torts (eg, assault and battery, false imprisonment, etc) cannot, by their nature, be committed against a corporation. A company may, however, sue for an injury to its reputation in the way of its business by libel or slander, such as, for example, an allegation that the company is insolvent[121].

[4.050] Where the tort complained of has its foundation in *negligence*, ie, breach of a duty of care[122], it is quite possible for the one act of negligence to amount both to breach of a duty owed to the company and, at the same time, to breach of a duty owed to a shareholder. This will be so if both the company and the shareholder can be regarded as 'neighbours'[123] whom the tortfeasor ought reasonably to have had in his contemplation when directing his mind towards the act or omission in question.

Where, however, a third party provides services involving skill, advice or judgment to a company, the duty of care owed by the provider of the service to the company will not, in general, extend to the shareholders – especially where the shareholder suffers only economic loss[124]. This is well illustrated in *McSweeney v Bourke*[125], where a financial consultant, engaged by a group of companies in financial difficulties, advised the group that one prudent course of action open to it was to obtain an injection of further capital from two of its controlling shareholders. The two shareholders in question had been in close consultation with the consultant during the formulation of his proposal. The group of companies obtained the investment from the shareholders in line with the consultant's proposal. When the group failed to recover from its financial difficulties, the two shareholders brought an action against the consultant for negligent misstatement giving rise to economic loss. Carroll J dismissed their action, holding on

118 See generally, McMahon & Binchy, *The Irish Law of Torts* (3rd edn, Bloomsbury Professional, 2000), Ch 39.

119 *Rainham Chemical Works Ltd (In Liquidation) v Belvedere Fish Guano Co Ltd* [1921] AC 465; *British Thomson-Houston Co v Sterling Accessories Ltd* [1924] 2 Ch 33.

120 *National Telephone Company Ltd v The Constables of St Peter Port* [1900] AC 317. See Jenkins, 'Corporate Liability in Tort and the Doctrine of Ultra Vires' (1970) 5 Ir Jur (ns) 11.

121 *South Hetton Coal Co v North Eastern News Association* [1894] 1 QB 133; *Irish People's Assurance Society v Dublin City Assurance Co* [1929] IR 25; *D & L Caterers and Jackson v D'Ajou* [1945] KB 364. *Gormanstown Equestrian Centre Ltd v Anglo Irish Bank Corporation plc* (14 July 1994, unreported) CC, Judge McGuinness.

122 See generally McMahon & Binchy, *The Irish Law of Torts* (3rd edn, Bloomsbury Professional, 2000), Ch 6.

123 See Lord Atkin's famous *dictum* in *Donoghue v Stevenson* [1932] AC 562 at 580.

124 See *Securities Trust Ltd v Hugh Moore & Alexander Ltd* [1964] IR 417; *Hedley Byrne & Co Ltd v Heller & Partners Ltd* [1964] AC 465; and, generally, McMahon & Binchy, *The Irish Law of Torts* (3rd edn, Bloomsbury Professional, 2000), Ch 10.

125 *McSweeney v Bourke* (24 November 1980, unreported) HC, Carroll J.

the facts that the consultant had not been negligent in any way[126]. She added, however, that if the consultant had been negligent, his negligence could only have been in relation to his client, the group of companies, and not to the two shareholders. She explained:

> '[I]rrespective of contract, the adviser has a primary duty of care to the client and there may or may not be a duty to third parties. If the advice given is not given negligently *vis-à-vis* the client in the first instance but is given with all due care, there is no breach of duty to the client. If an adviser is not negligent *vis-à-vis* the client and does not purport to advise any person other than the client, I do not see how a third party who knows the advice given to the client and who carries out the steps outlined in that advice (ultimately to his own detriment) can claim that the advice was negligent in relation to him ... [T]he only reliance the two shareholders, as such, could place on the advice was that it was good advice for the group as a whole. They were intended to act on the advice but in the context that the advice was given with the interest of the group in mind. Once [the consultant] did not hold himself out as advising the shareholders as well as the group there was no additional duty placed on [him] to add any words of warning in relation to the risks attached to further capital investment in the group. There is no evidence that [the consultant] undertook an additional and separate duty of advising the shareholders, as such, with a conflicting interest[127].'

Controlling shareholders should seek independent assurances from parties advising the company before relying on advice given to the company – or they should seek independent advice from third parties. This, as shall be seen[128], is of particular importance where reliance is placed by the shareholders on advice given to the company by its accountants or auditors. Similar steps should also be taken where other services are provided to the company, as may be seen from *Verderame v Commercial Union Assurance Co plc*[129]. There, a company engaged the services of an insurance broker to obtain insurance cover. The broker obtained cover in the name of one of the controlling shareholders. When some of the company property was subsequently stolen, the controlling shareholder-director was unable to recover on the policy because he had no insurable interest in the stolen property[130]. Instead, he and his wife, a fellow controlling shareholder-director, sued the insurance broker for damages for loss of business, alleging that the broker owed them a duty of care when effecting insurance for the company. The Court of Appeal unequivocally rejected the contention that any such duty of care existed. Balcombe LJ explained:

> '... the directors are seeking to go behind the corporate status of the company. In effect they are saying to the brokers, 'By failing to arrange proper insurance cover for the company you broke a duty which you owed to us as directors and shareholders of the company and you are liable to us for our loss of emoluments' ... if this submission were to succeed the principles of the leading case of *Salomon v Salomon & Co Ltd* would become a dead letter[131].'

The fact that the company was a small private company made no difference to the court. Nourse LJ added:

---

[126] *McSweeney v Bourke* (24 November 1980, unreported) HC at p 22 of the transcript.

[127] *McSweeney v Bourke* (24 November 1980, unreported) HC at pp 17–18 of the transcript.

[128] See Ch 17, *Financial Statements, Auditors and Annual Return*, at para **[17.330]** *et seq*.

[129] *Verderame v Commercial Union Assurance Co plc* [1992] BCLC 793.

[130] See para **[4.037]**.

[131] *Verderame v Commercial Union Assurance Co plc* [1992] BCLC 793 at 802.

> 'It being accepted that there was a contract between the brokers and the company alone, the proposition that the brokers also came under a duty of care in tort to the directors is not only novel but to my mind startling. If it was sustained it would have very wide-ranging consequences, not only in relation to insurance brokers, but also to others who provide services to small private companies, for example, solicitors, accountants, estate agents and so forth. Not only would it pierce the corporate veil on a vast scale, it would lead to quite unjustifiable procedural impracticabilities and rights or potential rights of double recovery. In my view it is simply unarguable that a duty of care can arise in such circumstances[132].'

[4.051] A corporation may also, of course, be sued in respect of torts committed by it. The fact that a company's objects clause does not contemplate commission of tortious acts does not enable the company simply to avoid liability on the grounds that the activity complained of is *ultra vires*[133]. To say otherwise would be 'to say that no corporation can ever be sued for a public wrong'[134], and that would be absurd. Similarly, where the tort occurs in connection with the commission of an *ultra vires* activity (eg, where a bus knocks someone down and the bus is owned and operated by a company whose objects do not contemplate the operation of a bus business), a claim in tort will not be prohibited[135].

[4.052] Most commonly, a company's tortious liability arises *vicariously* through the operation of the principle of *respondeat superior*. Where a wrong is committed in the course of the company's employees' activities, the company will be vicariously liable as employer in much the same way as a natural employer would, regardless of whether the company consented to the particular act in question[136]. The company may be entitled to an indemnity from the servant or agent in such circumstances[137]. On the other hand, some torts may properly be said to be the result of the company's *own* acts – such as where they are done or authorised under the direction of the board of directors or the shareholders in general meeting. In such cases the courts will look to the actions of those who control the company. In *Lennard's Carrying Co v Asiatic Petroleum Co*[138], Viscount Haldane LC said:

> 'My lords, a corporation is an abstraction. It has no mind of its own any more than it has a body of its own; its active and directing will must consequently be sought in the person of somebody who for some purposes may be called an agent, but who is really the directing mind and will of the corporation, the very ego and centre of the personality of the corporation ... [T]he fault or privity is the fault or privity of somebody who is not merely a servant or agent for whom the company is liable upon the footing of *respondeat superior*;

132 *Verderame v Commercial Union Assurance Co plc* [1992] BCLC 793 at 804.

133 See Jenkins, 'Corporate Liability in Tort and the Doctrine of Ultra Vires' (1970) 5 Ir Jur (ns) 11; Goodhart, 'Corporate Liability in Tort and the Ultra Vires Doctrine' (1926) 2 Cam LJ 350; Warren, 'Torts by Corporations in Ultra Vires Undertakings' (1925) Cam LJ 180.

134 *Per* Avory J in *Campbell v Paddington Corporation* [1911] 1 KB 869 at 875.

135 See Jenkins, 'Corporate Liability in Tort and the Doctrine of Ultra Vires' (1970) 5 Ir Jur (ns) 11 at pp 17–19.

136 See, eg, *Pearson & Son Ltd v Dublin Corporation* [1907] 2 IR 27. See generally McMahon & Binchy, *The Irish Law of Torts* (3rd edn, Bloomsbury Professional, 2000), para 35.10 *et seq*.

137 *Lister v Romford Ice and Cold Storage Co Ltd* [1957] AC 555.

138 *Lennard's Carrying Co v Asiatic Petroleum Co* [1915] AC 705.

> but somebody for whom the company is liable because the action is the very action of the company itself[139].'

The above statement of principle was quoted with approval by McCarthy J in *Taylor v Smith*[140], and was later applied by the Supreme Court in *Superwood Holdings plc and Others v Sun Alliance and London Plc Assurance plc and Others*[141] with the qualification that the directing mind and will of a corporation was not necessarily that of the person or persons who had general management and control since the directing mind and will could be found in different persons in respect of different activities[142]. The Supreme Court in *Superwood* accepted the artificiality of the approach 'in seeking to force complex and varying corporate structures into a uniform human mould'[143]. One notable shortcoming of the doctrine, which was alluded to by the Supreme Court, is that where power is diffused through a corporation it may be impossible to identify any one person as representing the directing mind and will.

[4.053] The principle is well illustrated in *The Lady Gwendolen*[144], where a ship owned by Arthur Guinness & Son Co (Dublin) Ltd was involved in a collision through failure to use radar during heavy fog. The ship had failed to use radar largely because the captain had never been fully instructed in its use. The company was vicariously liable for the captain's negligence, but ss 502 and 503 of the Merchant Shipping Act 1894 allowed the company's liability to be limited if the damage occurred without the 'actual fault or privity' of the company. The court was able to find such fault or privity by the company by looking at its management structure. The responsibility for transport and transport staff had been delegated by the board of directors to an assistant managing director, who was at fault by having failed to ensure that the captain was properly instructed. His fault was imputed as the actual fault of the company; and the company, accordingly, could not limit its liability under the Mercantile Shipping Act of 1894. Therefore, where the tort complained of requires malicious intent to be proved, or where some defence[145] to an action in tort requires that the act not be done maliciously, the courts will show no hesitation in imputing the malice of the controllers of the company to the company itself. It appears that proof of the company's liability in tort does not automatically prove that all the controlling members of the company are liable as well unless they can be shown to have actually participated in the commission of the tort or they have authorised or directed its commission[146].

[4.054] Where a company is identifiable with only one person as its directing mind and will it cannot, thus, rely on any fraud thus imputed to it as a ground for suing a third

[139] *Lennard's Carrying Co v Asiatic Petroleum Co* [1915] AC 705 at 713–714.

[140] *Taylor v Smith* [1991] IR 142 at 166.

[141] *Superwood Holdings plc and Others v Sun Alliance and London Plc Assurance plc and Others* (27 June 1995, unreported) SC.

[142] Following *El Ajou v Dollar Land Holdings plc and Another* [1994] 2 All ER 685.

[143] See Ussher, *Company Law in Ireland* (1986), p 39.

[144] *The Lady Gwendolen* [1965] 2 WLR 91.

[145] Eg, the defence of qualified privilege to an action in defamation; see generally McMahon & Binchy, *The Irish Law of Torts* (3rd edn, Bloomsbury Professional, 2000), para 34.134 *et seq*.

[146] *Rainham Chemical Works Ltd (In Liquidation) v Belvedere Fish Guano Co Ltd* [1921] 2 AC 465; *Williams v Natural Life Health Foods Ltd* [1998] BCC 428.

party. This is well illustrated in *Stone & Rolls Ltd (In Liquidation) v Moore Steven*[147], where a shadow director, the sole directing mind and will of the company, had used the company to procure frauds on a number of banks, effectively lining his own pockets at their, and the company's, expense. The liquidator of the company subsequently sued the company auditors on behalf of the company on the basis that they had failed to discover the dishonest nature of the transactions. Lord Phillips, for the bare majority in the House of Lords, considered that the controller's fraud was the company's fraud and the company's claim should be denied as a base claim under the principle of *ex turpi causa*, on the basis that the company's directing mind and will had 'filled it with turpitude' and there was no innocent participator within the company[148]. The company was effectively the fraudster so far as Lord Philips was concerned. Some commentators have questioned, however, whether the company ought to have been regarded as one with the controller once it entered liquidation whereupon its assets belonged no longer in effect to the controller but to its creditors[149].

(iii) Crime

[4.055] The topic of corporate criminal liability is considered here under the following headings:

(I) Corporations as prosecutors;
(II) Justifications for holding corporations criminally liable;
(III) Practical limitations of corporate criminal liability;
(IV) Principles of attribution of corporate criminal liability;

(I) Corporations as prosecutors

[4.056] An important common law power of members of the public is the power to institute criminal prosecutions – whether or not they themselves have been the victims – as 'common informers'[150]. This power to act as a common informer at common law, however, is not available to corporations[151]. In *Cumann Luthchleas Gael Teo v District Justice Windle*[152], Dublin Corporation, acting as a common informer, had obtained an order from the respondent sending the GAA forward for criminal trial for breaches of the Fire Services Act 1981 arising out of its occupation and management of its premises at Croke Park. The Supreme Court quashed the order, Finlay CJ saying:

> a body corporate cannot, under a general common law principle, prosecute as a common informer or a private prosecutor either in relation to summary offences or in relation to indictable offences up to the stage of return for trial.

---

147 *Stone & Rolls Ltd (In Liquidation) v Moore Steven* [2009] AC 1391.

148 *Stone & Rolls Ltd (In Liquidation) v Moore Steven* [2009] AC 1391 at 1462.

149 See Ferran, 'Corporate Attribution and the Directing Mind and Will' (2011) 127 LQR 239. Ferran argues that the anthropomorphic convolutions of the case distracted the court from the real question – the scope of duty of the auditors.

150 See *The People v Roddy* [1977] IR 177.

151 Statute can confer express power on corporate agencies to prosecute, however – see Horan, *Corporate Crime* (2011, Bloomsbury Professional), at para 4.029 *et seq.*

152 *Cumann Luthchleas Gael Teo v District Justice Windle* [1994] 1 IR 533.

(II) Justifications for holding corporations criminally liable

[4.057] Though companies may not prosecute at common law, it is well established that in appropriate circumstances they may *be prosecuted*, whether vicariously or personally, for criminal offences. The field of corporate criminal liability is fraught, however, with theoretical and practical difficulties[153], and outside of the regulatory regimes imposed by statute for the protection of health and safety, the environment, or the security of financial markets, for example, there is no real tradition in Ireland of companies being prosecuted for general crimes[154].

The criminal law has traditionally been concerned primarily with the responsibility of individuals rather than organisations. Old aphorisms that corporations are not capable of being subjected to the criminal law since it punishes 'violations of the social duties that belong to men and subjects'[155], and corporations cannot be expected to have a conscience when they have 'no soul to be damned, and no body to be kicked'[156] have partially fallen from favour in the modern context since corporations can be and are subjected to the criminal law under the regulatory regime. A fundamental difficulty remains, however – should the general focus of criminal law be confined to the individuals acting within the company rather than the company itself?

[4.058] Proponents of corporate criminal responsibility argue that the synergies of corporate organisation are not fully reflected in an individualistic approach. Many companies, it is argued, promote themselves as distinct *personae*, through advertising or otherwise. To fail to attach blame to the publicly perceived wrongdoer creates a perception that the real wrongdoer is getting away with criminal activity. Conversely, it is argued that a conviction of an individual within the company should not result in automatic conviction of the company itself absent significant corporate participation in the crime or absent substantial policy considerations such as would justify the imposition of liability on one person (ie, the corporation) for the acts of another (ie, the individual)[157]. Such policy considerations are considered justified under our legal tradition only in the regulatory field.

Secondly, it is said that a focus on individual wrongdoers within the corporate structure deflects attention from the fact that corporations may have a 'momentum and dynamic'[158] of their own which seriously influences individual conduct. As against such concerns, it is said that all human activity – whether within the corporate environment or otherwise – is influenced by a variety of factors (social and cultural, familial,

---

153 See generally Wells, *Corporations and Criminal Responsibility* (2nd edn, Oxford University Press, 2001); Fisse & Braithwaite, *Corporations, Crime and Accountability* (1993, Cambridge University Press); Horan, *Corporate Crime* (2011, Bloomsbury Professional).

154 See Law Reform Commission, *Consultation Paper on Corporate Homicide* (2002); *Report on Corporate Killing* (LRC 77-2005); and Horan, *Corporate Crime* (2011, Bloomsbury Professional).

155 *Per* Denman LCJ in *R v Great North of England Railway Company* (1846) 9 QB 315 at 326.

156 *Per* Edward, First Baron Thurlow (1731–1806), Lord Chancellor. See Coffee, 'No Soul to Damn: No Body to Kick:' An Unscandalised Inquiry into the Problem of Corporate Punishment' (1981) 79 Mich L Rev 386.

157 *Re Article 26 and the Employment Equality Bill 1996* [1997] IR 321.

158 Ashworth, *Principles of Criminal Law* (6th edn, Oxford University Press, 2009).

institutional, political, economic, etc)[159]. Such external influences do not offer a defence to individual liability, though they can be given substantial weight in mitigation of sentence.

A third, related, argument is that it just may not be possible to attach liability to any individual within a corporation since the fault may lie in the system of management – a '*management failure*' – so that the responsibility for the conduct is dispersed throughout the organisation and diluted rather than concentrated in any individual[160]. In such cases nobody – corporation or individual – can be prosecuted. The fundamental question in such cases, however, is whether management failure is an inherently criminal thing, or whether it ought to be so where it has serious or fatal consequences – particularly given that 'management failure' is difficult to define. Within the relatively new science of organisational understanding there is still no uniform concept of what exactly management failure is[161]. If management failure is considered to be a mischief, as all accept it is, it can be argued, then, that it is better to tackle it at its roots by introducing measures designed to improve management practices (eg, the system of education monitoring and supervision employed by the Health and Safety Authority in the context of safety related issues, or the Corporate Governance Codes following the *Turnbull*, *Cadbury* and *Hempel Reports* in the context of investor protection)[162].

[4.059] The role of the criminal law in supporting such measures is arguably to follow with sanction for serious breach of the regulatory code rather than to impose vague prohibitions on under-understood areas of activity; but such arguments seem to be losing ground to the political will in the realm of corporate activity resulting in death. In 1996, the Law Commission of England and Wales proposed a new offence of homicide aimed specifically at corporations[163]. Following a decade of debate, the new crime finally made it onto the statute books in the Corporate Manslaughter and Corporate Homicide Act 2007. The offence, called 'corporate manslaughter' in England, Wales and Northern Ireland, and 'corporate homicide' in Scotland, is committed where the way in which a corporation's[164] activities are managed or organised causes death, or amounts to a gross breach of a relevant duty of care owed by the organisation to the deceased[165].

---

159 See Wells, *Corporations and Criminal Responsibility* (2nd edn, Oxford University Press, 2001), pp 147 *et seq*.

160 See Fisse & Braithwaite, *Corporations, Crime and Accountability* (1993, Cambridge University Press), Chs 1 & 4; Wells, *Corporations and Criminal Responsibility* (2nd edn, Oxford University Press, 2001), pp 70 and 148. The Law Commission of England and Wales proposed, in 1996, a new offence of homicide aimed specifically at corporations. The offence, 'corporate killing,' would be committed where a 'management failure' was a cause of death and the failure fell far below what could reasonably have been expected of the corporation; this is addressed in further detail at **[4.059]** below.

161 See Wells, *Corporations and Criminal Responsibility* (2nd edn, Oxford University Press, 2001), Ch 8.

162 See Ch 29, *Public Limited Companies and SEs*, at para **[29.089]**.

163 Law Commission of England and Wales, *Legislating the Criminal Code: Involuntary Manslaughter* (4 March 1996) Law Comm 237 (HC 171).

164 The Law Commission recommended that the offence would be limited to corporations; but the Act as enacted extends beyond corporations to partnerships, government departments, and police forces – Corporate Manslaughter and Corporate Homicide Act 2007, s 1(2).

165 Corporate Manslaughter and Corporate Homicide Act 2007, s 1(1).

Substantial involvement by senior management in the organisation of the relevant activity is required before liability can be imposed. The Irish Law Reform Commission has followed suit; in its 2005 Report on *Corporate Killing*[166] it recommended a new offence of 'corporate manslaughter' which would be committed, according to clause 3 of the Commission's Draft Corporate Manslaughter Bill, as follows:

> '(1) Where an undertaking causes the death of a human person by gross negligence that undertaking is guilty of an offence called 'corporate manslaughter'.
>
> (2) An undertaking causes death by gross negligence where
>
> (a) it owed a duty of care to the deceased human person;
>
> (b) it breached that duty of care in that it failed to meet the standard of care in subsection (3);
>
> (c) the breach of duty was of a very high degree and involved a significant risk of death or serious personal harm; and
>
> (d) the breach of duty caused the death of the human person.
>
> (3) The standard of care required of the undertaking is to take all reasonable measures to anticipate and prevent risks to human life, having due regard to the size and circumstances of the undertaking.'

The Draft Bill goes on in sub-clause 3(5) to identify the matters which should go towards determining whether an undertaking has breached the requisite standard of care:

> '(5) In assessing whether the undertaking breached the standard of care in subsection (3) the court shall have regard to any or all of the following
>
> (a) the way in which the activities of the undertaking are managed or organised by its high managerial agents;
>
> (b) the allocation of responsibility within the undertaking;
>
> (c) the procedural decision-making rules of the undertaking;
>
> (d) the policies of the undertaking;
>
> (e) the training and supervision of employees by the undertaking;
>
> (f) the response of the undertaking to previous incidents involving a risk of death or serious personal harm;
>
> (g) the stated and actual goals of the undertaking;
>
> (h) the adequacy of the communications systems within the undertaking including systems for communicating information to others affected by the activities of the undertaking;
>
> (i) the regulatory environment in which the undertaking operates, including any statutory duties to which the undertaking is subject;
>
> (j) any assurance systems to which the undertaking has subscribed;
>
> (k) whether the undertaking was operating within the terms of a contract or licence made or granted under legislation.'

The Law Reform Commission's' proposals have not made it onto the statute books, though there have been political murmurings that they will ultimately receive legislative force[167], which is hardly surprising given the widespread more general concern about

166 LRC 77–2005.

167 See Horan, *Corporate Crime* (2011, Bloomsbury Professional), para 1.49.

white collar crime in the wake of the banking collapse; but such promises have not yielded results to date.

[4.060] Even if management failure is to be criminalised, whether it results in death or some other wrong, there remains the issue of whether it is the corporation itself or the individuals within it who should be penalised – or both? The United Kingdom has gone down the purely corporate route; s 18 of the Corporate Manslaughter and Corporate Homicide Act 2007 provides that 'an individual cannot be guilty of aiding, abetting, counselling or procuring the commission of an offence of corporate manslaughter'. The Irish proposals adopt the opposite tack by prescribing dual offences; under clause 4 of the Law Reform Commission's Draft Bill, a high managerial agent of an undertaking convicted of corporate manslaughter can be convicted personally of an offence of 'grossly negligent management causing death' where they knew or ought to have known of the risk but failed to take reasonable steps to eliminate it.

Though this may raise an apparent spectre of double jeopardy in some circumstances, particularly where ownership and control are closely held, the Irish courts have not been afraid to fix criminal liability on both the company and its directors, particularly where statute so permits. In *DPP v Roseberry Construction Ltd*[168], the Court of Criminal Appeal upheld fines of £200,000 against a construction company in respect of breaches of the Health and Safety Acts which resulted in a fatality on site. The company had appealed the fines on the basis that they were excessive, and that the principal of the company had also been convicted and fined in respect of the same breaches. Hardiman J, delivering the judgment of the court, stressed that there would be no double counting where the director and the company were separate legal entities, stating as follows[169]:

> 'A number of points are made, some relating to points of principle, some relating to the specific circumstances of the case. One in particular, we think requires attention. It is to the effect that the penalties imposed, bearing in mind that the principal of the company was also fined, amount in some degree to double counting because, as counsel for the accused said, the director, Mr McIntyre, and the accused were basically the same thing. That is a point of view on which it is, perhaps, important to express an opinion. There is no obligation on any person conducting a trade, whether it is the building trade or any other business, to incorporate the business which he is conducting. He is entitled to trade, as no doubt he started, in his own name and to bear personally the risks attaching to that, namely the commercial risks. The director, as many other people, chose not to do this but to incorporate a company for the purpose of interposing the company between himself and various liabilities which might arise in the course of business. That is a thing which a person is fully entitled to do. If someone sued the director in respect of the liabilities of the accused, one can assume the director or his lawyers would be quick to point out that these are two completely different entities. He has drawn down the veil of incorporation, the effect of which is to render him, except in restricted circumstances arising under the Companies Acts, safe from liability for the accused's debts.
>
> The same must clearly apply in reverse in circumstances like these. The director and the accused are not 'basically the same thing'. The accused may be a creation of the director's, but it is created with the express purpose of being a separate entity. Moreover, s 48 of the Act of 1989, as counsel for the prosecutor points out, specifically provides for the liability

[168] *DPP v Roseberry Construction Ltd* [2003] 4 IR 338.

[169] *DPP v Roseberry Construction Ltd* [2003] 4 IR 338 at 339.

> of an individual who is a director in addition to the liability of a company. That is plainly provided by a statute to which the court must give effect. The director and the accused were separately charged in recognition of that distinction and we cannot at all see that it is a point suggestive of an error in principle that an entity which the director, also an accused, expressly created to be separate from himself should be separately pursued in relation to this matter.'

[4.061] Finally, it is sometimes argued that corporations should be the subject of criminal responsibility because it is they, rather than their individual constituents, who are best placed to prevent or remedy the defects in their operations which led to the incident. Such 'rehabilitative' arguments assume, of course, that corporations will react to criminal sanction by mending their ways and by adopting remedial policies. There is no evidence of such a trend, however. Corporations, like any other offender, measure the impact of criminal sanction against a variety of scales: the risk of offending; the risk of detection; the cost of compliance; and the cost of sanction *versus* the potential for profit, etc. Such balancing exercises are a function in the response to all criminal liability, and they vary little whether the offence is part of a regulatory regime or part of the 'mainstream' criminal law. Accordingly, the 'rehabilitative' argument is of little assistance in the argument that the criminal liability of corporations should be extended beyond the regulatory regime – where, as it happens, there is greater scope for the imposition of remedial measures

(III) Practical limitations of corporate criminal liability

[4.062] Beyond such fundamental difficulties, the circumstances in which companies will be criminally liable are limited by a number of practical considerations.

First, certain crimes, such as bigamy or rape, cannot physically be attributed to corporations without absurdity. That is not to say, however, that they could not be made criminally liable as secondary parties for such crimes. For example, where a film company supervises intercourse between a fifteen-year-old girl and a fifteen-year-old boy, there seems to be no reason why the company and its controllers could not be convicted as secondary parties to unlawful sexual intercourse.

Secondly, punishments involving death, corporal punishment, or imprisonment are incapable of being suffered by corporations[170]. Therefore, a company cannot be convicted of crimes, such as murder, which carry mandatory sentences of imprisonment. Indeed, the only possible *direct* punishment for companies in the modern Irish repertoire of criminal penalties seems to be a fine or an order for sequestration[171]. The use of the fine is sometimes criticised[172]. It is argued that companies are well placed to 'buy their way out of justice,' and that fines in any event punish innocent shareholders rather than

---

[170] See *The King (Cottingham) v The Justices of County Cork* [1906] 2 IR 415, *per* Johnson J at 427; *Pearks, Gunston and Tee Ltd v Ward* [1902] 2 KB 1; *Hawke v E Hulton & Co* [1909] 2 KB 93; *R v The Daily Mirror Newspapers Ltd* (1922) 16 Cr App R 131.

[171] Sequestration is the appropriate order where a company is in contempt of court: *Re Hibernia National Review* [1976] IR 388: see Ch 6, *Corporate Civil Litigation*, at para **[6.100]**.

[172] See, eg, Wells, *Corporations and Criminal Responsibility* (2nd edn, Oxford University Press, 2001), p 31.

the 'real' wrongdoers – the management. For corporate criminal liability to have full effect there is a real need for novel sentencing solutions[173].

(IV) Principles of attribution of corporate criminal liability

[4.063] Most regulatory offences for which corporations can be prosecuted are offences of *strict liability*, so it is not necessary for the prosecution to prove any mental attitude or *mens rea* on the part of the offender[174]. The strict liability approach is of particular significance in the prosecution of corporate defendants because it dispenses with the need to attribute to the corporation the *mens rea* of some individual closely associated with it[175]. Furthermore, the liability is commonly *direct* rather than vicarious. Professor JC Smith has explained it thus:

> 'Where a statutory duty to do something is imposed upon a particular person (here, 'an employer') and he does not do it, he commits the *actus reus* of an offence. It may be that he has failed to fulfil his duty because his employee or agent has failed to carry out his duties properly but this is not a case for vicarious liability. If the employer is held liable, it is because he, personally, has failed to do what the law requires him to do and he is personally, not vicariously, liable. There is no need to find someone – in the case of a company, the 'brains' and not merely the 'hands' – for whose act the person with the duty can be held liable. The duty on the company in this case was to 'ensure' – ie to make certain – that persons are not exposed to risk. They did not make it certain. It does not matter how; they were in breach of their statutory duty and, in the absence of any requirement of *mens rea*, that is the end of the matter[176].'

Some of the offences are qualified, however, by a defence of 'reasonable practicality'.'[177] In *R v Gateway Foodmarkets Ltd*[178], the Court of Appeal held that the onus is on the defence to prove that such reasonably practicable precautions have been taken. The court further held that the 'identification doctrine' and 'directing mind and will' concepts[179] have no application in establishing such a defence. Accordingly, the corporation will be liable for breaches of the Health and Safety Acts by any persons for whom it is responsible, even where there had been no failure to take practical precautions at higher levels of management. In *Gateway*, the company was convicted of the offence of failing in its duty to ensure, as far as reasonably practicable, the health and safety of its employees when an employee at a supermarket site fell to his death down an unguarded lift shaft. The company had employed an experienced and highly reputable firm of lift contractors to maintain the lift, and the head office was unaware of an informal arrangement at store level whereby company employees would themselves adjust the lift

173 See, eg, the Law Reform Commission,' *Report on Corporate Killing* (LRC 77–2005), which proposes a variety of penalties including fines, remedial orders, community service orders, adverse publicity orders, and restraining orders and injunctions.

174 *R v British Steel plc* [1995] 1 WLR 1356.

175 See para **[4.065]**.

176 *R v British Steel plc* [1995] Crim LR 654 at 655.

177 Eg, s 6(1) of the Safety, Health and Welfare at Work Act 1989 provided that 'it shall be the duty of every employer to ensure, so far as is reasonably practicable, the safety, health and welfare at work of all his employees'.

178 *R v Gateway Foodmarkets Ltd* [1997] 2 Cr App R 40.

179 Ie, the prevailing concepts involved in the attribution of liability to corporations for crimes requiring *mens rea;* see further para **[4.065]**.

mechanism when it became stuck. The employee was killed when carrying out this informal procedure. The Court of Appeal found that the failure at store level was attributable to the company without need to consider whether head office knew or ought to have known of the informal procedures.

Corporations cannot evade liability for offences under the regulatory regimes merely by issuing injunctions at board level prohibiting illegal activity; what is required is a proactive response at all levels of operation. In *R v British Steel plc*[180], the Court of Appeal rejected the company's argument that taking reasonable care at board level should lead to an acquittal. In that case a worker for an independent contractor was killed because of the collapse of a steel platform during a repositioning operation which a competent supervisor would have recognised was inherently dangerous. The defence was that the workmen had disobeyed instructions and, even if the supervisor was at fault, the company at the level of its directing mind had taken reasonable care. An appeal against conviction was dismissed by the Court of Appeal. Steyn LJ said[181]:

> 'If it be accepted that Parliament considered it necessary for the protection of public health and safety to impose, subject to the defence of reasonable practicability, absolute criminal liability, it would drive a juggernaut through the legislative scheme if corporate employers could avoid criminal liability where the potentially harmful event is committed by someone who is not the directing mind of the company ... That would emasculate the legislation.'

[4.064] A corporation will occasionally be *vicariously* liable for the crimes of its employees and agents committed within the scope of their employment where a natural person would similarly be vicariously liable. Although at common law there is not generally any vicarious liability for criminal acts[182], a company may be made vicariously liable for public nuisance at common law[183], or indeed where a statute provides for vicarious criminal liability[184]. Where the offence for which the company is to be made vicariously liable is a crime of strict liability the company may easily be found guilty[185]. The essential prerequisite is that the offence concerns an activity such as 'selling', 'offering' or 'using' which falls within the scope of the employee's or agent's activities[186]. Where the company is to be made vicariously liable for an offence which *does* require a *mens rea* to be proved – such as intent to defraud the revenue[187] – the courts will impose liability provided that the *mens rea* in question is not so personal to the perpetrator as to break the link between the company and its servant or agent[188].

---

[180] *R v British Steel plc* [1995] 1 WLR 1356. The approach of the Court of Appeal was endorsed by the House of Lords in *R v Associated Octel Co Ltd* [1996] 1 WLR 1543.

[181] *R v British Steel plc* [1995] 1 WLR 1356 at pp 1362–1363.

[182] *Tesco Supermarkets Ltd v Natrass* [1972] 2 AC 153, *per* Diplock LJ at 199.

[183] *R v Great North of England Railway Company* (1846) 9 QB 315.

[184] *Griffiths v Studebakers Ltd* [1924] 1 KB 102.

[185] *R v Birmingham and Gloucester Railway Co* (1841) 2 QB 47; *R v Great North of England Railway Co* (1846) 2 Cox CC 70.

[186] See *Pearks, Dunston & Tee Ltd v Ward* [1902] 2 KB 1; *Tesco Stores Ltd v Brent London Borough Council* [1993] 2 All ER 718.

[187] *Mousell v London & North Western Railway Co* [1917] 2 KB 836.

[188] Where the company is found personally criminally liable, the individual perpetrators may also be found liable as secondary parties: *McMahon v Murtagh* [1982] ILRM 342; *DPP v Roberts* [1987] IR 268.

Thus, in *R v Cory Brothers & Co*[189] Finlay J quashed an indictment against a limited company which contained a count of manslaughter, partly, it seems, because the offence was too personal to the individual perpetrator to be attributed to the company. However, in *R v ICR Haulage Ltd*[190], Stable J pointed out that this was a branch of the law which had developed and, if the matter came before the courts today, the result might well be different[191].

[4.065] A corporation will be *personally*, as opposed to vicariously, liable for criminal activity where the criminal act and the state of mind of a controlling officer or officers can be identified or attributed to the corporation in the same way as the tortious acts and intent of controlling officers can be attributed to a company[192]. As Denning LJ explained in *HL Bolton (Engineering) Ltd v TJ Graham & Sons Ltd*[193]:

> 'A company may in many ways be likened to a human body. They have a brain and nerve centre which control what they do. They also have hands which hold the tools and act in accordance with directions from the centre. Some of the people in the company are mere servants and agents who are nothing more than hands to do the work and cannot be said to represent the mind or will. Others are directors and managers who represent the directing mind and will of the company, and control what they do. The state of mind of these managers is the state of mind of the company and is treated by the law as such.'

In the Canadian Supreme Court in *Canadian Dredge & Dock Co Ltd v R*[194], Estey J put the principle thus:

> 'The identity doctrine merges the board of directors, the managing director, the superintendent, the manager or anyone else delegated by the board of directors to whom is delegated the governing executive authority of the corporation, and the conduct of any of the merged entities is thereby attributed to the corporation.'

The courts often encounter what is considered by many to be difficulty in applying the '*identification doctrine*' to find the 'directing mind and will of the company'. The problem, if it be such, is that not every person who exercises some managerial discretion can be said to control the company. Thus, in *HL Bolton (Engineering) Ltd v TJ Graham & Sons Ltd*[195], where the company was charged with an offence under the Trade Descriptions Act 1978 (UK), it was held not to be personally liable since the commission of the offence was due to the act or default of a branch supermarket manager and the company had hundreds of supermarkets, ie, the branch manager was the hands, and not the brains, of the company. Similar difficulty was encountered in *R v P & O European Ferries (Dover)*[196], a prosecution arising out of the capsize of the car

189 *R v Cory Brothers & Co* [1927] 1 KB 810.

190 *R v ICR Haulage Ltd* [1944] KB 551.

191 *R v ICR Haulage Ltd* [1944] KB 551 at 556. In *R v P&O European Ferries (Dover) Ltd* (1991) 93 Cr App R 72, it was accepted that a company may be *personally* liable for manslaughter. See further Law Reform Commission, *Consultation Paper on Corporate Homicide* (2002).

192 See para **[4.052]**.

193 *HL Bolton (Engineering) Ltd v TJ Graham & Sons Ltd* [1957] 1 QB 159 at 173.

194 *Canadian Dredge & Dock Co Ltd v R* (1985) 19 DLR (4d) 314 at 336–337.

195 *HL Bolton (Engineering) Ltd v TJ Graham & Sons Ltd* [1972] AC 153.

196 *R v P & O European Ferries (Dover)* (1991) 93 Cr App R 72. The company had been slated in an official inquiry arising out of the disaster as having been 'infected with the disease of sloppiness' from top to bottom: (contd.../)

ferry *Herald of Free Enterprise* at Zeebrugge, when the assistant bosun and the chief officer were found not to be sufficiently high up in the management hierarchy of the company for their carelessness to be held against the company. Who then is high enough to think and act as the company? In *Tesco Supermarkets Ltd*, Lord Reid said:

> 'Normally the board of directors, the managing director and perhaps other superior officers of a company carry out functions of management and speak and act as the company. Their subordinates do not[197].'

Viscount Dilhorne felt that the person should be one who:

> '... is in actual control of the operations of a company or part of them and who is not responsible to another person in the company for the manner in which he discharges his duties in the sense of being under others[198].'

Lords Diplock and Pearson felt that only persons drawing their authority from the memorandum of association (whether directly, or indirectly through the positive sanction of the board of directors or the general meeting) could be said to represent the will of the corporation. Lord Diplock identified them as:

> 'those natural persons who by the memorandum and articles of association or as a result of action taken by the directors or by the company in general meeting pursuant to the articles are entrusted with the exercise of the powers of the company[199].'

Clearly the person who will be identified as representing the company must be a *directive* rather than an *executive* employee or agent of the company[200]. But the exact limits of this are uncertain. An uncontroversial case is *Director of Public Prosecutions v Kent and Sussex Contractors Ltd*[201], where a transport manager knowingly produced a false return under certain Defence Regulations in order to acquire petrol coupons. The Divisional Court held that there was ample evidence that the company had done the act in question through the only person who could act or speak or think for it. That decision was approved in *R v ICR Haulage Ltd*[202], where a company and nine other persons were convicted of common law conspiracy to defraud, it being held that the fraudulent acts of the managing director were the fraudulent acts of the company. The conspiracy was thus between the company, acting through its managing director, and the nine others.

A more controversial case, however, is *Moore v I Bresler Ltd*[203], where a company was convicted of making certain returns in respect of UK purchase tax, which were false in material particulars, with intent to deceive contrary to the Finance (No 2) Act 1940

[196] (\...contd) Sheen, *the Merchant Shipping Act, 1894, mv Herald of Free Enterprise, Report of Court No 8074* (1987), para 14.1. Similar difficulty was encountered in the prosecution of Great Western Trains Company for manslaughter following the Southall rail crash in England in which seven persons lost their lives. No member of senior management could be identified as having had the requisite gross negligence to fix the company with liability for manslaughter: see *Attorney General's Reference (No 2 of 1999)* [2000] QB 796.

[197] *HL Bolton (Engineering) Ltd v TJ Graham & Sons Ltd* [1972] AC 153 at 171.

[198] *HL Bolton (Engineering) Ltd v TJ Graham & Sons Ltd* [1972] AC 153 at 187.

[199] *HL Bolton (Engineering) Ltd v TJ Graham & Sons Ltd* [1972] AC 153 at 200.

[200] Glanville Williams, *Criminal Law, The General Part* (1953, Stevens), at p 857.

[201] *Director of Public Prosecutions v Kent and Sussex Contractors Ltd* [1944] 1 KB 146.

[202] *R v ICR Haulage Ltd* [1944] KB 551.

[203] *Moore v I Bresler Ltd* [1944] 2 All ER 515.

(UK). The returns were physically made by the company secretary and the sales manager of a branch of the company *in their own interests* and with the intention of defrauding the company itself. Viscount Caldecote LCJ found that[204]:

> 'These two men were important officials of the company, and when they made statements and rendered returns which were proved in this case, they were clearly making those statements and giving those returns as the officers of the company, the proper officers to make those returns. Their acts, therefore, as indeed the Recorder seems to have been prepared to agree, were the acts of the company. It is only because, for some reason which I am not able to fathom, he thinks that they have converted the goods of the company and made them their own and so acted without authority, that the Recorder came to the conclusion that the appeal ought to be allowed. How he came to base his decision upon the fallacious reasoning contained in his opinion, if I may say so with great respect to him, I do not know. It is sufficient for us, I think, to say that he went wrong on a point of law and on the facts stated in this case these two people acting as officers of the company made the company liable for the offence which was committed.'

The decision has been heavily criticised as going too far[205]. In *Canadian Dredge & Dock Co Ltd v R*[206], Estey J observed:

> 'Where the corporation benefited or was intended to be benefited from the fraudulent or criminal activities of the directing mind, the rationale for the identification rule holds. Where the delegate of the corporation has turned against his principal, the rationale fades away'.

Nevertheless, the acts at least involved the company secretary. *Re Kent and Sussex Contractors*[207] may, on another reading, appear more doubtful since that case involved merely a transport manager.

A practical consequence of the 'identification doctrine' is that it is far easier to convict small closely-knit companies that it is to convict larger ones having diffuse organisational structures. The outcome of the *P&O case*[208], for example, seems to contrast starkly with that of *R v Kite and OLL Ltd*[209], where an outdoor leisure company was convicted of manslaughter for the death of a canoeist during a negligently managed canoeing expedition. The company was essentially a one-man operation, and the company's liability was established automatically upon his conviction for manslaughter in connection with the same events since he was its managing director and directing mind and will – its 'brains' and its 'hands.'

[4.066] The narrow focus of the identification doctrine may be contrasted with the broader principles of attribution which have been developed since *Tesco* by the English Courts to deal with statutory offences by corporations. In *Re Supply of Ready Mixed Concrete (No 2)*[210], the House of Lords found companies to be in contempt of court

204 *Moore v I Bresler Ltd* [1944] 2 All ER 515 at 517.

205 Glanville Williams, *Criminal Law, The General Part* (1953, Stevens), p 859; Welch, 62 LQR 345 at 360.

206 *Canadian Dredge & Dock Co Ltd v R* (1985) 19 DLR (4d) 314.

207 *Re Kent and Sussex Contractors* [1944] 1 KB 146.

208 *P&O case* (1991) 93 Cr App R 72.

209 *R v Kite and OLL Ltd* (8 December 1994) Winchester Crown Court, (1994) The Independent, 9 December.

210 *Re Supply of Ready Mixed Concrete (No 2)* [1995] 1 AC 456.

when their employees implemented anti-competitive practices in breach of injunctions against the company and the Restrictive Practices Act 1976 (UK). The Law Lords held that the employees were carrying on the business of the company in the course of their employment, and liability would attach despite instructions from senior management – the directing mind and will – not to engage in such practices.

A similar approach was adopted by the Privy Council in *Meridian Global Funds Management Asia Ltd v Securities Commission*[211], where a company was convicted for failing to issue a notice disclosing a substantial shareholding contrary to New Zealand securities legislation. The shares were acquired by employees acting on behalf of the company, but without the knowledge of the board of directors and the managing director. Lord Hoffmann held that where the 'primary' principles of attribution of responsibility, such as those derived from the company's constitution or implied by company law, would defeat the intended application of a particular provision to companies, it is necessary for the courts to devise a special rule of attribution which will give effect to the provision[212]. What that rule should be depends in each case on an interpretation that is appropriate to the offence involved and the policies behind it. In the instant case, the rule of attribution should not require consideration of whether the board and managing director knew of the infringements, since such an interpretation would defer any enforceable reporting obligation until senior executives became aware.

Meridian was considered significant in the law relating to corporate criminal liability not merely because it involved a displacement of the identification principle in favour of a broader approach in cases where statutory provisions are concerned, but because the purposive approach to attribution gave recognition to the complexities of diffuse management structures and the fact that corporations do not always operate on a purely hierarchical or vertical model[213]. Its promise was short lived, however; in *Re Attorney General's Reference (No 2 of 1999)*[214], the Court of Appeal firmly rejected the argument that *Meridian* admitted of any principle of attribution other than the identification doctrine in the general criminal liability of corporations. Rose J, speaking for the court, said that 'Lord Hoffmann's speech in *Meridian* … is a re-statement, not an abandonment, of existing principles'.'[215]

As for this country, there has yet to be a firm pronouncement on whether the Irish courts will embrace *Meridian*. The High Court was invited to apply the *Meridian* principles in *Fyffes plc v DCC plc*[216], where one of the questions for the court was whether the knowledge of a tipster could be attributed to a corporate tipee in the context of insider dealing under s 108 of the CA 1990. The plaintiff in that case, Fyffes plc, contended that alleged price sensitive information in the possession of the CEO of DCC plc, James Flavin, could be attributed to DCC plc using the *Meridian* principles.

211 *Meridian Global Funds Management Asia Ltd v Securities Commission* [1995] 2 AC 500.

212 *Meridian Global Funds Management Asia Ltd v Securities Commission* [1995] 2 AC 500 at 507.

213 See, eg, Gray, 'Company Directors and Ignorance of the Law' (1996) 17 Co Law; Grantham, 'Corporate Knowledge: Identification or Attribution?' (1996) 59 MLR 732; and Robert-Tissot, 'A Fresh Insight into the Corporate Criminal Mind: Meridian Global Funds Management Asia Ltd v Securities Commission' (1996) 17 Co Law 99.

214 *Re Attorney General's Reference (No 2 of 1999)* [2000] QB 796.

215 *Re Attorney General's Reference (No 2 of 1999)* [2000] QB 796 at 814.

216 *Fyffes plc v DCC plc* [2009] 2 IR 417.

Laffoy J outlined Lord Hoffmann's principles but expressed no view on them, finding instead that the wording of s 108 did not admit such a proposition because to attribute insider knowledge in that manner would render the knowledge requirement in s 108 superfluous.

[4.067] While it has been held that a company may be guilty in conspiring with others[217], the English courts have held that the company cannot conspire with the person who represents the controlling mind and will of the company, because conspiracy requires two minds. In *R v Mc Donnell*[218], Nield J observed:

> '... in the particular circumstances here, where the sole responsible person in the company is the defendant himself, it would not be right to say that there were two persons or two minds. If it were otherwise, I feel it would offend against the basic concept of a conspiracy, namely, an agreement of two or more to do an unlawful act and I think it would be artificial to take the view that the company, although it is clearly a separate legal entity, can be regarded here as a separate person or a separate mind, in view of the admitted fact that this defendant acts alone so far as these companies are concerned ..'.

That case was concerned with criminal conspiracy. The Irish Supreme Court, however, has taken the opposite view as far as civil conspiracy is concerned, and it would seem logically that the same view could be applied to criminal conspiracy[219]. This view was expressed in *Taylor v Smyth*[220], where the question was whether Mr Smyth could conspire with companies he controlled and in which he was the only active participant. McCarthy J noted that *R v McDonnell* had not been extended to civil cases, and then went on to hold that Mr Smyth had in fact and in law conspired with his companies. He said:

> 'In principle, it would seem invidious, for example, that the assets of a limited company should not be liable to answer for a conspiracy where its assets had been augmented as a result of an action alleged to constitute the conspiracy. Essentially, it would be permitting the company to lift its corporate veil if and when it suits ... I see no reason why the fact that one individual controls the company of limited liability should give immunity from suit to both that company and that individual in the case of an established arrangement for the benefit of both company and individual to the detriment of others. If such were the case, it would follow that a like arrangement to the advantage of two companies of limited liability, both controlled by the same individual, would give an equal immunity from suit to both companies and so on.'

(iv) Constitutional rights and duties

[4.068] The Irish courts, in contrast to some other jurisdictions[221], have adopted a measured approach in according to corporations the personal rights guaranteed by the Constitution. The caution stems largely from the notion that some of those rights are an emanation of natural law, which is a system of rights derived from man's inherent

---

217 *DPP v Kent and Sussex Contractors Ltd* [1944] 1 KB 146.

218 *R v Mc Donnell* [1966] 1 QB 233.

219 See MacCann, 'Companies and Conspiracy' (1990) ILT 197.

220 *Taylor v Smyth* [1991] IR 142.

221 See 'Constitutional Rights of the Corporate Person' (1982) 91 Yale LJ 1641; O'Neill, *Constitutional Rights of Companies* (2007).

humanity[222]. The right to equality, for example, is guaranteed by Article 40.1 of Bunreacht na hÉireann, which provides:

> 'All citizens shall, as human persons, be held equal before the law. This shall not be held to mean that the State shall not in its enactments have due regard to differences of capacity, physical and moral, and of social function.'

Corporations are considered by the courts to be unable to rely on the constitutional protection of this right since they are not human persons; as Walsh J observed in *Quinn's Supermarket Ltd v Attorney General*[223]:

> '... under no possible construction of the Constitutional guarantee could a body corporate or any entity but a human being be considered to be a human person for the purposes of this provision[224].'

The same can be said of the right to communicate, which has been held to exist by virtue of man's human personality[225] and cannot be enjoyed by corporations. Certain other constitutional rights are of no personal relevance to corporations; eg, the right to *habeas corpus*[226]; the right to inviolability of the dwelling[227]; and the unenumerated rights to marry and found a family[228], to marital privacy[229], and to bodily integrity[230]. There seems to be no bar, however, on the corporation acting to protect such constitutional rights *of others* once it is shown to have sufficient *locus standi*[231].

[4.069] The 'inherent humanity' approach would not in principle extend to all personal rights guaranteed by the Constitution; eg, the personal right to property. Article 40.3.2° of *Bunreacht na hÉireann* provides:

> 'The State shall, in particular, by its laws protect as best it may from unjust attack and, in the case of injustice done, vindicate the life, person, good name and property rights of every citizen.'

---

222 See generally, Kelly, Hogan & Whyte, *The Irish Constitution* (3rd edn, Butterworths, 1994) at pp 671 *et seq*; but *cf Caldwell v Mahon* [2007] 3 IR 542 and *Digital Rights Ireland Ltd v Minister for Communications* [2010] 3 IR 251 where a limited right of privacy in business communications was held to exist.

223 *Quinn's Supermarket Ltd v Attorney General* [1972] IR 1.

224 *Quinn's Supermarket Ltd v Attorney General* [1972] IR 1 at p 14. In *Abbey Films Ltd v Attorney General* [1981] IR 158, a company alleged that certain legislation was an unconstitutional breach of the equality guarantee because it required a company to retain a solicitor whereas individual citizens could appear in person. The Supreme Court, sidestepping the issue of whether the company could rely on that guarantee, held that even if it could, the differing treatment would be justified according to differences in capacity and social function.

225 *Attorney General v Paperlink Ltd* [1984] ILRM 373.

226 Article 40.4.2°.

227 Article 40.5. 'Dwelling' appears to refer only to the living quarters of a human person. See *The People (Attorney General) v O'Brien* [1965] IR 142; *DPP v Corrigan* [1986] IR 190; *O'Mahony v Shields* (22 February 1988, unreported) HC.

228 *Murray v Attorney General* [1985] IR 532.

229 *McGee v Attorney General* [1974] IR 284.

230 *Ryan v Attorney General* [1965] IR 294.

231 Eg, *Quinn's Supermarket Ltd v Attorney General* [1972] IR 1; *Educational Company of Ireland v Fitzpatrick* [1961] IR 323.

Prior to 1969, the ability of bodies corporate to rely on these provisions was not questioned in decisions in which the constitutionality of legislation was challenged by such bodies[232], though in that year O'Keeffe P adverted to the question in *East Donegal Co-Operative Livestock Mart Ltd v Attorney General*[233] merely as follows:

> 'Artificial persons may possibly not be entitled to rely on the constitutional guarantees … (although they have been held to be so entitled in the United States).'

In *Private Motorists' Provident Society v Attorney General*[234], Carroll J reasoned that the property rights guaranteed by Article 40.3.2° are incapable of being enjoyed by corporations since those rights are, she reasoned, in turn derived from Article 43 of the Constitution, which recognises that 'man, in virtue of his rational being, has the natural right, antecedent to positive law, to the private ownership of external goods' and corporations do not enjoy such inherent humanity[235]. The Supreme Court in that case was less unequivocal, and did not express any opinion as to whether the corporation, as a creature of positive law, enjoyed the constitutional guarantees accorded to citizens, but Carroll J's reasoning was later applied by Murphy J in the High Court in *Chestvale Properties Ltd v Glackin*[236].

The decision in the *Private Motorist's* case gave rise to the use of an artificial practice to circumvent the problem. In that case this was done by joining a member of the corporation as a co-plaintiff, who, as a natural person and a citizen, could maintain an action on the grounds that *his* constitutionally guaranteed property rights constituted by his membership of the corporation would be indirectly affected if the corporation were injured. This indirect means of protecting the corporation and its members against unconstitutional attack was open to criticism[237], however, and appeared to contradict the approach of the courts in respect of the invocation of other constitutional rights by companies[238].

[4.070] In *Iarnród Éireann v Ireland*, Keane J (as he then was) challenged Carroll J's doubts in the *Private Motorists* case[239] about the ability of corporations to invoke the

---

232 *Attorney General v Southern Industrial Trust* (1957) 94 ILTR 161; *Educational Company of Ireland Ltd v Fitzpatrick (No 2)* [1961] IR 345.

233 *East Donegal Co-Operative Livestock Mart Ltd v Attorney General* [1970] IR 317.

234 *Private Motorists' Provident Society v Attorney General* [1983] IR 339.

235 *Private Motorists' Provident Society v Attorney General* [1983] IR 339 at 349.

236 *Chestvale Properties Ltd v Glackin* [1993] 3 IR 35 at 45. In *MMDS Television Ltd and Suir Nore Relays Ltd v South East Community Deflector Association Ltd and Kirwan* [1997] IEHC 60, an application for an interlocutory injunction relating to a planning matter, the argument was raised before Carroll J that the plaintiffs, being corporate bodies, had no constitutional rights. The learned judge did not consider the issue, however, deciding in the plaintiff's favour on other grounds. See also *Carrigaline Community TV v Minister for Transport Energy and Communications and Others* (10 November 1995, unreported) HC, Keane J; *Cork Communications Ltd and Kerr v Dennehy and Others* (4 October 1993, unreported) HC, Lynch J.

237 See Courtney, *The Law of Private Companies* (1st edn, 1994), at para 3.056. Also Ussher, *Company Law in Ireland* (1986, Sweet & Maxwell), at pp 54–56.

238 See para **[4.061]**.

239 *Private Motorists case* [1983] IR 339.

constitutionally guaranteed property rights in Article 40.3.2°[240]. Keane J reasoned, following a number of Supreme Court decisions[241], that the property rights guaranteed by Article 40.3.2° are *not* derived from Article 43, since the latter is concerned with the institution of private property (the sanctity of which institution the State guarantees only to human persons). He said[242]:

> 'It is, accordingly, clear that the rationale on which Carroll J based her rejection of the *locus standi* of the corporate plaintiff in *Private Motorists' Provident Society v Attorney General* [1983] IR 339 can no longer be supported. In contrast to Article 40, s 1 and Article 43, Article 40, s 3, sub-s 2, in enumerating the rights which are thereby guaranteed, refers simply to 'the property rights of every citizen'. If the decision in *PMPS* is to be supported, it must be on the ground that the 'property rights of every citizen' thereby guaranteed are confined to rights enjoyed by the citizens as human persons.
>
> Undoubtedly, some at least of the rights enumerated in Article 40, s 3, sub-s 2 – the rights to life and liberty – are of no relevance to corporate bodies and other artificial legal entities. Property rights are, however, in a different category. Not only are corporate bodies themselves capable in law of owning property, whether movable or immovable, tangible or intangible. The 'property' referred to clearly includes shares in companies formed under the relevant companies' legislation which was already a settled feature of the legal and commercial life of this country at the time of the enactment of the Constitution. There would accordingly be a spectacular deficiency in the guarantee to every citizen that his or her property rights will be protected against 'unjust attack', if such bodies were incapable in law of being regarded as 'citizens', at least for the purposes of this Article, and if it was essential for the shareholders to abandon the protection of limited liability to which they are entitled by law in order to protect, not merely their own rights as shareholders but also the property rights of the corporate entity itself, which are in law distinct from the rights of its members.
>
> Article 43 undoubtedly treats the general right of private property, the abolition of which in its entirety is expressly prohibited, as one inhering in 'man in virtue of his rational being' and, in that sense, as being 'antecedent to positive law', including the Constitution itself. But it does not necessarily follow that the property rights of the individual citizens which are protected against 'unjust attack' by Article 40, s 3 are confined to rights enjoyed by human persons. Had the framers of the Constitution wished to confine the comprehensive guarantee in Article 40, s 3 in that manner, there was nothing to prevent them including a similar qualification to that contained in Article 40, section 1.'

The learned judge went on to reveal the deficiencies of the approach commonly adopted since the *Private Motorists'* case of joining a human co-plaintiff:

> 'The present case demonstrates that the restriction on the property rights of the citizen which would logically result from confining the protection of Article 40, s 3 to individual citizens would not necessarily be eased in every case by joining the shareholders as plaintiffs in the proceedings. If this case were to depend on the *locus standi* of the second plaintiff, it would appear that his property rights as an individual arising out of his ownership of one share in the first plaintiff are of so nominal a nature as not to afford him any such *locus standi*. It is unnecessary at this point to consider how many other corporate

240 *Iarnród Éireann v Ireland* [1996] 3 IR 321.

241 The learned judge relied on the Supreme Court's judgments in *Blake v Attorney General* [1982] IR 117 and *Attorney General v Southern Industiral Trust Ltd* (1957) 94 ILTR 161.

242 *Iarnród Éireann v Ireland* [1996] 3 IR 321 at 344–345.

bodies would be in a similarly impotent state, although they would clearly include some in the private sector, such as companies limited by guarantee. It is sufficient to say that, although the strategy adopted in *Private Motorists' Provident Society v Attorney General* [1983] IR 339 of joining the shareholder as a plaintiff was accepted by the Supreme Court as obviating any constitutional difficulty that might have arisen in that case, it is of critical importance that the Court expressly refrained from holding that the corporate plaintiff had no *locus standi*. In the result, I consider that I am not bound to hold that where, as here, it is not possible to make effective use of such a strategy, the claim of a corporate plaintiff must necessarily fail[243].'

Keane J concluded that the expression 'every citizen' in Article 40.3.2° is not confined to citizens in their capacity as human beings, and that artificial legal entities must also be protected by the laws of the State against unjust attacks on their property rights. It is peculiarly the role of the courts to vindicate the property rights of such entities in accordance with Article 40.3.2°. The Supreme Court in *Iarnród Éireann v Ireland*[244] declined, however, to consider the *locus standi* issue[245].

[4.071] The other personal rights guaranteed by Article 40, including the *unenumerated rights* judicially identified as emanating from Article 40.3.1°[246], are conferred simply on 'citizens' without expressly requiring that the citizens be human persons. Are these rights conferred on corporations?[247] It has been argued[248] that if this were so it would be to make too odd and arbitrary a distinction between those rights and the others protected by the Article[249], but the courts have recognised that corporations may invoke such rights.

The personal unenumerated[250] right of access to the courts[251] was invoked by a company in *Bula Ltd v Tara Mines Ltd*[252], where Murphy J rejected the defendant's

243 *Iarnród Éireann v Ireland* [1996] 3 IR 321 at pp 345–346.

244 *Iarnród Éireann v Ireland* [1986] 3 IR 370.

245 Keane J's reasoning was applied by the High Court *in Lancefort Ltd v An Bord Pleanála, Ireland, Attorney General and Treasury Holdings Ltd (Notice Party)* (6 June 1997, unreported) HC, Morris J; *An Blascaod Mór Teoranta and Others v Commissioners of Public Works in Ireland and Others and Minister for the Arts Culture and the Gaéltacht* (27 February 1998, unreported) HC, Budd J; *Lancefort Ltd v An Bord Pleanala, Ireland and the Attorney General and Treasury Holdings Ltd (Notice Party)* (12 March 1998, unreported) HC, McGuinness J; *Daly v The Revenue Commissioners* [1995] 3 IR 1.

246 See generally Casey, *Constitutional Law in Ireland* (3rd edn, 2000).

247 It may be argued that a corporation is a 'citizen' since it is capable of having a nationality: see, for example, *Daimler Co Ltd v Continental Tyre and Rubber Co (Great Britain) Ltd* [1916] 2 AC 307.

248 By Ussher, *Company Law in Ireland* (1986, Sweet & Maxwell), at pp 53–54.

249 In support of his submission, Ussher cites Costello J in *Attorney General v Paperlink* [1984] ILRM 373 at 385, where the learned judge advised that the courts should not, in interpreting the Constitution, 'place the same significance on differences in language used in two succeeding sub-paragraphs as would, for example, be placed on differently drafted sub-sections of a Finance Act. A purposive, rather than a literal approach ... is appropriate.' See also *Cafolla v Ireland* [1986] ILRM 177 at 183.

250 First recognised in *Macauley v Minister for Posts and Telegraphs* [1966] IR 345.

251 See *SEE Co Ltd v Public Lighting Services Ltd* [1987] ILRM 255 at 258. But the right of a company to *appear in court*, as opposed to its right of access to the courts, is restricted; see Ch 6, *Corporate Civil Litigation*, at para **[6.066]**.

252 *Bula Ltd v Tara Mines Ltd* [1987] IR 85.

argument that the plaintiff (a body corporate) should make out a *prima facie* case before being granted an order for the inspection of the defendant's mining activities, saying:

> 'It is the right of citizens under the Constitution to have access to the courts for the resolution of justiciable controversies ... If, then, a citizen is free to institute proceedings he must be at least equally free to invoke the procedures of the court to present his case properly. In my view the right of a party to seek and obtain an order for inspection (or indeed an order for discovery which may be equally burdensome) is in no way dependent upon the court being satisfied as to the strength of the plaintiff's case[253].'

Again, in *Society for the Protection of Unborn Children (Ireland) Ltd v Coogan*[254], where the plaintiff was a company limited by guarantee formed with the object of protecting human life, particularly the life of the unborn, the Supreme Court held that the company had sufficient *locus standi* to commence proceedings to enforce compliance with the provisions of Article 40.3.3° of the Constitution (which deal with the right to life of the unborn). Walsh J said:

> 'One of the fundamental political rights of the citizen under the Constitution, indeed one of the most valued of his rights, is that of access to the courts ... The citizen's right of access to the courts in the appropriate case will include not only access in defence of his own personal and direct rights which are being threatened by the executive or by his fellow citizens, but also the right to seek to restrain the acts of the executive or other persons from breaching the constraints imposed by the Constitution if the public interest requires that such breaches or attempted breaches should be restrained[255].'

The fact that the 'citizen' in this case happened to be a limited company did not prevent the court from finding that it had a constitutional right of access to the courts. More recently, in *Irish Penal Reform Trust Ltd v Governor of Mountjoy Prison*[256] Gilligan J explained the apparent contradiction thus:

> '[W]hether or not *SPUC v Coogan* [1989] IR 734 was indeed restricted to the right to present argument on behalf of the unborn child is not wholly relevant to the present case. The simple fact is that *Cahill v Sutton* [1980] IR 269 allows, in plain terms, for the relaxation of the personal standing rules where those prejudiced may not be in a position to adequately assert their constitutional rights. It does not restrict this category of persons to the living, the dead or the unborn nor does it give any indication of what category of person may not be in a position to adequately assert their constitutional rights. If a person is incapable of adequately asserting his constitutional rights for whatever reason, I am of the view that *Cahill v Sutton* would support a relaxation of the personal standing rules, provided the relevant person or body is genuine, acting in a bona fide manner, and has a defined interest in the matter in question.'

[4.072] The mere existence of a constitutional right of access to the courts does not guarantee that the corporate constitutional litigant will have *locus standi* in any given case: it must further be shown that the corporation has a *bona fide* interest to invoke the constitutional right. This was explained in the context of the corporate constitutional

---

[253] *Bula Ltd v Tara Mines Ltd* [1987] IR 85 at 92–93.

[254] *Society for the Protection of Unborn Children (Ireland) Ltd v Coogan* [1989] IR 738.

[255] *Society for the Protection of Unborn Children (Ireland) Ltd v Coogan* [1989] IR 738.

[256] *Irish Penal Reform Trust Ltd v Governor of Mountjoy Prison* [2005] IEHC 305.

litigant by Walsh J in the Supreme Court in *Society for the Protection of Unborn Children (Ireland) Ltd v Coogan*[257]:

> 'In a case such as this the essential question is have the plaintiffs a *bona fide* interest to invoke the protection of the courts to vindicate the constitutional right [of the unborn] in question. It would be an ironic situation if our law, which permits a citizen to bring a petty thief before the courts even though the citizen himself is not a victim of the theft, could yet deem the citizen unqualified to invoke the court's protection to prevent the destruction of the constitutional right to life.'

Thus, in *Lancefort Ltd v An Bord Pleanála, Ireland and the Attorney General and Treasury Holdings Ltd*[258], where a limited company was formed to pursue judicial review proceedings generally and, more particularly, to challenge the constitutionality of s 14(8) of the Local Government (Planning and Development) Act 1976, while at the same time affording the true applicants a shield against an award of costs, McGuinness J held that while the corporate plaintiff enjoyed *locus standi* to pursue a judicial review application in respect of a planning decision, it lacked *locus standi* on the constitutional issue:

> '… I find the learned Keane J's survey and analysis [in the *Iarnród Éireann* case] both impressive and convincing and I would accept that in principle a corporate body, or juristic person, can possess *locus standi* to impugn legislation by invoking the relevant provisions of the Constitution.
>
> However, that is not the end of the matter. The second question then arises as to whether the Applicant in the present proceedings has 'sufficient interest' in the proceedings in the sense used in *Cahill v Sutton* [1980] IR 269 to acquire the necessary *locus standi* …
>
> In the instant case the Applicant seeks to rely on Article 43 of the Constitution. While in its Statement of Grounds the Applicant relies on the reference in Article 43.2 to the concepts of social justice and the common good, this must be seen in the context of the main purpose of the Article which is to uphold the right of private property and to forbid its abolition. The Applicant is a company limited by guarantee with effectively no assets. It maintains no commercial or profit making activity which could enable it to acquire property. It owns no property in the area affected by the proposed development – or indeed anywhere else. It was not an objector to the planning permission at the time nor did it take any part in the oral hearing by the inspector appointed by An Bord Pleanála. It was not even in existence at the time of An Bord Pleanála's decision on 11 December, 1996. At the time of An Bord Pleanála's decision, therefore, the Applicant was neither a property owner in the area affected by the development nor an upholder of social justice and the common good which was affected by that decision. The applicant cannot be compared with SPUC in *the SPUC v Coogan* case: it is by no means impossible that a Plaintiff whose actual property interests were affected by this or any other decision of An Bord Pleanála could mount a challenge to the impugned section. In the context of social justice and the common good there were a number of individual objectors to both the planning authority's decision and to An Bord Pleanála's decision who could as Plaintiffs challenge the Section.

---

[257] *Society for the Protection of Unborn Children (Ireland) Ltd v Coogan* [1989] IR 738.

[258] *Lancefort Ltd v An Bord Pleanála, Ireland and the Attorney General and Treasury Holdings Ltd* (12 March 1998, unreported) HC, McGuinness J.

> The Applicant also cannot be compared with Iarnród Éireann, the corporate plaintiff in the case of that name. Iarnród Éireann was definitely and seriously financially affected by the legislation which it sought to challenge.
>
> It does not appear to me that the Applicant has established the proper interest to provide it with *locus standi* to challenge Section 14(8) of the 1976 Act.'

The use of the corporate form exclusively as a means of shielding constitutional litigants from potential awards of costs will, consequently, result in *locus standi* being denied.

[4.073] The constitutional right to freedom of expression under Article 40.6.1°i has also been invoked by companies to allow the dissemination of factual information in appropriate circumstances. The matter of the company's expression rights was skirted in *Attorney General v Paperlink Ltd*[259], where the constitutional claim was maintained by the directors and members of the company, it being accepted that the company had no constitutionally guaranteed personal rights on which to found a cause of action. But in *Attorney General for England and Wales v Brandon Books Publishers Ltd*[260], Carroll J held that the defendant had a constitutional right under Article 40.6.1°i to publish information which does not involve any breach of copyright provided that the public interest in this jurisdiction is not affected by the publication and there was no breach of confidentiality.

[4.074] More recently, in *Digital Rights Ireland Ltd v Minister for Communications*[261], the High Court considered the rights of a company to invoke the constitutional and European rights to privacy; family life; travel and communication; to privileged communication; and to travel confidentially. McKechnie J granted the plaintiff *locus standi* to bring an *actio popularis* and further granted the plaintiff's motion for a reference to the European Court of Justice. The learned judge noted that, in deciding *locus standi,* it was only necessary for the court to determine that a limited company might avail of such rights, not the extent or breadth of those rights. He further noted that the fact that the plaintiff company had an interest in the matter which, though separate and distinct from its members' interests, might overlap with them, in no way precluded the company from relying on an interest it held in its own right. In that regard he held that a company had a right to privacy in respect of business transactions; but that this right, given the legal and factual nature of such artificial persons, would inevitably be narrower than that applicable to natural persons, and might be limited by the exigencies of the common good, with the threshold for such interference being relative and specific to the case or circumstances. He found, however, that a company could not enjoy the right to travel as it is incorporeal.

[4.075] Whatever about a corporation's constitutional rights, there is no doubt that the corporation, as a creature of positive law, is obliged to observe constitutional *duties*[262]. Breach of the duty may even give rise to an award of compensation against the company. Thus, in *Meskell v CIÉ*[263], where the defendant company made membership of a trade

[259] *Attorney General v Paperlink Ltd* [1984] ILRM 373.

[260] *Attorney General for England and Wales v Brandon Books Publishers Ltd* [1986] IR 579.

[261] *Digital Rights Ireland Ltd v Minister for Communications* [2010] IR 251.

[262] See, eg, *Irish Times Ltd and Others v Ireland* [1998] 1 IR 359; *Byrne v Judge Scally and Dublin Corporation* [2000] IEHC 72, Ó Caoimh J.

[263] *Meskell v CIÉ* [1973] IR 121.

union a condition of employment, the company was held to have breached the plaintiff employee's constitutional right of dissociation[264], and was made liable to pay such damages as might, upon inquiry, be proved to have been sustained by him.

(v) Legal rights and duties

[4.076] As a legal person, the corporation is capable of enjoying rights and being the subject of duties and obligations – just as natural persons can. Indeed, for the purposes of legislation, bodies corporate are treated as falling within the definition of 'person' wherever that word appears in an enactment[265]. Where a statute does not clearly stipulate whether its provisions are to apply to companies, the courts will consider the general background and purpose of the legislation in question[266].

Certain statutes, however, prohibit companies from acting in situations where natural persons are permitted to act. The Companies Acts prohibit companies from acting as company directors[267], examiners[268], liquidators[269] and receivers[270], and other statutes forbid them from providing services as solicitors[271], doctors or dentists[272], or veterinary surgeons[273]. A certificate of personal fitness to operate bookmaking premises may not be held by a company[274].

(e) Privileges and obligations

[4.077] A consequence of gaining separate legal personality is that it may alter relations between the enterprise and the world at large – including the company's relations *vis-à-vis* its controllers. Consequently, a sole trader who incorporates his business may find himself to be an employee of the legal person he has created, and may thereby become entitled to avail of the statutory protection given to employees. A good illustration is *Lee v Lee's Air Farming Ltd*[275], in which Mr Lee, who held the beneficial interest in all of the shares in the defendant company, and who was also its sole governing director, was employed by it as a salaried pilot. When he was killed while flying on company work, his wife claimed compensation under the New Zealand Worker's Compensation Act 1922 as the widow of a 'worker' of the company. The Privy Council, applying *Salomon's* case, held that she should succeed. The company and Lee were separate legal persons,

---

264 Which is a necessary corollary of the right to freedom of association under Article 40.6.1°iii of *Bunreacht na hÉireann*: *Educational Company Ltd v Fitzpatrick (No 2)* [1961] IR 345.

265 Section 18(c) of the Interpretation Act 2005 provides that: '"person" shall be read as importing a body corporate (whether a corporation aggregate or a corporation sole) and an unincorporated body of persons, as well as an individual, and the subsequent use of any pronoun in place of a further use of "person" shall be read accordingly.'

266 See, for example, *R (Cottingham) v The Justices of Cork* [1906] 2 IR 415.

267 Section 176 of the CA 1963.

268 Section 28 of the C(A)A 1990.

269 Section 300 of the CA 1963.

270 Section 314 of the CA 1963.

271 Section 64 of the Solicitors Act 1954.

272 Sections 59 and 61 of the Medical Practitioners Act 1978; s 52 of the Dentists Act 1985.

273 Section 47 of the Veterinary Surgeons Act 1931.

274 Section 4(1) of the Betting Act 1931. A natural person may, however, hold such a certificate as agent for the company: *McDonnell v Reid* [1987] IR 51.

275 *Lee v Lee's Air Farming Ltd* [1961] AC 12.

and the mere fact that Lee was governing director of the company should not preclude him from entering into a contract of service with it – even though, paradoxically, this duality of roles could lead to Lee, as governing director, giving orders to himself as an employee.

Reasoning similar to that applied in *Lee's* case was employed recently by the Court of Appeal in *Secretary of State for Trade and Industry v Bottrill*[276] to hold that the controlling shareholder director of a small insolvent company was entitled to redundancy payments under the Employment Rights Act 1996 (UK) despite the argument that as controlling shareholder he could have prevented his own dismissal. Lord Woolf MR added, however, that the courts should inquire into whether the company was established purely for the fraudulent motive of entitling the director to redundancy payments. The learned Master of the Rolls suggested that the size of the individual's shareholding should be taken into account as an indicator of whether such a motive existed. A literal application of this test could lead unfairly to the separate legal personality of small companies being ignored, and the benefits of *Lee's* case being denied[277].

It follows from *Lee's* case that a controlling shareholder may maintain an action against the company where a winding up of the company would cause the breach of a service contract between the shareholder and the company. In *Fowler v Commercial Timber Co Ltd*[278], it was held that such an action for breach of contract would not be precluded by the fact that the shareholder had voted in favour of the winding up.

[4.078] Another good example of how the incorporation of a company may be used to gain a privilege which would have been unavailable to the individual shareholders is to be found in *Farrar v Farrars Ltd*[279]. In that case it was held that a mortgagee may exercise his power of sale by selling the property which forms the subject matter of the mortgage to a company of which he is the controlling shareholder – despite the rule that he may not sell the property to himself[280] or to an agent or nominee acting on his behalf[281].

[4.079] The separate legal personality of the company may also be relied upon effectively to avoid obligations which would otherwise fall on the controlling shareholders. However, it is advisable to tread warily, for the courts may find it necessary to disregard the separate personality of the company where incorporation is used fraudulently to evade existing legal obligations[282]. But where the legal relation does not amount to an obligation, or where the intention is to avoid *future* obligations, incorporation can be a successful avoidance mechanism. In *Roundabout Ltd v Beirne*[283], a limited company – 'Marian Park Inn Ltd', owned and operated a public house when, in

276 *Secretary of State for Trade and Industry v Bottrill* [2000] 1 All ER 915. *Cf Buchan v Secretary of State for Employment* [1997] BCC 145.

277 See Howell, 'Salomon under Attack' (2000) 21 Co Law 312.

278 *Fowler v Commercial Timber Co Ltd* [1930] 2 KB 1.

279 *Farrar v Farrars Ltd* (1888) 40 Ch D 395.

280 *Henderson v Astwood* [1894] AC 150.

281 *Downes v Grazebrook* (1817) 3 Mer 200.

282 See Ch 5, *Disregarding Separate Legal Personality*, at para **[5.039]** *et seq*.

283 *Roundabout Ltd v Beirne* [1959] IR 423.

May 1958, all of the staff joined a trade union. The controllers of the company, unwilling to operate with a unionised staff, caused the company to close the public house and to dismiss all the staff. The union, arguing that the closure was effected to force staff-members to leave the union, responded by placing a peaceful picket on the premises, something it was entitled to do under the Trade Disputes Act 1906. Meanwhile, the controllers of the company formed a second company, called 'Roundabout Ltd', of which they were permanent directors with a controlling interest in its shares. Roundabout Ltd then leased the public house from the first company. Three new non-union barmen were made directors of Roundabout Ltd, and it was they who carried out the day-to-day business of the public house when it opened for business three weeks after its closure. Since the new company had no employees (only barmen-directors, who, under the articles of association of the company, could be removed by the controllers at any time) it could not be classed as an 'employer'; consequently it could not be the subject of a trade dispute. The new company then sought an injunction against the union to restrain the picketers on the basis that the business was being conducted by a different legal person to that with which the ex-employees had a trade dispute. Dixon J, granting the injunction said:

> 'The new company is in law a distinct entity, as is the old company. Each company is what is known as a legal person. I have to regard the two companies as distinct in the same way as I would regard two distinct individuals. I must, therefore, proceed on the basis that a new and different person is now in occupation of the premises and carrying on business there.'

[4.080] It should be noted that the European Communities (Safeguarding of Employees' Rights on Transfer of Undertakings) Regulations 1980[284] automatically transfer any obligations arising under collective agreements entered into by the transferor to the transferee of a business undertaking. Incorporation may not, therefore, be used to evade obligations under collective agreements.

Limited liability

[4.081] Limited liability is an extremely significant consequence of incorporation, and one of the principal reasons why most businesses decide to incorporate in the first place. It must be stressed at the outset that it is only the members' liability which is limited – the company remains liable down to its last penny for all its debts and liabilities.

[4.082] By definition, the expression 'limited liability' connotes some form of liability. The expression is sometimes incorrectly used to describe the 'immunity' (which connotes no liability whatsoever) which members enjoy from direct liability to the company's creditors. As we have seen[285], the members of the company are not liable to the company's creditors in respect of the company's obligations, since the company's obligations are separate and distinct from those of its members[286]. This 'immunity'

---

284 SI 303/1980. See generally Kerr & Whyte, *Irish Trade Union Law* (1985, Professional Books), at pp 158–159.

285 At para **[4.041]** *et seq.*

286 Statute and common law have intervened, however, to provide for situations in which the members' immunity from liability for corporate debts may be eroded; see Ch 5, *Disregarding Separate Legal Personality.*

stems from the separate legal personality of the company, and as such, it exists regardless of whether the company is registered with or without limited liability. Clearly, then, it is not this immunity to which the Companies Acts refer when they speak of limited liability – though the immunity is, of course, a consequence of incorporation of paramount importance.

[4.083] What the expression 'limited liability' refers to in fact is the *liability* of the members towards the company, rather than towards the company's creditors. This liability is of statutory origin, and does *not* stem from the fact that the company is a separate legal person. Where the company is liable for its obligations to third parties, it is entitled to look to its members for a contribution to enable it to discharge its obligations. The limit to the members' liability to contribute to the company is stated in the company's memorandum, and it is calculated by reference 'to the amount, if any, unpaid on the shares respectively held by them'[287]. If the shareholders have additionally undertaken in the memorandum to guarantee the company, their liability is limited to the amount which they 'respectively thereby undertake to contribute to the assets of the company in the event of its being wound up'.'[288] The extent of a shareholder's liability to contribute in a winding up is further regulated by s 207(1) of the CA 1963 which provides:

> 'In the event of a company being wound up, every present and past member shall be liable to contribute to the assets of the company to an amount sufficient for payment of its debts and liabilities, and the costs, charges and expenses of the winding up, and for the adjustment of the rights of the contributors among themselves ... subject to the following qualifications:
>
> (a) a past member shall not be liable to contribute if he has ceased to be a member for one year or more before the commencement of the winding up;
>
> (b) a past member shall not be liable to contribute in respect of any debt or liability of the company contracted after he ceased to be a member;
>
> (c) a past member shall not be liable to contribute unless it appears to the court that the existing members are unable to satisfy the contributions required to be made by them in pursuance of this Act;
>
> (d) in the case of a company limited by shares, no contribution shall be required from any member exceeding the amount, if any, unpaid on the shares in respect of which he is liable as a present or past member ...[289]'

The liability of shareholders to contribute to the assets of the company is thus limited to the amount, if any, unpaid on their shares[290]. This liability exists both while the company is a going concern[291], and also continues where the company is being wound up. Where the liability is limited by guarantee in the memorandum of association, it is limited to the amount undertaken to be contributed in the guarantee – but the guarantor is not

---

[287] Section 5(2)(a) of the CA 1963.

[288] Section 5(2)(b) of the CA 1963.

[289] Paragraphs (e), (f) and (g) of the subsection deal with companies limited by guarantee; policies of insurance; and dividends and profits due to a member, respectively. For an outline of the history leading to the introduction of limited liability to company law see Ch 1, *The Private Company in Context*, at para **[1.056]** *et seq*.

[290] See generally, Ch 25, *Realisation and Distribution of Assets in a Winding Up*, at para **[25.130]**.

[291] See Ch 8, *Shares and Membership*, at para **[8.093]** *et seq*.

obliged to pay under the guarantee until the company is being wound up[292]. By way of contrast, where the company is registered as an unlimited company, the members' liability to contribute to the assets of the company is unlimited[293].

[4.084] It may be observed that limited liability is not logically a necessary attribute of separate legal personality but is, rather, a statutory development[294]. In *Revenue Commissioners v Bank of Ireland*[295], Murnaghan J observed:

> 'There is at common law no liability upon the members of a body corporate in respect of the debts and liabilities of the body corporate, and such liability in respect of the corporate acts must be created by statute[296].'

This principle was again to the fore in the English case of *Maclaine Watson v Department of Trade and Industry*[297], where Lord Templeman observed that[298]:

> '... by custom or by legislation the members of some corporations in some countries are not free from personal liability. But no such custom exists in the United Kingdom as a general rule and s 4 of the Partnership Act 1890, which preserves for a Scottish partnership some of the benefits of incorporation and some of the attributes of an unincorporated association, does not prove the existence of any general custom in any part of the United Kingdom that members of a corporation or of a body analogous to corporations shall be liable for the debts of the corporation. Parliament, of course, may provide that members of a corporation shall bear liability for or shall be bound to contribute directly or indirectly to payment of the debts of the corporation to a limited or an unlimited extent in accordance with express statutory provisions. The history of the Companies Acts illustrates the power of Parliament, if it pleases, to impose some liability on shareholders as a condition of the grant of incorporation.'

Transferability of interests

[4.085] One of the significant advantages of incorporation as a registered company is that the members' interests may easily be transferred. This is especially so where, as with the private company, the company has a share capital. The transfer and registration of shares is discussed in detail in Ch 9, so at this stage we may simply observe that a member's shares are items of his personal property[299], the transfer and registration of which in the transferee's name relieves the transferor of all[300] of his obligations to the company, and which places the transferee in the shoes of the transferor. The transfer of shares in a private company must, of course, be subject to restrictions on transfer and the public may not be invited to participate[301].

---

292 Section 207(1)(e) of the CA 1963.

293 Except as regards past members who ceased to be members over a year before the commencement of the winding up: s 207(1)(a) of the CA 1963.

294 See Ch 1, *The Private Company in Context*, at para **[1.063]**.

295 *Revenue Commissioners v Bank of Ireland* [1925] 2 IR 90.

296 [1925] 2 IR 90 at 108.

297 *Maclaine Watson v Department of Trade and Industry* [1990] BCLC 102.

298 [1990] BCLC 102 at 108–109.

299 See, generally, Ch 8, *Shares and Membership*.

300 Subject, of course, to the possibility of liability under s 207(1)(a) of the CA 1963 where a winding up follows within a year and the shares were not fully paid up.

301 Section 33(1) of the CA 1963; see Ch 1, *The Private Company in Context*, at para **[1.133]** and Ch 9, *Share Transfer*, at para **[9.016]**.

The significance of the ease of transfer of interests may be understood by contrasting it with the transfer of interests in a partnership or the transfer of a sole trader's interests. The transfer of a partner's interest does not entitle the person to whom the interest is transferred to interfere in the management or administration of the partnership business or affairs, or to require any accounts of the partnership transactions, or to inspect the partnership books[302]. The transferee of the transferring partner's interest is only entitled to receive the share of the profits to which the transferring partner would otherwise have been entitled[303]. Unless the partners have agreed otherwise, the transferee may only be admitted as a partner if all the other partners agree[304]. Notably, the transferring partner will continue to be liable for the obligations of the firm until the firm's creditors agree to release him[305].

The sole trader who wishes to transfer his interest will also encounter difficulty. Many of the existing obligations of the sole trader will be personal in nature and may not be easily transferred to others without the agreement of the parties to whom the obligations are owed.

Perpetual succession

[4.086] As one writer has observed[306]: 'one of the principal advantages of an artificial person is that it is not susceptible to "'the thousand natural shocks that flesh is heir to'".' Since a company only ceases to exist as a legal person upon the occurrence of one of the dissolving events referred to earlier[307], its existence remains unaffected by the insanity, bankruptcy, or other incapacities of any or all of its members. Likewise, where all the members of the company die, the company will survive[308] – though its membership will necessarily fall below the statutory minimum until the registration of some new persons as members under a transfer by the deceased's executors or administrators.

Perpetual succession has particular advantages where the sale of a business is concerned as the company remains there to perform existing contracts whereas when a sole trader or a firm of partners sells a business as a going concern problems may arise concerning the performance of existing contracts and the validity of contracts entered into by customers ignorant of the change of ownership.

Common seal

[4.087] Section 18(2) of the CA 1963 requires the company to have a common seal. The use of the common seal is discussed in further detail in Ch 7[309].

Floating charges

[4.088] Banks and financial institutions often prefer to lend to a company than to a sole trader or firm of partners because a company registered under the Companies Acts is

302 Section 31(1) of the Partnership Act 1890.
303 Section 31(2) of the Partnership Act 1890.
304 Section 24(7) of the Partnership Act 1890.
305 Section 17(2) and (3) of the Partnership Act 1890.
306 Gower, *Principles of Modern Company Law* (5th edn, 1992) at p 92.
307 See para **[4.020]**.
308 See, for example, *Re Tedman Holdings* [1967] QR 561.
309 Ch 7, *Corporate Contracts, Capacity and Authority*, at para **[7.014]**.

capable of granting a floating charge over its assets to secure the company's indebtedness. A *charge*, very simply, is an equitable interest in goods which entitles the chargee to look to the goods for repayment in the event of a default by the debtor. A *floating charge* may be described as an equitable charge which floats or hovers over the assets from time to time which match a certain description, eg, 'stock in trade'; 'book debts and other debts', etc, but which does not restrict the company's ability to deal with the charged assets in the usual course of business until something occurs to cause the charge to become crystallised or fixed. Where, prior to such crystallisation, the assets which are subject to the charge are sold and replaced with new assets of that description the floating charge attaches to those new assets. A *fixed charge*, by way of contrast, attaches to specific, identifiable and defined property and restricts the ability of the company to deal with, or dispose of, the assets which are subject to the charge[310].

[4.089] A floating charge may not, in practice, be granted by a sole trader or a partnership; though legally speaking there is no prohibition on their doing so. It is impractical for them to do so because a charge given by an individual or partnership over personal chattels[311] amounts to a *bill of sale* within the meaning of the Bills of Sale (Ireland) Acts 1879–1883 (which do not apply to companies)[312] and must therefore comply with certain registration formalities[313]. If not registered with a detailed inventory of the charged chattels in the form required by the 1883 Act, the bill of sale, the security *and the loan* will be invalid[314] – indeed, this will be so if the inventory supplied is not very specific about the precise identity of the chattels. Thus, in *Davies v Jenkins*[315], an inventory which stated 'Stock: 2 Horses, 4 Cows' was held not to satisfy the Acts' requirements, and in *Witt v Banner*[316], an inventory describing two paintings by reference to the place in which they were hanging was held to be equally inadequate. The requisite specificity would be impossible to achieve in the case of a floating charge by a sole trader or partnership because the charged assets would be changing from day to day[317].

310 The topic of floating and fixed charges is discussed more fully in Ch 18, *Corporate Borrowing: Debentures and Security*.

311 'Personal chattels' is defined in s 4 of the Bills of Sale (Ireland) Act 1879. Notably, the definition does not include interests in land, shares or interests in the stock, funds or securities of a government or an incorporated company, or *choses in action*. Ships are excluded from the definition by the Mercantile Marine Act 1955, as are agricultural machines, stock and crops by s 36(1) of the Agricultural Credit Act 1978.

312 Section 17 of the Bills of Sale (Ireland) Act 1879 (Amendment) Act 1883; *Re Standard Manufacturing Co* [1891] 1 Ch 627.

313 See Ch 19, *Corporate Borrowing: Registration of Charges*, at para **[19.068]**.

314 Section 9 of the Bills of Sale (Ireland) Act 1879 (Amendment) Act 1883.

315 *Davies v Jenkins* [1900] 1 QB 133.

316 *Witt v Banner* (1887) 20 QBD 794.

317 A second impediment to the creation of floating charges by sole traders and partnerships was the doctrine of 'reputed ownership' which applied in the bankruptcy of individuals. Under this doctrine the court was empowered to order the sale and disposal of any goods or chattels of which the bankrupt was the 'reputed owner' for the benefit of the creditors, despite the interests of floating charge holders: Irish Bankrupt and Insolvent Act 1857, s 313. The doctrine was repealed and not replaced by the Bankruptcy Act 1988.

Formation of large associations

[4.090] A practical consequence of incorporation under the Companies Acts is that it enables members to form an association consisting of more than 20 persons, with a view to the acquisition of gain, which would otherwise have been prohibited by s 376 of the CA 1963. This provides:

> 'No company, association or partnership consisting of more than twenty persons shall be formed for the purpose of carrying on any business (other than the business of banking), that has as its object the acquisition of gain by the company, association or partnership, or by the individual members thereof, unless it is registered as a company under this Act or is formed in pursuance of some other statute[318].'

A private company, however, may not as a general rule have more than 99 members[319].

Taxation

[4.091] A major consequence of incorporation is the differing tax treatment which companies receive as opposed to individuals and partnerships. A comprehensive analysis of the taxation advantages of incorporation is beyond the scope of this work. However the following features may briefly be noted: first, companies are taxed on the whole of their income and capital gains under a single rate of corporation tax[320], whereas individuals are taxed separately on their income and capital gains and at varying rates. Second, the controlling shareholders of the company should also note that company directors are not insurable as employees for the purposes of calculating pay related social insurance (PRSI) contributions, and may, consequently, be entitled to reduced social insurance benefits.

It is of note that incorporation of an existing activity carried out for the benefit of the public does not *per se* render the company liable to rates as a profit making company: in *Port of Cork Company v The Commissioner of Valuation*[321], Kearns J overturned a decision of the Valuation Tribunal that the incorporation of the Port of Cork Company, which was previously vested in the Cork Harbour Commissioners and exempt from rates, meant that the port area was to be run on a commercial basis and subject, therefore, to rates. Kearns J noted that the sole shareholder was the Minister, and all dividends were payable into the Exchequer in the public interest, and the company had no beneficial interest in the charges it levied but had to devote them to the maintenance of the public harbour. In such circumstances the company was emphatically not a private profit making company.

Other consequences of incorporation

[4.092] To the list of consequences already discussed may be added the *practical* statutory consequences of incorporation already listed in Ch 2, namely: the requirements to carry on an activity within the State; to deliver certain particulars to the

[318] Section 13 of the C(A)A 1982, however, permits partnerships consisting of more than 20 solicitors or qualified accountants.

[319] Section 33(1) of the CA 1963.

[320] Taxes Consolidation Act 1997, s 21.

[321] *Port of Cork Company v The Commissioner of Valuation* [2003] IESC 47.

Revenue Commissioners; to maintain certain registers; to have at least two directors and a secretary; to display certain information; and to make annual returns to the CRO[322].

A further major consequence of incorporation is the application of doctrines such as the *ultra vires* rule[323], and the rules governing the raising and maintenance of capital[324], to companies.

[322] See Ch 17, *Financial Statements, Audit and Annual Return*.

[323] See Ch 7, *Corporate Contracts, Capacity and Authority*, at para **[7.045]**.

[324] See Ch 10, *The Maintenance of Capital*.

Chapter 5

Disregarding Separate Legal Personality

Introduction

[5.001] This chapter is concerned with situations in which the separate legal personality of a private company may be disregarded. It will be recalled that in *Salomon's* case[1] it was not only established that an incorporated company was a legal person, but also that it was a *separate and distinct* legal person from its members. Therefore, companies should not be regarded as agents or trustees of their members (or vice versa), and the motives of those who form a company should be of no consequence to its separate corporate existence.

[5.002] Many jurists have described the principle of separate legal personality through the use of metaphors such as 'mask,' 'cloak,' 'shell,' and, most popularly, 'veil' of incorporation[2]. The terms 'lifting the veil' or 'piercing the veil' are frequently used to describe situations in which the separate legal personality of a company is disregarded[3]. Even the courts have shown a penchant for such imagery[4]. The problem, however, is that the use of such vague metaphorical language often obscures precisely which aspect of the principle of separate legal personality (if any) is in issue. As Cardozo J said in an American case[5], 'metaphors are in law to be narrowly watched, for starting as devices to liberate thought, they often end by enslaving it'. The 'veil' image, for example, has been described as 'a singularly unhelpful and confusing metaphor[6]' because it gives the impression that regard may never be had to the identity and character of those who control a company when its affairs are in issue – an impression which is falsely grounded[7]. The use of such metaphors will be avoided in this chapter.

---

§ *This chapter has been contributed by G Brian Hutchinson.*

1 *Salomon v Salomon and Co Ltd* [1897] AC 22. See Ch 4, *Incorporation and its Consequences*, at para **[4.026]** *et seq*.

2 For a detailed list of metaphors in this context see Pickering, 'The Company as a Separate Legal Entity' (1968) 31 MLR 481 at p 482.

3 See, for example, Davies (ed), *Gower's Principles of Modern Company Law* (6th edn, Sweet & Maxwell, 1997); Forde, *Company Law* (4th edn, Round Hall, 2007).

4 See para **[5.040]** *et seq*.

5 *Berkley v Third Avenue Railway* (1926) 50 ALR 599 at 604.

6 Keane, *Company Law* (4th edn, Bloomsbury Professional, 2007), at p 126.

7 Keane, *Company Law* (4th edn, Bloomsbury Professional, 2007), at p 126. The learned author points out that the great principle underlying modern companies legislation is the requirement that the identity of those who control the company should be ascertainable to the public. In that regard see Ch 8, *Shares and Membership*, at para **[8.127]** *et seq*.

[5.003] What has sometimes been overlooked is the fact that *Salomon's* case itself recognises the possibility of departure from the principle of separate legal personality. Lord Halsbury said that the principle was to be of application *provided that* there was:

> '... no fraud and no agency and if the company was a real one and not a fiction or a myth[8].'

A company, thus, is a legal person which should not *per se* be regarded as an agent or trustee of its members (or vice versa), and the motives of those who formed it should not *per se* affect its separate corporate existence. Where additional factors exist, the separate legal personality of the company may be disregarded. This chapter is primarily concerned with identifying those additional factors.

[5.004] In the first edition[9] we noted that as the law then stood the courts had failed to identify in a systemic manner the additional factors permitting the disregard of the separate legal personality of a company. This failure produced an amorphous and unprincipled body of jurisprudence where each case was treated, to a large degree, on its own merits and according to convenience rather than legal principle. An Australian judge described the situation thus:

> 'The threshold problem arises from the fact that there is no common, unifying principle which underlies the occasional decision of courts to pierce the corporate veil. Although an *ad hoc* explanation may be offered by a court which so decides, there is no principled approach to be derived from the authorities[10].'

Decided cases contain abundant reference to metaphors such as 'veil,' 'façade,' 'cloak,' 'alias,' 'alter ego,' 'agent,' 'fiction,' 'instrumentality,' 'puppet,' and 'sham'[11] which do not serve to enlighten. Attempts by commentators to disentangle and rationalise the cases in the hope of identifying a unifying underlying principle have resulted in little more than the unhelpful observation that the courts will disregard the principle of separate legal personality where some injustice is intended, or would result, to a party dealing with the company or its members[12]. Thus, in *Re A Company (1985)*[13], the English Court of Appeal stated:

> 'In our view the cases ... show that the court will use its power to pierce the corporate veil if it is necessary to achieve justice irrespective of the legal efficacy of the corporate structure ...'

The 1970s and 1980s in particular had witnessed a tendency in the courts to disregard the separate legal personality of companies by giving regard to the economic realities of

---

8 *Salomon v Salomon and Co Ltd* [1897] AC 22 at 22–23.

9 Courtney, *Law of Private Companies* (1st edn, Butterworths, 1994), at para [4.015].

10 *Per* Rogers AJA in *Briggs v James Hardie & Co Pty Ltd* [1989] 16 NSWLR 549 at 567, cited by Farrar, Furey & Hannigan, *Farrar's Company Law* (3rd edn, Butterworths, 1991) at p 73.

11 See Pickering, 'The Company as a Separate Legal Entity' (1968) 31 MLR 481.

12 See *eg* Gallagher & Zeigler, 'Lifting the Corporate Veil in the Pursuit of Justice' [1990] JBL 292; Pickering, 'The Company as a Separate Legal Entity' (1968) 31 MLR 481 at p 22. For an empirical study of the circumstances in which the English Courts have disregarded the separate legal personality of companies, including a comparison with American and Australian studies in the field, see Mitchell, 'Lifting the Corporate Veil in the English Courts: An Empirical Study' (1999) 3 CFILR 15.

13 *Re A Company (1985)*[1985] BCLC 333 at 337, 338.

the situation rather than legal formality on the basis that the 'justice of the case' so required[14]. Though the courts were cautious in the application of this approach, it gave the impression that *Salomon's* case was losing importance.

[5.005] The intervening years, however, have witnessed a concerted effort on the part of the English and Irish courts (and some commentators) to restate the importance of *Salomon's* case in an attempt to restore principle to this area. In his 1997 Hamlyn Lecture on *Salomon's* case, Lord Cooke of Thorndon revealed this trend, saying:

> 'In the main, the concept that a duly incorporated limited liability company, if not a real thing, is at least not to be identified with its shareholders, has been faithfully followed by British and other Commonwealth courts ever since *Salomon's* case. But there has been some gnawing away at the edges of the doctrine, a process commonly described as piercing or lifting the corporate veil. I believe that there is only one broad class of cases where this is truly consistent with the *Salomon* reasoning. They are all cases where, under enactments such as those against fraudulent or wrongful trading, or on the permissible interpretation of an enactment or contract, or for the purposes of the common law or equitable principles against fraud or oppression or relating to agency, it is necessary to look at what has happened in fact, rather than in form[15].'

The Court of Appeal in *Adams v Cape Industries*[16] held that the courts were not generally free to disregard separate legal personality on the vague and elusive 'justice of the case' criterion; Gower[17] summarises the decision as giving rise to the conclusion that the courts may only disregard the separate legal personality of a company in the following circumstances:

(a) when the court is construing a statute, contract or other document;

(b) when the court is satisfied that a company is a 'mere façade' concealing the true facts; or

(c) when it can be established that the company is an authorised agent of its controllers or its members, corporate or human.

Adams was followed by Walker J in *Re Polly Peck International plc (In Administration) (No 4)*[18], where the learned judge added that the courts must look to the legal substance of any transaction and not its economic substance when deciding whether the company is a mere façade, regardless of any perceived injustice that arose when the company became insolvent. Again in *Ord v Belhaven Pubs Ltd*[19] the Court of Appeal indicated that the disregard by the courts of the separate legal personality of companies should be exercised with restraint, and generally should only occur where some impropriety is found.

[14] See para **[5.051]**.

[15] Lord Cooke of Thorndon, *Hamlyn Lectures – Turning Points of the Common Law* (1997, Sweet & Maxwell) p13. See, for example, *Trustor AB v Smallbone et al (No 2)* [2001] 3 All ER 987 where *Re A Company* [1985] BCLC 333 was not followed.

[16] *Adams v Cape Industries* [1990] Ch 433. See para **[5.048]**.

[17] Davies (ed), *Gower's Principles of Modern Company Law* (6th edn, Sweet and Maxwell, 1997).

[18] *Re Polly Peck International plc (In Administration) (No 4)* [1996] 2 All ER 433. See para **[5.060]**.

[19] *Ord v Belhaven Pubs Ltd* [1998] 2 BCLC 447. See para **[5.044]**.

The Irish Supreme Court, in *Allied Irish Coal Supplies Ltd v Powell Duffryn International Fuels Ltd*[20], showed similar restraint, holding that the principles enunciated by the House of Lords in *Salomon's* case remain the '*corner stone of company law*'[21] and that the proposition that the assets of a parent company should be generally available to meet the liabilities of a trading subsidiary was so fundamentally at variance with those principles as to be 'wholly unstateable'[22].

[5.006] In *Fyffes plc v DCC plc*[23], Laffoy J affirmed that:

> 'It has been a fundamental principle of Irish company law since the decision of the House of Lords in *Salomon v Salomon & Co* [1897] AC 22 that a company registered under the Companies Acts is an artificial legal entity separate and distinct from the members, whether natural or corporate persons, of which it is composed.'

She went on to quote with approval Keane's[24] summary of the principles of law in this area as follows:

> '(1) The rule in *Salomon's* case is still the law. The company and its shareholders are separate legal entities and the courts normally cannot infer from the degree of control exercised by a shareholder a relationship of principal and agent or beneficiary and trustee between the shareholders and the company.
>
> (2) The courts, however, will not permit the statutory privilege of incorporation to be used for a fraudulent, illegal or improper purpose. Where it is so misused, the court may treat the company thus incorporated as identical with its promoters.
>
> (3) In certain cases, where no actual misuse of the privilege of incorporation is involved, the courts may nonetheless infer the existence of an agency or trust if to do otherwise would lead to injustice or facilitate the avoidance of tax liability.
>
> (4) In the case of a group of companies, the court may sometimes treat the group as one entity, particularly where to do otherwise would have unjust consequences for outsiders dealing with companies in the group.
>
> (5) The rule in *Salomon's* case does not prevent the court from looking at the individual members of the company in order to determine its *character* and *status* and where it legally resides.'

This summary continues to be welcome as a principled map of the prevailing legal landscape, and it can be expected to continue to have a significant effect on future judicial decisions. It is submitted that, *for the future*, the true principles of *Salomon's* case will better be reflected by the abandonment of the '*justice of the case*' criterion, as there is nothing in *Salomon's* case to suggest such a special rule. It is further submitted that the true principle of *Salomon's* case is that, where the corporate form has not in fact been misused and where statute does not expressly allow the disregard of separate legal personality, *ordinary* principles of contract, agency, or the law of trusts, etc, should be

---

20 *Allied Irish Coal Supplies Ltd v Powell Duffryn International Fuels Ltd* [1998] 2 IR 519. See para **[5.045]**.

21 *Allied Irish Coal Supplies Ltd v Powell Duffryn International Fuels Ltd* [1998] 2 IR 519 *per* Murphy J at 535, approving the comments of Laffoy J in the High Court in the case.

22 *Allied Irish Coal Supplies Ltd v Powell Duffryn International Fuels Ltd* [1998] 2 IR 519 at 537.

23 *Fyffes plc v DCC plc* [2009] IR 417.

24 Keane, *Company Law* (4th edn, Bloomsbury Professional, 2007) pp 139–140.

applied when inferring the existence of a connecting relationship between the members of a company and the company itself. It is not sufficient to suggest, for example, that a company can be regarded as the agent of its members simply because injustice might otherwise be done – injustice would likewise be done to the company, its members, and its creditors were the courts to ignore the ordinary legal formalities in establishing an agency relationship[25].

[5.007] Some have suggested that the legislature should lay down definite rules in this area[26]. As shall be seen, however, the legislature has not responded to such pleas; though it has provided for disregard of separate legal personality in a number of particular circumstances[27].

The manner in which separate legal personality may be disregarded

[5.008] The separate legal personality of a company may be disregarded in a number of different ways, and to varying degrees. It may be, and commonly is, disregarded without ignoring the fact that the company still exists as a legal person – instead, the *separateness* of its existence is compromised by the identification of the company with its members, or by regarding it as an agent or trustee for them. Four means of disregarding the separate legal personality of a company have been identified[28], and it is to these which discussion now, briefly, turns.

First, the separate legal personality of the company may be disregarded merely by looking at its controlling members in order to characterise it, ie, to attribute to it some characteristic, such as residence, negligence, or *mens rea*, which cannot comfortably be associated with a purely metaphysical entity having no physical manifestation. In such cases, the legal existence of the company is not ignored, but the separateness of its existence is compromised to the extent that the characteristics of its controllers are attributed to it[29].

Second, the separate legal personality of the company may be disregarded by making other persons, particularly its members, *in addition to the company itself*, responsible for the debts and other obligations of the company. It should be noted that such disregard is not limited merely to making *members alone* liable for the company's debts; other persons who are *not members* may also be made liable[30]. Again, in such cases, the legal

25 See the comments of Murphy J in *Allied Irish Coal Supplies Ltd v Powell Duffryn International Fuels Ltd* [1998] 2 IR 519 at 537; also those of Walker J in *Re Polly Peck International plc (In Administration) (No 4)* [1996] 2 All ER 433.

26 'The Legislature might, but no Court could possibly, lay down a hard and fast rule ...': *Daimler v Continental Tyre & Rubber Co* [1916] 2 AC 307, *per* Lord Parker at 346; see also Wedderburn, 'Multinationals and the Antiquities of Company Law' (1984) 47 MLR 87 at 90.

27 See para **[5.073]** *et seq*.

28 See Ottolenghi, 'From Peeping Behind the Corporate Veil to Ignoring it Completely' (1990) 53 MLR 338. The author describes these four means as 'peeping behind the veil,' 'penetrating the veil,' 'extending the veil,' and 'ignoring the veil,' respectively.

29 See, for example, *The King (Cottingham) v The Justices of County Cork* [1906] 2 IR 415, discussed at para **[5.072]**.

30 See, for example, s 297A(1)(b) of the CA 1963, discussed in detail in Ch 15, *Duties of Directors and Other Officers*, at para **[15.126]** *et seq* which empowers the court to impose personal liability for the company's debts and other liabilities on '*any person* ... knowingly a party to the carrying on of any business of the company with intent to defraud ...' (italics added). See also *O'Keeffe v Ferris* [1993] 3 IR 165, *per* Murphy J at 174.

existence of the company is not forgotten, but the separateness of its existence is compromised to the extent that its responsibilities are *shared*, whether jointly or severally, with other persons. Such disregard of separate legal personality is most commonly permitted by legislative provision[31], though the same effect can be obtained through contract[32] or agency[33], and through the courts' power to order enforcement of its orders against anyone in respect of another's obligation[34].

Third, the separate legal personality of the company may be disregarded by regarding it as a mere constituent of a larger legal entity, such as a group of companies. In such cases the legal existence of the company is not ignored, but its identity is consumed by a larger entity. This kind of disregard is sometimes employed by the courts where a group of corporate entities is regarded as a 'single economic unit'[35]. Certain legislative provisions permit similar disregard[36]. In such cases, the disregard directly affects the other members of the larger entity, notably, one of the company's principal members – its 'parent' or holding[37] company.

The final type of disregard of the separate legal personality of the company involves ignoring the existence of the company completely, so that liability will fall on some other person – often a member. The courts have regularly stated that they will disregard the legal personality of a company in this manner where it is erected merely as a 'sham,' 'device,' or 'façade' designed as a means to defraud or to avoid a person's existing legal obligations[38]. Unfortunately the courts have been unable to come up with uniform criteria for identifying whether a company is such a sham, device or façade, etc. Furthermore, in many cases where these circumstances *have* been identified by the courts, the courts have then proceeded to give a determination of the case which could be justified *without* disregarding the separate legal personality of the company[39]. Disregard of the existence of the company has the disadvantage of estopping a court from directing orders against the company itself, and it has been suggested that, as a means of preventing or remedying injustice, it goes too far[40].

With whom will the company be identified?

[5.009] When the separate legal personality of a company is disregarded, the question becomes: with whom will it be identified? The answer varies depending on the manner

31 See the statutory provisions discussed at para **[5.073]** *et seq*.

32 Such as a contract of guarantee. See para **[5.015]**.

33 Agents who do not disclose the fact that they are acting as agents may be made liable for the obligations of their principals. See para **[5.027]**.

34 See para **[5.063]**.

35 See, for example, *Power Supermarkets Ltd v Crumlin Investments Ltd et al* (22 June 1981, unreported) HC, Costello J, discussed at para **[5.052]**.

36 See, for example, s 141 of the CA 1990, considered in detail in Ch 25, *Realisation and Distribution of Assets in a Winding Up*, at para **[25.119]** *et seq*. The section permits two or more related companies to be wound up as though they were a single company.

37 On holding companies and subsidiary companies see generally Ch 12, *Groups of Companies*.

38 See, for example, *Jones v Lipman* [1962] 1 All ER 442, and *Gilford Motor Company Ltd v Horne* [1933] Ch 939, both discussed at para **[5.040]** *et seq*.

39 See, for example, *Cummings v Stewart* [1911] 1 IR 236, discussed *ibid*.

40 Ottolenghi, 'From Peeping Behind the Corporate Veil to Ignoring it Completely' (1990) 53 MLR 338 at 351.

of disregard, but in most situations the focus shifts to the controllers of the company[41]. The persons or entities most likely to be identified with a company where the company's separate legal personality is disregarded are its day-to-day controllers, whether they are directors of the company or not[42]. This factor should be of particular concern to the many Irish private companies which are beneficially owned and controlled by only one person, and is of even greater significance to the sole member of a single-member private limited company[43].

It is essential to note, however, that control is *not* the determining factor in the decision to disregard the separate legal personality of a company[44]. Some additional circumstances must be shown to exist which would justify the controllers being identified with the company. It is to a review of these circumstances that discussion now turns.

The circumstances in which separate legal personality may be disregarded

[5.010] The circumstances in which the separate legal personality of a company may be disregarded are considered in this chapter under the following headings:

[A] Contract, Tort, Agency and Trusts.
[B] Misuse of the Corporate Form.
[C] Single Economic Entities.
[D] Injunctions and Orders.
[E] Characterisation.
[F] Statute.

[A] CONTRACT, TORT, AGENCY AND TRUSTS

[5.011] *Salomon's* case established that a company is to be regarded as a separate legal person, and that a company is not *per se* to be regarded as entitled to or responsible for the rights and obligations of its members, and *vice versa.* The law has long recognised, however, that persons (natural or artificial) are generally free to assume the rights and responsibilities of others through ordinary principles of contract, tort, agency or trusts. Thus, for example, a person can become responsible for the debts of another by agreeing to a guarantee; a person can become responsible in tort to another where they have personally assumed a duty of care; a principal will be responsible to another for the acts of his agent; and a beneficiary under a trust will be entitled to property held by another in trust. The law also recognises that such relationships can arise unwittingly – the parties to an agency or a trust, for example, do not have to appreciate that they are entering such a relationship, though they commonly do. Here, we consider the circumstances in which such relationships may arise under the following headings:

---

41 See especially *Smith, Stone & Knight Ltd v Birmingham Corporation* [1939] 4 All ER 116, discussed at para **[5.024]**.

42 See *Gilford Motor Co v Horne* [1933] Ch 939, discussed in further detail at para **[5.041]**, where the controller was neither a director nor even a member of the company.

43 See Howell, 'Salomon under Attack' (2000) 21 Co Law 312.

44 *Allied Irish Coal Supplies Ltd v Powell Duffryn International Fuels Ltd* [1998] 2 IR 519.

1. Contracts;
2. Torts;
3. Agency;
4. Trusts.

Contracts

[5.012] The separate legal personality of a company is subject to easy circumvention by agreement. There is no legal objection to an agreement whereby a member agrees to be liable in respect of the company's obligations – provided the normal formalities for the making of such agreements are observed[45]. Most institutional lenders, for example, would insist on the director-members of smaller private companies contracting around the separate (limited) liability of the company by getting them to agree to personal guarantees or other securities – so that they assume personal responsibility for the debts of the company.

Likewise, a company may agree to be liable for the obligations of its members if the usual formalities are observed – provided, however, that the transaction is not *ultra vires*[46]; beyond the scope of the directors' authority[47]; does not amount to a fraudulent preference[48]; and does not amount to a breach of statutory regulations governing transactions between directors and companies[49].

[5.013] The courts will be slow to imply such agreements, however, as both the High Court and Supreme Court noted in *Sweeney v Duggan*[50]. The plaintiff in that case was seriously injured whilst employed by a quarrying company. His action in negligence against the company succeeded, but the company went into voluntary liquidation during the proceedings and was unable ultimately to satisfy the judgment against it. The plaintiff then commenced proceedings against the defendant, who was principal shareholder in the company and quarry manager within the meaning of the Mines and Quarries Act 1965. The two broad planks of his case against the defendant were that in reality he was the company (or its *alter ego*) and that as quarry manager he owed the plaintiff duties in contract and tort to take reasonable care to ensure that the company had adequate insurance cover to meet any claims in respect of injuries to employees. Barron J in the High Court refused to hold the defendant liable, saying:

> 'Neither of these matters is a ground for imposing liability on the defendant personally. He is in law a different person from the company and there are no circumstances from which it could be inferred that the company was a sham or should be treated as an instrument of fraud. Undoubtedly, as quarry manager the defendant was personally liable for breach of any of the statutory duties imposed upon the holder of that office. But such duties relate only to safety. There is no statutory duty of the type which the plaintiff seeks to establish … The reality of the plaintiff's claim is that the defendant was the person in control of the company. He can certainly have no greater liability than that of the company

45 See *Ford & Carter Ltd v Midland Bank Ltd* (1979) 129 New L J 543.

46 See Ch 7, *Corporate Contracts, Capacity and Authority*, at para **[7.045]**.

47 See Ch 7, *Corporate Contracts, Capacity and Authority*, at para **[7.099]** *et seq*.

48 Section 286 of the CA 1963, as amended. See Ch 25, *Realisation and Distribution of Assets in a Winding Up*, at para **[25.081]** *et seq*.

49 See, generally, Ch 16, *Statutory Regulation of Directors' Transactions*.

50 *Sweeney v Duggan* [1991] 2 IR 274.

> itself. However it does seem to me that perhaps this claim should be answered by saying that to allow it as against the defendant would in effect be depriving the defendant of his protection under company law and to nullify all the essential principles of that law.'

Each case will, however, turn on its own facts and in *Shinkwin v Quin-Con Ltd and Quinlan*[51], a case said by Fennelly J to bear a superficial resemblance to *Sweeney*, a manager was held to be liable in tort for an employee's injuries[52].

[5.014] The types of agreement which cause the separate legal personality of a company to be disregarded include:

(a) Personal guarantees;
(b) Indemnities;
(c) Comfort letters;

A few brief points may now be made in respect of each.

(a) Personal guarantees

[5.015] It is common for lending institutions to require personal guarantees from third parties, often director-members, where a company seeks credit facilities. A guarantee is a contract whereby a person agrees to become answerable *himself* to the lending institution in the event that the company fails to meet its obligations. In many Irish private companies the directors will be members, and the contract of guarantee may be viewed by the lending institution as a means of circumventing the separate legal personality of the company and the limited liability of the member. A detailed review of the law relating to guarantees is outside the scope of this work[53]; however, the following features may briefly be noted:

(a) A guarantee must be evidenced in writing[54].
(b) A guarantee is an *ancillary* obligation, ie, no obligation arises under it until the company has defaulted. Additionally, anything which terminates the company's obligation (eg, release[55], notice of death, bankruptcy, insanity, misrepresentation, etc) likewise terminates the guarantor's obligations. However, standard form letters of guarantee issued by lending institutions frequently modify this principle[56].

---

51 *Shinkwin v Quin-Con Ltd and Quinlan* [2001] 1 IR 514.

52 See para **[5.018]**.

53 See further Johnston, *Banking and Security Law in Ireland* (1998, Butterworths), Ch 9; Breslin, *Banking Law in the Republic of Ireland* (2nd edn, Round Hall, 2006); Marks & Moss, *Rowlatt on Principal and Surety* (6th edn, Sweet & Maxwell, 2011); Goode, *Legal Problems of Credit & Security* (4th edn, Sweet & Maxwell, 2008); Donnelly, *Law of Banks and Credit Institutions* (2000, Round Hall); Donnelly, *Law of Credit and Security* (2011, Round Hall).

54 Section 2 of the Statute of Frauds (Ireland) 1695. See generally Clark, *Contract Law in Ireland* (6th edn, Round Hall, 2008), Ch 4. The equitable doctrine of part performance may not generally be relied upon where guarantees are concerned: *Madison v Alderson* (1883) 8 App Cas 467; *cf Steadman v Steadman* [1976] AC 536.

55 See, however, *Tempany v Royal Liver Trustees Ltd* [1984] ILRM 273, where it was held that where a liquidator disclaims any of the company's continuing obligations, under s 290 of the CA 1963, the disclaimer will *not* relieve the guarantor of his obligations under the guarantee.

56 See *Moschi v Lep Air Services* [1973] AC 331; *Heald v O'Connor* [1971] 2 All ER 1105; *Yeoman Credit v Latter* [1961] 2 All ER 294; *Garrard v James* [1925] Ch 616.

(c) Standard letters of guarantee issued by lending institutions may stipulate that the guarantee is a 'continuing security'. By this it is meant that the guarantor agrees to guarantee not only the company's liability in respect of the initial advance, but also in respect of any future advances made to the company. In contractual terms, a continuing guarantee is a standing offer which is accepted by the lending institution each time a new advance is made[57]. The offer may be revoked by the guarantor in respect of future advances before acceptance by notifying the lending institution in accordance with the provisions of the guarantee[58]. In *Bank of Ireland v McCabe*[59], the Supreme Court held that a continuing security clause in a standard letter of guarantee could be ousted by oral agreement between the parties at the time of contracting.

(d) Since it is an agreement, a guarantee may be invalidated by want of capacity, or by mistake, misrepresentation, duress, undue influence, etc. The circumstances in which guarantees are given may render them susceptible to invalidation on grounds of misrepresentation[60] or duress and undue influence[61]. Lending institutions will normally require a guarantor to sign a declaration that he has been given an opportunity to obtain independent legal advice to mitigate the chances of such invalidation[62]. Guarantees may also be avoided by statute[63].

Standard form letters of guarantee regularly contain covenants by the guarantor entitling the lending institution to enforce the guarantee by exercising a lien over any monies held by it in the guarantor's account; by setting-off the amount due under the guarantee against those monies; or by exercising any other form of security right (eg, mortgage of the family home) it may have against the guarantor. Where the guarantor is himself a creditor of the company, the lending institution may additionally require him to agree to subordinate any security he holds in the company's assets in favour of a security held by the institution. Under such a subordination agreement, the guarantor agrees not to realise his security until any securities held by the lending institution in the company's assets have been realised in full[64].

---

57 *Lloyds v Harper* (1880) 16 Ch D 290.

58 See *Bradbury v Morgan* (1862) 1 H & C 249; *Bradford Old Bank v Sutcliffe* [1918] 2 KB 833; *Morrisson v Barking Chemicals Ltd* [1919] 2 Ch 325.

59 *Bank of Ireland v McCabe* (19 December 1994) SC.

60 See *Lloyds Bank v Bundy* [1975] QB 326.

61 See *Barclay's Bank v O'Brien* [1993] 4 All ER 417; *Bank of Ireland v Smyth* [1993] 2 IR 102. See Sanfey, 'Undue Influence and the "Tender Treatment" of Wives' (1994) CLP 99.

62 See *CIBC Mortgages v Pitt* [1993] 4 All ER 433 and *Banco Exterior Internaçional v Mann* [1995] 1 All ER 936. For a discussion of the legal principles surrounding the giving of independent legal advice see Johnston, *Banking and Security Law in Ireland* (1998, Butterworths), Ch 8.

63 See Courtney, 'The Latest Hazard to Guarantees: Inter-Company Guarantees and s 31 of the CA 1990' (1991) Gazette ILSI 261, and Ch 16, *Statutory Regulation of Directors' Transactions*; also Johnston, *Banking and Security Law in Ireland* (1998, Butterworths), pp 626 *et seq;* and Breslin, 'Guarantees under Attack' (1996) CLP 243.

64 On debt subordination generally see Wood, *The Law of Subordinated Debt* (1990, Sweet & Maxwell).

(b) Indemnities

[5.016] Lending institutions may additionally require an *indemnity* from the controlling members of a company seeking credit facilities. Strictly speaking, an indemnity differs from a guarantee in that it is a *primary* obligation, personal to the individual and independent of the company's obligation. Most standard form letters of guarantee contain provisions creating the same effect as an indemnity – thus rendering the distinction between guarantees and indemnities somewhat academic[65]. Indeed the current practice is for banks to describe their standard suretyship agreement as a 'guarantee and indemnity'. An indemnity need not, however, be evidenced in writing[66].

(c) Comfort letters

[5.017] Where credit facilities are sought by a subsidiary[67] of a holding company, a lender may seek a comfort letter from the holding company instead of a full guarantee. The comfort letter will usually state that the holding company will not reduce its shareholding in the subsidiary during the term of the loan; that it will ensure that the subsidiary remains in a position to repay the loan; and that it will not do anything which could result in the subsidiary defaulting in its repayments under the loan[68]. The terms of such comfort letters vary from case to case, as does their legal effect[69].

A comfort letter, depending upon its terms, may have the effect of creating a binding contractual obligation on the holding company to observe any terms making it liable for the default of the subsidiary. Indeed, in appropriate circumstances, an officer of a company may even become personally liable for the commitment given in a comfort letter[70]. In order to avoid such liability, the letter should not evidence an intention to create legal relations[71]. In *Kleinwort Benson Ltd v Malaysia Mining Corporation*

---

65 *Moschi v Lep Air Services* [1973] AC 331; *Heald v O'Connor* [1971] 2 All ER 1105; *Yeoman Credit v Latter* [1961] 2 All ER 294; *Garrard v James* [1925] Ch 616. Also, s 25(1) of the CA 1990 interprets 'guarantee' as including 'indemnity' for the purposes of Part III of that Act, which concerns transactions between a company and its directors.

66 See, for example, *Barnett v Hyndman* (1840) 3 Ir LR 109, where an indemnifier was held liable on an oral promise to indemnify.

67 On holding and subsidiary companies see Ch 12, *Groups of Companies*.

68 See, for example, the terms of the letter examined in *Re Atlantic Computers Ltd (In Liquidation); National Australia Bank Ltd v Soden* [1995] BCC 696.

69 For more detailed discussion on the topic see Johnston, *Banking and Security Law in Ireland* (1998, Butterworths), paras 9.123–9.130. For a comparative review see Trichardt, 'Chameleonic Documents in Law – A Comfort Letter Trilogy' (2001) 16 BJIB & FL 416; Von Diessl, 'US Comfort Letters: Purpose and Content' (2001) PLC 45; and Vernerson, 'Sweden: Company Law – Letters of Comfort – Recent Case Law' (1996) ECL 58.

70 See *Paulger v Butland Industries Ltd* [1989] 3 NZLR 549, where the managing director of D Ltd, which was facing financial difficulties, circulated a letter, written on the firm's letterhead, in which he asked for the 'tolerance' of all creditors whilst a certain deal concerning the acquisition of a part of the firm's business by another entity was being finalised. He advised that D Ltd 'would make good all outstanding matters within 90 days' and added: 'The writer personally guarantees that all due payments will be made.' The Court of Appeal of New Zealand confirmed the finding of the Master on summary judgment that the letter constituted a personal guarantee.

71 A mere statement that 'This letter is not intended to create any legal obligations' will not be conclusive: *Wilson Smithett & Cape Sugar v Bangladesh Sugar and Food Industries* [1986] 1 Lloyds' Rep 378.

Berhad[72], a comfort letter stated, *inter alia*, that 'It is our policy to ensure that the business of [the subsidiary] is at all times in a position to meet its liability to you'. At first instance, Hirst J held that the letter evidenced an intention to be legally bound, and consequently, was actionable. The Court of Appeal, however, overturned Hirst J's findings on the basis that the letter confined itself to a representation of existing fact, ie, 'it *is* our policy'. It would seem, then, that careful phrasing of the acknowledgements contained in the letter, and use of the present tense, might avoid the creation of a contractual obligation. The decision has been criticised, however, as a 'semantic and textual analysis' in the Australian courts[73].

Torts

[5.018] A third party (eg, director, member, controller) may become responsible for the torts (ostensibly) of a company where it is found to owe an 'independent duty' to the victim[74]. Whether such an independent duty exists depends upon the elements of the tort in question, and will involve an inquiry into the centrality of the third party in the events generating corporate liability. Where the third party has knowingly authorised, directed or procured the tort in question, personal liability may be imposed[75]. In *Fairline Shipping Corporation v Adamson*[76], the plaintiff claimed damages for negligence sustained to ships' provisions which were not kept adequately refrigerated. The defendant, who was managing director of the company providing the cold storage, denied liability arguing that sole responsibility lay with the company. Kerr J noted that the mere fact that the defendant was managing director of a company, and that the company alone was the contracting party, did not mean that the director's personal duty to the plaintiff was excluded. On the evidence it was clear that the defendant was the only director to concern himself with the goods following delivery to the cold store, which was in his personal ownership. Correspondence indicated that he, rather than the company, was responsible for storage. Kerr J imposed personal liability on the defendant, saying:

> '… the defendant … assumed and owed a duty of care to the plaintiff in respect of storage of their goods in his premises and was in breach of that duty with the result that the plaintiff's goods were damaged[77].'

A significant element in the decision is that the managing director had positively, personally and voluntarily assumed (and not excluded) a duty to the plaintiff.

A similar approach was taken by the Supreme Court in *Shinkwin v Quin-Con Ltd and Quinlan*[78]. There, the plaintiff lost three fingers and part of his thumb when his hand slipped and came into contact with the circular saw that he had been operating. The

---

72 *Kleinwort Benson Ltd v Malaysia Mining Corporation Berhad* [1989] 1 All ER 785. See also Chemco *Leasing SPA v Rediffusion* [1987] FTLR 201.

73 *Banque Brussels Lambert SA v Australian National Industries Ltd* (1989) 21 NSWLR 502.

74 See generally Hawke, *Corporate Liability* (2000, Sweet & Maxwell), Ch 4.

75 *Rainham Chemical Works Ltd and Others v Belvedere Fish Guano Co Ltd* [1921] 2 AC 465; *Wah Tat Bank Ltd v Chan Cheng Kum* [1975] AC 507; *Reitzman v Grahame-chapman and Derustit Ltd* (1950) 68 RPC 25.

76 *Fairline Shipping Corporation v Adamson* [1975] 1 QB 180.

77 *Fairline Shipping Corporation v Adamson* [1975] 1 QB 180 at 191.

78 *Shinkwin v Quin-Con Ltd and Quinlan* [2001] 1 IR 514.

plaintiff succeeded in the High Court against the defendant employer-company and also against the second defendant who was the manager of the factory. It was held that the second defendant, who was the sole owner of the company, had failed in his duty by not providing proper training or warnings in relation to the operation of the saw. The decision of the High Court was appealed to the Supreme Court. Fennelly J reduced the question of liability to whether the manager had involved himself 'so closely in the operation of the factory and, in particular, in the supervision of the plaintiff as to make himself personally liable for any of the acts of negligence which injured the plaintiff'. Fennelly J went on to note the significance of the manager being in undisputed control of the factory. In finding the manager liable in negligence, Fennelly J said:

> '… the second defendant, on the particular facts of this case, placed himself in a relationship of proximity to the plaintiff. He had personally taken on a young and untrained person to work in a factory managed by him and personally put him to work upon a potentially dangerous machine over which he exercised control to the extent of giving some though completely inadequate instructions to the workers. He was bound to take appropriate steps to warn the plaintiff of such obvious dangers … In his supervision and instruction of the plaintiff, he failed to do these things and was consequently negligent.'

This case did not involve the 'lifting of the veil' of incorporation. Fennelly J made it quite clear that the claim was made directly in negligence, 'not as employer or as shareholder but as a person who had placed himself by his own actions in such a relationship to the plaintiff as to call upon himself the obligation to exercise care'.

[5.019] In *Williams v Natural Life Health Foods*[79], the plaintiffs approached a one-man company, which operated franchises in the retail health food sector, with a view to obtaining a franchise. The defendant managing director, Mr Mistlin, advised them of his expertise and experience in the sector, and he produced for them various financial projections predicting their turnover and profits. In the event, turnover and profits failed to match the projections, and the plaintiffs sued the company for damages in respect of financial loss arising from negligent misstatement. The company was later wound up, and Mistlin was joined as second defendant. The Court of Appeal found Mistlin liable on an application of the ordinary principles of negligent misstatement in tort, given his substantial participation in the events. The House of Lords, however, reversed that decision, holding that an independent duty on the part of Mistlin could only arise if he had positively and voluntarily assumed responsibility so that a special relationship of care could be said to exist between him and the plaintiffs. The primary focus in that regard had to be on the personal exchanges between Mistlin and the plaintiffs. The House of Lords held that while the plaintiffs had been given a brochure promoting the company's expertise as being derived from Mistlin's own expertise, that was insufficient to constitute a voluntary assumption of responsibility on Mistlin's part. Applying an objective test, their Lordships held that the plaintiffs could not reasonably have relied on the brochure as constituting a voluntary assumption of personal liability by Mistlin.

[79] *Williams v Natural Life Health Foods* [1998] 2 All ER 577.

Agency

[5.020] Although a company is not *per se* to be treated as the agent or trustee of its members, there is also no objection in principle to a company agreeing to act and be treated as an agent or trustee of its members. And, of course, as shall be seen, the corollary whereby members who are directors or other officers of the company agree to act as agents, in particular circumstances, of the company is an essential feature of all companies[80].

[5.021] An agent is a person who has authority to do acts affecting the legal position of another person, termed the principal. When an agent acts on behalf of his principal, the law treats the act as being that of the principal himself, and renders the principal liable for it[81].

A comprehensive treatment of the law of agency is beyond the scope of this work[82]; suffice it to say that agents commonly obtain the authority to alter their principal's legal position from an *agency agreement*, to which both the agent and the principal are parties. Where the agent is a company and the principal is a member, the agency agreement has the effect of circumventing the company's separate legal personality to the extent that the member, as principal, will be liable for the acts of the company, his authorised agent.

Little controversy can be said to arise where there exists an express agency agreement whereby a company agrees to act as a member's agent, because the principal's liability for the acts of the agent must clearly have been in the contemplation of both parties to the agreement when they first entered into it[83]. Greater controversy arises, however, concerning the extent to which the courts are prepared to *infer*, in the absence of an express agency agreement, that a company is in fact the agent of its member who is its principal. There remains, however, another situation in which the members of a company may be made personally liable for the company's obligations through the operation of the law of agency. That is where the member is acting as agent of the company and he fails to disclose that he is acting on the company's behalf.

[5.022] Specific aspects of the law of agency insofar as it concerns the separate legal personality of companies are considered here under the following headings:

(a) Implied agency;

(b) Undisclosed agency.

---

80 See Ch 7, *Corporate Contracts, Capacity and Authority*, at para **[7.099]** *et seq*.

81 The maxim *qui facit per aliam facit per se* (he who does through another does by himself) applies.

82 See Fridman, *Law of Agency* (7th edn, Butterworths, 1996); Reynolds, *Bowstead on the Law of Agency* (19th edn, Sweet & Maxwell, 2010).

83 See for example *Rainham Chemical Works Ltd v Belvedere* [1921] 2 AC 465, where an agency agreement provided that a company should take possession of land as an agent of its members; also *Southern v Watson* [1940] 3 All ER 439, where a company agreed, as part of a contract for the purchase of the business of its incorporators, to act as agent for the incorporators in the fulfilment of their outstanding commitments stemming from the time when they ran the business in the form of a partnership.

(a) Implied agency

[5.023] Though a company is not to be regarded *per se* as the agent of its members, there is nothing to prevent the *creation* of an agency relationship between the two. Some controversy has arisen about the extent to which the courts are willing to imply that a company is an agent of its members.

[5.024] In *Smith, Stone and Knight v Birmingham Corporation*[84], a subsidiary of the plaintiff company took over a waste business. The waste business was carried out on land owned by the plaintiff. The subsidiary was beneficially owned by the plaintiff company, and it was treated in day-to-day running as a mere department of the plaintiff's business. The arrangement between the subsidiary and the plaintiff company was such that the plaintiff company was entitled to all the profits of the subsidiary without any need for a dividend to be declared[85]. When the lands of the parent company were compulsorily acquired by the defendant corporation, the plaintiff successfully claimed compensation in respect of the disturbance caused to the subsidiary. Atkinson J accepted that the subsidiary was carrying on business as the agent of the plaintiff company. He observed:

> '[T]he corporation rest their contention on *Salomon's* case and their argument is that the waste company was a distinct legal entity. It was in occupation of the premises, the business being carried on in its name, and the claimant's only interest in law was that of holders of the shares. It is well settled that the mere fact that a man holds all the shares in a company does not make the business carried on by the company his business, nor does it make the company his agents for the carrying on of the business. That proposition is just as true if the shareholder is itself a limited company. It is also well settled that there may be such an arrangement between the shareholders and a company as will constitute the company the shareholders' agent for the purpose of carrying on the business and make the business the business of the shareholders[86].'

The learned judge considered that six factors should be weighed in determining whether such an agency may be deemed to exist, namely:

- Were the profits of the subsidiary treated as the profits of the holding company?
- Were the persons who were conducting the business of the subsidiary appointed by the holding company?
- Was the holding company the 'head and brains' of the trading venture?
- Did the holding company govern the adventure?
- Were the profits made by the subsidiary company made by the skill and direction of the holding company?
- Was the holding company in effective and constant control of the subsidiary?

---

84 *Smith, Stone and Knight v Birmingham Corporation* [1939] 4 All ER 116.

85 On shareholders' entitlements to dividends see Ch 8, *Shares and Membership*, at para **[8.073]** *et seq.*

86 *Smith, Stone and Knight v Birmingham Corporation* [1939] 4 All ER 116 at 120.

Atkinson J considered that all six questions should be answered in the plaintiff's favour. He continued:

> 'Indeed, if ever one company must be said to be the agent or employee or tool or *simulacrum* of another, I think the waste company was in this case a legal entity because that is all that it was. There was nothing to prevent the claimants at any moment saying 'we will carry on the business in our own name.' They had but to paint out the waste company's name on the premises, change their business paper and form and the thing would have been done. I am satisfied that the business belonged to the claimants; they were, in my view, the real occupiers of the premises.'

Notably, most of Atkinson J's criteria for the determination of an agency relationship between a subsidiary and its holding company concentrate on the issue of *control* of the subsidiary's day-to-day operations. If such a criterion is to be applied to every case in which the day-to-day affairs of a company are controlled by a member, then a significant number of companies may be regarded as agents of their members, and the principle of separate legal personality would be the exception rather than the rule. The courts, however, seem reticent to imply such agency where the company is controlled by a natural person, and most cases in which agency has been implied have been concerned with subsidiaries and holding companies.

[5.025] Some explanation for this may be found in *Munton Bros Ltd v Secretary of State*[87], where the facts were not dissimilar to the *Smith, Stone & Knight* case. A parent company made a claim for compensation in respect of criminal damage done to the property of its subsidiary, alleging that the loss was really its own because of the close relationship between the two companies. The subsidiary's business was to make up cloth supplied by the parent company and return the cloth to it. Its finances were arranged so that it never made a profit or incurred a loss in any year. Gibson J found in favour of the parent company, holding that the subsidiary was in fact its agent. He observed that while the courts are extremely reluctant to hold that a company is its shareholder's agent or acts as trustee for them, even though the shareholder may be a sole proprietor:

> '... the same objections do not apply where it is sought to demonstrate that a subsidiary company is in fact the agent of its parent company because the conception of incorporation remains intact.'

While the learned judge's words may be taken as an indication of the courts' reluctance to regard companies as agents of their *natural* members, and of the courts' readiness to regard companies as agents of their *corporate* members, the learned judge's reasoning is less than convincing, because the concept of incorporation remains intact where a company is treated as agent of its member *regardless* of the member's attributes. This flaw deprives the observations as to the reluctance of the courts to regard companies as agents of their natural members of much weight.

[5.026] A case where a subsidiary has been found to be an agent of its parent or holding company is *Firestone Tyre and Public Co v Llwellin*[88]. In that case, an American company formed a wholly-owned subsidiary in England for the purpose of manufacturing tyres and supplying them to the European market. The English company

[87] *Munton Bros Ltd v Secretary of State* [1983] NI 369.

[88] *Firestone Tyre and Public Co v Llwellin* [1957] 1 All ER 561.

received the payment for the tyres, and, after deducting a sum representing 5% of the payment, transferred the balance to the American company. When the American company was assessed for English tax on the profits of the business, it sought to deny liability on the basis that it was a legal person separate from its subsidiary. Indeed, the circumstances of the case seemed to lie in its favour: the English company was independent in its day-to-day operations, and only one of the English company's directors was also a director of the American company. Nevertheless, the Court of Appeal and the House of Lords found the English company to be an agent of the American company on the basis of the actual manner in which the companies had arranged their affairs. In the Court of Appeal, Evershed MR said:

> 'My conclusion does not involve the proposition that [the subsidiary], instead of being an independent legal entity, is a mere branch of [the American company]; but [the subsidiary], though a separate entity, is in fact wholly controlled by [the American company], and in the making of what may be described as [the American company's] proprietary branded articles it acts under the close direction of [the American company] in all respects, and in selling those articles to [the American company's] customers it does so on terms fixed by [the American company], so that after allowing [the subsidiary] its costs and a percentage thereon the whole of the profits on the transactions go to [the American company][89].'

Similarly, in *Re FG (Films) Ltd*[90], a company was incorporated in England to enable films produced in its name to qualify as British under the Cinematograph Films Act 1938 (UK). The company was promoted by an American company. Two of its three directors were English, one of whom was also the president of the American company. The third director, an American, held 90% of the company's issued shares. The English company contracted with its American parent to make the film in question, but the money for the purpose was to be found by the American company, and all contracts and arrangements for making the film were made by the American company in the name of the English company. It was clear, then, that the English company was undercapitalised for the business which it conducted under the guise of a separate legal entity. The court held that the film did not qualify as British, because it had not been made by the English company at all; what little the English company did, it did as a mere nominee of the American company.

[5.027] More recently, in *Redfern v O'Mahony*[91], Mc Govern J acknowledged the implied agency principle, postulating that it might be open to the plaintiffs in that case to argue that the court should infer the existence of an agency or trust on the part of a company established to hold the shares in another company. The learned judge cited the

---

89 *Cf Kodak Ltd v Clark* [1902] 2 KB 450, where an English company held 98% of the shares in its American subsidiary. The court refused to hold that the subsidiary was agent of the English company so as to render the latter liable for tax on the subsidiary's profits. In the course of his judgment, Phillimore J said (at 459): 'A company may control another company; but it does not necessarily follow because an individual controls the company, or the company controls the individual, that the business carried on by the person or company controlled is necessarily a business carried on by the controller; and particularly is that the case when the machinery of companies is used and the controller is a company.'

90 *Re FG (Films) Ltd* [1953] 1 All ER 615.

91 *Redfern v O'Mahony* [2010] IEHC 253.

passage from Laffoy J's judgment in *Fyffes plc v DCC plc* quoted above[92]. However, the learned judge found on the facts that the agreement sought to be enforced by the plaintiff had become rescinded regardless of any such agency or trust.

(b) Undisclosed agency

[5.028] Where the agents of a company fail to disclose that they are acting on behalf of the company, they will, under ordinary principles of agency, become personally liable for their acts – even though, legally speaking, the acts are done by the company[93]. As far as the third party is concerned, the agent is really a principal, dealing in his own name, and on his own behalf, and there is no obligation on the third party to inquire whether there is an undisclosed principal. At common law, both the agent and the undisclosed principal, once discovered, may be sued upon contracts concluded in such circumstances[94]. These principles apply, however, only where the existence of the principal has not been disclosed *at all*, at the time the contract is concluded. If the agent represents that he is acting as agent of a principal, but misdescribes or misidentifies the principal, the principal will not be undisclosed, and the agent will not be liable[95]. The Companies Acts expand upon these common law principles, however, by providing for liability of the company's agents in certain circumstances where they have misdescribed or misidentified their principal. These circumstances are examined in further detail at para **[5.081]** below.

Trusts

[5.029] There is no legal objection to a company formally agreeing to act as trustee for all or some of its members, provided all the requisite formalities are observed[96]. But even where no such formal trust may be found, the courts will, on occasion, disregard the separate legal personality of a company so as to *imply* that it acts as trustee for its members. This approach is most clearly evident in those cases concerning incorporated social clubs.

[5.030] In *Re Parnell GAA Club Ltd*[97], McWilliam J found that the club held its stock and assets on trust for its members. Accordingly, when it sold drink to the members, the 'sale' was really a distribution of the members' common property. Such a distribution would not require an intoxicating liquor licence. The learned judge quoted from Lord

---

92 See para **[5.006]**.

93 See generally Goodhart & Hamson, 'Undisclosed Principals in Contract' (1931) 4 Cam LJ 320; Müller-Frienfels, 'The Undisclosed Principal' (1953) 16 MLR 299; *Fridman, Law of Agency* (7th edn, Butterworths, 1996) at pp 228–244.

94 *Short v Spackman* (1831) 2 B & Ad 962; *Hersom v Bernett* [1955] 1 QB 98. The obligations of the principal and agent are not joint. Once the third party discovers the existence of the undisclosed principal he must elect whether to sue the principal or the agent, and once a final judgment has been obtained by the third party against one, he cannot then sue the other: *Kendall v Hamilton* (1879) 4 App Cas 504. Similarly, a settlement with one may discharge the other: *Coates v Lewes* (1808) 1 Camp 444.

95 *Finzel, Berry & Co v Eastcheap Dried Fruit Co* [1962] 1 Lloyd's Rep 370.

96 See, for example, *Bayworld Investments v McMahon* [2004] 2 IR 199 where a company was established to act as bare trustee of lands for the incorporators.

97 *Re Parnell GAA Club Ltd* [1984] ILRM 246.

Hewart's judgment in *Trebanog Working Men's Club v MacDonald*[98], where it was said that:

> '... once it is conceded that a members' club does not necessarily require a licence to serve its members with intoxicating liquor because the legal property in the liquor is not in the members themselves, it is difficult to draw any legal distinction between the various legal entities which may be entrusted with the duty of holding the property on behalf of the members, be it an individual, or a body of trustees, or a company formed for the purpose, so long as the real interest in the liquor remains, as it clearly does, in the members of the club. In this connection, there is no magic in the expression 'trustee' or 'agent'. What is essential is that a holding of property by the agent or trustee must be a holding for and on behalf of, and not a holding antagonistic to, the members of the club.'

[B] MISUSE OF THE CORPORATE FORM

[5.031] Misuse of the corporate form can occur in a variety of ways. Here we consider the topic under the following headings:

1. Concealment of impropriety.
2. Mismanagement.
3. Evasion of existing legal obligations.
4. Avoidance of future legal obligations.

Concealment of impropriety

[5.032] In many instances the courts have threatened to disregard the separate legal personality of a company where to do otherwise would result in the use of the corporate personality as a cloak to conceal impropriety.

[5.033] The case of *Re Darby; ex parte Brougham*[99] serves as an example of judicial disregard of the separate legal personality of a company where the company was being used to conceal fraudulent profits. Darby and Gyde, both of whom were undischarged bankrupts, registered a company in Guernsey in the Channel Islands. That company then promoted and registered a second company in England. Finances were raised by the English company on foot of debentures, and these monies were paid to the Guernsey company, where they were distributed directly to Darby and Gyde. When the English company failed, its liquidator claimed in Darby's bankruptcy for the secret profits Darby and Gyde had made through the Guernsey company. The court allowed the liquidator's claim, rejecting the argument that the profits had been made by the Guernsey company and not Darby himself.

98 *Trebanog Working Men's Club v MacDonald* [1940] 1 KB 576. See also *Newell v Hemmingway* (1888) 60 LT 544.

99 *Re Darby; ex parte Brougham* [1911] 1 KB 95. See also *R v Goodwin* (1980) 71 Cr App R 97, where a bankrupt who had obtained credit for himself through the vehicle of a company was held to have committed an offence under the UK equivalent of s 129 of the Bankruptcy Act 1988, even though normally the offence is not committed if the credit is obtained for another person.

[5.034] Likewise, in *Re Bugle Press Ltd*[100], the use of a company as a device to expropriate a minority was struck down by the courts as a 'hollow sham,' but in that case the impropriety complained of consisted of an attempt to abuse a fundamental principle of company law, namely that a majority of shareholders should not, unless permitted by the articles, be allowed to expropriate a minority. Section 209(1) of the English Companies Act 1948 – their equivalent of s 204(1) of the CA 1963[101] – permitted a company which had acquired a 90% shareholding in a takeover of another company to compulsorily acquire the remaining 10%, unless the court, in its discretion, thought fit to order otherwise. Two majority shareholders of Bugle Press Ltd, holding 90% of its issued share capital, formed a company, which then made a takeover bid for all the shares of Bugle Press Ltd. The purpose of this was to enable the company to compulsorily acquire the shareholding of a third minority shareholder under s 209. The third shareholder applied to the court for relief. Harman LJ disregarded the separate legal personality of the new company, describing it as nothing but a 'little hut' built around the two shareholders and 'a bare faced attempt to evade that fundamental rule of company law which forbids the majority of shareholders unless the articles so provide, to expropriate the minority'[102].

[5.035] A not dissimilar instance of disregard of the separate legal personality of a company formed for a fraudulent purpose is the case of *Re Shrinkpak Ltd*[103]. In that case, a company, Shrinkpak Ltd, was established using monies which had been fraudulently converted from the use of a company which had gone into voluntary liquidation, Contract Packaging Ltd. Both companies were under the control of the same person, Mr Waldner, and Barron J found that the liquidation of Contract Packaging Ltd and the subsequent establishment of Shrinkpak Ltd had been choreographed by Waldner so as deliberately to defraud the creditors of Contract Packaging Ltd. The learned judge granted an order winding up Shrinkpak Ltd on the application of the liquidator of Contract Packaging Ltd.

[5.036] In *Re (H) (Restraint Order: Realisable Property)*[104], the Court of Appeal allowed the separate legal personality of a company to be disregarded where the company's owners had used the company as a device or façade to conceal criminal activities, including fraud on the Commissioners of Customs and Excise. A receiver appointed to the assets of the controllers under s 77 of the English Criminal Justice Act 1988 was permitted to treat the company's assets as the 'realisable property' of the controllers. Likewise, in *Trustor AB v Smallbone (No 3)*[105] receipt by a company of funds was treaded as receipt of those funds by its owner-director. The funds were caused to be paid to it by its owner-director who was using the company as a vehicle to siphon off substantial funds from another company of which he was also managing director.

---

[100] *Re Bugle Press Ltd* [1961] Ch 270. The case is also examined in Ch 9, *Share Transfer*, at para **[9.101]** *et seq*.

[101] See Ch 9, *Share Transfer*, at para **[9.087]**. Note that in Ireland the magic figure is 80%.

[102] *Re Bugle Press Ltd* [1961] Ch 270 at 288.

[103] *Re Shrinkpak Ltd* (20 December 1989, unreported) HC, (1989) Irish Times, 21 December. See also the related decision in *Re Contract Packaging Ltd* (1992) Irish Times, 16, 17 & 18 January, discussed in Ch 15 *Duties of Directors and Other Officers*, at para **[15.122]**.

[104] *Re (H) (Restraint Order: Realisable Property)* [1996] 2 All ER 391.

[105] *Trustor AB v Smallbone (No 3)* [2001] 3 All ER 987.

Mismanagement

[5.037] Where the controllers of a company have been guilty only of *mismanagement*, it appears that the courts will not disregard the separate legal personality of the company so as to make them personally liable for the company's obligations. In *Dublin County Council v Elton Homes Ltd*[106], a company which had been granted planning permission for a housing development went into liquidation before it was able to comply with the conditions of the planning permission. The plaintiff County Council sought an injunction under s 27 of the Local Government (Planning and Development) Act 1976 compelling the company *and* its directors, Mr Keogh and Mr English, to carry out the necessary works. Barrington J refused the plaintiff's application, saying:

> 'What is suggested is that because they were directors of the company at the time when the company obtained planning permission that they should be ordered to complete the development at their own expense. I am not saying that there might not be a case where the court would be justified in making such an order. If the case were one of fraud, or if the directors had siphoned off large sums of money out of the company, so as to leave it unable to fulfil its obligations, the court might be justified in lifting the veil of incorporation and fixing the directors with personal responsibility. But that is not this case. The second and third named respondents appear to be fairly small men who having failed in this particular enterprise are now back working for others. The worst that can be imputed against them is mismanagement.
>
> They gave personal guarantees to the insurance company which supplied the bond for £10,000 and to the company's bankers. They therefore stand to lose heavily arising out of the transaction. Moreover ... the liquidator and his officials entertain no suspicion that there has been any impropriety on the part of the directors in dealing with the assets of the company.
>
> It appears to me that Mr Keogh and Mr English traded with the benefit of limited liability in this case and that in the absence of any evidence of impropriety on their part, I would not be justified in attempting to make them liable for the default of the company.'

[5.038] Again, in *Dublin County Council v O'Riordan*[107], even though the affairs of the company had been carried on with 'scant disregard for the requirements of the Companies Acts,' Murphy J refused to grant an injunction against the company's directors requiring them personally to fulfil the planning obligations of the company since no evidence of 'fraud or the misapplication of monies' had been established. That case was relied upon by Hamilton P in *Dunlaoghaire Corporation v Park Hill Developments*[108], where the learned judge refused to grant an injunction against a director of the respondent company. It was contended by the applicant in that case that the company and Mr Parkinson Hill, the director, were indistinguishable in law because: in contravention of s 131 of the CA 1963, no annual general meeting was ever held; no formal directors' meeting was ever convened; no director's fees or dividends on his

---

[106] *Dublin County Council v Elton Homes Ltd* [1984] ILRM 297.

[107] *Dublin County Council v O'Riordan* [1986] ILRM 104.

[108] *Dunlaoghaire Corporation v Park Hill Developments* [1989] IR 447. See also *Ellis v Nolan* [1983] IEHC 38, where McWilliam J refused to grant an injunction under s 27 of the Local Government (Planning and Development) Act 1976 against a director in respect of whom no 'fraud, misrepresentation, improper application of money or negligence' had been established.

shares were paid to Mr Kearns, the other director; in contravention of s 148 of the CA 1963 no financial reports were ever issued to the shareholders; Mr Parkinson Hill was the only person with knowledge of the financial affairs of the company; and Mr Parkinson Hill was in total control of the company and managed it without regard for the requirements of the Companies Acts. Hamilton P observed[109]:

> 'I have no doubt, having heard the evidence of [Mr Parkinson Hill], that he was in effective control of the first respondent and he failed to comply with the requirements of the Companies Act 1963, but I have found no evidence of any fraud or misrepresentation on his part; any siphoning off or misapplication of the funds of the said company; nor of negligence in the carrying out of the affairs of the said company ... As I have found no evidence of any impropriety by the second respondent in the conduct of the affairs of the first respondent, I am satisfied that he traded with the benefit of limited liability in this case and I would not be justified in attempting to make him personally responsible for the admitted default of the first respondent.'

It should be noted that despite the reluctance of the courts to disregard the separate legal personality of a company where the controllers are guilty of mismanagement, the legislature has also made provisions to protect creditors of the company from abuse of the corporate form through either fraudulent or reckless trading. These are considered in further detail in Ch 15, below[110].

Evasion of existing legal obligations

[5.039] The courts have shown an apparent willingness to disregard the separate legal personality of a company where to do otherwise would allow a controller to evade an existing legal obligation. Such a case is *Cummings v Stewart*[111], where Cummings entered into a patent licensing agreement whereby he agreed to license his patent for reinforced concrete to Stewart. Clause 2 of the agreement required Stewart to pay Cummings a minimum sum annually in respect of royalties. Clause 5 of the agreement forbade Stewart from subletting, assigning, or transferring the licence without Cummings's consent; but the clause also contained a proviso permitting Stewart to transfer the licence to any limited company he might form to carry on his business or the business connected with the licence. Stewart was unable to make a profit from his use of the patents, and, in an attempt to evade his liability to Cummings for royalties on the patents, he transferred the licence to a limited company formed by him. It was not intended that this new company should work the patents. Cummings successfully claimed that Stewart should be regarded as being liable for all arrears of royalty payments, *including those due for the period during which the licence was held by the company.* Meredith MR said:

> 'In my opinion, the Companies (Consolidation) Act 1908 embodies a code framed (*inter alia*) for the purposes of preserving and enforcing commercial morality and it would be strange indeed, if that code could be turned into an engine for the destruction of legal obligations and the overthrow of legitimate and enforceable claims. The most casual reader of the speeches of the House of Lords in the case of *Salomon v Salomon & Co*

---

109 [1989] IR 447 at 450–452.

110 See Ch 15, *Duties of Directors and Other Officers*, at para **[15.096]** *et seq*.

111 *Cummings v Stewart* [1911] 1 IR 236.

> cannot fail to observe that there is nothing in any of those speeches contrary to the view that I have just expressed ...
>
> The defendant says he has formed the company within the meaning of [clause 5 of the licensing agreement] and that the intention with which the company was formed and with which the two holders of £1 shares come into this concern is not for me, and I have no right to comment on it. I have no right at all except for the fact that it is demonstrated that the company was formed not to carry on the business of the plaintiff – not, in the words of the proviso, to carry on the business 'connected with and arising out of said patents and this licence', but for the purpose of extinguishing the patent rights or at all events – and this is sufficient to justify the plaintiff in persisting in his claim in this case – for the purpose of refraining from carrying on any work connected with the reinforced concrete patents of the plaintiff.'

The fact that no order appears to have been made against the company, coupled with the opening sentiments expressed in the passage quoted, would suggest that the learned Master of the Rolls was prepared to ignore completely the existence of the company. On the other hand, it has been suggested that this was not a case of disregard of separate legal personality at all, but was, rather, a case of mere contractual interpretation[112]. Nevertheless, other cases involving avoidance of existing legal obligations illustrate some disregard by the courts of the separate legal personality of a company.

[5.040] The decision in *Mastertrade (Exports) Ltd et al v Phelan et al*[113] shows that there must be some evidence that a company was used 'as an engine for the destruction of legal obligations or the overthrow of legitimate or enforceable claims'. The facts there were that P sold 50% of his interest in the Master Meat Group of companies to T and subsequently, in breach of their joint venture agreement, T disposed of his shares to G. P was not aware that T had disposed of his shares to G. After the Group encountered financial difficulties P and T entered into negotiations; T's agents in fact acted on behalf of G. P offered to acquire the group for £2.5m but a counteroffer of £2.75m was made and under the terms of the joint venture agreement, that became binding. Subsequently, P commenced proceedings against T, G and the Master Meat Group of companies. These companies countered with an action against P, alleging 32 allegations of misappropriations by P. The application before the court was brought by P to strike out the proceedings against him by the Master Meat Group of companies having regard to G's alleged wrongdoing. In particular, P alleged that the effect of the actions was to ensure that an entirely unlawful and improper benefit would be obtained by G as beneficial owner of the companies because although the companies' complaints against P predated G's involvement, G would still benefit from any award made. P also contended that G's alleged wronging constituted fraud and was a factor the court must consider in lifting the corporate veil. Murphy J refused to disregard the companies' separate legal personality saying that the respondent companies 'have not been in breach of any agreement, have not induced a breach of an agreement nor are in any way tainted with illegality, deceit or fraud. They are the proper plaintiffs in relation to the allegations that they make in these proceedings.' In finding that the companies were not used as an engine for the destruction of legal obligations or the overthrow of legitimate or enforceable claims (as referred to in *Cummings v Stewart*) Murphy J also held that

112 Ussher, *Company Law in Ireland* (1986) at p 27.

113 *Mastertrade (Exports) Ltd et al v Phelan et al* [2001] IEHC 172.

whilst there may have been concealment, which did mislead the public, 'there is no evidence before the Court that the sole object of the concealment was to "cheat and mislead the public"'[114]. Having regard to the documentary evidence before the court, Murphy J concluded that it was inappropriate to lift the corporate veil and he refused to strike out the proceedings.

[5.041] One case where the courts have disregarded the separate legal personality of a company is *Jones v Lipman*[115]. In that case, Lipman entered into a legally enforceable contract to sell his house to Jones. Subsequently, Lipman changed his mind, and, in an attempt to avoid having to convey the house to Jones, he acquired a ready-made company, which had been incorporated with the object of acquiring land, and transferred the house to it. Lipman was the beneficial owner of all the shares of the company. Russell J, awarding specific performance to Jones and thereby compelling Lipman to sell the house, said that the company was[116]:

> 'the creature of the first defendant, a device and a sham, a mask which he holds before his face in an attempt to avoid recognition by the eye of equity.'

An order for specific performance was also made against the company. This last fact indicates that the learned judge was not prepared to ignore altogether the existence of the company he had so recently described as a sham; but appears to have disregarded its separate legal personality to the extent that he considered the company to be bound by the obligations of a member. Sadly, the terms 'device,' 'sham,' and 'mask' serve merely to cloud the true reasoning in the case, and it has been suggested that the outcome in that case might have been achieved by applying more conventional legal methods[117].

[5.042] In the *Jones* case, orders were directed against both the company and its controlling member. In *Gilford Motor Co Ltd v Horne*[118], the use of a company to avoid existing legal obligations caused the courts to make an order against the company and a person who was *not* one of its members. In that case, Horne's contract of employment contained a covenant whereby he agreed that should he leave their employment he would not compete with the plaintiff employers for a period of six years from 1 September 1928. Before this period had expired, Horne left the plaintiff's employ. A week later his wife and son set up a company to carry on business in competition with the plaintiff. Horne was neither a registered shareholder nor a director of the company, but it acted in accordance with his instructions[119]. The plaintiff succeeded in obtaining an injunction against Horne *and* the new company, restraining them from carrying on business in competition. Lord Hanworth said that the new company[120]:

> 'was formed as a device, a stratagem in order to mask the effective carrying on of the business of Mr Horne. The purpose of it was to try to enable him under what is a cloak or

---

114 An expression used in *Scott v Brown, Douring McNab and Company* (1892) 2 QB 724.

115 *Jones v Lipman* [1962] 1 All ER 442.

116 *Jones v Lipman* [1962] 1 All ER 442 at 445.

117 Ussher, *Company Law in Ireland* (1986) at p 28.

118 *Gilford Motor Co Ltd v Horne* [1933] Ch 939.

119 Nowadays, he would be classed as a 'shadow director'; see Ch 13, *Corporate Governance: Management by the Directors*, at para **[13.055]**.

120 *Gilford Motor Co Ltd v Horne* [1933] Ch 939 at 956.

a sham to engage in business in respect of which he had a fear that the plaintiffs might intervene and object ...'

[5.043] An even less convincing though nonetheless similar finding was made in *Creasey v Breachwood Motors Ltd*[121]. In that case a company, Breachwood Welwyn Ltd, wrongfully dismissed Creasey, its general manager. Creasey then commenced an action for wrongful dismissal against the company. The company ceased trading, paid off all its creditors apart from Creasey, and transferred its assets to a new company, Breachwood Motors Ltd. Creasey subsequently obtained judgment against Breachwood Welwyn Ltd which by then had no assets. Richard Southwell QC, sitting as deputy High Court judge in the Queens Bench Division, held that the takeover of Breachwood Welwyn Ltd's assets by the new company was carried out by the directors in total disregard of their duties as such, and in an attempt to ensure that Creasey would not recover anything if successful in his claim. Accordingly, he disregarded the separate identity of Breachwood Motors Ltd and allowed Creasey to proceed in enforcing his judgment for wrongful dismissal against it. The decision may be criticised[122], however, on the basis that the facts did not justify a finding that the arrangement between Breachwood Welwyn Ltd and Breachwood Motors Ltd was a façade concealing the actual facts. The directors were under a common law duty to act *bona fide* and in the best interests of the company as a whole. By transferring the business to Breachwood Motors Ltd and paying off all the old company's *existing* creditors, they were able to produce a stronger balance sheet in the members' interest. If there was evidence of a fraudulent motive or desire on the part of the incorporators of the new company to evade an existing legal obligation, it was not relied upon by the learned judge in his reasoning; nor was it suggested that the new company was established as a façade concealing the true facts. Unfortunately, the new company, Breachwood Motors Ltd, decided not to defend the case, so the reasoning was not challenged. It is also important to note that the court decided merely that Breachwood Motors Ltd, the new company, could be substituted as a defendant in Creasey's action against his former employer – no liability was imposed on the directors. *Creasey's* case was rejected by the Court of Appeal in *Ord v Belhaven Pubs Ltd*[123], considered below.

[5.044] Though not traditionally viewed as such, the decision of Costello J in *Power Supermarkets Ltd v Crumlin Investments Ltd and Dunnes Stores (Crumlin) Ltd*[124] may be seen as an Irish example of judicial willingness to ignore the separate legal personality of a company when its substantial purpose and effect is to evade an existing legal obligation. The decision was made at a time when the 'single economic entity' theory was in vogue, and the major part of the judgment is devoted to an application of the then popular view that the separate identity of companies in a group could be ignored where the 'justice of the case' so required. What is clear from the learned judge's reasoning in the case is that the justice of the case required the group to be regarded as a single entity in that case because to do otherwise would lead to the evasion

121 *Creasey v Breachwood Motors Ltd* [1993] BCLC 480.

122 See Png, 'Lifting the Veil of Incorporation: Creasey v Breachwood Motors: A Right Decision for the Wrong Reasons' (1999) 20 Co Law 122.

123 *Ord v Belhaven Pubs Ltd* [1998] 2 BCLC 447.

124 *Power Supermarkets Ltd v Crumlin Investments Ltd and Dunnes Stores (Crumlin) Ltd* (22 June 1981, unreported) HC.

of an existing legal obligation to respect the terms of a commercial lease. The case is considered in further detail at para **[5.053]** below.

[5.045] An important element in the decision of whether to disregard the separate legal personality of a company for evasion of legal obligations is whether, as a matter of fact, the company was incorporated for that purpose, and whether the true facts were concealed. In *Ord v Belhaven Pubs Ltd*[125], the facts (which may be likened to those in *Creasey's* case, above) were that the plaintiffs bought a 20-year lease of a public house from Belhaven Pubs Ltd and subsequently claimed that the vendor had misrepresented the turnover and profitability of the pub. They commenced proceedings against the company in 1991. In 1992, however, following a general collapse in property values, the defendant's parent company decided to restructure group operations with the ultimate effect that, by 1995, the assets of Belhaven Pubs Ltd had been bought by other members of the group at a price in excess of the net book value, and its creditors had been satisfied, so that the company became nothing more than a dormant company, having no assets and no liabilities. The Court of Appeal allowed an appeal against an order of the English High Court that the parent company be substituted as defendant in the plaintiffs' action against Belhaven Pubs Ltd. The Court of Appeal held that nothing improper had been done by the directors and there was no evidence to suggest that the company was a mere façade or that the true facts were concealed.

[5.046] Another Irish analogue is to be found in the case of *Allied Irish Coal Supplies Ltd v Powell Duffryn International Fuels Ltd*[126]. In that case, the plaintiff alleged that the defendant, a wholly-owned subsidiary of Powell Duffryn plc, was in breach of a commercial contract to supply coal. When the plaintiff later became aware that the parent company was about to sell the subsidiary it sought an order joining the parent as co-defendant. Laffoy J in the High Court rejected the application, noting that the plaintiff had traded with the defendant knowing that it was a subsidiary, and that there was no suggestion of any privity of contract between the plaintiff and the parent company. The learned judge concluded that the mere fact alone that the defendant subsidiary was financially dependent on its parent was insufficient to render the parent responsible for the contractual obligations of the subsidiary:

> 'The proposition advanced by the plaintiff seems to me to be so fundamentally at variance with the principle of separate corporate legal personality laid down in *Salomon v Salomon & Co* [1897] AC 22, and the concept of limited liability, that it is wholly unstateable.'

The Supreme Court upheld Laffoy J's decision. Murphy J, contrasting *Power Supermarkets Ltd v Crumlin Investments Ltd and Dunnes Stores (Crumlin) Ltd,* pointed to the fact that the defendant subsidiary company was more than a mere shell; it carried on a very substantial business and its employees reported to the board of the subsidiary rather than directly to the board of the parent.

[5.047] The courts have shown themselves willing to disregard the separate legal personality of a company where it has been used to avoid statutory obligations, or where it would otherwise frustrate the purpose of a statute. In *Merchandise Transport Ltd v*

125 *Ord v Belhaven Pubs Ltd* [1998] 2 BCLC 447.

126 *Allied Irish Coal Supplies Ltd v Powell Duffryn International Fuels Ltd* [1998] 2 IR 519.

British Transport Commission[127], a holding company attempted to use its subsidiary company[128] as a vehicle to avoid a statutory provision designed to protect the public from unfair competition. The provision prohibited licensed public hauliers from using their vehicles to carry their *own* goods; and private hauliers were likewise prohibited from using surplus capacity to carry the goods of others. The holding company wished to transfer vehicles which it owned and used privately to a subsidiary engaged in the public haulage business. The subsidiary was to use the vehicles to carry the holding company's goods, and to use surplus capacity to carry third parties' goods. An application by the subsidiary for a public haulier's licence was refused by the licensing authority, and the refusal was upheld by the Court of Appeal, because to grant the licence would put the holding company in the position of a manufacturer who could use his own vehicles to deliver his goods and then solicit return loads from the public. Here, the court disregarded the separate legal personality of the subsidiary by looking at the motives of its controllers.

[5.048] A similar approach appears to have been adopted by the Supreme Court in *The State v District Justice Donnelly*[129], where the holders of a wine licence established a company, to which they transferred the premises. They were the company's only directors and shareholders, and they had formed the company in the hope that they could transfer to it the licence which had been indorsed twice already, and which, if it continued in their hands, was about a suffer a third indorsement, whereupon it would be revoked. The transfer of the licence required a *certificate of no objection* from the District Justice[130], and the Justice refused to issue such a certificate. The Supreme Court upheld the refusal, stating that the wide discretion given to the Justice by the Revenue Act 1862 justified him in disregarding the separate legal personality of the company by examining the motivations of those who had formed it.

Avoidance of future legal obligations

[5.049] The courts will *not*, however, disregard the separate legal personality of a company where it is used merely to avoid prospective or *future* obligations. This is evident in the judgment of the House of Lords in *Adams v Cape Industries*[131]. In that case, Cape Industries, a large multinational company based in England, was engaged in the asbestos industry. At one stage, Cape had a supply subsidiary (the North American Asbestos Corporation) in America, but after that company was involved in a $20 million settlement for injuries suffered by its employees, it was put into liquidation and its operations taken over by CPC. CPC was an American company which was established with financial assistance from Cape. Though not a subsidiary of Cape, CPC was instructed from time to time by AMC, a Liechtenstein incorporated company, which acted as Cape's agent.

---

127 *Merchandise Transport Ltd v British Transport Commission* [1962] 2 QB 173.

128 On holding and subsidiary companies see Ch 12, *Groups of Companies*, at para **[12.008]** *et seq*.

129 *The State v District Justice Donnelly* (1977) Irish Times, 5 November, noted by Ussher, *Company Law in Ireland* (1986) at p 33.

130 Section 15 of the Revenue Act 1862.

131 *Adams v Cape Industries* [1990] Ch 433.

In a subsequent tort action, workers at the CPC asbestos plant who had suffered illness as a result of exposure to asbestos obtained judgment in default against Cape in the American courts to the tune of some $15.64 million, and sought to have the judgment enforced in the English courts. In order to succeed in their application, they had to establish either that Cape had established and maintained, at its own expense, a fixed place of business in America and for more than a minimal time carried on business there through its servants and agents, or that Cape had, through its representative, carried on business at some fixed place in America. The plaintiffs contended that Cape had carried on business in America through CPC, which, they said, though not technically a subsidiary of Cape, was established and controlled indirectly by Cape in an attempt to evade future tortious liability.

The Court of Appeal found that CPC had indeed been established with a view to minimising the appearance of Cape's involvement in the sale of asbestos in America, and also with a view to lawfully reducing the possibility of Cape being made liable for US taxes or for future tort claims. But the court was equally satisfied that CPC was an independent corporation, wholly-owned by its chief executive, and carrying on its *own* business in America. Slade LJ said[132]:

> 'We do not accept as a matter of law that the court is entitled to lift the corporate veil as against a defendant company which is the member of a corporate group merely because the corporate structure has been used so as to ensure that the legal liability (if any) in respect of particular future activities of the group (and correspondingly the risk of enforcement of that liability) will fall on another member of the group rather than the defendant company. Whether or not this is desirable, the right to use a corporate structure in this manner is inherent in our corporate law ... [Counsel for the plaintiffs] urged on us that the purpose of the operation was in substance that Cape would have the practical benefit of the group's asbestos trade in the United States ... without the risks of tortious liability. This may be so. However, in our judgment Cape was in law entitled to organise the group's affairs in that manner and (save in the case of AMC to which special considerations apply) to expect that the court would apply the principle of [separate legal personality].'

[5.050] An earlier Irish analogue is to be found *Roundabout Ltd v Beirne*[133], where the High Court held that a company which was incorporated with a view to evading potential future pickets was in law a distinct entity not to be identified with its predecessor. The case is considered in detail in Ch 4, above.[134]

[C] THE SINGLE ECONOMIC ENTITY

[5.051] In the 1970s and 1980s, the courts put forward a novel apparent justification for disregarding the separate legal personalities of related companies. In a number of cases the courts disregarded the separate legal personality of the company *where justice requires*[135] by regarding it as a mere constituent of a larger legal entity, or 'single

132 *Adams v Cape Industries* [1990] Ch 433 at 544.

133 *Roundabout Ltd v Beirne* [1959] IR 423. See Ch 4 *Incorporation and its Consequences,* at para **[4.079]**.

134 See Ch 4, *Incorporation and its Consequences,* at para **[4.079]**.

135 See *Power Supermarkets Ltd v Crumlin Investments Ltd et al* (22 June 1981, unreported) HC, Costello J, discussed at para **[5.053]**.

economic entity'. This kind of disregard may be distinguished from the implied agency cases discussed earlier, for where a number of companies are regarded as a single legal entity, only one legal person is recognised, whereas agency recognises the existence of two persons. This means of disregarding separate legal personality has been employed in the past by the Irish courts, and has received approval in general terms from the Supreme Court[136], but its scope has severely been restricted by the English Court of Appeal[137], and more recently by the Irish Supreme Court[138]. The recent trend of the courts reveals a significant reluctance to introduce any general rule of disregard of the separate legal personality of companies in groups beyond those enunciated in *Salomon's* case.

The single economic entity approach never took root firmly in Ireland. Though it was taken in its time as evidence of a new exception to *Salomon's case*, it appears now that the courts will only apply it to determine who should be identified with a company when its separate legal personality is being disregarded in accordance with the *Salomon* principles.

[5.052] The 'single economic entity' approach has its roots in an observation of Gower's that there was 'evidence of a general tendency to ignore the separate legal entities of companies within a group, and to look instead at the economic entity of the whole group'[139]. This statement was accepted without question by Lord Denning in *DHN Food Distributors Ltd v Tower Hamlet London Borough Council*[140], a case which arose out of a compulsory acquisition of property. A holding company conducted business on land owned by one of its wholly-owned subsidiaries. When the Council compulsorily acquired the land, the holding company entered a claim for compensation in respect of the disturbance caused to it. The Court of Appeal upheld the claim for compensation. Lord Denning MR held that the court could look to the economic entity of the whole group and treat the business as being carried on by that group. He said[141]:

> 'We all know that in many respects a group of companies are treated together for the purpose of general accounts, balance sheet and profit and loss account. They are treated as one concern. Professor Gower in his book on company law says: 'there is evidence of a general tendency to ignore the separate legal entities of various companies within a group, and to look instead at the economic entity of the whole group'. This is especially the case when a parent company owns all the shares of the subsidiaries, so much so that it can control every movement of the subsidiaries. These subsidiaries are bound hand and foot to the parent company and must do just what the parent company says ... This group is virtually the same as a partnership in which all the three companies are partners. They should not be treated separately so as to be defeated on a technical point ... They should not be deprived of the compensation which should justly be payable for disturbance. The

---

136 *Re Bray Travel and Bray Travel (Holdings) Ltd* (13 July 1981) SC, discussed at para **[5.053]**.

137 *Adams v Cape Industries* [1990] Ch 433.

138 *Allied Irish Coal Supplies Ltd v Powell Duffryn International Fuels Ltd* [1998] 2 IR 519.

139 Gower, *Principles of Modern Company Law* (3rd edn, Stevens & Son, 1969) at p 216. Perhaps the effect which the author's remarks had on subsequent jurisprudence prompted him to take the especially measured view which appears in later editions of his work. See para **[5.005]**.

140 *DHN Food Distributors Ltd v Tower Hamlet London Borough Council* [1976] 3 All ER 462.

141 *DHN Food Distributors Ltd v Tower Hamlet London Borough Council* [1976] 3 All ER 462 at 467.

> three companies should, for present purposes, be treated as one and the parent company, DHN, should be treated as that one.'

Lord Denning MR also found that the holding company was entitled to compensation on other grounds, namely, that the subsidiary had given an irrevocable licence to the holding company to conduct business on the land, and that this licence conferred an equitable interest in the land on the holding company. Goff and Shaw LJJ were of the view that the case should be decided on the basis that the holding company was the owner in equity of the property under a resulting trust. Nevertheless, it was Lord Denning's observations concerning the disregard of separate legal personality which attracted later attention to the case.

[5.053] Lord Denning's views on the disregard of separate legal personality were adopted in Ireland by Costello J in *Power Supermarkets Ltd v Crumlin Investments Ltd and Dunnes Stores (Crumlin) Ltd*[142]. In that case, Crumlin Investments Ltd were landlords of a large shopping centre. Power Supermarkets Ltd, controllers of the Quinnsworth chain of supermarkets, entered into a lease of one of the units in the shopping centre. Since it was important to Power Supermarkets Ltd that no other large supermarket should be allowed to set up in the shopping centre in competition with them, Crumlin Investments Ltd covenanted, *inter alia*:

> 'not during the term to grant a lease for or to sell or permit or suffer the sale by any of its tenants or so far as within [Crumlin Investments Ltd's] control any sub or under tenants of groceries or food products in or over an area exceeding 3000 square feet in any one unit ... forming part of the shopping centre ...'

The shopping centre failed in those early days to be a financial success for Crumlin Investments Ltd, and the company decided to sell it. A sale was agreed with Cornelscourt Shopping Centre Ltd, and the sale was subsequently carried out by way of a transfer of all the shares in Crumlin Investments Ltd to Cornelscourt Shopping Centre Ltd. Cornelscourt Shopping Centre Ltd was one of the Dunnes Stores group of companies, operators of a rival chain of stores. The 150 or so individual companies making up the Dunnes Stores group were, in many respects, only notionally separate companies. All the affairs of the group were managed by members of the Dunne family. It was vital from the Dunne family's point of view that a Dunnes Stores retail outlet be established in the shopping centre. The family policy was that a new company should operate each separate retail unit, and so a new company, Dunnes Stores (Crumlin) Ltd, was incorporated for the purposes of acquiring a lease in the shopping centre and establishing a retail outlet there in direct competition with Power Supermarkets Ltd. Upon incorporation of this new company, Cornelscourt Shopping Centre Ltd caused Crumlin Investments Ltd to convey the freehold of a large unit in the shopping centre to Dunnes Stores (Crumlin) Ltd for a nominal consideration, and without any of the usual covenants which would accompany a transaction of this kind when carried out between strangers at arm's length.

When Dunnes Stores (Crumlin) Ltd began to trade in the shopping centre, Power Supermarkets Ltd sought an injunction restraining them. Costello J found for the

---

[142] *Power Supermarkets Ltd v Crumlin Investments Ltd and Dunnes Stores (Crumlin) Ltd* (22 June 1981, unreported) HC, Costello J. See Hannigan, 'Piercing the Corporate Veil' (1983) DULJ (ns) 111.

plaintiffs, holding that Dunnes Stores (Crumlin) Ltd were bound by the covenant contained in the plaintiff's lease, *even though* they were not a party to that lease. He found that the covenant was a restrictive covenant, the burden of which, according to well established principles, ran with the land. Significantly, he also found that Dunnes Stores (Crumlin) Ltd were bound by the terms of the lease to which they were not formally a party because Dunnes Stores (Crumlin) Ltd, Crumlin Investments Ltd, and Cornelscourt Shopping Centre Ltd were all part of a single economic entity. Having cited the views of Lord Denning MR and Shaw LJ in *DHN Ltd v Tower Hamlets London Borough Council*, Costello J continued:

> 'It seems to me to be well established ... that a court may, if the justice of the case so requires, treat two or more related companies as a single entity so that the business notionally carried on by one will be regarded as the business of the group or another member of the group if this conforms to the economic and commercial realities of the situation. It would, in my view, be very hard to find a clearer case than the present one for the application of this principle. I appreciate that Crumlin Investments is a property owning not a trading company but it is clear that the creation of the new company and the conveyance to it of the freehold interest in a unit in the shopping centre were means for carrying out the commercial plans of the Dunne family in the centre. The enterprise had a two-fold aspect (a) the creation of a new retail outlet for the Dunnes Stores Group in the shopping centre and (b) the enhancement of the rents in the centre as a whole which the creation of such an outlet would hopefully produce. To treat the two companies as a single economic entity seems to me to accord fully with the realities of the situation. Not to do so could involve considerable injustice to the plaintiffs as their rights under the covenant might be defeated by the mere technical device of the creation of a company with a £2 issued capital which had no real independent life of its own. If it is established that the covenant is breached there should in my opinion be an injunction against both defendants.'

[5.054] This passage was, along with Lord Denning's observations in the *DHN* case, subsequently cited with approval by the Supreme Court in *Re Bray Travel and Bray Travel (Holdings) Ltd*[143], and may thus still be regarded as a correct statement of the law in this jurisdiction. In that case, the court granted an injunction to the liquidator of Bray Travel Ltd freezing the assets of its subsidiaries. Henchy and Kenny JJ, with whom Hederman J concurred, both observed that the injunction was equally justified on ordinary tracing principles without the necessity for disregarding the separate legal personality of the company, there being evidence that the company had transferred properties to its subsidiaries at a gross undervalue[144].

[5.055] A common feature of all of the cases discussed in the two preceding paragraphs is that in each case the disregard of the separate legal personality of the companies was justified on traditional grounds in accordance with the principles in *Salomon's* case.

---

143 *Re Bray Travel and Bray Travel (Holdings) Ltd* (13 July 1981) SC. The judgment was delivered *ex tempore* and no written judgments were handed down. Its value as an authority may be questioned to this extent. The case is, however, noted by Keane, *Company Law* (4th edn, Bloomsbury Professional, 2007) at p 135, and *Ussher*, *Company Law in Ireland* (1986) at p 52, fn 65–66. See also MacCann, *A Casebook on Company Law* (1991, Butterworth Ireland) at pp 135–136. The 'justice' criterion was also applied by Barron J in *H Albert De Bary & Co NV v TF O'Mullane et al* (2 June 1992, unreported) HC, but without much explanation.

144 See Courtney, *Mareva Injunctions and Related Interlocutory Orders* (1998, Butterworths) at pp 9–19.

[5.056] Accordingly, in *Rex Pet Foods Ltd v Lamb Bros (Dublin) Ltd et al*[145], Costello J refused to disregard the separate legal personalities of a group of companies under common ownership or control. The case arose on a claim by the receiver and manager of Rex Pet Foods Ltd that its assets and the assets of the defendant companies should be aggregated and that the businesses of all the companies should be treated as one. Lamb Bros (Dublin) had acquired a 52% shareholding in Rex Pet Foods Ltd. Some of Lamb Bros (Dublin)'s directors joined Rex Pet Foods' board of directors, but the management of Rex Pet Foods Ltd remained unaltered. A number of contracts were entered into between Rex Pet Foods and Lamb Bros (Dublin) whereby the defendant group of companies became sole distributors for Rex Pet Foods' goods, and under which the defendants would supply management services to Rex Pet Foods. Separate books of account were maintained by the companies. When Rex Pet Foods got into financial difficulties Lamb Bros (Dublin) acquired the remaining shares in Rex Pet Foods. At this stage there were some management changes to Rex Pet Foods whereby managers from the defendant group joined its board. When Rex Pet Foods went into receivership, the receiver sought to have the assets of all the companies treated as one. Costello J, refusing the application, said:

> 'It is alleged that the plaintiff company should be regarded merely as a branch of the defendant group as its manufacturing arm because, firstly, the defendants discharged the creditors of the plaintiff company from time to time. The evidence establishes that this in fact occurred ... but this to my mind did not in any way affect the separate legal entity of the plaintiff company and was a normal enough arrangement for companies trading in a group such as these companies were trading. Secondly, it is suggested that the claim is supported by the fact that invoices from suppliers of the plaintiff company were sent direct to the defendant company. Factually this is so. From time to time creditors of the plaintiff company, in particular suppliers of goods and raw materials to the plaintiff company, sent invoices to one or other of the defendant companies but this does not raise any claim or sustain any claim that the two companies should be treated as one legal entity. It does perhaps, reflect some confusion but not to the extent which would justify the claim now being made on the plaintiff's behalf. Thirdly, it is suggested that the management of the plaintiff company was such that the claim being made is justified. The management changed in the way I have indicated. The explanation for the change is a reasonable one and in my view does not of itself justify the claim that has been made. Fourthly, it was suggested that there were no regular meetings of the board of directors of the plaintiff company. There were meetings of the board of directors and meetings were held up to March 1982. Thereafter it seems that no inference such as is being sought to be drawn arises from the fact that the board of directors comprised members of the parent company for this is a situation which is normal and is to be found where a group of companies is controlled by a parent company.
>
> Finally, the point was raised that the defendant company was sole distributor for the plaintiff company, but this was a situation which was in no way unique or which raises the inference which the plaintiffs seek to raise.
>
> The question arises whether all these factors taken together raise the inference sought to be raised but I cannot agree that this is so. There have been some cases which counsel have referred me to where the courts have treated companies as being one legal entity but

[145] *Rex Pet Foods Ltd v Lamb Bros (Dublin) Ltd et al* (5 December 1985, unreported) HC, Costello J.

these have been cases in which the facts are very different to those which the evidence establishes in the circumstances of this case.

So in my view the plaintiffs have failed to make out a case which would justify me in making the declaration which is sought. I should add that even if the situation were different and there were circumstances in which the court should regard these companies as being one for some reason or other, this would not justify the court making another order which, indeed, is a separate order in relation to the aggregation of assets because it seems to me there has been *no evidence to suggest that any funds of the plaintiff company were siphoned off into any of the defendant companies in such circumstances as would raise an equitable claim to the assets of any of the defendant companies* ...[146]'

Much seems to have been made by Costello J of the fact that no equitable claim to the assets of any of the defendant companies arose, and he refused to disregard the separate legal personality of the plaintiff company on that basis. If an equitable claim had been established permitting such disregard of the company's separate legal personality, then doubtless it would have been actionable in equity without a need to disregard separate legal personality.

[5.057] Likewise, in *The State (McInerney & Co Ltd) v Dublin County Council*[147], Carroll J refused to regard two subsidiaries of the same holding company as part of a single economic entity so that one could, when refused planning permission, compel the defendant Council to purchase lands owned by the other. No recognised legal relationship between the subsidiaries could be identified which might establish a proprietary relationship in the first subsidiary. Had a proprietary interest been found, it is submitted, there would have been grounds other than the single economic entity principle upon which to afford the applicants relief. The learned judge said:

'In my opinion the corporate veil is not a device to be raised and lowered at the option of the parent or group. The arm which lifts the corporate veil must always be that of justice. If justice requires (as it did in the *DHN* case) the courts will not be slow to treat a group of subsidiary companies as one. But can it be said that justice requires it in this case? We have here a parent company with 30 subsidiary companies forming the McInerney Group. According to Mr Cody, the finance director of the parent company, it is group policy, depending on circumstances to operate in the name of one of these companies on various sites throughout the country. He says that McInerney Construction Ltd (the registered owner) has no resources other than those supplied by another subsidiary. The purchase moneys were provided by the applicant, it being the intention that such moneys be repaid in due course out of the proceeds of realisation.

When those averments are considered, it appears to me that here is a group of companies operated so as to maximise the benefits to be gained from the individual corporate identity of each subsidiary. If the purchase money was to be repaid out of the proceeds of realisation, it follows that the profits or losses remained with the registered owner. If the development was not profitable the loss would be confined within the assets of that one company ... In my opinion this is not a case where justice demands that the corporate veil be lifted ... It is not for a corporate group to claim that the veil should be lifted to illuminate one aspect of its business while it should be left *in situ* to isolate the individual actions of its subsidiaries in other respects.'

---

146 Italics added.

147 *The State (McInerney & Co Ltd) v Dublin County Council* (12 December 1984, unreported) HC, Carroll J.

[5.058] As Carroll J observed in *The State (McInerney & Co)* case, a controller must not be allowed to disregard the separate legal personality of a company simply when it suits him. In *Gresham Industries Ltd v Cannon*[148], Finlay P refused to regard a company and its controller as a single economic entity. He refused to allow a debtor to set off, against a debt which was owed to a creditor, a debt owed by that creditor to Paulcar Ltd, one company in a group of companies, all of which were beneficially owned by the debtor. He said:

> 'It seems to me ... a fundamental principle of the law that if a person decides to obtain and use the benefit of trading through limited liability companies and if for any purposes whether the limitation of his liability, tax purposes or otherwise he transfers assets from one company to another or makes drawings from one company and invests them in his own name in another company that he cannot subsequently be heard to ignore the existence of the legal entities consisting of the different companies and to look upon the entire transaction as a personal one ... All these claims were put forward by the defendant upon the basis that he was the effective beneficial owner of Paulcar Ltd which he asserted was a solvent company and that therefore he must be identified with the rights and liabilities of Paulcar Ltd as if they were his own rights and liabilities and that therefore he was entitled to these as a set-off or credit against the amounts due by him to the plaintiff company in liquidation ... I am satisfied that as a matter of law even a 100% beneficial shareholder in a company cannot for the purposes of the settling of an account between him and another individual or company be identified with the company[149].'

[5.059] English authorities suggest that the justice of the case will only permit a company to be regarded as part of a single economic entity where it is established merely as a 'façade' to conceal improprieties, or where the court is interpreting a statute or contract. Doubts about the scope of Lord Denning's observations in the *DHN* case were expressed in the English House of Lords by Lord Keith of Kinkel in *Woolfson v Strathclyde Regional Council*[150], where he said:

> 'I have some doubts whether ... the Court of Appeal properly applied the principle that is appropriate to pierce the corporate veil only where special circumstances exist indicating that it is a mere façade concealing the true facts.'

[5.060] In *Adams v Cape Industries*[151], discussed above, the Court of Appeal determined:

> 'the relevant parts of the judgments in the *DHN* case ... must, we think, likewise be regarded as decisions on the relevant statutory provisions for compensation even though these parts were somewhat broadly expressed and the correctness of the decision was doubted by the House of Lords in *Woolfson v Strathclyde Regional Council* ...'

The Court of Appeal concluded that:

> 'save in cases which turn on the wording of particular statutes or contracts, the court is not free to disregard the principles of *Salomon v Salomon* merely because it considers that

---

148 *Gresham Industries Ltd v Cannon* (2 July 1980, unreported) HC, Finlay P.

149 *Gresham Industries Ltd v Cannon* (2 July 1980, unreported) HC, Finlay P at p 19 of the transcript. Contrast *Munton Bros Ltd v Secretary of State* [1983] NI 369 where Gibson LJ stated that the members of a group may apply to have their separate legal personality disregarded where justice so requires.

150 *Woolfson v Strathclyde Regional Council* (1978) SC 90.

151 *Adams v Cape Industries* [1990] Ch 433 at 536. See para **[5.049]**.

> justice so requires. Our law, for better or worse, recognises the creation of subsidiary companies which though in one sense the creatures of their parent companies, will nevertheless under the general law fall to be treated as separate legal entities with all the rights and liabilities which would normally attach to such legal entities.'

[5.061] *Adams* was followed by Walker J *Re Polly Peck International plc (In Administration) (No 4)*[152], where the learned judge added that the courts must look to the legal substance of any transaction and not its economic substance when deciding whether the company is a mere façade, regardless of any perceived injustice that arose when the company became insolvent.

In that case, the court was required to determine the legal status of a wholly owned subsidiary company which had been established within the Polly Peck group as a special-purpose financial vehicle, to raise funds through bond issues from the group. The subsidiary had a very small paid up capital (which would not have covered even the transaction costs); it had no independent management; and had no bank account or separate financial records. Once it received funds pursuant to a bond issue, the subsidiary on-loaned the money to its holding company. The holding company guaranteed the subsidiary's obligations and pursuant to the relevant agreements became the principal obligor in regard to the bonds. The holding company went into administration and in the subsequent scheme of arrangement it was provided that no creditor should prove more than once in respect of any scheme claim. The subsidiary company then itself went into liquidation and sought to claim from the scheme supervisors for sums on-loaned to the holding company. Banks which had taken up the bonds also lodged claims against the holding company pursuant to its guarantees. The supervisors, after accepting most of these claims by the banks, applied to the court for directions as to whether the subsidiary company was entitled to maintain a claim in the arrangement separate to those of the banks in respect of which it was essentially the same debt.

Walker J held that the claims of the subsidiary and of the banks were *not* so closely connected as to be, in substance, claims in respect of the same debt. He observed that it was not open to the court to disregard the principle of separate corporate personality and treat a closely integrated group of companies as a single economic unit on the basis merely of perceived injustice, particularly in cases where the separate legal existence of these companies assumed greater importance once they became insolvent. One company in the group could not properly be considered to be a nominee or agent of another, since neither agency nor nomineeship could be inferred simply because a subsidiary company has a small paid up capital and has a board of directors all or most of whom are also directors or senior executives of its holding company.

The court held that full force had to be given to the legal meaning of the documents in question, for to regard them otherwise would be to deprive them of any legal meaning and would be at variance with the intentions of the parties. Nor was the subsidiary a sham. Walker J thought that there was a considerable difference between the creation and operation of a single-purpose financial vehicle, and the creation of a sham or façade simply to cloak the true character of certain transactions.

---

152 *Re Polly Peck International plc (In Administration) (No 4)* [1996] 2 All ER 433.

[5.062] The Irish courts, as has been stated above, have reaffirmed the importance of *Salomon's* case in cases where the single economic entity approach has been argued. In *Allied Irish Coal Supplies Ltd v Powell Duffryn International Fuels Ltd*[153], discussed above, both the High Court and the Supreme Court rejected any possibility of a general rule that the mere existence of a close relationship between companies in a group could lead *per se* to their separate legal personalities being disregarded. What is especially interesting in the judgment of Murphy J in the Supreme Court in that case is his consideration of Costello J's decision in *Power Supermarkets Ltd v Crumlin Investments Ltd and Dunnes Stores (Crumlin) Ltd*[154]. Murphy J said:

> '... apart from the distinctions which may be drawn between this and other cases, the crucial feature of *Power Supermarkets Ltd v Crumlin Investments Ltd* is that Costello J did not purport to question the authority of *Salomon v Salomon & Co* [1897] AC 22. Indeed no reference was made to that case in the course of his judgment nor, as far as I am aware, the argument on which it was based. Again it is clear from the judgment in *Rex Pet Foods Ltd v Lamb Brothers (Ireland) Ltd* ... that Costello J had not intended in *Power Supermarkets Ltd v Crumlin Investments Ltd* to lay down any revolutionary principle of law.
>
> While it would be impossible to say that there are no circumstances in which the members of a company, whether corporate or individual, could not conduct, or purport to conduct the business of a company in such a way as to render their assets liable to meet claims in respect of the business normally carried out by the company, I believe that this would be an altogether exceptional state of affairs and difficult to reconcile with the seminal judgment in *Salomon v Salomon & Co* ...

This serves to strengthen the proposition that the Supreme Court is keen to relegate the single economic entity approach to circumstances in which the exceptions identified in *Salomon's* case are shown to exist. It is submitted that that is where it rightly belongs.

[5.063] The door has not been firmly shut, however. In *Fyffes plc v DCC plc*[155], Laffoy J gave thorough consideration to the authorities in Ireland and England. The central issue in that case was whether DCC plc was liable to Fyffes plc for insider dealing under Part V of the CA 1990 in relation to the sale of its shareholding in Fyffes plc, given that the CEO of DCC plc was also a non-executive director of Fyffes plc and had access to internal management accounts forecasting a drop in profits. For tax reasons, DCC plc sold its shares in Fyffes plc at no profit to a related company, Lotus Green Ltd, which then became resident in the Netherlands before selling on the shares. The High Court was asked to find that Lotus Green Ltd and DCC were part of the same single economic entity so that Lotus Green could be held to account to Fyffes under Part V of the CA 1990. After a lengthy consideration of the authorities, Laffoy J stated as follows:

> 'On the basis of the foregoing analysis of the pleadings, the submissions made by the parties, the authorities and commentary on the authorities, I have come to the following conclusions:-
>
> (1) As a matter of law, Lotus Green may be regarded as having acted as the agent of DCC in relation to the holding and disposal of the shares in Fyffes, if to do

153 *Allied Irish Coal Supplies Ltd v Powell Duffryn International Fuels Ltd* [1998] 2 IR 519. See para **[5.046]**.

154 See para **[5.044]**.

155 *Fyffes plc v DCC plc* [2009] 2 IR 417.

otherwise would lead to an injustice. Whether it should be, depends on whether the inference is factually justified. This is to be determined having regard to all of the facts, including the nature of its interest in the shares, and the relationship between Lotus Green and DCC. The views of the human agents of the companies are not in any way determinative of the question.

(2) As a matter of law, Lotus Green and DCC may be treated as a single entity as regards the sale of the shares in Fyffes and the generation of the profit therefrom for the purpose of preventing the avoidance of the availability of an effective remedy under s 109 and thus preventing an injustice to parties with a remedy under s 109, if DCC is liable to account. It should be so treated if the plaintiff has established that:-

(a) an evidential basis exists for finding that, as regards the holding and disposal of the shares, to borrow the terminology used by Murphy J in *Lac Minerals Ltd v Chevron Mineral* [1995] 1 ILRM 161, there was a factual identification of the acts of Lotus Green and DCC; and

(b) not to so treat the companies would allow the DCC Group to evade its obligations under Part V.

In relation to the point at (a), the plaintiff argued that the companies in the DCC Group could have, but did not in fact, arrange their affairs so as to ensure that factual identification did not take place. In relation to the point at (b), the plaintiff did not and, on the evidence could not, assert that the purpose of the incorporation of Lotus Green and the hiving off of the shares to it was to avoid liability under Part V. The sole objective was to mitigate the tax liability of the DCC Group. However, the reality of the situation is that by defending the plaintiff's statutory claim on the basis that DCC made no profit from the sale of the shares, if DCC was precluded from dealing by virtue of s 108(6) and Lotus Green was not, the DCC Group would effectively evade liability under s 109, if the profit generated by Lotus Green on the Share Sales were not treated as the profit of DCC. To recognise this reality is to give a purposive meaning to Part V in the light of the Directive[156].

Though the injustice concept raises its head in the learned judge's judgment, the approach is actually very measured. It is of note that Laffoy J did not acknowledge a general power to ignore the separate legal personality of the members of the economic group; rather, she required that an injustice first has to be proved. In this case, it would require proof of a factual identification of the acts of the members of the group as being the same acts, and proof that there would otherwise be an evasion of existing legal liability. There is nothing new in that decision and although Cooke J in *Goode Concrete v CRH plc*[157] mooted the possibility of lifting the veil on the 'justice of the case' ground in an application for security for costs against an unlimited company with limited liability shareholders,[158] he did not do so because the limited companies in question were foreign companies[159].

[5.064] The European courts, however, have held on more than one occasion that the EU Commission enjoys a degree of discretion in the choice of which company in the group ought to have a fine imposed on it for breaches of EU competition law. In *BPB*

---

156 *Fyffes plc v DCC plc* [2009] 2 IR 417 at 495.

157 *Goode Concrete v CRH plc* [2012] IEHC 116.

158 See Ch 6, *Corporate Civil Litigation*, at **[6.025]**.

159 See para **[5.039]** *et seq*.

Industries and British Gypsum[160], the Court of First Instance confirmed the Commission's decision to impose fines on a subsidiary, 'whilst it is indeed true that the Commission could have imposed those fines on the parent company'[161]. And in *Commercial Solvents*[162], the Court of Justice established that the Commission can choose to impose the fine jointly and severally on a parent company and its subsidiary. While such decisions on the face of them appear to indicate a general disregard of the principles of *Salomon's* case, it must be remembered that EU competition law focuses on economic personality rather than legal personality by directing its provisions to 'undertakings' rather than to individuals or companies[163].

[D] INJUNCTIONS AND ORDERS

[5.065] The courts retain an inherent jurisdiction to order enforcement of their judgments or orders against *any* person whom they think ought to be named therein to ensure observance of the order. In such cases the courts may disregard the separate legal personality of the company and issue an order or injunction against its directors or controlling members, in addition to the company itself, in order to ensure that the company meets its obligations. This is well illustrated in cases involving injunctions under s 160 of the Planning and Development Act 2000[164], though the principle is the same for many other types of order. In *Dublin County Council v Elton Homes Ltd*[165], Barrington J observed:

> 'Let me say at once that I think it may be quite proper, in certain circumstances to join the directors of a company as respondents when an application is made by a planning authority against a company pursuant to the provisions of s 27 ... There may be many cases particularly in the case of small companies where the most effective way of ensuring that the company complies with its obligations is to make an order against the directors as well as against the company itself. But in such a case the order against the directors would be a way of ensuring that the company carried out its obligations. A body corporate can only act through its agents and the most effective way of ensuring that it does in fact carry out its obligations might be to make an order against the persons in control of it.'

[5.066] It has recently been settled, however, that the jurisdiction to extend injunctions and orders to incorporators in this way does not extend to making 'fall-back' orders against members and directors of polluting companies under the Waste Management Acts – at least where the directors or members are not themselves polluters. In *Environmental Protection Agency v Neiphin Trading Ltd*[166], Edwards J in the High Court held that the 'polluter pays' principle behind the Waste Framework Directive[167] had not been fully implemented in Ireland and in any event did not automatically render the

---

160 *BPB Industries and British Gypsum* Case T- 65/89 [1993] ECR II-442.

161 *BPB Industries and British Gypsum* Case T- 65/89 [1993] ECR II-442.

162 *Commercial Solvents* Joined Cases 6 and 7/73 [1974] ECR 254.

163 See Wils, 'The Undertaking as Subject of EC Competition Law and the Imputation of Infringements to Natural or Legal Persons' (2000) 25 EL Rev 99.

164 Formerly s 27 of the Local Government (Planning and Development) Act 1976.

165 *Dublin County Council v Elton Homes Ltd* [1984] ILRM 297. See para **[5.037]**.

166 *Environmental Protection Agency v Neiphin Trading Ltd* [2011] IEHC 67.

167 Council Directive 2008/98/EC.

controllers of polluting companies severally liable for the pollution brought about by their companies. He stated:

> '… the Court cannot disregard the fundamental nature of the separate legal personality principle and ... in the absence of an express statutory abridgment of that principle, the Court should lean against an interpretation permitting the corporate veil to be pierced. This is in the interests of legal certainty, a very important principle underpinning our law … although a jurisdiction does already exist to lift the veil of incorporation in the case of a company being used for a fraudulent or other improper purpose that jurisdiction, which is of long standing, is intended to ensure (a) that a statutory privilege is not abused, and (b) that the Court's own process is not abused. Every Court is entitled as a matter of inherent jurisdiction to seek to protect its own process and may in an appropriate case lift the corporate veil to ensure that its orders are not frustrated by a cynical and strategic reliance on the principle of separate corporate personality by the directors (or shareholders) of a company. Whenever, under the planning code, a Court has seen fit to lift the corporate veil in the case of s 27 Orders formerly, and now s 160 Orders, it has invariably done so to that end. If the polluter pays principle only required the lifting of the veil in similar circumstances s 57 and s 58 could be harmoniously interpreted on the basis that the necessary jurisdiction already exists and is of long standing. However, it demands more than that. It demands that the polluter should pay in all circumstances which may require the veil to be lifted in any case where a company cannot comply, even in cases where the shareholders/directors are not fraudulently or improperly attempting to hide behind the company. The jurisprudence of the Irish Courts has long set its face against such an incursion. Absent the existence of a fraudulent or improper purpose the Courts will not lift the corporate veil unless authorised to do so by statute[168].'

The decision contradicted and in many respects overruled[169] the practice of making fall-back orders against the directors of insolvent corporate polluters, started ten years earlier by O'Sullivan J in *Wicklow County Council v Fenton*[170]. In that case O'Sullivan J had stated:

> 'The domestic law in relation to limited liability of companies would, in my opinion, frustrate or at least fail fully to implement the objectives of the relevant directives if it precluded the making of an order against directors in circumstances where the company in question, having first been directed by the court to comply with such orders, was not in a position for financial or other reasons so to do. In my view, in order to ensure the full application of the 'polluter pays' principle, whereby those responsible even indirectly for causing environmental pollution should pay for it rather than leave it to an innocent party or the community to do so, the court must be in a position to make orders directly against directors in such circumstances, and the domestic company law of limited liability should be suspended and the veil of incorporation lifted in order to ensure the full application of this principle and other objectives of the European waste directives. To hold otherwise

168 At para 6.50 *et seq* of the judgment.

169 The High Court decision is of equal jurisdiction with earlier decisions establishing the fall back order jurisdiction. The decision arguably may carry more authority as it arose as a preliminary question of law. Though the last word rests with the Supreme Court, no appeal was made in this case.

170 *Wicklow County Council v Fenton* [2002] 4 IR 44. See also *Minister for the Environment v Irish Ispat Ltd* [2005] 2 IR 338; *Cork County Council v O'Regan* [2009] 3 IR 39; *Laois County Council v Scully* [2006] 2 IR 292; *Wicklow County Council v O'Reilly* [2006] IEHC 265, [2007] IEHC 71.

> would, in my opinion, mean that innocent parties (local authorities or the public) would have to 'pay' (if only by accepting pollution of their environment without remedy), whereas those individuals who are at least indirectly responsible for it would be beyond the reach of Irish domestic law. That is not, in my opinion, a transposition into the Irish law of the European Directives. Accordingly, a 'fall-back' order may be made against individual directors and/or shareholders where a company cannot comply with a primary order[171].'

The *Neiphin Trading* judgment has not quite spelled the end of fall-back orders, however. In *John Ronan and Sons v Clean Build Ltd (in liquidation) and Others*[172], following a comprehensive review of the authorities, Clarke J held that polluter pays liability could still be fixed on directors and shareholders who were personally complicit in polluting. He stated:

> 'Insofar as the polluter pays principle forms part of the landscape of environmental law in this jurisdiction, the tenor of Edwards J's decision is that its scope does not extend to the provision of a jurisdiction on the courts to make 'fall back' orders against individuals who have no connection with environmental pollution other than their position as either director or shareholder of a company found liable under the 1996 Act. In short, the 'polluter pays' principle cannot, in the view of Edwards J, be used to infer provisions into the law which simply are not there. This finding, however, does not suggest that the polluter pays principle should not be given any consideration *at all* by the court nor does it address circumstances where a director or shareholder is found to be independently liable under the 1996 Act. Accordingly the principles set out in *O'Regan* in my view represent the present state of the law on the question of 'independent' as opposed to 'fall back' liability for those actively involved in a company[173].'

Clarke J found on the evidence before him that two of the directors were on-site and exercised personal supervisory functions whilst the polluting operations were being carried out. He concluded that they were thus directly and personally involved in the ongoing waste operation and deserved to bear responsibility for the wrongs which occurred during their watch. A third director, however, played a substantially non-executive role and had no practical involvement in the waste operations; no order was made against him.

[5.067] The converse scenario, whereby the court issues an order or injunction against a company in respect of the obligations of its controlling members, is likewise possible. In *TSB Private Bank International SA v Chabra and Another*[174], a *Mareva* injunction was made against a company even though the cause of action was not against it, but rather was against its controlling shareholder. Mummery J found that the court had jurisdiction so to order, saying:

> 'In the present case there are two defendants. There is one defendant, Mr Chabra, against whom the plaintiff undoubtedly has a good arguable cause of action: the claim on the guarantee. That is justiciable in the English court; Mr Chabra is amenable to the jurisdiction of the English court to make a final judgment against him on the guarantee.

171 *Wicklow County Council v Fenton* [2002] 4 IR 44 at 68.

172 *John Ronan and Sons v Clean Build Ltd (in liquidation) and Others* [2011] IEHC 350.

173 *John Ronan and Sons v Clean Build Ltd (in liquidation) and Others* [2011] IEHC 350 at para 6.18.

174 *TSB Private Bank International SA v Chabra and Another* [1992] 2 All ER 245.

> The claim for an injunction to restrain disposal of assets by Mr Chabra is ancillary and incidental to that cause of action. In my judgment, the claim for a similar injunction against the company is also ancillary and incidental to the claim against Mr Chabra and the court has power to grant such an injunction in an appropriate case. It does not follow that, because the court has no jurisdiction to grant a *Mareva* injunction against the company, if it were the sole defendant, the court has no jurisdiction to grant an injunction against the company as ancillary, or incidental, to the cause of action against Mr Chabra ... I agree that such course of action is an exceptional one, but I do not accept that it is one that the court has no jurisdiction to take.'

The granting of the injunction against the company was, according to the judge, the most practical form of relief in the circumstances[175].

[E] CHARACTERISATION

[5.068] The courts regularly look behind the separate legal identity of a company in order to attribute to it a human characteristic required by law. It must be stressed that in such circumstances the courts *do not* ignore the separate legal existence of the corporation; rather, they examine its background in order to be able to say more about its separate personality. A number of such instances may be examined as follows:

1. Residence;
2. Culpability and *mens rea*;
3. Character for licensing purposes.

Residence

[5.069] Questions of residence arise very frequently, especially in relation to taxation, when, for example, a company is registered in one country and makes profits in another[176]. The actual residence of companies incorporated in Ireland is now irrelevant for the purposes of the Tax Acts and the Capital Gains Tax Acts. This is because s 82(2) of the Finance Act 1999 provides that subject to certain limited exceptions, '...a company which is incorporated in the State shall be regarded ... as resident in the State'[177]. *Actual residence*, however, continues to be relevant, for example, to companies not incorporated in Ireland and for companies that come within the exceptions to s 82(2). The governing factor for determining the actual residence (as opposed to deemed residence) of a company is the place where its *control* abides[178]; but in each case

---

175 See also *Re A Company* [1985] BCLC 333 and *International Credit and Investment Co (Overseas) Ltd v Adham* [1998] BCC 134 and, generally, Courtney, *Mareva Injunctions and Related Interlocutory Orders* (1998, Butterworths) at para [4.20] *et seq*.

176 See Goldstein, 'The Residence and Domicile of Corporations with Special Reference to Income Tax' (1935) 51 LQR 684; Corrigan, 'Place of Abode Test in Establishing Tax Residence' (1988) 6 ILT 106.

177 See Ch 2, *Incorporation by Registration*, at para **[2.045]**.

178 The residence of a company is less easy to establish than its *nationality* or *domicile*, both of which are determined simply by reference to the *place* of incorporation. Domicile may be determined by reference to other criteria for the purposes of certain legislation; see, for example, s 13(2) of the Jurisdiction of Courts and Enforcement of Judgments (European Communities) Act 1988 which provides that for the purposes of that legislation the domicile of a company is determined by where the corporation has its seat. See also Gill, 'The Seat of a Company and the EEC Judgments Convention' (1988) ILT 30.

it is a question of fact as to who actually controls the company, and the courts will disregard the separate legal personality of the company to find the answer to that question.

[5.070] The test for determining actual residence was established in *De Beers Consolidated Mines Ltd v Howe*[179]. The issue in that case was whether a South African registered company was resident for tax purposes in England. Lord Loreburn, in the House of Lords, rejected the argument that a company resides where it is registered and nowhere else, and said:

> 'Now, it is easy to ascertain where an individual resides, but when the inquiry relates to a company, which in a natural sense does not reside anywhere, some artificial test must be applied ... In applying the conception of residence to a company, we ought, I think, to proceed as nearly as we can upon the analogy of an individual. A company cannot eat or sleep, but it can keep house and do business. We ought, therefore, to see where it really keeps house and does business. An individual may be of foreign nationality, and yet reside in the United Kingdom. So may a company ... I regard that as the true rule; and the real business is carried on where the central management and control actually abides[180].'

The head office of the company was in Kimberly, South Africa, and it was there that the general meetings of the company were held. Some of the directors also lived in Kimberly and directors' meetings were occasionally held there. But it was clearly established that the majority of directors and life governors of the company resided in England. The main directors' meetings were held there, at which all the important business of the company, such as negotiation of contracts, determination of policies of disposal of assets and the working of the mines, the application of profits, and the appointment of directors, were decided. Thus, since the company was controlled from England, it was held to reside there.

[5.071] In *John Hood & Co Ltd v Magee*[181], a company was held to be controlled by its shareholders in general meeting. Accordingly, it was held to be resident in Belfast, where the general meetings took place, rather than New York, where its managing director resided. Madden J referred to Lord Loreburn's test for residence in the *De Beers* case, and continued:

> 'Applying the test supplied by Lord Loreburn I ask in the first instance where does this company keep house? Assuredly in Belfast, for here the registered office must be, under the provisions of the memorandum of association, and here the general meetings of the company are in fact held. Where does it do business? Some of the business transactions are carried on in Ireland and some in New York, and this divided business leaves unsolved the question which Lord Loreburn regards as the true test as to where the real business is carried on. This, he says, is where the central management and control actually abides. In my opinion, the central management and control of this company abides with the general meeting of shareholders in Belfast, where the registered office of the company is situated and where the general meetings of the company are held ... If the shareholders in general meeting were to consider it more in the interests of the company that the managing director should reside where the goods in which they deal are manufactured and bought,

179 *De Beers Consolidated Mines Ltd v Howe* [1906] AC 455. See Young, 'The Legal Personality of a Foreign Corporation' (1906) 22 LQR 178.

180 *De Beers Consolidated Mines Ltd v Howe* [1906] AC 455 at 458.

181 *John Hood & Co Ltd v Magee* [1918] 2 IR 34.

> they might refuse to re-elect him, except on the terms of his residing in Belfast. Adopting the analogy suggested by Lord Loreburn, the movement would proceed from the heart and brain of the organisation in Belfast by which the action of its organs is controlled[182].'

The shareholders' power to remove and replace the managing director, thus, was indicative of where the control of the company actually resided.

[5.072] The importance of this kind of control was also in evidence in the celebrated First World War case of *Daimler v Continental Tyre Co*[183], where the matter of residence was considered for purposes other than taxation. The issue in that case was whether the defendant, a British registered company, should pay the debt it owed the plaintiff, another British registered company, even though directors and shareholders of the defendant company were all German residents. The Proclamation against Trading with the Enemy Act 1914 (UK) forbade trade with enemies and rendered contracts with the enemy void, but as regards companies it stated that 'in the case of incorporated bodies, enemy character attaches only to those incorporated in an enemy country'. The courts of first instance found that the defendants should pay the plaintiff, since the legislation in question set out the decisive factor in determining the character of the plaintiff company. On appeal, however, the House of Lords found the plaintiff company to be an enemy[184]. Lord Parker, with whom Lords Paramoor and Kinnear, and Viscount Mersey, agreed, said:

> 'The acts of a company's organs, its directors, managers, secretary and so forth, functioning within the scope of their authority, are the company's acts and may invest it definitively with enemy character. It seems to me that similarly the character of those, who can make and unmake those officers, dictate their conduct mediately or immediately, prescribe their duties and call them to account, may also be material in a question of the enemy character of the company. If not definite and conclusive, it must at least be *prima facie* relevant, as raising a presumption that those who are purporting to act in the name of the company are in fact, under the control of those whom it is their interest to satisfy ... [A] company may assume an enemy character. This will be the case if its agents or the persons in *de facto* control of its affairs ... are resident in an enemy country ... The character of individual shareholders cannot of itself affect the character of the company ... [it] may, however, be very material on the question of whether the company's agents, or the persons in *de facto* control of its affairs, are in fact adhering to, taking instructions from, or acting under the control of enemies. This materiality will vary with the number of shareholders who are enemies and the value of their holding[185].'

Thus, the residence of the company's principal officers will be of prima facie importance in determining the residence of a company, but the extent to which they are controlled, removable, and replaceable, by the other members of the company may cause the focus to shift to the persons exercising such control.

[5.073] From the foregoing examination of the manner in which the courts disregard the separate legal personality of a company in order to determine its actual residence it

---

182 *John Hood & Co Ltd v Magee* [1918] 2 IR 34 at 49–50.

183 *Daimler v Continental Tyre Co* [1916] 2 AC 307.

184 The finding on this matter, admittedly, was *obiter*, since the court's main ground for allowing the appeal was its finding that the secretary of the plaintiff company had no authority to commence litigation in the company name.

185 *Daimler v Continental Tyre Co* [1916] 2 AC 307 at 345.

should be clear that a company may, at one and the same time, be resident in a number of jurisdictions. This will be so where its control is exercised from a number of different states[186]. It should also be noted that in *Unit Construction Ltd v Bullock*[187] it was held that a stipulation in the company's constitution that it was to be managed only from a specified jurisdiction was not conclusive as regards its place of residence.

Culpability and *mens rea*

[5.074] The circumstances in which the courts will look to the character of a company's controllers in order to attribute the company with culpability or *mens rea* have already been discussed in detail in Ch 4, above[188].

Character for licensing purposes

[5.075] Certain licensing statutes require the applicant to be of 'good character', and where a company is the applicant the courts will look for that character in the character of the company's agents or controllers. Such was the case in *The King (Cottingham) v The Justices of County Cork*[189], where the issue was whether a wholesale beer dealer's licence could be granted to a brewing company, Beamish and Crawford Ltd, when one of the prerequisites of granting such a licence was that the applicant be of good character. The company was granted a licence by the judges of the Petty Sessions District of Macroom, the licence stating that the magistrates found the company to be of 'good character, and that their house in the Main Street, Macroom ... has been conducted in a peaceable and orderly manner in the past year ...'. The licence was objected to by Mr Cottingham, the District Inspector, and he obtained a conditional order of *certiorari* to quash the licence. Palles CB found no difficulty in refusing to make the order absolute. He said:

> 'the only difficulty which presents itself ... [is] the alleged impossibility of an incorporated company being able to have a good character, or a character at all. But I cannot appreciate the difficulty. I cannot see why a public Company cannot have a character. No doubt it has no soul; but it can act by others, and through others do acts which in the case of a natural person would affect conscience, and be the foundation of that reputation which the law knows as 'character', be it good or bad. It can be guilty of fraud, of malice, and of various criminal offences, some of commission, others of omission; some punishable summarily, others by indictment. 'Character' as used in the section means 'reputation.' Reputation is acquired by conduct. *The conduct of the authorised agents of a company is its conduct. Why should not that conduct give rise to a reputation as to its character, good, bad, or indifferent?*[190]'

[186] *Swedish Central Railway v Thompson* [1925] AC 495; *Egyptian Delta Land & Investment Co Ltd v Todd* [1929] AC 1.

[187] *Unit Construction Ltd v Bullock* [1960] AC 351.

[188] See Ch 4, *Incorporation and its Consequences*, at para **[4.063]** *et seq*.

[189] *The King (Cottingham) v The Justices of County Cork* [1906] 2 IR 415. See also *R v LCC, ex parte London and Provincial Electric Theatres Ltd* [1915] 2 KB 466 where a local authority was held justified in its decision not to renew a cinematograph licence held by an English company because most of its shares were held by Germans and three of its six directors were Germans.

[190] *The King (Cottingham) v The Justices of County Cork* [1906] 2 IR 415 at 422–423 (italics added). See also *The State (Hennessy and Chariot Inns Ltd) v Commons* [1976] IR 238; and *McMahon v Murtagh Properties Ltd* (20 October 1981, unreported) HC, Barrington J, where this passage was cited with approval.

Thus, where 'good character' is sought to be established, the courts may disregard the separate legal personality of the company by examining the conduct of its agents.

[F] STATUTE

[5.076] Private companies are creatures of statute; thus, the principles which pertain to them may be modified by statute, provided the modification is made within the bounds permitted by the Constitution. The legislature has introduced a number of statutory provisions which cause the principle of separate personality to be disregarded in particular circumstances. A number of such provisions appear in the Companies Acts and secondary legislation implementing EU company law directives. More are contained in taxation legislation. The principal legislative provisions requiring disregard of the separate legal personality of companies are discussed here as follows:

1. The Companies Acts;
2. Other legislation.

The Companies Acts

[5.077] The Companies Acts provide for several instances in which the separate legal personality of a private company may be ignored. Some of these provisions require a company to be identified with other companies in a group. For example, groups of companies will be required to show accounts which reflect the financial position of the group as a whole[191]. Similarly, the court appointing an examiner to a company is empowered to appoint an examiner to other related companies[192].

Other provisions provide for several instances in which members, directors, or other officers may be made personally liable for the debts or other obligations of the company. Many of these provisions are not directed specifically at members, but at directors or other officers. The making of persons other than members personally liable for corporate debts and obligations is one of the most extreme forms of disregard of the principle of separate legal personality.

Some of the more significant provisions of the Companies Acts which create personal liability[193] will be considered here under the following list of headings, which is not exhaustive:

(a) Reduction of number of members below the legal minimum;
(b) Failure to state correctly the company's name;
(c) Breach of restriction or disqualification order;
(d) Failure to meet capital requirements;
(e) Failure to keep proper records;
(f) Unreasonably inaccurate declaration of solvency;
(g) Liquidation of related companies;
(h) Fraudulent or reckless trading.

---

191 See Ch 17, *Financial Statements, Audit, and Annual Return*, at para **[17.144]** *et seq*.

192 See Ch 22, *Examinerships*, at para **[22.051]** *et seq*.

193 See generally MacCann, 'Personal Liability for Corporate Debts' (1991) ILT 206 and (1991) ILT 232.

(a) Reduction of number of members below the legal minimum

[5.078] Section 36 of the CA 1963 provides:

> 'If at any time the number of members of a company is reduced, in the case of a private company, below two, or, in the case of a public company, below seven, and it carries on business for more than 6 months while the number is so reduced, every person who is a member of the company during the time that it so carries on business after those 6 months and knows that it is carrying on business with fewer than two members, or seven members, as the case may be, shall be severally liable for the payment of the whole debts of the company contracted during that time, and may be severally sued therefor.'

The application of this section to private companies limited by shares has been discontinued by the EC(SMPLC)R 1994[194], reg 7(1) of which provides that s 36 of the CA 1963 shall not apply to a private company limited by shares or by guarantee. It should be noted that s 36 continues to apply to unlimited private companies. Regulation 7(2) further provides that:

> 'Without prejudice to paragraph (1), a person who, before the coming into force of these regulations, is liable by virtue of s 36 of the CA 1963 (Members severally liable for debts where business carried on with fewer than, in the case of private company, two members) for the payment of the debts of a private company limited by shares or by guarantee, shall not be so liable for the payment of the company's debts contracted on or after the date on which these regulations come into force.'

Regulation 7(2) is, thus, a transitional provision, continuing the application of s 36 of the CA 1963 to acts done prior to 1 October 1994 by a private company with fewer than two members.

[5.079] It must be stressed at the outset that a company continues to exist as a legal person despite any reduction in membership below the legal minimum, even where no members remain[195]. Since s 36 makes only the remaining members – not the withdrawing members – liable, it has no application where there are no members left. In such circumstances, however, it appears that a single new member will be caught by the section for the debts of the company incurred until a second member joins to bring the number of members back up to the statutory minimum. It should also be noted that the remaining member must *know* that the company is carrying on business with fewer than two members.

The personal liability imposed by the section is several – thus, the creditors of the company may proceed directly against the liable member. But such liability arises only in respect of those debts of the company which have been contracted for subsequent to the expiration of six months from the reduction in membership. This seems to encompass only pecuniary obligations of a contractual nature, and would not include other liabilities such as claims for damages in tort or claims arising under statute, eg, claims for damages for unfair dismissal. In addition, where a member does incur liability under the section he will be entitled to seek an indemnity from the company since the company, as a separate legal person, remains primarily liable for the debt[196].

---

194 SI 275/1994.

195 See Ch 4, *Incorporation and its Consequences*, at para **[4.020]**.

196 *Brook's Wharf Ltd v Goodman Brothers* [1937] 1 KB 534.

[5.080] There is much to be said in favour of the disapplication of s 36 to all private limited companies. In *Nisbet v Shepherd*[197], Moulton, one of the members of a two-member company, Moulton & Co Ltd, transferred his shares to the other member, Shepherd, and resigned as director. This transfer was duly recorded in the company's register of members. No other transfer of shares was made until 1990 when Shepherd transferred a single share to his wife so that a resolution for the winding up of the company could be made. The liquidator successfully applied to have Shepherd made liable under the UK equivalent of s 36. The Court of Appeal rejected Shepherd's argument that the transfer of Moulton's shares to him was defective[198]. Hoffmann LJ observed:

> 'I have considerable sympathy with the appellant, who has fallen into a trap created by an ancient and obsolete rule. Section [36 of the CA 1963] requires that a company should have at least two members. In default of compliance it strips the remaining member of the protection of limited liability. The rule goes back to s 48 of the Companies Act 1862 when the minimum number of members was seven. This reflects the evolution of company law from partnership, but the reason why it has survived through successive Companies Acts is obscure. It seems to serve no purpose in protecting the public or anyone else[199].'

The section continues to apply to unlimited private companies, and to public companies. It is to be hoped that future legislation might remove it from the statute books altogether[200].

(b) Failure to state correctly the company's name

[5.081] Section 114(4) of the CA 1963 provides that if an officer of a company or any person on its behalf:

> 'signs or authorises to be signed on behalf of the company any bill of exchange, promissory note, endorsement, cheque or order for money or wherein its name is not mentioned [in legible characters] ... he shall be liable to a fine ... and shall further be personally liable to the holder of the bill of exchange, promissory note, cheque or order for money or goods for the amount thereof unless it is duly paid by the company.'

Section 114(5)[201] continues:

> 'The use of the abbreviation 'Ltd' for 'Limited' or 'Teo' for 'Teoranta' or 'plc' for 'public limited company' or 'cpt' for 'cuideachta phoiblí theoranta' shall not be a breach of the provisions of this section.'

The effect of these provisions is that where the correct and full registered name of the company does not appear on a bill of exchange, promissory note, cheque or order for money or goods[202] the signatory will be personally liable to pay the holder[203] if the

---

197 *Nisbet v Shepherd* [1994] 1 BCLC 300.

198 See further Ch 9, *Share Transfer*, at para **[9.006]**.

199 *Nisbet v Shepherd* [1994] 1 BCLC 300 at 305.

200 The CLRG, *First Report* (2001) recommends the repeal of s 36 of the CA 1963: recommendation 4.9.3.

201 As amended by Schedule 1, para 13 of the C(A)A 1983.

202 But not an order for the supply of services, as Gower, *Principles of Modern Company Law* (3rd edn, Stevens & Son, 1969) notes at p 116.

203 The holder is the person to whom the document is addressed and who is to benefit by it: *Civil Service Co-Operative Society Ltd v Chapman* (1914) TLR 376.

company defaults in payment – even though the holder has not been misled by the misdescription. Thus, in *Atkins & Co v Wardle*[204], where a company whose registered name was 'South Shield Salt Water Baths Co Ltd' was described in a bill of exchange as 'Salt Water Baths Co Ltd', the directors who had signed the bill on the company's behalf were held to be personally liable to the holder of the bill. Similar principles were applied in *Nassau Steam Press v Tyler*[205], where 'The Bastille Syndicate Ltd' was described as 'Old Paris and Bastille Syndicate Ltd'. Two examples of the harshness of the rule are *Barber & Nicholls Ltd v R & G Associates (London) Ltd*[206] and *Hendon v Adelman*[207]. In the former case, liability was imposed where '(London)' was left out of the company name on a cheque; in the latter case liability was imposed on a cheque where '&' was left out of the company name, 'L & R Agencies Ltd'. The use of the abbreviation 'Co' for 'Company' has been held not to offend against the provisions[208], but a failure to indicate by the use of the appropriate word at the end of the company's name that the liability of the members is limited will fall foul of these statutory requirements[209].

The officer or agent will be liable under s 114(4) of the CA 1963 even where the misdescription of the company's name in the document is made by the holder of the document, because it is the duty of the officer or agent to ensure that the name is accurately stated on the document before he signs it or authorises it to be signed. Thus, in *Lindholst & Co A/S v Fowler*[210], where bills of exchange prepared by the plaintiffs referred to a company named 'Corby Chicken Co Ltd' simply as 'Corby Chicken Co', the defendant, who had signed the bills on behalf of the company without correcting the misdescription, was made personally liable on the bills. By way of contrast, in *Durham Fancy Goods Ltd v Michael Jackson (Fancy Goods) Ltd*[211], where a bill of exchange was drawn by the plaintiffs on the defendant company, and the bill and the form of acceptance had both been prepared by the plaintiffs, the plaintiffs were held to be estopped from invoking the personal liability of the signatory for a misdescription of the company as 'M Jackson (Fancy Goods) Ltd'. In the *Lindholst* case, Donaldson MR distinguished the decision in the *Durham Fancy Goods* case on the basis that in that case the form of words for the acceptance had been prescribed by the plaintiffs and they were estopped by what they had prescribed whereas in the case before him the form of words for the acceptance had not been prescribed by the plaintiffs.

Clearly then, the officers and agents of a company must take great care to ensure that the company name is accurately stated *before* signing or authorising the signature of a bill of exchange, promissory note, cheque or order for money or goods. A mistake of the slightest nature may expose them to personal liability – whether or not they knew of the misdescription. The courts have made it clear that they will provide little assistance *after*

204 *Atkins & Co v Wardle* (1889) 61 LT 23.

205 *Nassau Steam Press v Tyler* (1894) 70 LT 376.

206 *Barber & Nicholls Ltd v R & G Associates (London) Ltd* (1981) 132 NLJ 1076.

207 *Hendon v Adelman* (1973) 117 JJ 631.

208 *Banque de l'Indochine v Euroseas Group Finance Co Ltd* [1981] 3 All ER 198.

209 *Penrose v Martyr* (1858) EB & E 499; *British Airways Board v Parish* [1979] 2 Lloyd's Rep 361; *Blum v OPC Repartition SA* [1988] BCLC 170.

210 *Lindholst & Co A/S v Fowler* [1988] BCLC 166.

211 *Durham Fancy Goods Ltd v Michael Jackson (Fancy Goods) Ltd* [1968] 2 QB 839.

signature: rectification will not be granted where the motive is to avoid personal liability under s 114(4)[212].

[5.082] The liability of the officer or agent is dependent upon his being a signatory to the document in question or his having authorised the signature of the document. If there is no signature on behalf of the company there can be no liability[213]. Where there is such a signature, but it is sought to impose personal liability not on the actual signatory but on the person who authorised the signing of the document, it must be shown that he not only authorised the signing of the document but also authorised it to be signed in such a way that the name of the company did not properly appear thereon[214]. The giving of such authority may, however, be inferred by the courts in appropriate circumstances, such as where the person who authorised the signature knew at the time of a misprint of the company's name on the document[215].

If the signatory is authorised to act on behalf of the company, the company will remain primarily liable on the document, despite the misdescription, so long as it can be identified[216]. The officer's or agent's liability under s 114(4), then, is *secondary* or collateral to that of the company. It is not in the nature of a guarantor's or surety's liability; thus the defences which are available to guarantors and sureties are not available[217]. And, it would appear, the signatory may be entitled to recover an indemnity from the company itself in respect of any personal liability incurred[218].

(c) Breach of restriction or disqualification order

[5.083] Part VII of the CA 1990 is designed to prevent the directors of a company which is in an insolvent liquidation from forming a new company and carrying on business as before. To this end, ss 150[219] and 160[220] of the CA 1990 provide for the making of a *restriction order* and a *disqualification order* against directors, shadow directors, and other officers of the company, in appropriate circumstances. These are discussed in further detail in Ch 28. Contravention of either order may render a person liable for the debts and liabilities of the company. Such liability qualifies as an exception to the principle that others, particularly members, are not normally to be made liable for the debts and other obligations of the company. Personal liability for contravention of these orders may arise in two ways:

(i) where the restricted or disqualified person contravenes the order *in person*; or

(ii) where another person acts on the directions of a restricted person.

---

212 *Blum v OCP Repartition SA* [1988] BCLC 170; *Rafsanjan Pistachio Producers v Reiss* [1990] BCLC 352.

213 *Oshkosh B'Gosh Inc v Dan Marbel Inc Ltd* [1989] BCLC 507.

214 *John Wilkes Footwear Ltd v Lee International Footwear Ltd* [1985] BCLC 444.

215 [1985] BCLC 444.

216 *Goldsmith (Sicklesmere) Ltd v Baxter* [1970] Ch 85.

217 *British Airways Board v Parish* [1979] 2 Lloyd's Rep 361.

218 Following *Brook's Wharf and Bull Ltd v Goodman Brothers* [1937] 1 KB 534. Such a right will, more often than not, prove worthless, since the company will (if the holders are choosing to move against the officers of the company rather than the company itself) probably be insolvent.

219 See further Ch 28, *Compliance and Enforcement*, at para **[28.062]** *et seq*.

220 See further Ch 28, *Compliance and Enforcement*, at para **[28.148]** *et seq*.

(i) Restricted or disqualified person acting in person

[5.084] Section 163(3) of the CA 1990 provides that where any person who is subject to these restrictions or disqualifications acts in breach of them, and the company with which he then became concerned commences an insolvent winding up either while he is involved or within 12 months of his so being involved, then:

> 'the court may, on the application of the liquidator or any creditor of the company, declare that such person shall be personally liable, without any limitation on liability, for all or any part of the debts or other liabilities of the company incurred in the period during which he was acting in such a manner or capacity.'

(ii) Acting on the directions of a disqualified person

[5.085] Where a director, officer, member of a committee of management, or trustee of any company acts *in accordance with the instructions* of a restricted or disqualified person while knowing that they are so restricted or disqualified, he will be guilty of an offence under s 164(1) of the CA 1990. In addition, s 165(1) of the CA 1990 provides that any person convicted under s 164(1) for acting in accordance with the directions of a *disqualified*[221] person will automatically become 'personally liable for the debts of the company concerned incurred in the period during which he was so acting'. He may, however, seek such relief from this personal liability as the court, having regard to the circumstances of the case, considers to be just and equitable[222].

Curiously, the liability of persons acting on the directions of disqualified persons seems to arise independently of whether the company is insolvent – even though the disqualified persons themselves only become personally liable if the company enters an insolvent liquidation. Whether the solvency of the company is a factor which will spur the courts to grant relief from the rigours of s 165(1) remains to be seen.

(d) *Failure to meet capital requirements*

[5.086] Where a person becomes the subject of restrictions under s 150 of the CA 1990 he may not accept appointment or act in any manner, whether directly or indirectly, as a director or secretary or take part in the promotion or formation of any company unless the company satisfies certain capital requirements. Furthermore, he must, within the 14 days immediately preceding such appointment or so acting, send to the registered office of the company a notice stating that he is subject to such restrictions[223]. If, having received such notification, the company carries on business without fulfilling these capital requirements within a reasonable period and subsequently enters an insolvent liquidation, then, by virtue of s 163(4) of the CA 1990:

> 'the court may, on the application of the liquidator or any creditor or contributory of the company, declare that any person who was an officer of the company while the company so carried on business and who knew or ought to have known that the company had been so notified shall be personally responsible, without any limitation of liability, for all or any part of the debts or other liabilities of the company as the court may direct.'

---

221 Notably, conviction for acting on the instructions of a restricted person does not attract the operation of s 165.

222 Section 165(2) of the CA 1990.

223 Section 155(5) of the CA 1990. See Ch 28, *Compliance and Enforcement*, at para **[28.071]**.

This personal liability, unlike the liability of a restricted or disqualified person under s 163(3) of the CA 1990[224], is not restricted to the debts or other liabilities of the company arising during any specific period. The persons made personally liable may, however, apply to the court for such relief, in whole or in part, from personal liability as to the court, having regard to the circumstances of the case, appears fit[225].

(e) Failure to keep proper records

[5.087] Section 202 of the CA 1990 requires every company to keep proper books of account, whether in the form of documents or otherwise (for example, on computer). These requirements are discussed in detail in Ch 17[226], *post*.

Where a company has contravened s 202, and the court is satisfied that the contravention has either:

(i) contributed to the company's inability to pay all of its debts; or
(ii) resulted in substantial uncertainty as to the assets and liabilities of the company; or
(iii) substantially impeded the orderly winding up of the company,

then, under s 204 of the CA 1990, the court may, on the application of the liquidator or any creditor or contributory of the company, impose personal liability for the debts and other liabilities of the company without limitation on any one or more officers and former officers of the company who are in default. The principles governing such liability are discussed further in Ch 15, below[227].

(f) Unreasonably inaccurate declaration of solvency

[5.088] A statutory *declaration of solvency*, made by the directors in the prescribed form, will be required for a members' voluntary winding up[228]. The particulars required to be stated in such declarations are discussed elsewhere in this work[229].

[5.089] Where such a declaration has been made, and it is subsequently proved to the satisfaction of the court that the company is unable to pay its debts, s 256(8) of the CA 1963 provides that:

> 'the court on the application of the liquidator or any creditor or contributory of the company may, if it thinks it proper to do so, declare that any director who was a party to the declaration without reasonable grounds for the opinion that the company would be able to pay its debts in full within the period specified in the declaration shall be personally responsible, without limitation of liability, for all or any of the debts or other liabilities of the company as the court may direct[230].'

The only defence available to the director against such personal liability is to show that he had reasonable grounds for making the declaration; and it is to be presumed until the contrary is shown that there were no such reasonable grounds for the opinion[231]. What

[224] See para **[5.084]**.
[225] Section 163(5) of the CA 1990.
[226] See also Ch 17, *Financial Statements, Audit and Annual Return*, at para **[17.005]** *et seq*.
[227] See Ch 15, *Duties of Directors and Other Officers*, at para **[15.131]**.
[228] See Ch 23, *Winding Up Companies*, at para **[23.010]** *et seq*.
[229] See Ch 23, *Winding Up Companies*, at para **[23.004]** *et seq*.
[230] Section 256(8) of the CA 1963, inserted by s 128 of the CA 1990.
[231] Section 256(9) of the CA 1963, as amended by s 128 of the CA 1990.

amounts to reasonable grounds is not altogether clear, since there appear to be no judicial decisions on this point[232]. But one thing is clear: directors should take the utmost care and should seek independent professional advice[233] before making a declaration of solvency. This is especially so considering that where the debts are not paid or provided for in full within the period stated in the declaration the court may also make such further directions as it thinks proper to give effect to the declaration of personal liability[234]. This could, it has been suggested[235], include charging all or part of the company's debts and other liabilities on the assets of the defaulting directors.

(g) Liquidation of related companies

[5.090] The principles enunciated by Costello J in *Power Supermarkets Ltd v Crumlin Investments Ltd*[236] are to a large extent reflected in ss 140 and 141 of the CA 1990. Section 140 of the CA 1990 allows the court to order a company to make a contribution to the liquidator of a *related company* equivalent to the debts of that company. Section 141 of the CA 1990 allows the court to order, where two or more related companies are being wound up, that the companies be wound up together as if they were the one company. Each of these provisions is considered in detail in Ch 25, *post*[237].

(h) Fraudulent or reckless trading

[5.091] Section 297A of the CA 1963, as inserted by s 138 of the CA 1990, provides that if, during the course of a winding up or an examinership, a person is found to have been guilty of reckless or fraudulent trading, the court may declare such person to be personally responsible, without limitation of liability, for all or any part of the debts or other liabilities of the company as the court may direct. The circumstances in which such a declaration may be made are discussed in further detail in Ch 15, below.

Other legislation

[5.092] Among other legislative provisions which involve disregard of the principle of separate legal personality are the Capital Gains Tax Act 1975, the Taxes Consolidation Act 1997, and the Capital Acquisitions Tax Consolidation Act 2003, as amended. A detailed review of these complex provisions lies outside the scope of this work; however, it may be observed that the provisions endeavour to prevent persons from using companies to conceal taxable personal income and gains. The provisions place heavy emphasis on the degree of control a person exercises over a company, and a special

---

232 Nor, indeed, does there appear to be any judicial decision on what was meant by reasonable grounds under the old s 256 of the CA 1963 (now repealed and replaced by s 128 of the CA 1990) which provided for criminal penalties, as opposed to civil liability, in such circumstances: see *Keane*, *Company Law* (4th edn, Bloomsbury Professional, 2007) at para 40.7.

233 From an independent practising liquidator, if possible, since it will most likely be the liquidator of the company who will raise any subsequent challenges to the accuracy of the statement.

234 Section 256(10) of the CA 1963 as amended by s 128 of the CA 1990.

235 MacCann, 'Personal Liability for Corporate Debts' (1991) ILT 206 and (1991) ILT 232 at p 234.

236 *Power Supermarkets Ltd v Crumlin Investments Ltd* (22 June 1981, unreported) HC; See para **[5.052]**.

237 See Ch 25, *The Realisation and Distribution of Assets in a Winding-Up*, at para **[25.119]** *et seq.*

feature of the legislation is the concept of a 'close company,' which, broadly speaking, is a company under the control of five or fewer persons, or under the control of its directors[238]. A large number of Irish private companies fall within this definition. Onerous taxation regulations govern the provision of benefits or loans by a close company to its controllers.

[5.093] A trend in many regulatory statutes is the inclusion of provisions rendering company directors, secretaries, managers and other such officers personally criminally liable where the company is shown to have committed an offence. Such provisions adopt a common formula:

> 'Where an offence committed by a body corporate … is proved to have been committed with the consent or connivance of, or to have been attributable to any neglect on the part of any director, manager, secretary or other similar officer of the body corporate or a person who was purporting to act in any such capacity, he as well as the body corporate shall be guilty of that offence and shall be liable to be proceeded against and punished accordingly.'

Provisions of this nature are to be found, for example, in the Safety, Health and Welfare at Work Act 2005, s 80, and the Competition Act 2002, s 26(6)[239]. Similar provisions are to be found in statutes extending at least as far back as the Customs Consolidation Act 1876[240]. They have been described by the English courts as 'parasitic'[241] because they make substantial inroads into the principle of the separate legal personality, and, it seems, they have been introduced by the legislature with scant regard for the principles of *Salomon's* case, so dear to the courts.

[5.094] It should be noted, however, that the provisions do not impose automatic or strict liability on the directors, etc[242]. The onus on the prosecution is to prove first that the company committed the offence. There does not have to be a corporate conviction however, so that if the company is disbanded or wound up so that there is no undertaking left to convict, personal liability might still be imposed if the prosecution proves that an offence was committed by the company while in existence[243]. There is no advantage, therefore, in hurriedly winding-up a company[244] in the hope that personal liability might thereby be avoided.

[5.095] The prosecution must also prove that the individual *consented* to or *connived* at the corporate offence, or that it was attributable to their *neglect*. Various definitions of

238 Section 430 of the Taxes Consolidation Act 1997.

239 See Hutchinson, 'Criminal Liability of Directors, Managers and Other Similar Officers Under the Competition Amendment Act, 1996' (1997) 4 CLP 47.

240 Customs Consolidation Act 1876, 39 & 40 Vict c 36, ss 191 & 259; also the Merchandise Marks Act 1877, 50 & 51 Vict c 28, ss 2(2) and 5 as amended, and the Stamp Act 1891, 54 & 55 Vict c 39, s 13. More recent examples from the Irish Statute Books include the Redundancy Payments Act 1966, s 52; the Protection of Employment Act 1977, s 21(3); the Factories Act 1955, s 100(5); and the Office Premises Act 1958, s 31(4).

241 Per Evans LJ in *R v Wilson* [1997] 1 All ER 119.

242 *Huckerby v Elliott* [1970] 1 All ER 189.

243 See *R v Dickson & Another* [1991] Crim LR 854, [1991] BCC 719.

244 And, perhaps, transferring its business to another company.

consent and connivance in the context of provisions such as these have been given by the courts over the years, and the following propositions emerge:

- consent and connivance both involve some *deliberate* and *conscious* complicity in the acts constituting the offence[245];
- a person consents to the commission of an offence by his company when he is '*well aware of it and he agrees to it*'[246];
- *consent* requires simply that you consent to the doing of the acts; you do not have to know that the acts were criminal[247];
- '*connivance* ... suggests to my mind some form of knowledge by the defendant that something was wrong, because you cannot connive at something unless you have mental knowledge that something is going wrong'[248].

The upshot of these statements of principle is that in order to consent to or connive at acts constituting an offence one must *know* of those acts. In other contexts in the criminal law the term connivance has been held to connote 'wilful shutting of the eyes', 'wilful blindness', 'purposefully abstaining from ascertaining'; 'wilfully abstaining from knowing'; 'deliberately refraining from making enquiries the results of which he might not care to have' and 'shutting his eyes to the obvious'[249]. In order to connive, therefore, there must have been facts (which one purposefully ignored) which would raise suspicion or would put one on inquiry.

Neglect, which may be proved in the alternative, requires proof of a breach of duty. Whether a duty exists depends on the individual's position in the company and his professional responsibilities. Such duties may properly be delegated to another. In *Huckerby v Elliott*[250], the Court of Appeal allowed an appeal against the conviction of a director who, it was held, had properly left matters of licensing to another director of the company. Lord Parker CJ said[251]:

> '... I know of no authority for the proposition that it is the duty of a director to, as it were, supervise his co-directors or to acquaint himself with all the details of the running of the company.'

Not all such delegation will relieve the individual of neglect however. If the individual knew of the particular circumstances of the corporate offence, or had reasonable grounds to believe that it might be committed, he would be obliged to act to prevent it. In *Hirschler v Birch*[252], accordingly, the defendant director was convicted for neglect for failing to consult an authoritative source before confirming a purchase of high level brake lights, the legality of which was open to doubt in the UK. Nor will the mere issuing of injunctions at board level prohibiting illegal activity necessarily relieve an

245 *Southend Borough Council v White* (1991) 156 JP 463.
246 *Huckerby v Elliott* [1970] 1 All ER 189.
247 *R v McMillan Aviation* (4 June 1981) Crown Court, Kingston upon Thames.
248 *R v McMillan Aviation* (4 June 1981) Crown Court, Kingston upon Thames, *per* Reuben J; also *Secretary of State for Trade v Markus* [1976] AC 35.
249 See Edwards, *Mens Rea in Statutory Offences* (1955, MacMillan & Co) pp 196–203.
250 *Huckerby v Elliott* [1970] 1 All ER 189.
251 *Huckerby v Elliott* [1970] 1 All ER 189 at 194.
252 *Hirschler v Birch* [1987] RTR 13.

individual of liability[253]. The size of the company will be of significance. In *Lewis v Bland*[254], a managing director was acquitted on a charge of neglect giving rise to the corporate offence of providing false particulars of car servicing contrary to the Trade Descriptions Act 1968. The company in question was a large company, and the court felt that the managing director was entitled to delegate work to his senior staff and could expect that the work would be conducted in accordance with his instructions.

[5.096] Even though some other legislative provisions do not so clearly permit disregard of the separate legal personality of a company, it has been suggested by Lord Diplock, in the House of Lords in *Dimbleby & Sons v National Union of Journalists*[255], that a purposive interpretation of the provisions of a statute may give rise to the inference that parliament intended the provision to permit such disregard. He observed:

> 'My Lords, the reason why English statutory law, and that of all other trading countries, has long permitted the creation of corporations as artificial persons distinct from their individual shareholders and from that of any other corporation even though the shareholders of both corporations are identical, is to enable business to be undertaken with limited financial liability in the event of the business proving to be a failure. The 'corporate veil' in the case of companies incorporated under the Companies Acts is drawn by statute and it can be pierced by some other statute if such other statute so provides: but in view of its *raison d'être* and its consistent recognition by the courts since *Salomon v Salomon and Co Ltd* [1897] AC 22, one would expect that any parliamentary intention to pierce the corporate veil would be expressed in clear and unequivocal language. I do not wholly exclude the possibility that even in the absence of express words stating that in specified circumstances one company, although separately incorporated, is to be treated as sharing the same legal personality of another, a purposive construction of the statute may nevertheless lead inexorably to the conclusion that such must have been the intention of Parliament.'

Indeed, the learned judge's observations reveal that which has already become apparent from earlier discussion in this chapter, namely, that the courts may, when construing the provisions of a statute, find it necessary to ignore the separate legal personality of a company in order to give effect to the statutory provisions.

253 *Southend Borough Council v White* (1991) 156 JP 436.

254 *Lewis v Bland* [1985] RTR 171.

255 *Dimbleby & Sons v National Union of Journalists* [1984] 1 WLR 427 at 435.

Chapter 6

Corporate Civil Litigation

[6.001] As was considered in Ch 4, *Incorporation and Its Consequences*, one of the consequences of incorporation is that a company can sue and be sued in its own name. In very many respects, the laws of civil litigation apply to companies as they apply to individuals. In many other respects, however, the laws (and more often the practice and procedures) applicable to proceedings commenced by or taken against companies can differ markedly to those applicable to individuals or partnerships. Although corporate litigation is not generally perceived to be a distinct area of company law, it is thought to be a useful clustering of issues that are illustrative of the principles of company law in a practical setting or, if you like, applied company law. Here, the following issues are considered:

[A] The Proper Plaintiff where a Company is Wronged.

[B] Authority to Institute Proceedings by Companies.

[C] Service of Proceedings.

[D] Security for Costs.

[E] Discovery and Interrogatories against Companies.

[F] Appearance in Court by Companies.

[G] Enforcement of Judgments and Orders against Companies.

[A] The Proper Plaintiff where a Company is Wronged

[6.002] The proper plaintiff in an action in respect of a wrong alleged to be done to a company is, *prima facie*, the company[1]. This is the primary consequence of the rule in *Foss v Harbottle*[2], and as a principle of company law ranks alongside the principle of separate legal personality, conclusively established in *Salomon's* case[3]; indeed, it can be viewed as an inevitable consequence of the principle of separate legal personality. In *O'Neill v Ryan et al*[4], O'Flaherty and Blayney JJ cited, *inter alia*, the following passage from the English Court of Appeal's decision in *Prudential Assurance Co Ltd v Newman Industries Ltd*:

> '[The rule in *Foss v Harbottle*] is not merely a tiresome procedural obstacle placed in the path of a shareholder by a legalistic judiciary. The rule is the consequence of the fact that a corporation is a separate legal entity … The company is liable for its contracts and torts;

---

1 See *Prudential Assurance Co Ltd v Newman Industries Ltd* [1982] 1 Ch 204 at 210 *per* Jenkins LJ.

2 *Foss v Harbottle* (1843) 2 Hare 461.

3 *Salomon v Salomon & Co* [1897] AC 22.

4 *O'Neill v Ryan et al* [1993] ILRM 557.

the shareholder has no such liability. The company acquires causes of action for breaches of contracts and torts which damage the company. No cause of action vests in the shareholder[5].'

Suffice it to say for present purposes that it is well established that where a wrong is committed against a company (eg, breach of contract, a tort, etc) it will be the company, and not its shareholders or others, who will have *locus standi* to bring proceedings[6]. The converse is equally true and a company will not be the proper defendant where one of its directors commits a tort, unless the company is as a matter of law vicariously liable for the tort[7]. As fundamental as this principle is, it can be overlooked particularly in small private companies involving proprietary-directors who have a tendency to confuse corporate property (in all of its forms) with their own personal property.

[6.003] The importance of joining, in litigation, all relevant parties is illustrated by *Re New Ad Advertising Ltd*[8]. In that case a petition was brought alleging oppression pursuant to s 205 of the CA 1963, where the only named party was the company, although the details of the oppression were directed against a Mr McNulty whom it was alleged was the controlling force in the company. Mr McNulty was not, however, jointed as a notice party and was not in any other sense a party to the petition proceedings. Notwithstanding this, the High Court ordered Mr McNulty to pay over a total of £67,200 being the value that had been placed on the petitioner's shareholding in the company. On appeal to the Supreme Court, O'Flaherty J said:

> '… the petition proceeded on the basis, presumably, that there was such an identity of interest between the company and Mr McNulty that, in effect, any order that was being made would be on the basis that Mr McNulty *was* the company: this seems to be the way that the case was approached. There is no doubt that the company and Mr McNulty availed of the same firm of solicitors. But it is trite law to say that the identity of a company is distinct from the individuals who comprise it: that is *Salomon v Salomon & Co* [1897] AC 22. While in modern company legislation there is a tendency on occasion to allow the veil to be lifted on a corporation, that companies have a separate existence is still basic law[9].'

The result was that the Supreme Court ordered Mr McNulty to be made a notice party to the proceedings, that he be furnished with all documents in the case and that he should be given an opportunity to put in a defence if he was of such a mind.

[6.004] The doctrine of *res judicata* operates to estop parties from denying not only the state of affairs established by a judgment but also the grounds upon which that judgment was based; *res judicata* can be either cause of action estoppel or issue estoppel. One

---

5 *Prudential Assurance Co Ltd v Newman Industries Ltd* [1982] 1 Ch 204 at 224.

6 This principle is consistently applied: see, for example, *DBP Construction Ltd et al v ICC Bank plc et al* (21 May 1998, unreported) SC, Keane J, *nem diss*. There, Keane J said 'in the light of the rule in *Foss v Harbottle* [1843] 2 Hare 461 as applied by this court in *O'Neill v Ryan et al* [1993] ILRM 557, [the individual plaintiffs], as shareholders and directors of the company, could not recover losses which were in fact the losses of the company itself' (at p 24 of the judgment).

7 *Crofter Properties Ltd v Genport Ltd (No 3)* [2002] IEHC 26, McCracken J.

8 *Re New Ad Advertising Ltd* (26 March 1998, unreported) SC, O'Flaherty and Lynch JJ.

9 *Re New Ad Advertising Ltd* (26 March 1998, unreported) SC at pp 4 and 5 of the judgment.

question that arises in the context of company law is whether a company will be estopped from taking proceedings against a defendant in circumstances where a director and shareholder of the company has previously taken an action in the same matter that was determined against him by a court. This was the issue at stake in *Belton v Carlow County Council; Prendergast & Prendergast (third parties)*[10]. In that case a factory owned by WJ Prendergast & Son Ltd (the company) was destroyed by fire. The third parties were shareholding directors of the company. The company had brought a claim for compensation under the Malicious Injuries Act 1981 and had been successful in the Circuit Court but unsuccessful, on appeal, to the High Court. The defendant county council had asserted that the fire had been deliberately started by the third parties. Subsequently, the plaintiff (who was the owner of an adjoining premises that had been damaged by the fire) sought and received compensation from the Circuit Court. The defendant county council claimed to be indemnified by the third parties in respect of the decree of £4,500. The question that arose was whether the third parties were estopped by the earlier High Court judgment from litigating the issue as to whether they had deliberately started the fire. One of the key issues to be determined by the Supreme Court was whether there was sufficient 'privity of interest' between the company and the third parties as to satisfy the requirements of issue estoppel. After noting the definition of privity given by Lord Lowry LCJ in *Shaw v Sloan*[11] that 'a party is the privy of another by blood, title or interest when he stands in his shoes and claims through or under him', Keane J stated that the enquiry in hand was solely concerned with whether there was 'privity of interest'. Keane J held:

> 'Assuming that the third parties are the owners of all the shares in the company and are the only directors (as to which there is no finding of fact in the case stated), I am satisfied that there is no such privity of interest between them and the company. It has, of course, been settled law since the decision in *Salomon v Salomon* that the company on the one hand and its shareholders on the other are separate and distinct legal entities. Moreover, while the interest of the company and its controlling shareholders may very often coincide, that is not always the case. The interest of the shareholder is to receive a dividend, in the event of the company's profits allowing it to be paid, and to share in any surplus assets of the company on a winding-up. The company's affairs must, however, be conducted by the directors, not merely in the interests of the shareholders, but of those of any persons who may have an interest in its financial well being: specifically the creditors, whether secured or unsecured. In the event of the company becoming insolvent (and it should be said that there is no evidence that this was at any stage the case with this company) the latter's interests will become paramount: see the decision of this court in *Re Frederick Inns Ltd* [1991] ILRM 582.'

Keane J went on to say that even assuming that the third parties had some control over the proceedings brought by the company, their interests were not identical to the company's: 'the proceeds of a successful application would become the assets of the company and would fall to be dealt with in accordance with the memorandum and articles and the applicable legislation.' On this point Keane J concluded:

10 *Belton v Carlow County Council; Prendergast & Prendergast (third parties)* [1997] 2 ILRM 405.

11 *Shaw v Sloan* [1982] NI 393.

> 'Similarly, in the event of the application being unsuccessful, the consequent liability for costs would be that of the company alone and in no sense the personal liability of the third parties. By contrast, in the present proceedings, the third parties alone will be liable, in the event of the local authority's claim succeeding and the company has no interest, present or contingent, in the outcome.'

On that basis Keane J answered the case stated in the negative and found that the third parties were *not estopped* from adducing facts to establish the cause of the fire on the company's premises.

[6.005] It would have been difficult for the Supreme Court to have permitted the invocation of an old doctrine which would have had the effect of denying individuals the right to defend allegations made against them that would have rendered them liable to pay compensation. In few cases involving companies and their shareholders is justice so acutely balanced. Yet, the decision of the Supreme Court in *Belton* clearly establishes that a shareholding in a company is not *per se* sufficient to give rise to the privity of interest necessary to invoke the doctrine of *res judicata*. An example of a different approach is seen in the English decision in *Barakot Ltd v Epiette Ltd*[12]. In that case, the controlling director of the plaintiff company *personally* sued the defendant for repayment of a loan allegedly made by him for £1.2m on foot of an oral agreement. This claim had been dismissed because at the time of the alleged agreement, the defendant company had not been incorporated. The plaintiff company subsequently instituted proceedings for the repayment of the loan against the defendant company, which applied to have the proceedings struck out on the basis of the doctrine of *res judicata*, by virtue of the parties' identities. It was held by a deputy High Court judge that the doctrine of *res judicata* did apply because there was sufficient identity between the plaintiff and its controlling director to ground privity of interest by reason of the fact that the plaintiff company was wholly owned by the controlling director and there was also sufficient identity of subject matter. It is thought that, intellectually, the decision of the Supreme Court in *Belton* (which of course represents the law in Ireland) is to be preferred.

[B] Authority to Institute Proceedings by a Company

[6.006] Where model reg 80 of Table A is adopted[13], the authority to institute any legal proceedings will be vested in the board of directors as, by this regulation, the members delegate the general power of management to the directors. Unless the directors have previously delegated the authority to institute proceedings to the CEO or a committee of the board or some other person, a resolution should be passed by the directors at a properly convened and constituted meeting of the board of directors authorising such action. Where it is found that a meeting of the directors was not properly held, as in the case of *Re Aston Colour Print Ltd*[14], any purported decision to commence proceedings – in that case a petition to have an examiner appointed to the company – can be invalidated.

---

12 *Barakot Ltd v Epiette Ltd* [1997] 1 BCLC 303.

13 See Ch 13, *Corporate Governance: Management by the Directors*, at para **[13.127]** *et seq*.

14 *Re Aston Colour Print Ltd* (21 February 1997, unreported) HC, Kelly J. See Ch 14, *Corporate Governance: Meetings*, at para **[14.109]**.

[6.007] Even where model reg 80 has been adopted by a company (and its management thereby delegated to its directors) it is arguable that its members may, notwithstanding, *direct* the directors to institute legal proceedings. This is because the delegation of the powers of management to directors is, *inter alia*, subject to 'such directions, being not inconsistent with the aforesaid regulations or provisions, as may be given by the company in general meeting'. There is a view that because there is no specific, express, delegation of power to directors to institute legal proceedings, the effect is to permit the members to make a 'direction' to the directors in that regard[15]. This point can be significant where a company's members wish the company to institute proceedings but where its directors are not inclined to do so; rather than take the more drastic step of removing the directors, the members may in general meeting (or by written resolution) purport to issue a direction to institute proceedings.

[6.008] Where there are no directors (or none, at least, capable of acting) the authority to institute proceedings will revert to a company's members. In such circumstances, an ordinary resolution must be passed in general meeting or, where allowed by the company's articles, by means of a written resolution pursuant to s 141(8) of the CA 1963 or, in the case of a single-member private limited company, a written decision pursuant to reg 9 of the EC(SMPLC)R 1994. As in the case of a directors' meeting, a members' meeting at which it is proposed to pass a resolution authorising the institution of proceedings must be validly convened and held. Where a meeting is not properly constituted, any litigation instituted might be found to be unauthorised: see *Colthurst and Tenips Ltd v La Touche Colthurst and Colthurst*[16].

[6.009] Once a company goes into liquidation, its directors' powers to institute legal proceedings are displaced and any litigation can only be instituted by the company's liquidator. In an official winding up, the liquidator is empowered to bring or defend legal proceedings in the name and on behalf of the company, subject to the sanction of the court or committee of inspection[17]. The exercise of an official liquidator's powers to bring or defend litigation on a company's behalf is subject to the control of the court and any creditor or contributory may apply in relation to any exercise of those powers[18]. The difference between directors' and liquidators' powers to continue proceedings was commented upon by Laffoy J in *Re Greendale Developments Ltd*[19] in the following terms:

> 'The decision of the court on a contested application to continue proceedings under s 231 is qualitatively different from the decision of a board of directors of a solvent company in relation to prosecuting litigation. The decision of the board of directors should be informed by the interests of the company, not by the sectional interests of individual shareholders or creditors. Once a winding-up order is made, the company is doomed to extinction. The winding up process is the process of the administration of the assets of the company: their collection, realisation and distribution in discharge of the liabilities of the company to the creditors and of the entitlement of its contributories in accordance with the

15 See Ch 13, *Corporate Governance: Management by the Directors*, at para **[13.133]**.

16 *Colthurst and Tenips Ltd v La Touche Colthurst and Colthurst* [2000] IEHC 14, McCracken J. See Ch 14, *Corporate Governance: Meetings*, at para **[14.039]**.

17 Section 231(1) of the CA 1963. See Ch 24, *Liquidators*, at para **[24.029]**.

18 Section 231(3) of the CA 1963.

19 *Re Greendale Developments Ltd* (28 July 1997, unreported) HC, Laffoy J.

scheme of priorities prescribed in the Companies Acts. Insofar as the Companies Acts give an entitlement to a creditor or a contributory to be heard by the court in relation to a matter arising in the winding up, in my view, the court is required to have regard to the sectional interest of that creditor or contributory and, in particular, to the protection of his legal entitlement to a distribution from the assets of the company as defined by the Companies Acts[20].'

Liquidators' powers to bring and defend proceedings by and on behalf of companies are considered in detail in Ch 24, *Liquidators*[21].

[C] SERVICE OF PROCEEDINGS

[6.010] In order to commence legal proceedings in the District, Circuit or High Courts, it is necessary, after *issuing* the papers, to *serve* the requisite process[22] on the defendant in the action. In this section we consider service on companies formed and registered under the Companies Acts[23].

[6.011] The service of proceedings (and, for that matter, any *document*) on companies registered under the Companies Acts is governed by s 379(1) of the CA 1963, which provides:

> 'A document may be served on a company by leaving it at or sending it by post to the registered office of the company or, if the company has not given notice to the registrar of companies of the situation of its registered office, by registering it at the office for the registration of companies.'

For example, a High Court summary summons applicable to a simple contract debt can validly be served on a company by sending it by ordinary post to its registered office. If the Companies Registration Office ('CRO') has not been notified of the company's registered office, the summons may be sent to the CRO itself[24]. In *National Gas Engine Co Ltd v Estate Engineering Co Ltd*[25], it was held that 'summons' in this regard includes 'default summons'. Service need not be by post[26], and a summons can simply be 'left at' the company's registered office. Service on a company's solicitor will only be good service where the solicitor has been authorised by the company to accept service[27].

---

20 *Re Greendale Developments Ltd* (28 July 1997, unreported) HC at pp 7 and 8 of the judgment.

21 At para **[24.029]**.

22 In the District Court, a civil process; in the Circuit Court, a civil bill; and the High Court, a summons (summary, special or plenary) or an originating notice of motion. See, generally, Courtney, *Mareva Injunctions and Related Interlocutory Orders* (1998) at paras [8.14]–[8.24].

23 Service of proceedings on foreign companies with an established place of business in the State; and foreign companies that have established a branch within the State are considered in Ch 34, *External Companies and Branches*, at paras **[34.024]** and **[34.039]**, respectively.

24 *Cf Bank of Ireland v North City Providers Ltd* (1953–1954) Ir Jur Rep 16, where Murnaghan J allowed service on the directors at their home addresses where a company had ceased to occupy its registered office and place of business.

25 *National Gas Engine Co Ltd v Estate Engineering Co Ltd* [1913] 2 IR 474.

26 The question of service by fax remains contentious: see Hall, 'Service of Documents by Fax' (1989) Gazette ILSI 318.

27 *Re Denver United Breweries Ltd* (1890) 63 LT 96.

[6.012] The decision in *O'Shea v DPP*[28] shows that while service on a body corporate may be effected through service on an officer of that body corporate, service on an individual in that individual's own right, cannot be effected by service on a body corporate of which he is a director. In that case Murphy J said:

> 'Service on a company secretary is good service on the company. It is not good service on a director of the company. While an argument could be made that service on a director, as agent of the company (see s 8 of the Companies Act 1963 and SI No 163 of 1973) is service on the company, the reverse cannot be so. The company is not an agent of the director or member of the company.'

The facts in that case were that a defendant (who happened to be director of a company) was to be prosecuted for certain road traffic offences. Summonses were served on his workplace and, in his absence, were served by the police on another person at his workplace. The defendant was convicted of the offences and this was upheld in the Circuit Court. The defendant sought a judicial review of this decision and Murphy J held that he had not been properly served and remitted the matter back to the District Court. In that case the service provision under consideration was Ord 47, r 2(a) of the District Court Rules 1948[29] which deals with individuals. Murphy J's comment that service on a company secretary is good service needs to be contextualised. Service on a company secretary of a company within the meaning of s 2 of the CA 1963 is not, *per se*, good service. Where the company is a company to which s 379 applies, the provisions of s 379 must be complied with. This can involve addressing the notice to the company secretary, *but must involve* 'leaving it at or sending it by post to the registered office of the company', etc.

[6.013] Where a company actually operates from its registered office no injustice can result from s 379 of the CA 1963. However, in reality, very many private companies have as their registered office the office of their accountant or solicitor which is normally the office where the company was formed. In such cases, the company obviously does not operate from its registered office. Consequently, a summons could validly be served on a company at its registered office without the company ever being, in fact, aware of service. This potential for injustice is compounded by s 379(2) of the CA 1963, which provides:

> 'For the purposes of this section, any document left at or sent by post to the place for the time being recorded by the registrar of companies as the situation of the registered office of a company shall be *deemed* to have been left at or sent by post to the registered office of

---

28 *O'Shea v DPP* (30 November 2000, unreported) HC, Murphy J.

29 This provided: 'A summons may be served on a defendant to whom it is directed by delivering to him a copy thereof issued for service or by leaving such copy for him at his last or most usual place of abode, or at his office, shop, factory, home or place of business with the husband or wife of the defendant or with the child or other relative (residing with the defendant) … or with any agent, clerk or servant of the defendant, or with the person in charge of the house or premises wherein the defendant usually resides, provided that any person (other than the defendant himself) with whom such copy is left for the defendant is not under sixteen years of age and is not the complainant'. This was amended by Ord 5 of the District Court Rules (No 1) 1962 (SI 7/1962). These rules have now been replaced by the District Court Rules 1997. Service on companies is now addressed in Ord 6, which mirrors the wording of s 379 of the CA 1963.

the company notwithstanding that the situation of its registered office may have been *changed*[30].'

This subsection deems a document to have been served on a company once it is left at or posted to the company's registered office. However, the presumption may be rebutted in appropriate circumstances, where, for example, it is proved that the document never in fact reached its destination. Such were the circumstances in *Re J Bird Moyer & Co (Ireland) Ltd*[31], where an Irish registered company was sued by an American company for £6,446 5s 10d. The American company sent the summons to the registered office of the Irish company by registered mail, but the letter was retained by the Post Office and was never delivered. The American company subsequently obtained summary judgment in default of appearance and proceeded to register the judgment as a judgment mortgage against the Irish company's property. When the Irish company was being wound up, the liquidator sought to have the judgment mortgage set aside. Budd J, in granting the relief sought by the liquidator, held that the presumption was rebutted in this case because of the admitted fact that the summons had not in fact been delivered to the registered office. Thus, he held, time had not begun to run for the entry of an appearance and so the summary judgment in default of appearance had been wrongly awarded.

[D] Security for Costs

[6.014] When a limited company appears as plaintiff in any proceedings, s 390 of the CA 1963 allows the defendant to apply to court for an order requiring the plaintiff company to provide *security for costs*[32]. As Denham J said in the Supreme Court decision in *Superwood Holdings plc v Sun Alliance and London Insurance plc*[33], the purpose of s 390 is:

> '... to protect defendants from litigation by corporate bodies who are not a mark for the costs of such litigation.'

Where an order for security for costs is granted, the plaintiff company must pay into court a sum that can be looked to, in order to discharge the defendant's costs, should the defendant be successful in defending the proceedings. The effect of s 390 is that the court may, at its discretion[34], stay proceedings commenced by a limited company until such time as *sufficient*[35] security for the defendant's costs has been provided. Section 390 provides:

> 'Where a limited company is plaintiff in any action or other legal proceeding, any judge having jurisdiction in the matter, may, if it appears by credible testimony that there is

30 Italics added.

31 *Re J Bird Moyer & Co (Ireland) Ltd* 98 ILTR 202.

32 See generally: Buttimore, *Security for Costs* (1999); Delany, 'Security for the costs of Discovery' (2005) 1(1)JCPP 3; Delany, 'Security for Costs in Relation to Corporate Plaintiffs' (2000) ILT 58; Milman, 'Security for Costs; Limited Liability in Litigation' (1995) Palmer's In Company, Issue 10/1995, 16 November 1995; and Doolan, 'The Insolvent Company and Security for Costs' (1986) ILT 218.

33 *Superwood Holdings plc v Sun Alliance and London Insurance plc* [2002] IESC 22, Denham J.

34 As to the court's discretion, see para **[6.041]** *post*.

35 See para **[6.057]** *post*.

reason to believe that the company will be unable to pay the costs of the defendant if successful in his defence, require sufficient security to be given for those costs and may stay all proceedings until the security is given.'

Section 390 gives the High Court jurisdiction to grant an order for security for costs against a limited company. An order for security for costs affords protection to defendants who might incur substantial legal costs in successfully defending an action, only to be faced with an impecunious limited liability plaintiff company or a person living outside the jurisdiction[36]. Where the plaintiff is an individual, as opposed to a limited company, the only grounds upon which he may be required to give security for costs is where he resides outside of the State or where one appeals an order or judgment made by a court[37]. As Keane J held, however, in *Pitt v Bolger*[38], the discretion to order security for costs against a person resident outside of the State will never, save in the most exceptional of circumstances, be exercised against an EU resident plaintiff[39]. The High Court of Northern Ireland in *McAteer v Lismore*[40] has rejected the claim that an order for security for costs infringed article 6 of the European Convention on Human Rights, holding that it was a proportionate response designed to safeguard defendants' rights. Before embarking upon a review of the jurisdiction to grant orders for security for costs against limited companies, we shall first consider the circumstances in which such orders will be granted against non-resident natural plaintiffs.

The jurisdiction to order security for costs against non-residents

[6.015] The rules relating to applications for security for costs against non-resident plaintiffs (whether natural persons or bodies corporate) are set out in Ord 29 of the RSC 1986[41] which provides:

'1. When a party shall require security for costs from another party, he shall be at liberty to apply by notice to the party for such security; and in case the latter shall not, within forty-eight hours after service thereof, undertake by notice to comply therewith, the party requiring the security shall be at liberty to apply to the Court for an order that the said party do furnish such security.

2. A defendant shall not be entitled to an order for security for costs solely on the ground that the plaintiff resides in Northern Ireland.

3. No defendant shall be entitled to an order for security for costs by reason of any plaintiff being resident out of the jurisdiction of the Court, unless upon a satisfactory affidavit that such defendant has a defence upon the merits.

4. A plaintiff ordinarily resident out of the jurisdiction may be ordered to give security for costs though he may be temporarily resident within the jurisdiction.

---

36 In relation to security for costs in proceedings brought by foreign plaintiffs see Binchy, *Conflicts of Law* (1988, Butterworths), pp 652–669.

37 Order 58, r 17 of the RSC 1986. See para **[6.015]** *post*.

38 *Pitt v Bolger* [1996] 1 ILRM 68. See also *Lough Neagh Exploration Ltd v Morrice et al* (27 August 1997, unreported) HC, Laffoy J.

39 Or, indeed, since the enactment of the Jurisdiction of the Courts (Enforcement of Judgments) Act 1988, outside the European Union: see *De Bry v Fitzgerald* [1990] 1 All ER 561; but *cf Berkley Administration Inc v McClelland* [1990] 1 All ER 959.

40 *McAteer v Lismore* [2000] NI 477.

41 See Ó Floinn, *Practice and Procedure in the Superior Courts* (2nd edn, 2008) at pp 273–280.

5. If a person brings an action for the recovery of land after a prior action for the recovery of the same has been brought by such person or by any person through or under whom he claims, against the same defendant, or against any person through or under whom he defends, the Court may at any time order that the plaintiff shall give to the defendant security for the defendant's costs, whether the prior action has been disposed of by discontinuance or by non-suit or by judgment for the defendant.
6. Where the Court shall have made an order that a party do furnish security for costs, the amount of such security and the time or times at which, and the manner and form in which, and the person or persons to whom, the same shall be given shall, subject to rule 7, be determined by the Master in every case.
7. Where a bond is to be given as security for costs, it shall, unless the Master shall otherwise direct, be given to the party or person requiring the security, and not to an officer of the Court. Provided that in any matrimonial cause or matter where security for costs is to be given by bond the bond shall be given to the Master.'

The two jurisdictions were recently considered by Clarke J in *Boyle and Boyle v McGilloway*[42]. As shall be seen below, Ord 29 is relevant to *non-resident* bodies corporate, against which application cannot be made under s 390 because they are not 'companies' within the meaning of s 2 of the CA 1963[43].

The justification for treating limited companies differently to individuals

[6.016] The law is less favourable to limited liability companies than it is to individuals, since, regardless of whether they are resident in the State, they may be ordered to give security for costs where there is reason to believe that they may be unable to pay the defendant's costs. It is public policy, rather than any rational imperative that has decided that a corporate plaintiff's winding-up does not carry sufficient stigma as to dissuade the institution of frivolous proceedings. The rationale for this discrimination between natural and corporate plaintiffs seems to draw largely on the stigma that is perceived to accompany an individual's bankruptcy. The prospect of bankruptcy may deter an individual litigant from taking frivolous proceedings, whereas a person behind a limited company – who may, after all, have their total liability limited to as little as one cent – has do direct financial loss should the company lose the action. Nevertheless, as Murphy J observed in *Bula Ltd v Tara Mines Ltd*[44]:

> 'It is clear beyond doubt that section 390 aforesaid may impose a serious handicap on an impecunious limited liability company where a lack of funds would not create the same problem for an individual litigant.'

In *Harrington et al v JVC (UK) Ltd*[45], O'Hanlon J cited with approval the following passage from the decision of Megarry VC in *Pearson v Naydler*[46]:

---

42 *Boyle and Boyle v McGilloway* [2006] IEHC 37.

43 See para **[6.026]**.

44 *Bula Ltd v Tara Mines Ltd* [1987] IR 494.

45 *Harrington et al v JVC (UK) Ltd* (16 March 1995, unreported) HC, O'Hanlon J.

46 *Pearson v Naydler* [1977] 3 All ER 531.

'In the case of a limited company, there is no basic rule conferring immunity from any liability to give security for costs. The basic rule is the opposite; s 447 [of the English Companies Act 1948] applies to all limited companies, and subjects them to the liability to give security for costs. The whole concept of the section is contrary to the rule developed by the cases that poverty is not to be made a bar to bringing an action. There is nothing in the statutory language (the substance of which goes back at least as far as the Companies Act 1862, s 69) to indicate that there are any exceptions to what is laid down as a broad and general rule for all limited companies. Nor is it surprising that there should be such a rule. A man may bring into being as many limited companies as he wishes, with the privilege of limited liability; and s 447 provides some protection for the community against litigious abuses by artificial persons manipulated by natural persons. One should be slow to whittle away this protection as one should be to whittle away a natural person's right to litigate despite poverty.'

It is clear that the courts will therefore try to maintain a balance between the interests of limited liability companies and those of defendants when considering applications for orders for security for costs.

Constitutionality and human rights

[6.017] There is a *prima facie* argument that, to the extent that an order for security for costs operates to prevent a plaintiff from litigating to vindicate a civil right – whether to property or good name or otherwise – it is unconstitutional[47]. The Irish courts have, however, consistently rejected any suggestion that s 390 of the CA 1963 is unconstitutional[48], and it is thought that this must be correct since the privilege of limited liability is open to abuse if the directors of a limited company can inflict the costs of defending a perhaps frivolous or vexatious litigation on a blameless defendant. Moreover, it would seem entirely appropriate (and not unconstitutional discrimination) to distinguish between a corporate plaintiff and a natural plaintiff since the latter will have the spectre of personal bankruptcy operate as a disincentive to expose him or herself to the costs of unworthy litigation[49]. Indeed, it is to some extent an open question as to whether companies (as distinct from their shareholders) enjoy rights under the Constitution[50].

[6.018] The European Convention on Human Rights has recently opened up a further avenue of hope for limited liability companies with limited ability to pay their defendants' costs. In *Superwood Holdings plc et al v Sun Alliance and London Insurance plc et al*[51], a declaration was sought that s 390 was repugnant to the Constitution and/or in the alternative was incompatible with the European Convention for the Protection of Human Rights and Fundamental Freedoms ('ECHR') and in particular article 6 concerning access to the courts and article 1 of the first protocol on property rights. Because the plaintiff had not given notice of the proceedings to the

47 See O'Neill, *The Constitutional Rights of Companies* (2007) at p 222–227.

48 *Salih v General Accident* [1987] IR 628; *Superwood Holdings plc v Ireland* [2005] 3 IR 398.

49 See *Lismore Homes Ltd v Bank of Ireland Finance Ltd* [1992] 2 IR 57 at 62.

50 See *Framus Ltd v CRH plc* [2004] 2 IR 20 and, generally, O'Neill, *The Constitutional Rights of Companies* (2007).

51 *Superwood Holdings plc et al v Sun Alliance and London Insurance plc et al* [2005] 3 IR 398.

Human Rights Commission, Murphy J found the court could not decide the matter but he went on to make the following observations, *obiter dicta*:

> It seems to this court that the provisions of section 390 fall clearly within the margin or appreciation enjoyed by the State in legislating for a balance between litigants. The restriction does pursue a legitimate aim and there is a reasonable relationship or proportionality between the means employed and the aim sought to be achieved to regulate limited liability plaintiffs' rights of action.[52]

In *Tolstoy Miloslavsk v United Kingdom*[53], the European Court of Human Rights said that the courts must take a 'tentative view' of the overall merits of the substantive proceedings when considering applications for security for costs but also found it was not disproportionate to impose a total bar on an appellant's right to the Court of Appeal if security required was not lodged within 14 days. The *Tolstoy* case was raised in a later application in *Superwood Holdings plc et al v Sun Alliance and London Insurance plc et al*[54], and there, Quirke J made no finding on the question as to whether the principles applicable to applications for security for costs have been affected by the *Tolstoy* decision. It is hard to see how the convention on 'human rights' can have any application to an artificial person and, even if it were to apply, what it would add in a jurisdiction governed by a written Constitution.

The test for an order for security for costs under s 390 of the CA 1963

[6.019] The following simple test proposed by Morris J in *Inter Finance Group Ltd v KPMG Peat Marwick*[55] has been frequently cited by both the High and Supreme Courts in security for costs' applications:

> '1. In order to succeed in obtaining security for costs an initial onus rests upon the moving party to establish:
>
> (a) that he has a prima facie defence to the plaintiff's claim, and
> (b) that the plaintiff will not be able to pay the moving party's costs if the moving party be successful;
>
> 2. In the event that the above two facts are established then security ought to be required unless it can be shown that there are specific circumstances in the case which ought to cause the court to exercise its discretion not to make the order sought. In this regard the onus rests upon the party resisting the order.
>
> The most common examples of such special circumstances include cases where a plaintiff's inability to discharge the defendant's costs of successfully defending the action concerned flow from the wrong allegedly committed by the moving party or where there has been delay by the moving party in seeking the order sought. The list of special circumstances referred to is not, of course, exhaustive.'

[6.020] The circumstances in which security for costs will be ordered against a limited company may be stated in the following, sequential, test where references to the '*plaintiff company*' are to the limited liability company against whom an application for

---

52 *Superwood Holdings plc et al v Sun Alliance and London Insurance plc et al* [2005] 3 IR 398 at 420.

53 *Tolstoy Miloslavsk v United Kingdom* (1995) 20 EHRR 432.

54 *Superwood Holdings plc et al v Sun Alliance and London Insurance plc et al* [2006] IEHC 123.

55 *Inter Finance Group Ltd v KPMG Peat Marwick* (29 June 1998, unreported) HC, Morris J.

security for costs is brought and references to '*defendant*' are to the party who brings the application for security for costs:

(a) Section 390 of the CA 1963 can be invoked by the defendant in any *action or other legal proceedings* where the plaintiff company is a *limited liability company* within the meaning of s 2 of the CA 1963.

(b) The plaintiff company will normally be a plaintiff who institutes proceedings but can include an *appellant* (who might be a plaintiff or defendant in an action) or a *counterclaiming defendant*, for a substantial amount, or a *notice party* in judicial review proceedings[56].

(c) The defendant will normally be a defendant to proceedings brought by the plaintiff company but can include such other persons as are added to an action commenced by the plaintiff company, who might be liable to have costs, should the plaintiff company be unsuccessful.

(d) There is an onus of proof on the defendant who invokes s 390 to establish by *credible testimony* that there is a proven or admitted inability to discharge the defendant's costs, should the plaintiff company fail in its action[57].

(e) There is also an onus of proof on the defendant to satisfy the court that he has a *prima facie* defence to the plaintiff company's claim[58].

(f) The jurisdiction to order a plaintiff company to give security for costs is discretionary, and is not available to a defendant as of right; and notwithstanding that the defendant discharges all of the foregoing proofs, the court may decline to make an order of security for costs if the plaintiff company can satisfy it that *special circumstances* exist. These *include*:

  (i) the *bona fides* of the plaintiff company and defendant;

  (ii) the strength of the plaintiff company's case;

  (iii) whether the plaintiff company's insolvency has been caused by the defendant;

  (iv) whether the plaintiff company seeks to vindicate the public interest;

---

56 *Usk and District Residents Association Ltd v The Environmental Protection Agency* [2006] 1 ILRM 363.

57 The following passage from MacCann & Courtney, *Companies Acts 1963–2006* (2008, Bloomsbury Professional) at 661 was said to succinctly set out the matters to be proven by the applicant and where the burden of proof lies by Laffoy J in *Ronbow Management Company Ltd v Sorohan Builders Ltd et al* [2010] IEHC 60: 'Firstly, there is an onus on the applicant to establish by credible evidence an inability, on the part of the respondent company, to discharge the costs of the applicant. Secondly, there is an onus on the applicant to satisfy the court that he has a *prima facie* defence. Once the court is satisfied of these two matters, the burden of proof is then placed on the respondent company, who must satisfy the court that 'special circumstances' exist, such that the court should exercise its discretion not to order security for costs. The court can take into account the strength of the plaintiff's case in determining whether to order security for costs. However, the strength of the plaintiff's case will not, on its own, be a ground for refusing an order for security for costs, unless the strength is such as to show that the defendant has no real defence.'

58 *Usk and District Residents Association Ltd v The Environmental Protection Agency* [2006] 1 ILRM 363.

(v) the existence of a personal co-plaintiff;

(vi) whether the defendant has delayed in applying for security for costs.

(h) If satisfied that it is proper to make an order for security for costs, the court must determine what it considers to be *sufficient security.*

The commentary that follows will explore each of the foregoing limbs and sub-limbs of the test for an order for security for costs.

(a) Section 390 may be invoked in any 'action or other legal proceedings'

[6.021] Although s 390 of the CA 1963 is not expressly confined to *civil* actions or proceedings, it is in that context that the section has, to date, invariably been invoked; it is conceivable that a limited company in proceedings other than civil might be ordered to give security for a respondent's costs. The same words as used in the similar English provision, s 726(1) of the English Companies Act 1985, were given a wide interpretation in *Re Unisoft Group*[59]. There, 'action' was considered to be broad enough to include a petition for unfair prejudice so that a corporate petitioner under s 459 of the English 1985 Act could be ordered to give security for costs. That this is the law in Ireland has been put beyond question by the decision in *USK District Residents Association Ltd v The Environmental Protection Agency and Greenstar Recycling Holdings Ltd (notice party)*[60] where the Supreme Court (per Clarke J) held that:

> 'While the section speaks of 'plaintiff' and 'defendant' it is clear that the intent of the section is that it should apply not only to an 'action' but also to 'other legal proceedings'. It is not contested that the section can apply to any form of proceeding. For example in *Village Residents Association Ltd v An Bord Pleanála (no 2)* [2004] 4 IR 321; [2001] 2 ILRM 22, Laffoy J made an order for security for costs in favour of a respondent as against an applicant for judicial review. Similarly, it seems to me that any person or body who is a necessary party to judicial review proceedings, even though termed a 'notice party' rather than a 'respondent' comes within the scope of a 'defendant' for the purposes of s 390.'

[6.022] In *PDC (Moate) Ltd AIB plc*[61], it was confirmed that an application brought by the official liquidator of the plaintiff company pursuant to s 280 of the CA 1963 seeking the court's determination as to what interest, if any, the plaintiff company had in certain lands was an 'other legal proceeding' within the meaning of s 390 of the CA 1963 and the defendant could invoke s 390 and apply for security for costs to be provided by the liquidator.

[6.023] In *Dublin International Arena Ltd v Campus & Stadium Ireland Development Ltd et al*[62], it was claimed that security for costs could not be sought by reason of the EU Remedies Directive as such an order would compromise its effectiveness. The plaintiff company making this contention sought to rely on the judgment of the ECJ in

---

59 *Re Unisoft Group* [1994] BCC 11.

60 *USK District Residents Association Ltd v The Environmental Protection Agency and Greenstar Recycling Holdings Ltd (notice party)* [2006] 1 ILRM 363.

61 *PDC (Moate) Ltd AIB plc* [2008] IEHC 281.

62 *Dublin International Arena Ltd v Campus & Stadium Ireland Development Ltd et al* (26 May 2004, unreported) HC, Ó Caoimh J.

Universalebau v Ensor Gunsbethrieba Simmering[63] and the principle of effectiveness in European Community law whereby national rules of procedure must not render the application of Community law impossible or excessively difficult. In making orders for security for costs, Ó Caoimh J held that the principles of equivalence or effectiveness did not preclude the making of the application.

[6.024] It may also be noted that it is not necessary that an applicant for an order for security for costs under s 390 must first ask the plaintiff to provide them, only proceeding by motion upon receiving a refusal. This was established in *Lancefort Ltd v An Bord Pleanála et al*[64] where Morris J found that the requirement in Ord 29, r 1 of the RSC (that a demand to the plaintiff for security must have been made before applying to court for an order) was *not* a precondition to an application under s 390 of the CA 1963.

(b) The plaintiff company must have limited liability

[6.025] An application for security for costs may not be brought against an unlimited company, because of the express words used in s 390 of the CA 1963 which applies only to limited companies.[65] An application for security for costs cannot be brought under s 390 against an unlimited company even if its members are all limited liability companies[66]. In *Goode Concrete v CRH plc*[67] Cooke J refused to adopt a purposive approach' to override the 'clear and obviously deliberate terms' of s 390 and declined to lift the veil on the 'justice of the case' ground because, in that case, the unlimited company's members were limited *foreign* companies. Before s 390 can be invoked, the members of the plaintiff company must have limited liability. Normally, liability will be limited by shares, but it was held in *R v Westminster ex p Mayfair Residents*[68] that companies limited by guarantee can also be ordered to provide security under the English equivalent to s 390 of the CA 1963 and this is accepted in Ireland too[69].

[6.026] Section 390 does not apply to all 'bodies corporate' and is expressly confined to limited liability '*companies*' as defined by s 2 of the CA 1963[70]. In England and Wales it has been held that s 726 of the English Companies Act 1985 does not apply to companies that are incorporated in Northern Ireland[71] and, similarly, s 390 does not apply to Northern Ireland registered companies or indeed to any body corporate other than a company that is formed and registered in the State or an existing company. So, in *Harrington v JVC (UK) Ltd*[72] O'Hanlon J said:

---

63 *Universalebau v Ensor Gunsbethrieba Simmering* (1999) ECJ C470.

64 *Lancefort Ltd v An Bord Pleanála et al* (23 January 1997, unreported) HC, Morris J.

65 *ABM Construction v Habbingly Ltd* [2012] IEHC 61.

66 See, further, Ch 31, *Unlimited Companies*, at para **[31.015]** *et seq*.

67 *Goode Concrete v CRH plc* [2012] IEHC 116.

68 *R v Westminster ex p Mayfair Residents* (1991) English High Court, unreported but referenced in Milman, 'Security for Costs; Limited Liability in Litigation' (1995) Palmer's In Company, Issue 10/1995, 16 November 1995.

69 In *Usk and District Residents Association Ltd v The Environmental Protection Agency* [2006] 1 ILRM 363, the plaintiff company was limited by guarantee.

70 See Ch 1, *The Private Company in Context*, at para **[1.156]** *et seq*.

71 *DSQ Properties v Lotus Cars* [1987] 1 WLR 127; *cf Wilson Vehicle Distribution Ltd v Colt Car Co Ltd* [1984] BCLC 93.

72 *Harrington v JVC (UK) Ltd* (16 March 1995, unreported) HC, O'Hanlon J.

> 'As the statutory provision relates only to situations in which a limited company incorporated within the jurisdiction is plaintiff in any action or other legal proceeding, and there is reason to believe that the company will be unable to pay the costs of the defendant if successful in his defence, the application for this relief can only be sought as against the second and third-named plaintiffs and not against the first-named plaintiff who is suing in his personal capacity, or against the fourth-named plaintiff, which is a company incorporated in Northern Ireland[73].'

The matter arose again in *Windmaster Developments Ltd v Airoglen Ltd and another*[74] where at the hearing for the purpose of assessing the amount of security for costs (ie, after an order for security had been made) it was contended that because the plaintiff was registered in England and Wales, s 390 did not apply as that section only applied to Irish companies. McCracken J refused to consider the matter of jurisdiction anew because first, he had already determined the matter which the plaintiff was not permitted to reopen; second, no evidence of the plaintiff's status as an English registered company was put before the court; and third, the plaintiff had not raised the matter at the original hearing. Accordingly, whilst in that case an order pursuant to s 390 was, apparently, made against an English registered company, it was in very exceptional (even, accidental) circumstances. It is clearly the case that s 390 applies only to 'companies' which expression has, by virtue of s 2 of the CA 1963, a very clear and precise meaning[75].

[6.027] It should be noted, however, that even if s 390 of the CA 1963 cannot be invoked, one may seek to place reliance upon Ord 29 of the RSC which can be invoked against either corporate or individual plaintiffs who are ordinarily resident outside of the jurisdiction. So, in *Lough Neagh Exploration Ltd v Morrice et al*[76] although the plaintiff was not a company within the meaning of s 2 of the CA 1963 (being a company incorporated pursuant to the laws of Northern Ireland) application for security for costs was brought pursuant to Ord 29, r 1. Further, where application is made under Ord 29 the results may not be all that different than if it were made under s 390 since, in that case, Laffoy J said:

> 'However, it is common case that, in broad terms, the same principles govern the determination whether a plaintiff should be ordered to furnish security for a defendant's costs under s 390 and under Ord 29[77].'

In *Harlequin Property (SVG) Ltd and another v O'Halloran and O'Halloran*[78], Clarke J held that where the court determines to exercise its discretion and make an order for security for costs against a non-resident body corporate pursuant to Ord 29, the court should ordinarily treat the non-resident body corporate on a par with an Irish company,

---

73 *Harrington v JVC (UK) Ltd* (16 March 1995, unreported) HC at p 15 of the judgment.

74 *Windmaster Developments Ltd v Airoglen Ltd and another* (10 July 2000, unreported) HC, McCracken J.

75 See *Harlequin Property (SVG) Ltd and another v O'Halloran and O'Halloran* [2012] IEHC 13, Clarke J, considered at para **[6.025]** *post*.

76 *Lough Neagh Exploration Ltd v Morrice et al* (27 August 1997, unreported) HC, Laffoy J.

77 *Lough Neagh Exploration Ltd v Morrice et al* (27 August 1997, unreported) HC at pp 1 and 2 of the judgment.

78 *Harlequin Property (SVG) Ltd and another v O'Halloran and O'Halloran* [2012] IEHC 13, Clarke J.

the subject of s 390, and should order that *full* security for costs be provided, rather than apply the one-third rule normally applicable to individual foreign plaintiffs. Clarke J analysed the basis of the jurisdiction to grant security and held that:

> '... such analysis seems to me to support the view that the justice of an application for security for costs under Order 29 made against a corporate foreign plaintiff should lead to that corporate foreign plaintiff being required to put up the same type of security as an Irish corporate plaintiff would have to. I should emphasise that the logic of that position only holds true in circumstances where the court makes the order for security for costs against the foreign corporate plaintiff on the same grounds as the court would make an order for security for costs against an Irish corporate plaintiff, ie, that the relevant corporate plaintiff would be unable to pay costs in the event of losing. There may well be circumstances where an Irish court would direct security against a foreign corporate plaintiff solely on the basis that that foreign corporate entity was based outside the jurisdiction and had no assets inside this or any other relevant jurisdiction. In such a case, it is difficult to see how any legitimate distinction could be drawn between a foreign corporate plaintiff and a foreign individual plaintiff. Where, however, as here, the court has already been satisfied that the tests for the making of an order for security under s 390 of the 1963 Act were met, save only for the fact that the corporate entity concerned was not Irish, then it seems to me that there is a compelling logic in applying the same regime for the calculation of the amount of security required as would apply arising out of a successful application for security under s 390 of the 1963 Act.
>
> For that reason alone, I am satisfied that it is appropriate to approach the fixing of security on the facts of this case on the basis of full security rather than by the application of the one-third practice[79].'

[6.028] It was Ireland's membership of the European Union that prompted Keane J in *Pitt v Bolger*[80] to say that the discretion under Ord 29 to order security for costs against a person resident outside of the State will never, save in the most exceptional of circumstances, be exercised against an EU resident plaintiff. What of the position in relation to applications under Ord 29 against EU registered bodies corporate? The English Court of Appeal in *Chequepoint SARL v McClelland and another*[81] decided that there is jurisdiction to order an EU registered body corporate to provide security for costs in an action in England in such a way as not to constitute unlawful discrimination contrary to EU law. Its reasoning was because a similar power could be exercised against an English company under s 726 of the English Companies Act 1985. It is thought that a limited liability EU legal entity that commences an action in Ireland is amenable to Ord 29 where it is not resident in Ireland. By the same token, where such an EU body corporate *is* resident in Ireland, an order cannot be made under Ord 29.

[6.029] The question of the residence of a body corporate was considered by the English High Court in *Re Little Olympian Each Ways Ltd*[82]. Like Ord 29, r 4 of the RSC, Ord 23, r 1(1)(a) of the English Rules refers to a plaintiff being 'ordinarily resident' outside of

79 *Harlequin Property (SVG) Ltd and another v O'Halloran and O'Halloran* [2012] IEHC 13, Clarke J at paras 4.15, 4.16.

80 *Pitt v Bolger* [1996] 1 ILRM 68. See also *Lough Neagh Exploration Ltd v Morrice et al* (27 August 1997, unreported) HC, Laffoy J.

81 *Chequepoint SARL v McClelland and another* [1997] 1 BCLC 117.

82 *Re Little Olympian Each Ways Ltd* [1994] 4 All ER 561.

the jurisdiction. In that case, Lindsay J held that a corporate plaintiff will be ordinarily resident outside of the jurisdiction if the central control and management of the company actually abides and is exercised overseas[83].

(c) The plaintiff company can be a 'plaintiff', an 'appellant' or a 'counter-claiming defendant'

[6.030] The most usual situation in which a plaintiff company will be faced with an application for security for costs is where it is the *plaintiff* in an action. By reason of the reference to 'any action or other legal proceedings' it is thought to be clear that s 390 can be invoked against a company that is appealing a decision of a court of first instance[84]. This view was accepted by the Supreme Court in *Bula Ltd et al v Tara Mines Ltd et al*[85]. In that case Lynch J had, in the High Court, found against the plaintiff on the substantive issues. The plaintiffs, however, appealed that decision to the Supreme Court and the defendants then brought motions to the Supreme Court seeking orders for security for costs against the corporate plaintiffs (pursuant to s 390 of the CA 1963) and against both the corporate and individual plaintiffs (pursuant to Ord 58, r 17 of the RSC). Whilst Ord 58, r 17 makes express provision for the making of an order for security for costs on an appeal[86], Keane J saw no jurisdictional issues in making an order under both s 390 and Ord 58, r 17, saying:

> '… this is clearly a case in which an order providing for security for costs should be made under Ord 58, r 17. I am also satisfied that, in the case of the corporate plaintiffs, it would be reasonable to make such an order under s 390 of the Companies Act 1963. An application for security under that section was made at a far earlier state of the proceedings and refused by Murphy J in the High Court on the ground that [the plaintiff] had made out an arguable case that their insolvency was the result of the wrongdoing of the defendants, a conclusion which was upheld on appeal by this court … The position at this stage, however, is radically different: there has been a prolonged trial in the High Court in the course of which the claim that the insolvency of [the plaintiff] was caused by the wrongdoing of the defendant was rejected. While the plaintiffs are, of course, entitled to challenge that conclusion on the hearing of the appeal, the trial judge's findings, coupled with the other circumstances discussed at an earlier stage of this judgment, make it clear that this is a case in which the corporate plaintiffs should be required to furnish security for costs[87].'

It is thought that s 390 can be invoked in any action or other legal proceedings in which it is possible to have costs awarded against the plaintiff to the defendant.

---

83 Following *De Beers Consolidated Mines Ltd v Howe* [1906] AC 455 and *Unit Construction Co Ltd v Bullock* [1959] 3 All ER 831. See, generally, Ch 5, *Disregarding Separate Legal Personality*, at para **[5.070]**.

84 *Cf Electro Services Ltd v Issa Nicholas (Grenada) Ltd* [1998] 1 WLR 202 where the Privy Council held that s 584 of the Grenada Companies Act only permitted the making of an order for security for costs in respect of first instance proceedings although it was acknowledged that in exceptional circumstances the court had an inherent jurisdiction to order security for costs.

85 *Bula Ltd et al v Tara Mines Ltd et al* (26 March 1998, unreported) SC, Keane J, *nem diss*.

86 Order 58, r 17 provides: 'Such deposit or other security for the costs to be occasioned by any appeal shall be made or given as may be directed under special circumstances by the Supreme Court.'

87 *Bula Ltd et al v Tara Mines Ltd et al* (26 March 1998, unreported) SC at p 28 of the judgment.

[6.031] Where an appellate court is asked by an appealing plaintiff to exercise its discretion against making an order for security for costs, the circumstances which should be taken into account were stated by McCarthy J in *SEE Company Ltd v Public Lighting Services*[88] to be:

> 'Without attempting to make an exhaustive list, it would seem relevant to consider such matters as:
>
> (i) Has a *prima facie* case been made to the effect that the inability identified by the section flows from the wrong allegedly committed by the party seeking the security?
>
> (ii) Is there an arguable case stated in the notice of appeal?
>
> (iii) Has there been undue delay by the moving party?
>
> Countervailing circumstances would include the very fact that the insolvent company has lost the case in the High Court and is now an appellant.'

The question of the exercise of the court's discretion to make or decline an order for security for costs is considered in detail below[89]. It is important to note here, however, that in *Lismore Homes Ltd v Bank of Ireland Finance Ltd*[90] Barron J elaborated on the meaning of the second point, namely, whether there is an arguable case in the notice of appeal. He said:

> 'What may or may not be an arguable case has not been precisely defined in the cases. However it would seem to me that since the application is heard on affidavit that there must be at least a case which would be sufficiently strong as that which would entitle a defendant in a motion for liberty to enter final judgment to be permitted to defend[91].'

Barron J later added that 'once an arguable case has been established the strength of that case is immaterial unless it leads to showing that in reality the defendant has no real defence'[92]. The first[93] and third[94] points of this test are considered below. The test was applied in *Superwood Holdings plc et al v Sun Alliance and London plc et al*[95] where an order for security for costs was made against an appellant plaintiff company.

(d) The defendant includes a notice party

[6.032] The typical applicant for an order for security for costs is the defendant in the action or other legal proceedings commenced by the plaintiff. Other persons too, who are not strictly 'defendants', may apply for security for costs as described in *USK District Residents Association Ltd v The Environmental Protection Agency and Greenstar Recycling Holdings Ltd (notice party)*[96]. In *Broadnet Ireland Ltd v Office of*

---

88 *SEE Company Ltd v Public Lighting Services* [1987] IRLM 255.

89 See para **[6.041]** *post.*

90 *Lismore Homes Ltd v Bank of Ireland Finance Ltd* (11 February 1998, unreported) SC, Barron J.

91 *Lismore Homes Ltd v Bank of Ireland Finance Ltd* (11 February 1998, unreported) SC at p 14 of the judgment.

92 As to the defendant's defence: see para **[6.038]**.

93 See para **[6.047]**.

94 See para **[6.055]**.

95 *Superwood Holdings plc et al v Sun Alliance and London plc et al* [1995] 3 IR 303.

96 *USK District Residents Association Ltd v The Environmental Protection Agency and Greenstar Recycling Holdings Ltd (notice party)* [2006] 1 ILRM 363; see para **[6.021]**, *ante.*

the Director of Telecommunications Regulation and Eircom plc[97], the plaintiff company in a security for costs motion had applied for a broadband fixed wireless point to multi-point access licence and had been advised that it had been unsuccessful. The plaintiff company had then sought a judicial review of the decision of the Director of Telecommunications Regulation. By subsequent order of the court, Eircom was joined as a defendant and three other companies (who were successful in their applications for a licence) were joined as notice parties in the judicial review proceedings. Five motions were brought for, *inter alia*, security for costs. These were brought by the Director of Telecommunications Regulation, Eircom and three notice parties. Laffoy J noted that it was all but conceded that the Director of Telecommunications Regulation was entitled to security for costs but the plaintiff contested any order in favour of Eircom and the notice parties. The plaintiff contended that as the core issue on the substantive application was apparent bias on the part of the Director of Telecommunications Regulation, in which it was not alleged that the other parties were implicated, those parties had no role to play in the resolution of the core issue and that if they wished to participate in the substantive application, the plaintiff should not be required to give security for the costs of that participation, which it considered to be unnecessary. Laffoy J noted that Ord 84, r 22 of the RSC required that the originating notice of motion in judicial review proceedings 'must be served on all persons directly affected'. Laffoy J held:

> 'It is not disputed that these parties are directly affected and it was on that basis that they were joined in the proceedings as notice parties and, in the case of Eircom, as a respondent. If these parties are directly affected and have a right to be served with the proceedings, they have a right to participate in the proceedings and to be heard in order to protect their respective interests … The fact that in this case the alleged wrongdoer, the Director, is defending the proceedings, in my view, cannot as against the acknowledged innocent parties who are directly affected by the proceedings, Eircom and the Notice Parties, constitute a special circumstance for refusing to award security for costs to those parties.'

Laffoy J went on to note that even if it was subsequently found by the trial judge on deciding costs that the notice parties only required limited participation, the plaintiff would not be prejudiced as it would be entitled to a return of any surplus of the funds lodged in court by way of security.

(e) The defendant's onus to adduce credible testimony of the plaintiff's inability to pay costs

[6.033] It is a prerequisite to making an order under s 390 that it appears by *credible testimony* that there is reason to believe that a plaintiff company will be unable to meet the costs of a successful defendant[98]. The requisite testimony will concern the solvency (or, more appropriately, the insolvency) of the plaintiff company. In its initial consideration of whether there is reason to believe that a plaintiff company will be unable to pay the costs of the defendant if successful in his defence, the court will be exclusive concerned with the plaintiff company's factual ability to pay and not with the reasons why it might be unable to pay. Once it is established that the plaintiff is likely to

97 *Broadnet Ireland Ltd v Office of the Director of Telecommunications Regulation and Eircom plc* [2000] 3 IR 281, Laffoy J.

98 *Ronbow Management company Ltd v Sorohan Builders Ltd et al* [2010] IEHC 60.

be unable to pay the defendant's costs, the court has jurisdiction to make an order under s 390. Where it is alleged that the plaintiff's impecuniosity has been caused by the defendant's wrongdoing, the onus will be on the plaintiff company to prove that to the court. Moreover, this will merely be a *special circumstance* as to why the court might exercise its discretion against making an order and establishing that the plaintiff company's inability is due to the defendant will not mean that an order will be declined automatically; this and other special circumstances are considered below[99]. In this section, however, we are concerned with the initial enquiry into the plaintiff's solvency.

[6.034] The essence of the enquiry into whether there is reason to believe that the plaintiff will be unable to pay the defendant's costs is the plaintiff company's solvency. Insolvency may either be proved by the defendant or conceded by the plaintiff[100] and the latter course is taken with surprising frequency[101]. Where the plaintiff company is a 'shelf-company' which has no significant assets it has been held by the Supreme Court that:

> 'it follows therefore, that, undoubtedly if the applicant [ie, plaintiff company] is unsuccessful in its claim before the High Court, it will be unable to pay the costs of the defendant and it therefore appears to be clearly within the jurisdiction of the High Court to make the order for security for costs[102].'

Where insolvency is not admitted, it will be necessary to enquire into the plaintiff's finances. In *Bula Ltd v Tara Mines Ltd*[103], Murphy J said:

> 'However, I do not think it is necessary for me to enter into a detailed analysis of the assets and liabilities of Bula Ltd. All that the section requires is that it should appear by credible testimony 'that there is *reason to believe* that the company would be unable to pay the costs of the defendant if successful in his defence[104].'

Where solvency is hotly disputed, however, it will be necessary to outline the financial situation of the plaintiff. The plaintiff's alleged inability to pay the defendant's costs was disputed in *Irish Press plc v EM Warburg Pincus & Company International Ltd*[105]. In that case McGuinness J considered the assets and liabilities of the plaintiff and of its seven subsidiaries. The learned judge found that some of the companies did hold valuable assets and, notwithstanding that they were held by legal entities separate from the plaintiff, included them in reckoning the plaintiff's ability to meet any order for costs. McGuinness J said:

---

99 See para **[6.044]**.

100 *Per* Finlay CJ in *Jack O'Toole Ltd v MacEoin Kelly Associates* [1986] IR 277 at 283; see *also Campbell Seafoods Ltd v Brodene Gram A/S* (21 July 1994, unreported) HC, Costello J.

101 See, for example, *Bula Ltd v Tara Mines Ltd* [1987] IR 494; *SEE Co Ltd v Public Lighting Services Ltd* [1987] ILRM 255; *Society for the Protection of Unborn Children (Ireland) Ltd v Grogan* [1992] ILRM 461; *Comhlucht Páipear Ríomhaireachta Teo v Údarás na Gaeltachta* [1990] ILRM 266.

102 Per Keane CJ in *Hot Radio Co Ltd v IRTC and NP* (14 April 2000, *ex tempore*) at p 2 of the judgment.

103 *Bula Ltd v Tara Mines Ltd* [1987] IR 494.

104 *Bula Ltd v Tara Mines Ltd* [1987] IR 494 at 498.

105 *Irish Press plc v EM Warburg Pincus & Company International Ltd* (12 March 1997, unreported) HC, McGuinness J.

> 'While Irish Press plc is not in a particularly happy position and while its assets appear to be diminishing, it is not insolvent and continues to hold reasonably substantial assets through its subsidiary companies. I must also take account of the fact that Mr McHugh, a partner in the firm of Messrs Deloitte and Touche, who is not a director or member of the plaintiff company but the audit partner with overall responsibility for the plaintiff's audit, is prepared as a professional accountant with full knowledge of the plaintiff's financial affairs to aver that in his opinion the assets of the plaintiff will be sufficient to discharge the costs of the defendants[106].'

In that case the defendant's application for an order that the plaintiff should provide security for its costs was refused because of the factual finding that the plaintiff company would be able to meet the defendant's costs.

[6.035] The estimated amount of the defendant's costs will be in respect of the present action. In *Irish Press plc v EM Warburg Pincus & Company International Ltd*[107], the defendant submitted that the possible costs of an appeal to the Supreme Court should also be considered. This was rejected by McGuinness J who held:

> 'It is my view that I am here dealing only with an action in this court and the costs that may arise therefrom. It is too uncertain a matter to look into the future to try to assess the plaintiff's ability to meet the costs of a putative appeal to the Supreme Court which may not in fact take place. If there is such an appeal, an appropriate application in regard to costs may be brought to the Supreme Court itself, as has been done in previous cases[108].'

One such previous case in point is *Bula Ltd et al v Tara Mines Ltd et al*[109]. At the trial of the action an order for security for costs was refused. In the trial of the substantive issues, the defendant was successful. The plaintiff, however, appealed to the Supreme Court and once again the defendant applied for an order that the plaintiff company provide security for costs. This time the Supreme Court acceded to the defendant's new application that security for costs be provided for the appeal. Generally, the precise amount of the defendant's costs will not be known at the hearing of the motion for security for costs and it will frequently happen that if a defendant is successful in his application, the actual amount of costs will be fixed by the Master of the High Court, although it may come back to the High Court[110]. The question of 'sufficient security' is considered below[111].

[6.036] The appropriate time in respect of which the court must determine inability to pay a defendant's costs is when the defendant has been successful in his defence. This was held to be the correct interpretation of s 390 by O'Neill J in *Ochre Ridge Ltd v Cork Bonded Warehouses Ltd and Port of Cork Company Ltd*[112]. In that case the plaintiff's

---

106 *Irish Press plc v EM Warburg Pincus & Company International Ltd* (12 March 1997, unreported) HC, McGuinness J at p 17 of the judgment.

107 *Irish Press plc v EM Warburg Pincus & Company International Ltd* (12 March 1997, unreported) HC, McGuinness J.

108 *Irish Press plc v EM Warburg Pincus & Company International Ltd* (12 March 1997, unreported) HC, McGuinness J at p 10 of the judgment.

109 *Bula Ltd et al v Tara Mines Ltd et al* (26 March 1998, unreported) SC, Keane J, nem diss.

110 See, for example, *Windmaster Developments Ltd v Airoglen Ltd and Kelly* (10 July 2000, unreported) HC, McCracken J.

111 See para **[6.057]**.

112 *Ochre Ridge Ltd v Cork Bonded Warehouses Ltd and Port of Cork Company Ltd* (20 December 2000, unreported) HC, O'Neill J.

solvency was contested and the plaintiff argued that no evidence has been adduced which would prove on the balance of probabilities that it was insolvent as at the time of the making of the security for costs application. The plaintiff also argued that it had a valuable asset, namely the benefit of the contract in dispute that was worth £775,000. O'Neill J held that the appropriate reference point for determining ability to pay was the time when the defendant was successful in his defence. Accordingly, if the defendant were successful, the plaintiff would not be entitled to the benefit of the contract and so it appeared to the learned judge 'to be probable' that it would have no assets or income out of which to meet an order for costs.

[6.037] Where an action is brought by a company after commencement of its liquidation, the costs of a successful defendant against the company will rank in priority to the claims of all creditors (other than creditors secured by a mortgage or charge). This is because, as McCarthy J explained in *Comhlucht Páipear Ríomhaireachta Teo v Údarás na Gaeltachta*[113], it would be:

> 'a great injustice if a company were free, after liquidation, to maintain an action for the benefit of the general body of creditors and, if unsuccessful, successfully to contend that the costs of the successful litigant against the company should only rank *pari passu* with the claims of the creditors.'

Accordingly, where a company that is in the course of being wound up has sufficient funds to pay the defendant's costs, the defendant will not normally be granted an order that the company being wound up must provide security for the defendant's costs. This will be the case even where the company is insolvent in the sense that its liabilities exceed its assets, provided that what assets it has are sufficient to pay the defendant's costs. In this way, money otherwise earmarked for unsecured or preferential creditors will instead of going to them, be earmarked for the defendant's costs[114]. Priority aside, where a company that is in the course of being wound up would not be able to pay the defendant's costs, then normal principles will apply.

(f) The defendant's onus to establish a prima facie defence

[6.038] There is an onus on a defendant, who brings an application under s 390, to show that he has a *prima facie* defence to the plaintiff's claim[115]. Whilst s 390 does not require that the applicant for security for costs swears a satisfactory affidavit that the defendant has a defence on its merits, nevertheless, it is customary for defendants to produce evidence of at least a *prima facie* defence[116]. This requirement is more established in the context of an application under Ord 29; so in *Fares v Wiley*[117] it was held by the Supreme Court that a defendant who establishes a *prima facie* defence to a claim made by a plaintiff residing outside of the State, has a *prima facie* right to an order for security for

---

[113] *Comhlucht Páipear Ríomhaireachta Teo v Údarás na Gaeltachta* [1990] ILRM 267 at 274.

[114] See the discussion by McGuinness J in *Irish Press plc v EM Warburg Pincus & Company International Ltd* (12 March 1997, unreported) HC, McGuinness J at pp 8 and 9 of the judgment.

[115] *Ronbow Management company Ltd v Sorohan Builders Ltd et al* [2010] IEHC 60; *Inter Finance Group Ltd v KPMG Peat Marwick* (29 June 1998, unreported) HC, Morris J; *Wexford Rope and Twine Company Ltd v Gaynor and Modler* (6 March 2000, unreported) HC, Laffoy J.

[116] See *Hidden Ireland Heritage Holidays Ltd v Indigo Services Ltd* [2005] 2 ILRM 498.

[117] *Fares v Wiley* [1994] 2 IR 379.

costs[118]. Lynch J in the Supreme Court in *Lismore Homes Ltd v Bank of Ireland Finance Ltd et al*[119]formulated the *prima facie* defence requirement in different terms, namely:

> 'The strength or otherwise of the parties' case is not an appropriate consideration unless the plaintiff's case is unanswerable in which circumstance security should be refused[120].'

As McCarthy J observed in *Comhlucht Páipear Ríomhaireachta Teo v Údarás na Gaeltachta*[121]:

> 'The fact that the plaintiff appears to have a very strong case is not a ground for refusing an order for security, unless the strength is such as to show that the defendant has no real defence.'

A plaintiff's case will not be 'unanswerable' where a defendant establishes that he has a *prima facie* defence. The courts will look simply at whether each side has a *prima facie* case without turning a blind eye to the obvious. If the plaintiff has what appears to be an unanswerable case, no order will be made[122]. An example at the other extreme is provided by *Kerry Tree Ltd et al v Sun Alliance and London Insurance plc*[123]. There, Carroll J granted the order for security sought by the defendant, holding that the plaintiff's 'claim for damages for delay in paying damages' was not known in law and that as a result the plaintiff did not have a stateable claim either in contract or in tort.

[6.039] Although the onus lies on the defendant to establish that he has a *prima facie* defence, this may be admitted by the plaintiff[124] or the defendant's averment of a good defence not contested[125]. Where this is not admitted by the plaintiff, the defendant will have to show that he has a *prima facie* defence and that the plaintiff's case is, therefore, answerable. It is not appropriate to adduce voluminous evidence on a motion for security for costs which, it must be remembered, is an interlocutory application. In *Bula Ltd v Tara Mines Ltd*[126], Murphy J explained as follows:

> '... I repeat now that it is no part of my function as I see it to forecast the outcome of the litigation or to prejudice the facts or express an interim view on the questions of law involved. On behalf of the defendants it was argued that the weakness of the plaintiff's case is a factor to which regard should be had. Whilst it must be established that the

[118] This decision was referred to by Laffoy J in *Lough Neagh Exploration Ltd v Morrice et al* (27 August 1997, unreported) HC, immediately after commenting that in broad terms the same principles govern the determination of applications brought under both s 390 and Ord 29.

[119] *Lismore Homes Ltd v Bank of Ireland Finance Ltd et al* (11 February 1998, unreported) SC, Lynch, Barrington and Barron JJ. It will be noted that all three judges gave written judgments.

[120] *Lismore Homes Ltd v Bank of Ireland Finance Ltd et al* (11 February 1998, unreported) SC, Lynch, Barrington and Barron JJ at p 8 of the judgment.

[121] *Comhlucht Páipear Ríomhaireachta Teo v Údarás na Gaeltachta* [1990] ILRM 266, at 275.

[122] See, for example, *Society for the Protection of Unborn Children (Ireland) Ltd v Grogan* [1992] ILRM 461; *Irish Commercial Society Ltd v Plunkett* [1985] IR 1.

[123] *Kerry Tree Ltd et al v Sun Alliance and London Insurance plc* [2001] IEHC 144, Carroll J.

[124] See *Beauross Ltd v Kennedy* (18 October 1995, unreported) HC, Morris J at p 3 of the judgment.

[125] See *Johnstown Ltd v Thiennez Ltd* [2001] IEHC 44, McCracken J.

[126] *Bula Ltd v Tara Mines Ltd* [1987] IR 494 at 501.

plaintiffs do have an arguable case it does not seem to me that it is either necessary or proper to evaluate the prospects of success.'

In *Lismore Homes Ltd v Bank of Ireland Finance Ltd et al*[127], an application which involved an appeal to the Supreme Court and gave rise to three judgments from that court, Barrington J said:

> 'The most important thing to remember about an application for security for costs is that it is an interlocutory motion. It will usually be made when the facts of the dispute have yet to be established. Our law recognises an oral hearing and cross-examination as the primary method of resolving disputed questions of fact. It is dangerous to attempt to resolve such questions on affidavit unless there is objective evidence which points conclusively in one direction or the other. Normally there is no reason why a motion for security for costs should occupy four days in the High Court or seven days in the Supreme Court as happened in this case[128].'

[6.040] Where the strength of the parties' claims is in contention, a balance must be struck. In *Inter Finance Group Ltd v KPMG Peat Marwick*[129], the plaintiff had conceived an idea of developing a software package that would assist large organisations in running their accounts' departments. The plaintiff had entered into a contract with the defendant under which the defendant agreed to design a software package to the plaintiff's specification. Subsequently, the plaintiff sued the defendant claiming that it had, in breach of contract, purported to sell and install the software system in a number of other sites, had held itself out as owner of the software system and had failed to take the necessary steps to put the plaintiff in a position to exploit the software package. On the motion for security for costs, Morris J held that there was an onus on the defendant to establish, *inter alia*, 'that he has a *prima facie* defence to the plaintiff's claim'. On this point Morris J considered the plaintiff's claim that it was part of the contract that it would become beneficially entitled to the software package; the defendant claimed that since the contract was silent on the point, it as author of the software package was beneficially entitled to it. Morris J held on the *prima facie* defence point:

> '… I am satisfied, for the purposes of determining this application, that the beneficial ownership in the programme was not affected by any term of any contract entered into between the parties. It remains therefore to decide, at the hearing of this action, in whom the beneficial ownership is vested. Both … [parties] … claim beneficial ownership. Each has supported their claim with a variety of arguments and submissions.
>
> In determining the issue, for the purposes of this motion, I am satisfied that the defendants have established a *prima facie* defence to the plaintiff's claim. I consider it is undesirable to elaborate upon the nature of this defence as to do so might well prejudice the ultimate

---

127 *Lismore Homes Ltd v Bank of Ireland Finance Ltd et al* (11 February 1998, unreported) SC, Lynch, Barrington and Barron JJ. It will be noted that all three judges gave written judgments.

128 *Lismore Homes Ltd v Bank of Ireland Finance Ltd* (11 February 1998, unreported) SC at p 5 of the judgment. Barrington J went on to cite with approval the decision of Sir Nicholas Browne-Wilkinson VC in *Porzelac KG v Porzelac (UK) Ltd* [1987] 1 WLR 420 at 423 and of Purchas LJ in *Trident International Freight Services v Manchester Ship Canal Company* [1990] BCLC 263 at 271 and noted that the quoted passages had been expressly approved of by O'Hanlon J in *Shortt v Ireland* [1996] 2 IR 195.

129 *Inter Finance Group Ltd v KPMG Peat Marwick* (29 June 1998, unreported) HC, Morris J.

> hearing. Accordingly, I am of the view that the defendants have overcome the second of the two necessary proofs in order to succeed in this motion[130].'

Again, in *Wexford Rope and Twine Company Ltd v Gaynor and Modler*[131] the question of whether the defendant had a *prima facie* defence was considered. There, the plaintiff had sued the defendants (who were former directors of the plaintiff company) for, *inter alia*, damages for breach of fiduciary duty, breach of contract, fraud and passing off. Barr J held that he was satisfied that the defendants had met the condition that they establish a *prima facie* defence to the plaintiff's claim. It is interesting to see that Barr J struck the balance between overcoming this evidential hurdle and not determining the substantive matter, by speaking in terms of the defendants' contentions having the 'appearance of credibility'.

(g) Judicial discretion and 'special circumstances'

[6.041] The jurisdiction to make an order for security for costs under s 390 of the CA 1963 is entirely discretionary. A defendant cannot demand as of right that an order is made against a plaintiff. In *Peppard & Co Ltd v Bogoff*[132], Kingsmill Moore J observed in relation to the predecessor of s 390 that:

> '… the section does not make it mandatory to order security for costs in every case where the plaintiff company appears to be unable to pay the costs of a successful defendant, but that there still remains a discretion in the court which may be exercised in special circumstances[133].'

As McCarthy J said in *SEE Company Ltd v Public Lighting Services Ltd*[134], the 'discretionary nature of the order is emphasised when read in the light of the constitutional right of access to the courts'. The importance of the discretionary nature of the remedy cannot be over-emphasised. In *Irish Press plc v EM Warburg Pincus & Company International Ltd*[135], McGuinness J said she got the impression from reading the Irish judgments on security for costs that the courts have tended to lean against the making of such orders. McGuinness J went on to refer to the comments of McCarthy J as follows:

> 'While I accept, as was submitted by counsel for the defendants in this case, that the constitutional right of access to the courts is primarily available to natural persons and that the courts must be careful not to render s 390 nugatory, it seems to me that in his judgment the learned McCarthy J is expressing the general tenor of judgments in this court and in

---

130 *Inter Finance Group Ltd v KPMG Peat Marwick* (29 June 1998, unreported) HC, Morris J at pp 5 and 6 of the judgment.

131 *Wexford Rope and Twine Company Ltd v Gaynor and Modler* (6 March 2000, unreported) HC, Barr J.

132 *Peppard & Co Ltd v Bogoff* [1962] IR 180.

133 *Peppard & Co Ltd v Bogoff* [1962] IR 180 at 188. The learned judge repeated this view in *Personal Service Laundry Ltd v The National Bank Ltd* [1964] IR 49 at 62. His *dictum* in the latter case was cited with approval in the English Court of Appeal in *Sir Lindsay Parkinson & Co Ltd v Triplan Ltd* [1973] 2 All ER 273.

134 *SEE Company Ltd v Public Lighting Services Ltd* [1987] ILRM 255 at 258.

135 *Irish Press plc v EM Warburg Pincus & Company International Ltd* (12 March 1997, unreported) HC, McGuinness J.

the Supreme Court in regard to security for costs under s 390 of the Companies Act 1963[136].'

Whilst it is thought that the learned judge put the case against making orders for security for costs somewhat too far, it is clear that the court will actively exercise its discretion and endeavour to do so in the interests of justice. Moreover on appeal, the appellate court's discretion will be exercised independently of the lower court[137].

[6.042] In *West Donegal Land League Ltd v Údarás na Gaeltachta*[138], Geoghegan J said in the Supreme Court that the case law on s 390 establishes that notwithstanding the insertion of the word 'may', the court in the absence of special circumstances and as a matter of appropriate exercise of its discretion will in a given case order security for costs in the circumstances provided for by the section.

[6.043] The burden of proving that special circumstances exist lies on the plaintiff company. This is because it will be the plaintiff company's assertion that special circumstances exist and that although the defendant might be *prima facie* entitled to an order, an order should not in fact be made because of these *special circumstances*. As Finlay CJ observed in *Jack O'Toole Ltd v MacEoin Kelly Associates*[139]:

> '... if the plaintiff-company seeks to avoid an order for security for costs ... it must, as a matter of onus of proof, establish to the satisfaction of the judge the special circumstances which would justify the refusal of an order.'

The onus of proof will, therefore, shift from the defendant to the plaintiff company once the defendant has established that the plaintiff company is unlikely to be able to pay the defence costs and that the defendant has a *prima facie defence*[140]. So, in *Wexford Rope and Twine Company Ltd v Gaynor and Modler*[141], Barr J said:

> 'Where it is established, as in the instant case, that the defendants appear to have a *prima facie* defence to the claim or claims made against them the onus passes to the plaintiff company to satisfy the court on the balance of probabilities that there are *special circumstances* which the court should take into account and accept in exercising its discretion whether or not to accede to the defendant's application for security for costs[142].'

It is to those matters, which have to date been considered *special circumstances*, that next we turn.

---

136 *Irish Press plc v EM Warburg Pincus & Company International Ltd* (12 March 1997, unreported) HC, McGuinness J at p 18 of the judgment.

137 *Lismore Homes Ltd v Bank of Ireland Finance Ltd et al* (11 February 1998, unreported) SC, Lynch, Barrington and Barron JJ (Barron J at p 13 of his judgment).

138 *West Donegal Land League Ltd v Údarás na Gaeltachta* [2007] 1 ILRM 1, cited with apparent approval by Denham J in *Dublin International Arena Ltd v Campus & Stadium Ireland Development Ltd an others* [2008] 1 ILRM 496.

139 *Jack O'Toole Ltd v MacEoin Kelly Associates* [1986] IR 277 at 283.

140 *Ochre Ridge Ltd v Cork Bonded Warehouses Ltd and Port of Cork Company Ltd* (20 December 2000, unreported) HC, O'Neill J.

141 *Wexford Rope and Twine Company Ltd v Gaynor and Modler* (6 March 2000, unreported) HC, Barr J.

142 *Wexford Rope and Twine Company Ltd v Gaynor and Modler* (6 March 2000, unreported) HC at p 4 of the judgment; italics added.

[6.044] The reported judgments show that the following matters have been held to constitute so-called *special circumstances*:

- (i) The defendant's lack of *bona fides*;
- (ii) The plaintiff company's insolvency having been caused by the defendant;
- (iii) The plaintiff company seeking to vindicate the public interest;
- (iv) The existence of a personal co-plaintiff;
- (v) The defendant's delay in applying for an order for security for costs[143].

The significance of these special circumstances is that, notwithstanding the fact that the defendant has proved everything required by s 390[144] and seems to be *prima facie* entitled to an order for security for costs, the court may still exercise its discretion and refuse to order the plaintiff company to provide security. Though the recognised '*special circumstances*' are undoubtedly well developed and said by Geoghegan J in *West Donegal Land League Ltd v Údarás na Gaeltachta*[145] to be 'limited', it was observed in *Millstream Recycling Ltd v Tierney and another*[146] by Charleton J that:

> 'Since the discretion of the court on a motion for security for costs is delineated by existing case law, it is important to note that the categories are not closed in respect of which a special reason for not ordering security as against a company likely to be unable to pay costs where the defendant has shown a real prospect of a defence[147].'

(i) The defendant's lack of bona fides

[6.045] Defendants commonly seek security for costs against corporate plaintiffs as a first line of defence in the hope that the plaintiff company will be put off from continuing with the proceedings. Consequently, if there is evidence that an application for security for costs is not *bona fide*, as, for example, where the defendant has made a partial admission or lodgment into court[148], the court may refuse to grant the order.

[6.046] Where a defendant has established a *prima facie* defence, the court will be loath to find that the defendant lacks *bona fides* in making application for security for costs. This was one of the matters alleged in *Village Residents Association Ltd v An Bord Pleanála and McDonald's Restaurants of Ireland Ltd*[149]. There, the plaintiff company had been incorporated for the very purpose of seeking judicial review of the first defendant's decision to grant planning permission to the second defendant (McDonalds) for a change of use from a hotel to a restaurant with a drive-through facility. The incorporators were residents in the locality of the drive-through restaurant. As a special

---

143 This list of five special circumstances in the 2nd edn of this book (2002) at p 281 was cited by Denham J in the Supreme Court in *Dublin International Arena Ltd v Campus & Stadium Ireland Development Ltd an others* [2008] 1 ILRM 496.

144 As set out in paras **[6.019]–[6.040]**.

145 *West Donegal Land League Ltd v Údarás na Gaeltachta* [2007] 1 ILRM 1, cited with apparent approval by Denham J in *Dublin International Arena Ltd v Campus & Stadium Ireland Development Ltd an others* [2008] 1 ILRM 496.

146 *Millstream Recycling Ltd v Tierney and another* [2010] IEHC 55 at para 33.

147 See also *Interfinance Group Ltd v KPMG* (29 June 1998, unreported) HC, Morris P, where it was noted that 'The list of special circumstances referred to is not of course, exhaustive'.

148 *Sir Lindsay Parkinson & Co Ltd v Triplan Ltd* [1973] 2 All ER 273.

149 *Village Residents Association Ltd v An Bord Pleanála and McDonalds Restaurants of Ireland Ltd* (23 March 2000, unreported) HC, Laffoy J.

circumstance, the plaintiff company argued that the order for security for costs should not be granted as the true purpose was to stifle its legitimate claim. This was rejected by Laffoy J who said:

> 'It is quite clear that the impetus for the incorporation of the applicant, and I think it is reasonable to infer that its immediate sole *raison d'être* was to constitute a vehicle for bringing these proceedings. By its very nature, the applicant can have no assets or finances other than those its members put into it or procure for it.'

Laffoy J went on to note that the members of the plaintiff company could finance the company to meet the order and found that the action would only come to a halt if they failed to do so. It should be noted that in *Lancefort Ltd v An Bord Pleanála*[150] Keane J had, in the Supreme Court, recognised the right of persons to organise themselves as a company with limited liability to shield themselves against an order for costs but had noted the existence of s 390 and the corresponding right of defendants to apply for an order for security for costs.

(ii) The plaintiff's insolvency having been caused by the defendant

[6.047] The fact that the insolvency of the plaintiff company has been caused by the defendant's actions has proven to be the most contentious and frequently relied upon *special circumstance* that the court is asked to accept as a basis for refusing the defendant's application that the plaintiff company provide security. Kingsmill Moore J observed in the seminal decision of the former Supreme Court in *Peppard and Co Ltd v Bogoff*[151], that in such circumstances:

> '... to order security would be to allow the defendants to defend an action by reason of an impecuniosity which they have themselves wrongfully and deliberately produced, a result which a court would strive to avoid.'

This defence to an otherwise proven application for an order that security be provided is a classic example of the exercise of the court's discretion to achieve justice between the parties. In the *Peppard* case, Kingsmill Moore J referred to *Gill All Weather Bodies Ltd v All Weather Motor Bodies Ltd*[152], where Maugham J was reported as saying:

> 'The section only confers a discretion on the court. There may be many cases where a company is insolvent, and yet the court would not order security to be lodged. I will take as an example of a defendant-company which is alleged to have stolen the plaintiff company's business. It is quite clear that the court would not ask the plaintiff-company to give security.'

So, in *SEE Company Ltd v Public Lighting Services Ltd*[153], the Supreme Court refused to make an order for security for costs where it found that accountants' and auditors' evidence linked the failure of certain equipment (in respect of which the claim was being made against the defendants) with the financial collapse of the company[154].

---

150 *Lancefort Ltd v An Bord Pleanála* [1998] 2 ILRM 401.

151 *Peppard and Co Ltd v Bogoff* [1962] IR 180 at 187. See *also Personal Service Laundry Ltd v National Bank Ltd* [1964] IR 49 at 62.

152 *Gill All Weather Bodies Ltd v All Weather Motor Bodies Ltd* 77 Law Journal 123.

153 *SEE Company Ltd v Public Lighting Services Ltd* [1987] ILRM 255.

154 See also *Bula Ltd v Tara Mines Ltd* [1987] IR 494, and *Aquila Design v Cornhill Insurance* [1988] BCLC 134, where, after the plaintiff's factory was burnt down, the defendant insurance company refused to pay on the policy, thus causing the plaintiff's insolvency.

Likewise, in *Campbell Seafoods Ltd v Brodene Gram A/S*[155], the plaintiff company admitted that it would be unable to meet the defendant's costs in the event of a successful defence, and it attributed this inability to the defendant's actions. The plaintiff alleged that machinery which it had acquired in reliance upon the defendant's representations as to fitness for purpose was, in fact, grossly unsatisfactory for the purposes for which it was required, and that this had led ultimately to the appointment of a receiver. Costello J accepted the plaintiff company's contention and refused to make an order for security for costs. Again, in *Inter Finance Group Ltd v KPMG Peat Marwick*[156], Morris J said that it is 'well settled that the plaintiff must do more than merely state this to be a fact. It must support this assertion with details', and the judge concluded that the evidence adduced in that case, far from supporting the allegation, had discredited it[157].

[6.048] Most recently, a test has been formulated which will be of further assistance to the courts in determining whether a plaintiff company should succeed in its claim that this special circumstance exists which makes in inappropriate to order security for costs. In *Connaughton Road Construction Ltd v Laing O'Rourke Ireland Ltd*[158], Clarke J said that for a plaintiff company to succeed in proving that his inability to pay stems from the wrongdoing asserted, four propositions must necessarily be true:

> '(1) That there was actionable wrongdoing on the part of the defendant (for example, a breach of contract or tort);
>
> (2) that there is a causal connection between that actionable wrongdoing and a practical consequence or consequences for the plaintiff [company];
>
> (3) that the consequence(s) referred to in (2) have given rise to some specific level of loss in the hands of the plaintiff which loss is recoverable as a matter of law (for example, by not being too removed); and
>
> (4) that the loss concerned is sufficient to make the difference between the plaintiff being in a position to meet the costs of the defendant in the event that the defendant should succeed, and the plaintiff not being in such a position.'

In *Citywide Leisure Ltd et al v IBRC Ltd*[159], McGovern J applied this test in an application for security for costs, resisted by the plaintiff company on the grounds that its insolvency was caused by the defendant. In so doing, the learned judge found the defendant's evidence of the plaintiff company's prior inability to pay its debts compelling and concluded that the plaintiff company had failed to show any credible evidence to link its inability to pay costs with the defendant's conduct[160].

---

155 *Campbell Seafoods Ltd v Brodene Gram A/S* (21 July 1994, unreported) HC, Costello J.

156 *Inter Finance Group Ltd v KPMG Peat Marwick* (29 June 1998, unreported) HC, Morris J.

157 *Inter Finance Group Ltd v KPMG Peat Marwick* (29 June 1998, unreported) HC, Morris J at pp 6 and 7 of the judgment.

158 *Connaughton Road Construction Ltd v Laing O'Rourke Ireland Ltd* [2009] IEHC 7.

159 *Citywide Leisure Ltd et al v IBRC Ltd* [2012] IEHC 220.

160 See also, *CMC Medical Operations Ltd v VHI* [2012] IEHC 232 where Cooke J also applied Clarke J's test and again found insufficient evidence of a causal link between the plaintiff company's inability to pay and the defendant's alleged wrongdoing.

[6.049] It is necessary that a plaintiff company claiming this special circumstance of insolvency due to the defendant's wrongdoing must make out a *prima facie* case of the matters alleged and described in Clarke J's test in *Connaughton Road Construction*[161]. It has been said, time after time, that a mere 'bald assertion' by the plaintiff company that its insolvency has been brought about by the defendant will not suffice[162]. In *Jack O'Toole Ltd v MacEoin Kelly Associates*[163], Finlay CJ said:

> 'It is clear that s 390 of the Act of 1963 deals with the situation where an insolvent company is suing for damages or money due. That very circumstance in itself would appear to me to make it probable that in a very high majority of cases which would come within that section recovery of the amount claimed would make a significant contribution towards the solvency of the company concerned and a corollary of that is that its insolvency is being probably contributed to, though possible not entirely caused, by the delay in the payment of the amount alleged to be due.
>
> Having regard to these circumstances, it does not seem to me a sufficient discharge of the onus of proof which I deem to be on a company against whom an application is made under section 390, to make a mere bald statement of fact that the insolvency of the company has been caused by the wrong the subject-matter of the claim. On the facts of this instant case, in particular, it seems to me that if the plaintiff company were to satisfy even the duty of establishing a prima facie special circumstance, it would be necessary for some accounts, even though they might be in an informal form, such as bank accounts or the state of a bank overdraft, of the plaintiff company to be produced. It seems to me that some information would necessarily have to be established as to what other sources of income the plaintiff company had at the material time when this contract was being concluded. Apart from a mere statement that the company was in the course of building houses for the Dublin County Council, no concept at all of the extent of that contract or the monies due and owing or capable of being earned on it has been afforded[164].'

The reason why a 'bald' or 'vague' assertion will not suffice is because there is an onus on the plaintiff company that asserts the defendant's wrongdoing has caused its 'impoverished condition' to prove that assertion[165]. The reference in the decided cases to a *prima facie* case that the plaintiff company's inability is caused by the defendant is a reasonable marker that the plaintiff must overcome[166]. *Millstream Recycling Ltd v*

---

161 See *Harrington et al v JVC (UK) Ltd et al* (16 March 1995, unreported) HC, O'Hanlon J at p 18 of the judgment.

162 In *Lismore Homes Ltd v Bank of Ireland Finance Ltd et al* (11 February 1998, unreported) HC, Lynch J at p 29 of the judgment.

163 *Jack O'Toole Ltd v MacEoin Kelly Associates* [1986] IR 277.

164 At 284; cited as being the relevant law on this point by the Supreme Court (per Barron J) in *Lismore Builders Ltd v Bank of Ireland Finance Ltd et al* (11 February 1998, unreported) SC, Lynch, Barrington and Barron JJ.

165 See, for example, *Harrington et al v JVC (UK) Ltd et al* (16 March 1995, unreported) HC, O'Hanlon J.

166 See, for example, *Wexford Rope and Twine Company Ltd v Gaynor and Modler* (6 March 2000, unreported) HC, Barr J, where despite adducing some evidence of this defence to an order for security for costs, Barr J held that the plaintiff's evidence did not go 'sufficiently far as to establish a prima facie case that the fall in profits was caused by the wrong doing on the part of the defendants or either of them. The alternative case which they put forward was at least equally credible.'

Tierney and another[167] provides an example of a situation where security for costs were refused and where the court found that the plaintiff company's assertion that its insolvency has been caused by the defendant did not amount to a bald assertion and was one of the reasons why security for costs was refused. There, the plaintiff was suing the defendants who had supplied it with oil for a pig-feed processing machine which had contaminated the foodstuffs and the pigs fed with it, severely damaging the reputation of Irish pork products.

In *Johnstown Ltd v Thiennez Ltd et al*[168], the plaintiff company did not establish to McCracken J's satisfaction that its insolvency had been caused by the defendants and the learned judge found that the direct cause of the plaintiff's financial problems arose from the refusal of an insurance company to pay monies to the plaintiff. On the other hand, in *Beauross Ltd v Kennedy*[169] Morris J said that he had no doubt but that the plaintiff had established a *prima facie* case that its inability to pay the defendant's costs had arisen from the wrong allegedly committed by the defendant. In that case the plaintiff's case against the defendant was that he had, as a director of another company, traded recklessly; the plaintiff was a creditor of the company of which the defendant was a director. The essence of the plaintiff's case was that the defendant had made representations to the plaintiff which were designed to induce it to continue to provide credit to the company in circumstances where he ought to have known that such were unrealistic. Morris J said of the evidence adduced by the plaintiff:

> 'I am satisfied that the plaintiff has fulfilled this requirement in this case. It is not necessary for him, in my view, to answer every criticism or query raised by the defendant on these accounts. This may well arise at a future date and indeed I may say at this stage many of the criticisms raised by the defendant would appear to me to require answers. However, on the level of proof which is required of the plaintiff at this stage, I am satisfied that he has established special circumstances which the court in its discretion should exercise in his favour[170].'

In *Irish Conservation and Cleaning Ltd v International Cleaners Ltd*[171], the plaintiff company's action against the defendant claimed it was owed over £377,000 in respect of works done and services rendered. The defendant was the plaintiff company's only customer and the plaintiff company's directors had been employees of the defendant. The plaintiff had ceased to trade owing to its financial difficulties and it was not disputed that, if unsuccessful, it would be unable to pay the defendant's costs. The plaintiff company resisted an application for an order for security for costs on the grounds that there were special circumstances, those circumstances being that the very financial situation which rendered them unable to pay the defendant's costs was created by the defendant's failure to pay their accounts in a timely manner. The Supreme Court found that what the plaintiff company was saying was 'if that issue is resolved against us in the High Court so be it, but if it is resolved in favour of us in the High Court it would

167 *Millstream Recycling Ltd v Tierney and another* [2010] IEHC 55.

168 *Johnstown Ltd v Thiennez Ltd et al* [2001] IEHC 44, McCracken J.

169 *Beauross Ltd v Kennedy* (18 October 1995, unreported) HC, Morris J.

170 *Beauross Ltd v Kennedy* (18 October 1995, unreported) HC, Morris J at pp 7 and 8 of the judgment.

171 *Irish Conservation and Cleaning Ltd v International Cleaners Ltd* (19 July 2001, unreported) SC, Geoghegan and Murray JJ, and Keane CJ.

inevitably follow that indeed the very inability on our part to provide security for costs is due by the actions of the defendants'. Keane CJ identified that as the real issue and said:

> 'Neither the High Court nor this Court on this motion can determine that issue. It will have to be resolved in the proceedings, but it would in effect mean that if the Court was to accede to the application for security for costs that it would be resolving that very issue against the plaintiffs. It would be holding that there was no set of special circumstances in this case of the nature alleged by the plaintiff which brought about their particular financial difficulties.'

Keane CJ refused to make an order for security for costs and affirmed the earlier order of the High Court. In *James Elliott Construction Ltd v Irish Asphalt Ltd*[172], Clarke J found that although there was a credible basis for suggesting that the plaintiff would not be able to meet the full costs of the proceedings, that state of affairs was due to the wrong alleged (the supply of infill material containing pyrite) and refused an application for security for costs.

[6.050] If the plaintiff company was already insolvent before the events forming the basis of the action, it is not acceptable to allege that the defendant's wrongdoing caused (or even contributed to or increased) the plaintiff company's inability to pay the likely costs. So in *Lismore Homes Ltd v Bank of Ireland Finance Ltd et al*[173] Lynch J said:

> 'If the plaintiff is insolvent before the events complained of then the plaintiff cannot resist the claim for security for costs on the basis that the defendant contributed to or increased the insolvency[174].'

This was one of the reasons why the Supreme Court in that decision upheld an order for security for costs brought by some of the defendants – a receiver to the plaintiff company and auctioneer who sold the company's property – because it was held that the company could not sustain the argument that the first defendant bank had caused the insolvency and simultaneously claim that the receiver appointed to the company (by the bank) had also wronged the company so as to make it unable to pay the defendants' costs. Where a plaintiff company is unsuccessful at trial, appeals that decision, and the defendant seeks security for costs for the appeal[175], the plaintiff company will be hard pressed to convince the Supreme Court that the plaintiff's inability to pay the defendant's costs was as a result of the defendant's wrongdoing. So in *Bula Ltd et al v Tara Mines Ltd et al*[176], Keane J said, after noting that an application for security for costs had been refused by the High Court at trial upon the judge accepting that the plaintiffs had made out an arguable case that their insolvency was the result of the defendants' wrongdoing:

---

172 *James Elliott Construction Ltd v Irish Asphalt Ltd* [2010] IEHC 234 (Clarke J).

173 *Lismore Homes Ltd v Bank of Ireland Finance Ltd et al* (11 February 1998, unreported) SC, Lynch, Barrington and Barron JJ (*per* Lynch J).

174 At p 8 of the judgment. See also *Lough Neagh Exploration Ltd v Morrice* (27 August 1997, unreported) HC, where Laffoy J held that the plaintiff was in substantially the same financial position prior to the commission of the acts complained of on the part of the defendant as it was at the time of the hearing for security for costs.

175 See para **[6.030]** *ante*.

176 *Bula Ltd et al v Tara Mines Ltd et al* (26 March 1998, unreported) SC, Keane J, *nem diss*.

> 'The position at this stage, however, is radically different: there has been a prolonged trial in the High Court in the course of which the claim that the insolvency of the [first plaintiff] was rejected. While the plaintiffs are, of course, entitled to challenge that conclusion on the hearing of the appeal, the trial judge's findings, coupled with the other circumstances discussed at an earlier stage of this judgment, make it clear that this is a case in which the corporate plaintiffs should be required to furnish security for costs[177].'

This is an eminently sensible decision: the converse – that an appellate court would completely disregard the finding of a full trial hearing – would be perverse.

[6.051] In *Lismore Homes Ltd v Bank of Ireland Finance Ltd et al*[178], Barron J stressed the need for a plaintiff company, appealing to the Supreme Court having been unsuccessful in the High Court action, who is alleging that the defendant's wrongdoing caused his impecuniosity, to establish, *inter alia*, that there:

> 'is a prima facie case of a causal connection between the wrong alleged and the inability to furnish security for costs[179].'

On this point, which was identified by Barron J as the real issue on the appeal, the learned judge said it was necessary to establish how the plaintiffs had come to arrive at their present financial situation. As against the five defendants, Barron J held that there was *prima facie* evidence to support the plaintiff company's allegation that its business collapsed because of the manner in which it was managed by an employee of the second defendant accountants who was answerable to the first defendant bank and that security would not be ordered for their costs. Barron J refused to find a causal connection between the plaintiff's' insolvency and the third, fourth and fifth defendants (quantity surveyors, estate agents and receivers respectively) and he made an order that they would get security for their costs. Barrington J concurred with this result based on the same reasons. The minority judgment of Lynch J would have given all five defendants orders for security for costs as on the evidence he found that the plaintiffs had made no more than bald assertions against them.

(iii) The plaintiff company seeking to vindicate the public interest

[6.052] Another factor which may influence the court in the exercise of its discretion is where the plaintiff seeks to litigate a matter of such gravity and importance as to transcend the interests of the parties actually before the court or where it is in the interests of the common good that the law on a point be clarified so as to enable it to be administered in the instant case and in future cases[180]. It is only in exceptional cases, however, that this will be a real factor that will influence the court's discretion. This special circumstance was rejected in both *Broadnet Ireland Ltd v Office of the Director of Telecommunications Regulation and Eircom plc*[181] and *Village Residents Association*

---

177 *Bula Ltd et al v Tara Mines Ltd et al* (26 March 1998, unreported) SC, Keane J, *nem diss*, at p 28 of the judgment.

178 *Lismore Homes Ltd v Bank of Ireland Finance Ltd et al* (11 February 1998, unreported) SC, Lynch, Barrington and Barron JJ (*per* Barron J).

179 *Lismore Homes Ltd v Bank of Ireland Finance Ltd et al* (11 February 1998, unreported) SC, Lynch, Barrington and Barron JJ (*per* Barron J) at p 13 of the judgment.

180 See *Moone et al v Attorney General (No 2)* [1929] IR 544; *Fallon v An Bord Pleanála* [1992] 2 IR 380 and *Lancefort Ltd v An Bord Pleanála* [1998] 2 ILRM 401.

181 *Broadnet Ireland Ltd v Office of the Director of Telecommunications Regulation and Eircom plc* [2000] 3 IR 281, Laffoy J.

Ltd v An Bord Pleanála and McDonald's Restaurants of Ireland Ltd[182]. Assertions of this ground as a special circumstance will not be permitted to override legitimate commercial interests. This proposition was made clear by Keane CJ in the Supreme Court in *Hot Radio Co Ltd v IRTC and NP*[183]. There, the former Chief Justice said:

> 'Now in cases involving planning considerations, it is undoubtedly the case that this court has on more than one occasion indicated that the court would be concerned that in the case of decisions of public importance concerning planning and development and the environment, affecting the interests of the public in many ways, bodies who are formed solely for the purpose of protecting the public interest, voluntary associations, should not be unduly and unfairly impeded in bringing challenges to the decisions of bodies such as An Bord Pleanála or planning authorities before the courts. That may also arise in other branches of the law but this is plainly not such a case because, while undoubtedly the public have a considerable interest in seeing that the provisions of this type of legislation are operated in a fair, and as people like to say nowadays, in a transparent manner and which is very right and no one would question, I think, that it is anything but appropriate that persons in the position of the disappointed applicants in this case should, if they have an arguable case, be in a position to bring it before the court, the fact remains at the end of the day that there are commercial interests at stake in this case … They are doing it in their own interest and there is nothing wrong with that. But they are not to be equated with the sort of applicants who have been looked on benevolently by the courts in other areas of law, who are doing a public service by litigating matters which would otherwise not be litigated and who have simply not the financial resources to meet orders for costs given against them[184].'

In that case Keane CJ upheld an order for security for costs against a disappointed applicant (being a shelf company) for an independent radio licence, in circumstances where it sought a judicial review of the IRTC's decision not to grant it a licence[185].

[6.053] In *Millstream Recycling Ltd v Tierney and another*[186], Charleton J equated the public interest with the discovery of the facts concerning the contamination with dioxins of pig meat and the damage caused to the reputation of Irish pork products. Having been blamed publicly for causing the contamination, the plaintiff company had:

> 'a case to make that they were not responsible for this, but that they acted as they had always done and had it not been for the oil supplied by the defendants that their pig food products would have continued to enjoy the high reputation for quality that they assert was their entitlement. I would find it impossible, where they have made out a case that the ruination of their business and reputation was caused by the defendant to make an order that undermines or removes their right to litigate[187].'

---

182 *Village Residents Association Ltd v An Bord Pleanála and McDonalds Restaurants of Ireland Ltd* (23 March 2000, unreported) HC, Laffoy J.

183 *Hot Radio Co Ltd v IRTC and NP* (14 April 2000, ex tempore) SC, Keane CJ.

184 *Hot Radio Co Ltd v IRTC and NP* (14 April 2000, ex tempore) SC, Keane CJ at p 3 of the judgment.

185 In *Salthill Properties Ltd and Cunningham v Royal Bank of Scotland plc et al* [2010] IEHC 31, it was held that no issues of significant public importance were likely to arise. It had been contended that the important point concerned the obligations of a bank which is, at the same time, acting as a vendor of property in its capacity as a mortgagee in possession and as lender to the purchaser of the property.

186 *Millstream Recycling Ltd v Tierney and another* [2010] IEHC 55.

187 *Millstream Recycling Ltd v Tierney and another* [2010] IEHC 55 at para 36.

In those circumstances Charleton J said it was clear to him that 'the determination of the facts behind the scandal transcends the individual claims and counterclaims of the parties' and meant that the 'litigation must proceed'[188] and should not be prevented by the plaintiff company's inability to provide security for costs.

(iv) The existence of a personal co-plaintiff

[6.054] Where the plaintiff company has a natural (ie, human) co-plaintiff, a further complication arises. On the one hand, the individual's fear of the stigma accompanying bankruptcy might be thought to come into play, so that neither the court nor the defendant need be concerned about frivolous litigation. In *Peppard and Co Ltd v Bogoff*[189], Kingsmill Moore J said:

> 'There is no doubt that where an application for security for costs is made on the ground that a plaintiff is outside the jurisdiction it will be refused if there is another plaintiff within the jurisdiction who would be answerable for costs ... There is, as far as I have been able to ascertain, no case in which this principle has been applied where the ground for seeking security was based on the section of the Companies Act and not on residence without the jurisdiction, but in principle the same arguments would seem applicable in both cases.'

On the other hand, the natural co-plaintiff might also be impecunious, so that the fear of having nobody to answer for costs remains. Thus, in *Bula Ltd v Tara Mines Ltd*[190], Costello J said the involvement of a human co-plaintiff should:

> '... have no direct bearing on the question of whether a corporate co-plaintiff would be required to give security. It might be argued, however, that the position would be different if it was shown that the individual plaintiffs were a good mark because it is only in that way that their inclusion would provide an answer to the defendant's concern of facing proceedings against an impecunious corporate body.'

The learned judge was concerned that 'nominal' co-plaintiffs could be named as parties 'in the confidence that they were so impecunious that an order for costs against them would no more increase their problems than solve those of the defendants'. However, the fact that the same scenario may arise in respect of a human plaintiff resident abroad, whereby 'a man of straw' lends his name to that plaintiff's action, was not addressed.

It is submitted that the correct approach lies somewhere between the two views outlined in these cases, and that the courts should ascertain whether the individual co-plaintiff is *bona fide* rather than a 'good mark'[191]. Certainly, it would seem essential to establish that the natural co-plaintiff has a stateable case in his personal right against the defendant and has not been added to the action as a ruse. In *Salthill Properties Ltd and Cunningham v Royal Bank of Scotland plc et al*[192], the High Court struck the balance in

188 See also *County Monaghan Anti-Pylon Ltd v Eirgrid plc* [2012] IEHC 103.

189 *Peppard and Co Ltd v Bogoff* [1962] IR 180.

190 *Bula Ltd v Tara Mines Ltd* [1987] IR 494.

191 See *In Bonis Mooney* [1938] IR 354 at 358 where Hanna J stressed the importance of establishing the *bona fides* of a resident individual co-plaintiff when deciding whether or not to order security for costs against a non-resident individual plaintiff.

192 *Salthill Properties Ltd and Cunningham v Royal Bank of Scotland plc et al* [2010] IEHC 31 (Clarke J).

the manner suggested above and Clarke J said that it is for the party placing reliance on the existence of the individual co-plaintiff to show that the individual plaintiff is a good mark. In that case, it was found that no such evidence had been produced and given that there were existing judgments against the individual co-plaintiff which the Sheriff had been unable to execute, such tended to establish that he would not, personally, be a good mark[193].

(v) The defendant applicant's delay in applying for an order for security for costs

[6.055] Excessive delay on the part of the defendant may likewise indicate a lack of genuine concern about the plaintiff's ability to pay costs[194]. It is well established that where it is shown that a defendant has been guilty of *unreasonable delay* in bringing an application for security for costs, this is something that may constitute a special circumstance that is cognisable by the court when exercising its discretion[195]. This *special circumstance* was articulated by Morris J, in *Beauross Ltd v Kennedy*[196], in the following terms:

> '… as I understand the principle it is this. If the party seeking security has delayed to such an extent as to commit the other party to an amount and a level of costs which it would never have become committed to had it known that it was to be required to provide security for costs and thereby altered its position to its detriment, then the court will not make the order[197].'

In *Hidden Ireland Heritage Holidays Ltd v Indigo Service Ltd*[198], Fennelly J said in the Supreme Court:

> 'A review of the authorities shows that delay in applying for security may, depending on the circumstances, be a ground for refusing security. The court will look at the facts of the particular case, the impact of the delay, other surrounding circumstances and, in the end, will seek to find a fair balance.'

This particular, special circumstance is, therefore, in the nature of an estoppel, which prevents a defendant from prejudicing a plaintiff company that *alters its position* on the basis of the defendant's actions. In that case, the plaintiff company was a creditor of a company that had become insolvent and the defendant was a director of that company, who the plaintiff was pursuing for reckless trading. Morris J noted that there had been a time lapse from mid-November 1994 to late February 1995. Although that was a relatively short period, Morris J held that this was a basis for refusing the defendant the order for security for costs that had been sought because 'comprehensive legal costs had been incurred in [that] short period of time' due to the defendant's attendance and cross-

---

193 *Salthill Properties Ltd and Cunningham v Royal Bank of Scotland plc et al* [2010] IEHC 31 at paras 7.1 and 7.2.

194 *Lismore Homes Ltd v Bank of Ireland Finance Ltd* [1992] ILRM 798.

195 *Oakes v Lynch* (27 November 1953, unreported) SC and *SEE Company Ltd v Public Lighting Services Ltd* [1987] ILRM 266.

196 *Beauross Ltd v Kennedy* (18 October 1995, unreported) HC, Morris J.

197 *Beauross Ltd v Kennedy* (18 October 1995, unreported) HC, Morris J at p 8 of the judgment.

198 *Hidden Ireland Heritage Holidays Ltd v Indigo Service Ltd* [2005] 2 IR 115 at 122. See also *Ronbow Management Company Ltd v Sorohan Builders Ltd et al* [2010] IEHC 60.

examination before the Master of the High Court on the substantive issues. It is implicit that, if the defendant had wanted to seek an order for security for costs, he ought to have done so before the plaintiff company had embarked upon the litigation process, thereby incurring its own costs.

[6.056] It is necessary that a plaintiff company should be proved to have 'altered its position' in order to successfully invoke this shield to an order for security for costs. So, in *Village Residents Association Ltd v An Bord Pleanála and McDonald's Restaurants of Ireland Ltd*[199], Laffoy J held that there was no evidence that the plaintiff company had 'altered its position to its detriment'. Accordingly, the plaintiff company's invocation of this defence as a basis for refusing an order for security for costs was rejected. The message is clear: to successfully invoke *unreasonable delay* as a defence to an otherwise *prima facie* case for granting security for costs, the plaintiff company must have altered its position as a direct result of the defendant's inertia.

(h) The amount required as security

[6.057] Once an order for security for costs has been made by the court, it falls to the Master of the High Court to fix the sum which the plaintiff company will be required to in fact provide as security[200]. The security, as Kingsmill Moore J observed in *Thake v Soares et al*[201], is *not* 'intended either as an indemnity against all costs or as an encouragement to luxurious litigation'. Until recently, the practice was that the amount fixed by way of security would approximate to one-third of the amount which it would cost the defendant to defend the proceedings; although this practice was departed from in particular circumstances[202]. The general rule of one-third was, however, turned on its head by the decision of McCracken J in *Lismore Homes Ltd v Bank of Ireland Finance Ltd et al*[203]. There, the statutory expression of 'sufficient security' was interpreted to mean such security as must approximate to the (full) probable costs of the defendant, should he succeed. In that case, which had a long and chequered history, McCracken J set his task as deciding what constituted '*sufficient security*', and in that regard accepted the distinction between s 390 and Ord 29 – as determined in *Thalle v Soares et al* – as being governed by a deciding factor, namely, 'the wording of the section when contrasted with the rule', quoting Kingsmill Moore J as follows:

> 'The statute lays down reasonably precise instructions as to the measure of security while the rule makers and the judges seem studiously to have avoided any approach to definitiveness, leaving each case to be decided by an uncontrolled discretion[204].'

McCracken J went on to cite the consideration of the expression '*sufficient security*' in the English Court of Appeal decision in *Innovare Displays plc v Corporate Broking Services Ltd*[205] where Leggatt LJ said, *inter alia*:

---

199 *Village Residents Association Ltd v An Bord Pleanála and McDonalds Restaurants of Ireland Ltd* (23 March 2000, unreported) HC, Laffoy J.

200 Order 29, r 6,of the RSC.

201 *Thake v Soares et al* [1957] IR 152 at 194.

202 See, for example, *Fallon v An Bord Pleanála and Burke* [1991] ILRM 779.

203 *Lismore Homes Ltd v Bank of Ireland Finance Ltd et al* (24 March 2000, unreported) HC, McCracken J.

204 *Lismore Homes Ltd v Bank of Ireland Finance Ltd et al* (24 March 2000, unreported) HC, McCracken J at p 2 of the judgment.

205 *Innovare Displays plc v Corporate Broking Services Ltd* (1991) BCC 726.

> 'However, the section does not mean, in my judgment, complete security. It can only mean security of a sufficiency in all the circumstances of the case to be just.'

McCracken J held that the statutory nature of s 390 and the use of the words '*sufficient security*' were significant. The learned judge went on to hold:

> 'It is certainly arguable that the use of the word 'may' in s 390 gives a general discretion to the court, but on the whole I think it more likely that that word refers to the *making of the order for security for costs* rather than the amount thereof. In other words, even if there is credible testimony that there is reason to believe the company will be unable to pay the costs, there is still a discretion in the court whereby an order for security for costs may be refused. If the discretion was intended to be in relation to the amount, I think the word '*sufficient*' would not have been used, but it is in the section and it must have a meaning. The question can be posed: *sufficient for what?* I think that question is answered in the section by saying '*for those costs*', that is the costs of the defendant if successful in his defence. This seems to me to be the only logical construction of the section. Where the court orders security for costs to be given in other circumstances, such as where the plaintiff is out of the jurisdiction, it is customary to require security of approximately one-third of the probable costs. I do not see how under any circumstances this could be called '*sufficient security*' and I think the section can only mean that the security required must approximate to the probable costs of the defendant should he succeed[206].'

This interpretation of 'sufficient security' was questioned, but followed, by the Supreme Court (*per* Keane CJ) in *Hot Radio Co Ltd v IRTC and NP*[207] where the Chief Justice found that even though McCracken J was speaking *obiter dictum*, it was just in the instant case to order the full measure of security 'because there is no suggestion that the action would be stifled by the award of security for costs in the sum actually awarded as opposed to awarding security for costs in the more conventional measure of one-third'[208]. Keane CJ's concern with awarding full costs was that the plaintiff's action might be stifled, and bears out the overriding concern of the judiciary when confronted with applications for security for costs, that a plaintiff company's constitutional rights to access to the courts are not unjustly limited. There can be no other reason for the existence of so many written judgments of both the High and Supreme Court on a topic that is normally disposed of as a matter of mere practice and procedure.

[6.058] Any remaining questions as to the meaning of 'sufficient security' appeared to have been put beyond doubt by the Supreme Court in the actual appeal against McCracken J's decision in *Lismore Homes v Bank of Ireland*[209]. In delivering the judgment of a five-judge court, Murphy J reviewed the Irish and English authorities and concluded that the plain meaning of the words 'sufficient security' were inescapable.

> 'The word 'sufficient' in its plain meaning signifies adequate or enough and it is directly related in the section to the defendant's costs. The section does not provide – as it might

206 *Lismore Homes Ltd v Bank of Ireland Finance Ltd et al* (24 March 2000, unreported) HC, McCracken J at p 3 of the judgment. Italics added.

207 *Hot Radio Co Ltd v IRTC and NP* (14 April 2000, unreported) SC, Keane CJ, *nem diss*.

208 *Hot Radio Co Ltd v IRTC and NP* (14 April 2000, unreported) SC at p 7 of the judgment. In *Windmaster Developments Ltd v Airoglen Ltd and Kelly* (10 July 2000, unreported) HC, McCracken J applied the same test as to the amount of security in ordering that the full amount of the defendant's costs should be provided for.

209 *Lismore Homes v Bank of Ireland* [2001] IESC 79, [2001] 3 IR 536.

> have – a sufficient sum 'to meet the justice of the case' or some such phrase as would give a general discretion to the Court. Harsh though it may be, I am convinced that 'sufficient security' involves making a reasonable estimate or assessment of the actual costs which it is anticipated that the defendant will have to meet. Much of the injustice which may be anticipated by the operation of the section can be avoided by the application of the established principles in granting or withholding the order for security. Insofar as the quantum of the security may be oppressive in a case where security is in fact ordered this must be seen in the context in which it arises. It applies only to limited liability companies who are shown to be insolvent. Legislation has conferred many benefits on limited liability companies including, in particular, the very limitation and it is not surprising to find that some burdens are likewise case by the legislature on corporators who enjoy those advantages. It is with hesitation that I disagree with the conclusions reached by the Court of Appeal in England[210] but I am greatly comforted to find myself in full agreement with the views expressed by Kingsmill Moore J in *Thalle v Soares* so many years ago.'

Murphy J went on to hold that he considered the assessment made by the trial judge to be as realistic an assessment as could be made and rejected the plaintiff's appeal (and the defendant's cross-appeal on the quantum of costs).

[6.059] Considerable doubt, however, was cast upon the certainty of the Supreme Court's position by Keane CJ giving the subsequent decision of that court in *Mooreview Developments Ltd v William Fanagan Ltd*[211]. In that case the plaintiff company could only put up €100,000 of the €330,000 security ordered by the High Court. Although Keane CJ dismissed the appeal, he did say:

> 'There are, of course, circumstances where, given that it is a discretionary order, the court may not require the sufficient security to consist of the entire amount of the costs although again the cases make it clear that the court is not, in such cases, normally confined to the measurement of approximately one-third of the estimated costs. It can require the company to provide security in the full amount of the costs. It is clear that one ground on which the court might refrain from exercising its jurisdiction is where the action would be stifled if such an order were to be made.'

This represents a more measured approach and would avoid the scenario envisaged in an earlier edition of this book where it was suggested that where the effect of requiring full security was to stifle a plaintiff company's action, it remained to be seen whether the courts would opt to exercise their discretion against making any order.

[6.060] In *Harlequin Property (SVG) Ltd and another v O'Halloran and O'Halloran*[212], it was held by Clarke J that a non-resident body corporate should be in the same position as a resident company and when the court decides to exercisc its jurisdiction to order security for costs under Ord 29 against a non-resident body corporate, it is appropriate to order that *full security* is provided rather than simply one-third.

---

210 In *Innovate Displays plc v Corporate Broking Services Ltd* [1991] BCC 174; *Roburn Construction Ltd v William Irwin (Slough) & Co Ltd* [1991] BCC 726; *Unisoft Group Ltd (No 2)* [1993] BCLC 532 and *Keary Developments Ltd v Tarmac Construction Ltd* [1995] 2 BCLC 400.

211 *Mooreview Developments Ltd v William Fanagan Ltd* (9 June 2004, unreported) SC.

212 *Harlequin Property (SVG) Ltd and another v O'Halloran and O'Halloran* [2012] IEHC 13, Clarke J.

[E] Discovery and Interrogatories against Companies

[6.061] 'Discovery is a process generally available in civil proceedings whereby one party may, by way of certain pre-trial devices, obtain information in writing and on oath from the opposite party in the proceedings[213].' Interrogatories is a pre-trial process whereby one party can obtain an order directing the opposite party in the proceedings to answer on affidavit a series of written questions relating to the matter in question[214]. Order 31 of the RSC deals generally with discovery and interrogatories. In the case of interrogatories against companies and other bodies corporate, Ord 31, r 5 provides:

> 'If any party to a cause or matter be a body corporate or a joint stock company, whether incorporated or not, or any other body of persons, empowered by law to sue or be sued, whether in its own name or in the name of any officer or other person, any opposite party may apply for an order allowing him to deliver interrogatories to any member or officer of such corporation, company, or body, and an order may be made accordingly.'

It will be noted that this rule prevents members (and indeed directors and other officers) from relying on the fact that a company is a separate legal entity to resist an order for interrogatories. That said, it is important to appreciate that where interrogatories are directed at officers and members, such persons will be answering *on behalf of the company* and not on their own behalf. This is clear from the following comments of Walsh J in the Supreme Court decision in *J and LS Goodbody Ltd v The Clyde Shipping Company Ltd*[215]:

> '*Prima facie* the secretary is the person to whom they [the interrogatories] should be delivered and in the absence of any order to the contrary it is to be assumed that that was what was intended in the present case. It is important to bear in mind, however, that it is not the secretary who is being interrogated but the company. The secretary is not answering for himself but for the company and in doing so he must get such information as he can from the other servants of the company who have personally conducted the transaction in question and have personal knowledge of the facts sought. The secretary's function is to give the answer of the company. When the secretary answers on the basis of information obtained from other servants of the company he is answering according to information. On behalf of the company he is bound to answer according to information and belief acquired or formed from personal knowledge or from information obtained from others who are servants or agents of the company and have acquired the information in that capacity[216].'

---

213 Cahill, *Discovery in Ireland* (1996, Roundhall) at p 1. See also Ó Floinn, *Practice and Procedure in the Superior Courts* (2nd edn, Bloomsbury Professional, 2008) at p 236 *et seq* and Courtney, *Mareva Injunctions and Related Interlocutory Orders* (1998, Butterworths) at p 373 *et seq*.

214 See *Mercantile Credit Company of Ireland and Highland Finance (Ireland) Ltd v Heelan* [1994] ILRM 406 and, generally, Courtney, *Mareva Injunctions and Related Interlocutory Orders* (1998, Butterworths) at p 399 *et seq*.

215 *J and LS Goodbody Ltd v The Clyde Shipping Company Ltd* (9 May 1967, unreported) SC, Walsh J, Ó Dálaigh CJ concurring.

216 *J and LS Goodbody Ltd v The Clyde Shipping Company Ltd* (9 May 1967, unreported) SC at p 5 of the judgment.

In *Money Markets International Stock Brokers Ltd v Fanning et al*[217], O'Sullivan J held that where information can be said to be properly at the disposal of people to whom interrogatories are directed, it matters not that 'they are being interrogated as individuals rather than as officers of a company'. In either case, persons may not avoid giving answers to interrogatories merely on the grounds that the subject matter thereof is not within their personal knowledge[218]. Generally, a party is only obliged to disclose documents that are in his possession, custody or power. The general rule is that documents held by one separate legal entity will not be discoverable by another separate legal entity unless an agency can be established[219].

[6.062] It should also be noted that in an action against a company, directors and other officers and members can be made amenable to so-called third-party discovery, pursuant to Ord 31, r 29[220]. Notwithstanding a company's separate legal personality, it will not always be appropriate to consider the company a third party for the purposes of discovery in an action between warring shareholder-directors. *Re Murray Consultants Ltd and Nocrumb Ltd; Horgan v Murray and Milton*[221] concerned a number of points that arose in discovery motions. The first point raised by the petitioner was that the respondents had failed to refer to files of advices received by the *companies* by several categories of third-party advisors. O'Sullivan J said:

> 'The relevance of the documents sought being accepted, the precise question is whether these are within the power or possession of the respondents who claim that these are advices given to a third party, (namely the companies referred to in the title of these proceedings) and not to themselves. It is submitted that the petitioner can bring a third party discovery motion compelling the relevant companies to furnish him with the documents but that the respondents themselves should not be obliged in these proceedings as part and parcel of the general obligations under discovery principles to refer to these documents and to produce them for the petitioner.
>
> This case is a 'Section 205' petition. The petitioner alleges that the affairs of the above entitled companies have been operated oppressively against him by the two respondents. I do not think the company is a 'third party' in the usual sense of that term in these circumstances. If the advices furnished to the companies are relevant, as I have held, then they should be produced as part of discovery unless they are privileged. In my opinion the documents are within the power of the respondents in the circumstances of this case and they should be referred to in the affidavit and I so direct[222].'

---

217 *Money Markets International Stock Brokers Ltd v Fanning et al* [2000] IEHC 15, [2000] 3 IR 215, O'Sullivan J.

218 See, for example, *Re Holborne Investments Trust Ltd* (1991) Irish Times, 9 October (Barron J) where a managing director was ordered to make full discovery of both his own and the company's assets and liabilities, in circumstances where a *Mareva* injunction preventing the company, the director and his wife from reducing their assets below £300,000 had been made.

219 *Johnson v Church of Scientology, Mission of Dublin Ltd et al* [2001] IESC 25. *Cf Northern Bank Finance v Charlton* (26 May 1977, unreported) HC, Finlay P.

220 See Courtney, *Mareva Injunctions and Related Interlocutory Orders* (1998, Butterworths) at p 381.

221 *Re Murray Consultants Ltd and Nocrumb Ltd; Horgan v Murray and Milton* (9 October 1998, unreported) HC, O'Sullivan J.

222 *Re Murray Consultants Ltd and Nocrumb Ltd; Horgan v Murray and Milton* (9 October 1998, unreported) HC at p 2 of the judgment.

So, in that s 205 petition, it was held that advices to the company are discoverable unless they are privileged.

[6.063] Ordinarily, *legal professional privilege* entitles a legal entity that has received legal advice to refuse to disclose that advice to any other legal entity. It is, however, a well established rule of practice, in the case of companies, that as stated by Harman J in *Re Hydrosan Ltd*[223]:

> 'There is no doubt that matters passing between solicitors to a company and a company are *prima facie* entitled to be produced to all shareholders of the company.'

This is the so-called *disclosure rule*. The basis of this rule is trustee law[224]. The rule was rationalised by Simonds J in *Dennis & Sons Ltd v West Norfolk Farmers' Manure and Chemical Co-Op Co Ltd*[225] where he quoted from the 1943 English Annual Practice note:

> 'A *cestui que trust* … is entitled to see cases and opinions submitted and taken by the trustee for the purpose of the administration of the trust; but where stated and taken by the trustees not for that purpose, but for the purpose of their own defence in litigation against themselves by the *cestui que trust* they are protected …[226].'

The fact that the *disclosure rule* is based on principles of trust law was re-emphasised in *CAS (Nominees) Ltd et al v Nottingham Forest plc et al*[227] where Evans-Lombe J said:

> 'As the authorities show the rule is based on principles of trust law, an analogy being drawn between the position of directors as fiduciaries and trustees. As the authorities show, directors though not properly described as trustees of the assets of the company within their charge, none the less owe fiduciary duties to the shareholders which prevent them from applying those assets save for the purposes of the company. Directors are subject to the same duty to shareholders regardless of the size of the company concerned[228].'

The exception to the *disclosure rule*, as instanced by Simonds J in the passage quoted above, is referred to as the 'Rule in *Woodhouse & Co*[229]'. The exception to the rule is, perhaps, as important as the rule itself. In *Woodhouse*, Phillimore LJ and Lush J took it to be a clear exception to the *disclosure rule* (ie, that where a company takes the opinion of counsel and pays for it out of the funds of a company a shareholder has a right to see it) that it does not apply where the company has brought an action against a shareholder. In *Re Hydrosan Ltd*[230], however, it was held by Harman J that for the purposes of the exception to the rule, a petition to wind-up a company on the 'just and equitable' grounds, was not properly to be regarded as hostile litigation because the nature of such allegations involved wrongs by those in control of the company rather than by the

---

223 *Re Hydrosan Ltd* [1991] BCLC 418 at 420f.

224 *Tugwell v Hooper* (1847) 10 Beav 348.

225 *Dennis & Sons Ltd v West Norfolk Farmers' Manure and Chemical Co-Op Co Ltd* [1948] 2 All ER 94.

226 *Dennis & Sons Ltd v West Norfolk Farmers' Manure and Chemical Co-Op Co Ltd* [1948] 2 All ER 94 at 96.

227 *CAS (Nominees) Ltd et al v Nottingham Forest plc et al* [2001] 1 All ER 954.

228 *CAS (Nominees) Ltd et al v Nottingham Forest plc et al* [2001] 1 All ER 954 at 959.

229 Rule in *Woodhouse & Co* (1914) 30 TLR 559.

230 *Re Hydrosan Ltd* [1991] BCLC 418 at 420f.

company itself, even though such a petition might produce severe results. The *disclosure rule* has been refined to state that a shareholder in a company is entitled to obtain from it otherwise privileged documents provided that they relate to the *company's administration* and not to litigation between the parties. In that case it was also held that a further exception to the disclosure rule arose where, from the nature of the relations between the parties, it was reasonable to be contemplated that litigation would arise.

[6.064] It was established in *CAS (Nominees) Ltd et al v Nottingham Forest plc et al*[231] that the disclosure rule applies to *all* companies and not just small private companies. In that case the facts were that at an EGM of the shareholders in the first defendant company, the shareholders approved of an agreement relating to the disposal of shares in a wholly-owned subsidiary. The claimants in the case were minority shareholders who contended that the agreement was unfairly prejudicial to them and, in the proceedings that they instituted, they sought disclosure of certain documents between the first defendant company and its legal advisers which had come into existence in connection with the first defendant's board of directors' decision to support the agreement to dispose of the shares in the subsidiary and the preparations for the EGM. At that time the directors had realised that litigation was likely and all of the defendants contended that the documents were protected by legal professional privilege and not amenable to disclosure. The claimant minority shareholders sought to rely upon the *disclosure rule* but the defendants claimed that it only applied to 'small private companies'. That contention that the *disclosure rule* was confined to small private companies was categorically rejected by Evans-Lombe J who held that:

> 'Nothing in the *Woodhouse & Co* case or the subsequent authorities down to and including *Re Hydrosan Ltd* supports the proposition that the rule is to be differently applied depending on the size and importance of the company concerned … Directors are subject to the same duty to shareholders regardless of the size of the company concerned[232].'

In that case it was held that the documents had been created by the company's lawyers for the purpose of procuring the first defendant to take certain actions and that it had been anticipated that such might give rise to litigation in which the claimant minority shareholders would challenge the propriety of those actions. In the instant proceedings – in which the first defendant appeared in a nominal capacity so as to be bound by any court order in the substantive issue – it was held that there was no reason why the claimant minority shareholders should not be entitled to see the advice and guidance given to the board by the company's solicitors when those transactions had been embarked upon. In this respect the claim of legal professional privilege was rejected.

[6.065] In *Re Hydrosan Ltd*[233], the facts were that, after a petition alleging unfair prejudice had been presented, the petitioner then applied orders for discovery. The basis of that petition was the petitioner's complaint that the company's money had been expended in defending an earlier unfair prejudice petition. First, the petitioner sought discovery of solicitors' bills arising from the earlier petition. Second, the petitioner sought discovery of documents relative to a certain 'rights issue' proposed by the company in a particular circular. The English registrar had ruled that none of these

---

[231] *CAS (Nominees) Ltd et al v Nottingham Forest plc et al* [2001] 1 All ER 954.

[232] *CAS (Nominees) Ltd et al v Nottingham Forest plc et al* [2001] 1 All ER 954 at 959.

[233] *Re Hydrosan Ltd* [1991] BCLC 418.

documents were discoverable and the petitioner appealed to the English High Court. Harman J accepted the propriety of the *discovery rule* and that there were exceptions (a) where there was hostile litigation between the company and its shareholder (but finding that a petition to have a company wound up on the just and equitable ground was not hostile litigation in that sense) and (b) where from the nature of the relations between the parties it was reasonable to contemplate that litigation would arise. In respect of the first ground he held that all documents relating to the earlier petition were discoverable and in relation to the second he held that all documents and communications *prior* to the circular and notice of meetings relating to the proposed rights issue were discoverable, coming within the general rule relating to discovery of documents between a company and its shareholders.

[F] Appearance in Court

[6.066] A consequence of the corporate right to sue and be sued is that a company cannot appear in court except through its solicitor or counsel[234]. In *Battle v Irish Art Promotion Centre Ltd*[235], the managing director and majority shareholder of the defendant company applied to the court for leave to defend an action against the company on foot of an alleged debt, on the grounds that the company had not the means to employ counsel and that a successful judgment in default of defence would reflect badly on his personal reputation. The Supreme Court refused his application on the basis that the company was a different person, separate and distinct from its controlling shareholder. Ó Dálaigh CJ explained:

> '... in the absence of a statutory exception, a limited company cannot be represented in court proceedings by its managing director or other officer or servant. This is an infirmity of the company which derives from its very nature. The creation of the company is the act of its subscribers; the subscribers, in discarding their own *personae* for the *persona* of the company, doubtless did so for the advantages which incorporation offers to traders. In seeking incorporation they thereby lose their legal right of audience which they would have as individuals; but the choice has been their own. One sympathises with the purpose which the appellant has to mind, to wit, to safeguard his business reputation; but, as the law stands, he cannot as major shareholder and managing director now substitute his *persona* for that of the company. The only practical course open to him would, it appears, be for him personally to put the company in funds for the purpose of presenting its defence[236].'

It appears that this prohibition does not amount to a breach of a constitutional right of access to the courts[237].

[6.067] The principle outlined in the *Battle* case may undoubtedly be the cause of great hardship, especially where the cost to the shareholder of personally putting the company

[234] Unless the company is being prosecuted on indictment, when it may appear in court by a representative appointed by the company: s 382 of the CA 1963. See para **[6.070]** *post*.

[235] *Battle v Irish Art Promotion Centre Ltd* [1968] IR 252; the principle in which was acknowledged by Hogan J in *NO2GM Ltd v Environmental Protection Agency* [2012] IEHC 369.

[236] *Battle v Irish Art Promotion Centre Ltd* [1968] IR 252 at 254.

[237] *Abbey Films Ltd v Attorney General* [1981] IR 158.

in funds to employ lawyers is great. There are signs, however, that the courts may be able to depart from the strict rule where hardship would otherwise be caused. In *Arbuthnot Leasing Ltd v Havelet Leasing Ltd*[238], Scott J in the English Companies Court concluded, after a review of many authorities, including the *Battle* case, that while companies cannot appear in court except through their advocate, the courts have the inherent power to permit *any* person to appear as advocate for a litigant if the exceptional circumstances of the case so warrant. Thus, another party to the case, such as a shareholder, may be permitted to address the court both on behalf of the company as well as on his own behalf. Scott J stated:

> 'One of the great topical questions concerning the administration of justice in England is what, if anything, can be done about the burdens that exceptionally heavy legal costs lay on ordinary individuals who find themselves (not always, I accept, through no fault of their own) enmeshed in litigation. The financial implications faced by individuals who become parties to complex civil litigation are very serious. The cost burden is one that the courts should endeavour, in so far as is consistent with principle and practice, to mitigate ... In all these circumstances I can see no reason why a director should not, in an appropriate case (I would certainly not say in every case and I emphasise 'in an appropriate case'), be allowed to become a party to litigation in which the company of which he is director is defendant in order to make an application in that litigation in relation to orders which have been made against that corporate defendant. Take as an example an action in which the company is the only defendant and a *Mareva* injunction has been granted against the company freezing its assets. Why should not a person who stands in relation to that corporate defendant [as beneficial owner of all the shares in the company] be permitted to become a party to the action and to apply in person for a variation or discharge of the injunction? I can see no sound reason of practice, procedure or policy which obliges the court to say to the director who desires to make such an application, 'your only remedy is to put your hand in your pocket and instruct solicitors and counsel to appear on the company's behalf.' I repeat, I see no reason why an individual should be forced to incur the horrendous cost of commercial litigation if he is willing to appear in person[239].'

This discretionary approach has been followed in other common law jurisdictions, such as Australia, as the decision of the Supreme Court of Western Australia in *Eastern Metropolitan Regional Council v Four Seasons Construction Pty Ltd*[240] shows. In that case, after reviewing *Arbuthnot Leasing Ltd* and a number of Australian authorities[241], the court exercised its discretion to permit a former director to represent the company. A distinction was, however, made in that case between 'defending an action' and 'appearing for a company'. Unlike the Irish Rules of the Superior Courts 1986, the

---

238 *Arbuthnot Leasing Ltd v Havelet Leasing Ltd* [1990] BCLC 802.

239 *Abbey Films Ltd v Attorney General* [1981] IR 158 at 108–109. See also *Re a Company, ex parté F Ltd* [1991] BCLC 567.

240 *Eastern Metropolitan Regional Council v Four Seasons Construction Pty Ltd* (13 July 2000, unreported) Western Australia Supreme Court.

241 Cases reviewed were: *Hubbard Association of Scientologists International v Anderson & Just* [1972] VR 340; *Bay Marine Pty Ltd v Clayton Country Properties Pty Ltd* (1986) 8 NSWLR 104; *Molnar Engineering Pty Ltd v Burns* (1984) 3 FCR 68; *ACT General Cleaning Pty Ltd v Naoum* (1996) 67 FCR 361; *Alice Springs Abattoirs Pty Ltd v Northern Territory of Australia* (1996) 134 FLR 440; *Schagen v The Queen (1993) 8 WAR 410; and NR & NJ Gardiner & Sons Pty Ltd v Osborne Cold Stores (WA) Pty Ltd* (1988) 7 SR (WA) 62.

Western Australia Rules of Court expressly provide that a defendant to an action which is a body corporate may not enter an appearance in the action or defend it otherwise than by a solicitor. Applying this distinction, the court held that an individual could *not* submit affidavits in relation to a security for costs application as such would be to allow him to defend the proceedings. The court also held it had no jurisdiction to make any exception to this because it was a rule of court. The court went on, however, to permit the individual to *appear* as advocate on behalf of the company, having satisfied itself that that was one of the rare and exceptional circumstances where such should be permitted[242].

[6.068] Whether the Irish courts will be so willing to depart from the strict rule in *Battle* remains to be seen. There was some evidence of a relaxation of the rule (or at the least, evidence of judicial pragmatism) in the Supreme Court's decision in *DBP Construction Ltd, Hennerty & Hennerty v ICC Bank plc et al*[243]. In that case, the first plaintiff company and the Hennertys (who were the company's sole shareholding-directors) were unsuccessful in a High Court action for negligence, breach of duty and breach of contract in respect of the sale of the plaintiff company's premises. The company and the Hennertys lodged an appeal and at the hearing of the appeal the company was not represented by solicitor or counsel. In the written submissions of two of the defendants, objection was taken to the *locus standi* of the Hennertys to conduct an appeal on behalf of the company. Nevertheless, in giving the decision of the Supreme Court, Keane J reviewed extensively the findings of the trial judge and concluded that the Supreme Court could not interfere with the findings of fact and that, accordingly, the trial judge was correct in holding that there was no negligence, breach of duty or breach of contract. Keane J said:

> 'While the merits of the case were fully argued before us and it is, accordingly, appropriate that the court should come to a conclusion on them, it must, of course, be pointed out that, having regard to the decision of this court in *Battle v Irish Art Promotion Centre Ltd* [1968] IR 252 Mr Hennerty was not entitled to represent the company on the hearing of this appeal[244].'

---

242 The court held (at para 55 of the judgment): 'The weight of the evidence establishes on the balance of probabilities that the company is impecunious and cannot afford or arrange legal representation. Mr Mavlian is closely involved with the affairs of the company and has a legitimate interest in making known to those called upon to adjudicate upon the current procedural issues his view of the matters in controversy and his detailed knowledge of the history of the dispute. As mentioned earlier, I am also influenced by the precept that a party in litigation should generally not be denied an opportunity to be heard. In the exceptional circumstances of this case, where there is a very close affinity between the party to the litigation and the person who is to speak on the company's behalf, bearing in mind that the company has undertaken one project only, and that Mr Mavlian was directly involved in the implementation of the project in question, the precept I have just mentioned weighs in favour of leave being granted.

243 *DBP Construction Ltd, Hennerty & Hennerty v ICC Bank plc et al* (21 May 1998, unreported) SC, Keane J, *nem diss*.

244 *DBP Construction Ltd, Hennerty & Hennerty v ICC Bank plc et al* (21 May 1998, unreported) SC at pp 23 and 24 of the judgment.

Later, Keane J said of this and other points, that in view of the conclusions already reached, he did not find it necessary to express any view on those arguments. Accordingly, it may be concluded, that where an Irish court has substantive grounds for finding against a company, it will do so in preference to non-suiting its directors who seek to represent the company in person[245].

[6.069] It must, of course, be noted that an appeal of an earlier decision that was fully argued is more amenable to this pragmatic approach. Indeed, it is unlikely that a court of first instance would adopt the approach taken by the Supreme Court. In practice, therefore, a company which cannot afford a solicitor or counsel should seek financial assistance from its shareholders who share an interest in the success of the company.

[6.070] An exception of sorts arises where a company is charged with an indictable criminal offence and it may, by virtue of s 382 of the CA 1963, appear in court by a representative. The representative may answer questions, enter any plea, and exercise any right of objection or election on the company's behalf. The representative must be authorised by the company to appear on its behalf. Any natural person may be appointed to act as a representative, but he must be appointed in writing – although the appointment need not be under seal. Where a natural person is to be returned for trial for an indictable offence, it is generally necessary that he appear *in person*, so that questions may be put to him[246]. This rule no longer applies to companies, however, since s 382(2) of the CA 1963 empowers the District Judge to proceed, in the absence of a representative, to take depositions and to send the company forward for trial.

[G] Enforcing Judgments and Orders Against a Company.

[6.071] Common law and statute provide a variety of means by which judgments and orders may be enforced. Generally, the same principles apply in relation to enforcement against companies as apply to enforcement against natural persons. The aim here is to highlight the idiosyncrasies of and peculiarities in the enforcement of judgments and orders obtained against companies. In considering the issues arising, it is considered useful to distinguish between the enforcement of money judgments from the enforcement of court orders and non-money judgments.

(a) Enforcing money judgments against companies

[6.072] Many remedies for the enforcement of money judgments have no appreciable differences in their application to companies as compared with natural persons. Examples here include, orders for possession (in the case of secured creditors), receivers by way of equitable execution, garnishee orders, charging orders, stop notices on shares, etc[247]. Some examples of remedies, where there are peculiarities in their application to companies, include:

---

245 See also *Re Motor Racing Circuits Ltd* (31 January 1997, unreported) SC, Blayney J, nem diss.

246 See *The State (Batchelor & Co Ireland Ltd) v O'Leannain* [1957] IR 1, where, prior to the enactment of s 382 of the CA 1963, Murnaghan J held that a company could not be returned for trial on indictment because it could not appear 'in person'.

247 On receivers by way of equitable execution and garnishee orders, see generally, Courtney, *Mareva Injunctions and Related Interlocutory Orders* (1998, Butterworths) at paras [10.77] *et seq* and [10.83] *et seq*, respectively.

(i) Seizure and sale of goods by the sheriff;

(ii) Judgment mortgages;

(iii) Winding up;

(iv) Sequestration.

The primary difference between money judgments and non-money judgments is that the remedies of attachment and committal are not available in the case of judgments that require defendants to pay money[248].

(i) Seizure and sale of goods by the sheriff

[6.073] The primary method of enforcement of a judgment for the payment of money, whether into court or otherwise, is for the judgment creditor to obtain an order directed to the sheriff[249] commanding him to seize whatever goods are within his bailiwick belonging to the judgment debtor and to procure the sum due, including interest and costs, out of their sale[250]. In the High Court, the order directed to the sheriff is known as a writ of *fieri facias* (commonly abbreviated to '*fi fa*'); in the Circuit Court it is known as an execution order against the goods, and in the District Court the decree of the court itself is sent to the sheriff for execution. There are few peculiarities in the law on this method of judgment enforcement as it applies to companies. The clearest difference in the law as it applies to companies is contained in s 292 of the CA 1963, which provides that where the execution is for €25.39 or upwards, the sheriff must, *after* disposing of the seized assets, hold the proceeds for 14 days to allow for notice of a winding up of the company to be served on him. If such notice is served within that time, he must, after the deduction of his costs, pay the balance to the liquidator, who is entitled to retain it as against the execution creditor. If, however, the sheriff receives notice of the winding up *before* the sale or the completion of the execution by the receipt or the recovery of the full amount of the levy, he must deliver the goods or any money received to the liquidator without deducting the costs of the execution[251]. The costs of the execution will be a first charge on the goods or the monies so delivered, and the liquidator may sell the goods or a sufficient part thereof in order to satisfy the charge[252].

[6.074] Where a judgment creditor issues execution proceedings against a company and the company is subsequently wound up, then, under s 291 of the CA 1963, the judgment creditor shall not be entitled to retain the benefit of the execution against the liquidator in the winding up of the company unless he has completed the execution before commencement of the winding up. An execution will be deemed to be completed only where the goods have been seized and sold, or, in the case of land, where it is seized[253]. Where, however, an execution creditor has received the proceeds of the execution prior

[248] Order 42, r 7 of the RSC.

[249] Or, outside of Dublin or Cork, the County Registrar.

[250] See Ord 42, rr 13–25, and Appendix F, Part II, of the RSC 1986; Ord 33 of the Rules of the Circuit Court; and r 136 of the District Court Rules.

[251] Section 292(1) of the CA 1963. See Ch 25, *Realisation and Distribution of Assets in a Winding Up*, at para **[25.056]** *et seq*.

[252] Section 292(1) of the CA 1963. See Ch 25, *Realisation and Distribution of Assets in a Winding Up*, at para **[25.056]** *et seq*.

[253] Section 291(5) of the CA 1963.

to the commencement of the winding up, his judgment will have been discharged to that extent, and he may keep the proceeds even though the remainder of the execution has not been completed[254]. At any time after the presentation of the petition and before the winding up the court may, under s 217 of the CA 1963, restrain any action or proceeding, including execution proceedings[255], against a company.

(ii) Judgment mortgages

[6.075] A judgment creditor may apply to have his judgment or order converted into a mortgage against the land of the company under the Judgment Mortgage (Ireland) Act 1850, as amended by the Judgment Mortgage (Ireland) Act 1858[256], provided that the judgment or order requires the payment of a sum of money to the judgment creditor[257]. There are no special conditions on the registration of judgment mortgages against companies as opposed to natural persons, but it should be noted that a judgment mortgage over property comprised in a previously crystallised floating charge will rank subordinate to that floating charge[258]. It may also be noted that where a judgment mortgage is obtained against a company, s 102(1) of the CA 1963[259] provides that two copies (certified by the Land Registry or Registry of Deeds) of the affidavit required for the purpose of registering the judgment mortgage should be delivered by the judgment creditor to the company within 21 days after the date of registration; and within three days from the receipt thereof, the company must deliver one copy to the registrar of companies[260].

(iii) Winding up

[6.076] One means of enforcing a judgment that is exclusive to company debtors is a creditor's ability to petition to have the company wound up. This is comprehensively considered in Ch 23, *Winding-up Companies*.

(iv) Sequestration

[6.077] Sequestration can be used as a remedy in the case of a money judgment, but treatment of this remedy is deferred to its use in the enforcement of court orders (such as injunctions) and other non-money judgments[261].

---

254 *Re Andrew, ex parte Official Receiver* [1937] Ch 122.

255 *Re Artistic Colour Printing Co* (1880) 14 Ch D 502; see also *Pierce v Wexford House Co* [1915] 2 IR 310.

256 See generally Wylie, *Irish Land Law* (4th edn, Bloomsbury Professional, 2010) at p 867 *et seq.*

257 Sections 27 and 28 of the Debtors (Ireland) Act 1840; s 6 of the Judgment Mortgage (Ireland) Act 1850.

258 *Eyre v McDowell* (1861) 9 HL Cas 619.

259 See, generally, Ch 19, *Corporate Borrowing: Registration of Charges*, at para **[19.085]**.

260 The Land Registry and the Registry of Deeds are also obliged to deliver a copy of the affidavit to the registrar of companies.

261 See para **[6.100]**.

(b) *Enforcing court orders and judgments*[262]

[6.078] The enforcement of court orders and judgments against companies is regulated by Ord 42, r 32 of the RSC 1986[263]. This provides:

> 'Any judgment or order against a company wilfully disobeyed may, by leave of the court, be enforced by sequestration against the corporate property, or by attachment against the directors or other officers thereof, or by order of sequestration of their property.'

Central to the operation of Ord 42, r 32 is that a judgment or order must be '*wilfully disobeyed*', a matter considered in detail below[264]. Where a judgment or order is not wilfully disobeyed, the party who obtained it against the company will have to look elsewhere to enforce the judgment or order. Further, a company's inability to pay a money judgment against it will not result in 'wilful disobeyance' and will not give rise to its officers being attached[265]. The most obvious example of a court order is an injunction of any nature but there may also be a statutory basis for making an order. In *The Environmental Protection Agency v Neiphin Trading Ltd et al*, it has been held that that there is no jurisdiction to make 'fall-back' orders (where the veil of incorporation is lifted and directors and shareholders of a company are personally ordered to comply with an order) under the Waste Management Act 1996[266].

[6.079] In this section the following issues are considered:

(i) Proving 'wilful disobeyance' of judgments and orders by companies;
(ii) The standard of proof: beyond reasonable doubt;
(iii) Wilful disobeyance due to employees' acts or omissions;
(iv) Breach of undertakings given in lieu of court orders;
(v) Attachment of a company's officers;
(vi) Sequestration of companies' and their officers' assets;
(vii) Fining companies and their officers.

(i) Proving 'wilful disobeyance' of judgments and orders by companies

[6.080] The use of the word 'wilful' in Ord 42, r 7 of the RSC and in the English RSC, prior to 1965, has proven troublesome[267] and was removed from the English Rules in 1965. The correct meaning of the expression is seen in the judgment of Warrington J in *Stancomb v Trowbridge*[268] where he said in a passage quoted with approval in *The Competition Authority and The Licensed Vintners Association*[269] by McKechnie J:

---

262 The remainder of this chapter is based upon Ch 12 of Courtney, *Mareva Injunctions and Related Interlocutory Orders* (1998, Butterworths).

263 See Ó Floinn, *Practice and Procedure in the Superior Courts* (2nd edn, Bloomsbury Professional, 2008) at p 399.

264 See para **[6.080]**.

265 See para **[6.081]**.

266 See Ch 5, *Disregarding Separate Legal Personality*, at para **[5.066]**.

267 See Courtney, *Mareva Injunctions and Related Interlocutory Orders* (1998, Butterworths) at para [12.24] to [12.26] where the decisions in *AG v Walthamstow UDC* [1895] 11 TLR 533; *Fairclough & Sons v Manchester Ship Canal Co (No 2)* [1897] WN 7; and *Stancomb v Trowbridge UDC* [1910] 2 Ch 190 are considered.

268 *Stancomb v Trowbridge* [1910] 2 Ch 190.

269 *The Competition Authority and The Licensed Vintners Association* [2009] IEHC 439.

> '... if a person or a corporation is restrained by injunction from doing a particular act, that person or corporation commits a breach of the injunction, and is liable for process for contempt, if he or it in fact does the act, and it is no answer to say that the act was not contumacious in the sense that, in doing it, there was no direct intention to disobey the order ...
>
> I think the expression 'wilfully' ... is intended to exclude only such casual or accidental and unintentional acts ...'

This interpretation was endorsed by the English House of Lords in *Heatons Transport (St Helens) Ltd v Transport and General Workers' Union*[270], which was also cited with approval by McKechnie J in *The Competition Authority and The Licensed Vintners Association*[271], where Lord Wilberforce said that Warrington J's view as to the meaning of 'wilful':

> '... has thus acquired high authority. It is also the reasonable view, because the party in whose favour an order of a court has been made is entitled to have it enforced, and also the effective administration of justice normally requires some penalty for disobedience to an order of a court if the disobedience is more than casual or accidental or unintentional.'

It is thought that this is the correct interpretation of the meaning and significance of 'wilful', and that Ord 42, r 32 of the RSC would be so construed by the Irish courts. Support for this view can be taken from the Supreme Court's decision in *Irish Shell Ltd v Ballylynch Motors Ltd and Morris Oil Company Ltd*[272], where Ord 42, r 32 was in issue. There, Costello P had found three of the directors of the second defendant company to be in contempt of court and had fined each of them £1,000. Their contempt arose from an injunction made by the High Court which restrained the second defendant company from providing to the first defendant company or any other persons, motor fuels for resale from premises bearing the plaintiff's livery, trademark and logo and which were also under contract to the plaintiff for the exclusive sale of 'Shell' brand motor fuels. In breach of the injunction the second defendant had supplied motor fuels to a third party whose premises was also under contract with the plaintiff for the exclusive sale of 'Shell' products. The defence tendered was that the third party, who had been supplied by the second defendant, had represented that it was out of contract with the plaintiff. On appeal to the Supreme Court the second defendant's directors' counsel argued that none of the directors were wilfully in breach of the injunction, as was required by Ord 42, r 32[273]. The plaintiff's counsel contended that the directors had a duty to be aware of what was being done by their company and that because they had taken no steps in that behalf, they were, accordingly, answerable for the breach of the injunction[274]. In his judgment for the Supreme Court Lynch J held that Costello P was entitled to conclude that the second defendant had wilfully disobeyed the order and that

---

270 *Heatons Transport (St Helens) Ltd v Transport and General Workers' Union* [1972] 3 All ER 101.

271 *The Competition Authority and The Licensed Vintners Association* [2009] IEHC 439.

272 *Irish Shell Ltd v Ballylynch Motors Ltd and Morris Oil Company Ltd* (5 March 1997, unreported) SC, Lynch J, *nem diss*.

273 Relying upon *Ronson Products Ltd v Ronson Furniture Ltd* [1966] 2 All ER 381 and *Halsbury's Laws of England* (Simmonds edn) Vol 9 at p 26.

274 Relying upon Borrie & Lowe, *The Law of Contempt* (Butterworths) at p 567 *and Biba Ltd v Stratford Investments Ltd* [1972] 3 All ER 1041.

the directors were liable to attachment or fine in lieu thereof. He said that once the second defendant had been requested to supply motor fuels to a premises which bore the plaintiff's 'Shell' logo then:

> '... they must as a matter of common sense make all necessary and proper enquiries to ensure that the premises are no longer tied to the plaintiffs and are free to accept the second defendant's motor fuels. If a company operating tied premises in the plaintiff's livery, trademark and logo requests the second defendants to supply motor fuels to them for resale it is wholly inadequate to rely solely upon that company's assurances that they are not tied ...
>
> Nothing whatever was done by the [appellant directors] to check the accuracy and reliability of the assurances given to them by the consignee company ... and to ensure that a delivery of motor fuels to them did not contravene the order ...[275]'

A breach of an injunction will be 'wilful' if it is anything other than casual, accidental or unintentional. 'Wilful' is not to be construed as intentional; a careless disregard as to whether a court order is respected or breached can amount to a wilful breach. On the contrary, the applicable test is objective. In *The Competition Authority and The Licensed Vintners Association*[276], McKechnie J said that in that case it was not disputed by the parties 'that no distinction should be made between "disobeyance" *simpliciter* and "wilful disobeyance" for the purposes of determining breach: Order 42, rule 32'.

[6.081] In *Sligo Corporation v Cartron Bay Construction Ltd, Maguire and Maguire*[277], the applicant local authority applied for an order of attachment and sequestration against the first respondent company and the second and third respondents who were two of its directors. The application arose out of the failure to complete certain works detailed in a schedule to a previous High Court order, in accordance with a planning permission that had been issued to the respondent company. The required works related to a particular housing estate and included works relating to roads, footpaths, sewers and manholes. The applicant local authority claimed that the company had failed to comply with the terms of the order and asserted its belief that the respondent company and its directors were in 'wilful disobedience' of the court's order. It was also claimed that the disobedience with the order was not caused by reason of any negligence or mismanagement but by premeditated wilfulness and an anxiety to frustrate the applicant's rights and those of the residents. Moreover, it was claimed that the directors had an intimate knowledge of the company's affairs and that they were solely responsible for deciding the recalcitrant policy of wilful disobedience. In addition to denying all impropriety and asserting that the court order had not been wilfully disobeyed, it was contended that the company was insolvent and therefore unable to carry out the terms of the order. Citing *Lewis v Pontypridd Caerphilly and Newport Railway Company*[278], Ó Caoimh J accepted that an order or judgment cannot be said to have been wilfully disobeyed if compliance was impossible on account of a lack of

---

[275] *Irish Shell Ltd v Ballylynch Motors Ltd and Morris Oil Company Ltd* (5 March 1997, unreported) SC, Lynch J, *nem diss* at pp 5 and 6 of the transcript.

[276] *The Competition Authority and The Licensed Vintners Association* [2009] IEHC 439.

[277] *Sligo Corporation v Cartron Bay Construction Ltd, Maguire and Maguire* [2001] IEHC 94, Ó Caoimh J.

[278] *Lewis v Pontypridd Caerphilly and Newport Railway Company* 1 ITLR 203.

funds. It was, however, also noted that the burden of proving impossibility of compliance rested on the company and its directors[279]. Ó Caoimh J concluded that the company's directors had not accounted to the company for certain money, that this had resulted in the company being unable to pay for the construction of the works in question and, on that basis, that a case had been made for the sequestration and attachment of the respondents.

[6.082] In order for a company to wilfully breach a court order or judgment, it must be *on notice* of the terms of that order or judgment. Service of any order or judgment on a company is regulated by s 379 of the CA 1963, considered above[280]. In addition to formally *serving* a company with the terms of an order or judgment, it is thought that persons who obtain such orders are well advised to seek to place a company's directors and other officers *on actual notice* of the order or judgment and to indicate to them that, if the injunction is breached, they may be attached and fined and their property sequestrated.[281]. Unlike England and Wales, there is no Irish equivalent to Ord 45, r 7 of the English Rules of the Supreme Court 1965, which provide, *inter alia*, for the personal service of a court order, such as an injunction, on an officer of the company. The indication on the face of a court order, that a person is liable to be imprisoned for breach of the order, is termed a 'penal notice'[282].

(ii) The standard of proof: beyond reasonable doubt

[6.083] The standard of proof required to find that a defendant has breached an injunction or other order of the court – and thereby committed civil contempt of court – could either be the usual criminal standard of 'beyond reasonable doubt' or the usual civil standard of 'on the balance of probabilities'. In England[283], it has been established that the standard of proof required to be shown in order that a defendant be found to be in contempt of court is that applicable to criminal cases, namely, '*beyond all reasonable doubt*'[284], and McKechnie J in *The Competition Authority and The Licensed Vintners Association*[285] held that this is also the standard of proof in Ireland[286]. In that case, both sides agreed that given the criminal nature of contempt proceedings, the standard of

---

279 See *Guilford Borough Council v Smith et al* (1993) The Times, 18 May.

280 See para **[6.011]**.

281 For an instances where directors were fined where their company breached the terms of an injunction (not a *Mareva*) see *Irish Shell Ltd v Ballylynch Motors Ltd* (5 March 1997, unreported) SC.

282 The foregoing paragraph is, in the main, a verbatim transcript of para [12.14] of Courtney, *Mareva Injunctions and Related Interlocutory Orders* (1998, Butterworths).

283 See generally, Lowe & Sufrin, *Borrie & Lowe The Law of Contempt* (3rd edn, Butterworths, 1996) at p 565–569.

284 See also *Re Bramblevale Ltd* [1970] Ch 128; see Courtney, *Mareva Injunctions and Related Interlocutory Orders* (1998, Butterworths) at para [12.21].

285 *The Competition Authority and The Licensed Vintners Association* [2009] IEHC 439.

286 See also *Muller v Shell E&P Ireland Ltd* [2010] IEHC 238, *Brightwater v Allen & Robert Walters Ltd* [2005] IEHC 155 (Laffoy J); *Cooke v Cooke & Cooke* [1919] 1 IR 227 at 249 and *Orion Pictures Corporation v Hickey* (18 January 1991, unreported) HC, at p 2 of the judgment where Costello J said, of the defendant in a motion for committal for contempt of court (through breach of an *Anton Piller* order), that he was '... satisfied beyond a reasonable doubt that Mr Hickey was in very serious contempt of both of these orders'.

proof in relation to facts is beyond reasonable doubt. However, the Competition Authority argued that once the facts had been established or otherwise admitted to that level, the follow-on question of whether, as a matter of law, there had been a contempt can be determined by reference to the civil standard – the balance of probabilities. McKechnie J refused to follow the line of authority[287] which supported a twin standard approach, instead preferring the authorities which made it clear that the relevant standard is beyond reasonable doubt and that applied to all matters at issue, both factual and legal[288]:

> 'The overwhelming preponderance of case law is to this effect: *Re Bramblevale Ltd* is a clear-cut example espousing the higher standard: *National Irish Bank Ltd* is a clear-cut example of the application of this standard in practice; Keane J, as he then was, despite very strong circumstantial evidence of a breach, refused to attach as the required matters had not been established beyond a reasonable doubt. The only contrary view of note is Millett J's decision in *Chelsea Man plc* where the standard of '*degree and impression*' is suggested. If that view cannot be explained by reference to its own facts, and if the citation of *Bramblevale* and *Dean* to the court would have made no difference, then respectfully I would have to prefer the alternative view. I believe that the criticism offered of that decision by Arlidge, Eady & Smith is sound and accords with established practice. Moreover, I have to say that even if this area had not been touched by authority, I would have come to the same conclusion on first principles[289].'

(iii) Wilful disobeyance due to employees' acts or omissions

[6.084] Where it is found that a court order or judgment, directed at a company, is 'wilfully disobeyed', it must also be shown that the conduct which led to the breach was the *act of the company* and not, say, the act of an employee of the company acting outside the scope of his employment or, to use the colloquial favoured in this context, 'on a frolic of his own'[290]. Although a company can only act through its directors, officers and employees, not every act of its directors, officers or employees can be attributed to the company[291]. It seems reasonably straightforward that where a company's board of directors causes a company to act in breach of an injunction or other court order, the company itself will be found to have been in breach of the order and in contempt of court[292]. What is less clear is where the breach of an injunction or other court order is occasioned by the actions of persons, such as employees, who may not have authority to bind the company. Moreover, the legal consequences which follow

---

287 *Chelsea Man plc v Chelsea Girl Ltd* [1988] FSR 217.

288 *National Irish Bank Ltd v Graham* [1994] 1 IR 215; *Dean v Dean* [1987] 1 FLR 55; and *Re Bramblevale Ltd* [1970] Ch 128.

289 *The Competition Authority and the Licensed Vintners Association* [2009] IEHC 439 at para 27 of the judgment.

290 *Cf Stancomb v Trowbridge UDC* [1910] 2 Ch 190. In the course of his judgment in that case Warrington J had said of a body corporate that: 'Such a body can only act by its agents or servants, and I think, if the act is in fact done, it is no answer to say that, done, as it must be, by an officer or servant of the council, the council is not liable for it, even though it may have been done by the servant through carelessness, neglect, or even in dereliction of his duty.'

291 See generally, Ch 7, *Corporate Contracts, Capacity and Authority*, at para **[7.100]** *et seq*.

292 A company's directors or other officers may also be liable for the breach: see para **[6.095]**.

where a company's shareholders vote in such a manner as to cause their company to breach a court order or undertaking is considered below[293].

[6.085] Where the act or omission which amounts to a breach of the injunction or other court order is caused by a company's employee, as opposed to a director or senior manager with power to bind the company, difficult questions are raised. Should a company be found to be in contempt of court if its directors or other senior management expressly instruct the company's employees not to act in breach of a court order? This was the question in issue in *Director General of Fair Trading v Smiths Concrete Ltd*[294]. In that case, the company was subject to orders of the Restrictive Practices Court which restrained it from, *inter alia*, 'giving effect to or enforcing or purporting to enforce, whether by itself, its servants or agents or otherwise', agreements with other companies relating to the supply of ready-mixed concrete in contravention of s 35(1) of the UK's Restrictive Practices Act 1976. It was held by the Court of Appeal that the company itself did not breach the order because, *inter alia*, there should be a *mens rea* on the part of the contemnor. There, Lord Donaldson MR said:

> 'It is an essential prerequisite to a finding of contempt that the factual basis shall have been proved beyond all reasonable doubt and that there shall have been *mens rea* on the part of the alleged contemnor. *Mens rea* in this context does not mean a wilful intention to disobey the court's order, but an intention to do the act which constitutes the disobedience with knowledge of the terms of the order, although not necessarily an understanding that the act is prohibited[295].'

In relation to a company's employees, the Court of Appeal, *per* Lord Donaldson MR said:

> 'Whether X is doing an act by the instrumentality of its servants or agents will depend upon the scope of their mandate. This will be judged in the light of reality rather than form. If X should have appreciated that the servant or agent would be likely to do the prohibited act unless dissuaded by X, the act will be regarded as being within the scope of that mandate if X has not taken all reasonable steps to prevent it. Such steps may in appropriate cases involve far more than express prohibition and extend to elaborate monitoring and compliance machinery and procedures and the creation of positive incentives designed to dissuade the servant or agent.
>
> If the mandate of the servant or agent has been effectively restricted, *ie* all reasonable steps have been taken to achieve this objective, X may nevertheless be answerable to third parties for damage suffered in consequence of the acts of the servant or agent, if it can be said that X put him in a position to do them. This is to be distinguished from answerability for acts done by X personally through the instrumentality of his servants or agents and does not involve a disobedience by X of the court's orders or any liability in contempt[296].'

This was the state of the art English judicial thinking on this point when the first edition of this work was published. The decision of the Court of Appeal was, however, overruled by the House of Lords in *Re the Supply of Ready Mixed Concrete (No 2);*

---

293 See *Northern Counties Securities Ltd v Jackson & Steeple Ltd* [1974] 2 All ER 625 and generally, at para **[6.090]**.

294 *Director General of Fair Trading v Smiths Concrete Ltd* [1991] 4 All ER 150.

295 *Director General of Fair Trading v Smiths Concrete Ltd* [1991] 4 All ER 150 at 168.

296 *Director General of Fair Trading v Smiths Concrete Ltd* [1991] 4 All ER 150 at 168.

Director General of Fair Trading v Pioneer Concrete (UK) Ltd and another[297]. Following the Court of Appeal's decision, certain other companies, which had at first instance been found to be in contempt of court for breach of the order, were given leave to appeal out of time and were successful before the Court of Appeal[298]. The matter eventually came before the House of Lords. After reviewing the authorities against[299] and for[300] finding the companies liable for contempt of court, the House of Lords held that where a breach of a court order is committed by an employee, a company will be liable for the breach even though the employee was expressly forbidden by the company to do the act prohibited by the court order, provided that the employee was acting within the scope of his employment. In so holding, Lord Nolan expressly endorsed the decision of Warrington J in *Stancomb v Trowbridge UDC*[301] and held that Lord Wilberforce's judgment in *Heatons Transport (St Helens) Ltd v Transport and General Workers' Union*[302]was not inconsistent with Warrington J's decision. Lord Nolan said:

> 'Given that liability for contempt does not require any direct intention on the part of the employer to disobey the order, there is nothing to prevent an employing company from being found to have disobeyed an order 'by' its servant as a result of a deliberate act by the servant on its behalf. In my judgment, the decision in *Stancomb v Trowbridge UDC* is good law and should be followed in the present case.'

It is thought that to find a company liable for contempt for its employees' acts or omissions, *in circumstances where there is clear evidence that the company expressly prohibited those employees from doing such acts*, is wrong in principle and it is further submitted that the decision of the House of Lords in *Re the Supply of Ready Mixed Concrete (No 2)* ought not be followed in Ireland.

[6.086] The following criticisms may be made of the House of Lords' decision in *Re the Supply of Ready Mixed Concrete (No 2)*[303]. In the first place, the *Stancomb* case is only authority for the proposition that the sole significance attaching to the word 'wilfully' is to exclude casual, accidental and unintentional acts which constitute disobedience. Secondly, Warrington J did not say that a company or other body corporate would be in contempt of court where its employees acted in breach of a court order in circumstances where those in authority expressly prohibited such employees from doing such acts. Thirdly, it is thought that there is much sense in the following statement of the law by

---

297 *Re the Supply of Ready Mixed Concrete (No 2); Director General of Fair Trading v Pioneer Concrete (UK) Ltd and another* [1995] 1 All ER 135.

298 *Re the Supply of Ready Mixed Concrete (No 2); Director General of Fair Trading v Pioneer Concrete (UK) Ltd and another* [1994] ICR 57.

299 The earlier Court of Appeal decision in *Smith's case* [1994] 4 All ER 150; *Tesco Supermarkets Ltd v Natrass* [1971] 2 All ER 127.

300 *Rantzen v Rothchild* (1865) 14 WR 96; *Stancomb v Trowbridge UDC* [1910] 2 Ch 190; *Heatons Transport (St Helens) Ltd v Transport and General Workers' Union* [1972] 3 All ER 101.

301 *Stancomb v Trowbridge UDC* [1910] 2 Ch 190.

302 *Heatons Transport (St Helens) Ltd v Transport and General Workers' Union* [1972] 3 All ER 101.

303 See Courtney, *Mareva Injunctions and Related Interlocutory Orders* (1998, Butterworths) at para [12.30]. This paragraph has been reproduced verbatim.

Slade J in *Hone v Page*[304] (a passage cited with approval by the Court of Appeal in *Attorney General for Tuvalu and another v Philatelic Distribution Corp Ltd et al*[305]):

> 'I think that a man must be deemed to do a relevant act 'by his servants or agents'... if (a) the persons who did the acts were his servants or agents, (b) the acts were done in the course of the service or agency, and (c) he either (i) authorised the acts or (ii) could reasonably have foreseen the possibility of such acts and failed to take all reasonable steps to prevent them.'

It would seem that the House of Lords paid no regard at all to basic agency principles[306]. Fourthly, the 'deliberate act' of a company's employee cannot, in justice, be the sole determinant for holding that company to have been in contempt of court. Matters such as whether the employee was acting within the course of his employment, his or her 'apparent competence'[307] and whether the company *genuinely* exhorted the employee not to act in breach of an injunction or other order of the court *must* be material considerations. It is thought that where these circumstances are found to exist, the appropriate finding is that the company as principal is not in contempt of court, although the employee personally may well be in contempt of court as a third party who knowingly obstructs or frustrates the object of the injunction or other order[308].

(iv) Breach of undertakings given in lieu of court orders

[6.087] In *The Competition Authority and The Licensed Vintners Association*[309], McKechnie J held that:

> 'for the purpose of enforcement no distinction arises between an undertaking, an injunction and a court order: all can be treated as equal for attachment and sequestration purposes.'

McKechnie J quoted with approval the following passage from the decision of Sir John Donaldson MR in *Hussain v Hussain*[310]:

> 'Let it be stated in the clearest possible terms that an undertaking to the court is as solemn, binding and effective as an order of the court.'

---

304 *Hone v Page* [1980] FSR 500.

305 *Attorney General for Tuvalu and another v Philatelic Distribution Corp Ltd et al* [1990] 2 All ER 216 at 222.

306 See generally Wickins & Ong, 'Confusion Worse Confounded: The End of the Directing Mind Theory?' [1997] JBL 524.

307 Where a firm of solicitors employed an 'apparently competent' solicitor it was found that they had taken all reasonable care and that they were not in contempt of court: see the decision of Skinner J in *TDK Tape Distributor (UK) Ltd v Videochoice Ltd et al* [1985] 3 All ER 345.

308 The liability of companies *as third parties* to a court order or judgment in respect of the default of their employees is considered in Courtney, *Mareva Injunctions and Related Interlocutory Orders* (1998, Butterworths) at paras [12.38]–[12.42], generally, but with particular emphasis on *Mareva* injunctions.

309 *The Competition Authority and The Licensed Vintners Association* [2009] IEHC 439.

310 *Hussain v Hussain* [1986] 1 All ER 961 at 963. Also cited was *London & Birmingham Railway v Grand Junction Canal Co* (1835) 1 Ry CA 224.

In *AG v Wheatley & Co Ltd*[311], Warrington J said:

> 'The practice of the Court of Chancery was not to treat an undertaking as distinct from an injunction with regard to breach, and for the purpose of enforcing an undertaking that undertaking is equivalent to an order – that is to say, an undertaking, if broken, would involve the same consequences on the persons breaking the undertaking as would their disobedience to an order for an injunction[312].'

Undertakings given on behalf of companies raise particular issues. Insofar as it is accepted that an undertaking by a company has the same effect as a court order, it was held in England in *Biba Ltd v Stratford Investments Ltd*[313] that the Rules of the Supreme Court should be construed as applying to undertakings. In Ireland, under the RSC, it is a prerequisite to a company, or its directors or other officers, being sanctioned for contempt of court that the order of the court has been '*wilfully disobeyed*'[314].

[6.088] An undertaking given by or on behalf of a company must be properly authorised by those with authority in the company. In most private companies the board of directors will be the most appropriate organ to authorise (by resolution) the giving of an undertaking. A company's board may, however, delegate the actual authority to any person to give such an undertaking. It is thought that a director of a private company, present in court at the hearing of an application may be said to have ostensible (if he does not, in fact, have actual) authority to bind his company[315]. By contrast, an ordinary employee would not have ostensible authority, although if properly authorised, he may have the actual authority to give an undertaking. An undertaking given by a company's solicitor or counsel is enforceable against a company because they are the company's agents in the cause or matter.

[6.089] Notwithstanding English authority, apparently to the contrary[316], it is thought that a company will not be liable in contempt for breaching an undertaking *in lieu* of an injunction or other court order where breach is occasioned by employees acting contrary to express instructions. It is thought that the situation whereby a company fails to take 'adequate and continuing steps to ensure'[317] that its obligations under an undertaking are complied with, must be distinguished from a situation whereby a company's employees

311 *AG v Wheatley & Co Ltd* (1903) 48 Sol Jo 116. Applied in *Biba Ltd v Stratford Investments Ltd* [1972] 3 All ER 1041.

312 Warrington J went on to cite *London and Birmingham Railway Co v Grand Junction Canal Co* (1835) 1 Ry & Can Cas 224 where it was said that: '... an undertaking is equivalent to an injunction, and, if violated, may be the subject of an application to this court.'

313 *Biba Ltd v Stratford Investments Ltd* [1972] 3 All ER 1041.

314 Order 42, r 32 of the RSC, see para **[6.078]**.

315 On actual and ostensible authority of corporate officers see Ch 7, *Corporate Contracts, Capacity and Authority*, at para **[7.100]**.

316 In *Re Garage Equipment Associations' Agreement* (1964) LP 4 RP 491, Megaw J said (at 504): 'The court is prepared to accept that none of the officers of the company individually knew or realised that an undertaking given to the court was being broken or had been broken. But that does not in any way detract from the fact that the company – and this motion is only concerned with the company – was in contempt of court by these things being done when an undertaking had been given on behalf of the company and the company was aware of the existence of that undertaking.'

317 *Re Galvanised Tank Manufacturers' Association's Agreement* [1965] 2 All ER 1003.

cause an undertaking to be breached when acting outside the scope of their employment[318].

[6.090] It has been held that where a company's shareholders cause a company to act in breach of an undertaking they, the shareholders, will not be liable for contempt of court[319]. In *Northern Counties Securities Ltd v Jackson & Steeple Ltd*[320], the defendant company undertook to the court to use its best endeavours to apply for a stock exchange quotation, and within 28 days of such quotation being obtained, to allot and issue shares to the plaintiff and not to increase the authorised share capital of the company or to do any other thing requiring the shareholders' authority in general meeting. Subsequently, the defendant company discovered that the stock exchange required that the issue of shares be subject to the consent of the 'company in general meeting'. The defendant company's directors initially failed to give notice of an extraordinary general meeting. At the plaintiff's prompting, they did eventually convene the meeting. Contrary to the company's undertaking the resolutions proposed (i) that the company's share capital be increased by 370,000 ordinary shares ranking *pari passu* as to dividend with the existing ordinary shares; and (ii) that the directors be authorised to issue those shares fully paid to the plaintiff. The text of the proposed resolutions was accompanied by a circular which stated that having taken a leading counsel's advice on the court order and the company's undertaking, the shareholders were free to vote as they wished. The directors also said that they were making no recommendation to the shareholders and were leaving the decision on how to vote to their individual judgment. Moreover, the directors advised that if the resolutions were passed the company would have to pay £300,873 for an asset it had acquired from the plaintiff but that if they were not passed, the cost would be approximately £183,873. The plaintiff objected to the terms of what was circulated by the directors to the shareholders. Walton J held that the circular did not comply with the undertaking of the company to use its best endeavours to have the shareholders pass a resolution to issue shares to the plaintiff and that it ought to have been couched in more positive terms; he also held, *inter alia*, that the resolution to increase the company's share capital was a breach of the company's undertaking. More significantly for present purposes, however, was the finding by Walton J that the shareholders would *not* be in contempt of court if they voted against the resolution to issue shares to the plaintiff. In distinguishing the position of a director who votes, at a *directors' meeting*, against his company complying with a court order or undertaking to court, Walton J rejected the submission that a shareholder who votes, at a *members' meeting*, against a course of action required to comply with a court order or undertaking would be 'a step taken by him knowingly which would prevent the company from fulfilling its undertaking to the court'[321]. Walton J said:

> 'When a director votes as a director for or against any particular resolution in a directors' meeting, he is voting as a person under a fiduciary duty to the company for the proposition that the company should take a certain course of action. When a shareholder is voting for or against a particular resolution he is voting as a person owing no fiduciary duty to the company who is exercising his own right of property to vote as he thinks fit.

---

[318] *Cf Re the Supply of Ready Mixed Concrete (No 2)* [1995] 1 All ER 135.

[319] The principle here is equally applicable to a Court order made against a company.

[320] *Northern Counties Securities Ltd v Jackson & Steeple Ltd* [1974] 2 All ER 625.

[321] *Northern Counties Securities Ltd v Jackson & Steeple Ltd* [1974] 2 All ER 625 at 635a.

> The fact that the result of the voting at the meeting (or subsequent poll) will bind the company cannot affect the position that in voting he is voting simply as an exercise of his own property rights.
>
> ... a director is an agent, who casts his vote to decide in what manner his principal shall act through the collective agency of the board of directors; a shareholder who casts his vote in general meeting is not casting it as an agent of the company in any shape or form. His act, therefore, in voting as he pleases cannot in any way be regarded as an act of the company[322].'

In so finding he concluded:

> 'It is, I think, equally clear that the shareholders are not abetting the company to commit a contempt of court; the company is, indeed, by convening the requisite meeting and putting a positive circular before the members duly complying with the obligations which rest on it. It will have done its best, and the rest is in the lap of the gods in the shape of the individual decisions of the members.
>
> It would, of course, be otherwise if one could envisage any circumstances in which an order was made by the courts on a company to do something, for example, to increase its capital (as distinct from using its best endeavours to increase its capital), which must of necessity involve the shareholders voting in a particular manner. But I at any rate cannot envisage any ordinary resolution (as distinct from, for example, a situation where all the shareholders were before the court and bound by the order) where such an order would ever be made[323].'

[6.091] This decision might at first appear to be at odds with the general principle that a third party will be in contempt of court for aiding and abetting the breach of a court order or obstructing or frustrating a court order[324]. All other things being equal, however, it is thought that there is no conflict between these two principles. First, an individual shareholder who casts his vote in such a manner as to *indirectly* cause a company to act in breach of a court order is acting in furtherance of his own property rights – it would be unjust to expect a shareholder who is not directly party to the matter which gave rise to the court order or undertaking by the company to sacrifice his own interests in favour of another party's interests. Second, it may be considered that a court order or undertaking in such circumstances *implicitly* acknowledges that the company will abide by same to the extent that such is within its own remit – because it must be acknowledged that a shareholder can act in his own interests, to so act cannot be a contempt of court.

[6.092] In circumstances where a company's shareholders are different persons to a company's directors, it is thought that the foregoing manifestly represents good law. What may be seen as less clear is where the directors and shareholders are one and the same persons, as may be the case in a small, closely-held private company, which may even be run on the basis of a 'quasi-partnership'. In such a case it may be argued that it would be unconscionable for the directors, wearing their shareholders' hats, to cast their vote in such a manner as to cause the company to breach a court order or undertaking.

---

322 *Northern Counties Securities Ltd v Jackson & Steeple Ltd* [1974] 2 All ER 625 at 635e-g.

323 *Northern Counties Securities Ltd v Jackson & Steeple Ltd* [1974] 2 All ER 625 at 636a-b.

324 See Courtney, *Mareva Injunctions and Related Interlocutory Orders* (1998, Butterworths) at para [12.31] *et seq*.

To that extend, the finding by Walton J in *Northern Counties Securities Ltd v Jackson & Steeple Ltd*[325] that a director may, wearing his shareholder's hat, vote as he pleases, can be doubted. He said there that:

> 'I think that a director who has fulfilled his duty as a director of a company by causing it to comply with an undertaking binding on it is nevertheless free, as an individual shareholder, to enjoy the same unfettered right of voting at general meetings of the members of the company as he would have if he were not also a director.'

Where, on the facts of a case, the directors' conduct is found to be fraudulent or unconscionable, it is thought that it is open to a court to disregard which particular 'hat' a person is wearing on the same grounds as a court can disregard a company's separate legal personality. In so finding that a director-shareholder is in contempt of court, the court would, in effect, be lifting the corporate veil on grounds of fraud or circumvention of an existing legal obligation[326].

[6.093] Another possible situation where a company's shareholders may be found to be in contempt of court is where they vote to cause a company to breach a court order or undertaking, without any personal gain, and where the dominant purpose of their action was spiteful or malicious. Were this basis to be found sufficient to deem shareholders to be in contempt of court, it could apply to large companies with unconnected membership and not be confined to small closely-held companies. One practical problem with this ground as a basis for finding shareholders in contempt of court is that it is notoriously difficult to establish a 'dominant intention'.

[6.094] It should also be remembered that a person who is a director or controlling shareholder in a company can be made the subject of a court order if their acts or omissions may them a joint tortfeasor with their company. In *Tommy Hilfiger Europe Inc and another v Derek McGarry t/a 'Lifejacket' and others*[327], Carroll J made an order personally against the first defendant, citing with approval the following passage in *MCA Records Inc et al v Charly Records Ltd*[328] from the decision of Chadwick LJ:

> '... there is no reason why a person who happens to be a director or controlling shareholder of a company should not be liable with the company as a joint tortfeasor if he is not exercising control through the constitutional organs of the company and the circumstances are such that he would be so liable if he were not a director or a controlling shareholder. In other words, if, in relation to the wrongful acts which are the subject of complaint, the liability of the individual as a joint tortfeasor with the company arises from his participation or involvement in ways which go beyond the exercise of constitutional control, then there is no reason why the individual should escape liability because he would have procured those same acts through the exercise of constitutional control ...'

Given that it appears that the first defendant to the proceedings was Mr McGarry, it is not clear from the judgment why this issue arose. Moreover, it is submitted that before any order can be directed at any person, whether it be a company, a director or a

---

325 *Northern Counties Securities Ltd v Jackson & Steeple Ltd* [1974] 2 All ER 625.

326 On the grounds for lifting the veil and disregarding a company's separate legal personality, see Ch 5, *Disregarding Separate Corporate Personality*, at para **[5.039]**.

327 *Tommy Hilfiger Europe Inc and another v Derek McGarry t/a 'Lifejacket' and others* [2005] IEHC 66 (Carroll J).

328 *MCA Records Inc et al v Charly Records Ltd* [2003] 2 BCLC 93.

shareholder, there must be a substantive cause of action in existence against that person and proceedings in being.

(v) Attachment of a company's officers

[6.095] It will be noticed that Ord 42, r 32 of the RSC only makes provision for attachment and not the 'more stringent remedy'[329] of committal[330] of a company's officers. An order for *attachment* directs the person against whom the order is directed to be brought before the court to answer the contempt in respect of which the order is issued[331]. An order for *committal* directs that upon the arrest of the person against whom the order is directed, he 'shall be lodged in prison until he purge his contempt and is discharged pursuant to further order of the Court'[332]. It has been said, however, that the only practical difference between attachment and committal concerns the manner of enforcement: attachment was enforced by the sheriff and committal was enforced by the tipstaff[333]. Even this distinction no longer holds true in Ireland, since the rules provide that every order of attachment or committal shall be directed to the Commissioner and members of An Garda Síochána[334]. In the case of an application for an order of either 'attachment' or 'committal' the effect may be the same: the contemnor may be committed to prison. Order 44, r 4 of the RSC concerns *attachment*. It provides:

> 'When the person against whom an order of attachment is directed is brought before the Court on his arrest, the Court may either discharge him on such terms and conditions as to costs or otherwise as it thinks fit or commit him to prison for his contempt either for a definite period to be specified in the order, or until he shall purge his contempt and be discharged by further order of the Court.'

In the case of an order of attachment, an alleged contemnor is brought before the court to answer his contempt. He is thereby given an opportunity, prior to being incarcerated, to explain his actions or omissions which are alleged to have caused the court's order to have been breached[335]. An order of committal directs that a contemnor be summarily lodged in prison: he will not have an opportunity to answer his contempt unless he applies to vary the order. Although it may well transpire to be the prelude to committal, an 'attachment' order can therefore be considered to be a lesser order than a 'committal'

---

329 *Per* Ronan LJ in *Cooke v Cooke & Cooke* [1919] 1 IR 227 at 241.

330 As to the distinction between 'attachment' and 'committal' see Courtney, *Mareva Injunctions and Related Interlocutory Orders* (1998, Butterworths) at para [12.54].

331 Order 44, r 1.

332 Order 44, r 2.

333 *R v Lambeth County Court Judge and Jonas* (1887) 36 WR 475.

334 Order 44, r 7.

335 See, for example, *M Ltd v T* (1991) Irish Times, 19 September (Johnson J). There Johnson J ordered that the defendant be brought to court to explain why he should not be sent to prison for failing to comply with an order of Carroll J which directed him to make discovery on oath concerning various goods within 14 days from the making of the order. The plaintiff claimed that it had never been paid by the defendant or the company of which he was manager for tea and coffee making equipment which it had supplied and which was valued at over STG£99,000. It appears from the newspaper report that the plaintiff had obtained the order from Carroll J as ancillary relief to either a *Mareva* application or a claim for a proprietary injunction and the *Irish Times* report said that Carroll J has also made an order restraining the sale of or disposing of any interest in goods which had been supplied by the plaintiff.

order[336]. An order for either committal or attachment for contempt of court requires the leave of the court which is applied for by motion on notice, save in the case of a criminal contempt 'in the face of the Court'[337]. The purpose of a contemnor's imprisonment is considered only to be *coercive*: the court has made an order which the contemnor has not obeyed and, in these circumstances, the contemnor is liable to be visited with an indefinite term of imprisonment until he agrees to comply with the order or the plaintiff agrees to his release[338]. In *Shell E&P Ireland Ltd v McGrath et al*[339], Finnegan P held that in civil proceedings committal for contempt was primarily coercive but in cases of serious misconduct, the High Court had jurisdiction to punish the contemnor in order to vindicate the authority of the court.

[6.096] Where a company wilfully disobeys an injunction or other court order those persons liable to be attached are its directors and other officers. 'Officer' of a company is defined by s 2 of the CA 1963 to include its directors and the company secretary[340]. Where a director or other officer of a company actively assists the company in disobeying an injunction or other court order he will be in contempt of court, as would any third party, on the basis that he has either aided and abetted the breach of the court's order or obstructed or frustrated the court's order[341]. This much is clear from cases such as *Ronson Products Ltd v Ronson Furniture Ltd*[342] and *Biba Ltd v Stratford Investments Ltd*[343].

[6.097] The circumstances in which a director or other officer can be attached for his company's breach of a court order must, however, be distinguished from cases where the director or other officer does not actively participate in the breach of the order or undertaking[344] given by the company. The question here is whether a director or other officer who has not actively participated in the breach of a court order and who has adopted a purely passive role will be liable to be attached. The English authorities are, on this point, equivocal. On the one hand, in *Director General of Fair Trading v Buckland and another*[345] Anthony Lincoln J held that a person is not liable in contempt merely by virtue of his office, ie, by simply being a director. In so finding he said:

> '... I reach the conclusion that Ord 45, r 5 does not render an officer of a company liable in contempt by virtue of his office and his mere knowledge that the order sought to be enforced was made. Resort can be had to r 5 only if he can otherwise be shown to be in

336 See *Piper v Piper* [1876] WN 202.

337 Order 44, r 3.

338 *The State (Commins) v McRann* [1977] IR 78 at 89.

339 *Shell E&P Ireland Ltd v McGrath et al* [2006] IEHC 108, [2007] 1 IR 671.

340 'Officer' will also include persons who hold offices that are created by and recognised in a company's memorandum and articles of association, eg, treasurer, chief executive, etc, even where such persons are not also directors: see Ch 13, *Corporate Governance: Management by the Directors*, at para **[13.003]**.

341 See generally, Courtney, *Mareva Injunctions and Related Interlocutory Orders* (1998, Butterworths) at para [12.31] *et seq.*

342 *Ronson Products Ltd v Ronson Furniture Ltd* [1966] 2 All ER 381.

343 *Biba Ltd v Stratford Investments Ltd* [1972] 3 All ER 1041 at 1045c.

344 As to attachment of directors and other officers following the breach of an undertakings by a company see *Biba Ltd v Stratford Investments Ltd* [1972] 3 All ER 1041.

345 *Director General of Fair Trading v Buckland and another* [1990] 1 All ER 545.

contempt under the general law of contempt. In the circumstances set out in the preliminary issue neither Mr Buckland nor Mr Stone could be liable in contempt in the absence of mens rea or an actus reus[346].'

On the other hand, in *Biba Ltd v Stratford Investments Ltd*[347], the director whom it was sought to be found in contempt was a solicitor who had taken only a superficial interest in the day-to-day affairs of the defendant company and had nothing to do with staffing, advertising, selling or stocking. There, although it was accepted that he had, as director, played a 'purely passive role', Brightman J held that he was liable to proceedings for contempt, although he failed to support his finding with reasons. In Ireland, it is thought that 'wilful disobeyance' is a prerequisite to finding an individual officer in contempt.

[6.098] The decision of Anthony Lincoln J in *Buckland* was, however, distinguished by Woolf LJ in the Court of Appeal decision in *Attorney General for Tuvalu and another v Philatelic Distribution Corp Ltd et al*[348]. In that case, the defendant company contracted with the plaintiff government to design, produce and sell Tuvalu postage stamps. The plaintiff government subsequently suspected that the security printer company (which was owned by the defendant's managing director) had deliberately printed flawed stamps; the plaintiff government obtained injunctions restraining the managing director and his companies from producing any more Tuvalu stamps or selling or dealing in stamps or other articles of philately or printing materials bearing the name Tuvalu. The injunction was subsequently varied and the managing director and the defendant both undertook not to make use of the printing materials. Prior to the variation of the injunction, an employee of the defendant company gave an order to the security printer to produce stamps and the printing materials were used to this end. The plaintiff government proceeded against a number of persons, including the managing director of the defendant company for contempt of court and the employee who ordered the stamps. The managing director was found to be in contempt of the injunction by, *inter alia*, causing or permitting the further production of Tuvalu stamps after the injunction was made and also in giving the later undertaking without making sure than no prohibited stamps were on order or were in the process of being printed. The managing director was fined £3,000 and committed to prison for three months. It was against this that he appealed to the Court of Appeal. In the Court of Appeal judgment, delivered by Woolf LJ, it was held:

> 'In our view where a company is ordered not to do certain acts or gives an undertaking to like effect and a director of that company is aware of the order or undertaking he is under a duty to take reasonable steps to ensure that the order or undertaking is obeyed, and if he wilfully fails to take those steps and the order or undertaking is breached he can be punished for contempt. We use the word 'wilful' to distinguish the situation where the director can reasonably believe some other director or officer is taking these steps[349].'

---

[346] *Director General of Fair Trading v Buckland and another* [1990] 1 All ER 545 at 549j.

[347] *Biba Ltd v Stratford Investments Ltd* [1972] 3 All ER 1041.

[348] *Attorney General for Tuvalu and another v Philatelic Distribution Corp Ltd et al* [1990] 2 All ER 216. This was cited in passing in *Cork County Council v CB Readymix Ltd and Cronin* (15 June 1999, unreported) HC, McGuinness J.

[349] *Attorney General for Tuvalu and another v Philatelic Distribution Corp Ltd et al* [1990] 2 All ER 216 at 222c.

Later, it was said:

> 'There must, however, be some culpable conduct on the part of the director before he will be liable to be subject to an order of committal under Ord 45, r 5; mere inactivity is not sufficient[350].'

In this regard the Court of Appeal distinguished *Buckland* on the grounds that, there, no finding of culpable conduct on the part of the director had been found and the decision should not be taken as meaning that a director must actively participate in the breach before he is liable in contempt. A director's failure to supervise or investigate or his deliberate blindness will be regarded as being 'wilful' and he may be found to be in contempt[351].

[6.099] Where the court deems imprisonment to be the appropriate punishment for a contempt of court, it was held by Finnegan P in Shell *E&P Ireland Ltd v McGrath et al*[352] that it should be for a definite term.

(vi) Sequestration of companies' and their officers' assets

[6.100] Sequestration is 'essentially penal in effect'[353]. It is a 'process of contempt'[354] by which a person or persons known as *sequestrators* are empowered to take a contemnor's property into their possession until such time as the contemnor purges his contempt. Sequestration of an individual defendant's assets is facilitated by Ord 43, r 2 of the RSC which provides:

> 'Where any person is by any judgment or order directed to pay money into Court or to do any other act in a limited time, and after due service of such judgment or order refuses or neglects to obey the same according to the exigency thereof, the person prosecuting such judgment or order shall, at the expiration of the time limited for the performance thereof, be entitled, without obtaining any order from the Court for that purpose, to issue an order of sequestration in the Form No 17 in the Appendix F, Part II, against the estate and effects of such disobedient person.'

Sequestration is primarily available as a remedy to a plaintiff where a defendant or other person breaches a *mandatory* court order or injunction. Sequestration is also available to enforce a judgment or order for the recovery of property other than land[355]. Although sequestration in these circumstances is 'of right', ie, without the leave of the court, before issuing an order for sequestration against a contemnor, the plaintiff must apply to the Master of the High Court to approve one or more sequestrators and to obtain directions as to his or their security and accounting[356].

[6.101] A person appointed a sequestrator is an officer of the court. As a process, sequestration can only ever be effective against a contemnor of substance. Upon his appointment, a sequestrator will take possession of a contemnor's real and personal

---

350 *Attorney General for Tuvalu and another v Philatelic Distribution Corp Ltd et al* [1990] 2 All ER 216 at 223e.

351 *Re Galvanized Tank Manufacturers' Association's Agreement* [1965] 2 All ER 1003 cited.

352 *Shell E&P Ireland Ltd v McGrath et al* [2006] IEHC 108, [2007] 1 IR 671.

353 *Larkins v NUM* [1985] IR 671 at 688.

354 *Pratt v Inman* (1889) 43 Ch D 175 at 179; *Romilly v Romilly* [1963] 3 All ER 607 at 609F-G.

355 Order 42, r 6.

356 Order 43, r 3.

estate and collect, receive and get into his hands the rents and profits of the real estate and personal estate and keep same in his possession until such time as the contemnor purges his contempt. Unlike a fine, which is considered below[357], sequestration does not permit the indefinite retention of a contemnor's assets. This was made clear in *Con-Mech Ltd v Amalgamated Union of Engineering Workers*[358], where Sir John Donaldson MR said:

> 'If someone is fined the money is lost to him for ever. If his assets are sequestrated the money remains his but he cannot use it. The money stays in the sequestrator's possession until the court orders what shall be done with it. The man can come to court at any time and ask for the money to be returned to him, but if he does so the court will require some explanation of his conduct[359].'

While a sequestrator has possession of a contemnor's assets, he owes the contemnor a duty of care in respect of those assets[360].

[6.102] Sequestration *as of right* arises where a company neglects or refuses to obey a judgment or order requiring the payment of money into court, or requiring the doing of any act within a limited time. In such case, the person prosecuting is, by virtue of Ord 43, r 2, of the RSC:

> '... entitled, without obtaining any order from the court for that purpose, to issue an order of sequestration.'

It must be stressed that the judgment or order which has been disobeyed must require either the payment of money into court or the doing of an act within a limited time (and, of course, in the case of the latter, the time limit must have expired).

[6.103] Where a company 'wilfully disobeys'[361] a judgment or order of the court, Ord 42, r 32 of the RSC provides that the judgment or order may, by leave of the court, be enforced, *inter alia*, by *sequestration against the corporate property or by order of sequestration of its directors' or other officers' property.* Here, however, sequestration is not 'of right' and must be by leave of the court. Any judgment or order against a company may be enforced by sequestration with the leave of the court if it has been wilfully disobeyed. Significantly, in appropriate circumstances the sequestration may be against the property of the *directors or other officers* as well as that of the company: Ord 42, r 32 of the RSC. Where a company is in wilful disobedience of any judgment or order, enforcement may be brought against the company by way of sequestration, or against the company's directors or officers by way of attachment or sequestration.

(vii) Fining companies and their officers

[6.104] The RSC 1986 are silent as to the jurisdiction to fine a person or a company who or which is found to be in contempt of court. It is, however, accepted practice that the

357 See para **[6.104]**.

358 *Con-Mech Ltd v Amalgamated Union of Engineering Workers* [1973] ICR 620 at 627.

359 See further Lowe & Sufrin, *Borrie & Lowe The Law of Contempt* (3rd edn, Butterworths, 1996) at p 606 *et seq* where this and other cases such as *Australian Consolidated Press Ltd v Morgan* (1965) 112 CLR 483 are considered.

360 *Inland Revenue Commissioners v Hoogstraten* [1984] 3 All ER 25.

361 See para **[6.080]**.

High Court has jurisdiction to impose a fine where it considers attachment, committal, or sequestration to be inappropriate. The jurisdiction to impose a fine *in lieu* of attachment or committal was considered by Cross J in *Phonographic Performance Ltd v Amusement Caters (Peckham) Ltd*[362]. There, he said:

> 'I cannot for myself see the logic of saying that in a case of civil contempt the court has no alternative to sending the defendants to prison ... I think that the court must have power, if there has been contumacious behaviour, to impose the lesser penalty of a fine[363].'

Where a company's directors are being fined for their company's contempt of court it has been said by the English Court of Appeal in *McMillan Graham Printers v RR (UK) Ltd*[364] that each individual director's circumstances should be examined separately and that the directors should not be fined jointly and severally.

[6.105] In *Irish Shell Ltd v Ballylynch Motors Ltd and Morris Oil Company Ltd*[365], the Supreme Court, *per* Lynch J, held that the President of the High Court had power to fine a defaulting company's directors *in lieu* of attachment[366]. Furthermore, Ord 44, rr 4 and 5 of the RSC provide that with regard to attachment and committal, the court may discharge a person 'on such terms and conditions as to costs *or otherwise* as it thinks fit'. It is thought that this is broad enough to empower the making of a fine *in lieu* of imprisonment[367].

---

362 *Phonographic Performance Ltd v Amusement Caters (Peckham) Ltd* [1963] 3 All ER 493.

363 [1963] 3 All ER 493 at 497.

364 *McMillan Graham Printers v RR (UK) Ltd* [1993] TLR 152.

365 *Irish Shell Ltd v Ballylynch Motors Ltd and Morris Oil Company Ltd* (5 March 1997, unreported) SC, Lynch J, *nem diss*. See also *Phonographic Performances Ltd v Amusement Caterers (Peckham) Ltd* [1963] 3 All ER 493 where Cross J said (at 497): 'I cannot for myself see the logic of saying that in a case of civil contempt the court has no alternative to sending the defendants to prison ... I think that the court must have power, if there has been contumacious behaviour, to impose the lesser penalty of a fine.'

366 At p 6 of the transcript.

367 Order 36, r 22 of the RSC provides that the officer having the management of the Central Office of the High Court is the proper officer to make entries and render accounts of all fines or penal sums imposed by the court.

Chapter 7

Corporate Contracts, Capacity and Authority

[7.001] While natural persons are said to be 'only flesh and blood', they can think and act for themselves[1]. Companies, on the other hand, cannot think and act for themselves and are totally reliant upon natural persons to think and act for them. To grasp this point at the outset is not merely to acknowledge the obvious, but is to understand the central theme of this chapter: the involvement of human agents is a prerequisite to corporate contracting.

[7.002] Corporate contracts are considered in this chapter in four sections:

- [A] Corporate Contracts: Form and Formalities.
- [B] Pre-Incorporation Contracts.
- [C] Contractual Capacity and *Ultra Vires*.
- [D] The Authority of Corporate Agents.

Section [A] of this chapter examines the nature of the corporate contract and the basic legal formalities required to create a binding corporate contract. Section [B] considers pre-incorporation contracts, ie, contracts which purport to be made by a company prior to its incorporation. The remaining two sections look at two fundamental limitations on corporate contracting. Section [C] considers corporate contractual capacity and, in particular, the consequences where a company acts outside of its objects clause, or *ultra vires*. Finally, Section [D] addresses the application of the law of agency to corporate contracts which arises by virtue of the fact that a company can only act through its human agents.

[A] Corporate Contracts: Form and Formalities

[7.003] Of the thousands of contracts entered into every day by companies, the vast majority are concluded without formality, often orally, and the majority that are in writing tend to be signed 'for and on behalf of' companies by their agents. Formalities are at a minimum and as a general rule the company seal is not required to bind the company. Section 38 of the CA 1963 provides the form which corporate contracts may take, and in so doing makes a threefold distinction: those required to be under seal, those required to be in writing and those which may be oral or parol. The changes to contract law effected by the Electronic Commerce Act 2000 ('ECA 2000') are considered as part of the treatment of written contracts and contracts that require to be under seal.

---

1 See the colourful passage from the judgment of Buckley J in *Continental Tyre & Rubber Co (GB) Ltd v Daimler & Co* [1915] 1 KB 893 at 916, quoted at para **[7.099]** *post*.

[7.004] Here, the form and formalities of corporate contracts are considered under the following headings:

1. Oral contracts.
2. Written contracts.
3. Contracts and other instruments required to be under seal.
4. The requirement to have a seal.
5. Attestation of the company seal.
6. Delivery of a deed by a company.
7. Execution by power of attorney.

Oral contracts

[7.005] Section 38(1)(c) of the CA 1963 provides the general rule that all contracts which can be made orally, or by parol, by an individual can also be made orally by a company, acting through its authorised agents. The authority of the contracting corporate agent to enter into contracts on behalf of the company is considered in Section [D], below[2].

[7.006] Not all contracts which can be made orally by an individual should be made orally by a company. The Companies Acts provide that certain contracts entered into by companies with certain persons *must* be in writing, or evidenced in writing, notwithstanding the provisions of s 38 of the CA 1963 and the ordinary laws of contract. An example is provided by the EC(SMPLC)R 1994[3]. Regulation 13(1) provides that, save in respect of contracts entered into in the ordinary course of a company's business[4]:

> 'where a single-member company enters into a contract with the sole member of the company and the sole member also represents the company in the transaction, whether as a director or otherwise, the company shall, unless the contract is in writing, ensure that the terms of the contract are forthwith set out in a written memorandum or are recorded in the minutes of the first meeting of the directors of the company following the making of the contract.'

Although the company and every officer of the company who is in default will be guilty of an offence where reg 13(1) is not complied with[5], the failure to comply will *not* affect the validity of that contract[6]. Furthermore the provisions of reg 13 are expressed to be without prejudice to any other enactment or rule of law applicable to contracts between a company and its director[7].

---

2 At para **[7.099]**, *et seq*.

3 SI 275/1994.

4 Regulation 13(2) of the EC(SMPLC)R 1994. Were it otherwise, the sole member of a company that operates a newsagent would be required to have a written contract to buy a newspaper from the company!

5 Regulation 13(3) of the EC(SMPLC)R 1994.

6 Regulation 13(5) of the EC(SMPLC)R 1994.

7 Regulation 13(4) of the EC(SMPLC)R 1994.

Written contracts

[7.007] Section 38(1)(b) of the CA 1963 provides that:

> a contract which if made between private persons would be by law required to be in writing, signed by the parties to be charged therewith, may be made on behalf of the company in writing, signed by any person acting under its authority, express or implied.

Where the law requires a contract entered into by an individual to be in writing and signed, such a contract entered into by a company must also be in writing and signed. An example of a contract required to be in writing is a contract which is going to operate over a number of years as seen in *Henley Forklift (Ireland) Ltd v Lansing Bagnall & Co Ltd et al*[8]. The principle here is clear: corporate contracts are on a par with individual contracts.

[7.008] Many diverse types of contract are required by law to be made or evidenced in writing: examples include contracts for the sale of land or an interest therein; contracts of guarantee (but not indemnity); contracts that are not intended to be performed within one year[9]; and legal assignments of choses in action[10], etc[11]. The requirement that a contract be in writing under hand (as opposed to oral or under seal) arises from statute, the agreement of the parties, or in equity[12]. Although these contracts are merely required to be *evidenced* in writing, in practice these contracts are actually made in writing.

[7.009] The dual requirements of 'in writing' and 'signed' are both affected by the ECA 2000. Section 19 of the ECA 2000 permits certain[13] contracts that would otherwise be required to be in writing, to be instead in electronic form[14]. Section 19 provides:

---

8 *Henley Forklift (Ireland) Ltd v Lansing Bagnall & Co Ltd et al* [1979] ILRM 257, where O'Higgins CJ said in relation to the contract in question: 'I find it very difficult to say in the circumstances whether the suggested execution of this scheduled agreement by any of the companies involved was such as to comply with the provisions of s 38 of the Companies Act 1963. It was, by reason of its terms, an agreement which was going to operate over a number of years and therefore was required to be in writing.'

9 Section 2 of the Statute of Frauds (Ireland) 1695 (7 Will 3 c 12), provides: '... no action shall be brought ... whereby to charge the defendant upon any special promise to answer for the debt, default or miscarriage of another person, or to charge any person upon an agreement made upon consideration of marriage, or upon any contract or sale of lands, tenements or hereditaments or any interest in or concerning them, or upon any agreement that is not to be performed within the space of one year from the making thereof, unless the agreement upon which such action shall be brought, or some note or memorandum thereof, shall be in writing, and signed by the party to be charged therewith, or some other person thereunto by him lawfully authorised.' Other examples of contracts which must be in writing are consumer lending contracts within the meaning of Part III of the Consumer Credit Act 1995.

10 Section 28 of the Supreme Court of Judicature Ireland Act 1877.

11 See further, Kearney, 'Execution of Commercial Documents' (1994) 16 DULJ 1 at pp 6, 7.

12 There is no common law requirement that any contract be in writing 'under hand' because, as Kearney, 'Execution of Commercial Documents' (1994) 16 DULJ 1, points out at p 5, the common law required instruments in writing to be executed under seal.

13 Not all contracts can be concluded electronically: see s 10 of the ECA 2000, considered post at **[7.020]**.

14 See Coleman, 'The Irish Electronic Commerce Bill 2000' (2000) 7 CLP 139.

> '(1) An electronic contract shall not be denied legal effect, validity or enforceability solely on the grounds that it is wholly or partly in electronic form, or has been concluded wholly or partly by way of an electronic communication.
>
> (2) In the formation of a contract, an offer, acceptance of an offer or any related communication (including any subsequent amendment, cancellation or revocation of the offer or acceptance of the offer) may, unless otherwise agreed by the parties, be communicated by means of an electronic communication.'

This section confirms the acceptability of 'electronic form' for contracts that would otherwise require to be 'in writing'. Generally, matters required to be 'in writing' may now be in electronic form[15]. In addition, s 13(1) of the ECA 2000 modifies the meaning of what has traditionally been taken to be meant by 'signed' and recognises an 'electronic signature'[16]. It provides:

> 'If by law or otherwise the signature of a person or public body is required (whether the requirement is in the form of an obligation or consequences flow from there being no signature) or permitted, then, subject to *subsection (2)*, an electronic signature may be used.'

Subsection (2) enshrines the principle of consent. Where a signature is required or permitted to be given to a person who is not (and does not act for) a 'public body'[17] that person must consent to the use of an electronic signature. A public body must also consent but can also specify that an electronic signature conforms to certain information technology and procedural requirements[18].

[7.010] Because of the curiously inverted operation of s 38(1)(b) of the CA 1963, since s 19(1) of the ECA 2000 permits individuals to conclude certain contracts electronically,

---

15 Section 12(1) of the ECA 2000: see para **[7.019]** (fn).

16 'Electronic signature' is defined by s 2(1) of the ECA 2000 to mean 'data in electronic form attached to, incorporated in or logically associated with other electronic data and which serves as a method of authenticating the purported originator, and includes an advanced electronic signature'. An 'advanced electronic signature' is defined by the same section to mean 'an electronic signature (a) uniquely linked to the signatory, (b) capable of identifying the signatory, (c) created using means that are capable of being maintained by the signatory under his, her or its sole control, and (d) linked to the data to which it relates in such a manner that any subsequent change of the data is detectable'.

17 'Public body' is defined by s 2(1) of the ECA 2000 to mean: '(a) a Minister of the Government or a Minister of State, (b) a body (including a Department of State but not including a non-government organisation) wholly or partly funded out of the Central Fund or out of moneys provided by the Oireachtas or moneys raised by local taxation or charges, or (c) a commission, tribunal, board or body established by an Act or by arrangement of the Government, a Minister of the Government or a Minister of State for a non-commercial public service or purpose'.

18 Section 13(2)(a) of the ECA 2000 provides: an electronic signature may be used as provided in *subsection (1)* only – 'where the signature is required or permitted to be given to a public body or to a person acting on behalf of a public body and the public body consents to the use of an electronic signature but requires that it be in accordance with particular information technology and procedural requirements (including that it be an advanced electronic signature, that it be based on a qualified certificate, that it be issued by an accredited certification service provider or that it be created by a secure signature creation device) – if the public body's requirements have been met and those requirements have been made public and are objective, transparent, proportionate and non-discriminatory'.

s 38(1)(b) applies this law to companies. Those contracts that are excluded from the operation of ss 12 to 23 of the ECA 2000, specifically relevant to companies[19], are the law governing the creation, execution, amendment, variation or revocation of trusts[20]; the law governing the making of an affidavit or a statutory or sworn declaration, or requiring or permitting the use of one for any purpose[21]; and the law governing the manner in which an interest in real property (including a leasehold interest in such property) may be created, acquired, disposed of or registered 'other than contracts (whether or not under seal[22]) for the creation, acquisition or disposal of such interests'[23]. That latter exclusion thus draws a distinction between *contracts* for the acquisition or disposal of interests in real property (which can be concluded electronically) on the one hand and instruments that actually effect the disposal or acquisition of interests in real property on the other, such as conveyances, assignments and transfers (which cannot be concluded electronically as they do not attract the protection of ss 12 to 23). Accordingly, all of the examples cited earlier[24] of contracts that require to be in writing and signed may be concluded electronically.

[7.011] Where contracts are required to be made or evidenced in writing it is sufficient in law for any person so authorised by the company to sign either the contract or a written memorandum of the contract 'for and on behalf' of the company. A similar requirement pertains in the case of an electronic contract. The meaning of 'signing' was considered by Finnegan J in *Dundalk AFC Interim Company Ltd v The FAI National League*[25]. There, Finnegan J quoted with approval the following passage from the decision of Romer LJ in *London County Council v Vitamins Ltd*[26]:

> It is established in my judgment as a general proposition that at common law a person sufficiently 'signs' a document if it is signed in his name and within his authority by somebody else and in such case the agent's signature is treated as being that of the principal.

Where a director signs on behalf of a company his authority must derive from the board of directors who will have the authority to manage the company under model reg 80 of Table A[27]. An authorised person's authority need not be in writing[28]. It will suffice for the authorised person to 'rubber stamp' such contracts. In *McDonald v John Twiname Ltd*[29], Evershed MR said:

---

19 Also excluded are wills, codicils and other testamentary instruments, enduring powers of attorney and the rules practices and procedures of a court or tribunal: see s 10(1) of the ECA 2000.

20 Section 10(1)(a)(ii) of the ECA 2000.

21 Section 10(2)(c) of the ECA 2000.

22 As to sealing, see para **[7.014]** *post*.

23 Section 10(1)(b) of the ECA 2000.

24 See para **[7.008]** *ante*.

25 *Dundalk AFC Interim Company Ltd v The FAI National League* [2001] 1 IR 434, Finnegan J.

26 *London County Council v Vitamins Ltd* [1955] 2 All ER 229 at 232.

27 See Ch 13, *Corporate Governance: Management by the Directors*, at para **[13.127]** *et seq*.

28 *Coles v Trecothick* (1804) 9 VES 234, cited by Finnegan J in *Dundalk AFC Interim Company Ltd v The FAI National League* [2001] 1 IR 434.

29 *McDonald v John Twiname Ltd* [1953] 2 All ER 589 at 594A.

'A limited company can sign a document by means of some duly authorised person putting its printed signature to it or impressing the printed name of the company on it. That will suffice as a proper execution except in cases where the common seal must be affixed ...'

It may be obvious, but where an agent contracts 'for and on behalf of' a company, they should sign just that, ie, 'A for and on behalf of A & B Company Ltd'. The absence of these qualifying words could leave the contracting agent personally liable to perform the contract. Moreover, the exact registered name of all companies should be correctly stated in all contracts. If a spelling or other typographical error is made, resulting in A purporting to contract for and on behalf of a non-existent entity, the error may not be fatal provided that there is no misrepresentation or uncertainty[30]. In *F Goldsmith (Sicklesmere) Ltd v Baxter*[31], Stamp J said:

'I would find it impossible to hold that a company incorporated under the Companies Acts has no identity but by reference to its correct name, or that, unless an agent acts on its behalf by that name, or a name so nearly resembling it that it is obviously an error for that name, he acts for nobody.'

This limited saver[32] ought not to encourage complacency, and the general rule is that precision is required to avoid such a contract being held to be void for uncertainty. Moreover, by virtue of s 114(4) of the CA 1963, the failure to correctly state the company's name in a written contract can render the company's agent personally liable. This has already been discussed at length in Chapter 5[33].

[7.012] To use the abbreviation 'Co' for the word 'company' has been held to be an insufficient deviation to cause personal liability to be imposed pursuant to s 114(4) on officers of the company who use or authorise the use of that abbreviation. This was the case in *Banque de I'Indochine et de Suez SA v Euroseas Group Finance Co Ltd et al*[34] where Goff J said:

'"Co" is an abbreviation of "Company"... we all know this to be true as a matter of ordinary commercial usage, 'Co' is a generally and commonly accepted abbreviation of the word 'Company', and is so to such an extent that it is treated as equivalent to 'Company' and there is no possibility of it meaning anything else[35].'

---

30 See Ch 5, *Disregarding Separate Legal Personality*, at paras **[5.081]–[5.082]**.

31 *F Goldsmith (Sicklesmere) Ltd v Baxter* [1969] 3 All ER 733 at 736 G. In this case a Mr Brewster, director of F Goldsmith (Sicklesmere), Ltd, purported to contract 'for and on behalf of Goldsmith Coaches (Sicklesmere), Ltd.' The defendant refused to complete the sale arguing that there was no such legal entity. Stamp J rejected this and gave the order for specific performance sought.

32 *F Goldsmith (Sicklesmere) Ltd v Baxter* [1969] 3 All ER 733 at 737G, where Stamp J said '... it is not essential to the validity of a contract made on behalf of a limited company that the company should be described with precision ...'. However, in an age when there are very many companies with very similar sounding names, particularly containing initials, precision should be striven for. See also *Badgerhill Properties Ltd v Cottrell* [1991] BCLC 805 at 813.

33 Ch 5, *Disregarding Separate Legal Personality*, at para **[5.081]** *et seq*.

34 *Banque de I'Indochine et de Suez SA v Euroseas Group Finance Co Ltd et al* [1981] 3 All ER 198.

35 *Banque de I'Indochine et de Suez SA v Euroseas Group Finance Co Ltd et al* [1981] 3 All ER 198 at 201(b-c).

It is thought that s 114 of the CA 1963 will operate to impose personal liability, only where it is shown that the other contracting party was misled to their detriment[36].

[7.013] The decision of the English case in *R (on the application of Mercury Tax Group Ltd & another) v HMRC & Co*[37] is a salutary reminder that a deed or contract should be complete before it is signed. In that case it was held that the transfer of signature pages from an earlier incomplete version of a deed to the final amended version was not effective.

Deeds and contracts required to be under seal

[7.014] Section 38(1)(a) of the CA 1963 provides that contracts which are required by law to be in writing and to be *under seal* in the case of an individual, 'may be made on behalf of the company in writing under the common seal of the company'[38]. Whilst this provided for equality of contractual formality between companies and individuals[39], the Companies Acts formulation has now been surpassed by s 64(1) of the Land and Conveyancing Law Reform Act 2009 (the 'LCLRA 2009') which provides that any rule of law which required either a seal for the valid execution of a deed by an individual or authority to deliver a deed to be given by deed is abolished. The effect is to render redundant s 38(1)(a) of the CA 1963 in its application to 'deeds'; it will, however, continue to apply in the case of other contracts required to be under seal.

[7.015] The focus of the new law is now on the formalities for *deeds*, and s 64(2) of the LCLRA 2009 makes explicit provision for the formalities for deeds executed by companies:

> 'An instrument executed after the commencement of this chapter is a deed if it is–
>
> (a) described at its head by words such as 'Assignment', 'Conveyance', 'Charge', 'Deed', 'Indenture', 'Lease', 'Mortgage', 'Surrender' or other heading appropriate to the deed in question, or it is otherwise made clear on its face that it is intended by the person making it, or the parties to it, to be a deed, by expressing it to be executed or signed as a deed,
>
> (b) executed in the following manner ...
>
> (ii) if made by a company registered in the State, it is executed under the seal of the company in accordance with its Articles of Association ...
>
> and
>
> (c) delivered as a deed by the person executing it or by a person authorised to do so on that person's behalf.'

---

36 See *Badgerhill Properties Ltd v Cottrell* [1991] BCLC 805.

37 *R (on the application of Mercury Tax Group Ltd & another) v HMRC & Co* [2008] EWHC 2721.

38 As with written and oral contracts, a contract which is under seal can be 'varied or discharged in the same manner in which it is authorised' to be made: s 38(3) of the CA 1963.

39 It should be noted that as with s 38(1)(c) and (b) of the CA 1963 the provision here is not couched in mandatory terms. Rather, the provisions of the section are facilitatory, through the use of the word 'may'.

Since the commencement of the LCLRA 2009, in order for a company to execute a deed, therefore, three elements must be present:

- the document must be described as a deed, etc, at its head or this must be otherwise clear to the person or persons making it; and
- it must be executed under the company's seal *in accordance with its articles of association*; and
- it must be delivered as a deed.

The fundamental point here is that the validity of execution of a deed by an Irish company will turn on whether the execution complies with the company's articles of association. Accordingly, there is now a separate regime applicable to the execution of deeds by companies; whereas individuals no longer need to seal deeds, Irish registered companies are required to execute a deed using their common seal[40]. There are separate provisions for bodies corporate registered in the State that are not companies[41] and also for foreign bodies corporate[42]. The new requirements in relation the formalities for companies making deeds does not prevent a company from appointing an attorney under a power to execute a deed on behalf of the company.

[7.016] Contracts that are required to be executed as deeds are, in the main, contracts that dispose of an interest in land. Section 62(1) of the LCLRA 2009 provides that:

> 'Subject to *section 63*, a legal estate or interest in land may only be created or conveyed by a deed.'

Accordingly, where a company creates or conveys a legal estate or interest in land, it must use a deed and comply with s 64(2)(b)(ii) of the LCLRA 2009.

[7.017] Section 63 of the LCLRA 2009 carves out, from the foregoing general rule, a number of instruments which relate to a legal estate or interest in land but which are not required to be deeds. These are:

> '(a) an assent by a personal representative;
> (b) a surrender or other conveyance taking effect by operation of law;
> (c) a disclaimer not required to be by deed;
> (d) a grant or assignment of a tenancy not required to be by deed;
> (e) a receipt not required to be by deed;
> (f) a vesting order of the court or other competent authority; or
> (g) any other conveyance which may be prescribed.'

It follows that where a company executes any of the foregoing, it may do so in writing and is not required to comply with s 64(2)(b)(ii) of the LCLRA 2009.

[7.018] One type of contract which continues to require to be executed by an individual under seal and so, by operation of s 38(1)(a) of the CA 1963, by a company under seal

40 Note, this does not mean that a company cannot execute a deed where it has created a power of attorney in favour of an individual since, in those circumstances, the deed would be made by an individual on behalf of the company and so governed by s 64(2)(b)(i) of the LCLRA 2009: see para **[7.030]** *post*.

41 See s 64(1)(b)(iii) of the LCLRA 2009.

42 See s 64(1)(b)(iv) of the LCLRA 2009.

are contracts of guarantee[43] where there is no valuable consideration[44]. Certain other instruments executed by individuals, that are not deeds, are also required to be under seal[45]. These include: security bills of sale[46]; transfers and mortgages of Irish registered ships or shares in ships[47]; perfection of share certificates where so required by a company's articles of association; transfers of shares (in some cases)[48]; execution of bonds[49]; extensions of the standard contract and tort limitation period from 6 to 12 years; avoiding the need for consideration; and effecting a legal assignment of a chose in action under s 28 of the Supreme Court of Judicature Ireland Act 1877[50]. A power of attorney is no longer required to be under seal[51] nor is it necessary to impress the seal in order for a company to authenticate documents[52].

[7.019] Section 16 of the ECA 2000 purports to facilitate the sealing of documents by electronic means. Section 16(1) provides:

> 'If by law or otherwise a seal is required to be affixed to a document (whether the requirement is in the form of an obligation or consequences flow from a seal not being affixed) then, subject to *subsection (2)*, that requirement is taken to have been met if the document indicated that it is required to be under seal and it includes an advanced electronic signature, based on a qualified certificate, of the person or public body by whom it is required to be sealed.'

The law on electronic sealing has never developed and in the 12 years since the ECA 2000 became law, it is thought that there has rarely, if ever, been an electronic sealing by an Irish company. The other requirement for a deed or instrument to be under seal – that it is in writing – is addressed by s 12(1) of the ECA 2000[53]. As in the case of ordinary electronic contracts, s 16(2) again enshrines the principle of consent. Where a document

---

43 *Cf* a guarantee which is supported by consideration, which does *not* have to be under seal: *Re PMPA Garage (Longmile) Ltd et al* [1992] ILRM 337 at 345.

44 *Drimmie v Davies* [1899] 1 IR 176, which held that promises under seal between partners were enforceable without the need to show consideration. See Clark, at p 36; see Cheshire Fifoot & Furmston, *Law of Contract* (12th edn, Butterworths, 1986) at p 26.

45 See, generally, Kearney, 'Execution of Commercial Documents' (1994) 16 DULJ 1 at p 3, 4.

46 Note, the Bills of Sale Acts do not, per se, apply to companies: see generally, Ch 19, *Corporate Borrowing: Registration of Charges*, at para **[19.046]**.

47 Section 31 of the Merchant Shipping Act 1894.

48 See Ch 9, *Share Transfer*, at para **[9.011]**.

49 See *British India Steam Navigation Co v IRC* (1881) 7 QBD 165 at 173 *per* Lindley J.

50 As Kearney, 'Execution of Commercial Documents' (1994) 16 DULJ 1 at p 5fn points out, although s 28 refers to an assignment 'in writing, under the hand of the assignor', in *Re A Debtor's Summons* [1929] IR 136 Murnaghan J in the Supreme Court said (at 151) that an assignment 'would in the case of a company require to be under seal because the seal of an incorporated body is the equivalent of the hand of a natural person'.

51 See para **[7.030]** *post*.

52 Section 42 of the CA 1963 provides that a document or proceeding may be authenticated by being signed by a director, secretary or other authorised officer.

53 Section 12(1) provides: 'If by law or otherwise a person or public body is required (whether the requirement is in the form of an obligation or consequences flow from the information not being in writing) or permitted to give information in writing (whether or nor in a form prescribed by law) then, subject to *subsection (2)*, the person or public body may give the information in electronic form, whether as an electronic communication or otherwise.'

to be under seal is required or permitted to be given to a person who is not (and does not act for) a 'public body'[54] that person must consent to the use of an advanced electronic signature based on a qualified certificate. A public body must also consent but it can also specify that an advanced electronic signature conforms to certain information technology and procedural requirements[55]. The essential difference between ordinary contracts and documents under seal is that whereas the former can be concluded with an electronic signature *simpliciter*, documents under seal require an advanced electronic signature[56] based on a qualified certificate[57]. It is opined that where a company seeks to utilise s 16 of the ECA 2000 its articles of association ought to envisage such a means for sealing documents. This is because reg 115 is in the nature of an internal control on the use of a seal: where a company's articles require (as in reg 115) two persons to attest the use of the seal, it is to be assumed that two persons, rather than one, are required for reasons of control. Therefore, whilst because of s 16 of the ECA 2000, the validity of an electronic sealing may not be disputed, the question of corporate authority is not addressed by s 16: an officer acting alone who causes a document to be sealed electronically may well be liable for breach of duty by acting beyond his authority and in breach of the company's articles of association.

[7.020] Not all deeds and instruments that require to be under a company's seal can be sealed electronically. For many private companies, the most frequent use of the seal is in relation to the acquisition or disposal of real property, and from s 10(1)(b) of the ECA 2000, it is clear that s 16 is without prejudice to the law governing the manner in which an interest in real property may be created, acquired, disposed of or registered.

[7.021] Again, it should be noted that s 16 of the ECA 2000 applies to companies 'by proxy' since although it does not specifically mention companies, by virtue of s 38(1)(a) of the CA 1963 the laws relating to the sealing of deeds and documents by individuals is applied to companies.

The requirement to have a seal

[7.022] Section 114(1)(b) of the CA 1963 provides that every company 'shall have its name engraven in legible characters on its seal'. This is the common seal referred to in s 18(2) of the CA 1963, which provides that on becoming incorporated a company shall, *inter alia*, have a common seal. The use of the term 'common seal', distinguishes the

54 'Public body' is defined by s 2(1) of the ECA 2000: see para **[7.009]** *ante*.

55 Section 16(2)(a) of the ECA 2000 provides: an advanced electronic signature based on a qualified certificate may be used as provided in subsection (1) only – 'where the document to be under seal is required or permitted to be given to a public body or to a person acting on behalf of a public body and the public body consents to the use of an electronic signature but requires that it be in accordance with particular information technology and procedural requirements (including that it be an advanced electronic signature, that it be based on a qualified certificate, that it be issued by an accredited certification service provider) – if the public body's requirements have been met and those requirements have been made public and are objective, transparent, proportionate and non-discriminatory'.

56 See para **[7.009]** *ante* (fn).

57 Section 2(1) of the ECA 2000 defines 'qualified certificate' to mean a certificate which meets the requirements set out in Annex I of the ECA 2000 and is provided by a certification service provider who fulfils the requirements set out in Annex II of the ECA 2000.

basic form of seal from an 'official seal'[58] (which can be used for transacting business outside the State: s 41 of the CA 1963). These are the only two possible forms of seal in the case of a private company[59]. Despite the uncertainty[60], in principle it is thought that there can be no objection to a company having two or more common seals (ie, duplicate seals) which all comply with s 114(1)(b) of the CA 1963. Such a scenario might be expedient in a large company (most likely a PLC) which has a high volume of deeds that require to be sealed so that, for example, two directors in Dublin might validly attest one seal whilst two other directors in Cork may attest a second seal, provided that all executions are authorised by the directors in accordance with the company's articles of association.

[7.023] A company whose objects include the transaction of business outside the State may, if authorised by its articles[61], have an official seal for use in any territory, district or place not situate in the State: s 41(1) of the CA 1963. The official seal must be a facsimile of the common seal of the company with the addition on its face of the name of every territory, district or place where it is to be used. A deed or other instrument to which an official seal is duly affixed shall bind the company as if it has been sealed with the common seal of the company[62]. Where a company has an official seal, it may by writing under its common seal[63] authorise any person appointed for the purpose in that territory, district or place to affix the seal to any deed or document to which the company is party in that place[64]. The authority of a person so appointed will last for the period specified in the appointment or, if no period is specified, until the notice of revocation or determination of the agent's authority has been given to the person dealing with him[65]. The person affixing any such official seal shall by writing under his hand certify on the deed or other instrument to which the official seal is affixed, the date on which and place at which it is so affixed[66].

---

58 If a company decides to have an 'official seal', s 41 of the CA 1963 provides that it 'shall be a facsimile of the common seal of the company with the addition on its face of the name of every territory, district or place where it is to be used'.

59 It should be noted that a company other than a private company may, by s 3 of the C(A)A 1977, also have a 'securities seal': see Ch 29, *Public Companies and SEs*, at para **[29.035]**.

60 Note that the matter was considered by the English Law Commission in its report, *Execution of Deeds and Other Documents by or on behalf of Bodies Corporate* (1998) Law Com No 253, considered in Millerchip, 'Execution of Deeds and Documents – Proposals for Clarity' (1998) Practical Law for Companies 41. After noting that there was considerable uncertainty as to whether companies could have duplicate seals, it concluded that it would not recommend that companies should be permitted to have more than one common seal.

61 The requisite authority will be present where model reg 82 of Table A is adopted.

62 Section 41(2) of the CA 1963.

63 Note the anomaly in that since the Powers of Attorney Act 1996, it is no longer necessary as a matter of law to appoint an attorney by deed under seal: see para **[7.030]** *post*.

64 Section 41(3) of the CA 1963.

65 Section 41(4) of the CA 1963.

66 Section 41(5) of the CA 1963.

Attestation of the common seal

[7.024] Usually, a company's articles of association make provision for the affixing and attestation of the company seal. It was held by the High Court in *Safeera Ltd v Wallis and O'Regan*[67] that the failure to execute a conveyance of property in accordance with a company's articles will mean that the conveyance will *not be effective* to convey the company's interest in the property. This decision has been given further authority by s 68(2)(b)(ii) of the LCLRA 2009 which makes compliance with the provisions of a company's articles of association paramount in determining the validity of the execution of a document by a company. The sealing requirements in any particular company will depend, entirely, upon its particular articles of association[68], which must always be consulted since, because they are public documents, persons will be taken to have constructive notice of their provisions[69].

(a) Regulation 115 of Table A of the First Schedule to the CA 1963

[7.025] It is usual for a private company to adopt the provisions of model reg 115 of Table A. Regulation 115 provides:

> 'The seal shall be used only by the authority of the directors or of a committee of directors authorised by the directors in that behalf, and every instrument to which the seal shall be affixed shall be signed by a director and shall be countersigned by the secretary or by a second director or by some other person appointed by the directors for that purpose.'

The first point to note is that the seal must only be used by the *authority of the directors or of a committee of directors*. This means that individual directors may not take it upon themselves to affix the seal and sign and countersign it. The board of directors (or a committee thereof) must always *authorise* the use of the seal which means authorising the entering into by the company of the contract or deed to which it is affixed.

Where a person holds both the offices of director and secretary, his sole signature will not suffice: s 177 of the CA 1963[70]. It is not necessary under the model regulation for either a director or the secretary to physically affix the seal and the physical affixing can be effected by someone else[71]; neither is it required to be affixed in the presence of the signatories[72]. When the sealing provisions in a company's articles are observed, and the corporate officers have the requisite authority to act for the company, then the deed so sealed will be invalidated only where it contravenes the law or is *ultra vires* the

---

67 *Safeera Ltd v Wallis and O'Regan* (12 July 1994) HC, Morris J.

68 It is possible that a company's articles could require *all* of the company's directors and the secretary to attest the company seal.

69 On constructive notice of the memorandum and articles of association, see para **[7.119]** *post.*

70 *Re Stainless Pipeline Supplies (IRL) Ltd; Tyner v Lafferty and another* [2010] IEHC 318 (Laffoy J). *Cf Re David Wright & Co Ltd* (1905) 39 ILT 204.

71 See *Savage River Pty Ltd v Fordcorp Industries Pty Ltd* (14 August 1998, unreported) Supreme Court of Victoria.

72 Note, in this respect, model reg 115 differs from model reg 76 of Table A of the C(C)A 1908 which requires the seal to be affixed in the presence of two directors and the secretary. See para **[7.027]** *post.*

company's objects clause[73]. Where the provisions of the articles of association are not observed, the purported execution will be defective. In *Re Stainless Pipeline Supplies (IRL) Ltd; Tyner v Lafferty and another*[74], a company purported to appoint a proxy to vote at a creditors' meeting pursuant to Ord 74, r 75 of the RSC 1986. The notes to Form 21 and Form 22 require the form of proxy, in the case of a corporation, to be, *inter alia*, 'under its common seal ...'. Although the appointor-company's articles of association were in the form of model reg 115, *only one* of its directors signed the proxy to which the common seal had been affixed. Laffoy J held that the proxy was not executed in accordance with Ord 74, r 75 because, *inter alia*, the purported signing of the proxy was not in conformity with the company's own articles of association.

[7.026] Where the sealing provisions in a company's articles are not observed, and the company or its liquidator seeks to avoid the contract, an outsider[75] may be able to enforce the contract where he satisfies the requirements of the rule in *Turquand's* case[76] or comes within reg 6 of the European Communities (Companies) Regulations 1973 ('EC(C)R 1973')[77]. Where there is no evidence of the directors resolving to sanction the use of the seal, the rule in *Turquand's* case may be invoked: *Ulster Investment Bank Ltd v Euro Estates Ltd and Drumkill Ltd*[78]. In *Re Motor Racing Circuits Ltd*[79], an appeal was brought to the Supreme Court against the trial judge's finding that an irregularity in the execution of a debenture created by the company (it would appear to have been claimed that one of the persons who attested the seal was not in fact a director) was covered by the rule in *Turquand's* case. Blayney J said:

> 'The position under the articles of association of the company is that the seal had to be affixed in the presence of the director and the secretary of the company. If one looks at the manner in which the debenture was executed it is clear that it purports to have been executed by a director and the secretary. In so far as the bank was concerned, all they were required to check was that the debenture appeared to have been executed in accordance with the requirements of the articles of association. The bank was not required to investigate as to whether the particular individual who executed as a director was in fact a director or whether the particular individual who executed as the secretary was in fact the secretary. They were entitled to assume that what is called the internal management of the company has been correctly complied with[80].'

73 *Power v Hoey* (1871) 19 WR 916.

74 *Re Stainless Pipeline Supplies (IRL) Ltd; Tyner v Lafferty and another* [2010] IEHC 318 (Laffoy J).

75 The term 'outsider' is often used to denote persons who deal with the company.

76 *Royal British Bank v Turquand* (1855) 5 EL & BL 248, considered post at para **[7.121]**.

77 SI 163/1973: see para **[7.129]**, *et seq*.

78 *Ulster Investment Bank Ltd v Euro Estates Ltd and Drumkill Ltd* [1982] ILRM 57, considered at para **[7.122]**, *post*.

79 *Re Motor Racing Circuits Ltd* (31 January 1997, unreported) SC, Blayney J, *nem diss*.

80 At p 6, 7 of the judgment. The internal management rule (ie, the rule in Turquand's case) is considered in detail at para **[7.121]** *post*.

Similarly, where a debenture was attested by a solicitor acting under a power of attorney and countersigned by the secretary in contravention of the company's articles[81], the equivalent UK provision to reg 6 saved the validity of the debenture[82].

(b) Regulation 76 of Table A of the First Schedule to the Companies (Consolidation) Act 1908

[7.027] Particular care should be taken when attending to the sealing of a deed or document by a company formed and registered under the Companies (Consolidation) Act 1908 ('C(C)A 1908') for, although a company formed and registered under the C(C)A 1908 is treated as being a 'company' within the meaning of s 2 of the CA 1963, unless expressly disapplied, its governing articles of association will be Table A of the First Schedule to the C(C)A 1908[83]. A trap for the unwary is provided by old model reg 76 of Table A of the C(C)A 1908. This provides:

> 'The seal of the company shall not be affixed to any instrument except by the authority of a resolution of the board of directors, and in the presence of at least two directors and of the secretary or such other person as the directors may appoint for that purpose; and those two directors and the secretary or other person as aforesaid shall sign every instrument to which the seal of the company is so affixed in their presence.'

Accordingly, where sealing is regulated by that regulation three signatures must appear: of *two* directors *and* of the secretary (or another person appointed for that purpose). Moreover, the seal must be affixed *in the presence of* the two directors and secretary or other person, something which is not required by reg 115. This requirement can cause difficulties where such companies execute deeds under execution blocks which opt for the more modern formulation of 'Given under the common seal' rather than the traditional 'Present when the common seal was affixed hereto' is used since the former will not evidence compliance with reg 76 and raise the spectre that the execution was not in accordance with the company's articles of association, the basic requirement for a document to be a deed as provided for by s 64(2)(b)(ii) of the LCLRA 2009.

[7.028] Regulation 76 of Table A of the C(C)A 1908 was considered by the High Court in *Safeera Ltd v Wallis and O'Regan*[84]. In that case – which arose out of a vendor and purchaser's summons – the defendant purchasers had refused to complete the purchase of a property on the ground that a deed on title had not been properly executed. Under the deed in question, a company that had been incorporated under the C(C)A 1908 had purported to convey the property to the plaintiff vendor. The point was that the deed had only been countersigned by *one* director and the secretary. Although the plaintiff

---

81 The articles were in the same form as the Irish model reg 115. While reg 115 provides that 'some other person appointed by the directors' may countersign, this is an alternative to the secretary countersigning and not an alternative to a director signing. It should further be noted that in Ireland there is no prohibition on the directors granting a power of attorney even where the articles do not expressly authorise this: *Industrial Development Authority v Moran* [1978] IR 159.

82 *TCB Ltd v Gray* [1986] 1 All ER 587. For a short note see Fish, (1987) Gazette ILSI 287. See para **[7.131]** *post*.

83 See *Re Sean Hussey, A Bankrupt* (23 September 1987, unreported) HC, Hamilton P at p 6 of the transcript.

84 *Safeera Ltd v Wallis and O'Regan* (12 July 1994, unreported) HC, Morris J.

vendor's solicitor had initially contended that the defendant purchasers were not entitled to look behind the deed and were to assume that the seal had been properly affixed, eventually, the conveyance had been countersigned by a second director. However, although it was no longer disputed that there was a valid conveyance in existence, the issue remained of relevance in determining interest and costs on the delay in closing the sale. The plaintiff vendor's counsel contended that since the CA 1963 had repealed the C(C)A 1908, one must construe s 324 of the CA 1963[85] as applying Table A of the CA 1963 to companies formed under the 1908 Act. It was also contended that it was appropriate to interpret the Companies Acts as mercantile documents and on that construction and upon the application of Table A of the CA 1963 to the C(C)A 1908, the execution of the deed 'was at all times valid and properly attested'. This argument did not find favour with Morris J who said:

> 'I reject this argument. In my view the position is clear. The indenture was not executed in accordance with the articles of association and was not effective to convey the company's interest in the property to the vendors.
>
> The Land Purchase Act 1925 clarified this matter in the United Kingdom where at s 74 it provided, in favour of a purchaser, that a deed should be deemed to be duly executed by a corporation aggregate if its seal had been affixed thereto in the presence of and attested by a clerk, secretary or other permanent officer or his deputy or a member of the board of directors, council or other governing body of the corporation had been affixed to a deed attested by persons purporting to be persons holding office as aforesaid, the deed should be deemed to have been executed in accordance with the requirements of the section and to have taken effect accordingly. However, I accept as a correct statement of the law the statement at p 531 of the 13th edition of Volume 1 of *Emmett on Title* that 'as regards deeds executed before 1926 and also cases not coming within subsection (1) above, it will still be necessary to inspect the articles of association or other authority for the purpose of ascertaining how the seal should have been affixed and to see that it has been so affixed'.
>
> Since no section corresponding to s 74 exists in this jurisdiction in my view the onus still remains upon a company to strictly comply with its articles of association in the affixing and attestation of its seal and upon a purchaser investigating title to ensure such compliance[86].'

Morris J held that the purchasers had been justified in refusing to complete the contract up to and including the date upon which they were informed that the third signatory to the seal had been added. A matter not considered in that case was where the beneficial or equitable interest in the property lay up to the valid execution of the deed by adding a third signatory. In such a case, notwithstanding that the legal title to the property in question remains vested in the company, where that company has been paid full consideration for the property, it seems clear that the purchaser will be the equitable or beneficial owner. So if, for example, the company that defectively executes a deed subsequently goes into liquidation, the property the subject matter of the deed would be

---

85 Section 324(1) of the CA 1963 provides: 'Subject to subsection (2), in the application of this Act to existing companies, it shall apply in the same manner – (a) in the case of a limited company ... as if the company had been formed and registered under this Act as a company limited by shares ...'

86 *Safeera Ltd v Wallis and O'Regan* (12 July 1994, unreported) HC, Morris J at pp 3, 4 of the judgment. Italics added.

owned beneficially by a purchaser who has paid full consideration and would not be available for distribution as part of the company's assets, being effectively held on trust[87].

Delivery of deed by a company

[7.029] After a company has caused its common seal to be affixed to a deed, the deed may not be effective until such time as it has been *delivered*. Where a deed is held in *escrow* the effect is to suspend its delivery, and therefore its effectiveness[88]. 'Deliver' has a technical meaning and a deed may be delivered even though it has not been physically handed over[89]. In the case of deeds executed by individuals, the practice is to recite in the deed that it has been 'signed, sealed and delivered', and it has been held that this is *prima facie* evidence that the person delivered the deed[90]. Where a company executes a deed, the attestation clause will usually provide 'present when the common seal of X Ltd was affixed hereto'. Although 'delivery' is not expressly mentioned, there was a rebuttable presumption at common law that the affixing of the common seal imports delivery[91]. Wylie[92] reasoned that, whilst arguable that a company cannot deliver a deed as an escrow[93], there is no reason in principle why a company (or other corporation) cannot deliver a deed in escrow if it so wishes, provided its intention is made clear[94]. Legislative effect has been given to this view by s 65(1) of the LCLRA 2009 which now provides that any rule of law to the effect that the affixing of a corporate seal to an instrument effects delivery by that body corporate is abolished. Section 65(2) goes on to provide that an instrument created by a body corporate in accordance with s 64(2)(b) is capable of operating as an escrow in the same circumstances and with the same consequences as an instrument executed by an individual.

Execution by power of attorney

[7.030] Section 15(2) of the Powers of Attorney Act 1996 (the 'POAA 1996') provides that a power of attorney is not required to be made under seal. This is, however, without prejudice to any requirement in or under any other enactment as to the execution of instruments by bodies corporate: s 15(3) of the POAA 1996. Section 40(1) of the CA 1963 facilitates a company granting a power to any person to act on the company's behalf *outside* the State. It provides:

---

87 For property held in trust on a liquidation, see Ch 25, *The Realisation and Distribution of Assets in a Winding Up*, at para **[25.149]** *et seq*.

88 See Wylie & Woods, *Irish Conveyancing Law* (3rd edn, 2005) at para [18.129].

89 *Evans v Grey* (1882) 9 LR Ir 539.

90 *Evans v Grey* (1882) 9 LR Ir 539 *per* Sullivan MR at 546.

91 See Wylie & Woods, *Irish Conveyancing Law* (3rd edn, 2005) at para [18.133] where the cases of *McArdle v Irish Iodine Co* (1864) 15 ICLR 146 and *Willis v Jermin* (1590) Cro Eliz 167 are cited in authority.

92 Wylie & Woods, *Irish Conveyancing Law* (3rd edn, 2005) at para [18.133].

93 *Gartside v Silkstone* (1882) 21 Ch D 762.

94 *Lloyd's Bank v Bullock* [1896] 2 Ch 192 and *Beesly v Hallwood Estates Ltd* [1961] Ch 105 cited by Wylie.

'A company may, by writing under its common seal, empower any person, either generally or in respect of any specified matters, as its attorney, to execute deeds on its behalf in any place outside the State.'

Accordingly, an appointment of an attorney under s 40(1) (ie, to execute deeds *outside* the State) must be under a company's common seal. When a deed is executed by an attorney pursuant to a valid power of attorney, such a deed is as binding on the company as if it were executed under the company's common seal[95]. A deed signed by a duly appointed attorney is *made* by the attorney, and not by the company on whose *behalf* it is made. Accordingly, where a deed is executed by a company acting through an attorney who is an individual, the provisions of s 64(2)(b)(i) of the LCLRA 2009 is the appropriate regime to be followed.

[7.031] Any doubts that a company could appoint an attorney to act on its behalf *within the State* were dispelled by the decision in *Industrial Development Authority v Moran*[96], where it was decided that s 40(1) of the CA 1963 was intended to clarify the law as to a company's power to act by attorney *outside* of the State, and that its specificity did not lead to an inference that a company could not act by attorney *within* the State. Therefore, Kenny J held that 'a company has power to act by attorney to execute deeds within the State'. As to the exercise of the power, he cited *Palmer's Company Precedents*[97]:

'Whether, however, in any particular case the directors of a company have power to execute a power of attorney on the company's behalf depends on the article. The general rule is *delegatus non potest delegare*. But directors are generally invested with wide general powers, and in virtue of such powers they are usually in a position to grant a power of attorney: otherwise the sanction of a general meeting must be obtained.'

Although Kenny J held that an article with the equivalent wording to the present model reg 80[98] was sufficient to empower the directors to appoint an attorney, where model reg 81 is adopted, a company will have specific authority to appoint an individual or a company to act as its attorney. Regulation 81 provides:

'The directors may from time to time and at any time by power of attorney appoint any company, firm or person or body or persons, whether nominated directly or indirectly by the directors, to be the attorney or attorneys of the company for such purposes and with such powers, authorities and discretions (not exceeding those vested in or exercisable by the directors under these regulations) and for such period and subject to such conditions as they may think fit, and any such power of attorney may contain such provisions for the protection of persons dealing with any such attorney as the directors may think fit, and may also authorise any such attorney to delegate all or any of the powers, authorities and discretions vested in him.'

It is curious that this regulation can be interpreted to mean that the directors may appoint an attorney by resolution as opposed to under the seal of the company[99]. It is thought

95 Section 40(2) of the CA 1963.

96 *Industrial Development Authority v Moran* [1978] IR 159 at 164 *per* Kenny J.

97 *Palmer's Company Precedents* (17th edn, 1956) Vol 1 at p 950.

98 See para **[7.112]** *post*, and Ch 13, *Corporate Governance: Management by Directors*, at para **[13.127]** *et seq*.

99 The CLRG's *First Report* (2000–2001), recommendation 4.8.13 at p 70 recommends that reg 81 be repealed on the grounds that an attorney can already be appointed under reg 80.

that the creation of a power in favour of a person to act as a company's attorney within the State (as opposed to outside of the State) does not require to be by deed under seal. Since no enactment prescribes the manner of execution of a power of attorney by a company for use within the State, and since s 38(1)(a) of the CA 1963 equates companies with individuals, s 15(3) of the POAA 1996 has no application and so s 15(2) applies, meaning that such a power of attorney is not required to be made under the company's common seal. Notwithstanding this, it is thought to be prudent for companies to appoint all donees of powers under their common seals since any such appointment would be susceptible to challenge were the donee, by chance, to execute a deed outside of the State.

[7.032] The execution of instruments by the donee of a power (ie, the attorney) has been clarified by s 17 of the POAA 1996. Section 17(1) provides that the donee of a power of attorney may (a) execute any instrument with his own signature and, where sealing is required, his own seal and (b) do any other thing in his own name by the authority of the donor of the power. This section goes on to provide that 'any instrument executed or thing done in that manner shall be as effective as if executed or done by the donee with the signature and seal, or, as the case may be in the name of the donor'. As to the execution of conveyances by a donee for a donor company, s 17(2) provides:

> 'A person who is authorised under a power of attorney to convey any estate or interest in property in the name or on behalf of a corporation sole or aggregate may either execute the conveyance as provided in *subsection (1)* or, as donee of the power, execute the conveyance by signing his or her name as acting in the name or on behalf of the corporation in the presence of at least one witness and, in the case of a deed, by affixing his or her own seal, and such execution takes effect and is valid in like manner as if the corporation had executed the conveyance.'

It has been suggested by a leading conveyancer that whenever a conveyance of real property is executed by an attorney on behalf of a corporation, it is prudent to use the special method of execution provided for in s 17(2) rather than the general method provided for in s 17(1)[100]. The same author suggests that best practice in relation to the execution of deeds by an attorney for a company (or other body corporate) is that:

- the deed is prepared in the company's name;
- the attestation clause states that the deed is executed on behalf of the company by the attorney; and
- the attorney executes by writing in his own hand: 'AB (the donor company) by its attorney CD (the donee)' who then signs his or her own name[101].

[7.033] Where a company (or other body corporate – not being a corporation sole) is appointed as an attorney, whether for an individual or another body corporate, the attorney company (or donee) may appoint a person for the purpose of executing the deed or other instrument in the name of the donor company: s 17(3) of the POAA 1996. Moreover, that subsection also provides that where an instrument appears to be executed by a person so appointed then, in favour of a purchaser, the instrument is deemed to have been executed by the person, unless the contrary is shown.

---

100 See Gallagher, *Powers of Attorney Act 1996* (1998) at p 23.

101 Gallagher, *Powers of Attorney Act 1996* (1998) at p 23.

[7.034] Powers of attorney should not be given lightly. Although a company may revoke a power of attorney, protection is afforded to the donee[102] and third parties who deal with the donee[103] where they are unaware that the power has been revoked. Moreover, s 20(1) of the POAA 1996 provides that where a person (whether a natural person or a company) creates a power of attorney which is expressed to be irrevocable and given to secure (a) a proprietary interest of the donee of the power, or (b) the performance of an obligation owed to the donee, then for the duration of the interest or obligation, the power shall not be revoked by the donor without the consent of the donee or even by the winding up or dissolution of the donor company[104].

[B] PRE-INCORPORATION CONTRACTS

[7.035] Business opportunities often arise unexpectedly. Sometimes it may not be practical for individuals to form or acquire a company before the exigencies of business require a contract to be signed.

To take an example. A new shopping centre is in the course of construction and the developers are approaching potential tenants. A and B are interested in starting up a business for themselves and agree in principle to take a 35-year lease, and their solicitors are furnished with all necessary documentation. The centre is due to open in two months, and it will take that time for A and B to fit out the unit. The developers' solicitors insist that an agreement for lease[105] be signed before allowing A and B to occupy the unit to fit it out. Time is of the essence. A and B do not have a company, and moreover, are not yet decided as to whether they want to take the lease in their own names or that of a company. *Tempus fugit*. In such circumstances A and B may sign the agreement for lease 'for and on behalf of A and B Company Ltd'. If they do form such a company, in due course the company can, by virtue of s 37 of the CA 1963, take the lease by resolving to ratify the agreement for lease. However, if A and B decide to take the lease in their own personal names, in the absence of an express agreement to the contrary, they can sue and be sued on foot of the agreement for lease.

Prior to the coming into force of s 37 of the CA 1963, the implications of signing 'for and on behalf of' an unincorporated company were a legal quagmire. In this section pre-incorporation contracts are considered under the following headings:

1. The old quagmire.
2. Section 37 of the CA 1963.
3. The liability of corporate agents.
4. Limitations on the application of s 37 of the CA 1963.

The old quagmire

[7.036] The problems that existed before 1963 were based on two principles of the law of contract. The first principle was privity of contract: on the facts of our example, the

[102] Section 18(1) of the POAA 1996.

[103] Section 18(2) of the POAA 1996.

[104] See, further, Ch 20, *Corporate Borrowing: Receivers*, at para **[20.039]**.

[105] An *agreement for lease* is a contract whereby a tenant agrees to take, and a landlord agrees to give, a lease of a premises at a future date.

company 'A and B Company Ltd' could not sue or be sued in law or in equity[106] on the agreement for lease since it was not party to that contract. The second principle was the rules governing the ratification of contracts in the law of agency. Agency was at first thought to be the solution to the problems raised by the rule on privity of contract, and into this round hole a square peg was hammered. If A and B could be said to be the agents of A and B Company Ltd, could not the company as principal, ratify the agreement for lease-contract? The answer was 'No'. It is a basic principle of ratification that a principal can only ratify an agent's actions where the principal itself could have entered into the contract at that time: A and B Company Ltd could not have entered into the agreement for lease since it did not itself exist at the time the agreement for lease was entered. The principles governing the ratification of contracts were stated by Wright J in *Firth v Staines*[107] to be as follows:

> 'To constitute a valid ratification three conditions must be satisfied: first, the agent whose act is sought to be ratified must have purported to act for the principal; secondly, at the time the act was done the agent must have had a competent principal; and, thirdly at the time of ratification the principal must be legally capable of doing the act himself.'

Although now modified in the context of pre-incorporation contracts, the principles of ratification set out in *Firth v Staines* continue to apply to ratification of contracts generally in Ireland[108].

Section 37 of the CA 1963

[7.037] The problematic second condition for ratification of pre-incorporation contracts in *Firth v Stains* was reversed by s 37(1) of the CA 1963. As far as pre-incorporation contracts are concerned, only the first and third conditions in *Firth v Stains* now remain. Section 37(1) of the CA 1963 provides:

> 'Any contract or other transaction purporting to be entered into by a company prior to its formation or by any person on behalf of the company prior to its formation *may be ratified* by the company after its formation and thereupon the company shall become bound by it and entitled to the benefit thereof as if it had been in existence at the date of such contract or other transaction and had been a party thereto[109].'

Several points arise for consideration. First, the section is not confined to 'contracts' but applies to 'transactions', which includes conveyances, trusts, covenants, but not (it has been held) grants of planning permission[110]. Second, s 37(1) not only applies to transactions entered into by persons 'on behalf of' a company, but also to transactions where an unincorporated company *itself* purports to enter into the transaction.

[7.038] Post-incorporation ratification of pre-incorporation contracts may be effected by either the resolution of the board of directors or of the members of the company in general meeting. The authority of both the board and the members to ratify will depend

---

106 See Vaughan Williams LJ in *Re English Colonial Produce Co Ltd* [1906] 2 Ch 435.

107 *Firth v Staines* [1897] 2 QB 70 at 75.

108 *Bank of Ireland v Rockfield* [1979] IR 21.

109 Italics added.

110 See *State (Finglas Industrial Estate Ltd) v Dublin County Council* [1983] IESC 8, where a planning permission was held not to be a ratifiable *transaction* within the meaning of s 37 of the CA 1963.

upon what the articles of association of a given company provide. Under model reg 80[111] the powers of management of the company are given to the directors. Where this is adopted by a company the appropriate organ to ratify a pre-incorporation contract will be the company's board of directors.

[7.039] In *HKN Invest OY v Incotrade PVT Ltd et al*[112], Costello J made a number of interesting observations on the question of corporate ratification of pre-incorporation contracts. In the first place he held that ratification may be effected informally:

> 'I do not think that any formal meeting to ratify must be shown to have taken place before [s 37] can be applied. Each case must depend on its own facts, but it seems to me that ratification can in certain circumstances occur informally, for example, in a one man company[113] where after incorporation the controlling shareholder, implements the contract without the benefit of a formal board meeting[114].'

In that case, Costello J felt that he could not infer ratification of the pre-incorporation contracts from the mere acceptance by the principal shareholder of sums paid by commission. Costello J also held that in appropriate circumstances a company's liquidator could ratify a pre-incorporation contract under s 231(2)(i) of the CA 1963[115]. This was appropriate in the instant case and meant, according to Costello J, that:

> 'Ratification in this case will mean that as a matter of law the pre-incorporation contracts will have existed from their date of execution – it will not affect the rights of either party arising from the manner in which the contract has or has not been performed since then[116].'

[7.040] The facts in *HKN Invest OY v Incotrade PVT Ltd et al* were that two German nationals came to Ireland, established a bogus loan brokerage, defrauded a number of Irish and foreign nationals and departed 'this country hurriedly only a few steps ahead of the Irish and German police. They left behind them a number of angry creditors and a cluster of legal problems as to who is now entitled to the benefit of certain assets which they failed to take with them[117].' The plaintiffs were judgment creditors of both the individuals and their company. The liquidator of the fraudsters' company claimed the assets left behind for the benefit of the company's creditors. The fraudsters incorporated the defendant company but prior to its incorporation had carried on business. Persons who had conducted business with the company and had entered into contracts in respect of loans to be obtained and commission to be paid believed that the fraudsters had been acting on the company's behalf. The main fraud appears to have been that the fraudsters would undertake to procure a loan and would in return obtain a commission. In most cases this commission was paid to the defendant company on foot of contracts entered into *before* the company had been incorporated. One of the fraudsters opened a personal bank account and caused the commission, payable to the defendant company, to be paid

---

[111] See Ch 13, *Corporate Governance: Management by the Directors*, at para **[13.127]**.

[112] *HKN Invest OY v Incotrade PVT Ltd et al* [1993] 3 IR 152. See Steen, 'Constructive Trusts and Pre-Incorporation Contracts: A Reappraisal' (2004) 11 (1) DULJ 260.

[113] A reference to *de facto* single-member companies.

[114] *HKN Invest OY v Incotrade PVT Ltd et al* [1993] 3 IR 152 at 160.

[115] See Ch 25, *Realisation and Distribution of Assets in a Winding Up*, at para **[25.010]**.

[116] *HKN Invest OY v Incotrade PVT Ltd et al* [1993] 3 IR 152 at 161.

[117] *HKN Invest OY v Incotrade PVT Ltd et al* [1993] 3 IR 152 at 155.

into this account. Sums continued to be paid into the fraudster's personal account even after the company's incorporation and no monies were transferred from the personal account to the company's account. Some of the monies in the personal accounts were used to purchase two Mercedes cars and a Porsche car which were registered in the fraudsters' personal names. The matter before Costello J was, who was beneficially entitled to the remainder of the monies in the personal account?

Having held that the liquidator of the company was entitled to ratify the pre-incorporation contracts, Costello J went on to hold that the company was *beneficially entitled* to the commission paid to the fraudsters, who held such payments under a constructive trust[118]. Costello J said:

> 'It seems to me therefore that the court should hold that the promoter of a company who received payment on behalf of a company which he is incorporating and pursuant to a pre-incorporation contract which the company is empowered to ratify holds the commission as a constructive trustee for the company[119].'

Costello J also said that this would remain the case even if the company did not ratify the contract as the monies obtained were held on trust for the company.

Liability of corporate agents

[7.041] Once a contract or other transaction has been validly ratified the company will become bound by its terms and its agents normally will drop out of the picture. However, prior to ratification, s 37(2) of the CA 1963 provides:

> '... the person or persons who purported to act in the name or on behalf of the company shall in the absence of any express agreement to the contrary be personally bound by the contract or other transaction and entitled to the benefit thereof.'

A similar UK provision was considered in the case of *Phonogram Ltd v Lane*[120]. In that case Lord Denning MR construed the word 'purports' (note that s 37 uses the word 'purported') as not implying any question that the outsider should believe that the company was in existence. So, it can be common knowledge to all contracting parties that at the time the contract is entered into there is no company in existence. However, it is important to note that an agent will be liable where the company is ultimately not formed and there is no *express* agreement that he is not to be liable. It is clear from s 37(2) of the CA 1963 that the persons who purport to act in the name of an incorporated company are 'entitled to the benefit' of the contract or other transaction (in the absence of agreement to the contrary). In *Badgerhill Properties Ltd v Cottrell*[121], the obvious point was made that for the transaction in question to be ratifiable, it must purport to be made by the company in question.

---

118 *HKN Invest OY v Incotrade PVT Ltd et al* [1993] 3 IR 152 at 162, citing *Hussey v Palmer* [1972] 3 All ER 744 as authority.

119 *HKN Invest OY v Incotrade PVT Ltd et al* [1993] 3 IR 152 at 163.

120 *Phonogram Ltd v Lane* [1981] 3 All ER 182. This interpreted s 9(2) of the European Communities Act 1972 (UK), which provided that where a contract purports to be made by a company, or an agent on behalf of the company, prior to incorporation, subject to any agreement to the contrary, the person who purported to act for the company or as agent for it is personally liable.

121 *Badgerhill Properties Ltd v Cottrell* [1991] BCLC 805 at 813.

[7.042] Before the enactment of s 37(2) of the CA 1963, the liability of corporate agents prior to the incorporation of the company and ratification of the transaction was uncertain. In *Kelner v Baxter*[122], three agents purported to buy wine 'on behalf of' a company which had not been incorporated. In due course the company was formed, the wine was delivered and drunk and, as if *in vino veritas*, the company went into liquidation before the wine had been paid for. The three agents were held to be personally liable. In the oft quoted words of Erle CJ:

> 'Where a contract is signed by one who professes to be signing 'as agent', but who has no principal existing at the time, and the contract would be altogether inoperative unless binding on the person who signed it, he is bound thereby: and a stranger cannot by a subsequent ratification relieve him from that responsibility[123].'

While in that case the individual agents sought to avoid liability, the quagmire was such as to render the outcome of every case a matter of speculation. So in *Newborne v Sensolid (Great Britain) Ltd*[124], the hapless Mr Newborne was unsuccessful in seeking to *enforce* a pre-incorporation contract. His error was not signing 'for and on behalf of' the company. Rather, he signed his own name over the name of the company, thus making it unclear as to whether he signed for himself, as agent for the company to be, or as a future director of the company. As the company could not in law ratify the contract, and the court could not decide in what capacity Mr Newborne had signed, it was held that the whole contract was void for uncertainty. It is to be welcomed that s 37(2) renders such case law obsolete in the context of pre-incorporation contracts entered by companies to which the Companies Acts apply[125].

Limitations on the application of s 37 of the CA 1963

[7.043] The reference in s 37 of the CA 1963 to a 'company' must be strictly construed. A strict construction of s 37 precludes a foreign company, which enters into a contract in Ireland prior to its foreign formation and registration, from relying upon its provisions. This is because 'company' is defined by s 2 of the CA 1963 as meaning 'a company formed and registered under this Act, or an existing company'[126]. Section 37 will not extend to companies outside of the s 2 definition[127]. This was indeed the construction given to the similar English section[128] in *Rover International Ltd v Cannon Film Sales Ltd*[129] where it was held that it had no application to foreign companies. Harman J held:

---

122 *Kelner v Baxter* (1866) LR 2 CP 174.

123 *Kelner v Baxter* (1866) LR 2 CP 174 at 183.

124 *Newborne v Sensolid (Great Britain) Ltd* [1954] 1 QB 45.

125 Section 37(1) and (2) is applied to certain unregistered companies by s 377 of the CA 1963. Compare the old 'half-solutions' such as the company re-entering a new contract on the same terms after its incorporation, or entering a conditional contract; both of which exposed people to the vicissitudes of trusting the other contracting party to co-operate. These may still have relevance where a transaction does not fall within s 37 of the CA 1963: see **[7.043]** *et seq post*.

126 See Ch 1, *The Private Company in Context*, at para **[1.156]**.

127 Section 37(3) of the CA 1963 provides specifically that the section's application is not of general application to *all* companies, providing that the section should 'not apply to a company incorporated before the operative date'.

128 Section 36(4) of the Companies Act 1985 (UK).

129 *Rover International Ltd v Cannon Film Sales Ltd* [1987] BCLC 540.

> 'In my judgment, that contention [ie, that it was intended the provision should apply to foreign companies since the common law applied the 'pre-incorporation' rule to both United Kingdom and foreign companies] does not create a sufficient context to show a 'contrary intention' so that s 36(4) would refer to companies wherever incorporated. Parliament has plainly legislated for United Kingdom companies and the subsection is effective in that regard. I do not find any convincing reason for believing that Parliament intended to legislate for foreign companies[130].'

It may be noted that in England pre-incorporation contracts made by foreign companies, including Irish companies, are now treated as having been validly created if done in the manner prescribed by the law of the country in which the company is incorporated[131].

[7.044] A further limitation arises where a contract purports to be made by a company which was once incorporated, but which is subsequently struck off the register of companies. In *Cotronic (UK) Ltd v Dezonie et al*[132], it was held that the similar English provision had no application where a company had been dissolved. It has also been held in *Oshkosh B'Gosh Inc v Dan Marbel Inc Ltd*[133] that the similar English section has no application to a situation where a company changes its name, and trades before a new certificate of incorporation on change of name has issued. It is thought that in both situations s 37 of the CA 1963 would be held to have no application to contracts entered into by a company in such circumstances.

[C] CONTRACTUAL CAPACITY AND *ULTRA VIRES*

The objects clause and *ultra vires*

[7.045] Section 6(1)(b) of the CA 1963 provides that the memorandum of association must state 'the objects of the company'. Accordingly, every company has to have an *objects clause*, which states the purposes for which the company was formed and the legitimate activities it can pursue.

When a company purports to enter into a contract which is neither expressly nor impliedly in furtherance of its objects, such a contract is said to be *ultra vires*, or beyond the company's capacity[134]. Such contracts are void at common law. In *Ashbury Railway Carriage and Iron Co v Riche*[135], a company was incorporated with, the object, *inter alia*, of making and selling railway carriages. Without regard to the company's objects, its directors purported to contract to buy a concession for constructing a railway in Belgium. It was held by the House of Lords that the contract was *ultra vires* and void and, furthermore, was unratifiable by the shareholders because the contract was a nullity. Today, while *ultra vires* contracts remain unratifiable[136], s 10 of the CA 1963 permits the alteration of the objects clause.

---

130 *Rover International Ltd v Cannon Film Sales Ltd* [1987] BCLC 540 at 543.

131 Foreign Companies (Execution of Documents) Regulations 1994 (UK), SI 1994/950.

132 *Cotronic (UK) Ltd v Dezonie et al* [1991] BCLC 721. See 'Editorial' (1991) 12 Co Law 113.

133 *Oshkosh B'Gosh Inc v Dan Marbel Inc Ltd* [1989] BCLC 507.

134 See generally MacCann, 'The Capacity of a Company' (1992) ILT 79 and 151.

135 *Ashbury Railway Carriage and Iron Co v Riche* (1875) LR 7 HLC 653.

136 See *Northern Bank Finance Corporation Ltd v Quinn and Achates Investment Company* [1979] ILRM 221.

[7.046] The rationale of the doctrine of *ultra vires* was and remains the protection of the company's shareholders and creditors. Indeed, received wisdom is that it is thought to be part and parcel of limited liability that, upon a company being incorporated, its activities should be confined to its stated objects. In fact the doctrine often does more harm than good. As we shall see, the effects of the doctrine have been considerably modified by s 8 of the CA 1963[137]. Moreover, the Company Law Review Group has recommended that the doctrine be disapplied to private companies limited by shares which should be given the same contractual capacity as a natural person and this is what has been provided for in the draft Companies Bill published in 2011[138].

Restraining *ultra vires* activities

[7.047] So established is the doctrine of *ultra vires* that there is a statutory right to have recourse to the courts for an injunction to prevent a company from acting *ultra vires*. Section 8(2) of the CA 1963 provides:

> 'The court may, on the application of any member or holder of debentures of a company, restrain such company from doing any act or thing which the company has no power to do.'

It may appear to be somewhat anomalous to confine *locus standi* to members and debenture-holders. Members – Yes; debenture-holders – Yes; but what about other creditors? On the one hand, one may think that this ought to be extended to all creditors; on the other hand, however, one would not wish the legislature to afford a right of recourse to the courts to nominal unsecured creditors, with a frivolous or vexatious claim against a company. The anachronism is, however, found in the reference to 'debenture-holders' and it might be more appropriate to refer to 'secured and preferential creditors'. In exercising its discretion to make an order under this section the courts will apply the same principles as in an application for any interlocutory injunction[139]. In *McGilligan and Bowen v O'Grady et al*[140], O'Donovan J, in the High Court, had granted an injunction against the third defendant, a company which was restrained from 'acting *ultra vires* the objects set forth in its memorandum of association and, in particular, from engaging in activities that did not come within those objects'[141]. The company had wished to become involved in a manufacturing process and although such was not expressly permitted by its objects clauses, there was power to 'do all such other things as are incidental or conducive to the attainment of the above objects or any of them' which it was thought *might* permit the company to engage in manufacturing. At a meeting of the members to amend the objects clause the requisite qualified majority to pass a special resolution was not forthcoming and it was against this background that O'Donovan J restrained the company from acting *ultra vires*. That part[142] of the order was discharged on appeal to the Supreme Court. Keane J held that he was not satisfied that the balance of convenience required the company to be restrained from becoming

---

[137] See para **[7.080]** *post*.

[138] See para **[7.096]** *post*.

[139] As to which see, Courtney, *Mareva Injunctions and Related Interlocutory Orders* (1998, Butterworths) at paras [5.03]–[5.11].

[140] *McGilligan and Bowen v O'Grady et al* [1999] 1 IR 346.

[141] *McGilligan and Bowen v O'Grady et al* [1999] 1 IR 346 at 348.

[142] See further Ch 11, *Shareholders' Remedies*, at para **[11.069]**.

involved in a manufacturing process and that irreparable damage could be caused to the company.

Contractual capacity

[7.048] In this section the following issues relating to corporate *capacity* to contract are considered:

- (a) Judicial construction of the objects clause.
- (b) Classifying corporate capacity.
- (c) Substantive objects or ancillary powers?
- (d) Express ancillary powers: conditions on their exercise.
- (e) The significance of conditions on the exercise of powers.
- (f) Implied ancillary powers.
- (g) Gratuitous dispositions of company property.
- (h) Section 8 of the CA 1963.
- (i) Regulation 6 of the EC(C)R 1973.
- (j) Corporate enforcement of *ultra vires* contracts.
- (k) Recovery of money given *ultra vires*.
- (l) Reform of the doctrine of *ultra vires*.

(a) Judicial construction of the objects clause

[7.049] In view of the drastic effects which can result from a contract being *ultra vires*[143], draughtsmen submit companies for registration with a veritable plethora of 'so-called' objects. The hope is that whatever activity the company might possibly engage in will be *intra vires*. Hence, the 'admirable brevity' of the objects clause seen in the model objects clause in Table A bears no relation to the realities of life[144]. In the early days, the judiciary was not impressed by the multiplicity of so-called objects with which companies were formed. It was felt that such a practice was contrary to the spirit of the Companies Acts, since it defeated the purpose of requiring a company to set out, up-front, what it was formed to do. Thus, Lord Wrenbury in *Cotman v Brougham*[145] spoke of the '*pernicious practice*', namely that of:

> '... registering memoranda of association which, under the clause relating to objects contained paragraph after paragraph not specifying or delimiting the proposed trade or purpose ...'

What follows is an analysis of the 'cat and mouse' game played by the judiciary and the draughtsmen. The following are considered:

- (i) The main objects rule;
- (ii) The independent objects clause;
- (iii) The '*Bell Houses*' clause.

---

143 See Shapira, 'Ultra Vires Redux' (1984) LQR 468.

144 See Ussher, *Company Law in Ireland* (1986, Sweet & Maxwell) at p 112.

145 *Cotman v Brougham* [1918] AC 514; [1918–19] All ER Rep 265.

(i) The main objects rule

[7.050] The judiciary could not declare elongated objects clauses to be void on account of the statutory predecessors of s 5 of the C(A)A 1983. Like s 5, these provided that a company's certificate of incorporation shall be *conclusive evidence* that:

> '... all the requirements of the Companies Acts in respect of registration and of matters precedent and incidental thereto have been complied with ...[146]'

Although the registrar of companies might try to refuse to register a company which contains an elongated objects clause, thus far this has not been done, presumably because the registrar's right to do so is far from clear. As for the judiciary, as Lord Finlay LC said in *Cotman v Brougham*[147], 'all the courts can do is construe the memorandum as it stands'.

[7.051] Judicial construction has been inventive and of devastating effect. The particular device used by the courts to defend what they perceived to be the legislative intention was the *ejusdem generis* rule of interpretation, which says that, when *particular* words are followed by *general* words, the general words are limited so as to have the same import implicit in the particular words. Accordingly, where the perceived 'main objects' of a company were followed by wider powers, the latter would be construed as being capable only of exercise in furtherance of the 'main objects'. This is the essence of the main objects or 'substratum rule'. The rule was described in *Anglo-Overseas Agencies Ltd v Green*[148] as follows:

> '... where the memorandum of association expresses the object of the company in a series of paragraphs, and one paragraph, or the first two or three paragraphs, appear to embody the 'main object' of the company, all the other paragraphs are treated as merely ancillary to the 'main object', and as limited or controlled thereby.'

Not only will a contract, which is not in furtherance of the main objects, be *ultra vires*, but so also might a company, which does not pursue its main objects, be wound up for failure of substratum: *Re German Date Coffee Co Ltd*[149]. But the draughtsmen were not to be outdone.

(ii) The independent objects clause

[7.052] The draughtsmen rallied by devising so-called *independent objects clauses* which oust the main objects rule. A typical independent objects clause provides:

> 'It is hereby expressly declared that each sub-clause of this clause shall be construed independently of the other sub-clauses hereof, and that none of the objects mentioned in

[146] On the conclusiveness of the certificate of incorporation see Ch 4, *Incorporation and its Consequences*, at para **[4.004]** *et seq*.

[147] *Cotman v Brougham* [1918–19] All ER 265 at 267.

[148] *Anglo-Overseas Agencies Ltd v Green* [1961] 1 QB 1; [1960] All ER 244.

[149] *Re German Date Coffee Co Ltd* [1882] 20 Ch 169; [1881–85] All ER 372. Here a company acquired a Swedish patent for manufacturing a substitute for coffee from dates. The objects expressly referred to a German patent and Lindley LJ said (at 375): '... the real object of this company ... was to manufacture a substitute for coffee in Germany under a patent which is valid according to German law. All the rest is subordinate to that main object and that is what the people subscribe their money for ...'

> any sub-clause shall be deemed to be merely subsidiary to the objects mentioned in any other sub-clause.'

The validity of such a clause was upheld by the House of Lords in *Cotman v Brougham*[150], on the basis that the registrar of companies had issued the company (that had been registered with such an objects clause) with a certificate of incorporation which was conclusive evidence as to the validity of the contents of the memorandum of association[151]. In that case the objects clause contained 35 sub-clauses which, if valid, would have permitted the company to pursue almost any object. Were it not for the insertion of an independent objects clause, the main object would have been found to be the development of rubber plantations. However the 12th sub-clause permitted the buying of stocks or shares in any company. The 30th sub-clause was an independent objects clause which said that all sub-clauses should be construed as substantive clauses. The company underwrote and had allotted to it shares in an oil company. Problems arose when the oil company was wound up and the company was placed on the list of contributories. In spite of protests to the contrary from both sides of the bench, it was held that the contract in respect of the shares was *intra vires* the company. Almost begrudgingly, Lord Wrenbury held:

> 'The language of c 13(30) is such that I cannot say that such a transaction was *ultra vires* because it was not ancillary to or connected with or in furtherance of something which I find elsewhere in the company's memorandum to have been "its business".'

An independent objects clause is found in the objects clause of most companies formed today.

(iii) The 'Bell Houses' clause

[7.053] A '*Bell Houses*' clause – so called after a case of that name[152] – gives a company the capacity to pursue any business which the directors believe would be advantageous to the company[153]. Accordingly, the company's capacity to pursue a particular business will be determined by the directors' subjective discretion. An example is:

> 'To carry on any other trade or business which can, in the opinion of the board of directors, be advantageously carried on by the company in connection with or as ancillary to any of the above businesses or the general business of the company, or further any of its objects.'

In *Bell Houses Ltd v City Wall Properties Ltd*[154], the principal business set out in the company's memorandum was the development of housing estates. However, the objects clause contained a clause which empowered the directors to pursue any business they considered advantageous to the company. The objects clause also contained an independent objects clause similar to that in the *Cotman* case. The company contracted to introduce a financier to another company for a procuration fee. The Court of Appeal held that in view of the clause used, the transaction was *intra vires*. Danckwerts LJ said that the impact of the clause was:

---

150 *Cotman v Brougham* [1918] AC 514.

151 *Cotman v Brougham* [1918] AC 514 at 267, *per* Lord Finlay LC.

152 *Bell Houses Ltd v City Wall Properties Ltd* [1966] 2 All ER 674.

153 See Wedderburn, (1966) MLR 191 and Pollock, (1966) CLJ 174.

154 *Bell Houses Ltd v City Wall Properties Ltd* [1966] 2 All ER 674.

> '... to make the *bona fide* opinion of the directors sufficient to decide whether an activity of the plaintiff company is *intra vires*[155].'

When this clause is coupled with an independent objects clause, the potential ambit of the doctrine of *ultra vires* is considerably reduced: almost any object can validly be pursued.

(b) Classifying corporate capacity

[7.054] Companies' objects clauses frequently contain a multiplicity of sub-clauses. The courts have held that not all of these sub-clauses may actually be substantive *objects* which the company can pursue, independently. Some sub-clauses may be found to be mere ancillary powers which are incapable of being exercised otherwise than in furtherance of the company's substantive objects. Moreover, it may be found that in addition to these *express clauses* the company will have *implied* powers, ancillary to the company's substantive objects. The labelling of the various combinations is threefold:

(i) Substantive objects;
(ii) Express ancillary powers;
(iii) Implied ancillary powers.

(i) Substantive objects or ancillary powers?

[7.055] Most companies formed today have in excess of 20 sub-clauses within their objects clause. Many are merely *ancillary powers*, which a company would be implied to have, eg, the power to borrow, provide security in respect of borrowings, etc. The effects of the 'main objects' rule and the use by draughtsmen of the 'independent objects' clause have already been considered[156]. How do these bear on the question of whether or not something is an object or a power?

Whether a particular sub-clause is properly a substantive object or an ancillary power will, in every case, be a matter of construction for the courts. It has been held in *Rolled Steel Products (Holdings) Ltd v British Steel Corporation et al*[157] that some sub-clauses are *incapable* of constituting a substantive object. Where this is found to be the case, the sub-clause in question must be construed as being an express ancillary power. In the *Rolled Steel* case, Slade LJ said:

> '... the question whether [the sub-clause which, *inter alia*, allowed the company to give guarantees] of RSP's memorandum contains a separate independent object of the company is purely one of construction of that memorandum. The decision of the House of Lords in *Cotman v Brougham* [1918] AC 514, [1918–19] All ER 265 requires that, in answering it, full force must be given, so far as possible, to the provision at the end of [the objects clause] which directs that each sub-clause shall be construed independently of the other sub-clauses. I accept counsel's submission ... that [the sub-clause which, *inter alia*, allowed the company to give guarantees] must be treated as containing a substantive object unless either (i) the subject matter of this sub-paragraph is by its nature incapable of constituting a substantive object (as was the power to borrow in *Re Introductions* ...), or (ii) the wording of the memorandum shows expressly or by implication that the sub-clause was intended merely to constitute an ancillary power only ...[158].'

---

155 *Bell Houses Ltd v City Wall Properties Ltd* [1966] 2 All ER 674.
156 See paras **[7.050]** and **[7.052]** *ante*.
157 *Rolled Steel Products (Holdings) Ltd v British Steel Corporation* [1985] 3 All ER 52.
158 *Rolled Steel Products (Holdings) Ltd v British Steel Corporation* [1985] 3 All ER 52 at 81.

Slade LJ, while accepting that a company could have as its main object the giving of guarantees, held that on the true construction of the objects clause in that case, the giving of guarantees was but an ancillary power and not a substantive object[159].

[7.056] The distinction between 'true objects' and 'mere powers' has been made in many cases. In *Re Horsley & Weight Ltd*[160], Buckley LJ said:

> 'It has now long been a commercial practice to set out in memoranda of association, a great number and variety of "objects", so called, some of which (for example, to borrow money, to promote the company's interests by advertising its products or services or to do acts or things conducive or incidental to the company's objects) are by their very nature incapable of standing as independent objects which can be pursued in isolation as the sole activity of the company. Such "objects" must, by reason of their very nature, be interpreted merely as powers incidental to the true objects of the company and must be so treated notwithstanding the presence of a separate objects clause ... Where there is no separate objects clause, some of the express 'objects' may upon construction fall to be treated as no more than powers which are ancillary to the dominant or main objects of the company[161].'

It seems clear that not even the presence of a separate or independent objects clause can 'save' what purports to be an object from being construed as a power *if in fact that is what it is*. Often, the giving of guarantees will be the action under scrutiny[162]. This may happen where Company A gives a guarantee to a bank in respect of money loaned to Company B. Unless the companies are members of a group of companies, it might be argued that Company A acted *ultra vires* in that it only had power to give guarantees in furtherance of its own objects. If, on construction of its objects clause, the giving of guarantees is found to be only an ancillary power the next question to be asked is, what is the significance of this distinction?

(ii) Express ancillary powers: exercise conditional on the existence of commercial benefit

[7.057] While express ancillary powers can be subject to express limitations which go to the very root of the power itself, the most common express limitation is that they are expressly said to be exercisable only 'as may seem expedient for the furtherance of the objects of the company'[163], ie, that there is *commercial benefit* to the company. However, even if they are not so qualified, such limiting conditions will always be implied[164].

---

159 *Rolled Steel Products (Holdings) Ltd v British Steel Corporation et al* [1985] 3 All ER 52, where Slade LJ said: 'The references in [the sub-clauses] to the giving of credit and to customers of and persons having dealings with the company, make it additionally clear that the sub-clause in its context was intended to comprise merely a series of ancillary powers.'

160 *Re Horsley & Weight Ltd* [1982] 3 All ER 1045. See generally, (1983) MLR 204.

161 *Re Horsley & Weight Ltd* [1982] 3 All ER 1045 at 1050.

162 On inter-company guarantees see generally, Andrews & Millett, *Law of Guarantees* (1992, Longman) at pp 138–139.

163 *Per* Slade LJ in *Rolled Steel Products* [1985] 3 All ER 52.

164 *Rolled Steel Products (Holdings) Ltd v British Steel Corporation et al* [1985] 3 All ER 52 at 84a, where Slade LJ referred to *Re Introductions Ltd* [1969] 1 All ER 887 and *Re David Payne & Co Ltd* [1904] 2 Ch 608 at 612.

Hence, express ancillary powers are *always conditional* and the board of directors must ensure that they are only exercised in furtherance of the objects of the company.

[7.058] Difficulties can arise in respect of groups of companies. One question that has arisen is whether there is commercial benefit to one member of the group where it enters into a guarantee for the benefit of another member of the group[165]? An example of where the power to guarantee in such circumstances was found to be exercised in furtherance of the objects of a company is *Re PMPA Garage (Longmile) Ltd et al*[166]. In that case, a number of members in a group of companies gave guarantees for the benefit of another company (PMPS) in return for a loan to only some of them. While recognising that the giving of guarantees can sometimes be a substantive object, it was stated that in this case it could not be so described, and was merely an ancillary power of all the companies[167]. The questions which arose were, first, could a guarantee in respect of very substantial sums advanced to associate companies benefit the guarantor companies, and, second, was there an abuse by the directors of their powers in giving guarantees without ostensibly receiving consideration? Murphy J said that the purpose of the guarantees was to secure payment to the PMPS by all members of the group of the amounts loaned by the PMPS, although he admitted that it was not easy to see why companies which did not get a loan from the PMPS gave guarantees. For example, there was no record of the directors of one of the companies having directed their minds to whether or not the execution of the guarantee could in some way further the business interests of that company or in any way resound to its benefit. However, this was no surprise to the judge who recognised the automatic nature of such decision making: in practice such resolutions would be prepared in advance by a company's solicitors. Murphy J further recognised that while directors of subsidiary companies cannot be excused from discharging their duties to the company of which they are directors:

> '... the analysis which the director or directors make of routine problems and the nature of the record made of the ultimate decisions must vary with the circumstances of particular cases and the dearth of records and even the failure of the directors to address problems which others can see clearly with the benefit of hindsight cannot be necessarily condemned as an abuse of fiduciary duty. It is clear ... that those having control of the business interests of the companies constituting the group discussed the business problems on a day to day basis and fitted their decisions into the complex corporate structure that existed ... there was considerable co-operation between the garage companies. One company which had surplus funds might transfer it to another in need. One company would, as one might expect, transfer potential customers to another. But as to the PMPS advances and the guarantees therefor [it was] simply explained that the PMPS required, as the auditors advised, further security for the advances made to the individual members of the group and this was given on the basis that it was 'one for all and all for one' ... There were advantages and disadvantages of acting in the group. 'You guaranteed others and others guaranteed you[168].'

---

165 See, generally, Price, 'Intra-Group Guarantees – Who Benefits?' (1997) Practical Law for Companies 15.

166 *Re PMPA Garage (Longmile) Ltd et al* [1992] ILRM 337.

167 *Re PMPA Garage (Longmile) Ltd et al* [1992] ILRM 337 at 340, where Murphy J cited with approval *Rolled Steel Products (Holdings) Ltd v British Steel Corporation* [1985] 3 All ER 52.

168 *Re PMPA Garage (Longmile) Ltd et al* [1992] ILRM 337 at 342, 343.

Having thus examined the circumstances of this particular case, Murphy J concluded that:

> 'In the nature of things companies associated with each other as parent and subsidiary or through common shareholders or who share common management and common titles or logos can not safely ignore the problems of each other. Even the most independently minded director of any such related company seeking to advance the interests of a particular company would necessarily recognise that he should and perhaps must protect the interests of the group as a whole or else take steps to secure that the particular company disassociates itself from the group.
>
> In the circumstances of the present case it seems to me that whilst the directors of the Debtor Companies [the guarantors] may have accepted the need to give the guarantee without giving serious consideration to the benefits or burdens which could arise therefrom that their almost intuitive reaction to the request from the auditors for such a guarantee and its renewal each year *was justifiable as a matter of law* although as a matter of commerce it ultimately proved a disaster for the Debtor Companies.'

Accordingly, Murphy J held that the act of giving guarantees by certain companies in a group in respect of loans to other members of the group was *intra vires* the guarantor companies. It should be noted, however, that Murphy J also found that the purported lending by the PMPS to different companies within the group was *ultra vires* the PMPS[169].

[7.059] Establishing commercial benefit is more difficult when a guarantee is given to a person other than a company that is part of the same group, particularly where the person who benefits from the guarantee is a director or person connected with a director of the guarantor company. Although it is now possible for a company to enter into a guarantee in such circumstances without breaching s 31 of the 1990 Act, by following the validation procedure provided for in s 34, it is necessary to establish and state, *inter alia*: 'the benefit which will accrue to the company directly or indirectly from entering into the guarantee or providing the security[170].'

(c) The significance of conditions on the exercise of powers

[7.060] The significance of express or implied conditions attaching to an express ancillary power has given rise to great confusion. Until relatively recently, it was thought that the exercise of an express ancillary power for a purpose not in furtherance of a company's main objects was *ultra vires* the capacity of the company[171]. Implicit in this old school of thought is the idea that the doctrine of constructive notice should be extended, and the outsider deemed to have notice not only of the company's objects clause but also of the existence of a condition attached to the exercise of a power and to whether or not the condition was fulfilled. This analysis, it is submitted, imposes too

---

169 The fact that the PMPS was registered under the Industrial and Provident Societies Act 1893 was central to Murphy J's finding that the lending was ultra vires: the PMPS's power to lend was limited to members and 'on receiving proper security therefor'. See para **[7.067]**, *post*.

170 Section 34(3)(e) of the CA 1990, as inserted by s 78 of the CLEA 2001. See Ch 16, *Statutory Regulation of Directors' Transactions*, at para **[16.085]** *et seq*.

171 See generally, *Re Introductions Ltd* [1968] 2 All ER 1221; *Thomas Williamson Ltd v Bailieborough Co-Operative Agricultural Society Ltd* (31 July 1986, unreported) HC *per* Costello J.

onerous a burden on an outsider dealing with the company, who ought only to suffer where he has notice of the directors' misfeasance. Since a wrongful exercise of any express ancillary power will result from the directors' abuse of their powers, it is thought that it is more appropriate to apply the legal principles relating to the authority of corporate agents to the resulting legal problem[172]. If the outsider can be saved by the rule in *Turquand's* case, or by reg 6 of the EC(C)R 1973, then the outsider ought to be able to enforce the transaction. If he cannot be saved, the transaction should fall as being a case where the directors abused their delegated powers, *to the knowledge of the outsider*.

[7.061] The new school of thought holds that the exercise of an express power contrary to the express or implied conditions attached to its exercise will always be *intra vires* the capacity of the company. Central to this analysis is the idea that an outsider is entitled to assume that the directors of a company will only exercise their powers, and those of the company, in furtherance of the company's objects. However, whilst the exercise of the power will not be *ultra vires*, the transaction at the centre of a wrongful exercise of that power will be unenforceable by an outsider where he is aware of the abuse by the directors of their powers and their lack of authority to authorise such a transaction[173]. A power is, of itself, neutral. It can be put to either *ultra* or *intra vires* purposes. Since it is the function of the directors to *channel* the exercise of a power, a strong case can be made for saying that where the exercise of a power is not in furtherance of the company's main objects, the validity of the exercise of that power should be determined by reference to the legal principles applicable to the authority of corporate agents.

(i) The old school of thought on express powers

[7.062] The old school may be said to have thought that where the board of directors did not exercise express powers in furtherance of the objects of the company (through either *mala fide* intentions or simple non-advertence to the question) such an exercise was *ultra vires* the capacity of the company. So in *Thomas Williamson Ltd and Another v Bailieborough Co-Operative Agricultural Society Ltd*[174], it was contended that the guarantee given by the defendant co-operative was invalid. It was this guarantee which the receiver of the plaintiff company wished to enforce. The co-operative's power to guarantee was expressly conditional, being limited to:

> '... where the giving of such guarantee is in the opinion of the Board of Directors directly or indirectly conducive or incidental to the business or trade of the Society.'

Costello J interpreted this to mean that:

> 'The Society could, therefore, only enter into certain types of guarantees, namely, those in respect of which the opinion referred to in [the rules] has been expressed by the board of directors; any other type of guarantee would be *ultra vires* the Society's powers[175].'

---

172 See para **[7.099]** *et seq, post*.

173 See *Rolled Steel Products (Holdings) Ltd v British Steel Corp et al* [1985] 3 All ER 52.

174 *Thomas Williamson Ltd and Another v Bailieborough Co-Operative Agricultural Society Ltd* (31 July 1986, unreported) *per* Costello J.

175 *Thomas Williamson Ltd and Another v Bailieborough Co-Operative Agricultural Society Ltd* (31 July 1986, unreported) *per* Costello J at p 13 of the transcript.

In *Re Introductions Ltd*[176], a similar view was taken. In that case the company was incorporated for the purpose of offering tourist services to visitors to Britain from 1951 to 1953 and for providing accommodation to tourists. From then until 1958 its business was the provision of deckchairs and amusement machines for tourists. Late in 1958, 398 of its 400 shares changed hands, as did the composition of the board of directors. In 1960, the only business pursued was pig-breeding. However, the company needed finance and borrowed money from the National Provincial Bank Ltd, which was actually aware of both the objects clause and the actual business pursued. Contrary to the old adage of 'where there's muck, there's luck', the pig-breeding business came a cropper and the company was placed in liquidation. At trial, the issue arose as to whether or not the borrowing was *ultra vires* the company's capacity.

It was clear that the pig-breeding business was *prima facie ultra vires*, but the bank sought to rely on one of the sub-clauses in the company's objects clause, which provided, *inter alia*, that the company could borrow money. It argued that when read in conjunction with the independent objects clause, it meant that any act of borrowing was *per se intra vires*. At trial, Buckley J construed the sub-clause as being an ancillary power and not a substantive object, and said:

> '... the moneys that were borrowed from the bank were not borrowed for legitimate purposes of the company; they were borrowed for *ultra vires* activities.'

This case and others seemed to support the belief that where such ancillary powers are exercised in circumstances other than in pursuit of the company's substantive objects, such an exercise is *ultra vires* and void.

(ii) The new school of thought on express powers

[7.063] More recent case law views the foregoing analysis as based on a flawed understanding of the relationship between actions which are truly *ultra vires* a company's capacity and those which are an abuse of the directors' powers. Some current judicial thinking views *any* exercise of express ancillary powers as being *intra vires*[177].

A contract resulting from an exercise of an express ancillary power can founder if the directors exercise it in circumstances which are not in furtherance of that company's objects. Though not *ultra vires* the capacity of the company, to exercise a power otherwise than in furtherance of the company's objects is an abuse of the directors' powers, since directors must always act *bona fide* and in the interests of the company. If an outsider acts in good faith and is unaware of the internal irregularity, the contract will be enforceable against the company[178]. On the other hand, if outsiders do not act in good faith, or are aware of the abuse of the directors' powers[179], the company will not be estopped from denying the contract because the outsider had notice of the irregularity.

---

[176] *Re Introductions Ltd* [1968] 2 All ER 1221.

[177] *Rolled Steel Products (Holdings) Ltd v British Steel Corp et al* [1985] 3 All ER 52

[178] Under the rule in *Turquand's* case, or reg 6 of the EC(C)R 1973. While the memorandum and articles of association are public documents of which the outsider is deemed to have notice, they: '... would find, not a prohibition from [for example] borrowing, but a permission to do so on certain conditions', *per* Jervis CJ in *Royal British Bank v Turquand* (1856) 6 E & B 327; [1843–60] All ER Rep 435.

[179] As the bank was in *Re Introductions Ltd*. See also *Re MJ Cummins Ltd; Barton v Bank of Ireland* [1939] IR 60.

This is the principle of law which led to the unfortunate use of the phrase, '*ultra vires* the powers of the directors'. Using *ultra vires* in this context is inaccurate and ought to be laid to rest. '*Ultra vires*' in company law should be reserved to cases involving transactions or activities that are outside of a company's contractual capacity and ought never be used in the context of an abuse of directors' powers.

[7.064] The switch in judicial thinking is clearest in the English Court of Appeal decision in *Rolled Steel Products (Holdings) Ltd v British Steel Corp et al*[180]. In that case, two directors of the plaintiff company caused the company to give a guarantee with a supporting charge in respect of the debts of another company owned by one of its directors. The plaintiff company had an express power to guarantee, namely:

> 'to lend and advance money or give credit to such persons, firms or companies and on such terms as may seem expedient, and in particular to customers of and others having dealings with the company, and to give guarantees or become security for any such persons, firms or companies.'

There was also an independent objects clause in the memorandum of association. As was seen above[181], Slade LJ construed the foregoing clause as being an ancillary power to, *inter alia*, give guarantees. The qualifying words 'as may seem expedient', were interpreted as meaning 'as may seem expedient for the furtherance of the objects of the company'[182]. Here the crucial point emerges. The court held that the giving of guarantees *per se* was *intra vires* the capacity of the plaintiff company. Whether or not the exercise of the power to guarantee was in furtherance of the objects of the company did *not* affect the company's capacity to guarantee. Slade LJ was at pains to distinguish the use of the phrase *ultra vires* and clearly discouraged its usage in circumstances other than in respect of corporate capacity.

Of assistance to Slade LJ was the judgment of Buckley J in *Re David Payne & Co Ltd, Young v David Payne & Co Ltd*[183]. In that case the company had an express power to borrow, and did so, issuing a debenture to secure a loan. Later, the company's liquidator sought to have the debenture declared *ultra vires* because there was evidence that, contrary to the express condition attached to the power, the borrowing was not for the purposes of the company's business. While Buckley J did say 'a corporation cannot do anything except for the purposes of its business, borrowing or anything else; everything else is beyond its power, and is *ultra vires*', Slade LJ interpreted[184] this as the use of the phrase '*ultra vires*' in the sense of '*ultra vires* the directors' powers' or abuse of their powers. Slade LJ was fortified in his interpretation by the conclusion of Buckley J that:

> 'If this borrowing was made ... for a purpose illegitimate so far as the borrowing company was concerned, that may very well be a matter on which rights may arise between the shareholders and directors of that company. It may have been a wrongful act on the part of the directors. But I do not think that a person who lends to the company is by any words such as these required to investigate whether the money borrowed was for a proper

[180] *Rolled Steel Products (Holdings) Ltd v British Steel Corp et al* [1985] 3 All ER 52; [1986] 1 Ch 246.
[181] At para **[7.052]** *ante*.
[182] *Rolled Steel Products (Holdings) Ltd v British Steel Corp et al* [1985] 3 All ER 52 at 81f.
[183] *Re David Payne & Co Ltd, Young v David Payne & Co Ltd* [1904] 2 Ch 608.
[184] *Rolled Steel Products (Holdings) Ltd v British Steel Corp et al* [1985] 3 All ER 52 at 82h.

> purpose or an improper purpose. The borrowing being effected, and the money passing to the company, the subsequent application of the money is a matter in which the directors may have acted wrongly; but this does not affect the principal act, which is the borrowing of the money.'

The decision in *Re Introductions Ltd* was distinguished likewise by Slade LJ who said that what was meant there was that the borrowing was *ultra vires* the directors' powers, in that it was an abuse of their powers, but was not *ultra vires* the capacity of the company.

[7.065] Where an outsider enters into a transaction with a company *knowing* that the directors are wrongfully exercising their powers, the transaction will not be enforceable by him. Slade LJ observed:

> 'The directors of the borrowing company in fact had no authority from the company to take the loan and grant the debenture because these transactions were not effected for the purposes of the company. Nevertheless as a general rule, a company incorporated under the Companies Acts holds out its directors as having the ostensible authority to do on its behalf anything which its memorandum of association, expressly or by implication, gives the company the capacity to do. In *Re David Payne & Co Ltd* the company's memorandum gave it the capacity to borrow. As a matter of construction of the company's memorandum, the court was not prepared to construe the words 'for the purposes of the company's business' as limiting its corporate capacity, but construed them simply as limiting the authority of the directors. In the absence of notice to the contrary, the lenders would thus have to assume, on the authority of the principle in [*Turquand's* case] and on more general principles of the law of agency, that the directors of the borrowing company were acting properly and regularly in the internal management of its affairs and were borrowing for the purposes of the company's business ... However, a party dealing with a company cannot rely on the ostensible authority of its directors to enter into a particular transaction, if he knows they in fact have no such authority because it is being entered into for improper purposes. Neither the rule in *Turquand's* case nor the more general principles of the law of agency will avail him in such circumstances ... The various passages in the judgments in both courts in the *David Payne* case which refer to the extent of the lender's obligations (if any) to inquire as to the purposes for which the loan is to be used, in my opinion, are not directed at all to the corporate capacity of the borrowing company: they are directed to the right of the lender to rely on the ostensible authority of the borrower's directors[185].'

That the validity of such contracts is to be governed by the law of agency was earlier stated in *Charterbridge Corp Ltd v Lloyds Bank Ltd*[186]. This proposition received the

[185] *Rolled Steel Products (Holdings) Ltd v British Steel Corp et al* [1985] 3 All ER 52 at 83e–j.

[186] *Charterbridge Corp Ltd v Lloyds Bank Ltd* [1969] 2 All ER 1185 at 1189. Pennycuick J said: 'The memorandum of a company sets out its objects and proclaims them to persons dealing with the company and it would be contrary to the whole function of a memorandum that objects unequivocally set out in it should be subject to some implied limitation by reference to the state of mind of the parties concerned. Where directors misapply the assets of their company, that may give rise to a claim based on breach of duty. Again a claim may arise against the other party to the transaction, if he has notice that the transaction was effected in breach of duty. Further, in a proper case, the company concerned may be entitled to have the transaction set aside. But all that results from the ordinary law of agency and has not of itself anything to do with the corporate powers of the company.'

obiter dictum support of Johnston J in *Re MJ Cummins Ltd: Barton v Bank of Ireland*[187]. There, a Mr Cummins obtained a loan from the defendant bank to enable him to purchase the shares in a company which subsequently changed its name to MJ Cummins Ltd. That company then borrowed from the defendant bank and used the proceeds of the loan to discharge the indebtedness of Cummins to the bank on foot of the first loan. The loan by the company was *ultra vires* its objects clause. In fact the company exercised 'its general borrowing powers,' an ancillary power of the company which was subject to the implied condition that any exercise of this power had to be in furtherance of its objects clause. Johnston J held that:

> '[T]his exercise by the company of its borrowing powers was ... clearly an act *ultra vires* the powers of the company, and it is contended on behalf of the liquidator that the bank, at the time when they advanced this sum were well aware that the company was exceeding its powers and that no valid debt was thereby incurred which ... can be relied upon by the bank.
>
> Now, there are certain propositions of the law which have been advanced on behalf of the bank with which I entirely agree. For instance, it is the law that while a proposed lender in his dealings with a public company must be presumed to have notice of the provisions of its memorandum and articles of association, he is not called upon in the case of a company which has a general power of borrowing, to make any inquiries as to the purpose of the loan in order to make sure that that purpose is within the powers of the company. That proposition is very conveniently illustrated in the case of In *Re David Payne & Co Ltd*, where it was further decided that knowledge on the part of the lender that the money was intended to be misapplied will avoid the loan ...
>
> The main question in the case, therefore, is whether the bank had knowledge of the wrongful purpose for which this money was being raised: and, having analysed all the circumstances connected with the loan, I am satisfied that not only had the bank the fullest knowledge of that purpose, but the local Agent of the bank ... was the person who arranged the ingenious plan by which the loan was carried through ...[188]'

The foregoing analysis seems firmly predicated upon the law of agency, since the enforceability of the transaction turned on whether the bank had knowledge of the wrongful purpose of the loan, ie, the abuse by the directors of their powers.

[7.066] The distinction between *ultra vires* a company's capacity and an abuse of the directors' powers has been accepted by Blayney J in *Parkes & Sons Ltd v Hong Kong and Shanghi Banking Corporation*[189]. In that case Collier, owner of a company called Walsh Kavanagh & Company Ltd, acquired control of the plaintiff company ('Parkes'). Later, the stock and premises of Parkes were destroyed by fire, and the business of Parkes was transferred to the premises of Walsh & Kavanagh & Company Ltd ('Walsh'). Walsh owed the defendant bank £200,000 and Mr Collier guaranteed the indebtedness of the company up to this sum. Shortly after, the company ceased trading and its entire stock was bought by Parkes. The defendant bank pressed for repayment of the money owed, and eventually, Parkes, *inter alia*, gave a guarantee to the defendant bank, supported by a mortgage over its property. At this point in time, both companies were insolvent. Eventually, Parkes was wound up and, *inter alia*, Hamilton P ordered

[187] *Re MJ Cummins Ltd: Barton v Bank of Ireland* [1939] IR 60.

[188] *Re MJ Cummins Ltd: Barton v Bank of Ireland* [1939] IR 60 at 64.

[189] *Parkes & Sons Ltd v Hong Kong and Shanghi Banking Corporation* [1990] ILRM 341.

that the question of whether or not the guarantee and mortgage were *ultra vires* Parkes should be tried in liquidation proceedings.

Blayney J held that the guarantee and mortgage were not *ultra vires* Parkes simply because the company was insolvent at the time they were made. In respect of the case before him, he said:

> 'the court is not being asked to consider whether Mr Collier, as director of [Parkes], was in breach of duty, but whether the guarantee and mortgage were *ultra vires* [Parkes][190].'

Having said that, simply because a company is insolvent, does not mean that any disposition of its assets is *ultra vires*, Blayney J held:

> 'While a disposition in such circumstances may constitute a breach of duty on the part of the directors, it does not follow that it would be *ultra vires* the company[191].'

Here the distinction between *ultra vires* the company, and abuse of the directors' powers, was recognised[192]. In *Re Frederick Inns Ltd*[193], the Supreme Court, *per* Blayney J, also distinguished between an abuse of directors' powers from questions of corporate capacity[194].

[7.067] Certain ancillary powers will contain express limitations on their exercise which are so fundamental as to mean that they are properly described as *limited powers*. An example of such a limited power is seen in *Re PMPA Garage (Longmile) Ltd et al*[195], where the power to lend was:

> 'To advance or lend to members or others ... any of the capital or other monies of the Society on receiving proper security therefor.'

In that case, the Private Motorists Provident Society Ltd ('PMPS') lent money to a number of subsidiary companies in return for unsecured guarantees. When the PMPS and other subsidiary companies were wound up, the liquidator of the PMPS sought to recover the sums due on the guarantees but this was disputed by the liquidators of the other companies on the grounds, *inter alia,* that the guarantees by the other companies were *ultra vires* as was the lending by the PMPS. Murphy J held that the giving of the guarantees by the other companies in the group was *intra vires*[196]. Accordingly, the remaining question concerned the validity of the loan advances made by PMPS to the other companies in the group.

---

190 *Parkes & Sons Ltd v Hong Kong and Shanghi Banking Corporation* [1990] ILRM 341 at 349.

191 *Parkes & Sons Ltd v Hong Kong and Shanghi Banking Corporation* [1990] ILRM 341 at 349.

192 In support of this proposition, see Keane, *Company Law* (4th edn, 2007) at para 12.05.

193 *Re Frederick Inns Ltd* [1994] 1 ILRM 387.

194 *Re Frederick Inns Ltd* [1994] 1 ILRM 387 at 398 where Blayney J cited with approval Slade LJ in *Rolled Steel Products* where he distinguished both situations in the context of recovery of assets wrongly transferred by a company. In this regard he quoted the following passage of Slade LJ: 'The *Belmont* principle thus provides a legal route by which a company may recover its assets in a case where its directors have abused their fiduciary duties and a person receiving assets as a result of such abuse is on notice that they have been misapplied. The principle is not linked in any way to the capacity of the company; it is capable of applying whether or not the company had the capacity to do the acts in question.'

195 *Re PMPA Garage (Longmile) Ltd et al* [1992] ILRM 337.

196 See para **[7.058]**, *ante*.

The argument in respect of the alleged *ultra vires* lending was that the advances were made to persons who were not members of the PMPS and, moreover, were made without any security, real or personal. It is important to note that but for a particular statutory provision[197], the PMPS would not have power to lend at all. Murphy J held that for the PMPS to advance monies in these circumstances was *ultra vires* the PMPS. It is submitted that it is because of the fundamental restriction, coupled with the statutory provisions governing the powers of industrial and providential societies, that the exercise of this power by the PMPS was *ultra vires*. In effect, the power was a limited power *ab initio* and so differed fundamentally from those express ancillary powers considered above[198].

(f) Implied ancillary powers

[7.068] Although companies are invariably incorporated with voluminous objects clauses, the truth is that this results more from a nervous adherence to practice than from legal necessity. It has long been the case that the courts will *imply* powers to a company which 'may fairly be regarded as incidental to, or consequential upon', a company's express objects[199].

Certain powers are obviously incidental and necessary, eg, borrowing to finance the company's main business, hiring employees, acquiring business premises[200]. Others have traditionally been contentious: corporate gifts[201] and other gratuitous payments, such as political donations, pensions, sponsorships, scholarships and even redundancy payments in excess of those required by law.

[7.069] Whether or not any given power will be implied depends upon whether or not its exercise can be said to be reasonably *incidental* to the furtherance of the company's objects. This test will determine the very existence of an implied power and is the *sole* test today notwithstanding the case of *Re Lee Behrens & Co*[202] where Eve J set out a tripartite test:

> '... whether [gratuitous payments] may be made under an express or implied power, all such grants involve an expenditure of the company's money, and that money can only be spent for purposes reasonably incidental to the carrying on of the company's business, and the validity of such grants is to be treated as is shown in all the authorities by the answers to three pertinent questions: (i) Is the transaction reasonably incidental to the carrying on of the company's business? (ii) Is it a bona fide transaction? and (iii) Is it done for the benefit and to promote the prosperity of the company[203]?'

197 Section 40 of the Industrial and Provident Societies Act 1893.

198 Although the lending was ultra vires the PMPS, Murphy J allowed the liquidator of the PMPS recover the amounts loaned: *Re PMPA Garage (Longmile) Ltd (No 2)* [1992] ILRM 349. See para **[7.089]** *et seq, post*.

199 *Attorney General v Great Eastern Railway* (1880) 5 App Cas 473.

200 In *Halifax Building Society v Meridian Housing Association Ltd* [1994] 1 BCLC 540, it was held by Arden J that the development of office units was a transaction of a category that was capable of being performed as reasonably incidental to the defendant's main objects which were that of carrying 'on the industry, business or trade of providing housing or any associated amenities'.

201 Bastin, 36 Conv (ns) 89.

202 *Re Lee Behrens & Co* [1932] All ER 889, [1932] 2 Ch 46.

203 *Re Lee Behrens & Co* [1932] All ER 889 at 891A–B.

The reality is that the foregoing passage confuses corporate incapacity (*ultra vires*) with an abuse of the directors' powers. Limbs (ii) and (iii) are heresy when the existence of an implied power is in question[204]. All that now remains of the test is whether or not the exercise of a power is reasonably incidental to or consequential upon the company's substantive objects.

(g) Gratuitous dispositions of company property

[7.070] It is in the context of alleged gratuitous dispositions of company property that the doctrine of *ultra vires* is often frequently considered in modern judgments. Here the following issues are considered:

(i) Implicit power to make a gratuitous disposition where reasonably incidental;
(ii) Express object or power to make a gratuitous disposition;
(iii) No express object and not in furtherance of the company's interests.

(i) Implicit power to make a gratuitous disposition where reasonably incidental

[7.071] In appropriate circumstances the power to make a gratuitous disposition can be *implied*. In *Parke v Daily News Ltd*[205], a company sold its newspaper business for £2m, which had constituted its main business. It subsequently purported to give £1.5m to its then redundant employees in the form of pensions and retirement plans. It was held that these *ex gratia* payments were not permitted by the company's express objects and the company had no implied power to give them. As Plowman J said:

> '... the essence of this matter is this, that the directors of the defendant company are proposing that a very large part of its funds should be given to its former employees in order to benefit those employees rather than the company ...'

Hence the payments were not reasonably incidental to or consequential upon the company's objects.

[7.072] As Keane J said in *Re Greendale Developments Ltd*[206], 'it has been settled law since the decision in *Hutton v West Cork Railway Co*[207] that a company cannot spend money or dispose of its property except for purposes which are reasonably incidental to the carrying on of the business of the company'[208]. In *Hutton v West Cork Railway Co*, it was held that it could not be said that there was any implied power to give gratuities to servants or directors of the company. While *prima facie* the gratuities were in the interests of the company because goodwill was generated, this did not apply here since

---

[204] In *Rolled Steel Products (Holdings) Ltd v British Steel Corp and Others* [1985] 3 All ER 52 at 81–82, [1986] 1 Ch 246, Slade LJ said of Eve J's test that it: '... should, in my opinion, now be recognised as being of no assistance and indeed positively misleading when the relevant question is whether a particular gratuitous transaction is within a company's corporate capacity.' See also *Northern Bank Finance Corporation Ltd v Quinn and Achates Investment Company* [1979] ILRM 221 where Keane J said the observations of Rowen LJ in *Hutton* 'may have been taken too far in *Re Lee, Behrens and Co*', and went on to refer to *Charterbridge*.

[205] *Parke v Daily News Ltd* [1962] Ch 927, [1962] 2 All ER 929.

[206] *Re Greendale Developments Ltd* (20 February 1997, unreported) SC, Keane J, *nem diss*.

[207] *Hutton v West Cork Railway Co* [1883] 23 Ch D 654.

[208] *Re Greendale Developments Ltd* (20 February 1997, unreported) SC, Keane J, *nem diss* at p 22 of the judgment.

the company was being wound up. On the general issue of corporate charity, Bowen LJ said:

> 'A railway company, or the directors of the company, might send down all the porters at a railway station to have tea in the country at the expense of the company. Why should they not? It is for the directors to judge, provided it is a matter which is reasonably incidental to the carrying on of the business of the company and a company which always treated its employees with Draconian severity ... would soon find itself deserted ... The law does not say that there are to be no cakes and ale, but that there are to be no cakes and ale except such as are required for the benefit of the company ... Charity has no business to sit at boards of directors qua charity. There is, however, a kind of charitable dealing which is for the interest of those who practice it, and to that extent and in that garb (I admit not a very philanthropic garb) charity may sit at the board, but for no other purpose.'

In that case corporate charity was not reasonably incidental to or consequential upon the company's objects since the company was being wound up. When a company is solvent it will usually be the case that gratuitous dispositions to charities or a company's employees or officers will be found to pass the foregoing test, such dispositions being tantamount to money spent on public relations or remuneration, respectively.

(ii) Express object or power to make a gratuitous disposition

[7.073] The general rule is that a company cannot make a gratuitous disposition of its property unless such a disposition is an express object in a company's memorandum of association. It has already been noted that certain forms of disposition – such as a guarantee – will rarely properly fall to be construed as a true object and will almost invariably be a 'mere' power which must be exercised in a manner that is in furtherance of an express object[209]. Other dispositions can, however, be express objects and where they are expressly authorised by the objects clause, they will not be *ultra vires*. So in *Re Horsley & Weight Ltd*[210], Oliver J said:

> 'The objects of a company do not need to be commercial, they can be charitable or philanthropic; indeed, they can be whatever the original incorporators wish, provided that they are legal. Nor is there any reason why a company should not part with its funds gratuitously or for non-commercial reasons if to do so is within its declared objects ... Of course if the memorandum of association expressly or by implication provides that an express object only extends to acts which benefit or promote the prosperity of the company, regard must be paid to that limitation; but where there is no such express or implied limitation, the question whether an act done within the terms of an express object of the company will benefit or promote the prosperity of the company or of its business is ... irrelevant.[211]'

In *Barclays Bank plc et al v British & Commonwealth Holdings plc*[212], Harman J said that in *Brady v Brady*[213] Nourse LJ had accepted that the law 'imposes a limit on even an

[209] See para **[7.055]** *ante*.

[210] *Re Horsley & Weight Ltd* [1982] 1 Ch 442.

[211] *Re Horsley & Weight Ltd* [1982] 1 Ch 442 at 450, 452.

[212] *Barclays Bank plc et al v British & Commonwealth Holdings plc* [1996] 1 BCLC 1.

[213] *Brady v Brady* [1988] BCLC 20.

express power such as he envisaged to give away all a company's assets so that such a power could only be exercised by a company with available distributable profits'[214].

[7.074] The courts will strictly construe any object which it is claimed authorises a company to make a gratuitous disposition of its property. The decision in *Re Frederick Inns Ltd et al*[215] is instructive in this regard. In that case three companies – *Frederick Inns Ltd, The Rendezvous Ltd* and *The Graduate Ltd* – all operated public houses in Dublin and were wholly-owned subsidiaries of Motels Ltd. All companies were in a constant state of indebtedness to, *inter alia*, the Revenue Commissioners, and owed in total, by June 1986, *circa* £2.8 million. Meetings were held between the company's representatives and the Revenue Commissioners, but the revenue were dissatisfied and threatened to wind up each of the four companies. A further meeting was held and it was decided that the public houses owned by Frederick Inns Ltd, The Rendezvous Ltd and The Graduate Ltd would be sold and the proceeds of sale paid to the Revenue Commissioners. In total, £1.2 million was paid over. In the High Court Lardner J found that this money was appropriated in reduction of the tax liabilities of not only these four companies, but also the tax liabilities of six other companies which were also subsidiaries of Motels Ltd. The liquidator contended that 'when any company is insolvent it is beyond its powers gratuitously to alienate its property or to make a gift to a third party out of its assets'[216]. After citing the most basic principle of company law, the concept of separate legal personality[217], Lardner J held:

> Insofar as payments to the Revenue were made by companies out of their assets, which exceeded their liabilities for tax, and were intended to be applied in reduction of the tax liabilities of other companies in the group, they can only be regarded as voluntary payments made without consideration for the benefit of third parties and as such in the

[214] *Barclays Bank plc et al v British & Commonwealth Holdings plc* [1996] 1 BCLC 1 at 17a. See, further, Ch 10, *The Maintenance of Capital*, at para **[10.099]**.

[215] *Re Frederick Inns Ltd et al* [1991] ILRM 582 (HC) and [1994] 1 ILRM 387 (SC).

[216] *Re Frederick Inns Ltd et al* [1991] ILRM 582 at 588. Reliance for this was placed upon *Hutton v West Cork Railway Company* (1883) 23 Ch D 654; *Parke v Daily News* [1962] 2 All ER 929; and *Charterbridge Corporation Ltd v Lloyds Bank Ltd* [1970] Ch 407.

[217] *Re Frederick Inns Ltd et al* [1991] ILRM 582 at 587 where, Lardner J said: 'A fundamental attribute of a company in Irish law is that of corporate personality. A company is a legal entity distinct from its members, capable of enjoying rights and of being subject to duties which are not the same as those enjoyed or borne by its members. This was finally established in *Salomon v Salomon and Company Ltd* (1897) AC 22 and the principle has been recognised and applied in many decisions of the Irish courts. Generally speaking this principle and the statutory rules of company law in which the principle is implicit apply to the relationship between holding companies and subsidiaries and to transactions between them and third parties. The assets of such companies are treated as owned by them legally and beneficially as distinct legal entities. And except where circumstances enable a court to discover an agency or trustee relationship between them, a holding company is not treated as owner of its subsidiaries' assets. And the liabilities of companies which are members of the same group are those of the individual companies which incur them. There is no common group liability for the obligations of individual members of the group imposed by law. The principle is reflected in many aspects of company law; for example in s 147 of the Companies Act 1963 every company (whether a holding company or a subsidiary) is required to keep proper books of account which must include accounts of all sums of money received and expended by the company ...'

absence of any evidence that such excess payments were for the benefit of the paying companies they are clearly *ultra vires*[218].

Lardner J also held that there was a breach of the directors' duties in applying the proceeds of sale as they did[219]. He concluded: 'that payment to the Revenue Commissioners by any of the companies of any sum in excess of its particular tax liability was *ultra vires* the paying company insofar (a) as it effected a gratuitous reduction or alienation of its assets and (b) it was done when the company was insolvent[220].'

[7.075] The decision of Lardner J was appealed to the Supreme Court[221]. Blayney J giving the judgment of the court dismissed the appeal. On the question of the gratuitous dispositions of funds in the reduction of the liabilities of other companies, Blayney J held that those payments were *ultra vires* because they were not within the contemplation of the companies' objects that were relied upon by the Revenue Commissioners. Of the two clauses[222] claimed to give the companies the power to pay other companies' debts, Blayney J said:

> 'In my opinion neither of these clauses gives the power to pay the debts of an associate company, which is what happened here. What the first clause gives is a power 'to establish or promote or concur in establishing or promoting' another company in certain circumstances. That could not be construed as a power to pay the debts of another company. And the second clause gives the power 'to purchase or otherwise acquire and undertake all or any part of the … liabilities … of any company etc.' The companies here were neither 'purchasing' nor 'acquiring and undertaking' the liabilities of the other companies. They were paying part of their debts. This clause did not give any power to do this[223].'

---

218 *Re Frederick Inns Ltd et al* [1991] ILRM 582 at 588, supported by reference to *Trevor v Whitworth* [1887] 12 AC 414; *Hutton v The West Cork Railway Company Ltd* (1883) 23 Ch D 654; and *Roper v Ward* [1981] ILRM 408.

219 See generally, Ch 15, *Duties of Directors and Other Officers*. It is important to note that the reference to the abuse by the directors of their powers and their duty owed to the creditors on the insolvency of a company and the question of *ultra vires* were treated very separately by Lardner J. In this the eternal distinction between corporate capacity and directors' authority was underscored.

220 *Re Frederick Inns Ltd et al* [1991] ILRM 582 at 591.

221 *Re Frederick Inns Ltd et al* [1994] 1 ILRM 387.

222 The clauses were: '(1) To establish or promote or concur in establishing or promoting any other company whose objects shall include the acquisition and taking over of all or any assets and liabilities or, or the promotion of which shall be in any manner calculated to advance directly or indirectly the objects or interests of this company, and to acquire and hold, or dispose of shares, stock or securities of, and guarantee the payment of any securities issued or any other obligation of any such company. (2) To purchase or otherwise acquire and undertake all or any part of the business, property, liabilities and transactions of any person, firm or company carrying on or proposing to carry on any business which this company is authorised to carry on, or possessed of property suitable for the purpose of the company or to promote any company or companies for the above purpose.'

223 *Re Frederick Inns Ltd et al* [1994] 1 ILRM 387 at 393, 394.

Blayney J also rejected the submission that the power to lend money could be relied upon to validate the payments, and concluded that the payments were *ultra vires*[224].

(iii) No express object and not in furtherance of the company's interests

[7.076] It will be difficult, if not impossible, to uphold the validity of a gratuitous disposition by a company where its objects clause contains no express object to make such a disposition, the payments were not for the benefit of the company and the disposition is not paid from 'distributable profits'[225]. In *Aveling Barford Ltd v Perion*[226], Hoffmann J said:

> 'A company can only lawfully deal with its assets in furtherance of its objects. The corporators may take assets of the company by way of dividend, or with the leave of the court, by way of reduction of capital, or in a winding up. They may of course acquire them for full consideration. They cannot take assets out of the company by way of voluntary disposition, however, described, and if they attempt to do so, the disposition is *ultra vires* the company[227].'

In *Brady v Brady*[228], Nourse LJ said:

> 'In its broadest terms the principle is that a company cannot give away its assets. So stated, it is subject to the qualification that in the realm of theory a memorandum of association may authorise a company to give away all its assets to whomsoever it pleases, including its shareholders. But in the real world of trading companies, charitable or political donations to widows of ex-employees and the like apart, it is obvious that such a power would never be taken. The principle is only a facet of the wider rule, the corollary of limited liability, that the integrity of a company's assets, except to the extent allowed by its constitution, must be preserved for the benefit of all those who are interested in them, most pertinently its creditors[229].'

Harman J cited both of these decisions in *Barclays Bank plc et al v British & Commonwealth Holdings plc*[230], and accepted that a company cannot make a gratuitous disposition of its assets save where this is for the benefit of its business (and so not really gratuitous) or where it is made out of distributable profits with the approval of its shareholders applied very widely[231].

[7.077] This same issue was at the centre of the decision in *Re Greendale Developments Ltd*[232] which concerned an appeal from an order of the High Court that a director of a company was obliged to repay over £435,000 to the company's liquidator. The circumstances were that the company had three equal shareholders: Mr and Mrs Fagan

---

224 As to the reliance placed by the Revenue Commissioners on s 8 of the CA 1963, see para **[7.083]** *post*.

225 Within the meaning of s 45 of the C(A)A 1983: see Ch 10, *The Maintenance of Capital*, at para **[10.089]** *et seq*.

226 *Aveling Barford Ltd v Perion* [1989] BCLC 626. See Ch 10, *The Maintenance of Capital*, at para **[10.099]** *et seq*.

227 *Aveling Barford Ltd v Perion* [1989] BCLC 626 at 631.

228 *Brady v Brady* [1988] BCLC 20.

229 *Brady v Brady* [1988] BCLC 20 at 38.

230 *Barclays Bank plc et al v British & Commonwealth Holdings plc* [1996] 1 BCLC 1.

231 *Barclays Bank plc et al v British & Commonwealth Holdings plc* [1996] 1 BCLC 1 at 17.

232 *Re Greendale Developments Ltd* (20 February 1997, unreported) SC, Keane J, *nem diss*.

and Mr Burgess; Mr Fagan and Mr Burgess were its directors. The company had been formed to carry out a development at Islandbridge, Dublin and 80 houses had been built and sold, as also had an office building on the site. Following disputes between Mr Fagan and Mr Burgess, Mr Burgess presented a s 205 petition; Mr Fagan countered with a petition to wind up the company on the just and equitable ground and the company was wound up. The liquidator appointed to the company formed the view that substantial sums were owed by Mr Fagan to the company and instituted proceedings for misfeasance pursuant to s 298 of the CA 1963. It was as a result of these proceedings that the High Court order was made against Mr Fagan and this was appealed to the Supreme Court. On appeal it was argued by Mr Fagan's counsel that all payments made to Mr and Mrs Fagan or benefits obtained had been made with the assent of all the shareholders, with the result that the misfeasance proceedings were misconceived and since there was no evidence that the company had been insolvent, the payments could not constitute any form of wrongdoing or breach of trust. On the question of the assent of the shareholders to the impugned transactions, Keane J in the Supreme Court accepted the propriety of the principle summarised by Kingsmill Moore J in *Buchanan Ltd and another v McVey*[233] that where all corporators agree to a certain course of action, such is an act of the company and binds the company subject to two prerequisites:

> '(1) that the transaction to which the corporators agree should be *intra vires* the company;
>
> (2) that the transaction should be honest.'

It was in these circumstances that Keane J considered whether the making of payments by a solvent company to its director was *ultra vires*. Two very important aspects of the circumstances in this case should be noted. First, Keane J noted that *ex hypothesi* the company had obtained no benefits whatever from the impugned payments but that it was, nevertheless, contended that the payments were *intra vires*. Second, there was no express object or authorisation in the memorandum or articles of association to make the payments in question and it appears there was no attempt to argue that any of the company's objects envisaged the making of such payments[234]. As Keane J said, were it otherwise, 'different considerations might apply'[235].

[7.078] Keane J addressed the issue by noting that it was 'settled law' since the decision in *Hutton v West Cork Railway Company* that a company cannot spend money or dispose of its property except for purposes that are reasonably incidental to the carrying on of the company's business. Thus, having noted that the transaction was not 'expressly authorised' by the company's objects clause, Keane J discarded any suggestion that it

233 *Buchanan Ltd and another v McVey* [1954] IR 89: see Ch 14, *Corporate Governance: Meetings*, at para **[14.093]**.

234 See Forde, *Company Law* (3rd edn, Round Hall Sweet & Maxwell, 1999) at p 103 where he states that the objects clause of Greendale Developments Ltd said that the company could 'grant … gratuities, bonuses or other payments to the officers … or the dependants or connections of such persons'. This is, however, irrelevant since it was not argued and the judgment proceeded on the basis that there was no authority in the objects clause for such payments.

235 *Re Greendale Developments Ltd* (20 February 1997, unreported) SC, Keane J, *nem diss* at p 23 of the judgment.

could be said that the company had an *implied power* to effect the transaction[236] because it received no benefit. The genesis of the Supreme Court's finding that the payments by the company were *ultra vires* was that there was no express or implied power for the company to make payments of the sort made to the director. Mr Fagan's counsel's purported reliance upon the principle that all of the corporators of a solvent company can do that which they like to its assets fell down on the simple fact that for that principle to operate, the thing which is done must be *intra vires*. Equally, there is no conflict between Keane J's judgment and that of Gavan Duffy P in *Re SM Barker Ltd*[237] upon which Mr Fagan's counsel relied heavily. In that case it was held that misfeasance proceedings did not lie against shareholders who had caused a company to voluntarily release a number of debts due to it by the company's three directors. The judgment of Gavan Duffy P was, however, predicated on the fact that in that case the voluntary release of indebtedness was not *ultra vires*; in *Re Greendale Developments Ltd*, it was found as a matter of fact that the payments made there were *ultra vires*. As Keane J said:

> '*Re SM Barker Ltd* is, accordingly, not authority for the proposition that a company may spend money or apply property for purposes which are *ultra vires* the company provided all the shareholders agree to the *ultra vires* transaction ...
>
> On the proved or admitted facts of this case, the impugned payments were made by the company to or for the benefit of the appellants in circumstances where the company derived no benefit in return. They were not expressly authorised by the memorandum or articles of association of the company. They were, accordingly, *ultra vires* the company and their fundamental illegality cannot be cured by the fact, if it be the fact, that all the shareholders assented to each and every one of the payments in question[238].'

The decision in *Re Greendale Developments Ltd* was clearly in accordance with sound legal principle and established authority[239]. As far back as 1931, the principles in issue were considered by Orde JA in *Plain Ltd v Kenley*[240]:

> '... a limited joint stock company cannot do what it likes with its property ... It cannot lawfully give away its property, either to shareholders or others. I am speaking broadly, because there are cases where, in the interests of its own business, a company may [make gifts] but transactions of that character either depend upon the fact that they are prudent and proper expenditures or are made out of accumulated profits and with the consent of the shareholders[241].'

The suggestion that, if shareholders can agree to a company acting *ultra vires*, the *ultra vires* action will not be improper, is entirely misplaced and results from a failure to recognise the legitimate interests of creditors and the fact that the doctrine of *ultra vires* is intended to protect *both* shareholder *and* creditors. Only the existence of the clearest of express objects to make gratuitous dispositions – which will, of course, be a matter of

---

236 In addition to citing the *Hutton* case, Keane J cited *Re Lee, Behrens and Company Ltd* [1932] 2 Ch 46; *Parke v Daily News Ltd* [1962] Ch 927; and *Roper v Ward et al* [1981] ILRM 408.

237 *Re SM Barker Ltd* [1950] IR 123.

238 *Re Greendale Developments Ltd* (20 February 1997, unreported) SC, Keane J, *nem diss* at pp 27, 28 of the judgment.

239 For a contrary view, see Forde, *Company Law* (3rd edn, Round Hall Sweet & Maxwell, 1999) at pp 104–107. Dr Forde appeared for the Fagans, who lost the appeal.

240 *Plain Ltd v Kenley* [1931] 1 DLR 468.

241 *Plain Ltd v Kenley* [1931] 1 DLR 468 at 479.

public record, will allow companies to gratuitously divest themselves of their assets in favour of their owners and controllers. Even then, dispositions can only be made out of 'distributable profits', the validity of which will also turn upon whether the consent of the shareholders has been given. The fallacy lies in elevating shareholder consent to the sole prerequisite. Were it otherwise, creditor protection measures such as the controls on loans to directors[242], capital maintenance rules[243], the very concept of 'distributable profits'[244], and the statutory declaration of solvency in a winding up would all be rendered meaningless. Moreover, *vires* aside, all dispositions of corporate property must be made for the benefit of the company; where not made for the benefit of the company, the directors may be found to have acted in breach of their duties to the company, as fiduciaries.

[7.079] In *Ridge Securities Ltd v IRC*[245], Pennycuick J said:

> 'A company can only lawfully deal with its assets in furtherance of its objects. The corporators may take assets out of the company by way of dividend or, with leave of the court, by way of reduction of capital, or in a winding up. They may of course acquire them for full consideration. They cannot take assets out of the company by way of voluntary distribution, however described, and, if they attempt to do so, the disposition is ultra vires the company.'

This statement of the law was cited with approval by the United Kingdom's Supreme Court in *Progress Property Company Ltd v Moorgarth Group Ltd*[246]. In this case shares in a company which owned property were disposed of for STG£4 million less than their market value; the error arose from the mistaken belief that the properties were subject to a repairing clause which, had they been so subject, would have reduced the market value by that amount. Because a shareholder in the company had benefitted, the question arose as to whether the sale at below market value constituted an unlawful distribution which was *ultra vires*. The United Kingdom's Supreme Court held that it had been found that the sale had been genuine.

(h) Section 8 of the CA 1963

[7.080] Section 8(1) of the CA 1963 provides:

> 'Any act or thing done by the company which if the company had been empowered to do the same would have been lawfully and effectively done, shall, notwithstanding that the company had no power to do such act or thing, be effective in favour of any person relying on such act or thing who is not shown to have been actually aware, at the time when he so relied thereon, that such act or thing was not within the powers of the company, but any director or officer of the company who was responsible for the doing by the company of such act or thing shall be liable to the company for any loss or damage suffered by the company in consequence thereof.'

---

242 Section 31 of the CA 1990.

243 See generally, Ch 10, *The Maintenance of Capital*.

244 Section 45 of the C(A)A 1983.

245 *Ridge Securities Ltd v IRC* [1964] 1 All ER 275 at 288.

246 *Progress Property Company Ltd v Moorgarth Group Ltd* [2011] 2 All ER 432 at 435.

This statutory provision tempers the severity of the doctrine of *ultra vires* as seen in cases such as *Re Jon Beauforte (London) Ltd*[247]. There, the company's main object was to operate the business of costumiers and gown makers. Contrary to this it carried on the business of veneer panel makers. The transaction in issue was a contract to supply coke from a fuel merchant, a substance which could apparently be used in either business. Because of the fact that the company's objects clause was a matter of public knowledge, being registered in a public registry, and because the notepaper on which the order was sent to the fuel merchant was headed 'Veneered Panel Manufacturers,' the fuel merchant was held to have constructive notice of the *ultra vires* purpose for which the coke was intended, and so the contract was unenforceable and was not admitted as a debt when the company went into liquidation. Today, the doctrine of constructive notice is ousted and the contract would only be unenforceable if the fuel merchant was *actually aware* of the *ultra vires* purpose for which the coke was to be used.

[7.081] On the foregoing analysis of express ancillary powers, the scope of s 8 of the CA 1963 must now be seen to have been considerably reduced. Only the pursuit of non-objects and the purported exercise of powers not stated in the objects clause will attract the doctrine of *ultra vires*, and so be capable of being mitigated by s 8 of the CA 1963. Section 8 of the CA 1963 may most usefully be considered by parsing its provisions:

(i) Lawfully and effectively done;
(ii) In favour of any person;
(iii) Actually aware.

(i) Lawfully and effectively done

[7.082] The use of these words show that acts or things prohibited by the Companies Acts and the general law of the land cannot be validated by s 8(1) of the CA 1963. Accordingly, a contract which unlawfully assists the purchase of the company's own shares cannot be saved: *Bank of Ireland Finance Ltd v Rockfield Ltd*[248]. The use of the word *effectively*, shows that contracts void for uncertainty or other defect can not be validated.

[7.083] 'Lawfully and effectively done' was interpreted by the Supreme Court in *Re Frederick Inns Ltd et al*[249]. There, on the facts considered above[250], Lardner J in the High Court had said of s 8(1) of the CA 1963 that:

> '[b]y its terms this section refers to acts or things done which, if the company had been empowered to do the same, would have been lawfully and effectively done. I do not find the section capable of assisting the Revenue Commissioners in relation to companies which were insolvent, to their knowledge, even if one supposes that in the present case these companies had been empowered by their memoranda and articles to make gratuitous payments to or for the benefit of third parties out of their assets (and it is a supposition which in this case is so inconsistent with some of the basic principles of company law as to be hardly made). For insolvent companies such payments constitute a misapplication of the companies' assets and could not have been lawful or effective as against the general

---

[247] *Re Jon Beauforte (London) Ltd* [1953] 1 All ER 634.
[248] *Bank of Ireland Finance Ltd v Rockfield Ltd* [1979] IR 21.
[249] *Re Frederick Inns Ltd et al* [1994] 1 ILRM 387.
[250] See para **[7.074]** *ante*.

> unsecured creditors, since they would effectively defraud them of assets to which the creditors were entitled to have recourse.'

This was upheld by Blayney J in the Supreme Court. He also held that at the time the *ultra vires* payments were made by the companies to the Revenue Commissioners, the companies were insolvent. Moreover, the learned judge held that one effect of a company being insolvent was that 'the company had ceased to be the beneficial owner of its assets with the result that directors would have had *no power* to use the company's assets to discharge the liabilities of other companies'[251]. He held that in consequence:

> '... I think it is clear that it could not be held that the payments by the four companies were 'lawfully and effectively done'. At the time the payments were made, the four companies were under the management of their directors pending imminent liquidation. Because of the insolvency of the companies the shareholders no longer had any interest. The only parties with an interest were the creditors. The payments made could not have been lawful because they were made in total disregard of their interests. And since the payments were not lawfully made, the Revenue Commissioners cannot rely on s 8 of the Companies Act 1963 to remedy the fact that the payments were *ultra vires*[252].'

The effect of the Supreme Court's decision is that *ultra vires* dispositions of assets cannot be rendered effective by s 8 where the company is *insolvent*. The decision in *Re Frederick Inns Ltd* was on that basis distinguished by Laffoy J in *Ulster Factors Ltd v Entonglen Ltd and another*[253], the facts of which are considered below[254]. There the liquidator of a company had sought to claim that payments made to a third party (at the request of a person who was director and secretary of the company) was *ultra vires* and that no reliance could be placed on s 8 of the CA 1963. Since the company was not insolvent at the time the payments were made, Laffoy J held that reliance upon s 8(1) was not precluded.

[7.084] The decision in *Re Frederick Inns Ltd* greatly curtails the scope of s 8(1) of the CA 1963. The preclusion of reliance upon s 8, to make effective *ultra vires* dispositions of corporate assets when a company is insolvent, totally emasculates s 8(1). The propriety of the act or thing that is done must not be assailable on any other ground; s 8(1) will only excuse the act or thing being *ultra vires* the company's capacity. Precluding reliance upon s 8, to make effective something that is beyond a company's capacity, on account of directors' breaches of duty, confuses corporate *capacity* with directors' *authority*.

(ii) In favour of any person

[7.085] The reference to 'in favour of any person' shows that s 8 is not confined to 'outsiders', but can also apply to 'insiders', such as directors. Although from an evidential stance it will be hard to show that insiders were not 'actually aware' of the lack of company power, their reliance on s 8(1) is not *per se* automatically excluded.

---

251 *Re Frederick Inns Ltd et al* [1994] 1 ILRM 387 at 396. Italics added.

252 *Re Frederick Inns Ltd et al* [1994] 1 ILRM 387 at 397.

253 *Ulster Factors Ltd v Entonglen Ltd and another* (21 February 1997, unreported) HC.

254 See para **[7.105]** *post*.

(iii) Actually aware

[7.086] In ordinary speech, *actual awareness* indicates an advertence to something and the consequent realisation of the consequences. In law, however, it has been decided that a person will be found to be 'actually aware' in law where they see something but do not, as a matter of fact, appreciate its consequences.

In *Northern Bank Finance Company Ltd v Quinn and Achates Investment Co*[255], the defendant company purported to enter into a contract of guarantee with the plaintiff bank on behalf of a Mr Quinn. Keane J held that the guarantee was *ultra vires* because the memorandum of association 'conferred neither expressly nor by implication any power on the Company to execute a Guarantee for the purpose of securing the payment of a bank loan to Mr Quinn'[256]. Nevertheless, the bank sought to rely on s 8(1) of the CA 1963, arguing it was not actually aware of the corporate incapacity. However, the bank's solicitor had been sent the memorandum and articles of association. Although the solicitor could not recall reading them, Keane J found that:

> 'I think that the probabilities are that [the solicitor] did read the objects clause ... and came to the conclusion that the execution of the Guarantee and the mortgage was within the powers of the company[257].'

Having so held, Keane J said s 8(1) did not apply, as:

> 'The bank, because of the knowledge of their Agent ... which must be imputed to them, were aware of the objects of the company[258].'

To the argument that this was not the 'actual awareness' contemplated by the section, Keane J said:

> 'I think it is clear that the section was designed to ensure that ... persons who had entered into transactions in good faith with the company without ever reading the memorandum and accordingly with no actual knowledge that the transaction was *ultra vires* were not to suffer. I can see no reason in logic or justice why the legislature should have intended to afford the same protection to persons who had actually read the memorandum and simply failed to appreciate the lack of vires[259].'

Keane J concluded by saying that:

> '... where a party is shown to have been actually aware of the contents of the memorandum but failed to appreciate that the company was not empowered thereby to enter the transaction in issue, s 8(1) has no application[260].'

---

[255] *Northern Bank Finance Company Ltd v Quinn and Achates Investment Co* [1979] ILRM 221.

[256] *Northern Bank Finance Company Ltd v Quinn and Achates Investment Co* [1979] ILRM 221 at 226. Even with the recent developments in respect of express ancillary powers, such a view would still be correct today as the power to guarantee was in relation to 'the company', and furthermore, it appears there was no independent objects clause.

[257] *Northern Bank Finance Company Ltd v Quinn and Achates Investment Co* [1979] ILRM 221 at 228.

[258] *Northern Bank Finance Company Ltd v Quinn and Achates Investment Co* [1979] ILRM 221 at 229.

[259] *Northern Bank Finance Company Ltd v Quinn and Achates Investment Co* [1979] ILRM 221 at 229.

[260] *Northern Bank Finance Company Ltd v Quinn and Achates Investment Co* [1979] ILRM 221 at 230.

Even at its most restrictive, this decision provides that a person who has not seen the memorandum will have the protection of s 8(1) of the CA 1963. Academic focus has largely been on Keane J's restrictive construction of the section, and the decision has been criticised on this basis[261]. Criticism has principally been directed at the finding that the clear meaning of the words 'actually aware', were ignored and treated as if the section had, instead, referred to a person having *actual notice*. In law, actual, constructive and imputed notice have very particular meanings[262]. 'Notice' does not mean 'awareness'. If being 'actually aware' of the provisions of a company's memorandum of association was intended to equate with 'actual notice' of such, one would have thought that the legislature ought to have used the words 'actual notice'.

As the law stands, a person who has not seen a company's memorandum and articles will be protected by s 8(1). Ironically, a person who reads a company's memorandum and articles of association, but fails to understand the lack of *vires*, will not be protected by s 8(1). Notwithstanding this, it is not recommended that constitutional documents are ignored[263].

(i) Regulation 6 of the EC(C)R 1973

[7.087] Regulation 6 of the EC(C)R 1973 was introduced into Irish law as a result of Article 9 of the First EU Directive on Company Law[264]. The regulation concerns defects both in corporate agents' authority *and* in corporate capacity. Just as the rule in *Turquand's* case is overlapped by reg 6, also overlapped is s 8(1) of the CA 1963. However, while there is an overlap, s 8(1) provides more protection to persons dealing with the company. First, the requirement of 'good faith' in the regulation imposes a greater standard of care than does 'actually aware', even on its restrictive interpretation, because the former would seem to impose a duty to investigate. Second, reg 6 only affords protection where one deals with the board of directors or a registered person[265]. Third, the regulation applies only to *limited* companies. Regulation 6 is considered in detail in the context of corporate authority, below[266].

---

261 Ussher, *Company Law in Ireland* (1986, Sweet & Maxwell) at p 126; see also Ussher, (1981) DULJ 76.

262 Wylie, *Irish Land Law* (4th edn, Bloomsbury Professional, 2008) at para 3.069.

263 See Johnston, *Banking and security Law in Ireland* (1998, Butterworths) at para [18.40].

264 SI 163/1973. See Ch 1, *The Private Company in Context*, at para **[1.113]**.

265 It was for this reason that the Revenue Commissioners could not rely upon reg 6 of SI 163/1973 in *Re Frederick Inns Ltd* [1994] 1 ILRM 387. Blayney J said (at 394) that: 'I think it is clear that none of the companies had any person registered under the regulations as a person authorised to bind the company, so if the Revenue Commissioners are to get the benefit of the article [reg 6 of the EC(C)R 1973] they would need to show that the payment to them was a transaction entered into by the board of directors of each of the companies. There is no evidence of this in any of the affidavits filed by either side. The payment appears to have been agreed to be made as a result of informal meetings between accountants acting on behalf of the companies and Mr Patrick Burke acting on behalf of the Revenue Commissioners. In these circumstances it seems to me that the Revenue Commissioners cannot rely on Article 6 as validating the payment.'

266 See para **[7.172]** *et seq, post*.

(j) Corporate enforcement of ultra vires contracts

[7.088] It might seem logical that if a company wishes to enforce a contract which is invalid according to its objects clause it should be able to amend its objects clause. However, in law a company cannot ratify an *ultra vires* act[267]. Furthermore, s 8(1) of the CA 1963 affords no remedy to the company as its saving provisions apply only in favour of any person relying on an act or thing done by a company. Although an *ultra vires* contract is void at common law, where s 8(1) can be relied upon the contract is unilaterally enforceable at the option of the person dealing with the company.

(k) Recovery of money given by a company ultra vires

[7.089] It has long been debated whether or not a company that has lent or advanced money in an *ultra vires* transaction can recover that money. The matter was addressed in detail by the High Court in *Re PMPA Garage (Longmile) Ltd et al (No 2)*[268]. This judgment arose out of the earlier finding by Murphy J, considered *ante*[269], that certain loans made by the PMPS were *ultra vires*. As to the rights of the parties in these circumstances, Murphy J held that 'there are four possible solutions': that the loans were unenforceable; recoverable in an action *in rem*; recoverable on the basis of quasi-contract; or recoverable on the basis of an estoppel. Each of the four possible solutions is next considered in turn.

(i) Unenforceable[270]

[7.090] This alternative provides that because the lending of the money was *ultra vires*, the loan is unenforceable and the borrowers can retain benefit of the loan for themselves. In *Re PMPA Garage (Longmile) Ltd et al (No 2)*[271], Murphy J dismissed this as a solution in the following terms:

> 'The monstrous injustice which would flow from the acceptance of such an audacious proposition would certainly render it unattractive to any court seeking to achieve justice in accordance with law.'

Accordingly, the learned judge rejected the argument that a party who holds money paid on foot of an *ultra vires* contract can retain it, although he noted that the authorities differ as to the means which a court can avail of to restore such property to the company who gave it.

(ii) Recoverable in an action in rem – constructive trusts and the Belmont principle[272]

[7.091] In *Re PMPA Garage (Longmile) Ltd et al (No 2)*[273], Murphy J accepted the existence of this remedy which allows the lender to recover property in an action *in rem*

[267] *Ashbury Railway Carriage & Iron Co v Riche* (1875) LR 7 HLC 653; and *Re Balgooley Distillery Co* (1886) 17 LR Ir 239.

[268] *Re PMPA Garage (Longmile) Ltd et al (No 2)* [1992] ILRM 349.

[269] See para **[7.058]** and **[7.067]** *ante*.

[270] *Re PMPA Garage (Longmile) Ltd et al (No 2)* [1992] ILRM 349 at 351.

[271] *Re PMPA Garage (Longmile) Ltd et al (No 2)* [1992] ILRM 349.

[272] *Re PMPA Garage (Longmile) Ltd et al (No 2)* [1992] ILRM 349 at 351.

[273] *Re PMPA Garage (Longmile) Ltd et al (No 2)* [1992] ILRM 349.

on the basis that the monies available were never validly lent and as such remained the property of the lender. This solution has the disadvantage that the lender cannot recover interest on those sums and can only recover that which can be specifically traced and identified. This was established in the case of *Sinclair v Brougham*[274], where the facts bore an extraordinary resemblance to the facts of the case in question, save that in issue there was *ultra vires* borrowing while in the *PMPA* case the question concerned *ultra vires* lending. In *Sinclair*, it was said that the doctrine of *ultra vires* excluded any claim *in personam* and, accordingly, in the words of Viscount Haldane LC:

> '... the only possible remedy for the person who has paid the money would on principle appear to be *in rem* and not *in personam*, a claim to follow and recover specifically any money which could be earmarked as never having ceased to be his property. To hold that a remedy will lie *in personam* against a statutory society, which by hypothesis cannot in the case in question have become a debtor or entered into any contract for repayment, is to strike at the root of the doctrine of ultra vires as established in the jurisprudence of this country[275].'

Murphy J also noted that this case rejected the possibility that such monies could be recovered on a quasi-contract basis, based on the principle of unjust enrichment and a promise implied by law to repay.

[7.092] In *Re Frederick Inns Ltd*[276], the Supreme Court considered the principle enunciated in *Belmont Finance Corporation Ltd v Williams Furniture Ltd*[277]. The *Belmont* principle states that where the directors of a company breach their fiduciary duties and misapply company funds and those funds come into the hands of a stranger to the trust with knowledge (actual or constructive) of the breach, the stranger cannot conscientiously retain them against the company unless he has some better equity[278]. In applying the *Belmont* principle to the *ultra vires* payments in favour of the Revenue Commissioners, Blayney J said:

> 'The *ultra vires* payments in the present case were made on the authority of the directors of the four companies and, being *ultra vires*, they constituted a misapplication by the directors of the companies' funds ... This misapplication was a breach by the directors of their fiduciary duties and the monies were received by the Revenue Commissioners with constructive knowledge of the breach since, if they had read the memorandum of association of the four companies, as they could have done since they are documents of public record, they would have seen that the companies had no power to make the payments. It follows in my opinion that the Revenue Commissioners are constructive

274 *Sinclair v Brougham* [1914] AC 398.

275 *Sinclair v Brougham* [1914] AC 398 at 414.

276 *Re Frederick Inns Ltd* [1994] 1 ILRM 387.

277 *Belmont Finance Corporation Ltd v Williams Furniture Ltd* [1980] 1 All ER 393.

278 The *Belmont* principle does not turn on corporate capacity but the abuse of fiduciary duties. In *Re Frederick Inns Ltd*, Blayney J quoted the following passage from Slade J in *Rolled Steel Products* where he said: 'The *Belmont* principle thus provides a legal route by which a company may recover its assets in a case where its directors have abused their fiduciary duties and a person receiving assets as a result of such abuse is on notice that they have been misapplied. The principle is not linked in any way to the capacity of the company; it is capable of applying whether or not the company had the capacity to do the acts in question.'

> trustees of the sums which were the subject of the *ultra vires* payments and must repay them to the official liquidator for each of the companies[279].'

This was applied in *Ulster Factors Ltd v Entonglen Ltd and Maloney*[280]. In that case the liquidator of the first defendant company sought to impugn a transaction whereby it had authorised the plaintiff to pay a sum to a firm of Northern Irish solicitors. Laffoy J was not satisfied that the liquidator had established that the payment was *ultra vires* or, if it was, that s 8(1) of the CA 1963 would not be available. Laffoy J held that even if the liquidator was right on both counts, the *Belmont* principle as applied by the Supreme Court in *Re Frederick Inns Ltd* was not available. The learned judge said:

> 'Under the *Belmont* principle, as applied by the Supreme Court, what renders the recipient of or the dealer with funds which are being misapplied in breach of the fiduciary duties of the directors of a company liable as a constructive trustee is knowledge, actual or constructive, of the breach of trust. The factual position in this matter is that on the morning of 21 June 1990 the plaintiff acknowledged that it held at least IR£37,839.83 which, in accordance with the terms of the Agreement, was payable at the request of the company to the company or to its order and, later that morning, the plaintiff received a request on the letter-heading of the company showing its trading name and signed by a director of the company, who was also the financial director and secretary of the company, to make a payment equivalent to IR£37,839.83 to Messrs King & Gowdy and the plaintiff duly made that payment. Even if the payment was *ultra vires* the company and in breach of the directors' fiduciary duties, it is clear from the evidence that Mr Murray did not have actual knowledge of the purpose for which the payment was being made or of the breach. The agreement specifically provided that the plaintiff was objected to make payments to third parties at the request of the company. There was no obligation on the plaintiff to enquire as to the purpose for which any payment which the company requested the plaintiff to make to a third party was being made or to satisfy itself that the payment was *intra vires* the company and, even if the payment was *ultra vires*, constructive knowledge of a breach of trust cannot be imputed to the plaintiff for failure to make such enquiries[281].'

(iii) Recoverable on basis of quasi-contract[282]

[7.093] In *Re PMPA Garage (Longmile) Ltd et al (No 2)*[283], Murphy J noted that recovery on the basis of quasi-contract was at conflict with the decision in *Sinclair v Brougham*, 'inasmuch as it does involve recognising the availability of an action other than an action *in rem*', but the learned judge went on to recognise the evolution of the law relating to quasi-contract. Referring to *East Cork Foods v O'Dwyer Steel*[284], Murphy J noted that there Henchy J had said:

> 'the plaintiff succeeds in this type of action because, it is said, the law imputes a promise to pay the debt ... In most cases it is in the teeth of the facts to impute to the debtor a promise to pay ... Nowadays, however, when the forms of action have long since been

---

279 *Ulster Factors Ltd v Entonglen Ltd and Maloney* [1994] 1 ILRM 387 at 399.

280 *Ulster Factors Ltd v Entonglen Ltd and Maloney* (21 February 1997, unreported) HC, Laffoy J. See para **[7.122]** *post*.

281 *Ulster Factors Ltd v Entonglen Ltd and Maloney* (21 February 1997, unreported) HC, Laffoy J at pp 8, 9 of the judgment.

282 *Re PMPA Garage (Longmile) Ltd et al (No 2)* [1992] ILRM 349 at 353.

283 *Re PMPA Garage (Longmile) Ltd et al (No 2)* [1992] ILRM 349.

284 *East Cork Foods v O'Dwyer Steel* [1978] IR 103.

> buried, the concept of implied contract is an unreal and outdated rationale for the action for money had and received. Judges in modern times generally prefer to look at the reality of the situation rather than engage in the pretence that the defendant has promised to pay the debt[285].'

Thus, the need[286] for an express or imputed promise to pay is no longer a necessary ingredient of the action for money had and received. Accordingly, Murphy J said:

> '... there is no impediment in availing of that remedy against a corporate body to recover monies received by it as a result of a transaction which was outside its corporate powers[287].'

As to the case in hand, Murphy J said that the difference between the parties in dispute was whether the PMPS could recover the monies on a basis other than an action *in rem* or a contract between the parties.

(iv) Recoverable on the basis of an estoppel

[7.094] In *Re PMPA Garage (Longmile) Ltd et al (No 2)*[288], the fourth possible solution was that the PMPA companies were committed to repaying the money to the PMPS by virtue of their promises to repay. As authority for this proposition, Murphy J first referred to the decision of the English Court of Appeal in *Re Coltman*[289], which allowed recovery of monies in similar circumstances. However whilst this decision has been criticised[290], Murphy J referred to an Australian decision, *Re KL Tractors Ltd*[291], where the company concerned bought machinery from the Commonwealth Government of Australia. When the company subsequently become insolvent, its creditors disputed the right of the Commonwealth to recover, arguing that the contract was *ultra vires* the company. In what was 'very solid judicial support for the estoppel-type argument', it was held that the company could not plead *ultra vires* to avoid payment of the debt due and owing[292].

[7.095] Having thus canvassed the four possible alternatives, Murphy J admitted that the conflicting, but persuasive, authorities placed him in considerable difficulty. He concluded, however:

> 'I recognise the force of the simple cogent proposition that a body corporate cannot enforce a contract which it never had the capacity to make. It is demonstrated with equal clarity that all judicial authorities have set their face against any party who seeks to

---

285 *East Cork Foods v O'Dwyer Steel* [1978] IR 103 at 110.

286 Note that Murphy J held that he would in any event have imputed such a promise on the facts of the case in hand.

287 *Re PMPA Garage (Longmile) Ltd et al (No 2)* [1992] ILRM 349 at 354.

288 *Re PMPA Garage (Longmile) Ltd et al (No 2)* [1992] ILRM 349.

289 *Re Coltman* [1881] 19 Ch D 64.

290 For not recognising the authority of *Ashbury Railway Carriage and Iron Co v Riche* (1875) LR 7 HL 653. See also the decision of Mocatta J in *Bell Houses Ltd v City Wall Properties Ltd* (1966) 1 QB 207, which although reversed on appeal, held at first instance that money paid was not recoverable.

291 *Re KL Tractors Ltd* (1961) 106 CLR 318.

292 Murphy J also referred to the Alberta Supreme Court of Canada in *Breckenridge Speedway Ltd* 64 DLR 488 and the Supreme Court of Canada in *Rolland v La Caisse d'Economie Notre-Dame de Quebec* (1895) 24 SCR 405.

> prevent the recovery from him of goods or monies which he has retained under an *ultra vires* transaction. The precise grounds on which such claims have been defeated have varied over the century during which the debate has spasmodically taken place but the result has been the same. No court would permit the manifest injustice which such a contention would involve ... There is no inconsistency between the proper application of the *ultra vires* doctrine and the recovery by means of an action *in rem* or on a quasi contractual basis of monies or goods in the hands of the party receiving the same in consequence of the transaction. The problem which must be faced is whether there is any other basis on which such goods can be recovered. It seems to me that the alternative basis is something akin to an *estoppel*[293].'

The basis of this finding can only be that the courts will not countenance injustice when it is within their power to prevent it. In the case in hand it was held that the PMPS was entitled to be admitted as creditor of the PMPA companies, since it would be unconscionable to allow the borrowing companies to rely on any want of authority to lend by the PMPS.

(l) Reform of the doctrine of ultra vires

[7.096] The traditional reason why a company had to have an objects clause was, first, to make its shareholders aware of its objectives, and second, to let its creditors know the nature of its business[294]. In this day and age such reasons are anachronistic. For both creditors and shareholders, the modern realities of company practice, as opposed to company law, have meant that the doctrine has done more harm than good. If the decision in *Rolled Steel Products* is followed, the scope of the doctrine of *ultra vires* will be greatly diminished[295].

[7.097] In the United Kingdom, s 35 of the Companies Act 1985[296] attempts to abolish the doctrine of *ultra vires*. One way could have been to dispense with the requirement to have an objects clause at all thus allowing a company to do as it pleased. This was not the chosen reform. Rather, s 35 (as amended) provided that:

> 'the validity of an act done by a company shall not be called into question on the ground of lack of capacity by reason of anything in the company's memorandum.'

It has been suggested[297] that such a reform seems the most just solution in that while the doctrine of *ultra vires* cannot now apply in the UK, nevertheless, a director who is responsible for the company pursuing an object, which is not within the capacity of the company, will be guilty of an abuse of power. Hence, English legislative focus has been on the imposition of responsibility on the internal management of the company: a previously *ultra vires* act will not invalidate the contract but will ground an action against the directors, at the suit of the company's members.

---

293 *Re PMPA Garage (Longmile) Ltd et al (No 2)* [1992] ILRM 349 at 362. Italics added.

294 See Pennington, (1983) 8 Co Law at 103, 104, where the 'Prentice Report on *Ultra Vires*' is reviewed.

295 Note Clark, (1985) 6 Co Law 155 who says: 'the modern corporation will effectively have full contractual capacity.'

296 As amended by s 108 of the Companies Act 1989 (UK).

297 Pennington, *Pennington's Company Law* (6th edn, Butterworths, 1990) at p 97.

[7.098] In Ireland, the Company Law Review Group has recommended that the doctrine of *ultra vires* be abolished for *private companies limited by shares*, which accounts for some 89% of all companies registered. The Review Group's recommendation is that such companies should 'be given the legal capacity of a natural person'[298]. The draft Companies Bill published in 2011 gives effect to this recommendation by providing in s 38(1) of the draft Bill that in the case of the new model private company:

> '... notwithstanding anything contained in its constitution a company shall have, whether acting inside or outside of the State –
>
> (a) full and unlimited capacity to carry on and undertake any business or activity, do any act or enter into any transaction; and
>
> (b) for the purposes of *paragraph (a)*, full rights, powers and privileges.'

This will be subject only to the company not being thereby relieved from any duty or obligation under any enactment or the general law, eg, where a business or activity is regulated, the company must comply with the enactment or law which provides for that regulation. It is important to note that it is proposed that it will be the new model private company limited by shares only, that will not have an objects clause: PLCs, unlimited companies, guarantee companies and private companies limited by shares which elect to have an objects clause (to be known as *designated activity companies* or 'DACs'), etc, will all continue to have an objects clause in their memoranda of association.

[D] The Authority of Corporate Agents

[7.099] Although a company is a separate legal entity[299], because of both *de jure* and *de facto* limitations, it does not have the same contractual capabilities as human persons. The most colourful expression of this is found in the *dictum* of Buckley J in *Continental Tyre & Rubber Co (GB) Ltd v Daimler & Co*[300] where he said:

> 'The artificial legal person called the corporation has no physical existence. It exists only in contemplation of law. It has neither body, parts, nor passions. It cannot wear weapons nor serve in wars. It can be neither loyal nor disloyal. It cannot compass treason. It can be neither friend nor enemy. Apart from its corporators it can have neither thoughts, wishes, nor intentions, for it has no mind other than the mind of the corporators.'

The root-source of corporate authority in general, and contractual authority in particular, lies with the members of a company. However, it is usual for the members to divest themselves of almost all power through the adoption of model reg 80[301]. By model reg 80, the members delegate the management of the company to the board of directors. The board may in turn delegate its authority to a managing director where model reg 112 has been adopted; and indeed, most companies delegate further authority to others such as employees.

The company's members can, where permitted by the articles of association, resolve in general meeting to enter into a contract. In practice, however, this is not the norm, and

[298] The CLRG's *First Report* (2000–2001), recommendation 10.9.2 at p 226.

[299] *Salomon v Salomon & Co Ltd* [1897] AC 22. See generally Ch 4, *Incorporation and its Consequences*, at para **[4.026]**.

[300] *Continental Tyre & Rubber Co (GB) Ltd v Daimler & Co* [1915] 1 KB 893 at 916.

[301] See Ch 13, *Corporate Governance: Management by the Directors*, at para **[13.127]**.

the vast majority of contracts are entered into by the board or the managing director (or others under their authority) without reference to the members. The board or managing director will be acting on delegated authority as agents for the company. Where authority is not delegated to the directors, and where the members resolve to enter into a contract, the only restrictions on their authority are the company's constitutional documentation and the general law. However, where the directors enter into a contract on behalf of a company they can only act within their *permitted delegated authority*. Much of the case law on the authority of corporate agents is consequently concerned with situations where the chain of authority breaks down. The issues which arise here for consideration are examined under the following headings:

1. Actual and implied authority of corporate agents.
2. Ostensible authority of corporate agents.
3. The usual and ostensible authority of particular corporate organs.
4. Constructive notice of public documents.
5. The indoor management rule.
6. The scope of the rule in *Turquand's* case.
7. European intervention: EC(C)R 1973.

Actual and implied authority of corporate agents

[7.100] The legal principles applicable to the actual authority of corporate agents are found in the laws of agency[302]. Where an agent acts within the limits of his *actual* authority and the capacity of the company[303], the company as principal will be bound by all contracts entered into by the agent[304]. The basis of *actual authority* is the 'consensual arrangement' between the company and the agent[305]. No special formalities are required to appoint an agent[306]. In the case of corporate employees, the basis of the consensual arrangement will usually be rooted in their contract of employment. It should also be

[302] See *Halsbury's Laws of England* (4th edn, 1974) Vol 1; Frideman, *The Law of Agency* (6th edn, Butterworths, 1990); *Bowstead & Reynolds on Agency* (16th edn, 1996) and Cheshire Fifoot & Furmston, *Law of Contract* (12th edn, Butterworths, 1986) at p 469.

[303] The company will not be bound by the ultra vires acts of an agent: *Thomas Williamson Ltd and another v Bailieborough Cooperative Agricultural Society Ltd* (31 July 1986, unreported) HC, per Costello J, considered at para **[7.062]**, *post*.

[304] *Freeman & Lockyer v Buckhurst Park Properties (Mangal) Ltd* [1964] 2 QB 480. Diplock LJ said (at 502, 503): 'An "actual" authority is a legal relationship between principal and agent created by a consensual agreement to which they alone are parties. Its scope is to be ascertained by applying ordinary principles of construction of contracts, including any proper implications from the express words used, the usages of trade, or the course of business between the parties. To this agreement the contractor is a stranger; he may be totally ignorant of the existence of any authority on the part of the agent. Nevertheless, if the agent does enter into a contract pursuant to the "actual" authority, it does create contractual rights and liabilities between the principal and the contractor.'

[305] *Kett v Shannon & English* [1987] ILRM 364 at 366 *per* Henchy J, following Diplock LJ in *Freeman & Lockyer v Buckhurst Park Properties (Mangal) Ltd* [1964] 2 QB 480.

[306] Section 38 of the CA 1963. That said, however, a *commercial agent,* within the meaning of the European Communities (Commercial Agents) Regulations 1994 (SI 33/1994), must be appointed, or his appointment evidenced, in *writing*: reg 5.

noted that an agent may have *implied actual authority.* In *SMC Electronics Ltd v Akhter Computers Ltd et al*[307], the following passage[308] was cited with approval:

> 'An agent who is authorised to do any act in the course of his trade, profession or business as an agent has implied authority to do whatever is normally incidental, in the ordinary course of such trade, profession or business, to the execution of his express authority, but not to do anything which is unusual in such trade, profession or business, or which is neither necessary nor incidental to the execution of his express authority.'

In *Thomas Williamson Ltd and Another v Bailieborough Co-operative Agricultural Society Ltd*[309], Costello J said:

> 'Actual authority can be expressly conferred on a company's board of directors or it can be *expressly* conferred by the board of directors on an agent or it can *impliedly* be conferred by them on an agent. Thus when a board of directors appoints a 'managing director' or a 'secretary' it impliedly confers on the person so appointed the powers usually associated with holders of such offices[310].'

Where an agent's authority is conferred in ambiguous terms, his company might be bound by his actions where he acts reasonably and in good faith[311]. The concern of company law and agency is with the authority of corporate officers and corporate organs. The basis of the consensual arrangement between the agent and principal company will be found in the company's articles of association, the resolutions of its members and directors and any contracts between the company and its agents. However, even where there exists no actual authority based on a consensual arrangement, the company may still be bound by an agent's actions where the agent is found to have acted within his *ostensible* or *apparent* authority[312].

Ostensible authority of corporate agents

[7.101] Actual and ostensible authority were distinguished by Henchy J in the Supreme Court in *Kett v Shannon & English*[313] where he said:

---

307 *SMC Electronics Ltd v Akhter Computers Ltd et al* [2001] 1 BCLC 433.

308 From *Bowstead & Reynolds on Agency* (16th edn, 1996) art 30.

309 *Thomas Williamson Ltd and Another v Bailieborough Co-operative Agricultural Society Ltd* (31 July 1986, unreported) HC, *per* Costello J.

310 *Thomas Williamson Ltd and Another v Bailieborough Co-operative Agricultural Society Ltd* (31 July 1986, unreported) HC, *per* Costello J at p 8 of the transcript.

311 In *SMC Electronics Ltd v Akhter Computers Ltd et al* [2001] 1 BCLC 433, the English Court of Appeal cited with approval the following passage from *Bowstead & Reynolds on Agency* (16th edn, 1996) art 26, p 116 at para 3-106: 'Where the authority of an agent is conferred in such ambiguous terms, or the instructions given to him are so uncertain, as to be fairly capable of more than one construction, an act reasonably done by him in good faith which is justified by any of those constructions is deemed to have been fully authorised, though the construction adopted and acted upon by him was not that intended by the principal.'

312 In *Ulster Factors Ltd v Entonglen Ltd and Maloney* (21 February 1997, unreported) HC, Laffoy J, it was held that, although the director in question did not have actual authority to make certain payments under scrutiny, he did in fact have ostensible authority: see para **[7.105]** *post*.

313 *Kett v Shannon & English* [1987] ILRM 364 at 366.

> 'Actual authority exists when it is based on an actual agreement between the principal and the agent ... Ostensible authority, on the other hand, derives not from any consensual arrangement between the principal and the agent, but is founded on a representation made by the principal to the third party which is intended to convey, and does convey, to the third party that the arrangement entered into under the apparent authority of the agent will be binding on the principal.'

The doctrine of apparent or ostensible authority may be seen as a form of estoppel which prevents the company from denying an agent's *ostensible* authority, which the company represented the agent as having. The law views the company as 'misrepresenting' the agent's authority, or lack of it. In consequence the company is estopped from later denying that agent's authority to bind the company. Implicit in this analysis is that there must be a representation from someone with actual authority[314].

[7.102] The definition of ostensible authority set out by Henchy J in *Kett v Shannon & English* is a paraphrase of the universally cited *dictum* of Diplock LJ in *Freeman & Lockyer v Buckhurst Park Properties (Mangal) Ltd*[315]. In this, the leading case on ostensible authority, the facts were that the defendant company was formed by Kapoor to buy and sell an estate of land. The articles of the company provided that the directors could appoint a managing director. Although Kapoor, who was a director, acted to the knowledge of the other directors as if he were managing director, he had never been formally appointed as such. When Kapoor engaged the plaintiff architects to apply for planning permission to develop the estate of land, the question which arose was whether the company was liable on the contract to pay their fees. It was held that the company was liable to pay their fees, because Kapoor had *ostensible or apparent authority* to engage the plaintiffs since the board had *represented* that he was the managing director who had the actual authority to bind the company in a contract.

[7.103] If an outsider is to enforce a contract against a company by arguing that the agent who made it had ostensible authority to contract, the matters set out by Diplock LJ in *Freeman & Lockyer v Buckhurst Park Properties (Mangal) Ltd*[316] must be proved:

> '(1) that a representation that the agent had authority to enter on behalf of the company into a contract of the kind sought to be enforced was made to the contractor;
>
> (2) that such representation was made by a person or persons who had 'actual' authority to manage the business of the company either generally or in respect of those matters to which the contract relates;
>
> (3) that he (the contractor) was indeed induced by such representations to enter into the contract, that is, that he in fact relied upon it; and
>
> (4) that under its memorandum or articles of association the company was not deprived of the capacity either to enter into a contract of the kind sought to be

[314] On corporate representations, see para **[7.104]**, *post*.

[315] *Freeman & Lockyer v Buckhurst Park Properties (Mangal) Ltd* [1964] 2 QB 480.

[316] *Freeman & Lockyer v Buckhurst Park Properties (Mangal) Ltd* [1964] 2 QB 480. Diplock LJ said (at 503): 'An "apparent" or "ostensible" authority ... is a legal relationship between the principal and the contractor created by a representation, made by the principal to the contractor, intended to be and in fact acted upon by the contractor, that the agent has authority to enter on behalf of the principal into a contract of a kind within the scope of the "apparent" authority, so as to render the principal liable to perform the obligations imposed upon him by such contract.'

> enforced or to delegate authority to enter into a contract of that kind to the agent[317].'

It is well established that this is a correct statement of the law in Ireland[318]. Each of these requirements in order to establish that a person had ostensible authority is next considered, namely:

(a) Corporate representations;
(b) The actual authority of the representor;
(c) Relying on the representation;
(d) The contract was within the permitted capacity and authority of the company.

(a) Corporate representations

[7.104] In *United Bank of Kuwait Ltd v Hammond & Ors*[319], Lord Donaldson MR said:

> '... it is trite law that an agent cannot ordinarily confer ostensible authority on himself. He cannot pull himself up by his own shoelaces ...'[320]

In order for the doctrine of ostensible authority to apply, the *company* must represent or 'hold the agent out as having' authority to do the act in question. No amount of 'self-representation' by the 'agent' will estop the company: *ESS-Food Eksportlagtiernes Sallgsforening v Crown Shipping (Ireland) Ltd*[321]. That this represents Irish law was made clear by the Supreme Court in *Kett v Shannon & English*, where Henchy J cited with approval *Freeman & Lockyer*, and went on to quote the following passage from the *dictum* of Goff LJ in *Armagas Ltd v Mundagas SA*[322]:

> 'It appears from that judgment [*Freeman & Lockyer*] that ostensible authority is created by a representation by the principle, to the third party that the agent has the relevant authority, when acted on by the third party, operates as an estoppel, precluding the principal from asserting that he is not bound. The representation which creates ostensible authority may take a variety of forms, but the most common is a representation by conduct, by permitting the agent to act in some way in the conduct of the principal's business with other persons, and thereby representing that the agent has the authority which an agent so acting in the conduct of his principal's business usually has.'

---

317 *Freeman & Lockyer v Buckhurst Park Properties (Mangal) Ltd* [1964] 2 QB 480, *per* Diplock LJ at 506.

318 See, for example, *Kett v Shannon & English* [1987] ILRM 364 and *Ulster Factors Ltd v Entonglen Ltd and Maloney* (21 February 1997, unreported) HC, Laffoy J.

319 *United Bank of Kuwait Ltd v Hammond & Ors* [1988] 1 WLR 1051 at 1066.

320 See also *AG for Ceylon v Silva* [1953] AC 461 at 479.

321 *ESS-Food Eksportlagtiernes Sallgsforening v Crown Shipping (Ireland) Ltd* [1991] ILRM 97. Of the requirement for a corporate representation, Costello J said (at 108): 'This means that although Ballybay [the agent] in this case certainly represented to the defendants [the outsider] that they had authority from third parties to enter into the contract on their behalf this is of no avail to the defendants – they must show some representation made by the plaintiffs which now estops them from denying the existence of the contract and the term conferring a right of lien on the defendants. But no such representation was made by the plaintiffs in this case and none can be inferred from their conduct ...'

322 *Armagas Ltd v Mundagas SA* [1985] 3 All ER 795 at 805.

The most common way in which a company *represents* is by conduct: the other directors hold the agent out as having the usual authority of a person in a particular position, or holding a particular office[323]. The paradigm situation is where a director acts like a managing director, and the company (ie, the other directors) acquiesces in outsiders believing this. Where a director has 'the airs' of a managing director and the company acquiesces in outsiders so believing that he is, the outsider can assume that the person has as much power as a real managing director would usually have in *that* company[324].

[7.105] In *Ulster Factors Ltd v Entonglen Ltd and Maloney*[325], it was held that a 'tacit representation' by a company's board of directors that a particular director had authority to authorise a draw-down of funds could bind the company. The dispute in that case was between the plaintiff and the defendant company's liquidator, who challenged the validity of a payment made by the plaintiff to the order of the defendant company, to a third party on foot of a factoring agreement. In return for the defendant company assigning all of its debts to the plaintiff, the plaintiff agreed, on request, to make payment 'to or to the order of' the defendant company of a sum not exceeding the balance available to it under the terms of the agreement. By side-letter it was agreed that the defendant-company would advise the plaintiff as to which of its officers had been nominated to 'call off factor's funds' and these terms were accepted by the defendant company by the same two directors who had countersigned the affixing of its seal to the factoring agreement. Moreover, the factoring agreement also provided that the defendant company would provide the plaintiff with the names and specimen signatures of all persons authorised to sign documents on its behalf. Laffoy J found that notwithstanding these agreements, no instructions or written mandate as to the formalities to be complied with in relation to the draw-down of funds was ever given to the plaintiff. Laffoy J also found that for a period of three years, in all but three draw-downs (one of which was the disputed one) the plaintiff had been instructed to make the payments directly to the defendant company. The draw-down that was disputed concerned an instruction from a Mr Holland to the plaintiff to make a cheque in the sum of STG£35,000 payable to a firm of Northern Irish solicitors. Mr Holland, who was a director, financial director and secretary of the defendant company, faxed the plaintiff, directing that the sum be paid to 'King Goddy Solicitors'. The plaintiff queried this by telephone and on foot of this received a second fax, amending the instruction to read 'King and Gowdy Solicitors'. Mr Holland signed both faxes. The plaintiff complied with the instruction and paid the money to the designated solicitors and sent a statement, recording the draw-down, to the defendant company. The statement was not queried.

[323] See *Allied Pharmaceutical Distributions Ltd v Walsh* [1991] IR 8 at 17, *per* Barron J. The totality of a company's conduct must always be considered: *Ebeed v Soplex Refson* [1985] BCLC 404; *First Energy (UK) Ltd v Hungarian International Bank Ltd* [1993] BCLC 1409.

[324] The reason for the stress on 'in that company' is because, as we shall see post, an outsider will be deemed to have constructive notice of the company's articles of association which will say what authority a managing director will have in that company. This is because the articles are 'public documents', and any member of the public can examine them in the CRO. See para **[7.119]**.

[325] *Ulster Factors Ltd v Entonglen Ltd and Maloney* (21 February 1997, unreported) HC, Laffoy J. See Linnane, 'Corporate Capacity and Ostensible Authority and their "Inextricable" Entwinement on Display' (2000) 7 CLP 37.

Over six months' later, the defendant company's then secretary, at the request of its auditors, requested a copy of the cheque for STG£35,000, which the then secretary thought had been paid to 'Gaul & Knowlton Solicitors'. The plaintiff furnished the copy of the cheque, pointing out the correct name of the payee. Again, this was not queried by the defendant company. Business continued to be transacted between the plaintiff and the defendant company until the company was wound-up. The defendant company's liquidator realised the debts due to the defendant company, and paid over to the plaintiff all of them, with the exception of the STG£35,000, which he disputed. The liquidator contended that that payment was *ultra vires* and also made without the authority of the defendant company[326]. The defendant company's managing director testified that Mr Holland in fact had no authority to direct payments of funds to third parties on his own because his authority was as one of two signatories.

[7.106] On this evidence, Laffoy J held that Mr Holland did not have actual authority. The learned judge went on to find, however, that Mr Holland had ostensible authority and that she was satisfied that the four conditions laid down by Diplock LJ in *Freeman and Lockyer v Buckhurst Park Properties (Mangal) Ltd* had been fulfilled, in that:

> '(1) there was a representation that Mr Holland, as a director and as company secretary, had authority to request draw down of funds to the company or to a third party,
>
> (2) such representation was made by the board of directors of the company, which had actual authority under its articles of association to manage its business,
>
> (3) the plaintiff actually relied on such representation, and
>
> (4) under its memorandum or articles of association, the company was not deprived of the capacity to request payment of its funds to a third party or to delegate authority to do so[327].'

As to the nature of the representation by the defendant company that Mr Holland had authority to request draw down of the funds to the third parties, Laffoy J said:

> 'The representation on which the ostensible authority of Mr Holland, as a director and as company secretary, was founded was a tacit representation. The Agreement specifically provided for monies due to the company being drawn-down either by payment to the company directly or to a third party. The Agreement itself and the terms and conditions contemporaneously agreed to by the company in relation to the method of the operation of the Agreement required the company to advise the plaintiff as to which officers of the company had authority to draw-down funds due to the company. The evidence establishes that in the early stages of the operation of the Agreement it was verbally agreed, in the context of a draw-down of funds to the company, that draw-downs would be advised by the directors and the company secretary. In the operation of the Agreement prior to [the disputed draw-down], subject to one exception, every draw-down was requested by one officer of the company only. In failing to communicate to the plaintiff that draw-downs to the order of the company were to be authorised in a different manner to draw-downs into the company, in my view, the company tacitly represented that all draw-downs were to be authorised in the same manner – by one officer of the company[328].'

[326] The ultra vires claim was considered ante at para **[7.083]** and **[7.092]** *post*.

[327] *Ulster Factors Ltd v Entonglen Ltd and Maloney* (21 February 1997, unreported) HC, Laffoy J at p 10 of the judgment.

[328] *Ulster Factors Ltd v Entonglen Ltd and Maloney* (21 February 1997, unreported) HC, Laffoy J at pp 10, 11 of the judgment.

Laffoy J found that the fact that the first authorisation to make a payment to the order of the company (in the nature of a payment to a director) had been authorised by both the managing director and Mr Holland, did not negate that tacit representation as it was made in the early stages of the agreement and, being a payment to a director, might well have been perceived as being in a special category. Laffoy J also thought it significant that the propriety of the payment in question was not questioned for some considerable time, and, ultimately, only after the commencement of the winding up. Accordingly, Laffoy J upheld the validity of the payment on the grounds that a director and company secretary had ostensible authority to authorise it. It can be seen that the court will normally look to the totality of a company's express and tacit representations and not confine its remit to what is normal or usual authority for a particular agent[329].

(b) The actual authority of the representor

[7.107] The person or organ which makes the representation must themselves have the actual authority to make such a representation either generally, or in respect of the particular transaction in issue[330]. In a company where model reg 80 is adopted, the board will be entrusted to manage the business of the company and so will have the requisite actual authority to represent an agent as having authority. In the absence of such a provision in the articles, residual actual authority can only lie with the members of the company: *Mahony v East Holyford Mining Co*[331].

(c) Relying on the representation

[7.108] The third condition in *Freeman & Lockyer* is that the outsider must have relied upon the representation if the company is to be estopped from disclaiming the transaction. To admit in evidence that one did not rely on the representation is fatal to establishing that a company is bound by ostensible authority of one of its officers[332].

(d) The contract was within the permitted capacity and authority of the company

[7.109] Not only must the representor have actual authority to enter into the transaction in hand, but so too must the company have the *capacity* to enter into such a transaction. The fourth condition in *Freeman & Lockyer* is that the company's objects clause must allow a contract of the sort made by the agent. This is but a reminder that contracts which are *ultra vires* the company's powers are void. So in *Thomas Williamson Ltd & Another v Bailieborough Co-operative Agricultural Society Ltd*, Costello J did not have to decide whether or not the board had held out the financial controller and chief executive as having power to enter into contracts of guarantee (or authorise others to do

---

329 See, for example, *Ebeed and another (trading as Egyptian International Foreign Trading Co) v Soplex Wholesale Supplies Ltd and another (The Raffaella)* [1985] BCLC 404.

330 So in *British Bank of the Middle East v Sun Life Assurance Co of Canada* [1985] BCLC 78, it was found by the House of Lords that the representors did not themselves have the actual authority to make the representation.

331 *Mahony v East Holyford Mining Co* (1875) LR 7 HL 869; see also *Kilgobbin Mink and Stud Farms Ltd v National Credit Company Ltd* [1980] IR 175 and generally, Ch 13, *Corporate Governance: Management by the Directors*, at para **[13.127]**.

332 See *Dunn v MBS Distribution Ltd* (1990) EAT/132/89, 12 June 1990 (UK).

so) because he held that such contracts of guarantee were *ultra vires* the defendant society.

[7.110] Accordingly, even where all other elements exist, a person will not have ostensible authority to do something that is *ultra vires* the company's capacity or precluded by the company's articles of association. Outsiders will be deemed to be aware of any such restrictions on capacity and authority in companies' memoranda and articles of association because these are documents of public record of which they will be deemed to have *constructive notice*. Constructive notice is considered below[333].

The usual and ostensible authority of particular corporate organs

[7.111] It is important to consider what the *usual* authority of any given corporate agent is, and this can be gleaned from the articles of association of the particular company. In view of the fact that it is open to a company to vary its articles of association from those set out in Table A, what follows is necessarily a specific analysis of the powers given to various corporate officers in a company which has adopted the model articles in Table A. The authority of the following organs and officers is next considered:

(a) The board of directors;
(b) The managing director;
(c) The chairman of the board;
(d) Directors;
(e) The company secretary;
(f) The sole member of a single-member private company.

(a) The board of directors

[7.112] The model articles in Table A confer a wide variety of powers on the board of directors ('the board')[334]. Of these, reg 80 is the widest, providing:

> 'The business of the company shall be managed by the directors, who may ... exercise all such powers of the company as are not, by the Act or by these regulations, required to be exercised by the company in general meeting ...'

It is common for most companies incorporated today to adopt reg 80 in an undiluted form[335]. Accordingly, the board potentially has the widest possible actual authority to enter into contracts on behalf of the company. Even where a particular board does not have actual authority, it may be found that it has *ostensible authority*. In *Mahony v East Holyford Mining Co*[336], the articles provided that the directors of the company should manage the business of the company and that all sums paid on behalf of the company were to be paid by cheque, signed as directed by the board. The subscribers to the articles acted as directors, and one acted as secretary although nobody was ever formally appointed to these posts. A letter to a bank claimed that the board had resolved that cheques would be signed by two of three named directors and countersigned by the secretary. A cheque was drawn and the bank which honoured it was protected when the

---

333 See para **[7.119]** *post*.

334 See generally, Table A, Part I, First Schedule to CA 1963, arts 79 to 90.

335 See, Ch 13, *Corporate Governance: Management by the Directors*, at para **[13.127]**.

336 *Mahony v East Holyford Mining Co* (1875) LR 7 HL 869; [1874–80] All ER 427.

company sought to avoid liability. The board of directors had acted within the ostensible authority which could have been conferred upon them by the articles and the company was estopped from avoiding liability.

[7.113] Regulation 79 of Table A, which permits borrowing, is a very important power of the board. However, it is usual to exclude this from a company's articles as it contains restrictions on the directors' powers to borrow[337]. It is usual for the model articles to be amended on incorporation to give to the directors an unfettered power to borrow, in anticipation of a lending institution requiring a company to have this at a later stage[338]. However, one can never assume that model reg 79 has been dropped, and an examination of the articles of every company must be undertaken[339]. In *Re Shannonside Holdings Ltd*[340], the company's articles of association contained a model reg 79 type restriction on the directors' powers to borrow. This provided that the directors could not borrow in excess of the company's issued share capital without first obtaining the consent of the company's members in general meeting. What is noticeable is that Costello J held *obiter dictum* that 'in the absence of express notice' outsiders would not be bound where the directors borrowed in excess of the company's issued share capital[341]. This decision is considered further, below[342].

(b) The managing director

[7.114] Where reg 112 of the model articles is adopted, the directors can delegate their authority to the managing director or, as they are more commonly referred to today, the chief executive officer[343]. In such a case the potential for actual authority of the managing director is high, and practice shows that it is usual to adopt reg 112 in full. One can only assume that the managing director has as much authority as the board has and so one should ensure that reg 80 also exists. Where both model regs 80 and 112 exist, the managing director will have very wide usual authority. Because a managing director's ostensible authority is very wide, a person who is represented as being a managing director will be assumed to have a wide *ostensible authority* too. Thus in the *Freeman & Lockyer* case, although one of the directors had not in fact been appointed managing director, he acted as such and it was represented by the company that he was managing director. Accordingly, it was held that he had the ostensible authority of a

---

337 See Ch 3, *Constitutional Documentation*, at para **[3.051]**.

338 A standard replacement for reg 79 is: 'The directors may exercise all the powers of the company to borrow money, and to mortgage or charge its undertaking, property and uncalled capital, or any part thereof and to issue debentures, debenture stock and other securities, whether outright or as security for any debt, liability or obligation of the company or of any third party without any limit.'

339 *Eg Re Burke Clancy & Co Ltd* (23 May 1974, unreported) HC *per* Kenny J especially at pp 10, 11 of the transcript. There an equivalent to reg 79 provided that the directors could not borrow in excess of the nominal issued share capital without the sanction of the members in meeting.

340 *Re Shannonside Holdings Ltd* (20 May 1993, unreported) HC, *per* Costello J.

341 *Re Shannonside Holdings Ltd* (20 May 1993, unreported) HC, *per* Costello J at p 7 of the transcript.

342 See para **[7.120]** *et seq*.

343 Note, however, that Table A makes no reference to chief executive officers or 'CEOs', so a person who acts as and is held out as a CEO will have no usual authority in accordance with model articles.

managing director. A further example is *Hely-Hutchinson v Brayhead Ltd*[344] where the chairman of the board acted as *de facto* managing director of a company. The articles would have permitted the appointment of a managing director, but none was ever appointed. The company entered into an arrangement to assist the plaintiff's company and bought £100,000 of shares from the plaintiff who was appointed a director of the company. Later the chairman signed letters to the plaintiff 'on behalf of' Brayhead Ltd purporting to indemnify him against a personal guarantee he had given for a loan of £50,000 to his company. The chairman further purported, on behalf of Brayhead Ltd, to guarantee a personal loan given by the plaintiff to his company in the amount of £45,000. When the company became insolvent, the plaintiff honoured his guarantee to the bank but the company refused to indemnify him, arguing that the chairman had no authority to sign the letters. The Court of Appeal held that the chairman had implied actual authority:

> 'implied from the circumstance that the board by their conduct over many months had acquiesced in his acting[345].'

This decision is open to criticism for engendering further confusion in an already confused area and it is submitted that it ought to have been decided on the basis of ostensible authority. It could not be said that the test for the finding of 'implied actual authority' was satisfied since the acts of the chairman were not 'necessary and incidental' to his chairmanship[346].

(c) The chairman of the board

[7.115] Regulation 104 of the model articles provides that 'the directors may elect a chairman of their meetings ...'. While sometimes the office of chairman can have wide-ranging actual authority[347], this will only arise because the chairman has been given a high degree of authority by the articles of association of the company in question. The primary role of a chairman is to preside over meetings of the board of directors, the chairman's remit being governance and process and not normally extending to operational matters.

It was held in *Kilgobbin Mink and Stud Farms Ltd v National Credit Company Ltd*[348] that a chairman had both ostensible and *implied actual authority* to request the company's landlord to pay £8,500 into the account of another company in return for surrendering the company's lease in circumstances in which it seemed that the articles of that company had no potential for conferring such wide authority on the chairman. The decision has been criticised[349] on the ground, *inter alia*, that there was no corporate representation that the chairman had the authority to do what he did. Apart from saying that the decision was one decided on its own facts, it may have been that since a

---

[344] *Hely-Hutchinson v Brayhead Ltd* [1968] 1 QB 549.

[345] *Hely-Hutchinson v Brayhead Ltd* [1968] 1 QB 549 at 584, *per* Lord Denning MR.

[346] See *Halsbury's Laws of England*, (4th edn, 1974) Vol 1 at p 441.

[347] A chairman had 'full and complete plenipotentiary powers' in *Nash v Lancegaye Safety Glass (Ireland) Ltd* (1958) 92 ILTR 11.

[348] *Kilgobbin Mink and Stud Farms Ltd v National Credit Company Ltd* [1980] IR 175.

[349] See Keane, *Company Law* (2nd edn, 1991) at para 12.14.

company resolution was required to surrender the lease[350] the authority of the board was in question. Hence, while an agent cannot as a rule 'hold himself out' it may be possible to say that the chairman, who held 49,999 of the 50,000 shares in the company, could be said to have acted *qua* member in representing himself as a chairman to the outsider. The finding may, of course, simply have been wrong. The reality is that, in general, the chairman will have very little potential actual authority under the Table A model articles of association[351].

(d) Directors

[7.116] As to the ostensible authority of other officers, a director has little or no potential actual authority in the model articles, other than the authority to attest the company seal in model reg 115. Whether or not any given director has more authority will depend on that company's articles.

(e) The company secretary

[7.117] Similarly, the secretary has little actual authority in the model articles (and so, little ostensible authority), but again, this will depend on the circumstances of any given case[352]. Any actual authority enjoyed by a company secretary will have been given to him by the company. It may be noted, however, that being a company's chief administrative officer, a secretary will have ostensible authority to enter into certain contracts on behalf of the company, eg, employing staff, ordering office machinery and stationery, etc[353].

(f) The sole member of a single-member private company

[7.118] The sole member of a single-member private company[354] would appear to have no ostensible authority in his capacity as member. In such companies there may well be a tendency for the sole member to think that he has full plenipotentiary powers for the company, but this will remain wishful thinking unless the company's articles of association vest such powers in him. Even at that, where reg 80 is adopted and delegates the management of the company to its directors, a sole member's ostensible authority may derive from his status as a *shadow director*, and not as a member[355].

Constructive notice of public documents

[7.119] The foregoing analysis of ostensible authority has been predicated on the basis that the outsider is aware of the actual authority conferred upon the company's officers and organs by its articles of association. By virtue of the doctrine of constructive notice, whether or not an outsider is in fact aware of what the articles say, in law he will be

350 *Kilgobbin Mink and Stud Farms Ltd v National Credit Company Ltd* [1980] IR 175 at 176.

351 Note however that s 145(2) of the CA 1963 provides that where a chairman signs the minutes of a board meeting, such is a standing representation that the meeting was held, and of what happened.

352 See *Panorama Developments (Guilford) v Fidelis Furnishing Fabric Ltd* [1971] 2 QB 711.

353 See Palmer's *Company Law* (Sweet & Maxwell) at p 8226, para 8.1107.

354 As permitted by the EC(SMPLC)R 1994. See generally, Ch 1, *The Private Company in Context*, at para **[1.143]**.

355 See Ch 13, *Corporate Governance: Management by the Directors*, at para **[13.127]** *et seq*.

deemed to be aware of the provisions in a company's articles of association[356]. The rationale is that, since the documents are public, the public is on notice of their existence, and the public is further deemed to be aware of their contents[357]. Thus, for example, a person dealing with a company is deemed to be aware:

– that a given company does not have a reg 112 type regulation, so that a person purporting to be the managing director has no ostensible authority, since in that company, there can be no managing director!
– that a particular company has no reg 80 type regulation, so that the board has no potential actual authority to manage the business of the company,
– that a particular company has an unmodified reg 79 type regulation, and that the members must pass a resolution if the directors are to borrow in excess of the issued share capital.

In its unmodified form, the doctrine of constructive notice of a company's articles has the potential to lead to draconian consequences.

[7.120] The *obiter dictum* finding by Costello J in *Re Shannonside Holdings Ltd*[358], that an outsider would not be bound by the provisions of a company's articles of association unless he has *express notice* of their provisions, is thought not to be a sufficient authority to displace the albeit unruly but firmly established doctrine of constructive notice. Although it would be difficult to argue against the common sense of such a stance, it is thought that the learned judge was mistaken in his application of the legal principles applicable to *ultra vires* acts to the law applicable to the authority of corporate agents. In so finding Costello J said:

> 'Once the company in general meeting had decided to issue this debenture, even if it was for a sum in excess of the issued share capital, there was nothing *ultra vires* in the company so deciding to do this and so there was nothing *ultra vires* in the issuing of the debenture. Even if this was not so, I accept the submissions made on behalf of the [debenture-holder]. I am not satisfied on the evidence that [the debenture-holder] had any express notice of [the article which restricted the directors' borrowing powers]. It seems to me that I would have to have some evidence on which to conclude that [the debenture-holder had] some express notice of that article before I could adopt the submissions made on behalf of [the creditor seeking to set the debenture aside]. In the absence of express notice, the debenture granted to [the debenture-holder] could not be invalidated even if the directors had exceeded their powers, which they had not, in my opinion[359].'

---

356 See *MJ Cummins Ltd; Barton v Bank of Ireland* [1939] IR 60 at 64 (see para **[7.065]**, *ante*, where Johnston J is quoted) and also: *Mahony v East Holyford Mining Co* (1875) 7 HL 869 at 893; *Ernest v Nicholls* (1857) 6 HL Cas 401 at 419; and *Re Jon Beauforte (London) Ltd* [1953] 1 All ER 634. A company's memorandum and articles of association are public documents in the sense that any member of the public can visit the CRO, and see, *inter alia*, a copy of these documents, a copy of the company's certificate of incorporation, all accounts filed and special resolutions passed.

357 For a justifiably critical analysis, see Ussher, *Company Law in Ireland* (1986, Sweet & Maxwell) at pp 148–151.

358 *Re Shannonside Holdings Ltd* (20 May 1993, unreported) HC.

359 *Re Shannonside Holdings Ltd* (20 May 1993, unreported) HC at pp 6, 7 of the transcript.

It is respectfully submitted that the fact that the creation of the debenture was not *ultra vires* the company's capacity had no bearing on the question of the directors' *authority* to issue a debenture in excess of the company's issued share capital. It is further suggested that the subsequent references to 'express notice' of the company's articles must be viewed in the context of transactions which might be *ultra vires* but capable of being saved by reliance on s 8 of the CA 1963[360].

The indoor management rule[361]

[7.121] Thankfully, the doctrine of constructive notice has been modified at common law by the rule in *Royal British Bank v Turquand*[362]. This relieves outsiders from any duty to satisfy themselves that any *internal requirement* necessary to perfect an agent's actual authority has been complied with. In *Turquand's* case, a company issued a bond to borrow money under seal. Its rules authorised this to be done where an ordinary resolution was passed. However, no such resolution was passed. Subsequently, the company argued that the bearer of the bond could not enforce it because it had constructive notice of the requirement in the company's articles that a resolution must be passed in support of the issuing of such a bond. This argument was rejected and it was held that the company was bound by the bond because, on reading the company's rules, an outsider:

> '... would find, not a prohibition from borrowing but a permission to do so on certain conditions. Finding that the authority might be made complete by a resolution, he would have a right to infer the fact of a resolution authorising that which on the face of the document appeared to be legitimately done[363].'

In *Re Motor Racing Circuits Ltd*[364], Blayney J said in the Supreme Court:

> '... *Turquand's* case says that where a matter appears to be regular then the party dealing with the company is not affected if in fact by reason of some error in the internal management of the company there is an irregularity[365].'

In that case the validity of a debenture given by a company was challenged on the basis that although the company's seal had been affixed to the debenture, one or other of the counter-signatories was not in fact a director or secretary. The Supreme Court upheld the validity of the debenture on the basis that the bank (in whose favour the debenture had been created) was 'entitled to assume that what is called the internal management of the company had been correctly complied with'[366].

In *ACC Bank plc v McCann & Griffin*[367], Hogan J said:

---

[360] On the doctrine of ultra vires and the effects of s 8 of the CA 1963, see para **[7.081]** *ante*.

[361] See generally, McCormack, 'The Indoor Management Rule in Ireland' (1985) Gazette ILSI 17 and Prentice, 'The Rule in *Turquand's* case' (1991) MLR 14.

[362] *Royal British Bank v Turquand* (1856) 6 E & B 327, [1843–60] All ER Rep 435.

[363] *Royal British Bank v Turquand* (1856) 6 E & B 327, [1843–60] All ER Rep 435 at 437, 438.

[364] *Re Motor Racing Circuits Ltd* (31 January 1997, unreported) SC, Blayney J, *nem diss*.

[365] *Re Motor Racing Circuits Ltd* (31 January 1997, unreported) SC, Blayney J, *nem diss* at p 7 of the judgment.

[366] *Re Motor Racing Circuits Ltd* (31 January 1997, unreported) SC, Blayney J, *nem diss* at p 7 of the judgment.

[367] *ACC Bank plc v McCann & Griffin* [2012] IEHC 236; the decision in *Ruben*.

> 'The rule in *Turquand* reflects the principle that, generally speaking, a third party is entitled to rely as against the company on the validity of acts done or resolutions passed or documents executed by or on behalf of the company without the necessity of inquiring whether the company complied with its own memorandum and articles of association or other associated procedural rules, such as the presence of a quorum or the appointment of officers[368].'

In that case Hogan J said that the rule in *Turquand* was so embedded in the fabric of the common law that it became the 'law' that was carried over by Article 50.1 of the Constitution. The facts in this case were that a director of a company, who had guaranteed certain loan facilities from ACC Bank, resisted a demand under the guarantee on the ground, *inter alia*, that an amendment to the loan facility (increasing the interest rate) had not been approved by him as a director. Hogan J accepted that minutes of a meeting purporting to show him in attendance were false and his signature on the amendment letter had been forged. Despite this, ACC Bank sought to rely on the rule in *Turquand*: the minutes of a meeting purported to show approval and the signatures of the other directors were properly affixed. Hogan J held that the bank could rely on the rule in *Turquand* and that the fact the document contained a forgery did not oust the application of the rule[369]. Applying the test suggested by Keane[370], Hogan J said:

> 'In the present case, the company plainly had the capacity to enter into a loan arrangement of this kind (thus satisfying the first limb of *Turquand*) and unless ACC can be shown to have had actual knowledge of that forgery, Killorglin would be bound by the resolution and the company minutes which were tendered to the bank on its behalf. Nor was the transaction *patently* irregular and there were no circumstances to excite suspicion.'

However, the learned judge went on to find that the bank could not invoke *Turquand* against the director-guarantor, only against the company, saying:

> '32. To my mind, in these circumstances, the lender – and not the surety – should bear this loss. There are several reasons for this conclusion. First, the whole tenor and language of the rule in *Turquand* is that it protects the third party in its dealing against the *company* and persons holding themselves out as agents of the company. In the present case we know that the February, 2008 resolution was handed to Ms Catriona O'Driscoll (who a senior banking manager within a specialised business unit of ACC based in Cork) by Brian Fitzgerald, another director of the company in early March, 2008.
>
> 33. That in itself is sufficient to bind Killorglin as against ACC for the purposes of the rule in *Turquand* and the persons who acted as agents of the company for that purpose would be estopped vis-à-vis the bank from asserting the invalidity of the resolution. But the rule in *Turquand* only operates in favour of the third party as *against the company*. The invalid resolution would, of course, bind the directors qua directors so far as the general law of agency and estoppel is concerned. While Mr McCann might – perhaps – be bound as against a third party in his capacity as a director of Killorglin in the circumstances just described, he is not sued in that capacity, but, to repeat, he is rather sued as guarantor. Neither the operation of the rule in *Turquand* or the doctrines of estoppel or agency have any application to him in that capacity.'

---

368 *ACC Bank plc v McCann & Griffin* [2012] IEHC 236 at para 21.

369 See para **[7.123]** *post*.

370 Keane, *Company Law* (4th edn, 2007) at para [12.41] quoted in para **[7.123]** *post*.

Accordingly, the amendment was found to be valid as against the company (which was required to pay the higher interest rate) but ineffective as against the director-guarantor (who was still liable as surety on the original loan facility, but at the original, lower, interest rate).

[7.122] The rule in *Turquand's* case has been applied in many other Irish cases. In *Allied Irish Banks Ltd v Ardmore Studios International (1972) Ltd*[371], a lending bank had notice, through the company's articles of association, that the company had three directors and that two directors were required for a quorum. The bank was given a copy of a resolution signed by a director and the secretary *cum* managing director. This certified that a meeting had been held at which a resolution had been passed which allowed, *inter alia*, the company to borrow from the bank. The company then drew a cheque and the bank honoured it. However, there was an irregularity in the meeting which had been held to pass the resolution. Although two directors had attended the meeting, in fact a third director had not been given notice of the meeting. Finlay J said that this along with other invalid procedures were, merely, 'classic examples of an irregularity in the internal management of the company'[372]. Accordingly the bank was permitted to rely on the rule in *Turquand's* case and the company was held to be bound to repay the bank[373]. Similarly in *Ulster Investment Bank Ltd v Euro Estates and Drumkill Ltd*[374] a mortgage was invalidly sealed by reason of the fact that there had been no valid directors' meeting to approve and authorise the sealing of the mortgage deed because the meeting had been invalid by reason of being inquorate. Nevertheless Carroll J held that the bank was:

> '... entitled to rely on the rule in the *Royal British Bank v Turquand* and to assume that the mortgage prepared by it and which on its face is duly executed in accordance with the articles, is the deed of the company[375].'

---

371 *Allied Irish Banks Ltd v Ardmore Studios International (1972) Ltd* (30 May 1973, unreported) HC, *per* Finlay J.

372 *Allied Irish Banks Ltd v Ardmore Studios International (1972) Ltd* (30 May 1973, unreported) HC, *per* Finlay J at p 8 of the transcript.

373 Finlay J accepted that the rule in *Turquand's* case was more far-reaching than the case in hand. Referring to *Duck v The Tower Galvanising Co Ltd* [1901] 2 KB 314 Finlay J said: 'The facts ... were that a debenture had been issued by the defendant company without authority, no directors of the company having been appointed and no resolution to issue debentures having been passed. The holder of the debenture, however, had, on the findings of the court, no notice of any irregularity in the issue of the debenture. It was there held that the debenture was good and prevailed over the rights of an execution creditor. It seems to me that the irregularities found to have existed in the case which I have just quoted were far more fundamental than those which I assumed to exist in this case.'

374 *Ulster Investment Bank Ltd v Euro Estates and Drumkill Ltd* [1982] ILRM 57.

375 *Ulster Investment Bank Ltd v Euro Estates and Drumkill Ltd* [1982] ILRM 57 at 67 Carroll J cited with approval the judgment of Lindley LJ in *County of Gloucester Bank v Rudry Merthyr Steam and House Coal Colliery Co* [1895] 1 Ch 629 where he said (at 636) that: 'Here the directors may make any quorum they like – it may be two, or it may be three. They did apparently appoint three. The mortgage in question is under the seal of the company, signed by two directors and countersigned by the secretary. Now what could anybody think of that? What is there to put them upon inquiry? (contd.../)

It is significant that Carroll J held that the bank had not disentitled itself to rely on the rule in *Turquand's* case by requiring in its facility letter the right to receive and approve copies of the various board resolutions authorising the borrowing[376].

The scope of the rule in *Turquand's* case

[7.123] While *Turquand's* case will certainly save certain transactions, there are limits to its scope and operation[377]. Many of the so-called 'exceptions' to the rule are but examples of its definitional limits. Where, for example, an agent acts beyond his ostensible authority, the rule in *Turquand's* case cannot redeem the situation for an outsider, since one may only assume that an agent has the authority associated with the officer whom he is held out as being. Similarly, there must be reliance by an outsider on the articles which show the potential authority of any given agent. Thus in *Rama Corporation Ltd v Proved Tin & General Investments Ltd*[378], a director of the defendant company, who had no actual authority to do so, contracted with the plaintiff company. The defendant company's articles provided that the directors could delegate power to one director but since there had been no reliance upon the articles by the plaintiffs, who had not read them, they could not enforce the contract against the defendant company. Constructive notice of the articles will not suffice: there must be actual reliance on the existence of the power to delegate. The other limitations on the scope of the rule in *Turquand's* case are:

(a) where the irregularity is of public record;

(b) the outsider must act in good faith.

It has now been put beyond doubt in Ireland that the forgery of a document is not an exception to the rule in *Turquand's* case[379]. The decision of the English House of Lords in *Ruben v Great Fingall Consolidated*[380] was authority for the proposition that where a

---

375 (\...contd) What is there to give them notice of anything irregular? If a person looked at the deed and looked at the articles he would not see anything irregular at all; he would be at liberty to infer, and any one in the ordinary course of business would infer, that if the directors had appointed a quorum they appointed the two who signed that deed. But supposing that three were wanted, he is not bound to go and look at the directors' minutes; he has no right to look at them except as a matter of bargain. The directors' minutes unless he knows what they are, do not affect him at all. There is nothing irregular on the face of the deed even taken with the articles – there is nothing illegal in it. As to a plea of *non est factum*, that could not be sustained for a moment and I have not the slightest doubt myself that that deed is as good as any deed that ever was sealed.'

376 See also the judgment of McWilliam J in *Re Irish Grain (Trading Board) Ltd* (26 November 1984, unreported) HC and the Supreme Court decision of Lynch J in *Hyland v Ireland et al* [1998] IESC 28, *nem diss* at p 7 of the judgment. In *Clark v Cutland* [2003] 4 All ER 733, the English Court of appeal, somewhat surprisingly, found that payments made by directors to trustees in respect of their remuneration were without legal effect because the articles provided that the company in general meeting must approve such payments. It does not seem that the rule in *Turquand* was considered.

377 See Prentice, (1991) LQR 14.

378 *Rama Corporation Ltd v Proved Tin & General Investments Ltd* [1952] 1 All ER 554.

379 *ACC Bank plc v McCann & Griffin* [2012] IEHC 236.

380 *Ruben v Great Fingall Consolidated* [1906] AC 439.

document had been forged by an officer of the company a person relying on that forgery could not invoke the indoor management rule against the company. In that case a company secretary forged share certificates which were presented to stock brokers who transferred £20,000 to the secretary. The stockbrokers were unsuccessful in suing the company for the return of the £20,000. Lord Loreburn LC said:

> 'The forged certificates are a pure nullity. It is quite true that persons dealing with limited liability companies are not bound to inquire into their indoor management, and will not be affected by irregularities of which they had not notice. But this doctrine, which is well established, applies only to irregularities that otherwise might affect a genuine transaction. It cannot apply to a forgery.'

Keane[381] has pointed out that the transaction in question did not fall within the rule in *Turquand* because a company secretary would not normally be empowered to enter into such a transaction and opines that the rule should apply in the case of a forged document where: '(a) the transaction was within the ostensible authority of the company's agent and was not *patently* irregular; (b) the outsider was unaware of the forgery and (c) there were no circumstances to excite suspicion.'

In *ACC Bank plc v McCann & Griffin*[382], the facts of which are given above, after describing the rule in *Turquand*, Hogan J went on to note that the director-guarantor had sought to invoke the forgery as an exception to *Turquand* on the authority of *Ruben*. Hogan J held that while the rule in *Turquand* was so embedded in the fabric of the common law to have been carried over by Article 50.1 of the Constitution, the decision in *Ruben* was not, and referring to Lord Loreburn's comments, quoted above, that:

> '... irrespective of the technical status of these comments (ie regardless of whether they are pure dicta or, alternatively, form part of the ratio), it could not possibly be said that the decision had achieved the unquestioned status and importance which has attached to *Turquand*, a decision which still remains to this day as a central feature of the entire edifice of company law[383].'

Hogan J went on to expressly approve the passage in Keane, quoted above, saying:

> 'Freed thus of any precedential constraints, I would not be disposed to follow the decision in *Ruben* insofar as it suggests fraud automatically destroys the operation of the rule in *Turquand*, since, in my view, it is inconsistent with the underlying rationale of that rule. Indeed, in his concurring judgment, Lord Davey suggested ([1906] AC 434 at 447) that the person dealing with the shares 'could always apply' to the shareholders to inquire whether the signatures appearing on the share certificates were genuine. This suggestion is, with respect, so unrealistic – certainly in modern conditions – that in its own way it graphically demonstrates just how far the House in *Ruben* had failed to grasp the underlying principle in *Turquand*. On that view, Jervis CJ might just as well have said in *Turquand* that any third party was put on inquiry to see that the resolution authorising the company's borrowings had been duly passed[384].'

---

[381] Keane, *Company Law* (4th edn, 2007) at para [12.41].

[382] *ACC Bank plc v McCann & Griffin* [2012] IEHC 236.

[383] *ACC Bank plc v McCann & Griffin* [2012] IEHC 236 at para 26.

[384] *ACC Bank plc v McCann & Griffin* [2012] IEHC 236 at para 27.

(a) Where the irregularity is of public record

[7.124] While *Turquand's* case allows one to assume that internal matters necessary to perfect authority have been done, it cannot apply to situations where the act needed to perfect authority becomes an act of public record. Consequently, where a company's articles require a resolution of the members to be passed before the directors can borrow above a certain amount, whether the rule in *Turquand's* case will apply depends upon the nature of the required resolution. Although one can assume that an ordinary resolution was passed, one cannot assume that a special resolution was passed. This is because a copy of any special resolution passed must, pursuant to s 143(4)(a) of the CA 1963 be registered in the CRO, and once registered become a document of public record. Once something becomes a matter of public record, the rule in *Turquand's* case ceases to apply.

In *Irvine v Union Bank of Australia*[385], the company's articles required the members to pass a special resolution authorising the directors to borrow in excess of a specified amount. The directors caused the company to borrow an amount in excess of the specified amount without the sanction of the members by special resolution. It was held that the rule in *Turquand's* case did not apply because the outsider had constructive notice that a special resolution had not been passed in accordance with the company's articles, since no copy had been filed in the CRO.

(b) The outsider must act in good faith

[7.125] Where a person is *actually aware* that a company's internal procedures have not been followed, he cannot rely upon the rule in *Turquand's* case because the rule only assists those who deal with the company in good faith. This limit on the scope of the rule will often, but not inevitably[386], mean that *insiders* cannot rely on the rule because they ought to know whether or not the articles of association have been complied with. Thus, in *Cox v Dublin City Distillery Co (No 2)*[387], a company's articles required a quorum of two directors and further precluded directors from voting on matters in which they were personally interested. Notwithstanding this, the directors issued debentures, both to themselves and to others, as security for advances. Barton J held that the debentures in favour of the 'outsiders' were valid by virtue of the rule in *Turquand's* case and that the company was estopped from denying their validity. However, the loans to the directors were held not to be binding on the company because the directors were aware of the company's articles and thus could not rely on *Turquand's* case:

> 'The resolution was a nullity, and the two other directors cannot be regarded as outsiders who took without notice of the board's meetings.'

---

[385] *Irvine v Union Bank of Australia* (1877) 2 Ap Cas 366 (Privy Council).

[386] Sometimes the duty of directors to ensure compliance with the company rules is elevated to a rule that *Turquand's* case can never assist 'insiders': *Morris v Kanssen* [1946] AC 459. However, *cf Hely-Hutchinson v Brayhead Ltd* [1968] 1 QB 549, where the plaintiff, although a director, was permitted to enforce a contract against his company by relying on the rule.

[387] *Cox v Dublin City Distillery Co (No 2)* [1915] IR 345. See also *Howard v Patent Ivory Manufacturing Co* [1883] 3 Ch D 156.

In this case, the resolutions were invalid because two of the three directors were personally interested and because the meeting was inquorate.

[7.126] Similarly, where the contract is of an exceptional nature, the outsider may be on notice that there may be an irregularity and so under a duty to satisfy himself that the company's articles were indeed complied with. Again, the central point is that the outsider should deal in good faith. Accordingly, in *AL Underwood Ltd v Bank of Liverpool & Martins*[388], the director of the plaintiff company endorsed cheques which were made payable to the plaintiff company into his *own* bank accounts with the defendant bank. The receiver to the plaintiff company successfully sued the defendant bank in conversion. The bank was prohibited from relying on *Turquand's* case because it failed to make ordinary enquiries as to the director's actions. As Bankes LJ said, '... the strangeness of his conduct ... is material'[389]. In the case of *Houghton & Co v Nothard Lowe & Wills Ltd*[390], a director entered into a contract with an outsider which entitled the outsider to sell goods owned by the company and to keep the proceeds to secure another debt of the company. Here the transaction was so unusual as to put the outsider on inquiry as to whether the contract was authorised. The outsider failed to make reasonable inquiries and consequently the company was held not to be bound by the contract purportedly made by the director on the company's behalf.

European intervention: the EC(C)R 1973

[7.127] The EC(C)R 1973[391] brought Article 9(2) of the First EU Council Directive on Company Law (68/151 of 9 March 1968) into Irish law. The regulations have the effect of modifying the doctrine of constructive notice in two respects.

(a) Regulation 10 of the EC(C)R 1973

[7.128] Regulation 10 has the effect of limiting those documents of which an outsider will be deemed to have constructive notice. In respect of those documents listed in reg 4[392], a company cannot rely on these documents as against a person dealing with the company *unless* either notice has been published in the Companies Registration Office Gazette[393] of their delivery to the registrar of companies, or the person dealing with the

388 *AL Underwood Ltd v Bank of Liverpool & Martins* [1924] All ER 230, [1924] 1 KB 775.

389 *AL Underwood Ltd v Bank of Liverpool & Martins* [1924] All ER 230 at 234E.

390 *Houghton & Co v Nothard Lowe & Wills Ltd* [1927] 1 KB 246, [1927] All ER 97.

391 SI 163/1973.

392 Regulation 4(1) provides that notice that the following documents have been delivered to the registrar of companies *shall* be published in the Companies Registration Office Gazette: (a) any certificates of incorporation; (b) memoranda and articles of association or charters; (c) documents amending/altering the documents at (b); (d) the amended text of the memoranda and articles; (e) returns relating to directors/change in directors; (f) returns regarding persons other than the board of directors, authorising such other persons to enter transactions binding the company and changes in respect of such persons; (g) annual returns; (h) notice of, or change in, the registered office; (i) any winding up order; (j) any order for the dissolution of the company; (k) returns by liquidator of final meeting on winding-up. Regulation 4(2) provides that notice of the foregoing shall be published within six weeks of the relevant delivery.

393 The requirement to publish in *Iris Oifigiúil* was replaced by a requirement to publish in the Companies Registration Office Gazette by reg 5 of the EC(C)R 2004 (SI 839/2004).

company had knowledge of them[394]. Although the list of documents is very comprehensive it at least has the effect that persons dealing with the company have certainty as to what documents they shall be deemed to have notice of. The effects of the regulation are, in theory, that simple filing in the CRO will not be sufficient in itself to put a person dealing with the company on notice: now notice of the delivery must also be published in the Companies Registration Office Gazette. In practice, once these documents are delivered to the CRO, the registrar of companies arranges for their publication in the Companies Registration Office Gazette.

(b) Regulation 6 of the EC(C)R 1973

[7.129] Regulation 6, when read in conjunction with reg 10, modifies the doctrine of constructive notice. It provides:

> 'In favour of a person dealing with a company in good faith, any transaction entered into by any organ of the company, being its board of directors or any person registered under these regulations as a person authorised to bind the company, shall be deemed to be within the capacity of the company and any limitation of the powers of that board or person, whether imposed by the memorandum or articles of association or otherwise, may not be relied upon as against any person so dealing with the company.'

Furthermore, there is a presumption[395] that the person dealing with the company acted in *good faith*. Regulation 6 raises several points for consideration.

[7.130] In the first place, reg 6 does not affect the doctrine of ostensible authority because it only applies to transactions entered into by the board of directors and persons registered under the regulations. This prevents a person from relying upon the regulations where he transacts with a body which he *mistakenly thinks* is the board of directors or believes to be a person registered under the regulations. The regulations only apply where one transacts with any organ of the company '*being* its board of directors or any person registered ...'. In *Smith v Henniker-Major & Co*[396], it was held by Rimer J that s 35A of the English Companies Act 1985[397] did not apply to validate a resolution passed by an inquorate board of directors. In that case one director purported to resolve in favour of an assignment of a cause of action from the company to himself. By reason of the company's articles, the meeting was inquorate. Rimer J held that in such circumstances it could not be said that the board of directors had in fact acted at all.

It should be noted that the case law on ostensible authority remains intact. Rather, it is the doctrine of constructive notice which has been modified by the EC(C)R 1963 in that now qualifications in the articles on the *authority* of the board of directors or person

---

394 Regulation 10 provides also that as regards: 'transactions taking place before the sixteenth day after the date of publication, they shall not be relied upon against a person who proves that it was impossible for him to have knowledge of them.'

395 Regulation 6(2) of the EC(C)R 1973.

396 *Smith v Henniker-Major & Co* (unreported) English HC, transcript HC 0102108 noted by Howell, 'Section 35A of the Companies Act 1985 and an Inquorate Board: One Won't Do' (2002) 23 Co Law 96.

397 This provides: 'In favour of a person dealing with a company in good faith, the power of the board of directors to bind the company, or authorise others to do so, shall be deemed to be free of any limitation under the company's constitution.'

registered under the EC(C)R 1973 will not upset a transaction entered into by a person acting in good faith.

[7.131] In the second place, reg 6 applies only to persons dealing *in good faith*[398]. Clearly, insiders as well as outsiders can act in good faith. While there are no Irish authorities in point, the concept of dealing in good faith in this context has received consideration by the English courts. In *International Sales and Agencies Ltd & another v Marcus*[399], Lawson J said:

> '... the test of good faith in somebody entering into obligations with a company will be found either in proof of his actual knowledge that the transaction was *ultra vires* the company or where it can be shown that such a person could not in view of all the circumstances, have been unaware that he was party to a transaction *ultra vires*.'

A more pragmatic view of the law was taken by Browne Wilkinson VC in *TCB Ltd v Gray*[400]. In that case the company's articles required that all debentures securing a loan were to be under seal, with the usual attestation provisions[401]. While the secretary did sign, the other signatory was a solicitor acting under a power of attorney. *Inter alia*, it was argued that the debenture was invalid because a director ought to have attested the company seal. The plaintiff bank successfully relied upon the English provision similar to reg 6. Notwithstanding that the bank did not look at the company's articles, it was held that it had acted in good faith:

> 'The last words of the second part of the sub-section expressly provide that good faith is to be presumed; the second part further provides that the person dealing with the company is *not* bound to inquire as to limitations on the powers of directors. In my judgment it is impossible to establish lack of 'good faith' within the meaning of the section solely by alleging that inquiries ought to have been made which the second part of the sub-section says need not be made[402].'

While the existence of the requirement that a person must act in good faith means that there is no blanket protection, it is submitted, as has been suggested elsewhere, that[403] a subjective honesty is required: the fact that a *reasonable man* may have done otherwise than the person dealing with the company did is but an evidential factor in deciding whether or not good faith existed[404]. It is thought that good faith must also have been influential in the decision of *Smith v Henniker-Major & Co*[405] since there, not only was it possible to find out that a quorum for directors' meetings was two and that only one

---

398 For further consideration of good faith or bona fides and an analysis of case law, in the context of s 38(1)(b) of the CA 1990 see Ch 16, *Statutory Regulation of Directors' Transactions*, at para **[16.105]**.

399 *International Sales and Agencies Ltd & another v Marcus* [1982] 3 All ER 551.

400 *TCB Ltd v Gray* [1986] 1 All ER 587.

401 As *per* model reg 115.

402 *TCB Ltd v Gray* [1986] 1 All ER 587 at 596 e –f. Italics added.

403 See Ussher, *Company Law in Ireland* (1986, Sweet & Maxwell) at pp 135, 136.

404 *Cf Crowley v Flynn* (13 May 1983, unreported) HC *per* Barron J where it was suggested that in good faith implied that a person would take reasonable steps and was not absolved from all enquiry.

405 *Smith v Henniker-Major & Co* (unreported) English HC, transcript HC 0102108 noted by Howell, 'Section 35A of the Companies Act 1985 and an Inquorate Board: One Won't Do' (2002) 23 Co Law 96.

person had in fact attended the board meeting but also the person who sought to rely upon the protection was himself a director.

[7.132] In the third place, it is not clear that an Irish court in the interpretation of reg 6 would find that it may be invoked by 'insiders'. It is though that in the absence of statutory assistance along the lines of the UK legislation, it would be very tempting for an Irish court to follow *Cox v Dublin City Distillery Co (No 2)*[406], where it was held that 'insiders' could not rely on the *Rule in Turquand* where a provision in a company's articles was not followed[407]. The English High Court in *EIC Services Ltd and Another v Phipps & Others*[408] found that s 35A of the UK's Companies Act 1985 could be relied upon by 'insiders'. In that case bonus shares were issued to existing members in breach of the company's own articles of association. It may be significant, however, that the English legislation seems specifically to envisage reliance on their provision by 'insiders' as it is provided that: 'A person shall not be regarded as acting in bad faith by reason only of his knowing that an act is beyond the powers of the directors under the company's constitution[409].'

[7.133] In the fourth place, reg 6 refers to 'any transaction'. This means that its scope is wider than mere contract. However, it is not necessary that the transaction be validly authorised by the company; indeed, it is fundamental to the nature of the regulation's intention that it be a 'purported transaction'[410].

[7.134] Fifthly, it should be noted that in accordance with reg 3, the regulations only affect *limited liability* companies. Consequently, the regulations do not have application to all three types of private company and can only be invoked in transactions with limited liability companies.

[7.135] Finally, in *Coöperatieve Rabobank 'Vecht en Plassengebied' BA v Minderhoud (receiver in bankruptcy of Mediasafe BV)*[411], the European Court of Justice held that the rules governing the enforceability of acts as against third parties by a company's relevant organs where there is a conflict of interest fall outside the normative framework of article 9 of the First Council Directive on Company Law (68/151 of 9 March 1968), which was implemented in Ireland by SI 163/1973. Previously, the Advocate General had held that article 9 did not afford protection where there was a conflict of interest, saying that it:

> '... concerns only the enforceability of the limits, laid down by law, the statutes or resolutions of the company, on the powers conferred on the company representatives.

---

406 *Cox v Dublin City Distillery Co (No 2)* [1915] IR 345. See also *Howard v Patent Ivory Manufacturing Co* [1883] 3 Ch D 156.

407 See para **[7.125]** *ante*.

408 *EIC Services Ltd and Another v Phipps & Others* [2003] BCC 931.

409 Section 35A(2)(b) of the English Companies Act 1985.

410 See *TCB Ltd v Gray* [1986] 1 All ER 587 at 596g–h.

411 *Coöperatieve Rabobank Vecht en Plassengebied BA v Minderhoud (receiver in bankruptcy of Mediasafe BV)* [1998] 2 BCLC 507.

> … A conflict of interests entails a defect of intention on the part of the representative, thus preventing him from lawfully carrying out certain acts because the *contemplatio domini* is absent[412].'

In that case a Dutch company's articles provided that in the event of a conflict of interests between the company and its directors, those director(s) without a conflict would be empowered to bind the company; and moreover, where there was only one director or if all of the directors had a conflict of interest, the company should be represented in such transactions by a 'board of commissioners'. The company had only one director and he caused the company to enter into a transaction that involved a conflict with his own interests. On the company's insolvency, the receiver appointed sought to avoid the transaction and he succeeded in avoiding the transaction in the Dutch courts. On appeal to the Dutch Supreme Court, the question was referred to the European Court of Justice. The Advocate General held that article 9 had no application to a conflict of interests so that the person who would have been affected by the avoidance of the transaction could not use it as a shield. This was upheld by the European Court of Justice, which stated:

> '… the rules governing enforceability as against third parties of acts done by members of company organs in circumstances where there is a conflict of interest with the company fall outside the normative framework of the First Directive and are matters for the national legislature[413].'

Accordingly, it would seem that on its true interpretation article 9 of the First Directive cannot be relied upon by a third party to enforce a transaction or arrangement entered into by a company in circumstances where the board of directors had a conflict of interest. In such circumstances, the third party's defence would seem to be confined to the rule in *Turquand's* case[414]. In some respects this decision is similar to that of the Irish courts in their interpretation of 'lawfully and effectively done' as used in s 8 of the CA 1963[415]. The international judicial trend is to refuse protection in cases where there is an abuse of directors' powers.

---

412 *Coöperatieve Rabobank Vecht en Plassengebied BA v Minderhoud (receiver in bankruptcy of Mediasafe BV)* [1998] 2 BCLC 507 at 511a–d.

413 *Coöperatieve Rabobank Vecht en Plassengebied BA v Minderhoud (receiver in bankruptcy of Mediasafe BV)* [1998] 2 BCLC 507 at 516de.

414 See para **[7.080]** *ante*.

415 See para **[7.121]** *ante*.

Chapter 8

Shares and Membership

Introduction

[8.001] Although a company is legally a separate person from the members who constitute it[1], it has no practical[2] or physical existence without its members, for the company is really nothing more than a conglomeration of their mutual rights, interests and obligations.

In a private company limited by shares, a shareholder (ie, a person who holds a share in the company) is a member[3] of the company whose liability is limited to the extent of his investment in the share capital of the company. Every private company is required to have a share capital and to limit the maximum number of members to 99[4]. Each member contributes to the share capital of the private company by taking shares in it; secure in the knowledge that his liability to contribute to the assets of the company in the event of a winding-up will be limited to the amount, if any, left unpaid on his shares[5]. In relation to the private company, then, it has been observed that the terms 'member' and 'shareholder' are synonymous[6]. This statement is not unimpeachable – for a subscriber to the memorandum of association will become a member upon incorporation of the company before becoming a shareholder; and a person who acquires a share or shares upon transfer or transmission does not become a member until his name is entered in the register of members[7].

[8.002] Most of the rights, interests, and obligations associated with shares stem from the fact that a shareholder, properly registered as such, is a member[8]. Accordingly, this chapter is divided into two sections: [A] Membership; and [B] Shares.

§ *This chapter has been contributed by G Brian Hutchinson.*

1 See Ch 4, *Incorporation and its Consequences*, at para **[4.023]** *et seq*.

2 The company will, however, continue to exist legally even though it may have no members, for a company only ceases to exist as a separate legal person upon the occurrence of one of the circumstances detailed in Ch 4, at para **[4.002]**.

3 Provided, on becoming a shareholder, his name has been entered on the register of members; see para **[8.006]** *et seq*, *post*.

4 Section 33(1) of the CA 1963; See generally Ch 1, *The Private Company in Context*, at para **[1.133]**.

5 Section 207 of the CA 1963; see, however, Ch 5, *Disregarding Separate Legal Personality* for exceptions to this statement.

6 Schmitthoff (ed), *Palmer's Company Law* (24th edn, Stevens & Sons, 1987) at p 791.

7 See para **[8.006]** *et seq*.

[A] MEMBERSHIP

[8.003] The rights, interests and obligations of a shareholder are to a large extent dependent upon the shareholder's status as a member of the private company. Membership will be examined here under the following headings:

1. What constitutes membership?
2. Persons who may become members.
3. The register of members.
4. Cesser of membership.

What constitutes membership?

(a) Definition of member

[8.004] Section 31 of the CA 1963 is unequivocal as to what constitutes a member of a private company. A member of a private company is someone who either:

(i) is an original subscriber of the memorandum of association[9]; or

(ii) has agreed to become a member and whose name has been entered on the register of members[10].

Only persons who fall into one of these categories acquire full status as members[11]. In this respect s 31 of the CA 1963 provides for a very specific and restricted meaning of the term 'member' which excludes beneficial owners and persons whose shares are held by nominees[12]. Each category will now be examined in further detail.

(i) Subscribers of the memorandum

[8.005] Section 31(1) of the CA 1963 provides:

> 'The subscribers of the memorandum of a company shall be deemed to have agreed to become members of the company, and, on its registration, shall be entered as members on its register of members.'

The effect of this subsection is that the subscriber becomes a member *automatically* upon registration of the company. This will be so even if his name is not subsequently entered on the register of members[13]. No allotment[14] of shares to the subscriber is

---

8 For an examination of the rights of a 'bare' shareholder whose name has not been entered on the register of members see para **[8.032]** *post* and generally Ch 9, *Share Transfer*.

9 Section 31(1) of the CA 1963.

10 Section 31(2) of the CA 1963.

11 See Schmitthoff (ed), *Palmer's Company Law* (24th edn, Stevens & Sons, 1987) at p 792; also *Nicol's case* (1885) 29 Ch D 421.

12 In *Re Irish Life and Permanent Group Holdings plc* [2012] IEHC 89, Feeney J held that for the purposes of s 11(1) of the Credit Institutions (Stabilisation) Act 2012, the word 'member' as used in that provision (even in the context of a company to which the Companies Acts applied) had a sufficiently broad meaning as to embrace not only registered members but also persons who held shares through nominees and that the meaning of 'members' for the purposes of s 11(1) of that enactment should not be confined to that in s 31 of the CA 1963.

13 *Nicol's case* (1885) 29 Ch D 421; *Alexander v Automatic Telephone Co* [1900] 2 Ch 56.

14 See para **[8.050]** *post*.

required to make him a member[15]; but in *Mackley's* case[16], it was held that it will no longer be possible to regard the subscriber as a member if *all* the authorised shares have been issued to others without any shares being allotted to the subscriber.

While failure to enter the subscriber's name on the register of members is not fatal to a subscriber's membership, it amounts, nevertheless, to the commission of a criminal offence for which the company and every officer may be punished by a fine[17].

(ii) Other persons

[8.006] Section 31(2) of the CA 1963 provides:

> 'Every other person who agrees to become a member of the company, and whose name is entered in its register of members, shall be a member of the company.'

Therefore, in order for a person who is not a subscriber to the memorandum to become a member, two conditions must be fulfilled:

(a) he must *agree* to become a member; and

(b) his name must be entered in the register of members.

Both conditions must be fulfilled; merely agreeing to become a member does not make that person a member[18]. Likewise, where a person's name is entered on the register of members *without* his consent, he is not bound by it, and he may apply to have the register rectified and his name removed from it[19]; though he may, in certain circumstances, be *estopped* from denying his membership of the company[20].

(b) Membership agreements

[8.007] There is no difference in law between an agreement to become a member and any other type of agreement. All that is required is a valid offer and valid acceptance[21]. An agreement to take shares will constitute an agreement to become a member. In general, no formal requirements need be fulfilled by an agreement to become a member, eg, it need not be in writing, but the articles may, in particular circumstances, require certain formalities to be met. Model reg 31 of Table A, for example, requires a person, who has become entitled to a share by way of *transmission*[22] and who elects to register as member himself, to 'deliver or send to the company a notice in writing signed by him stating that he so elects'.

(c) Estoppel

[8.008] In the absence of formal agreement to become a member, a person may still be regarded as a member through the operation of estoppel if his name is entered on the

---

15 *Evan's case, Re London, Hamburg and Continental Exchange Bank* (1867) 2 Ch App 427.

16 *Mackley's case* (1875) 1 Ch D 247.

17 Section 116(9) of the CA 1963, as amended by s 240 of the CA 1990. On the register of members see para **[8.017]** *post*.

18 See *Re a Company* (No 003160 of 1986) [1986] BCLC 391 at 393; *Nicol's case* (1885) 29 Ch D 421.

19 See para **[8.022]** *post*.

20 See para **[8.008]**.

21 See generally Clark, *Contract Law in Ireland* (6th edn, Round Hall, 2008), Ch 1.

22 See Ch 9, *Share Transfer*, at para **[9.025]** *et seq*.

register of members. Estoppel can operate in two ways to make a member of someone who has not consented to the entry of his name on the register of members.

First, entry of names in the register entitles persons examining the register to rely on the truth of its contents; and they may subsequently rely on the results of their examination. As Lord Cranworth observed in *Oakes v Turquand*[23]:

> 'When the legislature enabled shareholders to limit their liability, not merely to the amount of their shares but to so much of that amount as should remain unpaid, it is obvious that no creditor could safely trust the company without having a means of ascertaining, first, who the shareholders might be, and, secondly, to what extent they might be liable ... The legislature took care to provide the register as a means of enabling persons dealing with the company to know to whom and to what they might trust.'

The person who knows that his name has been placed in the register of members without his consent will be treated as a member if he does not act quickly to have his name removed because the entry of his name on the register has the effect 'of inducing other persons to alter their position'[24], eg, they may extend credit to the company or they may subscribe for shares in it. Delay in seeking rectification of the register will estop the person so registered from denying his membership[25].

Second, where a person whose name has been entered on the register of members without his consent does some act which is consistent with membership he will be estopped from denying his membership and from having the register rectified. In *Linz v Electric Wire Co of Palestine*[26], Linz, an allottee of shares under a void allotment, sold the shares to third parties who were subsequently registered as members of the company. Linz then sought to recover from the company the money she had paid it for the shares, on the basis that she had not become a member because of the invalidity of the allotment. She was estopped from suing the company for the return of her consideration because, having sold the shares, she had acted in a manner consistent with membership.

Persons who may become members

(a) Natural members

[8.009] The law places few restrictions on natural persons becoming members. Foreigners may become members[27]. Likewise, a bankrupt may become a member, and his bankruptcy will not inhibit his membership rights[28]. Minors and persons of unsound mind may become members, but contracts by them for the purchase of shares will be subject to the ordinary rules of contractual capacity which pertain to persons not *sui juris*[29]. A minor enjoys all the benefits of membership, provided he appears on the register of members, until such time as the contract for the purchase of his shares is

---

23 *Oakes v Turquand* (1867) LR 2 HL 325 at 366.

24 *Per* Lord Cairns in *Lawrence's case, Re Cachar Co* (1867) LR 2 Ch 412 at 417.

25 *Sewell's case, Re New Zealand Banking Corporation* (1868) 3 Ch App 131; *Re Scottish Petroleum Co* (1883) 23 Ch D 413; *Re Railway Timetables Publishing Co* (1889) 42 Ch D 98.

26 *Linz v Electric Wire Co of Palestine* [1948] AC 371. See also *Crawley's case* (1869) LR 4 Ch 322.

27 *Princess of Reuss v Bos* (1871) LR 5 HL 176.

28 *Morgan v Gray* [1953] Ch 83; *Birch v Sullivan* [1957] 1 WLR 1247.

29 See generally, Clark, *Contract Law in Ireland* (6th edn, Round Hall, 2008).

repudiated by either himself or the company[30]. A company's constitutional documents may, however, exclude certain persons from becoming shareholders. Furthermore, as shall be seen[31], the articles of a private company usually give the directors a broad discretion to refuse to register any person as a member.

(b) Corporate members

[8.010] A company may become a member of another company provided its objects so permit[32]. If the company in which membership is sought is neither the company itself nor its holding company, no further restrictions apply. There are significant restrictions, however, on the extent to which a company can become a member in itself by acquiring its own shares[33]. Likewise, a company cannot be a member of its holding company unless certain requirements are met.

The following matters in relation to corporate members are considered here as follows:

- (i) Subsidiaries and holding companies;
- (ii) Section 32 of the CA 1963;
- (iii) Exceptions to the prohibition contained in s 32 of the CA 1963;
- (iv) Section 224 of the CA 1990;
- (v) Formalities required to be met for s 224 to apply;
- (vi) Treatment of shares held by subsidiary.

(i) Subsidiaries and holding companies[34]

[8.011] Section 224 of the CA 1990 permits a subsidiary to acquire and hold shares in its holding company once authorised to do so in advance, and provided certain capital safeguards are met. The section largely supersedes s 32 of the CA 1963, which lays down a blanket prohibition, subject to specified exceptions, on a subsidiary becoming a member in its holding company. Section 32 remains in force, however.

Where membership of a subsidiary in its holding company is in issue, a two pronged examination will thus be required. First, it must be determined whether the membership falls within one of the exceptions to s 32 of the CA 1963. If it does, then the matter will end there. But if it does not, it must, secondly, be determined whether the membership is permitted in accordance with s 224 of the CA 1990. Each of these statutory provisions may now be considered in turn.

(ii) Section 32 of the CA 1963[35]

[8.012] Section 32(1) of the CA 1963 provides:

> 'Subject to the provisions of this section, a body corporate cannot be a member of a company which is its holding company, and any allotment of shares in a company to its subsidiary shall be void.'

---

30 *Capper's case* (1868) LR 3 458; *Pugh and Sharman's case* (1872) LR 13 566.

31 See Ch 9, *Share Transfer*, at para **[9.042]** *et seq*.

32 *Re Barned's Banking Co* (1867) LR 3 Ch 105.

33 See Ch 10, *The Maintenance of Capital*, at para **[10.024]** *et seq*.

34 On subsidiary and holding companies see further Ch 12, *Groups of Companies*.

35 See, further, Ch 10, *The Maintenance of Capital*, at para **[10.036]** *et seq*.

A nominee of the subsidiary is likewise prohibited from becoming a member of the subsidiary's holding company[36]. If the holding company is not a company limited by shares (eg, a guarantee company or an unlimited company without a share capital) then the reference to shares is to be construed as a reference to the interests of members, whatever the form of that interest[37]. The rationale behind the prohibition contained in s 32(1) is the prevention of companies from trafficking in their own shares by indirect means[38].

(iii) Exceptions to the prohibition contained in s 32

[8.013] There are four exceptions to the prohibition on a subsidiary becoming a member of its holding company. Three of these may be relied upon by most companies; the fourth, however, is applicable only to companies which were subsidiaries on or before 5 May 1959. The exceptions are as follows.

First, the prohibition does not extend to situations where a subsidiary is a personal representative under a will or an intestacy[39].

Second, the prohibition does not extend to situations where the subsidiary is a trustee, unless the holding company, or a subsidiary of the holding company, is beneficially interested in the trust, except by way of security issued in the ordinary course of a business which includes the lending of money[40].

Third, a company which is a member of another company and subsequently becomes a subsidiary of that other company is not prohibited from continuing to be a member of that company[41]. It may even acquire further shares in the holding company – but only if those shares are issued to it for no consideration in the course of a capitalisation by the holding company[42]. The holding company may, when making an offer of shares to its members, sell any shares which the subsidiary could have taken up by virtue of its membership of the holding company, and pay the subsidiary the proceeds of the sale instead[43]. Furthermore, the subsidiary is prohibited from voting at meetings of the holding company or at class meetings of the holding company's shareholders[44]. The subsidiary is, thus, deprived of one of the advantages ordinarily associated with being a member[45].

Fourth, a subsidiary which was a member of a holding company on 5 May 1959 is not prevented from continuing as member of its holding company[46], but the same restrictions apply to that company as apply to the subsidiary considered in the previous exception.

---

36 Section 32(7) of the CA 1963.

37 Section 32(9) of the CA 1963.

38 See Schmitthoff (ed), *Palmer's Company Law* (24th edn, Stevens & Sons, 1987) at para 50-09; Ussher, *Company Law in the Republic of Ireland* (1986) at p 104.

39 Section 32(2) of the CA 1963.

40 Section 32(2) of the CA 1963.

41 Section 32(5) of the CA 1963.

42 Section 32(5) of the CA 1963.

43 Section 32(8) of the CA 1963.

44 Section 32(6) of the CA 1963.

45 On voting rights see para **[8.081]** *et seq, post.*

46 Section 32(3) of the CA 1963.

(iv) Section 224 of the CA 1990

[8.014] Section 224 of the CA 1990 provides:

> 'Notwithstanding ss *32 and 60* of the CA 1963 a company may, subject to the provisions of this section, acquire and hold shares in a company which is its holding company.'

The first point of note in relation to this provision is that it only permits a subsidiary to acquire *shares* in its holding company. The holding company must, therefore, be a company limited by shares before the provision may be relied upon; if it is not, then the subsidiary will be prohibited from becoming a member by s 32 of the CA 1963 unless the membership falls within the permitted exceptions to that section.

(v) Formalities required to be met for s 224 to apply

[8.015] Two formalities must be satisfied before a subsidiary may rely on the provisions of s 224(1) and hold shares in its holding company. Failure to comply with these requirements may render the directors of the subsidiary personally liable to repay the total amount paid by the subsidiary for the shares[47].

First, a contract for the acquisition of the shares must be authorised in advance both by the subsidiary and its holding company[48]. If the shares are to be purchased on a recognised stock exchange and subject to a marketing agreement, then an *ordinary resolution*[49] of the general meetings of both the holding and the subsidiary company authorising the acquisition will suffice[50]. If, however, the shares are to be acquired in some other manner, such as in a private sale, or if the subsidiary proposes to enter into a contract whereby it will be obliged to take shares in its holding company on the occurrence of some contingency, *special resolutions*[51] will be required from both companies authorising the contracts[52]. In all cases, the authority may be revoked, varied or released only by the passing of a resolution of the kind which was necessary to authorise the acquisition in the first place[53].

Second, the consideration paid by the subsidiary for the shares in its holding company may only come out of those profits of the subsidiary which are available for distribution[54]. When calculating the profits which are available for distribution for the purposes of acquiring shares in its holding company, the subsidiary may not take into

---

47 Section 225 of the CA 1990.

48 Section 224(3) of the CA 1990. Notably, such authority will only be required where the shares are to be acquired under a contract; if there is no contract – say, for example, the shares are a gift from the holding company – no advance authority appears to be required. In most cases, however, some kind of contract will be involved.

49 On ordinary resolutions generally see Ch 14, *Corporate Governance: Meetings*, at para **[14.082]**.

50 See also ss 212 and 215 of the CA 1990.

51 On special resolutions see Ch 14, *Corporate Governance: Meetings*, at para **[14.084]** *et seq*.

52 Sections 224(3), 212, 213, and 214 of the CA 1990. The special resolution will not be effective unless a copy of the proposed contract or, if it is not in writing, a memorandum of its terms, is available for inspection at the registered offices of the companies for at least 21 days before each meeting respectively, and at the meetings themselves: s 213(5).

53 Sections 213(2), 215(1), and 214(2) of the CA 1990, respectively.

54 Section 224(2) of the CA 1990. On the availability of profits for distribution see Ch 10; *The Maintenance of Capital*, at para **[10.089]** *et seq*.

account any profits attributable to any shares in the subsidiary which are held by the holding company, insofar as they are profits relating to the period before the holding company became a member of the subsidiary[55].

(vi) Treatment of shares held by subsidiary

[8.016] Once a subsidiary acquires shares in its holding company, two restrictions apply to how it may deal with them. First, the subsidiary's profits available for distribution must be treated as being reduced by the total cost of the shares acquired[56]. Second, the subsidiary may not exercise any voting rights in respect of the shares acquired by it in the holding company, and any purported exercise of those rights will be void[57]. This prevents the directors of the holding company from controlling the voting rights of shares held by the subsidiary in order, say, to perpetually vote themselves into office.

Regarding a holding company in which a subsidiary has acquired shares, the holding company must, for the purposes of preparing its consolidated accounts[58], treat the shares held by the subsidiary in the same manner as treasury shares[59].

The register of members

(a) Form and location of the register[60]

[8.017] According to s 116 of the CA 1963[61], every company is required to keep a register of members (the 'register'). The register may be kept either 'by making entries in bound books or by recording the matters in question in any other manner'[62] or 'by recording the matters in question otherwise than in a legible form so long as the recording is capable of being reproduced in a legible form'[63] (eg, electronically)[64]. Where the register is not kept in a bound book, 'adequate precautions' must be taken for guarding against falsification and facilitating its discovery[65]. Failure to take such precautions renders the company and every officer in default liable to a class C fine[66].

55 Section 224(4) of the CA 1990.

56 Section 224(2)(b)(i) of the CA 1990.

57 Section 224(2)(b)(iii) of the CA 1990.

58 See Ch 17, *Financial Statements, Audit & Annual Return*, at para **[17.144]** *et seq*.

59 Section 224(2)(b)(ii) of the CA 1990. On treasury shares generally, see para **[8.113]** *post*.

60 See, generally, McGowan-Smyth & Daly, *Irish Company Secretary's Handbook* (2011, Bloomsbury Professional) at p 679.

61 As amended by s 20 of the C(A)A 1982.

62 Section 378(1) of the CA 1963.

63 Section 4(1) of the C(A)A 1977.

64 Section 18 of the Electronic Commerce Act 2000 ('ECA 2000') overlaps here, allowing registers to be kept in electronic form. The CLRG has noted the potential for confusion between the Companies Acts and the ECA 2000, and recommended that the latter should prevail in all respects in so far as it concerns corporate registers. See the CLRG, *First Report*, at para 4.48 *et seq*.

65 Section 378(2) of the CA 1963. What is meant by 'adequate' in these circumstances is not elaborated upon.

66 Section 378(2) of the CA 1963, as amended and to be read in accordance with s 6(3) of the Fines Act 2010.

The register is required to be kept at the company's registered office except when work is being done on it at another office of the company or an office of some person (eg, the company's solicitor or accountant) who undertakes work on the register on behalf of the company[67]. The register must not be kept in any place outside the State[68], and the company is required to notify the registrar of companies of the place where the register is kept and of any change in that place[69]. Failure to comply with any of these requirements will render the company and every officer in default, and, if the books are being looked after by an agent of the company, the agent, liable to a class C fine[70]. In practice, many private companies have been guilty of less than strict compliance with these requirements.

(b) Inspection of the register

[8.018] The register is open to inspection by *anyone*, whether they are members of the company or not. The register must be open for public inspection for at least two hours each day to any member free of charge and to any other person upon payment of a reasonable fee not to exceed six cent[71]. The register can be closed for inspection when the company has advertised in a newspaper circulating in the district of the company's registered office that the register will be closed[72]. The register may not be closed for more than 30 days in each year[73].

Any member or other person may obtain a copy of the register from the company on payment of a sum not to exceed three cent per one hundred words or fraction thereof[74]. Such copy must be sent to the member or other person requesting it within 10 days[75].

Failure to comply with inspection requirements will render the company, every officer in default, and, where the register is being looked after by an agent, the agent, liable to a class C fine[76]. A refusal by the company to allow inspection or copying must be distinct and definite before such liability will arise[77].

---

[67] Section 116(5) of the CA 1963, but solicitors, accountants and others are not entitled to claim a lien on the register of members since they are required by the Act to be kept open for inspection at the registered office or at such other place where the work of maintaining them is carried out: *Re Capital Fire Insurance Association* (1883) 24 Ch D 408; *DTC (CNC) Ltd v Gary Sargent* [1996] 2 All ER 369.

[68] Section 116(6) of the CA 1963.

[69] Section 116(7) of the CA 1963.

[70] Section 116(9) of the CA 1963, as amended and to be read in accordance with s 6(3) of the Fines Act 2010.

[71] Section 119(1) of the CA 1963. The section describes the maximum amount as being 'one shilling' which, following decimalisation, converted to 5 new pence, now 6.34 cent. The provisions of s 119 of the CA 1963 regarding the inspection of the register and index do not apply to investment companies: s 260(1) of the CA 1990.

[72] Section 121(1) of the CA 1963.

[73] Section 121(1) of the CA 1963.

[74] Section 121(2) of the CA 1963. The Act describes the maximum fee for this purpose as 'sixpence,' which upon decimalisation converted to two-and-a-half new pence. That, in turn, converts to 3.17 cent.

[75] Section 121(2) of the CA 1963.

[76] Section 119(3) of the CA 1963, as amended and to be read in accordance with s 6(3) of the Fines Act 2010.

[77] *R v Wiltshire and Berkshire Canal Navigation* (1835) 3 Ad & El 477.

In cases of refusal or default the court may by order compel an immediate inspection of the register or direct that the copies required shall be sent to the persons requiring them[78]. The court's power is discretionary, however, and even though as a general rule the court will make a mandatory order to give effect to a legal right, there may be something special in the circumstances of a case which would lead the court to refuse to compel inspection, though terms and conditions may be attached to the order for inspection which will protect the interests of both sides[79].

It has been held that the person seeking to inspect the register need not specify his reasons for so doing[80]. In recognition of the need to protect shareholders from being contacted for an improper purpose, the Companies Act 2006 (UK) has made access to companies' registers of members subject to a 'proper purpose' test[81]. There are no plans for similar legislation in Ireland as of yet.

Moreover, inspection of the register cannot be refused on the ground that the applicant is the solicitor for parties who are engaged in litigation against the company, even though the inspection is in the interests of the applicant's clients and not in the interests of the company or any individual member of the company[82].

The right to inspect, and to receive copies of, the register terminates upon a winding up[83].

(c) Particulars to be registered

[8.019] Section 116 of the CA 1963 provides that the register must contain the following particulars:

> '(a) the names and addresses of the members, and ... a statement of the shares held by each member, distinguishing each share by its number so long as the share has a number, and ... the amount paid or agreed to be considered as paid on the shares of each member;
>
> (b) the date at which each person was entered in the register as a member;
>
> (c) the date at which any person ceased to be a member.'

The register should also contain details of the class of share held by each member[84]. The particulars detailed in para (a) are required to be entered on the register within 28 days of the conclusion of the agreement to become a member, or, in the case of a subscriber to the memorandum, within 28 days after the registration of the company[85].

---

78 Section 119(4) of the CA 1963.

79 *Pelling v Families Need Fathers Ltd* [2001] EWCA Civ 1280.

80 *Holland v Dickson* (1888) 37 Ch D 669; *Davies v Gas Light and Coke Co* [1909] 1 Ch 248, aff'd [1909] 1 Ch 708.

81 Sections 116–119 of the Companies Act 2006 (UK).

82 *Re Kent Coalfields Syndicate* [1898] 1 QB 754.

83 *R v Wiltshire and Berkshire Canal Navigation* (1835) 3 Ad & El 477.

84 *Re Performing Rights Society Ltd* [1978] 2 All ER 712. Where shares are held electronically under CREST, the register must also distinguish the number of shares held by a member in uncertificated form – CA 1990 (US) Regs 1996; see Ch 29, *Public Limited Companies and SEs*, at para **[29.036]**.

85 Section 116(2) of the CA 1963.

(d) Legal significance of the particulars registered

[8.020] Section 124 of the CA 1963 provides that the register of members 'shall be *prima facie* evidence' of any of the matters authorised or directed by the Companies Acts to be inserted in it. The fact that it is *prima facie* evidence of the matters contained therein (and *not conclusive* evidence) means that a person relying on the contents of the register must remember that a person's name may have been improperly entered on the register because of some mistake, misrepresentation or accident, and that the name may subsequently be removed.

(e) Registration of changes in particulars

[8.021] The company should register any changes in the registered details, such as change of ownership, name, address, etc, of which it has notice, lest the register should be as untrue as if false particulars had been registered in the first place[86]. Such registration should be carried out by the company secretary or the person appointed to keep the register, but no changes may be made without the prior approval of the board of directors[87].

(f) Rectification of the register

(i) Rectification by the company

[8.022] The company has a statutory power to rectify any error or omission in the register by s 122(5) of the CA 1963. Such rectification may be made without an application to the court, but rectification will not be allowed to affect adversely any person unless he agrees to the rectification being made[88]. The rectification will be made by the company secretary or the person appointed to keep the register, but no rectification may be made without the prior approval of the board of directors[89]. Notice of the rectification must be sent to the registrar of companies within 21 days of rectification if the error or omission appeared in any document previously sent to her[90].

(ii) Rectification through the court

[8.023] Section 122 of the CA 1963 also gives the court the power to order rectification of the register where:

> '(a) the name of any person is, without sufficient cause, entered in the register of members or omitted therefrom in contravention of ... s 116; or
>
> (b) default is made in entering on the register within the period fixed by ... s 116 of the fact of any person having ceased to be a member.'

An application for rectification in such circumstances may be made to the court by any aggrieved person, member of the company, or, indeed, the company itself. The court's power to make an order under the section is discretionary[91], and the court has the power

---

86 See generally, Doyle, *The Company Secretary* (2nd edn, 2002) and McGowan-Smyth & Daly, *Irish Company Secretary's Handbook* (2011, Bloomsbury Professional).

87 *Wheatcroft's case* (1873) 29 LT 324; *Chida Mines Ltd v Anderson* (1905) 22 TLR 27.

88 Section 122(5) of the CA 1963.

89 See para **[8.021]** *ante*.

90 Section 122(5) of the CA 1963.

91 *Trevor v Whitworth* (1887) 12 App Cas 409, *per* Lord Macnaghten at 440.

to decide any question of the title of any party to the application and may decide any question necessary or expedient to be decided for the rectification of the register[92]. The court may award compensation for any loss suffered by the aggrieved person[93]. If costs are to be awarded against individual directors as opposed to the company, those directors should be named as respondents to the proceedings[94].

[8.024] The court's power to examine title in an application under s 122 makes the application attractive whenever a dispute arises concerning the title to shares[95]. The application to the court for rectification may be invoked to compel the company to register particulars which it has improperly neglected or refused to register. In this regard it provides an appropriate procedure to the transferee of shares whom the directors refuse to register as a member of the company[96]. The court's power is discretionary[97], however, and as shall be seen, it may prove very difficult to show that the directors acted 'without sufficient cause'[98] or in bad faith, as is required to be proved

---

92 Section 122(3) of the CA 1963.

93 Section 122(3) of the CA 1963.

94 *Morgan v Morgan Insurance Brokers Ltd* [1993] BCLC 676.

95 See, generally, Ch 9, *Share Transfer,* at para **[9.066]** *et seq*; *Banfi Ltd v Moran* [2006] IEHC 257; and *Re Hoicrest Ltd, Keane v Martin* [2000] 1 BCLC 194.

96 On the power of the directors to refuse the register a transfer of shares see Ch 9, *Share Transfer*, at para **[9.042]** *et seq*.

97 *Re Olde Court Holiday Hostel Ltd* [2006] IEHC 424.

98 MacCann & Courtney, *Companies Acts 1963–2009* (2010, Bloomsbury Professional), list the following circumstances as warranting rectification of the register: 1. Where the company removed the name of one person from the register and entered the name of another on foot of a forged share transfer: *Davis v Bank of England* [1824] 2 Bing 393; *Sloman v Bank of England* [1845] 14 Sim 475; *Re Bahia and San Francisco Railway* (1868) LR 3 QB 584; *Barton v London and Northwestern Railway* (1888) 38 ChD 144; *Welch v Bank of England* [1955] Ch 508; 2. Where the company has wrongfully forfeited shares: *Re Ystalyfera Gas Co* [1887] WN 30; 3. Where the applicant was induced to acquire the shares and to become a member as a result of an untrue statement in a prospectus or as a result of some other misrepresentation: *Stewart's Case* (1886) 1 Ch App 574; *Component's Tube Co v Naylor* [1900] 2 IR 1; 4. Where the directors' power to refuse to register a transfer or transmission of shares has lapsed: *Re Inverdeck Ltd* [1998] 2 BCLC 242; 5. Where shares have been allotted to members other than the applicant in breach of pre-emption provisions: *Re Thundercrest Ltd* [1995] 1 BCLC 117; 6. Where the directors have, in breach of the provisions of the articles, wrongfully refused to register a transfer or transmission of shares: *Banfi Ltd v Moran & ors* [2006] IEHC 257; *Re New Cedos Engineering Co Ltd* [1994] 1 BCLC 797; 7. Where a purported transfer of shares had been registered by the company notwithstanding the fact that the purported transfer was unauthorised by the true owner, was unsupported by any consideration and was not effected pursuant to properly executed share transfer forms: *International Credit and Investment Co (Overseas) Ltd v Adham* [1994] 1 BCLC 66; 8. Where due to an administrative oversight, a transfer of shares from one person to another was not recorded in the register of members: *Re New Millenium Experience Co Ltd* [2004] 1 BCLC 19; *Re Fagin's Bookshop plc* [1992] BCLC 118; 9. Where a company issued a share certificate to an individual in respect of a particular number of shares but then failed to record that holding in the register: *Alipour v UOC Corp* [2002] 2 BCLC 770; 10. Where a company had effected an unlawful bonus issue of shares; *Re Cleveland Trust plc* [1991] BCLC 424; 11. Where shares were transferred in breach of restrictive provisions contained in the articles of association: *Re Picadilly Radio plc* [1989] BCLC 683.

by the section, if the articles give the directors a general power to refuse to register a transfer[99]. The circumstances in which such an application might succeed are examined in the next chapter. Likewise, rectification may be sought to compel the company to register particulars where the company, acting on foot of a forged share transfer, has removed the name of the real owner and entered another's name[100], or where shares have been improperly forfeited[101]. Damages in such cases will include the amount of declared dividends which the applicant would otherwise have received together with interest[102].

An application under this section may also be used to compel the company to remove particulars from the register. Thus, an application may succeed where registration has been effected on foot of a misrepresentation[103], unless a winding up has commenced[104], and in such cases damages may be measured as the amount paid for the shares together with interest thereon[105].

Failure to apply for rectification within a reasonable time, or otherwise acting inconsistently with his grievance, may estop the aggrieved person from proceeding with his application for rectification[106].

An order for rectification may be made by the court notwithstanding the fact that the company has been wound up, unless it results in the rescission of an allotment and a consequent reduction in the overall number of contributories[107].

(g) Beneficial interests

[8.025] The *register of members* is only concerned with legal title to shares. Section 123 of the CA 1963 succinctly provides that:

> 'No notice of any trust, express, implied or constructive, shall be entered on the register or be receivable by the registrar.'

In *Rearden v Provincial Bank*[108], Porter MR explained that the intention of the section is:

> 'to spare the company the responsibility of attending any trusts or equities whatever attached to their shares, so that they might safely and securely deal with the person who is registered owner, and with him alone, recognising no other person and no different right; freeing them, in short, from all embarrassing inquiries into conflicting claims as to shares, transfers, calls, dividends, right to vote and the like; and enabling them to treat the registered shareholder as owner of the shares for all purposes, without regard to contract as between himself and third persons.'

This provision facilitated the *de facto* one-man company before the advent of the *de jure* single-member private limited company with the introduction of the EC(SMPLC)R

---

99 *Re Olde Court Holiday Hostel Ltd* [2006] IEHC 424.

100 *Re Bahia and San Francisco Railway* (1868) LR 3 QB 584.

101 *Re Ystalyfera Gas Co* [1887] WN 30. On forfeiture of shares, see para **[8.123]**.

102 *Sri Lanka Omnibus Co Ltd v Perera* [1952] AC 76.

103 *Stewart's case* (1886) 1 Ch App 74; *Components Tube Co v Naylor* [1900] 2 IR 1.

104 *Oakes v Turquand* (1867) LR 2 HL 325.

105 *Re Metropolitan Coal Consumers' Association, ex parte Wainwright* [1890] WN 3.

106 See para **[8.023]** *ante*.

107 Section 235(1) of the CA 1963. See *Re New Millenium Experience Co Ltd* [2004] 1 BCLC 19; *Oakes v Turquand* (1867) LR 2 HL 325; *Tennant v City of Glasgow Bank* (1880) 5 App Cas 317.

108 *Rearden v Provincial Bank* [1896] IR 532.

1994. A shareholder may appear in the register of members as owner of all but one share in the company, and his nominee, holding the remaining share on behalf of, or on trust for, the majority shareholder, may appear in the register as the other shareholder. The company, thus, had the requisite minimum two members formerly required for a private company, but it was under the effective control of only one. Only the person registered can be made liable by the company in respect of payment for the shares or to contribute in a winding up.

The prohibition on the entry of trusts in the register of members also has the effect of making it less attractive for banks and other lending institutions to take equitable mortgages or charges of the shares as security for advances. This is because the registered owner of the shares can pass a good title to the shares to a *bona fide* purchaser for value without notice – thus depriving the lender of his security[109].

[8.026] Section 123 of the CA 1963 must be read in conjunction with model reg 7 of Table A, which provides:

> 'Except as required by law, no person shall be recognised by the company as holding any share upon any trust, and the company shall not be bound by or be compelled in any way to recognise (even when having notice thereof) any equitable, contingent, future or partial interest in any share or any interest in any fractional part of a share (except only as by these regulations or by law otherwise provided) and any other rights in respect of any share except an absolute right to the entirety thereof in the registered holder: this shall not preclude the company from requiring the members or a transferee of shares to furnish the company with information as to beneficial ownership of any share when such information is reasonably required by the company.'

The effect of this article, in conjunction with s 123 of the CA 1963, is to permit the company to ignore all equitable interests in its shares. The regulation goes beyond the statutory provision in that it relates not merely to registration of the equitable right but also to recognition of the right.

[8.027] It may also be observed that the provision does not prevent a company, if it so desires, from recognising an equitable interest in a share[110], though it may not, of course, enter the interest so recognised on the register of members because of s 123 of the CA 1963.

[8.028] It should be stressed that the provisions of s 123 and model reg 7 *do not* prevent the creation of beneficial interests in the shares of a company. In *Société Générale de Paris v Walker*[111], James Walker, the registered owner of 100 shares in a tram company, created two equitable charges over the shares. The first charge arose by virtue of an equitable deposit of the share certificates with a Mr James Scott Walker as security for advances. The second and subsequent charge was in favour of the Société Générale de Paris and arose on foot of a blank transfer form duly executed in their favour as security for advances. The Société tried to register as members of the tram company but were unsuccessful because they could not show that they possessed the share certificates. A dispute then arose as to whether the Société or the executors of James Scott Walker (by

[109] *Société Generalé de Paris v Walker* (1885) 11 App Cas 20; *Ireland v Hart* [1902] 1 Ch 522.

[110] The article merely provides that the company is not 'bound,' nor can it be 'compelled,' to recognise the interests to which it refers.

[111] *Société Générale de Paris v Walker* (1885) 11 App Cas 20.

then deceased) had priority of equitable security interests. The Société argued that since a share is a *chose in action*[112], and since priority of interests in *choses in action* is given to the first person to notify the debtor or fund-holder (or, in this case, the company) of his interest, then they should take in priority. By attempting to have their name entered in the register of members, they had been first to notify the company of their interest. The courts, however, held that the normal rules governing priorities of interests in *choses in action* did not apply to interests in shares. In the course of his judgment in the Court of Appeal, which was later affirmed by the House of Lords, Lindley LJ stated:

> 'If a shareholder in a company governed by the Companies Act ... does not transfer his shares, but agrees to transfer them or to hold them on trust for another, either absolutely or by way of security, there can be no doubt as to the validity of the agreement, nor as to the effect of it as between the parties to it. As between them the agreement or trust can be enforced; but as regards the company the shareholder on the register remains shareholder still. He is the person to exercise the rights of a shareholder, for example, to vote as such, to receive dividends as such, and to transfer the shares. On the other hand, he, and he alone, is liable for calls, and to be put on the list if contributories of the company is wound up.'

Thus, although the company may safely ignore the equitable interests of others in the shares held by a registered member, the interests remain valid as between the trustee and the *cestui que trust*. In *Re Harvard Securities Ltd*[113], it was further held that the law governing the equitable interests so created in the shares will normally be the *lex situs* – the law of the place of incorporation.

[8.029] Despite the provisions of s 123 of the CA 1963 and model reg 7 of Table A, a company will *not* be allowed to ignore beneficial interests of which it has actual notice[114]. In *Rearden's* case[115], Mr Barry, a trustee holding shares in the bank to which Mrs Rearden was beneficially entitled, became personally indebted to the bank. The bank had been told, in the course of correspondence, that Mr Barry held the shares on trust for Mrs Rearden, but despite this notification it nevertheless sought to exercise a lien[116] over the shares in respect of Mr Barry's personal debt. The bank argued that the combined effect of s 30 of the Companies Act 1862 (the precursor to s 123 of the CA 1963) and Clause 8 of its articles of association (the precursor to model reg 7 of Table A) was to permit the bank to ignore *all* equitable interests – even those of which it had been notified – so that it could exercise a lien on the shares in respect of the personal debts of the registered owner. The courts, however, found otherwise. Porter MR explained:

> 'It is right and necessary that a company should not be mixed up with outside claims and disputes. The company is to have one person, or one set of persons, alone to deal with as shareholders; and it is to be unaffected by trusts, equities and the like, which they have no means of determining or knowing anything about. In such cases, apart from s 30 and special articles of association, they really could not protect themselves. But this immunity

---

112 See para **[8.038]** *post*.

113 *Re Harvard Securities Ltd* [1997] 2 BCLC 369.

114 Though again, of course, it may not enter them on the register: s 123 of the CA 1963.

115 *Rearden v Provincial Bank of Ireland* [1896] IR 532. See also *MacKereth v Wigan Coal and Iron Co Ltd* [1916] 2 Ch 293; *McGrattan v McGrattan* [1985] NI 28.

116 On liens over shares, see para **[8.121]** *post*.

> can have no reason to support it when it is claimed that the company may, for its own benefit, ignore facts within its own knowledge, as by creating liens in its own favour, contrary to good faith ... *In both cases the language is, I think, intended for the protection of the company; not to enable it to commit frauds; or knowingly take the benefit of them*[117].'

On appeal to the Court of Appeal, Palles CB added:

> 'The effect and operation of the section, and of clause No 8 does not extend to extinguish or affect any obligation to which the company would otherwise have been subjected by reason of its own unconscientious conduct, although notice of the trust might be a material element in arriving at the conclusion that the conduct of the company was against conscience. The mere fact of notice does not convert the company into trustees for the persons whose beneficial interest they have notice; but if, having that notice, they advance money to the trustee, on the security of the trust property, their conduct is not protected by the section and they participate in a breach of trust. So, too, they seek to commit a breach of trust by claiming, under colour of a lien created after such notice, to appropriate to the payment of their own debt property which to their knowledge is trust property. Property thus acquired they cannot be permitted to hold against the *cestui que trust*.'

This principle was more recently to the fore again in *McGrattan v McGrattan*[118], where a resolution which had been carried with the votes of trustees of shares was held to be null and void because the company had knowledge of the fact that the trustees, in so voting, were acting in breach of trust.

[8.030] Although beneficial interests may not be recorded in the register of members, the beneficial interests of directors and secretaries must be disclosed and recorded in a register specially kept for that purpose. Likewise, the beneficial interests of other persons may be required to be disclosed on foot of a court order – though no register recording the fruits of such disclosure appears to be required. The topic of disclosure of interests in shares is considered at para **[8.127]** below.

Protection of beneficial interests

[8.031] Order 46 of the Rules of the Superior Courts 1986 ('RSC 1986') provides a mechanism whereby persons beneficially entitled to shares may protect their interests. Under this mechanism, the beneficiary, having filed a 'stop notice' and an affidavit of their interest in the Central Office of the High Court, may serve a copy of the stop notice and affidavit on the company, thus notifying it of his interest[119]. The company, in turn, upon receipt of the stop notice, must thereafter notify the beneficiary of any attempt by the legal owner to transfer the shares or to pay the dividends[120] payable thereon to another, and must delay the transfer or payment for eight days in order to allow the beneficiary to take steps to protect his position[121].

---

117 *Rearden v Provincial Bank of Ireland* [1896] IR 532, at 567–568. Italics added.

118 *McGrattan v McGrattan* [1985] NI 28.

119 Order 46, rr 5–11, 13, of the RSC 1986. See also Ch 9, *Share Transfer*, at para **[9.038]**.

120 On dividends see para **[8.073]** *et seq, post*.

121 Order 46, r 12.

Limits of beneficial interests

[8.032] Beneficial ownership of a share cannot necessarily be equated with membership of the company. In *Re Via Networks Ireland Ltd*[122], Keane CJ stated:

> 'It is undoubtedly the case that a person who has become entitled to be registered as a shareholder may be unable to exercise any of his rights as a shareholder until his name has been entered on the register.'

Thus, if the share is registered in the name of a nominee or trustee, that nominee or trustee, rather than the beneficial owner, will be regarded as the member and will be entitled to exercise the rights associated with that position, as well as bearing the burden thereof[123].

(h) Cesser of membership

[8.033] Membership may cease in many ways, each of which is considered in its proper context elsewhere in this work. Here it is necessary only to list the principal modes of cesser of membership and to add, as a rule of thumb, that membership may be treated as subsisting as long as the member's name appears on the register of members, with the consequence that failure on the part of the outgoing member to ensure prompt removal of his name from the register may result in the creation of an estoppel[124]. The principal ways in which membership ceases include cesser:

- upon *dissolution* of the company[125];
- upon *transfer* of shares (whether voluntarily or compulsorily) and entry of the transferee's name on the register of members[126];
- upon *transmission* of shares by operation of law upon death or bankruptcy and entry of another's name on the register of members in place of the deceased or bankrupt member or on merger under the EC(CBM)R 2008[127];
- upon *redemption* of shares by the company[128];
- upon *forfeiture* or *surrender* of shares[129];
- upon sale by the company on foot of a *lien on shares*[130];
- upon *rescission*, for misrepresentation, of the contract for the acquisition of the shares[131];

[122] *Via Networks Ireland Ltd* [2002] 2 IR 47.

[123] *Re Munster Bank; Dillon's Claim* (1886–87) 17 LR Ir 341; *Casey v Bentley* [1902] 1 IR 376, 387; *Re Allied Metropole Hotel Ltd* (19 December 1988, unreported) HC (Gannon J) noted by MacCann, 'Locus Standi and Section 205 of the Companies Act 1963' (1989) 7 ILT 195; *Re Via Net Works Ireland Ltd* [2002] 2 IR 47; *Re A Company* [1986] BCLC 391; *Re Quickdome Ltd* [1988] BCLC 370. *Cf Re Irish Life and Permanent Group Holdings PLC and the Credit Institutions Stabilization Act 2010* [2012] IEHC 89 concerning the meaning of 'member' in the context of the Credit Institutions (Stabilisation) Act 2010.

[124] See para **[8.008]** *ante*.

[125] See Ch 4, *Incorporation and its Consequences*, at para **[4.020]**.

[126] See further Ch 9, *Share Transfer*, at para **[9.006]** *et seq*.

[127] See further Ch 9, *Share Transfer*, at para **[9.025]** *et seq*.

[128] See further Ch 10, *The Maintenance of Capital,* at para **[10.041]** *et seq*.

[129] See further para **[8.123]** *et seq*, *post*.

[130] See para **[8.121]** *post*.

[131] See para **[8.007]** *ante*.

- upon *repudiation*, by a minor, of the contract to take the shares[132];
- upon foot of a *court order*, such as an order under s 205(3) of the CA 1963 ordering the purchase of the shares of an oppressed minority by the company[133];
- upon a *takeover* by an 80% shareholder exercising his power under s 204 of the CA 1963 to acquire compulsorily the shares of a dissentient minority[134];
- upon a *sale of assets in a liquidation* to another company in consideration for shares or like interests in the other company – under s 260 of the CA 1963 the liquidator may elect to purchase the shares of a shareholder who does not wish to take shares in the other company[135].

[B] SHARES

[8.034] Shares are considered here in the following manner:

1. The legal nature of shares.
2. Formal requirements relating to shares.
3. Allotment of shares.
4. Shareholders' rights and duties.
5. Classes of shares.
6. Conversion of shares.
7. Liens on shares.
8. Forfeiture and surrender of shares.
9. Disclosure of interests in shares.

The legal nature of shares

[8.035] A share is an intangible accumulation of rights, interests and obligations. It is not a document – though a document (ie, a share certificate) is used to certify that a person has the rights, interests and obligations of a shareholder[136]. The courts appear reticent when it comes to giving an exact description of the legal nature of shares; but certain features of shares are, by now, well established. Those features are examined here in the following manner:

(a) A share confers no interest in the company's assets;
(b) A share is an interest in the nature of personalty;
(c) A share is a *chose in action*;
(d) A share confers contractual rights and obligations;
(e) A share confers an interest in the company itself;
(f) A share confers statutory rights and obligations;
(g) A share confers interests and rights protected by the Constitution.

---

132 See para **[8.009]** *ante*.

133 See Ch 11, *Shareholders' Remedies*, at para **[11.079]** *et seq*.

134 On compulsory acquisitions of shares see Ch 9, *Share Transfer*, at para **[9.087]** *et seq*.

135 See generally Ch 21, *Schemes of Arrangement and Reconstructions*, at para **[21.066]**.

136 See para **[8.047]** *post*.

(a) A share confers no interest in the company's assets

[8.036] It used to be thought that a shareholder held beneficial ownership of the company's property, or, in other words, that the company held its assets on trust for the members[137]. This view stemmed from the fact that the property and assets of old deed of settlement companies were vested in trustees to hold for the benefit of the members[138]. But the modern company cannot *ipso facto* be regarded as a mere trustee for its members because of the separate legal existence which it enjoys – this was the crux of *Salomon's* case[139]. Where the company holds property, it holds it in its own right. The shareholders have no interest in the property or any particular part of it. As Kenny J observed in *Attorney General for Ireland v Jameson*[140]:

> 'No shareholder has a right to any specific portion of the company's property, and save by, and to the extent of, his voting power at a general meeting of the company, cannot curtail the free and proper disposition of it.'

Thus, in *Short v Treasury Commissioners*[141], a case concerning the valuation of shares according to regulations which provided for payment of their value 'as between a willing buyer and a willing seller,' the Court of Appeal rejected the argument that the shares should be valued according to the value of the company's assets and undertaking, since:

> 'The shareholders are not in the eye of the law part-owners of the undertaking. The undertaking is something different from the totality of the shareholdings[142].'

(b) A share is an interest in the nature of personalty

[8.037] It follows from the foregoing that the nature of the share is not affected by the nature of the corporate assets, whether those assets are in the nature of real property or personal property[143]. In fact, s 79 of the CA 1963 expressly states that:

> 'The shares or other interest of any member in a company shall be personal estate, transferable in a manner provided in the articles of the company, and shall not be of the nature of real estate.'

In *Lee & Co (Dublin) Ltd v Egan (Wholesale) Ltd*[144], it was argued that a contract for the sale of shares in a company owning land should be subject to the rule in *Bain v Fothergill*[145] so that only nominal damages could be recovered by the intending

---

137 *Child v Hudson's Bay Co* (1723) 2 P Wms 207; *Harrisson v Pryse* (1740) Barn Ch 324.

138 See generally Ch 1, *The Private Company in Context*, at para **[1.077]**.

139 *Salomon v Salomon & Co* [1897] AC 22; See generally Ch 4, *Incorporation and its Consequences*, at para **[4.026]** *et seq*.

140 *Attorney General for Ireland v Jameson* [1904] 2 IR 644 at 671. See also *Kerry Co-operative Creamery Ltd v An Bord Bainne Co-Op Ltd* [1990] ILRM 664.

141 *Short v Treasury Commissioners* [1948] 1 KB 116.

142 *Short v Treasury Commissioners* [1948] 1 KB 116, *per* Evershed J at 124. On the valuation of shares generally see Ch 9, *Share Transfers*, at para **[9.117]** *et seq*.

143 See Rice, 'The Legal Nature of a Share' (1957) 21 Conv (ns) 433.

144 *Lee & Co (Dublin) Ltd v Egan (Wholesale) Ltd* (18 October 1979, unreported) HC, Kenny J.

145 *Bain v Fothergill* (1874) LR 7 HL 158. See generally Wylie, *Irish Conveyancing Law* (1978, Professional Books) at pp 573–579.

purchaser. Kenny J rejected that argument, observing[146] that that rule applies to the sale of land only, and not to the sale of shares in a company which owns land.

(c) A share is a chose in action

[8.038] Shares belong to that class of personal property known as *choses in action*[147]. What exactly a chose in action constitutes may be difficult to define, since the term is used to describe a wide range of interests. A simple description of a chose in action is an intangible interest which one can only protect by legal action rather than by taking possession of a physical thing[148]. Shares are affected by many of the idiosyncrasies which apply to the transfer or assignment of choses in action generally[149]. For example, shares do not come within the definition of 'goods' under the Sale of Goods Act 1893[150]. As shall be seen in the next chapter[151], the transfer or assignment of shares is also subject to its own peculiar rules. Thus, unlike other choses in action, the legal title to shares may not be passed simply by notifying the company of the transfer[152].

(d) A share confers contractual rights and obligations

[8.039] One feature of shares which is repeatedly focused upon by the courts is the fact that shares embody contractual rights. The contractual rights and obligations associated with shares stem from the shareholder's status as a member of the company and the so-called 's 25 contract'[153]. This contract 'of the most sacred character'[154] has already been considered in detail[155]. The contractual aspect of the interests constituted by a share was emphasised by Farwell J in his respected definition of a share in *Borlands Trustee Co v Steele*[156]:

> 'A share is the interest of a shareholder in the company measured by a sum of money, for the purpose of liability in the first place, and of interest in the second, but also consisting of a series of mutual covenants entered into by all the shareholders *inter se* in accordance with [s 25 of the CA 1963]. The contract contained in the articles of association is one of the original incidents of the share.'

---

146 *Lee & Co (Dublin) Ltd v Egan (Wholesale) Ltd* (18 October 1979, unreported) HC, Kenny J, at p 3 of the transcript.

147 *Colonial Bank v Whinney* (1886) 11 App Cas 426; *Re VGM Holdings* [1942] Ch 235. See also *Halsbury's Laws of England* (4th edn), Vol 6, at para 6.

148 See *Re Cuff Knox (deceased)* [1963] IR 263, *per* Kingsmill Moore J at 291.

149 On the assignment of choses in action generally see Bell, *Modern Law of Personal Property in England and Ireland* (1989, Butterworths) Ch 15.

150 Section 62 of the Sale of Goods Act 1893 defines 'goods' as including 'all chattels personal other than things in action and money' (italics added). See also *Lee & Co (Dublin) Ltd v Egan (Wholesale) Ltd* (18 October 1979, unreported) HC, Kenny J.

151 See Ch 9, *Share Transfer*, at para **[9.006]** *et seq*.

152 *Ireland v Hart* [1902] 1 Ch 522.

153 Arising under s 25 of the CA 1963.

154 *Per* Ross J in *Clark v Workman* [1920] IR 107 at 112.

155 See Ch 3, *Constitutional Documentation*, at para **[3.092]** *et seq*.

156 *Borlands Trustee Co v Steele* [1901] 1 CH 279 at 288. See also *Provincial Bank of Ireland Ltd v O'Connor* (23 July 1973) HC, Kenny J.

In *Attorney General for Ireland v Jameson*[157], Kenny J amplified this definition, saying of a shareholder's rights and obligations that:

> 'He is entitled to a share of the company's capital and profits, the former ... being measured by a sum of money which is taken as the standard for the ascertainment of his share of the profits. If the company disposes of its assets, or if the latter be realised in a liquidation, he has a right to a proportion of the amount received after the discharge of the Company's debts and liabilities. In acquiring these rights – that is, in becoming a member of the company – he is deemed to have simultaneously entered into a contract under seal to conform to the regulations contained in the articles of association ... Whatever obligations are contained in those articles, he accepts the ownership of the shares and the position of a member of the company, bound and controlled by them. He cannot divorce his money interest, whatever it may amount to, from those obligations. They are inseparable incidents attached to his rights, and the idea of a share cannot, in my judgment, be complete without their inclusion.'

The *terms of issue* of a share enumerate the particular contractual rights associated with the share, but these terms must be authorised by the memorandum or the articles of association.

(e) A share confers an interest in the company itself

[8.040] Shareholders are *members* of the company, and membership constitutes an interest *in the company itself*[158]. That a share confers an interest in the company itself is evident in Farwell J's definition in the *Borland's Trustee* case[159]. This interest stems from the contractual rights associated with membership, but it is more than a mere contractual right *in personam*[160]. Rather, it is a right *in rem*. In other words, the shareholder not only has rights *against* the company but he also, as member, has rights *in* the company itself. He, along with the other shareholders, owns the company, and, depending upon the extent of the interest he possesses, he has a hand in controlling its activities. The extent of his interest in the company is determined by reference to the contractual rights conferred by the memorandum and articles and the Companies Acts. Thus, Russell LJ, in *IRC v Crossman*[161], described a share as follows:

> 'It is the interest of a person in the company, that interest being composed of rights and obligations which are defined by the Companies Act and by the memorandum and articles of association of the company.'

In *Kerry Co-operative Creamery Ltd v An Bord Bainne Co-Op Ltd*[162], Costello J explained the shareholder's interests in a similar manner, emphasising that they are property rights[163]:

---

157 *Attorney General for Ireland v Jameson* [1904] 2 IR 644 at 671.

158 Though not, of course, its assets. See para **[8.036]** *ante*.

159 See para **[8.039]** *ante*.

160 See *North Western Railway v M'Michael* (1851) 5 Exch 114; *Cork and Bandon Railway v Cazenove* (1847) 10 QB 935; *Steinberg v Scala (Leeds) Ltd* [1923] 2 Ch 452.

161 *IRC v Crossman* [1937] AC 26 at 66.

162 *Kerry Co-operative Creamery Ltd v An Bord Bainne Co-Op Ltd* [1990] ILRM 664.

163 *Kerry Co-operative Creamery Ltd v An Bord Bainne Co-Op Ltd* [1990] ILRM 664 at 714. See also *Poole v Middleton* (1861) 29 Beav 646; *Private Motorist's Provident Society Ltd & Moore v Attorney General* [1984] ILRM 988.

> 'The shareholder has rights which can properly be regarded as property rights (*PMPS Ltd & Moore v Attorney General* [1984] ILRM 88) but their nature and extent are to be ascertained by reference to the contract it has entered into with the society whose terms are contained in the society's rules.'

As property rights, the rights conferred on an individual member by a share may be exercised independently of the will of the majority of shareholders[164], and they are protected by the Constitution[165]. It is the fact that a shareholder holds property in the company itself which distinguishes him from a debenture-holder who has rights against the company, and, if the debenture is secured, in the company property, but who has no rights in the company itself. Shareholders' contractual rights are considered more fully at para **[8.071]** below.

(f) A share confers statutory rights and obligations

[8.041] Apart from those rights which are conferred on shareholders by the company's memorandum and articles, the Companies Acts confer certain other individual and collective rights on shareholders as members of the company. These are considered at para **[8.086]** post.

(g) A share confers interests and rights protected by the Constitution

[8.042] The interests conferred by a share are interests which are protected by the Constitution. In *Kerry Co-operative Creamery Ltd v An Bord Bainne Co-Op Ltd*[166], both the Society and Mr Moore, one of its major shareholders, sought a declaration that s 5(2) of the Industrial and Provident Societies (Amendment) Act 1978, which prohibited the Society from accepting or holding deposits, constituted an unjust attack on their constitutional property rights. Carroll J, in the High Court, for reasons discussed in Ch 4[167], dismissed the Society's application; but in relation to Mr Moore's application she said[168]:

> 'Mr Moore is a shareholder in the Society. He invested his money with other shareholders in a society incorporated under the law which is entitled to carry on business *intra vires*. If the business of the society is affected by the Act of 1978 in such a way that the property rights of Mr Moore are affected, then he is entitled, *prima facie*, to make a claim that his constitutional rights that are protected by Article 40, s 3, and Article 43 have been infringed. Ownership of shares is one of the bundle of rights which constitute ownership of private property: *per* Mr Justice Kenny at p 84 of the report of *Central Dublin Development Association v The Attorney General* (1969) 109 ILTR 69.'

Carroll J's reference to 'ownership of shares' may be taken as a reference to the interests conferred by a share, since there was no question of the offending legislation divesting

---

164 *Carruth v ICI Ltd* [1937] AC 707, *per* Maugham LJ at 765. It is important here, however, to distinguish a shareholder's personal rights from the rights of the company as a whole; See Ch 11, *Shareholders' Remedies*, at para **[11.103]**.

165 See para **[8.042]** *post*.

166 *Kerry Co-operative Creamery Ltd v An Bord Bainne Co-Op Ltd* [1983] IR 339.

167 See Ch 4, *Incorporation and its Consequences,* at para **[4.069]**.

168 *Kerry Co-operative Creamery Ltd v An Bord Bainne Co-Op Ltd* [1983] IR 339 at 349.

Mr Moore of his ownership of the shares in question. That was how the Supreme Court approached the matter on appeal. Delivering the court's judgment, O'Higgins CJ said[169]:

> '[A]s a shareholder and to the extent of his investment, Mr Moore has an interest in the Society and contractual rights arising therefrom. This interest and these contractual rights are property rights which belong to Mr Moore and they are capable of being harmed by injury done to the Society. The Court, therefore, rejects the submission made on behalf of the Attorney General that, as a shareholder in the Society, Mr Moore has no property rights capable of being invoked for the purposes of Article 40, s 3, of the Constitution.'

Apart from providing a convenient mechanism for indirectly enforcing rights which are not available to a company, it has been suggested[170] that the constitutionally protected property rights conferred by shares may also open the door for another exception to the rule in *Foss v Harbottle*[171], which is discussed in Ch 11, *post*.

Formal requirements relating to shares

[8.043] Every share is required to have a nominal value[172], and, unless certain conditions are met, to be numbered[173]. In addition, each shareholder is entitled to a share certificate[174], certifying his title to the shares held by him unless the conditions of issue otherwise provide. Each of these matters will now be considered in turn.

(a) Nominal value of shares

[8.044] Section 6(4) of the CA 1963 requires the memorandum of a private company (or any other company having a share capital) 'to state the amount of share capital with which the company proposes to be registered, and the division thereof into shares of a fixed amount'[175]. In *Re Scandinavian Group plc*[176], Harman J held that the division into shares of a fixed amount need not be expressed in the currency of the realm – a foreign currency is equally acceptable[177].

The monetary value given to a share by the memorandum is referred to as its *nominal* or *par* value, for it need not represent the amount actually paid on the share and rarely does it reflect the true price which the share might obtain upon transfer or transmission[178]. The nominal value of a share, as may be seen from Farwell J's definition

169 *Kerry Co-operative Creamery Ltd v An Bord Bainne Co-Op Ltd* [1983] IR 339 at 359.

170 See MacCann, 'The Rule in *Foss v Harbottle*, Recent Developments' (1990) 8 ILT 68 at 72.

171 *Foss v Harbottle* (1843) 2 Hare 461.

172 Section 6(4) of the CA 1963.

173 Section 80 of the CA 1963.

174 Section 86 of the CA 1963.

175 The share capital as stated in the memorandum represents the limit of the capital which the company is authorised to issue, not the amount of capital actually issued; see Ch 3, *Constitutional Documentation*, at para **[3.017]**.

176 *Re Scandinavian Group plc* [1987] 2 WLR 752.

177 *Cf* Keane, *Company Law* (4th edn, Bloomsbury Professional, 2007), at para 17.07, where the learned author suggests that the better view is that the amount should be expressed in the local currency, in euros and cents.

178 On the valuation of shares upon transfer or transmission see Ch 9, *Share Transfer*, at para **[9.117]**.

of a share in the *Borland's Trustee* case[179], serves merely as a yardstick by which the strength of the rights, interests and obligations of the shareholder may be measured.

'No par' shares

[8.045] Other jurisdictions, such as the USA and Canada, have allowed companies to issue *no par* shares, whereby a shareholder's rights, interests and obligations are measured as a fraction of the aggregate, without a misleading nominal value being attributed to the share capital and the individual shares in a manner which serves to confuse unsophisticated parties dealing with the company. While there is something to be said in favour of such measures, they would only compound confusion unless all companies were required to dispense with their shares having a nominal value. The Company Law Review Group, in its *Second Report*, recommended that Ireland should express support for and work towards the possibility of introducing no par value shares at the appropriate EU forums, but stopped short of recommending that Ireland should dispense with par value shares[180]. Although various commentators[181] and company law committees[182] have favoured the introduction of no par shares on this side of the Atlantic, nothing has yet come of their recommendations.

(b) Numbering of shares

[8.046] Section 80 of the CA 1963 requires each share to be distinguished by an appropriate number, unless all the issued shares, or all the issued shares of a particular class, are fully paid up and rank *pari passu* (ie, carry equal rights of participation in the benefits of membership) for all purposes and provided that those conditions continue to exist. In practice, those conditions usually exist in private companies, and, consequently, the numbering of shares is frequently dispensed with. Where shares are numbered the number does not, of course, appear on the share itself – since a share is not a tangible item – rather, the number of each share held by a member is registered in the register of members, and may also be recorded on the share certificate[183].

(c) Share certificates

[8.047] Under s 86 of the CA 1963, each shareholder is to be furnished with a share certificate which is *prima facie* evidence of his title to the shares held by him[184]. The share certificate must be completed and ready for delivery within two months of the

179 See para **[8.039]** *ante*.

180 CLRG, *Second Report,* para 7.5.7.

181 Eg, Gower, *Principles of Modern Company Law* (5th edn, Sweet & Maxwell, 1992) at p 242.

182 Eg, The Gedge Committee, Cmnd 9112 (1954); The Jenkins Committee, Cmnd 1749 (1962), at paras 32–34. An attempt to introduce them in the UK in 1967 failed; see Cmnd 5391, at para 49. Note, however, that an *investment company* within the meaning of Pt III of the CA 1990 may have, in effect, no par shares. See Ch 29, *Public Limited Companies and SEs*, at para **[29.144]**.

183 Section 116(1)(a) of the CA 1963.

184 Section 87 of the CA 1963. Under s 239(3) of the CA 1990, however, the Minister is empowered to make regulations dispensing with the obligation of a company to issue certificates and providing for alternative procedures. The CA 1990 (US) Regs 1996 provide for electronic share dealings in uncertificated securities; see further Ch 29, *Public Limited Companies and SEs*, at para **[29.062]**.

allotment or transfer[185]. It is not necessary that a separate certificate be issued for each share held by the shareholder. Failure to comply with the requirements governing share certificates will render the company and its officers liable to make good the default, and the directors may be made liable to cover the costs of making good such default[186].

(i) Liability of the company for false information in certificate

[8.048] The company may be liable to third parties who suffer damage in respect of incorrect information appearing in share certificates. The company's liability in such circumstances stems from the equitable doctrine of estoppel. Under this doctrine, any person who makes or authorises a representation as to a certain fact is bound to accept the truth of that fact as regards a third party who relies upon it. In *Re Bahaia and San Francisco Railway Co*[187], Cockburn LJ said of a share certificate that it:

> 'is a declaration by the company to all the world that the person in whose name the certificate is made out, and to whom it is given, is a shareholder in the company, and it is given by the company with the intention that it shall be so used by the person to whom it is given, and acted upon in the sale and transfer of shares.'

Thus, the company will be liable to any person who purchases the share in good faith on the strength of the information contained in the certificate[188]. The purchaser in such circumstances will not be entitled, however, to have his name entered on the register of members – the original person named in the certificate will remain on the register – but the company must pay damages to the purchaser. Likewise, in the past it has been held that where a certificate states that the shares are fully paid up, the company cannot make a call[189] on the shareholder in respect of any amount actually unpaid on the share[190]. This decision has now, however, been superseded by s 27 of the C(A)A 1983 which prohibits the issue of shares at a discount[191].

It need hardly be said that the issue of share certificates is a matter which requires the utmost care and attention, for the company may incur serious liability as a result of an incorrect certificate.

(ii) Forged certificates

[8.049] The company will not, of course, be liable to third parties where the third party is aware of the fact that the information contained in the share certificate is incorrect, since no estoppel is created[192]. Likewise, the company will not be liable in respect of a share certificate which has been forged by a person having no authority to issue such a certificate, because the information contained therein does not amount to a

185 Section 87 of the CA 1963. A transfer for these purposes means a transfer which is duly stamped and otherwise valid and not one which the company is entitled to refuse to register and has not registered. See also Ch 9, *Share Transfer*, at para **[9.008]**.

186 Section 86(3) of the CA 1963.

187 *Re Bahaia and San Francisco Railway Co* (1868) LR 3 QB 584 at 595.

188 *Re Bahaia and San Francisco Railway Co* (1868) LR 3 QB 584; *Balkis Consolidated Co v Tomkinson* [1893] AC 396.

189 See para **[8.094]** *et seq*, *post*.

190 *Burkinshaw v Nicholls* (1878) 3 App Cas 1004.

191 See Ch 10, *The Maintenance of Capital*, at para **[10.108]** *et seq*.

192 *Re Caribbean Co* (1875) 10 Ch App 614.

representation which is made or authorised by the company as was held to be the case in *Ruben v Great Fingall Consolidated*[193]; however, there it was the company secretary who perpetrated the 'wicked fraud' as it was described by Lord Macnaghten. A certificate which is issued by the company secretary without first obtaining the requisite authority of the board of directors may be regarded as a forgery[194], but this will depend upon whether the secretary can be viewed as having no ostensible authority to issue the certificate[195].

By contrast, however, if a share certificate were to be issued by persons who were directors and therefore had ostensible authority to issue share certificates, even if the signatures attesting the seal on the share certificate had been forged and provided the outsider was unaware of the forgery and there were no circumstances to excite suspicion, on the authority of *ACC Bank plc v McCann and Griffin*[196] the rule in *Turquand's* case can apply to estop the company from denying the validity of the forged share certificate[197].

Allotment of shares[198]

[8.050] There are three principal ways in which a person may become a shareholder: namely, upon *allotment* of newly issued shares by the directors of a company; upon *transfer* by an existing shareholder; or upon *transmission* from an existing shareholder. A share is to be taken as having been allotted in a company when a person acquires an unconditional right to be included in the register of members in respect of that share[199]. Transfer and transmission of shares are considered in Ch 9, *post.* In this section, the allotment of shares by the company will be considered, and the following issues will be examined:

- (a) Directors' authority to allot shares;
- (b) The mechanics of allotment;
- (c) Statutory pre-emption rights on allotment;
- (d) Consideration for shares on allotment;
- (e) The court's power to rectify a defective allotment.

(a) Directors' authority to allot shares

[8.051] Model reg 5 of Table A gives the directors the authority to make an allotment; however, this must be read in the light of s 20 of the C(A)A 1983 which provides that the directors shall not exercise the power of the company to allot shares unless they are authorised to do so either by the company in general meeting or by the articles of association.

---

193 *Ruben v Great Fingall Consolidated Co* (1875) 10 Ch App 614.

194 *South London Greyhound Racecourses Ltd v Wake* [1931] 1 Ch 496.

195 See Ch 7, *Corporate Contracts: Capacity and Authority*, at para **[7.101]**

196 *ACC Bank plc v McCann and Griffin* [2012] IEHC 236.

197 See Ch 7, *Corporate Contracts: Capacity and Authority*, at para **[7.123]**.

198 See McGowan-Smyth & Daly, *Irish Company Secretary's Handbook* (2011, Bloomsbury Professional) at pp 750–760.

199 Section 2(2) of the C(A)A 1983.

Such authority may be given either for a particular allotment or it may be given unconditionally; but in either case it must state the maximum number of shares to be allotted and the date (not exceeding five years from the date of incorporation or the date of the resolution) upon which the authority will expire[200]. After the authority has expired, the directors may still make an allotment to any person who entered into an agreement with the company before the authority expired. The authority given may be revoked, varied, or renewed for a further five years by an ordinary resolution of the company, even though this may have the effect of varying the company's articles of association. In practice, where articles of association are amended the opportunity is often taken to 'reset' the five-year authorisation.

An allotment in contravention of s 20 of the C(A)A 1983 remains valid; but any director knowingly and wilfully involved in the contravention will be guilty of an offence. The section does not apply to the allotment of shares pursuant to an employee share scheme, nor to a right to subscribe for or to convert any security into shares.

[8.052] In exercising their powers of allotment, the directors are required to act *bona fide* and in the best interests of the company. In *Nash v Lancegaye (Ireland) Ltd*[201], the plaintiff, and certain proxies he had obtained, accounted for approximately 51% of the voting shares in the defendant company, the remaining 49% or so being held by a Mr Ryan and his associates. Ryan and his associates dominated the board of directors, and when differences arose between Ryan and the plaintiff, a fresh issue of shares was authorised by the board, allotted in such a way as to give Ryan and his associates 51% of the issued voting shares. Dixon J found that the resolutions authorising the allotment were not made in good faith. No agenda or notice of any resolution was circulated before the directors' meeting; and the only heading appearing on the notice circulated at the meeting under which the matter could be discussed was 'capital position' – an item appearing on the agenda of nearly every meeting. The plaintiff's plea for an adjournment to afford further consideration of the matter was summarily rejected. All these factors combined to indicate that the directors' true motive in making the allotment was to maintain their control over the affairs of the company and to defeat the wishes of the existing majority of shareholders[202].

[8.053] Moreover, directors of a private company must respect the limits on offering shares or debentures in the company for sale to the public. Section 21 of the C(A)A

---

200 Section 20(3) of the C(A)A 1983.

201 *Nash v Lancegaye (Ireland) Ltd* (1958) 92 ILTR 11. See also *Hogg v Cramphorn Ltd* [1966] 3 WLR 254; *Smith (Howard) Ltd v Ampol Petroleum Ltd* [1974] AC 821; *Clemens v Clemens Brothers Ltd* [1976] 2 All ER 268; *Bamford v Bamford* [1969] 2 WLR 1107; *G and s Doherty Ltd v Doherty* (19 June 1969, unreported) HC, Henchy J; *Mills v Mills* (1938) 60 CLR 150; *Harlowe's Nominees Pty Ltd v Woodside (Lakes Entrance) Oil Co NL* (1968) 121 CLR 483; *Teck Corporation Ltd v Millar* (1972) 3 DLR (3d) 288; *Punt v Symons and Co Ltd* [1903] 2 Ch 506; *Piercy v s Mills and Co Ltd* [1920] 1 Ch 77; *Whitehouse v Carlton Party Ltd* [1976] 2 All ER 268.

202 Contrast *Re Jermyn Street Turkish Baths Ltd* [1971] 1 WLR 1042 where, in return for desperately needed cash, a director was allotted shares giving her control of the company. The net effect of the allotment, coupled with the director's management prowess, was the saving of the company. The Court of Appeal held the allotment to have been *bona fide* and for the benefit of the company as a whole.

1983, as amended[203], makes any officer who acts in default guilty of an offence, though the section does not extend to offers or allotments of shares to *qualified investors* or to 99 or fewer persons, or both, within the meaning of the Prospectus Directive[204].

(b) The mechanics of allotment

[8.054] Often, few formal steps are observed in the allotment of shares. However, since an allotment involves a contract for the sale of shares, a number of legal principles apply to each step taken in it. Once the directors agree to make an allotment, a person may apply to them for shares. Such an application, whether made orally or in writing, amounts to an *offer*, and it will be subject to the normal legal principles applying to offers in contract[205]. For example, the application may be revoked by the applicant at any reasonable time up to acceptance. In the private company, this offer is often accepted by conduct, ie, by issuing the applicant with a share certificate which indicates his title to the shares[206]. It may also be accepted by the company when the offeror is notified, whether orally or in writing, that he has been allotted the shares for which he has applied. Mere posting of a written notice of allotment will, it appears, amount to acceptance[207]. Shares shall be taken to have been allotted when a person acquires an unconditional right to be included in the company's register of members in respect of those shares[208].

It is also possible to issue a *renounceable letter of allotment*, under which the person to whom the shares have been allotted may renounce the allotment in favour of another. These are relatively rare as far as private companies are concerned.

[8.055] Within one month of the allotment, the company must, under s 58(1)(a) of the CA 1963, make a return to the registrar of companies stating the number and nominal amount of the shares comprised in the allotment; the names and addresses of the allottees; and the amount, if any, paid or due and payable on each share. Great care should be taken in making this return on a *Form B5* to the registrar of companies because it will be treated by the registrar as formally representing the new amount of the company's issued share capital. Where, through accident, the issued share capital is overstated, the registrar will not permit a correctional refilling and takes the view, shared by the High Court[209], that such might amount to a reduction in share capital and so requires a court order directing the registrar to show the lower amount of issued share capital on the registrar.

(c) Statutory pre-emption rights on the allotment of shares

[8.056] It will be recalled that a private company is not permitted to offer its shares to the public[210]. This requirement is, to some extent, enhanced by the provisions of s 23 of

203 By s 8 of the IFCMPA 2006, with purported retrospective effect from 1 July 2005.

204 See Ch 32, *Prospectus, Market Abuse and Transparency Law*, at para **[32.006]** *et seq*.

205 See Clark, *Contract Law in Ireland* (6th edn, Round Hall, 2008) Ch 1.

206 On share certificates, see para **[8.047]** *ante*.

207 *Household Fire Insurance Co v Grant* (1879) 4 Ex D 216.

208 Section 2(2) of the C(A)A 1983.

209 See *Air France Aircraft Leasing v Registrar of Companies* (30 April 2007, unreported) HC, Laffoy J.

210 See Ch 1, *The Private Company in Context*, at para **[1.133]**

the C(A)A 1983, which gives the existing members of a private company a statutory *pre-emption* right, in proportion to their existing shareholding, on the allotment of new shares. These pre-emption rights may, in the case of a private company, however, be ousted by the provisions of the memorandum or articles. A pre-emption right is a right of first refusal, which arises either by way of statute or by way of agreement[211]. Under the statutory scheme, the offer of shares to existing shareholders must be served in the same way as notices[212] and must state a period of not less than 21 days during which the offer may be accepted and during which the offer may not be withdrawn[213].

The Companies Acts do not contain any provisions regulating how the company may deal with shares which have not been taken up by existing members under the statutory pre-emption scheme. This should be dealt with in the company's memorandum and articles of association or in the resolution authorising the allotment. The relevant provision should stipulate whether the company is to be permitted to offer the 'refused' shares to persons who are not already members or whether it must first offer those shares to existing members.

[8.057] The memorandum and articles of a private company may exclude generally the operation of s 23 of the C(A)A 1983[214]. Furthermore, even where the section is not excluded generally, the articles or a special resolution may exclude the section in respect of a particular allotment[215]. The notice of the meeting at which such a special resolution is to be passed must contain a written statement from the directors explaining their reasons for departing from the statutory pre-emption scheme, and the amount to be paid to the company in respect of the shares to be allotted. There is nothing, of course, to prevent a company from providing for its own pre-emption scheme in its memorandum or articles. In such cases, the statutory system will not apply, but any offers under the company's own scheme must still be made in the manner described above, or else they will be of no effect[216].

[8.058] Statutory pre-emption rights are *not* given:

- to the holders of *preference shares* which, as respects dividend and capital, carry a right to participate only up to a specified amount in a distribution[217];
- when the allotment is in respect of an *employees' share scheme*[218];
- when the allotment is an allotment of *preference shares* which, as respects dividend and capital, carry a right to participate only up to a specified amount in a distribution[219];
- when the allotment is to be paid for, either wholly or partly, in *non-cash consideration*[220];

---

211 As to pre-emption rights on transfer of shares see Ch 9, *Share Transfer*, at para **[9.069]** *et seq*.

212 See Ch 14, *Corporate Governance: Meetings*, at para **[14.040]** *et seq*.

213 Section 23(7) and (8) of the C(A)A 1983.

214 Section 23(10) of the C(A)A 1983.

215 Section 24 of the C(A)A 1983.

216 Section 23(9) of the C(A)A 1983; see para **[8.051]** *ante*.

217 Section 23(13) of the C(A)A 1983. As to preference shares, see para **[8.102]** *et seq*, *post*.

218 Section 23(6) of the C(A)A 1983. On employees' shares, see para **[8.115]** *post*.

219 Section 23(13) of the C(A)A 1983.

220 Section 23(4) of the C(A)A 1983. On consideration for allotments, see para **[8.060]** *et seq*, *post*.

– where the memorandum or articles of a private company, or a special resolution of the general meeting of a private company, *exclude* the operation of s 23 of the C(A)A 1983[221];

– where the memorandum or articles provide for the *company's own pre-emption scheme*[222].

[8.059] Failure to comply with the statutory requirements as to pre-emption will render the company and every officer who knowingly authorised or permitted the contravention jointly and severally liable to compensate any person to whom the offer should have been made[223]. Proceedings in respect of contravention may not, however, be commenced after the expiration of two years from the delivery to the registrar of companies of the return of allotments in question[224]. It may be observed that contravention of the statutory provision does not invalidate the allotment itself.

(d) Consideration for shares on allotment

[8.060] Shares may be issued for either a cash payment or for some other form of consideration. The allottee need not necessarily be required to pay the full amount of the consideration upon allotment – he may be allowed to pay in instalments, or he may be allowed to keep his money until it is needed by the company, when it can look to him for payment by way of a *call*[225]. He will normally be liable in a winding up only to the extent of any sums due or owing on his shares, and if he has transferred the shares to another person and that other person is registered as a member, then the new member becomes liable to pay the sums due. Here, the following issues in the consideration for shares on allotment are considered:

(i) The meaning of 'cash';
(ii) Non-cash consideration;
(iii) Issue of shares at a discount;
(iv) Issue of shares at a premium.

(i) The meaning of 'cash'

[8.061] Section 2(3)(a) of the C(A)A 1983 provides:

> 'a share in a company shall be taken to have been paid up (as to its nominal value or any premium on it) in cash or allotted for cash if the consideration for the allotment or the payment up is in cash received by the company or is a cheque received by the company in good faith which the directors have no reason for suspecting will not be paid or is the release of a liability of the company for a liquidated sum or is an undertaking to pay cash to the company at a future date.'

Accordingly, an undertaking to pay cash at a future time is considered to be the same as a cash payment. Moreover, 'cash' includes foreign currency[226].

---

221 Sections 23(10) and 24(1) and (2) of the C(A)A 1983.
222 Section 24(2) and (9) of the C(A)A 1983.
223 Section 23(10) of the C(A)A 1983.
224 Section 23(13) of the C(A)A 1983.
225 See para **[8.094]** *et seq*, *post*.
226 Section 2(3)(a) of the C(A)A 1983.

(ii) Non-cash consideration

[8.062] Shares in private companies may be paid for in kind[227]; s 26 of the C(A)A 1983 expressly provides:

> 'shares allotted by a company and any premium payable on them may be paid up in money or money's worth (including goodwill and expertise).'

Where shares are allotted for a consideration other than cash, the company must, under s 58(1)(b) of the CA 1963, deliver to the registrar of companies the contract constituting the title of the allottee to the shares, or, if it is not in writing, particulars of the contract, and a return stating the number and nominal amount of the shares so allotted, the extent to which they are to be treated as paid up, and the consideration for which they have been allotted. Delivery of these particulars to the registrar must be effected within one month of allotment. Default in the delivery of particulars within the prescribed period renders every officer in default to a class C fine[228], but the time for delivery of any document under the section may be extended by the court if it is satisfied that the omission was accidental or due to inadvertence or that it is just and equitable to grant relief[229]. The Company Law Review Group has recommended the repeal of s 58 in so far as it required details of unwritten contracts for the sale of shares for non-cash consideration to be filed[230].

Goods or services will constitute good consideration for shares provided the company is prepared to accept them as payment. Thus, in *McCoy v Greene*[231], the provision of mediation services to a company which had been split by a family dispute was found to constitute valid consideration for an allotment. However, since under ordinary principles of contract law 'past consideration is no consideration,'[232] services already performed, or services which the allottee is already bound to render to the company under an earlier contract with it, will not constitute valid consideration[233]. An allotment in consideration of the release of a debt due to the allottee by the company will be regarded as an allotment for cash, so no return to the registrar will be required[234]; but an allotment by way of accord and satisfaction will be regarded as an allotment for non-cash consideration[235].

[8.063] Ordinary principles of contract law forbid the courts from inquiring into the adequacy of consideration[236] and the same principles apply to consideration given for

227 *Re Heyford Co, Pell's Case* (1869) 5 Ch App 11; *Re Wragg Ltd* [1897] 1 Ch 796; *Re Leinster Contract Corporation* [1902] 1 IR 349; *McCoy v Greene* [1984] IEHC 70 (Costello J).

228 Section 58(3) of the CA 1963.

229 Section 58(4) of the CA 1963.

230 CLRG, *Second Report*, para 7.7.10.

231 *McCoy v Greene* (19 January 1984) HC, Costello J.

232 See Clark, *Contract Law in Ireland* (6th edn, Round Hall, 2008) Ch 2.

233 *Re Eddystone Marine Insurance Co* [1893] 3 Ch 9; *Re Leinster Contract Corporation* [1902] IR 349.

234 Section 2(2) of the C(A)A 1983; see para **[8.061]** *ante* and *Larocque v Beauchemin* [1897] AC 358.

235 *Re Johannesburg Hotel Co, ex parte Zoutpansberg Prospecting Co* [1891] 1 Ch 119.

236 See Clark, *Contract Law in Ireland* (6th edn, Round Hall, 2008) Ch 2. *Pilmer v Duke Group Ltd* [2001] 2 BCLC 773.

shares. Thus, in *Re Leinster Contract Corporation*[237], where shares were allotted in return for certain patents, the court refused to set aside the allotment even though the patents proved ultimately to be valueless. In *Re Wragg Ltd*[238], where a business run by two partners was acquired by a company formed by them in consideration of a sum of money and the allotment to them of fully paid up shares, the court refused to accede to the liquidator's argument that the shares be treated as unpaid because the business had been overvalued by £18,000. Lord Lindley said:

> 'It is not the law that persons cannot sell property to a limited company for fully paid-up shares and make a profit by the transaction. We must not allow ourselves to be misled by talking of value. The value paid to a company is measured by the price at which the company agrees to buy what it thinks is worth its while to acquire. While the transaction is unimpeached, that is the only value to be considered.'

However, where *convertible debentures* (ie, debentures[239] which give the holder the right to convert his interest into shares in the company) are to be converted, the amount to be paid up, or actually paid up, on the debenture must at least equal the nominal value of the share into which it is to be converted – otherwise the conversion would amount to the issue of a share at a discount[240].

(iii) Issue of shares at a discount

[8.064] There is a general prohibition on the issue of shares at a discount, ie, at a price below their nominal value, because such an issue causes a reduction of the company's share capital. The issue of shares at a discount is considered in Ch 10[241].

(iv) Issue of shares at a premium

[8.065] While there is a general prohibition on the issue of shares at a discount, there is nothing to prevent a company from issuing shares at a *premium*, ie, at a price higher than their nominal value. In private companies it is particularly common to issue shares at a premium, since the price of the share will normally reflect the value of the business. A premium obtained from the issue of shares is *not*, however, part of the company's trading profit; instead, it is treated like the capital of the company and it is transferred to a special account called the *share premium account*.

[8.066] Section 62 of the CA 1963 requires all such premia to be transferred into the share premium account and provides that the rules governing the maintenance of capital apply to the share premium account in the same way as they apply to the paid up share capital of the company. The section goes on to permit four applications of the share premium account:

(a) paying up unissued shares of the company and issuing them to members of the company as fully paid up *bonus* shares;

---

237 *Re Leinster Contract Corporation* [1902] IR 349.

238 *Re Wragg Ltd* [1897] 1 Ch 796.

239 On debentures see further Ch 18, *Corporate Borrowing: Debentures and Charges*, at para **[18.018]** *et seq*.

240 *Mosley v Koffyfontein Mines Ltd* [1904] 2 Ch 108. On the prohibition against issue of shares at a discount see Ch 10, *The Maintenance of Capital*, at para **[10.108]** *et seq*.

241 See Ch 10, *The Maintenance of Capital*, at para **[10.108]** *et seq*.

(b) writing off the preliminary expenses of the company;

(c) writing off the expenses of, or the commission paid on, any issue of shares or debentures in the company;

(d) providing for the premium payable on redemption of any redeemable preference shares pursuant to s 220 of the CA 1990, or of any debentures of the company.

[8.067] Where shares in one company are allotted in consideration for shares in another company, and the nominal value of the shares in the allotting company is lower than the actual value of the shares in the allottee company, the difference in value constitutes a premium which must be transferred to the share premium account. This is so even though the difference represents profits made by the allottee company prior to the acquisition of its shares by the allotting company[242]. These pre-acquisition profits may not be distributed by the allotting company in any subsequent dividend, because to do so would amount to an unauthorised application of the share premium account[243]. English law, in line with the expectations of the accounting profession, has been altered to allow such distribution[244]; no such changes have been made in Ireland.

(d) The court's power to rectify a defective allotment

[8.068] Section 89 of the CA 1963, as amended[245], empowers the court to declare that the creation, issue or acquisition of shares in the capital of a company shall be valid for all purposes if the court considers it just and equitable to do so. The declaration may be made upon application to the court by the company, any holder or former holder of such shares or any member or former member or creditor, or the liquidator, of the company[246].

[8.069] In *Re Sugar Distributors Ltd*[247], an application was made to validate an allotment of 900,000 redeemable preference shares in Sugar Distributors Ltd to Irish Sugar plc following findings by a court appointed inspector that the necessary meetings to increase the authorised share capital by an amount sufficient to enable the allotment had not in fact taken place. The goal of the allotment was to make Sugar Distributors Ltd a 90% subsidiary of Irish Sugar plc so that Sugar Distributors Ltd could avail of the lower manufacturing tax rate of income tax. Counsel for Sugar Distributors Ltd argued that despite the lack of formality, the agreement of all relevant stakeholders was in place, and that it was just and equitable for the court to validate the allotment. Keane J, however, held that the discretion under s 89 is one which must be exercised in a judicial manner and in accordance with appropriate criteria and having regard to the underlying policy of the section which is to prevent possible hardship to persons who innocently subscribe for or pay for shares and who find that they may have spent their money for no

242 *Henry Head & Co v Ropner Holdings Ltd* [1952] Ch 124; *Shearer (Inspector of Taxes) v Bercain Ltd* [1980] 3 All ER 295. See Ussher, 'Doubts Remain on *Shearer v Bercain*' (1982) 3 Co Law 28.

243 *Henry Head & Co v Ropner Holdings Ltd* [1952] Ch 124; *Shearer (Inspector of Taxes) v Bercain Ltd* [1980] 3 All ER 295.

244 Sections 131–134 of the Companies Act 1985 (UK).

245 Section 227 of the CA 1990.

246 Section 89(1) of the CA 1963.

247 *Re Sugar Distributors Ltd* [1995] 2 IR 194.

return because of a defect in the relevant transaction of which they had no knowledge and could not be expected to have had any knowledge. He stated:

> 'That policy is quite clear. A share in a company is, in effect, a bundle of proprietary rights which can be sold or exchanged for money or other valuable consideration. If it should transpire that shares were created, issued or transferred in circumstances which gave rise to doubts as to the validity of the transaction in question, persons who had innocently subscribed or paid for the shares could find that they had spent their money for no return, because of a defect in the relevant transaction of which they had no knowledge and could not be expected to have any knowledge. It seems clear that s 89 was enacted in order to enable the possible hardship involved to such persons to be avoided, if it could be done in a manner which would not be unjust or inequitable having regard to the interests of any other persons who were or might be affected by the transactions in question[248].'

Moreover, the learned judge held that the court must only validate the transaction if it is possible to do so in a manner which will not produce unjust or inequitable results having regard to the interests of any other persons who were or might be affected by the transaction in question. In this case, the interests of the revenue were at stake. Keane J held that the section cannot be invoked where the purpose of the application is to retrospectively validate seriously irregular transactions and thereby obtain for the company a tax advantage to which it would not otherwise have been legitimately entitled.

[8.070] In *Re Lake Communications Ltd*[249], however, Laffoy J granted an order declaring a defective allotment to be valid. In that case, a share-for-share swap agreement between the corporate members of a group of companies was found to be defective because the authorised share capital of the petitioner company, Lake Communications Ltd, was never increased to enable a valid allotment of shares to be swapped under the share-for-share swap agreement with the sole shareholder in the company, Inter-Tel Lake Limited; moreover, no valid resolution authorising the allotment was ever passed. Laffoy J gave full consideration to Keane J's judgment in *Re Sugar Distributors*, and also to a number of Australian authorities[250], before finding that the facts in the case before her warranted the making of the order validating the allotment. She stated:

> 'Returning to the question whether it would be just and equitable to validate the creation of the necessary shares and their allotment to the Sole Member pursuant to s 89, I am satisfied that it would. This application is non-contentious and could not be otherwise. The only parties affected are the Petitioner and the Sole Member. No third party could be prejudiced by the validating of the increase in the authorised share capital of the Petitioner and the allotment to the Sole Member. There is no shareholder other than the Sole Member. No creditor could be prejudiced. I am satisfied that the objective of the transactions embodied in the Exchange Agreements was to effect a restructuring within the Mitel Group, not to gain a tax advantage. Having regard to the evidence, and, in particular, the evidence furnished to the Revenue Commissioners with a view to obtaining relief from stamp duty on the share transfers to the Petitioner, I consider it reasonable to infer that the validation of the transaction would not involve any prejudice to the Revenue

248 *Re Sugar Distributors Ltd* [1995] 2 IR 194 at 207.

249 *Re Lake Communications Ltd* [2011] IEHC 455.

250 *Re Farnell Electronic Components Pty Ltd* (1997) 25 ACSR 345; *Moran v Moranco Enterprises Pty Ltd* (1996) 22 ACSR 65; *Re Onslow Salt Pty Ltd* (2003) 45 ACSR 322.

Commissioners. There are no public policy considerations which would militate against validating the increase in the authorised share capital of the Petitioner or the allotment to the Sole Member. On the contrary, public policy would seem to dictate that the Sole Member, which is a limited company, should be put in the position of validly obtaining what it bargained for under the Exchange Agreements, lest its members or creditors be prejudiced by its defective title to 283,745 ordinary shares in the Petitioner. I accept that the failure to take the formal steps to increase the share capital of the Petitioner in accordance with law and to effect a valid allotment to the Sole Member pursuant to the Exchange Agreements was due to an oversight in July 2009 in the implementation of complex transactions. I think the probability is that the oversight is attributable to the solicitor who was dealing with the matter at the time, who has since ceased to be employed by the Petitioner's solicitors. As submitted by counsel for the Petitioner, validation of the allotment could not be regarded as a charter for careless implementation of regulatory and contractual formalities in relation to company transactions[251].'

As there were no third parties prejudiced by the validation of the allotment, and there were no public policy issues, Laffoy J further found it that it was unnecessary to give any party notice of the petition before making the order.

Shareholders' rights and duties

[8.071] Shareholders' rights and interests are determined by reference to the terms of issue of their shares, which, in turn, must be authorised by the company's constitutional documents and any necessary resolutions. Model reg 2 of Table A provides simply that shares may be issued 'with such rights or restrictions as the company may by ordinary resolution determine'. In each case, a shareholder's rights should be determined by reference 'to the terms of the instrument which contains the bargain which they have made with the company and each other'[252]. Too much reliance should not be placed on judicial decisions dealing with the rights of shareholders in other companies, unless the clause or term in question is identical[253].

[8.072] The principal rights that shares generally confer are:

(a) the right to *dividend*, if, while the company is a going concern, a dividend is duly declared;

(b) the right to attend and *vote* at meetings of the company;

(c) the right, in the winding up of the company, after the payment of the company's debts, to receive a proportionate part of the *capital* or otherwise participate in the distribution of the assets of the company; and

(d) statutory rights to notices, information, and to seek relief against the company, which are conferred by the Companies Acts.

Each of the above will now be considered in turn; then consideration will be given to the duties of a shareholder.

---

251 *Re Lake Communications Ltd* [2011] IEHC 455 at para 4.6 of the judgment.

252 *Scottish Insurance Corp v Wilson & Clyde Coal Co* [1949] AC 462 at 488.

253 *Cork Electric Supply Co v Concannon* [1932] IR 314.

(a) Dividend

[8.073] A dividend is a distribution out of a company's profits[254] to its members. Every company has the implied power, subject to any restrictions which may be imposed by its memorandum, to apply its profits to the distribution of a dividend amongst its members. This inherent power of a company to divide its profits amongst its members is a reflection of the fact that companies are vehicles through which profits may be made. That said, however, there is no legal obligation on the company to pay a dividend, even where there are sufficient distributable profits available, unless the company's constitutional documents provide otherwise. As Lord Davey said in *Burland v Earle*[255]:

> 'Their Lordships are not aware of any principle which compels a joint stock company while a going concern to divide the whole of its profits among its shareholders. Whether the whole or any part should be divided, or what portion should be divided and what portion retained, are entirely questions of internal management ... and the court has no jurisdiction to control or review their decision[256].'

Dividends are considered here under the following headings:

- (i) Entitlement to dividend where the company is a going concern;
- (ii) Forfeiture of dividend;
- (iii) Entitlement to dividend where the company is being wound up;
- (iv) Declaration of dividend;
- (v) Form of dividend.

(i) Entitlement to dividend where the company is a going concern

[8.074] A shareholder has no right to dividend while the company is a going concern until the dividend is *declared and payable*[257]. Once it is declared and payable, however, the shareholder is entitled to sue the company for arrears of his proportion as a contract debt in the same way as an ordinary creditor of the company may sue for a debt[258]. This debt is one which is personal to the shareholder; thus, after a dividend has been declared, a transfer of the share and registration of the transferee as a member of the company does not entitle the transferee to sue the company for the dividend. Whether he may sue the transferor, however, depends upon the terms of the transfer[259].

The holders of *preference shares* will generally be entitled to claim arrears of a declared dividend out of subsequently declared dividends in priority to ordinary shareholders. Preference shares are examined at para **[8.102]** below.

---

[254] The profits available for such a distribution are considered in Ch 10, *The Maintenance of Capital,* at para **[10.089]**.

[255] *Burland v Earle* [1902] AC 83,at 95.

[256] The court, since the introduction of s 205 of the CA 1963, now appears to have some power of control in relation to dividends; see para **[8.078]** *post* and, generally, Ch 11, *Shareholders' Remedies*.

[257] *Re Drogheda Steampacket Co Ltd* [1903] IR 512; *Bond v Barrow Haematite Steel Co* [1902] 1 Ch 353.

[258] *Re Drogheda Steampacket Co Ltd* [1903] IR 512; *Bond v Barrow Haematite Steel Co* [1902] 1 Ch 353; *Re Belfast Empire Theatre of Varieties* [1963] IR 41. The company does not hold the unclaimed dividend on trust for the shareholder.

[259] *Black v Homersham* (1878) 4 Ex D 24; *Re Wimbush* [1940] Ch 92.

[8.075] The time limit for the bringing of an action against a company in respect of dividends is 12 years from the date of declaration or the declared date of payment, whichever is the later. In *Re Belfast Empire Theatre of Varieties*[260], a case where a company was unable to pay declared dividends to a number of shareholders who could not be traced, Kenny J explained:

> 'Section 11(1) of the Statute of Limitations 1957 provides:- 'The following actions shall not be brought after the expiration of six years from the date on which the cause of action accrued ... (*a*) actions founded on simple contract', while sub-s 5 of the same section provides:- 'The following actions shall not be brought after the expiration of twelve years on which the cause of action accrued ... (*a*) an action on an instrument under seal...'.The right of [a member of] a company to receive dividends is conferred by the articles of association of the company; it is a right derived from the contract which the articles create between the company and each of its members ... and although the contract is not sealed by each member or by the company, the effect of [s 25 of the CA 1963] is that the contract binds the company and the members as if it were under seal. The appropriate statutory period is the period of twelve years ...'

The 12-year limitation period has been forsaken by the English courts in favour of the six-year period applicable to simple contract debts. In *Re Compania de Electricidad de la Provencia de Buenos Aires Ltd*[261], Slade J held that the right of a shareholder to a properly declared dividend was a simple contract debt, since although s 14 of the Companies Act 1985 (UK) (which is materially the same as s 25 of the Irish CA 1963) deems the contractual effect of the articles to be under seal, it does not state that the company is deemed to have sealed the contract but only that the members are deemed to have sealed it. It remains to be seen whether the Irish courts will follow this decision.

(ii) Forfeiture of dividend

[8.076] The articles may provide for the forfeiture of dividends which are not claimed within a period less than 12 years. Such clauses will be construed strictly by the courts. In *Ward v Dublin North City Milling Co Ltd*[262], a limited company provided in its articles that 'Notice of each dividend declared shall be given to each member in the manner hereinafter mentioned, and all dividends unclaimed for three years after having been declared may by a resolution of the directors be forfeited for the benefit of the company'. Although notices of meetings at which dividends were to be declared were sent to one of two joint owners of certain shares (who was known to be dead), none were sent to the other joint owner. When the latter died, his executrix brought an action for arrears of dividends stretching back over five years. Upholding her claim, O'Connor MR said[263]:

> 'I read this article as meaning that the unclaimed dividends to be forfeited are dividends of which notice has been given, for I cannot read the earlier part of the article apart from the latter. Arts 140 and 141 prescribe how notices are to be given ... Now, provisions such as these in arts 140 and 141 are absolutely necessary for the convenient despatch of business and a company's protection. But they should not be used dishonestly or unfairly, and if the

260 *Re Belfast Empire Theatre of Varieties* [1963] IR 41.

261 *Re Compania de Electricidad de la Provencia de Buenos Aires Ltd* [1980] Ch 146.

262 *Ward v Dublin North City Milling Co Ltd* [1919] 1 IR 5.

263 *Ward v Dublin North City Milling Co Ltd* [1919] 1 IR 5 at 11.

officers of a company have actual knowledge that one of two joint shareholders is dead, and if with that knowledge present to their mind they issue notices to the deceased shareholder and no notice to the surviving registered shareholder, the company is in such default that it cannot rely upon a formal notice which in substance is no notice. That would be a perversion of the purpose for which the articles were framed.'

Furthermore, although the time limit for the bringing of an action against the company in respect of dividend has passed, the company may, by its conduct, revive the right of action. In *Re Compania de Electricidad de la Provencia de Buenos Aires Ltd*[264], Slade J held that a balance sheet showing an entry acknowledging unclaimed arrears of dividend may amount to an acknowledgment which will revive the right of action, provided that the person claiming the right can prove receipt of the relevant accounts. In such circumstances the time limit will begin afresh from the date of acknowledgement[265].

(iii) Entitlement to dividend where the company is being wound up

[8.077] A shareholder's entitlement to a dividend can arise only before a winding up commences. Declared dividends cease to be debts owed by the company once a winding up occurs, and the shareholder's right to sue in respect of the dividend is deferred until the debts owed to the company's ordinary creditors have been satisfied. This is because the capital available for distribution in the form of dividend ceases in a liquidation to be 'profit' and becomes instead part of the assets to be distributed in the winding up. In *Wilson (Inspector of Taxes) v Dunnes Stores (Cork) Ltd*[266], Kenny J explained this principle as follows:

> '[W]hile what is distributed to the members in a winding up may be identified as having been profits, it is not distributed as profits but as a distribution in the winding up of the company or (as some call it) surplus assets. In a winding up of a company there may be liabilities which are related to the amount of the profits made before the company went into liquidation or the articles may confer on some shareholders a right to a dividend related to the amount of the profits before the company goes into liquidation but these are cases of the discharge of liabilities incurred before liquidation. What remains after discharge of liabilities is distributed among the shareholders not as profits but as surplus assets or as a distribution in the winding up. All the cases are consistent with this view and, on close examination, they refute the contention that what is distributed in a winding up is in any sense profits of the company[267].'

This does not mean that the shareholder loses his entitlement to the dividend; it may be taken into account in calculating the extent of the shareholder's right of participation in the distribution of assets in the winding up. To this end, s 207(1)(g) of the CA 1963 provides:

> 'a sum due to any member of the company, in his character of a member, by way of dividends, profits or otherwise, shall not be deemed to be a debt of the company, payable to that member in a case of competition between himself and any other creditor not a

---

264 *Re Compania de Electricidad de la Provencia de Buenos Aires Ltd* [1980] Ch 146.

265 Section 56 of the Statute of Limitations 1957.

266 *Wilson (Inspector of Taxes) v Dunnes Stores (Cork) Ltd* (22 January 1976) HC, Kenny J.

267 *Wilson (Inspector of Taxes) v Dunnes Stores (Cork) Ltd* (22 January 1976) HC, Kenny J at p 8 of the transcript. See also *IRC v Blott* [1920] 2 KB 657; *IRC v Burrell* [1924] 2 KB 52; *Re Lafayette* [1950] IR 100; and *Re Imperial Hotel (Cork) Ltd* [1950] IR 115.

> member of the company, but any such sum may be taken into account for the purpose of the final adjustment of the rights of the contributories among themselves.'

As shall be seen, the articles and the terms of issue of certain preference shares entitle the holders to rank ahead of other shareholders in the distribution of assets in a winding up[268].

(iv) Declaration of dividend

[8.078] The Companies Acts do not provide who shall declare a dividend nor do they stipulate when a dividend shall become payable; these are matters of internal management. Model reg 116 of Table A provides simply that:

> 'The Company in general meeting *may* declare dividends, but no dividend shall exceed the amount recommended by the directors[269].'

Since the recommendation of the general meeting must not exceed the amount, if any, recommended by the directors, the directors have, effectively, the last say as to when a dividend is to be declared and how much is to be made available for that purpose. There is no way in which the shareholders can force the directors to recommend a dividend[270]. The general meeting may get around this difficulty, however, by removing the directors through an ordinary resolution under s 182 of the CA 1963[271], or by altering the articles through a special resolution under s 15 of the CA 1963[272]. A failure by the directors to declare dividends may, in any event, amount to *oppression* within the meaning of s 205 of the CA 1963, where, for example, the directors cause themselves to be paid excessive salaries which consume the profits which would otherwise be available for distribution in the form of dividend. The wide discretion given to the courts to award relief for a breach of that section may include the power to order that a dividend be declared[273].

Model reg 117 of Table A also allows, but does not require, the directors to pay *interim* dividends. It provides:

> 'The directors may from time to time pay to the members such interim dividends as appear to the directors to be justified from the profits of the company.'

The power of the directors to pay interim dividends does not require the sanction of the general meeting.

(v) Form of dividend

[8.079] Dividends are *prima facie* payable in cash; but, if the articles permit, a company may pay them by the distribution of non-cash assets such as shares, debentures or specific items of property[274]. Model reg 123 of Table A authorises the payment of dividend by cheque.

---

268 See para **[8.108]** *et seq, post*.

269 Italics added.

270 See, eg, *Scott v Scott* [1943] 1 All ER 582.

271 See Ch 13; *Corporate Governance: Management by the Directors*, at para **[13.077]** *et seq*.

272 See Ch 3; *Constitutional Documentation*, at para **[3.056]** *et seq*.

273 See generally Ch 11, *Shareholders' Remedies*, at para **[11.073]** *et seq*.

274 *Hoole v Great Western Railway* (1867) 3 Ch App 262. The articles of public companies may commonly give their shareholders the choice of electing to take shares in the company in lieu of cash dividends.

(b) Attendance and voting at meetings

[8.080] The mechanics of calling and attending meetings of the company is considered in Ch 14[275]. Unless a company's articles otherwise provide, notice of general meetings must be given to every shareholder of the company[276], even where the terms of issue of the shares and the articles confer no right on the shareholder to attend or to vote[277]. At common law, a meeting will be invalid unless each shareholder entitled to receive notice of the meeting has done so[278]. It is usual, therefore, for the articles to provide that accidental failure to give notice, or the non-receipt of notice, shall not invalidate the meeting[279].

A body corporate which is a member may authorise, by resolution of its directors, such person as it thinks fit to act as its representative at any meeting of the company[280]. The representative is not a proxy and therefore there is no need to notify the company of his appointment before the meeting.

[8.081] Every shareholder who appears on the register of members and who is entitled to attend meetings of the company is also entitled to vote on any questions which are to be decided by the meeting, unless the terms of issue of their shares and the company's constitutional documents otherwise provide. It is not uncommon, however, for the terms of issue and the articles to restrict or abrogate the voting rights associated with certain classes of shares; conversely, some shares may be given loaded voting rights[281].

(i) Show of hands

[8.082] Questions arising at meetings are to be decided, in the first place, by a show of hands[282]. This is a common law rule which applies automatically unless the company's constitutional documents provide otherwise[283], and it is one which is repeated in model reg 59 of Table A. In the absence of a contrary provision in the company's memorandum or articles, each shareholder will be entitled on a show of hands to *only one vote*, regardless of the size of his shareholding[284].

(ii) Poll

[8.083] A show of hands is often a very inadequate means for determining the wishes of the whole company; accordingly, common law and statute[285] both provide that a shareholder may demand a *poll*. Where voting takes place by poll, every member has

---

275 See Ch 14, *Corporate Governance: Meetings*.

276 Section 134(a) of the CA 1963.

277 *Re MacKenzie & Co Ltd* [1916] 2 Ch 450.

278 *Smyth v Darley* (1849) 2 HL Cas 789.

279 See Ch 14, *Corporate Governance: Meetings*, at para **[14.048]** *et seq*.

280 Section 139 of the CA 1963. If the body corporate is in liquidation, it is the liquidator who makes the appointment: *Hillman v Crystal Bowl Amusements Ltd* [1973] 1 All ER 379.

281 See para **[8.110]** *post*.

282 See Ch 14, *Corporate Governance: Meetings*, at para **[14.062]** *et seq*.

283 *Re Horbury Bridge Co* (1879) 11 Ch D 109.

284 See also model reg 63 of Table A.

285 Section 137 of the CA 1963. See Ch 14, *Corporate Governance: Meetings*, at para **[14.067]** *et seq*.

one vote in respect of each share held by him, unless the articles otherwise provide[286]. Model reg 63 of Table A repeats the one share/one vote principle, but model reg 62 gives the chairman a casting vote where there is equality of votes. In practice, a poll is usually conducted by each shareholder signing a piece of paper stating whether he is for or against the motion and the number of votes held by him.

Section 137 of the CA 1963 renders void any provision in the articles[287] that excludes the right to demand a poll on any question other than the election of a chairman or adjournment, or that requires a demand for a poll to be made by more than four[288] members having the right to vote at the meeting. Moreover, s 137(1)(b) provides that any provision that makes a demand for a poll ineffective shall also be void where such a demand is made by:

- members representing not less than 10% of the total voting rights of all members entitled to vote at the meeting;
- members holding shares paid up to the extent of not less than 10% of the total sum paid up on all the shares conferring a right to vote at the meeting.

Model reg 59 of Table A is more generous in allowing for a poll where demanded by at least three members. Where there are less than three shareholders who wish to demand a poll, they may, in advance of the meeting, vest some of their shares in nominees and obtain their proxies[289] for the meeting; but they may encounter difficulty if the directors refuse to register the nominees in the register of members[290].

A poll does not have to be preceded by a vote on a show of hands[291], but where it is, a poll duly demanded nullifies the show of hands[292]. Neither does the poll have to take place there and then unless the articles otherwise provide. Model articles 60 and 62 of Table A allow the poll to be taken 'in such manner as the chairman directs' and 'at such time as the chairman of the meeting directs' unless the poll relates to a question of the election of a chairman or an adjournment, when it must take place 'forthwith'. A postponement of the meeting until a subsequent day upon which a poll is to be held is not an adjournment[293].

(iii) Proxies

[8.084] At common law, there is no right to vote by proxy. However, as will be seen in Ch 14[294], this position has been modified by s 136 of the CA 1963.

286 Section 134(e) of the CA 1963.

287 Notably, there seems to be no prohibition on such a provision appearing in the memorandum. Such a provision would not, apparently, be contrary to common law either: *R v Wimbledon Local Board* (1882) 8 QBD 459.

288 The section refers to 'not less than five' members.

289 See para **[8.084]** *post*.

290 See Ch 9, *Share Transfer*, at para **[9.042]** *et seq*.

291 *Re Credit Finance Bank plc* (9 June 1989) HC, Costello J.

292 *Anthony v Seger* (1879) 1 Haag Cas Con 9.

293 *R v Chester* (1843) 1 Ad & El 342.

294 See Ch 14, *Corporate Governance: Meetings*, at para **[14.074]** *et seq*.

(c) Participation in a winding up

[8.085] Where a company is being wound up, once the creditors and the expenses of the liquidator have been paid, shareholders are returned their capital investment in the shares and any remaining property of the company is distributed among the shareholders in proportion to their rights and interests in the company, unless the articles otherwise provide[295]. Where the memorandum (as opposed to the articles) provides that no part of the assets is to be distributed to the members, the surplus assets are still distributable amongst the members[296]. Where, however, the memorandum further provides that the surplus assets are to be distributed in a special manner, such as to a charity, the courts have given effect to the provision notwithstanding the absence of equivalent provisions in the articles[297].

Prima facie, the distribution of surplus assets is to be in proportion to the nominal value of each share[298], and, as has been seen[299], sums due to a member which are not treated as creditors' claims in the liquidation (eg, dividends, etc) are to be taken into account when adjusting the rights of shareholders to participate in the surplus. The articles and terms of issue of some shares may provide for preferential rights of participation in a winding up; see para **[8.108]** *et seq, post*. The topic of distribution in a winding up is considered in further detail in Ch 25[300].

(d) Shareholders' statutory rights

[8.086] Apart from the principal rights of shareholders discussed above, the Companies Acts also confer a number of ancillary rights, which include the following:

- to receive a copy of the memorandum and articles of association and any Act of the Oireachtas which alters the memorandum[301];
- to inspect and obtain copies of the minutes of general meetings and resolutions[302];
- to inspect and receive a copy of the registers kept by the company, such as the register of members[303], the register of directors and secretaries[304], and the register of directors' shareholdings[305];
- to receive copies of balance sheets and directors' and auditors' reports[306];

---

295 See s 275 of the CA 1963.

296 *Re Merchant Navy Supply Association Ltd* (1947) 177 LT 386.

297 *Liverpool and District Hospital for Diseases of the Heart v Attorney General* [1981] 1 All ER 994.

298 *Re London India Rubber Company* (1868) LR 5 Eq 519.

299 At para **[8.077]** *ante*.

300 See Ch 25, *Realisation and Distribution of Assets on Liquidation*.

301 Section 29 of the CA 1963.

302 Section 143(3) (in respect of copy special resolutions) and s 146(2) (in respect of minutes of general meetings) of the CA 1963.

303 Section 119 of the CA 1963.

304 Section 195 of the CA 1963.

305 Section 190 of the CA 1963.

306 Section 159 of the CA 1963.; see generally Ch 17, *Financial Statements, Audit and Annual Return*.

- to demand and receive the balance sheets of a subsidiary company for the preceding 10 years[307];
- to exercise pre-emption rights where the company proposes to allot unissued equity securities which are to be wholly paid up in cash[308];
- to petition the court for the winding up of the company[309];
- to petition the court for relief in cases of oppression[310].

(e) Shareholders' 'personal' rights

[8.087] Not all the rights associated with a share may be enforced by the shareholder in his personal or individual capacity. Yet the classification of certain rights as personal is of particular importance, for, as shall be seen in Ch 11[311], company law has established a rule (known as the rule in *Foss v Harbottle*) that an individual shareholder cannot generally initiate proceedings in respect of a wrong done to the company, rather than to him personally. This is so even though the wrong suffered by the company will almost certainly impinge upon his rights as a shareholder. This rule is of no application where the individual is alleging that the wrong has been done to him *personally*[312].

[8.088] Neither the courts nor the legislature have provided a uniform formula for identifying whether a right associated with a share is personal or otherwise. At this juncture, it may prove useful to consider situations in which shareholders have been held to have personal rights. An examination of the case law shows that personal rights arise in at least the following situations:

(i) where those rights stem from the 's 25 contract' and the particular right is considered *too fundamental to the individual* to be allowed to be abrogated by the majority of shareholders;

(ii) where those rights stem from the directors' fiduciary duties in the course of *direct dealings* between the directors and the individual shareholder;

(iii) where the right is given to the shareholder *by statute*.

A brief examination of these categories will now follow. However, it must be stressed that the list is neither conclusive nor closed – for these are no more than miscellaneous examples of situations in which a shareholder's rights have been held to be personal and actionable by a shareholder individually.

(i) Section 25 rights

[8.089] Shareholders have contractual rights by virtue of s 25 of the CA 1963 which makes them party to a contract with the company and the other shareholders which is contained in the memorandum and articles of association – provided that the right is given to them *qua* member, and not in another capacity such as solicitor or accountant of the company[313].

---

307 Section 154 of the CA 1963.

308 Section 23 of the C(A)A 1983; see para **[8.056]** *ante*.

309 Section 213 of the CA 1963; see generally Ch 23, *Winding up Companies*.

310 Section 205 of the CA 1963; see generally Ch 11, *Shareholders' Remedies*.

311 See Ch 11, *Shareholder's* Remedies, at para **[11.103]** *et seq*.

312 See, eg, *Edwards v Halliwell* [1950] 2 All ER 1064, *per* Jenkins LJ at 1067.

313 See Ch 3, *Constitutional Documentation*, at para **[3.099]** *et seq*.

Many of these rights stem from the articles of association of the company, and, as has already been seen[314], many breaches of the articles can subsequently be regularised by ratification by the majority. In such circumstances, the courts will be slow to let an individual shareholder proceed against the company or the member in breach, because to do so would be to 'interfere in the domestic affairs of a company or association on the ground of mere irregularity in form in the conduct of those affairs'[315]. The following examples, however, have been held to be breaches of the articles which could not subsequently be regularised:

(a) breach of rules which provide that subscriptions may only be increased with the consent of a two-thirds majority of members[316];

(b) breach of articles requiring the directors to purchase an outgoing member's shares[317];

(c) breach of articles providing that no decision of the board of directors should be valid where either of two particular directors dissented[318].

To the extent that actions (for injunction and declaration) by individual shareholders in respect of these breaches were permitted, the breaches may be described as breaches of the shareholders' *personal* rights; but it must be stressed that the shareholder in each case was attempting to protect his personal interests, and not those of the company as a whole.

Where rights stem from the objects clause in the memorandum of association, retrospective regularisation will not be permitted[319]. In such cases it is well established that an individual shareholder can bring injunctive or declaratory proceedings to restrain the company from acting *ultra vires* in breach of its objects[320].

[8.090] A shareholder's vote is an individual contractual right stemming from the company's constitutional documents. It is a kind of property right, which he may use as he pleases. Where the company denies him this right he may obtain an injunction or take some other form of legal action to restrain the company from so acting. In *Pender v Lushington*[321], Jessel MR proclaimed:

> In all cases of this kind, where men exercise their rights of property, they exercise their rights from some motive adequate or inadequate and I have always considered the law to be that those who have the rights of property are entitled to exercise them, whatever their motives may be for such exercise... This is an action by Mr Pender himself. He is a member of the company and whether he votes with the majority or the minority he is entitled to have his vote recorded – an individual right in respect of which he has a right to sue ... He has a right to say, 'Whether I vote in the majority or minority, you shall record my vote, as that is a right of property belonging to my interest in this company and if you refuse to record my vote I will institute legal proceedings against you to compel you.'

---

314 See Ch 3, *Constitutional Documentation*, at para **[3.085]** *et seq*.

315 *Per* Jenkins LJ in *Edwards v Halliwell* [1950] 2 All ER 1064.

316 *Per* Jenkins LJ in *Edwards v Halliwell* [1950] 2 All ER 1064.

317 *Rayfield v Hands* [1960] Ch 1.

318 *Quin & Axtons v Salmon* [1909] 1 Ch 311.

319 See Ch 7, *Corporate Contracts, Capacity and Authority*, at para **[7.045]** *et seq*.

320 *Simpson v Westminster Palace Hotel* (1860) 8 HLC 712; *Smith v Croft (No 2)* [1988] Ch 114.

321 *Pender v Lushington* (1877) 6 Ch D 70.

> What is the answer to such an action? It seems to me it can be maintained as a matter of substance and that there is no technical difficulty in maintaining it ...'

(ii) Directors' fiduciary duties

[8.091] Case law has also established that in certain circumstances the directors owe certain fiduciary duties[322] to individual shareholders personally. This normally arises where the directors are involved in direct dealings with the shareholder concerned.

The issue first arose in *Percival v Wright*[323]. In that case, the directors were involved in negotiating the sale of the company's undertaking to third parties. Without disclosing the negotiations to certain shareholders, they purchased those shareholders' shares. When the shareholders learnt of the negotiations (which, in the event, were abortive) they sought to rescind the sale of their shares to the directors. Swinfen-Eady J rejected their claim on the basis that, on the facts, there had been no breach of duty – which suggests that a personal duty was in fact owed to the shareholders, but was not breached.

The duty was again recognised in *Allen v Hyatt*[324], where the directors, who were negotiating an amalgamation of the company with a third party, represented to certain shareholders that they would act, in effect, as agents for them. Those shareholders then gave the directors options to purchase the shares. The directors subsequently exercised these options at a profit and claimed to be entitled to retain that profit. The Privy Council found that the directors' actions amounted to a breach of a fiduciary duty owed to the shareholders concerned and made them accountable to those shareholders for the profits.

It may be observed, in any event, that in many private companies there is little likelihood of problems such as these arising because the shareholders and the directors will often be the same persons.

(iii) Statutory rights

[8.092] The statutory rights given to shareholders (listed at para **[8.086]** above) are enjoyed, exercisable, and enforceable by a shareholder in his personal capacity.

(f) Shareholders' duties

[8.093] The principal duty of the shareholder, *qua* shareholder, is to pay the company the amount, if any, which remains outstanding in respect of the price[325] agreed for the share in the original allotment[326]. Such monies become payable by the shareholder when a *call* is made upon him by the company, or, where the terms of issue provide for payment in instalments, when the dates stated in the terms have arrived. Where shares are to be paid for by instalments, model reg 19 of Table A provides that all the provisions of the articles regulating payment of interest and expenses, forfeiture or other matters shall apply as if such sum had become payable by virtue of a call.

---

[322] See Ch 15, *Duties of Directors and Other Officers*, at para **[15.024]** *et seq*.

[323] *Percival v Wright* [1902] Ch 421.

[324] *Allen v Hyatt* (1914) TLR 444. See also *Coleman v Myers* [1977] 2 NZLR 225.

[325] The price will exceed the nominal value of the share where it is issued at a premium; see para **[8.066]** *ante*.

[326] See para **[8.060]** *ante*.

A shareholder's liability for past and future calls continues where the company is being wound up, since the uncalled amount forms part of the assets to be made available for distribution in the liquidation. In the private company, it may be recalled, a shareholder's liability to contribute to the company in a winding up is restricted to the amount, if any, unpaid on his shares[327].

Apart from the foregoing duty, the other duties of shareholders include the duty to account to the company for any dividend received in contravention of the rules governing profits available for distribution; and the duty to answer personally for the company's liabilities where statute or common law require. These topics are considered elsewhere in this book[328].

[8.094] The shareholder's liability in respect of a call is contractual in nature, stemming from the terms of issue and the s 25 contract. After a call has been made and it has matured into a debt, the amount due on foot of the call may not be recovered by the company after the expiration of 12 years from the date upon which it became due[329].

The liability of a shareholder for future calls on his shares is transferred to any shareholder who takes the share by way of transfer or transmission once the latter's name is entered on the register of members, even though he may be a minor[330]. Where shares are transferred to a minor, however, the transferring shareholder continues to be liable for all future calls for so long as the minor is registered as a member. The company may not waive its right to uncalled capital if the waiver would cause the company to receive less than the nominal value of the shares, because to do so would result in the issue of those shares at a discount in breach of the rules of capital maintenance[331].

[8.095] The procedure for the making of calls is usually contained in the articles. Model regs 15 to 21 of Table A contain provisions in relation to calls which are adopted by most private companies. Under those articles, the power to make calls from time to time is given to the directors, provided that no call shall exceed one-fourth of the nominal value of the share or be payable at less than one month from the date fixed for payment of the last preceding call[332]. Each shareholder is required to pay, subject to receiving at least 14 days' notice) the amount of every call made on him to the persons and at the times and places fixed by the directors[333]. If a call is not paid before or on the date appointed by the directors, it carries interest at such rate not exceeding 5% *per annum* as the directors may determine[334].

The power of the directors to make calls must be exercised in good faith and for the benefit of the company as a whole[335]. Where it is exercised *mala fide*, an injunction may be obtained to restrain the call[336]. Such relief may be difficult to obtain in practice,

327 See Ch 4, *Incorporation and its Consequences*, at para **[4.081]**.

328 See Ch 10, *The Maintenance of Capital*, at para **[10.104]**, and Ch 5, *Disregarding Separate Legal Personality*, at para **[5.076]** *et seq*, respectively.

329 Section 25(2) of the CA 1963.

330 *Cork and Bandon Railway v Cazenove* (1847) 10 QB 935.

331 See, generally, Ch 10, *The Maintenance of Capital*.

332 Regulation 15, Table A.

333 Regulation 15, Table A.

334 Regulation 18, Table A.

335 *Alexander v Automatic Telephone Co* [1900] 2 Ch 56.

336 *Odessa Tramways v Mendel* (1878) 8 Ch D 235.

however, since the onus of proving bad faith rests on the shareholder[337]. Calls should be made *pari passu* unless the articles otherwise provide, and should certainly not favour a shareholder who is a director above the other shareholders. Although model reg 20 of Table A allows directors to differentiate between the holders of shares as to the amount of calls to be paid and the time of payment, the principle of equal calls should still not be departed from unless there is very good reason[338]. Furthermore, the resolution of the directors making the call must be passed at a properly convened directors' meeting, and a proper entry must be made in the minutes; otherwise the call may be invalid[339].

[8.096] The directors, if the articles permit, may also receive payment in advance of calls from any shareholders willing to advance such sums, and may credit the sum with interest not to exceed a specified percentage *per annum*. The amount of interest allowed must not be excessive[340]. Model reg 21 of Table A permits directors to receive payment in advance of calls and permits the directors to pay such interest not exceeding 5% *per annum* (unless the company in general meeting otherwise directs) as may be agreed upon by the directors and the shareholder paying in advance. Such powers must be exercised *bona fide* and in the best interests of the company. Thus, in *Sykes'* case[341], where the directors of an insolvent company exercised the power to accept payment in advance of calls in respect of their own shares, and then used the money obtained to pay their own directors' fees, it was held that the power was not exercised in good faith. The entire transaction was held to be ineffectual and the directors were held to remain liable on their shares.

[8.097] The articles generally provide for the forfeiture of shares for non-payment of calls. The topic of forfeiture is considered at para **[8.123]** post.

Classes of shares

(a) Preliminary presumptions

[8.098] All shares are presumed, *prima facie*, to rank *pari passu*, so that each share is presumed to carry the same rights, interests and obligations as every other share. This principle was expressed by Lord Macnaghten in *Birch v Cropper, Re Bridgewater Navigation Co*[342], as follows:

> 'Every person who becomes a member of a company limited by shares of equal amount becomes entitled to a proportionate part in the capital of the company, and, unless it be otherwise provided by the regulations of the company, entitled as a necessary consequence, to the same proportionate part in all the property of the company ...'

Often, it is simply the size of a shareholding which distinguishes the extent of a shareholder's interests and obligations from those of the other shareholders in the company.

---

337 *Odessa Tramways v Mendel* (1878) 8 Ch D 235.

338 *Galloway v Halle Concerts Society Ltd* [1915] 2 Ch 233.

339 *Garden Gully United Quartz Mining Co v McLister* (1875) 1 App Cas 39; *Cornwall Mining Co v Bennett* (1860) H & N 423.

340 *Poole, Jackson and Whyte's case* (1879) 9 Ch D 322.

341 *Sykes' case* (1872) LR 13 Eq 255.

342 *Birch v Cropper, Re Bridgewater Navigation Co* (1899) 14 App Cas 525 at 543.

But where, for example, a company issues shares to persons who merely invest in the company without participating in its management, the company may wish to restrict the rights held by that shareholder, despite the size of his shareholding[343]. This it may do once the memorandum or articles permit the creation of different *classes* of shares with differing rights, since the rights associated with a share stem, largely, from the memorandum and articles in the first place.

(b) Power to create different classes of shares

[8.099] The power to create different classes of shares must appear in either the memorandum or the articles. The power may, but need not necessarily[344], be provided for in the capital clause of the memorandum[345]. More commonly, it is dealt with in the articles, for they are easier to alter than the memorandum. Therefore, model reg 2 of Table A provides:

> 'Without prejudice to any special rights previously conferred on the holders of any existing shares or class of shares, any share in the company may be issued with such preferred, deferred or other special rights or such restrictions, whether in regard to dividend, voting, return of capital or otherwise, as the company may from time to time by ordinary resolution determine.'

In *Andrews v Gas Meter Co*[346], it was held that where the power to create different classes of shares appears in the articles it must not conflict with any provision of the memorandum which expressly requires equality amongst all shareholders. Where such a conflict arises, the provisions of the memorandum will take precedence, but the memorandum itself may be altered to remove the requirement of equality amongst all shareholders. In *Campbell v Rofe*[347], the Privy Council summarised the principles governing the power to create different classes of shares as follows:

> 'While the memorandum must state the amount of capital, divided into shares of a certain fixed amount, provision as to the character of the shares and rights to be attached to them is more properly made by the articles of association, which may be altered from time to time by special resolution of the company. If equality of the shareholders is expressly provided in the memorandum, that cannot be modified by the articles of association. If nothing is said in the memorandum, the articles of association may provide for the issue of the authorised capital in the form of preference shares; if the articles do not so provide, or do provide for equality *inter socios*, the power to issue preference shares may be obtained by alteration of the articles.'

In *Re Powell Cotton's Settlement, Henniker Major v Powell Cotton*[348], Roxburgh J held that it was possible to have sub-classes within a class of shares; but this was not a company law case, and the better view seems to be that each sub-class should be regarded as a separate class[349].

---

343 Or, indeed, it may wish to enlarge certain of the rights associated with the share to encourage the shareholder to invest.

344 *Andrews v Gas Meter Co* [1897] 1 Ch 361.

345 See Ch 3, *Constitutional Documentation*, at para **[3.017]**.

346 *Andrews v Gas Meter Co* [1897] 1 Ch 361.

347 *Campbell v Rofe* [1933] AC 91 at 98.

348 *Re Powell Cotton's Settlement, Henniker Major v Powell Cotton* [1957] Ch 159.

349 See *Re Hellenic and General Trust Ltd* [1975] 3 All ER 382.

(c) *Particular categories of shares*

[8.100] Different classes of shares are usually given distinguishing descriptions, such as 'ordinary shares,' 'preference shares,' and 'deferred shares,' or, quite commonly, 'A shares,' 'B shares,' 'A ordinary shares,' 'B ordinary shares,' etc. It must be stressed that the company is free to choose whatever description it wishes, and the law does not apply any rigid meaning to the description. The company's register of members should show the class of shares of each member[350].

Whatever the label given to a class of shares, company law has established a number of presumptions governing the extent of preferred rights in the absence of stipulation to the contrary. It may prove useful here to attempt a categorisation of some of the more common types of share. Accordingly, the following types of share will be considered here:

- (i) Ordinary shares;
- (ii) Preference shares;
- (iii) Redeemable shares;
- (iv) Deferred or founders' shares;
- (v) Treasury shares;
- (vi) Bonus shares;
- (vii) Employee shares.

(i) Ordinary shares

[8.101] The description 'ordinary shares' is sometimes used to describe that class of shares which confer on their holders the residual rights which have not been conferred on other classes. There should be no mystery about the description – it is simply a means of distinguishing the shares from other classes of shares of restricted or preferred status. Where no separate classes of shares have been created, then all shares may be thought of as ordinary shares.

The rights and duties already considered will normally attach to ordinary shares; but, as has been seen, the rights and duties to be carried by shares are matters for the company. In every case, the terms of issue of the shares and the company's constitutional documents should be referred to when seeking to establish the extent of the shareholder's rights and duties.

(ii) Preference shares

[8.102] The description 'preference shares' is used to describe shares which carry preferential rights over those of the other classes of shares. Such preferential rights may be in respect of any of the rights and duties already discussed; the most common types of preference shares being either:

- (I) preferred as to dividend;
- (II) preferred as to capital;
- (III) preferred as to voting.

Any combination of the above preferences is, of course, possible. However, where the articles and the terms of issue of preference shares confer a preference in respect of only

[350] *Re Performing Rights Society Ltd* [1978] 2 All ER 712.

some of these rights, they do not imply a preference as regards the other rights, because of the principle expressed by Lord Macnaghten in *Birch v Cropper*[351], that *prima facie* all shares rank equally.

(I) Preferred as to dividend

[8.103] Shares which are preferred as to dividend usually entitle the shareholder to be paid his dividend in priority to the ordinary shareholders. The terms of issue of such shares commonly express the preferential right as a right to a percentage *per annum* of the nominal amount of the share. Thus, for example, '10% preference shares' might carry a right to a fixed dividend amounting to 10% of the nominal amount of the share each year. The fact that the right to a preferential dividend is expressed to arise annually should not, however, be taken as meaning that the dividend is to be payable annually, for the terms of issue normally entitle the shareholder to claim his dividend only when a dividend has been declared by the directors. A contrary intention may, however, be divined from the relevant documents. In *Re Lafayette Ltd*[352], the company's articles provided:

> 'The holders of the preference shares shall be entitled to receive out of the profits of the company a cumulative preferential dividend for each year of 6 per cent per annum on the amount for the time being paid on the preference shares held by them respectively, such dividend shall be cumulative, and arrears thereof shall be the first charge on the subsequent profits of the company.'

Kingsmill Moore J held that the effect of the articles was to give the preference shareholders:

> 'a right to their dividend, irrespective of any declaration, and again without any declaration, automatically charge arrears of preference dividends on any future profits[353].'

So, the articles there entitled the preferential holders to a dividend even where one had not been declared by the directors. It should be noted, however, that in order to be payable, the dividend had to come from profits, which nowadays would be referred to as 'distributable profits'.

[8.104] A preferential right as to a dividend is presumed to be a right to a *cumulative* dividend[354]. This means that if a dividend is not declared in any particular year, or if there is a shortfall in the payment in respect of a previously declared preferential dividend, then, when a dividend *is* declared, the shareholder may claim the arrears as well as his dividend in priority to the ordinary shareholders. This presumption can be rebutted by wording which indicates that the dividend is non-cumulative or that the dividend is to be paid only out of the 'profits available for dividends' of a particular year[355].

[8.105] Whether arrears of undeclared cumulative preference dividend are payable in a winding up depends upon the wording of the articles and the terms of issue. If the

---

351 *Birch v Cropper* (1889) 14 App Cas 525.

352 *Re Lafayette Ltd* [1950] IR 100.

353 *Re Lafayette Ltd* [1950] IR 100 at 112.

354 *Webb v Earle* (1875) LR 20 Eq 556; *Re F de Jong and Company Ltd* [1946] Ch 211.

355 *Adair v Old Bushmills Distillery* [1908] WN 24.

wording makes it clear that the entitlement extends to a winding up, the preference shareholders will be entitled to those arrears. Where the preference shares are also preferred as to capital[356] but the articles and the terms of issue are silent as to whether arrears of undeclared preference dividend are payable in a winding up, the courts may nevertheless imply an entitlement to such arrears[357]. Where the preference shareholder's entitlement to dividend depends upon the existence of 'profits available for dividend', the shareholder's preferential right to arrears ceases, because 'profits' are no longer regarded as such where a winding up occurs[358].

[8.106] Claims for arrears of cumulative preference dividend may not be discharged in a winding up until the claims of non-member creditors have been discharged in full[359]. Section 207(1)(g) of the CA 1963 provides that such claims shall not be payable to a member in competition between himself and any other creditor who is not a member of the company. Such claims may, however, be discharged in priority to the claims of the ordinary shareholders. In *Re Imperial Hotel (Cork) Ltd*[360], the articles gave preference shareholders a right to an annual 6% cumulative dividend, including all arrears, 'independent of any recommendation by the board of directors and independent of any declaration of dividend by the company in general meeting'. Gavan Duffy J construed those provisions as giving rise to a *debt*, accruing annually, owed by the company to the preference shareholders. This debt, he found, survived the winding up of the company and was payable by the liquidator in preference to claims for arrears by the ordinary shareholders, but was deferred to the claims of the non-member creditors. He said:

> 'If in every financial year showing profits the company, under its articles, owed a dividend to its preference shareholders without any recommendation or declaration, it incurred a debt to those members under their contract with the corporate body, when the board declared the net profits, if not before ...
>
> I have not overlooked the rule that dividends, properly so called, are not payable on a winding up, when, after payment of the liabilities, the mass of a company's assets, whatever their separate provenance, comes to be allocated among the members entitled; but that rule is immaterial here, if the application of the surplus assets under the [articles'] code for liquidation does not come into play at all, until the debt due to the preference shareholders is discharged out of the moneys available for its payment; and that is the position. I find that the claimants are seeking to enforce payment of a debt due to them by the company; I find that that is one of the liabilities that the liquidator ... is bound to discharge before he distributes the company's property among the members ...; and I find that this liability is in the peculiar position of not being payable *pari passu* with the liabilities generally, because the claimant's debt is deferred debt, not payable in competition with those creditors who are not members of the company, by virtue of [s 207(g) of the CA 1963].'

---

356 See para **[8.108]** *post*.

357 *Re F de Jong & Co Ltd* [1946] Ch 211; *Re E W Savory Ltd* [1951] 2 All ER 1036.

358 *Re Crichton's Oil Co* [1902] 2 Ch 86. See *Wilson (Inspector of Taxes) v Dunnes Stores (Cork) Ltd*, discussed at para **[8.077]** *ante*.

359 Section 207(1)(g) of the CA 1963; see para **[8.077]** *ante*.

360 *Re Imperial Hotel (Cork) Ltd* [1950] IR 115. See also *Re WJ Hall & Co Ltd* [1909] 1 Ch 521, *per* Swinfen-Eady J at 527; and *Re Spanish Prospecting Co Ltd* [1911] 1 Ch 92, *per* Farwell LJ at 107.

[8.107] Shares which are preferred as to dividend are presumed to be *non-participatory* unless the company's constitutional documents and the terms of issue provide otherwise. This means that once the preference shareholders have been paid their fixed dividend they are not entitled to participate in the distribution of the remaining profits along with the ordinary shareholders. Thus, where the profits available for distribution are large, the ordinary dividends may well exceed the preference dividends in value.

In *Will v United Lankat Plantations Co*[361], preference shareholders who had already been paid their preferential dividend of 10% *per annum* sought to participate *equally* with the ordinary shareholders in the distribution of the remaining profits made available for dividend, arguing that the principle in *Birch v Cropper*[362] required equality between all shareholders unless the contrary was stated. The House of Lords rejected their argument on the basis that an expression of preferential rights in relation to one or more of the particular rights of shareholders (eg, dividend, capital, voting, etc) must be taken as an exhaustive definition of those rights. Lord Haldene said[363]:

> '... when you turn to the terms on which the shares are issued you expect to find all the rights as regards dividends specified in the terms of issue. And when you do find these things prescribed it certainly appears to me unnatural to go beyond them.'

This presumption may, of course, be rebutted by appropriate wording[364].

(II) Preferred as to capital

[8.108] Shares which are preferred as to capital entitle the shareholder to have his capital investment in the company repaid in full before the ordinary shareholders are returned their capital in a winding up. As has been seen, however, such preferential entitlement must be created by express provision, because of the presumption expressed in *Birch v Cropper* that *prima facie* all shares rank *pari passu*[365].

[8.109] Shares carrying preferred rights as to return of capital are presumed to be *participatory*, ie, after the return of their capital, the shareholders are presumed to be entitled to participate in the distribution of any surplus assets in the winding up along with the other shareholders. This presumption was found to exist in *Birch v Cropper*, and was applied by the Supreme Court in the case of *Cork Electric Supply Co Ltd v Concannon*[366]. In that case, the preference shareholders were given preferred rights as to dividend (which were expressed to be non-participatory) and preferred rights as to return of capital. The company was being wound up and its assets compulsorily acquired by the ESB, and the company sought directions from the High Court as to whether the preference shareholders' rights of participation should be confined to those contained in the articles or whether they had any further rights of participation in the winding up.

---

361 *Will v United Lankat Plantations Co* [1914] AC 11.

362 *Birch v Cropper* (1889) 14 App Cas 525. See para **[8.098]** *ante*.

363 *Will v United Lankat Plantations Co* [1914] AC 11 at 17.

364 See, eg, *Steel Company of Canada Ltd v Ramsay* [1931] AC 270; *Re Isle of Thanet Electricity Supply Co Ltd* [1950] Ch 161.

365 *Birch v Cropper* (1889) 14 App Cas 525; see para **[8.098]** *ante*.

366 *Cork Electric Supply Co Ltd v Concannon* [1932] IR 314.

Johnson J held that the statement of the rights in the articles should be considered exhaustive; but on appeal the Supreme Court reversed his decision. Kennedy CJ said[367]:

> '... the right to participate in a distribution of surplus assets on a winding up will be taken from preference shareholders by a clause in the Articles of Association delimiting their rights exhaustively to the exclusion of any other rights and ... the question whether a particular clause does so exhaust the rights attached to the preference share exhaustively and exclusively is a question of construction of the particular Articles of Association in each case ...'

The court found that no limitation on the right of the preference shareholders to participate in the distribution of surplus assets in a winding up existed in the articles, and, thus, held the preference shareholders entitled so to participate.

In England, however, this presumption has been departed from in favour of a presumption along the lines of *Will v United Lankat Plantations Co*[368], ie, that a statement of a preference shareholder's right to participate in capital in a winding up will be exhaustive[369]. This approach has been said to reflect the view, commonly held in the commercial world, that a preference share is more like a debenture than a share, since it carries a fixed return[370]. Whether the Irish Supreme Court will move towards this approach remains to be seen.

(III) Preferred as to voting

[8.110] Shares preferred as to voting have created little controversy and few special presumptions pertain to them[371]. Shares which are preferred as to capital or dividend are commonly given no voting rights, or are given voting rights only where their dividend is in arrears, but the extent of voting rights depends in each case on the terms of issue of the shares in question.

(iii) Redeemable shares

[8.111] Preference shares, commonly carrying a right to a fixed dividend, resemble debentures in many ways, and are regarded by companies and business people as a form of quasi-loan capital. In order to enable companies to continue to treat preference shares in a like manner to debentures, s 64 of the CA 1963 permitted the issue of *redeemable preference shares*, which allowed the company to obtain a capital injection when necessary, which could be redeemed or paid-off when finances improved. Special conditions applied to the redemption of redeemable preference shares. That section has now been repealed by s 220 and replaced by s 207 of the CA 1990. Under s 207, a

367 *Cork Electric Supply Co Ltd v Concannon* [1932] IR 314 at 328.

368 *Will v United Lankat Plantations Co* [1914] AC 11; see para **[8.107]** *ante*.

369 *Scottish Insurance Corporation v Wilsons and Clyde Coal Company* [1949] AC 462; *Prudential Assurance Co v Chatterly Whitfield Collieries Co Ltd* [1949] AC 462; *Re Isle of Thanet Electricity Supply Co Ltd* [1950] Ch 161. See Rice, 'Capital Rights of Preference Shares' (1962) Conveyancer (ns) 115; Pickering, 'The Problem of the Preference Share' (1963) 26 MLR 499.

370 See Keane, *Company Law* (4th edn, Bloomsbury Professional, 2007) at para 17.49; Schmitthoff (ed), *Palmer's Company Law* (24th edn, Stevens & Son, 1987), at pp 559–560.

371 As to the uses to which weighted voting rights may be put see Ch 3, *Constitutional Documentation*, at para **[3.053]**.

company may, if authorised by its articles, issue redeemable ordinary or preference shares. The company cannot have only redeemable shares, and redemption can only take place if the shares are fully paid up. The conditions for the redemption of redeemable shares are discussed in further detail in Ch 10[372].

(iv) Deferred or founders' shares

[8.112] Shares in this category, virtually obsolete nowadays, were at one time commonly given to the founders of the enterprise which became the company. They carried special rights, such as rights to a fixed dividend, which were deferred in priority to the ordinary shares in order to encourage others to invest in the shares of the company.

(v) Treasury shares

[8.113] Where shares are redeemed, the company, instead of cancelling them, may retain them as treasury shares[373]. While retained as treasury shares, the company will be unable to exercise the rights as to dividend and voting associated with the shares. The idea of a treasury share is of US origin, and it has been observed that it is of little practical utility in this jurisdiction[374].

(vi) Bonus shares

[8.114] A 'bonus issue' (or 'capitalisation issue') of shares occurs where the company capitalises profits or revenue reserves or some permissible fund, such as the share premium account or the capital redemption reserve fund, and applies the proceeds in paying up bonus shares which are then given, normally, to existing members in proportion to their entitlement to dividend[375]*!* A capitalisation of this nature is essentially an accounting exercise which reduces the company's reserves but increases its share capital. One advantage of a bonus issue is that the funds in the share premium account may be applied to the funding of the issue – so that the shareholders receive the benefits of that account – whereas they may not be distributed by way of dividend. A bonus share, therefore, is a fully or partly paid up share in the company, paid for by the company out of permissible funds.

(vii) Employees' shares

[8.115] Unlike some other jurisdictions, such as France, there is no legal requirement on companies in Ireland to allot shares to their employees. Some companies, however, take the view that allotting shares to their employees encourages them to participate more wholeheartedly in the company's affairs. Employees may find the possibility of participating in the profits of the company, and voting on its decisions, attractive. Accordingly, companies may wish not only to allot shares to their employees, but also to assist them in purchasing shares. The legislature has responded in a number of ways to the desires of companies to assist their employees in the purchase of shares in the company.

---

372 See Ch 10, *The Maintenance of Capital*, at para **[10.041]** *et seq*.

373 See Ch 10, *The Maintenance of Capital*, at para **[10.043]**.

374 Keane, *Company Law* (4th edn, Bloomsbury Professional, 2007) at p 150.

375 See model reg 130A of Table A, inserted by para 24 of the First Schedule to the C(A)A 1983.

First, a variety of tax relief incentives and reliefs from employer pay related social insurance contributions facilitate certain schemes for the purchase of shares in a company by its employees[376]. Second, the statutory prohibition, contained in s 60 of the CA 1963, on a company assisting the purchase of its own shares does not apply where a company *provides money* in accordance with any scheme for the time being in force under which its shares are to be held by, or on behalf of, its employees (including directors who are salaried employees), former employees, or the employees of its subsidiary[377]. Nor does it apply to *loans* made by the company to *bona fide* employees (but not employees who are directors) to enable them to acquire shares in the company or its holding company[378].

Third, as has already been observed[379], the statutory pre-emption rights given to the general body of shareholders by s 23 of the C(A)A 1983 do not arise where the allotment is in respect of employee share schemes. An employee share scheme is defined by s 2(1) of the C(A)A 1983 as:

> 'any scheme for the time being in force, in accordance with which a company encourages or facilitates the holding of shares or debentures in the company or its holding company by or for the benefit of employees of former employees of the company or of any subsidiary of the company including any person who is or was a director holding a salaried employment or office in the company or any subsidiary of the company.'

Whether or not a company should issue employee shares is a matter entirely for the company itself; but in making such a decision it should weigh up the benefits of employee participation against the non-desirability of employees hinging all their prospects on the fortunes of the company.

Conversion of shares

[8.116] As was observed in Ch 3[380], s 68 of the CA 1963 permits a company, if so authorised by its articles, *inter alia*, to:

(a) consolidate and divide all or any of its share capital into shares of larger amount than its existing shares; or

(b) convert all or any of its paid up shares into stock, and re-convert that stock into paid up shares of any denomination; or

(c) subdivide its shares, or any of them into shares of smaller amount than is fixed by the memorandum, so however, that in the subdivision the proportion between the amount paid and the amount, if any, unpaid on each reduced share shall be the same as it was in the case of the share from which the reduced share is derived.

Model arts 40 to 45 of Table A provide that these alterations may be effected by ordinary resolution. It should also be remembered that the standard notification and disclosure requirements in relation to alteration of the company's constitutional documents also

376 See generally McAvoy, *Irish Income Tax 2012* (Bloomsbury Professional) Division 11.3 *et seq*.

377 Section 60(13)(b) of the CA 1963.

378 Section 60(13)(c) of the CA 1963.

379 See para **[8.056]** *ante*.

380 See Ch 3, *Constitutional Documentation*, at para **[3.031]**.

apply to these alterations[381]. Notice of any of the above conversions must be sent to the registrar of companies within one month of the conversion[382]. Failure to notify the registrar in the prescribed manner will render the company and every officer in default liable to a class C fine[383].

(a) Consolidation

[8.117] Consolidation means converting a number of shares into a new share of aggregate nominal value; eg, the conversion of five €1 shares into one €5 share. This procedure is quite uncommon nowadays, but may be used where long established companies wish to make their shares less unwieldy – because, say, inflation has caused there to be little point in having 10 cent shares; because decimalisation or the introduction of the euro have intervened; or because certain denominations of currency, such as half-pennies, have been withdrawn from circulation. Consolidation has no financial impact on the shareholders, who now hold fewer shares but of greater nominal value, but it may affect their voting power in a poll.

(b) Conversion of shares into stock, and vice versa

[8.118] Shares may be converted into stock if they are fully paid up. Though it is uncommon to do so nowadays, they may be so converted to allow the stock to be dealt with in fractions. While this may be of some use to public companies whose shares are traded on the stock exchange, it is of little use to a private company which may not offer its shares to the public. Stockholders are given the same rights, privileges and advantages as if they held the shares[384].

(c) Subdivision

[8.119] Subdivision is merely the converse of consolidation. For example, the holder of one €5 share may find his shareholding converted into five €1 shares. This is usually done to improve the marketability of shares when a company feels that the nominal value of its shares is too high, though occasionally it may be done to change the control of the company[385].

Conversion into redeemable shares

[8.120] Section 210 of the CA 1990 permits a company, subject to the rules governing variation of rights and the alteration of a company's constitutional documents, to convert any of its shares into redeemable shares. A shareholder may notify the company before the conversion of his wish not to have his shares so converted. If he notifies the company in this manner, his shares may not be converted, and any attempt to convert them may be struck down by the courts.

No conversion of shares into redeemable shares will be permitted if as a result of the conversion the nominal value of the issued share capital which is not redeemable would be less than one-tenth of the total issued share capital of the company.

---

381 See Ch 3, *Constitutional Documentation,* at para **[3.056]** *et seq.*

382 Section 69 of the CA 1963.

383 Section 69(2) of the CA 1963, as amended by Schedule 1 to the C(A)A 1982.

384 See model reg 42 of Table A.

385 See *Greenhalgh v Arderne Cinemas Ltd* [1946] 1 All ER 512.

Liens on shares

[8.121] Model reg 11 of Table A provides:

> 'The company shall have a first and paramount lien on every share (not being a fully paid share) for all monies (whether immediately paid or not) called or payable at a fixed time in respect of that share but the directors may at any time declare any share to be wholly or in part exempt from the provisions of this regulation. The company's lien on a share shall extend to all dividends payable thereon.'

A lien is a right to withhold possession of an item of property, such as a share, until payment has been received either in respect of that piece of property (in which case the lien is described as 'particular') or in respect of some other claim which the person exercising the lien has against the owner of the property (in which case the lien is described as 'general'). A company has no power to exercise a lien at all over its shares in respect of monies outstanding on them or in any other respect unless the power to do so is expressly provided for in the articles, and where so provided it is presumed, unless the contrary is shown to have been agreed, that the lien is particular and not general[386].

[8.122] The company's lien will be enforceable against the shareholder in priority to all other claims (eg, charges in favour of third parties) which may exist against the share[387] unless the company has notice of the other interests[388]. Enforcement of the lien normally involves a sale of the share to third parties[389]. Model reg 12 of Table A provides that the company may sell any shares on which it has a lien if it gives 14 days notice to the shareholder and is not paid by him within that period. Of course the shareholder may be unwilling to execute a transfer[390] of the shares to the purchaser. Thus, model reg 13 of Table A authorises the directors to appoint some other person to execute a transfer of the shares to the purchaser.

Forfeiture and surrender of shares

(a) Forfeiture

[8.123] Model regs 33 to 39 of Table A empower the directors, by resolution, to forfeit shares in the event of the member failing to pay any call or instalment of a call on the day appointed for payment thereof. Such provisions are regarded as being penal in nature, and must be observed strictly or else the forfeiture will be invalid[391]. Fourteen days' notice to the member will be required, and the notice must state that in the event of

---

386 *Re Dunlop* (1882) 21 Ch D 583.

387 *New London and Brazilian Bank v Brocklebank* (1882) 21 Ch D 302.

388 *Rearden v Provincial Bank of Ireland* [1896] 1 IR 532; *Bradford Banking Co v Briggs* (1886) 12 App Cas 29.

389 See, however, *G & s Doherty Ltd v Doherty and Another* (4 April 1968 & 19 June 1968) HC, Henchy J; (19 December 1969) SC, noted by O'Dowd, (1989) 11 DULJ 120, where a lien was enforced by attaching special terms to an allotment of new shares, requiring the recalcitrant shareholder to pay any amounts outstanding on his existing shares before taking up the new shares.

390 See Ch 9, *Share Transfer*, at para **[9.006]**.

391 *Johnson v Lyttle's Iron Agency* (1877) 5 Ch D 687.

payment not being made within that period, the shares in respect of which the liability arose will be liable to be forfeited.

[8.124] A forfeited share may be sold or otherwise disposed of in any manner which the directors think fit; however, at any time prior to the forfeiture the directors may cancel the forfeiture notice on such terms as the directors think fit. Since the recalcitrant shareholder may refuse to return the share certificate in respect of the shares to the company, and since he may even attempt to deal with the forfeited shares by relying on the share certificate, model reg 38 provides that a statutory declaration by a director or the company secretary that a share has been forfeited is to be conclusive evidence of the facts stated therein against all persons claiming entitlement to the shares. The article also provides that any irregularity or invalidity in the forfeiture proceedings is not to affect the title of any person taking the forfeited shares under a sale or other disposition by the directors.

[8.125] Model reg 37 of Table A provides that a person whose shares have been forfeited shall cease to be a member. Notwithstanding such cesser, the regulation provides that he is to continue to be liable for all monies outstanding on the date of forfeiture until such time as the monies have been paid to the company in full. The company does not have the power to annul a forfeiture and reinstate the shareholder as member without the shareholder's agreement[392].

(b) Surrender

[8.126] A shareholder may surrender his share to the company in order to avoid the formalities of forfeiture, provided the articles permit, and provided those provisions as to surrender are strictly observed. Failure to observe the provisions as to surrender constitutes an unlawful reduction of capital[393].

Disclosure of interests in shares

[8.127] The fact that beneficial interests may not be entered on the register of members would make it easy for directors and other officers, having inside knowledge about the affairs of the company, to buy and sell shares in the company through nominees without anyone noticing or being able to discover otherwise. This would, for example, enable the insider to acquire the shares of other members, secure in the knowledge that the shares can be sold at a large profit in an impending takeover of which the other members are unaware. As has already been observed[394], s 53 of the CA 1990 requires directors and secretaries to notify the company of any interests they may have in the shares or debentures of the company, and the company is required to keep a register for this purpose, ie, the register of directors' and secretaries' share interests. 'Interests' for these purposes is defined broadly to encompass virtually every kind of legal or equitable interest in a share.

---

392 *In Re Exchange Trust Ltd, Larkworthy's Case* [1903] 1 Ch 711.

393 *Bellerby v Rowland & Marwood's SS Co* [1902] 2 Ch 14. On the acquisition of own-shares for nil consideration as permitted by s 41(2) of the C(A)A 1983, see Ch 10, *The Maintenance of Capital*, at para **[10.018]** *et seq*.

394 See Ch 13, *Corporate Governance: Management by the Directors*, at para **[13.095]** *et seq*.

[8.128] Part IV of the CA 1990 also provides for a procedure enabling a wide variety of persons to obtain information about interests held by other persons in shares (or debentures) of the company. For this procedure to be put in motion, a court order must first be obtained. The order, called a *disclosure order*, may be applied for by any person who has 'a financial interest' in the company – which includes members, contributories, creditors, employees, co-adventurers, examiners, lessors, lessees, licensors, licensees, liquidators or receivers, of either the company itself or a related company[395]. The applicant must give 10 days' notice of his application to the company, and to the person to whom the order is intended to be directed[396].

(a) Scope of disclosure order

[8.129] A disclosure order may require the person to whom it is addressed to give the court written particulars of his past and present interests in shares of the company, and, so far as such information lies within his knowledge, particulars of any other interests subsisting in the shares during the time at which he was interested, and of the identity of the person who became interested when he ceased to be interested[397].

[8.130] The interests which must be disclosed by the addressee of a disclosure order include 'any interest of any kind whatsoever in the shares'[398], and specifically include the interests of a beneficiary under a trust[399], a purchaser under a contract[400], and a person who, though not a shareholder, is entitled to exercise or control the exercise of the rights of the shareholder[401]. A person will also be deemed to be interested where his spouse or minor child is interested, or where a body corporate which is accustomed to act in accordance with his instructions, or in which he controls more than one-third of the voting power, is interested[402].

[8.131] The following need *not* be disclosed:

- where property is held on trust, an interest in reversion or remainder, or of a bare trustee, or any discretionary interest[403];
- interests subsisting under unit trusts or UCITS[404];
- interests in schemes under s 46 of the Charities Act 1961[405];

---

395 On what constitutes a 'related company' see Warnock, 'Inter-Company Relationships and Section 31 of the CA 1990' (1994) CLP 243. See generally Ch 25, *Realisation and Distribution of Assets on Liquidation*.

396 Section 99 of the CA 1990.

397 Section 100(1) of the CA 1990.

398 Section 77 of the CA 1990, as applied by s 100(3) of the CA 1990.

399 Section 77(2) of the CA 1990. A person on whose behalf a nominee holds shares is, thus, caught by the section.

400 Section 77(4)(b) of the CA 1990.

401 Section 77(4)(b) of the CA 1990.

402 Section 72 of the CA 1990.

403 Section 78(1)(a) of the CA 1990.

404 Section 78(1)(b)(i) of the CA 1990.

405 Section 78(1)(b)(ii) of the CA 1990.

- life interests under irrevocable settlements where the settlor has no interest in the income or the property[406];
- 'exempt security interests,' ie, interests held as security for a loan by a bank, insurance company, trustee savings bank, post office savings bank, or stockbroker carrying on business on a recognised stock exchange[407];
- interests held by the President of the High Court under s 13 of the Succession Act 1965[408];
- interests held by the Accountant of the High Court pursuant to the Rules of Court[409];
- any other interests exempted by the Minister[410].

(b) Powers of the court in relation to disclosure orders

[8.132] The court may only make a disclosure order if it deems it just and equitable to do so and if it is of the opinion that the financial interest of the applicant is or will be prejudiced by the non-disclosure of any interest in the shares or debentures of the company[411]. The court may impose such restrictions or conditions on the rights attaching to the shares in respect of which the order is made as it sees fit[412]; but any person affected by conditions or restrictions may apply to the court for relief[413]. The court may subsequently, on cause shown, vary or rescind a disclosure order, or, if it is of the opinion that it would be just and equitable to do so and that the financial interests of the applicant would not be prejudiced, it may exempt any person or persons, share or class of shares, interest or class of interests, or debenture or class of debentures from the requirements of a disclosure order[414].

[8.133] The order must identify the person to whom it is directed and must give his address[415]. Notice of the making of an order must be given, within seven days of its making, by the applicant to the company, the registrar of companies, shareholders or debenture-holders not resident in Ireland where the court considers they should be notified, and any such other person as the court sees fit[416]. Notice must also be published in two daily newspapers circulating in the district of the company's registered office[417].

---

406 Section 78(1)(c) and s 78(3) of the CA 1990.

407 Section 78(1)(d) and s 78(4) of the CA 1990. See also the Companies (Stock Exchange) Regulations 1990, SI 337/1990.

408 Section 78(1)(e) of the CA 1990.

409 Section 78(1)(f) of the CA 1990.

410 Section 78(1)(g) of the CA 1990. No regulations creating new categories have been made to date.

411 Section 98(5) of the CA 1990.

412 Section 101(4) of the CA 1990.

413 Section 101(5) of the CA 1990.

414 Section 101(3) of the CA 1990.

415 Section 103(1) of the CA 1990.

416 Section 102 of the CA 1990.

417 Section 102 of the CA 1990.

Any information given to the court in compliance with the order must be given by an officer of the court to the applicant and to the company, unless the court otherwise directs[418].

(c) Consequences of contravention of a disclosure order

[8.134] Where a person fails to fulfil the obligations required by a disclosure order, or provides information which is false, no right or interest of any kind whatsoever in respect of any shares or debentures of the company held by him may be enforced, whether directly or indirectly, by action or legal proceeding, unless the court is satisfied upon an application for relief by any person that such default was accidental, or due to inadvertence or some other sufficient cause[419]. Notably, no criminal sanctions apply to contravention – however, breach of the order may also render the offender liable to contempt proceedings, including attachment and, ultimately, committal to prison[420].

418 Section 102 of the CA 1990.

419 Section 104 of the CA 1990.

420 See Ord 44 of the RSC 1986.

Chapter 9

Share Transfer

Introduction

[9.001] In private companies, shares are normally transferred by the registered owner ('transferor') or someone on his behalf, executing a stock transfer form in favour of the purchaser ('transferee'). However, in order to comply with the statutory definition of a private company, the articles of association of every private company must restrict the right of shareholders to transfer their shares[1]. Sometimes, the shareholders will go one step further and enter into a shareholders' agreement which will typically include extensive restrictions on the transfer of shares[2]. Restrictions will often extend not only to the transfer of shares, but also to their transmission and mortgaging. The transmission of shares is where shares pass by operation of law. The traditional means by which shares pass by operation of law are on a member's death or bankruptcy, to his personal representatives or the official assignee in bankruptcy, respectively[3], but increasingly, shares are passing by operation of law on the merger of companies[4].

[9.002] Restrictions on the transfer of shares may be categorised as being either general or specific in nature. The objective of transferring shares is to place the transferee in the same position as the transferor *vis-à-vis* membership rights. As shall be considered below, to pass full title in shares, the transferee must not only be named in the stock transfer form, but must also have his name entered in the register of members by the company's directors. General restrictions are usually in the nature of the power to refuse to register shares, which is vested in the directors[5]. Specific restrictions on the transfer of shares invariably take the form of pre-emption rights, or rights of first refusal on the sale of shares usually in favour of the company's existing members. Pre-emption rights usually require proposing transferors first to offer their shares to the other members of the company before transferring them to outsiders.

[9.003] Where the transferee intends to acquire the entire of the company's business, perhaps the greatest choice facing him is the share/asset purchase quandary. This involves deciding whether to purchase all of the company's shares from the shareholders, or to purchase all of the company's assets and undertaking from the

---

1 Section 33(1)(a) of the CA 1963. See generally, Ch 1, *The Private Company in Context*, para **[1.134]**.

2 For restrictions in shareholders' agreements, see para **[9.069]**. For shareholders' agreements, see generally, Ch 3, *Constitutional Documentation*, para **[3.106]**.

3 See para **[9.027]** *et seq.*

4 See para **[9.032]**.

5 See para **[9.042]** *et seq.*

company itself. Where it is decided to purchase the shares in a private company, a share purchase agreement should be prepared setting out the rights of the transferee and obligations of the transferor. Although this chapter is concerned only with the law relating to the transfer of shares, the factors influencing the choice between a share purchase and an asset purchase are outlined below[6].

[9.004] Where the transferor and the transferee agree upon the consideration to be paid for the shares in sale, the valuation of shares will not be in issue. In cases where the consideration for the shares cannot be agreed or where the articles or a shareholders' agreement contain a valuation mechanism, recourse may be had to the courts by the transferee or transferor. The valuation of shares may arise also where the court makes an order to buy or sell shares pursuant to s 205 of the CA 1963. The valuation of shares is considered below[7].

[9.005] The law of the transfer, transmission and general alienation of shares in private companies is considered here under the following sections:

- [A] The mechanics of share transfer.
- [B] Transferability and restrictions.
- [C] Transmission of shares by operation of law.
- [D] Security over shares.
- [E] Directors' powers to refuse registration.
- [F] Pre-emption rights on share transfer.
- [G] Compulsory transfers of shares.
- [H] Share purchase agreements.
- [I] The valuation of shares in private companies.

[A] The Mechanics of Share Transfer

The requirement for a 'proper instrument of transfer'

[9.006] Save in public companies, whose shares can be in uncertificated form[8], and in transfers by operation of law, in order to effect a transfer of shares[9] the transferor must execute a proper instrument of transfer[10]. Model reg 23 of Part I of Table A of the First Schedule to the CA 1963 ('Table A') provides:

---

6 See para **[9.108]** *et seq*.

7 See para **[9.117]** *et seq*.

8 See para **[9.010]**.

9 See Johnston, *Banking and Security Law in Ireland* (1998), Ch 16; McGowan-Smyth & Daly, *Irish Company Secretary's Handbook* (2011, Bloomsbury Professional), Ch 14; Doyle, *The Company Secretary* (1994), Ch 7; Nicholson, *Table A Articles of Association* (1997), pp 53–73.

10 Contrast a contract for the sale of shares which can be oral: *Bowlby v Bell* (1846) 3 CB 284. In *Guardian Builders Ltd v Sleecon Ltd and Berville Ltd* (18 August 1988, unreported), HC, Blayney J distinguished a contract for the sale of shares from a contract for the sale of land and held that the former contract would not be within the Statute of Frauds (Ireland) 1695. See generally, Clark, *Contract Law in Ireland* (3rd edn, 1992), Ch 4.

'Subject to such of the restrictions of these regulations as may be applicable, any member may transfer all or any of his shares by instrument in writing in any usual or common form or any other form which the directors may approve.'

The requirement[11] for a written instrument to transfer shares derives from s 81(1) of the CA 1963, which provides:

'Subject to subsection (2), and notwithstanding anything in the articles of a company, it shall not be lawful for the company to register a transfer of shares in or debentures of the company unless a proper instrument of transfer has been delivered to the company.'

One question that arises is whether the phrase 'proper instrument of transfer' as used in s 81 of the CA 1963 implies that a transfer must be stamped. Where, for example, it is certified on the instrument of transfer that no duty is payable because, for example, the transferee is the beneficial owner and so only the bare legal title is being transferred, the instrument will be, indisputably, a proper instrument of transfer. But what of a situation where stamp duty is payable and has not been paid? It is thought, on balance, that it is lawful for a company to register an instrument transferring shares on which stamp duty has not been paid. In *Nisbet v Shepherd*[12], the English Court of Appeal had to consider whether the registration of a stock transfer form which omitted the consideration and which had not been stamped had been validly registered. Leggatt LJ said:

'The question is whether that omission [particulars of the consideration] in particular prevented the stock transfer form from constituting a proper instrument. In my judgment, the phrase does not mean an instrument complying in all respects with statutory requirements. In this context, 'proper' means no more than 'appropriate' or 'suitable'. What it had to be suitable for was stamping ... That would no doubt have required the addition to the document of the amount of the consideration, so that the stamp duty might be ascertained, but because the document sufficiently recorded the transaction, the defects in the form were mere irregularities. It was an instrument chargeable with stamp duty. It was, therefore, a proper instrument, and the registration of the transfer was not invalid[13].'

It is thought that the foregoing is the correct interpretation of the phrase 'proper instrument of transfer'. The failure to stamp a stampable document does not invalidate that document, as stamping is simply a revenue requirement[14]. In *Re Charles Kelly Ltd; Kelly v Kelly and another*[15], Laffoy J quoted with approval the decision in *Nisbet v*

11 So, for example, when the Minister for Finance was obliged to nationalise Anglo Irish Bank Corporation plc, s 5(2) of the Anglo Irish Bank Corporation Act 2009 ('AIBCA 2009') states that s 5(1), which provides that 'all shares in Anglo Irish Bank are transferred to the Minister', 'transfers the shares in Anglo Irish Bank *without the necessity for any instrument*'. Because of the unusualness of a nationalisation, the matter was put beyond doubt by s 14(4)(a) of the AIBCA 2009 which disapplies s 81 of the CA 1963 to the bank and also s 4 of the AIBCA 2009 which provides that the AIBCA 2009 has effect 'notwithstanding anything in (a) the Companies Acts or any other enactment, or (b) the memorandum and articles of Anglo Irish Bank'.

12 *Nisbet v Shepherd* [1994] 1 BCLC 300. See also *Re Paradise Motor Co Ltd* [1968] 2 All ER 625 at 630, *per* Danckwerts LJ and *Powell v London and Provincial Bank* [1893] 2 Ch 555.

13 *Nisbet v Shepherd* [1994] 1 BCLC 300 at 305.

14 See *Re Motor Racing Circuits Ltd* (31 January 1997, unreported), SC, Blayney J, *nem diss*, considered in Ch 18, *Corporate Borrowing: Debentures and Security*, para **[18.039]**.

15 *Re Charles Kelly Ltd; Kelly v Kelly and another* [2010] IEHC 38, Laffoy J.

Shepherd and the foregoing passage from the second edition of this book, before applying them as the law and finding that the company in that case was entitled to register the petitioner as a member notwithstanding that the transfer in question was unstamped.

[9.007] This is not to say that companies are not obliged to have any regard to whether or not a stampable instrument of transfer has in fact been stamped. For one thing, s 129(1) of the Stamp Duties Consolidation Act 1999 provides:

> 'If any person whose office it is to enrol, register, or enter in or on any rolls, books, or records any instrument chargeable with duty, enrols, registers, or enters any such instrument not being duly stamped, such person shall incur a penalty of [€630].'

So, while a company can register an unstamped transfer that is chargeable with stamp duty, an *officer* of the company *whose office is to register the instrument of transfer* (eg, a company secretary) can be liable to a penalty. It is notable, though, that the act of registration is not a criminal offence and merely attracts a penalty. Moreover, if someone other than an officer registers the unstamped transfer, that person is not liable to a penalty. Finally, where the instrument is not chargeable to duty because, say, no beneficial interest passes or because of the application of a group exemption, no penalty will be attracted.

[9.008] However, while it may be considered to be settled law that a company has a right to register an unstamped instrument of transfer, a company has no duty to issue a share certificate following receipt of an unstamped instrument of transfer. This is because s 86(1) of the CA 1963 provides in connection with the duties of a company in relation to the issue of share certificates following, *inter alia*, a transfer of shares:

> 'The expression 'transfer' for the purpose of this subsection means a transfer duly stamped and otherwise valid, and does not include such a transfer as the company is, for any reason, entitled to refuse to register and does not register.'

[9.009] Where fully paid shares are transferred, a standard pre-printed stock transfer form as permitted by the s 2 of the Stock Transfer Act 1963 (the 'STA 1963') is invariably used. Section 2(1) of the STA 1963 provides that shares 'may be transferred by means of an instrument under hand in the form set out in the First Schedule to this Act'. This is, however, permissive not mandatory and, accordingly, shares can be validly transferred without using the form provided for in the STA 1963. This is borne out by s 2(3) of the STA 1963, which states that 'nothing in this section shall be construed as affecting the validity of any instrument which would be effective to transfer securities apart from this section'. The pro forma stock transfer form provided for in the STA 1963 makes provision for certification as to whether or not stamp duty is payable.

[9.010] Whilst the operation of the Companies Act 1990 (Uncertificated Securities) Regulations 1996[16] is not expressly confined to public companies, in practice, it is. Indeed, the free transferability of shares in uncertificated (or, indeed, any) form is anathema to private companies which, by definition, must restrict the transfer of shares[17]. It is opined that, in a private company, it is not open to the directors to resolve

---

16 SI 68/1996.

17 Section 33(1)(a) of the CA 1963.

that title to shares of a class issued or to be issued may be transferred by means of a 'relevant system' pursuant to reg 8(2) of the 1996 Regulations.

Execution of the instrument of transfer

[9.011] In the case of an individual, a stock transfer form can be executed under hand. In the case of a body corporate transferor of shares, it is debatable whether the form must be executed under hand or under seal. Although s 2(1) of the STA 1963 clearly states that shares 'may be transferred by means of an instrument under hand in the form set out in the First Schedule to this Act', the form in the said First Schedule[18] contains a note 'a body corporate should execute this transfer under its common seal or otherwise in accordance with applicable statutory requirements'. It is thought that the prescribed stock transfer form is not required to be under seal where executed by companies, for a number of reasons. First, the express reference to 'under hand' in s 2(1) of the STA 1963 leans firmly against execution under seal. Second, the equation of individuals with companies, in s 38(1)(a) of the CA 1963 as to when a seal is required[19] to be used by companies would support the interpretation that sealing under hand is sufficient. Third, the use of 'should' as opposed to 'must' in the prescribed form may be evidence that sealing is advisable but not mandatory. Of course, it is open to a transferee to seek to insist that a stock transfer form be executed under seal.

[9.012] Although model reg 22 of Table A provides that a transfer should also be executed by the transferee, private companies limited by shares will almost invariably amend model reg 22 to dispense with the necessity of the transferee also executing the transfer. This amendment will also remove any discrepancy between a company's articles of association and s 2 of the STA 1963 which provides that a transfer of shares need only be executed by the transferor. The execution of a stock transfer form need not be attested[20]. Unpaid or partly paid shares are not covered by the STA 1963 which provides, in s 2(4) that 'this section applies to fully paid up transferable registered securities'[21].

The transferee's obligations on transfer

[9.013] Upon the execution of a share transfer, the transferor is obliged to give the transferee the share certificate(s) relating to the shares transferred. A transferor of shares is also obliged to:

> '... execute a valid transfer of the shares and hand the same to the transferee, and do all that is necessary to enable the transferee to insist with the company on his right to be registered a member in respect of such shares[22].'

Unless a contract for the sale of shares specifically provides otherwise, the general rule is that a transferor is not obliged to procure the registration of the shares in the name of

---

18 As inserted by the Stock Transfer (Forms) Regulations 1996 (SI 263/1996).

19 See Ch 7, *Corporate Contracts, Capacity and Authority*, para **[7.014]**.

20 Section 2(2) of the STA 1963.

21 See model reg 23.

22 *Skinner v The City of London Marine Insurance Corporation* (1885) 14 QBD 882 at 887, *per* Brett MR.

the transferee[23]. Notwithstanding this general rule, a transferor, who was a director, has been held to be obliged to vote in favour of the registration of the transferee as a member of the company[24].

[9.014] Prudent transferees who purchase shares will require that a share purchase agreement is also prepared and executed. The *raison d'être* of a share purchase agreement is the protection of the transferee. It is sought to achieve this by the reduction to writing of warranties and indemnities from the transferor. Share purchase agreements are considered below[25].

[9.015] Where a transferor sells only some of his shares or sells all of his shares to different transferees, practical difficulties prevent him from handing over his share certificate to the transferee(s). In such cases the company may certify the transfer(s) pursuant to s 85 of the CA 1963. Such certification by the company is a representation to *bona fide* purchasers that the company has been furnished with such documents as are necessary to prove the transferor's *prima facie* title to the shares. As considered in the previous chapter, the company concerned may be liable where, on foot of a forged share transfer, it issues a share certificate[26].

[B] TRANSFERABILITY AND RESTRICTIONS

[9.016] The transfer of shares involves the consideration of a number of diverse matters. Although shares are *prima facie* transferable, by definition, private companies must impose restrictions on the transfer of their shares. Here the following matters are considered:

1. Shares are transferable but subject to restrictions.
2. The rationale for restrictions in private companies.
3. Registration by the directors.
4. Transferees' position pending registration.

Shares are transferable but subject to restrictions

[9.017] Shares in private companies are *prima facie* transferable. Section 79 of the CA 1963[27] provides that:

> 'The shares or other interest of any member in a company shall be personal estate, transferable in manner provided by the articles of the company, and shall not be of the nature of real estate.'

---

[23] For the consequences of the directors refusing to register a share transfer, see para **[9.027]** *et seq*.

[24] *Lee & Company (Dublin) Ltd v Egan (Wholesale) Ltd* (27 April 1978, unreported) HC at p 10, *per* Kenny J.

[25] See para **[9.108]**. For specialised treatments see: Sinclair, *Warranties and Indemnities on Share Sales* (2nd edn, 1989); Patterson, *Private Company Share Sale Manual* (2nd edn, 1990); Longman, *Commercial Series*; and Wine, *Buying & Selling Private Companies and Businesses* (3rd edn, 1986).

[26] See Ch 8, *Shares and Membership*, para **[8.047]**.

[27] For further consideration, see Ch 4, *Incorporation and its Consequences*, para **[4.085]**.

It is crucial to recognise that s 79 cannot be read in isolation and in particular does not confer an absolute unfettered right to transfer shares. Rather, the provisions of other sections of the Companies Acts and a company's articles must also be considered. Notwithstanding the principle of transferability in s 79, restrictions on either the transfer of shares or the registration of the transferee as a member are intrinsic to private companies.

[9.018] In *Weston*'s case[28], Selwyn LJ said of the materially similar[29] s 22 of the Companies (Consolidation) Act 1908 ('C(C)A 1908') that it:

> '... merely refers the company to their own articles for determining the manner in which that transfer shall be effected, but leaves the general right to transfer to stand upon the provisions of the Act.'

Referring to this, in *Re Hafner*[30], the learned Black J said of s 22 of the C(C)A 1908:

> '... I think the section is plain itself, that a statutory right of transfer is given independently of the articles, but a right which may or may not be restricted by the articles. This is shown by the fact that articles cannot validly confer upon the directors a power to refuse to allow a member of the company to transfer his shares at all to anybody ...
>
> The statute confers what Selwyn LJ called a general right of transfer, and what the statute has given, the articles cannot take away. On the other hand, the words of the sub-section which follow the word 'transferable' are 'in manner provided by the articles of the company,' and it is well settled that these latter words permit of various restrictions being imposed by the articles upon the general statutory right of transfer. It is by virtue of this power held to be given by s 22, [s 79 of the CA 1963] that a private company restricts the transfer of its shares by its articles, which, indeed, it is bound to do under s 121, [s 33 of the CA 1963] such restriction being one of the essential ingredients of a private company[31].'

Accordingly, while shares *per se* are transferable, shares in private companies must contain restrictions. These restrictions are to be found in the company's articles[32].

[9.019] Restrictions on the transfer of shares in private companies have been held not to fall foul of the rule against perpetuities. In *AG for Ireland v Jameson*[33], the alienation of shares was governed by an elaborate series of provisions in the company's articles. *Inter alia*, shares could only be transferred to members of the company where a member was willing to purchase the shares at the 'fair value thereof'. Fair value was defined as the sum of £100 per share or such other sum as was from time to time fixed as the fair value

28 *Re Smith, Knight & Co* (1868) LR 4 Ch App 20 at 30.

29 Section 22 of the C(C)A 1908 omitted the final words of s 79 of the CA 1963: 'and shall not be of the nature of real estate'.

30 *Re Hafner* [1943] IR 426.

31 *Re Hafner* [1943] IR 426 at 448.

32 Although restrictions are also found in shareholders' agreements, where adopted, such restrictions are optional.

33 *AG for Ireland v Jameson* [1904] IR 644. For an analysis of the policy considerations involving the question of the inalienability of shares, see Andre, 'Restrictions on the Transfer of Shares: A Search For A Public Policy' (1979) Tulane L Rev 776, where the case law of Louisiana is analysed. The differences between the corporations considered there and the Irish private company are striking.

by resolution of the company in general meeting. When a member who held 750 shares died, his estate became liable to pay estate duty. His executors valued his shares on the basis of the right of pre-emption and the restrictions on transfer contained in the articles, ie, £100 per share. The Revenue Commissioners sought a declaration from the court that the value of the shares was the value which they would obtain if they were sold on the open market. The Revenue Commissioners argued, *inter alia*, that the restrictions on share transfer in the articles were invalid either as infringing the rule against perpetuities or as being repugnant to the right of alienation inherent in absolute ownership. Kenny J rejected these suggestions, holding as follows:

- that it was only the shares which were subject to restrictions on alienation and not the company's assets;
- that shareholders' rights are enjoyed by entering into a statutory contract under seal and shareholders' rights are inseparable from shareholders' obligations;
- that there is no interest in land, legal or equitable, vested in the members or the members' executors; and
- that there existed no absolute prohibition on the alienation of shares[34].

The rationale for restrictions in private companies

[9.020] Restrictions on the transfer of shares in private companies exist for reasons beyond mere compliance with s 33(1) of the CA 1963. Restrictions on share transfers are frequently adopted by promoters of their own volition because a restriction on the transfer of shares is sympathetic to the underlying structure of many private companies. It is common for restrictions in the articles or shareholders' agreements in many private companies to extend further than the statutory requirement. Often the restrictions placed on the transfer of shares are the result of very elaborate and complex feats of draughtsmanship. The practical necessity for restrictions on the transfer of shares is underscored by the statutory restrictions on a company purchasing or assisting the purchase of its own shares in order to maintain control and prevent outsiders from entering the circle of members[35].

[9.021] Intrinsic to many Irish private companies are the ties of friendship, quasi-partnership, mutuality and kinship which exist between their members. The involuntary admission of an outsider to such a close circle could destroy the very fabric of the company and shatter a quasi-partnership understanding. As Lord Greene MR observed in *Re Smith and Fawcett Ltd*[36] of the directors' power to refuse registration:

> 'Private companies are in law separate entities just as much as are public companies, but from the business and personal point of view they are much more analogous to partnerships than to public corporations. Accordingly, it is to be expected that in the articles of such a company the control of the directors over the membership may be very strict indeed.'

---

34 See also *Borland's Trustee v Steel, Bros & Co Ltd* [1901] 1 Ch 279; *Casey v Bentley* [1902] 1 IR 376 and *London & South–Western Railway Co v Gomm* 20 Ch D 562.

35 See the *dictum* of Lord Macnaghten in *Trevor v Whitworth* [1887] 13 App Cas 409 at 428 and 436.

36 *Re Smith and Fawcett Ltd* [1942] 1 Ch 304 at 306.

Furthermore, restrictions on the transfer of shares can assist the maintenance of the status quo by restricting existing members from acquiring additional shares and so perhaps obtaining a controlling interest. Indeed, even in jurisdictions such as England and Wales where statutory restrictions on the transfer of shares in private companies have been abolished, the existence and importance of restrictions in private companies have continued regardless[37].

Registration by the directors

[9.022] A transfer of shares is inchoate until the transferee is registered as a member of the company[38]. In *Tangney v The Clarence Hotels Company Ltd*[39], Johnston J said '[a] transfer is not legally complete until the transferee has been registered in the books of the company ...'. Accordingly, while the transferee has certain equitable or beneficial rights to the shares, his legal title is not perfected until his name is placed on the company's register of members[40]. It is the transferee's responsibility to procure the registration of the transfer[41]. Directors have both powers and duties in regard to the refusal of registrations of share transfers. Where the articles give the directors a veto to refuse the registration of shares, the directors will have a power of refusal. On the other hand, the directors have a duty to refuse registration where there is non-compliance by a transferring member with a pre-ordained pre-emption procedure in the company's articles. There exists a considerable amount of case law on the directors' powers and duties of refusal to register share transfers, which is considered below[42].

Transferees' position pending registration

[9.023] In principle, at any given time, only one person should be beneficially entitled to enjoy whatever rights attach to particular shares in a company[43]. This is particularly true of voting rights. By reason of this principle, before the transferor is removed from the register of members and the transferee is registered as a member, the transferee has none

---

37 See Schmitthoff (ed), *Palmer's Company Law* (24th edn, 1987), para 40.14 and Fox & Bowen, *The Law of Private Companies* (1991), pp 63, 64.

38 See *Powell v London and Provincial Bank* [1893] 2 Ch 555 where Lindley LJ said at 560 that '... in order to acquire the legal title to stock or shares in companies governed by the Companies Clauses Consolidation Act you must have a deed executed by the transferor, and you must have that transfer registered. Until you have got both you have not got the legal title in the transferee.' This passage was cited with approval by Barron J in *Kinsella v Alliance and Dublin Consumers' Gas Company* (5 October 1982, unreported) HC at p 10 of the transcript.

39 *Tangney v The Clarence Hotels Company Ltd* [1933] IR 51 at 61.

40 On the register of members, see Ch 8, *Shares and Membership*, para **[8.017]** *et seq*.

41 See *Skinner's case* (1885) 14 QBD 882, cited with approval by Johnston J in *Tangey v The Clarance Hotels Company Ltd et al* [1933] IR 51 at 59, 60.

42 See para **[9.042]**.

43 Where shares are in joint-ownership, the model articles restrict the rights attaching to the senior joint-owner: see, eg, model reg 64 which provides that 'the vote of the senior who tenders the vote ... shall be accepted'.

of the rights of membership[44]. This was found to be the position in *Kinsella v Alliance and Dublin Consumers' Gas Company*[45], where Barron J held that:

> 'Persons entitled to stock must be registered in the register of shareholders. Until they are, they are not entitled to vote. This is a well established principle and I would be wrong not to follow it[46].'

Accordingly, the applicant transferees were unsuccessful in their claim to be entitled to exercise the voting rights attaching to the shares transferred to them which had not yet been registered in their names. The fact that the transfers had been lodged with the company for registration did not alter the rule. It is thought that this common law rule may be displaced and that a company's articles may provide to the contrary so as to afford unregistered transferees with full rights of membership exercisable through the registered member. Moreover, as is considered below[47], a transferee who has paid for shares enjoys equitable or beneficial rights to those shares.

[9.024] A number of cases show that the position of a transferee pending registration can be precarious. Care must be taken to apply for registration as soon as possible since pending registration a transferee has only equitable rights to the shares. Where another person also has an equity in the same shares, the rule governing priorities is that where the equities are equal, the first in time prevails[48]. This rule is said to apply unless the transferee has 'a present, absolute, unconditional right to have the transfer registered'[49]. In *Moore v NW Bank*[50], Romer J interpreted the foregoing statement as referring to a situation where an unregistered transferee acquires the full status of a shareholder or at least where all formalities have been complied with, there being only some purely administrative act remaining to be done by the company which the company could not refuse to do[51]. An example might be where the directors have voted in favour of the transferee's registration and only the perfection of the transferee's title remains, by his name being physically entered in the register of members.

Where a transferee cannot be registered as a member of a company by reason of a failure to comply with pre-emption rights, it is thought that his position pending registration is especially precarious. The attitude of the courts appears to be firmly in

---

44 Contrast s 205(6) of the CA 1963, which gives the personal representatives of a deceased member *locus standi* to petition the court under s 205(1). See generally, Ch 11, *Shareholders' Remedies*.

45 *Kinsella v Alliance and Dublin Consumers' Gas Company* (5 October 1982, unreported) HC, *per* Barron J.

46 *Kinsella v Alliance and Dublin Consumers' Gas Company* (5 October 1982, unreported) HC at p 12.

47 See para **[9.065]**.

48 *Moore v NW Bank* [1891] 2 Ch 599 at 602 *per* Romer J. See also *Ireland v Hart* [1902] 1 Ch 522; and *Société Generale de Paris v Walker* (1885) 11 App Cas 20, *per* Lord Selborne. See generally, Keane, *Equity and the Law of Trusts in the Republic of Ireland* (1988), para 5.04.

49 *Per* Lord Selborne in *Société Generale de Paris v Walker* (1885) 11 App Cas 20 at 29.

50 *Moore v NW Bank* [1891] 2 Ch 599.

51 See also *Re Rose* [1949] Ch 78; *Milroy v Lord* (1862) 4 De GF & J 264; *Re Fry, Chase National Executors & Trustees Corp v Fry* [1946] Ch 312.

favour of assisting the enforcement of pre-emption agreements and recognising the rights of those to whom the shares should be offered[52].

[C] TRANSMISSION OF SHARES BY OPERATION OF LAW

[9.025] Section 81(2) of the CA 1963 provides:

> 'Nothing in subsection (1) shall prejudice any power of the company to register as shareholder or debenture holder any person to whom the right to any shares in, or debentures of the company, has been transmitted by operation of law.'

Accordingly, the need for the delivery of a proper instrument of transfer, in order to register the transfer of a share, is without prejudice to a company's power to register as shareholder[53] any person to whom the right to any shares in the company[54] have been transmitted *by operation of law*. There are at least three means by which shares in a private company can be transmitted by operation of law:

1. Transmission on death;
2. Transmission on bankruptcy; and
3. Transmission on a merger

The transmission of shares on death

[9.026] Where the title to shares passes by transmission – by operation of law – on the death of a member, it is typical for the articles to provide that the same restrictions shall apply as apply in the case of an *inter vivos* transfer of shares. Consequently, it is common for the directors' power to refuse to register the shares to apply in the case of a transmission[55]. Similarly, where pre-emption rights exist, they are commonly expressed in articles to apply to a deceased member's personal representatives who will, in consequence, be obliged to comply with such provisions[56].

[9.027] The principle that only one person should be legally entitled to particular shares holds good in the case of the transmission of shares. Model reg 29 provides that the:

> '... survivor or survivors where the deceased was a joint holder, and the personal representatives of the deceased where he was a sole holder, shall be the *only persons recognised by the company as having any title* to his interest in the shares.[57]'

Personal representatives cannot be said to be in a similar position to transferees, as the rights of a personal representative *per se* are only legal[58]. The production of a grant of

52 See *Lee and Co (Dublin) Ltd v Egan (Wholesalers) Ltd* (27 April 1978, unreported) HC, *per* Kenny J; *Re Champion Publications Ltd* (4 June 1991, unreported) HC; and *Tett v Phoenix Property and Investment Co Ltd* [1987] BCLC 149. *Cf Hawks v McArthur* [1951] 1 All ER 22.

53 Or, debenture-holder.

54 Or, debentures of the company.

55 See model reg 30, at para **[9.029]**. In *Re Hackney Pavilion Ltd* [1924] 1 Ch 276, it was held that where the articles provided that the beneficiary of a deceased member's shares was entitled to be registered unless the directors declined registration, the beneficiary was entitled to be registered where the board of directors was deadlocked on the question of refusing registration.

56 *Re Benfield Greig Group plc* [2000] 2 BCLC 488.

57 Italics added.

58 It should be remembered that model reg 29 can be deleted or amended prior to incorporation.

probate or letters of administration must be accepted by the company as sufficient evidence of the personal representative's title in the shares[59]. A transfer of a share of a deceased member made by his personal representative shall, although the personal representative is not a member, be as valid as if he had been such a member at the time of execution of the transfer: s 82 of the CA 1963.

[9.028] A personal representative has two options. On the one hand, he can elect to ask to be registered himself; on the other, he can elect to ask to have another person registered as the holder of the shares and entered in the register as a member. These options are addressed in model reg 31, which provides:

> 'If the person so becoming entitled elects to be registered himself, he shall deliver or send to the company a notice in writing signed by him stating that he so elects. If he elects to have another person registered, he shall testify his election by executing to that person a transfer of the share. All the limitations, restrictions and provisions of these regulations relating to the right to transfer and the registration of transfers of shares shall be applicable to any such notice or transfer as aforesaid as if the death or bankruptcy of the member had not occurred and the notice or transfer were a transfer signed by that member.'

So, whether a personal representative elects[60] to be registered or not, model regs 30[61] and 31 provide that the directors have the same right to decline or suspend registration as if the death (or bankruptcy) had not occurred. In either case, a personal representative should execute a stock transfer form on behalf of the deceased's estate in favour of either the personal representative or the transferee. In *Re Greene*[62], the company's articles provided that a shareholder's shares would be transferred automatically on death. It was held that this was impermissible and that the transferor's personal representatives must execute a share transfer form.

[9.029] Model reg 30 of Table A provides:

> 'Any person becoming entitled to a share in consequence of the death or bankruptcy of a member may, upon such evidence being produced as may from time to time properly be required by the directors and subject as hereinafter provided, elect either to be registered himself as holder of the share or to have some person nominated by him registered as the transferee thereof, but the directors shall, in either case, have the same right to decline or suspend registration as they would have had in the case of a transfer of the share by that member before his death or bankruptcy, as the case may be.'

The registration of a transfer executed by a personal representative is subject to the directors' discretion, where, of course, the articles give the directors such discretion[63]. In *Village Cay Marine Ltd v Acland (Barclays Bank plc third party)*[64], the Privy Council held that personal representatives were not in a more privileged position than ordinary transferors, saying:

---

59 Section 87 of the CA 1963.

60 Where a personal representative elects to be registered, model reg 31, where adopted, will govern the mechanics of registration. See *Stothers v William Steward (Holdings) Ltd* [1994] 2 BCLC 266.

61 See para **[9.029]**.

62 *Re Greene* [1949] 1 All ER 167.

63 See para **[9.042]**.

64 *Village Cay Marine Ltd v Acland (Barclays Bank plc third party)* [1998] 2 BCLC 327.

> '[The articles of association] expressly say that applications for registration by personal representatives or trustees in bankruptcy, either of themselves...or of a nominated person...shall be treated as if they were transfers. They were accordingly subject to the [directors'] discretion...in the same way as any other transfer ...[65].'

Under common form articles of association – where the registration of all share transfers is made subject to the directors' unfettered discretion – the registration of a transfer, executed by a personal representative, will be at the directors' discretion. Where, however, the articles of association direct that transfers to a particular class of person are not subject to the directors' discretion, then registration of a transfer by a personal representative in favour of a member of such class will not be subject to the directors' discretion, by reason of the use of the words 'have the same right to decline ... as they would have had in the case of a transfer of the share by that member before his death'. This distinction was made clear in *Stothers v William Steward (Holdings) Ltd*[66]. In that case the company's articles provided that a transfer by a member to one of the following classes of member was not subject to the directors' general discretion to refuse registration: another existing member; a privileged relation (as defined); and trustees to be held upon family trusts (as defined). Upon the death of a shareholder, it was held by the English Court of Appeal that since the directors could not have refused to register a transfer by a member to his wife (who fell to be defined as a 'privileged relation'), the directors could not refuse to register a transfer from a deceased member's personal representatives in favour of that deceased member's wife[67].

[9.030] Pending registration, a personal representative has certain rights that are indicative of his fiduciary position and duty to account to the beneficiaries of the deceased shareholder[68]. Common form articles provide that a personal representative is entitled to receive notice of members' meetings[69]. Personal representatives cannot, however, vote at such meetings unless registered as members. In *Arulchelvan and Wright v Wright*[70], the question arose as to whether a meeting attended by a deceased's personal representatives was quorate and whether resolutions passed thereat were valid. It was contended that the personal representatives of a deceased shareholder were to be counted as shareholders at meetings. It was sought to support this contention by the fact that model reg 136 entitles personal representatives to be given notice of general meetings; that the articles of association must be construed together[71]; that a transmission of shares was to be treated differently from a transfer of shares[72]; that one member may be counted as two if he holds in different capacities[73]; and that s 141 of the CA 1963, which relates to a special resolution being passed by not less than 75% of the votes cast, draws a distinction between members entitled to vote and those not entitled to

65 *Village Cay Marine Ltd v Acland (Barclays Bank plc third party)* [1998] 2 BCLC 327 at 336.

66 *Stothers v William Steward (Holdings) Ltd* [1994] 2 BCLC 266.

67 See also the final 24 words of model reg 31 para **[9.028]**.

68 *Gabbett v Lawder* (1883) 11 LR Ir 295.

69 Model reg 136(b).

70 *Wright v Wright* (7 February 1996, unreported) HC, Carroll J.

71 *Stothers v William Stewart (Holdings) Ltd* [1994] 2 BCLC 266 cited.

72 *Moodie v W & J Shepherd (Bookbinders) Ltd* [1949] 2 All ER 1044 cited.

73 *Neil M'Leod & Sons* [1967] SLT 46 cited.

vote, which could therefore refer to personal representatives. This was rejected by Carroll J who held:

> 'A 'member' is defined by section 31 of the 1963 Act. Unless his name is on the register of members, he is not a member. A personal representative who is entitled to be registered as a member of a company does not become a member unless his name is entered on the register of members. A personal representative is recognised as having title to the deceased member's interest in his shares (regulation 29) and is entitled to the same dividends and other advantages to which he would be entitled if he were the registered holder (regulation 32). But before being registered as a member in respect of a share he is not entitled in respect of it to exercise any right conferred by membership in relation to meetings of the company (see: Regulation 32, Part I of Table A).
>
> The regulations seem eminently clear to me. The right to attend a meeting is conferred by membership, as is the right to speak and to vote. Since the first and third defendants have not been registered as members, they could not be counted as forming part of the quorum at the two meetings in question. And since no valid quorum was present, no business was transacted[74].'

The general rule under the model articles is that 'a person becoming entitled to a share' has the same entitlement to dividends and other advantages attaching to shares as he would have, were he registered, save the right to vote[75].

Transmission of shares on bankruptcy

[9.031] On a person being adjudicated bankrupt any shares he holds in any company will automatically vest in the official assignee in bankruptcy by virtue of s 44(1) of the Bankruptcy Act 1988[76]. It is common for companies' articles to provide that the same restrictions shall apply on a member's bankruptcy as apply on death or the *inter vivos* transfer of shares. Private companies commonly adopt model regs 30, 31 and 32, already considered in the context of the transmission of shares on a member's death[77].

Transmission on a merger[78]

[9.032] As mergers under the European Communities (Cross-Border Mergers) Regulations 2008 (the 'EC(CBM)R 2008')[79] become more common[80], shares in Irish companies are being transferred by operation of law. Such mergers involve all of the assets and liabilities of one company being transferred to another company, referred to as the 'successor company', and where shares in an Irish company are comprised in

---

74 *Wright v Wright* (7 February 1996, unreported) HC, Carroll J at pp 8–9 of the transcript.

75 Model reg 32.

76 See Sanfey & Holohan, *Bankruptcy Law and Practice* (2012, Round Hall) at ch 6.

77 See para **[9.028]** to **[9.029]**.

78 Although a case can be made out for categorising the change in ownership of shares arising from the merger of companies as a *transfer* of the shares, because the transfer takes effect by operation of law, it is thought that the more natural classification is as a *transmission*.

79 SI 157/2008. See MacCann & Courtney, *Companies Acts 1963–2009* (2010, Bloomsbury Professional) at pp 2585–2629.

80 It is understood that there have been upwards of 50 cross-border mergers registered with the CRO.

those assets, they too will transfer by operation of law[81]. Although it is possible to make a case for saying that an instrument of transfer should be executed, it is thought that the better view is that the transfer happens by virtue of the merger, not by virtue of an instrument of transfer. The effect of the merger will be to transfer the equitable and beneficial interest in the shares to the successor company; however, the successor company will not automatically become the registered member of the shares until its name has been entered in the register of members. This is recognised by reg 19(2) of the EC(CBM)R 2008[82]. Accordingly, the successor company must present evidence that the shares have transferred by operation of law to the company in which the shares are held, requesting the directors to register the successor company as the registered member of the shares.

Because transmission by merger is relatively new to Irish law, some questions are unresolved. For example, is it the case, as it is for transmission by death or bankruptcy, that the directors' right to refuse registration of a successor company as member continues? On the one hand it might be argued that given the dissolution of the transferor company, the shares can only be held by the successor company which should be taken to have been registered. On the other hand, in no other circumstances are the restrictions on transfer of shares in private companies set aside, so why should they be set aside on merger? Inherent in the chose in action that is a share in a private company is that it can only be transferred in accordance with the restrictions imposed by its articles of association. Although few existing companies' articles of association currently make provision for transfer or transmission by merger, it is thought that the general restriction on transfer contained in reg 3 of Table A[83], which allows the directors to decline to register any transfer or any share, applies to transmission by merger too.

[9.033] So, assuming that they are minded to register the successor company as a member, what evidence should the directors of an Irish company whose shares have transferred by merger require? Where the merger takes effect under Irish law – which will be the position where the successor company is an Irish company – it is thought that it is sufficient to provide the directors with a copy of the court order made under reg 14(1) of the EC(CBM)R 2008, and that, in reliance upon that order and s 81(2) of the CA 1963, the directors may lawfully register the successor company on the register of members in respect of those shares. Unlike transmission on death or bankruptcy, Table A makes no provision for merger, and it is thought that it would not be unreasonable for the directors to propose to the members an amendment to the articles of association making express provision for the procedures applicable on the registration of shares following a merger.

In the case of a merger that takes effect under a foreign law, the directors of the Irish company need to be more careful, and the reference in s 81(2) of the CA 1963 to

---

81 For example, reg 19(1)(a) of the EC(CBM)R 2008 provides that '... the consequences of a cross-border merger are that, on the effective date – *all the assets and liabilities of the transferor companies are transferred to the successor company*'.

82 Regulation 19(2) of the EC(CBM)R 2008 provides: 'The successor company shall comply with filing requirements and any other special formalities required by law (including the law of another EEA State) for the transfer of the assets and liabilities of the transferor companies to be effective in relation to other persons.'

83 See para **[9.043]** *post*.

'operation of law' cannot be assumed to refer to a foreign law. It is thought that a strong argument can be made that s 81(2) of the CA 1963 will apply where the law in question is that of another EU Member State and the merger has taken effect under Council Directive No 2005/56/EC of 26 October 2005. Prudent directors will insist upon receiving a legal opinion from a practicing lawyer in the jurisdiction in which the merger has taken place, confirming that it is effective to transfer the shares in the Irish company. Again, a provision in the articles of association specifying the evidence required would be very helpful. In cases of mergers effective under non-EU law, it may well be appropriate for the directors to require the successor company to obtain an order of the Irish courts recognising the foreign merger court order.

[D] Security Over Shares

[9.034] Another form of alienation of shares is where the registered owner creates a mortgage over his shares[84]. Although often regarded by lending institutions as a less than perfect security, shares in private companies may be mortgaged and charged at law or in equity[85].

Legal mortgage of shares

[9.035] A legal mortgage of shares involves the transfer of the legal title in shares to the mortgagee and the registration of the mortgagee as legal owner and full member of those shares[86]. By reason of s 123 of the CA 1963, the mortgagor's equity of redemption cannot be recorded in either the transfer instrument or the register of members[87]. A mortgagee of shares can, however, register a *stop notice*, considered below[88]. Accordingly, the transfer to the mortgagee must be outright, giving the mortgagee all of the rights to vote and to dividend which attach to the shares. On the release of the security the shares must be re-transferred[89], giving rise to a double stamp duty liability. If the mortgagee becomes the registered shareholder before it advances money to the borrower, it can avoid the potential problems of pre-emption rights and of approaching the directors to be registered as a member on a foreclosure, both of which may be problematic in the case of equitable mortgages[90]. Where the conditions of s 155(3)(d) of the CA 1963 are met, the legal transfer of shares by a holding company to a lending institution may not sunder the relationship of holding company and subsidiary[91]. Written

84 See generally, Johnston, *Banking and Security Law in Ireland* (1998), Ch 16 and Lingard, *Bank Security Documents* (3rd edn, 1993), Ch 15.

85 Shares may also be *charged* and a debenture or deed of charge executed by the registered owner of the shares in favour of a chargee. The effect is to give the charge holder equitable rights over the shares in the private company. For the reasons set out at para **[9.037]** *et seq*, this is considered to be a below average security.

86 See generally, Bell, *Modern Law of Personal Property in England and Ireland* (1989), p 183 (where mortgages are considered) and p 173 (where charges are considered).

87 See Ch 8, *Shares and Membership*, para **[8.017]**.

88 See para **[9.038]**.

89 *Tutt v Mercer* (1725) 2 Bro PC 563; *Langton v Waite* (1868) LR 6 Eq 165; and *Ellis & Co's Trustees v Dixon–Johnson* [1925] AC 489.

90 See Johnston, 'Bank Finance – Searching for Suitable Security' (1994) CLP 3 at 5–6.

91 See Ch 12, *Groups of Companies*, at para **[12.026]**.

deeds of mortgage and charge over shares will typically permit the mortgagor to vote the shares and receive any dividends payable thereon, for as long as the mortgagor is not in default[92].

Equitable mortgage of shares

[9.036] An equitable mortgage of shares typically arises where the mortgagor executes a blank stock transfer form and gives a power of attorney in favour of the mortgagee to complete the form at a later time, and deposits the share certificate with the mortgagee[93]. It is established that this transaction operates as an equitable mortgage and not a pledge of the share certificate, which is merely evidence of title: a share is a *chose in action* and cannot be pledged[94]. Where share certificates are deposited with a mortgagee, the onus of proof rests with the mortgagee to show that the deposit was intended to be as security[95]. In the absence of a written mortgage deed, a power of sale will be implied upon reasonable notice being given to the defaulting mortgagor[96].

[9.037] Where a blank stock transfer form is taken, the mortgagee should also obtain a power of attorney[97] to enable it to complete the blank transfer. In *Powell v London and Provincial Bank*[98], Lindley LJ held that in the absence of a power of attorney a bank,

---

92 See further, Johnston, *Banking and Security Law in Ireland* (1998), pp 554–555.

93 No particular form of document is needed to create an equitable mortgage over shares. As Chernov J said in the Supreme Court of Victoria decision in *Whiting Inc v Prudential Bache Securities Australia Ltd and another* [1998] VSC 86 (18 September 1998), para 31 of the judgment: 'To create an equitable mortgage, no particular form of words is necessary. An equitable mortgage of legal property is based upon a contract between the parties. If that contract or agreement is supported by valuable consideration, equity treats it as an agreement to create a legal mortgage, and where consideration has been given … specific performance is available and the equitable maxim whereby equity regards as done that which ought to be done operates, thereby creating immediately a security in the property in question.'

94 In *Harold v Plenty* [1901] 2 Ch 314 at 316, Cozens-Hardy J said the deposit of a share certificate was properly construed as an *equitable mortgage* and not a pledge, saying that: 'I do not think that this is properly a case of pledge. A share is a chose in action. The certificate is merely evidence of title ... I think I cannot treat the plaintiff as a mere pledgee. The deposit of the certificate by way of security for the debt ... seems to me to amount to an equitable mortgage, or, to an agreement to execute a transfer of the shares by way of mortgage.' See also *Stubbs v Slater* [1910] 1 Ch 632 and *London and Midland Bank v Mitchell* [1899] 2 Ch 161. It may, however, be that a pledge exists in respect of the share certificate itself, as a document of title.

95 See *Re Alton Corporation* [1985] BCLC 27 at 31, 32 where Megarry VC stressed the need to find an agreement to create a mortgage in the context of the deposit of a land certificate.

96 On reasonable notice, see *Deverges v Sandeman, Clark & Co* [1902] 1 Ch 579 and *Stubbs v Slater* [1910] 1 Ch 632.

97 A letter of authority will suffice where a pre-printed stock transfer form is permitted under the Stock Transfer Act 1963 and a power of attorney is only strictly necessary where the transfer must be by deed under seal. For reasons given above, a power of attorney is most certainly to be preferred. On the alteration of deeds without authority, see the *Rule in Pigot's Case* (*Winchcombe v Pigot* (1614) 2 Bulst 246) as recently applied by the High Court of Northern Ireland in *Northern Bank Ltd v Laverty* [2001] NI 315.

98 *Powell v London and Provincial Bank* [1893] 2 Ch 555.

with which a stock certificate and blank transfer had been deposited, was not entitled to complete the blank forms. In *Powell*, the trustee of a trust had made the deposit, and although the bank had no notice of the trust, the beneficiaries of the trust were held to have priority[99]. The power of attorney should be expressed to be irrevocable and, where given to secure a proprietary interest of the donee of the power of the performance of an obligation owed to the donee, will attract the benefit of s 20(1) of the Powers of Attorney Act 1996. A power within the meaning of that section cannot be revoked, without the donee's consent, for as long as the interest or obligation remains undischarged. Neither will the donor's death, incapacity, bankruptcy, winding up or dissolution revoke the power of attorney.

One difficulty with an equitable mortgage of shares is that should the mortgagee seek to enforce its security, it may be thwarted by the directors refusing registration of the share transfer or by pre-emption rights in the articles or a shareholders' agreement of which the mortgagee has notice[100]. For this reason, a mortgagee may insist upon the articles being amended to ensure that it will have an automatic right to be registered as a member, carved out of the directors' veto, in the event that the security is enforced.

Protection for mortgagees – stop notices[101]

[9.038] An equitable mortgagee of shares can bolster his position by serving a stop notice on the company. This is facilitated by Ord 46, rr 5–13 of the RSC 1986[102], which enable a person claiming an interest in shares in a company to serve notice on the company itself, restraining the transfer of stock or shares and/ or the payment of dividends. The legal basis for Ord 46 is s 23 of the Debtors (Ireland) Act 1840, which provides:

> '… If any person against whom any judgment shall have been entered up in any of … [the] … superior courts at Dublin shall have any Government Stock, Funds or Annuities, or any Stock or Shares of or in any public company in Ireland (whether incorporated or not), standing in his name in his own right, or in the name of any person in trust for him, it shall be lawful for the Court … on the application of any judgment creditor, to order such Stock, Funds, Annuities or Shares or any of them or such part thereof respectively as he shall think fit, shall stand charged with the payment of the amount for which the judgment shall have been so recovered and interest thereon; and such order shall entitle the judgment creditor to all such remedies as he would have been entitled to if such charge had been made in his favour by the judgment debtor …'

---

99 See also *Ireland v Hart* [1902] 1 Ch 522.

100 Equitable mortgagees are well advised to insist upon the articles of the company being amended to provide that the directors are obliged to register a transfer of shares in their favour: see Lingard, *Bank Security Documents* (3rd edn, 1993), para 15.24 for a form of article. It must be remembered, though, that a company cannot contract that it will not alter its articles: see Ch 3, *Constitutional Documentation*, para **[3.037]**, although it may be possible to injunct its shareholders where they act contrary to a contract not to cause the articles to be altered. Regard should also be had to pre-emption clauses, be they contained in the articles or in shareholders' agreements.

101 See generally, Johnston, *Banking and Security Law in Ireland* (1998), pp 555–559.

102 SI 15/1986.

The procedure for obtaining a charging order is contained in s 24 of the 1840 Act which, so far as relevant, provides:

> '… in order to prevent any person against whom judgment shall have been obtained from transferring, receiving, or disposing of any Stock, Funds, Annuities or Shares hereby authorised to be charged for the benefit of the judgment creditor under an order of a Court or Judge … every order of any such Court or Judge, charging any Government Stock, Funds or Annuities, or any Stock or Shares, in any Public Company under this Act, shall be made in the first instance *ex parte* and without any notice to the judgment debtor, and shall be an order to show cause only; and such order … if any Stock or Shares of or in any Public Company standing in the name of the judgment debtor in his own right, or in the name of any person in trust for him, is or are to be affected by any such order, shall in like manner restrain such Public Company from permitting a transfer thereof; and that if after notice of such order to the person or persons to be restrained thereby, or in case of corporations to any authorised agent of such corporation, and before the same order shall be discharged or made absolute such corporation or person shall permit any such transfer to be made, then and in such case the corporation or such person or persons so permitting such transfer shall be liable to the judgment creditor for the value or amount of the property so charged and so transferred; … and that no disposition of the judgment debtor in the meantime shall be valid or effectual as against the judgment creditor; … and further that unless the judgment debtor shall, within a time to be mentioned in such order show to one of the said Courts, or the Judge thereof, sufficient cause to the contrary, the said order shall after proof of notice thereof to the judgment debtor, his attorney or agent, be made absolute; provided that any such Court or Judge shall, upon the application of the judgment debtor, or any person interested, have full power to discharge or vary such order, and to award such costs, upon such application, as such Court or Judge may think fit.'

Furthermore, s 132 of the Common Law Procedure Act 1853 empowers the court to make an order of attachment in similar circumstances to those in which a charging order may be made under s 24 of the 1840 Act.

[9.039] A stop notice is obtained by the notice and a grounding affidavit being filed in the Central Office of the High Court, and serving a duplicate of the filed notice and an attested copy affidavit on the company at its registered office. The effect of this is that after service of the notice, it is unlawful[103] for the company to permit the specified shares to be transferred or to pay dividends on the shares. The company is obliged to notify the person named in the notice upon receiving a request to transfer the shares and to wait eight days before registering the transfer. Even where a stop notice lapses, it is possible that the equitable mortgagee's interests may continue to be protected by reason of the fact that the company has notice of its interest and a company's right to exercise a lien is suspended[104]. All of this is notwithstanding s 123 of the CA 1963 which prohibits companies from entering notice of any trust, express, implied or constructive, on the register. Where an equitable mortgagee of shares gives a stop notice, it has been held that such constitutes the taking of the necessary steps to perfect its title by putting the company on notice of its interest in the shares[105].

---

103 Order 46, r 10 of the RSC.

104 *Rearden v Provincial Bank of Ireland* [1896] 1 IR 532, considered in Ch 8, *Shares and Membership*, para **[8.026]**.

105 See *Re Morrissey and Morrissey* [1961] IR 442.

[9.040] In *Honniball v Cunningham and BPI Property Company Ltd*[106], the plaintiff obtained a judgment against the defendant for €850,000 and, pursuant to an application under Ord 46, r 1 of the RSC 1986, the plaintiff obtained an order charging the defendant's share in a company called BPI Property Company Limited. Later, an application was made to have a receiver appointed by way of equitable execution in respect of the share or its proceeds, and the application which came before Laffoy J was brought by the defendant to have the charging order and appointment of the receiver discharged. After reviewing the statutory jurisdiction to make a charging order in ss 23 and 24 of the 1840 Act, Laffoy J said:

> 'What is clear from an analysis of s 24 is that a charging order made by the court on foot of an *ex parte* application under the power conferred by ss 23 and 24 is not an absolute order; it is an order to show cause only. Counsel for both parties are *ad idem* that that is the correct interpretation of the provisions. Further, the order should stipulate a date within which the judgment debtor should show cause why the charging order should not be made. Accordingly, it would appear that in providing that the order made on foot of a motion *ex parte* shall be absolute in the first instance, Ord 46, r 1 purports to exceed the jurisdiction conferred by the statute. As regards the order made on 3rd October, 2006, it was not described in terms as an absolute order. Nonetheless, it was deficient in not providing a time limit within which the defendant should show cause. Fortunately, the fact that the application to appoint the receiver by way of equitable execution was returnable for 6th October, 2006 obviated any injustice to the defendant, because counsel for the defendant was able to inform the court on that day that it was proposed to apply to court to have the charging order discharged.'

Laffoy J went on to note that the defendant had submitted that the court had no power to make a charging order under s 23 of the Act of 1849 because the company was a private company and not a public company. This argument was, however, rejected by Laffoy J on the basis that the concept of 'private company' did not exist when the Act of 1840 or 1853 was passed and because the parliamentary intention in using the epithet 'public' before 'company' was to capture a company which had the attributes of publicity[107].

[9.041] Stop orders have become more common since the economic crisis has resulted in banks seeking to enforce more judgments than ever against defaulting borrowers. One way to enforce a judgment is to seek to charge shares held by the judgment-debtor in companies. In November 2007, and on a number of occasions thereafter, the High Court went further than to just create a charge over shares, and directed the registrar of companies to place on the file of the company whose shares had been charged, notice of the charging order having been made. The Company Law Review Group has recommended[108] that the Companies Acts be amended to provided that no order affecting a shareholder or debenture-holder shall be accepted by the registrar of companies for registration on the file of the company that issued the shares or debentures.

---

106 *Honniball v Cunningham and BPI Property Company Ltd* [2006] IEHC 326, Laffoy J.

107 Laffoy J relied on the decision in *MacIntyre v Connell* 1 Sim NS 225 and s 6 of the Interpretation Act 2005.

108 *Report of the Company Law Review Group, 2010–2011* at para 3.1.6.

[E] DIRECTORS' POWERS TO REFUSE REGISTRATION

[9.042] The directors' power to refuse registration of a share transfer is clearly a restriction directed at the registration of the transfer and not at the transfer of the share itself. The directors' power to refuse registration can take many forms. On the one hand there is model reg 3 of Table A, Part II, considered below[109]. This is a completely unfettered power with little by way of guidance as to how it should be exercised by the directors. Alternative restrictions empower the directors to refuse to register shares unless they are being transferred to existing members; or transferred or transmitted to family members of the transferring, bankrupt or deceased member; or to existing employees of the company. Such restrictions focus on the status of the transferee. Other restrictions focus on the qualities of the transferee, such as financial strength and other personal attributes. In all cases the powers of the directors to refuse registration must be exercised *bona fide* and for the benefit of the company as a whole. In addition, the powers of the directors will lapse unless exercised, whether for or against registration, within a reasonable period of time. Where a member-transferor feels that the directors have exercised their powers oppressively it is open to him to institute proceedings under s 205 of the CA 1963. In this section, the foregoing matters are considered under the following headings:

1. The model reg 3 restriction.
2. The transferee's status.
3. The transferee's qualities.
4. The *bona fides* of the directors.
5. The lapsing of the directors' powers.
6. Relief under s 205 of the CA 1963.
7. The consequences of declining registration.
8. The procedure for challenging a refusal to register.

The model reg 3 restriction

[9.043] The most common restriction on the transfer of shares in private companies is a provision in the articles which empowers the directors to veto the registration of any transfer. Model reg 3 of Part II of Table A provides:

> 'The directors may, in their absolute discretion, and without assigning any reason therefor, decline to register any transfer of any share, whether or not it is a fully paid share.'

The essence of this restriction on transfer is the power of the directors to decline the registration of a share transfer without giving reasons for their decision. This is the most unfettered of powers. Where registration is refused on the basis of model reg 3, the prospective transferee has few grounds upon which to contest the directors' decision. The only real basis for challenge is to claim that the directors have abused their powers. While the duties of directors are considered in detail in Ch 15[110], the *bona fides* of the exercise of directors' powers in the context of declining registration of share transfers is further considered here.

---

[109] See para **[9.043]** *et seq.*

[110] See Ch 15, *Duties of Directors and Other Officers*.

[9.044] The difficulty in setting aside an exercise of the directors' powers is seen in *Re Smith and Fawcett Ltd*[111], where the articles of the company concerned provided that the directors could in their absolute discretion refuse to register any transfer of shares. The company had two shareholders and directors, Smith and Fawcett, who each held 4,001 shares. On Fawcett's death, his son, as executor of the will, applied to be registered as member in respect of his father's 4,001 shares. Smith refused, offering to purchase 2,000 of the shares and agreeing to register the remaining 2,001 shares in Fawcett Jr's name. Fawcett Jr unsuccessfully applied to the court to have all 4,001 shares registered in his name and the decision of the court was affirmed by the Court of Appeal. In the course of his judgment Lord Greene MR said of the model reg 3 type power:

> 'There is nothing, in my opinion, in principle or in authority to make it impossible to draft such a wide and comprehensive power to directors to refuse to transfer as to enable them to take into account any matter which they conceive to be in the interests of the company, and thereby to admit or not to admit a particular person and to allow or not to allow a particular transfer for reasons not personal to the transferee but bearing on the general interests of the company as a whole – such matters, for instance, as whether by their passing a particular transfer the transferee would obtain too great a weight in the councils of the company or might even perhaps obtain control ... In the present case the article is drafted in the widest possible terms[112], and I decline to write into that clear language any limitation other than a limitation which is implicit by law, that a fiduciary power of this kind must be exercised bona fide in the interests of the company. Subject to that qualification, an article in this form appears to me to give the directors what it says, namely, absolute and uncontrolled discretion[113].'

Lord Greene MR rejected the argument that the directors' refusal to register a transfer of shares must always be limited to matters personal to the transferee[114]. That the directors were prepared to register 2,001 shares, but not 4,001, may have indicated that there was no personal objection to Fawcett J, but this fact did not affect or determine the directors' discretion to refuse to register whatever number of shares they wished.

[9.045] Another feature of the model reg 3 restriction is that the directors are not obliged to give reasons for declining to register a share transfer. It has been observed that these words 'are in fact surplusage'[115] by reason of the fact that directors, like trustees, are not obliged to assign reasons for their decisions. This general rule was acknowledged by Black J in *Re Hafner*[116]. In that case the directors of a company declined to register the plaintiff as a member of the company and refused to give reasons for their decision, astutely choosing to rely on the blanket power to refuse registration contained in the

---

111 *Re Smith and Fawcett Ltd* [1942] 1 Ch 304.

112 The article in question in *Smith and Fawcett Ltd* provided simply that: 'The directors may at any time in their absolute and uncontrolled discretion refuse to register any transfer of shares ...'

113 *Re Smith and Fawcett Ltd* [1942] 1 Ch 304 at 308; this passage was cited with approval by Laffoy J in *Banfi Ltd v Moran et al* [2006] IEHC 257.

114 This is, of course, unless a company's articles provide that such is to be the case.

115 Ussher, *Company Law in Ireland* (1986), p 191.

116 *Re Hafner* [1947] IR 426.

articles[117]. Black J recognised the general rule that the directors were entitled to remain mute, saying:

> 'It is well settled that under such an article as this the directors may refuse to register a transfer. It is equally well settled that the directors' power in this regard is a fiduciary one and must be exercised in the interest of the company as a whole. They must not exercise it arbitrarily, capriciously, or corruptly. They are not bound to assign their reasons, and the court is not entitled to infer merely from their omission to do so that their reasons were not legitimate[118].'

Although the general rule[119] is that directors are not obliged to give reasons for declining to register a transfer or transmission of shares, there are exceptions to the rule. In *Re Hafner*, Black J put the matter succinctly:

> 'Hedged round with the privilege of remaining mute and the prima facie presumption of rectitude, the astutely silent director may well consider himself all but invulnerable. No need to speak and no unfavourable inference from reticence – that is the settled rule. Yet, like many another settled rule, I am persuaded that it is not proof against possible exceptions[120].'

Having considered Chitty J's judgment in *Bell*'s case[121], Black J concluded that 'in order to interfere the court must not only find that the directors had an invalid motive, but it must also find that they had no valid motive that might be itself sufficient'[122]. The rule that the directors are not obliged to assign reasons for their decisions ceases to be good where an invalid reason for declining to register the shares is proved to the satisfaction of the court. Black J accepted that the purpose of the directors acting as they did was to compel the plaintiff to sell his shares to them at an undervalue and to prevent him from questioning the directors' voting themselves large emoluments. It was held on this point that the acceptance of the allegation of an improper motive was sufficient to enable the court to draw an inference from the directors' silence[123].

[9.046] The significance of the exceptions to the rule that directors are not obliged to assign reasons for declining to register a transfer are somewhat equivocal. To come within the exception recognised by Black J in *Re Hafner,* a transferee who is refused registration must establish an improper motive on the part of the directors which cannot be explained by reference to some valid motive. Where a *prima facie* case of invalid motive, otherwise inexplicable, is established, it is logical that the court will require some explanation from the directors. Where the directors remain silent and they do not counter the *prima facie* case, it seems inevitable that the transferee should succeed in establishing that the directors acted in bad faith. However, to establish a *prima facie* case

---

117 Regulation 6 of the company's articles of association provided: 'The directors may, in their absolute and uncontrolled discretion and without assigning any reason, refuse to register any transfer of shares, and clause 20 of Table "A" shall be modified accordingly.'

118 *Re Hafner* [1947] IR 426 at 439.

119 See also *Re Dublin North City Milling Co Ltd* [1909] 1 IR 179 at 184 where Meredith MR said that although he disliked mystery, the directors were entitled in law 'to hold their tongues'.

120 *Re Hafner* [1947] IR 426 at 440.

121 *Re Bell Brothers Ltd* 7 TLR 689.

122 *Re Hafner* [1947] IR 426 at 441.

123 See also *Clark v Workman* [1920] 1 IR 107 at 118.

of improper motive is tantamount to proving that there was an abuse of the directors' powers and, accordingly, the exception to the rule that directors may remain mute may be seen as being of little practical value.

[9.047] Directors are not confined to the reasons they give at the time of a refusal: *Village Cay Marine Ltd v Acland (Barclays Bank plc third party)*[124]. In that case, P owned the entire issued share capital in the plaintiff, Village Cay Marine Ltd, which owned certain development land. Pursuant to a joint venture agreement for the residential development of the land a joint venture company – Landac Development Ltd ('the JVC') – was incorporated, P holding 49 shares and A holding 51 shares. A made a loan of $150,000 to the JVC, which it passed to the plaintiff in return for an option to require the grant of sub-leases of the proposed residential units to its nominees. P died and his 49 shares passed to his widow. Subsequently, the plaintiff granted underleases to a company nominated by the JVC. The shares in the plaintiff were subsequently acquired by E from P's widow. E also acquired the 49 shares in the JVC, P's administrators executing a transfer. A, the sole director of the JVC, declined to register E as a shareholder, saying in a letter that he did not regard it as beneficial to the company to involve third parties in its ownership at that stage of the development. At trial, further reasons for the refusal were given and it was accepted by the court that A was entitled to refuse to register the transfer on the basis of his knowledge that the plaintiff was over-indebted to banks and because it was owned by a holding company which could result in its beneficial ownership changing without the JVC's knowledge. The British Virgin Islands Court of Appeal reversed this but the trial judge's decision was, on appeal to the Privy Council, restored in this respect. The Privy Council, per Lord Hoffmann, held that there was no rule of law by which directors are confined to the reasons they have given. In so finding the Privy Council distinguished and explained – on the construction of the particular article – the *dictum* of Lord Cozens-Hardy MR in *Re Bede Steam Shipping Co Ltd*[125] where he had said that 'the directors ought not to be allowed to state their reason in the certificate itself to the transferee and then to say that was not the only reason, but they had other and different reasons'[126]. The Privy Council went on to accept that A's reasons were *bona fide* and not 'obviously unreasonable', saying:

> '[The JVC] was a vehicle for a joint venture in the nature of partnership and it is not obviously unreasonable that [A] should have concerns about the financial standing of a prospective new partner or the possibility that he might lose any practical form of control over further transfers of the beneficial ownership in the shares[127].'

The transferee's status

[9.048] The transferee's status will often be deemed a relevant, or indeed the determining factor, in the directors' exercise of their discretion to admit or decline the registration of a transfer of shares. In many private companies, existing members are

124 *Village Cay Marine Ltd v Acland (Barclays Bank plc third party)* [1998] 2 BCLC 327.

125 *Re Bede Steam Shipping Co Ltd* [1917] 1 Ch 123.

126 *Re Bede Steam Shipping Co Ltd* [1917] 1 Ch 123 at 135.

127 *Village Cay Marine Ltd v Acland (Barclays Bank plc third party)* [1998] 2 BCLC 327 at 339.

accorded a favoured position in that it is sometimes provided that restrictions do not apply to transfers between members[128].

In many Irish private companies, restrictions are expressed not to apply to a member's family. An example of such an exception based on the transferee's status is that model reg 3 of Part II of Table A is sometimes amended to provide that any share may be transferred to a member's, or deceased member's, spouse, child or grandchild[129]. Such exceptions to the directors' general right to decline registration are not as popular as positive pre-emption rights in favour of spouses, children and other family members of deceased or existing shareholders.

[9.049] Another possible exception to the directors' general power to refuse registration are transfers of shares to the company's employees. Such restrictions are appropriate where the company concerned is run on co-operative, or extended partnership, principles. Again, it is more usual to protect employees through a positive pre-emption right in their favour, rather than a carve-out from the directors' power to refuse registration.

The transferee's qualities

[9.050] Even where existing members are not expressly excluded from the operation of restrictions on transfer, it has been held that the restrictions will not apply to members where the directors' power to refuse registration is referable to the transferee's status as being a 'desirable person'. In *Tangney v The Clarence Hotels Company Ltd*[130], the articles of the company provided, *inter alia*, that members proposing to transfer shares had to notify the directors of the proposed transferee's name and address and that '... if the directors are of opinion that the proposed transferee is not a desirable person to admit to membership, they may decline to register the transfer of any such share ...'.

In that case, the plaintiff, Denis Tangney, had been a shareholder and member of the company for many years. However, on his purchasing further shares, the directors of the company refused to register those shares in his name on the ground that he was not a 'desirable person' to admit to membership. Johnston J noted that although the directors were entitled to decline registration, their power was not unlimited[131]. Rather, their power turned upon whether a proposed transferee was a desirable person. He held that an existing member's application for registration of additional shares could not be declined by the directors.

[9.051] Where the articles provide that the directors may decline registration if 'in their opinion it is contrary to the interests of the company that the proposed transferee should be a member thereof', the directors may only have regard to the transferee's personal

[128] *Jarvis Motors (Harrow) Ltd and another v Carabott and another* [1964] 1 WLR 1101.

[129] For further comment on a variation of this clause, see Ussher, *Company Law in Ireland* (1986), p 193, fn 66.

[130] *Tangney v The Clarence Hotels Company Ltd* [1933] IR 51.

[131] *Tangney v The Clarence Hotels Company Ltd* [1933] IR 51 at 62. Of the power to decline registration in the case of undesirable persons, Johnston J said at 62–63: 'It seems to me that that clause was intended to meet the case of a stranger proposing to come into the family, as it were.'

qualities. In *Re Bede Steam Shipping Company Ltd*[132], where the articles so provided, it was held by the Court of Appeal that the directors could not decline to register shares on the ground that the person was an existing shareholder who already held a large shareholding or because registration would increase the number of shareholders and so alter the balance of power. Lord Cozens-Hardy held[133] that where a company's articles contain such a provision:

> 'You may look and see personally who the transferee is. There may be personal objections to him: it may be because he is an uncertain person, or it may be that he is acting in the interests of a rival company, or something of that kind. All those things are fairly incidental in the word 'personal'; but to seek to say 'We will not accept any transfer of a single share from a particular shareholder who holds a large number' is, it seems to me, an abuse of the power which was conferred by the clause in the articles[134].'

It should be noted that the directors' lack of power to decline registration turned entirely upon the construction of the actual restriction in that company's articles.

The *bona fides* of the directors

[9.052] Irrespective of the wording of any particular restriction which empowers directors to decline to register shares, directors, as fiduciaries, must exercise their powers *bona fide* and for the benefit of the company as a whole[135]. Lord Greene MR said in *Re Smith and Fawcett Ltd*[136] that the principles to be applied to the directors' discretion to decline registration of a share transfer were clear:

> 'They must exercise their discretion bona fide in what they consider – not what a court may consider – is in the interests of the company, and not for any collateral purpose[137].'

Although the exercise of the power to refuse to register shares lies within the directors' subjective discretion, it is within the courts' competence to review the result of an exercise of their power where it is established that the directors of a company have acted otherwise than *bona fide* and for the benefit of the company.

[9.053] The leading modern Irish authority on the exercise of directors' discretion on approving the transfer of shares is *Banfi Ltd v Moran et al*[138]. The facts in this case were that the plaintiff, Banfi Limited, was the *beneficial owner* of 16,525 of the 88,777 issued ordinary shares in a company called Emerald Group Holdings Limited (Emerald), the fifth defendant. The 16,525 shares were registered in the name of ICT Nominees Limited but in trust for the plaintiff on foot of a declaration of trust. At the plaintiff's behest, ICT Nominees Limited executed a stock transfer form in favour of the plaintiff; this was done by ICT Nominees Limited's two directors, Mr Moran and Ms Ray, who were also directors of Emerald. Following this in May 2003, the plaintiff presented the transfer to the directors of Emerald for registration. At that time, there were three

---

132 *Re Bede Steam Shipping Company Ltd* [1917] 1 Ch 123.

133 Following Mellish LJ in *Ex p Penny* LR 8 Ch 446.

134 *Re Bede Steam Shipping Company Ltd* [1917] 1 Ch 123 at 133.

135 See generally, Ch 15, *Duties of Directors and Other Officers*, para **[15.027]**.

136 *Re Smith and Fawcett Ltd* [1942] 1 Ch 304.

137 *Re Smith and Fawcett Ltd* [1942] 1 Ch 304 at 306.

138 *Banfi Ltd v Moran et al* [2006] IEHC 257, Laffoy J.

directors – Mr Moran, Ms Ray and Mr Kavanagh. The plaintiff's director who swore its affidavit (Mr Hasslacher) had also been a director of Emerald but had ceased to be one at the time the transfer was presented for registration. The company subsequently wrote to the plaintiff advising that the board had concluded that the decision to register or refuse to register should only be taken following certain clarifications. A further letter also sought information and documents but these were not furnished by the plaintiff. On this point Laffoy J noted that the lack of a response had to be seen in the context of proceedings brought under s 205 of CA 1963, which were pending having been brought by the plaintiff and Mr Hasslacher, where one of the issues was that since neither were members, neither had standing to maintain the proceedings. Ultimately, in September 2003 the board of Emerald reached a unanimous decision that, in accordance with article 7 – which was materially identical to model reg 3 – it would decline to register the transfer from ICT to the plaintiff. The board minute recorded that the decision had been made after the board had 'considered the correspondence and the impact of the registration on all interested parties'. The first respondent, Mr Moran, in his affidavit averred that the decision had been taken *bona fide* in the interests of the company (Emerald); the third respondent, Mr Kavanagh, concurred in his affidavit and cited the failure to receive cooperation from the plaintiff regarding the request for information. The plaintiff, through its director Mr Hasslacher, claimed on affidavit that the directors' refusal to enter the name of the plaintiff on the register of members had been actuated by fraud and *mala fides* on the part of the respondents, the alleged ultimate motivation being to enable Mr Moran and Ms Ray to continue to divert business from a subsidiary to another company controlled by them, something they strenuously denied.

[9.054] The application in *Banfi* came before the High Court by way of an application by the plaintiff to have Emerald's register of members rectified pursuant to s 122 of CA 1963. In considering the law applicable to the determination of the issue whether a transferee of shares was refused registration as a member of a company 'without sufficient cause', Laffoy J summarised the relevant principles as set out in the second edition of this work[139] and applied them in the following terms:

139 Laffoy J said: '(1) The exercise of the directors' power to refuse to register must be gauged by reference to the relevant regulation in the company's articles of association, which may take many forms. However, in all cases the powers of the directors to refuse registration must be exercised *bona fide* and for the benefit of the company as a whole (Courtney, *The Law of Private Companies* (2nd edn, 2002) at para 16.037). (2) Where, as here, the material part of the relevant regulation replicates verbatim model Reg 3 of Table A, Part II, the directors have the most unfettered of powers (Courtney, para 16.038). The breadth of the discretion given in an article so worded was recognised by Lord Greene MR in *In re Smith and Fawcett Ltd* [1942] 1 Ch 304 in the following passage in his judgment (at p 308): "In the present case the article is drafted in the widest possible terms, and I decline to write into that clear language any limitation other than a limitation, which is implicit by law, that a fiduciary power of this kind must be exercised *bona fine* in the interests of the company. Subject to that qualification an article in this form appears to me to give the directors what it says, namely, an absolute and uncontrolled discretion." (3) The Table A, Part II model permits the directors to decline registration without giving any reasons for their decision. As Courtney points out (at para 16.040) it was recognised by Black J in *In re Hafner* [1947] IR 426 (at p 440) that there are exceptions to that general rule. However, in this case, the respondents gave reasons in the minute of the meeting of 17th September, 2003 and in the affidavits filed by them in these proceedings. (contd.../)

> 'Applying the foregoing principles, the crucial question in determining whether the refusal of the board of the Company to register the plaintiff was without sufficient cause is whether or not, in exercising their discretion under article 7, the members acted bona fide in what they considered to be in the interests of the Company as a whole. To succeed on this application to have the register rectified, the plaintiff must discharge the burden of proving that they did not.'

While noting that the directors could have elected to stay silent, they did not and broke their silence by putting in evidence contemporaneous documentation and by adducing affidavit evidence as to why they refused to register. Laffoy J analysed the evidence adduced by both the defendants and the plaintiff before concluding that she was:

> '... satisfied that the real reason for the refusal to register the plaintiff as a member was to ensure that the plaintiff would never have standing to prosecute such proceedings against Mr Moran and Ms Ray. The plaintiff's beneficial shareholding represented the interest of Mr Hasslacher in the Company, which interest had existed since 1989. Since 1995 at least, and perhaps earlier, ICT held that interest in trust for the plaintiff and through the plaintiff for Mr Hasslacher. Mr Moran and Ms Ray were the directors of ICT and, as such, owed fiduciary duties to ICT, to the plaintiff and Mr Hasslacher. From 1995 those arrangements were formalised in the declaration of trust in 1995 and remained unchanged thereafter. What changed in the relationship of the human agents of the plaintiff and ICT was that in

139 (\...contd) Accordingly, unlike the *Hafner* case, this is not a case in which the plaintiff has to penetrate the total reticence of the directors. As Courtney points out (at para 16.042), the directors are not confined to the reasons they gave at the time of the refusal: *Village Cay Marine Ltd v Ackland (Barclays Bank Plc third party)* [1998] 2 BCLC 327. (4) As to the nature of the court's jurisdiction under s 122 and the process the court is required to engage in, I agree with the view expressed in Courtney (at para 16.048) that is to review the result of the exercise of their power by the directors where it is established that they have acted otherwise than *bona fide* and for the benefit of the company. In *In re Smith and Fawcett Ltd* Lord Greene MR emphasised the subjectivity of the discretion which is reposed by an article on the lines of the article at issue here in the directors. He stated (at p 306): "They must exercise their discretion *bona fide* in what they consider – not what the court may consider – is in the interests of the company, and not for any collateral purpose." In *In re Hafner*, on appeal to the Supreme Court, Sullivan CJ recorded (at p 470) a concession made by counsel for the defendants that the power conferred by the directors by the relevant article was a fiduciary power to be exercised *bona fide* in the interests of the company, the exercise of which might be controlled by the court if there was evidence which justified the conclusion that the directors had acted improperly. Later in his judgment Sullivan CJ, having adverted to the difficulty which the plaintiff faced in seeking to establish that the actions of the directors was not a *bona fide* exercise of their fiduciary power because the directors were not obliged to assign any reason for their refusal to register, went on to identify the burden placed on the plaintiff as follows (at p 471): "And accordingly the plaintiff had to adduce evidence of relevant circumstances from which the court could legitimately infer that the directors had acted improperly." The Supreme Court affirmed the finding of Black J in that case, which was a witness action, that the directors' exercise of their discretion was actuated by an illegitimate motive (to facilitate payment of exorbitant emoluments to themselves) and, as such, was not a *bona fide* discharge of their fiduciary duty. (5) As is pointed out in *Courtney* (at para 16.056), the rights of a transferor of shares are not entirely dependent upon common law principles. If the directors have exercised their powers in a manner oppressive to, or in disregard of, a transferor-member's interests he may bring a petition under s 205. Further, the personal representative of a deceased member has *locus standi* by virtue of s 205(6).'

> 2002 Mr Hasslacher initiated the s 205 proceedings against Mr Moran and Ms Ray. The proper inference to be drawn from the conduct of the defence of the s 205 proceedings by Mr Moran and Ms Ray, in my view, is that the reason for the refusal to register the plaintiff as a member was to ensure that the pending proceedings would be struck out and that the plaintiff would not be in a position to initiate any further proceedings under s 205.'

Having satisfied herself as to the reason why registration was refused, Laffoy J then turned to consider whether in refusing to register the plaintiff as a member so as to ensure it could not prosecute the s 205 proceedings, the directors were acting *bona fide* in the interests of the company as a whole. On this point, the learned judge determined that the directors had been acting in their own interests, and not those of the company:

> 'I have no doubt that the proper inference to draw from the evidence and, in particular, the evidence as to the defence of the then pending s 205 proceedings, is that Mr Moran and Ms Ray were motivated by self interest, not the interest of the company as a whole, in participating in the decision to refuse to register the plaintiff.
>
> ... Mr Moran and Ms Ray could, if they wished, ensure that the interests of the plaintiff are protected by enabling it to pursue the remedies which are open to all shareholders since 1963, the remedies available under s 205, either through the trustee which is the registered owner of the shares, or by allowing it to become registered. They have effectively closed off one avenue by the decision to refuse to register the transfer to the plaintiff and they are in control of the other avenue. Having regard to the position they have adopted in relation to registering the transfer, and given their position as directors of ICT, the registered owner of the plaintiff's shares, it is reasonable to assume that ICT as a transferor member will not be pursuing the statutory remedies available under s 205 on behalf of the plaintiff. Through ICT, and in the face of their fiduciary duties, Mr Moran and Ms Ray have maintained a stranglehold on the plaintiff's shareholding in the Company and have wholly stymied the plaintiff in pursuing the statutory redress which is available to all shareholders. I have no doubt, on the evidence, that in participating and, in effect, carrying the resolution to refuse to register the plaintiff as a member they were pursuing their own self interests, not the interests of the Company as a whole.'

Laffoy J held that a delay of two years in bringing application under s 122 of the CA 1963 was insufficient, in the circumstances, to prejudice the company or bar relief under that section and ordered that the register of members be rectified by showing the plaintiff as the registered owner of the 16,525 shares in Emerald.

[9.055] In *Popely v Planarrive Ltd*[140], a bitter feud existed between the plaintiff, on the one side, and his wife, children and nephew on the other, arising from his wife's discovery that he had had extra-marital relationships with two women, each of whom had borne him a child. Upon the plaintiff submitting certain shares that he had acquired, for registration, the directors refused to register but did not inform the plaintiff of this fact (this aspect of the decision is considered below[141]). On the question of the directors' *bona fides* in refusing registration and whether it was in the company's interests, it was contended by the plaintiff's counsel that the decision was taken for personal, not company, reasons and that personal feelings were so strong that the directors could never have acted *bona fide* in the company's interests and ought to have resigned and allowed new directors to make the decision. Laddie J rejected this, saying:

---

140 *Popely v Planarrive Ltd* [1997] 1 BCLC 8.

141 See para **[9.061]**.

> 'Particularly in small private companies there are likely to be ebbs and flows of personal relationships between directors and shareholders. Opposing camps may form. Relationships may become strained. But such common occurrences do not mean that the directors are to be disqualified from exercising powers which may have impact on other directors or shareholders …'

In such companies the directors will normally have private views as to the suitability of new shareholders. It would be unrealistic and unworkable in many cases to require the directors to disqualify themselves in relation to the issue of registration of shareholdings merely because such views exist. No doubt if it can be shown that those private and personal feelings have been allowed to overcome the directors' views as to what is *bona fide* in the interests of the company, then a decision taken to refuse registration may be impeached. But if, say, directors believed that registration of a new shareholder's shares would give him control of the company and that that would not be in the interests of the company because he was a fraudster and liar, the decision to refuse registration could not be challenged simply because the new shareholder had defrauded all of the current directors. The fact that the directors had a personal dislike of the new shareholder would not alter the fact that their decision was taken *bona fide* in the interests of the company[142].' On reviewing the evidence, Laddie J found that any reasonable board would have been likely to have taken the same decision as the directors had taken.

[9.056] In *Re Hafner*[143], it was established that the directors had acted in bad faith. In that case the directors of the company declined to register the plaintiff as a member of the company. In his claim the plaintiff had asserted that the directors had declined to register him because, were he a member, he would be in a position to query the 'bloated emoluments'[144] paid to the directors. Black J accepted that this was the real reason (or primary purpose) why the directors had declined registration and concluded that:

> '... if, and so far as, the defendants' refusal to register the plaintiff was based upon the discretion given them by Art 6[145] it was not the result of a bona fide or legitimate exercise of their discretion and if it cannot be justified apart from Art 6, it cannot be justified at all[146].'

That finding was subsequently upheld by the Supreme Court[147].

[9.057] In *Re Dublin North City Milling Company*[148] the transferee was refused registration, even though he was an existing member. The facts of the case were that a Mr Edward Spicer held 25 shares in Dublin North City Milling Company but the directors of the company refused to register him in respect of a further 20 shares which he had acquired. The articles of the company provided that the transferee had to be approved of by the board of directors. One of the directors swore an affidavit stating that

---

142 *Popely v Planarrive Ltd* [1997] 1 BCLC 8 at 15–16.

143 *Re Hafner* [1943] IR 426.

144 *Re Hafner* [1943] IR 426 at 443.

145 Regulation 6 of the company's articles of association provided: 'The directors may, in their absolute and uncontrolled discretion and without assigning any reason, refuse to register any transfer of shares, and clause 20 of Table "A" shall be modified accordingly.'

146 *Re Hafner* [1943] IR 426 at 445.

147 *Re Hafner* [1943] IR 426 at 471, *per* Sullivan CJ.

148 *Re Dublin North City Milling Company* [1909] 1 IR 179.

although the plaintiff had previously been registered as a member, having considered the matter carefully, the directors thought it detrimental and injurious to the company, its property and business to register a further transfer of shares in the plaintiff's name. Although the plaintiff already held 25 shares, he was managing director of another company, John Spicer & Co Ltd, millers and bakers.

Meredith MR considered that the Court of Appeal decision in *Re Coalport China Company*[149] summed up the 'true guiding principle' upon which the court should act. Meredith MR quoted with approval the judgment of Lindley LJ in that case, where he said[150]:

> '... I have not the slightest doubt that the court has ample power to control the refusal of directors, or the exercise by them of their power to refuse, provided there is some evidence which justifies the court in coming to the conclusion that they have not done their duty; but in the absence of all such evidence, the court has no right to presume – it is contrary to the ordinary principles of justice to do so – that they have done wrong, but it must be presumed that they have done right.'

Although Meredith MR admitted that he 'disliked mystery', he said that he thought it wise to refuse to compel directors to disclose their reasons for accepting or declining to register a transfer. He went on to say:

> '... I am of the opinion that the law allows the directors to hold their tongues. It allows them to say that everything was done honestly and bona fide in the interests of their company; and they have unanimously decided that it is not for the interest or advantage of the Company that their shares should be transferred to Mr Spicer: and according to my view I have no power to make them say more[151].'

Had the applicant made any clear charge of corruption, conspiracy or dishonesty, such would have been examined by the court. Indeed such might on the authority of Black J in *Re Hafner* justify a departure from the general rule that no implication can be drawn from the directors' silence[152]. The burden of proof in such matters is clearly on the rejected transferee. As Meredith MR said, '[e]ach transferee who demands registration of a transfer must allege and prove some indirect motive on the part of directors in refusing application. The fact that he is already a shareholder does not prove this'[153].

The lapsing of the directors' powers

[9.058] Directors are obliged to exercise their powers within a reasonable period of time of such powers arising. Where the directors neither effect nor decline registration of a share transfer within a reasonable period, their power to do so will lapse and the transferee will become entitled to be registered automatically. The reason for this can be seen in the fact that shares are *prima facie* transferable. It has been held that a transferor has a basic right to transfer his shares in a company[154], albeit one which can be ousted

149 *Re Coalport China Company* [1895] 2 Ch 404.

150 *Re Coalport China Company* [1895] 2 Ch 404 at 409.

151 *In Re Dublin North City Milling Company* [1909] IR 179 at 184.

152 See para **[9.045]** *et seq*.

153 *In Re Dublin North City Milling Company* [1909] IR 179 at 183.

154 See *Re Discoverers Finance Corporation Ltd, Lindlar's case* [1910] 1 Ch 312 where Buckley LJ held, *inter alia*, that if the articles of association do not contain any restrictions, shareholders have the right the transfer their shares. See also *Stothers v William Steward (Holdings) Ltd* [1994] 2 BCLC 266.

where the directors, in accordance with the articles, validly decline the registration of a share transfer. It must be questioned, however, whether this is good law in the context of a private company since the law provides that the transfer of shares must be subject to restrictions. Subject to this, it seems to be accepted that where the directors' powers to refuse registration lapse, the right of a transferee to be registered is resurrected.

[9.059] An example of where the transferee's right to become registered as a member was resurrected in the face of directors' inertia is *Re Hackney Pavilion Ltd*[155]. In that case the executrix of a deceased member sought to be registered as a member of the company. The directors of the company had an absolute right to decline registration under the company's articles. A meeting of the company's board of directors was called, but the two-man board was divided on the issue, there being no provision for a casting vote. Accordingly the resolution was neither approved nor rejected. Astbury J held that the directors had not declined to register the executrix's shares as the directors' power to decline registration must actively be exercised by a vote of the board of directors. In such a case the right of the transferee to be registered is resurrected, and this is the status quo which has precedence where the directors' powers are not exercised[156].

[9.060] What will be considered to be a reasonable period of time, will depend upon the circumstances of each case. It is generally accepted, however, that a period of two months from the date on which the transfer is lodged for registration is reasonable[157]. This is because s 84 of the CA 1963 requires the company to notify a transferee within two months that his application has been refused by the directors, if that be the case. In *Re Swaledale Cleaners Ltd*[158], where the directors had delayed in either effecting or declining registration for four months, it was held that the directors' power to decline to register a transfer had lapsed and that the transferee was entitled to be registered as a member of the company. This rule continues to be applied[159].

[9.061] In *Popely v Planarrive Ltd*[160], a distinction was drawn between a situation where the directors do not exercise their discretion within two months and a situation where the directors do exercise their discretion within two months, but do not inform the transferee. The facts in this case, set out above[161], were that the plaintiff submitted shares

155 *Re Hackney Pavilion Ltd* [1924] 1 Ch 276.

156 See also *Moodie v W & J Shepherd (Bookbinders) Ltd* [1949] All ER Rep 1044 where the principle was again applied, the court holding that the directors could only exercise their right to decline registration by passing a resolution to that effect: a mere failure to pass a resolution was not a formal exercise of the right to decline registration. In this case the deceased member's executors were held to be entitled to be registered as members since the directors had not exercised their power to decline registration.

157 See *Re New Cedos Engineering Co Ltd* [1994] 1 BCLC 797.

158 *Re Swaledale Cleaners Ltd* [1968] 1 WLR 1710.

159 So in *Re Inverdeck Ltd* [1998] 2 BCLC 242, where the directors of a company failed to either register or refuse to register a transfer of shares within two months from its being lodged for registration, Carnwath J held that they had lost the power to refuse to register. This was notwithstanding that one of the directors claimed to be part beneficial owner of the shares in transfer, although it was said that registration would not prevent his asserting his beneficial ownership.

160 *Popely v Planarrive Ltd* [1997] 1 BCLC 8.

161 See para **[9.055]**.

for registration in his name. Were he so registered, he would have obtained control of the company as a shareholder with the entitlement to control the board of directors. The articles provided that the directors had an absolute discretion as to registration and also provided that if they refused to register shares they should send the transferee notice to this effect within two months from the date the transfer was lodged with them. Upon the plaintiff lodging the transfer with the directors, they refused to register it but failed to inform him of their decision. Consequent upon this happening, the plaintiff applied to have the share register rectified[162]. Laddie J found that although the directors had not notified the plaintiff of their decision to refuse registration, they had exercised their discretion within the requisite two months. He said:

> 'When a company's articles of association include an article like art 14[163] in this case, the directors' power to refuse to register will be narrowly construed. If they fall outside the time limit implicitly set in the articles then their decision is a nullity. That is all that was being considered in *Re Swaledale Cleaners Ltd*. As all the judgments in that case make clear, at the time the directors took their decision to refuse registration they had no power to take it. However, quite different considerations apply in a case where the decision is taken within the time set by the articles. If that happens then the decision itself is not a nullity. The subsequent failure to notify the shareholder in accordance with the procedure and timetable set by the articles may well expose the directors to civil[164] and criminal[165] liabilities, but I do not see how that failure can relate back so as to turn a proper exercise of the directors' powers into a nullity[166].'

Laddie J went on to say that it might be open to a court to find an estoppel where the delay in notification was so long and where the shareholder took actions on the assumption that he had been registered, but that had not been advanced in the instant case.

Relief under s 205 of the CA 1963

[9.062] It should be remembered that the rights of a transferor of shares are not entirely dependent upon common law principles. Where the directors have exercised their powers in a manner oppressive to, or in disregard of, a transferor-member's interests he may bring a petition under s 205 of the CA 1963. Although normally only members of a company have standing to petition the court for s 205 relief, an exception exists in the case of deceased members' personal representatives, who are given *locus standi* by s 205(6)[167].

---

162 See para **[9.066]**.

163 Regulation 14 provided: 'The directors may, in their absolute discretion and without assigning any reason therefor, decline to register the transfer of a share, whether or not it is a fully paid share …'

164 Presumably this refers to the breach of the 's 25 contract'. Where an existing shareholder's application for registration of additional shares is refused, a civil action might be maintained; however, where the applicant-transferee is not a member it is thought that he would not be privy to the s 25 contract, although the existing shareholder who purported to transfer the shares to him would have privity of contract.

165 The failure to send to a transferee, within two months of lodgement of transfer, notice of refusal: s 84(1) of the CA 1963.

166 *Popely v Planarrive Ltd* [1997] 1 BCLC 8 at 15a–c.

167 See Ch 11, *Shareholders' Remedies*, para **[11.052]**.

[9.063] Section 205 of CA 1963 is considered in detail in Ch 11. However, its possible application to situations where the directors of a closely-held private company unreasonably decline to register a share transfer should be remembered. The necessity for restrictions on the transfer of shares in closely-held companies has been discussed above[168]. The converse is that a quasi-partner should be able to dispose of his interest in the business venture. The result must be a balancing of interests. Where the directors cannot or will not strike the appropriate balance, the courts may be asked to do so.

The consequences of declining registration

[9.064] Where a share transfer is executed by the transferor but the directors of the company decline to register the transferee as a member of the company, a binding contract to sell the shares continues to exist[169]. The contract to sell the shares cannot be avoided unless the contract is expressly made conditional upon the transferee's registration.

[9.065] In the case of an unlimited public company, it has been held that there exists no implied term in a contract for the sale of shares that the transferee will be registered as a member of the company: *Casey v Bentley*[170]. In that case the transferee paid the transferor the consideration due under the contract for the sale of the shares in the public company, upon the transferor giving the transferee an executed transfer and the share certificate. The directors of the company were entitled to decline to register a transfer under the company's articles, and this they duly did upon the share transfer being presented for registration. The transferor issued proceedings claiming specific performance of the contract and an order that the transferee should be ordered to procure the shares to be registered in his own, or some other person's, name. Later, the transferor amended the proceedings seeking an indemnity and rescission of the contract. At trial, Madden J held that there was a condition subsequent in the contract that the transferee would be registered and the failure to do this meant that the transferor was entitled to treat the contract as at an end and that the shares should be re-transferred to the transferor on the return of the purchase money.

The Court of Appeal overruled Madden J by a majority, holding that the contract for the sale of shares on the Stock Exchange did not import an undertaking by the transferor that the company would register the share transfer. Lord Ashbourne noted that the reason for the transferor's concern was that she continued to have an exposure since she remained a member of an unlimited company but yet she was paying over the dividend on the 'sold' shares to the unregistered transferee.

The distinction between contracts made on the Stock Exchange from those made off it was crucial to the reasoning of the Court of Appeal[171]. Although this case is authority for the proposition that there is no implied term as to registration in contracts for the sale of shares on the Stock Exchange, that principle does not necessarily extend to the sale of shares in private companies. In the case of a contract for the sale of shares in a private company, there is a strong case for implying a term that the contract is conditional upon

---

[168] See para **[9.020]**.

[169] See *Skinner v City of London Marine Insurance Corp* (1885) 14 QBD 882.

[170] *Casey v Bentley* [1902] 1 IR 376.

[171] *Casey v Bentley* [1902] 1 IR 376 at 386–387, where Lord Ashbourne cited *Fry on Specific Performance*.

the transferee's registration as a member of the company. Depending upon the type of private company, there may well exist considerable overlap between those who own the shares and those who manage the company. It was established in *Lee & Company (Dublin) Ltd v Egan (Wholesale) Ltd*[172] that a director who sells shares must vote in favour of the transferee's registration as a member.

Where registration is refused by the directors and the transferee has paid over the purchase price of the shares, the transferor remains the legal owner of the shares but is a trustee of the shares for the transferee who is the equitable owner[173]. By this rule of law, where consideration has passed the registered transferor must account to the unregistered transferee for dividends paid and must vote to the order of the unregistered transferee[174].

The procedure for challenging a refusal to register[175]

[9.066] Procedurally, where a transferee is declined registration, he will commonly seek rectification of the company's register of members under s 122(1) of the CA 1963. Section 122(1) provides:

> 'If—
>
> (a) the name of any person is, without sufficient cause, entered in the register of members or omitted therefrom, in contravention of subsections (1) and (2) of section 116; or
>
> (b) default is made in entering on the register within the period fixed by subsection (3) of section 116 the fact of any person having ceased to be a member;
>
> the person aggrieved, or any member of the company, or the company, may apply to the court for rectification of the register.'

On application being made, the court may either refuse or order rectification[176] of the register, and it may also order the payment by the company of compensation for any loss suffered by any party aggrieved[177]. On an application under s 122 the court may decide any question of title. The s 122 procedure is without prejudice to a company's own right to rectify its own register[178]. In bringing an application for rectification it is imperative

[172] *Lee & Company (Dublin) Ltd v Egan (Wholesale) Ltd* (27 April 1978, unreported) HC, *per* Kenny J at p 10.

[173] *Stevenson v Wilson* (1907) SC 445 and *Hawks v McArthur* [1951] 1 All ER 22.

[174] See *Musselwhite v CH Musselwhite & Son Ltd* [1962] Ch 964, considered at para **[9.074]**.

[175] See also generally, Ch 8, *Shares and Membership*, para **[8.017]**.

[176] Where rectification is ordered, s 122(4) of the CA 1963 provides: 'In the case of a company required by this Act to send a list of its members to the registrar of companies, the court when making an order for rectification of the register shall by its order direct notice of the rectification to be given to the registrar.'

[177] Section 122(2) of the CA 1963.

[178] Section 122(5) of the CA 1963 provides: 'A company may, without application to the court, at any time rectify any error or omission (whether occurring before, on or after the operative date) in the register but such a rectification shall not adversely affect any person unless he agrees to the rectification made. The company shall, within 21 days, give notice of the rectification to the registrar of companies if the error or omission also occurs in any document forwarded by the company to him.'

that the company, whose register it is sought to have rectified, be joined as a party[179]. It has been observed[180] that these utilitarian provisions fill a gap in shareholder protection legislation, since the Companies Act 1985 (UK) cannot be invoked by prospective or former members wishing to assert membership rights. With the exception of personal representatives[181], the same can be said of s 205 of the CA 1963.

[9.067] Rectification can be ordered under s 122(1)(a) of the CA 1963 only where a member's name is entered or omitted 'without sufficient cause'. As Laffoy J said in *Re Olde Court Holiday Hostel Ltd; Trehy v Murtagh et al*[182]:

> 'In broad terms, the jurisdiction to rectify is a discretionary remedy, which empowers the court to rectify particulars which have been entered in the register "without sufficient cause"'.

In that case, rectification of the register was sought to show that Mrs Murtagh held 1,500 €1 shares at €1 and €99 premium and not 50,000 €1 shares issued at nominal value as recorded in the register of members. Laffoy J was inclined to the view that the registration of the 50,000 allotment had been made 'without sufficient cause' but due to a host of conflicting evidence, which the learned judge described as being a 'mess', Laffoy J was not prepared to say, on the evidence presented to her, that there was 'sufficient cause' to register Mrs Murtagh as owner of 1,500 shares either! The application was, therefore, adjourned to enable the liquidator to address the specific issues raised by Laffoy J.

[9.068] Where application is made for rectification based on the directors' refusal to register by reason of, for example, the failure to respect pre-emption rights or because the directors have absolute discretion to refuse registration, either of these grounds may give rise to 'sufficient cause' for the refusal. The interaction between the UK's provisions similar to s 122(1) and (2) of the CA 1963 has been the subject of recent consideration by the English courts. Section 122(3) of the CA 1963 provides:

> 'On an application under this section the court may decide any question relating to the title of any person who is a party to the application to have his name entered in or omitted from the register, whether the question arises between members or alleged members, or between members or alleged members on the one hand and the company on the other hand, and generally may decide any question necessary or expedient to be decided for rectification of the register.'

In *Keene v Martin*[183], the English Court of Appeal held that the fact that a proper share transfer does not exist, does not automatically preclude the court from proceeding under s 122(1), as s 122(3) empowers the court to decide questions of title. At trial (reported as *Re Hoicrest Ltd*[184]), Judge Rich QC had held that no ground for registration existed until the applicant could show legal title, which the company had failed to register. He had

179 See *Autodata v Gibbons* (13 July 2000, unreported), SC (NSW).

180 Milman, 'Rectifying Share Registers' (1998) Palmer's *In Company*, Issue 10/98 20 November 1998.

181 See Ch 11, *Shareholders' Remedies*, para **[11.052]**.

182 *Re Olde Court Holiday Hostel Ltd; Trehy v Murtagh et al* [2006] IEHC 424.

183 *Keene v Martin* [2000] BCC 904; [2000] TLR 777.

184 *Re Hoicrest Ltd* [1998] 2 BCLC 175.

also held that the English equivalent to s 122(3) did not enlarge the jurisdiction conferred by s 122(1)[185]. This was rejected by the Court of Appeal, which found that an over-concentration on the equivalent to s 122(1) does not give full effect to the wide powers of the court under sub-s (3), and that it was circular to contend that sub-s (3) was subject to the prior limitations in sub-s (1). Mummery LJ said:

> 'The answer is to be found, in my view, in an appreciation of the distinction between jurisdiction and discretion. Jurisdiction to rectify is conferred by subsection (1). A general discretionary power is conferred on the court by subsection (3) so that a court, to which an application to rectify is made may, on such application, '… decide any question relating to the title of a person who is a party to the application to have his name entered in or omitted from the register … and generally may decide any question necessary or expedient to be decided for rectification of the register.'
>
> There is such a question here: the title of Mr Keene to the 49 shares which he claims should be registered in his name. It is true that … Mr Keene must establish that he has title to be entered in the register as a member in respect of the 49 shares. But, if there is a dispute about that title, subsection (3) empowers the court 'on such an application' to decide that question. It is true that the court would not make an order which required the company or its board to act in contravention of s 183 [of the Companies Act 1985 (UK); s 81(1) of the CA 1963] or the articles. But that inhibition on making an order does not prevent the court from resolving, prior to deciding whether or not to make an order for rectification, relevant disputes about the entitlement to the shares[186].'

The Court of Appeal did, however, go on to caution against the exercise of the discretion to determine title disputes in what are, essentially, summary proceedings, and indicated that proceedings for a declaration might often be more appropriate. In that case directions were made for the trial on the preliminary issue of whether the parties had agreed that 49 of the shares in the company would be held by the defendant on trust for the plaintiff, pending repayment of a loan by the defendant to the company.

[F] Pre-Emption Rights on Share Transfer

[9.069] In addition to the directors' rights to decline registration of share transfers, the articles of private companies commonly include pre-emption rights or rights of first refusal[187]. Because pre-emption clauses are creatures of the draughtsmen, any definition

---

[185] Judge Rich QC said: 'Subsection (3) of the section seems to be to be very clear. The first half makes clear that the court may decide any question relating to the title of a party "to have his name entered or omitted". [It is suggested] that this latter phrase is concerned only with title, that is ownership, legal or equitable, of the shares. In my view the words "to have his name entered" cannot be disregarded. That is the title which Cotton LJ found in *Wernher*'s case. These words do not enlarge the jurisdiction to rectify when the company itself would be powerless to alter the register.' In *Re Kimberley North Block Diamond Co, ex p Wernher* (1888) 59 LT 579, Cotton LJ said: 'Section 35 of the Companies Act 1862 imposes no limit on the jurisdiction thereby conferred on the court, though there may be cases in which it is not desirable that it should be executed.' It may be noted, though, that there the applicant had had a transfer executed in his favour.

[186] *Keene v Martin* [2000] BCC 904 at 908B–E.

[187] Where a shareholders' agreement exists, pre-emption rights are very commonly included and form an integral part of such agreements.

can only be general. However, it can be said that a pre-emption clause confers rights, usually in favour of existing members or the directors[188] of the company, which entitle them, usually on a pro rata basis, to a right of first refusal to buy the shares which are for sale before they can be offered to an outsider. The primary purpose of a pre-emption provision is to control the admission of members to a private company and to obstruct the unregulated admission of outsiders to the circle of members. Pre-emption rights on the transfer of shares should be distinguished from pre-emption rights on allotment of shares, considered in Ch 8[189].

[9.070] The following is a form of pre-emption clause which might be found in a private company's articles or a shareholders' agreement[190]:

'(a) The legal, equitable, beneficial or other interest in a share (hereinafter called 'a Share' or 'Shares') shall not be transferred unless the following provisions are complied with.

(b) Any member or any other person entitled to a Share by reason of the death or bankruptcy of any member or by operation of law who wishes to transfer a Share (hereinafter called 'the Proposing Transferor') shall give notice in writing to the company (hereinafter called 'a Transfer Notice'). Every such Transfer Notice shall constitute the directors as the Proposing Transferor's agents for the sale of the Shares specified in the Transfer Notice at a price to be agreed upon by the Proposing Transferor and the directors or in the absence of such agreement, at the price which the company's auditors shall certify to be, in their opinion, the fair value thereof, but without discounting or giving a premium to the value because the Shares constitute a minority or majority interest in the company[191], if that is the case ('the Share Price').

(c) A Transfer Notice served or deemed[192] to be served by a Proposing Transferor shall be irrevocable, save with the consent of the directors who may impose such conditions as they think fit in their absolute discretion.

(d) The certificate of the company's auditors as to the Share Price shall be final and binding upon all parties.

(e) When the Share Price has been determined in accordance with the provisions of clause (b) hereof, the directors shall within 7 days by notice in writing, offer to the existing members of the company the Shares specified in the Transfer Notice at the Share Price pro rata to their existing shareholdings in the company. Such

[188] See *Dean v Prince* [1954] 1 Ch 409, considered at para **[9.127]**.

[189] See Ch 8, *Shares and Membership*, para **[8.056]**.

[190] This clause is intended merely as an example of its genre and may not be suitable for use in some companies. It is not intended for use as a precedent.

[191] This may be considered appropriate in a quasi-partnership private company but perhaps inappropriate to other forms of private company: see generally para **[9.122]** *et seq*.

[192] In *Re Sedgefield Steeplechase Company (1927) Ltd; Scotto v Petch et al* [2000] 2 BCLC 211; [2000] TLR 107, it was held that an agreement for the sale of shares that expressly precluded the purchaser from requiring the vendor to do anything which would contravene the company's pre-emption provisions, did not demonstrate the necessary intention to transfer the legal title so as to trigger the pre-emption rights. Lord Hoffmann also held that a shareholder who had done nothing inconsistent with an intention to comply with the existing provisions, at the appropriate moment, could not be required to serve a transfer notice before he had entered into arrangements which placed him under a contractual obligation to execute and deliver a transfer in violation of the rights of pre-emption.

offer shall be open to the existing members for a period of 28 days from the date of the offer (hereinafter called 'the Acceptance Period'). If within the Acceptance Period the existing members apply for all or any of the Shares specified in the Transfer Notice the directors shall allocate the Shares, or such of them as are applied for, to the existing members in proportion or pro rata to their existing shareholdings in the company, as nearly as may be.

(f) If the existing members accept the offer within the Acceptance Period, the directors shall forthwith send a written notice to the Proposing Transferor (hereinafter called 'the Acceptance Notice') of the acceptance and shall specify in the Acceptance Notice the completion date which shall be not more than 28 days from the date of the Acceptance Notice and details of the completion date for the sale of the Shares.

(g) The Proposing Transferor shall be bound to complete the sale of the Shares specified in the Transfer Notice in accordance with the terms of the Acceptance Notice and where the Proposing Transferor refuses or fails for any reason whatsoever to complete the sale of the Shares, the directors shall be deemed and are hereby appointed the Proposing Transferor's attorney with full power to execute, complete and deliver in the name and on behalf of the Proposing Transferor, a transfer of the Shares or such as are applied for to the existing members of the company on receipt of the Share Price. Upon the payment of the Share Price to the directors:

   (i) the transferee shall obtain good title to the Shares and shall be entitled to insist upon being registered as a member of the company; and

   (ii) the company shall pay the Share Price into a separate bank account and shall hold same on trust for the Proposing Transferor.

(h) If the existing members or any or all of them do not within the Acceptance Period accept the offer to purchase the Shares specified in the Transfer Notice, then the Proposing Transferor may on payment of the Share Price transfer all or any of those Shares which are not applied for by the existing members to a person who is not a member of the company (hereinafter called 'a Non-Member') PROVIDED THAT

   (i) the directors shall be satisfied that the Non-Member is a person whom it is desirable to admit to membership of the company and unless they are so satisfied, shall not register the Non-Member as a member of the company,

   (ii) the directors shall be satisfied that the Proposing Transferor does not transfer the Shares at a price less than the Share Price and that the transfer is a bona fide sale for the consideration stated in the transfer.

(i) The restrictions on the transfer of Shares contained in this article shall not apply to any transfer approved in writing by all the members.

(j) For the purposes of this article the following shall be deemed to give rise to and are deemed to be the service of a Transfer Notice:

   (i) any direction by a member renouncing his right to an allotment of shares,

   (ii) any sale or other disposition of any equitable or beneficial interest in a share whether for consideration or otherwise and whether or not effected by an instrument in writing,

   (iii) the death or bankruptcy of any member,

   (iv) in the case of a member which is a body corporate, 7 days before its going into liquidation, except a members' voluntary winding up for the purpose of a reconstruction or amalgamation, or, 7 days before the appointment of a receiver to the corporate member, or 7 days before an Examiner is appointed to the Company.

(k) Subject to compliance with the foregoing sub-clauses, the directors shall register any transfer made in pursuance of these provisions but shall refuse to register any other transfer.'

[9.071] The foregoing clause is given to exemplify the sort of matters with which pre-emption clauses are concerned. The basic philosophy behind the clause is that a member who wants to sell his shares in the company must first offer them to the existing members in proportion to their existing shareholding. The pre-emption clause set out above contains a number of features common to many such clauses. First, there is a prohibition on the transfer of a share or any interest in a share, save in accordance with the provisions of the clause. Second, concepts central to the operation of the pre-emption procedure are defined, eg 'Transfer Notice', 'Proposing Transferor', etc. Third, the person desiring to transfer his shares must serve notice of his wish to sell his shares on the directors of the company who are thereby constituted his agent for the sale of the shares. Fourth, the price to be paid for the shares is the price agreed by the transferor and the directors, or in default of agreement, by the company's auditors whose determination of the shares' value is binding on all parties. Fifth, the existing members of the company are offered the shares for sale in proportion to their existing shareholdings. Sixth, strict time limits apply to the procedure. Seventh, if the existing members do not take up the shares on sale, the transferor may sell them to a non-member, subject to the directors' powers to veto such in particular situations. Eighth, certain circumstances will give rise to the deemed service of a transfer notice. Finally, provision is made for compulsory transfers of shares in particular specified circumstances.

[9.072] Pre-emption rights are a very important control on the transfer of shares in Irish private companies. Such clauses have been the subject of judicial scrutiny in a number of cases[193]. Pre-emption clauses are considered here as follows:

1. The need for pre-emption rights in private companies.
2. The judicial construction of pre-emption clauses.
3. Application to beneficial interests in shares.
4. The enforceability of pre-emption rights.

The need for pre-emption rights in private companies

[9.073] It is primarily because of the limitations of model reg 3 of Part II of Table A type restrictions on the registration of share transfers that some private companies favour the adoption of pre-emption rights. Although the directors can generally veto the registration of a share transfer, model reg 3 does not prohibit a member from transferring the equitable interest in his shares, whether outright[194] or by way of mortgage[195]. Although the equitable transferee or mortgagee may not be the registered owner of the shares in the company, it is well established that where consideration has

[193] See Hannigan, 'Share Transfer Problems in the Private Company' (1990) 11 Co Law 170, for an overview of some recent decisions of the Courts of England and Wales.

[194] *Musselwhite v CH Musselwhite & Son Ltd* [1962] Ch 964.

[195] *Wise v Landsell* [1921] 1 Ch 420.

passed, the legal owner holds the shares in trust. In this way control of a company can pass without the directors' consent.

[9.074] The decision in *Musselwhite v CH Musselwhite & Son Ltd*[196] demonstrates the weakness of the model reg 3 type restriction on the transfer of shares. In *Musselwhite,* the company had four shareholders: the plaintiff husband and wife held 3,599 shares and 1 share respectively, and the defendant husband and wife held 3,599 shares and 1 share respectively. The plaintiff husband was managing director and the other three shareholders were directors of the company. The plaintiff husband and wife agreed to sell their shares in the company and in another company to the defendants for £10,000, to be paid partly by way of instalments. It was also agreed that the transfers of the shares should be executed and, together with the share certificates, deposited with the company's solicitors until payment in full had been made to the plaintiffs. This was done but a dispute arose when the defendants erroneously believed that the plaintiffs were not entitled to receive notice of general meetings of the company, when in fact they remained on the register of members. When a general meeting was called without the plaintiffs being given notice, the plaintiffs applied, *inter alia*, for a declaration that the meeting was invalid.

Russell J rejected the defendants' contention that the plaintiffs were not entitled to notice of general meetings of the company. For as long as the plaintiffs were unpaid vendors in respect of their shares, they remained members of the company and were entitled to receive notice of meetings of the company. In this regard Russell J held that an unpaid vendor was in no weaker a position than a mortgagee:

> 'The purchaser acquires the beneficial interest subject to the vendor's lien; the mortgagor retains the beneficial interest subject to the charge in favour of the mortgagee, in the form of an equity of redemption. In the one case the mortgagee is deliberately put on the register to safeguard his money lent: in the other case the vendor is deliberately left on the register until all is paid to safeguard his purchase-money due.
>
> In my judgment an unpaid vendor of shares remaining on the register after the contract for sale retains vis-à-vis the purchaser the prima facie right to vote in respect of those shares[197].'

Conversely, where consideration has passed but the transferee has not been registered, the transferor will hold the shares in trust for the transferee and will be compelled to account for dividends paid in respect of the shares and to vote to the order of the transferee[198]. It is in this way that the reins of control in a company may change hands notwithstanding the directors' powers to refuse registration.

[9.075] The decision in *Musselwhite* was distinguished by the High Court in *O'Gorman v Kelleher*[199]. In this case, the plaintiffs and defendants were all directors of a company. The defendants were together entitled to 56.25% of the shares. The defendants had previously offered to buy the plaintiffs' shares and this offer was accepted but subsequently withdrawn when financial arrangements did not come through. The

196 *Musselwhite v CH Musselwhite & Son Ltd* [1962] Ch 964.

197 *Musselwhite v CH Musselwhite & Son Ltd* [1962] Ch 964 at 987.

198 *Ward and Henry's case* (1867) 2 Ch App 431; *Stevenson v Wilson* (1907) SC 445; and *Hawks v McArthur* [1951] 1 All ER 22.

199 *O'Gorman v Kelleher* (19 July 1999, unreported) HC, Carroll J.

plaintiffs then offered to buy the first defendant's shareholding and the plaintiffs claimed that he agreed to sell his shareholding for £5.2 million. The first defendant disputed this. Subsequently, the defendants gave notice of their intention to remove certain persons as directors of the company and the proposed meeting was injuncted by interim order. On the interlocutory application the plaintiffs sought, *inter alia*, an injunction restraining the defendants from exercising rights in respect of the 160,000 ordinary shares that were alleged to be the subject of the agreement. Carroll J noted that if there was (as alleged) an enforceable agreement the effect would be to shift the balance of the voting power from the defendants to the plaintiffs. Citing *Musselwhite*, the defendants argued that even if the plaintiff was to succeed in the specific performance of the alleged contract for the sale of the shares, it was not open to the court to restrict the right of a registered owner to vote whichever way he wanted. Carroll J noted that there it was held that the 'unpaid vendors were entitled to exercise their voting rights in respect of the shares (it not being alleged that the rights would be exercised so as to damage the subject matter of the purchase)'. The learned judge distinguished the facts there from those in hand, saying:

> 'Here it is clear that the voting rights attached to the shares, the subject matter of the alleged contract, are being used to oust Michael O'Gorman, one of the purchasers, which is damaging to the plaintiffs' interests. If an unpaid vendor of shares were to vote deliberately so as to damage the purchaser, or contrary to the interests of the purchaser, who is the beneficial owner, it seems to me that he should be restrained by the court of Equity[200].'

It is thought to be sound law for the courts of equity to restrain a paid vendor of shares from exercising the voting rights attaching thereto to the detriment of the purchaser. Whether a purchaser who has not parted with any consideration ought to be afforded protection is a more difficult matter. Some support can be found for saying that the voting rights of a vendor under an uncompleted contract are in abeyance, at least for certain purposes. In *Michaels v Harley House (Marylebone) Ltd*[201], Robert Walker LJ considered shareholders' rights to vote for the purposes of the definition of holding company and subsidiary company. There, he said:

> 'A registered shareholder who is absolute beneficial owner can vote as he pleases, subject only to rather imprecise constraints imposed by company law (see *Smith v Croft (No 2)* [1987] 3 All ER 909 at 957–958). A registered shareholder who is a nominee must vote in accordance with the directions of the absolute beneficial owner, to whom his voting rights are attributed. A registered shareholder who is vendor under an uncompleted contract is in an intermediate position, a fiduciary but not a nominee, and his voting rights are for the purposes of s 736 [of the Companies Act 1985 (UK), which defines parent and subsidiary company] in abeyance.'

It would seem that the Irish (and perhaps the English) courts are prepared to protect a purchaser who has not parted with the consideration for the shares on the basis that the vendor is in a fiduciary relationship to the purchaser and the purchaser has an equity as a result of the unconcluded contract.

---

200 *O'Gorman v Kelleher* (19 July 1999, unreported) HC at p 4.

201 *Michaels v Harley House (Marylebone) Ltd* [1999] 1 All ER 356. See further Ch 12, *Groups of Companies*, para **[12.023]** *et seq*.

The judicial construction of pre-emption clauses

[9.076] Clauses which confer pre-emption rights on members can fall to be construed by the courts, directly or indirectly, in a number of situations. Pre-emption rights may result in a direct judicial hearing where application is made under Ord 83 of the RSC 1986, which facilitates application to be made to court for the determination of any question of construction arising under a written instrument. Pre-emption rights may fall to be indirectly construed by the courts in a variety of situations: in a minority shareholders' remedy action under s 205 of the CA 1963; and where decisions of the company are called into question by its members on the basis that the articles or a shareholders' agreement have been breached[202].

[9.077] In *McAuliffe v Lithographic Group Ltd*[203], the Supreme Court considered a member's right to purchase shares which was conferred by a pre-emption clause in a shareholders' agreement. In the High Court Costello J had construed a clause in a shareholders' agreement as requiring the plaintiff and his wife to purchase the shares held by the defendant in a company called Mac Publishing Ltd. The appeal to the Supreme Court arose from this decision. The facts of the case were that the McAuliffes and the defendant had entered into a shareholders' agreement whereby the McAuliffes purchased 40% and the defendant purchased 60% of the shares in the company. O'Flaherty J said it was clear that each party was given a right of pre-emption, entitling them to purchase the other party's shares. The problem which required resolution in the case was whether the obligation to purchase the shares was a mutual obligation or a unilateral obligation.

When, pursuant to the clause, the defendant company served a purchase notice on the McAuliffes, the McAuliffes did not accept the offer but served their own purchase notice on the defendant. Were the obligation to purchase the shares mutual, the first in time would have prevailed. Costello J had held that the obligation was mutual and that the McAuliffes were obliged to purchase the defendant's shares. O'Flaherty J accepted that the clause in hand 'was quite a confused provision'[204]. However he acknowledged that the court must come to grips with the clause as best it may. He held that the clause imposed an obligation on the defendant to purchase the McAuliffes' shares and that the only binding purchase notice was the one served by the McAuliffes. Accordingly, the decision of the High Court was reversed. The importance of this case is that the wording of the pre-emption clause in hand was decisive; a cautionary note for the legal draughtsman.

[9.078] There is a tendency for the courts to construe pre-emption clauses strictly[205]. Shares are *prima facie* transferable, and where the right to transfer is curtailed, the courts will strictly construe all restrictions. This is exemplified by the English Court of

---

202 See generally, Ch 11, *Shareholders' Remedies*.

203 *McAuliffe v Lithographic Group Ltd* (2 November 1993, unreported) SC, ex tempore recorded judgment *per* O'Flaherty J.

204 *McAuliffe v Lithographic Group Ltd* (2 November 1993, unreported) SC at p 10.

205 In *The Ocean Coal Company Ltd v The Powell Duffryn Steam Coal Company Ltd* [1932] 1 Ch 654, a pre-emption clause obliged any member desiring to sell his shares to notify the directors of the number of shares, the price and the proposed transferee and provided that the directors must offer such shares at that price to the existing members. (contd.../)

Appeal decision in *Safeguard Industrial Investments Ltd v National Westminster Bank Ltd*[206]. The plaintiff investment company and a deceased member of the company together held one-sixth of the issued shares in the subject company, M Wright & Sons Ltd. The remainder of the shares were held by the deceased member's two cousins and one of the cousin's two children, Y and Z. By his will the deceased member appointed the defendant bank as executor and named Y and Z as beneficiaries. The company's articles contained pre-emption rights in favour of the existing members where shares were transferred. No restriction was stated to apply to the transmission of shares[207]. The beneficiaries, Y and Z, directed the executor bank not to transfer the shares to them, preferring to rely on the bank's acknowledgement that it held the shares on trust for Y and Z. At trial the plaintiff unsuccessfully argued that the bank was bound to serve a transfer notice after it had completed the administration of the deceased member's estate and purported to assent to the vesting of the beneficial interest in the shares in Y and Z. The Court of Appeal upheld the trial judge's decision, holding that on a true construction of the articles the bank was not obliged to serve a transfer notice and that until such was served the pre-emption machinery could not be triggered. Furthermore it was held that the term 'transfer' only embraced the legal title to shares and not the equitable title[208]. It is because of decisions such as this that most properly-drafted pre-emption clauses are expressed to apply to the transmission of shares and, as shall be considered next, restrictions on the transfer of shares are deemed to apply to the disposal of an equitable interest in addition to a legal interest.

[9.079] Where a pre-emption clause contains a time limit within which action must be taken, this will be construed strictly by the courts. An example of this is *Re New Cedos Engineering Co Ltd*[209], where Oliver J held that a deceased member's personal representatives were only bound to transfer the shares where, within three months of receiving notice of the member's death, the company found a member willing to purchase the shares at fair value.

Application to beneficial interests in shares

[9.080] As has been seen, it was held by the Court of Appeal in *Safeguard Industrial Investments Ltd v National Westminster Bank Ltd*[210] that the pre-emption clause in question applied only to transfers of the legal interest in a share, and did not extend to

---

205 (\...contd) It was further provided that if the shares or any of them were not so accepted, the proposing transferor could sell to the transferee of his choice. It was held by Farwell J that a subsequent offer to buy less than 4% of the shares at even the stated price was not sufficient and that the proposing transferor was entitled to sell all of the shares to the proposed transferee of his choice.

206 *Safeguard Industrial Investments Ltd v National Westminster Bank Ltd* [1982] 1 All ER 449.

207 *Safeguard Industrial Investments Ltd v National Westminster Bank Ltd* [1982] 1 All ER 449 at 451, *per* Oliver LJ.

208 See also *Hunter v Hunter* [1936] AC 222 and *Lyle & Scott Ltd v Scott's Trustees* [1959] 2 All ER 661.

209 *Re New Cedos Engineering Co Ltd* [1994] 1 BCLC 797.

210 *Safeguard Industrial Investments Ltd v National Westminster Bank Ltd* [1982] 1 All ER 449.

the equitable interest in shares. As Harmon LJ said in *Re Swaledale Cleaners Ltd*[211], in a passage noted by Roderick Murphy J in *Phelan v Goodman*[212]:

> 'If the right of transfer, which is inherent in property of this kind, is to be taken away or cut down, it seems to me that it should be done by language of sufficient clarity to make it apparent that this was the intention.'

The case law on this point is somewhat ambiguous[213]. It was said in the first edition of this book[214] that the dominant view was that that a simple prohibition on the transfer of shares will not prevent the disposition of the equitable or beneficial interest in shares[215]. Since then, the balance may be said to have tipped in favour of construing a restriction on transfer as preventing the equitable interest being transferred. In *Phelan v Goodman*[216], it was held by the High Court that the disposition of a person's equitable interest in shares was in breach of a prohibition in the articles of association on the 'transfer' of shares without first offering them to the other member. In so finding, Roderick Murphy J quoted the following passage from Lord Keith in *Lyle and Scott Ltd v Scotts Trustees*[217]:

> 'A share is of no value to anyone without the benefits it confers. A sale of a share is sale of the beneficial rights that it confers, and to sell or purport to sell the beneficial rights without the title to the share is, in my opinion, in plain breach of the provisions of [the relevant article].'

The learned High Court judge also quoted the following passage from Lord Keith, and in so doing, illustrated the attitude he took to the argument that legal and beneficial title could be distinguished for the purposes of pre-emption rights:

> 'A shareholder who has transferred, or pretended to transfer, the beneficial interest in a share to a purchaser for value is merely endeavouring by a subterfuge to escape from the peremptory provisions of the Article.'

In *Phelan v Goodman,* the High Court would not countenance a technical argument that sought to distinguish legal from beneficial title. The company in that case had, however, only two shareholders and it remains to be seen whether future cases might not seek to distinguish this decision on the grounds that it ought to be confined to companies with so few members.

[9.081] *Hawks v McArthur*[218] is, however, authority for the proposition that a simple restriction on share transfer will not prevent the equitable interest in the shares passing where full consideration has passed to the transferor. The articles of the company

211 *Re Swaledale Cleaners Ltd* [1968] 1 WLR 1710. See also *Scotto v Petch* (20 January 2000), English High Court.

212 *Phelan v Goodman* (11 September 2001, unreported) HC.

213 See *Lyle & Scott Ltd v Scott's Trustees* [1959] 2 All ER 661, and generally, Stedman & Jones, *Shareholders' Agreements* (2nd edn, 1990), pp 23–26.

214 Courtney, *The Law of Private Companies* (1st edn, 1994), para **[10.057]**.

215 For a distinction between *equitable* and *beneficial* ownership, see *J Sainsbury plc v O'Connor (Inspector of Taxes)* [1990] STC 516, *per* Millett J.

216 *Phelan v Goodman* (11 September 2001, unreported) HC.

217 *Lyle and Scott Ltd v Scotts Trustees* [1959] AC 763 at 785.

218 *Hawks v McArthur* [1951] 1 All ER 22.

contained rights of pre-emption. Notwithstanding the pre-emption rights in the articles, a retiring director, McArthur, executed two transfers of shares, one in favour of the chairman and one in favour of the manager of the company. The chairman and the manager paid McArthur the full purchase price for the shares, although they had not been registered as owners of the shares. The plaintiff, who was a member of the company, obtained a money judgment against McArthur and converted this into a charging order on his shares. The chairman and the manager of the company, who had paid the full price for the shares, claimed that notwithstanding that the pre-emption rights had not been complied with, they held the beneficial interest in the shares and that the charging order was ineffective.

Vaisey J reluctantly[219] upheld the manager's and the chairman's contention. The decisive factor was that they had both paid McArthur full consideration. Vaisey J considered that he could not bring himself to suppose that they got nothing from the bargain. Having accepted that the chairman and the manager had rights, the remaining question was that of priorities: McArthur had legal rights; the plaintiff with his charging order had an equity or quasi-equitable rights; and the chairman and the manager had equitable rights. In the clash between the equitable rights Vaisey J held that the first in time prevailed and reluctantly held for the manager and the chairman, whom he felt had acted in almost scandalous disregard of the company's articles[220].

[9.082] This decision appears to conflict with *Lee & Company (Dublin) Ltd v Egan (Wholesale) Ltd*[221], where Kenny J did not acknowledge that the purchaser had any equitable rights in shares which were contracted to be sold in breach of a company's pre-emption right provisions. The decision in *Lee & Company* may be distinguished on a number of grounds. First, a transfer of shares had not been executed, there being only a contract for the sale of the shares. Second, the purchaser had thought he was buying all the shares in the company when in fact the vendor did not own all the shares and so the purchaser may not have been well served had it been declared that he had merely an equitable interest in only some of the company's shares[222]. Finally, the purchaser had not yet paid the vendor for the shares as is required to claim an equitable interest.

[9.083] It has been held that that no rights, whether legal or equitable, can arise in favour of the equitable mortgagee where pre-emption rights are bypassed. Authority for this proposition is *Hunter v Hunter*[223], where Lord Atkin said:

> 'The effect of art 17 in my opinion is to provide the means and the only means by which a member of the company can form an agreement for the sale of shares, which can only be constituted by the act of the secretary as agent for seller and purchaser declaring a contract to be concluded at the price fixed by the auditor. That was not done in that case, and in my

---

[219] *Hawks v McArthur* [1951] 1 All ER 22 at 27g–h.

[220] See also *Theakston v London Trust plc et al* [1984] BCLC 390 where 'transfer' in the pre-emption clause in hand was defined by Harman J (at 397) as referring to actions disposing of the legal ownership of shares and 'not to mere dealings with equitable interests in the shares'.

[221] *Lee & Company (Dublin) Ltd v Egan (Wholesale) Ltd* (27 April 1978, unreported) HC, *per* Kenny J, considered at para **[9.084]**.

[222] To have equitable rights in only some of the shares in a private company is a less than desirable position to be in, especially if the other shareholders are opposed to one's admission.

[223] *Hunter v Hunter* [1936] AC 222. See *Re Hafner* [1943] IR 426, *per* Black J.

> opinion no rights arose between the bank and Harry Hunter under any contract of sale either equitable or legal[224].'

As a general proposition it must be doubted that the distinction between equitable mortgagees and other transferees can be sustained. Perhaps the matter should turn upon whether or not the transferee (or equitable mortgagee) had actual notice of the pre-emption provisions[225]. In view of the ambiguities in the law, when drafting a pre-emption clause extreme caution should be exercised. Although it would seem that a simple prohibition on the transfer of shares is sufficient to prevent an equitable mortgagee from acquiring either legal or beneficial title in shares, such might be ineffective to prevent the passing of the equitable or beneficial interest to a transferee for value. When restricting the transfer of a share it may be desirable to define share in the articles or in a shareholders' agreement as including the legal and beneficial and equitable interest in the share.

The enforceability of pre-emption rights

[9.084] Where the articles or a shareholders' agreement contain pre-emption rights, the courts of Ireland and the UK have shown that they will vigorously defend the rights of a company's members to first refusal to purchase the shares in the company[226]. One of the clearest examples is *Lee & Company (Dublin) Ltd v Egan (Wholesale) Ltd*[227]. In that case the articles of the defendant company included a right of pre-emption in favour of the existing members[228]. There were four members: Mr Roe who held 7,100 shares, his wife who held 900 shares, Mr Wallace who held 800 shares and Mr Mulligan who held two shares. Mr Roe was anxious to retire from the business and entered into negotiations, through an auctioneer, with a Mr Conroy who was managing director of the plaintiff company, Lee & Company (Dublin) Ltd. Conroy believed that Roe owned 90% of the shares in the company and that he had authority to sell all the issued shares. A purchase price of £205,000 was agreed, the parties thinking in terms of the assets and liabilities of the company although Roe had no authority to sell all the shares in the company. Roe contracted to sell all the shares in the company to Conroy; the contract was not conditional and although the terms were never put in writing, they were set out in a letter to Roe dictated by the auctioneer. The fact that articles gave the other members the right to acquire Roe's 7,100 shares in priority to any other person was overlooked. Problems arose when Roe sought more money for the shares in the company. Conroy refused to pay more and sought an order for specific performance of the contract to sell the shares.

Kenny J held that the proper form of relief was to declare that the contract for the sale of the 7,100 shares owned by Roe ought to be performed. However, Kenny J held

---

224 *Hunter v Hunter* [1936] AC 222 at 261.

225 *Actual notice* is to be preferred to *constructive notice* in this context: were the pre-emption machinery contained in a company's articles, it is possible that because the articles are public documents, everybody would have constructive notice of their provisions.

226 See *Attorney General for Ireland v Jameson* [1904] 2 IR 644.

227 *Lee & Company (Dublin) Ltd v Egan (Wholesale) Ltd* (27 April 1978, unreported) HC, *per* Kenny J.

228 For the actual wording of the particular clause, see *Lee and Company (Dublin) Ltd v Egan (Wholesale) Ltd* (27 April 1978, unreported) HC, pp 2–5.

that if the plaintiff decided to purchase the shares, Roe, the proposing transferor, had to give notice under the company's articles to the company's other members of the fixed price which had been agreed with Conroy. The right of first refusal of the existing members was thus vindicated by the court. Any other member of the company was accordingly entitled to purchase Roe's shares in accordance with the pre-emption machinery. Only if no other member elected to purchase the shares within the specified time period could Roe execute a transfer of shares in favour of Conroy. This decision clearly affords the members of the company, who have rights of first refusal, with equitable rights, or at the very least, equities. In *O'Gorman v Kelleher*[229], where an alleged contract to sell shares was claimed to be in breach of the company's pre-emption provisions, Carroll J declined to find that the pre-emption rights would render the contract inoperable. Following *Lee & Company Dublin Ltd v Egan Wholesale Ltd*, Carroll J found that Kenny J had held that the 'proper form of relief in such a case was to declare that the contract ought to be performed subject to the pre-emption rights of the members of the company'[230].

[9.085] The willingness of the court to enforce the rights of pre-emption is seen also in Blayney J's judgment in *Re Champion Publications Ltd*[231]. In that case, the articles contained pre-emption rights in favour of existing members and Blayney J ordered that certain transfers be set aside because they were not carried out in accordance with the articles. The form of the pre-emption clause employed by the company was one which is in relatively common use in Ireland, and is favoured by a number of company formation firms. The part of the clause under examination concerned the method in which shares being transferred should be offered to the company's existing members. The clause provided that the members of the company in general meeting could make, and from time to time vary, the procedure to be followed and the rights of the members. It went on to provide that unless otherwise determined, 'every such share shall be offered to the members in such order as shall be determined by lots drawn in regard thereto and the lots shall be drawn in such manner as the directors think fit'. Blayney J refused to construe this so as to give the directors a free reign and held that it was the sensible course 'to allow the members themselves to decide the appropriate rules which should be formulated and in accordance with which shares contained in a transfer notice should be offered to the members'.

[9.086] In *Tett v Phoenix Property and Investment Co Ltd*[232], the defendant company's articles contained pre-emption rights in favour of existing members and their families on both the transfer and transmission of shares. When a member died, her executors were instructed to sell her shares by the beneficiary under her will. Due to a misunderstanding, notice was served on the company's other members advising them that 23 shares were on offer; in fact the deceased member had held 113 shares in the company. When the other members refused what they thought was an offer of 23 shares, the executors believed that the offer to sell all 113 of the shares had been rejected by the

---

229 *O'Gorman v Kelleher* (19 July 1999, unreported) HC, Carroll J. The facts are given at para **[9.075]**.

230 *O'Gorman v Kelleher* (19 July 1999, unreported) HC at p 5.

231 *Re Champion Publications Ltd* (4 June 1991, unreported) HC, Blayney J.

232 *Tett v Phoenix Property and Investment Co Ltd* [1986] BCLC 149.

existing members and they agreed to sell the shares to the plaintiff, Tett. The directors of the company refused to register the transfer in favour of the plaintiff on the basis that the pre-emption provisions had not been complied with properly. The directors then took the step of advising the members that a further 90 shares were in fact being offered, and before the trial of the matter at least one member indicated an interest in purchasing the shares. At trial Vinelott J ordered the company to register Tett as a member of the company. This was reversed by the Court of Appeal. The first question to be determined was identified by Slade LJ as being: did the clause on its true construction impose a valid and enforceable condition which has to be satisfied if the executors were to have the right to transfer the 90 shares to a non-member of the company? Slade LJ said that the clause was valid and effective:

> 'This condition was that the executors should have first taken reasonable steps to give all other members and their specified relatives a reasonable opportunity to make an offer to purchase the shares at a fair value to be determined by the auditors in default of agreement and that no such offer should have been made ... I am satisfied that the executors before executing the transfer of their shares, did not take reasonable steps to give even the other members of the company a reasonable opportunity to make such an offer[233].'

Although there were certain uncertainties with the clause, it was held to contain a sufficiently clear express restriction to cut down the prima facie right to transfer shares[234]. On account of the non-compliance with the required procedure, the directors were entitled to refuse to register the shares in the plaintiff's name.

[G] Compulsory Transfers of Shares

[9.087] Shares may be transferred compulsorily in three ways:

- in accordance with the provisions in a company's articles;
- by statute, pursuant to s 205 of the CA 1963(3); or
- also by statute, pursuant to s 204 of the CA 1963.

Section 205 of CA 1963 is considered in Ch 11, *Shareholders' Remedies*. At this point, compulsory transfer under the articles and under s 204 of the CA 1963 are considered.

Compulsory transfer under the articles

[9.088] Sometimes the articles of private companies will provide that a member is obliged to transfer his shares upon the occurrence of certain events. One of the earlier cases which upheld the validity and enforceability of such a clause was *Borland's Trustee v Steel Brothers & Co Ltd*[235]. Extreme caution should be exercised by the members in altering the articles to provide for the compulsory transfer of a member's shares, lest the alteration be set aside as being *mala fide* and not in the interests of the company as a whole[236]. Even where the articles provide *ab initio* for the compulsory

[233] *Tett v Phoenix Property and Investment Co Ltd* [1986] BCLC 149 at 161.

[234] *Tett v Phoenix Property and Investment Co Ltd* [1986] BCLC 149 at 157 recognised by Slade LJ, referring to *Re Swaledale Cleaners Ltd* [1968] 3 All ER 619 and *Greenhalgh v Mallard* [1943] 2 All ER 234. See also Robert Goff LJ at 163.

[235] *Borland's Trustee v Steel Brothers & Co Ltd* [1901] 1 Ch 279.

[236] See generally, Ch 3, *Constitutional Documentation*, para **[3.067]** *et seq*.

transfer of a member's shares, the courts will construe such provisions strictly. Where a member's shares are expropriated in an oppressive manner, he may petition the court under s 205 of the CA 1963[237].

[9.089] Although there is no compulsory transfer of shares clause in the model articles, some companies' articles provide that the following acts are triggers for requiring the compulsory transfer of shares:

- death;
- bankruptcy;
- conviction of an indictable offence;
- insanity or other mental incapacity;
- the commencement of a winding up or the appointment of a receiver or an examiner, where the member is a body corporate;
- the change in the control of a member which is a body corporate;
- the member's ceasing to be a director or an employee of the company;
- the disposal or attempted disposal of the equitable or beneficial ownership in shares in the company.

It is possible to include a compulsory transfer clause in a pre-emption clause[238]. Where this is done, the occurrence of one of the foregoing events can be deemed to constitute the service of a transfer notice in respect of that member's shares. Upon the service of that transfer notice, the usual pre-emption rights mechanism will then come into operation.

[9.090] When shares are compulsorily transferred it is prudent to provide that they are valued in a just and equitable manner. Where the auditors are entrusted with the valuation of shares sold pursuant to the pre-emption rights clause, it is often appropriate to apply the same valuation provisions to compulsory transfers. In *Re Castleburn Ltd*[239], the company concerned was a quasi-partnership private company. In addition to having pre-emption rights, there was a compulsory transfer provision. This provided that any member who was a director or employee and who ceased to be such could be compelled by a majority of the other members to sell his shares. When one of the original promoters, who was a director and the owner of 44% of the shares, was removed as an employee and a director, the compulsory transfer provisions were triggered. The valuation by the company's auditors, which discounted their value on the basis that they were a minority shareholding, was upheld as being reasonable by the court.

The valuation of shares in private companies is considered in more detail below[240].

Compulsory transfer under s 204 of the CA 1963

[9.091] In particular limited circumstances, a member can be compelled by statute to transfer his shares[241]. The power to acquire shares from members arises under s 204 of the CA 1963. Section 204(1) provides an enabling mechanism whereby one company,

237 See generally, Ch 11, *Shareholders' Remedies*, at para **[11.006]** *et seq*.

238 See para **[9.070]** at sub-clause (j).

239 *Re Castleburn Ltd* [1991] BCLC 89.

240 See para **[9.117]**.

241 See generally, Clarke, *Takeovers and Mergers Law in Ireland* (1999), p 326 *et seq*.

('the transferee-company') can compulsorily acquire shares held by members of another company ('the target company') where its offer to purchase the shares in the target company has been accepted by at least 80% of its members. The effect of s 204 is to facilitate a complete and efficient takeover of the target company by the transferee-company. Its exclusive application to takeovers is borne out by the fact that only a company[242] can compulsorily acquire the shares in the target company; a human person has no standing under s 204 to acquire shares compulsorily. It is important to note, however, that the transferee-company need not be a 'company' within the meaning of s 2 of the CA 1963, but the transferor or target company must be an Irish company within the meaning of s 2: *Re Fitzwilton plc; Duggan v Stoneworth Investment Ltd*[243].

[9.092] Although s 204 of the CA 1963 is a legitimate and useful means of taking over a company, if abused, it has the potential to give rise to unjust results. Even the notional agreement of members, which can by implication be said to exist when shares are compulsorily acquired in accordance with a company's articles, does not exist in a s 204 acquisition. Accordingly, it is only proper that the courts should construe s 204 strictly. Here it is proposed to consider the issues that arise in the context of s 204 under the following headings:

(a) The mandatory statutory requirements.

(b) The court's discretion.

(a) The mandatory statutory requirements

[9.093] Section 204(1) of the CA 1963 provides:

> 'Subject to subsection (2), where a scheme, contract or offer involving the acquisition by one company, whether a company within the meaning of this Act or not (in this section referred to as 'the transferee-company') of the beneficial ownership of all the shares (other than shares already in the beneficial ownership of the transferee-company) in the capital of another company, being a company within the meaning of this Act (in this section referred to as 'the transferor company') has become binding or been approved or accepted in respect of not less than four-fifths in value of the shares affected not later than the date 4 months after publication generally to the holders of the shares affected of the terms of such scheme, contract or offer, the transferee-company may at any time before the expiration of the period of 6 months next following such publication give notice in the prescribed manner to any dissenting shareholder that it desires to acquire the beneficial ownership of his shares, and when such notice is given the transferee-company shall, unless on an application made by the dissenting shareholder within one month from the date on which the notice was given, the court thinks fit to order otherwise, be entitled and bound to acquire the beneficial ownership of those shares on the terms on which under the scheme, contract or offer, the beneficial ownership of the shares in respect of which the scheme, contract or offer has become binding or been approved or accepted is to be acquired by the transferee-company.'

[242] Section 204(1) of the CA 1963. In this regard, it should also be noted that only 'companies' within the meaning of s 2 of the CA 1963 can have their shares compulsorily acquired. For the provisions of s 2 of the CA 1963, see Ch 1, *The Private Company in Context*, para **[1.156]** *et seq*.

[243] *Re Fitzwilton plc; Duggan v Stoneworth Investment Ltd* [2000] 2 ILRM 263. There the transferee-company was a British Virgin Islands company; the target or transferor company was an Irish company.

In order to acquire the shares held by dissident shareholders, the transferee-company must publish details of the terms of the scheme, contract or offer generally to the holders of the shares affected by the scheme. The transferee-company's offer must relate to all of the shares in the company since the terms of s 204(1) do not extend to partial offers. It is only when a scheme, contract or offer ('the offer') has become binding or has been approved or accepted by the holders of 80%[244] in value of the shares in the target company that the compulsory transfer of shares can be triggered. It is usual for offers to be made conditional upon the transferee-company receiving acceptances from the requisite four-fifths[245]. This offer must have been accepted by and become binding on the holders of the 80% not later than four months after the publication of the terms of the offer to the shareholders. Once notice has been served, dissenting shareholders become obliged to sell, and the transferee-company becomes obliged to purchase the shares[246]. Where, on application by the transferee-company, all of the mandatory statutory requirements have been met, dissenting shareholders will be bound to sell and the transferee-company will be bound to acquire the remaining shares. A dissenting shareholder must act without delay in making objection because the offer will become binding on him without the sanction of the court unless he makes application to court within one month of receiving the notice aforesaid. The terms offered to dissenting shareholders (including the consideration) must be the same as those which the assenting shareholders received[247].

[9.094] Section 204(2) and (3) of the CA 1963 provides:

> '(2) Where shares in the transferor company are, at the date of such publication, already in the beneficial ownership of the transferee-company to a value greater than one-fifth of the aggregate value of those shares and the shares affected, subsection (1) shall not apply unless the assenting shareholders besides holding not less than four-fifths in value of the shares affected are not less than three-fourths in number of the holders of those shares.
>
> (3) For the purpose of this section, shares in the transferor company in the beneficial ownership of a subsidiary of the transferee-company shall be deemed to be in the beneficial ownership of the transferee-company, the acquisition of the beneficial ownership of shares in the transferor company by a subsidiary of the transferee-company shall be deemed to be the acquisition of such beneficial ownership by the transferee-

244 *Four-fifths* is the phrase used in s 204 of the CA 1963.

245 See further, Clarke, *Takeovers and Mergers Law in Ireland* (1999), pp 330, 331 where the Takeover Rules' provisions are also noted.

246 Section 204(4) of the CA 1963.

247 Section 204(1) of the CA 1963 provides: 'Where the scheme, contract or offer provides that an assenting shareholder may elect between 2 or more sets of terms for the acquisition by the transferee company of the beneficial ownership of the shares affected, the notice given by the transferee company under subsection (1) shall be accompanied by or embody a notice stating the alternative sets of terms between which assenting shareholders are entitled to elect and specifying which of those sets of terms shall be applicable to the dissenting shareholder if he does not before the expiration of 14 days from the date of the giving of the notice notify to the transferee company in writing his election as between such alternative sets of terms, and the terms upon which the transferee company shall under this section be entitled and bound to acquire the beneficial ownership of the shares of the dissenting shareholder shall be the set of terms which the dissenting shareholder shall so notify or, in default of such notification, the set of terms so specified as applicable.'

company and shares shall not be treated as not being in the beneficial ownership of the transferee-company merely by reason of the fact that those shares are or may become subject to a charge in favour of another person.'

Therefore, s 204(1) is subject to sub-s (2), which applies where at the date of publication of the terms of the offer, the transferee company already has in its beneficial ownership, more than 20% of the aggregate value of the shares in the company and the affected shares. In such circumstances the transferee-company cannot apply for an order under sub-s (1) unless those who are agreeable to sell their shares not only hold 80% in value of the shares but are also together not less than 75% of the holders of those shares[248].

(b) The court's discretion

[9.095] Where a dissenting shareholder applies for relief from compulsory acquisition of his shares, the court has discretion where it thinks fit to order otherwise. It is notable that the court's discretion is not confined to a stark choice between confirmation and veto. Rather, it can make *any order it thinks fit*, and so could order that the dissenting shareholders be paid more than the assenting shareholders. That said, however, in general, the court will either confirm or veto the takeover. In exercising its discretion, it will have regard to a number of matters, which are considered here as follows:

(i) Disclosure of full particulars.
(ii) The onus of proof.
(iii) The *bona fides* and independence of the transferee-company.

(i) Disclosure of full particulars

[9.096] A transferee-company must disclose full details of the proposed transaction in publishing the terms of the offer to the target company's shareholders[249]. In *Securities Trust Ltd v Associated Properties Ltd and Estates Development Ltd*[250], McWilliam J said:

> 'I do not know what is the reason for the provisions of s 204 of the 1963 Act or why it should be thought desirable that minority shareholders may be compulsorily bought out, but I am of opinion that, on a compulsory purchase of this nature, the people whose shares are being compulsorily purchased are entitled to be given full particulars of the transaction, its purpose, the method of carrying it out and its consequences. The purpose

[248] Shares in the target company which are in the beneficial ownership of a subsidiary of the transferee-company are deemed to be in the beneficial ownership of the transferee-company: s 204(3) of the CA 1963.

[249] *Cf Re Evertite Locknuts Ltd* [1945] 1 Ch 220 where Vaisey J said (at 224–225): 'I do not see how I can listen to the plea of the applicant, who refuses to tell me whether he regards the offer as fair or unfair, but merely asks the court to say that he is not bound, because he might have had more information than in fact was offered to him as to circumstances which were, or might have been, relevant when he was considering the terms of the offer he had received ... it cannot be right that one shareholder, owning one seven-hundredth part of the shares affected, should be entitled to stand out against the decision of the 699/700ths of the share capital, merely because he has, as he thinks, been left somewhat in the dark in regard to the material facts.'

[250] *Securities Trust Ltd v Associated Properties Ltd and Estates Development Ltd* (19 November 1980, unreported) HC, *per* McWilliam J.

> of the transaction and its consequences have not yet been disclosed and the method of carrying it out was not disclosed to the persons concerned[251].'

It was unnecessary to make an order in that case because the parties settled the action. Although it has been observed that this case marks a slight lightening of the burden on dissenting shareholders[252], this test is thought to be correct in the context of some private companies. Where there exist mutuality and understanding between a company's shareholders, and especially where the company is in the nature of a quasi-partnership, the deprivation of relief to a dissenting shareholder must be withheld sparingly.

(ii) The onus of proof

[9.097] Where the statutory provisions embodied in s 204 of the CA 1963 have been complied with, case law establishes that the onus is on the dissenting shareholder to establish unfairness[253]. An early case in point is *Re Hoare and Co Ltd*[254], where the transferee-company made an offer to the shareholders in the target company to acquire their shares. The holders of 99.62% of the total issued share capital in the target company had accepted the offer. Although remaining shareholders holding 0.24% went on to agree to compulsory purchase, 0.14% refused and they made application to court seeking a declaration that their shares could not be acquired compulsorily. Maugham J refused the declaration sought and ordered the sale of their shares. As to the court's exercise of its discretion, he said:

> '... the mere circumstance that the sale or exchange is compulsory is one which ought not to influence the court. It has been called an expropriation, but I do not regard that phrase as being very apt in the circumstances of the case. The other conclusion I draw is this, that again prima facie the court ought to regard the scheme as a fair one inasmuch as it seems to me impossible to suppose that the court, in the absence of very strong grounds, is to be entitled to set up its own view of the fairness of the scheme in opposition to so very large a majority of the shareholders who are concerned. Accordingly, without expressing a final opinion on the matter, because there may be special circumstances in special cases, I am unable to see that I have any right to order otherwise in such a case as I have before me, unless it is affirmatively established that, notwithstanding the views of a very large majority of shareholders the scheme is unfair. There may be other grounds, but I see no other grounds available in the present case for the interference of the court[255].'

---

251 *Securities Trust Ltd v Associated Properties Ltd and Estates Development Ltd* (19 November 1980, unreported) HC at pp 9–10 of the transcript. In the earlier case of *McCormick v Cameo Investments Ltd* [1978] ILRM 191 McWilliam J had said (at 193): 'I consider it unsatisfactory that they and I do not understand the full implications of the scheme and that a full and simple statement, elucidating the ramifications of the group or groups of companies involved and the purpose and effect of this scheme, has not been made, but I am only concerned with the scheme as it stands and the provisions of the statute enabling it to be put through, and, the statutory provisions being complied with, the onus is on the applicants to establish that it is unfair to them ...'

252 See Ussher, *Company Law in Ireland* (1986), p 300. At p 298 the author says: '[i]n dealing with these applications the courts reflect the attitude of the section itself which is, put bluntly, that 80 per cent of the offerees cannot be wrong, or, put another way, the resisting minority are merely being difficult.'

253 *Re Walls Properties Ltd; Walls v PJ Walls Holdings Ltd* [2007] IESC 41.

254 *Re Hoare and Co Ltd* (1933) 150 LT 374.

255 *Re Hoare and Co Ltd* (1933) 150 LT 374 at 375.

Maugham J's judgment has been applied in many subsequent cases[256]. Where a large company with diverse membership is concerned, the reasoning of Maugham J is unimpeachable. However, reflected in his own allusion to 'special circumstances' and 'other grounds' is the recognition that the onus of proof may not be as strong on a dissenting shareholder in all cases. In *Re Hoare*, the shareholdings were many and diverse. It should not be seen as settled that the same onus will be placed on dissenting shareholders in a private company with fewer members.

[9.098] In *McCormick v Cameo Investments Ltd*[257], the applicants were the personal representatives of a deceased shareholder in the target company who had dissented and made application under s 204(1) of the CA 1963. The scheme had been accepted by the holders of 90% of the shareholders of the target company. The applicants made a number of objections: that the provisions of s 60 of the CA 1963 had been breached; that the target company had made a loan of £800,000 to the transferee-company which had not been repaid at the date of the notice to them under s 204(1); and that the purported acquisition of their shares was oppressive and unfair to them. McWilliam J held that s 60 had not been breached[258] and that the making of an unsatisfactory decision by the directors was not oppressive. In the context of s 204, McWilliam J applied Maugham J's decision in *Re Hoare* and held that the onus of proving that the scheme was unfair rested with the applicants. They did not prove to his satisfaction that the scheme was unfair, and he rejected the arguments that the shares were worth more than was being offered and that it was a bad time to sell their shares as the market was poor or that there was evidence of oppression (or bad faith)[259]. From the facts of the case it would seem that the company concerned could not be said to have been of the quasi-partnership type and such does not appear to have been pleaded. In different circumstances, it is thought that such a plea might shift the onus, as in *Re Bugle Press Ltd*, discussed below, particularly where the applicants can also make out a case to have the company wound up on just and equitable grounds.

[9.099] In *Re Bugle Press Ltd*[260], which concerned a company in which there were only three shareholders, Buckley J said:

> 'In a case of this kind it seems to me that the onus must clearly be on the other side, and it must be incumbent on the majority shareholders to satisfy the court that the scheme is one with which the minority shareholders ought reasonably to be compelled to fall in[261].'

This was cited by the Supreme Court in *Re Fitzwilton plc; Duggan v Stoneworth Investment Ltd*[262] but Murphy J went on to note that, in general, the onus falls on a dissenting shareholder to satisfy the court that it is an appropriate case in which to 'order

[256] In *Evertite Locknuts Ltd* [1945] 1 Ch 220, Vaisey J applied the principles in *Re Hoare*; as did McWilliam J in *McCormick v Cameo Investments Ltd* [1978] ILRM 191, citing also *Grierson, Oldham & Adams Ltd* [1968] 1 Ch 17.

[257] *McCormick v Cameo Investments Ltd* [1978] ILRM 191.

[258] See Ch 10, *The Maintenance of Capital*, para **[10.046]**.

[259] On bad faith, see para **[9.100]**.

[260] *Re Bugle Press Ltd* [1961] 1 Ch 270. See para **[9.101]**.

[261] *Re Bugle Press Ltd* [1961] 1 Ch 270 at 227.

[262] *Re Fitzwilton plc; Duggan v Stoneworth Investment Ltd* [2000] 2 ILRM 263.

otherwise'[263] and that it is reasonable as a matter of fact and established as a matter of law[264] that 'the Court should pay great attention to the views of the majority who have accepted the bid'[265]. Murphy J went on to say:

> 'The Court of Appeal in England in the *Bugle* case held that the fact that the promoters of the transferee-company held 90% of the shares in the transferor company shifted the onus from the applicant to the respondents. A 27% shareholding would not necessarily have the same effect. On the other hand, it would clearly follow that the acceptance of an offer by the shareholders in the transferor company who were also associated directly or indirectly with the transferee-company would not carry the same weight or influence as acceptance by shareholders wholly independent of the transferee-company. In the present case the learned judge of the High Court adopted the prudent course of assuming – without deciding – that the onus lay on the respondents to prove that the offer made was a fair one and that the court should not exercise its discretion by 'ordering otherwise'[266].'

The facts in *Re Fitzwilton plc* are considered, and the factors that influenced the Supreme Court in upholding the trial judge's decision not to 'order otherwise', are considered below[267]. In *Re Walls Properties Ltd; Walls v PJ Walls Holdings Ltd*[268], the applicant also sought to invoke the *dictum* in *Re Bugle Press* to reverse the onus but this was rejected by Finnegan J in the Supreme Court[269].

(iii) The bona fides and independence of the transferee-company

[9.100] In establishing the *bona fides* of the transferee-company the courts will look at a number of factors such as the independence of the assenting shareholders and the intentions of the transferee-company. In *Esso Standard (Inter-America) Inc v JW Enterprises*[270], the Supreme Court of Canada refused to sanction a compulsory transfer of shares where the holding company of the transferee-company held over 96% of the shares in the target company. Its reason for doing so was based on the perceived lack of independence in the assenting shareholder, by reason of the connection between the transferee-company and the assenting shareholders in the target company.

[9.101] A blatant example of a sham is provided by *Re Bugle Press Ltd*[271]. In that case an attempt was made to rely on a section similar to s 204 of the CA 1963 to expropriate a

---

[263] Citing *McCormick v Cameo Investments Ltd* [1978] ILRM 191. See also *Elkington v Vockbay Pty Ltd* 10 ACSR 785 at 793–794 and *Super John Pty & Ors v Marsford Investments Pty Ltd* (18 April 1997) Federal Court of Australia.

[264] Citing *Securities Trust Ltd v Associated Properties Ltd* (19 November 1980, unreported) HC (McWilliams J).

[265] *Re Fitzwilton plc; Duggan v Stoneworth Investment Ltd* [2000] 2 ILRM 263 at 274.

[266] *Re Fitzwilton plc; Duggan v Stoneworth Investment Ltd* [2000] 2 ILRM 263 at 275.

[267] See para **[9.102]**.

[268] *Re Walls Properties Ltd; Walls v PJ Walls Holdings Ltd* [2007] IESC 41.

[269] Finnegan J said: 'In the present case the learned High court judge held that it is clearly distinguishable from *In Re Bugle Press Ltd* in that there is no element of sham not was the outcome of the offer a foregone conclusion and that accordingly the onus of proof remained on the appellant.'

[270] *Esso Standard (Inter-America) Inc v JW Enterprises* (1963) 37 DLR 598.

[271] *Re Bugle Press Ltd* [1960] 3 All ER 791. See also Ch 5, *Disregarding Separate Legal Personality*, para **[5.034]**.

minority shareholder in the target company, Bugle Press Ltd. The majority shareholders in the target company formed another company which became the transferee-company. The transferee-company served notice on all the shareholders in the target company of its desire to acquire their shares. The majority shareholders naturally agreed to transfer their shares in the target company, thus giving the transferee-company the requisite percentage to enable it to require any dissenting shareholders to transfer their shares[272]. The minority shareholder refused to transfer his shares and sought a declaration that he was not obliged to transfer his shares. The Court of Appeal made the declaration sought. Harman LJ, in a judgment which concurred with that of Lord Evershed MR, said:

> 'In my judgment this is a barefaced attempt to evade that fundamental rule of company law which forbids the majority of shareholders, unless the articles so provide, to expropriate a minority. It would be all too simple if all one had to do was to form a £2 company and sell to it one's shares, and then force the outsider to comply ... no serious attempt to comply with the section has ever been made here ... [t]here is no sign anywhere of any scheme or contract ... and therefore the section does not begin to operate[273].'

Lord Evershed MR said:

> 'Even, therefore, though the present case falls strictly within the terms of [the English provision, similar to s 204 of the CA 1963], the fact that the offeror, the transferee-company, is for all practical purposes entirely equivalent to the nine-tenths of the shareholders who have accepted the offer, makes it in my judgment a case in which, for the purposes of exercising the court's discretion, the circumstances are special – a case, therefore, of a kind contemplated by Maugham J, to which his general rule would not be applicable[274].'

It is thus clear that the courts will not allow s 204 of the CA 1963 to be used as an unlawful method of expropriation. So notorious is the decision in *Re Bugle Press Ltd* that it would be a very foolhardy individual who would attempt to mimic the machinations of the majority shareholders in that case.

[9.102] The independence of accepting shareholders was extensively reviewed by the Supreme Court in *Re Fitzwilton plc; Duggan v Stoneworth Investment Ltd*[275] where it was held that independence of shareholding is not an actual requirement, but merely a factor to be considered in the court's exercise of its discretion. The facts were that Fitzwilton plc, a company quoted on the Dublin and London Stock Exchanges, was owned as to 27.6% of its ordinary shares by Dr AJF O'Reilly and Mr PJ Goulandris and their immediate families. These men formed Stoneworth Investments Ltd, an investment company in the British Virgin Islands ('Stoneworth') and offered to buy the ordinary shares in Fitzwilton at 50 pence a share and the preference shares at £1 per share. This offer was accepted by 47% of the shareholders who, together, held 84% of the ordinary shares in Fitzwilton. Thereafter, Stoneworth notified the holders of the remaining 16% of the ordinary shares that, having obtained the requisite four-fifths (80%) of the ordinary shares, it intended to compulsory acquire the outstanding 16% in reliance upon

---

[272] The requisite percentage under s 209 of the Companies Act 1948 (UK) was 90%.

[273] *Re Bugle Press Ltd* [1960] 3 All ER 791 at 796F.

[274] *Re Bugle Press Ltd* [1960] 3 All ER 791 at 795H.

[275] *Re Fitzwilton plc; Duggan v Stoneworth Investment Ltd* [2000] 2 ILRM 263; see Lysaght, 'The Compulsory Acquisition of Shares' (2000) 21 Co Law 221.

s 204 of the CA 1963. The plaintiff, who held 10 ordinary shares (0.0001% of the ordinary share capital) objected and applied to the High Court, asking that the court 'order otherwise' than to sanction the proposal.

The essence of the plaintiff's objection was that the requisite four-fifths had not been acquired. He asserted that by applying a teleological rather than literal interpretation[276], Stoneworth was not the true owner of the 84% of ordinary shares as it was O'Reilly's and Goulandris's 'alter ego', since Stoneworth was owned by them and they owned 27.6% of the shares in Fitzwilton. The court was urged to 'tear aside the corporate veil' and to treat O'Reilly and Goulandris as being identical with Stoneworth in construing s 204(2), with the result that Stoneworth would not then have acquired the requisite four-fifths' shareholding. In the alternative it was argued that the court should not exercise its discretion because the majority of acceptances of the offer was achieved only by treating O'Reilly and Goulandris as separate and distinct from Stoneworth, when, he claimed, this did not correspond with the commercial reality of the situation.

[9.103] The decisions in *Esso Standard (Inter-America) Inc v JW Enterprises*[277] and *Re Bugle Press Ltd* were both cited by the plaintiff. Stoneworth, on the other hand, relied upon the decisions in *Sammel v President Brand Gold Mining Co Ltd*[278] and *Blue Metal Industries Ltd v Dilley*[279]. Beginning with the decision in *Re Bugle Press Ltd*, Murphy J analysed and contextualised all four decisions. On *Re Bugle Press Ltd* Murphy J noted that Harman LJ was critical of the procedure adopted by the majority shareholders to expropriate the minority shareholding, describing the procedure in the following terms:

> '... the transferee-company was nothing but a little hut built round his two co-shareholders, and the so-called scheme was made by themselves as directors of that company with themselves as shareholders and the whole thing, therefore is seen to be a hollow sham[280].'

This was essentially what the plaintiff in *Re Fitzwilton plc* wanted the court to find and to then disregard shares held by Stoneworth in computing the four-fifths requirement. Murphy J rejected this finding, pointing out the importance of the basis on which the *Bugle* case was decided, namely, the complete absence of evidence from the transferee-company substantiating the valuation of the shares which the applicant sought to challenge[281] and not just on account of the fact that the shareholders in the transferee-

---

276 On a literal interpretation s 204(2) did not apply to cause the 27.6% of ordinary shares held by O'Reilly and Goulandris to be discounted as these shares were not held by the transferee-company, Stoneworth.

277 *Esso Standard (Inter-America) Inc v JW Enterprises* (1963) 37 DLR 598.

278 *Sammel et al v President Brand Gold Mining Co Ltd* (1963) 37 DLR (2d).

279 *Blue Metal Industries Ltd v Dilley* [1970] AC 827.

280 *Re Bugle Press Ltd* [1961] 1 Ch 270 at 288, [1960] 3 All ER 791.

281 Murphy J quoted the following passage from the conclusion of Lord Evershed MR ([1961] 1 Ch 270 at 288): 'It was then for the transferee company to show that nevertheless there was some good reason why the scheme should be allowed to go on. The transferee company, whether because the two members did not wish to go into the witness-box and be cross-examined or for some other reason, did not file any evidence at all; they merely purported to rely on a copy of a valuation said to have been made on their behalf by a firm of chartered accountants. That valuation was not sworn to, nobody was able to cross-examine the authors of it and there is in my judgment no case [to answer]. The minority shareholder has nothing to knock-down; he only has to shout and the walls of Jericho fall flat.'

company were not independent. Murphy J next considered the Supreme Court of Canada's decision in *Esso Standard (Inter-America) Inc v JW Enterprises*[282], quoting from the decision of Judson J, where he stressed the importance of shares being 'independently held' in the transferee-company[283]. Murphy J rejected that this favoured the plaintiff, saying:

> 'If the phrase 'and that this 90% must be independently held' with which that quotation concludes was intended to convey or reinforce what Judson J had previously said as to the value of a transfer between closely related companies as an indication of the propriety of the transaction, I would respectfully agree with it. If, on the other hand, the learned judge was deciding that the section did not apply where the majority of the shares in respect of which the offer was made were held by a company associated with the transferee-company I would not accept that it is a proper interpretation of s 204 of the Irish Act nor does it accord, in my view, with the judgments in the *Bugle* case[284].'

Murphy J then turned to the South African decision in *Sammel v President Brand Gold Mining Co Ltd*[285], and said that the judgment of the court delivered by Trollip JA was helpfully and correctly summarised in the head note to the judgment in the following terms:

> 'Section 103 of the [South African] Act does not require for its applicability that the holders of the nine-tenths majority of countable shares must be independent of or disinterested in the transferee-company. If such a majority does accept a take-over made in pursuance of a scheme or contract the existence of any connection, interest or dependence between that majority and the transferee-company is merely a factor to be taken into account by the court in exercising its discretion under the section, the weight to be given to it depending upon the circumstances of each case.'

Murphy J went on to hold that the foregoing passage represents a correct statement of the law as to the proper interpretation of s 204(1) of the CA 1963[286].

[9.104] The relationship between s 204(1) and s 204(2) of the CA 1963 was next considered and Murphy J held that there was no ambiguity in their interpretation, saying:

> 'The legislature determined clearly and unequivocally to apply the relevant subsections to the beneficial ownership of shares of the transferor-company other than shares 'already in the beneficial ownership of the transferee-company'. Subsection (3) extended that exclusion by providing that shares in the beneficial ownership of a subsidiary of the

282 *Esso Standard (Inter-America) Inc v JW Enterprises* (1963) 37 DLR 598.

283 Judson J had said (at 604): 'We have here 90% ownership in Standard Oil (New Jersey). The promoting force throughout is obviously that of Standard Oil and not its subsidiary. A transfer of shares from Standard Oil to Esso Standard is meaningless in these circumstances as affording any indication of a transaction which the court ought to approve as representing the wishes of 90% of the shareholders. This 90% is not independent. On this ground alone I would reject the appeal and hold that the section contemplates the acquisition of 90% of the total issued shares of the class affected and that this 90% must be independently held.'

284 *Re Fitzwilton plc; Duggan v Stoneworth Investment Ltd* [2000] 2 ILRM 263 at 272.

285 *Sammel v President Brand Gold Mining Co Ltd* (1963) 37 DLR (2d).

286 Murphy J held that the purposive approach taken by the Privy Council in *Blue Metal Industries Ltd v Dilley* [1970] AC 827 was undertaken to resolve a conflict between the New South Wales Interpretation Act and the actual terms of s 185 of their Companies Act.

transferee-company should not be deemed to be in the beneficial ownership of the transferee-company itself. It is curious, as Mr Lyndon MacCann pointed out at p 201 of his book on the *Companies Acts 1963–1990* that the deeming provisions were not extended to the case where shares in the transferor company were held by a holding company of the transferee-company. However, it is the very fact that the particular exclusionary provisions are expressed to relate to shares in the beneficial ownership of the transferee-company and that the legislature consciously extended that exclusion to capture only shares in a subsidiary which makes it impossible to infer an intention to exclude other categories of share holdings. Moreover, the legislature must have addressed very consciously the particular terms in which the excluded share holdings were described. Those terms differ significantly from the comparable provisions contained in s 8 of the Companies Act [1959] which had been enacted only four years earlier. Furthermore even if s 204 expressly provided or this Court were, contrary to my views, to infer that shares in the holding company were deemed to be in the beneficial ownership of its subsidiary, that would not carry the applicant in the present case. The 27% of the ordinary shares which he asks the court to treat 'as if' they were in the beneficial ownership of the transferee-company were not held by its holding company but by the shareholders therein. It is clear that the shares in question are not in the beneficial ownership of Stoneworth as a matter of fact or law. It is equally clear that they are not deemed by the provisions of s 204 to be in the beneficial ownership of Stoneworth. In those circumstances I can find no basis on which the court would be justified for the purpose of s 204(1) or (2) as treating those shares 'as if' they were in that ownership[287].'

[9.105] In upholding the refusal to order otherwise – and thereby upholding the expropriation of the dissenting minority – Murphy J listed the nine distinct factors in that case, which had entitled the trial judge to refuse to order otherwise[288]. It may be noted that costs were awarded against the plaintiff in this case, a fact which has provoked one commentator to forecast that 'the High Court and Supreme Court have almost certainly ensured that they will not again be troubled by applications by dissenting shareholders dissatisfied by the terms of takeover bids'[289].

[9.106] The principles described in the foregoing paragraphs from decisions of the Irish and English courts were affirmed by the Supreme Court in *Re Walls Properties Ltd and Thornhill Properties Ltd; Walls v PJ Walls Holdings Ltd*[290]. The facts of this case were that the appellant held 10% of the issued share capital in Walls Properties Ltd

---

287 *Re Fitzwilton plc; Duggan v Stoneworth Investment Ltd* [2000] 2 ILRM 263 at 274.

288 These were (at 275): '1. The offer was accepted by the overwhelming majority of shareholders. 2. The acceptance included all of the major institutional and all of the substantial shareholders in the transferor company. 3. The bankers, Deutsche Morgan Grenfel, advised the independent directors that the offer was fair and reasonable. 4. NCB Stockbrokers likewise expressed the opinion that the offer was "full and fair". 5. The independent directors, whose independence has been scrutinised by the Take-over Panel, unanimously recommended and accepted the offer in respect of the shares held by them. 6. Perhaps more important in relation to the offer price was the fact that it reflected a very significant premium over the then market price. 7. The objections of Mr Duggan to the bid were investigated by the Take-over Panel and rejected. 8. The involvement of the O'Reilly Group in the transferee company was clearly and fully disclosed in all of the offer documentation. 9. That Mr Duggan held a mere ten ordinary shares in Fitzwilton representing 0.0001% of that share capital.'

289 See Lysaght, 'The Compulsory Acquisition of Shares' (2000) 21 Co Law 221 at 224.

290 *Re Walls Properties Ltd; Walls v PJ Walls Holdings Ltd* [2007] IESC 41.

('Properties') and just under 10% of the issued share capital in Thornhill Properties ('Thornhill') and it was sought to compulsorily acquire his shares in both companies. He also held 10% of the voting shares in PJ Walls Holdings Ltd ('Holdings'). Holdings made an offer to acquire all of the shares in Properties and Thornhill, and all of their shareholders (representing 90% and 90.91% of the issued share capital, respectively), except the appellant, agreed to the sale. The appellant objected to the invocation of s 204 of the CA 1963 on a number of grounds, including, that the offer price was substantially below the true value, the time given for acceptance was too short, a valuation of the companies' worth was not given to the shareholders, information on the scheme was not forthcoming and the expropriation of the appellant's shares would be in breach of the pre-emption clause in the articles of association of Properties. Smyth J in the High Court concluded that the offer was not unfair to the applicant who appealed to the Supreme Court.

[9.107] The Supreme Court also found for the respondents and dismissed the appellant's appeal, finding that the appellant had not discharged the onus of proof. The Supreme Court held that although the acceptance of an offer by shareholders who are associated directly or indirectly with the transferee-company will not carry the same weight or influence as acceptance by shareholders wholly independent of the transferee-company, in the instant case the court rejected the appellant's contention that the acceptance of the offers was a sham and that there was no independent majority. The Supreme Court also held that the fact that some aspects of a scheme are open to valid criticism does not amount to unfairness as would justify the scheme being considered to be unfair. One particular objection raised by the appellant concerned the fact that the articles of association of Properties contained a pre-emption clause which provided, *inter alia*, that a share could not be transferred to a non-member for as long as any member was willing to purchase the share at fair value. They also provided that if any member attempted to dispose of shares other than in accordance with the articles, that member would be deemed to have served the company with a transfer notice in respect of the shares. The appellant contended that because Holdings was not a member, the pre-emption rights were triggered and Properties ought to have acted in accordance with the articles. On this point Finnegan J noted the appellant's contention:

> 'The consequence of this, it is argued, is that Holdings in relation to shares transferred to it can take no greater interest than the transferors are entitled to pass and accordingly holds those shares subject to the appellant's right of pre-emption which entitles him to acquire not only a number of those shares proportionate to his own shareholding but also the like proportion of those shares which have not been taken up by other members. Further those members who have transferred their shares have thereby waived their right of pre-emption and the effect of this is that Holdings could not obtain four fifths by value of the issued share capital as required by section 204 and would not be in a position to issue a notice under section 204(1). In support of the argument reliance was placed on *Lee & Company (Dublin) Ltd v Egan (Wholesale) Ltd*, the High Court (Kenny J, 27th April 1978).'

Finnegan J, however, distinguished the decision in *Lee & Company (Dublin)*, saying:

> 'In that case the articles of association of *Egan (Wholesale) Ltd* contained broadly similar provisions conferring rights of pre-emption. The second named defendant who owned 90% of the issued share capital in the company agreed the sale of the entire issued share capital. There were three other shareholders. The second named defendant repudiated the agreement for sale and this action for specific performance was taken. In short Kenny J

held that the plaintiff was entitled to specific performance of the agreement insofar as it related to the second named defendant's shares only but also to damages, or alternatively, not to proceed with the purchase and seek damages only. In the course of his judgment, however, Kenny J said that the obligation on the second named defendant under the pre-emption provisions must be complied with.'

Finnegan J went on to reject the applicability of a company's articles of association where an application is made under s 204 of the CA 1963 on the grounds that a company's memorandum and articles of association are, by reason of s 25 of the CA 1963, subservient to the Companies Acts:

> 'In the course of argument before this court there was extensive argument as to the proper construction of the provisions of Article 7. However in my opinion it is unnecessary to consider those provisions in detail having regard to the clear statutory provision contained in section 25(1) of the 1963 Act. In the event of any conflict between the provisions of the Companies Acts and a provision in the Articles of Association the former will prevail. Section 204(1) of the Act of 1963 is triggered by a scheme, contract or offer involving the acquisition 'of the beneficial ownership of all the shares' of a transferee company. As is clear from *Lee and Company (Dublin) Ltd v Egan Wholesale Ltd* a shareholder notwithstanding pre-emption provisions in the Articles of Association may enter into a binding and enforceable contract for the sale of the shares notwithstanding non-compliance by him with pre-emption provisions affecting the shares. Upon each shareholder accepting the offer of Holdings a binding agreement in respect of those shares came into existence. The beneficial interest in those shares passed to Holdings upon a binding agreement coming into existence. *Hawks v McArthur* [1951] 1 All ER 22, *Re Hafner, Olhausen v Powderly* [1943] IR 426 at 453 *et seq*. The provisions of the articles of association, article 7 operate as between the shareholder and the company but also between the transferor and transferee of shares to the extent that the pre-emption provisions prevent the legal estate in the shares passing: the beneficial ownership as between transferor and transferee however passes. Once the statutory proportion of the issued share capital came into the beneficial ownership of Holdings its entitlement to invoke section 204 arose. At this time the conflict between the pre-emption provisions and the statutory entitlement of Holdings under section 204 came into conflict but having regard to the provisions of section 25(1) of the Act of 1963 this conflict is resolved in favour of Holdings. It was so held by the learned trial judge and I am satisfied that he was correct in so holding.'

[H] Share Purchase Agreements

[9.108] A company's business may be acquired in either of two ways: by the purchase from the shareholders of their shares in the company or by the purchase from the company itself of the company's property, assets and undertaking. This is the share/asset purchase quandary, spoken of at the outset of this chapter. Although a full treatment of the two methods of acquiring a business is beyond the scope of this work, it is proposed to outline briefly the nature of a share purchase agreement[291]. First, however, we examine the relative merits of the share purchase versus the asset purchase.

[291] The following books provide a specialised treatment of the topic: Wine, *Buying & Selling Private Companies & Businesses* (3rd edn, 1986); Sinclair, *Warranties and Indemnities on Share Sales* (2nd edn, 1989, Longman Commercial Series); and Patterson, *Private Company Share Sale Manual* (2nd edn, 1990, Longman Commercial Series).

The relative merits of the share purchase versus the asset purchase

[9.109] The advantages of a share purchase may be summarised as follows:

- there may be tax savings and, in particular, a stamp duty saving since, where real property used for commercial purposes is sold stamp duty is payable at 2%[292] – by contrast, the standard rate of stamp duty payable on a share purchase is 1%;
- where the company is well established, the goodwill and identity of the company may more easily be preserved on a share transfer.

[9.110] The advantages of an asset purchase may be summarised as follows:

- the purchaser can be selective and purchase only those assets which he wants;
- the company's liabilities are not included in the purchase, one of the greatest disadvantages of a share purchase[293]; and
- the legal procedure and documentation involved in an asset purchase are generally more standardised and commonplace than in a share purchase.

The nature of a share purchase agreement

[9.111] Where it is agreed to purchase the shares in a private company[294] two documents are required: a simple share transfer form and a share purchase agreement. The purpose of a share purchase agreement is to afford protection to the transferee. The need for protection may be said to stem from the target company's separate legal personality. Where the target company has been trading for a number of years, there is the possibility that it may have hidden tax liabilities, law suits, contractual commitments, labour relation difficulties, defective title to its properties, etc. The title to the target company's shares will not disclose any of the foregoing problems and liabilities because such problems and liabilities belong directly to the company. Where a transferee purchases the shares in the company those problems become his problems.

(a) Disclosure letters

[9.112] Transferees will usually seek to be provided with detailed information of all matters affecting the company by being given a so-called 'disclosure letter'. Because the transferee of shares is not protected by any statutory provisions he must protect himself by insisting that the transferor provide him with warranties and indemnities, discussed below. The subject matter of the warranties and indemnities provided by the transferor will often be dictated by the contents of the disclosure letter. Accordingly, disclosure

---

[292] In respect of residential property, where the value is up to €1m the rate is 1% and is 2% thereafter. Previously, the rates (and the gap between commercial and residential rates) were significantly greater and stamp duty on commercial property was as high as 6% and on residential property as high as 9%.

[293] When a business is acquired by purchasing the entire issued share capital in the company, the new owners of the company stand in no better a position than did the old owners. All debts, liabilities, claims and demands against the company whilst the old owners owned the company will continue to exist on the change of ownership. The separate legal personality of the company is uninterrupted and unaffected by the change in shareholdings.

[294] The sale of shares in quoted public limited companies ('PLCs') is not normally accompanied by a share purchase agreement.

letters can serve to put the transferee on notice of matters adversely affecting the company (and so affect the value of the shares being acquired) and also bind the transferor to the veracity of its contents which can be seen as representations to the transferee[295].

(b) Warranties on share sales

[9.113] The transferee seeking protection from hidden liabilities will require the transferor to make certain warranties in relation to the company's affairs. Warranties involve the transferor of the shares giving the transferee certain assurances in relation to all potential liabilities of the company concerned. In addition to creating a legal liability between the transferor and transferee, it has been accepted that the giving of warranties also serves to bring all factors affecting the value of the shares to the transferee's attention[296]. In practice, warranties may also serve to further the transferor's interests since problems that are identified may be excluded from the warranties, and this fact will commonly be reflected in the consideration paid for the shares.

[9.114] The warranties typically given by the transferor fall into the following generic categories:

- Taxation warranties;
- Property warranties;
- Company's constitutional documents warranties;
- Accounting and financial warranties;
- Labour warranties;
- Contractual and trading warranties.

Depending upon the company in question, while all of the foregoing warranties will be important, some will be more important than others. Taxation warranties are of particular importance in almost all companies. These will span the entire ambit of taxation and address corporation tax, capital acquisitions tax, capital gains tax, value added tax, stamp duty, etc. Property warranties can also be of enormous importance where the company owns any real property. Although it is possible for the transferee to rely entirely upon the property warranties offered by the transferor, it is more usual for the transferee's solicitor to conduct a full investigation of title to the property by raising objections and requisitions on title. Alternatively, the transferor's solicitor may certify that the company has good and marketable title to the property.

[9.115] It is common to delimit warranties in terms of time, and the share purchase agreement may provide that any claims must be brought within a period of, say, three years[297]. Where, having warranted something to be the case, and within the prescribed time limit, it later transpires that the warranty is materially false, the transferor becomes

---

295 For an example of the matters addressed in a disclosure letter, see Wine, *Buying & Selling Private Companies & Businesses* (3rd edn, 1986), Appendix C.

296 See Sinclair, *Warranties and Indemnities on Share Sales* (2nd edn, 1989), Ch 1, 'History and Function of Warranties and Indemnities'.

297 Certain warranties, such as those in relation to taxation matters, may be extended in some cases to six years.

liable to compensate the transferee[298]. The transferee may face difficulties where he has paid the full consideration to the transferor and subsequently discovers that there has been a breach of a warranty given[299]. For this reason transferees sometimes require security. This is commonly achieved by an agreed retention from the total consideration which will only be released after a certain period of time. Alternatively, the transferor may be required to effect insurance against a breach of a warranty.

(c) Indemnities on share sales

[9.116] Indemnities from the transferor are usually limited to taxation matters. It has been noted[300] that, originally, indemnities were only given by the transferor in respect of specific secondary taxation liabilities. This is now usually extended to all taxation liabilities of the company and indemnities are often given to the transferee and the company itself.

[I] THE VALUATION OF SHARES IN PRIVATE COMPANIES

[9.117] The valuation of shares[301] can be a contentious exercise in a number of distinct situations. Disputes as to the basis of valuation can arise where a member, who wants to sell his shares, is compelled to offer them for sale to existing members pursuant to a pre-emption clause. Similarly, where an event arises which compels a member to transfer his shares, disputes as to the value of such shares can arise. In addition, where a member is obliged to transfer his shares pursuant to a court order under s 205 of the CA 1963 the value of the interest to be transferred often becomes an issue. In this section it is proposed to consider the legal rules which apply to share valuations in private companies under the following headings:

1. The principles of share valuation.
2. Discounting share value for a minority holding.
3. Establishing fair value.
4. The appropriate valuation date.

The principles of share valuation

[9.118] The valuation of a shareholding in a private company may be said to involve a two-fold process:

(a) Determination of a company's total worth; and
(b) Assessment of the value of the shareholding.

The responsibility for the valuation of a shareholding will often be given to the company's auditors or to some independent accountant. Where the value of shares

---

298 See *Eurocopy plc v Teesdale* [1992] BCLC 1067, which concerns a claim that the warrantors had failed in breach of warranty to disclose all relevant facts in the disclosure letter.

299 On warranty claims generally, see Fagan & McKendrick, 'Corporate Warranty Claims – How They Should be Handled' (1995) PLC 15.

300 Stedman & Jones, *Shareholders' Agreements* (2nd edn, 1990), p 3.

301 Clarke, *Takeovers and Mergers Law in Ireland* (1999), p 10 *et seq*; Giblin, *Valuation of Shares in Private Companies* (3rd edn, The Institute of Taxation in Ireland, 1999); see also Fox & Bowen, *The Law of Private Companies* (1991), Ch 14, 'Valuing Shares in Private Companies'.

cannot be agreed, conflicting valuations by opposing expert valuers will commonly result[302]. Where the matter cannot be resolved amicably and results in a court hearing, the valuation of the shareholding may be determined by the court[303].

(a) Determination of a company's total worth

[9.119] The determination of the total worth of a company can be a most difficult task, with conflicting evidence being adduced by both parties. Private companies can be valued in a number of different ways. One way is to value the company as a going concern. Whether or not a company can be said to be a going concern will obviously depend upon the finances of the company in question[304]. An interesting consideration of the fate of one company is seen in the judgment of O'Hanlon J in *Re Clubman Shirts Ltd*[305]. This case arose as a result of an order previously made under s 205 of the CA 1963 that the petitioner's shares in the company be bought out[306]. In all of the circumstances, O'Hanlon J concluded that he was not prepared to say that the petitioner's shares should be valued on the basis that the company should be regarded as a going concern on the valuation date. In that case the company was running at a loss and was unable to meet its liabilities as they fell due. Because of this, O'Hanlon J said:

> '... I take the view that the Petitioner's shareholding as of the 31 July 1980, was unsalable in the open market; had no value if assessed on a dividend yield or earnings yield basis, and the Petitioner must fall back on a net asset valuation basis to support a claim for payment when the shares are to be acquired by the parties resisting his claim[307].'

O'Hanlon J went on to say that in the circumstances, the company's assets should properly be valued on a 'break-up' basis and not in relation to their value to a company which could continue in business as a going concern. Even on this basis he could not readily establish their value and he was convinced that they were of no great value. Due to the deficiencies in the evidence he was, however, unwilling to hold that the shares were worthless. In the circumstances he measured the value of the shares at 60 pence each and he refused to award interest, although over 10 years had passed since the finding of oppression. He considered that in striking the figure of 60 pence he may have erred on the side of generosity.

[9.120] The valuation of shares has been considered in a number of Irish cases. The first of these was *Colgan v Colgan*[308], a case which also arose on foot of an application under s 205 of the CA 1963. The companies in question were part of a very successful group of companies which owned a considerable number of unencumbered properties in and around Dublin, including the Lucan Spa Hotel and the County Bars Lucan. Costello J

---

302 An example in point being *Irish Press plc v Ingersoll Irish Publications Ltd* (13 May 1994, unreported) HC, *per* Barron J.

303 See *Colgan v Colgan & Colgan* (22 July 1993, unreported) HC, *per* Costello J; *Re Clubman Shirts Ltd* [1991] ILRM 43, *per* O'Hanlon J; and *Irish Press plc v Ingersoll Irish Publications Ltd* (13 May 1994, unreported) HC, *per* Barron J.

304 See generally, *Buckingham v Francis* [1986] 2 All ER 738.

305 *Re Clubman Shirts Ltd* [1991] ILRM 43.

306 *Re Clubman Shirts Ltd* [1983] ILRM 323.

307 *Re Clubman Shirts Ltd* [1991] ILRM 43 at 54.

308 *Colgan v Colgan* (22 July 1993, unreported) HC, *per* Costello J.

had the benefit of a valuation report on all of the companies' properties and found that the combined valuation figures totalled £7,370,000. From this figure Costello J deducted the sum of £300,000 to allow for current liabilities over current creditors. He then held that the share value should be calculated by reference to the net asset value of the group without deduction. This case is also important for holding that there should not be a discounting for a minority interest. The second case was *Irish Press plc v Ingersoll Irish Publications Ltd*[309]. The principal difficulty there was that conventional methods of valuation were considered unsatisfactory on account of the company's business and financial situation. The valuations from both the petitioner and the respondent, while different, were both non-asset based. In the end Barron J valued the companies without fully accepting the method advanced by either party's valuer. Generally, the market for shares in private companies will be very limited and accordingly a valuation based on the price payable by a willing buyer and a willing seller may be fraught with artificiality[310]. Where shares are valued on the basis of an order to purchase under s 205 of the CA 1963, it has been held in *Re Clubman Shirts Ltd*[311] that sub-s (3) of that section confers a wide discretion on the courts, having regard to all the circumstances of the case, in arriving at a fair valuation. In *Re New-Ad Advertising Company Ltd*[312], Laffoy J ordered that a shareholding director, whom she found to have engaged in oppressive conduct, should purchase the petitioner's shares. As to the value of the shares, the learned judge said:

> 'The evidence [of the accountant], is that, as explained in his report, ordinarily the value of a company is obtained by reference to its net asset position at a given date together with a review of its dividend policy over a period of three to five years. In this case there was insufficient evidence to show what the assets of the company were and no dividends were paid. In the alternative, what has to be done is to establish what the income of the company ought to have been and from this to reconstruct what the net asset position would have been if the income to which the company was entitled had been received[313].'

In that case, the latter method was adopted by Laffoy J in valuing the petitioner's 10% shareholding in the company.

(b) The assessment of the value of the shareholding

[9.121] Once the net worth of a company has been established, the second step is to ascertain the value of the shareholding in question. The fundamental question here will be: should the shares in question be valued on a pro rata basis, or should the shareholding be subject to a discount or a premium to reflect the fact that a minority or majority shareholding is being transferred?

---

309 *Irish Press plc v Ingersoll Irish Publications Ltd* (13 May 1994, unreported) HC, *per* Barron J.

310 For a discussion of the concept of 'willing seller', see *Shortt v Treasury Commissioners* [1948] AC 534. See also *Attorney General v Jameson* [1904] 2 IR 644.

311 *Re Clubman Shirts Ltd* [1991] ILRM 43 at 53 where O'Hanlon J approved of *Re Bird Precision Bellows Ltd* [1985] 3 All ER 523 at 529, *per* Oliver LJ.

312 *Re New-Ad Advertising Company Ltd* (1 July 1997, unreported) HC, Laffoy J.

313 *Re New-Ad Advertising Company Ltd* (1 July 1997, unreported) HC at p 14.

(c) Discounting share value for a minority holding

[9.122] It is generally accepted that in a quasi-partnership private company, a minority shareholding should not be discounted, nor a majority shareholding attributed a premium[314]. Rather, in quasi-partnership companies, all shareholdings should be valued on a pro rata basis. This has been accepted as the law in Ireland by Costello J in *Colgan v Colgan and Colgan*[315] where the learned judge said:

> '... all the authorities indicate that there should not be a discount when dealing with a quasi-partnership[316].'

[9.123] The traditional position was that a minority shareholding would not be discounted when it was sold pursuant to a court order under s 205 of the CA 1963. The rationale for this is seen in *Re Bird Precision Bellows Ltd*[317], where Nourse J said at trial:

> 'I would imagine that in a majority of cases where purchase orders are made under s 75 [s 205 of the CA 1963] in relation to quasi-partnerships the vendor is unwilling in the sense that the sale has been forced upon him. Usually he will be a minority shareholder whose interests have been unfairly prejudiced by the manner in which the affairs of the company have been conducted by the majority. On the assumption that the unfair prejudice has made it no longer tolerable for him to retain his interest in the company, a sale of his shares will invariably be his only practical way out short of a winding up. In that kind of case it seems to me that it would not merely not be fair, but most unfair, that he should be bought out on the fictional basis applicable to a free election to sell his shares in accordance with the company's articles of association, or indeed on any other basis which involved a discounted price. In my judgment the correct course would be to fix the price pro rata according to the value of the shares as a whole and without any discount, as being the only fair method of compensating an unwilling vendor of the equivalent of a partnership share. Equally, if the order provided, as it did in *In re Jermyn Street Turkish Baths Ltd* [1970] 1 WLR 1194, for the purchase of the shares of the delinquent majority, it would not merely not be fair, but most unfair, that they should receive a price which involved an element of premium[318].'

On the authority of more recent decisions, including that of Laffoy J in *Re Skytours Travel Ltd; Doyle v Bergin*[319], it is thought that the correct approach is to confine the non-application of a discount to cases where the companies are quasi-partnerships so that the general rule is that there should be a discount for a minority interest *unless* the company is a quasi-partnership.

[9.124] In *Re Bird Precision Bellows Ltd*[320], the company was established for the purpose of combining the expertise of one man (Bird) in the manufacture of precision bellows with the experience of two other men (Armstrong and Nin) in management, finance and industrial matters. All three were also directors of the company. After about

---

314 See generally, Fox, 'Valuing Minority Holdings in Private Companies' (1985) 129 SJ 456.

315 *Colgan v Colgan and Colgan* (22 July 1993, unreported) HC.

316 *Colgan v Colgan and Colgan* (22 July 1993, unreported) HC at p 7. See also *Profinance Trust SA v Gladstone* [2000] 2 BCLC 516.

317 *Re Bird Precision Bellows Ltd* [1984] Ch 409; for the Court of Appeal see [1986] 2 WLR 158.

318 *Re Bird Precision Bellows Ltd* [1984] Ch 409 at 430.

319 *Re Skytours Travel Ltd; Doyle v Bergin* [2011] IEHC 517.

320 *Re Bird Precision Bellows Ltd* [1986] 2 WLR 158, [1984] Ch 409, CA (Nourse J).

five years, the company's business prospered but the relationship of mutual c between the shareholders began to deteriorate. Following the calling of an extra general meeting, Armstrong and Nin were removed as directors. Armstrong an petitioned the court under s 75 of the Companies Act 1980 (UK), which was broadly similar to our s 205 of the CA 1963, providing a remedy where the affairs of the company were conducted in a manner unfairly prejudicial to them. The relief sought by the petitioners was to have their shares purchased by the respondents at the fair value thereof. At trial Nourse J found that there was no universal rule applicable to the valuation of shares. He did, however, as considered in the last paragraph, hold that in valuing a shareholding in a quasi-partnership private company, a pro rata approach should be adopted and no discount should be made for the fact that a minority shareholding was being valued.

[9.125] The converse is, however, also true and where the company is not a quasi-partnership, then even where the shares are being sold by order of the court, a discount should be applied to the valuation of a minority shareholding. The valuation of shares in the context of a s 205 petition was comprehensively considered by Laffoy J in *Re Skytours Travel Ltd; Doyle v Bergin*[321]. After declaring that the affairs of the company were being conducted in a manner oppressive to the petitioner, Laffoy J determined that she proposed to make an order that the respondent be compelled to purchase the petitioner's share in the company. In approaching the question of the valuation of the oppressed petitioner's share, the starting point taken by Laffoy J was the decision in *Re Greenore Trading Co Ltd* where Keane J determined that the shares should be purchased at a 'fair price' which he held could include an element of compensation for the injury inflicted by the oppressors. The learned judge also noted that the Supreme Court in *Irish Press plc v Ingersoll Irish Publications Ltd*[322] acknowledged that compensation could be paid in limited circumstances where incidental to the main relief and reflective of the court's determination of what would be a fair price for the shares. Laffoy J noted that the 'discount or no-discount' issue had been considered in a number of United Kingdom decisions[323] before finding:

> 'I am persuaded by the decisions of the courts of the United Kingdom to which I have referred above that it is only in the case of a quasi-partnership company or where some other exceptional circumstance exists that a minority shareholding should be valued on a non-discounted basis where the Court has directed that the petitioner's minority shareholding should be purchased by the respondent shareholder or by the company pursuant to s 205(3) of the Act of 1963. In this case, the company is not, and never was, a quasi-partnership company. There is nothing in the circumstances of the case which would justify a non-discounted basis of valuation of the petitioner's shareholding. Accordingly, in the valuation process, in order to fix a fair price, the appropriate discount, having regard to the minority nature of the petitioner's shareholding, must be applied[324].'

In that case, Laffoy J considered that it was appropriate to apply a discount of 50% in valuing the petitioner's shareholding in the company.

---

321 *Re Skytours Travel Ltd; Doyle v Bergin* [2011] IEHC 517.

322 *Irish Press plc v Ingersoll Irish Publications Ltd* [1995] 2 IR 175.

323 *Strahan v Wilcock* [2006] 2 BCLC 555; *Irvine v Irvine* [2006] 4 All ER 102; and *Fowler v Gruber* [2010] 1 BCLC 563.

324 *Re Skytours Travel Ltd; Doyle v Bergin* [2011] IEHC 517 at para 4.13.

Establishing fair value

[9.126] Where a shareholders' agreement or a company's articles provide for an extra-judicial mechanism for the valuation of shares, the courts generally decline jurisdiction and insist upon the parties exhausting the ordained procedure[325]. Establishing the fair value of shares will often be a task entrusted to the company's auditors. Often the document referring the determination of a shareholding's fair value to the company's auditors will provide that the auditors' certification will be conclusive evidence[326]. Save where there is manifest error, mistake or proof of some improper motive[327] or where the auditors give reasons for their valuation[328], the auditors' valuation will not be questioned by the courts[329]. The justification for this is that upon joining the company the members implicitly accept the provisions in a company's articles or internal rules. As Lord Denning MR said in *Campbell v Edwards*[330], albeit in another context[331]:

> 'If two persons agree that the price of property should be fixed by a valuer on whom they agree, and he gives that valuation honestly and in good faith, they are bound by it. Even if he has made a mistake they are bound by it. The reason is because they have agreed to be bound by it. If there were fraud or collusion, of course, it would be very different. Fraud or collusion unravels everything. It may be that if a valuer gives a speaking valuation – if he gives reasons or his calculations – and you can show on the face of them that they are wrong it might be upset.'

It has been held that such provisions in articles of association also bind deceased members' executors by virtue of the deceased's adherence to the articles[332].

[9.127] One of the leading authorities on the concept of fair value is *Dean v Prince*[333]. There, the court held on the preliminary issue of jurisdiction that notwithstanding that an auditor's determination is conclusive, there was jurisdiction to review the valuation in that case by reason of the fact that the auditor had, in an attempt to achieve agreement, given reasons for his determination of the shareholding's fair value. The facts were that on the death of a director and controlling shareholder, his shares were subject to compulsory sale to the surviving directors of the company, at a price to be certified by an auditor as a fair value. The auditor certified a fair value for the deceased director's shareholding, but went further and stated his reasons for not valuing the company as a going concern on account of consistent losses. At trial, Harman J held the valuation invalid and not binding because the auditor had not attributed a premium to the shareholdings to reflect the fact that they represented a majority and controlling interest in the company.

The finding of Harman J was rejected by the Court of Appeal, which held that the auditor was correct in not attributing a premium to the value of the shares, which should

325 See *XYZ Ltd* (1986) 2 BCC 520.

326 See para **[9.128]**.

327 *Collier v Mason* (1858) 25 Beav 200, *per* Sir John Romilly MR and *Johnston v Chestergate Hat Manufacturing Co Ltd* [1915] 2 Ch 338, *per* Sargant J. See also *Re Benfield Greig Group plc* [2000] 2 BCLC 488.

328 *Burgess v Purchase & Sons (Farms) Ltd* [1983] 1 Ch 217, considered at para **[9.128]**.

329 See also *Arenson v Arenson* [1972] 2 All ER 939 concerning valuer's liability.

330 *Campbell v Edwards* [1976] 1 WLR 403 at 407.

331 The context of this decision was landlord and tenant law.

332 *Re Benfield Greig Group plc* [2000] 2 BCLC 488.

333 *Dean v Prince* [1954] 1 Ch 409.

be valued pro rata to the company's worth[334], and that he had rightly rejected valuing the company on the basis of a going concern because of the losses suffered[335].

[9.128] Caution should to be exercised by auditors in valuing a company's shares pursuant to a pre-emption type provision that requires them to establish the fair value of a shareholding. Where acting as an expert, an auditor's determination can only be impugned in the limited circumstances set out above[336], unless the auditor states the basis of the valuation. Another case in point is *Burgess v Purchase & Sons (Farms) Ltd*[337]. There, the executors of a deceased member notified the company of their desire to sell the deceased member's shares pursuant to a pre-emption clause in the company's articles. Upon the happening of this the company became the executors' agent for the sale of the shares to any existing member at their fair value which was to be determined by the company's auditors. The auditors' determination was expressed to be final, binding and conclusive. Notwithstanding that the auditors could simply have advised the executors of the value they had assessed, they went on to explain by letter how they had arrived at that value. Nourse J held that 'a speaking valuation' could be impugned notwithstanding that the articles provided that it was final, binding and conclusive.

The appropriate valuation date

[9.129] Two broad situations must be distinguished in fixing the appropriate date for the valuation of shares in a private company, namely:

- where shares are valued pursuant to the company's articles or a shareholders' agreement;
- where shares are valued pursuant to an order of court, such as an order under s 205 of the CA 1963.

[9.130] Where shares are valued pursuant to the company's articles or a shareholders' agreement, the valuation date will be governed by the terms of the instrument giving rise to the valuation. On the valuation of shares pursuant to a pre-emption clause it will typically be provided that the valuation date will be either the date of the deceased member's death[338], the date of the service of a transfer notice by a proposing transferor, or the occurrence of an event giving rise to the compulsory sale of a member's shares[339].

[9.131] Difficulties can arise where an order for the sale of shares is made pursuant to s 205 of the CA 1963. If there can be said to be a general rule[340] it is that shares ordered

334 *Dean v Prince* [1954] 1 Ch 409 at 427–428 *per* Lord Denning.

335 In this regard it was accepted that although the company's worth had increased since the valuation date, this was irrelevant because the material date for the valuation was the date of the member's death, *per* Evershed MR at 416.

336 At para **[9.126]**.

337 *Burgess v Purchase & Sons (Farms) Ltd* [1983] 1 Ch 216.

338 See, eg, *Dean v Prince et al* [1954] 1 Ch 409.

339 See, eg, *Re Castleburn Ltd* [1991] BCLC 89.

340 It is not accepted that there is a general rule. In *Profinance Trust SA v Gladstone* [2000] 2 BCLC 516, it was held that there was no *prima facie* rule that the date of the court's order was the appropriate date on which to value a minority shareholding for purchase by the majority shareholder. See also *Re Regional Airports Ltd* [1999] 2 BCLC 30; and *Re DR Chemicals Ltd* (1989) 5 BCC 39.

to be bought should be valued as at the date of the making of the order. This is seen in the judgment of Nourse J in *Re London School of Electronics Ltd*[341] where he said:

> 'If there were to be such a thing as a general rule, I myself would think that the date of the order or the actual valuation would be more appropriate than the date of the presentation of the petition or the unfair prejudice. Prima facie an interest in a going concern ought to be valued at the date on which it is ordered to be purchased. But whatever the general rule might be it seems very probable that the overriding requirement that the valuation should be fair on the facts of the particular case would, by exceptions, reduce it to no rule at all[342].'

[9.132] Case law demonstrates that the general rule has been departed from in a great many situations. In addition to the date the shares are ordered to be purchased[343], the courts have fixed the appropriate valuation date to be:

- the date of the oppression[344];
- the date of the petition if there had been no oppression[345];
- the date of valuation when the petitioner had previously unreasonably rejected fair offers to purchase the shares[346]; and
- a date a few weeks before the court's order to purchase the shares[347].

[9.133] Barron J held that different considerations apply to the fixing of a valuation date where an order is made under s 205 of the CA 1963 against a party who has acted oppressively, ordering him to sell his shares to an oppressed petitioner. In the course of his judgment in *Irish Press plc v Ingersoll Irish Publications Ltd*[348] Barron J said:

> 'It has been submitted on behalf of the respondent that the date of presentation of the petition should be the date at which the shares should be valued. This may be the correct approach when the wrongdoer is being compelled to buy the shares but not if their value has already fallen by that date by reason of the oppression. A totally different situation arises when it is the wrongdoer who is being compelled to sell his shares. His actions have caused loss and the value of the shares has gone down. This factor must be reflected in the price which the petitioner will be required to pay for the respondent's shares. Here this fall has taken place, not only in the value of the respondent's shares but also in the value of the petitioner's shares. Clearly the appropriate date for valuing the respondent's shares must be the date of valuation. In addition, additional compensation must be provided for any drop in value of the petitioner's shares[349].'

The learned judge ordered that the appropriate valuation date was to be 21 December 1993, five days after he delivered the judgment in which he found that there had been oppression. Notwithstanding the Supreme Court's subsequent finding that compensation

---

341 *Re London School of Electronics Ltd* [1983] 3 WLR 474.

342 *Re London School of Electronics Ltd* [1983] 3 WLR 474 at 484B–C.

343 *Re Sunrise Radio* [2010] 1 BCLC 367 and *Profinance Trust SA v Gladstone* [2002] 1 BCLC 141, cited by Laffoy J in *Re Skytours Travel Ltd; Doyle v Bergin* [2011] IEHC 517.

344 *Re Clubman Shirts Ltd* [1983] ILRM 323; *Re OC (Transport) Services Ltd* [1984] BCLC 251.

345 *Scottish Co-operative Wholesale Society Ltd v Meyer* [1959] AC 324.

346 *Re A Company (No 002567 of 1982)* [1983] 1 WLR 927.

347 *Colgan v Colgan & Colgan* (22 July 1993, unreported) HC, *per* Costello J.

348 *Irish Press plc v Ingersoll Irish Publications Ltd* (16 December 1993, unreported) HC.

349 *Irish Press plc v Ingersoll Irish Publications Ltd* (16 December 1993, unreported) HC at p 85.

cannot be awarded pursuant to s 205(3) of the CA 1963[350], it is thought that Barron J's comments on the appropriate valuation date remain valid.

[9.134] In *Re Skytours Travel Ltd; Doyle v Bergin*[351], Laffoy J noted that while the general rule should be the date of the order, it has been departed from on a number of occasions and the learned judge cited the authorities last mentioned. Finding that there was little or no material difference in the outcome were the court to adopt the date of the presentation of the petition rather than the date of the order to purchase the shares, Laffoy J determined that the real issue was whether the valuation should be by reference to 2003 accounts or more recent accounts. In the end, the judge determined that the proper course was to determine the value by reference to the most recent accounts, which she referred to as the so-called 'straightforward' method:

> 'The so called 'straightforward' approach seems to me to be a fair method of valuing the petitioner's shareholding. It is reasonable to assume that, but for the actions of the respondent which I have found to constitute oppression, the asset value of the company would be in the region of €2.3m greater than it is. That approach is in line with the approach adopted by Keane J in *Re Greenore Trading Co Ltd,* although that authority indicates that the petitioner should also be refunded the par value which he paid for his shares. The other methodologies deployed by the experts certainly did not produce any fairer figure. Accordingly, I find that, for the purposes of applying s 205(3), the value of the shareholding of the petitioner, before discount, is €115,000. However, in the light of the view I have expressed earlier in para 4.13, that value must be discounted. The evidence of both Mr Traynor and Mr Dawson was that the minority discount rate would be in the region of 40% to 60%. In view of the size of the petitioner's shareholding, I consider it appropriate to apply a discount of 50%[352].'

[350] See Ch 11, *Shareholders' Remedies*, para **[11.074]**.

[351] *Re Skytours Travel Ltd; Doyle v Bergin* [2011] IEHC 517.

[352] *Re Skytours Travel Ltd; Doyle v Bergin* [2011] IEHC 517 at para 5.4.

Chapter 10

The Maintenance of Capital

Introduction

[10.001] This chapter is concerned with the rules of share capital maintenance. A company can acquire finance in one of three ways. In the first place it can acquire loan capital by borrowing money from either internal sources (members or directors) or external sources (lending institutions or private investors). This method of acquiring capital and the company law issues involved are considered in Chs 18, 19 and 20[1]. In the second place, a company can acquire capital through the issue of shares. This is referred to as *share capital* and it is the maintenance of share capital that is the concern of this chapter. Share capital is generally intended to be permanently[2] invested in a company for the life of the company. Here, a distinction may be drawn between the owner of the share capital, who may change, and the capital itself, which will generally remain intact. Loan capital, on the other hand, especially from external sources, is not intended to be permanently invested: loans mature and are repaid. In the third place, it must be remembered that a company can acquire capital by successfully conducting its business and making profits on its investments.

The rationale behind share capital maintenance rules

[10.002] It has always been a basic principle of company law that throughout a company's corporate existence its share capital must remain intact. The traditional rationale for the maintenance of capital is to ensure that a company's creditors can rely upon the existence of the company's share capital to satisfy their claims on a winding up. Furthermore, share capital maintenance rules are designed to protect shareholders from other shareholders, or classes of shareholders, redeeming their shares and getting back their capital.

[10.003] Companies acquire share capital through the issue of shares. The basic rationale for prohibiting a company from buying back its own shares is that the liability of a member of a private limited company is limited to the amount, if any, unpaid on the shares which he holds: were a member permitted to take back the share capital which he contributed to the company, the statutory liability contained in s 207 of the CA 1963 would be obviated[3]. Although the liability imposed by s 207 on the members of many private companies is largely illusory in practice, this would seem to continue to be the

1 Ch 18 *Corporate Borrowing: Debentures and Security*; Ch 19, *Corporate Borrowing: Registration of Charges*; and Ch 20, *Corporate Borrowing: Receivers*.

2 Subject to the permitted methods of share capital reduction, considered below.

3 See Ch 25, *Realisation and Distribution of Assets in Winding Up*, para **[25.130]**.

primary rationale behind the rules on capital maintenance. A judicial expression of the rationale behind share capital maintenance rules is seen in *Guinness v Land Corporation of Ireland*[4], where Cotton LJ said of a predecessor of s 207 of the CA 1963 that it:

> '... provides that in the case of a company limited by shares being wound up, no contribution shall be required from any member exceeding the amount if any unpaid on the shares in respect of which he is liable as a present or past member; that the capital of the company as mentioned in the memorandum is to be the fund which is to pay the creditors in the event of the company being wound up. *From this it follows that whatever has been paid by a member cannot be returned to him* ... [Capital] ... is, of course liable to be spent or lost in carrying on the business of the company, but no part of it can be returned to a member so as to take away from the fund to which the creditors have a right to look as that out of which they are to be paid[5].'

This is the basic rationale which underlies the rules of share capital maintenance. However, as shall be considered, in no other area of company law is the traditional rationale underlying the law more divorced from the commercial reality.

Private companies and capital maintenance rules

[10.004] The notion that the subscribed share capital in a private company is a creditors' fund will frequently be little more than a nonsense in many private companies. While a company may well have an *authorised* share capital of €1m divided into one million €1 shares, its *issued* share capital will often be as little as €1: because a private company may have as few as one shareholder, the result is that the 'creditors' fund' may be as little as €1[6]. Accordingly, there is a vast difference between private companies and public limited companies ('PLCs') because, by virtue of s 19 of the C(A)A 1983, PLCs must have a minimum *issued* share capital of €38,092.14[7]. However, the rules of capital maintenance still have relevance to many private companies because of the fact that the *nominal* value of a share will not, in a successful company, reflect the actual *market value* of that share. Accordingly, where a company has an issued share capital of two €1 shares, but an actual value (total assets *less* total liabilities) of €100,000, each €1 share may have a market value of €50,000. If the company was allowed to buy back one of its two issued €1 shares at market value, the company's worth would fall from €100,000 to €50,000.

[10.005] The foregoing example demonstrates that rules on capital maintenance exist to ensure that the capital of a company is preserved by preventing the distribution of assets to members. Here the notion of *distributable profits*, as defined by s 45 of the C(A)A 1983, is important. As will be considered below, the controls on a company acquiring its

---

4 *Guinness v Land Corporation of Ireland* (1882) 22 Ch D 349.

5 *Guinness v Land Corporation of Ireland* (1882) 22 Ch D 349 at 373.

6 Indeed, a company's share capital can be as little as one cent, ie, one one-cent share issued to the sole member of a single-member private limited company as permitted by the EC(SMPLC)R 1994 (SI 275/1994).

7 It should be noted, however, that not all of the minimum issued share capital of €38,092.14 must be fully paid up, and it is sufficient that only one quarter of the nominal value of shares be paid up: ss 6(3)(b) and 28(1) of the C(A)A 1983. See Ch 29, *Public Limited Companies and SEs*, para **[29.011]**.

own shares[8], redeeming its own shares[9] or paying a dividend on its shares[10], all provide that such potential reductions of capital can be funded only from a company's distributable profits.

[10.006] The only departure from the general principle that a private company is not obliged by law to have a minimum issued share capital is the situation envisaged by s 150(3) of the CA 1990[11]. This provides that where a court makes an order restricting a director or other officer of an insolvent company which goes into liquidation, any other company in which the restricted person acts as director or secretary or in which the restricted person is concerned or takes part in its promotion or formation, must meet certain minimum capital requirements. In the case of a private company, the minimum nominal value of the allotted share capital is €63,486.90, which together with any premium must be fully paid up in cash.

[10.007] Although the rationale behind the maintenance of capital in private companies is somewhat of an anomaly, practitioners will frequently encounter the rules on capital maintenance. Some of the most common situations where caution must be exercised include situations where it is proposed:

- to purchase a dissident shareholder's holding in order to maintain control;
- to acquire a business by means of a share purchase as opposed to an asset purchase; where the loan for the acquisition is guaranteed or otherwise secured by the company;
- to divide profits at the end of a joint venture; and
- to pay dividends to the company's members.

It must be remembered that the rules of capital maintenance continue to apply even where the company concerned has few, or even no, creditors.

[10.008] Capital maintenance rules have traditionally been considered to be a shield for shareholders. The rationale was that a shareholder who advanced monies for shares in the company was entitled to assume that his fellow shareholders would not dilute their shareholding in the company. Attempting to rationalise the rules of capital maintenance in the context of single-member companies[12] is consequently rendered even more difficult.

[10.009] If a schism occurs in a quasi-partnership type private company and if one of the members wants to separate from the others, where the remaining members cannot muster sufficient personal finances to buy him out, it may be suggested that the company would either buy back that member's shares or finance the purchase of his shares by the remaining members. This situation could also arise where, in an attempt to maintain control of a private company and to avoid a member selling his shares to an outsider, the remaining members seek to cause the company to purchase the departing member's shares by relying on whatever pre-emption rights are contained in the

8 See para **[10.013]**.

9 See para **[10.041]**.

10 See para **[10.089]** *et seq*.

11 See Ch 28, *Compliance and Enforcement*, para **[28.069]**.

12 As permitted by the EC(SMPLC)R 1994: see generally Ch 1, *The Private Company in Context*, para **[1.143]** *et seq*.

company's articles of association or in a shareholders' agreement[13]. However, it has been made clear as far back as 1887 in the leading case of *Trevor v Whitworth*[14] that the quite reasonable end of maintaining control in a private family company will not justify breaches of the capital maintenance rules. Lord Herschell said that one suggestion as to why the company in that case bought back its own shares was because the company:

> '... was intended to be a family company, and that the directors wanted to keep the shares as much as possible in the hands of those who were partners, or who were interested in the old firm, or of those persons whom the directors thought they would like to be amongst this small number of shareholders. I cannot think that the employment of the company's money in the purchase of shares for any such purpose was legitimate ... I can quite understand that the directors of a company may sometimes desire that the shareholders should not be numerous, and that they should be persons likely to leave them with a free hand to carry on their operations. But I think it would be most dangerous to countenance the view that, for reasons such as these, they could legitimately expend the moneys of the company to any extent they please in the purchase of its shares. No doubt if certain shareholders are disposed to hamper the proceedings of the company, and are willing to sell their shares, they may be bought out; but this must be done by persons, existing shareholders, who can be induced to purchase the shares, and not out of the funds of the company[15].'

The purchase of a company's shares in circumstances where the remaining shareholders wish to retain control of the company must be financed by persons other than the company itself. This was stated in trenchant terms by Lord Macnaghten who said:

> 'If shareholders think it worth while to spend money for the purpose of getting rid of a troublesome partner who is willing to sell, they may put their hands in their own pockets and buy him out, though they cannot draw on a fund in which others as well as themselves are interested. That, I think, is the law and that is the good sense of the matter[16].'

Whatever about the 'good sense' of the rule of law which prevents a company from buying back the shares of a disenchanted member, problems are caused for many private companies where the pockets of the individual shareholders are not deep enough to finance the buy-out of such a dissenting member.

[10.010] One of the more frequently encountered situations where the capital maintenance rules meet commercial practice is where it is proposed to buy the business of a private company by means of a share purchase, as opposed to an asset purchase[17]. Often, the purchasers will propose to finance the purchase of the shares through a lending institution which will be asked to accept, as security for the advance, a charge over the assets of the company. Because in such circumstances the company will be providing financial assistance for the purchase of its own shares, extreme care must be exercised. As shall be considered below[18], s 60 of the CA 1963 prohibits a private company from providing such financial assistance, whether directly or indirectly, unless certain steps are taken.

---

13 See, generally, Ch 9, *Share Transfers*.

14 *Trevor v Whitworth* (1887) 12 App Cas 409. See para **[10.014]**.

15 *Trevor v Whitworth* (1887) 12 App Cas 409 at 417.

16 *Trevor v Whitworth* (1887) 12 App Cas 409 at 436.

17 See Ch 9, *Share Transfers*, para **[9.108]** *et seq*.

18 See para **[10.046]** *et seq*.

Overview of capital maintenance rules

[10.011] The rules of capital maintenance, as they apply to private companies, shall be considered in this chapter under the following headings:

[A] Acquisition by a company of its own shares.

[B] Acquisition of shares in holding company.

[C] Redemption of shares.

[D] Assisting the purchase of a company's own shares.

[E] Court ordered capital reduction.

[F] Distributions and the payment of dividends.

[G] Miscellaneous capital maintenance rules.

[10.012] It has long been recognised that no matter what the legislature provides, nothing can prevent a company from suffering a capital loss in the course of trading[19]. However, where a company does suffer a serious loss of capital, the directors of that company are under a duty, by s 40 of the C(A)A 1983, to call an EGM of the members[20].

[A] Acquisition by a Company of its Own Shares

[10.013] Companies can directly or indirectly acquire their own shares. Here, the following issues in connection with the acquisition of a company's own shares are considered:

1. The common law prohibition on the purchase of own shares.
2. The statutory prohibition on acquiring own shares.
3. Exceptions to the prohibition on acquiring own shares.
4. Acquiring shares in a company's holding company.

The common law prohibition on the purchase of own shares

[10.014] It is a long-established rule at common law that a company may not purchase its own shares[21]. The cornerstone of the common law is *Trevor v Whitworth*[22]. In that case the executors of the late Mr Whitworth, a shareholder in James Schofield & Sons Ltd, sold back the shares which he had held in the company *to* the company. This was permitted by the company's articles of association. When the company subsequently went into liquidation, the executors sought to recover from the company the balance of the purchase price which was outstanding on the shares. This was resisted by the liquidator and the case eventually came before the House of Lords. It was held that because the purchase of a company's own shares was not permitted by the objects

---

19 See *Guinness v Land Corporation of Ireland* (1882) Ch D 349, cited at para **[10.014]** and *Trevor v Whitworth* (1887) 12 App Cas 409.

20 See Ch 14, *Corporate Governance: Meetings*, at para **[14.017]**.

21 See generally, Brennan, *A Company Purchasing its Own Shares* (1991); McCormack, *The New Companies Legislation* (1991), pp 40–61; and for a specific analysis of private companies acquiring their own shares, see Fox & Bowen, *The Law of Private Companies* (1991), pp 150–168.

22 *Trevor v Whitworth* (1887) 12 App Cas 409. For a more recent application, see *Barclays Bank plc et al v British & Commonwealth Holdings plc* [1996] 1 BCLC 1.

clause, the purchase of the company's own shares was *ultra vires*. Moreover, it was held by the House of Lords that whether or not the acquisition by a company of its own shares was authorised by its objects clause, the act of purchasing its own shares was in itself repugnant to the law. After referring to the law on the reduction of capital[23], Lord Watson said:

> 'One of the main objects contemplated by the legislature, in restricting the power of limited companies to reduce the amount of their capital as set forth in the memorandum, is to protect the interests of the outside public who may become creditors. In my opinion the effect of these statutory restrictions is to prohibit every transaction between a company and a shareholder, by means of which the money already paid to the company in respect of his shares is returned to him, unless the court has sanctioned the transaction. Paid-up capital may be diminished or lost in the course of the company's trading; that is a result which no legislation can prevent; but persons who deal with, and give credit to a limited company, naturally rely upon the fact that the company is trading with a certain amount of capital already paid up, as well as the responsibility of its members for the capital remaining at call; and *they are entitled to assume that no part of the capital which has been paid into the coffers of the company has been subsequently paid out, except in the legitimate course of its business*[24].'

The case of *Guinness v Land Corporation of Ireland*, quoted above[25], was cited with approval. An old Irish case which restated the common law prohibition is *Re Irish Provident Assurance Company Ltd*[26]: that case demonstrates that the acquisition by a company of its own shares often arises in circumstances where it is agreed that one of the shareholders in a company should leave and his shares be acquired. There, differences of opinion arose between a company and one of its shareholders who also happened to be its managing director. A deal was struck and it was agreed that his shares would be purchased by the company for £2,000 in return for his waiving any claim he had against the company and agreeing not to compete with the company. It was held by Palles CB that the agreement was void because part of the consideration was the purchase by a company of its own shares. These authorities continue to hold good and prevent own-share purchase by a company unless a transaction can be brought within one of the statutory exceptions[27].

The statutory prohibition on acquiring own shares

[10.015] The old common law rule that a company cannot purchase its own shares was given statutory expression in s 72(1) of the CA 1963. It simply provided that:

> 'Except insofar as this Act expressly permits, it shall not be lawful for a company limited by shares ... to purchase any of its shares or reduce its share capital in any way.'

---

23 Considered in Ch 3, *Constitutional Documentation*, para **[3.033]** *et seq*.

24 *Trevor v Whitworth* (1887) 12 App Cas 409 at 423, 424. Emphasis added.

25 See para **[10.003]**.

26 *Re Irish Provident Assurance Company Ltd* [1913] IR 352 (Court of Appeal).

27 *Re RW Peak (Kings Lynn) Ltd* [1998] BCC 596.

In what can only be seen as a spurt of 'blind' European fervour, the Oireachtas enacted a second statutory prohibition on a company acquiring its own shares in the guise of s 41(1) of the C(A)A 1983[28]. This provides:

> 'Subject to the following provisions of this section, no company limited by shares or limited by guarantee and having a share capital shall acquire its own shares (whether by purchase, subscription or otherwise).'

It should be stressed that neither provision prohibits *unlimited private companies* (or for that matter, public unlimited companies) from acquiring their own shares[29].

[10.016] The direct acquisition of own shares can be distinguished from a situation where a company acquires shares in a company whose principal asset comprises of shares in the acquiring company. In *Acatos & Hutcheson plc v Watson*[30], it was held by the English High Court that, as a general principle, a company is not precluded by either the common law rule in *Trevor v Whitworth* or statute[31] from acquiring the shares of another company in circumstances where the sole asset of the company whose shares are acquired is shares in the acquiring company[32]. This decision is soundly based on the fundamental principle of company law, established in *Salomon v A Salomon & Co Ltd*[33] and consistently applied by the Irish courts, that a company's separate legal personality should be respected. Although in the instant case the acquiring company's shares were not *directly* held, Lightman J recognised that the economic effect was the same and did sound a caution:

> 'I should add that, whilst such a purchase by one company of a shareholder in it is not absolutely prohibited, in view of the potential for abuse and for adverse consequences for shareholders and creditors, the court will look carefully at such transactions to see that the directors of the acquiring company have acted with an eye solely to the interests of the acquiring company (and not for example to the interests of the directors) and have fulfilled their fiduciary duties to safeguard the interests of shareholders and creditors alike[34].'

In that case there were legitimate reasons for adopting the proposed course of action, which included the mitigation of taxes otherwise payable on a restructure. The independent directors of the acquiring company had obtained legal and accounting advice that the proposed transaction was in the interests of both the plaintiff and its shareholders. In particular, it should be noted, that the shares in the acquiring company

28 As Ussher, *Company Law in Ireland* (1986), p 315 has most aptly said, 'Statute is not required to repeat itself for emphasis'.

29 See Ch 31, *Unlimited Companies*, at para **[31.021]**.

30 *Acatos & Hutcheson plc v Watson* [1995] 1 BCLC 218.

31 Section 143(1) of the CA 1985 (UK) which provides, in terms similar to s 41(1) of the C(A)A 1983, that: 'Subject to the following provisions, a company limited by shares ... shall not acquire its own shares, whether by purchase, subscription or otherwise.'

32 See also the supporting Australian authorities cited with approval by Lightman J: *Dyason v JC Hutton Pty Ltd* (1935) Argus LR 419; August *Investments Pty Ltd v Poiseidon Ltd and Samin Ltd* [1971] 2 SASR 71; and *Trade Practices Commission v Australian Iron & Steel Pty Ltd* (1990) 22 FCR 305; 92 ALR 395.

33 *Salomon v A Salomon & Co Ltd* [1897] AC 22.

34 *Acatos & Hutcheson plc v Watson* [1995] 1 BCLC 218 at 225b–c.

had not deliberately been transferred to a shelf company with the sole intention of evading the statutory and common law prohibition on the acquisition of a company's own shares. In a case where a dummy company is incorporated with the sole or dominant intention of evading the prohibition on own-share acquisition, it is thought that a court would be sorely tempted to lift the veil of incorporation and deem the transaction a sham[35]. Insofar as the result of such a transaction is that the company whose shares are acquired *in toto* thereby becomes a subsidiary of the acquiring company in circumstances where it holds shares in, what has become, its holding company, regard must be had to s 32 of the CA 1963. It is thought that s 32(1) does not prevent such an acquisition because s 32(1) only renders void any allotment or transfer of shares in a company to its subsidiary: this must be read as referring to any future allotment or transfer. Moreover, s 32(4) expressly provides that the section shall not prevent a company, which at the date it becomes a subsidiary is already a member of the acquiring company, from continuing to be a member[36].

Exceptions to prohibition on acquiring own shares

[10.017] Prior to the enactment of the CA 1990, there were a number of recognised exceptions under the CA 1963 and the C(A)A 1983 to the statutory prohibitions on own-share purchase. If s 41(1) of the C(A)A 1983 repeated the prohibition in s 72 of the CA 1963 against the acquisition of a company's own shares, s 41 also provides in sub-s (2) and (4) a useful summary of the exceptions to the rule:

(a) the acquisition of fully paid shares otherwise than for valuable consideration pursuant to s 41(2) of the C(A)A 1983;

(b) the redemption of preference shares pursuant to s 65 of the CA 1963[37];

(c) the acquisition of any shares in a reduction of capital duly made pursuant to s 72 of the CA 1963, s 72[38] as recognised by s 41(4)(b) of the C(A)A 1983;

(d) the purchase of shares on foot of remedial court orders under s 15 of the C(A)A 1983, or s 10 or 205 of the CA 1963[39];

(e) the forfeiture of any shares, or the acceptance of any shares surrendered in lieu, in pursuance of the articles of association for failure to pay any sum payable in respect of those shares[40]; and

(f) the redemption or purchase of shares pursuant to Part XI of the CA 1990, as recognised by s 41(4)(a) of the C(A)A 1983.

Before treating the exceptions provided for at (f) – the purchase of shares and redemption of shares in accordance with Part XI of the CA 1990 – which are considered in detail below[41], we shall first review the exceptions at (a) to (e).

---

35 On lifting the veil, see Ch 5, *Disregarding Separate Legal Personality.*

36 See further McGee, *Share Capital* (1999), pp 3 and 115. See, further, para **[10.036]** *et seq*.

37 Section 41(4)(a) of the C(A)A 1983. Furthermore, it should be noted that the redemption or purchase of shares pursuant to Part XI of the CA 1990 now forms part of this exception by virtue of s 232(a) of the CA 1990, which amends s 41(4)(a) of the C(A)A 1983.

38 Section 41(4)(b) of the C(A)A 1983.

39 Section 41(4)(c) of the C(A)A 1983.

40 Section 41(4)(d) of the C(A)A 1983.

41 On the purchase of shares pursuant to Part XI of CA 1990, see para **[10.023]** *et seq*, and on the redemption of shares, see [C] Redemption of Shares, at para **[10.041]** *et seq*.

(a) The acquisition of fully paid shares for no consideration

[10.018] There is no prohibition on a company acquiring its own shares from a shareholder provided (a) the shares are fully paid up; and (b) the company does not give valuable consideration for the shares. Section 41(1) of C(A)A 1983 can sometimes provide a neat way of tidying up loose ends. The rationale is simple: if the company does not pay for the shares, then its capital is being maintained so there is no policy against it acquiring its own shares for no valuable[42] consideration. It is important to note, however, that shares thus acquired by a company are *not* treasury shares because only shares as come into a company's ownership by operation of s 207 or s 211 of the CA 1990 are properly called 'treasury shares': s 209(1) of the CA 1990. As such, there is no statutory power either to cancel shares acquired under s 41(2) of the C(A)A 1983 or re-issue them as there is with true treasury shares[43]. While the position is different for PLCs[44], where a private company acquires its own shares for no consideration, the result is that the shares are in limbo: they cannot be treated as treasury shares or cancelled. Similarly, their rights to vote and to dividend are not automatically suspended and where a company acquires its own shares pursuant to s 41(2) it should consider making appropriate provision in its articles of association. Despite the absence of any express statutory power, it is thought that shares acquired in this manner can be re-issued or transferred; again, appropriate provision should be made in the company's articles of association which in the absence of a statutory regime are the appropriate place to have such rules.

(b) The redemption of shares pursuant to s 65 of the CA 1963

[10.019] Section 65 of the CA 1963 gives companies power to redeem preference shares that were issued before 5 May 1959 and is mentioned here for completeness only.

(c) Acquisition pursuant to a s 72 of the CA 1963 reduction of capital

[10.020] The alteration of the capital clause contained in a company's memorandum of association is considered in Ch 3[45]. It is important to realise that although a special resolution of the members of the company in general meeting is necessary, so too is confirmation by the court under s 72(2) of the CA 1963. It has been noted[46] that this provision is primarily concerned with the protection of the company's creditors thereby underscoring the notion that a company's capital is its 'creditors' fund'.

(d) Purchase of shares on foot of remedial court orders

[10.021] A court may order a company to purchase its own shares from a shareholder pursuant to the court's powers under s 15 of the C(A)A 1983, and ss 10 and 205 of the CA 1963. Section 15(7) of the C(A)A 1983 provides that the High Court can order a

---

42 Share acquired pursuant to s 41(2) of the C(A)A 1983 should be transferred by deed under seal to avoid being set aside on grounds of no consideration.

43 Sections 208 and 209(4) of the CA 1990. See para **[10.024]** *post*.

44 PLCs are required by s 43 of the C(A)A 1983 to dispose of or cancel shares it thus acquires beneficially within three years: see Ch 29, *Public Limited Companies and SEs*, at para **[29.074]**.

45 See Ch 3, *Constitutional Documentation*, para **[3.033]** *et seq*.

46 See Ussher, *Company Law in Ireland* (1986), p 339.

PLC, which converts to a private company, to purchase the shares of dissenting shareholders[47]; s 10(6A) of the CA 1963 provides that the High Court can order a company, which changes its objects clause, to purchase the shares of dissenting shareholders[48]; and s 205(3) of the CA 1963 confers a similar power to order a company to purchase its own shares where the affairs of the company or powers of the directors are being exercised in a manner oppressive to a member or in disregard of a member's interests[49].

(e) Forfeiture of shares

[10.022] Companies may forfeit unpaid or party paid shares where the shareholders fails to pay on a call made by the directors in accordance with a company's own articles of association. The rationale is similar to the acquisition of shares for no consideration pursuant to s 41(2) of the C(A)A 1983: there is no diminution in the company's capital in acquiring the shares as it does not pay anything for them[50].

Acquisition of own shares pursuant to Part XI of the CA 1990

[10.023] The most far-reaching, non-judicial means whereby a company may lawfully acquire by purchase its own shares from its shareholders is where it does so in accordance with the statutory regime provided for in Part XI of the CA 1990. Here, the following issues are considered:

(a) Own-share purchase under s 211 of the CA 1990.
(b) Funding can only come from distributable profits.
(c) Authorised by articles of association.
(d) The requirement for a special resolution.
(e) Contingent purchase contracts.
(f) Statutory safeguards.
(g) Repudiation by company and effect of winding up.
(h) Ministerial regulations.

(a) Own-share purchase under s 211 of the CA 1990

[10.024] In relative terms, the regime applicable to the purchase by a company of its own shares, as provided for in Part XI of the CA 1990, is of recent origins. The key provision which enables a company to acquire its own shares is s 211 which provides:

> '(1) Subject to the following provisions of this Part, a company may, if so authorised by its articles, purchase its own shares (including any redeemable shares).

---

47 See Ch 29, *Public Limited Companies and SEs*, at para **[29.019]** *et seq*.

48 See Ch 3, *Constitutional Documents*, at para **[3.027]**.

49 See Ch 11, *Shareholders' Remedies*, at para **[11.083]**.

50 On forfeiture of shares, see Ch 8, *Shares and Membership*, at para **[8.123]** *et seq*.

(2) Sections 207(2)[51], 208[52] and 209[53] shall apply in relation to the purchase by a company under this section of any of its own shares as those sections apply in relation to the redemption of shares by a company under section 207.

(3) A company shall not purchase any of its shares under this section if as a result of such purchase the nominal value of the issued share capital which is not redeemable would be less than one tenth of the nominal value of the total issued share capital of the company.'

The permitted mechanism by which a private company limited by shares or by guarantee can acquire its own shares is by means of an '*off-market purchase*' pursuant to s 213 of the CA 1990. Section 212 of the CA 1990 defines an off-market purchase as being one where the shares are purchased either:

(a) otherwise than on a recognised Stock Exchange; or

(b) on a recognised Stock Exchange but are not subject to a marketing arrangement on that Stock Exchange.

A company's shares are subject to a marketing arrangement on a recognised Stock Exchange if either they are listed on that Stock Exchange, or, the company has been afforded facilities for dealing in those shares to take place on that Stock Exchange without prior Stock Exchange permission for individual transactions and without limit as to the time during which those facilities are to be available[54]. The most common example of an off-market purchase will be a private contract whereby the company enters into an agreement with one of its shareholders to acquire some or all of that shareholder's shares in the company.

[10.025] Section 211(2) of the CA 1990 provides that s 207(2) also applies to own-share purchases. Re-stating s 211(2) and applying s 211(3)[55] to own-share purchases results in the following conditions for private companies:

'(a) No own-shares shall be purchased by a company at any time when the nominal value of the issued share capital which is not redeemable is less than one tenth of the nominal value of the total issued share capital of the company.

(b) No such shares shall be purchased unless they are fully paid.

(c) The terms of purchase must provide for payment on purchase.

(d) Subject to condition (e), no such shares shall be purchased otherwise than out of profits available for distribution.

(e) Where the company proposes to cancel shares on their purchase pursuant to section 208, such shares may also be purchased out of the proceeds of a fresh issue of shares made for the purposes of purchase.

(f) The premium, if any, payable on the purchase of shares, must, have been provided for out of the said profits of the company provided however where the shares were issued at a premium, any premium payable on their purchase (being a redemption to which condition (e) applies) may be paid out of the proceeds of a

51 See para **[10.041]**.

52 See para **[10.042]**.

53 See para **[10.043]**.

54 Section 212(2)(a) and (b) of the CA 1990. See further, Ch 29, *Public Limited Companies and SEs*, at para **[29.069]**.

55 Although s 207(2) of the CA 1990 is applied in its entirety by s 211(2), s 207(2)(a) is effectively substituted by s 211(3) which is reflected in condition (a).

fresh issue of shares made for the purposes of the purchase, up to an amount equal to—

(i) the aggregate of the premiums received by the company on the issue of the shares purchased, or

(ii) the current amount of the company's share premium account (including any sum transferred to that account in respect of premiums on the new shares),

whichever is the less, and in any such case the amount of the company's share premium account shall, not withstanding anything in section 62(1) of the Principal Act [ie, CA 1963] be reduced by a sum corresponding (or by sums in the aggregate corresponding) to the amount of any payment made by virtue of this paragraph out of the proceeds of the issue of the new shares.'

(b) Funding can only come from distributable profits

[10.026] Section 211(2) of the CA 1990 provides that ss 207(2), 208 and 209 (which primarily apply to the redemption of shares) also apply to own-share purchases and so, by extension, the requirement in s 207(2)(d)(i) of the CA 1990 that the consideration paid for shares that are acquired by a company must come from '*profits available for distribution*'[56]. Furthermore, it should be noted that a company may use only distributable profits to fund premia or other payments upon an acquisition or redemption of shares as made clear by s 218(1) and (2) of the CA 1990, which provides that payments from a source other than distributable profits is unlawful.

(c) Authorised by articles of association

[10.027] In order to be able to purchase its own shares, a private company must first be authorised to do so by its articles of association. In England, this is considered to be an essential prerequisite and one that cannot be overridden by an informal resolution[57], and it is thought that this is likely to be followed in Ireland[58].

(d) The requirement for a special resolution

[10.028] The first step in a private company acquiring its own shares is that the members in general meeting must pass a special resolution authorising the terms of the proposed off-market contract of purchase[59]. This special resolution[60] must be passed *before* the contract to purchase a company's own shares is entered into, and any such authority may be varied, revoked or from time to time renewed by special resolution. Although the fact that a special resolution is required ensures that a qualified majority of members are in agreement that the company purchase its own shares, a further safeguard is provided by s 213(3) of the CA 1990. This provides that the special resolution:

'... shall not be effective for the purposes of this section if any member of the company holding shares to which the resolution relates exercises the voting rights carried by any of

56 See para **[10.089]** *et seq*.

57 See Ch 14, *Corporate Governance: Meetings*, para **[14.093]** *et seq*.

58 See *R W Peak (Kings Lynn) Ltd* [1998] BCC 597.

59 Section 213(2) of the CA 1990.

60 By s 213(4) of the CA 1990, notwithstanding anything in s 137 of the CA 1963 or in a company's articles, any member can demand a poll on such a special resolution.

> those shares in voting on the resolution and the resolution would not have been passed if he had not done so.'

Furthermore, a special resolution shall *not be effective* unless a copy of the proposed contract of purchase (or a written memorandum of the contract, where the proposed contract is oral) is available for inspection by members of thc company both at the meeting itself, and at the registered office of the company for at least 21 days before the extraordinary general meeting ('EGM') at which the special resolution is proposed[61]. Any memorandum of the terms of a contract for the purchase of shares must include the names of any members who hold shares to which the contract relates and a copy of the contract which is made available must have annexed to it a written memorandum specifying any such names which do not appear in the contract itself[62]. The members in general meeting may agree to a variation of an existing contract to purchase shares only if the variation is authorised by special resolution before the variation is agreed to by s 213(7) of the CA 1990. Retrospective validation of a variation is not permitted. Whilst a company cannot assign its rights under a contract to purchase its shares, it can release its rights. In such a case, a private company is required to pass a further special resolution[63].

[10.029] It is clear that the nature and timing of the requisite special resolution is closely regulated. In England it has been held that the principle in *Re Duomatic Ltd* cannot override the statutory formalities involved in own-share purchases. *Re RW Peak (Kings Lynn) Ltd*[64] concerned an application for rectification of a company's register of members. The applicant had sold his shares in a company back to the company pursuant to an agreement signed by himself and the only other member of the company. The applicant sought to have this sale set aside on the grounds that it was invalid by reason of the rule in *Trevor v Whitworth*, by virtue of s 143 of the Companies Act 1985 (UK) and the fact that the validation procedure, permitted by Part V, Chapter VII of that Act, had not been followed. Against this, it was argued that the effect of the company's only two members signing the agreement under which the shares were bought back was tantamount to compliance by reason of the principle in *Re Duomatic Ltd*[65]. Lindsay J considered the problem from the perspective of the written resolution procedure; had that been utilised as permitted in England by s 381A of the Companies Act 1985 (UK), two resolutions would have been required: one to amend the articles of association and the other to authorise the proposed share purchase contract. That the similar English legislation (s 164(2) of the Companies Act 1985 (UK)) requires the resolution to be passed *before* the entering into of a contract for the purchase of shares was found to be fatal to the purported reliance on the *Duomatic* principle. Lindsay J said:

> 'If, on the hypothesis of any such written procedure being used, the only signed paper, instead of being two such resolutions, had been the contract itself, then, even if its language were generously to be regarded as if it were also effective as an alteration to the articles and as a resolution approving the company's entry into the contract, its effect

61 Section 213(5) of the CA 1990.

62 Section 213(6) of the CA 1990.

63 Section 217 of the CA 1990.

64 *Re RW Peak (Kings Lynn) Ltd* [1998] BCC 596.

65 *Re Duomatic Ltd* [1969] 2 Ch 365.

> could hardly antedate the entry into itself and hence it could not be regarded as a resolution passed '*before* the contract is entered into' within s 164(2). The contract would thus not have been approved 'in advance' within s 164(2) …
>
> If that is right then it is evidence that, in relation to such a supposed case, Parliament would have preserved and have retained as determinative of the efficacy of the related transactions at least some of the requirements of s 164, even in cases where written assent had been given by the only persons or person … who by statute is to have a voice in the decision of whether or not the company should enter into the particular contract to buy its own shares. That being so, can it sensibly be the case that, where there has been no approval of the contract *in advance* but where the shareholder whose shares are being bought also assents, and therefore brings assents up to 100% of the membership of the company, a transaction, ineffective in reliance upon s 381A, is thereupon to be given efficacy?
>
> I cannot think that Parliament can be taken to have countenanced an application of the *Duomatic* principle such that a transaction, even less formal than a written resolution under s 381A and which would have been ineffective as such, would become effective merely by reason of the further assent of the remaining shareholder, [the applicant], a person excluded by statute from having his votes on the subject counted had there been a vote (s 164(5)), and whose signature of approval was rendered unnecessary to any written resolution had there been one … A transaction otherwise ineffective, had s 381 been deployed in a corresponding way, would, were that so, have become effective upon the decision of the very person whom statute requires not to have a voice in its favour. So anomalous would that be that in the circumstances, rather than my ruling upon the application of the *Duomatic* principle more generally, I reject its applicability to cure this particular transaction[66].'

It is thought that an Irish court, interpreting s 211 of the CA 1990 and s 14(8) of the CA 1963 would reach a similar conclusion[67].

[10.030] An interesting variation on the same theme, of compliance with the statutory regime, arose for consideration in *Vision Express (UK) Ltd v Wilson*[68]. The facts were that a 'Tomlin order'[69] had been made which provided, *inter alia*, that the plaintiff company would purchase certain shares (in itself) from the defendant by a particular date and for a particular price. The purchase did not complete by the specified date so as to facilitate compliance with the statutory requirements where a company purchases its own shares. The defendant claimed that the plaintiff company was in breach of the Tomlin order; the plaintiff company refuted this. The defendant also claimed that the Tomlin order was a contract for the sale and purchase of the shares, which was illegal because no special resolution had been passed in advance. The instant case arose from the plaintiff company's request that a clause be implied into the Tomlin order to the

---

66 *Re RW Peak (Kings Lynn) Ltd* [1998] BCC 596 at 603C–H.

67 On written resolutions, see generally, Ch 14, *Corporate Governance: Meetings*, para **[14.090]** *et seq*.

68 *Vision Express (UK) Ltd v Wilson* [1998] BCC 173.

69 A 'Tomlin order' is an order of a court which directs that all further proceedings in a matter be stayed upon specified terms (set out in a schedule to the order) save for the purpose of enforcing the said terms with liberty to apply for that purpose. The origin of the order is an English practice direction issued following the decision of Tomlin J in *Dashwood v Dashwood* [1927] WN 276. See, generally, Hardiman, 'Settlement of Actions' (1998) 5 CLP 247 at 253.

effect that the order was '… subject (in so far as necessary) to compliance with statutory provisions for the purchase by the company of its own shares'. In these circumstances, Judge Levy QC held that the court should do all it can to uphold an agreement which parties in litigation have come to unless there are obvious illegalities and that he would imply the terms sought by the plaintiff company, with the result that there was no illegality with the agreement.

(e) Contingent purchase contracts

[10.031] The agreement by a company to purchase its own shares need not be acted upon immediately. So, the provisions considered above also apply to '*contingent purchase contracts*', defined by s 214(1) of the CA 1990 as meaning contracts entered into by a company which do not amount to a contract to purchase its shares but under which the company may become entitled or obliged to purchase those shares. So, a 'put' and 'call' contract is permitted, provided that the provisions contained in s 213(2)(7) of the CA 1990 are complied with in full.

(f) Statutory safeguards

[10.032] Part XI of the CA 1990 embodies certain additional safeguards in respect of own-share acquisition by companies. These focus primarily on the disclosure to the public of particulars of contracts for own-share purchase. Section 222 of the CA 1990 provides that copies of the purchase contracts must be kept at the company's registered office for a period of 10 years after full performance of the contract, and that they must be made available for public inspection. Failure to comply can render the officers of the company liable to a fine or imprisonment or both. Another safeguard is seen in s 226 of the CA 1990 which provides that within 28 days of a company purchasing its own shares, it must deliver to the registrar of companies a return in the prescribed form stating each class purchased, the number and nominal value of the shares and the date upon which they were delivered back to the company. Again, failure to comply means that every officer who is in default is guilty of an offence.

(g) Repudiation by company and the effect of winding up

[10.033] A company that enters into a contract to purchase its own shares can repudiate the contract without a shareholder being able to sue the company for damages: s 219(2) of the CA 1990. Moreover, s 219(3) provides:

> 'The court shall not grant an order for specific performance of the terms of redemption or purchase of the shares to which this section applies if the company shows that it is unable to meet the cost of redeeming or purchasing the shares out of profits available for distribution.'

Although this provision weakens the enforceability of contracts for the purchase of a company's own shares, it is consistent with the spirit of the legislation which only permits a company to purchase shares out of distributable profits[70].

[10.034] Where the winding up of a company commences before a contract to purchase its shares has been completed, the contract may be enforced against the company by s 219(4) of the CA 1990. Where this happens, the shares purchased are to be treated as

---

70 On distributable profits see para **[10.089]** *et seq*.

cancelled. However, to this provision there are two exceptions, and s 219(4) shall *not* apply if:

- the terms of the purchase provide for the purchase to take place at a date later than that of the commencement of the winding up (namely, the date of the presentation of the petition to have the company wound up); or
- the company could not have lawfully made a distribution equal in value to the price at which the shares were to have been purchased between the date on which the purchase was to have taken place and the commencement of the winding up.

Section 219(6) of the CA 1990 provides that any payment made pursuant to sub-s (4) shall rank, in order of priority, *after* the payment of all other debts and liabilities of the company other than any due to members in their capacity as members, and if other shares have rights, after those shareholders' claims have been satisfied. However, any such payments shall rank in priority over any amounts due to members in satisfaction of their rights whether as to capital or income as members.

(h) Ministerial regulations

[10.035] Section 228(1) of the CA 1990 empowers the Minister for Jobs, Enterprise and Innovation to make regulations by way of statutory instrument in respect of the purchase by a company of its own shares, just as he may make such regulations in respect of treasury shares, above[71], or a company purchasing shares in its holding company. Without prejudice to the generality of the Minister's power to make regulations, s 228(2) of the CA 1990 provides that such regulations may provide, in particular, for the following matters:

- the class or description of shares which may (or may not) be purchased or sold;
- the price at which they may be purchased or sold;
- the timing of such purchases or sales;
- the method by which the shares may be purchased or sold; or
- the volume of trading in the shares which may be carried out by companies.

Failure to comply with such Ministerial regulations means that the company and every officer in default shall be guilty of an offence[72].

[B] ACQUISITION OF SHARES IN HOLDING COMPANY

[10.036] There is a general rule that a subsidiary company (or a subsidiary's nominee)[73] cannot become a member of its own holding company[74] expressed in s 32(1) of CA 1963 which provides that 'a body corporate cannot be a member of a company which is its holding company, and any allotment or transfer of shares in a company to its subsidiary

---

71 See para **[10.043]** *et seq*.

72 Section 228(3) of the CA 1990.

73 Section 32(7) of the CA 1963. See also Ch 8, *Shares and Membership*, at paras **[8.011]** to **[8.016]**.

74 If the holding company is limited by guarantee or unlimited, references in s 32 to shares, whether or not it has a share capital, shall be construed as including references to interests of members as such, whatever that form of interest: s 32(9) of the CA 1963.

shall be void'. While the general rule has been greatly diminished by the operation of s 224(1) of the CA 1990, which is considered below, even s 32 of the CA 1963 contains an extensive list of circumstances when a body corporate can lawfully be a member of its holding company:

(a) where the subsidiary is a personal representative[75];

(b) where the subsidiary is a trustee unless the holding company or a subsidiary thereof is beneficially interested under the trust (other than by way of security for the purposes of a transaction entered into by the holding company in the ordinary course of a business which includes the lending of money)[76];

(c) if the subsidiary was a member of its holding company on 5 May 1958 it may continue to be a member[77];

(d) if the subsidiary was already a member of a company, which subsequently becomes its holding company, then it may continue to be a member[78];

(e) if the subsidiary was already a member of a company, which subsequently becomes its holding company, the subsidiary is not prevented from accepting and holding further shares in the capital of the holding company if allotted to it in consequence of a capitalisation by the holding company and if the terms are such that the subsidiary is not involved in any obligation to make any payment or give other consideration for such further shares[79].

Except where a subsidiary is a personal representative or trustee, where a subsidiary is a member of its holding company it shall not have a right to vote at meetings of the holding company or any class of members thereof[80]. It is also important to note that for the purposes of s 32 of the CA 1963, the meaning of 'subsidiary' and 'holding company' is as provided in s 155 of the CA 1963[81].

[10.037] The most far-reaching exception to the general rule stated in s 32(1) of the CA 1963 is s 224(1) of the CA 1990, which provides that, notwithstanding ss 32[82] and 60 of the CA 1963, a company[83] may, subject to the provisions of that section, acquire and

75 Section 32(2) of the CA 1963.

76 Section 32(2) of the CA 1963.

77 Section 32(3) of the CA 1963.

78 Section 32(4) of the CA 1963.

79 Section 32(5) of the CA 1963. Where a holding company offers new shares to its existing shareholders for value such that its subsidiary cannot avail of s 32(5), then the holding company may sell on behalf of the subsidiary such shares and pay the proceeds of sale to the subsidiary: s 32(8) of the CA 1963.

80 Section 32(6) of the CA 1963.

81 See Ch 12, *Groups of Companies*, at para **[12.008]**.

82 Note, though, that s 224 of the CA 1990 does not apply to shares held by a subsidiary in its holding company in the circumstances permitted by s 32 of the CA 1963: s 224(5) of the CA 1990. Neither does s 224 of the CA 1990 (except sub-s (2)(b)(iii)) apply to shares subscribed for, purchased or held by a subsidiary in its holding company pursuant to s 9(1) of the Insurance Act 1990: s 224(6) of the CA 1990.

83 The reference to 'a company' here is deemed, by reg 4(4) of the EC(PLCS)R 1997, to include a body corporate. Moreover, for the purposes of Part XI of the CA 1990, in addition to the circumstances set out in s 155 (1) of the CA 1963, a limited company (including a body corporate) (contd.../)

hold shares in a company which is its holding company. Section 224(2) of the CA 1990 provides that the acquisition and holding by a subsidiary under sub-s (1) of shares in its holding company shall be subject to the following conditions:

> '(a) The consideration for the acquisition of such shares shall be provided for out of the profits of the subsidiary available for distribution.
>
> (b) Upon the acquisition of such shares and for so long as the shares are held by the subsidiary—
>
> (i) the profits of the subsidiary available for distribution shall for all purposes be restricted by a sum equal to the total cost of the shares acquired;
>
> (ii) the shares shall, for the purposes of the consolidated accounts prepared by the holding company in accordance with sections 150 to 152 of the Principal Act, be treated in the same manner as is required in respect of shares held as treasury shares under section 43A of the Act of 1983 (inserted by section 232 (c) of this Act); and
>
> (iii) the subsidiary shall not exercise any voting rights in respect of the shares and any purported exercise of those rights shall be void.'

Distributions and the meaning of profits available for distribution are considered in detail later[84]. Section 224(3) of the CA 1990 provides that a contract for the acquisition (whether by allotment or transfer) by a subsidiary of shares in its holding company shall not be entered into without being authorised in advance both by the subsidiary and its holding company and the provisions of ss 212–217 are applied, with the necessary modifications, to the granting, variation, revocation and release of such authority. This means that a special resolution is required in a private sale as would be undertaken by a private company[85]. In the context of s 224, a subsidiary's profits available for distribution shall not include the profits attributable to any shares in the subsidiary for the time being held by the subsidiary's holding company so far as there are profits for the period before the date on or from which the shares were acquired by the holding company[86].

[10.038] Section 224 of the CA 1990 has been extended by reg 5 of the European Communities (Public Limited Companies Subsidiaries) Regulations 1997 (the 'EC(PLCS)R 1997')[87]. In the case of private companies that fall within the definition of a '*public company subsidiary*'[88], reg 5(2) provides that such companies may not, despite

---

83 (\...contd) 'shall also be deemed to be a subsidiary of a public limited company if, but only if, the public limited company is itself a shareholder or member of it and controls alone, pursuant to an agreement with other shareholders or members, a majority of the shareholders' or members' voting rights in the company in question': reg 4(1) of the EC(PLCS)R 1997. Moreover, for the purposes of Part XI of the CA 1990, a PLC exercises its control indirectly where the control of a subsidiary is exercised through another subsidiary, pursuant to s 155(1)(b) of the CA 1963: reg 4(3) of the EC(PLCS)R 1997.

84 See para **[10.089]** *post*.

85 An ordinary resolution suffices where the shares are to be purchased on a recognised Stock Exchange and subject to a marketing agreement.

86 Section 224(4) of the CA 1990.

87 SI 67/1997.

88 A public company subsidiary is defined by reg 5(1) of SI 67/1997 as being a subsidiary of a PLC.

what s 224(2) provides, subscribe for the shares of their parent public company or purchase shares in their parent public company which are not fully paid. So, a public company subsidiary may not subscribe for shares in its parent PLC even though it has sufficient distributable profits available and if it does so it commits a criminal offence and the subscription will be void[89]. It can purchase such shares by transfer, however, but only if they are fully paid shares. There are also restrictions on such companies availing of the validation or whitewash procedure under s 60(2) of the CA 1963 and this is considered below[90].

[10.039] Where a public company subsidiary purchases, subscribes for or holds shares in its parent public company, and:

- the shares were not fully paid when they were purchased, or
- the authorisation required by s 224(3) of the CA 1990 has not been obtained, or
- the shares are held as treasury shares in excess of the limit referred to in s 209(2) of the CA 1990, or
- the purchase or subscription was in contravention of reg 5(2)(c) of the EC(PLCS)R 1997,

then, reg 5(5) of the EC(PLCS)R 1997 provides that, unless the shares or any interest of the public company subsidiary in them are previously disposed of, the provisions of s 43(3) of the C(A)A 1983 shall apply to the public company subsidiary in respect of such shares[91]. This is expressed to be without prejudice to any other requirements contained in or penalties imposed by the Companies Acts.

[10.040] The EC(PLCS)R 1997 are expressly stated not to affect or prohibit certain subscriptions and allotments[92]. An offence under the EC(PLCS)R 1997 is punishable, on

---

89 Regulation 5(3) of the EC(PLCS)R 1997. Where, in contravention of reg (2)(a) of the EC(PLCS)R 1997, a nominee of a public company subsidiary subscribes for shares in a parent public company, the shares will be treated as being held by the nominee on his own account and the public company subsidiary will be regarded as having no beneficial interest in them and the provisions of s 42(2)(6) of the C(A)A 1983 are applied, with any necessary modifications.

90 See para **[10.067]**.

91 With the modification that the 'relevant period' in relation to any shares shall be 12 months and with any other necessary modifications. On s 43 of the C(A)A 1983, see Ch 29, *Public Limited Companies and SEs*, at para **[29.074]**.

92 These are provided in reg 5(6) of the EC(PLCS)R 1997: '(a) the subscription for, acquisition or holding of, shares in its parent public company by a public company subsidiary where the public company subsidiary is concerned as personal representative or where it is concerned as trustee unless the parent public company or a subsidiary thereof is beneficially interested under the trust and is not so interested only by way of security for the purposes of a transaction entered into by it in the ordinary course of a business which includes the lending of money; (b) the allotment to, or holding by, a public company subsidiary of shares in its parent public company in the circumstances set out in section 32(5) of the Principal Act [ie, the CA 1963], but where the shares so allotted are held as treasury shares and the nominal value of treasury shares held by the public company subsidiary exceeds the limit referred to in section 209(2) of the Act of 1990 then, unless the shares or any interest of the public company subsidiary in them are previously disposed of, the provisions of section 43(3) of the Companies (Amendment) Act, 1983, (contd.../)

summary conviction, by a class C fine or to imprisonment for a term not exceeding six months, or both[93]. Where an offence has been committed by a public company subsidiary and it is proved to have been committed 'with the consent or connivance of or to be attributable to any neglect on the part of a person being a director, manager, secretary, or a person purporting to act in any such capacity', or a member where the affairs of the company are managed by its members, that person too shall be guilty of an offence[94].

[C] Redemption of Shares

[10.041] Section 207 of the CA 1990 allows a company to issue redeemable shares[95]. Redeemable shares lack the permanency normally associated with share capital. Companies are, however, only permitted to issue and redeem redeemable shares provided that the following conditions are met:

- the issue and redemption of redeemable shares is authorised by the company's articles of association[96]; and
- the *nominal value of issued share capital which is not* redeemable is not less than one-tenth (10%) of the nominal value of the total issued share capital of the company[97]; and
- the shares redeemed are fully paid[98]; and
- the terms of redemption provide for payment on redemption[99]; and
- the funds used to finance the redemption must be from profits which are available for distribution[100]; and
- where shares are cancelled pursuant to s 208 of the CA 1990, such shares may also be redeemed out of the proceeds of a fresh issue of shares made for the purposes of redemption[101]; and

92 (\...contd) shall with the modification that the relevant period in relation to any shares shall be 3 years and with any other necessary modifications, apply to the public company subsidiary in respect of such shares; (c) the subscription, acquisition or holding of shares in its parent public company by a public company subsidiary where the subscription, acquisition or holding is effected on behalf of a person other than the person subscribing, acquiring or holding the shares, who is neither the parent public company itself nor a subsidiary within the meaning of Part XI of the Act of 1990 of the said parent public company; (d) the subscription, acquisition or holding of shares in its parent public company by a public company subsidiary which is a member of an approved stock exchange specified in section 17(2) of the Stock Exchange Act, 1995 (No 9 of 1995), acting in its capacity as a professional dealer in securities in the normal course of its business.'

93 Regulation 5(7) of the EC(PLCS)R 1997.

94 Regulation 8(a) and (b) of the EC(PLCS)R 1997.

95 On 'redeemable shares', see Ch 8, *Shares and Membership*, at para **[8.111]**.

96 Section 207(1) of the CA 1990.

97 Section 207(2)(a) of the CA 1990.

98 Section 207(2)(b) of the CA 1990.

99 Section 207(2)(c) of the CA 1990.

100 Section 207(2)(d)(i) of the CA 1990. See para **[10.089]** *et seq.*

101 Section 207(2)(d)(ii) of the CA 1990.

- any premium payable on the redemption of the shares must be paid out of profits available for distribution[102]; and
- where shares were issued at a premium, any premium payable on their redemption (being a redemption involving the cancellation of shares pursuant to s 208 of the CA 1990 and the fresh issue of shares for that purpose) may be paid out of the proceeds of a fresh issue of shares made for the purposes of the redemption, up to an amount equal to the aggregate of the premiums received by the company on the issue of the shares redeemed, or the current amount of the company's share premium account, whichever is less. In any such case the amount of the company's *share premium account*[103] shall, notwithstanding s 62(1) of the CA 1963, be reduced by a sum corresponding to the amount of any payment made by virtue of this provision out of the proceeds of the issue of the new issue[104].

Where an existing company wishes to issue redeemable shares, it must ensure that its articles of association authorise the issue of redeemable shares. Furthermore, subject to the conditions outlined in s 210 of the CA 1990, a company may convert any of its shares into redeemable shares.

[10.042] Where a company decides to redeem its shares it is presented with a number of options as to what to do with them. In the first place, a company may cancel them after redeeming them. Cancellation of redeemable shares is governed by s 208 of the CA 1990. Where shares are cancelled, the company's issued share capital is reduced, but the authorised share capital is maintained as it was before. Central to the maintenance of capital principle is the notion of a company's *capital redemption reserve fund*. Into this fund the company must pay the proceeds of the redemption. Where the redemption is funded from profits, a sum equal to the amount by which the company's issued share capital is reduced must be paid into the company's capital redemption reserve fund. Where the redemption is in whole or in part funded by a fresh issue of shares, and the *amount* of money obtained is less than the amount required to redeem the shares, then the difference must be paid from profits into the company's capital redemption reserve fund.

[10.043] In the second place, upon redeeming its shares a company may retain them, instead of cancelling them, in which case they become *treasury shares*[105]. This is facilitated by s 209(2)(a) of the CA 1990, which provides that the nominal value of treasury shares held by a company at any one time may not exceed 10% of the company's nominal issued share capital. The creation of treasury shares is an alternative to cancelling redeemed shares. A treasury share is different from all other types of share. The principal difference lies in its ownership. Central to the notion of a share is that some person or body corporate holds it, giving that person a share in the company. A treasury share on the other hand is not owned by anyone other than the company and may be seen as existing in a state of limbo. Accordingly, although a treasury share may

---

102 Section 207(2)(e) of the CA 1990.

103 For a company's share premium account, see para **[10.111]**.

104 Section 207(2)(f) of the CA 1990.

105 See Ch 8, *Shares and Membership*, para **[8.113]**.

carry voting rights and the right to a dividend, such may not be exercised while the company holds it[106].

[10.044] Treasury shares may be reissued or cancelled[107]. Where reissued by private companies, s 209(6) of the CA 1990 provides that a certain price must be obtained. The 'reissue price range', which is set by the members of the company in general meeting, sets a maximum and minimum price which must be obtained before any contract is formed for the reissue of treasury shares[108]. Where the treasury shares, which are reissued, are derived in whole or in part from *shares purchased by the company*, the reissue price range of the whole or such part of those shares must be determined by special resolution of the company passed at the meeting at which the resolution authorising the purchase has been passed and such determination shall remain effective with respect to those shares for the requisite period[109]. Where treasury shares, which are reissued, are derived in whole or in part from *shares redeemed by the company*, the reissue price range must be determined by special resolution of the company passed before any contract for the reissue of those shares is entered into and such determination shall remain effective for the requisite period[110]. The company may, from time to time by special resolution, vary or renew a determination of the reissue price range with respect to particular treasury shares before any contract for reissue of those shares is entered into, and any such variation or renewal shall remain effective as a determination of the reissue price range of those shares for the requisite period of time[111]. Requisite period is defined as the period of 18 months from the date of the passing of the resolution determining the reissue price range or varying or renewing such determination, or such lesser period of time as the resolution may specify[112]. A reissue of treasury shares in contravention of s 209(6) of the CA 1990 will render the reissue unlawful[113].

By s 228(1) of the CA 1990, the Minister for Jobs, Enterprise and Innovation may make regulations governing the sale by companies of their own shares which are held as treasury shares. The Minister's regulations may relate either to companies in general or to a particular category or class of company. In this way, it is open to the Minister acting by statutory instrument to differentiate between public and private companies.

[10.045] Sections 218 of the CA 1990 (payments with respect to purchase or redemption of own shares), 219 (effect of failure to purchase or redeem a company's own shares) and 228 (ministerial power to make regulations in respect to purchase/redemption of a company's own shares) all apply to the redemption of redeemable shares. These also apply to the acquisition of a company's own shares and are considered next.

106 Section 209(3) of the CA 1990.
107 Section 209(4) of the CA 1990.
108 Section 209(6)(a) of the CA 1990.
109 Section 209(6)(b) of the CA 1990.
110 Section 209(6)(c) of the CA 1990.
111 Section 209(6)(d) of the CA 1990.
112 Section 209(6)(e)(ii) of the CA 1990.
113 Section s 209(7) of the CA 1990.

[D] Assisting the Purchase of Own Shares

[10.046] One of the most common ways in which a company can inadvertently breach the rules of capital maintenance is by directly or indirectly providing financial assistance for the purchase of its own shares[114]. The basic prohibition is contained in s 60(1) of the CA 1963, which provides that subject to certain exceptions:

> '... it shall not be lawful for a company to give, whether directly or indirectly and whether by means of a loan, guarantee, the provision of security or otherwise, any financial assistance for the purpose of or in connection with a purchase or subscription made or to be made by any person of or for any shares in the company, or where the company is a subsidiary company, in its holding company.'

The integrity of the basic prohibition is maintained despite a number of exceptions to the section, which do not detract substantially from the general prohibition. The exceptions to s 60(1) of the CA 1963 are considered here as follows:

1. Section 60 of the CA 1963 and private companies.
2. The consequences of contravening s 60(1) of the CA 1963.
3. The meaning of 'financial assistance'.
4. The validation procedure: resolution and declaration.
5. Dividends and lawful liabilities: s 60(12) of the CA 1963.
6. Miscellaneous exceptions: s 60(13) of the CA 1963.

Section 60 of the CA 1963 and private companies

[10.047] The application of s 60 of the CA 1963 to private companies is best illustrated by way of an example. A company, which shall be termed 'Borrowings Ltd', decides to acquire the business of another company called 'Investment Properties Ltd', which owns a property portfolio worth €1m. In order to minimise stamp duty, which would otherwise be payable at 2% of €1m[115], Borrowings Ltd decides to acquire indirectly the property portfolio by purchasing the shares in Investment Properties Ltd from its shareholders, as opposed to purchasing its assets from the company. By doing this Borrowings Ltd will own the assets (and liabilities) of the company, *but only indirectly*; the title to those assets being vested in the separate legal entity which is Investment Properties Ltd. Borrowings Ltd strikes an agreement with the shareholders of Investment Properties Ltd to purchase their shares for €1m, which a credit institution agrees to advance to it. Although Borrowings Ltd cannot itself offer any security for the loan, its controllers know that after acquiring Investment Properties Ltd, it can cause Investment Properties Ltd to offer its assets as security for the loan from the credit institution.

Before the credit institution issues its facility letter, it will ensure that one of the special conditions of the letter will be that 'all of the provisions of s 60 of the CA 1963 are complied with in all respects'. This is because in providing security for the purchase of its own shares, Investment Properties Ltd would be directly providing financial

---

114 See Johnston, *Banking and Security Law in Ireland* (1998), paras [18.13]–[18.29]; Cotter, 'Section 60 of the Companies Act 1963' (2000) 7 CLP 111; and MacCann, 'Section 60 of the Companies Act 1963: Law and Procedure' (1994) 1 CLP 74.

115 See Ch 9, *Share Transfer*, para **[9.109]**.

assistance (ie, to Borrowings Ltd) for the purchase of the shares in Investment Properties Ltd. Unless the provisions of s 60 of the CA 1963 are complied with in all respects the provision of security by Investment Properties Ltd to the credit institution would be voidable. Regard should also be had to s 31 of the CA 1990, as to which see Ch 16[116].

The consequences of contravening s 60(1) of the CA 1963

(a) Criminal consequences

[10.048] The criminal sanction for the contravention of s 60(1) is set out in s 60(15) of the CA 1963[117]. This provides that where a company acts in breach of the prohibition every officer who is in default is liable, on summary conviction, to imprisonment for a term not exceeding six months or to a class C fine, or both. Where convicted on indictment, an officer in default is liable to imprisonment for a term not exceeding two years or to a fine of €6,348.70, or both.

(b) Civil consequences – voidability

[10.049] For there to be a breach of s 60 of the CA 1963 there must be a finding of fact that the company concerned has directly or indirectly financed the acquisition of its own shares[118]. Where the prohibition in s 60(1) is contravened, s 60(14) of the CA 1963 provides that:

> 'Any transaction in breach of this section shall be voidable at the instance of the company against any person (whether a party to the transaction or not) who had notice of the facts which constitute such breach[119].'

In *Lombard & Ulster Banking Ltd v Bank of Ireland*[120], it was noted by Costello J that the consequence of a contravention of s 60(14) of the CA 1963 is that the transaction is merely *voidable* against persons having notice of the facts constituting the breach, and is not *void ab initio*. Accordingly, it is a matter for the company, which provides such financial assistance, to seek to avoid the transaction in question. Where a company, which has unlawfully provided financial assistance in connection with the purchase of its own shares, goes into liquidation, the liquidator of the company may seek to have the transaction set aside in order to swell the company's assets[121]. However, it should be stressed that a contravening transaction is merely *voidable* against persons *who have notice* of the facts that constitute the breach.

---

116 See Ch 16, *Statutory Regulation of Directors' Transactions*, at para **[16.055]**.

117 As amended by s 15 of the C(A)A 1983.

118 *McCormick et al v Cameo Investments Ltd* [1978] ILRM 191 at 194.

119 Note, by way of exception, s 218(1) of the National Asset Management Agency Act 2009 provides that s 60 of the CA 1963 shall not invalidate or render void or voidable as against NAMA or a NAMA group entity or their successors in title, an 'acquired bank asset' which can include a guarantee or charge or other financial support a company may have given in connection with the purchase of its own shares.

120 *Lombard & Ulster Banking Ltd v Bank of Ireland* (2 June 1987, unreported) HC *per* Costello J.

121 See Ch 25, *Realisation and Distribution of Assets in Winding Up*, para **[25.137]**.

[10.050] In *Quinn and ors v Irish Bank Resolution Corporation Ltd and another*[122], it was suggested that a breach of s 60 of the CA 1963 might justify the invocation of a plea of illegality in contracts. In that case the wife and five adult children of Sean Quinn sought to rely on an alleged breach of s 60 and of the Market Abuse Regulations[123] in aid of their claims for declarations of invalidity, unenforceability and no legal effect in respect of any charge on shares and personal guarantees given by them relating to loans made by the former Anglo Irish Bank corp to Sean Quinn and entities belonging to him. In his preliminary ruling on this point, Charleton J said the core of the decision was on whether the Market Abuse Regulations and s 60 'are confined as to remedy only to those criminal sanctions and responses in civil law as set out in legislation, or whether ... a general principle of illegality with an effect on the various contracts underpinning the loans, the guarantees and share charge, may be called in aid by them'. Charleton J said that he was

> '... not persuaded that s 60 of the Companies Act 1963 which forbids a company from purchasing its own shares or from offering financial assistance in that regard, is self-contained in its remedies and cannot impact on public policy. In a case such as that pleaded herein, the general law of illegality of contracts is entitled to respond in an appropriate and proportionate way so that loss caused through the manipulation of the share price of Anglo to those directly at the receiving end of that conduct, namely the Quinns, can be appropriately responded to.'

It is thought that it would be perverse to turn a provision of law, designed to protect a company's capital and creditors, against the company to deprive it of its right to recover a loan made in contravention of s 60 or the guarantee of such a loan. The possible wrongdoing by a company's directors should not be equated with the wrongdoing of the company. Where a director of a company causes a company to make a loan in breach of s 60 of the CA 1963 and a third party guarantees that loan, there is no public policy interest in voiding that loan or guarantee. On the contrary, the public interest firmly lies on the company recovering the monies which its director wrongly caused the company to advance since the purpose of s 60 is to prevent the company's capital from being depleted. This is entirely consistent with why s 60(14) provides that transactions in breach are voidable *at the instance of the company*: they will only be voidable where the company will benefit from voiding them and the company may elect not to void them where such is beneficial to the company.

(c) The meaning of 'any transaction'

[10.051] The meaning of 'any transaction' as used in s 60(14) of the CA 1963 was considered in *CH (Ireland) Inc (in liquidation) v Credit Suisse Canada*[124], the facts of which are set out below[125]. McCracken J said:

> 'A transaction in breach of the section must be one which is in breach of *subsection (1)*, which is the giving of financial assistance for the purpose of or in connection with the purchase or subscription of shares. Furthermore, it must be a transaction whereby the

---

[122] *Quinn and others v Irish Bank Resolution Corporation Ltd and another* [2012] IEHC 36, Charleton J.

[123] See Ch 32, *Prospectus, Market Abuse and Transparency Law*, at para **[32.058]** *et seq.*

[124] *CH (Ireland) Inc (in liquidation) v Credit Suisse Canada* [1999] 4 IR 542 (McCracken J).

[125] See para **[10.057]**.

> company gives the financial assistance. Furthermore, the use of the word 'transaction' in the subsections dealing with the making of a declaration by the directors refers in both *subsections (4)* and *(5)* to 'the company having carried out the transaction whereby such assistance is to be given'. In my view the only transaction which can be attacked under *subsection (1)* is a transaction directly involving the company[126].'

Applying this to the facts of the case in hand, McCracken J held that the relevant transaction there was the depositing of monies by or at the direction of the company and the consideration for that deposit. In that case, McCracken J found that there had been a provision of financial assistance in connection with the purchase of a company's own shares and that there was 'actual notice' of the facts that constituted the breach. The order of the court was to declare void the deposit of the monies by CHI with CSZ as security and the consideration for that deposit. The declaration was, however, made only as against CSC – a party to the proceedings – and not against any other company involved.

[10.052] In *Re Ravenshaw Ltd*[127], a company called White Lace Limited borrowed £2.7m from First Active plc on the security of a mortgage debenture. White Lace then made this money available to Ravenshaw, which it used to purchase the shares held by two individuals (Mr Deane and Mr Cassidy) in White Lace for £3m. Laffoy J said that there was breach of s 60 when White Lace borrowed, gave security and then advanced the sum of £2.7m to Ravenshaw by way of financial assistance for the purchase of the shares, and that the civil remedy in s 60(14) was available to White Lace at that stage. The learned judge went on, however, to reject the claim that the effect of s 60(14) was to render voidable the completion of the share purchase agreement and the transfer of the shares in White Lace by the individuals to Ravenshaw. Laffoy J said that this was not a 'transaction directly involving the company' (ie, White Lace) which was voidable and, after quoting the passage from the decision of McCracken J in *CH (Ireland) Inc (in liquidation) v Credit Suisse Canada*[128], stated:

> 'A transaction is the action of conducting business which involves exchange or interaction between parties. The completion of the share purchase agreement, the payment of the purchase consideration, and the taking of the transfer of the shares in White Lace was carried out on the one side by Mr Deane and Mr Cassidy and on the other side by [Ravenshaw Limited]. It was not carried out by, nor was it a transaction directly involving, White Lace. Apart from that, even if it could be proved that Mr Deane and Mr Cassidy, as one side of the transaction involving the transfer of the shares, had actual notice of the facts which constituted the breach of s 60(1), as required by s 60(14), which seems highly unlikely, it simply defies reason and common sense to suggest at this remove that any benefit could be gained by any person, natural or corporate, on Mr Fahy's side of the transaction by seeking to have the transfer of the shares to the Company made void, which would result in the shares reverting to Mr Deane and Mr Cassidy, presumably on return of the IR£3m purchase consideration by them[129].'

---

126 *CH (Ireland) Inc (in liquidation) v Credit Suisse Canada* [1999] 4 IR 542 at 556.

127 *Re Ravenshaw Ltd* [2012] IEHC 37, Laffoy J.

128 *CH (Ireland) Inc (in liquidation) v Credit Suisse Canada* [1999] 4 IR 542 (McCracken J).

129 *Re Ravenshaw Ltd* [2012] IEHC 37 at para 5.6.

(d) The meaning of 'notice'

[10.053] In order for a company to avoid a transaction, which is in breach of s 60(1) of the CA 1963, against any person it must be shown that the person concerned had notice of the facts which constitute such breach. 'Notice', in this context has been held to mean *actual notice*. Accordingly, in *Bank of Ireland Finance Ltd v Rockfield Ltd*[130] Kenny J in the Supreme Court held that:

> 'The notice referred to in s 60(14) is actual notice and not constructive notice. As there has been considerable confusion as to the meaning of the terms 'actual notice' and 'imputed notice' and 'constructive notice' – a confusion which has been pointed out by many judges and text-book writers – I wish to say that I use the term 'actual notice' as meaning in this case that the plaintiff bank, or any of its officials, had been informed either verbally or in writing, that part of the advance was to be applied in the purchase of shares in the defendant company, or that they knew facts from which they must have inferred that part of the advance was to be applied for this purpose ... I include in 'actual notice' cases where the agent gets actual notice of the equity[131].'

In particular, Kenny J refused to extend the doctrine of constructive notice to s 60(14) of the CA 1963, citing with approval the case of *Manchester Trust v Furness*[132]. In the *Manchester Trust* case, Lindley J, who was acknowledged by Kenny J to be 'a great authority upon company law', said:

> '... as regards the extension of the equitable doctrines of constructive notice to commercial transactions, the courts have always set their faces resolutely against it. The equitable doctrines of constructive notice are common enough in dealing with land and estates, with which the court is familiar; but there have been repeated protests against the introduction into commercial transactions of anything like an extension of those doctrines, and the protest is founded on perfect good sense. In dealing with estates in land title is everything and it can be leisurely investigated; in commercial transactions possession is everything and there is not time to investigate title; and if we were to extend the doctrine of constructive notice to commercial transactions we should be doing infinite mischief and paralysing the trade of the country[133].'

The fact that the transaction in question involved a mortgage of land was found to be immaterial; the learned judge held that it would be a ludicrous interpretation to read s 60(14) in one sense for financial assistance without security, and in another sense when a mortgage is involved.

[10.054] In the *Rockfield* case, two men wished to acquire an hotel and obtained an agreement from the plaintiff bank to advance £170,400, the bank's security being the equitable deposit of the land certificate of the hotel. The bank understood that the hotel would in time be conveyed to a company called either 'Rockville Ltd' or 'Rockfield Ltd'. In fact the company was called Rockfield Ltd, it owned the hotel, and the deal involved the purchase of the company's shares by the two borrowers. A first advance of

[130] *Bank of Ireland Finance Ltd v Rockfield Ltd* [1979] IR 21.

[131] *Bank of Ireland Finance Ltd v Rockfield* Ltd [1979] IR 21 at 37. Kenny J quoted with approval Snell's *Principles of Equity* (27th edn), where 'imputed notice' was defined as: '... where his agent as such in the course of the transaction has actual or constructive notice of the equity'.

[132] *Manchester Trust v Furness* [1895] 2 QB 539.

[133] *Manchester Trust v Furness* [1895] 2 QB 539 at 545.

£150,000 was made by the bank, which the borrowers used to purchase the shares in Rockfield Ltd. The second advance was used to repay part of the initial advance. When the borrowers acquired control of the company, they authorised the deposit of the land certificate of the hotel with the plaintiff bank by way of equitable mortgage by deposit of title deeds. The bank was aware that stamp duty at 1% was being paid on the acquisition, indicating a share transfer and not a transfer of land. The bank was also aware that the defendant company had applied for and had obtained planning permission in respect of the land. On the second[134] question to be determined, Kenny J said:

> 'This is the first case, as far as I know, in which the meaning of sub-s 14 of s 60 has been considered by any court in this country. The onus of proving that the money was advanced for the purchase of shares in the defendant company lies on the person who alleges this. The plaintiffs do not have to prove that they had no notice of the facts which constituted a breach of s 60. What has to be established is that the plaintiffs had notice when lending the money that it was to be used for the purchase of shares in the defendant company. The fact which constituted such breach in this case was the application of £150,000 to the purchase of the shares in the defendant company. As the purchase followed the loan, the defendants must establish that the plaintiffs knew at the time when they made the loan that it was to be applied for this purpose. If they got notice of this subsequently, that is irrelevant[135].'

As noted earlier[136], Kenny J rejected the application of the doctrine of constructive notice and, in so doing, the Supreme Court tempered the effects of s 60(14) of the CA 1963. However, notice of the 'facts which constitute such breach' should be distinguished from notice of a breach. Section 60(14) uses the former expression and, consequently, even where a person does not have actual notice of a breach, it may be argued that they had notice of *facts which constitute* a breach. It is significant, however, that notwithstanding that the plaintiff bank knew that the stamp duty was estimated at 1%, this fact was held by the Supreme Court *not* to be notice that the money was to be applied to purchase shares in the defendant company. Accordingly, the Supreme Court held that the defendant company was not entitled to avoid the transaction since the plaintiff bank did not have notice of the facts which constituted a breach of s 60(1).

[10.055] In *Lombard & Ulster Banking Ltd v Bank of Ireland*[137], certain persons came together with a view to acquiring indirectly a school house by purchasing the shares in the company which owned it. The plaintiff bank agreed to finance the acquisition of the shares in the company, its security being a guarantee supported by a charge over the school building from the company. Although at the time of the advance the bank was assured that the procedure set out in s 60(2) of the CA 1963[138] had been complied with, it later transpired that this was not the case. In fact a special resolution of the members was not passed, nor had a statutory declaration of solvency been sworn by the company's directors. Costello J held that there had indeed been a breach of s 60(1) but that such merely rendered the transaction voidable against persons who had notice of the facts

---

134 He also considered the question of ratification by the company, and held that this had been validly done.

135 *Bank of Ireland Finance Ltd v Rockfield Ltd* [1979] IR 21 at 36–37.

136 See para **[10.053]**.

137 *Lombard & Ulster Banking Ltd v Bank of Ireland* (2 June 1987, unreported) HC *per* Costello J.

138 See para **[10.067]**.

which constituted the breach. Costello J considered that there were three questions to be answered on the matter of notice.

First, he rejected the liquidator's contention that the phrase 'transaction in breach of the section' meant the carrying out of a transaction prohibited by s 60(1) of the CA 1963 and that since the plaintiff bank knew that the transaction was prohibited by s 60(1), it had sufficient notice to enable the company to avoid the guarantee and charge. In order for a company to avoid a transaction, it is necessary to show that the bank knew of the facts which resulted in non-compliance with the section. It is not sufficient that it merely knows of the fact that a transaction that would contravene s 60(1) if the validation procedure is not followed, is proposed.

Second, Costello J held that the company, or its liquidator, must establish as a matter of probability that the bank had notice that there was non-compliance with the exceptions to s 60(1). Therefore, the onus is on the liquidator or the company to prove his or its case. The failure to show that a person had actual notice will mean that a guarantee, mortgage, charge or other security, is enforceable and cannot be avoided by the company.

Third, the learned judge applied the meaning of notice decided by the Supreme Court in *Bank of Ireland Finance Ltd v Rockfield Ltd*, and held that in order for the bank to have notice, it must have had actual notice, meaning:

> '(a) that they or their officials actually knew that the required procedures were not adopted or that they knew facts from which they must have inferred that the company had failed to adopt the required procedures, or (b) that an agent of theirs actually knew of the failure or knew facts from which he must have inferred that a failure had occurred ... 'Constructive Notice' of the failure is not sufficient for sub-s (14).'

From the foregoing it is clear that the authorities on the meaning of notice have found that it is actual notice and that this includes the notice of an agent.

[10.056] In *Re Cognotec Ltd*[139], a sum of US$10m was loaned by Barclays Bank Ireland plc for the purpose of financial assistance in connection with the purchase or acquisition of a company's own shares as part of a reorganisation of the company which involved one of its shareholders selling its shares to the remaining shareholders. The structure involved one group company borrowing the money and the company, Cognotec Limited, guaranteeing that loan and providing a debenture containing a fixed and floating charge as security. The company purported to follow the validation procedure in s 60(2) of the CA 1963[140] but a copy of the directors' statutory declaration of solvency was not delivered to the registrar of companies within 21 days after the date on which the financial assistance was given owing to an oversight by the company's own solicitors who did not act for the bank. McGovern J found that the bank did *not* have actual notice of the breach:

> 'Any failure to deliver the statutory declaration for registration within the time allowed only taints the validation procedure and becomes relevant if the bank had actual notice. Although I was referred to the decision in *Re NL Electrical Ltd, Ghosh and another v 3i* [1994] 1 BCLC 22, which dealt with the consequences of failing to deliver particulars to the Companies Registration Office, it is not necessary to consider its application in this

139 *Re Cognotec Ltd* [2010] IEHC 309.

140 See para **[10.067]** *post*.

> jurisdiction in circumstances where the Bank did not have notice of the failure to deliver the declaration for registration. Nor do I have to construe subsection (14) to determine whether it could have been the intention of the legislature that a failure to deliver the declaration for registration would have the effect contended for by the company[141].'

McGovern J concluded that the debenture was valid, as was the appointment of a receiver thereunder, and that neither were invalidated by any breach of s 60 of the CA 1963.

[10.057] The question of notice – and in particular notice of the facts that constitute the breach – was considered in *CH (Ireland) Inc (in liquidation) v Credit Suisse Canada*[142]. The facts, like many of these cases, are somewhat convoluted. The applicant company was in liquidation and was suing by its liquidator. The litigation concerned a transaction whereby the respondent company ('CSC') made a loan of £18.8m to Castor Holdings Ltd ('Castor') which was secured by a 'payment obligation' from CSC's holding company, Credit Suisse ('CSZ'). Castor utilised the borrowed money to subscribe for shares in a company called CH Investments (New Brunswick) Inc ('CHNB'). CHNB, in turn, used the money to subscribe for shares in the applicant company ('CHI'). CHI then deposited the purchase monies with CSZ, indemnified CSZ against any liability on foot of its payment obligation to CSC, and pledged the deposited monies as security. CSZ then guaranteed the repayment of the loan made by CSC to Castor. In addition, CHI guaranteed all liabilities of Castor to either CSZ or CSC. It was CHI's liquidator's contention that the monies paid by CHNB to CHI as a subscription for shares were deposited by CHI effectively as the ultimate security for the monies advanced by CSC to Castor, and that this was a breach of s 60 of the CA 1963. McCracken J held that the depositing of monies by CHI with CSZ was to ensure that CSC (on CSZ's effective direction) would advance monies to Castor and then to CHNB to enable it to purchase the shares in CHI, and that the foregoing constituted 'financial assistance'[143]. However, McCracken J did not believe that the only or main purpose of the guarantee given by CHI was to give financial assistance for the purchase of shares.

Turning to s 60(14) of the CA 1963, McCracken J considered the meaning of 'any transaction in breach of this section' as used therein and held that in the relevant transaction there was the depositing of monies by or at the direction of the company and the consideration for that deposit[144]. McCracken J noted that a transaction is only voidable under s 60(14) against any person who had notice of the facts which constitute the breach of s 60(1), and that the onus was on the liquidator to prove that CSC had such notice. After reviewing the finding of the Supreme Court in *Bank of Ireland Finance Ltd v Rockfield Ltd*[145] and the requirement that '*actual notice*' be shown, McCracken J considered the facts of the case in hand and found that CSC did in fact have actual notice of the facts that constituted the breach of s 60(1), ie, it knew that:

---

141 *Re Cognotec Ltd* [2010] IEHC 309 at para 18.

142 *CH (Ireland) Inc (in liquidation) v Credit Suisse Canada* [1999] 4 IR 542.

143 See further, para **[10.058]**.

144 See para **[10.051]**.

145 *Bank of Ireland Finance Ltd v Rockfield Ltd* [1979] IR 21; see para **[10.054]** *ante*.

- the monies it was advancing to Castor were going to be paid on to CHNB to acquire shares in CHI and that the words 'reference: capital subscription' had been used in correspondence;
- that CHI was going to make a fiduciary deposit with CSZ;
- that the fiduciary deposit was to be security for the payment obligation or guarantee by CSZ to CSC; and
- that the payment obligation or guarantee by CSZ to CSC was to cover the monies being advanced.

McCracken J concluded that CSC had actual notice that the monies they were advancing were going to be ultimately used by CHNB to acquire shares in CHI and that those monies were being secured by a payment obligation or guarantee by CSZ which was countersecured by the deposit of the same monies by CHI with CSZ. McCracken J went on to say:

> 'As probably the most important link, or perhaps as it would be put by CSC as the weak link, in this argument, was the reference to capital subscription in the payment directions. I should comment on this further. The evidence of Mr McFarland was that as far as he was concerned this was simply a note put into the request by Castor and by CHNB respectively for the purpose of giving information to their auditors, and that it was of no relevance to CSC. However, even if one accepts that that was what Mr McFarland thought at the time, that does not take away from the fact that it is a clear statement of fact which directly informed CSC that the money was going to be used to subscribe for shares. I can appreciate that Mr McFarland may not have thought this was of any relevance, as of course I fully accept that Mr McFarland was totally unaware of the provisions of s 60 of the Companies Act 1963. However, what s 60(14) relates to is a person having notice of the facts which constitute the breach of s 60. It does not require that the person who had notice of the facts also had notice that it was in law a breach of s 60, or indeed that such person was aware of the existence of s 60. I am quite satisfied that CSC had notice of the facts which constituted the breach, and no doubt had they been aware of the provisions of s 60, they would have been aware that there was a breach of that section[146].'

Ignorance of the law can never be a defence; hence what is only relevant is actual notice of the facts that constitute a breach of the prohibition against financial assistance.

The meaning of 'financial assistance'

[10.058] Section 60(1) of the CA 1963 provides that it shall not be lawful for a company to give 'financial assistance' for the purpose of or in connection with a purchase or subscription made or to be made by any person of or for the shares in the company or its holding company. In examining the meaning of 'financial assistance' the following points are considered:

(a) The express forms of 'financial assistance'.

(b) The breadth of the prohibition: 'otherwise' and 'in connection with'.

(c) Warranties and covenants that constitute financial assistance.

(d) Actual versus potential financial assistance.

---

146 *CH (Ireland) Inc (in liquidation) v Credit Suisse Canada* [1999] 4 IR 542 at 558–559.

(a) The express forms of 'financial assistance'

[10.059] In *Charterhouse Investment Trust Ltd v Tempest Diesels Ltd*[147], in a passage quoted with approval by McCracken J in *CH (Ireland) Inc (in liquidation) v Credit Suisse Canada*[148], Hoffmann J said:

> 'There is no definition of giving financial assistance in the section, although some examples are given. The words have no technical meaning and their frame of reference is in my judgment the language of ordinary commerce. One must examine the commercial realities of the transaction and decide whether it can properly be described as the giving of financial assistance by the company, bearing in mind that the section is a penal one and should not be strained to cover transactions which are not fairly within it[149].'

The express statutory examples referred to are 'by means of a loan, guarantee, the provision of security or otherwise'.

[10.060] In *CH (Ireland) Inc (in liquidation) v Credit Suisse Canada*, the facts of which are given above[150], it was held that the only or main purpose of the applicant company depositing monies was to ensure that monies would be advanced to enable the applicant company's shares be purchased. Therefore, McCracken J held that the applicant company had clearly given financial assistance within the meaning of s 60 of the CA 1963. In *Re Northside Motor Co Ltd; Eddison v Allied Irish Banks*[151], an individual owned half of the shares in a company and wished to acquire the remainder. The defendant bank advanced finance to another company which was owned by the individual, the bank's security being the provision by the plaintiff company of a guarantee of the repayment of the loan taken out by the second company. Costello J held that the company had provided financial assistance for the purchase of its own shares because the transaction involved a promise to make a pecuniary payment to the bank if the borrower company defaulted in its obligations.

[10.061] One of the most recent Irish judicial considerations of the term 'financial assistance' was against the somewhat unexpected backdrop of s 36 of the Public Health (Tobacco) Act 2002, which creates the offence of giving financial assistance to a person in consideration of, *inter alia*, the promotion of a tobacco product. In *The Health Service Executive v PJ Carroll & Company Ltd*[152], Kearns J, after quoting the passage

---

147 *Charterhouse Investment Trust Ltd v Tempest Diesels Ltd* [1986] BCLC 1.

148 *CH (Ireland) Inc (in liquidation) v Credit Suisse Canada* [1999] 4 IR 542.

149 *Charterhouse Investment Trust Ltd v Tempest Diesels Ltd* [1986] BCLC 1 at 10. Hoffmann J went on to say (in a passage also quoted by McCracken J): 'The *Belmont* case shows that the sale of an asset by a company at a fair value can properly be described as giving financial assistance if the effect is to provide the purchaser of its shares with the cash needed to pay for them. It does not matter that the company's balance sheet is undisturbed in the sense that the cash paid out is replaced by an asset of equal value. In the case of a loan by a company to a credit worthy purchaser of its shares, the balance sheet is equally undisturbed but the loan plainly constitutes giving financial assistance. It follows that if the only or main purpose of such a transaction is to enable the purchaser to buy the shares, the section is contravened.'

150 See para **[10.057]**.

151 *Re Northside Motor Co Ltd; Eddison v Allied Irish Banks* (24 July 1985, unreported) HC, Costello J.

152 *The Health Service Executive v PJ Carroll & Company Ltd* [2012] IEHC 147, Kearns P.

from the decision of Hoffmann J in *Charterhouse Investment Trust Ltd v Tempest Diesels Ltd*, and that Aldous LJ had said in *British and Commonwealth Holdings plc v Barclays Bank plc*[153] had said that the words, 'financial assistance', are 'not words which have any recognised legal significance', went on to find that their use in the context of s 36 Public Health (Tobacco) Act 2002 were ambiguous and, being a criminal offence, should be in language that was clear and certain. In that case, it was held that the giving of a €30 voucher in the context of a cigarette promotion did not constitute financial assistance.

(b) The breadth of the prohibition: 'otherwise' and 'in connection with'

[10.062] Whether financial assistance can be said to have been provided will, in each case, depend upon the facts of the particular transaction. As Lord Denning MR said in *Wallersteiner v Moir*[154] 'you look to the company's shares and see into whose hands they have got. You will soon see if the company's money has been used to finance the purchase.' Such a broad statement can be substantiated by considering that the prohibition in s 60(1) of the CA 1963 is not just confined to the express forms of financial assistance in s 60(1), but also refers to financial assistance 'otherwise' provided. So too is the connection, between whatever the financial assistance given and the purchase or subscription of own shares or shares in a company's holding company, widely drafted. Section 60(1) refers to the financial assistance being 'for the purpose of or in connection with'. As *Johnston* has said: 'the reference to "directly or indirectly" and the words "in connection with" are such as to render s 60 applicable to many transactions which are not at first sight obviously apparent[155].' It is significant that the words 'in connection with' have been dropped from the English section that regulates the provision of financial assistance for the purchase of shares[156] and that the Company Law Review Group has recommended the same in Ireland, a recommendation accepted in the published draft Companies Bill[157].

[10.063] The words 'in connection with' were considered in the Australian case of *Sterileair Pty Ltd v George Ralph Papallo and another*[158]. In that case, D Ltd was owned

[153] *British and Commonwealth Holdings plc v Barclays Bank plc* [1986] BCLC 1 at 10.

[154] *Wallersteiner v Moir* [1974] 3 All ER 217.

[155] Johnston, *Banking and Security Law in Ireland* (1998) at 18.14.

[156] Section 151 (1) of the Companies Act 1985 (UK) provides: 'Subject to the following provisions of this Chapter, where a person is acquiring or is proposing to acquire shares in a company, it is not lawful for the company or any of its subsidiaries to give financial assistance directly or indirectly for the purpose of the acquisition before or at the same time as the acquisition takes place.' Moreover, s 152(1) provides '(a) "financial assistance" means – (i) financial assistance given by way of gift, (ii) financial assistance given by way of guarantee, security or indemnity … (iii) financial assistance given by way of a loan … (iv) any other financial assistance given by a company the net assets of which are thereby reduced to a material extent or which has no net assets'. Section 152(2) provides that 'net assets' means 'the aggregate of the company's assets, less the aggregate of its liabilities …'. The differences are apparent; the English legislation is clearly less onerous than s 60(1) of the CA 1963.

[157] See s 80 of the draft Companies Bill.

[158] *Sterileair Pty Ltd v George Ralph Papallo and another* [1998] 1446 Federal Court of Australia (16 November 1998).

as to 75% by the defendants and as to 25% by W. The defendants loaned D Ltd Aust$100,000. Subsequently, W acquired the plaintiff company, which was a shelf company. At this time the defendants and W were in dispute but notwithstanding, the first defendant became a director and shareholder in the plaintiff company. After discussions, it was agreed that D Ltd's assets and liabilities (including the debt to the defendants) would be transferred to the plaintiff company and a new loan agreement would be drawn up between the plaintiff and the defendants. After the loan agreement was executed, the first defendant resigned from the plaintiff company, transferred his share in that company to W's nominee and he and the second defendant also resigned from D Ltd and transferred their shares in D Ltd. The plaintiff company subsequently sought to void the loan agreement on the ground, *inter alia*, that it breached the Australian Corporations Law by involving the giving of financial assistance for the purpose of or in connection with the acquisition of the plaintiff company's shares. This was rejected at trial and that finding was upheld by the Federal Court of Australia, where the court held:

> 'Not only was there in our opinion no 'financial assistance' for the acquisition of the share, there was not the necessary purpose of connection which s 205 [of the Australian Corporations Law] requires. (Counsel for [the plaintiff company] put his case only on the 'in connection with' limb of the section.) While the covenant of [the plaintiff company] under the loan agreement undoubtedly involved a 'diminution in the company's resources' (see *Burton v Palmer* [1980] 2 NSWLR 878 at 881), that was for the purpose of, or in connection with, the acquisition of the assets of [D Ltd]. The commercial reality was that for [W's] vehicle, [the plaintiff company], to get access to the business of [D Ltd] so that he could carry it on free from interference by [the defendants], [the plaintiff company] had to take over [D Ltd's] debt to them. Viewed in this light, the acquisition of [the first defendant's] share in [the plaintiff company] was no more than a tidying up[159].'

Later the court said:

> 'We think therefore that it is not enough to satisfy the 'in connection with' requirement to say, as counsel for [the plaintiff company] argued, that 'but for' the [plaintiff company's] covenant to pay the [defendants], the transfer of [the first defendant's] one $1 share to [W's nominee] would not have taken place. Whilst 'but for' considerations are material, they are not conclusive – the issue remains whether in a practical business sense financial assistance was given by the company in connection with the acquisition of its shares[160].'

(c) Warranties and covenants that constitute financial assistance

[10.064] It is sometimes questioned whether the giving of covenants, representations and warranties by a company in a share purchase/subscription agreement can amount to the provision of financial assistance in connection with the purchase of or subscription for its shares. It has been noted, though, that there are two views on this point[161]. One, seen in *Charterhouse Investment Trust Ltd v Tempest Diesels Ltd*[162], is that such does not

---

159 *Sterileair Pty Ltd v George Ralph Papallo and another* [1998] 1446 Federal Court of Australia (16 November 1998) at p 7.

160 *Sterileair Pty Ltd v George Ralph Papallo and another* [1998] 1446 Federal Court of Australia (16 November 1998) at p 9.

161 See Cotter, 'Section 60 of the Companies Act 1963' (2000) 7 CLP 111.

162 *Charterhouse Investment Trust Ltd v Tempest Diesels Ltd* [1986] BCLC 1.

amount to financial assistance as they are not financial in nature, merely contractual representations, albeit that they may ultimately have financial implications where a court of law finds that there has been a breach and awards damages. In the New South Wales case of *Burton v Palmer*[163], Mahony J said:

> 'The fact that a company undertakes obligations, absolute or contingent, in connection with the proposal for the transfer of its shares does not of itself constitute the giving of financial assistance. As I said, the fact that a company facilitates a proposal for such a transfer will not involve it necessarily in contravention of s 67. Thus, a company may answer requests for information relevant to the proposed transfer knowing that it does so in circumstances such that it will be liable for damages if, for lack of care, the information is incorrect (*cf Mutual Life and Citizens' Assurance Co Ltd v Evatt* [1971] 1 All ER 150, [1971] AC 793). But, by answering such requests, the company does not thereby give financial assistance. There may, of course, be circumstances in which the obligations entered into by a company are entered into for a collateral purpose: in such circumstances it may be that the company will, in the particular case, be giving financial assistance. But, collateral purpose aside, if s 67 is to be relevant, there must be more than the incurring, in connection with the transfer of shares, of an obligation which may involve the company in the payment of money. The obligation must be such that it is properly to be categorised as financial assistance. An obligation of a different kind, eg, an obligation to permit inspection of books and records, will not constitute the giving of financial assistance simply because, if it is broken, the company will be liable to pay damages. I do not mean by this that the relevance of s 67 is to be determined by a schematic analysis of the obligation undertaken. The words 'financial assistance' are words of a commercial rather than a conveyancing kind and the form of the obligation or transaction will not be conclusive. Thus a loan ostensibly given by a third party may, in the context of a 'round robin' of cheques, be seen as financial assistance in connection with the sale of shares: see *Wallersteiner v Moir* [1974] 3 All ER 217. And a loan given by the company after the sale has completed may, in particular circumstances be such: in the example given in the Greene Report, the Act might be contravened: cf *Glennon v Comr of Taxation* (1972) 127 CLR 503 at 510. Similarly, a warranty given with the intention that the company will be called upon to pay damages and to provide funds in connection with the transfer of its shares will contravene the section.'

This is considered to be the better view and is supported by the decision of the English Court of Appeal in *Barclays Bank plc v British & Commonwealth Holdings plc*[164]. In that case it was agreed that a major shareholder in a public company would, instead of placing such a large number of shares on the market, have the shares converted to redeemable shares, which would be redeemed in four tranches. This scheme of arrangement was approved by court. To safeguard the shareholder against the company not redeeming the shares, a special purpose company was formed and the shareholder given an option to sell the shares to that company, which was financed by a number of banks. As part of the arrangement the company whose shares were being sold covenanted to maintain certain asset rates. After the redemption of two tranches, the company redeeming the shares went into administration and the shareholder exercised its option to call upon the special purpose company to acquire the shares. The financing banks then claimed damages from the company for, *inter alia*, breach of the covenant to

163 *Burton v Palmer* [1980] 2 NSWLR 878 at 889–890.

164 *Barclays Bank plc v British & Commonwealth Holdings plc* [1996] 1 BCLC 1.

maintain the particular agreed asset rates. One of the questions that arose was whether the company had, in giving the covenants to the banks, provided *financial assistance* for the purchase of its own shares. The English Court of Appeal held, after quoting the passage in *Burton v Palmer* (quoted above):

> 'That statement of the way to approach s 67 of the Australian Companies Act 1961 is, I believe, applicable to s 151 of the 1985 Act. No doubt, as pointed out by Mahony J, there will be cases where the court will look behind the form to see whether there was a collateral purpose and if so conclude that financial assistance was provided; this is not such a case. The purpose of the covenants in the option agreement was to assure [the vendor of the shares]. The covenants were bona fide covenants the performance of which did not involve giving financial assistance. The fact that breach of the covenants might render [the company whose shares were being redeemed] liable to damages did not mean that [it] gave financial assistance thereby[165].'

Even allowing for the difference between s 151 of the Companies Act 1985 (UK) and s 60 of the CA 1963 (and, especially, the absence of 'in connection with' in the English Act) it is thought that this represents the law in Ireland. Covenants, representations and warranties can amount to financial assistance in particular cases[166], but not unless that is the dominant purpose behind them.

(d) Actual versus potential financial assistance

[10.065] In England there is also a tendency to interpret particular agreements and transactions in such a way as not to contravene s 151 of the Companies Act 1985 (UK)[167]. In *Parlett v Guppys (Bridport) Ltd*[168], the plaintiff was chairman and managing director of the defendant company and three other family companies; none of the companies were in a formal group. In 1988 it was agreed the plaintiff would, in return for an annual salary of £100,000, a pension and a bonus of 25% of the group of companies' profits, transfer his shares in one of the companies (Guppys (Estates) Ltd) into the joint names of himself and his sons. The companies agreed to share the cost of providing the package to the plaintiff, but did not set a percentage contribution. This operated for a number of years and some three years' later the plaintiff executed stock transfer forms in blank. These were subsequently completed in favour of another of the companies in the 'group', Guppys (Bridport) Ltd. Some five months later, in December 1991, the plaintiff issued proceedings against his sons and the nominee company, claiming the balance of salary and bonus owed to him. The defendants contended that the agreement was unenforceable as it amounted to the provision of financial assistance by Guppys (Estates) Ltd in connection with the purchase of its own shares. It was held by the Court of Appeal that the agreement was not unenforceable as it did not have to be performed in a manner that contravened s 151(1) of the Companies Act 1985 (UK). This could have been done had Guppys (Estates) Ltd (the company whose shares were being sold) not contributed to the plaintiff's package; instead the other companies privy to the

165 *Barclays Bank plc v British & Commonwealth Holdings plc* [1996] 1 BCLC 1 at 41.

166 As to when 'break fees' (ie, a sum agreed to be paid by a bidder to a target company in the event of specified events occurring which prevent a takeover bid proceeding) see: Charnley & Breslin, 'Break Fees: Financial Assistance and Directors' Duties' (2000) 21 Co Law 269.

167 *Brady v Brady* (1988) BCC 390.

168 *Parlett v Guppys (Bridport) Ltd* [1996] 2 BCLC 34; [1996] BCC 299.

agreement – Guppys (Bridport) Ltd, Guppys (Properties) Ltd and Guppys (Builders) Ltd – could have provided the funds. Nourse LJ said:

> '... the directors of Bridport and Properties could, at the date of the 1988 agreement, reasonably and prudently have made provision for the whole cost to be borne by those two companies and, in discharge of their contractual and statutory duties to [the plaintiff] and Estates respectively as identified in *Lawlor v Gray*, they were bound to do so. On that footing there was no reduction in the net assets of Estates and no financial assistance within s 151(1)[169].'

The reference to *Lawlor v Gray*[170] was to the English Court of Appeal's finding that an agreement which could have been, but did not have to be, performed in breach of a statutory provision, would be interpreted as not coming within its ambit. This was followed (although not expressly) in *Vision Express (UK) Ltd v Wilson*[171] in the context of the statutory provisions concerning the purchase of own shares. There it was held again that where an agreement could be performed in alternative ways, one lawful and the other not, it was presumed that the parties would perform it in accordance with the lawful means. In Ireland too this approach has been taken. So, in *McGill and another v Bogue*[172] the Supreme Court refused to strike out an application for specific performance of a share purchase agreement, which it was claimed contravened s 60(1) of the CA 1963 because it envisaged a company providing security in connection with the purchase of its own shares. Keane CJ refused to strike out the application because, *inter alia*, it could be argued that what had been envisaged was that when the share purchase was complete, the company would then provide financial assistance in the nature of security but strictly in compliance with the validation procedure in s 60(2).

The validation procedure: resolution and declaration

[10.066] The principal exception to the prohibition in s 60(1) of the CA 1963 is the validation procedure – or 'whitewash' procedure as it is sometimes referred to in England – contained in s 60(2)–(11) of the CA 1963. The validation procedure is considered under the following headings:

(a) The validation procedure in practice.
(b) Not all companies can utilise the validation procedure.
(c) The directors' statutory declaration.
(d) The shareholders' special resolution.
(e) The importance of strict compliance in Ireland.
(f) The validation procedure cannot be utilised retrospectively.
(g) Shareholder protection.

(a) The validation procedure in practice

[10.067] Section 60(2) of the CA 1963 provides that the s 60(1) prohibition on a company providing financial assistance in connection with the purchase of its own shares shall not apply where:

---

169 *Barclays Bank plc v British & Commonwealth Holdings plc* [1996] 1 BCLC 1 at 45c–d.

170 *Lawlor v Gray* (10 July 1979, unreported) English Court of Appeal.

171 *Vision Express (UK) Ltd v Wilson* [1998] BCC 173.

172 *McGill and another v Bogue* (11 July 2000, unreported) SC.

- the directors of the company swear a statutory declaration of solvency containing the matters detailed below[173]; and
- the members in general meeting pass a special resolution, not more than 12 months before the financial assistance is provided, giving the directors authority to provide such financial assistance[174]; and
- the company has forwarded, with each notice of the extraordinary general meeting where the special resolution is to be considered, a copy of a statutory declaration, which complies with s 60(3) and (4) of the CA 1963[175]; and
- the company delivers, within 21 days after the date on which the financial assistance is given, a copy of the directors' statutory declaration of solvency to the registrar of companies for registration[176]; and
- where the members do not unanimously vote in favour of the special resolution, the assistance must not be provided before 30 days after the special resolution is passed, or, until any application made to court has been disposed of by the court[177].

This is the traditional validation procedure that should still be followed as the norm. A more streamlined procedure may be followed where the proposed financial assistance is *unanimously approved* of by the company's members, and the company's articles of association contains a model reg 6 type provision (from Part II of Table A). In such cases, the following procedure might be adopted:

- the directors of the company swear a statutory declaration of solvency; and
- the members unanimously sign a written resolution, not more than 12 months before the financial assistance is provided, giving the directors authority to provide such financial assistance[178]; and
- appended to the written resolution is a copy of a statutory declaration, which complies with s 60(3) and (4) of the CA 1963[179]; and
- the company delivers, within 21 days after the date on which the financial assistance is given, a copy of the directors' statutory declaration of solvency to the registrar of companies for registration[180].

These are the *key features* of the validation procedure. To understand where, when and how they arise in practice, an example is considered useful.

[10.068] Returning to the example given above[181] of Investment Properties Ltd providing a guarantee and security in connection with the purchase of its own shares, s 60(2) of the CA 1963 might be utilised in the following manner. Two individuals, A and B, who own all of the shares in Investment Properties Ltd, have agreed to sell their

[173] See para **[10.071]**.
[174] Section 60(2)(a) of the CA 1963.
[175] Section 60(2)(b) of the CA 1963, as substituted by s 89(1) of the CLEA 2001.
[176] Section 60(2)(b) of the CA 1963.
[177] Section 60(7) of the CA 1963.
[178] Section 60(2)(a) of the CA 1963.
[179] Section 60(2)(b) of the CA 1963 as inserted by s 89(a) of the CLEA 2001.
[180] Section 60(2)(b) of the CA 1963, as inserted by s 89(a) of the CLEA 2001.
[181] See para **[10.047]**.

shares to Borrowings Ltd, a shelf company owned and controlled by C and D, for €1m. C and D have arranged for Borrowings Ltd to borrow all of the monies from a credit institution on the security of the guarantee of Investment Properties Ltd and a mortgage debenture over its property portfolio. On the closing of such transaction, a typical chronology of events might be:

- The solicitors for A and B, and C and D (and both companies) will, in advance of the completion, agree the share transfer documentation, and C and D will conduct (through their solicitors, accountants and tax advisers) a due diligence of the affairs of Investment Properties Ltd[182].
- On the day of completion, A and B and their solicitors, and C and D and their solicitors will attend at the offices of the lending bank[183].
- The solicitors for the share vendors (A and B) and the solicitors for Borrowings Ltd and C and D will prepare to close the share sale; A and B's solicitor will pass over all documentation (eg, share certificates, stock transfer forms in favour of Borrowings Ltd, share purchase agreement, to mention but a few of the documents involved).
- The bank will then advance the €1m by way of a loan to Borrowings Ltd *after* Borrowings Ltd has executed a debenture. (Borrowings Ltd may not have any assets at this point in time and the reason for the debenture will be to acquire a floating security over the shares in Investment Properties Ltd which will shortly be acquired by Borrowings Ltd.) Typically, the personal guarantees of C and D will also be required.
- Borrowings Ltd will then pay to A and B the consideration for the shares in Investment Properties Ltd.
- A and B (the shareholders in Investment Properties Ltd) may then execute a form of declaration of trust in favour of Borrowings Ltd. By this A & C will confirm that, although they continue to be the legal owners of the shares pending registration of the stock transfer, having received payment for the shares, they hold the shares in trust for Borrowings Ltd. The intention of this is to make Borrowings Ltd the holding company of Investment Properties Ltd so as to avoid any possible contravention of s 31 of the CA 1990 when it comes to Investment Properties Ltd giving security later on[184].
- Borrowings Ltd's auditors may then often be required to give the bank a certificate that Investment Properties Ltd is a subsidiary of Borrowings Ltd as defined by s 155 of the CA 1963.

---

182 See Ch 9, *Share Transfer*, para **[9.108]**.

183 The necessity to meet in the early morning to ensure there is time to file the directors' statutory declaration in the CRO no longer applies since the statutory declaration no longer needs to be filed the same day. Section 60(2)(b) of the CA 1963, as substituted by s 89(a) of the CLEA 2001, now provides that a copy of the statutory declaration must be delivered to the registrar 'within 21 days after the date on which the financial assistance was given'.

184 Borrowings Ltd will be the holding company of Investment Properties Ltd by reason of s 155(3)(b)(i) of the CA 1963: see, generally, Ch 12, *Groups of Companies*, para **[12.022]** *et seq*. On s 31 of the CA 1990, see Ch 16, *Statutory Regulation of Directors' Transactions*, para **[16.055]** *et seq*.

- Borrowings Ltd's directors (C and D) will then be appointed as directors of Investment Properties Ltd by A and B who will meet as directors and appoint C and D as such. Immediately thereafter the existing directors of Investment Properties Ltd (A and B) will resign, expressly stating that they have no claims for compensation for loss of office or under any contract of employment.
- C and D (as sole directors of Investment Properties Ltd) will then swear a statutory declaration of solvency for Investment Properties Ltd in accordance with s 60(2)–(5) of the CA 1963[185].
- In the example given, where there is unanimous agreement to the provision of financial assistance, the written resolution procedure as envisaged by s 141(8) of the CA 1963, as now permitted by s 60(6) of the CA 1963[186], may be availed of to pass the requisite special resolution. If this is utilised, the copy statutory declaration must be appended to the written special resolution. The written special resolution must then be signed by A and B (who are still the sole registered shareholders in Investment Properties Ltd). Although not strictly necessary, the cautious practitioner might seek to have the beneficial owner of the shares in Investment Properties Ltd, namely Borrowings Ltd, also execute the written special resolution under seal.
- The written special resolution should approve the provision of financial assistance in connection with the purchase of the company's (ie, Investment Properties Ltd's) shares. If there is any doubt as to the capacity of Investment Properties Ltd to give a guarantee in favour of what is now its holding company (Borrowings Ltd) this opportunity may also be taken to pass a second special resolution to alter and bolster its objects clause[187].
- C and D, the sole directors of Investment Properties Ltd, will then meet as directors and pass a board resolution in favour of entering into the guarantee and providing a mortgage debenture as security over its assets in respect of Borrowings Ltd's loan from the bank. Section 35 of the CA 1990 will operate to exempt the guarantee and the provision of security from the provisions in s 31 of the CA 1990, to the extent to which it might be thought that they apply.
- C and D will then, as directors of Investment Properties Ltd, cause it to execute the bank's guarantee and mortgage debenture in favour of the bank.
- Within 21 days of the entering into of the guarantee and mortgage debenture by Investment Properties Ltd, a copy of the directors' statutory declaration must be delivered to the registrar of companies in the CRO[188].

Where the written resolution procedure cannot be availed of (because, for example, some of the shareholders are unavailable) there will need to be additional steps. So, for example, an EGM will need to be convened after the directors swear the statutory declaration of solvency. Thereafter, C and D (as directors of the Investment Properties

---

185 See para **[10.071]**.

186 As substituted by s 89(b) of the CLEA 2001.

187 See Ch 7, *Corporate Contracts, Capacity and Authority*, para **[7.045]**.

188 Of course, particulars of both charges, created by both companies, must be delivered to the CRO within 21 days of their creation: s 99(1) of the CA 1963. See, generally, Ch 21, *Corporate Borrowing: Registration of Charges*.

Ltd) would be required to give short notice of an EGM for the purpose of passing the requisite special resolution, and this will require the consent of Investment Properties Ltd's auditors[189]. As the only registered members will still be A and B (Borrowings Ltd not yet being registered), they will, upon the direction of Borrowings Ltd as the sole equitable and beneficial owner of the shares, pass the requisite special resolution at a general meeting. The resolution will approve the giving of authority to the directors to provide financial assistance in connection with the purchase of Investment Properties Ltd's shares.

Although where there is unanimous agreement to proceed with the provision of financial assistance, the validation procedure will be very much a paper exercise, only the foolhardy would attempt to short-circuit the statutory procedures. As Costello J said in *Lombard & Ulster Banking Ltd v Bank of Ireland*[190], where reliance is placed on these exceptions 'then strict compliance with the procedures is necessary'.

(b) Not all companies can utilise the validation procedure

[10.069] It should be noted at the outset that the validation procedure may *not* be utilised by PLCs. Section 60(15A) of the CA 1963 provides that sub-ss (2)– (11) shall not apply to a PLC originally incorporated as such or to a company registered or re-registered as a PLC under the C(A)A 1983 unless a special resolution as provided for in s 60(2) of the CA 1963 was passed before the company's application for registration or re-registration. Other companies that are precluded from availing of the validation procedure exception to the prohibition in s 60(1) include investment companies[191] and companies whose directors have been restricted pursuant to s 150 of the CA 1990[192].

[10.070] Although the general rule is that private companies can utilise the validation procedure, a private company which is a 'public company subsidiary' is precluded from providing financial assistance, in accordance with the validation procedure, for the purchase of or subscription for shares in its 'parent public company'[193].

(c) The directors' statutory declaration

[10.071] Section 60(2)(a) of the CA 1963 requires that any financial assistance provided must be given under the authority of a special resolution. Section 60(2)(b) of the CA 1963 provides that the prohibition in s 60(1) shall not apply where, in addition to the special resolution being passed:

> 'the company has forwarded with each notice of the meeting at which the special resolution is to be considered or, if the procedure referred to in subsection (6) is followed, the company has appended to the resolution, a copy of a statutory declaration which complies with subsections (3) and (4) and also delivers, within 21 days after the date on which the financial assistance was given, a copy of the declaration to the Registrar of Companies for registration.'

---

189 See Ch 14, *Corporate Governance: Meetings*, para **[14.041]**.

190 *Lombard & Ulster Banking Ltd v Bank of Ireland* (2 June 1987, unreported) HC, *per* Costello J.

191 Section 260(1) of the CA 1990.

192 Section 155(2) of the CA 1990. See, further, Ch 28, *Compliance and Enforcement*, para **[28.070]**.

193 Regulation 5(2)(c) of the EC(PLCS)R 1997 (SI 67/1997). See para **[10.038]**.

The statutory declaration referred to in s 60(2)(b) must be made by a majority of the directors of the company. Although this statutory declaration is essentially one of *solvency*, it also contains reference to other matters. The statutory declaration of the directors must contain the following matters[194]:

- the form which such assistance is to take;
- the persons to whom such assistance is to be given;
- the purpose for which the company intends those persons to use such assistance; and
- that the directors have made a full inquiry into the affairs of the company and that, having done so, have formed the opinion that the company, having carried out the transaction whereby such assistance is to be given, will be able to pay its debts in full as they become due (ie, that the company is solvent).

The directors' statutory declaration must be made at a meeting of the directors held not more than 24 days before the meeting of the members at which the requisite special resolution is to be passed[195]. In practice, it is common for this declaration to be made on the same day as the financial assistance is provided. Furthermore, the declaration must be made by two directors where a company has only two directors or, by a majority of the directors where there are more than two[196]. There is a strong incentive for the directors to ensure that their statutory declaration is correct since s 60(5) of the CA 1963 provides that the prohibition in s 60(1) shall not apply where, in addition to the special resolution being passed:

> 'Any director of a company making the statutory declaration without having reasonable grounds for the opinion that the company having carried out the transaction whereby such assistance is to be given will be able to pay its debts in full as they become due, shall be liable to imprisonment for a period not exceeding 6 months or to a [class C fine] or to both; and if the company is wound up within the period of 12 months after the making of the statutory declaration and its debts are not paid or provided for in full within the period of 12 months after the commencement of the winding up, it shall be presumed until the contrary is shown that the director did not have reasonable grounds for his opinion.'

The severity of the punishment in s 60(5) is one reason why it will be the *new* directors of the company providing the financial assistance who will swear the declaration of solvency, and not the *old* directors. Because they will have nothing further to do with the company, the old directors will be reluctant to expose themselves to the presumption in s 60(5) where the company is wound up insolvent within the following 12 months. Logically, it would seem to be more appropriate for the old directors and members to implement the s 60(2) validation procedure; where the new directors and members implement the procedure, the timing of the transaction becomes paramount and the loan to purchase the shares will be have to occur momentarily before the provision of security.

194 Section 60(4)(a)(d) of the CA 1963.

195 Section 60(3) of the CA 1963.

196 Section 60(3) of the CA 1963.

(d) The shareholders' special resolution

[10.072] An example of the operative part of the special resolution might be:

> 'In connection with the purchase by Borrowings Ltd of all of the ordinary (and preference) shares in Investment Properties Ltd, it is HEREBY RESOLVED by way of a special resolution and for the purposes of s 60(2)(a) of the Companies Act 1963 that Investment Properties Ltd should enter into a guarantee and provide security in the form of a Mortgage Debenture incorporating a floating charge and several fixed charges to include a specific fixed charge over its property in folio 12345678F Co Dublin (the 'Security') in favour of Big Bank PLC, bankers to Borrowings Ltd, to secure a loan to Borrowings Ltd, in circumstances where the provision of the Security constitutes the provision of financial assistance within the meaning of s 60(1) of the Companies Act 1963.'

Section 89 of the CLEA 2001 substituted the following for the original s 60(6) of the CA 1963: 'The special resolution referred to in subsection (1)(a) may be passed in accordance with section 141(8).' Accordingly, since 1 October 2001, the written resolution procedure[197] can be availed of to pass the special resolution, and the formal convening and holding of a general meeting, whether on full or short notice, can be avoided. Prior to this change, it was common to rely upon the provisions in the CA 1963 that permit the convening and holding of a members' EGM on short notice with the company's auditor's consent[198]. In this way, the resolution of the company's members and the declaration of solvency of the company's directors may both happen at the same meeting, shortly before the company provides the financial assistance in connection with the purchase of its own shares.

(e) The importance of strict compliance in Ireland

[10.073] It is important to recognise that there are differences in the form of (and judicial attitude to) the validation procedure between England and Ireland. Accordingly, great care must be taken of some English authorities that suggest that strict compliance with the validation procedure is not absolutely necessary[199], notwithstanding the decision in *Re Cognotec Ltd*[200], where it was held that although the statutory declaration of the directors had not been filed in the CRO within the prescribed time, the debenture could not voidable against a bank which did not have actual notice of the fact that the

[197] Ch 14, *Corporate Governance: Meetings*, para **[14.090]**.

[198] Ch 14, *Corporate Governance: Meetings*, para **[14.041]**.

[199] See, however, *Re SH & Co (Realisations) 1990 Ltd* [1993] BCLC 1309, where Mummery J stressed the need for strict compliance with the prescribed statutory procedure whereby companies may provide financial assistance in connection with the purchase of their own shares. In this case the statutory declaration sworn by the directors failed to provide details of the debenture which the company intended to provide. Although Mummery J found that the detail of the particulars provided satisfied the statutory requirements, it was a borderline case. In *Re RW Peak (Kings Lynn) Ltd* [1998] BCC 596, Lindsay J held that a failure to comply with the provisions of the Companies Act 1985 (UK) in the context of the *purchase of own shares* (as distinct from providing financial assistance in connection with the purchase of own shares) could not be overridden by the principle in *Re Duomatic Ltd* [1969] 2 Ch 365 on informal resolutions.

[200] *Re Cognotec Ltd* [2010] IEHC 309.

validation procedure had been breached[201]. An example of the attitude of the English Courts is *Re NL Electrical Ltd, Ghosh v 3i plc*[202], where a company provided financial assistance in connection with the purchase of its own shares within the meaning of s 156 of the Companies Act 1985 (UK). The directors of the company made a statutory declaration but did so in the form prescribed by an obsolete statutory instrument. In addition, a copy of the declaration was not delivered within the time limits prescribed by s 156 of the Act[203]. Notwithstanding these defects Harman J held that they were insufficient to render the financial assistance unlawful under the English legislation.

[10.074] In stark contrast stands the decision of Costello J in *Lombard & Ulster Banking Ltd v Bank of Ireland*[204], where it was held that the validation procedure in s 60(2) had not been complied with even though the shareholders had authorised their solicitor to take all necessary steps to enable the company to provide financial assistance for the purchase of its own shares, and the shareholders had agreed informally to what was done. In the words of the learned judge:

> 'The section makes illegal the granting of financial assistance (as defined) and if exemption for a transaction in breach of sub-s (1) is claimed because of the adoption of the procedures laid down in sub-s (2) and (3) and (4) then strict compliance with the procedures is necessary. It is not sufficient to show that all the shareholders had authorised their solicitor to take the necessary steps and that they subsequently ratified what in fact was done. If the procedural requirements were not adopted the transaction is an illegal one, if in fact it involved that granting of financial assistance contrary to sub-s (1).'

In so holding, Costello J rejected the application of the line of authorities on informal agreement by shareholders[205] to the statutory exception contained in s 60(2)[206]. In view of Costello J's judgment, it is thought Mummery J's advice that '[i]n future solicitors responsible for completing such a statutory declaration should err on the side of caution'[207] is equally applicable to solicitors in this jurisdiction[208].

(f) The validation procedure cannot be utilised retrospectively

[10.075] In *Re Northside Motor Co Ltd; Eddison v Allied Irish Banks*[209], an individual owned half of the shares in the plaintiff company and wished to acquire the remainder.

---

201 See para **[10.056]** *ante*.

202 *Re NL Electrical Ltd, Ghosh v 3i plc* [1994] 1 BCLC 22.

203 A copy of the declaration was delivered to the English Companies House 30 days after it had been made, which was clearly outside the 15-day statutory limit.

204 *Lombard & Ulster Banking Ltd v Bank of Ireland* (2 June 1987, unreported) HC, *per* Costello J.

205 *Best illustrated by Cane v Jones* [1980] 1 WLR 1451. See also, *Re Duomatic Ltd* [1969] 2 Ch 365; *Re Bailey Hay* [1971] WLR 1352; and *Re Gee and Co (Woolich) Ltd* [1975] Ch 52. See generally, Ch 14, *Corporate Governance: Meetings*, para **[14.093]**.

206 Cf *Re Shannonside Holdings Ltd* (20 May 1993, unreported) HC, where, in different circumstances, Costello J appears to have accepted the principle that all of a company's members may informally alter a company's articles of association. See Ch 14, *Corporate Governance: Meetings*, para **[14.094]**.

207 *Re SH & Co (Realisations) 1990 Ltd* [1993] BCLC 1309 at 1318h.

208 On solicitors' liabilities and whether solicitors owed a company a duty of care, see *BDG Roof-Bond Ltd v Douglas et al* [2000] BCC 770.

209 *Re Northside Motor Co Ltd; Eddison v Allied Irish Banks* (24 July 1985, unreported) HC, Costello J.

The defendant bank advanced finance to another company, which was owned by the individual, the bank's security being the provision by the plaintiff company of a guarantee of the repayment of the loan taken out by the second company. The bank later became aware that the procedure set out in s 60(2) had not been followed, and it demanded that the company pass the appropriate special resolution, and that the directors make the requisite declaration of solvency. These were done. Later, the company was called upon to honour its guarantee and paid money over to the plaintiff bank. Subsequently, the company was wound up and the liquidator sought the recovery of the money paid on foot of the guarantee. It was accepted by Costello J that the company had provided financial assistance for the purchase of its own shares because the transaction involved a promise to make a pecuniary payment to the bank if the borrower company defaulted in its obligations. Costello J held that the declaration and special resolution could not retrospectively validate the breach of s 60(1) and held that the liquidator was entitled to the recovery of the money paid by the company on foot of the guarantee.

[10.076] A person who is the beneficiary of a corporate transaction which is in breach of s 60(1) is placed in a very difficult position where facts constituting a breach of s 60(1) *subsequently* come to their notice. The judgment of Costello J in *Re Northside Motor Co Ltd* makes it clear that one cannot retrospectively validate a transaction through compliance with sub-s (2). What is unclear from that judgment is whether the bank in question had notice of the facts which constituted a breach of s 60(1) *at the time* the guarantee was given. Where a bank or other person does not have the requisite notice at the time the transaction is entered into, the transaction may not subsequently be avoided by the company or its liquidator. The taking of steps to regularise the situation – even where these are proved to be ineffective – ought not to retrospectively jeopardise a person's position[210].

(g) Shareholder protection

[10.077] Section 60(8) of the CA 1963 enables a shareholder, who does not approve of the provision of financial assistance, to apply to court for relief in the form of an order for the cancellation of the special resolution. Where such an application is made to court, the special resolution shall have no effect, except to the extent, if any, to which it is confirmed by the court. Those shareholders who are entitled to make application to court are the holders of 10% in nominal value of the company's issued share capital or any class thereof[211]. The equitable principle of estoppel finds statutory form in s 60(10) of the CA 1963, which provides that those who consented to or voted for the special resolution may not make an application under s 60(8). The only procedural provision in respect of this application[212] provides that the application must be made within 28 days after the date of the passing of the special resolution, and may be made on behalf of

[210] Even had it been possible retrospectively to validate the transaction, Costello J held that the statutory declaration of solvency of the directors was 'materially inaccurate and misleading' and the members' special resolution invalid since its factual statements were incorrect, averring that the ownership of the shares were held by persons who were not in fact the owners.

[211] Section 60(9) of the CA 1963.

[212] Section 60(11) of the CA 1963.

those entitled to make application by one person whom they appoint in writing for the purpose.

Dividends and lawful liabilities: s 60(12) of the CA 1963

[10.078] Section 60(12) of the CA 1963 provides:

> 'Nothing in this section shall be taken to prohibit the payment of a dividend properly declared by a company or the discharge of a liability lawfully incurred by it.'

It is thought that the sort of transaction envisaged by the 'discharge of a liability lawfully incurred', is one where a company pays a person for a *bona fide* debt (whether for goods, services or otherwise) and that person uses those proceeds to acquire shares in that company. Notwithstanding that a somewhat different situation arose in *Eccles Hall Ltd v Bank of Nova Scotia*[213], Murphy J found that s 60(12) provided 'a complete answer to the plaintiffs' claim'[214] that the provision of finance to acquire shares in such a circumstance was contrary to s 60(1).

[10.079] In *Eccles Hall Ltd v Bank of Nova Scotia*[215], the plaintiff company, Eccles Hall Ltd ('Eccles Hall'), which was owned by Mr K and Mrs K, was the owner of a Knocklofty House. Mr K agreed to sell to Mr L 500 shares (being 50% of the company's equity share capital) for £180,000 and to redeem a mortgage affecting the property with the proceeds; Mr L agreed to advance £156,250 to Eccles Hall to complete the development of the property and it was agreed that that sum would be secured by a charge over most of the property, from the company in favour of Mr L. It was also acknowledged that Mr K had loaned the company £180,000. Subsequently the company purported to increase its share capital by the creation of an additional 40,000 ordinary shares of £1 each and 359,000 10% cumulative preference shares of £1 each, and to allot Mr K and Mr L 179,5000 of those preference shares. The company's records supporting the allotment of shares were scant. Later still, two charges were created in favour of Mr L, secured on the property. Just over a year later the relationship between Mr K and Mr L deteriorated dramatically and resulted in a breakdown in communications. To resolve the impasse, an accountant sought to negotiate an arrangement, in effect to ascertain a price at which Mr L could be bought out of the company and also to find some way of financing that purchase and further development of the property. He was successful in brokering a deal and it was agreed that in consideration of £300,000 Mr L would, *inter alia*, transfer his interest in the share capital of the company to Mr K and vacate the two mortgages that he held. In his judgment, Murphy J said that it was essential to recognise that the agreement brokered was arrived at by reference to the amount 'put up' by Mr L in connection with thc transaction, and that he was concerned to be repaid the full amount contributed by him, whether by way of advance or investment in the company or as a result of the purchase of shares; and that the negotiations did not involve the discussion of the then value of the company's properties, less still the value of a 50% shareholding.

As Mr K did not have sufficient personal resources to finance the purchase, the accountant eventually found a willing purchaser, a Mr B. Mr B negotiated a facility with

---

213 *Eccles Hall Ltd v Bank of Nova Scotia* (3 February 1995, unreported) HC, Murphy J.

214 *Eccles Hall Ltd v Bank of Nova Scotia* (3 February 1995, unreported) HC at p 18.

215 *Eccles Hall Ltd v Bank of Nova Scotia* (3 February 1995, unreported) HC, Murphy J.

the first defendant – the Bank of Nova Scotia. The result was that Mr B would purchase a 50% beneficial interest in the company, Mr L was to get £325,000 of which Mr B was to put up £100,000 and the Bank of Nova Scotia was to provide the remaining £225,000 to complete the purchase of the shares. The transaction proceeded as follows: the company, Eccles Hall, obtained a mortgage loan of £350,000 and an overdraft facility of £25,000. These were secured by a first fixed and floating charge over its assets with the exception of certain time-share units and the personal guarantees of Mr B, Mr K and Mrs K. The acquisition of Mr L's shares and the repayment of loans made by him to Eccles Hall was structured thus: the bank loaned the sum of £225,000 to a company called Paramount Enterprises Ltd ('Paramount'), a company wholly owned by Mr B. Paramount would then lend the £225,000 that it had borrowed to Eccles Hall which would charge its assets in favour of Paramount and that Paramount would in turn grant a sub-mortgage to the bank. Paramount would also obtain the sum of £100,000 from Mr B. The result of the various transactions ultimately effected was as follows:

- Mr L received £350,000; Paramount obtained 50% of the issued share capital in Eccles Hall;
- Eccles Hall's indebtedness to Mr L was discharged;
- Mr B provided £100,000 to the transactions and the Bank of Nova Scotia provided the remainder; and
- Eccles Hall provided security for the monies advanced, otherwise than those from Mr B.

[10.080] Subsequently, an official liquidator was appointed to Eccles Hall and he challenged the validity of the security given by it, which he contended constituted the provision of security for the purpose of or in connection with the purchase of its own shares. Murphy J rejected that s 60 had been breached by reason of the fact that Mr L's shares were not sold for £325,000, as initially envisaged, but for a mere £50. Although there was some dispute as to what the true value of the shareholding was, Murphy J said:

> 'Whilst the potential value of the shareholding is not without relevance, it is only a peripheral consideration in the present case. I am satisfied that the sum paid to secure the withdrawal of Mr L from the venture was not related to the value of his shareholding but to the amount of his contribution or the cost to him of his investment in the enterprise[216].'

Murphy J went on to note that the official liquidator had sought to rely upon a number of case authorities: Irish[217], English[218] and South African[219]. He pointed out that the importance of the Irish cases was the decision in *Bank of Ireland Finance Ltd v Rockfield* which determined the meaning of 'notice' as used in s 60(14) to mean 'actual notice' as opposed to and distinct from 'constructive notice'. As to the English and South African cases he said that they established the following propositions:

> '1. That such legislation being punitive in its nature 'should not be strained to cover transactions which are not fairly within it'.

[216] *Eccles Hall Ltd v Bank of Nova Scotia* (3 February 1995, unreported) HC at p 12.

[217] *Bank of Ireland Finance Ltd v Rockfield* [1979] IR 21; *Northside Motor Company Ltd: Eddison v Allied Irish Banks Ltd* (24 July 1985, unreported) HC, Costello J.

[218] *Charterhouse Investment Trust Ltd v Tempest Diesels Ltd* [1986] BCLC 1.

[219] *Gradwell Property Ltd v Rostra* [1959] 4 SA 419.

2. That the words 'in connection with' are of wide import. Indeed it was submitted on behalf of the plaintiffs that it was the wide ambit of that phrase which resulted in its deletion from the UK amending provisions of 1981.
3. That commercial transactions negotiated between a company and a person intending to purchase shares therein might constitute the provision of 'financial assistance'. Certainly the purchase by a company of an asset from the intending purchaser at an inflated price would constitute such assistance. In addition it would seem that the purchase of an asset at a fair price or any other sound commercial transaction negotiated at arm's length might constitute the giving of financial assistance if the purpose of such purchase or transaction was to put the purchaser in funds to buy shares in the company entering into the transaction.
4. That the legislation might be breached by the provision of financial assistance to the vendor of the shares as distinct from the purchaser thereof[220].'

Murphy J repeated his belief that the vast bulk of the payment to Mr L represented the repayment of the company's indebtedness to him: 'The Bank had no notice and indeed I do not believe that it was the case that any part of the moneys provided by them was to be used for the purpose of purchasing shares in Eccles Hall Ltd[221].'

[10.081] Murphy J went on to find that s 60(12) of the CA 1963 provided a complete answer to the plaintiff's claim because the payments made by the company (with money borrowed by the company and secured on its assets) were to discharge debts owed by the company to the shareholder. Notwithstanding this decision[222], it is thought that great care must be taken in satisfying oneself that a particular transaction falls squarely within the terms of, and intentions behind, s 60(12). Insofar as it is possible, the consideration for a share purchase should be kept separate from the repayment of a loan. The value attributable to the share purchase must reflect the true value and an appropriate valuation should always be obtained[223]. The fact that in the *Eccles Hall* case the vendor's shares were sold for a nominal sum of £50 and the balance paid in discharge of the company's indebtedness shows, in the words of Murphy J, an 'apparently extraordinary fall in the value of the 50% shareholding in Eccles Hall between February 1989 and May 1989 from £325,000 to £50'[224]. It is difficult to concur with Murphy J's conclusion that 'whilst the potential value of the shareholding is not without relevance, it is only a peripheral consideration in the present case'[225].

[10.082] Irrespective of other considerations, if s 60(12) of the CA 1963 is to be of relevance, the liability that is discharged must be a liability of the company, which engages in activity that would otherwise be prohibited financial assistance. So, in

---

[220] *Eccles Hall Ltd v Bank of Nova Scotia* (3 February 1995, unreported) HC at pp 16, 17.

[221] *Eccles Hall Ltd v Bank of Nova Scotia* (3 February 1995, unreported) HC at p 17.

[222] The findings in *Eccles Hall Ltd* have been questioned by Breslin, *Banking Law in the Republic of Ireland* (1998), p 691: 'It is, with respect, hard to reconcile the decision with the wide ambit of section 60(1). Even if the discharge of the debt is part of the overall share purchase transaction, the granting of security to secure a loan to discharge that indebtedness is at least an indirect provision of financial assistance in connection with the purchase of the shares.'

[223] See Ch 9, *Share Transfer*, para **[9.117]** *et seq*.

[224] *Eccles Hall Ltd v Bank of Nova Scotia* (3 February 1995, unreported) HC at p 11.

[225] *Eccles Hall Ltd v Bank of Nova Scotia* (3 February 1995, unreported) HC at p 12.

Armour Hick Northern Ltd v Armour Trust Ltd[226] it was held that where company A owed money to company B, the discharge of that liability by company C (a subsidiary of company A) contemporaneously with the sale by company B of its shares in company A was outside the English equivalent to s 60(12).

[10.083] The fundamental principle, before s 60(12) of the CA 1963 will operate to exempt the discharge of a lawful liability incurred by a company from the prohibition in s 60(1), must be that the liability is *bona fide* incurred. The use of the word 'lawful', in the context of s 8(1) of the CA 1963, has been interpreted to mean not in breach of directors' duties[227], and there is no reason to distinguish its meaning in s 60(12)[228].

The payment of dividends from distributable profits is considered below[229].

Miscellaneous exceptions: s 60(13) of the CA 1963

[10.084] Section 60(13) of the CA 1963 provides that the general prohibition contained in s 60(1) shall not be taken to prohibit:

- the lending of money by a company in the ordinary course of its business; or
- the provision by a company, in accordance with any scheme for the time being in force, of money for the purchase of or subscription for fully paid shares in the company or its holding company where such is for the benefit of its employees or former employees of either it or a subsidiary. This exception includes a director holding salaried employment in either the company or a subsidiary; or
- the making by a company of loans to persons, other than directors, *bona fide* in the employment of the company or a subsidiary with a view to enabling them to purchase or subscribe for fully paid shares in the company or its holding company to be held by them as beneficial owners.

The foregoing exceptions are self-explanatory. Extreme care must be exercised where the company proposes to assist directors, and persons connected with them, to purchase shares in the company; regard must also be had to s 31 of the CA 1990, as to which see Chapter 16.

[E] COURT ORDERED CAPITAL REDUCTION

[10.085] The Companies Acts provide for certain situations in which the courts may *order* the reduction of a company's capital by ordering the company to purchase its own shares. Here, the following provisions, which enable the court to order the reduction of a company's capital, are considered:

1. Section 10(6A) of the CA 1963;
2. Section 205(3) of the CA 1963;
3. Section 15 of the C(A)A 1983.

[226] *Armour Hick Northern Ltd v Armour Trust Ltd* [1980] 3 All ER 833.

[227] *Re Frederick Inns Ltd et al* [1994] 1 ILRM 387.

[228] In *Belmont Finance Corporation Ltd v Williams Furniture Ltd* [1979] Ch 250, an asset was acquired by a company at a grossly inflated value and the proceeds were then used to acquire the company's own shares. This was held by the Court of Appeal to be the unlawful provision of financial assistance in connection with the purchase of its own shares.

[229] See para **[10.089]**.

Section 10(6A) of the CA 1963

[10.086] Section 10(1) of the CA 1963 enables a company to alter its objects clause[230]. Section 10(6A) of the CA 1963 provides that where application is made to court in circumstances where a company has by special resolution altered its objects clause, the court may, *inter alia*:

> '... provide for the purchase by the company of the shares of any members of the company and for the reduction accordingly of the company's capital and may make such alterations in the memorandum and articles of association of the company as may be required in consequence of that provision.'

The purpose behind this provision is to enable dissenting shareholders to be bought out where the majority of the company's shareholders decide to change its direction by altering its object clause. Implicit in s 10(6A) is the recognition that the majority of shareholders may not have sufficient resources to finance the purchase of the dissenting shareholders' shares. That such an order by the court may be made 'on such terms and conditions as it thinks fit' is thought to be a sufficient safeguard to ensure that the rights of creditors will not be prejudiced by any order for the reduction of capital.

Section 205(3) of the CA 1963

[10.087] A similar provision, which also enables dissenting shareholders to have their shares acquired by the company, is s 205(3) of the CA 1963. The protection of minority shareholders' interests is considered in Ch 11, where the statutory right of shareholders to apply to court for relief is discussed. One of the powers of the court is to make an order:

> '... for the purchase of the shares of any members of the company by other members of the company or by the company and in the case of a purchase by the company, for the reduction accordingly of the company's capital, or otherwise.'

Again, implicit in s 205(3) is the recognition that dissenting shareholders, whether they are a minority or a majority, can have their shares acquired in circumstances where the remaining shareholders have insufficient resources to acquire their shares. It is especially just that an oppressed minority should not be prejudiced by the majority's impecuniosity.

Section 15 of the C(A)A 1983

[10.088] Section 15 of the C(A)A 1983 is concerned with a situation where the members of a PLC pass a special resolution to have the company re-registered as a private company under s 15. Section 15 is essentially a safeguard, which enables members to object to court and to have the special resolution cancelled by court. The court can make an order either cancelling or confirming the resolution, and again any order made may, if the court thinks fit, provide for the purchase by the company of the shares of any member and the consequent reduction of the company's capital.

---

230 See Ch 3, *Constitutional Documentation*, para **[3.036]** *et seq*.

[F] DISTRIBUTIONS AND THE PAYMENT OF DIVIDENDS

[10.089] Section 45(1) of the C(A)A 1983[231] provides that:

> 'A company shall not make a *distribution* (as defined by section 51) except out of profits available for the purpose[232].'

This does not require companies to make distributions to their members from distributable profits; where, however, distributions are made to members, they must be from distributable profits. In this section we consider the following:

(a) The meaning of distribution.

(b) The meaning of 'profits available for distribution'.

(c) Determining whether profits are available for distribution.

(d) To be a distribution, it must be made to a 'member', qua member.

(e) Disguised distributions.

(f) Liability of directors for unlawful distributions.

(g) Liability of members for unlawful distributions.

(a) The meaning of distribution

[10.090] 'Distribution' is defined by s 51 of the C(A)A 1983[233] as meaning every description of distribution of a company's assets to members of the company, whether in cash or otherwise, with the exception of the following distributions:

- an issue of shares as fully or partly paid bonus shares;
- the redemption of preference shares pursuant to s 65 of the CA 1963, out of the proceeds of a fresh issue of shares made for the purpose of the redemption;
- the redemption or purchase of shares under Part XI of the CA 1990, out of the proceeds of a fresh issue of shares made for the purpose of the redemption or purchase and the payment of any premium out of the company's share premium account on a redemption under s 220 of the CA 1990;
- the reduction of share capital by extinguishing or reducing the liability of any of the members on any of its shares in respect of share capital not paid up or by paying off paid up share capital; and
- a distribution of assets to members of the company on its winding up.

Accordingly, the prohibition in s 45(1) of the C(A)A 1983 on a company making a distribution otherwise than out of profits available for the purpose is subject to a number of exceptions, many of which have been considered previously.

---

231 See generally, Power, *Accounting Law and Practice for Ltd Companies* (1983), Ch 14.

232 Whether or not directors are obliged to apply profits that are available to pay dividends to capital is a matter for individual companies' articles of association. So, in *Kehoe v The Waterford and Limerick Railway Company* (1888) LR 21 (Ire) Ch 221 an injunction to restrain the defendant company and its directors from paying dividends (declared and passed) to the preference shareholders before first replacing certain railway wagons was refused by Porter MR where the directors were under no legal obligation to set aside a fund for maintenance of capital assets.

233 As amended by s 232 of the CA 1990.

[10.091] It should be noted that insofar as the prohibition under s 45 applies to 'distributions', it includes the payment of dividends. Dividends have been considered previously in Ch 8[234]. The payment of dividends by private companies is less entrammeled by restrictions than public companies. The rules on the payment of dividends by private companies have been succinctly summarised by Power[235]:

> 'Private limited companies may pay dividends:
>
> (i) out of net realised profits,
>
> (ii) but must make up past losses first,
>
> (iii) need not cover net unrealised losses, and
>
> (iv) may use unaudited interim accounts to justify payments.
>
> Such accounts need not be filed with the registrar of companies.'

[10.092] Great care should be taken when using the word 'distribute' in relation to a company's assets in commercial agreements or even in articles of association. In *Igote Ltd v Badley Ltd*[236], a share subscription agreement that had been entered into by the parties provided that in any financial period of 12 months' duration, the company would 'distribute' at least £40,000 to the parties. The agreement went on to provide that such 'shall be *distributed* to the first subscriber and thereafter a similar amount shall be *distributed* to the second subscriber. Any dividend in excess of such amounts shall be split between the shareholders in proportion to their holdings of ordinary shares.' It was held by the Supreme Court that this was to be interpreted, not as a simple obligation to pay, but rather as an obligation to distribute monies by way of dividend which could only be paid out of distributable profits. Murphy J said:

> 'The learned trial judge expressed the view that the ordinary and natural meaning of the word "distribute" as used in the paragraph in question was "pay". I would respectfully disagree with that view. The *Shorter Oxford Dictionary* gives the primary definition of "distribute" as "to deal out or bestow in proportions or shares amongst many; to allot or apportion as his share to each".'

In those circumstances it was held that the use of the word 'distribute' suggested the payment of a dividend, meaning that such could be paid, only, from distributable profits[237].

(b) The meaning of 'profits available for distribution'

[10.093] Central to s 45(1) of the C(A)A 1983 is that only distributions 'out of profits available for the purpose' are permitted. Section 45(2) of the C(A)A 1983 defines profits available for distribution as meaning a company's:

> '... accumulated, realised profits, so far as not previously utilised by distribution or capitalisation, *less* its accumulated, realised losses, so far as not previously written off in a reduction or reorganisation of capital duly made.'

---

234 Ch 8, *Shares and Membership*, para **[8.073]** *et seq*.

235 Power, *Accounting Law and Practice for Limited Companies* (1983), p 129.

236 *Igote Ltd v Badley Ltd* [2004] 4 IR 511.

237 See also *MacPhearson and another v European Strategic Bureau Ltd* [2002] BCC 39.

Realised and unrealised profits and losses are not defined by the Companies Acts, although in a scattered way, certain subsections of s 45 provide assistance to those desirous of understanding the rules on distributions. The central rationale behind these rules is that the only assets which a company can distribute are those assets which in the case of an individual very roughly accord with his 'disposable income'. Distributions cannot be made out of capital assets, only out of 'realised profits'.

[10.094] For those unfamiliar with accounting terminology, the concepts of 'accumulated realised profits' and 'accumulated realised losses'[238] can pose some difficulty. In essence, what a company can distribute are those profits remaining after its total losses for the current and previous years are subtracted from its total profits for the current and previous years. The distributable profits may be loosely described as unencumbered profits or 'real profits' as opposed to 'artificial profits'. By so legislating, an attempt has been made to ensure that a company's capital is maintained in situations where a company makes a distribution. The question of whether a distribution may be made by a company is to be determined by reference to the relevant items in the company's accounts[239].

[10.095] In *Re Irish Life and Permanent plc*[240], Clarke J cited the following passage from the decision of Fetcher Moulton LJ in *Re Spanish Prospecting Company*[241]:

> 'The word 'profits' has in my opinion a well-defined legal meaning, and this meaning coincides with the fundamental conception of profits in general parlance, although in mercantile phraseology the word may at times bear meanings indicated by the special context which deviates in some respects from this fundamental signification. 'Profits' implies a comparison between the state of a business at two specific dates usually separated by an interval of a year. The fundamental meaning is the amount of gain made by the business during the year. This can only be ascertained by a comparison of the assets of the business at the two dates … We start, therefore, with this fundamental definition of profits, namely, if the total assets of the business at the two dates to be compared, the increase which they show at the later date as compared with the earlier date (due allowance of course being made for any capital introduced into or taken out of the business in the meanwhile) represents in strictness the profits of the business during the period in question.'

This passage had previously been approved in Ireland by Kenny J in *Wilson v Dunnes Stores (Cork) Ltd*[242]. Clarke J summarised the principles applicable to the meaning of 'profits' as follows:

---

[238] On what is to be treated as a realised loss see s 45(4) of the C(A)A 1983.

[239] Section 49(1) of the C(A)A 1983. See generally Ch 17, *Financial Statements, Audit & Annual Return.*

[240] *Re Irish Life and Permanent plc* [2009] IEHC 567, Clarke J.

[241] *Re Spanish Prospecting Company* [1911] Ch 92.

[242] *Wilson v Dunnes Stores (Cork) Ltd* (1976) (22 January 1996, unreported) HC. See also *Meagher v Meagher* [1962] IR 96. Other judicial definitions of profit referred to by Clarke J included R*ushden Heel Company Ltd v Keane* [1946] 2 All ER 141 where Atkinson J said: 'Profits consist of a sum arrived at by adding up the receipts of a business and by deducting all the expenses and losses, including depreciation and the like, incurred in carrying on the business'; and *McClelland v Hyde* [1942] NI 1 where Babington LJ said: 'The word "profits" generally speaking means the excessive returns over outlay, but in commercial agreements, its meaning may be and often is restricted to annual pecuniary profits as would ordinarily appear in a profit and loss account.'

> 'A. The current assets of a commercial entity (and in principle, these comments would apply equally to a partnership or other trading entity as they would to a company) must, in logic, represent either the accumulated capital invested into the business or company (that is, all of the capital invested less any capital taken out) together with the accumulated net undistributed profits of the business (that is, all of the profits less all of the losses less any profits distributed, in whatever way might be appropriate, to the investors).
>
> B. In this context, the term profits includes both what might, for Revenue purposes, be described as capital gains or income.
>
> C. In principle, the term 'profits' reflects a change in the assets of the entity concerned not explained by a movement in the capital invested in the entity. Obviously if further capital is invested, or if capital is returned to the investors, then that will explain a movement in the assets of the entity which does not derive from the entity having made profits. However, when any appropriate allowance is made for further investment or return of capital, then the remaining change in the assets of the entity must be its profits (or, in the case that there be a diminution, its losses).
>
> D. Profits over any particular period (which will, of course, be most commonly calculated on a yearly basis) amount, therefore, to the change in the assets for the period in question which cannot be explained by a movement in the capital invested[243].'

The learned judge went on to conclude:

> '7.10 It seems to me to follow from the provisions of s 148 of the 1963 Act that profits, for the purposes of a company incorporated under that Act, and, therefore, profits for the purposes of considering whether distribution under s 45 can take place, must mean profits calculated in accordance with the relevant applicable accountancy standards. It follows, therefore, that it is movements in the assets of the company by reference to such standards that needs to be considered in the context of determining whether profits, within the meaning of the Act, can be said to have occurred.'

In *Re Irish Life and Permanent plc*[244], the meaning of what was a distributable profit was considered in the context of a scheme of arrangement. The background was that under a proposed scheme of arrangement under s 201 of the CA 1963, Irish Life and Permanent plc (Old IL&P) was to become a subsidiary of a new company (New IL&P). This was to be done by cancelling and extinguishing Old IL&P's share capital (excepting seven nominal shares) and the whole of the resulting reserve being applied in allotting and paying up, in full and at nominal or par value, a number of new shares in Old IL&P and issuing them to New IL&P so that it became the holding company. The total book value of the equity of Old IL&P was €3,584m; the 'fair value' of the equity was €1,578m and the par value of the new shares issued by New IL&P was €89m. Accounting rules required that the balance sheet of New IL&P show its investment in Old IL&P as being its total equity (ie, €3,584m). The actual nominal value of share capital received by New IL&P was €89m and the actual share premium on those shares was the difference between the nominal value and the fair value, that is €1,489m. Accordingly, there was €1,584m on the other side of the balance sheet which meant, to make it balance, a figure of €2,006m was required to be recorded as an 'other reserve'. The question

243 *Re Irish Life and Permanent plc* [2009] IEHC 567, Clarke J at para 7.9.

244 *Re Irish Life and Permanent plc* [2009] IEHC 567, Clarke J.

Clarke J had to determine was the status of that 'other reserve' which he found was to be considered an asset of New IL&P (since why else would it be on its balance sheet):

> '8.6 On the assumption, therefore, that the other reserve must represent some form of asset of the company, then it seems to follow from the fundamental definition of profit derived from the case law, that the other reserve must either amount to part of the net capital of the company (that is all capital contributed and not returned) or alternatively, must represent part of the net accumulated and undistributed profits of the company (that is all profits less all losses less any distributed profits). It is difficult to see how there is any other box into which the other reserve can fit without doing a complete injustice to the fundamental definition of profit as set out in the case law.'

The learned judge rejected that the other reserve should be considered to be capital and held that it was in law a 'distributable profit' of New IL&P:

> '9.1 I could see no even theoretical basis for an argument in favour of treating the other reserve as net undistributed capital. New ILP received its assets, in substance, by being able to subscribe for the shares in old ILP created as part of the scheme and paid up by the cancellation of the existing shares. Those existing shares had their market value. In substance, the shareholders allowed, by virtue of the scheme, new ILP to acquire shares in old ILP in return for being given an equivalent amount of shares in new ILP. The 'investment' by the shareholders, as a matter of reality, was the value of their shareholding which in substance was its market value. The other reserve was in addition to that sum. In those circumstances it is very hard to see how there could be any basis for treating it as capital. On the other hand there is a sense (albeit somewhat artificial), on which it could be said that the other reserve could be treated as a profit. The effect of the accountancy standards to which I have referred means that an investment by new ILP in obtaining the shares of old ILP for a value which, in substance, is of the order of €1.6BN must be written, at least initially, into the books of new ILP, at a value of approximately €3.6BN. While it is highly artificial to put it this way, there is at least a sense in which one could regard that fact as giving rise to an instantaneous profit in that an investment of €1.6BN acquires an asset which, while worth €1.6BN, has to be written into the books of the company in a manner which reflects the company as having assets of €3.6BN. It is only a profit in that sense. It only arises because the transaction requires the additional €2BN to be written into the books of the company. It is not a profit in any real or tangible sense. However, it seems to me that it can properly be regarded as a profit deriving from the need, in order to conform with company law, that the additional €2M requires to be written into the books of the company as a result of the transaction.
>
> 9.2 In that sense it seemed to me that treating the other reserve as a profit did less injustice to a logical approach to the company's accounts than treating it as net unreturned capital. For the reasons which I have already set out, I was persuaded that to regard the other reserve as being neither net accumulated unreturned capital or net accumulated undistributed profits still less as not being an asset at all, would do a level of injustice to the logic of the situation which could not be stood over. It followed that the other reserve had, therefore, in my view, to be treated as either capital or profit. It seemed to me that treating the other reserve as profit did less injustice to first principles than any other possible approach. It was for those reasons that I was satisfied that the other reserve was profit for the purposes of s 45.'

The converse may also apply and where the total equity in a company (ie, the book value) is in fact lower than its fair value, then on the basis of Clarke J's decision, it would have to be treated as a 'loss'. Although Clarke J stated that the profit was a 'realised profit', he offered no authority or reasons for so doing and it is thought that this might be open to further examination should the matter come before the courts again. In the context of the converse situation, where a reserve must be treated as a loss, it is thought that such a loss should be treated as an 'unrealised loss' and not as a 'realised loss'[245].

(c) Determining whether profits are available for distribution

[10.096] Section 49(1) of the C(A)A 1983 provides that the question of whether a distribution may be made by a company without contravening s 45, and the amount of any distribution which may be so made shall be determined by reference to the relevant items as stated in the relevant accounts as defined in s 49(2), and s 45 shall be treated as contravened in the case of a distribution unless the requirements of this section about those accounts are complied with in the case of that distribution. 'Relevant accounts' in the case of any particular distribution are said by s 49(2) to be:

> '(a) except in a case falling within paragraph (b) or (c), the last annual accounts that is to say, the accounts prepared in accordance with the requirements of the Principal Act [ie, the CA 1963] (and, where applicable, in accordance with the requirements of Article 4 of the IAS Regulation) which were laid in respect of the last preceding financial year in respect of which accounts so prepared were laid;
>
> (b) if that distribution would be found to contravene the relevant section if reference were made only to the last annual accounts, such accounts (interim accounts) as are necessary to enable a reasonable judgment to be made as to the amounts of any of the relevant items[246];
>
> (c) if that distribution is proposed to be declared during the company's first financial year or before any accounts are laid in respect of that financial year, such accounts (initial accounts) as are necessary as aforesaid.'

Accordingly, it is open to a company to use its last annual accounts and *interim accounts*, being management accounts which bridge the gap between the present and the last annual accounts; interim accounts alone can be used where a company proposes a distribution in its first year of trading when no annual accounts have yet been prepared.

[10.097] Where the last annual accounts constitute the *only* relevant accounts (ie, where no interim accounts are used), s 49(3) of the C(A)A 1983 provides that:

> '(a) those accounts must have been properly prepared or have been so prepared subject only to matters which are not material for the purpose of determining, by reference to the relevant items as stated in those accounts, whether that distribution would be in contravention of the relevant section[247];

---

245 *Cf* ICAEW Technical Release 02/10 at 9.40 which would indicate that such a loss should be taken to be a realised loss.

246 Section 49(9) of the C(A)A 1983 provides that: '"relevant item" means the following amounts as dealt with in the company's relevant accounts— (a) profits, losses, assets and liabilities, (b) where the company prepares Companies Act individual accounts, any provisions mentioned in the Companies (Amendment) Act 1986 or any provisions mentioned in the Sixth Schedule to the Principal Act (depreciation, diminution in value of assets, retention to meet liabilities, etc), (c) where the company prepares IFRS individual accounts, provisions of any kind, and (d) share capital and reserves.'

247 Section 49(8) of C(A)A 1983 provides that where 'subsection (3)(a), (5)(a) or (6)(a) applies to the relevant accounts, section 45(5) shall not apply for the purposes of determining whether any revaluation of the company's fixed assets affecting the amount of the relevant items as stated in those accounts has taken place, unless it is stated in a note to those accounts (contd.../)

(b) the auditors of the company must have made a report under section 163 of the Principal Act in respect of those accounts;

(c) if, by virtue of anything referred to in that report, the report is not an unqualified report[248], the auditors must also have stated in writing[249] (either at the time the report was made or subsequently) whether, in their opinion, that thing is material for the purpose of determining, by reference to the relevant items as stated in those accounts, whether that distribution would be in contravention of the relevant section; and

(d) a copy of any such statement must have been laid before the company in general meeting.'

For accounts to be 'properly prepared' they must comply with s 49(9)[250]. Where interim management accounts are prepared for a proposed distribution, s 49(5) sets out the following requirements:

---

[247] (contd.../)—(a) that the directors have considered the value at any time of any fixed assets of the company without actually revaluing those assets; (b) that they are satisfied that the aggregate value of those assets at the time in question is or was not less than the aggregate amount at which they are or were for the time being stated in the company's accounts; and (c) that the relevant items affected are accordingly stated in the relevant accounts on the basis that a revaluation of the company's fixed assets which by virtue of section 45(5) included the assets in question took place at that time.'

[248] Section 49(9) provides that: '"unqualified report" in relation to any accounts of a company, means a report, without qualification, to the effect that in the opinion of the person making the report the accounts have been properly prepared; and for the purposes of this section, accounts are laid if section 148 of the Principal Act has been complied with in relation to those accounts.'

[249] Section 49(4) of the C(A)A 1983 provides that: 'A statement under subsection (3)(c) suffices for the purposes of a particular distribution not only if it relates to a distribution which has been proposed but also if it relates to distributions of any description which include that particular distribution, notwithstanding that at the time of the statement it has not been proposed.'

[250] Section 49(9) provides that '*properly prepared*' means, in relation to any accounts of a company, 'that the following conditions are satisfied in relation to those accounts, that is to say—(a) in the case of annual individual accounts, that they have been properly prepared in accordance with the Principal Act, (b) in the case of interim or initial accounts that they comply with the requirements of section 148 and either section 149 or 149A (inserted by the European Communities (International Financial Reporting Standards and Miscellaneous Amendments) Regulations 2005) of the Principal Act, where applicable, and any balance sheet comprised in those accounts has been signed in accordance with section 156 of the Principal Act; and (c) in either case, without prejudice to the foregoing, that, except where the company is entitled to avail itself, and has availed itself, of any of the provisions of Part III of the Sixth Schedule to the Principal Act— (i) so much of the accounts as consists of a balance sheet gives a true and fair view of the state of the company's affairs as at the balance sheet date; and (ii) so much of those accounts as consists of a profit and loss account gives a true and fair view of the company's profit or loss for the period in respect of which the accounts were prepared.' Section 49(10) also provides that for the purpose of para (b) of the definition of 'properly prepared' in sub-s (9), s 148 and either s 149 or 149A of the Principal Act, where applicable, of, and the Sixth Schedule to the Principal Act shall be deemed to have effect in relation to interim and initial accounts with such modifications as are necessary by reason of the fact that the accounts are prepared otherwise than in respect of a financial year. See, generally, Ch 17, *Financial Statements, Audit and Annual Return*.

> '(a) the accounts must have been properly prepared or have been so prepared subject only to matters which are not material for the purpose of determining, by reference to the relevant items as stated in those accounts, whether that distribution would be in contravention of the relevant section;
>
> (b) a copy of those accounts must have been delivered to the registrar of companies;
>
> (c) if the accounts are in a language other than the English or Irish language, a translation into English or Irish of the accounts which has been certified in the prescribed manner to be a correct translation must also have been delivered to the registrar.'

It is also provided that for the purpose of determining by reference to particular accounts whether a proposed distribution may be made by a company, this section shall have effect, in any case where one or more distributions have already been made in pursuance of determinations made by reference to those same accounts, as if the amount of the proposed distribution was increased by the amount of the distributions so made[251].

(d) To be a distribution, it must be made to a 'member', qua member

[10.098] In order for s 45(1) of the C(A)A 1983 to regulate a payment by a company, the payment must be made to a member or a nominee of a member in the person's capacity as a member. A payment by a company to a person who is not a member of the company (or in any way connected with a member) will not require to be made from distributable profits. The payment by a company of a lawful debt, for example, will not be invalidated by reason of s 45 even where the company is insolvent after the payment has been made or the financial effect is to wipe out its capital. A payment to a member's nominee, such as to a company owned and controlled by that member, may fall to be treated as being a distribution to that member[252].

(e) Disguised distributions

[10.099] The rule that members may only receive distributions from distributable profits operates to restrict the return of capital to members. The fact that a distribution can only be made from distributable profits implies that following the distribution, the company's coffers should not be bare. Accordingly, even where a company's creditors have been paid off and it is sought to close a solvent company, s 45 of the C(A)A 1983 can compel the company to go into members' voluntary liquidation rather than pursue any shortcuts to dissolution such as voluntary strike off. It is no answer to s 45(1) of the C(A)A 1983 to say that the payment by the company to its members was *intra vires* because it was authorised by its objects clause[253]; that its directors were expressly authorised by its

---

[251] Section 49(7) of the C(A)A 1983.

[252] See, for example, *Aveling Barford Ltd v Perion Ltd et al* [1989] BCLC 626; (1989) 5 BCC 677.

[253] See Ch 7, *Corporate Contracts, Capacity and Authority*, at para **[7.076]**. Sometimes the older decisions (ie, before the Second EU Directive required a statutory prohibition on distributions other than from distributable profits) characterise the mischief of returning capital as being *ultra vires*. So in *Ridge Securities Ltd v IRC* [1964] 1 All ER 275 Pennycuick J said: 'A company can only lawfully deal with its assets in furtherance of its objects. The corporators may take assets out of the company by way of dividend or, with leave of the court, by way of reduction of capital, or in a winding up. They may of course acquire them for full consideration. (contd.../)

articles of association to make such payments and so were not in breach of their duties; or, indeed, that the company's shareholders unanimously consented to the payment: the rule that distributions to members must be from distributable profits is inflexible, even in these circumstances[254].

[10.100] The English Supreme Court, *per* Lord Walker SCJ recently said in *Progress Property Company Ltd v Moorgarth Group Ltd*[255]:

> 'A limited company not in liquidation cannot lawfully return capital to its shareholders except by way of a reduction of capital approved by the court. Profits may be distributed to shareholders (normally by way of dividend) but only out of distributable profits computed in accordance with the complicated provisions of the Companies Act 2006 (replacing similar provisions in the Companies Act).'

In this case, a vendor subsidiary of a holding company sold shares in another company to a sister subsidiary. The consideration paid allowed for a £4m reduction in the price to allow for a perceived liability which, in fact, it transpired was non-existent. Subsequently, the holding company disposed of its interest in the vendor subsidiary, whereupon the new owners caused an action to be brought alleging that the vendor subsidiary had breached the English equivalent to s 45 on the ground that the consideration paid for the shares was at such a significant undervalue that it amounted to an unlawful return of the vendor company's capital to its member. The trial judge dismissed the plaintiff's claim and rejected that there was an unlawful return of capital whenever a company had entered into a transaction with a shareholder which resulted in a transfer of value not covered by distributable profits regardless of the purposes of the transaction. The English Court of Appeal also dismissed the claim, accepting that there was a genuine belief that the price was market value, that there was no knowledge or intention that the shares should be disposed at an undervalue, and that the transaction was a genuine commercial sale. The English Supreme Court also rejected the appeal and upheld the transaction finding that the court should always look to the substance of the transaction, and not the form, and where, as here, the price paid was genuinely believed to be the market price, then although the effect might have been to reduce the vendor subsidiary's capital, the intention was not to return capital and so the transaction stood. Lord Walker SCJ was loath to decide between a subjective or an objective test in determining whether the sale of the shares was an unlawful return of capital. He did, however, say that if there was a stark choice between a subjective and objective test then 'the least satisfactory choice would be to opt for the latter' and:

> '[27] ... But in cases of this sort the court's real task is to inquire into the true purpose and substance of the impugned transaction. That calls for an investigation of all the relevant

---

253 (\...contd) They cannot take assets out of the company by way of voluntary disposition, howsoever described, and, if they attempt to do so, the disposition is ultra vires the company.' This statement of the law is correct but only where the objects clause has not been expressly amended to authorise a voluntary disposition. Unlike the doctrine of *ultra vires*, however, a disposition in breach of s 45 cannot be prospectively validated by special or unanimous resolution of the members.

254 See, generally, Micheler, 'Disguised Returns of Capital – An Arm's Length Approach' [2010] CLJ 151.

255 *Progress Property Company Ltd v Moorgarth Group Ltd* [2011] 2 All ER 432.

> facts, which sometimes include the state of mind of the human beings who are orchestrating the corporate activity.
>
> [28] Sometimes their states of mind are totally irrelevant. A distribution described as a dividend but actually paid out of capital is unlawful, however technical the error and however well-meaning the directors who paid it. The same is true of a payment which is on analysis the equivalent of a dividend ... If a controlling shareholder simply treats a company as his own property, as the domineering master-builder did in *Re George Newman & Co* [1895] 1 Ch 674, his state of mind (and that of his fellow-directors) is irrelevant. It does not matter whether they were consciously in breach of duty, or just woefully ignorant of their duties. What they do is enough by itself to establish the unlawful character of the transaction.
>
> [29] The participants' subjective intentions are however sometimes relevant, and a distribution disguised as an arm's length commercial transaction is a paradigm example. If a company sells to a shareholder at a low value assets which are difficult to value precisely, but which are potentially very valuable, the transaction may call for close scrutiny, and the company's financial position, and the actual motives and intentions of the directors, will be highly relevant. There may be questions to be asked as to whether the company was under financial pressure compelling it to sell at an inopportune time, as to what advice was taken, how the market was tested, and how the terms of the deal were negotiated. If the conclusion is that it was a genuine arm's length transaction then it will stand, even if it may, with hindsight, appear to have been a bad bargain. If it was an improper attempt to extract value by the pretence of an arm's length sale, it will be held unlawful. But either conclusion will depend on a realistic assessment of all the relevant facts, not simply a retrospective valuation exercise in isolation from all other inquiries.'

The transaction stood because in substance it was not a return of capital, but a genuine commercial transaction albeit one based on a very wrong assumption as to the value of the asset the subject of the transaction.

[10.101] In contrast is the infamous decision of Hoffmann J in *Aveling Barford Ltd v Perion Let et al*[256], where it was held that the substance of the transaction in that case did on the evidence amount to an unlawful return of capital. In that case, a Singapore businessman called Dr Lee Kin Tat was the direct or indirect shareholder in a company called Aveling Barford Limited ('Aveling') and he procured the sale by Aveling of a country house on 18 acres to a company called Perion which was also owned by Dr Lee. The property had development potential and had been valued by one valuer at £650,000 and by another, for mortgage purposes, at £1,150,000. The consideration for the sale to Perion was a mere £350,000 with provision for a further £400,000 if the property was sold within a year for more than £800,000. In fact, the property sold for £1,500,000 within a year. In approaching the legal issues involved, Hoffmann J said in a passage quoted by Lord Walker SCJ in *Progress Property Company Ltd v Moorgarth Group Ltd*[257]:

> 'Whether or not the transaction is a distribution to shareholders does not depend exclusively on what the parties choose to call it. The court looks at the substance rather than the outward appearance[258].'

---

256 *Aveling Barford Ltd v Perion Ltd et al* [1989] BCLC 626, (1989) 5 BCC 677.

257 *Progress Property Company Ltd v Moorgarth Group Ltd* [2011] 2 All ER 432.

258 *Aveling Barford Ltd v Perion Ltd et al* [1989] BCLC 626 at 631.

There, the substance of the transaction was found not to be a sham, but a 'false dressing' and, referring to the decision in *Rolled Steel Products*, Hoffmann J said:

> 'It is clear however that Slade LJ excepted from his general principle cases which he described as involving a 'fraud on creditors' (see [1985] 3 All ER 52 at 86). As an example of such a case, he cited *Re Halt Garage*. Counsel for the defendants said that frauds on creditors meant transactions entered into when the company was insolvent. In this case Aveling Barford was not at the relevant time insolvent. But I do not think that the phrase was intended to have such a narrow meaning. The rule that capital may not be returned to shareholders is a rule for the protection of creditors and the evasion of that rule falls within which I think Slade LJ had in mind when he spoke of a fraud on creditors. There is certainly nothing in his judgment to suggest that he disapproved of the actual decisions in *Re Halt Garage* or *Ridge Securities*. As for the transaction not being a sham, I accept that it was in law a sale. The false dressing it wore was that of a sale at arm's length or at market value. It was the fact that it was known and intended to be a sale at an undervalue which made it an unlawful distribution[259].'

Hoffmann J concluded that the sale to Perion was not a genuine exercise of the company's power under its memorandum to sell its assets. It was a sale at a gross undervalue for the purpose of enabling a profit to be realised by an entity controlled and put forward by its sole beneficial shareholder:

> 'This was as much a dressed-up distribution as the payment of excessive interest in *Ridge Securities* or excessive remuneration in *Halt Garage*. The company had at the time no distributable reserves and the sale was therefore ultra vires and incapable of validation by the approval or ratification of the shareholder. The fact that the distribution was to Perion rather than to Dr Lee or his other entities which actually held the shares in Avling Barford is in my judgment irrelevant.'

The reason unlawful distributions are problematic for companies is because they are prohibited by a statutory provision which does not provide for an exemption. It is thought that it is unhelpful to characterise unlawful distributions as being *ultra vires*; certainly, the doctrine of *ultra vires* can be addressed by specifically amending a company's objects clause to specifically allow the distribution in question.

[10.102] Another example of a disguised transaction can be seen in *MacPherson and another v European Strategic Bureau Ltd*[260]. In that case a shareholders' agreement that provided for the payment to departing shareholders of a percentage of profits earned from contracts on which they had worked, was held by Ferris J[261] not to be an unlawful distribution within the meaning of s 263(1) of the Companies Act 1985 (UK). This was, however, reversed on appeal. The Court of Appeal held that in order for a payment to a member to be found not to be a distribution on account of it being made to the member in another capacity (eg, as director, employee or creditor) the payment should be made pursuant to a *bona fide* transaction entered into for the benefit, and to promote the prosperity, of the company as opposed, for example, to effect an informal winding up.

---

259 *Aveling Barford Ltd v Perion Ltd et al* [1989] BCLC 626 at 633.

260 *MacPherson and another v European Strategic Bureau Ltd* [2002] BCC 39.

261 *MacPherson v European Strategic Bureau Ltd* [1999] TLR 144.

(f) Liability of directors for unlawful distributions

[10.103] Directors who cause a company to pay dividends contrary to statute are accountable to the company for such unlawful payments. In *Flitcroft's Case, Re Exchange Banking Company*[262], directors of a company presented accounts to shareholders which showed debits as assets and so encouraged the shareholders to approve payments of dividends. The English Court of Appeal held that the directors were liable to repay the dividends to the company[263]. *Re Sharpe*[264] bears out the principle that the board of directors (as the body that authorises an unlawful payment) is liable to repay that amount. As Lindley LJ said:

> 'As soon as the conclusion is arrived at that the company's money has been applied by the directors for the purposes which the company cannot sanction, it follows that the directors are liable to replace the money, however honestly they may have acted. Whether they can in turn get it back from those persons who receive it is another matter, but their own liability to restore it is now clearly settled[265].'

In *Bairstow v Queens Moat Houses plc*[266], the English Court of Appeal (*per* Robert Walker LJ) said:

> 'The basic rules about lawful and unlawful dividends, developed from the earliest days of company law and now elaborated in accordance with Community legislation, exist not only for the protection of creditors but also for the protection of shareholders. If directors cause a company to pay a dividend which is ultra vires and unlawful because it infringes these rules, the fact that the company is still solvent should not be a defence to a claim against the directors to make good the unlawful distribution[267].'

In that case it was also held that the directors' liability was not limited to the difference between the unlawful dividends and the amount of dividends that could lawfully have been paid, but extended to the full amount paid. This was because although not trustees, directors were in a closely analogous position because of their fiduciary duties and trustee-like responsibilities. Accordingly, it was held that the directors in that case were liable for deliberately, and, in one case, dishonestly, paying dividends out of the company's funds which were in their stewardship[268]. Neither could the directors in that case obtain relief under the English equivalent of s 391 of the CA 1963[269].

(g) Liability of members for unlawful distributions

[10.104] Where a company makes a distribution to its members in contravention of s 45(1) of the C(A)A 1983, and where at the time of the distribution a member beneficiary knows or has reasonable grounds for believing that it is so made, that member shall by s 50 of the C(A)A 1983 be liable to repay what he receives to the

---

262 *Flitcroft's Case, Re Exchange Banking Company* (1882) LR 21 Ch D 519.

263 On directors' liability for unlawful payments, see also *Dovey v Cory* [1901] AC 477.

264 *Re Sharpe; Masonic and General Life Assurance Company v Sharpe* [1892] Ch 154.

265 *Re Sharpe; Masonic and General Life Assurance Company v Sharpe* [1892] Ch 154 at 165, 166.

266 *Bairstow v Queens Moat Houses plc* [2001] EWCA Civ 712, [2001] 2 BCLC 531.

267 *Bairstow v Queens Moat Houses plc* [2001] 2 BCLC 531 at 546, para [44].

268 *Cf Target Holdings v Redferns* [1995] 3 All ER 785.

269 See, further, Ch 15, *Duties of Directors and Other Officers*, para **[15.088]**.

company[270]. Where the member who receives an unlawful distribution is a director or other officer of the company there must be a strong presumption that he or she has reasonable grounds for believing that it is unlawful. Where a member receives a non-cash distribution, he shall be liable to pay the company a sum equal to the value of the distribution.

[G] MISCELLANEOUS CAPITAL MAINTENANCE RULES

[10.105] There exist a number of other situations where there is a potential for the capital of a company to be reduced. Here the following issues are considered:

1. Forfeiture of unpaid or partly paid shares.
2. Issuing shares at a discount.
3. Liens on shares.
4. Shares issued at a premium.

Forfeiture of unpaid or partly paid shares

[10.106] Model regs 33–39 of Table A concern the *forfeiture* of shares that are unpaid or partly paid[271]. These regulations provide that if a member fails to pay any call or instalment of a call on the day appointed for payment, the directors may serve a notice on the member and require payment on the call or instalment, together with interest[272]. The notice to a member should name a further day at least 14 days after the service of the notice, and state that unless payment is made by that day, the shares in respect of the call are liable to be forfeited[273]. The directors may, by model reg 36, sell a forfeited share or otherwise dispose of it on such terms and conditions as they think fit and at any time before forfeiture, the forfeiture notice may be cancelled on such terms as the directors think fit. The actual act of forfeiture is effected by a resolution of the directors[274]. Model reg 37 states:

> 'A person whose shares have been forfeited shall cease to be a member in respect of the forfeited shares, but shall, notwithstanding, remain liable to pay to the company all monies which, at the date of forfeiture were payable by him to the company in respect of the shares, but his liability shall cease if and when the company shall have received payment in full of all such monies in respect of the shares.'

Model reg 38 provides that a statutory declaration that the declarant is a director or secretary of the company and that a share has been duly forfeited on a date stated in the declaration is conclusive evidence of the facts therein as against all persons claiming to be entitled ot the share.

---

[270] Authorities here include *Precision Dippings Ltd v Precision Dippings Marketing Ltd* [1986] Ch 447; *Bairstow v Queens Moat Houses plc* [2001] 2 BCLC 531; and *It's a Wrap (UK) Ltd v Gula and another* [2006] EWCA 544. See also Payne, 'Unjust Enrichment, Trusts and Recipient Liability for Unlawful Dividends' (2003) LQR 583.

[271] See also Ch 8, *Shares and Membership*, para **[8.123]** *et seq.*

[272] Regulation 33 of Table A.

[273] Regulation 34 of Table A.

[274] Regulation 35 of Table A.

[10.107] Section 41(4)(d) of the C(A)A 1983 expressly provides that the restrictions on a company acquiring its own shares shall not prevent a company from forfeiting its shares.

Issuing shares at a discount

[10.108] There is a general prohibition on a company issuing shares at a discount. The reason for concern is that where shares are issued at a discount, the result is that the company will end up having less actual capital than if it had issued shares at full price, and at the same time, it will appear to outsiders that the company has received full payment for its shares[275]. Such a situation is worse than where shares are issued and partly paid for, since in such a case, there is a further unpaid liability outstanding. Where shares are issued at a discount, the shares held are not subject to any further claim for payment.

[10.109] The issuing of shares at a discount is prohibited by s 27(1) of the C(A)A 1983. This provides that '... the shares of a company shall not be allotted at a discount'. Where this prohibition is breached, the allottee is liable to pay the company the difference between the amount paid and the amount actually due, together with interest[276].

Liens on shares

[10.110] A lien on shares is a security right in favour of a company which allots shares to a shareholder in respect of amounts remaining unpaid on those shares[277]. Liens on shares held in private companies remain unregulated, notwithstanding the restrictions imposed on public companies by s 44 of the C(A)A 1983[278]. Such a situation is envisaged by common form model articles of association, and in particular regs 11–14. Accordingly, model reg 11 provides that a company has a first and paramount lien on all unpaid shares, subject to express exclusion by the directors, and model reg 12 gives the company an express power of sale of such shares. One common modification of the model articles of association is the inclusion of fully paid shares being subject to this lien in respect of all debts due by members to the company[279].

Shares issued at a premium

[10.111] Often, companies will issue shares at a premium[280]. Where shares are issued by a company at a premium, whether for cash or otherwise, s 62(1) of the CA 1963[281] provides:

---

275 See *Ooregram Gold Mining Co of India v Roper* [1892] AC 92, where it was said that a shareholder could '… purchase immunity from liability beyond a certain limit on terms that there shall be and remain a liability up to that limit'.

276 Section 27(2) of the C(A)A 1983.

277 See Ch 8, *Shares and Membership*, para **[8.121]** *et seq.*

278 See Ch 29, *Public Limited Companies and SEs*, para **[29.122]** *et seq.*

279 See *Allen v Gold Reefs of West Africa Ltd* [1900] 1 Ch 656.

280 This is a matter for the company, and companies are not obliged to issue shares at a premium: *Lowry (Inspector of Taxes) v Consolidated African Selection Trust Ltd* [1940] 2 All ER 545.

281 As amended by para 11 of Sch 1 of the C(A)A 1983 and s 231(1) of the CA 1990.

> '... a sum equal to the aggregate amount or value of the premium on those shares shall be transferred to an account, to be called 'the share premium account', and the provisions of this Act relating to the reduction of the share capital of a company shall, except as provided in this section and s 207(2) of the Companies Act 1990[282] apply as if the share premium account were paid up share capital of the company.'

Accordingly, where shares are issued at a premium it is not the full consideration received which must be paid into the share premium account, only the amount received which is in excess of the nominal value of the shares. Monies held in a company's share premium account are not available for distribution[283].

[10.112] A company's *share premium account* may be utilised in any of the four circumstances provided for in s 62(2) of the CA 1963, namely:

- in paying up unissued shares of the company (other than redeemable shares) to be allotted to members of the company as fully paid bonus shares[284];
- in writing off the preliminary expenses of the company;
- in writing off the expenses of, or the commission paid or discount allowed on, any issue of shares or debentures of the company;
- in providing for the premium payable on redemption of any redeemable preference shares in pursuance of s 220 of the CA 1990, or of any debentures of the company.

In *Henry Head & Co Ltd v Ropner Holdings Ltd*[285], the defendant company was incorporated for the acquisition, for amalgamation purposes, of two shipping companies which had previously been carried on separately under the same management. The means employed was that the shareholders in the two shipping companies sold their shares in exchange for shares in the new holding company. Each shareholder got one new share in the new holding company in exchange for each old share in the shipping companies. In consequence, although the new holding company had an authorised and issued share capital of £1,719,606, the real value of the shares was approximately £7m because the shares in each of the two companies were worth more than the nominal value of their shares. In these circumstances the directors were advised that the sum of circa £5m had to be placed in the company's share premium account. The directors of the company objected to this because they were seriously fettered in their use of this money by virtue of the equivalent UK provision to s 62 of the CA 1963. Although Harman J was willing to limit the operation of the section he was constrained by the clear wording of the section and said:

---

282 See para **[10.041]**.

283 In *Shearer (Inspector of Taxes) v Bercain Ltd* [1980] 3 All ER 295, it was held that monies paid into a holding company's share premium account after the holding company issued its shares (nominal value of £4,100) in return for the entire issued share capital in two other companies (worth £96,000) were not distributable by the holding company. This was so although most of the value in the shares of the other two companies represented undistributable profits. Because it was held that the money in the share premium account was not distributable, this money was not taxable. See Ussher, 'Doubts Remain on *Shearer v Bercain*' (1982) 3 Co Law 28.

284 On bonus shares see Ch 8, *Shares and Membership*, para **[8.114]**.

285 *Henry Head & Co Ltd v Ropner Holdings Ltd* [1952] Ch 124.

> 'I have every desire to reduce the effect of this section to what I cannot help thinking would be more reasonable limits, but I do not see my way of limiting it in that way. It is not stated to be a section which only applies after the company has been in existence a year or after the company has acquired assets or when the company is a going concern, or which does not apply on the occasion of a holding company buying shares on an amalgamation. Whether that is an oversight on the part of the legislature or whether it was intended to produce the effect it seems to have produced, is not for me to speculate. All I can say is that this transaction seems to me to come within the words of the section, and I do not see my way to holding as a matter of construction that it is outside it.'

Since s 62 of the CA 1963 is identical in all material respects to the section under consideration, s 56 of the Companies Act 1948 (UK), it is thought that an Irish court would be bound to follow this decision[286]. In Ireland, however, the provisions of s 149(5) of the CA 1963 should be noted[287]. This states that the profits and losses attributable to any shares in a subsidiary held by its holding company may be treated in the holding company's accounts as revenue profits or losses, *provided that* the directors and the auditors of the company are satisfied and so certify that it is fair and reasonable and does not prejudice the rights and interests of any person.

286 Section 56 of the Companies Act 1948 (UK) was modified by s 37 of the Companies Act 1981 (UK) to provide an exemption in these circumstances.

287 See also Ch 17, *Financial Statements, Audit & Annual Returns*, para **[17.194]**.

Chapter 11

Shareholders' Remedies

Introduction to shareholders' remedies

[11.001] This chapter is concerned with situations where relations between shareholders and directors, and between shareholders *inter se*, break down. In company law there exists a general rule, known as 'the rule in *Foss v Harbottle*', which states that where a company is wronged, the only person who can sue to redress that wrong is the company. This can cause considerable difficulty for minority shareholders where the directors and a majority of the other shareholders refuse to sue to redress the wrong to the company. The rationale of the rule is that the will of the majority of the shareholders ought to prevail. In a private company, particularly where the shareholders can be said to be quasi-partners, majority rule is more difficult to justify. It is for this reason that s 205 of the Companies Act 1963 ('CA 1963') has become the most important shareholders' remedy, allowing shareholders to seek redress from the courts in cases where they are oppressed or their interests are disregarded. Section 205 allows petitioners to avoid the artificialities of the rule in *Foss v Harbottle* as it applies to private companies. In this work s 205 is elevated from being a mere statutory exception to the rule in *Foss v Harbottle* to being centre stage in this discussion of shareholders' remedies. It should, in addition, be remembered that there are other remedies available to shareholders as follows:

(a) Petitioning to wind up on just and equitable grounds.
(b) Miscellaneous statutory remedies in particular situations.
(c) Shareholders' personal rights.

(a) Petitioning to wind up on just and equitable grounds

[11.002] Another remedy, potentially more potent than s 205 of the CA 1963, that is also available to disgruntled shareholders, is to petition the court to have the company wound up on *just and equitable* grounds under s 213(f) of the CA 1963. Frequently, application is made to the High Court under ss 205 and 213(f) in 'double-harness'. Section 213(f) of the CA 1963 and the principles of winding up on just and equitable grounds are considered in Ch 23[1].

(b) Miscellaneous statutory remedies in particular situations

[11.003] The Companies Acts afford several statutory remedies to shareholders in particular situations, primarily those involving serious constitutional changes and capital

[1] See Ch 23, *Winding Up Companies*, para **[23.091]** *et seq.*

reorganisations. Shareholders may apply to court for relief in the following instances, all of which are considered elsewhere in this book:

- on the alteration of the objects clause[2];
- on the alteration of the articles of association, whether in respect of individual members' rights[3] or class rights;
- on the provision of financial assistance in connection with the purchase of a company's own shares[4];
- on the entering into of a guarantee or the provision of security in connection with a loan, quasi-loan or credit transaction in favour of a 'relevant person'[5];
- in a scheme of arrangement[6];
- in a reconstruction on a voluntary liquidation[7]; and
- on the compulsory acquisition of shares[8].

(c) Shareholders' personal rights

[11.004] Finally, by virtue of their membership of a company, shareholders have *personal rights* by virtue of the articles of association and the Companies Acts. These rights are enforceable by the shareholders personally, and the rule in *Foss v Harbottle* does not apply to such actions. The personal rights of shareholders have been considered in Ch 8 above[9]; but in this chapter the rights of members to vindicate their personal rights are distinguished from the rule in *Foss v Harbottle*.

[11.005] The primary shareholders' remedies, which are considered in this chapter, are addressed as follows:

[A] Oppression and Disregard of Interests.
[B] The Rule in *Foss v Harbottle*.
[C] Derivative Actions and Exceptions to *Foss v Harbottle*.

[A] Oppression and Disregard of Interests[10]

[11.006] Section 205 of the CA 1963 provides a company's shareholders with their most powerful and far-reaching remedy against the company and its directors in cases of oppression and disregard of their interests. This statutory remedy was first introduced in Ireland in 1963 and, despite the dearth of early cases, has established itself today as the

2 Ch 3, *Constitutional Documentation*, para **[3.026]**.
3 Ch 3, *Constitutional Documentation*, para **[3.056]**.
4 Ch 10, *The Maintenance of Capital*, para **[10.077]**.
5 Ch 16, *Statutory Regulation of Directors' Transactions*, para **[16.083]**.
6 Ch 21, *Schemes of Arrangement and Reconstructions*, para **[21.050]** *et seq.*
7 Ch 21, *Schemes of Arrangement and Reconstructions*, para **[21.067]**.
8 Ch 9, *Share Transfer*, para **[9.087]** *et seq.*
9 Ch 8, *Shares and Membership*, para **[8.087]**.
10 See generally, MacCann, 'Minority Shareholder Protection: Sections 205 and 213(f) of the Companies Act, 1963' (1995) Dli – The Western Law Gazette 85.

remedy most frequently resorted to by shareholders[11]. Many cases[12] demonstrate the effectiveness of s 205 actions in cases where relationships in quasi-partnership companies have broken down. Section 205 is of particular utility where the members of a quasi-partnership type private company fail to cater prospectively for their relations in a shareholders' agreement[13].

[11.007] Section 205(1) of the CA 1963 provides:

> 'Any member of a company who complains that the affairs of the company are being conducted or that the powers of the directors of the company are being exercised in a manner oppressive to him or any of the members (including himself), or in disregard of his or their interests as members, may apply to the court for an order under this section.'

This subsection demonstrates the fundamental objective of s 205: to provide members with relief where the *affairs of the company or the powers of the directors* are being conducted or exercised *oppressively or in disregard of their interests*. Here, s 205 shall be considered in the following manner:

1. The nature of the remedy.
2. Oppression.
3. Disregarding members' interests.
4. 'Affairs of the company' and 'powers of directors'.
5. Quasi-partnership companies and 'legitimate expectations'.
6. The *locus standi* to petition.
7. Abuse of process and inordinate delay in prosecuting petitions.
8. The position of the company.
9. *In camera* applications.
10. Remedies: restraining the removal of a shareholding-director.
11. Remedies: ending the matters complained of.
12. Costs of the petition.
13. The unfairly prejudicial remedy contrasted.
14. Contracting-out of s 205.

The nature of the remedy

[11.008] Section 205 of the CA 1963 may be resorted to in a wide variety of situations. In the context of quasi-partnership private companies, perhaps the paradigm situation in which s 205 is invoked is where one or more of the quasi-partner-members believes that the affairs of the company or the powers of the directors are being exercised *oppressively*, or in *disregard of his interests*. Of course s 205 has a wider application, and any member, whether he is a quasi-partner or not, can make application under the section. Where it is shown to the court's satisfaction that s 205 relief is available, the

---

11 See generally, Temple-Lang, 'Minority Shareholder Protection Under Irish Law' (1974) NILQ 387.

12 Such as *Colgan v Colgan* (22 July 1993, unreported) HC and *Irish Press plc v Ingersoll Irish Publications Ltd* (15 December 1993, unreported) HC.

13 *Cf Irish Press plc v Ingersoll Irish Publications* (15 December 1993, unreported) HC, where there was in fact a substantial shareholders' agreement in existence.

court has wide powers. Accordingly, the court is empowered to order any of the following courses of action:

- that the oppressor buy the petitioner's shares;
- that the petitioner buy the oppressor's shares;
- that the company buy either party's shares;
- that the company's memorandum and/or articles of association are amended to provide as the court directs; or
- that the company be wound up.

These remedies are considered below[14].

[11.009] Section 205 petitions are a messy and expensive business. Putative petitioners would do well to heed the words of Murphy J in *Re Murray Consultants Ltd and Nocrumb Ltd; Horgan v Murray and Milton*[15] where he said:

> 'It has been observed before that there is a surprising parallel between matrimonial proceedings and proceedings under section 205 of the 1963 Act[16]. They both involve an examination of the conduct of the parties over a period of years and usually a determination by them to assert rights rather than solve problems. It may well be that the disparate forms of litigation are frequently fuelled by a bitterness borne of rejection: matrimonial or commercial. In neither discipline can the courts persuade the parties that it is in their best interests to direct their attention to solving their problems rather than litigating them.'

Oppression

[11.010] At this point, the concept of oppression is considered. The study of oppression involves the consideration of a number of matters:

(a) The test for oppression.
(b) Oppression need not be *qua* member.
(c) Isolated acts of oppression.
(d) Fraudulent and unlawful transactions.
(e) Oppressive management.
(f) Exclusion from management.
(g) Non-consultation with shareholders.
(h) Technical oppression.

(a) The test for oppression

[11.011] The concept of *oppression* is relatively new in company law, having first being introduced by the Companies Act 1948 (UK). In *Re Greenore Trading Company Ltd*[17], Keane J acknowledged that 'oppressive conduct' for the purposes of the corresponding

[14] At para **[11.073]**.

[15] *Re Murray Consultants Ltd and Nocrumb Ltd; Horgan v Murray and Milton* [1997] 3 IR 29 at 42.

[16] Sentiment echoed by O'Flaherty J in *New Ad Advertising Ltd* (26 March 1998, unreported) SC at p 3.

[17] *Re Greenore Trading Company Ltd* [1980] ILRM 94 at 100–101.

s 210 of the English 1948 Act meant the exercise of the company's authority '... in a manner burdensome, harsh and wrongful'[18].

Acceptance of this definition of oppressive conduct is seen in the judgment of Viscount Simonds in *Scottish Co-operative Wholesale Society Ltd v Meyer*[19]. In that case, a subsidiary company was formed by a co-operative society, in which the plaintiff company became a minority shareholder. The plaintiff became a minority shareholder in the subsidiary to facilitate the co-operative society because without the plaintiff's involvement a licence would have been required for the manufacture of raylon. When the law relating to such licences changed, the co-operative no longer needed the plaintiff as a minority shareholder and it sought to buy the plaintiff's shares. When the plaintiff refused to sell its shares, the co-operative transferred the subsidiary's business into its own name, rendering the subsidiary's shares valueless. The plaintiff succeeded in its action under s 210 of the Companies Act 1948 (UK) and the court ordered that the co-operative buy out the plaintiff's shares at the value they would have been, had the subsidiary's assets not been dissipated. In the course of his judgment, Viscount Simonds said:

> '... it appears to me incontrovertible that the society have behaved to the minority shareholders of the company in a manner which can justly be described as "oppressive". They had the majority power and they exercised their authority in a manner "burdensome, harsh and wrongful" – I take the dictionary meaning of the word.'[20]

In *Re Greenore Trading Company Ltd*[21], a company had three shareholders – the petitioner, a Mr Boyle and a Mr Vanlandeghem – each of whom owned 8,000 £1 shares. Shortly after the company was formed, a resolution was passed that no one shareholder should hold more than 8,000 shares in the company. Some years later, when the company was encountering financial difficulties, Vanlandeghem contributed £10,000 to it in return for a further 10,000 shares in the company. Subsequently, Boyle agreed to sell his shares to Vanlandeghem for £22,500, made up of £8,000 from Vanlandeghem, being par value for the shares, and £14,500 from the company as a severance payment. The petitioner brought proceedings under s 205 claiming that Vanlandeghem was using his control of the company in a manner that was oppressive. The petitioner sought, *inter alia*, the winding up of the company or an order requiring the oppressor to buy his shares. Keane J noted that the payment by the company of the £14,500 was contrary to s 60 of the CA 1963 and 'constituted conduct of such a nature as to justify, and indeed require, the making of an order under s 205(3)'[22]. Through his influence, Vanlandeghem had caused the company to part with its assets to provide indirect financial assistance to enable him purchase the company's shares. As Keane J said:

18 In *Re Charles Kelly Ltd; Kelly v Kelly & Kelly (No 2)* [2011] IEHC 349, Laffoy J noted that this had come to be the established meaning of oppression.

19 *Scottish Co-operative Wholesale Society Ltd v Meyer* [1959] AC 324.

20 *Scottish Co-operative Wholesale Society Ltd v Meyer* [1959] AC 324 at 342. For a recent case concerning alleged 'unfairly prejudicial' conduct in the context of parent companies and their subsidiaries, see *Nicholas v Soundcraft Electronics Ltd* [1993] BCLC 360.

21 *Re Greenore Trading Company Ltd* [1980] ILRM 94.

22 *Re Greenore Trading Company Ltd* [1980] ILRM 94 at 100.

'The patent misapplication of the company's monies for the purpose of giving Mr Vanlandeghem a dominant position in its affairs seems to me to be properly described as "burdensome, harsh and wrongful" *quoad* the petitioner[23].'

[11.012] An objective standard will be used in determining whether particular conduct should be deemed to be burdensome, harsh and wrongful. In the first Irish case to consider s 205 of the CA 1963, *Re Irish Visiting Motorists' Bureau Ltd*[24], Kenny J said:

'The affairs of a company may be conducted or the powers of the directors may be exercised in a manner oppressive to any of the members although those in charge of the company are acting honestly and in good faith. If one defines oppression as harsh conduct or depriving a person of rights to which he is entitled, the person whose conduct is in question may believe that he is exercising his rights in doing what he does. One of the most terrifying aspects of human history is that many of those whom we now regard as having been oppressors had a fanatical belief in the rightness of what they were doing. The question then when deciding whether the conduct of the affairs of a company or the passing of a resolution is oppressive is whether, judged by objective standards, it is.'[25]

The foregoing passage also makes clear that it is not necessary for the court to make any finding of *wrongdoing* in order to uphold a complaint under s 205, as was recently noted by Finlay Geoghegan J *Emerald Group Holdings Ltd & Banfi Ltd v Moran et al*[26].

[11.013] Although the conduct complained of is to be judged by objective standards, what will be oppressive will vary from company to company. What might be oppressive in the context of a quasi-partnership company may not be oppressive in a private company with unconnected membership. In *Crindle Investments v Wymes*[27], it was held that the rejection of offers to compromise proceedings in circumstances where such constituted 'an improvident gamble' amounted to oppression and a disregard of the interests of other shareholders within the meaning of s 205 of the CA 1963. In *Re Charles Kelly Ltd*; *Kelly v Kelly & Kelly (No 2)*[28], Laffoy J said:

'11.5 Objectively assessing the evidence in support of the petitioner's allegations of oppression, which has been comprehensively outlined above, must lead to the conclusion that the "burdensome, harsh and wrongful" test has been met in this case. The first respondent's conduct in purporting to suspend the petitioner, in whatever capacity, from the company, on its own, meets the test. Taking an overall view of the evidence, and having regard to the combination of factors relied on by the petitioner as constituting oppression, in my view, the test is met. While, as I have indicated, the petitioner's conduct, to put it mildly, has been reprehensible on occasion, I have come to the conclusion that, to some extent, but not totally, that conduct is excusable because the petitioner was provoked by the first respondent.

11.6 Apart from that, as has been clearly illustrated, there has been a total breakdown of the relationship between the petitioner and the first respondent in every capacity in which they are involved with the company, as executives, as shareholders and as directors and I

---

23 *Re Greenore Trading Company Ltd* [1980] ILRM 94 at 101.

24 *Re Irish Visiting Motorists' Bureau Ltd* (7 February 1972, unreported) HC.

25 *Re Irish Visiting Motorists' Bureau Ltd* (7 February 1972, unreported) HC at p 33.

26 *Emerald Group Holdings Ltd & Banfi Ltd v Moran et al* [2009] IEHC 440, Finlay Geoghegan J.

27 *Crindle Investments v Wymes* [1998] 4 IR 578 at 582 where Keane J noted an earlier decision of Murphy J in the High Court (at p 7).

28 *Re Charles Kelly Ltd; Kelly v Kelly & Kelly (No 2)* [2011] IEHC 349.

find that the first respondent must bear most of the responsibility for that state of affairs. This is not mere "technical oppression" in the sense in which that expression is used in Courtney (*op cit*) at para 19.027. It is a state of affairs which has been primarily brought about by the conduct of the first respondent.

11.7 Accordingly, prior to listing the matter for further hearing on 9th February 2011, I had made the following findings of which the parties were informed at the hearing on that day:

(a) that the first respondent has exercised his powers as a director of the company in a manner oppressive to the petitioner within the meaning of s 205(1), and

(b) that there has been a total breakdown in the relationship of the petitioner and the first respondent at every level, both business and personal, that they are deadlocked to the extent that they are incapable of running the company properly together and that the situation is irretrievable and requires to be remedied by the Court in accordance with s 205(3) or otherwise.'

(b) Oppression need not be qua member

[11.014] One of the many problems with s 210 of the Companies Act 1948 (UK) was that the oppression suffered by a member had to be suffered by him in his capacity as a member, or *qua member*. This was established by a series of cases[29]. However, the provision which replaced s 210 – s 459 of the Companies Act 1985 (UK) – has been afforded a wider interpretation[30]. Further, in Ireland, s 205(1) of the CA 1963 provides that the court can grant relief where a member proves that the affairs of the company are being conducted, or that the powers of the directors of the company are being exercised, in a manner oppressive to him or *any of the members* (including himself).

[11.015] Implicit authority for the proposition that oppression can be suffered by a member in his capacity *as a director* is found in *Re Murph's Restaurants Ltd*[31]. The facts of this case are considered in detail in Ch 23[32]. Of interest here is the fact that the petitioner's claim was based on his oppression in his capacity as a director of the

[29] Eg, *Elder v Elder* (1952) SC 49; *Re Lundie Brothers Ltd* [1965] 1 WLR 1051; and *Re Westbourne Galleries Ltd* [1971] 2 WLR 618.

[30] See, eg, *Tay Bok Choon v Tahanson Sdn Bhd* [1987] BCLC 472 and *R & H Electrical Ltd v Haden Bill Electrical Ltd* [1995] 2 BCLC 280. *Cf Re JE Cade & Son Ltd* [1992] BCLC 213 where Warner J refused to make an order under s 459 of the Companies Act 1985 (UK) where the company concerned occupied a farm owned by a minority shareholder and refused to deliver up possession. See also *Re Alchemea Ltd* [1998] BCC 964 where it was found that any alleged unfairly prejudicial conduct did not affect the petitioner's interests as a member in any material respect in circumstances where the company had been established as a cooperative under which members, like employees, could hope to derive nothing but wages, discretionary bonuses and expenses. In *Gamlestaden Fastigheter AB v Baltic Partners Ltd et al* [2007] 4 All ER 164, the Privy Council held that Jersey law that was substantially identical to s 459 did not preclude the grant of relief simply on the ground that the relief would not benefit an applicant in his capacity as member where the purpose of the application was to have money lost due to mismanagement repaid to the company in order to make it available to the member but in his capacity as a creditor of the company.

[31] *Re Murph's Restaurants Ltd* [1979] ILRM 141. See Ussher, 'Company Law – Oppression, Justice and Equity' (1979–80) DULJ 92.

[32] See Ch 23, *Winding Up Companies*, para **[23.094]**.

company. At the interlocutory hearing McWilliam J refused the order seeking to have the company wound up, saying that ss 205 and 213(g) of the CA 1963 only apply to members in their capacity as members. In that case the petitioner was both a shareholder and a director of the company. His complaint was, *inter alia*, that he was removed as a director of the company by the other two directors. At the actual hearing of the action Gannon J did not doubt his jurisdiction to make an order under s 205, although in the circumstances he ordered that the company be wound up under s 213(f) of the CA 1963[33]. A definitive judicial statement from the Irish courts is awaited on this point, but it is thought on a literal interpretation of s 205(1) that it will be found that relief for oppression is not confined to members acting *qua* member.

(c) Isolated acts of oppression

[11.016] It is now generally accepted that an isolated act of oppression can give rise to relief under s 205 of the CA 1963: *Re Williams Group Tullamore Ltd*[34], *per* Barrington J. Often, the matters complained of can be said to be ongoing. In the *Williams* case, Barrington J said:

> '... in the present case we are dealing with a transaction which is ongoing at the date of the hearing of this petition in the sense that it is one which will be implemented if the petitioners do not obtain the relief they are seeking[35].'

In that case the company's authorised share capital was divided into 250,000 ordinary shares of £1 each and 150,000 8% preference shares of £1 each. There were 133,540 ordinary shares and 133,540 preference shares issued in the company. On the basis of the rights attaching to both classes of share, the ordinary shareholders fared much better than the preference shareholders on foot of the dividend paid. The company's directors decided to adjust the position by allowing the preference shareholders to participate in the profits of the company and a resolution was passed in general meeting to make a distribution of £267,000 between all of the shareholders. The ordinary shareholders, who could not vote at this meeting, petitioned the court on the grounds that the preference shareholders' actions were oppressive.

Barrington J held that the petitioners were entitled to relief under s 205 of the CA 1963 because, although it could not be said that the ordinary shareholders were oppressed, the transaction was in objective disregard to the ordinary shareholders' interests. As authority for the proposition that an isolated transaction can give rise to relief under s 205 of the CA 1963, Barrington J cited the judgment of Kenny J in *Re*

---

33 In *R & H Electrical Ltd and another v Haden Bill Electrical Ltd* [1995] 2 BCLC 280, the petitioner claimed to have been unfairly prejudiced by reason of his having been removed as a director in circumstances where a company controlled by the petitioner was a creditor of the subject company and was prejudiced. Robert Walker J said that the court should take a broad view of the petitioner's interest when considering the capacity in which a petitioner complained. There, it was found that the petitioner had a 'legitimate expectation' (see para **[11.035]**) of being able to participate in the management of the company for as long as the loan was outstanding to his company.

34 *Re Williams Group Tullamore Ltd* [1985] IR 613. *Cf Re Westbourne Galleries Ltd* [1970] 3 All ER 374 and *Re Greenore Trading Company Ltd* [1980] ILRM 94.

35 *Re Williams Group Tullamore Ltd* [1985] IR 613 at 620.

Westwinds Holding Company Ltd[36]. In the *Westwinds* case, considered below, the sale of the company's assets was found to constitute oppression. After reciting the first in a series of acts by the oppressor, Kenny J said:

> 'The sale of the lands at Knocknacarra was an exercise by the directors of their powers in a manner which was fraudulent and oppressive to the petitioner and was in total disregard of his interest as a member of the company. On *this ground alone* the conditions for the exercise of the powers of the court under s 205(3) have been fulfilled[37].'

By way of contrast, in *Re Greenore Trading Company Ltd*[38] Keane J said that an isolated act of oppression will not normally be sufficient to justify relief[39]. He overcame that requirement in that case by finding 'a multiplicity of unlawfulness in the same one act in order to raise it to the level of oppressive conduct'[40]. Although sometimes a distinction is drawn between lawful and unlawful actions, it is thought that such a distinction is artificial and that an isolated act of oppression or disregard of members' interests will be sufficient to grant relief[41].

(d) Fraudulent and unlawful transactions

[11.017] *Re Westwinds Holding Company Ltd*[42] provides one of the most vivid and dramatic examples of a case in which the Irish High Court found the petitioner to have been oppressed. The facts of the case are worthy of extensive summary. The company in question was incorporated in 1964 to take over the business of builders and public works contractors carried on by a Martin Hession, the promoter and defendant in the subsequent action. The company's articles of association provided for the appointment of a 'governing director', Hession, and went on to give him weighted voting rights. Two shares were issued in the company, one in Hession's name and one in another person's name. The following year Hession held discussions with the petitioner, on foot of which the second shareholder transferred her share to the petitioner who in turn was appointed director and the company secretary. Subsequently, at the offices of a solicitor, the petitioner, Hession and an auditor met. The solicitor made a written record of what transpired, and Kenny J noted that it had been agreed, *inter alia*, that 4,998 shares were to be issued to Hession in return for assets which were to become the company's property; 4,999 shares were to be issued to the petitioner for cash; Hession was to become chairman and the petitioner the company secretary; that there was to be no governing director; and that Hession and the petitioner were to be permanent directors. The company subsequently acquired three acres of land at Knocknacarra, Galway. Some time later two of these three acres were sold to a company in which Hession owned almost all the shares. The deed of transfer to that company bore the seal of Westwinds Holding Company Ltd but the petitioner's signature had been forged by Hession. The two acres were again sold on to another company in which Hession was the owner of

36 *Re Westwinds Holding Company Ltd* (21 May 1974, unreported) HC.

37 *Re Westwinds Holding Company Ltd* (21 May 1974, unreported) HC at p 17. Emphasis added.

38 *Re Greenore Trading Company Ltd* [1980] ILRM 94 at 101.

39 Citing *Re Westbourne Galleries* [1970] 1 WLR 1378.

40 Ussher, *Company Law in Ireland* (1985), p 261.

41 Ussher, *Company Law in Ireland* (1985), p 261.

42 *Re Westwinds Holding Company Ltd* (21 May 1974, unreported) HC.

most of the shares. Subsequently, Hession disposed of his shares in that company to another individual for £15,000.

There was also a second transaction, whereby Hession caused Westwinds Holding Company Ltd to guarantee the overdraft of another company owned indirectly by him. Hession provided the bank concerned with a minute of a meeting, purportedly signed by Hession and the petitioner. Kenny J accepted that the petitioner's signature was a forgery. Even the prescribed form used to deliver to the CRO particulars of the equitable charge created by the company contained the forged signature of the petitioner. Kenny J said that he was:

> '... convinced that the petitioner would never have agreed to the creation of this charge and that he did not get notice of the meeting because Mr Martin Hession wished to conceal the business being transacted.'[43]

A number of meetings were purportedly held, the minutes of which were not signed by the petitioner. Finally, Hession purported to hold a meeting appointing himself company secretary and removing the petitioner as secretary and director of the company.

[11.018] Kenny J found that the sale of the lands at Knocknacarra was made at a gross undervalue 'and was a fraud on the other member of the company' and that the 'sale benefited Mr Martin Hession only at the expense of the company and the petitioner'[44]. As has been noted above[45], Kenny J held that this ground alone was adequate to justify an order under s 205 of the CA 1963(3). Similarly, the mortgage created by the company was not for the benefit of the company or the petitioner, but was to Hession's benefit. Again this was found to be an exercise of the directors' powers which was oppressive to the petitioner, being in total disregard of his interest as a member. Kenny J held that the appropriate remedy was to make an order directing Hession to purchase the petitioner's shares, to be valued on the basis that the lands sold were still the property of the company, and without regard to the fact that there existed restrictions on the transfer of shares in the company.

[11.019] Conduct does not need to be unlawful to be oppressive. In *Re Clubman Shirts Ltd*[46], O'Hanlon J found that the petitioner had been oppressed notwithstanding that the respondents had not acted unlawfully[47].

(e) Oppressive management

[11.020] It is sometimes said that mere incompetence or mismanagement of a company's affairs will not *per se* amount to oppression within the meaning of s 205 of the CA 1963. An authority in point is *Re Five Minute Car Wash Service Ltd*[48]. In that case the petitioner, who was a former director of the company, took proceedings under s 210 of the Companies Act 1948 (UK). The petitioner alleged that the managing

---

43 *Re Westwinds Holding Company Ltd* (21 May 1974, unreported) HC at p 12.

44 *Re Westwinds Holding Company Ltd* (21 May 1974, unreported) HC at pp 16, 17.

45 See para **[11.016]**.

46 *Re Clubman Shirts Ltd* [1983] ILRM 323.

47 There had been a number of breaches of the Companies Acts such as failure to file accounts, hold annual general meetings and to furnish copies of the register of members and accounts, however such were found not to amount to oppression ([1983] ILRM 323 at 325).

48 *Re Five Minute Car Wash Service Ltd* [1966] 1 All ER 242.

director conducted the affairs of the company with complete disregard of the interests of any shareholders other than his wife and himself. Buckley J refused to find that there was oppression because, *inter alia*, even if the managing director was unwise, inefficient and careless in the performance of his duties as managing director there was no suggestion that he had acted unscrupulously, unfairly or with any lack of probity or had overborne or disregarded the wishes of the board of directors or that his conduct was harsh, burdensome or wrongful towards any member of the company.

[11.021] In *Re Clubman Shirts Ltd*[49] O'Hanlon J held:

> 'I would not classify as oppressive conduct within the meaning of the Act, the omission to comply with the various provisions of the Act referable to the holding of general meetings and the furnishing of information and copy documents. These were examples of negligence, carelessness, irregularity in the conduct of the affairs of the company, but the evidence does not suggest that these defaults or any of them formed part of a deliberate scheme to deprive the petitioner of his rights or to cause him loss or damage[50].'

Similarly in *McCormick v Cameo Investments Ltd*[51], McWilliam J held that mere mismanagement by the directors of the company was not sufficient to constitute oppression. In contrast, in *Re a Company (No 00789 of 1987) ex p Shooter*[52], Harman J held that a repeated failure to hold annual general meetings and to lay accounts before the members was conduct unfairly prejudicial to the interests of all the members. It is thought that irregularity in the conduct of a company's affairs will be oppressive where it is part of a *deliberate* scheme.

[11.022] One of the most striking cases of tyranny in the management of a company is *Re Harmer*[53]. In that case the sons of an octogenarian, Harmer Snr, who had incorporated his successful stamp-dealing business, grew increasingly frustrated by his totalitarian management of the company in which they were shareholders. Harmer Snr was deemed to be the company's 'governing director', but the office had no special or distinctive rights or powers. The sons alleged that Harmer Snr ran the business as if he owned it himself, disregarding the resolutions and wishes of the board of directors and the interests of the shareholders. An example of his actions was that he unilaterally, and against the wishes of the directors, founded an unprofitable branch of the business in Australia. The Harmer sons succeeded both at trial and in the Court of Appeal in establishing that there had been oppression.

[11.023] In *Irish Press plc v Ingersoll Irish Publications Ltd*[54], the respondent was found to have acted in furtherance of its own agenda in managing the subject company. The background to the case was that in 1989 the petitioner and respondent agreed to enter into a partnership to manage three newspapers, *The Irish Press*, *The Evening Press* and *The Sunday Press*. To that end two companies were formed – Irish Press Newspapers Ltd and Irish Press Publications Ltd – in which the petitioner and respondent held equal

---

49 *Re Clubman Shirts Ltd* [1983] ILRM 323.

50 *Re Clubman Shirts Ltd* [1983] ILRM 323 at 327.

51 *McCormick v Cameo Investments Ltd* [1978] ILRM 191.

52 *Re a Company (No 00789 of 1987) ex p Shooter* [1990] BCLC 384.

53 *Re HR Harmer Ltd* [1958] 3 All ER 689.

54 *Irish Press plc v Ingersoll Irish Publications Ltd* (15 December 1993, unreported) HC.

shareholdings. The parties also entered into a subscription and shareholders' agreement and a management agreement. Under the management agreement the respondent was engaged by Irish Press Newspapers Ltd. Although the relationship was initially good, it deteriorated and culminated in the petitioner instituting proceedings under s 205 of the CA 1963. The petitioner claimed, *inter alia*, that although management services ceased to be provided by the respondent, the respondent insisted upon the continuance of the management agreement; the respondent acted in furtherance of its own interests and contrary to the interests of the subject companies; and the respondent had acted oppressively towards the petitioner. In a lengthy judgment, Barron J found that the respondent had acted oppressively. Having quoted extensively from the case of *Scottish Cooperative Wholesale Society v Meyer*[55] he held that there were parallels between it and the case in hand and that:

> 'What it shows is that where a deliberate plan to damage the interests of a company is carried out by a shareholder in the manner by which it exercises its power to conduct the affairs of the company, such behaviour is oppression ...
>
> Here there is also a deliberate plan. Though it was not a plan to destroy the business of the company, it was a plan of action against the interests of the petitioner and was carried out by the manner in which the affairs of the companies were exercised[56].'

The failure by the respondent to properly operate the management agreement, which was held to be a repudiation of the agreement, was central to the finding of oppression. Barron J went on to hold that after the management agreement had come to an end:

> '... insistence that it still subsisted was oppression. But the real *complaint was the de facto* take over of the companies. This in reality was the placing in position of nominees by the respondent for the purpose of the interests of the respondent and not in the interests of the company. That is also oppression. Neither was done *bona fide*. Both were done in wilful disregard of the interests of the companies[57].'

Barron J ordered the respondent to sell its shares in the companies to the petitioner at a price to be determined by the court[58]. Although on appeal to the Supreme Court it was held that damages could not be awarded pursuant to s 205(3) of the CA 1963, the foregoing findings were not disturbed.

[11.024] One particular issue in petitions alleging oppression in the management of a company concerns the position of *nominee directors*[59]. The duty of nominee directors was considered in the judgment of Viscount Simonds in *Scottish Cooperative Wholesale Society v Meyer*[60], which was cited with approval by Barron J in *Irish Press plc v Ingersoll Irish Publications Ltd* above. Viscount Simonds, in a passage quoted by Barron J[61], said that nominee directors were not entitled to remain silent and inactive

---

55 *Scottish Cooperative Wholesale Society v Meyer* [1959] AC 324.

56 *Irish Press plc v Ingersoll Irish Publications Ltd* (15 December 1993, unreported) HC at pp 79, 80.

57 *Irish Press plc v Ingersoll Irish Publications Ltd* (15 December 1993, unreported) HC at p 81.

58 See *Irish Press plc v Ingersoll Irish Publications Ltd* (13 May 1994, unreported) HC, *per* Barron J. See Ch 9, *Share Transfer*, para **[9.133]**.

59 See generally Ch 15, *Duties of Directors and Other Officers*, para **[15.045]** *et seq.*

60 *Scottish Cooperative Wholesale Society v Meyer* [1959] AC 324.

61 *Irish Press plc v Ingersoll Irish Publications Ltd* (13 May 1994, unreported) HC at p 77.

with full knowledge of the majority shareholder's intention to strip the company of its assets. He said:

> 'They were the nominees of the Society and, if the Society doomed the Company to destruction, it was not for them to put out a saving hand. Rather, they were to join in that work, and, when a frank and prompt statement to their co-Directors might have enabled them to retrieve its fortunes, they played their part by maintaining silence. That is how they conducted the affairs of the Company, and it is impossible to suppose that that was not part of the deliberate policy of the Society. As I have said, nominees of a parent Company upon the Board of a subsidiary company may be placed in a difficult and delicate position. It is, then, the more incumbent on the parent company to behave with scrupulous fairness to the minority shareholders and to avoid imposing upon their nominees the alternative of disregarding their instructions or betraying the interests of the minority. In the present case the Society pursued a different course. It was ruthless and unscrupulous in design and it was effective in operation, and, as I have said, it was promoted by the action or inaction of the nominee directors[62].'

Commenting on the nominee directors appointed by the respondent in the *Irish Press plc* case, Barron J said:

> 'The position of nominee directors can be a difficult one if they disagree with the views of the person or body appointing them. Their duty is to act in the interests of the company. They have also got a duty to act on the instructions of their nominating party. But acting in the interests of the company is no more than acting in the interests of all its shareholders. If what they are asked to do involves seeking to damage the interests of one section of the shareholders in favour of another then as a director they have a duty not to do that. However, if what they are required to do is merely something that they themselves personally think is not the way to approach the matter then they must give way. There is nothing wrong with the appointing body or party from having a view as to where the interests of the company lie and ensuring that its nominees follow that direction provided that in so doing they are not seeking to damage anybody else's interest in the company.'

Nominee directors are frequently appointed to the boards of joint-venture companies, which can sometimes be found to be quasi-partnership companies. Barron J's comments in this regard are extremely instructive and are cautionary words for both nominee directors and for those who appoint them[63].

(f) Exclusion from management

[11.025] To exclude a director from the management of the company can amount to oppression in certain circumstances. This is apparent from the decision of Gannon J in *Re Murph's Restaurants Ltd*[64] where he said '... the purported exclusion of [the petitioner] by the [respondents] in an irregular and arrogant manner is undoubtedly oppressive'[65].

In that case, the respondent directors had resolved to dismiss the petitioner as a director of the company, offering him three months' salary. In *Re Ghyll Beck Driving Range Ltd*[66], it was held that a petitioner (a shareholding director) who had been

62 *Scottish Cooperative Wholesale Society v Meyer* [1959] AC 324 at 341.

63 See further Ch 15, *Duties of Directors and Other Officers*, para **[15.047]** *et seq.*

64 *Re Murph's Restaurants Ltd* [1979] ILRM 141.

65 *Re Murph's Restaurants Ltd* [1979] ILRM 141 at 152.

66 *Re Ghyll Beck Driving Range Ltd* [1993] BCLC 1126.

excluded from a joint venture, which it was contemplated would be managed by all four participants, was unjustly excluded and that his exclusion had destroyed the trust between the parties[67]. It is believed that in similar circumstances such conduct could amount to oppression[68].

[11.026] The exclusion of a shareholding director from the management of a quasi-partnership company may be found to destroy the trust, confidence and mutuality which theretofore subsisted. However, in *O'Neill v Phillips*[69], the facts of which are set out below[70], it was held that a shareholder in a quasi-partnership company does not have 'a stark right of unilateral withdrawal'[71] where trust and confidence breaks down. On this point it was said:

> 'Such breakdowns often occur (as in this case) without either side having done anything seriously wrong or unfair. It is not fair to the excluded member, who will usually have lost his employment, to keep his assets locked in the company. But that does not mean that a member who has not been dismissed or excluded can demand that his shares be purchased simply because he feels that he has lost trust and confidence in the others. I rather doubt whether even in partnership law a dissolution would be granted on this ground in a case in which it was still possible under the articles for the business of the partnership to be continued. And as Lord Wilberforce observed in *Re Westbourne Galleries Ltd* [1973] AC 360 at 380B, one should not press the quasi-partnership analogy too far: "A company, however small, however domestic, is a company not a partnership or even a quasi-partnership"[72].'

In an Irish context it is important to remember that before the remedies provided for in s 205(3) of the CA 1963 can be invoked, oppression or disregard of interests within the meaning of s 205(1) must first be established.

(g) Non-consultation with shareholders

[11.027] Although the directors' non-consultation with a company's shareholders will not *per se* amount to oppressive conduct, it may do so in certain circumstances. In quasi-partnership private companies, non-consultation can be indicative of a breakdown in the mutual trust associated with such companies. In *Re Clubman Shirts Ltd*[73], the petitioner claimed that he was oppressed by the respondent directors because they had, *inter alia*, completed a transaction whereby the *entire* business of the company was transferred to

---

67 See also *Re Elgindata Ltd* [1991] BCLC 959 where the petitioner's expectation to take part in the management of the company was in issue. See also *Re Apollo Cleaning Services Ltd; Richards v Lundy et al* [1999] BCC 786.

68 In *Re Eurofinance Group Ltd* (16 June 2000, unreported) English High Court, Pumfrey J the exclusion of the petitioner from the management of a banking consultancy company amounted to unfair prejudice. See also *Re Tottenham Hotspur plc* [1994] 1 BCLC 655 for an example in the breakdown of a personal relationship between the company's chief executive and chairman.

69 *O'Neill v Phillips* [1999] BCC 600.

70 See para **[11.039]**.

71 *O'Neill v Phillips* [1999] BCC 600 at 611H.

72 *O'Neill v Phillips* [1999] BCC 600 at 612B. To the extent to which *Re Apollo Cleaning Services Ltd; Richards v Lundy et al* [1999] BCC 786 found otherwise, it should not be considered as correctly decided.

73 *Re Clubman Shirts Ltd* [1983] ILRM 323.

another company without the petitioner's knowledge or consent. O'Hanlon J held that in such circumstances:

> '[a] minority shareholder is entitled to have such a transaction, completed without his knowledge or consent, subjected to the closest scrutiny to ensure that he has been dealt with fairly by those who controlled the destinies of the company[74].'

(h) Technical oppression

[11.028] Section 205 of the CA 1963 provides a very useful remedy where the relationship between shareholders has broken down. Where oppression is found, the court has many options open to it, although the usual order is for the purchase or sale of either party's shares. An order to wind up a company under s 213(f) of the CA 1963 on the ground that such is *just and equitable* may have disastrous consequences for all concerned. In practice, parties in dispute have occasionally *agreed* that the court has jurisdiction to make an order under s 205. In *Colgan v Colgan & Colgan*[75], Costello J began his *ex tempore* judgment by saying:

> 'I think that the court has jurisdiction on the evidence before it under s 205 of the Act. The parties agreed that I can make an order under this section, and I have jurisdiction to do so. I do not think that I need give any final conclusion as to the nature of the oppression that occurred.
>
> In that case very serious disputes arose. Certain actions were taken arising from these disputes and these actions do mean that I have got jurisdiction under the section to do what is fair between the parties to bring an end to the situation which exists. I do not think that my jurisdiction to do so has been challenged[76].'

In that case, Costello J noted that the father of the petitioner and respondents had 'built up a fine commercial empire'[77], but that unfortunate differences had arisen amongst his sons, the successors to his enterprises. The empire consisted of a number of prime properties, including a number of hotels and public houses in Dublin, all unencumbered by mortgages. Costello J acknowledged that nobody wanted a winding-up order to be made, and in this, it is opined, he was objectively right. Had five hotels/public houses simultaneously come onto the property market, their realisable value, and the value of the shares in the companies concerned, would have been greatly diminished. The relief claimed by the petitioner was an order requiring his brother respondents to buy out his shares, and Costello J concluded that the respondents should be required to buy out the petitioner at a valuation determined by him based on submissions from the parties' respective accountant valuers[78].

It is thought that the approach adopted by the learned Costello J was particularly suited to the case in hand. Whether the parties were satisfied with the valuation placed on the shares in sale is one thing; that it was appropriate for the court to end the matters complained of by ordering the purchase of the petitioner's shares seems indisputable.

---

74 *Re Clubman Shirts Ltd* [1983] ILRM 323 at 325.

75 *Colgan v Colgan & Colgan* (22 July 1993, unreported) HC.

76 *Colgan v Colgan & Colgan* (22 July 1993, unreported) HC at p 1.

77 *Colgan v Colgan & Colgan* (22 July 1993, unreported) HC.

78 With regard to the valuation of the shares, see generally Ch 9, *Share Transfer*, para **[9.117]**.

Disregarding members' interests

[11.029] The second situation in which a member can petition the court under s 205 of the CA 1963 is where the affairs of the company or the powers of the directors are being exercised in *disregard of his interests*. Although, disregard of members' interests seems to be an easier ground than oppression upon which to succeed, the majority of Irish cases have turned upon whether or not there has been oppression.

[11.030] The reference to 'disregard of his or their *interests* as members' is wider than referring to a disregard of one's *rights* as a member[79]. This has been recognised in England in the context of s 459 of the Companies Act 1985 (UK). In *Re Sam Weller & Sons*[80], Peter Gibson J observed:

> 'The word 'interests' is wider than a term such as 'rights', and its presence as part of the test of s 459(1) to my mind suggests that Parliament recognised that members may have different interests, even if their rights as members are the same[81].'

The reference to 'interests' enables the court to have regard to the widest possible matters, unconnected with the petitioner's purely legal rights as a member of the company.

[11.031] The leading Irish case on conduct in disregard of members' interests is *Re Williams Group Tullamore Ltd*[82]. The facts of that case are considered above[83]. There, Barrington J held that the preference shareholders in the company had acted within their formal powers and had acted honestly in resolving to allow the distribution between all shareholders; their conduct was found to be neither burdensome, harsh, wrongful nor lacking in probity or fair dealing and consequently did not amount to oppression. However, Barrington J recognised that there was an alternative to finding oppression:

> 'It is perhaps worth noting that the Irish section offers relief not only when the affairs of the company are being conducted in an oppressive manner but also (and alternatively) where they are being conducted *in disregard of the interests of some member or members*[84].'

Of the resolutions passed by the preference shareholders, Barrington J said that it appeared to him that they:

> '... were carried in disregard of the interests of the ordinary shareholders. It appears to me that the implementation of these resolutions is an ongoing matter in the company and justifies the view that the affairs of the company are being conducted in disregard of the interests of the ordinary shareholders. I fully accept that the proposal put forward in the resolution ... was put forward in good faith. Nevertheless, it appears to me that it is in objective disregard of the interests of the ordinary shareholders and that to persist in implementing it would, in the circumstances, be oppressive to the ordinary shareholders[85].'

---

79 See MacCann, *Butterworth Ireland Companies Acts 1963–1990* (1993), p 203, *Note* 41.

80 *Re Sam Weller & Sons* [1990] BCLC 80.

81 *Re Sam Weller & Sons* [1990] BCLC 80 at 85b–c.

82 *Re Williams Group Tullamore Ltd* [1985] IR 613.

83 See para **[11.016]**.

84 *Re Williams Group Tullamore Ltd* [1985] IR 613 at 620. Emphasis added.

85 *Re Williams Group Tullamore Ltd* [1985] IR 613 at 622.

Although the learned judge grounded his jurisdiction to make an order on the basis that the affairs of the company were being conducted in disregard of the interests of the ordinary shareholders, it is remarkable that he tagged onto his view the observation that to implement the resolutions would be *oppressive*. It is thought that it was unnecessary to find that the implementation of the resolutions would be oppressive: sufficient jurisdiction existed to make an order pursuant to s 205 of the CA 1963 on the finding that the affairs of the company were being conducted in disregard of the ordinary members' interests.

[11.032] A petitioner claiming that the powers of the directors or the affairs of the company are being conducted in disregard of his interests as a member must show that the damage suffered was *qua* member or in his capacity as a member. The operative part of s 205(1) of the CA 1963 refers to 'in disregard of his or their interests *as members*'. As was considered above, oppression can be claimed by a member in his capacity as member or in some other capacity, such as director[86].

'Affairs of the company' and 'powers of directors'

[11.033] Where a petition is brought under s 205 of the CA 1963, the oppression or the disregard of interests must result from either the conduct of the *affairs of the company* or the exercise of the *powers of the directors*. The '*powers of the directors*' refers to the directors' exercise of their delegated powers of management which typically arises on foot of reg 80 of Table A. In *Re Charles Kelly Ltd*; *Kelly v Kelly & Kelly (No 2)*[87], Laffoy J characterised the conduct complained of by the petitioner as relating to the exercise by the first respondent of the 'powers of the directors':

> '... the acts on his part complained of, such as the proposed suspension of the petitioner, or defaults alleged against him, such as his failure to co-operate in the finalisation of accounts and submission of annual returns or to address the need to curb the costs of the business, were acts or omissions which were either done, or should have been done, by him in his capacity as a director.'

Laffoy J noted that the petitioner's case was that the first respondent's power as a director was being exercised by the first respondent in a manner which was both oppressive to the petitioner and is in disregard of the petitioner's interest as a member of the company. Laffoy J was not inclined to accept that argument that the petitioner's interests as a member were damaged by the first respondent exercising his powers as a director. Laffoy J said that in 'reality, the true basis of the petitioner's claim for relief under sub-s (1) of s 205 is that the first respondent is exercising his powers as a director of the company in a manner which is oppressive to the petitioner'.

[11.034] The 'affairs of the company' refers to the conduct of the member shareholders when acting together as corporators[88]. An example in point from decided case law is *Re Williams Group Tullamore Ltd*, where the passing of the resolution by the preference shareholders was found to be in disregard of the interests of the ordinary shareholders.

---

86 See para **[11.014]**.

87 *Re Charles Kelly Ltd; Kelly v Kelly & Kelly (No 2)* [2011] IEHC 349.

88 Cited by Laffoy J in *Re Charles Kelly Ltd; Kelly v Kelly & Kelly (No 2)* [2011] IEHC 349.

In the Australian case of *Weatherall v Satellite Receiving Systems (Australia) Pty Ltd*[89], the equal shareholders in the respondent company agreed to admit W as third equal shareholder and director in consideration of his investing US$250,000 in the company. A third party company ('UST') agreed by deed to procure the allotment to W of one-third of the shares in the company and his appointment as director upon his paying UST the consideration on the respondent company's account, which UST would remit to the respondent company. Although only US$150,000 was received and remitted to the respondent company, W was allotted the shares and appointed as a director. The petitioner alleged oppression. It was held, in these circumstances, that W's failure to pay UST had nothing to do with his position as a director or member so as to constitute the company's 'affairs', and that the failure to pay the remaining US$100,000 was not 'corporation-related'. In *Re Leeds United Holdings plc*[90], it was held that the petitioner had no right to expect that another shareholder would not sell his shares without the consent of the petitioner, as such did not relate to the company's 'affairs'.

Quasi-partnership companies and 'legitimate expectations'

[11.035] Quasi-partnership companies[91] are referred to in various places throughout this book[92]. Where a relationship of *equality, mutuality, trust, and confidence*[93], based on a personal relationship[94], subsists in a private company[95] it may be appropriate that it be considered as a quasi-partnership[96]. Such a finding may result in members and directors being found to be restrained on equitable grounds from enforcing rights found in the 'black letter of the law'. In such companies, acts and omissions may be found to amount to oppression or disregard of members'[97] interests, by reason of equitable

89 *Weatherall v Satellite Receiving Systems (Australia) Pty Ltd* [1999] Federal Court of Appeal 218 (12 March 1999).

90 *Re Leeds United Holdings plc* [1996] 2 BCLC 545.

91 See, generally, Twomey, *Partnership Law* (2000) at [8.68] *et seq.* See also Prime & Scanlan, *The Law of Private Limited Companies* (1996), p 298.

92 See Ch 1, *The Private Company in Context*, para **[1.151]** and Ch 23, *Winding Up Companies*, para **[23.093]**.

93 See *Re Murph's Restaurant Ltd* [1979] ILRM 141 at 151.

94 See *Re Astec (BSR) plc* [1999] BCC 59 where Jonathan Parker J found (at 86) that in order to give rise to an equitable constraint based on 'legitimate expectations' 'what is required is a personal relationship or personal dealings of some kind between the party seeking to exercise the legal right and the party seeking to restrain such exercise, such as will affect the conscience of the former'. One of the best examples of a personal relationship is seen in *Re Apollo Cleaning Services Ltd; Richards v Lundy* [1999] BCC 786 and *Re Legal Costs Negotiators Ltd* [1999] BCC 547 where pre-existing partnerships had been converted into limited companies.

95 In England, it has been said that there was no room for 'legitimate expectations' in public companies: *Re Blue Arrow plc* (1987) 3 BCC 618 at 623; *Re Astec (BSR) plc* [1999] BCC 59 at 87D.

96 In *Third v North East Ice & Cold Storage Co Ltd* [1998] BCC 242, it was held that where a company was a quasi-partnership, but circumstances changed rendering it not a quasi-partnership, 'legitimate expectations' would be displaced.

97 It is possible that some members will be found to be quasi-partners and some will not: see *Re Planet Organic Ltd* [2000] 1 BCLC 366.

considerations; formal rights may be forced to give way to equitable principles implied from the law of partnership[98].

[11.036] Quasi-partnerships have been found to exist, notwithstanding the provisions of s 1(2)(a) of the Partnership Act 1890, which provides that the relationship between members of a registered company 'is not a partnership within the meaning of this Act'. Although there is a *presumption* that those who choose to incorporate have elected for the legislation governing companies to govern their relationship, that presumption can be rebutted by clear evidence[99]. An example of where the court found that the three shareholders in a company, which had been incorporated over 20 years' previously, were not in a partnership arrangement, is *Horgan v Murray and Milton*[100]. This case concerned an application to strike out plenary proceedings seeking various declarations, including one that the plaintiff was a partner of the two defendants[101]. In striking out the proceedings, O'Sullivan J said:

> 'I cannot agree that there is any indication on the pleadings that clear evidence will be advanced to show that obligations or rights apart from or additional to those arising under the companies code were contemplated or agreed between the parties. On the contrary, [the plaintiff's counsel] has accepted in argument that the relationship between the parties under what is an independently subsisting partnership relationship are precisely the same as those which exist between them as fellow shareholding members of the company. In my view this is no case for a partnership: these parties conceived and promoted a public business to be conducted through the medium of [the company].'

[11.037] The existence of formalised agreements – such as shareholders' agreements – will generally operate to preclude the implication of unstated expectations, although this will not always be conclusive[102]. In England, it has been found to be possible for one member of a company to be considered a 'junior partner' to another member who was the 'dominant senior partner' so that despite the absence of complete equality, the company could still be considered to be a quasi-partnership where the characteristics of such a company had been found to exist[103].

[11.038] One twist to this is the categorisation of such equitable considerations as giving rise to so-called 'legitimate expectations'. Some English authorities have discussed how,

98 In *Irish Press plc v Ingersol Irish Publications Ltd* (15 December 1993, unreported) HC, at p 70 of the judgment, Barron J said: 'Where there are equal shareholdings in a company and where the reality is that the shareholders have entered into a partnership the court will where necessary apply the principles of partnership law.'

99 See the decision of Murphy J in *Crindle Investments v Wymes* [1998] 4 IR 567 at 576 where he said: '… I believe that the presumption must be that parties who elect to have their relationship governed by corporate structures rather than, say, a partnership, intend their duties – and where appropriate their rights and remedies – to be governed by the legal provisions relating to such structures and not otherwise. It would require, in my view, reasonable clear evidence to impose obligations on directors or shareholders above and beyond those prescribed by legislation or identified by long established legal principles.'

100 *Horgan v Murray and Milton* [1999] IEHC 65, O'Sullivan J.

101 There already existed s 205 proceedings and other plenary proceedings for wrongful dismissal in being.

102 See, eg, *Re A Company (No 002015 of 1995)* [1997] 2 BCLC 1.

103 See *Quinlan v Essex Hinge Co Ltd* [1996] 2 BCLC 417.

in such companies, a member may be entitled to have certain *legitimate expectations*, over and above those to which he would be entitled as a matter of strict contract and statute law[104]. Lord Hoffmann in *O'Neill v Phillips* described the term[105], as follows:

> 'In *Re Saul D Harrison & Sons plc* [1994] BCC 475 at 490A I used the term "legitimate expectation", borrowed from public law, as a label for the "correlative right" to which a relationship between company members may give rise in a case when, on equitable principles, it would be regarded as unfair for a majority to exercise a power conferred upon them by the articles to the prejudice of another member. I gave as an example the standard case in which shareholders have entered into association upon the understanding that each of them who has ventured his capital will also participate in the management of the company. In such a case it will usually be considered unjust, inequitable or unfair for a majority to use their voting power to exclude a member from participation in the management without giving him the opportunity to remove his capital upon reasonable terms. The aggrieved member could be said to have had a 'legitimate expectation' that he would be able to participate in the management or withdraw from the company[106].'

Lord Hoffmann went on to express his own misgivings with the term he had applied to quasi-partnership companies:

> 'It was probably a mistake to use this term, as it usually is when one introduces a new label to describe a concept which is already sufficiently defined in other terms. In saying that it was "correlative" to the equitable restraint, I meant that it could exist only when equitable principles of the kind I have been describing would make it unfair for a party to exercise rights under the articles. It is a consequence, not a cause, of the equitable restraint. The concept of a legitimate expectation should not be allowed to lead a life of its own, capable of giving rise to equitable restraints in circumstances to which the traditional equitable principles have no application. That is what seems to have happened in this case[107].'

Despite Lord Hoffmann's misgivings, 'legitimate expectations' remains a useful label with which to describe certain shareholders' hopes, although it must be remembered that it is just a label for oppressive conduct or disregard of interests and is not an independent cause of action.

[11.039] The facts in *O'Neill v Phillips* were that O'Neill had been an employee of Pectel Ltd, a construction company, who had risen through the ranks to become a shareholding director, holding 25% of the company's shares. Phillips was the other director and holder of 75% of the shares in the company. O'Neill alleged that, as a result of informal discussions, he had been led to believe that he would receive a full 50% shareholding in Pectel Ltd, upon the company achieving certain targets. Upon Phillips retiring, O'Neill became sole director and upon the company prospering, O'Neill was credited with half the profits by Phillips, who voluntarily waived a third of his 75% entitlement to dividends. During this time a number of relevant events happened: the

---

104 See *O'Neill v Phillips* [1999] BCC 600; *Re Astec (BSR) plc* [1999] BCC 59; *Re Pectel Ltd* [1998] BCC 405 (the Court of Appeal decision in *O'Neill v Phillips); Richards v Lundy; Re Apollo Cleaning Services Ltd* [1999] BCC 786; *Third v North East Ice & Cold Storage Co Ltd and another* [1998] BCC 242.

105 *O'Neill v Phillips* [1999] BCC 600.

106 *O'Neill v Phillips* [1999] BCC 600 at 609, 610.

107 *O'Neill v Phillips* [1999] BCC 600 at 610.

company's share capital was increased by £100,000 by contributions in the proportion of 25:75; O'Neill guaranteed the company's bank account, secured by a charge on his residence; and Phillips indicated in principle his willingness to increase O'Neill's shareholding to 50% upon certain net-asset targets being achieved. Things turned sour when the construction industry went into recession. Phillips became dissatisfied with O'Neill's management of the company and resumed personal command. At one particular meeting Phillips criticised O'Neill's management and said that he would no longer receive 50% of the profits, just the 25% to which he was entitled as a 25% shareholder. O'Neill terminated his guarantee and arranged to set up a competing business in Germany (where Pectel Ltd also had operations). O'Neill then petitioned under s 459 of the Companies Act 1985 (UK), alleging unfairly prejudicial conduct by Phillips. O'Neill lost at trial but succeeded in the Court of Appeal[108] where it was found that despite the absence of a concluded agreement between the parties, O'Neill had a 'legitimate expectation' that he would receive a further 25% of the company's shares from Phillips when targets were reached.

[11.040] The House of Lords allowed the appeal and dismissed O'Neill's petition. Lord Hoffmann accepted that the Court of Appeal had found that the company had acquired the characteristics identified as commonly giving rise to equitable restraints upon the exercise of powers under articles, namely:

- an association formed on the basis of a personal relationship which involved mutual confidence;
- an understanding that certain shareholders would participate in the management of the business; and
- restrictions on the transfer of shares[109].

Lord Hoffmann held that it would have been unfair had O'Neill been excluded from participation in the management of the company without affording him the chance to sell his shares. Despite this the House of Lords went on to find that O'Neill had not been excluded from participating in the company's management, nor had he been driven out of the company. Lord Hoffmann found:

> '... the Court of Appeal said that Mr O'Neill had a legitimate expectation of being allotted more shares when the targets were met. No doubt he did have such an expectation ... and no doubt it was legitimate, or reasonable, in the sense that it reasonably appeared to happen. Mr Phillips had agreed in principle, subject to the execution of a suitable document. But this is where I think that the Court of Appeal may have been misled by the expression 'legitimate expectation'. The real question is whether in fairness or equity Mr O'Neill had a right to the shares. On this point, one runs up against what seems to me the insuperable obstacle of the judge's finding that Mr Phillips never agreed to give them. He made no promise on the point. From which it seems to me to follow that there is no basis, consistent with established principles of equity, for a court to hold that Mr Phillips was behaving unfairly in withdrawing from the negotiation. This would not be restraining the exercise of legal rights. It would be imposing upon Mr Phillips an obligation to which he never agreed. Where, as here, parties enter into negotiations with a view to a transfer of shares on professional advice and subject to a condition that they are not to be bound until

[108] *Re Pectel Ltd* [1998] BCC 405; also reported as *Re a Company (No 00709 of 1992)* [1999] 2 BCLC 739.

[109] See *Re Westbourne Galleries Ltd* [1973] AC 360.

a formal document has been executed, I do not think it is possible to say that an obligation has arisen in fairness or equity at an earlier stage.'

The same reasoning applies to the sharing of profits. The judge found as a fact that Phillips made 'no unconditional promise about the sharing of profits'[110].

Lord Hoffmann went on to find that Phillips had not acted unfairly. It would seem that the notion of 'legitimate expectations', as applied before the House of Lords' decision, bore some considerable relation to the doctrine of promissory estoppel[111]. As observed earlier, it is considered wise to confine its usage to a mere descriptive term for existing, independent, equitable obligations. The House of Lords' reluctance to interfere in a statutory and contractual relationship is thought to be both understandable and correct.

[11.041] Notwithstanding the discrediting of the label, 'legitimate expectations' in a quasi-partnership company, where there are personal relationships and understandings[112], which give rise to equitable considerations over and above legal and statutory rights, the courts are more likely to deem *unconscionable* acts and omissions to be oppressive or in disregard of members' interests[113].

The *locus standi* to petition

[11.042] Only certain persons have *locus standi* to petition the court for relief under s 205 of the CA 1963. Those who have *locus standi* are the following:

(a) Members of the company.
(b) Personal representatives of deceased members.

[11.043] Section 205(2) of the CA 1963 provides that the Minister for Jobs, Enterprise and Innovation can apply for an order under s 205 'in a case falling within sub-s (3) of s 170 of the 1963 Act. Sections 165–173 of the CA 1963, which governed the appointment of an inspector to a company, have now been repealed by s 6 of the CA 1990. Section 12 of the CA 1990 roughly corresponds to the repealed s 170 of the CA 1963. However, s 12 of the CA 1990 makes no specific mention of s 205 of the CA 1963 and makes no provision for the Minister's right to apply for an order under s 205. Although the Minister does not have express *locus standi* to seek relief under s 205 of the CA 1963, the thought was expressed in the last edition of this book that s 20(1) of the Interpretation Act 1937 might allow s 205(2) to be construed as referring to s 12 of the CA 1990.[114] The 1937 Act has since been repealed and replaced by the Interpretation Act 2005, and it is more difficult now to arrive at the same conclusion[115].

---

110 *O'Neill v Phillips* [1999] BCC 600 at 610H–611B.

111 See McDermott, *Contract Law* (2001), pp 136–148.

112 See *Re a Company (No 002015 of 1996)* [1997] 2 BCLC 1.

113 See, eg, the seminal *Re Murphs Restaurants Ltd* [1979] ILRM 141.

114 Section 20(1) of the Interpretation Act 1937 provides: 'Whenever any statute or portion of a statute is repealed and re-enacted, with or without modification, by an Act of the Oireachtas, references in any other statute or in any statutory instrument to the statute or portion of a statute so repealed and re-enacted shall, unless the contrary intention appears, be construed as references to the portion of such Act of the Oireachtas containing such re-enactment.'

115 Section 26(2)(f) of the Interpretation Act 2005 provides: 'Where an enactment ("former enactment") is repealed and re-enacted, with or without modification, by another enactment ("new enactment"), the following provisions apply ... (contd.../)

(a) Members of the company

[11.044] Any member of the company may petition the court for relief under s 205 of the CA 1963. Save as considered below, it is a prerequisite that the petitioner has been registered as a member of the company and that his name appears on the register of members[116]. A person whose name still appears on the register of members but who has disposed of his beneficial interest in the shares cannot, however, petition for s 205 relief. The Supreme Court has made this clear in *Re Via Net Works Ireland Ltd*[117]. In that case the respondents were s 205 petitioners who had agreed in a shareholders' agreement to transfer their shares to the appellants in the subject company. Giving the judgment of the court, Keane CJ held that the respondents did not have *locus standi* to petition under s 205. He said:

> 'Section 205 is a valuable protection against the misuse by shareholders, usually constituting the majority, of their powers in a manner which is oppressive to the other shareholders or fails to have regard to their interests. Persons, such as the respondents, who have voluntarily disposed of their entire shareholding in a company could not conceivably have been contemplated by the legislature as persons who would be entitled to relief under the section. Nor is it any answer to say that, because the respondents have not transferred their shares, as they are contractually bound to do, they remain registered as members of the company. It is undoubtedly the case that a person who has become entitled to be registered as a shareholder may be unable to exercise any of his rights as a shareholder until his name has been entered on the register. But it does not follow that a person who, conversely, has voluntarily divested himself of all his shares in the company, but remains on the register must be treated as a member of the company for all purposes. I have no doubt that, when the legislature enacted s 205(1), it was not envisaged that persons without any interest in the company but who, for whatever reason, remained on the register as members would be entitled to present a petition grounded on alleged oppression of them as members.'

Similarly, in *Banfi Ltd v Moran et al*[118] a beneficial owner of shares to whom the shares had in fact been transferred, although the transfer had not been registered, failed in its attempt to bring a s 205 petition on the grounds that it was not a member of the company.

[11.045] The decision in *Re Via Net Works Ireland Ltd*[119] could, if taken literally, lead to injustice. It could not, for example, have been intended to suggest that a trustee of shares was debarred from petitioning under s 205 although he was not beneficially entitled to the shares. Equally, where the articles provide for the compulsory transfer of shares, it could not have been intended that once triggered an aggrieved transferor who claims that

[115] (\...contd) (f) a reference in any other enactment to the former enactment shall, with respect to a subsequent transaction, matter or thing, be read as a reference to the provisions of the new enactment relating to the same subject-matter as that of the former enactment, but where there are no provisions in the new enactment relating to the same subject-matter, the former enactment shall be disregarded in so far as is necessary to maintain or give effect to that other enactment.'

[116] See Ch 8, *Shares and Membership*, para **[8.017]**.

[117] *Re Via Net Works Ireland Ltd* (23 April 2002, unreported) SC.

[118] *Banfi Ltd v Moran et al* [2006] IEHC 257. See Ch 9, *Share Transfer*, at para **[9.053]**.

[119] *Re Via Net Works Ireland Ltd* (23 April 2002, unreported) SC.

the effect of the expropriation was oppressive was denied the right to petition under s 205. In such a case it could be argued that the transferor had voluntarily agreed to the transfer because he became a member on the basis of the company's articles of association, which contained a compulsory transfer clause. It is thought that where the oppression or disregard of interest alleged is the expropriation of the petitioner's shares, the decision in *Re Via Net Works Ireland Ltd* will not preclude the petition being heard under s 205.

[11.046] 'Member' has the meaning assigned to it by s 31 of the CA 1963[120]. A person to whom shares have been transferred but whose name has not been entered by the directors on the register of members cannot petition under s 205 of the CA 1963[121]. An example in point is *Re Quickdome Ltd*[122] where the petitioner, a Mrs O'Callaghan, claimed to be entitled to present a petition under s 459 of the Companies Act 1985 (UK). Her only claim to be a member was that she possessed a stock transfer form which had been executed in blank[123]. It was held that she had no standing to present the petition. It is important to note that unlike s 205, s 459 of the 1985 Act did allow an unregistered transferee to present a petition. However, Mervyn Davies J rejected her contention that she was even an unregistered transferee. Similarly, company employees[124] and ex-members of a company[125] cannot rely on s 205.

[11.047] The beneficial owners of shares in a company who are not the registered members of the company do not have *locus standi* to petition under s 205. This remains the law despite the decision in *Re Irish Life Group Holdings plc*[126], where a beneficial owner of shares in Irish Life was considered to be a member for the purposes of applying under s 11(1) of the Credit Institutions (Stabilisation) Act 2010 to challenge a direction order made by the Minister for Finance under that Act. Distinguishing the 2010 Act from s 31 of the CA 1963, Feeney J said:

> 'The definition of member in the 1963 Act is a technical definition directly relevant and applicable to the provisions of that Act in relation to the governance of companies.
>
> 26. The Court is satisfied that the word 'member' as used in s 11(1) of the 2010 Act does not on an objective interpretation have only one potential meaning nor does it have an obvious meaning. Where, as in this case, there are alternative literal meanings capable of being applied to the word "member" it can be properly said that the word "member" as used in s 11(1) is ambiguous.'

Accordingly, where shares are held in a dematerialised form or held under depository receipts, the beneficial holder will not be a member within the meaning of s 31 of the

---

120 See *Re Allied Metropole Hotel Ltd* (19 December 1988, unreported) HC, *per* Gannon J.

121 *Re A Company (No 003160 of 1986)* [1986] BCLC 391. See generally Ch 10, *Share Transfers in Private Companies*.

122 *Re Quickdome Ltd* [1988] BCLC 370.

123 On stock transfer forms executed 'in blank' see the comments of Mervyn Davies J at 374–375 and *Re A Company (No 003160/1986)* [1986] BCLC 391. See generally, Ch 9, *Share Transfer*, at para **[9.006]**.

124 *Jaber v Science and Information Technology Ltd* [1992] BCLC 764.

125 *Re Baltic Real Estate Ltd (No 1)* [1993] BCLC 498.

126 *Re Irish Life Group Holdings plc* [2012] IEHC 89, Feeney J.

CA 1963 and the decision in *Re Irish Life Group Holdings plc*[127] will provide no succour.

[11.048] In *Re Charles Kelly Ltd; Kelly v Kelly and another*[128], the petitioner and respondant were brothers who had for years conducted and managed the affairs of the company on the basis of acknowledging their equal shareholding in the company and their entitlement to share equally in its management. The petition did not disclose that the petitioner was a member of the company or state his shareholding and so a preliminary issue was whether the petitioner was a 'member' so as to have *locus standi* to bring the petition. In the event it was held by Laffoy J that the petitioner was a member and entitled to bring s 205 proceedings[129].

[11.049] The petitioning member does not have to be a *minority* member, notwithstanding the heading, 'Minorities', to the section. In *Re Westwinds Holding Company Ltd*[130], Kenny J dismissed the respondent's claim that the section had no application on account of the fact that the petitioner was an equal shareholder with the respondent:

> 'The word "minority" does not appear in any part of the section and the heading is merely a convenient way of describing the majority of cases in which the section will apply. In addition, Martin Hession was governing director and under Article 42 had five votes on a show of hands or on a poll for each share of which he was the holder, while every other member was to have one vote for every hundred shares held by him. Although the two share-holders held an equal number of shares, the petitioner was certain to be out-voted and so was a minority[131].'

In so holding, Kenny J may be said to have been 'hedging his bets'. After holding that it was irrelevant to the wording of the section that a petitioner should be a minority, he went on to hold that the petitioner was a minority through the operation of a *Bushell v Faith*-type clause. It is thought that a petitioner needs only to be a member, and not necessarily a minority member. In *Irish Press plc v Ingersoll Irish Publications Ltd*[132], it is notable that the petitioner and respondent were equal 50-50 shareholders in the joint-venture companies[133].

[11.050] Although a petitioner should be a member of the company, it is not necessary that his complaint should be in respect of conduct affecting him in his capacity *qua* member. In this regard it is crucial to distinguish between complaints based on oppression and those based on a disregard of interests. As has already been considered, whilst complaints based on disregard of interests must be made *qua* member[134], complaints based on oppression can and have been made in the petitioner's capacity as a

---

[127] *Re Irish Life Group Holdings plc* [2012] IEHC 89, Feeney J.

[128] *Re Charles Kelly Ltd; Kelly v Kelly and another* [2010] IEHC 38, Laffoy J.

[129] See Ch 9, *Share Transfer*, at para **[9.006]**.

[130] *Re Westwinds Holding Company Ltd* (21 May 1974, unreported) HC.

[131] *Re Westwinds Holding Company Ltd* (21 May 1974, unreported) HC at p 20.

[132] *Irish Press plc v Ingersoll Irish Publications Ltd* (16 December 1993, unreported) HC.

[133] See also *Re Baltic Real Estate Ltd (No 1)* [1993] BCLC 498 where Knox J refused to strike out a petition simply because it was brought by a majority shareholder since it was arguable that a case could be made out.

[134] See para **[11.014]**.

director[135]. Moreover, in *Emerald Group Holdings Ltd & Banfi Ltd v Moran et al*[136] it was held by Finlay Geoghegan J that a member can complain of conduct which happened when it was not a registered member and only a beneficial owner, provided it becomes a member before presenting the petition:

> 'It does not appear to me that there is anything in the section which precludes Banfi complaining of conduct allegedly oppressive to it or in disregard of its interests as a member, which commenced at a time that it was the beneficial owner of shares, albeit not a member of the company, provided, of course that prior to the presentation of the petition it is a member of the company, and that the oppressive conduct to it or conduct in disregard of its interests as a member is continuing ...'

It is thought that the corollary is that where the oppression or disregard has ceased that the time a beneficial owner becomes a member that he will not have grounds for presenting a petition based solely on discontinued past oppression when he was not a member.

[11.051] Although, in general, those who have *locus standi* to petition the court for relief under s 205 of the CA 1963 may do so whenever they wish, petitions are blocked in certain circumstances by s 5(4) of the C(A)A 1990. This provides that:

> 'Complaints concerning the conduct of the affairs of the company while it is under the protection of the court shall not constitute a basis for the making of an order for relief under s 205 of the Principal Act [ie, the CA 1963].'

It is thought that this must be strictly construed and that, accordingly, relief may still be granted for complaints concerning the exercise of the *powers of the directors* (whether by the directors or, indeed, by an examiner) of a company under examination[137].

(b) Personal representatives of deceased members

[11.052] Were s 205 of the CA 1963 confined to *members* it would mean that under common form articles of association[138] the personal representatives of a deceased member could not rely on the section unless the directors acceded to their registration as members. Where the personal representatives were aggrieved, the directors would understandably be reluctant to register them as members. However, s 205(6) provides that the personal representatives of deceased members have standing to petition the court for relief. It provides:

> 'The personal representatives of a person who, at the date of his death was a member of a company, or any trustee of, or person beneficially interested in, the shares of a company by virtue of the will or intestacy of any such person, may apply to the court under *subsection (1)* for an order under this section and, accordingly, any reference in that subsection to a member of a company shall be construed as including reference to any such personal representative, trustee or person beneficially interested as aforesaid or to all of them.'

---

135 See para **[11.015]** and particularly *Re Murph's Restaurants Ltd* [1979] ILRM 141.

136 *Emerald Group Holdings Ltd & Banfi Ltd v Moran et al* [009] IEHC 440, Finlay Geoghegan J.

137 On examinerships, see further Ch 22, *Examinerships*.

138 Regulation 3 of Table A: see generally, Ch 9, *Share Transfer*, at para **[9.042]** *et seq*.

There are no reported Irish cases involving such an application by a deceased member's personal representatives[139]. It should be noted, however, that in addition to personal representatives, trustees and persons beneficially interested in shares under a member's will or by intestacy also have standing. Accordingly, where such a person is refused registration by the directors of the company, it is open to them to petition the court for relief under s 205.

Abuse of process and inordinate delay in prosecuting petitions

[11.053] Upon the presentation of a petition under s 205 of the CA 1963 it may be open to the respondents to apply to have the petition struck out as being vexatious or otherwise constituting an abuse of process. One of the first Irish applications of this kind was made in *Re Murray Consultants Ltd and Nocrumb Ltd; Horgan v Murray and Milton*[140]. In this case the respondents applied to have a s 205 petition struck out as being an abuse of process and claimed that since the primary relief sought by the petitioner was to be bought out, that could be done more beneficially by adopting a procedure for the valuation of shares which was contained in the company's articles of association. In the High Court Barron J refused to find that the petition was an abuse of process. In his judgment:

> 'Before the issue of proceedings can amount to an abuse of the process of the court, it seems to me that there must be some element of impropriety. So if a plaintiff who has a valid claim which has been admitted seeks to continue proceedings for further relief to which such plaintiff could not in any circumstances be entitled that would be an abuse of the process of the court. It is upon this basis that the respondents maintain that the petitioner would be abusing the processes of the court by refusing to accept the offer to value the shares being made by them[141].'

Barron J accepted that if the articles of association contained a specific provision as to what should happen in the circumstances, to refuse to rely on the articles would be an abuse of process[142]. He noted that in England it had been held that a petition should not be struck out where there was impropriety on the part of the respondent[143] or where there was any risk to the petitioner that a proper valuation would not be made of his shareholding[144]. Barron J declined the respondents' application for four reasons:

---

[139] For an English example, see *Re a Company* [1983] 2 All ER 36. See also *Re Jermyn Street Turkish Baths Ltd* [1971] 3 All ER 184.

[140] *Re Murray Consultants Ltd and Nocrumb Ltd; Horgan v Murray and Milton* [1997] 3 IR 23 (HC) and 29 (SC).

[141] *Re Murray Consultants Ltd and Nocrumb Ltd; Horgan v Murray and Milton* [1997] 3 IR 23 at 27.

[142] As held in *Re a Company* [1987] BCLC 562.

[143] *Re a Company; ex p Kremer* [1989] BCLC 365. There Hoffmann J said (at 368) '... there might be cases of impropriety on the part of the respondent which had so affected the value of the shares in the company as to make it inappropriate for the matter to be dealt with by a straightforward valuation.'

[144] *Re a Company; ex p Holden* [1991] BCLC 597. There, Harman J said (at 603): 'A petitioner is entitled to refuse to accept a risk – any risk – in an accountant's valuation of his interest if such risk can be seen to be one that would depreciate in any way the valuation.'

- the articles did not provide for an involuntary sale;
- the articles form a contract between the shareholders and no party can impose altered terms on another party without their prior consent;
- no court valuation would arise unless oppression had been established; and
- the petitioner was seeking an equitable remedy and the level of the valuation to be determined by the court will take into account the court's view of the appropriate level of compensation having regard to the circumstances giving rise to the proceedings[145].

[11.054] On appeal, by a 2-to-1 majority, the Supreme Court upheld Barron J's decision and refused to strike out the petition. The majority judgment, given by Murphy J, reviewed in some detail several relevant English authorities[146]. Murphy J concluded that in those cases in which petitions had been struck out, there was no oppression or wrongdoing proven. He held:

> 'If oppression had actually taken place … or was alleged, I believe that a court, in this jurisdiction at any rate, would not strike out the petition as being an abuse of process of the court. It is difficult to see how the court could be satisfied that the precise remedy offered by the oppressor was the appropriate means by which to bring to an end the oppression if it had occurred[147].'

Murphy J refused to strike out the instant petition. He noted that the petitioner was asserting oppression 'above and beyond the mere breakdown of the previously harmonious relationship' and also asserting that the respondents' actions represent a deliberate and calculated decision by them to further their own ambitions and to oppress the petitioner. The court held that these assertions were for the trial judge to decide and that it was inappropriate to strike out the petition.

[11.055] In *Re Vitara Foods Ltd*[148], a petition alleging unfairly prejudicial conduct was struck out on the ground of want of prosecution which amounted to an abuse of process. Lindsay J held that an application could be struck out where there was intentional and contumelious delay (which possibly included conduct amounting to an abuse of court) and proof of inordinate and inexcusable delay by a petitioner which gave rise to a

[145] In this latter respect Barron J noted that whilst *Irish Press plc v Ingersoll Irish Publications Ltd* [1995] 2 IR 175 had decided that damages as a common law remedy are not available to a s 205 petitioner, the Supreme Court had accepted that where a shareholder is bought out the price can include an element of compensation, as relief incidental to the main relief.

[146] *Re a Company* [1986] BCLC 362; *Re a Company* [1987] BCLC 94; *Re a Company* [1989] BCLC 365; *Re a Company* [1983] 1 WLR 927; *Re a Company* [1987] BCLC 563; *Re a Company* [1987] BCLC 80; *Re a Company; ex p Holden* [1991] BCLC 597; *Re a Company* [1996] 2 BCLC 192; and *Virdi v Abbey Leisure et al* [1990] BCLC 342.

[147] *Re Murray Consultants Ltd and Nocrumb Ltd; Horgan v Murray and Milton* [1997] 3 IR 29 at 40–41. See also *North Holdings Ltd v Southern Tropics Ltd; Re a Company No 004837 of 1998* [1999] BCC 746 where the Court of Appeal refused to strike out a petition alleging unfairly prejudicial conduct on the grounds that allegations that the company's assets had been used to capitalise and develop the respondent's business might extend to an account for profits and so the offer to purchase the petitioner's shares following a share valuation was not sufficient to remove any potential unfair prejudice.

[148] *Re Vitara Foods Ltd* [1999] BCC 315.

substantial risk that there would not be a fair trial[149]. In *Arrow Nominees Inc v Blackledge*[150], it was held that a petition would not be automatically struck out where a petitioner committed a fraud on the court by disclosing forged documents if there was no substantial risk that a fair trial of the petitioner's claim would not follow. Evans-Loambe J held that to strike out such a petition where the court took the view that a fair trial would follow was likely to be a breach of Article 6.1 of the European Convention on Human Rights[151]. Application to strike out a petition may also be made where it is presented by a company without the authority of its directors[152].

[11.056] In *Re Walsh Western Computer Services Ltd*[153], proceedings were issued in 1997 alleging oppression and seeking various remedies under s 205, relying on allegations of events that occurred between 1998 and 1995. In November 1998 points of claim were delivered; particulars arising were sought and the points of defence were delivered in April 2001. No reply was delivered by the petitioner. In April 2008 the petitioner delivered a notice of intention to proceed and eight months later voluntary discovery was sought seeking 28 categories of documentation covering periods from 1987 to 1996. Hedigan J granted the application by the respondents to have the petition struck out for inordinate and inexcusable delay. Noting that the petitioner had accepted the delay was inordinate, Hedigan J went on to find it was also inexcusable and rejected that the petitioner's without prejudice negotiations justified the delays:

> 'It is the case that such without prejudice negotiations may "stop the clock" in terms of the delay of which a respondent can complain in a motion of this kind. However, it does not remove the significance of lengthy delay and its implications for the due administration of justice. It must be borne in mind that, pursuant to the State's obligations under Article 6 of the European Convention on Human Rights, there is an overall public interest in the conclusion of litigation within a reasonable time. In the present proceedings, it is, of course, the case that settlement negotiations only provide an explanation in respect of a limited period of the delay. A lengthy four-year period (2001–2005) remains for which insufficient excuse has been put forward by the petitioner. I therefore find that the delay in this case was inexcusable.'

Hedigan J also considered that the balance of justice was against the continuance of the proceedings, citing prejudice to the respondents which was evident from the large volume of documentation of some antiquity and the fact that the recollection of witnesses would be diminished considerably. He also noted a matter specific to delay in s 205 petitions:

> 'A further factor influencing the court's discretion is that the company in respect of which the s 205 petition was brought has now been dissolved. That renders the usual remedy under s 205 of an order for the purchase of shares in the company inoperable. While the petitioner has sought damages in his claim, an action for damages is improbable in the context of s 205 proceedings. I am also guided by the State's obligations under Article 6 of

---

[149] See also *Re Marchday Group plc* [1998] BCC 800.

[150] *Arrow Nominees Inc v Blackledge* [2000] 1 BCLC 709.

[151] See also *Logicrose Ltd v Southend United Football Club Ltd* (1988) Times, 5 March and *Re Swaptronics Ltd* (1998) Times, 17 August.

[152] *Re Oriental Gas Co Ltd* [2000] 1 BCLC 209.

[153] *Re Walsh Western Holdings Ltd; Meehan v Walsh Western Holdings Ltd and Enright* [2009] IEHC 505, Hedigan J.

> the European Convention on Human Rights to ensure that justice is done as expeditiously as possible. This legal duty is, of course, a facet of the public interest in the due administration of justice, which demands that litigation be concluded in a reasonable time. Having regard to the circumstances of the present case, I am satisfied that the petitioner failed to act with due expedition and that there would be a real risk of an unfair trial if the case was allowed to proceed. The balance of justice demands that it be dismissed on grounds of inordinate and inexcusable delay, though it is with due reluctance and consideration that the court does so.'

In *Wolfe and another v Wolfe et al*[154], although Finlay Geoghegan J found that there had been an inordinate and inexcusable delay in prosecuting s 205 proceedings, the balance of the interests of justice was in favour of permitting the plaintiffs to proceed, but the learned judge only allowed this on a conditional and limited basis, namely, that the proceedings would be dismissed unless a certificate of readiness was delivered and filed prior to a specified date[155].

The position of the company

[11.057] Disputes under s 205 of the CA 1963 are typically between the members *inter se* or the members and the directors. The separate legal entity which is the company will usually not play an active part in the litigation, although for practical reasons it may be separately represented at a s 205 hearing. In the particular context of disputes involving the exclusion of quasi-partners from the company's management it will be wrong for the company's controllers to utilise the company's resources in connection with the proceedings.[156] In *Re Milgate Developments Ltd*[157], it was held that there was no justification for the companies concerned to incur expenditure in proceedings under s 459 of the Companies Act 1985 (UK) where the dispute was one between the shareholders based on the petitioner's exclusion from the companies' management. In *Re Murph's Restaurants Ltd*[158], Gannon J, after ordering that the company should be wound up, held that the company itself should bear its own costs, as they were *not* related to those of the respondents.

[11.058] In *Re Murray Consultants Ltd and Nocrumb Ltd; Horgan v Murray and Milton (No 2)*[159], the petitioner in an action under s 205 of the CA 1963 brought a discovery motion, objecting to the fact that the respondents had failed to refer to files of advice given to the companies involved by several categories of third-party advisers. In ordering that the advices be discovered, O'Sullivan J held:

> 'It is submitted that the petitioner can bring a third party discovery motion compelling the relevant companies to furnish him with the documents but that the respondents themselves should not be obliged in these proceedings as part and parcel of the general obligations

---

154 *Wolfe and another v Wolfe et al* [2006] IEHC 106, Finlay Geoghegan J.

155 In *Re Martialone Ltd; Hennessy v Griffin and ors* [2009] IEHC 570, Laffoy J dismissed all but one of the petitioner's claims against the respondents.

156 The first three sentences of this paragraph were expressly approved by Laffoy J in *Re Charles Kelly Ltd; Kelly v Kelly and Charles Kelly Ltd* [2012] IEHC 335 at para 5.

157 *Re Milgate Developments Ltd* [1993] BCLC 291.

158 *Re Murph's Restaurants Ltd* [1979] ILRM 141 at 155.

159 *Re Murray Consultants Ltd and Nocrumb Ltd; Horgan v Murray and Milton (No 2)* [1999] 1 ILRM 257.

under discovery principles to refer to these documents and to produce them for the petitioner.

> This is a "section 205" petition. The petitioner alleges that the affairs of the above entitled companies have been operated oppressively against him by the two respondents. I do not think the company is a "third party" in the usual sense of that term in these circumstances. If the advices furnished to the companies are relevant, as I have held, then they should be produced as part of discovery unless they are privileged[160].'

In the light of O'Flaherty J's comments in *Re New-Ad Advertising Company Ltd*[161], the correctness of disregarding the company's separate legal personality is open to question and it is thought that, when in doubt, the company should be joined in the action whether as a respondent or notice party.

[11.059] Minority shareholders would do well to remember the so-called 'disclosure rule', which might be of assistance in obtaining copies of legal advice given to the company. In *Re Hydrosan Ltd*[162], Harman J said that 'There is no doubt that matters passing between solicitors to a company and a company are prima facie entitled to be produced to all shareholders of the company.' This has been considered in Ch 6[163].

In camera applications

[11.060] The basic rule governing the hearing of actions is set out in Article 34.1 of *Bunreacht na hÉireann*:

> 'Justice shall be administered in Courts established by law by judges appointed in the manner provided by this constitution, and, save in such special and limited cases as may be prescribed by law, shall be administered in public.'

One of the 'special and limited cases' referred to therein is s 205(7) of the CA 1963 which provides:

> 'If, in the opinion of the court, the hearing of proceedings under this section would involve the disclosure of information the publication of which would be seriously prejudicial to the legitimate interests of the company, the court may order that the hearing of the proceedings or any part thereof shall be in camera.'

In recent years there have been two Supreme Court decisions on the principles of law applicable to an application for proceedings to be *in camera*[164].

---

160 *Re Murray Consultants Ltd and Nocrumb Ltd; Horgan v Murray and Milton (No 2)* [1999] 1 ILRM 257 at 259–260.

161 *Re New-Ad Advertising Company Ltd* (26 March 1998, unreported) SC, at p 6 *per* O'Flaherty J.

162 *Re Hydrosan Ltd* [1991] BCLC 418 at 420f. See also *Dennis & Sons Ltd v West Norfolk Farmers' Manure and Chemical Co-Op Co Ltd* [1948] 2 All ER 94 and *Tugwell v Hooper* (1847) 10 Beav 348.

163 See Ch 6, *Corporate Civil Litigation*, at para **[6.063]**.

164 *Re R Ltd* [1989] ILRM 757 and *Irish Press plc v Ingersoll Irish Publications Ltd* [1993] ILRM 747. For an analysis of *Re R Ltd* see Daly, 'Lifting the Veil of Secrecy' (1990) Dlí – The Western Law Gazette 11. See also *Criminal Assets Bureau v MacAviation Ltd et al* [2010] IEHC 121 where the principles established in those cases were applied.

[11.061] The law applicable to the hearing of applications under s 205(7) of the CA 1963 *in camera* was conveniently summarised by Finlay CJ in *Irish Press plc v Ingersoll Irish Publications Ltd*[165]:

'1. The court cannot even commence to exercise a discretion under s 205(7) unless it is of opinion that the hearing of the proceedings or of some particular part of the proceedings would involve the disclosure of information the publication of which would be seriously prejudicial to the legitimate interests of the company.

2. If it is of opinion that such a situation exists the court may then enter upon an investigation as to whether it should exercise its discretion under s 205(7) to hold the case *in camera*. In so doing, it will, however, be involved in considering a fundamental constitutional right vested in the public, namely, the administration of justice in public, and it cannot, therefore, make an order under s 205(7) merely on the consent of all the parties concerned in the petition before it.

3. The additional matter which a court would have to be satisfied of in order to direct a hearing of the whole or part of the petition otherwise than in public would be that a public hearing of the whole or of that part of the proceedings would prevent justice being done.

4. In reaching a conclusion as to whether this test has been satisfied in any particular case, it would be appropriate for the court, having regard to the terms of the provisions of Article 34.1 of the Constitution, to construe s 205(7) bearing in mind that the entitlement of the Oireachtas pursuant to Article 34.1 to prescribe by law for the administration of justice otherwise than in public is confined to special and limited cases.

5. It would appear to me to be probable that in most instances, at least, a successful application for a hearing *in camera* pursuant to s 205(7) would be:

   (a) where the party seeking an *in camera* hearing is the petitioner, by establishing to the satisfaction of the court that, by reason of the making known to the public of information concerning the company involved, notwithstanding the very wide and varied jurisdiction which by virtue of s 205(3) the court would have to redress the wrong inflicted upon the petitioner by oppression, if that was proved, by reason of the extent of the damage to the asset consisting of the petitioner's shareholding in the company concerned that the court was incapable by reason only of the publication of the proceedings or some part thereof to render a just remedy to the wronged petitioner, or

   (b) where the party seeking an *in camera* hearing is the respondent by establishing to the satisfaction of the court that by reason of the making known to the public of information concerning the company involved in the course of the hearing of the petition that even if the petition were to be dismissed by the court and the respondent awarded costs against the unsuccessful petitioner, that by reason of the extent of the damage to the asset consisting of the respondent's shareholding in the company concerned, or if the company were the respondent by reason of the damage to its value, that the court would, merely by dismissing the petition with costs, be incapable, by reason only of the publication of the proceedings, from rendering a just remedy to the wrongfully sued respondent, or

165 *Irish Press plc v Ingersoll Irish Publications Ltd* [1993] ILRM 747 at 754–755.

(c) by proving that either the petitioner to further his claim or the respondent to defend himself against the claim of the petitioner, in reasonable prudent protection of the asset which he owned consisting of his shareholding in the company, would be obliged to abstain from tendering evidence which would probably influence the resolution of the issues and the achieving of a just result by the court, by reason of the fact that the publication of it would do such damage, (irrespective of the result of the case and the remedy which he might obtain from the court) to the asset consisting of his shareholding so as to outweigh the advantage of succeeding in the petition.

Although Finlay CJ formulated the law applicable to s 205(7) applications into five points, it is thought that before the courts can exercise their discretion under s 205(7), a twin test must be satisfied.

[11.062] Section 205(7) of the CA 1963 has been consistently construed strictly[166]. It is now well established that in order to have s 205 proceedings heard *in camera* an applicant must prove two matters to the court's satisfaction:

- that the hearing of the proceedings in public would involve the disclosure of information the publication of which would be seriously prejudicial to the legitimate interests of the company; this is a statutory condition precedent to the exercise of the court's discretion[167]; and
- that the hearing in public of the whole or that part of the proceedings which it is sought to have heard *in camera* would fall short of doing justice.

These two limbs are conjunctive: both must be proven to the court's satisfaction by the applicant.

[11.063] The first limb of this test is a difficult obstacle for an applicant to overcome. In *Re R Ltd*[168], the majority decision of the Supreme Court, delivered by Walsh J, noted that it had been agreed between the parties in dispute that the information in question related to the company's five-year business plan to the programme of the company, to details of its accounts and of one particular transaction and its commercial terms. Having considered the matters in question, Walsh J held that it was a condition precedent to the exercise of the court's discretion that the disclosure of these matters would seriously prejudice the company's legitimate interests. It was held on the facts that the first limb of the test was *not* met.

[11.064] In *Irish Press plc v Ingersoll Irish Publications Ltd*[169], the judgments of Finlay CJ and Blayney J both concurred that there was not sufficient evidence to satisfy the first limb of the test. Blayney J in particular was most systematic in addressing the details of the company which had previously been published. Having reviewed the matters which had already been reported in the national newspapers, he concluded that in the circumstances the public was already aware of much of the companies' financial

---

166 See the majority judgment of Finlay CJ in *Irish Press plc v Ingersoll Irish Publications Ltd* [1993] ILRM 747 at 754.

167 *Per* Walsh J, giving the majority judgment of the Supreme Court in *Re R Ltd* [1989] ILRM 757 at 766.

168 *Re R Ltd* [1989] ILRM 757.

169 *Irish Press plc v Ingersoll Irish Publications Ltd* [1993] ILRM 747.

affairs and that the publication of audited accounts would not seriously prejudice the legitimate interests of the companies. Having so found, Blayney J held that it was not necessary to consider the second limb.

[11.065] A good example of where the court held that it *would* be prejudicial to the company's legitimate interests to hear a s 205 petition in public is thought to be the case of *Re Bula Holdings; Roche v Wymes*[170]. Because it was held *in camera* neither the judgment of the High Court or Supreme Court was made public and the only references are in a related case involving the same parties. It can be surmised, however, that because the essence of the complaint of oppression/disregard of interests concerned the failure to compromise third-party litigation involving Tara Mines Ltd, Bula Holdings' legitimate interests would have been prejudiced had its shareholders' divergent views on the litigation between it and Tara Mines Ltd been made public.

By way of contrast is *Re Skytours Travel Ltd; Doyle v Bergin*[171], which provides an example of where disclosure would not be prejudicial to a company's interests. There, the information sought to be suppressed was that the respondent had acknowledged that he appropriated monies belonging to the company to his own use and that, following a revenue audit, he had made a voluntary disclosure to the revenue. Laffoy J found it was impossible to conclude that the publication of the disclosure of that information heard in open court would be seriously prejudicial to the legitimate interests of the company.

[11.066] The second limb of the test is whether a hearing in public would prevent justice being done. The justification for this second limb arises from the requirement that all derogations from the principle enunciated by Article 34.1 must be construed strictly. This second limb is particularly difficult to overcome. The onus is firmly placed on the applicant to prove to the satisfaction of the court that to have the petition heard in public would prevent justice being done.

Remedies: restraining the removal of a shareholding director

[11.067] The exclusion from management by the removal or intended removal of a shareholding director as a director can form the basis of a claim of oppression under s 205 of the CA 1963. In *Gilligan and Bowen v O'Grady*[172], the Supreme Court denied the sanctity of members' rights to remove a director, pursuant to s 182 of the CA 1963[173], and upheld the jurisdiction to restrain by injunction the removal of a director pending the hearing of a s 205 petition.

[11.068] A few months before the Supreme Court's decision in *Gilligan*, the High Court had decided in *Re SIAC Construction Ltd; Feighery v Feighery*[174] that there was no jurisdiction to enjoin the removal of a director pending the hearing of a s 205 petition. In that case the petitioner was a minority shareholder and director in a construction company where he had been employed for 16 years. His petition alleged oppression and in particular pointed to the convening of an extraordinary general meeting ('EGM') to

[170] See references thereto in *Crindle Investments v Wymes* [1998] 4 IR 578.

[171] *Re Skytours Travel Ltd; Doyle v Bergin* [2010] IEHC 531.

[172] *Gilligan and Bowen v O'Grady* [1999] 1 IR 346. See Dunleavy, 'The Power of Shareholders to Remove Directors under Section 182 of the Companies Act, 1963' (1999) Bar Review 265.

[173] See Ch 13, *Corporate Governance: Management by the Directors*, para **[13.077]**.

[174] *Re SIAC Construction Ltd; Feighery v Feighery* (25 February 1998, unreported) HC, Laffoy J.

consider a resolution to remove him as director. The petitioner claimed that the company had been operated as a quasi-partnership and that there was an understanding that he would be employed as a director for his working life. By way of interlocutory relief to preserve the status quo the petitioner sought an injunction to restrain his removal as director. Laffoy J refused to grant the injunction and in arriving at her decision noted the decision in *Bentley-Stevens v Jones*[175], where Plowman J had rejected that *Re Westbourne Galleries Ltd*[176] was authority for the jurisdiction to grant an injunction to interfere with shareholders' statutory right to remove a director. Laffoy J also noted the distinction between an injunction to restrain directors from excluding another director from office, on the one hand, from an injunction which interferes with shareholders' statutory power to remove directors, without prejudice to directors' rights (if any) to damages[177]. Laffoy J held that she did not have jurisdiction to override the shareholders' statutory power in s 182 of the CA 1963 to remove the petitioner as a director.

[11.069] In *Gilligan and Bowen v O'Grady*[178], the first plaintiff was managing director of Business and Trading House Investment Company Ltd ('BTH') which was in the business of arranging investment funds on behalf of various people under the Business Expansion Scheme. BHT decided to invest in Premier International Trading House Ltd ('PITH'); and it, PITH and the Bank of Ireland entered into an agreement (the 1989 Agreement) under which the Bank of Ireland applied for shares to the value of £600,000 on behalf of a number of investors. Under that agreement, BTH was to be kept fully informed of PITH's business and its financial affairs, and the first plaintiff and another person were appointed directors of PITH. The first defendant was chairman, chief executive and secretary of Premier International Merchandising Ltd ('PIM'); the first and second defendants controlled the votes of at least a simple majority of the shareholders in PITH and PIM. The first plaintiff held circa 1% of the shares in PIM. Subsequent to the 1989 Agreement the bank and BTH wished to realise their investments but since the 1989 Agreement contained no exit mechanism, a sub-committee was formed by PITH's board of directors and discussions took place with another company ('Seamar Ltd') that was in the same business as PITH. The first plaintiff was also a director of Seamar Ltd. In the Supreme Court Keane J found that the proposal became a source of acrimony between the parties to the proceedings. Subsequently, in 1995, the shareholders in PITH accepted an offer made by PIM to exchange their shares in PITH for an equivalent shareholding in PIM together with a loan note for £2.38 in respect of every seven shares held by them in PITH. As a result, PITH became a wholly-owned subsidiary of PIM and the first plaintiff was appointed non-executive director of PIM. Disagreements between the first plaintiff and the first and second defendants ultimately led to the convening of an EGM of PIM for the purpose of considering a resolution that the first plaintiff be removed as director. This led to the plaintiffs instituting proceedings and presenting a petition pursuant to s 205 of the CA 1963 claiming that the affairs of PIM were being conducted in a manner oppressive to the plaintiffs and in disregard of their interests; the relief sought was an

175 *Bentley-Stevens v Jones* [1974] 1 WLR 638.

176 *Re Westbourne Galleries Ltd* [1973] AC 360.

177 Citing *Palmer's Company Law* (24th edn, 1987), p 901.

178 *Gilligan and Bowen v O'Grady* [1999] 1 IR 346. See Dunleavy, 'The Power of Shareholders to Remove Directors under Section 182 of the Companies Act, 1963' (1999) Bar Review 265.

order directing PIM to purchase the beneficial shareholding of each of the petitioners or in the alternative an order winding up the company. The plaintiffs successfully applied for an injunction in the High Court to restrain the removal of the first plaintiff as director of the company. In so deciding, O'Donovan J distinguished the earlier decision of Laffoy J in *Feighery v Feighery*[179], accepting the plaintiffs' submission that by virtue of the 1989 Agreement, the first plaintiff was a director not merely to represent his own interests as shareholder but also to represent the interests of the Business Expansion Scheme investors. O'Donovan J held:

> 'There is no doubt in my mind that, in the absence of the said agreement of 25 July 1989, having regard to the decision of Laffoy J in *Feighery v Feighery*, these plaintiffs have no right to the injunctive relief sought herein. In this regard, I am satisfied that, were he a director of PITH and PIM in the ordinary sense in which one might be on the board of a limited company, I have no jurisdiction to deprive the shareholders of either company of the opportunity of considering resolutions to remove him from their respective boards. However, I think that there is substance to Mr Shipsey's submission that, by virtue of the terms of that agreement, Mr McGilligan is a director of each company; not merely in his own interests, but also representing the interests of BTH and the BES investors and in this regard, by the way, I think that there is also substance to the argument that, after the takeover of PITH by PIM in 1995, the rights and interests of BTH and the Bank under the said agreement of 1298 were transferred to PIM … I think that, in the event that a court were to conclude that BTH and the BES investors, through their nominee, the Bank were entitled to be represented on the boards of PITH and PIM by Mr McGilligan, the decision of Laffoy J in *Feighery v Feighery et al* is of no relevance in this case because she was only concerned with the rights of shareholders to remove a director who had no such special entitlement to be on the board of the company with which she was concerned.'

Accordingly, O'Donovan J granted the injunction sought, restraining the shareholders from removing the first plaintiff as a director of PIM and PITH.

[11.070] The Supreme Court rejected the defendants' appeal. Keane J did not seek to try to distinguish the case of *Feighery v Feighery* or *Bentley-Stevens v Jones* and instead contented himself with finding that they should not be followed to the extent that they held that there was no jurisdiction to make an injunction in such matters. After reviewing the purpose of s 205, Keane J held[180]:

> 'Why then should the court, on an application for an interlocutory injunction, be unable to restrain the company from removing a director pending the hearing of a petition under s 205 where he has established that there is a serious question to be tried as to whether his exclusion from the affairs of the company constitutes conduct which would entitle the shareholders to relief under s 205? It should be noted that in *Bentley-Stevens v Jones* there do not appear to have been any proceedings in existence under the English equivalent of s 205 at the time the application for an interlocutory injunction was made. However, apart from that consideration, I am bound to say, with all respect, that I do not understand why it should be thought that, because the relief sought in the interlocutory proceedings is not the same as the relief which will ultimately be sought in the s 205 proceedings, an interlocutory injunction should not be granted on that ground alone. If it is desirable, in accordance with the principles laid down in the *American Cyanamid Company* and *Campus Oil* cases, to preserve the plaintiff's rights pending the hearing of the s 205

[179] *Feighery v Feighery* (25 February 1998, unreported) HC, Laffoy J.

[180] *Gilligan and Bowen v O'Grady* [1999] 1 ILRM 303 at 319.

> proceedings and the balance of convenience does not point to a different conclusion, I see no reason why interlocutory relief should not be granted. To cite but one example, the relief granted in many *Mareva* cases is very often not the relief which is sought in the substantive proceedings. I am satisfied that, to the extent that *Bentley-Stevens v Jones* and *Feighery v Feighery et al* suggest a different view of the law, they should not be followed.'

Keane J went on to find that, in that case, the balance of convenience favoured the granting of an injunction to preserve the status quo pending the outcome of the substantive proceedings[181].

[11.071] It will not, however, invariably be the case that a shareholding director's removal will be restrained pending the outcome of s 205 proceedings. So, in *Re Avoca Capital Holdings*[182] although Clarke J found that a shareholding employee-director had established that there was a serious question to be tried, he went on to find that the balance of convenience favoured the company and declined the injunction on the basis that it was not in the overall interests of the company to have the petitioner involved in the board's decision making. Indeed, it is thought that this will be the norm, save in cases of quasi-partnership where all parties have an equal interest in the venture.

[11.072] The converse to the removal of a director – the appointment of another director – which can also alter the status quo pending the outcome of the substantive proceedings can additionally be prevented by injunction of the court[183].

Remedies: ending the matters complained of

[11.073] Section 205(3) of the CA 1963 provides in the widest possible terms that the court has power to *end the matters complained of*. Accordingly, where conduct oppressive or in disregard of a member's interests is found to exist:

> '... the court may, with a view to bringing to an end the matters complained of, make such order as it thinks fit, whether directing or prohibiting any act or cancelling or varying any transaction or for regulating the conduct of the company's affairs in future, or for the purchase of the shares of any members of the company or by the company and in the case of a purchase by the company, for the reduction accordingly of the company's capital, or otherwise.'

It is thought that the enormous width of the court's power is encapsulated in the words 'make such order as it thinks fit'. Although the particular powers set out in s 205(3) are themselves extensive, they ought not be viewed as being exhaustive. The court's general power must not be viewed as prejudiced by the specificity of its particular powers. This is, of course, subject to the important limitation that the court may not award damages for oppression or disregard of members' interests, as established by the Supreme Court in *Irish Press plc v Ingersoll Irish Publications Ltd*[184] and discussed further below. Here, the following matters are considered:

(a) Section 205(3) of the CA 1963 does not permit a general award of compensatory damages.

---

181 Another injunction sought to restrain the company from becoming involved in a manufacturing process was refused.

182 *Re Avoca Capital Holdings* [2005] IEHC 302, Clarke J.

183 See *Corbett v Corbett* [1998] BCC 93.

184 *Irish Press plc v Ingersoll Irish Publications Ltd* [1995] 2 IR 175.

(b) Section 205(3) of the CA 1963 does not justify orders requiring persons to desist from litigation.
(c) Futile orders will not be made.
(d) Permissible orders under s 205 of the CA 1963(3) 'to end the matters complained of'.

(a) Section 205(3) of CA 1963 does not permit a general award of compensatory damages

[11.074] The Supreme Court in *Irish Press plc v Ingersoll Irish Publications Ltd*[185], the facts of which have been given previously[186], held that s 205(3) of the CA 1963 does not empower the court to award damages for oppression. In the High Court Barron J had held:

> 'Having regard to the nature of the oppression and the consequential losses to the companies as a result, the nature of the relief must be designed not only to bring an end to the matters complained of, but also to compensate the petitioner and the companies for the losses sustained. This can best be done by directing a purchase of the respondent's shareholding.
>
> ... The price to be paid for such shares shall be the present value of the respondent's shareholding having regard to the terms of the subscription and shareholders' agreement but not to the terms of the management agreement on the basis that there shall have been made good in money terms all actual financial loss to the company by reason of the oppression. In addition the petitioner shall be entitled to recover from the respondent the drop in value of its shareholding upon the same basis and the value of its shareholding on the 14 November 1991 being a date contemporaneous with the commencement of the oppression but before it commended having regard to the terms of both agreements[187].'

Subsequently, the High Court made, *inter alia*, the following orders:

– that Ingersoll should repay £6m to Irish Press Newspapers Ltd ('IPN') and Irish Press Publications Ltd (IPP) and £2.75m to Irish Press plc ('PLC');
– Ingersoll's shareholdings were valued at £2.25m and PLC was to pay this sum to Ingersoll after the sums of £6m and £2.75m were paid by Ingersoll; and
– all shares held by Ingersoll in IPN and IPP were to be transferred to PLC.

On appeal to the Supreme Court, Ingersoll claimed, *inter alia*, that the court had no power to award damages in a s 205 petition.

[11.075] The Supreme Court held that the order to transfer the shares from Ingersoll to PLC would, of itself, 'bring to an end the oppression complained of' and went on to find that the court had no power to order the payment of compensation. Blayney J held:

> 'The relief which may be given under the section is that the Court may make such order as it thinks fit "with a view to bringing to an end the matters complained of". The Court is not at large as to what it may do. Whatever order it makes must have this object. It must be

[185] *Irish Press plc v Ingersoll Irish Publications Ltd* [1995] 2 IR 175.
[186] See para **[11.023]**.
[187] *Irish Press plc v Ingersoll Irish Publications Ltd* (15 December 1993, unreported) HC at p 84.

made with a view to bringing to an end whatever it was that was causing the oppression[188].'

Blayney J went on to say:

'Could it be said that the order directing [Ingersoll] to pay £6 million to IPN and IPP and the £2.5 million to PLC was made with a view to bringing to an end the oppression of which PLC had complained? In my opinion it could not. The object of the order was clearly something quite different. It was to compensate IPN and IPP for the loss suffered by those companies and to compensate PLC for the reduction in the value of its shareholding. The object quite clearly was not to bring to an end the oppression which the learned trial judge had found to exist. The object was to compensate the three companies for the consequences of the oppression. Even if no other order had been made by the High Court, that would still have been the position, but the fact that [Ingersoll] was directed to transfer its shares to PLC, and that this put an end to the oppression, as referred to earlier, puts it beyond doubt that the order for the payment of compensation could not have also have been made with a view to bringing to an end the matters complained of. That object had already been achieved by the direction to transfer the shares.'

This finding is open to the criticism that it divorces the notion of a partial remedy from a complete remedy.

[11.076] It is important to note, though, that the decision of the Supreme Court does not *entirely* rule out an element of compensation when taken in conjunction with an order for the purchase of shares. Blayney J went on to recognise that in both *Re Greenore Trading Co Ltd*[189] and *Scottish Co-operative Wholesale Society Ltd v Meyer*[190] there had been an element of compensation in the courts' orders. Blayney J distinguished both of these cases from the case in hand on the grounds that in those cases the element of compensation was incidental to the main relief which was the purchase of shares. Blayney J expressed the distinction in the following terms:

'While compensation was included in the relief given in each of these two cases, it was given in an extremely limited context – where the oppressor had been directed to purchase the shares of the oppressed shareholder, and where the compensation resulted from the court's determination of what would be a fair price for the shares in the particular circumstances. The element of compensation was incidental to the main relief which was

188 *Irish Press plc v Ingersoll Irish Publications Ltd* [1995] 2 IR 175.

189 *Re Greenore Trading Co Ltd* [1980] ILRM 94. There Keane J had said (at 102): '… it is clear that in prescribing the basis on which the price is to be calculated, the Court can, in effect, provide compensation for whatever injury has been inflicted by the oppressors.'

190 *Scottish Co-operative Wholesale Society Ltd v Meyer* [1959] AC 324. There Lord Denning had said (at 369): 'One of the most useful orders mentioned in the section – which will enable the court to do justice to the injured shareholders – is to order the oppressor to buy their shares at a fair price; and a fair price would be, I think, the value which the shares would have had at the date of the petition, if there had been no oppression. Once the oppressor has bought the shares, the company can survive. It can continue to operate. That is a matter for him. It is no doubt, true that an order of this kind gives to the oppressed shareholders what is in effect money compensation for the injury done to them; but I see no objection to this. The section gives a large discretion to the court and it is well exercised in making the oppressor make compensation to those who have suffered at his hands.'

> the purchase of the shares. The cases are not authority for a general right to compensation for loss resulting from oppression…[191].'

Blayney J also went on to reject as a general proposition that damages might be awarded under s 205(3) of the CA 1963. In this regard he said:

> 'It was also submitted that the provisions of section 205(3) were so wide that they would permit damages to be awarded. I am unable to agree. Firstly, an award of damages would not satisfy the condition that the order be made 'with a view to bringing to an end the matter complained of', secondly, an award of damages is a purely common law remedy for a tort, breach of statutory duty or breach of contract, and acts of oppression would not come within any of these categories, and finally, if the Oireachtas had intended to include the remedy of damages as one of the reliefs which could have been granted, there would have been no difficulty in doing so, and it is quite clear that this was not done[192].'

Whilst this passage is open to criticism[193] it is thought that the die has been cast and that it is unlikely, in the near future, that the courts in Ireland will recant. It is equally clear, though, that the price at which shares may be ordered to be purchased may contain an *incidental* element of compensation for the oppression suffered by the vendor of the shares.

(b) Section 205(3) does not justify orders to desist from litigation

[11.077] In *Crindle Investments v Wymes*[194], an order was sought in proceedings under s 205 of the CA 1963 to require the defendants, whether as directors or personal litigants, to join in the acceptance of an offer in other proceedings, which had then been made to compromise those proceedings. In the High Court Murphy J declined to make such an order and this was upheld by the Supreme Court on appeal. Finlay CJ said:

> 'Having regard to the constitutional right to litigate and having regard in addition to the fact that the particular form of litigation with which we are involved in this case in part at least is a claim be it valid or otherwise, that constitutional rights of property have been interfered with, it seems to me that s 205 of the Act of 1963, so clearly designed and expressed to deal with the affairs of a company, could not by implication include the right to prevent a citizen from litigation. If it were established in any case that members of a company in addition to acts of oppression or disregard of interests to other members were maintaining or intending to institute proceedings which constituted an abuse of the process of the court in the sense that it was not being done for a valid intention or hope of obtaining relief but rather for some other indirect or improper motive then it might well be that the court might be entitled to intervene but, if it were, it would appear more probable that it could be entitled to intervene in order to prevent an abuse of its own processes. However, I am not satisfied that it is possible on the facts in this case and having regard to the terms of s 205 to grant the additional relief sought by the petitioner.'

Accordingly, it can be concluded that only in the rarest of cases will a court, on foot of s 205, order respondents to desist from exercising their constitutional right to litigate.

---

191 *Irish Press plc v Ingersoll Irish Publications Ltd* [1995] 2 IR 175 at 190.

192 *Crindle Investments v Wymes* [1995] 2 IR 175 at 190.

193 See Courtney, *Company Law Review 1995* (1996), pp 18–19.

194 *Crindle Investments v Wymes* SC, per Finlay CJ (*in camera*) but noted at [1998] 4 IR 578, [1998] 2 ILRM 275.

(c) *Futile orders will not be made*

[11.078] The court will only grant relief to a petitioner under s 205(3) of the CA 1963 where its order can bring to an end the matters complained of: the court will decline its jurisdiction under s 205 where it believes that it cannot make an order which will have this end result. In *Re Murph's Restaurants Ltd*[195], Gannon J declined to exercise his jurisdiction under s 205(3) because, although he had found that the petitioner had been oppressed, he held that:

> 'It is clear from the evidence that there is no form of order of the nature indicated in s 205(3) which could bring to an end the matters complained of by [the petitioner] in the proceedings or which could regulate the affairs of the company for the future. It appears to me that the circumstances in which by order under s 205 the court may direct the purchase of the shares of a member by other members or by the company are circumstances in which the court would do so 'with a view to bringing to an end the matters complained of' by the person applying to the court. It is my opinion that in that case the fundamental relationship between [the petitioner and the respondents was so] sundered that proceedings under s 205 would not in any circumstances be appropriate[196].'

On the facts of the case in question Gannon J ordered that the company be wound up. Central to this decision was the fact that the company was a quasi-partnership company and that the relationship between the quasi-partners had broken down irretrievably.

(d) *Permissible orders under s 205(3) 'to end the matters complained of'*

[11.079] In *Re Forest Mill Investments Ltd; MacAvin v Fleming*[197], the petitioner claimed that she had been oppressed by the defendants. The petitioner claimed to have been ousted from her position as marketing director (holding 50% of the company's shares) by the first defendant, who owned the remaining 50%, and the second defendant, who was also a director. The allegations were denied. Since the petition had been filed the company had been placed into liquidation and the High Court dismissed the petition for oppression on that basis. In dismissing the petitioner's appeal Barron J said:

> 'Where the conduct whether of the majority in general meeting or of the directors is oppressive of any shareholder, the Court has power to regulate the matter in one of three ways. It can direct that the decisions leading to the oppression be reversed or amended; it can direct a purchase of the shares of any member; or it can direct a winding up of the company[198].'

Notwithstanding the reduction of the means of granting relief into three ways, it is thought to be convenient to consider particular relief in the following order:

(i) Purchasing the petitioner's shares.

(ii) Purchasing the respondent's shares.

(iii) The company purchasing shares.

---

195 *Re Murph's Restaurants Ltd* [1979] ILRM 141.

196 *Re Murph's Restaurants Ltd* [1979] ILRM 141 at 152.

197 *Re Forest Mill Investments Ltd; MacAvin v Fleming* (14 July 1998, unreported) SC, Barron J, *nem diss.*

198 *Re Forest Mill Investments Ltd; MacAvin v Fleming* (14 July 1998, unreported) SC at p 4.

(iv) Cancellation and variation of transactions.

(v) Alteration of constitutional documents.

(vi) Other relief except damages.

(i) Purchasing the petitioner's shares

[11.080] An order for the purchase of the petitioner's shares is the most commonly invoked remedy to end the matters complained of. Examples of cases in point include: *Re Greenore Trading Company Ltd*[199]; *Re Clubman Shirts Ltd*[200]; *Re Westwinds Holding Company Ltd*[201]; *Colgan v Colgan & Colgan*[202]; and *Re OC (Transport) Services Ltd*[203]. The principles upon which the shares will be valued have been considered in Ch 9[204].

[11.081] An important procedural point to remember is that all persons against whom an order to purchase the petitioner's shares may be made, must be named parties in the petition or, at the very least, notice parties. In *New-Ad Advertising Company Ltd*[205], a petition alleging oppression was brought in which the only named party was the company. After the company sold all of its assets, the company advised that it did not wish to defend the proceedings and asked that the defence which it had previously delivered be struck out. Costello P held that a Mr McNulty, a director and majority shareholder in the company, had acted oppressively towards the petitioner and in disregard of his interests as a member. Costello P said:

> 'The usual order in a case of this kind is that the company or the oppressor should buy out the minority shareholder at a value the shares would have had but for the oppressive conduct. Alternatively, an order to wind up the company can be made. However, in this case it would not be just to order the winding up of the company because no relief would be given to the petitioner. Similarly, I see no point in ordering that the company should buy the petitioner's shares because the company has no assets with which to purchase them. In order to ensure that justice is done, it seems to me that the wrongdoer – in this instance Mr McNulty – should buy the petitioner's shares at the value which they would have had but for the oppressive conduct to which I have briefly referred.
>
> I am aware of the fact that Mr McNulty has not been jointed as a notice party but he must have known that such an order might be sought, particularly in view of the fact that he, as a director, was instrumental in selling all the assets of the company. He must have been aware that it was highly likely, as claimed in the petition, that an order would be made against him personally. However, Mr McNulty did not seek separate representation. He could have brought a motion seeking to be separately jointed but he did not do so. It would therefore be unjust not to order that Mr McNulty, who was the person who committed the acts of which complaint is made, should remedy the injustice. And as Mr McNulty

199 *Re Greenore Trading Company Ltd* [1980] ILRM 94.

200 *Re Clubman Shirts Ltd* [1983] ILRM 323 and [1991] ILRM 43.

201 *Re Westwinds Holding Company Ltd* (21 May 1974, unreported) HC.

202 *Colgan v Colgan & Colgan* (22 July 1993, unreported) HC.

203 *Re OC (Transport) Services Ltd* [1984] BCLC 251.

204 See Ch 9, *Share Transfer*, at para **[9.117]**.

205 *New-Ad Advertising Company Ltd* (1 July 1997, unreported) HC, Costello P; (26 March 1998, unreported) SC.

> decided to sell the company's assets and not to contest the petition, it seems to me that it would be wrong for the court not to make the order sought by the petitioner[206].'

Costello P went on to assess the value of the shares on the evidence presented and ordered McNulty to pay £67,200 to the petitioner in return for the petitioner's shares in the company. McNulty subsequently applied to be made a notice party but this was refused by Costello P who informed him that it was too late. On appeal to the Supreme Court it was held that McNulty should then be made a notice party to the proceedings and should be furnished with all documents in the case and given an opportunity to enter a defence if he was so minded. In the course of his judgment O'Flaherty J said that based on the basic constitutional principles of *audi alteram partem* and the necessity to give a party against whom allegations are being made the opportunity to take part in the proceedings, it was a matter of 'elementary and fundamental justice that Mr McNulty should have been a party to the proceedings'[207].

(ii) Purchasing the respondent's shares

[11.082] In *Irish Press plc v Ingersoll Irish Publications Ltd*[208], on finding that the petitioner had been oppressed, the High Court ordered that the respondent sell its shares to the petitioner. This was one of the few occasions on which the High Court ordered that the petitioner should be at liberty to purchase the respondent wrongdoer's shares[209]. In *Brenfield Squash Racquets Club Ltd*[210], Rattee J said in the English High Court that it would only be in exceptional circumstances that a majority shareholder would be obliged to sell his shares to an unfairly prejudiced minority.

(iii) The company purchasing shares

[11.083] Section 205(3) of the CA 1963 empowers the court to order that the company itself should purchase the petitioner's or the respondent's shares. This may be the only remedy available where a party who is ordered to purchase the other's shares lacks the necessary resources and the company cannot avail of the validation procedure under s 60(2) of the CA 1963 and provide financial assistance for the purchase of its own shares by the party ordered to buy the shares[211]. In such circumstances, it is acknowledged by the wording of s 205(3) that the company's capital may be reduced and allows the court to so order. Where the funds to purchase shares come other than from distributable profits, the court must be extremely cautious lest the interests of the company's creditors' are prejudiced. In *Re Charles Kelly Ltd*; *Kelly v Kelly & Kelly*

206 *New-Ad Advertising Company Ltd* (1 July 1997, unreported) HC at pp 10–11.

207 *New-Ad Advertising Company Ltd* (26 March 1998, unreported) SC at p 6. O'Flaherty J also warned against the tendency to approach such matters on the basis that a controlling shareholder and director *is* the company and remarked that it was trite law to say that the identity of a company is distinct from the individuals who comprise it: *Salomon v A Salomon & Co* [1897] AC 22 (at p 4).

208 *Irish Press plc v Ingersoll Irish Publications Ltd* (15 December 1993, unreported) HC.

209 *Cf* Ussher, *Company Law in Ireland* (1985), pp 267–268, where the author criticises the situation whereby the wrongdoers could be left in 'sole control of the field of battle'.

210 *Brenfield Squash Racquets Club Ltd* [1996] 2 BCLC 184.

211 For distributable profits see Ch 10, *The Maintenance of Capital*, para **[10.089]** *et seq*.

(No 2)[212], Laffoy J ordered that the company would purchase the first respondent's shares and that the memorandum and articles of association be altered accordingly, following a market valuation to be carried out by Deloitte & Touche.

(iv) Cancellation and variation of transactions

[11.084] On a number of occasions the High Court has cancelled or varied transactions which have occurred. This remedy will frequently be coupled with an order to purchase either the respondent's or petitioner's shares[213]. Resolutions passed by the members have been cancelled by the court upon finding oppression or disregard of interests[214]. Sometimes it will not be necessary to cancel or vary a transaction which has been found to be oppressive because the court will order that the respondent purchase the petitioner's shares, and it will go on to value the shares on the basis that the impugned transaction never took place[215].

(v) Alteration of constitutional documents

[11.085] A less frequently employed remedy is for the court to order that the company's constitutional documents (ie, its memorandum and articles of association) should be amended to safeguard the petitioner's rights. Perhaps one reason for such infrequent use is because such a remedy may only provide temporary relief: in the many companies where s 205 of the CA 1963 proceedings are taken the members will be quasi-partners and the institution of proceedings will mark the end of the mutuality which characterises such relationships. Where the court orders that the company's constitutional documents are to be altered, they may not subsequently be altered again without the consent of the court[216].

(vi) Other relief except damages

[11.086] It is considered that the relief which the court can grant is unlimited, with the important proviso that *damages* may not be awarded[217]. Examples of extreme relief can be seen in a number of cases. An example is *Re HR Harmer Ltd*[218], where the English Court of Appeal ordered that the octogenarian respondent be excluded from the management of the company[219].

Costs of the petition

[11.087] Ordinarily, costs follow the event and this is no different in s 205 proceedings. The question of costs was considered by Laffoy J in *Re Skytours Travel Ltd; Doyle v*

212 *Re Charles Kelly Ltd; Kelly v Kelly & Kelly (No 2)* [2011] IEHC 349.

213 *Re Westwinds Holding Company Ltd* (21 May 1974, unreported) HC, *per* Kenny J.

214 *Re Williams Group Tullamore Ltd* [1985] IR 613 and *Re Irish Visiting Motorists' Bureau Ltd* (7 February 1972, unreported) HC.

215 Eg, *Re Westwinds Holding Company Ltd* (21 May 1974, unreported) HC, *per* Kenny J.

216 Section 205(4) of the CA 1963.

217 See para **[11.074]** *et seq*.

218 *Re HR Harmer Ltd* [1958] 3 All ER 689. See para **[11.022]**.

219 See the *ex tempore* judgment in *Re Christy Kenneally Communications*, noted by MacCann, *Butterworth Ireland Companies Acts 1963–1990*, p 204 where Costello J disqualified the respondents from acting as directors and replaced them with court-appointed directors.

Bergin (No 2)[220]. In that case, Laffoy J had previously held in favour of the petitioner[221], having declared that the affairs of the company were being conducted in a manner oppressive to the petitioner and in disregard of his interests, and making an order directing the respondent to purchase the petitioner's shares for €58,769.74. The respondent objected to paying all of the petitioner's costs on two grounds. The first ground was that the petitioner had not succeeded on all issues. Laffoy J rejected this ground on the basis that the legal arguments advanced on the points lost concerning the valuation of the petitioner's shareholding had not unnecessarily elongated the proceedings. The respondents succeeded in avoiding paying all of the petitioner's costs on the second ground, however, by reason of Ord 99, r 1A(1)(b) of the RSC 1986[222] and the fact that the respondent had issued a so-called *Calderbank* letter which offered to acquire the petitioner's shareholding for €75,001 in staggered payments. Adopting as a useful test that set out by Sir Thomas Bingham MR in *Roache v Newsgroup Newspapers Ltd*[223], Laffoy J noted that the petitioner's response to the respondent's claim for costs to be awarded against the petitioner from the date of the letter was threefold. First, it was contended that the plaintiff had a legitimate interest in pursuing his claim for a declaration with a view to disconnecting himself from what was alleged was a gross fraud perpetrated by the respondent; second, it was claimed that there was a 'public dimension' to s 205 which incentivises a member of the company to expose through litigation a serious fraud; and third, it was contended that the petitioner was justified in rejecting the phasing of payment for his shares.

Laffoy J rejected the first argument advanced by the petitioner on the grounds that, subject to one qualification, the letter offered to pay an amount in excess of the fair value ascribed by the court to the shares, when the petitioner's claim was for an order directing that the shares be acquired at fair value. Moreover, a declaration distancing the petitioner from wrongdoing was not something that was necessary to bring to an end the oppression. Laffoy J also rejected the second argument on the ground that there is no public dimension to s 205 of the CA 1963.

Laffoy J went on to say that Ord 99, r 1A(1)(b) of the RSC 1986 allowed the court to depart from the normal rule that costs follow the event but said that in any particular case 'it may not be sufficient to base a conclusion that it is just to deprive a party who has rejected an offer to satisfy the whole or part of the claim and who as a matter of

---

220 *Re Skytours Travel Ltd; Doyle v Bergin (No 2)* [2011] IEHC 518, Laffoy J.

221 *Re Skytours Travel Ltd; Doyle v Bergin* [2011] IEHC 517, Laffoy J. See also para **[11.065]** *ante*.

222 Order 99, r 1A(1)(b) of the RSC 1986 provides: 'The High Court, in considering the awarding of the costs of any action (other than an action in respect of a claim or counterclaim concerning which a lodgment or tender offer in lieu of lodgment may be made in accordance with Order 22) or any application in such an action, may, where it considers it just, having regard to the terms of any offer in writing sent by any party to any other party or parties offering to satisfy the whole or part of that other party's (or those other parties') claim, counterclaim or application.'

223 *Roache v Newsgroup Newspapers Ltd* (1992) CAT 1120: 'The judge must look closely at the facts of the particular case before him and ask: Who, as a matter of substance and reality, has won? Has the plaintiff won anything of value which he could not have won without fighting the action through to a finish? Has the defendant substantially denied the plaintiff the prize which the plaintiff fought the action to win?'

substance and reality, has not achieved anything more than he was offered as a result of the decision of the Court, of the costs which accrued after the date of the offer'. In exercising her discretion, Laffoy J ordered that the respondent should pay the petititoner's costs other than the valuation evidence costs. The basis for this was because of the four-day trial, a period of two days was taken up with evidence of the issue of liability under s 205 which, had it been admitted by the respondent, would have saved considerable time and cost.

The unfairly prejudicial remedy contrasted[224]

[11.088] At this point it is appropriate to consider briefly the statutory remedies for shareholders in England and Wales[225]. Because of the tendency to consider the case law of England and Wales and to cite such case law in the Irish courts, it is important to set out the differences between their statutory remedy and ours. Although English case law is extremely useful, it must be relied upon with caution. Section 210 of the Companies Act 1948 (UK) was the closest statutory remedy to s 205 of the CA 1963, employing the concept of '*oppression*'. The present English provision is s 994(1) of the Companies Act 2006 (UK). This provides:

> 'A member of a company may apply to the court by petition for an order under this Part on the ground—
>
> (a) that the company's affairs are being or have been conducted in a manner that is unfairly prejudicial to the interests of members generally or of some part of its members (including at least himself), or
>
> (b) that an actual or proposed act or omission of the company (including an act or omission on its behalf) is or would be so prejudicial.'

A number of comparisons with s 205 of the CA 1963 may be made.

[11.089] First and most significantly, s 994(1) of the Companies Act 2006 (UK) employs the test of *unfairly prejudicial* instead of *oppression*[226]. Second, there is no reference to the exercise of the *powers of the directors*. Third, the s 994(1) remedy is expressed to apply to actual or *proposed* acts or *omissions*. While these are the main differences, others exist[227].

---

224 See generally, Griffin, 'The Statutory Protection of Minority Shareholders: Section 459 of The Companies Act 1985' (1992) 13 Co Law 83; Hollington, *Minority Shareholders' Rights* (1990), Ch 4, 'The Unfair Prejudice Remedy'; and Gower, *Principles of Modern Company Law* (1992), p 662 *et seq*.

225 Griggs & Lowry, 'Minority Shareholder Remedies: A Comparative View' [1994] JBL 463, for a comparative consideration of shareholders' remedies in England, Canada and the United States.

226 See *Re a Company (No 00477 of 1986)* [1986] BCLC 376; *Re Bovey Hotel Ventures Ltd* (31 July 1980, unreported) High Court England & Wales, Nourse J; and see generally, Griffin, 'The Statutory Protection of Minority Shareholders: Section 459 of The Companies Act 1985' (1992) 13 Co Law 83 and Griggs & Lowry, 'Minority Shareholder Remedies: A Comparative View' [1994] JBL 463 at 466–468.

227 Eg, unregistered transferees of shares in the company have *locus standi* to petition under s 994(2) of the Companies Act 2006 (UK).

[11.090] The draft Companies Bill published in 2011, it has been announced, will be published as a formal Bill in late 2012. It proposes to substantially re-enact s 205 of the CA 1963, which has so well served the interests of members of Irish companies. Section 209(1) of the draft Bill provides:

> 'Any member of a company who complains that the affairs of the company are being conducted or that the powers of the directors of the company are being exercised –
>
> (a) in a manner oppressive to him or her or any of the members (including himself or herself); or
>
> (b) in disregard of his or her or their interests as members,
>
> may apply to the court for an order under this section.'

One particular amendment which is proposed is that the court will be expressly authorised to order the payment of compensation: s 209(3)(d) of the draft Bill.

Contracting out of s 205

[11.091] It has been established in England and Wales that there is nothing inherently contrary to public policy for shareholders to agree that their disputes should be referred to arbitration[228]. It is thought that where shareholders agree, whether in a shareholders' agreement or articles of association, to refer disputes to arbitration and thereby limit the right to apply to court for relief under s 205 of CA 1963, that there is no reason why the Irish courts would not give effect to that agreement. On a separate point, where shareholders agree to insert provisions in articles of association which might appear to be unfair or to manifestly disadvantage one shareholder or class of shareholders (eg, exclusion from a discretionary dividend) such as might incline a court to consider the exercise of such provisions to be oppressive or in disregard of interests, there may well be reason to expressly declare in the articles that the exercise of such powers is acknowledged not to constitute conduct within s 205.

[B] THE RULE IN *FOSS V HARBOTTLE*

[11.092] The rule in *Foss v Harbottle*[229] is one of the most established principles in company law. It has, however, been the cause of considerable confusion. The confusion has resulted largely from the failure to recognise that the rule has two *limbs*:

- the first is that where the company has been wronged, the company, and not its shareholders is the proper person to institute proceedings;
- the second is that an individual shareholder, or shareholders, may not bring proceedings to overturn a decision of the company where that decision is one which a majority of the members may confirm.

There is a further complication: members have *personal rights* which are always capable of being enforced by the members personally. In this section, the law is considered under a number of headings:

---

[228] *Fulham Football Club (1987) Ltd v Rochards and another* [2011] EWCA Civ 855, [2012] 1 BCLC 335. *Cf Exeter City Association Football Club Ltd v Football Conference Ltd* [2004] All ER 1179 which the Court of Appeal in *Fulham* overruled.

[229] *Foss v Harbottle* (1843) 2 Hare 461.

1. The principles behind the rule.
2. The rule in *Foss v Harbottle*.
3. The rule summarised.
4. Corporate rights distinguished from members' personal rights.
5. Personal rights and personal actions distinguished.

The principles behind the rule

[11.093] The basis of the rule in *Foss v Harbottle* is that the company is an independent legal entity which is separate from its shareholders[230]. Accordingly, wrongs committed against the company are generally actionable only by the company and not by its members. A further basis of the rule is that the members of a company generally[231] agree to majority rule in their relations *inter se*. Minority shareholders in a company are obliged to respect the decision of the majority. In common sense, nothing more could be expected. As in any democracy, the corporate enfranchised must dictate the direction of the company. Although minority members undoubtedly have rights, their wishes must not override the *bona fide* wishes of the majority. The traditional rule must, however, be qualified where the majority acts inequitably. The two fundamental principles considered above are the basis of the rule which, although diluted by the many exceptions thereto and overridden by s 205 of the CA 1963, still retains a certain vitality and importance. Commenting on the leading cases of *Foss v Harbottle*, *Prudential Assurance Co Ltd v Newman Industries Ltd (No 2)*[232] and *Burland v Earle*[233], O'Flaherty J said in *O'Neill v Ryan*[234]:

> 'The reasons are clear for the requirement established by this line of authority: otherwise there would be a multiplicity of actions, oppressive litigation and the company would cease to have proper control of its corporate destiny[235].'

[11.094] The rationalisation of the rule in *Foss v Harbottle* on the basis of the company's separate legal personality, as seen in the judgment of the English Court of Appeal in *Prudential Assurance Co Ltd v Newman Industries Ltd (No 2)* and the Supreme Court's endorsement thereof in *O'Neill v Ryan*, is indicative of a 'back to basics' approach. Notwithstanding that s 205 of the CA 1963 has driven a horse and four through the rule, the Supreme Court's recent endorsement of the rule has ensured its immediate survival in Irish company law.

The rule in *Foss v Harbottle*

[11.095] The rule in *Foss v Harbottle* has its origins in the now relatively dated case of *Foss v Harbottle*[236]. The facts of the case were that a company was formed by Act of the English Parliament for the purposes of acquiring approximately 180 acres of land in

---

230 See generally, Ch 4, *Incorporation and Its Consequences*, para **[4.026]** *et seq*.

231 In certain circumstances, majority rule is tempered by the weighting of certain members' voting rights, as illustrated by the case of *Bushell v Faith* [1970] AC 1099.

232 *Prudential Assurance Co Ltd v Newman Industries Ltd (No 2)* [1982] Ch 204.

233 *Burland v Earle* [1902] AC 83.

234 *O'Neill v Ryan* [1993] ILRM 557.

235 *O'Neill v Ryan* [1993] ILRM 557 at 559. See also the majority judgment of Blayney J at 570.

236 *Foss v Harbottle* (1843) 2 Hare 461.

Manchester. It was intended to develop the land by planting it in an ornamental and park-like manner and building houses with attached gardens. The land was purchased from one of the 13 defendants, a Joseph Denison, who had acquired the land only after the project had been agreed upon in principle. On foot of advertisements, the plaintiffs, Richard Foss and Edward Starkie Turton, subscribed for two shares and 12 shares respectively in the joint-stock company. Subsequently, to avail of the advantages of limited liability[237], application was successfully made for an Act of incorporation, and The Victoria Park Company began life.

The plaintiffs alleged, *inter alia*: first, that the defendants, who had been appointed directors in the company, purchased the lands from themselves for the use of the company and had charged the company an exorbitant consideration; and second, had raised finance for the company in a manner not authorised by its powers under the Act of incorporation since they created mortgages over the company's lands.

[11.096] The decision of the Vice-Chancellor in *Foss v Harbottle* incorporates a number of legal principles. The most important for present purposes is that where a company suffers a wrong, it is the company and not its shareholders which is the proper plaintiff in any subsequent action. Wigram VC said:

> 'It was not, nor could it successfully be argued, that it was a matter of course for any individual members of a corporation thus to assume to themselves the right of suing in the name of the corporation. In law, the corporation and the aggregate members of the corporation, are not the same thing for purposes like this; and the only question can be, whether the facts alleged in that case justify a departure from the rule which *prima facie* would require that the corporation should sue in its own name and in its corporate character, or in the name of someone whom the law has appointed to be its representative[238].'

Wigram VC justified the principle of majority rule on the basis that:

> '... whilst the supreme governing body, the proprietors at a special general meeting assembled, retain the power of exercising the functions conferred upon them by the Act of incorporation, it cannot be competent to individual corporators to sue in the manner proposed by the plaintiff on the present record. This in effect purports to be a suit by cestui que trusts, complaining of a fraud committed or alleged to have been committed by persons in a fiduciary character. The complaint is, that those trustees have sold lands to themselves, ostensibly for the benefit of the cestui que trusts. The proposition I have advanced is, that although the Act should prove to be voidable, the cestui que trusts may elect to confirm it. Now, who are the cestui que trusts in that case? The corporation, in a sense, is undoubtedly the cestui que trust; but the majority of the corporators at a special general meeting assembled, independently of any general rules of law upon the subject, by the very terms of the incorporation in the present case, has power to bind the whole body, and every individual corporator must be taken to have come into the corporation upon the terms of being liable to be so bound. How then can this court act in a suit constituted as this is, if it is to be assumed, for the purposes of the argument, that the powers of the body of the proprietors are still in existence, and may lawfully be exercised for a purpose like that I have suggested? Whilst the court may be declaring the acts complained of to be void at the suit of the present plaintiffs, who in fact may be the only proprietors who disapprove

[237] Joint-stock companies were denied limited liability until the passing of the Limited Liability Act 1855. See Ch 1, *The Private Company in Context*, para **[1.072]**.

[238] *Foss v Harbottle* (1843) 2 Hare 461 at 490–491.

of them, the governing body of proprietors may defeat the decree by lawfully resolving upon the confirmation of the very acts which are the subject of the suit. The very fact that the governing body of proprietors assembled at the special general meeting may so bind even a reluctant minority, is decisive to show that the frame of this suit cannot be sustained whilst that body retains its functions. In order then that this suit may be sustained, it must be shown either that there is no such power as I have supposed remaining in the proprietors, or, at least, that all means have been resorted to and found ineffectual to set that body in motion ...[239].'

In summary, under common form articles of association the management of the company is delegated to the company's directors and the company's directors act for the company which is the proper plaintiff in an action for a wrong committed against the company. The members of the company have the power to appoint and remove the board of directors and where the directors act in a manner at variance with the wishes of a majority of the members, the members are competent to remove the board, and to appoint a more sympathetic board in their stead.

The rule summarised

[11.097] In *Glynn and McCabe v Owen et al*[240], Finlay Geoghegan J said:

'Central to the rationale underlying the rule in *Foss v Harbottle* and the exceptions to it is that the courts should not interfere with the internal management of a company. It is a matter for the majority of the board of directors or shareholders to determine in an appropriate case whether litigation should be commenced by, and in the name of, a company against an allegedly wrongdoing director or shareholder (at least where the alleged wrongdoers are not in control of the company).'

[11.098] In *Prudential Assurance Co Ltd v Newman Industries Ltd (No 2)*[241], the Court of Appeal remarked that 'the classic definition of the rule in *Foss v Harbottle* is stated in the judgment of Jenkins LJ in *Edwards v Halliwell*'[242]. *Edwards v Halliwell* concerned the internal rules of a trade union which provided that the contributions of members should be as per the tables set out in the articles, unless these were varied by a members' ballot. Despite this rule, a delegate meeting of the trade union, without taking any members' ballot, increased the members' union subscriptions. The plaintiff members sought a declaration that this alteration of the rules was invalid. Jenkins LJ found that the rights infringed were members' *personal rights* and that, accordingly, *Foss v Harbottle* had no application to the case. In a passage quoted with approval by the Supreme Court in *Balkanbank v Taher*[243], Jenkins LJ said:

'The rule in *Foss v Harbottle*, as I understand it, comes to no more than this. First the proper plaintiff in an action in respect of a wrong alleged to be done to a company or association of persons is, prima facie, the company or association of persons itself. Secondly, where the alleged wrong is a transaction which might be made binding on the company or association and on all its members by a simple majority of its members, no individual member of the company is allowed to maintain an action in respect of that

239 *Foss v Harbottle* (1843) 2 Hare 461 at 493–494.

240 *Glynn and McCabe v Owen et al* [2007] IEHC 328, [2012] IESC 15.

241 *Prudential Assurance Co Ltd v Newman Industries Ltd* [1982] 1 Ch 204 at 210.

242 *Edwards v Halliwell* [1950] 2 All ER 1064.

243 *Balkanbank v Taher* (19 January 1995, unreported) SC at p 35 of the judgment.

> matter for the simple reason that, if a mere majority of the members of the company or association is in favour of what has been done, then *cadit quaestio*, no wrong has been done to the company or association and there is nothing in respect of which anyone can sue. If, on the other hand, a simple majority of members of the company or association is against what has been done, then there is no valid reason why the company or association itself should not sue. In my judgment, it is implicit in the rule that the matter relied on as constituting the cause of action shall be a cause of action properly belonging to the general body of corporators or members of the company or association as opposed to a cause of action which some individual member can assert in its own right[244].'

[11.099] In *Prudential Assurance Co Ltd v Newman Industries Ltd (No 2)*, the Court of Appeal summarised Jenkins LJ's statement of the rule in *Foss v Harbottle* in five propositions:

> '(1) The proper plaintiff in an action in respect of a wrong alleged to be done to a corporation is, *prima facie*, the corporation.
>
> (2) Where the alleged wrong is a transaction which might be made binding on the corporation and on all its members by a simple majority of the members, no individual member of the corporation is allowed to maintain an action in respect of that matter because, if the majority confirms the transaction, *cadit quaestio*; or, if the majority challenges the transaction, there is no valid reason why the company should not sue.
>
> (3) There is no room for the operation of the rule if the alleged wrong is ultra vires the corporation, because the majority of members cannot confirm the transaction.
>
> (4) There is also no room for the operation of the rule if the transaction complained of could be validly done or sanctioned only by a special resolution or the like, because a simple majority cannot confirm a transaction which requires the concurrence of a greater majority.
>
> (5) There is an exception to the rule where what has been done amounts to fraud and the wrongdoers are themselves in control of the company. In that case the rule is relaxed in favour of the aggrieved minority, who are allowed to bring a minority shareholders' action on behalf of themselves and all others. The reason for this is that, if they were denied that right, their grievance could never reach the court because the wrongdoers themselves, being in control, would not allow the company to sue[245].'

Points (3)–(5) are the so-called 'exceptions' to the rule in *Foss v Harbottle*, and are considered below. As shall be considered next, it is important to delimit the scope of the rule.

Corporate rights distinguished from members' personal rights

[11.100] Several judicial interpretations of the rule in *Foss v Harbottle* have engendered confusion for over 150 years[246]. The primary source of confusion has been the failure to

---

244 *Edwards v Halliwell* [1950] 2 All ER 1064 at 1066.

245 *Prudential Assurance Co Ltd v Newman Industries Ltd* [1982] 1 Ch 204 at 210–211.

246 The most notable cases are *Mozley v Alston* (1847) 1 Ph 790 and *MacDougall v Gardiner* (1875) 1 Ch D 13. For a commentary, see Ussher, *Company Law in Ireland* (1986), pp 166–167, where the confusion is attributed as being a failure to distinguish duties owed to the company from internal irregularities. See also Gower, *Principles of Modern Company Law* (5th edn, 1992), p 643 *et seq*.

distinguish actions by a member seeking to vindicate the *company's corporate rights* from actions by a member seeking to vindicate that *member's personal rights*[247]. A member's personal rights are always enforceable against his company by virtue of s 25 of the CA 1963. As has been considered in Ch 3, s 25 creates a statutory contract between a member and his company and the company and its members[248].

[11.101] This confusion was encouraged by cases such as *MacDougall v Gardiner*[249]. In that case the articles of association of the company provided that a poll could be demanded on the question of whether a general meeting could be adjourned by five shareholders. At a general meeting, an adjournment of the meeting was moved and accepted by the chairman. A poll was demanded by the members[250]. However the chairman ruled that there would not be an adjournment. One of the shareholders issued proceedings against the company and its directors both on his own behalf and on behalf of all of the other shareholders. It was alleged that the course taken at the meeting by the chairman was the result of collusion with the directors with a view to stifling discussion and that the directors were intending to carry out certain measures injurious to the company. A declaration was sought that the chairman's conduct was illegal and improper together with an injunction restraining the directors from carrying out the proposed arrangements without submitting them to the shareholders for approval. The Court of Appeal held that the action could not be sustained as it infringed the principles laid down in *Foss v Harbottle* and *Mozley v Alston*[251]. In short, the court would not interfere in the internal management of the company[252] even if that meant refusing to vindicate a member's personal rights. It is submitted that *MacDougall v Gardiner* makes bad law.

[11.102] Recognition of the members' right to vindicate their own personal rights has, however, been clearly recognised in a number of cases. In *Pender v Lushington*[253], the articles of association of the company provided that the votes of nominee shareholders would be counted at a general meeting. Contrary to this provision in the articles, the chairman of the company refused to count the votes of the plaintiff's nominees with the result that a resolution proposed by the plaintiff was not carried. The plaintiff applied, in both his own name and that of the company, for an injunction to restrain the directors from acting on foot of the invalid resolution. Jessel MR said in the course of his judgment that:

> 'This is an action by Mr Pender for himself. He is a member of the company and whether he votes with the majority or the minority he is entitled to have his vote recorded – an individual right in respect of which he has a right to sue. That has nothing to do with the question like that raised in *Foss v Harbottle* and that line of cases. He has a right to say, 'Whether I vote in the majority or minority, you shall record my vote, as that is a right of

---

[247] For members' personal rights see Ch 8, *Shares and Membership*, para **[8.041]** *et seq.*

[248] See Ch 3, *Constitutional Documentation*, para **[3.092]**.

[249] *MacDougall v Gardiner* (1875) 1 Ch D 13.

[250] On polls see Ch 14, *Corporate Governance: Meetings*, para **[14.067]**.

[251] *Mozley v Alston* (1847) 1 Ph 790.

[252] In *Carlen v Drury* (1812) 1 V & B 154, Lord Eldon said 'This court is not required on every occasion to take the management of every playhouse and brewhouse in the Kingdom.'

[253] *Pender v Lushington* (1877) 6 Ch D 70.

> property belonging to my interest in this company and if you refuse to record my vote I will institute legal proceedings against you to compel you.' What is the answer to such an action? It seems to me it can be maintained as a matter of substance and that there is no technical difficulty in maintaining it ...'

A similar conclusion was arrived at in *Edwards v Halliwell*[254]. There, in respect of the plaintiffs' rights not to have their membership subscriptions increased unless pursuant to a ballot, Jenkins LJ said:

> 'Those rights, these members claim, have been invaded. The gist of the case is that the personal and individual rights of membership of each of them have been invaded by a purported, but invalid, alteration of the tables of contributions. In those circumstances, it seems to me the rule in *Foss v Harbottle* has no application at all, for the individual members who are suing sue, not in the right of the union, but in their own right to protect from invasion their own individual rights as members[255].'

Although sometimes considered to be an exception to the rule in *Foss v Harbottle*, the right of members to sue to vindicate their personal rights as members is entirely divorced from the rule.

Personal rights and personal actions for reflective loss distinguished

[11.103] The cases cited in the preceding paragraphs clearly demonstrate that a member can sustain an action to vindicate his personal *rights* as a member of the company. Action to vindicate the personal rights accorded a member under the company's articles of association and the Companies Acts[256] must be distinguished from a member instituting proceedings in respect of a diminution in the value of his shareholding, or a personal action unrelated to his personal rights. The general rule is that shareholders may not sue to recover for what is termed *reflective loss* in the value of their shares as only the company has the right to sue for the actual loss to it[257]. The rule against reflective loss is conceptually different from the rule in *Foss v Harbottle*; as one commentator[258] has observed, the 'former concerns a shareholder's attempt to recover losses consequent on damage to the company, while the latter concerns actions to recover losses to the company for damage to the company'.

[11.104] In *Prudential Assurance Co Ltd v Newman Industries Ltd (No 2)*[259], the plaintiff company, which was a minority shareholder in the defendant company, brought a derivative action[260] and a personal action against the defendant and two of its directors. The personal action alleged that the directors had acted fraudulently, causing the value

---

254 *Edwards v Halliwell* [1950] 2 All ER 1064.

255 [1950] 2 All ER 1064 at 1067.

256 See Ch 8, *Shares and Membership*, para **[8.041]**.

257 See, generally, Ahern, 'The Rules Against Shareholders' Recovery of Reflective Loss' (2005) 12(6) CLP 163; Griffen, 'Shareholder Remedies and the No Reflective Loss Principle: Problems Surrounding the Identification of a Membership Interest' [2010] JBL 461; and Lee Suet Lin, 'Barring Recovery for Diminution in Value of Shares on the Reflective Loss Principle' (2007) Camb LJ 537.

258 Ahern, 'The Rules Against Shareholders' Recovery of Reflective Loss' (2005) 12(6) CLP 163 at 163.

259 *Prudential Assurance Co Ltd v Newman Industries Ltd (No 2)* [1982] Ch 204.

260 See para **[11.108]**.

of the company to diminish. The Court of Appeal held on this point, in a passage cited with approval by Blayney J in the majority Supreme Court decision in *O'Neill v Ryan*[261], that:

> 'In our judgment the personal claim is misconceived. It is of course correct, as the judge found and Mr Barlett did not dispute, that he and Mr Laughton, in advising the shareholders to support the resolution approving the agreement, owed the shareholders a duty to give such advice in good faith and not fraudulently. It is also correct that if directors convene a meeting on the basis of a fraudulent circular, a shareholder will have a right of action to recover any loss which he has been personally caused in consequence of the fraudulent circular; this might include the expense of attending the meeting. But what he cannot do is to recover damages merely because the company in which he is interested has suffered damage. He cannot recover a sum equal to the diminution in the market value of his shares, or equal to the likely diminution in dividend, because such a 'loss' is merely a reflection of the loss suffered by the company. The shareholder does not suffer any personal loss. 'Loss' is through the company, in the diminution in the value of the net assets of the company, in which he has (say) a 3% shareholding. The plaintiff's shares are merely a right of participation in the company on the terms of the articles of association. The shares themselves, his right of participation, are not directly affected by the wrongdoing. The plaintiff still holds all the shares as his own absolutely unencumbered property. The deceit practised upon the plaintiff does not affect the shares; it merely enables the defendant to rob the company[262].'

The following passage from the Court of Appeal's decision was also cited by both O'Flaherty[263] and Blayney JJ[264]:

> 'A personal action would subvert the rule in *Foss v Harbottle* and that rule is not merely a tiresome procedural obstacle placed in the path of a shareholder by a legalistic judiciary. The rule is the consequence of the fact that a corporation is a separate legal entity. Other consequences are limited liability and limited rights. The company is liable for its contracts and torts; the shareholder has no such liability. The company acquires causes of action for breaches of contracts and torts which damage the company. No cause of action vests in the shareholder. When the shareholder acquires a share he accepts the fact that the value of his investment follows the fortunes of the company and that he can only exercise his influence over the fortunes of the company by the exercise of his voting rights in general meeting. The law confers on him the right to ensure that the company observes the limitations of its memorandum of association and the right to ensure that other shareholders observe the rule, imposed upon them by the articles of association[265].'

Blayney J opined that the foregoing passage is a correct statement of the law in regard to the status of a shareholder in a limited liability company[266].

[11.105] Notwithstanding that disgruntled shareholders in Irish private companies tend to rely on s 205 of the CA 1963, the rule in *Foss v Harbottle* has been accepted and continues to be applied in the Irish courts[267]. Acceptance of the rule is seen in the

---

[261] *O'Neill v Ryan* [1993] ILRM 557 at 569.

[262] *Prudential Assurance Co Ltd v Newman Industries Ltd (No 2)* [1982] Ch 204 at 222.

[263] *O'Neill v Ryan* [1993] ILRM 557 at 559 (minority judgment).

[264] *O'Neill v Ryan* [1993] ILRM 557 at 569–570 (majority judgment).

[265] *Prudential Assurance Co Ltd v Newman Industries Ltd (No 2)* [1982] Ch 204 at 224.

[266] *O'Neill v Ryan* [1993] ILRM 557 at 570.

[267] See *Duggan v Bourke et al* (30 May 1986, unreported) HC, *per* Costello J.

decision of the Supreme Court in *O'Neill v Ryan*[268], where the High Court decision of Lynch J was confirmed[269]. The plaintiff claimed, *inter alia*, damages and other relief for breach of contract and wrongful dismissal against the first and second defendants in the action. The claim arose from the plaintiff's allegation that the four last-named defendants had caused damage to Ryan Air Ltd, thereby reducing the value of his shareholding in that company. The defendants brought a motion to have the plaintiff's action dismissed or stayed on the basis that the pleadings disclosed no reasonable cause of action. In the High Court, Lynch J dismissed the plaintiff's action against the four last-named defendants. This was upheld by the Supreme Court which endorsed the rule in *Foss v Harbottle* and went on to endorse the judgment of the Court of Appeal in *Prudential Assurance Co Ltd v Newman Industries Ltd (No 2)*, holding that the members of a company could not sue on account of a diminution in the value of their shareholding. As such, the position in Ireland is that shareholders may not recover reflective loss.

[11.106] In *Stein v Blake*[270], the first defendant was a 50% shareholder and the sole director (as permitted under English law) of a group of companies in which the plaintiff held the other 50% of the shares. The transaction in issue was one under which the assets belonging to the group of companies were transferred into the ownership of various other companies controlled by the first defendant. The plaintiff objected, claiming that in breach of the first defendant's fiduciary duty and the companies' articles of association, the first defendant had misappropriated the assets by causing the assets to be sold at an undervalue. The plaintiff claimed that this action had deprived him of the ability to sell his shares at their fair value and that this had caused him personal loss. At trial, it had been held that the plaintiff had no cause of action in respect of any losses suffered by the group of companies in which he was shareholder and that those companies were the proper plaintiffs in any action against the defendants. This was upheld by the English Court of Appeal. There, Millett LJ distinguished *Heron International v Lord Grade*[271], where the Court of Appeal had recognised that breach of directors' fiduciary duties may cause loss to the shareholders because 'they are deprived of the opportunity of realising their shares to greater advantage'[272]. Millett LJ pointed out that in the *Heron* case the court had been addressing a situation where, as a result of a breach of duty of care on the part of directors to advise their shareholders in relation to a prospective takeover bid, the plaintiff had been induced or compelled to dispose of his shares to a bidder at an undervalue. Millett LJ observed that in such a case 'no wrong is done to the company. Its assets are not depleted; its coffers remain unaffected.' On the distinction between the two scenarios, Millett LJ said:

> 'The distinction is between (i) loss sustained by a shareholder by a diminution in the value of his shares by reason of the misappropriation of the company's assets, and (ii) loss caused directly to a shareholder who has been induced to part with the shares at an

268 *O'Neill v Ryan* [1993] ILRM 557.

269 The judgment of Lynch J is reported at [1990] ILRM 140.

270 *Stein v Blake* [1998] 1 All ER 724. See also *Giles v Rhind* [2001] TLR 497 and *Johnson v Gore Wood & Co* [2001] 2 WLR 72.

271 *Heron International v Lord Grade* [1983] BCLC 244.

272 *Heron International v Lord Grade* [1983] BCLC 244 at 262.

> undervalue. The shareholder has a personal cause of action to recover in respect of the second type of loss, but not the first[273].'

Applying these principles to the case in hand, Millett LJ found that the wrong complained of had been done, if to anyone, to the companies whose assets were allegedly misappropriated. He concluded:

> 'In my judgment, this case indicated the distinction which must be made. Directors owe fiduciary duties to their company to preserve and defend its assets and to the shareholders to advise them properly so that they are not induced or compelled to part with their shares at an undervalue. No doubt other fiduciary duties are also owed to both the company and to its shareholders. Shareholders may suffer loss in the event of a breach of either duty, but in the first case the loss consists of a diminution of the value of their shares, is fully reflected in the loss suffered by the company, and is fully compensated by restitution to the company. In the second case the company suffers no loss. Its assets are unaffected, though they are changed from physical assets to a chose in action consisting of a claim against the wrongdoers[274].'

It is thought that, with the exception of the final sentence, the foregoing paragraph clearly expresses the distinction between a claim by the company and a claim by shareholders. The final sentence does not, however, make clear sense: where shareholders are induced to sell their shares at an undervalue the company's assets are not changed from physical assets to choses in action and it is thought that Millett LJ must have been referring to the nature of the shareholders' claims, although this too is not without difficulty since shareholders' interests in shares are, by definition, choses in action, and never were physical assets.

[11.107] The refusal to allow a member to take a personal action against the directors in respect of the diminution of his shareholding or in respect of some other breach of the directors' duties is open to criticism on a number of grounds. First, the refusal fails to take on board the developments in the law of negligence and the greatly expanded categories of duties of care. Indeed the Supreme Court has accepted that directors can owe duties to creditors, upon the company becoming insolvent[275]. Moreover, as discussed in the context of Ch 15, the Supreme Court in *O'Neill v Ryan et al* made no mention of the fact that there is case law to suggest that shareholders can be owed duties by the directors in certain circumstances[276]. Secondly, it was recognised in *Private Motorists' Provident Society v Attorney General*[277] that the shareholders in a company have certain constitutional rights in respect of their shareholding[278].

---

[273] *Stein v Blake* [1998] 1 All ER 724 at 729g.

[274] *Stein v Blake* [1998] 1 All ER 724 at 730c.

[275] *Re Frederick Inns Ltd* [1994] 1 ILRM 387.

[276] See Ch 15, *Duties of Directors and Other Officers*, para **[15.019]**.

[277] *Private Motorists' Provident Society v Attorney General* [1983] IR 339.

[278] See generally, Ch 4, *Incorporation and its Consequences*, para **[4.068]** *et seq.*

[C] DERIVATIVE ACTIONS AND EXCEPTIONS TO *FOSS V HARBOTTLE*

Preliminary considerations

[11.108] It now falls to consider the supposed[279] five recognised exceptions to the rule in *Foss v Harbottle,* and the procedural mechanism of the derivative action. On a practical level, it should be remembered that the derivative action and the exceptions to *Foss v Harbottle* are normally only relied upon by members where they cannot bring themselves within s 205 of the CA 1963.

[11.109] The exceptions to the rule in *Foss v Harbottle* amount to a recognition that the rule does not prevent a member from bringing either of two types of action. First, a member is entitled to bring a personal action to vindicate an infringement of his personal rights. Second, a member *may* be entitled to bring a derivative action on behalf of the company. This may seem peculiar in that the analysis here of *Foss v Harbottle* has been predicated on the basis that the rule has *no* application to where a member's personal rights have been infringed. The reason for including this now as an exception to the rule is in recognition of the traditional view that actions to vindicate a member's personal rights are an exception to the rule[280]. Whether there is a real significance in this distinction or whether it can be passed off as an exercise in semantics does not detract from the fact that it engenders confusion. Before considering the supposed exceptions to the rule in *Foss v Harbottle* it is proposed to first consider the most usual procedural means of enforcing those exceptions: the derivative action.

The derivative action

[11.110] Where a wrong is committed against a company, whether by outsiders or by the directors, the proper plaintiff in the subsequent action is the company. As Kelly J said in *Connolly v Seskin Properties Ltd and ors*:[281]

> 'The reason for the rule is that, in law, a company is a legal person with its own corporate identity. That identity is separate and distinct from its directors and shareholders.'

The decision to institute proceedings will typically be taken by the company's board of directors which will usually be empowered to manage the company's business under model reg 80[282]. The problem for minority shareholders can arise in two particular situations:

- where the directors are themselves responsible for the wrong done to the company and refuse to take action against themselves; or
- where the aggrieved member or members cannot muster sufficient voting power in general meeting to compel the directors to institute proceedings.

---

[279] It shall be argued that when one properly distinguishes the rule in *Foss v Harbottle* from a company's members' right to sue to vindicate their personal rights, the traditionally accepted *exceptions* are in some cases, not exceptions, but examples of situations in which the rule has no application whatsoever.

[280] Endorsed by the Supreme Court in *O'Neill v Ryan* [1993] ILRM 557.

[281] *Connolly v Seskin Properties Ltd* [2012] IEHC 332 at para 2.

[282] See generally, Ch 13, *Corporate Governance: Management by the Directors*, para **[13.127]** where model reg 80 is considered in detail.

Such situations arise less frequently in private companies than in public companies with large membership where the division of powers between members and directors is a reality. The central question at issue in deciding whether a minority member should be permitted to bring a derivative action is whether, unless the action is brought, a wrong committed against the company would otherwise go unredressed.

(a) The nature of a derivative action

[11.111] Although the rule in *Foss v Harbottle* precludes individual members from instituting proceedings where the company has been wronged, the rule does have a number of exceptions. Where such exceptions can be relied upon, a member or members may be allowed to institute a derivative action. A derivative action is where a shareholder, as representative of all of the other shareholders[283], institutes proceedings *on behalf of the company* in an attempt to redress a wrong perpetrated against the company. In *Wallersteiner v Moir (No 2)*[284], Lord Denning MR set out the general rule and the rationale for permitting derivative actions:

> 'It is a fundamental principle of our law that a company is a legal person, with its own corporate identity, separate and distinct from the directors or shareholders, and with its own property rights and interests to which alone it is entitled. If it is defrauded by a wrongdoer, the company itself is the one person to sue for the damage. Such is the rule in *Foss v Harbottle* ... The rule is easy enough to apply when the company is defrauded by outsiders. The company itself is the only person who can sue. Likewise, when it is defrauded by insiders of a minor kind, once again the company is the only person who can sue. But suppose it is defrauded by insiders who control its affairs – by directors who hold a majority of the shares – who then can sue for damages? Those directors are themselves the wrongdoers. If a board meeting is held, they will not authorise the proceedings to be taken by the company against themselves. If a general meeting is called, they will vote down any suggestion that the company should sue them themselves. Yet the company is the one person who is damnified. It is the one person who should sue. In one way or another some means must be found for the company to sue. Otherwise the law would fail in its purpose. Injustice would be done without redress[285].'

Accordingly, wrongs done to the company may be redressed by the minority members bringing a derivative action on the company's behalf[286]. In practice the company itself will be named as a party to the proceedings so as to ensure that any order made by the court may be enforced by or against the company.

It is important to remember that in a derivative action a shareholder acts in a non-personal capacity, namely, he acts not only for himself but also for all the other shareholders. Accordingly, it was held in *Cooke v Cooke*[287] that where a shareholder sought to join in one action a claim for relief in his personal capacity with a derivative claim as representative of all of the other shareholders, leave was required to join those causes of action.

---

283 See *Cooke v Cooke* [1997] 2 BCLC 28.

284 *Wallersteiner v Moir (No 2)* [1975] 1 QB 373.

285 *Wallersteiner v Moir (No 2)* [1975] 1 QB 373 at 390A–D. This passage was cited by Irvine J in *Fanning v Murtagh et al* [2008] IEHC 277; see para **[11.116]** *post*.

286 See generally, *East Pant Du United Lead Mining Co v Merryweather* (1864) 2 Hem & M 254, *Mason v Harris* (1879) 11 Ch D 97 and *Menier v Hooper's Telegraph* (1874) 9 Ch App 350.

287 *Cooke v Cooke* [1997] 2 BCLC 28.

(b) The twin test to bring a derivative action

[11.112] In *Prudential Assurance Co Ltd v Newman Industries Ltd (No 2)*[288], it was held by the English Court of Appeal that before a minority shareholder should be permitted to bring a derivative action on behalf of the company he:

> '... ought at least be required before proceeding with his action to establish a *prima facie* case (i) that the company is entitled to the relief claimed, and (ii) that the action falls within the proper boundaries of the exception to the rule in *Foss v Harbottle*[289].'

The reason for this procedural hurdle was said by the Court of Appeal to be that it cannot be right to subject the company to a lengthy court action[290] only to decide whether the plaintiff had a proper right of action. Keane J in *Crindle Investments v Wymes*[291] appears to have accepted the propriety of the Court of Appeal's procedural requirements in *Newman*.

[11.113] In the *Newman* case[292], the facts were that two companies, Newman and TPG, were substantial shareholders in each other. When TPG encountered financial difficulties, a rescue plan was put together by a Mr Barlett and a Mr Laughton, who held prominent positions of management in both companies. It was proposed that Newman would buy the entire of TPG's assets, save its shares in Newman, at a price to be determined by Newman's auditors. To comply with Stock Exchange regulations, a circular was sent to the shareholders in both companies, convening separate general meetings and explaining the mechanics of the proposed transaction. Prudential Assurance, a minority shareholder in Newman, took objection to the proposed purchase price for TPG's assets and took further objection to the contents of the circular, claiming that it was difficult and misleading. Despite Prudential's protestations, the resolution approving of the transaction was passed by a small majority. At this point Prudential instituted proceedings against Newman: a personal action on its own and in other capacities, and a derivative action on behalf of the company. At the preliminary hearing, Vinelott J, in a judgment[293] much criticised by the Court of Appeal, held that Prudential could proceed with its claim. At the subsequent trial[294] Vinelott J held that Prudential could bring a derivative action on behalf of Newman, and justified this on the basis of the fifth exception to the rule in *Foss v Harbottle*, considered below[295], namely that 'the interests of justice do require that a minority action should be permitted'[296].

[11.114] What followed was an appeal to the Court of Appeal which delivered such a lengthy judgment that only Chapter 5 (the law) and Chapter 7 (conclusions) were

---

288 *Prudential Assurance Co Ltd v Newman Industries Ltd (No 2)* [1982] 1 Ch 204.

289 *Prudential Assurance Co Ltd v Newman Industries Ltd (No 2)* [1982] 1 Ch 204 at 221, 222.

290 The *Newman* case lasted 64 days.

291 *Crindle Investments v Wymes* [1998] 4 IR 578 at 594. See further para **[11.140]**.

292 Considered by Gower, *Principles of Modern Company Law* (5th edn, 1992), under the heading of 'The "Calamitous" *Newman* case', at 647, although he attributes the label to the Court of Appeal at [1982] Ch 224 at 235C.

293 *Prudential Assurance Co Ltd v Newman Industries Ltd* [1981] Ch 229.

294 *Prudential Assurance Co Ltd v Newman Industries Ltd* [1981] Ch 257.

295 See para **[11.140]**.

296 *Prudential Assurance Co Ltd v Newman Industries Ltd* [1981] Ch 257 at 327B.

reported in the Chancery Reports. The personal actions brought by Prudential were unsuccessful, as considered above[297]. Because Vinelott J had allowed the derivative action to proceed and because this had not been appealed, the Court of Appeal refused to reopen the matter, saying that it would amount to 'a grave injustice to all parties to increase the already horrendous costs of this litigation by allowing time for argument on an interesting but irrelevant point'[298]. And so, despite the lengthy judgment, the law remained unsettled as to the principles of law applicable to derivative actions. What was put forward, though, was the twin test for establishing whether a member has standing to bring a derivative action, which has been set out above[299] and which has been applied in a number of subsequent English decisions such as *Smith v Croft (No 3)*[300].

[11.115] In *Glynn and McCabe v Owen et al*[301], considered post[302], Finlay Geoghegan J said that she agreed with the principles stated by Lord Denning in *Wallersteiner v Moir (No 2)*[303]. In *Fanning v Murtagh et al*[304], the plaintiff sought leave to issue a derivative action on behalf of Smart Telecom plc on the ground that it was alleged that the first three defendants had perpetrated a fraud in the minority by procuring the purchase of assets and undertaking of the company at an undervalue. After citing the passage from the decision of Lord Denning MR in *Wallersteiner v Moir (No 2)*[305], quoted above[306], Irvine J went on to quote the following passage from the decision of Gibson LJ in *Barrett v Duckett*[307]:

> '1. The proper plaintiff is prima facie the company.
>
> 2. Where the wrong or irregularity might be made binding on the company by a simple majority of its members, no individual shareholder is allowed to maintain an action in respect of that matter.
>
> 3 There are however recognised exceptions, one of which is where the wrongdoer has control which is or would be exercised to prevent a proper action being brought against the wrongdoer: in such a case the shareholder may bring a derivative action (his rights being derived from the company) on behalf of the company.
>
> 4 When a challenge is made to the right claimed by a shareholder to bring a derivative action on behalf of the company, it is the duty of the court to decide as a preliminary issue the question whether or not the plaintiff should be allowed to sue in that capacity.
>
> 5. In taking that decision it is not enough for the court to say that there is no plain and obvious case for striking out; it is for the shareholder to establish to the

[297] See para **[11.104]**.
[298] *Prudential Assurance Co Ltd v Newman Industries Ltd* [1982] Ch 204 at 220.
[299] See para **[11.113]**.
[300] *Smith v Croft (No 3)* [1987] BCLC 355.
[301] *Glynn and McCabe v Owen et al* [2007] IEHC 328, [2012] IESC 15.
[302] See para **[11.135]**.
[303] *Wallersteiner v Moir (No 2)* [1975] 1 QB 373.
[304] *Fanning v Murtagh et al* [2008] IEHC 277, Irvine J.
[305] *Wallersteiner v Moir (No 2)* [1975] 1 QB 373.
[306] See para **[11.111]** *ante*.
[307] *Barrett v Duckett* [1995] 1 BCLC 243.

satisfaction of the court that he should be allowed to sue on behalf of the company.

6. The shareholder will be allowed to sue on behalf of the company if he is bringing the action bona fide for the benefit of the company for wrongs to the company for which no other remedy is available. Conversely if the action is brought for an ulterior purpose or if another adequate remedy is available, the court will not allow the derivative action to proceed.'

Irvine J stated her view of the Irish law on derivative actions thus:

> 'The decision of Finlay Geoghegan J is, I conclude, authority for the proposition that notwithstanding the fact that there are no rules in this jurisdiction which require a minority shareholder who wishes to bring a derivative action on behalf of the company to apply to the court for its sanction, that it may choose to do so, and indeed this has been the approach adopted by the plaintiff on this application. It is also to be inferred from her judgment that if a minority shareholder brings such an application to the court, the court must be satisfied that there are reasonable grounds for permitting the action to proceed and the intended plaintiff must demonstrate that those proceedings are prudent and in the interest of the company.'

In the absence of rules of court at that time, Irvine J went on to improvise and observed the logic in requiring intended plaintiffs to establish the basis for bringing a derivative action.[308] Irvine J concluded that a plaintiff seeking leave to issue derivative proceedings should present the following proofs to the court:

> '(i) An affidavit in which the plaintiff will set out the nature and extent of the evidence available to support his claim to *locus standi* and also to his right to the relief claimed on behalf of the company;
>
> (ii) Where the claim is dependent upon expertise beyond that of the plaintiff, the substance of that evidence should be provided to the court in a suitable form; and
>
> (iii) A brief opinion of counsel certifying that, based upon the evidence set out at (i) and (ii) above, the plaintiff has a realistic prospect of success in the action.
>
> If the court concludes, on the basis of the evidence and material referred to above, that the plaintiff has discharged the appropriate burden of proof, it should then proceed to consider whether there are any discretionary matters which would, nonetheless, justify the refusal of the relief sought.'

In that case Irvine J considered the evidence concerning whether a wrong had been done to the company, whether it had been done at a time when the company was controlled by the alleged wrongdoers and whether those wrongdoers had benefitted from their alleged wrongdoing. The learned judge held that there was insufficient evidence of all three

308 Irvine J said: '... I nonetheless believe that there is an onus on the plaintiff on an application such as the present one to set out for the court and the proposed defendants, the nature and extent of the evidence available to support the intended proceedings, subject of course to the plaintiff's right to supplement that evidence at trial. In particular, where the case to be made on behalf of the company is likely to depend on expertise beyond that held by the plaintiff then the court should, unless there are special circumstances to justify its absence, expect to be furnished with the substance of that evidence on the leave application. Whilst such proofs cannot be stated to be mandatory absent rules of court governing such applications, the court is firmly convinced that the plaintiff's prospects of succeeding on such an application should depend on the nature and extent of the evidence which he chooses to place before the court.'

matters and concluded that the plaintiff had not established to the satisfaction of the court that it would be prudent or in the company's interests to maintain the intended derivative action and accordingly refused the application.

(c) Ord 15, r 38: the procedure in bringing a derivative action

[11.116] Since the decision in *Fanning v Murtagh et al*[309] the position in Ireland has changed following the enactment of the Rules of the Superior Courts (Derivative Actions) 2010[310] which insert a new Ord 15, r 38 of the RSC 1986. Order 15, r 38(1), defines 'derivative action' to 'include any action in which a claim is made on behalf of a company by a member of that company'. It is opined that where the application is brought in relation to a company within the meaning of s 2 of the CA 1963, by 'member' is meant a member within the meaning of s 31 of the CA 1963 and will not admit a person having a beneficial interest in shares.[311] Order 15, r 38(2) provides that a derivative action may not be commenced without the leave of the High Court, given in accordance with r 38.

An application for leave to commence a derivative action must be made by way of originating notice of motion, entitled *In the matter of an intended derivative action*, seeking–

- the leave of the Court to commence the derivative action;
- where relevant, an order requiring the company to indemnify the applicant in respect of the whole or part of the costs and expenses reasonably incurred by the applicant in conducting the derivative action (including any costs for which the applicant may be liable in such action), and
- any interim relief of an urgent nature.

The primary change in procedure introduced by the new rules of court is to formalise in a supporting affidavit the *ad hoc* requirements suggested by Irvine J in *Fanning v Murtagh et al*[312]. Order 15, r 38(5) now requires the support of an affidavit:

(i) setting out the nature and extent of the evidence available to support the applicant's claim to be a person entitled to bring the intended derivative action;

(ii) setting out the nature and extent of the evidence available to support the applicant's assertion that the company is entitled to make the claim to which the intended derivative action relates, and where such evidence is of an expert or technical nature, the substance of that evidence shall be provided to the Court in a report of a qualified person verified by its author and exhibited to the grounding affidavit, or in other suitable form;

(iii) setting out the basis of the deponent's belief as to the existence of the facts or circumstances referred to in paragraphs (i) and (ii);

(iv) specifying the efforts, if any, made by the applicant to cause the company to prosecute the claim concerned;

---

309 *Fanning v Murtagh et al* [2008] IEHC 277, Irvine J.

310 SI 503/2010.

311 Note that r 38 applies *mutatis mutandis* to other bodies corporate with members and not just to companies: Ord 15, r 38(17) and (18) of the RSC 1986.

312 *Fanning v Murtagh et al* [2008] IEHC 277, Irvine J.

(v) setting out the basis on which it is alleged that it is reasonable and prudent in the interests of the company that the applicant be given leave to commence the intended derivative action;

(vi) including evidence, where available, of the views of members other than the applicant;

(vii) to which is exhibited an opinion of counsel as to whether the applicant has a realistic prospect of success in the intended derivative action; and

(viii) to which is exhibited a draft of the summons or other originating document, and a draft of any statement of claim, in the intended derivative action.

A respondent served with such an originating notice of motion who intends to oppose the application may file a replying affidavit setting out his grounds of opposition, verifying any facts or circumstances relied on, and the applicant may reply to that.[313] On the return date the court may direct service on other members or persons, give directions as to filing and delivery of further affidavits, make other orders to ascertain the views of the members (eg it may order that general meetings are convened) give directions that any substantial disputes are determined by way of plenary hearing, require written submissions, and other matters.[314]

Where the court determines to grant leave to commence the derivative action, it may:

(a) direct service of notice of the application on any other member or other person, including mode of service and the time allowed for such service (and the Court may for that purpose adjourn the hearing or further hearing of the application to a date specified);

(b) give directions as to the filing and delivery of any further affidavits;

(c) make such orders and give such directions (including a direction that a meeting of members take place) as it considers appropriate for the purpose of ascertaining the views of members whose interest in the subject matter of the proposed derivative action is independent of that of the applicant and the respondent;

(d) where the court has directed in accordance with the preceding paragraph that a meeting of members shall take place, give directions as to the convening and conduct of the meeting and for the reporting to the Court of the proceedings at the meeting;

(e) give a direction that the application be determined by way of plenary hearing, where it appears to the Court that the subject matter of the application is likely to involve a substantial dispute of fact or it is otherwise necessary or desirable in the interests of justice (and the Court may for that purpose make orders and give directions in relation to the exchange of pleadings or points of claim or defence between the parties);

(f) give directions as to the furnishing by the parties to the Court and delivery of written submissions;

(g) give directions as to the publication of notice of the hearing of the application and the giving of notice in advance of such hearing to any person other than a

[313] Ord 15, r 38(8) and (9) of the RSC 1986.

[314] Ord 15, r 38(11) of the RSC 1986.

party to the proceedings who desires to be heard on the hearing of the application;

(h) hear and determine any application for relief of an interlocutory nature, whether in the nature of an injunction or otherwise.

[11.117] In *Connolly v Seskin Properties Ltd, Whelan and Whelan*[315], a matter of an intended derivative action, Kelly J noted that the applicant and respondents had complied with the requirements of Ord 15, r 38 of the RSC 1986. In that case the applicant was one of three directors, the other two being the Whelans and he held 49% of the shares in the first respondent company. The applicant sought to bring a derivative action on behalf of Seskin Properties Ltd on the grounds that it was owed over €5,300,000 by Maplewood Developments, a company allegedly owned and controlled by the Whelans. The applicant claimed that the reason why the Whelans had allowed the debt to accrue and had not instituted proceedings against Maplewood Developments was not based on the interests of the Seskin Developments Ltd. On the evidence, Kelly J determined that the prospects of success against Maplewood Developments in any derivative action were poor and heard that it had a good prospect of succeeding on its counterclaim that the €5,300,000 allegedly owed was due to an error in the underlying contract and also that, even if he was wrong, it had no assets to discharge any judgment. In those circumstances, Kelly J held that he did not believe that a court would be persuaded to find that the decision of the Whelans not to sue was in breach of their fiduciary duties owed to Seskin. On that ground alone, the application failed.

(d) The indemnity for costs

[11.118] Where a member is successful in a derivative action he will drop out of the action and the court will award judgment in favour of the company[316]. It is important to note that the member who instigates a derivative action may discontinue it at his own behest without the consent of his supposed principal[317]. The question of costs looms large for a member about to embark upon the institution of a derivative action. In *Wallersteiner v Moir (No 2)*[318], Lord Denning MR said:

> '... the minority shareholder, being an agent acting on behalf of the company, is entitled to be indemnified by the company against all costs and expenses reasonably incurred by him in the course of the agency. This indemnity does not arise out of a contract express or implied, but it arises on the plainest principles of equity. It is analogous to the indemnity to which a trustee is entitled from his cestui que trust who is *sui juris*: see *Hardoon v. Belilios* [1901] AC 118 and In *re Richardson, Ex parte Governors of St. Thomas's Hospital* [1911] 2 KB 705. Seeing that, if the action succeeds, the whole benefit will go to the company, it is only just that the minority shareholder should be indemnified against the costs he incurs on its behalf. If the action succeeds, the wrongdoing director will be ordered to pay the costs: but if they are not recovered from him, they should be paid by the company. And all the additional costs (over and above party and party costs) should be taxed on a common fund basis and paid by the company: see *Simpson and Miller v British Industries Trust Ltd*

[315] *Connolly v Seskin Properties Ltd and ors* [2012] IEHC 332, Kelly J.

[316] *Spokes v Grosvenor Hotel Co Ltd* [1897] 2 QB 124. See also *Wallersteiner v Moir (No 2)* [1975] 1 QB 373 at 391–392 *per* Lord Denning MR.

[317] *Re Alpha Co Ltd* [1913] 1 Ch 203.

[318] *Wallersteiner v Moir (No 2)* [1975] 1 QB 373.

(1923) 39 TLR 286. The solicitor will have a charge on the money recovered through his instrumentality: see section 73 of the Solicitors Act, 1974.

But what if the action fails? Assuming that the minority shareholder had reasonable grounds for bringing the action – that it was a reasonable and prudent course to take in the interests of the company – he should not himself be liable to pay the costs of the other side, but the company itself should be liable, because he was acting for it and not for himself. In addition he should himself be indemnified by the company in respect of his own costs even if the action fails. It is a well known maxim of the law that he who would take the benefit of a venture if it succeeds ought also to bear the burden if it fails. *Qui sentit commodum sentire debet et onus*. This indemnity should extend to his own costs taxed on a common fund basis.

In order to be entitled to this indemnity, the minority shareholder soon after issuing his writ should apply for the sanction of the court in somewhat the same way as a trustee does: see *In re Beddoe, Downes v Cottam* [1893] 1 Ch 547, 557–558. In a derivative action, I would suggest this procedure: the minority shareholder should apply ex parte to the master for directions, supported by an opinion of counsel as to whether there is a reasonable case or not. The master may then, if he thinks fit, straightaway approve the continuance of the proceedings until close of pleadings, or until after discovery or until trial (rather as a legal aid committee does). The master need not, however, decide it ex parte. He can, if he thinks fit, require notice to be given to one or two of the other minority shareholders – as representatives of the rest – so as to see if there is any reasonable objection. (In this very case another minority shareholder took this very point in letters to us.) But this preliminary application should be simple and inexpensive. It should not be allowed to escalate into a minor trial. The master should simply ask himself: is there a reasonable case for the minority shareholder to bring at the expense (eventually) of the company? If there is, let it go ahead[319].

Lord Denning MR went on to say that before being given leave to commence an action on behalf of the company, a putative plaintiff should first make application to the Master's Court for directions, supported by counsel's opinion as to whether such an action is reasonable. Although Lord Denning MR did say that application should be made *ex parte*, the English Court of Appeal has cast fatal doubts on this in *Prudential Assurance Co Ltd v Newman Industries Ltd (No 2)*.

[11.119] The importance of recognising early in proceedings that one's cause of action is to be framed as a derivative action is seen in the Supreme Court's decision in *Balkanbank v Taher*[320]. The facts in that case were that the plaintiff had commenced proceedings against the defendants alleging, *inter alia*, breach of trust, breach of duty and fraud by some of them against a joint venture company – Balkan International Ltd – in which the plaintiff company was a shareholder. The essence of the dispute concerned the draw down and subsequent utilisation of the proceeds of credit facilities by Balkan International Ltd. In the High Court it had been held that the defendants had not been guilty of fraud or breach of duty in drawing down the credit facilities and that any irregularity in the utilisation of the credit facilities was actionable only by Balkan

---

319 *Wallersteiner v Moir (No 2)* [1975] 1 QB 373 at 391G–H. This was endorsed by Buckley LJ who said (at 403G): 'It seems to me that in a minority shareholder's action, properly and reasonably brought and prosecuted, it would normally be right that the company should be ordered to pay the plaintiff's costs so far as he does not recover them from any other party.'

320 *Balkanbank v Taher et al* (19 January 1995, unreported) SC.

International Ltd, not the plaintiff, by reason of the operation of the rule in *Foss v Harbottle*. Notwithstanding that the proceedings had been commenced in the plaintiff's own name, the trial judge gave liberty to amend the statement of claim to include a derivative action, brought on behalf of the company based on the 'fraud on a minority'[321] exception to the rule in *Foss v Harbottle*. The defendants appealed against this on the basis that to make such a change in the proceedings was unfairly prejudicial to their defence. The Supreme Court agreed and allowed the appeal. In the course of his judgment Hamilton CJ found that the change was radical and not minor in nature and seriously prejudiced the defendants, and that such was not in accordance with fair procedures which require that a party to an action be given notice of the nature of a claim and an adequate opportunity of defending all aspects thereof. Hamilton CJ also noted that the plaintiff's original claim, as pleaded, required the establishment of fraud and that the High Court had found that the plaintiff had failed to establish fraud; however, in a derivative action 'they were merely required to establish that, without any element of dishonesty or criminality, monies entrusted to the defendants/appellants for a particular purpose were used by them for some other purpose'[322].

[11.120] Order 15, r 38(3)(b) of the RSC 1986 now expressly recognises the possibility that the court may order the company to indemnity the member bringing a derivative action, but this merely reflects the position at common law. In *Fanning v Murtagh et al*[323], Irvine J said that:

> 'It seems to follow that once a court sanctions a plaintiff to maintain derivative proceedings, then, even if those proceedings are ultimately unsuccessful, there is a high likelihood that the plaintiff will obtain an indemnity in respect of his costs from the company.'

In that case Irvine J held that the plaintiff had not established to the court's satisfaction that it would be prudent or in the company's interests to maintain the derivative action and so no indemnity as to costs was given. In the earlier case of *Glynn v McCabe (No 2)*[324], Finlay Geoghegan J was asked for an indemnity against the companies as to costs by the plaintiffs who she had previously held could not maintain a derivative action based on the 'fraud on a minority' exception to the rule in Foss v Harbottle[325]. While agreeing with the principles set out by Lord Denning in *Wallersteiner v Moir (No 2)*, quoted above[326], the learned judge refused an indemnity to the plaintiffs in that case on the grounds that the plaintiffs had not sought leave to commence the derivative action and had opposed the determination of their entitlement to pursue the derivative claim as a preliminary issue.

---

[321] See para **[11.129]** *et seq.*

[322] *Balkanbank v Taher et al* (19 January 1995, unreported) SC at p 39.

[323] *Fanning v Murtagh et al* [2008] IEHC 277, Irvine J.

[324] *Glynn v McCabe et al (No 2)* [2007] IEHC 452.

[325] See para **[11.129]** *post*.

[326] In the passage quoted at para **[11.111]** *ante*.

The exceptions to the rule in *Foss v Harbottle*

[11.121] Traditionally[327], the textbooks say that there are four exceptions to the rule in *Foss v Harbottle*[328]. To these has been added a less settled fifth exception. The five *possible* exceptions are said to be:

(a) Where an *ultra vires* or illegal act is perpetrated.
(b) Where more than a bare majority is required to ratify the 'wrong' complained of.
(c) Where the members' personal rights are infringed.
(d) Where a fraud has been perpetrated upon a minority by those in control.
(e) Where the justice of the case requires a minority to be permitted to institute proceedings.

Notwithstanding the cold response[329] to suggestions of the fifth exception, it may be argued that it is at least as deserving of recognition as the traditional four exceptions. In that the fifth exception recognises the inherent jurisdiction of the courts to remedy unconscionable conduct, it is thought that it is well placed and deserving of recognition as a *true* exception to the rule. Indeed the *justice of the case* is perhaps the true reason for permitting all derivative actions to subsist, the other four exceptions being variations on this theme.

(a) Ultra vires and illegal acts[330]

[11.122] Notwithstanding the rule in *Foss v Harbottle,* an individual member may either:

(a) seek an injunction to prevent the company committing an ultra vires act[331]; or
(b) where an *ultra vires* act has been committed, sue on behalf of the company for a declaration that the act was *ultra vires*[332].

This is an exception to both limbs of the rule in *Foss v Harbottle,* which exalts majority rule: a simple majority of the members cannot ratify action which is outside the company's capacity, and which is consequently *ultra vires*[333], and, it would appear, also that where a wrong is committed to the company, the company is the proper plaintiff[334].

---

327 See eg, Keane, *Company Law* (3rd edn, 2000), para 26.10.

328 However, in the current edition of Keane, *Company Law* (4th edn, 2007) at 26.04 the learned author opines that there are three exceptions, the infringement of personal rights not being an exception at all since the rule is of no relevance where there is no wrong done to the company.

329 See the *dicta* of the Court of Appeal in *Prudential Assurance Co Ltd v Newman Industries Ltd (No 2)* [1982] 1 All ER 354 and *Estmanco Ltd v GLC* [1982] 1 All ER 437.

330 See Ch 7, *Corporate Contracts, Capacity and Authority*, para **[7.045]** *et seq*.

331 See s 8(2) of the CA 1963; *Simpson v Westminister Palace Hotel Co* (1860) 8 HL Cas 712; *Maunsell v Midland Great Eastern (Ireland) Rly Co* (1863) 1 Hem & M 130; *Spokes v Grosvenor Hotel Co* [1897] 2 QB 4; and *Hoole v Great Western Rly Co* (1867) 3 Ch App 262.

332 See *Hennessy v National Agricultural and Industrial Development Association* [1947] IR 159; *Spokes v Grosvenor Hotel Co* [1897] 2 QB 124; and *Salomons v Laing* (1850) 12 Beav 377.

333 *Ashbury Railway Carriage and Iron Co v Riche* (1875) LR HL 653; *Buchanan Ltd v McVey* [1954] IR 89; and *Re Balgooley Distillery Co* (1886) 17 LR Ir 239; and see generally Ch 7, *Corporate Contracts, Capacity and Authority*, para **[7.045]**.

334 See *Smith v Croft (No 3)* [1987] BCLC 355.

[11.123] A number of decisions have held that an individual member has a *personal right* to take an action to restrain the commission of an *ultra vires* act[335]. In *Simpson v Westminister Palace Hotel Co*[336], Lord Campbell LC said:

> 'The funds of a joint stock company established for one undertaking cannot be applied to another. If an attempt to do so is made, this act is ultra vires, and although sanctioned by all the directors and by a large majority of the shareholders, any single shareholder has a right to resist it, and a court of equity will interpose on his behalf by injunction ...'.

This common law statement has statutory backing in s 8(2) of the CA 1963, which provides:

> 'The court may on the application of any member or holder of debentures of a company, restrain such company from doing any act or thing which the company has no power to do.'

On the traditional analysis, this is seen as a common law/statutory exception to the rule in *Foss v Harbottle*. It is thought that such an analysis is misfounded and that this situation is in reality also an example of a situation to which the rule has no application in the first place. Rather, to sue to prevent the commission of an *ultra vires* act is a personal right of a company's members.

[11.124] Where an *ultra vires* act has taken place, it was held in *Hennessy v National Agricultural and Industrial Development Association*[337] that a member of the company may apply to court for a declaration to that effect. Similarly, a member may bring a derivative action to have an *ultra vires* act set aside and to recover money wrongly paid, as in *Russell v Wakefield Waterworks Co*[338]. There is authority that different principles apply to where a member institutes proceedings to have an *ultra vires* transaction set aside as opposed to where proceedings are taken to prevent the commission of a threatened *ultra vires* act[339]. On this analysis, a member's right to sue is by way of derivative action, and not by way of vindication of his personal rights. In *Smith v Croft (No 3)*[340], Knox J said:

> '... the whole doctrine whereby a minority shareholder is permitted to assert claims on behalf of the company, is rooted in a procedural expedient, and adopted to prevent a wrong going without redress. Where what is sought is compensation for the company for loss caused by ultra vires transactions the wrong, in my judgment, is a wrong to the company which has the substantive right to redress. Where the minority shareholder is

---

335 *Hutton v West Cork Rly Co* (1833) 23 Ch D 654.

336 *Simpson v Westminster Palace Hotel Co* (1860) 8 HL Cas 712. See also *Hoole v Great Western Railway Co* (1867) LR 3 Ch App 262 where Lord Cairns LJ said: '... if the arrangement which has been proposed is legal, is *intra vires*, the company, through their general meetings, have power to carry it into effect; if on the other hand, it is *ultra vires*, if it is illegal, any member of the company may dissent from it, and has a right to appeal to this court to be protected against its effects ...'

337 *Hennessy v National Agricultural and Industrial Development Association* [1947] IR 159.

338 *Russell v Wakefield Waterworks Co* (1875) LR 20 Eq 474.

339 See *Smith v Croft et al (No 3)* [1987] BCLC 355. This has been accepted by Pennington, *Pennington's Company Law* (6th edn, 1990), p 655, but found to be 'unconvincing' by Keane, *Company Law* (3rd edn, 2000), para 26.12.

340 *Smith v Croft et al (No 3)* [1987] BCLC 355 at 389.

seeking to prevent an ultra vires transaction or otherwise seeking to enforce his personal substantive rights, the wrong which needs redress is the minority shareholder's wrong[341].'

Such a distinction seems excessively legalistic. The principles of law applicable to the so-called exceptions to the rule in *Foss v Harbottle* are already a quagmire. It should also be noted that Knox J in *Smith v Croft (No 3)* held that a minority shareholder may be prevented from bringing a derivative action where a majority of the minority shareholders oppose the action being taken. It is difficult to reconcile this with Knox J's acceptance of the fact that *ultra vires* actions are not ratifiable[342]: if acts are not ratifiable, why should any disgruntled member be prevented from instituting proceedings?

[11.125] A member is at liberty to institute proceedings in respect of apprehended illegal acts or where illegal acts have been committed. The leading Irish authority on this exception is *Cockburn v Newbridge Sanitary Steam Laundry Company*[343]. The facts of that case were that the company's managing director paid bribes to officials in the War Office in return for lucrative contracts with the company. Two of the company's shareholders instituted proceedings to compel the managing director to pay the bribes to the company; the other shareholders were not inclined to such action. The managing director's defence was that any proceedings against him should be brought in the name of the company and because 'the company' was not disposed to bringing such proceedings no action against him was possible. O'Brien LC dismissed the defence that the matters complained of related to the company's 'internal management'. He went on to say:

> 'The rule of law and of good sense laid down in *Foss v Harbottle* is indisputable, but is subject to the exception that where the acts complained of are of a fraudulent character, or beyond the powers of the company, the action may be maintained by a shareholder suing on behalf of himself and the other shareholders, the company being made a defendant in the action ...[344].'

The learned judge held also that it was 'not within the power of the company either to make, ratify or adopt a proceeding of the scandalous character sought to be cloaked over in the present case by ... resolution', and was satisfied that the plaintiffs were entitled to the relief sought[345].

---

341 Support for the distinction was found in the Court of Appeal judgments in *Towers v African Tug Co* [1904] 1 Ch 558.

342 *Smith v Croft et al (No 3)* [1987] BCLC 355 at 384e.

343 *Cockburn v Newbridge Sanitary Steam Laundry Company* [1915] 1 IR 237.

344 See also *Buchanan Ltd v McVey* [1954] IR 89 where a fraud on the Revenue Commissioners was held to be unratifiable by the company.

345 Holmes LJ said in the course of his judgment: 'There is, however, one well-recognised exception to this rule [ie, the rule in *Foss v Harbottle*]. Where the question involves the investigation of misconduct or criminality on the part of the company and one or more of its officers, or something ultra vires the company itself, the arm of the law cannot be stayed by the rule of law to which I have referred.' When the company's shareholders subsequently refused to make the managing director account for the bribes, further application was made to court. This resulted in the making of an order for the winding up of the company on just and equitable grounds: see *Re Newbridge Sanitary Steam Laundry Ltd* [1917] 1 IR 67 and, generally, Ch 23, *Winding Up Companies*, para **[23.091]**.

(b) *Transactions unratifiable by a bare majority*

[11.126] This exception may be said to derive from that limb of the rule which exalts *majority rule* in conflicts between shareholders. Where a bare majority of members purports to ratify an act which in fact requires the sanction of a special resolution, a dissenting member is not prohibited by the rule in *Foss v Harbottle* from bringing proceedings. Similarly where inadequate notice is given of a proposed resolution at a general meeting of the company any member can bring a derivative action to prevent the company from acting on any resolution passed[346].

[11.127] Where a bare majority of a company's members purports to act in breach of the company's memorandum or articles of association or purports to ratify a breach[347], a member can institute proceedings to restrain such a breach[348]. In such circumstances the majority must either abide by the articles of association or alter them in accordance with law. Where the alteration is not *bona fide* and in the interests of the company as a whole, the body of law considered in Ch 3, above, may be invoked by the minority[349].

(c) *Actions for infringement of personal rights*

[11.128] Although this has been considered to be an exception to the rule in *Foss v Harbottle*, it is thought that this is not an exception at all, but rather an example of a situation in which the rule has no application whatsoever. Actions to vindicate a member's rights have been considered above and are entirely divorced from the rule[350].

(d) *Fraud on a minority by those in control*[351]

[11.129] This is the clearest and most exceptional case where the rule in *Foss v Harbottle* will not apply, and has even been identified as the only true exception to the rule[352]. Accordingly, notwithstanding the rule, a minority of the company's shareholders may take a derivative action on behalf of the company where the majority in *control* of the company perpetrates a *fraud* on the minority. This is an exception to both limbs of the rule which provides that only the company has *locus standi* to take action on foot of a wrong committed against the company and that the will of the majority should prevail. In *Smith v Croft (No 3)*[353], Knox J said:

> 'Ultimately the question which has to be answered in order to determine whether the rule in *Foss v Harbottle* applies to prevent a minority shareholder seeking relief as plaintiff for the benefit of the company is: 'Is the plaintiff being prevented improperly from bringing

---

346 *Baillie v Oriental Telephone and Electric Co Ltd* [1915] 1 Ch 503; [1914–15] All ER Rep 1420.

347 *Edwards v Halliwell* [1950] 2 All ER 1064.

348 *Mosely v Koffyfontein Mines Ltd* [1911] 1 Ch 73 and *Salomon v Quinn and Axtens Ltd* [1909] 1 Ch 311.

349 See Ch 3, *Constitutional Documentation*, at para **[3.056]** *et seq.*

350 See para **[11.103]**. For members' personal rights, see Ch 8, *Shares and Membership*, **[8.041]** *et seq.*

351 See generally, Wedderburn, 'Shareholders' Rights and the rule in *Foss v Harbottle*' [1958] Cam LJ 93.

352 See Farrar, *Farrar's Company Law* (3rd edn, 1991), p 449.

353 *Smith v Croft (No 3)* [1987] BCLC 355.

> these proceedings on behalf of the company?' If it is an expression of the corporate will of the company by an appropriate independent organ that is preventing the plaintiff from prosecuting the action he is not improperly but properly prevented and so the answer to the question is No. The appropriate independent organ will vary according to the constitution of the company concerned and the identity of the defendants who will in most cases be disqualified from participating by voting in expressing the corporate will.'

What constitutes fraud on a minority has been considered in many cases. In *Connolly v Seskin Properties Ltd and ors*[354] Kelly J said:

> 'It has been found to exist in different situations involving different degrees of moral turpitude. In *Pavlides v Jensen* [1956] Ch 565, Dankwerts J speaks of the observations of Lord Davey in the case of *Burland v Earle* [1902] AC 83, as confining the cases in which a derivative action can be brought "to those in which the acts complained of are of a fraudulent character (in which he includes appropriation by a majority in fraud of the minority of the shareholders) or beyond the powers of the company.'

The learned Kelly J then opined:

> 'It would, given the ever changing circumstances of modern commercial life, be unwise to attempt to identify what might or might not constitute fraud on a minority in any given case. What can be said, however, is that it usually involves some element of moral turpitude."[355]

[11.130] This exception can only provide relief to the company concerned: it is not intended to provide the minority shareholders with relief[356]. This exception must be clearly distinguished from situations where a minority institutes proceedings on foot of an alteration of a company's articles of association by a majority which does not act *bona fide* and in the interests of the company as a whole: in such situations the minority's remedy will usually be a *personal action*[357]. The alteration of the articles of association in such circumstances has been considered in Ch 3[358].

[11.131] The case law which has built up around this exception typically involves the *expropriation* or *appropriation*, to use two expressions found in other textbooks, of corporate property by a majority which is in a controlling position. Other cases involve situations where a majority supports the directors who act in breach of their fiduciary duties, or negligently or *mala fide* in the exercise of their powers. Again, it is important to distinguish the case law proper to a consideration of this exception to the rule from cases concerning the expropriation by majority shareholders of minority shareholders' shares in a company. In such cases a derivative action is usually inappropriate, the expropriated members having a personal action against the majority.

---

[354] *Connolly v Seskin Properties Ltd and ors* [2012] IEHC 332, Kelly J.

[355] *Connolly v Seskin Properties Ltd and ors* [2012] IEHC 332, Kelly J at para 63.

[356] *Ferguson v Wallbridge* [1935] 3 DLR 66 (Privy Council). It has been noted by Wedderburn, 'Shareholders' Rights and the rule in *Foss v Harbottle*' [1958] Cam LJ 93 that the standard of service to be delivered to the company has not been very high.

[357] *Greenhalgh v Arderne Cinemas* [1950] 2 All ER 1120 and *Sidebottom v Kershaw Leese & Co Ltd* [1920] 1 Ch 154.

[358] Ch 3, *Constitutional Documentation*, at para **[3.056]**.

[11.132] One of the leading cases on the fraud on a minority exception is *Menier v Hooper's Telegraph Works Ltd*[359]. In that case the defendant company manufactured telegraph cable. Another company was formed with the intention that the defendant would supply cable to that company which would then lay a transatlantic telegraph cable. The necessary government concession was obtained and was held by a trustee on behalf of the company. Subsequently, the defendant began to supply its cable to a third party at a better price and procured a trustee who held the requisite government concession to transfer this concession to the third party. To thwart the company from instituting proceedings to recover the government concession, the defendant procured the passing of a resolution that the company be placed into voluntary liquidation. A liquidator, friendly to the defendant, was appointed who would not sue the defendant for what it had done. The unfortunate Menier was a minority shareholder in the company who, presumably outraged at the scam which had been perpetrated, brought a derivative action on behalf of the company against the defendant to make it account for its fraudulent profit. It was held that Menier had standing to bring the derivative action against the defendant, James LJ saying:

> 'The minority of the shareholders say in effect that the majority has divided the assets of the company, more or less, between themselves, to the exclusion of the minority. I think it would be a shocking thing if that could be done, because if so the majority might divide the whole assets of the company, and pass a resolution that everything must be given to them, and that the minority should have nothing to do with it. Assuming the case to be as alleged in the bill, then *the majority have put something into their pockets at the expense of the minority.* If so, it appears to me that the minority have a right to have their share of the benefits ascertained for them in the best way in which the court can do it, and given to them[360].'

This case demonstrates many of the factors properly associated with the *fraud on a minority* exception to the rule:

- The defendant majority perpetrated a *fraud* against the minority and the company.
- The defendant was in *control* of the company.
- The wrong committed to the company was unredressed and unless a derivative action was permitted, no proceedings could have been instituted.

It is proposed next to consider the concepts of *control* and *fraud*, the basic ingredients of the *fraud on a minority* exception. In addition, the other essential constituent – that *the defendant must derive benefit* – is also considered.

(i) Control

[11.133] The first constituent element in this exception to the rule is the requirement that the minority shows that those who have perpetrated the fraud are *in control* of the company[361]. To show that the majority holds in excess of 50% of the shares in the

359 *Menier v Hooper's Telegraph Works Ltd* (1874) 9 Ch App 350.

360 *Menier v Hooper's Telegraph Works Ltd* (1874) 9 Ch App 350 at 353. Emphasis added.

361 See *Prudential Assurance Co Ltd v Newman Industries Ltd (No 2)* [1982] 1 Ch 204; *Birch v Sullivan* [1958] 1 All ER 56; *Russell v Wakefield Waterworks Co* (1875) LR 20 Eq 474; and *Pavlides v Jensen* [1956] 2 All ER 518.

company which carry voting rights is the simplest way of satisfying this requirement. Where control is exercised by a majority through the use of nominees, trusts, etc, it is thought that the court can cut through the facade to the heart of where *de facto* control lies. Where simple voting control cannot be established, Fairweather J's[362] old test still has merit, namely that the minority shareholder:

> '... must *account for the fact that the company has not seen fit to bring action on its own behalf.* This may be done by showing that the company has refused to allow the action to be brought on its own behalf, or that, by reason of the wrongdoer being in control of the company at the time of bringing the action, it would be idle to apply to the company.'

In *Smith v Croft (No 3)*[363], Knox J held that the word 'control' was placed in inverted commas by the Court of Appeal in *Prudential Assurance Co Ltd v Newman Industries Ltd (No 2)*[364] 'because it was recognised that voting control by the defendants was not necessarily the sole subject of investigation'.

[11.134] In *Smith v Croft (No 3)*, Knox J went on to say that a further consideration exists, even after control is established. This further requirement is that the court must have regard to the views of other disinterested minority shareholders. Knox J said:

> '... I remain unconvinced that a just result is achieved by a single minority shareholder having the right to involve a company in an action for recovery of compensation for the company if all the other minority shareholders are for disinterested reasons satisfied that the proceedings will be productive of more harm than good. If the argument of counsel for the plaintiffs is well founded, once control by the defendants is established the views of the rest of the minority as to the advisability of the prosecution of the suit are necessarily irrelevant. I find that hard to square with the concept of a form of pleading originally introduced on the ground of necessity alone in order to prevent a wrong going without redress[365].'

In that case Knox J had regard to the views of an independent shareholder and concluded that the interests of the company would not be best served by allowing the action to proceed.

[11.135] In *Glynn and McCabe v Owen et al*[366], the two plaintiffs and first three defendants were directors of two companies, Fatstrippa Corporation Limited and Fatstripper Holdings Limited. The plaintiffs' derivative action on behalf of the companies formed on the basis of the 'fraud on a minority' exception to the rule in *Foss v Harbottle* failed on the grounds that the alleged wrongdoers were not shown to have been in control of the company. In the High Court, Finlay Geoghegan J noted that the plaintiffs submitted that the court should apply a broad concept of 'control' and rely upon the test applied by Jessel MR in *Russell v Wakefield Waterworks Co*[367]:

---

362 *Fisher v St John Opera House Co* [1937] 4 DLR 337 at 342 (emphasis added), quoted approvingly by Wedderburn, 'Shareholders' Rights and the rule in *Foss v Harbottle*' [1958] Cam LR 93 at 95.

363 *Smith v Croft (No 3)* [1987] BCLC 355 at 403b.

364 *Prudential Assurance Co Ltd v Newman Industries Ltd (No 2)* [1982] 1 All ER 354 at 364.

365 *Smith v Croft (No 3)* [1987] BCLC 355 at 403e–f.

366 *Glynn and McCabe v Owen et al* [2007] IEHC 328, [2012] IESC 15.

367 *Russell v Wakefield Waterworks Co* (1875) LR 20 Eq 474 at 482.

'It is not necessary that the corporation should absolutely refuse by vote at the general meeting, if it can be shewn either that the wrong-doer had command of the majority of the votes, so that it would be absurd to call the meeting; or if it can be shewn that there has been a general meeting substantially approving of what has been done; or if it can be shewn from the acts of the corporation as a corporation, distinguished from the mere acts of the directors of it, that they have approved of what has been done, and have allowed a long time to elapse without interfering, so that they do not intend and are not willing to sue. In all those cases the same doctrine applies, and the individual corporator may maintain the suit.'

The learned judge went on to note that in *Prudential Assurance Company* the Court of Appeal said:

'… what is meant by 'control', which embraces a broad spectrum extending from an overall absolute majority of votes at one end, to a majority of votes at the other end made up of those likely to be cast by the delinquent himself plus those voting with him as a result of influence or apathy.'

Finlay Geoghegan J stated that she agreed with the above approaches and that 'what constitutes "control" must be determined in a common sense way in the context of the relevant facts and company structure'.

[11.136] In that case, the plaintiffs made a series of allegation concerning the third defendant director of the companies alleging negligence, breach of duty and breach of fiduciary duty. Although on finding that there was no allegation that the third defendant had wrongly benefitted at the expense of the company, it was not strictly necessary to consider whether he should be considered to be a part of a group of shareholders or directors 'in control' of the companies, the learned judge went on to opine that he should not be so regarded:

'The third defendant became a director and shareholder of the fourth and fifth named defendants at the behest of the plaintiffs with whom he had prior business connections. He has no business or other links with the first and second defendants. For the reasons set out above and having regard to the evidence, much of which is not in dispute and the actions taken by the board and in particular the third defendant from November, 2004 until the commencement of proceedings in September, 2005, I have concluded that the plaintiffs have failed to satisfy me on the normal balance of probabilities that he forms part of a controlling majority of either of the Companies applying the broad concept of "control" set out above.'

(ii) Fraud on the minority

[11.137] There exist many general judicial statements of what a majority of shareholders is not permitted to do: they may not 'appropriate to themselves money, property or advantages which belong to the company or in which the other shareholders are entitled to participate'[368] or may not 'put something into their pockets at the expense of the minority'[369]. The ordinary meaning of the word '*fraud*' has little application to the concept of 'fraud on the minority'. Rather, as *Keane* has said[370], '"fraud" in this context does not necessarily involve any element of dishonesty, let alone criminality'. This has

368 *Per* Lord Davey in *Burland v Earle* [1902] AC 83 at 93.

369 *Per* James LJ in *Menier v Hooper's Telegraph Works* (1874) LR 9 Ch App 350.

370 See Keane, *Company Law* (4th edn, 2007), para 26.09.

been endorsed by the Supreme Court in *Balkanbank v Taher*[371]. Fraud on a minority has been found to exist in a number of diverse situations, involving varying degrees of moral turpitude.

[11.138] In *Estmanco (Kilner House) Ltd v Greater London Council*[372], the defendant, the GLC, had incorporated a non-profit making company with the object of selling long leases of refurbished council flats to GLC tenants. Although the GLC retained control of the company, it was intended that the company would manage the blocks of flats and that each owner would become a shareholder in the company. Until all of the leases were sold, flat-owning shareholders had no voting rights attaching to their shares. An agreement was entered into between the company and the GLC on these terms. Following an election, the GLC had a change of political heart and no longer believed home-ownership to be a desirable social goal. Consequently, the GLC acted in breach of the agreement between it and the company. Two directors of the company caused the company to institute proceedings against the GLC for breach of the agreement. The GLC convened a general meeting of the company and procured the passing of a resolution to discontinue the legal action. A shareholding flat-owner sought to take over, by way of a derivative action, the proceedings which had been instituted by the company. Sir Robert Megarry VC held that the GLC as a majority shareholder could not exercise its voting rights selfishly and:

> '... with impunity ... injure his voteless fellow shareholders by depriving the company of a cause of action and [thereby] stultifying the purpose for which the company was formed[373].'

Although the GLC's actions were contrary to company law they could hardly be said to be truly *fraudulent* in the recognised sense of that word[374].

[11.139] A more blatant example of where a majority was found to have committed a fraud on the minority is seen in *Cook v Deeks*[375]. In that case the directors of a company, in gross disregard of their fiduciary duties to the company, diverted a contract belonging to the company to themselves. Mindful of their duties to the company, the directors, who together held a majority of the shares in the company, caused a resolution to be passed, approving of the transaction. The plaintiff, who was a minority shareholder, was successful in bringing a derivative action. Of the purported absolving resolution, the Privy Council held:

> '... a resolution that the rights of the company should be disregarded in this matter would amount to forfeiting the interests and property of the minority of shareholders in favour of the majority and that by the votes of those who are interested in securing the property for themselves.'

---

371 *Balkanbank v Taher* (19 January 1995, unreported) SC.

372 *Estmanco (Kilner House) Ltd v Greater London Council* [1982] 1 All ER 437.

373 *Estmanco (Kilner House) Ltd v Greater London Council* [1982] 1 All ER 437 at 448.

374 In *Daniels v Daniels* [1978] Ch 406, a derivative action against the company's directors and majority shareholders was successful where they had caused the company to sell company land to themselves at an undervalue, although in that case fraud was not found.

375 *Cook v Deeks* [1916] 1 AC 554.

Such an example of *fraud on a minority* may be classified as an unratifiable appropriation of corporate property. Other examples include negligence[376], although some instances of negligence have been held to be ratifiable, and thus not amenable to a minority shareholder's derivative action[377].

(iii) The defendant must derive benefit

[11.140] This constituent of the exception was mooted by the Supreme Court in *Crindle Investments v Wymes*[378]. The facts of that complicated and drawn-out case were succinctly summarised by Keane J in the Supreme Court who referred throughout to the plaintiffs as 'the R Group' and the defendants as 'the W Group'. Over 25 years prior to the decision the R Group and the W Group bought certain lands near Navan under which there lay a vast and valuable ore body. The ore body extended under adjoining lands and had been discovered by another company, Tara Mining Ltd ('Tara') which had been given a lease by the State. The State subsequently acquired a 49% interest in Bula Ltd ('Limited'), a company formed by the R Group and the W Group to exploit the ore body. Limited borrowed substantial sums from several banks, which took security from Limited and personal guarantees from the personal plaintiffs. There were considerable delays in exploiting the ore body and the banks ultimately appointed a receiver-manager to Limited and obtained judgment against the personal plaintiffs in the R Group. Subsequently, Limited, an associated company called Bula Holdings ('Holdings'), the personal plaintiffs and defendants instituted proceedings against Tara and the State for, *inter alia*, conspiracy to cause economic loss, trespass, etc ('the Tara Proceedings') and later against the receiver, four of the banks and a firm of consultant mining engineers for, *inter alia*, negligence ('the Bank Proceedings'). Some seven years later, in 1993, the Tara Proceedings were dismissed by Lynch J – this decision was still under appeal. Some eleven years later, in 1997, the Bank Proceedings were heard by Barr J but after a time he was informed that the plaintiffs accepted that if Lynch J's decision was upheld on appeal, the Bank Proceedings would also fail unless they could succeed on a particular Statute of Limitations point. In the circumstances, Barr J adjourned the Bank Proceedings to await the outcome of the appeal[379].

Differences had arisen between the R Group and the W Group and in 1993 a s 205 petition had been presented by the R Group, based on the manner in which the W Group (which held 60% of the shares in Holdings) was conducting the litigation and the manner in which possible compromises were being addressed. The s 205 petition was held *in camera*. Murphy J held that the actions of the W Group in rejecting particular offers of compromise in both proceedings was 'an improvident gamble' and amounted to oppression and a disregard of the interests of the other shareholders within the meaning of s 205 of the CA 1963. On appeal, the Supreme Court upheld this finding. It was ordered that the petitioning R Group should be in control of the negotiations on behalf of Holdings to settle the proceedings and should be entitled to settle them by negotiation if possible on terms broadly similar to those offered but no less

376 *Daniels v Daniels* [1978] Ch 406.

377 *Pavlides v Jensen* [1956] 2 All ER 518.

378 *Crindle Investments v Wymes* [1999] 4 IR 578.

379 The claim against the engineers was resolved and the proceedings against them were struck out.

advantageous unless agreed to by all of Holdings' members or approved by the High Court. The R Group also sought an order to require all of the parties, whether as directors or as personal litigants, to join in the acceptance of an offer which had then been made to compromise the proceedings (if still available). This was because the defendants in both the Tara Proceedings and the Bank Proceedings had indicated that they were unwilling to enter into any compromise unless all the plaintiffs *including the personal plaintiffs* were bound by the settlement. Murphy J declined to make such an order, a decision upheld on appeal by the Supreme Court.

The personal claims, which had been asserted in the Tara Proceedings and the Bank Proceedings by the R Group, were withdrawn. The W Group's personal claims – in the Tara Proceedings for monies lent to Holdings, embarrassment, etc, and in the Bank Proceedings to have the securities and personal guarantees set aside and for damages – were maintained.

[11.141] The R Group also instituted plenary proceedings against the W Group in an attempt to force the W Group to withdraw their personal claims. These plenary proceedings alleged, first, that the W Group owed a fiduciary duty to the R Group and that the maintenance and perseverance in the individual claims to the detriment of Limited and Holdings constituted a breach of trust. Second, it was contended that the exercise of the W Group's constitutional rights to assert individual claims was an abuse of the constitutional rights of the R group. In the High Court, Murphy J rejected the R Group's claims in the plenary proceedings. The subject matter of the instant case was an appeal from that decision. Keane J held that there was no fiduciary duty owed by the W Group, as alleged, as the requisite confidence and trust did not subsist between the parties at the relevant times. The R Group's next claim was that they could rely upon the damage allegedly caused to Holdings and Limited by the conduct of the W Group in pursuing their personal claims and were not prevented from so doing by the rule in *Foss v Harbottle* by reason of the fourth and fifth exceptions. Keane J noted the ambit of the fourth exception, as stated in *Burland v Earle*[380], and the fact that it was not necessary to establish fraudulent conduct in the criminal sense, noting that there was, even, some doubt as to whether fraud in any sense needed to be established[381]. Keane J held,

---

380 *Burland v Earle* [1902] AC 83. There he said: 'The cases in which the minority can maintain such an action are … confined to those in which the acts complained of are of a fraudulent character or beyond the powers of the company. A familiar example is where the majority are endeavouring directly or indirectly to appropriate to themselves money, property, or advantages which belong to the company, or in which the other shareholders are entitled to participate …'

381 Here Keane J noted the observations of Templeman J in *Daniels v Daniels* [1978] Ch 406 at 413 where he said: 'The authorities which deal with simple fraud on the one hand and gross negligence on the other do not cover the situation which arises where, without fraud, the directors and majority shareholders are guilty of a breach of duty which they owe to the company and that breach of duty not only harms the company but benefits the directors. If majority shareholders can sue if there is fraud, I see no reason why they cannot sue where the action of the majority and the directors, though without fraud, confers some benefit on those directors and majority shareholders themselves. It would seem to be quite monstrous – particularly as fraud is so hard to plead and difficult to prove – if the confines of the exception to *Foss v Harbottle* were drawn so narrowly that directors could make a profit out of their negligence.'

however, that the R Group's claim was bound to fail for failure to show that the W Group would derive benefit from the alleged wrongdoing. On this point he said:

> 'Should there be no reasonable offer forthcoming and approved by the court, the maintenance by the defendants of their personal claims will not constitute any form of wrongdoing *quoad* the company or anyone else. If there were such an offer forthcoming and the defendants maintained their personal claims, *no benefits would flow to the individual defendants – an essential constituent of the exceptions to the rule – since they would only derive such a benefit in the event of a victory in the Tara and Bank proceedings or a compromise of both*. In either event, far from any damage being caused to the company, benefits would accrue to it as a result of the persistence of the W Group in maintaining their claims and declining to co-operate in any offers of settlement, however ill-judged that course of conduct might now appear to be. This, even on the widest construction of the exceptions to the rule in *Foss v Harbottle* the maintenance of the personal claims does not come within them[382].'

It is significant that Keane J also questioned the form of procedure adopted by the R Group in pursuing what was in substance, although not in form, a derivative action. In this regard Keane J seems to have accepted the requirement in *Prudential Insurance Company v Newman Industries Ltd (No 2)*[383] that before such an action can proceed 'the fact of control by the alleged wrongdoers and a good *prima facie* case must first be established'[384].

[11.142] In *Glynn and McCabe v Owen et al*[385], the absence of any allegation that one of the defendants had wrongly benefitted at the expense of the company was sufficient grounds to preclude the plaintiffs from coming within this exception to the rule in *Foss v Harbottle*.

(e) Where justice requires a derivative action to be brought

[11.143] A number of cases have suggested that there exists a fifth exception to the rule in *Foss v Harbottle*[386]. This fifth exception to the rule is, however, less well established than the foregoing motley miscellany of supposed exceptions. In *Heything v Dupont*[387], Harmond LJ said:

> 'There are cases which suggest that the rule is not a right one and that an exception will be made where the justice of the case demands it.'

In *Moylan v Irish Whiting Manufacturers Ltd*[388], Hamilton J quoted this passage with approval and went on to say that:

---

382 *Crindle Investments v Wymes* [1999] 4 IR 578 at 594. Emphasis added.

383 *Prudential Insurance Company v Newman Industries Ltd (No 2)* [1982] Ch 204.

384 *Crindle Investments v Wymes* [1999] 4 IR 578 at 594. It may be noted that Keane J also rejected the R Group's claims, based on negligence and infringement of constitutional rights.

385 *Glynn and McCabe v Owen et al* [2007] IEHC 328, [2012] IESC 15.

386 See *Russell v Wakefield Waterworks Co* (1875) LR 20 Eq 474–480 which was cited with apparent approval by the Supreme Court in *O'Neill v Ryan* [1993] ILRM 557; *Edwards v Halliwell* [1950] 2 All ER 1064, 1067; *Baillie v Oriental Telephone and Electric Co Ltd* [1915] 1 Ch 503 at 518; *Cotter v National Union of Seamen* [1929] 2 Ch 58 at 69; and *Heything v Dupont* [1964] 1 WLR 843 at 851.

387 *Heything v Dupont* [1964] 1 WLR 843.

388 *Moylan v Irish Whiting Manufacturers Ltd* (14 April 1980, unreported) HC.

> 'Having regard to the provisions of Bunreacht na hÉireann, I am satisfied that an exception to the rule must be made when the justice of the case demands it.'

On the facts of the particular case, the learned judge was not required to rely on this exception and so his comments were *obiter dictum*[389].

[11.144] Although the issue was raised before the Supreme Court in *O'Neill v Ryan*[390], Blayney J was not required to pronounce upon its validity[391], because the nature of the plaintiff's claim was such that it fell totally outside the rule in *Foss v Harbottle*. Similarly, in *Crindle Investments v Wymes*[392], the Supreme Court *per* Keane J acknowledged the existence of 'the less solidly' and 'less securely' based fifth exception, but did not directly pronounce upon its validity. The fifth exception was considered by the Court of Appeal in *Prudential Assurance Co Ltd v Newman Industires Ltd (No 2)*[393] to be an impractical test to adopt. However, as Knox J observed in *Smith v Croft (No 3)*[394]:

> 'But the fact that such a yardstick would or might be unsatisfactory because it does not give a practical guide to the limits of the rule and its exceptions, does not detract from the fact that the whole doctrine whereby a minority shareholder is permitted to assert claims on behalf of the company, is rooted in a procedural expedient, and adopted to prevent a wrong going without redress.'

This passage contains the correct focus on the nature of the derivative action and the exceptions to the rule in *Foss v Harbottle*. If the *justice of the case* criterion would provide a nebulous exception to the rule, it would be in good company with the other four *supposed* exceptions. The Supreme Court's references to the fifth exception, albeit neutral references, indicated until recently that should a suitable case arise, the court might be unlikely to recoil from its application.

[11.145] In *Glynn and McCabe v Owen et al*[395], Finlay Geoghegan J quoted the following passage from Keane[396]:

---

389 In *Biala PTY v Mallina Holdings Ltd* [1993] ACFR 785, the Supreme Court of Western Australia concluded: 'The courts should not shrink from determining whether the justice of the case should allow a shareholder to proceed with a derivative action. Equity is concerned with substance and not form, and it was contrary to principle to require round minority shareholders to bring themselves within the boundaries of well recognised exceptions and to deny jurisdiction even where an unjust or unconscionable result may otherwise ensue. It was desirable to allow a minority shareholder to bring a derivative claim where the justice of the case clearly demanded that such a claim be brought, irrespective of whether the claim falls within the confines.' This passage was quoted by Irvine J in *Fanning v Murtagh et al* [2008] IEHC 277, but ultimately doubted.

390 *O'Neill v Ryan* [1993] ILRM 557.

391 Blayney J said (at 566) that: 'it was submitted that there was a fifth exception and [that the plaintiff] came within it. Such exception was where it was necessary to permit an exception "in the interests of justice." In my opinion, however, there is no need to consider whether such an exception exists as I am satisfied that for other reasons the plaintiff's claim to come within an exception to the rule in *Foss v Harbottle* is untenable ...'

392 *Crindle Investments v Wymes* [1999] 4 IR 578.

393 *Prudential Assurance Co Ltd v Newman Industries Ltd (No 2)* [1982] Ch 204; [1982] 1 All ER 354 at 366.

394 *Smith v Croft (No 3)* [1987] BCLC 355 at 389.

395 *Glynn and McCabe v Owen et al* [2007] IEHC 328, [2012] IESC 15.

'While the view was advanced in earlier editions of this book that the Irish courts might be reluctant to extend the exceptions to the rule, that is probably to err on the side of caution. While it is true that the wide import of the term "fraud" enables most deserving cases to avail of the third exception where the other two are not available, there is probably no good reason why the courts should not carve out further exceptions if justice so requires. Not only should the judicial comments in support of that view already cited be borne in mind; it is also worth noting that in the two seminal cases of *Foss v Harbottle* itself and *Edwards v Halliwell*, Wigram V-C and Jenkins LJ both observed that the rule should not be applied so in rigorous a fashion in any case as to lead to injustice.'

Finlay Geoghegan J agreed with that formulation saying:

'I respectfully agree that the formulation of the rule in the earlier cases makes clear that it should not be applied in such a way as to lead to injustice. Nevertheless, the entitlement of a shareholder to pursue by way of derivative action a claim for and on behalf of a company is an exception to an "elementary principle" as referred to above. As such, it should not be broadly or liberally applied. A very strong case would have to be made out. It would also have to be consistent with the principles underlying the rule in *Foss v Harbottle* and the exceptions to it. These include the reluctance of the courts to interfere in the internal management of a company.'[397]

Finlay Geoghegan J went on to hold that the plaintiffs did not establish the existence of any injustice or interests of justice on the facts disclosed. In the Supreme Court, O'Donnell J, after finding that the plaintiffs had not advanced any serious argument as to why that conclusion should be overturned, went on to say:

'Assuming for present purposes that such a jurisdiction exists, it would require some compelling facts. Furthermore, in my view, account should be taken of the rule in *Foss v Harbottle*, and the exceptions to it, was a judicial fashioned remedy for the difficulties faced by minorities in companies. The development of more sophisticated shareholders' agreements and the development of a specific statutory remedy for oppression by a majority, have reduced the need for a wide-ranging exception to the rule[398].'

This passage indicates judicial reluctance at the highest level to extend the exceptions to the rule and it is thought now that it would take extraordinary facts to provoke the Supreme Court to acknowledge the existence of the justice of the case exception.

---

396 Keane, *Company Law*, (4th edn, Bloomsbury Professional, 2007), para 26.20.

397 In *Connolly v Seskin Properties Ltd and ors* [2012] IEHC 332, Kelly J concurred with this statement From Finlay Geoghegan J's judgment.

398 In *Fanning v Murtagh et al* [2008] IEHC 277, Irvine J also said she remained to be convinced that Finlay Geoghegan J's decision in *Glynn* was as submitted by the plaintiff definitive authority of her acceptance of the justice of the case rule. Irvine J counseled against accepting the fifth ground, saying of the rule in *Foss v Harbottle*: 'The rule is intended to ensure that minority shareholders, unhappy with the management of a company, are not in a position to engage in litigation unless they can, at the outset of the proceedings, establish their *locus standi* as an exception to the rule. If such exceptions include "where the justice of a case so requires" the court, where such a plea is advanced, will end up hearing possibly all of the facts of the action, in what has been described in many of the authorities as a full dress rehearsal on a preliminary issue, before it can decide whether the plaintiff has the *locus standi* to maintain the action at all.'

Chapter 12

Groups of Companies

[12.001] The commercial reality of business is that a great many corporate enterprises operate as groups of companies, comprised of two or more individual companies. It is very common to utilise a group structure. This is true whether in the context of a large public limited company with a plethora of divisional subsidiaries or a small private company, which is a holding company and has just one subsidiary company. The aim of this chapter is to consider the circumstances in which companies will, primarily[1] for the purposes of company law, be treated as being part of a group of companies, consisting of a holding company and its subsidiaries. In addition, a number of issues, which are specific to groups of companies, are considered here. The matters considered are:

1. Significance of the holding–subsidiary relationship in company law.
2. The definition of holding company in company law.
3. The definition of subsidiary in company law.
4. Definitions of undertakings, parent undertakings and subsidiary undertakings for group accounting purposes.
5. Capital maintenance definitions of parent public companies and public company subsidiaries.
6. Taxation definitions of holding and subsidiary companies.
7. Select issues in the holding–subsidiary relationship.

Significance of the holding–subsidiary relationship in company law

[12.002] In Ireland and England, there is no distinct body of law applicable to groups of companies; the Companies Acts apply generally to groups of companies[2]. There are, however, consequences for companies in a group[3]. Some consequences involve possibly negative *impositions*, which do not apply to standalone companies – for example, the regulation of accounting in corporate groups[4] or lifting the veil at common law[5]. Other consequences allow group companies to avail of *exemptions* that do not apply to standalone companies – for example, s 35 of the CA 1990 which disapplies the prohibitions in s 31 of the CA 1990 to certain transactions and arrangements between group

---

1 Note, however, that, for purposes of comparison, the definition of holding company and subsidiary company in taxation legislation is considered at para **[12.043]** *et seq*.

2 See, generally, Wainman, *Company Structures* (1995, Sweet & Maxwell) at ch 6 'Groups of Companies'; Farrar & Hannigan, *Farrar's Company Law* (4th edn, Butterworths, 1998) at p 529; Forde, *Company Law* (3rd edn, Round Hall Sweet & Maxwell, 1999) at p 562.

3 See Schmitthoff & Wooldridge, *Groups of Companies* (1991, Sweet & Maxwell).

4 See Ch 17, *Financial Statements, Audit and Annual Return,* at para **[17.144]** *et seq*.

5 See, generally, Ch 5, *Disregarding Separate Legal Personality*, at para **[5.051]** *et seq*.

companies[6]. Where the law provides exceptions, lawyers and their clients will seek to bring themselves within those exceptions. In this chapter, some of the many ways in which stand-alone companies can be brought into a group, are considered. An important caveat is appropriate: the slightest tinkering with the ownership and control of the shares in a company can, for the non-tax lawyer, have unforeseen financial repercussions and the creation of a group of companies must always be considered in totality, the short term advantage in availing of a particular regime weighted against the accounting and taxation implications of a re-structure.

[12.003] The Companies Acts do not contain any definition of 'group of companies'. Accordingly, it is necessary to consider the definitions of the constituent elements of any group of companies, namely the meanings of 'holding' company and 'subsidiary' company. The practitioner must always be conscious of the eternal difference between the legal definition of a 'group of companies' and the vernacular meaning of that expression. So, for example, a businessman who holds the legal and beneficial ownership in all of the shares issued in five companies might legitimately refer to those companies as his 'group'. Because, however, the common connection is him, a natural person, and not a body corporate, his enterprise will not be a 'group of companies' within the meaning of s 155 of the CA 1963. The potential for confusion is exacerbated by the fact that a partnership which controls a company may, for the purposes of group accounts, be deemed that company's parent undertaking by reason of the application of the European Communities (Companies: Group Accounts) Regulations 1992 ('the EC(C:GA)R 1992')[7] to 'undertakings' and not just to bodies corporate[8].

[12.004] It is also important to recognise at the outset that a shareholding that gives rise to a holding-company/subsidiary relationship for the purposes of the Companies Acts, will not necessarily be sufficient for the purpose of enabling those companies to avail of certain advantages in revenue law which distinguishes between degrees of parent–subsidiary. The threshold degrees of connection and control in revenue law are outlined below[9].

[12.005] The term 'related company' is employed by the Companies Acts in the context of investigations[10], examinerships[11], and contribution and pooling orders in windings up[12]. A related company will not, *per se*, be a holding company or a subsidiary company within the meaning of s 155 of the CA 1963 as in each case the definition of 'related company' is wider than that contained in s 155. Companies and other bodies corporate can be *connected*, but only with a director and not another body corporate[13]. The term

---

6 See Warnock, 'Inter-Company Relationships and Section 31 of the Companies Act, 1990' (1994) 1 CLP 243 and, generally, Ch 16, *Statutory Regulation of Directors' Transactions*, at para **[16.055]** *et seq*.

7 SI 201/1992.

8 See para **[12.030]** *post*.

9 See para **[12.043]** *post*.

10 See Ch 27, *Investigations and Inspectors*, at para **[27.022]**.

11 See Ch 22, *Examinerships*, at para **[22.051]**.

12 See Ch 25, *The Realisation and Distribution of Assets in a Winding Up*, at para **[25.120]**.

13 Section 26(2) of the CA 1990. See, generally, Ch 16, *Statutory Regulation of Directors' Transactions*, at para **[16.003]**.

'associated company' or 'associated undertaking' is relevant in the context of company accounts[14], but not in the case of s 155 of the CA 1963 which governs the general company law definition of holding and subsidiary company.

The definition of holding company in company law

[12.006] 'Holding company' is circularly defined by s 155(4) of the CA 1963 in the following terms:

> 'For the purposes of this Act, a company shall be deemed to be another's holding company if, but only if, that other is its subsidiary.'

The consequence of this is that it is the definition of 'subsidiary', which will determine whether or not a company will be another's holding company.

[12.007] Ordinarily where the Companies Acts refer to a 'company', the reference is to a company within the meaning of s 2 of the CA 1963[15]. For the purposes of s 155 of the CA 1963, however, it is important to note that s 155(5) provides that '"company" includes any body corporate'. Accordingly, to take as an example of a body corporate that is not a 'company' for the purposes of s 2 of the CA 1963, a company formed and registered in accordance with the laws of England and Wales, such an entity will be a 'company' for the purposes of s 155 and can be either the holding company or subsidiary company of an Irish registered company[16].

The definition of subsidiary in company law

[12.008] 'Subsidiary company' is defined by s 155(1) of the CA 1963. This provides:

> 'For the purposes of this Act, a company shall, subject to *subsection (3)*[17], be deemed to be a subsidiary of another if, but only if—
>
> (a) that other—
>
> (i) is a member of it and controls the composition of its board of directors, or
>
> (ii) holds more than half in nominal value of its equity share capital, or
>
> (iii) holds more than half in nominal value of its shares carrying voting rights (other than voting rights which arise only in specified circumstances); or
>
> (b) the first-mentioned company is a subsidiary of any company which is that other's subsidiary.'

For general purposes of company law, there are, therefore, four circumstances in which one company shall be deemed to be the subsidiary of another company (the holding company). The issues that arise are now considered as follows:

(a) The 'golden share': a member controlling the composition of the board of directors.

[14] See Ch 17, *Financial Statements, Audit and Annual Return*, at para **[17.197]**.

[15] See Ch 1, *The Private Company in Context*, at para **[1.156]** *et seq.*

[16] Note that s 2(3) of the CA 1963 provides that 'references in this Act to a body corporate or to a corporation shall be construed as not including a corporation sole, but as including a company incorporated outside the State'.

[17] See para **[12.022]** *post.*

(b) Holding more than half in nominal value of the equity share capital or of the shares carrying voting rights.
(c) Shares held and powers exercisable in a fiduciary capacity, as nominee or pursuant to a debenture or trust.
(d) A subsidiary of a subsidiary.
(e) Wholly-owned subsidiaries.

(a) The 'golden share': a member controlling the composition of the board of directors

[12.009] It can sometimes come as a surprise to learn that a company can be deemed to be another company's subsidiary in circumstances where the holding company holds only one share in the subsidiary. The requirement in s 155(1)(a)(i) of the CA 1963 is twofold: a company shall be another's holding company if it is, first, a *member* of the subsidiary and, second, if it *controls the composition of its board of directors*. Membership, which is considered in Ch 8[18], arises from either being an original subscriber of the memorandum of association or having agreed to become a member and having one's name entered on the register of members. Every shareholder whose name is entered on the register of members is a member. For the purposes of s 155(1)(a)(i) it matters not that a company is the holder of just one of 10,000 shares issued – provided it is registered as a member, it passes the first limb.

[12.010] It is clear, therefore, that in order to be the holding company of another company under this limb, the holding company must be a member of the subsidiary within the meaning of s 31 of the CA 1963. In *Enviroco v Farstad Supply A/S*[19], the English Court of Appeal had to consider, *inter alia*, the meaning of the words '... is a member of it and controls, alone, pursuant to an agreement with other members, a majority of the voting rights in it'[20]. In that case the would-be holding company had charged its shares to a bank under a deed of pledge which required, *inter alia*, the shares to be registered in the name of the bank or its nominee. The English High Court had found that even though the would-be holding company's name was not entered in the register of members, because the shares had been pledged as security, a purposive construction was required to be applied to avoid the commercial absurdity of a holding company being able to conceal the fact that it had a subsidiary by pledging its shares. This was rejected by the Court of Appeal which held that membership was a status derived from the entry of the shareholder's name in the register of members and that the would-be holding company was unable to achieve that status because the bank was the registered member of the shares.

[12.011] The second limb contains the substantive basis for transforming such a potentially minor participant in a company into that company's holding company. To be another company's holding company, a corporate member must *control the composition of the subsidiary's board of directors*. Notwithstanding the fact that the first limb of the test is passed if the holding company is a nominal member, since the second limb

---

18 See Ch 8, *Shares and Membership*, at para **[8.003]** *et seq*.

19 *Enviroco v Farstad Supply A/S* [2010] 2 All ER 1013. See Lan, 'The Curious Case of a Subsidiary' (2012) 128 LQR 351.

20 Section 736(1) of the Companies Act 1985 (UK).

requires that member to control the board of directors, the most obvious circumstances in which the complete test will be passed is where a corporate member holds in excess of 50% of the issued equity share capital where all shares carry equal voting rights, for this will, all things being equal, permit that member to control the composition of the company's board of directors.

[12.012] As noted above, however, it will equally suffice for a corporate member to hold just one of, for example, 10,000 shares issued provided that the rights attaching to that one share entitle its holder to control the composition of the company's board of directors. This position is permitted by the definition afforded to '*control*' and companies' freedom to issue shares with *weighted* voting rights. Section 155(2) of the CA 1963 defines 'control' for the purposes of s 155(1):

> 'For the purposes of *subsection (1)*, the composition of a company's board of directors shall be deemed to be controlled by another company if, but only if, that other company by the exercise of some power exercisable by it without the consent or concurrence of any other person can appoint or remove the holders of all or a majority of the directorships; but for the purposes of this provision that other company shall be deemed to have power to appoint to a directorship in relation to which any of the following conditions is satisfied—
>
> (a) that a person cannot be appointed thereto without the exercise in his favour by that other company of such a power as aforesaid; or
>
> (b) that a person's appointment thereto follows necessarily from his appointment as director of that other company.'

The significance of s 155(2) is that the key factor in determining 'control' is the entitlement to *exercise some power without the consent or concurrence of any other person*. The source[21] of that power is irrelevant. It is also significant that the test in s 155(1)(a)(i) will be passed where there is power to appoint or remove the holders of a *majority* of the directorships. Finally, it may be noted that by containing a 'deeming' provision, s 155(2) operates to assist, rather than defeat, the creation of a parent–subsidiary relationship. So, the power to appoint to a directorship is *deemed* to exist where *either* of two situations exists. The first is where a person cannot be appointed as a director without the holding company exercising its power; the second is where a person's appointment as a director to the subsidiary 'follows necessarily' from his or her appointment as director of the holding company.

[12.013] There are a number of ways in which a corporate member holding just one share of, for example, the 10,000 issued shares can have the unilateral power to control the composition of the company's board of directors. In the first instance, the articles of association can provide that the holder of a particular class of shares is exclusively entitled to control the composition of the company's board of directors and the holders of all other classes of shares are expressly not so entitled. In *Bushell v Faith*[22], the House of Lords upheld the propriety of such 'golden shares'. An alternative source of a corporate member's entitlement to exercise the power to control the board of directors is a shareholders' agreement. This is because the source of the power is not confined to

21 See para **[12.013]** *post*.

22 *Bushell v Faith* [1970] AC 1099. See Ch 3, *Constitutional Documentation*, at para **[3.053]** *et seq*.

rights intrinsic to particular shares; the power can be contractual[23], whether by way of a shareholders' agreement or otherwise, and will be effective for the purposes of s 155(1)(a)(i) provided it is enforceable.

[12.014] In the Australian case of *Mount Edon Gold Mines (Aust) Ltd v Burmine Ltd*[24], it was stated that the most important feature of the power was that it must be legally enforceable. Accordingly, it was held that a practical or *de facto* power giving rise to control by reason of a significant shareholding (but legally insufficient shareholding to amount to an overall majority, if all persons entitled to attend and vote were to do so) would *not* satisfy the test under their similar legislation[25]. In that case White J said of the similarly worded Australian provision that:

> '… each of the three sub-paragraphs of para (a) is concerned with legal power. It is difficult to see how, in the absence of a legal power, a body corporate could be said to control the composition of the board of another body corporate, by virtue of what it in fact does, when another body holds more than one-half the maximum number of votes that might be cast at a general meeting of the company. To take a hypothetical example, suppose that the shares of a company are held as to 80% by shareholder A, as to 15% by shareholder B and as to 5% by shareholder C, and that, perhaps as the result of apathy, shareholder A is customarily absent from general meetings of the company. In the result, shareholder B is accustomed to appoint his nominees to the board of directors of the company and to remove directors of the company as it may decide, whether or not shareholder C agrees. In such a case, if the plaintiff is correct, the company is a subsidiary of shareholder B, a situation that is liable to change on short notice if shareholder A decides at any time to exercise its rights. In my opinion, it cannot correctly be said, in the hypothetical case envisaged, that shareholder B controls the composition of the board of the company[26].'

Burmine was followed by the Supreme Court of New South Wales in *Bluebird Investments Pty Ltd et al v Graf et al*[27] where it was held that the test for determining control of a subsidiary was one of *legal control* and not a present (*de facto*) ability to control. There, Santow J said:

> 'The test … is solely one of "control" not "present ability". This ordinarily connotes something intrinsically more durable and binding than an adventitious voting coalition, not reinforced by any legally enforceable arrangement. Such a coalition would be readily capable of changing at each shareholder meeting, providing additional reason for avoiding such a test falling short of legal enforceability, unless the language were clear[28].'

23 In *Kolotex Hoisely (Australia) Pty Ltd v Federal Commission of Taxation* (1973) 130 CLR 64, Mason J said: '(c)entral to the concept of control of a company is the capacity to control a general meeting. That capacity rests on majority voting power and it matters not whether the majority voting power is, or is not, attached to shares.'

24 *Mount Edon Gold Mines (Aust) Ltd v Burmine Ltd* (1994) 12 ACLC 185.

25 *Cf Re Federal Capital Press of Australia Pty Ltd et al* [1995] ACTAAT 102 (1 February 1995) where the Australian Administrative Appeals Tribunal distinguished *Mount Edon Gold Mines (Aust) Ltd v Burmine Ltd* and found that 'effective control' was sufficient for purposes of taxation law.

26 *Mount Edon Gold Mines (Aust) Ltd v Burmine Ltd* (1994) 12 ACLC 185 at 196.

27 *Bluebird Investments Pty Ltd et al v Graf et al* (1994) 12 ACLC 724.

28 *Bluebird Investments Pty Ltd et al v Graf et al* (1994) 12 ACLC 724 at 726.

[12.015] The capacity in which a power is exercisable is all-important. The foregoing assumes that the power to control the composition of the board of directors is not exercisable:

- in a fiduciary capacity;
- as nominee for some other person; or
- pursuant to a security debenture or trust.

The effect of a power being exercisable in a fiduciary capacity, or as nominee, or on foot of a security is considered below[29].

[12.016] Although equally applicable to s 155(1)(a)(ii) and (iii), it is readily apparent from s 155(1)(a)(i) that a company may be a subsidiary of another company whilst at the same time 'being controlled' by another person, whether a natural person or a body corporate. Section 155 does not prevent a company from being the subsidiary of two separate and unrelated holding companies[30]. It is also trite[31] to say that a company can be a subsidiary but yet 'controlled' by a director of that company within the meaning of s 26 of the CA 1990 for the purposes of, for example, ss 29 or 31 of the CA 1990[32].

(b) Holding more than half in nominal value of the equity share capital or of the shares carrying voting rights

[12.017] It is convenient to consider together, the two bases for the existence of the holding–subsidiary company relationship that are set out in s 155(1)(a)(ii) and (iii). Three distinct issues arising here require elaboration:

(i) More than half in nominal value;
(ii) 'Of equity share capital';
(iii) 'Of shares carrying voting rights'.

(i) More than half in nominal value

[12.018] More than half is self-explanatory: a holding company must hold *more than* 50% (eg, 50.0001% plus) in nominal value. The nominal value of shares is the monetary value assigned to a share in a company's memorandum of association; it is 'nominal' in the sense that it may bear no relation to the actual commercial value of a share in a company[33].

(ii) 'Of equity share capital'

[12.019] For the purposes of s 155 of the CA 1963, 'equity share capital' is defined by sub-s (5) to mean:

---

29 See para **[12.022]** *post*.

30 Warnock, 'Inter-Company Relationships and Section 31 of the Companies Act 1990' (1994) 1 CLP 243 at 244.

31 It is trite in the sense that ss 34 and 35 of the CA 1990 purport to exclude certain transactions and arrangements involving holding companies and subsidiary companies in circumstances where, since a body corporate cannot in Ireland be a director, it can only be a 'person connected with a director' which, in the case of a body corporate, is established by showing that it is 'controlled by a director'.

32 See Ch 16, *Statutory Regulation of Directors' Transactions*, at para **[16.003]** *et seq*.

33 See, generally, Ch 8, *Shares and Membership*, at para **[8.044]** *et seq*.

> '... in relation to a company, its issued share capital *excluding* any part thereof which, neither as respects dividends nor as respects capital, carries any right to participate beyond a specified amount in a distribution.' (Emphasis added.)

Accordingly, to be a holding company under s 155(1)(a)(ii) a company must hold more than half in *nominal value* of the subsidiary's *issued* equity share capital. Not all of a company's issued equity share capital is reckonable for this purpose; issued share capital that does not have the right to participate in dividends or capital beyond a specified amount in a distribution must be excluded from the computation. An example of such share capital might be certain preference shares that entitle the holder to a higher dividend than ordinary shareholders but which limit the holder's rights to participate beyond a certain limit (as regards dividends or capital) in a distribution[34]. It is thought that the limitation must be as regards both dividends *and* capital; a limitation in respect of either dividends or capital alone is insufficient to render such share capital unreckonable for the purposes of s 155 of the CA 1963.

(iii) 'Of shares carrying voting rights'

[12.020] Section 155(1)(a)(iii) provides that a company will be another's holding company where it 'holds more than half in nominal value of its shares carrying voting rights (other than voting rights which arise only in specified circumstances'. There is no statutory definition of the meaning of 'shares carrying voting rights', but the meaning is self-apparent. To be reckonable, the putative holding company's holding must be of shares which carry voting rights in *all circumstances* and not, for example, shares which have no voting rights on, say, a resolution to appoint or remove directors. Section 155(1)(a)(iii) is silent on the effect, if any, of different classes of shares having loaded or weighted voting rights in circumstances where all shares do have voting rights.

(c) Shares held and powers exercisable in a fiduciary capacity, as nominee or pursuant to a debenture or trust

[12.021] Were s 155 to have not given guidance as to when, for the foregoing purposes, a share will be considered to be 'held' or a power considered to be 'exercisable by', great confusion would have been occasioned due to the myriad capacities in which property can be held and powers exercisable. Not only must holding as 'legal' and 'equitable/beneficial' owner be distinguished, so also must holding in a 'fiduciary capacity' be distinguished from holding as a 'nominee' as must rights accruing pursuant to a debenture or trust[35].

[12.022] For the purposes of s 155(1), where a company holds shares or exercises a power in a fiduciary capacity, the rule is that such shares or power will be treated as *not* held or exercisable by it. Section 155(3)(a) and (b) provide:

> 'In determining whether one company is a subsidiary of another—
>
> (a) any shares held or power exercisable by that other in a fiduciary capacity shall be treated as not held or exercisable by it;

---

34 On the different rights that may attach to shares see Ch 8, *Shares and Membership*, at para **[8.072]** *et seq*.

35 On the splitting of legal and equitable/beneficial ownership, see Ch 9, *Share Transfer*, at para **[9.080]** *et seq*.

(b) subject to paragraphs (c) and (d), any shares held or power exercisable—

(i) by any person as a nominee for that other (except where that other is concerned only in a fiduciary capacity); or

(ii) by, or by a nominee for, a subsidiary of that other, not being a subsidiary which is concerned only in a fiduciary capacity;

shall be treated as held or exercisable by that other …'[36]

To take an extreme example: if company A holds all of the equity share capital in company B, but does so in a fiduciary capacity or as nominee for X, company A will not be company B's holding company. A *nominee* is someone in whose name shares are registered, but who is not the beneficial or equitable owner of those shares: a nominee is a bare trustee. Holding shares in a *fiduciary capacity* will arise where the registered owner has sold those shares to a purchaser: pending the registration of the purchaser as registered owner of the shares, the vendor will hold the shares in a fiduciary capacity. In both cases, s 155(3) of the CA 1963 requires that the 'nominee' or 'fiduciary' cannot be considered the holder of the shares or of the power to control the board of directors for the purposes of s 155(1).

[12.023] The meaning of holding of shares in a fiduciary capacity or as nominee was considered by the English Court of Appeal in *Michaels and another v Harley House (Marylebone) Ltd*[37]. In that case a company, called Taylor Woodrow Property Co Ltd ('Property'), owned a building in which the plaintiffs' flat was located. The plaintiffs sought to claim rights under landlord and tenant legislation. In 1992, Property agreed to sell the building to its subsidiary, Taylor Woodrow Development Ltd ('Development'). Development paid Property but title in the building rested with Property. Subsequently, in 1993, two transactions were effected:

(a) Development agreed to sell the building to its subsidiary, Harley House (Marylebone) Ltd ('Marylebone') for stg£15.75m and, to this end, agreed to lend Marylebone that sum to enable it to complete the purchase.

(b) On the same day, Development entered into an agreement with Frogmore Estates plc ('Frogmore') to sell to Frogmore the two £1 issued shares held by Development in Marylebone and also the loan notes.

The share sale agreement was expressed to be dependent upon the prior completion of the property sale agreement. At a pre-completion meeting the parties' solicitors signed an escrow agreement which provided that the transfer of the building would be completed before the transfer of the shares and the necessary transfers were executed in escrow. Completion was ultimately effected and the transfers lodged for registration.

[12.024] The plaintiffs' application was for an order against Marylebone, obliging it to disclose full particulars of the terms and dates of all transactions whereby Property agreed to transfer ownership and control of the building to Marylebone. The plaintiffs also sought a declaration that the transfer involved a 'relevant disposal' within the meaning of s 4 of the Landlord and Tenant Act 1987 (UK). In the course of his judgment Robert Walker LJ said:

---

36 Paragraphs (c) and (d) are considered at para **[12.026]** below.

37 *Michaels and another v Harley House (Marylebone) Ltd* [1999] 1 BCLC 670.

> 'It is … common ground that persons within the Taylor Woodrow group and the Frogmore group and their respective legal advisers set about producing a scheme under which they could achieve the commercial substance of a sale of the freehold in [the building] while in form and in law (as they hoped) avoiding triggering any relevant disposal for the purposes of the 1987 Act[38].'

Robert Walker LJ noted that a disposal would not be a 'relevant disposal' if made to an 'associated company', which was defined by the English Landlord and Tenant Act 1987 by reference to ss 736 and 736A of the English Companies Act 1985. Section 736A(5) provided: 'rights held by a person in a fiduciary capacity shall be treated as not held by him…' The net question (for present purposes) was whether Marylebone was Development's subsidiary at the time of the disposal. It was contended that Marylebone was not Development's subsidiary because:

> '… rights held by [Development] in [Marylebone] were held in a fiduciary capacity pursuant to the uncompleted share sale agreement[39].'

At trial, it had been held by Lloyd J that Marylebone *was* Development's subsidiary at the time of the disposal and that it followed that the disposal was not a 'relevant disposal' within the meaning of the English Landlord and Tenant Act 1987. Lloyd J had held that on the conclusion of the share sale agreement, Development had held the shares in Marylebone on trust for Frogmore but did not hold the voting rights in the shares in a fiduciary capacity within the meaning of s 736A(5). Lloyd J had held:

> '… this is not an ordinary trust and there is authority that, even where shares are the subject of an uncompleted, unconditional contract (as here), it is the vendor who can decide how to cast the relevant votes and he is not subject in this respect to any direction from the purchaser (see *Musselwhite v CH Musselwhite & Son Ltd* [1962] 1 All ER 210). It was argued in that case that the vendor, in exercising its voting powers in respect of the shares at any general meeting was, by virtue of the beneficial ownership of the purchaser in the shares, bound to comply with the directions of the purchaser as to how to vote, except in respect of a direction which would affect the value of the lien of the unpaid vendor, so that the vendor was (apart from that exception) in the same position as a bare trustee. Russell J rejected this argument and held that the unpaid vendor of share remaining on the register after the contract retains, vis-à-vis the purchaser, the prima facie right to vote in respect of those shares (see [1962] 1 All ER 201 at 208). He could, no doubt, be restrained by injunction, or made liable after the event in damages, if the right were exercised in a manner inconsistent with the contract. But it seems to me that it is impossible to say, in those circumstances, that he holds the voting rights in a fiduciary capacity for the purchaser even if, because of the doctrines of equity, he holds the shares themselves in a fiduciary capacity. This is consistent with the proposition that the vendor's trusteeship of the property agreed to be sold does not extend to the pre-completion fruits of the property, or give the purchaser a right to possession. For that reason, it seems to me, [it cannot be established] that the terms and circumstances of the contracts have the result that when the transfer of the building was executed unconditionally, [Marylebone] was other than a subsidiary …[40].'

---

38 *Michaels and another v Harley House (Marylebone) Ltd* [1999] 1 BCLC 670 at 674.

39 *Michaels and another v Harley House (Marylebone) Ltd* [1997] 2 BCLC 166 at 172i *per* Lloyd J.

40 *Michaels and another v Harley House (Marylebone) Ltd* [1997] 2 BCLC 166 at 178f–179b.

As Robert Walker LJ was later to comment[41], Lloyd J made a clear distinction 'between the shares themselves and the voting rights, which he seems to have regarded as equivalent or analogous to "fruits" of the shares, or to a right to possession of the shares'.

[12.025] The decision of Lloyd J was appealed to the English Court of Appeal. It was held that Lloyd J had erred in holding that Development did not hold the voting rights in Marylebone *in a fiduciary capacity* for Frogmore. Robert Walker LJ distinguished the case of *Musselwhite* on the grounds that, there, Russell J had upheld the unpaid vendor's '*prima facie* right' to vote in respect of shares registered in his name but that the case was not authority for the proposition that an unpaid vendor did not owe a purchaser a fiduciary obligation. Robert Walker LJ succinctly summarised the law in England in the following terms:

> 'A registered shareholder who is absolute beneficial owner can vote as he pleases, subject only to rather imprecise constraints imposed by company law (see *Smith v Croft (No 2)* [1987] 3 All ER 909 at 957–958). A registered shareholder who is a nominee must vote in accordance with the directions of the absolute beneficial owner, to whom his voting rights are attributed. A registered shareholder who is vendor under an uncompleted contract is in an intermediate position, a fiduciary but not a nominee, and his voting rights are for the purposes of s 736 in abeyance[42].'

It was, therefore, held that once Development had executed the uncompleted contract, its shares were held in a *fiduciary capacity* and its voting rights in respect of the shares in Marylebone were in abeyance and, therefore, Marylebone was *not* its subsidiary[43].

[12.026] Section 155(3)(c) and (d) of the CA 1963 provide:

> 'In determining whether one company is a subsidiary of another—
>
> ...
>
> (c) any shares held or power exercisable by any person by virtue of the provisions of any debentures of the first-mentioned company or of a trust deed for securing any issue of such debentures shall be disregarded;
>
> (d) any shares held or power exercisable by, or by a nominee for, that other or its subsidiary (not being held or exercisable as mentioned in paragraph (c)) shall be treated as not held or exercisable by that other if the ordinary business of that other or its subsidiary, as the case may be, includes the lending of money and the shares are held or power is exercisable as aforesaid by way of security only for the purposes of a transaction entered into in the ordinary course of that business.'

Section 155(3)(c) requires that shares held or powers exercisable by any person by virtue of the provisions of a debenture given by the company or of a trust deed for securing any issue of debentures, must be disregarded.

41 *Michaels and another v Harley House (Marylebone) Ltd* [1999] 1 BCLC 670 at 680f.

42 *Michaels and another v Harley House (Marylebone) Ltd* [1999] 1 BCLC 670 at 682d–e. See, further, Ch 9, *Share Transfer*, at para **[9.074]**.

43 Although the consequence was that the disposal was a 'relevant disposal' for the purposes of the English Landlord and Tenant Act 1987, the court exercised its discretion (as permitted under the 1987 Act) and rejected the appeal on the grounds that the plaintiffs had not acted sufficiently promptly.

The effect of s 155(3)(d) is to preclude a bank or other financial institution from being deemed to be the holding company of a subsidiary whose shares are transferred by its holding company to that bank, its subsidiary or its nominee as security for a loan. So, even if all of the equity share capital in a wholly-owned subsidiary are transferred by a holding company to a bank as security for a loan, the bank will *not* become the holding company of the subsidiary by reason of s 155(3)(d) of the CA 1963. However, it is important to note that s 155(3)(d) does not operate to preserve the relationship of holding company and subsidiary that existed prior to the transfer of shares which will be sundered once the transfer has taken place since the former holding company will no longer be a member of it or hold shares in it and so cannot satisfy any of the limbs in s 155(1)(a) of the CA 1963.

[12.027] The law in the UK is different in relation to how shares held as security are treated[44] but notwithstanding these differences, the English Court of Appeal decision in *Enviroco v Farstad Supply A/S*[45] demonstrates the consequences which can follow where a holding company transfers the shares it holds in its subsidiary to a bank as security. In *Enviroco v Farstad Supply A/S*[46], the English Court of Appeal considered the former UK provision, s 736A(7) of the Companies Act 1985 (UK), which provided:

> 'Rights attached to shares held by way of security shall be treated as held by the person providing the security – (a) where apart from the right to exercise them for the purpose of preserving the value of the security, or of realising it, the rights are exercisable only in accordance with his instructions; (b) where the shares are held in connection with the granting of loans as part of normal business activities and apart from the right to exercise them for the purpose of preserving the value of the security, or of realising it, the rights are exercisable only in his interests[47].'

In that case the former holding company had charged its shares to a bank under a deed of pledge which required, *inter alia*, the shares to be registered in the name of the bank or its nominee. The question for the court was whether that fact meant that the would-be holding company could satisfy the requirement to be a member in s 736(1) of the 1985 Act ie, '... is a member of it and controls, alone, pursuant to an agreement with other members, a majority of the voting rights in it'. It was held that membership of a company was not one of the 'rights' described in ss 736A(6)[48] and 736A(7), and that it (ie, membership) was not a right as such at all but a status derived from the entry of the shareholder's name in the register of members. Because the holding company was no longer a member or held shares, it could not continue to be a holding company.

(d) A subsidiary of a subsidiary

[12.028] Section 155(1)(b) of the CA 1963 provides that a company shall be another company's subsidiary where 'the first-mentioned company is a subsidiary of any

---

44 See s 1159 of the Companies Act 2006 (UK).

45 *Enviroco v Farstad Supply A/S* [2010] 2 All ER 1013.

46 *Enviroco v Farstad Supply A/S* [2010] 2 All ER 1013.

47 Paragraph 7 of the Sixth Schedule to the Companies Act 2006 (UK) has replaced s 736A(7) of the Companies Act 1985 (UK).

48 Section 736A(6) provided: 'Rights held by a person as nominee for another shall be treated as held by the other; and rights shall be regarded as held as nominee for another if they are exercisable only on his instructions or with his consent or concurrence.'

company which is that other's subsidiary'. So, a subsidiary of a company that is itself a subsidiary of a third company, is deemed to be a subsidiary of the third company.

(e) Wholly-owned subsidiaries

[12.029] There are subsidiaries and there are subsidiaries. In places the Companies Acts refer to 'wholly-owned subsidiaries'. This term is defined for a particular purpose by s 150(5) of the CA 1963:

> '… a body corporate shall be deemed to be the wholly-owned subsidiary of another if it has no members except that other and that other's wholly-owned subsidiaries and its or their nominees.'

If the 'and' is read as a conjunction, it would seem to imply that a wholly-owned subsidiary must have two members. It must be remembered, of course, that s 150(5) dates from a time when the only single-member company was the *de facto* kind, one shareholder being the other's nominee. Section 150(5) is, however, expressly stated to be 'for the purposes of *this* section', ie, s 150 of the CA 1963 which concerns the obligation to lay group accounts before a holding company[49]. One can only speculate at what precisely the legislature means by the reference to 'wholly-owned subsidiary' in s 29(6) and (7)(a) of the CA 1990[50], where the term is used but not defined.

Definitions of undertakings, parent undertakings and subsidiary undertakings for group accounting purposes

[12.030] The obligation to prepare group accounts is considered in Ch 17[51]. That obligation arises under the EC(C:GA)R 1992[52] and turns upon an entity being a 'parent undertaking', which is defined as 'an undertaking that has one or more subsidiary undertakings'[53]. The EC(C:GA)R 1992 apply to an 'undertaking', which is defined by reg 3(1) as meaning:

> 'a body corporate, a partnership, or an unincorporated body of persons engaged for gain in the production, supply or distribution of goods, the provision of a service or the making or holding of investments.'

Just as s 155 of the CA 1963, in applying to bodies corporate, expands its scope beyond 'companies' within the meaning of s 2 of the CA 1963, so too are the EC(C:GA)R 1992 widely cast.

[12.031] Central to the definition of 'parent undertaking' is the definition ascribed to 'subsidiary undertaking'. This is defined by reg 4(1), which provides:

> 'For the purposes of these Regulations, an undertaking shall be deemed to be a subsidiary of another, if but only if—
>
> (a) that other—
>
> (i) holds a majority of the shareholders' or members' voting rights in the undertaking, or

[49] See Ch 17, *Financial Statements, Audit and Annual Return*, at para **[17.144]**.

[50] See Ch 16, *Statutory Regulation of Directors; Transactions*, at para **[16.037]**.

[51] See Ch 17, *Financial Statements, Audit and Annual Return*, at para **[17.144]** *et seq*.

[52] SI 201/1992.

[53] Regulation 3(1) of the EC(C:GA)R 1992.

(ii) is a shareholder or member of it and controls the composition of its board of directors, or

(iii) is a shareholder or member of it and controls alone, pursuant to an agreement with other shareholders or members, a majority of the shareholders' or members' voting rights; or

(b) that other has the right to exercise a dominant influence over it—

(i) by virtue of provisions contained in its memorandum or articles, or

(ii) by virtue of a control contract; or

(c) that other has a participating interest in it and—

(i) that other actually exercises a dominant influence over it, or

(ii) that other and the subsidiary undertaking are managed on a unified basis; or

(d) the undertaking is a subsidiary of any undertaking which is that other's subsidiary undertaking.'

There are a number of similarities between the EC(C:GA)R 1992 and s 155 of the CA 1963; there are, however, also a number of major differences. The principal differences concern the two extra circumstances in which one entity will be deemed the subsidiary of another entity. Regulation 4(1)(b) operates to deem one undertaking the subsidiary of another where that other has the right to exercise a 'dominant influence' over it. Regulation 4(1)(c) contains a basis that is even more removed than those in s 155, namely, where that other has a *participating interest* in the undertaking. It is also noteworthy that the EC(C:GA)R 1992 refer to 'parent' undertakings as opposed to 'holding' undertakings, the term used in s 155 of the CA 1963. Such is the interchangeability of both terms in common speech, that it is not safe to assume that use of either expression refers to a group within the meaning of either the CA 1963 or the EC(C:GA)R 1992. The salient features of the reg 4 definition are next considered:

(a) Controlling the composition of the board of directors.
(b) Shares held/powers exercisable by 'nominees'.
(c) Circumstances in which voting rights shall be discounted.
(d) The meaning of 'dominant influence'.
(e) The meaning of 'participating influence'.
(f) The meaning of 'associated undertaking'.

(a) Controlling the composition of the board of directors

[12.032] Regulation 3(2) expressly provides that the definition of 'control' in s 155 of the CA 1963 applies to the use of that term in the EC(C:GA)R 1992:

> 'In determining whether one undertaking controls the composition of the board of directors of another for the purposes of paragraph 1 (a) (ii), subsection (2) of section 155 of the CA 1963 shall apply to undertakings subject to these Regulations as it applies to companies subject to that section.'

In this respect, the issues considered above are equally applicable to the EC(C:GA)R 1992[54].

54 See para **[12.012]** *ante*.

(b) Shares held/powers exercisable by 'nominees'

[12.033] The EC(C:GA)R 1992 also distinguish between shares held and powers exercisable by persons who are both the legal and beneficial owner from those who are nominees, and so bare trustees. Regulation 3(3) provides:

> 'For the purposes of paragraph (1) (a)—
>
> (a) subject to paragraphs (c) and (d), any shares held or power exercisable—
>
> (i) by any person as a nominee for that other; or
>
> (ii) by, or by a nominee for, a subsidiary undertaking of that other, not being the subsidiary undertaking whose shares or board of directors are involved;
>
> shall be treated as held or exercisable by that other,
>
> (b) any shares held or power exercisable by that other or a subsidiary undertaking of that other, on behalf of a person or undertaking that is neither that other nor a subsidiary undertaking of that other shall be treated as not held or exercisable by that other,
>
> (c) any shares held or power exercisable by that other or a nominee for that other or its subsidiary undertaking shall be treated as not held or exercisable by that other if they are held as aforesaid by way of security provided that such power or the rights attaching to such shares are exercised in accordance with instructions received from the person providing the security,
>
> (d) any shares held or power exercisable by that other or a nominee for that other or its subsidiary undertaking shall be treated as not held or exercisable by that other if the ordinary business of that other or its subsidiary undertaking, as the case may be, includes the lending of money and the shares are held as aforesaid by way of security provided that such power or the rights attaching to such shares are exercised in the interests of the person providing the security.'

One of the most significant differences between s 155 and the EC(C:GA)R 1992 is that the EC(C:GA)R 1992 are silent on the consequence of shares being held in a fiduciary capacity, as distinct from shares being held by a nominee. So, it would seem that the shares of a registered shareholder, who is a vendor-undertaking under an uncompleted contract, which will be held in a fiduciary capacity but not as a nominee, are considered to be held by the vendor-undertaking and not held in abeyance, as they would under s 155[55]. Again, the effect of this is to mean that undertakings will be deemed to be in a group for group accounting purposes in circumstances where they would not be a group within the meaning of s 155 of the CA 1963.

(c) Circumstances in which voting rights shall be discounted

[12.034] Regulation 4(4) details three specific circumstances where the total of the voting rights of shareholders or members in a subsidiary undertaking shall be reduced. It provides:

> 'For the purposes of paragraphs (1)(a)(i) and (iii), the total of the voting rights of the shareholders or members in the subsidiary undertaking shall be reduced by the following:—

55 *Michaels and another v Harley House (Marylebone) Ltd* [1999] 1 BCLC 670. See para **[12.023]** *ante*.

(a) the voting rights attached to shares held by the subsidiary undertaking in itself, and

(b) the voting rights attached to shares held in the subsidiary undertaking by any of its subsidiary undertakings, and

(c) the voting rights attached to shares held by a person acting in his own name but on behalf of the subsidiary undertaking or one of its subsidiary undertakings.'

(d) The meaning of 'dominant influence'

[12.035] One of the grounds by which an undertaking shall, under the EC(C:GA)R 1992, be deemed to be a subsidiary undertaking is where another undertaking has the right to exercise a *dominant influence* over it. The key to whether or not a dominant influence exists is whether one undertaking has the right to give directions 'with respect to the operating and financial policies' of another. That this is the guiding feature is made clear by reg 4(5), which provides

> 'For the purposes of paragraph 1(b) an undertaking shall not be regarded as having the right to exercise a dominant influence over another undertaking unless it has a right to give directions with respect to the operating and financial policies of that other undertaking which its directors are obliged to comply with.'

It seems clear that, in order to be reckonable, an undertaking must have a legally enforceable *right* to give directions. A *de facto* 'right' will not suffice.

[12.036] Of particular significance is the fact that an undertaking will be deemed by this provision to be the parent undertaking of another *without being a member or holding any shares in the other undertaking*. This basis for the creation and subsistence of a parent–subsidiary relationship is unique to the EC(C:GA)R 1992 and does not have a parallel in s 155 of the CA 1963. Accordingly, two companies that are required to prepare group accounts solely on the basis of the deeming provision in reg 4(1)(b) of the EC(C:GA)R 1992 will not be a holding and subsidiary company for the purposes of s 155 of the CA 1963 and will not, for example, be able to avail of the benefits of being in a group for general company law purposes. The EC(C:GA)R 1992 state that the dominant influence can arise by virtue of either of two means: (a) provisions in its memorandum or articles (reg 4(1)(b)(i)); or (b) by virtue of a control contract (reg 4(1)(b)(ii)).

[12.037] The reference to the right to exercise a dominant influence, by virtue of provisions contained in a body's memorandum or articles, would seem to refer to the memorandum or articles of the subsidiary undertaking. The circumstances in which reg 4(1)(b)(i) alone will give rise to a parent–subsidiary relationship are thought to be rare because, under Irish law, a right conferred by the memorandum and articles on a party who is not a member of the company is not enforceable[56].

[12.038] The other way in which an undertaking will be considered to have a 'dominant influence' is where it has the right to exercise such by virtue of a 'control contract': reg 4(1)(b)(ii). The meaning of a 'control contract' is provided by reg 4(6):

---

[56] *Eley v Positive Government Security Life Assurance Co* (1876) 1 Ex D 88 and s 25 of the CA 1963. See Ch 3, *Constitutional Documentation*, at para **[3.092]** where the case law that interprets s 25 is considered.

> 'A 'control contract' as specified in paragraph 1(b) means a contract in writing conferring such a right which—
>
> (a) is of a kind authorised by the memorandum or articles of the undertaking in relation to which the right is exercisable, and
>
> (b) is permitted by the law under which that undertaking is established.'

An undertaking will, therefore, be the subsidiary undertaking of another undertaking where there is a contract, which gives the parent the right to exercise a 'dominant influence', without the parent ever having to hold shares in or be a member of the subsidiary.

(e) The meaning of 'participating influence'

[12.039] Another basis by which an undertaking will be deemed to be a parent undertaking is where it has a participating interest in, and *actually*[57] exercises, a 'dominant influence' or where both undertakings are managed on a unified basis. This basis is also foreign to the general definition in s 155 of the CA 1963. Regulation 35(1) defines what is meant by a 'participating interest':

> 'A 'participating interest' means a qualifying capital interest held by one undertaking in another on a long term basis for the purpose of securing a contribution to that undertaking's own activities by the exercise of control or influence arising from or related to that interest.'

Unlike the 'dominant influence' basis considered above, to give rise to a parent–subsidiary relationship on this basis, the parent must have an interest in the capital of the subsidiary. Regulation 35(2) goes on to define what is meant by a 'qualifying capital interest' in the following terms:

> '(a) in relation to an undertaking with share capital means an interest in shares comprised in the allotted share capital of that undertaking,
>
> (b) in relation to an undertaking with capital but no share capital means an interest conferring rights to share in the capital of the undertaking,
>
> (c) in relation to an undertaking without capital means interests—
>
> (i) conferring any right to share in the profits or liability to contribute to the losses of the undertaking, or
>
> (ii) giving rise to an obligation to contribute to the debts or expenses of the undertaking in the event of a winding up; and
>
> (d) includes an interest which is convertible into a qualifying capital interest as well as an option to acquire any such qualifying capital interest.'

Regulation 35(3) provides that where an undertaking holds a qualifying capital interest in another undertaking and such an interest represents 20% or more of all such interests in the other undertaking it shall be presumed to hold that interest on the basis and for the purpose mentioned in reg 35(1) unless the contrary is shown[58].

---

57 See para **[12.040]** *post*.

58 Regulation 35(4) provides that the percentage of qualifying capital interests held in an undertaking with share capital shall be the percentage that the nominal value of the shares held represents of the nominal value of the allotted share capital of that undertaking. Regulation 35(5) provides that for the purpose of this regulation an interest held on behalf of an undertaking shall be treated as held by it. (contd.../)

[12.040] In addition to having a participating interest, the holder of such an interest must *actually exercise a dominant influence*. 'Dominant influence' has been considered above and it was observed that to be cognisable, reg 4(5) required it to be, *inter alia*, a legally enforceable right to give directions with respect to operating and financial policies. This is watered-down in the context of the nature of the dominant influence required where the holder has a 'participating interest'. Thus, reg 4(7) provides that reg 4(5) shall not be read as affecting the construction of the expression 'actually exercises a dominant influence' in reg 4(1)(c).

(f) The meaning of 'associated undertaking'

[12.041] Another category of association, which arises from the EC(C:GA)R 1992, is that of an 'associated undertaking'[59]. Regulation 35 provides:

> '(1) For the purposes of these Regulations an 'associated undertaking' means an undertaking in which an undertaking dealt with in the group accounts has a participating interest and over whose operating and financial policy it exercises a significant influence and which is not—
>
> (a) a subsidiary undertaking of the parent undertaking, or
>
> (b) a joint venture proportionally consolidated in accordance with Regulation 32.
>
> (2) Where an undertaking holds 20 per cent or more of the voting rights in another undertaking, it shall be presumed to exercise such an influence over it unless the contrary is shown.'

Moreover, reg 35(3) provides that paras (3) and (4) of reg 4 shall apply in determining for the purposes of this regulation whether an undertaking holds 20% or more of the voting rights in another undertaking.

Capital maintenance definitions of parent public company and public company subsidiary

[12.042] The European Communities (Public Limited Companies Subsidiaries) Regulations 1997 ('EC(PLCS)R 1997')[60] extend the meaning of 'subsidiary', as defined by s 155 of the CA 1963, for the purposes of Part XI of the CA 1990, which deals with the acquisition of own shares and shares in a company's holding company[61]. Regulation 4(1) of the EC(PLCS)R 1997 provides:

---

58 (\...contd) Moreover, reg 35(6) provides that for the purposes of reg 35, as it applies in relation to the expression 'participating interest' in reg 4(1)(c) (subsidiary undertaking): '(a) there shall be attributed to an undertaking any interests held by any of its subsidiary undertakings, and (b) the references in paragraph (1) to the purpose and activities of an undertaking include the purpose and activities of any of its subsidiary undertakings and of the group as a whole.' Finally, reg 35(7) provides that in the balance sheet and profit and loss formats set out in the Schedule to the 1986 Act, as amended by the Schedule to these regulations, 'participating interest' does not include an interest in a group undertaking.

59 For the significance of associated undertakings, see Ch 17, *Financial Statements, Audit and Annual Return*, at para **[17.197]**.

60 SI 67/1997.

61 See, generally, Ch 10, *The Maintenance of Capital*, at para **[10.038]** *et seq*.

> 'For the purposes of Part XI of the Act of 1990, in addition to the circumstances where a company (including a body corporate) is deemed to be a subsidiary of a public limited company by virtue of section 155 of the CA 1963, a limited company (including a body corporate) within the meaning of paragraph (2) shall also be deemed to be a subsidiary of a public limited company if, but only if, the public limited company is itself a shareholder or member of the said limited company and controls alone, pursuant to an agreement with other shareholders or members, a majority of the shareholders' or members' voting rights in the company in question.'

This extended definition borrows from the EC(C:GA)R 1992, considered above[62], the expression, a 'majority of the shareholders' or members' voting rights'. Again, it is important to note that where a company is deemed to be the subsidiary of another company (a parent public company) for the purposes of Part XI of the CA 1990, solely by reason of the EC(PLCS)R 1997, it will not be a subsidiary within the meaning of s 155 of the CA 1963 and may not avail of the advantages conferred by other provisions of the Companies Acts which are expressed to apply to a group of companies within the meaning of s 155 of the CA 1963.

Taxation definitions of holding and subsidiary companies

(a) Corporation tax

[12.043] The Taxes Consolidation Act 1997 ('TCA 1997') distinguishes between three different types of subsidiaries[63], based on different degrees of ownership. The different types of subsidiary are:

(a) A 51% subsidiary;

(b) A 75% subsidiary;

(c) A 90% subsidiary.

Section 9(1) of the TCA 1997 provides:

> 'For the purposes of the Tax Acts, except where otherwise provided, a company shall be deemed to be—
>
> (a) a '51 per cent subsidiary' of another company if and so long as more than 50 per cent of its ordinary share capital is owned directly or indirectly by that other company,
>
> (b) a '75 per cent subsidiary' of another company if and so long as not less than 75 per cent of its ordinary share capital is owned directly or indirectly by that other company,
>
> (c) a '90 per cent subsidiary' of another company if and so long as not less than 90 per cent of its ordinary share capital is directly owned by that other company.'

The main distinction between the three categories of subsidiary is that in the case of 90% subsidiaries, the shares must be *directly* owned by the holding company. In the case of both 51% and 75% subsidiaries, it is sufficient that the requisite percentage of shares held in the subsidiary is owned *directly or indirectly* by the holding company. 'Owned directly or indirectly' is defined by s 9(2) of the TCA 1997 as meaning:

---

62 See para **[12.030]** *et seq*, *ante*.

63 See, generally, Feeney, *The Taxation of Companies 2012* (2012, Bloomsbury Professional) at p 32 *et seq*.

'owned whether directly or through another company or other companies or partly directly and partly through another company or other companies.'

The reference to 'ownership' is defined to mean 'beneficial ownership'[64].

[12.044] For the purposes of s 9 of the TCA 1997 the amount of ordinary share capital of one company owned by a second company through another company or other companies, or partly directly and partly through another company or other companies, shall be determined in accordance with sub-ss (5) to (10)[65]. These rules are:

'(5) Where, in the case of a number of companies, the first directly owns ordinary share capital of the second and the second directly owns ordinary share capital of the third, then, for the purposes of this section, the first shall be deemed to own ordinary share capital of the third through the second and, if the third directly owns ordinary share capital of a fourth, the first shall be deemed to own ordinary share capital of the fourth through the second and third, and the second shall be deemed to own ordinary share capital of the fourth through the third, and so on.

(6) In this section—

- (a) any number of companies of which the first directly owns ordinary share capital of the next and the next directly owns ordinary share capital of the next but one and so on, and, if there are more than 3, any 3 or more of them, are referred to as a 'series';
- (b) in any series—
  - (i) that company which owns ordinary share capital of another through the remainder is referred to as 'the first owner';
  - (ii) that other company the ordinary share capital of which is so owned is referred to as 'the last owned company';
  - (iii) the remainder, if one only, is referred to as an 'intermediary' and, if more than one, are referred to as 'a chain of intermediaries';
- (c) a company in a series which directly owns ordinary share capital of another company in the series is referred to as an 'owner';
- (d) any 2 companies in a series of which one owns ordinary share capital of the other directly, and not through one or more of the other companies in the series, are referred to as being directly related to one another.

(7) Where every owner in a series owns the whole of the ordinary share capital of the company to which it is directly related, the first owner shall be deemed to own through the intermediary or chain of intermediaries the whole of the ordinary share capital of the last owned company.

(8) Where one of the owners in a series owns a fraction of the ordinary share capital of the company to which it is directly related, and every other owner in the series owns the whole of the ordinary share capital of the company to which it is directly related, the first owner shall be deemed to own that fraction of the ordinary share capital of the last owned company through the intermediary or chain of intermediaries.

(9) Where—

- (a) each of 2 or more of the owners in a series owns a fraction, and every other owner in the series owns the whole, of the ordinary share capital of the company to which it is directly related, or

---

64 Section 9(3) of the TCA 1997.

65 Section 9(4) of the TCA 1997.

(b) every owner in a series owns a fraction of the ordinary share capital of the company to which it is directly related,

the first owner shall be deemed to own through the intermediary or chain of intermediaries such fraction of the ordinary share capital of the last owned company as results from the multiplication of those fractions.

(10) Where the first owner in any series owns a fraction of the ordinary share capital of the last owned company in that series through the intermediary or chain of intermediaries in that series, and also owns another fraction or other fractions of the ordinary share capital of the last owned company, either—

(a) directly,
(b) through an intermediary which is not a member, or intermediaries which are not members, of that series,
(c) through a chain or chains of intermediaries of which one or some or all are not members of that series, or
(d) in a case where the series consists of more than 3 companies, through an intermediary which is a member, or intermediaries which are members, of the series, or through a chain or chains of intermediaries consisting of some but not all of the companies of which the chain of intermediaries in the series consists,

then, for the purpose of ascertaining the amount of the ordinary share capital of the last owned company owned by the first owner, all those fractions shall be aggregated and the first owner shall be deemed to own the sum of those fractions.'

[12.045] It is beyond the scope of this book to consider the consequences in taxation law of a subsidiary being deemed to be in any of the three categories recognised by the TCA 1997. Suffice it to say that the availability of various reliefs under the TCA 1997 is determined by reference to which category a subsidiary belongs[66].

(b) Stamp duty

[12.046] It may also be noted here that exemptions and relief from certain stamp duties[67] between group companies is not based on the s 155 of the CA 1963 definition[68]. Rather, the exemption and relief applies as respect dispositions between 'associated bodies'. 'Associated bodies' are defined by s 79(3) of the Stamp Duties Consolidation Act 1999 ('SDCA 1999')[69] as:

'that is, one was the beneficial owner of not less than 90 per cent of the ordinary share capital of the other, or a third such body was the beneficial owner of not less than 90 per cent of the ordinary share capital of each and that this ownership was ownership either directly or through another body corporate or other bodies corporate, or partly directly and partly through another body corporate or other bodies corporate, and subsections (5) to

66 See Feeney, *The Taxation of Companies 2012* (2012, Bloomsbury Professional).

67 Namely: (a) conveyance or transfer on sale of stocks or marketable securities; (b) conveyance or transfer on sale of a policy of insurance or a policy of life insurance where the risk to which the policy relates is located in the state; and (c) conveyance or transfer on sale of any property (eg, land and buildings) other than stocks or marketable securities or a policy or insurance or a policy of life insurance: s 79(1) of the SDCA 1999.

68 See, generally, Donegan & Friel, *Irish Stamp Duty Law* (2nd edn, Butterworths, 1998) at pp 169–182.

69 As amended by s 136 of the Finance Act 2003.

(10) of section 9 of the Taxes Consolidation Act, 1997, shall apply for the purposes of this section as if—

(a) references to company were references to a body corporate,

(b) references to companies were references to a bodies corporate.'

Moreover, s 79(3A) of the SDCA 1999 provides:

> 'For the purposes of *subsection (3)* 'ordinary share capital', in relation to a body corporate, means all the issued share capital (by whatever name called) of the body corporate, other than capital the holders of which have a right to a dividend at a fixed rate, but have no other right to share in the profits of the body corporate.'

Accordingly, the SDCA 1999 creates a fourth category of subsidiary for the purposes of stamp duty exemption and relief, namely a 90% subsidiary in which the shares are held, whether directly or indirectly. Section 79(4) of the SDCA 1999 provides that, in addition to meeting the conditions in sub-s (3), at the time of the execution of the otherwise stampable instrument, the holding company must be beneficially entitled to not less than 90% of any profits available for distribution to the shareholders of the subsidiary *and* to not less than 90% of any assets of the subsidiary[70] for distribution to its shareholders on a winding up[71]. It should be noted that there are other qualifying conditions too (eg, that the consideration is not paid directly or indirectly by an outsider)[72].

Select issues in the holding-subsidiary relationship

[12.047] Throughout this book there are references to specific issues that apply only or primarily to groups of companies. These issues are best considered in the context of their natural generic environment. It is thought, however, that three group-specific issues should be alluded to here, by reason of their fundamental importance to groups of companies.

(a) The sanctity of the separate legal personality of group companies;

(b) Holding company's liability for subsidiary's negligence;

(c) Group companies' directors' and holding companies' duties.

(a) The sanctity of the separate legal personality of group companies

[12.048] The general circumstances in which the courts have disregarded separate corporate personality have been considered in detail in Ch 5[73], as have the circumstances when the courts have treated a group of companies as a single economic entity[74]. It is

70 Or, if the disposition is between two subsidiaries, that a third-party holding company is entitled to not less than 90% of any profits available for distribution to the shareholders of each and to not less than 90% of any assets available for distribution to the shareholders of each on a winding up.

71 Section 79(4)(a) and (b) of the SDCA 1999. The percentage to which a body corporate is beneficially entitled of any profits available for distribution and of any assets on a winding-up means 'the percentage to which the first body corporate is, or would be, so entitled either directly or through another body corporate or other bodies corporate or partly directly and partly through another body corporate or other bodies corporate'. See also s 79(8) of the SDCA 1999.

72 See, further, Donegan & Friel, *Irish Stamp Duty Law* (2nd edn, Butterworths, 1998).

73 See Ch 5, *Disregarding Separate Legal Personality.*

useful, however, to mention here the general or orthodox[75] principle that a parent company and its subsidiaries are to be treated as separate entities. So, in *Re Frederick Inns Ltd*[76], Lardner J said (and the Supreme Court endorsed):

> 'A fundamental attribute of a company in Irish law is that of corporate personality. A company is a legal entity distinct from its members, capable of enjoying rights and of being subject to duties which are not the same as those enjoyed or borne by its members. This was finally established in *Salomon v Salomon and Company Ltd* [1897] AC 22 and the principle has been recognised and applied in many decisions of the Irish courts. Generally speaking this principle and the statutory rules of company law in which the principle is implicit apply to the relationship between holding companies and subsidiaries and to transactions between them and third parties. The assets of such companies are treated as owned by them legally and beneficially as distinct legal entities. And except where circumstances enable a court to discover an agency or trustee relationship between them, a holding company is not treated as owner of its subsidiaries' assets. And the liabilities of companies which are members of the same group are those of the individual companies which incur them. There is no common group liability for the obligations of individual members of the group imposed by law. The principle is reflected in many aspects of company law; for example in s 147 of the Companies Act 1963 every company (whether a holding company or a subsidiary) is required to keep proper books of account which must include accounts of all sums of money received and expended by the company ...[77].'

An example of the statutory recognition of group companies' separate legal personality is seen in s 17(1)(b) of the C(A)A 1986. That provision exempts subsidiaries that arc private companies from certain requirements of the C(A)A 1986 provided their holding company has entered into an irrevocable guarantee of their subsidiaries' liabilities, the clear implication being that a holding company is not automatically liable for its subsidiaries' liabilities.

[12.049] In *Allied Irish Coal Supplies Ltd v Powell Duffryn International Fuel Ltd*[78], after noting that ss 150–154 of the CA 1963 require, in certain circumstances, the production of group accounts, the Supreme Court (*per* Murphy J) said that whilst that legislation recognised that trading parents and subsidiaries 'may require to be viewed as an economic entity but there is no question of that legislation making the assets of one company within the group liable for the debts of another'[79].

---

74 See para **[5.051]** *et seq*.

75 See Milman, 'Groups: Recurrent Issues of Status' (1997) Palmer's In Company, Issue 2/97.

76 *Re Frederick Inns Ltd et al* [1991] ILRM 582 (HC); [1994] 1 ILRM 387 (SC).

77 *Re Frederick Inns Ltd et al* [1991] ILRM 582 at 587.

78 *Allied Irish Coal Supplies Ltd v Powell Duffryn International Fuel Ltd* (19 December 1997, unreported) SC.

79 *Allied Irish Coal Supplies Ltd v Powell Duffryn International Fuel Ltd* (19 December 1997, unreported) SC at p 12 of the judgment. In *Allied Irish Coal Supplies Ltd v Powell Duffryn International Fuels Ltd* (19 June 1996, unreported) HC, Laffoy J rejected the notion that the companies there were a single economic entity and held that the principle 'cannot be utilised to render the assets of a parent company available to meet the liabilities of a trading subsidiary to a party with whom it has traded'. (contd.../)

The distinction between 'legal substance' and 'economic substance' has also been made in England: in *Re Polly Peck International plc (in administration)*[80], Robert Walker J said:

> '... I think that [counsel] is in one sense assuming what he seeks to prove, since the unjust or inequitable result which he asserts does not occur unless the group is recognised as being in substance a single economic entity, whose constituent members' internal rights and obligations are to be disregarded. But the authorities to which I have already referred show that substance means legal substance, not economic substance (if different), and that ... the separate legal existence of group companies is particularly important when creditors become involved. Injustice may be in the eye of the beholder, but I do not perceive any obvious injustice – certainly not such as the court can remedy – in the unpredictable consequences that may follow from the unforeseen insolvency of a large international group of companies such as the Polly Peck group[81].'

There will be circumstances where a group of companies can be found to be a single economic entity such as to justify the disregard of their separate corporateness, but these will be exceptional[82]. This has recently been restated by the learned Clarke J in *IBB Internet Services Ltd and ors v Motorola*[83], where he said:

> '1.1 The fact that companies are regarded as having a separate legal existence or personality to their shareholders is, perhaps, the most fundamental aspect of corporate law in many countries including Ireland. That separation between companies and their shareholders confers many advantages, most particularly where the company has limited liability so that, in the ordinary way, the company's debts remain with the company and cannot be visited on the shareholders. The shareholders may lose their investment in the case of insolvency but not more. There are, of course, certain limited circumstances where the courts have been prepared to go behind the corporate structure (by engaging in what is sometimes referred to as lifting the corporate veil), but those circumstances are rare and closely defined. Our law, therefore, maintains, largely to the advantage of those who wish to engage in commerce through companies, a strict distinction between a company and those who may be involved in it such as its shareholders or, indeed, directors elected by those shareholders to run the company.
>
> 1.2 It needs to be noted that one of the consequences of that clear distinction is that, where the promoters of a corporate enterprise choose to run their business through a series of companies, each of those companies has a separate legal existence and personality separate not just from the ultimate beneficial owners but also one from the other. It is, of course, a matter of choice for the promoters as to what corporate structure they wish to put in place at the outset. However, where those promoters choose to form a group of

79 (\...contd) This was upheld by the Supreme Court (*per* Murphy J), who said that the proposition that the assets of a parent company should be available to meet the liabilities of a trading subsidiary was so fundamentally at variance with the principle of separate corporate personality as to be wholly unstatable.

80 *Re Polly Peck International plc (in administration)* [1996] 2 All ER 433.

81 *Re Polly Peck International plc (in administration)* [1996] 2 All ER 433 at 488e–g.

82 See generally *DHN Food Distributors Ltd v Tower Hamlet London Borough Council* [1976] 3 All ER 462; *Power Supermarkets Ltd v Crumlin Investments Ltd and Dunnes Stores (Crumlin) Ltd* (22 June 1981, unreported) HC; *Re Bray Travel and Bray Travel (Holdings) Ltd* (13 July 1981, unreported) SC; *Rex Pet Foods Ltd v Lamb Bros (Dublin) Ltd et al* (5 December 1985, unreported) HC; *Adams v Cape Industries* [1990] Ch 433; discussed in Ch 5, *Disregarding Separate Corporate Personality*, at para **[5.051]** *et seq*.

83 *IBB Internet Services Ltd and ors v Motorola* [2011] IEHC 504.

connected companies, the relevant promoters concerned create a situation where there are a number of separate corporate entities each with its own separate legal existence and personality but where there may be some form of interlocking shareholding arrangements which give it its group structure. There may be many reasons why those behind a commercial enterprise choose not just to establish a company through which to carry on their enterprise, but choose to establish a number of interlocking companies within a group. One must assume that, at least in most cases, the division of the company's assets and business into separate companies is considered to have an advantage. This may well be so, not least, perhaps, because each separate company has its own limited liability. It follows that, again ordinarily and subject to very limited exceptions, the debts of one company cannot be visited on another company within the group unless there are in place obligations, such as cross guarantees, whereby the liabilities of one company are guaranteed by others.'

In that case, the defendant successfully applied to have the plaintiffs' statement of claim struck out on the ground that some of the proposed plaintiffs were companies in the plaintiffs' group which did not have themselves a clear cause of action against the defendant. As Clarke J said:

'While there have been some cases where a plaintiff has been able to pursue damages against different companies within the same group on the basis that the group operated as a single economic entity, it does not necessarily follow that the same argument works in reverse so as to permit a claim to be made by, in substance, a group of companies, even though only some of those companies are contracting parties while losses were suffered by others.'

[12.050] In *Ringway Roadmarking v Adbruf Ltd*[84], the terms of a contract provided that either party could terminate it if a controlling shareholding in a party to the agreement passed to a new owner. The defendant company wished to increase its prices to the plaintiff company under the contract but the plaintiff declined. With the intention of triggering the provision in the contract that gave rise to its termination, the defendant company's holding company transferred its shares in the defendant company to another subsidiary. It was held that although the ownership of the shares in the defendant company has been transferred, to read 'new owner' as referring to a subsidiary company, which had bought shares from the holding company, did not reflect the purpose and intention of the parties. Accordingly, the defendant company was held not to be entitled to terminate the contract.

(b) Holding company's liability for subsidiary's negligence

[12.051] In very particular circumstances, a holding company may be found liable in negligence on behalf of a subsidiary company on the basis that the conduct giving rise to the breach of duty was under the control of the holding company. This was the 'fact-specific' finding of the English High Court in *Chandler v Cape plc*[85], which was upheld by the Court of Appeal[86]. There, Arden LJ said:

---

84 *Ringway Roadmarking v Adbruf Ltd* [1998] 2 BCLC 625.

85 *Chandler v Cape plc* [2011] EWHC 951; see Griggin, 'Establishing a Holding Company's Duty of Care to an Employee of a Subsidiary without the need to Life the Corporate Veil' (2011) Co LN August 2011.

86 *Chandler v Cape plc* [2012] EWCA Civ 525.

> '... this case demonstrates that in appropriate circumstances the law may impose on a parent company responsibility for the health and safety of its subsidiary's employees. Those circumstances include a situation where, as in the present case, (1) the businesses of the parent and subsidiary are in a relevant respect the same; (2) the parent has, or ought to have, superior knowledge on some relevant aspect of health and safety in the particular industry; (3) the subsidiary's system of work is unsafe as the parent company knew, or ought to have known; and (4) the parent knew or ought to have foreseen that the subsidiary or its employees would rely on its using that superior knowledge for the employees' protection. For the purposes of (4) it is not necessary to show that the parent is in the practice of intervening in the health and safety policies of the subsidiary. The court will look at the relationship between the companies more widely. The court may find that element (4) is established where the evidence shows that the parent has a practice of intervening in the trading operations of the subsidiary, for example production and funding issues.'

It is clear that this case does not make a radical departure from the established circumstances in which the courts will disregard a subsidiary's separate legal personality. The facts were that a subsidiary and its holding company, an asbestos producer, were based on the same site, cooperated closely and shared the same group medical advisor. When an employee of the subsidiary developed asbestosis and could not claim against the subsidiary (which had been dissolved) or its insurance policy, it was held that the holding company, in that case, owed a duty of care to the employee. The Court of Appeal was at pains to stress that the subsidiary's separate legal personality was not being disregarded; liability was imposed on the holding company only because its actions amounted to taking on a direct duty of care to its subsidiary's employees.

(c) Group companies' directors' and holding companies' duties

[12.052] Directors' duties are primarily owed to the company of which they are directors[87] and it follows from the principle in *Salomon* that the duties owed by directors of group companies are to their individual companies. This can sometimes result in directors of group companies being placed in a 'difficult and delicate position'[88] which will be exacerbated where the subsidiary is not wholly-owned by its parent. A stark example of an abusive relationship is provided by *Scottish Co-operative Wholesale Society Ltd v Meyer and another*[89], where it was observed that:

> '… in all the evidence I have not been able to find the least trace that they [the directors] regarded themselves as owing any duty to the company of which they were directors. They were the nominees of the society and, if the society doomed the company to destruction, it was not for them to put out a saving hand. Rather, they were to join in that work, and, when a frank and prompt statement to their co-directors might have enabled them to retrieve its fortunes, they played their part by maintaining silence[90].'

---

87 *Percival v Wright* [1902] 2 Ch 421. See, generally, Ch 15, *Duties of Directors and Other Officers*, and, on nominee directors, para **[15.006]**.

88 See *Scottish Co-operative Wholesale Society Ltd v Meyer and another* [1959] AC 324 at 341 *per* Viscount Simonds.

89 *Scottish Co-operative Wholesale Society Ltd v Meyer and another* [1959] AC 324.

90 *Scottish Co-operative Wholesale Society Ltd v Meyer and another* [1959] AC 324 at 341.

The position of and duties owed by nominee directors have been considered in another chapter[91]. What is clear is that where a subsidiary company is fraudulently abused through the actions or at the sufferance of its nominee directors, not only will those directors be accountable, but so too will the holding company which appointed them. In the *Meyer* case, it would seem that there was a special relationship between the company and the society which was analogous to partnership in substance, though not law[92]. This will not be so in every case. Neither is it true, in every case, that the apparently gratuitous act or omission by a subsidiary in favour of its holding company will mean that there has been an actionable (or even moral) breach of duty. In *Re PMPA Garage (Longmile) Ltd et al*[93], Murphy J observed:

> 'In the nature of things companies associated with each other as parent and subsidiary or through common shareholders or who share common management and common titles or logos cannot safely ignore the problems of each other. Even the most independently minded director of any such related company seeking to advance the interests of a particular company would necessarily recognise that he should and perhaps must protect the interests of the group as a whole or else take steps to secure that the particular company disassociates itself from the group.'

Equally it is thought that there will be occasions when it will be legitimate for the directors of a subsidiary (or holding company) to sacrifice either company's short term interests for the good of the group[94].

---

[91] See Ch 15, *Duties of Directors and Other Officers*, at para **[15.045]** *et seq*.

[92] See Lower, 'Good Faith and the Partly-Owned Subsidiary' [2000] JBL 232 at 246, 247.

[93] *Re PMPA Garage (Longmile) Ltd et al* [1992] ILRM 337.

[94] See Lower, 'Good Faith and the Partly-Owned Subsidiary' [2000] JBL 232 at 245.

Chapter 13

Corporate Governance: Management by the Directors

Introduction

[13.001] In any company, the theoretical baseline is that corporate governance is divided between the members in general meeting and the directors acting as a board. One of the central concepts in company law is the distinction between corporate *ownership* and corporate *management*[1]. Ownership is considered in Ch 8, *Shares and Membership*. In this chapter, corporate *management* and those responsible for management, the *directors* and other officers, are considered. In the context of private companies, it is important to recognise that the distinction between ownership and management remains the baseline and that corporate governance is divided between the members and the directors. However, while this is the *de jure* position, the *de facto* position will often be that the directors and the members will be one and the same persons. In this sense, the division of powers can be something of a sham, since the players on both sides are quite often the same persons. The formalities imposed on directors and members that may seem to do no more than pay homage to the apparent sham, can – especially when relations are harmonious – be a source of irritation (or even jest) in small companies where the members and directors are one and the same people. Where, however, relations become acrimonious, these same formalities can become a battleground for warring factions, each side scrutinising the running of the company for transgressions of the Companies Acts and culpability on the other's part.

[13.002] In this chapter, corporate governance and the management of companies by the directors is considered in four separate sections:

[A] Officers.
[B] The Directors.
[C] The Secretary.
[D] Delegating Managerial Power to the Directors.

---

1 For commentary on how even more acute these issues become in public companies, see, generally, Clarke, 'Corporate Responsibility in Light of the Separation of Ownership and Control' [1997] 19 DULJ 50.

[A] OFFICERS

Who are officers?

[13.003] Persons holding official positions in relation to companies and other bodies corporate are referred to as 'officers' although, in the case of private companies, the designation has become secondary to two particular types of officer, namely directors and secretaries. Section 2(1) of the CA 1963 offers a non-exhaustive, or inclusive[2], definition of 'officer' as, '*in relation to a body corporate includes a director or secretary*'. Accordingly, directors and secretaries are but two examples of officers. The generic meaning of 'officer' in the context of a body corporate is someone who holds an office. In *Glover v BLN Ltd*[3], Kenny J said:

> 'The characteristic features of an office are that it is created by Act of the National Parliament, charter, statutory reg, articles of association of a company or of a body corporate formed under the authority of a statute, deed of trust, grant or by prescription, and that the holder of it may be removed if the instrument creating the office authorises this.'

The positions of directors and secretaries are that they are both offices which are created by the Companies Acts and, in the case of many companies, also by companies' articles of association. The reason why the definition of officer in s 2(1) of the CA 1963 is non-exhaustive is in recognition of the fact that other offices may be created by companies' articles of association. Although rarely will the articles of association of private companies create additional offices this is not so unusual in guarantee companies where clubs' articles of association will create offices such as treasurer, honorary secretary or president. Regulation 104 of Table A makes clear that the position of chairman is an office[4] but since most articles will provide that only persons who are already office holders (ie, directors) may be chairman there is little significance to the existence of this office since its holder will already be an officer. As a working definition, for the purposes of the Companies Acts, an 'officer' is a person who is a director, secretary, auditor or who holds any other office that has been created by a company's memorandum or articles of association.

[13.004] Auditors are officers by reason of the fact that the position they hold is described by s 160(1) of the CA 1963 as an office:

> '... every company shall at each annual general meeting appoint an auditor or auditors to hold *office* from the conclusion of that until the conclusion of the next annual general meeting.' (Emphasis added.)

In determining whether an auditor was an officer within the meaning of the comparable English provisions, as Lord Parker CJ said in *R v Shacter*[5], 'it can well be asked what office an auditor is being appointed to unless it is an office in the company, and what officer he becomes unless it be an officer of the company'. In that case it was held that a

---

2 *R v Shacter* [1960] 2 QB 252 at 255 *per* Lord Parker CJ.

3 *Glover v BLN Ltd* [1973] IR 388 at 414 *per* Kenny J.

4 Regulation 104 provides: 'The directors may elect a chairman of their meeting and determine the period for which he is to hold office ...'.

5 *R v Shacter* [1960] 2 QB 252 at 255 *per* Lord Parker CJ.

person appointed to fill the office of auditor is an officer whereas an auditor appointed *ad hoc* for a limited purpose is not[6]. In *Re Western Counties Steam Bakeries and Milling Co*[7], Lindley LJ said:

> 'An auditor may or may not be an officer of a company. So may anybody else – eg, a banker or solicitor. Prima facie such persons are not officers. See as to bankers, *Re Imperial Land Co of Marseilles* (LR 10 Eq 298): as to solicitors, *Carter's Case* (31 Ch D 496). But if appointed to an office under the company, and if they act in that office as officers of the company, they will be officers ... That was decided in the case of *Re Liberator Permanent Benefit Building Society* (71 LT (NS) 406) and no irregularity in their appointment, would, I conceive, avail them. But to be an officer there must be an office, and an office imports a recognised position with rights and duties annexed to it, and it would be an abuse of words to call a person an officer who fills no such position either de jure or de facto, but who happens to do some of the work which he would have to do if he were an officer in the proper sense of the word.'

Accordingly, whilst a person or firm appointed as being a company's independent auditors for the purposes of s 160(1) of the CA 1963 will be an officer, a person employed as an internal auditor is, in the absence of some unusual provision in its articles of association, most unlikely to be found to be an officer.

[13.005] Where a company's articles of association create the office of 'chief executive officer' and provide that it may be filled by a person other than someone appointed as a director, the incumbent officeholder will be an 'officer' of the company. A relatively recent phenomenon in banking companies (which can be private companies) is the creation of new offices such as 'chief risk officer' by the amendment of companies' articles of association to empower the directors to fill such offices.

The consequences of being an officer

[13.006] An officer of a company will have such rights and obligations as are provided for in the provisions of the articles of association creating that office. In addition, an officer who is not a director (and so who has no power to manage the company) can be liable in certain circumstances for breaches of the Companies Acts. This is because many of the offences created by the Companies Acts are expressed to apply to 'the company and every officer of the company who is in default'. The liability of officers and the concept of 'officer in default' are considered in Ch 28[8].

[13.007] Officers of companies may also be disqualified under s 160 of the CA 1990. For the purposes of a disqualification application, officer is defined in s 159 of the CA 1990 and: 'includes any director, shadow director, or secretary of the company'. In *The Director of Corporate Enforcement v D'Arcy*[9], the respondent was head of the financial advice and services division but was not a director, shadow director or secretary of the

---

6 *R v Shacter* [1960] 2 QB 252; *Re London and General Bank* [1895] 2 Ch 166; *Re Kingston Cotton Mill Co* [1896] 1 Ch 6; and *Re Western Counties Steam Bakeries and Milling Co* [1897] 1 Ch 617. See also *Mutual Reinsurance Co Ltd v Peat Marwick Mitchell & Co* [1996] BCC 1010.

7 *Re Western Counties Steam Bakeries and Milling Co* [1897] 1 Ch 617.

8 See Ch 28, *Compliance and Enforcement,* at para **[28.033]** *et seq.*

9 *The Director of Corporate Enforcement v D'Arcy* [2006] 2 IR 163.

company bank. The ODCE contended that a person in an elevated management position such as the respondent came within the meaning of the term 'officer' and in this respect relied upon the English Court of Appeal decision in *Re a Company*[10]. In that case, the Court of Appeal was dealing with an appeal from a decision of Vinelott J in the High Court who had refused an application made by the English Director of Public Prosecutions under s 441 of the Companies Act 1948 (UK) which enabled the Director of Public Prosecutions to apply to the High Court for a type of search warrant on showing reasonable cause to believe that any person had, while an officer of a company, committed an offence in connection with the management of the company's affairs and that evidence of the commission of the offence was to be found in any books or papers of or under the control of the company. Lord Denning MR said in the Court of Appeal (in a passage quoted by Kelly J in *D'Arcy*):

> 'The word "officer" in relation to a body corporate is defined in section 455 of the Act. Not really "defined": for it only "includes a director, manager, or secretary." Its meaning may depend on the context in which it is used and in this case on the whole phrase ... "while an officer of a company, committed an offence in connection with the management of the company's affairs ...". The officer here referred to is a person in a managerial situation in regard to the company's affairs. I would not restrict these words too closely. The general object of the Act is to enable the important officers of the State to get at the books of the company when there has been a fraud or wrongdoing. It seems to me that whenever anyone in a superior position in a company encourages, directs or acquiesces in defrauding creditors, customers, shareholders or the like, then there is an offence being committed by an officer of the company in connection with the company's affairs.'

In a concurring judgment Shaw LJ said in relation to the decision of Vinelott J:

> 'He also considered that the party said to be an officer of the company of whom it was alleged that he had committed some offence in connection with the management of the company's affairs was not to be regarded as an officer or a manager within the definition in section 455 of the Companies Act 1948. The expression "manager" should not be too narrowly construed. It is not to be equated with a managing or other director or a general manager. As I see it, any person who in the affairs of the company exercises a supervisory control which reflects the general policy of the company for the time being or which is related to the general administration of the company is in the sphere of management. He need not be a member of the board of directors. He need not be subject to specific instructions from the board. If he fulfils a function which touches the central administration of the company, that is sufficient in my view to constitute an "officer" or "manager" of the company for the purposes of section 441 of the Act.'

It is submitted that to thc cxtent that the decision in *Re a Company* is authority for the proposition that a person in an elevated management position is, without more, an 'officer' of a company within the meaning of s 2 of the CA 1963 or s 159 of the CA 1990, it is wrong, and the Supreme Court decision in *Glover v BLN Ltd*[11] represents the law in Ireland. Whilst a certain degree of flexibility might be expected in the case of an application for a form of search warrant (intrusive and all as that is) such a loose interpretation of a long-used term would be completely untenable in the context of an application to disqualify a person or convict a person of a criminal offence.

---

10 *Re a Company* [1980] Ch 138.

11 *Glover v BLN Ltd* [1973] IR 388 at 414 *per* Kenny J.

[13.008] Although Kelly J did say in *D'Arcy* that he thought the ODCE's assertion was 'probably correct' he did not make a finding on the matter and instead considered the application for disqualification under s 160(2)(e) of the CA 1990 whereby any 'person' and not just an 'officer' may be disqualified. Similarly in *The Director of Corporate Enforcement v Boner*[12], the respondent was not a director or secretary but had held a number of positions in National Irish Bank: a regional manager with responsibility for 19 branches, reporting to the general manager of retail banking; the head of retail reporting to the chief executive; and chief manager–retail reporting to the general manager–banking. After quoting the passage from the decision of Lord Denning MR, also quoted by Kelly J, Murphy J said:

> 'While this decision of the English Court of Appeal refers to criminal proceedings, there seems to be no logical reason why it should be restricted and not include investigations by inspectors appointed by the court. It may be somewhat tautological to say that the management of the company is entrusted to the directors when, in reality there are those in a superior position in a company who may encourage, direct or acquiesce in defrauding creditors, customers, shareholders or the like. The court has to recognise the reality of the power and responsibility of senior management in large public or private companies who have particular expertise and authority, as distinct from the division between directors of companies formed under the Joint Stock Companies Act in the 19th Century who employed administrators to implement their bidding[13].'

This might well be a justification for revisiting of the definition of 'officer' in statute by the legislature, but it does not, it is submitted, justify a court finding that a person who was neither a director or a secretary or held a position created by the company's constitution is an officer so as to impose penalties, whether in the nature of a disqualification or of a criminal conviction.

[B] The Directors[14]

[13.009] As we have seen, directors are officers. The term 'director', however, has no technical meaning. It is defined by s 2(1) of the CA 1963 to include 'any person occupying the position of director by whatever name called'. As seen above, the powers of management are delegated by the members to the directors and, therefore, those who occupy the position of director are those persons who are appointed to manage the business of the company. The definition of 'director' is robust. Were the members not to delegate management to the directors and, instead, to exercise the powers of management themselves, they could also be said to 'occupy the position of directors' and would be accountable under the Companies Acts just as properly appointed, or *de jure* directors would. However, it is almost invariably the case that the board of directors will be the organ within a company which is the recipient of the members' delegated powers. While the members in general meeting retain certain powers, it is the board of directors which, under the model articles, is deemed to have the important powers of

12 *The Director of Corporate Enforcement v Boner* [2008] IEHC 151 (Murphy J).

13 *The Director of Corporate Enforcement v Boner* [2008] IEHC 151 at para 5.1 of the judgment.

14 See, generally, Sealy et al (eds), *British Company Law and Practice* (2010; loose leaf, Sweet & Maxwell) at 29,001.

management of the business of the company. However, the board itself has no separate existence and is but the sum of its directors.

[13.010] In this section, the following issues concerning directors are considered:

1. Two directors, one EEA-resident, and all natural persons.
2. Persons disqualified from and restricted in becoming directors.
3. The number of directorships that can be held by one person.
4. The formal appointment of directors.
5. Types of formally appointed directors.
6. *De facto* directors.
7. Shadow directors.
8. The remuneration of directors.
9. Ceasing to be a director.
10. Disclosures concerning directors and secretaries.

Two directors, one EEA-resident, and all natural persons

(a) Two directors

[13.011] Every company, including single-member companies, must have at least two directors[15], and while there is no statutory upper limit on the number of directors that can be appointed to a company, a company's articles of association may set a maximum number[16]. A director of a company may also be its secretary: s 175 of the CA 1963. However, s 177 of the CA 1963 provides that where the law requires something to be done by or to both a director and the secretary, this will not be satisfied by its being done by or to the same person acting both as director and as, or in place of, the secretary. The most obvious example of this is the attestation of the company seal; where the articles require two directors or one director and the secretary, an attestation by one person alone who is both director and secretary will be invalid.

(b) At least one EEA-resident director

[13.012] One of a series of measures taken to prevent Ireland being used as a jurisdiction of incorporation of choice by nefarious foreigners, is s 43(1) of the Companies (Amendment) (No 2) Act 1999 (the 'C(A)(No2)A 1999'). The background to this was the utilisation of Irish registered non-resident (IRNR) companies in international money laundering and various other scams in foreign countries, as far apart as Mexico and Latvia and many in between. Although essentially tax driven, the vicw takcn was that company law changes were also required to prevent these non-resident Irish companies from tarnishing Ireland's international reputation[17]. Though clearly motivated by the best of intentions, the remedial legislation makes for tortuous reading, trying to batten down the hatches whilst provisioning, simultaneously, for fire escapes, necessitated by EU membership. Section 43(1) provided that, subject to certain exceptions, *at least one* of the directors for the time being of a newly incorporated

15 Section 174 of the CA 1963.

16 Model reg 97 of Table A provides that the members can by ordinary resolution increase or decrease the number of directors.

17 See generally, Ch 2, *Incorporation by Registration*, at para **[2.045]**.

company shall, from 18 April 2000[18], be a person who is resident in the State[19]. With effect from 12 July 2009, however, s 43 was amended[20] so that the requirement is now for at least one director to be a resident of a Member State of the European Economic Area or EEA[21]. The failure to comply renders the company and every officer in default guilty of an offence[22], and summary proceedings may be brought and prosecuted by the registrar of companies[23]. Moreover, a defaulting company may be struck off the register[24].

[13.013] Section 44(8) of the C(A)(No2)A 1999 provides that so far as it is the person's residence in the State that falls to be determined for the purposes of s 43, a person is resident in the State at a particular time ('the relevant time') if:

> '(a) he or she is present in the State at–
>
> (i) any one time or several times in the period of 12 months preceding the relevant time ('the immediate 12 month period') for a period in the aggregate amounting to 183 days or more, or
>
> (ii) any one time or several times–
>
> (I) in the immediate 12 month period, and
>
> (II) in the period of 12 months preceding the immediate 12 month period ('the previous 12 month period'),
>
> for a period (being a period comprising in the aggregate the number of days on which the person is present in the State in the immediate 12 month period and the number of days on which the person was present in the State in the previous 12 month period) in the aggregate amounting to 280 days or more,
>
> or
>
> (b) that time is in a year of assessment (within the meaning of the Taxes Consolidation Act, 1997) in respect of which the person has made an election under s 819(3) of that Act.'

Moreover, notwithstanding s 44(8)(a)(ii), where in the immediate 12-month period concerned a person is present in the State at any one time or several times for a period in the aggregate amounting to not more than 30 days, the person shall not be resident in the State for the purposes of s 43 and no account shall be taken of the period for the purposes of the aggregate mentioned in s 44(8)(a)(ii)[25]. References to a person being present in the State mean being 'personally present in the State' and a person is deemed to be present for a day if the person is present at the end of the day[26].

---

18 The commencement date for s 43(1) of the C(A)(No2)A 1999: SI 61/2000.

19 In the case of companies formed and registered under the CA 1963 and existing companies (as defined by s 2 of the CA 1963), companies had 12 months from 18 April 2000 to ensure that at least one of their directors was a person resident in the State: s 43(2) of the C(A)(No2)A 1999.

20 Section 43 was amended by s 10(1) of the Companies (Amendment) Act 2009 ('C(A)A 2009').

21 Member State of the EEA means a state that is a contracting party to the Agreement on the European Economic Area signed at Oporto on 2 May 1992, as amended for the time being: s 43(16) of the C(A)(No2)A 1999.

22 Section 43(13) of the C(A)(No2)A 1999.

23 Section 43(14) of the C(A)(No2)A 1999.

24 Section 43(15) of the C(A)(No2)A 1999: see generally Ch 26, *Strike Off and Restoration*.

25 Section 44(9) of the C(A)(No2)A 1999.

26 Section 44(10)(a) and (b) of the C(A)(No2)A 1999.

[13.014] The main exception to the general rule that every company must have at least one director who is a person resident in a Member State of the EEA is set out in s 43(3). This provides that the general rule in sub-ss (1) and (2) will not apply to a company that holds a bond, in the prescribed form, in force to the value of €25,394.76[27]. This bond must provide for payment to a person nominated by the registrar of companies or the Revenue Commissioners of a sum of money to discharge the whole or part of the company's liability in respect of certain fines and penalties. The fines and penalties to which the bond must relate are:

(a) a fine, if any, imposed on the company in respect of an offence under the Companies Acts, committed by it, being an offence that is prosecutable by the registrar of companies; and

(b) a fine, if any, imposed on the company in respect of an offence under s 1078 of the Taxes Consolidation Act 1997 committed by it, being an offence that consists of a failure by the company to deliver a statement which it is required to deliver under s 882 of that Act or to comply with a notice served on it under s 884 of that Act; and

(c) a penalty, if any, which the company has been held liable to pay under s 1071 or 1073 of the Taxes Consolidation Act 1997.

The nominated person is obliged by s 43(3) to apply any sum that becomes so payable to such fine or penalty. The nominated person is obliged to keep all proper and usual accounts, including an income and expenditure account and a balance sheet of all monies received by him on foot of the bond and of all disbursements made by him[28]. The Minister for Jobs, Enterprise and Innovation may, following consultation with the Minister for Finance, the Revenue Commissioners and other concerned or interested persons, prescribe that arrangements in relation to bonds shall only be entered into with persons of a prescribed class or classes; the Minister may also prescribe the form of the bond and the minimum term of the bond[29]. Where a company is required to have such a bond it must append it to the statement required by s 3 of the C(A)A 1982 (where there is no resident director on the company's incorporation); to any notification by a person ceasing to be a director that the company has no directors resident in a Member State of the EEA (as required by s 43(9) of the C(A)(No2)A 1999); to its annual return where during the period to which it relates, none of the directors has the requisite residence (unless notification has already been made under s 43(9))[30]. As noted, where a person ceases to be a director and he knows that he was the only director with the requisite residence at that time, he is under a direct obligation to notify in writing the registrar of companies of those facts[31]. Where a former director fails to comply with the

27 In addition to the sum of €25,394.76, the bond must also make provision for the payment of a sum of money (not exceeding such sum as the Revenue Commissioners and the Minister for Jobs, Enterprise, and Innovation may sanction) for the purpose of defraying such expenses as may have been reasonably incurred by the nominated person in carrying out his duties under s 43(3) of the C(A)(No2)A 1999.

28 Section 43(6) of the C(A)(No2)A 1999.

29 Section 43(7) of the C(A)(No2)A 1999.

30 Section 43(8) of the C(A)(No2)A 1999.

31 Section 43(9) of the C(A)(No2)A 1999. Such notification is deemed not, of itself, to be regarded as constituting defamatory matter: s 43(10) of the C(A)(No2)A 1999.

aforementioned requirement, he shall become jointly and severally liable with the company to pay any of the fines or penalties referred to in sub-s (3) above, that are subsequently imposed upon the company[32]. Section 43(4) of the C(A)(No2)A 1999 exempts the bond from the laws of champerty.

[13.015] A further, discretionary, exemption from the requirement that every company must have at least one director who is a person resident in a Member State of the EEA is provided for in s 44(1) of the C(A)(No2)A 1999, which states that sub-ss (1) and (2) of s 43 shall not apply 'in relation to a company in respect of which there is in force a certificate under this section'. Such a certificate may be granted by the registrar of companies, on application being made in the prescribed form, where the registrar has been tendered proof[33] that:

> '… the company has a real and continuous link with one or more economic activities that are being carried on in the State.'

An example of a case where the registrar may grant such a certificate might be where a foreign multinational incorporates an Irish company in connection with the multinational locating a factory or other industry in Ireland. In such a case, the registrar may exempt the Irish company from the requisite residency requirement. A written statement[34] to the company from the Revenue Commissioners made within two months of application for a certificate which states that the revenue has 'reasonable grounds to believe that the company has a real and continuous link with one or more economic activities being carried on in Ireland' is deemed to be proof for the registrar[35]. Where the registrar, in consequence of information that has come into her possession, is of opinion that the company has ceased to have such a link, she must revoke the certificate[36], and likewise if the revenue obtains such information, it may (but is not obliged) to give notice in writing of this to the registrar[37]. Where the registrar receives such notice from the revenue, such is deemed to constitute information in her possession[38].

(c) Only natural persons can become directors

[13.016] In Ireland, only natural persons can become directors of companies, as s 176(1) of the CA 1963 prohibits companies from having a body corporate as a director. It should be noted that there is no prohibition under the Companies Acts on an Irish company (or indeed any body corporate) from becoming a director of a company in a jurisdiction which permits corporate directors: the prohibition is on Irish companies having as a director, a body corporate. Accordingly, an Irish company can validly be a director of a company incorporated in another jurisdiction where the laws of that

32 Section 43(11) of the C(A)(No2)A 1999, which goes on to provide that any such fine or penalty may be recoverable by the registrar of companies or the Revenue Commissioners, as appropriate, from the former director, as a simple contract debt in any court of competent jurisdiction.

33 Section 44(3) of the C(A)(No2)A 1999.

34 Within the meaning of s 44(5) of the C(A)(No2)A 1999.

35 Section 44(4) of the C(A)(No2)A 1999.

36 Section 44(6) of the C(A)(No2)A 1999.

37 Section 44(7) of the C(A)(No2)A 1999.

38 Section 44(7) of the C(A)(No2)A 1999.

jurisdiction do not prevent companies from having as directors, bodies corporate, eg, an Irish company may validly be the director of a company formed and registered in England and Wales.

Persons disqualified from and restricted in becoming directors

[13.017] The office of director requires no *formal* qualifications[39]. Qualifications, such as they are, are purely *negative* and the Companies Acts merely state that certain persons may not become directors, or may only do so subject to specific restrictions. A four-fold classification can be made between:

(a) Persons debarred from being directors;
(b) Qualification shares;
(c) Persons restricted in their directorships; and
(d) Disqualification of directors and others.

(a) Persons debarred from being directors

[13.018] An undischarged bankrupt cannot lawfully become a director, and for a bankrupt to do so is a criminal offence: s 183 of the CA 1963[40]. It was held in *R v Brockley*[41] that to act as a company director whilst being an undischarged bankrupt is an absolute offence of strict liability and that it was no defence for the accused to claim that he genuinely believed that he had been discharged as a bankrupt before becoming a company director. A person convicted of an indictable offence concerning his involvement with a company or of fraud or dishonesty can be prevented by the courts from being a director of a company[42]. It should also be noted that an auditor is debarred from being a director of the company of which he is auditor[43].

(b) Qualification shares

[13.019] As a general rule, a director is not required to hold so-called 'qualification shares' in a company. While reg 77 of Table A allows a company to have a shareholding qualification for its directors, it goes on to provide that where the company in general meeting does not fix any, none shall apply. Under s 180 of the CA 1963, a director, who by resolution of the members is required to have a share qualification, must obtain and maintain such shares within two months from his appointment or a lesser time if the company's articles so provide. It may of course be provided in the articles that a share qualification is a condition precedent to the appointment of a director. It should be noted that this issue will not generally arise since, in many Irish private companies, the directors will perhaps themselves be the only shareholders of the company.

(c) Persons restricted in their directorships

[13.020] The law relating to the making of restriction orders pursuant to s 150 is comprehensively addressed in Ch 28[44], and it is sufficient to simply note here the

39 See Ch 15, *The Duties of Directors and Other Officers*, at para **[15.078]**.
40 As amended by s 169 of the CA 1990.
41 *R v Brockley* [1994] 1 BCLC 606.
42 Section 160(1) of the CA 1990.
43 Section 162(5) of the CA 1963, as amended by s 6 of the C(A)A 1982.
44 See Ch 28, *Compliance and Enforcement*, para **[28.062]** *et seq.*

existence of the restriction. Section 150 of the CA 1990 provides that, subject to certain qualifications in sub-s (2), on an insolvent company being wound up, the court *shall declare* that a person to whom the chapter applies shall not for five years:

> '... be appointed or act in any way, whether directly or indirectly, as a director or secretary or be concerned or take part in the promotion or formation of any company unless it meets the requirements set out...'

In the case of a private company, these requirements are set out in s 150(3) of the CA 1990, which provides that any company in which such a person is involved should have a nominal value of allotted[45] and fully paid up, in cash, share capital of €63,486.90[46]. On application being made to court, the court may grant relief to a *restricted company* under s 157 of the CA 1990. Before a 'restricted' person accepts an appointment as a director or secretary in another company, he must, within 14 days of his appointment or of his so acting, notify that company that he is a restricted person[47]. This latter provision will prove inappropriate in many Irish private companies, since, far from it being the case that a restricted person will be 'head-hunted' by an innocent company looking for a director, it is quite likely that it will be the restricted director himself who will form the company which will, by his involvement, thereby become a *restricted company.*

(d) Disqualification of directors and others[48]

[13.021] The law relating to the making of disqualification orders pursuant to s 160 is comprehensively addressed in Ch 28[49], and it is sufficient to again note here that persons who are disqualified may not act as directors of companies.

The number of directorships that can be held by one person

[13.022] In addition to the requirement that Irish companies have at least one EU or EEA resident director[50], another measure taken to curb the abuse of Irish companies was to limit the number of directorships which any one person can hold. The perceived danger was that by requiring one Irish (or, now, EU or EEA) resident director, unscrupulous Irish residents might have facilitated the foreign controllers of companies wishing to locate in Ireland by allowing their name go forward and to act as a multiple nominee director. An acute example of what might have been is seen in the case of *Official Receiver v Vass and another*[51]. There, Blackburne J disqualified a resident of the jurisdiction of Sark who had acted as nominee director to 1,313 companies and as company secretary to 513 companies. When one of the companies went into liquidation two years after its formation owing over £571,000 disqualification proceedings were taken against the nominee director. Blackburne J held that in holding himself out as a director to so many companies the person had abrogated his responsibilities for those

---

45 See s 156 of the CA 1990 as to the requirements for allotting shares in a restricted company.

46 Section 150(3)(a)(ii) of the CA 1990 as amended by s 41(1)(b) of the CLEA 2001. See also s 158 of the CA 1990, which empowers the Minister for Jobs, Enterprise and Innovation to vary the amounts mentioned in s 150(3).

47 Section 150(5) of the CA 1990.

48 Linnane, 'Restrictions on and Disqualification of Directors' (1994) ILT 132.

49 See Ch 28, *Compliance and Enforcement*, para **[28.148]** *et seq.*

50 See para **[13.012]** *ante*.

51 *Official Receiver v Vass and another* [1999] BCC 516.

companies by merely acting as a nominee and that he deserved to be disqualified for a substantial period.

[13.023] Section 45(1) of the C(A)(No2)A 1999 provides that a person shall not, at a particular time, be a director or shadow director[52] of more than 25 companies. It will be noted that this provision is directed at the person, not the company, and that an Irish company may have more than 25 directors, unlikely though that might be. It is an offence for a person to become a director of one or more companies in contravention of the limit in s 45(1)[53], and such person may be summarily prosecuted by the registrar of companies[54]. Any appointment of a person as a director to a company in breach of s 45(1) is void[55], but the legislation attempts to provide that the first 25 directorships shall not become unlawful or be rendered void or cease to have effect by reason of a subsequent invalid appointment[56]. Where a director holds in excess of 25 directorships after the commencement of s 45[57], the appointments having been made before the commencement of s 45, at the expiry of 12 months following its commencement, such appointments in excess of the 25-directorship limit, shall cease to have effect[58]. Where appointments of a person as director to two or more companies are made simultaneously and their timing is incapable of being distinguished, their timing will be deemed to be as per their order of registration under the Companies Acts[59].

[13.024] Just as there are exceptions to the general rule that every company must have at least one EU or EEA resident director, so too are there exceptions to the general rule that no person may hold more than 25 directorships. Section 45(3) of the C(A)(No2)A 1999 provides that in reckoning whether a person has 25 directorships, the following directorships are not to be included, namely directorships of:

- public limited companies[60];
- public companies (eg, companies limited by guarantee without a share capital)[61];

52 Section 45(2) of the C(A)(No2)A 1999 provides that in subsection (1) – but not any other subsection of s 45 – 'director' includes a 'shadow director' within the meaning of the CA 1990.

53 Section 45(8). Each appointment in excess of the 25-directorship limit is deemed to constitute a separate contravention: s 45(11)(a) of the C(A)(No2)A 1999.

54 Section 45(13) of the C(A)(No2)A 1999.

55 Section 45(9) of the C(A)(No2)A 1999.

56 Section 45(11)(b) of the C(A)(No2)A 1999.

57 18 April 2000: SI 61/2000.

58 Section 45(10) of the C(A)(No2)A 1999. Subsection (11)(c) provides that: 'in determining whether one particular appointment referred to in subsection (10), as distinct from another such appointment, has ceased to have effect by virtue of that subsection or whether a person's remaining in office under one such appointment, as distinct from another such appointment, constitutes an offence under subsection (8), the provisions of this section (other than subsection (3)(b), (5), (6), (7) and (8)) shall be deemed to have been in operation at the time of the making of that appointment.'

59 Section 45(12) of the C(A)(No2)A 1999.

60 Section 45(3)(a)(i) of the C(A)(No2)A 1999.

61 Section 45(3)(a)(ii) of the C(A)(No2)A 1999; public company means as within the meaning of the C(A)A 1983.

- companies in respect of which a s 44(2) certificate is in force[62]; and
- any company that is the holder of a licence under s 9 of the Central Bank Act 1971 or exempt from holding such a licence or that is referred to in the Second Schedule to the C(A)(No2)A 1999, *provided* that before assuming such a directorship, and following notice[63] to the registrar of companies, the registrar certifies that such company is within one of these categories or the Minister for Jobs Enterprise and Innovation directs that such a company is not to be included amongst the companies that shall be reckoned for the purposes aforesaid[64].

It should be noted that if a person is director of both a holding company and its subsidiary, those two (or more if there is more than one subsidiary) directorships are treated as one directorship for the purposes of reckoning the number of directorships a person holds[65]. There was also a transitional provision in respect of the period from commencement of the section to 12 months after commencement[66].

The formal appointment of directors

[13.025] First, it may noted that the restrictions contained in s 179 of the CA 1963 on the appointment of or advertisement for directors do not apply to private companies by virtue of sub-s (5)(b). The statutory restrictions on the appointment of a director to a private company are, relatively speaking, minimal. A person can be formally appointed a director of a company in either of two ways. In the first place, the person can be appointed as one of the first directors of a company; in the second place, a person can be

---

62 Section 45(3)(a)(iii) of the C(A)(No2)A 1999.

63 Such notice may be delivered to the registrar of companies before the person concerned becomes a director of the company to which the notice relates: s 45(7) of the C(A)(No2)A 1999.

64 Section 45(3)(b)(i) and (ii) of the C(A)(No2)A 1999. The registrar of companies may accept as sufficient evidence that the company falls within a recognised category, a statutory declaration in the prescribed form to that effect made by an officer of the company of the putative director: s 45(5). An appeal to the Minister for Jobs Enterprise and Innovation can be taken from the refusal of the registrar to issue a certificate. The Minister may either (a) confirm the registrar's decision; (b) certify that the company falls within a category; or (c) direct that the company shall not be included: s 45(6). The direction referred to in s 45(6)(c) can only be made where the director was a director of the company before the commencement of s 45, the Minister forms the opinion that the section would result in serious injustice or hardship for the director, and the giving of the direction would not operate against the common good.

65 Section 45(3)(c) of the C(A)(No2)A 1999.

66 Section 45(4) of the C(A)(No2)A 1999 provides: 'Without prejudice to subsection (3), in reckoning, for the purposes of subsection (1), the number of companies of which the person concerned is a director at a particular time, being a time that is before the expiration of the period of 12 months from the commencement date of this section, there shall not be included any company of which the person is a director at that time if he or she was such a director immediately before such commencement.' The effect would appear to have been to disapply the 25-directorship limit for a 12-month period following commencement, but only in respect of directorships held prior to commencement, ie, no new directorships in excess of the limit could be taken on after commencement.

appointed a director to an existing company. In either case it is a prerequisite that the person first consents to becoming a director.

(a) Consent to act as a director

[13.026] A person is required to *consent* on a statutorily prescribed form to his or her appointment as a director to either a new[67] or an existing company[68]. In addition, and statutory form aside, a person must *in fact* consent to acting as a director in a particular company. One of the issues here concerns age. The Companies Acts prescribe neither a minimum nor a maximum age requirement for company directors. In the context of minors, the fact that directors must consent to act as such must (as a matter of practical fact) require the director to be of a sufficient age, maturity and education to understand the nature of the consent. It is a sad fact of life that many parents have put forward their infant children to act as directors of the companies they control. The ability of a two-year-old to sign, let alone to understand, the nature of such a consent is not even debatable. But where does one draw the line? If age alone is the criterion by which the consent is to be assessed, one can only say with certainty that an 18-year-old will be deemed to give a valid consent. But what about a 17-year-old, or a 15-year-old of above average intelligence? The result is to place the CRO in an invidious position, to accept or reject the validity of the consent. Even where the CRO registers a minor director, the validity of the consent given is open to challenge, subsequently. The CLRG has recommended and s 128 of the draft Companies Bill provides that no person can be appointed a director unless he or she is 18 years of age.

[13.027] Of course, consent to act as a director may be vitiated for other reasons. Where a person signs the consent on the appropriate statutory form, this will be strong *prima facie* evidence that he has in fact consented to act as a director – for the purposes of both the statutory requirement and his agreement to act generally as a director of a particular company. In this regard the decision in *Re CEM Connections Ltd*[69] is instructive. The facts in that case were that the English official receiver applied to have a woman disqualified from acting as a director and the question arose as to whether she had been formally appointed as a director of the company. There was no evidence that the woman had been appointed as a director of the company at any meeting of the company. As proof that she had been a director, however, the official receiver sought to rely upon the fact that she had signed the statutory consent to act as a director. The woman accepted that the signature was hers but claimed that at the time she had not knowingly signed it. Hers was, by any standard, a sorry story and the vitiating factors asserted were many: her grandfather, to whom she had been very close, had just died; her mother was seriously ill with cancer; and she herself was clinically depressed, anorexic and addicted to cocaine. In addition to signing the statutory consent, she also acknowledged that the signature on the company's VAT registration form and bank mandate was hers. However, it was claimed that that had been signed the day after she had tried to commit suicide and at a time when she claimed that she did not know whether she was 'coming or going'. Mr Registrar Rawson said:

> 'In my judgment, for the appointment of a director of a company to be valid it is necessary that the person appointed should give informed consent to that appointment … I do not

---

67 Section 3(3) of the C(A)A 1982.

68 Section 195(7) of the CA 1963.

69 *Re CEM Connections Ltd* [2000] BCC 917.

> think that the cases on non est factum are of any real assistance in resolving this question. The fact that a person signs a form of consent is, of course, strong prima facie evidence that consent was given, but it is not in my view conclusive and may be rebutted by evidence which indicates that the signature was obtained without the person signing the document appreciating what he or she was doing. I am satisfied that Miss Prowse did not realise that she was giving consent to being appointed a director …[70]'

In these circumstances, the disqualification application was dismissed. It is thought, however, that where a person's capacity is impaired at the time of signing the statutory consent or agreeing to become a director, he will only be excused if he removes himself from the position as soon as capacity is regained. If a person does not recant and if, upon regaining capacity, he continues to hold himself out as a director and continues to 'occupy the position' of director, that person is likely to be deemed a *de facto* director[71].

(b) Appointment as a first director

[13.028] The formal appointment of a director is governed by a company's articles of association; reg 75 of Table A provides that the number of directors and the names of the first directors shall be determined in writing by the subscribers of the memorandum of association, or a majority of them. As noted above, s 3(1) of the C(A)A 1982 requires that the names of the first directors and secretary, and their consent[72] to their appointment must be sent to the CRO with the memorandum of the company. Such persons are then deemed to have been appointed as directors by the subscribers[73]. Regulation 92 of Table A, which provides for the retirement of directors at the first annual general meeting ('AGM'), is usually deleted by most private companies[74]. Where this article is retained and an AGM is not, for whatever reason, held or is held and the reappointment of directors is overlooked, the result can give rise to considerable ambiguity as to the status of the directors[75].

(c) Appointments to an existing company

[13.029] Directors can, of course, also be formally appointed subsequent to a company's formation, and whether or not a person has been formally appointed a director is a matter of fact[76]. Post-incorporation, directors are usually appointed either by resolution of the company's members in general meeting or by resolution of the existing directors, acting as a board[77]. Where at a general meeting it is proposed by persons other than the

---

70 *Re CEM Connections Ltd* [2000] BCC 917 at 919.

71 See para **[13.045]** *post*. The liabilities of reluctant directors who might be said to contract a 'sexually transmitted debt' is considered in Ch 15, *Duties of Directors and Other Officers*, at para **[15.049]**.

72 Section 3(3) of the C(A)A 1982.

73 Section 3(5) of the C(A)A 1982.

74 As are regs 93, 94 and 95 of Table A.

75 See, for example, *Phoenix Shannon plc et al v Purkey et al* (7 May 1997, unreported) HC, Costello J; considered in Ch 14, *Corporate Governance: Meetings*, at para **[14.013]**.

76 See, for example, *Linden Ltd v Glenon* [2007] IEHC 59 (McGovern J).

77 Articles of association may provide for an appointment to be effected by notice of a third party; this is a reasonably common provision in the articles of a subsidiary in favour of its ultimate holding company (which may not be a member where there is an intermediate holding company).

directors to appoint a person as a director (other than a retiring director), notice should be sent to the company's registered office, signed by the proposing member, not less than three nor more than 21 days before the meeting: reg 96 of Table A. Where the members in general meeting remove[78], by ordinary resolution, a director, the vacancy thereby created may be filled at that meeting or if not so filled may be filled as a casual vacancy[79] by the board of directors. Section 181 of the CA 1963 provides that at a general meeting, directors must be elected individually unless the members unanimously agree to vote them in *en bloc*[80].

[13.030] Regulation 98 of Table A provides that casual vacancies can be filled by the board of directors who can (subject to the total number of directors not exceeding any limit imposed by the articles) also appoint an additional director; in either case, their appointment will last until the next AGM. Where a director is appointed by the existing directors, a resolution of the directors at a board meeting is required[81]. In practice, for very many private companies, this is by far the most frequent way in which directors are appointed.

[13.031] Whether or not a person is appointed on a company's incorporation, as a first director, or subsequently, to an existing company, he will only be a formally appointed, or *de jure* director where his appointment is in accordance with the company's articles of association. So, for example, for a person to be appointed as a formal director to fill a casual vacancy, his appointment requires a formal resolution of the board of directors, pursuant to reg 98 of Table A. Moreover, his appointment must comply with all other requirements contained in the articles, for example, that he holds any requisite share qualification, as envisaged by model reg 77 (where adopted). If a person's appointment does not comply with such requirements, he will not be a formally appointed director although, as is considered below, he may be found to be a *de facto* director[82].

[13.032] Companies are obliged to notify the registrar of companies, within 14 days, from the happening of any change among its directors or in its secretary[83]. Although the failure to notify a change in directors is an offence, the actual validity of a director's appointment is unaffected by the failure and where a director is appointed on foot of a board resolution, the appointment will date from the passing of the resolution or such other time specified in the resolution. Judicial recognition of this long-standing position is seen in the decision of Jacob J in *POW Services Ltd and another v Clare et al*[84] where he said:

---

78 See para **[13.077]** *post*.

79 Section 182(5) of the CA 1963. A person appointed a director in place of a removed director shall be treated, for the purpose of determining the time at which he or any other director is to retire, as if he had become a director on the day on which the person in whose place he is appointed was last appointed director: s 182(6) of the CA 1963.

80 See *Moylan v Irish Whiting Manufacturers Ltd* (14 April 1980, unreported) HC, *per* Hamilton J, where the validity of the appointment of the directors of a company was doubted since they had been appointed *en bloc*, without evidence that there was a unanimous resolution.

81 See, generally, Ch 14, *Corporate Governance: Meetings*, at para **[14.124]** *et seq*.

82 See para **[13.045]** *post*.

83 Section 195(6)(a) of the CA 1963.

84 *POW Services Ltd and another v Clare et al* [1995] 2 BCLC 435.

> 'The general rule is that the fact of registration or not has nothing whatever to do with whether a person is in fact a director or company secretary. Subject to one exception there is no deeming provision arising from registration. It is the company, acting by the procedures under the articles, which makes or sacks a director or company secretary. There are statutory requirements for registration of the persons whom the company has made a director or secretary with sanctions for non-compliance. It may well be that where a company has permitted registration of a person who is not in fact a director or secretary, the company would be estopped as against a third party who relied upon the registration from denying it, but that is as far as the matter goes. The only exception relates to the first directors and secretaries. By s 13(5) of the 1985 Act[85] the persons named on the appropriate form (Form 10) as these persons are deemed to be such[86].'

This statement of law has been accepted by the Irish High Court as representing the law in Ireland[87]. Unless the Companies Acts provide otherwise, a requirement for the registration of a particular matter does not touch upon the validity of that matter and is solely intended to facilitate the inspection of a public register.

Types of formally appointed directors[88]

[13.033] In corporate practice, businessmen often add an adjectival label to formally appointed directors. Some have a statutory basis and some do not. To the uninitiated, these can be confusing. Here, the different types of formally appointed directors are considered:

(a) Managing directors;
(b) Chairmen;
(c) Executive directors;
(d) Non-executive directors;
(e) Nominee directors;
(f) Caretaker directors;
(g) Alternate directors;
(h) Associate directors.

(a) Managing directors

[13.034] The articles of association of companies will frequently provide that the board of directors may appoint one of themselves as a managing director with such powers as are delegated to him or her. Regulation 110 of Table A provides that:

> 'The directors may from time to time appoint one or more of themselves to the office of managing director for such period and on such terms as to remuneration and otherwise as

85 Section 3(5) of the Irish C(A)A 1982 also deems the persons specified in the form delivered to the CRO, as having been appointed as the first directors and secretaries.

86 *POW Services Ltd and another v Clare et al* [1995] 2 BCLC 435 at 440, 441.

87 In *Mattimoe et al v Uniprop Ltd* (15 March 2010), HC, an application heard by Finlay Geoghegan J where the decision in *POW Services Ltd* was opened to the court, Finlay Geoghegan J acknowledged that a director's resignation is effected by his letter of resignation and not by whether it had been filed in the CRO.

88 See generally, Lipton & Hertzberg, *Understanding Company Law* (9th edn, LCB Information Services, 2000) (an Australian publication) at pp 236–240.

> they think fit, and, subject to the terms of any agreement entered into in any particular case, may revoke such appointment …'

Table A provides that managing directors are not subject to the normal rules as to rotation of directors[89] but their appointment will be automatically terminated if they cease to be directors, for any reason. Their remuneration shall be as the directors determine[90]. Under model articles, managing directors will have such powers as the directors determine: reg 112 of Table A provides:

> 'The directors may entrust to and confer upon a managing director any of the powers exercisable by them upon such terms and conditions and with such restrictions as they may think fit, and either collaterally with or to the exclusion of their own powers, and may from time to time revoke, withdraw, alter or vary all or any of such powers.'

It is this standard provision which, if adopted, will result in persons held out as managing directors having ostensible or apparent authority to exercise all of the powers of management that would ordinarily be exercisable by the board of directors[91]. In *Shirlaw v Southern Foundries (1926) Ltd*[92], Lord Greene MR said:

> 'A managing director is … a director to whom the board, being empowered to do so by the articles of association, delegates its powers of management, or some of them, and this delegation is usually, if not invariably, made subject to the overriding authority of the board. Management here means management of the company's business, or part of it, as the case may be. There is no delegation of the remaining powers of the board. Such important matters [as] the financial policy of the company, the dividends to be declared and the issue of new shares are all reserved to the board.'

The precise powers retained by the board of directors will depend upon the arrangements made in particular companies, but 'outsiders' to the company will not normally have notice of these as the articles will be silent, and the matter one of internal management.

[13.035] Today, many companies are electing to have *chief executive officers* rather than managing directors. In practice, these two positions and titles can be used interchangeably and technically the only difference is that a chief executive officer or CEO can hold their office without being a director whereas a managing director must, by definition, be a director.

(b) Chairmen

[13.036] The board of directors may appoint a chairman[93]; notwithstanding perceived political correctness, in the absence of a company's articles expressly so providing, the term 'chairperson' has no reference point in company law. The function of a chairman is largely confined to corporate governance, namely, the management of directors' and members' meetings. In the Australian case of *AWA Ltd v Daniels*[94], Rogers CJ said:

---

89 See para **[13.074]** *post*.

90 Regulation 111 of Table A.

91 See, further, Ch 7, *Corporate Capacity and Authority*, at para **[7.114]** *et seq*.

92 *Shirlaw v Southern Foundries (1926) Ltd* [1939] 2 All ER 113.

93 Regulation 104 of Table A.

94 *AWA Ltd v Daniels* (1992) 10 ACLC 933.

> 'The chairman is responsible to a greater extent than any other director for the performance of the board as a whole and each member of it. The chairman has the primary responsibility of selecting matters and documents to be brought to the board's attention, for formulating the policy of the board and promoting the position of the company.'

Model articles do not confer any particular powers of management on chairmen and, accordingly, they do not have any particular ostensible or usual authority over and above that of ordinary directors[95].

(c) Executive directors

[13.037] The position of executive director has no statutory definition. In simple terms, an executive director is a director who participates in the day-to-day management of a company. Executive directors will – especially in larger companies – usually be employed by their company on a full-time basis and be in receipt of a salary (as opposed to simply directors' fees).

(d) Non-executive directors

[13.038] A non-executive director is a director who does not have a contract of service with the company and has no role in the day-to-day management of a company. The position of a non-executive director (or 'NED') had, until recently[96], no statutory definition or reference point. In the case of private companies that are public-interest entities[97] and, as such, required to have audit committees under reg 91(3) of the European Communities (Statutory Audits) (Directive 2006/43/EC) Regs 2010 ('EC(SA)(D)R 2010')[98], it is provided that the members of such committees shall include not less than two independent directors:

> 'that is to say, directors—
>
> (a) the terms of appointment of whom indicate or state that they are being appointed in a non-executive capacity; and
>
> (b) who otherwise possess the requisite degree of independence (particularly with regard to each of them satisfying the condition in paragraph (4)) so as to be able to contribute effectively to the committee's functions.'

Regulation 91(4) sheds further light on the meaning of independence, providing that the condition in para (3)(b):

> 'Is that each director there referred to does not have, and at no time during the period of 3 years preceding his or her appointment to the committee did have—
>
> (a) a material business relationship with the public-interest entity, either directly, or as a partner, shareholder, director or senior employee of a body that has such a relationship with the entity; or
>
> (b) a position of employment in the public-interest entity.'

---

95 See, further, Ch 7, *Corporate Capacity and Authority*, at para **[7.115]** *et seq*.

96 Although s 205B of the CA 1990 required certain companies to have audit committees and for that purpose had a qualifying test for directors which prevented them from being employees, that provision was never commenced and has been superseded by the EC(SA)(D)R 2010.

97 Within the meaning of reg 3 of the EC(SA)(D)R 2010. See Ch 29, *Public Limited Companies and SEs*, at para **[29.086]**.

98 SI 220/2010.

The position of non-executive director is, therefore, a sub-set of being an independent director so that every independent director must be a non-executive director although not every non-executive director will be an independent director.

[13.039] The role of a non-executive director is therefore confined to the boardroom, where he will receive information from the executive directors and managers of the company. The value of non-executive directors is in their input to decisions of the company which are widely thought to be enhanced by their impartiality, objectivity and independence[99]. The duties of non-executive directors are considered in Ch 15[100].

(e) Nominee directors

[13.040] A nominee director is a director who is 'expected to act in accordance with some understanding or arrangement which creates an obligation or mutual expectation of loyalty to some person or persons other than the company as a whole'[101]. This term does not have a statutory definition. Nominee directors do not owe any lesser duties to their company than do other directors and their particular predicament is considered in Ch 15[102].

(f) Caretaker directors

[13.041] Caretaker directors are directors who were appointed by shareholders who have subsequently disposed of their shares in circumstances where the new shareholders are likely to replace the existing directors with their own nominees. This so-called type of director has been recognised in a number of Australian[103] and New Zealand[104] cases. As in the case of nominee directors, caretakers do not owe any lesser duties to their company. It has, however, been suggested that the powers of such directors might be found to be limited – particularly where a members' meeting has been called at which they may be voted from office. In such an event it has been suggested that caretaker directors may be restrained from taking decisions that are fundamental or significant, outside of the ordinary course of the company's day-to-day business and which are not otherwise necessary for the proper running of the company[105]. It remains to be seen whether an Irish court would accept that such limitation on directors' powers exists, or even recognises the concept of 'caretaker director'.

---

99 See Mercer, 'Non-Executive Directors: Watchdogs, Oracles or Fall-Guys?' (1992) PLC 15 for an excellent, early, commentary on the then, recent phenomenon in the appointment of non-executive directors to listed PLCs.

100 See Ch 15, *Duties of Directors and Other Officers,* at para **[15.042]**. See, generally, *Re Dublin Sports Cafe Ltd* [2008] IESC 66 and *Re Tralee Beef and Lamb Ltd* [2008] IESC 1.

101 Companies and Securities Review Committee (NSW, Australia), *Nominee Directors and Alternate Directors*, Report No 8 (2 March 1989) at p 7. See Ahern, 'Nominee Directors' duty to Promote the Success of the company: Commercial Pragmatism and Legal Orthodoxy' (2011) 127 LQR 118; and Kelly, 'The Nominee Director, His Duties to the Company and to His Appointor and Whether they can be modified by Agreement' (2010) CLP 23.

102 See Ch 15, *Duties of Directors and Other Officers,* at para **[15.045]**.

103 *Paringa Mining and Exploration Co PLC v North Flinders Mines Ltd et al* (1989) 7 ACLC 153.

104 *Utilicorp NZ Inc v Powerer New Zealand Ltd* (1997) 8 NZCLC 261.

105 *Woonda Nominees Pty Ltd et al v Chng et al* (19 October 2000) Western Australia Supreme Court.

(g) Alternate directors

[13.042] An alternate or substitute director does not hold office in his own right. An alternate director is a person appointed to act in the place of a director when that director is unable to act. Regulation 9 of Part II of Table A enables the appointment of an alternate director and, in this respect, the model articles of private and public companies are different. Regulation 9 provides:

> 'Any director may from time to time appoint any person who is approved by the majority of the directors to be an alternate or substitute director. The appointee, while he holds office as an alternate director, shall be entitled to notice of meetings of the directors and to attend and vote thereat as a director and shall not be entitled to be remunerated otherwise than out of the remuneration of the director appointing him. Any appointment under this reg shall be effected by notice in writing given by the appointer to the secretary. Any appointment so made may be revoked at any time by the appointer or by a majority of the other directors or by the company in general meeting. Revocation by an appointer shall be effected by notice in writing given by the appointer to the secretary.'

Where appointed, an alternate director will, where this article is adopted, only hold office for as long as the principal director, whom he represents, determines.

(h) Assignee directors

[13.043] Directors who assume office as the result of the assignment of that office by another director are a rare creature indeed. Section 199 of the CA 1963 envisages the office of director being assigned, and provides that where the articles of association so permit (and it may be noted that model articles make no provision one way or the other) any assignment of the office of director will be of no effect 'unless and until it is approved by a special resolution of the company' in general meeting.

(i) Associate directors

[13.044] The term 'associate director' has no statutory definition or particular meaning. One leading English commentator[106] has said of the practice of appointing associate directors that it is normally 'to allow the person concerned the dignity and standing of a title which included the word "director", without conferring upon him the full authority and duties of a director'. In *Secretary of State for Trade and Industry v Tjolle et al*[107], Jacob J recognised that the title 'director' can be used as a motivational tool and its usage did not necessarily mean that a person was holding herself out as a director. Notwithstanding that employees so labelled may not be penalised for corporate failure, their companies may be exposed. Although an associate director does not have the same actual authority enjoyed by an ordinary director, it is thought that a company that so designates individuals, may well expose itself to a finding that such persons have the same ostensible or apparent authority as an ordinary director and may thus find itself bound by their actions.

---

[106] Sealy et al (eds), *British Company Law and Practice* (1983; loose leaf, CCH.New Law) at 28-250.

[107] *Secretary of State for Trade and Industry v Tjolle et al* [1998] BCC 282.

De facto directors

[13.045] *De facto* directors are persons 'occupying the position of director'[108] but who have not been formally or validly appointed as directors[109]. It has been noted that the concept is as old as the Companies Clauses Consolidation Act of 1845 which defined directors to include 'all persons having the direction of the undertaking whether under the name of directors, managers, committee of management, or under any other name'[110]. The reasons for extending the definition of 'directors' to include persons who occupy the position of director have been expressed to be:

> '... to impose legal duties on a person described therein and to give other persons, including the company itself, legal rights against such a person. The justification for this is no doubt that, in some way, the powers or conduct of the person, or the practical necessities of commercial life, if the device of the limited liability company is to play a part in such life, warrants so treating the person[111].'

The justification for preventing persons who occupy the position of director but who have not in law been appointed director from evading responsibility for their acts or omissions is clear. What is not so clear, however, is the test for establishing a *de facto* directorship.

[13.046] An example of the traditional circumstances in which a person was found to be a *de facto* director is where he has been appointed a director but where his appointment does not satisfy other requirements of a company's articles of association, for example, where he does not hold a requisite share qualification. In that event such a person's appointment will be invalid, but if he assumes the position of director, he can be found to be a *de facto* director. This was precisely the issue in hand in what must be one of the earliest cases in which an individual was deemed to be a *de facto* director, *Re Canadian Land Reclaiming and Colonizing Co*[112]. In that case, Sir George Jessel MR said of two persons who had been appointed as directors, and had acted as such, but who lacked the share qualification required by their company's articles of association:

> 'No doubt they were not properly elected, and were, therefore, not *de jure* directors of the company; but that they were *de facto* directors of the company is equally beyond all question. The point I have to consider is whether the person who acts as *de facto* director is a director within the meaning of this section, [s 165 of the Companies Act 1862, which made officers liable for misfeasance] or whether he can afterwards be allowed to deny that he was a director within the meaning of this section. I think he cannot. We are familiar in the law with a great number of cases in which a man who assumes a position

---

[108] Section 2(1) of the CA 1963 in its definition of director refers to persons 'occupying the position of director'.

[109] See, Noonan & Watson, 'Examining Company Directors through the Lens of De Facto Directorship' [2008] JBL 587; and Watts, 'De Facto Directors' (2011) 127 LQR 162 and Yap, 'De Facto Directors and Corporate Directorships', [2012] JBL 579.

[110] Noonan & Watson, 'Examining Company Directors through the Lens of De Facto Directorship' [2008] JBL 587 at 589 where the history of the position and its development are explored.

[111] *Per* Madgwick J in *Deputy Commissioner of Taxation v Austin* (27 August 1998) Federal Court of Australia.

[112] *Re Canadian Land Reclaiming and Colonizing Co* (1880) 14 Ch D 660.

cannot be allowed to deny in a Court of Justice that he really was entitled to occupy that position. The most familiar instance is that of executor *de son tort*. In like manner, it seems to me, in an application under this section, the *de facto* director is a director for the purposes of the section[113].'

Although this decision was delivered over 120 years ago, little judicial attention was given to *de facto* directors until the 1980s when the courts of England and Wales were called upon to disqualify persons who were *de facto* directors. Prior to the 1980s, the circumstances in which it was alleged that a person was a *de facto* director was confined to people whose appointment to the office of director was in some way defective. As Lord Collins SCJ said in *Revenue and Customs Commissioners v Holland*[114]:

> 'For almost 150 years *de facto* directors in English law were persons who had been appointed as directors but whose appointment was defective, or had come to an end, but who acted or continued to act as directors. There was a striking judicial innovation in *Re Lo-Line Electric Motors Ltd* [1988] 2 All ER 692 and *Re Hydrodam (Corby) Ltd* [1994] 2 BCLC 180 (endorsed by the Court of Appeal in *Re Kaytech International plc* [1999] 2 BCLC 351) by which (at the risk of over-simplification) persons who were held to be part of the corporate governance of a company, even though not directors, could be treated as directors for the purposes of statutory provisions relating to such matters as wrongful trading by, and disqualification of, directors.'

Although in Ireland s 297 of the CA 1963 provides that *de facto* directors could be made personally liable for fraudulent trading, where they were involved in the 'carrying on [of the company's] business' in a fraudulent manner, there have to date been no decisions on this point[115]. Most of the English judicial authorities next considered derive from applications to disqualify from acting as director, persons who were alleged to have been *de facto* directors[116]. This trend is apparent in Ireland too since the assertion by the High Court of a jurisdiction to make restriction orders under s 150 of the CA 1990 against persons who are found to be *de facto* directors[117]. One manifestation of this is the

---

[113] *Re Canadian Land Reclaiming and Colonizing Co* (1880) 14 Ch D 660 at 664, 665. See also *Corporate Affairs Commission v Drysdale* (1978) 141 CLR 236 where the Australian courts found that a director, who had been deemed to retire at an AGM but who had continued to participate in the management of the company, was a *de facto* director.

[114] *Revenue and Customs Commissioners v Holland* [2010] UKSC 51, [2011] 1 All ER 430; [2010] 1 WLR 2793. See Watts, 'De Facto Directors' (2011) 127 LQR 162.

[115] Note also that s 178 of the CA 1963 provides that actions of directors shall be valid notwithstanding that there may be a defect in their appointment. However, in *Morris v Kanssen* [1946] AC 459 it was decided that this merely covered 'slips or irregularities' in the appointment of a director and did not refer to 'a total absence of appointment'.

[116] In one of the first decisions on this point, *Re Lo-Line Electric Motors Ltd* (1988) 4 BCC 415 at 422, Sir Nicholas Browne-Wilkinson VC said: '... the plain intention of Parliament in s 300 [of the English Companies Act 1985] was to have regard to the conduct of a person acting as a director, whether validly appointed, or just assuming to act as a director without any appointment at all.'

[117] See *Re Vehicle Imports Ltd* (23 November 2000, unreported) HC, Murphy J; *Re Gasco Ltd* (5 February 2001, unreported) HC, Murphy J; and *Re Lynrowan Enterprises Ltd* (31 July 2002, unreported) HC, O'Neill J; and, generally, Ch 28, *Compliance and Enforcement*, at para **[28.076]** *et seq*.

reference in a series of recent Irish enactments to the concept by precluding certain persons in certain circumstances from being found to be *de facto* directors[118].

(a) The English authorities on the test for de facto directorship

[13.047] One of the leading modern authorities on the meaning of *de facto* director is the decision of Millett J in *Re Hydrodam (Corby) Ltd*[119], which is also the leading authority on the meaning of shadow directors. In that case Millett J said that the terms '*de facto*' director and 'shadow director' do *not* overlap; they are in most cases mutually exclusive alternatives. Of a *de facto* director, Millett J said:

> 'A *de facto* director is a person who assumes to act as a director. He is held out as a director by the company, and claims and purports to be a director, although never actually or validly appointed as such. To establish that a person was a *de facto* director of a company it is necessary to plead and prove that he undertook functions in relation to the company which could properly be discharged only by a director. It is not sufficient to show that he was concerned in the management of the company's affairs or undertook tasks in relation to its business which can properly be performed by a manager below board level.
>
> A *de facto* director, I repeat, is one who claims to act and purports to act as director, although not validly appointed as such.'

It has been said that this case is the basis for the two different tests which were developed in the English courts for *de facto* directorship: the 'holding out test' and the 'equal footing test' which have been described thus:

> 'The equal footing test focuses on the involvement of the putative director in the 'corporate governing structure'. The holding out test has two requirements. The second, less contentious requirement was essentially the same as the equal footing test. In involves an inquiry into whether the putative *de facto* director undertook functions in relation to the company that properly could only be discharged by a director. The first requirement of the holding out test was that the person, with his or her consent, has to have been held out or represented by the company and perceived by outsiders to be a director[120].'

It is thought, however, that far from being two different tests, both enquiries can be useful in determining the status of a putative *de facto* director.

[13.048] In *Re Richborough Furniture Ltd*, Lloyd QC said:

> 'It seems to me that for someone to be made liable to disqualification … as a *de facto* director, the court would have to have clear evidence that he had been either the sole person directing the affairs of the company (or acting with others all equally lacking in

---

[118] One of the first enactments in which this was done was in s 21(1) of the Anglo Irish Bank Corporation Act 2009 which provided that while the Minister for Finance or his nominees was a member of that bank, none of a list of persons (which included the Minister or his nominee) was to be taken to be 'what is known as a *de facto* director'. See also s 15(3) of the National Asset Management Agency Act 2009 which provides that for the purposes of that section 'a *de facto* director is a person who is determined to have been a director of a company although not formally or validly appointed to the position'; and s 49 of the Credit Institutions (Stabilisation) Act 2010.

[119] *Re Hydrodam (Corby) Ltd* [1994] 2 BCLC 180, [1994] BCC 161.

[120] Noonan & Watson, 'Examining Company Directors through the Lens of De Facto Directorship' [2008] JBL 587 at 604.

> valid appointment, as in *Morris v Kassen* [1946] AC 459) or, if there were others who were true directors, that he was acting on equal footing with the others in directing affairs of the company. It also seems to me that, if it is unclear whether the acts of the person in question are referable to an assumed directorship, or to some other capacity such as a shareholder or, as here, consultant, the person in question must be entitled to the benefit of the doubt[121].'

It is thought that the foregoing test cannot alone provide the solution and in isolation is not the correct test for the finding that a person was, or was not, a *de facto* director. In other cases such as *Secretary of State v Tjolle*[122], the equal footing approach was followed but, indicative of the utility of both tests, in this case Jacob J said there was not one single test:

> '… it may be difficult to postulate any one decisive test. I think what is involved is very much a question of degree. The court takes into account all the relevant factors. Those factors include at least whether or not there was a holding out by the company of the individual as a director, whether the individual used that title, whether the individual had proper information (eg management accounts) on which to base decisions, and whether the individual had to make major decisions and so on. Taking all these factors into account, one asks 'was this individual part of the corporate governing structure?', answering it as a kind of jury question. In deciding this, one bears very much in mind why one is asking the question. That is why I think the passage I quoted from Millett J is important. There would be no justification for the law making a person liable to misfeasance or disqualification proceedings unless they were truly in a position to exercise the powers and discharge the functions of a director. Otherwise they would be made liable for events over which they had no real control, either in fact or law[123].'

It is thought that this is the correct approach. The difficulty with the judicial analysis in the foregoing decisions is that there is an implicit assumption that the person, whose status is in question, disputes that he is or was a *de facto* director. Any truly generic test for *de facto* directors must recognise that the person whose status is in question may also actually claim that he is or was a *de facto* director. In *Kaytech International plc*, the trial judge, Jacob J, had found that the person in question had been a *de facto* director and this was upheld on appeal. Robert Walker LJ said that that conclusion seemed to him to be inevitable and incontrovertible, having regard to the nature of the evidence heard. The evidence included that the person had been the moving spirit in giving instructions for the incorporation of the company; had pretended to raise the necessary capital; had described himself as a director on at least one occasion; and had allowed himself to be held out as a joint founder and chief executive at a meeting with suppliers.

(b) The Irish authorities on the test for de facto directorship

[13.049] The leading Irish authority on the test for *de facto* directorship is *Re Lynrowan Enterprises Ltd*[124]. In that case, O'Neill J found that a person, though not validly appointed a director of a company, may be said to be a *de facto* director and thus deemed to be 'a director' within the meaning of s 2(1) of the CA 1963, and therefore amenable to restriction under s 150 of the CA 1990 in the following circumstances:

---

121 *Re Richborough Furniture Ltd* [1996] BCC 155 at 169, 170.

122 *Secretary of State v Tjolle* [1998] 1 BCLC 333.

123 *Secretary of State v Tjolle* [1998] BCC 282 at 290.

124 *Re Lynrowan Enterprises Ltd* [2002] IEHC 90.

'1. Where there is clear evidence that that person has been either the sole person directing the affairs of the company; or

2. Is directing the affairs of the company with others equally lacking in valid appointment; or

3. Where there were other validly appointed directors that he was acting on an equal or more influential footing with the true directors in directing the affairs of the company.

4. In the absence of clear evidence of the foregoing and when there is evidence that the role of the person in question is explicable by the exercise of a role other than director, the person in question should not be made amenable to the *Section 150* restriction.

5. Where the object of the Section is the protection of the public from dishonest or irresponsible persons the absence of a valid appointment should not permit an escape from the restriction in *Section 150*. It would be nonsensical if a person who had been validly appointed a director was to be treated differently to someone who lacked valid appointment but nevertheless assumed in all other respects the role of director. I would agree that "*liability cannot sensibly depend upon the validity of the defendant's appointment*".

6. In the light of all of the foregoing then in my view the Companies Acts 1963 to 1990 recognise and embrace in the provision of *Section 2(1)* of the Act of 1963 and *Section 150* of the Act of 1990, the concept of the "*de facto* director".'

On the facts, O'Neill J went on to find that one of the respondents was a *de facto* director[125].

[125] 'The evidence does however satisfy me, on the balance of probabilities that James V Mealy was a *de facto* director of the company. From October 1996 until April of 1998 the evidence establishes to my satisfaction that James V Mealy had virtual complete control over the affairs of the company and the only other director James A Mealy had virtually no involvement in its affairs during that time. This fact is most visibly illustrated by the fact that during that period James V Mealy carried out all bank transactions for the company. Whilst it could be said that the carrying out of bank transactions is not necessarily indicative of the role of a director, I am satisfied that in the context of the affairs of this company and the fact that its affairs could only have been directed either by James A Mealy or James V Mealy the fact that all of these transactions were carried out by James V Mealy points to him having a decisive role in the direction of the affairs of the company. This conclusion, I think is fortified by the fact that James V Mealy was the authorised signatory for the purposes of the bank account whereas James A Mealy was not. The fact that James A Mealy could not have written a cheque drawn on the company tends to persuade me that his role in the company was nominal only. In his evidence before the Master he appeared to readily accept that, and his lack of knowledge of the affairs of the company seemed to confirm that position. Thus the only person who could have exercised direction over the affairs of the company was James V Mealy and there is ample evidence, in the conduct of the banking transactions of the company the inclusion of the company in advertisements for James V Mealy's own company to support this conclusion. The evidence establishes that 80% of the business done by the company was with the Futon and Fabric Workshop Limited a company in which James V Mealy appears to be the principal shareholder and director. On its own, this fact would not be decisive in persuading me that James V Mealy was a director of the company but in combination with the other evidence it tends to paint a picture of control and direction of the affairs of the company by James V Mealy. I have therefore come to the conclusion that James V Mealy was a *de facto* director of the company and is therefore amenable to the restriction in *Section 150*.'

[13.050] In the second edition of this book the opinion was expressed that it was erroneous to require that a person whom it is alleged is a *de facto* director must either be the sole person directing the company or act with others on an equal footing[126]. On reflection, it is thought that the test is properly construed by reading points 1, 2 and 3 as *alternatives*[127]. It is thought that O'Neill J's description in points 1 to 3 of the necessary roles, in the alternative, of a putative *de facto* director is accurate and correct. It recognises as alternatives that a putative *de facto* director can be the sole director but need not be; that the person might be one of many, none of whom have authority or one of a number of people, some of whom have been lawfully appointed without necessarily having a more influential role[128].

[13.051] It is also thought that O'Neill J's recognition of the importance of a putative *de facto* director not being in a role other than director was a very perceptive insight into the dilemma of determining who should and should not be considered a *de facto* director. Indeed, some nine years later, the English Supreme Court has come to the same conclusion in *Revenue and Customs Commissioners v Holland*[129]. In that case, by majority, it was held that the defendant, Mr Holland, was not a *de facto* director in circumstances where he was a director of a 'corporate director' (a concept permitted under English company law) of a number of other companies (referred to as the composite companies, being the companies in respect of which it was claimed he was a *de facto* director). The majority of the Supreme Court held that Mr Holland was not a *de facto* director because he 'was doing no more than discharging his duties as the director of the corporate director ... everything that he did was done under that umbrella'[130]. In effect, they applied the test proposed by O'Neill J that the role of the person was 'explicable by the exercise of a role other than director'. Lord Walker said:

> 'If the question is, as I believe, whether Mr Holland was part of the corporate governing structure of the composite companies and whether he assumed a role in those companies which imposed on him the fiduciary duties of a director, then I would answer that he was not.
>
> ... There is no material to suggest that Mr Holland was doing anything other than discharging his duties as the director of the corporate director of the composite companies. It does not follow from the fact that he was taking all the relevant decisions that he was part of the corporate governance of the composite companies or that he assumed fiduciary duties in respect of them. If he was a de facto director of the composite companies simply because he was the guiding mind behind their sole corporate director, then that would be so in the case of every company with a sole corporate director[131].'

---

126 Courtney, *The Law of Private Companies* (2nd edn, 2002) at para [13.054].

127 The correct interpretation was in fact noted by McKechnie J in *Re Horcroft Developments Ltd* [2009] IEHC 580 who, referring to *The Law of Private Companies*, said: 'On one reading of *Re Lynrowan* it might be thought that a positive finding could only be made if one or more of the three sets of circumstances mentioned were met, but if not, no such finding could result.'

128 The test was applied by MacMenamin J in *Re Kelly Technical Services (Ireland) Ltd* [2005] IEHC 421.

129 *Revenue and Customs Commissioners v Holland* [2010] UKSC 51, [2011] 1 All ER 430; [2010] 1 WLR 2793. See Watts, 'De Facto Directors' (2011) 127 LQR 162.

130 *Revenue and Customs Commissioners v Holland* [2011] 1 All ER 430 at 448 (*per* Lord Hope).

131 *Revenue and Customs Commissioners v Holland* [2011] 1 All ER 430 at 464 (*per* Lord Walker).

The minority judgments of the court would have found Mr Holland a *de facto* director on the basis that it was enough if he in fact directed the composite companies' activities.

[13.052] It is thought that the decision of the majority in *Holland* was correct and that to re-characterise Mr Holland's involvement in the governance of the composite companies would have been, in the words of Lord Collins, 'an unjustifiable judicial extension of the concept of *de facto* director'[132]. Holland did what he did in the discharge of his duties as a director of the corporate director; his involvement in the management of the composite companies was explicable by reference to his being a director of the corporate director. He had, in effect, a lawful excuse to be involved in the management of the composite directors and that involvement did not require him personally to be a director of the composite companies. Indeed, this decision's focus on the *capacity* in which an alleged *de facto* director acts has a parallel in the case of shadow directors: there, even though a person ticks all the boxes for being deemed a shadow director, he or she will not be a shadow director where his or her advice is given in a professional *capacity.* Liquidators, examiners, receivers and others whose duties may on occasion overlap those of directors should not be considered to be *de facto* directors[133]. It follows that where a person's involvement in the management of a company is carried out in a legitimate capacity other than as a director, the courts should be slow to re-characterise that involvement as amounting to *de facto* directorship.

[13.053] In order to find that a person is a *de facto* director, it is submitted that in addition to establishing one of the three matters referred to in the judgment of O'Neill J in *Re Lynrowan Enterprises Ltd*, the following test applies, namely that:

1. Although the person was not, in fact, a formally appointed director, he 'occupied the position of director'; and
2. The company held him out as a director and he acquiesced in this or, in the alternative, he held himself out as a director and the company acquiesced in this.

It is thought that in order to be a *de facto* director, it is essential to show that a person was held out as such. In *Re Kelly Technical Services (Ireland) Ltd*[134], McKechnie J was not prepared to say that the foregoing was always essential, although it would always be of considerable weight:

> 'It seems to me on this point that a comparative assessment, as to power and influence between a true and *de facto* director, is not required in any formal sense: although evidentially a *de facto* director must be a person of considerable influence so as to exercise a similar power and authority as a true director. It is more likely I think that no one test is decisive but that all relevant factors must be considered, as Jacob J did in *Secretary for State for Industry v Tjolle* [1998] BCC 282, later endorsed by Walker LJ in *Re Kaytech International plc, Portier v Secretary of State for Trade and Industry* [1999] BCC 390. Undoubtedly one such factor, always of considerable weight, is whether the person in question, with the approval of the true directors or a majority of them, held himself out as

132 *Revenue and Customs Commissioners v Holland* [2011] 1 All ER 430 at 453.

133 Indeed, in *Cahill v Grimes* [2002] IESC 12 the Irish Supreme Court considered that a person who occupies the position of liquidator though never formally appointed could be a '*de facto* liquidator'.

134 *Re Kelly Technical Services (Ireland) Ltd* [2005] IEHC 421.

> a director or was allowed by the company to do so. But there are others. In the final analysis I would respectfully share the view of Finlay Geoghegan J, who in *Re First Class Toy Traders Ltd; Gray v McLoughlin, McLoughlin & Tuohy* [2004] IEHC 421 described as the critical issue whether the person has assumed the status and function of a director.'

In *Re First Class Toy Traders Ltd; Gray v McLoughlin*[135], Finlay Geoghegan J concluded that a respondent (Mr Tuohy) was a *de facto* director listing seven reasons, which included that the two *de jure* directors considered him to have acted as a director, that he had the description of finance director, that he met regularly with the two *de jure* directors at what were characterised as board meetings, that he was a cheque signatory and had responsibility for the company's finance function without being an employee.

[13.054] Factors that can indicate that a person has assumed the status and function of a director include:

(a) The person had been appointed by the directors or members in general meeting as a director, but his appointment was invalid on grounds that it did not comply with the Companies Acts (eg, because he was disqualified by operation or law or court order from acting as director or a restriction order had been made against him, etc) or by virtue of the company's articles of association (eg, because he did not hold qualification shares, his appointment as director meant that the number of directors was in excess of the maximum number ordained by the articles, etc);

(b) The person sought to be called (or he acquiesced in the title of) a 'director', with or without an adjectival[136] label, but especially where the title 'managing director'[137] is used[138];

(c) The person was an authorised signatory on the company's bank mandates[139];

(d) The person attended board meetings by invitation or by uncontested choice, or was otherwise one of those who took managerial decisions, whether by formal resolution or otherwise on matters reserved for the board of directors or, where

135 *First Class Toy Traders Ltd; Gray v McLoughlin* [2004] IEHC 289 (Finlay Geoghegan J).

136 See *Re First Class Toy Traders Ltd; Gray v McLoughlin* [2004] IEHC 289 (Finlay Geoghegan) where a person was described as a 'finance director'. As to the various adjectival labels that a director may have, see para **[13.033]** *et seq*, *ante*.

137 See, for example, in *Secretary for State for Trade and Industry v Jones et al* [1999] BCC 336, where on appeal it was held that the title 'joint managing director' had a significance far greater than that accorded it by the district judge.

138 Evidence of title alone will not normally suffice. In *Re Red Label Fashions Ltd* [1999] BCC 308, it was held that although there was evidence that a woman was described in draft accounts as a director, there was no clear or unequivocal reference or indication that she 'was or acted as a director rather than as a manager or dutiful wife' (at 313) *per* Lightman J. See also *Secretary for State for Trade and Industry v Tjolle et al* [1998] BCC 282, where Jacob J held that there, the use of the title 'director' did not necessarily mean that the person was holding herself out as a director and could have been merely a motivational tool for staff to do better.

139 The fact that a person was a signatory on the company's bank mandate alone should not, however, suffice as this is not the exclusive preserve of directors and could be done by an employee or manager in a company's finance department; see, however, *Re Sykes (Butchers) Ltd* [1998] 1 BCLC 110. See also *Re Lynrowan Enterprises Ltd* where the carrying out of all banking transactions was a factor in finding an individual a *de facto* director.

the articles permitted the appointment of a managing director, he acted as such and took decisions permitted to be taken by a managing director;

(e) The person held a substantial shareholding in the company in circumstances where one or more of the foregoing circumstances also existed[140].

The foregoing is a non-exhaustive list of some of the circumstances in which it is thought that a recalcitrant (or indeed, desirous) person may be found to be (or to have been) a *de facto* director.

Shadow directors

[13.055] A shadow director[141] is a person who is neither formally appointed, nor necessarily held out as a director, but to whom certain sanctions and regulations, normally reserved for directors, can be applicable. Shadow directors existed in Ireland long before the passing of the Companies Act 1990, although they were only christened as such by s 27 of the CA 1990, which defines a shadow director as:

> '... a person in accordance with whose directions or instructions the directors of a company are accustomed to act ... unless the directors are accustomed so to act by reason only that they do so on advice given by him in a professional capacity.'

Section 195(12)(a) of the CA 1963, however, always required every company to keep a register of formally appointed directors and the persons, not then christened, 'in accordance with whose directions or instructions the directors of a company are accustomed to act'. A finding that a person is a shadow director can have far-reaching consequences for the individual concerned: he or she can, for example, be made liable for reckless trading, can be made the subject of a disqualification[142] or restriction[143] order and will be subject to the s 31 of the CA 1990 prohibition of loans, quasi-loans, credit transactions and guarantees and the provision of security in connection with such loans, quasi-loans and credit transactions.

[13.056] Shadow directors are considered under the following sub-headings:

(a) The professional advice exception;

(b) The proofs required to establish a person is a shadow director;

---

140 Evidence of a substantial shareholding should not alone be considered sufficient. It is considered to ignore the realities of many private companies to entirely disregard evidence of shareholding as was done by Rimer J in the trial decision in *Re Kaytech International plc* [1999] BCC 390 at 401 on the grounds that where a model reg 80 type article is adopted and management delegated to the directors, evidence of shareholding is irrelevant. Indeed in *Secretary for State for Trade and Industry v Jones et al* [1999] BCC 336, it was held that where a substantial shareholder in a small company wished to take an active part in running the company's affairs in order to protect his investment, that raised the question as to whether in so doing he might not be constituting himself as a *de facto* director.

141 See further Ch 15, *Duties of Directors and Other Officers*, at para **[15.097]** *et seq*. See also Noonan & Watson, 'The Nature of Shadow Directorship: Ad Hoc Statutory Intervention or Core Company Law Principle?' [2006] JBL 763 and Kemp & Handforth, 'Shadow Directors: Keeping on the Sidelines' [2011] Practical Law for Companies.

142 Section 159 of the CA 1990.

143 Section 149(5) of the CA 1990. See *Re Lynrowan Enterprises Ltd* [2002] IEHC 90; *Re Hocroft Developments Ltd* [2009] IEHC 580; *Re Worldport Ireland Ltd* [2008] IESC 68.

(c) 'Directed or instructed';
(d) 'Acted in accordance with such directions or instructions';
(e) 'Were accustomed so to act';
(f) Can bodies corporate be shadow directors?

(a) The professional advice exception

[13.057] Before considering who is a shadow director, it is necessary to consider who will *not* be deemed to be such. The 'professional advice' exception means that a person who gives directions or instructions to the directors of a company on foot of which they are accustomed to act, but who does so only by way of advice given in a professional capacity, will not be deemed to be a shadow director. It is important to note that a person can act in many capacities and it is only where a person acts in a *professional capacity* that he or she can invoke this exception. In the Irish decision in *Re Vehicle Imports Ltd (in liquidation)*[144], a liquidator sought to have an order pursuant to s 150 of the CA 1990 made against the company's accountant. The liquidator was satisfied that the accountant had a significant involvement in and control over the management of the company's business during its short trading life and that the accountant had – on his own evidence – received substantial monies in that period. Murphy J held that although the evidence in relation to the accountant fell short of constituting him a shadow director, the uncontroverted evidence of a director that the director had signed blank cheques to be filled in by the accountant 'does sit with the definition of shadow director in s 27' of the CA 1990. Murphy J accepted that the accountant could well have a plausible explanation but in the absence of a denial that he was a shadow director in his affidavit, Murphy J made an order pursuant to s 150 of the CA 1990 against the accountant on the basis that he was a shadow director, granting a stay of 21 days to enable the accountant to make application if he deemed fit.

(b) The proofs required to establish a person is a shadow director

[13.058] The proofs required to be established in order to find that a person is a shadow director were set out by Millett J in *Re Hydrodam (Corby) Ltd*[145]. In the course of his judgment he said:

> 'To establish that a defendant is a shadow director of a company it is necessary to allege and prove:
>
> (1) who are the directors of the company, whether *de facto*[146] or *de jure*[147];
> (2) that the defendant directed those directors how to act in relation to the company or that he was one of those persons who did so;
> (3) that those directors acted in accordance with such directions; and
> (4) that they were accustomed so to act.

144 *Re Vehicle Imports Ltd (in liquidation)* (6 December 2000, unreported) HC, Murphy J.

145 *Re Hydrodam (Corby) Ltd* [1994] 2 BCLC 180, [1994] BCC 161. Whilst consistently referred to as *Hydrodam* in the BCLC (Butterworths Company Law Cases) series, it is referred to as *Hydrodan* in the BCC (CCH's British Company Cases) series.

146 See para **[13.045]** *ante*.

147 See para **[13.024]** *et seq ante*.

> What is needed is, first, a board of directors claiming and purporting to act as such; and secondly, a pattern of behaviour in which the board did not exercise any discretion or judgment of its own, but acted in accordance with the directions of others[148].'

In keeping with s 27 of the CA 1990, to this formulation should be added, at point (2), that the defendant 'directed *or instructed*' the directors how to act. Notwithstanding the English Court of Appeal's decision in *Secretary of State for Trade and Industry v Deverell*[149], which qualifies, to an extent, the decision in *Re Hydrodam*, it is thought that this test represents good law as far as the definition of shadow director in the context of s 27 of the CA 1990 is concerned. The concepts of *de jure* director and *de facto* director have been considered previously. In relation to these proofs it is (2), (3) and (4) that give rise to further concern and which are next considered.

[13.059] The leading Irish case on shadow directors is the decision of McKechnie J in *Re Hocroft Developments Ltd*[150]. Summarising the principles applicable to determining whether someone is a shadow director, the learned judge said:

> '1. The question of whether a person is a "shadow director" is purely a question of statutory interpretation with the normal applicable rules of construction applying:
>
> 2. The interpretation of the phrase will be influenced by:-
>
>   (i) The purpose of the relevant provisions of the Companies Act 1990, where that definition is to be found (s 27(1)), and
>
>   (ii) The fact that a shadow director so found is identified with a duly appointed director for Companies Act purposes, which include:-
>
>   (a) Transactions involving directors where conflicts of interest arises,
>
>   (b) The restriction/disqualification provisions of ss 150 and 160 of the Companies Act 1990, as amended,
>
>   (c) Insider trading formerly under Part V of the Companies Act 1990, now covered by market abuse under Part 4 of the Investment Funds, Companies and Miscellaneous Provisions Act 2005, and
>
>   (d) Fraudulent and reckless trading under ss 297 and 297A of the Companies Act 1963, as inserted by ss 137 and 138 of the Companies Act 1990 and under ss 33 and 34 of the Companies (Amendment) Act 1990.
>
> 3. For a finding to be made there must be directors of a company, either *de jure* or *de facto* and, in addition, two further requirements must be met:-
>
>   (i) Firstly that directions/instructions were given by the person in question, and
>
>   (ii) Secondly, that the true directors (or majority) were accustomed to act upon such instructions or directions.
>
> 4. These conditions, in addition to being conjunctive are interlinked by cause and effect: the implementation must be causatively connected to the communication.
>
> 5. The making of such communication and the reliance thereon must be by force of habit, that is habitual: they must be repetitive, customary and recurring: they must

148 *Re Hydrodam (Corby) Ltd* [1994] 2 BCLC 180 at 183.

149 *Secretary of State for Trade and Industry v Deverell* [2000] BCC 1057.

150 *Re Hocroft Developments Ltd* [2009] IEHC 580.

be part of the usual course of things. Or, as said, they must constitute "*a well established practice or pattern*" of behaviour. (Forde & Kennedy "*Company Law (4th Ed)*" para 613). On the other hand if either the communication, reliance or both are infrequent, rare or occasional they will not come within the section.

6. The nature or character of the communication, however so labelled, couched or phrased, must, by objective assessment, be such as to equate with the ordinary meaning of the words direction or instruction. It must have an obligatory or imposing force or command behind it. This may be self evident or may be deducible from the habitual responses of the directors.
7. Any communication falling short of this standard is excluded, including advices "*per se*".
8. Advices given by a person in a professional capacity ("professional advice"), including those upon which directors are accustomed to act, are for the avoidance of doubt, expressly excluded: professional advice is to be understood in context.
9. The nature of the affected business must be of a type in respect of which the directors would as a matter of course act executively. The scope of the affected business, must be such as to demonstrate a real influence over a wide ranging area of the company's affairs; although not its total affairs.
10. The above analysis is to be judged by the entire circumstances as presented. Factors such as motive, intention, expectation etc, are all useful to consider but not decisive. Neither is the ability to show, in all cases, an abdication of independence greater than that envisaged above, or that the company or the subject person took steps to conceal his true role. The weight of each admissible and material factor is relative and degree based. Finally,
11. Where the involvement of the person in question is explicable, or at least equally explicable, by the exercise of a role other than that of director, a positive finding should not be made.'

In *Devona Ltd; Pyne v Vandeventer*[151], Dunne J applied points 4–6 of McKechnie J's test to find that a respondent was not a shadow director. In that case it was contended that the fourth respondent was a shadow director and liable to be restricted in circumstances where the directors of the company relied on him in the amendment of the statement of affairs prepared on the company being wound up. The alleged shadow director was a former employee book keeper and company secretary who had been redundant for seven months when the directors prepared the original statement of affairs but he was consulted when the company's accountants, who were owed money, provided little assistance to the directors. The alleged shadow director pointed out that the company owed some further debtors and the directors amended the statement by the further sum of €200,000. Dunne J observed:

> 'Could it be said in those circumstances that they acted on the instructions/directions of the fourth named respondent? Given the role of the third named respondent as the person who was responsible for the financial affairs of the company and to whom the fourth named respondent stated on affidavit that he reported in respect of book keeping matters, it is somewhat surprising that the third named respondent who has, after all, an accepted responsibility in this regard did not and was not apparently in a position to supply the missing details. Nevertheless, on its own, the involvement of the fourth named respondent in the preparation of the amended statement of affairs is not such that I would be of the

[151] *Devona Ltd; Pyne v Vandeventer* [2012] IEHC 263.

view that the test set out above has been met by the applicant. I am not satisfied that it is the case that the fourth named respondent directed the directors of the company how to act in relation to the company and that the directors acted in accordance with his directions and that they were accustomed so to act. If I can revert to the principles set out by McKechnie J at paras 4, 5 and 6 as referred to above, I think it is clear that there is a cause and effect element in relation to the statement of affairs in the sense that the directors acted on the communication of the fourth named respondent, but it is impossible to say that there is the element of force of habit in relation to the conduct of the directors vis-à-vis the fourth named respondent as a general proposition. As set out by McKechnie J at para 5 of the principles "the making of such communication and the reliance thereon must be by force of habit that is habitual: they must be repetitive, customary and recurring: they must be part of the usual course of things". There is simply no evidence before the court of anything that falls into the description of habitual communication and reliance thereon.'

The learned judge want on to say that while the alleged shadow director was in a managerial position within the company, was the company secretary and was very much involved in financial matters as the person responsible for book keeping, these facts described his role in the company and did not inculpate him as a shadow director.

(c) 'Directed or instructed'

[13.060] One of the key questions concerning shadow directors is whether or not they must be more dominant than a company's *de facto* or *de jure* directors. In *Re Unisoft Group Ltd*[152], Harman J said that:

'… the shadow director must be, in effect, the puppet-master controlling the actions of the board. The directors must be (to use a different phrase) the 'cat's-paw'[153] of the shadow director. They must be people who act on the directions or instructions of the shadow director …'.

In the first edition of this book it was suggested that to be a shadow director a person must be in a higher position of authority than an ordinary director and that perhaps the required standard of authority could best be described as being akin to that of a 'managing director'[154]. This was the view taken by Judge Cooke at first instance in the case of *Secretary of State for Trade and Industry v Deverell*[155]. He said:

'Directions or instructions are both words with a mandatory effect. Coupled with the word 'accustomed' they … contemplate a situation where the board has cast itself in a subservient role to the 'shadow' ie it does what it is told or to borrow an expression from trust law it 'surrenders its discretion' to the shadow. Being accustomed to follow what somebody says does not of itself make what is said a direction/instruction … what the court has to find, whether on direct evidence or inference, is that the board does what [the shadow] tells it and exercises no (or at least no substantial) independent judgment[156].'

---

152 *Re Unisoft Group Ltd* [1994] BCC 766.

153 The use of such epithets has been discouraged by Morritt LJ in *Secretary of State for Trade and Industry v Deverell* [2000] BCC 1057 at 1068 on the basis that such imply 'a degree of control both of quality and extent over the corporate field in excess of what the statutory definition requires'.

154 See Courtney, *The Law of Private Companies* (1994, Butterworths) at para [7.055].

155 *Secretary of State for Trade and Industry v Deverell* [2000] BCC 1057.

156 *Secretary of State for Trade and Industry v Deverell* [2000] BCC 1057 at 1066.

In the Court of Appeal, Morritt LJ doubted Judge Cooke's view that the board of directors should be subservient to the shadow director. He said:

> 'It will, no doubt, be sufficient to show that in the face of 'directions or instructions' from the alleged shadow director the properly appointed directors or some of them cast themselves in a subservient role or surrendered their respective discretions. But I do not consider that it is necessary to do so in all cases. Such a requirement would be to put a gloss on the statutory requirement that the board are 'accustomed to act in accordance with' such directions or instructions. It appears to me that Judge Cooke, in looking for the additional ingredient of a subservient role or the surrender of discretion by the board, imposed a qualification beyond that justified by the statutory language[157].'

It is thought that this cannot be taken as a correct interpretation of s 27 of the CA 1990 and that the interpretation placed on the similar words used in the English legislation by Judge Cooke and Harman J are to be preferred as being correct. The legislation is unequivocal: the real directors must act in accordance with the 'directions or instructions' of the shadow director. The statutory words must be given their natural and unstrained meaning and ought not to be construed otherwise[158]. For a person to be found to be a shadow director of a company, he or she must 'direct or instruct' the real directors as to how they act, ie, how they exercise their powers as directors, and to that extent the real directors must be subservient to the 'shadow'.

[13.061] In *Secretary of State for Trade and Industry v Deverell*[159], Morritt LJ held that non-professional advice – which does not constitute a direction or instruction – can come within the definition, saying, 'the proviso excepting advice given in a professional capacity appears to assume advice generally is or may by included. Moreover the concepts of "direction" and "instruction" do not exclude the concept of "advice" for all three share the common feature of "guidance"[160].' It is thought that this is incorrect. Section 27 of the CA 1990 plainly requires a shadow director to issue 'directions or instructions': 'advice' is not part of the primary requirement; all that s 27 says on 'advice' is that such, given in a professional capacity, is insufficient to render its maker a shadow director. The significance of the professional advice exception can be grasped by accepting that a professional adviser does not direct or instruct a company on what it should do: he *advises* the company on what he perceives, in his professional judgment, to be the best course of action. The legislature clearly intended to preclude such 'advice' from being construed, as a result of linguistic gymnastics of the sort seen in the judgment of Morritt LJ, a reckonable 'direction or instruction' for the purposes of s 27 of the CA 1990.

---

157 *Secretary of State for Trade and Industry v Deverell* [2000] BCC 1057 at 1067.

158 In the Court of Appeal in *Deverell*, Morritt LJ expressly said (at p 1067) that: 'the definition of a shadow director is to be construed in the normal way to give effect to the parliamentary intention ascertainable from the mischief to be dealt with and the words used. In particular the purpose of the Act is the protection of the public and as the definition is used in other legislative contexts it should not be strictly construed because it also has quasi-penal consequences …'

159 *Secretary of State for Trade and Industry v Deverell* [2000] BCC 1057.

160 *Secretary of State for Trade and Industry v Deverell* [2000] BCC 1057 at 1067.

[13.062] In *Fyffes plc v DCC plc et al*[161], Laffoy J considered the decision of Morritt LJ and the commentary in the preceding paragraph of the second edition of this work and said:

> 'It is difficult to state in the abstract the legislative intent which underlies the rather terse definition contained in s 27. However, in the light of the submissions in this case I make the following observations. First, it seems to me that it is implicit in s 27 that the directions or instructions emanating from the alleged shadow director must have an imperative quality. It may be that advice, in a given factual context, will have an imperative quality. If that is the case, it would explain the apparent oddity to which counsel for the plaintiff pointed: why the legislature thought it necessary to exclude advice given in a professional capacity, if advice does not come within the expression "directions or instructions". Therefore, for a communication of any type to constitute a direction or instruction, it must have an imperative quality ...'

In *Re Hocroft Developments Ltd*[162], McKechnie J noted that whereas Morritt LJ had held that non-professional advice is included, Laffoy J 'was of the view that, for advice to be included, it has to carry the same "imperative quality" as any other communication'[163]. McKechnie J, however, seemed more inclined to the view that only a communication that amounts to a direction or instruction comes within the section, saying:

> '67. As normally understood, "advice" or "the giving of advice" means to recommend, to propose, or to suggest. A "direction or instruction" is materially more compelling than simply a proposal or a suggestion. Therefore, again as normally understood, there is a distinction between both. It could never have been intended that the section should posit varying thresholds. Accordingly, one only should apply and the other, if possible, differentiated, but if not, at least explained. If the lower standard of "guidance" was intended as the qualifying level, why use the more demanding threshold, which it should be noted, is included as part of the rule, whereas advice is part of the exception. To accept guidance as the entry point would, in my view, significantly undermine one of the two key aspects of the section, namely the communication aspect; it would promote the lesser meaning and relegate the greater. In addition it would expand the scope and applicability of the section in a way that was never intended. It would undermine the well-structured proportionality within the section between upholding the public interest and recognising the far reaching consequences, on both the civil and criminal side, which a defaulting director may have to face. I, therefore, cannot accept that a communication which cannot be properly described as a 'direction or instruction' comes within the section.
>
> 68. There is another reason for this view, which becomes clear if the *proviso* is given its ordinary and natural meaning as applied in the context of company and corporate affairs. Advice given by a professional in that capacity, or "professional advice" so described, is readily and notoriously recognised for what it is by those who have recourse to it. A professional consulted as such, may have many services to offer, one of which is the giving of advice; but I doubt very much if another is the giving of directions or instructions. This *proviso* in my opinion, whilst inserted for the avoidance of doubt and therefore not strictly necessary, was designed to exclude from the section advices, as commonly understood, given by a professional person in that capacity. Such a person, even if the board was accustomed to act upon his advice, should not, by reason of that only, be designated as a shadow director. The phrase in my view was intended to apply in

161 *Fyffes plc v DCC plc et al* [2005] IEHC 477.

162 *Re Hocroft Developments Ltd* [2009] IEHC 580.

163 *Re Hocroft Developments Ltd* [2009] IEHC 580 at para 66 of the judgment.

this way. If it was otherwise the relationship between business and professions would have to be re-appraised. It was never intended to affect the rule: it was to deal with the *proviso* only. As understood there is no conflict between the rule and the exception. If however, notwithstanding this view, it still becomes necessary to render the *proviso* compatible with the rule, I would unhesitatingly support the approach of Laffoy J in *Fyffes*, in that regard[164].'

(d) 'Acted in accordance with such directions or instructions'

[13.063] The real directors of the company in question must, *in fact*, act in accordance with the shadow director's directions or instructions. This means that a person will not be found to be a shadow director, even if he or she gives directions or instructions, if the real directors do not, *in fact*, act in accordance with such directions or instructions. As Finn J said in *Australian Securities Commission v AS Nominees Ltd*[165], the idea of the section is that 'the third party [shadow director] calls the tune and the directors dance in their capacity as directors'[166].

[13.064] In *Secretary of State for Trade and Industry v Deverell*[167], Morritt LJ held that whether any particular communication from an alleged shadow director, whether by words or by conduct, is to be classified as a direction or instruction, 'must be objectively ascertained by the court in the light of all the evidence'[168]. It is thought that this is a correct statement of the law and that the subjective intentions of an alleged shadow director – unlike, perhaps, those of a *de facto* director – are irrelevant, as are the subjective impressions of the real directors who receive such a direction or instruction. As Morritt LJ said, 'In many, if not most, cases it will be sufficient to prove the communication and its consequence. Evidence of understanding or expectation may be relevant but it cannot be conclusive.' In *Fyffes plc v DCC plc et al*[169], Laffoy J said:

> '... just because there is consideration by the board interposed between the direction, instruction or imperative advice does not mean that the act of the board is not to be taken into account in applying s 27, if the board acts in accordance with the direction, instruction or imperative advice. If it were otherwise, the effect of s 27 could be seriously diluted, particularly because of the difficulty inherent in making an objective assessment as to why the board acted in the manner it did.'

(e) 'Were accustomed so to act'

[13.065] Section 27 of the CA 1990 expressly envisages that the actual directors of a company must not only act on a shadow director's directions or instructions, but must be 'accustomed so to act'. The plain meaning is that the shadow director must have issued more than one direction or instruction that was acted upon: there must be a *pattern*. It is thought that it is clear that a *single* direction or instruction, acted upon by a company's actual directors, is not sufficient to cause the person who gave that direction or instruction being deemed to be a shadow director. It is thought, however, that whilst a

---

164 *Re Hocroft Developments Ltd* [2009] IEHC 580 at paras 67 and 68 of the judgment.

165 *Australian Securities Commission v AS Nominees Ltd* (1995) 133 ALR 1, (1995) 13 ACLC 1822.

166 *Australian Securities Commission v AS Nominees Ltd* (1995) 133 ALR 1 at 52.

167 *Secretary of State for Trade and Industry v Deverell* [2000] BCC 1057.

168 *Secretary of State for Trade and Industry v Deverell* [2000] BCC 1057 at 1067.

169 *Fyffes plc v DCC plc et al* [2005] IEHC 477.

solitary 'direction or instruction' is insufficient, it is not necessary that the real directors act in accordance with *all* directions or instructions given by the alleged shadow director. This was accepted by Laffoy J in *Fyffes plc v DCC plc et al*[170] where she said:

> '... s 27 does not require that the board should always act on the directions and instructions if a shadow directorship is to exist. That is indicated by a requirement that the board should be accustomed so to act.'

The decision in *Australian Securities Commission v AS Nominees Ltd*[171] is also instructive. There, Finn J said:

> '... the reference in the section to a person in accordance with whose directions or instructions the directors are "accustomed to act" does not in my opinion require that there be directions or instructions embracing all matters involving the board. Rather, it only requires that, as and when the directors are directed or instructed, they are accustomed to act as the section requires[172].'

Later in his judgment, Finn J said:

> 'The question the section poses is: Where, for some or all purposes, is the locus of effective decision making? If it resides in a third party ... and if that person cannot secure the 'adviser' protection ... then it is open [to the court] to find that the person is a [shadow director].'

A single or solitary direction or instruction will not make the alleged shadow director the locus of effective decision making. Section 27 of the CA 1990 requires a pattern of cause (direction or instruction) and effect (action on foot of same). This was accepted to be the legislative intent of the similar legislative provision by Morritt LJ in *Secretary of State for Trade and Industry v Deverell*[173]. As McKechnie J said in *Re Hocroft Developments Ltd*[174], 'the making of such communication and the reliance thereon must be by force of habit, that is habitual: they must be repetitive, customary and recurring: they must be part of the usual course of things[175].

(f) Can bodies corporate be shadow directors?

[13.066] In *Ex parte Copp*[176], the question of whether a bank could be deemed a 'shadow director' arose in the context of wrongful trading[177], and it was held by the English court that a sustainable case had been made out that the bank was a shadow director[178]. Previous editions of this book wrestled with the question of whether a body corporate can be a shadow director. In the first edition of this book it was suggested that

---

170 *Fyffes plc v DCC plc et al* [2005] IEHC 477.

171 *Australian Securities Commission v AS Nominees Ltd* (1995) 133 ALR 1, (1995) 13 ACLC 1822.

172 *Australian Securities Commission v AS Nominees Ltd* (1995) 133 ALR 1 at 52.

173 *Secretary of State for Trade and Industry v Deverell* [2000] BCC 1057 at 1067.

174 *Re Hocroft Developments Ltd* [2009] IEHC 580.

175 *Devona Ltd; Pyne v Vandeventer* [2012] IEHC 263.

176 *Ex parte Copp, Re a Company (No 005009 of 1987)* [1989] BCLC 12.

177 In England and Wales it was decided to penalise those who engaged in 'wrongful trading', while in Ireland, 'reckless trading' was introduced: see Ussher, *Company Law in Ireland* (1986, Sweet & Maxwell) at p 530.

178 See further Ch 15, *Duties of Directors and Other Officers*, at para **[15.110]**.

whilst s 27 of the CA 1990 defines a shadow director as a 'person' in accordance with whose directions or instructions the directors of a company are accustomed to act, it was arguable that a body corporate could not be a shadow director[179]. In the second edition[180] the view was expressed that whatever about a body corporate incorporated in a foreign jurisdiction, an Irish company (within the meaning of s 2 of the CA 1963) could be a shadow director. The reason given for that view was because although s 176 of the CA 1963 prohibits a company from having a body corporate as a director, it does not prohibit an Irish company from acting as a director[181]. It was noted, though, that some residual injustice must, however, remain in the notion that an Irish company can be visited with the penalties liable to be imposed upon shadow directors, since they cannot lawfully benefit from being the *de jure* director of an Irish company[182].

[13.067] In *Re Worldport Ireland Ltd*[183], O'Leary J considered whether a body corporate, whether incorporated inside or outside of the jurisdiction, could be a shadow director for the purposes of an application for restriction under s 150 of the CA 1990. It was held that there was no reason based on s 176(1) of the CA 1963 why a body corporate could not be a shadow director for the purposes of s 150 of the CA 1990. The decision was based on the fact of the word 'person': s 11(d) of the Interpretation Act 1937[184] stated that 'person' 'shall, unless the contrary intention appears, be construed as importing a body corporate (whether a corporation aggregate or a corporation sole) ...'; s 176(1) of the CA 1963 did not prohibit a company from becoming a director as a matter of inherent lack of capacity, since the Act provided a short transition period upon its enactment during which a body corporate could act as a director; and s 27 of the CA 1990 recognised shadow directors as a separate category to directors. In *Fyffes plc v DCC plc*[185], Laffoy J followed this approach:

> 'The issue whether a body corporate can be a shadow director arose in the *Worldport* case in the context of an application by a liquidator for a restriction order under s 150 of the Act of 1990, which is contained in Part VII of that Act, as amended, against a body corporate incorporated outside the jurisdiction. Section 176(1) of the Act of 1963 provides that a company shall not have as a director of a company a corporate body. It was argued by the body corporate against whom the restriction order was sought that, as it was disqualified from appointment as a director of the company, it could not be a shadow director because such status was only attainable by a person with the capacity to be appointed a director.
>
> While the manner in which the concept of shadow director is incorporated in Part VII differs from the manner in which it is incorporated in Part V, for the purposes of both parts

[179] See Courtney, *The Law of Private Companies* (1st edn, 1994) at para [13.082].

[180] See Courtney, *The Law of Private Companies* (2nd edn, 2002) at para [13.067].

[181] See para **[13.016]** *ante*.

[182] In the Australian case of *Standard Chartered Bank of Australia Ltd v Antico* (1995) 13 ACLC 1381, it was held by the New South Wales Supreme Court that a holding company was a shadow director of its subsidiary because of the extent of control it exercised over the subsidiary's board of directors in which the subsidiary's directors had acquiesced.

[183] *Re Worldport Ireland Ltd* [2005] IEHC 467.

[184] Now, s 18(c) of the Interpretation Act 2005 provides that 'person': 'shall be read as importing a body corporate (whether a corporation aggregate of a corporation sole) ...'

[185] *Fyffes plc v DCC plc* [2005] IEHC 477.

the meaning of shadow director is to be found in s 27, which I have quoted earlier. I respectfully agree with and adopt the reasoning of O'Leary J as to the significance of the manner in which the legislature has established the status or office of shadow director in s 27, the use of the formula that a person who falls within the definition 'shall be treated … as a director' for the purposes of the legislation. The language is highly suggestive of an intention on the part of the legislature that the concept of shadow director is distinct from, and not merely a sub-set of, the office of director. O'Leary J found support for that proposition in Part VII of the Act of 1990 in which the application of the provisions of that Part in relation to restriction and disqualification was effected by the terminology that the relevant Chapter "applies to shadow directors as it applies to directors".'

[13.068] The Supreme Court in *Re Worldport Ireland Ltd*[186] considered both decisions. Of the decision of O'Leary J, Fennelly J said he was satisfied:

'... that the learned judge was correct in his primary conclusion on the interpretation of the relationship between section 150 of the Act of 1990 and section 176 of the Act of 1963. The appellant's case is that it follows from the prohibition of a body corporate from being a director of a company that a body corporate cannot be a shadow director for the purposes of section 27(1) of the Act.

23. That argument is based on the fallacy that section 27 is concerned with persons who formally hold the position of director. The learned judge rightly held "that shadow directors are not a sub-set of the office of directors but entirely separate…". The section is addressed to persons who, in many if not most cases, will not hold any formal title as director. The shadow director is a "person in accordance with whose directions or instructions the directors of a company are accustomed to act…". A finding that a person is a shadow director is a finding about how that person is accustomed to behave in relation to the company. It is quite unrelated to and distinct from the observance of any formalities concerning that person's appointment or election as a director. No such formalities are required. There is nothing inconsistent about finding a person to be a shadow director for the purposes of section 27 and the fact that the person is legally ineligible to hold the position of director.

24. The learned judge was quite right to test the proposition by reference to the prohibition in section 183 of the Act of 1963 on an undischarged bankrupt from becoming a director without the leave of the court. In fact, that section makes it an offence for an undischarged bankrupt to act as a director. So, presumably the election of an undischarged bankrupt may conceivably be valid, though unlawful. Nonetheless, if the appellant's submissions were correct, an undischarged bankrupt would be free to direct all the dealings of the formal directors and give all instructions as to how the company was to be run, without committing any offence contrary to section 183 and without being treated as a shadow director for the purposes of section 27 and, hence, liable to the imposition of a restriction pursuant to section 150.'

Turning to the decision of Laffoy J in *Fyffes plc*, Fennelly J said:

'In that judgment, the learned judge applied the reasoning of O'Leary J in his judgment in the present case. Following a detailed analysis of the statutory provisions, she concluded as follows: "The word 'director' is defined as including a shadow director within the meaning of s 27. The drafting technique employed in Part V, in my view, was not intended to, and does not affect the proper interpretation of s 27. By virtue of s 11(c) of the Act of 1937, the word 'person' in s 27 is to be construed as including a company unless the

[186] *Re Worldport Ireland Ltd* [2008] IESC 68.

> contrary intention appears. I can discern no contrary intention in Part V of the Act of 1990. Interpreting the word 'person' in s 27 as importing a company is not in any way inconsistent with s 176 of the Act of 1963. The latter provision precludes a company from having a body corporate as a director; the former identifies the type of person who, by reference to the manner in which he acts vis-à-vis the company, is to be treated as a director."
>
> 26. I would respectfully agree with that statement of the law. I should add that her conclusion with regard to the effect of the Interpretation Act on section 27 does not determine the interpretation of section 150, discussed below.'

The Supreme Court then concluded that a body corporate may be a shadow director.

[13.069] The Supreme Court went on, however, to find that a body corporate could not be a shadow director for the purposes of s 150 of the CA 1990. This finding was made on the basis that in all cases, it was necessary under s 11(c) of the Interpretation Act 1937 to have regard to the context since it provides that 'person' will include a body corporate 'unless the contrary intention appears'. The basis for finding that there was a contrary intention in the case of s 150 of the CA 1990 is considered in the context of restriction orders[187].

The remuneration of directors

[13.070] As officers, the directors of a company are not automatically entitled to be remunerated for their services[188]. To be entitled to remuneration, the directors' contract for services or of employment must authorise payment to directors. Model reg 76 provides that the remuneration and expenses of the directors shall be determined by the members in general meeting of the company, a convenient provision in view of the fact that, as repeatedly pointed out, the directors will in most Irish private companies be the shareholding-members[189]. A provision in the articles that there be a fixed sum paid to the directors seems to be insufficient unless the members pass a resolution or the director can show an express or implied contract: *Re New British Iron Co*[190]. However, once the members of a company pass a resolution to the effect that a sum or sums should be paid to the directors, then the directors can sue the company for such sums as a debt due and owing from the company[191]. Where the director does not have a controlling or even a substantial interest in a company, then it is best for him to have an express contract of employment. Where all else fails, a director may be able to claim payment on a *quantum meruit* basis[192].

---

187 See Ch 28, *Compliance and Enforcement*, at para **[28.079]**.

188 *Hutton v West Cork Railway Co* (1883) 23 Ch D 654.

189 Members may not amend a company's articles of association so as to remove a directors' entitlement to accrued remuneration, but a prospective amendment may be valid: *Swabey v Port Darwin Gold Mining Co* (1889) 1 Meg 385. See MacCann, *A Casebook on Company Law* (1991, Butterworth Ireland) at p 415.

190 *Re New British Iron Co* [1989] 1 Ch 324.

191 *Re Richmond Gate Property Co Ltd* [1964] 2 All ER 936.

192 *Craven-Ellis v Cannons Ltd* [1936] 2 KB 403. See generally, Clark, *Contract Law in Ireland* (3rd edn, Sweet & Maxwell, 1992) at p 487 *et seq*.

[13.071] Section 28 of the CA 1990 imposes restrictions on directors' service contracts with a company[193]. Subsection (2) provides:

> 'This section applies to any term by which a director's employment with the company of which he is the director or, where he is the director of a holding company his employment within the group is to continue, or may be continued, otherwise than at the instance of the company (whether under the original agreement or under a new agreement entered into in pursuance of the original agreement), for a period exceeding five years during which the employment—
>
> (a) cannot be terminated by the company by notice, or
>
> (b) can be so terminated only in specified circumstances.'

In accordance with sub-s (1) a company shall not incorporate in an employment agreement such a term, unless the term is first approved by a resolution of the company in general meeting and, in the case of a director of a holding company, by a resolution of that company in general meeting. To avoid a situation where contracts are terminated and new ones entered into, sub-s (3) provides for an anti-avoidance measure whereby the period of employment in the further agreement is added to the unexpired period of the original agreement. Before the general meeting at which it is proposed to pass such a resolution, a written memorandum setting out the proposed agreement incorporating the relevant term must be available for inspection by members of the company for not less than 15 days before the meeting at the company's registered office and also at the meeting itself[194]. Any term in an agreement in contravention of s 28 shall, to the extent of the contravention, be void, and in respect of agreements within the meaning of sub-s (3), shall be deemed to contain a term entitling the company to terminate it at any time by the giving of reasonable notice[195]. The effects of s 28 of the CA 1990 would seem destined to be of far greater significance for public companies than private companies. In private companies where the shareholders and directors are one and the same people, it will merely add a further paper procedure that must be complied with.

Ceasing to be a director

[13.072] The circumstances in which a person can cease to be a director and the issues attendant upon such cessation are next considered as follows:

(a) Resignation;
(b) Retirement by rotation;
(c) The removal of directors;
(d) Notification to CRO of cessation of a directorship;
(e) Compensation on loss of office.

(a) Resignation

[13.073] A director may, of his or her own volition, resign as a director at any time by giving notice to the company. Where model reg 91(e) of Table A[196] is adopted, this will

---

[193] By s 28(7) of the CA 1990, 'employment' is deemed to include employment under a contract *for services*.

[194] Section s 28(4) of the CA 1990.

[195] Section s 28(5) of the CA 1990.

[196] See para **[13.075]** *post*.

be expressly provided for but, even in the absence of such an article, this provision will apply as a general rule of law. It was held in *POW Services Ltd and another v Clare et al*[197] that whether a company has notice of the resignation of a director is a question of fact and in that case, the fact that all of a company's directors had notice of a director's letter of resignation was sufficient, notwithstanding that it had not been served upon the company's registered office. This decision is also authority for the fact that resignation is a matter entirely between the director and his company and the validity of a resignation is entirely unaffected by whether or not notice of the director's resignation has been filed in the CRO[198].

(b) Retirement by rotation

[13.074] Under the model articles of association, provision is made for the retirement by rotation of directors. Model reg 92 provides:

> 'At the first annual general meeting of the company all the directors shall retire from office, and at the annual general meeting in every subsequent year, one-third of the directors for the time being, or, if their number is not three or a multiple of three, then the number nearest one-third shall retire from office.'

Regulations 93 to 100 also make provision for the rotation of directors. Such articles will usually be unsuitable in private companies, especially where ownership and management are not divorced. In such companies it may, following legal review, be prudent to purge these provisions from the articles because unforeseen consequences can flow where such an article exists and, for example, an AGM is not, for whatever reason, held or is held but the reappointment of directors overlooked[199].

(c) The removal of directors

(i) Automatic removal

[13.075] Directors can be automatically removed if they are made the subject of a disqualification order under s 160 of the CA 1990[200]. In addition, model reg 91 of Table A provides that the office of director shall be vacated if the director:

> '(a) ceases to be a director by virtue of s 180 of the Act; or
>
> (b) is adjudged bankrupt in the State or in Northern Ireland or Great Britain or makes any arrangement or composition with his creditors generally; or
>
> (c) becomes prohibited from being a director by reason of any order made under s 184 of the Act; or
>
> (d) becomes of unsound mind; or
>
> (e) resigns his office by notice in writing to the company; or
>
> (f) is convicted of an indictable offence unless the directors otherwise determine; or
>
> (g) is for more than 6 months absent without permission of the directors from meetings of the directors held during that period.'

---

[197] *POW Services Ltd and another v Clare et al* [1995] 2 BCLC 435.

[198] See generally, para **[13.083]** *post*.

[199] See *Re Consolidated Nickel Mines Ltd* [1914] 1 Ch 883; *cf* Phoenix *Shannon plc et al v Purkey et al* (7 May 1997, unreported) HC, Costello J, both of which are considered in Ch 14, *Corporate Governance: Meetings*, at para **[14.012]** *et seq*.

[200] See Ch 28, *Compliance and Enforcement*, at para **[28.148]**.

Companies will sometimes adopt a modified version of this provision. One common change is to provide that a director of a single-member company can be removed by notice in writing served on the company by the sole member. A variation on this theme is to permit the removal of a director by a company's holding company serving a written notice. The latter provision can be especially useful in a group situation where directors hold office in subsidiaries at the behest of the parent since it will enable such director's removal without having to convene an EGM to pass an ordinary resolution for which extended notice will be required unless the resolution is proposed by the board of the company on which the director sits[201].

(ii) Removal by directors

[13.076] Sometimes articles will provide that a director can be removed by notice in writing given by all of his or her fellow directors. A lower threshold is also possible and where the articles of a company so permit, a director may be removed by resolution of a simple majority of the board of directors. Where the directors resolve to expel one of their number from the board of directors, they must exercise this power *bona fide* and in the interests of the company and not for ulterior purposes: *Lee v Chou Wen Hsien et al*[202]. Of course, where a director has rights under a contract of employment or in a quasi-partnership company, removal will be without prejudice to the director's rights.

(iii) Removal by members

[13.077] It is a basic principle of company law that the shareholders of a company can dismiss or remove a director by passing an ordinary resolution in a general meeting. So, s 182(1) of the CA 1963 provides:

> 'A company may by ordinary resolution remove a director before the expiration of his period of office notwithstanding anything in its articles or any agreement between it and him, so, however, that this subsection shall not, in the case of a private company, authorise the removal of a director holding office for life.'

Life directors, notwithstanding that they are permanently appointed by the memorandum or articles of association, can only be ousted from office by a special resolution which alters the company's constitutional documents, unless the memorandum of association itself prohibits their removal[203]. Where the resolution of the members to oust a director is invalid or the director is deprived of his statutory rights to notice, he may seek an injunction declaring that his removal was invalid. In *Coubrough v James Panton & Co Ltd*[204], an ordinary resolution was passed instead of the special resolution (as required under that particular company's articles) and accordingly the removal of the director was declared invalid. Similarly, an injunction may be sought to prevent the holding of an EGM for the purposes of passing such a resolution to remove a director where the notice of the EGM is invalid[205].

---

201 See Ch 14, *Corporate Governance: Meetings*, at para **[14.044]** *et seq*.

202 *Lee v Chou Wen Hsien et al* [1985] BCLC 45.

203 Section 28(3) of the CA 1963. See Ch 3, *Constitutional Documentation*, at para **[3.053]**.

204 *Coubrough v James Panton & Co Ltd* [1965] IR 272.

205 See *Currie v Cowdenbeath Football Club Ltd* [1992] BCLC 1029 (Court of Sessions), where *inter alia*, this grounded the granting of the Scottish equivalent of an interlocutory injunction.

[13.078] A unanimous written *resolution*, which can in other circumstances be used to pass an ordinary resolution in accordance with s 141(8) of the CA 1963 where the company's articles contain reg 6 of Table A, may not be utilised to remove a director because s 141(8)(c) excludes its use for the purposes of s 182 of the CA 1963. Accordingly, in a multi-member private company a general meeting will have to be convened and an ordinary resolution proposed and passed in order to remove a director[206]. In the case of a single-member private limited company, however, the sole member may take a written *decision* within the meaning of reg 9(1) and (3) of the EC(SMPLC)R 1994. Whereas s 141(8)(c) of the CA 1963 excludes the use of the written resolution procedure for the purposes of both s 182 of the CA 1963 (removal of directors) and s 160 of the CA 1963 (removal of auditors), reg 9(2) of the EC(SMPLC)R 1994 only excludes the use of the written *decision* procedure in the case of s 160 of the CA 1963. Care should be taken, however, to make clear that the sole member is making a written decision pursuant to reg 9 of the EC(SMPLC)R 1994 and not passing a written resolution pursuant to s 141(8) of the CA 1963.

[13.079] Shareholding-directors may also bolster the likelihood of their staying in office through the use of a *Bushell v Faith*[207] clause in the articles of association. Such clauses can give certain members loaded voting rights which apply generally or simply where it is proposed to dismiss a director. Accordingly, the articles of association could provide that on a vote to dismiss a director, the voting rights of the director concerned are loaded, thus allowing him to thwart any resolution to remove him. Furthermore, shareholding-directors may enter into a shareholders' agreement containing a similar provision. Alternatively, the directors may simply retain sufficient shares, holding either legal or equitable/beneficial title, to ensure that they retain sufficient control over the company.

[13.080] Although a company acting through its members has an express statutory right to dismiss a director, certain factors may deter shareholders from exercising this power[208]. It is inappropriate to consider at length those disincentives rooted in labour law, and treatment here is confined to specific company law issues. However, it should be said that while s 182(1) *allows* the member-shareholders to dismiss, s 182(7) of the CA 1963 provides that the right to compensation or damages payable to the director in respect of the determination of his appointment remains intact. To have rights against the company, a director must have been employed on a contractual basis as opposed to having been merely appointed as a director by resolution. Where there is such a contract, either express or implied, and the director is dismissed in contravention of that contract, or in breach of the terms of the Unfair Dismissals Acts, or simply wrongfully dismissed[209], then the director's right to compensation may be invoked[210]. Essentially, the

---

206 See Ch 14, *Corporate Governance: Meetings*, at para **[14.092]**. This is unless the articles of association permit the removal of a director by means other than an ordinary resolution, eg, by the service of notice by a subsidiary's ultimate holding company.

207 *Bushell v Faith* [1970] AC 1099. See Ch 3, *Constitutional Documentation*, at para **[3.053]**.

208 See Ussher, *Company Law in Ireland* (1986, Sweet & Maxwell) p 91 *et seq*. And see generally, Ch 11, *Shareholders' Remedies*, at para **[11.067]** et seq.

209 *Glover v BLN Ltd* [1973] IR 388.

210 *Industrial Yarns Ltd v Greene* [1984] ILRM 15; *Carvill v Irish Industrial Bank Ltd* [1968] IR 325; *Read v Astoria Garage (Streatham) Ltd* [1952] Ch 637; *Glover v BLN Ltd* [1973] IR 388.

question of compensation may be reduced to a finding that there were terms in the appointment of the director which were irreconcilable with the right of summary dismissal.

[13.081] In a private quasi-partnership type private company, there is a danger that summary dismissal could give rise to an application by the dismissed director-shareholder for an order pursuant to s 213(f) of the CA 1963, directing that the company be wound up on just and equitable grounds[211]. Indeed, a director could seek relief under s 205 for oppression[212].

[13.082] A number of recent Irish cases have considered the correct interpretation of s 182 of the CA 1963 in circumstances where the director of a private company, who has commenced proceedings under s 205 of the CA 1963, claiming oppression, seeks an injunction to prevent his removal[213]. In *Feighery v Feighery et al*[214], Laffoy J had, in the High Court, held:

> 'In my view, even assuming that the petitioner has an arguable case of relief under s 205 and an arguable case that that the respondents as shareholders and directors, owe him fiduciary duties and are in breach of those duties, I must nonetheless be satisfied that I have jurisdiction to override the shareholders' statutory power under s 182 to remove the petitioner from the board. I am not satisfied that I have such jurisdiction …[215].'

The Supreme Court in *McGilligan & Bowen v O'Grady et al* did not follow this decision[216]. After stating that the effect of s 205 of the CA 1963 was to curb the majority's power to act in a manner which was harsh and oppressive, Keane CJ held:

> 'Why then should the court, on an application for an interlocutory injunction, be unable to restrain the company from removing a director pending the hearing of a petition under s 205 where he has established that there is a serious question to be tried as to whether his exclusion from the affairs of the company constitutes conduct which would entitle shareholders to relief under s 205?
>
> It should be noted that in *Bentley-Stevens v Jones* [1974] 1 WLR 638 there does not appear to have been any proceedings in existence under the English equivalent of s 205 at the time the application for an interlocutory injunction was made. However, apart from that consideration, I am bound to say, with all respect, that I do not understand why it should be thought that, because the relief sought in the interlocutory proceedings is not the same as the relief which will ultimately be sought in the s 205 proceedings, an interlocutory injunction should not be granted on that ground alone. If it is desirable, in accordance with the principles laid down in the *American Cyanamid Company* and *Campus Oil* cases[217], to preserve the plaintiff's rights pending the hearing of the s 205

211 See *Ebrahimi v Westbourne Galleries* [1973] AC 360; and for an Irish example, *Re Murph's Restaurants Ltd* [1979] ILRM 141. See generally Ch 23, *Winding Up Companies*, at para **[23.091]**.

212 See Ch 11, *Shareholders' Remedies*, at para **[11.006]** *et seq*.

213 See Dunleavy, 'The Power of Shareholders to Remove Directors Under s 182 of the Companies Act 1963' (1999) Bar Law Review 265.

214 *Feighery v Feighery et al* (25 February 1998, unreported) HC, Laffoy J.

215 *Feighery v Feighery et al* (25 February 1998, unreported) HC, Laffoy J at p 28 of the judgment.

216 *McGilligan & Bowen v O'Grady et al* (5 November 1998, unreported) SC.

217 As to which, see generally, Courtney, *Mareva Injunctions and Related Interlocutory Orders* (1998, Butterworths) at paras [5.03]–[5.10].

> proceedings and the balance of convenience does not point to a different conclusion, I see no reason why interlocutory relief should not be granted to cite but one example, the relief in many Mareva cases is very often not the relief which is sought in the substantive proceedings. I am satisfied that, to the extent that *Bentley-Stevens v Jones* and *Feighery v Feighery et al* suggest a different view of the law, they should not be followed[218].

It should be stressed that it will not be every case in which the shareholders' statutory right to remove a director will be restricted by injunction and that the Supreme Court's decision would appear to be confined to injunctions sought as ancillary relief in a s 205 petition[219].

(d) Notification to CRO of cessation of a directorship

[13.083] Section 195(6) of the CA 1963 imposes a duty on *companies* to notify the CRO within 14 days from the happening of any change among its directors or secretary. Originally, s 195(8) allowed directors the right to file notice of their resignation where their former company was remiss in complying with s 195(6). This was not particularly liked by the CRO because the result was, in many cases, a proliferation of registered companies without any apparent directors. In consequence, s 195 was amended by s 47 of the C(A)(No2)A 1999, which introduced new subsections (11A) to (11E). The main change is now contained in s 195(11A), which provides:

> 'If a company fails to send, in accordance with subsection (6), a notification, in the prescribed form, to the registrar of companies of the fact of a person's having ceased, for whatever reason, to be a director or secretary of the company and of the date on which that event occurred that person may serve on the company a notice—
>
> (a) requesting it to send forthwith the notification of that matter, in the prescribed form, to the registrar, and
>
> (b) stating that if the company fails to comply with that request within 21 days of the service of the notice on it, he will forward to the registrar of companies and to every person who, to his knowledge, is an officer of the company a copy of any notice of resignation by him as a director or secretary of the company or any other documentary proof of his having ceased to be such a director or secretary together with—
>
> (i) in the case of the registrar of companies, such additional information as may be prescribed (which may include a statutory declaration made by the person stating the names of the persons who, to his knowledge, are officers of the company), and
>
> (ii) in the case of every other person as aforesaid, a written request of the person that he take such steps as will ensure that the failure of the company to comply with the notice continues no further.'

The effect of this subsection is that where a company does not comply with its obligation to notify the CRO, the rights of a director or secretary to make notification is preserved but made expressly subject to such director or secretary complying with

---

218 *McGilligan & Bowen v O'Grady et al* (5 November 1998, unreported) SC at p 27, 28 of the judgment. An injunction was also granted in *O'Gorman et al v Kelleher et al* (19 July 1999, unreported) HC, Carroll J, where there were s 205 proceedings in train.

219 See *Re Avoca Capital Holdings* [2005] IEHC 302 and, further, Ch 11, *Shareholders' Remedies*, at para **[11.071]**.

certain conditions. The main condition is that the ex-director or ex-secretary must first request the company to notify the CRO and state that, if it fails to do so within 21 days, the ex-director or ex-secretary will send to the CRO and to every person who is to his knowledge an officer of the company, a copy of his resignation (or other documentary proof of his cessation to act as director or secretary)[220] together with such additional information as the CRO might require. The CRO will require a statutory declaration stating the names of the person who 'to his knowledge' are officers of the company. The ex-director or ex-secretary must also send to those whom he believes to be officers, a written request that they take such steps as will end the failure of the company to comply with the notice.

[13.084] Where the company does not comply with the ex-director's or ex-secretary's request, he can proceed to notify the CRO[221]. There was a concern that to misrepresent an individual as being a director of a company that was, say, insolvent or known to be engaged in nefarious activity, might expose the ex-director or ex-secretary to an action for defamation, so it is expressly provided that any representation made will not, of itself, constitute defamatory matter[222]. Any person may give notice (accompanied by such proof as may be prescribed) of the death of a director or secretary[223].

[13.085] The sole purpose behind this provision is to try to ensure that companies will have some persons registered as their directors. Of course, if there are no directors remaining that cannot stop an ex-director or ex-secretary from demanding that the register be amended accordingly, it just makes matters more difficult. No doubt the additional bureaucracy was considered justified by the greater good of making it difficult for registered companies to appear to have no directors.

(e) Compensation on loss of office

[13.086] Section 186 of the CA 1963 provides that the approval of the members of a company is necessary for the payment of compensation by a company to a director for loss of office. It provides:

---

[220] Section 195(11C) of the CA 1963 provides: 'No notice of resignation or other documentary proof of a person's having ceased to be a director or secretary of a company which is forwarded to the registrar of companies by that person (other than such a notice or other proof which is forwarded by him under and in accordance with subsections (11A) and (11B), or section 43(9) of the Companies (Amendment) (No 2) Act 1999) shall be considered by the registrar.'

[221] Section 195(11B) of the CA 1963 provides: 'If a company fails to comply with a request made of it under a notice referred to in subsection (11A) the person who served the notice may forward to the registrar of companies and to every person who, to his knowledge, is an officer of the company a copy of the notice of resignation or other documentary proof referred to in subsection (11A) if, but only if, there is forwarded together with that notice or proof, in the case of the registrar, the additional information referred to in that subsection and, in the case of every other person as aforesaid, the written request referred to in that subsection.'

[222] Section 195(11D) of the CA 1963 provides: 'No additional information referred to in subsection (11A)(b)(i) that is included in a notice of resignation or other documentary proof referred to in this section which is forwarded, under and in accordance with the foregoing provisions, to the registrar of companies shall, of itself, be regarded as constituting defamatory matter.'

[223] Section 195(11E) of the CA 1963.

> 'It shall not be lawful for a company to make to any director of the company any payment by way of compensation for loss of office, or as consideration for or in connection with his retirement from office, without particulars relating to the proposed payment (including the amount thereof) being disclosed to the members of the company and the proposal being approved by the company in general meeting.'

It is necessary to consider s 186 by reference to s 189(3) of the CA 1963, which provides that references in s 186 to payments to any director of a company *by way of compensation for loss or office or as consideration for or in connection with his retirement from office*, include:

> '... payments to him by way of compensation for loss of office as director of the company or for the loss, while director of the company, or on or in connection with his ceasing to be a director of the company of any other office in connection with the management of the company's affairs or of any office as director or otherwise in connection with the management of the affairs of any subsidiary company but do not include any *bona fide* payment by way of damages for breach of contract or by way of pension in respect of past services, and for the purposes of this subsection 'pension' includes any superannuation allowance, superannuation gratuity or similar payment.'

[13.087] Here, the following issues in the payment of compensation to directors are considered:

(a) Payments caught by s 186 of the CA 1963;
(b) Payment of damages for breach of contract;
(c) Payment of pensions;
(d) The mechanics of compliance: disclosure and resolution;
(e) Payments made in connection with the transfer of undertaking or property.

(i) Payments caught by s 186 of the CA 1963

[13.088] Accordingly, payments to the director of a company in the following three circumstances *prima facie* fall within s 186 of the CA 1963 and require the authorisation of an ordinary resolution of the members in general meeting:

– payments by way of compensation for loss of office as director of the company;
– payments for the loss (whether while a director or on, or in connection with, ceasing to be a director) of any other office in connection with the management of the company's affairs; and
– payments for the loss (whether while a director or on, or in connection with, ceasing to be a director) of any office as director or otherwise in connection with the management of the affairs of any subsidiary company.

A payment to a director who is stepping down as a director is obviously caught; also caught is a payment to a director who is continuing as a director but ceasing to hold an executive capacity in the company or a subsidiary. A payment by a company to a director of a subsidiary company will fall outside s 186 provided that person is not also a director of the company making the payment.

[13.089] Whether or not something is a 'payment' is a matter of fact. The materially identical UK provision[224] was considered by the Scottish Court of Session in *Mercer v*

[224] Section 312 of the Companies Act 1985 (UK).

Heart of Midlothian plc[225]. The facts in that case were that Mercer had been a majority shareholder and chairman of the defendant football club and part of the agreement that he would be elected life president was that he would be granted certain privileges including seats in the directors' box at a football stadium on match days, access to the boardroom and a car park pass. When Mercer retired shortly thereafter, the board of directors sought to withdraw his privileges on the grounds that, pursuant to s 312 of the Companies Act 1985 (UK), they had not been approved by the members. It was held that the payments in question were not within the contemplation of s 312 for two reasons. In the first place, it was held that the directors had regarded the privileges as being conferred on the life president and they were firmly attached to his future enjoyment of that position – not his leaving office. In the second place, it was held that although the privileges were of benefit to the recipient, it was not obvious that it would actually cost the defendant anything to allow Mercer to enjoy them; accordingly, it was held that the privileges did not constitute a 'payment'.

(ii) Payment of damages for breach of contract

[13.090] Certain payments are also expressly excluded from the operation of s 186 by reason of s 189(3), namely 'any *bona fide* payment by way of damages for breach of contract or by way of pension in respect of past services'. The classic example of this will be where a director sues or threatens to sue his company for breach of his contract of employment and the company is forced, or compromises the litigation, and agrees to pay damages. In those circumstances the proposed payment does not have to be disclosed to the members of the company nor approved by the company in general meeting.

[13.091] The leading case on damages for breach of contract is the Privy Council decision in *The Taupo Totara Timber Co Ltd v Rowe*[226] where an identical New Zealand provision was considered. There, it was decided that the wording of the section involves:

> '... a prohibition on uncovenanted payments as contrasted with payments which the company is legally obliged to make.'

In that case it was noted that the respondent, as well as being a director, was an employee and had a service contract which provided that in certain events, which might not happen, he could become contractually entitled to a sum of money, on resignation or dismissal, the amount of which was not fixed by the contract and could only be ascertained when the event happened. The payment to a director under such a contract was held to fall outside the prohibition because it was a contractually agreed payment. This decision was followed in *Lander v Premier Pict Petroleum Ltd*[227], where a company's managing director had a service contract, the terms of which were amended by a supplemental agreement to provide that the managing director would be entitled to terminate his contract and receive compensation should there be a chance of control of the company. It was held that there was no basis for distinguishing the facts from those in *Taupo* and the payment was found to be valid without disclosure to and resolution of the members.

---

225 *Mercer v Heart of Midlothian plc* (2001) SLT 945, noted by Goddard, (2002) 23 Co Law 23.

226 *The Taupo Totara Timber Co Ltd v Rowe* [1977] 3 All ER 123, [1978] AC 537.

227 *Lander v Premier Pict Petroleum Ltd* [1998] BCC 248.

(iii) Payment of pensions

[13.092] Another payment excluded from the operation of s 186 by virtue of s 189(3), is 'any *bona fide* payment … by way of pension in respect of past services'. Moreover, it is provided that for the purposes of that subsection, 'pension' includes any superannuation allowance, superannuation gratuity or similar payment.

(iv) The mechanics of compliance: disclosure and resolution

[13.093] Where a payment comes within s 186 of the CA 1963, compliance can be achieved in either of two ways. Disclosure of the proposed payment and its amount must be made to all of the members and not just those with voting rights[228]. Where the members are to be asked to approve of the payment at a general meeting at which an ordinary resolution is proposed to be passed, the disclosure must be made in the notice convening the meeting and not just at the meeting[229]. Approval may also be given by unanimous written resolution of the members entitled to vote where this is permitted by the company's articles of association. The disclosure there should be made in the written resolution and where there are other members who do not have voting rights, a letter of disclosure should be sent to them. In all cases the disclosure must be made *prior* to the payment being made. The Scottish Court of Session in *Mercer v Heart of Midlothian plc*[230] also held that the disclosure in a company's accounts of any payments within the contemplation of the section could not be said to be disclosure and approval because disclosure to and approval by members was required to be *prior* to the making of any such payments, not *ex post facto*.

(v) Payments made in connection with the transfer of undertaking or property

[13.094] It should also be noted that it is unlawful, in connection with the transfer of the whole or any part of the undertaking or property of a company, for any payment to be made to a director by way of compensation for loss of office or as consideration for or in connection with his retirement from office, without the prior disclosure to, and approval by, the members in general meeting[231].

Disclosures concerning directors and secretaries

[13.095] A company is obliged to disclose certain aspects of its relationship with its directors and secretary. These disclosure requirements may be considered under the following two headings:

(a) The register of directors and secretary.

(b) The disclosure and registration of directors' and others' interests.

[228] *Re Duomatic Ltd* [1969] 1 All ER 161.

[229] *Kaye v Croydon Tramways Co* [1898] 1 Ch 358.

[230] *Mercer v Heart of Midlothian plc* (2001) SLT 945, noted by Goddard, (2002) 23 Co Law 23.

[231] Section 187 of the CA 1963. It should also be noted that tax free payments to directors are also prohibited: s 185 of the CA 1963.

(a) Register of directors and secretary

[13.096] Section 195 of the CA 1963 provides that every company shall keep at its registered office a register of its directors and secretary, which should keep the prescribed details of such officers. Within 14 days of any change in either the directors or secretary or any change in any of the particulars in the register, the company[232] must send the registrar of companies notification in the prescribed form[233]. Where the notification is of the appointment of a person as director or secretary/joint secretary, then the new officers must sign a consent[234].

[13.097] The register of directors and secretary must be kept open for inspection for not less than two hours per day during business hours, subject to whatever reasonable restrictions the company's articles of association or resolution of the members in general meeting may impose[235]. Those who may inspect the register are the members of the company, who may do so without charge, and the general public, on payment of a nominal fee. Section 195 imposes a duty on the directors and secretary to give information to the company in writing to enable the company to comply with the section[236]. A refusal to permit inspection, or any default in complying with the operative sub-sections is liable to be visited by a fine on the company and every officer who is in default[237].

[13.098] The matters required to be detailed in relation to each *director* are set out in s 195(2) of the CA 1963. These are as follows:

(i) his present forename, surname and any former names[238];

(ii) his date of birth;

(iii) his usual residential address;

(iv) his nationality;

(v) his business occupation, if any; and

(vi) particulars of other directorships of other bodies corporate, Irish or foreign, past or present.

It is unnecessary to record particulars of other directorships that have not been held by a director during the 10 years preceding inspection. Also excluded are directorships of bodies corporate of which the company is or was a wholly-owned subsidiary, or which are or were wholly-owned subsidiaries either of the company or of another body corporate of which the company is or was the wholly-owned subsidiary[239].

---

232 Section 195(8) of the CA 1963 provides that a person who has ceased to be a director may himself notify the registrar of companies.

233 Section 195(6) of the CA 1963.

234 Section 195(7) of the CA 1963.

235 Section 195(10) of the CA 1963.

236 Section 195(11) of the CA 1963. A person who fails to comply with this is guilty of an offence and liable to a fine.

237 Section 195(12) of the CA 1963, which provides for a class C fine and class E daily default fine. Subsection (13) provides that the court may by order compel an immediate inspection of the register.

238 Section 195(15) of the CA 1963.

239 Section 195(3) of the CA 1963.

[13.099] The matters required to be detailed in relation to the *secretary* are set out in s 195(4) of the CA 1963 and are considered below[240].

(b) Disclosure and registration of directors' and secretaries' interests in shares and debentures

[13.100] Prior to the Companies Act 1990 directors were only obliged to register with the company their interests in shares and debentures to which they held the legal title. On account of there being no obligation to register their interest in shares to which they held equitable or beneficial title, it was considered that this was a black spot on the register. This has now been addressed by Part IV of the CA 1990 (which applies to directors, shadow directors[241] and the secretary). The effect of Part IV of the CA 1990 has been to turn an arc light on the black spot and it is generally considered by practitioners that the disclosure requirements in Part IV have placed a significant and disproportionate burden of compliance on companies, their shareholders and officers[242]. In this section, the law relating to the disclosure and registration of directors' and secretaries' interests in shares and debentures is considered under the following headings:

(i) The obligation on becoming a director or secretary;
(ii) The obligation while occupying the office of director or secretary;
(iii) Interests which must be disclosed – general;
(iv) Interests which must be disclosed – family interests;
(v) Interests which can be disregarded;
(vi) The mechanics of notification;
(vii) The consequences of failing to comply;
(viii) The register of interests;
(ix) Notification of stock exchange;
(x) Investigation of suspected contravention of ss 53 and 64.

(i) The obligation on becoming a director or secretary

[13.101] Section 53(1) of the CA 1990 imposes an obligation on a person who on becoming[243] a director, shadow director or secretary of a company is then interested in shares in or debentures of the company and certain other bodies corporate to notify the company in writing of:

(a) the subsistence of his interests at that time,
(b) of the number of shares of each class in, and the amount of debentures of each class of the company or the holding or subsidiary company.

Shares and debentures in the company must be notified; so also must any shares or debentures in the company's holding company or a subsidiary of the company's holding

---

240 See para **[13.125]** *ante*.

241 Section 53(9) of the CA 1990.

242 See, Nolan, 'Disclosure of Interests in Securities under Part IV of the Companies Act 1990' (2000) 7 CLP 31.

243 The section also applied to directors and secretaries holding such interests when the section was commenced on 1 August 1991, by SI 117/1991.

company. The holding company or sister subsidiary need not even be Irish companies since the section refers to 'any other body corporate'. The obligation does not, however, apply to shares in a body corporate which is the wholly-owned subsidiary of another body corporate[244].

[13.102] The obligation to notify an interest must, if the person knows of the existence of the interest on the day he or she becomes a director, be fulfilled before the expiration of five days beginning the day next following the day he or she is appointed to office; where he or she is unaware that they have a notifiable interest, it must be fulfilled before the expiration of five days beginning with the day next following that on which the interest comes to his or her knowledge[245]. In computing the five days, a day that is a Saturday, Sunday or public holiday is not to be included[246].

(ii) The obligation while occupying the office of director or secretary

[13.103] A person who occupies the office of director, shadow director or secretary and who whilst holding that office acquires share or debentures is also under a notification obligation. Section 53(2) provides that such a director, etc, must notify the company in writing of the occurrence of the following events and the date on which it occurred:

> '(a) any event in consequence of whose occurrence he becomes, or ceases to be, interested in shares in, or debentures of, the company or any other body corporate, being the company's subsidiary or holding company or a subsidiary of the company's holding company;
>
> (b) the entering into by him of a contract to sell any such shares or debentures;
>
> (c) the assignment by him of a right granted to him by the company to subscribe for shares in, or debentures of, the company; and
>
> (d) the grant to him by another body corporate, being the company's subsidiary or holding company or a subsidiary of the company's holding company, of a right to subscribe for shares in, or debentures of, that other body corporate, the exercise of such a right granted to him and the assignment by him of such a right so granted;
>
> stating the number or amount, and class, of shares or debentures involved.'

The obligation is extensive and will apply where a director or secretary buys or sells shares (or debentures), contracts to do so, or gets options to subscribe for shares in the company, its holding company (even if foreign) or its sister subsidiary. The obligation does not, however, apply to shares in a body corporate which is the wholly-owned subsidiary of another body corporate[247].

[13.104] The delivery to a person's order of shares or debentures in fulfilment of a contract for the purchase thereof by him or in satisfaction of a right of his to call for delivery thereof, or failure to deliver shares or debentures in accordance with the terms of such a contract or on which such a right falls to be satisfied, shall be deemed to constitute an event in consequence of the occurrence of which he ceases to be interested

244 Section 53(10) of the CA 1990.

245 Section 56(1) of the CA 1990.

246 Section 4(2) of the CA 1990.

247 Section 53(10) of the CA 1990.

in them, and so shall the lapse of a person's right to call for delivery of shares or debentures[248].

[13.105] The obligation, under s 53(2)(a) of the CA 1963, to notify arising as a result of a director or secretary entering into a contract for the purchase of share or debentures will not be discharged in the absence of inclusion in the notice of a statement of the price to be paid by him under the contract[249]. The obligation under s 53(2)(b) to notify the entering into by him of a contract to sell any such shares or debentures is taken not to be discharged in the absence of inclusion in the notice of the price to be received under the contract[250]. The obligation under s 53(2)(c) to notify a company of the assignment of a right granted by the company to subscribe for shares or debentures of the company is taken not to be discharged in the absence of inclusion in the notice of a statement of the consideration (or absence of consideration) for the assignment[251]. The obligation under s 53(2)(d) to notify the assignment of a right is taken not to be discharged in the absence of inclusion in the notice of a statement of the consideration (or absence of consideration) for that assignment[252].

[13.106] In relation to options, where under s 53(2)(d) a director or secretary is obliged to notify a company of a grant of a *right to subscribe* for shares or debentures, the obligation will not be taken to be discharged in the absence of inclusion in the notice of a statement of the following matters:

- (a) the date on which the right was granted,
- (b) the period during which or time at which the right is exercisable,
- (c) the consideration for the grant (or, if it be the case that there is no consideration, that fact), and
- (d) the price to be paid for the shares or debentures[253].

It is because the obligation to notify the grant of options arises where the company itself grants those options to a director that the CLRG considered that the law is in need of reform. It is also provided that where under s 53(2)(d) a director or secretary is obliged to notify a company of the *exercise of a right* granted to subscribe for shares or debentures, the obligation will not be taken to be discharged in the absence of inclusion in the notice of a statement of:

- (a) the number of shares or amount of debentures in respect of which the right was exercised, and
- (b) if it be the case that they were registered in his or her name, that fact, and, if not, the name or names of the person or persons in whose name or names they were registered,

together (if they were registered in the names of two persons or more) with the number of amount thereof registered in the name of each of them[254]. In all cases, reference to

[248] Section 54(13) of the CA 1990.
[249] Section 57(1) of the CA 1990.
[250] Section 57(1) of the CA 1990.
[251] Section 57(2) of the CA 1990.
[252] Section 57(2) of the CA 1990.
[253] Section 57(3) of the CA 1990.
[254] Section 57(4) of the CA 1990.

consideration includes any consideration other than money given or received in respect of any such interest[255].

[13.107] The obligation to notify an interest must, if at the time at which the event occurs the person knows of the occurrence, be fulfilled before the expiration of the period of five days beginning with the day next following that on which it occurs; otherwise, it must be fulfilled before the expiration of the period of five days beginning the day next following that on which the occurrence of the event comes to his or her knowledge[256]. In computing the five days, a day that is a Saturday, Sunday or public holiday is not to be included[257].

(iii) Interests which must be disclosed – general

[13.108] It is not only the full legal title to shares or debentures which qualifies as a notifiable interest and a reference to an interest in shares or debentures is read as including a reference to any interest of any kind whatsoever and there shall be disregarded any restraints or restrictions to which the exercise of any right attached to the interest is or may be subject[258].

[13.109] A person will be taken to have an interest in shares or debentures in all of the following scenarios:

– where he or she is the beneficiary of a trust comprised of any interest in those shares or debentures[259];

– where he or she has entered into a contract to purchase shares or debentures (for cash or otherwise)[260];

– where he or she is entitled to exercise or control the exercise of any right conferred by the holding of shares or debentures, even though he or she is not the registered holder[261]; a person will be taken to be so entitled if he or she has a right (whether or not subject to conditions), the exercise of which would make him so entitled or is under an obligation (whether so subject or not), the fulfilment of which would make him so entitled[262] (acting as a proxy to vote at a specified meeting, etc, or acting as a body corporate's authorised representative at any meeting or class meeting of a company does not, however, confer an interest[263]);

– where a body corporate is interested in the shares or debentures and that body corporate or its directors are accustomed to act in accordance with that person's directions or instructions[264];

---

255 Section 58(5) of the CA 1990.
256 Section 56(2) of the CA 1990.
257 Section 4(2) of the CA 1990.
258 Section 54(2) of the CA 1990.
259 Section 54(3) of the CA 1990.
260 Section 54(4)(a) of the CA 1990.
261 Section 54(4)(b) of the CA 1990.
262 Section 54(8) of the CA 1990.
263 Section 54(9) of the CA 1990.
264 Section 54(5)(a) of the CA 1990.

- where body corporate X is interested in the shares or debentures and that person is entitled to exercise or control the exercise of one-third or more of the voting power at general meetings of body corporate X[265];
- where body corporate X is interested in the shares or debentures and body corporate Y is entitled to exercise or control the exercise of any of the voting power at general meetings of body corporate X and that person is entitled to exercise or control the exercise of one-third or more of the voting power at general meetings of body corporate Y[266];
- where a person has a right (whether absolute or conditional) to call for delivery of the shares or debentures to himself or to his order otherwise than by virtue of having an interest under a trust[267] (rights or obligations to subscribe for any shares or debentures, however, shall not be taken for the purposes of s 54(7) to be rights to acquire, or obligations to take, any interest in shares or debentures[268]);
- where a person has a right (whether absolute or conditional) to acquire an interest in shares or debentures or is under an obligation to take an interest in share or debentures, otherwise than by virtue of having an interest under a trust[269] (again, rights or obligations to subscribe for any shares or debentures, however, shall not be taken for the purposes of s 54(7) to be rights to acquire, or obligations to take, any interest in shares or debentures[270]);
- where a person has a joint interest in shares or debentures[271];
- where the interest in shares and debentures is unidentifiable[272].

(iv) Interests which must be disclosed – family interests

[13.110] It is not only interests that a director or secretary has in shares or debentures which is notifiable; the obligation in s 53(1) and (2) will also extend to interests held by the following:

(a) the spouse of a director or secretary of a company (not him or herself being a director or secretary) and the spouse's interests will be treated as being those of the director or secretary;

(b) the minor child of a director or secretary (not him or herself being a director or secretary) and again that child's interests being treated as being those of the director or secretary[273].

265 Section 54(5)(b) of the CA 1990.

266 Section 54(6) of the CA 1990 provides: 'Where a person is entitled to exercise or control the exercise of one-third or more of the voting power at general meetings of a body corporate and that body corporate is entitled to exercise or control the exercise of any of the voting power at general meetings of another body corporate (the "relevant voting power"), then, for the purposes of subsection 5(b), the relevant voting power shall be taken to be exercisable by that person.'

267 Section 54(7)(a) of the CA 1990.

268 Section 54(10) of the CA 1990.

269 Section 54(7)(b) of the CA 1990.

270 Section 54(10) of the CA 1990.

271 Section 54(11) of the CA 1990.

272 Section 54(12) of the CA 1990.

273 Section 64(1)(a) and (b) of the CA 1990.

Contracts, assignments or rights of subscription entered into, exercised or made by or grants made to the spouse or minor children of a director or secretary shall be treated as having been entered into, exercised or made by, etc., the director or secretary[274]. Sections 54 and 55 of the CA 1990 are said to have effect for the interpretation of s 64(1) and (2) and s 53(8) and (9) for the purposes of s 64[275].

[13.111] A director or secretary is by s 64(3) of the CA 1990 under an obligation, independent to s 54(1) and (2), to notify the company in writing of the occurrence, while he or she is director or secretary, of either of the following events:

(a) the grant to his or her spouse or minor child by the company, of a right to subscribe for shares in or debentures of the company; or

(b) the exercise by the spouse or minor child of such a right granted by the company.

When giving a notice under s 64(3), there shall be stated:

(a) in the case of the grant of a right, the like information as is required by s 53 to be stated on the grant to him or her by another body corporate of a right to subscribe for shares or debentures of that other body corporate; and

(b) in the case of the exercise of a right, the like information as is required by s 53 to be stated on the exercise of a right granted by another body corporate to subscribe for shares or debentures of that other body corporate[276].

The obligation imposed by s 64(3) must be fulfilled before the expiration of the period of five days beginning with the day next following that on which the occurrence of the event that gives rise to it comes to his knowledge[277] and the failure to fulfil the obligation within the proper period is an offence[278]. This is an important point because it bears out that the obligation is conditional upon the director or secretary becoming aware of the doings of his or her spouse and minor children.

(v) Interests which can be disregarded

[13.112] Certain interests can be disregarded for the purposes of s 54 and ss 56 to 58. Accordingly, the following interests in shares or debentures are not relevant and, where held by a director, etc, do not have to be notified:

1. an interest in reversion or remainder or of a bare trustee and any discretionary interest where property is held in trust and shares or debentures are comprised in that property[279];
2. an interest that subsists by virtue of holding units in certain unit trusts and UCITS[280];

---

[274] Section 64(2) of the CA 1990.

[275] Section 64(7) of the CA 1990.

[276] Section 64(4) of the CA 1990.

[277] Section 64(5) of the CA 1990.

[278] Section 64(6) of the CA 1990.

[279] Section 55(1)(a) of the CA 1990.

[280] Section 55(1)(b)(i)(I)–(III) of the CA 1990.

3. an interest that subsists by virtue of a scheme made under s 46 of the Charities Act 1961[281];
4. an interest for life under a settlement in the case of which the property comprised in the settlement consists of or includes shares or debentures and the settlement is irrevocable and the settler has no interest in any income arising under or property comprised in the settlement[282];
5. an interest in shares or debentures held by a member of a recognised stock exchange carrying on business as a stock broker which is held by way of security only for the purposes of a transaction entered into by the person or body concerned in the ordinary course of business of such person or body[283];
6. such interests, or interests of such a class as may be prescribed for the purposes of this paragraph by regulations made by the Minister[284]; and
7. interests in shares or debentures arising by virtue of s 54(4)(b) by reason only that a person has been appointed a proxy to vote at a specified meeting of a company or of any class of its members and at any adjournment of that meeting, or has been appointed by a body corporate to act as its representative at any meeting of a company or of any class of its members[285].

(vi) The mechanics of notification

[13.113] The notifications required to be made pursuant to s 53(1) and (2) must be in writing. Moreover, the obligations imposed by s 53(1) and (2) shall be treated as not being fulfilled unless the notice by means of which it purports to be fulfilled is expressed to be given in fulfilment of that obligation[286]. An obligation to make a notification under Chapter 1 of Part IV is treated as not being fulfilled unless the notice by means of which it purports to be fulfilled identifies him and gives his address[287]. While a shadow director is obliged to make a notification where he or she falls within the obligations, the making of a notification shall not, in itself, be proof that the person is a shadow director[288]. Where a director, etc, appoints an agent to acquire or dispose of shares for him, he must secure that the agent notifies him immediately upon an acquisition or disposal to enable the director to comply with his obligations[289].

(vii) The consequences of failing to comply

[13.114] The failure to comply with s 53(1) or (2) of the CA 1990 is a criminal offence[290] which, because no punishment is specified, means that it is, by virtue of s 240(1) of the CA 1990, capable of being tried both summarily and on indictment.

---

281 Section 55(1)(b)(ii) of the CA 1990.
282 Section 55(1)(c) and (3) of the CA 1990.
283 Section 55(1)(d) of the CA 1990.
284 Section 55(1)(e) of the CA 1990.
285 Section 55(2) of the CA 1990.
286 Section 53(8) of the CA 1990.
287 Section 58(2) of the CA 1990.
288 Section 53(9) of the CA 1990.
289 Section 58(1) of the CA 1990; the failure to comply with this is an offence: s 58(7).
290 Section 53(7) of the CA 1990.

[13.115] There are also civil consequences in failing to make the required notification within the prescribed time limits. Section 58(3) provides:

> 'Where a person fails to fulfil, within the proper period, an obligation to which he is subject by virtue of section 53, no right or interest of any kind whatsoever in respect of the shares or debentures concerned shall be enforceable by him, whether directly or indirectly, by action or legal proceeding.'

This consequences does not, however, apply to an obligation in relation to a person ceasing to be interested in shares or debentures, with the consequences that the rights of an acquiring third party will be unaffected by a breach of s 53[291]. Section 58(3) is peculiar in its effect. It provides that the rights or interests in such shares and debentures are not removed, voided or rendered incapable of being respected by the company; rather, it is open to a company to decide whether or not to continue to pay dividends and extend voting rights to the holder of shares that have not been notified. Where a director is happy that the company will recognise his rights, he may decide to do nothing. If, on the other hand, the director wants to remove the company's unilateral right to choose whether or not to recognise his rights in the shares, he may apply to court for judicial relief. So, where any right or interest is so restricted:

> '... any person in default under that subsection or any other person affected by such restriction may apply to the court for relief against a disability imposed by or arising out of subsection (3) and the court on being satisfied that the default was accidental, or due to inadvertence, or some other sufficient cause, or that on other grounds it is just and equitable to grant relief, may grant such relief either generally, or as respects any particular right or interest on such terms and conditions as it sees fit.'

While there are wide grounds available for seeking relief, the court is enjoined from granting relief it is appears that the default has arisen as a result of any deliberate act or omission on the part of the applicant[292].

(viii) The register of interests[293]

[13.116] Every company is obliged to keep a register for the purposes of recording interests disclosed pursuant to s 53 of the CA 1990[294]. Moreover, there is a statutory obligation on a company, which receives information from a director or secretary in fulfilment of an obligation imposed by s 53, to enter in the register, against the name of that person, that information and the date of the entry[295]. Companies are obliged to enter in the register details of rights granted to directors or secretaries to subscribe for shares or debentures[296] and details as to the exercise of such rights[297]. Section 60 of the CA 1990 prescribes certain matters relating to the register, and ss 61 and 62 make provision for the removal of entries from the register.

---

291 Section 58(6) of the CA 1990.

292 Section 58(5) of the CA 1990.

293 See generally, McGowan-Smyth & Daly, *Irish Company Secretary's Handbook* (2011, Bloomsbury Professional) at pp 692–702.

294 Section 59(1) of the CA 1990.

295 Section 59(2) of the CA 1990.

296 Section 59(3) of the CA 1990.

297 Section 59(4) of the CA 1990.

(ix) Notification of stock exchange

[13.117] Whenever a private company with debentures (ie, which has a debt listing) which is listed on the stock exchange is notified of any matter by a director or secretary in consequences of the fulfilment of an obligation imposed by ss 53 or 64 and that matter relates to debentures for which dealing facilities are provided, the company is obliged to notify the stock exchange of that matter[298]. This obligation must be fulfilled by the company before the end of the day next following that on which it arises[299] and the failure to comply is an offence for the company and every officer in default[300].

(x) Investigation of suspected contravention of ss 53 and 64

[13.118] The Director of Corporate Enforcement can appoint an inspector where he believes that there are circumstances suggesting that contraventions may have occurred in relation to shares and debentures of a company of ss 30, 53 or 64(3)–(5) to investigate whether such contraventions occurred[301].

[C] THE SECRETARY[302]

The requirement to have a secretary

[13.119] By s 175 of the CA 1963, every company, including single-member companies, must have a secretary, who may be one of the directors. In addition, s 175(2) provides:

> 'Anything required to be done by or to the secretary may, if the office is vacant or there is for any other reason no secretary capable of acting, be done by or to any assistant or deputy secretary or, if there is no assistant or deputy secretary capable of acting, by or to any officer of the company authorised generally or specially in that behalf by the directors.'

It should be noted that the prohibition[303] against companies having a body corporate as a director has no parallel in the case of secretaries, and indeed many incorporated companies provide secretarial services for many other Irish companies. Although it is permissible for a company to have more than one secretary[304], it would be unusual for a private company to have more than one secretary.

Appointment and cessation

[13.120] It should be noted that no formal qualifications are required to become the secretary of a private company[305]. The name of the first secretary must be notified to the

---

298 Section 65(1) of the CA 1990.

299 Section 65(2) of the CA 1990.

300 Section 65(3) of the CA 1990.

301 Section 66 of the CA 1990. See Ch 27, *Investigations and Inspectors*, at para **[27.018]**.

302 See generally, McGowan-Smyth & Daly, *Irish Company Secretary's Handbook* (2011, Bloomsbury Professional) at Ch 1.

303 Section 176(1) of the CA 1963.

304 Section 195(4) of the CA 1963.

305 *Cf* public limited companies: see Ch 29, *Public Limited Companies and SEs*, at para **[29.084]**.

CRO in the Form A1, as in the case of a company's first directors[306], accompanied by their consent to act as such[307]. The subsequent appointment of a company secretary will be in accordance with the articles of association of each company and changes must be notified to the CRO[308]. In this regard, it is common for companies to adopt reg 113 of Table A. This provides:

> 'The secretary shall be appointed by the directors for such term, at such remuneration, and upon such conditions as they think fit; and any secretary so appointed may be removed by them.'

Companies are obliged to notify the CRO of any cessation in the office of secretary and where the company fails to do this, an ex-secretary may effect notification, subject to the provisions of s 195(11A) of the CA 1963, considered above[309].

Status and remuneration

[13.121] A company's secretary, like its directors, is an office holder[310]. A company secretary's entitlement to remuneration and conditions of appointment will be set by the directors. A company secretary can have, but does not have to have, a contract of service or employment with the company.

Functions and duties

[13.122] The Companies Acts do not prescribe the function or duties of the company secretary; rather, this is the preserve of the board of director of a given company. It can be said, however, that in practice the functions and duties of a company secretary are essentially administrative, as opposed to managerial[311]. They typically involve the keeping of the various registers required to be kept under the Companies Acts[312]. In many private companies no clearly defined office of secretary will exist and many companies charge the performance of statutory tasks to the other 'secretary' who answers the telephone and does the typing! However, in the current environment of corporate compliance, companies who acquiesce in such practices do so at their peril[313].

[13.123] In *Barnett, Hoares & Co v South London Tramways Co*[314], Lord Esher MR said:

> 'A secretary is a mere servant; his position is that he is to do what he is told and no person can assume that he has any authority to represent anything at all.'

Commenting upon this passage, Lord Denning MR, in *Panorama Developments (Guilford) Ltd v Fidelis Furnishing Fabrics Ltd*[315], noted that times have changed since it

---

306 Section 3(1)(b) of the C(A)A 1982. See Ch 2, *Incorporation by Registration*, at para **[2.038]**.

307 Section 3(3) of the C(A)A 1982.

308 Section 195(6) of the CA 1963.

309 See para **[13.083]** *et seq*, *ante*.

310 See para **[13.003]** *ante*.

311 See Keane, *Company Law* (4th edn, Bloomsbury Professional, 2007) at para 28.02.

312 See Ch 2, *Incorporation by Registration*, at para **[2.037]** *et seq*.

313 See, generally, Ch 28, *Compliance and Enforcement*.

314 *Barnett, Hoares & Co v South London Tramways Co* (1887) 18 QBD 815 at 817.

315 *Panorama Developments (Guilford) Ltd v Fidelis Furnishing Fabrics Ltd* [1971] 3 All ER 16.

was uttered by Lord Esher in 1887. Lord Denning MR observed that the company secretary is a 'much more important person nowadays', being an officer with extensive duties and responsibilities. While this may be true in large private companies or plcs, it hardly reflects the reality in the vast majority of Irish private companies.

One of the great potential injustices of the Companies Acts is s 383(3) of the CA 1963 which provides that:

> 'It is the duty of each director and secretary of a company to ensure that the requirements of the Companies Acts are complied with by the company.'

The business of the management of companies will invariably be delegated by reg 80 of Table A to the directors and that fact justifies their inclusion in s 383(3); the secretary, on the other hand, will be empowered only to do that which is delegated to him by the board of directors. The potential injustice is that it is fundamentally unfair to make somebody responsible for matters that are entirely outside of his or her control[316]. This was recognised in *Wicklow County Council v O'Reilly et al*[317] by Clarke J who refused to join a company secretary in a 'fallback' order[318] concerning environmental pollution saying:

> 'Even a generous interpretation of the authorities and the underlying EU law could not in my view extend the jurisdiction to the making of orders against a company secretary as secretary. In that capacity the person concerned has no role of control or management over the company's affairs.'

The duties of the secretary are considered in Ch 15[319].

Disclosure requirements for secretaries

[13.124] Section 195(4) of the CA 1963 requires the *register of directors and secretaries* to contain the following particulars in relation to the secretary:

(a) in the case of an individual, his name, former names and his usual residential address;

(b) in the case of a body corporate, its name and registered office.

Company secretaries are also required to disclose their interests in shares held in the company, the details of which are set out in Part IV of the CA 1990, and considered in the context of company directors, above[320].

---

316 This is a matter which has been recognised by the CLRG and which is to be addressed in the forthcoming Companies Bill: compare s 220 (dealing with directors' duties) with s 223 (dealing with the secretary's duty).

317 *Wicklow County Council v O'Reilly et al* [2006] IEHC 265 (Clarke J).

318 It has recently been held in *The Environmental Protection Agency v Neiphin Trading Ltd et al* [2011] IEHC 67 that there is no jurisdiction to make 'fallback' orders (where the veil of incorporation is lifted and directors and shareholders of a company are held liable under the Waste Management Act 1996): see further Ch 5, *Disregarding Separate Legal Personality*, at para **[5.066]**.

319 Ch 15, *Duties of Directors and Other Officers*, at para **[15.154]** *et seq*.

320 See para **[13.100]** *et seq*, *ante*.

[D] DELEGATING MANAGERIAL POWER TO THE DIRECTORS

Root authority begins with the members

[13.125] Root, or residual, authority in a company vests in the members by virtue of s 18(2) of the CA 1963[321]. This provides, *inter alia*, that:

> 'From the date of incorporation ... the subscribers of the memorandum, together with such other persons as may from time to time become members of the company, shall be ... capable forthwith of exercising all the functions of an incorporated company ...'

Accordingly, the members of a company are entitled to appoint the board of directors and to dictate, whether *ab initio* or by future alteration, the specific provisions in the company's articles and memorandum of association. In this way the members are the *root authority* in a company. It should be remembered that the members are free to adopt any internal regulations they see fit and are certainly not obliged to adopt the model articles of association contained in Table A of the First Schedule. It is, for example, possible – albeit extremely unlikely in practice – that a company might be incorporated which leaves all power with the members, and does not make any delegation of powers to the directors[322]. Typically, however, the members will adopt the model articles and reg 80 of Table A, which is the cornerstone of corporate governance. Ironically, the very document to which the members give life typically emasculates them by operating to divest them of the powers of management. What can be given can also be taken away and having considered the usual delegation of the powers of management to the directors, this section shall then consider the circumstances in which members' powers can resurface.

Delegation of powers of management to the directors

[13.126] The vast majority of private companies incorporated in Ireland contain reg 80[323] (imported from Part 1 of Table A of the First Schedule to the CA 1963) in their articles of association. This most important of articles provides:

> 'The business of the company shall be managed by the directors, who may pay all expenses incurred in promoting and registering the company and may exercise all such powers of the company as are not, by the Act or by these regs, required to be exercised by the company in general meeting, subject, nevertheless, to any of these regs, to the provisions of the Act and to such directions, being not inconsistent with the aforesaid regs or provisions, as may be given by the company in general meeting; but no direction given by the company in general meeting shall invalidate any prior act of the directors which would have been valid if that direction had not been given.'

Therefore, unlike in certain other jurisdictions, in Ireland (and the United Kingdom) the source of the powers of boards of directors derives from the members of companies and

---

321 See Flynn, 'The Power to Direct' [1991] 13 DULJ 101.

322 In such an extreme situation, the company would still be required to have two formally appointed directors and the members are likely to be considered to be *de facto* directors by reason of their exercising powers normally delegated to directors.

323 Individual provisions in the articles of association contained in Table A are referred to as 'regulations' which is abbreviated here to 'reg' or 'regs'; particular provisions of a particular company's own articles of association are usually referred to as 'article' or 'articles'.

not from statute[324]. The effect of reg 80 of Table A is to vest the powers of management of the company's business in the directors, *exclusively*. Subject to the reservations contained in reg 80, considered below[325], and the members' ability to amend reg 80 by special resolution, the members cede to the directors the powers of management. So in *Howard Smith Ltd v Ampol Petroleum Ltd*[326], Lord Wilberforce said:

> 'The construction of a limited company normally provides for directors, with powers of management, and shareholders with defined voting powers having power to appoint the directors, and to take, in general meetings, by majority vote, decisions on matters not reserved for management ... directors, within their management powers, may take decisions against the wishes of the majority of shareholders, and indeed the majority of shareholders cannot control them in the exercise of these powers while they remain in office[327].'

This principle was applied in *Scott v Scott*[328]. There, the members passed, in general meeting, two resolutions: one as to the interim payment of dividends before the dividends were declared and the other as to the investigation of the company's financial affairs. It was held that both resolutions were invalid as they were attempts to usurp the powers of the directors given by the articles to determine the financial direction of the company.

[13.127] Regulation 80 of Table A delegates the powers to the 'directors', making no mention of the *board of directors*. However, the fact that a company must have at least two directors (s 174 of the CA 1963), that the directors will generally act by majority (reg 101) and that reg 80 delegates powers to the 'directors', plural, means that the delegation is to the board of directors. The vast majority of the boards of Irish and other common law countries' companies are *unitary* or *one-tier boards*. A *unitary board* is comprised of both executive and non-executive directors and is responsible for both running the business and ensuring compliance with strategies, policies and law.

In a *two-tier board* the two functions are separated so that there is a management board[329] and a supervisory board[330]. Whereas in the unitary model, where non-executive directors have been appointed, they will exercise a quasi-supervisory role in relation to executive directors, challenging the business, in a two-tier board there is a complete separation between management and supervision. Even without any statutory provisions facilitating an Irish company having a two-tier board, it is possible to create such a structure in a company's articles of association.

---

324 See Watson, 'The Significance of the Source of the Powers of Boards of Directors in UK Company Law' [2011] JBL 597.

325 At para **[13.130]**

326 *Howard Smith Ltd v Ampol Petroleum Ltd* [1974] AC 821.

327 *Howard Smith Ltd v Ampol Petroleum Ltd* [1974] AC 821 at 837.

328 *Scott v Scott* [1943] All ER Rep 582.

329 Wooldridge, 'The Management Board of German Public Companies' (2012) 33 Co Law 152.

330 See Wooldridge, 'The Composition and Functions of German Supervisory Boards' (2011) 32 The Company Lawyer 190; Sihler, 'The Tree Be Known by Its Fruits: One-tier or two-tier boards?' (2010) Boardroom 18; Belcher & Naruisch, 'The Evolution of Business Knowledge in the Context of Unitary and Two-Tier Board Structures' (2001) JBL 443.

[13.128] It should also be noted, for completeness, that in many companies the powers of management, delegated to the directors by reg 80, will be further delegated by the directors to managers and employees of the company. This delegation will take effect either by resolution of the board of directors or, where a managing director has been appointed (or other director conferred with authority to make such a delegation) by his authorised act in favour of the employee. Where directors effect such a delegation of managerial power, they have a duty to ensure it is properly exercised and they will remain accountable for any misuse of the delegated power[331].

The express reservations of power to members in reg 80 of Table A

[13.129] The delegation of the powers of management is, however, subject to the three express qualifications contained in reg 80, ie, it is:

(a) subject to the Companies Acts,
(b) subject to the other regulations in the articles of association[332], and
(c) subject to *directions* given by the members in general meeting where such are not inconsistent with the Companies Acts or the other regulations of the company's articles of association.

Of these three qualifications, (c) causes most controversy. The fact that the members do not, under model articles, fully divest themselves of all powers gives rise to the problem of the division of powers. Two distinct areas of debate are opened. The first is, in view of the extensive delegation of power to the board of directors, what powers remain with the members acting in general meeting? The second is, what is the effect of the members being empowered to give directions to the directors?

(a) Subject to the Companies Acts

[13.130] Even where reg 80 has been adopted, the Companies Acts provide that certain fundamental matters of corporate governance still require the assent of the members. This can be rationalised on the grounds that certain matters are so fundamental as to require the sanction of the *owners* of the company. In most private companies, the members and the directors will be one and the same, but nevertheless the law requires them to implement certain actions by voting in general meeting, wearing their members' hats. An example is where it is proposed that a company provide financial assistance in connection with the purchase of its own shares pursuant to s 60 of the CA 1963[333]. In this instance, the directors alone cannot legally sanction the action: the members of the company are required to pass a *special resolution*. Similarly, s 29 of the CA 1990 requires the members to pass an *ordinary resolution* to sanction a substantial property transaction between a director and the company.

---

[331] See Ch 15, *The Duties of Directors and Other Officers*, at para **[15.052]** *et seq*.

[332] Of course, if the articles of a company specifically give the members certain powers, or fetter the exercise of certain powers of the directors by making member-consent a prerequisite, the powers of management of the company by the directors are thus qualified.

[333] See Ch 10, *The Maintenance of Capital*, at para **[10.046]** *et seq*.

(b) Subject to other regulations in the articles of association

[13.131] The clearest example of a provision in the articles of association that confers a power on directors, subject to a claw-back in favour of the members, is model reg 79. The undiluted version of this article provides, *inter alia*, that the directors may exercise all the company's powers to borrow provided that the amount of the monies borrowed shall not exceed the nominal amount of the share capital of the company for the time being issued, '*without the previous sanction of the company in general meeting*', ie, by ordinary resolution of the members. As considered in a previous chapter, this article is typically modified on incorporation to give the directors an unfettered power to borrow[334]. In those rare companies where model reg 79 has been adopted, and the directors borrow in excess of the limits prescribed therein, it has been held that the members may ratify such unauthorised borrowing where the act of borrowing was itself within the capacity of the company, ie, where it was not *ultra vires*[335].

(c) Subject to directions given by the members

[13.132] The delegation to the directors of the power to manage is subject to the proviso contained in reg 80 that the directors' powers are subject to:

> '... such directions, being not inconsistent with the aforesaid regulations or provisions, as may be given by the company in general meeting ...'

The effects of this qualification and the extent to which the members in general meeting can control the directors have been the subject of some speculation[336]. It should be noted at the outset that any *directions* made by the members to the directors will not invalidate prior acts of the directors[337].

[13.0133] Regulation 80 must be considered in its historical context. Prior to the passing of the CA 1963, companies adopted a slightly different article under previous legislation. This provided that the members could give *regulations* as opposed to *directions*[338]. Indeed, the corresponding English modern provision still contains the word 'regulations', and, consequently, English case law must be viewed with caution. Judicial interpretation of the words 'such regulations' has held that the exclusive management of the company is vested in the directors and that the shareholders cannot interfere in the exercise of the directors' powers unless the shareholders amend the articles of association by inserting a new 'regulation', the effect of which is to wholly or partially oust the directors' powers of management. The old authorities in the United Kingdom[339] were applied in *Breckland Group Holdings Ltd v London and Suffolk*

---

334 See Ch 3, *Constitutional Documentation*, at para **[3.051]**.

335 See, for example, *Irvine v The Union Bank of Australia* (1877) 2 App Cas 366.

336 For a view which sees reg 80 as being a potential power base for the members, see Temple Lang, 'Shareholder Control in Irish Companies' (1973) Gazette ILSI 241; and for a contrary view see Ussher, 'Directing the Directors' (1975) Gazette ILSI 303. See generally, Ussher, *Company Law in Ireland* (1986, Sweet & Maxwell) pp 85–91 and Flynn, 'The Power to Direct' [1991] 13 DULJ 101.

337 Model reg 80.

338 Regulation 71 of the Companies (Consolidation) Act 1908.

339 *John Shaw & Sons (Salford) Ltd v Shaw* [1935] 2 KB 113; *Salmon v Quin & Axtens Ltd* [1909] AC 442; *Automatic Self-Cleansing Filter Syndicate Co Ltd v Cunningham* [1906] 2 Ch 34.

Properties Ltd et al[340]. In that case, the members of a company sought an injunction to prevent its directors from passing a board resolution to ratify the action of commencing a law suit. Harman J refused the injunction on the basis that:

> '... where matters are confided by the articles such as Article 80 to the conduct of the business by the directors, it is not a matter where the general meeting can intervene ... The principle, as I see it, is that Article 80 confides the management of the business to the directors and in such a case it is not for the general meeting to interfere[341].'

This case marks the present state of the English courts' interpretation of their corresponding model article to our reg 80. In *Alexander Ward and Co Ltd v Samyang Navigation Co Ltd*[342], Lord Kilbrandon said that:

> '... the directors, and no one else, are responsible for the management of the company, except in the matters specifically allotted to the company in general meeting.'

This interpretation means that exclusive power vests in the directors, save in respect of functions which are specifically reserved to the members in general meeting.

[13.134] Irish authorities have similarly interpreted the predecessor of model reg 80, which used the phrase 'such regulations'. In *Clark v Workman*[343], Ross J said:

> '... the powers given to directors are powers delegated to the directors by the company, and when once given the company cannot interfere in the subject-matter of the delegation unless by special resolution.'

However, the use of 'such directions' in the modern reg 80 of Table A casts some doubt on whether the management of the company exclusively vests in the directors. The word 'directions' might imply the members' directive, other than by an actual special resolution, the effect of which is to amend the articles of association by the insertion of a new article or 'regulation'. Although the judgment of Buckley LJ in *Gramophone and Typewriter Ltd v Stanley*[344] shows the deficiency in the use of the word 'regulations', so too does it demonstrate the significance of the use of the word 'directions'. In the course of his judgment Buckley LJ said:

> '... even a resolution of a numerical majority at a general meeting of the company cannot impose its will upon the directors when the articles have confided to them the control of the company's affairs. The directors are not servants to obey directions given by the shareholders as individuals; they are not agents appointed by and bound to serve the shareholders as their principals. They are persons who may by the regulations be entrusted with the control of the business, and if so entrusted they can be dispossessed from that control only by the statutory majority which can alter the articles[345].'

---

340 *Breckland Group Holdings Ltd v London and Suffolk Properties Ltd et al* [1989] BCLC 100.

341 *Breckland Group Holdings Ltd v London and Suffolk Properties Ltd et al* [1989] BCLC 100 at 106.

342 *Alexander Ward and Co Ltd v Samyang Navigation Co Ltd* [1975] 2 All ER 424; see also *Scott v Scott* [1943] 1 All ER 582.

343 *Clark v Workman* [1920] IR 107. See also *Nash v Lancegaye Safety Glass (Ireland) Ltd* (1958) ILTR 11 at 26, *per* Budd J.

344 *Gramophone and Typewriter Ltd v Stanley* [1980] 2 KB 89, [1908–10] All ER Rep 833.

345 *Gramophone and Typewriter Ltd v Stanley* [1980] 2 KB 89 at 105–106.

[13.135] The result of the use of the word 'directions' can be said to be as follows[346]: the members can direct the directors to do or refrain from doing certain acts only where to do so is not inconsistent with the articles of that company. Hence, where the articles themselves (apart from reg 80) expressly give the directors certain powers, the members cannot act in disregard of those powers by directing the directors as to how such powers should be exercised[347]. Accordingly, the members cannot direct the directors to register shares against their wishes, where model reg 3 of Part II has been adopted[348] or to pay an interim dividend where model reg 117 of Part I is adopted or a final dividend where model reg 116 of Part I is adopted. This approach has been confirmed as the correct approach by the High Court in *Ryanair Ltd v Aer Lingus Group plc*[349]. In this case the plaintiff, Ryanair, held 29.82% of the defendant, Aer Lingus's, issued share capital. Ryanair wrote to Aer Lingus relying on s 133B of the CA 1963, inserted by the Shareholders' Rights Directive[350], wishing to table two resolutions at its forthcoming AGM. The first resolution sought to declare the shareholders' belief that the company should declare and pay a dividend of €30m and the second sought to declare the shareholders' belief that no further payments should be made to the company's employees' pension scheme without prior shareholder approval[351]. Aer Lingus refused to table the resolutions on the grounds that the right to table resolutions under s 133B was not an absolute right and was subject to the articles of association, company and other law. Aer Lingus contended that the two resolutions were bad in law and could not, if passed, be lawfully implemented.

The reason why it was contended the first resolution was bad in law was because the directors had recommended that no dividend be paid for that year and article 111 of Aer Lingus's articles of association prohibited the company from declaring dividends by

---

346 See Ussher, *Company Law in Ireland* (1986, Sweet & Maxwell) at p 87 *et seq*.

347 These two sentences were cited by the defendant in *Ryanair Ltd v Aer Lingus Group plc* [2011] IEHC 170 and the principles applied by McGovern J in his decision.

348 In *Scott v Scott* [1943] All ER 582 at 584, Lord Clauston, after referring to a reg 117 type regulation, (which provides that 'The directors may from time to time pay to the members such interim dividends as appear to the directors to be justified by the profits of the company') said: 'It is quite clear, accordingly, that the payment of an interim dividend is a matter which, by that article, is placed within the exclusive power of the directors, unless I can find some other article which limits that ... I do not think it is suggested that, if this was a resolution for the payment of an interim dividend, that it could possibly be held to be valid, it having been passed by the company in general meeting. If it was, then the annual general meeting impinged upon the sphere of activity which, in the most express terms, is confined to the directors.'

349 *Ryanair Ltd v Aer Lingus Group plc* [2011] IEHC 170 (McGovern J).

350 See Ch 29, *Public Limited Companies and SEs*, at para **[29.103]**.

351 The resolutions provided: '(1) In view of the company's substantial cash reserves, which have increased by €56.5m during the year to €885m, and the two recent payments of €25m to the ESOT and €30m to the Revenue Commissioners arising from payments made to 715 staff under the 2009 Greenfield Programme, shareholders believe that the company should declare and pay a dividend of €30m for the year ended 31st December, 2010. (2) In view of the recent €25.3m payment to the ESOT and the €30m payment to the Irish Revenue, and the company's confirmation that its pension schemes operate on a defined contribution basis, shareholders believe that no further payments should be made either to the ESOT, or to any company pension schemes over and above the existing defined contribution rates, without prior shareholder approval.'

ordinary resolution in excess of the amount recommended by the directors. Accordingly, although its articles of association contained an article materially identical to reg 80, conferring power on the directors to manage its business *subject to such directions given in general meeting*, it was contended that the members in general meeting could not by resolution override that recommendation. It was contended that the second resolution was bad in law because the power to determine what, if any, pension benefits the company will provide had been entrusted to the directors by the articles of association so that the members in general meeting could not, by ordinary resolution, seek to override or fetter that exclusive power.

The learned McGovern J concluded as follows:

> 'I accept the submissions of the defendant that the directors have recommended to the members that no dividend be paid and that the first of the proposed resolutions by the plaintiff seeks to circumvent Article 111. This is not permissible. The Company was entitled to refuse to put this resolution before the AGM since it was not within the power of the members by ordinary resolution to declare a dividend which exceeds the amount recommended by the directors. In this case, the directors were recommending no dividend.
>
> I also accept the submissions of the defendant concerning the second proposed resolution on the pension scheme ... The board has been given power to determine what (if any) pension benefits the Company will provide and to determine what payments are to be made to the Company's pension scheme. Since this power is given to the directors under the Articles of Association, the members, in general meeting, cannot, by ordinary resolution, seek to override or fetter that exclusive power. If the directors cannot or will not exercise a power vested in them, then the general meeting may do so. But that has not happened here. The Court of Appeal in *Automatic Self-Cleansing Filter Syndicate Co v Cuninghame* [1906] 2 Ch 34, stated clearly that the division of powers between the board of directors and the company in general meeting depended, in the case of registered companies, entirely on the construction of the articles of association, and that, where powers had been vested in the board, the general meeting could not interfere with their exercise. The articles were held to constitute a contract by which the members had agreed that the directors should manage certain aspects of the company's affairs. In *Scott v Scott* [1943] 1 All ER 582, it was held that resolutions of a general meeting which might be interpreted either as directions to pay an interim dividend or as instructions to make loans were nullities in circumstances where the relevant powers have been delegated to the directors. The second resolution proposed by the plaintiff also offends against this principle, since it seeks to usurp or override the powers of the directors specifically given to them under the articles of association[352].'

[13.136] An example of where the Irish article might allow the members to direct the directors is where the members wished the directors to do something outside of the *management of the business* or otherwise expressly delegated to the directors. It has been opined that members may direct the directors to commence or desist from litigation because the power to commence litigation is not *specifically* delegated to the directors but this will depend upon whether litigating may be said to be outside of the management of the business. Accordingly, the powers of members may be said, in practice, to be dependent upon chance: they can only give directions to the directors upon matters that the articles have not exclusively remitted to the directors. That said, it is thought that maximum latitude will be given by the courts to the expression 'the

352 *Ryanair Ltd v Aer Lingus Group plc* [2011] IEHC 170 at paras 17 and 18.

business of the company', which is what reg 80 entrusts to the management of the directors.

[13.137] Where the directors refuse to follow the members' wishes, one solution may be for the members to muster sufficient support to pass a special resolution amending the articles. In this respect, the Irish reality is in practice not all that different to the scenario outlined in *John Shaw & Sons (Salford) Ltd v Shaw*[353], where it was said that:

> 'The only way in which the general body of the shareholders can control the exercise of the powers vested by the articles in the directors is *by altering their articles* ...'

Only by altering by special resolution the articles of association of a company can the members safely reassume the powers of management in the company. Where a separation of corporate powers exists the members will seldom have to exercise their legislative powers in this manner. This is because the directors' knowledge of the members' power to regain control will often be sufficient to ensure they comply with the members' wishes because, otherwise, there is every reason to expect that they (the directors) will be ousted by ordinary resolution[354]. More frequently, there will not be a complete separation of corporate powers, and disputes may arise where the members are not a united body and some or all of their number are also the company's directors.

The resurgence of members' powers

[13.138] Notwithstanding that the members delegate most of their powers to the directors, the members' powers may resurface. The three most common occasions when this will happen are:

(a) Where there are no directors capable of acting;
(b) Where the directors exceed their delegated authority;
(c) Where directors act in breach of their duties.

(a) Where there are no directors capable of acting

[13.139] In the first place, the members will always be the persons to whom power *reverts in default*. So, where the directors resign or die or become incapacitated, it is the members to whom power will revert in default. An example of this 'power in default' is seen in *Mahony v East Holyford Mining Co*[355], where it was held that where there was no official board of directors the members of the company had the power to 'hold out' certain of their number as being directors. The ability to hold out persons as something that they are not, is the essence of authority. Similarly, in *Alexander Ward and Co Ltd v Samyang Navigation Co Ltd*[356], two individuals issued a summons against the defendant company on behalf of the plaintiff company which had no directors. The defendant company later sought to have the action set aside on the ground that the plaintiff company had not authorised the action. The plaintiff company contended that it was open to the company subsequently to ratify the action under ordinary principles of

---

353 *John Shaw & Sons (Salford) Ltd v Shaw* [1935] All ER 456 at 464, *per* Greer LJ.

354 In accordance with s 182(1) of the CA 1963: see para **[13.077]** *ante*.

355 *Mahony v East Holyford Mining Co* (1875) LR 7 HL 869, considered in Ch 7, *Corporate Contracts, Capacity and Authority*, at para **[7.107]**.

356 *Alexander Ward and Co Ltd v Samyang Navigation Co Ltd* [1975] 2 All ER 424.

agency. The articles of association of the plaintiff company contained a reg 80 type regulation which delegated the powers of management to the directors. Lord Hailsham held that where no directors had been appointed, residual authority to do such things reverted to the members in general meeting. Accordingly, the action on behalf of the company was capable of ratification. He said:

> 'In my opinion at the relevant time the company was fully competent ... to raise proceedings ... The company could have done so either by appointing directors or as I think by authorising proceedings in general meeting which, in the absence of an effective board, has a residual authority to use the company's powers ... it was competent to do so, and in my view it was therefore a competent principal ...[357].'

(b) Where the directors exceed their delegated authority

[13.140] The second set of circumstances in which the members' powers resurface is where the directors exceed their delegated authority. An example in point is the case of *Re Burke Clancy & Co Ltd*[358]. In that case, the directors of the company purported to borrow more money than they were authorised, under the articles of association, to borrow[359]. However, the members of the company approved of the accounts of the company in general meeting. Of this, Kenny J said:

> 'It is established law that the members of a company may ratify acts which are outside the powers of the directors but are *intra vires* the company ... the approval of the accounts showing the amount borrowed was a ratification by the company of the action of the directors in borrowing an amount in excess of the [authorised limit][360].'

In one of the decisions relied upon by Kenny J, *Grant v United Kingdom Switchback Railways Company*[361], the articles of a company authorised the sale of part of its undertaking to another company; they also contained a provision prohibiting any director from voting in respect of any contract in which he was interested. The directors of the company caused the company to enter into a contract for the sale of part of its undertaking to another company, of which all of the directors of the first company, except one, were also directors. At a general meeting of the company an ordinary resolution was passed approving and adopting the agreement for sale. Lindley LJ held that the adoption of the contract was within the objects of the company, did not amount to an alteration of the articles of association and thus could be sanctioned by an ordinary, as opposed to a special, resolution. He said:

> 'The appellant contends that the company could not ratify this contract except by special resolution. In my opinion that contention is unfounded. There is a broad distinction

---

[357] *Alexander Ward and Co Ltd v Samyang Navigation Co Ltd* [1975] 2 All ER 424 at 428.

[358] *Re Burke Clancy & Co Ltd* (23 May 1974, unreported) HC.

[359] See the present reg 79, which limits the borrowing powers of the directors, to borrow an amount which does not exceed the issued share capital. This is typically deleted by companies upon formation, but if it is not deleted *ab initio*, when that company decides to approach a bank to borrow money, then the bank or other financial institution will insist that it is deleted. See also *Re Shannonside Holdings Ltd* (20 May 1993, unreported) HC, *per* Costello J.

[360] *Re Burke Clancy & Co Ltd* (23 May 1974, unreported) HC at pp 9, 10 of the transcript. Kenny J followed the cases of *Irvine v Union Bank of Australia* (1877) 2 App Cas 366 and *Grant v United Kingdom Switchback Railways Company* (1888) 40 Ch D 135.

[361] *Grant v United Kingdom Switchback Railways Company* (1888) 40 Ch D 135.

> between altering the articles and merely saying 'this act was not authorised by the articles, but we will ratify it'. The shareholders can ratify any contract which comes within the powers of the company, and this contract clearly does, for the articles expressly authorise selling any part of the undertaking of the company[362].'

The *raison d'être* for the members in general meeting being able to validate unauthorised acts of the directors which are *intra vires* the company's capacity is because the directors' powers derive from the members. The members of a company cannot, however, ratify acts that are *ultra vires* the company[363]. Were the directors to cause the company to engage in *ultra vires* activities, then not only would they be exceeding the ambit of the authority conferred upon them by the members, but they would also be acting beyond the company's capacity to act. After the commencement of a company's winding-up, a liquidator is competent to ratify acts done without authority[364].

(c) Where directors act in breach of their duties

[13.141] The third set of circumstances in which the inherent powers of the members may resurface is where the members ratify breaches of directors' duties at any time before a company is wound up. In most circumstances, the members in general meeting can absolve the directors of their wrongdoings, provided those wrongdoings are *intra vires*. A good example of this is seen in *Bamford and another v Bamford et al*[365]. In that case, 90% of a company's authorised capital had been issued and the articles provided that the power to issue shares was vested in the directors. When a takeover bid was made, the directors allotted the remaining 10% of the unissued capital at par value to a principal distributor of the company's products. The plaintiffs – who were two shareholders in the company – instituted proceedings, claiming that the allotment was invalid as in making the allotment the directors had not acted *bona fide*, but with an improper motive, namely to stymie the takeover bid. The directors responded by convening an extraordinary general meeting of the company and despite the plaintiffs issuing further proceedings for a declaration that any ratifying resolution would be invalid, a majority of the company's members passed an ordinary resolution, ratifying the allotment of the unissued 10% of the company's shares by the directors. At trial, Plowman J held that the directors' allotment was capable of being ratified and that the actions of the members in ratifying the allotment had validated it, and this was upheld by the Court of Appeal. Harman LJ said:

> 'I am expressing the view which I have held throughout – that this is a tolerably plain case. It is trite law, I had thought, that if directors do acts, as they do every day, especially in private companies, which, perhaps because there is no quorum, or because their appointment was defective, or because sometimes there are no directors properly appointed at all, or because they are actuated by improper motives, they go on doing for years, carrying on the business of the company in that way in which, if properly

---

[362] *Grant v United Kingdom Switchback Railways Company* (1888) 40 Ch D 135 at 139, 140.

[363] *Ashbury Railway Carriage and Iron Co v Riche* (1875) LR 7 HL 256. For criticism of the members' inability to ratify *ultra vires* acts, see Ussher, *Company Law in Ireland* (1986, Sweet & Maxwell) at p 131.

[364] *Alexander Ward & Co Ltd and another v Samyang Navigation Co Ltd* [1975] 1 WLR 673.

[365] *Bamford and another v Bamford et al* [1970] 1 Ch 212.

> constituted, they should carry it on, and then they find that everything has been so to speak wrongly done because it was not done by a proper board, such directors can, by making a full and frank disclosure and calling together the general body of the shareholders, obtain absolution and forgiveness of their sins; and provided the acts are not ultra vires the company as a whole everything will go on as if it had been done all right from the beginning. I cannot believe that that is not a commonplace of company law. It is done every day. Of course, if the majority of the general meeting will not forgive and approve, the directors must pay for it[366].'

Moreover, the English Court of Appeal in that case rejected the contention that a special resolution was required to ratify the wrongs of directors. The wrong there involved an action (allotment of shares) that was within the contemplation of the articles of association; it was only 'wrong' because the directors exercised their powers to allot shares for an improper purpose. In these circumstances, Russell LJ said that since it would be a matter for the company by ordinary resolution to decide whether to proceed against the directors for compensation for misfeasance, the company could validly decide by ordinary resolution not to institute proceedings. This, he said, supported entirely the view that an ordinary resolution 'would be effective, having as it would in substance the same purpose and effect as a resolution not to bring the proceedings to avoid the allotment'[367].

[13.142] The members need not wait until there has been a breach of duty, and they can act in anticipation of a breach of duty and prospectively release the directors from their duties. Perhaps the best example of this is seen in the leading case on directors' conflicts of interest: *Regal (Hastings) Ltd v Gulliver*[368]. There, Lord Russell said of the options open to the directors whom, it was held, had made a profit from their relationship with their company that:

> 'They could, had they wished, have protected themselves by resolution (either antecedent or subsequent) of the Regal shareholders in general meeting. In default of such approval, the liability to account must remain.'

It should be noted, however, that while the members in general meeting may absolve the directors of breaches of their duties to the company, they cannot release the directors of breaches of duties owed to individual members or to a minority of shareholders[369]. There is a principle that an act authorised by all of the shareholders is in law an act of the company[370]. In *Re D'Jan of London Ltd*[371], Hoffmann LJ held that that principle required that the shareholders should have, whether formally or informally, mandated or ratified the act in question and that it was not enough that they *probably would have ratified* if they had known or thought about it before the appointment of a liquidator[372].

---

366 *Bamford and another v Bamford et al* [1970] 1 Ch 212 at 237, 238.

367 *Bamford and another v Bamford et al* [1970] 1 Ch 212 at 242G.

368 *Regal (Hastings) Ltd v Gulliver* [1967] 2 AC 134, the facts of which are considered in Ch 15, *Duties of Directors and Other Officers*, at para **[15.058]**.

369 For members' personal rights see Ch 8, *Shares and Membership*, at para **[8.089]** and Ch 11, *Shareholders' Remedies*, at para **[11.103]**.

370 *Multinational Gas and Petrochemical Co v Multinational Gas and Petrochemical Services Ltd* [1983] Ch 258.

371 *Re D'Jan of London Ltd* [1993] BCC 646.

372 *Re D'Jan of London Ltd* [1993] BCC 646 at 648.

Chapter 14

Corporate Governance: Meetings

[14.001] Where the managers (the directors) and the owners (the shareholder-members) of a company are different people, the holding of meetings of both members and directors will be the cornerstone of sound corporate governance, providing a focal point for directors' accountability. It is a statutory requirement that all companies (except single-member private limited companies)[1] *must* hold an annual general meeting ('AGM') of their members; extraordinary general meetings ('EGMs') will be required from time to time where the statutory approval of members (by ordinary or special resolution) is required for particular matters. As was considered in the previous chapter, the management of companies is invariably vested in the directors; meetings of the directors, whether formal or informal, will be required in order to take particular decisions in the management of companies.

[14.002] The practice of corporate governance in many Irish private companies differs greatly from the prevailing practices in public companies, particularly those regulated by the Irish Stock Exchange[2]. More often than not, the pomp and ceremony of formal meetings of the board of directors and of the members, as portrayed in television drama, bears no relation to the practice of meetings in small Irish private companies. For a substantial number of Irish private companies, meetings of the members and of the directors will more often be held in the public house or over the breakfast table than in any 'boardroom'. Formal notice of meetings, in particular, is often forgotten unless a company is involved in a transaction with a credit institution, which makes the observance of formalities a prerequisite to the draw-down of loan facilities.

[14.003] Another feature of many Irish private companies is that the relationship between members and directors is frequently blurred by reason of their being one and the same people. This duality of roles can even result in participants at meetings not being sure whether they are attending a members' general meeting or a directors' meeting[3]. This recognition of the reality for many companies should not be taken as an endorsement of such practices; the formalities imposed by the Companies Acts must be complied with and defective practices can result in resolutions that were thought to have been passed, being set aside. This chapter considers meetings of both members and directors.

---

1 See para **[14.006]** *post*.

2 See Ch 29, *Public Limited Companies and SEs*, at para **[29.089]** *et seq* where the requirements of *The Combined Code* are discussed.

3 See, for example, *Re Aston Colour Print Ltd* (21 February 1997, unreported) HC, considered at para **[14.125]** *post*.

[A] MEMBERS' MEETINGS[4]

[14.004] Members' general meetings are the fora at which the will of a company's members can be elicited, decisions reserved to members taken and at which members are formally provided with certain information on the company. With the exception of the AGM, which is a statutory requirement, the holding of members' meetings is largely at the discretion of the company[5]. One of the most common – although not exclusive – reasons for convening EGMs is for the purposes of 'considering and if thought proper, adopting' a particular resolution. With a few notable exceptions[6], most resolutions can be passed without holding a members' meeting by using the unanimous *written resolution* procedure, facilitated by s 141(8) of the CA 1963[7]. In appropriate cases, where the articles of association[8] so permit, s 141(8) can substantially alleviate what might be considered, not unreasonably, excessive bureaucracy in small companies. The unanimous written resolution procedure and resolutions in general are considered below[9]. Even more dynamic is the *written decision* mechanism open to the sole member of a single-member private limited company, which is facilitated by reg 9 of the EC(SMPLC)R 1994[10].

[14.005] In this section the legal issues arising in members' meetings are considered under the following headings:

1. The annual general meeting.
2. Extraordinary general meetings.
3. Notice of members' meetings.
4. Notice of business to be conducted at a meeting.
5. The quorum.
6. Postponing and adjourning meetings.
7. Voting at members' meetings.
8. Minutes of members' meetings.
9. Resolutions.

---

4 See generally, Cordes et al, *Shackleton on The Law and Practice of Meetings* (12th edn, Sweet & Maxwell, 2011) at pp 105–220; and Davies et al, *Modern Law of Meetings* (2nd edn, Jordans, 2009).

5 An exception is the requirement to convene an EGM where a company suffers a serious capital loss: s 40 of the C(A)A 1983.

6 Resolutions to appoint or remove auditors (s 160 of the CA 1963) or to remove directors (s 182 of the CA 1963) cannot be passed as written resolutions: see para **[14.092]**.

7 In the case of single-member private limited companies, an alternative to the written resolution procedure is the written decision procedure facilitated by reg 9 of the EC(SMPLC)R 1994.

8 This is where model reg 6 of Part II of Table A, or a bespoke equivalent, is adopted.

9 See para **[14.090]** *post*.

10 Only decisions to remove auditors may not be taken by written decision; see para **[14.088]** *post*.

The annual general meeting

[14.006] It is mandatory[11] that every multi-member company holds an AGM, and s 131(1) of the CA 1963 provides that companies *must*, in each calendar year[12], hold an AGM. The primary requirement in s 131(1) for an *annual* general meeting is further limited – and not relaxed[13] – by the requirement that not more than 15 monthly intervals may elapse between AGMs. There is one exception to this general rule, contained in s 131(2), which provides that so long as a company holds its first AGM within 18 months of its incorporation, it is not obliged to hold an AGM in the year of its incorporation or in the following year[14].

[14.007] The AGM in private companies is considered under five sub-headings:

- (a) The purpose of the AGM;
- (b) AGMs must generally be held within the State;
- (c) Ministerial direction to call an AGM;
- (d) Possible consequences where AGM not held;
- (e) AGMs in single-member private limited companies.

(a) The purpose of the AGM

[14.008] Historically, the AGM was intended to give the investing public an opportunity to meet the directors of their company, to receive certain information and to ask questions. In many private companies (especially those where the directors and members are one and the same) little remains of this rationale; indeed the Company Law Review Group has recommended that all companies except public limited companies ('PLCs') should be permitted to dispense with holding an AGM where the members unanimously so resolve[15]. The purpose behind the statutory obligation on companies to hold an AGM is primarily to provide an annual forum at which the directors can comply with their statutory duties. Accordingly, in each financial year, company directors must lay before the company's members in general meeting the annual financial statements (ie, accounts), the directors' report and the auditors' report on the financial statements. It is thought, however, that the requirement to lay financial statements before members at an AGM only arises where there are financial statements to be laid and that an AGM can be validly held without laying financial statements before the members. It would seem unnecessarily restrictive to prevent a general meeting held, say, three months after

---

11 An elective, as opposed to mandatory, regime applies in the case of single-member private limited companies: see para **[14.014]** *post*.

12 'Year' has been held to mean a *calendar year* and not a period of 12 months from the date of incorporation: *Gibson v Barton* (1875) QB 329; see also s 21 of the Interpretation Act 2005 where in Part 1 of the Schedule, 'year' when used in an enactment is defined thus: 'when used without qualification, means a period of 12 months beginning on the 1st day of January in any year.'

13 This does not mean that companies are entitled to hold their AGM every 15 months, as the primary obligation is that an AGM is held *each calendar year*. So, for example, if a company holds an AGM on 30 November 2001, its next AGM must be held not later than 31 December 2002 (a period of only 13 months), since there must be an AGM in the calendar year 2002.

14 Section 131(1) and (2) is mirrored by model reg 48 of Part 1 of Table A.

15 See the CLRG, *First Report* (2000–2001), recommendation 4.5.6 at p 66.

incorporation from being a company's AGM for that year by reason only of the fact that it would be impractical to have prepared and audited financial statements to lay before that meeting. The requirement to lay financial statements before members is considered in detail in Ch 17[16]. Moreover, where a company's articles of association require directors to retire by rotation, the election or re-election of directors will typically occur at the AGM.

[14.009] Model reg 53 of Table A provides that all business that is transacted at an AGM shall be deemed to be 'special business' with the exception of declaring a dividend, the consideration of the accounts, balance sheets and reports of the directors and auditors, the election of directors in the place of those retiring, the re-appointment of the retiring auditors and the fixing of the remuneration of the auditors. The question of whether something constitutes ordinary business or special business at an AGM is of diminishing relevance[17].

(b) AGMs must generally be held within the State

[14.010] By virtue of s 140 of the CA 1963, and reg 47 of Table A, the AGM of a company must be held within the State[18]. This, however, is subject either to the company's articles providing otherwise, a resolution being passed in general meeting or the members' unanimously resolving in writing that it be held elsewhere[19].

(c) Ministerial direction to call an AGM

[14.011] Under the CA 1963, a member of a company can request the Minister for Jobs, Enterprise and Innovation to call or direct the calling of an AGM, but such requests are rare[20]. Section 131(3) provides:

> 'If default is made in holding a meeting of the company in accordance with *subsection (1)*, the Minister may, on the application of any member of the company, call or direct the calling of a general meeting of the company and give such ancillary or consequential directions as the Minister thinks expedient, including directions modifying or supplementing in relation to the calling holding and conducting of the meeting, the operation of the company's articles, and it is hereby declared that the directions which may be given under this subsection include a direction that one member of the company present in person or by proxy shall be deemed to constitute a meeting.'

---

16 See Ch 17, *Financial Statements, Audit and Annual Returns*, at para **[17.017]** *et seq*.

17 See para **[14.051]** *post* where the relevance of special business in the context of notice periods is considered.

18 Section 140(1) provides: 'Subject to subsection (2), the annual general meeting of a company shall be held in the State and any business transacted at a meeting held in breach of this requirement shall be void unless—(a) either all the members entitled to attend and vote at such meeting consent in writing to its being held elsewhere or a resolution providing that it be held elsewhere has been passed at the preceding annual general meeting; and (b) the articles do not provide that the annual general meeting shall be held in the State.' This is, however, subject to s 140(2), which provides: 'Subsection (1) shall not apply to the first annual general meeting of a company held on or after the operative date.'

19 See s 140(1) and (2) of the CA 1963.

20 Section 131(3)–(5) of the CA 1963.

The obligation is placed upon the company and its officers to hold the meeting by virtue of s 131(6), and where a failure to hold the meeting is detected, the company and its officers can be fined[21]. Although the instances of criminal prosecutions under the Companies Acts have been rare, prosecutions are not unknown.[22]

(d) Possible consequences where AGM not held

[14.012] In certain circumstances the failure to hold an AGM may, depending upon the company's articles of association's provisions on rotation and retirement of directors, mean that some or all of the directors will cease to hold office. In *Kansen v Rialto (West End) Ltd*[23], the company's articles of association were materially identical to reg 92 of Table A, which provides:

> 'At the first annual general meeting of the company all the directors shall retire from office, and at the annual general meeting in every subsequent year, one-third of the directors for the time being, of if their number is not three or a multiple of three, then the number nearest one-third shall retire from office.'

In that case, the court heard that an AGM at which a certain Mr Cromie should have retired as director, was not held in the year 1942. It was determined that he had vacated office on 31 December 1941 by reason of this article. Similarly in *Re Zinotty Properties*[24], it was held that the effect of a materially identical article was that since no AGMs had been held, the original directors must be deemed to have retired.

The clearest example of this in action is seen in *Re Consolidated Nickel Mines Ltd*[25]. In this case, a company's directors made claims for remuneration against the company's liquidator but the liquidator denied the claims on the grounds that the directors had vacated office. The basis of the liquidator's contention was that the company's articles provided that 'At the ordinary meeting in 1906 all directors and in every subsequent year one-third of all the directors shall retire from office. A retiring director shall retain office until the dissolution of the meeting at which his successor is elected.' No general meetings were held in either 1906 or 1907 and it was held that the meaning of that particular article was that:

> '... the holding of office of director was only to last until the end of 1906, or until the earlier date on which the ordinary meeting for that year was held ... The duty of the directors was to call a meeting in 1906 and 1907, and they cannot take advantage of their own default in that respect and say that they still remain as director[26].'

---

21 Section 131(6) of the CA 1963. See *Smedley v Registrar of Joint Stock Companies* [1919] 1 KB 97.

22 See, for example, *Re Muckross Park Hotel Ltd* (21 February 2001) DC, reported in (2001) Irish Times, 22 February, where it was reported that a company and its directors were successfully prosecuted for failing to hold an AGM of the company in 1999. This was despite having been notified of their breach by the Department of Jobs, Enterprise and Innovation on a number of occasions. The defendants were fined a total of £1,200 and ordered to pay expenses of £400 at Killarney District Court.

23 *Kansen v Rialto (West End) Ltd* [1944] Ch 346.

24 *Re Zinotty Properties* [1984] 1 WLR 1249. See also *Alexander Ward and Co Ltd v Samyang Navigation Co Ltd* (1973) SLT 80.

25 *Re Consolidated Nickel Mines Ltd* [1914] 1 Ch 883.

26 *Re Consolidated Nickel Mines Ltd* [1914] 1 Ch 883 at 888.

[14.013] This line of authority was distinguished by Costello J in *Phoenix Shannon plc et al v Purkey et al*[27]. In that case, the defendants were co-opted to the board of the plaintiff company and the existing directors, with the exception of the second and third plaintiffs (who between them held 81% of the issued share capital) resigned. The directors were co-opted under the company's article 92, a bespoke article which provided:

> 'The directors may from time to time and at any time appoint any person to be a director either to fill a casual vacancy or as an additional director provided that the total number of directors shall not exceed the maximum number fixed by or in accordance with these Articles. Subject to the provisions of the Acts, a director so appointed shall hold office only until the commencement of the annual general meeting following next after his appointment, when he shall retire. A director who retires under this article shall be eligible for re-appointment at the meeting at which he retires[28].'

No AGM was held in the year 1996 and the plaintiffs argued that the effect was that all six directors who had been co-opted in 1996 had automatically vacated office by reason of article 92. At trial, in support of this contention, the plaintiffs relied upon the decision in *Re Consolidated Nickel Mines Ltd.* The second plaintiff conceded that he too had vacated office because of his obligation to retire by rotation. The third plaintiff then purported to exercise his powers under the company's articles[29] to co-opt the second plaintiff back as a director and together they co-opted four more directors. The defendants – the six directors who had been co-opted in 1996 – disputed that they had been automatically retired by reason of the failure to hold the AGM and, despite the authorities cited in the previous paragraph, Costello J agreed with the defendants, finding that they had not vacated office by reason of the failure to hold an AGM in 1996. Costello J said:

> 'I agree that the 'annual general meeting next following' the date of co-option referred to in article 92 must refer to the annual general meeting which should be held under article 52 and section 131 [of the CA 1963]. But the article is silent as to what is to happen if the directors fail in their duty to convene the meeting. In effect the plaintiff requires the court to imply a provision in article 92 to the effect that should the directors fail to convene an annual general meeting as required by the article the co-opted directors will automatically vacate office on the last day on which the meeting should lawfully have been held[30].'

Costello J assigned two reasons for deciding that the court should not imply such a provision. In the first place, he found it significant that s 131(3) of the CA 1963 makes express provision as to what is to happen should the directors default in convening an annual general meeting and said that:

> 'These provisions not only provide a practical remedy should the directors fail to convene an annual general meeting but also a means by which the default can be legally rectified

---

27 *Phoenix Shannon plc et al v Purkey et al* [1998] 4 IR 597.

28 The company's bespoke article was largely based on what is model reg 98 of Part I of Table A.

29 The company's article in question was article 106 which broadly corresponded to reg 103 of Table A.

30 *Phoenix Shannon plc et al v Purkey et al* [1998] 4 IR 597 at 603.

> ... In the light of this express statutory provision should default occur I do not think the court should imply into the article the suggested provision of automatic resignations[31].'

The second reason Costello J gave for refusing to imply such a provision into the company's article 92 was because the company's bespoke article dealing with the circumstances in which the office of director shall be vacated did not cite, as a ground, the failure to hold an AGM. Costello J went on to say that the same arguments applied to the company's article dealing with rotation of directors.

Having thus determined the matter in favour of the defendants, Costello J went on to review the UK authorities considered above[32]. Costello J distinguished the decision in *Re Consolidated Nickel Mines Ltd*[33] on the basis that there, the articles provided that all of the directors would retire at the AGM to be held in 1906 and that in every subsequent year one-third would resign. Costello J said that he agreed with the construction placed upon the company's articles in that case but said:

> 'The court decided that the ordinary and natural meaning of the words used in the article was that, having specified the year in which the directors were to resign, vacation of office would occur at the end of that year, even if the company failed to hold an annual general meeting at which the resignations would formally take place. The construction does not assist the court in construing an entirely different clause, one which provides for the resignation of co-opted directors not in a specified year but at the happening of a future event, the 'annual general meeting next following' their appointment. In *In re Consolidated Nickel Mines Ltd* [1914] 1 Ch 883, *the court constr*ued the article in accordance with the words used – in this case the court is required to imply a provision into the relevant article ...'

Costello J held that the decision in *Consolidated Nickel Mines* was of no assistance and meant he did not have to qualify his views on the articles of the plaintiff company; he went on to dismiss, also, the relevance of the other authorities mentioned above. Costello J seemed at pains to prevent the plaintiffs from deriving benefit from the *Consolidated Nickel Mines* line of authorities without going so far as to expressly decline to follow them. It may be that the learned judge believed that the justice of the case leaned against the plaintiffs using the failure to hold an AGM as a convenient way of ousting the defendants. It is thought that this decision gives rise to considerable uncertainty and it is not clear whether an Irish court would interpret reg 92 of Table A to mean that a failure to hold an AGM results in automatic retirement or not.

(e) AGMs in single-member private limited companies

[14.014] Notwithstanding s 131 of the CA 1963, reg 8(1) of the EC(SMPLC)R 1994[34] provides:

> 'The sole member of a single-member company may decide, in the manner provided for in regulation 9, to dispense with the holding of annual general meetings and, if he or she does so, s 131 of the Principal Act [ie, the CA 1963] shall not apply to the company.'

---

31 *Phoenix Shannon plc et al v Purkey et al* [1998] 4 IR 597 at 604.

32 See para **[14.012]** *ante.*

33 *Re Consolidated Nickel Mines Ltd* [1914] 1 Ch 883.

34 SI 275/1994.

Regulation 8(1) is an elective provision, whereby the sole member of a single-member company can hold or dispense with holding an AGM if he so wishes. The sole member or the company's auditor may subsequently call an AGM under reg 8(3), which provides:

> 'In any year in which an annual general meeting would, but for a decision pursuant to paragraph (1) be required to be held, and in which no such meeting has been held, the sole member or the auditor of a single-member company may, by notice to the company not later than three months before the end of the year, require the holding of an annual general meeting in that year.'

When such notice is given to the company, the provisions of s 131 of the CA 1963 are again applied with respect to the calling of the meeting and the consequences of default[35]. It may be noted here[36] that corporate accounting requirements in the Companies Acts that require accounts[37] and other matters to be laid before the AGM are deemed to be satisfied where such accounts and reports are sent to the sole member within 21 days before the appropriate date[38], in accordance with s 159 of the CA 1963[39].

Extraordinary general meetings

[14.015] An EGM has the potential to be the most dynamic of the two varieties of members' meetings since it will be convened where it is proposed to do something new, even if not quite 'extraordinary', in the vernacular sense of that word. Under model reg 53, all business shall be deemed 'special' that is transacted at an EGM[40]. Four particular circumstances in which EGMs can be called are next considered:

(a) EGMs convened by the directors;
(b) EGMs convened on the requisition of qualified members;
(c) EGMs convened by order of the court;
(d) EGMs convened on the requisition of retiring auditors.

(a) EGMs convened by the directors

[14.016] Model reg 50 of Table A provides that an EGM can be called in either of two ways. In the first place, under reg 50, the directors of the company may call an EGM. Model reg 50 goes on to provide:

> '... If at any time there are not within the State sufficient directors capable of acting to form a quorum, any director or any 2 members of the company may convene an extraordinary general meeting in the same manner as nearly as possible as that in which meetings may be convened by the directors.'

An EGM may be called at the directors' behest where, for example, they wish to obtain the prior approval of the members as required under the Companies Acts (eg, for a substantial property transaction within the meaning of s 29 of the CA 1990) before

35 Regulation 8(4) of the EC(SMPLC)R 1994.
36 See further Ch 17, *Financial Statements, Audit and Annual Return*, at para **[17.019]**.
37 Section 148 of the CA 1963.
38 As defined by reg 8(9) of the EC(SMPLC)R 1994.
39 Regulation 8(5) of the EC(SMPLC)R 1994.
40 As to the significance of this, see para **[14.051]** *post*.

taking a certain course of action. Ordinarily, a general meeting convened by the directors ought to be allowed to proceed notwithstanding that somebody disputes a particular member's entitlement to vote at that meeting, the appropriate course of action being to challenge the decision of the meeting rather than the holding of the meeting[41].

[14.017] By virtue of s 40 of the C(A)A 1983, directors are *obliged* to convene an EGM where a company suffers a serious loss of capital; members are not, however, require to attend the EGM or, indeed, to take any action. Section 40(1) of the C(A)A 1983 provides that:

> '... where the net assets of a company are half or less of the amount of the company's called up share capital, the directors of the company shall, not later than 28 days from the earliest day on which that fact is known to a director of the company, duly convene an extraordinary general meeting of the company for a date not later than 56 days from that day for the purpose of considering whether any, and if so what, measures should be taken to deal with the situation.'

Clearly, not only is there an obligation on the directors to convene such a meeting, but the directors also have a statutory duty to consider what should be done. In so providing, the legislature has imposed a positive obligation on such a company's directors which prevents them from ignoring the situation faced by the company. What is also clear, however, is that should the members or the directors decide to do nothing, there is nothing which can be done to force them to take action.

[14.018] Section 40(2) of the C(A)A 1983 provides that where there is a failure to convene an EGM, each of the directors of the company who knowingly and wilfully authorises or permits the failure to hold the meeting, or who knowingly and wilfully authorises or permits the failure to hold the meeting during the period in which it should be held, is guilty of an offence.

(b) EGMs convened on the requisition of qualified members

[14.019] The second circumstance in which an EGM may be called, envisaged by reg 50, is pursuant to s 132 of the CA 1963. Section 132(1), which empowers a member, or several members, holding not less than 10% of the paid up share capital with voting rights of the company (qualified members) to compel the directors of a company to call an EGM[42], provides:

> 'The directors of a company, notwithstanding anything in its articles, shall, on the requisition of members of the company holding at the date of the deposit of the requisition not less than one-tenth of such of the paid up capital of the company as at the date of the deposit carries the right of voting at general meetings of the company, or, in the case of a company not having a share capital, members of the company representing not less than one-tenth of the total voting rights of all the members having at the said date a right to

---

41 In particular cases, however, the court may injunct the holding of a general meeting: see, for example, *Finnegan v Barrett*, an application reported in (2005) Irish Times, 23 November (Smyth J), where an injunction was granted restraining the holding of a company's EGM where the beneficial ownership of shares was in dispute.

42 *Re Downs Wine Bar Ltd* [1990] BCLC 839.

> vote at general meetings of the company, forthwith proceed duly to convene an extraordinary general meeting of the company[43].'

The formal requirements are that the requisition for an EGM must be signed by the requisitionists[44] and deposited at the registered office of the company and may consist of several documents in like form each signed by one or more requisitionists[45]. However, directors, faced with a members' requisition, should have regard to both the subject matter of the requisitioned meeting and, also, the manner in which it is summoned.

[14.020] The Shareholders' Rights Directive, which was transposed in Ireland by the Shareholders' Rights (Directive 2007/36/EC) Regulations 2009[46], introduced significant changes to the law in this area for companies whose shares are traded on a regulated market, but these changes do not apply to private companies[47].

[14.021] A member's requisition for an EGM should not misrepresent the circumstances which the member requisitioning the EGM holds out as the reason therefor. However, some latitude will be granted to members in respect of what they represent to be the case when seeking support for the requisitioning of an EGM. The facts in *Rose v McGivern et al*[48] were that the plaintiff was a member of the Royal Automobile Club Ltd (a friendly society) and he wrote a letter to other members of the company, proposing that it be demutualised. It was further proposed that an EGM be summoned and that two resolutions be put to the meeting: the first resolution to elect a new board of directors; and the second resolution to authorise the board to proceed with the demutualisation. The plaintiff's letter received sufficient support from the members to require the directors to convene and hold an EGM. It was held by Neuberger J that the fact that the plaintiff's letter to his fellow members might have given the impression that the company's directors were against the sale of the company's subsidiary's assets – which the directors denied was the case – merely expressed the plaintiff's opinion. Neuberger J said:

> '... I have reached the conclusion that this [the 'impression' given by the plaintiff] is not a ground for validly challenging the March letter which gave rise to the requisitions. First, the March letter does not state in terms the attitude of the board [of the subsidiary]. It merely identifies [the plaintiff's] opinion at the date of the March letter as to the likely attitude of the board ... In other words, the sentence centrally complained of is a statement

43 This is underscored by s 134 of the CA 1963 which provides: 'The following provisions shall have effect in so far as the articles of the company do not make other provision in that behalf— ... (b) two or more members holding not less than one-tenth of the issued share capital or, if the company has not a share capital, not less than 5 per cent in number of all the members of the company may call a meeting.'

44 Where the requisite number of shares is held jointly, the requisition must be signed by all of those entitled to those shares: *Patenwood Keg Syndicate Ltd v Pearse* [1906] WN 164.

45 Section 132(2) of the CA 1963.

46 SI 316/2009.

47 See Ch 29, *Public Limited Companies and SEs*, at paras **[29.099]** *et seq*.

48 *Rose v McGivern et al* [1998] 2 BCLC 593.

> of opinion on the part of the person seeking the requisitions on an assumed state of facts based on past knowledge. The letter represented [the plaintiff's] honest opinion[49].'

Neuberger J held that the requisitions obtained for summoning the EGM were properly obtained and so were valid.

[14.022] A members' requisition must state the objects of the meeting. Great care should be taken in framing the objects of the meeting because at the meeting no business, other than that stated in the requisition, may be introduced by other members (as opposed to introduced by the directors)[50] for consideration at a meeting so requisitioned. Again, the case of *Rose v McGivern et al*[51], the facts of which have just been considered, is instructive. There, Neuberger J held that the proposals for resolutions, put forward by the plaintiff, could not constitute the subject matter of valid resolutions as they were too vague and ambiguous. In particular, he found that resolution (a) failed to identify the persons to be elected as directors, the exact size of the board, or which members of the old board were to be removed. In addition, resolution (b) failed too as, *inter alia*, it was meaningless as the board of the company had the power, regardless of such a resolution, to demutualise. Member-requisitionists would do well to bear this in mind and to consult with lawyers before attempting to frame the resolutions which they seek to propose at an EGM requisitioned by them. The notice of the business intended to be conducted at a meeting (AGM or EGM) is considered further, below[52]. In *Ball v Metal Industries Ltd et al*[53], it was held that it was not competent to put a resolution to remove a director before an EGM of a company convened pursuant to the equivalent provision of the Companies Act 1948 (UK) where that matter was not covered by the terms of the requisition and where the directors had not convened the meeting for that particular purpose.

[14.023] The directors of a company would be ill-advised to ignore a properly constituted requisition. Section 132(3) provides that:

> 'If the directors do not within 21 days from the date of the deposit of the requisition proceed duly to convene a meeting to be held within 2 months from the said date, the requisitionists, or any of them representing more than one half of the total voting rights of all of them, may themselves convene a meeting, but any meeting so convened shall not be held after the expiration of 3 months from the said date[54].'

---

49 *Rose v McGivern et al* [1998] 2 BCLC 593 at 601, 602.

50 *Ball v Metal Industries Ltd* [1957] SLT 124. This case also suggests (at 125) that 'it would be perfectly competent for the board of a company when they are sending out a notice convening an extraordinary general meeting pursuant to s 132 [of the English Companies Act 1948] to incorporate in the notice provisions relating to business which could competently have been put before the company by the directors at an extraordinary general meeting of the company …'.

51 *Rose v McGivern et al* [1998] 2 BCLC 593.

52 See para **[14.050]** *post*.

53 *Ball v Metal Industries Ltd et al* [1957] SLT 124.

54 Note that s 132(6) of the CA 1963 provides: 'For the purposes of this section, the directors shall, in the case of a meeting at which a resolution is to be proposed as a special resolution, be deemed not to have duly convened the meeting if they do not give such notice thereof as is required by section 141.'

Where a meeting is convened by the requisitionists it must be convened in the same manner as nearly as possible as that in which meetings are to be convened by directors[55]. In England, it has been held that where the directors simply *convened a meeting* they were not in breach of the provisions of the English section notwithstanding that they did not actually hold the meeting until some months later[56]. The position is different in Ireland in that not only must the directors convene a meeting within 21 days from the date of the requisition, but they must convene a meeting to be actually held within two months from the date of the deposit of the members' requisition to hold the meeting. Where the directors fail to convene an EGM and the member-requisitionists decide to convene it themselves, they should be careful to comply with the provisions of the Companies Acts, lest any meeting they convene and hold be declared invalid for want of compliance with the requisite formalities. So, for example, the Supreme Court of New South Wales in *Howard v Mechtler*[57] declared that an EGM held by requisitionists was invalid because the notice convening the meeting was short of that required by statute. In that case, however, it was held that to convene a meeting for 6.00pm on the 30 December was not an inherently unreasonable time.

(c) EGMs convened by order of the court

[14.024] A problem can arise where the holding of an EGM is thwarted because the other member or members do not attend a convened meeting, resulting in the meeting being inquorate. In such circumstances, s 135(1) of the CA 1963 can be invoked. This provides that:

> 'If for any reason it is impractical to call a meeting of a company in any manner in which meetings of that company may be called, or to conduct the meeting of the company in manner prescribed by the articles or this Act, the court may either of its own motion or of any member of the company who would be entitled to vote at the meeting, order a meeting of the company to be called, held and conducted in such manner as the court thinks fit, and where any such order is made may give such ancillary or consequential directions as it thinks expedient; and it is hereby declared that the directions that may be given under this subsection include a declaration that one member of the company present in person or by proxy shall be deemed to constitute a meeting[58].'

---

55 Section 132(4) of the CA 1963. Section 134(5) provides: 'Any reasonable expenses incurred by the requisitionists by reason of the failure of the directors duly to convene a meeting shall be repaid to the requisitionists by thc company and any sum so repaid shall be retained by the company out of any sums due or to become due from the company by way of fees or other remuneration in respect of their services to such of the directors as were in default.'

56 See *McGuinness et al v Bremmer plc et al* [1988] BCLC 673, following *Re Windward Islands (Enterprises) UK Ltd* [1983] BCLC 293. Note that s 386 of the Companies Act (UK) 1985 has been amended by Schedule 19, para 9 of the Companies Act (UK) 1989 so that the directors will be deemed not to have convened a meeting where they hold it more than 28 days after the notice convening it.

57 *Howard v Mechtle* (16 March 1999) New South Wales Supreme Court 232.

58 It should be noted that the wording here is narrower than the corresponding UK provision in s 306 of the Companies Act 2006 (UK), which also permits the court to order a meeting of the directors of a company: see *Re Sticky Fingers Restaurant Ltd* [1992] BCLC 84.

This is an exceptional jurisdiction and one that will be exercised sparingly on account of the judiciary's reluctance to interfere in the internal affairs of companies[59]. Where the court's jurisdiction is invoked, it has the consequence that:

> 'Any meeting called, held and conducted in accordance with an order under *subsection (1)* shall for all purposes be deemed to be a meeting of the company duly called, held and conducted[60].'

[14.025] The general rule is that one person cannot by him or herself hold a meeting[61]. A member may, however, be permitted by order of the court under s 135 to convene and hold a meeting by himself. It was emphasised, however, in *Arulchelvan and another v Wright et al*[62] that the general rule was that there cannot be a 'meeting' held by just one person. The facts of the case were that MW was the 100% beneficial owner of Company A. The legal ownership of the shares in Company A were held by MW (as to 49%), by the first defendant (as to 49% but in trust for MW) and by two solicitors (as to 2%, again in trust for MW). MW was also the 50% legal and beneficial owner of another company, Company B; its other shareholder being the first defendant. After MW died, probate of his will was granted to the first and third defendants who were named as his executors. MW had been a director of both companies; after his death the directors were the two plaintiffs and the first defendant and meetings were not held. Subsequently, the first and third defendants (MW's executors) and the first defendant in her own right as a member, convened EGMs of both Company A and Company B for the purpose of co-opting the second and third defendants to the boards of both companies. Notwithstanding that only one member (the first defendant) was present it was insisted that the meeting was quorate and the resolutions were passed. Whilst the executors had served notice of election to be registered as members the directors had not made a decision and the two month period had not elapsed. The plaintiffs successfully challenged the validity of the meeting and the resolutions purportedly passed, and Carroll J held that the meetings were not quorate[63]. In the event that they were unsuccessful on that point, the defendants had also sought an order under s 135 of the CA 1963 for the convening of an EGM with a declaration that one member was deemed to constitute the meeting. On this point Carroll J said:

> 'The basic general rule is that there cannot be a meeting held by one person. Section 135 of the 1963 Act specifically provides that where the court on its own motion orders a meeting of the company to be held it can direct that one member of the company present in person or by proxy be *deemed* to constitute a meeting. While there are some exceptions to the general rule (eg such as where one person holds all of a class of shares) the exceptions do not in my opinion extend to the case where there is only one voting shareholder in a company and where the shares of a deceased member have not yet been registered in the name of a personal representative[64].'

59 See note by Milman, 'The Courts and Company Meetings' (1997) Palmer's In Company, Issue 8/97, 18 September 1997.

60 Section 135(2) of the CA 1963.

61 *Re London Flats Ltd* [1969] 1 WLR 711.

62 *Arulchelvan and another v Wright et al* (7 February 1996, unreported) HC, Carroll J.

63 See para **[14.055]** *post*.

64 *Arulchelvan and another v Wright et al* (7 February 1996, unreported) HC, Carroll J at p 9 of the judgment.

Carroll J went on to say:

> 'I will not order a meeting to be held under s 135 on my own motion as I think that it is premature to do so. The directors have yet to consider and deal with the application of the first and third defendants to be registered as members. If this application is granted, the problem concerning the holding of general meetings is solved. If their application to be registered is refused, the defendants can apply under s 205 of the 1963 Act, with all that entails[65].'

It is thought that Carroll J's decision was undoubtedly correct and that an order under s 135 with a declaration that one member would constitute the meeting was inappropriate there. This decision should not, however, be too narrowly construed, particularly the exceptions to the general rule that there cannot be a meeting held by one person. In *Re El Sombrero*[66], the applicant member held 90% of the issued shares, where the two directors who held the remaining 10% thwarted the holding of a members' meeting. Wynn Parry J made an order under the corresponding English section because otherwise the applicant member would have been unable to exercise his statutory right to remove the directors. More recently, in the case of *Re Opera Phonographic Ltd*[67], Morritt J exercised his discretion and ordered a meeting to be convened and held in similar circumstances.

[14.026] The making of an order under s 135 is discretionary, and, as was observed by Kenny J in *Angelis v Algemene Bank Nederland (Ireland) Ltd*[68], the court's power will not be exercised where there is no evidence that the directors of the company have shown themselves unwilling to comply with the requisition for the meeting. If, of course, there are no directors, the matter will be more straightforward. In *Re The Cambridge Group plc*, an *ex tempore* application to the Irish High Court, reported in *The Irish Times*[69], it was said that application was brought by 12% of the company's shareholders to convene an EGM. The report stated that the once publicly quoted company appeared to have no directors following their resignation and that of the company secretary and in these circumstances Kinlen J granted the application, agreeing to direct the convening of an EGM for a particular date, time and venue[70].

[14.027] The facts in *Re British Union for the Abolition of Vivisection*[71] provide a classic example of the sort of situations in which s 135 was intended to be of assistance. In this case, the applicant company (the BUAV) was a company limited by guarantees which

---

65 *Arulchelvan and another v Wright et al* (7 February 1996, unreported) HC, Carroll J at pp 9, 10 of the judgment. The unreported judgment actually refers to s 105 in the final sentence but it is thought this is a misprint.

66 *Re El Sombrero* [1958] 3 All ER 1, [1958] Ch 900.

67 *Re Opera Phonographic Ltd* [1989] BCLC 763. See also *Re H & R Paul & Son Ltd* (1974) 118 Sol Jo 166, where the court held that the requirement to have a quorum for a meeting could not be allowed 'to frustrate the wishes of the majority'.

68 *Angelis v Algemene Bank Nederland (Ireland) Ltd* (4 July 1974, unreported) HC *per* Kenny J.

69 *Re The Cambridge Group plc* (1998) Irish Times, 10 February (Kinlen J).

70 See also *Re Kenoughty Ltd*, an application reported in (1995) Irish Times, 16 October (Carroll J), where an order under s 135 was sought by a director and member of a company in circumstances where the only other director and member's whereabouts were unknown and the purpose of the EGM was to appoint another director.

71 *Re British Union for the Abolition of Vivisection* [1995] 2 BCLC 1.

opposed vivisection. Its articles of association only permitted voting by members in person, not permitting proxies. Its membership was, however, seriously factionalised, some of the factions being very militant. A previous AGM was long and confrontational and a previous EGM for the purpose of introducing voting by proxy had degenerated into tumult so badly that the police had had to intervene and close the meeting, apprehending a breach of the peace. The BUAV's board of directors brought an application under the similar English provision for an order that the court convene a meeting to vote on a special resolution to alter the company's articles of association to permit voting by proxy and that the only persons entitled to attend this meeting should be the board (known in BUAV as its executive committee). However, the voting on the resolution to alter the articles by the company's *other members* should be by way of postal ballot and that the requirement for personal attendance in the company's articles should be dispensed with. Rimer J granted the application, saying that because of the genuine apprehension of violence it was clear to the court that it was impracticable to hold a meeting of the members in person as required by the company's articles.

[14.028] Section 135 of the CA 1963 can also have application where all persons concerned are willing to convene and hold a meeting, but where problems arise in complying with the Companies Acts. An example of a non-contentious application can be seen in *Re Waterford Foods plc*, another *ex tempore* Irish order. There, because of the postal dispute in mid-1992, the company felt it would be impractical to advise all its shareholders of a forthcoming EGM to consider proposed acquisitions of shares in other companies. The directors had agreed to make the share acquisitions subject to ratification by the company's members in general meeting. In lieu of postal notification, Lardner J gave leave to the company to advertise notice of the meeting in the national newspapers and some weekly newspapers in the South East[72]. Failure to take the prudent step of making such an application to court could have resulted in any subsequent ratification being impugned.

[14.029] It has been held by the English Court of Appeal that the similar UK provision[73] was *procedural* in nature and was not intended (and should not be used) to resolve a deadlock between two equal shareholders by affecting substantive voting rights[74]. The facts in *Ross v Telford and another*[75] were that there were two companies, whose only directors and equal shareholders were an estranged husband and wife. As the quorum for meetings of the directors and members was two, there was deadlock. The husband had claimed that the wife had fraudulently amassed undisclosed assets at the expense of one of the companies but this claim was rejected in the acrimonious divorce proceedings. Subsequently, having commenced proceedings in the company's name against the wife, the husband sought to have the initiation of these proceedings ratified and to this end sought an order under the English provision, requiring the convening of an EGM for the purposes of considering and voting on a resolution to appoint a third

72 On the service of notices on members, see model regs 133–136 of Table A.

73 Section 371 of the Companies Act 1985 (UK).

74 See *Wheeler v Ross* [2011] EWHC 2527 (Ch); *Hussain v Wycombe Islamic Mission and Mosque Trust Ltd* [2011] EWHC 971 (Ch); and *Smith v Butler and another* [2011] EWHC 2301 (Ch), [2012] 1 BCLC 444.

75 *Ross v Telford and another* [1998] 1 BCLC 82. See also *Re Woven Rugs Ltd* [2002] 1 BCLC 324.

director for a period of one year. This application was granted and the judge ordered that the third director (the husband's representative) could attend and vote at the EGM. This was appealed to the Court of Appeal, which allowed the appeal. Nourse LJ accepted counsel's argument that the provision:

> '... is a procedural section not designed to affect substantive voting rights or to shift the balance of power between shareholders in a case where they have agreed that power shall be shared equally and where the potential deadlock is something which must be taken to have been agreed on with the consent and for the protection of each of them[76].'

Nourse LJ also pointed out that this section has nothing whatsoever to do with board meetings and is exclusively concerned with meetings of members.

[14.030] In *BML Group Ltd v Harman*[77], the Court of Appeal refused to convene an EGM where it would have been contrary to a shareholders' agreement which had been entered into by the company's shareholders. The shareholders' agreement provided that a members' meeting would not have a quorum unless a 'B' shareholder was present. The requisitionists held in excess of 50% of the shares carrying voting rights and wished to dismiss two of their opponent directors. In this they were thwarted by the only 'B' shareholder who refused to attend any members' meetings. The Court of Appeal reversed the decision of first instance and refused to convene a meeting of the members. To do so, it was held, would be in breach of the freely contracted shareholders' agreement and the rights of the 'B' shareholder which were akin to rights entrenched in a company's articles of association. Accordingly, where there is an agreement or arrangement which confers a right in the nature of a class right to one shareholder, the court will not make an order if the effect is to infringe that class right[78].

[14.031] It may be taken as established in the United Kingdom that the court will be slow to exercise its discretionary jurisdiction where the purpose is to break a deadlock which the members deliberately created in order to balance their respective rights, and in

---

76 A similar application was brought in the Irish High Court in *Re a Company*, an ex tempore application reported in (1997) Irish Times, 18 November (Costello P). There, application was brought for an order directing the convening of an EGM and an order that one director of the company be deemed a valid meeting. The sole directors and shareholders of the company were an estranged husband and wife. The applicant husband claimed that the company was in financial difficulties and was required to dispose of certain property but that his spouse, the other director and shareholder, had refused to agree to the sale and that he had attempted to convene an EGM to discuss the situation and appoint a third director but his spouse had refused to attend. The newspaper report stated that the applicant's spouse's counsel claimed that she objected to the appointment of the third director, whom it was claimed was in a relationship with the applicant and was 'perhaps the reason for the marital breakdown'. On hearing that the spouse had agreed to attend a board meeting to discuss the sale of the company's property, Costello P made no order but gave liberty to re-enter in the event of agreement not being reached on the sale of the property.

77 *BML Group Ltd v Harman* (1994) Times, 8 April (Court of Appeal).

78 In *Vectone Entertainment Holding Ltd v South Entertainment Ltd* [2005] BCC 123, it was found that there was nothing in a shareholders' agreement which gave a right to equal board representation and indeed the shareholders had a right to appoint additional directors. Neither was there anything in the nature of a class right or substantive right conferred by the agreement which would be overridden by a court order and in those circumstances an order was made.

such a situation the appropriate remedy may be to apply under s 205 of the CA 1963 for relief from oppression or disregard of interests. In *Alvona Developments Ltd v The Manhattan Loft Corporation (AC) Ltd*[79], a joint-venture company was owned 70:30 by two shareholders, each of whom, it had been agreed orally, would be entitled to appoint one director. When one of the directors resigned, the other director refused to act save on the joint instructions of the two shareholders. The 70% shareholder exercised its rights to convene an EGM but the 30% shareholder refused to attend so that the meeting was inquorate and incapable of doing business. The 70% shareholder then sought an order under the English equivalent of s 135 for an EGM where the quorum would be one. The purpose of the EGM was either to remove the sole director and appoint replacement directors or to appoint additional directors, and the 70% shareholder asserted its right to control the board as a majority shareholder. The English High Court dismissed the application and, referring to the *Harman* decision, found that there:

> '... it is reiterated that the articles can be overridden under s 371 and the right of a member to choose not to attend a meeting does not amount to a right to veto or a right to frustrate the wishes of a majority. As is shown by the *re Opera Photographic Ltd* (1989) 5 BCC 601 the court on the facts was able to resolve the deadlock by a meeting under s 371 as an alternative to the presentation of a petition under s 459 of the Companies Act 1985. Morritt J (as he then was) plainly considered it appropriate on that case to make an order to break the deadlock. A desire to break the deadlock whilst commendable is not of itself a justification for making an order under s 371 as the *Ross* case demonstrates[80].'

Peter Smith J went on to acknowledge the limitations of the section saying:

> 'The section was plainly intended to be a procedure to be invoked summarily (and thus speedily). Nevertheless that apparently simplified procedure has been overturned by the application of class rights and other matters in my view by the courts. Whilst this might involve arguments that were capable of being ventilated under s 459 petition it is clear that the courts have allowed arguments that could be used under s 459 petition to be deployed on a s 371 application[81].'

(d) EGMs convened on the requisition of retiring auditor

[14.032] Section 186(1) of the CA 1990 provides that a notice served by a resigning auditor (pursuant to s 185 of the CA 1990) may also requisition the convening of a general meeting by the directors of the company. The purpose of such a meeting is to receive and consider such account and explanation of the circumstances connected with the auditor's resignation as the resigning auditor may wish to give to the meeting. Where such a requisition is made the directors of the company must, within 14 days of the service on the company of the auditor's notice, proceed to convene a general meeting for a day not more than 28 days after such service[82]. Where the reason for the auditor's resignation is due to circumstances, which the auditor considers should be brought to the notice of the members or creditors, the auditor may request the directors to circulate to

---

79 *Alvona Developments Ltd v The Manhattan Loft Corporation (AC) Ltd* [2006] BCC 119.

80 *Alvona Developments Ltd v The Manhattan Loft Corporation (AC) Ltd* [2006] BCC 119 at 130 (para 44). The reference to *Ross* is to *Ross v Telford* [1997] BCC 945.

81 *Alvona Developments Ltd v The Manhattan Loft Corporation (AC) Ltd* [2006] BCC 119 at 132 (para 58).

82 Section 186(2) of the CA 1990.

the company's members prior to any requisitioned meeting[83] a further statement prepared by the auditor of circumstances connected with his resignation, which he considers should be brought to the members' notice[84]. The directors of a company so requested *must* record the fact of the statement having been made in the notice convening the meeting and members must be sent a copy of the statement[85]. So as to protect innocent companies against gratuitously vindictive auditors, s 186(4) of the CA 1990 allows companies and other aggrieved persons to apply to court and for the court to excuse the company from having to issue such a statement, where:

> '… the court is satisfied that the rights conferred by this section are being abused to secure needless publicity for defamatory matter and the court may order the company's costs on an application under this section to be paid in whole or in part by the auditor concerned notwithstanding that he is not a party to the application.'

The similar English section was considered by Lightman J in *Jarvis plc et al v PricewaterhouseCoopers*[86]. In that case, a company applied to court to be excused from issuing its auditors' statement and although the company subsequently discontinued its application, the auditors contended that the court should consider the matter. Lightman J held that the effect and purpose of this provision was to impose:

> '… upon auditors an important duty in the public interest and in the interest of the persons interested and indirectly of creditors and the investing public: to make a statement. Indeed, it is a duty of such importance that a failure to comply constitutes a criminal offence. The auditor is the judge of whether there are relevant circumstances: he must exercise his judgment and, uninfluenced by any collateral considerations, make up his own mind and state whether he considers that there are circumstances which ought to be brought to the attention of the persons interested to whom for this purpose he must owe a duty of care. He is uniquely placed to judge. The requirement is not designed to protect the auditors or give the auditors an opportunity to say something which protects their goodwill or reputation when they cease to be the auditors, and the court will presume that the auditors who make a statement under [the section] are acting in faithful discharge of their duty and not in pursuit of any private or collateral interest, unless the contrary is shown[87].'

In that case, it was held that the effect of the discontinuance of the company's application was to bring the matter to an end and, specifically, it was held that the court was not required to issue a decision on the matter. It was also held that the company was liable to pay the auditors' costs on an indemnity basis.

Notice of members' meetings

[14.033] In this section, the following matters concerning the convening of members' meetings and the notice required to be given are considered:

---

83 And, indeed, other general meetings: a general meeting at which apart from the notice his term of office would expire, *or*, a general meeting at which it is proposed to fill the vacancy caused by the auditor's resignation.

84 Section 186(3) of the CA 1990.

85 Section 186(3) of the CA 1990.

86 *Jarvis plc et al v PricewaterhouseCoopers* [2001] BCC 670.

87 *Jarvis plc et al v PricewaterhouseCoopers* [2001] BCC 670 at 677.

(a) The requirements of a notice;
(b) Those who should receive notice;
(c) Notice periods for AGMs and EGMs;
(d) Extended notice;
(e) Accidental omission to give notice;
(f) Summary of notice provisions.

(a) The requirements of a notice

[14.034] A notice issued by a company must state the date, time and venue of the meeting and the purpose of the meeting, something usually fulfilled by itemising the agenda for the meeting[88]. The general rule is that only business that has been described in the notice for a meeting may be transacted at that meeting. There is one exception to that rule which is that, technically, a notice is not required to set out matters that constitute 'ordinary business' and is only required in respect of matters that are 'special business'[89].

(b) Those who should receive notice

[14.035] Section 134(a) of the CA 1963 requires that, subject to a company's articles of association, all members – as defined by s 31 of the CA 1963[90] – should receive notice of a meeting[91]. To be entitled to receive notice, a member's name must have been entered in the register of members. This is considered further, below, in the context of those entitled to vote at general meetings[92].

[14.036] It should be noted that the personal representatives of a deceased member and the official assignee of a bankrupt member are entitled, under model reg 136 of Table A, to receive notice of every general meeting. Personal representatives and the official assignee in bankruptcy are not, however, entitled to vote and will not be counted for the purposes of determining whether the meeting is quorate[93].

[14.037] Sometimes a company's articles of association will confer the express right on directors to receive notice of and attend general meetings. It is thought that, as the company's agents, the directors will be aware of when a general meeting is to be held without receiving notice and are entitled to attend general meetings, not as a result of any personal right, but in the capacity of representing the company. Indeed, where a general meeting is convened by the directors, it would give rise to an absurdity if the people who convened a meeting were not entitled to attend or only entitled to attend by

88 See reg 51 of Table A.

89 See para **[14.051]** *post*.

90 See Ch 8, *Shares and Membership*, at para **[8.004]** *et seq*.

91 Section 134 of the CA 1963 provides that: 'The following provisions shall have effect in so far as the articles of the company do not make other provision in that behalf—(a) notice of the meeting of a company shall be served on every member of the company in the manner in which notices are required to be served by Table A and for the purpose of this paragraph "Table A" means that Table as for the time being in force.'

92 See para **[14.061]** *post*.

93 See *Arulchelvan and Wright v Wright et al* (7 February 1996, unreported) HC, Carroll J considered at para **[14.057]** *post*.

accident of also being members. Members can attend and be silent; it would be a queer general meeting if the directors attended and said nothing or, queerer still, were not permitted to attend at all! Although the Companies Acts are silent[94] on the directors' right to receive notice of and to attend general meetings, it is thought that they will, as directors, have notice of a proposed general meeting and that directors have both a right and perhaps even a duty to attend general meetings.

[14.038] Notice of general meetings must also be given to the company's auditors. By virtue of s 193(5) of the CA 1990[95], the auditors of a company are entitled to attend and to receive notices and other communications relating to any general meeting of a company, which any member of the company is entitled to receive. Moreover, the same section entitles auditors to be heard at any general meeting, which they attend on any part of the business of the meeting, which concerns them as auditors. Moreover, s 186(5) of the CA 1990 provides that an auditor of a company who has resigned shall be permitted to attend (and shall receive notices[96] of) the AGM at which, but for his resignation as auditor, his term of office would have expired and any EGM at which it is proposed to fill the vacancy caused by his resignation or convened by him pursuant to s 186(1) of the CA 1990[97]. An auditor also has a right to be heard at any such meeting on any part of the business of the meeting that concerns him as a former auditor of the company.

[14.039] Save in the case of an accidental omission to give notice[98], a meeting held for which notice was not given to those entitled to notice, will be invalid. An example of this is seen in *Colthurst and Tenips Ltd v La Touche Colthurst and Colthurst*[99]. The plaintiffs in the proceedings in hand sought the recission of an earlier settlement and of an earlier court consent order in which the parties purported to settle various outstanding disputes. The second plaintiff company was owned as to 49% of its shares by the first plaintiff, 1% by his wife and the remaining 50% by his mother, the second defendant. The shareholders were also the company's three directors. The second defendant claimed

---

94 It is implicit, however, from a number of provisions of the Companies Acts and Table A that directors will be present at general meetings and entitled to attend such meetings: s 182(3) of the CA 1963 provides that a director, who is being removed from office, is entitled to require that his representations to members be read out at the meeting and this is 'without prejudice to his *right* to be heard orally'. Since the right to be heard orally implies personal attendance and since s 182 does not confer that right, it can be implied that directors have a right to attend. This contrasts with auditors who have been removed, who are given an express right to attend the next general meeting: s 161(2A) of the CA 1963. Moreover, reg 56 of Table A (which does not confer an express right on directors to attend general meetings) provides that the chairman of the board shall chair a general meeting and if he is not present, the directors present shall elect one of their number to chair the meeting. Again, it cannot be that the regulation is predicated on their accidental attendance *qua* member; so it also implies that directors will be in attendance as of right.

95 And model reg 136 of Part I of Table A.

96 And other communications relating to any such meeting as a member would be entitled to receive.

97 See para **[14.032]** *ante*.

98 See para **[14.048]** *post*.

99 *Colthurst and Tenips Ltd v La Touche Colthurst and Colthurst* (9 February 2000, unreported) HC, McCracken J.

that the instant proceedings had never been authorised by her as a director nor had the second plaintiff company resolved to set aside the settlement. In what McCracken J described as a charade, the first plaintiff had sought to 'put a gloss of legality on issuing these proceedings in the name of the company' by authorising the plaintiffs' solicitors to issue the proceedings by letter. The operative part of the letter provided that the husband and wife as 'directors and shareholders' authorised the solicitors to issue the proceedings. What in fact happened was that a meeting of the directors had been convened for the purposes of convening an EGM, the purpose of which was to authorise the issue of the proceedings. No notice of either the directors' meeting or the EGM had been given to the second defendant director and 50% shareholder. The minutes of the EGM provided that the resolution to initiate proceedings had been proposed and seconded and passed on a show of hands. McCracken J said that the only explanation he was given for the failure to give the notices was that the first plaintiff and his wife were aware that the second-defendant would vote against the resolution, but were also aware that they would out-vote her. The judge also noted that the first plaintiff claimed that he had been advised by his accountants not to give his mother notice. McCracken J found that claim 'astonishing':

> 'both that in general his accountant would not have been aware of the necessary formalities in calling an extraordinary general meeting, and in particular that he would advise a director and 50% shareholder would not be notified of either a directors' meeting or a general meeting of the company in which it was intended to pass a resolution authorising the company to issue proceedings against her.'

This, the judge found, was a deliberate attempt to prevent the defendants from finding out about the plaintiffs' intention to issue proceedings against them. On the consequences of the failure to give notice, McCracken J said:

> 'Lest there be any doubt as to the validity of the meeting … I would point out that it purported to be an extraordinary general meeting of the company, and that under s 134 of the Companies Act 1963 notice of a meeting of the company must be served on every member of the company, and further under s 193 of the Companies Act 1990 the auditor of the company is entitled to attend any general meeting of the company and to receive all notices in relation thereto. In view of the statutory provisions, quite clearly the resolution which was purported to be passed is invalid, and the second plaintiff has no standing in these proceedings[100].'

This must, of course, be contrasted with an accidental omission to give notice of a meeting[101].

(b) Notice periods for AGMs and EGMs

(i) Standard notice

[14.040] In the case of all companies, s 133 of the CA 1963 provides that at least 21 days' notice must be given in writing for an AGM. In the case of a private company, at least *seven days'* notice must be given in writing for an EGM[102]. It is important to note,

[100] *Colthurst and Tenips Ltd v La Touche Colthurst and Colthurst* (9 February 2000, unreported) HC, McCracken J at p 8 of the judgment.

[101] See para **[14.048]** *post*.

[102] Or, for any unlimited company. Note that in the case of a plc at least 14 days' notice of an EGM is required to be given: see Ch 29, *Public Limited Companies and SEs*, at para **[29.098]**.

however, that seven days' notice for an EGM only applies where it is not proposed to pass a special resolution at the EGM: otherwise, 21 days' notice is required. Section 133(2) provides:

> 'Save in so far as the articles of a company make other provision in that behalf (not being a provision avoided by *subsection (1)*) a meeting of the company (other than an adjourned meeting) may be called—
>
> (a) in the case of the annual general meeting by 21 days' notice in writing; and
>
> (b) in the case of a meeting (other than an annual general meeting or a meeting for the passing of a special resolution) ... by 7 days' notice in writing, where it is a private company ...'

Any provision in a company's articles of association that provides for shorter notice shall be void[103]. Consequently, model reg 4 of Part II of Table A[104], which will usually be adopted by most private companies, contains the same notice periods[105]. It is implicit, however, that a particular company may provide for longer notice and so it is always important to ascertain from a company's articles whether Table A applies. By 'notice' is meant what is termed '*clear notice*'. So, reg 4 of Part II of Table A provides that 'notice shall be exclusive of the day on which it is served or deemed to be served and of the day for which it is given'. Articles of association will invariably provide that notice is deemed to be served in certain situations, eg, when posted, notice is deemed to be served 24 hours after postage[106]. In computing notice, the day it is deemed to be served is excluded as is the day that the meeting is actually held so that there are in the case of a seven-day notice period, seven *clear days* between the date it is deemed to have been served and the date of the meeting.

(ii) Short notice – AGMs and EGMs where special resolutions are not proposed

[14.041] Section 133(3) of the CA 1963 contains a very important proviso to the prescriptive provisions of sub-ss (1) and (2) as regards notice for meetings (both AGMs and EGMs). This provides:

---

103 Section 133(1) of the CA 1963 provides: 'Any provision of a company's articles shall be void in so far as it provides for the calling of a meeting of the company (other than an adjourned meeting) by a shorter notice than—(a) in the case of the annual general meeting, 21 days' notice in writing; and (b) in the case of a meeting (other than an annual general meeting or a meeting for the passing of a special resolution) 14 days' notice in writing where the company is neither a private company nor an unlimited company and 7 days' notice in writing where it is a private company or an unlimited company.'

104 Which applies in the case of a private company. Note that reg 51 of Table A, Part I, applies only to public companies limited by shares.

105 Thus reg 4 provides: 'Subject to sections 133 and 141 of the Act, an annual general meeting and a meeting called for the passing of a special resolution shall be called by 21 days' notice in writing at the least and a meeting of the company (other than an annual general meeting or a meeting for the passing of a special resolution) shall be called by 7 days' notice in writing at the least. The notice shall be exclusive of the day on which it is served or deemed to be served and of the day for which it is given and shall specify the day, the place and the hour of the meeting and, in the case of special business, the general nature of that business and shall be given in a manner authorised by these regulations to such persons as are under the regulations of the company entitled to receive such notices from the company.'

106 See para **[14.048]** *post*.

> 'A meeting of a company shall, notwithstanding that it is called by shorter notice than that specified in *subsection (2)* or in the company's articles, as the case may be, be deemed to have been duly called if it is so agreed *by the auditors of the company and by all the members entitled to attend and vote* thereat.'[Emphasis added.]

Short notice can mean anything from six days to six hours – there are no limitations on how short, short notice, can be. The basis for this provision – the consent of the auditors and of *all* members entitled to attend and vote – is the old notion that all of a company's members can waive a protection intended for them. Requiring the consent of all members, however, renders the section a limited concession to the exigencies of commercial life[107]. The reason why the auditor's consent is also required is because s 193 of the CA 1990 and model reg 136 of Table A requires that companies give notice of general meetings to their auditors. It is also very important to remember the limitations of the short notice provisions in s 133(3): the short notice procedure here does *not* apply to meetings at which special resolutions are passed.

(iii) Short notice – special resolutions

[14.042] While the 21 days' notice required for a special resolution can be abridged, the basis for that abridgement is not s 133(2). The requirements in relation to special resolutions are considered in detail, below,[108] but for completeness short notice for special resolutions is mentioned here. Central to the definition of a special resolution is that it is passed at a meeting of which 'not less than 21 days' notice, specifying the intention to propose the resolution as a special resolution, has been given': s 141(1) of the CA 1963. A resolution can, however, in accordance with s 142(2), still be a special resolution where it is proposed and passed at a meeting of which less than 21 days' notice has been given where:

> '... it is so agreed by a majority in number of the members having the right to attend and vote at any such meeting being a majority together holding not less than ninety per cent in nominal value of the shares giving that right ...[109].'

[14.043] Accordingly, if the directors of a company wish to put a special resolution to the members but believe that 21 days is too long, they may convene an EGM (whether on the standard seven days' notice, or, on shorter notice with the consent of all the members and the auditors) specifying the intention to propose the resolution as a special resolution. At the meeting, the directors would then seek the agreement of the members in accordance with s 142(2), which requires:

- a majority of the members entitled to vote including those absent from the meeting to support the resolution;
- that majority to hold not less than 90% of the nominal value of the shares giving that right to vote.

---

[107] *Cf* s 141(8) of the CA 1963, *post* at para **[14.090]**, which permits unanimous written resolutions.

[108] See para **[14.085]**, *post* where s 141(2) of the CA 1963 is considered.

[109] In the case of companies what do not have a share capital (eg, guarantee companies) the requirement is that the supporting members should represent 'not less than ninety per cent of the total voting rights at that meeting of all the members'.

In the event of securing that agreement, the special resolution can then be put to the meeting. In such a case, the auditors of the company are not required to consent to the passing of the special resolution on short notice.

(c) Extended notice

[14.044] Perhaps the best way of describing extended notice is by saying what it is not: extended notice is not longer notice by a company to its members of a meeting. Extended notice refers to the notice given *by* a member *to* the company of the intention to put a particular resolution to a general meeting and to that extent is a misnomer in comparison with *standard notice* or *short notice* both of which refer to notice given *by* companies *to* members. Extended notice is required to be given to a company where a member proposes:

- a resolution at an AGM, appointing as auditor a person other than a retiring auditor or providing expressly that a retiring auditor shall not be re-appointed[110];
- a resolution at an AGM or EGM, removing an auditor before the expiration of his term of office[111];
- a resolution at an AGM or EGM of a company filling a casual vacancy in the office of auditor; and
- any resolution at an AGM or EGM to remove a director under s 182(1) of the CA 1963 or to appoint somebody instead of a director so removed at the meeting at which he is removed[112].

These four types of resolution are referred to here as an 'extended notice resolution'. Section 142(1) of the CA 1963 describes what must happen in order for an extended notice resolution to be valid:

> 'Subject to *subsection (2)*, where by any provision hereafter contained in this Act extended notice is required of a resolution, the resolution shall not be effective unless (except when the directors of the company have resolved to submit it) notice of the intention to move it has been given to the company not less than 28 days before the meeting at which it is moved, and the company shall give its members notice of any such resolution at the same time and in the same manner as it gives notice of the meeting or, if that is not practicable, shall give them notice thereof, either by advertisement in a daily newspaper circulating in the district in which the registered office of the company is situate or in any other mode allowed by the articles, not less than 21 days before the meeting.'

Accordingly, it is clear that where the board of directors resolves to convene an AGM or EGM and put to that meeting an extended notice resolution, nothing additional is required in order for the resolution to be effective, and it can be put to the meeting in the same way as any resolution. Where, however, the initiative to put such a resolution to a general meeting comes from the members of the company and not the directors, s 142(1) imposes a procedure to be followed by both the company and the member.

---

110 Section 161(1)(a) of the CA 1963.

111 Section 161(1)(b) of the CA 1963.

112 Section 182(2) of the CA 1963.

[14.045] Where a member wishes to propose an extended notice resolution, the member must notify the company of his intention to propose it 28 days before the meeting at which it is to be moved. Section 142 does not, it must be remembered, confer any substantive right to convene a meeting at which to consider such a resolution and the only right a member has in this regard is that provided by s 132 of the CA 1963[113]. Since a member has no means of knowing when an EGM will be convened by the directors (which can be called on either 21 days' notice if special resolutions are to be considered or seven days' notice if ordinary resolutions are to be considered), s 142 is in effect a 'blocker' which prevents members from springing extended notice resolutions at AGMs or EGMs.

[14.046] Companies cannot, however, thwart members from putting extended notice resolutions by immediately convening a meeting to be held less than 28 days after it receives the notice; technically, it could convene an EGM to consider a special resolution the day it receives the notice so that the member's notice would have been given less than 28 days before that EGM. This is prevented by s 142(2) which provides:

> 'If, after notice of the intention to move such a resolution has been given to the company, a meeting is called for a date 28 days or less after the notice has been given, the notice though not given within the time required by *subsection (1)* shall be deemed to have been properly given for the purposes of that subsection.'

Where a company receives a notice under s 142(1) from a member, it must give its other members notice of such resolution at the same time and in the same manner as it gives notice of the meeting or if this is not practicable, it shall give notice by advertisement or in some other way permitted by the articles not less than 21 days before the meeting.

[14.047] Where the members (or member in the case of a holding company) wish to reserve the right to remove directors and do so outside of s 142, this can be achieved be providing in the articles, for example, that a director is automatically removed from office upon service by the member of a notice to that effect on the company. Sections 162, 182 and 142 only regulate *resolutions* put to general meetings and not any other means of removing directors or auditors.

(d) Accidental omission to give notice

[14.048] Reg 52 of the model articles provides that:

> 'The accidental omission to give notice of a meeting to, or the non-receipt of notice of a meeting by, any person entitled to receive notice shall not invalidate the proceedings at the meeting.'

Furthermore, reg 133 provides that where notice is sent by post, service of the notice shall be deemed to be effected 'by properly addressing, prepaying and posting a letter containing the notice, and to have been effected in the case of the notice of a meeting at the expiration of 24 hours after the letter containing the same is posted'. This has, however, been interpreted in England as not entitling those who serve such notices to disregard reality. Thus, in *Bradman v Trinity Estates plc*[114] a company sent to its members notice of an impending meeting during a postal strike. Those shareholders

---

113 See para **[14.019]** *ante*.

114 *Bradman v Trinity Estates plc* [1989] BCLC 757.

who lived within London were notified by courier, but those outside London were mailed their notices, and it transpired that, in some cases, the notices did not arrive until after the meeting had been held. As in the Irish model articles, the articles of the company allowed notices to be served by post[115]. One shareholder sought an injunction to restrain the holding of the meeting on the grounds, *inter alia*, that the meeting had not been validly summoned under the provisions of the company's articles. It was held by Hoffmann J that the equivalent article to the Irish reg 133 was open to an interpretation other than a literal interpretation. In particular, it was arguable that in the circumstances of a postal dispute, the posting of notices could not be deemed to have been effective service on all the shareholders. It was also convenient to grant an injunction because if it subsequently transpired that the meeting had been convened invalidly, it would be very difficult to unravel business transacted thereat. In the instant case he granted an injunction preventing the meeting from being held, and suggested that the chairman should adjourn it[116].

(e) Summary of notice provisions

[14.049] The Companies Acts provide for different notice provisions where it is proposed to consider a special resolution as opposed to an ordinary resolution. The provisions of the CA 1963 may be summarised thus:

- In the case of an AGM, 21 days' notice must be given whether or not a special resolution is proposed[117].
- Although in the case of an EGM only seven days' notice is generally required, where it is proposed to consider a special resolution, 21 days' notice is required[118].
- An AGM or EGM can be held on short notice where all of the members and the auditors so consent – but this does not abrogate the 21 days' notice requirement for special resolutions[119];
- In the case of a special resolution, notice of less than 21 days' may be given for the meeting at which it has been passed where a majority of the company's members who are entitled to vote and who hold not less than 90% of the nominal value of the shares, so agree[120];
- Save where proposed by the directors, members proposing an extended notice resolution[121] must give the company 28 days' notice of his or her intention to propose such a resolution[122].

---

115 Regulation 133 of Part I, Table A, First Schedule to the CA 1963. However, the articles of that company also allowed notices to be served by an alternative method, where there was a 'total suspension or curtailment of postal services'.

116 See *Re Waterford Foods plc* (1992) Irish Times, 12 May, at para **[14.028]** *ante*.

117 Section 133(2) of the CA 1963. See para **[14.040]** *ante*.

118 Section 141(1) of the CA 1963. See para **[14.042]** *ante* and **[14.085]** *post*.

119 Section 133(3) of the CA 1963.

120 Section 141(2) of the CA 1963. See para **[14.042]**.

121 See para **[14.044]** *ante*.

122 Section 142 of the CA 1963.

Notice of business to be conducted at a meeting

[14.050] The notice requirements for the convening of members' meetings last considered concern simple notice of the *fact that a meeting is intended to be held*. Here we examine notice of the *business that it is proposed to consider* at meetings. Where the business before the meeting will be either 'special business' or a special resolution, notice of the intention to transact such specific business must also be given in the notice convening the meeting[123].

(a) Notice of special business

[14.051] Although the concepts of '*special business*' and '*ordinary business*' are becoming obsolete terms in the context of the law of meetings, they will remain of some importance for as long as the model articles of association contain reference to them. Model reg 51 provides that the notice of meetings shall '... specify ... in the case of special business, the general nature of that business'. As to what constitutes 'special business', reg 53 of Table A provides:

> 'All business shall be deemed special that is transacted at an extraordinary general meeting, and also all that is transacted at an annual general meeting, with the exception of declaring a dividend, the consideration of the accounts, balance sheets and the reports of the directors and auditors, the election of directors in the place of those retiring, the re-appointment of the retiring auditors and the fixing of the remuneration of the auditors.'

In theory, there is no need for a notice of an AGM to set out any of the matters referred to in reg 53 as the members are deemed to have notice of the provision in the articles and so of the agenda items[124]; practice is, however, to detail not only the matters to be considered but also the order in which they are to be considered in an agenda. The notice required to be given of special business does not need to be as detailed or exact as in the case of a proposed special resolution, and it has been held that a general indication of the business is sufficient[125]. However, care should be taken as where insufficient particulars of the special business to be conducted are given, an injunction to restrain the holding of the meeting may be obtained[126].

(b) Notice of special resolutions

[14.052] Where it is proposed to pass a special resolution, s 141(1) of the CA 1963 provides that the notice should also specify the wording of the proposed special resolution[127]. In the English case of *Re Moorgate Mercantile Holdings Ltd*[128], Slade J held that:

---

[123] Cordes et al, *Shackleton on the Law and Practice of Meetings* (12th edn, 2011) at pp 41–43.

[124] *Choppington Collieries v Johnson* [1944] 1 All ER 762. See generally, *Shackleton on the Law and Practice of Meetings* (12th edn, 2011) at p 40.

[125] In *Betts & Co Ltd v Mcnaghten* [1910] Ch 430, it was held that notice of an intention to propose the appointment of three directors was broad enough to cover the appointment of an additional two directors where the resolution was so amended at the meeting.

[126] See *Jackson v Munster Bank* (1884–85) 13 LR 118.

[127] See para **[14.084]** *post*.

[128] *Re Moorgate Mercantile Holdings Ltd* [1980] 1 All ER 40.

> '... if a special resolution passed at a general meeting is to be valid, it must be the same resolution as that which the requisite notice has specified the intention to propose ... If, however, there is any difference whatsoever of substance between the two I would not, in the absence of authority, have regarded the later resolution, which was actually passed, as having been preceded by proper notice ...'.

In that case, a special resolution purportedly passed by a company's members was held not to have been validly passed as it differed not only in form but also in substance from the one set out in the notice for the meeting. Unless the difference between the proposed resolution which has been notified and the actual resolution laid before the members is of a mere grammatical or clerical nature or otherwise inconsequential[129], the notice given may be deemed to be invalid[130]. Where notice of a special resolution has been given, its terms may be amended by ordinary resolution moved at the meeting provided that the terms of the resolution as amended will still be such that adequate notice of the intention to pass the same can be considered to have been given[131]. Such a waiver by the members was found not to have been given in *Re Moorgate Mercantile Holdings Ltd*[132]. Moreover, in that case it was held by Slade J that in giving notice of a special resolution to be passed, nothing would be achieved by the addition of such words as 'with such amendments and alterations as shall be determined on at the general meeting'. Special resolutions are considered in more detail, below[133].

(c) Other matters

[14.053] Whether a meeting (AGM or EGM) is convened by the directors or by the members (pursuant to s 132 of the CA 1963, considered above[134]) it beholds those convening it or requisitioning its convening to represent accurately the basis for the need to propose resolutions. This has already been considered in the circumstances of members requisitioning an EGM but the principle applies equally to where directors convene a meeting for the purposes of passing a resolution. In *Re European Home Products plc*[135], Mervyn Davies J held that it was not easy to secure the court's confirmation for resolutions passed on the strength of a circular that contained inaccurate information; in that case the court made an exception since it found that although reasonable shareholders could have been misled, they were not in fact misled. The finding in the case must be seen as very much the exception, and every care should be taken to accurately represent the facts upon which shareholders are asked to base their judgment when voting on a resolution.

---

129 See *Re Willaire Systems plc* [1987] BCLC 67.

130 It has been said that '[a]s far as ordinary resolutions are concerned, there is a greater latitude for amendments to be proposed and passed at a general meeting, even though they were not notified to members in advance in the same way as the original resolution': Jones & Jacobs, *Company Meetings: Law and Procedure* (1991, Longman) at p 93. See *Baillie v Oriental Telephone & Electric Co Ltd* [1915] 1 Ch 503. *Cf Henderson v Bank of Australasia* (1890) 45 Ch D 330.

131 Section 141(5) of the CA 1963.

132 *Re Moorgate Mercantile Holdings Ltd* [1980] 1 All ER 40.

133 See para **[14.085]** *post*.

134 See para **[14.019]** *ante*.

135 *Re European Home Products plc* (1988) 4 BCC 779.

[14.054] Issues arise where notice of a resolution has been given and on the holding of the meeting it is desired to amend the resolution to be put to the meeting. Where notice has been given of an *ordinary resolution*, it can be amended at the meeting provided that the proposed change does not alter the essential intention of the original resolution[136]. A resolution to wind up a company where notice was given of a resolution to wind up the company for the purpose of a reconstruction, has been held to be invalid[137]. On the other hand, a resolution to wind up a company and appoint X as liquidator instead of winding up and appointing Y as liquidator has, however, been held to be valid[138]. A stricter test applies in the case of an amendment to a *special resolution*, and in such cases, there can be no amendment to the substance (however slight) of the resolution of which notice was given[139].

The quorum

[14.055] Every company may validly decide in its own articles the requisite quorum for a general meeting of the company[140] but, by virtue of s 134(c) of the CA 1963, unless the articles of the company provide otherwise, the quorum shall be two. Under model reg 5, the quorum for a general meeting of the members of a private company limited by shares is two members, 'present in person or by proxy'. Section 134(c) of the CA 1963 provides that (in so far as the articles of the company do not make other provision in that behalf):

> '… in the case of a private company two members, and in the case of any other company three members, personally present shall be a quorum.'

Model reg 55 provides that 'if within half an hour from the time appointed for the meeting a quorum is not present, the meeting, if convened upon the requisition of members, shall be dissolved'. If otherwise convened, 'it shall stand adjourned to the same day in the next week, at the same time and place or to such other day and at such other time and place as the directors may determine, and if at the adjourned meeting a quorum is not present within half an hour from the time appointed for the meeting, the members present shall be a quorum'. Where a quorate meeting is convened, it was held in *Re Hartley Baird Ltd*[141] that where members leave during the course of the meeting, it will remain validly constituted and subsequent decisions taken will be valid. It may be observed that in *Re Hartley Baird* the company's articles required a quorum of 10 members; in the case of a company requiring a quorum of two members and where only one member is left, it is questionable as to whether the courts would uphold business subsequently transacted[142].

---

136 See generally Cordes et al, *Shackleton on the Law and Practice of Meetings* (12th edn, Sweet & Maxwell, 2011) at pp 182, 183.

137 *Re Teele & Bishop* (1901) 70 LJ 409.

138 *Re Trench Tubeless Tyre Co* [1900] 1 Ch 408.

139 *Re Moorgate Mercantile Holdings* [1980] 1 All ER 40, considered at para **[14.052]**.

140 The requisite quorum for a members' meeting may be agreed between the members in a shareholders' agreement: *BLM Group Ltd v Harman* (1994) Times, 8 April (Court of Appeal).

141 *Re Hartley Baird Ltd* [1954] Ch 143.

142 See *Re London Flats Ltd* [1969] 1 WLR 711.

[14.056] In the case of single-member companies, reg 10 of the EC(SMPLC)R 1994[143] provides:

> 'Notwithstanding any provision to the contrary in the articles of a single-member company, one member present in person or by proxy shall be a quorum.'

Notwithstanding s 134(c) of the CA 1963, in the case of single-member companies, reg 10 shall apply as otherwise a meeting could never be held or, more importantly, the business required to be transacted at a meeting could not be transacted. Except as provided for by s 135 of the CA 1963 and reg 10, above, it has been held that a single person cannot as a rule constitute a quorate meeting[144].

[14.057] A meeting will not be quorate where the quorum is two members and only one member is present, even if a deceased member's executors are present. This was confirmed by Carroll J in *Arulchelvan and another v Wright et al*[145] on the grounds that by virtue of s 31 of the CA 1963, a person is not a member unless his name is on the register of members and, specifically, that a personal representative is not a member until such time as he is registered as such. Interpreting the articles of association, Carroll J held that although a personal representative is recognised as having title to a deceased member's shares (reg 29) and is entitled to dividends (reg 32) he is not entitled to exercise any right conferred by membership (reg 32). Carroll J went on to hold that as the deceased member's personal representatives had not been registered as members, they could not be counted as forming part of the quorum and since no quorum was present, no business had been transacted at the purported meeting.

Postponing and adjourning meetings

[14.058] In *Smith v Paringa Mines Ltd*[146], it was held that a company's directors may not *postpone* a general meeting that has been validly convened, unless the articles of association expressly empower them to so postpone. In that case, a company's directors convened an AGM. Later that day one of its shareholders (who was also a director) initiated proceedings against the company and, on learning of this, the directors purported to postpone the AGM pending the outcome of the litigation. The shareholder wrote to the company and advised that he had taken advice that the AGM could not be postponed and advertised in the press that the AGM would be held. On the appointed day for the AGM the shareholder (and others) attended but the directors and secretary did not. At this meeting the shareholder and certain others were elected directors and the existing directors and secretary voted out of office. The case arose out of the plaintiff shareholders' action against the old directors and secretary in which an order was sought directing them to deliver-up the company's books, records and seal. The court granted the order sought, finding that the AGM had been validly convened, and held and that it could not be postponed. Kekewich J held:

---

143 SI 275/1994.

144 See *Arulchelvan and another v Wright et al* (7 February 1996, unreported) HC, Carroll J at para **[14.025]** *ante*; *Re London Flats Ltd [1969] 1 WLR 711*; and *Sharp v Dawes* [1876] 2 QBD 26.

145 *Arulchelvan and another v Wright et al* (7 February 1996, unreported) HC, Carroll J.

146 *Smith v Paringa Mines Ltd* [1906] 2 Ch 193.

> '… it was not competent for the board to postpone the meeting. The articles provide for the adjournment of a general meeting in certain events, but they contain no provision for postponement. It is said that the directors must be able to postpone the meeting because they may fix the time and place at which the meeting is to be held; but in my opinion that is not so. On the other hand, if the directors had power to postpone, and a meeting adverse to the directors was called, they might postpone it for a week or a month, or perhaps *sine die*[147].'

Where a meeting has been convened, and circumstances arise which make it undesirable to hold the meeting, then – in the absence of the articles expressly providing for postponement – the appropriate course of action would be to meet but then immediately adjourn the meeting *sine die*[148].

[14.059] Adjournment of meetings is regulated by model reg 58 which states:

> 'The chairman may, with the consent of any meeting at which a quorum is present, and shall if so directed by the meeting, adjourn the meeting from time to time and from place to place, but no business shall be transacted at any adjourned meeting other than the business left unfinished at the meeting from which the adjournment took place. When a meeting is adjourned for 30 days or more, notice of the adjourned meeting shall be given as in the case of an original meeting. Save as aforesaid it shall not be necessary to give any notice of an adjournment or of the business to be transacted at an adjourned meeting.'

[14.060] Where a resolution is passed at a meeting of a company which had been adjourned at an earlier meeting, the resolution shall for all purposes be treated as having been passed on the date on which it was in fact passed and shall not be deemed to have been passed on any earlier date[149]. It was held in *Holmes and another v Keyes et al*[150] that a resolution on which a poll was taken had been passed on the date the result became known. In that case a poll was taken on the election of directors on 23 December but the result was not known until 24 December. The directors, who were obliged to hold qualification shares within two months of their appointment, only acquired their shares on 24 February of the following year. The question arose as to whether they had acquired them within the requisite period of two months. The Court of Appeal held that the directors had been elected on 24 December, the date upon which the result became known. Jenkins LJ held:

> 'In my judgment, the ascertainment of the result should be considered as part of the poll, and, consequently, there can be no appointment of a director by a general meeting until the result of the poll is ascertained. It is only then that the appointment can become in any sense effective. I think that, in effect, the meeting should be treated as continuing until the result of the voting on the poll is ascertained. Unless the appointment begins when the result of the poll is ascertained and on no earlier date, it would be impossible for the company to know who its directors were. It seems to me that produces a really quite impossible result[151].'

---

147 *Smith v Paringa Mines Ltd* [1906] 2 Ch 193 at 197, 198.

148 See Cordes et al, *Shackleton on The Law and Practice of Meetings* (12th edn, 2011) at p 147.

149 Section 144 of the CA 1963.

150 *Holmes and another v Keyes et al* [1959] 1 Ch 199.

151 *Holmes and another v Keyes et al* [1959] 1 Ch 199 at 216.

Voting at members' meetings

[14.061] To be entitled to vote at a general meeting, a member's name must be registered in the register of members[152]. In this respect, a company is not obliged to await the registration of particular persons as shareholders and members before convening and holding a meeting. There is no obligation on the chairman of a meeting to adjourn it pending the registration of share transfers, in order to facilitate a person acquiring voting rights[153]. The decision as to when to hold a general meeting is, however, an exercise of directors' powers which must be exercised in a *bona fide* manner and there is authority for saying that the company must have some regard for the interests of its shareholders[154]. Here, the following issues are considered:

(a) 'One member one vote' or one vote per share;

(b) Voting on a poll;

(c) Voting by representatives;

(d) Voting by proxy.

(a) 'One member one vote' or one vote per share

[14.062] Voting at general meetings will be effected in either of two ways: on a show of hands or on a poll. The norm is on a show of hands, which will apply unless a poll is called[155]. Where voting is by a show of hands, the general rule is that of 'one member one vote'; on a poll the general rule is one vote for each share held. Model reg 63 states:

> 'Subject to any rights or restrictions for the time being attached to any class or classes of shares, on a show of hands every member present in person and every proxy shall have one vote, so, however, that no individual shall have more than one vote, and on a poll every member shall have one vote for each share of which he is the holder.'

Section 134(e) of the CA 1963 provides that, in so far as the articles of the company do not make other provision in that behalf, in the case of a company originally having a share capital, every member shall have one vote in respect of each share or each £10 of stock held by him, and in any other case, every member shall have one vote. Of course it is open to companies to decide what voting rights each share or class of share shall have and in what circumstances such arises[156]. If there is an equality of votes, whether on a show of hand or on a poll, the chairman of the meeting at which the show of hands takes

---

152 Section 31 of the CA 1963. Where the articles of association prescribe a procedure for admission as a member, it must be followed. In *POW Services Ltd and another v Clare et al* [1995] 2 BCLC 435, it was held an EGM had not been validly constituted because admission to membership required a decision of the company's council as to whether a person should be admitted, and the procedure adopted was defective since it conferred membership on a virtual automatic administrative basis which was insufficient to comply with the company's articles.

153 *Kinsella et al v Alliance and Dublin Consumers Gas Company et al* (5 October 1982, unreported) HC *per* Barron J: see Ch 9, *Share Transfer*, at para **[9.023]**.

154 In *Cannon v Trask* (1875) 20 Eq 669, an injunction was granted restraining the holding of an AGM in circumstances where the directors had convened the AGM several weeks earlier than was usual and before the plaintiff's voting rights under recently effected transfers had been registered.

155 Model reg 59. See para **[14.067]** *post*.

156 *Bushell v Faith* [1970] AC 1099.

place or at which the poll is demanded, shall be entitled to a second or casting vote[157]. This is the default in most companies' articles but it will usually be removed in a joint venture company.

[14.063] On a vote on a show of hands, the amount of shares held by a member will not, unless the articles provide otherwise, add to or take from his voting power, the general rule being one member, one vote[158]. Unless a poll is demanded[159], model articles of association provide that a declaration by the chairman that a resolution has, on a show of hands, been carried or carried unanimously, or by a particular majority, or lost, and an entry to that effect in the book containing the minutes of the proceedings of the company shall be conclusive evidence of the fact without proof of the number or proportion of the votes recorded in favour of or against such resolution: model reg 59. A similar provision to model reg 59 was interpreted in *Re Hadleigh Castle Gold Mines Ltd*[160]. In that case, Cozens Hardy J held that in the absence of fraud, or the valid requisition of a poll, the declaration of the chairman of a meeting that a special resolution has been passed, is conclusive. The learned judge said that:

> '… "unless a poll is demanded by at least five members a declaration of the chairman that the resolution has been carried shall be deemed conclusive evidence of the fact without proof of the number or proportion of the votes recorded in favour of or against the same". "Conclusive" seems to me to be a clear word … I cannot regard "conclusive" as equivalent to "sufficient". I think the legislature intended, in the case of a special or extraordinary resolution, that the chairman's declaration should be conclusive unless challenged by means of a poll demanded by five members[161].'

[14.064] On a vote on a show of hands, it is not possible to split one's vote. Accordingly, it was held in *McGrattan v McGrattan*[162] that where a member of a company held shares in his own right and also held shares in trust, where he voted at a general meeting on a show of hands, his vote could not be split so that he must be taken to have voted both his own shares and the shares he held in trust by raising his hand and voting. For this reason, where a shareholder holds shares on trust for different persons, and receives divergent instructions on how to vote those shares, he should call for a poll to be taken.

[14.065] Care must be taken, however, not to be complacent when following such an apparently informal voting method as a 'show of hands'. In *Re The Citizens' Theatre Ltd*[163], an EGM was convened to consider a special resolution to effect a change in the company's memorandum. The resolution was proposed and seconded and when there was no counter motion the chairman, without calling for a show of hands, declared that the resolution had been passed as a special resolution. It was held that as there had been no show of hands, the resolution had not been effectively submitted to the meeting and

---

157 Model reg 61.

158 See Ch 3, *Constitutional Documentation*, at para **[3.053]**.

159 See para **[14.068]** *post*.

160 *Re Hadleigh Castle Gold Mines Ltd* [1900] 2 Ch 419.

161 *Re Hadleigh Castle Gold Mines Ltd* [1900] 2 Ch 419 at 421, 422. Note that Cozens Hardy J distinguished *Young v Sough African and Australian Exploration and Development Syndicate* [1896] 2 Ch 275.

162 *McGrattan v McGrattan* [1985] NI 28.

163 *Re The Citizens' Theatre Ltd* (1948) SC 14.

that, in those circumstances, reliance could not be placed upon wording similar to model reg 59.

[14.066] Model articles provide that where there are joint holders of shares, the vote of the senior (as determined by the order of the joint holders' names in the register of members) who tenders a vote, whether in person or by proxy, shall be accepted[164]. Again, the model articles disenfranchise any member where there are outstanding calls or other sums immediately payable by him in respect of the shares he holds[165]. Objections to the qualification of voting members can only be raised at the meeting or adjourned meeting at which they vote and every vote not disallowed shall be valid; objections must, by the model articles, be referred to the chairman whose decision is final and conclusive[166].

(b) Voting on a poll

[14.067] In the Irish High Court decision in *Duggan v The Governor and Company of the Bank of Ireland*[167], McCracken J described the purpose of a poll:

> 'It is important to recognise the purpose of the taking of a poll at meetings of shareholders or stockholders. Largely for reasons of convenience, if a motion is put to a general meeting, it is initially decided on a show of hands, on the basis that each person present has one vote, irrespective of the number of shares they hold. When that result is known, normally any member … [or number of members, depending upon the articles] … or the chairman may demand a poll. This is frequently done where the persons who are defeated on a show of hands feel that in fact they have a greater shareholding than those who succeeded. In the present case, the chairman decided to hold a poll because he was not prepared to determine whether the resolution has been passed or not on a show of hands. However, the essence of a poll is that, instead of there being a principle of one vote for each shareholder, there is one vote for each share … Thus the purpose of a poll is to allow those with the greatest financial interest in the company ultimately to determine the outcome of any vote[168].'

Unlike a vote on a show of hands – where the rule of *one member one vote* applies – in the case of a vote on a poll, the general rule (subject to the articles) is *one vote per share*.

[14.068] An article that excludes the right to demand a poll on any question other than the election of the chairman of the meeting is void[169]; provided, however, that companies can (within certain parameters)[170] regulate when a poll can be demanded. The usual

---

164 Model reg 64.

165 Model reg 66.

166 Model reg 67.

167 *Duggan v The Governor and Company of the Bank of Ireland* (29 July 1998, unreported) HC, McCracken J.

168 *Duggan v The Governor and Company of the Bank of Ireland* (29 July 1998, unreported) HC, McCracken J at p 4 of the transcript.

169 Section 137(1) of the CA 1963.

170 Section 137(1)(b) of the CA 1963 provides that a demand for a poll cannot be deemed ineffective where it is made '(i) by not less than five members having the right to vote at the meeting, or (ii) by a member or members representing not less than one-tenth of the total voting rights of all the members having the right to vote at the meeting, or (iii) by a member or members holding shares in the company conferring a right to vote at the meeting, being shares on which an aggregate sum has been paid up equal to not less than one-tenth of the total sum paid up on all the shares conferring that right'.

manner in which the calling of a poll is regulated is provided for in model reg 59, which provides:

> 'At any general meeting a resolution put to the vote of the meeting shall be decided on a show of hands unless a poll is (before or on the declaration of the result of the show of hands) demanded—
>
> (a) by the chairman; or
>
> (b) by at least three members present in person or by proxy; or
>
> (c) by any member or members present in person or by proxy and representing not less than one-tenth of the total voting rights of all the members having the right to vote at the meeting; or
>
> (d) by a member or members holding shares in the company conferring the right to vote at the meeting being shares on which an aggregate sum has been paid up equal to not less than one-tenth of the total sum paid up on all the shares conferring that right …'

In addition to providing for the conclusiveness of a chairman's declaration, this article also provides that a poll may be withdrawn. In *The Second Consolidated Trust Ltd v Ceylon Amalgamated Tea & Rubber Estates Ltd et al*[171], it was held that the right of a chairman to demand a poll was not a personal right and that the chairman of a meeting had an obligation to demand a poll where such was necessary to give effect to the real sense of the meeting.

[14.069] Where a poll is demanded by members, it should be noted that a proxy's demand counts equally with that of a member because an instrument of proxy is deemed by s 137(2) to confer authority to demand or join in demanding a poll[172]. On a poll, a member entitled to more than one vote need not, if he votes, use all his votes or cast all the votes he uses in the same way[173]. The manner in which a poll is taken will, under model articles, be as directed by the chairman[174]; where, however, the poll is taken on the election of a chairman, it shall be taken forthwith, but otherwise a poll will be taken at such time as the chairman directs, whether before or after any other business.[175] The result of a poll is deemed to be the resolution of the meeting[176].

[14.070] In *Duggan v The Governor and Company of the Bank of Ireland*[177], the defendant company – that is, established by charter and not a company to which the Companies Acts apply, automatically[178] – proposed to amend its articles of association (known in the case of the defendant company as its bye-laws) to provide that on a poll,

171 *The Second Consolidated Trust Ltd v Ceylon Amalgamated Tea & Rubber Estates Ltd et al* [1943] 2 Ch 567.

172 See also model reg 72 of Table A.

173 Section 138 of the CA 1963.

174 Model reg 60 of Table A.

175 Model reg 62 of Table A.

176 Model reg 60 of Table A.

177 *Duggan v The Governor and Company of the Bank of Ireland* (29 July 1998, unreported) HC, McCracken J.

178 The Governor and Company of the Bank of Ireland is an 'unregistered company' within the meaning of s 377 of the CA 1963, to which the provisions set out in the Ninth Schedule to the CA 1963, as amended, apply.

each member should have one vote for each £1 of ordinary stock of the defendant company without limit. This had the effect of removing a 'cap' then contained in the bye-laws limiting a member's right to vote *to the extent that he held stock exceeding 1%* of the defendant company's shares. At the AGM the resolution was considered by the meeting, a number of people from the floor spoke against the resolution and the plaintiff put forward an amendment that would have had the effect of retaining the cap but increasing it to 3% of stock. On a vote on a show of hands, the chairman refused to call the vote on the basis that it was too tight to call and that he did not see a discernible majority either way. Accordingly, the chairman called a poll, saying:

> 'There are 122,803,863 votes in favour of the resolution for supporting the directors. Only those who oppose the resolution need vote, to speed up the process. If you wish to vote No, you may get a ballot from the stewards along each row and if you have any query, ask the stewards[179].'

The plaintiff asked in respect of the 120 million qualified votes, could the defendant company's proxy exercise all the one-percents and was told they had been vetted and approved by the auditors. Those who wished to vote were given a ballot paper, the votes were cast and counted and ultimately the chairman declared the resolution carried, saying that the final position was that there were circa 122.8 million for and 0.68 million against. As regard the expeditious means employed by the chairman – only inviting votes from those who wished to vote against the resolution – and after noting that one of the bye-laws gave the chairman the discretion to direct how the will of those with a majority financial interest was to be determined, McCracken J said of the chairman, that:

> 'He was, of course, aware that he held such a large number of proxies that the resolution was in fact going to be passed, however he had an obligation to allow those who disagreed with the resolution to exercise their vote. I think it is unfortunate that he tried to cut corners by only seeking votes against the resolution, but that does not necessarily invalidate the poll or affect the question of whether he did in fact exercise the votes contained in the proxies. In my view the discretion given to him was so wide as to allow him to give the discretion which he gave …[180].'

It seems clear that it would, accordingly, be prudent on a poll to invite both those for and against a resolution to vote.

[14.071] In *Duggan v The Governor and Company of the Bank of Ireland*[181], another point raised by the plaintiff was whether in fact the chairman had cast the votes to which he was, undoubtedly, entitled to cast, pursuant to proxies received. In this case the chairman had simply said 'there are 122,803,863 votes in favour of the resolution for supporting the directors'. McCracken J had no doubt but that the chairman had *intended* to exercise the votes and that this was clear to everybody present at the meeting. McCracken J said of the words used by the chairman that:

---

179 *Duggan v The Governor and Company of the Bank of Ireland* (29 July 1998, unreported) HC, McCracken J at p 2 of the transcript.

180 *Duggan v The Governor and Company of the Bank of Ireland* (29 July 1998, unreported) HC, McCracken J at p 4, 5 of the transcript.

181 *Duggan v The Governor and Company of the Bank of Ireland* (29 July 1998, unreported) HC, McCracken J.

> 'I do not think that could be interpreted as anything other than his exercising the vote contained in those proxies. It should be noted that he did not merely state that he held proxies of this number of votes, but he specifically said that there were those number of votes in favour, and he said it having already declared that there was going to be a poll. In that context, I think there was a clear exercise of the votes by him[182].'

The final question considered by McCracken J was whether the casting of votes by a proxy is required to be in writing. In this respect the learned judge said:

> 'I know of no general proposition, nor is there anything contained in the bye-laws [articles of association], which require votes in a poll to be cast in writing. The only reason why there might be such an implied requirement would be to ensure that there is a record of the votes cast. In the present cast there was such a record, as the proxies existed and were in writing, and furthermore were actually signed by the stockholders themselves. If there is any need for there to be a record in writing of votes cast at a poll, and I do not have to determine that matter, any such requirement is satisfied by the existence of the proxy documents which are of course available to the scrutineers who are counting the votes[183].'

It is recommended that wherever any decision (particularly an exercise of discretion) is taken, it is preferable that there is a written record of that decision. A simple letter from the chairman or other person entitled to act as proxy, indicating that he is casting those votes in favour of or against the resolution in question, is thought to be desirable.

(c) Voting by representatives

[14.072] Not all members will be able to vote in person and in certain limited instances, members may appoint *representatives*. Persons of unsound mind may vote, on a show of hands or on a poll, by their committee, receiver, guardian or other person appointed by the court, and such persons may, in turn, like bodies corporate, also appoint proxies[184].

[14.073] In the case of members that are bodies corporate, s 139(1)(a) of the CA 1963 provides that a body corporate may:

> 'if it is a member of a company, by resolution of its directors or other governing body authorise such person as it thinks fit to act as its representative at any meeting of the company or at any meeting of any class of members of the company[185].'

A person authorised as aforesaid shall be entitled to exercise the same powers on behalf of the body corporate which he represents as that body corporate could exercise if it were an individual member, creditor or holder of debentures of the company[186]. Where a corporate member is in liquidation, the liquidator may appoint a person to represent it[187]. A body corporate may, instead of appointing a representative, appoint a proxy. It should be noted that there are differences between a corporate representative and a proxy appointed by a body corporate, eg, a representative's appointment need not be notified

[182] *Duggan v The Governor and Company of the Bank of Ireland* (29 July 1998, unreported) HC, McCracken J at p 5 of the transcript.

[183] *Duggan v The Governor and Company of the Bank of Ireland* (29 July 1998, unreported) HC, McCracken J at p 5 of the transcript.

[184] Model reg 75 of Table A

[185] This is echoed in model reg 74 of Table A.

[186] Section 139(2) of the CA 1963.

[187] See *Hillman v Crystal Bowl Amusement Ltd* [1973] 1 WLR 162.

ahead of the meeting whereas a proxy's must. While both natural and legal persons can appoint proxies, only bodies corporate can appoint representatives. Blanchard J explained the rationale for this in *Mauri Development Corporation Ltd v Power Beat International Ltd*[188] thus:

> 'A corporation, which is an entirely abstract concept, clearly cannot attend meetings in person so in its case the legislation provides for attendance on its behalf by a representative who acts as the agent of the company and can do anything at the meeting which the corporation could have done if it were a human shareholder.
>
> A corporation is thereby given an advantage not available to a human being, who cannot be represented at a meeting except by means of a proxy … in respect of whom a notice of appointment has to have been given to the company up to 48 hours prior to the meeting, if the articles so provide[189].'

In that case, a company's board of directors appointed a person as its *proxy* 'to attend and act on its behalf' at an EGM of the company in which it was a shareholder and the proxy was given verbal instructions as to how to vote. The member company made a failed attempt to fax a proxy through to the company holding the EGM. Subsequently, the 'proxy' attended the meeting, signed in as agent of the member company and addressed the meeting as the 'representative' of the member company; he signed the polls on the resolutions under consideration as 'proxy' of the member company. The chairman of the meeting disallowed his votes for want of compliance with the relevant statute and the company's articles. It was held by the New Zealand High Court that the person had attended the meeting not only as a purported proxy, but also as a representative within the meaning of s 143 of the New Zealand Companies Act 1955 (which was materially identical to s 139(1)(a) of the CA 1963). In so finding, the court held that the right to attend and vote depended upon whether the member company had validly resolved to authorise him to act as representative and that this was a matter of fact. Unlike the CA 1963 or the model articles therein, the articles of the company holding the EGM provided that where a representative was appointed, the chairman of the meeting could seek evidence of a representative's authority. However, here the court held that the chairman and board knew full well that he was not a proxy – since no proxy form had been appointed – and that under the articles he was only obliged to produce evidence of his authority if so called upon by the chairman. Blanchard J went on to say:

> 'The right to vote does not depend upon the evidence offered (if any) but rather upon whether a valid resolution of the shareholder appointing the representative has in fact been passed. Further, if no objection is taken to the representation and no inquiry made as to the status of the representative prior to the declaration by the chairman of the result of the poll, the representative must be taken to have validly cast the vote of the corporate shareholder. The company cannot later rely upon a ground of invalidity not then specified by the chairman[190].'

---

188 *Mauri Development Corporation Ltd v Power Beat International Ltd* [1995] 2 NZLR 568.

189 *Mauri Development Corporation Ltd v Power Beat International Ltd* [1995] 2 NZLR 568 at 574.

190 *Mauri Development Corporation Ltd v Power Beat International Ltd* [1995] 2 NZLR 568 at 576, citing *ANZ Nominees Ltd v Allied Resources Corporation Ltd* (1984) 2 ACLC 783 at 788 as authority for the last sentence.

While the model Irish articles of association are silent on a company's authority to seek evidence of a representative's authority, it seems clear that the chairman of a meeting can seek such to establish not only a purported representative's authority, but also his *bona fides*. One learned English commentator has said that 'the company may be unwise to debar the representative from attending and voting unless it has, after careful enquiry, formed the view that no resolution had been passed'[191]. It is thought, however, that it is more accurate to say that to allow a person to attend and vote without careful enquiry would be imprudent.

(*d*) *Voting by proxy*

[14.074] Section 136(1) of the CA 1963 and model reg 68 provide that members entitled to attend and vote at a meeting (whether a general meeting or a class meeting) may cast their votes in person or *by proxy*[192]. Moreover, a member's proxy (a contraction of 'procuracy'[193]) shall have the same right as the member to speak at the meeting and to vote on a show of hands and on a poll[194]. Unless the articles provide otherwise, members of companies not having a share capital are not entitled to appoint proxies and, in every company, unless the articles provide otherwise, members are not entitled to appoint more than one proxy[195]. Where members have a right to appoint proxies, a statement to this effect must appear with reasonable prominence on the notice calling the meeting[196]. Companies cannot insist upon receiving an instrument appointing a proxy or other document necessary to show the validity of or otherwise relating to the appointment of a proxy more than 48 hours before a meeting or adjourned meeting[197]. Model reg 70 makes provision for proxies to be delivered not less than 48 hours before the meeting at which a member appoints a proxy. Companies are also prohibited from inviting, at the company's expense, only certain members to appoint a particular person as their proxy[198].

---

191 Cordes et al, *Shackleton on The Law and Practice of Meetings* (12th edn, 2011) at p 156.

192 Statutory intervention (initially s 39 of the Joint Stock Companies Act 1856) modified the common law rule that shareholders could only attend and vote at meetings in person, save to the extent that the articles provided otherwise: *Harben v Phillips* (1883) 23 Ch D 14. See also Ahern & Maher, 'The Continuing Evolution of Proxy Representation' [2011] JBL 125.

193 *Mauri Development Corporation Ltd v Power Beat International Ltd* [1995] 2 NZLR 568 at 575.

194 See generally, Jones & Jacobs, *Company Meetings: Law and Procedure* (1991, Longman) at p 76.

195 Section 136(2)(a) and (b) respectively.

196 Section 136(3) of the CA 1963. Default renders the company and every officer in default liable to be fined.

197 Section 136(4) of the CA 1963.

198 Section 136(5) provides: 'Subject to subsection (6), if for the purpose of any meeting of a company invitations to appoint as proxy a person or one of a number of persons specified in the invitations are issued at the company's expense to some only of the members entitled to be sent a notice of the meeting and to vote thereat by proxy, every officer of the company who knowingly and wilfully authorises or permits their issue as aforesaid shall be liable to a class C fine.' This is subject to sub-s (6), which provides: 'An officer shall not be liable under subsection (5) by reason only of the issue to a member at his request in writing of a form of appointment naming the proxy or of a list of persons willing to act as proxy if the form or list is available on request in writing to every member entitled to vote at the meeting by proxy.'

[14.075] Model reg 69 provides that the instrument appointing a proxy must be in writing under the hand of the appointer or of his attorney duly authorised in writing, or, if the appointer is a body corporate, either under seal or under the hand of an officer or attorney duly authorised. Moreover, a proxy need not be a member of the company. An instrument appointing a proxy shall be in the form set out in model reg 71 (or a form as near thereto as circumstances permit). The model articles do not require that proxies be attested by a witness, but this may vary from company to company[199].

[14.076] Companies will generally be afforded a measure of comfort where they act on foot of proxies. So model reg 73 provides:

> 'A vote given in accordance with the terms of an instrument of proxy shall be valid notwithstanding the previous death or insanity of the principal or revocation of the proxy or of the authority under which the proxy was executed or the transfer of the share in respect of which the proxy is given, if no intimation in writing of such death, insanity, revocation or transfer as aforesaid is received by the company at the office before the commencement of the meeting or adjourned meeting at which the proxy is used.'

Were it otherwise, it would be very unsafe for companies to act on foot of proxies.

Minutes of members' meetings

[14.077] There is a statutory obligation on a company *as soon as may be* to cause minutes of all proceedings of general meetings to be entered in books kept for that purpose[200]. Where minutes have been made of the proceedings at any general meeting in accordance with s 145(3) of the CA 1963, then:

> '... until the contrary is proved, the meeting shall be deemed to have been duly held and convened, and all proceedings had thereat to have been duly had, and all appointments of directors or liquidators shall be deemed to be valid[201].'

Model reg 89 obliges the directors to cause minutes to be made in books provided for the purpose, *inter alia*, of all resolutions and proceedings at all meetings of the company. Where signed by the chairman of the meeting (or by the chairman of the next succeeding meeting), all minutes made in accordance with s 145 are *prima facie* evidence of the proceedings[202].

[14.078] Section 145(1) of the CA 1963 requires[203] that every company shall as soon as may be cause minutes of all proceedings of general meetings to be entered in books kept for that purpose. Extreme care should be taken when recording the minutes of a meeting so as to ensure, not only that all decisions taken are properly recorded but also that the record does not appear to show (through sloppy drafting, carelessness or loose use of language) any illegality or impropriety, not least because s 145(3A) of the CA 1963 provides:

---

199 See, for example, *Harben v Phillips* [1883] Ch 14.

200 Section 145 of the CA 1963.

201 Section 145(3) of the CA 1963.

202 Section 145(2) of the CA 1963. See *Re Indian Zoedone Co* (1884) 26 Ch D 70; *Re Fireproof Doors* [1916] 2 Ch 142; and *Kerr v John Mottram Ltd* [1940] 1 Ch 657.

203 Section 145(4) provides that the company and every officer of the company who is in default shall be liable to a fine.

> 'A company shall, if required by the Director, produce to the Director for inspection the book or books kept in accordance with subsection (1) and shall give to the Director such facilities for inspecting and taking copies of the contents of the book or books as the Director may require.'

Not alone will the Director of Corporate Enforcement be empowered to demand sight of minutes, but so too will the proceedings at the meeting be deemed, by s 145(3), to be duly had.

[14.079] Section 146(1) of the CA 1963 provides that the books containing the minutes of proceedings of any general meeting of a company shall be kept at the registered office of the company, and shall during business hours (subject to such reasonable restrictions as the company may by its articles or in general meeting impose, so that not less than two hours in each day be allowed for inspection) be open to the inspection of any member without charge[204]. Default renders the company and every officer in default liable to be fined[205]. It is also significant that where there is a refusal or default under s 146, the court may by order compel an inspection of the books in respect of all proceedings of general meetings or direct that copies be sent to the persons requiring them[206].

[14.080] Section 134(d) of the CA 1963 provides that, in so far as the articles of a company do not make other provision in that behalf, any member elected by the members present at a meeting may be chairman thereof. Model reg 56 provides that: 'The chairman, if any, of the board of directors shall preside as chairman at every general meeting of the company, or if there is no such chairman, or if he is not present within 15 minutes after the time appointed for the holding of the meeting or is unwilling to act, the directors present shall elect one of their number to be chairman of the meeting.' Model reg 57 provides: 'If at any meeting no director is willing to act as chairman or if no director is present within 15 minutes after the time appointed for holding the meeting, the members present shall choose one of their number to be chairman of the meeting.'

Resolutions

[14.081] Resolutions are the means used to effect decisions of the members of a company in general meeting[207]. A duly passed resolution represents the will of the majority of a company's members, or in the case of a special resolution, the will of a qualified majority of members. Unless a company's articles of association so provide, there is no requirement for resolutions to be proposed and seconded. The various aspects to members' resolutions are considered here as follows:

(a) Ordinary resolutions;
(b) Special resolutions;

---

[204] Where a member requires a copy of the minutes, he 'shall be entitled to be furnished within 7 days after he has made a request in that behalf to the company with a copy of any such minutes as aforesaid at a charge not exceeding one shilling for every 100 words': s 146(2).

[205] Section 146(3) of the CA 1963.

[206] Section 146(4) of the CA 1963.

[207] Note that in single-member companies a written decision of the sole member is used: see para **[14.088]** *post*.

(c) Decisions by sole members of single-member private companies;
(d) The written resolution procedure;
(e) *Re Duomatic*: the unanimous consent of members to a course of action;
(f) Filing of resolutions.

(a) Ordinary resolutions

[14.082] To pass an ordinary resolution, a simple majority of the members present in person or by proxy and entitled to vote must vote in favour of the resolution. Abstainers are not counted[208]; it is sufficient that a simple majority *in number* of those who actually vote, vote in favour of the resolution. In *Bushell v Faith*[209], Lord Upjohn said of the term 'ordinary resolution':

> 'An ordinary resolution is not defined nor used in the body of the Act of 1948 though the phrase occurs in some of the articles of Table A in the First Schedule to the Act. But its meaning is, in my opinion, clear. An ordinary resolution is in the first place passed by a bare majority on a show of hands by the members entitled to vote who are present personally or by proxy and on such a vote each member has one vote regardless of his shareholding. If a poll is demanded then, for an ordinary resolution still only a bare majority of votes[210] is required[211].'

If there are 10 shareholders, all being entitled to vote, an ordinary resolution will be passed if five abstain, two vote against and three vote in favour. The ordinary resolution demonstrates one of the most fundamental principles of company law: majority rule, as seen in cases such as *Foss v Harbottle*. In an age of exceptions and ubiquitous 'special circumstances', it is important to remember that the general rule in a company is that the will of a majority shall prevail. The norm is that companies are democracies and, save to the extent to which their articles of association provide otherwise[212], the minority will be bound by the will of the majority acting *bona fide*.

[14.083] As compared with special resolutions, ordinary resolutions are typically required to carry out routine, non-contentious business. That said, their importance should not be underestimated and it should be remembered that all that is required to legitimate an action outside the directors' authority, is an ordinary resolution. Where the Companies Acts refer *simpliciter* to the company in general meeting being permitted or required to do something, such will be effected by an ordinary resolution.

(b) Special resolutions

[14.084] Although for either an ordinary or a special resolution to be passed a majority is required to vote in favour of the resolution, the essential difference between an ordinary and a special resolution is that in the case of an ordinary resolution a bare

208 *Re William Dixon Ltd* (1948) SLT 423.

209 *Bushell v Faith* [1970] AC 1099.

210 Calculated on the basis of one vote per share and not one vote per member.

211 *Bushell v Faith* [1970] AC 1099 at 1108.

212 As Lord Upjohn went on to say, in *Bushell v Faith* [1970] AC 1099 at 1108, 1109: 'But whether a share or class of shares has any vote upon the matter and, if so, what is its voting power upon the resolution in question depends entirely upon the voting rights attaching to that share or class of shares by the articles of association.'

majority of over 50% is required, while for a special resolution a qualified majority of *75%* is required[213].

[14.085] Section 141(1) of the CA 1963 defines what is meant by a special resolution:

> 'A resolution shall be a special resolution when it has been passed by not less than three-fourths of the votes cast by such members as, being entitled so to do, vote in person or, where proxies are allowed, by proxy at a general meeting of which not less than 21 days' notice, specifying the intention to propose the resolution as a special resolution, has been duly given.'

A special resolution, therefore, involves *three* distinct elements: first, it must be passed by 75% of the members entitled to vote; second, 21 days' notice must be given of the intention to pass the resolution; and third, the intention of proposing the resolution as a special resolution must have been given. The 21 days' notice requirement is, however, mitigated by sub-s (2), which provides that a special resolution can be passed on short notice:

> 'A resolution may be proposed and passed as a special resolution at a meeting of which less than 21 days' notice has been given if it is so agreed by a majority in number of the members having the right to attend and vote at any such meeting being a majority together holding not less than ninety per cent in nominal value of the shares giving that right or, in the case of a company not having a share capital, together representing not less than ninety per cent of the total voting rights at that meeting of all the members[214].'

To be effective, those who invoke this remedial provision must appreciate the fact that they are invoking it. In *Re Pearce Duff & Co Ltd*[215], Buckley J said:

> 'Section 141(2) of the Companies Act 1948 [UK], requires 21 days' notice in the case of a special resolution, with the proviso as to resolutions being passed on short notice which is to be found in that subsection. In my judgment, that proviso requires the persons who agree to a resolution being passed on short notice to appreciate that the resolution is being passed on short notice and to agree to its being so passed with that consideration in their minds[216].'

In that case, over 90% of the members of a company consented at a general meeting to receiving short notice there and then of a special resolution ancillary to the special resolution in respect of which the meeting had been convened. In fact, the directors had given short notice for the primary resolution and it was held that the members' consent to short notice for the second would not be taken as consent for the short notice that had been given for the primary resolution[217].

[14.086] Notice will be deemed to be duly given and the meeting duly held when the notice is given and the meeting is held in the manner provided for by the Companies Acts or the company's articles of association[218]. At any meeting at which a special

213 Section 141(1) of the CA 1963.

214 See para **[14.042]** *ante*.

215 *Re Pearce Duff & Co Ltd* [1960] 1 WLR 1014.

216 *Re Pearce Duff & Co Ltd* [1960] 1 WLR 1014 at 1016.

217 In that case, the two resolutions were in fact upheld on the grounds that the unanimous written consent of the members was subsequently obtained.

218 Section 141(4) of the CA 1963.

resolution is submitted to be passed, a declaration of the chairman that the resolution is carried shall, unless a poll is demanded, be conclusive evidence of the fact without proof of the number or proportion of the votes recorded in favour of or against the resolution[219].

[14.087] Those matters that are specifically required by the Companies Acts to be effected by special resolution are:

- alteration of the articles of association[220];
- most alterations of the memorandum of association – namely the alteration of the objects clause[221], the name clause[222], the capital clause (but only where the effect is to reduce the share capital)[223], rendering unlimited the liability of directors[224], and any other clause that could be in the articles of association[225];
- the variation of class rights attaching to classes of shares[226];
- conversions – from private company to plc[227], from unlimited (public) company to plc[228], from plc to private company[229], limited companies to unlimited companies[230], and unlimited companies to limited companies[231];
- the provision of financial assistance in connection with own-share purchase[232];
- approving a scheme of arrangement[233];
- resolving that a company be wound up by court[234];
- resolving in favour of a members' voluntary winding-up[235];
- the disapplication of statutory pre-emption rights on allotment[236];
- setting the price of treasury shares[237];
- the purchase off-market of own shares[238] and of shares in a holding company[239];

219 Section 141(3) of the CA 1963. See also *Re Graham's Morocco Co* [1932] SC 269. Where manifest error is shown the chairman's declaration may be set aside: *Re Caratal (New) Mines Ltd* [1902] 2 Ch 498.
220 Section 15 of the CA 1963.
221 Section 10 of the CA 1963.
222 Section 23 of the CA 1963.
223 Section 72 of the CA 1963.
224 Section 198 of the CA 1963.
225 Section 28 of the CA 1963.
226 Section 38 of the C(A)A 1983.
227 Section 9 of the C(A)A 1983.
228 Section 11 of the C(A)A 1983.
229 Section 14 of the C(A)A 1983.
230 Section 52 of the C(A)A 1983.
231 Section 53 of the C(A)A 1983.
232 Section 60 of the CA 1963.
233 Section 210 of the CA 1963.
234 Section 213 of the CA 1963.
235 Section 251 of the CA 1963.
236 Section 24 of the C(A)A 1983.
237 Section 209 of the CA 1990.
238 Section 213 of the CA 1990.
239 Section 224 of the CA 1990.

- the provision of guarantees and security in connection with loans, quasi-loans and credit transactions in favour of directors of a company, its holding company or persons connected with such directors[240].

These are the main circumstances in which special resolutions of the members in general meeting are required.

(c) Decisions by sole members of single-member private companies

[14.088] In single-member companies it would be absurd to require the sole member to go through the motions of 'passing a resolution'. Consequently, it was necessary for the EC(SMPLC)R 1994 to provide that decisions of the members normally effected by resolutions can instead be taken by *written decisions* of the sole member. Regulation 9(1) provides:

> 'Subject to paragraph (2), all the powers exercisable by a company in general meeting under the Companies Acts or otherwise shall be exercisable, in the case of a single-member company, by the sole member without the need to hold a general meeting for that purpose.'

Again, this provision is not mandatory and it is open to a sole member to hold a general meeting. Regulation 9(2) provides that the foregoing paragraph does not entitle the sole member to exercise the power to remove an auditor[241]. The issue of *resolutions* is addressed by reg 9(3), which provides that, subject to reg 9(2):

> '... any provision of the Companies Acts which—
>
> (a) enables or requires any matter to be done or to be decided by a company in general meeting, or
>
> (b) requires any matter to be decided by a resolution of the company,
>
> shall be deemed to be satisfied, in the case of a single-member company, by a decision of the member which is drawn up in writing and notified to the company in accordance with this Regulation.'

Because the provisions in reg 9 are not mandatory, the sole member of a private company may (a) take a written decision as permitted by reg 9; (b) pass a written resolution in accordance with s 141(8)(a) where permitted by the articles[242]; or (c), unlikely though it may be, hold an AGM or EGM and pass a resolution at that meeting by a show of hands or poll.

[14.089] Where the sole member of a single-member company takes a decision which may be taken by the company in general meeting, he must provide the company with a written record of that decision, unless the decision is taken by way of written resolution which he has already forwarded to the company[243]. The company is obliged to record and retain such resolutions in a book or other suitable means maintained for the purpose[244]. Where the decision taken would ordinarily be required to be notified to the

---

[240] Section 34 of the CA 1990, as substituted by s 78 of the CLEA 2001.

[241] Sections 160(2)(b), 160(5) and 160(6) of the CA 1963. See Ch 17, *Financial Statements, Audit and Annual Return*, at para **[17.338]**.

[242] See para **[14.090]** *post*.

[243] Regulation 9(4) of the EC(SMPLC)R 1994.

[244] Regulation 9(5) of the EC(SMPLC)R 1994.

registrar of companies, this must be done by the company within 15 days[245]. The failure by a sole member to notify the company as set out above, does not affect the validity of any decision referred to above[246].

(d) The written resolution procedure

[14.090] At common law it was always the case that the unanimous agreement of the shareholders in a company, expressed informally, was sufficient to adopt a resolution and, indeed, this remains good law. The Jenkins Committee recommended that there should be an express statutory provision governing such matters, which should provide that a resolution in writing signed by all of the members would have the same effect as an ordinary or special resolution. The recommendation was that total informality would be formalised by a lesser informality, which required writing. This became law in s 141(8)(a) of the CA 1963, which provides:

> 'Notwithstanding anything to the contrary in this Act, in any case in which a company is so authorised by its articles, a resolution in writing signed by all the members for the time being entitled to attend and vote on such resolution at a general meeting ... shall be as valid and effective for all purposes as if the resolution had been passed at a general meeting of the company duly convened and held, and if described as a special resolution shall be deemed to be a special resolution within the meaning of this Act.'

It will be noted that in order to avail of s 141(8), a company must be so authorised by its articles of association. In this regard model reg 6 of Part II of Table A provides:

> 'Subject to s 141 of the Act, a resolution in writing signed by all the members for the time being entitled to attend and vote on such resolution at a general meeting (or being bodies corporate by their duly authorised representatives) shall be as valid and effective for all purposes as if the resolution had been passed at a general meeting of the company duly convened and held, and if described as a special resolution shall be deemed to be a special resolution within the meaning of the Act.'

Unless expressly excluded by a company's articles of association, this will automatically apply in the case of private companies, incorporated under the Companies Acts. It should be noted that there is no similar provision in the Companies (Consolidation) Act 1908 and care should be taken when dealing with companies incorporated under that Act as the model articles contained in the First Schedule to the CA 1963 do not automatically apply to such companies[247].

[14.091] The written resolution procedure can be used to pass both ordinary resolutions and special resolutions. Section 141(8) of the CA 1963 is intended to give effect to the unanimous voice of those whose authorisation is required to pass a resolution. It follows that even though a simple majority of members is all that is required in order to pass an ordinary resolution, *all* of the members entitled to attend and vote on the resolution must sign the written resolution if s 141(8) is to be utilised. Where the written resolution procedure is followed, a resolution will be deemed to have been passed on the date on which it was signed by the last member to sign. Moreover, 'where the resolution states a date as being the date of his signature thereof by any member the statement shall be

245 Regulation 9(6) of the EC(SMPLC)R 1994.

246 Regulation 9(8) of the EC(SMPLC)R 1994. A failure to comply with para (4) will render the sole member liable to a fine, and a failure to comply with paras (5) or (6) will render the company liable to a class C fine: reg 9(7) of the EC(SMPLC)R 1994.

247 See *Safeera Ltd v Wallis & O'Regan* (12 July 1994, unreported) HC, Morris J.

prima facie evidence that it was signed by him on that date'[248]. Where the resolution passed is a special resolution or other designated resolution, it should be filed in accordance with s 143(1) of the CA 1963, considered below[249].

[14.092] It is important to remember that the written resolution procedure may not be utilised for passing all resolutions. By its very terms, its application is excluded in the case of resolutions for any of the purposes of ss 160 or 182[250]. Moreover, the practice of the legal community was to interpret s 60(6) of the CA 1963 as implicitly excluding the application of s 141(8)(a)[251], thereby precluding its use on the passing of a special resolution authorising the provision of financial assistance in connection with the purchase of a company's own shares. Any doubts over the use of the written resolution procedure when utilising the validation procedure in s 60 have now been dispelled by s 89(b) of the CLEA 2001[252]. Notwithstanding the limited exclusions, the written resolution procedure provides private companies with a welcome relief from the otherwise prescriptive formalities of the Companies Acts.

(e) The 'Buchanan principle': unanimous consent of members to a course of action

[14.093] The unanimous agreement of members, whether express or implied from their acts or omissions, can have the same consequences as if the members had passed a formal resolution to that effect. It cannot be said, however, that such an agreement amounts to a resolution that complies with the Companies Acts, as there is no written record of a resolution, nor document that can be filed. This is especially so in the case of resolutions that require to be filed pursuant to s 143 of the CA 1963. In effect, an estoppel arises from the members' unanimous agreement against the company and, indeed, any subsequently dissenting member[253]. The estoppel that arises from the unanimous agreement of members has come to be known in the UK as the *Duomatic* principle[254], but given that our own Supreme Court put forward the same principle some 15 years earlier, it seems appropriate to refer to it here as the *Buchanan* principle. In *Buchanan Ltd and another v McVey*[255], Kingsmill Moore J said:

---

248 Section 141(8)(b) of the CA 1963.

249 See para **[14.100]** *post*.

250 Section 141(8)(c) of the CA 1963.

251 See Ch 10, *The Maintenance of Capital*, at para **[10.068]**.

252 Section 89(b) of the CLEA 2001 substituted the old s 60(6) for the following new s 60(6): 'The special resolution referenced in subsection (1)(a) may be passed in accordance with section 141(8).'

253 In *Re Greenore Trading Co Ltd* [1980] IRLM 94, it was argued that an allotment of shares was invalid because it had not been authorised by the board of directors in accordance with the articles, but by the members in general meeting. All of the members who were entitled to be present at the directors' meeting were present, and the petitioner had not challenged the decision for some time. Keane J held that: 'The Petitioner is clearly estopped in my opinion, from asserting the irregularities of a transaction which he tacitly approved of when it was being implemented, which does not offend against any principle of law and which was entirely for the benefit of the company and indeed its creditors.'

254 See, generally, Burton, 'Dispensing with Formalities: The Duomatic Principle' (2000) 21 Company Lawyer 186 and Cabrelli, '*BDG Roof Bond Ltd v Douglas*: Further Observations on the Application of *Re Duomatic* Relief' (2001) 22 Company Lawyer 130.

255 *Buchanan Ltd and another v McVey* [1954] IR 89.

'If all the corporators agree to a certain course then, however informal the manner of their agreement, it is an act of the company and binds the company subject only to two pre-requisites: *Re Express Engineering Works Ltd* [1920] 1 Ch 466, *Parker and Cooper Ltd v Reading* [1926] 1 Ch 975[256].

The two necessary pre-requisites are (1) that the transaction to which the corporators agree should be *intra vires* the company; (2) that the transaction should be honest: *Parker and Cooper Ltd v Reading* [1926] 1 Ch 975.'

The decision of Kingsmill Moore J was cited with approval by the Supreme Court in *Re Greendale Developments Ltd*[257], although in that case, it was deemed not to apply because the court found that the agreements in question were *ultra vires* the company's capacity.

In *Re Duomatic Ltd*[258], the case which gave its name to the principle as applied in the UK, a company's articles of association made the payment of compensation to a director for loss of office, conditional upon the members authorising this by resolution; in addition the members were required to determine the directors' remuneration. A claim by the company's liquidator for the repayment of a sum paid on a director's loss of office and for the repayment of certain remuneration paid to the company's directors, by reason of neither having been approved by the company's members in general meeting, failed. Buckley J held:

'... where it can be shown that all shareholders who have a right to attend and vote at a general meeting of the company assent to some matter which a general meeting of the company could carry into effect, that assent is as binding as a resolution in general meeting would be[259].'

[14.094] In *Cane v Jones*[260], the court applied the '*Duomatic* principle' and held that an unsigned shareholders' agreement was sufficient to override a company's articles of association, and to deprive the chairman of the board of directors of his casting vote. It was acknowledged to be a basic principle of company law that all the corporators of a company, acting together, can do anything that is *intra vires* the company, and the statutory provisions on the alteration of the articles did affect this position[261]. In *Parker*

---

256 In *Parker and Cooper Ltd v Reading* [1926] 1 Ch 975 at 982, Astbury J had said: '... where a transaction is *intra vires* the company and honest, the sanction of all the members of the company, however expressed, is sufficient to validate it, especially if it is a transaction entered into for the benefit of the company itself.'

257 *Re Greendale Developments Ltd* (20 February 1997, unreported) HC *per* Keane J, *nem diss.*

258 *Re Duomatic Ltd* [1969] 2 Ch 365.

259 *Re Duomatic Ltd* [1969] 2 Ch 365 at 373,

260 *Cane v Jones* [1981] 1 All ER 533; see also Ch 3, *Constitutional Documentation*, at para **[3.085]**. See also *Re Horsley & Weight Ltd* [1982] 3 All ER 1045; *Re Oxted Motor Co* [1921] 3 KB 32; and *Re Fletcher Hunt (Bristol) Ltd* [1989] BCLC 109.

261 In *Re Shannonside Holdings Ltd* (20 May 1993, unreported) HC, Costello J said: 'In my opinion, non-compliance with ... reg [47] does not invalidate any resolutions passed at the meeting. It seems to me that the members of the company can mutually decide to have meetings anywhere they like, even though the Articles indicate that they are to be held in the State. Should they decide to hold meetings outside the State, they are entitled to do so provided there is agreement. If there was no formal indication that such agreement was forthcoming, it would be clear that it was to be implied in the circumstances of this case.'

and Cooper Ltd v Reading, Astbury J went so far as to say that the unanimous consent was sufficient even if the members did not all meet together in one place, but merely discussed it and agreed 'to it one with another separately'[262]. The decision of the English Court of Appeal in *Schofield v Schofield*[263] emphasises, however, the need for there to be an actual agreement to treat a meeting (for which insufficient notice had been given) as being valid. Such agreement can be 'express or by implication, verbal or by conduct, given at the time or later, *but nothing short of unqualified agreement, objectively established, will suffice*'[264].

[14.095] Where the legal and beneficial or equitable ownership of shares is split, there is authority for the proposition that the *Duomatic* principle can be invoked where there is the agreement of the *beneficial* owners of shares. So in *Deakin and another v Faulding and another*[265], Hart J rejected the submission that 'as a matter of law, the assent of the shareholder himself must be proved, and that it was not sufficient simply to show that assent had been given by the beneficial owner of a share held by a nominee'[266]. Hart J said that he did not see why as a matter of principle it should be regarded as correct and that where a person 'has an equity to compel a consent, I see no reason why equity should not have regard to the position of the beneficial as opposed to the legal owner in its application of the rule'.

[14.096] The authorities were extensively and carefully considered in the decision of Finlay Geoghegan J in *Kerr et al v Conduit Enterprises Ltd*[267]. The facts of this case concerned a lease granted to a company by two directors of the company; no formal resolution had been passed as required by s 29 of the CA 1990[268] and the company's new controllers subsequently sought to treat the lease as void. Although Finlay Geoghegan J held that, on the facts, the company had *not* acquired a non-cash asset of the requisite value from its directors, the learned judge went on to consider whether, if it had been found that s 29 did apply, s 29 had been complied with. As a matter of fact, Finlay Geoghegan J found that all the shareholders with a right to both attend and vote at a general meeting of the defendant company had, albeit at a meeting of a board of directors, agreed to and authorised the defendant to enter into the lease prior to its execution. On those facts, it was submitted by counsel for the plaintiffs that the *Duomatic* principle applied whereas counsel for the company submitted that the court should not follow the *Duomatic* principle as to do so would do violence to the words of s 29(1) of the CA 1990.

Finlay Geoghegan J said that the since the decision of the High Court and Supreme Court in *Buchanan Ltd v McVey*[269] it appears settled law that the informal agreement of

---

262 *Parker and Cooper Ltd v Reading* [1926] Ch 975 at 984.

263 *Schofield v Schoflield* [2011] EWCA Civ 154, [2011] 2 BCLC 319.

264 In *Tulsesence Ltd; Rolfe v Rolfe* [2010] EWHC 244, [2010] 2 BCLC 525, Newey J did not accept that a 'shareholder's mere internal decision can of itself constitute assent for *Duomatic* purposes'. [Emphasis added]

265 *Deakin and another v Faulding and another* [2001] EWHC (Ch) 7.

266 *Re New Cedos Engineering Co Ltd* [1994] 1 BCLC 797 had been cited as authority for that proposition.

267 *Kerr et al v Conduit Enterprises Ltd* [2010] IEHC 300.

268 See Ch 16, *Statutory Regulation of Directors' Transactions*, at para **[16.022]** *et seq*.

269 *Buchanan Ltd v McVey* [1954] IR 89.

all the shareholders to do something which is honest and *intra vires* the company is to be regarded as an act of the company and does not require a formal resolution by the company in general meeting. After reviewing the decision in *Re Duomatic* the learned judge said:

> 'Whilst the principle, as stated by Buckley J in *Re Duomatic Ltd* is expressed in slightly different terms to its expression by Kingsmill Moore J in the High Court and Maguire CJ in the Supreme Court in *Buchanan Ltd v McVey*, it is, in substance the same principle. Insofar as the Irish decision refers to 'all the corporators', that must be a reference to all shareholders with a right to both attend and vote at a general meeting of the company and it appears to me that it follows that if, in accordance with *Buchanan Ltd v McVey*, the agreement of all the corporators is to be treated as an act of the company, then it must also be treated as binding as a resolution in general meeting, which is the normal way in which shareholders would act[270].'

Finlay Geoghegan J noted that in the United Kingdom, the *Duomatic* principle had been applied to statutory requirements such as s 320 of the Companies Act 1985 (UK) (the equivalent of s 29 of the CA 1990)[271]. In the instant case, the learned judge held that s 29 of the CA 1990 did not evidence an intention by the Oireachtas to preclude a court from applying to the express requirement for a resolution of a general meeting, a principle which the Supreme Court considered in 1954 to be settled law saying:

> 'The fact that the Oireachtas did not specify any special requirements in relation to the holding of the general meeting or any special requirements in relation to a resolution passed for the purposes of section 29(1), including registration in the Companies Registration Office, appears to me to demonstrate that there was no intention to interfere with the principle considered in *Buchanan Ltd v McVey* to be settled law. Insofar as the Oireachtas required approval of a majority of shareholders with a right to vote by a resolution of the company in general meeting, that is, of course, the normal way in which shareholders of a company should take formal decisions. However it does not evidence an intention to preclude the agreement of all shareholders with a right to vote being treated as effective as a resolution in general meeting in accordance with the principle determined in *Buchanan Ltd v McVey* to be settled law[272].'

It might be surmised, from this, however, that were a statutory requirement to require the passing of a special resolution, the particulars of which are required to be delivered to the CRO, the decision might be different.

[14.097] Another significant finding of Finlay Geoghegan J in *Kerr et al v Conduit Enterprises Ltd*[273] was that the *Buchanan* principle could apply even if there were other shareholders who were entitled to attend but not vote at general meetings:

> 'The second matter to which I wish to refer in the application of the principle as stated by the Supreme Court in *Buchanan Ltd v McVey* to the facts herein is not a matter relied upon by counsel for the defendant, correctly, in my view. The evidence is that Enterprise Ireland was, in 1997, the holder of non-voting preference shares in the defendant. In accordance with Article 2(d) of the Articles of Association, it did have a right to receive notice of and to attend but not to vote at general meetings of the Company. However, the undisputed

270 *Kerr et al v Conduit Enterprises Ltd* [2010] IEHC 300 at para 43 of the judgment.

271 *NBH Ltd v Hoare* [2006] EWHC 73 (Ch), Park J.

272 *Kerr et al v Conduit Enterprises Ltd* [2010] IEHC 300 at para 47 of the judgment.

273 *Kerr et al v Conduit Enterprises Ltd* [2010] IEHC 300.

evidence of Mr Young, in his witness statement to the Court, was that Enterprise Ireland was also notified and approved of the move to Block V, East Point, and was directly involved in securing an Enterprise Ireland Area Certificate required by the defendant prior to the Lease being signed in 1997. In such factual circumstances, it does not appear that the existence of a preference shareholder with a right to receive notice of and attend but not vote at a meeting of the company precludes the Court, in accordance with *Buchanan Ltd v McVey*, treating the approval of all the ordinary shareholders to the arrangement to enter into the Lease as a resolution of the Company in general meeting, for the purposes of section 29(1) of the Act of 1990[274].'

[14.098] The fact that an estoppel might arise should, however, never be considered a sufficient basis for deliberately proceeding in a manner that is *prima facie* at variance with the requirements of company law. The *Buchanan* principle is best regarded as a remedial shield, the successful reliance upon which can never be guaranteed. So in *Re RW Peak (Kings Lynn) Ltd*[275], a company purchased its own shares contrary to the English statutory provisions on own-share purchase. In particular, the articles of association made no provision for the purchase of its own shares. Lindsay J held that the purported own-share purchase was void and that the provisions in the Companies Act 1985 (UK) could not be overridden by the *Duomatic* principle. One of the reasons given was that the statutory protection in question was intended to protect 'future shareholders'. It must be questioned whether the interests of future shareholders should be considered since persons becoming shareholders should take the company as it is. In *Demite Ltd v Protec Health Ltd*[276], Park J said that he was not convinced that s 320 of the English Companies Act 1985 – which is similar to s 29 of the Irish CA 1990 and regulates substantial property transactions between directors and their companies – could be satisfied by a *Duomatic* type assent. It is thought, however, that even on a restrictive application of the *Duomatic* principle, there is no reason why it should not apply in such a case since the statutory provision is exclusively concerned with shareholder protection.[277]

[14.099] Although it may be argued that the realities of the Irish private company should be accommodated by law, there are valid reasons for requiring the members to resolve in writing to carry out certain acts. Thus, where the resolution changes the company's constitution, unless there is something in writing, the registrar of companies cannot record the change, in order to make it ascertainable by the public. Accordingly, a balance must be struck between the exigencies of private company business, the necessary administration of the CRO and the interests of creditors and, indeed, members.

274 *Kerr et al v Conduit Enterprises Ltd* [2010] IEHC 300 at para 52 of the judgment.

275 *Re RW Peak (Kings Lynn) Ltd* [1998] BCC 596.

276 *Demite Ltd v Protec Health Ltd* [1998] BCC 638.

277 In applying the *Duomatic* principle, the English court in *BDG Roof Bond Ltd v Douglas* [2000] 1 BCLC 401 at 417 observed that the provision that the company's members had waived (making available a share repurchase agreement at the company's registered office) involved 'no element of creditor protection at all'. See also *Precision Dippings Ltd v Precision Dippings Marketing Ltd* [1985] 3 WLR 812, where a different treatment for provisions designed to protect creditors was mooted.

(f) Filing of resolutions

[14.100] Special resolutions and certain ordinary resolutions must, within 15 *days* of their passing, be forwarded to the registrar of companies for recording: s 143(1) of the CA 1963[278]. Those ordinary resolutions that must be forwarded to the registrar of companies for recording are listed in s 143(4) as being:

- resolutions which have been agreed to by all the members of a company, but which, if not so agreed to, would not have been effective for their purpose unless they had been passed as special resolutions;
- resolutions or agreements which have been agreed to by all the members of some class of shareholders but which if not so agreed to, would not have been effective for their purpose unless they had been passed by some particular majority or otherwise in some particular manner, and all resolutions or agreements which effectively bind all the members of any class of shareholders though not agreed to by all those members;
- resolutions increasing the share capital of a company;
- resolutions that a company be wound up voluntarily passed under s 251(1)(a) or (c) of the CA 1963;
- resolutions attaching rights or restrictions to any share;
- resolutions varying any such rights or restrictions;
- resolutions classifying any unclassified share;
- resolutions converting shares of one class into shares of another class;
- resolutions of the directors of a company passed by virtue of ss 12(3)(a) and 43(3) of the C(A)A 1983.

In this way such resolutions become *public documents*, and the public at large will be deemed to have constructive notice of their contents. Failure to register a resolution to which the section applies does *not* taint the validity of the resolution, which will have full force and effect without being registered. It should be noted, however, that a failure to file a copy of a resolution renders the company and every officer in default liable to a fine[279].

[14.101] There is also a requirement that where articles have been registered, a copy of every such resolution or agreement for the time being in force shall be embodied in or annexed to every copy of the articles issued after the passing of the resolution or the making of the agreement[280]. Members are entitled to receive a copy of every such resolution or agreement[281].

---

278 Section 143(1) of the CA 1963 provides: 'A printed copy of every resolution or agreement to which this section applies shall, within 15 days after the passing or making thereof, be forwarded to the registrar of companies and recorded by him.'

279 Section 143(5) of the CA 1963. Subsection (6) provides that the failure to comply with sub-s (2) or (3) renders the company and every officer of the company who is in default liable to a fine not exceeding €1.27 for each copy in respect of which default is made. Moreover, sub-s (7) provides that for the purposes of sub-ss (5) and (6) a liquidator of a company shall be deemed to be an officer of the company.

280 Section 143(2) of the CA 1963.

281 Section 143(3) of the CA 1963, which provides that this is in return for the payment of one shilling or such less sum as the company may direct.

[B] Directors' Meetings[282]

[14.102] The law governing the convening and holding of meetings of members is very prescriptive. Both statute and the model articles of association are purposefully intended to safeguard members' rights to attend and vote at general meetings and to thwart any attempt by company directors to stymie the exercise of these rights. Moreover, it is important to bear in mind that general meetings of members are invariably sporadic, almost ritualistic events when the owners of a company are asked to either note certain statutory matters (as in the case of an AGM) or decide an important course of action for the company, where such a decision is reserved for the members' judgment (as in the case of an EGM, or, indeed at an AGM). Directors' meetings are usually far more frequent and informal affairs. These are the fora at which the *day-to-day* management decisions for a company are taken – especially where a company's board is comprised of executive directors who are personally involved in the management of the company. In consequence of this, the law relating to directors' meetings, such as it is, is far less prescriptive in terms, for example, of the notice required, notice of business to be conducted thereat, etc. In place of rigid notice provisions, and in deference to the exigencies of commerce, the key requirement underlying the law on directors' meetings is *reasonableness*.

[14.103] In this section, directors' meetings shall be considered under the following headings:

1. Regulation of directors' meetings.
2. Convening and notice of a directors' meeting.
3. Holding directors' meetings.
4. The business transacted.
5. The quorum.
6. The chairman.
7. Adjourned meetings.
8. Minutes of directors' meetings.
9. Resolutions and voting.

Regulation of directors' meetings

[14.104] The regulation of directors' meetings is largely a matter for the directors themselves. Such provisions in the Companies Acts as concern meetings of directors tend to be in the nature of model articles – that can be amended or purged by a company – rather than prescriptive statutory requirements. Accordingly, reg 101 of Table A provides:

> 'The directors may meet together for the dispatch of business, adjourn and otherwise regulate their meetings as they think fit. Questions arising at any meeting shall be decided

[282] See generally, Cordes et al, *Shackleton on The Law and Practice of Meetings* (12th edn, 2011) at paras 22-01–23-11; Jones & Jacobs, *Company Meetings: Law and Procedure* (1991, Longman) at pp 105–193. For a brief overview of Irish law see Maloney & Spellman, *The Law of Meetings* (1999) at pp 148–151. See also, Creamer & Michie, 'Board Meetings: Best Practice and New Trends' (1997) *Practical Law for Companies 31* for an excellent review of law and modern practice of directors' meetings.

> by a majority of votes. Where there is an equality of votes, the chairman shall have a second or casting vote. A director may, and the secretary on the requisition of a director shall, at any time summon a meeting of the directors. If the directors so resolve, it shall not be necessary to give notice of a meeting of directors to any director who, being resident in the state, is for the time being absent from the state.'

This omnibus regulation is adopted by most private companies incorporated in Ireland today. The desirability of leaving the organisation of directors' meetings to directors is evident in the fact that, unlike the many articles that govern aspects of members' meetings, as regards directors' meetings, the one article addresses voting, casting votes, the convening of meetings and notice of meetings.

Convening and notice of a directors' meeting

[14.105] Regulation 101 of Table A provides that the directors may meet together as they think fit. Any one director may, of his own right, summon a meeting, and the company secretary must summon a meeting where a director requisitions a meeting. Unlike members' meetings, there is no express statutory equivalent to s 135 of the CA 1963[283] that enables persons to apply to court to requisition a directors' meeting. There are two reasons for this absence of specific jurisdiction. In the first place, any one director can summon a directors' meeting. Secondly, an impasse on the board of directors can be cured by the members in general meeting voting out the existing board and replacing it, so it can be said that the members' ability to requisition a general meeting is sufficient recourse.

[14.106] Model articles are silent on the length of notice required to be given for a directors' meeting. This is in recognition of the fact that the exigencies of business may dictate that, in particular circumstances, the directors of a company may be required to meet on a daily basis. Notwithstanding the absence of a fixed notice period, notice must be given to directors of forthcoming meetings and if notice is not given to all directors entitled to receive notice, any meeting held will be deemed irregular and any business purportedly effected deemed a nullity[284]. Here, common sense accords with the law, and it was held in *Holland et al v McGill et al*[285] that *due notice*, namely reasonable notice, must be given. In addition, there is no requirement in the model articles that notice be given of the business which it is proposed to conduct at a directors' meeting. However, as seen in the *Holland* case, a director will have cause to complain where he can show that he was misled as to the business which it was proposed to transact or consider at a meeting. Where what was transacted would have been done in any event through the force of majority voting, and in the absence of any finding of abuse of directors' powers, the meeting may not be invalidated[286]. An old example of the need for reasonable notice is seen in *Re Homer District Consolidated Gold Mines; ex p Smith*[287]. There a company had invited application for 106,000 preference shares in the company but had resolved

---

283 See s 371 of the English Companies Act 1985, considered in *Ross v Telford and another* [1998] 1 BCLC 82. *Cf Re Sticky Fingers Restaurant Ltd* [1992] BCLC 84.

284 *Re Portuguese Consolidated Copper Mines Ltd* [1889] 42 Ch 160.

285 *Holland et al v McGill et al* (16 March 1990, unreported) HC, Murphy J.

286 *Holland et al v McGill et al* (16 March 1990, unreported) HC, Murphy J at p 12 *et seq* of transcript.

287 *Re Homer District Consolidated Gold Mines; ex p Smith* (1888) 39 Ch 546.

that there would be no allotment until at least 14,000 had been applied for. The company had five directors and the articles provided that the quorum was two. Upon receiving applications for some 3,000 shares, one of the directors sought the approval of the board to reverse its earlier decision and to allot the circa 3,000 shares applied for. A board meeting was called on a particular day at 2 pm, on a few hours' notice. It was attended by two directors who purported to resolve that the earlier resolution be cancelled and that the shares applied for should be allotted. Of the three directors who did not attend, one was absent from the jurisdiction (and so not entitled to notice under the company's articles) another received notice but had said he could not make the meeting until 3 pm and the third did not receive the notice until the day after the meeting had been held. North J held that the allotments of shares were invalid and did not bind the company because the meeting had been improperly constituted without adequate notice of either the meeting or the business intended to be considered at the meeting[288].

[14.107] Where reg 101 of Table A is adopted, it will not be necessary to give notice of a meeting to any director who, being resident in the State, is for the time being absent from the State, *provided that the directors have previously resolved that such be the case*. If the directors do not so resolve, the default position is that all directors must receive notice. Whilst there is some ambiguity, it is thought that reg 106 will not override the requirement for a quorum and that even where the directors have previously so resolved, a valid meeting cannot take place (nor written resolution be passed) where the number of directors within the State is insufficient to make up the quorum[289].

[14.108] Resolutions passed and decisions taken at an invalidly convened, held and constituted board meeting can be subsequently validated by a valid board meeting. Alternatively, they can be ratified by the members in general meeting[290].

Holding directors' meetings

[14.109] If a meeting is to be a valid meeting of the board of directors, those present should appreciate or have a basis for appreciating that fact, the chairman of the board should chair it, and it should be referred to as such in notices convening it[291]. Notwithstanding this, it has long been established that directors' meetings can be held in informal circumstances[292]. One of the inherent difficulties of informal regimes, however, is that there can be uncertainty as to whether a particular meeting was, in fact, a directors' meeting or some other kind of meeting. Whether or not a board meeting had taken place was one of the issues before the High Court in *Re Aston Colour Print Ltd*[293].

---

288 *Cf La Compagnie de Mayville v Whitley* [1896] 1 Ch 788, which suggests that it is not necessary to specify in a notice convening a directors' meeting, the business that it is intended will be transacted thereat.

289 See also *Hood Sailmakers Ltd v Axford and another* [1996] 4 All ER 830, considered at para **[14.126]** *post*.

290 See *Bamford and another v Bamford et al* [1970] 1 Ch 212 and *Re D'Jan of London Ltd* [1993] BCC 646. See further, Ch 13, *Corporate Governance: Management by the Directors*, at para **[13.143]**.

291 *Re Aston Colour Print Ltd* (21 February 1997, unreported) HC, Kelly J.

292 See *Smith v Paringa Mines* [1906] 2 Ch 193, where a valid board meeting was held to have taken place in the corridor outside a director's office.

293 *Re Aston Colour Print Ltd* (21 February 1997, unreported) HC, Kelly J.

It was claimed that a directors' petition to have a company placed under the protection of the court had not been authorised by the company's board of directors because there had neither been a board meeting nor an authorising resolution. Kelly J heard that meetings, known as executive or management meetings, had been held, attended by the company's two directors with some or all of its shareholders and its financial controller, on a weekly basis to discuss the day-to-day running of the company. No formal notices were issued convening these meetings. The meeting under scrutiny was to consider the company's financial difficulties. The company's options – more investment, the appointment of a liquidator or the appointment of an examiner – were all discussed. The meeting was attended by the company's only two formally appointed directors (C and B), two shareholders (McC and P) and by its financial controller (L). P, one of the shareholders present, chaired the meeting. Subsequently, a petition was presented in the names of the two directors, to have an examiner appointed. One of the directors, B, did not regard the meeting as having been a board meeting and irrespective of the nature of the meeting held (it was not disputed that there had been a meeting) did not believe a decision had been taken to appoint an examiner. Giving four reasons, Kelly J concluded that the meeting in question was not a board meeting:

> '1. Whilst board meetings may be held on an informal basis, the directors must at least appreciate or have a basis for appreciating that they are attending such a meeting[294]. Mr B did not so appreciate, nor was there any reason why he should. The meeting was not so described; it did not differ from other management or executive meetings; it was not chaired by the chairman of the board.
>
> 2. If the meeting was that of the board, why was it not chaired by [C]? He was the chairman of the board yet it was Mr P, a non-director, who presided at the meeting.
>
> 3. Mr L [the financial controller], who is a man of some experience on the financial side, told me in evidence that he did not consider that he was attending a board meeting of the company.
>
> 4. Mr P who chaired the meeting, as he did the other executive meetings, believed he was presiding over a meeting of the company in general meeting which subsequently became a board meeting, to quote his evidence. But subsequent to what? And when did this change occur? And how was Mr B to know when the metamorphosis occurred[295]?'

This case underscores the importance of observing what might at first appear to be mere formalities[296].

[14.110] Modern technology facilitates, with ease, meetings to take place over the telephone, provided that all persons participating can hear each other. The question is whether this is sufficient to come within the expression, the directors may '*meet together*' as provided for in reg 101. There is old authority for the proposition that the directors need not be in the same physical location at the time they reach a decision, but the possibilities of audio or audio-visual meetings could not have been even dreamed of

---

[294] See, for example, *Barron v Potter* [1914] 1 Ch 895.

[295] *Re Aston Colour Print Ltd* (21 February 1997, unreported) HC, Kelly J at pp 6, 7 of the judgment.

[296] See Canniffe, 'More than Mere Formalities: *Re Aston Colour Print Ltd and the Companies Acts*' (1997) 4 Commercial Law Practitioner 280.

in 1871[297]. Modern authority is provided by the Australian case of *Bell v Burton*[298] in which Tadgell J said:

> 'No doubt there is no necessity nowadays – if there ever was – that directors should gather physically together at a directors' meeting. In appropriate circumstances they can meet by assenting to a document, or by telephone, video link, or other electronic means which caters for a meeting of their minds.'

This was adopted by Santow J in *Wagner v International Health Promotions*[299], who went on to say: 'I agree that the words "meet together" connote a meeting of minds made possible by modern technology and not of bodies.' Both of these cases were followed by the Federal Court of Australia in *GIGA Investments Pty Ltd (in admin) v Ferguson*[300], which added:

> 'In my view, provided that each participating director is able to be aware of the contributions to the meeting made by each other director, and to contribute himself or herself to the meeting without significant impediment, it is not of importance that the meeting together of the directors is achieved with the assistance of the telecommunications industry. I conclude that directors can, generally speaking, meet together by video links or by using telephone conference connections. A meeting of two directors only can by analogy of reasoning, in my view, generally speaking, be held using an ordinary telephone connection.'

[14.111] Although there is, therefore, authority for saying that the expression 'meet together' as used in reg 101 encompasses telephone and other electronic meetings because it means a meeting of minds, it is preferable to expressly provide for such in a company's articles of association. The wording of such an article might provide:

> 'A meeting of the directors or of a committee of the board of directors may consist of a conference between some or all of the directors (including any alternate directors) who are not all in one place, but each of whom is able (directly or by means of telephonic, video or other electronic communication) to speak to each of the others and to be heard by each of the others and:
>
> (a) a director (or an alternate director) taking part in such a conference shall be deemed to be present in person at the meeting and shall be entitled to vote and be counted in a quorum accordingly; and
>
> (b) such a meeting shall be deemed to take place where the largest group of those participating in the conference is assembled, or, if there is no such group, where the chairman of the meeting then is; and

---

297 See *Re Bonelli's Telegraph Company; Collie's Claim* (1871) LR 12 EQ 246, where a letter committing the company to a course of action was found to be a decision of the company in circumstances where it was signed by each of the directors, some in different locations.

298 *Bell v Burton* (1993) 12 ACSR 325. *Cf* the earlier Australian cases of *Re Southern Resources* (1989) 15 ACLR 770 at 792–794 and *Magna Crete Ltd v Douglas-Hill* (1988) 48 SASR 565 at 603, where Perry J concluded that a company's articles did not contemplate a telephone meeting.

299 *Wagner v International Health Promotions* [1994] 12 ACLC 986.

300 *GIGA Investments Pty Ltd (in admin) v Ferguson* [1995] 13 ACLC 1050.

(c) the word 'meeting' where used in these articles of association in the context of a meeting of the company's directors or committee of directors shall be construed accordingly[301].'

The adoption of such an article will remove any uncertainty arising from simply relying upon the line of cases that affords a 'meeting of the minds' interpretation to the phrase 'meet together'.

The business transacted

[14.112] Depending upon the size of a company, pre-board meetings may be held to determine the agenda for the next board meeting. Individual directors should raise, with the chairman, items for consideration, as it is the chairman who will normally determine the agenda. As to the business transacted at meetings, the directors can take items on the agenda in whatever order they wish[302]. Obstructive directors can be suspended if their conduct is so disorderly as to impede the proceedings at a board meeting[303].

The quorum

[14.113] Model reg 102 of Table A provides that the quorum necessary for the transaction of the business of the directors may be fixed by the directors, and unless so fixed shall be two. The general rule is that no business may be conducted at a meeting of the board of directors unless there is a quorum present. Some companies will provide in their articles of association that there should be a minimum number of directors, eg, five directors. Where the number of directors falls below that minimum number, the continuing directors may continue to act, where model reg 103 is adopted, provided that if, due to a death or vacancy, the number of directors falls below the number necessary for a quorum, no business may be transacted at a directors' meeting, except for the purpose of increasing the number of directors to satisfy the quorum or of summoning a general meeting of the company[304].

[14.114] The general rule is that there must be a *disinterested quorum*, by which is meant those directors making up the quorum are not personally interested in, say, a transaction under consideration. However, it should be noted that most private

---

[301] See the very interesting article by Creamer & Michie, 'Board Meetings – Best Practice and New Trends' (1997) Practical Law for Companies 31 at 34. As early as 1991, Irish companies were amending their article of association to facilitate telephonic meetings: see (1991) Irish Times, 17 April, where it was reported that Woodchester Investments plc proposed the following new regulation for its articles: 'Any director or alternative director may participate in a meeting of the directors or any committee of the directors by means of a conference telephone or of other telecommunications equipment by means of which all persons participating in the meeting can hear each other and such participation in a meeting shall constitute presence in person at the meeting.' This was subsequently passed by special resolution of the shareholders in general meeting.

[302] *Re Cawley & Co* [1888] 42 Ch 209.

[303] *Barton v Taylor* [1886] 11 App Cas 197.

[304] See *Re Scottish Petroleum Company* (1882) 23 Ch D 413; *In Re Bank of Syria* (1901) 1 Ch 115; but note also *In Re Alma Spinning Company (Bottomley's case)* (1880) 16 Cr D 681, where it was confirmed that the continuing directors could only continue to act where the articles of association contain a reg 103 type provision.

companies will have adopted reg 7 of Part II, which provides that directors can vote in respect of any contract, appointment or arrangement in which they are interested and shall be counted in the quorum present at the meeting.

[14.115] In Ireland, it remains the law that every company must have at least two directors. As noted earlier, this position was unchanged by the EC(SMPLC)R 1994. It may be noted, however, that in jurisdictions – such as England and Wales – where one director companies are permitted, it has been held that self-dealing transactions, which require directors to disclose their interests in particular transactions, continue to apply, even though this requires a director to disclose to himself his interest in a particular transaction[305]!

The chairman

[14.116] Regulation 104 of Table A provides that:

> 'The directors may elect a chairman of their meetings and determine the period for which he is to hold office, but if no such chairman is elected, or, if at any meeting the chairman is not present within 5 minutes after the time appointed for holding the same, the directors present may choose one of their number to be chairman of the meeting.'

Accordingly, the 'chairman' referred to in reg 101 can be appointed in accordance with reg 104, and apart from having the casting vote, his formally prescribed functions are few. One role of the chairman is signing the minutes of meetings; when signed by the chairman, the minutes are *prima facie* evidence of what took place at a meeting[306]. Where a chairman's period of office is not specified, the other directors can remove the chairman and appoint an alternative[307] subject to any right the chairman may have under any executive contract.

Adjourned meetings

[14.117] Where a resolution is passed at a meeting of the directors which had been earlier adjourned, the resolution shall for all purposes be treated as having been passed on the date on which it was in fact passed and shall not be deemed to have been passed on any earlier date[308].

Minutes of directors' meetings

[14.118] Section 145(1) of the CA 1963 requires[309] that the minutes of all proceedings at meetings of directors and of committees of directors should be entered in a minute book as soon as may be possible. Regulation 89 enumerates the matters that should be entered in the minutes of directors' meetings, these being:

---

305 See *Neptune (Vehicle Washing Equipment) Ltd v Fitzgerald* [1995] 1 BCLC 352, where Lightman J held that it was necessary for a sole director to show that he had declared to himself, his interest in a transaction at a director's meeting.

306 Section 145(2) of the CA 1963. See *Re Indian Zoedone Co* (1884) 26 Ch D 70; *Re Fireproof Doors* [1916] 2 Ch 142; and *Kerr v John Mottram Ltd* [1940] 1 Ch 657.

307 *Foster v Foster* [1916] 1 Ch 532.

308 Section 144 of the CA 1963.

309 Section 145(4) of the CA 1963 provides that the company and every officer of the company who is in default shall be liable to a fine.

- all appointments of officers made by the directors;
- the names of the directors present at each board meeting and of any committee meetings;
- all resolutions and proceedings at members' meetings and at all meetings of the directors and of committees of directors.

Section 145(3A) of the CA 1963 empowers the Director of Corporate Enforcement to obtain copies of all minutes[310].

[14.119] Board minutes are *approved* by the board of directors acting as a body and by majority. Board minutes are *evidenced as having been approved* by the signature of the chairman. A chairman does not exercise an independent judgment in signing minutes – where the chairman is satisfied that the minutes were approved by the board of directors, his or her only role is to evidence that fact by signing them. Where the minutes are signed by the chairman of the meeting (or by the chairman of the next succeeding meeting) the minutes shall be evidence of the proceedings[311]. A further consequence of keeping minutes is that until the contrary is proved, the meeting shall be deemed to have been duly held and convened, and all proceedings had thereat to have been duly had, and all appointments of directors or liquidators shall be deemed to be valid[312].

[14.120] Where meetings are held informally, there will often be no record of the meeting other than individual directors' recollections. Minutes of meetings, where taken, tend to be mechanical formulae to satisfy statutory requirements or the requirements of lending institutions which require a written record of certain board decisions before advancing finances. This was recognised in *Re PMPA Garage (Longmile) Ltd (No 1)*[313] where Murphy J said[314]:

> '... one would not expect to find in any case the minute book of a company recording divergent views of directors and managers in relation to commercial documentation. The minute book of Longmile records, as does probably most minute books of comparable companies, the basic decisions which must be taken in accordance with the requirements of the Companies Acts from time to time. I think it may be assumed confidently that minutes of this nature and any record of any decision or resolution made for statutory or financial purposes would be prepared in advance by the secretary in case of routine matters or by legal advisers in relation to more important matters but in either event the purpose of the meeting would be to approve a preordained formula so that the minutes would reflect that formula and not the discussion, if any, which might take place.'

It is very important that basic minutes are kept. Where no record exists of what has taken place, directors can find themselves exposed, especially when a board's decisions become the subject of judicial scrutiny in establishing the motive behind taking a particular course of action[315]. It should also be noted that the general rule applied to

---

310 See para **[14.078]** *ante*.

311 Section 145(2) of the CA 1963.

312 Section 145(3) of the CA 1963.

313 *Re PMPA Garage (Longmile) Ltd (No 1)* [1992] ILRM 337.

314 *Re PMPA Garage (Longmile) Ltd (No 1)* [1992] ILRM 337 at 342.

315 See *Re Shrinkpak Ltd* (20 December 1989, unreported) HC *per* Barron J, reported in (1989) Irish Times, 21 December 1989.

minutes is that they should record 'decisions not discussions'[316] so that whilst decisions *must* be recorded, deliberations *may* be recorded. There are exceptions to this rule too and an industry regulator may require a greater level of detail where companies are engaged in a particular sphere of activities[317]. In the case of ordinary companies, ultimately, whether minutes record decisions only or also include deliberations is a matter to be decided upon by the board of directors itself, acting by majority if needs be, under the authority of reg 101 of Table A, which provides that the directors shall regulate their meetings as they think fit.

[14.121] Once approved by the directors, board minutes may not be amended, in any circumstances, including to correct purported typographical errors[318]. What has been approved by the board has been approved, and just as a contract, when signed, cannot be amended by a third party to correct a misspelling, neither can minutes. Just as approved minutes cannot be amended post approval, neither can signed board minutes be amended, in any circumstances, including to correct typographical amendments. Where, after minutes have been approved or signed by the chairman, it transpires that they are inaccurate in any respect, the correct procedure is to raise the inaccuracy at a board meeting and put a resolution to that meeting to amend or rescind the decision to approve those minutes. The original minute remains on the record, however, and must never be amended or destroyed. Rather, it remains on the record but is surpassed by the subsequent decision that it was incorrect. It is important to distinguish errors in the minutes from errors in the proceedings. Where there is an error in the proceedings at a meeting (eg, it is asserted that X is Y when it is in fact Z) and this is recorded in the minutes, those minutes will not contain an error since they accurately reflect those proceedings.

Committees

[14.122] In the absence of an empowering article, there can be no delegation by the board to a committee[319]. Regulation 105 of Table A provides that directors may delegate any of their powers to committees consisting of such member or members of the board as they think fit; any committee so formed shall, in the exercise of the powers so delegated, conform to any regulations that may be imposed on it by the directors.

316 On the lackadaisical approach of many small Irish private companies to keeping minutes, see the comments of Murphy J in *Irish Microforms Ltd v Browne* (3 April 1987, unreported) HC.

317 The Central Bank's *Corporate Governance Code for Credit Institutions and Insurance Undertakings* (2010) provides (at cl 15.3) 'Detailed minutes of all board meetings shall be prepared with all decisions, discussions and points for further actions being documented. Dissensions or negative votes shall be documented in terms acceptable to the dissenting person or negative voter. The minutes of meetings shall provide sufficient detail to evidence appropriate board attention, the substance of discussions and their outcome and shall be agreed at the subsequent board meeting. Minutes shall also document the attendance or non-attendance of members of the board.'

318 Amending a board minutes after it has been approved may constitute an offence under s 243(1) of the CA 1990. This provides that an officer of a company who 'falsifies, or is privy to the … falsification of any book or document affecting or relating to the property or affairs of [a company], or makes or is privy to the making of a false entry therein, shall, unless he proves that he had no intention to defeat the law, be guilty of an offence.'

319 *Howard's Case* (1866) 1 Ch 561.

Committees may elect their own chairs[320]. Committees may meet and adjourn as they think proper and questions arising at any meeting shall be determined by a majority of votes of the members present, and where there is an equality of votes, the chairman shall have a second or casting vote[321]. There is authority for the proposition that a sole director can validly constitute a committee[322].

[14.123] It should be noted that reg 105 only provides for the creation of committees composed exclusively of directors. Companies may provide that committees can be composed of non-directors too, and may restrict the rights of non-directors by denying them voting rights or confining their attendance to that by invitation only. The delegation of powers to committees comprised of person who are not directors can raise important governance issues since it could give rise to a situation where people who are not accountable in law are empowered to take binding decisions.

Resolutions and voting

[14.124] Formal decisions of the board of directors are referred to as resolutions. In *Municipal Mutual Insurance Ltd v Harrop et al*[323], Rimer J said:

> 'The fundamental principle is, however, that a company is an artificial legal person the validity of whose operations is governed by its constitution. The ordinary rule is that the acts of a company's board must be authorised by resolutions properly passed at a duly convened board meeting. If the directors purport to act in accordance with the decisions of their majority, but without the prior authority of a board meeting, their acts are not those of either the board or the company[324].'

In that case, it was held that a company's directors had not amended the rules of a pension scheme, which required the passing of a resolution. Rimer J held that an oral assent in response to a memorandum sent to the board was not a resolution which satisfied the company's articles.

(a) Formal resolutions at board meetings

[14.125] The general rule on voting at directors' meetings is that each director has one vote and that voting will take place by a show of hands. Regulation 101 of Table A provides that all questions are to be decided by simple majority and that where there is an equality of votes, the chairman will have a second or casting vote[325]. It is unusual even in plcs for actual formal voting to take place, companies preferring to proceed on the basis of consensus. In *Re Aston Colour Print Ltd*[326], the facts of which have been considered above[327], Kelly J went on to consider whether a resolution of the board had been passed. To the extent that he had already decided that a board meeting had not been

[320] Model reg 106 of Table A.

[321] Model reg 107 of Table A.

[322] *Re Fireproof Doors Ltd* [1916] 2 Ch 142.

[323] *Municipal Mutual Insurance Ltd v Harrop et al* [1998] 2 BCLC 540.

[324] *Municipal Mutual Insurance Ltd v Harrop et al* [1998] 2 BCLC 540 at 551b–c. *Re East Norfolk Tramways Co, Barber's Case* (1877) 5 Ch D 963, cited.

[325] Unless the chairman has been invalidly appointed: *Clark v Workman* [1920] 1 IR 107.

[326] *Re Aston Colour Print Ltd* (21 February 1997, unreported) HC, Kelly J.

[327] See para **[14.109]** *ante*.

held, this aspect of his judgment is *obiter*, but nonetheless instructive. Having noted that there was no formal resolution and certainly no vote taken, he went on to say:

> 'A decision by a board of directors to take such a step [ie, presenting a petition to appoint an examiner] must be made in a manner which makes the will of the board clear. The usual way to do that is by the proposal of a resolution and its being voted upon[328].'

Accordingly, formal resolutions should be proposed[329] and should be voted upon at a properly convened board meeting and, if passed, recorded in the minutes as having been adopted by the board. In that case, Kelly J found there had been no formal resolution nor, indeed, any informal resolution put to the meeting and he believed that what had occurred was that 'there was a general understanding arrived at between four of the five people present at the meeting'. Kelly J concluded:

> 'But the fifth person was of course the second director. He did not appreciate what was to happen. The level of informality was such that I do not think that he can be blamed or criticised for this. There was no resolution put before him nor was there any question put in such a way as to alert him as to what was to occur. Such being so, I do not accept that there was any resolution, formal or informal, passed by the board[330].'

(b) Written resolutions without a board meeting

[14.126] Directors' resolutions may also be passed as written resolutions as is provided for in reg 109 of Table A which states:

> 'A resolution in writing signed by all the directors for the time being entitled to receive notice of a meeting of the directors shall be as valid as if it had been passed at a meeting of the directors duly convened and held.'

The effect of this article is to dispense with the need to convene and hold a board meeting, in order to have a resolution passed. Accordingly, it will suffice if a resolution is in writing and signed by all of the directors. It is thought that even if a particular director is not entitled to vote on a particular resolution, his signature to the resolution will still be required, as the regulation refers to a resolution 'signed by *all the directors*' without qualification. It should be noted, though, that reg 109 will not override a company's quorum requirements. So, in *Hood Sailmakers Ltd v Axford and another*[331] one director of a two-director company purported to pass a written resolution by signing it himself. His co-director was at that time out of the jurisdiction and the company's articles provided that where directors were out of the jurisdiction, they need not receive notice of a director's meeting. The company's articles of association included regulations that were identical to the Irish reg 109 (on written resolutions) and the Irish reg 102 (on quorum)[332]. Its regulation on notice of directors' meetings differed from the Irish reg 101[333] in that it simply stated that it was not necessary to give notice 'to any

---

328 *Re Aston Colour Print Ltd* (21 February 1997, unreported) HC, Kelly J at p 8 of the judgment.

329 Sometimes a practice exists of seconding a proposed resolution. This is not required by law or indeed most company's articles of association; the requirement for proposers and seconders is usually found in the rules of unincorporated associations.

330 *Re Aston Colour Print Ltd* (21 February 1997, unreported) HC, Kelly J at p 8 of the judgment.

331 *Hood Sailmakers Ltd v Axford and another* [1996] 4 All ER 830.

332 See para **[14.113]** *ante*.

333 See para **[14.105]** *ante*.

director for the time being absent from the United Kingdom', so that this applied automatically, without the need for the directors to resolve that this be the case, as is required in Ireland where reg 101 is adopted without modification. Carnwath J said:

> 'It seems to me that [reg 109] is ambiguous. The reference to the meeting being 'duly convened and held' could be taken as a reference, not only to the establishment of the meeting, but also to the validity of the business conducted at it. On the other hand, it might simply be indicating that the document is to be treated as equivalent to a meeting, without prejudice to any other requirement relating to the actual business transacted at it. I note that [reg 102] refers specifically to the quorum required 'for the transaction of business'. This tends to suggest that, even if the meeting is validly convened and held, the requirement for a quorum is to be treated as a separate matter relating to the particular items of business on which reliance is placed. This view also accords with what I take to be the purpose of the provisions. As suggested by the textbooks[334], the object of [reg 109] appears to be to avoid the need for a meeting where it would otherwise be superfluous. It does not appear to be directed to making a fundamental change to the quorum requirements. It would be odd if a director could evade the quorum requirements simply by waiting for his fellow director or directors to leave the country[335].'

The same conclusion appears to have been independently arrived at by the Scottish Court of Session in *Davidson & Begg Antiques Ltd v Davidson*[336], a judgment handed down a few weeks prior to Carnwaith J's decision. In that case, the company's articles made similar provision to those just discussed. In reliance upon them, one of the company's two directors resolved by written resolution that the company would institute proceedings against the other director, the other director being absent from the jurisdiction. Lord Roger held that the proceedings had been commenced on the basis of a resolution that did not comply with the company's quorum requirements. Specifically, he held that the equivalent to reg 109, which commenced 'a resolution in writing signed by all of the directors', suggested the need for more than one signature and also that it had to be read in the context of the other articles. Moreover, he held that the company had set a quorum 'for the transaction of the business of the directors', that the initiation of litigation was part of the company's business and so the quorum requirement applied to any resolution in that context. In reconciling the apparent conflict, Lord Roger said of the equivalent to reg 102 that its terms are more general than simply laying down the quorum for a meeting of the directors, since it prescribes the quorum 'for the transaction of business of the directors'. He found:

> 'Especially since other regulations refer specifically to meetings of the directors, the inference must be that [reg 102] has been framed deliberately in these wider terms in order to cover any means by which the directors are to transact business. [Regulation 102] therefore applies to business transacted by means of resolutions under [reg 109]. The result is that a resolution under [reg 109] is valid provided not only that it is signed by all the directors who are entitled to receive notice of a meeting but also that the number of directors signing is at least two [where that is the quorum][337].'

---

334 Carnwath J had previously referred to Gower, *Principles of Modern Company Law* (5th edn, 1992) at p 160; Pennington, *Pennington's Company Law* (7th edn, 1995) at p 768; and Schmitthoff (ed), *Palmer's Company Law* (1993) Vol 2 at para 8.301.

335 *Hood Sailmakers Ltd v Axford and another* [1996] 4 All ER 830 at 834e–g.

336 *Davidson & Begg Antiques Ltd v Davidson* [1997] BCC 77.

337 *Davidson & Begg Antiques Ltd v Davidson* [1997] BCC 77 at 80D.

It is thought that this is the correct interpretation of these articles and that neither article 109 nor 101 can override a company's quorum requirements.

[14.127] The decisions in *Hood Sailmakers Ltd* and *Davidson & Begg Antiques Ltd* both concerned the recognised exception to the rule that a director who is resident in the State is not entitled to notice of a board meeting if he or she is out of the State. This rule is a limited concession to expedience since it effectively excludes a director who is accountable for all decisions taken by the company from the decision-making process. In theory, it would seem to be possible for a company's articles of association to provide for *majority* written decisions of directors to take effect as resolutions. Provided that appropriate safeguards were built in (for example, the prompt notification of the decision by the directors who did not sign the resolution) a dissenting director would not be in a materially different position than if they had at a physical board meeting voted against a particular resolution and lost.

(c) Unanimous acts of the directors

[14.128] In *Municipal Mutual Insurance Ltd v Harrop et al*[338], Rimer J recognised that there was an exception to the general rule that resolutions must be either formal or written. Where the directors act unanimously in a matter, without either the prior sanction of a resolution of the board or a unanimous *written* resolution, there is authority for saying that their acts will, ordinarily, still be regarded as those of the company[339]. In *Harrop*, it had been sought to extend that exception to a situation where a certain course of action was not unanimous, but this was rejected by Rimer J who said of the exception that:

> '… its essence is unanimity. Once an inroad is made into it so as to enable it to operate where there is something less than unanimity, the need for board meetings might as well be dispensed with altogether[340].'

It is thought that this principle, such as it is, should only ever be considered to be a shield, and that full formality (or, at the very least, the informality permitted by the articles) should never be sacrificed in reliance upon it.

---

338 *Municipal Mutual Insurance Ltd v Harrop et al* [1998] 2 BCLC 540.

339 *Runciman v Walter Runciman plc* [1992] BCLC 1084.

340 *Municipal Mutual Insurance Ltd v Harrop et al* [1998] 2 BCLC 540 at 551b.

Chapter 15

Duties of Directors and Other Officers

Introduction

[15.001] The duties owed by directors and other officers to their company are wide and diverse[1]. The source of such duties is found at common law, in equity and in statute. In many Irish private companies, the directors will often be the shareholders of the company. Consequently, directors' recognition of their duties as directors will often be blurred by the belief that their shareholdings entitle them to the company's assets. Sometimes the only interest which directors will look after will be their own self-interest. Into what has become, for many directors, this misguided reality, intrude the Companies Acts, the common law and equity, which together impose a myriad of duties on company directors and other officers. While the draft Companies Bill published in June 2011 proposes to give effect to the recommendations of the Company Law Review Group by codifying directors' duties, for the moment, the source of their duties is scattered across statute and case law.

[15.002] This chapter is mainly concerned with the duties owed by company directors. In law a director stands in a fiduciary position[2] to the company of which he is an officer. The duties of all fiduciaries can be onerous. A fiduciary may be defined, simply, as a person in a special relationship of trust to another, whether a real person, or a legal person. No matter who is the subject of the fiduciary duties[3], the same principle applies: a fiduciary must act in a manner which is legally becoming of his office and which places the interests of the subject ahead of his own. Consequently, in many private companies where the directors are themselves the only shareholders, there is a real potential for conflict between their legal duties as directors and their selfish interests as shareholders.

[15.003] In this chapter, the duties of directors and other officers are considered in five sections:

- [A] The Subject of Directors' and Other Officers' Duties.
- [B] Duties of Directors at Common Law.
- [C] Directors' Statutory Duties Arising on Insolvency.
- [D] Secretaries' Duties.
- [E] Promoters' Duties.

---

1 See, generally, Keane, *Company Law* (4th edn, Bloomsbury Professional, 2007) at p 368; Ahern, *Directors' Duties Law & Practice* (2009, Round Hall).

2 For an analogy of a director's status with that of a fiduciary, see the comments of Farwell J in *Re City Equitable Fire Insurance Co Ltd* [1925] Ch 407. For a recent work on the duties of fiduciaries, see Stafford & Richie, *Fiduciary Duties: Directors and Employees* (2008, Jordans).

3 On the relevance of the law of 'trustee and beneficiary', to the law of 'director and company', see para **[15.024]** *post*.

It is the duty of each director and secretary 'to ensure that the requirements of the Companies Acts are complied with by the company'[4]. The myriad of statutory duties, both negative and positive, many of which are also criminal offences, are considered in Ch 28[5]. It should also be noted that the duties of company liquidators (voluntary and official) are considered separately in Ch 24[6], and the duties of auditors are considered in Ch 17[7].

[A] The Subject of Directors' and Other Officers' Duties

[15.004] The general rule has always been that directors' duties are owed to the company itself, and not to the shareholders, creditors or employees of the company. In this section the following matters are considered:

1. The general rule: duties are owed to the company.
2. The expansion of directors' duties.

The general rule: duties are owed to the company

[15.005] Directors have long been considered to stand in a fiduciary relationship to their company, and accordingly to owe duties to their company[8]. The rationale for directors being in a fiduciary relationship to the company is that, *inter alia*, they are *agents* of the company and the relationship of agent and principal will give rise to fiduciary duties[9]. Where directors act in breach of their duties, the general rule is that the so-called 'proper plaintiff' in an action against the directors is the company itself[10]. Where the directors and the shareholders are one and the same persons, the duality of roles will often have the effect of preventing the company from taking legal action against errant directors. Action to enforce directors' duties is more likely to be taken where the company acts at the instigation of a liquidator, examiner or receiver. Furthermore, it should be recognised that the happiest of families and friendships can fall apart, especially where there is money at stake, and even where there are only two shareholding directors, one of the duo can embark upon a solo career in breach of his duties as a director. In such cases the problem of to whom the directors' duties are owed takes on a very real significance, because for the company to take action, common form articles of association require a majority of the directors to instigate litigation[11]. However, there appears to be an increasing number of exceptions[12] and clarifications[13] to the general principle that directors' duties are only owed to the 'company'.

---

4 Section 383(3) of the CA 1963.

5 See Ch 28, *Compliance and Enforcement*, at para **[28.030]** *et seq*.

6 See Ch 24, *Liquidators*, at para **[24.020]** *et seq*.

7 See Ch 17, *Financial Statements, Audit and Annual Returns,* para **[17.312]** *et seq*.

8 See MacCann, 'Directors' Duties: To Whom Are They Owed?' (1991) ILT 3 and 30.

9 *Dawson International plc v Coats Paton plc* [1989] BCLC 233 at 243 *per* Lord Cullen. See para **[15.007]** *post*.

10 *Foss v Harbottle* (1843) 2 Hare 461. See generally Ch 11, *Shareholders' Remedies*, at para **[11.092]** *et seq*.

11 See reg 80 of Table A.

12 See para **[15.009]** *post*.

13 See *Brunninghausen v Glavanics* (1999) 32 ACSR 294, considered at para **[15.023]** *post*.

[15.006] The case of *Percival v Wright*[14] is the accepted authority for the proposition that directors' duties are owed to the company and *not* to its shareholders. In that case, the plaintiff shareholders sold their shares to three directors of the company. They discovered later that the directors intended to sell the entire of the company's undertaking to another person at a greatly inflated share price to that received by the plaintiffs. Although the sale never proceeded, had it done so, the directors would have profited handsomely. The plaintiffs alleged that the directors were in breach of their fiduciary relationship to the plaintiffs *as shareholders* through not disclosing the fact that it was proposed to sell the company at a greater price. It was held by Swinfen Eady J that no fiduciary duty was owed to the shareholders in such circumstances, that the directors had the power to negotiate the sale of the company and that the shareholders were deemed to be aware of the powers of the directors. Accordingly, the directors were under no obligation to disclose their negotiations to the plaintiff shareholders.

[15.007] The Court of Session in *Dawson International plc v Coats Paton plc*[15] restated this general rule. In that case, the directors of the plaintiff and defendant companies agreed that the plaintiff company should take over the defendant company by way of a share purchase. It was further agreed that the directors of the defendant company would recommend the plaintiff company's bid to the defendant's shareholders and that the directors of the defendant company would not assist any other prospective purchaser. In breach of this agreement, the defendant's directors co-operated with a different purchaser and the plaintiff company sued the defendant company's directors for breach of the agreement. The defendant's directors claimed in their defence that they owed a duty to the shareholders of the defendant company to advise them of the advantages and disadvantages of all takeover bids. It was held that the directors owed no such duty to the shareholders and that their duties were owed to the company itself. Consequently, their only concern should have been which takeover bid was in the best interests of the company. Lord Cullen said:

> 'It is well recognised that directors owe fiduciary duties to the company. Thus the directors have the duty of fiduciaries with respect to the property and funds of the company ... These fiduciary duties spring from the relationship of the directors to the company, of which they are its agents ... In contrast I see no good reason why it should be supposed that directors are, in general, under a fiduciary duty to the shareholders, and in particular current shareholders with respect to the disposal of their shares in the most advantageous way. The directors are not normally the agents of the current shareholders ... The cases and other authorities to which I was referred do not seem to me to establish any such fiduciary duty [to the shareholders] ...
>
> What is in the interests of current shareholders who are sellers of their shares may not necessarily coincide with what is in the interests of the company. The creation of parallel duties could lead to conflict. *Directors have but one master, the company*[16].'

It should be remembered that the company in question was a *public limited company*. Although the principle that directors' duties are owed to the company remains true in the case of private companies, it is suggested that in private companies it is more likely that

14 *Percival v Wright* [1902] 2 Ch 421.

15 *Dawson International plc v Coats Paton plc* [1989] BCLC 233.

16 *Dawson International plc v Coats Paton plc* [1989] BCLC 233 at 243. Italics added.

the directors may (by virtue of collateral contracts) be found to be the agents of the shareholders and consequently to owe fiduciary duties to the shareholders[17].

The expansion of directors' duties

[15.008] The current trend would seem to be towards the broadening of directors' duties in favour of persons beyond the company. Although the Supreme Court has refused to stretch the expansion to include shareholders' interests in the value of their shareholdings[18], recent developments have extended directors' duties to creditors[19] and, by statute, to employees and members[20]. In particular circumstances, the legislature can extend this further as it did, for example, in the Credit Institutions (Stabilisation) Act 2010. There, s 48(1) provides that in the performance of their functions the directors of a relevant institution[21] 'shall have a duty to have regard to the matters mentioned in s 4(f)'[22] of that Act and, in sub-s (2), that that duty is owed to the Minister for Finance on behalf of the State and takes priority over any other duty of the directors to the extent of any inconsistency. The Credit Institutions (Stabilisation) Act 2010 was emergency legislation which gave the Minister emergency powers to stabilise the crisis in Irish banking, and the foregoing example of an extension of directors' duties by statute may be considered as being very much an the exception to the general rule.

[15.009] It is proposed to consider the extension of directors' duties to the following categories of persons:

(a) Duties to creditors.
(b) Duties to employees and members.
(c) Duties to shareholders.

(a) Duties to creditors

[15.010] A series of Irish judgments have held that when a company is insolvent, even if not in liquidation, the directors of the company will owe a duty to the company's creditors[23]. The principle relied upon by the Irish judges in all of these judgments was

---

17 See para **[15.019]** *post*.

18 *O'Neill v Ryan* [1993] ILRM 557. See Ch 11, *Shareholders' Remedies*, at para **[11.104]** *et seq*.

19 When a company becomes insolvent: *Re Frederick Inns Ltd* [1994] 1 ILRM 387, see para **[15.013]** *post*.

20 Directors must have regard to the interests of employees: s 52(1) of the CA 1990, see para **[15.018]** *post*.

21 Relevant institution, as defined by s 2(1), includes a number of private companies limited by shares.

22 Those matters were the purposes of the Act being to facilitate the availability of credit in the economy of the State, to protect the State's interests in respect of guarantees given, to protect the interest of taxpayers, to restore confidence in the banking sector and to underpin Government support measures in relation thereto and to align the activities of relevant institutions and the duties of their officers and employees with the public interest and the other purposes of the Act.

23 *Parkes v Hong Kong & Shanghai Bank Corp* [1990] ILRM 341, *per* Blayney J (High Court); *Re Frederick Inns Ltd* [1991] ILRM 582 *per* Lardner J (High Court) and [1994] 1 ILRM 387 *per* Blayney J (Supreme Court); *Jones et al v Gunn et al* [1997] 2 ILRM 245, *per* McGuinness J.

explained by Street CJ in the Court of Appeal in New South Wales in *Kinsella v Russell Kinsella Property Ltd*[24] where he said:

> 'In a solvent company the proprietary interests of the shareholders entitled them as a general body to be regarded as the company when questions of the duty of directors arise. If, as a general body they authorise or ratify a particular action of the directors there can be no challenge to the validity of what the directors have done. But where a company is insolvent the interests of the creditors intrude. They become prospectively entitled, through the mechanism of liquidation, to displace the power of the shareholders and the directors to deal with the company's assets. It is in a practical sense their assets and not the shareholders' assets that, through the medium of the company, or under the management of the directors pending either liquidation, return to solvency, or the imposition of some alternative administration[25].'

This principle may be taken as representing the modern Irish law on the duties owed by directors to an insolvent company's creditors, having been cited with approval by Blayney J in the Supreme Court decision in *Re Frederick Inns Ltd*[26]. One consequence, identified by McGuinness J in *Jones et al v Gunn et al*[27], is that the directors of an insolvent company 'may not make payments which benefit either closely connected companies or themselves personally to the detriment of the general and independent creditors'. It is submitted that this is merely illustrative, and is not an exhaustive statement of directors' duties to creditors arising on insolvency.

[15.011] As will be considered, those Irish judgments as have cited the foregoing passage in *Kinsella* have taken it as authority for the imposition of duties on directors of insolvent companies, in favour of creditors. There is another interpretation open, as identified by Tulson J in *Yukong Line Ltd of Korea v Rendsburg Investments Corp of Liberia et al (No 2)*[28]. In that case, it was held that the transfer of assets in disregard of creditors' interests was a breach of duty owed to the company, the only redress for which was the statutory remedies available in any liquidation. The judge concluded:

> 'Where a director, or person having the management, of an insolvent company acts in breach of his duty to the company by causing assets of the company to be transferred in disregard of the interests of its creditor or creditors, under English law he is answerable through the scheme which Parliament has provided. In my judgment he does not owe a direct fiduciary duty towards an individual creditor, nor is an individual creditor entitled to sue for breach of the fiduciary duty owed by the director to the company[29].'

In *Colin Gwyer & Associates Ltd and another v London Wharf (Limehouse) Ltd et al*[30], it was held that where two directors resolved in favour of settling legal proceedings involving the company which was insolvent, they did not have regard to the interests of

---

24 *Kinsella v Russell Kinsella Property Ltd* [1986] 4 NSWLR 722.

25 *Kinsella v Russell Kinsella Property Ltd* [1986] 4 NSWLR 722 at 730.

26 *Re Frederick Inns Ltd* [1994] 1 ILRM 387.

27 *Jones et al v Gunn et al* [1997] 2 ILRM 245 at 263.

28 *Yukong Line Ltd of Korea v Rendsburg Investments Corp of Liberia et al (No 2)* [1998] 4 All ER 82.

29 *Yukong Line Ltd of Korea v Rendsburg Investments Corp of Liberia et al (No 2)* [1998] 4 All ER 82 at 99e–f.

30 *Colin Gwyer & Associates Ltd and another v London Wharf (Limehouse) Ltd et al* [2002] EWHC 2748, [2003] 2 BCLC 152.

the creditors of the company, and so were in breach of their fiduciary duties *to the company*. The resolution to settle proceedings was declared void. It is thought that the interpretation given by the Irish courts is to be preferred.

[15.012] The first[31] Irish judgment to recognise this principle was that given by Blayney J in *Parkes v Hong Kong & Shanghai Bank Corp*[32]. The facts in that case have already been given in Ch 7[33], but in summary the issue was, *inter alia*, whether the fact that a company was insolvent meant that a disposition of its assets was *ultra vires*. The liquidator relied upon the English case of *West Mercia Safetywear Ltd v Dodd*[34]. In that case, the defendant was a director of the plaintiff company and another company, which was a wholly-owned subsidiary of the former. The plaintiff company owed the defendant £30,000, and although an accountant advised both companies not to operate their bank accounts, the defendant transferred £4,000 from the plaintiff's account into the account of the other company. Later, both companies went into liquidation, and the liquidator of the plaintiff company issued misfeasance proceedings against the defendant, alleging, *inter alia*, that the defendant owed a fiduciary duty to the plaintiff company. This was accepted by the Court of Appeal, which held that the director:

> '... was guilty of breach of duty when, for his own purposes, he caused the £4,000 to be transferred in disregard of the interests of the general creditors of this insolvent company.'

In the *Parkes* case, Blayney J went on to cite the principle of law stated by Street CJ in the *Kinsella* case, but although he quoted both cases with approval, the learned judge went on to distinguish them from the case in hand. In both cases, he said, the question concerned breach of directors' duties or abuse of directors' authority, while in the case in hand the question concerned lack of corporate capacity, or the doctrine of *ultra vires*. In addition, Blayney J distinguished the case in hand by saying:

> '... the defendant in the *West Mercia* case was aware that the company whose money he transferred was insolvent whereas, in the present case, there is no evidence that [the defendant] knew the claimant company was insolvent[35].'

It would appear that in the *Parkes* case Blayney J accepted the distinction between *solvent* and *insolvent* companies, and that the directors of insolvent companies owed duties to that company's creditors. This distinction marked a novel departure in company law, since it represented the first inroad in Irish common law corporate jurisprudence to the general principle that officers' duties are only owed to their company.

[15.013] The other landmark Irish case on the duties of directors to creditors where a company is insolvent is *Re Frederick Inns Ltd*[36], where, in both the High Court and the

31 An earlier statement of the Irish law on directors' duties to creditors is found in the judgment of O'Hanlon J in *Byrne v Shelbourne FC Ltd* [1984] IEHC 11, where he said: '... before any limited company can dispose of all its assets, it must do the best it can for the creditors and explore all reasonable possibilities of obtaining a better offer before selling out to a particular bidder.' In that case, the plaintiff unsuccessfully claimed that the company made a sale at an undervalue to the detriment of the creditors, of which he was one.

32 *Parkes v Hong Kong & Shanghai Bank Corp* [1990] ILRM 341.

33 Ch 7, *Corporate Capacity and Authority*, at para **[7.066]**.

34 *West Mercia Safetywear Ltd v Dodd* [1988] BCLC 250.

35 *Parkes v Hong Kong & Shanghai Bank Corp* [1990] ILRM 341 at 349.

36 *Re Frederick Inns Ltd* [1991] ILRM 582 (HC) and [1994] 1 ILRM 387 (SC). See Fealy, 'The Role of Equity in the Winding Up of a Company' [1995] 17 DULJ 18.

Supreme Court, Street CJ's statement of principle was cited with approval. In this case, the directors of a group of companies caused certain of those companies to sell their principal assets and to pay the Revenue Commissioners not only the individual company's debts, but also debts owed by other companies within the group, in flagrant disregard of the concept of separate legal personality. After citing the judgments of Street CJ in the *Kinsella* case and of Dillon LJ in the *West Mercia* case, Lardner J in the High Court held that the statements of law therein seemed to him:

> 'to be consonant with the intent of Irish company legislation and to be appropriate and applicable to insolvent companies in Irish law. In my judgment therefore the payments to the Revenue which are in question were also misapplications of the respective companies' assets because they were made when the companies were insolvent and the payments were in disregard of the rights and interests of the general creditors[37].'

Lardner J also said that:

> '... the payments to the Revenue which are in question were made by the authority of the directors of the respective companies in breach of the duty which the company *and the directors* owed to the general creditors of these insolvent companies[38].'

The Revenue Commissioners unsuccessfully appealed to the Supreme Court against Lardner J's decision. Blayney J, who gave the Supreme Court's judgment, held that the company's directors owed duties to the company's creditors when the company became insolvent. After citing an old authority[39] for the proposition that a company's property is *trust property* when a company is being wound up, Blayney J said:

> 'It is clear from this case that as soon as a winding-up order has been made the company ceases to be the beneficial owner of its assets, with the result that the directors no longer have power to dispose of them. Where, as here, a company's situation was such that any creditor could have caused it to be wound up on the ground of solvency, I consider that it can equally well be said that the company had ceased to be the beneficial owner of its assets with the result that the directors would have had no power to use the company's assets to discharge the liabilities of other companies. Once the company clearly had to be wound up and its assets applied *pro tanto* in discharge of its liabilities, the directors had a duty to the creditors to preserve the assets to enable this to be done, or at least not to dissipate them[40].'

After referring to the judgment of Street CJ in the *Kinsella* case, Blayney J adopted and followed the statement of principle quoted above[41]. Indicative of the strength of the principle that directors of an insolvent company owe duties to creditors is Blayney J's conclusion that the directors *could not lawfully and effectively* have made the payments

---

37 *Re Frederick Inns Ltd* [1991] ILRM 582 at 590.

38 *Re Frederick Inns Ltd* [1991] ILRM 582 at 589; italics added.

39 *Re Oriental Inland Steam Co* (1874) 9 Ch App 557, cited by Templeman J in *Ayerst v C & K (Construction) Ltd* [1974] 1 All ER 676.

40 *Re Frederick Inns Ltd* [1994] 1 ILRM 387 at 396. Note that in *Commissioner of Taxation v Linter Textiles Australia Ltd* [2003] FCAFC 63 (14 April 2003), the Federal Court of Australia held that where a holding company was in liquidation the shares it held in a subsidiary did not cease to be in its 'beneficial ownership'.

41 See para **[15.010]** *ante*.

to the Revenue Commissioners. Thus, where directors act in breach of their duties to the creditors of an insolvent company their actions will properly be termed *unlawful*.

[15.014] In *Hughes v Hitachi Koki Imaging Solutions Europe*[42], Clarke J relied on the decision in *Re Frederick Inns* to justify the granting of a *Mareva* injunction against an insolvent company even though there was no evidence that the directors intended to dispose of the company's assets with a view to evading its obligations or to frustrate the anticipated order of the court. In that case, a company which owed the plaintiff a sum of money arising from disability payments due to her was winding down its Irish business and did not appear to be making provision for her contingent claim. Clarke J said after considering *Re Frederick Inns* that he was:

> '... satisfied that, in principle, it is open to a plaintiff to seek a *Mareva* type injunction in circumstances where it can be shown that an insolvent corporate entity intends to deal with its assets in a manner which would be in breach of the obligations on the company and its directors to ensure that those assets are maintained in a fashion which would enable them to be applied in accordance with corporate insolvency law.'

This decision is considered further in Ch 25.

[15.015] It is only where a company is insolvent that directors will owe duties to creditors. In *Parkes v Hong Kong & Shanghai Bank Corp*[43], Blayney J appears to have adopted a subjective test by distinguishing the facts of the case in hand case from those in the *West Mercia* case, saying that there was no evidence that the defendant in the *Parkes* case *knew* that the company was insolvent[44]. This may now be taken as settled law in Ireland, and in *Re DSC Ltd, Fitzpatrick v Henley*[45] MacMenamin J said:

> 'In *Re Frederick Inns Ltd* [1994] ILRM 387 the Supreme Court had to consider the question of the duties of directors in a situation where a company was being wound up and where any creditor could have had it wound up on the ground of insolvency. Blayney J in giving the judgment of the court, found that in such circumstances the directors owed a duty to the creditors to preserve the assets to as to enable them to be applied *pro tanto* in discharge of the liabilities of the company. There can be little doubt therefore that amongst the important duties of directors is one to ensure that when it becomes clear that a company is insolvent, the assets are preserved and dealt with in accordance with the requirements of the Companies Acts[46].'

[15.016] It may be noted that while the authorities in England are equivocal they are leaning towards the finding of a duty to the creditors of a company by the directors[47]. Several commonwealth cases also strongly endorse this trend. The extension of the duty

42 *Hughes v Hitachi Koki Imaging Solutions Europe* [2006] IEHC 233.

43 *Parkes v Hong Kong & Shanghai Bank Corp* [1990] ILRM 341.

44 *Parkes v Hong Kong & Shanghai Bank Corp* [1990] ILRM 341 at 349.

45 *Re DSC Ltd, Fitzpatrick v Henley* [2006] IEHC 179.

46 *Re DSC Ltd, Fitzpatrick v Henley* [2006] IEHC 179 at para 35.

47 See *Lonrho v Shell Petroleum Ltd* [1980] 1 WLR 627; *Multinational Gas & Petrochemical Co v Multinational Gas & Petrochemical Services Ltd* [1983] 3 WLR 492; *Charterbridge Corp Ltd v Lloyds Bank Ltd* [1969] 2 All ER 1185; *Re Halt Garage (1964) Ltd* [1982] 3 All ER 1016; and *Re Horsley & Weight Ltd* [1982] 3 All ER 1045. The cases of *West Mercia Safetywear Ltd v Dodd* [1988] BCLC 250 and *Winkworth v Edward Baron Developments Ltd* [1987] 1 All ER 114 must be distinguished. (contd.../)

can be explained on the basis of the general extension of the duty of care to one's neighbours in tort law. In the New Zealand case of *Nicholson v Permakraft (NZ) Ltd*[48], Cooke J heard a misfeasance suit[49] against the directors of a company resulting from the distribution to shareholders of a profit arising from the revaluation of certain properties owned by the company. On the facts, it was held that the directors had no reason to doubt the solvency of the company and so the remainder of the judgment is *obiter dictum*. Even so, the learned judge's rationale for the directors owing a duty of care is instructive. It was said that the creditors of a company are entitled to consideration in the following circumstances: where the company is insolvent; where it is near insolvent; where it is of doubtful solvency; and where a proposed course of action places the creditors in jeopardy, based on business ethics and upon general principles of the duty of care[50].

[15.017] It is interesting to note that Cooke J believed that where the shareholders *ratify* the actions of the directors the acts done cannot be challenged by the liquidator or creditors. Perhaps time will show that the inherent power of the shareholders to ratify the actions of directors will be confined to situations where the company is *solvent*, and that the concept of solvency will surpass the notion of the commencement of the winding up as the sole determinant of the shareholders power to do this[51]. In the context of the Irish private company, where the directors will often be the shareholders, it is submitted that if the expansion of the duties owed by directors to creditors is to have any teeth, this further step must be taken, and the shareholders cannot be permitted to ratify the wrongs of the directors when the company is insolvent. It must not be forgotten, however, that the need for such a shift is to some extent obviated by the enactment of the provisions on

---

47 (\...contd) In the latter case, the House of Lords *per* Lord Templeman said: '... a company owes a duty to its creditors, present and future. The company is not bound to pay off every debt as soon as it is incurred and the company is not obliged to avoid all ventures which involve an element of risk, but the company owes a duty to its creditors to keep property inviolate and available for the repayment of its debts. The conscience of the company is confided to its directors. A duty is owed by the directors to the company and to the creditors of the company to ensure that the affairs of the company are properly administered and that its property is not dissipated or exploited for the benefit of the directors themselves to the prejudice of the creditors.' This case was cited with approval in *Jones et al v Gunn et al* [1977] 2 ILRM 245 at 260.

48 *Nicholson v Permakraft (NZ) Ltd* [1985] 1 NZLR 242.

49 See para **[15.149]** *post*.

50 Note that Sealy, *Cases and Materials in Company Law* (4th edn, Butterworths, 1989) at p 250 believes that Cooke J's judgment is too wide.

51 Such may be said to be implicit in the judgment of Blayney J in *Re Frederick Inns Ltd* [1994] 1 ILRM 387 at 396 where he quoted from the judgment of James LJ in Re *Oriental Inland Steam Co* (1874) 9 Ch App 557 who said: 'The English Act of Parliament has enacted that in the case of a winding-up the assets of the company so wound up are to be collected and applied in discharge of its liabilities [there is a similar provision in s 235 of the CA 1963]. That makes the property of the company clearly trust property. It is property affected by the Act of Parliament with an obligation to be dealt with by the proper officer in a particular way. Then it has ceased to be beneficially the property of the company; and, being so, it has ceased to be liable to be seized by the execution creditors of the company.'

reckless trading, since the difference between trading recklessly and breaching a duty to creditors is narrow[52].

(b) Duties to employees and members

[15.018] The statutory duty introduced by the CA 1990 that directors should have regard to the interests of the company's employees and members is of dubious value to its intended beneficiaries. Section 52 of the CA 1990 provides:

> '(1) The matters to which the directors of a company are to have regard in the performance of their functions shall include the interests of the company's employees in general, as well as the interests of its members.
>
> (2) Accordingly, the duty imposed by this section on the directors shall be owed by them to the company (and the company alone) and shall be enforceable in the same way as any other fiduciary duty owed to a company by its directors.'

Truly, what the legislature gave by sub-s (1), it took away by sub-s (2). What began as a flame of potentially far greater significance than the Supreme Court's extension of directors' duties to creditors of an insolvent company in *Re Frederick Inns Ltd*[53], became a wet squib. The net effect of s 52 may be said to be: directors are obliged to have regard to the interests of employees and members *but* the recipients of the statutory favour may not themselves enforce the directors' duty. Only where an altruistic liquidator is appointed to the company may the duty to employees be vindicated; only where the aggrieved members can muster sufficient voting power in general meeting to *compel* the directors to have regard to them, may the duty owed to them by s 52 be vindicated[54]. The difficulty of course with extending the categories of persons with *locus standi* to sue directors is the possibility of a multiplicity of actions, something which, in this litigious age, must be a concern.

(c) Duties to shareholders

[15.019] Judicial attempts to expand directors' duties to shareholders have been varied and can often be seen as stopgap attempts to avoid an inequity or injustice caused by the general rule that duties are only owed to the company[55]. Such attempts can best be seen as a recognition of the principle that, although directors are agents of the company and in consequence *automatically* owe fiduciary duties to the company, there is no rule of law that directors cannot also be agents of the shareholders and so stand in a fiduciary relationship to them[56]. Keane J put the matter thus in the Supreme Court decision of *Crindle Investments et al v Wymes et al*[57]:

> 'There can be do doubt that, in general, although directors of a company occupy a fiduciary position in relation to the company, they do not owe a fiduciary duty, merely by virtue of their offices, to the individual members. That was the effect of the decision in the

52 See para **[15.096]** *post*.

53 *Re Frederick Inns Ltd* [1994] 1 ILRM 387. See para **[15.013]** *ante*.

54 See Ch 13, *Corporate Governance: Management by the Directors,* at para **[13.138]** *et seq*.

55 See *Colman v Myers* [1977] 2 NZRL 225 considered at para **[15.021]** *post*.

56 See *Re Chez Nico (Restaurants) Ltd* [1992] BCLC 192; *Platt v Platt* [1999] 2 BCLC 745; *Peskin and another v Anderson et al* [2000] 2 BCLC 1; and *Brunninghausen v Glavanics* (1999) 32 ACSR 294.

57 *Crindle Investments et al v Wymes et al* [1998] 2 ILRM 275.

leading case of *Percival v Wright* [1902] 2 Ch 421 but it has been emphasised in subsequent decisions that, in particular circumstances, a company director may indeed be in a position where he owes a fiduciary duty to individual shareholders. A helpful example is the decision of the New Zealand Court of Appeal in *Coleman v Myers* [1977] 2 NZLR 225, which is referred to in the judgment under appeal[58].'

In that case, the Supreme Court held that mutual trust and confidence was not a feature of the relationship between the parties which led to the proceedings and, accordingly, no fiduciary duties were owed by the defendant directors to the members. Again, in the English case of *Peskin and another v Anderson et al*[59], Neuberger J said:

> 'I am satisfied, both as a matter of principle and in light of the state of the authorities, that *Percival v Wright* [1902] 2 Ch 421 is good law in the sense that a director of a company has no general fiduciary duty to shareholders. However, I am also satisfied that, in appropriate and specific circumstances, a director can be under a fiduciary duty to a shareholder. It seems to me that as a general proposition a director's primary fiduciary duty to shareholders (a) would involve placing an unfair, unrealistic and uncertain burden on a director and (b) would present him frequently with a position where his two competing duties, namely his undoubted fiduciary duty to the company and his alleged fiduciary duty to shareholders, would be in conflict[60].'

So in *Platt and another v Platt*[61], a case involving three brother shareholders, it was held that the defendant brother shareholder did owe fiduciary duties to his brothers, the plaintiffs. The circumstances giving rise to this duty were that the defendant had induced the plaintiffs to sell their shares to him for a nominal amount at a time when the company was in financial difficulties. The defendant had told the plaintiffs that this was necessary to enable the business to be sold at the insistence of BMW and that if the sale did not proceed their shares would be re-transferred. The defendant refused to transfer the shares back and when he eventually sold the business himself, the plaintiffs successfully sued for, *inter alia*, breach of fiduciary duty.

[15.020] The clearest situation in which directors will stand in a fiduciary relationship to the shareholders is where they expressly undertake certain obligations to the shareholders. Authority here is *Allen v Hyatt*[62], where the directors of a company induced the shareholders to give them options to buy their shares, on the pretext that this would assist the directors who were negotiating an amalgamation with another company. A dispute arose when, upon the terms of the amalgamation being agreed, the directors exercised the options to sell the shares and made a personal profit. It was held by the Privy Council that the directors were obliged to account to the shareholders for the profit made by them. Viscount Haldane LC distinguished this case from the general rule that directors' duties were owed to the company, saying:

> 'The [directors] appeared to have been under the impression that [they] were entitled in all the circumstances to act as though they owed no duty to individual shareholders. No doubt the duty of the directors was primarily one to the company itself. It might be that in

58 *Crindle Investments et al v Wymes et al* [1998] 2 ILRM 275 at 288.

59 *Peskin and another v Anderson et al* [2000] 2 BCLC 1. The decision was upheld by the Court of Appeal: [2001] 1 BCLC 372.

60 *Peskin and another v Anderson et al* [2000] 2 BCLC 1 at 14c–e.

61 *Platt and another v Platt* [1999] 2 BCLC 745.

62 *Allen v Hyatt* (1914) 30 TLR 444 (Privy Council).

> circumstances such as those in *Percival v Wright* they could deal at arm's length with a shareholder. But the facts in the present case were widely different from those in *Percival v Wright*, and their Lordships thought that the directors must here be taken to have held themselves out to the individual shareholders as acting for them on the same footing as they were acting for the company itself, that was, as agents ...[63]'

Because of the factual finding of agency, the court was able to hold that the directors stood in a fiduciary relationship to the shareholders.

[15.021] It has been said that the 'traditional authorities are now on the retreat'[64], and evidence that the Irish courts may be inclined towards extending directors' duties to shareholders is seen in *Securities Trust Ltd v Associated Properties Ltd*[65]. In that case, McWilliam J suggested that the directors of a company were 'to some extent in a fiduciary position' to the shareholders who were entitled to be given reasonably full particulars by the directors of a takeover of the company being proposed to be financed by the company itself[66]. In the New Zealand case of *Coleman v Myers*[67], the retreat of the general rule that directors' duties are only owed to the company is also evident. Of particular interest is that the case concerned a family-type private company. One of the defendant directors acquired a controlling interest in the company and the plaintiff minority shareholders were forced to sell their shares by virtue of a statutory provision, similar to s 204 of the CA 1963[68], whereupon the plaintiff shareholders alleged that the directors were in breach of fiduciary duties owed to them. In the New Zealand Court of Appeal, the fact that the company was a closely-held private company was crucial to the court in deciding that the directors were in a fiduciary position to the shareholders, since the latter often looked to the directors for advice. By withholding information on the value of the shares, the directors were found to have breached their duty to the shareholders. It is submitted that the true authority of this case is that directors are not automatically precluded from standing in a fiduciary relationship to the shareholders of a company, and where they are agents of the shareholders they may, on the facts of the case, be in a fiduciary position to them. As Woodhouse J said:

> 'In my opinion it is not the law that anybody holding the office of director of a limited liability company is for that reason alone to be released from what otherwise would be regarded as a fiduciary responsibility owed to those in the position of shareholders of the same company ... it is my opinion that the standard of conduct required from a director in relation to dealings with a shareholder will differ depending upon all the surrounding circumstances and the nature of the responsibility which in a real and practical sense the director has assumed towards the shareholder[69].'

This would seem to be an eminently sensible position to adopt, because unlike the position between a director and his company, the relationship between a director and a

---

63 *Cf Dawson International plc v Coats Paton plc* [1989] BCLC 233, considered at para **[15.007]** *ante*.

64 See Ussher, *Company Law in Ireland* (1986) at p 205.

65 *Securities Trust Ltd v Associated Properties Ltd* (19 November 1980, unreported) HC.

66 See also *Heron International Ltd v Lord Grade* [1983] BCLC 244, where it was held that a duty can be owed to shareholders where a takeover bid has been made.

67 *Coleman v Myers* [1977] 2 NZLR 225.

68 See Ch 9, *Share Transfer*, at para **[9.097]** *et seq*.

69 *Coleman v Myers* [1977] 2 NZLR 225 at 324.

shareholder does not *per se* give rise to fiduciary duties: such will only arise where there are special circumstances which give rise to a fiduciary duty[70]. Whether or not a fiduciary duty exists will, therefore, depend upon the circumstances in each case. As Neuberger J said in *Peskin and another v Anderson et al*[71] useful guidance as to whether a fiduciary duty exists is seen in the observations of Millett LJ in *Bristol and West Building Society v Mothew*[72] where he said:

> 'A fiduciary is someone who has undertaken to act for or on behalf of another in a particular matter in circumstances which give rise to a relationship of trust and confidence. The distinguishing obligation of a fiduciary is the obligation of loyalty. The principal is entitled to the single-minded loyalty of his fiduciary. The core liability has several facets. A fiduciary must act in good faith; he must not make a profit out of his trust; he must not place himself in a position where his duty and his interest may conflict; he may not act for his own benefit or the benefit of a third person without the informed consent of his principal. This is not intended to be an exhaustive list, but it is sufficient to indicate the nature of fiduciary obligations[73].'

[15.022] In private companies, the relationship between the directors and the shareholders can sometimes ground a fiduciary relationship[74]. The *dicta* in *Coleman v Myers*[75] clearly show the possibility of a fiduciary relationship arising in the context of a private company. In a passage, cited with approval by Keane J in the Supreme Court in *Crindle Investments et al v Wymes et al*[76], Woodhouse J said:

> '... the courts can and should find some practical means of giving effect to sensible and fair principles of commercial morality in the cases that come before them; and while it may not be possible to lay down any general test as to when the fiduciary duty will arise for a company director or to prescribe the exact conduct which will always discharge it when it does, there are nevertheless some factors that will usually have an influence upon a decision, one way or the other. They include, I think, dependence upon information and advice, the existence of a relationship of confidence, the significance of some particular transaction for the parties and, of course, the extent of any positive action taken by or on behalf of the director or directors to promote it. In the present case each one of those matters had more than ordinary significance and when they are taken together they leave me in no doubt that each of the two directors did owe a fiduciary duty to the individual shareholders[77].'

It may be noted, however, that in *Peskin and another v Anderson et al*[78], Neuberger J cautioned against compartmentalising a type of company – such as a private company or

---

70 See *Re Chez Nico (Restaurants) Ltd* [1992] BCLC 192. See also *Platt v Platt* [1999] 2 BCLC 745 and *Peskin and another v Anderson et al* [2000] 2 BCLC 1.

71 *Peskin and another v Anderson et al* [2000] 2 BCLC 1. The decision was upheld by the Court of Appeal: [2001] 1 BCLC 372.

72 *Bristol and West Building Society v Mothew* [1996] 4 All ER 698.

73 *Bristol and West Building Society v Mothew* [1996] 4 All ER 698 at 711–712.

74 See Keane, *Equity and the Law of Trusts in the Republic of Ireland* (1988, Butterworths), at Ch 29.

75 *Coleman v Myers* [1977] 2 NZLR 225.

76 *Crindle Investments et al v Wymes et al* [1998] 2 ILRM 275 at 288.

77 *Coleman v Myers* [1977] 2 NZLR 225 at 325.

78 *Peskin and another v Anderson et al* [2000] 2 BCLC 1. The decision was upheld by the Court of Appeal: [2001] 1 BCLC 372.

a family company – and saying that fiduciary duties to shareholders can only arise in such companies and not in others[79].

[15.023] In *Brunninghausen v Glavanics*[80], the New South Wales Court of Appeal refused to follow *Percival v Wright*[81] and found that the directors did owe a duty to the company's shareholders. The circumstances were that the company had two shareholding directors and, following a disagreement, one became passive in the running of the company. The other director agreed to buy the passive director's shares, but did not disclose that he was in discussions with a third party concerning the sale of the entire shareholding. The passive director was paid 10 times less for his shares than the active director obtained from the third party. Handley JA held that the decision in *Percival v Wright* did not stand in the way of the recognition of a fiduciary duty by directors. This case went further than both *Coleman v Myers* and *Allen v Hyatt*. Unlike *Coleman v Myers*, there was no relationship of actual trust and confidence and no such relationship invited by the defendant director; unlike *Allen v Hyatt*, the defendant director had not placed himself in a fiduciary relationship with the shareholders akin to that owed by agents to principals[82]. Handley JA's reasoning is compelling. Whilst the statement that directors owe a duty to their company is undoubtedly correct and its validity is undiminished, he said that:

> 'Any statement that the defendant owed a duty to the company in relation to his dealings with the plaintiff over his shares is meaningless. Such a duty would lack all practical content. The company could not suffer any loss from the breach of such a duty, and had no interest in its loyal and disinterested performance. Where a director's fiduciary duties are owed to the company this prevents the recognition of concurrent and identical duties to its shareholders covering the same subject matter. *However this should not preclude the recognition of a fiduciary duty to shareholders in relation to dealings in their shares where this would not compete with any duty owed to the company*[83].'

This is precisely what Handley JA went on to find, namely: that directors can owe a fiduciary duty 'to the shareholders where there are negotiations for a takeover or an acquisition of the company's undertaking' which 'would require the directors to loyally promote the joint interests of all shareholders.' A conflict that might arise would be if they sought to prefer their personal interests to the joint interest, and Handley JA said that this was 'the very conduct which would be proscribed by the duty'[84]. On the facts it was found that the defendant director did owe the plaintiff, as shareholder, a fiduciary duty which had been breached by his non-disclosure of the negotiations for the sale of the company's assets before the purchase of the plaintiff's shares.

---

79 *Peskin and another v Anderson et al* [2000] 2 BCLC 1 at 15a–b.

80 *Brunninghausen v Glavanics* (1999) 32 ACSR 294. See 'Comment, The Last Rites for *Percival v Wright*' (2000) 21 Co Lawyer 261.

81 *Percival v Wright* [1902] 2 Ch 421.

82 *Brunninghausen v Glavanics* (1999) 32 ACSR 294 at para 53 of the judgment.

83 *Brunninghausen v Glavanics* (1999) 32 ACSR 294 at para 58 of the judgment. Emphasis added.

84 *Brunninghausen v Glavanics* (1999) 32 ACSR 294 at para 106, 107 of the judgment.

[B] DUTIES OF DIRECTORS AT COMMON LAW

The nature and source of directors' common law duties

[15.024] Having explored the question of to whom the fiduciary duties of the directors are owed, it next falls to examine the nature of such fiduciary duties. The fiduciary duties of directors may be reduced to three broad principles:

- Directors must exercise their powers[85] in good faith and in the interests of the company as a whole;
- Directors are not allowed to make an undisclosed personal profit from their position as directors, and must account[86] for any profit which they secretly derive from their position;
- Directors are obliged to carry out their functions with due care, skill and diligence[87].

The sources[88] of directors' duties are diverse. They can be summarised as follows:

- *Duties arising from a director's position as an agent* – Since a company must act through its agents, the directors under common form articles of association[89] are appointed the company's agents. As agents, the directors have fiduciary obligations to their principal, the company.
- *Duties arising from a director's status as a trustee and fiduciary* – Company directors are in charge of property which is not their own and, accordingly, they are quasi-trustees for the legal owner: the company[90]. As trustees, directors are also fiduciaries.
- *Duties arising from a director's status as an employee* – Directors may have a written or oral contract of employment and will thus owe the normal duties owed by employees to their employer. While not fiduciary in nature, an employee owes duties of loyalty and fidelity which are important concepts in the context of competition with the company.
- *Duties* arising from a director's proximity to a 'neighbour' – By virtue of Lord Atkin's analysis in *Donoghue v Stevenson*[91], directors may be said to owe a duty of care in tort to those who are their neighbours, and so must take reasonable care to avoid acts or omissions which they can reasonably foresee would be liable to injure their neighbour.

The diverse sources of directors' duties have been recognised by the Company Law Review Group, which has said:

---

85 Ie, the powers expressly delegated to them by the shareholders of the company pursuant to the company's articles of association, and powers which directors implicitly have.

86 To 'account' in law has a very specific meaning: see Keane, *Equity and the law of Trusts in the Republic of Ireland* (2nd edn, Bloomsbury Professional, 2011) at [22.01] *et seq*.

87 See para **[15.029]** *et seq post*.

88 See generally, Loose & Yelland, *The Company Director* (6th edn, Jordans, 1987) at Ch 4.

89 Typically, reg 80: see Ch 13, *Corporate Governance: Management by the Directors*, at para **[13.127]**.

90 See *JJ Harrison (Properties) Ltd v Harrison* [2001] EWCA Civ 1467, [2002] 1 BCLC 162.

91 *Donoghue v Stevenson* [1932] AC 562.

> 'the fiduciary duties of directors have been enunciated on a case by case basis rather than in a codified form … the Review Group has come firmly to the view that inaccessibility and incomprehensibility of the law concerning the duties of directors can be remedied by their being stated in statute law. Such inaccessibility and incomprehensibility can in practice be a disincentive to compliance or a ready excuse to the indolent who have no wish to comply with such duties[92].'

[15.025] At the outset it is important to remember that only persons who *are directors* owe directors' duties. So, a person who is a 'director elect' will not, generally, owe the duties to a company of which he is a prospective director[93]. Directors' duties will, however, be owed by *de facto* directors, executive and non-executive directors, and nominee directors[94]. In this section the following aspects of directors' duties at common law are considered:

1. The exercise of directors' powers.
2. Fiduciary duties: conflicts of interests.
3. Fiduciary duties: competition with the company.
4. Directors' duties of skill, care and diligence.

The exercise of directors' powers

[15.026] The powers of directors must be exercised *bona fide* and in the interests of the company. This test for the proper exercise of directors' power also applies in other circumstances, such as in the exercise of the shareholders' powers to alter a company's constitutional documentation[95]. Eight specific matters are considered here:

(a) Acting in the interests of the company as a whole;
(b) Good faith;
(c) The exercise of independent discretion and fetters on discretion;
(d) The duties of executive and non-executive directors;
(e) The duties of nominee directors;
(f) Token directors in family companies and 'sexually transmitted debt';
(g) The delegation of directors' powers;
(h) The consequences of abuse of directors' powers.

(a) Acting in the interests of the company as a whole

[15.027] The concept of the *company as a whole* has been examined in Ch 3[96]. In essence, this means, in the first place, the company as a separate legal entity, and in the second place, the shareholders as a whole. It is submitted that in the context of a private company it is central to the nature of such ventures that the company as a whole ought to mean the shareholders as a whole because this recognises that the shareholders have

---

92 See the Company Law Review Group's *First Report* (2000–01), at para 11.3.1, p 238. See, further, s 225 of the draft Companies Bill where there is a proposed statement of the principal fiduciary duties of directors.

93 *Lindgen et al v L & P Estates Ltd* [1968] 1 Ch 572.

94 See para **[15.045]** *post*.

95 See Ch 3, *Constitutional Documentation*, at para **[3.067]** *et seq*.

96 See Ch 3 *Constitutional Documentation*, at para **[3.070]** *et seq*.

ultimate ownership of a company. In *G & s Doherty Ltd v Doherty*[97], Henchy J said of the exercise of the directors' powers to issue shares:

> '... directors are in a fiduciary position, and must exercise their power *bona fide* for the benefit of the company as a whole, that is to say, the shareholders as a whole: see *Greenhalgh v Arderne Cinemas Ltd* [1951] 1 Ch 286 at page 291. Where, as in the present case, directors issue shares for the ulterior purpose of benefiting themselves to the detriment of other shareholders, then it cannot be said that the issue of shares is *bona fide* or for the benefit of the company as a whole.'

This reference to fiduciary duties being owed to 'the shareholders as a whole' does not detract from the principle that those duties are owed to the *company.* Rather, such a statement is indicative of a recognition of the reality that the shareholders are the ultimate owners of the separate entity which is the company.

[15.028] It follows from this that directors must not exercise their powers in furtherance of their own personal interests. In practice, often the most blatant flouting of this duty is relatively common, particularly where proprietary directors 'forget' that the company's assets are not theirs. Directors may not misapply their companies' assets in favour of themselves or their nominees[98] or acquire assets at an undervalue[99]. A straightforward example of this is seen in *Re Ashclad Ltd; Forrest v Harrington and Culleton*[100], where upon the expiry of a financial lease of valuable machinery a company was entitled to acquire the machinery for the nominal sum of £121. Instead of the company acquiring the machinery for that amount, one of its directors paid the £121 and subsequently claimed, after the company had gone into liquidation, that the machinery was not a company asset. This was rejected by Geoghegan J who held that because the director owed the company a fiduciary duty, he was a bare trustee of the machinery and the judge made an order vesting the machinery in the company's liquidator[101].

(b) Good faith

[15.029] Directors must exercise the powers which are entrusted to them in good faith, or *bona fide.*[102] The exact meaning of the phrase *in good faith* appears to be relatively straightforward. Where a director exercises his powers, his *intention* is the paramount consideration. In determining a director's intention, a court will take cognisance of the evidential circumstances surrounding the director's action[103]. The question of good faith usually arises in the negative in deciding not what is the proper exercise of the directors' powers but rather what constitutes an abuse of the directors' powers.

---

[97] *G & s Doherty Ltd v Doherty* (19 June 1969, unreported) HC *per* Henchy J.

[98] *Gwembe Valley Development Co Ltd v Koshy and another* [1998] 2 BCLC 613.

[99] *Daniels v Daniels* [1978] Ch 406.

[100] *Re Ashclad Ltd; Forrest v Harrington and Culleton* (5 April 2000, unreported) HC, Geoghegan J.

[101] *Re Ashclad Ltd; Forrest v Harrington and Culleton* (5 April 2000, unreported) HC, Geoghegan J at p 17 of the judgment.

[102] See generally Ch 9, *Share Transfer*, at para **[9.052]** where the exercise of directors' powers in good faith is considered in the context of refusing to register a share transfer.

[103] See *Re Smith & Fawcett Ltd* [1942] 2 All ER 542 at 543, where Lord Greene MR said of the exercise of directors' powers that: 'They must exercise their discretion *bona fide* in what they consider not what the court may consider to be in the interests of the company ...'

[15.030] In determining a director's intention, many cases have made it clear that the courts will not interrogate the directors[104]. In *Re North City Milling Co Ltd*[105], Meredith MR said:

> 'I am of the opinion that the law allows the directors to hold their tongues. It allows them to say that everything was done honestly and *bona fide* in the interest of their company ... and according to my view I have no power to make them say more.'

In *Re Hafner*[106], Black J said of the directors' failure to explain the reasons for their actions:

> 'They are not bound to assign their reasons, and the court is not entitled to infer merely from their omission to do so that their reasons were not legitimate. Hedging around with the privilege of remaining mute and the prima facie presumption of rectitude the astutely silent director who wishes to exercise [his powers] illegitimately may well consider himself all but invulnerable.'

However, silence in the face of questions does not result in mandatory answering, but can lead to an adverse inference (namely bad faith) being drawn by the courts.

[15.031] The duty imposed on directors to act *bona fide* in the interests of the company is a subjective duty[107]. As Jonathan Parker J said in *Regentcrest plc v Cohen and another*[108]:

> 'The question is not whether, viewed objectively by the court, the particular act or omission which is challenged was in fact in the interests of the company; still less is the question whether the court, has it been in the position of the director at the relevant time, might have acted differently. Rather, the question is whether the director honestly believed that his act or omission was in the interests of the company. The issue is as to the director's state of mind. No doubt, where it is clear that the act or omission under challenge resulted in substantial detriment to the company, the director will have a harder task in persuading the court that he honestly believed it to be in the company's interest; but that does not detract from the subjective nature of the test[109].'

In *Regentcrest*, it had been claimed that a director had not acted *bona fide* in the interest of the company in waiving a contractual provision which would have entitled the company to claim £1.5m against the vendors of land to the company. In that case it was held that there were good commercial reasons for agreeing to release the vendor from the strict contractual provisions and that the director had not been in breach of his fiduciary duties.

[15.032] One way of determining a director's *bona fides* is to look to his perceived intentions. Another means is to scrutinise the proper purpose of the powers exercised. A

---

104 For example, see *Re Dublin North City Milling Co Ltd* [1909] 1 IR 179; *Re Hafner, Olhausen v Powderley* [1948] IR 426; *Clark v Workman* [1920] 1 IR 107. See also, Ussher, *Company Law in Ireland* (1986) at p 222 *et seq*.

105 *Re Dublin North City Milling Co Ltd* [1909] 1 IR 179.

106 *Re Hafner* [1943] IR 426.

107 *Re Smith & Fawcett Ltd* [1942] 1 All ER 542 at 543; Bristol *and West Building Society v Mothew* [1996] 4 All ER 698 at 712. See Keay, 'Good Faith and Directors' Duty to Promote the Success of their Company' (2011) 32 Co Law 138.

108 *Regentcrest plc v Cohen and another* [2001] 2 BCLC 80.

109 *Regentcrest plc v Cohen and another* [2001] 2 BCLC 80 at 105b–d; para 120.

wide variety of powers are given to directors and the essence of the delegation of such powers by the members is that the directors should use such powers in furtherance of the objects of the company. However, powers, being intrinsically neutral, can be put to either good or bad purposes.

Since any exercise of power can have two or more purposes, in deciding whether or not a power was properly or improperly exercised, the courts will look at the *substantial purpose* behind the exercise. Consequently, in *Smith (Howard) Ltd v Ampol Petroleum Ltd*[110] Lord Wilberforce said that the court must:

> '... examine the substantial purpose for which it was exercised, and ... reach a conclusion whether that purpose was proper or not. In doing so it will necessarily give credit to the bona fide opinion of the directors, if such is found to exist, and will respect their judgment as to matters of management; having done this, the ultimate conclusion has to be as to the side of a fairly broad line on which the case falls.'

In the context of private companies, where often the same persons will be both the directors and the shareholders, it is difficult to believe that the exercise of all the directors' powers will be altruistically directed to further the company's interest[111].

[15.033] Of all directors' powers, the power to issue new shares has given rise to the most litigation. This is because intrinsic to the exercise of such power is the potential to alter the control of the company. The case of *G & s Doherty Ltd v Doherty*[112] illustrates how the issue of shares can marginalise certain shareholders. Where this happens, the directors' resolution authorising the exercise of the power to allot shares is liable to be set aside as being an abuse of power, and so invalid. In *Nash v Lancegaye (Ireland) Ltd*[113], an allotment of shares was made in favour of one shareholder. The result was that he obtained 51% of the shares in the company. While it was conceivable that the allotment could have been made for the benefit of the company (ie, to increase its capital), it was held that it was an abuse of the directors' fiduciary powers and so the resolution authorising it was invalid. Recognising that the exercise of a power could have a dual purpose, Dixon J held:

> 'Having the two-fold object ... of conferring a privilege or advantage on [one shareholder] and also increasing the voting strength of [that shareholder], is it of any avail to the defendant directors that they may also have had the object, other things being equal, of benefiting the company. This was certainly not their sole object and I cannot say that it, in

110 *Smith (Howard) Ltd v Ampol Petroleum Ltd* [1974] AC 821.

111 See *Mills v Mills* (1938) 60 CLR 150, where the directors made an issue of bonus shares out of company profits, instead of by way of dividend. The incidental effect of this was that the managing director's voting power was increased, but it was held that this was not the substantial purpose of the exercise of the directors' powers, which was to act in the interests of the company. Latham CJ said that a director is not: '... required by law to live in an unreal region of detached altruism and to act in a vague mood of ideal abstraction from obvious facts which must be presented to the mind of any honest and intelligent man when he exercises his powers as a director. It would be setting up an impossible standard ...'

112 *G & s Doherty Ltd v Doherty* (4 April 1968, unreported) HC. See Ch 3, *Constitutional Documentation*, at para **[3.072]**.

113 *Nash v Lancegaye (Ireland) Ltd* (1958) 92 ILTR 11.

> fact, contributed to their decision. Even if it did, it was conceded in argument that would not suffice to validate the resolutions if the motives were partly improper[114].'

In other cases, the directors' exercise of the power to allot fresh shares has been found to have been predominantly motivated by *bona fide* motives[115]. An example is the case of *Re Jermyn Street Turkish Baths Ltd*[116], where the allotment of shares to a director which gave her a majority stake in the company was held to be valid in that it was part of a rescue package for the company, and very much in the interests of the company.

[15.034] One contentious area concerns allotments which are designed to fight off takeover bids for the company's shares. In *Hogg v Cramphorn Ltd*[117], an allotment in such circumstances was held to be invalid as a breach of the directors' fiduciary duties. Buckley J said:

> 'Accepting, as I do, that the board acted in good faith and that they believed that the establishment of a trust would benefit the company and that avoidance of the acquisition of control by [an outsider] would also benefit the company. I must still remember that the essential element of the scheme, and indeed its primary purpose, was to ensure control of the company by the directors and those whom they could confidently regard as their supporters.'

However, *Teck Corporation Ltd v Millar*[118] has suggested that the matter is not cut and dried, because the directors may reasonably:

> '... consider who is seeking control and why. If they believe that there will be substantial damage to the company's interests if the company is taken over, then the exercise of their powers to defeat those seeking a majority will not necessarily be categorised as improper. I think the courts should apply the general rule in this way: the directors must act in good faith. Then there must be reasonable grounds for their belief. If they say that they believe there will be substantial damage to the company's interests, then there must be reasonable grounds for that belief. If there are not, that will justify a finding that the directors were actuated by an improper purpose.'

Most private companies will act prospectively and prevent such a situation arising by providing for pre-emption rights in their articles of association or in a shareholders' agreement. The effect of such provisions is that one shareholder cannot sell his shares without first offering them, usually on a *pro rata* basis, to the existing shareholders[119].

(c) The exercise of independent discretion and fettering discretion[120]

[15.035] Company directors have a positive duty to exercise their discretion, and inaction by directors in circumstances where action is required in order to further their

---

114 See also *Whitehouse v Carlton Hotel Party Ltd* [1976] 2 All ER 268.

115 See *Mutual Life Insurance Co of New York v The Rank Organisation Ltd* [1985] BCLC 11, and *Afric Sive Ltd v Gas and Exploration Ltd* [1989] IEHC 35, *per* Carroll J.

116 *Re Jermyn Street Turkish Baths Ltd* [1971] 1 WLR 1042.

117 *Hogg v Cramphorn Ltd* [1966] 3 All ER 420.

118 *Teck Corporation Ltd v Millar* (1972) 33 DLR 288.

119 See Ch 9, *Share Transfer*, at para **[9.069]**.

120 See generally, Courtney, 'Fettering Directors' Discretion' (1995) 16 Co Lawyer 227 and Keay, 'The Duty of directors to Exercise Independent Judgment' (2008) 29 Co Law 290. See also Reece Thomas & Ryan, *The Law and Practice of Shareholders' Agreements* (1999, Butterworths) at pp 69–78.

company's interests will amount to a breach of duty[121]. This duty requires directors to exercise their judgment and discretion in relation to whether there are sufficient reserves to pay dividends[122], in the approval of the drawing of company cheques[123], etc. Often, the failure to exercise discretion will leave directors liable in negligence for breach of their duties of care, skill and diligence, considered below[124]. When exercising their discretion, directors are required to exercise an independent judgment. Regard can be had to the interests of others[125], such as members and employees, but decisions must be based on the individual director's independent judgment.

[15.036] The general rule is that directors, as fiduciaries, may not, in their capacity as directors[126], fetter their discretion to make an independent judgment, ie, to agree that they will act in a particular way into the future. Problems can arise, however, where the exigencies of business require directors to agree to a future course of action. This can arise on the entering into of share sale agreements, shareholders' agreements and joint-venture agreements. Examples here include: agreeing to convene and hold meetings for the purpose of allotting shares in particular amounts to particular persons[127]; agreeing to vote in favour of the registration of a share transfer[128]; agreeing not to declare a dividend for a particular period[129]; or, generally, having taken a particular business decision, agreeing not to reverse that decision[130].

[15.037] The leading Irish case on the exercise of directors' powers in bad faith, *Clark v Workman*[131], is also authority for the proposition that directors cannot fetter their discretion. The facts there were that the directors of a private company approved of a transfer of shares by a majority shareholder to a non-member. The chairman of the board of directors had promised the outsider transferee that he would do all that he could to obtain board approval for the transfer. The plaintiff shareholders argued that this was wrong because the board had inadequate time to consider the matter and had acted in breach of its fiduciary duty by fettering its sacred discretion to act in the best interests of the company. Ross J stated that 'in all cases *bona fides* is the test of the valid exercise of powers by trustees'[132], and that an opportunity for deliberation of a proposed exercise of

---

121 See, generally, Gregory, 'Directors' Duty to Exercise Discretion' (1998) *Special Report*, British Company Law Library Service, CCH for a very useful analysis of this aspect of directors' duties.

122 *Leeds Estate Building and Investment Co v Shepherd* (1887) 36 Ch D 787.

123 *Re Railway and General Light Improvement Col Marzetti's Case* (1880) 42 LT 206.

124 See para **[15.074]** *post*.

125 See para **[15.018]** *post*.

126 Persons may, however, fetter their discretion in their capacity as members or other non-fiduciary capacity as members are generally free to act as they wish: *Northern Counties Securities Ltd v Jackson & Steeple Ltd* [1974] 2 All ER 625. See also *Coronation Syndicate Ltd v Lilkienfield* (1903) TS 489, where a South African court made this distinction in the context of a comparison with directors and their duties.

127 See, for example, *Thorby v Goldberg* [1965] 112 CLR 597, considered at para **[15.040]** *post*.

128 See, for example, *Clark v Workman* [1920] 1 IR 107, considered at para **[15.037]** *post*.

129 Such may be a covenant in a joint-venture agreement.

130 As in *Fulham Football Club Ltd v Cabra Estates plc* [1994] 1 BCLC 363.

131 *Clark v Workman* [1920] 1 IR 107.

132 *Clark v Workman* [1920] 1 IR 107 at 113.

power was required in law. This was found not to be present notwithstanding that the result would have such an important bearing on the future of the company[133]. In view of the fact that an uncontradicted statement of a witness showed that the chairman director had promised to use his best endeavours to approve of the transfer of shares to the outsider it was held that this must be taken to represent the motives and intentions of the chairman director. Accordingly, Ross J said:

> 'By acting thus he had fettered himself by a promise to the [outsider] and had disqualified himself from acting bona fide in the interests of the company ...[134].'

Thus, the general rule must be that, being in a fiduciary position, directors should not contract, undertake or otherwise agree in advance to exercise their discretionary powers in a particular way[135]. So, in *John Crowther Group plc v International plc*[136] the plaintiff instituted proceedings against the defendant company when its directors recommended to the company's shareholders not to accept a bid made by the plaintiff for the defendant company's shares. The circumstances were that the directors had entered into a prior agreement with the plaintiff to, *inter alia*, procure the satisfaction of the conditions in the agreement but had changed their recommendation to the shareholders when a more attractive bid was received. Vinelott J held in favour of the defendant company on the grounds that the directors' obligations under the agreement must be read in the light of their duties to act in the interests of the company. He said:

> 'The terms of the agreement must clearly be read in the light of the fact known to all parties that directors owe a fiduciary duty to act in the interests of their company … and to make full and honest disclosure to shareholders before they vote on such a resolution. It seems to me that it must have been understood by all that if the undertaking was to use reasonable endeavours to procure the passing of the resolution it was necessarily subject to anything which the directors had to do in pursuance of that fiduciary duty … It seems to me plain beyond question that directors are under a duty to disclose the facts to the shareholders[137].'

Later, Vinelott J said that it was for the directors to decide what was in the best interests of the company and to take whatever steps they consider in furtherance of that[138].

---

133 *Clark v Workman* [1920] 1 IR 107 at 113. Ross J said: 'It is a strong proposition to assert that a majority is to overbear and stifle a minority when the intention is to do such a serious thing as to give a controlling interest in one company to another company that is engaged in the same line of business, and that may be to some extent a rival company.'

134 *Clark v Workman* [1920] 1 IR 107 at 118.

135 See, for example, the dissent of Lord Denning MR in *Boulting v Association of Cinematography, Television and Allied Technicians* [1963] 2 QB 606 at 626 where he said: 'It seems to me that no one, who has duties of a fiduciary nature to discharge, can be allowed to enter into an engagement by which he binds himself to disregard those duties or to act inconsistently with them. No stipulation is lawful by which he agrees to carry out his duties in accordance with the instructions of another rather than on his own conscious judgment; or by which he agrees to subordinate the interests of those whom he must protect to the interests of someone else.'

136 *John Crowther Group plc v International plc* [1990] BCLC 460.

137 *John Crowther Group plc v International plc* [1990] BCLC 460 at 464.

138 See also *Rackham v Peel Foods Ltd* [1990] BCLC 895; *Motherwell v Schoof* [1949] 2 WWR 529, [1949] 4 DLR 812; *Alder v Dobie and Gallop* (8 April 1999) Supreme Court of British Columbia (Burnyeat J).

[15.038] There are, however, exceptions to this general rule and it is fallacious to suggest that directors can never agree to fetter their discretion. Case law indicates that there are at least two possible justifications for directors to agree to fetter their discretion. In the first place, it is open to the members of a company to release directors from the strict application of the general rule. This was confirmed by majority in the English Court of Appeal in *Boulting v Association of Cinematography, Television and Allied Technicians*[139], which is also authority for the proposition that this directors' duty cannot be used as a shield by the directors: 'it is a sword and as such only can it be used by the person entitled to the benefit of it, and he may sheath the weapon'[140]. Thus, in that case it was not open to directors to assert the general rule as such was the sole preserve of the company[141]. In order for directors to be validly released, however, the company acting by its shareholders must fully understand what they are approving[142].

[15.039] In the second place, it is submitted that directors may validly and lawfully decide, at the time when they enter into a contract, what is in the best interests of their company and to this end, agree to fetter their future discretion. Authority here is the decision of the English Court of Appeal in *Fulham Football Club Ltd et al v Cabra Estates plc*[143]. The facts in this case were that a subsidiary of the defendant company which owned the freehold in certain lands applied for planning permission to develop the lands for residential purposes. The plaintiff company, through another subsidiary, had a leasehold interest in the lands. The local council also wished to develop the lands for its own purposes and issued a compulsory purchase order (CPO) in respect of the lands and itself applied for planning permission. An agreement was entered into between the defendant company and its subsidiary and the plaintiff company and its directors and shareholders, concerning the future development of the lands, under which the plaintiff company was to receive a large amount of money. Contemporaneous to the entering into of this agreement, the plaintiff company's directors and shareholders entered into a letter of undertaking whereby they agreed to use their powers and rights as directors and members to ensure that:

- the plaintiff company would do nothing to prevent the withdrawal of the existing CPO and would not support any new CPO as might be substituted therefor;
- the plaintiff company would not object to the current planning applications on behalf of the defendant or any other applications for redevelopment of the land; and
- the plaintiff company would, if called upon by the defendant company, write to the planning authority and the English Secretary of State, in support of the defendant company's application for development of the land for residential purposes.

---

[139] *Boulting v Association of Cinematography, Television and Allied Technicians* [1963] 2 QB 606.

[140] *Boulting v Association of Cinematography, Television and Allied Technicians* [1963] 2 QB 606 at 637.

[141] See also the Canadian case of *Ringuet v Bergeron* (1960) 24 DLR (2d) 449.

[142] *Knight v Frost et al* [1999] 1 BCLC 364.

[143] *Fulham Football Club Ltd et al v Cabra Estates plc* [1994] 1 BCLC 363.

Following an inquiry into the CPO and the planning applications, the CPO was not confirmed and both planning applications were refused. The defendant company's subsidiary made a fresh application, which was refused, and following this a further public enquiry was held. At this time the plaintiff company did not wish to be bound by the undertaking that had been given, and instituted proceedings seeking a declaration that they were entitled to give such evidence at the inquiry as they considered to be in the plaintiff company's best interests. The plaintiff company also refused to provide a letter of support for the defendant company's subsidiary's revised application. It was argued, *inter alia*, by the plaintiff company that the undertaking was unenforceable as it conflicted with its directors' fiduciary duties.

At trial, Chadwick J rejected the contention that the undertaking was in breach of the directors' duties. He said:

> 'It is said … [that] … an obligation which seeks to fetter the exercise by directors of their fiduciary duties in the future is unenforceable as a matter of law. Whether or not that would be so in circumstances where the obligation is assumed by directors in that capacity alone, there is, in my judgment, no such principle where the obligation is assumed by directors who are at the time, and intend to continue to be, together the only members of the company; or where it is assumed with the approval of all those who are the members of the company[144].'

Chadwick J also rejected the plaintiff company's contention that there ought to be implied into the undertaking, a limitation that the directors would not thereby be required to do anything that would be inconsistent with their fiduciary duties. In distinguishing the cases of *Crowther* and *Rackham*, considered above[145], Chadwick J held there was no room for such an implication where the undertaking was given by persons who had been acting in their capacity as members[146].

[15.040] Both of the points upon which Chadwick J had held against the plaintiff company were appealed to the Court of Appeal. Whilst upholding the decision of Chadwick J, Neill LJ rejected his reasons, namely that the members could release the directors from their strict duties. He did this on the grounds that directors owed common law duties to creditors[147] and because there were statutory duties to employees[148]. This finding is open to criticism[149] on the grounds that (a) duties to creditors only arise where companies are insolvent[150]; and (b) duties to employees are only enforceable by the company and directors can, therefore, be released by the company acting through its members. Neill LJ preferred a more general reason for upholding Chadwick J's decision. He said:

> 'It is trite law that directors are under a duty to act bona fide in the interests of their company. However, it does not follow from that proposition that directors can never make a contract by which they bind themselves to the future exercise of their powers in a

144 *Fulham Football Club Ltd et al v Cabra Estates plc* [1994] 1 BCLC 363 at 376.

145 At para **[15.037]**.

146 *Fulham Football Club Ltd et al v Cabra Estates plc* [1994] 1 BCLC 363 at 375, 376.

147 See para **[15.010]** *ante*.

148 See para **[15.018]** *ante*.

149 See Courtney, 'Fettering Directors' Discretion' (1995) 16 Co Lawyer 227 at 234, 235.

150 See para **[15.013]** *ante*.

> particular manner, even though the contract taken as a whole is manifestly for the benefit of the company. Such a rule could well prevent companies from entering into contracts which were commercially beneficial to them[151].'

Neill LJ relied heavily on the decision of the Australian case of *Thorby v Goldberg*[152]. There, Kitto J had said:

> 'There are many kinds of transactions in which the proper time for the exercise of directors' discretion is the time of the negotiation of the contract, not the time at which the contract is to be performed. A sale of land is a familiar example. Where all the members of a company desire to enter as a group a transaction such as that in the present case[153], the transaction being one which requires action by the board of directors for its effectuation, it seems to me that the proper time for the directors to decide whether their proposed action will be in the interests of the company as a whole is the time when the transaction is being entered into, and not the time when their action is required. If at the former time they are bona fide of the opinion that it is in the interests of the company that the transaction should be entered into and carried into effect, I see no reason in law why they should not bind themselves to do whatever under the transaction is to be done by the board[154].'

In the *Fulham Football Club Case*, Neill LJ found that the directors had exercised their discretion at the time of entering into the agreement and giving the undertaking and had concluded such was in the best interests of their company. Moreover, he found that the plaintiff company had received substantial benefits from the original agreement and that it could not be said that the directors had acted improperly in agreeing to fetter the future exercise of their discretion.

[15.041] Where it is proposed to enter into a contract or other agreement, which clearly does fetter directors' discretion, or could be so construed, good corporate housekeeping would suggest that a transparent and recorded procedure is followed. Without attempting to be definitive, companies should ensure:

- that the directors explicitly acknowledge that they are agreeing to fetter their fiduciary discretion and in particular consider whether such is in the company's best interests;
- where it is decided to proceed, the decision (and, perhaps departing from the normal rules of minute taking, their deliberations) should be minuted and the minutes of the board meeting signed by the chairman;
- it may be prudent to allude to the directors' decisions in the recitals to the contract or other agreement; and
- if practicable, a resolution in support of the proposed course of action by the members of the company might be procured.

(d) The duties of executive and non-executive directors

[15.042] The Companies Acts have not, traditionally, differentiated between executive directors and non-executive directors[155] or applied a different test to the duties and

---

151 *Fulham Football Club Ltd et al v Cabra Estates plc* [1994] 1 BCLC 363 at 392.

152 *Thorby v Goldberg* [1965] 112 CLR 597.

153 A transaction involving the demolition and redevelopment of a building.

154 *Thorby v Goldberg* [1965] 112 CLR 597 at 605, 606.

155 See Ch 13, *Corporate Governance: Members and Directors*, at para **[13.038]** *et seq.*

responsibilities owed by either category of director. The traditional position can be seen in the High Court decision in *Re Dublin Sports Cafe Ltd*[156], where Peart J said in the context of an application under s 150 of the CA 1990 to restrict one of the two directors of a company that was wound up insolvent:

> '... the fact that he was a non-executive director is neither here nor there. He was a director and as such shares the responsibility to ensure that all is in order, and I venture to suggest that in a company where there are but two directors, the obligation on the non-executive director is even higher than a non-executive director of a much larger company who may have certain identifiable and particular responsibilities within the company, but who may rely on other directors to carry out their particular functions, even though he would be remiss not to be concerned and satisfied as a member of the board of directors that all the affairs of the company were being properly attended to.
>
> In the present case, one director, the first named respondent, was basically running the company in Dublin on a day to day basis, while the second named respondent, the main financial backer, was in British Columbia. In my view it was not responsible behaviour for the second named respondent not to make absolutely certain that all books and records were being maintained ...'

There is, however, some recent evidence of a rethink and that the Irish courts may be open to acknowledging that executive directors have different duties to non-executive directors.

[15.043] The first cases in which this was considered was in the Supreme court in *Re Tralee Beef & Lamb Ltd*[157]. Again, this concerned an appeal against the decision of the High Court to restrict a director of a company that had been wound up insolvent. The director in question was a non-executive who had been appointed at the behest of an investor in the company. The Supreme Court allowed the appeal and set aside the order of the High Court imposing restrictions on him. In the course of his judgment, Hardiman J noted that the High Court had relied upon the decision of Parker J in *Re Baring plc*[158], considered below[159], but went on to question its application to smaller companies and non-executive directors, saying:

> 'This is an interesting case and amply repays study. But it concerned a vast company and the judgment extends from p 433 to p 620 of the Report, and incorporates its own separate Table of Contents. Barings was a company run with a high degree of formality, as one would expect having regard to its size and the vast sums of money it dealt in. The managerial responsibilities of each of the executive Directors implicated in the case were established in evidence in some very considerable detail: all had specific responsibilities in relation to Leeson's (the fraudulent employee) department. Moreover, all relevant directors were Executive directors. In my view, apart from any general amplification of the words of Shanley J, there is a yet unmet need to make authoritative findings after full debate, as to the respective duties of an Executive and a non-executive director and,

156 *Re Dublin Sports Cafe Ltd* [2005] IEHC 458.
157 *Re Tralee Beef & Lamb Ltd* [2008] IESC 1.
158 *Re Baring plc* [1999] 1 BCLC 433.
159 See para **[15.053]** *post*.

perhaps, a non-executive director appointed (as the appellant was) for a particular and specific purpose. But this has yet to occur.

I would not be prepared simply to apply the *Baring's* criteria, without such argument, to all these classes of director, or to assume that their common law duties are identical. I am slightly uneasy that, in this case, there may have been an assimilation in particular of the position of a non-executive director to that of an executive one. Such an approach might derive some support from the judgment of Roderick Murphy J in *Vehicle Imports Ltd (in liquidation)* (Unreported, High Court, 23rd November 2000), but it is not explicit and in any event there does not appear to have been argument on the topic of the duties of the different classes of director, mentioned above.

I do not consider that this case, or that of *Vehicle Imports*, mandates the assimilation of the position of a non-executive director to that of an executive in terms of their common law duties. The position of a highly paid executive director of a vast Bank may be of limited use in considering the common law duties of a non-executive director, appointed to keep BES investors informed, of a small company.

Clearly, in applying words of general application from a decision relating to so vast a corporation, care must be taken to avoid being unrealistic in relation to a small meat company in rural Ireland run effectively, so the evidence in this case goes, by one man. This was Mr Delaney, the sole executive director.'

In the appeal of the High Court decision discussed above in *Re Dublin Sports Cafe Ltd*[160], the Supreme Court again sought to distinguish the position of executive and non-executive directors, Finnegan J saying:

'The duties of directors *inter se* may differ and in particular the duties of a non-executive director may not be co-extensive with those of an executive director. Each case will turn upon its own circumstances: *Re Tralee Beef and Lamb Ltd* [2008] IESC 1.'

[15.044] So how do the duties of executive and non-executive directors differ? While the Supreme Court has clearly indicated that it believes a differentiation is justified, it has provided no direct guidance on the nature of that differentiation. It is thought that 'different' does not necessarily mean 'lesser' and that there is a case to be made for the law evolving along the basis of executive directors being more responsible for ensuring that the company's business operates appropriately and non-executive directors more responsible for overseeing executive directors and executive employees by holding them to account for the company's operations. Supervision and oversight are the key controls which non-executive directors can and should bring to the boardroom. To take an example. If there is an employee failure in the maintenance of accounting records, an executive director to whom the employees responsible report should be called to account for his management of those employees (or their managers) and of the company's systems and processes. A non-executive director, on the other hand, might reasonably be excused to account for such operational matters but, equally reasonably, be called to account for his oversight of the robustness of the auditing of the company's operational processes and policy on the employment of competent personnel.

160 *Re Dublin Sports Cafe Ltd* [2008] IESC 66.

(e) The duties of nominee directors[161]

[15.045] A nominee director is a director who is 'expected to act in accordance with some understanding or arrangement which creates an obligation or mutual expectation of loyalty to some person or persons other than the company as a whole'[162]. A director nominated by another person will not automatically owe duties to that person. In *Re Neath Rugby Ltd*[163], the English Court of Appeal held that:

> '... the fact that a director of a company has been nominated to that office by a shareholder does not, of itself, impose any duty on the director owed to his nominator. The director may owe duties to his nominator if he is an employee or officer of the nominator, or by reason of a formal or informal agreement with his nominator, but such duties do not arise out of his nomination, but out of a separate agreement or office[164].'

[15.046] The nominee director can, however, find himself caught between a rock and a hard place being contemporaneously under some obligation to a third party and continuing to owe the same duties to the company as any other director. Traditionally, the courts have been loath to acknowledge the commercial reality of nominee directors and have considered it wrong to have regard to anyone's interest but the company's. This is most vividly illustrated by the views of Street J in the Australian case of *Bennets v Board of Fire Commissioners of New South Wales*[165], where he said:

> 'It is entirely foreign to the purpose for which this or any other board exists to contemplate a member of the board being representative of a particular group or a particular body. Once a group has elected a member he assumes office as a member of the board and becomes subject to the overriding and predominant duty to serve the interests of the board in preference, on every occasion upon which any conflict might arise, to serving the interests of the group which appointed him. With this basic position there can be no room for compromise[166].'

This has been described as imposing a standard that makes the position of nominee directors impossible.[167] The position of nominee directors is perhaps most precarious in the context of a joint venture, where two separate companies come together to jointly pursue a particular business opportunity and form a third company for that purpose. Where each of the joint venturers nominates, say, a director each, one must ask whether it is realistic to think that these directors will have no regard for the wishes of their

---

161 See, generally, Boros, 'The Duties of Nominee and Multiple Directors' (1989) 10 Co Lawyer 211 and (1990) 11 Co Lawyer 6; Crutchfield, 'Nominee Directors: The Law and Commercial Reality' (1991) 12 Co Lawyer 136; Yeung, 'Corporate Groups: Legal Aspects of the Management Dilemma' [1997] Lloyd's Maritime and Commercial Law Quarterly 208; and Reece, Thomas & Ryan, *The Law and Practice of Shareholders' Agreements* (1999, Butterworths) at p 78.

162 Companies and Securities Review Committee (NSW, Australia), *Nominee Directors and Alternate Directors*, Report No 8 (2 March 1989) at p 7.

163 *Re Neath Rugby Ltd* [2010] BCC 597.

164 *Re Neath Rugby Ltd* [2010] BCC 597 at 605.

165 *Bennets v Board of Fire Commissioners of New South Wales* (1967) 87 WN (NSW) 307.

166 *Bennets v Board of Fire Commissioners of New South Wales* (1967) 87 WN (NSW) 307 at 311.

167 See Crutchfield, 'Nominee Directors: The Law and Commercial Reality' (1991) 12 Co Lawyer 136 at 137.

appointing joint venturer. The directors of a joint venture company are in such an invidious position that there is a strong case to put the matter beyond doubt in statute.[168]

[15.047] In *Irish Press plc v Ingersoll Irish Publications Ltd*[169], Barron J took a more commercially focused and sympathetic approach to the plight of the nominee director, saying:

> 'The position of nominee directors can be a difficult one if they disagree with the views of the person or body appointing them. Their duty is to act in the interests of the company. They have also got a duty to act on the instructions of their nominating party. But acting in the interests of the company is no more than acting in the interests of all its shareholders. If what they are asked to do involves seeking to damage the interests of one section of the shareholders in favour of another then as a director that have a duty not to do that. However, if what they are required to do is merely something that they themselves personally think is not the way to approach the matter then they must give way. There is nothing wrong with the appointing body or party having a view as to where the interests of the company lie and ensuring that its nominees follow that direction provided that in so doing they are not seeking to damage anybody else's interest in the company[170].'

In the foregoing passage Barron J recoiled from the absolutist position of Street J in the *Bennets* case. In the Australian case of *Levin v Clark*[171], it was held that a nominee director could act primarily in the interests of his principal and take steps to enforce his principal's security, the reasoning being that the duty could be modified by the company's constitutional documents and the members' wishes[172]. It is thought that this decision accords more with the realities of commercial life[173]. However, in the House of Lords decision in *Scottish Cooperative Wholesale Society Ltd v Meyer and another*[174], in a passage quoted by Barron J, Viscount Simonds said that nominee directors were not

---

168 See Lower, 'Do We Need a Joint Venture Act?' (1995) Palmer's In Company, Issue 5/95 (17 May 1995) where the author refers to s 131(4) of the New Zealand Companies Act which expressly allows the constitution of a joint venture company to be altered so that nominee directors can act in the best interests of their appointor even where this is not in the best interests of the joint venture company. Note that the Company Law Review Group in its *First Report* (2000–2001) has recommended that 'a director appointed or nominated for appointment by a member with an entitlement to so appoint or nominate under the articles of association or a shareholders' agreement may have regard to the interests of that member': see para 11.3.7 at p 241. Effect has been given to that recommendation in s 225(3) and (4) of the draft Companies Bill.

169 *Irish Press plc v Ingersoll Irish Publications Ltd* (16 December 1993, unreported) HC.

170 *Irish Press plc v Ingersoll Irish Publications Ltd* (16 December 1993, unreported) HC at p 77 of the transcript.

171 *Levin v Clark* [1962] NSWR 686.

172 See Boros, 'The Duties of Nominee and Multiple Directors' (1989) 10 Co Lawyer 211 at p 214.

173 See MacCann, (1991) ILT 104 at p 106, and see also *Berlai Hestia (NZ) Ltd v Fernyhough* [1980] 2 NZLR 150 where it was said that where a director is appointed nominee by a particular group of shareholders he may also owe duties to them. *Cf Kuwait Asia Bank EC v National Mutual Life Nominees Ltd* [1991] 1 AC 187 at 222 where the Privy Council said of nominee directors that 'they could not plead any instruction from the bank (that appointed them) as an excuse for breach of their duties …'

174 *Scottish Cooperative Wholesale Society Ltd v Meyer and another* [1959] AC 324.

entitled to remain silent and inactive with full knowledge of the majority shareholder's intention to strip the company of its assets. It is interesting that Viscount Simonds extended his comments to the appointor of the nominee directors and said it was 'incumbent on the parent company to behave with scrupulous fairness to the minority shareholders and to avoid imposing upon their nominees the alternative of disregarding their instructions or betraying the interests of the minority'[175]. In conclusion, it is thought, on the authority of Barron J, that whilst a nominee director will owe duties to his company, he can have regard to his appointor's interests where this does not harm any other party's interests. As Stanley Burnton LJ said in *Re Neath Rugby Ltd*[176]:

> '... an appointed director, without being in breach of his duties to the company, may take the interests of his nominator into account, provided that his decisions as a director are in what he genuinely considers to be the best interests of the company.'

[15.048] The decision of the English High Court in *Re Southern Counties Fresh Foods Ltd, Cobden Investments Ltd v RWM Langport Ltd et al*[177] is authority for the proposition that where all the shareholders of a company agree, a nominee director's duties may be qualified. Warren J summarised the applicable law as follows:

> '… the position of a nominee director is, I conclude, as follows.
>
> a. First, he owes the same duties to the company as any other director.
> b. Secondly, he owes his duties as a director to the company alone.
> c. Thirdly, the company is entitled to expect from the director his best independent judgment.
> d. However, fourthly, these duties can be qualified in the case of a nominee director just as they can be qualified in the case of any other director. In particular, such duties (except perhaps for certain core duties) can be qualified by the unanimous assent of the shareholders.
> e. But, fifthly, it is doubtful whether, as a matter of English law, it is possible to release a director from his general duty to act in the best interests of the company.
> f. Sixthly, even if it is possible to do so, it would require strong evidence to demonstrate that that had been done, ideally an express written agreement signed by all of the shareholders. The onus must lie on those saying that the general rule has been attenuated or, to use another word, relaxed, as a result of unanimous shareholder approval to demonstrate that such approval has been given. And, I must add, they must show the extent to which the general rule has been relaxed.
> g. Seventhly, however, I see no reason in principle why in relation to specific areas of interest, a director should not be released from his fiduciary duty to give his best independent judgment to the company. In particular, if a director is charged with negotiating on behalf of his appointor an agreement with the company where the interests of his appointor and the company are opposed, the shareholders can unanimously agree that he may conduct such negotiation without regard to the interests of the company. But if that were to be done, it might be expected that the

175 See, Lower, 'Good Faith and the Partly-Owned Subsidiary' [2000] JBL and, further, Ch 12, *Groups of Companies*, at para **[12.052]**.

176 *Re Neath Rugby Ltd* [2010] BCC 597.

177 *Re Southern Counties Fresh Foods Ltd, Cobden Investments Ltd v RWM Langport Ltd et al* [2008] EWHC 2810; see Kelly, 'The Nominee Director, his Duties to the Company and his Appointor, and whether they can be Modified by Agreement' [2010] CLP 23.

> director concerned would, by the same agreement, be precluded from discussions of the board relating to the negotiations and certainly from voting on the issue.
>
> But whatever can be said as a matter of generality, I consider that the extent of the duties of a director in such a situation are very much fact-specific. The general duty is clear; the difficult question is the extent to which the duty is qualified. That qualification will depend critically on the context of the relationship and the particular action which is said to constitute a breach of duty[178].'

Where it is sought to qualify the duties of a nominee director the unanimous agreement of the shareholders must be obtained; for a majority to force its will on a minority in this regard will, it is thought, result in a finding of oppression under s 205 of the CA 1963. The unanimous agreement can be recorded in a shareholders' agreement or the articles of association can be amended to so qualify the directors' duties. Where the articles are amended, it is thought that the effect will be to bind subsequent shareholders since they will have notice of the departure from the general rule and be taken to have voluntarily acquired their shares subject to the qualification and be estopped from petitioning under s 205; shareholders acquiring their share by transmission can have rights or expectations no greater than those of the shareholder who agreed to such a qualification.

(f) 'Token directors' in family companies and 'sexually transmitted debt'

[15.049] Although nominee directors are expected to act on an understanding or arrangement which creates an obligation or mutual expectation of loyalty to some person, the concept most certainly does not, *per se*, imply that the nominee director will abdicate all responsibility in relation to the company's management. It is thought that a different label is required for such directors, and that '*token director*' is more apt. A token director is a nominee director who abdicates all responsibility for the company's management and whose sole purpose in being a director is to meet the statutory requirement that all companies must have at least two directors. A token director can sometimes assume that position at the behest of his or her spouse. In *Re Hunting Lodges Ltd*[179], Carroll J said of the wife of one of the directors concerned, who was a nominee director, that in the context of fraudulent trading[180] she could not:

> '... evade liability by claiming that she was only concerned with minding her house and looking after the children. If that was the limit of the responsibilities she wanted, she should not have become a director of the company, or having become one she should have resigned. Any person who becomes a director takes on the responsibilities and duties, *particularly where there are only two* ... A director who continues as a director but abdicates all responsibility is not lightly to be excused[181].'

A more liberal approach is apparent in the Supreme Court of New South Wales decision in *Southern Cross Interiors Pty Ltd and another v Deputy Commissioner of Taxation et al*[182]. There, the liquidator of a company sought to have payments made by the company

---

178 *Re Southern Counties Fresh Foods Ltd, Cobden Investments Ltd v RWM Langport Ltd et al* [2008] EWHC 2810 at paras 67 and 68 of the transcript.

179 *Re Hunting Lodges Ltd* [1985] ILRM 75.

180 See para **[15.116]** *et seq post*.

181 See also *Cronje No v Stone* (1985) (3) SA 597 (T) considered at para **[15.106]** *post*.

182 *Southern Cross Interiors Pty Ltd and another v Deputy Commissioner of Taxation et al* [2001] NSWSC 621 (31 August 2001).

to the Australian Revenue Commissioners declared unlawful as an 'unfair preference'. The Revenue Commissioners, in addition to defending the liquidator's claim, sought a declaration that the company's two directors (a husband and wife) should be declared liable to indemnify the Revenue Commissioners on grounds of having traded whilst the company was insolvent. The wife director sought to defend the claim against her by relying upon a provision in Australian legislation that created the defence of not taking part in the management of the company for a 'good reason'. The wife director contended that she had only accepted the appointment at her husband's request, that she had been unaware of the duties of a company director and that it was for those reasons that she had not participated in the management of the company. The essence of her claim was that she had only agreed to become a director because of the trust and confidence she had placed in her husband. The court held that the wife director had established 'good reason' for not participating in the management of the company. Palmer J said:

> 'I hold that [the wife director] accepted appointment as a director of [the company] with no understanding at all of the duties and responsibilities which that office entailed. That lack of understanding was not due to any fault on her part. Her husband failed to explain to her anything of the responsibilities which directorship involved and did not suggest that she seek advice or further information. She accepted the appointment at his request because of the trust and confidence which she had in him, believing, at his suggestion, that the appointment was only a formal requirement. She did not participate in the management of the company because she did not believe that she was required to do so. That belief was induced by her husband's statements at the time he requested her to become a director and by his subsequent conduct in not discussing the company's affairs with her. She acted upon that belief because of the trust and confidence she placed in her husband because she thought that he was knowledgeable in such matters. Nothing was brought to her attention during her directorship which should have put her upon enquiry as to [the company's] financial position or as to her responsibilities as a director[183].'

There is, of course, no such defence as 'good reason' to an action for reckless trading in Irish law. Nevertheless, the foregoing represents the other end of the spectrum in the approach to token directors' liabilities to that seen in *Re Hunting Lodges Ltd*[184]and it remains to be seen whether it will find favour, generally, in relation to actions against token directors. Somewhat surprisingly, in *Re Lynrowan Enterprises Ltd*[185], an application to have persons restricted under s 150 of the CA 1990, O'Neill J declined to make a restriction order for the following reason:

> 'All of the evidence before the Court suggests that [the first respondent] although a de jure director of the company took no part whatsoever in its affairs and does not appear to have been expected so to do. In those circumstances in the absence of any evidence of specific irresponsibility or dishonest behaviour on his part I am of the view that the granting of the relief sought against him would be inappropriate and I make no declaration pursuant to s 150(1) in respect of [the first respondent].'

---

183 *Southern Cross Interiors Pty Ltd and another v Deputy Commissioner of Taxation et al* [2001] NSWSC 621 at para 137 of the judgment.

184 *Re Hunting Lodges Ltd* [1985] ILRM 75.

185 *Re Lynrowan Enterprises Ltd* (31 July 2002, unreported) HC, O'Neill J.

One might have thought that allowing one's name be used as a token director of a company in circumstances where one was not expected to take part in the affairs of the company is, and of itself, an act of gross irresponsibility. It is thought that the approach taken by Carroll J in *Re Hunting Lodges* is to be preferred.

[15.050] What was particularly novel about the decision in *Southern Cross Interiors Pty Ltd and another v Deputy Commissioner of Taxation et al*[186] was the judicial recognition afforded to the so-called phenomenon of 'sexually transmitted debt' or the less salacious 'emotionally transmitted debt'. This has been described by the Australian Law Reform Commission in the following terms:

> 'The key feature of sexually transmitted debt is the relationship of dependence and the emotional ties that dominate the transaction. These are often found, for example, in wife/husband, parent/child and de facto relationships. The dependent party in the relationship accepts responsibility for the other party's debt primarily because of that relationship. If the other party becomes unable or unwilling, for example, through bankruptcy or divorce, to meet the debt, the dependent party is liable for that debt. In that way the debt is 'transmitted' to the dependent party. A useful generic definition of sexually transmitted debt is the transfer of responsibility for a debt incurred by a party to his/her partner in circumstances in which the fact of the relationship, as distinct from an appreciation of the reality of the responsibility for the debt, is the predominant factor in the partner accepting liability[187].'

As a phenomenon, sexually transmitted debt has a wider application than company law. In *Southern Cross Interiors Pty Ltd and another v Deputy Commissioner of Taxation et al*, Palmer J held it was applicable to cases where wives (not, it will be noted, 'spouses')[188] become directors at their husbands' behest, saying:

> '… if a woman, inexperienced in business and completely unaware of the responsibilities of company directorship, is told by her husband, whom she trusts and believes to be honest and to be knowledgeable in such matters, that some formality requires her to be appointed as a director to a family company and that management of the company may be left entirely to him, then, in my view, she has a 'good defence' for not participating in management for such time as she remains in ignorance of her duties[189].'

Palmer J's view that recognition of sexually transmitted debt will not undermine the policy of the law that those who accept office as director are expected to act with

---

[186] *Southern Cross Interiors Pty Ltd and another v Deputy Commissioner of Taxation et al* [2001] NSWSC 621 (31 August 2001).

[187] *Equality Before the Law: Women's Equality* (1994) Report No 69 Part II at para 13.4.

[188] Much of the legal commentary on this phenomenon is feminist in origin. A sample of the legal literature in Australia includes: Fehlberg, *Sexually Transmitted Debt* (1997, Clarendon Press); Bailey, 'Sexually Transmitted Debts: Criticisms and Prospects for Reform' (1999) 8(4) Aukland University Law Review 1001, Kaye, 'Equity's Treatment of Sexually Transmitted Debt' (1997) 5(1) Feminist Legal Studies 35; Howell, 'Sexually Transmitted Debt: a Feminist Analysis of Laws Regulating Guarantors and Co-Borrowers' (1995) 4 Australian Feminist Law Journal 93; Baron, 'The Free Exercise of Her Will: Women and Emotionally Transmitted Debt' (1995) Law in Context 23; and Fehlberg, 'Money and Marriage: Sexually Transmitted Debt in England' (1997) 11 International Journal of Law, Policy and Family 320.

[189] *Southern Cross Interiors Pty Ltd and another v Deputy Commissioner of Taxation et al* [2001] NSWSC 621 at para 135 of the judgment.

competence and diligence in discharging the duties of their office is debatable. Whether this defence for token directors is just and proper or whether it is a charter that ignores culpability and furthers the in vogue 'nobody-is-to blame' culture is a moot point. It is this writer's view that rather than operate as a defence to negligently acting as a second statutory director, the fact that some spouses are prevailed upon to meet a statutory minimum of two directors should instead cause us to consider whether private companies should be required to have two directors[190].

(g) The delegation of directors' powers

[15.051] In many private companies it will commonly be the case that the directors are executives in their company, responsible alone or with employees for its day-to-day management. The larger the company, however, the greater the likelihood that the directors will be forced to delegate some of their powers to others. As shall be considered, the delegation of powers does not exonerate directors from their responsibilities or mitigate the duties they owe to their company.

[15.052] A particularly vexed question arises where one director relies upon another director to perform the first director's functions. While it is undoubtedly true that a director can rely upon his co-directors, it has been suggested that where a director does so, but fails to investigate the activities being undertaken, that director may very well cross the line and breach his duty. Irish authority here is *Jackson v Munster Bank Ltd*[191], where a director was held liable for breach of duty when he did not make proper enquiry upon being put on notice of irregular loans. Mere objection has been held to be insufficient, and to be certain of absolution, a director would be best advised to cease participation in the company.

[15.053] A more recent Irish case to consider this issue is the High Court decision of *Re Vehicle Imports Ltd*[192], where Murphy J held that the obligation[193] to keep proper books of account was not limited to where one director had a reputed responsibility for keeping the books and that the responsibility was a joint and separate liability on each of the directors. In the course of that case – which concerned s 150 of the CA 1990 and is considered in detail in Ch 28 – Murphy J adopted the head note to the judgment of Jonathan Parker J in *Re Barings plc et al (No 5); Secretary of State for Trade and Industry v Baker et al (No 5)*[194]. This states:

190 See the Company Law Review Group's *First Report* (2000–2001), recommendation 11.8.11 at p 247 where it is recommended that private companies limited by shares should be permitted to have just one director.

191 *Jackson v Munster Bank Ltd* (1885) 15 LR Ir 356.

192 *Re Vehicle Imports Ltd* (23 November 2000, unreported) HC, Murphy J.

193 Whilst this comment may have been made in the light of s 202(10) of the CA 1990 – which criminalises the failure to keep proper books of account and applies to every person who is a director of a company – it is thought to have a more wide spread application.

194 *Re Barings plc et al (No 5); Secretary of State for Trade and Industry v Baker et al* (No 5) [1999] 1 BCLC 433. See Parry, 'Delegation of Directors' Duties after Re Barings plc' (1999) CCH's Company Law News, Issue 25, 11 February 1999.

'(a) Each individual director owed duties to the company to inform himself about its affairs and to join with his co-directors in supervising and controlling them[195].

(b) Subject to the articles of association of the company, a board of directors might delegate specific tasks and functions. Some degree of delegation was almost always essential if the company's business was to be carried on efficiently; to that extent, there was a clear public interest in delegation by those charged with the responsibility for the management of a business[196].

(c) The duty of an individual director, however, did not mean that he might not delegate. Having delegated a particular function it did not mean he was no longer under any duty in relation to the discharge of that function, notwithstanding that the person to whom the function had been delegated appeared both trustworthy and capable of discharging the function.

(d) Where delegation had taken place the board (and the individual directors) remained responsible for the delegated function or functions and retained a residual duty of supervision and control. The precise extent of that residual duty will depend on the facts of each particular case, as will the question of whether it had been breached.

(e) A person who accepted the office of director of a particular company undertook the responsibility of ensuring that he understood the nature of the duty a director was called upon to perform. That duty would vary according to the size and business of that particular company and the experience or skills of the director held himself or herself out to have in support of appointment to the office. The duty included that of acting collectively to manage the company[197].

(f) Where there was an issue as to the extent of a director's duties and responsibilities in any particular case, the level of reward which he was entitled to receive or which he might reasonable have expected to receive from the company might be a relevant fact in resolving that issue. It was not that the unfitness depended on how much he was paid. The point was that the higher the level of reward, the greater the responsibilities which might reasonably be expected (prima facie, at least) to go with it[198].

(g) The following general propositions could be stated[199] with respect to the director's duties:

    (i) Directors had, both collectively and individually, a continuing duty to acquire and maintain a sufficient knowledge and understanding of the

[195] Jonathan Parker J quoted from the decision in *Re Westmid Packing Services Ltd* [1998] 2 BCLC 646 where Woolf MR went on to say (at 654): 'It is of the greatest importance that any individual who undertakes the statutory and fiduciary obligations of being a company director should realise that these are inescapable personal responsibilities.'

[196] The authority here was *Dovey v Corey* [1901] AC 477, where Halsbury LC said (at 486): 'The business of life could not go on if people could not trust those who are put in a position of trust for the express purpose of attending to details of management.'

[197] The authority given here was *Daniels v Anderson* (1995) 16 ACSR 607; see para **[15.079]** *post*.

[198] *Re Barings plc; Secretary of State for Trade and Industry v Baker* [1998] BCC 583.

[199] The authorities cited by Jonathan Parker J were: *Re Brazilian Rubber Plantations and Estates Ltd* [1911] 1 Ch 425; *Re City Equitable Fire Insurance* [1925] Ch 407; *Re Norman Holding Co Ltd* [1991] BCLC 1; *Re D'jan of London Ltd, Copp v D'jan* [1994] BCLC 561; *Bishopsgate Investment Management Ltd v Maxwell (No 2)* [1993] BCLC 1282; *Martin v Webb* 110 US 7; *Briggs v Spaulding* 141 US 132; *Rankin v Cooper* 149 F 1010; *Atherton v Anderson* 99 F 2nd 883; and *Federal Deposit Insurance Corp v Bierman* 2 Fed Rep (3rd series) 1424.

company's business to enable them properly to discharge their duties as directors.

(ii) Whilst directors were entitled (subject to the articles of association of the company) to delegate particular functions to those below them in the management chain, and to trust their competence and integrity to a reasonable extent, the exercise of the power of delegation did not absolve a director from the duty to supervise the discharge of the delegated functions.

(iii) No rule of universal application can be formulated as to the duty referred to in (ii) above. The extent of the duty, and the question whether it had been discharged, depended on the facts of each particular case, including the director's role in the management of the company[200].'

As Murphy J said, this is indeed a convenient summary of directors' duties on delegation[201] although as seen above[202]in *Re Tralee Beef & Lamb Ltd*[203], Hardiman J cautioned against the general application of these principles to all companies in all circumstances. In the absence of specific restrictions, directors can – and often, probably should – delegate particular duties to employees and others. It must always be borne in mind, however, that overall *accountability* is not delegable and just as a tenant remains responsible to his landlord where he carves out a sub-lease in favour of a sub-tenant, so too does a director remain *accountable* to his company where he delegates the performance of some or all of his duties to others.

(h) The consequences of abuse of directors' powers

[15.054] Where directors abuse their powers, then the consequence is that any action taken is invalid, but can be cured by the company in general meeting ratifying the actions of the directors[204]. Where an outsider enters into a contract which is an abuse of the directors' powers, provided that he does not have notice of the abuse, the company will remain bound: *Rolled Steel Products Ltd v British Steel Corporation Ltd*[205].

Fiduciary duties: conflicts of interests

[15.055] The principle that a director shall not place himself in a position whereby his paramount duty to the company comes into conflict with his own personal interests arises from his status as a fiduciary *vis-à-vis* his company. Here we consider situations where a director abuses his position, fails to disclose a personal interest and gains a personal advantage. Other situations involve transactions and arrangements between a director and his company and the many statutory provisions that regulate such transactions and arrangements are considered in Ch 16[206].

---

200 *Re Barings plc et al (No 5); Secretary of State for Trade and Industry v Baker et al* (No 5) [1999] 1 BCLC 433 at 435, 436.

201 *Re Vehicle Imports Ltd* (23 November 2000, unreported) HC, Murphy J at p 10 of the transcript.

202 See para **[15.043]** *ante*.

203 *Re Tralee Beef & Lamb Ltd* [2008] IESC 1.

204 See Ch 13, *Corporate Governance: Management by the Directors*, at para **[13.142]**.

205 *Rolled Steel Products Ltd v British Steel Corporation Ltd* [1985] 3 All ER 52.

206 Ch 16, *Statutory Regulation of Directors' Transactions*.

[15.056] Being a *fiduciary*, a director is bound to avoid a situation whereby his own personal interests conflict with those of the company[207]. One judicial statement of this principle is found in *Bray v Ford*[208], where Lord Herschell said:

> 'It is an inflexible rule of a Court of Equity that a person in a fiduciary position, such as the respondent's, is not, unless otherwise expressly provided, entitled to make a profit; he is not allowed to put himself in a position where his interest and duty conflict. It does not appear to me that this rule is, as has been said, founded upon principles of morality. I regard it rather as based on the consideration that, human nature being what it is, there is danger, in such circumstances, of the person holding a fiduciary duty being swayed by interest rather than duty, and thus prejudicing those whom he was bound to protect. It has, therefore, been deemed expedient to lay down this positive rule. But I am satisfied that it might be departed from in many cases, without any breach of morality, without any wrong being inflicted, and without any consciousness of wrongdoing[209].'

In *Aberdeen Rly Co v Blaikie Bros*[210], Lord Cranworth said that no fiduciary:

> '... shall be allowed to enter into engagements in which he has, or can have, a personal interest conflicting, or which may possibly conflict, with the interests of whose whom he is bound to protect[211].'

Accordingly, the principle that directors must avoid conflicts of interest is a general one, designed to counteract human nature, and is especially applicable in a private company in which the directors and the shareholders are one and the same. However, as this is but an application of the general fiduciary principle of agent and principal or trustee and beneficiary, it follows that the company can make an informed and free decision to release the fiduciary-director from his duty. Provided that the breach of a director's duty does not involve an act which is *ultra vires*, the company can prospectively or retrospectively release a director from his obligations by absolving him of his wrongdoing in general meeting[212].

[15.057] In *Bhullar et al v Bhullar and another*[213], Jonathan Parker LJ in the English Court of Appeal said in a case where directors of a company purchased a property without informing the company of the existence of the opportunity to acquire it that:

> 'In a case such as the present, where a fiduciary has exploited a commercial opportunity for his own benefit, the relevant question, in my judgment, is not whether the party to whom the duty is owed (the company, in the instant case) has some kind of beneficial interest in the opportunity: in my judgment that would be too formalistic and restrictive an approach. Rather, the question is simply whether the fiduciary's exploitation of the opportunity is such as to attract the application of the rule[214].'

---

207 See MacCann, 'Directors' Fiduciary Duties' (1991) ILT 80, 81.

208 *Bray v Ford* [1896] AC 44 at 51–52, [1895–9] All ER Rep 1009 at 1011.

209 This quotation was cited with approval by the Court of Appeal in *Guinness plc v Saunders* [1990] 1 All ER 652 at 660. See also *Aberdeen Railway Co v Blaikie Bros* (1854) 1 Macq 461.

210 *Aberdeen Rly Co v Blaikie Bros* [1854] 1 Macq 461.

211 *Aberdeen Rly Co v Blaikie Bros* [1854] 1 Macq 461 at 471.

212 See generally, *Re Burke Clancy & Co Ltd* (23 May 1974, unreported) HC *per* Kenny J.

213 *Bhullar et al v Bhullar and another* [2003] 2 BCLC 241.

214 *Bhullar et al v Bhullar and another* [2003] 2 BCLC 241 at 252.

The test to be applied in determining whether the rule had been breached is whether a reasonable man, looking at the relevant facts and circumstances, would think that there was a real sensible possibility of conflict[215].

(a) The general rule: no profit

[15.058] The principle that a director cannot gain, or profit, from his fiduciary position is best illustrated by the leading case of *Regal (Hastings) v Gulliver*[216]. There, the plaintiff company was in the cinema business, owning one cinema, which the directors decided to sell. The directors decided that it would be best to sell the cinema as part of a chain and so they decided to acquire a number of other cinemas and to sell them all together. To this end, a subsidiary company was formed having a share capital of £5,000, divided into 5000 £1 shares. The landlord of two other cinemas would only offer leases to the new company if the new company had a *paid up* share capital of £5,000, or alternatively, if the directors would provide personal guarantees. The directors were not inclined to provide such guarantees and the plaintiff company could not afford to raise any more than £2,000. Consequently, the plaintiff company subscribed for £2,000 worth of shares in the new company and the directors personally subscribed for £3,000 worth of shares in the new company. The new company then acquired a lease of the two cinemas. Ultimately, it was decided to sell the shares in both companies rather than selling the assets themselves, and in this way the cinemas were indirectly sold. Upon the sale of the shares in the new company, the entire profit did not accrue to the plaintiff company, but instead to the new company's shareholders. Of course, this meant that the directors made a personal profit since they held some of the shares in the new company. The matter became contentious when it was discovered by the new owners of both companies that the directors had made such profits through their office, and the new owners alleged that the directors had breached their fiduciary duties to the company.

It was held by the House of Lords that the directors were obliged in law to account for the profit made by them. In the words of Viscount Sankey, the directors:

> '... were in a fiduciary position and their liability to account does not depend upon proof of mala fides. The general rule of equity is that no one who has duties of a fiduciary nature to perform is allowed to enter into engagements in which he has or can have a personal interest conflicting with the interests of those whom he is bound to protect. If he holds any property so acquired as trustee, he is bound to account for it to his *cestui que trust*[217].'

Lord Russell said of fiduciaries, in a passage cited with approval by Clarke J in *Allied Irish Bank plc and ors v Diamond and ors*[218]:

> 'The rule of equity which insists on those, who by use of a fiduciary position make a profit, being liable to account for that profit, in no way depends on fraud, or absence of bona fides; or upon such questions or considerations as whether the profit would or should otherwise have gone to the plaintiff, or whether the profiteer was under a duty to

[215] *Boarman v Phipps* [1966] 3 All ER 721 at 756; *Bhullar et al v Bhullar and another* [2003] 2 BCLC 241 at 253.

[216] *Regal (Hastings) v Gulliver* [1942] 1 All ER 378.

[217] *Regal (Hastings) v Gulliver* [1942] 1 All ER 378 at 381. The case of *Keech v Sandford* (1726) Sel Cas Ch 61 was cited as authority for this point.

[218] *Allied Irish Bank plc and ors v Diamond and ors* [2011] IEHC 505.

> obtain the source of the profit for the plaintiff, or whether he took a risk or acted as he did for the benefit of the plaintiff or whether the plaintiff has in fact been damaged or benefited by his action. The liability arises from the mere fact of a profit having, in the stated circumstances, been made. The profiteer, however honest and well-intentioned, cannot escape the risk of being called upon to account.'

Accordingly, the motives of the directors were immaterial to the outcome: in the course of their management of the company they entered into a transaction from which they made a personal profit. As fiduciaries, the directors were obliged to account for that profit.

[15.059] Since there were no *mala fides* on the part of the directors, it seems on first sight that the decision in the *Regal (Hastings)* case was harsh. However, had the directors formally notified the company of the proposal, they could have been released from their fiduciary duty by the members of the company passing a resolution (either antecedent or subsequent) to the directors' actions[219]. Where a director purports to disclose his interest in a particular matter to the members, that disclosure must be sufficient as to enable the members to make an informed decision as to whether or not to release the director from his duty[220]. In the context of many private companies, the directors will often also be the shareholders, and so it could be said that obtaining the shareholders' absolution is a mere technicality. However, since even in a two-director, 50–50 shareholding company, one director could act in breach of the quasi-partnership relationship of trust, the point is far from moot[221].

[15.060] The general rule will not, however, apply where the company is aware that its directors are involved in exit-negotiations with a third party and the company expressly tells its directors that it is not interested in knowing of their private negotiations. In *Framlington Group plc and another v Anderson et al*[222], three directors decided to leave their company to join a competitor in circumstances where their contracts of employment permitted them to join or set up a competing business on leaving. The company to which they were going agreed with their company to acquire part of its business, represented by the clients who were serviced by the three directors. The plaintiff company received by way of consideration, shares in the company. The three directors were told by the company not to take part in these negotiations and were further told that the company was not interested in hearing about the terms of their remuneration package. Subsequently, on learning that the three directors had received shares in the company to which they were going, the plaintiff claimed that they had been in breach of their fiduciary duty which, it was alleged, was to assist the plaintiff obtain the best price possible for its assets. It also claimed that they had earned secret profits and that they were accountable to it for the profits they had made. The plaintiff's action failed and it was held that the three directors had not, in the circumstances, been in breach of their duties because their company had expressed itself to be disinterested in their negotiations.

---

219 *Regal (Hastings) v Gulliver* [1942] 1 All ER 378 at 389d–e.

220 *JJ Harrison (Properties) Ltd v Harrison* [2001] 1 BCLC 158.

221 Similarly, in a single-member company, one of the two directors could embark on a personal frolic to the detriment of the company.

222 *Framlington Group plc and another v Anderson et al* [1995] 1 BCLC 475.

[15.061] The failure of directors to inform their fellow directors that they were the subject of a determined attempt by a potential competitor to get them to leave to join the competitor's enterprise was found to be a breach of duty in *British Midland Tool Ltd v Midland International Tooling*[223].

(b) Rejected business opportunities

[15.062] It would seem to be sensible for the law to relax directors' liability to account in circumstances where the company's board of directors has considered the transaction but rejected it. There seems to be nothing wrong in principle in permitting one of the directors to personally take up that rejected transaction or contract. In law where the company *bona fide* rejects a business opportunity, and one of the directors takes it for himself, then the director will not be liable to account for any profits made. This is borne out by *Peso Silver Mines Ltd v Cropper*[224]. In that case, one of the directors of the plaintiff company became aware that several mining claims were up for sale. He advised the board of directors of this and they decided not to acquire the claims because of cash-flow difficulties. The director, who was a geologist, formed a syndicate involving some of the other directors, and together they acquired the mining claims for themselves. The control of the plaintiff company changed, and the new owners were peeved that the syndicate of directors had made a profit out of an opportunity which was the company's initially and which had come to the directors' notice in the course of their work for the plaintiff company. However, it was held by the Supreme Court of Canada that the case was distinguishable from the *Regal (Hastings)* case since in the *Peso* case the company had rejected the 'business chance'. Consequently, the court refused an order to compel the directors to account for the profit[225].

[15.063] Some commentators[226] have espoused the general principle that directors should be obliged to account for any profits made where their self-interests conflict with those of the company. This view satisfies itself with the knowledge that the entrepreneurial director could always have disclosed his intentions to the company, and obtained its prior approval. There is much merit in this view since the principal difficulty with a more lenient approach is that it is dependant upon the court being able to satisfy itself that the board acted *bona fide* in rejecting the contract. Indeed, there is authority to suggest that the decision in *Peso Silver Mines* may not be followed in England where the strict duty to account was recently restated in *Gencor ACP Ltd et al v Dalby et al*[227]. In that case, the plaintiffs were three group companies engaged in the design, manufacture and sale of asphalt plant and equipment. After the group was taken over, its new owners investigated certain transactions and instituted proceedings against the defendants who were the group's managing director (previously a substantial

223 *British Midland Tool Ltd v Midland International Tooling* [2003] 2 BCLC 523.

224 *Peso Silver Mines Ltd v Cropper* (1966) 58 DLR 1.

225 See *Queensland Mines Ltd v Hudson* (1978) 18 ALR 1, and generally, MacCann (1991) ILT 104 at 105, for a thorough analysis of the cases and principles involved.

226 See Ussher, *Company Law in Ireland* (1986) at p 215, and MacCann, (1991) ILT 104 at 105.

227 *Gencor ACP Ltd et al v Dalby et al* [2000] 2 BCLC 734. See Li, 'The Peso Silver Case: An Opportunity to Soften the Rigid Approach of the English courts on the Problem of Corporate Opportunity' (2011) 32 Co Law 68 where the case is made that *Peso Silver* should be recognised in English law.

shareholder in the group) and the company secretary, alleging misfeasance in the misapplication of group money and assets and in diverting business opportunities. It was claimed, in particular, that the managing director had arranged for orders by foreign companies for second-hand refurbished plant and equipment and for equipment ancillary to plant previously supplied by the group to be placed with a company controlled by him. The sales of such second-hand equipment were often to group customers; group notepaper was often used for correspondence; and group staff had sometimes been used to fit the second-hand equipment. The managing director sought to excuse his actions on the grounds that the group did not, itself, deal in second-hand equipment. Rimer J rejected this, holding:

> 'The principles are well established. It is no answer to them that the company could not or would not have taken up the business opportunity that the director took up for his own benefit. Nor is it an answer that the director's own skill or property were also used in the course of making the profit. The only escape from potential accountability is the obtaining of the prior approval of the company's shareholders after full disclosure of all the facts and circumstances[228].'

In so holding, Rimer J expressly purported to apply the principle in *Regal (Hastings) Ltd v Gulliver*. Whether the Irish courts will depart from the strict rule in *Regal (Hastings) Ltd* has been expressly left open by Clarke J in *Parolen Ltd v Doherty and Lindat Ltd*.[229]

[15.064] Where, however, a company has not even had a chance to consider the business opportunity and where there is no disclosure, the law is clear in providing that the director will be bound to account for any profit gained. This point is illustrated by the case of *Industrial Development Consultants v Cooley*[230] where Mr Cooley, the managing director of the plaintiff company tried, on behalf of the company, to secure a construction contract with the Eastern Gas Board, an English public body. Whilst Cooley was unsuccessful from the view point of the company, he himself very much impressed the gas board, who offered the contract to him in his private capacity. Feigning illness, Cooley resigned his position as managing director of the plaintiff company and took up a job as project manager with the gas board. The plaintiff then sought to make Cooley account for the profit made by him. He refused, countering that there was no breach of fiduciary duty and that at best the plaintiffs could only get

---

[228] *Gencor ACP Ltd et al v Dalby et al* [2000] 2 BCLC 734 at 741, para [17].

[229] *Parolen Ltd v Doherty and Lindat Ltd* [2010] IEHC 71. This case concerned an application for security for costs; it was noted by Clarke J that 'the most rigorous application of the strict rule that directors must account to a company for any gain which they make is to be found in *Regal (Hastings) Ltd v Gulliver* [1942] 1 All ER 378. However, both academic commentators and the courts of other common law jurisdictions (not least the Canadian Courts – see *Canadian Aero Services v O'Malley* [1974] SCR 592) have criticised an over strict approach whose application might have the potential to create an inequitable situation whereby the relevant company obtained a windfall gain. A full consideration of the precise circumstances, if any, in which it might be appropriate to depart from a strict application of the rule is something which, in my view, could only be determined after a full trial. At the level of principle I cannot conclude, therefore, that the law in this jurisdiction, properly analysed, may not include some exceptions to the strict rule and that should the facts turn out to be as Mr Doherty asserts them to be, this case might not come within such a legitimate departure from the strict rule.'

[230] *Industrial Development Consultants v Cooley* [1972] 2 All ER 162.

damages, although they did not suffer any damage since they could not have obtained the contract themselves in any event. It was held that there was a fiduciary duty owed, *and* there had been a breach of that duty by the director in using for his own ends the information obtained by him while working for the company[231]. Accordingly, the director was ordered to account for all personal profit made by him.

[15.065] In *Re Allied Business and Financial Consultants Ltd*[232], it was held that where a director takes up an opportunity in relation to a business not in fact carried on by a company that there would be no breach of the 'no conflicts' rule. That case would have created an exception to the 'no conflicts rule' based on the scope of a company's business. Such an approach was roundly rejected by the English Court of Appeal decision in *O'Donnell v Shanahan*[233]. In that case, it was held that where directors had obtained the information which they subsequently used to acquire an interest in property and would only have known of that opportunity by virtue of being directors of the company, whether or not the opportunity was inside or outside the company's business was immaterial and resulted in the directors being in breach of the 'no conflict' and 'no profit' rules. Distinguishing the law of partnership[234] from the law applicable to directors, Rimer LJ said:

> 'The statements of principle in the authorities about directors' fiduciary duties make it clear that any inquiry as to whether the company could, would or might have taken up the opportunity itself is irrelevant; so also therefore must be a 'scope of business' inquiry. The point is that the existence of the opportunity is one that it is relevant for the company to know and of which the director has a duty to inform it. It is not for the director to make his own decision that the company will not be interested and to proceed, without more, to appropriate the opportunity for himself. His duty is one of undivided loyalty and this is one manifestation of how that duty is required to be discharged[235].'

Again, in *Termascan Ltd v Norman*[236] it was held that a director is precluded from taking any property or business advantage of the company, especially where he was a participant in the negotiations, even after his resignation, if the resignation was prompted or influenced by a desire to acquire for himself any maturing business opportunity[237].

[15.066] In *Hunter Kane Ltd v Watkins*[238], the following principles (that were described by Brooke LJ in the English Court of Appeal in *Plus Group Ltd v Pyke*[239]) were set out:

> '1. A director, while acting as such, has a fiduciary relationship with his Company. That is he has an obligation to deal towards it with loyalty, good faith and avoidance of the conflict of duty and self-interest.

---

231 See also *Canadian Aero Service Ltd v O'Malley* [1973] 40 DLR 371, where a similar situation occurred.

232 *Re Allied Business and Financial Consultants Ltd* [2009] BCC 517.

233 *O'Donnell v Shanahan* [2009] BCC 822.

234 At trial, the judge had relied on *Aas v Benham* [1891] 2 Ch 244.

235 *O'Donnell v Shanahan* [2009] BCC 822 at 843.

236 *Termascan Ltd v Norman* [2011] BCC 535.

237 Expressly applying *CMS Dolphin Ltd v Simonet* [2002] BCC 600; *Hunter Kane Ltd v Watkins* [2003] EWHC 186; and *Foster Bryant Surveying Ltd v Bryant* [2007] BCC 804.

238 *Hunter Kane Ltd v Watkins* [2003] EWHC 186.

239 *Plus Group Ltd v Pyke* [2002] 2 BCLC 201.

2. A requirement to avoid a conflict of duty and self-interest means that a director is precluded from obtaining for himself, either secretly or without the informed approval of the Company, any property or business advantage either belonging to the Company or for which it has been negotiating, especially where the director or officer is a participant in the negotiations.
3. A director's power to resign from office is not a fiduciary power. He is entitled to resign even if his resignation might have a disastrous effect on the business or reputation of the Company.
4. A fiduciary relationship does not continue after the determination of the relationship which gives rise to it. After the relationship is determined the director is in general not under the continuing obligations which are the feature of the fiduciary relationship.
5. Acts done by the directors while the contract of employment subsists but which are preparatory to competition after it terminates are *not necessarily* in themselves a breach of the implied term as to loyalty and fidelity.
6. Directors, no less than employees, acquire a general fund of skill, knowledge and expertise in the course of their work, which is plainly in the public interest that they should be free to exploit it in a new position. After ceasing the relationship by resignation or otherwise a director is in general (and subject of course to any terms of the contract of employment) not prohibited from using his general fund of skill and knowledge, the 'stock in trade' of the knowledge he has acquired while a director, even including such things as business contacts and personal connections made as a result of his directorship.
7. A director is however precluded from acting in breach of the requirement at 2 above, even after his resignation where the resignation may fairly be said to have been prompted or influenced by a wish to acquire for himself any maturing business opportunities sought by the Company and where it was his position with the Company rather than a fresh initiative that led him to the opportunity which he later acquired.
8. In considering whether an act of a director breaches the preceding principle the factors to take into account will include the factor of position or office held, the nature of the corporate opportunity, its ripeness, its specificness and the director's relation to it, the amount of knowledge possessed, the circumstances in which it was obtained and whether it was special or indeed even private, the factor of time in the continuation of the fiduciary duty where the alleged breach occurs after termination of the relationship with the Company and the circumstances under which the breach was terminated, that is whether by retirement or resignation or discharge.
9. The underlying basis of the liability of a director who exploits after his resignation a maturing business opportunity 'of the Company' is that the opportunity is to be treated as if it were the property of the Company in relation to which the director had fiduciary duties. By seeking the exploit the opportunity after resignation he is appropriating to himself that property. He is just as accountable as a trustee who retires without properly accounting for trust property.
10. It follows that a director will not be in breach of the principle set out as point 7 above where either the Company's hope of obtaining the contract was not a 'maturing business opportunity' and it was not pursuing further business orders nor where the director's resignation was not itself prompted or influenced by a wish to acquire the business for himself.

11. As regards breach of confidence, although while the contract of employment subsists a director or other employee may not use confidential information to the detriment of his employer, after it ceases the director/employee may compete and may use know-how acquired in the course of his employment (as distinct from trade secrets – although the distinction is sometimes difficult to apply in practice).

(c) The remedies available where directors wrongly profit from their office

[15.067] The normal remedy available to companies where directors wrongly profit from their office will be an account for profits. There must be a reasonable connection between the breach of duty and the profits for which it is sought to make a fiduciary accountable[240]. The underlying basis of a director's liability for exploiting a business opportunity is that the opportunity is treated as if it were the company's property and the director becomes a constructive trustee of the fruits of his abuse[241]. In the Australian High Court in *Chan v Zacharia*[242], Deane J had said, of the duties of a fiduciary:

> '… the principle of equity is that a person who is under a fiduciary obligation must account to the person to whom the obligation is owed for any benefit or gain (i) which has been obtained or received in circumstances where a conflict or a significant possibility of conflict existed between his fiduciary duty and his personal interest in the pursuit or possible receipt of such a benefit or gain or (ii) which was obtained or received by use or by reason of his fiduciary position or of opportunity or knowledge resulting from it. Any such benefit or gain is held by the fiduciary as constructive trustee …'

The English Court of Appeal in *Paragon Finance plc v DB Thakerar & Co*[243] and in *JJ Harrison (Properties) Ltd v Harrison*[244] has observed that where a director receives property in breach of trust he is described as a constructive trustee but in a different position to a 'stranger' who acquires trust property. On the fiduciary duties of directors Chadwick LJ said in *JJ Harrison (Properties) Ltd v Harrison*[245]:

> '… a director, on appointment to that office, assumes the duties of a trustee in relation to the company's property. If, therefore, he takes possession of that property, his possession 'is coloured from the first by the trust and confidence by means of which he obtained it'. His obligations as a trustee *in relation to that property* do not arise out of the transaction by which he obtained it for himself. The true analysis is that his obligations as a trustee in relation to that property predate the transaction by which it was conveyed to him. The conveyance of the property to himself by the exercise of his powers in breach of trust does not release him from those obligations. He is trustee of the property because it has become vested in him; but his obligations to deal with the property as a trustee arise out of his pre-existing duties as a director; not out of the circumstances in which the property was conveyed.'

---

240 See *CMS Dolphin Ltd v Simonet and another* [2001] 2 BCLC 704.

241 *CMS Dolphin Ltd v Simonet and another* [2001] 2 BCLC 704.

242 *Chan v Zacharia* (1984) 154 CLR 178 at 198; quoted with apparent approval by Morritt LJ in *Don King Productions Inc v Warren* [2000] 1 BCLC 607 at 629.

243 *Paragon Finance plc v DB Thakerar &* [1999] 1 All ER 400.

244 *JJ Harrison (Properties) Ltd v Harrison* [2001] EWCA Civ 1467, [2002] 1 BCLC 162.

245 *JJ Harrison (Properties) Ltd v Harrison* [2001] EWCA Civ 1467, [2002] 1 BCLC 162 at 175, para [29].

[15.068] The Irish decision in *Aerospares Ltd v Thompson et al*[246] shows that an account for profits will not be the invariable result and that damages alone may be found to be the appropriate remedy. In that case, Kearns J agreed to grant a *Mareva* injunction to the plaintiff company against the defendants in circumstances where the first two defendants were former directors of the plaintiff company who, it was alleged, had diverted monies from the company to their own use. The plaintiff's contention was that the first three defendants had perpetrated a fraud against the plaintiff by diverting monies due to the plaintiff from its customers and trading connections to the fourth defendant using an account in the name of the fifth defendant. The fifth defendant was a company incorporated in the Seychelles that had exactly the same name as the plaintiff. In addition, the plaintiff claimed further for as then unascertained losses for business allegedly poached by the first three defendants, both whilst still working for the plaintiff and thereafter. Kearns J found that while the plaintiff might well recover damages, it would not extend to profits obtained over a virtually indefinite period from a 'poached client'. Kearns J distinguished the case in hand from *Canadian Aeroservices v O'Malley*[247], where two senior officers were ordered to return profits made to their company after they had established the benefit of a contract with a former customer of their company. Kearns J said:

> 'That situation seems quite different to the instant case where two of the three first named defendants were on routine service contracts terminable by one month's notice in writing, in a non-exclusive area of commercial trade and where in any event they could not have been restrained from competing for the same business under either the terms of their employment of under the Competition Acts. Accordingly, while the plaintiff company may well recover damages in this case, it seems to me that such damages must in reality be confined to 'poached' business … rather than the ongoing indefinite time contended for[248].'

Whether such a distinction will be maintained in future cases on this point remains to be seen.

[15.069] Transactions entered into by directors with their companies in breach of their duties can be set aside by the company, subject to the defence of laches, acquiescence and the rights of *bona fide* third parties acquired for value without actual notice of the breach[249]. It should be noted, however, that the English Court of Appeal in *JJ Harrison (Properties) Ltd v Harrison*[250] disallowed the defence of laches and a defence based on the Limitations Act 1980 (UK) to a claim for breach of trust against a director on the grounds that it was not intended to permit a trustee to retain something that he ought not to have.

---

246 *Aerospares Ltd v Thompson et al* (13 January 1999, unreported) HC, Kearns J.

247 *Canadian Aeroservices v O'Malley* [1973] 40 DLR 371.

248 *Aerospares Ltd v Thompson et al* (13 January 1999, unreported) HC, Kearns J at p 12 of the transcript.

249 See *Aberdeen Railway Co v Blaikie Bros* (1854) 1 Macq 461; *Movites Ltd v Bulfield* [1988] BCLC 104 and *JJ Harrison (Properties) Ltd v Harrison* [2001] 1 BCLC 158.

250 *JJ Harrison (Properties) Ltd v Harrison* [2001] EWCA Civ 1467, [2002] 1 BCLC 162.

Directors' duties: competition with the company

[15.070] As a general principle, it is not *per se* a breach of a director's fiduciary duties to be involved in a business which competes with that of his company[251]. The leading authority on an analogous point (concerning the law relating to trustees) is the Irish case of *Moore v M'Glynn*[252] where Chatterton VC said that he was:

> '... not prepared to hold that a trustee is guilty of a breach of trust in setting himself up in a similar line of business in the neighbourhood, provided that he does not resort to deception, or solicitation of custom from persons dealing at the old shop.'

In that case, an executor and trustee was put in charge of the deceased's shop, which he held in trust and ran for the beneficiaries of the trust. When he set up in business himself, the question arose as to whether or not he was in breach of his trust. It was held that he was not *per se* in breach of his trust, provided that he did not divert custom from the 'trust shop' to his own shop[253]. The leading English authority on this point is *London and Mashonaland Exploration Co v New Mashonaland Exploration Co*[254]. The entire judgment reads:

> 'Chitty J said, even assuming that Lord Mayo had been duly elected chairman and director of the plaintiff company, there was nothing in the articles which required him to give any part of his time, much less the whole of his time, to the business of the company, or which prohibited him from acting as a director of another company; neither was there any contract, express or implied, to give his personal services to the plaintiff company and to no other company. No case had been made out that Lord Mayo was about to disclose to the defendant company any information that he had obtained confidentially in his character of chairman; the analogy sought to be drawn by the plaintiff company's counsel between the present case and partnerships was incomplete; no sufficient damage had been shown, and no case had been made for an injunction; the application was wholly unprecedented, and must be dismissed with costs.'

The general principle that it is not *per se* a breach of a director's fiduciary duty to compete with his company has been criticised by a number of commentators[255].

[15.071] The issue of conflict of interests must always be borne in mind by a director of a company in such situations. The basis for the application of this principle to the office of company director is because both directors and trustees are *fiduciaries*. So, in *Spring Grove Services (Ireland) Ltd v O'Callaghan et al*[256] Herbert J said:

> 'A director of a company owes strict obligations of good faith, fair dealing and honesty to the company of which he is a director. Aspects of these obligations commonly referred to

---

251 *Bell v Lever Brothers Ltd* [1932] AC 161.

252 *Moore v M'Glynn* [1894] 1 IR 74 at 89.

253 However, Chatterton VC held that while there was no breach of trust, there was an inconsistency in the trustee's interests under the trust and his own self-interest, and so removed him from the office of trustee.

254 *London and Mashonaland Exploration Co v New Mashonaland Exploration Co* [1891] WN 165.

255 See, for example, Christie, 'The Director's Fiduciary Duty Not to Compete' [1992] 55 Modern Law Review 506.

256 *Spring Grove Services (Ireland) Ltd v O'Callaghan et al* (31 July 2000, unreported) HC, Herbert J.

as 'fiduciary duties', include a duty not to compete with the company, a duty to act in the best interests of the company and a duty not to use confidential information obtained as such director otherwise than for the benefit of the company.'

[15.072] Where a director is employed under a contract of employment, or service contract, he will have certain duties to his company employer. For example, where a director has a *written* contract of employment, there may be an express restraint of trade, non-competition and anti-solicitation clause in his contract[257]. In addition, whether a director's contract is in writing or not, the director employee owes *implied duties* of fidelity and loyalty to his company employer for so long as the contract of employment is in existence[258].

[15.073] The duty of fidelity owed by an employee will often surface in the context of the abuse of confidential information which is learnt by the director employee in the course of his employment. It is important to note that where information cannot be classified as a 'trade secret' or 'confidential information' the common law duty of fidelity will not survive the termination of employment. In *Faccenda Chicken Ltd v Fowler*[259], the defendants, who were former employees (but not directors) of the plaintiff company, were sued when they began to compete with the plaintiff company by selling fresh chickens from refrigerated vans. The information used by them in their business included: the company's pricing policy, customers' names and addresses, routes taken by salesmen and other such matters. Using this information they proceeded to undercut the plaintiff company. It was held that the plaintiff company could not invoke an implied term of fidelity because the contract of employment had ended, and so the information used could not be classified as being legally confidential[260].

Breach of the implied duty of fidelity may justify the dismissal of an employee director. In *Fairbrother v Stiefel Laboratories (Ireland) Ltd*[261], the dismissal of an employee was held to be fair where he had double-jobbed with his wife, another pharmaceutical researcher, who had her own business making a product similar to that made by her husband's employers[262].

---

257 See Brearley & Bloch, *Employment Covenants and Confidential Information* (1993, Butterworths); Cheshire, Fifoot & Furmston, *Law of Contract* (12th edn, Butterworths, 1991), Ch 12.

258 *Cf Dawnfleet Ltd t/a TES Technology v Shorte and McGowan*, reported in (1991) Irish Times, of 6 September, where an interim injunction was granted to the plaintiff company restraining the defendant directors (who resigned) from competing with the company until the end of the required notice from terminating their employment. The order granted also required the directors to hand over confidential documents in their possession, not to destroy it, to refrain from soliciting customers and suppliers obtained from the company's confidential information and from publishing matters defamatory to the plaintiff company. Both directors had been responsible for marketing and sales. See also, Wedderburn, *The Worker and The Law* (3rd edn, Penguin Books, 1986) at p 183.

259 *Faccenda Chicken Ltd v Fowler* [1986] 1 All ER 617.

260 See *The Pulse Group Ltd an another v O'Reilly and another* [2006] IEHC 50 (Clarke J) where it was accepted as clear law that: 'the only enduring obligation on the part of an employee after his employment has ceased is one which precludes the employee from disclosing a trade secret.'

261 *Fairbrother v Stiefel Laboratories (Ireland) Ltd* (1985) UD665/1985. See also, *Mulchrone v Feeney* (1983) UD1023/1982.

262 See also, *Conachey v Little Chic Knitwear* (1985) UD342/85.

Directors' duties of care, skill and diligence

[15.074] Directors owe duties of care, skill and diligence to their company[263]. A director must not act negligently or conduct the business of his company in an inept manner. These duties arise not only from the directors' fiduciary duties as agents, and from the fact that directors will often be employees, but also because directors owe duties of care in tort to persons who forseeably rely on their actions. Like other directors' duties, these are primarily owed to the company, but can sometimes be owed to third parties. It has been said[264] that unlike the principles involved in fiduciary duties which are largely prohibitive or negative, the duties under discussion here are in the nature of positive duties. As regards the enforcement of these duties it will invariably be the case that the controllers of a company will be slow to sue *themselves*. Often, action will only be taken against inept directors where, upon a company being wound up, a liquidator instigates such action or, alternatively, where following a change in a company's ownership, the control of the company shifts to outsiders. It will frequently be the case that directors' duties of care skill and diligence will be enforced by s 298 of the CA 1963, in a misfeasance suit[265]. It is proposed to consider the various facets of such duties as follows:

(a) General principles of care, skill and diligence;
(b) Qualifications: their presence or absence;
(c) The need for diligence;
(d) Reliance on others for advice;
(e) Tortious liability to third parties.

(a) General principles

[15.075] In the absence of an indemnity of the type envisaged by model reg 138[266], a company director is liable in tort for negligent behaviour. One of the oldest statements on this point is found in the case of *Charitable Corporation v Sutton*[267], where Lord Hardwicke said:

> '[Directors] may be guilty of acts of commission or omission, of malfeasance or non-feasance ... By accepting a trust of this sort, a person is obliged to execute it with fidelity and reasonable diligence; and it is no excuse to say that they had no benefit from it, but that it was merely honorary; and therefore, they are within the case of common trustees.'

---

263 See generally, Trebilcock, 'The Liability of Company Directors For Negligence' (1969) 32 MLR 499; Stanton & Dugdale, 'Recent Developments in Professional Negligence – IV: Directors' Liability' (1982) NLJ 251; Loose & Yelland, *The Company Director* (6th edn, Jordans, 1987) at para 4.8; Keane, *Company Law* (4th edn, Bloomsbury Professional, 2007) at para 29.29; and Ussher, *Company Law in Ireland* (1986) at p 228 *et seq*.

264 See Loose & Yelland, *The Company Director* (6th edn, Jordans, 1987) at para 4.8.1.

265 Note that in *Re B Johnson & Co (Builders) Ltd* [1955] Ch 634 it was suggested that so called 'mere-common-law-negligence' would not ground a misfeasance suit and that the negligence involved would have to have been such as to force the company into liquidation.

266 See para **[15.091]** *post*.

267 *Charitable Corporation v Sutton* (1742) 2 Atk 400 at 405, 406.

In that case, 50 committee members of a company formed by charter were found liable for losses to the company which were occasioned by the failure of a person who was employed by the corporation to require adequate security for loans made to impecunious peasants. However, this promising start, from the viewpoint of the imposition of liability, plummeted in subsequent cases. The 'low point'[268] has been said to be the case of *Turquand v Marshall*[269], where the so-called *business management rule* came into vogue[270]. According to Lord Hatherley LC, provided that the directors acted *bona fide* and within their authority they could not be liable for loss occasioned to the company. In that case, the directors had caused the company to make a loan to one of their number, who subsequently died insolvent without repaying the loan. The directors were held not to have been negligent or liable for the loss to the company. Subsequent judicial statements have tempered the extremities of both the 'high' and 'low' points of directors' negligence. The current thinking is that it remains difficult to establish actionable negligence, and the standard of care required of directors has certainly not kept pace with developments in the law of tort since the landmark case of *Donoghue v Stevenson*[271]. It may also be noted that even where negligence is proven, the court may grant relief under s 391 of the CA 1963[272].

[15.076] The leading case on directors' duties in the context of negligence remains *Re City Equitable Fire Insurance Co Ltd*[273]. The facts there were that the company concerned had lost £1.2m because of bad investments and the fraudulent activity of one director, a 'daring and unprincipled scoundrel'. When the company went into liquidation, it was sought to make the other honest directors personally liable for the losses of the company. Although the action ultimately failed because of a specific exclusion in the company's articles of association for losses not caused by the wilful neglect or default of the directors, the judgment of the learned Romer J remains instructive. The essence of his judgment (which is worthy of being quoted *in extenso*) was that to establish directors' duties in the context of negligence:

> '... it is necessary to consider not only the nature of the company's business, but also the manner in which the work of the company is in fact distributed between the directors and other officials of the company, provided that this distribution is a reasonable one in the circumstances, and is not inconsistent with the provisions of the articles of association. In discharging the duties of his position thus ascertained a director must, of course[274],
>
> (a) act honestly; but he must also exercise some degree of both skill and diligence ...
>
> (b) The care that he is bound to take has been described ... as 'reasonable care' to be measured by the care an ordinary man might be expected to take in the circumstances on his own behalf ...

---

268 See Trebilcock, 'The Liability of Company Directors For Negligence' (1969) 32 MLR 499 at p 500.

269 *Turquand v Marshall* (1869) LR 4 Ch App 376.

270 See Rhoads, 'Personal Liability of Directors for Corporate Mismanagement' (1916) 65 U of Pa LR 128.

271 *Donoghue v Stevenson* [1932] AC 562.

272 See para **[15.088]** *et seq*, *post*.

273 *Re City Equitable Fire Insurance Co Ltd* [1925] Ch 407.

274 In the interests of clarity the *dictum* is broken down into point form, with sections of text omitted. The reader is referred to the actual judgment of Romer J at [1925] Ch 407, 408.

(c) A director need not exhibit in the performance of his duties a greater degree of skill than may reasonably be expected from a person of his knowledge and experience[275].

(d) A director is not bound to give continuous attention to the affairs of his company. His duties are of an intermittent nature to be performed at periodical board meetings, and at meetings of any committee of the board upon which he happens to be placed. He is not however, bound to attend all such meetings though he ought to attend whenever, in the circumstances, he is reasonably able to do so.

(e) In respect of all duties that, having regard to the exigencies of business, and the articles of association, may properly be left to some other official, a director is, in the absence of grounds for suspicion, justified in trusting that official to perform such duties honestly.'

The most contentious of these is the principle encapsulated in (c), namely that the standard of care appropriate to a company director is a subjective standard. Subjectivity in this context has been interpreted as meaning that an idiot, provided he is honest, can avoid liability. The existence of professional and quasi-professional qualifications among company directors will mean that their actions will be judged by standards which accord with their increased subjective ability. The effect is that the modern spread of education and the rise of the executive director will mean that there is an increasing probability that liability may be imposed on modern directors.

[15.077] There is modern precedent for findings of negligence against directors. In *Daniels et al v Daniels et al*[276], Templeman J held that the disposal of company land to a director for its probate value (£4,250) where he subsequently sold the land for £120,000 was negligence and the minority shareholders could bring an action against him, notwithstanding that there was no actual fraud. In *Cohen and another v Selby and another*[277], the Court of Appeal allowed an appeal against a trial judge's finding that a director had been negligent in delegating to his then 19-year-old son the decision of whether or not to effect insurance against loss or theft in respect of stock that was outside the UK. Having purchased jewellery worth some £393,000, the jewellery had been stolen or lost in the course of a ferry crossing. The company was subsequently wound up insolvent. The Court of Appeal held that the pleaded case against the director went no further than to allege negligence in delegating to his son the power to decide whether or not to insure the company's property outside of the UK, that the allegation of breach of duty lay not in the decision to delegate *per se* but in the decision to delegate to the 19-year-old director and student, and that in the circumstances there was no evidence touching upon the 19-year-old director's unsuitability.

(b) Qualifications: their presence or absence

[15.078] In law, a company director may be as thick as two short planks. The palpable lack of business acumen seen in two of the directors in *Re Brazilian Rubber Plantations*

[275] As Romer J said by way of an example, 'A director of a life insurance company, for instance, does not guarantee that he has the skill of an actuary or physician'.

[276] *Daniels et al v Daniels et al* [1978] 2 All ER 89.

[277] *Cohen and another v Selby and another* [2001] 1 BCLC 176.

& Estates Ltd[278] could still be equalled today. There, Neville J described two of the directors in the following terms:

> 'Sir Arthur Aylmer was absolutely ignorant of business. He only consented to act because he was told the office would give him a little pleasant employment without incurring any responsibility. HW Tugwell was a partner in a firm of bankers in a good position in Bath; he was seventy-five years of age and very deaf; he was induced to join the board by representations made to him …'

Neville J went on to hold that neither of the directors was liable in negligence when the company lost substantially after investing badly in the speculative business of rubber plantations in North Brazil. Thus, it was said of a director that he was:

> '... not bound to bring any special qualifications to his office. He may undertake the management of a rubber company in complete ignorance of everything connected with rubber, without incurring responsibility for the mistakes which may result from such ignorance.'

This may be seen as the 'country gentleman syndrome', since the older cases are typically concerned with the squire turned businessman whose company got into dire straits[279].

[15.079] However, while the foregoing remains true in theory, the modern practice is for directors to have more qualifications than in the past and the modern trend is for company directors to have a certain business acumen. While qualifications are not necessary their presence will raise the standard of care which an educated director will be expected to exercise. In what has been described as a case involving an exhaustive analysis[280] of directors' duties of skill, care and diligence, *Daniels v Anderson*[281], the Supreme Court of New South Wales said:

> 'A person who accepts the office of director of a particular company undertakes the responsibility of ensuring that he or she understands the nature of the duty a director is called upon to perform. That duty will vary according to the size and business of the particular company *and the experience or skills that the director held himself or herself out to have in support of appointment to the office*. None of this is novel. It turns upon the natural expectations and reliance placed by shareholders on the experience and skill of a particular director.'

So whilst a director may in fact be intellectually challenged, he may forfeit his immunity on this basis if he musters the intelligence to dupe the company into believing that he has particular experience or skills.

[15.080] In *ASIC v Vines*[282], Austin J said that the *Daniels* case 'established an objective duty, broadly in the region of competence, arising out of the director's duty of diligence' which was enhanced where a directorial appointment is based on a special skill. In *ASIC v Healey*[283], the Federal Court of Australia endorsed this approach, Middleton J saying:

278 *Re Brazilian Rubber Plantations & Estates Ltd* [1911] 1 Ch 425.

279 See *Re Denham & Co* (1884) 25 Ch D 752.

280 *Per* Jonathan Parker J in *Re Barings plc et al (No 5); Secretary of State for Trade and Industry v Baker et al (No 5)* [1999] 1 BCLC 433 at 488b.

281 *Daniels v Anderson* (1995) 16 ACSR 607 at 668. Emphasis added.

282 *ASIC v Vines* [2003] NSWSC 1095 at para 30. See also *ASIC v Rich* [2009] NSWSC 1229.

283 *ASIC v Healey* [2011] FCA 717.

> 'In my view, the objective duty of competence requires that the directors have the ability to read and understand the financial statements, including the understanding that financial statements classify assets and liabilities as current and non-current, and what those concepts mean. This classification is relevant to the assessment of solvency and liquidity. Equally, a director should have an understanding of the need to disclose certain events post balance sheet date[284].'

In that case, a number of executive and non-executive directors were found to be in breach of their duties in not taking reasonable steps to focus and consider the content of the company's financial statements. The foregoing passage has to be contextualised, however, because in that jurisdiction, it was provided in statute that a director must exercise their powers and discharge their duties with the degree of care and diligence that a reasonable person would exercise if he or she were a director of a company in the company's circumstances and occupied the office held by and had the same responsibilities with the company as the director[285].

(c) The need for diligence

[15.081] The degree of *diligence* required of a director is dependent upon his abilities and is subjectively ascertained. Again, the older cases show the evolution of responsibilities from a very low point, the case of *Re Cardiff Savings Bank (the Marquis of Bute's* case)[286] being an example in point. In that case, the Marquis became president of a bank at the tender age of six months, inheriting the office from his father in a singularly blatant display of nepotism. Of course, the diligence which could have been expected of the child Bute could not have been much. His involvement in the affairs of the company did not keep pace with his own development, and his diary only permitted him to attend one meeting after he reached the age of majority. Some 20 years later the liquidator of the company sought to make the adult Bute liable to reimburse the funds which were fraudulently taken from the company by one of the officials of the bank. It was held by Stirling J that he was not liable, was not expected to attend board meetings, and indeed the fact that he received regular notice of the company's meetings meant that he could assume that business was being transacted as usual!

[15.082] An Irish case on the question of directors' diligence is *Jackson v Munster Bank Ltd*[287]. There the respondent bank lent money to several of its own directors notwithstanding that loans to directors were proscribed by the bank's articles of association. One of the directors, whom it was sought to have made personally liable for the lending, did not participate in the meetings at which the loans were sanctioned. In fact the bank had two branches, one in Dublin and one in Cork. The director concerned worked in Dublin and had attended meetings held there. However, it was in Cork that the meetings were held at which the loans were sanctioned. His liability was in fact ultimately held to be limited. He was not liable for the loss arising from the Cork meeting, but was liable in respect of a subsequent loss because he was shown a letter which should have alerted him to the possibility of the 'systematic fraudulent

---

284 *ASIC v Healey* [2011] FCA 717 at para 124.

285 Section 189(1) of the Australian Corporations Act 2001.

286 *Re Cardiff Savings Bank (the Marquis of Bute's case)* [1892] 2 Ch 100.

287 *Jackson v Munster Bank Ltd* (1885) 15 LR Ir 356.

misappropriation of the property of the bank', and because of his inertia, from this point onward he was held to be liable. Had he been more diligent, he might have escaped liability entirely.

[15.083] The modern position must be taken to be tempered, and whether or not a director is guilty of not being diligent must depend upon the circumstances of each case. Clearly, where the director is a professional person and he abdicates his responsibilities to the company resulting in the management of the company being left to another director who causes losses to be incurred, there is a strong likelihood that the inert director will be held responsible; as the directors were in the case of *Dorchester Finance Co Ltd v Stebbing*[288]. There, two professional men, who were non-executive directors, were made liable for the debts of the company occasioned when a third director caused the company to make loans which were never repaid. While it would seem that such liability may be restricted to instances in which, had the directors intervened, loss would have been avoided[289], indications to date are that the Irish courts might impose a stricter liability[290]. The directors of an Irish 'two-person' or single-member private company should exercise great caution and where an active role is not taken, resignation should be seriously considered. Indeed it seems there are greater duties of diligence owed in the context of a private company than in a public company[291]. This is particularly true because of the rules concerning disqualification of directors, reckless trading and the general possibilities of incurring personal liability which loom ominously before all directors, shadow directors and non-participating nominee directors alike. An even more recent example is the case of *Re Contract Packaging Ltd*[292], where Flood J imposed personal liability on the wife of one of the directors under s 297 of the CA 1963 for fraudulent trading and s 298 of the CA 1963 for breach of fiduciary duty. Indeed, it was ordered that the family home of the husband and wife directors be delivered up to the liquidator. Although these examples of increased liability do not arise from tortious duties it is thought they are still relevant to the present discussion.

[15.084] When a director is present at a meeting it is no defence for him to claim to have not been listening, asleep or otherwise inattentive while the meeting was being held and when improper decisions were taken by the other directors. It is one thing not to be present, but once present, one cannot claim not to have paid attention: *Land Credit Co of Ireland v Lord Fermoy*[293].

(d) Reliance on others for advice

[15.085] Not only is a director permitted to obtain, and rely upon, advice from other officers (*Re City Equitable Fire Insurance Co Ltd)*, but he is also obliged to *seek* such

288 *Dorchester Finance Co Ltd v Stebbing* [1989] BCLC 498, a case which was heard in 1977 but went unreported for 12 years. See also, (1980) 1 Co Law 38.

289 See Trebilcock, 'The Liability of Company Directors For Negligence' (1969) 32 MLR 499.

290 See, for example, *Re Hunting Lodges Ltd* [1985] ILRM 75 considered at para **[15.049]** *ante*.

291 See also *Brenes & Co v Downie* (1914) SC 97 at 104.

292 *Re Contract Packaging Ltd* (16 January 1992, unreported) HC *per* Flood J, reported in (1992) Irish Times, 17 January. The author wishes to thank Mr Michael McInerney, Solicitor for bringing this case to his attention.

293 *Land Credit Co of Ireland v Lord Fermoy* (1870) LR 5 Ch App 763.

advice[294]. Where a director signs a company cheque, Romer J stated in *Re City Equitable Fire Insurance Co Ltd* that the director should satisfy himself that there is an authorising resolution, which should preferably specify the proposed payee. It has been said that such suggestions are impracticable for large companies[295].

(e) Tortious liability to third parties

[15.086] The question of a director being held liable to third parties is a difficult one and its answer is largely dependent upon the extension of the general principles of foreseeable liability in the law of negligence. Here, we are concerned with liability to outsiders of the company. In *WB Anderson & Sons v Rhodes*[296], a director was held liable for negligently supervising the accounts of his company and for not realising that one of the company's debtors had amassed dangerously large debts to the company. The buyer of shares in the company was thus duped, as was a subsequent third party supplier who was told that the company was financially healthy[297]. However, it was said in *Mutual Citizens' Assurance Co Ltd v Evatt*[298] that for a person to be liable to third parties the person must give his advice in a professional capacity meaning that a director must hold himself out as having the requisite knowledge to advise the third party.

[15.087] In *Williams and another v Natural Life Health Foods Ltd and another*[299], the English House of Lords overruled a Court of Appeal decision that would have had significant adverse consequences for directors of companies. The Court of Appeal had held[300] that a franchisee had been persuaded to take on a franchise in reliance upon the personal expertise of the director of the franchisor company and that there were special circumstances that displaced the presumption that the company alone was responsible. This was reversed by the House of Lords, which held, on the evidence, that there was an insufficient relationship between the franchisee and the director as to result in the director assuming responsibility. It further held that the appropriate test was an objective test as to whether or not the franchisee (who claimed the director had made representations) could reasonably rely on the director's assumption of personal liability in respect of the representations. Lord Steyn said:

> 'In the present case a triangular position is under consideration: the prospective franchisees, the franchisor company, and the director. In such a case where the personal liability of the director is in question the internal arrangements between a director and his company cannot be the foundation of a director's personal liability in tort. The enquiry must be whether the director, or anybody on his behalf, conveyed directly or indirectly to

---

294 See *Fry v Tapson* (1884) 28 Ch D 268, where directors were said to be correct in seeking independent advice in respect of the valuation of a property which it was proposed to take as security for a mortgage.

295 See Loose & Yelland, *The Company Director* (6th edn, Jordans, 1987) at para 4.8.2.

296 *WB Anderson & Sons v Rhodes* [1967] 2 All ER 850.

297 See also *Hedley Byrne & Co Ltd v Heller & Partners Ltd* [1963] 2 All ER 575.

298 *Mutual Citizens' Assurance Co Ltd v Evatt* [1971] 1 All ER 150.

299 *Williams and another v Natural Life Health Foods Ltd and another* [1998] BCC 428. For comment on the House of Lords' decision, see Milman, 'Personal Liability of Directors: Aiding an Enterprise Culture?' (1999*) Palmer's In Company*, Issue 2/99, 12 February 1999.

300 For comment, on the Court of Appeal decision see Milman, 'Directors Under Fire' (1997) Palmer's In Company, Issue 4/97, 16 April 1997.

> the prospective franchisees that the director assumed personal responsibility towards the prospective franchisees[301].'

It was also held that the director could not be regarded as a joint tortfeasor with the company as to do so would expose directors, officers and employees of companies carrying on business to a plethora of new tort claims[302]. Whether a director owes an 'independent duty' will depend upon the facts of the case, and in *Shrinkwin v Quinn-Con Ltd*[303] it was held that a director had placed himself in a relationship of proximity to the plaintiff.

Judicial relief for directors and indemnities

(a) Judicial relief for directors and other officers

[15.088] Section 391 of the CA 1963 confers discretion on the court to relieve directors from liability in certain circumstances. It provides:

> '(1) If in any proceeding for negligence, default, breach of duty or breach of trust against an officer of a company or a person employed by a company as auditor, it appears to the court hearing the case that that officer or person is or may be liable in respect of the negligence, default, breach of duty or breach of trust, but that he has acted honestly and reasonably, and that, having regard to all the circumstances of the case, including those connected with his appointment, he ought fairly to be excused for the negligence, default, breach of duty or breach of trust, that court may relieve him, either wholly or partly from his liability on such terms as the court may think fit.
>
> (2) Where any such officer or person as aforesaid has reason to apprehend that any claim will or might be made against him in respect of any negligence, default, breach of duty or breach of trust, he may apply to the court for relief, and the court on any such application shall have the same power to relieve him as under this section it would have had if it had been a court before which proceedings against that person for negligence, default, breach of duty or breach of trust had been brought.
>
> (3) Where any case to which subsection (1) applies is being tried by a judge with a jury, the judge, after hearing the evidence, may, if he is satisfied that the defendant ought in pursuance of that subsection to be relieved, either in whole or in part, from the liability sought to be enforced against him, withdraw the case in whole or in part from the jury, and direct judgment to be entered for the defendant on such terms as to costs or otherwise as the judge may think proper.'

Section 391 of the CA 1963 would seem not to have received scrutiny by an Irish court[304]. The circumstances in which relief may be granted are seen in a number of

---

301 *Williams and another v Natural Life Health Foods Ltd and another* [1998] BCC 428 at 433. Lord Steyn gave, as an example where this had been proved, *Fairline Shipping Corp v Adamson* [1975] QB 180.

302 *Cf AWA Ltd v Daniels* [1995] 16 ACSR 607 where an Australian court held that directors can be guilty of negligence and thus joint tortfeasors. For comment, see Marks, 'Taking Responsibility: The New Regime for Directors' (1998) In House Lawyer 36.

303 *Shrinkwin v Quinn-Con Ltd* [2001] 1 IR 514. See further, Ch 5, *Disregarding Separate Legal Personality*, at para **[5.018]**.

304 For a concise note on the invocation of the similar English provision in the courts of England and Wales, see and Linklater, 'Section 727 Relief From Liability – Redundant or Relevant' (2002) Company Law Newsletter, Issue 3/2002.

English decisions. In *Duckwari plc v Offerventure Ltd and another (No 2)*[305], Nourse LJ held that a statutory liability arising under s 322(3)(b) of the English 1985 Act (see s 29 of the Irish CA 1990) was 'a liability in respect of default' within the meaning of the equivalent English section (s 727 of the English 1985 Act)[306]. In *Coleman Taymar Ltd et al v Oakes and another*[307], however, it was stated that relief under the similar English provision[308] could be granted in respect of a liability occasioned by a breach of fiduciary duty or arising out of an account for profits or an inquiry as to damages[309].

[15.089] It is an absolute precondition to the grant of relief under s 391 of the CA 1963 that a supplicant officer has acted 'honestly and reasonably'[310]. But how does the latter reference to 'reasonableness' sit against a claim for relief where the officer has been negligent? Interpreting the similar English provision, s 727 of the Companies Act 1985 (UK), Hoffmann LJ said in *Re D'Jan of London Ltd*[311] that the section:

> '… gives the court a discretionary power to relieve a director wholly or in part from liability for breaches of duty, including negligence, if the court considers that he acted honestly and reasonably and ought fairly to be excused. It may seem odd that a person found to have been guilty of negligence, which involves failing to take reasonable care, can ever satisfy a court that he acted reasonably. Nevertheless, the section clearly contemplates that he may do so and it follows that conduct may be reasonable for the purposes of s 727 despite amounting to lack of reasonable care at common law.'

In *Bairstow et al v Queens Moat Houses plc et al*[312], a director was found to be liable for unlawfully paying dividends where the company had insufficient distributable reserves. Nelson J said that 'even if under the rules of negligence a director ought to have known of the facts which rendered the payments unlawful, the court may nevertheless relieve him from liability if considering his personal situation it was reasonable that he did not in fact know'. The 'guilty of negligence but relieved on account of reasonableness' paradox can therefore be resolved by focussing upon the degree of culpability of the director's conduct. In that case, Nelson J said that 'if his conduct was honest but he was nevertheless guilty of negligence, he might still be relieved from liability if his negligence was not gross but the "kind of thing which could happen to any busy man"'[313]. The court did not grant relief because it found that the directors had not acted

305 *Duckwari plc v Offerventure Ltd and another (No 2)* [1999] BCC 11 (Court of Appeal).

306 See Ch 16, *Statutory Regulation of Directors' Transactions*, at para **[16.022]**.

307 *Coleman Taymar Ltd et al v Oakes and another* [2001] 2 BCLC 749.

308 Section 727(1) of the English Companies Act 1985.

309 *Cf* in *Customs and Excise Commissioners v Hedon Alfa Ltd* [1981] 1 QB 81, it was held that relief under the similar English provision was only available in respect of a claim against a director for breach of duty, negligence default or trust in an action brought by the company.

310 *National Trustees Co of Australia v General Finance Co of Australia* [1905] AC 373. See also *Bairstow et al v Queens Moat Houses plc* [2001] EWCA Civ 712, [2001] 2 BCLC 531 where the English Court of Appeal held that 'honesty and reasonableness are absolutely necessary preconditions' and held that it was not open to a judge, having found former directors to have been guilty of dishonesty in preparing false accounts, to find that they had acted honestly and reasonably in paying any dividends on the strength of those accounts.

311 *Re D'Jan of London Ltd* [1993] BCC 646 at 648H–649B.

312 *Bairstow et al v Queens Moat Houses plc et al* [2001] EWCA Civ 712, [2001] 2 BCLC 531.

313 At para 1.035, incorporating a quotation from Hoffmann LJ in *Re D'Jan of London Ltd* [1993] BCC 646 at 649C.

honestly or reasonably. In *Re Brian D Pierson (Contractors) Ltd*[314], the court excused directors from liability for certain misfeasance claims, but not others. There it was held that a failure to obtain payment for goodwill in selling part of the company's business could not be regarded as *reasonable* but the making redundant of two senior employees was reasonable, although only to the extent that proper redundancy payments had been granted to them.

[15.090] The position is, therefore, a legislative fudge that vests in the courts a discretion to take all circumstances into account in deciding whether or not to make an officer personally liable. The court is indeed expressly directed by s 391 to have 'regard to all the circumstances of the case'. So in *Coleman Taymar Ltd et al v Oakes and another*[315] it was said:

> 'It does not follow that merely because a director has acted (subjectively) honestly and (objectively) reasonably the court is bound to excuse him. Proof that a director has acted honesty and reasonably are preconditions of the court's jurisdiction. Once the conditions are fulfilled, the court must consider whether in all the circumstances the director ought fairly to be excused, and if so may (not must) relieve him either absolutely or partly on the terms the court thinks fit[316].'

In that case, a director had used company confidential information to negotiate the purchase of leases personally, had failed to disclose his interest to the company and had competed with the company. It was found that the company was entitled to an inquiry as to any benefit that had accrued to the director from the breach of duty and to nominal damages for the director's breach of contract. It was, however, held that the director was entitled to relief from liability for engaging in competition since he had acted honestly and reasonably.

(b) Indemnities for directors and other officers

[15.091] Directors may not rely upon provisions in companies' articles of association which have the effect of exempting or indemnifying company officers from any liability in respect of negligence, default, breach of duty or breach of trust[317]. Section 200(1) of the CA 1963 provides:

> '(1) Subject as hereinafter provided, any provision whether contained in the articles of a company or in any contract with a company or otherwise for exempting any officer of the company or any person employed by the company as auditor from, or indemnifying him against, any liability which by virtue of any rule of law would otherwise attach to him in respect of any negligence, default, breach of duty or breach of trust of which he may be guilty in relation to the company shall be void, so, however, that—
>
> (a) nothing in this section shall operate to deprive any person of any exemption or right to be indemnified in respect of anything done or omitted to be done by him while any such provision was in force; and
>
> (b) notwithstanding anything in this section, a company may, in pursuance of any such provision as aforesaid, indemnify any such officer or auditor against any

[314] *Re Brian D Pierson (Contractors) Ltd* [1998] BCC 26.

[315] *Coleman Taymar Ltd et al v Oakes and another* [2001] 2 BCLC 749.

[316] *Coleman Taymar Ltd et al v Oakes and another* [2001] 2 BCLC 749 at 770.

[317] See Passmore, 'Directors' Indemnities' (1995) 16 Company Lawyer 243.

> liability incurred by him in defending proceedings, whether civil or criminal, in which judgment is given in his favour or in which he is acquitted, or in connection with any application under section 391 in which relief is granted to him by the court.'

Accordingly, a company can be bound to indemnify an officer for that officer's legal costs incurred in civil or criminal proceedings taken against him provided he is successful in defending such proceedings. Companies cannot, however, be bound by any provision in the articles of association or a contract which exempt or indemnify a director. Moreover, it is not just present directors who are caught by s 200: sub-s (5) provides that a reference in the section to an officer or auditor includes any *former* or current officer or auditor.

[15.092] There are, however, limits to the scope of s 200 of the CA 1963[318], and it does not prevent companies from giving their directors an indemnity of sorts. Model form articles of association provide such an indemnity in reg 138 of Part I of Table A:

> 'Every director, managing director, agent, auditor, secretary and other officer for the time being of the company shall be indemnified out of the assets of the company against any liability incurred by him in defending any proceedings, whether civil or criminal, in relation to his acts while acting in such office, in which judgment is given in his favour or in which he is acquitted or in connection with any application under section 391 of the Act in which relief is granted to him by the court.'

Although the general rule is that the articles are only enforceable between the company and its members, *qua* member, *inter se*, the courts have been easily satisfied that the indemnity in reg 138 has been incorporated into contracts between companies and their directors and auditors[319].

[15.093] While any provision in a contract or articles exempting a director from liability in the circumstances described in s 200 is void, this does not preclude a company from *actually* exempting or indemnifying an officer where it believes this to be in its own best interests. Whereas an officer may not enforce such a provision in a contract, the section does not prevent companies from voluntarily agreeing to exempt or indemnify an officer. So what the provision actually does is to remove any certainty or comfort that an officer may derive from a contract for exempting or indemnifying him. Also, s 200 does not render void a contract which provides for an exemption or indemnity in respect of an officer of that company's holding company, subsidiary company or sister subsidiary company. In such circumstances, normal fiduciary duties on disclosure of conflicts and other provisions concerning self-dealing would have to be complied with but subject to that, such an indemnity or exemption could be granted without breaching s 200 of the CA 1963.

(c) Directors' and officers' liability insurance

[15.094] For years there was a question mark over directors' and officers' insurance: did s 200 of the CA 1963 render such insurance void? This question was finally answered in

---

318 See Gregory, 'The Scope of the Companies Act 1948, Section 205' (1983) 98 LQR 413; Birds, 'Permissible Scope of Excluding Articles' [1976] 39 MLR 394.

319 See *John et al v Price Waterhouse and another* [2001] TLR 533.

the negative by an amendment to s 200, through the insertion of sub-ss (2) to (4) which now provide:

> '(2) Notwithstanding subsection (1), a company may purchase and maintain for any of its officers or auditors insurance in respect of any liability referred to in that subsection.
>
> (3) Notwithstanding any provision contained in an enactment, the articles of a company or otherwise, a director may be counted in the quorum and may vote on any resolution to purchase or maintain any insurance under which the director might benefit.
>
> (4) Any directors' and officers' insurance purchased or maintained by a company before the date on which the amendments made to this section by the Companies (Auditing and Accounting) Act 2003 came into operation is as valid and effective as it would have been if those amendments had been in operation when that insurance was purchased or maintained.'

[C] Directors' Statutory Duties Arising on Insolvency

[15.095] Generally, all directors owe a statutory duty to their companies to ensure that the requirements of the Companies Acts are complied with by the company[320]. This section is concerned with the statutory duties owed by directors where a company becomes insolvent. The following matters are considered:

1. Reckless trading.
2. Criminal fraudulent trading.
3. Civil fraudulent trading.
4. Personal liability for failure to keep proper books of account.
5. Section 251 of the CA 1990: invocation of statutory remedies where a company is not being wound up.
6. Misfeasance.

Reckless trading

[15.096] The civil remedy of reckless trading arising out of proceedings under the C(A)A 1990 was first introduced by s 33 of that Act. This has now been repealed by s 138 of the CA 1990 which inserted s 297A of the CA 1963. Proceedings for reckless trading can arise in two distinct circumstances[321]:

(a) during an examinership; or
(b) during a winding up.

Before considering the circumstances in which proceedings for reckless trading can be brought, it is proposed to first consider the actual principles of law applicable to reckless trading.

[15.097] The principal section on reckless trading is s 297A of the CA 1963, which provides that:

---

320 Section 383(3) of the CA 1963 as replaced by s 100 of the CLEA 2001.

321 See Flynn, 'Reckless Trading' (1991) ILT 186; MacCann, 'Reckless Trading Revisited' (1993) ILT 31; Kettle, 'Improper Trading in Ireland and Britain' (1994) ILT 91. For a prospective analysis of the possibilities of reckless trading coming into Irish law, see Ussher, *Company Law in Ireland* (1986) at p 530 *et seq*.

> (1) If in the course of winding up of a company or in the course of proceedings under the Companies (Amendment) Act 1990, it appears that—
>
> (a) any person was, while an officer of the company, knowingly a party to the carrying on of any business of the company in a reckless manner ...
>
> the court, on the application of the receiver, examiner, liquidator or any other creditor or contributory of the company, may, if it thinks it proper to do so, declare that such person shall be personally responsible without any limitation of liability, for all or any part of the debts or other liabilities of the company as the court may direct.'

Irish law thereby encompasses the concept whereby the officers, including the directors and shadow directors[322] of a company can be made personally liable for the debts of the company where it is shown that they acted *recklessly*. The first question which must be addressed on an application for reckless trading is: was the respondent a party to the carrying on of the business in a reckless manner?

(a) The meaning of 'knowingly' and 'reckless'

[15.098] Before personal liability can be imposed upon an officer it must be shown that he has been *knowingly* a party to the carrying on of any business of the company in a *reckless* manner. Under this heading, the circumstances in which a person can be found to have *in fact* been knowingly reckless are considered. This contrasts with the situation where a person may not have been in fact knowingly reckless but where he is deemed in law to have been reckless[323].

[15.099] The meaning of the word *reckless* poses great difficulties of interpretation. Traditionally, a person would only be said to be reckless if he actually contemplated the particular consequences of his actions, and went on to consciously run the risk of such consequences ensuing. This is known as the *Cunningham* test of recklessness[324]. However there is another possible test, known as the *Cauldwell* test[325] which holds that a person will be reckless even where he does not appreciate the risks consequential upon his actions, where such risks would have been appreciated by a reasonable man. The difference between the two tests is that the former is subjective and the latter objective. The leading Irish case on recklessness is in the context of criminal law: *People v Murray*[326]. In that case, the Supreme Court delivered five opinions, each of which involved different tests of recklessness. One foreign judgment on recklessness, which comes from the Republic of South Africa, is *State v Goertz*[327]. That case concerned the meaning of recklessness in the context of the South African provision of reckless trading[328]. There, an objective test was favoured and it was not necessary for the person to have actually adverted to the risk involved, it being merely required that the person 'acted recklessly judged by the standards of reasonable businessmen'.

---

322 Section 297A(10) of the CA 1963.

323 See para **[15.103]** *et seq*, *post*.

324 *R v Cunningham* [1957] 2 All ER 412.

325 *R v Cauldwell* [1982] AC 341.

326 *People v Murray* [1977] IR 360. See McAleese, 'Just What is Recklessness?' (1981) DULJ 29.

327 *State v Goertz* (1980) (1) SA 269.

328 Section 424(1) of the Companies Act 1973 (RSA).

[15.100] The leading Irish decision on reckless trading is *Re Hefferon Kearns Ltd*[329]. The facts were that the respondents in the proceedings for personal responsibility for the debts and liabilities of the company were the directors of an ill-fated building company called Hefferon Kearns Ltd. Incorporated in 1988, it commenced trading in 1989 with an issued share capital of £202, the majority of the shares being held by the respondent directors. The company had three main contracts, in respect of construction work at Simmonscourt, Malahide and Rathgar. Six months after the company commenced trading, management accounts were prepared, which showed that to June 1989, the company had suffered a net loss of £73,101. In his judgment, Lynch J remarked that while indicating insolvency:

> '... the summer had arrived: the company had good contracts on hand: and the defendants as directors, having considered the position, were confident that the losses could be reversed and were proved right in that the audited accounts for the year ending the 31st December 1989 showed a net loss of only £8,113[330].'

Optimism had reasonably prevailed. Because of the loss in 1989 the directors sought and obtained bi-monthly management accounts so as to keep the trading position of the company under control and scrutiny. Those accounts, up to 31 July 1990, showed total losses (including the losses carried from 1989) of £142,507. In the opinion of Lynch J, the accounts 'indicated a very serious crisis as to the viability of the company at that time'[331]. Previously, in May of 1990, two of the directors had borrowed £45,000 personally which was indirectly used to finance the company and the net effect of which was to result in their incurring personal liability 'in order to improve the company's cash flow'[332].

The directors usually met for an informal directors' meeting each Monday. Immediately after the building trade holidays in August 1990, the directors met and considered the position of the company in the light of the accounts available. It was agreed that an urgent review of the company's trading position was required and it was resolved at that meeting that each of the four respondent directors would be assigned different tasks, the cumulative effect of which was designed to examine work on hand. At that meeting it was decided to continue trading to give priority to the Rathgar contract but to complete the others and to try to control and reduce costs in so far as possible. The company's auditors were also instructed to prepare further accounts, on a doomsday basis, so as to assist the directors in deciding whether the company was viable.

The directors managed to discharge debts to the end of August, but realised by mid-September that they would have great difficulty in meeting payments at the end of September. Accordingly, another meeting was convened for 17 September 1990, at which one of the directors collapsed and was removed to hospital. On his discharge from

329 *Dublin Heating Company Ltd v Hefferon et al* (14 January 1993, unreported) HC *per* Lynch J at p 44 of the transcript.

330 *Dublin Heating Company Ltd v Hefferon et al* (14 January 1993, unreported) HC *per* Lynch J at pp 5,6 of the transcript.

331 *Dublin Heating Company Ltd v Hefferon et al* (14 January 1993, unreported) HC *per* Lynch J at p 6 of the transcript.

332 *Dublin Heating Company Ltd v Hefferon et al* (14 January 1993, unreported) HC *per* Lynch J at p 7 of transcript.

hospital on 27 September the meeting was reconvened at his home (against medical advice). At that meeting their review was completed: the contracts at Simmonscourt and Malahide would be abandoned or rescinded and Rathgar would be pursued as the best chance to get money for their creditors. It was also decided that two of the directors would commence approaching creditors individually in an attempt to secure their co-operation for a moratorium. The minutes of the meeting indicated that achieving fairness amongst the creditors was paramount in the directors' minds.

The meetings with the company's creditors did not run smoothly and creditors began calling on some of the directors at their homes. Lynch J accepted one director's description of this as 'involving extreme pressure and a nightmare'[333]. Eventually, it was resolved that individual meetings with the creditors were futile, and so it was resolved to call a general meeting of the creditors. At that meeting the creditors by a majority decided to apply for the appointment of an examiner. The application was successful, an examiner was appointed and arising from that appointment, proceedings for reckless trading were instituted against the four director respondents under s 33 of the C(A)A 1990.

[15.101] Having set out in full s 33 of the C(A)A 1990, and the submissions by both the plaintiffs and the defendants, Lynch J reviewed the meaning of 'reckless'. In particular, he noted[334] that the Supreme Court considered the meaning of 'reckless' in *Donovan v Landys Ltd*[335] and that Kingsmill Moore J had quoted Megaw J in *Shawinigan v Vokins*[336], which Lynch J said seemed to him 'to go to the root of the matter and to constitute the best and most realistic test of recklessness which has yet been propounded in cases of Tort'. What Kingsmill Moore J (and Lynch J) thought worthy of quoting *in extenso* was the following:

> 'In my view reckless means grossly careless. Recklessness is gross carelessness – the doing of something which in fact involves a risk whether the doer realises it or not: and the risk being such having regard to all the circumstances that the taking of that risk would be described in ordinary parlance as reckless. The likelihood or otherwise that damage will follow is one element to be considered not whether the doer of the act actually realised the likelihood. The extent of the damage which is likely to follow is another element not the wisdom or folly happens to foresee. If the risk is slight and the damage which will follow if things go wrong is small it may not be reckless however unjustified the doing of the act may be. If the risk is great and the probable damage great recklessness may readily be a fair description however much the doer may regard the action as justified and reasonable. Each case has to be viewed on its own particular facts and not by reference to any formula. The only test in my view is an objective one. Would a reasonable man knowing all the facts and circumstances which the doer of the act knew or ought to have known describe the act as reckless in the ordinary meaning of that word in ordinary speech? As I have said my understanding of the ordinary meaning of that word is a high degree of carelessness[337].'

333 *Dublin Heating Company Ltd v Hefferon et al* (14 January 1993, unreported) HC *per* Lynch J at p 14 of the transcript.

334 *Dublin Heating Company Ltd v Hefferon et al* (14 January 1993, unreported) HC *per* Lynch J at p 41 of the transcript.

335 *Donovan v Landys Ltd* [1963] IR 441.

336 *Shawinigan v Vokins* [1961] 1 WLR 1206.

337 *Shawinigan v Vokins* [1961] 1 WLR 1206 at 1214.

The foregoing test of recklessness is expressly *objective* and follows that described in *R v Cauldwell*, above[338]. What is notable is that having implicitly adopted this to be the appropriate meaning of the word 'reckless' in s 33(1), Lynch J went on to hold that such could not be juxtaposed onto reckless trading within the meaning of that section. Thus he said:

> 'The inclusion of the word 'knowingly' in sub-s (1) (a) of s 33 must have been intended by the Oireachtas to have some effect on the nature of the reckless conduct required to come within the sub-section. I think that its inclusion requires that the director is party to carrying on the business in a manner which the director knows very well involves an obvious and serious risk of loss or damage to others and yet ignores that risk because he does not really care whether such others suffer loss or damage or because his selfish desire to keep his own company alive overrides any concern which he ought to have for others[339].'

In the present case, Lynch J held that there was no evidence of recklessness within the meaning of the section and that he was not satisfied that the directors were *knowingly* a party to the carrying on of any business of the company in a reckless manner within the meaning of s 33(1)(a). Indeed, on the contrary he found that the directors were: concerned about the effects of a forced liquidation on creditors and traded in the hope and belief they would do better by the company so trading than by immediate liquidation; had diligently tried to achieve profitable trading; had guaranteed the company's debt; and were willing to surrender their shareholding in another company for the benefit of Hefferon Kearns Ltd. Accordingly, this first test for reckless trading, whilst appearing to be objective, must be construed in the light of the word 'knowingly', and is thus tempered by subjectivity.

[15.102] The reference in s 297A(2)(a) to having regard 'to the general knowledge, skill and experience that may reasonably be expected of a person in his position' is not, however, relevant to the consideration of whether a person is reckless within the meaning of s 297A(1)(a). As Finlay Geoghegan J held in *Re PSK Construction Ltd; Kavanagh v Killeen and Higgins*[340], s 297A(2) is directed at 'additional circumstances in which an officer may be *deemed* to have been knowingly a party to the carrying on of any business'[341]. In that case an application was made to, *inter alia*, find two directors liable for reckless trading arising from the decision to keep the company's business going by under-declaring and under-paying to the Revenue Commissioners. The applicant contended that that decision had been taken to the knowledge of each respondent and was an obvious and serious risk of loss or damage to creditors which was ignored by reason of a desire to keep the company alive. On the evidence, Finlay Geoghegan J held that the applicant had established that the first respondent, Mr Killeen, as a matter of probability must have known that if he continued trading by under-declaring and under-paying tax, such a decision involved an obvious and serious risk of loss or damage to creditors. However, it was found that the applicant had not

338 See para **[15.099]** *ante*.

339 *Dublin Heating Company Ltd v Hefferon et al* (14 January 1993, unreported) HC at p 42 of the transcript.

340 *Re PSK Construction Ltd; Kavanagh v Killeen and Higgins* [2009] IEHC 538.

341 *Re PSK Construction Ltd; Kavanagh v Killeen and Higgins* [2009] IEHC 538 at para 28. Emphasis added.

established as a matter of probability that the other director, Ms Higgins (an executive director who did not hold a senior position)[342] had sufficient knowledge about the financial position of the company at the relevant time.

(b) Deemed reckless trading

[15.103] Even if a person is not, in fact, found to have been knowingly a party to the carrying on of business in a reckless manner, he can be *deemed in law* to have been reckless in either of the two circumstances detailed in s 297A(2) of the CA 1963. This subsection provides:

> 'Without prejudice to the generality of sub-s (1)(a), an officer of a company shall be deemed to have been knowingly a party to the carrying on of any business of the company in a reckless manner if—
>
> (a) he was a party to the carrying on of such business and, having regard to the general knowledge, skill and experience that may reasonably be expected of a person in his position, he ought to have known that his actions or those of the company would cause loss to the creditors of the company, or any of them, or
>
> (b) he was a party to the contracting of a debt by the company and did not honestly believe on reasonable grounds that the company would be able to pay the debt when it fell due for payment as well as all its other debts (taking into account the contingent and prospective liabilities).'

This was considered by Lynch J in *Re Hefferon Kearns Ltd (No 2)*[343] who, after finding no recklessness in fact, said of s 33(2) of the C(A)A 1990 (now s 297A(2) of the CA 1963):

> 'Sub-s (2) does not affect or extend the meaning of sub-s (1)(a) but it extends the application of sub-s (1)(a) to the cases mentioned in paragraphs (a) and (b) of sub-s (2) even though the director was not guilty of reckless trading within the meaning of sub-s (1)(a) itself as interpreted by me above. Sub-s (2) deems a director to be guilty of reckless trading in the circumstances set out in paragraphs (a) and (b) and that presupposes that otherwise he would not be so guilty[344].'

Interpreting this provision involving 'deemed recklessness' Lynch J considered that the essential question was whether a person ought to have known that his actions or those of the company would cause loss to the creditors of the company or any of them. Lynch J said it was crucial to a finding of *deemed* reckless trading that there be found:

> '... knowledge or imputed knowledge that the ... defendant's actions or those of the company *would* cause loss to creditors: it is not sufficient that there might be some worry or uncertainty as to the ability to pay all creditors. The requirement is that the ... defendant knew or ought to have known that his actions or those of the company would cause loss to creditors[345].'

---

342 Ms Higgins sought to describe herself as a 'non-executive' director, by which she means that she was an employee of the company (and so, *ipso facto* an executive director) but had no executive or management role, who acted under Mr Killeen's direction.

343 *Re Hefferon Kearns Ltd (No 2)* (14 January 1993, unreported) HC.

344 *Re Hefferon Kearns Ltd (No 2)* (14 January 1993, unreported) HC at p 44 of the transcript.

345 *Re Hefferon Kearns Ltd (No 2)* (14 January 1993, unreported) HC at p 45 of the transcript.

While this is an objective test, on the facts of the case Lynch J found that the director concerned 'had good reason to believe that the company would be able to pay all its creditors falling due for payment' at the relevant time, 'had reasonably expected extra monies' arising from the company's contracts, and that the directors 'reasonably expected that no further losses would be incurred on those contracts but rather gains ... ' Accordingly, there was no evidence within s 297A(2)(a) by which to deem the directors guilty of reckless trading. In *Re PSK Construction Ltd; Kavanagh v Killeen and Higgins*[346], Finlay Geoghegan J also refused to deem a director who held a junior position in the company to have been knowingly a party to the carrying on of the company's business in a reckless manner. In this respect, it would seem that having knowledge that the company was engaged in tax evasion (the under-declaring of income and under-payment of tax) on a temporary basis is not sufficient, *per se*, to justify a finding of deemed recklessness.

[15.104] Section 297A(2)(b) sets out the second limb of the second test by which a person may be *deemed* to have been knowingly guilty of reckless trading. Where a person did not honestly believe on reasonable grounds that the company would be able to pay its debts, as they fell due, he will be deemed to have been knowingly guilty of reckless trading. Of the application of this ground, Lynch J said that he was:

> '... not satisfied that as at the 29th of August 1990 and the weeks immediately thereafter the ... defendant did not honestly believe on reasonable grounds that the company would be able to pay the debt when it fell due for payment as well as its other debts (taking into account the contingent and prospective liabilities).'

Here too, although an objective test applied, Lynch J held on the facts of the case that the individual director concerned honestly believed that, *at that time*, the debts of the company could be paid as they fell due. *After that time* (28 September), the continued trading of the company was still:

> 'mainly in the interests of the creditors because ... [he] ... believed that an immediate winding-up would be far more detrimental to creditors than continuing to trade ...'

However, Lynch J went on to hold that by continuing to trade after 28 September the director was *deemed to have traded recklessly*. This was the case although the director had acted honestly and *bona fide* in what appeared to be the best interests of the creditors. The learned judge said that the director:

> '... was in fact a party to the contracting of debts, by the company at a time when he knew that those debts, together with all the other debts of the company, including contingent and prospective liabilities, could not be paid by the company as they fell due. In these circumstances in respect of the period from the 28th of September to the 11th of October 1990 the ... defendant falls within the ambit of paragraph (b) of sub-s (2) though not necessarily within the ambit of paragraph (a) because he believed that the loss (if any) to be caused to creditors or any of them would be less than immediate liquidation[347].'

Notwithstanding that the defendant was guilty of reckless trading, albeit of the *deemed* variety, Lynch J went on to absolve him by invoking his discretionary jurisdiction

---

[346] *Re PSK Construction Ltd; Kavanagh v Killeen and Higgins* [2009] IEHC 538.

[347] *Re PSK Construction Ltd; Kavanagh v Killeen and Higgins* [2009] IEHC 538 at p 47 of the transcript.

provided in the equivalent of s 297A(6) which is similar to that in s 391 of the CA 1963[348].

The judgment of Lynch J is welcome not least for its understanding of the realities of commercial life. Indeed, the judgment may be seen as a reaction against the rigours of s 297A(2)(b). In the course of his judgment Lynch J said[349]:

> 'Paragraph (b) of sub-s (2) appears to be a very wide ranging and indeed draconian measure and could apply in the case of virtually every company which becomes insolvent and has to cease trading for that reason. If, for example, a company became insolvent because of the domino effect of the insolvency of a large debtor, it would be reasonable for the directors to continue trading for a time thereafter to assess the situation and almost inevitably they would incur some debts which would fall within paragraph (b) before finally closing down. It would not be in the interests of the community that whenever there might appear to be any significant danger that a company was going to become insolvent, the directors should immediately cease trading and close down the business. Many businesses which might well have survived by continuing to trade coupled with remedial measures could be lost to the community.'

It is submitted that where a company gets into difficulties which, it is thought, may result in the company having to cease business, it would be prudent for the directors to record and minute all business decisions taken in as detailed a fashion as possible up to the time of cessation of trading. This would have the effect of focusing the minds of the directors on the harsh realities of their plight, hastening the demise of a hopelessly insolvent company, and providing the directors with a documentary record of the last weeks which could become evidence of their *bona fides* in any future reckless trading proceedings.

(c) The requirement that the company is insolvent

[15.105] Section 297A(3)(a) provides that a court can only grant a declaration of personal responsibility if the requirements provided for in s 214 (a), (b) or (c) of the CA 1963 apply to the company concerned. By this is meant that the company is unable to pay its debts (of at least €1,269.74) when demanded under the 21-day demand procedure[350], or execution on the company is returned unsatisfied, or it is proved to the court that the company is unable to pay its debts.

(d) The meaning of 'a party' and 'business'

[15.106] In respect of all possible respondents to an action for reckless trading, s 297A(1)(a) provides that they must have been 'knowingly a party to the carrying on of any business of the company in a reckless manner'. Previously, we have considered the meaning of 'knowingly' and 'reckless'. Two further concepts now require examination.

The first is that the respondent must have been 'a party to' the reckless conduct. As we have already seen, the view taken by some of the Irish High Court judges is such as to indicate that where a person becomes a director, they undertake the responsibilities and duties of directors. In *Re Hunting Lodges Ltd*[351] (a case which concerned fraudulent trading), Carroll J accepted the meaning of to be 'a party to' as indicating no more than

---

348 See para **[15.088]** *ante* and para **[15.112]** *post*.

349 *Re Hefferon Kearns Ltd (No 2)* (14 January 1993, unreported) HC at p 47 of the transcript.

350 See Ch 23, *Winding Up Companies*, at para **[23.075]**.

351 *Re Hunting Lodges Ltd* [1985] ILRM 75.

'participates in', 'takes part in' or 'concurs in', as was stated by Pennycuick VC in *Maidstone Buildings Provisions Ltd*[352]. Carroll J went on to observe, and apparently adopt, Pennycuick VC's observation that some positive steps were required. It remains to be determined whether or not inert disinterest will constitute being *knowingly* a party. In the South African case of *Cronje No v Stone*[353], a director, who was also a large shareholder in the company, never became actively involved in the business of the company. It was held that she had recklessly refrained from exercising proper control over the company and that her inertia had facilitated the mismanagement by her co-director.

[15.107] The second concept is the 'carrying on of the business[354] of the company'. It is thought that one single act of recklessness will constitute the carrying on of a company's business in a reckless manner. So in *Re Hunting Lodges Ltd*[355] Carroll J said (in the context of fraudulent trading) that:

> 'In the course of the conduct of its affairs, a company will have many different aspects of its business. One single transaction can properly be described as 'business of the company' and so also can constituent parts of a transaction[356].'

This seems a common sense approach since, were it otherwise, then one large transaction alone could not ground proceedings, whereas several minor ones could[357]. Support for this view is found in *Morris v Banque Arabe et Internationale d'Investissment SA (No 2)*[358]. In that case, Neuberger J held – in the context of fraudulent trading – that while it was necessary to prove that a respondent had participated in the fraudulent acts of the company, it was not necessary to show that such a person carried on or assisted in carrying on the company's business.

(e) The requirement to be an applicant

[15.108] Furthermore, s 297A(3)(b) provides that an applicant, being a creditor or contributory or any person on whose behalf application is made, must have:

> '... suffered loss or damage as a consequence of any behaviour mentioned in subs (1).'

In the absence of such proof, a court has no power to grant a declaration of personal responsibility against a respondent[359]. It should be noted that the meaning of 'creditor'

---

352 *Maidstone Buildings Provisions Ltd* [1971] 3 All ER 363 at 368.

353 *Cronje No v Stone* (1985) (3) SA 597 (T).

354 '... most any form of activity, apart from one pursued for pleasure or as a hobby can be described as "business",' *per* Mann J in *Corfield v Stenvwaus Garage Ltd* (1985) RTR 109 at 117.

355 *Re Hunting Lodges Ltd* [1985] ILRM 75.

356 See also *Re Gerard Cooper Chemicals Ltd* [1978] 2 All ER 49 at 53.

357 See also *Re Sarflax Ltd* [1979] 1 All ER 529 at 534 where Oliver J held: '... I feel quite unable to say that the expression "carrying on any business" in the section is necessarily synonymous with actively carrying on trade or that the collection of assets acquired in the course of business and the distribution of the proceeds of those assets in the discharge of business liabilities cannot constitute the carrying on of "any business" for the purposes of the section.'

358 *Morris v Banque Arabe et Internationale d'Investissment SA (No 2)* [2000] TLR 749.

359 See Lynch J in *Re Hefferon Kearns Ltd (No 2)* at pp 48 and 49 of the transcript. In that case insufficient proof was adduced to the court that the claimants had suffered loss or damage as a consequence of the behaviour of the respondents mentioned in s 33(1) of the C(A)A 1990.

in the context of fraudulent trading was considered in *R v Smith*[360]. In that case, the English Court of Appeal gave the broadest possible interpretation of the meaning of 'creditor', saying, *obiter dictum*, that it included contingent and prospective creditors who might come into existence after the fraudulent trading had commenced.

[15.109] Where a creditor relies upon s 297A(2)(b), above, then by s 297A(4) the court shall have regard to whether or not that creditor was at the time that the debt was incurred:

> '... aware of the company's financial state of affairs and, notwithstanding that awareness, nevertheless assented to the incurring of the debt[361].'

This will be a question of fact to be decided in each case[362]. Applicants under this provision can give evidence themselves or call witnesses[363]. Where the Director of Corporate Enforcement applies under s 251 of the CA 1990 for an order under s 297A, s 251(4)(a) provides that s 297A(7)(b) of the CA 1963 shall apply in relation to any order made pursuant to an application brought by the Director, except that no order shall be made in favour of the Director 'otherwise than as to his costs and expenses'.

(f) Potential respondents

[15.110] Section 297A(1)(a) of the CA 1963 is expressly directed at persons who are, or were, officers of the company. The term 'officers', for the purposes of the section is deemed, by s 297A(10), to include any auditor, liquidator, receiver, or shadow director. In *Ex parte Copp*[364], the question of whether a bank could be deemed a 'shadow director' arose in the context of wrongful trading under English law[365]. When the company concerned exceeded its overdraft, the lending bank sought security and successfully obtained a fixed charge on the company's book, and other, debts. This was done in furtherance of a report which was commissioned by the bank. Also in furtherance of the report, the bank appointed a receiver. Eventually, the company went into liquidation. *Inter alia*, the liquidator to the company sought an order that the bank concerned was a shadow director of the company and had *traded wrongfully*. One of the grounds relied upon by the liquidator was that, 'at an early stage, the bank was aware that the company was insolvent with no reasonable prospect of avoiding insolvent liquidation'[366]. On the facts, Knox J held that the claim against the bank was sustainable,

[360] *R v Smith* [1996] 2 BCLC 109.

[361] Section 297A(4) of the CA 1963. The use of the word 'assented' seems to indicate that consent in the formal written sense is unnecessary, and that mere tacit awareness is sufficient for the court to take cognisance. See *DKG Contracting Ltd* (1990) (UK) where it was held that ignorance of a company's financial position was no defence to proceedings for wrongful trading under s 214 of the Insolvency Act 1986 (UK), see (1990) Irish Times, 13 December.

[362] In *Re Hefferon Kearns Ltd (No 2)* at p 31 of transcript, Lynch J found that the plaintiffs were not sufficiently aware of the company's financial state of affairs to be affected by s 33(4) of the C(A)A 1990, which was equivalent to s 297A(4) of the CA 1963.

[363] Section 297A(5) of the CA 1963.

[364] *Ex parte Copp* [1989] BCLC 12; *Re a Company (No 005009 of 1987)*.

[365] In England and Wales it was decided to penalise those who engaged in 'wrongful trading', while in Ireland, 'reckless trading' was introduced: see Ussher, *Company Law in Ireland* (1986) at p 530.

[366] *Ex parte Copp* [1989] BCLC 12 at 18.

and that it was possible that the bank may have been a shadow director which had traded wrongfully.

[15.111] Another potential class of respondents are *nominee directors*[367]. In *Kuwait Asia Bank EC v National Mutual Life Nominees Ltd*[368], the Privy Council considered the question of nominee directors. In that case, a company operated as a money broker, accepting deposits from the public. To protect investing depositors, the respondent company was appointed trustee, to which the company covenanted to provide information. The appellant bank, which was a shareholder in the company, nominated two persons as directors. A depositor sued the respondent company for breach of trust and on this action being settled, the respondent sought contribution from, *inter alia*, the appellant bank. It was alleged that the nominee directors had acted in breach of their duties of care, skill and diligence and other statutory duties to the company. Following from this, the respondent alleged that the appellant bank was vicariously liable for the actions of its employee nominee directors. It was held by the Court of Appeal that the facts disclosed a cause of action. It was against this decision that the appellant appealed to the Privy Council. The Privy Council held that there was not a good arguable case against the appellant bank, refusing to hold that the bank was vicariously liable for the acts or omissions of its employees, or that the appellant bank was a shadow director:

> 'In the performance of their duties as directors ... [the two directors] were bound to ignore the interests and wishes of their employer, the [appellant] bank. They could not plead any instruction from the bank as an excuse for breach of their duties to [the company] and [the respondent]. Of course, if the bank exploited its position as employees of [the two directors] to obtain an improper advantage for the [appellant] bank or to cause harm to [the respondent] then the [appellant] bank would be liable for its own misconduct. But there is no suggestion that the [appellant] bank behaved with impropriety. Its duty to refrain from exploiting its influence over its employees is not different in principle from the duty of a father not to exploit his influence over a son who is a director or the duty of a businessman not to exploit his influence over a business associate who is a director[369].'

Where the person who nominates a director causes the nominee to *wrongly* fetter his discretion as a fiduciary, that person may be vicariously liable for the actions of the nominee directors. This will not invariably be the case: directors may fetter the future exercise of their powers where this is in the company's interests[370].

(g) Defences to reckless trading

[15.112] Section 297A(6) of the CA 1963 provides a quasi-subjective defence. This provides that where it appears to the court, that an officer:

> 'acted honestly and responsibly in relation to the conduct of the affairs of the company or any matter or matters on the ground of which such declaration is sought to be made, the

---

367 See *Cronje No v Stone* (1985) (3) SA 597, and see generally, Flynn, 'Reckless Trading' (1991) ILT 186, for an excellent analysis of the comparative law on this question. As to so-called 'token directors', see para **[15.049]** *ante*.

368 *Kuwait Asia Bank EC v National Mutual Life Nominees Ltd* [1990] 3 All ER 404, [1990] BCLC 868. See also *Re Tasbian Ltd (No 3)* [1991] BCLC 792.

369 *Kuwait Asia Bank EC v National Mutual Life Nominees Ltd* [1990] 3 All ER 404 at 424.

370 *Fulham Football Club Ltd v Cabra Estates plc* [1994] 1 BCLC 363. See para **[15.039]** *ante*.

court may, having regard to all the circumstances of the case, relieve him either wholly or in part, from personal liability on such terms as it may think fit.'

Consequently, where it appears to the court that a person acted honestly and responsibly in relation to the conduct of the affairs of the company, the court may by s 297A(6), relieve him in whole or in part from personal liability on such terms as it may think fit. This jurisdiction was first invoked in *Re Hefferon Kearns Ltd (No 2)*[371] by Lynch J who considered that it was not proper to impose personal responsibility for the debts of the company on the defendant directors. The 'draconian' effect of s 297A(2)(b) of the CA 1963 was considered by the judge to justify the exercise of this discretion:

> 'I think that it is because sub-s (2) and especially paragraph (b) is so wide-ranging that sub-s (6) was included ... The English Insolvency Act 1986 at s 214(3) is not quite as widely drafted as sub-s (6) ... and accordingly in the *Produce Marketing Consortium* case it was held that, while the court could take account of the absence of any fraudulent intent so as to lessen the amount ordered to be paid by the directors, unless the evidence showed that the directors had taken every step to minimize loss to creditors that they ought to have taken, an order should be made against them. It seems to me that the expression 'acted honestly and responsibly in relation to the conduct of the affairs of the company' is wider than the corresponding provisions in sub-s (3) of s 214 of the English Act and the court in this jurisdiction is given specific power to relieve such a director from any personal liability whatsoever.
>
> I am satisfied that the ... defendant acted honestly and responsibly in relation to the conduct of the affairs of the company to such an extent that having regard to all the circumstances of the case I relieve him wholly from any personal liability without imposing any terms[372].'

Through this interpretation, the judiciary have retained their discretion in the face of very strict statutory guidelines on the circumstances in which a person will be deemed to have been a party to the carrying on of the company's business in a reckless manner[373].

(h) The scope of the court's order

[15.113] Section 297A(7)(a) of the CA 1963 empowers the court when making an order for personal responsibility to:

> '... give such further directions as it thinks proper for the purpose of giving effect to that declaration and in particular may make provision for making the liability of any such person under the declaration a charge on any debt or obligation due from the company to him, or on any mortgage or charge or any interest in any mortgage or charge on any assets of the company held by or vested in him or any company or person on his behalf, or any person claiming as assignee from or through the person liable or any company or person acting on his behalf, and may from time to time make such further order as may be necessary for the purpose of enforcing any charge imposed under this subsection.'

In addition, by virtue of s 297A(7)(b), the court may:

> 'provide that sums recovered under this section shall be paid to such person or classes of persons, for such purposes, in such amounts or proportions at such time or times and in such respective priorities among themselves as such declaration may specify.'

---

371 *Re Hefferon Kearns Ltd (No 2)* (14 January 1993, unreported) HC *per* Lynch J.

372 *Re Hefferon Kearns Ltd (No 2)* (14 January 1993, unreported) HC at p 48 of transcript.

373 See para **[15.107]** *ante*.

Consequently, where a company owes an officer who has been made personally responsible for the company's debts, any sum of money, the court can order that the sum can be made the subject of a charge. Moreover, the court can order that any mortgage or charge held by him, or a person (human or artificial claiming on his behalf, or any person claiming to be an assignee) can be itself made the subject of a charge. Hence, this section empowers the court to create a *security* in respect of the personal responsibility imposed upon an officer.

(i) The date of the conduct complained of

[15.114] It has been conclusively established that the provisions on reckless trading are *not* retrospective, ie, only conduct after the passing of the two 1990 Companies Acts, (31 August 1990 for the C(A)A 1990, and 1 August 1991 for the CA 1990) can be considered for the purposes of reckless trading proceedings. This was confirmed in *Re Hefferon Kearns Ltd (No 1)*[374]. There, Murphy J reviewed the nature of retrospective legislation and concluded that having regard to Article 15.5 of the Constitution[375]:

> 'In my view reckless trading is now an infringement of the law and to declare retrospectively innocent actions as constituting that wrong would necessarily amount to a breach of Article 15. Accordingly it seems to me for that reason also to be clear that the Oireachtas did not intend (nor could it have intended) to make s 33 operate retrospectively[376].'

Re Hefferon Kearns Ltd (No 2)[377] established that not only is conduct prior to the coming into force of the legislation not cognisable, but where a person is guilty of reckless trading, neither can he be made personally liable for debts or liabilities incurred before the coming into effect of the legislation.

(j) Reckless trading proceedings in an examinership

[15.115] Section 33 of the C(A)A 1990 enabled proceedings to be taken for reckless trading in circumstances where a company had been placed in examinership. This has now been repealed by s 180(3) of the CA 1990 and replaced by s 138 of the CA 1990 which inserted s 297A of the CA 1963. The appropriateness of a provision on reckless trading during an examination of a company has been questioned, both by practitioners[378] and by the court in *Re Hefferon Kearns Ltd*[379]. In that case, Murphy J said:

---

374 *Re Hefferon Kearns Ltd (No 1)* [1992] ILRM 51.

375 Which provided that, 'The Oireachtas shall not declare Acts to be infringements of the law which were not so at the date of their commission.'

376 *Re Hefferon Kearns Ltd* [1992] ILRM 51 at 59.

377 *Re Hefferon Kearns Ltd (No 2)* (14 January 1993, unreported) HC at p 29 of transcript.

378 See (1991) Irish Times, 6 April, where Mr Peter Fitzpatrick (the first Irish examiner) is reported as having said that: 'My view is that litigation is not compatible with reconstruction ... The aspects of fraudulent or reckless trading are those which will more likely be found within the company which is beyond financial redemption and are issues which would more appropriately be left for pursuit by any subsequent receiver or liquidator rather than by an examiner.'

379 *Re Hefferon Kearns Ltd* [1992] ILRM 51.

'As already demonstrated the 1990 [Amendment] Act is designed essentially to empower the courts to appoint a new form of officer as examiner of a company enjoying certain statutory powers in the hope that by so doing it may be possible to preserve as a going concern a company which would be wound up otherwise. In practice a successful examinership would appear to entail a moratorium whilst the examiner conducted an examination and designed proposals under which creditors would compromise existing claims so as to facilitate the survival of the business. It is difficult to reconcile that scheme of things with a situation in which a creditor (amongst others) could pursue an officer of a company on the basis of an allegation of reckless trading at a time when the company is deemed to be under the protection of the court. It is even more difficult to reconcile the institution of such proceedings with the embargo imposed on proceedings and execution by Paragraph (f) of subs (2) of s 5 of the [C(A)A 1990]. However these apparently conflicting provisions must be reconciled.'

Murphy J went on to reconcile the provisions by saying that s 5, which prevents proceedings from being taken generally when a company is under the protection of the court, does not prevent a creditor from taking proceedings for reckless trading, although he felt that evidentially, it would be difficult for a creditor to derive benefit from s 33 and that it was difficult to envisage the effective operation of s 33 otherwise than in the context of insolvent liquidation. It remains the case, however, that s 297A of the CA 1963 can be invoked in either the course of a winding-up or in the course of proceedings under the C(A)A 1990.

Civil fraudulent trading

[15.116] Section 297A of the CA 1963[380] provides a civil remedy for fraudulent trading in addition to the civil remedy for reckless trading considered above[381]. Section 297A(1) provides:

'If in the course of winding up of a company or in the course of proceedings under the Companies (Amendment) Act 1990, it appears that—

(b) any person was knowingly a party to the carrying on of any business of the company with intent to defraud creditors of the company, or creditors of any other person or for any fraudulent purpose;

the court, on the application of the receiver, examiner liquidator or any creditor or contributory of the company, may, if it thinks it proper to do so, declare that such person shall be personally responsible, without any limitation of liability, for all or any part of the debts or other liabilities of the company as the court may direct.'

Central to understanding s 297A(1)(b) is that the test for fraudulent trading is *doubly subjective*. Before personal responsibility can be imposed[382] it must be proved that the person alleged to have traded fraudulently: (a)was *knowingly* a party to the (b) carrying on of any business of the company[383] (c) with *intent to defraud* creditors of the company

[380] As inserted by s 138 of the CA 1990.

[381] See para **[15.096]** *et seq ante*.

[382] Note that those who can be made personally responsible for fraudulent trading are the same individuals who can be made personally responsible for reckless trading, namely: directors, secretaries, and 'officers', as defined by s 297A(10) to include an auditor, liquidator, receiver or shadow director.

[383] *Morris v Banque Arabe et Internationale d'Investissment SA (No 2)* [2000] TLR 749; see para **[15.107]** *ante*.

or of any other person or for any other *fraudulent purpose*. The use of 'knowingly' imports a subjective test into reckless trading[384]. In the case of fraudulent trading the requirement that there also be shown an intention to defraud provides a second, even stronger, subjective test.

(a) The intention to defraud

[15.117] The requirement of an *intention to defraud* has beleaguered liquidators in their pursuit of delinquent officers of Irish companies. The difficulty in proving fraudulent trading is because of the subjective nature of the test. In the case of *Re William C Leitch Bros Ltd*[385], Maugham J said[386]:

> 'In my opinion, I must hold with regard to the meaning of the phrase carrying on business 'with intent to defraud creditors' that, if a company continues to carry on business and to incur debts at a time when there is, to the knowledge of the directors, no reasonable prospect of the creditors ever receiving payment of those debts, it is in general a proper inference that the company is carrying on business with intent to defraud.'

This test requires that the directors had actual knowledge that there was no reasonable chance that the creditors of the company would be paid[387]. Similarly, in *Re White & Osmond (Parkinstone) Ltd*[388] Buckley J said:

> '... there is nothing wrong in the fact that directors incur credit at a time when, to their knowledge, the company is not able to meet all its liabilities as they fall due. What is manifestly wrong is if the directors allow a company to incur credit at a time when the business is being carried on in such circumstances that it is clear that the company will never be able to satisfy its creditors. However, there is nothing to say that directors who genuinely believe that the clouds will roll away and the sunshine of prosperity will shine upon them again and disperse the fog of their depression are not entitled to incur credit to help them to get over the bad time.'

Consequently, for a person[389] to be held personally responsible for the debts of the company on the grounds of fraudulent trading, it is necessary to prove a subjective intention to defraud[390]. A mere 'intention to prefer' one creditor over another does not amount to an 'intention to defraud'[391].

---

384 See para **[15.101]** *ante*.

385 *Re William C Leitch Bros Ltd* [1932] All ER 892.

386 *Re William C Leitch Bros Ltd* [1932] All ER 892 at 895, of his widely quoted but only two page judgment.

387 Lingard, *Corporate Rescues and Insolvencies* (2nd edn, Butterworths, 1989) at para 2.9. See also *Re Patrick & Lyon Ltd* [1933] Ch 786, where Maugham J also held that fraudulent trading requires 'actual dishonesty involving, according to current notions of fair trading among commercial men, real moral blame'.

388 *Re White & Osmond (Parkinstone) Ltd* (30 June 1960, unreported) UK HC *per* Buckley J.

389 It should be noted that, unlike in reckless trading, persons other than 'officers' can be respondents in an action for fraudulent trading. Section 297A(1)(b) of the CA 1963 refers to 'any person' who was knowingly a party to the carrying on of any business of the company, with intent to defraud creditors.

390 See also *Hardie v Hanson* (1960) 105 CLR 451 (Australia), where Dixon CJ stressed the need for: '... the intent to defraud creditors must be express or actual and real: nothing constructive, imputed or implied will do.'

391 See *Re Sarflax Ltd* [1979] 1 All ER 529 at 535f.

[15.118] In *O'Keeffe v Ferris*[392], the plaintiff sought a declaration that the old s 297(1) of the CA 1963 was unconstitutional since it created a criminal offence which was not minor in nature and that it should only be tried before a jury. The plaintiff also claimed that, even if it did create only a civil cause of action, it could not be pursued unless and until the conclusion of criminal proceedings under s 297(3). This was rejected by Murphy J who held that the old s 297(1) did not create a criminal offence and that the section was properly construed as creating only a civil wrong. He also held that civil proceedings need not be postponed pending a criminal prosecution. In the course of his judgment Murphy J held:

> 'The subsection confers a wide discretion on the court and it must be assumed that the court will exercise those powers, not merely in a responsible but also in a constitutional fashion. If the Constitution does require that in civil proceedings the burden imposed on the defendants should in general be commensurate with the loss suffered by the plaintiff (or the class whom the plaintiff represents) then it must be assumed that the subsection will be so construed and applied[393].'

This was upheld by the Supreme Court[394] which held (*per* O'Flaherty J) that 'the section does not create a criminal offence; it does not involve civil proceedings being dressed up to involve criminal procedures and the sanctions available do not trench on the Constitution in any respect[395]'.

[15.119] It has been held that whilst it is imperative to establish an intention to defraud, it is not a pre-condition to a finding of such intent or purpose that the victim had in fact relied on the fraud[396].

(b) Proving fraudulent trading

[15.120] Proving fraudulent trading is a difficult, although not impossible task, as is illustrated by five Irish cases in which successful actions were taken. The first of these is *Re Kelly's Carpetdrome Ltd*[397], where debts were incurred by the company at a time when it failed to keep proper books of account and where records were actually destroyed. Indeed, assets were actually transferred to other companies when the main creditor, the Revenue Commissioners, began to pursue the company vigorously. Costello J held that it was proper in the circumstances for personal responsibility for the debts of the company to be imposed, not only on the officers, but also on persons who beneficially owned the company. In respect of one outsider (being neither a director nor a member) Costello J ordered that he too was personally responsible for the debts of the company[398].

In *Re Aluminium Fabricators Ltd*[399], the fraud involved the keeping of two sets of books of account, one for the benefit of the controllers of the company and the other for

---

392 *O'Keeffe v Ferris* [1994] 1 ILRM 425. See Duffy, 'Fraudulent Trading and the Decision in O'Keeffe v Ferris' (1994) CLP 255.

393 *O'Keeffe v Ferris* [1994] 1 ILRM 425 at 432.

394 *O'Keeffe v Ferris* (19 February 1997, unreported) SC.

395 *O'Keeffe v Ferris* (19 February 1997, unreported) SC at p 12 of the judgment.

396 *Morphites v Bernasconi et al* [2001] 2 BCLC 1.

397 *Re Kelly's Carpetdrome Ltd* (1 July 1983, unreported) HC *per* Costello J.

398 See Ussher, *Company Law in Ireland* (1986) at p 520.

399 *Re Aluminium Fabricators Ltd* [1984] ILRM 399.

the Revenue Commissioners. The intention and effect of this was to enable the controllers of the company to siphon-off company assets for their own benefit, to the obvious detriment of the creditors. Again, it was held by O'Hanlon J that an order for full personal responsibility for the debts of the company should be made against those responsible.

[15.121] The most helpful case is that of *Re Hunting Lodges Ltd*[400]. There, a single act – namely the sale at an under value of Durty Nellies public house, the company's principal asset – was deemed to constitute fraudulent trading[401]. The company sold the public house, disguising the true price of the sale by paying a substantial part of the consideration to one of the directors 'under the counter'. Although the sale price was £480,000, a secret payment of £160,000 was also paid by the purchaser to the controllers. This money was then lodged by one of the directors into various building society accounts. This single fraudulent act was held to constitute the carrying on of the company's business in a fraudulent manner. There was an intention to defraud found by Carroll J who said:

> 'In my opinion, in order for the section to apply it is *not* necessary that there should be a common agreed fraudulent intent. If each of the participants acts for a fraudulent purpose then each may be liable.'

In the case of all four parties, a fraudulent intent was found namely defrauding the creditors, defrauding the revenue of stamp duty and depriving the company of money which rightly belonged to it.

[15.122] Another case is *Re Contract Packaging Ltd*[402]. There the liquidator to the company learnt through his investigations into the company's affairs of several instances of fraudulent trading. Amongst the instances of fraud detected were the existence of a number of deposit accounts which were excluded from the company's audited accounts, books and records. The money in these accounts had been siphoned off by some of the directors, action which resulted in the Revenue Commissioners being defrauded and company funds being misappropriated. In total over £384,000 was discovered in these accounts and the beneficiaries of withdrawals from them were one particular director (Mr W), a company controlled by him (Shrinkpak Ltd), and genuine creditors. The liquidator had evidence that Mr W withdrew over £160,000 for his own personal use. Furthermore, the liquidator unearthed a VAT fraud, whereby the value of goods at point of importation was underestimated, a second invoice stating the true value issued by the company, and VAT credits sought on the basis of the second invoice. Evidence was also heard that when the company became insolvent, in addition to money being misappropriated by the directors, company business was diverted to Shrinkpak Ltd, W's company. The court also heard that the equitable ownership of the company's premises was fraudulently diverted to Shrinkpak Ltd. It was held by Flood J that it was proper to impose personal liability under s 297 of the CA 1963 on some of the directors involved. So it was ordered that Mr W and his common law wife give up their home to the liquidator[403], and W was also ordered to give his interest in a Jaguar car, two boats and funds held in various financial institutions to the liquidator.

---

400 *Re Hunting Lodges Ltd* [1985] ILRM 75.

401 See para **[15.126]** *post*.

402 See (1992) Irish Times, of 16, 17, 18 January.

403 Note though that in respect of the family home, a stay was put on the order for two months when Flood J heard that the family were homeless: (1992) Irish Times, 17 January.

[15.123] In *Re PSK Construction Ltd; Kavanagh v Killeen and Higgins*[404], Finlay Geoghegan J found that a director who had knowingly under-declared the amounts due to the Revenue Commissioners for PAYE/PRSI and RCT over a series of months had done so for a fraudulent purpose and that the claim under s 297A(1)(b) against the director had been made out.

(c) The beneficiary of an award

[15.124] In *Re Esal (Commodities) Ltd and another v Punjab National Bank*[405], it was held by the English Court of Appeal that any recovery for fraudulent trading had to be in favour of the company's liquidator and not an individual shareholder. Where an individual shareholder (or indeed creditor) successfully brings an action any award will, at the court's discretion, be for the benefit of the general body of shareholders and creditors.

[15.125] Where the Director of Corporate Enforcement applies under s 251 of the CA 1990 for an order under s 297A, s 251(4)(a) provides that s 297A(7)(b) of the CA 1963 shall apply in relation to any order made pursuant to an application brought by the Director, except that no order shall be made in favour of the Director 'otherwise than as to his costs and expenses'.

The extent of personal responsibility imposed for reckless or fraudulent trading

[15.126] The extent of personal responsibility imposed by the court will depend upon the circumstances of each case. Thus, while full liability for the debts of the company was imposed in both the *Re Kelly's Carpetdrome Ltd* and *Re Aluminium Fabricators Ltd* cases, the extent of judicial discretion is seen in the judgment of Carroll J in *Re Hunting Lodges Ltd*[406]. There, there were four respondents, Mr and Mrs Porrit, Mr O'Connor and a company called Plage Services Ltd (PS Ltd) which was owned by Mr O'Connor. The actions of each were stated by Carroll J[407] to be as follows:

> 'Mr Porrit – ... participated from start to finish. He was involved in all the negotiations; he required the payment on the side; he produced at closing the resolution of the directors authorising the sale at £480,000; he countersigned the affixing of the seal to the conveyance; he took the additional £160,000 and he opened the accounts with the building society under false names.
>
> Mrs Porrit – ... participated in the sale. While she denied any knowledge of the resolution of the directors, she attended at the closing of the sale and countersigned the affixing of the seal to the conveyance without objection. She signed a false name to the signature cards in respect of the building society accounts. Therefore, she took an active part in the closing of the sale and the disposition of part of the purchase money.
>
> Mr O'Connor – ... participated in the sale up to and including the closing. He negotiated directly with Mr Porrit and agreed to provide the money on the side. He co-operated by providing the three bank drafts in false names together with cash and the endorsed bank draft for the deposit and handed them over secretly to Mr Porrit without the knowledge of their solicitors or the company's auditor.

---

404 *Re PSK Construction Ltd; Kavanagh v Killeen and Higgins* [2009] IEHC 538.

405 *Re Esal (Commodities) Ltd and another v Punjab National Bank* [1997] 1 BCLC 705.

406 *Re Hunting Lodges Ltd* [1995] ILRM 75.

407 *Re Hunting Lodges Ltd* [1995] ILRM 75 at 83.

> PS Ltd – ... is the actual vehicle which Mr O'Connor used to take the conveyance. It was therefore a party to the sale at closing.'

Having established the requisite element of fraudulent intent, Carroll J decided that it was proper to make a declaration of personal responsibility for the debts of the company. She then went on to consider the extent to which the participants should be made personally liable, stressing the importance of looking at the entire circumstances of the case. That the imposition can be punitive in nature was accepted *ab initio*[408]. However, looking at all the circumstances, Carroll J apportioned the extent of personal liability on the basis of individual culpability. Thus, in the case of Mr Porrit she held that he:

> '... should be personally responsible without any limitation for all the debts of the company. The benefit of limited liability should, in my opinion, be totally withdrawn and he should be put in the same position as if he were a trader carrying on business personally.'

Accordingly not only was he liable for the sums siphoned off from the company, but also *all* of the other debts of the company. Since the Revenue Commissioners were owed over £750,000, this decision is a prime example of the punitive discretion of the High Court in such matters.

However, in respect Mrs Porrit, her liability was somewhat less, ie, all of the debts of the company not exceeding the value of advancements made by her husband six years thence, a decision which has been criticised as exposing Mrs Porrit to a double indemnity[409]. Mr O'Connor and Plage Services Ltd fared best of all and their liability was only in the sum of £12,000, jointly and severally. This figure represented the cash sum given by Mr O'Connor which had disappeared.

[15.127] In *Re PSK Construction Ltd; Kavanagh v Killeen and Higgins*[410], Finlay Geoghegan J found the first respondent director to have traded recklessly and fraudulently in under-declaring and under-paying to the Revenue Commissioners. In considering whether to make a declaration of personal responsibility, without any limitation of liability, for all or any part of the debts or other liabilities of the company, the learned judge noted the importance of the principle of proportionality expressed by O'Flaherty J in *O'Keeffe v Ferris*[411] that '[a]ny sanction imposed should be proportionate to the wrongdoing that has been made out'. In that case, the extent of the declaration of personal liability for the company's debts was fixed at €1,604,526 which was considered in the circumstances to be appropriate notwithstanding that the company's total debts were in excess of that amount.

---

408 Carroll J relied on the judgment of Maugham J in *Re William C Leith Bros Ltd* [1932] All ER 892 at 896 where he said: 'I am inclined to take the view that [the corresponding section in England and Wales] is in the nature of a punitive provision, and that where the court makes such a declaration in relation to "all or any of the debts or other liabilities of the company", it is in the discretion of the court to make an order without limiting the order to the amount of the debts of those creditors proved to have been defrauded by those acts of the director in question, though, no doubt, the order would in general be so limited.'

409 See Ussher, *Company Law in Ireland* (1986), at pp 522, 523.

410 *Re PSK Construction Ltd; Kavanagh v Killeen and Higgins* [2009] IEHC 538.

411 *O'Keeffe v Ferris* [1997] 3 IR 463 at 473.

Criminal fraudulent trading

[15.128] Section 297 of the CA 1963 provides that it is a criminal offence to trade fraudulently.[412] Thus s 297(1) provides:

> 'If any person is knowingly a party to the carrying on of the business of a company with intent to defraud creditors of the company or creditors of any other person or for any fraudulent purpose, that person shall be guilty of an offence.'

On summary conviction the penalty is imprisonment for 12 months and, or in the alternative, a class C fine. On conviction on indictment, the penalty is a term of imprisonment not exceeding seven years and/or a fine not exceeding €111,102.08[413]. Fraudulent trading is an offence for which a suspect can be arrested without warrant and detained for six hours (and a further six in certain circumstances) for questioning under s 4 of the Criminal Justice Act 1984.

[15.129] The first successful prosecution for fraudulent trading occurred in 1996. This arose from the case of *Re Mark Synnott (Life and Pensions) Brokers Ltd*. The facts as emerged from the newspaper reports[414] were that over a number of years a brokerage business had consistently mismanaged clients' funds. Investors had been attracted to Mr Synnott's company on foot of its claims of having discovered a brilliant investment strategy which could net returns of at least 20% *per annum*. It transpired, however, that moneys received for investment were in fact often simply put into a bank account and when an investor was looking for a return, money was simply withdrawn from the bank account. It emerged that the company had been trading at a loss for at least eight years. Many investors successfully applied for *Mareva* injunctions to restrain the dissipation of the managing director's assets[415]. Arising from these facts a director of the company, Mark A Synnott, was prosecuted for fraudulent trading in the Circuit Court in *People (DPP) v Mark A Synnott*[416]. The report in *The Irish Times* stated that charges against Synnott alleged that between 2 September 1990 and 3 June 1991 he was knowingly a party to the carrying on of the business of the company with intent to defraud the creditors of the company by falsely pretending that he, as director, was engaged in the *bona fide* business of investing monies entrusted to him when he knew that the company was insolvent. Synnott was also charged with fraudulently converting two sums of money to his own use, one in 1990 and one in 1991. Three of the charges were admitted from a total of 39 on the indictment and a *nolle prosequi* was entered on the remaining charges. The defendant was sentenced to four years and three months imprisonment and disqualified from acting as a director.

---

412 See generally, Ussher, *Company Law in Ireland* (1986) at p 516 and Pennington, *Corporate Insolvency Law* (1991, Butterworths) at p 229.

413 Section 297(2) of the CA 1963 as amended by ss 6 and 9 of the FA 2010.

414 For newspaper coverage of various interlocutory and interim applications and orders (eg, for *Mareva* injunctions) in the *Synnott* case, see (1991) Irish Times, 15, 18, 19, 25, 27 June; 3, 4, 6, 9 July; and 6, 7, 8, 9 November.

415 See Courtney, *Mareva Injunctions and Related Interlocutory Orders* (1998, Butterworths) at [6.50].

416 *People (DPP) v Mark A Synnott* (7 May 1996) CC, Judge Cyril Kelly.

[15.130] In *Aktieselskabet Dansk Skibsfinansiering v Brothers et al*[417], the Hong Kong Court of Final Appeal held that the offence of fraudulent trading requires proof that someone carried on the business of the company with a fraudulent intention and that the other directors whom it was sought to make liable were knowingly party to that fraud. As in civil fraudulent trading, considered next, it was stated that the question of 'fraud' was subjective in that the defendant must have been dishonest. The court also held that an inquiry into the conduct of the particular defendants was required in preference to invoking the concept of the 'hypothetical decent honest man'. It is thought that this is preferable to the approach taken by the English Court of Appeal in *R v Grantham*[418]. In that case, involving a criminal prosecution, the accused's intentions seem to have been objectively ascertained. Lord Lane CJ held than in order to prove an 'intent to defraud', actual 'fraud' is unnecessary, and it is sufficient that a respondent obtained credit from a creditor, where he knew there was no good reason for believing that the company would have funds to repay the credit when it became due, or soon after. Referring to the *dicta* of Buckley J quoted above[419], Lord Lane said:

> 'In so far as Buckley J was saying that it is never dishonest or fraudulent for directors to incur credit at a time when, to their knowledge, the company is not able to meet all its liabilities as they fall due, we would respectfully disagree ... In the present case it was open to the jury to find, if not inevitably that they would find, that whoever was running this business was intending to deceive or was actually deceiving [the creditor] into believing that he would be paid in 28 days or shortly thereafter, when they knew perfectly well that there was no hope of that coming about. He was plainly induced thereby to deliver further [goods] on credit. The potential or inevitable detriment to him is obvious[420].'

It is by no means certain that an Irish court would follow the reasoning of the English Court of Appeal even in the context of a criminal prosecution, particularly in view of the clear wording of the section.

Personal liability for failure to keep proper books of account

[15.131] Section 202(1) of the CA 1990 provides that every company must keep proper books of account that:

- correctly record and explain the transactions of the company;
- will at any time enable the financial position of the company to be determined with reasonable accuracy;
- will enable the directors to ensure that any balance sheet, profit and loss account or income and expenditure account of the company complies with the requirements of the Companies Acts; and
- will enable the accounts of the company to be readily and properly audited.

---

417 *Aktieselskabet Dansk Skibsfinansiering v Brothers et al* [2001] 2 BCLC 324.

418 *R v Grantham* [1984] 3 All ER 166.

419 See para **[15.117]** *ante*.

420 *R v Grantham* [1984] 3 All ER 166 at 170e–j.

In *Re Rayhill Property Company Ltd; Conroy v Corneill and Corneill*[421], Smyth J quoted the following passage from the decision of *Maloe Construction Limited v Chadwick Lovegrove and Beor*[422]:

> 'These accounting records every company must cause to be 'kept'. It has been held by the Court of Appeal in *R v Bennett and another* [1985] 2 NZCLC 96-034 that the word 'kept' is not limited to retaining or storing such records as happen to come into possession. It imports as well the obligation to create those records necessary to conform to the description in subs (1) and (2) which are not already in existence and retained.
>
> The records must speak for themselves. The must, without more, do or enable to be done, the matters spelt out in the four paragraphs of subs (1). It does not avail a company to say, as was said here, that those objectives could be achieved by reference to the accounting records available, plus further information and explanations that can be furnished by a company officer or employee.
>
> The records themselves do not have to show the financial position to the company. They must be such that they will, at any time, enable that position to be determined. This requirement is not complied with if the company keeps only basis accounting records such as cheque books, deposit books, bank statements, invoices and the like. It may be that using such basic records an accountant could construct further records that would enable the financial position of the company to be determined. But the section requires that this basic accounting information should be assembled and recorded in such a way that the record itself will not only enable the financial position to be determined, but will enable that to be done *at any time* ...'

In *Re Rayhill Property Company Ltd* one of the directors was made personally liable in the amount of €203,334, Smyth J having found that there was a causative connection between the failure to keep the proper books and records and the inability to pay debts. It was found that no meaningful proper records were available as such 'bits and scraps' of information as the liquidator was able to work up into a set of records clearly indicated that the company could not pay its debts.

The duty in s 202(1) of the CA 1990 is fully considered in Ch 17. In this chapter the concern is the personal liability that can be visited upon officers of a company where s 202(1) is breached.

(a) The power to declare officers personally liable where proper books of account not kept

[15.132] Section 204(1) of the CA 1990 provides:

> '(1) Subject to subsection (2)[423], if—
>
> (a) a company that is being wound up and that is unable to pay all of its debts has contravened section 202, and
>
> (b) the court considers that such contravention has contributed to the company's inability to pay all of its debts or has resulted in substantial uncertainty as to the

[421] *Re Rayhill Property Company Ltd; Conroy v Corneill and Corneill* (7 October 2003, unreported) HC, Smyth J.

[422] *Maloe Construction Ltd v Chadwick Lovegrove and Beo* [1986] 3 NZCLC 99.

[423] Section 204(2) of the CA 1990 provides: 'On the hearing of an application under this subsection, the person bringing the application may himself give evidence or call witnesses.'

> assets and liabilities of the company or has substantially impeded the orderly winding up thereof,
>
> the court, on the application of the liquidator or any creditor or contributory of the company, may, if it thinks it proper to do so, declare that any one or more of the officers[424] and former officers of the company who is or are in default shall be personally liable, without any limitation of liability, for all, or such part as may be specified by the court, of the debts and other liabilities of the company.'

The object of this section was stated by Shanley J in *Mehigan v Duignan; Re Mantruck Services Ltd*[425] not to be the removal of the benefit of limited liability and the placing of the person (on whom liability is imposed) in the same position as if he were a sole trader. This is because those against whom such a declaration can be made are not confined to officers, but extend beyond executives, and can embrace a company's auditors and members of a company.

[15.133] Upon making such a declaration, the court's powers are far-reaching. Section 204(3)(a) provides that the court may:

> '... give such directions as it thinks proper for the purpose of giving effect to the declaration and in particular may make provision for making the liability of any such person under the declaration a charge on any debt or obligation due from the company to him, or on any mortgage or charge or any interest in any mortgage or charge on any assets of the company held by or vested in him or any company or other person on his behalf, or any person claiming as assignee[426] from or through the person liable under the declaration or any company or person acting on his behalf, and may from time to time make such further order as may be necessary for the purpose of enforcing any charge imposed under this subsection.'

The court's power to declare that an officer is personally liable where there has been a breach of s 202 is without prejudice to the fact that such a person may be criminally liable under s 202(10)[427].

(b) The imposition of personal liability is discretionary

[15.134] It does not follow, automatically, that where a company has failed to keep proper books of account as required by s 202 of the CA 1990, a declaration of personal liability will be made against its officers. Section 204(4) provides a defence:

> 'The court shall not make a declaration under subsection (1) in respect of a person if it considers that—

---

424 In s 204 of the CA 1990, the term 'officer' is deemed to *include*: 'a person who has been convicted of an offence under s 194, 197 or 242 in relation to a statement concerning the keeping of proper books of account by the company.'

425 *Mehigan v Duignan; Re Mantruck Services Ltd* [1997] 1 ILRM 171. For comment, see Sanfey, 'Personal Liability of Directors under Section 204 of the Companies Act 1990' (1996) The Bar Review 50.

426 Section 204(3)(b) of the CA 1990 defines 'assignee' to *include*: 'any person to whom or in whose favour, by the directions of the person liable, the debt, obligation, mortgage or charge was created, issued or transferred or the interest created, but does not include an assignee for valuable consideration (not including consideration by way of marriage) given in good faith and without notice of any of the matters on the ground of which the declaration is made.'

427 Section 204(5) of the CA 1990.

(a) he took all reasonable steps to secure compliance by the company with section 202, or

(b) he had reasonable grounds for believing and did believe that a competent and reliable person, acting under the supervision or control of a director of the company who has been formally allocated such responsibility, was charged with the duty of ensuring that that section was complied with and was in a position to discharge that duty.'

It should be noted, however, that in *Re Vehicle Imports Ltd*[428], Murphy J held that the obligation[429] to keep proper books of account was not limited to where one director had a reputed responsibility for keeping the books and that the responsibility was a joint and separate liability on each of the directors. Accordingly, whilst delegation to a competent person will be a defence to an application to have one made personally responsible for a company's debts, it will not be a defence to a criminal prosecution or indeed any comfort, necessarily, in an application to have a director restricted under s 150 of the CA 1990.

[15.135] In *Rayhill Property Company Ltd; Conroy v Corneill and Corneill*[430], the liquidator of a company which was involved in the ownership and operation of Clonmannon Retirement Village sought a declaration to make the mother and son directors personally liable for the company's debts pursuant to s 204 of the CA 1990. In that case, one of the directors denied that books of account had not been kept and sought to invoke the defence in s 204(4) by asserting that a competent and reliable person had been charged with that duty. This was rejected by Smyth J who found that the person in question was in fact a management consultant and not a book keeper and was not engaged by either the company or the directors to keep proper books of account in the manner required by s 202 of the CA 1990 and that the director did not have reasonable grounds for believing to the contrary.

(c) The proofs required for an order under s 204

[15.136] The first case in which s 204 of the CA 1990 was considered was *Re Mantruck Services Ltd; Mehigan v Duignan*[431], where Shanley J usefully set out the proofs required for an order under s 204. The facts of this case were that Mantruck Services Ltd was placed into creditors' voluntary liquidation, which was subsequently converted into an official liquidation. An employee of the official liquidator collected some books and records of the company from its premises. He did not collect certain books referred to as the 'red cathedral books'; those that he did receive were delivered to the liquidator's solicitor. Later, the High Court ordered the directors to deliver-up all books, records, documents and assets of the company to the official liquidator. This order had been sought by the official liquidator after he had examined the books and records received from the voluntary liquidator and having formed the view that there were 'significant

428 *Re Vehicle Imports Ltd* (23 November 2000, unreported) HC, Murphy J.

429 On pain of criminal sanction in the light of s 202(10) of the CA 1990 – which criminalises the failure to keep proper books of account and applies to every person who is a director of a company.

430 *Rayhill Property Company Ltd; Conroy v Corneill and Corneill* (7 October 2003, unreported) HC, Smyth J.

431 *Mehigan v Duignan; Re Mantruck Services Ltd* [1997] 1 ILRM 171.

and extensive' omissions in the company's records and that these resulted in substantial uncertainty as to the company's assets and liabilities that had impeded its orderly winding up. No further records were forthcoming and the respondent declared that proper books and records were duly made available to the official liquidator. At the hearing of a motion to have the respondent restricted under s 150 of the CA 1990 and an order for personal liability under s 204, it was indicated by the respondent that there might be certain other records at the company's old premises. The motion was adjourned and an order made that these be delivered up; following this, 28 computer disks and the five red cathedral books were recovered. The applicant liquidator continued to assert that certain basic information was still missing covering a period of some 18 months. The liquidator claimed that because of this he could not determine the company's financial position, that the company could not be readily and properly audited, there was no proper record of the assets and liabilities, no proper record of invoices and no proper record of money received or expended. The liquidator also claimed that these omissions impeded the orderly winding up of the company and gave evidence that some 80% of the time spent by him and his staff related to efforts to overcome these deficiencies. The respondent claimed that additional information was available on the computer disks and that he had thought that the 'red cathedral books' had been given to the voluntary liquidator.

[15.137] Shanley J made an order under s 204(1) against the respondent, restricted to 80% of the liquidator's costs in overcoming the deficiencies occasioned by the absence of proper books and records. Shanley J held that the requisite proofs, before an order could be made under s 204 were:

> '(a) The company in question is being wound up.
>
> (b) The company is unable to pay all its debts.
>
> (c) The company has contravened s 202.
>
> (d) Such contravention has contributed to the company's inability to pay all of its debts or has resulted in substantial uncertainty as to the assets and liabilities of the company or has substantially impeded the orderly winding up of the company.
>
> (e) The officer (or former officer) of the company knowingly and wilfully authorised or permitted the contravention by the company of s 202, or, the 'officer' is a person convicted under ss 194, 197 or 242 in relation to a statement concerning the keeping of proper books of account[432].'

Focusing on proof (d), Shanley J held:

> 'The section, on its face, does not require that there be any causal relationship between the s 202 contravention and the liability declared under s 204. Nor does the section, on its face, make any allowance for different degrees of blameworthiness which might attend contraventions of s 202. As to the absence of a causal connection between a contravention of s 202 and the liability imposed under s 204, there may well be a significant number of situations where the contravention bears little or no relationship to the amount of the debts of the insolvent company. For example, where the insolvency is the direct result of unwise foreign exchange transactions and it is discovered that the auditors and directors have knowingly and consistently *undervalued* the assets of the company (thereby resulting in a contravention of s 202) such that, while insolvent, the company's indebtedness is less than it would have been had the assets been properly valued. Where such an undervaluation

432 *Mehigan v Duignan; Re Mantruck Services Ltd* [1997] 1 ILRM 171 at 187.

> results in substantial uncertainty as to the assets of the company or substantially impedes the orderly winding up of the company liability under s 204 is established, yet it would be clearly unjustifiable in principle to impose liability for all the debts of the company … On the other hand, where a particular contravention of s 202 can be seen to have a particular financial consequence resulting in a particular debt of the insolvent company, it is difficult to see how it could be argued that imposing liability for such a debt works any injustice[433].'

Shanley J concluded that although s 204 could be read as to permit the imposition on a person of unlimited liability for all of a company's debts such could, where the s 202 contravention has not in itself resulted in any loss to the company but has substantially impeded the orderly winding up of the company, constitute an unjust attack on the person's personal rights. Accordingly, the court must exercise its discretion in a responsible and constitutional fashion and have regard to the extent to which the officer's involvement in the s 202 contravention resulted in financial loss and, if it did, whether or not such losses were reasonably foreseeable by the officer as a consequence of the contravention. Shanley J said that only in exceptional circumstances would liability be imposed where the contravention of s 202 did not result in loss or for losses not reasonably foreseeable as a consequence of the breach of s 202. Shanley J said that he thought that the three factors suggested by Tompkins J in *Maloc Construction Ltd v Chadwick*[434] – causation, culpability and duration – in his interpretation of the almost identical provisions of the New Zealand legislation, were relevant to the principles that should guide the court's discretion and in assessing liability under s 204 of the CA 1990. As to the standard of proof, Shanley J considered this to be in the context of a civil wrong and held that no higher degree of probability of a contravention of s 202 is required than in any other civil wrong.

On the facts of the case in hand, Shanley J held that the company was in contravention of s 202 of the CA 1990 for some period of time and that the respondent was an officer of the company who had wilfully authorised and permitted the contraventions and could not avail of any defence under s 204(4). He concluded that he should exercise his discretion and declare the respondent personally liable for 80% of the cost of the liquidator's time as the losses that flowed from that expenditure of time were reasonably foreseeable as a consequence of the contravention of s 202.

[15.138] The decision in *Mehigan v Duignan* was followed by Geoghegan J in *Re Ashclad Ltd; Forrest v Harrington and Culleton*[435]. In this case, the official liquidator (who took the action) found deficiencies to a greater or lesser degree in the available bank statements, purchases' book, sales ledger, cheque payments' books, PAYE and PRSI records, audited accounts for certain years and VAT records. Geoghegan J said that as a consequence of these deficiencies, there was quite obviously substantial uncertainty as to the company's assets and liabilities and its orderly winding up was being impeded. Again, the liquidator estimated that 80% of his time related to his efforts to assess the company's books and records and to overcome deficiencies. Geoghegan J did not find the respondent's evidence impressive, particularly in relation to the explanations proffered for certain discrepancies in monies belonging to the company. He concluded

433 *Mehigan v Duignan; Re Mantruck Services Ltd* [1997] 1 ILRM 171 at 188, 189.

434 *Maloc Construction Ltd v Chadwick* [1986] 3 NZCLC 99.

435 *Re Ashclad Ltd; Forrest v Harrington and Culleton* (5 April 2000, unreported) HC, Geoghegan J.

that as a matter of probability sums amounting to at least £100,000 had been wrongly withdrawn from the company and appropriated for other purposes. Geoghegan J went on to say:

> 'I have read and considered the judgment of Shanley J in *Mehigan v Duignan* [1997] 1 IR 341. I broadly accept the approach which he adopted and the principles which he said had to be applied particularly having regard to the Constitution. To some extent he lays down quite a strict onus of proof in relation to causality. But the facts of that case are not the same as the facts of this case and I am satisfied that as a matter of probability the liabilities of the company were very substantially affected by cash withdrawals which were not for the benefit of the company[436].'

Geoghegan J went on to declare that the respondent be made personally liable to the extent of £112,000 for the company's debts. His grounds were that the company had failed to keep proper books of account as required by s 202 of the CA 1990, that such contravention had resulted in substantial uncertainty as to the company's assets and liabilities and/or had impeded the orderly winding up of the company and/or contributed to the company's inability to pay all of its debts.

[15.139] In *Re Dev Oil and Gas Ltd; Jackson v Devlin*[437], a company carried on business as an oil and gas sales company which sold petrol, red diesel, gas and home heating oil, on a retail and wholesale basis. Finlay Geoghegan J concluded, on the evidence presented, that it did not keep proper books of account that correctly recorded and explained the transactions of the company and enabled the financial position to be determined with reasonable accuracy. After considering the judgment of Shanley J in *Mantruck Services Ltd; Mehigan v Duignan* and the facts of the case before her, Finlay Geoghegan J declared that she was satisfied that the company's contravention of s 202 contributed to its inability to pay all of its debts and had resulted in substantial uncertainty as to the assets and liabilities of the company. In declaring the respondent personally liable, the learned judge set his liability at 68% of the company's liabilities on the basis that the liquidator would have expected to have recovered 70% of the company's debts but only recovered 1.85% on account of the failure to keep proper books and records.

[15.140] In *Re PSK Construction Ltd; Kavanagh v Killeen and Higgins*[438], Finlay Geoghegan J had found that the first respondent director had traded both recklessly and fraudulently but that the second respondent director had not. The liquidator also brought an application under s 204 of the CA 1990 for failure to keep proper books of account. On this point the learned judge said:

> '52. On the facts of this application, I am not satisfied that the applicant has established the necessary causal link between his inability to recover certain of the debts of the Company and the failure of the Company to maintain its books in accordance with the requirements of s 202 of the Companies Act, 1990. The collection of debts due on construction contracts in the winding up of a construction company is notoriously difficult. I could not be satisfied, on the facts stated in the affidavit, that the inability of the

436 *Re Ashclad Ltd; Forrest v Harrington and Culleton* (5 April 2000, unreported) HC, Geoghegan J at p 15 of the judgment.

437 *Re Dev Oil and Gas Ltd; Jackson v Devlin* [2008] IEHC 252.

438 *Re PSK Construction Ltd; Kavanagh v Killeen and Higgins* [2009] IEHC 538.

applicant is caused by the absence of the books and records. It is not disputed, however, on behalf of the respondents, that the applicant incurred additional expenses in the liquidation of €21,447 in relation to the reconstitution of books, and I am satisfied that a claim pursuant to s 204 in respect of this amount has been made out. Both respondents were directors of the Company. The directors are ultimately responsible for the proper keeping of books of account. I have concluded that both respondents must be considered to be in default in failing to ensure that the Company kept proper books of accounts in accordance with s 202 and neither of the respondents have put facts before the Court which entitle them to avail of the potential defences in s 204(4).

53. The applicant is entitled pursuant to s 204(1) to a declaration that the respondents are jointly and severally liable in the sum of €21,447 in respect of additional expenses incurred in the liquidation, which is a liability of the Company. As this sum is a quite separate and distinct sum to that already declared pursuant to s 297A against Mr. Killeen, it must stand as a separate declaration.'

Section 251 of the CA 1990: invocation of statutory remedies where a company is not being wound up

[15.141] It is not a prerequisite to issuing proceedings for fraudulent trading, failing to keep proper books of account, etc, that a company is being wound up. Section 251 of the CA 1990 facilitates the invocation of various statutory remedies where a company is insolvent[439] even though it is not being wound-up. Section 251 applies to companies which are not being wound up but where:

- execution or other process issued on a judgment, decree or order of any court in favour of a creditor of the company is returned unsatisfied in whole or in part; or
- it is proved to the satisfaction of the court that the company is unable to pay its debts, taking into account the contingent and prospective liabilities of the company;

and where it appears to the court that the reason or principal reason for its not being wound up is the insufficiency of its assets.

The purpose of this provision is to confer jurisdiction upon the court to make any one of a series of orders that could otherwise only be made where a company is being wound up, thereby making the directors of a hopelessly insolvent company amenable to the court. The legislative intention was to provide redress in cases of the so-called *scorched earth* syndrome[440], which refers to a situation where the directors of a company so deplete its assets as to make it unattractive for any creditor to cause a liquidator to be appointed because of the absence of funds in the hope that nobody will investigate any wrongdoing and pursue the directors. This provision is examined under the following headings:

[439] Ie, where the company is unable to pay its debts, taking contingent and prospective liabilities into account, *or* where the company has had execution or other process issued on judgment which is returned unsatisfied: s 251(1) (a) and (b) of the CA 1990.

[440] See the *Report of the Working Group on Company Law Compliance and Enforcement* (1998) at para 4.42 (the 'McDowell Report').

(a) Those with *locus standi* to apply under s 251.
(b) The orders that can be made under s 251.
(c) The insufficiency of assets as a precondition to jurisdiction.
(d) The operation of the section.

(a) Those with locus standi to apply under s 251

[15.142] The original s 251 was silent as to who could apply for an order. It would seem, however, that creditors and members must have jurisdiction to apply for an order under s 251 as these are the two constituencies most likely to be adversely affected by corporate wrongdoing. The Director of Corporate Enforcement also has *locus standi* to apply for an order by reason of s 251(2A)[441], which provides:

> 'The Director may apply to the court pursuant to this section for an order or judgment, as the case may be, under any of the sections which apply to a company to which this section relates.'

Accordingly, it is only the Director who has express *locus standi* to bring application under this provision. The role of this Director in this regard very much remains to be seen, particularly as regards those provisions that facilitate the making of an order rendering directors personally liable for some or all of a company's debts, as the McDowell Group clearly stated that 'the Director's right to seek a declaration of personal liability or damages pursuant to s 251 should not extend to receiving or distributing any assets as may be recovered from persons pursuant to the relevant sections, as the Group considers this to be a matter for aggrieved creditors'[442]. In this regard it is to be noted that s 251(4)(a) provides that s 297A(7)(b) of the CA 1963[443] shall apply in relation to any order made pursuant to an application brought by the Director, except that no order shall be made in favour of the Director 'otherwise than as to his costs and expenses'. The rights of the 'aggrieved creditors', mentioned in the McDowell Report, are, however, vindicated and s 251(4)(b) provides:

> 'A person having a claim against the company may apply for an enforcement order for a share of any sums or assets recovered or available following a successful action by the Director pursuant to subsection (2A), provided that the order is sought within a period of one month from the date of judgment on behalf of the Director.'

In view of the very short limitation period, it is important that aggrieved creditors closely follow any action for recovery taken by the Director, lest they be statute barred in seeking an enforcement order for a share of sums or assets recovered or available.

(b) The orders that can be made under s 251

[15.143] Section 251(2) of the CA 1990 permits a court to hear application for any of the following orders:

---

441 Inserted by s 54(b) of the CLEA 2001.

442 See the *Report of the Working Group on Company Law Compliance and Enforcement* (1998) at pp 60, 61, point 8 of Annex 4.1.

443 Section 297A(7)(b) provides that on making a declaration the court may: 'provide that sums recovered under this section shall be paid to such person or classes of persons, for such purposes, in such amounts or proportions at such time or times and in such respective priorities among themselves as such declaration may specify.'

(a) an order directing the return of assets improperly transferred[444];

(b) a contribution order[445];

(c) a restriction order[446];

(d) criminal failure to keep proper books of account[447];

(e) civil failure to keep proper books of account[448];

(f) inspection of books by creditors or contributories of the company[449];

(g) power to summon persons for an examination[450];

(h) an order against property as a result of an examination[451];

(i) the arrest of absconding persons[452];

(j) fraud by officers of companies in liquidation[453];

(k) criminal fraudulent trading[454];

(l) civil fraudulent trading[455];

(m) power to assess damages against directors[456].

The orders that can be sought under s 251 are the essential tools of any liquidators' armoury which facilitate the furnishing of information, preservation of assets and recovery of assets in cases of wrongdoing.

[15.144] One apparent gap in s 251 is that proceedings for reckless trading are not permissible under the section. *Inter alia*, s 251(2)(b) of the CA 1990 provides that 'the provisions of the CA 1963 mentioned in the Table to this section' shall apply notwithstanding that the company is not being wound up. This Table provides, *inter alia*, that s 297A of the CA 1963 shall apply but delimits its application by the further description: 'Civil liability for fraudulent trading'. Section 297A contains two limbs: civil liability for fraudulent trading *and* civil liability for reckless trading. Accordingly, if one applies a strict construction to this provision, the specific reference prejudices the general reference and precludes an applicant from relying on s 251 to ground an

444 Section 139 of the CA 1990. See Ch 27, *Realisation and Distribution of Assets on Liquidation*, at para **[27.103]**.

445 Section 140 of the CA 1990. See Ch 27, *Realisation and Distribution of Assets on Liquidation*, at para **[27.119]**.

446 Section 149 of the CA 1990. See Ch 28, *Compliance and Enforcement*, at para **[28.062]**.

447 Section 203 of the CA 1990. See Ch 17, *Financial Statements, Audit and Annual Returns*, at para **[17.012]**.

448 Section 204 of the CA 1990. See para **[15.131]** *ante*.

449 Section 243 of the CA 1963.

450 Section 245 of the CA 1963, as amended by s 126 of the CA 1990. See Ch 27, *Realisation and Distribution of Assets on Liquidation*, at para **[27.024]**.

451 Section 245A of the CA 1963 as inserted by s 127 of the CA 1990.

452 Section 247 of the CA 1963. See Ch 27, *Realisation and Distribution of Assets on Liquidation*, at para **[27.043]**.

453 Section 295 of the CA 1963.

454 Section 297 of the CA 1963.

455 Section 297A of the CA 1963 as inserted by s 138 of the CA 1990, and s 297 of the CA 1963 as inserted by s 137 of the CA 1990.

456 Section 298 of the CA 1963 as amended by s 142 of the CA 1990.

application for reckless trading where the company is not in liquidation or under the protection of the court.

(c) The insufficiency of assets as a precondition to jurisdiction

[15.145] The grounds which must be satisfied in order for s 251 to become operational are similar in part to the grounds for petitioning to have a company wound up under s 213 of the CA 1963. It is submitted that proving to the court that the company is unable to pay its debts is likely to be the most common reason relied upon to ground a s 251 application. Essential to the success of any application is that the reason or principal reason for the company not being wound up is the insufficiency of its assets. Since the main reason for a liquidation is to enable the orderly realisation and distribution of assets, it follows that where there are insufficient assets, there operates a strong financial disincentive to commencing costly liquidation proceedings. However, a court will not accede to a request under s 251 if there are sufficient assets available for the economical winding up of the company. It is submitted that this ground will be strictly adhered to by the courts to prevent abuse of this innovative legislative device.

[15.146] In *Alba Radio Ltd v Haltone (Cork) Ltd*[457], an order for examination under s 245 of the CA 1963 was sought pursuant to s 251 and it was argued, *inter alia*[458], that it had not been proved that that company had not been wound up by reason of insufficiency of its assets. Prior to the commencement of the CA 1990 the plaintiff had obtained a judgment against the defendant company. On this point Barron J said:

> 'The evidence shows that the judgment obtained by the plaintiff has not been satisfied at all and that such assets as may have belonged to the defendant company have been transferred to the company presently using the same premises. In the absence of any denial as to the facts alleged in the [plaintiff's affidavit], I am satisfied that the company is unable to pay its debts and that the reason it is not being wound up is the insufficiency of its assets[459].'

(d) The operation of the section

[15.147] It was held in *Jones and Tarleton v Gunn et al*[460] that s 251 was not retrospective. In that case, because the transactions complained of were completed prior to the commencement of s 251 of the CA 1990, and because the company was not being wound up, the plaintiffs' claim under ss 297A and 298 of the CA 1963 must fail because their application in circumstances where a company was not being wound up would involve retrospection.

[15.148] Not every order made under s 251 will, however, violate the rule against retrospection. So, in *Alba Radio Ltd v Haltone (Cork) Ltd*[461] application was brought under s 251 for an examination order under s 245 of the CA 1963 against a person who was a director of a company that was not being wound up. The plaintiff company had obtained a judgment against the defendant company prior to the commencement of

---

457 *Alba Radio Ltd v Haltone (Cork) Ltd* (1 June 1995, unreported) HC, Barron J.

458 As to retrospectivity, see para **[15.114]** *post*.

459 *Alba Radio Ltd v Haltone (Cork) Ltd* (1 June 1995, unreported) HC, Barron J at p 3 of the judgment.

460 *Jones and Tarleton v Gunn et al* [1997] 2 ILRM 245.

461 *Alba Radio Ltd v Haltone (Cork) Ltd* (1 June 1995, unreported) HC, Barron J.

s 251 of the 1990 Act. To the director's claim that to make an order pursuant to s 245, under s 251, would be to give the CA 1990 retrospective effect, Barron J held:

> 'There is nothing new in that procedure [ie, an order for examination under s 245 of the CA 1963]. What is new is that the application can be made even though the company is not being wound up. In effect what s 251 is doing is to permit a form of procedure which existed before the passing of the Act to be adopted in slightly different circumstances. Admittedly until the Act was passed, it was necessary to put the company into liquidation or to have a provisional liquidator appointed before the relief could be obtained. In my view that is not creating a retrospective effect to the section.
>
> Whether or not an Act is retrospective in its effect is determined by the proper construction of the provisions of that Act. Where rights have been acquired or duties imposed in respect of completed transactions prior to the passing of the Act in question, then those rights or those duties cannot be affected by the Act unless it is to be retrospective in its operation. In the present case there is no right vested in [the director] not to be examined under s 245 of the CA 1963 unless the company is being wound up. Because the law has been altered as to the circumstances in which an application may be made under s 245 and its provisions have been altered to some extent does not mean that the Act is being operated retrospectively[462].'

It followed that Barron J granted in part the order sought. The question was left open as to whether any order seeking to impose personal liability which might be sought, subsequently, would involve retrospection.

Misfeasance

[15.149] Section 298(1) of the CA 1963 provides[463]:

> 'Subsection (2) applies if in the course of winding up a company it appears that any person who has taken part in the formation or promotion of the company, or any past or present officer, liquidator, receiver or examiner of the company, has misapplied or retained or become liable or accountable for any money or property of the company, or has been guilty of any misfeasance or other breach of duty or trust in relation to the company.'

Section 298(2) provides:

> 'The court may, on the application of the liquidator, or any creditor or contributory, examine into the conduct of the promoter, officer, liquidator, receiver or examiner, and compel him—
>
> (a) to repay or restore the money or property or any part thereof respectively with interest at such rate as the court thinks just, or
>
> (b) to contribute such sum to the assets of the company by way of contribution in respect of the misapplication, retainer, misfeasance or other breach of duty or trust as the court thinks just.'

This section can be invoked 'in the course of winding up a company' or under s 251 of the CA 1990[464]. It must be remembered that s 298 is merely a procedural measure and

---

462 *Alba Radio Ltd v Haltone (Cork) Ltd* (1 June 1995, unreported) HC, Barron J at p 3, 4 of the judgment.

463 As amended by s 142 of the CA 1990.

464 See para **[15.141]** *ante*.

does not impose any additional duties on officers, nor confer any additional remedies on creditors[465]. Section 298 enables existing duties of officers to be enforced[466].

[15.150] Section 298 of the CA 1963 can only be used against an officer who has been guilty of a breach of trust which has caused his company to suffer a pecuniary loss[467]. That pecuniary loss must arise from the officer's breach of duty. In *Re SM Barker Ltd*[468], the three directors (and beneficial shareholders) of a company caused the company to voluntarily release a number of simple contract debts due to the company, arising out of transactions between the company and them in their personal capacities. Later, they sold their shares to another group of persons. When the company went into insolvent liquidation, the official liquidator sought an order under a section similar to s 298 of the CA 1963 for a declaration that the former directors were liable to contribute to the assets of the company by way of restitution or as damages for misfeasance. It was held that no order would be made since the gains made by the directors were made in their personal capacity, and not *qua* director nor *qua* trustee of the shareholders. Gavin Duffy J held:

> 'To succeed in this motion the liquidator must prove damage to the company at the hands of the respondent directors. So far, I think no such damage has been proved, unless the cancellation in the Latchmans' interest of an asset worth nearly £12,000, as I assume, so that the company thereafter had nothing to show for that asset, is itself such an actual loss as to justify this claim under [s 298 of the CA 1963]. At this point, it cannot be stressed too emphatically that on the evidence the three Latchmans were in truth the owners of the entire share capital, so that they were at liberty to do virtually whatever they chose, short of acting dishonestly or *ultra vires*. The transaction was the honest result of negotiations between the Latchmans and an external group of businessmen, eager for their own ends to gain control of the company and its assets without paying an excessive price for the shares which carried control. And I discern no moral obliquity in the deeds and omissions of the Latchmans as directors in this transaction ...
>
> Here was a small private company, owned and controlled by a family group, who acted unanimously, and in concert with the incoming members about to replace them, at the ... meetings, and what they did they did in good faith and in natural reliance for the technical mechanics of their operations and of the deal upon an accountant-auditor belonging to a firm of high repute. However improvident the resolution releasing the Latchmans' indebtedness and however regrettable the failures to observe the requirements and formalities of company law, quite beyond their ken, I think, the outstanding fact is the fact

[465] In *Re Kirby's Coaches Ltd* [1991] BCLC 414, it was held by Hoffmann J that a petitioner did not specifically have to plead misfeasance, and it could arise at trial for the first time

[466] See *Re Irish Provident Assurance Company Ltd* [1913] IR 352, where Cherry LJ said of the old section similar to s 298, that 'it applies only to cases where a cause of action would, independently of the section, exist, at the suit of the company', and went on to quote *Cavendish-Bentinck v Fenn* [1887] 12 AC 652 at 669: '... it has been settled, and I think rightly settled, that that section creates no new offence, and that it gives no new rights, but only provides a summary and efficient remedy in respect of rights which, apart from that section, might have been vindicated either in law or in equity.'

[467] See *Re B Johnson & Co (Builders) Ltd* [1955] 2 All ER 775.

[468] *Re SM Barker Ltd* [1950] IR 123.

> that the true owners of the property, acting with the full assent of their prospective assignees, all concurred at the two meetings and throughout in every step taken[469].'

Hence, only losses occasioned by breach of directors' duties can be pursued under s 298[470]. An example of an order being made under s 298 is seen in *Re Contract Packaging Ltd*[471]. After finding that the directors were, *inter alia*, in breach of their fiduciary duties, Flood J declared that pursuant to the section, two of the directors held a house (their family home) in trust for their company, and ordered that they convey it to the liquidator.

[15.151] It should be noted that where confusion is caused because of the intermingling of a 'sole director's' assets with those of the company thereby provoking a liquidator to take misfeasance proceedings, it is open to the court to exercise its discretion and hold the director concerned liable for the costs of the action. This is what happened in *Re David Ireland & Co Ltd*[472], where the sole controller and beneficial owner of a company intermingled his personal finances with those of the company and treated the company's bank account as if it were his own. In fact the man concerned acted honestly, and always ensured that the company was reimbursed. Nevertheless, because it was his 'messing' which provoked the bewildered liquidator to institute misfeasance proceedings, he was held liable to pay the costs of the liquidator in taking the proceedings. In the words of Fitzgibbon LJ:

> 'It has been said that this is 'an extremely hard order'. The hardship, if any, is the result of the 'one man company' system. In my opinion anyone who chooses to give the support of his name as a director to a company of that class, and who neglects his duty by allowing 'one man' to do as he pleases, and actively assists him by paying away the company's money at will, deserves to bear the expense of investigating what has been done, and any practical judicial lesson against undertaking such directorships should not be lightly set aside by a Court of Appeal[473].'

Such has been said to remain 'a salutary reminder in the Ireland of today in which mere figurehead second directors are compulsory'[474]. Indeed, one could go further and say that not only is it a salutary reminder to figurehead or token[475] directors, but also to *all* controllers involved in conducting business through a private company, who tend to be most astute at realising the advantages of the limited liability company, but ignorant of the duties owed by corporate officers and, particularly, by directors.

---

469 Gavan Duffy J (at 135 *et seq*) went on to state that the actions were not *ultra vires*.

470 See also *Derek Randall Enterprises Ltd v Randall* [1991] BCLC 379.

471 *Re Contract Packaging Ltd* (16 January 1992, unreported) HC *per* Flood J reported in (1992) Irish Times, 17, 18 January.

472 *Re David Ireland & Co Ltd* [1905] IR 133.

473 *Re David Ireland & Co Ltd* [1905] IR 133 at 141.

474 See Ussher, *Company Law in Ireland* (1986) at p 241.

475 See para **[15.049]** *et seq*, *ante*.

[D] SECRETARIES' DUTIES

[15.152] The appointment and powers of the company secretary have been considered in Chapter 13[476]. In *Barnett, Hoares & Co v South London Tramways Co*[477], Lord Esher MR said:

> 'A secretary is a mere servant; his position is that he is to do what he is told and no person can assume that he has any authority to represent anything at all.'

Commenting upon this passage, Lord Denning MR in *Panorama Developments (Guilford) Ltd v Fidelis Furnishing Fabrics Ltd*[478] noted that times have changed since it was first mooted by Lord Esher in 1887. Lord Denning observed that the company secretary is a 'much more important person nowadays', being an officer with extensive duties and responsibilities. While Lord Denning's comments are indeed true in the context of public limited companies and large private companies, they hardly reflect the reality in the vast majority of small Irish private companies.

[15.153] The secretary is the chief *administrative* officer of a company; by not having a *management* role as of right, it follows that his duties are equally circumscribed in terms of scope and to whom they are properly owed. It is important to consider, however, the actual duties and powers conferred on secretaries in any particular company. In the vast majority of small Irish private companies the office of secretary will be held by a person who is also a director. Large and medium-sized private companies will frequently employ the services of a legal or accountancy firm to act as company secretary and to perform the requisite secretarial functions.

The subject of secretaries' duties

[15.154] The duties of secretaries are only owed to the separate legal entity that is the company: *Kelly v Kelly*[479]. Unlike the law in relation to directors, there has been no judicial extension of secretaries' duties to persons other than the company, such as shareholders, creditors, or employees. This is explained by reason of the fact that a company secretary is not, *qua* secretary, involved in the management of a company.

Secretaries' common law duties

[15.155] On account of the secretary's limited managerial role, his duties are also limited. As with any employee, a secretary has duties of fidelity and confidentiality. A secretary can be restrained by injunction from disclosing confidential information or trade secrets belonging to his company[480]. The company secretary owes the company duties of skill, care and diligence and can be liable in negligence for failure to exercise the necessary skill, care and diligence. Because a company secretary does not, usually or *ex officio*, have powers of management or decision making, it is thought that a company

---

[476] See Ch 13, *Corporate Governance: Management by the Director*, at para **[13.119]** *et seq*. See generally, McGowan-Smyth & Daly, *Irish Company Secretary's Handbook* (2011, Bloomsbury Professional).

[477] *Barnett, Hoares & Co v South London Tramways Co* (1887) 18 QBD 815 at 817.

[478] *Panorama Developments (Guilford) Ltd v Fidelis Furnishing Fabrics Ltd* [1971] 3 All ER 16.

[479] *Kelly v Kelly* [1986] SLT 101.

[480] *Robb v Green* [1895] 2 QB 315.

secretary is not a fiduciary to the same extent as directors and that the secretary does not owe the same fiduciary duties as are owed by directors. As an employee, however, a secretary must not make a secret profit by virtue of his office. Whether it is correct to say, as the authors of *Palmer's Company Law* do, that the principle in *Regal (Hastings) v Gulliver* applies to company secretaries, is thought to be debatable[481]. This is because the secretary has neither a vote at meetings of the board nor even the right to participate in discussions. If the principles concerning conflict of interest were extended to secretaries, then why not also to ordinary employees?

Secretaries' statutory duties

[15.156] The Companies Acts provide that the company secretary is *expressly* named as the person responsible for certain specific matters, which *include*:

- ensuring (with the directors) 'that the requirements of the Companies Acts are complied with by the company'[482];
- co-signing (with a director) the annual return[483];
- certifying (with a director) the copy of the balance sheet to be annexed to the annual return as being a true copy[484];
- signing the certificate required in the case of a private company that the company has not issued any invitation to the public to subscribe for shares or debentures and where the number of members is over 50, that those persons over 50 are not reckonable in accordance with s 33 of the CA 1963 (with a director)[485];
- in a banking company, signing the balance sheet (with a director)[486];
- giving notice in writing to the company as soon as may be of such matters relating to himself and to his spouse and children as may be necessary for the purposes of s 190 (register of shareholdings)[487];
- giving information in writing to the company as soon as may be of such matters as may be necessary to enable the company to comply with s 195 of the CA 1963[488];
- giving notice to a person who is to become a director with unlimited liability of that fact[489];
- filing and verifying the statement of affairs required under s 224(1) of the CA 1963, where the court has made a winding up order or appointed a provisional liquidator[490];

481 *Palmer's Company Law* (Sweet & Maxwell) at p 8236; para 3.1118.
482 Section 383(3) of the CA 1963.
483 Section 127(1) of the CA 1963.
484 Section 128(1)(a) of the CA 1963.
485 Section 129 of the CA 1963.
486 Section 156(2) of the CA 1963.
487 Section 193(1) of the CA 1963.
488 Section 195(11) of the CA 1963, as inserted by s 51 of the CA 1990.
489 Section 197(2) of the CA 1963.
490 Section 224(2) of the CA 1963.

- submitting and verifying the statement of affairs required under s 319 of the CA 1963, where a receiver has been appointed[491];
- certifying (with a director) the copy of the balance sheet, profit and loss account, or auditor's report, as the case may be, laid before the annual general meeting of the company held during the period to which the return relates to be annexed to the annual return as being true copies[492];
- signing a written statement (with a director) which contains the information required to be given by s 16(1) of the 1986 Act, in lieu of being stated in a note to the accounts, to be annexed to the annual return[493];
- certifying (with a director) that the copy of the statement required by s 16(3)(b) of the 1986 Act annexed to the annual return is a true copy[494];
- certifying the copy of the report of the auditors under s 18(3) to be furnished to the registrar of companies as being a true copy[495];
- notifying the company in writing of the subsistence of his interests in shares or debentures and other information as required by s 53 of the CA 1990[496];
- disclosing interests in shares or debentures[497];
- notifying the company in writing if the secretary's spouse or children are granted a right to subscribe for shares in, or debentures of, the company and of the exercise by the spouse or minor child of such a right[498].

The foregoing statutory duties relate to matters that are exclusive duties of the company secretary in respect of which no other officer or person can perform.

[15.157] In addition, common form articles of association impose the following *express* duties on the company secretary:

- Summon a meeting of the directors, where called by a director[499];
- Countersigning (with a director) the affixing of the company's common seal where authorised by the directors or a committee thereof[500].

Again, the foregoing duties under standard form articles relate to matters that are exclusive duties of the company secretary in respect of which no other officer or person can perform.

[15.158] The Companies Acts impose a myriad of duties on companies. Where a company defaults, the company secretary is liable to be penalised as being an 'officer in default'[501].

491 Section 320(2) of the CA 1963.
492 Section 7(1)(a) of the 1986 Act.
493 Section 16(3)(a) of the 1986 Act.
494 Section 16(3)(b) of the 1986 Act.
495 Section 18(5) of the 1986 Act.
496 Section 53(1) and (2) of the CA 1990.
497 Section 63(1) and (5) of the CA 1990.
498 Section 64(3) of the CA 1990.
499 Regulation 101 of Part I of Table A of the First Schedule to the CA 1963.
500 Regulation 115 of Part I of Table A of the First Schedule to the CA 1963.
501 See Ch 28, *Compliance and Enforcement*, at para **[28.033]** *et seq*.

[15.159] Being a company's chief administrative officer, company secretaries will *in practice* be given a number of other duties. It is important to recognise that these are not statutory duties but, because they are commonly performed by company secretaries, they are noted here. These include:

- issuing notice of directors' meetings, collating the board pack to go to directors, attending and taking minutes;
- filing with the CRO and all other governmental agencies, all returns;
- keeping all statutory registers;
- administering share registrations;
- causing all notices to be published;
- receiving all correspondence and legal notices on behalf of the company.

The actual duties of individual company secretaries will vary according to the practices adopted by their particular board of directors. In many small Irish private companies, there must be a suspicion that the duties of company secretary are taken more lightly, perhaps, than is prudent.

[15.160] In *Re Hydro Klenze Ltd; Trehy v Rutherford et al*[502], Smyth J said in respect of a secretary who was also a director of a company in the context of s 150 of the CA 1990:

> 'As a director and secretary of the company, more particularly in his capacity as secretary, he was under a duty to maintain true and accurate records ...
>
> While accepting that small private companies do not have the resources of a plc and that much of the business of such companies is done on an informal basis – yet this does not absolve the directors, especially one who is a secretary of the company, from keeping things on a proper footing by the holding of meetings, however brief and keeping a proper record thereof.'

It is thought that where a director is also company secretary that that director will have an enhanced duty *as a director* to ensure that matters relating to the maintenance of records and minuting of meetings is looked after, if not by him, then by someone else within the company.

[E] PROMOTERS' DUTIES

Corporate promoters

[15.161] The persons who undertake the formation of a company are termed its *promoters*. Although often a promoter may be a professional advisor, it must not be forgotten in this context that A and B, who incorporated their garage business back in Ch 2[503], are in law also 'promoters'. It has been said[504] that a promoter is:

> '... one who undertakes to form a company with reference to a given project, and to set it going and who takes the necessary steps to accomplish that purpose.'

502 *Re Hydro Klenze Ltd; Trehy v Rutherford et al* [2007] IEHC 456.

503 See Ch 2, *Incorporation by Registration*, at para **[2.004]**.

504 *Twycross v Grant* (1877) CPD 469 at 541, *per* Cockburn CJ.

In the context of private companies, people who are involved in all but a purely professional or advisory capacity in the formation and ultimate registration of a company are liable in law to be deemed promoters.

Fiduciary duties of promoters

[15.162] Promoters owe fiduciary duties both to the shareholders and to the company itself. It has been said in *Whaley Bridge Calico Printing Co v Green & Smith*[505] that the duties owed by a promoter are based on general principles of equity. Thus, Bowen J said[506]:

> 'The relief afforded by equity to companies against promoters, who have sought improperly to make concealed profits out of the promotion, is only an instance of the more general principle upon which equity prevents the abuse of undue influence and of fiduciary relations. The term promoter is a term not of law, but of business, usefully summing up in a word a number of business operations familiar to the commercial world by which a company is generally brought into existence. In every case the relief granted must depend on the establishment of such relations between the promoter and the birth, formation and floating of the company, as render it contrary to good faith that the promoter should derive a secret profit from the promotion. A man who carries about an advertising board in one sense promotes a company, but in order to see whether relief is obtainable by the company what is to be looked to is not a word or name, but the acts and the relations of the parties.'

[15.163] Turning from the general to the specific; like a company director, a promoter is considered to be a trustee, so where he acquires assets 'on behalf of the company', he does so in trust[507]. The duties owed by a trustee are of a fiduciary nature. As such, a promoter is bound to account for any profits made. So in *Erlanger v New Sombrero Phosphate Co*[508], Lord Cairns said:

> '[The promoters] stand, in my opinion, undoubtedly in a fiduciary position. They have in their hands the creation and moulding of the company; they have the power of defining how, and when, and in what shape, and under what supervision, it shall start into existence and begin to act as a trading corporation.'

By accounting for profits is meant that where a company's promoter, for example, buys a piece of property he will be liable to account for any profits made where he sells that property to the company. A good example in point is the case of *Gluckstein v Barnes*[509], where a syndicate was formed to purchase a particular company. The syndicate, of which Gluckstein was a member, formed another company called the Olympia Company Ltd. A prospectus[510] was issued by the company and stated that the property was purchased for £180,000 and disclosed a profit of £40,000. However, what the prospectus did not disclose was that the syndicate had purchased the shares of the company at a price which was below the market value and as a result made an additional

---

505 *Whaley Bridge Calico Printing Co v Green & Smith* (1879) 5 QBD 109.

506 *Whaley Bridge Calico Printing Co v Green & Smith* (1879) 5 QBD 109 at 111.

507 For the duties of trustees, see Keane, *Equity and the Law of Trusts in the Republic of Ireland* (2nd edn, Bloomsbury Professional, 2011) at [10.01] *et seq.*

508 *Erlanger v New Sombrero Phosphate Co* [1878] 3 AC 1218 HL.

509 *Gluckstein v Barnes* [1900] AC 240.

510 See Ch 32, *Prospectus, Market Abuse & Transparency Law*, at para **[32.006]**.

profit of £20,000. When Olympia Company Ltd went into liquidation, the liquidator, mindful of the duties of promoters, sought to make the promoters account to the company for the additional profit as an undisclosed profit. The House of Lords held that the promoters were obliged to disclose the additional profit, to account to the company for it, and were accordingly bound to pay it to the liquidator. Although in that case the company was a public company, the rule that a promoter of a private company must disclose all profits to the shareholders of his company holds true. So where a person has a bright and apparently commercially viable idea, forms a company and invites his friends to join in with him to exploit this idea, and makes a 'secret profit' in the course of his promotional activities, he will be liable to account for this profit to the company and the other shareholders[511].

Breach of the promoter's fiduciary duty

[15.164] Where a promoter acts in breach of his fiduciary duties he will be liable to compensate the company. This is true whether the promoter acquired any property with a sale on to the company in mind, or not[512]. The remedies available to a company where a promoter acts in breach of his duties encompass the equitable, tortious and contractual.

[15.165] In equity, a claim can be made for recession of a contract prejudicial to the company, but this will only succeed where *restitutio in integrum* is possible[513]. An example of where restitution was held to be impossible is *Re Cape Breton*[514], where a number of individuals, one of whom was a director of the company concerned, financed the purchase of certain coal fields which were taken in the name of a nominee. After the company in question was formed, the nominee agreed to sell the coalfields to the company. The director never disclosed his interest to the company. When the company went into liquidation, the coalfield was sold at a loss. The liquidator sought to make the director liable for breach of duty and although the Court of Appeal accepted that the contract could previously have been rescinded, restitution at the date of the hearing was impossible because the coalfield had been sold by the company. Accordingly, the company could not rescind the contract to purchase the coalfield from the promoter's nominee.

[15.166] Where a promoter has acted in breach of his duties to a company, the company can claim restitution of the benefit obtained by the promoter. Such can be done in equity on the basis of a *constructive trust*. Where a promoter receives commission on pre-incorporated contracts he will hold this as constructive trustee and not as a fiduciary agent to the company: *HKV Invest OY v Incotrade PVT Ltd.* Such a trust arises where a trustee obtains a benefit or derives a profit to which he is not entitled from his trusteeship[515]. A promoter is a trustee of the company he promotes, and where he acts in

[511] See also *Re Leeds and Hanley Theatre of Varieties Ltd* [1902] 2 Ch 809.

[512] *Ladywell Mining Co v Brookes* [1887] 35 Ch D 400; and *Re Cape Breton Co* [1885] 29 Ch D 795.

[513] Ie, where all parties can be restored to their original position.

[514] *Re Cape Breton* [1885] 29 Ch D 795.

[515] See generally, Keane, *Equity and Trusts in the Republic of Ireland*, (2nd edn, Bloomsbury Professional, 2011), Ch 13, Constructive Trusts. See also *HKV Invest OY v Incotrade PVT Ltd* [1993] 3 IR 152 at 162 where Costello J cited *Hussey v Palmer* [1972] 1 WLR 1286.

breach of his duties, he will hold any profit or other benefit in trust for the company. In such a situation a company may seek a declaration from the court that such profit or other benefit is held in trust by the promoter for the company. It should also be remembered that a delinquent promoter may also be pursued in tort for deceit or negligent misstatement[516].

[15.167] A promoter can be pursued in misrepresentation for damages for breach of contract, or damages for breach of trust. An example of an action for damages is *Re Leeds and Hanley Theatre of Varieties Ltd*[517]. In that case, a director and promoter did not disclose his interest in a transaction with the company through a nominee third party. The Court of Appeal held that not only could the company retain the property, but the company was also entitled to recover damages from the promoter for breach of fiduciary duty. In the course of his judgment, Vaughan Williams J said:

> 'The authorities are not all perfectly conclusive that there is no remedy by way of an account for profits, but I prefer to say that, whether there is such a remedy or not, I am clear there is a remedy in the shape of damages.'

Insofar as this decision provides authority for promoters being liable in damages for breach of fiduciary duty, as opposed to breach of contract, it has been suggested that it is 'at least questionable'[518].

[15.168] The law of evidence may also provide a remedy in that a promoter may be estopped from denying that he purchased property on his own behalf. This is clear from *Jacobus Marler Estates Ltd v Marler*[519], where the House of Lords held that a promoter of a company could not assert that he bought property in his own capacity while acting as a promoter and was estopped from denying that the property was bought on behalf of the company.

[15.169] A 1972 Irish case concerning the duties of promoters and the foregoing principles, which was only unearthed in the late 1980s[520], is *Hopkins v Shannon Transport Systems Ltd*[521]. In that case, the plaintiff had a dream and floated the idea of a new project for a ferry across the Shannon. The support of another individual was secured when suitable vessels were located. Finance for the venture was sought from two sources: share subscriptions and grants from the Department of Finance. Unknown to some of the directors of the company, the plaintiff and the other individual, who were the promoters of the company, bought as a partnership some of the vessels which were subsequently sold to the company after it had been formed and registered. When the Department of Finance decided not to proceed, the plaintiff decided to pull out of the project. Later, he sought, through the courts, his share of the profits of the partnership. When the matter came before the High Court, Pringle J held that because they were

---

516 See McMahon & Binchy, *The Law of Torts* (3rd edn, Butterworth Ireland, 2000) at Chs 35 and 10, respectively.

517 *Re Leeds and Hanley Theatre of Varieties Ltd* [1902] 2 Ch 809.

518 Meagher, Gummow & Lehane, *Equity – Doctrines & Remedies* (3rd edn, Butterworths, 1992) at p 150. See also *Tracy v Mandalay Party Ltd* (1952) 88 CLR 215.

519 *Jacobus Marler Estates Ltd v Marler* [1916–17] All ER Rep 291.

520 See *O'Dowd* (1989) DULJ 120.

521 *Hopkins v Shannon Transport Systems Ltd* (10 January 1972, unreported) HC.

promoters, they were under a duty to make full disclosure, and so the contract entered by the company with the partnership was *voidable* at the instance of the company.

Promoters' transactions with a company

[15.170] Where there is *full disclosure* by a promoter of his interest or involvement in a contract entered by him with the company, his position will be safeguarded. The extent of the disclosure required by a promoter was examined in a number of cases, such as *Gluckstein v Barnes*[522] and *Erlanger v New Sombrero Phosphate Co*[523]. In the latter case, Lord Cairns said:

> 'I do not say that the owner of property may not promote and form a joint stock company, and then sell his property to it, but I do say that if he does he is bound to take care that he sells it to the company through the medium of a board of directors who can and do exercise an independent and intelligent judgment on the transaction[524].'

Caution should thus be exercised by promoters. Care must always be taken where an existing business is sold to a new company. Where an appropriate objects clause is adopted by the promoters and they as directors resolve in favour of the acquisition, they can be assured that they will not be guilty of a breach of their duties as promoters.

522 *Gluckstein v Barnes* [1900] AC 240.
523 *Erlanger v New Sombrero Phosphate Co* [1878] 3 AC 1218.
524 *Erlanger v New Sombrero Phosphate Co* [1878] 3 AC 1218 at 1236.

Chapter 16

Statutory Regulation of Directors' Transactions

[16.001] The fiduciary nature of the relationship between directors and their companies provides the justification for the statutory regulation of transactions and arrangements involving directors and their companies[1]. The legislature has ordained that common law fiduciary duties are not a sufficient protection of companies' assets when it comes to transactions involving directors and their companies. Directors are in a special position *vis-à-vis* their company and the temptation to abuse their position is particularly acute where the directors and shareholders are one and the same persons, as is often the case in private companies. In such companies, the usual control on directors abusing their position, namely the shareholders, does not exist. Where the directors and shareholders are one and the same persons the 'watchdog', that is, the shareholders acting in general meeting in the interests of the company (and in their own interests, indirectly) is stood down. Part III of the Companies Act 1990 ('the CA 1990') was described in the explanatory memorandum to the Bill as containing:

> 'a series of detailed provisions to deal with recognisable situations where a company director might be tempted to put his personal interest before that of the company.'

In so providing, Part III of the CA 1990 amplifies by statute the common law regulation of transactions involving directors and their companies; the principle, however, is as old as company law itself. As was said in *Re Duckwari plc*[2] in the context of the very similar English provisions:

> 'None of the provisions introduce any novel concept into the law for it has long been recognised that the relationship of a director to his company is a fiduciary one, akin to that between trustee and beneficiary, though not identical with it. The specific topic of sales by the company to its directors at an undervalue or purchases by the company from its directors at an inflated value had been the subject of a number of cases, of which *Daniels v Daniels* [1978]Ch 406 is an example, but it was not tackled by the legislature until the Companies Act 1980, section 48.'

The abuse which Part III of the CA 1990 seeks to curtail is the gratuitous use of corporate assets for the benefit of directors and persons connected with them, to the detriment of the company, its creditors and its members. The statutory regulation of transactions involving directors and their companies arises under three main statutory provisions: ss 29 and 31 of the CA 1990 (which are the two main regulatory provisions

---

1 See generally, Ch 15, *Duties of Directors and Other Officers*.

2 *Re Duckwari plc* [1997] 2 WLR 48 at 51 (*per* Judge Paul Baker QC).

3 Other transactions between directors and their companies that are regulated by Part III, and addressed in other chapters, are: s 28 of the CA 1990: directors' contracts of employment (Ch 13, *Corporate Governance: Management by the Directors*, at para **[13.071]**); and s 41: disclosure of substantial contracts (Ch 17, *Financial Statements, Audit and Annual Return*, at para **[17.113]**).

in Part III of the CA 1990) and s 194 of the CA 1963. Of the three provisions, ss 29 and 31 of the CA 1990 are the most far-reaching and comprehensive regulations.

[16.002] The provisions of ss 29 and 31 of the CA 1990 extend beyond directors to persons connected with directors, and this chapter begins by identifying all of the persons who are regulated by ss 29 and 31. Thereafter, the main regulatory provisions are considered.

[A] Directors and Persons Connected with Directors.

[B] Section 29 – Substantial Property Transactions.

[C] Section 31 – Loans, Quasi-loans, Credit Transactions, Guarantees and the Provision of Security in favour of Directors and other Relevant people.

[D] Disclosure of Interests in Contracts with Companies.

These statutory provisions are given particular prominence in this work because of the frequency with which they arise in the practice of Irish company law and the far-reaching consequences of contravention.

[A] DIRECTORS AND PERSONS CONNECTED WITH DIRECTORS

[16.003] Both ss 29 and 31 of the CA 1990 regulate transactions and arrangements between companies and their directors, directors of their holding company (if any) and persons connected with such directors. It is the inclusion of *persons connected with directors* which causes Part III of the CA 1990 to be a minefield. Three distinguishable classes of 'relevant person' – a non-statutory term that, when used in this chapter, includes directors and persons connected with directors – can be identified:

1. Directors of the company and of its holding company.
2. Natural persons that are connected persons.
3. Bodies corporate that are connected persons.

Each of these is now considered.

Directors of the company and of its holding company

[16.004] Both ss 29 and 31 of the CA 1990 apply to transactions and arrangements between companies and persons who are directors of such companies. 'Directors' here includes formally appointed or *de jure* directors[4] and *de facto*[5] directors. In addition, s 27(1) of the CA 1990 provides that Part III of that Act (containing ss 29 and 31) and s 194 of the CA 1963 apply to *shadow directors*[6].

[16.005] Sections 29 and 31 also regulate transactions and arrangements between a company and the directors of its holding company. The reference to 'holding company' means a company so defined in accordance with s 155 of the CA 1963[7]. Again, it is thought that the reference to a director of a holding company will include a person who

---

4 See Ch 13, *Corporate Governance: Management by the Directors*, at para **[13.025]** *et seq*.

5 See Ch 13, *Corporate Governance: Management by the Directors*, at para **[13.045]** *et seq*.

6 See Ch 13, *Corporate Governance: Management by the Directors*, at para **[13.055]** *et seq*.

7 See Ch 12, *Groups of Companies*, at para **[12.006]** *et seq*.

is either a *de jure* director, a *de facto* director or a shadow director of a company's holding company.

Natural persons that are connected persons

[16.006] Both ss 29 and 31 of the CA 1990 apply to transactions and arrangements between companies and 'persons connected with directors'. This was a new concept, introduced by the CA 1990. Section 26(1) of the CA 1990 defines the term as follows:

> 'For the purposes of this Part, a person is connected with a director of a company if, but only if, the person (not being himself a director of the company) is—
>
> (a) that director's spouse, civil partner within the meaning of the Civil Partnership and Certain Rights and Obligations of Cohabitants Act 2010, parent, brother, sister or child[8];
>
> (b) a person acting in his capacity as the trustee of any trust, the principal beneficiaries of which are the director, his spouse or any of his children or any body corporate which he controls; or
>
> (c) in partnership within the meaning of section 1(1) of the Partnership Act 1890, with that director.'

A practical s 29 example involving a connected person is that a company must obtain the approval of its members before it can convey a property to the child of one of its directors where the value of the property is in excess of €63,486.90[9]. Similarly, a s 31 example involving a connected person might be that a company cannot guarantee a loan made to the sister of one of its directors, unless the transaction comes within one of the exceptions to the s 31 prohibition[10]. It is also important to note that the spouses, civil partners, parents, brothers, sisters, children, etc of *shadow directors* are also persons connected with directors. Moreover, where a company is a subsidiary, the spouses, civil partners, parents, siblings, etc of the directors of the subsidiary's holding company will also be persons connected with directors.

[16.007] Where, for example, a director's spouse is also a director of a company, he or she will not be deemed to be a person connected with a director, whose dealings with the company are regulated on that basis. Instead, of course, a director's spouse's dealings with the company will be regulated on the basis that they are themselves directors of the

---

8 Section 168 and Part 3 of the Schedule to the Civil Partnership and Certain Rights and Obligations of Cohabitants Act 2010 ('CPCROCA 2010') amends s 26(1)(a) of the CA 1990. However, although s 26(1)(b) also refers to 'spouse', no such amendment is made to para (b). Someone seeking to assert that para (b) of s 26(1) applies to civil partners and the children of a civil partnership may seek to argue that s 97(1) of the CPCROCA 2010 has application; that provision provides: 'For the purposes of determining matters concerning ethics and conflicts of interests under any rule of law or enactment— (a) with respect to a person, a reference to a 'connected person' or a 'connected relative' of that person shall be construed as including that person's civil partner and the child of the person's civil partner who is ordinarily resident with the person and the civil partner'. This is not, however, very convincing since why would s 26(1)(a) be amended and s 26(1)(b) not? This certainly seems a shaky basis for imposing criminal liability or affecting civil rights.

9 See para **[16.022]** *post*.

10 See para **[16.065]** *post*.

company. If a director's spouse is a director of a subsidiary's holding company but not a director of the subsidiary, he or she will be a person connected with a director.

[16.008] The CLEA 2001 also clarified the meaning of 'partner' in s 26(1)(c). It has now been put beyond all doubt that by 'partner' is meant a business partner within the meaning of s 1(1) of the Partnership Act 1890[11] as distinct from a 'civil partner' which is included as a connected person by s 26(1)(a), inserted by the Civil Partnership and Certain Rights and Obligations of Cohabitants Act 2010 ('CPCROCA 2010').

[16.009] Regulation 12 of the EC(SMPLC)R 1994[12] used to operate to *deem* the sole member of a single-member company to be a connected person[13]. This has now been replaced[14] with a presumption by s 76(c) of the CLEA 2001, which inserted a new s 26(6) in the CA 1990, which provides:

> 'It shall be presumed for the purposes of this Part, until the contrary is shown, that the sole member of a single-member private limited company within the meaning of the European Communities (Single-Member Private Limited Companies) Regulations, 1994 (SI No 275 of 1994) is a person connected with a director of that company.'

Sole members will not automatically be deemed to be classed as persons connected with directors. Like all presumptions, the presumption created by s 26(6) of the CA 1990 is rebuttable. On the one hand, it can be said that the effect of s 26(6) is minimal since, whatever about a presumption, as a matter of fact a sole member can only be a person connected with a director if he (or it, in the case of a body corporate sole member) meets the requirements in s 26. Whilst this is, of course, true, the significance of the presumption is to shift the onus from the person claiming that a sole member is a connected person, to the sole member to refute that he, she or it, is a connected person.

Bodies corporate that are connected persons

[16.010] Companies are also prohibited from entering into certain transactions or arrangements *in favour of another body corporate*. This is because s 26(2) of the CA 1990 provides:

> 'A body corporate shall also be deemed to be connected with a director of a company if it is controlled by that director.'

It is significant that the term 'body corporate' is used and not merely 'company'. As has been considered in an earlier chapter, 'company' means an Irish company, ie, one formed and registered under the Companies Acts or an existing company[15]. '*Body corporate*', on the other hand, is more generic and refers to any entity that has a separate

---

11 See Twomey, *Partnership Law* (2000, Butterworths) at Ch 2.

12 SI 275/1994.

13 Whilst dealt with under the heading of 'natural persons that are connected persons' for convenience, it is of course the case that a sole member of a private limited company can be a body corporate.

14 Regulation 12 of the EC(SMPLC)R 1994 was repealed by reg 3 of the European Communities (Single-Member Private Limited Companies) Regulations, 1994 (Amendment) Regulations 2001, SI 437/2001.

15 Section 2 of the CA 1963: see Ch 1, *The Private Company in Context*, at para **[1.156]**.

existence from its members, eg, companies, building societies, industrial and provident societies, etc. Section 2(2) of the CA 1963 expressly states that references in the Companies Acts to a body corporate or to a corporation shall be construed as 'including a company incorporated outside the State'. The consequence is that an Irish company will be prohibited from entering into a transaction or arrangement of a kind envisaged by ss 29 or 31 of the CA 1990 *in favour of a foreign company* that is controlled by a director. Again, it should be noted that where a company is a subsidiary, regard must be had not only to bodies corporate that are controlled by directors of the subsidiary, but also to those that are controlled by directors of the subsidiary's holding company.

(a) The meaning of 'control'

[16.011] A body corporate will only be a person connected with a director if that director *controls* it. There is a statutory definition of 'control' in s 26(3) which provides:

> 'For the purposes of this section, a director of a company shall be deemed to control a body corporate if, but only if, he is, alone or together with any other director or directors of the company, or any person connected with the director or such other director or directors, *interested in* one-half or more of the equity share capital of that body or entitled to exercise or control the exercise of one-half or more of the voting power at any general meeting of that body.' (Italics added.)

The amended s 26(3)[16] has clarified an issue that caused trouble to practitioners trying to interpret the old version. The question was – where two directors of Company A are *equally* interested in all of the shares issued in Company B, could Company B be said to be 'controlled' by either director? The uncertainty stemmed from the fact that since both directors had an equal interest, it seemed that, individually, neither could be said to be interested in 'more than one half' of the equity share capital[17], as provided for in the original s 26(3). The revised wording now puts beyond doubt that, in such a situation, Company B will be deemed to be controlled by both directors and so Company B will be a person connected with both directors. The consequence of this is that transactions or arrangements entered into by Company A in favour of Company B will be regulated by Part III of the CA 1990.

[16.012] Where a director is interested in one-half or more of the equity share capital or entitled to exercise or control the exercise of one-half or more of the voting power at a general meeting of a body corporate, he will be deemed to control that body corporate. The other important change effected by the CLEA 2001 concerns aggregation of interests. So, in determining whether a body corporate is controlled by a given director, that director's interests will be aggregated with those of any other director or directors and also with those of any person connected with him or any other director or directors. It should be noted that this latter aggregation pool includes other bodies corporate which a director controls and, to some extent, overlaps with s 26(4)(b) of the CA 1990[18].

[16.013] It may also be noted that one of the two relevant aspects of 'control', *equity share capital* is assigned the same meaning as it has under s 155 of the CA 1963[19].

---

16 As substituted by s 76(b) of the CLEA 2001.

17 Or, indeed, entitled to control the exercise of 'more than one half' of the voting power as provided in the original s 26(3) of the CA 1990.

18 See para **[16.019]** *post*.

19 Section 26(4)(a) of the CA 1990. See Ch 12, *Groups of Companies*, at para **[12.019]**.

(b) 'Interested in' one-half or more of the equity share capital

[16.014] Where a person is the legal and beneficial owner of one-half or more of the shares in a body corporate, it will be connected with him. A person need not, however, be the legal and beneficial owner and lesser interests will satisfy the test of 'interested in one-half or more of the equity share capital of that body or entitled to exercise or control the exercise of one-half or more of the voting power at any general meeting of that body'. Section 54 of the CA 1990 defines the expression 'interested in' shares, for the purpose of s 26(3)[20].

[16.015] Where a director is interested in one-half or more of the shares in a body corporate it does not matter whether or not the director has full rights to the shares. Section 54(2) of the CA 1990 provides:

> 'Any reference to an interest in shares or debentures shall be read as including a reference to any interest of any kind whatsoever in shares or debentures; and accordingly there shall be disregarded any restraints or restrictions to which the exercise of any right attached to the interest is or may be subject.'

This means that where one-half or more of the shares in a body corporate are held, it is irrelevant that the holder or holders of the remaining shares *in fact* control the company. The person who holds one-half or more of the issued equity share capital is, in effect, deemed to control the company (or body corporate) for the purposes of s 26(3) and it will be a person connected with him for the purposes of s 26(2).

[16.016] Where shares are held by a trustee, it will be the real beneficiary who will be deemed to be 'interested in' them. Section 54(3) of the CA 1990 provides:

[20] Section 54 is subject to s 55 of the CA 1990, which expressly disregards certain interests: '(1) The following interests shall be disregarded for the purposes of section 54 and sections 56 to 58— (a) where property is held on trust and an interest in shares or debentures is comprised in that property, an interest in reversion or remainder or of a bare trustee and any discretionary interest; (b) an interest of a person subsisting by virtue of—(i) his holding units in— (I) a registered unit trust scheme within the meaning of section 3 of the Unit Trusts Act, 1972; (II) a unit trust to which section 31 of the Capital Gains Tax Act, 1975, as amended by section 34 of the Finance Act, 1977 relates; (III) an undertaking for collective investment in transferable securities, within the meaning of the European Communities (Undertakings for Collective Investment in Transferable Securities) Regulations, 1989 (SI 78/1989); (ii) a scheme made under section 46 of the Charities Act, 1961; (c) an interest for the life of himself or another of a person under a settlement in the case of which the property comprised in the settlement consists of or includes shares or debentures, and the conditions mentioned in subsection (3) are satisfied; (d) an interest in shares or debentures held by a member of a recognised stock exchange carrying on business as a stock broker which is held by way of security only for the purposes of a transaction entered into by the person or body concerned in the ordinary course of business of such person or body; (e) such interests, or interests of such a class, as may be prescribed for the purposes of this paragraph by regulations made by the Minister. (2) A person shall not by virtue of section 54(4)(b) be taken to be interested in shares or debentures by reason only that he has been appointed a proxy to vote at a specified meeting of a company or of any class of its members and at any adjournment of that meeting, or has been appointed by a body corporate to act as its representative at any meeting of a company or of any class of its members. (3) The conditions referred to in subsection (1) (c) are, in relation to a settlement— (a) that it is irrevocable, and (b) that the settlor (within the meaning of section 96 of the Income Tax Act, 1967) has no interest in any income arising under, or property comprised in, the settlement.'

> 'Where any property is held on trust and any interest in shares or debentures is comprised in that property, any beneficiary of that trust who, apart from this subsection, does not have an interest in the shares or debentures shall be taken to have such an interest; but this subsection is without prejudice to the following provisions of this section.'

The effect of this subsection is that if one-half or more of the shares in a body corporate are held in trust for a beneficiary, it is the beneficiary and not the trustee who is deemed to be interested in those shares.

[16.017] It follows, therefore, that in order for a person to be '*interested in*' shares, it is not necessary that legal title in the shares is actually vested in that person. Section 54(4) of the CA 1990 furthers the philosophy in s 54(3), last considered, by providing:

> 'A person shall be taken to have an interest in shares or debentures if—
>
> (a) he enters into a contract for their purchase by him (whether for cash or other consideration); or
>
> (b) not being the registered holder, he is entitled to exercise any right conferred by the holding of those shares or debentures or is entitled to control the exercise of any such right.'

This makes two distinct provisions the effect of both being to render reckonable inchoate interests. In the first place a person who has merely *contracted* to acquire one-half or more of the shares in a body corporate will be deemed to be interested in those shares. There is no restriction on this and it would seem to apply even if the existence of pre-emption rights might thwart a person's legal registration as a shareholder. In the second place s 54(4)(b) is a catch-all measure, whereby a person who is entitled 'to exercise any right conferred by the holding' or 'to control the exercise of any such right' will also be taken to have an interest in shares in circumstances other than where he has entered into a contract to acquire them (s 54(4)(a)) or where he is the beneficiary of any trust of them (s 54(3)). Section 54(7) provides further specific detail on when a person will be taken to be 'interested in' shares:

> 'A person shall be taken to have an interest in shares or debentures if, otherwise than by virtue of having an interest under a trust—
>
> (a) he has a right to call for delivery of the shares or debentures[21] to himself or to his order; or
>
> (b) he has a right to acquire an interest in shares or debentures or is under an obligation to take an interest in shares or debentures;
>
> whether in any case the right or obligation is conditional or absolute.'

It should be noted, however, that rights or obligations to subscribe for any shares or debentures shall not be taken for the purposes of subsection (7) to be rights to acquire, or obligations to take, any interest in shares or debentures' and that this is without prejudice to s 54(2).[22] Moreover, s 54(8) and (9) provide:

---

[21] Section 54(13) provides: 'Delivery to a person's order of shares or debentures in fulfilment of a contract for the purchase thereof by him or in satisfaction of a right of his to call for delivery thereof, or failure to deliver shares or debentures in accordance with the terms of such a contract or on which such a right falls to be satisfied, shall be deemed to constitute an event in consequence of the occurrence of which he ceases to be interested in them, and so shall the lapse of a person's right to call for delivery of shares or debentures.'

[22] Section 54(10) of the CA 1990.

'(8) For the purposes of subsection (4)(b) a person shall be taken to be entitled to exercise or control the exercise of any right conferred by the holding of shares or debentures if he has a right (whether subject to conditions or not) the exercise of which would make him so entitled or is under an obligation (whether so subject or not) the fulfilment of which would make him so entitled.

(9) A person shall not by virtue of subsection (4)(b) be taken to be interested in any shares or debentures by reason only that he has been appointed a proxy to vote at a specified meeting of a company or of any class of its members and at any adjournment of that meeting or has been appointed by a body corporate to act as its representative at any meeting of a company or of any class of its members.'

[16.018] Section 54(5) concerns situations where one body corporate is 'interested in' the shares in another body corporate. This provides:

'A person shall be taken to be interested in shares or debentures if a body corporate is interested in them and—

(a) that body corporate or its directors are accustomed to act in accordance with his directions or instructions; or

(b) he is entitled to exercise or control the exercise of more than half[23] of the voting power at general meetings of that body corporate.'

This is a particularly far-reaching measure. It means that Body Corporate A will be connected with a director of Body Corporate B if Body Corporate C is interested in more than one-half of the shares in Body Corporate A and the director is a shadow director of Body Corporate C or is entitled to exercise or control the exercise of more than half of the voting power at general meetings of Body Corporate C. This provisions rests uneasily with s 26(4)(b), considered in the next paragraph, in that there is some overlap with s 54(5)(b). Further elaboration is provided by s 54(6):

'Where a person is entitled to exercise or control the exercise of more than half[24] of the voting power at general meetings of a body corporate and that body corporate is entitled to exercise or control the exercise of any of the voting power at general meetings of another body corporate (the 'relevant voting power'), then, for the purposes of subsection (5)(b), the relevant voting power shall be taken to be exercisable by that person.'

Generally, it should be noted that where persons have a joint interest, each of them shall be deemed to have that interest[25] and it is provided that it is immaterial that shares or debentures in which a person has an interest are unidentifiable[26].

---

23 Section 26(5) directs that 'one-third or more', as appears in s 54, should be replaced by 'more than half' when s 54 is being applied to the construction of s 26(3). It would appear to be a minor oversight not to have amended s 26(5) to refer to 'one-half or more' when substituting the new s 26(3).

24 Section 26(5) of the CA 1990 directs that 'one-third or more', as appears in s 54, should be replaced by 'more than half' when s 54 is being applied to the construction of s 26(3). It would appear to be a minor oversight not to have amended s 26(5) to refer to 'one-half or more' when substituting the new s 26(3)

25 Section 54(11) of the CA 1990.

26 Section 54(12) of the CA 1990.

(c) Body corporate controlled by body corporate controlled by a director

[16.019] A body corporate that is controlled by a body corporate that is itself controlled by a director of a company will also be a person connected with such a director. This is apparent from the extensive definitions given to 'interested in' shares in s 54 of the CA 1990 which is applied to s 26(3) but is also the case pursuant to s 26(4)(b) of the CA 1990, which provides that:

> 'references to voting power exercised by a director shall include references to voting power exercised by another body corporate which that director controls.'

This means that where A Ltd is a wholly-owned subsidiary of B Ltd and B Ltd is controlled by a director of C Ltd, then A Ltd is a person connected with a director of C Ltd with the consequence that transactions between C Ltd and A Ltd will be regulated by ss 29 and 31 of the CA 1990.

(d) A subsidiary can be a body corporate controlled by a director

[16.020] A body corporate can be a subsidiary company – within the meaning of s 155 of the CA 1963[27] – and, contemporaneously, a body corporate controlled by a director within the meaning of s 26(2) of the CA 1990. It is, however, important to stress that a subsidiary will not invariably be a person connected with a director of its holding company. In the case of a wholly-owned subsidiary, such a subsidiary could only be a person connected with a director of its holding company if that director 'controlled' the holding company by, for example, being interested in all of the issued shares in the holding company.

Summary

[16.021] In the context of Part III of the CA 1990, the expression director and any person connected with a director includes all of the following persons:

Persons who are directors and other 'relevant people'	
• directors of a company; • shadow directors of a company; • directors of a holding company; • shadow directors of a holding company; • the spouse, civil partner, parent, brother, sister, child of a director of a company or of its holding company; • the partner of a director of a company or of its holding company; • trustees where the principal beneficiaries of the trust are a director (whether of the company or of its holding company), his spouse, any of his children or any body corporate he controls;	• a body corporate controlled by a director of a company or of its holding company; • a body corporate controlled by a body corporate that is itself controlled by a director of a company or of its holding company; • there is a presumption that the sole member of a single-member private limited company is a person connected with a director.

[27] See Ch 12, *Groups of Companies*, at para **[12.020]** *et seq*.

[B] Substantial Property Transactions[28]

[16.022] Section 29 of the CA 1990[29] is designed to provide protection to the *members of a company*, not its creditors. As Finlay Geoghegan J said in *Kerr et al v Conduit Enterprises Ltd*[30]:

> 'The purpose of section 29 of the Act of 1990 is to protect the shareholders of a company against directors entering into certain transactions with the company in which they have a personal interest, without the approval of at least those shareholders holding a simple majority of the voting shares ... The mischief sought to be avoided appears confined to the protection of shareholders with a right to vote[31].'

Section 29 achieves its goal by requiring the members of a company to approve, by means of an ordinary resolution, all substantial property transactions entered into between companies and their directors. It therefore provides a safeguard against directors abusing their position in corporate transactions involving themselves in their personal capacities. Section 29 is a derogation from the directors' powers to manage the business of the company, conferred by reg 80 of Table A.

[16.023] The failure to comply with s 29 is not a criminal offence; it does, however, render an unapproved transaction *voidable* at the instance of the company (and not *ab initio*[32]) and exposes the directors involved to unpleasant personal consequences[33]. Whilst the effect may be to maintain the value of a company's assets, any protection afforded to creditors is incidental and not by design. This is because s 29 does not prohibit any corporate transaction involving directors that the members of the company are not capable of approving by ordinary resolution. This remains the case even where the directors and the members are one and the same, meaning that two shareholding directors can approve of a substantial property transaction (wearing their members' hats) although it is to the manifest disadvantage of the company without contravening s 29 of the CA 1990[34]. Section 29 gives no voice to creditors in whether or not substantial property transactions between directors and their companies are validated. Where the members and directors are one and the same persons – as is frequently the case in many Irish persons – there will be no difficulty in complying with s 29 of the CA 1990 which, in such cases, is no more than a paper exercise. The real issue, however, is whether companies and their advisors *realise* that s 29 has application. As Hodgson J

---

28 See generally, Courtney, '"Substantial Property Transactions" Between Directors and Companies: Section 29 of the Companies Act 1990' (1996) 3 Commercial Law Practitioner 142; and for a note on s 320 of the Companies Act 1985 (UK) (now replaced by s 190 of the Companies Act 2006 (UK)) Milman, 'Problems with Substantial Property Transactions' (1998) Palmer's In Company, Issue 8/98 17 September 1998.

29 See Keane, *Company Law* (4th edn, Bloomsbury Professional, 2007) at para 27.79.

30 *Kerr et al v Conduit Enterprises Ltd* [2010] IEHC 300 (Finlay Geoghegan J).

31 At para 45.

32 See para **[16.046]** *post*.

33 See para **[16.049]** *post*.

34 Of course, regard must be had to the directors' common law duties, considered in Ch 15, *Duties of Directors and Other Officers* and otherwise unlawful transactions may be avoided on a winding-up: see generally Ch 25, *The Realisation and Distribution of Assets in a Winding Up*.

observed in *Joint Receivers and Managers of Niltan Carson v Hawthorne*[35] in the context of a 'family company'[36]:

> 'Plainly there would not have been the slightest difficulty in obtaining approval at the time, but as I have said, I am sure that Mr Nelson did not then know of the section at all[37].'

Where the members and directors are different persons and the members refuse to approve a particular transaction, the section is doing as was intended – providing a safeguard against directors' abuses – and cannot be objectively criticised for so doing. In *British Racing Drivers' Club Ltd and another v Hextall Erskine & Co (a firm)*[38], Carnwath J said of the purpose of the materially identical s 320 of the English Companies Act 1985 (now s 190 of the Companies Act 2006 (UK)):

> 'The thinking behind that section is that if directors enter into a substantial commercial transaction with one of their number, there is a danger that their judgment may be distorted by conflicts of interest and loyalties, even in cases where there is no actual dishonesty. The section is designed to protect a company against such distortions. It enables members to provide a check. Of course, this does not necessarily mean that the members will exercise a better commercial judgment; but it does make it likely that the matter will be more widely ventilated, and a more objective decision reached[39].'

Of course the transaction need not be a 'substantial commercial transaction', and s 29 has considerable implications for routine conveyancing where a director proposes to sell or lease property of the requisite value to or from a company.

[16.024] Section 29(1) of the CA 1990 has been in force since 1 February 1991; it does not apply to arrangements entered into before that date[40]. As to its territoriality, it is important to note that s 29, like Part III generally, has effect in relation to an arrangement whether or not that arrangement is governed by the law of the State or the law of another country[41]. The decisive criterion is that it only applies to arrangements entered into by an Irish *company*[42].

[16.025] Section 29 is now analysed under the following headings:

1. The regulation of substantial property transactions.
2. The meaning of 'non-cash asset'.
3. The meaning of 'requisite value'.
4. Exceptions.
5. Compliance by approving resolution.
6. The consequences of breaching s 29(1).
7. Liability of directors and others for breach.

---

35 *Joint Receivers and Managers of Niltan Carson v Hawthorne* [1988] BCLC 298.

36 *Joint Receivers and Managers of Niltan Carson v Hawthorne* [1988] BCLC 298 at 303j.

37 *Joint Receivers and Managers of Niltan Carson v Hawthorne* [1988] BCLC 298 at 320e–f.

38 *British Racing Drivers' Club Ltd and another v Hextall Erskine & Co (a firm)* [1996] 3 All ER 667.

39 *British Racing Drivers' Club Ltd and another v Hextall Erskine & Co (a firm)* [1996] 3 All ER 667 at 681, 681.

40 Section 25(7) of the CA 1990.

41 Section 25(8) of the CA 1990.

42 As defined by s 2 of the CA 1963.

The regulation of substantial property transactions

[16.026] Section 29(1) of the CA 1990 is a two-way valve. It regulates substantial property transactions in which a director acquires assets from his company *and* in which a company acquires assets from its director. It provides that, subject to certain exceptions[43]:

> '... a company shall not enter into an arrangement—
>
> (a) whereby a director of the company or its holding company or a person connected with such a director acquires or is to acquire one or more non-cash assets of the requisite value from the company; or
>
> (b) whereby the company acquires or is to acquire one or more non-cash assets of the requisite value from such a director or a person so connected;
>
> unless the arrangement is first approved by a resolution of the company in general meeting and, if the director or connected person is a director of its holding company or a person connected with such a director, by a resolution in general meeting of the holding company.'

The arrangement need not be contractually binding; it includes agreements and understandings[44]. It should also be noted that where a subsidiary company enters into an arrangement with a director or other relevant person, if that person also happens to be a director of the subsidiary's holding company, the members of the holding company will also be required to approve of the arrangement by resolution *even though the holding company does not itself enter into any arrangement with any person.*

[16.027] It is difficult to appreciate fully the scope of s 29 without also appreciating the meaning of the defined terms used therein. The concept of *a person connected with a director* is defined by s 26 of the CA 1990 and has been comprehensively considered in Section [A][45]. The statutory definitions of *non-cash assets* and *requisite value* are equally fundamental to understanding what transactions are affected by s 29 of the CA 1990.

The meaning of 'non-cash asset'

[16.028] As might be expected, 'non-cash asset' is defined by s 29(9)(a) as any property other than cash, and for the purposes of the definition, cash is deemed to include foreign currency. Moreover, any reference to the acquisition of a non-cash asset includes a reference to the creation or extinction of an estate or interest in, or a right over, any property and also a reference to the discharge of any person's liability other than a liability for a liquidated sum[46]. In *Re a Company No 0032314 of 1992; Duckwari plc v Offerventure Ltd*[47] the defendant company (which was controlled by a director of the plaintiff company) agreed to buy a freehold property, from a third party, for £495,000

---

43 See para **[16.036]** *et seq*, *post*.

44 In *Duckwari plc v Offerventure Ltd (No 2)* [1999] BCC 11 Nourse LJ said: '"Arrangement" is a word which is widely used by Parliament to include agreements or understandings having no contractual effect. Further there is no misuse of language in describing a transaction contemplated by such an agreement or understanding as one which is entered into "pursuant to" it.'

45 See para **[16.003]** *et seq*, *ante*.

46 Section 29(9)(b) of the CA 1990.

47 *Re a Company No 0032314 of 1992; Duckwari plc v Offerventure Ltd* [1995] BCC 89.

and paid a deposit of £49,500 to stakeholders. On completion of the sale, the property was in fact conveyed to the plaintiff company, which paid the balance of the purchase price and reimbursed the defendant company for the deposit. At trial it was held that there had been a transfer to the plaintiff of the defendant's interest under the contract of sale. This finding was, *inter alia*, appealed on the basis that the transaction did not involve the acquisition of an asset by the plaintiff from the defendant and that what had occurred was a novation of the contract. In the Court of Appeal, Millett LJ held, after quoting the then English equivalent of s 29(9)(b)[48], that 'it is arguable that Duckwari acquired an asset from Offerventure even if the transaction was carried out by novation'[49].

In *Micro Leisure Ltd v County Properties & Developments Ltd and another (No 1)*[50], the facts of which are given below[51], Lord Hamilton made the following observation on the English equivalent to s 29(9)(b):

> 'The concept of a person acquiring an asset from the company (or vice versa) imports, in my view, as a matter of ordinary language that immediately prior to the time of acquisition the asset is in existence – though, given that s 320 covers arrangements under which a party 'is to acquire' an asset, it may be that it can apply where an asset comes into existence between the making of the arrangement and the acquisition of the asset under it. [Section 29(9)(b) of the CA 1990] defines 'non-cash asset' as meaning any property or interest in property. That is, as Lord Osborne observed in *Lander v Premier Pict Petroleum & another* [1998]BCC 248 at 254, a comprehensive definition. That definition … does not, however, in my view embrace property or an interest in property which is brought into existence only by the 'acquisition' itself. It matters not that the property or interest in property then brought into existence is itself capable of transmission, by assignment or otherwise[52].'

In *Lander v Premier Pict Petroleum & another*[53], the plaintiff had claimed the right (under his contract of employment) to terminate his contract as managing director when another party obtained more than 50% of the company's equity share capital and in such an event he became entitled to a sum of three times his gross salary. The defendant company claimed, *inter alia*, that this was an arrangement concerning a substantial property transaction with a non-cash asset of the requisite value and was required to be approved by the company's members. Lord Osborne held, *inter alia*, that the nature of the rights in question was to cash payments which could not be described as 'property or interest in property other than cash' and so were not 'non-cash assets'.

---

48 Section 739(2) of the English Companies Act 1985.

49 *Re a Company No 0032314 of 1992; Duckwari plc v Offerventure Ltd* [1995] BCC 89 at 96.

50 *Micro Leisure Ltd v County Properties & Developments Ltd and another (No 1)* (19 January 1999, unreported) Scottish Court of Sessions.

51 See para **[16.034]** *post*.

52 *Micro Leisure Ltd v County Properties & Developments Ltd and another (No 1)* (19 January 1999, unreported) Scottish Court of Sessions at p 8 of the transcript.

53 *Lander v Premier Pict Petroleum & another* [1998] BCC 248 at 254.

The meaning of 'requisite value'

[16.029] Not all transactions involving the acquisition or disposal of non-cash assets come within the scope of s 29(1). '*Requisite value*' is defined by s 29(2), which provides that for the purposes of s 29, a non-cash asset is of the requisite value:

> '... if at the time the arrangement in question is entered into its value is not less than €1,269.74 but, subject to that, exceeds €63,486.90 or ten per cent of the amount of the company's *relevant assets* ...'

'*Relevant assets*' is in turn defined by s 29(2)(a) and (b) as being:

> '(a) except in a case falling within paragraph (b), the value of its net assets[54] determined by reference to the accounts prepared and laid in accordance with the requirements of section 148 of the CA 1963 in respect of the last preceding financial year in respect of which such accounts were so laid;
>
> (b) where no accounts have been prepared and laid under that section before that time, the amount of its called-up share capital.'

Since, frequently, private companies will not be capitalised by shares – eg, the subscription for and issue of one or two €1 shares is commonplace – for 'relevant assets' to amount to a meaningful figure in such companies, regard will have to be had to their annual accounts[55]. Where the value of relevant assets is in issue in a proposed transaction, it is thought prudent to have it certified by the company's auditors.

[16.030] The provisions on requisite value may be summarised thus. First, there is a *de minimis* provision – if the value of a non-cash asset is less than €1,269.74 it falls outside of s 29(1). If the value of the non-cash asset is greater than €63,486.90 *or* greater than 10% of the company's relevant assets – *whichever is the lesser*[56] – s 29(1) will apply. All transactions where the value of the non-cash assets exceeds €63,486.90 must comply with s 29(1). Where the value of the non-cash asset is between €1,269.74 and €63,486.90, whether or not the transaction is caught by s 29(1) will depend upon the value of its relevant assets. In a company where relevant assets are, say, €100,000, a transaction involving assets valued at more than €10,000 will be caught. By contrast, in a company with relevant assets of €634,869, all transactions involving assets the value of which do not exceed €63,486.90, will fall outside of s 29(1). It is clear from s 29(2) that the *punctum temporis* for the valuation of the non-cash asset is the time at which the arrangement is question is made[57].

---

54 Section 29(9) provides: '"net assets", in relation to a company, means the aggregate of the company's assets less the aggregate of its liabilities, and for this purpose "liabilities" includes any provision for liabilities or charges within paragraph 70 of the Schedule to the Companies (Amendment) Act, 1986.'

55 See Ch 17, *Financial Statements, Audit and Annual Return*, at para **[17.250]** *et seq*

56 Section 29(2) does not use the words '*whichever is the lesser*' but it is thought that this must be implied from the language used. This interpretation of the similar English legislation (s 48(2) of the Companies Act 1980, which pre-dates s 320 of the Companies Act 1985 and s 190 of the Companies Act 2006 (UK)) has been thus construed by Hodgson J in *Joint Receivers and Managers of Niltan Carson Ltd v Hawthorne* [1988] BCLC 298 at 321g. Finlay Geoghegan J in *Kerr et al v Conduit Enterprises Ltd* [2010] IEHC 300 at para 18 also accepted that it is the lesser of the two figures that is relevant.

57 See also *Lander v Premier Pict Petroleum & another* [1998] BCC 248 at 254.

[16.031] The leading Irish case on the valuation of non-cash assets in the context of substantial property transactions is *Kerr et al v Conduit Enterprises Ltd*[58]. The facts in this case were that in December 1997, the defendant company ('Conduit') took a 25-year lease at an annual rent of £240,785. The landlords under that lease were two directors and shareholders of Conduit, their spouses also being directors and shareholders. As such, s 29(1)(b) of the CA 1990 had *prima facie* application to the transaction whereby a company, Conduit, acquired a non-cash asset (the lease) from not one but two of its directors. Ownership of Conduit changed on many occasions from the time the lease was entered into until 2008, some 11 years later, when Conduit indicated that it proposed to treat the lease as void and surrender the property, the reason given being that the lease had been granted in breach of s 29. The first question which the High Court had to consider was whether the interest in property constituting the non-cash asset was of the requisite value.

[16.032] In considering the appropriate value to be ascribed to the lease entered into in December 1997, Finlay Geoghegan J noted that Conduit's counsel had relied upon the definition of the *value* of a transaction or *arrangement* for the purposes of Part III of the CA 1990. This provides that, for the purposes of Part III of the CA 1990, the value of an arrangement is:

> '… the price which it is reasonable to expect could be obtained for the goods, land or services to which the transaction or arrangement relates if they had been supplied at the time the transaction or arrangement is entered into in the ordinary course of business and on the same terms (apart from price) as they have been supplied or are to be supplied under the transaction or arrangement in question.'

The learned High Court judge rejected the application of this definition to establishing the value of a non-cash asset for the purposes of s 29, saying:

> 'Section 29 of the Act of 1990 is within Part III. However, whilst section 29(1) prohibits a company from entering into 'an arrangement' whereby the company acquires one or more non-cash assets of the requisite value, it is not the value of the *arrangement* which is relevant, but rather, the value of the *non-cash asset*, for the purposes of the application of section 29. Considering Part III of the Act of 1990, there is, in my view, a clear distinction made by the Oireachtas in the words used in sections 25 and 29 between, on the one hand, the value of 'a transaction or arrangement', as defined in section 25(4), and the value of 'a non-cash asset' for the purposes of section 29. Section 25 does not address the valuation of a non-cash asset for the purposes of section 29, and, accordingly, I have formed the view that it is not applicable to the valuation of the non-cash asset acquired by the defendant in entering into the lease in December 1997. It appears appropriate to note that a lease may constitute a credit transaction for the purposes of Part III of the Act of 1990 by reason of the definition of credit transaction in section 25(3)(b) as a transaction under which one party 'leases ... the use of land ... in return for periodical payments'. However, section 29 does not, of course, apply to a 'credit transaction' as defined, but rather, to the acquisition of a 'non-cash asset'[59].'

---

58 *Kerr et al v Conduit Enterprises Ltd* [2010] IEHC 300 (Finlay Geoghegan J).

59 *Kerr et al v Conduit Enterprises Ltd* [2010] IEHC 300 at para 20. Finlay Geoghegan J also found that s 25(5), which also refers to the value of a 'transaction or arrangement', does not apply to the valuation of a non-cash asset allegedly acquired in breach of s 29: see para 22.

Finlay Geoghegan J went on to conclude from this that the annual rental charge under the lease was *not* the relevant value for the purposes determining the value of the lease as a non-cash asset.

[16.033] Finlay Geoghegan J went on to hold that in the case of a non-cash asset that is a lease, its value is the *capital value of the lease*. In this respect the learned judge agreed with the decision of Lawison J in *Ultraframe (UK) Ltd v Fielding*[60] that where a company enters into a lease, as lessee, for the purposes of s 29 what it acquires as the non-cash asset is the lessee's interest in the property granted by the lease, ie, the estate or interest in the property which gives the tenant a right to exclusive possession and, *inter alia*, a right to assign its interest under the lease subject to the landlord's consent. Finlay Geoghegan J went on to hold that:

> 'In my view, the assignment value of the lease is similar to the capital value of the lessee's interest. If the defendant, as lessee, had, shortly after the grant of the lease, sought to realise the capital value of the lease granted to it, it could have done so by assigning, in accordance with clause 5.30 of the lease, with the consent of the landlord. [The expert valuer's] view is that there was no capital value to the defendant on such an assignment. The further relevant evidence of the nil capital value is the absence of the payment by the defendant of any premium or fine on the granting of the lease. Consistent with the nil capital value, the lease is not represented in the balance sheet of the defendant as an asset with a value[61].'

The learned judge concluded that Conduit had failed to establish that the value of the non-cash asset acquired by Conduit from two of its directors was in excess of £10,292

---

60 *Ultraframe (UK) Ltd v Fielding* [2005] EWHC 1638, [2006] FSR 17. In that case, Lewison J stated (at 1371, 1372): 'The essential question, therefore, is how to characterise the asset acquired by the company. Is it the lease; or is it the right to possession granted by the lease? First, on the face of it, the comparators are all capital sums, especially the company's net asset value, and its called-up share capital. In any comparison one would expect to compare like with like. That would indicate that one is looking for a capital value on the other side of the comparison. Second, a non-cash asset is described in terms of property or an interest in property. The property interest created by a lease is the lease itself. Third, a lease may be granted for an indeterminate period (eg an annual tenancy). If one is required to assess the aggregate of the rental payments that will fall due during the term of the lease, the practical problems will be acute. If, on the other hand, one is expected to undertake a discounted cash flow or a capitalisation of the rent at an appropriate rate, there would seem to be a lot of room for argument about value, which is unlikely to have been Parliament's intention. And if a lease is granted for a long fixed term at a modest rent, an assessment of the aggregate rental payments which will fall due during the term might bring the transaction within the scope of section 320. Since the purpose of the section is to deal with "substantial" property transactions, this would be surprising. Fourth, Hodgson J held in *Niltan Carson Ltd v Nelson* [1988] BCLC 298 that the periodic rent would appear in the company's accounts as a debit item and could not, therefore, represent its value for the purposes of the section. Fifth, contracts with directors require the director's interest to be disclosed either under the articles or under section 317 of the Companies Act or both; and consequently there is some control over a company entering into rack rent leases with a director ... I conclude, therefore, that the asset is properly characterised as the lease rather than the periodic value of the right to occupy; that the relevant value is its capital value.'

61 *Kerr et al v Conduit Enterprises Ltd* [2010] IEHC 300 at para 29.

(which the judge had previously established was 10% of Conduit's relevant assets) so that the lease had not been in breach of s 29 and so could not be avoided.

[16.034] The onus of establishing that a non-cash asset is of the requisite value is on the person who invokes the section[62]; this will generally be the company or its liquidator. Placing a value on a particular asset the subject matter of an arrangement will usually be straightforward. An example of where, however, this posed a particular difficulty was *Micro Leisure Ltd v Country Properties & Developments Ltd and another*[63]. There, it was held by Lord Hamilton in the Scottish Court of Session (Outer House) that s 320 of the Companies Act 1985 (UK) was to be broadly construed and the value of a particular asset meant the true market value of the asset to the director or person connected with him, as subjectively ascertained. The facts[64] in that case were that the plaintiff sourced land available for purchase and development. The defendant provided funds for its acquisition and in return would receive title to part of the property and a half share in the subsequent development of the property. The plaintiff took title at first but subsequently transferred it to the defendant, pursuant to an alleged trust, and thereafter the defendant mortgaged the entire of the property and then re-transferred a portion of it to the plaintiff, but subject to the mortgage in favour of a High Street bank. This occurred in 1993 and 1994, and at all material times the defendant was a person connected with a director of the plaintiff. Subsequently, in 1996, an agreement was put in place between the plaintiff and defendant whereby they agreed to develop lands owned by both companies, the development being carried out by the defendant and both companies sharing in the profits, the greater proportion going to the defendant. In *Micro Leisure Ltd v County Properties & Developments Ltd and another (No 1)*[65], it was held by Lord Hamilton that the 1996 agreement could, in certain circumstances, apply to the rights acquired by the first defendant but he went on to say that the existing pleadings did not contain averments apt to satisfy the statutory provisions. The instant case arose from the plaintiff's amended proceedings. On the question of the requisite value, Lord Hamilton noted that the first defendant company owned two sites, adjacent to the plaintiff's site. When taken together as one large site the plaintiff's site and one of the defendant's sites had a significantly greater value than had their values in isolation. The question to be determined was whether the non-cash asset had an 'objective market value' or a more subjective value, based on its utility to the director or person connected with a director. Lord Hamilton favoured the subjective approach, holding:

> 'Parliament has not defined the criteria by which "its value" in s 320(2), *ie* the value of the non-cash asset, is to be determined. That state of affairs is to be contrasted with definitions of "value" given for other statutory purposes. It is also to be contrasted with the prescribed criteria for determining whether the relevant threshold of value has been reached. The absence of definition suggests, in my view, that Parliament intended the value of the non-cash asset to be determined, having regard to the statutory purposes, in

62 *Joint Receivers and Managers of Niltan Carson v Hawthorne* [1988] BCLC 298.

63 *Micro Leisure Ltd v Country Properties & Developments Ltd and another* [2000] BCC 872.

64 As elicited from the earlier decision of Lord Hamilton in *Micro Leisure Ltd v County Properties & Developments Ltd and another (No 1)* (19 January 1999, unreported) Scottish Court of Sessions.

65 *Micro Leisure Ltd v Country Properties & Developments Ltd and another* (19 January 1999, unreported) Scottish Court of Sessions.

> the context of the particular circumstances of the transaction or arrangement. I figured in the course of argument a situation in which a company owned a strip of land which a director of it sought to acquire, the director already being proprietor of adjacent land. In circumstances in which it was quite evident both to the company (ie its board) and to the director that the land proposed to be acquired was a random strip, the acquisition of which would markedly enhance the development value of the director's existing property, it is difficult to see why the 'value' of the strip should, for the purposes of s 320(2), be assessed without reference to that circumstance. Otherwise, not only would the director be acquiring the strip at an advantageous price but the company would be failing to take advantage of the known circumstance that its property could on sale to a particular purchaser realise a significantly higher price than its value treated in isolation. That enhanced price would in such circumstances, in my view, represent the true market value or worth of the property. Such an example is not, in my view, so fanciful or unusual that taking account of it would distort the true purpose and intent of the statutory provisions[66].'

It is thought that the application of the finding in this decision must be limited to circumstances where no contract of sale has been executed by the parties and where the valuation of a particular non-cash asset is, to some extent, notional. The facts in the instant case were unusual as it was even arguable that the arrangement in question did not give rise to an arrangement within the meaning of the legislation.

[16.035] It should also be noted that where the value of a transaction or arrangement is not capable of being expressed as a specific sum of money (because the amount of any liability arising under the transaction is unascertainable, or for any other reason), it shall, whether or not any liability under the transaction has been reduced, *be deemed* to exceed €63,486.90[67].

Exceptions

[16.036] There are three exceptions which exempt certain transactions notwithstanding that non-cash assets of the requisite value are acquired from (or disposed of to) relevant people from companies. These are:

(a) Inter-group arrangements;
(b) Arrangements in insolvent windings up;
(c) Acquisitions by members acting '*qua* member'.

(a) Inter-group arrangements

[16.037] Section 29(7)(a) of the CA 1990 provides that neither of the two limbs in s 29(1) applies where non-cash assets are acquired by a holding company from a wholly-owned subsidiary, *or* by a wholly-owned subsidiary from its holding company, or by one wholly-owned subsidiary from another wholly-owned subsidiary. Implicit in this is the recognition that arrangements between companies will be caught by s 29(1) where one of the companies is controlled by a director of the other; and that *control* for the purposes of s 26(2) of the CA 1990 does not, *per se*, exclude a company that is controlled by a director within the meaning of s 26 from also being controlled by another company to the extent that it is its subsidiary within the meaning of s 155 of the

66 *Micro Leisure Ltd v Country Properties & Developments Ltd and another* [2000] BCC 872 at 874, 875.

67 Section 25(5) of the CA 1990.

CA 1963[68]. However, one should not assume that because a group relationship exists members of that group will automatically be persons connected with directors, and before looking to see whether s 29(7)(a) applies, one should first establish whether a particular company is in fact a person connected with a director. It is also important to note that not every transaction between a holding company and a subsidiary is automatically exempted. In order to avail of the s 29(7)(a) exemption, it is insufficient to merely show that the companies in the transaction are holding companies and subsidiaries, within the meaning of s 155 of the CA 1963. Only transactions involving *wholly-owned subsidiaries* can avail of the s 29(7) exemption. It should be noted that 'wholly-owned subsidiary' is not defined by s 29, and s 150(5) of the CA 1963[69] can be taken to be a guide *only* as to the meaning of wholly-owned subsidiary in the context of s 29(7) of the CA 1990[70]. It cannot, in particular, be assumed that a wholly-owned subsidiary for the purposes of s 29(7) can have more than one member although two members are acceptable for the purposes of s 150(5) of the CA 1963 where the second member is itself a wholly-owned subsidiary of the first member.

(b) Arrangements in insolvent windings up

[16.038] Section 29(7)(b) exempts arrangements for the acquisition of a non-cash asset where the arrangement is entered into by a company which is being wound up, 'unless the winding-up is a member's voluntary winding up'. This means that neither court appointed liquidators nor voluntary liquidators in creditors' voluntary windings up are required to comply with s 29(1) in disposing of assets to directors or other relevant people. A voluntary liquidator in a members' voluntary winding up must, however, comply with s 29(1) and the members must approve of any arrangements whereby directors (and other relevant people) are to acquire non-cash assets from the company, or vice versa. This exception underscores the purpose of s 29, namely, the protection of members, since where a company is insolvent its members can have no legitimate interest in the company's assets which, as has been said in another context, are held 'in trust' for the company's creditors[71].

[16.039] It has been held by the English High Court in *Demite Ltd v Protec Health et al*[72] that the former s 320 of the Companies Act 1985 (UK) applies to disposals by receivers of non-cash assets to directors or other relevant people[73]. The facts there were that Demite, the plaintiff company, had been established in 1995 by s and WP, who were its

---

68 See para **[16.020]** *ante*.

69 Section 150(5) of the CA 1963 provides: 'For the purposes of this section, a body corporate shall be deemed to be the wholly-owned subsidiary of another if it has no members except that other and that other's wholly-owned subsidiaries and its or their nominees.' See Ch 12, *Groups of Companies*, at para **[12.029]**.

70 See the Company Law Review Group's *First Report* (2000–2001), at para 6.11.4, p 108 where it is recommended that s 29(7)(a) should be amended to identify a 'wholly owned subsidiary' as per s 150(5) of the CA 1963.

71 See *Parkes v Hong Kong & Shanghai Bank Corp* [1990] ILRM 341 considered in Ch 15, *Duties of Directors and Other Officers*, at para **[15.012]**.

72 *Demite Ltd v Protec Health et al* [1998] BCC 638.

73 See Courtney, 'Receiverships in Ireland in the Wake of *Demite Ltd v Protec Health Ltd*' (1998) 5 CLP 255.

directors, with a view to exploiting a product called Z-Net which, when used with mattresses and pillows gave protection from house dust mites. Demite had three shareholders: Integro Fiduciaire Sarl, an offshore holding vehicle for s which held 58.5% of Demite's shares; Schroder Asia Nominees Ltd, an offshore holding company for WP which held 40.5% of Demite's shares; and P, a senior employee, who held 1% of Demite's shares. Demite borrowed £215,000 from L, a friend of WP, who contemporaneously lent £35,000 to a sister company called Pioneer Biosciences Ltd ('Pioneer'). Cross guarantees were given and Demite executed a debenture in favour of L. After Demite encountered financial difficulties the relationship between s and WP broke down. The holder of the debenture, L, appointed administrative receivers and the receivers sold Demite's business to the defendant, Protec Health Ltd ('Protec'). The case proceeded on the basis that Protec was a company controlled by WP and so was 'a person connected with a director'. Demite argued, *inter alia*, that the prior approval of its members was required before its business (a non-cash asset of the requisite value) was sold to a person connected with one of its directors and sought to have the sale voided. Protec argued that s 320 of the Companies Act 1985 (UK) did not apply to receivers and that, if it did apply, there had been prior approval by informal agreement. It was held by Park J that s 320 did apply and that the sale of Demite's business was voidable. In rejecting that he should *imply* an exception to s 320 in the case of a sale by a receiver to a relevant person, Park J said:

> 'For me to do that would be to go beyond anything that I can properly do as an exercise in construction of the statute, and to assume the role of a legislator. [Counsel for Protec and the receivers] say that section 320 should be construed so as to exclude sales by companies in receivership. In my judgment, however, the argument is effectively ruled out by section 321(2)(b), which I have quoted above. That creates an express statutory exception for sales by companies acting by liquidators (except in the case of members' voluntary windings-up). The presence of that provision leaves no room for me to find an implied statutory exception for sales by companies acting by receivers[74].'

In accepting that s 320 applied to the sale by Demite's receivers, Park J went on to reject Protec's assertion that there had been compliance by means of an informal shareholders' agreement. Neither did Park J consider that it was open to find that lapse of time (in seeking to avoid the sale) would operate to prevent avoidance and he was not prepared to imply such a fourth[75] exception to avoidance[76].

---

74 *Demite Ltd v Protec Health et al* [1998] BCC 638 at 646E. Park J also said (at 647B–C): 'I think that that is true, but it is not the case that, where there is a hole to be patched, the patch must exactly fit the hole. Statutory patches are commonly bigger than the holes. In any case, where an express exclusion from the section has been enacted for one kind of sale by insolvent companies – sales by companies in insolvent liquidation (see section 321(2)(b)) – I do not think that I can invent another one for a different kind of sale by insolvent companies – sales by companies in receivership.'

75 On bars to avoidance: see s 29(3) of the CA 1990, considered at para **[16.047]** *post*.

76 Protec successfully applied for leave to appeal but withdrew the appeal when faced with an application for security for costs. It subsequently applied for leave to appeal out of time but the Court of Appeal rejected this: *Demite Ltd v Protec Health Ltd et al (No 2)* (24 June1999)] English Court of Appeal, Gibson LJ.

[16.040] It is submitted that the decision in *Demite* ought not to be followed in Ireland[77]. In the first place, sales of company assets by receivers to officers, directors and persons connected with directors are already regulated by s 316A (3) of the CA 1963 and it would be an unnecessary duplication. To apply s 29 of the CA 1990 to such situations would be wrong in principle and there is a clear case for implying into s 29 that it only applies to arrangements by companies *where effected at the behest of their directors*. In this regard the pragmatism seen in the decision of Barr J in *Bula Ltd v Crowley et al*[78] is significant. In that case, commenting on the nature of a receivership, Barr J said:

> 'In practical terms vis-à-vis mortgagee and mortgagor the control over the company's assets exercised by the receiver amounts to possession of the debtor's secured assets by him which in turn in practical terms is possession by the mortgagee who appointed him.'

Secondly, Irish receivers have a statutory obligation to 'exercise all reasonable care to obtain the best price reasonably obtainable for the property as at the time of sale'[79]. Thirdly, the appointment of a receiver will often imply insolvency, and where a company is insolvent it is the interests of its creditors, not of its members, which require protection. Finally, it is an affront to common sense to apply s 29 to a sale by a receiver in circumstances where a company is insolvent, its members have nothing to protect and its creditors are left short. It is thought that the decision in *Demite* can be distinguished on the grounds that there, the debenture-holder was a personal friend of one of the directors and that it would not apply where a receiver is appointed by an entirely independent third party. If practitioners acting for debenture-holders believe that there is a possibility that, on a forced sale, the only interest in an asset being taken as security from a company is likely to come from the company's directors or other relevant people, it may be wise to insist upon members' prior approval to the creation of the debenture[80]. The Company Law Review Group recommendation that s 29 should be amended by the addition of a further exception of where a disposal of a company's assets is by a receiver has been included in s 235(4)(c) of the draft Companies Bill[81].

(c) Acquisitions by members acting 'qua member'

[16.041] Section 29(8) of the CA 1990 provides:

> 'Subsection (1)(a) shall not apply in relation to any arrangement whereby a person acquires or is to acquire an asset from a company of which he is a member if the arrangement is made with that person in his character as such member.'

---

77 For a fuller argument on this point, see Courtney, 'Receiverships in Ireland in the Wake of *Demite Ltd v Protec Health Ltd*' (1998) 5 CLP 255 at pp 259–261.

78 *Bula Ltd v Crowley et al* [2002] IEHC 4, Barr J.

79 Section 316A(1) of the CA 1963. See generally Ch 19, *Corporate Borrowing: Receivers*, at para **[19.051]** *et seq*.

80 The operative part of such a resolution might provide: 'We, being all of the members of ABC Ltd ('the company'), entitled to attend and vote at a general meeting to pass a resolution envisaged by section 29(1) of the Companies Act 1990 have seen a copy of a [mortgage] debenture with XYZ Bank plc which the company proposes to enter and HEREBY RESOLVE, for the purpose of section 29(1) to approve of any future sale of all or any of the company's assets by any receiver appointed pursuant to that mortgage debenture to any director of the company or person connected with a director of the company for whatever consideration is, at the time of the sale of the assets, the best price reasonably obtainable.'

81 See the Company Law Review Group's *First Report* (2000–2001) at para 6.11.4, p 108.

It is important to note that this exception only applies to one limb of the two-fold regulation of arrangements, namely those whereby a director or other relevant person acquires or is to acquire non-cash assets *from his company.* It has no application where companies acquire non-cash assets from directors. The only clear situation in which a person can be said to be acting *qua member* is in a voluntary winding up where a company's assets are distributed *in specie* amongst its members[82].

Compliance by approving resolution

[16.042] In order to comply with s 29(1) of the CA 1990, the members of the company must approve in advance of the proposed arrangement by passing an ordinary resolution. Thus s 29(1) provides that companies shall not enter into a substantial property transaction with a director or other relevant person:

> '... *unless the arrangement is first approved by a resolution* of the company in general meeting and, if the director or connected person is a director[83] of its holding company or a person connected with such a director, by a resolution in general meeting of the holding company.'

Where a company is a subsidiary company and it proposes to enter into an arrangement with a director or other relevant person, not only must its members approve of the arrangement by resolution, but so too must the members of its holding company give their approval *if the director or other relevant person* is a director of the holding company. Frequently, there will be common directors of subsidiary companies and holding companies and where a subsidiary enters into an arrangement with such a common director (or person connected with him) it will be the case that *two approving resolutions* will be required. This remains the case notwithstanding that the holding company does not itself actually enter into any arrangement[84].

[16.043] Although the section specifically refers to a resolution passed in general meeting, it will not be necessary to formally convene and hold a members' meeting where the company's articles of association incorporate model reg 6 of Part II of Table A[85] which entitles one to rely upon s 141(8) of the CA 1963[86]. Accordingly, where the

---

82 See Ch 25, *The Realisation and Distribution of Assets in a Winding Up*, at para **[25.196]**.

83 Note that not all 'connected persons' can be directors; specifically, bodies corporate cannot be directors of Irish companies.

84 An example of this is provided by *British Racing Drivers' Club Ltd and another v Hextall Erskine & Co (a firm)* [1996] 3 All ER 667, considered at para **[16.054]** *post*.

85 Private companies that adopt model reg 6 of Part II of Table A of the First Schedule to the CA 1963 will be authorised by their articles of association to pass informal resolutions. Regulation 6 provides: 'Subject to section 141 of the Act, a resolution in writing signed by all the members for the time being entitled to attend and vote on such resolution at a general meeting (or being bodies corporate by their duly authorised representatives) shall be as valid and effective for all purposes as if the resolution had been passed at a general meeting of the company duly convened and held.' See Ch 14, *Corporate Governance: Meetings*, at para **[14.090]**.

86 Section 141(8) of the CA 1963, provides that where a company is so authorised by its articles of association: '... a resolution in writing signed by all the members for the time being entitled to attend and vote on such resolution at a general meeting ... shall be as valid and effective for all purposes as if the resolution had been passed at a general meeting of the company duly convened and held ...'

company's articles of association so permit, all the members for the time being entitled to attend and vote on such a resolution may simply resolve in writing to approve of the arrangement[87]. The form the resolution takes will obviously depend upon the nature of the proposed transaction. The operative part of a simple form of written resolution might provide:

> 'We, being all of the members of ABC Ltd, entitled to attend and vote at a general meeting to pass a resolution envisaged by section 29(1) of the Companies Act 1990 HEREBY RESOLVE, for the purpose of that section, in favour of the proposed arrangement between ABC Ltd and Joe Bloggs, a director of ABC Ltd, whereby ABC Ltd is to acquire the property comprised in folio 12345 Co Dublin from Joe Bloggs for the sum of EURO€100,000. We make this written resolution in accordance with Regulation 6 of Part II of Table A of the First Schedule to the Companies Act 1963 which has been adopted into the articles of association of the ABC Ltd, as permitted by section 141(8) of the Companies Act 1963.'

Where reg 6 has not been adopted by a company it will be necessary for the company's directors to convene and hold an EGM of the company's members and to comply with the notice provisions for EGMs as provided for in the Companies Acts[88].

[16.044] In *Kerr et al v Conduit Enterprises Ltd*[89], it was held that the principle in *Re Duomatic* (or, in Ireland, *Buchanan Ltd v McVey*) can apply to satisfy a statutory requirement such as s 29 of the CA 1990. In the course of her judgment, Finlay Geoghegan J held that s 29 did not evidence an intention by the Oireachtas to preclude the application of the principles in those cases.

> 'I consider the principle to include the treatment of the agreement of all shareholders with a right to both attend and vote at a general meeting of the company as effective or as in the words of Buckley J in *Re Duomatic Ltd* 'as being tantamount to' a resolution of a general meeting of the company. I have concluded that section 29 of the Act of 1990 does not include an intention to so preclude the Court[90].'

In that case, it had been argued that even if the *Duomatic* principle had application, the evidence did not disclose approval of the 'arrangement' whereby the defendant was to acquire a lease, sufficient to meet the requirements of section 29(1). Finlay Geoghegan J held:

> '... I am satisfied that all ordinary shareholders, prior to the approval given as directors to the defendant entering the lease, were aware that the lessors included two directors and were aware of the key terms of the lease. That appears sufficient approval of the arrangement for the purposes of section 29(1). A proposed resolution to approve the arrangement would not appear to require greater knowledge of the shareholders[91].'

---

87 This procedure has been referenced in the Law Society's Conveyancing Committee's Practice Note on substantial property transactions: see 'Practice Notes' (1991) Gazette ILSI 419.

88 See Ch 14, *Corporate Governance: Meetings*, at para **[14.033]** *et seq*.

89 *Kerr et al v Conduit Enterprises Ltd* [2010] IEHC 300 (Finlay Geoghegan J). See also *NBH Ltd and another v Hoare et al* [2006] 2 BCLC 649; and *Conegrade Ltd v Clarke and Clarke* [2002] EWHC 2411 (Ch).

90 *Kerr et al v Conduit Enterprises Ltd* [2010] IEHC 300 at para 46. Finlay Geoghegan J found further support for this conclusion in s 5 of the Interpretation Act 2005.

91 *Kerr et al v Conduit Enterprises Ltd* [2010] IEHC 300 at para 51.

It was also held that the existence of a preferential shareholder (which had the right to receive notice of and to attend general meetings but not to vote) did not preclude the application of the *Duomatic* principle. While the High Court found as a matter of fact that the preferential shareholder was aware of the lease, it is thought that that fact was irrelevant as all that was required was the approval of those entitled to vote. Although not mentioned by the High Court, it is the case that auditors are entitled to receive notice of general meetings. This does not, however, preclude companies from passing resolutions without holding meetings where the written resolution procedure in s 141(8) of the CA 1963 is followed.

[16.045] Where s 29 applies in a conveyancing transaction, regard should be had to the Law Society's conveyancing committee's practice note[92]. The essence of the recommendation is that in transactions between a natural person and a body corporate and in transactions between bodies corporate a certificate should be included in the purchase deed showing that the parties are either not connected[93] or that they are connected and the requisite resolution has been passed by the appropriate company[94]. In other arrangements involving non-cash assets *other than real property* it is also prudent to insert a suitable certificate into the deed or other document which evidences that s 29 of the CA 1990 either does not apply or has been complied with.

The consequences of breaching s 29(1)

[16.046] Arrangements that contravene s 29(1) are not voidable *ab initio*[95]. So, in *Joint Receivers and Managers of Niltan Carson v Hawthorne*[96] Hodgson J said in respect of the predecessor of s 320 of the English Companies Act 1985:

> 'That subsection seems to me to show clearly that a contract entered into contrary to [s 29]is not illegal *ab initio*. It remains valid and binding until it is avoided at the instance of the company.'

Where a company acts in contravention of s 29(1) the arrangement entered into is deemed by s 29(3) to be *voidable* at the instance of the company. This is the primary remedy for unlawful arrangements. In *Re Duckwari plc*[97], Judge Paul Baker QC said:

---

92 'Practice Notes' (1991) Gazette ILSI 419.

93 The Law Society's recommended certificates are: 'IT IS HEREBY CERTIFIED for the purposes of s 29 of the Companies Act 1990 that the [vendor/purchaser] is not a director or a person connected with a director of A or its holding company', and 'IT IS HEREBY CERTIFIED for the purposes of s 29 of the Companies Act 1990 that the vendor and the purchaser are not bodies corporate connected with one another in a manner which would require this transaction to be ratified by resolution of either.'

94 The Law Society's recommended certificate here is: 'IT IS HEREBY CERTIFIED for the purposes of s 29 of the Companies Act 1990 that the transaction hereby effected has been approved by a resolution passed (at an Extraordinary General Meeting of the members of [A/B being the holding company of A]) or (as a written resolution of the members of [A/B being the holding company of A]).'

95 See *Re Hydro Klenze Ltd; Trehy v Rutherford et al* [2007] IEHC 456.

96 *Joint Receivers and Managers of Niltan Carson v Hawthorne* [1988] BCLC 298 at 322b.

97 *Re Duckwari plc* [1997] 2 WLR 48 at 53.

> 'The primary remedy of the company for a contravention of section 320 is avoidance of the arrangement and of any transaction entered into pursuant to it with consequential repayment of the money paid and retransfer of the asset.'

Not only will the 'arrangement' be voidable, but so too will 'any transaction entered into in pursuance of the arrangement (whether by the company or any other person)'.

[16.047] A company's ability to avoid an arrangement which does not comply with s 29(1) is dependent upon certain conditions being met. So, avoidance will not be permitted where:

> '(a) restitution of any money or other asset which is the subject-matter of the arrangement or transaction is no longer possible or the company has been indemnified in pursuance of subsection (4)(b) by any other person for the loss or damage suffered by it; or
>
> (b) any rights acquired bona fide for value and without actual notice of the contravention by any person who is not a party to the arrangement or transaction would be affected by its avoidance; or
>
> (c) the arrangement is, within a reasonable period, affirmed by the company in general meeting and, if it is an arrangement for the transfer of an asset to or by a director of its holding company or a person who is connected with such a director, is so affirmed with the approval of the holding company given by a resolution in general meeting.'

Accordingly, a company's ability to avoid an arrangement that contravenes s 29(1) is conditional upon a finding that none of the foregoing 'savers' apply. Section 29(3)(a) and (b) (which are identical to s 38(1)(a) and (b)) are examined in the context of loans and other transactions made in favour of directors and other relevant people[98]. The reference contained in s 29(3)(a) to s 29(4)(b) enables the company to make the director concerned and any other director of the company who authorised the arrangement, account for any gain made, whether directly or indirectly, and to indemnify the company for any loss or damage resulting from the arrangement or transaction, and this is considered below[99].

[16.048] Section 29(3)(c) again demonstrates the purpose behind the section: the safeguarding of members' interests since the members may retrospectively validate an otherwise voidable arrangement involving a company and its directors and other relevant people[100]. The ability of a company's members to retrospectively validate an arrangement is subject to their so resolving 'within a *reasonable* period'. No guidance is provided for what is meant by 'reasonable'. In *Re Duckwari plc (No 2)*[101], Judge Baker QC said of the reference to 'a reasonable period' that the term suggested to him:

---

98 See paras **[16.103]–[16.109]** *post*.

99 See para **[16.049]** *post*.

100 Of course, members may decline to retrospectively approve an arrangement. In *British Racing Drivers' Club Ltd and another v Hextall Erskine & Co (a firm)* [1996] 3 All ER 667, when a s 320 arrangement was put to the company's members they declined to give it their retrospective approval.

101 *Re Duckwari plc (No 2)* [1997] 2 WLR 48. Note: 'No 2' is not used in the official name of the case but is used here to distinguish the case from *Re a company No 0032314 of 1992; Duckwari plc v Offerventure Ltd* [1995] BCC 89. Note also that the decision of Judge Paul Baker QC in *Re Duckwari plc* was successfully appealed (on another point than that made here) to the Court of Appeal and is reported as *Duckwari plc v Offerventure Ltd (No 2)* [1999] BCC 11.

'... that avoidance has to be pursued promptly once members have been made aware of the transaction, otherwise there is no point in limiting the time within which members can affirm it.'

In *Demite Ltd v Protec Health Ltd et al*[102], Park J said of this passage, that 'If the judge is saying that the statutory right to avoid a transaction may be lost on grounds of passage of time alone, I respectfully disagree'. It is thought that Park J's analysis is correct and that the passage from Judge Baker's decision confuses (a) the members' right to affirm with (b) the company's right to avoid. Where s 29(1) is not complied with, it is voidable at the instance of the company, but valid until it is avoided; if, within a reasonable period of time, the members affirm the arrangement then it is no longer voidable and is valid. It follows that if the members' affirmation is not effected within a reasonable period of time, then the right to affirm it disappears; it does not follow from the language used in s 29 that the company must act promptly in avoiding the transaction. If the members do not act promptly their power to affirm disappears and the default position continues, namely, that the arrangement is voidable[103]. What will be reasonable in one situation will be unreasonable in another: what will be found to be a 'reasonable period' will vary from case to case[104]. It is thought, however, that the reasonable period will only begin to run from the time all of the members become aware of the transaction.

Liability of directors and others for breach

[16.049] Where an arrangement contravenes s 29(1), the director and other relevant people for whom it was made together with any other director who authorised the arrangement or transaction entered into in pursuance of such an arrangement can be made to account to the company for any gain made and to indemnify the company against any loss suffered. Section 29(4) of the CA 1990 provides:

> 'Without prejudice to any liability imposed otherwise than by this subsection, but subject to *subsection (5)*, where an arrangement is entered into with a company by a director of the company or its holding company or a person connected with him in contravention of this section, that director and the person so connected, and any other director of the company who authorised the arrangement or any transaction entered into in pursuance of such an arrangement, shall (whether or not it has been avoided in pursuance of *subsection (3)*) be liable—
>
> (a) to account to the company for any gain which he had made directly or indirectly by the arrangement or transaction; and
>
> (b) (jointly and severally with any other person liable under this subsection) to indemnify the company for any loss or damage resulting from the arrangement or transaction.'

The distinction between s 29(4)(a) and (b) is that (a) applies to a situation where, in breach of s 29(1)(a) a *gain is made by a director* or other relevant person arising from the acquisition of an asset from the company. On the other hand (b) applies where, in breach

102 *Demite Ltd v Protec Health Ltd et al* [1998] BCC 638 at 650.

103 See (1998) 5 CLP 255 at 258.

104 See the Company Law Review Group's *First Report* (2000–2001) at para 6.11.4, p 108. There, it is recommended that 'reasonable period' should be subject to ratification taking place at the next AGM and in any event not later than 15 months unless all of the members at any time unanimously consent in writing to the transaction.

of s 29(1)(b), a *loss is made by the company* arising from the acquisition of an asset from a director or other relevant person. In the former case the company's remedy is *an account* for the profit made, whereas in the latter case it is *an indemnity* for the loss suffered.

[16.050] The Court of Appeal extensively reviewed the then materially identical English provision in the leading English case on s 320 of the Companies Act 1985 (UK), *Duckwari plc v Offerventure Ltd and another (No 2)*[105]. The facts in that case were that the defendant (Offerventure) agreed to buy a freehold property for £495,000 and paid a deposit of £49,500 to the stakeholders. At the completion of the sale, by agreement with the plaintiff ('Duckwari'), the property was conveyed to Duckwari, which repaid the deposit to Offerventure. A director of Duckwari was also a director of Offerventure, and he and his wife owned all of the shares in Offerventure, making it a person connected with a director of Duckwari. The transaction was not approved by the members of Duckwari in general meeting as required by s 320 of the Companies Act 1985 (UK). Subsequently, Duckwari sought to avoid the transaction and sought to do so on the basis that it was a substantial property transaction within the meaning of s 320. Offerventure and the director argued that the transaction did not involve the acquisition of an asset by Duckwari from Offerventure, that the transaction involved a novation of the purchase contract, that the asset was not a non-cash asset, and that its value was not £49,500. As considered above[106], these arguments were rejected by the Court of Appeal. The subsequent proceedings were concerned with the consequence of the contravention of s 320, and, in particular, the ambit of the indemnity against loss and damage. In *Re Duckwari plc*[107], Judge Paul Baker QC was asked to determine the amount of compensation and damages payable to Duckwari pursuant to s 322(3) which is couched in similar terms to s 29(4) of the CA 1990. The judge held that the loss or damage suffered by a company must result from the transaction, 'not from the holding of the property acquired pursuant to it'[108]. He said:

> 'The primary remedy of the company for a contravention of s 320 is avoidance of the arrangement and of any transaction entered into pursuant to it with consequential repayment of the money paid and retransfer of the asset. The personal liability of the director or connected person is to account for profits and indemnify against losses. The statutory remedies are thus analogous to equitable remedies in which the common law rules as to damages play no part. We are not here concerned with a breach of any contractual or tortious duty, giving rise to an award of damages at common law. We are concerned with the unauthorised acquisition or disposal of a non-cash asset. This is akin to an unauthorised investment by a trustee, but with the difference that directors of a company can and are expected to take risks which would be unacceptable in the case of a

---

[105] *Duckwari plc v Offerventure Ltd and another (No 2)* [1999] BCC 11 (Court of Appeal). See also *Re Duckwari plc* [1997] 2 WLR 48 which was the decision of Judge Paul Baker QC which was successfully appealed to the Court of Appeal. The original case – *Re a Company No 0032314 of 1992; Duckwari plc v Offerventure Ltd* [1995] BCC 89 – where the decision of Robert Reid QC that the transaction in question was a substantial property transaction within the meaning of s 320 of the English 1985 Act involving a non-cash asset of the requisite value was upheld by the Court of Appeal.

[106] See para **[16.028]** *ante*.

[107] *Re Duckwari plc* [1997] 2 WLR 48.

[108] *Re Duckwari plc* [1997] 2 WLR 48 at 54B.

> trustee. Accordingly, as I see it, the mischief, and only mischief, addressed by these provisions is acquisitions[s] by the company at an inflated value or disposals by the company at an undervalue[109].'

He also held that a successful claim would call for the accounting to the company for any 'gain', not any 'profit'; and that the doctrine of mitigation had no place in a case under s 320. Accordingly, notwithstanding that the company had acquired the property in question for £495,000 and the fact that it was found that the value of the property in 1993 to the date of the judgment was £90,000, the loss or damage resulted from Duckwari retaining the property and not from the transaction.

[16.051] The decision of Judge Baker was successfully appealed to the Court of Appeal[110]. Nourse LJ said that an indemnity arises 'for any loss or damage resulting from the arrangement or transaction' and said such, in isolation, are capable of including *either* a loss incurred on realisation *or* a loss resulting from a fall in value of the acquired asset. Regard had to be had to the other provisions in ss 320 and 322 and the general law in order to see what sort of loss was intended to be included. Nourse LJ concluded that:

> 'Bearing in mind the evident purpose of ss 320 and 322 to give shareholders specific protection in respect of arrangements and transactions which will or may benefit directors to the detriment of the company, I am unable to construe s 322(3)(b) as denying the company a remedy which appears to flow naturally from a combination of s 320(1)(b) and the general law. No doubt it is possible to cite instances where Parliament has been held to take away with one hand what it appears to give with the other. But I cannot conceive that one would be found where the result was to give a narrow effect to provisions plainly intended to afford a protection and equally amenable to being given some wider effect[111].'

Nourse LJ went on to hold that the two defendants (Offerventure and the director with whom it was connected) were jointly and severally liable to make good to Duckwari the loss caused to it by the depreciation in value of the property. It is thought that Nourse LJ's interpretation is to be preferred.

[16.052] It is not every loss that will have to be indemnified or every gain accounted for under s 29(4) of the CA 1990. There is English authority for the proposition that in determining whether a gain was made in the sale of a non-cash asset by a director to a company, it is the market value at the time of the sale to the company as compared with the consideration actually paid on that sale that is relevant and not the consideration paid for the non-cash asset when it was first acquired by the director. In *NBH Ltd and another v Hoare et al*[112], a company (HWM) acquired a package of landfill sites from another company (C Limited) for £4,400,000. C Limited was a person connected with a director of HMW and so the acquisition ought to have been approved by HWM's shareholders. C Limited had previously acquired the landfill sites for £400,000. Subsequently, HMW disposed of the landfill sites and received some £5,020,000 for them. When the shares in HMW were sold and its control changed, it claimed against the director (Mr Hoare) who controlled C Limited the whole of the profit (in the region of £4,000,000) which C Limited had made on the assets. Park J rejected the claim that C Limited had made a

---

109 *Re Duckwari plc* [1997] 2 WLR 48 at 49E.

110 *Duckwari plc v Offerventure Ltd and another (No 2)* [1999] BCC 11.

111 *Duckwari plc v Offerventure Ltd and another (No 2)* [1999] BCC 11 at 19H–20A.

112 *NBH Ltd and another v Hoare et al* [2006] 2 BCLC 649.

gain of €4,000,000 'by the transaction' with HMW. In fact, he found that it had made a loss since before the transaction with HMW by which the landfill sites were sold, C Limited had an asset worth £5,500,000 but after the transaction it had only £4,400,000 in cash. He said:

> 'The next question is whether the £4m for which the claimants contend that Mr Hoare is liable to account to HWM is indeed a 'gain' of the type to which the section applies. In my judgment it is not. Arithmetically it is of course true that, if [C Limited] or a predecessor acquired the [landfill sites] for £400,000 in 1992 and sold them for £4.4m in 1997, there was a gain of £4m in one sense of the word. But in my judgment it is not a sense which should apply in this contest. The question is whether [C Limited] made a gain 'by' the transaction, and the transaction was not only the sale. The question is not, for example, whether a gain of any amount accrued to [C Limited] on an acquisition and disposal where the disposal was the sale to HWM ... on a realistic analysis, [C Limited] suffered a loss 'by' the transaction. Previously it had assets worth over £5.5m. By the transaction it ceased to have those assets and had £4.4m instead. It would be unreal and wholly out of line with the statutory purpose, to say that [C Limited] made a gain of £4m by the transaction.'

In justifying why it was outside the section to consider that C Limited and Mr Hoare had made a gain, Park J went on to say:

> 'Surely s 320(1)(a) is about cases where a director or a person connected with him purchases assets from a company at an undervalue, so that the director or connected person is in a position to make a gain at the expense of the company; that is the situation in which the director is liable to account to the company under s 322(3)(a). And conversely s 320(1)(b) is about cases where a director or a person connected with him sells assets to a company at an overvalue, so that the company is exposed to a loss which ought to have fallen on the director of the connected person; that is the situation in which the director is liable to indemnify the company under s 322(3)(b).'

[16.053] Where an arrangement is entered into in breach of s 29(1), it is a defence for a director to show that he took all reasonable steps to secure compliance. Section 29(5) provides:

> 'Where an arrangement is entered into by a company and a person connected with a director of the company or its holding company in contravention of this section, that director shall not be liable under *subsection (4)* if he shows that he took all reasonable steps to secure the company's compliance with this section and, in any case, a person so connected and any such other director as is mentioned in that subsection shall not be so liable if he shows that, at the time the arrangement was entered into, he did not know the relevant circumstances constituting the contravention.'

It should be noted that this defence does not apply to an arrangement entered into by a company *directly* with a director of that company or with a director of its holding company; sub-s (5) only applies where the arrangement is between 'a company *and a person connected with a director*'[113]. In precluding directors of the company and of its holding company from relying upon the defence the intention would appear to be that, as 'insiders' and officers, they ought to be aware of their duties under the Companies Acts. It is for this reason that, in *Duckwari plc v Offerventure Ltd and another (No 2)*[114], the

[113] See the comments of Judge Paul Baker QC in *Re Duckwari plc* [1997] 2 WLR 48 at 56E–F.

[114] *Duckwari plc v Offerventure Ltd and another (No 2)* [1999] BCC 11 (Court of Appeal).

director (with whom Offerventure was a connected person) could not seek relief under the equivalent English provision[115] and instead sought to rely upon the English equivalent to s 391(1) of the CA 1963[116], namely s 727(1) of the Companies Act 1985 (UK)[117]. In the Court of Appeal, Nourse LJ held that a liability arising under s 322(3)(b) of the English 1995 Act was 'a liability in respect of default within s 727'. A more difficult question is whether or not the existence of a *Ltd* specific defence in s 29(5) precludes a director from relying on the *general* defence in s 391. At trial, Judge Baker had held that the existence of specific defences to s 322 did not exclude the operation of the English s 727. Nourse LJ said he did not wish to restrict the application of s 727 unless it was necessary to do so and did not express a view[118]. It is thought that the limitation in the specific defence in s 29(5) of the CA 1990 to persons connected with directors, gives rise to a clear legislative intention to prevent directors from being excused liability and that an Irish court would be slow to permit a director to rely upon the general defence in s 391 of the CA 1963.

[16.054] As in the case of other statutory provisions where companies look to their professional advisers for guidance, persons other than directors and relevant people can also be liable in negligence where a company acts in contravention of s 29(1). In England a firm of solicitors was held liable in negligence for failing to properly advise a company of the necessity to comply with the materially identical s 320 of the Companies Act 1985 (UK). In *British Racing Drivers' Club Ltd and another v Hextall Erskine & Co (a firm)*[119], W was a director and chairman of the first plaintiff company and chairman of the second plaintiff company, which was a wholly-owned subsidiary of the first plaintiff company. The subsidiary entered into a joint venture with another company of which W was a substantial shareholder and which was a person connected with him. The company's solicitors did not advise that s 320 of the English Companies Act 1985 required the prior approval of the members of the first plaintiff company as the holding company of the company that entered into the substantial property transaction with the connected person. The second plaintiff company invested £5.3m. Subsequently, when the agreement was put to the members for their retrospective approval, the

---

115 Section 322(5) and (6) of the English Companies Act 1985.

116 See Ch 15, *Duties of Directors and Other Officers*, at para **[15.088]** *et seq*.

117 Section 727(1) of the English Companies Act 1985 provides: 'If in any proceedings for negligence, default, breach of duty or breach of trust against an officer of a company or a person employed by a company as auditor (whether he is or is not an officer of the company) it appears to the court hearing the case that that officer or person is or may be liable in respect of the negligence, default, breach of duty or breach of trust, but that he has acted honestly and reasonably, and that having regard to all the circumstances of the case (including those connected with his appointment) he ought fairly to be excused for the negligence, default, breach of duty or breach of trust, that court may relieve him, either wholly or partly, from his liability on such terms as it thinks fit.'

118 There, Nourse LJ noted that Judge Baker had exercised his discretion not to permit the director to rely on s 727(1) of the English 1985 Act. Assuming that s 727(1) did apply (without deciding the point) he went on to say that the arrangement in question was 'a one-sided arrangement detrimental to Duckwari' and that in the circumstances 'it cannot be said that [the director] acted reasonably or that he ought fairly to be excused' (at 21G).

119 *British Racing Drivers' Club Ltd and another v Hextall Erskine & Co (a firm)* [1996] 3 All ER 667.

members refused to approve of the arrangement and ordered the directors to extract themselves from the joint venture. Eventually, a settlement was agreed whereby W acquired the company's interest for £3.2m. In an action for negligence against the company's solicitors, it was held that the solicitors were liable for the loss, as had they given proper advice, and had the matter been referred to the shareholders for approval, the deal would not have gone ahead. Carnwath J said:

> 'It was [the company's solicitor's] duty to advise the board of the need to comply with s 320. By failing to do so he deprived the company of the protection which that section offers, namely the protection of the approval of the members in general meeting. It was certainly foreseeable that such a decision was likely to have produced a more informed and objective commercial judgment on the joint venture agreement. In my view, the loss on the shares, while directly caused by the directors' decision to make a bad investment, was fairly within the scope of the dangers against which, having regard to s 320, it was [the company's solicitor's] duty to provide protection. The defendants' negligence was accordingly an effective cause of the loss[120].'

This decision provides a salutary lesson for professional advisers on the dangers of overlooking the application of s 29 to a particular transaction.

[C] Loans, Quasi-loans, Credit Transactions, Guarantees and the Provision of Security in Favour of Directors and other Relevant People[121]

[16.055] Loans by private companies to directors have long been used as sweeteners whereby directors were indirectly remunerated by receiving benefits in kind. Often, such loans were never re-paid to the company, thereby depriving the company's creditors of available assets on the insolvent winding up of the company. For years this abuse went unregulated allowing some unscrupulous company controllers to line their pockets with money and assets through loans, quasi-loans, credit transactions, guarantees and the provision of security being made in their favour. Only when such transactions went beyond the somewhat uncertain and ill-drawn line provided by the case law on directors' duties, would the beneficiaries of such loans be brought to task. Another prime example of such abuses was where directors caused companies to create long leases reserving below market or even nominal rent of company property in favour of themselves or their nominees. The enactment of s 31 of the CA 1990 drastically changed the *laissez faire* approach to such transactions, so much so that, following its commencement on 1 February 1991, the status quo was entirely reversed and many *bona fide* commercial transactions were stymied.

---

[120] *British Racing Drivers' Club Ltd and another v Hextall Erskine & Co (a firm)* [1996] 3 All ER 667 at 682e.

[121] See generally: Courtney & Johnston, *Structuring Company Lending after the Company Law Enforcement Act 2001* (2001, Butterworths); Johnston, *Banking and Security Law in Ireland* (1998, Butterworths) at pp 626–631; and Breslin, *Banking Law in the Republic of Ireland* (1999, Gill & Macmillan) at pp 700–707. See also: Courtney, 'The Latest Hazard to Guarantees: The Effects of S.31, Companies Act 1990 on Inter-Company Guarantees' (1991) Gazette ILSI 261 and Courtney, 'Credit Transactions and Section 31 of the Companies Act 1990' (1994) CLP 17.

[16.056] Section 31 beleaguered businessmen and practitioners alike. The general consensus amongst the users of company law was that the balance had swung too far and had rendered many legitimate commercial (and more mundane) transactions either possible only after costly restructuring or, sometimes, simply impossible. This contrasted sharply with the position in England and Wales. Although there is similar English legislation – s 197 of the Companies Act 2006 (UK) which is the successor to s 330 of the Companies Act 1985 – this has never caused the same difficulties for English practitioners and businessmen because their regime, upon which, ironically, s 31 of the CA 1990 was originally based, has now been significantly diluted, distinguishes between public and private companies and recognises that the members may validate loans, etc.

[16.057] The first published government sponsored recognition that s 31 was in need of reform was in the *Report of the Working Group on Company Law Compliance and Enforcement*, more commonly known as the 'McDowell Report', which noted:

> '... the Company and Commercial Law Committee of the Law Society has for a number of years been proposing urgently needed change to Part III of the Companies Act, 1990, which deals with transactions involving directors and, in particular, to the effect of section 31 of the CA 1990 on credit institutions providing legitimate financial services to customers. The Law Society's concerns are shared by domestic credit institutions and have been the subject of considerable debate in legal and academic journals and circles[122].'

The Report which highlighted Ireland's dismal company law compliance (and enforcement) record also recognised legislative excesses and concluded that in a zero-tolerance environment, only reasonable laws would be on the statute books. The result was the inclusion of Part 9 in the Company Law Enforcement Act 2001 ('CLEA 2001') which remedied a number of the previous excesses and provided a more workable structure.

[16.058] The primary prohibition is contained in s 31(1) of the CA 1990, which provides:

> 'Except as provided by sections 32 to 37, a company shall not:
>
> (a) make a loan or quasi-loan to a director of the company or of its holding company or to a person connected with such a director;
>
> (b) enter into a credit transaction as creditor for such a director or a person so connected;
>
> (c) enter into a guarantee or provide any security in connection with a loan, quasi-loan or credit transaction made by any other person for such a director or a person so connected.'

It is impossible to even begin to understand the full import of these few lines of legislation without cross-referencing them to the various meanings and definitions afforded to particular terms used in Part III of the CA 1990. Section 31 may be summarised in the following manner:

- a *company* shall not;
- directly or *indirectly*;
- make or enter into any of five prohibited transactions and arrangements;

122 At para 5.9, p 64.

- to or for;
- a director or other relevant person;
- unless any of *five exceptions* apply.

Each of the italicised words has a particular significance and meaning and each shall be considered in turn; in addition, the consequences – both civil and criminal – of contravening the s 31 prohibition are considered.

[16.059] Section 31 and its related provisions are considered in this chapter as follows:

1. Section 31 prevents companies from making or entering into transactions or arrangements;
2. Anti-avoidance by preventing indirect activity;
3. The five prohibited transactions and arrangements;
4. The meaning of 'for' a director or other relevant person;
5. The application of s 31 to directors and other relevant people;
6. The five exceptions to the s 31 prohibition;
7. Civil consequences of contravention: voidability;
8. Civil consequences of contravention: account and indemnity;
9. Civil consequences of contravention: personal liability;
10. The criminal consequences of contravention.

Each of these will now be considered.

Section 31 prevents companies from making or entering into transactions or arrangements

[16.060] Unlike s 29(1) of the CA 1990, which regulates arrangements whereby a company acquires or disposes of non-cash assets from or to a director or other relevant person, s 31 is not a two-way valve and is only concerned with prohibited transactions or arrangements made or entered into *by a company.* So, to take the most straightforward prohibited transaction – a loan – a company cannot[123] make a loan to a director or other relevant person but there is nothing to prevent a director or other relevant person making a loan to a company. Similarly, a director can enter into a credit transaction – another prohibited transaction – in favour of a company and whilst such may fall to be regulated by s 29(1) of the CA 1990, s 31 is irrelevant to that transaction.

[16.061] Another important aspect under this heading is that when s 31 prohibits a *company* from making or entering into certain transactions and arrangements to or for directors and other relevant people, it refers to an Irish 'company' as defined by s 2 of the CA 1963[124]. So, a company incorporated in England, which does business in Ireland, can make a loan to one of its directors without s 31 of the CA 1990 having any relevance. Of course, that transaction may well be regulated by the similar – but far from identical – s 197 of the Companies Act 2006 (UK)[125].

---

[123] Subject to the express statutory exceptions. See para **[16.073]** *et seq post.*

[124] Note too that by s 377(1) of the CA 1963, the Ninth Schedule to the CA 1963 (which specifies Part III of the CA 1990) is applied to certain bodies corporate, *other than those mentioned in s 377(2)*. See, generally, Ch 1, *The Private Company in Context*, at para **[1.156]**.

[125] See para **[16.069]** *ante.*

Anti-avoidance by preventing indirect activity

[16.062] Section 31(1) prohibits companies from directly engaging in prohibited transactions and arrangements. Subsections (2) and (3) of s 31 operate to prohibit companies from *indirectly* taking part in such prohibited transactions and arrangements. Section 31(2) provides:

> 'A company shall not arrange for the assignment to it or the assumption by it of any rights, obligations or liabilities under a transaction which, if it had been entered into by the company, would have contravened subsection (1); but for the purposes of this Part the transaction shall be treated as having been entered into on the date of the arrangement.'

This operates, for example, to prohibit a company from taking an assignment of a loan made by another person to a director of that company because the company would itself be prohibited from making such a loan by reason of s 31(1). By treating the date of the transaction as the date of the assignment or assumption of rights, obligations or liabilities, it cannot be argued that a transaction effected before 1 February 1991 was not prohibited then, with a view to arguing that the assignment (or assumption) is not now prohibited. Moreover, s 25(7) of the CA 1990 provides that for the purposes of determining whether an arrangement is one to which s 31(2) applies, the transaction to which the arrangement relates shall, if it was entered into before the commencement of Part III, be deemed to have been entered into thereafter.

[16.063] A further measure of anti-avoidance is provided by s 31(3) of the CA 1990. This provides:

> 'A company shall not take part in any arrangement whereby—
>
> (a) another person enters into a transaction which, if it had been entered into by the company, would have contravened subsection (1) or (2); and
>
> (b) that other person, in pursuance of the arrangement, has obtained or is to obtain any benefit from the company or its holding company or a subsidiary of the company or its holding company.'

An example of the operation of this subsection might be where a third party makes a loan to the director of a company in circumstances where the third party obtains (or is to obtain) a benefit from the company. The '*benefit*' need not be an actual guarantee or an indemnity[126] (since these would be captured by s 31(1)(c) of the CA 1990) and could conceivably include a concession, indulgence, waiver of a company's legal entitlement or something else which benefits the third party. It does not appear to be a precondition that the giving of the benefit must be contrary to the company's interests. It should also be noted that the benefit need not come directly from the company: it is sufficient for the purposes of s 31(3) that the benefit comes from its holding company, or subsidiary or subsidiary of its holding company (ie, sister subsidiary).

The five prohibited transactions and arrangements

[16.064] Section 31(1) of the CA 1990 prohibits a company from doing any one of five things in favour of a director or other relevant person: (a) making a loan or (b) quasi-loan, (c) entering into a credit transaction as creditor or (d) entering into a guarantee in

[126] See para **[16.]** *post*.

connection with a loan, quasi-loan or credit transaction or (e) providing security in connection with a loan, quasi-loan or credit transaction.

(a) Loans

[16.065] Of all the prohibitions, the prohibition on making a loan is the most straightforward[127]. Although normally, when one speaks of 'loan', one assumes a cash-loan, a loan is not confined to cash. It is thought that any asset may be lent and that a loan of real or personal property, choses in action and, of course, cash will all be subject to the s 31(1)(a) prohibition. In *Tait Consibee (Oxford) Ltd v Tait*[128], it was held that where a loan is made to a director in breach of s 330 of the Companies Act 1985 (UK) the loan is illegal and is immediately recoverable by the company, irrespective of the terms and conditions on which it was made. This decision was followed in *Currencies Direct Ltd v Ellis*[129] where it was held that public policy did not prevent a company from recovering a loan that had been made to a director in breach of s 330 of the Companies Act 1985 (UK).

(b) Quasi-loans

[16.066] A company cannot make a quasi-loan in favour of a director or other relevant person. Section 25(2)(a) of the CA 1990 defines a quasi-loan as:

> 'a transaction under which one party ('the creditor') agrees to pay, or pays otherwise than in pursuance of an agreement, a sum for another ('the borrower') or agrees to reimburse, or reimburse otherwise than in pursuance of an agreement, expenditure incurred by another party for another ('the borrower')—
>
> (i) on terms that the borrower (or a person on his behalf) will reimburse the creditor; or
>
> (ii) in circumstances giving rise to a liability on the borrower to reimburse the creditor;'

Section 25(2)(b) states that any reference to the person to whom a quasi-loan is made is a reference to the borrower, and para (c) provides that the liabilities of a borrower under a quasi-loan include the liabilities of any person who has agreed to reimburse the creditor on behalf of the borrower. This definition tries to capture transactions which are loans in all but name, including where there is no formal agreement, whether written or oral, by which the company can be said to have agreed to repay the debts of any of the relevant people. An implicit understanding to discharge the debts of a director or other relevant person would accordingly seem to constitute a quasi-loan.

---

127 Section 31 of the CA 1990 crops up in the most unexpected of places. Whilst few might associate the boy-band 'Westlife' with s 31 of the CA 1990, it is interesting to note that it was alleged in the *Sunday Independent* of 1 April 2001 that a company controlled by members of 'Westlife' 'breached company law by dishing out too many directors' loans, according to latest accounts'. More recently, s 31 featured in the presidential election when it was reported that one of the candidates, Mr Sean Gallagher, had received a loan from his company that was allegedly in breach of s 31: see (2011) Irish Times, 20 October.

128 *Tait Consibee (Oxford) Ltd v Tait* [1997] 2 BCLC 349.

129 *Currencies Direct Ltd v Ellis* [2001] TLR 654.

(c) Credit transactions[130]

[16.067] A credit transaction is defined by s 25(3) of the CA 1990 as a transaction under which one party, defined as 'the creditor' (ie, a company):

> '(a) supplies any goods or sells any land under a hire-purchase agreement or conditional sale agreement;
>
> (b) leases or licences the use of land or hires goods in return for periodical payments;
>
> (c) otherwise disposes of land or supplies goods or services on the understanding that payment (whether in a lump-sum or instalments or by way of periodical payments or otherwise) is deferred.'

This is a very far-reaching definition. As regards *goods*, a company cannot: (a) supply goods under a hire-purchase agreement or conditional sale agreement; (b) hire goods in return for periodical payments; or (c) otherwise supply goods or services on the understanding that payment (whether in a lump-sum or instalments or by way of periodical payments or otherwise) is deferred to a director or other relevant person. As regards *real property* (eg, land), a company cannot: (a) sell any land under a conditional sale agreement; (b) lease or licence the use of land in return for periodical payments; or (c) otherwise dispose of land on the understanding that payment (whether in a lump-sum or instalments or by way of periodical payments or otherwise) is deferred to a director or other relevant person. One of the more common instances of credit transactions are leases of land, including a *bona fide* commercial or residential lease of land. Accordingly, a company may not grant a lease to any relevant person. The definitions in s 25(3)(a) and (b) are wide enough to include a conveyance where the full consideration is not paid to a company on the disposal of its interest, one indicator of which will be the absence or modification of the usual receipt clause in a purchase deed[131].

[16.068] Prior to the CLEA 2001 it had been thought to be strongly arguable that not all leases of land are credit transactions[132] and that long leases of say, 10,000 years which reserve a peppercorn rent do not properly fall to be termed as credit transactions. The reasoning was that where a long lease is granted in return for an initial capital payment it can not be said to be 'in return for periodical payments'. Any periodic payments made subsequent to the creation of such a lease are merely incidental to the real consideration passing. Such a view was further strengthened where the nominal rent reserved in the long lease is expressed to be 'if demanded'. This matter has been conclusively resolved by s 75 of the CLEA 2001, which amends s 25 of the CA 1990, by the insertion of a new sub-s (3A):

> 'For the purposes of this Part, a lease of land which reserves a nominal annual rent of not more than £10 is not a credit transaction where a company grants the lease in return for a premium or capital payment which represents the open market value of the land thereby disposed of by the company.'

---

130 See Courtney, 'Credit Transactions and Section 31 of the Companies Act 1990' (1994) CLP 17.

131 See Wylie & Woods, *Irish Conveyancing Law* (3rd edn, 2005) at paras [18.43], [18.44].

132 Courtney, 'Credit Transactions and Section 31 of the Companies Act 1990' (1994) CLP 17 at p 19.

This reflects the conveyancing reality of long leases, since usually, the sole reason for choosing to alienate property by way of a long lease, as opposed to a conveyance of the freehold, is to further the proper management of an apartment complex or retail development by facilitating the enforcement of positive covenants, eg, the payment of a service charge.

(d) *Guarantees in connection with loans, quasi-loans or credit transactions*[133]

[16.069] Section 31 also prohibits a company from entering into a guarantee in connection with a loan, quasi-loan or credit transaction made by any other person for a director of the company or of its holding company or to a person connected with such a director. It should be noted that 'guarantee' includes 'indemnity'.[134] Guarantees in respect of loans and quasi-loans can be most readily recognised. Where a lending institution makes a loan to a director of a company, that company cannot guarantee that loan unless one of the exceptions, considered below[135], can be invoked. The *prima facie* prohibition on companies entering into guarantees in respect of credit transactions made by other persons for directors and other relevant people has proven to be particularly problematic. Again, unless one of the exceptions applies, a company cannot guarantee the performance of, say, a 35-year lease granted by a third party to a company controlled by a director.

(e) *Providing security in connection with loans, quasi-loans or credit transactions*

[16.070] The prohibition on companies giving security in connection with loans, quasi-loans and credit transactions made by third parties for directors or other relevant people operates in the same way as the prohibition on guarantees. In practice, third party security will frequently involve both a guarantee and security. The specific prohibition on the provision of security operates to capture cases where no guarantee is given as, for example, in the case of a surety mortgage over land, which can charge the surety's lands and property with the repayment of a borrower's debt in the absence of a guarantee.

The meaning of 'for' a director or other relevant person

[16.071] It is important to note the meaning assigned to the expression, 'a transaction or arrangement made for a person'. This is relevant in the interpretation of, for example, s 31(1)(b), which prohibits a company from entering into a credit transaction as creditor '*for*' a director or relevant person and the interpretation of s 31(1)(c), which prohibits the entering into of guarantees and the provision of security in connection with loans, quasi-loans and credit transactions made by any third party '*for*' a director or relevant person[136]. Section 25(6) of the CA 1990 provides:

133 See Courtney, 'The Latest Hazard to Guarantees: The Effects of S.31, Companies Act 1990 on Inter-Company Guarantees' (1991) Gazette ILSI 261.

134 Section 25(1) of the CA 1990.

135 See para **[16.073]** *post*.

136 It is also relevant in the context of the definition of 'quasi-loan' (s 25(2)(a) of the CA 1990) and in the context of civil remedies for breach of s 31 (s 38(2)) and the imposition of personal liability in certain cases (s 39(1)).

'For the purposes of this Part, a transaction or arrangement is made for a person if—

(a) in the case of a loan or quasi-loan, it is made to him;

(b) in the case of credit transaction, he is the person to whom goods or services are supplied, or land is sold or otherwise disposed of, under the transaction;

(c) in the case of a guarantee or security, it is entered into or provided in connection with a loan or quasi-loan made to him or a credit transaction made for him;

(d) in the case of an arrangement to which s *31(2)* or *31(3)* applies[137], the transaction to which the arrangement relates was made for him; and

(e) in the case of any other transaction or arrangement for the supply or transfer of goods, land or services (or any interest therein), he is the person to whom the goods, land or services (or the interest) are supplied or transferred.'

Because of the specific definitions afforded to the expression 'a transaction or arrangement made for a person' it is thought that in the case of a dispute, the section must be strictly construed.

The application of s 31 to directors and other relevant people

[16.072] Section 31(1) does not operate, generally, to prevent companies from making loans or quasi-loans or entering into credit transactions or guarantees or providing security in connection with loans, quasi-loans and credit transactions. The prohibition only applies in circumstances where such transactions or arrangements are made to or for *directors of the company and other relevant people*. In summary, those persons for whom a company is prohibited by s 31(1) from making or entering into a prohibited transaction or arrangement are:

Persons who are directors and other 'relevant people'	
• directors of a company; • shadow directors of a company; • directors of a holding company; • shadow directors of a holding company; • the spouse, civil partner, parent, brother, sister, child of a director of a company or of its holding company; • the partner of a director of a company or of its holding company; • trustees where the principal beneficiaries of the trust are a director (whether of the company or of its holding company), his spouse, any of his children or any body corporate he controls;	• a body corporate controlled by a director of a company or of its holding company; • a body corporate controlled by a body corporate that is itself controlled by a director of a company or of its holding company; • there is a presumption that the sole member of a single-member private limited company is a person connected with a director.

The reader's attention is referred to the beginning of this chapter where the subjects of the statutory regulation provided for in Part III of the CA 1990 are considered in detail[138].

137 See paras **[16.062]** and **[16.063]** *ante*.

138 See para **[16.003]** *et seq, ante*.

The five exceptions to the s 31 prohibition

[16.073] It now falls to consider the five exceptions to the prohibition on a company entering certain transactions or arrangements in favour of directors or other relevant people under the following headings.

(a) Applicability of exceptions to prohibited transactions and arrangements.
(b) Section 32: the *de minimis* exception.
(c) Section 34: the validation procedure for guarantees and security.
(d) Section 35: the group exception.
(e) Section 36: directors' expenses.
(f) Section 37: business transactions.
(g) The repealed exception.

It should be noted that, unless otherwise stated, all references to 's 34 of the CA 1990' are to the 'new' s 34 of the CA 1990, as substituted by s 78 of the CLEA 2001, unless otherwise stated.

(a) Applicability of exceptions to prohibited transactions and arrangements

[16.074] There are in total five exceptions to the s 31 prohibition. However, whilst there are five aspects to the s 31 prohibition (loans, quasi-loans, credit transactions, guarantees and the provision of security), and there are five exceptions, not all five exceptions apply to all five aspects of the s 31 prohibition.

Prohibited Transactions or Arrangements	*Exceptions*
Loans, quasi-loans and credit transactions	ss 32, 35, 36 and 37
Guarantees and the provision of security in connection with loans, quasi-loans and credit transactions	ss 34, 35 and 36

In addition, not all five exceptions are available to all 'relevant people'.

'Relevant people'	*Exceptions*
Directors (de facto, de jure and shadow) of companies	ss 32, 34, 36 and 37
Directors (de facto, de jure and shadow) of companies' holding companies	ss 34 and 37
Natural persons that are connected persons	ss 32, 34 and 37
Bodies corporate that are connected persons	ss 32, 34, 35 and 37

(b) Section 32: the de minimis exception

[16.075] One of the most availed of exceptions in the context of loans to directors is s 32 of the CA 1990. This provides a *de minimis* exception, whereby if the value of an arrangement[139] is below a certain amount, it falls through the net on the grounds that it is

[139] Note, the *de minimis* exception is confined to 'arrangements' as defined. See para **[16.079]** *post*.

of insufficient value to justify the invocation of the s 31 prohibition. Section 32(1) provides that:

> '*Section 31* shall not prohibit a company from entering into an *arrangement* with a director or a person so connected with a director if—
>
> (a) the value of the arrangement, and
>
> (b) the total amount outstanding under any other arrangements entered into by the company with any director of the company, or any person connected with a director,
>
> together, is less than ten per cent of the company's *relevant assets*.' (Italics added.)

Two figures are fundamental to determining whether or not the *de minimis* exception applies: (i) the value of the arrangement; and (ii) the amount of the company's relevant assets.

[16.076] Looking first at the *value of the arrangement*, s 25(4) of the CA 1990 provides some assistance in determining what value means in either of the three possible arrangements that can be exempted by s 32. In the case of a loan, its value is the principal of the loan; in a quasi-loan it is the 'amount or maximum amount which the person to whom the quasi-loan is made is liable to reimburse the creditor'[140]. In the case of a credit transaction[141], its value is:

> '... the price which it is reasonable to expect could be obtained for the goods, land or services to which the transaction or arrangement relates if they had been supplied at the time the transaction or arrangement is entered into in the ordinary course of business and on the same terms (apart from price) as they have been supplied or are to be supplied under the transaction or arrangement in question.'

Where the value of a transaction or arrangement is not capable of being expressed as a specific sum of money, it shall be deemed to exceed €63,486.90.

[16.077] Turning next to the company's *relevant assets*, as referred to in s 32(1)[142], this expression has the meaning assigned to it in s 29(2) of the CA 1990. Section 29(2)(a) and (b) defines 'relevant assets' as:

> '(a) except in a case falling within *paragraph (b)*, the value of its net assets determined by reference to the accounts prepared and laid in accordance with the requirements of s 148 of the CA 1963 in respect of the last preceding financial year in respect of which such accounts were so laid;
>
> (b) where no accounts have been prepared and laid under that section before that time, the amount of its called-up share capital.'

In the case of many private companies, reliance upon para (b) will not provide it with much scope for reliance upon s 32. In the typical '€2 private company', it will mean that the amount permitted to be, for example, loaned to a director, will be 20 cent. Notwithstanding that companies are obliged to prepare accounts, there can be some

140 Section 25(4)(a) and (b).

141 Section 25(4) (c) is unhappily worded. Rather than specifically say 'credit transaction', it refers to a transaction or arrangement 'other than a loan or quasi-loan or a transaction or arrangement within *paragraph (d)* or *(e)*'. Of course, the effect of this is that it applies to more than just credit transactions, ie, any 'arrangement' for the purposes of s 29(1) of the CA 1990.

142 By virtue of s 32(2)(b) of the CA 1990.

delay in the preparation of accounts in many companies. Accordingly, if the *de minimis* exception is to be meaningful, the 10% will be of the company's net assets as determined by the profit and loss account/income and expenditure account spoken of in s 148 of the CA 1963.

[16.078] It may happen that a company's relevant assets are reduced either in the normal course of its business, or because they were deliberately inflated so as to bring an arrangement within the *de minimis* exception. Where this happens after an arrangement which is in breach of s 31 has been entered into and the company has relied upon s 32, the provisions of s 33 of the CA 1990 apply. Thus, s 33(2) provides:

> 'Where the directors of a company become aware, or ought reasonably to become aware, that there exists a situation referred to in *subs (1)*, it shall be the duty of the company, its directors and any persons for whom the arrangements referred to in that subsection were made, to amend, within two months, the terms of the arrangements concerned so that the total amount outstanding under the arrangements again falls within the percentage limit referred to in that subsection.'

Consequently, where the relevant assets are reduced and the amount of the transaction or arrangement is then no longer less than 10% of the company's relevant assets, the situation must be regularised within *two months*. Whilst the CA 1990 was silent on the consequences of relevant assets falling, s 77of the CLEA 2001 has introduced a new s 33(3) to the CA 1990 which provides:

> 'Where the terms of the arrangements referred to in subsection (2) are not amended within the period specified in that subsection, the arrangements shall be voidable at the instance of the company unless section 38(1)(a) or (b) applies.'

[16.079] Finally, turning to the application of the s 32 exception, it is by its very terms confined to 'arrangements'. For the purposes of s 32(1), s 32(2)(a) provides:

> '... a company enters an arrangement with a person if it makes a loan or quasi-loan to, or enters into a credit transaction as creditor for, that person.'

Accordingly, the '10% exception' has no application to guarantees or the provision of security and only applies to loans, quasi-loans and credit transactions. It should also be noted that s 32(1) prohibits a company from entering into an arrangement 'with a director or a person connected with a director'. It would seem, therefore, that the *de minimis* exception cannot be availed of where a company proposes to enter into an arrangement with a director (*de facto*, *de jure* or shadow) of that company's holding company or a person connected with such a director.

(c) Section 34: the validation procedure for guarantees and security

[16.080] In principle, there can be no public policy objection to a company making or entering into any transaction or arrangement in favour of anybody where (a) its creditors' interests are safeguarded and (b) the majority of its members consent. The 'new' s 34 of the CA 1990[143] exempts companies from the prohibition on entering into guarantees and providing security in favour of any relevant person, where the interests of the two fundamental constituencies – creditors and shareholders – are protected. Based on the procedure whereby certain companies can provide financial assistance in

143 As substituted by s 78 of the CLEA 2001. For the 'old' s 34, see para **[16.098]** *post*.

connection with the purchase of their own shares (s 60 of the CA 1963) the 'new' s 34 introduced a *validation procedure* which, if followed, will allow companies to enter into guarantees and provide security in connection with loans, quasi-loans and credit transactions made to relevant people. The validation procedure cannot be utilised to validate loans or quasi-loans, the relaxation in the CLEA 2001 being confined to transactions that involve only a *contingent* liability for companies.

[16.081] The operative part of this exception is contained in s 34(1) which provides:

> 'Section 31 does not prohibit a company from entering into a guarantee or providing a security in connection with a loan, quasi-loan or credit transaction made by any other person to a director of the company or of its holding company or to or for a person connected with such a director, if—
>
> (a) the entering into the guarantee is, or the provision of the security is given, under the authority of a special resolution of the company passed not more than 12 months previously; and
>
> (b) the company has forwarded with each notice of the meeting as which the special resolution is to be considered or, if the procedure detailed in subsection (6) is followed, the company has appended to the resolution, a copy of a statutory declaration which complies with subsections (2) and (3) and also delivers, within 21 days after the date on which the guarantee was entered into or the date on which the security was provided, as the case may be, a copy of the declaration to the registrar of companies for registration.'

It will be noticed that the validation procedure is very similar to that contained in s 60 of the CA 1963[144]. The various issues that arise in the context of the s 34 validation procedure are considered under the following headings:

(i) The special resolution.
(ii) The statutory declaration of solvency.
(iii) The independent person's report.
(iv) The consequences of swearing a declaration based on unreasonable grounds.

(i) The special resolution and shareholder protection

[16.082] The protection of shareholders – an essential feature of this exception – is provided by the requirement that the members must pass a special resolution approving of the giving of a guarantee and or security. Accordingly, there must be at least 75% shareholder support before a company can enter such a transaction in favour of a relevant person[145]. It will be noted that unlike the s 29 validation procedure, s 34 requires a qualified majority to approve of thc transaction.

The special resolution must be passed not more than 12 months before the transaction is entered into. This is to provide a measure of protection against a change in circumstances. Section 34(6) provides a very useful administrative procedure in that the special resolution referred to in s 34(1)(a) 'may be passed in accordance with s 141(8) of the CA 1963' ie, the written resolution procedure which has been considered in Ch 14[146]. The advantage of this is that where a company is so permitted by its articles of

---

[144] See, generally, Ch 10, *The Maintenance of Capital*, at paras **[10.066]** to **[10.077]**.

[145] On special resolutions generally, see Ch 14, *Corporate Governance: Meetings*, at para **[14.084]**.

[146] See Ch 14, *Corporate Governance: Meetings*, at para **[14.090]** *et seq*.

association, the special resolution may be passed by a written resolution, thereby avoiding the artificialities inherent in convening on statutory notice and thereafter holding a meeting of perhaps as few as one or two persons, who might also be the company's only directors.

[16.083] As in the case of the s 60 validation procedure, there is also additional shareholder protection, over and above the fact that a qualified majority must resolve in favour of a company entering into a guarantee or providing security in favour of a director or other connected person. First, unless the transaction is unanimously approved of by the members (ie, all of the members entitled to vote at general meetings of the company in favour of the special resolution), the company may not enter into the guarantee or provide the security before the expiry of 30 days after the passing of the resolution or, if an application is made to court, until the application has been disposed of by the court[147]. Second, members (who have *not* consented to, signed or voted in favour of the special resolution)[148] may make application to court for relief and where such application is made the special resolution shall not have effect except to the extent to which it is confirmed by the court[149]. The 'counter-counterbalance' to these safeguards is that the application by dissenting members must be brought within 28 days after the date on which the special resolution was passed[150] and an application must be made by the holders of not less in the aggregate than 10% in nominal value of the company's issued share capital or any class thereof[151]. Of course, where the written resolution procedure is adopted, none of the foregoing safeguards are relevant since s 141(8) of the CA 1963 requires unanimity.

(ii) The statutory declaration of solvency

[16.084] Creditor protection is provided by the requirement that the directors of a company proposing to enter into a guarantee or provide security in connection with a loan, quasi-loan or credit transaction in favour of a relevant person, must make a statutory declaration of solvency. The timing of the statutory declaration is regulated by s 34(2), which provides:

> 'The statutory declaration shall be made at a meeting of the directors held not earlier than 24 days before the meeting referred to in subsection (1)(b) or, if the special resolution is passed in accordance with subsection (6), not earlier than 24 days before the signing of the special resolution, and shall be made by the directors or, in the case of a company having more than 2 directors, by a majority of the directors.'

The content of the statutory declaration is also regulated by statute. Section 34(3) provides that the statutory declaration must state:

> '(a) the circumstances in which the guarantee is to be entered into or the security is to be provided;
>
> (b) the nature of the guarantee or security;

[147] Section 34(7) of the CA 1990.

[148] Members who have consented to, signed or voted for the special resolution are debarred from bringing application to court for relief: s 34(10).

[149] Section 34(8) of the CA 1990.

[150] Section 34(11) of the CA 1990 which goes on to state that the application may be made on behalf of the persons entitled to make the application by such one or more of their number as they may appoint in writing for the purpose.

[151] Section 34(9) of the CA 1990.

(c) the person or persons to or for whom the loan, quasi-loan or credit transaction (in connection with which the guarantee is to be entered into or the security is to be provided) is to be made;

(d) the purpose for which the company is entering into the guarantee or is providing the security;

(e) the benefit which will accrue to the company directly or indirectly from entering into the guarantee or providing the security; and

(f) that the declarants have made a full inquiry into the affairs of the company and that, having done so, they have formed the opinion that the company, having entered into the guarantee or provided the security, will be able to pay its debts in full as they become due.'

The requirements at (a) and (b) are self-explanatory. Requirement (c) involves the disclosure of the beneficiary of the guarantee and or security. Requirement (d) involves stating the purpose for which the company is entering into the guarantee or providing the security.

[16.085] Requirement (e) is very important. It requires the declaring directors to state the benefit that will accrue to the company (directly or indirectly) from entering into the guarantee or providing the security. Apart altogether from being a necessary disclosure, the effect of this requirement is to remind the declaring directors that a company should not enter into transactions where it does not itself derive benefit; for a company to give a gratuitous guarantee or security is likely to be both *ultra vires*[152] and in breach of the directors' duties[153]. It is thought to be insufficient to state that 'no benefit' will accrue to the company; it is implicit that some benefit must accrue since otherwise the legislature would have said 'the benefit (if any)' or, even, 'whether any benefit will accrue'. It is also thought to be unlikely that it could be claimed that any benefit would flow to the company where a guarantee is in respect of a loan made to a director or other relevant person, to enable him or it to set up a competing business or to further his exclusively personal interests. An example of benefit flowing to a company from its guaranteeing a loan from a bank to one of its directors, might be where the purpose of the loan is to on-lend the money to the company in support of its trading activities. In *Charterbridge Corp Ltd v Lloyds Bank Ltd*[154], Pennycuick J said of the meaning of benefit that:

> 'The proper test ... must be whether an intelligent and honest man in the position of a director of the company concerned, could, in the whole of the existing circumstances, have reasonably believed that the transaction was for the benefit of the company.'

Where the directors believe that the entering into of a guarantee or the provision of security is for their company's benefit, it would be prudent to ensure a minute to that effect is recorded. The requirement for there to be 'benefit' to the company strikes a good balance between the interests of directors, their companies and companies' creditors.

[16.086] The final requirement, (f), provides the essential creditor protection. This requires the directors to aver that they have made a full inquiry into the company's affairs and that, having done so, have formed the opinion that the company will be able

---

152 See Ch 7, *Corporate Contracts, Capacity and Authority*, at para **[7.045]** *et seq*.

153 See Ch 15, *Duties of Directors and Other Officers*, at para **[15.026]**.

154 *Charterbridge Corp Ltd v Lloyds Bank Ltd* [1969] 2 All ER 1185 at 1194.

to pay its debts in full as they become due. In other words, the company must be solvent following the entering into of the guarantee and or the provision of the security.

(iii) The independent person's report

[16.087] The possible temptation for directors to be overly optimistic about their company's solvency is addressed by s 34(4) which requires the directors' statutory declaration to be accompanied by a report drawn up in the prescribed form[155] by an independent person. To be an independent person, one must be qualified at the time of the report to be appointed or to continue to be the company's auditor[156]. The importance of the independent person's report is that is must state whether, in the opinion of the independent person, the statutory declaration is reasonable[157]. It may be noted that there is no such requirement in respect of a statutory declaration sworn by directors pursuant to the s 60 validation procedure. There are some concerns amongst auditors and the accounting profession that the independent person's report, as required by s 34 and as prescribed by statutory instrument, is too wide and might expose auditors to civil liability. Of particular concern is the open-ended nature of the directors' declaration[158]. Although the prescribed form cannot be added to or detracted from it is opined that auditors, anxious lest they incur civil liability, could legitimately attach a disclaimer to the prescribed form which will alert all readers as to the basis upon which they make the independent report.

(iv) The consequences of swearing a declaration based on unreasonable grounds

[16.088] It is with respect to the consequences of swearing a declaration based on unreasonable grounds that the s 34 validation procedure again departs significantly from the s 60 validation procedure. Where the directors of a company proposing to provide financial assistance in connection with the purchase of the company's own shares swear a declaration on unreasonable grounds and the company is wound up insolvent, the directors are liable to prosecution. In the case of the s 34 validation procedure the consequences of swearing a declaration that is based on unreasonable grounds are likely to be more of a deterrent than is the risk of prosecution as the directors run the risk of being made personally liable 'without limitation of liability, for all or any of the debts or other liabilities of the company': s 34(5)(a) of the CA 1990. So, where the directors make a statutory declaration 'without having reasonable grounds for the opinion that the company having entered into the guarantee or provided the security will be able to pay its debts in full as they become due' the court is empowered to make the directors personally liable on such application being made by a liquidator, creditor, member or contributory of the company. Moreover, where a company is wound up within 12 months after the making of the declaration and its debts are not paid or provided for in

155 As prescribed by the Companies Act, 1990 (Section 34) Regulations 2001, SI 439/2001.

156 Section 34(4)(a) of the CA 1990. On the qualifications to be a company's auditor, see Ch 17, *Financial Statements, Audit and Annual Return*, at para **[17.296]**.

157 Section 34(4)(b) of the CA 1990.

158 Strangely, this does not seem to have been an issue in relation to s 60(2) declarations by directors where companies assisted the purchase of their own shares which is also 'open-ended'.

full within 12 months after the commencement of the winding up, there is a statutory presumption 'until the contrary is shown, that the director did not have reasonable grounds for this opinion'[159].

(d) Section 35: the group exception

[16.089] The original s 35 exception only applied to transactions and arrangements made or entered into by a subsidiary in favour of its holding company[160]. It provided a complete exemption for such transactions and arrangements but was greatly limited by the fact that it did not exempt transactions or arrangements made or entered into by holding companies in favour of subsidiaries or by subsidiaries in favour of sister subsidiaries. The 'new' s 35[161] does not suffer from such disabilities. It provides:

> '*Section 31* shall not prohibit a company from—
>
> (a) making a loan or quasi-loan to any company which is its holding company, subsidiary or a subsidiary of its holding company or entering into a guarantee or providing any security in connection with a loan or quasi-loan made by any person to any company which is its holding company, subsidiary or a subsidiary of its holding company;
>
> (b) entering into a credit transaction as creditor for any company which is its holding company, subsidiary or a subsidiary of its holding company or entering into a guarantee or providing any security in connection with any credit transaction made by any other person for any company which is its holding company, subsidiary or a subsidiary of its holding company.'

Accordingly, it is now the case that any member of a group of companies can, in favour of another member of that group, make or enter into any of the five transactions or arrangements that are otherwise prohibited by the s 31 prohibition. It is thought that the use of the words 'for any *company* which is its holding company' in the first lines of both paras (a) and (b) does *not* limit the invocation of this exemption to transactions and arrangements made in favour of holding companies that are 'companies' within the meaning of s 2(1) of the CA 1963 and that it can be invoked where the holding company is a body corporate on the basis that the context requires company to be given a broader meaning in support of the use of the term holding company which by s 155(5) of the CA 1963 includes bodies corporate[162].

---

159 Section 34(5)(b) of the CA 1990.

160 Section 35 of the CA 1990, as originally enacted, provided that: '*Section 31* shall not prohibit a company from—(a) making a loan or quasi-loan to its holding company or entering into a guarantee or providing any security in connection with a loan or quasi-loan made by any person to its holding company; (b) entering into a credit transaction as creditor for its holding company or entering into a guarantee or providing any security in connection with any credit transaction made by any other person for its holding company.'

161 As amended by s 79 of the CLEA 2001. Section 79 of the CLEA 2001 provides: 'Section 35 of the Act of 1990 is amended by the substitution for "its holding company" (wherever occurring) of "any company which is its holding company, subsidiary or a subsidiary of its holding company".'

162 See further, MacCann & Courtney, *Companies Acts, 1963–2009* (2010, Bloomsbury Professional) at p 1204.

[16.090] It is fundamental to the invocation of s 35 that both companies (or bodies corporate) are part of a group within the meaning of s 155 of the CA 1963 which alone defines what constitutes a 'holding company' and a 'subsidiary company' for the purpose of s 35 of the CA 1990. The definitions of 'holding company' and 'subsidiary company' are considered in detail in Ch 12[163].

[16.091] To the first-time reader of Part III of the CA 1990 it is, on its face, an apparent contradiction to conceive of a subsidiary company being a 'person connected with a director' of a holding company. The assumption is that if a company is another's subsidiary it must be exclusively controlled by that other company and cannot be controlled by someone else for the purposes of s 26 of the CA 1990. The apparent contradiction dissipates, however, when one realises that on the proper construction of Part III of the CA 1990 and of s 155 of the CA 1963, it becomes clear that a given company can be a 'person connected with' a director and, contemporaneously, a subsidiary of another company. The two tests for control are not mutually exclusive. This said, one must not automatically assume that every subsidiary company (or holding company) will be a person connected with a director of its holding company (or subsidiary company) so that s 35 must be invoked to exempt an otherwise unlawful transaction or arrangement. This will not necessarily be the case. These issues have been considered above[164] at the beginning of this chapter.

[16.092] On the application of s 35, it is readily obvious that it can only apply where a company proposes to make or enter into an otherwise prohibited transaction or arrangement in favour of a *body corporate* and that s 35 has no application to relevant people who are natural persons. It should also be noted that it applies to all five transactions or arrangements that are prohibited by s 31.

(e) Section 36: directors' expenses

[16.093] Section 36 of the CA 1990 provides:

> '(1) *Section 31* shall not prohibit a company from doing anything to provide any of its directors with funds to meet vouched expenditure properly incurred or to be incurred by him for the purposes of the company or the purpose of enabling him properly to perform his duties as an officer of the company or doing anything to enable any of its directors to avoid incurring such expenditure.
>
> (2) Where a company enters into a transaction pursuant to *subs (1)*, any liability falling on any person arising from any such transaction shall be discharged by him within six months from the date on which it was incurred.
>
> (3) A person who contravenes *subs (2)* shall be guilty of an offence.'

At first, it would appear that the s 36 exception saves transactions which form part of everyday commercial, and especially, banking life such as where a company guarantees a director's credit card, or his petrol account, or loans him money to pay his hotel/restaurant expenses. However, on a closer reading of sub-s (2) it is seen that such 'loans' must be repaid to the company within six months from the date on which any liability was incurred. Failure to comply with this provision results in the director concerned

---

163 See Ch 12, *Groups of Companies,* at paras **[12.008]** to **[12.030]**.

164 See para **[16.003]** *ante*.

being guilty of an offence, and liable to be visited with the penalties set out in s 40 of the CA 1990, considered below[165].

[16.094] Section 36 has application to all five prohibited transactions or arrangements prohibited by s 31. It should be noted, however, that as regards those relevant people who may rely upon this exception, only the directors (*de facto* and *de jure*) and shadow directors of the company concerned, in whose favour a transaction or arrangement is made, come within s 36.

(f) Section 37: business transactions

[16.095] Section 37 of the CA 1990 provides:

> '*Section 31* shall not prohibit a company from making any loan or quasi-loan or entering into any credit transaction as creditor for any person if—
>
> (a) the company enters into the transaction concerned in the ordinary course of its business; and
>
> (b) the value of the transaction is not greater, and the terms on which it is entered into are no more favourable, in respect of the person for whom the transaction is made, than that or those which—
>
> (i) the company ordinarily offers, or
>
> (ii) it is reasonable to expect the company to have offered,
>
> to or in respect of a person of the same financial standing as that person but unconnected with the company.'

The reference to a company entering into a transaction in the *ordinary course of its business*[166] implies a certain 'usualness' for that company to enter into such a transaction. For a company to make a loan or quasi-loan in the ordinary course of its business may imply that the company is a financial services company, or if a loan to a director acting as a consumer, to be governed by the Consumer Credit Act 1995. A company would also require to have as one of its principal objects, the object of lending money, etc.

[16.096] It is also a requirement that such a transaction be made or entered into on terms which are no more favourable and for a value no greater than those which the company would both reasonably, and ordinarily, offer to others. Here, an objective test is applied by the use of the word 'reasonable', and so a transaction which has already been made in favour of an unconnected person may not be used as a touchstone, unless the transaction concerned is also objectively 'reasonable' for the company to have entered into.

[16.097] It is very important to recognise that s 37 applies to only three (loans, quasi-loans and credit transactions) of the five prohibited transactions or arrangements in the s 31 prohibition. Guarantees and the provision of security are excluded. It would seem, however, that s 37 can be invoked in transactions between a company and any relevant

---

165 See para **[16.118]** *post*.

166 A transaction will not be in the ordinary course of a company's business where the company has agreed to cease trading: *Re Ashmark Ltd (No 2)* [1990] ILRM 455. 'Insolvency' may also be relevant in deciding whether something is in the ordinary course of a company's business: *Williams v Quebrada Railway Land and Copper Co Ltd* [1895] 2 Ch 751, cited in *Murphy v Kirwan* (9 April 1992, unreported) HC *per* Costello J.

person, since it refers to a situation where a company makes a loan, quasi-loan or enters into a credit transaction, for 'any person'.

(g) The repealed exception

[16.098] The 'old' s 34 of the CA 1990, which was repealed by s 78 of the CLEA 2001, provided:

> 'Where a company is a member of a group of companies, consisting of a holding company and its subsidiaries, s *31* shall not prohibit that company from—
>
> (a) making a loan or quasi-loan to another member of that group; or
>
> (b) entering into a guarantee or providing any security in connection with a loan or quasi-loan made by any person to another member of the group;
>
> by reason only that a director of one member of the group is connected with another.'

In order to appreciate the intricacies of this exception, a number of concepts referred to therein require further consideration. This section was flawed in two fundamental respects. First, whilst it could be invoked in respect of loans and quasi-loans and guarantees and the provision of security in connection with such transactions, it could not be invoked in respect of credit transactions and guarantees and security in connection with credit transactions. Second, the final proviso – 'by reason only that a director of one member of the group is connected with another' – was nonsensical. This was because Part III did not elsewhere envisage or contain any definition of a situation where a *director* was connected *with a company*, ie, with another member of the group; s 26 only defines a situation where a person is deemed to be connected *with a director*.

[16.099] Because companies may have relied upon the repealed s 34 between 1 February 1991 and 30 September 2001, it is necessary to retain reference to it here. Again, it is important to note that the repealed s 34 only applied to where a company was part of a group of companies. This required one to have regard to s 155 of the CA 1963 and because 'group of companies' is not specifically defined, one must look to the meaning of 'holding' and 'subsidiary' companies.

Civil consequences of contravention: voidability

[16.100] There are three civil consequences for contravening s 31 of the CA 1990. The first is that, subject to certain 'savers', any contravening transaction or arrangement is voidable at the instance of the company. The second is that the directors (and other relevant people) are liable to indemnify the company for any loss it suffers and to account for any gain they make. The third consequence is that, in certain circumstances, certain people can be made personally liable if the company is subsequently wound up insolvent.

[16.101] The first civil consequence of the contravention of the prohibition contained in s 31 is drastic, in that s 38(1) provides that subject to certain exceptions:

> 'Where a company enters into a transaction or arrangement in contravention of s 31 the transaction or arrangement *shall be voidable at the instance of the company ...*'

It is important to note that the consequence of contravention is not that the offending transaction or arrangement is void, merely that it is voidable. This means that the company (whether acting by its directors, liquidator or shareholders) must take the step of voiding the transaction or arrangement and until that happens, it is valid. This distinction scuppered a defence to a claim by a liquidator to have loans repaid, where that defence was based on the six-year statutory limitation period in *Re Westminister Property Management Ltd (No 3); Boyden v Stern and another*[167]. In that case, the directors tried to argue that a liquidator's claim to repayment of loans made in breach of s 330 of the English 1985 Act was statute barred since, they claimed, the loans were repayable from the moment the monies had been drawn down. The English High Court rejected this argument on the ground that an unlawful loan was voidable not void and so would only become repayable when it was voided.

[16.102] A contravening transaction or arrangement will not, however, be voidable pursuant to s 38(1) of the CA 1990 where any one of the following savers can be relied upon:

(a) restitution of any money or any other asset which is the subject matter of the arrangement or transaction is no longer possible: s 38(1)(a); *or*

(b) the company has been indemnified in pursuance of sub-s (2)(b) for the loss or damage suffered by it: s 38(1)(a); *or*

(c) any rights acquired *bona fide* for value and without actual notice of the contravention by any person other than the person for whom the transaction or arrangement was made would be affected by its avoidance: s 38(1)(b).

These 'savers' from voidability must be distinguished from exceptions. Although a voidable transaction may be capable of being saved, it remains the case that there has been a contravention of s 31, which will have criminal consequences[168]. Where a transaction or arrangement can be brought within an exception, then there will have been no contravention of s 31.

(a) Restitutio in integrum is impossible

[16.103] A prohibited transaction shall not be rendered voidable at the instance of the company entering it where restitution of the money or other asset which is the subject matter of that transaction is no longer possible: s 38(1)(a) of the CA 1990. It would seem that this saver is somewhat anomalous in respect of both guarantees and the provision of security. It is certainly arguable that where a third party has, in good faith, made a loan to a director and that loan has been guaranteed by his company in breach of s 31, restitution is impossible unless the director can repay the loan to the third party.

(b) The indemnity

[16.104] Section 38(1)(a) of the CA 1990 provides that a transaction or arrangement will not be voidable where the company concerned 'has been indemnified' in pursuance of s 38(2)(b). What exactly is meant by an indemnity poses some difficulty, and can only be resolved in the light of judicial interpretation. The indemnity which is required to be given is to be in accordance with s 38(2)(b), which provides that where an arrangement or transaction is made in contravention of s 31 for a relevant person, such relevant people together with any other director of the company who authorised the transaction

167 *Re Westminister Property Management Ltd (No 3); Boyden v Stern and another* [2004] BCC 599.

168 See para **[16.118]** *post*.

or arrangement, shall (whether or not the transaction or arrangement has been avoided under s 38(1)) be:

> '(jointly and severally with any other person liable under this subsection) to indemnify the company for any loss or damage resulting from the arrangement or transaction.'

Such persons are also liable to account to the company for any gain made, directly or indirectly, by the transaction or arrangement: s 38(2)(a). The excusing circumstances set out in s 38(3)[169] ought to be borne in mind, although they will not directly affect the question of whether or not a transaction or arrangement can be avoided or saved under s 38.

This particular exception is not without difficulty. In the first place, one must ask what exactly does 'has been indemnified' mean? 'Indemnified' can *either* mean to merely give a certificate or 'paper indemnity' that the company which enters the transaction or arrangement will not suffer any loss *or* it can mean that the company has *actually* been compensated or reimbursed for any loss or damage suffered. If the latter is the case, it seems to suggest that the company which enters into a prohibited transaction or arrangement must have actually been compensated for the loss suffered[170].

(c) Bona fide and without actual notice

[16.105] Where the avoidance of the prohibited transaction or arrangement would affect any rights acquired *bona fide* for value and without actual notice of the contravention of s 31, being rights of persons other than the person for whom the transaction or arrangement was made, s 38(1)(b) provides that the transaction or arrangement *cannot be avoided*. This saver was invoked to prevent a transaction being voided in the case of *Ruby Property Company Ltd et al v Kilty and Superquinn*[171]. The facts in this case were that the second and third plaintiffs (both deceased at the hearing of the case) were a husband and wife who had owned the entire of the issued share capital in the first plaintiff ('Ruby') and were its only directors. Ruby's sole asset was a property, situate in Sutton, Co Dublin. The directors were indebted to a bank, and by a collateral mortgage debenture, dated 3 August 1990, Ruby had charged the Sutton property with repayment of all monies owed by the directors to the bank. After the directors defaulted in their obligations to the bank, the bank demanded repayment and when this was not received, appointed a receiver (the first defendant) to Ruby. After realising other security, which the directors had owned personally, the bank sought to recover the shortfall of £15,554.08 from Ruby and consequent upon this, the receiver sold the Sutton property

[169] Section 38(3) provides: 'Where an arrangement or transaction is entered into by a company and a person connected with a director of the company or its holding company in contravention of s *31* that director shall not be liable under *subs (2)* if he shows that he took all reasonable steps to secure the company's compliance with that section and, in any case, a person so connected and any other such director as is mentioned in the said *subs (2)* shall not be so liable if he shows that, at the time the arrangement or transaction was entered into, he did not know the relevant circumstances constituting the contravention.' See para **[16.047]** *ante*, where the similar defence in s 29(5) to a claim for an account or indemnity arising from a breach of s 29(1) is considered.

[170] See para **[16.110]** *post*.

[171] *Ruby Property Company Ltd et al v Kilty and Superquinn* (1 December 1999, unreported) HC, McCracken J.

to Superquinn. In the instant proceedings, Ruby sought, *inter alia*, declarations that the collateral mortgage had lapsed and had no validity or effect, and that the appointment of the receiver was invalid and an order that the conveyance of the Sutton property to Superquinn was of no effect.

On the s 31 point, Ruby argued that although it had given the security before the date upon which s 31 became operative, the terms of the loan had been revised post 1 February 1991 and this had created a new debt that 'in reality amounted to the giving of a new security'. It therefore contended that the collateral debenture contravened s 31(1)(c), being security given in connection with a loan to a director. McCracken J said that he thought it unlikely that the plaintiffs could succeed on that argument but acknowledged the possibility that more detailed evidence could lead to a finding that a new security had been given. McCracken J went on to point out that any such issue would be between Ruby and the bank, not between the plaintiffs and the defendants and that unless and until the transaction had been avoided, the debenture and the appointment of the receiver remained valid. McCracken J went on to say, however, that he was quite satisfied that even if the debenture had been in breach of s 31(1)(c) of the CA 1990, the plaintiffs would have no remedy against either of the defendants by reason of s 38(1)(b) of the CA 1990. On this point, he said:

> '… I have no doubt whatever that the Second Defendant [Superquinn] acquired the property *bona fide* and for value without actual notice of any contravention of s 31, if there has been such a contravention. Therefore, any challenge to the sale on the basis of a possible contravention of s 31 must fail[172].'

Accordingly, if a company seeks to set aside a transaction or arrangement for contravention of s 31 it should be aware that any subsequent purchaser is liable to seek to rely upon s 38(1)(b) and claim to be 'equity's darling'. Not everyone can, however, rely on this saver and four observations are apposite:

(i) Beneficiaries of the transaction or arrangement may not seek to rely upon s 38(1)(b)

[16.106] Only 'outsiders' can rely upon s 38(1)(b). The beneficiaries of a transaction or arrangement cannot rely on s 38(1)(b), and s 25(6) of the CA 1990 sets out the circumstances in which a transaction or arrangement is 'made for a person'[173]. Therefore, a director or other relevant person for whom a transaction or arrangement is made is disqualified from claiming to be a *bona fide* purchaser for value without actual notice.

(ii) A person must not have actual notice of the contravention

[16.107] A person's rights will only be saved if he does not have actual notice of the contravention. Actual notice imposes a lesser standard than does constructive notice, in that actual notice turns upon a person's subjective knowledge of a contravention. However, although this aspect of the saver is subjective, a person seeking to rely upon s 38(1)(b) will be precluded from adopting a blinkered approach. In *Agra Bank Ltd v Barry*[174], Lord Cairns said in the context of the doctrine of priorities:

---

172 *Ruby Property Company Ltd et al v Kilty and Superquinn* (1 December 1999, unreported) HC, McCracken J at p 7 of the transcript.

173 See para **[16.071]** *ante*.

174 *Agra Bank Ltd v Barry* (1874) LR 7 HL 135 at 149.

> 'Of course, you may have ... conduct so reckless, so intensely negligent, that you are absolutely unable to account for it in any other way than this, that by reason of a suspicion entertained by the person whose conduct you are examining that there was a registered deed before his, he will abstain from inquiring into the fact, because he is so satisfied that the fact exists, that he feels persuaded that if he did enquire, he must find it out.'

Actual notice has also been considered by the Supreme Court in *Bank of Ireland Finance Ltd v Rockfield Ltd*[175]. There, s 60(14) of the CA 1963 was under consideration[176], which provides that any transaction in breach of s 60(1) of the CA 1963 would be voidable against all persons with notice of the facts which constitute a breach. Kenny J held that the 'notice' referred to therein was 'actual notice'. Of interest is his comment that:

> '... I wish to say that I use the term 'actual notice' as meaning in this case that the plaintiff bank, or any of its officials, had been informed either verbally or in writing, that part of the advance was to be applied in the purchase of shares in the defendant company, or that they knew facts from which they must have inferred that part of the advance was to be applied for this purpose ... I include in 'actual notice' cases where the agent gets actual notice of the equity.'

In practice this has caused legal practitioners great difficulties: to what extent should a solicitor for a lending institution, desirous to lend money to a company, enquire into the circumstances of the loan, particularly where a guarantee and collateral security is being advanced by another company, which may or may not be a *relevant person*[177]. It has been opined elsewhere[178] that extreme caution must be exercised in striking the appropriate balance, and that it will often be the case that in the course of other routine enquiries made in the course of the transaction, facts will come to the knowledge of both a lending institution and its lawyer which may give them notice that the company which proffers the guarantee or security, is doing so in favour of a relevant person.

(iii) Rights must be acquired 'for value'

[16.108] Section 38(1)(b) is confined to non-gratuitous rights acquired, ie, only where a person has given consideration for the rights he acquired. Although counter intuitive, it has been held by the High Court that a person who receives money can be considered to be a 'purchaser'[179].

(iv) The requirement of bona fides[180]

[16.109] The person seeking to rely upon this saver must also have acted *bona fide*, ie, in good faith. The question left unanswered is whether 'good faith' implies a duty to

---

175 *Bank of Ireland Finance Ltd v Rockfield Ltd* [1979] IR 21 at 37.

176 See Ch 10, *The Maintenance of Capital*, at para **[10.053]**.

177 See Courtney, 'The Latest Hazard to Guarantees: The Effects of S.31, Companies Act 1990 on Inter-Company Guarantees' (1991) Gazette ILSI 261, on the question of inter-company guarantees.

178 Courtney, 'The Latest Hazard to Guarantees: The Effects of S.31, Companies Act 1990 on Inter-Company Guarantees' (1991) Gazette ILSI 261 at p 264.

179 *Re Headstart Global Fund Ltd v Citico Bank Nederland NC and another* [2011] IEHC 5 (Clarke J).

180 See Ch 7, *Corporate Contracts, Capacity and Authority*, at para **[7.131]** where 'good faith' in the context of reg 6(1) of the EC(C)R 1973 (SI 163/1973) is considered. It must be remembered that, by reg 6(2), there is a *presumption* that a person acts in good faith.

investigate and if it does, how does this lie with the 'actual notice' standard, since a duty to investigate is more consistent with constructive notice. In a different context, it was said in *International Sales and Agencies Ltd v Marcus*[181], by Lawson J, that:

> '... the test of good faith in somebody entering into obligations with a company will be found either in proof of his actual knowledge that the transaction was *ultra vires* the company or where it can be shown that such a person could not in view of all the circumstances, have been unaware that he was a party to a transaction *ultra vires*.'

This interpretation is essentially objective, meaning that it is open to a court to find that even though a person claims not to have had actual notice, the incredibility of such in the circumstances of the case could mean that the court may find that he did not, in law, act *bona fide*. In a number of situations the Irish courts have held that to act *bona fide*, a person must not turn their face against the possibility of something being improper[182]. It is thought that the twin requirements of 'without actual notice' and '*bona fide*' can only be reconciled by interpreting '*bona fide*' as merely requiring that the outsider must act honestly[183] and not recklessly. A duty to investigate should not be implied in circumstances where the legislature has clearly turned its face against constructive notice of a contravention.

Civil consequences of contravention: account and indemnity

[16.110] The second civil consequence of contravention of s 31 is that the person for whom a contravening transaction or arrangement was made, and any directors who authorised it, are liable to indemnify the company for any loss it suffers and to account to the company for any gain made. Section 38(2) of the CA 1990 provides:

> 'Without prejudice to any liability imposed otherwise than by this subsection but subject to subsection (3), where an arrangement or transaction is made by a company for a director of the company or its holding company or person connected with such a director in contravention of section 31, that director and the person so connected and any other director of the company who authorised the transaction or arrangement shall (whether or not it has been avoided in pursuance of subsection (1)) be liable—
>
> (a) to account to the company for any gain which he has made directly or indirectly by the arrangement or transaction; and

[181] *International Sales and Agencies Ltd v Marcus* [1982] 3 All ER 551 at 559. See also *TCB Ltd v Gray* [1986] 1 All ER 587.

[182] See also *In Re Vendor and Purchaser Act 1874; Crowley v Flynn* (13 May 1983, unreported) HC *per* Barron J. There, s 51(1) of the Succession Act 1965, which protects a 'purchaser' of a deceased person's estate from a personal representative, was interpreted as meaning a person who acts in 'good faith', and further that this meant that such person ought to make reasonable inquiries if the protection was to be successfully invoked. See also *Re Molyneau and White* 13 LR Ir 382.

[183] In the context of the Fraudulent Conveyances Act 1634 (10 Chas 1 Sess 2, c 3), Hamilton P, as he then was, held in *Re Thomas O'Neill, a bankrupt* [1989] IR 544, that: 'With regard to the use of the term "*bona fide*" or "in good faith" in th[at] statute ... I am satisfied that the use of the term must be taken to mean without notice of the intention to delay, hinder or defraud creditors of their lawful debts, rights and remedies.'

(b) (jointly and severally with any other person liable under this subsection) to indemnify the company for any loss or damage resulting from the arrangement or transaction.'

This provides an identical remedy to companies to that provided by s 29(4) of the CA 1990 where a substantial property transaction is entered into in contravention of s 29(1), and the English case law on their former s 322(3) of the Companies Act 1985, considered above[184], is equally relevant to interpreting s 38(2) of the CA 1990. It is also the case that a director may be relieved of liability where he can show that he took all reasonable steps to secure compliance with s 31. This is provided for by s 38(3), which states:

> 'Where an arrangement or transaction is entered into by a company and a person connected with a director of the company or its holding company in contravention of section 31 that director shall not be liable under subsection (2) if he shows that he took all reasonable steps to secure the company's compliance with that section and, in any case, a person so connected and any such other director as is mentioned in the said subsection (2) shall not be so liable if he shows that, at the time the arrangement or transaction was entered into, he did not know the relevant circumstances constituting the contravention.'

This has also been considered above[185] in the context of s 29(5) of the' CA 1990.

[16.111] In *Re Ciro Citterio Menswear plc*[186], it was held that a loan to a director in contravention of s 330 of the Companies Act 1985 (UK) did not automatically make the director a constructive trustee. It was said that a loan to a director was not *per se* the sort of transaction that was inevitably a misapplication of company money or a breach by a director of his trusteeship of company assets. The fact that a loan in breach of s 330 stood until it was avoided was inimical to the existence of a constructive trusteeship or to any form of tracing claim, at least in the absence of special circumstances. It was also said that s 341(2)(a) of the Companies Act 1985 (UK) (which was materially identical to s 38(2)(a) of the CA 1990) supported this as it seemed to presuppose the absence of constructive trusteeship because it expressly provided for what would otherwise be one of the consequences of constructive trusteeship, namely an obligation to account for gains made. It followed that an administrator's claim to a share in a property bought by a director, in part with money advanced by his company, failed.

[16.112] The similarly worded English provision on indemnification[187] was interpreted by the English Court of Appeal in *Neville v Krikorian*[188] as meaning that where a director was aware that his company operated a loan account in favour of another director in breach of s 330 of the Companies Act 1985 (UK), that director would be jointly and severally liable to repay all sums loaned after he became so aware even if he was unaware of the details of individual loans. Moreover, the director was also found to be in breach of duty in not taking steps to recover unlawful loans made before he had become aware of the breach and was liable to repay the difference between what could have been

184 See para **[16.049]** *ante*.

185 See para **[16.053]**. See in particular, *Duckwari plc v Offerventure and another (No 2)* [1999] BCC 11 (Court of Appeal).

186 *Re Ciro Citterio Menswear plc* [2002] EWHC 293 (Ch), [2002] 2 All ER 717.

187 Section 341(2)(b) of the Companies Act 1985 (UK).

188 *Neville v Krikorian* [2006] EWCA Civ 943, [2006] BCC 937.

recovered from the other director had such steps been taken and what could then be recovered.

Civil consequences of contravention: personal liability

[16.113] The third civil consequence of contravention of s 31 is that certain persons may be made personally liable for some or all of the company's debts in the event of its subsequently being wound up insolvent. Section 39(1) of the CA 1990 provides that where a company being wound up is insolvent a court may, if it thinks proper to do so, declare that any person for whose benefit *an arrangement of a kind described in s 32 was made* shall be personally liable without limitation of liability for all or certain specified debts and other liabilities of the company.

[16.114] It can immediately be seen that by use of the word 'arrangement', the application of s 39(1) is limited by reason of the reference to 'of a kind described in s 32'. This means only persons for whose benefit the following prohibited transactions are made may be personally liable:

- loans;
- quasi-loans;
- credit transactions.

Accordingly, it would seem that persons who benefit from guarantees and the provision of security are not liable to be made personally liable under s 39(1) because such are not 'arrangements' within the meaning of s 32.

[16.115] One question of interpretation which arises here is, can personal liability be imposed only where s 32 is relied upon? The reference to 'an arrangement of a kind described in section 32', can refer either to the more narrow interpretation of:

- an arrangement whereby the value of the arrangement is less than 10% of the company's relevant assets; *or*, the broader interpretation of:
- an 'arrangement' which is defined by s 32(2)(a), ie, the beneficiary of a loan, quasi-loan or credit transaction.

The significance of this distinction is that where the former is applied, it means that only persons who benefit from an arrangement which comes within the s 32, 'less than 10% exception', can be made personally liable under s 39. On the other hand, where the latter is applied, it means that anybody who benefits from a loan, quasi-loan or credit transaction, which is in contravention of s 31, may be made personally liable under s 39.

[16.116] It should also be noted that beneficiaries of an 'arrangement' are not automatically personally liable for the debts of a company where that company goes into insolvent liquidation. Rather, on the application of the liquidator or any creditor or contributory of the company, personal liability under s 39(1) *may* be imposed where:

> '... the court considers that any arrangement of a kind described in s *32* has contributed materially to the company's inability to pay its debts or has substantially impeded the orderly winding up thereof.'

While the simple fact that an arrangement was made for a beneficiary's benefit is sufficient to make them a respondent, it is necessary to prove that the arrangement made in their favour either contributed materially to the company's insolvency, or substantially impeded the orderly winding up of the company[189].

[16.117] A court can make an order under s 39(1), 'if it thinks it proper to do so'. Some guidance is given by sub-s (2) which provides:

> 'In deciding whether to make a declaration under *subs (1)*, the court shall have regard to whether, and to what extent, any outstanding liabilities arising under any arrangement referred to in that subsection were discharged before the commencement of the winding up.'

Clearly, where the beneficiary of an arrangement has entirely repaid or reimbursed the company, the court should have regard to this fact and be inclined to exercise its discretion against the making of an order under s 39.

Criminal consequences of contravention

[16.118] The contravention of s 31 is, by s 40 of the CA 1990, a criminal offence, s 40 providing:

> 'If a company enters into a transaction or arrangement that contravenes section 31, every officer of the company who is in default shall be guilty of an offence.'

Section 7 of the C(A)A 2009 replaced the original s 40 which had two subsections with the foregoing provision. Accordingly, it is no longer an offence to procure a company to enter into a transaction or arrangement knowing or having reasonable cause to believe that the company was thereby contravening s 31. The original offence of knowing, or having reasonable cause to believe, that the company was contravening s 31 has also been replaced with the '*officer in default*' formula. The intention is, therefore, that officers will, in accordance with s 383(1) of the CA 1963 be guilty of an offence where they authorise or, in breach of their duties as such officers, permit the default mentioned[190]. Section 383(2) provides that an officer shall be presumed to have permitted a default by the company unless he can establish that he took all reasonable steps to prevent it or that, by reason of circumstances beyond his control, he was unable to do so.

[16.119] The penalties prescribed for a person or corporation who commits either of the foregoing offences are set out in s 240 of the CA 1990. For either offence, on summary conviction, one is liable to a class C fine or, at the discretion of the court, to imprisonment for a term not exceeding 12 months, or both; on conviction on indictment one is liable to a fine not exceeding €22,220.42 or, again at the discretion of the court,

---

189 See *Re David Ireland & Co Ltd* [1905] IR 133, where a director's honest but confusing intermingling of his personal finances with those of the company provoked the liquidator of the company to issue misfeasance proceedings. See Ch 15, *Duties of Directors and Other Officers*, para **[10.149]**.

190 Although s 383(1) of the CA 1963 refers to a provision which provides that 'an officer of a company who is in default shall be liable to a fine or penalty', in fact s 40 does not so refer to an officer being liable to a fine or penalty but, rather, to a officer being guilty of an offence. Whether this minor mis-match would be sufficient to justify an acquittal of an officer so charged remains to be seen.

to a term of imprisonment not exceeding five years, or both[191]. Breach is, therefore, an indictable offence which is reportable by a company's auditors and also, because it can attract five years' imprisonment, means that a suspect can be arrested without warrant and detained under s 4 of the Criminal Justice Act 1984.

[16.120] Unlike a transaction or arrangement that comes within the exemptions listed above in ss 32–37, when there is a contravention of the prohibition in s 31 but it is not voidable by reliance on one of the savers in s 38, the transaction or arrangement remains a criminal offence.

[D] Disclosure of Interests in Contracts with Companies

[16.121] Section 194(1) of the CA 1963 imposes a duty on a director[192] who is in any way, whether directly or indirectly, interested in a contract or proposed contract with the company, to declare the nature of his interest at a meeting of the directors of the company. This states:

> 'It shall be the duty of a director of a company who is in any way, whether directly or indirectly, interested in a contract or proposed contract with the company to declare the nature of his interest at a meeting of the directors of the company[193].'

Like s 29 of the CA 1990, s 194 of the CA 1963 seeks to regulate self-dealing between companies and their directors. Whereas s 29 is pitched at substantial property transactions, s 194 appears at first sight to apply to *every* contract between a director and a company (and some with connected persons). Whereas s 29 of the CA 1990 requires the members to approve of a substantial property transaction, s 194 of the CA 1963 requires disclosure to be made to the other directors[194].

[16.122] On first reading, it appears that the obligation to disclose under s 194(1) of the CA 1963 applies in respect of *every contract* entered into by a company with a director irrespective of its size, value, nature or whether or not it was entered into in the ordinary course of the company's business as there is no *de minimis* exception. This would give rise to ludicrous consequences whereby a director of a company that operates a supermarket is required to disclose the contract for his weekly grocery shop! While there is an ability to give a 'general notice' this does not relate to particular types of contracts, but to contracts entered into with particular persons[195]. However, it is thought that this is not the correct interpretation. Although the primary obligation under s 194(1) makes an unqualified reference to any 'contract', there is evidence in s 194(2)[196] that the intention of the legislature is not to apply to every contract and that what is intended is that only contracts *that will be considered by the board of directors* are required to be

---

191 The classification of the fine and monetary amount have been amended by ss 6 and 9 of the FA 2010.

192 Section 194 of the CA 1963 has application to *shadow directors* by s 27(3) of the CA 1990.

193 As to conflicts of interest, see, generally, Ch 15, *Duties of Directors and Other Officers*, at para **[15.055]** *et seq.*

194 See, generally, MacDonald, 'The Companies Act 2006 and the Directors' Duty to Disclose' [2011] ICCLR 96.

195 See para **[16.129]** *post.*

196 See para **[16.127]** *post.*

disclosed. Contracts which may be entered into by employees on behalf of companies and that are entered into in the ordinary course of business are not contracts which would ordinarily be approved by the board of directors. The purpose of s 194(1) is the disclosure of a potential conflict of interest so that where a contract is being considered by the board of directors, a director who is directly or indirectly interested in that should declare his interest for the purpose of the discussion on that contract. The purpose of s 194(1) is not to require a director to tell his fellow directors that he purchased tea bags from an employee of the company. It is thought that the correct interpretation of the application of s 194(1) is to such contracts only that are required to be approved by the board of directors, ie, the entry of which is reserved to the board of directors.

The proposed new Companies Bill will, if enacted, confine the scope of the replacement provision to interests in contracts that can reasonably be regarded as likely to give rise to a conflict of interest[197].

The scope of s 194: to whom does it apply?

[16.123] Section 194 of the CA 1963 can apply to contracts entered into by companies with three persons or classes of person. First, s 194 applies, primarily, to contracts entered into by companies *with their own directors*. Second, in the case of transactions or arrangements of a kind described in s 31 of the CA 1990 (which are deemed to be contracts[198]), contracts between companies and *persons connected with directors* within the meaning of s 26 of the CA 1990 are also in scope. Third, contracts between companies and their *shadow directors* are in scope by virtue of s 27(3) of the CA 1990. In all cases, it is thought to refer to contracts with such persons or classes of persons as are considered by the board of directors.

The meaning of 'directly or indirectly, interested in a contract'

[16.124] Section 194(1) of the CA 1963 refers to a director being '*directly or indirectly, interested in a contract*'. A director will be *directly* interested in a contract where that contract is between the company and the director; a director will be *indirectly* interested in a contract where that contract is between the company and a nominee of a director where the director *is beneficially interested in the contact*.

There is no reason to say that a contract entered into with a company controlled by a director is a contract in which the director is indirectly interested since if the legislature wanted to include such a scenario, it would have applied the section generally to persons connected with a director, as it has done in certain situations. The ordinary meaning of the words 'directly or indirectly, interested in a contract' is, however, contorted by two statutory provisions which are next considered.

(a) Contracts are deemed to include transactions which are not contracts

[16.125] Section 47(1) of the CA 1990 provides that any reference in s 194 of the CA 1963 to a contract shall be construed as including a reference to any transaction or arrangement made or entered into on or after the commencement of this section – whether or not that transaction or arrangement constitutes a contract. Inexplicably, this

---

197 See s 228(2) of the draft Companies Bill.

198 By s 47(1) of the CA 1990: see para **[16.125]** *post*.

provision does not define what is meant by 'transaction or arrangement' despite the fact that in the subsection that follows, it does define 'transaction or arrangement' as being 'of a kind described in section 31'. Most likely a court would give the words 'transaction or arrangement' in sub-s (1) the same meaning but it is equivocal. If that meaning were to be implied, it would mean that were a company to give a third party a guarantee for a director's debts, that guarantee although not constituting a contract between the company and the director, being a transaction or arrangement of a kind described in s 31 of the CA 1990, is to be treated as if it were a contract and would be required to be disclosed by the director under s 194 of the CA 1963.

(b) Transactions and arrangements with connected persons are deemed to be contracts with directors

[16.126] Section 47(2) of the CA 1990 provides that for the purposes of s 194 of the CA 1963, a transaction or arrangement of a kind described in s 31 made by a company for a director or a person connected with such a director shall, if it would not otherwise be so treated (and whether or not prohibited by that section) be treated as a transaction or arrangement in which that director is interested. A number of observations can be made on this provision. First, this provision must be read in conjunction with s 47(1) of the CA 1990 which deems transactions and arrangements to be contracts for the purposes of s 194 of the CA 1963. Second, although s 194(1) of the CA 1963 is directed at contracts with directors, this provision extends its scope to contracts with persons connected with directors[199] of the company. It is important to remember that this does not mean that every contract with a person connected with a director such as a director's spouse comes within s 194(1): only those contracts that are deemed to be transactions or arrangements of a kind described by s 31 of the CA 1990. The ability to give a 'general notice' under s 194(3) that a director is to be regarded as interested in any contract which may after the date of the notice be made with a specified person who is connected with him within the meaning of s 26 of the CA 1990 must be construed in the light of s 47(2). Accordingly, s 194(3) does not mean that a director is to be taken to be automatically interested in all contracts entered into with connected persons, as the director's obligation to disclose arises in respect of transactions or arrangements that a company enters into with connected persons. Third, it does not matter that a transaction or arrangement within the meaning of s 31 is not prohibited by reason of the application of one of the exceptions in ss 32–37, it must still be disclosed for the purposes of s 194(1) of the CA 1963.

Making disclosure

[16.127] The key to discharging the duty imposed by s 194(1) is to disclose one's interest in the contract or proposed contract at a meeting of the directors. Section 194(2) of the CA 1963 is concerned with the timing of a director's declaration of interest. This recognises three different circumstances in which a director can be interested in a contract or proposed contract and prescribes the times at which such interests should be disclosed:

- in the case of a proposed contract – at the meeting at which the question of entering into the contract is first proposed;

199 For the meaning of persons connected with directors, see para **[16.003]** *ante*.

– in the case of a proposed contract where the director was not, at the date of the first meeting at which it was considered, interested – at the next meeting of the directors held after he became interested;
– in the case where a director becomes interested in a contract after it is made – at the first meeting of the directors held after the director became interested.

It is this provision which provides evidence of the true legislative intention, namely, that s 194 only applies to contracts that are required to be approved by the board.

[16.128] Section 194(4) provides that a notice shall be of no effect unless either given at a meeting of the directors or the director giving the notice takes reasonable steps to secure that it is brought up and read at the next meeting of the directors after it is given. Disclosure must be made at a meeting of directors and so it is technically insufficient to have disclosed an interest to all of the directors individually on separate occasions; moreover, the section does not provide that it is necessary that all directors of the company should be present at that meeting, and it is thought that if disclosure is made at a meeting of directors at which a quorum is present, it will be validly made for the purposes of s 194 of the CA 1963[200].

[16.129] As an alternative to making a specific disclosure, s 194(3) provides that a *general notice* may be given to the directors of a company which is deemed to be a sufficient declaration of interest. This provides that a general notice given to the directors of a company by a director to the effect that:

(a) he is a member of a specified company or a firm and is to be regarded as interested in any contract which may, after the date of the notice, be made with that company or firm; or

(b) he is to be regarded as interested in any contract which may after the date of the notice be made with a specified person who is connected with him (within the meaning of section 26 of the CA 1990);

shall be deemed to be a sufficient declaration of interest in relation to any such contract. Unlike specific declarations of interest under s 194(1), a general notice does not have to be given at a meeting of the directors but only 'to the directors of a company' so that a general notice may be given to all of the directors individually.

[16.130] In the case of shadow directors, disclosure is not made at a meeting of the directors but by a notice in writing to the directors. Section 27(3) of the CA 1990 provides that such notice can be either:

(a) a specific notice given before the date of the meeting at which, if he has been a director, the declaration would be required by s 194(2) of that section to be made; or

---

200 There may be a difference in consequence between the statutory requirement to disclose in s 194 of the CA 1963 and a director's fiduciary duty to disclose conflicts at common law. Whereas there is authority at common law for the propositions that disclosure should be to the full board (*Guinness plc v Saunders* [1988] 2 All ER 940) and that the directors to whom it is disclosed should not be themselves interested in the contract (*Hopkins v Shannon Transport Ltd* (10 July 1972, unreported) HC, Pringle J) the statutory provision does not expressly import either proposition so that neither will amount to a breach of s 194.

(b) a notice which under s 194(3) falls to be treated as a sufficient declaration of that interest or would fall to be so treated apart from the proviso;

and it is further provided that s 145 of the CA 1963 shall have effect as if the declaration had been made at the meeting in question and had accordingly formed part of the proceedings at that meeting.

The register of directors' interests and its inspection

[16.131] Section 194(5)(a) provides that declarations and interests must be kept in a book which is to be available for inspection by the officers and members of the company[201]. This book is referred to here as the register of directors' interests. Section 194(5)(a) provides:

> 'A copy of every declaration made and notice given in pursuance of this section shall, within 3 days after the making or giving thereof, be entered in a book kept for this purpose. Such book shall be open for inspection without charge by any director, secretary, auditor or member of the company at the registered office of the company and shall be produced at every general meeting of the company, and at any meeting of the directors if any director so requests in sufficient time to enable the book to be available at the meeting.'

Moreover, a company shall, if required by the Director of Corporate Enforcement, produce to the Director for inspection the register of declarations and notices, and must give the Director such facilities as he requires for inspecting and taking copies of the contents of the register[202].

The civil consequences of its breach

[16.132] Although the section is silent as to the civil consequences where a director does not declare his interest in a contract, it has been held that 'under the ordinary principles of general law'[203] the contract would be voidable at the company's instance, provided that the parties can be restored to their original position. This interpretation is assisted by s 194(7) which provides that nothing in the section shall be taken to prejudice the operation of any rule of law restricting directors from having any interest in contracts with the company.

[16.133] In *Hely-Hutchinson v Brayhead Ltd*[204], Lord Pearson said of the similar s 199 of the Companies Act 1948 (UK):

> 'It is not contended that section 199 in itself affects the contract. The section merely creates a statutory duty of disclosure and imposes a fine for non-compliance. But it has to be read in conjunction with article 99. The first sentence of that article is obscure. If a director makes or is interested in a contract with the company, but fails duly to declare his interest, what happens to the contract? Is it void, or is it voidable at the option of the

---

201 Failure to comply with sub-s (5) renders the company and every officer of the company in default, liable to a class C fine and the court may, by order, compel an immediate inspection or production: s 195(5)(b) of the CA 1963.

202 Section 194(5A) of the CA 1990 as inserted by s 2(b) of the C(A)A 2009.

203 See *Guinness plc v Saunders* [1990] BCC 205 at 217G and *Hely-Hutchinson v Brayhead Ltd* [1968] 1 QB 549 at 594.

204 *Hely-Hutchinson v Brayhead Ltd* [1968] 1 QB 549 at 594.

company, or is it still binding on both parties, or what? The article supplies no answer to these questions. I think the answer must be supplied by the general law, and the answer is that the contract is voidable at the option of the company, so that the company has a choice whether to affirm or avoid the contract, but the contract must be either totally affirmed or totally avoided and the right of avoidance will be lost if such time elapses or such events occur as to prevent rescission of the contract …'

Accordingly, not every breach of s 194(1) will render the contract to which it relates voidable. Where the articles of association of the company concerned permit directors to contract with the company, a failure to declare an interest in that contract in technical breach of s 194(1) may not result in that contract being invalidated. On the other hand, where the undisclosed contract constituted a conflict of interest as, for example, the sale of the cinemas in *Regal (Hastings) v Gulliver*[205], a failure to disclose can result in the invalidation of the contract for breach of director's duty[206].

[16.134] In *Craven Textile Engineers Ltd v Batley Football Club Ltd*[207], it was accepted that a director had not declared to his company his interest in a contract with his company. The contract had been performed and the company had work done for it and materials supplied to it. Clarke LJ held that it was inappropriate for the company to avoid the contract as the court could not restore the parties to the position they had been in before the work had been done and the materials supplied. In these circumstances, it was held that the company was obliged to pay on foot of the contract.

The criminal consequences of breach

[16.135] A breach of s 194 by a director is an offence which can render that director liable to a class C fine[208]. A company which fails to comply with s 194(5)(a) or (5A) and every officer of the company in default is guilty of an offence and liable to the same fine and, moreover, where required inspection or production is refused, the court may by order compel an immediate inspection or production[209].

205 *Regal (Hastings) v Gulliver* [1942] 1 All ER 378.

206 See, further, Ch 15, *Duties of Directors and Other Officers*, at para **[15.058]**.

207 *Craven Textile Engineers Ltd v Batley Football Club Ltd* [2001] BCC 679.

208 Section 194(6) of the CA 1963.

209 Section 194(5)(b) of the CA 1963.

Chapter 17

Financial Statements, Audit and Annual Return

Preliminary

[17.001] The Companies Acts contain detailed provisions regulating the maintaining of proper books of account, and the preparation, audit and disclosure of accounts, or as they have come to be called, *financial statements*[1]. The rationale for such regulation is that it is so important for all persons dealing with a company – whether shareholders, officers, creditors, or employees – that there be reliable and comprehensible financial information available regarding the company.

[17.002] The statutory regulation of accounting operates at three principal levels. First, every company is required to keep proper books of account, recording the company's assets, liabilities and transactions, and which give a 'true and fair view' of the state of affairs of the company. The books of account then form the basis for a company to prepare accounts – which it is required to do on a regular basis, and that follow prescribed formats which are familiar to the users of accounts – and for the audit of those accounts by qualified and independent auditors, who consider whether the accounts have been properly prepared, and give a true and fair view of the state of affairs of the company, and its profit or loss. Third, companies are required to disclose details of their accounts (and of the auditor's opinion) at regular intervals, both to their members, at the annual general meeting ('AGM'), and, usually, to the public at large, in the annual return filed with the registrar of companies in the Companies Registration Office ('CRO').

[17.003] The accounts prepared by a company are therefore among its most important, and most visible, links with its members and with the public at large, and any breach of the highly technical requirements set out in this chapter can have serious consequences, both in terms of direct penalties for the company and its officers, and in terms of reputational damage.

[17.004] The requirements are considered under the following headings, which mirror the proposed restructuring of the law relating to financial statements proposed in the draft Companies Bill:

[A] The Books of Account

[B] Financial Year

§ *This chapter has been contributed by Dáibhí O'Leary.*

1 Although *accounts* are now referred to as *financial statements*, this chapter will continue to make reference to accounts as this is the term which is used in the Companies Acts.

[C] The Annual Accounts.
[D] Group Accounts.
[E] Approval of Accounts.
[F] Directors' Report.
[G] Audit Requirement.
[H] Auditor's Report.
[I] Publication of Accounts.
[J] Annual Return.
[K] Exclusions, Exemptions and Special Arrangements with regard to Filing Obligation.
[L] Audit Exemption.
[M] Appointment of Statutory Auditors.
[N] Rights, Obligations and Duties of Auditors.
[O] Removal and Resignation of Auditors.
[P] Notification to Supervisory Authority of certain matters.

[A] THE BOOKS OF ACCOUNT

Introduction

[17.005] Section 202 of the CA 1990[2] requires that all companies must cause proper books of account to be kept, which set out the company's transactions in a correct and accurate manner, and facilitate the preparation and auditing of the company's annual accounts[3]. Section 202(1) provides[4]:

> 'Every company shall cause to be kept proper books of account, whether in the form of documents or otherwise, that —
>
> (a) correctly record and explain the transactions of the company,
>
> (b) will at any time enable the financial position of the company to be determined with reasonable accuracy,
>
> (c) will enable the directors to ensure that any annual accounts of the company comply with the requirements of the Companies Acts and, where applicable, Article 4 of the IAS Regulations, and
>
> (d) will enable the annual accounts of the company to be readily and properly audited.'

Such books must be 'kept on a continuous and consistent basis, that is to say, the entries therein shall be made in a timely manner and be consistent from one year to the next'[5].

Contents of the books of account

[17.006] Further to the requirements set out in the previous paragraph, and without prejudice to the generality of those requirements, the books of account are required to contain[6]:

---

2 Displacing s 147 of the CA 1963.

3 See generally MacCann, 'Duty to Keep Proper Books of Account' (1991) ILT 177.

4 Section 202(1) of the CA 1990.

5 Section 202(2) of the CA 1990.

6 Section 202(3) of the CA 1990.

'(a) entries from day to day of all sums of money received and expended by the company and the matters in respect of which the receipt and expenditure takes place,

(b) a record of the assets and liabilities of the company,

(c) if the company's business involves dealing in goods —

(i) a record of all goods purchased, and of all goods sold (except those sold for cash by way of ordinary retail trade), showing the goods and the sellers and buyers in sufficient detail to enable the goods and the sellers and buyers to be identified and a record of all the invoices relating to such purchases and sales,

(ii) statements of stock held by the company at the end of each financial year and all records of stocktakings from which any such statement of stock has been, or is to be, prepared, and

(d) if the company's business involves the provision of services, a record of the services provided and of all the invoices relating thereto.'

Section 202(4) of the CA 1990 states that the books of account must give a 'true and fair view of the state of affairs of the company and explain its transactions'[7]. This is however expressed as being in addition to the requirement that the books of account comply with sub-ss (1) to (3) of s 202, and therefore cannot be seen as qualifying the requirements of those subsections. In particular, there appears on a strict reading of s 202(3) to be no *de minimis* provision whereby minor errors might be tolerated. Accordingly it will be necessary to maintain high standards of book-keeping. The level of detail required can be seen from the example given by Smyth J in *Brosnan v Sommerville*[8] as cited below[9].

Location of the books of account

[17.007] The books of account must be kept either at the company's registered office, or at such other place as the directors think fit[10]. There is no obligation that the books of account be kept in the State, although significant additional requirements are imposed by s 202(6) of the CA 1990 where the books are kept at a place outside the State, in that:

> '... there shall be sent to and kept at a place in the State and be at all reasonable times open to inspection by the directors such accounts and returns relating to the business dealt with in the books of account so kept as will disclose with reasonable accuracy the financial position of that business at intervals not exceeding 6 months and will enable to be prepared in accordance with the Companies Acts (and, where applicable, Article 4 of the IAS Regulation) the company's accounts and any document annexed to those accounts giving information which is required by the said Acts and is thereby allowed to be so given.'

In practice, the above requirement to keep in the State such accounts and returns as will enable the preparation of the company's annual accounts[11] and the documents required to be annexed to those accounts[12] is likely to result in significant duplication, and

7 Section 202(4) of the CA 1990.

8 *Brosnan v Sommerville* [2007] 4 IR 135.

9 See para **[17.10]**.

10 Section 202(5) of the CA 1990.

11 See para **[17.017]** *et seq*.

12 See para **[17.250]** *et seq*.

therefore it seems that there would need to be strong reasons to keep the books of account outside the State before one would consider doing so.

Form of the books of account

[17.008] The books of account may be kept 'in the form of documents or otherwise'[13]. The books, and the accounts and returns required if the books are kept outside the State, must be kept either in written form in an official language of the State or so as to enable the books of account and the accounts and returns to be readily accessible and readily convertible into written form in an official language of the State[14]. Thus the books of account (and if applicable, the accounts and returns) may be kept on computer, and in such a case a 'hard copy' is not required to be kept at all times, so long as one may be produced when required. The books of account, and any accounts and returns, must be preserved by the company for a period of at least six years after the latest date to which they relate[15].

Inspection of the books of account

[17.009] The books of account, and any accounts and returns, must be made available in written form in an official language of the State at all reasonable times for inspection without charge by the officers of the company and by other persons entitled pursuant to the Companies Acts to inspect the books of account of the company[16]. This right of inspection is of particular importance to the directors of the company, as they need to be in a position to examine the books of account in order to perform properly their duties, including their duties to ensure that proper books of account are kept and to report on the annual accounts at the AGM[17]. The right to inspect the books of accounts may be enforced where necessary by means of an injunction[18] or by way of an application pursuant to s 371 of the CA 1963[19], which allows the court, on application by any member or creditor of the company, by the Director of Corporate Enforcement or by the registrar of companies, to make an order directing the company and any officer thereof to make good a default with a provision of the Companies Acts within a specified timeframe[20]. Therefore a director will only have standing to make an application pursuant to s 371 of the CA 1963 where that director is also a member or creditor of the company[21].

[17.010] It has further been held in *Healy v Healy Homes Ltd*[22] that a director exercising his right to inspect the books of account may be accompanied by an accountant, since it would be unreasonable to expect a director having no formal training in accountancy to be able to decide whether proper books of account were being kept. Kenny J stated in this case:

13 Section 202(1) of the CA 1990.
14 Section 202(7) of the CA 1990.
15 Section 202(9) of the CA 1990.
16 Section 202(8) of the CA 1990.
17 See para **[17.214]** *et seq*.
18 *Healy v Healy Homes Ltd* [1973] IR 209.
19 *Brosnan v Sommerville* [2007] 4 IR 135.
20 Section 371 of the CA 1963.
21 *Murray Browne Mulcahy Ltd v Companies Acts* [2010] IEHC 112.
22 *Healy v Healy Homes Ltd* [1973] IR 209.

> 'The purpose of [what is now s 202 of the CA 1990] is to compel companies to keep proper books of account: one of the ways in which this important object is achieved is by imposing an obligation on each director to make sure that this is being done. But a director who has not had a training in accountancy cannot decide whether proper books of account are being kept unless an accountant is allowed to inspect them; the phrase 'proper books of account' means books which give a true and fair view of the state of the company's affairs and which explain its transactions. It follows that a director's right to inspect books of account necessarily involves that an accountant nominated by him may do this. The accountant may do this when he is accompanied by the director or when the accountant has been given a written authority to do so, and he may be required to give a written undertaking that the knowledge which he gets will not be used for any purpose except in relation to the matter in connection with which he has been retained … The right of a director to inspect the books of a company when he has an obligation imposed on him the breach of which may involve him in criminal liability, necessarily implies that he has the right to employ a qualified agent to advise him. The question whether proper books are being kept is one on which an accountant is the only person qualified to advise as most directors would not be able to form a correct judgment on the matter. The director and his accountant are also entitled to make copies of the books of account or any part of them.'

Thus, the director need not even exercise his right in person; a qualified accountant or such other person having the necessary accounting training may exercise it on his behalf, provided that that person has written authority to do so, and gives, if requested to do so, a written undertaking to use the information he obtains only for the purpose of giving confidential advice to the director in relation to the matter in question. In addition, it was held in this case that the director and his agent are entitled to make copies of the accounts. The company will however be entitled to refuse the director access to the books of account – and the court will make no order to the contrary in this respect – where he is seeking access for the purpose of injuring the company or for some other improper purpose (eg, for the benefit of a competitor)[23].

The duty to provide access to the books of account is not satisfied by providing minimal information, but rather the information provided must be such as to render the company's transactions explicable. An example of the detail required was provided by Smyth J in *Brosnan v Sommerville*[24], in stating:

> '[If] "payments were made out of company funds through the intermingling of a company credit card and the Defendant's brother's personal credit card" the credit card and the credit card accounts of both the company and the Defendant or [his brother], if it be him, as well as the docket, invoice, statement, VAT statement, VAT returns and receipt of payment of VAT would all be embraced to enable a true and fair view of the company to be obtained and explain its transactions.'

The company's auditors are given an express statutory right of access at all reasonable times to the books of account[25]. The members of the company have no

---

23 *Oxford Legal Group Ltd v Sibbasbridge Services plc* [2008] 2 BCLC 381.

24 *Brosnan v Sommerville* [2007] 4 IR 135.

25 Section 193(3) of the CA 1990 refers to 'books, accounts and vouchers', but it is difficult to conceive of any case in which this would not be synonymous with 'books of account'.

statutory or common law right to inspect the books of account, and will only enjoy such a right if it is expressly conferred on them by the articles of association[26].

Liability for failure to keep proper books of account

Both civil and criminal penalties may be imposed on directors who fail to comply with their duties in relation to the keeping of proper books of account.

(a) Criminal liability

[17.011] Section 202(10) of the CA 1990 provides that a company which contravenes the requirements relating to proper books of account, and any director of such a company who fails to take all reasonable steps to secure compliance with these requirements, or who has by his own wilful act been the cause of any such default by the company, shall be guilty of an offence. Such an offence is punishable on summary conviction by the imposition of a class C fine[27] or, at the discretion of the court, by imprisonment for a term not exceeding 12 months, or both[28]. Upon conviction on indictment, a person guilty of such an offence shall be liable to a fine not exceeding €22,220.42 or imprisonment for a term not exceeding five years, or both[29]. As with all offences that carry a maximum term of five years' imprisonment, one should bear in mind that a person suspected of committing such an offence can be arrested without warrant and detained under s 4 of the Criminal Justice Act 1984[30]. Whether in relation to summary conviction, or conviction on indictment, it is expressly provided that a director may not be sentenced to imprisonment unless the court is of the opinion that the offence was committed wilfully[31].

In any proceedings against a director regarding a failure to take reasonable steps to secure compliance by a company with the requirements in respect of the keeping of proper books of account, it shall be a defence for that person to prove that he had reasonable grounds for believing, and did believe, that a competent and reliable person was charged with the duty of ensuring that those requirements were complied with and that that person was in a position to discharge that duty[32].

[17.012] Under s 203 of the CA 1990, where a company that is being wound up and that is unable to pay all of its debts has failed to meet the requirements in relation to the keeping of proper books of account, and the court considers that such contravention has either contributed to the company's inability to pay all of its debts, or has resulted in substantial uncertainty as to the assets and liabilities of the company, or has substantially

---

26 *Burn v New London & South Wales Coal Co* [1908] WN 209. It was suggested in *Re Clubman Shirts Ltd* [1983] ILRM 323, as cited by MacCann, 'Duty to Keep Proper Books of Account' (1991) ILT 177, that such a right might be found to exist under s 205 of the CA 1963, but O'Hanlon J. found in this case that the failure to furnish information constituted irregularity in the affairs of the company rather than oppressive conduct under s 205, and moreover did not expressly state that this right extended to books of account.

27 A class C fine is defined in s 3 of the Fines Act 2010 ('FA 2010') as 'a fine not exceeding €2,500'.

28 Section 240(1) of the CA 1990, as amended by the FA 2010.

29 Section 240(1) of the CA 1990, as amended by the FA 2010.

30 See Ch 28, *Compliance and Enforcement*, and in particular **[28.022]**.

31 Section 202(10)(b) of the CA 1990.

32 Section 202(10)(a) of the CA 1990.

impeded the orderly winding up of the company, then every officer of the company who is in default[33] shall be guilty of an offence. 'Officer', in this context, is expressly stated as including a director or secretary[34], but is not limited to such persons. Consequently, an auditor may be regarded as an officer of the company for the purposes of this section[35]. On summary conviction, the officer may be liable to a class C fine[36] or to imprisonment for a term not exceeding six months, or to both[37]. Upon conviction on indictment, the officer may be fined up to €22,220.42, or imprisoned for five years, or both[38].

It shall be a defence for an officer being prosecuted in such proceedings to prove that he took all reasonable steps to secure compliance with the obligation to keep proper books of account, or that he had reasonable grounds for believing, and that he did believe, that a competent and reliable person, acting under the supervision and control of a director of the company who has been formally allocated such responsibility, was charged with the duty of ensuring that proper books of account were kept and was in a position to discharge that duty[39].

(b) Civil liability

[17.013] Under s 204 of the CA 1990, where a company that is being wound up and that is unable to pay all of its debts has failed to keep proper books of account, and the court considers that such failure has contributed to the company's inability to pay its debts, or has resulted in substantial uncertainty as to the assets and liabilities of the company, or has substantially impeded the orderly winding up of the company, the court may declare that any one or more of the officers or former officers of the company who is or are in default shall be personally liable, without any limitation of liability, for all or a specified part of the debts or other liabilities of the company. This is in addition to the possibility of being found criminally liable[40]. In addition, the failure to keep proper books of account may also constitute reckless trading under s 297A of the CA 1990, which would also expose officers to potential personal liability. These consequences have already been examined in detail in Ch 15[41]. It is clear, however, that the potential personal liabilities for directors as a result of a company failing to keep proper books of account may be enormous.

---

33 Section 383 of the CA 1963 states that 'officer in default' means any officer who authorises, or who, in breach of his duty as such officer, permits the default; and an officer shall be presumed to have permitted a default by the company unless the officer can establish that he took all reasonable steps to prevent it, or, by reason of circumstances beyond his control, was unable to do so.

34 Section 2(1) of the CA 1963.

35 *R v Shacter* [1960] 2 QB 252.

36 A class C fine is defined in s 3 of the FA 2010 as 'a fine not exceeding €2,500'.

37 Section 203(1)(b)(i) of the CA 1990.

38 Section 203(1)(b)(ii) of the CA 1990.

39 Section 203(2) of the CA 1990.

40 Section 204(5) of the CA 1990.

41 See Ch 15, *Duties of Directors and Other Officers*, at para [**15.131**] *et seq.*

Concealment, destruction and falsification of books of account

[17.014] Section 243 of the CA 1990 provides, in relation to any book or document affecting or relating to the property or affairs of the company, that an officer of a company who:

(a) destroys, mutilates or falsifies any such book or document;

(b) is privy to the destruction, mutilation or falsification of any such book or document;

(c) makes or is privy to the making of a false entry in any such book or document;

(d) fraudulently parts with, alters or makes an omission in any such book or document; or

(e) is privy to fraudulent parting with, fraudulent altering or fraudulent making of an omission in, any such book or document,

shall be guilty of an offence (save where, in the case of (a) to (c) above, he proves that he had no intention to defeat the law). In each case, the officer shall be liable on summary conviction to a class C fine[42] or to imprisonment for a term not exceeding six months, or to both[43]; and upon conviction on indictment, the officer may be fined up to €22,220.42, or imprisoned for five years, or both[44].

[17.015] In addition to the general provisions above, s 293 of the CA 1963 sets out a number of offences which relate specifically to companies which are wound up, some of which are pertinent to the keeping of proper books of account. Section 293(1) of the CA 1963 provides:

> '... if any person, being a past or present officer of a company which at the time of the commission of the alleged offence is being wound up, whether by the court or voluntarily, or is subsequently ordered to be wound up by the court or subsequently passes a resolution for voluntary winding up —
>
> ...
>
> (c) does not deliver up to the liquidator, or as he directs, all books and papers in his custody or under his control belonging to the company and which he is required by law to deliver up; or ...
>
> (f) makes any material omission in any statement relating to the affairs of the company; or ...
>
> (h) after the commencement of the winding up prevents the production of any book or paper affecting or relating to the property or affairs of the company; or
>
> (i) within twelve months next before the commencement of the winding up or at any time thereafter conceals, destroys, mutilates or falsifies or is privy to the concealment, destruction, mutilation or falsification of any book or paper affecting or relating to the property or affairs of the company; or
>
> (j) within twelve months next before the commencement of the winding up or at any time thereafter makes or is privy to the making of any false entry in any book or paper affecting or relating to the property or affairs of the company; or

42 A class C fine is defined in s 3 of the FA 2010 as 'a fine not exceeding €2,500'.

43 Section 203(1)(b)(i) of the CA 1990.

44 Section 203(1)(b)(ii) of the CA 1990.

> (k) within twelve months next before the commencement of the winding up or at any time thereafter fraudulently parts with, alters or makes any omission in, or is privy to the fraudulent parting with, altering or making any omission in, any document affecting or relating to the property or affairs of the company; ...
>
> he shall ... be liable, on conviction on indictment, to imprisonment for a term not exceeding [5] years or to a fine not exceeding [€6,348.70] or to both, or ... on summary conviction, to imprisonment for a term not exceeding 6 months or to a [class C fine][45] or to both.'

For the purposes of this section, the term 'officer' includes any person in accordance with whose directions or instructions the directors of the company have been accustomed to act.

It is a good defence to a charge under para (c) or (f) if the accused proves that he had no intent to defraud[46], while acting fraudulently is expressly stated as being part of the charge at (k). Similarly, it is a good defence to a charge under paras (h), (i) and (j) of the subsection if he proves that he had no intent to conceal the state of affairs of the company or to defeat the law[47].

[B] Financial Year

[17.016] Section 2(1) of the CA 1963 provides that 'financial year' means

> 'subject to [s 2(1A)], in relation to any body corporate, the period in respect of which any profit and loss account of the body corporate laid before it in general meeting is made up, whether that period is a year or not.'

Section 2(1A) makes clear that the first financial year of a company commences on its date of incorporation and each subsequent financial year commences on the day after the end of the previous financial year. The resulting implication is that there shall be no periods of time in respect of which no accounts have been prepared. The definition of 'financial year' in the CA 1963 is therefore inextricably linked to the requirement in s 148(1) of that Act that the directors of every company prepare accounts for the company for each financial year 'on a date not later than 18 months after the incorporation of the company and subsequently once at least in every calendar year'.

A 'financial year' may therefore be either less or more than 12 months in duration. However, on the basis that (all other things being equal) it will cost more to prepare two sets of accounts for six-month periods than one set of accounts for a 12-month period, a company that persistently prepares accounts for financial years of less than 12 months will be acting inefficiently in this regard. In addition, while the provisions of s 148 of the CA 1963, read in isolation, would suggest that a financial year might be almost 24 months in duration (ie, if a company moved from a January to a December financial year-end date), this is constrained by the requirements in relation to AGMs[48] that the accounts be laid before the AGM of the company within nine months of the balance

45 As implicitly substituted by s 6 of the FA 2010; a class C fine is defined in s 3 of the FA 2010 as 'a fine not exceeding €2,500'.

46 Section 293(2) of the CA 1963.

47 Section 293(2) of the CA 1963.

48 See para **[17.249]** *post*; and See Ch 14 *Corporate Governance: Meetings*, at para **[14.006]**.

sheet date[49], that an AGM be held in each calendar year[50], and that not more than 15 months elapse between the holding of one AGM and that of the next[51].

In addition, where a company is required to file its accounts with its annual return[52], a change in its financial year-end date may require a change in its annual return date, and following such a change in the annual return date, a company will not be permitted to change again until five years have passed[53]. Accordingly it is likely that most companies will keep the same financial year-end date from one year to the next, and therefore maintain a 12-month financial year, unless there is a particular reason for doing otherwise.

[C] THE ANNUAL ACCOUNTS

Introduction

[17.017] As noted previously[54], the members of a company have no right under statute or at common law to inspect the company's books of account, unless the articles of association of the company expressly confer such a right upon them. Few companies include such a provision in their articles. However, one would expect most shareholders to consider it essential that they would be informed, periodically, of the state of the company's financial affairs. Accordingly, the Companies Acts require the directors of all companies to prepare certain accounts and reports, and to lay these before the AGM[55] of the company's members:

- a balance sheet as at the last day of the financial year[56];
- a profit and loss account for the financial year[57]; and
- a directors' report on the state of the company's affairs[58].

It should be noted that different terms may be used on occasion in substitution for the terms 'balance sheet' and 'profit and loss account'; notably, in respect of companies preparing accounts in accordance with international financial reporting standards[59], International Accounting Standard 1 refers to a 'statement of financial position' and 'statement of comprehensive income' respectively[60]. However the different terms do not signify any difference in respect of the purpose for which these statements are prepared and used. For the avoidance of confusion, the terms 'balance sheet' and 'profit and loss account' are used throughout this text, irrespective of the applicable accounting framework.

---

49 Section 148(7) of the CA 1963.

50 Section 131(1) of the CA 1963.

51 Section 131(1) of the CA 1963.

52 See para **[17.250]** *et seq*, *post*.

53 Section 127(10) of the CA 1963.

54 See para **[17.010]** *ante*.

55 See Ch 14, *Corporate Governance: Meetings*.

56 Section 149(1)(a) of the CA 1963.

57 Section 149(1)(b) of the CA 1963.

58 Section 158 of the CA 1963; See para **[17.214]** *et seq*, *post*.

59 See para **[17.024]** *post*.

60 International Accounting Standard 1, para 10.

In addition, where a company is a 'parent undertaking'[61], the directors shall also be required to prepare consolidated accounts for the group as a whole (referred to as group accounts)[62], detailing the state of affairs of that company and its subsidiary undertakings as a whole, and to lay these group accounts before the AGM at the same time as the individual company accounts[63].

Given that the members have no right of access to the books and records which form the basis for the annual accounts, they might be concerned as to whether they could reasonably place reliance on the accounts. This concern is addressed by providing for the appointment of a statutory auditor[64] to the company, save where an exemption from audit applies. A statutory auditor is required to make a report on the accounts (both individual and, if applicable, group accounts) laid before the company in general meeting[65], and that report must be read at the AGM of the company and be open to inspection by any member[66].

[17.018] Where a director of a company fails to take all reasonable steps to ensure compliance with the requirement to prepare accounts, that director will be, in respect of each offence, liable on summary conviction to imprisonment for a term of up to six months, or to a class D fine or to both[67]. It will, however, be a defence in any such proceedings for the director to prove that he had reasonable grounds to believe, and that he did believe, that a competent and reliable person was charged with the duty of seeing that the requirement was complied with and was in a position to discharge that duty[68]. Furthermore, a sentence of imprisonment may only be imposed if the court is of the opinion that the offence was committed wilfully[69].

[17.019] Every balance sheet and profit and loss account of the company must be approved by the board of directors[70], and signed on behalf of the directors by two of the directors of the company[71], before circulation. It is however made clear that while it is an offence to issue, circulate or publish a copy of a balance sheet or profit and loss account which has not been signed, this does not prohibit the issue, circulation or publication of a fair and accurate summary of any profit and loss account and balance sheet, or of the profit or loss figures for part of the company's financial year[72]. A copy of the accounts, together with a copy of the directors' and auditor's report, shall, not less than 21 days before the AGM, be sent to every member and debenture-holder of the company (regardless of whether they are entitled to notices of general meetings), and to any other person so entitled[73]. If the copies of the accounts are sent less than 21 days before the

61 Regulations 3 and 4 of the EC(C:GA)R 1992.
62 Section 150(1) of the CA 1963.
63 Section 150(9) of the CA 1963.
64 See para **[17.292]** *et seq, post.*
65 Section 193(1) of the CA 1990.
66 Section 193(2) of the CA 1990.
67 Section 148(11) of the CA 1963.
68 Section 148(11)(a) of the CA 1963.
69 Section 148(11)(b) of the CA 1963.
70 Section 157(1) of the CA 1963.
71 Section 156(1) of the CA 1963.
72 Section 156(4) of the CA 1963.
73 Section 159(1) of the CA 1963.

AGM, the accounts can be deemed to have been duly sent if it is so agreed by all the members entitled to attend and vote at the meeting[74]; specific provisions also apply in respect of single-member companies[75]. Failure to comply with any of these requirements renders the company and every officer in default liable to a class C fine[76]. In addition, every member and debenture-holder is entitled to have sent to him, without charge, copies of the preceding year's annual accounts[77]. Failure to comply within seven days of this demand being made will render the company and every officer in default liable to a class C fine[78] unless it is proved that the member made an earlier demand and was furnished with a copy[79].

[17.020] Regulation 8 of the European Communities (Single-Member Private Limited Companies) Regulations 1994 ('EC(SMPLC)R 1994') provides that the sole member of a single-member company may decide to dispense with the requirement to hold an AGM. Where it does so, the requirement that the directors lay before the AGM individual (and, where applicable, group) accounts, with a directors' report attached, and that the statutory auditors make a report on those accounts to the AGM, shall be deemed to be satisfied where they are sent to the sole member of the single-member company in accordance with the preceding paragraph not less than 21 days before the 'appropriate date'.

The 'appropriate date' is the last day of the month in which the anniversary falls of:

(a) the last AGM held in respect of the company, or
(b) the formation of the company, if it has not yet held an AGM[80].

If the decision to dispense with the AGM ceases to have effect, then the normal requirements as to the laying of the accounts and reports before the AGM will apply in respect of that financial year and subsequent financial years[81].

[17.021] Before considering the detailed obligations generally applicable to companies, one should note that not all companies are subject to the same obligations. First, 'medium-sized' and 'small' companies are exempted from some of the rigours of the requirements relating to the annual accounts[82]. In addition, a different regime historically applied to unlimited companies in respect of the preparation and disclosure of annual accounts. This could be explained by a belief that the need to make accounting information available to the public (and therefore to creditors) would be less pressing in the case of such companies, since the members thereof would not be in a position to hide behind the cloak of limited liability were the company to fall into insolvent liquidation[83].

---

74 Section 159(3) of the CA 1963.
75 See para **[17.020]**.
76 Sections 156(3), 157(2) and 159(5) of the CA 1963; a class C fine is defined in s 3 of the FA 2010 as 'a fine not exceeding €2,500'.
77 Section 159(4) of the CA 1963.
78 Sections 156(3), 157(2) and 159(5) of the CA 1963; a class C fine is defined in s 3 of the FA 2010 as 'a fine not exceeding €2,500'.
79 Section 159(5) of the CA 1963.
80 Regulation 8(9) of the EC(SMPLC)R 1994.
81 Regulation 8(7) of the EC(SMPLC)R 1994.
82 See para **[17.267]** *et seq, post*.
83 Section 207 of the CA 1963.

Therefore unlimited companies have not been subject to the same disclosure requirements as limited companies, and less detailed accounting requirements also applied[84].

It seems that a concern subsequently arose that a limited liability company might use an unlimited company as a cover for its activities so as to limit the amount of accounting information it makes public. To this end, the European Communities (Accounts) Regulations 1993 ('EC(A)R 1993') require certain unlimited companies[85] – for example, unlimited companies all of whose members are limited companies or their foreign equivalent – to meet the presentation and disclosure requirements which normally apply in respect of limited companies preparing Companies Act accounts[86]. Such companies will be subject to the requirements set out in this chapter.

Moreover, while unlimited companies outside the scope of the EC(A)R 1993 remain subject to the less detailed requirements set out in s 149 of the CA 1963 and the Sixth Schedule to the CA 1963[87], the same overriding obligation to give a 'true and fair view' applies in respect of the accounts of such unlimited companies as it does in respect of Companies Act accounts[88]. Therefore it is likely that, in practice, the annual accounts of unlimited companies will not be significantly different from those of limited companies[89].

[17.022] Each of the following shall now be considered in turn:

1. Accounting frameworks.
2. Companies Act individual accounts.
3. The balance sheet in Companies Act individual accounts.
4. The profit and loss account in Companies Act individual accounts.
5. Notes forming part of Companies Act individual accounts.
6. IFRS individual accounts.

Accounting frameworks

[17.023] Prior to the commencement of the European Communities (International Financial Reporting Standards and Miscellaneous Amendments) Regulations 2005 ('EC(IFRSMA)R 2005'), it was generally accepted that the requirement that the accounts of a company give a true and fair view[90] would be met when the accounts were prepared in accordance with the Standards of Standard Accounting Practice ('SSAPs'), issued until 1990 by the Accounting Standards Committee of the Consultative Committee of Accounting Bodies of the UK and Ireland, and the Financial Reporting Standards ('FRSs'), issued since 1990 by the Accounting Standards Board, the independent body which replaced the

84 As set out in the Sixth Schedule to the CA 1963.

85 Regulation 6 of the EC(A)R 1993.

86 Regulation 7(1) of the EC(A)R 1993.

87 While there would not seem to be any provision to preclude such a company preparing IFRS accounts, this would be considered highly unusual.

88 Section 149(2) of the CA 1963; the relevant term in respect of IFRS accounts is 'presented fairly'; para 18 of International Standard on Auditing (UK & Ireland) 700 states expressly that the terms 'true and fair view' and 'presented fairly' are equivalent.

89 See Ch 31, *Unlimited Companies*, at para **[31.023]** *et seq*.

90 As required by s 149(2) of the CA 1963 and s 3(1)(b) of the C(A)A 1986.

Accounting Standards Committee, which together are referred to as Irish generally accepted accounting practice ('Irish GAAP')[91].

[17.024] The EC(IFRSMA)R 2005 amended s 148 of the CA 1963 to require that a company prepare accounts for the company for each financial year ('individual accounts'),

> '(a) in accordance with section 149 (to be known and in this Act referred to as 'Companies Act individual accounts'), or
>
> (b) in accordance with international financial reporting standards and section 149A [of the CA 1963] (to be known and in this Act referred to as 'IFRS individual accounts')[92].'

Section 149 of the CA 1963 requires that Companies Act individual accounts give a true and fair view of the state of affairs of the company as at the end of the financial year, and of the profit or loss of the company for the financial year[93], and the understanding would continue to be that this would be met by compliance with Irish GAAP. In addition, limited companies (other than insurance undertakings or credit institutions) must comply with the detailed requirements of the C(A)A 1986[94].

Alternatively, the EC(IFRSMA)R 2005 provide for the use of an alternative accounting framework, being international financial reporting standards[95] ('IFRS'). A company looking to prepare its accounts under this framework must also comply with the requirements of s 149 of the CA 1963. The detailed requirements in respect of each of these frameworks are considered in the following sections.

A private limited company therefore effectively has the choice of two accounting frameworks[96], although restrictions apply in respect of this choice. First, a not-for-profit company or charity will only be permitted to prepare Companies Act (not IFRS)

---

91 See para **[17.026]** *et seq, post*.

92 Section 148(2) of the CA 1963 as amended by reg 4 of the EC(IFRSMA)R 2005.

93 Section 149(2) of the CA 1963.

94 Section 149(3)(a) of the CA 1963, in conjunction with the definition of 'company' (as not including an unlimited company) in s 1(1) of the C(A)A 1986.

95 Section 2(1) of the CA 1963 defines 'international financial reporting standards' as meaning 'international financial reporting standards within the meaning of [Regulation (EC) No 1606/2002], adopted from time to time by the European Commission in accordance with [Regulation (EC) No 1606/2002]'.

96 In theory, additional accounting frameworks may be available. Pursuant to s 1 of the C(MP)A 2009, certain parent undertakings are permitted to use US generally accepted accounting principles (as defined in the C(MP)A 2009) in the preparation of their individual and group accounts, to the extent that such use does not contravene any provision of the Companies Acts or of any regulations made thereunder; however, as one of the conditions for availing of this provision is that the company is subject to reporting to the Securities and Exchange Commission, it is extremely unlikely to apply to private companies; these provisions are addressed in detail in the context of public limited companies, in Ch 29, *Public Limited Companies and SEs*, at para **[29.118]** *et seq*. Secondly, s 2 of the C(MP)A 2009 empowers the Minister for Jobs, Enterprise and Innovation to make regulations that may prescribe other specified internationally recognised accounting standards, subject to specified criteria, but to date no such regulations have been made. Finally, s 260A of the CA 1990 allows an investment company within the scope of Part XIII of the CA 1990 to prepare its individual accounts in accordance with a specified alternative body of accounting standards.

accounts[97]. Secondly, once a company has prepared IFRS accounts for a financial year, it may not change to Companies Act accounts unless there is a relevant change in circumstances (eg, a change in ownership, or the company or its parent ceasing to have securities admitted to trading on a regulated market)[98].

Companies Act individual accounts

[17.025] Companies Act individual accounts must comply with the provisions of the Schedule to the C(A)A 1986[99], including following one of the formats set out in the Schedule[100]. The amounts to be included in the accounts are required to be determined in accordance with specified accounting principles[101], although this is subject to the overriding requirement that the accounts show a 'true and fair view of the state of affairs and profit or loss of the company'[102].

(a) 'True and fair view'

[17.026] The annual accounts must give a 'true and fair view' of the affairs of the company as at the end of the financial year, and of the profit or loss of the company for the financial year[103]. Where a balance sheet or profit and loss account that is drawn up in accordance with the prescribed formats and accounting principles of the C(A)A 1986 would not provide sufficient information to give a true and fair view of the state of affairs and profit or loss of the company, there is a requirement that:

> '... any necessary additional information shall be provided in that balance sheet or profit and loss account or in a note to the accounts[104].'

In addition, where compliance with the prescribed formats and accounting principles of the C(A)A 1986 would prevent the accounts from giving a true and fair view of the state of affairs and profit or loss of the company (even if additional information were given as in the preceding paragraph) the directors of the company are obliged to:

> '... depart from the requirements of the Schedule to [the C(A)A 1986] in preparing those accounts insofar as is necessary to [give a true and fair view][105].'

Details of the departure, the reasons, and the effect which the departure will have on the accounts must be included in a note to the accounts[106].

The effect of these requirements is that it is not merely sufficient to blindly comply with the requirements of the C(A)A 1986, but rather a company must constantly ask whether the accounts are giving a true and fair view of the state of affairs, and profit or loss, of the company.

---

97 Section 148(3) of the CA 1963.
98 Section 148(4) and (5) of the CA 1963.
99 Section 3(1)(a) of the C(A)A 1986.
100 Section 4(1) of the C(A)A 1986.
101 Section 5 of the C(A)A 1986; See para **[17.028]** *post*.
102 Section 3(1) of the C(A)A 1986.
103 Section 3(1)(b) of the C(A)A 1986.
104 Section 3(1)(c) of the C(A)A 1986.
105 Section 3(1)(d) of the C(A)A 1986.
106 Section 3(1)(e) of the C(A)A 1986.

[17.027] This, of course, raises the question as to the circumstances in which the accounts will be deemed to give a 'true and fair view' of the state of affairs and profit or loss of a company. This is not set out expressly in the Companies Acts, but it is generally accepted that Companies Act individual accounts will be deemed to give a true and fair view when they are prepared in accordance with Irish GAAP (as defined at para **[17.23]** above). Compliance with these standards in the preparation of the company accounts will be strong – but not conclusive – evidence that the accounts give a 'true and fair' view of the company's affairs. In the English case of *Lloyd Cheyham & Co Ltd v Littlejohn & Co*[107], Woolf J observed of the standards:

> 'While they are not conclusive, so that a departure from their terms necessarily involves a breach of the duty of care, and they are not as the explanatory foreword makes clear, rigid rules, they are very strong evidence as to what is the proper standard which should be adopted and unless there is some justification, a departure from this will be regarded as constituting a breach of duty. It appears to me important that this should be the position because third parties in reading the accounts are entitled to assume that they have been drawn up in accordance with the approved practice unless there is some indication in the accounts which clearly states that this is not the case.'

Adherence to the standards would thus seem to constitute prima facie evidence that the accounts portray a 'true and fair view'. In practice, then, adherence to the standards should be maintained wherever possible in the preparation of Companies Act individual accounts[108]. In some unusual circumstances, however, adherence to the standards may provide a distorted view of the company's financial position, in which case the overriding requirement of the 'true and fair view' must be preferred[109].

(b) Statutory accounting principles

[17.028] The amounts to be included in Companies Act individual accounts are to be determined in accordance with the following accounting principles:

> '(a) the company shall be presumed to be carrying on business as a going concern,
>
> (b) accounting policies shall be applied consistently from one financial year to the next,
>
> (c) the amount of any item in the accounts shall be determined on a prudent basis and in particular —
>
> (i) only profits realised at the balance sheet date shall be included in the profit and loss account, and
>
> (ii) all liabilities which have arisen in respect of the financial year to which the accounts relate, or a previous financial year, shall be taken into account, including those liabilities and losses which only become apparent between the balance sheet date and the date on which the accounts are signed in pursuance of section 156 of the CA 1963,

---

107 *Lloyd Cheyham & Co Ltd v Littlejohn & Co* [1987] BCLC 303; See also *Dovey v Corey* [1901] AC 477; *Dolan v AB Co Ltd* [1969] IR 247; *IRC v Duple Motor Bodies Ltd* [1961] 1 WLR 739.

108 This issues will obviously not arise in respect of IFRS individual accounts, where the requirement is that the accounts be prepared in accordance with IFRS, as stated in s 149A(1)(a) of the CA 1963, rather than that they give a true and fair view.

109 See Lasok & Grace, 'The True and Fair View' (1989) 10 Co Law 13; and McGee, 'The "True and Fair View" Debate: A Study in the Legal Regulation of Accounting' (1991) 54 MLR 874.

(d) all income and charges relating to the financial year to which the accounts relate shall be taken into account without regard to the date of receipt or payment,

(e) in determining the aggregate amount of any item the amount of each individual asset or liability that falls to be taken into account shall be determined separately, and

(f) in determining how accounts are presented within items in the profit and loss account and balance sheet, the directors of a company shall have regard to the substance of the reported transaction or arrangement, in accordance with generally accepted accounting principles or practice[110].

Realised profits, in the context of s 5(c) of the C(A)A 1986, are such profits as fall to be treated as realised profits in accordance with generally accepted accounting principles for the determination of realised profits at the time when the accounts are prepared[111]. It is also significant that s 5(e) requires that when determining the aggregate amount of an item in the accounts, each individual component of that item must be considered separately. This means, in effect, that a company may not offset gains and assets occurring within a particular item or group of items in the accounts, and a write down for diminution in value of each component item must be recorded when required.

[17.029] Departure from these principles is permitted if it appears to the directors of a company that there are special reasons necessitating such departure, but particulars of the departure, the reasons for it and its effect on the balance sheet and profit and loss account of the company must be stated in a note to the company's accounts[112]. In addition, as set out above[113], departure is *required* in the rare case where preparation in accordance with these principles would not give a true and fair view[114].

The balance sheet in Companies Act individual accounts

[17.030] The directors of every company must, on a date not later than 18 months after the incorporation of the company and subsequently once at least in every year prepare accounts[115]. Where the company prepares Companies Act individual accounts[116], these are required to include a balance sheet, made up to the last day of the financial year[117].

(a) The balance sheet formats

[17.031] For a limited company preparing Companies Act individual accounts, s 4(1) of the C(A)A 1986 requires that every balance sheet must show the items listed in either of the two balance sheet formats set out in Part I of the Schedule to the C(A)A 1986.

[17.032] The directors may choose which format to adopt, subject to the overriding requirement that the accounts must give a 'true and fair' view of the company's state of affairs[118]. Whichever format is used, however, the directors must adopt the same format

110 Section 5 of the C(A)A 1986.

111 Paragraph 72 of the Schedule to the C(A)A 1986.

112 Section 6 of the C(A)A 1986.

113 See para **[17.026]**.

114 Section 3(1)(d) of the C(A)A 1986.

115 Section 148(1) of the CA 1963.

116 See para **[17.125]** *ante*.

117 Section 149(1) of the CA 1963.

in subsequent years, unless, in their opinion, there are special reasons for a change[119]. Where such a change is made, the reasons for the change and full particulars of the change must be given in a note to the accounts in which the new format is adopted[120].

[17.033] Section 4 of the C(A)A 1986 also sets out additional rules in respect of the use of the formats in preparing the balance sheet. Thus, any item required in accordance with the formats may be shown in greater detail than required by the format adopted[121]. Secondly, any items to which an Arabic number (1, 2, 3, etc) is assigned in any of the formats may be combined where the individual amounts of such items are not material to assessing the state of affairs of the company, or where such combination facilitates the assessment (provided that in the latter case, disclosure of the individual amounts is set out in a note to the accounts)[122]. Thirdly, in respect of every item in the balance sheet, the corresponding amount for the previous financial year must be shown, and if it is not comparable, an adjustment must be made[123]. Fourthly, if there is no amount to be shown for an item in both the current financial year and the immediately preceding financial year, that item need not be included in the balance sheet[124]. Fifthly, amounts in respect of items representing assets may not be set off against items representing liabilities (or vice versa)[125]. The balance sheet may include an item representing or covering the amount of any asset or liability not covered by any of the items listed in the formats; however, preliminary expenses, expenses and commission on any issue of shares or debentures, and costs of research may not be treated as assets in the balance sheet[126]. Finally, the directors shall adapt the arrangement, headings and sub-headings required in respect of items to which an Arabic number is assigned in the format, in any case where the special nature of the company's business requires such adaptation[127].

[17.034] Format 2, as below, requires companies to adopt the following format in the preparation of the balance sheet:

ASSETS	LIABILITIES
A. Fixed Assets	***A. Capital and reserves***
I. Intangible assets:	*I. Called up share capital*
1. Development costs	*II. Share premium account*
2. Concessions, patents, licences trade marks and similar rights and assets	*III. Revaluation reserve*
3. Goodwill	
4. Payments on account	

[118] Section 3(1)(b) of the C(A)A 1986.
[119] Section 4(3) of the C(A)A 1986.
[120] Section 4(4) of the C(A)A 1986.
[121] Section 4(5) of the C(A)A 1986.
[122] Section 4(6) and (7) of the C(A)A 1986.
[123] Section 4(8) of the C(A)A 1986.
[124] Section 4(9) and (10) of the C(A)A 1986.
[125] Section 4(11) of the C(A)A 1986.
[126] Section 4(12) of the C(A)A 1986.
[127] Section 4(13) of the C(A)A 1986.

ASSETS	LIABILITIES
II. Tangible assets:	*IV. Other reserves*
1. Land and buildings	1. The capital redemption reserve fund
2. Plant and machinery	2. […][128]
3. Fixtures, fittings, tools and equipment	3. Reserves provided for by the articles of association
4. Payments on account and assets in course of construction	4. Other reserves
III. Financial assets:	*V. Profit and loss account*
1. Shares in group undertakings	[Minority Interest]
2. Loans to group undertakings	
3. Participating interests	
4. Loans to undertakings in which a participating interest is held	
5. Other investments other than loans	
6. Other loans	
B. Current Assets	***B. Provisions for liabilities***
I. Stocks:	1. Pensions and similar obligations
1. Raw materials and consumables	2. Taxation, including deferred taxation
2. Work in progress	3. Other provisions
3. Finished goods and goods for resale	***C. Creditors***
4. Payments on account	1. Debenture loans
II. Debtors:	2. Bank loans and overdrafts
1. Trade debtors	3. Payments received on account
2. Amounts owed by group undertakings	4. Trade creditors
3. Amounts owed by undertakings in which a participating interest is held	5. Bills of exchange payable
	6. Amounts owed to group undertakings
4. Other debtors	7. Amounts owed to undertakings in which a participating interest is held
5. Called up share capital not paid	
6. Prepayments and accrued income	8. Other creditors including tax and social welfare
III. Investments:	9. Accruals and deferred income
1. Shares in group undertakings	
2. […][129]	
3. Other investments	
IV. Cash at bank and in hand	

[17.035] There is no difference in the items required by Format 1 and Format 2 of the balance sheet formats. Format 1 has the same headers (with Roman numerals), and has the same items (with Arabic numbers) within those headers, save that 'Creditors' is split

[128] Item 2 deleted by s 233(2)(b) of the CA 1990.

[129] Item 2 deleted by s 233(2)(b) of the CA 1990.

into those falling due within and after one year; Format 1, however, orders those headers differently, as follows:

A. Fixed Assets

B. Current Assets

C. Creditors: Amounts falling due within one year

D. Net current assets (liabilities)

E. Total assets less current liabilities

F. Creditors: Amounts falling due after more than one year

G. Provisions for liabilities

H. Capital and reserves

Minority interest

The items for 'net current assets (liabilities)' and 'total assets less current liabilities' in Format 1 are subtotals. It should be noted that where Format 2 is adopted, while it does not require the split on the face of the balance sheet between 'creditors: amounts falling due within one year' and 'creditors: amounts falling due after more than one year', equivalent information has to be disclosed in a note to the accounts if not shown in the balance sheet[130].

[17.036] Regard must be had to the following matters when addressing each of the items required in the balance sheet. First, amounts in respect of concessions, patents, licences, trade marks and similar rights and assets can only be included under that heading in the balance sheet if either the assets were acquired for valuable consideration and are not required to be shown under goodwill, or the assets in question were created by the company itself[131]. Second, amounts in respect of goodwill may only be included to the extent that the goodwill was acquired for valuable consideration[132]. Third, as regards debtors, the amounts falling due after more than one year must be shown separately for each item included under that heading[133]. Fourth, the amounts of any convertible loans must be shown separately under debenture loans[134]. Fifth, as regards creditors, payments received on account of orders must be shown insofar as they are not shown as deductions from stocks[135]. Sixth, the amount for creditors in respect of taxation and social welfare must show the following separately[136]:

- Income tax payable on emoluments to which Chapter IV of the Income Tax Act 1967 applies;
- Any other income tax;
- Corporation tax;
- Capital gains tax;

130 Note 10 on the Balance Sheet Format, Part I of the Schedule to the C(A)A 1986.

131 Note 1 on the Balance Sheet Format, Part I of the Schedule to the C(A)A 1986.

132 Note 2 on the Balance Sheet Format, Part I of the Schedule to the C(A)A 1986.

133 Note 4 on the Balance Sheet Format, Part I of the Schedule to the C(A)A 1986.

134 Note 5 on the Balance Sheet Format, Part I of the Schedule to the C(A)A 1986.

135 Note 6 on the Balance Sheet Format, Part I of the Schedule to the C(A)A 1986.

136 Note 7 on the Balance Sheet Format, Part I of the Schedule to the C(A)A 1986.

– Value added tax; and

– Any other tax.

Seventh, as regards accruals and deferred income, the amount in respect of any government grants must be shown separately in a note to the accounts if it is not shown separately on the face of the balance sheet[137]. Finally, as regards called up share capital, the amount in respect of allotted share capital and the amount in respect of called up share capital which has been paid up must be shown separately[138].

(b) Statutory valuation rules

[17.037] The Companies Acts do not restrict companies to any one method of valuing assets, but allow for valuation at 'historic cost' (ie, by reference to the original purchase price or production cost)[139], at 'current cost' (ie, by reference to the current replacement cost)[140], or at 'fair value' (by reference to its market value)[141]. In *Carroll Industries plc v Ó Cualacháin*[142], the Revenue Commissioners challenged the valuation of assets on a current cost basis, on the basis that it would produce a smaller figure for taxable profits. Carroll J held that accounts prepared for taxation purposes must adopt an historic cost approach, as that was the accounting method envisaged by taxation legislation. However she added that, as regards accounts prepared for other purposes – eg, to be laid before the AGM – a company was free to choose its accounting method in the light of the nature of its business. Of course whatever the accounting basis adopted, the accounts must still provide a 'true and fair' view of the company's state of affairs[143].

[17.038] Part II of the Schedule to the C(A)A 1986 sets out the rules to be followed where valuation is carried out on an historic cost approach. Those rules are modified, where the company opts for a current cost approach, by the provisions of Part III of the Schedule, and where it adopts a fair value approach, by the provisions of Part IIIA of the Schedule. In either case, all assets must be categorised as being either 'fixed' or 'current'[144]. In addition, as referred to above[145], each individual asset must be valued separately[146].

(*i*) *Fixed assets*

[17.039] Fixed assets are defined as those assets which:

> '... are intended for use on a continuing basis in the company's activities[147].'

---

137 Note 8 on the Balance Sheet Format, Part I of the Schedule to the C(A)A 1986.

138 Note 9 on the Balance Sheet Format, Part I of the Schedule to the C(A)A 1986.

139 Part II of the Schedule to the C(A)A 1986.

140 Part III of the Schedule to the C(A)A 1986.

141 Part IIIA of the Schedule to the C(A)A 1986.

142 *Carroll Industries plc v OCualacháin* [1988] IR 705.

143 Section 3(1)(b) of the C(A)A 1986.

144 In accordance with the balance sheet formats set out in Part I of the Schedule to the C(A)A 1986, use of which is required by s 4(1) of the C(A)A 1986.

145 See para **[17.028]**.

146 Section 5(e) of the C(A)A 1986.

147 Paragraph 60 of the Schedule to the C(A)A 1986.

1. Historical cost rules

[17.040] Under the historic rules, a fixed asset must be shown at its purchase price or production cost[148]. In the case of any fixed asset having a limited useful economic life, this amount shall be reduced by depreciation so as to systematically write down that amount, over the period of the asset's useful economic life, to the residual value (if any) that it is estimated the asset will have at the end of the period of that life[149]. Purchase price means any consideration (whether in cash or otherwise) given by the company in respect of that asset[150], and includes any expenses incidental to its acquisition[151].

The production cost of a fixed asset comprises the price of raw materials and consumables used, and costs directly attributable to the production of the asset[152]. The production cost may also include a reasonable proportion of the costs indirectly attributable to the production of that asset, to the extent that those costs relate to the period of its production, and (providing that this is disclosed in a note to the accounts) interest on capital borrowed to finance the production of that asset[153].

If a reduction in value of a fixed asset is expected to be permanent, provision for such diminution in value *must* be made[154]. In addition, provision may be made for non-permanent diminution in fixed financial assets[155]. If the reason for any such provision ceases to apply (ie, there is an improvement in the value of the written-down fixed assets), the provision must be written back to the extent that it is no longer necessary, and any amount written back disclosed in a note to the accounts[156].

Additional rules apply to the valuation of fungible fixed assets (ie, assets which are substantially indistinguishable from one another)[157]. Tangible fixed assets which are constantly being replaced, the overall value of which is not material to assessing the company's state of affairs, and the quantity, value and composition of which are not subject to material variation may be included at a fixed quantity and value[158]. Development costs may only be included in a company's balance sheet, under 'fixed assets', in special circumstances, and if so included, disclosure must be made in the accounts as to the reason for treating those costs as a fixed asset, and the period over which the amount of the costs so capitalised is being or is to be written off[159].

Where goodwill is treated as a fixed asset, then, in addition to the foregoing rules, the amount of the consideration for any goodwill acquired by the company must be depreciated over a period (not exceeding the useful economic life of the goodwill) chosen by the directors, and disclosure must be made in the notes to the accounts as to the period so chosen and the reason for choosing that period[160].

---

148 Paragraph 5 of the Schedule to the C(A)A 1986.
149 Paragraph 6 of the Schedule to the C(A)A 1986.
150 Paragraph 71 of the Schedule to the C(A)A 1986.
151 Paragraph 14(1) of the Schedule to the C(A)A 1986.
152 Paragraph 14(2) of the Schedule to the C(A)A 1986.
153 Paragraph 14(3) of the Schedule to the C(A)A 1986.
154 Paragraph 7(2) of the Schedule to the C(A)A 1986.
155 Paragraph 7(1) of the Schedule to the C(A)A 1986.
156 Paragraph 7(3) of the Schedule to the C(A)A 1986.
157 Paragraph 15(6) of the Schedule to the C(A)A 1986.
158 Paragraph 13 of the Schedule to the C(A)A 1986.
159 Paragraph 8 of the Schedule to the C(A)A 1986.

[17.041] Where there is no record of the purchase price or production cost of any asset, or of the details required to determine that price or cost, or where it would cause unreasonable expense or delay to obtain any such record, the purchase price or production cost shall be deemed to be the value ascribed to it in the earliest available record of its value made on or after its acquisition or production by the company[161].

2. Alternative accounting rules

[17.042] Part III of the Schedule to the C(A)A 1986 allows alternative accounting rules (effectively, current cost accounting) in the valuation of fixed assets[162]. The following are the options in relation to fixed assets:

(a) Intangible fixed assets, other than goodwill, may be included at current cost;

(b) Tangible fixed assets may be included at:

  (i) current cost, or

  (ii) a market value determined as at the date of their last valuation;

(c) Financial fixed assets may be included at:

  (i) a market value determined as at the date of their last valuation; or

  (ii) a value determined on any basis which appears to the directors to be appropriate in the circumstances of the company[163].

[17.043] Where historical cost accounting is not employed, the items affected and the basis of valuation adopted in each case must be disclosed in a note to the accounts[164], and:

> 'In the case of each balance sheet item affected (except stocks) either —
>
> (a) the comparable amounts determined according to the historical cost accounting rules, or
>
> (b) the differences between those amounts and the corresponding amounts actually shown in the balance sheet in respect of that item,
>
> shall be shown separately in the balance sheet or in a note to the accounts[165].'

[17.044] Where any of these alternative accounting rules is used in the valuation of an asset, depreciation must be based on the value produced by that alternative rule rather than according to its purchase price or production cost[166]. The figure for depreciation in the profit and loss account may be either the amount written off the alternative value or the amount written off the historical cost; but where the amount provided for depreciation is that based on the historical cost amount, the amount of any difference between the two must be shown separately in the profit and loss account or in a note to the accounts[167].

---

160 Paragraph 9 of the Schedule to the C(A)A 1986.

161 Paragraph 16 of the Schedule to the C(A)A 1986.

162 Paragraph 19 of the Schedule to the C(A)A 1986.

163 Paragraph 19 of the Schedule to the C(A)A 1986.

164 Paragraph 21(2) of the Schedule to the C(A)A 1986.

165 Paragraph 21(3) of the Schedule to the C(A)A 1986.

166 Paragraph 20(1) of the Schedule to the C(A)A 1986.

167 Paragraph 20(3) of the Schedule to the C(A)A 1986.

[17.045] Any profit or loss arising on the revaluation of an asset on application of the alternative accounting rules must be credited or debited to a separate reserve, known as the 'revaluation reserve', and must be shown in the company's balance sheet under a separate sub-heading. The revaluation reserve must be reduced when the directors are of the opinion that the amounts standing to its credit are no longer necessary for the company's accounting policies, but an amount may only be transferred from the reserve to the profit and loss account if either the amount in question was previously charged to that account, or if it represents realised profit. The taxation treatment of the revaluation reserve must be disclosed in a note to the accounts[168].

3. Fair value accounting

[17.046] Financial instruments, including derivative financial instruments, may be accounted for by companies at fair value[169].

[17.047] Fair value in this context means its market value[170]. Where a reliable market value cannot readily be identified for a financial instrument but can be identified for its components or for a similar instrument, its fair value is to be determined by reference to those values. Where a reliable market value cannot readily be identified for any of the above, fair value is to be determined using generally accepted valuation models and techniques. If a fair value cannot be determined using any of the above, the assets must instead be measured using the historical cost or alternative accounting rules[171].

[17.048] The following financial instruments may not be accounted for at fair value[172], unless they are appropriately accounted for and the associated disclosure requirements made in accordance with IFRS[173]:

(a) non-derivative financial instruments which are liabilities, save where they are held as part of a trading portfolio;
(b) non-derivative financial instruments held to maturity;
(c) loans and receivables originated by the company and not held for trading purposes;
(d) interests in subsidiary undertakings, associated undertakings and joint ventures;
(e) equity instruments issued by the company;
(f) contracts for contingent consideration in a business combination; and
(g) financial instruments with such special characteristics that the instruments should be accounted for differently from other financial instruments.

[168] Paragraph 22 of the Schedule to the C(A)A 1986.
[169] Paragraph 22A of the Schedule to the C(A)A 1986.
[170] Paragraph 22B of the Schedule to the C(A)A 1986.
[171] Paragraph 22B of the Schedule to the C(A)A 1986.
[172] Paragraph 22A(2) and (3) of the Schedule to the C(A)A 1986.
[173] Meaning that they must be accounted for in accordance with international accounting standards as adopted by Commission Regulation 1725/2003 on or before 5 September 2006, and the associated disclosure requirements made as provided for in IFRS adopted in accordance with Regulation (EC) No 1606/2002.

A company may, in respect of any assets or liabilities which qualify as hedged items under a fair value hedge accounting system (or specified portions of those assets and liabilities), value those assets and liabilities at the amount required under that system[174].

[17.049] Where investment property and living animals and plants would be permitted under IFRS, to be included in accounts at fair value determined in accordance with IFRS, and where that value can reliably be determined, those assets may be included in Companies Act individual accounts at the same value[175].

(ii) Current assets

1. Historical cost rules

[17.050] Current assets are defined as those assets which are not intended for use on a continuing basis in the company's activities[176].

[17.051] Under the historical cost method, current assets must be stated at purchase price or production cost[177]. The same rules in respect of the calculation of the purchase price or production costs of fixed assets apply equally in determining those amounts in respect of current assets[178], save that it is expressly stated that distribution costs may not be included in the calculation of production costs of current assets[179].

The concept of depreciation does not apply to current assets, but if the net realisable value of any current asset is lower than the amount at which it is stated, the amount included in respect of that asset must be written down to its net realisable value[180]. Where there is a subsequent improvement in the net realisable value, the write-down must be written back to the extent that it no longer applies[181].

[17.052] The purchase price or production cost of stocks and all fungible assets (whether fixed or current) may be valued by the application of either:

- the first in, first out (FIFO) method; or
- a weighted average price method; or
- any method similar to these methods.

The method chosen must be one which appears to the directors to be appropriate in the circumstances of the company[182].Where the amount shown in respect of an asset pursuant to a method so permitted differs materially from the replacement cost of that asset as at the balance sheet date[183], or if the directors think it more appropriate, the most recent actual purchase price or production cost before the balance sheet date of assets in that class[184], the amount of the difference shall be disclosed in a note to the accounts[185].

---

174 Paragraph 22C of the Schedule to the C(A)A 1986.
175 Paragraph 22CA of the Schedule to the C(A)A 1986.
176 Paragraph 60 of the Schedule to the C(A)A 1986.
177 Paragraph 10 of the Schedule to the C(A)A 1986.
178 Paragraph 14 of the Schedule to the C(A)A 1986.
179 Paragraph 14(4) of the Schedule to the C(A)A 1986.
180 Paragraph 11(1) of the Schedule to the C(A)A 1986.
181 Paragraph 11(2) of the Schedule to the C(A)A 1986.
182 Paragraph 15(1) of the Schedule to the C(A)A 1986.
183 Paragraph 15(4) of the Schedule to the C(A)A 1986.
184 Paragraph 15(5) of the Schedule to the C(A)A 1986.

As in relation to tangible fixed assets[186], raw materials and consumables which are constantly being replaced, the overall value of which is not material to assessing the company's state of affairs and the quantity, composition and value of which are not subject to material variation may be included at a fixed quantity and value[187].

[17.053] Where any amount repayable on any debt owed by the company is greater than the value of the consideration received in the transaction giving rise to the debt, the amount of the difference may be treated as an asset. It must, however, be written off by reasonable amounts each year so that it is completely written off before repayment of the debt, and the amount not written off must be shown as a separate item in the company's balance sheet or disclosed in a note to the accounts[188].

[17.054] Again, where there is no record of the purchase price or production cost of an asset, or of the details required to calculate them, or where it would cause unreasonable expense or delay to obtain such records, the purchase price or production cost shall be deemed to be the value ascribed to it in the earliest available record of its value made on or after its acquisition or production by the company[189].

2. Alternative accounting rules

[17.055] Just as in relation to fixed assets, Part III of the Schedule to the C(A)A 1986 allows current cost accounting in the valuation of current assets, in providing that the following items may be included at current cost:

- stocks; and
- investments falling to be classified in the balance sheet as current assets[190].

[17.056] The same disclosures are required where current assets are included on a current cost basis as is the case where historical cost accounting is not employed for the valuation of fixed assets[191].

[17.057] In addition, the requirements set out[192] in relation to the establishment of a revaluation reserve in respect of a profit or loss arising on the revaluation of fixed assets on application of the alternative accounting rules will apply equally in respect of a profit or loss arising on the corresponding revaluation of current assets.

3. Fair value accounting

[17.058] The provisions above[193] whereby certain assets may be accounted for at fair value will apply equally where those assets are deemed to be current assets.

---

185 Paragraph 15(3) of the Schedule to the C(A)A 1986.

186 See para **[17.040]**.

187 Paragraph 13 of the Schedule to the C(A)A 1986.

188 Paragraph 12 of the Schedule to the C(A)A 1986.

189 Paragraph 16 of the Schedule to the C(A)A 1986.

190 Paragraph 19 of the Schedule to the C(A)A 1986.

191 See para **[17.043]**.

192 See para **[17.045]**.

193 See paras **[17.046]** to **[17.049]**.

The profit and loss account in Companies Act individual accounts

[17.059] As noted above in relation to the requirement to prepare a balance sheet[194], the directors of every company must, on a date not later than 18 months after the incorporation of the company and subsequently once at least in every year, prepare accounts[195]. Where the company prepares Companies Act individual accounts[196], these are required to include a profit and loss account[197].

[17.060] The general rules in respect of the format of the profit and loss account of a limited company preparing Companies Act individual accounts are similar to the rules in respect of the balance sheet of such a company[198].

[17.061] Every profit and loss account of such a company must show the items listed in any one of the four profit and loss accounts formats set out in Part I of the Schedule to the C(A)A 1986[199]. The directors may choose which format to adopt, subject to the overriding requirement that the accounts must give a 'true and fair' view of the profit or loss of the company for the financial year[200]. Whichever format is used, however, the directors must adopt the same format in subsequent years, unless, in their opinion, there are special reasons for a change[201]. Where such a change is made, the reasons for the change and full particulars of the change must be given in a note to the accounts in which the new format is adopted[202].

[17.062] Section 4 of the C(A)A 1986 also sets out the basic rules in respect of the use of the formats in preparing the profit and loss account. Thus, any item required in accordance with the formats may be shown in greater detail than required by the format adopted[203]. Secondly, any items to which an Arabic number (1, 2, 3, etc) is assigned in any of the formats may be combined where the individual amounts of such items are not material to assessing the profit or loss of the company, or where such combination facilitates the assessment (provided that in the latter case, disclosure of the individual amounts is set out in a note to the accounts)[204]. Thirdly, in respect of every item in the profit or loss account, the corresponding amount for the previous financial year must be shown, and if it is not comparable, an adjustment must be made[205]. Fourthly, if there is no amount to be shown for an item in both the current financial year and the immediately preceding financial year, that item need not be included in the profit or loss account[206]. Fifthly, amounts in respect of items representing income may not be set off

---

194 See para **[17.030]** *ante*.
195 Section 148(1) of the CA 1963.
196 See para **[17.125]** *ante*.
197 Section 149(1) of the CA 1963.
198 See para **[17.031]** *et seq, ante*.
199 Section 4(1) of the C(A)A 1986.
200 Section 3(1)(b) of the C(A)A 1986.
201 Section 4(3) of the C(A)A 1986.
202 Section 4(4) of the C(A)A 1986.
203 Section 4(5) of the C(A)A 1986.
204 Section 4(6) of the C(A)A 1986.
205 Section 4(8) of the C(A)A 1986.
206 Section 4(9) and (10) of the C(A)A 1986.

against items representing expenditure (or vice versa)[207]. The balance sheet may include an item representing or covering the amount of any income or expenditure not covered by any of the items listed in the formats[208]. Finally, the directors shall adapt the arrangement, headings and sub-headings required in respect of items to which an Arabic number is assigned in the format, in any case where the special nature of the company's business requires such adaptation[209].

[17.063] As noted above[210], there are four profit and loss account formats. There are no material differences between the items to be listed in Formats 1 or 3 (but only in the order in which they are laid out) and similarly for Formats 2 or 4.

[17.064] Formats 1 and 3 require companies to show the following items in the annual profit and loss account (these being set out in the order in which they are shown in Format 3); headings in italics do not appear in Formats 2 or 4:

Format 3	***Format 1***
A. Charges	
1. Cost of Sales	(2)
2. Distribution costs	(4)
3. Administration expenses	(5)
4. Amounts written off financial assets and investments held as current assets	(11)
5. Interest payable and similar charges	(12)
6. Tax on profit or loss on ordinary activities	(13)
7. Profit or loss on ordinary activities after taxation	
Minority Interest	
8. Extraordinary charges	(16)
9. Tax on extraordinary profit or loss	(18)
Minority Interest	
10. Other taxes not shown under the above items	(19)
11. Profit or loss for the financial year	
B. Income	
1. Turnover	(1)
2. Other operating income	(6)
3. Income for shares in group undertakings	(7)
4. Income from participating interests	(8)
5. Income from other financial assets	(9)
6. Other income receivable and similar income	(10)
7. Profit or loss on ordinary activities after taxation	

207 Section 4(11) of the C(A)A 1986.

208 Section 4(12) of the C(A)A 1986.

209 Section 4(13) of the C(A)A 1986.

210 See para **[17.061]** *ante*.

Format 3	***Format 1***
Minority Interest	
8. Extraordinary income	(15)
Minority Interest	
9. Profit or loss for the financial year	

[17.065] The numbers in the right-hand column above show the order in which the items are laid out in Format 1, showing the overlap between this format and Format 3. As can be seen from the above table, all substantive items are common to the two formats. The items from Format 3 without such an entry in the right-hand column are sub-total figures, such figures being set out at different points in Format 1, as follows:

Format 1

1. Turnover
2. Cost of Sales
3. Gross Profit or Loss
4. Distribution costs
5. Administration expenses
6. Other operating income
7. Income for shares in group undertakings
8. Income from participating interests
9. Income from other financial assets
10. Other income receivable and similar income
11. Amounts written off financial assets and investments held as current assets
12. Interest payable and similar charges
13. Tax on profit or loss on ordinary activities
14. Profit or loss on ordinary activities after taxation

Minority Interest

15. Extraordinary income
16. Extraordinary charges
17. Extraordinary profit or loss
18. Tax on extraordinary profit or loss

Minority Interest

19. Other taxes not shown under the above items
20. Profit or loss for the financial year

[17.066] Formats 2 and 4 require companies to show the following items in the annual profit and loss account (these being set out in the order in which they are shown in Format 4); headings in italics do not appear in Formats 1 or 3:

Format 4	***Format 2***
A. Charges	
1. Reduction in stocks of finished goods and in work in progress	(2*)
2. (a) Raw materials and consumables	(5)(a)
(b) Other external charges	(5)(b)
3. Staff costs:	(6)
(a) Wages and salaries	(6)(a)
(b) Social welfare costs	(6)(b)
(c) Other pension costs	(6)(c)
4. (a) Depreciation and other amounts written off tangible and intangible fixed assets	(7)(a)
(b) Exceptional amounts written off current assets	(7)(b)
5. Other operating charges	(8)
6. Amounts written off financial assets and investments held as current assets	(13)
7. Interest payable and similar charges	(14)
8. Tax on profit or loss on ordinary activities	(15)
9. Profit or loss on ordinary activities after taxation	
Minority Interest	
10. Extraordinary charges	(18)
11. Tax on extraordinary profit or loss	(20)
Minority Interest	
12. Other taxes not shown under the above items	(21)
13. Profit or loss for the financial year	
B. Income	
1. Turnover	(1)
2. Increase in stocks of finished goods and in work in progress	(2*)
3. Own work capitalised	(3)
4. Other operating income	(4)
5. Income for shares in group undertakings	(9)
6. Income from participating interests	(10)
7. Income from other financial assets	(11)
8. Other income receivable and similar income	(12)
9. Profit or loss on ordinary activities after taxation	
Minority Interest	

Format 4	***Format 2***
10. Extraordinary income	(17)
Minority Interest	
11. Profit or loss for the financial year	

[17.067] As in relation to Formats 1 and 3[211], the numbers in the right-hand column above show the order in which the items are laid out in Format 2, showing the overlap between the two formats. As can be seen from the above table, all substantive items are common to the two formats. The items from Format 4 without such an entry in the right-hand column are sub-total figures, as such figures are set out at different points as follows, in Format 2. The two items from Format 4 marked '2*' above are combined as item 2 in Format 2, as follows:

Format 2

1. Turnover
2. Variation in stocks of finished goods and in work in progress
3. Own work capitalised
4. Other operating income
5. (a) Raw materials and consumables

   (b) Other external charges
6. Staff costs:

   (a) Wages and salaries

   (b) Social welfare costs

   (c) Other pension costs
7. (a) Depreciation and other amounts written off tangible and intangible fixed assets

   (b) Exceptional amounts written off current assets
8. Other operating charges
9. Income for shares in group undertakings
10. Income from participating interests
11. Income from other financial assets
12. Other income receivable and similar income
13. Amounts written off financial assets and investments held as current assets
14. Interest payable and similar charges
15. Tax on profit or loss on ordinary activities
16. Profit or loss on ordinary activities after taxation

Minority Interest

17. Extraordinary income
18. Extraordinary charges

[211] See para **[17.065]** *ante*.

Format 2

19. Extraordinary profit or loss
20. Tax on extraordinary profit or loss

Minority Interest

21. Other taxes not shown under the above items
22. Profit or loss for the financial year

[17.068] 'Turnover' is defined as the amounts derived from the provision of goods and services falling within the company's ordinary activities, after deduction of trade discounts, value added tax, and any other taxes[212]. Cost of sales, distribution costs and administrative expenses must be stated after taking into account any necessary provisions for depreciation or diminution in the value of assets[213]. Income and interest from group undertakings must be shown separately from income and interest derived from other sources[214], and the amount of interest and charges payable to group undertakings must be shown separately from other interests and charges payable[215].

Every profit and loss account of a company shall show the amount of the profit or loss of the company on ordinary activities before taxation[216].

Notes to Companies Act individual accounts

[17.069] The matters to be set out in notes to Companies Act individual accounts are split between those relating to the balance sheet, the profit and loss account, and other matters, this seeming to be a logical approach. However there is no statutory obligation on a company to set out the notes in any particular order.

(a) Notes relating to the balance sheet

[17.070] In addition to the disclosure requirements set out above[217] in respect of statutory valuation rules, further details relating to the items shown in the balance sheet are required to be stated by way of notes to the accounts[218]. These matters relate to:

(i) Accounting policies;
(ii) Group undertakings;
(iii) Disaggregation of fixed assets;
(iv) Valuation according to historic cost rules;
(v) Valuation according to alternative valuation rules;
(vi) Fair valuation of assets and liabilities;
(vii) Development costs;
(viii) Goodwill;

212 Paragraph 75 of the Schedule to the C(A)A 1986.
213 Note 11 of the Notes on the Profit and Loss Account Formats, Schedule to the C(A)A 1986.
214 Note 12 of the Notes on the Profit and Loss Account Formats, Schedule to the C(A)A 1986.
215 Note 13 of the Notes on the Profit and Loss Account Formats, Schedule to the C(A)A 1986.
216 Section 4(14) of the C(A)A 1986.
217 See para **[17.037]** *et seq*, *ante*.
218 Paragraph 1 of the Schedule to the C(A)A 1986.

- (ix) Financial assets held as investments;
- (x) Loans given as financial assistance;
- (xi) Debt owed by company exceeding consideration received;
- (xii) Details of indebtedness;
- (xiii) Provision for taxation;
- (xiv) Taxation treatment of revaluation reserve;
- (xv) Share capital and debentures;
- (xvi) Shares and debentures held by subsidiary undertakings;
- (xvii) Reserves and provisions;
- (xviii) Restrictions on distributable profits;
- (xix) Dividends;
- (xx) Guarantees and other financial commitments.

(i) Accounting policies

[17.071] The accounting policies adopted by the company in determining the amounts to be included in respect of items shown in the balance sheet, including the policies with respect to the depreciation and diminution in value of assets, must be stated in the notes to the accounts[219].

(ii) Group undertakings

[17.072] If the company is a parent undertaking[220] within the meaning of the EC(C:GA)R 1992, the aggregate amounts of any items relating to:

- amounts attributable to dealings with or interests in any parent undertaking or fellow or subsidiary undertaking; or
- amounts attributable to dealings with or interests in any subsidiary undertaking of the company;

must be stated separately in the notes to the accounts if not shown separately in the balance sheet, in respect of the company's Companies Act individual accounts[221].

(iii) Disaggregation of fixed assets

[17.073] It was noted above[222] that items appearing with an Arabic number in the scheduled formats may be combined in the balance sheet where the individual amounts are not material to the assessment of the company's state of affairs, or where such combination facilitates that assessment. Where items shown under 'Fixed Assets' in the formats are combined in this way, the notes must state, in respect of each item[223]:

- The 'appropriate amount'[224] as at the beginning of the financial year and as at the balance sheet date, respectively;

---

[219] Paragraph 24(3) of the Schedule to the C(A)A 1986.

[220] See para **[17.134]** *post*.

[221] Paragraph 45 of the Schedule to the C(A)A 1986.

[222] See para **[17.033]** *ante*.

[223] Paragraph 29 of the Schedule to the C(A)A 1986.

[224] Being the purchase price or production cost, or the value as determined in accordance with the alternative accounting rules at para **[17.042]** *ante*, leaving out of account any provisions for depreciation or diminution in value.

- The effect on its value of any application of the alternative accounting rules[225], of acquisitions, disposals or transfers of assets during the year;
- The cumulative amount of provisions for depreciation or diminution in value of assets as at the beginning of the financial year and as at the balance sheet date, respectively;
- The amount of any provisions for depreciation or diminution in value made in the financial year;
- The amounts of any adjustments made in respect of depreciation or diminution in value during the financial year in consequence of the disposal of any assets;
- The amounts of any other adjustments made in respect of depreciation or diminution in value during the financial year.

(iv) Valuation according to historic cost rules

[17.074] Where interest on capital borrowed to finance the production of an asset is included in the calculation of production costs, a note to the accounts must disclose that fact[226]. In addition, where the purchase price or production cost of stocks or fungible assets is determined according to the FIFO or weighted average methods, or any similar methods, and the amount shown in respect of any item so valued differs materially from its replacement cost, the difference between the two values must be disclosed in a note to the accounts[227].

[17.075] Particulars must be given in the notes of any case where the purchase price or production cost of any asset is determined for the first time[228].

(v) Valuation according to alternative valuation rules

[17.076] Where the alternative valuation rules[229] are employed in the valuation of assets, the comparable amounts determined according to the historical cost accounting rules – ie, the amount which would be required to be shown in respect of that item, and the aggregate amount of cumulative provisions for depreciation or diminution in value which would be permitted or required in determining those amounts[230] – or the differences between those amounts and the corresponding amounts actually shown in the balance sheet in respect of that item must be shown separately in the balance sheet or in a note to the accounts[231].

[17.077] Where any fixed assets of the company, other than listed investments, are valued according to the alternative valuation rules, the notes to the accounts must also disclose the years (so far as they are known to the directors) in which the assets were severally valued and the several values. In the case of assets valued during the financial year, the names or particulars of qualification of any person who conducted any valuation, and the bases of valuation used, must also be stated[232].

---

225 See para **[17.042]** *ante*.
226 Paragraph 14(3) of the Schedule to the C(A)A 1986.
227 Paragraph 15(3) of the Schedule to the C(A)A 1986.
228 Paragraph 37(1) of the Schedule to the C(A)A 1986.
229 See para **[17.042]** *ante*.
230 Paragraph 21(4) of the Schedule to the C(A)A 1986.
231 Paragraph 21(3) of the Schedule to the C(A)A 1986.

(vi) Fair valuation of assets and liabilities

[17.078] Where financial instruments have been included at fair value[233], disclosures must be made[234] regarding:

(a) the significant assumptions and techniques underlying any valuation models and techniques the use of which was required in determining fair value;

(b) for each category of financial instruments, the fair value of the instruments in that category, and the amounts included in the profit and loss account, and credited to or debited from the fair value reserve, in respect of instruments in that category;

(c) for each class of derivative financial instrument, the extent and nature of the instruments including terms and conditions that may affect future cash flows;

(d) a table showing movements in the fair value reserve during the financial year.

[17.079] Where derivative financial instruments have not been included at fair value, there shall be stated:

(a) the fair value of the instruments in that class, if it can be determined; and

(b) the extent and nature of the instruments[235].

[17.080] Where a company is showing financial fixed assets, which could be stated at fair value, at a value in excess of this in its balance sheet, and has not made any provision for diminution in value of those assets, there shall be stated:

(a) the amount at which the individual assets, or appropriate groupings of those assets, is stated in the company's accounts;

(b) the fair value of those assets or groupings; and

(c) the reasons for not making provision for diminution in value[236].

[17.081] Where investment property or living animals and plants have been included at fair value, the balance sheet items and the bases of valuation adopted shall be disclosed in a note to the accounts. In the case of investment property, there shall be shown, either on the face of the balance sheet or in a note to the accounts, the amounts which would require to be shown for the asset, and for cumulative provisions for depreciation or diminution in value, under the historical cost accounting rules, and the differences between those amounts and the amounts actually shown in the balance sheet[237].

(vii) Development costs

[17.082] If development costs are capitalised in the balance sheet, a note to the accounts must disclose the period over which the amount so capitalised is being or is to be written off, and the reasons for capitalising the costs in question[238].

---

232 Paragraph 30 of the Schedule to the C(A)A 1986.

233 See para **[17.046]** *ante*.

234 Paragraph 31A of the Schedule to the C(A)A 1986.

235 Paragraph 31B of the Schedule to the C(A)A 1986.

236 Paragraph 31C of the Schedule to the C(A)A 1986.

237 Paragraph 31D of the Schedule to the C(A)A 1986.

238 Paragraph 8(2) of the Schedule to the C(A)A 1986.

(viii) Goodwill

[17.083] Where goodwill is included as an asset in the company's balance sheet, the period chosen for writing off the consideration for the goodwill, and the reason for choosing that period, must be disclosed in a note to the accounts[239].

(ix) Financial assets held as investments

[17.084] Disclosure must be made of the amount ascribable to listed investments, and a distinction made between investments listed on a recognised stock exchange and other listed investments. The notes must also set out the aggregate market value of the listed investments where it differs from this amount, and both the market and stock exchange value of any investments of which the market value is taken as being higher than the stock exchange value[240].

(x) Loans given as financial assistance

[17.085] Where a company has given a loan or loans for the purpose of or in connection with a purchase of or subscription for any shares in the company or, where the company is a subsidiary company, its holding company[241], it must disclose, in the notes to its financial statements, the aggregate amount of any outstanding loans made for those purposes[242]. The aggregate amount of any outstanding loans of this nature must be disclosed by way of note to the accounts, and a distinction made between loans permitted by the validation procedure, loans to employees, and loans to employees of a subsidiary[243]. It should be noted that this disclosure obligation only extends to loans, and does not require the disclosure of any other form of financial assistance which might be given for those purposes[244].

(xi) Debt owed by company exceeding consideration received

[17.086] Where any amount repayable on any debt owed by the company is greater than the value of the consideration received in the transaction giving rise to the debt, the amount of the difference may be treated as an asset but is required to be written off by reasonable amounts each year (to be completely written off before repayment of the debt) and is not shown as a separate item in the balance sheet, must be disclosed in a note to the accounts[245].

(xii) Details of indebtedness

[17.087] In respect of every item shown under 'creditors' in the balance sheet, the notes must state:

---

239 Paragraph 9 of the Schedule to the C(A)A 1986.

240 Paragraph 31 of the Schedule to the C(A)A 1986.

241 Pursuant to s 60 of the CA 1963; See Ch 10, *The Maintenance of Capital*, at para **[10.046]** *et seq*.

242 Paragraph 37(2) of the Schedule to the C(A)A 1986.

243 Paragraph 37(2) of the Schedule to the C(A)A 1986; the references to specific paragraphs of s 60 of the CA 1963 have been rendered out-of-date by subsequent amendments to s 60 of the CA 1963.

244 That is, despite the fact that such financial assistance would fall within the scope of s 60 of the CA 1963.

245 Paragraph 12 of the Schedule to the C(A)A 1986.

- the aggregate amount of any debts included under that item which are payable or repayable otherwise than by instalments and fall due for payment or repayment after the end of the period of five years beginning with the day next following the end of the financial year;
- the aggregate amount of any debts so included which are payable or repayable by instalments any of which fall due for payment after the end of that period, and the aggregate amount of instalments falling due after the end of that period;
- the aggregate amount of any debts included under that item in respect of which any security has been given;
- an indication of the nature of the securities so given[246].

[17.088] If any fixed cumulative dividends are in arrears, the amount of the arrears and the period for which each class of dividends is in arrears must be stated in the notes[247].

[17.089] As noted above[248], where Format 2 of the Balance Sheet Formats is adopted, the notes to the accounts must show separately, for each item falling under the heading 'Creditors', amounts falling due within one year and those falling due after one year[249].

(xiii) Provision for taxation

[17.090] The amount of any provision for taxation, other than deferred taxation, must be stated in a note to the accounts[250].

(xiv) Taxation treatment of revaluation reserve

[17.091] Where there is a revaluation reserve in the balance sheet, the taxation treatment of that reserve must be disclosed in a note to the accounts[251].

(xv) Share capital and debentures

[17.092] A company is required to disclose the following information in respect of its share capital:

(a) the authorised share capital;
(b) where shares of more than one class are allotted, the number and aggregate nominal value of shares of each class[252]; and
(c) in respect of any allotment during the financial year, the reason for that allotment and, in respect of each class of shares, the number and nominal value of shares issued and the consideration received for their allotment[253].

If any part of the allotted share capital consists of redeemable shares, the company must also disclose:

---

246 Paragraph 34 of the Schedule to the C(A)A 1986.
247 Paragraph 35 of the Schedule to the C(A)A 1986.
248 See para **[17.035]** *ante*.
249 Note 10 on the Balance Sheet Format, Part I of the Schedule to the C(A)A 1986.
250 Paragraph 33 of the Schedule to the C(A)A 1986.
251 Paragraph 22(5) of the Schedule to the C(A)A 1986.
252 Paragraph 26(1) of the Schedule to the C(A)A 1986.
253 Paragraph 27 of the Schedule to the C(A)A 1986.

(a) the earliest and latest dates on which the company has the power to redeem the shares;
(b) whether or not redemption is at the option of the company; and
(c) the premium (if any) payable on redemption[254].

In respect of debentures, a company must give the following information:

(a) in respect of any issue during the financial year, the reason for that issue and, in respect of each class of debentures, the amount issued and the consideration received for the issue;
(b) particulars of any redeemed debentures which the company has the power to re-issue; and
(c) the nominal amount of any debentures held by a nominee or trustee for the company, and the amount at which they are stated in the company's books of account[255].

(xvi) Shares and debentures held by subsidiary undertakings

[17.093] Where the company is a parent undertaking[256], and any shares in or debentures of it are held by a subsidiary undertaking or its nominee, the parent undertaking must disclose the number, description and amount of such shares and debentures in the notes to its accounts[257].

The disclosure obligation does not arise where the subsidiary undertaking is concerned only as personal representative or trustee, provided that where it holds the shares as trustee, neither the parent undertaking nor any subsidiary undertaking must be beneficially interested in those shares, save as security for the purposes of a transaction in its ordinary course of business[258].

(xvii) Reserves and provisions

[17.094] If movements in reserves and provisions do not appear on the balance sheet, then disclosure must be made in the notes of the amounts of reserves or provisions at the beginning of the financial year and at the balance sheet date, of any amounts transferred to or from the reserves or provisions during the financial year, and of the source and application of any amounts so transferred. In addition, particulars of each provision included in the item 'other provisions' in the balance sheet must be given in the notes where the amount of that provision is material[259].

(xviii) Restrictions on distributable profits

[17.095] Where a subsidiary acquires and holds shares in its holding company pursuant to s 224 of the CA 1990[260], there is a requirement that for so long as the subsidiary holds those shares, its profits available for distribution shall be restricted by a sum equal to the

---

254 Paragraph 26(2) of the Schedule to the C(A)A 1986.
255 Paragraph 28 of the Schedule to the C(A)A 1986.
256 Within the meaning of the EC(C:GA)R 1992; See para **[17.154]** *post*.
257 Paragraph 46(1) of the Schedule to the C(A)A 1986.
258 Paragraph 46(2) of the Schedule to the C(A)A 1986.
259 Paragraph 32 of the Schedule to the C(A)A 1986.
260 See Ch 10, *The Maintenance of Capital,* at para **[10.036]** *et seq*.

cost of the shares acquired[261]. Particulars of any such restriction must be stated in the notes to the accounts of the subsidiary[262].

(xix) Dividends

[17.096] The aggregate amount which is recommended for distribution by way of dividend must be stated in the notes[263].

(xx) Guarantees and other financial commitments

[17.097] Information must be disclosed in the notes to the accounts in respect of a range of financial commitments. First, particulars must be given of any charge on the assets of the company to secure the liabilities of any person, including, where practicable, the amount secured[264]. This is clearly in addition to the more detailed requirements in respect of the entry into a guarantee or provision of security in connection with a loan, quasi-loan or credit transaction made in favour of a director or person connected with such a director[265].

In addition, the following further information must be stated in the notes:

- The amount or estimated amount of any contingent liability not provided for;
- The legal nature of any such contingent liability not provided for;
- Whether any security has been provided in respect of such contingent liabilities and, if so, what[266];
- The aggregate or estimated amount of contracts for capital expenditure not provided for;
- The aggregate or estimated amount of capital expenditure authorised by the directors which has not been contracted for[267].

Information must also be disclosed in respect of pensions, as follows:

(a) particulars of any pension commitments, showing separately those provided for in the company's balance sheet and those not provided for (and also setting out separately any commitment relating to pensions payable to past directors of the company)[268];

(b) the nature of every pension scheme operated by or on behalf of the company, including whether each is a defined benefit or defined contribution scheme;

(c) whether each scheme is externally funded or internally financed; and

(d) the date of the most recent actuarial valuation (if any) of any pension costs and liabilities, and whether such valuation is available for public inspection[269].

Any of the above commitments which are undertaken on behalf of or for the benefit of:

---

261 Section 224(2)(b)(i) of the CA 1990.

262 Paragraph 32A of the Schedule to the C(A)A 1986.

263 Paragraph 37(3) of the Schedule to the C(A)A 1986.

264 Paragraph 36(1) of the Schedule to the C(A)A 1986.

265 See para **[17.113]** *et seq, post*.

266 Paragraph 36(2) of the Schedule to the C(A)A 1986.

267 Paragraph 36(3) of the Schedule to the C(A)A 1986.

268 Paragraph 36(4) of the Schedule to the C(A)A 1986.

269 Paragraph 36(5) of the Schedule to the C(A)A 1986.

(a) any parent undertaking or fellow subsidiary undertaking, or

(b) any subsidiary undertaking of the company,

must be shown separately from the other commitments, and commitments within (a) shall be shown separately from those within (b)[270]. Finally, particulars must be given of any other financial commitments which have not been provided for, and are relevant to assessing the company's state of affairs[271].

(b) Notes relating to the profit and loss account

[17.098] In addition to the items required to be shown on the face of the profit and loss account, further information relating to items covered in the profit and loss account is required to be shown by way of notes to the accounts[272]. These matters include the following:

(i) Accounting policies;
(ii) Particulars of turnover;
(iii) Particulars of staff;
(iv) Depreciation and diminution in value of fixed assets;
(v) Reconciliation of depreciation figures;
(vi) Improvements in the value of written down fixed assets;
(vii) Other items of income and expenditure (including directors' emoluments);
(viii) Interest payable and similar charges;
(ix) Particulars of tax;
(x) Extraordinary income or charges;
(xi) Foreign currencies;
(xii) Movements in profit and loss account.

(i) Accounting policies

[17.099] The accounting policies adopted by the company in determining the profit or loss of the company, including the policies with respect to the depreciation and diminution in value of assets, must be stated in the notes to the accounts[273].

(ii) Particulars of turnover

[17.100] Where in the course of a financial year a company, in the opinion of the directors, has carried on substantially different classes of business, or has supplied substantially different geographical markets, then the amount of turnover attributable to each class of business and/or each geographical market (as applicable) shall be stated in a note to the accounts.

In analysing the source of turnover (whether in terms of class or geographical market), the directors must have regard to the manner in which the company's activities are organised. If the directors are of the opinion that disclosure would be seriously prejudicial to the interests of the company then the disclosure need not be made, but the fact that the disclosure has not been made must be noted[274].

---

270 Paragraph 45A of the Schedule to the C(A)A 1986.
271 Paragraph 36(6) of the Schedule to the C(A)A 1986.
272 Paragraph 1 of the Schedule to the C(A)A 1986.
273 Paragraph 24 of the Schedule to the C(A)A 1986.
274 Paragraph 41 of the Schedule to the C(A)A 1986.

(iii) Particulars of staff

[17.101] The following information shall be given with respect to employees:

- the average number of persons[275] employed during the financial year;
- the average number of persons employed within each category of persons employed by the company.

The directors may choose whatever basis they wish (if any) for categorising the employees, having regard to the manner in which the company's activities are organised.

In addition, insofar as these amounts or any of them are not already stated in the profit and loss account, the aggregate amounts must be stated in the notes in respect of:

- wages and salaries;
- social welfare costs;
- pension costs[276].

'Wages and salaries' shall comprise payments made or costs incurred in respect of all persons employed by the company at any stage during the financial year. 'Social welfare costs' means any contribution to any State social welfare, social security or pension scheme or any fund or arrangement connected with such a scheme. 'Pension costs' include any other contributions established for the purpose of providing pensions for persons employed by the company, and any sums set aside or otherwise paid in respect of such schemes[277].

Given that Formats 1 and 3 do not cover these items in the profit and loss account, companies adopting Formats 1 or 3 without amendment will have to disclose these matters in the notes to the accounts.

(iv) Depreciation and diminution in value of fixed assets

[17.102] Where the profit and loss account is prepared by reference to Format 1 or 3, the notes must disclose the amounts of any provisions for depreciation or diminution in the value of tangible and intangible fixed assets[278]. Indeed, regardless of which of the four formats is adopted, any provisions for diminution in value of fixed assets and financial assets which are not shown separately in the profit and loss account shall be disclosed (either separately or in aggregate) in a note to the accounts[279].

(v) Reconciliation of depreciation figures

[17.103] If the alternative valuation rules are used in determining the value of an asset[280], but the amount of the provision for depreciation in the profit and loss account is the historical cost amount, the difference between the amount written off the alternative

275 As set out in para 42(4) of the Schedule to the C(A)A 1986, being the number, in respect of each week, of persons employed by the company under contracts of service for all or part of that week, added together and divided by the number of weeks in the financial year.

276 Paragraph 42 of the Schedule to the C(A)A 1986.

277 Paragraph 74 of the Schedule to the C(A)A 1986.

278 Note 14 of the Notes on the Profit and Loss Account Formats, Schedule to the C(A)A 1986.

279 Paragraph 7 of the Schedule to the C(A)A 1986.

280 See para **[17.042]** *ante*.

value and the amount written off the historical cost value must, if it is not shown in the profit and loss account, be shown in a note to the accounts[281].

(vi) Improvements in the value of written down fixed assets

[17.104] Where a provision for diminution in value had been made in respect of any fixed asset or financial asset, and the reasons for which this provision was made have ceased to apply to any extent, that provision shall be written back to the extent that it is no longer necessary; and if any amounts written back in this manner are not shown in the profit and loss account, they must be disclosed (either separately or in aggregate) in a note to the accounts[282].

(vii) Other items of income and expenditure (including directors' emoluments)

[17.105] Each of the following amounts shall be stated:

- The amounts respectively provided for the purchase of the company's share capital, for redemption of share capital and for redemption of loans[283];
- The amount of income from listed[284] and unlisted investments[285];
- Any amounts expended on research and development must likewise be stated in the notes; but where the directors are of the opinion that this would be prejudicial to the interests of the company, they need not make such a statement, but can simply state that such disclosure has not been made[286];
- The aggregate amounts of the emoluments of, and compensation in respect of loss of office to, directors, and compensation in respect of loss of office to past directors[287].

Both the CA 1963 and the CA 1990 contain further requirements as to disclosure by note of particulars relating to directors' emoluments and transactions and arrangements with directors. These requirements are considered below[288].

(viii) Interest payable and similar charges

[17.106] The amount of interest or any similar charges (excluding interest or charges on loans to the company from group undertakings) must be stated in the notes to the accounts in respect of each of the following:

- bank loans and overdrafts, and loans made to the company (other than bank loans and overdrafts) which –

[281] Paragraph 20(3) of the Schedule to the C(A)A 1986.

[282] Paragraph 7 of the Schedule to the C(A)A 1986.

[283] Paragraph 39(3) of the Schedule to the C(A)A 1986.

[284] As set out in para 66 of the Schedule to the C(A)A 1986, a 'listed investment' means an investment as respects which there has been granted a listing on a recognised Stock Exchange within the State or on any Stock Exchange of repute outside the State.

[285] Paragraph 39(4) of the Schedule to the C(A)A 1986.

[286] Paragraph 43 of the Schedule to the C(A)A 1986.

[287] Paragraph 39(6) of the Schedule to the C(A)A 1986.

[288] See para **[17.112]** *et seq post*.

- are repayable otherwise than by instalments and fall due[289] for repayment before the end of the period of five years following the end of the financial year of the company, or
- are repayable by instalments the last of which falls due for payment before the end of that period, and

– loans of any other kind made to the company[290].

(ix) Particulars of tax

[17.107] The following must be stated in the notes to the accounts:

– The basis on which the charge for corporation tax, income tax and other tax on profits (whether payable in or outside the State) is computed;

– Particulars of any special circumstances which affect liability in respect of taxation on profits, income or capital gains for the financial year concerned or for succeeding financial years;

– The amount of the charge for corporation tax, income tax and other taxation on profits or capital gains so far as charged to revenue, including taxation payable outside the State on profits (distinguishing where practicable between corporation tax and other taxation), distinguishing in each case between tax on profit or loss on ordinary activities, and tax on extraordinary profit or loss[291].

(x) Extraordinary income or charges

[17.108] Particulars of extraordinary income or charges arising in the financial year must be stated in the notes to the accounts. Furthermore, the effect of any transactions that (although arising on ordinary activities) are exceptional by virtue of size or incidence, must be stated in the notes[292].

(xi) Foreign currencies

[17.109] Where sums originally denominated in foreign currencies have been translated into euro, that fact and the conversion basis must be stated in the notes[293].

(xii) Movements in profit and loss account

[17.110] The notes to the profit and loss account of a company shall show:

(a) dividends paid (other than dividends for which a liability existed at the immediately preceding balance sheet date) or which the company is liable to pay;

(b) any transfers between the profit and loss account and other reserves;

(c) any increase or reduction in the balance on the profit and loss account since the immediately preceding financial year;

(d) the profit or loss brought forward at the beginning of the financial year;

---

289 As set out in para 67 of the Schedule to the C(A)A 1986, a loan (or an instalment of a loan) is to be treated as falling due for payment on the earliest date on which the lender could require (re)payment, if he exercised all options and rights available to him.

290 Paragraph 39 of the Schedule to the C(A)A 1986.

291 Paragraph 40 of the Schedule to the C(A)A 1986.

292 Paragraph 43 of the Schedule to the C(A)A 1986.

293 Paragraph 44(1) of the Schedule to the C(A)A 1986.

(e) the profit or loss carried forward at the end of the financial year[294].

(c) Other notes forming part of Companies Act individual accounts

[17.111] In addition to the above notes relating to specific items in the balance sheet and profit and loss account, disclosures are required to be made in respect of the following items:

(i) Directors' remuneration;

(ii) Transactions, arrangements and agreements with directors and connected persons;

(iii) Interests of director or secretary in the company's shares and debentures;

(iv) Remuneration of auditors;

(v) Related party transactions;

(vi) Off balance sheet items;

(vii) Additional disclosure requirements for certain group undertakings;

(viii) Subsidiary undertakings.

(i) Directors' remuneration

[17.112] The following information must be included regarding directors' remuneration:

(a) the aggregate amount of directors' emoluments;

(b) the aggregate amount of directors' or past-directors' pensions[295];

(c) the aggregate amount of any compensation to directors in respect of loss of office;

(d) the aggregate amount of any compensation to past-directors in respect of loss of office[296].

Section 191 of the CA 1963 defines the terms 'emoluments', 'pension' and 'compensation' broadly, and requires the inclusion of emoluments, pensions or compensations in respect of any subsidiary of the company. In addition, the company must distinguish, first, between emoluments, pensions or compensation in respect of the office of director, and other emoluments, pensions or compensation[297]; and second, between sums paid by or receivable from each of the company, the company's subsidiaries, and other persons[298]. Where the above requirements are not complied with, a specific obligation is imposed on the auditors, so far as they are reasonably able to do so, to include a statement in their report giving particulars of the non-compliance.

---

[294] Section 4(15) of the C(A)A 1986.

[295] The disclosures at (a) and (b) are as required by s 191 of the CA 1963.

[296] Regulation 39(6) of the Schedule to the C(A)A 1986 appears to require that the two compensation figures be shown separately.

[297] Paragraphs (2)(b), (3)(b) and (4)(b) of s 191 of the CA 1963. As to compensation for loss of office, See Ch 13, *Corporate Governance: Management by the Directors*, at para **[13.086]** *et seq*.

[298] Section 191(5) of the CA 1963.

(ii) Transactions, arrangements and agreements with directors and connected persons

[17.113] Section 41 of the CA 1990 requires that information be disclosed of certain substantial dealings with directors or connected persons[299], namely:

(a) Any transactions or arrangements 'of a kind described in s 31 of the CA 1990[300]' entered into by the company or a subsidiary of that company for a person who during the relevant period was a director, director of its holding company or a person connected to that director;

(b) Any agreements to enter into such a transaction or arrangement for such a director or connected person;

(c) Any other transactions or arrangements with the company or with a subsidiary of the company in which a person who during the relevant period was a director of the company or its holding company had, directly or indirectly a material interest.

The references to transactions or arrangements of a kind described in s 31of the CA 1990 comprise loans, quasi-loans, credit transactions, and guarantees and security in connection with such loans, quasi-loans and credit transactions[301].

It is rather less clear as to what should be included in para (c) above. If 'transaction' and 'arrangement' were given their ordinary meaning in English, they would cover practically any dealing between a company and a director. It is not certain, however, that they should be given their ordinary meaning given that both words are used elsewhere in Part III of the CA 1990 in a very particular way. That is, although s 47(1) of the CA 1990 provides that any reference in s 194 of the CA 1963 to a 'contract' shall be construed as including a reference to any transaction or arrangement, the converse is not provided, ie, it is not said that every reference to a 'transaction or arrangement' as used in s 41 of the CA 1990 shall be construed as including a reference to a contract. Therefore there is some support for saying that not every 'contract' will be a transaction or arrangement.

One certainty in respect of the meaning of s 41(1)(c) and (2)(c) is that it will include any transactions or arrangements directly between the company and a director or connected person, which have not already been caught under paras (a) or (b) of s 41(1) or s 41(2)[302].

The disclosure requirements apply whether or not:

(a) The transaction or arrangement was prohibited by s 31;

(b) The person for whom it was made was a director of the company or a connected person at the time it was made; or

(c) The company was a subsidiary at the time it was made[303].

---

[299] In relation to the definition of 'connected person', See Ch 16, *Statutory Regulation of Directors' Transactions,* at para **[16.003]** *et seq.*

[300] In relation to the transactions and arrangements which fall within the scope of this section, See Ch 16, *Statutory Regulation of Directors' Transactions,* at para **[16.055]** *et seq.*

[301] Section 31 of the CA 1990.

[302] By virtue of s 41(5) of the CA 1990.

[303] Section 41(8) of the CA 1990.

[17.114] In respect of a transaction, arrangement or agreement falling within the scope of the preceding paragraph, particulars of the principal terms of the transaction, arrangement or agreement are required to be given in notes to the accounts[304], including the following particulars[305]:

(a) a statement of the fact either that the transaction, arrangement or agreement was made or subsisted, as the case may be, during the financial year;

(b) the name of the person for whom it was made, and, where that person is or was connected with a director of the company or of its holding company, the name of that director;

(c) in the case of a transaction or arrangement under paragraph (1)(c) or (2)(c) of s 41 (ie, an 'other transaction or arrangement'), the name of the director with the material interest and the nature of that interest;

(d) in the case of a loan, or an agreement for a loan, or an arrangement relating to a loan, to set out details of the liability at the start and end of the period, of the maximum amount of that liability during the period, of any interest unpaid, and of any provision in respect of the loan;

(e) in the case of a guarantee or security or an arrangement relating to a guarantee or security, to set out details of the amount for which the company is liable at the start and end of the financial year, of the maximum amount for which it may become liable, and of the amount paid by the company;

(f) in the case of any other transaction, arrangement or agreement, the value of the transaction or arrangement (to which the agreement relates);

(g) the aggregate value of loans, quasi-loans and credit transactions to directors or connected persons at the end of the financial year concerned, expressed as a percentage of the company's relevant (net) assets at that time; and

(h) any amendment of the terms of any such arrangement.

[17.115] Where a company fails to comply with the above requirements, the company and every person who at the time of the default is a director of the company shall be guilty of an offence[306]. Such an offence is punishable on summary conviction by the imposition of a class C fine[307] or, at the discretion of the court, by imprisonment for a term not exceeding 12 months, or both[308]. Upon conviction on indictment, a person guilty of such an offence shall be liable to a fine not exceeding €22,220.42 or imprisonment for a term not exceeding five years, or both[309].

It is a defence in proceedings for such an offence to prove that one took all reasonable steps to secure compliance.

[17.116] There are a small number of complete exclusions from the above disclosure requirement. First, the requirements do not apply in respect of transactions, arrangements or agreements between one company and another in which a director of

304 Section 41(3) of the CA 1990.

305 Section 42 of the CA 1990.

306 Section 41(11) of the CA 1990.

307 A class C fine is defined in s 3 of the FA 2010 as 'a fine not exceeding €2,500'.

308 Section 240(1) of the CA 1990, as amended by the FA 2010.

309 Section 240(1) of the CA 1990, as amended by the FA 2010.

the first company (or its subsidiary or holding company) is interested only by virtue of his being a director[310]. It should be emphasised that this does not mean that a transaction between two companies is exempted if the companies have a common director; rather, it means that a transaction will be exempted if the only reason that it would otherwise be caught is that the companies have a common director. Second, the disclosure requirements do not apply in respect of a contract of service between a company and a director of that company or of its holding company[311]. Care should be taken in this respect in that the exclusion does not apply in respect of a contract of service between a company and a director of a subsidiary of that company. Finally, it is expressly stated that the disclosure requirements do not apply in respect of transactions, arrangements or agreements which either were not entered into during the relevant period and did not subsist at any time during the relevant period, or which were made before the section was commenced and which did not subsist thereafter[312] (which is exactly as one would expect in both respects).

[17.117] In addition, there are exclusions in respect of materiality. First, the disclosure requirements do not apply to loans, quasi-loans or credit transactions entered into by a company or subsidiary for a person who at any time during the relevant period was a director of the company (or holding company) or connected person, if the aggregate of the values of each arrangement for that director or any person connected with him less the amount by which the liabilities have been reduced did not at any time in the relevant period exceed €3,175[313].

Care should be taken in regard to this materiality provision, in that it does not match the *de minimis* exception in respect of the prohibition of loans, quasi-loans or credit transactions[314]. Thus, for example, were a company to have net assets of over €55,000, and make a loan of €5,000 to a director, having made no other loans, quasi-loans or credit transactions in favour of directors or connected persons, this would not contravene s 31 of the CA 1990 (as it would fall within the 10% exemption set out in s 32 of the CA 1990), but the company would be required to disclose the arrangement in the notes to the financial statements, as it exceeds €3,175. Secondly, the disclosure requirement in respect of a transaction or arrangement other than one of a kind described in s 31 of the CA 1990 only applies where the transaction or arrangement was one in which a director (of the company or of its holding company) had, directly or indirectly, a material interest[315]. That is, in respect of this exemption, the relevant consideration is not whether the transaction is itself material to the company, but whether the director's interest in it is material.

This meaning of 'materiality' – by reference to the director rather than to the company – is of course likely to lead to a much lower threshold than would otherwise be the case, in respect of any sizeable company. However an interest in such a transaction or arrangement is not material for these purposes if, in the opinion of the majority of the

310 Section 41(7)(a) of the CA 1990.

311 Section 41(7)(b) of the CA 1990.

312 Section 41(7)(c) and (d) of the CA 1990.

313 Section 45(1) of the CA 1990.

314 Section 32 of the CA 1990; See Ch 16, *Statutory Regulation of Directors' Transactions,* at para **[16.075]** *et seq.*

315 Section 41(1)(c) and (2)(c) of the CA 1990.

directors (other than that director), it is not material[316]. In addition, a *de minimis* provision also applies in relation to such a transaction or arrangement, in respect of the value of the transaction or arrangement itself, whereby the disclosure requirements will not apply in relation to any accounts prepared in respect of any relevant period, to any transaction or arrangement in which a director had, directly or indirectly, a material interest, if:

(a) the value of each transaction or arrangement in which that director has directly or indirectly a material interest and which was made after the commencement of that relevant period with the company or its subsidiaries, and

(b) the value of each such transaction or arrangement which was made before the commencement of that period less the amount by which the liabilities have been reduced,

did not at any time during the relevant period exceed in the aggregate €1,270 or, if more, did not exceed €6,350 or 1% of the company's net assets at the end of the relevant period (whichever is the less)[317].

Therefore if (say) a company had net assets of over €500,000, and made an arrangement of the type in para (1)(c) or (2)(c) of s 41 of the CA 1990, with a value of €5,000, in favour of a director, and had no other such arrangements in place, the arrangement would not be required to be disclosed in the accounts, notwithstanding the fact that the director's interest in that arrangement might be material to him.

[17.118] Finally, in addition to the disclosure requirements in respect of certain transactions with directors, an obligation arises where a company (or, if applicable, any subsidiary of the company) makes a loan or quasi-loan or enters into a credit transaction, or enters into a guarantee or provides security in connection with such a loan, quasi-loan or credit transaction, or enters into certain arrangements or assignments in respect of such a transaction, or makes an agreement to enter into any of the foregoing transactions or arrangements, with any officer other than a director of the company[318]. The obligation is that the company shall disclose the aggregate amount outstanding at the end of the relevant period in respect of such transactions, arrangements and agreements made for such officers, and the number of such officers with whom those transactions, arrangements and agreements were made[319]. There is a *de minimis* provision whereby disclosure shall not be required of such transactions, arrangements and agreements made for a particular officer where the aggregate amount outstanding at the end of the period in respect of the transactions, arrangements and agreements made for that officer does not exceed €3,174.35[320].

[17.119] In considering the above obligations, one should also bear in mind accounting requirements in respect of the disclosure of dealings with directors and connected persons ('related parties'). In UK and Irish GAAP, this is set out under Financial

[316] Section 41(5) of the CA 1990.

[317] Section 45(2) of the CA 1990.

[318] Section 43(1) of the CA 1990.

[319] Section 43(2) of the CA 1990.

[320] Section 43(3) of the CA 1990.

Reporting Standard 8, 'Related Party Disclosures' ('FRS 8') as issued in 1995 and updated in 2008. Under FRS 8, a party is related to an entity if:

(a) directly, or indirectly through one or more intermediaries, the party:

 (i) controls, is controlled by, or is under common control with, the entity (this includes parents, subsidiaries and fellow subsidiaries);

 (ii) has an interest in the entity that gives it significant influence over the entity; or

 (iii) has joint control over the entity;

(b) the party is an associate (as defined in FRS 9, 'Associates and joint ventures') of the entity;

(c) the party is a joint venture in which the entity is a venturer (as defined in FRS 9, 'Associates and joint ventures');

(d) the party is a member of the key management personnel of the entity or its parent;

(e) the party is a close member of the family of any individual referred to in subparagraph (a) or (d);

(f) the party is an entity that is controlled, jointly controlled or significantly influenced by, or for which significant voting power in such entity resides with directly or indirectly, any individual referred to in (d) or (e); or

(g) the party is a retirement benefit scheme for the benefit of employees of the entity, or of any entity that is a related party of the entity.

FRS 8 defines 'Key Management' as:

> 'Those persons having authority and responsibility for planning, directing and controlling the activities of the entity, directly or indirectly including any director (whether executive or otherwise) of that entity.'

[17.120] FRS 8 requires two levels of disclosure in the financial statements. First, it requires a disclosure of control (which is required irrespective of whether any transactions have taken place between the parties), setting out:

(a) the nature of the relationship with the related party;

(b) the name of the related party, and if different;

(c) the name of the ultimate controlling party.

Second, there is a requirement to disclose transactions and balances with related parties, setting out:

(a) the names of transacting parties;

(b) a description of the relationship between the parties;

(c) a description of the transactions;

(d) the amounts involved;

(e) the amounts due to or from related parties at the balance sheet date and provisions for doubtful debt;

(f) the amounts written off during the period arising from debts due to or from related parties;

(g) other information on the transactions necessary for the understanding of the financial statements ('true and fair view').

Additional obligations and provisions also apply in relation to licensed banks.

(iii) Interests of director or secretary in the company's shares and debentures

[17.121] The company must state, in the directors' report or the notes to its accounts for a financial year, in respect of each person who was a director or the secretary of the company at the end of that financial year:

(a) whether or not he was, at the end of that financial year, interested in shares in, or debentures of, the company or any body corporate being a holding company, subsidiary or sister company[321] of the company;

(b) if he was so interested:

  (i) the number and amount of such shares and debentures (setting out each body separately) in which he was then interested,

  (ii) whether or not he was, at the beginning of the financial year (or, if later, at the time of first becoming a director) interested in shares in, or debentures of, a relevant company;

  (iii) if he was, the number and amount of such shares and debentures (setting out each body separately) in which he was then interested[322].

This disclosure requirement does not therefore apply in respect of:

(a) a person who was a director or secretary of the company during the financial year but ceased to be such a director or secretary before the financial year-end; or

(b) a person who held shares in, or debentures of, a relevant company during the financial year but divested himself of such shares or debentures before the financial year-end.

(iv) Remuneration of auditors

[17.122] The EC(SA)(D)R 2010 have significantly increased the level of disclosure required regarding auditors' remuneration. Previously, a company was merely required to disclose the amount of the auditors' remuneration (including any sums paid by the company in respect of the auditors' expenses)[323], and no breakdown of this figure was required.

Under the new s 161D of the CA 1963[324], a company[325] is required to disclose in the notes to its annual accounts for a financial year the remuneration for all work carried out for that company, First, in respect of that financial year, and second, in respect of the preceding financial year. Remuneration is defined as including benefits in kind and payments in cash, and where all or part of the remuneration is in the form of a benefit in kind, the nature and estimated monetary value of the benefit must be disclosed. In addition, a breakdown of the above figures is required, with the figures in relation to the above being disclosed separately for each of the following categories of work:

[321] 'Sister company' is being used here to refer to a subsidiary of the company's holding company.

[322] Section 63(1) of the CA 1990.

[323] Paragraph 39(5) of the Schedule to the C(A)A 1986.

[324] Inserted by reg 120 of the EC(SA)(D)R 2010.

[325] Or a partnership falling within the scope of reg 6 of the EC(A)R 1993.

(a) the audit of individual accounts;

(b) other assurance services;

(c) tax advisory services;

(d) other non audit services.

Where the auditor of a relevant undertaking is a statutory audit firm, any work carried out by a partner in the firm or a statutory auditor on its behalf is considered for the purposes of this disclosure obligation to have been carried out by the audit firm. Where more than one auditor (whether a statutory auditor or a statutory audit firm) has been appointed as the auditor of a company in a single financial year, a separate disclosure must be made in the note to the accounts in respect of the remuneration of each of them.

[17.123] A company need not make the above disclosures where the company is to be treated as a small or medium-sized company[326] (although in the latter case, the company will be required to provide the above information in respect of auditors' remuneration to IAASA when requested so to do).

Alternatively, the disclosure obligation does not apply where the company is a subsidiary undertaking included in group accounts which a parent undertaking is required to, and does, prepare in accordance with the appropriate regulations, and where an equivalent disclosure is made in respect of that subsidiary undertaking in the notes to those accounts. The disclosure obligation required of a parent undertaking preparing group accounts is set out below[327].

[17.124] Where a relevant undertaking fails to comply with the above disclosure obligations, each company or other entity that forms all or part of that undertaking shall be guilty of an offence. Such an offence is punishable on summary conviction by the imposition of a class C fine[328] or, at the discretion of the court, by imprisonment for a term not exceeding 12 months, or both[329]. Upon conviction on indictment, a person guilty of such an offence shall be liable to a fine not exceeding €22,220.42 or imprisonment for a term not exceeding five years, or both[330].

(v) Related party transactions

[17.125] If the company has entered into transactions with related parties, and such transactions are material and were not concluded under normal market conditions, the following particulars shall be given in the notes to the company's accounts[331]:

(a) the amount of such transactions;

(b) the nature of the relationship; and

[326] In either case, in accordance with s 8(1) of the C(A)A 1986.

[327] See para **[17.189]**.

[328] A class C fine is defined in s 3 of the FA 2010 as 'a fine not exceeding €2,500'.

[329] Section 240(1) of the CA 1990, as amended by the FA 2010.

[330] Section 240(1) of the CA 1990, as amended by the FA 2010.

[331] Paragraph 36(1) of the Schedule to the C(A)A 1986 as amended by the European Communities (Directive 2006/46/EC) Regulations 2009 ('EC(D)R 2009'). Note that there are two paras 36 of the Schedule to the C(A)A 1986; it is thought that this is a typographical error in the EC(D)R 2009 and that this para should be titled para 36B.

(c) other information about the transaction which is necessary for an understanding of the financial position of the company.

Save in respect of a company whose securities are admitted to trading on a regulated market[332], the above particulars and information about individual transactions may be aggregated according to their nature, except where separate information is necessary for an understanding of the effects of the transactions on the financial position of the company[333]. The disclosure obligation shall not apply in respect of a transaction between a company and its wholly-owned subsidiary[334].

(vi) Off balance sheet items

[17.126] A company is required to set out in the notes to its accounts the nature and business purpose, and the financial impact, of any arrangements of the company that are not included in its balance sheet, if the risks or benefits of such arrangements are material, and to the extent that disclosure of those risks and benefits is necessary for assessing the financial position of the company[335].

(vii) Additional disclosure requirements for certain group undertakings

[17.127] Section 16 of the C(A)A 1986 requires that a company include a note to its accounts where, at the end of its financial year, the company, either:

(a) has a subsidiary[336]; or

(b) holds (including interests held by persons acting on behalf of the company) a qualifying interest of at least 20% in an undertaking other than a subsidiary ('an undertaking of substantial interest').

The note is required to set out the following information in relation to these entities (distinguishing between those at (a) and (b) above):

(i) the name and registered office of each entity and the nature of the business carried on by it;

(ii) the class of shares held by the company in each entity, and the proportion held by the company of the nominal value of the allotted shares of each such class in that entity;

(iii) the aggregate amount of the capital and reserves of the entity as at the end of the financial year of that entity ending with or last before the financial year-end of the company;

(iv) the profit or loss of the entity for the financial year of that entity ending with or last before the financial ycar-cnd of the company[337].

Paragraphs (iii) and (iv) above shall not apply in respect of an entity if the qualifying capital interest of the company in the subsidiary is included in the company's accounts or in a note thereto by way of the equity method of valuation, or if the entity is not

332 Paragraph 36(4) of the Schedule to the C(A)A 1986.

333 Paragraph 36(2) of the Schedule to the C(A)A 1986.

334 Paragraph 36(3) of the Schedule to the C(A)A 1986.

335 Paragraph 36A of the Schedule to the C(A)A 1986.

336 Within the meaning of s 155 of the CA 1963.

337 Section 16(1) of the C(A)A 1986.

required to publish its accounts and the qualifying capital interest does not amount to 50% of all such interests, or if the information is not material. In addition, paras (iii) and (iv) above shall not apply in respect of a subsidiary undertaking if it is dealt with in group accounts prepared by the company or a parent company of the company[338].

In addition, where a company is a member with unlimited liability of an undertaking[339], there is an obligation to include a note in the accounts of that company stating the name, the head or registered office, and the legal form of each such undertaking, unless such information is of negligible importance for the purpose of giving a true and fair view.

It should be noted that if the directors are of the opinion that to include the above information in the notes to the accounts would require a note of excessive length, then unless (in the opinion of the directors) the financial state of the entity has a substantial effect on the profit or loss, or financial position, of the company and its subsidiaries, the directors may instead set out that information in a separate statement which must be signed by one director and the secretary of the company, and which must be annexed to the annual return.

[17.128] The directors of a company to which these additional disclosure requirements relate do not have to state in their directors' report details of any change in the nature of the business of the company and its subsidiaries during the financial year so far as is material for the appreciation of the state of its affairs, or list the company's subsidiaries and any other bodies corporate in which the company has a beneficial shareholding of more than 20% of the shares carrying voting rights[340].

[17.129] The information above[341] may, in lieu of being stated in a note to the accounts, be given in a statement in writing signed by a director and the secretary of the company and annexed to the first annual return made by the company next after its accounts for that year are laid before the AGM of the company if, in the opinion of the directors, compliance with the section would required a note to the accounts of excessive length[342]. However, this mechanism may not be used where the directors of the subsidiary or undertaking of substantial interest are of the opinion that the financial state of their company or undertaking has a substantial effect on the profit or loss or the amount of assets of the parent company and its subsidiaries[343].

(viii) Subsidiary undertakings

[17.130] Where a company is a subsidiary undertaking[344], the following details must be stated in the notes concerning the parent undertakings of the largest and smallest group of undertakings for which group accounts are prepared and of which the company is a member[345]:

338 Section 16(2) of the C(A)A 1986.

339 The term 'undertaking' includes unincorporated bodies such as partnerships as well as companies.

340 Section 16(5) of the C(A)A 1986.

341 See para **[17.127]**.

342 Section 16(3)(a) of the C(A)A 1986.

343 Section 16(3)(b) of the C(A)A 1986.

344 Within the meaning of reg 4 of the EC(C:GA)R 1992.

345 Paragraph 46A of the Schedule to the C(A)A 1986.

- the name of the parent undertakings;
- the places of incorporation of the parent undertakings, if incorporated;
- the addresses of the principal places of business of the parent undertakings, if unincorporated;
- any addresses from where copies of the group accounts prepared by the parent undertakings may be obtained, if made available to the public.

IFRS individual accounts

[17.131] As stated above, IFRS individual accounts are defined as individual accounts prepared 'in accordance with international financial reporting standards and s 149A [of the CA 1963]'[346]. It is beyond the scope of this text to set out the requirements of IFRS. Section 149A of the CA 1963 requires that where IFRS individual accounts are prepared, the notes to those accounts must state that the accounts have been prepared in accordance with international financial reporting standards, and must also include in the notes to the accounts[347] specified information regarding the matters at (a) to (k) below. In addition, the notes to the accounts must set out details in respect of the remuneration of auditors, as at (l) below.

(a) Directors' remuneration

[17.0132] The disclosure obligations in this respect are set out in s 191 of the CA 1963 and para 39(6) of the Schedule to the C(A)A 1986, and are considered above[348].

(b) Transactions with directors and connected persons

[17.133] The disclosure obligations in this respect are set out in ss 41–45 of the CA 1990 and are considered above[349], save that the relevant accounting requirements are as set out under International Accountancy Standard 24 ('IAS 24'), most recently revised in November 2009, rather than under FRS 8.

The definitions of 'related party' and 'key management' in IAS 24 do not differ significantly from those in FRS 8; however, there are differences between IFRS and Irish GAAP in respect of the disclosure obligation. First, IAS 24 does not expressly require disclosure of the name of the related party but rather that disclosure should be categorised according to the relationship between the parties. Second, FRS 8 requires disclosure only of material transactions and exempts disclosures between a parent and a wholly-owned subsidiary; IAS 24 does not so provide.

(c) Interests of director or secretary in the company's shares and debentures

[17.134] The disclosure obligations in this respect are set out in s 63 of the CA 1990 and are considered at para **[17.121]** above.

---

346 Section 148(2)(b) of the CA 1963.

347 The disclosure obligation at (c) may alternatively be met by stating that information in the directors' report, as is also the case for a company preparing Companies Act individual accounts.

348 See para **[17.112]**.

349 See paras **[17.113]** to **[17.120]**.

(d) Details on group undertakings

[17.135] The disclosure obligations in this respect are set out in ss 16 and 16A of the C(A)A 1986 and are considered above[350].

(e) Details of share capital and debentures

[17.136] The disclosure obligations in this respect are set out in paras 26 to 28 of the Schedule to the C(A)A 1986 and are considered above[351].

(f) Restriction on the distributability of profits

[17.137] The disclosure obligations in this respect are set out in para 32A of the Schedule to the C(A)A 1986 and are considered above[352].

(g) Guarantees and other financial commitments

[17.138] The disclosure obligations in this respect are set out in para 36 of the Schedule to the C(A)A 1986 and are considered above[353].

(h) Financial assistance for the purchase of own shares

[17.139] The disclosure obligations in this respect are set out in para 37(2) of the Schedule to the C(A)A 1986 and are considered above[354].

(i) Details of staff numbers and remuneration

[17.140] The disclosure obligations in this respect are set out in para 42 of the Schedule to the C(A)A 1986 and are considered above[355].

(j) Shares and debentures held by subsidiary undertakings

[17.141] The disclosure obligations in this respect are set out in para 46 of the Schedule to the C(A)A 1986 and are considered above[356].

(k) Off balance sheet items

[17.142] The disclosure obligations in this respect are set out in para 36A of the Schedule to the C(A)A 1986 and are considered above[357].

(l) Remuneration of auditors

[17.143] The disclosure obligations in this respect are set out in s 161D of the CA 1963 and are considered above[358].

---

350 See paras **[17.127]** to **[17.129]**.

351 See para **[17.092]**.

352 See para **[17.095]**.

353 See para **[17.097]**.

354 See para **[17.085]**.

355 See para **[17.101]**.

356 See para **[17.093]**.

357 See para **[17.126]**.

358 See paras **[17.122]** to **[17.124]**.

[D] GROUP ACCOUNTS

Introduction

[17.144] Prior to 1 September 1992, the CA 1963 required that holding companies prepare group accounts dealing with the state of affairs and profit or loss of the company and its subsidiaries, and lay these accounts before the AGM of the company[359]. This obligation did not extend to private holding companies, provided that they made copies of all the subsidiaries' annual accounts available to every member on request[360], or to a holding company which was itself the wholly-owned subsidiary of another Irish company[361].

The group accounts were to comprise a consolidated balance sheet and a consolidated profit and loss account, but the directors were permitted to adopt a different form for the accounts (for example, showing separate sets of consolidated accounts for different subgroups within the group) where they were of the opinion that it would be better for the purpose of presenting the information[362]. The group accounts were required to give equivalent information as would be required in respect of individual company accounts.

[17.145] That regime still operates in respect of certain unlimited companies, being those which do not fall within the scope of reg 6 of the European Communities (Accounts) Regulations ('EC(A)R 1993')[363], ie, all the members of which are not limited companies or their foreign equivalent, or EEA unlimited companies (or their foreign equivalent) whose members are all such companies, or a combination of these[364].

[17.146] From 1 September 1992, the relevant legislative regime for all other companies in respect of the preparation of group accounts was the European Communities (Companies: Group Accounts) Regulations 1992 (SI 201/1992) (the 'EC(C:GA)R 1992'), which implement the EU Seventh Company Law Directive[365]. The most significant innovation was that the exemption by virtue of being a private company was removed. In addition, the scope of entities required to be consolidated in group accounts shifted from 'companies' to 'undertakings'[366]. As a result of the EC(C:GA)R 1992, a substantially greater number of entities were required to prepare consolidated accounts, and to lay these before the AGM at the same time as their own annual accounts were so laid.

[17.147] The EC(C:GA)R 1992 also prescribed the form which group accounts were to take, requiring that the group accounts *must* comprise a consolidated balance sheet, dealing with the state of affairs of the parent undertaking and its subsidiary undertakings as a whole; a consolidated profit and loss account, dealing with the profit or loss of the undertakings as a whole; and notes to the accounts giving additional information as

359 Section 150(1) of the CA 1963, prior to amendment.
360 Section 154 of the CA 1963, prior to amendment.
361 Section 150(2)(a) of the CA 1963, prior to amendment.
362 Section 151 of the CA 1963, prior to amendment.
363 SI 396/1993.
364 See Ch 31, *Unlimited Companies,* at para **[31.024]**.
365 Directive 83/349/EEC, 13 June 1983.
366 See **[17.154]** *post*.

provided by the EC(C:GA)R 1992. The consolidated accounts were required to combine in full the individual information contained in the separate accounts of each of the undertakings in the group, subject to adjustments which are required or permitted by the EC(C:GA)R 1992.

[17.148] The requirements in respect of the preparation of group accounts were further amended by Regulation (EC) No 1606/2002 of the European Parliament and of the Council on the application of International Accounting Standards (the 'IAS Regulation'), which requires that all companies with securities trading on a regulated market of an EEA State prepare their group accounts in accordance with international financial reporting standards adopted by the EU ('IFRS'). The IAS Regulation further provided that Member States were allowed to 'permit or require' companies which did not have securities so traded to use IFRS for the preparation of their group accounts. The EC(IFRSMA)R 2005 provide for a permissive regime in respect of such companies.

[17.149] Therefore, since the coming into force of the IFRS Regulations, the general rule for Irish companies that do not have securities admitted to trading on a regulated market of an EEA State, and that are required to prepare group accounts, is that they shall prepare either:

> '(a) group accounts in accordance with section 150A [of the CA 1963] (to be known and in [the CA 1963] referred to as 'Companies Act group accounts'), or
>
> (b) IFRS group accounts[367].'

The EC(C:GA)R 1992 now generally apply only to Companies Acts group accounts.

[17.150] The specific requirements in respect of disclosures in Companies Act group accounts and IFRS group accounts largely follow those prescribed in respect of Companies Act individual accounts and IFRS individual accounts respectively, but with necessary modifications to take into account the particular considerations relevant to group accounting.

[17.151] In respect of Companies Act group accounts, the EC(C:GA)R 1992 also contain special provisions as to whether an acquisition may be accounted for using the acquisition method or the merger method of accounting[368]. The EC(C:GA)R 1992 further make provision in regard to accounting for joint ventures, associated undertakings and participating interests, each as defined in the EC(C:GA)R 1992.

[17.152] Where a company which is a parent undertaking prepares group accounts (whether Companies Act group accounts or IFRS group accounts) in accordance with s 150 of the CA 1963, and the notes to the company's individual balance sheet show the profit and loss for the financial year determined in accordance with the C(A)A 1986 or s 149A of the CA 1963, the company will be exempted from the requirement to annex its individual profit and loss account or income statement to its annual return[369]. The notes to the consolidated accounts and to the individual accounts must disclose the fact that this exemption has been availed of[370].

367 Section 150(3) of the CA 1963.

368 See para **[17.190]** *et seq*.

369 Section 7(1A) of the C(A)A 1986.

370 Section 7(1B) of the C(A)A 1986.

[17.153] The following matters shall now be considered:

1. The obligation to prepare group accounts.
2. Exemptions from preparing group accounts.
3. Companies Act group accounts.
4. IFRS group accounts.

The obligation to prepare group accounts

[17.154] Following the amendments to the CA 1963 and the EC(C:GA)R 1992 effected by the IFRS Regulations, the primary obligation to prepare group accounts is set out in s 150 of the CA 1963, which provides that:

> 'Where at the end of its financial year a company is a parent company, the directors, as well as preparing individual accounts for a year, shall prepare consolidated accounts (to be known and in this Act referred to as 'group accounts') for the group for that year'.

The obligation to prepare accounts therefore applies to a 'parent company'. This is defined in s 2(1) of the CA 1963 as meaning:

> 'a company that has one or more subsidiary undertakings within the meaning of in [*sic*] the [EC(C:GA)R 1992].'

The meaning of 'undertaking,' 'parent undertaking' and 'subsidiary undertaking' has been considered in full detail in Ch 12[371]. The term 'undertaking' is broadly defined as meaning

> 'a body corporate, a partnership, or an unincorporated body of persons engaged for gain in the production, supply or distribution of goods, the provision of a service or the making or holding of investments[372].'

The EC(C:GA)R 1992 further provide[373] that

> 'an undertaking shall be deemed to be a subsidiary of another, if but only if—
>
> (a) that other—
>
> (i) holds a majority of the shareholders' or members' voting rights in the undertaking, or
>
> (ii) is a shareholder or member of it and controls the composition of its board of directors, or
>
> (iii) is a shareholder or member of it and controls alone, pursuant to an agreement with other shareholders or members, a majority of the shareholders' or members' voting rights; or
>
> (b) that other has the right to exercise a dominant influence over it—
>
> (i) by virtue of provisions contained in its memorandum or articles, or
>
> (ii) by virtue of a control contract; or
>
> (c) that other has the power to exercise, or actually exercises, dominant influence or control over it, or
>
> (ca) that other and the subsidiary undertaking are managed on a unified basis, or

371 See Ch 12, *Groups of Companies*, at para **[12.030]** *et seq*.

372 Regulation 3(1) of the EC(C:GA)R 1992.

373 Regulation 4(1) of the EC(C:GA) 1992.

(d) the undertaking is a subsidiary of any undertaking which is that other's subsidiary undertaking.

Therefore the bodies that are required to be consolidated in group accounts include not only companies, but also these other types of entities, whether incorporated or not and whether Irish or foreign.

It might be noted that the fact that the primary obligation to prepare consolidated accounts now applies (since the coming into force of the IFRS Regulations) to a 'parent company' rather than a 'parent undertaking', does not limit the number of entities required to prepare such accounts, as the obligation under the EC(C:GA)R 1992 only ever extended to:

- companies limited by shares[374];
- companies limited by guarantee[375];
- certain unlimited companies or partnerships[376].

[17.155] The directors of a holding company[377] must secure that the financial year of each of its subsidiaries coincides with its own, unless there are good reasons against this being the case[378]. The Minister may extend the financial year of a holding company or a subsidiary so that the subsidiary's financial year may end with that of the holding company[379]. In addition, where a company prepares Companies Act group accounts, these must be drawn up as at the same date as the annual accounts of the parent undertaking[380]. Where a company prepares Companies Act group accounts, if the financial year of a subsidiary undertaking differs from that of the parent undertaking, interim accounts must be drawn up by the subsidiary if the end of its financial year precedes the end of the parent undertaking's financial year by more than three months[381]. In addition, in respect of Companies Act group accounts, where the financial years of parent and subsidiary do not coincide, the reasons therefor and the dates must be disclosed in the parent's accounts and in any group accounts[382]. A parent undertaking preparing Companies Act group accounts is required to lay the group accounts before the AGM at the same time at which its own annual accounts are so laid[383].

Exemptions from preparing group accounts

[17.156] Certain parent undertakings are exempt from the requirement to prepare group accounts[384]. Four exemptions arise:

(a) Exemptions related to size of group;

---

374 Regulation 5(3)(a) of the EC(C:GA)R 1992.

375 Regulation 5(3)(b) of the EC(C:GA)R 1992.

376 See Ch 31, *Unlimited Companies,* at para **[31.024]**.

377 It should be noted that not all parent undertakings are holding companies; See Ch 12, *Groups of Companies,* at para **[12.035]** and para **[12.039]**.

378 Section 153(1) of the CA 1963.

379 Section 153(2) of the CA 1963

380 Regulation 26(1) of the EC(C:GA)R 1992.

381 Regulation 26(2) of the EC(C:GA)R 1992.

382 Paragraph 55 of the Schedule to the C(A)A 1986.

383 Regulation 5(1) of the EC(C:GA)R 1992.

(b) Exemptions for parent undertakings that are fully or 90% owned subsidiary undertakings of EEA undertakings;
(c) Exemptions for other parent undertakings that are subsidiary undertakings of EEA undertakings;
(d) Exemptions for parent undertakings that are subsidiary undertakings of non-EEA undertakings.

(a) Exemptions related to size of group

[17.157] This exemption is not unlike the exemptions which relate to 'small' and 'medium-sized' private companies in relation to their individual annual accounts. Only a parent undertaking which is a private company may avail of this exemption, whereby it will be exempt from the requirement to prepare group accounts in respect of any financial year and to lay those accounts before the AGM if at the balance sheet date for that financial year and the immediately preceding financial year, the group as a whole (ie, the parent and all of its subsidiary undertakings) satisfies two of the following three conditions:

- The balance sheet total of the group as a whole does not exceed €7,618,428;
- The amount of turnover of the group as a whole does not exceed €15,236,858;
- The average number of employees for the group as a whole does not exceed 250[385].

'Balance sheet total' in this context effectively means total assets, ie, before deducting any liabilities owed by the companies[386]. It would appear that the balance sheet total may be computed without reference to set-offs and other adjustments to be made in the preparation of group accounts where such accounts have not been previously prepared[387]. If this were not the case, companies would effectively be required to go through the process of preparing consolidated group accounts so as to ascertain whether they meet the exemption from having to prepare such accounts. Where the financial period to which the accounts relate is not in fact a year, the size exemption for turnover must be proportionally adjusted[388]. In the first financial year of becoming a parent undertaking, the exemptions may be calculated by reference to the figures for that year only[389]; subsequently the normal obligation to meet the requirements in both its present and immediately preceding financial year will apply. If it fails to meet the requirements in any subsequent financial year, it may avail of the exemption for that year – but may not rely on the exemption again until it has met the criteria in any immediately preceding financial year[390].

---

384 These exemptions are set out in the EC(C:GA)R 1992, and originally applied to the preparation of all group accounts. As a consequence of the EC(IFRSMA) R 2005, the exemptions are now expressed as applying to a parent undertaking that prepares Companies Act group accounts, but it appears that a view has generally been taken that the exemptions apply equally to a parent undertaking that prepares IFRS accounts.

385 Regulation 7(1) of the EC(C:GA)R 1992.

386 Regulation 7(2) of the EC(C:GA)R 1992.

387 Regulation 7(10) of the EC(C:GA)R 1992.

388 Regulation 7(4) of the EC(C:GA)R 1992.

389 Regulation 7(5) of the EC(C:GA)R 1992.

390 Regulation 7(7) of the EC(C:GA)R 1992.

[17.158] The size exemption may not be availed of where[391]:

- Any shares, debentures or other debt securities of the parent undertaking or one of its subsidiary undertakings have been admitted to trading on a regulated market of any EEA State[392]; or
- The parent undertaking or any of its subsidiary undertakings is an undertaking to which reg 6 of the EC(C:GA)R 1992 applies (ie, in general terms, a licensed bank, trustee savings bank, hire-purchase company, insurance company or other finance company).

(b) Exemptions for parent undertakings that are fully or 90% owned subsidiary undertakings of EEA undertakings

[17.159] The obligation to prepare consolidated group accounts and to lay them before the AGM shall not apply to a parent undertaking (the 'exempted parent') which is itself a wholly or more than 90% owned subsidiary undertaking of an undertaking established under the laws of an EEA State[393]. In the case of a non-wholly-owned exempted parent, the approval of the remaining shareholders in or members of the exempted parent for the exemption is required[394]. Shares held by directors in the exempted parent undertaking by virtue of operation of law or a provision in the exempted parent's articles of association must be disregarded in the above calculation[395]. The exemption is not available to any parent undertaking whose shares, debentures or debt securities have been admitted to trading on a regulated market of an EEA State[396].

[17.160] Furthermore, the following conditions must all be met[397]:

- The exempted parent and all of its subsidiary undertakings must be dealt with in group accounts prepared by a parent undertaking which is established under the law of an EEA State, and of which the exempted parent is a subsidiary undertaking (the 'EEA parent');
- The group accounts and directors' report of the EEA parent must be prepared and audited according to the law of the EEA State in which the EEA parent is established and in accordance with EEC Council Directive 83/349/EEC.
- The following must be annexed to the annual return of the exempted parent after the above group accounts have been prepared:
- The group accounts of the EEA parent;
- The directors' report of the EEA parent; and
- The report of the person responsible for auditing the accounts of the EEA parent.

---

391 Regulation 7(8) of the EC(C:GA)R 1992.

392 'Regulated market' is defined in s 8(13) of the C(A)A 1986 as having 'the meaning assigned to it by Article 4(1), point (14) of Directive 2004/39/EC', and means the markets set out in a list published each year by the European Commission. The list currently comprises the principal markets of each EEA State, while excluding some notable markets, such as London's AIM.

393 Regulation 8(1) of the EC(C:GA)R 1992.

394 Regulation 8(1)(b) of the EC(C:GA)R 1992.

395 Regulation 8(2) of the EC(C:GA)R 1992.

396 Regulation 8(4) of the EC(C:GA)R 1992.

397 Regulation 8(3) of the EC(C:GA)R 1992.

- The notes on the annual accounts of the exempted parent must disclose:
- The name and registered office of the EEA parent that draws up the above group accounts; and
- The exemption from the obligation to draw up group accounts and a directors' report.
- If the EEA parent's group accounts, directors' report or auditor's report are in a language other than the English language or the Irish language, a translation in the English language or the Irish language certified in the prescribed manner to be a correct translation is required to be annexed to each such document.

(c) Exemptions for other parent undertakings that are subsidiary undertakings of EEA undertakings

[17.161] A parent undertaking (the 'exempted parent') which is a subsidiary of another undertaking established under the law of an EEA State (the 'EEA parent'), but which does not qualify for the exemption above[398] (ie, which is not wholly or more than 90% owned by an EEA undertaking) may nonetheless avail of the exemption if the shareholders or members holding not less than 10% or more in aggregate of the nominal value of the total share capital of the exempted parent have not, at least six months prior to the end of its financial year, requested the preparation of group accounts[399]. The further conditions set out above[400] must be met[401], and again the exemption will not apply to a parent undertaking any of whose shares, debentures or other debt securities have been admitted to trading on a regulated market of an EEA State[402].

(d) Exemptions for other parent undertakings that are subsidiary undertakings of non-EEA undertakings

[17.162] A parent undertaking (the 'exempted parent') which is the subsidiary undertaking of an undertaking not established under the law of an EEA State (the 'non-EEA parent') shall be exempt from the requirement to prepare consolidated group accounts and to lay them before the AGM where:

(a) the exempted parent is a wholly-owned subsidiary of the non-EEA parent; or
(b) the non-EEA parent holds more than 50% of the shares in the exempted parent and notice requiring the preparation of group accounts has not been served on the exempted parent by shareholders holding in aggregate—
   (i) more than half of the remaining shares in the company, or
   (ii) 5%[403] of the total shares in the company[404].

The aforementioned notice must be served not later than six months after[405] the end of the financial year to which it relates.

---

[398] See para **[17.159]**.
[399] Regulation 9(1) of the EC(C:GA)R 1992.
[400] See para **[17.160]**.
[401] Regulation 9(2) of the EC(C:GA)R 1992.
[402] Regulation 9(3) of the EC(C:GA)R 1992.
[403] This is therefore lower than the 10% threshold required under reg 9 of the EC(C:GA)R 1992 in the case of an Irish parent undertaking having an EEA parent undertaking.
[404] Regulation 9A(1) of the EC(C:GA)R 1992.

As set out previously[406], shares held by directors in the exempted parent undertaking by virtue of operation of law or a provision in the exempted parent's articles of association must be disregarded in the above calculation[407]. In addition, shares held by a wholly-owned subsidiary of the non-EEA parent, or held on its behalf by such a wholly-owned subsidiary, shall be attributed to the non-EEA parent[408].

[17.163] Furthermore, the following conditions must all be met:

- The exempted parent and all of its subsidiary undertakings must be included in consolidated accounts for a larger group drawn up to the same date, or to an earlier date in the same financial year by the non-EEA parent[409];
- Those accounts and, where appropriate, the group's annual report must be drawn up in accordance with the provisions of the relevant EU Directives[410] (as modified or in a manner equivalent to consolidated accounts and annual reports so drawn up)[411];
- Those accounts must be audited by one or more persons authorised to audit accounts under the law under which the non-EEA parent is established;
- The exempted parent must disclose in its individual accounts that it is exempt from the obligation to prepare and deliver group accounts;
- The exempted parent must disclose in its individual accounts the name of the non-EEA parent and:
- the country in which the non-EEA parent is incorporated; or
- where the non-EEA parent is unincorporated, the address of its principal place of business;
- The exempted parent must deliver to the registrar, within the period allowed for delivering its annual accounts, copies of the group accounts and, where

405 Regulation 9A(2) of the EC(C:GA)R 1992; one should note that this differs from the requirement under reg 9 of the EC(C:GA)R 1992 in the case of an Irish parent undertaking having an EEA parent undertaking, whereby the notice must be served on the Irish parent undertaking at least six months *before* the end of the financial year.

406 See para **[17.159]**.

407 Regulation 9A(5) of the EC(C:GA)R 1992.

408 Regulation 9A(6) of the EC(C:GA)R 1992.

409 The wording of the references to dates in this condition (which are not included in regs 8 or 9) may preclude an Irish parent undertaking from availing of this exemption where the financial year for which it is seeking exemption is shorter than that of its parent. For example, if the Irish parent is seeking an exemption for 12-month accounts ending on 31 December, and the non-EEA parent is preparing 15-month accounts for that period ending on 31 March in the following year, then the accounts of the non-EEA parent will not meet this condition, as 31 March in the following year will not be 'the same date, or … an earlier date in the … financial year [of the exempted parent]'.

410 EEC Council Directive 83/349/EEC as modified, where applicable, by Council Directive 86/635/EEC or Council Directive 91/674/EEC.

411 There is accounting guidance (UITF 43, as issued in October 2006) to the effect that consolidated accounts prepared in accordance with the GAAP of the US, Canada, Japan, Australia, Hong Kong or South Africa will normally meet the test of equivalence with the above Directives, subject to considering the effect of any differences from IFRS as adopted by the EU.

appropriate, consolidated annual report of the non-EEA parent, together with the auditor's report on them; and

- If any document so delivered to the registrar is in a language other than the English language or the Irish language, a translation in the English language or the Irish language, certified in the prescribed manner to be a correct translation, is required to be annexed to each such document[412].

As at para **[17.159]** above, this exemption is not available to any parent undertaking whose shares, debentures or debt securities are admitted to trading on a regulated market of an EEA State[413].

Companies Act group accounts

[17.164] Save for particular exceptions, Companies Act group accounts prepared by companies limited by shares or by guarantee are required to comply with the EC(C:GA)R 1992[414], and the EC(C:GA)R 1992 supersede in this respect the corresponding provisions of the Companies Acts[415]. The aforementioned exceptions apply in the case of licensed banks, trustee savings banks, hire-purchase companies, insurance companies and other financial institutions and finance companies, which are permitted to depart from the provisions of the EC(C:GA)R 1992[416]. Certain unlimited companies and partnerships preparing Companies Act group accounts are also required to comply with the EC(C:GA)R 1992[417]. Save where otherwise stated, it is assumed for the purposes of this analysis that Companies Act group accounts will be required to comply with the EC(C:GA)R 1992.

(a) Form of Companies Act group accounts

[17.165] Companies Act group accounts are required to comprise:

> '(a) a consolidated balance sheet dealing with the state of affairs of the parent undertaking and its subsidiary undertakings (including those in liquidation) as a whole,
>
> (b) a consolidated profit and loss account dealing with the profit or loss of the parent undertaking and its subsidiary undertakings (including those in liquidation) as a whole, and
>
> (c) notes on the accounts giving additional information as provided for in the EC(C:GA)R 1992[418].'

The group balance sheet and profit and loss account must combine in full the information contained in the separate balance sheets and profit and loss accounts of the parent and subsidiary undertakings with adjustments required or permitted under the EC(C:GA)R 1992[419].

---

412 Regulation 9A(3) of the EC(C:GA)R 1992.

413 Regulation 9A(4) of the EC(C:GA)R 1992.

414 Regulation 5(3) of the EC(C:GA)R 1992.

415 Regulation 5(4) of the EC(C:GA)R 1992.

416 Regulation 6 of the EC(C:GA)R 1992.

417 See Ch 31, *Unlimited Companies,* at para **[31.024]**.

418 Section 150A(1) of the CA 1963 and reg 13 of the EC(C:GA)R 1992.

419 Regulation 16 of the EC(C:GA)R 1992.

[17.166] Companies Act group accounts are required to give a true and fair view of the state of affairs as at the end of the financial year, and of the profit or loss for the financial year, of the undertakings included in the consolidation as a whole[420]. To a significant extent, the provisions of the EC(C:GA)R 1992 are determinant as to what is required for Companies Act group accounts to give a true and fair view. However to the extent that the EC(C:GA)R 1992 are silent, as in relation to individual accounts[421], it is generally accepted that it will be necessary, in addition to meeting the express requirements of the EC(C:GA)R 1992, that the accounts be prepared in accordance with Irish GAAP[422].

[17.167] A subsidiary undertaking need not be included in Companies Act group accounts where its inclusion is not material for the purposes of giving a true and fair view. However where two or more undertakings each satisfy this requirement, they must nonetheless be included in the group accounts if taken together they are material for the purposes of giving a true and fair view[423]. In addition, the EC(C:GA)R 1992 provide that a subsidiary undertaking need not be included in group accounts where:

> '(a) severe long-term restrictions substantially hinder the parent undertaking in the exercise of its right over the assets or management of that subsidiary undertaking, or
>
> (b) the information necessary for the preparation of group accounts in accordance with the EC(C:GA)R 1992 cannot be obtained without disproportionate expense or undue delay, or
>
> (c) the shares of the subsidiary undertaking are held by the parent undertaking exclusively with a view to their subsequent resale[424].'

In regard to the restriction of rights as at (a), Irish GAAP requires exclusion rather than permitting it[425], and adds further detail in stating:

> 'The rights affected must be those by reason of which the undertaking holding them is the parent undertaking and without which it would not be the parent undertaking. Severe long-term restrictions justify excluding a subsidiary undertaking from consolidation only where the effect of those restrictions is that the parent undertaking does not control its subsidiary undertaking … Generally, restrictions are dealt with better by disclosure than non-consolidation. However, the loss of the parent undertaking's control over its subsidiary undertaking resulting from severe long-term restrictions would make it misleading to include that subsidiary undertaking in the consolidation[426].'

---

420 Section 150A(2) of the CA 1963 and reg 14(1) of the EC(C:GA)R 1992.

421 See **[17.026]** *et seq*, *ante*.

422 As defined at **[17.023]** *ante*, Irish generally accepted accounting practice is taken as meaning the Standards of Standard Accounting Practice ('SSAPs'), issued until 1990 by the Accounting Standards Committee of the Consultative Committee of Accounting Bodies of the UK and Ireland, and the Financial Reporting Standards ('FRSs'), issued since 1990 by the Accounting Standards Board, the independent body which replaced the Accounting Standards Committee.

423 Regulation 10 of the EC(C:GA)R 1992.

424 Regulation 11 of the EC(C:GA)R 1992.

425 Paragraph 25(a) of FRS 2, *Accounting for Subsidiary Undertakings*, as amended in June 2009.

426 Paragraph 78(c) of FRS 2, *Accounting for Subsidiary Undertakings*, as amended in June 2009.

A subsidiary undertaking so excluded should be treated as a fixed asset investment[427]. In addition, Irish GAAP significantly limits the scope of the exclusion at (b), providing that it only applies to subsidiary undertakings that are not material:

> 'Neither disproportionate expense nor undue delay in obtaining the information necessary for the preparation of consolidated financial statements can justify excluding from consolidation subsidiary undertakings that are individually or collectively material in the context of the group[428].'

Finally, Irish GAAP again requires, rather than permits, exclusion[429] where an interest in a subsidiary undertaking is held exclusively with a view to subsequent resale, defining such an interest as:

> '(a) an interest for which a purchaser has been identified or is being sought, and which is reasonably expected to be disposed of within approximately one year of its date of acquisition; or
>
> (b) an interest that was acquired as a result of the enforcement of a security, unless the interest has become part of the continuing activities of the group or the holder acts as if it intends the interest to become so[430].

Such an interest should be recorded in the consolidated financial statements as a current asset at the lower of cost and the net realisable value[431].

[17.168] Previously, the EC(C:GA)R 1992 required the exclusion of subsidiary undertakings from consolidation when their activities were so different from those of other undertakings to be dealt with in the group accounts that their inclusion would be incompatible with the obligation to give a 'true and fair view'[432]. However this provision has been deleted by the EC(IFRSMA)R 2005[433].

[17.169] If Companies Act group accounts drawn up in accordance with the EC(C:GA)R 1992 would not provide sufficient information to give a 'true and fair view', the accounts must give any necessary additional information[434]. Where (in exceptional circumstances) the preparation of group accounts in accordance with the EC(C:GA)R 1992 would prevent the accounts from giving a 'true and fair view' (even if additional information were provided), departure from the requirements of the EC(C:GA)R 1992 so far as is necessary to ensure that the accounts would give a true and fair view is required[435]. Any such departure must be disclosed by way of a note to the group accounts, giving details of the departure, explaining the reason therefor and the effect on the group accounts[436].

---

427 Paragraph 27 of FRS 2, *Accounting for Subsidiary Undertakings*, as amended in June 2009.

428 Paragraph 24 of FRS 2, *Accounting for Subsidiary Undertakings*, as amended in June 2009.

429 Paragraph 25(b) of FRS 2, *Accounting for Subsidiary Undertakings*, as amended in June 2009.

430 Paragraph 11 of FRS 2, *Accounting for Subsidiary Undertakings*, as amended in June 2009.

431 Paragraph 29 of FRS 2, *Accounting for Subsidiary Undertakings*, as amended in June 2009.

432 Regulation 12 of the EC(C:GA)R 1992.

433 Regulation 6(i) of the EC(IFRSMA)R 2005.

434 Regulation 14(2) of the EC(C:GA)R 1992.

435 Regulation 14(3) of the EC(C:GA)R 1992.

436 Regulation 14(4) of the EC(C:GA)R 1992.

(b) Format of Companies Act group accounts

[17.170] In general, the format rules which apply to the preparation of individual accounts will also apply to the preparation of Companies Act group accounts, with any necessary modifications[437]. In particular, with reference to the disclosure requirements for dealings with or interests in group undertakings:

- Any subsidiary undertaking of the parent undertaking not dealt with in the group accounts shall be treated as a subsidiary undertaking of the group; and
- If the parent undertaking is itself a subsidiary undertaking, the group is to be treated as a subsidiary undertaking of any parent undertaking of the parent undertaking, and any reference to fellow subsidiary undertakings shall be construed accordingly[438].

In addition, where the directors are of the opinion that undue expense would be incurred in showing separately different categories of stocks, namely raw materials and consumables, work in progress, finished goods and goods for resale, and payments on account, those items may be combined in the group balance sheet and shown as a single item under the heading 'Stocks'[439].

(c) Contents of Companies Act group accounts

[17.171] The contents of Companies Act group accounts bear many similarities to the requirements for Companies Act individual accounts, except that the figures shown will be consolidated for the group as a whole. In addition to the items required to be shown in the accounts by s 4 of the C(A)A 1986 and the Schedule to the C(A)A 1986, the Schedule to the EC(C:GA)R 1992 set out items that are particular to group accounts.

First, separate items in respect of 'Minority Interest' must be stated on the face of the consolidated balance sheet and consolidated profit and loss account[440]. The amount to be shown in the balance sheet in this respect shall be the amount of capital and reserves, and that in the profit and loss account shall be the amount of any profit or loss on ordinary activities and the amount of any profit or loss on extraordinary activities, attributable to shares in subsidiary undertakings dealt with in the group accounts held by or on behalf of persons other than the parent undertaking and its subsidiary undertakings[441].

Second, the items entitled 'participating interests' in an individual balance sheet shall be replaced in a consolidated balance sheet by two items, 'Interests in associated undertakings' and 'Other participating interests', while the items headed 'Income from participating interests' in an individual profit and loss account shall be replaced in a consolidated profit and loss account by 'income from interests in associated undertakings' and 'income from other participating interests' [442].

---

437 Regulation 15(1) of the EC(C:GA)R 1992.

438 Regulation 15(2) of the EC(C:GA)R 1992.

439 Regulation 15(3) of the EC(C:GA)R 1992.

440 Paragraphs 8 and 9 of the Schedule to the EC(C:GA)R 1992.

441 Paragraphs 8 and 9 of the Schedule to the EC(C:GA)R 1992.

442 Paragraph 10 of the Schedule to the EC(C:GA)R 1992.

[17.172] The group accounts must not take intra-group transactions into account, as to do so would give an inaccurate view of the group as a whole. Accordingly, reg 25 of the EC(C:GA)R 1992 requires the accounts to show the assets, liabilities, state of affairs as at the end of the financial year and profit or loss of the parent undertaking and its subsidiary undertakings dealt with in the group accounts as if they were a single undertaking. In particular:

- debts and claims between the undertakings dealt with in the group accounts must be eliminated from the accounts;
- income and expenditure relating to transactions between the undertakings dealt with in the group accounts must be eliminated from the accounts; and
- where profits and losses resulting from transactions between the undertakings dealt with in the group accounts are included in the book values of assets, they must be eliminated from the accounts;

but these requirements need not be complied with where the amounts involved are not material for the purpose of giving a 'true and fair view'[443].

[17.173] Where the composition of the undertakings dealt with in the group accounts has changed significantly in the course of the financial year, the group accounts must include information which makes the comparison of successive sets of group accounts meaningful[444].

[17.174] The valuation methods contained in ss 5 and 6 of the C(A)A 1986 and in the Schedule to the C(A)A 1986 must be applied in computing the amounts to be stated in Companies Act group accounts, and must be applied consistently within those accounts[445]. A parent undertaking must employ the same methods of valuation in drawing up Companies Act group accounts as it employs in the preparation of its individual accounts, unless departure is necessary to give a 'true and fair view', or unless it is the case that the parent undertaking prepares IFRS group accounts[446]. If the assets and liabilities of an undertaking to be dealt with in group accounts have been valued according to a different method to that being used by the group accounts, they must be revalued in accordance with the method used in the group accounts and included in the group accounts on that basis, unless such revaluation is immaterial, or unless there are special reasons for departing from this provision[447]. All departures must be stated in a note to the accounts[448]. Account must be taken in Companies Act group accounts of any difference on consolidation between the tax chargeable for the financial year and for preceding financial years and the amount of tax payable in respect of those years, provided that it is probable that the actual charge to tax will arise within the foreseeable future for one of the undertakings dealt with in the accounts[449].

443 Regulation 25 of the EC(C:GA)R 1992.
444 Regulation 27 of the EC(C:GA)R 1992.
445 Regulation 28 of the EC(C:GA)R 1992.
446 Regulation 29 of the EC(C:GA)R 1992.
447 Regulation 30 of the EC(C:GA)R 1992.
448 Regulation 29(3) of the EC(C:GA)R 1992.
449 Regulation 31 of the EC(C:GA)R 1992.

[17.175] The methods of consolidation of Companies Act group accounts are to be applied consistently from one financial year to the next, unless it appears to the directors that there are special reasons for departure, whereupon particulars of the departure, the reasons for it and its effect on the accounts must be disclosed in a note to the accounts[450].

(d) Notes to Companies Act group accounts

[17.176] In addition to the information required by the C(A)A 1986 to be stated by way of note to the accounts[451], the EC(C:GA)R 1992 require the notes to Companies Act group accounts to state certain additional information, in relation to:

(i) Acquisitions;

(ii) Foreign currencies;

(iii) Details of indebtedness;

(iv) Particulars of staff;

(v) Directors' remuneration;

(vi) Valuation of assets;

(vii) Transactions involving directors and others; and

(viii) Miscellaneous matters.

In addition, a parent undertaking preparing Companies Act group accounts is required to make certain disclosures in respect of the remuneration of auditors, which is addressed at (ix) below.

(i) Acquisitions

[17.177] The disclosure obligations in relation to acquisitions are discussed below[452].

(ii) Foreign currencies

[17.178] Where sums brought into any items shown in the balance sheet or profit and loss account in Companies Act group accounts were originally denominated in currencies other than the currency in which the group accounts are drawn up, the conversion basis on which the sums have been translated is to be stated[453].

(iii) Details of indebtedness

[17.179] The EC(C:GA)R 1992 require a statement in respect of the aggregate of the amounts shown in the balance sheet under the heading 'Creditors', distinguishing between debts payable, either by instalment or otherwise after five years from the financial year-end, and setting out the nature of securities given for those debts[454], which is the same as that required in respect of Companies Act individual accounts by para 34(1) of the Schedule to the C(A)A 1986[455].

450 Regulation 24 of the EC(C:GA)R 1992.

451 See **[17.069]** *et seq, ante*.

452 See para **[17.190]**.

453 Paragraph 13 of the Schedule to the EC(C:GA)R 1992.

454 Paragraph 14 of the Schedule to the EC(C:GA)R 1992.

455 See **[17.087]** *et seq, ante*.

(iv) Particulars of staff

[17.180] The regulations require the same information to be given in respect of persons employed by the undertakings dealt with in the group accounts as is required of individual companies by para 42 of the Schedule to the C(A)A 1986[456], except that the requirement is to set out the aggregate amount of staff costs (save insofar as this amount is stated in the group profit and loss account) rather than setting out separately wages and salaries paid, social welfare costs; and other pension costs. The average number of persons employed during the financial year by an undertaking proportionally consolidated must also be stated in Companies Act group accounts[457].

(v) Directors' remuneration

[17.181] The obligations set out in the C(A)A 1986 in relation to Companies Act individual accounts to make disclosures in respect of pension commitments, and emoluments and compensation in respect of loss of office to directors or past directors[458], apply equally to Companies Act group accounts. In the case of Companies Act group accounts, these disclosures are to encompass such commitments, emoluments and compensation relating to directors or past directors of the parent undertaking in respect of duties relating to the parent undertaking, to any of its subsidiary undertakings, to any undertakings proportionally consolidated, or to associated undertakings[459]. Significantly, the disclosure obligations set out in s 191 of the CA 1963 in respect of directors' emoluments shall not apply to Companies Act group accounts[460].

(vi) Valuation of assets

[17.182] Where financial instruments have been included at fair value pursuant to Part IIIA of the Schedule to the C(A)A 1986[461], Companies Act group accounts are required to state:

(a) the significant assumptions underlying the valuation models and techniques for determining the fair values;

(b) for each category of financial instrument, in respect of the instruments in that category:

  (i) the fair value of those instruments;

  (ii) the amounts included in the profit and loss account; and

  (iii) the amounts credited to or debited from the fair value reserve;

(c) for each class of derivative financial instrument, the extent and nature of the instruments including significant terms and conditions;

(d) a table showing movements in the fair value reserve during the year[462].

---

456 See **[17.101]** *ante*.

457 Paragraph 15 of the Schedule to the EC(C:GA)R 1992.

458 See **[17.112]** *et seq, ante*.

459 Paragraph 16(1) of the Schedule to the EC(C:GA)R 1992.

460 Paragraph 16(2) of the Schedule to the EC(C:GA)R 1992.

461 See **[17.046]** *et seq, ante*.

462 Paragraph 16A of the Schedule to the EC(C:GA)R 1992.

Where 'financial instruments at fair value' has not been applied, there shall be stated in respect of each class of derivative financial instrument:

(a) the fair value of the instruments in that class, if such a value can be determined; and

(b) the extent and nature of the instruments[463].

[17.183] Where the group has financial fixed assets that could be included at fair value, the amount at which those assets are included in the Companies Act group accounts is in excess of their fair value, and no provision has been made for the diminution in value of those assets in accordance with para 7(1) of the Schedule to the C(A)A 1986[464], the notes must state:

(a) the amounts at which the assets (either individually or grouped appropriately) are stated in the company's group accounts;

(b) the fair value of those assets or groupings; and

(c) the reason for not making a provision for diminution in value of those assets, including the nature of the evidence that provides the basis for the belief that the book value will be recovered[465].

[17.184] Where amounts have been included at fair value in Companies Act group accounts in respect of investment property or living animals and plants, the balance sheet items affected and the basis of valuation in the case of each item shall be disclosed in a note to those accounts. In addition, in the case of investment property, these shall be shown, either in the consolidated balance sheet or in a note to the Companies Act group accounts:

(a) the comparable amounts determined according to historical cost accounting rules (ie, the aggregate amount which would be required to be shown if the amounts to be included in respect of all the assets covered were determined according to those rules, and the aggregate amount of cumulative provisions for depreciation or diminution in value which would be permitted or required in determining those amounts according to those rules); and

(b) the differences between those comparable amounts and the corresponding amounts actually shown in the consolidated balance sheet in respect of that item[466].

(vii) Transactions involving directors and others

[17.185] The EC(C:GA)R 1992 extend the provisions of ss 41–43 of the CA 1990 to Companies Act group accounts[467]. Transactions, arrangements and agreements entered into by a director of the parent undertaking with an undertaking proportionally consolidated[468] or an associated undertaking[469] must also be stated[470]. It should be noted,

---

463 Paragraph 16B of the Schedule to the EC(C:GA)R 1992.

464 See **[17.047]** *ante*.

465 Paragraph 16C of the Schedule to the EC(C:GA)R 1992.

466 Paragraph 16D of the Schedule to the EC(C:GA)R 1992.

467 Paragraph 17(1) of the Schedule to the EC(C:GA)R 1992.

468 See **[17.196]** *post*.

469 See **[17.197]** *post*.

however, that ss 41–43 of the CA 1990 refer to holding companies and their subsidiaries rather than to parent undertakings and their subsidiary undertakings.

(viii) Miscellaneous matters

[17.186] The following information is to be given in relation to each undertaking dealt with in Companies Act group accounts (including the parent undertaking where appropriate):

(1) The name and registered office of the undertaking;
(2) The aggregate of the qualifying capital interests[471] held in that undertaking by the undertakings dealt with in the group accounts as a proportion of the total of such interests;
(3) Which of the provisions of reg 4 of the EC(C:GA)R 1992 gave rise to the undertaking being dealt with in the group accounts.

The information required by (3) above may be omitted where the undertaking has been dealt with in the group accounts by virtue of the parent undertaking holding or controlling alone a majority of the voting rights, or being a shareholder or member of it and controlling the composition of the board of directors, where the proportion of capital and the proportion of voting rights held are the same.

[17.187] The information referred to in (1) to (3) above is also to be given in respect of:

- Each undertaking which is excluded from the group accounts by virtue of the exemptions from consolidation[472];
- Each associated undertaking[473];
- Each undertaking that has been proportionally consolidated[474];
- Each undertaking of substantial interest[475].

In respect of each joint venture proportionally consolidated, the nature of the joint management must also be stated[476]. An undertaking of substantial interest for the purposes of this disclosure obligation is defined as an undertaking, other than a subsidiary undertaking, associated undertaking or joint venture, in which undertakings dealt with in the group accounts, or persons acting in their own name but on behalf of such undertakings, between them hold a qualifying capital interest[477] representing 20% or more of such interests[478].

[17.188] The nature of the joint management of each joint venture proportionally consolidated must be stated. In addition, the amount of capital, reserves, and profit or loss for each undertaking of substantial interest must be stated[479], unless it is of

---

470 Paragraph 17(2) of the Schedule to the EC(C:GA)R 1992.

471 See **[17.199]** *post*.

472 Paragraph 19 of the Schedule to the EC(C:GA)R 1992; See **[17.156]** *et seq, ante* in respect of the exemptions.

473 Paragraph 20 of the Schedule to the EC(C:GA)R 1992.

474 Paragraph 21 of the Schedule to the EC(C:GA)R 1992.

475 Paragraph 22 of the Schedule to the EC(C:GA)R 1992.

476 Paragraph 21(2) of the Schedule to the EC(C:GA)R 1992.

477 See **[17.199]** *post*.

478 Paragraph 22(1) of the Schedule to the EC(C:GA)R 1992.

negligible importance, or the undertaking is not required to attach a balance sheet to its annual return and the qualifying capital interest is less than 50%[480].

(ix) Remuneration of statutory auditors

[17.189] Where a parent undertaking is preparing Companies Act group accounts, it shall disclose in the notes to its consolidated accounts relating to each financial year the remuneration for all work carried out in respect of that financial year, and in respect of the preceding financial year, by the group auditor.

This remuneration shall, similarly to the disclosure in respect of individual accounts[481], be disclosed separately for each of the following categories of work:

(a) the audit of the group accounts;
(b) other assurance services;
(c) tax advisory services;
(d) other non-audit services.

As with individual accounts, where all or part of the remuneration is in the form of a benefit in kind, the nature and estimated monetary value of the benefit must be disclosed.

(d) Acquisition and merger accounting

[17.190] The EC(C:GA)R 1992 provide that one of two accounting methods must be employed where a subsidiary undertaking is acquired: namely the acquisition method and the merger method[482]. Where an undertaking becomes a subsidiary undertaking, that event is referred to in the regulations as its 'acquisition'[483]. An acquisition is to be accounted for by the acquisition method unless the conditions for accounting for it as a merger are met and the merger method of accounting is adopted[484]. Where the acquisition is of a group, as opposed to an individual undertaking, the following regulations apply with the necessary adaptations[485].

An acquisition is required to be accounted for by the acquisition method unless the conditions for accounting for it as a merger are met and the directors choose to adopt the merger method[486]. Those conditions for accounting for an acquisition as a merger are as follows:

- at least 90% of the nominal value of the relevant shares in the undertaking acquired is held by or on behalf of the undertakings dealt with in the group accounts;
- that 90% threshold was attained pursuant to the arrangement providing for the issue of equity shares by the undertakings dealt with in the group accounts; and
- the fair value of any consideration other than the issue of equity shares given pursuant to the arrangement by the undertakings dealt with in the group

479 Paragraph 21 of the Schedule to the EC(C:GA)R 1992.
480 Paragraph 22 of the Schedule to the EC(C:GA)R 1992.
481 See **[17.112]** *ante*.
482 Regulation 18 of the EC(C:GA)R 1992.
483 Regulation 17(1) of the EC(C:GA)R 1992.
484 Regulation 18 of the EC(C:GA)R 1992.
485 Regulation 23 of the EC(C:GA)R 1992.
486 Regulation 18 of the EC(C:GA)R 1992.

accounts did not exceed 10% of the nominal value of the equity shares issued[487].

The merger method is therefore allowed as an option where shares in a target undertaking are acquired in exchange for shares in the acquiring undertaking. 'Relevant shares' are those carrying unrestricted rights to participate both in distributions and in the assets of the undertaking upon liquidation[488].

(i) Acquisition accounting

[17.191] The acquisition method is defined as follows:

- The identifiable assets and liabilities of the undertaking acquired shall be included in the consolidated balance sheet at their fair values as at the date of acquisition. In this paragraph the 'identifiable assets or liabilities' means the assets or liabilities which are capable of being disposed of or discharged separately, without disposing of a business of the undertaking.
- The income and expenditure of the undertaking acquired shall be brought into the group accounts only as from the date of acquisition.
- There shall be set off against the acquisition cost of the interest in the shares of the undertaking held by the undertakings dealt with in the group accounts, the interest of the undertakings dealt with in the group accounts in the adjusted capital and reserves of the undertaking acquired.

The 'acquisition cost' means the amount of any cash consideration and the fair value of any other consideration, together with such amounts (if any) in respect of fees and other expenses of the acquisition as the parent undertaking may determine, and the 'adjusted capital and reserves' of the undertaking acquired means its capital and reserves at the date of the acquisition after adjusting the identifiable assets and liabilities of the undertaking to fair values as at that date. If the resulting amount is positive it must be treated as goodwill and treated in the manner in which goodwill is treated under the C(A)A 1986, but if it is negative it must be treated as a negative consolidation difference[489].

The EC(C:GA)R 1992 include a transition provision, which is extremely unlikely to have effect in any current situation, whereby where a parent undertaking acquired a subsidiary undertaking before 17 July 1992 (the date of introduction of the EC(C:GA)R 1992), but had not previously included that subsidiary in the group accounts, and there is no record of the fair values as at the date of acquisition of the identifiable assets or of the acquisition cost of the interest in shares of the acquired undertaking held by the undertakings dealt with in the group accounts, the earliest available record of those costs may be used. A similar provision applies where such records cannot be obtained without unreasonable expense or delay[490].

(ii) Merger accounting

[17.192] The merger method of accounting is defined as follows[491]:

487 Regulation 21(1) of the EC(C:GA)R 1992.

488 Regulation 21(2) of the EC(C:GA)R 1992.

489 Regulation 19 of the EC(C:GA)R 1992.

490 Regulation 20 of the EC(C:GA)R 1992.

- The assets and liabilities of the undertaking acquired shall be brought into the group accounts at the figures at which they stand in the undertaking's accounts, subject to any adjustment authorised or required by the EC(C:GA)R 1992.
- The income and expenditure of the undertaking acquired is to be included in the group accounts for the entire financial year, including the period before the acquisition.
- The group accounts shall show corresponding amounts relating to the previous financial year as if the undertaking had been included in the consolidation throughout that year.
- The nominal value of the issued share capital of the undertaking acquired held by the undertakings dealt with in the group accounts is to be set-off against the aggregate of:
  - (a) the appropriate amount in respect of shares issued by the undertakings dealt with in the group accounts as part of the merger arrangement in consideration for the acquisition of shares in the undertaking acquired; and
  - (b) the fair value of any other consideration for the acquisition of shares in the undertaking acquired, determined as at the date when those shares were acquired.
- The resulting amount is to be shown as an adjustment to the consolidated reserves.

[17.193] Therefore, under the merger method, the balance sheets of the undertakings are simply added together, the nominal value of the two sets of shares exchanged cancelling each other out as far as possible and the difference being provided for as an adjustment in reserves.

[17.194] No provision has been made for merger relief, which raises the question as to whether the merger method of accounting breaches the rules of capital maintenance[492]. In the English case of *Henry Head v Ropner Holdings Ltd*[493], it was held that in a share-for-share exchange, where the nominal value of the bidder's shares was less than the market value of the target's shares, the difference had to be transferred to a share premium account by virtue of the English equivalent of s 62(1) of the CA 1963. The amounts provided for in the share premium account do not constitute profits available for distribution. Thus, in the later English case of *Shearer (Inspector of Taxes) v Bercain Ltd*[494], where the merger method of accounting was used so that differences were transferred to distributable reserves, it was held that an unauthorised reduction of capital had occurred. This effectively prohibited the merger method of accounting in the UK, and legislative steps were taken to introduce merger relief[495]. The effect of this relief was to supplant the requirement that the subsidiary's pre-acquisition profits be transferred to a share premium account which can only be applied in special circumstances. Instead,

491 Regulation 22 of the EC(C:GA)R 1992.

492 See Ch 10, *The Maintenance of Capital,* at para [**10.112**] *et seq*.

493 *Henry Head v Ropner Holdings Ltd* [1952] Ch 124.

494 *Shearer (Inspector of Taxes) v Bercain Ltd* [1980] 3 All ER 295.

495 Sections 131–135 of the UK CA 1985, since repealed and replaced by ss 611–613 of the UK CA 2006.

the relief permits pre-acquisition profits to be distributed to the parent company which can then distribute them to the shareholders.

Although no such relief has been introduced in this jurisdiction, s 149(5) of the CA 1963, for which there was no English counterpart at the time of the *Henry Head* and *Shearer* decisions, provides that where the directors and auditors are satisfied and certify that it would be fair and reasonable and would not prejudice the rights of any person, the pre-acquisition profits or losses attributable to any shares in a subsidiary may be treated in the holding company's accounts as revenue profits or losses. Arguably, it would seem reasonable for the directors and auditors to so certify where the EC(C:GA)R 1992 permit merger accounting – provided, of course, that the parent undertaking is a holding company within the meaning of the CA 1963[496], and that the rights and interests of any person would not be prejudiced. In practice, however, there is very strong resistance from the accounting profession to provide such certification under s 149(5) of the CA 1963.

(iii) Disclosures in notes relating to acquisitions and mergers

[17.195] The EC(C:GA)R 1992 require the following disclosures concerning acquisitions of subsidiary undertakings to be made in the notes to Companies Act group accounts:

- As regards the positive or negative amount resulting under the acquisition method, the methods used in calculating those amounts and the reasons for any significant difference between such amounts for the financial year to which the group accounts refer and those for the preceding financial year; and
- As regards acquisitions taking place in the financial year:
  (a) the name and registered office of the undertaking acquired during the financial year, or where a group was acquired, the name and registered office of the parent undertaking of that group; and
  (b) whether the acquisition has been accounted for by the acquisition or the merger method of accounting[497].

It should be observed that the note disclosure requirements in Irish GAAP are more onerous, and that failure to observe these could amount to a breach of the 'true and fair view' requirement.

(e) Joint ventures

[17.196] Where a parent undertaking or one of its subsidiary undertakings dealt with in the group accounts manages another undertaking (the 'joint venture') jointly with one or more undertakings not dealt with in the group accounts, the joint venture may, if it is not a body corporate or a subsidiary undertaking of the parent undertaking, be proportionally consolidated in the group accounts in proportion to the rights in its capital held by the parent undertaking or the subsidiary undertakings dealt with in the group accounts as the case may be[498]. Where a joint venture is proportionally consolidated, the following information shall be stated in the notes to Companies Act group accounts[499]:

---

[496] See **[17.154]** *ante*.

[497] Paragraph 12 of the Schedule to the EC(C:GA)R 1992.

[498] Regulation 32(1) of the EC(C:GA)R 1992.

[499] See **[17.195]** *ante*.

(a) the name and registered office of the undertaking;

(b) the aggregate of the qualifying capital interests held in the joint venture by the undertakings dealt with in the group accounts as a proportion of the total of such interests; and

(c) the nature of the joint management of each joint venture[500].

Note that proportional consolidation in such circumstances is permitted, but is not mandatory. Where a joint venture is not proportionally consolidated, it is likely that it will be treated as an associated undertaking[501] or an undertaking of substantial interest[502].

(f) Associated undertakings

[17.197] The interest of an undertaking dealt with in Companies Act group accounts in an associated undertaking, and the amount of profit or loss attributable to such an interest, shall be shown in the group accounts by way of the equity method of accounting unless the amounts in question are immaterial for the purpose of providing a 'true and fair view,' and any goodwill must be dealt with in accordance with the provisions of the C(A)A 1986[503]. If the associated undertaking is itself a parent undertaking, the net assets and profits or losses to be taken into account are those of the associated-parent undertaking and its subsidiaries after the making of any consolidation adjustments[504].

[17.198] What constitutes the equity method of accounting is not defined in the EC(C:GA)R 1992; however, Irish GAAP sets out detailed provisions concerning the mechanics of equity accounting[505].

[17.199] An 'associated undertaking' is an undertaking in which an undertaking dealt with in the group accounts holds a qualifying capital interest on a long-term basis for the purpose of securing a contribution to that undertaking's own activities by the exercise of control or influence arising from or related to that interest (a 'participating interest'[506]), and over whose operating and financial policy it exercises a significant influence[507]. A 'qualifying capital interest' is defined as:

> '(a) in relation to an undertaking with share capital, an interest in shares;
>
> (b) in relation to an undertaking with capital but no share capital, an interest conferring rights to share in the capital;
>
> (c) in relation to an undertaking without capital, means interests—
>
> (i) conferring any right to share in the profits or liability to contribute to the losses of the undertaking; or
>
> (ii) giving rise to an obligation to contribute to the debts or expenses of the undertaking in the event of a winding-up; and

500 Paragraph 21 of the Schedule to the EC(C:GA)R 1992.

501 See **[17.197]** *post*.

502 See **[17.199]** *post*.

503 Regulation 33(1) and (3) of the EC(C:GA)R 1992.

504 Regulation 33(2) of the EC(C:GA)R 1992.

505 Paragraphs 31–37 of FRS 9.

506 Regulation 35(1) of the EC(C:GA)R 1992.

507 Regulation 34(1) of the EC(C:GA)R 1992.

(d) includes an interest which is convertible into a qualifying capital interest as well as an option to acquire any such qualifying capital interest[508].'

The associated undertaking must not be a subsidiary of the parent undertaking, or a joint venture which has been proportionally consolidated[509]. Where an undertaking holds 20% or more of the voting rights in another undertaking it is presumed to exercise a significant influence unless the contrary is shown[510].

[17.200] As set out above[511], information in respect of each associated undertaking concerning the name and registered office of that undertaking, and the aggregate of the qualifying capital interests held in that undertaking by undertakings dealt with in the group accounts as a proportion of the total of such interests, is required to be stated in the notes to Companies Act group accounts[512].

IFRS group accounts

[17.201] As stated above, IFRS group accounts are defined as group accounts prepared 'in accordance with international financial reporting standards'[513]. In addition, s 150B of the CA 1963 requires that where IFRS group accounts are prepared, the notes to those accounts must state that the accounts have been prepared in accordance with international financial reporting standards, and must also include in the notes to the accounts[514] specified information regarding the following matters:

(a) Directors' remuneration;
(b) Transactions with directors;
(c) Interests in shares and debentures;
(d) Details of group undertakings;
(e) Details of staff numbers and remuneration;
(f) Details of share capital and debentures;
(g) Restriction on distributability of profits;
(h) Guarantees and other financial commitments;
(i) Financial assistance for the purchase of own shares;
(j) Shares and debentures held by subsidiary undertakings;
(k) Off-balance sheet arrangements.

It should be noted that s 150B of the CA 1963, in setting out the information to be included in the notes to IFRS group accounts, includes an entry in respect of the remuneration of auditors. However the reference in s 150B(2)(k) of the CA 1963 to para

508 Regulation 35(2) of the EC(C:GA)R 1992.

509 Regulation 34(1)(a) and (b) of the EC(C:GA)R 1992.

510 Regulation 34(2) of the EC(C:GA)R 1992.

511 See para **[17.196]**.

512 Paragraph 20 of the Schedule to the EC(C:GA)R 1992.

513 Section 150(2)(a) of the CA 1963.

514 As for individual accounts as noted at **[17.121]** *ante*, the information at (c) may alternatively be set out in the directors' report (this is also the case where Companies Act group accounts are prepared).

39(5) of the Schedule to the C(A)A 1986 has been deleted by reg 4(3) of the EC(SA)(D)R 2010[515], and the only remaining reference in s 150B in this respect is to s 205D of the CA 1990. In addition, reg 120 of the EC(SA)(D)R 2010, which requires disclosures of the remuneration of statutory auditors, applies only to group accounts that are prepared in accordance with the EC(C:GA)R 1992, the European Communities (Credit Institutions: Accounts) Regulations 1992 (SI 294/1992) or the European Communities (Insurance Undertakings: Accounts) Regulations 1996 (SI23/1996)[516], and therefore does not apply to IFRS group accounts. It therefore appears that there is no statutory obligation in respect of the disclosure of auditors' remuneration in IFRS group accounts.

(a) Directors' remuneration

[17.202] A company preparing IFRS group accounts is required to meet the same disclosure obligation as a company preparing Companies Act group accounts, as set out in para 16 of the Schedule to the EC(C:GA)R 1992, and as addressed above[517]. In addition, a company preparing IFRS group accounts is expressly required also to meet the disclosure obligation in s 191 of the CA 1963[518]. This obligation is set out above in the context of individual accounts[519], and applies to IFRS group accounts *mutatis mutandis*.

(b) Transactions with directors

[17.203] A company preparing IFRS group accounts is required by virtue of para 17 of the Schedule to the EC(C:GA)R 1992 to disclose matters relating to ss 41–45 of the CA 1990. This obligation is set out above in relation to Companies Act group accounts[520], and applies equally to the preparation of IFRS group accounts.

(c) Interests in shares and debentures

[17.204] A company preparing IFRS group accounts is required to set out the disclosures required by s 63 of the CA 1990. This obligation is set out above in respect of individual accounts[521], and applies to IFRS group accounts *mutatis mutandis*.

(d) Details of group undertakings

[17.205] The disclosure obligation in this respect comprises, subject to reg 36 of the EC(C:GA)R 1992, the matters set out in paras 18 to 22 of the Schedule to the EC(C:GA)R 1992. This obligation is set out above in relation to Companies Act group accounts[522], and applies equally to the preparation of IFRS group accounts.

(e) Details of staff numbers and remuneration

[17.206] A company preparing IFRS group accounts is required to disclose the details required by para 15 of the Schedule to the EC(C:GA)R 1992. This obligation is set out above

---

515 Being, as defined at **[17.122]** *ante*, the European Communities (Statutory Audits) (Directive 2006/43/EC) Regulations 2010 (SI 220/2010).

516 Regulation 120(7) of the EC(SA)(D)R 2010.

517 See para **[17.181]**.

518 Section 150B(2)(a) of the CA 1963.

519 See para **[17.132]**.

520 See para **[17.185]**.

521 See para **[17.134]**.

522 See para **[17.186]** and **[17.187]**.

in relation to Companies Act group accounts[523], and applies equally to the preparation of IFRS group accounts.

(f) Details of share capital and debentures

[17.207] The disclosure obligation is as set out in paras 26 to 28 of the Schedule to the C(A)A 1986. This obligation is set out above in respect of individual accounts[524], and applies to IFRS group accounts with the necessary alterations.

(g) Restriction on distributability of profits

[17.208] A company preparing IFRS group accounts is required to set out the information required in para 32A of the Schedule to the C(A)A 1986. This obligation is set out above in respect of individual accounts[525], and applies to IFRS group accounts with the necessary alterations.

(h) Guarantees and other financial commitments

[17.209] A company preparing IFRS group accounts is required to make the disclosures required by para 36 of the Schedule to the C(A)A 1986. These disclosures are set out above in relation to individual accounts[526], and apply to IFRS group accounts with any required amendments.

(i) Financial assistance for the purchase of own shares

[17.210] The disclosure obligation in this respect is as set out in para 37(2) of the Schedule to the C(A)A 1986, and corresponds to the obligation addressed above in relation to individual accounts[527].

(j) Shares and debentures held by subsidiary undertakings

[17.211] A company preparing IFRS group accounts is required to meet the disclosure obligation in para 46 of the Schedule to the C(A)A 1986. The disclosure obligation is set out above in relation to individual accounts[528], and applies to IFRS group accounts with any necessary alterations.

(k) Off-balance sheet arrangements

[17.212] Regulation 7(1) of the European Communities (Directive 2006/46/EC) Regulations 2009 (SI 450/2009) require that the notes on the consolidated accounts prepared in respect of a parent undertaking and its subsidiary undertakings shall set out information relating to:

> '(a) the nature and business purpose of any arrangement that is not included in the consolidated balance sheet, and the financial impact of such arrangement if the risks or benefits arising from the arrangement are material, and in so far as the disclosure of such risks or benefits is necessary for assessing the financial position, taken as a whole, of the parent undertaking and its subsidiary undertakings included in the consolidated balance sheet, and

---

523 See para **[17.180]**.
524 See para **[17.136]**.
525 See para **[17.137]**.
526 See para **[17.138]**.
527 See para **[17.139]**.
528 See para **[17.141]**.

(b) subject to reg 7(2), transactions entered into by—

(i) the parent undertaking, or

(ii) a subsidiary undertaking of that parent undertaking included in the consolidation,

with related parties, if the transactions are material and have not been concluded under normal market conditions and the information shall include the amounts of such transactions, the nature of the related party relationship and other information about the transactions which is necessary for an understanding of the financial position, taken as a whole, of the parent undertaking and its subsidiary undertakings included in the consolidation.

Regulation 7(2) provides that a transaction referred to in para (1)(b) does not include an intra-group transaction. Information provided pursuant to reg (1)(b) above concerning individual transactions may be aggregated according to their nature, save where separate information is necessary for an understanding of the effects of the related party transactions on the financial position, taken as a whole, of the parent undertaking and its subsidiary undertakings included in the consolidation.

[E] APPROVAL OF ACCOUNTS

Signature and circulation of the balance sheet and profit and loss account

[17.213] Where the directors of a company prepare Companies Act individual accounts, every balance sheet and profit and loss account of the company, and where the directors prepare IFRS individual accounts, every balance sheet and income statement of the company, must be signed on behalf of the directors by two of them[529]. The signing is, however, only evidence that they have been approved by the board of directors, since two directors cannot unilaterally adopt the accounts. The formal adoption of the accounts must be done by resolution of the board of directors which may nominate two of its number to sign the accounts as required by s 156(1) of the CA 1963.

As well as the balance sheet, the accounts to be so approved comprise the profit and loss account, any group accounts, and the auditor's report, which must be annexed to the balance sheet prior to the approval and signing[530].

If any copy of a balance sheet or profit or loss account is issued, circulated, or published without compliance with the above requirements, the company and every officer of the company who is in default, shall be liable to a class C fine[531]. There is no prohibition[532], however, on the issue, circulation or publication of either:

(a) a fair and accurate summary of a balance sheet or profit and loss account and the auditor's report thereon, after the profit and loss account and balance sheet have been signed on behalf of the directors, or

(b) a fair and accurate summary of the profit or loss figures for part of the company's financial year.

529 Section 156(1) of the CA 1963.

530 Section 157(1) of the CA 1963.

531 Sections 156(3) and 157(2) of the CA 1963.

532 Section 156(4) of the CA 1963.

As set out below[533], the directors' report, and, where the corporate governance statement is produced in the form of a separate report, that report, must also be signed on behalf of the directors by two of the directors[534].

[F] Directors' Report

General obligation

[17.214] There is an obligation on every company preparing accounts (whether Companies Act accounts or IFRS accounts) that there shall be attached to the balance sheet laid before the AGM a *report by the directors* on the state of affairs of the company and, if it is a holding company, on the state of affairs of the company and its subsidiaries as a group[535]. The report must state[536]:

- the amount, if any, which the directors recommend should be paid by way of dividend, and the amount, if any, which they propose to carry to reserves[537];
- details of any change during the financial year in the nature of the business of the company or of its subsidiaries, or in the classes of business in which the company has a direct or indirect interest, so far as this is material for the appreciation of the state of the company's affairs[538];
- a statement of the measures taken by the directors to secure compliance with the requirement to keep proper books of account[539] and the exact location of those books[540];
- particulars of all contributions given for political purposes to an Irish-registered party, or to a party or individual contesting European, Dáil, Seanad, Irish local or Irish presidential elections where the aggregate donated to any particular person exceeds €5,079 in the financial year[541].

In the case of the few private companies that are licensed banks, the report must also include a copy of any 'disclosure issue notice' issued during the financial year under s 33AK of the Central Bank Act 1942[542].

Either the directors' report or the notes to the company's accounts must state whether a director or secretary was interested in shares or debentures of the company, its subsidiaries, its holding company, or subsidiaries of its holding company at the end of

---

533 See para **[17.221]**.

534 Section 158(2) and (6F) of the CA 1963.

535 Section 158(1) of the CA 1963.

536 The requirement under s 12(6) of the Safety Health and Welfare at Work Act 1989 that the directors' report also contain an evaluation of the extent to which the policy set out in a safety statement under Part II of that Act was fulfilled during the financial year has been removed by the repeal of that Act by the Safety, Health and Welfare at Work Act 2005, which imposes no corresponding obligation in respect of the directors' report.

537 Section 158(1) of the CA 1963.

538 Section 158(3) of the CA 1963.

539 See **[17.005]** *et seq, ante*.

540 Section 158(6A) of the CA 1963.

541 Section 26 of the Electoral Act 1997.

542 Section 158(6B) of the CA 1963.

the financial year, and, if so, the body or bodies and the number and amount of shares or debentures of each body held, distinguishing numbers and amounts held at the beginning of the financial year from those at the end[543].

[17.215] In addition, the directors' report must contain the following information[544]:

- a fair review of the development and performance of the business and the position of the company and of its subsidiary undertakings during the financial year, together with a description of the principal risks and uncertainties that the company and its subsidiary undertakings face, which shall be a balanced and comprehensive analysis, consistent with the size and complexity of the business, and shall include (to the extent necessary) an analysis of relevant key performance indicators;
- particulars of any important events since the end of the financial year which affect the company or its subsidiaries;
- an indication of likely future development, if any, in the business of the company and its subsidiaries;
- an indication of the research and development activities, if any, of the company or its subsidiaries;
- an indication of the existence of branches of the company located outside the State and the country in which each branch is located;
- in relation to the use by the company and its subsidiaries, if any, of financial instruments, and where material to the company and the group, the financial risk management objectives and policies of the company and the group, including the hedging policy for each major type of forecasted transaction, and the exposure of the company and the group to price risk, credit risk, liquidity risk and cash flow risk[545];

In addition, the directors' report must set out the following information regarding shares[546]:

- the number and nominal value of any of the company's own shares acquired by the company or by another person by way of forfeiture or surrender, or otherwise than for valuable consideration;
- the maximum number and nominal value of shares so acquired held at any time during the financial year;
- the number and nominal value of shares so acquired which are disposed of or cancelled during the financial year;
- the percentage of called-up share capital which any shares so acquired, disposed of, or cancelled represent;
- the reasons for the acquisition; and
- the amount or value of the consideration received in each case where any of the shares so acquired are acquired or disposed of for consideration.

---

543 Section 63 of the CA 1990.

544 Section 13(1) of the C(A)A 1986.

545 Section 13 of the C(A)A 1986.

546 Section 14 of the C(A)A 1986.

Additional obligations in respect of Companies Act group accounts

[17.216] In the case of a parent undertaking preparing group accounts in accordance with the EC(C:GA)R 1992 (ie, Companies Act group accounts), the directors' report is required[547] to contain, in addition to the information specified above[548], the following information as required by reg 37(1) of EC(C:GA)R 1992:

(a) a fair review of the development and performance of the parent undertaking and of its subsidiary undertakings, and of the position of the group as a whole, together with a description of the principal risks and uncertainties that the company and its subsidiary undertakings face, which shall be a balanced and comprehensive analysis, consistent with the size and complexity of the business, and shall include (to the extent necessary) an analysis of relevant key performance indicators;

(b) particulars of any important events since the end of the financial year which affect the parent undertaking or its subsidiary undertakings;

(c) an indication of likely future developments in the business of the parent undertaking and its subsidiary undertakings;

(d) an indication of the research and development activities, if any, of the parent undertaking or its subsidiary undertakings;

(e) the number and nominal value of shares in the parent undertaking held by the undertaking itself, by its subsidiary undertakings or by a person acting on behalf of those undertakings;

(f) in relation to the use by the parent undertaking and its subsidiary undertakings of financial instruments, and where material to the group, the financial risk management objectives and policies of the group, including the hedging policy for each major type of forecasted transaction, and the exposure of the group to price risk, credit risk, liquidity risk and cash flow risk.

The information required at (e) may instead be included in the notes to the group accounts[549].

Additional obligations in respect of IFRS individual and group accounts

[17.217] There is an obligation on companies preparing Companies Act[550] accounts to disclose, in the notes to the accounts, information in respect of subsidiaries and other bodies corporate. Accordingly, the obligation that would otherwise arise to disclose this information in the directors' report[551] is disapplied for such companies[552]. The obligation to set out this information in the directors' report therefore only applies in respect of IFRS accounts, in which case it is required[553] that the company lists every body corporate:

---

547 Regulation 37(1) of the EC(C:GA)R 1992.

548 See para **[17.214]**.

549 Regulation 37(2) of the EC(C:GA)R 1992.

550 Section 16 of the C(A)A 1986.

551 Section 158(4) of the CA 1963.

552 Section 16(5) of the C(A)A 1986.

(a) which is a subsidiary of the company; or

(b) in which the company has a beneficial shareholding of more than 20% in nominal value of the shares carrying voting rights.

The list shall distinguish between subsidiaries and other such bodies corporate, and shall state in relation to each its name, place of incorporation and the nature of the business carried on by it.

Additional obligation in respect of companies listed on a regulated market

[17.218] A company whose securities are admitted to trading on a regulated market[554] must include as a specific section of the directors report a corporate governance statement[555]. In the case of a private company, this can only apply to where it has issued debt securities which have been listed by being admitted to trading on a regulated market, as permitted since the commencement of the IFCMPA 2006[556]. For such companies, the directors' report must include, at least, all the following information[557]:

(a) a reference to:

  (i) the corporate governance code, being publicly available, to which either the company is subject or which it has voluntarily decided to apply; and

  (ii) all relevant information concerning corporate governance practices applied in respect of the company and additional to statutory requirements, where the information on such practices is available for inspection by the public;

(b) where the company departs, in accordance with a statutory provision or by choice, from the corporate governance code at (a)(i), an explanation as to the nature of the departure and of the reasons for that departure;

(c) a description of the main features of the internal control and risk management systems of the company in relation to the financial reporting process;

(d) where the company is subject to the European Communities (Takeover Bids (Directive 2004/25/EC) Regulations 2006 (SI 255/2006), the following information:

  (i) to the extent not already required to be disclosed pursuant to s 67 or s 91 of the CA 1990, in the case of each person with a significant direct or indirect holding of securities in the company, such details as are known to the company of the identity of the person, and the size and nature of the holding;

---

553 Section 158(4) of the CA 1963; but pursuant to s 158(6) of the CA 1963, this requirement shall not apply to a company which is principally engaged in the acquisition and underwriting of securities of companies carrying on a trade or industry in the State and which holds a certificate of exemption issued by the Minister ('Minister' currently refers to the Minister for Jobs, Enterprise and Innovation).

554 As noted at **[17.148]** *ante*, such a company may prepare either Companies Act individual accounts or IFRS individual accounts but, if it is a parent company, will be required to prepare IFRS group accounts.

555 Section 158(6C) of the CA 1963.

556 See Ch 18, *Corporate Borrowing: Debentures and Security*, at para **[18.021]**.

557 Section 158(6D) of the CA 1963.

(ii) in the case of each person who holds securities carrying special rights with regard to control of the company, the identity of the person, and the nature of the rights;

(iii) any restrictions on voting rights, including in particular limitations on voting rights, deadlines for exercising voting rights, and arrangements by which, with the company's cooperation, financial rights carried by securities are held by a person other than the holder of the securities;

(iv) any rules which the company has in force concerning appointment and replacement of directors, or amendment of the company's articles of association; or

(v) the powers of the company's directors, including in particular any powers in relation to the issuing or buying back by the company of its shares;

(e) a description of the operation of the shareholder meeting, the key powers of that meeting, shareholders' rights and the exercise of such rights; and

(f) the composition and operation of the board of directors and the committees of the board of directors with administrative, management and supervisory functions.

A company which does not have shares admitted to trading on a regulated market shall only be required to provide the information at (c) and (d) above, unless the company has issued shares which are traded in a multilateral trading facility[558].

[17.219] Rather than include the above information in the directors' report, it may be set out in a separate report[559], in which case that report must be attached to every balance sheet of the company, laid before the AGM, should be signed on behalf of the directors by two of them[560], and must be:

(i) published on the website of the company, and a statement that it has been so published included in the directors' report; or

(ii) annexed to the annual return, and certified by a director and the secretary as a true copy of the corporate governance statement laid or to be laid before the AGM[561].

[17.220] Where a company produces a corporate governance statement, the auditors of the company shall:

(a) establish that the company has produced a corporate governance statement, and that it contains the information at (a), (b), (e) and (f) above;

(b) provide an opinion as to whether or not the information given under (c) above is consistent with the outcome of their evaluation and testing of the relevant systems for the purposes of preparing their auditor's report;

---

558 Section 158(6I) of the CA 1963; 'multilateral trading facility' is defined in s 158(6J) of the CA 1963 as having the meaning assigned to it by Article 4(1) of Directive 2004/39, and in general terms means a trading system that facilitates the exchange of financial instruments between multiple parties.

559 Section 158(6E) of the CA 1963.

560 Section 158(6F) of the CA 1963.

561 Section 158(6G) of the CA 1963.

(c) provide an opinion as to whether or not the information given under (d) above is consistent.

Approval and signing of directors' report

[17.221] The directors' report, and, where the corporate governance statement is produced in the form of a separate report, that report, must also be signed on behalf of the directors by two of the directors[562]. As in relation to the signing of the accounts, there should be a resolution of the board of directors to nominate two of their number to sign the report[563].

Offences and penalties

[17.222] Failure to comply with a requirement imposed by ss 13 or 14 of the C(A)A 1986 renders the directors liable to conviction for an offence punishable on summary conviction by imprisonment for a term not exceeding six months or by a class C fine or to both. It will, however, be a defence in any such proceedings for a director to prove that he had reasonable grounds to believe, and that he did believe, that a competent and reliable person was charged with the duty of seeing that the requirements were complied with and was in a position to discharge that duty. Furthermore, a sentence of imprisonment may only be imposed if the court is of the opinion that the offence was committed wilfully[564].

[17.223] If any person, being a director of a company, fails to take all reasonable steps to secure compliance with the requirements of s 158 of the CA 1963, as set out above, he shall be guilty of an offence and shall be liable[565]:

(a) on summary conviction, to a class C fine, or imprisonment for up to 12 months, or both; or

(b) on conviction on indictment, to a fine of up to €22,220.42 or imprisonment for up to 5 years, or both.

[17.224] Where a directors' report is filed that does not comply with the requirements imposed by reg 37 of the EC(C:GA)R 1992, the parent undertaking and every officer of the company who is in default shall be liable on summary conviction to a class C fine[566].

[G] AUDIT REQUIREMENT FOR STATUTORY ACCOUNTS

Requirement to appoint an auditor

[17.225] Every company is required to appoint an auditor who must be either a statutory auditor or a statutory audit firm within the meaning of the EC(SA)(D)R 2010[567]. The procedure for the appointment and reappointment of auditors is addressed in further detail below[568], but it should be noted that it is principally the members who have the

---

562 Section 158(2) and (6F) of the CA 1963.

563 Section 158(2) and (6F) of the CA 1963.

564 Section 22(2) of the C(A)A 1986 and s 240(1) of the CA 1990.

565 Section 158(7) of the CA 1963.

566 Regulations 39 and 41(1) of the EC(C:GA)R 1992.

567 Section 2(1) of the CA 1963.

power to appoint or remove the auditor, and to fix his remuneration, and it is to them that the auditor owes a primary duty of care[569].

Requirement for the auditor to report on the accounts

[17.226] Unless the company avails of an exemption from the obligation to have its accounts audited[570], the auditors must make a report to the members of the company on the individual accounts examined by them, and on every balance sheet and profit and loss account or income statement, and all group accounts, laid before the company in general meeting during their tenure in office[571]. The items to be included in this report are considered in further detail below[572].

[H] AUDITOR'S REPORT

Requirement for auditors to report on the accounts

[17.227] Certain small companies satisfying specified criteria can opt out of the requirements to have their accounts audited[573]. Other than in such cases, however, s 193(1) of the CA 1990 provides:

> The auditors of a company shall make a report to the members on the accounts examined by them, and on every balance sheet and profit and loss account, and all group accounts, laid before the company in general meeting during their tenure of office.

Contents of the auditor's report

[17.228] The most important element of the auditor's report is that it must state whether, in their opinion[574], the annual accounts give a true and fair view[575] in accordance with the relevant financial reporting framework:

(i) in the case of individual accounts, of the state of affairs as at the end of the financial year, and profit or loss for the financial year, of the company; and

(ii) in the case of group accounts, of the state of affairs as at the end of the financial year, and profit or loss for the financial year, of the undertakings included in the consolidation as a whole, so far as concerns members of the company.

[17.229] The auditor's report must[576] additionally set out their opinion as to whether:

568 See para **[17.292]** *et seq.*

569 Under s 193(6) of the CA 1990, a person appointed as auditor of a company shall be under a general duty to carry out such audit with professional integrity.

570 Pursuant to Part III of the C(A)(No 2)A 1999; this is considered in detail at **[17.287]** *et seq, post.*

571 Section 193(1) of the CA 1990.

572 See para **[17.228]** *et seq.*

573 Pursuant to Part III of the C(A)(No 2)A 1999; this is considered in detail at **[17.287]** *et seq, post.*

574 Section 193(4D) of the CA 1990.

575 Section 193(4C) of the CA 1990.

576 Section 193(4A), (4B) and (4C) of the CA 1990.

- the annual accounts have been properly prepared in accordance with the requirements of the Companies Acts[577];
- the auditors have obtained all the information and explanations which, to the best of their knowledge and belief, are necessary for the purposes of their audit;
- proper books of account have been kept by the company;
- proper returns adequate for their audit have been received from branches of the company not visited by them;
- the company's balance sheet and (unless it is framed as a consolidated profit and loss account) profit and loss account are in agreement with the books of account and returns[578];
- there existed at the balance sheet date a financial situation which under s 40(1) of the C(A)A 1983[579] would require the convening of an extraordinary general meeting ('EGM')[580];

[17.230] The auditor's report must[581] also include:

(a) an introduction identifying the individual accounts, and, where appropriate, the group accounts, that are the subject of the audit and the financial reporting framework that has been applied in their preparation; and

(b) a description of the scope of the audit identifying the auditing standards in accordance with which the audit was conducted.

[17.231] In addition, if the obligation to disclose particulars of the following matters is not set out in a note to the accounts, the auditors are required, so far as they are reasonably able, to state the required particulars, the matters in question being:

- particulars relating to directors' emoluments, directors' or past-directors' pensions, and the amount of any compensation to directors or past-directors in respect of loss of office[582];
- particulars relating to transactions and arrangements[583] with directors, shadow directors and connected persons, agreements to enter into such transactions and arrangements, and other transactions and arrangements in which a director had a material interest[584].

[17.232] In respect of a company preparing Companies Act individual or group accounts, the auditors are additionally required to consider whether the information given in the directors' report relating to the financial year is consistent with the accounts prepared by the company for that year, and to state, in their report whether, in their opinion, this is the case[585].

---

577 Section 193(4A) of the CA 1990.

578 Section 193(4B) of the CA 1990.

579 That is, where the net assets of a company are half or less of the amounts of the company's called-up share capital; See Ch 14, *Corporate Governance: Meetings,* at para **[14.017]**.

580 Section 193(4C) of the CA 1990.

581 Section 193(4) of the CA 1990.

582 Section 191(8) of the CA 1963; See **[17.112]** *ante*.

583 Within the scope of s 31 of the CA 1990.

584 Section 46 of the CA 1990.

585 Section 15 of the C(A)A 1986.

(a) Form of the auditor's opinion

[17.233] In relation to each of the matters set out in s 193(4A) to (4D) of the CA 1990[586], the auditor's report is required[587] to contain a statement or opinion, which shall either be

(i) unqualified, or

(ii) qualified, including to the extent of an adverse opinion or disclaimer of opinion, where there is a disagreement or limitation in the scope of work,

and which shall include a reference to any matters to which the auditors wish to draw attention by way of emphasis without qualifying the report.

Auditing standards set out further detail in regard to the meaning of the above terms.

(i) Unqualified opinion

[17.234] International Standard on Auditing ('ISA') (UK & Ireland) 700 provides that an unqualified, or 'clean', audit opinion should be expressed when the auditor concludes that the financial statements have been prepared in accordance with the identified financial reporting framework, including the requirements of applicable law, and the financial statements give a true and fair view (or are presented fairly, in all material respects[588]). As set out above[589], the unmodified nature of such a report is not affected by the inclusion of an 'emphasis of matter' paragraph[590].

(ii) Qualified opinion

[17.235] A qualified opinion, other than to the extent of an adverse opinion or disclaimer of opinion, should be expressed when the auditor identifies misstatements, or is unable to obtain sufficient appropriate audit evidence on which to base the opinion, but concludes that the possible effects of misstatements identified, or in the latter case that may have gone undetected, are (individually or aggregated) material, but not pervasive, to the financial statements[591]. A qualified opinion should be expressed as being 'except for' the effects of the matter to which the qualification relates[592].

(iii) Adverse opinion

[17.236] An adverse opinion should be expressed when the effect of misstatements, individually or aggregated, are both material and pervasive to the financial statements[593].

(iv) Disclaimer of opinion

[17.237] A disclaimer of opinion should be expressed when the possible effect of a limitation on scope is so material and pervasive that the auditor has not been able to obtain sufficient appropriate audit evidence on which to base an opinion on the financial

586 See paras [17.228] and [17.229].

587 Section 193(4D) of the CA 1990.

588 ISA (UK & Ireland) 700, para 18.

589 See para **[17.233]**.

590 See **[17.239]** *post*

591 ISA (UK & Ireland) 705, para 7; See **[17.238]** *post* in relation to the meaning of 'material' and 'pervasive'.

592 ISA (UK & Ireland) 705, para 16.

593 ISA (UK & Ireland) 705, para 8.

statements, and concludes that the possible effects on the financial statements of undetected misstatements, if any, could be both material and pervasive[594]. A limitation on scope is defined as 'the auditor's inability to obtain sufficient appropriate evidence'[595], that is, as a restriction on ends rather than means. A limitation of scope may be imposed by circumstances (such as where the timing of the auditor's appointment is such that the auditor is unable to observe the counting of physical inventories). In such a case, the auditor should try to carry out reasonable alternative procedures to obtain evidence to support an unqualified opinion[596]. A limitation on scope may alternatively be imposed by management (such as where the terms of engagement specify that the auditor will not carry out any audit procedures that the auditor believes is necessary). If the auditor believes such a limitation on scope is likely to result in a disclaimer of opinion, they should not accept the engagement, or if they have already accepted the engagement, should consider resigning from it[597]. One should note that a statutory obligation to report to the appropriate regulators may apply where a significant limitation to scope is identified[598]. In addition, in relation to resigning from an engagement, there is a statutory obligation on auditors to give notice of their unwillingness to be re-appointed, where this is the case[599].

(v) Definition of 'material' and 'pervasive' effects

[17.238] The distinction between an unqualified and a qualified opinion rests on the materiality of the disagreement or limitation of scope in question, while the distinction between a qualified opinion and an adverse opinion or disclaimer of opinion is whether or not the effect of the qualification is pervasive. 'Material' has been defined in IFRS as follows:

> 'Omissions or misstatements of items are material if they could, individually or collectively, influence the economic decisions that users make on the basis of the financial statements. Materiality depends on the size and nature of the omission or misstatement judged in the surrounding circumstances. The size or nature of the item, or a combination of both, could be the determining factor[600].'

'Pervasive' is defined as follows:

> 'Pervasive effects on the financial statements are those that, in the auditor's judgment:
>
> (i) Are not confined to specific elements, accounts or items of the financial statements;
>
> (ii) If so confined, represent or could represent a substantial proportion of the financial statements; or
>
> (iii) In relation to disclosures, are fundamental to users' understanding of the financial statements[601].'

---

[594] ISA (UK & Ireland) 705, para 9.

[595] ISA (UK & Ireland) 705, para A8.

[596] ISA (UK & Ireland) 700, para 74.

[597] ISAs (UK & Ireland) 210, para 7, and 700, para 13.

[598] Section 185 of the CA 1990.

[599] Section 160(2)(c) of the CA 1963.

[600] IAS 1, para 7.

[601] ISA (UK & Ireland) 705, para 5.

However the existence of such definitions should not disguise the fact that whether a misstatement is 'material' or 'pervasive' is largely a subjective decision for the auditor, as shown by the use of the phrase 'in the auditor's judgment' in the definition of 'pervasive', and the reference to a number of different possible 'determining factor(s)' in the definition of 'material'. It is therefore not generally possible for any party other than the auditor to determine whether a particular set of circumstances will be seen by them as requiring a qualified opinion, or indeed an adverse opinion or disclaimer of opinion.

(vi) Emphasis of matter

[17.239] As stated above[602], the auditor's report 'shall include a reference to any matters to which the auditors wish to draw attention by way of emphasis'. Auditing standards therefore require that the auditors add a paragraph to their report to highlight any material matter identified regarding a going concern problem[603]. The auditors should also consider adding a paragraph to their report if there is a significant uncertainty, the resolution of which is dependent upon future events, and which may affect the financial statements[604]. An emphasis of matter paragraph is only ever used where the disclosure in the financial statements is adequate and not materially misstated (otherwise a qualified or adverse opinion is appropriate)[605]. An uncertainty is regarded as significant when it involves a significant level of concern about the validity of a matter whose potential effect on the financial statements is unusually great. Possible examples of significant uncertainties are the outcome of major litigation[606], or the valuation of assets for which no liquid market exists. The more recent auditing guidance states that the auditor should only include an emphasis of matter paragraph if the matter is 'fundamental to users' understanding of the financial statements'[607], which would appear to limit the use of such paragraphs. This would appear to be intentional; as stated, 'A widespread use of Emphasis of Matter paragraphs diminishes the effectiveness of the auditor's communication of such matters'[608].

[17.240] Finally, the more recent auditing guidance introduces the concept of an 'Other Matter paragraph' to highlight a matter other than those presented or disclosed in the financial statements that is relevant to users' understanding of the audit, the auditor's responsibilities or the auditor's report and is not prohibited by law or regulation. The example cited of where such a paragraph might be considered appropriate, namely – 'in the rare circumstance where the auditor is unable to withdraw from an engagement even though the possible effect of an inability to obtain sufficient appropriate audit evidence due to a limitation on the scope of the audit imposed by management is pervasive' – suggests that such a paragraph will only be used in very limited circumstances[609].

---

602 See para **[17.233]**.
603 ISA (UK & Ireland) 570, para 19.
604 ISA (UK & Ireland) 706, paras 1 and A1.
605 ISA (UK & Ireland) 706, para 6.
606 ISA (UK & Ireland) 706, para A1.
607 ISA (UK & Ireland) 706, para 6.
608 ISA (UK & Ireland) 706, para A2.
609 ISA (UK & Ireland) 706, para A5.

(b) Signature and dating of the auditor's report

[17.241] The auditor's report is required to state the name of the auditor and be signed and dated. Where the auditor is a statutory audit firm, the report shall be signed:

(a) by the statutory auditor (or, where more than one, each statutory auditor) designated by the statutory audit firm for the particular audit engagement as being primarily responsible for carrying out the audit, or

(b) in the case of a group audit, by at least the statutory auditor(s) designated by the statutory audit firm as being primarily responsible for carrying out the statutory audit at the level of the group,

in his or her own name, for and on behalf of, the audit firm[610].

The requirement that the auditor's report, where the audit was carried out by a firm, be signed by one or more individual auditors, rather than merely stating the handwritten name of the firm, has effect in respect of financial statements or financial years commencing after 20 May 2010[611].

Auditor's report to be read at the AGM

[17.242] The auditor's report must be read (though not necessarily by the auditors) at the AGM of the company, and shall be open to inspection by any member[612].

[I] Publication Of Accounts

Obligation to circulate accounts and reports

[17.243] In the case of a private company, a copy of each of the documents set out in the paragraph that follows, must[613] be sent to:

(a) every member of the company (whether or not that person is entitled to receive notices of general meetings of the company);

(b) every holder of debentures of the company (whether or not that person is entitled to receive notices of general meetings of the company); and

(c) every person, other than a member or holder of debentures of the company, who is entitled to receive notices of general meetings of the company.

[17.244] The documents referred to in the previous paragraph are a copy of:

(a) every balance sheet which is to be laid before the AGM;

(b) the profit and loss account required to be annexed to the balance sheet;

(c) so far as not incorporated in (a) or (b), any group accounts to be laid before the AGM;

(c) the directors' report; and

(d) the auditor's report[614].

---

610 Section 193(4G) of the CA 1990, as inserted by reg 57 of the EC(SA)(D)R 2010.

611 Regulation 2 of the EC(SA)(D)R 2010.

612 Section 193(2) of the CA 1990.

613 Section 159(1) of the CA 1963.

614 Section 159(1) of the CA 1963 and s 157 of the CA 1963; in respect of the requirement to lay documents before the AGM, See para **[17.249]** *post*.

[17.245] The documents described in the previous paragraph must be sent to the persons listed above[615] not less than 21 days before the date of the AGM, save that the documents shall be deemed to have been duly sent, (even if they were actually sent less than 21 days before the date of the meeting), if it is so agreed by all the members entitled to attend and vote at the meeting[616]. If there is default in complying with this requirement, the company and every officer of the company who is in default shall be guilty of an offence and liable to a class C fine[617].

Right to demand copies of accounts and reports

[17.246] Any member or holder of debentures of a company, whether or not that person is entitled to have sent to him copies of the company's balance sheets, shall be entitled to be furnished on demand without charge with a copy of the last balance sheet of the company, including every document required by law to be annexed thereto, together with copies of the directors' and auditor's report[618]. If a person makes a demand for such document, and the demand is not met within seven days of being made, the company and every officer of the company who is in default shall be guilty of an offence and liable to a class C fine, unless it is proved that the person has previously made a demand for and been furnished with a copy of that document[619].

[17.247] Where group accounts do not deal with a subsidiary of the company, any member of the company shall be entitled to be furnished without charge with a copy of the latest balance sheet of that subsidiary which has been sent to the members of the subsidiary, together with a copy of every document required by law to be annexed thereto and a copy of the directors' and auditor's reports[620]. Where any such document is not sent within 14 days after the member has made a request to the company, the company and every officer of the company who is in default are liable, in respect of an offence, to a class D fine, and the court may direct that the document required be sent to the member, unless it is proved that the person has previously made a demand for and been furnished with a copy of that document.[621]

Requirements in relation to publication of accounts

[17.248] 'Publish' and 'publication' in the context of these requirements refers to situations such as the publishing of accounts in a newspaper, rather than to the filing of accounts with the annual return[622]. If a company publishes full Companies Act individual accounts, it is required to publish its auditor's report[623], and it must indicate if group accounts have been prepared, and if so, where those group accounts can be obtained[624]. If it publishes abridged accounts, it must also file the special report that the

615 See para **[17.243]**.

616 Section 159(3) of the CA 1963.

617 Section 159(5) of the CA 1963.

618 Section 159(4) of the CA 1963.

619 Section 159(5) of the CA 1963.

620 Section 150(10)(a) of the CA 1963.

621 Section 150(10)(b) of the CA 1963.

622 In respect of the requirements regarding the annual return, See para **[17.250]** *post*.

623 Section 19(1) of the C(A)A 1986.

624 Section 19(3A) of the C(A)A 1986.

auditor is required to make in relation to such accounts[625]. If it publishes abbreviated accounts (ie, any balance sheet or profit and loss account, or summary or abstract thereof, otherwise than as a part of the full accounts), it must not publish the auditor's report, but must[626] publish a statement stating that the accounts are not full accounts, whether full accounts have been filed and audited, and whether the auditor's report was qualified[627] as to any matters, or included any emphasis of matter.

Similarly, if a company publishes full Companies Act group accounts, it is required[628] also to publish its auditor's report. If it publishes abbreviated accounts (ie, any group balance sheet or profit and loss account, or summary or abstract thereof, otherwise than as a part of the full accounts), it must not publish the auditor's report[629], but must[630] publish a statement stating that the accounts are not full accounts, whether full accounts have been filed and audited, and whether the auditor's report was qualified as to any matters, or included any emphasis of matter.

Accounts and reports to be laid before the company in general meeting

[17.249] The directors of every company must[631] lay the individual accounts of the company for each financial year before the AGM within nine months of the balance sheet date. In addition, the directors' report on the state of affairs of the company and, if it is a holding company, of the group, must[632] be attached to every balance sheet laid before the AGM. Where at the end of the financial year a company is a parent company, and is required to prepare group accounts, the directors of the company are required to lay those group accounts before the AGM of the company when the individual accounts are so laid[633]. Finally, as set out above[634], the auditor's report must be read at the AGM of the company[635].

[J] Annual Return

[17.250] Every company is required[636], at least once in every calendar year, to make a return (called the 'annual return') in the prescribed form[637] to the registrar of companies. The annual return makes available to the public information in relation to a company's affairs, such as the address of the registered office, the location at which important

625 Section 19(1A) of the C(A)A 1986; as regards 'abridged accounts' and the auditor's 'special report', see para **[17.267]** *et seq, post*.

626 Section 19(2) of the C(A)A 1986.

627 See para **[17.233]** *et seq, ante*.

628 Reg 40(1) of the EC(C:GA)R 1992.

629 Reg 40(3) of the EC(C:GA)R 1992.

630 Reg 40(2) of the EC(C:GA)R 1992.

631 Section 148(7) of the CA 1963.

632 Section 157 of the CA 1963.

633 Section 150(9) of the CA 1963.

634 See para **[17.242]**.

635 Section 193(2) of the CA 1990.

636 Section 125 of the CA 1963.

637 Article 4 of the Companies (Forms) Order 2011 (SI 94/2011) prescribes Form B1 as the form for the purpose of s 125 of the CA 1963.

records (eg, the register of members, register of directors' and secretary's interests in shares and debentures, and directors' service contracts) are kept, the identity of the directors, secretary, auditor and shareholders of the company, and details of authorised and issued share capital. In addition, there is generally an obligation that annual accounts, and the directors' report and auditor's report in relation to such accounts, be filed with the annual return.

[17.251] Prior to 31 December 1986 the obligation to file accounts did not apply to private companies[638]; however, a corresponding obligation was imposed on private companies limited by shares or guarantee by the C(A)A 1986[639]. The rigours of this obligation are however somewhat mitigated in the case of 'small' and 'medium-sized' private companies, as addressed at para **[17.267]** *et seq* below.

Time for filing of the annual return

[17.252] The annual return must be made at least once in every calendar year[640]. It must be made within 28 days of the company's annual return date ('ARD')[641]. Section 127 of the CA 1963 provides:

> '(1) The annual return of a company shall be made up to a date that is not later than its annual return date, except that the first annual return of a company incorporated after the commencement of section 46 of the Companies (Auditing and Accounting) Act 2003[642], shall be made up to the date that is its first annual return date.
>
> (2) Subject to subsection (3), the annual return shall be delivered to the registrar of companies—
>
> (a) in the case of the first annual return following the commencement date of a company incorporated before the commencement date – not later than 28 days after the annual return date or 3 months after the commencement date, whichever is the later, and
>
> (b) in any other case – not later than 28 days after the annual return date, unless it is made up to an earlier date in which case it shall be delivered to the registrar not later than 28 days after that earlier date.'

For companies incorporated on or after 1 March 2002, the first ARD is the day six months after the date of incorporation of the company[643]. For companies incorporated prior to 1 March 2002, the date is the anniversary of the date to which the then most recent annual return delivered to the registrar had been made up, or (if no such annual return had ever been delivered to the registrar) the day six months after the anniversary of the date of incorporation of the company[644]. In each case, subsequent ARDs will fall on the anniversary of that ARD[645], unless the ARD has been altered by the company, either by being brought forward to an earlier date or by being extended to a later date.

---

638 Section 128(4) of the CA 1963.

639 Section 7 of the C(A)A 1986.

640 Section 125(1) of the CA 1963.

641 Section 127(2) of the CA 1963.

642 The commencement date of s 46 of the C(A&A)A 2003 is 17 May 2004.

643 Section 127(6) of the CA 1963.

644 Section 127(5) of the CA 1963.

645 Section 127(5) and (6) of the CA 1963.

[17.253] The ARD shall be brought forward where the company makes an annual return up to a date earlier than the existing ARD, in which case the ARD shall thereafter be each anniversary of the date to which that return is made up, unless the company elects in the annual return to retain its existing ARD, or extends its ARD to a later date[646]. To extend the ARD to a later date, the company must deliver an annual return (without annexing accounts thereto) to the registrar not later than 28 days after the existing ARD, and must notify the registrar of the new ARD, which may be no later than six months after the existing ARD[647]. It should be noted that where a company has extended its ARD to a later date, it shall not be permitted to extend its ARD again until at least five years have passed[648]. In any case where it is proposed to extend the ARD of a company limited by shares, it is also important to remember that the accounts accompanying the return can predate the ARD by no more than nine months[649], and that a company is required to prepare accounts in every calendar year[650]. These obligations may substantially limit the ability of a company to extend its ARD. The ARD of a holding company or its subsidiary can also be extended with ministerial permission, and on the application or with the consent of the directors whose ARD is to be extended, to allow the ARDs of each to correspond[651].

[17.254] Where a company files its annual return electronically (whether using the CRO's online website, or company secretarial software approved by the CRO)[652], the same deadline applies for the filing of online information (ie, it must be filed not later than 28 days after the ARD). However the hard copy documentation (eg, accounts, directors' and auditor's report, along with a cover sheet generated by the software at the time of the online filing) need not be delivered until 28 days after the filing deadline; therefore the last date for delivering the company's accounts to the CRO is 56 days after either the ARD or (if earlier than the ARD) the date to which annual return is made up.

Consequences of failure to file annual return on time

[17.255] Late filing of the annual return will attract a penalty fee[653] (which includes an additional fee in respect of each day on which the failure to file the return continues) up to a maximum of €1,240. Furthermore, a failure by the company to comply with the filing requirements renders the company, every officer of the company who is in default, and any person in accordance with whose directions or instructions the directors of the company are accustomed to act and to whose directions or omissions the default is attributable, guilty of an offence[654]. Proceedings in relation to offences under the section may be commenced and prosecuted by the registrar of companies[655].

---

646 Section 127(8) of the CA 1963.

647 Section 127(9) of the CA 1963.

648 Section 127(10) of the CA 1963.

649 Section 7(1C) of the C(A)A 1986.

650 Section 148(1) of the CA 1963.

651 Section 153(2) of the CA 1963.

652 See **[17.261]** *post*.

653 Section 395(3) of the CA 1963, and the Eighth Schedule to the CA 1963.

654 Section 127(12) of the CA 1963.

655 Section 127(13) of the CA 1963.

Alternatively, the registrar has the option of issuing a notice to a person, or where the person believed to be in default is a company, to an officer of the company, setting out the obligation with which the person or company has failed to comply, inviting that person to remedy the default, and to pay an on-the-spot fine, within 21 days[656]. No prosecution may be commenced during that 21-day period; nor thereafter if the default is remedied and the fine paid during that period[657]. This allows the registrar to make companies and officers aware of the likelihood of prosecutions, without – at least initially – subjecting the registrar to the costs and effort of taking action in court.

Any document filed with the registrar which fails to comply with the requirements of any enactment (such as the requirement that the document be legible, be in the proper form, and state the registered number of the company[658]) may be rejected for filing[659]. The registrar may serve a notice on the person filing indicating the defect, and if not remedied within 14 days the original will be deemed not to have been delivered[660]. This may again result in the penalties in the preceding paragraph being imposed.

[17.256] The ultimate penalty for a failure to make annual returns is the possibility of strike-off. Where a company fails for one or more years to make an annual return, the registrar may take steps to have the company's name struck off the register of companies and to have the company dissolved[661]. These procedures are discussed in further detail in Ch 26][662]. The liability of every director, officer and member of the company will survive such dissolution, as will the court's power to wind up the company while struck off[663].

Contents and form of the annual return

[17.257] Section 125 of the CA 1963 requires the annual return to be 'in the prescribed form'. The Form B1 has been prescribed as the form for this purpose[664].

(a) Contents

[17.258] The following details must be contained in the annual return[665]:

- the company number;
- the name of the company;
- the date to which the return is made up. If the return is made up to a date earlier than the company's existing ARD[666], it must be stated whether the company

656 Section 66(1) of the CLEA 2001.
657 Section 66(2) of the CLEA 2001.
658 Section 248 of the CA 1990.
659 Section 249A(1) of the CA 1990.
660 Section 249A(2) of the CA 1990.
661 Section 12 of the C(A)A 1982.
662 See Ch 26, *Strike Off and Restoration*, at para **[26.006]** *et seq*.
663 See Ch 26, *Strike Off and Restoration* at para **[26.016]** *et seq*.
664 Article 4 of the Companies (Forms) Order 2011 (SI 94/2011).
665 Section 125 of the CA 1963 and the Schedule to the Companies (Forms) Order 2011 (SI 94/2011).
666 See para **[17.250]** *ante*.

wishes to retain the anniversary of its existing ARD, or wishes to change to the anniversary of the date of this return, for next year;

- the dates of commencement and of completion of the financial year of the accounts (if any)[667] annexed to the annual return;
- a statement of whether a company is claiming an audit exemption;
- the auditor registration number;
- the name, address and other details of the presenter (being the person to whom queries can be addressed in respect of the annual return);
- the address of the registered office of the company;
- the address of the place(s) where each of the register of members, register of debenture-holders and register of directors' and secretary's interests is kept, and where copies of directors' service contracts/memoranda of same (if applicable) are retained, if these are not kept at the registered office;
- the name (and any former name) and residential address of the company secretary;
- particulars of all donations for political purposes exceeding €5,079 in value made by the company in the year to which the return relates, including particulars sufficient to identify the value of each such donation and the person to whom the donation was made[668];
- the amount of the authorised share capital of the company and, for each class, the number and nominal value per share of shares into which it is divided;
- details of the issued share capital of the company, distinguishing first between issues for all-cash consideration and other issues, and in each case setting out, for each class, the number of shares, and the total nominal value, total premium and total amount (considered) paid;
- details of shares forfeited, shares or debentures issued at a discount or on which a commission was paid including share class, number of shares and amounts in each case;
- in respect of each person who held shares at any time from the date of the last return up to (and including) the date to which this return is made up:

    the name and address of that shareholder;

    the number of shares they held at the date of the annual return;

    in respect of each transfer of shares during the period between the annual returns, the number of shares transferred, date of transfer and particulars of the transferee;

- the name (and any former name), date of birth, residential address (and a statement as to EEA residency), business occupation, and nationality of each current director as at the date to which the annual return is made up;
- in respect of each such director, a list of other directorships held by them during the preceding 10 years, excluding 100% subsidiaries or 100% parent companies of the company; and
- a statement as to whether or not the company is a private company.

---

667 See para **[17.156]** *et seq, ante* and para **[17.267]** *et seq, post.*

668 As required by s 26 of the Electoral Act 1997.

[17.259] The form must be signed by a secretary and a director (not being the same person), to certify that the form sets out the required information, as at the date to which the annual return is made up[669].

(b) Form

[17.260] The Form B1 has been prescribed as the relevant form for the purpose of s 125 of the CA 1963[670], and is set out in full in the Schedule to the Companies (Forms) Order 2011. In addition, it is prescribed that the annual return (and any documents filed with it) must be easily legible and suitable for scanning and copying, and must meet specific requirements as to size, print and paper colour, paper weight and quality, binding and stapling, and manner of information insertion[671].

[17.261] An annual return may be completed, signed and delivered electronically to the registrar of companies. This may be done either by using the CRO's online filing website, www.core.ie, or by using particular secretarial software approved by the CRO[672]. One should note that in such cases, an additional 28-day period is permitted for the filing of hard copy documentation required to be annexed to the return (accounts, etc)[673], which may be useful in certain cases where time is an issue.

Documents to be annexed to the annual return

[17.262] Copies of the following documents are required[674] to be annexed to the annual return in respect of a company limited by shares or guarantee:

- the accounts of the company (ie, its balance sheet, profit and loss account and the notes to these accounts);
- the directors' report;
- the auditor's report.

Each of these documents must[675] be certified by both a director and the secretary to be a true copy of the document laid or to be laid before the AGM for the period to which the return relates. If the document is not in English or Irish it must be accompanied by a certified translation in one of those languages[676]. If any of the documents does not comply with the provisions required by law at the date of the relevant audit in respect of the form and contents of that document, it must be amended by the company to bring it into line with those provisions, and must contain a statement that it has been amended for those purposes[677].

---

669 Section 125 of the CA 1963 and the Schedule to the Companies (Forms) Order 2011 (SI 94/2011).

670 Article 4 of the Companies (Forms) Order 2011 (SI 94/2011).

671 Companies Act 1990 (Form and Content of Documents Delivered to the Registrar) Regulations 2002 (SI 39/2002).

672 See www.cro.ie in relation to the software that has been so approved.

673 See **[17.262]** *post*.

674 Section 7(1) of the C(A)A 1986.

675 Section 7(1) of the C(A)A 1986.

676 Section 7(1) of the C(A)A 1986.

677 Section 7(2) of the C(A)A 1986.

[17.263] If a company fails to comply with the above requirements, the company, and any officer in default, shall be guilty of an offence[678]. Such an offence is punishable on summary conviction by the imposition of a class C fine[679] or, at the discretion of the court, by imprisonment for a term not exceeding 12 months, or both[680]. Upon conviction on indictment, a person guilty of such an offence shall be liable to a fine not exceeding €22,220.42 or imprisonment for a term not exceeding five years, or both[681]. Summary proceedings in this regard may be brought by the registrar of companies[682]. Furthermore, where any person wilfully and knowingly makes a false statement in any of the documents, he will be liable on conviction on indictment to imprisonment for a term not exceeding five years or a fine not exceeding €6,349 or both, or on summary conviction, to imprisonment for a term not exceeding six months or a class C fine or both[683].

Exemptions from annexing documents to annual return

[17.264] First, where companies are exempt from preparing group accounts[684], the obligation to annex those documents to the annual return will obviously not apply.

[17.265] Second, special arrangements apply in respect of the filing obligations for what are termed 'small' and 'medium-sized' companies, and these are set out below[685].

[17.266] Finally, as set out above[686], where a parent undertaking[687] prepares consolidated accounts in accordance with s 150 of the CA 1963, and the required disclosures are made in the notes to the accounts, the company shall be exempt from the obligation to annex its individual profit and loss account or income statement to its annual return[688].

[K] EXCLUSIONS, EXEMPTIONS AND SPECIAL ARRANGEMENTS WITH REGARD TO FILING OBLIGATION

'Medium-sized' companies

(a) Definition of 'medium-sized' company

[17.267] A private company qualifies to be treated as a 'medium-sized' company for any financial year if, both in that year and in the immediately preceding financial year, it satisfies at least two of the following conditions:

- its balance sheet total did not exceed €7,618,438;
- its turnover did not exceed €15,236,857;
- its average number of employees did not exceed 250[689].

---

678 Section 22(1) of the C(A)A 1986.

679 A class C fine is defined in s 3 of the FA 2010 as 'a fine not exceeding €2,500'.

680 Section 240(1) of the CA 1990, as amended by the FA 2010.

681 Section 240(1) of the CA 1990, as amended by the FA 2010.

682 Section 22(1) of the C(A)A 1986.

683 Section 22(3) of the C(A)A 1986.

684 See para **[17.154]** *et seq ante*.

685 See para **[17.267]**.

686 See para **[17.152]**.

687 Within the meaning of regs 3 and 4 of the EC(C:GA)R 1992.

688 Section 7(1A) of the C(A)A 1986.

689 Section 8(3) of the C(A)A 1986.

[17.268] 'Balance sheet total' in this context effectively means total assets, ie, before deducting any liabilities owed by the companies[690]. 'Turnover' is defined in the Schedule as the amounts derived from the provision of goods and services falling within the company's ordinary activities, after deduction of trade discounts, value added tax, and any other taxes on those amounts[691]. Where the financial period to which the accounts relate is not in fact a year, the size exemption for turnover must be proportionally adjusted[692]. The average number of employees is computed by calculating the total number of persons under contracts of service with the company for each week of the financial year, adding the totals together, and dividing the result by the number of weeks in the financial year[693].

[17.269] In the first financial year since incorporation, the exemptions may be calculated by reference to the figures for that year only[694]; subsequently, the normal obligation to meet the requirements in both the company's present and immediately preceding financial year will apply. If it fails to meet the requirements in any subsequent financial year, it may avail of the exemption for that year – but may not rely on the exemption again until it has met the criteria in any immediately preceding financial year[695].

(b) Requirement to file 'abridged' accounts

(i) 'Abridged' balance sheet

[17.270] A 'medium-sized' private company is permitted to annex to its annual return an 'abridged' balance sheet[696]. In the case of a company preparing Companies Act individual accounts, the balance sheet will only be required to show those items preceded by letters or Roman numerals in Formats 1 and 2 of the Balance Sheet Formats set out in the Schedule to the C(A)A 1986, as well as specified other items[697].

Accordingly a Format 2 abridged balance sheet need only include the following items:

ASSETS	LIABILITIES
A. Fixed Assets	***A. Capital and reserves***
I. Intangible assets	I. Called up share capital
II. Tangible assets	II. Share premium account
III. Financial assets	III. Revaluation reserve
B. Current Assets	IV. Other reserves
I. Stocks	V. Profit and loss account
II. Debtors:	***B. Provisions for liabilities***

690 Section 8(4) of the C(A)A 1986.
691 Paragraph 75 of the Schedule to the C(A)A 1986.
692 Section 8(6) of the C(A)A 1986.
693 Section 8(9) of the C(A)A 1986.
694 Section 8(8) of the C(A)A 1986.
695 Section 9 of the C(A)A 1986.
696 Section 11(1) of the C(A)A 1986.
697 Section 11(2)(b) of the C(A)A 1986.

ASSETS	LIABILITIES
1. Trade debtors 2. Amounts owed by group undertakings 3. Amounts owed by undertakings in which a participating interest is held 4. Called up share capital not paid 5. Prepayments and accrued income III. Investments IV. Cash at bank and in hand	***C. Creditors:***

A Format 1 abridged balance sheet need only show the following items:

A. Fixed Assets

I. Intangible assets:

II. Tangible assets:

III. Financial assets:

B. Current Assets

I. Stocks:

II. Debtors:

1. Trade debtors
2. Amounts owed by group undertakings
3. Amounts owed by undertakings in which a participating interest is held
4. Called up share capital not paid
5. Prepayments and accrued income

III. Investments:

IV. Cash at bank and in hand

C. Creditors: Amounts falling due within one year

D. Net current assets (liabilities)

E. Total assets less current liabilities

F. Creditors: Amounts falling due after more than one year

G. Provisions for liabilities

H. Capital and reserves

I. Called up share capital

II. Share premium account

III. Revaluation reserve

IV. Other reserves

V. Profit and loss account

In each case above, the abridged balance sheet must show separately the amounts falling due within one year, and falling due after one year, in respect of:

- Amounts owed by group undertakings;
- Amounts owed by undertakings in which a participating interest is held.

In addition, a Format 2 abridged balance sheet must also show separately the amounts falling due within one year, and falling due after one year, in respect of:

- Debenture loans;
- Bank loans and overdrafts;
- Amounts owed to group undertakings;
- Amounts owed to undertakings in which a participating interest is held.

[17.271] In respect of the abridged balance sheet prepared by a company preparing Companies Act individual accounts, if the following items are not shown on the face of the balance sheet, they must be stated in the notes to the accounts[698]:

- Goodwill;
- Land and buildings;
- Plant and machinery;
- Fixtures, fittings, tools and equipment;
- Payments on account and assets in course of construction;
- Shares in group undertakings representing financial assets;
- Loans to group undertakings representing financial assets;
- Shares in undertakings in which a participating interest is held representing financial assets;
- Loans to undertakings in which a participating interest is held representing financial assets;
- Amounts owed by group companies;
- Amounts owed by undertakings in which a participating interest is held;
- Prepayments and accrued income;
- Shares in group undertakings representing investments;
- Debenture loans falling due within one year;
- Bank loans and overdrafts falling due within one year;
- Amounts owed to group undertakings falling due within one year;
- Amounts owed to undertakings in which a participating interest is held falling due within one year;
- Other creditors including tax and social welfare falling due within one year;
- Accruals and deferred income falling due within one year;
- Debenture loans falling due after one year;
- Bank loans and overdrafts falling due after one year;
- Amounts owed to group undertakings falling due after one year;
- Amounts owed to undertakings in which a participating interest is held falling due after one year;
- Other creditors including tax and social welfare falling due after one year;
- Accruals and deferred income falling due after one year.

698 Section 11(2)(b) of the C(A)A 1986.

[17.272] For a medium-sized 'private' company preparing IFRS individual accounts, the abridged balance sheet shall comprise the full balance sheet included in the IFRS individual accounts[699].

(ii) 'Abridged' profit and loss account

[17.273] A medium-sized private company is permitted to annex to its annual return an abridged profit and loss account or income statement[700].

For a company preparing Companies Act individual accounts, where Format 1 or 3 of the Profit and Loss Account Formats is adopted[701], the following items may be combined under the heading 'gross profit or loss' in an abridged profit and loss account[702]:

- Turnover;
- Cost of sales;
- Other operating income.

Where Format 2 or 4 of the Profit and Loss Account Formats is adopted, the following items may be combined under the heading 'gross profit or loss' in a short form profit and loss account[703]:

- Turnover;
- Reduction in stocks of finished goods and work in progress;
- Increase in stocks of finished goods and work in progress;
- Raw materials and consumables;
- Other external charges;
- Own work capitalised;
- Other operating income.

In addition, a company preparing such an abridged profit and loss account is relieved from the obligation to disclose particulars of turnover[704] in the notes to the accounts[705].

[17.274] Where a 'medium-sized' company prepares IFRS individual accounts, the directors may annex to the annual return an abridged income statement combining as one item the company's revenue, and:

(i) where expenses are classified by function, those expenses classified as 'cost of sales'; or

(ii) where expenses are classified by nature, changes in finished goods and work-in-progress and raw materials and consumables used[706].

---

699 Section 11(2)(a) of the C(A)A 1986.

700 Section 11(1) of the C(A)A 1986.

701 Part I of the Schedule to the C(A)A 1986.

702 Section 11(3)(b) of the C(A)A 1986.

703 Section 11(3)(b) of the C(A)A 1986.

704 As otherwise required by para 41 of the Schedule to the C(A)A 1986, and as set out at **[17.100]** *ante*.

705 Section 12(2)(b) of the C(A)A 1986.

706 Section 11(3)(b) of the C(A)A 1986.

(iii) Directors' statement

[17.275] The abridged balance sheet annexed to the annual return must also contain a statement by the directors that they have relied on specified exemptions, and that they have done so on the ground that the company is entitled to the benefit of those exemptions[707].

(iv) Special auditor's report

[17.276] Where a medium-sized company relies on the provisions permitting it to file abridged accounts, the company is required to file, rather than the auditor's report on the individual accounts of the company, a special report containing:

- a copy of a report stating that, in the opinion of the auditors of the company, the directors of the company are entitled to annex the abridged accounts to the annual return and that the accounts so annexed are properly prepared; and
- a copy of the report of the auditor on the individual accounts under s 193 of the CA 1990[708].

Each of the above reports must be certified by both a director and the secretary to be a true copy of that report[709].

'Small' companies

(a) Definition of 'small' company

[17.277] A private company qualifies to be treated as a 'small' company for any financial year if, both in that year and in the immediately preceding financial year, it satisfies at least two of the following conditions:

- its balance sheet total did not exceed €4.4 million;
- its turnover did not exceed €8.8 million;
- its average number of employees did not exceed 50[710].

It will be noted that all small companies are, by definition, also medium-sized companies and, accordingly, may avail of the reliefs available to medium-sized companies.

[17.278] The provisions above[711] in respect of the definitions of the terms used in determining whether a company is a 'medium-sized' company, and the provisions where the criteria are not met in a particular year[712], apply equally in determining whether a company is a 'small' company.

---

707 Section 18(2) of the C(A)A 1986.

708 Section 18(3)–(4) of the C(A)A 1986.

709 Section 18(5) of the C(A)A 1986.

710 Section 8(2) of the C(A)A 1986 as amended by the European Union (Accounts) Regulations 2012 (SI 304/2012).

711 See para **[17.268]**.

712 See para **[17.269]**.

(b) Requirement to file 'abridged' accounts

(i) 'Abridged' balance sheet

[17.279] A 'small' private company preparing Companies Act individual accounts is permitted to annex to its annual return an abridged balance sheet[713], which is only required to show those items preceded by letters or Roman numerals in Formats 1 and 2 of the Balance Sheet Formats set out in the Schedule to the C(A) A 1986. The only exception is that the item 'creditors' in a Format 2 abridged balance sheet must show separately amounts falling due within one year and those falling due after one year, while under either of the two formats has been adopted, the item 'debtors' must show separately amounts falling due within one year and after one year[714].

Accordingly a Format 2 abridged balance sheet need only include the following items:

ASSETS

A. Fixed Assets

I. Intangible assets

II. Tangible assets

III. Financial assets

B. Current Assets

I. Stocks

II. Debtors:

1. Falling due within one year
2. Falling due after one year

III. Investments

IV. Cash at bank and in hand

LIABILITIES

A. Capital and reserves

I. Called up share capital

II. Share premium account

III. Revaluation reserve

IV. Other reserves

V. Profit and loss account

B. Provisions for liabilities

C. Creditors:

1. Falling due within one year
2. Falling due after one year

A Format 1 abridged balance sheet need only show the following items:

A. Fixed Assets

I. Intangible assets:

II. Tangible assets:

III. Financial assets:

B. Current Assets

I. Stocks:

II. Debtors:

1. Falling due within one year
2. Falling due after one year

III. Investments:

---

713 Section 10(1) of the C(A)A 1986.

714 Section 10(2)(b) of the C(A)A 1986.

IV. Cash at bank and in hand

C. Creditors: Amounts falling due within one year

1. Falling due within one year
2. Falling due after one year

D. Net current assets (liabilities)

E. Total assets less current liabilities

F. Creditors: Amounts falling due after more than one year

1. Falling due within one year
2. Falling due after one year

G. Provisions for liabilities

H. Capital and reserves

I. Called up share capital

II. Share premium account

III. Revaluation reserve

IV. Other reserves

V. Profit and loss account

For a small 'private' company preparing IFRS individual accounts, the abridged balance sheet shall comprise the full balance sheet included in the IFRS individual accounts[715].

(ii) Notes to 'abridged' balance sheet

[17.280] The requirements for notes relating to the abridged balance sheet of a 'small' private company are considerably fewer than those relating to a full balance sheet. The only notes expressly required[716] to be annexed to the abridged balance sheet of a company preparing Companies Act individual accounts are:

- Accounting policies[717];
- Share capital and debentures[718];
- Valuation of financial instruments at fair value[719];
- Provision for taxation[720];
- Details of indebtedness[721];
- Foreign currency[722]; and
- Corresponding amounts[723].

---

[715] Section 10(2)(b) of the C(A)A 1986.

[716] Section 12(1)(b) of the C(A)A 1986.

[717] Paragraph 24 of the Schedule to the C(A)A 1986; see **[17.071]** and **[17.099]** *ante*.

[718] Paragraphs 26–27 of the Schedule to the C(A)A 1986; See **[17.092]** *ante*.

[719] Paragraph 31B–31C of the Schedule to the C(A)A 1986; See **[17.078]** *ante*.

[720] Paragraph 33 of the Schedule to the C(A)A 1986; see **[17.090]** *ante*.

[721] Paragraph 34 of the Schedule to the C(A)A 1986; see **[17.087]** *et seq ante*.

[722] Paragraph 44 of the Schedule to the C(A)A 1986; see **[17.109]** *ante*.

[723] Paragraph 44 of the Schedule to the C(A)A 1986; see **[17.110]** *ante*.

The notes expressly required[724] to be annexed to the abridged balance sheet of a company preparing IFRS individual accounts are:

- accounting policies[725];
- information in relation to the maturity of non-current liabilities and any security in respect of those liabilities; and
- the disclosures required by statute of IFRS individual accounts[726].

Caution should be exercised when preparing the notes relating to the abridged balance sheet, because certain particulars, eg, information regarding the period over which capitalised development costs are written off, must be included in the notes regardless of whether the item to which it relates is shown separately in the balance sheet[727].

(iii) Directors' statement

[17.281] As with a medium-sized company[728], the abridged balance sheet annexed by a small company to its annual return must also contain a statement by the directors that they have relied on specified exemptions, and that they have done so on the ground that the company is entitled to the benefit of those exemptions[729].

(iv) Exemption from filing profit and loss account and directors' report

[17.282] A 'small' private company is not required to annex to its annual return a copy of its profit and loss account, or of its directors' report[730].

(v) Special auditor's report

[17.283] As with a medium-sized company[731], where a 'small' company relies on the provisions permitting it to file an abridged balance sheet, the company is required to file, rather than the auditor's report on the individual accounts of the company, a special report containing:

- a copy of a report stating that, in the opinion of the auditors of the company, the directors of the company are entitled to annex the abridged accounts to the annual return and that the accounts so annexed are properly prepared; and
- a copy of the report of the auditor on the individual accounts under s 193 of the CA 1990[732].

Each of the above reports must be certified by both a director and the secretary to be a true copy of that report[733].

---

724 Section 12(1)(a) of the C(A)A 1986.

725 Paragraph 24 of the Schedule to the C(A)A 1986; see **[17.071]** and **[17.099]** *ante*.

726 Section 149A(2)(a)-(k) of the CA 1963; see **[17.131]** *et seq ante*.

727 Paragraph 8(2) of the Schedule to the C(A)A 1986.

728 See **[17.131]** *et seq ante*.

729 Section 18(2) of the C(A)A 1986.

730 Section 10(1) of the C(A)A 1986.

731 See **[17.267]** *ante*.

732 Section 18(3)–(4) of the C(A)A 1986.

733 Section 18(5) of the C(A)A 1986.

[17.284] One should also bear in mind that certain small companies may be able to avail of the exemption from audit, and if they do so, they will be exempt from the requirement to file a special auditor's report[734].

Exemption for subsidiary of EU parent undertaking

[17.285] Where a private company is a subsidiary undertaking of a private undertaking established under the laws of an EU Member State, the company shall, as respects any particular financial year, stand exempted from the obligation to annex its individual company accounts, and the auditor's report and directors' report in respect of those accounts, to its annual return, if all of the following conditions are satisfied[735]:

(a) Every person who is a shareholder of the company on the earlier of the date of the holding of the next AGM, or the next ARD, after the end of that financial year, shall declare his consent to the exemption;

(b) There is in force in respect of the whole of that financial year an irrevocable guarantee by the EU parent undertaking of all liabilities of the company in respect of that financial year, and notification in writing of the guarantee is sent by the company to every person at (a);

(c) The annual accounts of the company for that financial year are consolidated in the group accounts prepared by the EU parent undertaking and the fact that the company is availing of this exemption is disclosed in a note to the group accounts;

(d) A notice stating that the company has availed of this exemption in respect of that financial year, a copy of the guarantee and notification at (b), and a written declaration by the company that the condition at (a) has been complied with, is annexed to the annual return for the financial year made by the company to the registrar of companies;

(e) The group accounts of the parent undertaking are drawn up in accordance with the requirements of Council Directive 83/349/EEC of 13 June 1983 or in accordance with IFRS; and

(f) The group accounts of the parent undertaking are audited in accordance with Article 37 of the aforementioned Council Directive, and annexed to the annual return of the company.

[17.286] It should be stressed that the above exemption only relieves a company from annexing its individual company accounts to the annual return. Therefore, first, the company will still be obliged to prepare such individual company accounts and to lay them before the AGM. Second, if the company seeking the exemption is itself a parent undertaking, it will be required to prepare and file consolidated accounts, unless it can avail of an exemption in this respect[736].

734 Section 32(2) of the C(A)(No 2)A 1999. See **[17.287]** *et seq ante*.

735 Section 17 of the C(A)A 1986.

736 See **[17.156]** *ante* in respect of the exemptions from these requirements.

[L] AUDIT EXEMPTION

Exemption from the requirement to have accounts audited

[17.287] If a private limited company satisfies certain conditions in respect of a particular year, being that its turnover does not exceed €8.8m, its balance sheet total does not exceed €4.4m, and its average number of employees is not greater than 50, and if the directors of the company are of the opinion that it will meet those conditions again in the following financial year, the directors may elect (and must document that decision in the meeting minutes) to dispense with the requirement to appoint an auditor or to produce audited accounts in that following financial year[737]. A private limited company may avail of the exemption in its first financial year, if the directors are of the opinion that the conditions will be met in respect of that year; there will obviously be no requirement that the conditions were met in the preceding year[738]. The exemption cannot be availed of by a company which is a parent undertaking or a subsidiary undertaking, or by banking or insurance companies or companies within a group[739], nor can it be availed of by a company which has failed to comply with the requirements as to filing of an annual return[740].

[17.288] Given that the auditor has a duty to act in the members' interests, it would appear at first strange that the directors, and not the members, should be given the power to opt out of the requirement to have an auditor. However any member or members holding 10% in aggregate of the voting rights of a company have a right to veto the company availing of the exemption[741], which is exercised by serving a notice on the company, stating that that member or those members do not wish the exemption to be available to the company in a specified financial year[742]. That notice must be served no later than one month in advance of the end of the financial year in which the exemption, otherwise, would be claimed[743].

[17.289] The balance sheet of a company for a year in which it avails of the exemption must contain a statement by the directors, to appear in the balance sheet directly above the signatures of the directors (or if applicable, above any wording relating to the preparation of abridged accounts[744])[745]. This statement must state that the exemption is being availed of on the grounds that it satisfies the specified conditions, that no valid veto notice has been served on the company, and that the directors acknowledge the obligations of the Companies Acts to keep proper books of account and to prepare accounts that give a true and fair view of the state of affairs and profit or loss of the company[746].

---

737 Section 32 of the C(A)(No 2)A 1999, as amended by the Companies (Amendment) (No 2) Act 1999 (Section 32) Order 2012 (SI 308/2012).

738 Section 32(1)(b) of the C(A)(No 2)A 1999.

739 Section 32(3) of the C(A)(No 2)A 1999.

740 Section 32A of the C(A)(No 2)A 1999.

741 Section 32B of the C(A)(No 2)A 1999.

742 Section 33(1) of the C(A)(No 2)A 1999.

743 Section 33(2) of the C(A)(No 2)A 1999.

744 See **[17.267]** *et seq, ante*.

745 Section 33(5) of the C(A)(No 2)A 1999.

[17.290] If, in availing of the exemption, the office of a sitting auditor is to be terminated, the auditor must serve a notice on the company within 21 days including either:

(a) a statement to the effect either that there are no circumstances connected with the termination decision which should be brought to the attention of the members or creditors, or

(b) a statement setting out such circumstances.

The auditor must (within 14 days after serving notice on the company) send a copy of the notice to the registrar of companies, and if the statement sets out circumstances as at (b) above, the company must send a copy of the notice to every person entitled to be sent copies of the company's accounts[747].

[17.291] If the exemption should cease to have effect, the directors are required (and permitted) to appoint an auditor, as soon as may be, to fill the vacancy. If the directors fail to do so, the company in general meeting may do so. In either case, the auditor shall hold office until the conclusion of the next meeting of the company[748].

[M] APPOINTMENT OF STATUTORY AUDITORS

The requirement to appoint an auditor

[17.292] Every company is required to appoint an auditor or auditors at its AGM, to hold office from the conclusion of that AGM until the conclusion of the next AGM[749], save where the company avails of an exemption from audit pursuant to the C(A)(No 2)A 1999[750]. The term 'auditor' is defined as meaning either a statutory auditor (ie, an individual) or a statutory audit firm[751].

[17.293] The appointment of the auditor or auditors is principally a matter for the members in general meeting. The appointment of auditors need not be on the agenda of every AGM. A retiring auditor shall automatically be re-appointed without any resolution being passed, unless one of the following applies:

- he is not qualified for re-appointment[752];
- a resolution has been passed at that meeting appointing somebody instead of him;
- notice of a resolution to appoint somebody else instead of him has been given, but the proposed resolution cannot be passed because of the death, insanity, or disqualification of thc rcplacement;
- a resolution has been passed at that meeting providing expressly that he shall not be re-appointed;

746 Section 33(4) of the C(A)(No 2)A 1999.

747 Section 34 of the C(A)(No 2)A 1999.

748 Section 35 of the C(A)(No 2)A 1999.

749 Section 160(1) of the CA 1963.

750 See **[17.287]** *et seq*, *ante*.

751 Section 2(1) of the CA 1963, as amended by reg 4(1)(b) of the EC(SA)(D)R 2010; See **[17.296]** *post*.

752 See **[17.296]** *post*.

– he has given notice in writing of his unwillingness to be re-appointed[753].

[17.294] Where an AGM fails to appoint or re-appoint an auditor, the Minister[754] may appoint a person to fill the vacancy[755]. The company must, within one week of such an AGM, give notice of that fact to the Minister[756]. This provision is designed to ensure that companies do not frustrate the requirement to have an auditor by simply failing to appoint any auditors. Failure to notify the Minister renders the company and every officer in default liable to a class C fine[757].

[17.295] Not all appointments of auditors need be made at the AGM. The first auditors of the company may be appointed by the directors at any time before the first AGM, and if they fail to do so, the company in general meeting may make the appointment[758]. Similarly, casual vacancies in the office of auditor may be filled by the directors or by the company in general meeting, but while the vacancy continues, the surviving or continuing auditor or auditors may continue to act[759]. Extended notice must be given by a member of the intention to propose a resolution to fill a casual vacancy to a general meeting, and the company must, forthwith on receiving notice of such a resolution, send a copy thereof to the person (if any) whose ceasing to hold office occasioned the casual vacancy[760]. Finally, the company in general meeting may also appoint an auditor to replace an auditor removed from office at that meeting[761].

Qualification for appointment as auditor

[17.296] The EC(SA)(D)R 2010[762] define the term 'statutory audit' as 'an audit of individual or group accounts in so far as required by Community law'[763]. Statutory audits shall be carried out only by statutory auditors or statutory audit firms, being those that are approved under the EC(SA)(D)R 2010[764]. The EC(SA)(D)R 2010 define a 'statutory auditor' and a 'statutory audit firm' as, respectively, a natural person, or an audit firm, who or which (as applicable) is approved in accordance with the EC(SA)(D)R 2010 to carry out statutory audits[765]. The term 'auditor' when used in the Companies Acts means a statutory auditor or statutory audit firm within the meaning of the EC(SA)(D)R 2010[766].

[17.297] Regulation 21 of the EC(SA)(D)R 2010 provides that a person shall not:

753 Section 160(2)–(3) of the CA 1963.

754 'Minister' currently means the Minister for Jobs, Enterprise and Innovation.

755 Section 160(4) of the CA 1963.

756 Section 160(5A)(a)(i) of the CA 1963.

757 Section 160(5A)(b) of the CA 1963.

758 Section 160(6) of the CA 1963.

759 Section 160(7) of the CA 1963.

760 Section 161(1)–(2) of the CA 1963. On extended notice, See Ch 14, *Corporate Governance: Meetings*, at para **[14.044]**.

761 Section 160(2)(b) of the CA 1963; See **[17.338]** *et seq, post*.

762 Being, as defined at **[17.122]** *ante*, the EC(SA)(D)R 2010 (SI 220/2010).

763 Regulation 3(1) of the EC(SA)(D)R 2010.

764 Regulation 20 of the EC(SA)(D)R 2010.

765 Regulation 3(1) of the EC(SA)(D)R 2010.

766 Section 2(1) of the CA 1963.

(a) act as a statutory auditor;
(b) describe himself or herself as a statutory auditor; or
(c) so hold himself or herself out as to indicate, or be reasonably understood to indicate, that he or she is a statutory auditor,

unless he or she has been approved in accordance with the provisions of the EC(SA)(D)R 2010[767]. Regulation 22 of the EC(SA)(D)R 2010 provides that a firm shall not:

(a) act as a statutory audit firm;
(b) describe itself as a statutory audit firm; or
(c) so hold itself out as to indicate, or be reasonably understood to indicate, that it is a statutory audit firm,

unless it has been approved in accordance with the provisions of the EC(SA)(D)R 2010[768].

[17.298] Where a person contravenes the provisions in regs 21 or 22 of the EC(SA)(D)R 2010 or carries out a statutory audit while not being an auditor or audit firm, that person is guilty of an offence and is liable[769]:

(a) on summary conviction, to a class A fine; or
(b) on conviction on indictment to a fine not exceeding €50,000 or imprisonment for a term not exceeding 12 months or both.

Additional daily default penalties shall apply in cases of continued contravention[770].

Approval as statutory auditor

[17.0299] A person shall not be eligible for approval as a statutory auditor unless he or she is[771]:

(a) a member of a recognised accountancy body;
(b) a Member State auditor; or
(c) a third country auditor;

and in each case meets the required additional requirements.

(a) Member of a recognised accountancy body

[17.300] A 'recognised accountancy body' means a body of accountants recognised or deemed to be recognised under s 191 of the CA 1990[772]. There are currently six recognised bodies:

- ACCA – Association of Chartered Certified Accountants;
- ICAEW – Institute of Chartered Accountants in England & Wales;
- ICAI – Institute of Chartered Accountants in Ireland;
- ICAS – Institute of Chartered Accountants of Scotland;

767 Regulation 21 of the EC(SA)(D)R 2010.
768 Regulation 22 of the EC(SA)(D)R 2010.
769 Regulation 23(1) of the EC(SA)(D)R 2010.
770 Regulation 23(2) of the EC(SA)(D)R 2010.
771 Regulation 24 of the EC(SA)(D)R 2010.
772 Regulation 3(1) of the EC(SA)(D)R 2010.

- ICPAI – Institute of Certified Public Accountants in Ireland; and
- IIPA – Institute of Incorporated Public Accountants[773].

A person who is a member of such a body must also, to be eligible for approval, hold an appropriate qualification. An individual holds an appropriate qualification if he or she holds a qualification granted by a recognised accountancy body whose standards relating to training and qualifications meet the necessary standard[774].

(b) Member State auditor

[17.301] A 'Member State auditor' means an auditor approved in accordance with Directive 2006/43/EC by a competent authority of another Member State to carry out audits of annual or group accounts as required by Community law[775]. For such a person to be eligible for approval as a statutory audit in Ireland, it will additionally be necessary that they have passed an 'aptitude test' to demonstrate his or her knowledge of the enactments and practice relevant to statutory audits in Ireland[776], unless the competent authority is satisfied that he or she has otherwise demonstrated sufficient knowledge of such matters[777].

(c) Third country auditor

[17.302] A 'third country auditor' means a natural person who is entitled, under or by virtue of the laws, regulations or administrative provisions of a third country, to carry out audits of the individual or group accounts of a company incorporated in that third country. For such a person to be eligible for approval as a statutory audit in Ireland, it will again be necessary that he or she have passed an 'aptitude test' to demonstrate his or her knowledge of the enactments and practice relevant to statutory audits in Ireland[778], unless the competent authority is satisfied that he or she has otherwise demonstrated sufficient knowledge of such matters[779].

In addition, such a person shall not be approved as a statutory auditor unless reciprocal arrangements are in place with the third country in question, that is to say arrangements that enable, by virtue of the law of that third country, and on fulfilment by the statutory auditor concerned of requirements no more onerous than those that the statutory auditor would have to meet to be approved in Ireland, a statutory audit to carry out audits in that third country[780].

Approval as statutory audit firm

[17.303] A firm shall only be eligible for approval as a statutory audit firm if:

> '(a) the natural persons who carry out statutory audits in the State on behalf of the firm are approved as statutory auditors in accordance with [the EC(SA)(D)R 2010];

773 Section 191(3) of the CA 1990, as inserted by reg 10 of the EC(SA)(D)R 2010.
774 Regulation 26 of the EC(SA)(D)R 2010.
775 Regulation 3(1) of the EC(SA)(D)R 2010.
776 Regulation 24 of the EC(SA)(D)R 2010.
777 Regulation 30 of the EC(SA)(D)R 2010.
778 Regulation 24 of the EC(SA)(D)R 2010.
779 Regulation 30 of the EC(SA)(D)R 2010.
780 Regulation 112 of the EC(SA)(D)R 2010.

(b) the majority of the voting rights in the firm are held by—

(i) natural persons who are eligible for approval in the State or in any other Member State as statutory auditors; or

(ii) audit firms approved as statutory audit firms in the State or in any other Member State; and

(c) the majority of the members of the administrative or management body of the firm are—

(i) natural persons who are eligible for approval in the State or in any other Member State as statutory auditors; or

(ii) audit firms approved as statutory audit firms in the State or in any other Member State,

and for the avoidance of doubt, a majority, for the purposes of subparagraph (b) or (c), may be constituted by a combination of natural persons so eligible and audit firms so approved[781].

In summary, a statutory audit firm must be run by Irish or EEA statutory auditors or statutory audit firms, or a combination of them, and all individuals carrying out statutory audits on behalf of the firm must be statutory auditors.

[17.304] The Director of Corporate Enforcement may demand that a person acting as statutory auditor or audit firm, or purporting to have obtained approval under the EC(SA)(D)R 2010, produce evidence of his or her approval under the EC(SA)(D)R 2010. Failure to produce such evidence within 30 days of the demand (or such longer period as the director may allow) constitutes an offence, and the presumption of innocence is reversed so that the onus is placed on the accused to prove that the demand was complied with. A person who is guilty of an offence under this provision is liable, on summary conviction, to a class A fine, or on conviction on indictment, to a fine of up to €12,500[782].

[17.305] Since 20 May 2010, the registrar of companies has maintained a register which contains specified information in relation to statutory auditors and audit firms, and third country auditors and audit entities[783], as follows:

(i) Statutory auditors or third country auditor

- name and address of the auditor;
- registered number of the auditor;
- if applicable, the name, address, website address and registered number of the statutory audit firm by which the auditor is employed, or with whom he or she is associated;
- name and address of the competent authority responsible for the regulation of the auditor;
- if registered with one or more such authorities, particulars and number of registration as a statutory auditor, or with a third country authority;

781 Regulation 27 of the EC(SA)(D)R 2010.

782 Regulation 28 of the EC(SA)(D)R 2010.

783 Regulation 63 of the EC(SA)(D)R 2010.

- if the auditor is a Member State statutory auditor, the name and address of the competent authority responsible for approval, quality assurance, investigations, discipline and penalties, and public oversight, in relation to the auditor[784].

(ii) Statutory audit firms or third country audit entities

- name and address of the audit firm;
- registered number of the audit firm;
- legal form of the audit firm;
- contact details for the primary contact person in the audit firm;
- address of each office of the audit firm in the State, and website address of the audit firm;
- name of every individual approved as statutory auditor, who is employed by or associated as partner or otherwise with the audit firm;
- registered number of each such individual;
- name and address of the competent authority responsible for the regulation of the audit firm;
- names and addresses of the owners of, or as appropriate, shareholders in, the audit firm;
- names and addresses of the directors, or other members of the management structure (unless this comprises all partners);
- if the audit firm is a member of a network, that fact, a list of the names and addresses of member firms and affiliates of the network (or an indication of where that information is publicly available);
- if registered with one or more such authorities, particulars and number of registration as a statutory audit firm, or with a third country authority;
- if the audit firm is a Member State statutory audit firm, the name and address of the competent authority responsible for approval, quality assurance, investigations, discipline and penalties, and public oversight, in relation to the auditor[785].

The above apply in respect of a third country auditor or audit entity save in so much as any of them are inapplicable in the case of such an auditor or firm, as appropriate[786].

Each individual, firm and entity entered in the register shall be assigned an individual identification number[787].

An auditor or audit firm or third country auditor is required, as soon as may be after being approved as a statutory auditor or audit firm, to notify the relevant information to the competent authority, who shall notify the registrar of companies[788]. In addition, each statutory auditor and audit firm must, not later than one month after the event, notify the competent authority of any change in the information relating to them contained in the

784 Paragraph 1 of Schedule 1 to the EC(SA)(D)R 2010.

785 Paragraph 2 of Schedule 1 to the EC(SA)(D)R 2010.

786 Paragraph 3 of Schedule 1 to the EC(SA)(D)R 2010.

787 Paragraph 4 of Schedule 1 to the EC(SA)(D)R 2010.

788 Regulation 64 of the EC(SA)(D)R 2010.

public register[789]. In either of the above cases, the information notified is required to be signed by the statutory auditor, or on behalf of the statutory audit firm, as applicable[790].

Persons who may not act as auditor

[17.306] The general principle that the auditor should be independent of the entity it is auditing is set out at greater length in the EC(SA)(D)R 2010 than was previously the case. The overriding requirement is that, when carrying out a statutory audit, the statutory auditor, or the statutory audit firm (and every statutory auditor therein), must be independent of, and not be involved in the decision-taking of, the audited entity[791]. The EC(SA)(D)R 2010 set out specific provisions to secure this independence. A statutory auditor or audit firm shall not carry out a statutory audit if there exists any direct or indirect financial, business, employment or other relationship between the statutory auditor or audit firm (or a network to which he, she or it belongs) and the audited entity, from which an objective, reasonable and informed third party would conclude that the independence of the statutory auditor or audit firm is compromised[792]. In addition, if the statutory auditor or audit firm's independence is affected by threats, such as self-review, self-interest, advocacy, familiarity or trust or intimidation, the statutory auditor or audit firm shall apply safeguards to mitigate those threats; and if despite those safeguards the threats are so significant that their independence is compromised, the statutory auditor or audit firm shall not carry out the audit[793].

The EC(SA)(D)R 2010 also set out particular circumstances in which a statutory auditor or audit firm shall be disqualified from acting. Regulation 71(4) of the EC(SA)(D)R 2010 provides that a person shall not act as a statutory auditor if he or she is:

- an officer or servant of the company;
- a person who has been an officer or servant of the company during the period to which the accounts to be audited relate;
- a parent, spouse, brother, sister or child of an officer of the company;
- a person who is a partner of, or in the employment of, an officer of the company;
- a person who is disqualified, for any of the above reasons, from acting as auditor of any other body corporate which is a subsidiary, holding company, or subsidiary of the company's holding company, or would be so disqualified it the body corporate were a company;
- a person disqualified for any of the above reasons from acting as public auditor of an industrial and provident society which is a subsidiary, holding company, or subsidiary of the company's holding company; or
- a person in whose name a share in the company is registered (whether or not that person is the beneficial owner of the share)[794].

789 Regulation 66 of the EC(SA)(D)R 2010.
790 Regulation 67 of the EC(SA)(D)R 2010.
791 Regulation 70 of the EC(SA)(D)R 2010.
792 Regulation 71(1) and (2) of the EC(SA)(D)R 2010.
793 Regulation 71(3) of the EC(SA)(D)R 2010.
794 Regulation 71(4) of the EC(SA)(D)R 2010.

Similarly, reg 71(5) of the EC(SA)(D)R 2010 provides that a statutory audit firm (whatever its legal structure) shall not carry out a statutory audit if:

– any principal of the audit firm is an officer or servant of the company;
– any principal of the audit firm has been an officer or servant of the company during the period to which the accounts to be audited relate;
– the firm is disqualified, for any of the above reasons, from acting as auditor of any other body corporate which is a subsidiary, holding company, or subsidiary of the company's holding company, or would be so disqualified it the body corporate were a company; or
– the firm is disqualified for any of the above reasons from acting as public auditor of an industrial and provident society which is a subsidiary, holding company, or subsidiary of the company's holding company[795].

In addition, a person shall not carry out a statutory audit on behalf of a statutory audit firm if he or she is:

– A person in whose name a share in the company is registered (whether or not that person is the beneficial owner of the share); or
– A parent, spouse, brother, sister or child of an officer of the company[796].

[17.307] A person who is the subject or deemed to be the subject of a disqualification order[797] is also prohibited from being appointed to act as auditor of any company[798]. Where any such person becomes, or remains after 28 days from the making of the disqualification order, a partner in a firm of auditors, gives directions or instructions in relation to the conduct of any part of the audit of the accounts of a company, or works in any capacity in the conduct of the audit, he will be guilty of an offence. The disqualification order shall, upon conviction, be extended for a further 10-year period or such further period as the court, on the application of the prosecutor and having regard to all the circumstances of the case, may order[799].

Remuneration and expenses of auditors

[17.308] The remuneration and expenses of an auditor appointed by the Minister or by the directors is fixed by the person or persons who appoint him. Where the auditor is appointed by members, whether at the AGM or otherwise, the remuneration and expenses must be fixed at the AGM or in such manner as the company at the AGM shall determine[800]. Thus, the AGM may, and in practice commonly does, empower the directors to fix the auditors' remuneration and expenses.

[17.309] An auditor may, in appropriate circumstances, exercise a lien over the books of the company in respect of his fee. This may, however, be subject to a significant exception, in that the auditor may not exercise a lien over books and documents which are required by the articles of association to be kept in the possession of the company,

795 Regulation 71(5) of the EC(SA)(D)R 2010.

796 Regulation 71(6) of the EC(SA)(D)R 2010.

797 See Ch 28, *Compliance and Enforcement*, at para **[28.148]** *et seq.*

798 Section 160(1)(a) of the CA 1990.

799 Section 195 of the CA 1990.

800 Section 160(8) of the CA 1963.

since the central requirement of all valid liens is that possession of the subject matter of the lien is taken by the person exercising the lien with the consent of the debtor, and the directors would not have the power to validly provide such consent on behalf of the company. In *Re JJ Hopkins & Co*[801], the auditors claimed a lien over a number of books and documents belonging to the company. These included the petty cash book, the sales book, the debtors' ledger, the cash book, the cheques journal, certain creditors' ledgers and wages books, the nominal ledger, the share register, and the certificate of incorporation. The company's articles of association required the books of account to be kept at the company's registered office. On the application of the liquidator of the company for an order that the auditors were not entitled to exercise a lien, Dixon J, granting the order sought, said:

> '... lien is a matter of contract, and, if by reason of a prohibition in the articles of association, the directors of a company have no power to create a lien, there cannot be an implied contract. It has been said that the auditors are not bound by the articles of association but even if that is correct, it seems to me to be irrelevant. The articles of association restrict the power of the company to enter into the implied contract which is necessary to create a lien. It was submitted that a valid lien had been created because the books had been left with the auditors for a valid purpose. The purpose for which the books had been left with the auditors was a temporary purpose and it seems clear that the books would have to be returned to the company as soon as the purpose for which they had been left with the auditors was completed. There is no distinction in principle between books of account which come into the hands of the auditors for legitimate purposes and books of account which come into the possession of a solicitor. I think that the position is the same for solicitors and auditors. In either case, if the books are in the hands of an agent for a legitimate purpose, a lien may exist but it cannot arise when the books are of a type that are required by the articles of association of the company to be kept at the registered office of the company or are books like the register of members which are incapable of being the subject of a lien.'

Where an auditor successfully exercises a lien over the company's books or records, he may nevertheless be required to deliver up the books to any liquidator, provisional liquidator, or examiner of the company, but without prejudice to his rights under the lien[802].

[N] RIGHTS, OBLIGATIONS AND DUTIES OF AUDITORS

The rights and powers of auditors

[17.310] In addition to those rights which arise specifically upon resignation or removal, every auditor has a right of access at all reasonable times to the books, accounts and vouchers of the company, and is entitled in addition to require all officers and employees of the company to give such information and explanations which are within their knowledge or which they can procure, which he[803] thinks necessary for the performance

801 *In the Matter of J J Hopkins & Co Ltd* [1959] 93 ILTR 32, which followed the decision in *In Re Capital Fire Insurance Association* [1883] 24 Ch D 408 and *In Re Anglo Maltese Hydraulic Dock Co Ltd* [1885] 33 WR 652.

802 Section 244A of the CA 1963, and s 180(2) of the CA 1990.

803 This is a subjective decision, whereby the auditor decides what information, etc,. is necessary for the performance of his duties.

of his duties as auditor[804]. Any officer or employee who fails, within two days of the request being made, to give such information or explanations (being within their knowledge or which can be procured by them), will be guilty of an offence. Such an offence is punishable on summary conviction by the imposition of a class C fine[805] or, at the discretion of the court, by imprisonment for a term not exceeding 12 months, or both[806]. Upon conviction on indictment, a person guilty of such an offence shall be liable to a fine not exceeding €22,220.42 or imprisonment for a term not exceeding five years, or both[807]. It will be a defence, however, for a person to show that it was not reasonably possible for him to comply with the requirement within two days, but that he complied with the requirement as soon as was reasonably possible after the expiration of that time[808].

In addition, a person convicted of an offence in this respect may be made personally liable, without limitation of liability, for all or part of the company's debts and other liabilities in a winding up[809].

The provisions above apply equally where an officer of a company knowingly or recklessly makes a statement (whether orally or in writing) to the auditors of a company which is misleading, false or deceptive in a material particular, and which conveys, or purports to convey, any information or explanation which the auditors require under the Companies Acts, or are entitled to require, as auditors of the company[810].

Where a company (the 'holding company') has a subsidiary being a body corporate incorporated in the State, the subsidiary and its auditors have a duty to give to the auditor of the holding company such information and explanations as those auditors may reasonably require for the purpose of their duties as auditors of the holding company. Where the subsidiary is not incorporated in the State, the duty is on the holding company itself, to take all reasonable steps to obtain such information and explanations for the auditor[811]. If the company or an auditor of a subsidiary fails to comply with this requirement within five days, the company and every officer thereof who is in default, or the auditor, as the case may be, will be guilty of an offence. Such an offence is punishable on summary conviction by the imposition of a class C fine[812] or upon conviction on indictment to a fine not exceeding €22,220.42[813]. Again, it will be a defence for the defendant to show that it was not reasonably possible to comply with the requirement within five days, but that the defendant did comply with the requirement as soon as was reasonably possible after the expiration of that time[814].

There is old authority for the proposition that where an auditor is denied access to the books of account, they should report that matter to the members before taking a

---

804 Section 193(3) of the CA 1990.

805 A class C fine is defined in s 3 of the FA 2010 as 'a fine not exceeding €2,500'.

806 Section 240(1) of the CA 1990, as amended by the FA 2010.

807 Section 240(1) of the CA 1990, as amended by the FA 2010.

808 Section 197(4) of the CA 1990.

809 Section 204(1) of the CA 1990; See **[17.013]** *ante*.

810 Section 197(1)–(2) of the CA 1990.

811 Section 196(1) of the CA 1990.

812 A class C fine is defined in s 3 of the FA 2010 as 'a fine not exceeding €2,500'.

813 Section 240(2) of the CA 1990, as amended by the FA 2010.

814 Section 196(3) of the CA 1990.

court action to enforce their rights. In *Cuff v London and County Land & Building Co Ltd*[815], it was held that the courts will not order by mandatory injunction the company to produce the books of account to the auditor where the shareholders do not wish him to act.

[17.311] The auditor is also entitled to attend any general meeting of the company and to receive the same notices of, and communications relating to, meetings as the members. He has a right to be heard at all general meetings, annual or otherwise, on any part of the business of the meeting which concerns him as auditor[816]. Indeed, even where the sole member of a single-member company has decided to dispense with the holding of an AGM in a particular year, the auditor is empowered, by notice to the company not later than three months before the end of that year, to require the holding of an AGM in that year[817].

Status and duties of auditors

(a) Status

[17.312] An auditor is not normally an agent of the company, unless there are special provisions to this effect in his contract of engagement with the company. In *Re Transplanters (Holding Co) Ltd*[818], the applicant, one of two directors of the company, sought to prove as creditor in its liquidation, but his claim was opposed by the liquidator on the basis that the claim was statute-barred. The applicant pointed in evidence to two balance sheets of the company which made reference to the debt, signed by himself and his fellow director, and certified by the auditor. The applicant alleged that the references constituted an acknowledgement of the debt for the purposes of the Statute of Limitations, so that time began to run afresh from the date of the references. Wynn-Parry J held that the auditor's certificate was not such an acknowledgement, saying:

> 'In my view, an auditor of a company is (apart from any special contract, and there is none in this case) not an agent of the company, at any rate for the purpose of being able to bind the company by merely signing the normal certificate at the foot of the balance-sheet … No doubt, for certain purposes, the auditors may be regarded as servants of the company, so that the court will not, by mandatory injunction, force upon the company auditors whom the shareholders do not desire to act: see *Cuff v London and County Land and Building Co Ltd* [[1958] 1 WLR 822]. But apart again, as I say, from any special contract, the relations between the company and its auditors are governed by the provisions of the Companies Act, 1948, and their duty, as expressed by section 162 (1), is to make a report to the members on the accounts examined by them, and on every balance-sheet and every profit and loss account, and their report is to contain statements as to the various matters mentioned in the Ninth Schedule [to that Act] … I cannot spell out of their relations with the company, as to be extracted from the Companies Act, 1948, any authority to do anything in the nature of giving an acknowledgment within the Limitation Act, 1939, or any authority to do more than to perform the duties laid upon them as auditors by the Companies Act, 1948.'

815 *Cuff v London & County Land & Building Co Ltd* [1912] 1 Ch 440.
816 Section 193(5) of the CA 1990.
817 Regulation 8(3) of the EC(SMPLC)R 1994 (SI 275/1994).
818 *Re Transplanters (Holding Co) Ltd* [1958] 1 WLR 822.

The sources of the auditor's duties are the Companies Acts, the common law and any contract of engagement under which he is appointed, and his authority from the company extends merely to the performance of those duties and for those purposes only. If in the course of his audit he is fixed with constructive notice of matters not connected with the performance of his duties, that notice may not be imputed to the company[819].

However, while an auditor will not normally be an agent, he may be regarded as an officer of the company in relation to his duties, particularly where he has been guilty of, or has concurred in, the production of false or fraudulent accounts or the misappropriation of property. Accordingly, he may be made liable, either civilly or criminally, under any statutory provisions directed at 'officers'[820]. In *R v Shacter*[821], an auditor was convicted of larceny and misfeasance, offences which under the Larceny Acts and Companies Acts (UK) applied to officers. Parker CJ distinguished between auditors appointed to fill an office and those appointed *ad hoc* for a limited purpose, observing that the latter were not officers, but he could see no reason why the former should not be regarded as officers and made criminally liable as such. A corollary of this is that an auditor who is regarded as officer should be entitled to rely on statutory provisions which relieve officers from liability, such as the provision whereby the court may excuse officers for negligence, default, breach of duty or breach of trust, even prospectively, where he has acted honestly and reasonably and it appears to the court that he ought fairly to be so excused[822].

(b) Statutory duties

[17.313] The auditor's duties arise from statute, his contract of engagement, and the common law. His express statutory duties are five-fold:

- (i) To make a report to the members;
- (ii) To exercise professional integrity;
- (iii) To report failures to keep proper books of account;
- (iv) To disclose directors' emoluments if they do not appear in the accounts;
- (v) To report suspected indictable offences.

(i) To make a report to the members

[17.314] The auditor's principal statutory duty is to make a report to the members. Section 193(1) of the CA 1990 provides:

> The auditors of a company shall make a report to the members on the individual accounts examined by them, and on every balance sheet and profit and loss account or income statement, and all group accounts, laid before the company in general meeting during their tenure of office.

---

819 *Spackman v Evans* [1868] LR 3 HL 171.

820 See Ch 13, *Corporate Governance: Management by the Directors*, at para [**13.003**] *et seq*.

821 *R v Shacter* (1960) 44 Cr App R 42, citing *Re London General Bank* [1895] 2 Ch 166 and *Re Western Counties Steam Bakeries & Milling Co* [1897] 1 Ch 617.

822 Section 391 of the CA 1963. See Ch 15, *Duties of Directors and Other Officers*, at para **[15.088]**.

The statements required to be contained in the report have been considered above[823]. The statutory obligation to report to the members is not one which can be removed or limited by agreement or by the memorandum and articles. In *Newton v Birmingham Small Arms Co*[824], a special resolution changing the articles so as to provide that an internal reserve fund could be formed, and providing that it was to be the auditors' duty not to disclose any information with regard to it (to the shareholders or otherwise), was held to be invalid. Buckley J said:

> 'Any regulations which preclude the auditors from availing themselves of all the information to which under the Act they are entitled as material for the report which under the Act they are to make as to the true and correct state of the company's affairs, are, I think, inconsistent with the Act.'

(ii) To exercise professional integrity

[17.315] The auditor has a general duty to carry out his audit with 'professional integrity'[825]. As has been addressed above in the context of the auditor's report[826], the auditor is statutorily required to state, inter alia, whether proper books of account have been kept by the company, whether the company's balance sheet and profit and loss account are in agreement with the books of account, whether the information in the directors' report is consistent with the accounts, and whether the annual accounts give a 'true and fair view' of the state of affairs and profit or loss of the company or group (as applicable). Accordingly, it is not sufficient for the auditor merely to consider the annual accounts in isolation: rather, part of the auditor's reporting function is to carry out sufficient investigations to enable him to form an opinion as to the above matters. The Companies Acts do not elaborate further upon what is meant by 'professional integrity'. It seems, however, that compliance with the relevant accounting framework and auditing standards[827] will almost certainly amount to the exercise of 'professional integrity'.

(iii) To report failures to keep proper books of account

[17.316] Where an auditor forms the opinion that proper books of account are not being kept, save where the contraventions are minor or otherwise immaterial in nature, he is required by s 194(1) of the CA 1990 to serve by recorded delivery on the company a notice stating his opinion and, not less than seven days later, to notify the registrar of companies, who will forthwith notify the Director of Corporate Enforcement[828]. Failure by an auditor so to do renders him guilty of an offence.

[17.317] Where the auditor files a notice with the registrar of companies pursuant to s 194 of the CA 1990, the Director of Corporate Enforcement may require him to furnish information and an explanation of the reasons for the opinion, and to give the Director

---

823 See **[17.228]** *et seq, ante*.

824 *Newton v Birmingham Small Arms Co* [1906] 2 Ch 378.

825 Section 193(6) of the CA 1990.

826 See **[17.229]** *ante*.

827 International Standards on Auditing (UK and Ireland) and International Standard on Quality Control (UK and Ireland), which are based on the International Standards on Auditing (ISAs) and International Standard on Quality Control (ISQC) of the same titles that have been issued by the International Auditing and Assurance Standards Board (IAASB).

828 Section 194(1) of the CA 1990.

access to books and documents in the auditor's possession and control relating to the matter. Any written information given in response to a request of the Director will be admissible in subsequent legal proceeding as evidence of the facts stated therein, until the contrary is proved[829]. Failure to comply with the request of the Director constitutes an offence under s 194(4) of the CA 1990.

[17.318] An offence under s 194(1) or (4) of the CA 1990 is punishable on summary conviction by the imposition of a class C fine[830] or, at the discretion of the court, by imprisonment for a term not exceeding 12 months, or both[831]. Upon conviction on indictment, a person guilty of such an offence shall be liable to a fine not exceeding €22,220.42 or imprisonment for a term not exceeding five years, or both[832]. In addition, upon conviction the auditor may be made personally liable, without limitation of liability, for all or part of the company's debts and other liabilities in a winding up[833].

(iv) To disclose directors' emoluments if they do not appear in the accounts

[17.319] As has previously been noted[834], s 191 of the CA 1963 requires that detailed particulars of directors' emoluments be set out in the notes to the annual accounts. If such details are not disclosed, s 191(8) of the CA 1963 provides:

> '... it shall be the duty of the auditors of the company by whom the accounts are examined to include in the report thereon, so far as they are reasonably able to do so, a statement giving the required particulars.'

Obviously this duty will not apply where s 191 of the CA 1963 is disapplied, as is the case in respect of Companies Act group accounts[835].

(v) To report suspected indictable offences

[17.320] An auditor has a duty to report suspected indictable offences to the Director of Corporate Enforcement. Section 194(5) of the CA 1990 provides:

> 'Where, in the course of, and by virtue of, their carrying out an audit of the accounts of the company, information comes into the possession of the auditors of a company that leads them to form the opinion that there are reasonable grounds for believing that the company or an officer or agent of it has committed an indictable offence under the Companies Acts (other than an indictable offence under section 125(2) or 127(12)[836] of the [CA 1963]) the auditors shall, forthwith after having formed it, notify that opinion to the Director [of Corporate Enforcement] and provide the Director with details of the grounds on which they have formed that opinion.'

Failure so to do will itself constitute an offence[837], and it appears that the auditor is allowed no discretion as to whether to report the suspicion, even when the misconduct

829 Section 194(3A) of the CA 1990.

830 A class C fine is defined in s 3 of the FA 2010 as 'a fine not exceeding €2,500'.

831 Section 240(1) of the CA 1990.

832 Section 240(1) of the CA 1990.

833 Section 204(1) of the CA 1990; See **[17.013]** *ante*.

834 See **[17.112]** *ante*.

835 See **[17.181]** *ante*.

836 These provisions relate to default in filing the annual return.

837 Section 194(4) of the CA 1990.

has ceased. The penalties in relation to the failure to report are the same as for the obligations to report to the Director previously identified[838].

[17.321] No professional or legal duty of the auditor (such as, for example, a duty of client confidentiality) shall be regarded as breached by reason of compliance with the duty to report suspected indictable offences, nor will compliance expose the auditor to liability to members, creditors and other interested parties[839].

[17.322] The duty to report arises in the course of the auditing function, and so would seem to have no application where the suspicion is formed during non-audit work[840]. Moreover, the duty appears to end with the conclusion of duties as auditor. The duty creates certain difficulties for auditors. While the Director of Corporate Enforcement has published a list of indictable offences[841], which is likely to be of assistance, many of these are triable either summarily or upon indictment at the election of the prosecuting authorities. The auditor may obtain legal advice as to whether an indictable offence has been committed, but will not be entitled to rely conclusively on such legal advice.

(c) Common law duties

[17.323] If an auditor breaches duties contained in his contract of engagement, he may be made liable in contract for damages to the other party to the contract (ie, the company), provided that the other party can prove consequential loss. Such causation will often be difficult to prove since one would need to establish that the company would not have suffered as it did if it had not relied on the inaccurate figures, etc, which constitute the breach of duty. Individual members are not normally party to the contract of engagement, so an individual member may not sue the auditor in contract, unless he represents the company by way of a derivative action[842].

[17.324] The law of tort places a duty on the auditor not to breach his statutory duties, and to exercise reasonable skill and care in the performance of his duties, however they may arise. The standard of care required in such circumstances is 'to exercise such skill and care as a diligent, skilled and cautious auditor would exercise according to the practice of his profession'. In *Irish Woollen Co v Tyson*[843], Fitzgibbon LJ said:

> 'The measure of duty is the bringing of reasonable care and skill to the performance of the business directed to be done, having regard first to the contract of employment, then to the character of the business itself, to the remuneration of the defendant and to all the other circumstances of the case. In strict rule, however, the measure of the duty is to be ascertained by applying to all the circumstances of the case the best consideration so as to ascertain what ought to have been done under the circumstances.'

---

838 See para **[17.318]**.

839 Section 194(6) of the CA 1990.

840 See Decision Notice D/2006/2 issued by the Director of Corporate Enforcement, *Revised Guidance on the Duty of Auditors to Report Suspected Indictable Offences to the Director of Corporate Enforcement*, para 4.3 *et seq*.

841 *List of Offences pursuant to the Companies Acts 1963–2009*, issued by the Director of Corporate Enforcement.

842 See Ch 11, *Shareholders Remedies*, **[11.108]** *et seq*.

843 *Irish Woollen Co v Tyson* [1900] 26; See MacCann, *A Casebook on Company Law* (1991) at pp 489–90.

[17.325] Accordingly, the auditor must not certify as true that which he does not believe to be true, and he must make inquiries in relation to any irregularities which come to his attention which affect the performance of his duty. In *Re Kingston Cotton Mills Co (No 2)*[844], Lopes LJ said as follows:

> '… It is the duty of an auditor to bring to bear on the work he has to perform that skill, care, and caution which a reasonably competent, careful, and cautious auditor would use. What is reasonable skill, care, and caution must depend on the particular circumstances of each case. An auditor is not bound to be a detective, or, as was said, to approach his work with suspicion or with a foregone conclusion that there is something wrong. He is a watch-dog, but not a bloodhound. He is justified in believing tried servants of the company in whom confidence is placed by the company. He is entitled to assume that they are honest, and to rely upon their representations, provided he takes reasonable care. If there is anything calculated to excite suspicion he should probe it to the bottom; but in the absence of anything of that kind he is only bound to be reasonably cautious and careful.'

In this case it was therefore found that an auditor must be alert to irregularities which he may be expected to find in the performance of the audit, but that he need not search for them.

[17.326] The auditor must, however, be wary that mistakes might have been made. In *Fomento (Sterling Area) Ltd v Selsdon Fountain Co*[845], Lord Denning observed of an auditor that:

> His vital task is to take care to see that errors are not made, be they errors of computation, or errors of omission or commission, or downright untruths. To perform this task properly he must come to it with an inquiring mind – not suspicious of dishonesty, I agree – but suspecting that someone may have made a mistake somewhere and that a check must be made to ensure that there has been none.

[17.327] More recent decisions seem to indicate that the auditor will be required in the performance of his duties to make enquiries of customers and other third parties dealing with the company where he discovers an irregularity. In the *Irish Woollen Co* case[846], Holmes LJ was of the opinion that an auditor discovering irregularities is entitled to ask for explanations, but 'is not called to seek for knowledge outside the company or to communicate with customers or creditors. He is not an insurer against fraud or error.' Fitzgibbon LJ, however, was of the opinion that the auditor, though a watchdog, 'is bound to keep his eyes open and his nose, too. As in the case of the hound, the auditor will follow up this trail to the end[847].' In *Re City Equitable Fire Insurance Co*[848], Romer J held that an auditor could never be justified in omitting to make a personal inspection of company securities which were in improper hands. However, much depends here upon the prevailing standards of professional practice. Thus, in *Re Thomas Gerrard & Son Ltd*[849], where the explanations of a managing director as to irregular invoices concerning

[844] *Re Kingston Cotton Mills Co (No 2)* [1896] 2 Ch 279.

[845] *Fomento (Sterling Area) Ltd v Selsdon Fountain Co* [1958] 1 All ER 11.

[846] *Irish Woollen Co v Tyson* [1900] 26; See MacCann, *A Casebook on Company Law* (1991) at p 493.

[847] *Irish Woollen Co v Tyson* [1900] 26; See MacCann, *A Casebook on Company Law* (1991) at p 493.

[848] *Re City Equitable Fire Insurance Co* [1925] Ch 407.

[849] *Re Thomas Gerrard & Son Ltd* [1967] 2 All ER 525.

the purchases of stock had been accepted at face value by the auditor, Pennycuick J relied on expert evidence of prevailing practice in holding that the auditor had failed to perform his duties by not examining the suppliers' statements and, where necessary, communicating with the suppliers. Likewise, in *Kelly v Haughey Boland & Co*[850], Lardner J accepted that the standards of the profession have tended to become more exacting. He relied on accounting standards as evidence of the prevailing standard of care required of auditors in relation to stocktaking, and held that the auditor had not met those standards, even though the auditor in question had employed the same approach in the case as he might have legitimately employed 20 years' previously.

[17.328] The upshot of these cases, coupled with the statutory requirement to exercise 'professional integrity', is that auditors have a duty to maintain close adherence to the relevant accounting framework and to auditing standards. Professional standards may evolve and change over time so that the courts are bound to consider innovations and technical developments when assessing the standard of care required of auditors.

Civil liability of auditors

(a) Liability to the company

[17.329] As has been set out above[851], an auditor may be made liable by the company for breach of contract where he fails to observe the obligations imposed upon him by the contract of engagement, provided the company can prove consequential loss. Likewise, since the auditor is appointed by the company, his principal duty is to the company, and he may be made liable to the company in tort where his breach of duty causes loss[852]. As was also observed above, an auditor who has been convicted of an offence under s 194 of the CA 1990 may be made to contribute to the assets of the company in a subsequent insolvent liquidation[853].

(b) Liability to others

[17.330] An auditor's contractual liability to others depends upon whether the others are party to the contract. It may be recalled that an auditor's contract of engagement is normally between him and the company; accordingly, third parties, including shareholders and members, will not normally be entitled to rely on the contract. An auditor's liability to third parties in tort depends upon the existence of a duty of care owed to that party. Where a third party claims that reliance on inaccurate information negligently presented by the auditor led to economic loss, he must prove that he actually relied on the misstatement, and that:

- the loss was reasonably foreseeable;
- there was a sufficient degree of proximity between the auditor and the third party; and
- it was reasonable for the third party to rely on the accounts.

---

850 *Kelly v Haughey Boland & Co* [1989] ILRM 373.

851 See **[17.323]** to **[17.328]** *ante*.

852 *Candler v Crane Christmas* [1951] 1 All ER 426; *Caparo Industries plc v Dickman* [1990] 1 All ER 568.

853 See **[17.318]** *ante*.

[17.331] In *Kelly v Haughey Boland & Co*[854], the plaintiffs had wished to purchase the company to which the auditors had been appointed, and had been given copies of the audited accounts for the period 1973–1976. The figures contained therein were explained by the auditors during a number of meetings prior to completion of the purchase. Subsequent to completion, the plaintiffs sought to sue the auditors for damages in negligence in respect of inaccuracies in the accounts, arguing in particular that the auditors, in failing to attend the stocktaking, had not taken requisite care to ensure that stock figures were correct. Lardner J held for the plaintiffs. In doing so he relied on the words of Lord Morris in *Hedley Byrne & Co v Heller & Partners Ltd*[855] and those of Woolf J in *JEB Fasteners v Mark Bloom & Co*[856], where it was said:

> '… without laying down any principle which is intended to be of general application on the basis of the authorities which I have cited, the appropriate test for establishing whether a duty of care exists appears in this case to be whether the defendants knew or reasonably should have foreseen at the time the accounts were audited that a person might rely on those accounts for the purpose of deciding whether or not to take over the company and therefore could suffer loss if the accounts were inaccurate. Such an approach does place a limitation on those entitled to contend that there has been a breach of duty owed to them. First of all, they must have relied on the account and second, they must have done so in circumstances where the auditors either knew that they would or ought to have known that they might. If the situation is one where it would not be reasonable for the accounts to be relied on, then in the absence of express knowledge, the auditor would be under no duty. This places a limit on the circumstances in which the audited accounts can be relied on and the period for which they can be relied on, the longer the period which elapses prior to the accounts being relied on from the date on which the auditor gave his certificate, the more difficult it will be to establish that the auditor ought to have foreseen that his certificate would in those circumstances be relied on.'

Lardner J found that the plaintiffs met the foreseeable loss, proximity, and reasonable reliance tests outlined above, since the auditors were aware of an imminent sale when they audited the final set of accounts referred to, and ought to have foreseen in the previous year, that reliance might be placed on the accuracy of the accounts in a subsequent sale of the business. However, although the plaintiffs established that the auditors owed them a duty of care, they failed to prove that their loss was actually incurred as a result of reliance on inaccuracies negligently stated in the audited accounts, and the action failed.

[17.332] A similar conclusion was reached by Woolf J in the *JEB Fasteners* case[857], observing that even if the plaintiffs had known the true financial position of the company at the time, they would not have acted any differently. In that case, Woolf J held that, even though the auditor did not actually know that the plaintiffs were going to rely on the accounts, the auditor owed the plaintiffs a duty of care since he ought to have foreseen that the subsequent purchaser might rely on his work, being one of a class of persons, known or unknown to him, who might reasonably be expected to rely on the accuracy of his audit.

---

854 *Kelly v Haughey Boland & Co* [1989] ILRM 373.
855 *Hedley Byrne & Co v Heller & Partners Ltd* [1964] AC 465.
856 *JEB Fasteners v Mark Bloom & Co* [1981] 3 All ER 289.
857 *JEB Fasteners v Mark Bloom & Co* [1981] 3 All ER 289.

[17.333] The scope of the duty of care has been radically restricted in the UK in the case of *Caparo Industries plc v Dickman*[858]. In that case, the plaintiff bought shares in a company, Fidelity plc. The plaintiff's involvement with Fidelity occurred in three stages: at first, they were merely potential investors, relying on information in the public domain; later, they became shareholders and received copies of the shareholders' accounts; and finally, they became investors, by purchasing, in reliance upon the shareholders' accounts, shares in small batches on the open market until they could compel acceptance of their terms for the purchase of all the shares in Fidelity. Once they obtained control of Fidelity, they discovered its true worth, and issued proceedings against the defendant auditors.

At first instance, Sir Neil Lawson ruled that the auditors owed the plaintiffs no duty of care, either as potential investors, actual investors, or shareholders. Although the Court of Appeal overturned Sir Neil Lawson's finding on the duty of care to the plaintiffs as shareholders, the House of Lords restored his decision. The relationship as potential investor was not sufficiently proximate: Fidelity was a public limited company and its members could change from day to day. Moreover, the auditors did not know the plaintiffs' takeover plans when they became shareholders, nor ought they to have known then. As regards the plaintiffs' status as shareholder, their Lordships found that the auditors' statutory duties are owed to the shareholders as a whole – not to individual shareholders. The purpose of the audit was to protect the company itself. As a class the shareholders were determinate; but as individuals they could change identity from day to day and from time to time. To extend a duty to individual shareholders would open the auditor to liability for an indeterminate amount, for an indeterminate time, to an indeterminate class. The interests of the shareholders could be protected by the bringing of an action by, or on behalf of, the company, but not through individual action. Indeed, Lord Bridge found it difficult to see how a shareholder's interest could not adequately be protected through the bringing of an action on the company's behalf.

[17.334] The *Caparo* decision, and the cases which follow it, illustrate a turn away from the broad principles for identifying the existence of a duty of care which Lord Wilberforce laid down in *Anns v Merton London Borough Council*[859] and which have been upheld in by the Irish Supreme Court in *Siney v Dublin Corporation*[860]. To this extent it is questionable whether the Irish courts would be prepared to go a similar route. *Caparo* may be distinguished from the *Haughey Boland* case[861] on the basis that the auditors in the latter case actually knew the plaintiffs before they conducted the audit. Moreover, *Caparo* concerned a public limited company, and the relationship between auditors and shareholders or investors in a private company could hardly be more different. Private company auditors will often be aware of any on-going or prospective take over or investment negotiations, as in the *Haughey Boland* case, since they will be more acutely aware of the company's need for additional investment. Likewise, particularly in smaller private companies, banks and other lending institutions tend to rely more heavily on the audited accounts, as auditors may well know. Consequently, it is

858 *Caparo Industries plc v Dickman* [1990] 1 All ER 568.

859 *Anns v Merton London Borough Council* [1978] AC 728.

860 *Siney v Dublin Corporation* [1980] IR 400.

861 *Kelly v Haughey Boland & Co* [1989] ILRM 373.

easier to find foreseeability of loss, proximity, and reasonableness of reliance in a private company, and *Caparo* might be confined to its facts.

[17.335] Since *Caparo*, auditors have been found to owe a duty of care in a case where the price of shares in a transfer was fixed as a multiple of profits in audited accounts procured jointly by purchaser and vendor[862], and in a case where an auditor assumed responsibility for the accuracy of the accounts through statements to a prospective purchaser, knowing all the time that the accuracy of the accounts was the final consideration in the purchaser's decision whether or not to bid[863].

(c) Excluding liability

[17.336] An auditor cannot exclude his liability to the company, nor is it permitted for the company to indemnify him in respect of his liability to third parties:

> '... any provision whether contained in the articles of a company or in any contract with a company or otherwise for exempting any officer of the company or any person employed by the company as auditor from, or indemnifying him against, any liability which by virtue of any rule of law would otherwise attach to him in respect of any negligence, default, breach of duty or breach of trust of which he may be guilty in relation to the company shall be void ...[864]'

The auditor will, however, enjoy a limited right of indemnity from the company in respect of any liability incurred in defending proceedings, whether civil or criminal, in which judgment is given in his favour or in which he is acquitted, and in connection with any application for relief under s 391 of the CA 1963 or under s 42 of the C(A)A 1983[865]. Moreover, the company in general meeting may by resolution forgive or ratify a breach of duty by an auditor.

[17.337] Unless there is a contractual relationship between the parties, an exclusion clause in the contract of engagement will not exclude the auditor from liability to third parties to whom he owes a duty of care, because there will be no privity of contract. Where, however, a qualification is placed in the accounts, the exclusion clause may prove effective. In *John Sisk & Son v Flinn*[866], the plaintiffs wished to purchase a 75% shareholding in a company, it being agreed that the purchase price would be determined according to the company's accounts. The auditors knew of the plaintiff's plans when auditing the accounts. The books of account were not made available to the plaintiffs before the purchase, so there was no way in which they could verify the accuracy of the accounts. The audited accounts contained the following clause:

> 'We have obtained all the information and explanations which to the best of our knowledge and belief were necessary for the purpose of our audit except that stock and work in progress at the beginning and end of the financial period are as certified by the management and have not been physically observed.'

Finlay P found that although the auditors had prima facie failed to comply with the prevailing standards of recognised accounting practice in relation to the work in

---

862 *Galoo Ltd v Bright Grahame Murray Ltd* [1995] 1 All ER 16.

863 *ADT Ltd v BDO Binder Hamlyn* [1996] BCC 808.

864 Section 200 of the CA 1963.

865 See [**17.312**] *et seq, ante*.

866 *John Sisk & Son v Flinn* (18 July 1984, unreported).

progress figure, the clause in the accounts effectively excluded them from liability to the plaintiffs, because the defendants, seeing the statement, must have doubted whether the accounts contained the information sufficient to warrant reliance on them. The limits of such exclusions have not been judicially examined.

[O] Removal and Resignation of Auditors

Removal and replacement of auditors

[17.338] An auditor may be removed by ordinary resolution of the company in general meeting, and another auditor, nominated by any member of the company, may be appointed in his stead[867]. Alternatively, an auditor may be removed at the AGM if a resolution is passed appointing somebody as auditor instead of him, or providing expressly that he shall not be re-appointed[868]. In any of the above cases, extended notice[869] of the intended resolution must be given to the members[870]. When the company receives notice of a resolution in respect of any of the above cases, it must forthwith send a copy of the resolution to the auditor proposed to be removed, or not to be re-appointed[871]. In respect of the removal of the first auditor, the nomination for replacement must be notified to the members not less than 14 days before the date of the meeting[872]; notice must also be given to the members of the replacement for any other auditor[873].

With effect from 20 August 2010, s 161C(1) of the CA 1963 now provides that the passing of a resolution in any of the above cases shall not be effective with respect to the matter it provides for unless:

(a) in the case of resolution providing for the auditor's removal from office, there are good and substantial grounds for the removal related to the conduct of the auditor with regard to the performance of his duties as auditor of the company or otherwise; or

(b) in the case of any other resolution (ie, a resolution appointing as auditor someone other than the current auditor, or providing expressly that the current auditor shall not be re-appointed[874]), the passing of the resolution is, in the company's opinion, in the best interests of the company[875].

In addition, it is provided, in this context, that:

- diverging opinions on accounting treatments or audit procedures cannot constitute the basis for the passing of any such resolution; and

867 This is provided in respect of the first auditor of the company by s 160(6)(a) of the CA 1963, and in respect of any auditor other than the first auditor, by s 160(5) of the CA 1963.

868 Section 160(2)(b) of the CA 1963.

869 See Ch 14, *Corporate Governance: Meetings*, at para **[14.044]** *et seq*.

870 Section 161(1) of the CA 1963.

871 Section 161(2) of the CA 1963.

872 Section 160(6)(a) of the CA 1963.

873 Section 160(5) of the CA 1963.

874 Section 161C(2) of the CA 1963, as inserted by reg 62 of the EC(SA)(D)R 2010.

875 Section 161C(1) of the CA 1963, as inserted by reg 62 of the EC(SA)(D)R 2010.

– 'best interests of the company' do not include any illegal or improper motive with regard to avoiding disclosures or detection of any failure by the company to comply with the Companies Acts.

[17.339] It is conceivable that during the course of his audit, an auditor might uncover compromising information concerning the directors' handling of the company's financial affairs, or which would otherwise cause embarrassment to the directors. Safeguards have therefore been included to ensure that the members are fully informed in respect of any proposal to remove (or replace, or not re-appoint) the auditor.

[17.340] First, the auditor is permitted to make written representations, not exceeding a 'reasonable length', to the company, and may request the company to notify the members of his representations. Unless it is too late for it to do so, the company is then obliged to state in any notice of the resolution which it gives to the members the fact that such representations have been made to it, and must send a copy of the representations to every member to whom any notice of the meeting is or has been sent[876]. If copies of the representations are not so sent out to the members, whether because they have been received too late for circulation or because of the company's default, the auditor may, without prejudice to his right to be heard orally, require them to be read out at the meeting[877]. If the High Court finds, on application by the company or any aggrieved person, that the rights in respect of such representations are being abused to secure needless publicity for defamatory matter, the court may order that copies of the representations need not be sent out and that the representations need not be read out at the meeting[878].

[17.341] Second, an auditor who has been removed shall be entitled to attend the AGM at which, but for his removal, his term of office would have expired, and the general meeting at which it is proposed to fill the vacancy occasioned by his removal[879]. In addition, the auditor is entitled to receive all notices and other communications relating to any such meeting which a member of the company is entitled to receive, and to be heard at any general meeting on any business of the meeting which concerns him as former auditor of the company. This provision does not apply, however, to an auditor whose removal is consequent on the company availing of an exemption from audit under the C(A)(No 2)A 1999[880].

[17.342] With effect from 20 August 2010, where an auditor ceases to hold office between the conclusion of one AGM and the conclusion of the next, there is an obligation on both the auditor and the company to notify the Irish Auditing and Accounting Supervisory Authority[881]; this is set out in detail below[882].

876 Section 161(3) of the CA 1963.
877 Section 161(3) of the CA 1963.
878 Section 161(4) of the CA 1963.
879 Section 161(2A) of the CA 1963.
880 Section 34(5) of the C(A)(No 2)A 1999.
881 Pursuant to the new ss 161A and 161B of the CA 1963, as inserted by reg 62 of the EC(SA)(D)R 2010.
882 See para **[17.346]** *et seq*.

Resignation of auditor

[17.343] Section 185(1) of the CA 1990 permits an auditor to resign from office before the expiry of his term of appointment by serving notice in writing on the company. The resignation shall take effect on the date on which the notice is so served, or on such later date as may be specified in the notice. Prior to the enactment of this section, an auditor could only resign from office by notifying the company of his unwillingness to be re-appointed at the next AGM[883]; this option of course remains open to the auditor, but it is difficult to imagine any circumstances in which one would avail of it rather than simply resigning pursuant to s 185 of the CA 1990.

[17.344] A resigning auditor, or an auditor notifying the company of his unwillingness to be reappointed[884], is obliged to state in the notice of resignation the circumstances connected with his resignation which he considers ought to be brought to the attention of the members and creditors, or, if there are none, that no such circumstances exist[885]. Within 14 days of serving the notice on the company, the auditor must send a copy of the notice to the registrar of companies. In addition, unless the notice does not state any circumstances to be brought to the attention of the members and creditors of the company, the company must, within 14 days of service, send a copy of the notice to the registrar of companies and to every person entitled to receive copies of the annual accounts[886]. Failure by the auditor to make a statement in his notice, and failure by the company to circulate such notices, constitutes an offence, rendering the auditor, or the company and every officer in default as the case may be, liable on summary conviction to a class C fine[887] or to imprisonment for a term not exceeding 12 months, or to both[888], and on indictment to a fine not exceeding €22,220.42 or to imprisonment for a term not exceeding five years, or to both[889]. The company need not circulate the notice, however, if the High Court is satisfied, on the application of the company or any aggrieved person, that the notice contains material which has been included to secure needless publicity for defamatory matter[890].

[17.345] If a resigning auditor's notice contains a statement of circumstances as set out above, he is further entitled to requisition the convening by the directors of a general meeting of the company, for the purpose of receiving and considering such account and explanation as the auditor may wish to give of the circumstances connected with his resignation[891]. Where the auditor makes such a requisition in his notice, the directors must proceed, within 14 days of the service of the notice, to convene a general meeting for a day no later than 28 days after service of the notice[892].

---

883 Section 160(2)(c) of the CA 1963.

884 Section 185(5) of the CA 1990.

885 Section 185(2) of the CA 1990.

886 Section 185(3) of the CA 1990.

887 A class C fine is defined in s 3 of the FA 2010 as 'a fine not exceeding €2,500'.

888 Section 240(1) of the CA 1990, as amended by the FA 2010.

889 Section 240(1) of the CA 1990, as amended by the FA 2010.

890 Section 185(4) of the CA 1990.

891 Section 186(1) of the CA 1990.

892 Section 186(2) of the CA 1990.

The auditor shall be entitled to attend the general meeting convened pursuant to his requisition, any general meeting at which it is proposed to fill the vacancy occasioned by his requisition, and the AGM at which, but for his resignation, his term of office would have expired. In addition, the auditor is entitled to receive all notices and other communications relating to any such meeting which a member of the company is entitled to receive, and to be heard at any general meeting on any business of the meeting which concerns him as former auditor of the company[893].

If his notice of resignation contained a statement of circumstances which the auditor considered ought to be brought to the attention of the members and creditors, he may also require the company to circulate to the members a further statement of circumstances connected with the resignation, before any such general meeting. The company must state in any notice given to the members of the meeting that it has received such a further statement, and must send a copy of the statement to the registrar of companies and to every person entitled to receive copies of the company's annual accounts[894].

As in relation to the initial notice[895], failure by the company to circulate such notices constitutes an offence[896] rendering the company and every officer in default liable on summary conviction to a class C fine[897] or to imprisonment for a term not exceeding 12 months, or to both[898], and on indictment to a fine not exceeding €22,220.42 or to imprisonment for a term not exceeding five years, or to both[899]. Also as in relation to the initial notice, the company need not circulate the notice if the High Court is satisfied, on the application of the company or any aggrieved person, that the notice contains material which has been included to secure needless publicity for defamatory matter[900].

[P] Notification to Supervisory Authority of Certain Matters

[17.346] With effect from 20 August 2010[901], new ss 161A and 161B have been inserted into the CA 1963 by reg 62 of the EC(SA)(D)R 2010. These provisions impose a duty on the auditor and on the company respectively, to notify the Irish Auditing and Accounting Supervisory Authority (the 'supervisory authority') regarding the auditor's cessation of office.

[17.347] Section 161A of the CA 1963 requires that where during the period between the last AGM and the conclusion of the next AGM of a company, an auditor ceases to hold office either by virtue of s 160 (eg, his removal from office), or s 185 of the CA 1990 (his resignation from office), the auditor shall:

> '(a) in such form and manner as the Supervisory Authority specifies, and

893 Section 186(5) of the CA 1990.

894 Section 186(3) of the CA 1990.

895 As at **[17.344]** *ante*.

896 Section 186(6) of the CA 1990.

897 A class C fine is defined in s 3 of the FA 2010 as 'a fine not exceeding €2,500'.

898 Section 240(1) of the CA 1990, as amended by the FA 2010.

899 Section 240(1) of the CA 1990, as amended by the FA 2010.

900 Section 186(4) of the CA 1990.

901 Regulation 2 of the EC(SA)(D)R 2010.

(b) within 1 month after the date of that cessation,

notify the Supervisory Authority that the auditor has ceased to hold office[902].'

'Resignation' in this context includes an indication of unwillingness to be re-appointed at an AGM[903]. That notification shall be accompanied by:

(a) in the case of resignation of the auditor, the written notice served by the auditor on the company, notifying the company that he is resigning;

(b) in the case of removal of the auditor, a copy of any written representations made to the company[904], save where the court had found that the representations were intended to secure needless publicity for defamatory matter, and so such representations had not been circulated.

In the case of resignation, where the notice does not set out any circumstances to be brought to the notice of members or creditors of the company, the notification shall also be accompanied by a statement of the reasons for the auditor's resignation[905].

[17.348] Section 161B of the CA 1963 places a corresponding obligation on the company to notify the supervisory authority where the company's auditor ceases to hold office. In addition to the documents that an auditor is required to append to the notification under s 161A of the CA 1963[906], the company is required, in the case of removal of the auditor, to append the resolution for removal.

902 Section 161A(1) of the CA 1963, as inserted by reg 62 of the EC(SA)(D)R 2010.

903 Section 161A(4) of the CA 1963, as inserted by reg 62 of the EC(SA)(D)R 2010.

904 Under s 161(3) of the CA 1963.

905 Section 161A(3) of the CA 1963, as inserted by reg 62 of the EC(SA)(D)R 2010.

906 See **[17.347]** *ante*.

Chapter 18

Corporate Borrowing: Debentures and Security

Borrowing as a source of capital

[18.001] For the vast majority of Irish private companies there are three main ways in which they raise or acquire capital: by issuing shares[1], by generating profit or by borrowing money[2]. When many Irish private companies are incorporated, they are frequently capitalised to the princely sum of €1, representing one euro from the sole subscriber for one €1 share. It can be readily understood that this amount will not adequately capitalise a company's business. Accordingly, the first priority of a company on its incorporation is to acquire capital from another source to permit it to commence trading and, hopefully, to make a profit. Capital is typically acquired through the negotiation of finance internally, in the form of loans from its controllers or members, or externally, from financial institutions.

[18.002] Although it is now possible, provided certain conditions are met, for private companies to issue debt securities to the public, this is a very specialised activity[3]. In the case of a company with very little resources, it would be most unlikely for any commercial lending institution to advance facilities without first requiring security for the loan. Such security will often take the form of personal guarantees from the controllers of the company and, where the purpose of the loan is to acquire property with the funds provided, by the taking of a mortgage or charge over that property.

[18.003] The concern of this chapter is to consider the question of corporate capacity and authority to borrow, guarantee and provide security; the nature of the instruments of corporate borrowing; and the provision of different types of security in respect of that borrowing. This is done under the following headings:

[A] Corporate capacity and authority to borrow.

[B] Debentures and security.

---

1 See generally Ch 8, *Shares and Membership*.

2 There are, of course, other means available to companies to raise capital. More sophisticated companies can issue notes (whether domestically or internationally).

3 See s 33(1)(c) and 33(5) of the CA 1963, and para **[18.021]** *post*.

[A] Corporate Capacity and Authority to Borrow

The capacity to borrow, guarantee and secure

[18.004] Corporate capacity has already been considered at length[4]. However, it is necessary to recapitulate briefly on that treatment before embarking upon the consideration of corporate borrowing.

(a) The capacity to borrow

[18.005] A company's capacity to borrow will be found, expressly or implicitly, in its objects clause. Here one must reconsider the question of whether the act of borrowing is authorised by an express object, an express ancillary power or an implied ancillary power. Few private companies will actually engage in borrowing as their main business, and most companies will simply borrow in the course and furtherance of their business. The capacity or power to do this will be implied where the purpose of borrowing is reasonably incidental to the company's main objects[5].

[18.006] Problems in a company's capacity to borrow arise, typically, where the act of borrowing is neither a main object, nor reasonably incidental to the main objects of the company. A company's objects clause will often contain an express power to borrow. In such a case, notwithstanding the existence of an independent objects clause, the power to borrow can only be seen as an express ancillary power. Older case law suggested that where a company exercised the power to borrow other than in pursuit of its main objects, the act of borrowing was ultra vires, and void[6]. However, as considered above[7], the modern trend is to view the act of borrowing in such circumstances as being intra vires, but liable to be unenforceable as being an abuse of the directors' powers if the outsider is aware of the abuse[8].

(b) The capacity to guarantee

[18.007] Similar considerations apply to corporate guarantees. Although the giving of guarantees can be, in theory[9], a main object of a company[10], the giving of guarantees is more likely to be construed as being an express ancillary power. Most well-drafted objects clauses contain an express power to enter into guarantees. In certain circumstances, a company may be found to have an implied ancillary power to give guarantees where such is reasonably incidental to the furtherance of the company's main

---

4 See generally Ch 7, *Corporate Contracts: Capacity and Authority*, para **[7.045]** *et seq.*

5 See *Attorney General v Great Eastern Railway* (1880) 5 App Cas 473; *Re Lee Behrens & Co* [1932] 2 Ch 46, and generally, Ch 7, *Corporate Contracts, Capacity and Authority*, para **[7.068]**.

6 See *Re Introductions Ltd* [1968] 2 All ER 1221.

7 See Ch 7, *Corporate Contracts, Capacity and Authority*, para **[7.063]** *et seq.*

8 *Rolled Steel Products (Holdings) Ltd v British Steel Corp* [1985] 3 All ER 52.

9 The business of giving of guarantees, bonds and contracts of suretyship is highly regulated. Only assurance companies, banks and credit institutions can freely provide guarantees. See, further, Johnston, *Banking and Security Law in Ireland* (1998), p 268 *et seq.*

10 See *Rolled Steel Products (Holdings) Ltd v British Steel Corp* [1985] 3 All ER 52 at 81, *per* Slade LJ. See also the observations of Murphy J in *Re PMPA Garage (Longmile) Ltd* [1992] ILRM 337 at 340–341.

objects. Again, problems arise where the act of giving a guarantee can only be said to be an exercise of an express ancillary power in furtherance of an object other than the company's main object. Such a guarantee will on modern authority[11] be *intra vires* but unenforceable if the outsider is aware that the directors did not exercise the power in good faith.

[18.008] Guarantees entered into by companies in respect of loans and other transactions and arrangements made to or for directors and persons connected thereto (including inter-company guarantees) must also be considered in the light of s 31 of the CA 1990[12]. The essential point is that where a guarantee is entered into by a company for the benefit of certain relevant persons[13], it may be rendered voidable by virtue of s 38 of the CA 1990[14]. Other legislation relevant to the enforceability of corporate guarantees includes s 60 of the CA 1963, also considered above[15].

(c) The capacity to secure

[18.009] The foregoing comments in relation to borrowing and the giving of guarantees apply generally to the provision of security. Unless a company is, however, specially incorporated to provide security, the circumstances in which a company will have the provision of security as its main object will seldom arise in practice; the ability to provide security will almost invariably fall to be categorised as a power.

The authority to borrow, guarantee and secure

[18.010] Having established whether or not a company has the *capacity* to borrow, guarantee or secure, the next question is whether or not the officers who act for the company have the requisite *authority* to cause the company to borrow, enter into guarantees or provide security. The issue here is the extent of authority of a company's agents[16].

(a) The authority to borrow and secure

[18.011] The express authority for directors to borrow and secure is contained in reg 79 of Table A. However, it is common for this to be modified on incorporation[17], so that it will typically read (after modification) as follows:

---

11 *Rolled Steel Products (Holdings) Ltd v British Steel Corp* [1985] 3 All ER 52 at 81.

12 See Ch 16, *Statutory Regulation of Directors' Transactions*, para **[16.055]** *et seq.*

13 'Relevant persons' include directors and shadow directors of the company concerned, directors and shadow directors of that company's holding company and persons connected with the foregoing persons, namely a spouse, civil partner, parent, brother, sister, child, trustee, partner or a company controlled by the foregoing persons (ss 26 and 31(1) of the CA 1990). There is a presumption that the sole member of a single-member private limited company is a person connected with a director: s 26(6) of the CA 1990.

14 See generally, Ch 16, *Statutory Regulation of Directors' Transactions*, para **[16.100]** *et seq.*

15 Ch 10, *The Maintenance of Capital*, para **[10.046]** *et seq.*

16 See Ch 7, *Corporate Contracts: Capacity and Authority*, para **[7.099]** *et seq.*

17 The amendment is necessary so as to unfetter the power of directors, who otherwise could only borrow up to the nominal issued share capital of the company without obtaining authority from the members in general meeting. See Ch 3, *Constitutional Documentation*, para **[3.051]**.

> 'The directors may exercise all the powers of the company to borrow money, and to mortgage or charge its undertaking, property and uncalled capital, or any part thereof and to issue debentures, debenture stock and other securities, whether outright or as security for any debt, liability or obligation of the company or of any third party without any limit as to the amount.'

As noted in the next paragraph, this authority of directors will be implicitly subject to the directors exercising such powers *bona fide* and in the interests of the company[18].

(b) Authority to guarantee

[18.012] Directors will have power to give guarantees where they are expressly authorised to do so, or where the giving of guarantees is necessary to further the business of the company, and so can be said to be authorised by the general powers of management contained in reg 80[19] of Table A. Furthermore, it may be the case that the memorandum of association will authorise the directors to give guarantees 'where they see fit'. Whether or not the capacity to guarantee in the memorandum is so fettered, the power of directors to give guarantees will be implicitly subject to the directors exercising their powers *bona fide* and in the interests of the company.

[18.013] Where the directors do not exercise their authority to borrow, guarantee or secure bona fide and in the interests of the company, they abuse their authorised powers. Consequently, those acts, while not *ultra vires*, will be unenforceable where the outsider is either:

- aware of the abuse of authority, and so cannot rely on the rule in *Turquand's* case which would otherwise allow an outsider to assume that the internal rules, including the rule that powers are properly exercised, are in order[20]; or
- aware of the abuse of authority, and so does not have the requisite 'good faith' required for the EC(C)R 1973[21].

If the outsider is unaware of the fact that the directors have abused their authority, and in the absence of anything else untoward, the outsider should be able to call upon the company to honour the loan made and the guarantee or security given.

[B] Debentures and Security

The mechanics of secured borrowing

[18.014] The usual way in which a private company will obtain loan finance is through its directors approaching a lending institution and negotiating a loan facility. The principal matters under negotiation will usually be the amount of the facility, the interest to be paid, the term (ie, duration) of the facility, the security to be given by the company, and any other security which the lending institution requires, such as personal guarantees from the directors/shareholders, guarantees from associated companies or the assignment of a life policy on the lives of the principal directors. When a loan facility has been successfully negotiated, the lending institution will issue a *facility letter*

---

18 See Ch 15, *Duties of Directors and Other Officers*, para **[15.026]** *et seq.*

19 See Ch 13, *Corporate Governance: Management by the Directors*, para **[13.127]**.

20 See Ch 7, *Corporate Contracts, Capacity and Authority*, para **[7.121]** *et seq.*

21 SI 163/1973. Ch 7, *Corporate Contracts, Capacity and Authority*, para **[7.129]** *et seq.*

to the company's directors which will set out the terms of the facility to be granted. The directors will then consider the facility letter and arrange a directors' meeting to resolve in favour of accepting its terms and, in particular, resolving in favour of providing the required security. Evidence that the directors have done this will usually be provided by furnishing the lending institution with a certified copy of the minutes of the meeting whereby they resolved to accept the facility letter.

Certainly not later than this point in time[22], the respective legal advisers of both the lending institution and the borrowing company will become involved in the proposed transaction. The lending institution's solicitor will receive a copy of the facility letter and will in turn contact the borrowing company's solicitor. The lending institution's solicitor will then seek copies of the title to any real property being offered as security. In the majority of commercial loans to small and medium-sized Irish private companies, the lending institution's main security will be land and 'bricks and mortar'; floating charges too are taken – often on the understanding that they are 'for what they are worth'. However, where it is proposed to take personal property as security, the lending institution's solicitor will also seek information in respect of whatever personalty is to be mortgaged or charged. Upon receiving replies to these queries, he will then raise *requisitions and objections on title* in respect of the real property which will form the lending institution's security, information on the company[23], confirmation that insurance policies (if applicable) will be in place prior to draw-down of the facilities, and information on personal property which may form the basis of a floating charge.

When the lending institution's solicitor is satisfied that all matters are in order, a closing appointment will be arranged. Where the borrower company already owns the property being given as security the closing will be a straightforward two-way closing. In attendance will usually be both solicitors and the directors of the borrower company. Where the company is acquiring the property which it is mortgaging the closing will be a three-way closing because the vendor's solicitor will also attend. Title to the property being taken as security will be passed to the lending institution's solicitor and all security documentation will be executed under the seal of the company on the authority of the resolution accepting the facility letter, referred to above. Where searches[24]

22 Where the purpose of the facility involves something out of the ordinary, sometimes the solicitor for the lending institution will assist in the drafting of the facility letter.

23 Typically, the following documents are sought: a certified copy certificate of incorporation; a certified copy memorandum and articles of association; a certificate from the secretary of the company, stating the following information: (a) the names and addresses of directors of the company including those of any shadow directors; (b) the names and addresses of shareholders; (c) the company's registered office; (d) the nominal and issued share capital of the company; (e) confirmation no orders have been made or resolutions passed to wind up the company; (f) and that no charges have been created other than those that have been registered pursuant to s 99(1) of the CA 1963.

24 Searches carried out against a borrowing company will invariably be done by a law searching firm. The usual searches sought are: a *Registry of Deeds hand search* where unregistered real property is taken as security, or a *Land Registry folio search* where registered property is taken as security, a *planning search* against the property being taken as security, a *judgments search*, *Sheriff's Office search* against the borrower company and its directors and a *Companies Office search* against the borrower company to ascertain its status and particulars of any charges it has created. *Bankruptcy Office searches* may be made against the directors of the company, as may *CRO searches* to see if they have been restricted or disqualified.

disclose no adverse acts by or against the borrower and the lending institution's solicitor's requirements have been satisfied, the facility may then be drawn down.

[18.015] The remainder of this chapter is concerned with the law relating to debentures and other consensual security, granted by companies in the context of corporate borrowing. The following matters are discussed:

1. Facility letters.
2. The debenture defined.
3. Debentures as debt securities.
4. Transfer of debentures.
5. Secured debentures: the four kinds of consensual security.
6. Mortgages and charges, defined and distinguished.
7. All sums due debentures.
8. Creating the appropriate kind of security.
9. Fixed charges on book debts.
10. Fixed charges on deposit accounts.
11. Floating charges.
12. Negative pledge clauses.
13. Events which affect assets subject to floating charges.
14. Crystallisation of floating charges.
15. The causes of crystallisation.
16. The de-crystallisation of floating charges.

Facility letters

[18.016] A facility letter[25] is a letter from a lending institution addressed to the borrower which informs the borrower of the lender's willingness to advance credit facilities to the borrower and which sets out the terms and conditions of the facility. While it can be simple and succinct, a facility letter is a legal document and generally constitutes an offer by the lending institution to advance money on certain terms and conditions to the borrower, which can be accepted or rejected by the borrower.

[18.017] The contents of facility letters vary from lending institution to lending institution. One question which often arises is the extent and detail which the facility letter will devote to the legal terms of the advance, and whether or not such legal provisions should be catered for entirely in the security documentation, ie, the debenture. It is often considered to be best if the legal covenants as regards the actual protection of the security and rights of the lending institution are confined to the security documentation while financial covenants should be in the facility letter. One particular dilemma is whether or not to include a 'default clause' in the facility letter or in the security documents. On this point, Lingard[26] says:

---

[25] Otherwise known as a sanction letter, offer letter or loan agreement. See, generally, Johnston, *Banking and Security Law in Ireland* (1998) and Parsons, *Lingard's Bank Security Documents* (5th edn, 2011), Ch 5.

[26] Parsons, *Lingard's Bank Security Documents* (5th edn, 2011), para 5.2.

> 'There is much merit in putting default clauses in the security documents. Each facility letter must incorporate the default clause by reference, but well-drawn default clauses tend to be lengthy and are out of place in a short facility letter. From a marketing standpoint, it is undesirable to highlight the default clause and to repeat it each time a facility is granted.'

While lending institutions will be pleased where solicitors manage to draft a facility letter that is not off-putting, care must be taken to ensure that legal formalities are not sacrificed for aesthetic niceties. It is outside the scope of this work to consider further facility letters and the reader is referred to specialist texts[27].

The debenture defined[28]

[18.018] The term 'debenture' is often misunderstood and is commonly ascribed a far greater meaning than in fact it has. The definition provided in the CA 1963 sheds little light on the true meaning of the term[29]. In truth, a debenture is but the written acknowledgement of a debt by a company. In *Edmonds v Blaina Co*[30], Chitty J said of the meaning of debenture, that:

> 'The term itself imports a debt – an acknowledgement of a debt – and speaking of the numerous and varied forms of instruments which have been called debentures without anyone being able to say the term is correctly used, I find that generally, if not always, the instrument imports an obligation to pay. This obligation is in most cases at the present day accompanied by some charge or security[31].'

When people use the term 'debenture' they can mean:

- a written acknowledgement of a debt;
- an acknowledgement of a debt which incorporates a deed of mortgage and charge (commonly termed a 'mortgage debenture'); or
- an acknowledgement of a debt which includes a floating charge.

Often, people will mean all or a combination of the three.

[18.019] In the context of corporate borrowing by private companies, the modern debenture may be described as an instrument executed by or on behalf of[32] a company that acknowledges a debt, contains an obligation to repay that debt with interest, *will*

27 See Johnston, *Banking and Security Law in Ireland* (1998), Ch 7; and Parsons, *Lingard's Bank Security Documents* (5th edn, 2011).

28 See generally, Parsons, *Lingard's Bank Security Documents* (5th edn, 2011), Chs 7–12.

29 Section 2(1) of the CA 1963 defines 'debenture' to include 'debenture stock, bonds and any other securities of a company whether constituting a charge on the assets of the company or not'.

30 *Edmonds v Blaina Co* [1887] 36 Ch D 215 at 219.

31 See also *British India Co v IRC* [1881] 7 QBD 165; *Knightsbridge Estates Trust v Byrne* [1940] AC 613; and *Levy v Abercorris Co* [1887] 33 Ch D 260.

32 See *British India Co v IRC* [1881] 7 QBD 165, where a debenture was held to have been validly executed by two directors merely signing the debenture without the affixing of the common seal of the company. Note, though, that the company seal must be affixed where the debenture is executed as a deed or contains a mortgage over real property: see Ch 7, *Corporate Contracts, Capacity and Authority*, para **[7.014]** *et seq*.

usually create security and will contain a mechanism for enforcement in the event of default of repayment by the company.

[18.020] The person in whose favour a debenture is drawn (eg, usually, though not invariably, a bank or other credit institution) is termed a debenture holder. Whilst debenture holders, like shareholders, advance funds to a company, unlike shareholders, they do not become a member of the company, and remain 'outsiders'. Although in many Irish private companies the creation of debentures is almost invariably in favour of a lending institution, in return for that institution providing credit facilities to the company, a debenture can be drawn in favour of an individual, for example, a controller of the company, typically a director with a shareholding[33]. The concept of debenture stock is not really relevant to a discussion of corporate borrowing in the context of a private company, and must be distinguished in our present discussion. In practice, the issuing of debenture stock refers to a situation where, usually, a public limited company ('PLC') issues debentures and debenture stock certificates to the public.

Debentures as debt securities

[18.021] For a small number of private companies, however, a debenture can have quite a different meaning. Since 2006 it has been possible for private companies to issue *debt securities*, which are, in effect, debentures, which are listed on the official list of the stock exchange. This arises from the amendments to the definition of private company in s 33 of the CA 1963. So, while it remains the case that s 33(1)(c) requires that the articles of association of a private company must prohibit any invitation or offer to the public to subscribe for any shares, debentures or other securities of the company, s 33(5) of the CA 1963 provides that each of the following *offers of debentures* by a company, wheresoever made, shall not be regarded as falling within the prohibition in s 33(1)(c):

(a) an offer of debentures addressed solely to qualified investors,

(b) an offer of debentures addressed to fewer than 100 persons, other than qualified investors,

(c) an offer of debentures addressed to investors where the minimum consideration payable pursuant to the offer is at least €50,000 per investor, for each separate offer,

(d) an offer of debentures whose denomination per unit amounts to at least €50,000,

(e) an offer of debentures where the offer expressly limits the amount of the total consideration for the offer to less than €100,000,

(f) an offer of those classes of instruments which are normally dealt in on the money market (such as treasury bills, certificates of deposit and commercial papers) having a maturity of less than 12 months.

A number of private companies in the structured finance area have utilised these exemptions to issue bonds to the public, one of the more frequently used exemptions being where the bonds issued by the company have a minimum denomination of at least

33 Eg, *Salomon v A Salomon & Co* [1897] AC 22, considered in Ch 4, *Incorporation and Its Consequences*, para **[4.026]** *et seq.*

€50,000, which is usually the case for non-retail offerings to avoid the provisions of the Transparency Directive, the provisions of which are considered, generally, in Ch 32[34].

Transfer of debentures

[18.022] Debentures may be transferred by the debenture holder to some other person. The paradigm debenture created by a private company in favour of a lending institution will usually provide that it cannot be assigned by the borrowing company; although it may provide that the lending institution can transfer its interest[35]. Where a debenture is transferred, s 81 of the CA 1963 provides that the company cannot register the transfer unless a proper instrument of transfer has been delivered to the company[36].

[18.023] When a debenture is transferred, the law is that the transferee takes the debenture subject to any equities, ie, rights enjoyed by others, and so the assignee is in no better a position than the assignor: *Re Brown & Grogory Ltd*[37]. However, the case of *Hilger Analytical Ltd v Rank Precision Industries Ltd*[38] shows that a debenture can be transferred free from any equities which the company may have, where such is provided for in the debenture itself. In that case, the plaintiff purchased the defendant's entire business, which was the manufacture and sale of precision instruments. No money was paid, but the plaintiff gave the defendant a debenture comprising a fixed and floating charge over the plaintiff's assets. Later, the plaintiff company got into financial difficulties, and commenced proceedings against the defendant for, *inter alia*, misrepresentation, and claimed a set-off against the sums due under the debenture. Later still, the defendant assigned the debenture free from all equities to an associated company, which would have had notice of the plaintiff's claims. It in turn assigned the debenture to the defendant's holding company, both assignments appearing to be at market value. While it was accepted that, ordinarily, an assignee took subject to any equities, it was held that this was dependant upon the terms of the debenture itself: where the grantee company agreed with the original debenture holder that it should have the right to transfer its debenture free from equities, the court will give effect to this agreement. Harman J held:

> 'I accept the basic proposition of law that transferees of debentures are subject to equities, but that, by agreement, that position can be altered. On the true construction of this debenture the parties agreed to allow the debenture holder to transfer free of equities. The transfers in that case are both so expressed. In my judgment any creditor would wish to agree with his debtor that the instruments securing the debt shall be as freely negotiable as

---

34 On the Transparency Directive, see Ch 32, *Prospectus, Market Abuse and Transparency Law*, at para **[32.118]** *et seq*.

35 Such may be done by the lending institution where it is reorganising its business, and decides that one company within the group should hold all security taken by the lending institution. Well-drafted debentures will envisage the possibility of the future inclusion of the debenture and the loan it secures in a loan transfer and securitisation scheme. On securitisation generally, see Newby, 'Securitisation – A Lead Manager's Perspective' (2000) 7 CLP 264.

36 See Ch 9, *Share Transfer*, at para **[9.006]** where the requirement for the need for a proper instrument of transfer for shares is considered.

37 *Re Brown & Grogory Ltd* [1904] 1 Ch 827, and *Re Palmer's Decoration and Furnishing Co* [1904] 2 Ch 743; but *cf Re Goy & Co Ltd* [1900] 2 Ch 149.

38 *Hilger Analytical Ltd v Rank Precision Industries Ltd* [1984] BCLC 301.

possible. So far as the law permits this debenture is drawn so as to approximate to a negotiable instrument. The natural ambition of a creditor is thus satisfied by the terms of this debenture'[39].

Accordingly, whether or not a debenture can be transferred free from equities will depend upon its construction. Whether the benefit of a debenture, or, indeed, any other security document made in favour of a financial institution, can be transferred at all depends upon whether it contains the appropriate consents[40] on the borrower's part.

Secured debentures: the four kinds of consensual security

[18.024] While a debenture can be created which does not contain security, with the exception of debt securities, described above[41], it is almost unheard of in the context of modern commercial lending to private companies. The reason is simple, unless a loan is secured, then on a liquidation of the borrowing company, the lending institution is in no better a position than other unsecured creditors. The essence of the concept of a 'security' is that it means that the holder of that security is the person legally or equitably entitled to look to certain assets to satisfy the liabilities of the person who created the security. By 'consensual security' is meant security which is freely given by a company to the person entitled to rely upon the security and not, for example, security that arises by operation of law, eg, a judgment mortgage.

[18.025] As Millett LJ said in *Re Cosslett (Contractors) Ltd*[42]:

'There are only four kinds of consensual security known to English law:

(i) pledge;

(ii) contractual lien;

(iii) equitable charge and

(iv) mortgage.'

Initially[43], the common law recognised only three ways in which a company could give security over its assets. These were: first, the granting of a legal mortgage over the assets (whether realty or personalty) in the legal ownership of a company; second, the delivery to a creditor of corporate assets in the form of a pledge[44]; and third, the creation of a

39 *Hilger Analytical Ltd v Rank Precision Industries Ltd* [1984] BCLC 301 at 305.

40 For example, consent to disclosure of banker–customer information (where the debenture holder is a bank or other financial institution); consent to the disclosure of personal data under the Data Protection Act 1988; s 8 does not, however, apply where the data subject is a company.

41 See para **[18.021]** *ante*.

42 *Re Cosslett (Contractors) Ltd* [1997] 4 All ER 115. Although overruled by the House of Lords, the decision of the higher court does not affect the propriety of this statement of the law.

43 Before considering the modern law of corporate security, it is important to understand the broad historical development of the law of security. See generally Keeton & Sheridan, *Equity* (2nd edn, 1976), Ch IV, p 95 *ff*, for a detailed treatment of the gradual development of the 'mortgage' from a fettered common law concept to its rise through the intervention of equity.

44 See generally, Johnston, *Banking and Security Law in Ireland* (1998), Ch 12. See also Bell, *Modern Law of Personal Property in England and Ireland* (1989), Ch 8 at p 136 *et seq.* There Bell adopts the meaning of pledge as 'a transaction under which goods are delivered by a debtor (the pledgor) to his creditor (the pledgee) to be retained as security for the due discharge of the debt'.

contractual lien involving the company's authority to seize and sell its realty or personalty so as to recover the money lent from the proceeds of sale. Nowadays, the equitable charge has been added to the list of kinds of consensual security, and mortgages can be either legal or equitable.

(a) Pledge

[18.026] A pledge is a transaction under which a debtor (pledgor) delivers possession of goods (personalty) to his creditor (pledgee) to be retained by the pledgee as security and for as long as the pledgor has unsatisfied obligations to the pledgee[45]. A pledge is a *possessory security* in the sense that delivery of possession of the goods pledged must be given to the pledgee. Possession may be actual or constructive[46] where, for example, the pledgee holds documents of title to goods; there must, however, always be an intent to pledge[47]. A pledge confers a power of sale upon a pledgee in the event of the pledgor defaulting. In addition to the simplicity of its creation, one of the principal benefits of a pledge is that particulars of the pledge are not required to be delivered to the Companies Registration Office ('CRO') pursuant to s 99 of the CA 1963[48].

(b) Liens

[18.027] Liens are also a form of possessory security. A lien has been defined by Bell[49] in the following terms:

> 'A lien … is not a transaction, but a right. It is a right given to a person (the lienee) who is in possession of goods belonging to another (the lienor) under a contract for the provision of services relating to them, and it entitles him to retain possession until paid for his services.'

Liens may arise in a number of ways but above all else it is the *possession* and *delivery of possession* of goods which is crucial in determining the existence of a lien. First, liens may arise by operation of law, from the common law, equity and statute. Examples of these include the unpaid vendor's lien and the unpaid purchaser's lien and are considered in the next chapter in the context of whether such liens require to be registered under s 99 of the CA 1963[50]. Second, liens may arise by contractual arrangement between the

---

45 See generally, Bell, *Modern Law of Personal Property in England and Ireland* (1989), p 136.

46 See *Official Assignee of Madras v Mercantile Bank of India Ltd* [1935] AC 53 at 58.

47 *Dublin City Distillery (Great Brunswick Street, Dublin) Ltd v Doherty* [1914] AC 823.

48 As Johnston, *Banking and Security Law in Ireland* (1998), p 446 has pointed out, when taking a pledge, care must be taken not to inadvertently create a bill of sale which will be void for want of registration. On the distinction between a pledge and a bill of sale Johnston cites Lord Esher MR in *Re Hardwick* (1886) 17 QBD 690 at 697 where he said: '… the essence of a pledge is that the grantee says to the grantor, I will lend you money if and when you deposit certain goods with me. It is not, I will lend you money on the security of an authority to take possession of certain goods.' On the registration of bills of sale, see Ch 19, *Corporate Borrowing: Registration of Charges*, para **[19.046]** *et seq.*

49 Bell, *Modern Law of Personal Property in England and Ireland* (1989), Ch 8, p 136. For liens, see, generally, Bell, *Modern Law of Personal Property in England and Ireland* (1989), p 138 *et seq.* See also Hapgood, *Paget's Law of Banking* (11th edn, 1996), Ch 31.

50 Contractual liens may or may not be registrable under s 99 of the CA 1963. See, eg, *Re Hamlet International plc* [1998] 2 BCLC 164 and, generally, Ch 19, *Corporate Borrowing: Registration of Charges*, para **[19.024]**.

parties. The primary difference between a lien and a pledge is that while, in both cases, the holder of the security has possession of the goods, '... in the case of a lien the creditor retains possession of goods which had previously been delivered to him for some other purpose'[51]. In the Court of Appeal decision in *Re Cosslett (Contractors) Ltd*[52], the facts of which are considered below[53], Millett LJ said of the difference between a pledge and a lien that:

> '... in the case of a pledge the owner delivers possession to the creditor as security, whereas in the case of a lien the creditor retains possession of goods previously delivered to him for some other purpose[54].'

In that case it was held that the possession of the plant and materials in question was not attributable to any delivery of possession by way of lien. There, Millett LJ held that the company had brought (not *delivered possession*) the plant and materials onto the county council's site, exclusively, to enable it to use them in the completion of the construction works in question and that there was no question of it delivering them by way of lien:

> 'The council comes into possession of the plant and materials when it expels the company from the site leaving the plant and materials behind. But this does not amount to a voluntary delivery of possession by the company to the council … In my judgment, therefore, the council's rights are derived from contract, not possession and, in so far as they are conferred by way of security, constitute an equitable charge[55].'

(c) Equitable charge

[18.028] It was in the eighteenth and nineteenth centuries that equity developed two new forms of security, namely the equitable charge and the equitable mortgage. The essence of an *equitable charge*[56], in its application to commercial transactions, is that the lender and the borrower agree that in return for the lender making credit facilities available to the borrower, certain property will be available to satisfy the debt owing in the event of the borrower defaulting in repayment. From what was essentially a mere contractual obligation (which of itself confers no interest in the borrower's property) the charge became a security, which would be enforced in equity, as a proprietary interest.

[18.029] Equitable charges can be either *fixed* (on a specific asset or class or asset) or *floating* (over a body of assets). The fortunes of the holders of fixed and floating charges can differ immensely, particularly where the chargor company becomes insolvent. So, the holder of a fixed charge (having claim to identifiable property) has a higher priority than has the holder of a floating charge. By contrast, the holder of a floating charge is, first, dependent upon there being sufficient assets available within the class of assets that are subject to the floating charge to meet his debts, and, second, dependent upon not

---

[51] *Per* Millett LJ in *Re Cosslett (Contractors) Ltd* [1997] 4 All ER 115 at 126c. See also *Young v Matthew Hall Mechanical and Electrical Engineers Pty Ltd* (1988) 13 ACLR 399.

[52] *Re Cosslett (Contractors) Ltd* [1997] 4 All ER 115.

[53] See para **[18.071]**.

[54] *Re Cosslett (Contractors) Ltd* [1997] 4 All ER 115 at 126c.

[55] *Re Cosslett (Contractors) Ltd* [1997] 4 All ER 115 at 126e.

[56] See Coughlan, 'Equitable Mortgages and Charges' (1992) DULJ 171 and *O'Keeffe v O'Flynn Exhams and Partners and Allied Irish Bank* (31 July 1992, unreported) HC, Costello J. See also *Re TXU Europe Group plc (in administration)* [2004] 1 BCLC 519.

being leap-frogged by a debtor company's preferential creditors[57], eg, a policy of insurance, a share, etc.

(d) Mortgages: legal and equitable

[18.030] The early law of security only permitted the mortgaging of the legal interest in realty and personalty. In time, however, it came to be recognised that the equitable interest in both could also be mortgaged. Eventually it was recognised also that *choses in action* could be mortgaged. A chose in action 'is a known legal expression used to describe all personal rights of property which can be claimed or enforced by action, and not by taking physical possession'[58], eg, a policy of insurance, a share, etc.

[18.031] The *equitable mortgage* on the other hand developed where an agreement was reached to grant a legal mortgage, but there was in fact no legal instrument of mortgage. Here again, equity intervened and would, on application being made to court, grant a decree for specific performance of the agreement between the lender and the borrower[59]. Indeed, this remains the basis of many mortgages of land, where the borrower actually hands over the title deeds or land certificate to the property to the lender, who holds them until the loan is repaid. The act of depositing the deeds constitutes the 'agreement' between the parties[60].

Mortgages and charges, defined and distinguished

[18.032] The crucial distinction between a mortgage and a charge is that, unlike a mortgage, a charge does not operate to pass title in the secured assets to the chargee[61]. It is for that reason that all charges are said to be equitable: instead of getting legal title all that the chargee gets is the right in equity to look to the charged property for satisfaction of the secured debt[62]. In *Re Clare Textiles Ltd*[63], Costello J said:

> 'There is nothing special about the term 'charge'. It relates to a contract under the terms of which certain property is available as security to meet the performance of a liability, usually the payment of money. Its creation is dependent upon contract[64].'

---

57 See Ch 25, *The Realisation and Distribution of Assets in a Winding Up*, para **[25.183]** *et seq.*

58 *Per* Channell J in *Torkington v Magee* [1902] 2 KB 427. See also *Re Cuff Knox (deceased)* [1963] IR 263. On choses in action generally, see Bell, *Modern Law of Personal Property in England and Ireland* (1989), p 361 *et seq.*

59 See Farrell, *Specific Performance* (1994); and generally, Keane, *Equity and the Law of Trusts in the Republic of Ireland* (1988), para 16.01*ff* and Delaney, *Equity and the Law of Trusts in Ireland* (1996), p 434.

60 See Doyle, 'The Mortgage by Deposit for "Present and Future Advances"' (1990) Gazette of ILSI 141.

61 *London County and Westminster Bank Ltd* [1918] 1 KB 515. See also *Burlinson v Hall* (1884) 12 QBD 347 where Day J said: 'A charge differs altogether from a mortgage. By a charge the title is not transferred, but the person creating the charge merely says that out of a particular fund he will discharge a particular debt.'

62 In *Re Cosslett (Contractors) Ltd; Smith (Administrator of Cosslett (Contractors) Ltd v Bridgend County Borough Council* [2001] UKHL 58, [2002] 1 All ER 292, Lord Hoffmann said (at 303j; [41]): 'I do not see how a right to sell an asset belonging to a debtor and appropriate the proceeds to payment of the debt can be anything other than a charge.'

63 *Re Clare Textiles Ltd* (1 February 1993, unreported) HC.

64 *Re Clare Textiles Ltd* (1 February 1993, unreported) HC at p 2.

In *Re Charge Card Services Ltd*[65], Millett J said that:

> '... the essence of an equitable charge is that, without any conveyance or assignment to the chargees, specific property of the chargor is expressly or constructively appropriated to or made answerable for payment of a debt, and the chargee is given the right to resort to the property for the purpose of having it realised and applied in or towards payment of the debt. The availability of equitable remedies has the effect of giving the chargee a proprietary interest by way of security in the property charged[66].'

This definition was accepted by Finlay Geoghegan J in *Murray v Wilkin and Wilkin*[67]. In that case it was found that a solicitor's undertaking to discharge a sum owed out of the proceeds of sale of a particularly property[68] did not constitute an equitable charge: unlike an undertaking to hold title deeds for the benefit of another person, the undertaking in that case did not come within the above definition because it was not possible to construe it as even implicitly appropriating the property or as an agreement to make it answerable for the payment of the debt. In the words of Finlay Geoghegan J, at best it contained a representation that the property was in the process of being sold[69].

[18.033] It is no longer possible to create a legal mortgage over unregistered land by conveying title to a mortgagee, and now, one can only create a legal mortgage over unregistered land by a charge by deed. Section 89(1) of the Land and Conveyancing Law Reform Act 2009 ('LCLRA 2009') provides:

> 'A legal mortgage of land may only be created by a charge by deed and such a charge, unless the context requires otherwise, is referred to in this Part as a "mortgage", and "mortgagor" and "mortgagee" shall be read accordingly.'

Moreover, s 89(2) of the LCLRA 2009 provides what is *not* a legal mortgage as and from the commencement of Chapter 1 of Part 10 of the LCLRA 2009, namely:

> '(a) any instrument which would, but for the provisions of this section, convey a legal estate or interest in land by way of mortgage, or
>
> (b) any other transaction which under any instrument would operate, but for the provisions of this section, as a mortgage by conveyance of a legal estate or interest in land,
>
> does not create a legal mortgage.'

Accordingly, the formal conveyance, assignment or demise of the legal title to *real property* will no longer create a legal mortgage: now, a legal mortgage can only be created by a charge by deed. Providing that a mortgage is created by a charge may be considered to be a confusing tautology because what the section is in fact providing is that a mortgage of unregistered land is not in fact a mortgage (which involves the

---

65 *Re Charge Card Services Ltd* [1986] 3 All ER 289.

66 *Re Charge Card Services Ltd* [1986] 3 All ER 289 at 309.

67 *Murray v Wilkin and Wilkin* (31 July 2003, unreported) HC, Finlay Geoghegan J.

68 The undertaking provided: 'We hereby undertake on our clients' instructions to discharge the sum of £65,000 owing to your client out of the proceeds of sale of the above property when same are to hand.'

69 *Cf Anglo Irish Bank Corporation plc v Edward Kavanagh Maynooth Ltd* [2003] IEHC 113 (Gilligan J). See further, Ch 19, *Corporate Borrowing: Registration of Charges*, at para **[19.023]**.

transfer of title) but a charge. Such a deeming provision was needed if the term 'mortgage', so engrained in the vernacular of the public and practitioners alike, was to be retained in the vocabulary of security. This fundamental change to the law relating to the creation of security over unregistered land (ie, land registered in the Registry of Deeds) was intended to align the creation of security over unregistered land with that pertaining to the creation of security over registered land (ie, land registered in the Land Registry).

By contrast, however, the formal assignment or transfer of legal title to *personal property*, which is specifically identifiable at the time the mortgage is created, will create a legal mortgage over such personal property and the mortgagee becomes the legal owner of the mortgaged personal property. The mortgagor will be protected by equity which will imply the right of the mortgagor to redeem or recover the mortgaged property on repayment[70].

[18.034] An *equitable mortgage* may also be created[71] whereby the equitable mortgagee becomes the equitable owner of the mortgaged property[72], and s 89(6) of the LCLRA 2009 expressly provides that nothing in that section affects the creation of equitable mortgages of land. Equity will continue to protect the mortgagor by acknowledging his right to redeem the mortgage. An equitable mortgage may be created formally or informally; an informal equitable charge by the deposit of the title deeds of unregistered land or of personal property that is specifically identifiable from the title deeds deposited[73] can still be created. It has not, however, been possible to create an equitable charge in relation to registered land by the deposit of the land certificate since the commencement of s 73 of the Registration of Deeds and Title Act 2006 ('RDTA 2006')[74].

---

[70] Although the mortgagor will have a *legal right* to redeem the mortgage, this will often be on a specific date; the mortgagor will have the *equitable right* to redeem for an indefinite time: *Burrough v Cranston* (1840) 2 Ir Eq R 203. See Wylie, *Irish Land Law* (4th edn, Bloomsbury Professional, 2010) para 13.91 *et seq*; Baker & Langan, *Snell's Equity* (29th edn, 1990), p 391 *et seq*.

[71] See Coughlan, 'Equitable Mortgages and Charges' (1992) DULJ 171.

[72] On the distinction between an *equitable mortgage* and an *equitable charge*, see *O'Keeffe v O'Flynn Exhams and Partners and Allied Irish Banks* (31 July 1992, unreported) HC, Costello J, noted by Coughlan, 'Equitable Mortgages and Charges' (1992) DULJ 171. See also the decision of the Supreme Court [1994] 1 ILRM 137.

[73] See generally: Wylie, *Irish Land Law* (4th edn, 2010) at para [12.30]; *Russel v Russel* (1783) 1 Bro CC 269; *Eyre v McDowell* (1861) 9 HLC 619; *Re Hurley's Estate* [1894] 1 IR 488. See further, Johnston, *Banking and Security Law in Ireland* (1998), p 327–335 for an excellent review of the law and procedure on taking equitable deposits of title deeds. See also Hardiman, 'Deposit of Title Deeds' (1999) CLP 3 for a very perceptive analysis of the legal principles behind such security; Corscadded, 'Deposit of Title Deeds' (1953) 55 JIBI 253; and Doyle, 'The Mortgage by Deposit for "Present and Future Advances"' (1990) Gazette ILSI 141.

[74] Although s 73 of the RDTA 2006 preserved existing mortgages by deposit of land certificates, such mortgagees were required to register a lien in the Land Registry by 31 December 2009: s 73(1)(b)(ii), (2) and (3) of the RDTA 2006. See further, Wylie, *Irish Land Law* (4th edn, Bloomsbury Professional, 2010) at para [12.20].

[18.035] It is fundamental to a fixed charge that the charged property is *specifically identifiable*. In *Illingworth v Houldsworth*[75], the 'great Irish judge Lord Macnaughton [said] with his usual lucidity'[76]:

> 'A specific charge, I think, is one that without more fastens on ascertained and definite property or property capable of being ascertained and defined ...'

It should be noted that a fixed charge may be created over future property, ie, property which the chargor company acquires after the charge is created[77].

[18.036] An irrevocable agreement to grant a fixed charge operates to create an 'equitable' fixed charge. This was held to be the case in *Re Valley Ice Cream (Ireland) Ltd*[78]. In that case the company, the subject of its official liquidator's application, and certain associated companies were indebted to a creditor, Master Foods Ltd, in respect of goods supplied. To secure the indebtedness, the company agreed to provide the security set out in a debenture. The debenture provided in clause 5.4 that the company:

> '... irrevocably undertakes to [Master Foods Ltd] forthwith upon expiration or earlier determination of each lease to execute, or procure the execution of, a mortgage over the equipment to which the lease relates in the form attached hereto in the Fifth Schedule.'

The equipment referred to consisted of some vehicles and a large number of freezers located in various shops throughout the State. The vehicles and equipment were held by the company under leases, and at the expiration of each lease the company would be entitled to purchase the goods for a nominal sum. Therefore, at the time the debenture was created, the equipment was in the ownership of the lessor (Master Foods Ltd) and would continue to be in its ownership until the expiry of the leases. This was the reason why the company could only *undertake* to mortgage the equipment and could not then in fact mortgage the equipment. At the time of the application it was common case that there were a number of vehicles and freezers which came within clause 5.4 in respect of which no mortgage in the form set out in the fifth schedule to the debenture had been executed[79].

The net point to be decided was whether clause 5.4 created an equitable fixed charge or a floating charge over the equipment. Master Foods Ltd contended that it was the former; the official liquidator contended that it was the latter. On this point McCracken J said:

> 'Clause 5.4 clearly creates a legal and binding obligation on the Company to execute a mortgage as soon as any lease of equipment expires or terminates. It does not, and cannot, of itself create a legal mortgage over the equipment, as the equipment is not an asset of the Company at the time of execution of the debenture. However, at the moment that the lease of any one piece of equipment terminates or expires, there is no doubt that Master Foods

---

75 *Illingworth v Houldsworth* [1904] AC 355, cited with approval by the Supreme Court in *Welch v Bowmaker (Ireland) Ltd* [1980] IR 251 at 258, *per* Kenny J.

76 *Welch v Bowmaker (Ireland) Ltd* [1980] IR 251 at 258, *per* Kenny J.

77 *Welch v Bowmaker (Ireland) Ltd* [1980] IR 251.

78 *Re Valley Ice Cream (Ireland) Ltd* (22 July 1998, unreported) HC, McCracken J.

79 It was also heard that the Form 47 (the predecessor to the Form C1) which had been filed in the CRO in respect of the debenture, mistakenly referred to the mortgage, which the company undertook to execute, as being contained in the *first* schedule to the debenture. In fact it was contained in the *fifth* schedule. McCracken J found that this was of no material effect.

[Ltd] would be entitled to obtain an immediate order of specific performance to enforce the execution of a legal charge or mortgage. Furthermore, the form of the charge as set out in the fifth schedule to the debenture quite clearly is intended to create a fixed charge over the goods, as it specifically assigns the goods and the benefit of any insurance thereon. I think it is beyond doubt that the clear intention of this document is that there will be a fixed charge on the specific goods as soon as the document is executed. The only question, therefore, is whether an irrevocable agreement to grant such a fixed charge does of itself create an equitable fixed charge[80].'

After quoting with approval from Fisher & Lightwood's *Law of Mortgages*[81] McCracken J went on to hold:

'In the present case, there has not been a legal transfer of a proprietary interest, but there has been a binding undertaking to confer such an interest, which undertaking is specifically enforceable. I think it is entirely in keeping with the principles governing the creation of a fixed charge that such a charge should be created under these circumstances. The essence of a fixed charge is that property is irrevocably set aside in such a way that the creditor can have recourse to it to satisfy his debt. The clear intention of clause 5.4 was that, as each of the items came into the ownership of the company, it would immediately be subject to a legal charge in favour of Master Foods [Ltd], which was to be implemented by the execution of a deed. It is a well known maxim of equity, which is frequently enforced, that equity regards as being done that which ought to be done, and it is for this reason that the undertaking contained in clause 5.4 would be specifically enforceable. It must also be a consequence of the truth of that maxim that, while a legal charge may not have been created, equity will regard a charge as having been created because it ought to have been created under the terms of clause 5.4. That charge must be a fixed charge, as what clause 5.4 contemplates clearly is a fixed charge. Accordingly, I will grant a declaration that the debenture creates a fixed charge in equity over the leased assets to which it refers'[82].

This judgment shows just how easy it is to create a security interest in property. It is thought that the same conclusion could have been arrived at had the undertaking been

---

[80] *Re Valley Ice Cream (Ireland) Ltd* (22 July 1998, unreported) HC at pp 4–5.

[81] Fisher & Lightwood,' *Law of Mortgages* (10th edn), p 12 where it is stated: 'Generally, the essence of any transaction by way of mortgage is that a debtor confers upon his creditor a proprietary interest in property of the debtor, or undertakes in a binding manner to do so, by the realisation or appropriation of which the creditor can procure the discharge of the debtor's liability to him, and that the proprietary interest is redeemable, or the obligation to create it is defeasible, in the event of the debtor discharging his liability. If there has been no legal transfer of a proprietary interest but merely a binding undertaking to confer such an interest, that obligation, if specifically enforceable, will confer a proprietary interest in the subject matter in equity. An equitable mortgage is a contract which operates as a security and is enforceable under the equitable jurisdiction of the court. The court carries it into effect either by giving the creditor immediately the appropriate remedies, or by compelling the debtor to execute a security in accordance with the contract. It is applicable to all property of which a legal mortgage can be made, even where statute provides, as, for example, in the case of ships, a particular method for passing the legal property therein.' McCracken J noted that the first part of that statement is taken verbatim from the judgment of Buckley J in *Swiss Bank Corporation v Lloyds Bank Ltd* [1980] 2 All ER 419 at 426.

[82] *Re Valley Ice Cream (Ireland) Ltd* (22 July 1998, unreported) HC at p 6.

contained in a letter[83], as opposed to a debenture, provided, of course, that to be enforceable, s 99(1) of the CA 1963 must be complied with.

[18.037] Extreme care[84] should be taken in drafting a debenture that purports to create a fixed charge over property. Where the property charged is not properly identified, or where its identity is ambiguous, then it is likely that the charge will prove to be void and unenforceable where it purports to be *fixed*. Where property is intended to be the subject of a fixed charge but is not properly identified, and where the debenture or deed of charge creates a floating charge over all property of the company, the property may consequently only be subject to a floating charge, which ranks lower in priority to a fixed charge[85]. This is illustrated by *Re Hi-Fi Equipment (Cabinets) Ltd*[86] where a bank took a secured debenture which provided that the borrowing company charged 'by way of first fixed charge all future freehold and leasehold property of the company together with all buildings fixtures (including trade fixtures) and fixed plant and machinery from time to time thereon' and went on to give the bank a floating charge over all of its other assets. It was held that the reference to fixed plant and machinery implied that the plant and machinery was in some way firmly attached to the company's premises, and thus, since the plant and machinery in question was not attached to the company's premises, it did not form part of the assets subject to the fixed charge. On account of the deficiency in the assets available to satisfy the claims against the company, the plant and machinery in question were applied in satisfaction of other creditors' debts.

All sums due debentures

[18.038] It is more common for debentures to provide that they secure 'all sums due or to become due on any account or accounts, whether present or future' or, more generically, 'all present and future indebtedness'. The courts have, traditionally, applied a wide construction to such expressions and have held that 'debt' includes not merely present debts but liabilities that may mature into debts[87]. So in *Banner Lane Realisations v Berisford*[88] the Court of Appeal held that 'future indebtedness' includes not only a present obligation to pay a sum certain in the future, but also a 'present obligation to pay an unquantified sum in the future or on a contingency'[89].

[18.039] Nowadays, since 7 December 2006, stamp duty is not payable on mortgages[90]. Prior to that date, however, stamp duty was payable on mortgages where the amount secured exceeded €245,000 and duty was payable at a rate of 1% up to a maximum of

83 Either supported by valuable consideration or under seal.

84 *Cf Re Cimex Tissues Ltd* [1995] 1 BCLC 409 where it was found that, although the particular debenture in that case was in a number of ways 'ineptly drafted' it did not permit the chargor to dispose of the charged property without the chargee's consent and so, there was no reason to hold that the charge was other than what it was described as, namely, a fixed charge.

85 On *floating charges*, see para **[18.068]** *et seq*.

86 *Re Hi–Fi Equipment (Cabinets) Ltd* [1988] BCLC 65.

87 *Flint v Barnard* (1888) 22 QBD 90.

88 *Banner Lane Realisations v Berisford* [1997] 1 BCLC 380.

89 *Banner Lane Realisations v Berisford* [1997] 1 BCLC 380 at 388b–c.

90 Mortgages executed on or after 7 December 2006 are not liable to stamp duty and a return is not required.

€630. Under that old regime, where a financial institution advanced, say, €300,000 secured by an all-sums debenture and the financial institution subsequently advanced a further €100,000 all that was required to be done was to 'stamp-up' the debenture to cover a total indebtedness of €400,000. It was held by the Supreme Court that the validity of such an 'all sums due' debenture was not affected by its being 'stamped up' subsequent to the date of the presentation of a petition to have the chargor company wound up in *Re Motor Racing Circuits Ltd*[91]. In that case a chargee caused an 'all sums due' debenture to be stamped-up after a petition had been presented to have the company wound up. In the debenture, the company covenanted to pay to the chargee 'all such sums as may now be due or owing or at any time shall become due or owing'. In addition, the company also charged certain lands with all sums that might at any time be owing by the company. Blayney J said:

> 'The legal position is quite clear and that is initially such a debenture covers such amount as the mortgage is stamped in respect of but, where the amount exceeds the amount in respect of which the debenture is stamped, the bank is entitled to stamp up the debenture and that stamping up is simply a revenue requirement. The debenture from the beginning is valid to cover all sums which may at any time be due by the company to the bank. But if at any time the amount due under the debenture exceeds the amount in respect of which it has been stamped initially, the bank is free to increase the stamping so that the amount of the stamp duty will then cover the amount which is actually due at the time under the debenture.
>
> It is quite clear under the provisions of the Stamping Act and accordingly, the bank was perfectly free to stamp up the debenture so as to comply with the requirements of the Stamping Act. But as I said in the beginning the debenture itself covered all sums which at any time would be due by the company to the bank[92].'

There was, therefore, no problem with the bank stamping-up the debenture *after* the petition to wind up the company had been presented. The same reasoning should apply equally to where an 'all sums due' debenture or other charge is stamped-up after the passing of a resolution to wind up a company, to the appointment of an examiner or indeed in any other eventuality.

Fixed charges on book debts

[18.040] The advantage of being a fixed charge holder is that if the chargor company becomes insolvent and is placed into liquidation, the fixed chargee's position is more favourable than that of a floating chargee's position. Unlike the holder of a floating charge, the holder of a fixed charge *ordinarily* ranks ahead of the Revenue Commissioners and other preferential creditors[93]. Furthermore, although *all* securities are capable of being vitiated, unlike a floating charge, a fixed charge is not liable to be set aside where the company goes into liquidation within 12 months[94] of its creation.

---

91 *Re Motor Racing Circuits Ltd* (31 January 1997, unreported) SC, Blayney J, *nem diss*.

92 *Re Motor Racing Circuits Ltd* (31 January 1997, unreported) SC at pp 5, 6 of the judgment.

93 As shall be seen, para **[18.057]** *post*, in response to the courts' upholding the validity of fixed charges on book debts, the State responded by giving the Revenue Commissioners priority in respect of such fixed charges.

94 Or, in the case of a floating charge given to a 'connected person', within two years: s 288 of the CA 1963.

Consequently, credit institutions are more eager to take fixed charges than to take floating charges. It was the traditionally superior position of fixed charges, which provoked credit institutions to be imaginative in seeking to stretch the boundaries of the sort of assets that could be the subject of a fixed charge.

[18.041] Only in recent years has it been recognised that a fixed charge can be created over the book debts of a company[95]. As to what 'book debts' mean, in *Response Engineering Ltd v Caherconlish Treatment Plant Ltd*[96] Hogan J said the term means no more 'than future income which will accrue to the company by reason of the provision of goods and services to third parties by that company in the courts of its trade or business'. In *Ashcoin Ltd v Moriarty Holdings Ltd*[97] Hogan J held that the proceeds of a grant from a statutory agency were capable of amounting to a book debt within the meaning of a debenture. Book debts have been defined in *Palmer*[98] as:

> '... debts owing to the company concerned with and arising out of the company's trade or business, which are entered, or commonly would be entered in the ordinary course of business, in well kept books of such a trade or business.'

By their nature, book debts would seem to be incapable of being the subject of a fixed charge since they will not continue to be specifically identifiable: old book debts will be paid and new book debts will be created. Indeed, for years, it was generally thought that the only suitable means of taking security over book debts was by way of a *floating charge*. A series of cases have abandoned this position and now, when properly drafted[99], a fixed charge can be created over book debts. However, it should be noted at the outset that the primary rationale for creating fixed charges over book debts has, to a large extent, been rendered redundant by statute since, subject to certain limited exceptions, fixed charges on book debts do not have priority to the Revenue Commissioners[100].

(a) Judicial acceptance of the validity of fixed charges on book debts

[18.042] The first breakthrough case was the English case of *Siebe Gorman v Barclays Bank Ltd*[101]. In that case, a company created a debenture in favour of Barclays Bank, secured by way of legal mortgage over all its freehold and leasehold property and all fixed plant and machinery, present and future. In addition, the company further charged '... by way of first fixed charge all book debts and other debts now and from time to time due or owing to the company'.' Since the construction of such charges is all-important, the restrictions on dealing with its book debts placed on the company by the bank in the mortgage debenture in that case are worth quoting:

---

95 See Byrne & Tomkin, 'Charges on Book Debts – Siebe Gorman in Ireland' (1985) NLJ 443.

96 *Response Engineering Ltd v Caherconlish Treatment Plant Ltd* [2011] IEHC 345, [2012] 2 ILRM 67 at 79.

97 *Ashcoin Ltd v Moriarty Holdings Ltd* [2012] IEHC 365, Hogan J.

98 Schmitthoff (ed), *Palmer's Company Law* (24th edn, 1987), para 46–06. See also *Re Brian Tucker Ltd* [1990] 2 IR 549, considered in Ch 19, *Corporate Borrowing: Registration of Charges*, para **[19.060]**.

99 See generally, Houghton & Mercer, 'Fixed or Floating Charge? – Taking Security over Stock, Equipment and Other Movable Assets' (1995) PLC 43 for a thorough review of the concepts (and pointers) on taking an effective fixed charge over book debts.

100 See para **[18.057]**.

101 *Siebe Gorman v Barclays Bank Ltd* [1979] 2 Lloyd's Rep 142.

> 'During the continuance of this security the company ... shall pay into the company's account with the bank all moneys which it may receive in respect of the book debts and other debts hereby charged and shall not without the prior consent of the bank in writing purport to charge or assign the same in favour of any other person and shall if called upon to do so by the bank execute a legal assignment of such book debts and other debts to the bank.'

The court held that the effect of this clause was to create a fixed charge over the book debts of the company. Critical to the decision was the foregoing restriction on the rights of the chargor company to deal with its collected book debts. Had the company not been restricted in its right to deal with its collected book debts, Slade J would have been inclined to accept that the charge could be no more than a floating charge. However, in the circumstances, he concluded that[102]:

> '... it is perfectly possible in law for a mortgagor, by way of continuing security for future advances, to grant to a mortgagee a charge on future book debts in a form which creates in equity a specific charge on the proceeds of such debts as soon as they are received and consequently prevents the mortgagor from disposing of an unencumbered title to the subject matter of such charge without the mortgagee's consent ... I see no reason why the court should not give effect to the intention of the parties, as stated ... that the charge should be a first fixed charge on book debts. '

It is fundamental, however, to the finding that a particular charge over book debts is a fixed charge, that it was created *as such*. A charge which is created as a floating charge over book debts can never become a fixed charge, no matter how a receiver – appointed pursuant to the charge – may have come to hold them[103].

[18.043] The decision in *Siebe Gorman* is now of little more than historical interest in the United Kingdom since it was formally reversed by the House of Lords in *Re Spectrum Plus Ltd* in 2005[104]. As shall be considered below, just as the Irish Supreme Court found in *Re Keenan Brothers*[105] and *Re Holidair Ltd*[106], the House of Lords in Re Spectrum Plus Limited also found that the existence of actual restrictions which limited the company's ability to deal with its book debts consistent with a fixed charge, was more important than the mere intention of the parties.

(b) The importance of restrictions on the chargor's use of the debts

[18.044] If a charge over book debts is to be found to be a fixed charge it is crucial that the debenture should provide that the chargor company is *restricted* in its dealings with the collected book debts[107]. Where, as in *Re Armagh Shoes Ltd*[108], the debenture

---

102 *Siebe Gorman v Barclays Bank Ltd* [1979] 2 Lloyd's Rep 142 at 159.

103 *Re Pearl Maintenance Services Ltd; Re Pearl Building Contracts Ltd* [1995] BCC 657.

104 *Re Spectrum Plus Ltd* [2005] 2 BCLC 269.

105 *Re Keenan Bros Ltd* [1985] IR 401; [1985] BCLC 302 (HC) and [1986] BCLC 242 (SC).

106 *Re Holidair Ltd* [1994] 1 ILRM 481, considered by Connaughton, 'The Kentz Case – More Problems for Secured Lenders' (1994) CLP 110.

107 It was held in *William Gaskell Group Ltd et al v Highley (Nos 1, 2, 3)* [1994] 1 BCLC 197, *per* Morritt J, that the assignment of a fixed charge on book debts did not result in the charge becoming a floating charge since the same restrictions continued to bind the companies in question.

108 *Re Armagh Shoes Ltd* [1984] BCLC 405.

provided for no restrictions, the court will not imply restrictions and the charge will fall to be deemed a floating charge. Similarly, in *Re Brightlife Ltd*[109], although there was a prohibition on the chargor company selling, factoring or discounting the book debts in question, the absence of the positive requirement that the monies collected be paid into a separate bank account meant that the charge could only be a floating charge. This was because the absence of such a restriction meant that the company could use the assets as it wished; a freedom which is intrinsic to a floating charge, but anathema to a fixed charge. The nature of the restrictions placed on the chargor company was also found to be the decisive test by Barron J in *AH Masser Ltd v Revenue Commissioners*[110], who held that the restrictions were consistent with the security being a fixed charge. Although the restrictions were less extensive than those in *Re Keenan Bros Ltd*[111], Barron J held:

> 'Nevertheless it seems to me that the essential provision is the restriction on the mortgagor which prevents it from purporting to charge, assign or otherwise dispose of its book debts and other debts. I regard this provision as acknowledging that the debts are in equity the property of the mortgagee and so not available to the mortgagor in the ordinary course of its business[112].'

Today, such alone would not, in the light of recent Supreme Court pronouncements[113] and the decision of the House of Lords in *Re Spectrum Plus Ltd*[114], justify a finding that a charge over book debts is a fixed charge.

[18.045] A case considered by many to have been even stronger than *Siebe Gorman*[115], is *Re Keenan Bros Ltd*[116]. In that case the Supreme Court pronounced upon the validity of a fixed charge over book debts, and in the process reversed the High Court judgment of Keane J who had held that the charge in question was a floating charge. However it is clear that mere terminology, or labelling, will not be sufficient to make what is in reality a floating charge, a fixed charge[117]. Neither will the declared intention of the parties be sufficient to make a charge properly construed as a floating charge, a fixed charge. Rather, only on the true construction of the debenture in question will a charge on book debts be found to be a fixed charge. As in the cases cited in the preceding paragraph, the restrictions on the rights of the chargor company over the book debts were decisive in the determination of the question. There, the debenture provided that:

> 'The company shall pay into an account with the Bank designated for that purpose all moneys which it may receive in respect of the book debts and other debts hereby charged

109 *Re Brightlife Ltd* [1986] BCLC 418.

110 *AH Masser Ltd v Revenue Commissioners* [1978–1987] III ITR 706.

111 *Re Keenan Bros Ltd* [1985] IR 401. See para **[18.045]**.

112 *Re Keenan Bros Ltd* [1985] IR 401 at 552.

113 See para **[18.046]–[18.047]**.

114 *Re Spectrum Plus Ltd* [2005] 2 BCLC 269.

115 See *Re Brightlife Ltd* [1986] BCLC 418 at 423, *per* Hoffmann J.

116 *Re Keenan Bros Ltd* [1985] IR 401; [1985] BCLC 302 (HC) and [1986] BCLC 242 (SC).

117 See *Re Westmaze* (1998) (15 May 1998, unreported) HC (Eng); *CCH's Company Law Newsletter* (1998) Issue 11, 12 June 1998 where it was accepted that there mere fact that a charge was described as 'fixed' was not determinative of the question as to whether it was, in fact, fixed or floating.

> and shall not without the prior consent of the Bank in writing make any withdrawals or direct any payment from the said account.'

In the judgment of McCarthy J:

> 'In my view, it is because it was described as a specific or fixed charge and was intended to be such, that the requirement of a special bank account was necessary; if it were a floating charge payment into such an account would be entirely inappropriate and, indeed, would conflict with the ambulatory nature of the floating charge ...'[118]

In *Royal Trust Bank v National Westminster Bank plc*[119], Millett LJ said: 'while it is possible to distinguish between a capital asset and its income, I do not see how it can be possible to separate a debt or other receivable from the proceeds of its realisation.' It is thought that there is considerable merit in this observation. This has been reiterated by Lord Millett (as he later became) in the Privy Council in *Re Brumark Investments Ltd; Commissioner of Inland Revenue v Agnew*[120]. In that case he said, in relation to the question as to whether a debt or other receivable can be separated from its proceeds:

> 'While a debt and its proceeds are two separate assets, however, the latter are merely the traceable proceeds of the former and represent its entire value. A debt is a receivable; it is merely a right to receive payment from the debtor. Such a right cannot be enjoyed in specie; its value can be exploited only by exercising the right or by assigning it for value to a third party. An assignment or charge of a receivable which does not carry with it the right to the receipt has no value. It is worthless as a security[121].'

A fixed charge over book debts will operate as a charge on the uncollected book debts and if a company becomes insolvent, all uncollected book debts will be the subject of that charge and will be available to satisfy the chargee's debts. Where the proceeds are paid into a designated bank account, the chargee can also have a fixed charge on that account, but to be a fixed charge the account must be subject to restricted access and the chargor must not be able to withdraw without the chargee's permission. Alternatively, the account can be a 'trust account' where the chargee is the sole beneficial owner[122].

[18.046] The requirement that money collected be paid into a separate bank account is probably the most decisive factor in concluding that a charge on book debts is a fixed charge. Where a debenture provides that a separate bank account must be maintained, it has been held that it will not be fatal to the charge on book debts being deemed a fixed charge where the separate bank account is not *in fact* maintained. So, Finlay CJ held in *Re Wogan's (Drogheda) Ltd*[123] that:

> 'If a lender, having availed of a debenture in these terms as a concession delays the designation of a bank account or suspends for some period the operation of direct control over the bank account into which the proceeds of book debts is paid, thus permitting the company issuing the debenture to carry on trading in a more normal fashion than strict

---

[118] *Re Keenan Bros Ltd* [1985] IR 401 at 423, 424.

[119] *Royal Trust Bank v National Westminster Bank plc* [1996] 2 BCLC 682 at 704g–h.

[120] *Re Brumark Investments Ltd; Commissioner of Inland Revenue v Agnew* [2001] 2 BCLC 188, [2001] UKPC 28. See para **[18.053]**.

[121] *Re Brumark Investments Ltd; Commissioner of Inland Revenue v Agnew* [2001] 2 BCLC 188 at 204c–d, para [46].

[122] See Peterson, (2002) 23 Co Lawyer 24 at 25.

[123] *Re Wogan's (Drogheda) Ltd* [1993] 1 IR 157.

> compliance with the terms of a fixed charge would permit there does not appear to be any principle of law or justice which would deprive such a lender of the rights agreed by the debtor company of a fixed charge over the assets, whereas, a lender with a more draconian approach to the rights which were granted to it by a debenture would be in a more advantageous position[124].'

In that case, the terms of the debenture provided for, *inter alia*, the maintenance of a separate bank account. The clause in question provided:

> 'The company hereby covenants to pay into such banking account or accounts as may be designated for such purpose by the lender, and whether with the lender or with any other banking institution, designated by the lender, all monies which it may receive in respect of book debts and other debts or securities and not without the prior consent of the lender in writing to withdraw or deal with such monies or to assign or purport to assign the same in favour of any other person and if called upon to do so by the lender to execute a legal assignment of such book debts and other debts and securities to the lender.'

The requirement to have a designated bank account was held to be the decisive factor in determining whether the debenture created a fixed or floating charge over the company's book debts and the subsequent conduct of the parties was held not to be relevant for the purpose of construing the debenture[125]. In *Oakdale (Richmond) Ltd v National Westminster Bank plc*[126], a novel challenge was raised to the practice of insisting that book debts be paid into a designated bank account, based on Articles 85 and 86 of the EU Treaty which prevent anti-competitive practices. The challenge did not succeed. It was held by Chadwick J that the requirement that book debts be paid into the company's account with the chargee bank 'far from being anti-competitive, is necessary in order that the fixed charge over book debts which the company has sought to create should be effective'[127].'

[18.047] The subsequent Supreme Court decision in *Re Holidair Ltd*[128] is virtually impossible to reconcile with the decision in *Re Wogan's (Drogheda) Ltd*. In the *Holidair* case, the Kentz group of companies were placed under the protection of the court and an examiner was appointed. A dispute arose between the examiner and the company's main creditors who were debenture holders, *inter alia*, on whether their debentures created

---

[124] *Re Wogan's (Drogheda) Ltd* [1993] 1 IR 157 at 170–171.

[125] Following *Re Whitworth Street Estates Ltd* [1980] AC 583.

[126] *Oakdale (Richmond) Ltd v National Westminster Bank plc* [1997] 1 BCLC 63.

[127] *Oakdale (Richmond) Ltd v National Westminster Bank plc* [1997] 1 BCLC 63 at 75g. Similarly, Chadwick J upheld the prohibition in the debenture against selling, factoring, discounting or otherwise charging or assigning the book debts without the prior consent in writing of the bank, which he found to be an ancillary requirement to the requirement that the proceeds be paid into a specified account. On this point he said: 'The prohibition is not an absolute prohibition. It is a prohibition against dealing with debts without prior consent in writing of the bank. The requirement for prior consent ensures that the bank is given notice of what is proposed. It enables the bank to exercise its own commercial judgment in determining whether what is proposed will or will not prejudice its security and to reflect that determination by the giving or withholding of consent. The prohibition is necessary if the bank is to have the security which it sought and which the company was willing to provide' (at 76b).

[128] *Re Holidair Ltd* [1994] 1 ILRM 481, considered by Connaughton, 'The *Kentz* Case – More Problems for Secured Lenders' (1994) CLP 110.

fixed or floating charges over the company's book debts[129]. In the High Court, Costello J had held that on its proper construction, the debenture created a fixed charge over the company's book debts. This was reversed in the Supreme Court by Blayney J, who held that, upon its true construction, the debenture created a floating charge over the chargor company's book debts. This was so found notwithstanding the existence of a clause which provided that the chargee could designate a bank account into which the proceeds of book debts were to be paid. The clause in question provided, *inter alia*, that:

> 'With reference to the book debts and any other debts hereby charged, the companies shall pay into such accounts with the banks or any of them as the trustee [the banks] may from time to time select, all monies which they may receive in respect of such debts and shall not without the prior consent in writing of the trustee sell, factor, discount or otherwise charge, assign or dispose of the same in favour of any other person or purport so to do and the companies shall if called upon to do so by the trustee from time to time execute legal assignments of such book debts and other debts to the trustee in such form as the trustee shall require and at the companies' own expense[130].'

Blayney J rejected the notion that merely because the clause was described as a fixed charge it should be accepted as such unless there were other indications in the debenture consistent with this conclusion[131]. Moreover, he found that the charge under consideration had the three characteristics of a floating charge, as described by Romer J in *Re Yorkshire Woolcombers' Association Ltd*[132]. In particular, he found that the charge on book debts in the banks' debenture did not 'prevent the companies from using the book debts in the normal way for the purpose of carrying on their business'[133].' Finding that the existence of the particular clause in *Re Wogan's (Drogheda) Ltd*[134] 'clearly distinguishes that case from the present'[135], the learned judge concluded that the effect of the clause was to create a floating charge over the companies' book debts. The only significant difference between the two clauses was that the clause in *Re Wogan's (Drogheda) Ltd* specifically prohibited the company from withdrawing monies from the designated accounts[136]. Indeed, it appears that this was the only reasoning by which Blayney J could have found that the companies were not prohibited from using the book debts in the ordinary course of their businesses[137]. If this is so, it is within the power of the legal draftsman to ensure that such a fate will not befall all future fixed charges over book debts.

---

[129] A number of other issues are considered elsewhere: the effect of the negative pledge clause in the company's debenture on the examiner's powers to borrow without the debenture holders' consent: see para **[18.079]**; the effects of s 5(2)(d) of the C(A)A 1990 and the construction of s 29(3) of the C(A)A 1990 – see Ch 22, *Examinerships*, para **[22.073]** and **[22.085]**, respectively.

[130] *Re Holidair Ltd* [1994] 1 ILRM 481 at 491.

[131] Here, Blayney J relied on the High Court decision of Keane J in *Re Keenan Bros Ltd* [1985] BCLC 302.

[132] *Re Yorkshire Woolcombers' Association Ltd* [1903] 2 Ch 284. See para **[18.069]**.

[133] *Re Holidair Ltd* [1994] ILRM 481 at 493.

[134] See para **[18.046]**, *ante*, where the clause referred to is reproduced.

[135] *Re Wogan's (Drogheda) Ltd* [1994] ILRM 481 at 494.

[136] The Supreme Court decision in *Re Keenan Bros Ltd* [1986] BCLC 242 was distinguished in the same way.

[137] *Re Wogan's (Drogheda) Ltd* [1994] 1 ILRM 481 at 493.

[18.048] Since the House of Lords decision in *Re Spectrum Plus Ltd*[138], in the UK, the existence of real restrictions on the operation of a specified bank account into which book debts are to be paid, such as the blocking of unrestricted access to debit the account by the company until the facility secured by the charge has been repaid, is now essential to a charge on book debts being found to be a fixed charge. In that case a debenture provided for a fixed or specific charge over the company's book debts and other debts and provided:

> 'With reference to the book debts and other debts hereby specifically charged [the company] shall pay into [the company's] account with the Bank all moneys which it may receive in respect of such debts and shall not discount or otherwise charge or assign the same in favour of any other person or purport to do so and [the company] shall if called upon to do so by the Bank from time to time execute legal assignments of such book debts and other debts to the Bank.'

The company was, however, expressly permitted to draw on the account for its business expenses provided that the overdraft limit was not exceeded. In practice, after receiving the facility and entering into the debenture, the company opened the bank account and paid its book debts into the account and drew on the account for business purposes. When the company went into liquidation, the bank sought a declaration that the debenture created a fixed charge. The English High Court held that the charge was not a fixed charge, but a floating charge; this finding was, however, reversed by the English Court of Appeal which found the charge to be a fixed charge and it was from this decision that the House of Lords came to consider the matter.

[18.049] The House of Lords not only overruled the decision of the Court of Appeal in *Re Spectrum Plus Ltd*, but also the actual decision in *Siebe Gorman*. It found that there was no difference in legal substance between a charge expressed to be a fixed charge which comes into existence on the occurrence of a future event *or* the grant of a floating charge over a class of assets which could crystallise on the occurrence of a future event *or*, as was the case in hand, a charge expressed to be a fixed charge which permitted the chargor to use the charged assets in the ordinary course of its business until the occurrence of a future event. As Lord Scott said:

> 'The moneys in the bank account were assets subject to the charge. If the account had been treated as a blocked account, so long as it remained overdrawn, it would be easy to infer from a combination of that treatment and the description of the charge as a fixed charge that Spectrum had no right to draw on the account until the debit on the account had been discharged. But the account was never so treated. The overdraft facility was there to be drawn on by Spectrum at will. In the operation of the account there was never a suggestion that Spectrum needed to obtain the bank's consent before writing a cheque. The bank could, by notice, have terminated the overdraft facility, required immediate repayment of the indebtedness and turned the account into a blocked account. Pending such a notice, however, Spectrum was free to draw on the account. *Its right to do so was*

138 *Re Spectrum Plus Ltd* [2005] 2 BCLC 269. See Berg, 'The Cuckoo in the Nest of Corporate Insolvency: Some Aspects of the Spectrum Case' [2006] JBL 22; Catley, 'Floating Charges – Where are we after Spectrum Plus?' (2007) PLC 49; Pennington, 'Recent Developments in the Law and Practice relating to the Creation of Security for Companies' Indebtedness' (2009) 30 Co Law 163; and Wild, 'Spectrum and Leyland Daf: The Spectre of New Claims' (2005) 26 Co Law 10.

> *inconsistent with the charge being a fixed charge and the label placed on the charge by the debenture cannot, in my opinion, be prayed-in-aid to detract from that right.*
>
> 120. The correct conclusion, in my opinion, is that the debenture, although expressed to grant the bank a fixed charge over Spectrum's book debts, in law granted only a floating charge'[139].

By overruling *Siebe Gorman* and with it the basis for the standard English bank-debenture, this decision caused consternation amongst bankers and lawyers in the UK[140]. In truth, there was little new in this decision for Irish practitioners of company law who have understood, since the Supreme Court decision in *Re Holidair*, that substance is everything as are real restrictions on the chargor's use of property if a fixed charge is to be found over book debts[141].

(c) The chargee must exercise control as of legal right

[18.050] Another important feature in determining whether a particular charge over book debts is a fixed or floating charge is the legal basis of the chargee's control over the book debts. In *Re Double s Printers Ltd*[142], it was held that the fact that a chargee was a director of the chargor company and a signatory of the company's bank mandate was not sufficient to give rise to the requisite control over the chargor company's book debts. Jonathon Parker J held that:

> 'In order for the debenture to take effect as a fixed charge over present and future book debts, there must, it seems to me, be some right of control over the debts, or their proceeds, exercisable by [the chargee] in *his capacity as chargee*, and not in some other capacity, eg as a director of the company. The opportunity for [the chargee] to exercise de facto control of the company's bank account in his capacity as a director of the company is, in my view, *nihil as rem*. He might, after all, cease to be a director during the continuance of the security; or he might assign the debenture, in which event the assignee would not be in a position to exercise control. In any event, as a director, [the chargee] was at all material times under a fiduciary duty to the company to act bona fide in the interests of the company, and not for a collateral purpose such as the maintenance of his rights as chargee. I therefore conclude that, despite its description as a fixed charge, the charge over book debts created by the debenture takes effect not as a fixed but as a floating charge[143].'

---

139 *Re Spectrum Plus Ltd* [2005] 2 BCLC 269 at 313 (emphasis added). Subsequent decisions of the English courts have followed the principles in *Spectrum*: in *Re F2G Realisations Ltd* [2011] 1 BCLC 313, a chargor company's ability to draw freely on monies in a charged account meant it was consistent with being a floating charge, and see also *Re Beam Tube Products Ltd* [2006] BCC 615; by contrast, in *Russell-Cooke Trust Co Ltd v Elliott and others* [2007] 2 BCLC 637 the fact that a deed of charge prevented withdrawal of an asset from the security was found to be consistent only with a fixed charge, and see also *Re Harmony Care Homes Ltd* [2010] BCC 358.

140 So concerned was the bank that it argued that the decision should be found to be forward-looking only, an argument ultimately rejected by the House of Lords.

141 *Cf* Ali, 'Developments in Fixed and Floating Charges: Legal Principles, Policy Issues and Implications for Structured Financing' (2006) CLP 46.

142 *Re Double s Printers Ltd* [1999] BCC 303.

143 *Re Double s Printers Ltd* [1999] BCC 303 at 306–307.

Accordingly, for a charge to be a fixed charge on a company's book debts, the chargee must exercise the requisite control over the book debts as a matter of right or, *de jure*, in his capacity as chargee and not in any other *de facto* capacity.

(d) Hybrid charges on book debts

[18.051] The difficulty with fixed charges on book debts is that the restrictions and controls that must be imposed upon a company on how it deals with its book debts can be most inconvenient for the company. Indeed, the holder of the charge, too, is often happy to allow the company to deal with its book debts in the ordinary course of business – the real requirement being that in the event of the company's insolvency, its charge over those book debts that remain uncollected should have priority over any claim by the Revenue Commissioners. The best of both worlds is a fixed charge whilst the book debts are outstanding and a floating charge when they have been collected.

[18.052] The case of *Re New Bullas Trading Ltd*[144] broke new ground in allowing the creation of just such a hybrid charge on book debts. There, the charge provided that for as long as book debts remained uncollected, they were subject to a fixed charge but that as soon as they were paid into the designated bank account they became the subject of a floating charge[145]. The charge had the following features:

- the chargee could give instructions with respect to the manner in which the company dealt with the book debts and could also demand that the company assign the book debts to it;
- the chargor was obliged to pay the book debts into a designated bank account and the chargee could give directions with respect to the operation of the account;
- if the chargee failed to give directions in relation to the money in the designated account, then the moneys became released from the fixed charge and became subject to a floating charge, thereby permitting the company to deal with the money in the course of its ordinary business.

In the English Court of Appeal, Nourse LJ made it clear that the issue to be decided was whether the law allowed book debts to switch from being the subject of a fixed charge to being the subject of a floating charge. Pronouncing upon the validity of the debenture, Nourse LJ said:

> '... just as it is open to contracting parties to provide for a fixed charge on future book debts, so it is open to them to provide that they shall be subject to a fixed charge while they are uncollected and a floating charge on realisation. No authority to the contrary has been cited and, the principle being as spacious as it has been expressed to be, no objection is on that account sustainable. For these reasons, I would ... hold that the charge over book debts of the company, as created by the debenture, was, unless and until their proceeds were paid into the specified account, a valid fixed charge[146].'

[144] *Re New Bullas Trading Ltd* [1994] 1 BCLC 485.

[145] Nourse LJ observed (at 487) that: 'Here, for the first time in a reported case, the draftsman has deliberately and conscientiously set out to subject [the book debts] to a fixed charge while they are uncollected and a floating charge on realisation.'

[146] *Re New Bullas Trading Ltd* [1994] 1 BCLC 485 at 493.

The acceptance of such hybrid clauses was not universal. At the heart of the debate was the propriety of treating charges on book debts as being divisible from charges on the proceeds of book debts[147]. Another concern was with the chargor's ability to end the chargee's fixed charge by paying the proceeds of the book debts into a bank account. The issue was that a chargor should not, under a fixed security, be able to remove the charged assets from the chargee's security so as to be able to deal with the assets in the ordinary course of its business. Indeed, this concern goes back to the heart of the fixed/floating debate of the 1980s: the necessity for restrictions on the chargor's ability to deal with the book debts commensurate with a fixed security.

[18.053] The hybrid clause came to be used in debentures around the world, and it was in New Zealand that its demise began. In *Re Brumark Investments Ltd; Commissioner of Inland Revenue v Agnew,* the New Zealand Court of Appeal[148] and, subsequently, the Privy Council[149], both declined to follow *Re New Bullas Trading Ltd*[150]. The New Zealand Court of Appeal held that the charge (which was in all material respects identical to that in *Re New Bullas Trading Ltd*) was a *floating charge*. The trial judge, Fisher J, had drawn a distinction between the company's freedom to receive debts, thereby extinguishing the charge on the one hand and disposing of the debts to third parties on the other. This was not accepted by the Court of Appeal, and Gault J held:

> 'In the present case, by excluding from the purported fixed charge created by the debenture (until intervention by the bank) proceeds of book debts, the bank and the company were merely emphasising the freedom of the company to collect the book debts on its own account. That is the usual manner of dealing with book debts. That the company was contractually bound not to dispose of, create or allow any interest in the uncollected debts does not detract from that. As created this was a floating charge over book debts[151].'

The subsequent appeal to the Privy Council was dismissed. Giving the judgment of the Council, Lord Millett reviewed the history of the floating charge and the development of the fixed charge on book debts. He then turned to the hybrid charge that was upheld in *New Bullas Trading Ltd*, commenting:

> 'In every previous case the debenture had treated book debts and their proceeds indivisibly. Now for the first time in any reported case the draftsman set out deliberately to distinguish between them. As in the present case the debenture purported to create two distinct charges, a fixed charge on the book debts while they remained uncollected and a floating charge on their proceeds. It differed from the debenture in the present case only in

---

147 See Goode (1994) 110 LQR 592.

148 *Re Brumark Investments Ltd; Commissioner of Inland Revenue v Agnew* [2000] 1 BCLC 354.

149 *Re Brumark Investments Ltd; Commissioner of Inland Revenue v Agnew* [2001] 2 BCLC 188. See, generally, Berg, 'Brumark Investments Ltd and the "'Innominate Charge"' [2001] JBL 532; Tribe, 'The Privy Council and Brumark: A Lingering Shadow over Book Debts?' (2001) 22 Co Lawyer 318; Sealy, 'Thumbs Down for New Bullas "Down Under"' (2000) Company Law Newsletter; Issue 53; 9 May 2000; Sealy, 'Company Charges: New Bullas Overruled – But is this the End of the Story?' (2001) Company Law Newsletter; Issue 76; 29 June 2001.

150 The decision in *Re New Bullas Trading Ltd* was distinguished by Hart J in *Chalk v Kahn* [2000] 2 BCLC 361.

151 *Re Brumark Investments Ltd; Commissioner of Inland Revenue v Agnew* [2000] 1 BCLC 354 at 364i, para [34].

that the proceeds of the debts were not released from the fixed charge until they were actually paid into the company's bank account, whereas in the present case they were released from the fixed charge as soon as they were received by the company ... The intended effect of the debenture was the same in each case. Until the charge holder intervened the company could continue to collect the debts, though not to assign or factor them, and the debts once collected would cease to exist. The proceeds which took their place would be a different asset which has never been subject to the fixed charge and would from the outset be subject to the floating charge[152].'

Lord Millett said that the 'net question' was 'whether the book debts which were uncollected when the receivers were appointed were subject to a fixed charge or a floating charge'.

[18.054] The Privy Council made a number of findings. In the first place, it was held that Nourse LJ's observation in *Re New Bullas Trading Ltd* that 'an uncollected book debt is a natural subject of a fixed charge; but once it is collected, the proceeds being needed for the conduct of business, it becomes a natural subject of a floating charge' was 'unsound'. In the second place, the Privy Council disagreed with Nourse LJ's approach to interpretation that the question was one of construction and that the intention of the parties as gleaned from the terms of the debenture should prevail. On this point Lord Millett said:

'Their Lordships consider this approach to be fundamentally mistaken. The question is not merely one of construction. In deciding whether a charge is a fixed charge or a floating charge, the court is engaged in a two-stage process. At the first stage it must construe the instrument of charge and seek to gather the intentions of the parties from the language they have used. But the object at this stage of the process is not to discover whether the parties intended to create a fixed or a floating charge. It is to ascertain the nature of the rights and obligations which the parties intended to grant each other in respect of the charged assets. Once these have been ascertained, the court can then embark on the second stage of the process, which is one of categorisation. This is a matter of law. It does not depend on the intention of the parties. If their intention, properly gathered from the language of the instrument, is to grant the company rights in respect of the charged assets which are inconsistent with the nature of a fixed charge, then the charge cannot be a fixed charge however they may have chosen to describe it. A similar process is involved in construing a document to see whether it creates a licence or tenancy. The court must construe the grant to ascertain the intention of the parties: but the only intention which is relevant is the intention to grant exclusive possession ... So here, in construing a debenture to see whether it creates a fixed or a floating charge, the only intention which is relevant is the intention that the company should be free to deal with the charged assets and withdraw them from the security without the consent of the holder of the charge; or, to put the question another way, whether the charged assets were intended to be under the control of the company or of the charge holder[153].'

Turning from the general to the specific, the Privy Council rejected that the book debts were sufficiently under the chargee's control for the charge to be capable of being a fixed charge. In particular, Nourse LJ's reasoning that there was sufficient control was

---

152 *Re Brumark Investments Ltd; Commissioner of Inland Revenue v Agnew* [2001] 2 BCLC 188 at 199e–g, para [28].

153 *Re Brumark Investments Ltd; Commissioner of Inland Revenue v Agnew* [2001] 2 BCLC 188 at 200d–g, para [32].

rejected. Nourse LJ had said it was wrong to say that assets ceased to be subject to a fixed charge at the chargor's will, but rather that they ceased to be subject to a fixed charge because this is what the parties had agreed would happen in the debenture. It is opined that, objectively, there is nothing intrinsically wrong with Nourse LJ's reasoning and that the Privy Council was primarily motivated by the policy considerations in the pecking order of priorities in an insolvency rather than the pursuit of conceptual possibility.

[18.055] The Privy Council also discredited the suggestion that it was sufficient to prevent the chargor from alienating its book debts, for the purposes of establishing the requisite degree of control for a fixed charge, but that it was not necessary to go further and also prohibit it from collecting and disposing of them[154]. Lord Millett said of that proposition:

> 'It makes no commercial sense because alienation and collection are merely different methods of realising a debt by turning it into money, collection being the natural and ordinary method of doing so. A restriction on disposition which nevertheless allows collection and free use of the proceeds is inconsistent with the fixed nature of the charge; it allows the debt and its proceeds to be withdrawn from the security by the act of the company in collecting it[155].'

It was accepted that a company could exploit the characteristics inherent in the nature of the asset itself and that a wasting asset could be the subject of a fixed charge, provided always that whilst it subsists it cannot be destroyed or withdrawn from the security by the chargor[156]. The Privy Council also disapproved of the concept of two charges – one (fixed) over uncollected book debts and the other (floating) over the proceeds. As the influential company law commentator, Pennington, has observed, 'the conception of the proceeds of debts owing to a company as a separate item from the debts themselves was an impossibility'[157].

[18.056] The primary difficulty with the hybrid charge in *Re Brumark Investments Ltd* being a fixed charge was that the chargor was free to deal with the charged assets in a manner inconsistent with a fixed charge. As Lord Millett concluded:

> '… the debenture was so drafted that the company was at liberty to turn the uncollected book debts to account by its own act. Taking the relevant assets to be the uncollected book debts, the company was left in control of the process by which the charged assets were extinguished and replaced by different assets which were not the subject of a fixed charge and were at the free disposal of the company. That is inconsistent with the nature of a fixed charge[158].'

154 Cf *Re ASRS Establishment Ltd* [2000] 2 BCLC 631.

155 *Re Brumark Investments Ltd; Commissioner of Inland Revenue v Agnew* [2001] 2 BCLC 188 at 201, para [36].

156 *Re Brumark Investments Ltd; Commissioner of Inland Revenue v Agnew* [2001] 2 BCLC 188 at 201, para [37].

157 Pennington, 'Recent Developments in the Law and Practice relating to the Creation of Security for Companies' Indebtedness' (2009) 30 Co Law 163 at 165.

158 *Re Brumark Investments Ltd; Commissioner of Inland Revenue v Agnew* [2001] 2 BCLC 188 at 205, para [49].

The question remains – can a debenture be drafted that achieves what it was thought had been achieved by the *New Bullas Trading* debenture? And what of the position in Ireland? Ironically, the Supreme Court has distinguished between uncollected debts and their proceeds, albeit in circumstances unfavourable to the chargee. Following the decision in *Re Spectrum Plus Ltd*[159] and the approach taken by Finlay Geoghegan J in her impeccably constructed decision in *Re JD Brian Motors Ltd*[160], where the principles applicable to fixed charges on book debts were applied to determine whether express crystallisation charges were effective to create fixed charges, it seems that Irish and English law has never been closer on this point and that the decision in *Re Brumark Investments Ltd* is consistent with the evolved jurisprudence in Ireland.

(e) Legislative curtailment of the priority of fixed charges on book debts[161]

[18.057] Shortly after it was accepted by the Irish courts that a fixed charge could be created over book debts, s 115 of the Finance Act 1986 was enacted. This provided that a fixed charge over a book debt does *not* enjoy preference in priority to one preferential creditor, the Revenue Commissioners. This section was very convoluted. It provided that where a company, which had created a fixed charge over its book debts, was unable to pay certain taxes owed to the Revenue Commissioners, the Revenue Commissioners could serve a notice on the holder of the fixed charge whereupon the holder of the fixed charge would become liable to pay such sums. This was subject to the proviso that the fixed charge holder would not be liable to pay more than it had received from the company which had created the fixed charge, and did not apply to amounts received by the fixed charge holder before it was notified by the Revenue Commissioners that it was liable for the chargor company's liabilities.

[18.058] In March 1994, the Task Force for Small Business recommended that s 115 of the Finance Act 1986 be repealed[162]. As a result of this and other lobbying, the then Minister for Finance purported to reform the section so as to make fixed charges over book debts a more attractive security for banks, in the hope that there would be increased lending to small businesses. The result was s 174 of the Finance Act 1995,

---

[159] *Re Spectrum Plus Ltd* [2005] 2 BCLC 269. See Catley, 'Floating Charges – Where are we after Spectrum Plus?' (2007) PLC 49.

[160] *Re JD Brian Motors Ltd* [2011] IEHC 113.

[161] See Courtney, *Company Law Review, 1995* (1996), pp 33–40 and 'Editorial' (1995) 2 CLP 242.

[162] Task Force for Small Business, *Report*, pp 83 and 84: 'For many trading companies, their book debts are a major, if not the main, source of collateral that they can offer to banks in negotiating a loan. As a result of section 115, the value of book debts as a security has been considerably diminished. We discussed the effects of this provision with representatives of the associated banks. All indicated that it had had an adverse effect on their willingness to lend to small business and on the terms on which they did so. As we have noted already, the operation of the Section has also led to as greater emphasis on fixed asset-backed loans under the Small Business Expansion Loan Scheme than we consider desirable. We believe that the Revenue Commissioners have adequate powers with which to protect their interests. The effect of section 115 is to confer on them a kind of super preferential status which is neither necessary nor desirable. Though the legal position on book debts is similar in the United Kingdom, the authorities there have not legislated along the lines of section 115. We recommend that it should be repealed in the 1994 Finance Bill'.'

which amended the original s 115 by the substitution and addition of certain subsections.

[18.059] Such were the origins of s 1001 of the Taxes Consolidation Act 1997 ('TCA 1997'), which provides:

> '(2) Subject to this section, where a person holds a fixed charge (being a fixed charge created on or after the 27th day of May, 1986) on the book debts of a company (within the meaning of the Companies Act, 1963), such person shall, if the company fails to pay any relevant amount for which it is liable, become liable to pay such relevant amount on due demand, and on neglect or refusal of payment may be proceeded against in the like manner as any other defaulter.
>
> (3) This section shall not apply–
>
> (a) unless the holder of the fixed charge has been notified in writing by the Revenue Commissioners that a company has failed to pay a relevant amount for which it is liable and that by virtue of this section the holder of the fixed charge–
>
> (i) may become liable for payment of any relevant amount which the company subsequently fails to pay, and
>
> (ii) where paragraph (c) does not apply, has become liable for the payment of the relevant amount which the company has failed to pay,
>
> (b) to any amounts received by the holder of the fixed charge from the company before the date on which the holder is notified in writing by the Revenue Commissioners in accordance with paragraph (a), and
>
> (c) where within 21 days of the creation of the fixed charge the holder of the fixed charge furnishes in writing to the Revenue Commissioners the following details in relation to the charge–
>
> (i) the name of the company on whose book debts the charge has been created,
>
> (ii) the registration number of the company as issued by the Companies Registration Office to that company,
>
> (iii) the tax registration number of the company as issued by the Revenue Commissioners to that company,
>
> (iv) the date the fixed charge was created, and
>
> (v) the name and address of the holder of the fixed charge,
>
> to any relevant amount which the company was liable to pay before the date on which the holder notified in writing the Revenue Commissioners in accordance with paragraph (a)[163].
>
> (4) The amount or aggregate amount which a person shall be liable to pay in relation to a company in accordance with this section shall not exceed the amount or aggregate amount which the person has, while the fixed charge on book debts in relation to the company is in existence, received directly or indirectly from that company in payment or in part payment of any debts due by the company to the person.
>
> (5) The Revenue Commissioners may, at any time and by notice in writing given to the holder of the fixed charge, withdraw with effect from a date specified in the notice a notification issued by them in accordance with subsection (3); but such withdrawal shall not–

163 Paragraph (c) was substituted by s 120 of the Finance Act 2007 ('FA 2007'), with effect from 2 April 2007.

(a) affect in any way any liability of the holder of the fixed charge under this section which arose before such withdrawal, or

(b) preclude the issue under subsection (3) of a subsequent notice to the holder of the fixed charge.

(6) The Revenue Commissioners may nominate any of their officers to perform any acts and discharge any functions authorised by this section to be performed or discharged by the Revenue Commissioners.

If there were a prize for the most tortuous, rambling and cryptic legislative enactment, this would surely be a contender for first prize. The effect (and spirit) of this section is to punish those who dare to lend to small companies on the security of a fixed charge on book debts! By imposing a liability on a chargee to pay his chargor's liabilities to the Revenue Commissioners, it is possibly even unconstitutional.

[18.060] The approach of s 1001 of the TCA 1997 is to proceed by imposing a liability on the *holder* of a fixed charge on book debts to pay, in certain circumstances, his chargor's liabilities to the Revenue Commissioners and then to follow this with a series of qualifying provisos. The holder of a fixed charge on a company's book debts will, on due demand being made by the revenue, be liable to pay any PAYE and VAT[164] for which the chargor company is liable to the revenue, *unless* certain circumstances exist. Section 1001 goes considerably further than merely altering the long-established priority that a fixed charge holder prevails over all other creditors. The section can be described as a unilateral statutory indemnity whereby the holder of a fixed charge on book debts is forced to stand in his debtor's shoes.

[18.061] The first of four provisos to the chargee's liability is provided by s 1001(3)(a) of the TCA 1997. This provides that the chargee will not be liable to pay the chargor's liabilities for PAYE and VAT unless he has been so notified in writing by the Revenue Commissioners. The notification must provide that the chargor has defaulted and that the chargee may become liable for payment of any relevant amounts which the company subsequently fails to pay, or, if the third qualification does not apply, has already become liable for relevant amounts that the company has already failed to pay. The effect of this qualification is that s 1001 will only become operational at the instigation of the Revenue Commissioners.

[18.062] The second proviso is provided for in s 1001(3)(b) of the TCA 1997. This provides that the section does not apply to any amounts received by the chargee from the chargor before the chargee is notified in accordance with para 3(a), just considered. This proviso confuses the chargee's actual liability to pay anything with the extent of his liability. It would appear that this proviso provides that the chargee's liability does not apply to any amounts received by the chargee before he is notified as outlined. Therefore, regardless of the relevant amount that a chargee may be liable to pay, a chargee will only have to account for monies received by him after the Revenue Commissioners' notice is served on him.

[18.063] The third proviso, which was held out by the Department of Finance to be the panacea, is provided for in s 1001(3)(c) of the TCA 1997 (as substituted by s 120 of the

[164] Section 1001(1) of the TCA 1997 defines 'relevant amount' as amounts due under the PAYE system or VAT Acts.

FA 2007). This provides for a bastard procedure which seems intended to afford a chargee with some comfort where he notifies the Revenue Commissioners upon the creation of the fixed charge over the chargor's book debts. To avail of this, notification must be made within 21 days of the creation of the charge. The means of notification is by way of a copy to the Revenue Commissioners of the Form C1 that a chargee must deliver to the CRO within 21 days of the creation of a registrable charge pursuant to s 99 of the CA 1963. Where a chargee does this, then his liability for the chargor's liability for relevant amounts shall not apply 'to any relevant amount which the company was liable to pay before the date on which the [chargee] is notified in writing by the Revenue Commissioners in accordance with paragraph (a)'. Therefore, the amounts which the chargee is obliged to pay the Revenue Commissioners will, where this procedure is followed, only extend to subsequent relevant amounts. It is important to note that it is not relevant amounts which subsequently accrue, merely relevant amounts which the company fails to pay; so it would seem that relevant amounts which have accrued but are not actually due and owing are not excluded.

[18.064] The fourth proviso is provided for in s 1001(4) of the TCA 1997. This seeks to cap the extent of a chargee's liability. So, it is provided that the amount which a chargee shall be liable to pay:

> '... shall not exceed the amount or aggregate amount which that person has, while the fixed charge on book debts in relation to the said company is in existence, received, directly or indirectly, from that company in payment or in part payment of any debts due by the company to the person'.

The extent of a chargee's liability under s 1001(4) is draconian and, most probably, unconstitutional. The principal difficulty is the failure to recognise that companies may pay chargees amounts other than on foot of a fixed charge on book debts. Where a chargee also holds, say, a fixed mortgage and charge over lands and premises, whilst s 1001 does not assail the priority of that charge, it would seem to seek to affect the proceeds of sale by possibly requiring a chargee to pay to the Revenue Commissioners such proceeds in discharge of a chargor's tax liabilities. It is thought that s 1001 should simply be repealed once and for all.

Fixed charges on deposit accounts[165]

[18.065] Companies that have credit balances at banks and other financial institutions rightly regard such as being a valuable asset. Generically, such assets fall to be classified as *choses in action*. They do not, however, fall to be classified as book debts[166]. In *Re Brightlife Ltd*[167], Hoffmann J said:

---

165 See generally, Johnston, *Banking and Security Law in Ireland* (1998), Ch 15; and Breslin, *Banking Law* (2nd edn, 2007), 13-05, 13-05. See also, Hutchinson, 'Charge-Backs, Set-Off and Flawed Assets: Taking Security Over Self-Held Cash Deposits' (1996) 3 CLP 55; Randell-Kahn & Graham, 'Charge Backs: Charge Card Overruled' (1998) PLC 21; de Lacy, 'The Legality of Charge-Back Security Interests' (1998) *Palmer's In Company* Issue 5/98, 19 May 1998.

166 *Watson v Parapara Coal Co Ltd* (1915) 17 GLR 791; and *Perrins v State Bank of Victoria* (1991) 1 VR 749, cited in Gough, *Company Charges* (2nd edn, 1996), p 684.

167 *Re Brightlife Ltd* [1986] BCLC 418.

> '... I do not think that the bank balance falls within the term 'book debts or other debts' as it is used in the debenture. It is true that the relationship between banker and customer is one of debtor and creditor. It would not therefore be legally inaccurate to describe a credit balance with a banker as a debt. But this would not be a natural usage for a businessman or accountant. He would ordinarily describe it as 'cash at bank' ...'[168]

In the instant case Hoffmann J had further reason for finding that the cash balances of the company in question were not part of its 'book or other debts'. The debenture in that case provided that the company was prohibited from dealing with such debts without the chargee's consent 'otherwise than in the ordinary course of getting in and realising the same'. Hoffmann J held that a credit balance in a bank account could not sensibly be got in or realised and so, in that case, found that the company's cash in its bank account was not included in the term 'book or other debts'. Subsequently, in *Re Permanent Houses (Holdings) Ltd*[169] Hoffmann J stated that the previous case was not authority for the proposition that cash at the bank could never amount to a book debt and that it depended upon the wording of each debenture. Notwithstanding the legal reality that a credit balance in a bank account is indeed a debt owed by the bank to a company, current judicial thinking is that the creation of security over a company's 'book debts' will not operate to capture a credit balance in a bank account. That said, however, the prudent practitioner will, in anticipation of a judicial revision or the interpretation of a particular debenture, register a charge on a bank deposit as a charge on book debts in the CRO[170].

[18.066] Leaving to one side the nature of such assets, the observation of Millett J in *Re Charge Card Services Ltd*[171] that 'a charge in favour of a debtor of his own indebtedness to the chargor is conceptually impossible'[172] made lenders to companies very wary about taking security over cash in an account. This, of course, only applied to cases where a bank or other credit institution sought to take a charge over a company's money held in an account *held with* that bank or other credit institution. Many lenders sought to avoid Millett J's 'conceptual impossibility' by causing borrowing companies to deposit monies in subsidiary or otherwise associated companies before taking a charge over them. Others did, and still do, allow borrower companies to deposit monies with them but take security by obtaining an assignment of the debt, a charge over the account, a contractual set-off against monies borrowed and the making of the credit balance in the account a 'flawed asset'.

[18.067] The decision in *Re Charge Card Services Ltd* was reconsidered by the House of Lords in *Morris v Rayners Enterprises Inc; Morris v Agrichemicals Ltd; Re BCCI (No 8)*[173]. There, Lord Hoffmann noted the doctrine of 'conceptual impossibility', first

---

[168] *Re Brightlife Ltd* [1986] BCLC 418 at 422.

[169] *Re Permanent Houses (Holdings) Ltd* [1988] BCLC 563.

[170] See Johnston, *Banking and Security Law in Ireland* (1998), p 581 and Hutchinson, 'Charge-Backs, Set-Off and Flawed Assets: Taking Security Over Self-Held Cash Deposits' (1996) 3 CLP 55 at 57, 58 and *Re BCCI SA (No 8)* [1997] 4 All ER 568 at 577. *Cf Northern Bank Ltd v Ross* [1990] BCC 883. See, generally, Ch 19, *Corporate Borrowing: Registration of Charges*, para **[19.059]**.

[171] *Re Charge Card Services Ltd* [1986] 3 All ER 289.

[172] *Re Charge Card Services Ltd* [1986] 3 All ER 289 at 308.

[173] *Re BCCI (No 8)* [1997] 4 All ER 568.

propounded by Millett J, and went on to depart from the stringency of the rule of interpretation thus propounded, saying that there seemed to him '... no reason for preventing banks and their customers from creating charges over deposits if, for reasons of their own, they want to do so'[174]. Speaking obiter, Lord Hoffmann said:

> 'In a case in which there is no threat to the consistency of the law or objection of public policy, I think that the courts should be very slow to declare a practice of the commercial community to be conceptually impossible. Rules of law must obviously be consistent and not self-contradictory … But the law is fashioned to suit the practicalities of life and legal concepts like 'proprietary interest' and 'charge' are no more than labels given to clusters of related and self-consistent rules of law. Such concepts do not have a life of their own from which the rules are inexorably derived. It follows that in my view the letter was effective to do what it purported to do, namely to create a charge over the deposit in favour of BCCI'.

It is thought that the pragmatism witnessed in this judicial interpretation would find favour with the Irish courts and that there should be no prohibition on the creation of a charge, whether fixed or floating, over a credit balance at a credit institution which is the chargee in such a transaction[175]. That said, the cautious lender who takes security over a 'self-held' credit balance is likely to continue to take security by seeking a 'quadruple cocktail' in the form of a charge, an assignment, a right of set-off and a flawed asset.

Floating charges

(a) The nature and characteristics of a floating charge

[18.068] A floating charge is a charge over a company's present or future property, or classes of property, which hovers over that property until the moment of crystallisation whereupon the charge fastens onto the charged property or class of property, and becomes a quasi-fixed charge[176]. The 'crucial' distinction between a fixed charge and a floating charge has been described as relating to:

> '… the nature of the interest of the [chargee] in the charged property immediately created by the debenture before any crystallising event occurred. A fixed charge attaches to the charged property *in specie* either immediately or as soon as it is acquired by the chargor. The interest of a floating chargee is not specific prior to crystallisation. The floating

[174] *Re BCCI (No 8)* [1997] 4 All ER 568 at 577f.

[175] *Cf Re Euro Travel Ltd; Dempsey v The Governor and Company of the Bank of Ireland* (28 May 1984, unreported) HC [1963–93] Irish Company Law Reports 207 at 212 where Murphy J said: 'I find it difficult to accept the proposition that the company was purporting to charge monies in the hands of the bank itself with monies due by the company to the bank. This argument might have been more attractive when and so long as the sum of £75,000 was lodged by the company to the credit of the Bank of Ireland Finance Company Ltd, a legal entity separate from the respondents in the present proceedings.'

[176] The charge is a 'quasi-fixed charge' in the sense that although it becomes a fixed charge, it is in a different position to a charge which is fixed, *ab initio*. As we shall see, a floating charge can be upset in the order of priorities where it is created within 12 months, or two years in the case of a floating charge created in favour of a 'connected person', and a floating charge ranks after preferential creditors in priority.

> chargee is, in effect, given a security interest in the fund of assets over which the charge is created[177].'

In *Re JD Brian Ltd*[178], Finlay Geoghegan J observed that a floating charge is not defined for the purposes of the Companies Acts and 'it appears there is no one definition of a floating charge'[179].'

[18.069] The essence of a floating charge is that up until the moment of crystallisation the company is free to use the assets which are the subject of the charge in the ordinary course of its business. In the words of Lord Macnaghten in *Illingworth v Houldsworth*[180], unlike a specific or fixed charge, which fastens *ab initio* onto ascertained or definite property, a floating charge:

> '... is ambulatory and shifting in its nature, hovering over and so to speak floating with the property which it is intended to affect until some event occurs or some act is done which causes it to settle and fasten on the subject of the charge within its reach and grasp[181].'

From the view point of the chargor company, the principal advantage of the floating charge is that it allows the company to continue to have the use and enjoyment of the assets which are the subject matter of the floating charge for so long as it remains uncrystallised. This was made clear in the judgment which is most cited by the judiciary, *Re Yorkshire Woolcombers' Association Ltd*[182], where Romer J made a pragmatic speech which has long-lingered upon the lips of the judiciary:

> 'I certainly do not intend to attempt to give an exact definition of the term 'floating charge', nor am I prepared to say that there will not be a floating charge within the meaning of the Act, which does not contain all the three characteristics that I am about to mention, but I certainly think that if a charge has the three characteristics I am about to mention it is a floating charge. (1) If it is a charge on a class of assets of a company present and future; (2) if that class is one, which in the ordinary course of the business of the company, would be changing from time to time; and (3) if you find that by the charge it is contemplated that, until some future step is taken by or on behalf of those interested in the charge, the company may carry on its business in the ordinary way so far as concerns the particular class of assets I am dealing with.'

Floating charges are the most common form of floating security taken by creditors. It may be noted, however, that while it is possible to create a *floating mortgage*, they are not very common. The most common form of floating mortgage is a *floating chattel*

177 *Re Cimex Tissues Ltd* [1995] 1 BCLC 409 at 420, *per* Stanley Burnton QC, sitting as a deputy judge of the High Court.

178 *Re JD Brian Ltd* [2011] IEHC 113 and [2011] IEHC 383. For commentary, see Cuddihy, 'Floating charges – Express Crystallisation Clauses' (2011) CLP 135.

179 *Re JD Brian Ltd* [2011] IEHC 113 at para 16.

180 *Illingworth v Houldsworth* [1904] AC 355.

181 *Illingworth v Houldsworth* [1904] AC 355 at 358, approved of by Kenny J in *Welch v Bowmaker (Ireland) Ltd* [1980] IR 251 at 258.

182 *Re Yorkshire Woolcombers' Association Ltd* [1903] 2 Ch 284 at 295, being the judgment of the court of first instance in the case which on appeal was entitled *Illingworth v Houldsworth* [1904] AC 355.

mortgage. Floating chattel mortgages are most frequently used in agricultural lending where they are taken over a farmer's stock, plant and machinery[183].

[18.070] It should be noted that there is some controversy as to whether or not a floating charge takes immediate effect over the property charged, and merely allows the chargor company to continue to deal with the property until the moment of crystallisation, or, on the other hand, whether it is a future charge, which does not take effect until crystallisation. While it was the case that, previously, the former was the preferred view[184], a strong case can be made for the latter view[185]. It is submitted that the former is, logically, the more attractive view, in that upon the execution of a floating charge, a present charge comes into immediate effect, which requires registration under s 99(1) of the CA 1963. Although inchoate or dormant[186], a floating charge is very definitely a 'present charge' which is required to be registered within 21 days of its creation[187]. This view is supported by the decision of Blayney J in *Re Tullow Engineering (Holdings) Ltd*[188], where he held that a debenture which contained a floating charge over shares in another company constituted a present security[189] which was unaffected by the granting of an option to buy those shares. Blayney J quoted Buckley LJ in *Evans v Rival Granite Quarries Ltd*[190] where he said:

> 'A floating security is not a future security; it is a present security, which presently affects all the assets of the company expressed to be included in it ... A floating security is not a specific mortgage of the assets, plus a licence to the mortgagor to dispose of them in the course of his business, but is a floating mortgage applying to every item comprised in the security, but not specifically affecting any item until some event occurs ... which causes it to crystallise into a fixed security[191].'

Accordingly, Blayney J held that the shares all *remained* within the ambit of the floating charge, which did not crystallise until the appointment of a receiver. At that point, an

---

183 Floating chattel mortgages over agricultural stock must also be registered pursuant to the Agricultural Credit Act 1978.

184 Pennington, 'Genesis of a Floating Charge' (1960) 23 MLR 630.

185 See Gough, *Company Charges* (2nd edn, 1996), pp 135–137; and Goode, *Legal Problems and Security* (4th edn, Sweet & Maxwell, 2008) at p 126: 'it is now established that a floating charge creates an immediate, albeit, unattached security interest.'

186 In *Governments Stock and Other Securities Investment Co Ltd v Manila Railway Co* [1897] AC 81 at 86, Lord Macnaghten said: 'A floating security is an equitable charge on the assets for the time being of a going concern. It attaches to the subject charged in the varying condition in which it happens to be from time to time. It is of the essence of such a charge that it remains dormant until the undertaking charged ceases to be a going concern, or until the person in whose favour the charge is created intervenes.'

187 Section 99(1) of the CA 1963; see Ch 19, *Corporate Borrowing: Registration of Charges*, at para **[19.042]** *et seq.*

188 *Re Tullow Engineering (Holdings) Ltd* [1990] 1 IR 452.

189 *Re Tullow Engineering (Holdings) Ltd* [1990] 1 IR 452 at 458.

190 *Evans v Rival Granite Quarries Ltd* [1910] 2 KB 979 at 999.

191 See also *Wallace v Evershed* [1899] Ch 891 where Cozens-Hardy said (at 894): 'A floating security gives an immediate equitable charge on the assets, subject to a right to the company in the ordinary course and for the purposes of the business of the company, but not otherwise, to dispose of the assets as though the charge had not existed …'

equitable assignment of the shares to the debenture holder occurred[192]. More recently, in *Re JD Brian Ltd*[193] Finlay Geoghegan J said, without saying which was the correct view, that in the context of interpreting the CA 1963 it 'was well established, prior to 1963, that a floating charge creates an immediate, albeit unattached security interest, as explained by Buckley LJ in the passage cited above'.

[18.071] In *Smith (Administrator of Cosslett (Contractors) Ltd v Bridgend County Borough Council*[194], Lord Scott in the House of Lords acknowledged that not all floating charges are the same and said that some may be drafted so as to operate as a present charge and others to operate as a future charge. Of course, in practice, most debentures merely provide that a class of assets are charged 'by way of floating charge'. The point is largely moot and the House of Lords held that irrespective of the nature of the charge, it required to be registered as a floating charge upon its creation[195]. One question, to which there seems no immediately clear-cut answer, is whether a floating charge confers (on the holder) an equitable interest over the property of the chargor. Notwithstanding that the effect of crystallisation is to give effect to an equitable assignment in the assets, the subject matter of a floating charge, it is logically attractive to conclude that, pending crystallisation, the holder has some form of equitable interest in assets so charged[196]. On this point Gough[197] is instructive:

> 'Even before crystallisation, under a floating charge there is from the very moment of its creation a present security immediately in existence. For this reason enforcement remedies are available before crystallisation. It may appear contradictory that a floating charge should be both a present security and also a security under which the assignor is free to deal with the assets and under which the assignee gains no proprietary interest over present or future property. The contradiction is in fact apparent, rather than real. The very nature of the floating charge postulates both security for the chargee and commercial freedom for the chargor.

---

192 See *Re Interview Ltd* [1975] IR 382.

193 *Re JD Brian Ltd* [2011] IEHC 113 and [2011] IEHC 383. For commentary, see Cuddihy, 'Floating charges – Express Crystallisation Clauses' (2011) CLP 135.

194 *Smith (Administrator of Cosslett (Contractors) Ltd) v Bridgend County Borough Council* [2001] UKHL 58, [2002] 1 All ER 292. For comment, see Sealy, 'House of Lords Washes Floating Charges in Cosslett (Contractors) Ltd' (2001) Company Law Newsletter, (Issue 85; 12 November 2001).

195 Lord Scott said: 'I do not think, however, that this analysis bars the clause 63(1) future security rights from constituting a floating charge for s 395 registration purposes. In my opinion, a charge expressed to come into existence on the occurrence of an uncertain future event and then to apply to a class of assets that cannot be identified until the event has happened would, if otherwise valid, qualify for registration as a floating charge. The future charge would have the essential characteristic of floating, remaining dormant, until the occurrence of the specified event. It would, I think, come within the mischief sought to be dealt with by the s 395 requirement of registration of floating charges. For the same reasons, it would also, in my view constitute a floating charge for Insolvency Act 1986 purposes …' (at 307g–h; para [63]).

196 See, Forde & Kennedy, *Company Law* (4th edn, 2008) at para 20-66 where it is suggested that a chargee has some equitable interest in the assets charged prior to crystallisation.

197 Gough, *Company Charges* (2nd edn, 1996), pp 97, 98.

> … The combined features of a floating charge of a present security and a deferred proprietary interest for the chargee through lack of appropriation are fully consistent with general principle.'

It is thought that to describe pre-crystallisation rights as being 'proprietary'[198] is to overstate their importance[199]. If a label is to be attributed to the nature of the interest of a floating charge holder in the assets subject to such a charge, it is thought best described as 'an equity' and not 'an equitable interest'[200]. The definition of 'an equity', whether mere or naked, given by Kenny J in *Allied Irish Banks Ltd v Glynn*[201] seems apposite to the right in question. There, in distinguishing equitable interests from equities, Kenny J said: 'The main difference is, I think, that an "equity" does not create or give any estate in the land; it is a right against persons and is enforceable against those who were parties to the transactions which created it[202].' Certainly, a floating charge immediately creates rights that are enforceable against the chargor[203], but it is thought that the rights may, in certain circumstances, also be enforced against persons other than those who are parties to the transaction.

(b) The chargor's ability to deal with the charged property

[18.072] The ability of the chargor company to actually deal with the charged property, including the right to dispose of the property in the ordinary course of business, is clearly the most advantageous feature of the floating charge. In *Re Lakeglen*

---

198 In *Wily v George Partnership Banking Ltd* [1999] Federal Court of Appeal (29 January 1999) Finkelstein J said: 'One possible view of the effect of a floating charge is that it creates an immediate equitable interest over the property of the company and that the company is permitted (licensed) to deal with those assets free of the charge in order to carry on its business until the charge has crystallised … The opposing view is that because a floating charge does not specifically attract any asset until it crystallises into a fixed security it cannot confer a proprietary interest before crystallisation.' It was said, *obiter dictum*, that because the courts of equity will protect charged property, the rights of a floating charge holder are proprietary in nature.

199 *Cf* the views of Farrar & Hannigan, *Farrar's Company Law* (4th edn, 1998), p 633 where the authors take a different view.

200 In *Smith (Administrator of Cosslett (Contractors) Ltd v Bridgend County Borough Council* [2001] UKHL 58, [2002] 1 All ER 292, Lord Scott said that he did not think that the local authority, which he found to be secured by a floating charge, could be said to have had an equitable interest in the charged machinery. He said of their rights that they were a 'contractual operational right, not property rights' (at 307; para [62]).

201 *Allied Irish Banks Ltd v Glynn* [1973] IR 188 at 192.

202 Support for this view can be seen in the Australian case *of Landall Holdings Ltd v Caratti* [1979] WAR 97 where Wallace J said (at 114) '… the charge by way of floating charge or security, though equitable in nature, lies dormant ... Granted there is an equity created upon execution of the debenture charge in favour of the debenture holder but it is a *mere equity* and does not vest or become fixed until crystallisation' (emphasis added). See also *Latec Investments Ltd v Hotel Terrigal Pty Ltd* (1965) 113 CLR 265. Gough, *Company Charges* (2nd edn, 1996), p 230 supports this view of the nature of a floating chargee's right prior to crystallisation.

203 Eg *Re Woodroffes (Musical Instruments) Ltd* [1986] Ch 366 at 378 where an injunction was granted against the chargor to restrain it from dealing with the charged property otherwise than in the ordinary course of business.

Construction Co Ltd[204], the question which arose was whether a clause in a debenture in favour of some of the company's creditors created a fixed or floating charge. In charging the assets of the company, the debenture made certain assets subject to a fixed charge, and went on to further charge the company's 'book debts and all rights and powers of recovery thereof'. On account of the company having been insolvent when the debenture was created, the crucial question was whether the latter charge was fixed or floating. In his examination of the central question, Costello J said[205]:

> '... if it was intended that the charge was to remain dormant until some future date and that the company was permitted to go on receiving the book debts and using them until then, the security would contain the true element of a floating charge.'

In posing the central question[206], Costello J said that it was noticeable that the company concerned was a trading company and that the parties had expressly agreed that the company was permitted to carry on its business since 'in the normal course of affairs it would obviously create difficulties for a trading company if it were required to hand over to its mortgagees its book debts as it received them from time to time'[207]. He went on to cite and apply the test of Romer J in *Illingworth v Houldsworth*, and found that the charge over the book debts was a floating charge.

[18.073] It should also be noted that the test in *Illingworth v Houldsworth* is not, nor was it ever intended to be, exhaustive in detailing the traits of a floating charge. So, a charge can be a floating charge even where the company does not, in fact, dispose of the class of property so charged in the ordinary course of its business. Such is shown in *Welch v Bowmaker (Ireland) Ltd*[208]. There, a company created a debenture in favour of the defendant bank and gave a fixed charge over three parcels of property owned by the company specified in the schedule thereto, and a general charge on the company's undertaking and all its property and assets, present and future. There was, however, a condition in the debenture that, with regard to all of the company's specified property, the charge was to be a specific charge and with regard to other property, a floating charge. The company owned a fourth property which was not specified in the schedule to the debenture, and the question arose as to whether or not this was a fixed or floating charge. This became important when the company later gave an equitable mortgage on the fourth property to the Bank of Ireland. In the Supreme Court, Henchy and Parke JJ applied the old maxim, *generalia specialibus non derogant* (the general does not derogate from the particular), and held that the specification in respect of the first three properties ought to prevail, meaning that the fourth property was merely subject to a floating charge. This meant that Bowmaker lost priority to Bank of Ireland, as the latter had obtained a fixed equitable mortgage before Bowmaker's floating charge of the fourth property had crystallised. It is noticeable that although the company would not

---

204 *Re Lakeglen Construction Co Ltd* [1980] IR 347.

205 When he was referring to *Illingworth v Houldsworth* [1903] 2 Ch 284.

206 Namely, 'When they executed the debenture did the parties intend that in relation to its book debts the company was free to receive them and bring new book debts into existence as if the debenture had not been created – until such time as the debenture holder became entitled to intervene in the company's affairs?'

207 *Re Lakeglen Construction Ltd* [1980] IR 347 at 353.

208 *Welch v Bowmaker (Ireland) Ltd* [1980] IR 251.

ordinarily have disposed of land in the normal course of its business, the Supreme Court implicitly held by majority that this did not prevent the land from being the subject of a floating charge[209].

(c) Fixed or floating? – the Cosslett (Contractors) Ltd saga

[18.074] Whether or not a particular document or deed will give effect to the creation of a floating charge will depend upon its true construction. This is exemplified by *Re Cosslett (Contractors) Ltd*[210] (as the English Court of Appeal decision is reported) or *Smith (Administrator of Cosslett (Contractors) Ltd) v Bridgend County Borough Council*[211] (as the House of Lords' decision is reported). In this case, a company entered into a building contract with a local authority to carry out certain land reclamation works involving the processing of coal bearing shale. The company acquired two coal washing machines with an advance of £1.8 million from the local authority. The building contract[212] provided, *inter alia*, that all 'plant' owned by the company when on the site would be deemed to be the property of the local authority (clause 53). The contract also provided that in the event of the company's insolvency or abandonment of the contract, the local authority could enter upon the site and complete or employ another contractor to complete the works and could use such of the plant which had been deemed to become its property; the local authority could also, at any time, sell the plant and apply the proceeds of sale in or towards the satisfaction of any sums due under the building contract (clause 63). Some two years into the contract the company encountered financial difficulties and abandoned the site. The local authority invoked clause 63 and engaged another contractor to complete the works. Eventually, the local authority sold the two machines to the new contractor.

[18.075] When an administrator was appointed to the first company, he contended that the effect of the building contract was that the local authority had contractual rights over the plant that gave it a proprietary interest in the plant. He also contended that this proprietary interest amounted to an equitable 'security interest' which was a floating

---

209 Note the dissenting judgment of Kenny J who said (at 258) that: 'The land owned by the company is capable of being ascertained and defined and this satisfies Lord Macnaghten's definition of a specific charge. It certainly is not a class of asset which would be changing from time to time. I have no doubt that the debenture given to Bowmaker created a specific charge on the [fourth property].'

210 *Re Cosslett (Contractors) Ltd* [1997] 4 All ER 115. See Gregory, 'Floating Charge over Changing Asset – Statements of Principle' (1997) *CCH's Company Law Newsletter*, Issue 16, 11 September 1997.

211 *Smith (Administrator of Cosslett (Contractors) Ltd) v Bridgend County Borough Council* [2001] UKHL 58, [2002] 1 All ER 292. For comment, see Sealy, 'House of Lords Washes Floating Charges in Cosslett (Contractors) Ltd' (2001) Company Law Newsletter (Issue 85; 12 November 2001).

212 The contract was in standard English ICE (Institution of Civil Engineers Conditions of Contract) format. The fact that the clause in question was found to give rise to a floating charge was all the more incredible since this type of contract had been used for years without users suspecting that registration of a floating charge was required if the clause was not to be void. On registration of floating charges, see Ch 19, *Corporate Borrowing: Registration of Charges*, para **[19.066]**.

charge[213]. The local authority argued that no equitable charge had been created and, alternatively, that if a charge had been created it was a fixed or specific charge over the plant, which did not require registration[214]. Arising from the several proceedings instituted, the following findings were made:

- The administrator brought summary proceedings seeking the delivery up of the machinery to him. Parker J held[215] that the effect of clause 63 was to create an equitable charge over the machinery which was, because of the controls reserved over the machinery, a fixed charge not a floating charge.
- The administrator appealed this decision and the English Court of Appeal held[216] that the charge was properly construed as a floating charge and so, because it had not been registered, was void. The administrator, however, lost the appeal because it was also held that regardless of the validity of the charge, clause 63 gave the local authority the right to retain possession of the machinery until the works had been completed. This is referred to as the first Court of Appeal decision.
- After the local authority sold the machinery, the administrator instituted proceedings for conversion against the local authority on the basis that it had no authority to sell the machinery since the contract had created a charge that was void for want of registration. The administrator obtained summary judgment from Judge Toulmin QC.
- The local authority appealed against the order for summary judgment and the English Court of Appeal[217] set aside the summary judgment on the grounds that the 'charge' was not void for want of registration[218]. This is referred to as the second Court of Appeal decision.
- The administrator appealed against this decision to the House of Lords[219] which overruled the second Court of Appeal' decision and reinstated the order made by Judge Toulmin QC.

This legal saga gave rise to two really important issues concerning charges. The first issue, considered here, is whether the contract (clause 63) created a charge and, if so, whether that charge was fixed or floating. The second issue, considered in Ch 19, concerned the effect of the failure to register a registrable charge[220].

---

213 The basis of these contentions was, were the contract to have created a floating charge and were the floating charge not registered under CA 1985, s 395 (UK), it would be void as against the administrator.

214 As has been pointed out by Sealy, 'House of Lords Washes Floating Charges in Cosslett (Contractors) Ltd' (2001) Company Law Newsletter (Issue 85; 12 November 2001), it is curious that nobody contended that even if the charge was fixed it would still require to be registered as a charge which, had it been created by an individual, would require registration as a bill of sale.

215 *Re Cosslett (Contractors) Ltd* [1996] 4 All ER 46, [1996] 1 BCLC 407, [1996] BCC 515.

216 *Re Cosslett (Contractors) Ltd* [1997] BCC 724.

217 *Re Cosslett (Contractors) Ltd* [2000] BCC 1155.

218 This was a rather bizarre finding which was, in fact, reversed by the House of Lords at [2002] 1 All ER 292. See Ch 19, *Corporate Borrowing: Registration of Charges*, para **[19.007]**.

219 *Smith (Administrator) of Cosslett (Contractors) Ltd v Bridgend County Borough Council* [2001] UKHL 58, [2002] 1 All ER 292.

220 At para **[19.007]**.

[18.076] In the first Court of Appeal decision, the administrator's appeal was dismissed but it was held that a charge had been created, and that it was a floating charge. It was held that legal ownership in the plant did not pass to the local authority; neither did the contract constitute a possessory lien with a power of sale. After finding that the local authority's rights constituted an equitable charge, Millett LJ went on to hold that the charge was a floating charge, finding that the three characteristics of a floating charge identified by Romer LJ in *Yorkshire Woolcombers Association Ltd*[221] were all present. Of significance was his finding that:

> 'The chargor's unfettered freedom to deal with the assets in the ordinary course of his business free from the charge is obviously inconsistent with the nature of a fixed charge; but it does not follow that his unfettered freedom to deal with the charged assets is essential to the existence of a floating charge. It plainly is not, for any well-drawn floating charge prohibits the chargor from creating further charges having priority to the floating charge; and a prohibition against factoring debts is not sufficient to convert what would otherwise be a floating charge on book debts into a fixed charge …
>
> The essence of a floating charge is that it is a charge, not on any particular asset, but on a fluctuating body of assets which remain under the management and control of the chargor, and which the chargor has the right to withdraw from the security despite the existence of the charge. The essence of a fixed charge is that the charge is on a particular asset or class of assets which the chargor cannot deal with free from the charge without the consent of the chargee. The question is not whether the chargor has complete freedom to carry on his business as he chooses, *but whether the chargee is in control of the charged assets*[222].'

Millett LJ held that the contractual provision which prohibited the company from removing from the site plant and materials and from deploying them elsewhere did not have any relation to the local authority's security; it was designed to ensure that the company gave proper priority to the completion of the work and did not indicate that the charge was a fixed charge.

[18.077] The House of Lords in *Smith (Administrator of Cosslett (Contractors) Ltd) v Bridgend County Borough Council*[223] ultimately upheld the decision that clause 63 created a charge and also that the type of charge created was a floating charge. Lord Hoffmann said that he agreed with the reasons given by Millett LJ:

> 'I do not see how a right to sell an asset belonging to a debtor and appropriate the proceeds to payment of the debt can be anything other than a charge. And because the property subject to clause 63 (constructional plant, temporary works, goods and materials on the site) was a fluctuating body of assets which could be consumed or (subject to the approval of the engineer) removed from the site in the ordinary course of the contractor's business, it was a floating charge[224].'

---

221 *Yorkshire Woolcombers' Association Ltd* [1903] 2 Ch 284.

222 *Yorkshire Woolcombers' Association Ltd* [1903] 2 Ch 284 at 127d–f (emphasis added).

223 *Smith (Administrator of Cosslett (Contractors) Ltd) v Bridgend County Borough Council* [2001] UKHL 58, [2002] 1 All ER 292. For comment, see Sealy, 'House of Lords Washes Floating Charges in Cosslett (Contractors) Ltd' (2001) Company Law Newsletter (Issue 85; 12 November 2001).

224 *Smith (Administrator of Cosslett (Contractors) Ltd) v Bridgend County Borough Council* [2001] UKHL 58, [2002] 1 All ER 292 at 302j, para [41].

Notwithstanding Lord Hoffmann's confident, almost flippant, assertion as to the nature of the charge in hand, students and practitioners of company law can take some comfort that this outing to the House of Lords marked the end of a legal saga that had lasted several years.

(d) Floating charges are peculiar to companies

[18.078] In practice, floating charges tend only to be created by companies and other bodies corporate, and floating charges over personal chattels, within the meaning of the Bills of Sale Acts, cannot be created by an individual[225] without giving rise to considerable difficulties[226]. It is thought that there is no reason in theory or in practice why an individual cannot create a floating charge over 'non-personal chattels' such as classes of real property or of choses in action, or rights or interests therein. The High Court judgment of Keane J in *Re Keenan Bros Ltd*[227] shows the evolution and primary purpose of the floating charge:

> 'I think that one has to bear in mind at the outset that this form of charge made its first appearance in England as a by-product of the joint stock companies which began to flourish after the enactment of the Joint Stock Companies Act 1844. In order to borrow money, such companies offered as security not merely their fixed assets, but also assets which were regularly turned over in the course of business, such as the companies' stock in trade. It was obviously cumbersome and impractical to charge such assets specifically with the repayment of advances, since it would mean the constant execution and release of securities as the assets were disposed of and replaced. Hence the concept developed of a charge which did not attach to any specific assets of the company, remained dormant until the mortgagee intervened and in the interim did not prevent the mortgagor from using the assets in question in the ordinary course of his business.'

Stock, goods and other chattels and choses in action such as book debts are the assets most amenable to being the subject of a floating charge.

Negative pledge clauses

[18.079] Debentures often contain so-called 'negative pledge clauses' which provide that the chargor company shall not create any other charges or mortgages without the chargee's permission[228]. Negative pledge clauses seek to prevent chargors from creating subsequent fixed securities which would, in the absence of such clauses, have priority over the holders of a prior floating charge. Typically, a negative pledge clause will state *inter alia* that:

> 'The Company hereby covenants that it will not without the prior consent in writing of the Lender, create or attempt to create or permit to subsist any mortgage, debenture, charge or

---

225 There is authority that all *corporations* are excluded from the Bills of Sale Acts: *NV Slavenburg's Bank v Intercontinental Natural Resources Ltd et al* [1980] 1 All ER 955 at 975 per Lloyd J who said his preferred view of such an issue was 'that the Bills of Sale Acts apply to individuals only and not to corporations at all'.

226 See Ch 4, *Incorporation and its Consequences*, para **[4.088]**.

227 *Re Keenan Bros Ltd* [1985] IR 401 at 407.

228 See Gough, *Company Charges* (2nd edn, 1996), Ch 10 and Johnston, *Banking and Security Law in Ireland* (1998), p 470. See also Maxton, 'Negative Pledges and Equitable Principles' [1993] JBL 458.

> pledge upon or permit any lien or other encumbrance to arise on or affect the goodwill, undertaking, property, assets, revenue and rights hereby charged or any part thereof.'

However, such a clause in a debenture is only a contractual promise between a floating chargor and a floating chargee, and where the chargor acts in breach of it, eg, by creating a subsequent charge, the prior floating chargee will not, by virtue of the negative pledge clause, automatically have priority ahead of a subsequently created charge.

(a) Priority of floating charges accompanied by negative pledge clauses

[18.080] In Ireland[229], the question of priorities will be determined by whether or not the subsequent chargee had *notice* of the existence of the negative pledge clause[230]. Where a subsequent chargee (or purchaser) has actual notice of the existence of the negative pledge, it is settled law that they will be bound by it. In the High Court decision in *Re Salthill Properties Ltd*[231], Laffoy J cited with approval the following passage from Gough:

> 'Although creating no more than a negative contractual right, a restrictive clause can affect the quality of, and therefore bind, a subsequent proprietary interest through actual notice of the restriction. In equity it would be unconscionable to permit a subsequent third party to take his interest free of the restrictive right in spite of his actual knowledge that to do so would constitute a breach of a floating charge contract by the charger[232].'

This passage was quoted with apparent approval by the Supreme Court[233].

[18.081] Most debate turns upon whether or not constructive or imputed notice will suffice. The most authoritative Irish case in point is *Welch v Bowmaker (Ireland) Ltd*[234], where the Supreme Court, per Henchy J, held that:

> 'Counsel for [the defendant] has argued that ... the bank should be fixed with constructive notice of the provision in the debenture precluding the company from creating a mortgage (such as the bank got) which would have priority over the debenture. Since such a prohibition is more or less common form in modern debentures, there would be much to be said for applying the doctrine of constructive notice to such a situation were it not that it is settled law that there is no duty on the bank in a situation such as this to seek out the precise terms of the debenture ... Actual or express notice of the prohibition must be shown before the subsequent mortgagee can be said to be deprived of priority.

---

229 *Cf* the United Kingdom: CA 1985, s 464 (UK). In *AIB Finance Ltd v Bank of Scotland* [1995] 1 BCLC 185, the Scottish Court of Sessions construed CA 1985, s 464 (UK) as conferring priority to a floating charge over a fixed charge on land, in circumstances when both charges were created the same day, but where the floating charge contained a negative pledge clause. The reason why this was held to be the case was because when read against the statutory history, the negative pledge clause regulated ranking for the purposes of CA 1985, s 464 (UK) and its existence qualified the order of ranking of a fixed and floating charge.

230 For English authority that actual notice defeats the subsequent chargee's priority, see *Wilson v Kelland* [1910] 2 Ch 306; *English and Scottish Mercantile Investment Co Ltd* [1892] 2 QB 700; and *Re Castell and Brown Ltd* [1898] 1 Ch 315.

231 *Re Salthill Properties Ltd* (30 July 2004, unreported) HC, Laffoy J.

232 Gough, *Company Charges* (2nd edn, 1996) at p 228.

233 *Re Salthill Properties Ltd* [2006] IESC 35.

234 *Welch v Bowmaker (Ireland) Ltd* [1980] IR 251.

Whatever attractions there may be in the proposition that priority should be deemed lost because a duty to inquire further was called for but ignored, and that such inquiry would have shown that the company was debarred from entering into a mortgage which would have priority over the debenture, the fact remains that it would be unfair to single out the bank for condemnatory treatment because of their failure to ascertain the full terms of the debenture when what they did was in accord with judicially approved practice and when such a precipitate change in the law would undermine the intended validity of many other such transactions. If the proposed extension of the doctrine of constructive notice is to be made, the necessary change in the law would need to be made prospectively and, therefore, more properly by statute[235].'

From the judgment of Henchy J, it would appear that the factor which decided that the subsequent chargee would not lose priority was that it was 'settled law that there is no duty on a bank in a situation such as this to seek out the *precise terms* of the debenture'.

[18.082] Although it would seem clear that the doctrine of constructive notice will not be extended and that subsequent chargees will not be deemed to have constructive notice of the existence of a negative pledge clause, it is thought that, in practice, many subsequent chargees will have the *actual or express* notice spoken of by Henchy J in the passage last quoted. In practice, a subsequent chargee will invariably conduct a CRO search against the chargor company. Where the terms of a negative pledge have been inserted in a Form C1[236], the subsequent mortgagee will have *actual notice* of its existence. This will be *imputed* to the subsequent chargee through its solicitors or other legal advisers[237]. In such circumstances, it is thought that equity will prevent the subsequent chargee from obtaining priority. Moreover, there is authority that the burden of proof operates in favour of the prior floating charge[238].

[18.083] In *Re Salthill Properties Ltd*[239], a mortgage debenture provided that the chargor company shall not, *inter alia*, lease certain lands. In breach of this, the company created three leases over commercial units on the lands without the bank's consent. In the High Court, Laffoy J held that the onus of proof was on the subsequent lessees to show that they did not have actual notice and that they did not discharge that onus:

'It was submitted that the company and the lessee are two separate legal entities. That is undoubtedly the case. It was also submitted that the evidence did not establish that Mr

235 *Welch v Bowmaker (Ireland) Ltd* [1980] IR 251 at 256.

236 The form used to register a charge created by a company: see Ch 19, *Corporate Borrowing: Registration of Charges*, para **[19.103]**.

237 Indeed, it will almost certainly be the case that the solicitor acting for the subsequent mortgagee/chargee will have sight of a search of the CRO register, and may actually have in his possession the precise wording of the negative pledge clause. If he does not 'appreciate' the significance of this, then, presumably, the same reasoning as was applied by Keane J in *Northern Bank Finance Corporation v Quinn and Achates Investment Company* [1979] ILRM 221, would apply here too, so that the solicitor would be deemed to be actually aware of the negative pledge clause, and such knowledge imputed to his client.

238 See Gough, *Company Charges* (2nd edn, 1996), p 226 who cites *Kay Hian & Co (Pte) v Jon Phua Ooi Yong* [1989] 1 MLJ 284 and *Nymph Products Ltd v Heating Centre Pty Ltd* (1992) 7 ACSR 365. This has been accepted in Ireland by the Supreme Court: *Re Salthill Properties Ltd* [2006] IESC 35.

239 *Re Salthill Properties Ltd* (30 July 2004, unreported) HC, Laffoy J.

Cunningham controlled the company and that the control of the lessee, through its board of directors, was independent of Mr Cunningham. In my view, those arguments are specious in a context of the reality of the transactions between the company and the lessee at the end of December 1999 judged by documents which are properly before the court. Mr Cunningham, as a director of the company, witnessed the execution of the mortgage debentures, each of which contained clause 6. In the absence of evidence to the contrary, it must be assumed that he was aware of the contents of those instruments. On the day the leases were executed he obtained from the two shareholders of the lessee, Ms Hynes and Mr Quinn, declarations that proved that between them they held the entire share capital of the lessee in trust for Mr Cunningham. In return for each trustee shareholder becoming a director of the company, on the same day Mr Cunningham gave each full indemnity in respect of all costs, expenses and such like, including consequential fees, expenditure and VAT, in respect of or arising out of that office.

In my view, the core issue is whether the beneficial owner of the entire share capital of the lessee, who became the beneficial owner of the leasehold interest through the medium of the lessee, had actual notice of clause 6. I am satisfied that the evidence on the material facts, which I have just outlined and is not in controversy, clearly shows that he did. This conclusion does not impute any propensity to have anything other than proper regard for company law and regulation to the directors of the lessee. It merely reflects the reality of the situation which prevailed.

Accordingly, I am satisfied that the lessee has not discharged the onus of establishing that it did not have actual notice of clause 6.'

The decision of the High Court was upheld by the Supreme Court. Although it noted that objection was taken to the imputation of Mr Cunningham's knowledge to the company as actual knowledge rather than constructive knowledge, McCracken J did not consider it necessary to address this point given that the onus of proof had not been discharged. Even so, there is evidence that in the right case the courts will be pragmatic, as McCracken J did not preclude the possibility that Mr Cunningham's actual notice could be imputed saying that that 'depends on the closeness of the relationship between Mr Cunningham [and the lessee] and the extent of the control which he exercised over the affairs of [the lessee]'.

[18.084] The Supreme Court decision in *Re Holidair Ltd*[240] demonstrates a further weakness in negative pledge clauses. According to Finlay CJ, the effect of ss 7 and 9 of the C(A)A 1990 was that an examiner appointed to a company under the protection of the court can exercise his borrowing powers granted by the court without obtaining the consent of the debenture holders[241]. Section 18 of the C(A)(No 2)A 1999 does nothing to alleviate this. This amends s 7 of the C(A)A 1990 to allow examiners to repudiate contracts which provide that a company shall not, *inter alia*, 'create or permit to subsist any mortgage, charge, lien or other encumbrance or any pledge over the whole or any part of the property or undertaking of the company'[242].

---

240 *Re Holidair Ltd* [1994] 1 ILRM 481.

241 Ch 22, *Examinerships*, para **[22.098]** *et seq.*

242 Sections 7(5A)–7(5C) of the C(A)A 1990.

(b) Negative pledge clauses and competition law

[18.085] A novel challenge to debentures containing negative pledge clauses was made in *Oakdale (Richmond) Ltd v National Westminster Bank plc*[243]. In this case, the plaintiff was a small company which obtained its supplies from EU Member States, other than the UK. Its indebtedness to its bank was secured by an all sums due debenture which was expressed to be repayable on demand. The debenture created a specific fixed charge over the company's book and other debts and a floating charge over its other assets. Monies payable on foot of its book debts were required to be paid into its account with the chargee bank, and it was restrained from factoring, discounting, charging or assigning its book or other debts without the prior written consent of its bank, the chargee. Two loans under the UK Government's small firms loan guarantee scheme contained covenants prohibiting the company from borrowing and charging of assets. The company sued its chargee bank seeking, *inter alia*, a declaration that its loan arrangements and the debenture were void for being contrary to Articles 85 and 86 of the EU Treaty of Rome. The chargee bank countered for an injunction to restrain the company from paying its book debts into any account other than the chargor company's account with the chargee bank. The chargor company contended:

- that the restrictions and prohibitions against borrowing and charging assets were anti-competitive since the company was obliged to give security because it was locked into borrowings with the chargee bank;
- that the debenture was, itself, anti-competitive and void under Article 85 because it prevented the company from using property charged as security for a loan for further lending by a third party; and
- that the chargee bank had abused its dominant position contrary to Article 86.

These were, undoubtedly, novel and imaginative grounds for seeking to assail a standard form debenture and their formulation was, no doubt, occasioned by some necessity or other.

[18.086] Not surprisingly, Chadwick J held that the prohibition against borrowing and charging of assets without prior written consent was not anti-competitive for the reason that the company was always free to pay off its indebtedness to the chargee bank with money borrowed from another source and thereby freeing itself from the restriction in the debenture. Moreover, it was held that the requirement that the proceeds of book debts be paid into a designated account was occasioned by the requirement that control be exercised over fixed charges over book debts and it did not have as its object the prevention, restriction or distortion of competition within the EU. The restrictions in the small loans agreements (guaranteed by the UK Government) against unsecured borrowing without the bank's consent were held by Chadwick J to be a necessary incident of last resort lending and designed to enable the chargee bank to protect itself from a material change in the credit risk. In this respect Chadwick J held[244]:

> 'In assessing whether to lend to such a company it is likely to be highly material to evaluate at the time the decision is taken what other borrowing commitments the company has; that is to say it is necessary for the lender to understand the extent to which the

243 *Oakdale (Richmond) Ltd v National Westminster Bank plc* [1997] 1 BCLC 63.
244 *Oakdale (Richmond) Ltd v National Westminster Bank plc* [1997] 1 BCLC 63 at 76j–77b.

> company's continued trading is dependent on loan finance. A decision by a bank, made on the basis of material put before it at the time of that decision, would be undermined if the borrower was in a position to increase its borrowings without referring the matter back to the bank. A lender who lends on the basis that the borrower has no other borrowing commitments is concerned to ensure that he does not find, some six or 12 months later, that he is lending to a borrower who has incurred substantial other borrowing commitments.
>
> A restriction, therefore, that the bank must be approached for consent before the company incurs further borrowing may be seen as a necessary incident of the small firms loan guarantee scheme. It is necessary that a bank which is to participate in a scheme of last resort lending has the means to protect itself from a material change in the credit risk which it has agreed to undertake.'

It is opined that this reasoning will apply, with equal force, to most loans made by banks to companies where there is any credit assessment since a company's liabilities and repayment capacity are central to most decisions to lend. Finally, it was held that the company had not established an arguable case that the bank enjoyed a dominant position within the relevant market since it was one of a number of lenders to the small trading company sector, within the UK.

Events which affect assets subject to floating charges

[18.087] In the intervening period between when a company creates a floating charge and when it crystallises, the company may deal with its assets as it sees fit in the ordinary course of its business[245]. Where a company disposes of its assets and receives consideration, those assets will no longer be subject to the floating charge where the company retains bare legal title, pending the finalisation of the legal transfer of those assets[246].

[18.088] In the same way, third parties may cause steps to be taken against the chargor company which affect the assets of the company, including those assets which are subject to the floating charge[247]. This can happen in several ways, namely by the creation of subsequent charges, the application of the rules of set-off or by the existence of a lien[248].

(a) Subsequent mortgages and charges

[18.089] Since a floating charge is inchoate until the moment of crystallisation, if a company creates a subsequent fixed mortgage or charge over assets that are subject to a prior floating charge, the subsequent fixed mortgagee or chargee will have priority over

245 Subject, that is, to any provisions as to the general protection of the assets which may well be found in a modern well-drafted debenture.

246 In *Sharp v Woolwich Building Society* [1998] BCC 115, the House of Lords, on appeal from the First Division of the Inner House of the Court of Session of Scotland, held that where a company was paid the purchase price for an apartment it owned prior to the appointment of a receiver, the apartment was no longer part of the company's 'property and undertaking' and so took free of the floating charge.

247 Eg, when judgment is executed against a company, the judgment holder has priority over the holder of the uncrystallised floating charge.

248 See Parsons, *Lingard's Bank Security Documents* (5th edn, 2011) at paras 9.9.

the holder of the floating charge[249]. This will be the case unless the holder of the subsequent charge has notice of the existence of the prior floating charge, or has actual notice of the existence of a negative pledge clause[250]. Likewise, a subsequently created floating charge over part, but not all[251], of the assets of the class which is the subject of the first floating charge will have priority because the company has apparent authority to do this[252]. In a clash of priorities between floating charges it has been held that it is the date of crystallisation of the floating charges and not their date of creation that is critical[253]. The holder of a judgment registered as a judgment mortgage against a company's property which is subject to a floating charge will also have priority over the holder of the floating charge.

(b) Set-off

[18.090] The right to set-off arises[254] in favour of a debtor when the person or company to whom or which he owes money is also his debtor[255]. Before a floating charge crystallises, set-off can operate over assets that are subject to a floating charge, even if this means that those assets are consequently depleted. This is evidenced by the case of *Re Russell Murphy*[256] where Kenny J reviewed the law and held that:

> '... the debt due to the respondents was in existence when the receiver was appointed, and so the equitable assignment of the future asset (the right to payment of a terminal loss) was always subject to the right of set off[257].'

The converse situation should also be noted, however, namely, that where a floating charge has crystallised, then the right of set-off no longer exists[258].

(c) Liens

[18.091] Where a lien arises before a floating charge crystallises, the lien will take priority over the floating charge. This is true in respect of liens which are contractual or which arise by operation of law.

(d) Execution of judgment

[18.092] Where a plaintiff obtains a judgment against a company and proceeds to execute that judgment, the plaintiff will have priority over a floating charge which has not crystallised. Authority for this and its converse, namely, that a crystallised floating

---

249 See the judgment of North J in *Wheatley v Silkstone and Haigh Moor Coal Co* [1885] 29 Ch D 715 at 724.

250 *Welch v Bowmaker (Ireland) Ltd* [1980] IR 251; *Wilson v Kelland* [1910] 2 Ch 306; and *English and Scottish Mercantile Investment Co Ltd v Bruton* [1892] 2 QB 700.

251 *Re Benjamin Cope & Sons Ltd* [1914] 1 Ch 800.

252 *Re Automatic Bottle Makers Ltd* [1926] Ch 412.

253 *Griffiths v Yorkshire Bank* [1994] 1 WLR 1427.

254 Note that parties can contract out of their right to set-off: *Hong Kong and Shanghai Banking Corp v Kloecker & Co AG* [1989] BCLC 776.

255 See, generally, Donnelly, *The Law of Banks and Credit Institutions* (2000), pp 506–518.

256 *Re Russell Murphy* [1976] IR 15.

257 *Re Russell Murphy* [1976] IR 15 at 19. See also *Rother Iron Works Ltd v Canterbury Precision Engineers Ltd* [1974] QB 1, referred to by Kenny J.

258 See *Lynch v Ardmore Studios (Ireland) Ltd* [1966] IR 133, *per* Budd J.

charge will have priority over an unexecuted judgment is the decision of the High Court in *Lynch v Darlington Properties et al*[259]. In that case, the plaintiff had obtained judgment for over €64,000 against the first and second defendants on 20 April 2010, and on 7 May 2010 a receiver was appointed by a bank to both defendant companies. Peart J cited with approval the following passage from Keane:

> 'Where an unsecured creditor recovers judgment against the company but has not executed the judgment, the floating charge will have priority. Where, however, the creditor completely executes the judgment by a seizure or sale of the company's property before the charge crystallises, the floating charge loses its priority[260].'

Crystallisation of floating charges

[18.093] A floating charge may never crystallise, eg, where the debt secured by the floating charge is repaid. However, it may not 'float on' indefinitely and a time may come when it is said to crystallise. If this happens, it is as if a net drops over whatever assets the company has within the class or classes of assets, which are the subject of the floating charge. The *effect* is that the charge becomes a quasi-fixed charge[261]. As has been stated by Farrar in his frequently cited article[262], crystallisation is:

> '... the process whereby the charge attaches specifically to all the items of the class of mortgaged assets which the company owns at that date or subsequently acquires if future assets are within the scope of this particular charge. The latter assets become subject to a fixed charge as they come into existence. In relation to debts the fixed charge operates as an equitable assignment.'

The rights enjoyed by the holder of a floating charge are rights which exist in equity, and up until the moment of crystallisation are properly described as being *inchoate*[263]. After the occurrence of a crystallising event (considered next) the holder of the charge becomes entitled to fixed, tangible equitable rights. Existing assets within the ambit of the floating charge's net are said to be assigned to the holder of the charge, as are future assets which come into the class of property which is subject to the floating charge[264].

[18.094] Statute law in some jurisdictions expressly distinguishes between fixed charges originally created as such and quasi-fixed charges that were originally created as

---

259 *Lynch v Darlington Properties et al* [2011] IEHC 273.

260 Keane, *Company Law* (4th edn, Bloomsbury Professional, 2007) at para 20.50. Peart J also cited Fuller, *Corporate Borrowing: Law and Practice* (3rd edn, Jordans) at para 6.90 when it is said: 'The general rule is that a duly registered floating charge will rank after all prior and subsequent charges and other interests (legal or equitable) arising before crystallisation ...' and at para 6.91: 'Certain unsecured creditors also have priority over a floating charge. An execution creditor has priority if the execution is completed, or payment is made to avoid execution, before crystallisation, but not otherwise.'

261 Although it should be noted that it may be set aside where created within certain time scales, unlike a fixed charge.

262 Farrar, 'The Crystallisation of a Floating Charge' (1976) 40 Conv NS 397 at 398.

263 See Ussher, *Company Law in Ireland* (1986), p 431.

264 See *Lynch v Ardmore Studios (Ireland) Ltd* [1966] IR 133, and *Re Interview Ltd* [1975] IR 383, where Kenny J said: '[crystallisation] of a floating charge on the assets of a company operates as an equitable assignment of the property and goods owned by the company to the debenture holder'. See also *Tempany v Hynes* [1976] IR 101 at 116, *per* Kenny J.

floating charges. So, for example, s 251 of the Insolvency Act 1986 (UK) defines 'floating charge' to mean a 'charge which, as created, was a floating charge'. In Ireland, however, it was held in *Re JD Brian Ltd*[265] that where a floating charge crystallises and becomes a quasi-fixed charge, that fixed charge does not have priority over the Revenue Commissioners in an insolvent winding up because it is a floating charge within the meaning of s 285(7)(b) of the CA 1963. In this, the leading modern Irish decision on the nature and effect of floating charges, the liquidator of a company brought an application under s 280 of the CA 1963 for directions concerning the purported crystallisation of floating charges created in favour of Bank of Ireland. The debenture created a fixed charge over certain property identified in the schedule to the debenture and created a floating charge over all other property of the company and went on to provide in clauses 10 and 11:

> '10. The Bank, may, at any time, by notice in writing served on the Company, convert the floating charge contained in this Deed into a first fixed charge over all the property, assets and rights for the time being subject to the said floating charge or over so much of the same as is specified in the notice ...
>
> 11. The floating charge contained in this Deed shall in any event stand converted into a fixed charge automatically upon:
>
> (a) the filing of a petition for the winding up of the company;
>
> (b) the passing of a resolution for the winding up of the company;
>
> (c) the appointment of a receiver on behalf of the holders of any debentures of the company secured by a floating charge;
>
> (d) possession being taken of any property by or on behalf of the holders of any debentures of the company secured by a floating charge.'

In October 2009, Bank of Ireland served notice on the company converting the floating charge contained in the debenture into a fixed charge; in November 2009, the company was wound up following the presentation of a petition and an official liquidator was appointed. The company was insolvent and owed Bank of Ireland *circa* €16.25m; the liquidator anticipated realisations of between €12.5m and €14.5m, of which €2m related to assets the subject of the floating charge provisions. The official liquidator contended that the floating charge had crystallised in October 2009 and that the bank was entitled to all of the company's assets ahead of the preferential creditors. The Revenue Commissioners contended that regardless of whether or not the floating charge had crystallised prior to the commencement of the winding up, priority was to be given to the preferential claim; they also disputed that the floating charges had in fact crystallised and converted into fixed charges. In her judgment, Finlay Geoghegan J began by reviewing the terms of ss 220 and 285 of the CA 1963 before summarising the first issue as being one of the construction of s 285(7): should it be construed as meaning that the preferential debts rank ahead of the bank's claim to funds realised from the assets subject to the floating charge, irrespective of whether it crystallised prior to the commencement of the winding up or, should it be construed as meaning that such a priority only exists if the floating charge has not crystallised at the date of the commencement of the winding up?

---

265 *Re JD Brian Ltd* [2011] IEHC 113 and [2011] IEHC 383. For commentary, see Cuddihy, 'Floating charges – Express Crystallisation Clauses' (2011) CLP 135.

[18.095] Commenting upon what happens upon the crystallisation of a floating charge, Finlay Geoghegan J said:

> '18 ... As is sometimes said, the floating charge upon crystallisation becomes a fixed charge. However, no new charge is created by the company. The existing charge, the floating charge, created by the company, changes in nature and becomes a fixed charge. The nature of the security held by the debenture holder under the floating charge created by the company upon crystallisation changes, it ceases to float, and becomes a fixed charge over the charged property. In accordance with the general principles relating to fixed charges, upon the charge becoming fixed, there is an equitable assignment of the relevant assets to the debenture holder. Nevertheless, the right of the debenture holder to the charged assets derives from the floating charge created by the company. It is the nature of that right which is changed by the crystallisation.
>
> 19. If there were no relevant judicial authority on the construction of s 285(7) or a predecessor or similar section in the UK Companies Acts, I would have no hesitation in construing the section as giving priority to preferential debts over the claims of holders of debentures under floating charges which crystallise prior to the commencement of winding up. Further, I would construe the section as meaning that the preferential debts were entitled to be paid out of the realisation of assets subject to a floating charge in the debenture, notwithstanding that such floating charge crystallised prior to the commencement of winding up.'

Section 285(7) of the CA 1963 provides, in relation to preferential debts that:

> (7) The foregoing debts shall—
>
> (a) rank equally among themselves and be paid in full, unless the assets are insufficient to meet them, in which case they shall abate in equal proportions; and
>
> (b) so far as the assets of the company available for payment of general creditors are insufficient to meet them, have priority over the claims of holders of debentures under any floating charge created by the company, and be paid accordingly out of any property comprised in or subject to that charge.

Finlay Geoghegan J proceeded to give three reasons for so construing s 285(7) of the CA 1963. First, the priority given to preferential debts is 'over the claims of holders of debentures under any floating charge created by the company' and it followed that because the bank's *only* entitlement to the assets derived from the debenture containing the floating charge, its rights were subjudicated to the preferential debts. Finlay Geoghegan J said:

> 'Debentures, as already stated, is defined in s 2 to include 'any other securities of a company, whether constituting a charge on the assets of the company or not'. It appears to me that the phrase 'holders of debentures under any floating charge created by the company' is deliberately worded, having regard to the potentiality for a floating charge to crystallise and become a fixed charge so as to include persons who hold security of whatever nature, provided it is held under or by reason of a floating charge created by the company. It is the floating charge created by the Company which gives the Bank the right to make a claim to the assets. It is only the nature of the claim which changes post-crystallisation. The Bank's claim to the charged assets remains a claim as the holder of a debenture or security under the floating charge created by the company.'

Second, the learned judge noted that the word 'charge' in the phrase 'property comprised in or subject to that charge' refers to the floating charge created by the company, notwithstanding that by reason of crystallisation, such floating charge may have become fixed on such property prior to the commencement of the winding up. The third reason given for this construction was because of the absence in s 285(7) of any specification by the Oireachtas as to the date upon which the nature of the claims of 'holders of debentures under any floating charge' is to be ascertained. As the learned judge observed:

> 'if it was intended by the Oireachtas that this should be ascertained at the date of commencement of the winding-up, as is suggested by certain judicial authorities from other jurisdictions, then it appears to me that such date would have been specified by the Oireachtas, given that in s 285(1), they have clearly specified a date which is potentially a date other than the commencement of the winding up as the relevant date for the ascertainment of preferential claims[266].'

[18.096] Finlay Geoghegan J noted, however, that there were a number of relevant authorities from other jurisdictions. In *Re Griffen Hotel Company Ltd*[267], Bennett J construed a statutory provision materially identical to s 285(7) of the CA 1963[268] and held in favour of a bank over preferential creditors where the sums were secured by a floating charge which crystallised prior to the commencement of the company's winding up. Bennett J had said:

> 'In my judgment, subs (4)(b) of 264 only operates if at the moment of the winding up there is still a floating charge created by the company and it only gives the preferential creditors a priority over the claims of the debenture holders in any property which at that moment of time is comprised in or subject to that charge.
>
> In the present case the debenture held by the plaintiffs contained a floating charge over all the borrowers' property. On December 9, 1938, that charge ceased to float on the property and assets of which Mr Veale was appointed receiver. The charge on that day crystallised and became a fixed charge on any other assets of the borrowers. At the moment before the winding up order was made, the charge still floated over any other assets of the borrowers and over those other assets, if any, the preferential creditors as defined by subs (1) of s 264 have a priority over the claims of the plaintiffs by force of the provisions of the same section. This seems to be a corollary of the proposition established by *In re Lewis Merthyr Consolidated Collieries Ltd* [1929] 1 Ch 498.'

Finlay Geoghegan J was not persuaded by the foregoing, finding that Bennett J had not considered the meaning of 'the claims of holders of debentures under any floating charge created by the company', nor did he adequately explain why he considered the section only operated if there was still a floating charge created by the company. The learned judge also noted that the decision in *In re Lewis Merthyr Consolidated Collieries Ltd* did not concern the prior crystallisation of a floating charge and so Bennett J's conclusion could not be a corollary of that decision. The decision of Hoffmann J in *Re Brightlife Ltd*[269] was also noted and in particular his opinion of the purpose of legislation conferring priority on preferential creditors:

> 'One imagines that they were intended to ensure that in all cases preferential debts had priority over the holder of a charge originally created as a floating charge. It would be

---

266 *Re JD Brian Ltd* [2011] IEHC 113 at para 22 of the judgment.

267 *Re Griffen Hotel Company Ltd* [1940] 1 Ch 129.

268 Section 264(4)(b) of the Companies Act 1929 (UK).

269 *Re Brightlife Ltd* [1987] Ch 200.

difficult to think of any reason for making distinctions according to the moment at which the charge crystallised or the event which brought this about. But in *Re Griffin Hotel Co Ltd* [1941] Ch 129 revealed a defect in the drafting. It meant, for example, that if the floating charge crystallised before winding up, but otherwise than by the appointment of a receiver, the preferential debts would have no priority under either section ...'

Finlay Geoghegan J agreed with his observations as to the intent of the legislation but questioned whether there was indeed a 'defect' in the drafting at all or whether Hoffmann J was being polite as to the correctness of the decision in *Re Griffin Hotel Co*[270]. The learned judge went on to cite with approval the dissenting judgment of Barwick CJ in the High Court of Australia decision in *Stein v Saywell*[271] which considered ss 196 and 292(4) of the Australian Companies Act 1961 which, it was noted, were equivalent to ss 98 and 285(7) of the CA 1963. In conclusion, Finlay Geoghegan J said:

'I have concluded that I should not construe s 285(7) in accordance with the decision in *Re Griffin Hotel Company Ltd*. It is not binding on me. The primary obligation of this court is to construe the intention of the Oireachtas from the words used in the section. The fact that the decision at issue in *Re Griffin Hotel Company Ltd* and s 295(7) both have their legislative origin in similar provisions and most recently s 209 of the Companies (Consolidation) Act 1908, means that this court should give it careful consideration, which I have done. Nevertheless, I have concluded that I must respectfully decline to follow that decision. In my judgment, s 285(7) cannot be construed in accordance with the plain meaning of the words used so as to give it the meaning given in *Re Griffin Hotel Company Ltd*. I do not consider the reasoning of the decision persuasive. Insofar as it was followed in England in the decisions to which I have been referred, it appears to have been done so either by reason of precedent or without opposing submission. Hoffmann J was critical if it. Insofar as the High Court of Australia followed the decision for the reasons already explained, I do not find the majority judgments persuasive and prefer the reasoning of the dissenting judgment of Barwick CJ[272].'

The reasoning of Finlay Geoghegan J is both compelling and convincing and it is suggested represents the definitive interpretation on s 285(7) of the CA 1963 such that it cannot be contested that a quasi-fixed charge resulting from the crystallisation of a floating charge prior to the commencement of the liquidation of a company has priority over preferential creditors in the same way as a charge originally created as a fixed charge.

The causes of crystallisation

[18.097] Two eventualities are well established as causing a floating charge to *crystallise*: the appointment of a receiver to a chargor company, and the commencement of a chargor company's winding up. More contentious, however, are situations where a debenture purports to deem a floating charge to crystallise on the occasion of an event other than the established two, above. It is important to distinguish between situations

270 It was noted that in *Re Permanent Houses (Holdings) Ltd* [1988] BCLC 563 Hoffmann J had made clear his personal disagreement with the decision in *Re Griffin Hotel Co* but considered himself bound by it and bound to apply it despite finding the dissenting decision of Barwick CJ in *Stein v Saywell* [1969] 121 CLR 529 more persuasive.

271 *Stein v Saywell* [1969] 121 CLR 529 at 543.

272 *Re JD Brian Ltd* [2011] IEHC 113 at para 40 of the judgment.

where a debenture holder takes steps to cause a floating charge to crystallise and where it crystallises independently of any intervention by a debenture holder. Thus, the appointment of a receiver is an act of the debenture holder, while the commencement of a winding up may be an act independent of the debenture holder. *Ceasing to carry on business* can either be an event which is contained in the debenture and agreed to be an event which will crystallise a floating charge or could also be an event which will automatically cause the floating charge to crystallise.

(a) The appointment of a receiver

[18.098] It is beyond doubt that where a chargee causes a receiver to be appointed either by relying on the terms of the debenture or by order of the court, this will cause a floating charge to crystallise. One Irish authority on this point is *Halpin v Cremin*[273] where this was confirmed in the judgment of Lavery J[274]. The mere taking of steps to appoint a receiver will be insufficient to cause a floating charge to crystallise[275]. Where *another* debenture holder causes a receiver to be appointed to a company, this will usually have the effect of causing *all* floating charges created by that company to crystallise. This is because most debentures simply provide that the appointment of a receiver will cause the debenture holder's floating charge to crystallise and do not specify that the receiver must be appointed by them.

(b) The winding up of the chargor company

[18.099] Similarly, a floating charge will crystallise where the chargor company goes into liquidation and the process of winding up commences. The reason for this has been given by Warrington J in *Re Crompton & Co Ltd*[276] where he said:

> '... I think there can be no question at all that according to ordinary principles the winding up puts an end to the period of suspension; and the reason that it does that is that the effect of the winding up is to put an end to the floating nature of the security[277].'

A floating charge will crystallise whether a company is wound up by its members or creditors voluntarily, or compulsorily, by the court[278].

(c) Ceasing to carry on business[279]

[18.100] The fourth way in which a floating charge can crystallise is where the chargor company ceases to carry on business. While it has not been conclusively established in

---

273 *Halpin v Cremin* [1954] IR 19 at 24.

274 See also, *Re Panama, New Zealand and Australian Mail Co* (1870) 10 Ch D 530; *Nelson & Co v Faber & Co* [1903] 2 KB 367; *Evans v Rival Granite Quarries Ltd* [1910] 2 KB 979; *NW Robbie & Co v Witney Warehouse Co* [1963] 3 All ER 316; and *Farrar,* (1976) 40 Conv NS 397 at 398.

275 *Re Roundwood Colliery Co* [1897] 1 Ch 371.

276 *Re Crompton & Co Ltd* [1914] 1 Ch 954.

277 *Re Crompton & Co Ltd* [1914] 1 Ch 954 at 963.

278 See *Re Colonial Trusts Corp* (1879) 15 Ch D 465 and *Re Crompton & Co Ltd* [1914] 1 Ch 954 which applied the principle to a members voluntary winding up, even for the purposes of reconstruction of the company.

279 Gill, 'Ceasing to Carry on Business' and the Concept of Automatic Crystallisation of Floating Charges' (1986) ILT 160.

Ireland that such an event will cause a floating charge to crystallise, it is submitted that when it eventually falls to be decided by the Irish courts, it will be held to be a valid crystallising event[280]. The principle has now been accepted in England in *Re Woodroffes (Musical Instruments) Ltd*[281]. There, a company created a debenture in favour of a bank, which contained a first fixed charge over certain property and also a floating charge on all the undertakings and assets of the company, present and future, which were not affected by the fixed charge. The debenture allowed the bank to convert the floating charge into a fixed charge upon the bank giving notice to the company. Later, a second floating charge was created by the company in favour of one of the directors of the company, which provided that it too could become *fixed* by the debenture holder giving notice to the company. This second debenture and charge was created in violation of a negative pledge clause contained in the earlier debenture. Shortly afterwards, the director debenture holder gave the requisite notice that her debenture should crystallise. Some days later, the bank gave notice that all sums due on the debenture should be paid (although it did not give notice that its floating charge should crystallise) upon which the board of directors of the company resolved to invite the bank to appoint a receiver. The bank acted on this invitation. Later, the company went into liquidation and the net question was which floating charge should have priority, since the company's assets did not satisfy both claims. It was assumed that the director's floating charge had crystallised upon her giving notice to the company.

The bank advanced two main arguments. In the first place it was argued that when the director debenture holder gave notice that her charge should crystallise, this had the result that the bank's floating charge also crystallised, in that it should be implied into its debenture that crystallisation of a subsequent charge should also crystallise its charge. The giving of notice by the director debenture holder, it was argued, had the effect of determining the company's licence to use the assets forming the subject matter of the charge, which would have the effect of *automatically* crystallising its floating charge. Nourse J rejected this argument[282] saying that it appeared to run contrary to 'fundamental principles of the law of contract'. Indeed, he could not see that such action by the director debenture holder would necessarily cause the company to cease to carry on business. In effect, the motivation of Nourse J was that he was being asked to *imply* an automatic crystallisation clause on the happening of a certain event, into the debenture. This he refused to do, although as we shall see he accepted the validity of an *express* automatic crystallisation clause.

The second proposition of the bank is our present concern. In the words of Nourse J, it argued:

> '... that there was *in fact* a cessation of the company's business [on the giving of notice by the director debenture holder, or prior to its own action] and that that cessation caused an automatic crystallisation of the bank's floating charge[283].'

---

[280] It is also unclear as to its effectiveness in England, although Parsons, *Lingard's Bank Security Documents* (5th edn, 2011), para 9.20 says that: 'The better view is that a floating charge crystallises not only on the appointment of a receiver or the commencement of winding up but immediately a company ceases to carry on business as a going concern.' Cf Keane, *Company Law* (4th edn, 2007), para 20.69.

[281] *Re Woodroffes (Musical Instruments) Ltd* [1985] BCLC 227.

[282] *Re Woodroffes (Musical Instruments) Ltd* [1985] BCLC 227 at 231–232.

[283] *Re Woodroffes (Musical Instruments) Ltd* [1985] BCLC 227 at 232i.

This argument differs from the former, in that its acceptance hinged upon whether or not the judge accepted that cessation of business *in fact* caused a floating charge to crystallise. Having referred to several[284] authorities, Nourse J held that a factual cessation of business was a third circumstance (along with the appointment of a receiver and the commencement of a winding up) in which a floating charge would crystallise. While accepting that there were opinions which hold that 'automatic crystallisation clauses' are undesirable from a policy perspective, Nourse J held:

> 'On the state of the authorities it would be very difficult for me to question it, even if I could see a good reason for doing so. On the contrary, it seems to me that it is in accordance with the essential nature of a floating charge. The thinking behind the creation of such charges has always been a recognition that a fixed charge on the whole undertaking and assets of the company would paralyse it and prevent it from carrying on its business ... On the other hand it is a mistake to think that the chargee has no remedy while the charge is still floating. He can always intervene and obtain an injunction to prevent the company from dealing with its assets otherwise than in the ordinary course of its business. That no doubt is one reason why it is preferable to describe the charge as 'hovering', a word which can bear an undertone of menace, rather than as 'dormant'. A cessation of business necessarily puts an end to the company's dealings with its assets. That which kept the charge hovering has not been released and the force of gravity causes it to settle and fasten on the subject of the charge within its reach and grasp[285].'

Thus, where a company 'ceases to carry on business'[286], any floating charge created by that company will crystallise, in just the same way as it would were a receiver appointed or were the company wound up. While this is the law in England, and other Commonwealth countries, it remains to be seen whether this reasoning will be accepted in Ireland. More recently, in *Re The Real Meat Co Ltd*[287], it was held by Chadwick J that the effect of a company selling its business was to cause a floating charge to automatically crystallise because the sale of a company's business amounted to a cessation of business which was an implied ground for crystallisation.

[18.101] It has been questioned whether this is the law in Ireland[288]. Policy considerations aside, the bedrock of possible objection is *Halpin v Cremin*[289]. In that case, the plaintiff sought a declaration that he owned certain lands, formerly owned by the Listowel and Ballybunion Railway Company ('the company'), by virtue of a purchase made by him in 1942 and an order of the High Court which had vested in him

---

284 *Government Stock and other Securities Investment Co v Manila Rly Co* [1897] AC 81; *Hubbuck v Helms* (1887) 56 LJ Ch 536; *Robson v Smith* [1895] 2 Ch 118, *Re Victoria Steamboats Ltd* [1897] 1 Ch 228; *Davey & Co v Williamson & Sons Ltd* [1898] 2 QB 194; *Re Yorkshire Woolcombers' Association Ltd* [1904] AC 355; *Edward Nelson & Co Ltd v Faber & Co* [1903] 2 KB 367; *Evans v Rival Granite Quarries Ltd* [1910] 2 KB 979; and *Re Crompton & Co Ltd* [1914] 1 Ch 954.

285 *Re Woodroffes (Musical Instruments) Ltd* [1985] BCLC 227 at 233, 234.

286 As distinct from ceasing to be a going concern on which Nourse J did not comment, if there was a difference between the two concepts.

287 *Re The Real Meat Co Ltd* [1996] BCC 254.

288 See Ussher, *Company Law in Ireland* (1986) and Gill, 'Ceasing to Carry on Business and the Concept of Automatic Crystallisation of Floating Charges' (1986) ILT 160.

289 *Halpin v Cremin* [1954] IR 19.

the estate and interest theretofore vested in the company. The company had acquired those lands by virtue of an Act of 1886[290]. Two years later, the company executed a debenture in favour of the Debenture Corporation Ltd over the entire undertaking of the company. The company ran its last train in 1924, the track being removed from the land the following year. The defendant then entered on that land, and remained in exclusive and uninterrupted possession for many years. In 1928 the then owner of the debenture obtained a declaration that he was entitled to a lien or mortgage under the debenture on, *inter alia*, the lands in question. In 1942, the present plaintiff obtained the order referred to at the outset, but the defendant objected, claiming that he had acquired title through adverse possession. In the Circuit Court, the plaintiff lost his case for failing to show that the lands in question were part of the undertaking and premises owned by the company.

Lavery J held that nothing was done by the debenture holder or its successors and assigns to cause the floating charge to crystallise prior to when the squatter entered into adverse possession of the lands in question. In passing, he said[291] 'the charge becomes specific on the appointment of a receiver or on a winding up'. Since neither of these happened, Lavery J held that the floating charge had not crystallised. However, one cannot say with any conviction that this case is unequivocal authority for the proposition that a company's cessation of business does not cause a floating charge to crystallise.

[18.102] In the first place, it can only be implied into the judgment of Lavery J that the fact that the company ceased to carry on business prior to when the defendant squatter entered into occupation of the lands was not an event which in law would crystallise the floating charge. Nowhere in his judgment is this proposition canvassed by counsel for the plaintiff, nor indeed does Lavery J himself even allude to this point. Rather, that he made the point at all is pure surmise, particularly in that there is no statement that the appointment of a receiver, or a winding up are the sole events which cause crystallisation: he does not purport to be exhaustive. In the second place, while citing authorities such as *Government Stock v Manila Ry Co*[292] and *Evans v Rival Granite Quarries Ltd*[293] he did not allude to the fact that these suggested that ceasing to carry on business can cause a floating charge to crystallise: see *Re Woodroffes (Musical Instruments) Ltd*[294]. In the third place, the decision of Lavery J can be seen as indicative of a judiciary eager to give full effect to the legislative intent found in the statute similar to the modern s 13 of the Statute of Limitations 1957. Such legislative enactments are intended to 'quieten title to land' and avoid doubts as to ownership. In order to upset that intention he would presumably[295] have had to raise a point which was not raised before him in argument by counsel. It is submitted that the decision in the case can thus be explained. Finally, and most importantly, it is submitted that the fact that this decision was made in 1953 is of significance, particularly in view of the radical developments in both company and commercial law over even the last decade. In the view of the writer,

---

[290] 49 Vict, c vii.

[291] *Halpin v Cremin* [1954] IR 19 at 24.

[292] *Government Stock v Manila Ry Co* [1901] 1 Ch 326.

[293] *Evans v Rival Granite Quarries Ltd* [1910] 2 KB 979.

[294] *Re Woodroffes (Musical Instruments) Ltd* [1985] BCLC 227.

[295] 'Presumably', in view of the fact that while the argument of counsel is not reported in the law report, it is still possible that such could have been raised, though not reported.

the decision of *Halpin v Cremin* is not authority for the proposition that 'ceasing to carry on business' will not cause a floating charge to crystallise in Ireland[296].

(d) Express and automatic crystallisation clauses[297]

[18.103] An automatic or express crystallisation clause purports to deem in advance the occurrence of an event, other than the three preceding events, to cause a floating charge to crystallise. Such clauses are intended to mitigate the effects of the statutory limits placed on the floating charge and are to be found in most Irish debentures. Among those events which are commonly stated to cause automatic crystallisation are:

- the giving of notice by the debenture holder;
- an attempt to create a subsequent charge;
- any attempt by another to levy execution against the company;
- non-payment of loan instalments.

The mere service of notice on the chargor company that the floating charge is to crystallise forthwith, can cause a floating charge to crystallise where such is provided for in the instrument creating the floating charge[298]. The giving of notice can be seen as a withdrawal of the licence to deal with the assets which are the subject of the floating charge. Since the ability to deal with the assets which are subject to a floating charge is the very essence of a floating charge, the withdrawal of that licence necessarily changes the nature of the charge. Although the giving of notice has not traditionally been seen as a crystallising event, it seems clear that it must be such, because the withdrawal of the licence to use the assets in the normal course of business removes the basic trait which distinguishes a floating from a fixed charge.

[18.104] Unlike the appointment of a receiver and the commencement of a winding up which will take effect unless the charge itself provides to the contrary, the *giving of notice* will only be such an event where the charge itself expressly contains such a clause. In practice it will take the form of a 'notice of conversion clause' which empowers the charge holder to *convert* the floating charge into a fixed charge. In *Re Wogan's (Drogheda) Ltd*[299], clause 8 of the debenture in question provided, *inter alia*:

> 'If the lender shall by notice in writing make a demand on the company as provided for in clause 8E hereof then the floating charge created by clause 4E hereof shall immediately on service of such notice on the company become crystallised and be a specific fixed charge on ... [*inter alia*] ... all book debts and other debts and securities due to the company ...'

While the Supreme Court did not specifically comment upon the validity of this clause, Finlay CJ referred to clause 8 in the reasoning for his conclusion. It seems inconceivable that the Supreme Court could base its decision, albeit in part[300], on a clause which the law did not consider to be effective. Moreover, there is no sound policy reason why the giving of notice to that effect ought not effect crystallisation.

---

296 Note the comments of Gill, 'Ceasing to Carry on Business' and the Concept of Automatic Crystallisation of Floating Charges' (1986) ILT 160 at 161.

297 See Parsons, *Lingard's Bank Security Documents* (5th edn, 2011) para 9.26–9.32.

298 See Sealy, *Cases and Materials in Company Law* (4th edn, 1989), p 380.

299 *Re Wogan's (Drogheda) Ltd* [1993] 1 IR 157.

300 *Re Wogan's (Drogheda) Ltd* [1993] 1 IR 157 at 168.

[18.105] In *Re JD Brian Motors Ltd*[301], a debenture provided the following clause:

> '10. The Bank, may, at any time, by notice in writing served on the Company, convert the floating charge contained in this Deed into a first fixed charge over all the property, assets and rights for the time being subject to the said floating charge or over so much of the same as is specified in the notice. A notice under this clause may be served by the Bank only if in the sole judgment of the Bank, the Bank considers that the property, assets and rights described or referred to in the notice are in any way in jeopardy.'

Finlay Geoghegan J noted that one commentator[302] had criticised judicial treatment of the expression 'automatic crystallisation' as not being consistent, saying that sometimes the expression is used to refer to an event specifically agreed in the charge contract and in other cases to describe implicit crystallisation of the traditional kind developed in the older case law, eg, cessation of business and a charge-intervention event, including the appointment of a receiver manager, taking of possession as mortgagee and obtaining an injunction against company dealings with the charged assets. The learned High Court judge expressed the view that a clause of the kind contained in the debenture under scrutiny, which caused a floating charge to crystallise upon the giving of notice, was more correctly termed '*express crystallisation*':

> 'At issue in this application is an explicitly agreed crystallisation event which requires intervention by the charge, ie the services by the Bank of a notice pursuant to clause 10 of the Debenture. It appears preferable to refer to such crystallisation as '*express crystallisation*'. It is not truly automatic, in the sense that it does require charge action or intervention ie the service of a notice. It does, however, come within the type of crystallisation which, in some of the judicial decisions, has been referred to as 'automatic' and is not a traditional implicit crystallisation event.'

Of all the events which may cause a floating charge to crystallise, automatic crystallisation clauses are the most contentious. The essence of the objection is based on policy. As one commentator has observed[303]:

> 'There are two schools of thought on this question. One takes the view that the floating charge is not an established phenomenon having fixed characteristics, but is simply the creature of the draughtsman and that a creditor is free to strengthen his security in this way if he wants to. The other looks at the effect of such an arrangement on third parties and contends that it must be against public policy to have a charge crystallise in circumstances which may be unknown (and perhaps even unknowable) at the time, so that a company could not give a buyer a good title even though everyone was acting in good faith.'

Those opposed to the acceptance of automatic crystallisation clauses in charges include Keane[304], who says:

> 'It is thought, however, that this line of authority is unlikely to be followed in Ireland. The courts here will probably incline to the view that such automatic crystallisation would present problems for other creditors who would have no actual notice of the terms of the debenture and that any such doctrine would need to be the subject of considered legislation and regulation.'

---

301 *Re JD Brian Motors Ltd* [2011] IEHC 113.

302 Gough, *Company Charges* (2nd edn, Butterworths, 1996) at 232.

303 Sealy, *Cases and Materials in Company Law* (4th edn, 1989), p 380.

304 Keane, *Company Law* (3rd edn, 2000), para 20.67.

[18.106] In the last edition of this book a contrary view was expressed and it was said that it was hoped that, on full reflection, the Irish courts would accept the validity of such clauses[305]. This view was based on three objections to the contrary views expressed. In the first place, it was doubted that problems will necessarily be caused for creditors. Other opinion[306] suggests that notwithstanding that the chargor company will have no legal power to deal with the assets which were subject of a floating charge, but are not subject to a fixed charge, it remains the case that the company will have *ostensible authority* to deal with those assets. Indeed, a subsequent *bona fide* legal purchaser for value of such assets will, where the equities are equal, take priority over the prior equitable owner of a fixed charge[307]. It will only be where the subsequent purchaser has notice, actual or constructive, of the prior equitable floating (now fixed) charge, that he will be defeated.

In the second place, it was submitted that it would be misconceived for a court to impose additional restrictions on floating charges when the legislature has already made encroachments. Thus floating charges created within certain time periods before a company is wound up are liable to lose priority[308], and floating charges rank behind certain preferential creditors in priority[309]. For the courts to impose an additional limitation, in the form of a fetter on the freedom of the parties to contract, would, it is submitted, be judicial law-making and unconstitutional. This is in effect the view of Hoffmann J in *Re Brightlife Ltd*[310] who commented on existing legislative limitations thus:

> 'These limited and pragmatic interventions by the legislature make it in my judgment wholly inappropriate for the courts to impose additional restrictive rules on grounds of public policy. It is certainly not for a judge of first instance to proclaim a new head of public policy which no appellate court has even hinted at before. I would therefore respectfully prefer the decision of the New Zealand Supreme Court in *Re Manurewa Transport Ltd* [1971] NZLR 909, recognising the validity of a provision for automatic crystallisation, to the contrary dicta in the Canadian case[311] I have cited.'

Hoffmann J did not feel it was necessary to decide the question of the validity of the clause, although in the later *Re Permanent Houses (Holdings) Ltd*[312] he upheld the validity of such a clause which effected the crystallisation of a floating charge when a stated event of default occurred. Since the legislature can impose a third statutory restriction, it could provide that the Form C1, used to register charges created by a

---

305 See Courtney, *The Law of Private Companies* (2nd edn, Bloomsbury Professional, 2002), at para [20.095]. As considered below, this has now happened and Finlay Geoghegan J in *Re JD Brian Ltd* [2011] IEHC 113 has accepted the validity of automatic crystallisation clauses; see para **[18.107]** *post*.

306 See Goode, *Commercial Law* (1982), p 799.

307 See the discussion of priorities in equity, in Keane, *Equity and the Law of Trusts in the Republic of Ireland* (2nd edn, Bloomsbury Professional, 2011), Ch 5.

308 Section 288 of the CA 1963.

309 Section 285(2) of the CA 1963.

310 *Re Brightlife Ltd* [1986] BCLC 418 at 427–428.

311 *R v Consolidated Churchill Copper Corp Ltd* [1978] WLR 652.

312 *Re Permanent Houses (Holdings) Ltd* [1988] BCLC 56.

company, should note whether or not the charge includes an automatic crystallisation clause. Such would give any subsequent outsiders ample opportunity to enquire further.

In the third place, the floating charge is a creation of the draftsman, and as such is a *right* and does not exist by virtue of any *licence* granted by the legislature. As Hoffmann J said, 'I do not think that it is open to the courts to restrict the contractual freedom of parties to a floating charge ...'[313]. It is submitted that where a charge clearly contains an unequivocal automatic crystallisation[314] clause, there is no reason why the courts should not give effect to the parties' contractual agreement.

[18.107] In *Re JD Brian Ltd*[315], the question as to whether there was a principled objection in Irish law to automatic or express crystallisation was considered by Finlay Geoghegan J albeit *obiter dictum*. The learned judge noted the existence of the two schools of thought described by Sealy, the opposition of Keane J writing ex-judicially in his text book, the views expressed in the last edition of this work[316] and the decision of Hoffmann J in *Re Brightlife Ltd*[317]. In relation to the latter decision, Finlay Geoghegan J noted that there the question concerned the validity of the crystallisation effected by notice to the chargor, saying:

> 'The primary submission was that events of crystallisation were fixed by law and not by agreement of the parties. Those events were confined to (i) winding up; (ii) appointment of a receiver and (iii) ceasing to carry on business. It was submitted that only those three events would cause crystallisation, notwithstanding any agreement to the contrary. The common features of the events were that, in each case, the business of the company would cease, or at any rate, cease to be conducted by the directors.'

Finlay Geoghegan J noted Hoffmann J's conclusion that the commercial inconvenience of automatic crystallisation gives rise to a strong presumption that automatic crystallisation was not in fact intended and that, accordingly, very clear language will be required to show an intention that automatic crystallisation was intended. The learned judge said:

> 'On the public policy argument, the position, simply put, is that it is a matter for the Oireachtas and not the courts to intervene in order to avoid an unfair adverse impact on third party creditors from contractual arrangements which may be entered into between a debenture holder and a company. The Oireachtas has, of course, done so by enacting s 98 (in relation to receivers), s 99 (in relation to registration of certain charges) and s 285(7) (in relation to priority for certain debts on a winding up) referred to extensively above. I, again, respectfully agree with Hoffmann J that, having regard in particular to those interventions by the legislature, it is inappropriate for the courts to impose additional restrictive rules on grounds of public policy. Accordingly, on the first issue, for the very same reason set out by Hoffmann J, I am of the view that there is no rule of law which precludes parties to a debenture creating a floating charge agreeing, as a matter of

---

313 See Hoffmann J in *Re Brightlife Ltd* [1986] BCLC 418 at 427–428.

314 See the comments of Hoffmann J in *Re Permanent Houses (Holdings) Ltd* [1988] BCLC 563 at 567d–e.

315 *Re JD Brian Ltd* [2011] IEHC 113 and [2011] IEHC 383. For commentary, see Cuddihy, 'Floating charges – Express Crystallisation Clauses' (2011) CLP 135.

316 See Courtney, *The Law of Private Companies* (2nd edn, 2002) at para [20.095].

317 *Re Brightlife Ltd* [1987] Ch 200.

contract, that the flowing charge will crystallise upon the happening of an event or a particular step taken by the chargee[318].'

[18.108] However, while the principle that automatic crystallisation is lawful received the *obiter* support of the High Court, this decision also highlights the difficulties in the effectiveness of such a clause. As Finlay Geoghegan J said, 'whether the parties actually achieve their intention is a separate issue by reason *inter alia* of the Supreme Court decision in *Re Keenan Brothers*[319]'. Finlay Geoghegan J went on to note that it is not sufficient that a charge just be labelled as being a fixed charge and said:

> 'It appears to me, similarly, where a debenture expressly provides that a charge may, by service of a notice, effect a crystallisation of a floating charge over all the assets or specified assets, the mere fact that the debenture so provides does not of itself mean that the service of the notice, has the intended effect ie that the floating charge crystallises. In the words of McCarthy J 'mere terminology' used by the parties is not determinative of achieving the stated purpose ...
>
> 61. The issue is not, of course, whether the charge created by the debenture was a fixed or floating charge but, rather, whether the service of the notice provided for in Clause 10 of the Debenture does, in reality, what it purports to do, namely, 'convert the floating charge contained in this deed into a first fixed charge over all the property, assets and rights for the time being, subject to the said floating charge.' Similar to the approach of the Supreme Court in the above decisions, this Court must determine whether or not the effect of the service of the notice, pursuant to Clause 10, achieved what the parties intended it to achieve, namely, the conversion of the then floating charge into a first fixed charge over all the relevant property ... Further, in accordance with the decision in *Re Wogan's (Drogheda) Ltd*, it appears that this issue must be determined by a construction of the terms of the Debenture and the notice served, rather than any subsequent actions by either party.'

Finlay Geoghegan J found that if the service of the notice pursuant to clause 10 had in reality the effect of converting the floating charge over the book debts and stock in trade of the company into a first fixed charge on such assets, then it must also have effected an equitable assignment of such assets to the bank and the company would have lost the ability to deal in or dispose of those assets save as permitted by the bank. The presence or absence of restrictions in the debenture on the company's ability to deal with the assets formerly the subject of the floating charge but which were intended to become the subject of a fixed charge were, therefore, critical to whether the charge was fixed or floating.

[18.109] The High Court found it was not necessary to consider whether or not the restrictions in the debenture were appropriate to a fixed charge because it had already found that, either way, it would not have had priority to the preferential creditors. When, however, the liquidator indicated the decision would be appealed to the Supreme Court, the High Court considered it appropriate to address the issues so that all relevant issues could be before the Supreme Court. Accordingly, in *Re JD Brian Motors Ltd (No 2)*[320] Finlay Geoghegan J considered the effectiveness of the language used in the debenture

318 *Re JD Brian Ltd* [2011] IEHC 113 at para 56 of the judgment.

319 *Re Keenan Brothers* [1985] IR 401.

320 *Re JD Brian Motors Ltd (No 2)* [2011] IEHC 283 noted by Cuddihy, 'Floating Charges – Express Crystallisation Clauses' (2011) CLP 171.

by drawing heavily on the established jurisprudence applicable to the determination of whether a debenture creates a fixed or floating charge over book debts[321]. In approaching the construction of the debenture, she noted the Supreme Court's approval in *Analog Devices BV v Zurich Insurance*[322] of the summary by Lord Hoffmann of the proper approach to the construction of commercial contracts in *Investors Compensation Scheme v West Bromwich Building Society*[323] and summarised by Laffoy J in *UPM v BWG*[324] but stated that where the issue in question is whether a fixed or floating charge has been created, the court is also engaged in a two-stage process in accordance with the Privy Council's methodology in *Agnew v Commissioner on Inland Revenue*[325]. Finlay Geoghegan J said:

> 'In my judgment, it follows that the same approach should be taken to deciding whether or not the effect of the service of a notice, pursuant to Clause 10 of the Debenture, was to convert the floating charge created by the Deed over the stock-in-trade, cash-at-bank and book debts into a first fixed charge over such property. The court must, as a first step, construe the Debenture to ascertain the intention of the parties as to the rights and obligations granted to or imposed on each other in relation to the property subject to the floating charge after the service of a notice, pursuant to Clause 10 of the Debenture, referring to that property. Once this has been ascertained, the court should embark on the second stage and determine whether such rights and obligations are consistent with a fixed charge. If so, the notice will have the effect of converting the floating charge into a fixed charge. If not, it will not have achieved the stated intention and the property will remain subject to the floating charge[326].'

Applying this to the facts of the debenture in hand, Finlay Geoghegan J found that the intention to convert a floating charge into a fixed charge did not carry with it a necessary implication that the company was restricted from dealing in or disposing of any of the assets without the bank's consent and also found the debenture silent as to the bank's rights or the company's obligations following the purported conversion of the charge and nothing which restricted the company's entitlement to deal with or dispose of its stock in trade or use the proceeds of its book debts or cash at the bank. Moreover, the learned judge found the unqualified covenant in the debenture to 'carry on and conduct its business in a proper and efficient manner' to be inconsistent with the existence of a fixed charge on book debts, stock in trade and cash at bank. Finally, it was noted that clause 8 contained a prohibition on selling, assigning or otherwise disposing of property the subject of a fixed charge that was confined to property originally subject to a fixed charge, and not property which was subject to a floating charge which purportedly

---

321 See, generally, para **[18.044]** *ante*.

322 *Analog Devices BV v Zurich Insurance* [2005] 1 IR 274.

323 *Investors Compensation Scheme v West Bromwich Building Society* [1998] 1 WLR 896 at 912.

324 *UPM v BWG* [1999] IEHC 178 where Laffoy J said: 'The Court's task [in interpreting the documents which contain the parties' agreement] is to ascertain the intention of the parties and that intention must be ascertained from the language that they have used considered in the light of the surrounding circumstances and the object of the contract. Moreover, in attempting to ascertain the presumed intention of the parties, the Court should adopt an objective, rather than a subjective approach, and should consider what would have been the intention of reasonable persons in the position of the parties.'

325 *Agnew v Commissioner on Inland Revenue* [2001] 2 AC 710.

326 *Re JD Brian Motors Ltd (No 2)* [2011] IEHC 283 at para 13 of the judgment.

converted to a fixed charge. This was found to underscore the absence of a similar provision in relation to the property the subject of the purported quasi-fixed charge. So, while there was nothing in principle against a debenture having an express or automatic crystallisation provision, any such purported provision must be effective. In the instant case, Finlay Geoghegan J said:

> 'Accordingly, construing the Debenture, it appears from its provisions, that notwithstanding the provision for the service of a notice pursuant to Clause 10, when the Bank considers the property subject to the floating charge to be in jeopardy, there is no intention expressed therein that the Company should thereafter be restricted in its use of the property subject to the notice, other than pursuant to Clause 8. The company, in my judgment, in accordance with the terms of the Debenture, continued to be entitled to use such property for the proper carrying on and conduct of its business including selling stock in trade and making payments from cash at Bank and realised book debts without the necessity of obtaining the consent of the Bank for sale or other disposal. This entitlement is inconsistent with the existence of a first fixed charge over the stock-in-trade, cash-at-bank and book debts in favour of the Bank ... On a proper construction of the Debenture, the service of a notice, pursuant to Clause 10 thereof, does not have the effect of converting the property subject to the floating charge created by the Debenture into a first fixed charge over such property.'

Lessons can be learned from this decision, and debentures which provide for automatic or express crystallisation can be redrafted in the light of Finlay Geoghegan J's instructive comments in order to create effective conversion provisions.

De-cystallisation of floating charges

[18.110] Until recent times, it was a generally[327] held view that once a floating charge crystallised, it could not de-crystallise. The Supreme Court in *Re Holidair Ltd*[328] has turned this view on its head by holding that the appointment of an examiner pursuant to C(A)A 1990 will de-crystallise a crystallised floating charge. Having held[329] that the debenture in question created a floating charge over the companies' book debts, Blayney J acknowledged that it had crystallised upon the appointment of the receiver. However, he went on to hold that upon the appointment of an examiner, the crystallised floating charge de-crystallised. It is submitted that since floating charges are essentially matters of contract between the parties there is nothing in principle that should prevent the parties to a debenture from providing that a particular floating charge is *incapable* of de-crystallising, thereby distinguishing it from the floating charge (that was silent on that point) in *Re Holidair Ltd*. The decision in *Re Holidair Ltd* is considered further, and critiqued, in Ch 22[330].

---

327 See Gough, *Company Charges* (2nd edn, 1996), pp 404–407.

328 *Re Holidair Ltd* [1994] 1 ILRM 481.

329 See para **[18.047]**.

330 Ch 22, *Examinerships*, para **[22.074]–[22.078]**.

Chapter 19

Corporate Borrowing: Registration of Charges

Introduction

[19.001] It is vital to realise that before certain mortgages and charges will be valid, effective and have priority over subsequent mortgages and charges, they must be registered pursuant to the Companies Acts. Such charges are referred to here as registrable charges[1]. In this chapter the following issues are considered:

1. The register of charges.
2. The consequences of non-registration.
3. The conclusiveness of the certificate of registration.
4. Non-registrable security interests
5. Registrable charges.
6. Disguised registrable charges: retention of title clauses.
7. Judgment mortgages.
8. Charges over property outside of the State.
9. Late registration of registrable charges.
10. Registration.
11. Particulars required to be registered.
12. Satisfaction of charges.
13. The chargor company's obligations.

Charges created by external companies and charges created by foreign companies which have not registered as external companies, to which the *Slavenburg* file applies, are considered in Ch 34[2].

The register of charges

[19.002] Section 103 of the Companies Act 1963 ('CA 1963') prescribes that the registrar of companies shall keep, in relation to each company, a register of all charges which are required to be registered under Part IV of the CA 1963[3]. The basic principle to be remembered is that where a company creates a registrable charge[4], particulars of such

---

1. See Gough, *Company Charges* (2nd edn, 1996); Johnston, *Banking and Security Law in Ireland* (1998), Ch 17; Parsons, *Lingard's Bank Security Documents* (5th edn, 2011), Ch 3; and Schmitthoff (ed), *Palmer's Company Law* (24th edn, 1987), para 46–01 *et seq.*
2. Ch 34, *External Companies and Branches*, at para **[34.018]**.
3. Section 103 of the CA 1963 goes on to provide that the registrar of companies shall on payment of a fee – currently €40 – enter certain details in the register. This register is open to the public for inspection.
4. 'Registrable charge' refers to those charges described in s 99(2) of the CA 1963, and which are considered at para **[19.042]** *et seq.*

a charge must be delivered, in the prescribed form, to the registrar of companies at the Companies Registration Office ('CRO'). The failure to deliver particulars within the prescribed 21 days will render the mortgage or charge *void* against a liquidator of the company or any creditor of the company. The basic requirement and most far-reaching sanction is contained in s 99(1) of the CA 1963, which provides:

> 'Subject to the provisions of this Part, every charge created after the fixed date by a company, and being a charge to which this section applies, shall, so far as any security on the company's property or undertaking is conferred thereby, *be void against the liquidator and any creditor of the company*, unless the prescribed particulars of the charge, verified in the prescribed manner, are delivered to or received by the Registrar of Companies for registration in manner required by this Act within 21 days after the date of its creation, but without prejudice to any contract or obligation for repayment of the money thereby secured, and when a charge becomes void under this section, the money secured thereby shall immediately become payable. (Emphasis added.)'

(a) The rationale for the register of charges

[19.003] The rationale[5] behind the requirement that certain charges created by companies must be registered is to afford protection to creditors of the company by providing them with a means of discovering whether a particular company has secured creditors[6]. This protection is intended for both secured and unsecured creditors. However, this objective will not be realised unless subsequent creditors actually search against a company in the CRO. As Palmer has noted[7], the object of the legislation is to enable creditors to search the register. The result of such a search will show either that the company's property is encumbered or not with registrable charges. Thus, in the case of *Esberger & Son Ltd v Capital and Counties Bank*[8] Sargant J said that the object of registration was to:

> '... show what moneys are owing by the company on certain securities, so that the creditors may have some notion of how far the property of the company is unencumbered.'

Having this knowledge, the rationale continues that the creditor will then make an informed decision as to whether or not to deal with the company, eg, whether to extend credit to the company. Such a system of registration is not peculiar to companies. In the case of individuals, there is a somewhat similar, albeit infrequently used system under the Bills of Sale (Ireland) Acts 1879–1883[9]. However, even in the case of companies, while the object of the legislation aims for full consensual dealing by creditors with a company, the reality is somewhat different. In the first place, as we shall see below, not all security interests are registrable (not even all consensually created security interests). In the second place, to expect all creditors, particularly those who are unsecured such as suppliers of goods, to examine the register, assumes too much.

---

5 See generally Gough, *Company Charges* (2nd edn, 1996).

6 See *Re International Retail Ltd* (25 July 1974, unreported) HC, per Kenny J.

7 Schmitthoff (ed), *Palmer's Company Law* (24th edn, 1987), para 46.03.

8 *Esberger & Son Ltd v Capital and Counties Bank* [1913] 2 Ch 366 at 374.

9 See para **[19.047]** *et seq*.

(b) Notice of the register of charges

[19.004] In various places throughout this work[10] it has been noted that documents registered with the CRO are *public documents* and that third parties dealing with a company will, generally, be deemed to have constructive notice of matters which are registered. The general rule is true in the case of charges that are registered pursuant to s 99 of the CA 1963. Accordingly, persons who deal with a company will be deemed to have notice of the existence of charges that are duly registered[11].

[19.005] The exception to the general rule that the public has constructive notice of matters registered with the CRO is that it has been consistently held that the 'unruly horse'[12] of constructive notice does not extend beyond the particulars which have been recorded. The seminal Supreme Court decision in *Welch v Bowmaker (Ireland) Ltd and the Governor and Company of the Bank of Ireland*[13], which has been considered in Ch 18, decided that the public will not have constructive notice of negative pledge clauses[14], although this has been tempered by the decision of Laffoy J in *Re Salthill Properties Ltd*[15].

The consequences of non-registration

[19.006] Where particulars of a registrable charge are not delivered within 21 days of its creation, s 99(1) of the CA 1963 provides that it shall be void against the liquidator and any creditor of the company[16]. It is vital to realise that non-registration of a registrable charge will not entirely vitiate that charge, which will still be enforceable against the company[17], and indeed the sum secured by the charge will become immediately payable[18]. Rather, it is the case that if another creditor of the company exists, secured or unsecured, then the holder of the unregistered charge will not have priority over that other creditor[19]. In *Re Monolithic Building Co*[20], Phillimore LJ said of the predecessor of s 99(1) that:

---

10 See Ch 3, *Constitutional Documentation*, para **[3.112]** and Ch 7, *Corporate Contracts, Capacity and Authority*, para **[7.119]**.

11 See, eg, *Siebe Gorman & Co Ltd v Barclays Bank Ltd* [1979] 2 Lloyds Rep 142 at 615.

12 *Per* Parke J in *Welch v Bowmaker (Ireland) Ltd and the Governor and Company of the Bank of Ireland* [1980] IR 251.

13 *Welch v Bowmaker (Ireland) Ltd and the Governor and Company of the Bank of Ireland* [1980] IR 251.

14 See Ch 18, *Corporate Borrowing: Debentures and Security*, para **[18.079]** *et seq.* See also Johnston, *Banking and Security Law in Ireland* (1998), pp 611–616.

15 *Re Salthill Properties Ltd* (30 July 2004, unreported) HC, Laffoy J. See Ch 18, *Corporate Borrowing: Debentures and Security*, para **[18.083]**.

16 See *Re Clarets Ltd; Spain v McCann* [1978] ILRM 215 at 217, *per* Costello J, where there is a statement of the obvious effect of non-registration under s 99 of the CA 1963.

17 *Wright v Horton* [1887] 12 AC 371.

18 Section 99(1) of the CA 1963.

19 Of course priority will only be an issue where a company is insolvent and accordingly the security will stand as against the company when it is a going concern.

20 *Re Monolithic Building Co* [1915] 1 Ch 643.

'It makes void a security; not the debt, not the cause of action, but the security, and not as against everybody, not as against the company grantor, but against the liquidator, and against any creditor, and it leaves the security to stand as against the company while it is a going concern. It does not make the security binding on the liquidator as successor of the company[21].'

[19.007] The reference there to the fact that an unregistered charge is void but 'not as against *everybody*' was taken to peculiar lengths by the English Court of Appeal before they were reined-in by the House of Lords on appeal in *Smith (Administrator of Cosslett (Contractors) Ltd) v Bridgend County Borough Council*[22]. The facts in that case have been reviewed in Ch 18[23] and it is sufficient for present purposes to note that a contract was found to have unintentionally created a floating charge. In the Court of Appeal it had been said by Laws LJ that:

'… the failure to register the floating charge, which as this court found was constituted by cl 63, in my judgment conferred on the respondent administrator a purely adventitious potential claim *in specie* to recover or retain the plant as against the appellants if it lay in their hands after completion of the works. This inchoate claim had nothing to do with the true state of account between the company and the appellants as it would fall to be ascertained for the purposes of a just and reasonable approach to the administration or … liquidation of the company[24].'

The Court of Appeal went on to say that the only circumstances in which an unregistered charge would be void would be where a liquidator or administrator was suing *in his personal name* as, for example, under s 236 of the CA 1963[25]. This, of course, not only over-turned a century of received judicial wisdom (and legitimate expectation of the commercial community) but also made a total mockery out of the purpose of registration. It was not conceivable that it would stand. In the House of Lords, Lord Hoffmann stated that he considered that the grounds upon which the Court of Appeal had decided the case to be 'startling and unorthodox', rejecting as it had the accepted effects of a failure to register a registrable charge. To the extent that the Court of Appeal had said that an unregistered charge was void only as against a liquidator or, under English law, an administrator, acting personally this was overruled. Lord Hoffmann restated that an unregistered charge is 'void against a company acting by its liquidator'[26]. Moreover, Lord Scott said that where a security is barred from being enforceable because of non-registration, it is no part of equity to provide, via equitable set-off, an alternative security[27].

---

21 *Re Monolithic Building Co* [1915] 1 Ch 643 at 667–668.

22 *Smith (Administrator of Cosslett (Contractors) Ltd) v Bridgend County Borough Council* [2002] 1 All ER 292.

23 At para **[18.027]** *et seq.*

24 *Re Cosslett (Contractors) Ltd* [2000] 1 BCLC 775 at 791.

25 The English Court of Appeal specifically referred to the similar English provision, s 234 of the Insolvency Act 1986 (UK).

26 *Smith (Administrator of Cosslett (Contractors) Ltd) v Bridgend County Borough Council* [2002] 1 All ER 292 at para [21]. And, in England, as against a company in administration: see [2002] 1 All ER 292 at para [31].

27 *Smith (Administrator of Cosslett (Contractors) Ltd) v Bridgend County Borough Council* [2002] 1 All ER 292 at para [79].

[19.008] A registrable charge that is not registered will be void against a subsequent creditor even where that creditor is aware of the prior charge. Authority for this is again the case of *Re Monolithic Building Co*[28] where the subsequent encumbrancer, who registered his charge notwithstanding his knowledge of the existence of a prior unregistered mortgage, was held, by the Court of Appeal, to have priority. His knowledge of the prior charge did not preclude him from insisting on his rights as a registered debenture holder[29].

[19.009] Serious problems can arise where a charge is created which is not perceived to be a registrable charge and which is consequently not registered. As will be considered in some detail later in this chapter[30], a retention of title clause in a contract for the sale of goods can, in certain circumstances, be found to be a registrable charge. An example of the consequences that befall the holder of such a charge is found in *Carroll Group Distributors Ltd v G & JF Bourke Ltd*[31]. In that case, the plaintiff supplied goods to the defendant company under a contract that allowed four weeks' credit. The contract also contained a retention of title clause which provided that the property in the goods would remain with the plaintiff until the defendants had discharged all sums due to the plaintiff. The clause gave the defendant an express right to sell the goods, subject to the defendant company holding all proceeds of sale 'in trust' for the plaintiff. When the defendant company went into liquidation, the issue arose as to whether or not this retention of title clause constituted a registrable charge. Holding that this particular clause was properly construed as a registrable charge, Murphy J said:

> '... parties cannot escape the inference that a transaction constitutes a mortgage registrable under s 99 aforesaid by particular labels to the transaction. The rights of the parties and the nature of the transaction in which they engage must be determined from a consideration of the document as a whole and the obligations and rights which it imposes on both parties ... The description may be a material consideration but clearly it cannot be decisive. Specifically in relation to mortgages registrable under the Companies Acts it has been held that it is in the substance of the transaction as ascertained from the words used by the parties and the context in which the document is executed that determines registrability under the Companies Acts ... effectively [the defendant company] were creating or conferring a charge on the proceeds of sale in substitution for the right of property which [the plaintiff] had previously enjoyed. The charge so created required registration under s 99 of the Companies Act 1963 and in the absence of such registration was invalid[32].'

Accordingly, the plaintiff company lost any security interest it claimed because the retention of title clause was void against the liquidator and other creditors of the defendant company. What this case shows is that extreme caution ought to be exercised

28 *Re Monolithic Building Co* [1915] 1 Ch 643.

29 Cf *Re Clarets Ltd; Spain v McCann* [1978] ILRM 215 at 218 where Costello J distinguished this case from the case in hand. See also *Re Peleton Ltd* [2011] IEHC 479 where Laffoy J confirmed that this is the law.

30 See para **[19.071]** *et seq.*

31 *Carroll Group Distributors Ltd v G & JF Bourke Ltd* [1990] ILRM 285. For analysis, see Maguire, 'Romalpa Misinterpreted' (1989) DULJ 40 at 53 *et seq.*

32 *Carroll Group Distributors Ltd v G & JF Bourke Ltd* [1990] ILRM 285 at 290.

so as to ensure that any transaction does not result in a corporate party thereto unconsciously creating a registrable charge.

[19.010] In *Re Peleton Ltd*[33], a mortgage debenture was created but not registered in time. When this was realised, a fresh mortgage debenture was executed by the company for the bank, which debenture was not stamped. Laffoy J frowned on this practice and although the learned judge acceded to the application to allow late registration of the particulars of the original charge, her order was conditional upon the bank giving an undertaking to stamp the second charge and to undertake to court not to rely upon that second charge and to release it and to cause a satisfaction to be filed in the CRO.

The conclusiveness of the certificate of registration

[19.011] When the registrar of companies receives particulars of a registrable charge, the registrar will in due course issue a certificate of registration that the charge has been registered in accordance with s 99 of the CA 1963. Section 104 of CA 1963 provides that the certificate of registration is conclusive evidence that the requirements of Part IV of the CA 1963 have been complied with.

[19.012] The certificate of registration remains conclusive evidence even where the parties creating the charge act in a manner that was not contemplated by the legislature. Thus, in *Carroll Group Distributors Ltd v G & JF Bourke Ltd*[34] the plaintiff bank made loan facilities available to the defendant company ('Amurec') to enable it to purchase property. On the completion of the conveyance in November 1972, Amurec gave the deed of conveyance of, and the deed of mortgage and charge over, the property, along with documents of title, to the plaintiff bank's solicitors. Both deeds had been left undated. Amurec's solicitor gave an undertaking to give £3,500 to the plaintiff bank's solicitors for the stamping of the deeds. There was a delay in providing the stamp duty and, eventually, in March 1974 when the plaintiff bank's solicitors still had not received funds for stamping they decided to proceed and used their own funds, and so the conveyance and mortgage were stamped and dated 21 and 22 March 1974, respectively. The mortgage was then lodged with the registrar of companies who issued a certificate of registration. The certificate of registration of the charge certified that the date of the creation of the charge was 22 March 1974 and that the date of registration was 10 April 1974. The liquidator of Amurec contended that the plaintiff bank's charge was void because particulars of the charge had not been delivered to the registrar within the prescribed 21 days, as required by s 99(1) of the CA 1963. It was held by Hamilton J that the charge was valid because the certificate of registration was conclusive evidence that the requirements of Part IV of the CA 1963 had been complied with and in particular that the charge had been registered within the prescribed 21 days. In his judgment, he recited the wording of s 104 of the CA 1963 and accepted the argument of counsel for the plaintiff bank that since it was expressly stated to be conclusive as to the fact that the requirements of CA 1963 had been complied with, this included the time within which charges had to be registered. While he had considerable sympathy with the submissions of the liquidator, he found himself bound by the express provisions of

33 *Re Peleton Ltd* [2011] IEHC 479, Laffoy J.

34 *Lombard & Ulster Banking Ireland Ltd v Amurec Ltd* [1976–7] ILRM 222.

s 104. Thus he followed Pennycuick J in *Re Eric Holmes (Property) Ltd*[35] where he had held that the certificate was conclusive evidence that the delivery of particulars had been within 21 days, even though an incorrect date had been inserted. The reason why Hamilton J decided as he did was based on the fact that 'the wording of s 104 is clear and unambiguous'[36].' This decision was followed most recently by Laffoy J in *Re Investment Options and Solutions Ltd; Bank of Scotland (Ireland) Ltd v Investment Options and Solutions Ltd*[37].

[19.013] The rationale behind the conclusive evidence provision is seen in *Re CL Nye Ltd*[38], a case cited with approval by Hamilton J in the *Amurec* case. There again, a company had created a charge over property it had purchased and in February 1964 had handed the charge and the transfer to the solicitor for the chargee bank, undated for the purpose of the solicitor vetting the title for the bank. In March 1964, the solicitor reported that the security was good and the bank then lent to the company. Through an oversight, the charge was not registered and it was only on 3 July 1964 that particulars were delivered to the registrar of companies, stating that the charge had been created on 18 June 1964 (ie, a mere 15 days' previously). This was innocently accepted by the registrar and a certificate of registration was issued to the bank. The Court of Appeal held that the charge was valid, again on the basis that the certificate of the registrar was conclusive evidence that the requirements of the Companies Act had been complied with. In the course of his judgment, Harman LJ stated:

> 'In my judgment the certificate must be conclusive ... The whole point of creating the register under [s 99 of the CA 1963] is to give security to persons relying on the certificate. If it were possible to go behind the certificate and show that the date of creation of the charge made it out of time, no lender on the face of the charge could be secure and sure that it would not thereafter be attacked by somebody who could successfully prove that there was in fact an interval of more than twenty-one days between the charge's creation and its registration. This would be disastrous in my opinion and is not a view to be taken unless the language positively compels it[39].'

It is, therefore, accepted law that the certificate of registration of a charge is conclusive evidence that the relevant particulars were registered.

(a) The significance of mistakes in the Form C1

[19.014] The decision of Laffoy J in *Re Investment Options and Solutions Ltd; Bank of Scotland (Ireland) Ltd v Investment Options and Solutions Ltd*[40] is authority for the proposition that even where the particulars of the amount charged in the debenture are incorrect, this will not invalidate the certificate of registration. In that case, a charge was registered within the 21-day period but the date of its creation was misstated and the

35 *Re Eric Holmes (Property) Ltd* [1965] Ch 1052.

36 *Carroll Group Distributors Ltd v G & JF Bourke Ltd* [1990] ILRM 285.

37 *Re Investment Options and Solutions Ltd; Bank of Scotland (Ireland) Ltd v Investment Options and Solutions Ltd* [2010] IEHC 107 at para 6, quoting from p 225 of MacCann & Courtney, *Companies Acts 1963–2008*.

38 *Re CL Nye Ltd* [1970] 3 All ER 1061.

39 *Re CL Nye Ltd* [1970] 3 All ER 1061 at 1069.

40 *Re Investment Options and Solutions Ltd; Bank of Scotland (Ireland) Ltd v Investment Options and Solutions Ltd* [2010] IEHC 107.

incorrect date appeared in the certificate of charge. Laffoy J said that the form containing the particulars of the charge

> '... was received within twenty one days after the date of the creation of the charge, as required by s 99. Aside from the conclusiveness of the certificate of registration under s 104, I am satisfied that s 99(1), which provides that failure to deliver the prescribed particulars within twenty one days after creation of a charge '*shall, so far as any security on the company's property or undertaking is conferred thereby, be void against the liquidator and any creditor of the company*' could not be applied in this case so as to render the deed of mortgage and charge dated 22 June, 2001 void.'

This was also found to be the case in *Re Mechanisations (Eaglecliffe) Ltd*[41] which was followed by Costello J in *Re Shannonside Holdings Ltd*[42]. In that case, it was claimed that the company had created a debenture in favour of the estate of the late Mr Barrett, who was the promoter of the company and, also, who had advanced substantial sums to the company. On 25 May 1973, the directors of the company met in Chicago and agreed to grant a debenture to Mr Barrett. The debenture was then executed in favour of Mr Barrett. On 14 June 1973, Irish solicitors acting for the company filed a Form 47 (the predecessor to the Form C1) in respect of the debenture. The debenture was subsequently lost. Costello J accepted, on the balance of probabilities, that the debenture had been executed. One of the issues which also arose for consideration concerned the amount secured by the debenture. Costello J said:

> 'I now come to the terms of the debenture. In light of the submissions made by counsel it is perfectly clear that the debenture which is now lost was not limited to the sum of £200,000 which appears in Form 47. The explanation for that figure being in the debenture is, I think, to be found in the documents which indicate that it was to be stamped at this figure and that is why this figure was inserted in Form 47.
>
> One of the authorities to which I have been referred, *Re Mechanisations (Eaglescliffe) Ltd* [1964] 3 All ER 840, makes clear that what the court is required to do is to give effect to the document creating the charge and not to the particulars given in Form 47[43].'

Accordingly, while the certificate of registration will be conclusive evidence that particulars of the charge were delivered in accordance with the requirements of CA 1963, the actual terms of the debenture itself will always have precedence over the particulars contained in the Form C1[44].

[19.015] In *Re Valley Ice Cream (Ireland) Ltd*[45], the facts of which were considered in Ch 18[46], the liquidator of a company which had given an irrevocable undertaking to execute a mortgage on certain refrigerator equipment, challenged the registration of that charge. The basis of the challenge was that a Form 47 (the precursor to the Form C1) that had been filed in the CRO had incorrectly referred to '... the execution of a mortgage over the equipment in the form attached in the first schedule to the debenture';

41 *Re Mechanisations (Eaglecliffe) Ltd* [1964] 3 All ER 840.

42 *Re Shannonside Holdings Ltd* (20 May 1993, unreported) HC.

43 *Re Shannonside Holdings Ltd* (20 May 1993, unreported) HC at p 8.

44 See *National Provincial & Union Bank v Charnley* [1924] 1 KB 431 where the precursor to Form C1 had omitted to contain the categories of property that had been charged.

45 *Re Valley Ice Cream (Ireland) Ltd* (22 July 1998, unreported) HC, McCracken J.

46 See Ch 18, *Corporate Borrowing: Debentures and Security*, para **[18.036]**.

in fact, the draft mortgage which the company undertook to procure to be executed was contained in the *fifth schedule* to the debenture. On this point McCracken J said:

> 'It is suggested that this is misleading, as any creditor looking at the file in the companies office would not realise or understand the form of the mortgage to be executed. In my view, this is not relevant, as what is registered is the fact that there is an irrevocable undertaking to procure the execution of a mortgage over the equipment, and the equipment is clearly set out in the Form 47. What s 99 requires to be registered is particulars of the charge, not the form which the charge is to take. In my view, it is quite clear from what was registered that there was a charge in the form of an irrevocable undertaking to execute a mortgage over this equipment, and that satisfies s 99[47].'

It is thought that this was a pragmatic decision in which the validity of the charge was upheld in circumstances where to do so was just.

[19.016] A similar approach was taken in *Re Advantage Healthcare (T10) Ltd*[48]. In that case, a certificate of registration of charge issued which contained one company's name but another company's registered number. Lightman J rejected the argument that the charge was valid on account of the conclusiveness of the certificate of registration because in providing that the wrong company has complied with the statutory requirements as to the registration of a charge that it had not created, it was 'meaningless and worthless'. Lightman J went on, however, to find that the charge created by the company was valid, saying:

> 'The company's registered number is a detail which the applicant for registration is required to complete, but it cannot fairly be described as 'a particular of the charge' to be registered. It is a particular of the mortgagor. The explanation for the existence of the registered number is to be found in the Companies Act 1985, ss 705 and 706 [UK]. Section 705 requires the registrar to allocate to every company a number to be known as the company's registered number; and s 706(2) requires documents delivered to the registrar under any provision of the Companies Acts to state in a prominent position the registered number of the company to which it relates. Section 706(3) and (4) provides that, on receipt of a document not including such number, the registrar may (but not must) serve notice on the person by whom the document is delivered pointing out the non-compliance, whereupon (in default of delivery of a replacement document complying with this requirement) the original document shall be deemed not to have been delivered to him. The registrar served no such notice in this case, no doubt because he did not appreciate the error. In the absence of such notice, the particulars delivered by the company remain duly delivered to the registrar[49].'

As noted, below[50], it was suggested that a third party prejudiced by the error might have a cause of action against the registrar of companies or the company.

[19.017] Notwithstanding what might be taken as a concession to the human condition, the necessity for being nothing short of fastidiously accurate and timely in completing and filing the Form C1 cannot be over-stressed. Compliance with s 99 of the CA 1963 is one task in which pedantry is a definite virtue.

---

47 *Re Valley Ice Cream (Ireland) Ltd* (22 July 1998, unreported) HC at p 4.

48 *Re Advantage Healthcare (T10) Ltd* [2000] BCC 985.

49 *Re Advantage Healthcare (T10) Ltd* [2000] BCC 985 at 988c–d.

50 See para **[19.019]–[19.020]**.

(b) The limits to the decision in the Amurec case

[19.018] Notwithstanding the judgment of the High Court in *Lombard & Ulster Banking Ireland Ltd v Amurec Ltd,* an alternative line of authority exists, which was cited by counsel for the liquidator in that case. So in *Esberger & Son Ltd v Capital and Counties Bank*[51], a company deposited an undated charge with a bank, which, some months' later was dated and registered by the bank. Sargant J held that the charge was void because it was not registered within the 21-day limit. In his words:

> 'I feel that on the true meaning of that section the date of the creation of the mortgage or charge is the date when that instrument was executed and is not the date when any money is subsequently advanced, so as to make an effective charge for the amount of that money[52].'

This line of authority[53] is willing to ignore the conclusiveness of the certificate of registration and look behind it. As seen, however, this was not followed in the *Amurec* case.

[19.019] Another judgment which questions the sacrosanctity of the certificate of registration of charges is that of Mervyn Davies J in *R v Registrar of Companies, ex p Esal (Commodities) Ltd*[54]. There, he said that an error of law, made by the registrar of companies, could be subject to judicial review:

> '... the decision of the registrar may be reviewed if it can be shown that he made his decision to register (and issued his certificate) in consequence of, in the course of examining the facts, having asked himself the wrong questions[55].'

This was said in reliance on the notion that an error of law is always reviewable by the courts. However the modern trend in the English courts seems to be to follow the line of authority established in *Re CL Nye Ltd,* as did Hamilton J in the *Amurec* case. On appeal, the decision of Mervyn Davies J was overturned in *R v Registrar of Companies, ex p Central Bank of India*[56] and the view that the certificate of registration is conclusive was reaffirmed. In the words of Slade LJ:

> 'In the face of the 'conclusive evidence' provisions ... I am driven to the conclusion (which I think is strongly supported by the *Nye* decision) that [the relevant sections] on their true construction confer upon the registrar the power to decide finally and conclusively all ancillary questions, whether they be questions of fact or law, or mixed fact and law, which fall to be decided in determining whether the requirements of Part [IV] of the Act as to registration had been complied with in any given case. Even the clearest evidence that he had come to the wrong conclusion in answering any of these questions would not entitle anyone (except the Attorney General) to claim he acted beyond his powers, since [s 104 of the CA 1963] would preclude the court from considering such

---

51 *Esberger & Son Ltd v Capital and Counties Bank* [1913] 2 Ch 366.

52 *Esberger & Son Ltd v Capital and Counties Bank* [1913] 2 Ch 366 at 373.

53 See also *Re Defries N and Co Ltd* [1904] 1 Ch 366; *Re Stevenson* [1902] 1 IR 23 and [1903] 1 IR 403; and *Yolland v Husson & Birkett Ltd* [1908] Ch 152.

54 *R v Registrar of Companies, ex p Esal (Commodities) Ltd* [1985] BCLC 84. See generally O'Riordan & Pearce, 'The Conclusiveness of Certificates of Registration of Company Charges' (1986) ILSI Gazette 281.

55 *R v Registrar of Companies, ex p Esal (Commodities) Ltd* [1985] BCLC 84 at 97.

56 *R v Registrar of Companies, ex p Central Bank of India* [1985] BCLC 465.

evidence ... If these conclusions are correct, it must follow that even if the registrar erroneously registers a charge which should not have been registered and gives a consequent [s 104 of the CA 1963] certificate, such error may be incapable of correction[57].'

However, the judgment of Slade LJ went on to set out certain limitations to the scope of this principle, and so he went on to say:

'However, lest it be thought that this position may give rise to undue hardship or injustice, I would draw attention to two points. The first is the limited nature of the effect of registration and a consequent [s 104 of the CA 1963] certificate. It does not operate to confer validity on a charge which is invalid for reasons other than lack of registration. All it does is to give a chargee who has a valid charge protection against the statutory invalidation of that charge against a liquidator and creditors of the company which would occur by virtue of [s 99 of the CA 1963], if the company were to go into liquidation and the charge were unregistered ... Secondly, counsel for the registrar, has accepted that [s 104 of the CA 1963] does not bind the Crown, so that there might be nothing to prevent the Attorney General from interfering, if he saw fit, by way of an application for judicial review in what he considered an appropriate case, where evidence was available to show that the registrar had erred in the exercise of his functions as to registration. There is, therefore, in my opinion, no question of the registrar being wholly beyond the reach of the law.

Two special cases may arise on which I wish to express no concluded opinion in this present judgment, because it is not necessary to do so. The first is the hypothetical case where a purported certificate given by the registrar discloses an error on the face of it. It may well be that even the protection afforded by [s 104 of the CA 1963] would not operate in that situation. The second special situation might arise where the certificate had been obtained by fraud[58]. Even in that case a direct attack on the certificate would, at least prima facie, be ruled out by [s 104 of the CA 1963] ... though it might well be that the court would act *in personam* against the fraudulent party so as to prevent him taking advantage of the fraudulently obtained certificate ... and furthermore, a creditor personally damaged by the fraud might be able to take proceedings for damages ...'[59]

Thus, Slade LJ's *obiter dictum* is that while the certificate is conclusive, in special cases injured parties may have recourse to the courts. In the first place it is recognised that an error on the face of the document might be so manifestly wrong as to invalidate registration. This was the reasoning of the court in *Re Advantage Healthcare (T10) Ltd*[60]. The second situation envisaged by Slade LJ was that of a fraudulently obtained certificate of registration. Slade LJ acknowledged the possible availability of an action *in personam* against persons who have fraudulently obtained a certificate of registration of a charge. By their very nature, if successful, they only attach to the person and not the property, ie, the successful plaintiff would be an unsecured creditor of the defendant, a situation that is most undesirable where an insolvent company is involved. However, since such an action could be taken against a lending institution which has acted

---

57 *R v Registrar of Companies, ex p Central Bank of India* [1985] BCLC 465 at 490.

58 Note *Sun Tai Cheung Credits Ltd v AG of Hong Kong* [1987] 1 WLR 948 (Privy Council), *per* Lord Templeman.

59 *R v Registrar of Companies, ex p Central Bank of India* [1985] BCLC 465 at 490–491. The references to the CA 1963 replace the similar English provisions.

60 *Re Advantage Healthcare (T10) Ltd* [2000] BCC 985. See para **[19.016]**.

fraudulently, an aggrieved second charge holder may have a mark, should he be successful in establishing fraud. In establishing fraud here it is thought that, to be successful, the second charge holder would have to show that the charge holder, who had delivered particulars of a charge which he had dated out of time so as to come within the 21 days, was aware of the second charge holder's rights and consciously intended to thwart those rights. In particular it is thought that a second charge holder whose charge came into being *after* the coming into existence of the first charge holder's charge would be unlikely to be successful.

[19.020] In the absence of fraud a claim may still lie against the registrar of companies. In *Re Advantage Healthcare (T10) Ltd*[61], it was recognised by Lightman J in the English High Court that a third party who was prejudiced by an error might have a claim against the registrar (for registering the wrong particulars) or the company (for delivering, or allowing someone else to deliver, the wrong particulars)[62].

Non-registrable security interests

[19.021] The law provides that there are four kinds of consensual security which may be created: mortgages; charges; liens; and pledges. It is crucial to recognise at the outset that not all of these kinds of security interest are registrable pursuant to s 99 of the CA 1963. In order for mortgages and charges to be registrable they must be actually *created by* companies. Even still, not all charges are registrable. Moreover, liens and pledges are not, generally speaking, registrable. Here the following non-registrable security interests are considered:

(a) Charges which are not created by companies.
(b) Charges over proceeds of sale.
(c) Liens.
(d) Pledges.
(e) Trusts.
(f) Otherwise registrable charges provided as part of a financial collateral arrangement.

(a) Charges which are not created by companies

[19.022] It is important to note that s 99(1) of the CA 1963 refers to 'every charge created .... *by a company*'. Accordingly, where a charge arises other than through being created by a company, such as by operation of law[63], such a charge does *not* require to be registered[64]. It is this requirement – that in order for a charge to be registrable it must be created by a company – which is at the heart of the debate as to whether or not an aggregation type retention of title clause will constitute a 'registrable charge'[65]. Such an

---

[61] *Re Advantage Healthcare (T10) Ltd* [2000] BCC 985.

[62] See, also, *First City Corporation Ltd v Downsview Nominees Ltd* (1990) 5 NZCLC 66 at 303, [1990] 3 NZLR 265.

[63] See para **[19.024]** *et seq.*

[64] *Lovell Construction Ltd v Independent Estates plc* [1994] 1 BCLC 31.

[65] See para **[19.042]**.

express aggregation clause[66] was included in the contract for the sale of goods in *Kruppstahl AG v Quitmann Products Ltd*[67]. There, Gannon J said of this agreement that it, along with the other clauses:

> '... constitute an immediate assignment of future interests and an agreement for security for whatever indebtedness on the part of Quitmann to Krupps might later arise ...'[68]

In *Somers v Allen*[69], Carroll J said, in referring to the *Quitmann* case, that:

> '... this case therefore illustrates that a seller can make an effective reservation of title to goods prior to manufacture, but if he requires security over the manufactured goods the *buyer will have to grant him* this and this would require registration as a Bill of Sale[70].'

From the foregoing, it can be seen that the reason why an aggregation-type retention of title clause will be deemed a registrable charge, is because the purchaser company grants back a charge over the goods which have undergone a manufacturing process. The courts seem to have taken the view that when goods sold undergo a manufacturing process, the property in them passes to the purchaser company. Consequently, any security over those goods can only be *created by the company*, and so if it is within one of the heads of charge in s 99(2), it is a registrable charge under s 99(1).

(b) Charges over proceeds of sale

[19.023] Not all charges are registrable. By contrast with a mortgage or charge on land, a charge on *the proceeds of sale of lands* is not a registrable charge[71]. A charge on the proceeds of sale of land can arise where, pending the sale of a business premises and the proposed purchase of another, a lender advances bridging finance to the company to enable it to purchase the other property. The lender's security will often be to require a solicitor to give an undertaking to hold the proceeds of sale on trust for the lender until the existing premises is sold. Such a charge is not registrable because, while ostensibly a charge on land, it has been construed as a charge on *the proceeds of sale of land*[72]. This was decided in *Re Kum Tong Restaurant (Dublin) Ltd; Byrne v AIB Ltd*[73] where a company contracted to sell its business premises. To enable it to continue its business until the completion of the sale of the premises, AIB advanced money on the strength of the contract to sell its premises. The company undertook to hold the documents of title

---

66 Among the clauses in the contract, it was provided that: 'In the case of processing, blending and mixing of the reserved goods with other goods by the buyer, we acquire a joint title to the new goods in accordance with the ratio of the invoice value of the reserved goods to the invoice value of the other goods used. If our title lapses due to blending or mixing, the buyer assigns to us already at this stage his title to the new goods in accordance with the invoice value of the reserved goods, and holds them in trust for us, without charge.'

67 *Kruppstahl AG v Quitmann Products Ltd* [1982] ILRM 551.

68 *Kruppstahl AG v Quitmann Products Ltd* [1982] ILRM 551 at 559.

69 *Somers v Allen* [1984] ILRM 437.

70 *Somers v Allen* [1984] ILRM 437 at 441, emphasis added.

71 Such a charge may be registrable where it falls to be deemed a charge on a company's book debts if the company in question is a company which, in the ordinary course of its business, buys and sells land.

72 In practice, it may be noted that it is still common to register such a solicitor's letter of undertaking.

73 *Re Kum Tong Restaurant (Dublin) Ltd; Byrne v AIB Ltd* [1978] IR 446.

on trust for the bank and to hand over sufficient monies out of the proceeds of sale to redeem the bridging finance. Subsequently, an order was made to wind up the company, the sale being closed with the approval of the court, and the money placed on deposit, pending the direction of the court. The applicant, who was the liquidator to the company, claimed the money for the ordinary creditors, saying that the bank had a charge which was void for want of registration. McWilliam J rejected this contention, saying:

> 'I am satisfied that an equitable mortgage was created in favour of the bank. A difficulty arises as to what was mortgaged. In so far as a charge was created on the premises, it was void against the liquidator as it was not registered in accordance with the provisions of s 99 of the Companies Act 1963 but I have always understood that, as from the date of a contract for sale, the vendor's interest is converted into personalty, that in equity the lands are the purchaser's lands from the date of the contract, and that the vendor is only entitled to the purchase money with a lien on the lands for it. Section 99 of the Act of 1963 does not appear to require registration of a mortgage of the purchase price[74].'

In *Kum Tong*, the undertaking was found to constitute a charge which was not registrable as being a charge on land under s 99(2)(d) of the CA 1963 because it was a charge on the proceeds of sale of the company's land[75]. Although in that case, the charge was neither a charge on the company's book debts, it has been observed[76] that where a company is a property-investment company carrying on the business of buying and selling land, the creation of a charge on the proceeds of sale of the company's land might be registrable as constituting a charge on its book debts under s 99(2)(e) of the CA 1963. The undertaking in *Kum Tong* was distinguished from the undertaking given by a solicitor in *Murray v Wilken and Wilken*[77] which was to pay a specified sum out of the proceeds of the sale of a property when they were to hand. Finlay Geoghegan J said:

> 'The undertaking given in *Kum Tong* was an undertaking given when there was a contract for sale in place and included an undertaking 'to hold such documents of title ... in trust for the bank and to hand over sufficient monies out of the proceeds of sale ...'. Insofar as McWilliam J referred to a possible charge on the property, he did do in reliance upon the undertaking to hold the documents of title. The principal conclusion in the case related to the charge over the proceeds of sale which had come to hand ...'

(c) Liens

[19.024] Although liens confer proprietary rights they are not normally registrable under s 99 of the CA 1963. The reason for this is because, generally, they arise by operation of law[78]. Examples of liens include:

(i) Common law liens.

(ii) General liens: bankers' and solicitors' liens.

---

74 *Re Kum Tong Restaurant (Dublin) Ltd; Byrne v AIB Ltd* [1978] IR 446 at 448.

75 A similar conclusion was reached by Gilligan J in *Anglo Irish Bank Corporation plc v Edward Kavanagh Maynooth Ltd* [2003] IEHC 113.

76 See Ussher, *Company Law in Ireland* (1986), p 456.

77 *Murray v Wilken and Wilken* (31 July 2003, unreported) HC,Finlay Geoghegan J.

78 That liens are said to arise by operation of law is somewhat peculiar in that liens are properly classified as a kind of consensual security. In this respect the consensual nature can only be seen as deriving from the decision to first enter into a relationship which might give rise to the subsequent existence of a lien based on the nature of the relationship.

(iii) Equitable liens: purchasers' and unpaid vendors' liens.

(iv) Contractual liens.

(i) Common law liens

[19.025] A number of common law liens can be identified. They have their origins in the rule of law that merchants may retain customers' goods as security for payment for services rendered. As Bell[79] explains it, because innkeepers and common carriers were, in times' past, required by law to provide services to the public, this was balanced by the early recognition of liens over guests' belongings and goods carried. The list of situations in which common law liens will arise has, however, been established and is now fossilised. This explains why the list of situations giving rise to common law liens has 'an archaic flavour, and in part seems somewhat arbitrary'[80]. Common law liens include: the common carrier[81]; the sea carrier[82]; the innkeeper[83]; and the 'improver'[84]. None of these liens are registrable under s 99 of the CA 1963.

(ii) General liens: bankers' and solicitors' liens

[19.026] A general lien must be distinguished from a particular lien. Common law liens are examples of *particular* liens which entitle the lienee to retain goods as security for the services rendered in respect of those particular goods. By contrast a general lien allows the retention of goods as security until the lienee has been paid for past and present services rendered.

[19.027] One of the most common examples of a general lien is the bankers' lien[85]. A general banker's lien arises where securities are deposited with a bank unless there is an express or implied contract which is inconsistent with the lien, such as where title deeds are left with a bank for safe keeping[86]. Bankers' liens arose for consideration in the case of *Re Farm Fresh Frozen Foods Ltd*[87] where, in return for a cash advance from a bank, a company agreed to deposit title deeds with the bank, although the property was at the time already charged. When the company went into liquidation, the bank sought to rely on the general banker's lien. It was held by Keane J that there was no general banker's lien in that case, since it was negatived by the express intention of the parties to create an equitable mortgage. This was found to be the case, because the transaction amounted to

79 Bell, *Modern Law of Personal Property in England and Ireland* (1989), p 138.

80 Bell, *Modern Law of Personal Property in England and Ireland* (1989), p 139.

81 *George Barker (Transport) Ltd v Enyon* [1974] 1 WLR 462.

82 *Wolf v Sumners* (1811) 2 Camp 631.

83 This is now a statutory lien by reason of s 8 of the Hotel Proprietors Act 1963.

84 By 'improver' is meant someone who carries out work to goods. Bell, *Modern Law of Personal Property in England and Ireland* (1989), cites several examples as diverse as a mechanic who repairs a car, to accountants who draft ledgers and lawyers who work on documents.

85 See Breslin, *Banking Law* (2nd edn, 2007) at para 4-09–4-10.

86 *Brandao v Barnett* (1846) 12 Cl & Fin 787 at 806, cited with approval in *Re Farm Fresh Frozen Foods Ltd* [1980] ILRM 131 at 134. See generally, Hapgood, *Paget's Law of Banking* (1996), Ch 31.

87 *Re Farm Fresh Frozen Foods Ltd* [1980] ILRM 131.

an agreement to create an equitable mortgage which was void against the liquidator for want of registration[88].

[19.028] Solicitors' liens are another common form of general lien[89]. In *Re Galden Properties Ltd*[90], McCarthy J said:

> 'A solicitor holds a general or retaining lien; in that respects it differs from the ordinary lien derived from possession of the article to which there attaches a lien for payment of the charges in respect of that added value. A solicitor's lien attaches to all documents and other personal property in his possession as such solicitor and relates to all outstanding charges, as solicitor, not merely those in respect of the particular documents over which the lien is claimed. The lien entitles the solicitor to retain the documents, or the personal property, till payment of the full amount of the bill …'

A solicitor's lien over property extends only to costs incurred by the client against whom it is claimed. So a solicitor owed costs by certain companies was found to have no lien on the title deeds to premises owned by individuals even though the companies were wholly owned and controlled by those individuals[91]. A solicitor's lien cannot, however, arise in respect of title deeds where a solicitor is holding those deeds on accountable trust receipt[92].

(iii) Equitable liens: purchasers' and unpaid vendors' liens

[19.029] Equitable liens arise in circumstances where the lienee has no possession of the property the subject of the lien but where the rules of equity give rise to a lien on account of the parties' relationship. As Gough[93] has said, 'an equitable lien gives the creditor a proprietary interest, although there is no transfer of the beneficial ownership and although it exists as a security right independent of possession by contrast with a legal lien'. Neither a purchaser's lien nor an unpaid vendor's lien is registrable under s 99 of the CA 1963. Consequently, where a person enters into a contract to buy land from another, the purchaser has a lien (ie, a form of equitable charge) over the property in sale, to the extent of any deposit paid, which arises by operation of law. This is a purchaser's lien. Such a charge is not registrable by the purchaser against the vendor (where the vendor is a company). In addition, an unpaid vendor's lien, which entitles the vendor of property to a lien over the land in sale, to the extent of the outstanding purchase price, is also not registrable. Furthermore, where the vendor sells property to a

---

88 *Re Farm Fresh Frozen Foods Ltd* [1980] ILRM 131 at 136 where Keane J said: 'It follows that in the present case the documents of title came into the possession of the bank as equitable mortgagees and were not held by them at the relevant time on foot of any lien which survived the avoidance of the equitable mortgage for non-registration.'

89 See generally O'Callaghan, 'Safeguarding Solicitors' Fees' (1996) 3 CLP 167.

90 *Re Galden Properties Ltd* [1988] IR 213.

91 *Ring v Kennedy* [1999] 3 IR 316, (1997) ITLR 6 October 1997.

92 In *Re Galdan Properties Ltd* [1988] IR 213, McCarthy J rejected the argument that a solicitor's lien came into existence over title deeds in favour of a solicitor who held the deeds in question as a trustee for a bank (ie, on accountable trust receipt) because the solicitor's possession of the deeds was a highly qualified one which prevented the unilateral assertion of a solicitor's lien. See also the decision of Finnegan P in *Martin v Colfer and another* [2006] IEHC 124. *Cf Caldwell v Sumpters* [1972] Ch 478.

93 See Gough, *Company Charges* (2nd edn, 1996), p 501.

company, and a lending institution advances money to that company to buy the land in question, then by subrogation[94] the lending institution is entitled to the unpaid vendor's lien, to the extent of the advance made, over the property. Authority here is *Bank of Ireland Finance Ltd v DJ Daly Ltd*[95] where the plaintiff bank agreed to lend a sum of money to the defendant company to enable it to buy lands, secured by the defendant agreeing to deposit the title deeds to the property with the plaintiff bank as security for the loan. The sum was paid by the bank, and the defendant company paid almost all of that money over to the vendor of the property in question. In turn, the property was conveyed to the purchaser company, but the defendant company did not hand the deeds over, nor did it repay the loan to the bank. The plaintiff bank claimed, *inter alia*, that it was entitled by subrogation to the rights of the vendor of the property, ie, to the money paid over by the defendant company to the vendor which had been provided by the bank. McMahon J noted that Brightman J in *London Cheshire Co v Laplagrene Co*[96] had:

> '... held that an unpaid vendor's lien was the creature of the law; that it did not depend on contract but on the fact that the vendor had a right to a specific performance of his contract and that, accordingly, it was not registrable under s 95 of the Act of 1948. The learned judge pointed out that the provision in question had been in force since the Companies Act 1908, but no one had suggested that it was the practice for a vendor to register an unpaid vendor's lien when selling to a company. The lien is created on the formation of the contract of sale and the time for registration would expire twenty-one days thereafter. The lien is not discharged until the purchase money is paid on completion. If registration were necessary, every vendor selling to a company would be put to the inconvenience of having to register the unpaid vendor's lien as a matter of course on the off chance that circumstances might arise which would render it necessary for the vendor to rely on the unpaid vendor's lien. For the reasons of Brightman J I am satisfied that s 99 of the CA 1963 does not require registration of an unpaid vendor's lien arising on the purchase of property by a company[97].'

The bank was entitled to the unpaid vendor's lien by virtue of the doctrine of subrogation, and so had priority in the winding up. In *Highland Finance (Ireland) Ltd v Sacred Heart College, McEllin and Bank of Ireland*[98], the Supreme Court made clear that although it was settled law that a party who lends money to another to buy land is *prima facie* entitled by subrogation to the unpaid vendor's lien on the property for the amount of the advance, there were circumstances which might prevent or preclude the application of the doctrine of subrogation. In that case, it was found that subrogation was inconsistent with the parties' intentions and that justice and reason did not require that the doctrine be applied there.

[19.030] One particular form of purchaser's lien arises where a prospective purchaser pays a booking deposit in respect of the property which it is proposed to purchase.

---

94 Ie, the right to stand into the shoes of another and claim, as one's own, the rights which they enjoy. On the principles necessary for the right of *subrogation* to arise see *Highland Finance Ireland Ltd v Sacred Heart College of Agriculture Ltd* [1993] ILRM 260.

95 *Bank of Ireland Finance Ltd v DJ Daly Ltd* [1978] IR 79.

96 *London Cheshire Co v Laplagrene Co* [1971] Ch 499.

97 *Bank of Ireland Finance Ltd v DJ Daly Ltd* [1978] IR 79 at 84.

98 *Highland Finance (Ireland) Ltd v Sacred Heart College, McEllin and Bank of Ireland* [1997] 2 ILRM 87.

Again, such can amount to an equitable charge over the property which it is proposed to purchase, to the extent of the amount of the deposit. The case of *Re Barrett Apartments Ltd*[99] is instructive. In that case, putative purchasers paid booking deposits to a developer in respect of the apartments which they wished to buy following their construction. Subsequently, the developing company went into liquidation. The liquidator to the company alleged that the purchasers should only rank as unsecured creditors. However, the purchasers pointed out that in law they were entitled to a lien on the property. While the purchasers' contention was upheld in the High Court, the Supreme Court reversed the decision on the facts, holding that in the present case, there was no valid contract and that, consequently, there was no purchasers' lien.

(iv) Contractual liens

[19.031] Notwithstanding the central feature of a lien – namely, that it arises by operation of law – the general law recognises that liens can arise by virtue of express contract between parties. Such security interests are not registrable under s 99 of the CA 1963 for the simple reason that a lien is not a charge[100]; it is only a 'charge' (and by virtue of s 99(1)(a) of the CA 1963, a 'mortgage') that is registrable thereunder. In *Waitomo Wools (NZ) Ltd v Nelsons (NZ) Ltd*[101], Richmond J held that contractual liens are not registrable on the basis of the fundamental difference between a charge and a lien, namely that the latter relies exclusively on possession of the assets the subject matter of the security[102].

[19.032] In *Re Hamlet International plc (in administration)*[103], a freight forwarding and warehouse company (the applicant) sought leave to enforce its security under a general lien over stock held for and on behalf of two companies which were in administration. The applicant was owed over £1.8 million in respect of freight, warehousing and ancillary charges. The question which arose was whether the applicant's rights of lien coupled with its power of sale (granted under the British International Freight Association's and the Warehousing Association's conditions of sale) amounted to charges registrable under the former s 395 of the Companies Act 1985 (UK). The administrators of the two companies claimed that because of the contractual power of sale given to the applicant, the lien also given by those conditions was turned into a charge. It was held that the contractual right to retain possession and the right to sell did not operate to convert a lien to a charge. In the course of his judgment Eben Hamilton QC quoted from the last mentioned decision of Richmond J in *Waitomo Wools*:

---

99 *Re Barrett Apartments Ltd* (15 July 1983, unreported) HC, Keane J.

100 It is thought that the reference in s 44(1) of the C(A)A 1983 to 'a lien or other charge' cannot be taken as an indication that the legislature considers that a 'lien' was a 'charge'. Most likely there was a failure to distinguish their legal meaning and consequently treat them as synonymous. So, eg, the originally drafted s 5(2)(d) of the C(A)A 1990 appears to have assumed that mortgage, lien and pledge were included in the reference to 'charge'. Section 5(2)(d) was amended by s 14(b) of the C(A)(No 2)A 1999 and it now refers to 'mortgage, charge, lien or other encumbrance or a pledge of'.

101 *Waitomo Wools (NZ) Ltd v Nelsons (NZ) Ltd* [1974] 1 NZLR 484.

102 Cf *Re Wallis & Simmonds (Builders) Ltd* [1974] 1 All ER 561 at 573a–b, *per* Templeman J.

103 *Re Hamlet International plc (in administration)* [1998] 2 BCLC 164.

> '… I think that in its ordinary and generally accepted meaning the word 'charge' is apt only to describe a situation in which some particular property, real or personal, is appropriated or set aside in favour of someone who is given by law, or by agreement, will or otherwise, the right to resort to the property to satisfy or discharge some obligation … A charge involves some deduction from the right of ownership in the property rather than mere interference with the right to possession which is normally an incident of ownership. It is not a word which is apt to describe a purely possessory lien as opposed to a lien of a non-possessory nature such as an equitable lien … the most essential distinction [between legal possessory liens and any transaction which gives rise to a charge on the ordinary and accepted meaning of that word] is that a true possessory lien depends entirely on possession and is lost with the loss of possession. A charge, on the other hand, exists independent of possession and confers an interest in the property which carries with it a right to resort to the property (as opposed to merely detaining it) to satisfy or discharge some obligation secured by the charge'.

It was held that all that the applicant had was a contractual possessory lien. It was also considered significant that the goods in question were not delivered into the applicant's possession by way of security but in order that they could be distributed to the company's customers.

(d) Pledges

[19.033] Pledges of chattels given by companies are not registrable under s 99 of the CA 1963[104]; neither are genuine pledges of chattels given by individuals registrable under the Bills of Sale (Ireland) Acts 1879–1883[105].

(e) Trusts

[19.034] A trust created over assets belonging to a company where a charge is not created will not be registrable. So, for example, in *Associated Alloys Pty Ltd v Metropolitan Engineering & Fabrication Ltd*[106], considered below[107], it was held that a combined aggregation-proceeds of sale retention of title clause was found to be capable of being construed as a trust that is not required to be registered in order to be enforceable against a company's liquidator or creditors[108].

(f) Otherwise registrable charges provided as part of a financial collateral arrangement

[19.035] Directive 2002/47/EC of the European Parliament and of the Council of 6 June 2002 on financial collateral arrangements was intended to create an EU-wide regime for the provision of financial instruments and cash as collateral and where possession or

[104] *Highland Finance (Ireland) Ltd v Sacred Heart College, McEllin and Bank of Ireland* [1997] 2 ILRM 87.

[105] See Lord Esher MR's observations on the distinction between a pledge and a bill of sale in *Re Hardwick* (1886) 17 QBD 690 at 697, quoted in Ch 18, *Corporate Borrowing: Debentures and Security*, para **[18.026]**.

[106] *Associated Alloys Pty Ltd v Metropolitan Engineering & Fabrication Ltd* [1998] NSWSC 442 of 21 September 1998 (Supreme Court of New South Wales); [2000] HCA 25 of 11 May 2000 (High Court of Australia).

[107] See para **[19.047]**.

[108] See also, *Squires v AIG Europe (UK) Ltd* [2006] BCC 233.

control of the collateral passes to the collateral taker. The Directive has been implemented in Ireland by the European Communities (Financial Collateral Arrangements) Regulations 2010[109] (the 'EC(FCA)R 2010'). For present purposes, the Directive and the EC(FCA)R 2010 operate to exempt from the requirements of s 99(1), certain otherwise registrable charges (ie, charges that would otherwise be required to comply with that provision in order to be effective). The problem with the Directive and the EC(FCA)R 2010 is the lack of clarity around when an otherwise registrable charge created by an Irish company will be found not to be void under s 99(1) notwithstanding its non-registration despite being a charge of a kind described in s 99(2). Be warned, the Directive and the EC(FCA)R 2010 are ugly law.

[19.036] The operative provision which exempts certain otherwise registrable charges is reg 4(1) of EC(FCA)R 2010 which provides:

> 'Subject to paragraphs (2)[110] and (3)[111], the creation, validity, perfection, enforceability or admissibility in evidence of a financial collateral arrangement, or the provision of financial collateral under such an arrangement, does not depend on the performance of a formal act such as registration or notice to the debtor.'

Accordingly, 'formal act such as registration' for present purposes includes the delivery of particulars in relation to a registrable charge to the registrar of companies pursuant to s 99(1) of the CA 1963.

[19.037] Much of the difficulty with the exemption derives from the convoluted definition of '*financial collateral arrangement*' which is defined by reg 3(1) as meaning:

> '... a *title transfer financial collateral arrangement*[112] or a *security financial collateral* arrangement[113] (whether or not covered by a master agreement or by general terms and conditions).'

---

[109] SI 626/2010. The EC(FCA)R 2010 replaced the original European Communities (Financial Collateral Arrangements) Regulations 2004 (SI 1/2004).

[110] Regulation 4(2) provides that in the case of financial collateral that is or includes a credit claim, if, pursuant to the law of the State, the laws of another state would be applied to determine any of the matters referred to in paragraph (1) and, pursuant to the laws of that other state, that matter depends on the performance of a formal act such as registration or the giving of notice to the debtor, paragraph (1) does not affect the continued application of that requirement.

[111] Regulation 4(3) provides: paragraph (1) does not prejudice the application of these Regulations to financial collateral once that collateral has been provided if—(*a*) that provision is capable of being evidenced in writing, and (*b*) the relevant financial collateral arrangement is also capable of being evidenced in writing.

[112] Regulation 2(1) defines a *title transfer financial collateral arrangement* to mean: 'an arrangement under which a collateral provider transfers full ownership of, or full entitlement to, financial collateral to a collateral taker for the purpose of securing or otherwise covering the performance of relevant financial obligations, and includes a repurchase agreement.'

[113] Regulation 2(1) defines *security financial collateral arrangement* to mean: 'an arrangement under which a collateral provider provides financial collateral by way of security to or in favour of a collateral taker, and where the full or qualified ownership of, or full entitlement to, the financial collateral remains with the collateral provider when the security right is established.'

One clue as to what it is intended that the Directive is to cover is the reference to *financial collateral* in the definition of the two types of arrangement that can be a financial collateral arrangement. Unfortunately, the definition of *financial collateral* continues to be like peeling an onion (and is as likely to produce tears). Regulation 3(1) provides:

> '"financial collateral" means cash, financial instruments or credit claims provided under a financial collateral arrangement, but does not include shares in a company whose exclusive purpose is—
>
> (a) to own means of production that are essential for the collateral provider's business, or
>
> (b) to own real property.'

Accordingly, relevant charges are those over *cash* and certain types of *financial instruments*; 'financial instruments' are afforded a very extensive definition[114]. Therefore, where a charge is created by an Irish company over cash or the requisite type of financial instrument, then it will *not be registrable* provided the other conditions in the Directive and the EC(FCA)R 2010 are met.

[19.038] The EC(FCA)R 2010 only apply to charges given by persons who are '*collateral providers*' in favour of persons who are '*collateral takers*' and are primarily intended to legislate for complex financial arrangements between sophisticated parties. As one commentator has observed they '... provide that the provision of security for wholesale financial transactions – whether by outright transfer or charge – does not require any formal act of perfection to render the security effective'[115]. Whilst it is not disputed that this was the intention, it is thought that because of the way the regulations have been drafted, and in particular the meanings given in reg 4(2) to collateral providers and takers, it is possible for an 'ordinary company' to be a collateral provider and for an Irish bank to be a collateral taker in a humble commercial loan involving security over a bank account containing cash.

[19.039] The Directive and EC(FCA)R 2010 have not been considered by an Irish court and it seems that the first time the Directive and the similar UK regulations[116] were considered was in *Re F2G Realisations Ltd; Gray and another v GTP Group Ltd*[117]. In that case, the respondent entered into an agreement to provide debit card services to a company which sold floor coverings. The respondent collected payments by customers and deposited them into a trust account at a bank. Under a declaration of trust over the

---

114 Regulation 2(1) defines 'financial instruments' as meaning any of the following: (*a*) shares in companies; (*b*) securities equivalent to shares in companies; (*c*) bonds and other forms of debt instruments if negotiable on the capital market; (*d*) any securities (other than instruments referred to in subparagraphs (*a*) to (*c*)) that are normally dealt in and give the right to acquire any such shares, bonds or other securities by subscription, purchase or exchange; (*e*) any securities (other than instruments referred to in subparagraphs (*a*) to (*c*) and instruments of payment) that give rise to a cash settlement; (*f*) units in collective investment undertakings; (*g*) money market instruments; (*h*) claims relating to, or rights in or in respect of, shares, securities, bonds, and instruments of a kind referred to in subparagraphs (*a*) to (*d*);

115 Breslin, *Banking Law* (2nd edn, 2007, Thompson) at para 14-59.

116 UK's Financial Collateral Arrangements (No 2) Regulations 2003, SI 2003/3226.

117 *Re F2G Realisations Ltd; Gray and another v GTP Group Ltd* [2011] 1 BCLC 313.

account, the respondent agreed to transfer the balance in the account to the company without any deductions except for sums due to it in the event of the company defaulting on paying its fees or going into liquidation. When the company went into liquidation, the liquidators cancelled the debit card scheme and sought the transfer to them of *circa* £113,000; the respondent would only pay over £24,000 claiming to be entitled to the balance in respect of unpaid fees, loss of revenue and a termination fee. The liquidator' claimed that the trust constituted a registrable charge which was void for want of registration. The respondent company accepted that the trust was in fact a charge but argued (a) that it was a fixed charge and (b) that it was exempt from registration as a '*security financial collateral arrangement*' within the meaning of the Directive and the UK regulations. In response to the first question, Vos J in the English High Court held that the charge was a floating charge, not a fixed charge, since the respondent held the monies in the account on trust for the company which could draw them freely and the respondent was contractually bound to pay the monies over to the company on request, having no legal right to prevent payment being made when requested, until a default event occurred.

[19.040] In relation to the claim that the floating charge was not required to be registered by virtue of being a security financial collateral arrangement, Vos J held that the floating charge could not be regarded as falling within the definition of a 'security financial collateral arrangement' as provided for in the UK regulations. The UK regulations required the financial collateral to have been 'delivered, transferred, held, registered or otherwise designated so as to be in the possession or under the control of the collateral-taker or a person acting on its behalf' and Vos J found that the respondent did not have the requisite 'control' over the moneys in the account since until there was a default, the company was entitled to draw freely on them. It may be noted that although the definition of 'security financial collateral arrangement' in the EC(FCA)R 2010 appears to be different, in this respect it is the same because although it is defined to mean:

> 'an arrangement under which a collateral provider *provides financial collateral* by way of security in favour of, or to, a collateral taker, but only if the full ownership of the collateral remains with the collateral provider after the security right is established (emphasis added)'

the reference to '*provides financial collateral*' brings into play the definition of '*provision of financial collateral*' which reg 3(1) defines as meaning:

> 'the financial collateral that is or is to be delivered, transferred, held, registered or otherwise designated so as to be in the possession or under the control of the collateral taker or of a person acting on the collateral taker's behalf.'

Accordingly, the finding that control is required would be equally applicable in the interpretation of the EC(FCA)R 2010. In his decision, Vos J was highly influenced by Beale and others, *The Law of Personal Property Security*[118] where it was said:

> '10.29 ... We think the words 'possession or control' have to be interpreted in the light of Recital 10, which says that the Directive should apply only to arrangements that 'provide

[118] Beale, Bridge, Gllifer & Lomnicka, *The Law of Personal Property Security* (2007, Oxford University Press), Ch 10.

for some form of dispossession'. We consider that if the debtor retains the right to deal it is not 'dispossessed'. Therefore, a chargee who does not have negative control will not obtain the advantages of the [UK regulations]. This as we shall see has implications for floating charges over the financial collateral ...

10.48 Thus, it seems that the [UK regulations] will apply if a third party chargee under a floating charge has taken steps to crystallise the charge and has then notified the bank or other debtor of its assignment by way of (now) fixed charge; or has made some previous arrangement with the bank that on receipt of notification the bank will only pay money from the account on the directions of the chargee. When the chargee is the bank itself, it seems to suffest that the bank has blocked the account before the onset of insolvency[119].'

Vos J noted it had not been contended that the charge had crystallised prior to the onset of insolvency and rejected the contention that '*de facto*' or administrative control – which the respondent most likely had over the account – was sufficient, concluding that what the judge termed 'real legal control' was necessary.

[19.041] On the foregoing analysis, it would seem that floating charges over cash can never come within the Directive or the EC(FCA)R 2010 and where created by a company over any asset will always be registrable under s 99(1) CA 1963. Even where a floating charge crystallises and becomes a quasi-fixed charge, it would seem on the authority of Finlay Geoghegan J in *Re JD Brian Ltd*[120] that the resulting fixed charge might not be able to claim exemption under the Directive and the EC(FCA)R 2010 if it came into being on the back of an unregistered (and so void) floating charge[121].

Registrable charges

[19.042] Only those charges that are enumerated in s 99(2) of the CA 1963[122] are required by law to be registered. These 'registrable charges' are:

(a) Charges for the purpose of securing the issue of debentures.

(b) Charges on uncalled share capital of the company.

(c) Charges created or evidenced by an instrument which, if executed by an individual, would require registration as a bill of sale.

(d) Charges on land wherever situate, or any interest therein, but not including a charge for any rent or other periodical sum issuing out of land.

(e) Charges on book debts of the company.

(f) Floating charge.

(g) Charges on calls of shares.

(h) Charges on – or any shares in – a ship or aircraft.

(i) Charges on goodwill and other intellectual property.

It should be noted that s 99(10)(a) of the CA 1963 provides that 'charge' includes 'mortgage' for the purposes of Part IV of the CA 1963. It should also be remembered

---

119 Beale et al, *The Law of Personal Property Security* (2007, Oxford University Press) at paras 10.33 and 10.48.

120 *Re JD Brian Ltd* [2011] IEHC 113 and [2011] IEHC 383.

121 See Ch 18, *Corporate Borrowing: Debentures and Security*, at para **[18.094]**.

122 As amended by s 122 of the CA 1990.

that in order for a charge to be a registrable charge it must be created by the company. This feature of registrable charges is considered above[123].

[19.043] By virtue of s 99(2A) and (2B) of the CA 1963 the Minister for Jobs, Enterprise, and Innovation can, by statutory instrument, *add new* charges or remove or change the description of existing registrable charges. To date no order has been made under these provisions.

(a) Charges for the purpose of securing the issue of debentures

[19.044] This category of registrable charge is potentially very wide, since it could apply to any charge created which secures the issue of a single debenture. However, it has been held by the New Zealand Court of Appeal in *Automobile Association (Canterbury) Inc v Australasian Secured Deposits Ltd*[124] that the use of debentures in the plural, means that a charge securing the issue of a single debenture is not a registrable charge under this heading. Rather, this heading of registrable charge is only applicable to where a series of debentures are issued by a company, almost like an issue of shares. In Ireland, such a registrable charge may now be created by a private company following the amendment of s 33(1) of the CA 1963[125].

(b) Charges on uncalled share capital of the company

[19.045] The ambit of this category of registrable charge is confined to a charge on the shares in the chargor company itself. It has been identified as a noticeable gap in the legislation[126] that a company is not required to register charges which it creates over shares in a subsidiary company. Technically, this permits a company to transfer assets to a subsidiary and to then create a charge over the shares that it holds in the subsidiary, without having to register the charge in the CRO. In practice, this does not give rise to great abuses because charges on shares in Irish private companies are not a preferred form of security.

(c) Charges created or evidenced by an instrument which, if executed by an individual, would require registration as a bill of sale

[19.046] The inclusion in the Companies Acts of the requirement that certain charges must be registered to be enforceable, was not an original idea. Certain documents created by individuals in respect of their personal chattels were required to be registered under the Bills of Sale (Ireland) Acts 1879–1883[127]. Section 99(2)(c) of CA 1963 requires the registration of charges created or evidenced by an instrument which, if executed by an individual, would require registration as a bill of sale. The Bills of Sale

---

123 See para **[19.022]**.

124 *Automobile Association (Canterbury) Inc v Australasian Secured Deposits Ltd* [1973] 1 NZLR 417.

125 See s 99(8) of the CA 1963 which makes provision for registration of the issue of a series of debentures. See Ch 18, *corporate Borrowing: Debentures and Security*, at para **[18.021]**.

126 See *Fitzgerald*, (1968) Ir Jur 258; *McCormack*, (1984) ILT 67; and Ussher, *Company Law in Ireland* (1986), p 457.

127 See Maguire, 'The Bill of Sale: The Forgotten Relation' (1997) 4 CLP 3 for a thorough analysis of the provisions of the Bills of Sale (Ireland) Act 1879 and Bills of Sale (Ireland) Act (1879) Amendment Act 1883.

(Ireland) Act 1879 (the '1879 Act') and the Bills of Sale (Ireland) Act (1879) Amendment Act 1883 (the '1883 Act') were enacted with different purposes in mind. In *Manchester, Sheffield and Lincolnshire Railway Co v North Central Wagon Co*[128], Lord Herschell distinguished the different purposes behind the 1879 Act and the 1883 Act. Of the English Act, equivalent to the Irish 1879 Act, he said it was intended:

> '… for the protection of creditors, and to prevent their rights being affected by secret assurances of chattels which were permitted to remain in the ostensible possession of a person who had parted with his property in them. The bills were therefore made void only as against creditors or their representatives. As between the parties to them they were perfectly valid[129].'

And of the English Act, equivalent to the Irish 1883 Act, he said it was designed:

> '… to prevent needy persons being entrapped into signing complicated documents which they might often be unable to comprehend, and so being subjected by their creditors to the enforcement of harsh and unreasonable provisions.'

The Bills of Sale Acts' provisions on security bills do not apply directly to companies[130]; neither do the Acts apply, in toto, indirectly to companies. Rather, it is the case that where a company creates a 'charge' over 'personal chattels', that charge will be registrable if the charge amounts to a 'bill of sale' which, if created by an individual, would be registrable under the 1879–1883 Acts.

(i) The meaning of 'bill of sale' and the necessity for it to operate as a charge

[19.047] A bill of sale[131] is a document which transfers the property in goods from one person to another but permits the property to remain in the possession of the person

128 *Manchester, Sheffield and Lincolnshire Railway Co v North Central Wagon Co* (1888) 13 App Cas 554.

129 *Manchester, Sheffield and Lincolnshire Railway Co v North Central Wagon Co* (1888) 13 App Cas 554 at 560. In *Somers v Allen* [1984] ILRM 437, Carroll J said of the Bills of Sale (Ireland) Act 1879 that: 'The purpose of the Act was to prevent the owner of chattels defeating the claims of his creditors by making or giving a Bill of Sale which would entitle the holder or grantee to seize or take possession of chattels where those chattels remained in the possession or apparent possession of the giver.'

130 Section 17 of the Bills of Sale (Ireland) Act (1879) Amendment Act 1883 provides: 'Nothing in this Act shall apply to any debentures issued by any mortgage, loan, or other incorporated company, and secured upon the capital stock or goods, chattels, and effects of such company.' In *Re Standard Manufacturing Company* [1891] 1 Ch 627, it was held that the legislature could not have intended the Bills of Sale Act 1878 (UK) to apply to charges created by companies since registration of charges by such companies was governed by the Companies Clauses Acts 1845 and 1862. This was followed in Ireland in *Re Royal Marine Hotel Company Kingstown Ltd* [1895] 1 IR 368 and has been recently reaffirmed by the English Court of Appeal in *Online Catering Ltd v Acton* [2010] EWCA 58.

131 Section 4 of the Bills of Sale (Ireland) Act 1879 provides that: '… the expression "bill of sale" shall include bills of sale, assignments, transfers, declarations of trust without transfer, inventories of goods with receipt thereto attached, or receipts for purchase moneys of goods, and other assurances of personal chattels, and also powers of attorney, authorities or licences to take possession of personal chattels as security for any debt, and also any agreement, whether intended or not to be followed by the execution of any other instruments, by which a right in equity to any personal chattels or to any charge or security thereon shall be conferred, but shall not include the following documents: (contd.../)

transferring the goods. There are two types of bill of sale: security bills (given to secure the payment of money) and absolute bills (given other than to secure the payment of money). The 1879 Act applies to both security bills and absolute bills; the 1883 Act applies exclusively to security bills.

[19.048] In order for a charge to be registrable as a bill of sale under s 99(2)(c) of the CA 1963 it is necessary that it be a security bill – ie, in the nature of a charge to secure the repayment of money[132]. Accordingly, an absolute bill created by a company is not registrable under s 99(2)(c) because that subsection makes express reference to 'charges' created or evidenced by an instrument which if executed by an individual would require registration as a bill of sale. The usual authority cited is *Stoneleigh Finance Ltd v Phillips*[133] where Russell LJ said[134] of the English equivalent of s 99(2)(c) that:

> 'I would say at the outset that it is clear that this section has no application to a transaction unless it is one which operates to charge property as security for the payment of money ... it is not sufficient under s 99(2)(c) to find an instrument which if executed by an individual would require registration as a bill of sale; it is necessary also to find a charge. It is however what is in fact a charge in form an absolute assignment or by otherwise adopting a form which does not accord with the real transaction between the parties.'

That particular case concerned a hire-purchase agreement which, it was held, did not require to be registered under s 99(2)(c) and so was valid against the company's liquidator.

[19.049] Whilst it is a requirement that a bill of sale must operate to *charge* property, it is sufficient that it operates to *mortgage* property because s 99(10)(a) of the CA 1963 states clearly that for the purposes of Part IV 'charge' includes mortgage. However, these terms will on account of their long-established meaning be strictly construed and a *lien* or a *pledge* in respect of personal chattels will not be registrable under this (or any other)[135] head of charge[136].

(ii) Personal chattels defined

[19.050] The Bills of Sale Acts do not apply to all assets; they are exclusively concerned with *personal chattels*. Section 4 of the 1883 Act defines 'personal chattels' to mean:

---

131 (\...contd) that is to say, assignments for the benefit of the creditors of the person making or giving the same, marriage settlements, transfers or assignments of any ship or vessel or any share thereof, transfers of goods in the ordinary course of business or any trade or calling, bills of sale of goods in foreign parts or at sea, bills of lading, India warrants, warehouse-keepers certificates, warrants or orders for the delivery of goods, or any other documents used in the ordinary course of business as proof of the possession or control of goods, or authorising or purporting to authorise, either by indorsement or by delivery, the possessor of such documents to transfer or receive goods thereby repossessed.'

132 See Keane, *Company Law* (4th edn, 2007), para [21.15].

133 *Stoneleigh Finance Ltd v Phillips* [1965] 1 All ER 513.

134 *Stoneleigh Finance Ltd v Phillips* [1965] 1 All ER 513 at 525.

135 See para **[19.024]**.

136 On why liens, for example, do not come within s 99(2)(c), see *Waitomo Wools (NZ) Ltd v Nelsons (NZ) Ltd* [1974] 1 NZLR 484.

> 'goods, furniture, and other articles capable of complete transfer by delivery, and (when separately assigned or charged) fixtures and growing crops, *but shall not include* chattel interests in real estate, nor fixtures (except trade machinery as hereinafter defined), when assigned together with a freehold or leasehold interest in the land on which they grow, nor shares or interests in the stock, funds, or securities of any government, or in the capital or property of incorporated or joint stock companies, nor choses in action, nor any stock or produce upon any farm or lands which by virtue of any covenant or agreement or of the custom of the country ought not to be removed from any farm where the same are at the time of making or giving of such bill of sale.' [Emphasis added.]

Whilst stock and farm produce are excluded from the definition of *personal chattels* for the purposes of the Bills of Sale Acts, the registration of charges over such chattels (whether created by individuals or by companies) is regulated by the Agricultural Credit Act 1978. In *Somers v Allen*[137], Carroll J said of the 1879 Act that:

> 'The Act applies to Bills of Sale of personal chattels, whether absolute or subject to a trust, whereby the holder or grantee has power, with or without notice, either immediately or at any future time, to take possession of such chattels. There must be a maker or giver of the Bill of Sale and a holder or grantee of the Bill[138].'

That case concerned the issue of whether or not a particular retention of title clause was required to be registered under s 99(1) of the CA 1963 and in particular whether the clause was in fact a charge of the type described in s 99(2)(c) of the CA 1963. There, soya bean meal was sold to a company, subject to a so-called 'simple retention of title clause'[139]. The goods sold to the company were still identifiable, and it was held that the clause was not complex enough to create a charge over the goods in question. Accordingly, it was held that the clause was not an instrument which, if executed by an individual, would require registration as a bill of sale. The reason why the retention of title clause did not create a registrable charge was because the company did not, and could not, create[140] any charge because the clause did not permit the property in the goods to pass to the company.

(iii) Charges liable to be registered under this head

[19.051] It follows that where a company creates a charge in respect of personal chattels to which it holds title, then if an individual would be required to register such a charge under the Bills of Sale Acts, so too will the company under s 99(2)(c) of the CA 1963. Although retention of title clauses commonly fall to be registered under this head of charge, they are but one example of the sort of transaction caught. Also capable of being deemed registrable charges of the sort described by s 99(2)(c) are conditional sale agreements. Such an agreement is where a company is sold goods on the terms that it buys goods but charges them back to the vendor until the purchase monies in whole or in part have been paid. If there is a genuine sale or hiring transaction, or otherwise if there is no charge involved, then registration will not be required. Section 4 of the 1879 Act

---

137 *Somers v Allen* [1984] ILRM 437.

138 *Somers v Allen* [1984] ILRM 437 at 441.

139 See para **[19.071]** *et seq, post.*

140 For a charge to be a registrable charge it must have been *created* by a company: see para **[19.022]** *ante.*

provides that transfers of goods in the ordinary course of business are expressly excluded from being registrable charges under that legislation. Thus, it follows that in the case of a company, such transfers are also exempt from registration[141]. Although it has been argued in relation to retention of title clauses that, as their usage became more common, the basis upon which they were registrable as charges would collapse[142], nearly 20 years on from that observation, there has still been no suggestion of judicial acceptance. Indeed, if anything, the courts of Ireland and England – motivated by the perceived equity of *pari passu* amongst unsecured creditors and the preferential status of the Revenue Commissioners – are more likely to find retention of title clauses void against liquidators for being unregistered charges.

(d) Charges on land[143]

[19.052] The most popular (and by many considered the best) form of security is a first legal mortgage or a fixed charge over real property because, usually, land can be easily disposed of should the mortgagee or chargee wish to realise his security. A company which owns real property can create a mortgage or charge over its land in several ways[144]. In the case of registered land it can create a formal registered charge or an informal charge; in the case of unregistered land it can create a legal or equitable mortgage. In addition, a company may create a floating charge in respect of either registered or unregistered land[145]. All mortgages and charges over land, whether fixed or floating, legal or equitable and with or without the creation of a document, must be registered under s 99(2)(d) of the CA 1963. So too will an undertaking to create a mortgage or charge over land be registrable as such is itself an equitable charge[146].

[19.053] While it is beyond the scope of this book to consider in any detail the means by which a mortgage or charge over land can arise, the creation of charges over land is summarised in the next paragraph. Since the last edition of this book, significant changes to the law relating to the creation of legal mortgages over land have been brought about by the Land and Conveyancing Law Reform Act 2009 ('LCLRA 2009')[147]. The primary change is that all mortgages over land, whether the land be registered or unregistered, must be created by a charge only: no longer can a mortgage

---

141 See Green, *A Manual of the Law Relating to Bills of Sale in Ireland* (1882), p 129; Pearce, *The Bills of Sale Acts* (14th edn, 1926), pp 77–80.

142 See Ussher, *Company Law in Ireland* (1986), p 462; Farrar & Furey, (1976) CLJ 27; and the words of Lord Summer in *Dublin City Distillery Ltd v Doherty* [1914] AC 823 at 867 that from the Bills of Sale legislation: '... it is plain that the legislature intended to save certain documents, already known in commerce, and others which, by the usage of business, might come into existence notoriously and for the same or similar purposes'.

143 See Keane, *Company Law* (4th edn, Bloomsbury Professional, 2007), paras [21.18]–[21.26].

144 For the various means by which one can charge or mortgage real property, see Wylie, *Irish Land Law* (4th edn, Bloomsbury Professional, 2010), pp 745–884. See also Ch 18, *Corporate Borrowing: Debentures and Security*, para **[18.032]**.

145 See Ch 18, *Corporate Borrowing: Debentures and Security,* para **[18.068]**.

146 *Re Valley Ice Cream (Ireland) Ltd* (22 July 1998, unreported) HC, McCracken J and *Fullerton v Provincial Bank of Ireland* [1903] 1 IR 483.

147 See, generally, Wylie, *Irish Land Law* (4th edn, Bloomsbury Professional, 2010) at chs 12 and 13.

be created by conveyance or assignment[148]. The registration procedures are, however, different for registered and unregistered land.

[19.054] Charges of unregistered land should be registered pursuant to the Registration of Deeds and Title Act 2006 ('RDTA 2006'). Registration is effected by the completion and delivery of the prescribed form (a *Form 3*) to the Registry of Deeds which is under the management and control of the Property Registration Authority. Registration of the charge is required if the charge is to have priority. In the case of a legal mortgage of unregistered land, although such registration is not compulsory, the failure to register will mean that the mortgagee will lose priority. So, s 38(1) of the RDTA 2006 provides that deeds registered under Part 3 of that Act:

> 'are deemed and taken as good and effectual both in law and equity according to the priority determined by the serial numbers allocated to them pursuant to s 37 of that Act and shall, as regards any right, title, interest or liability arising from their execution, rank in priority among themselves according to the priority determined by the serial numbers so allocated.'

Moreover, by s 38(2) of the RDTA 2006, a deed which is not so registered is void against a registered deed affecting the land concerned. However, the foregoing priorities only apply to mortgages created by deed and an equitable mortgage by deposit of title deeds to unregistered land will be *unregistrable* unless a memorandum of equitable deposit is signed (whether by the chargor or chargee) so that an agreement to create a mortgage is registrable[149].

[19.055] Charges of registered land should be registered in the Land Registry under the Registration of Title Act 1964 as a burden of the mortgagor's folio. Since 1 March 2012, where a charge securing a specific amount is created on registered land, a Land Registry *Form 115* must be sent to the Land Registry; a *Form 114* is used for all sums charges securing present and future advances. The actual deed of charge is not filed in the Land Registry, however, only the form which is an abbreviated version or extract of the charge. The reason for registering a charge on registered land is to ensure that the chargee has priority over subsequent encumbrancers. Section 62 of the Registration of Title Act 1964 provides that:

> '... the instrument of charge shall operate as a mortgage by deed within the meaning of the Conveyancing Acts, and the registered owner of the charge shall, for the purpose of enforcing his charge, have all the rights and powers of a mortgagee under a mortgage by deed, including the power to sell the estate or interest which is subject of the charge.'

A fixed legal charge of land must be registered as a burden on the folio in the Land Registry. In the case of a floating charge, the predominant view is[150] that it cannot be registered as a burden, and so the holder of a floating charge can only enter a *caution* on

---

148 Section 89(1) of the LCLR 2009 provides: 'A legal mortgage of land may only be created by a charge by deed ...' By sub-s (2), any instrument which conveys a legal estate or interest in land by way of mortgage, etc, does not create a legal mortgage.

149 *Eyre v McDowell* (1861) 9 HL Cas 619.

150 See Keane, *Company Law* (4th edn, Bloomsbury Professional, 2007), para [21.30]. See also McAllister, *Registration of Title in Ireland* (1973), pp 191–192 and Fitzgerald, *Land Registry Practice* (1989), p 128.

the folio[151]. Upon its crystallisation a floating charge may be registered as a burden being a quasi-fixed charge[152]. Before a receiver exercises his powers under a debenture creating a floating charge, he should register the new quasi-fixed charge as a burden[153]. It is no longer possible for a chargor company to create an informal charge by depositing the land certificate to Irish lands with the chargee by reason of s 73 of the RDTA 2006[154].

[19.056] In all cases where a mortgage or charge is created over land by an Irish company the mortgage or charge must be registered under s 99(2) of the CA 1963. This is the case wherever the land is situate, even if outside the State, if created by an Irish company, it is registrable; although a charge on land for rent or other periodic sum issuing out of land is not registrable[155].

[19.057] Where a company does not create a charge, but acquires property which is already subject to a charge, s 101(1) of the CA 1963 provides:

> 'Where a company acquires any property which is subject to a charge of any such kind as would, if it had been created after the acquisition of the property, would have been required to be registered under this Part, the company shall cause the prescribed particulars of the charge, verified in the prescribed manner, to be delivered to the Registrar of Companies for registration in manner required by this Act within twenty-one days after the date on which the acquisition is completed ...'

Where such a charge is not registered its fate is akin to that of an unregistered judgment mortgage: an offence will have been committed, but the charge is not void. The sanction is again a class C fine by virtue of s 101(2) of the CA 1963[156]. As Gough says, because of this, there is a temptation for a creditor to claim that a charge is registrable under s 101 of the CA 1963 and not s 99 of the CA 1963, a claim 'which is particularly strong where a company purchases property using funds borrowed for the purpose either from the vendor himself or from a third party'[157]. The authorities[158] suggest that a charge will be registrable under s 101 and not s 99 where the vendor of land directly transfers that land to the chargee lender, as otherwise, the charge will normally arise out of an act of creation by the company.

[19.058] It may also be noted that s 99(7) of the CA 1963 states that the holding of debentures which entitles the holder of the debenture to a charge on land shall not be deemed to be an interest in land. It is thought that this relates to a series of debentures and not to one debenture which creates a charge.

---

151 Rules 131–145 of the Land Registration Rules 1972 (SI 230/1972).

152 Rule 4 of the Land Registration Rules 1986 (SI 310/1986).

153 *Re Mono Food Equipment Ltd* (21 May 1986, unreported) HC, Flood J.

154 See Ch 18, *Corporate Borrowing: Debentures and Security,* at para **[18.033]**.

155 Moreover, s 108 of the CA 1963 deems that s 10(1)(d) of the C(A)A 1907 and s 93(1) of the C(C)A 1908 never applied to a charge for any rent or other periodical sum issuing out of land.

156 As increased by s 15 of the C(A)A 1982.

157 See Gough, *Company Charges* (1978), p 230.

158 *Re Connolly Bros (No 2)* [1912] 2 Ch 25; *Church of England Building Society v Piskor* [1954] 1 Ch 553, [1954] 2 All ER 85; *Capital Finance Co Ltd v Stokes* [1968] 1 All ER 573, [1968] 3 All ER 625.

(e) Charges on book debts of the company

[19.059] As was considered in Ch 18, *Corporate Borrowing: Debentures and Security*, it is quite common for a company to create a charge over its book debts, whether present or future[159]. As was also seen, charges on book debts may be the subject of either a fixed or a floating charge. Book debts have been defined by Palmer[160] as:

> '... debts owing to the company concerned with and arising out of the company's trade or business, which are entered, or commonly would be entered in the ordinary course of business, in well kept books of such a trade or business.'

In *Response Engineering Ltd v Caherconlish Treatment Plant Ltd*[161], Hogan J provided one of the simple, yet powerfully incisive definitions:

> 'There is no doubt but that the phrase 'book debts' has, to the modern ear, something of a musty feel to it. The phase conjures up images of Victorian bookkeeping and ledger entries, the tales in relation to which form many a sub-plot of the great novels of Dickens and Trollope. Yet the term refers to no more than future income which will accrue to the company by reason of the provision of goods and services to third parties by that company in the course of its trade or business.'

In *Paul & Frank Ltd v Discount Bank (Overseas) Ltd*[162], Pennycuick J said that the test for whether something was a book debt was 'is it the practice to enter the debts in question in the ordinary course of business' in the company's books. In that case, the benefit of a contract was held not to be a book debt[163]. Where a company makes an assignment of a book debt for the purpose of securing a loan made to that company it will create a charge which is registrable under s 99(2)(e) of the CA 1963.

[19.060] A book debt is, however, more easily defined than its definition is applied to a given set of facts. In *Re Brian Tucker Ltd; Farrell v Equity Bank Ltd*[164], a company sought a cash advance from a bank to enable it to pay its insurance brokers the premiums due in respect of the company's insurance policies. This was advanced to the company and the company signed an irrevocable letter of authority to its brokers, authorising the brokers to pay over to the bank any monies received by the brokers on foot of such policies pending the repayment of the advance to the bank. It was expressly agreed that if the company was wound up, the bank could terminate the policies of insurance and take such part of the premium as may be refunded by the insurance

---

159 See *Re Keenan Brothers Ltd* [1985] IR 401; *Siebe Gorman & Co Ltd v Barclays Bank Ltd* [1979] 2 Lloyds Rep 142; *Re Wogan's (Drogheda) Ltd* [1993] 1 IR 157; *Re Holidair* [1994] 1 ILRM 481. See generally, Ch 18, *Corporate Borrowing: Debentures and Security*, at para **[18.045]** *et seq*. See also Johnston, *Banking and Security Law in Ireland* (1998), p 575.

160 Schmitthoff (ed), *Palmer's Company Law* (24th edn, 1987), p 739, referred to by Lynch J in *Re Brian Tucker Ltd* [1990] 2 IR 549. There, Lynch J cited the definition in *Halsbury's Laws of England* (4th edn) Vol 3, para 376, fn 2 and para 525, fn 4.

161 *Response Engineering Ltd v Caherconlish Treatment Plant Ltd* [2011] IEHC 345.

162 *Paul & Frank Ltd v Discount Bank (Overseas) Ltd* [1966] 2 All ER 922.

163 In *Northern Bank v Ross* [1991] BCLC 504, cash at a bank was held *not* to be a book debt; in *Re Brian Tucker Ltd* [1990] 2 IR 549, refunds of insurance premiums were held *not* to be a book debt; in *Re Kum Tong Restaurants (Dublin) Ltd* [1978] IR 446, the proceeds of the sale of land were held *not* to be a book debt.

164 *Re Brian Tucker Ltd* [1990] 2 IR 549.

company. The company went into liquidation and the liquidator claimed, *inter alia*, that there was no charge in favour of the bank, and in the alternative, that if there was a charge, it was void for want of registration as a book debt under s 99(2)(e) of the CA 1963. Lynch J cited the case of *Paul & Frank Ltd v Discount Bank (Overseas) Ltd*[165] and quoted Pennycuick J who said:

> 'It seems to me that, in order to ascertain whether any particular charge is a charge on book debts within the meaning of the section, one must look at the items of property which form the subject-matter of the charge at the date of its creation and consider whether any of those items is a book debt. In the case of an existing item of property, this question can only be answered by reference to its character at the date of creation. Where the item of property is the benefit of a contract and at the date of the charge the benefit of the contract does not comprehend any book debt, I do not see how that contract can be brought within the section as being a book debt merely by reason that the contract may ultimately result in a book debt[166].'

Lynch J accepted this view of the law, saying:

> 'The mere possibility that future refunds of premiums might become payable in amounts that were wholly unascertainable and might never arise at the date of the creation of the charge does not make that transaction a book debt which must be registered pursuant to s 99 of the 1963 Act[167].'

This does not mean that a future debt will not be registrable as a book debt, since, although it is unascertained it is the case that it will almost invariably arise after the creation of the charge.

[19.061] In *Response Engineering Ltd v Caherconlish Treatment Plant Ltd*[168], Hogan J was required to consider whether a solicitor's undertaking regarding future payments to be made to his client company constituted a charge over book debts within the meaning of s 99(2)(e) of the CA 1963. In that case, the plaintiff had obtained judgment against the defendant for over €225,000 plus costs; the defendant was in turn owed some €220,000 by Limerick County Council. The plaintiff obtained a conditional order of garnishee in respect of the €220,000 owed to the defendant but the defendant's bank, AIB, objected to the conditional order being made absolute, claiming that it had priority to the €220,000 on foot of an undertaking given to it by the defendant's solicitor. The defendant's solicitor explained that when practical completion of the works was carried out by the defendant for Limerick County Council, the Council would make the final payment to it of €220,000, before going on to say:

> '... my client, Caherconlish Treatment Plant Limited, require an overdraft facility in the amount of €305,000 and the same will be discharged in two payments ... as soon as the said payments come in from Limerick County Council I confirm that I have irrevocable instructions to lodge the said cheques to the [defendant's] account with AIB and I hereby undertake to do so.'

Hogan J noted that the undertaking had been given first in time and that, absent the question of whether particulars of the undertaking ought to have been delivered to the

---

165 *Paul & Frank Ltd v Discount Bank (Overseas) Ltd* [1966] 2 All ER 922.

166 *Paul & Frank Ltd v Discount Bank (Overseas) Ltd* [1966] 2 All ER 922 at 926.

167 *Re Brian Tucker Ltd* [1990] 2 IR 549 at 554.

168 *Response Engineering Ltd v Caherconlish Treatment Plant Ltd* [2011] IEHC 345.

registrar of companies, the undertaking would have priority ahead of the plaintiff's claim. In considering whether the sum owed by the County Council was a 'book debt', Hogan J distinguished the decision in *Re Brian Tucker Ltd; Farrell v Equity Bank Ltd*,[169] considered above[170], and the decision of McWilliam J in *Byrne v Allied Irish Banks Ltd*[171], and found that such a payment as was owed by the County Council '*classically amounts to a book debt within the meaning of this subsection*'[172].

[19.062] The essential trait which will give rise to a registrable charge on book debts is that the assignment of the book debts is intended to secure the repayment of a loan. The authorities on the question of whether or not a particular transaction will be deemed to be a charge on book debts show that each case must be viewed on its own particular facts. So in *Kent v Sussex Sawmills Ltd*[173] it was held that where a company obtained a loan from a bank secured by the company writing to a government department, authorising that department to pay moneys owed to the company due under a contract into the company's account at the bank, no outright assignment was intended. Rather, the letter from the company amounted to an equitable assignment by way of security and constituted a charge on the company's book debts. That charge was further found to be void for want of registration under the equivalent of s 99(2)(e) of the CA 1963[174]. This decision was cited with approval by Hogan J in *Response Engineering Ltd v Caherconlish Treatment Plant Ltd*[175], the facts of which have been considered above[176], when, after finding that the payment in respect of which the undertaking had been given was a book debt, the learned judge went on to consider whether the undertaking created a security interest by being an assignment by way of security or an absolute assignment. In this regard, Hogan J noted that in *Re Siebe Gorman Ltd*[177] a letter to a company's bankers irrevocably directing them to pay the proceeds of bills of exchange to a person was found to constitute an effective assignment of a debt and not a security interest. However, the learned judge found the solicitor's undertaking in this case to have been given by way of security. He said:

> '22. It is true that in the present case the undertaking was given in consideration of the provision of additional credit facilities and to that extent the present case roughly parallels the decision in *Siebe Gorman*, albeit that – and this is not an unimportant consideration in view of a working presumption which I will shortly mention – the assignment in the latter case was to a trading company and not to a bank. The real question, however, is whether the Council's debt had been effectively sold to AIB by way of assignment via the solicitor's undertaking or, alternatively, whether Caherconlish retained an equity of

[169] *Re Brian Tucker Ltd; Farrell v Equity Bank Ltd* [1990] 2 IR 549.

[170] See para **[19.060]** *ante*.

[171] *Byrne v Allied Irish Banks Ltd* [1978] IR 446.

[172] *Response Engineering Ltd v Caherconlish Treatment Plant Ltd* [2011] IEHC 345 at para 13 of the judgment.

[173] *Kent v Sussex Sawmills Ltd* [1946] All ER 638.

[174] Note that in *Re Welsh Irish Ferries Ltd* [1985] BCLC 327 it was held that a lien on sub-freights created by a company pursuant to a time charter in favour of a shipowner was registrable under the equivalent of s 99(2)(e) of the CA 1963.

[175] *Response Engineering Ltd v Caherconlish Treatment Plant Ltd* [2011] IEHC 345.

[176] See para **[19.061]** *ante*.

[177] *Re Siebe Gorman Ltd* [1979] 2 Lloyd's Reports 142.

> redemption in these moneys in (admittedly unlikely) event that the AIB debt were to be discharged, in whole or in part. I use the term 'effectively sold' advisedly, because in deference to the views expressed by Slade J in *Siebe Gorman* ([1979] 2 Lloyds's Law Reports 142 at 161), I would regard an assignment of debt for consideration (ie, the provision of credit facilities by either a trade creditor or a bank) as being tantamount to a sale, even if no formal purchase price is stipulated.
>
> 23. Given the presumption which must obtain in the ordinary banker/client relationship that the client enjoys the equity of redemption, absent a clear indication to the contrary, in my view, unlike the situation which was found to prevail on the facts in *Siebe Gorman*, that working presumption has not been displaced in the present case. It is true that Mr Potter's undertaking stated that he had 'irrevocable instructions to lodge the said cheques to Caherconlish Treatment Plant's account with AIB'. But this is in itself is not inconsistent with an equity of redemption. Nor do these words in themselves imply that the debt has actually been effectively sold by way of assignment in consideration of the extension of the overdraft facilities.
>
> 24. Again, if we test this proposition in the same manner as in *Kent Sawmills* and we must then ask ourselves what the situation would have been, if – *mirabile dictu* – the Caherconclish account had otherwise come into surplus. That question effectively answers itself. Even if Mr Potter's undertaking still applied in those unlikely but happy circumstances, all it meant was that the payment cheque from the Council had to be lodged in the company's account. It did not mean that these monies had thereby somehow become the property of the bank by way of windfall since there had, in fact, been no effective sale or assignment or the Council's payment to bank in return for the credit facilities. Putting this another way, the evidence coerces me to the view that the bank wanted security for its debt and it was not, in this instance at least, in the business of effectively purchasing the debt by providing additional overdraft facilities to Caherconlish.
>
> 25. For these reasons, I am of the view that the solicitor's undertaking was by way of security and not assignment. I will accordingly declare that the undertaking is void as against any creditor of the company for want of the registration of the security over the book debts of the company in the manner required by s 99(2)(e) of the 1963 Act.'

[19.063] In *Re Kum Tong Restaurants (Dublin) Ltd; Byrne v Allied Irish Banks Ltd*[178], a company, in the process of selling its premises, obtained a loan from the defendant bank to enable it to continue in business pending the sale. The company undertook:

> '… to hold such documents of title … in trust for the bank and to hand over sufficient monies out of the proceeds of the sale to redeem this bridging finance as soon as the sale is closed ...'

Subsequently, the company was wound up and the sale of its premises closed with court approval. The liquidator applied to the court to have the undertaking of the company set aside on the basis that it constituted a charge on the company's book debts which was void for want of registration under s 99(2)(e) of the CA 1963. It was held by McWilliam J that the proceeds of sale were indeed charged to the bank, but were not a book debt within the meaning of the section and so the order was made in favour of the bank. The reason for McWilliam J's decision was that upon the company contracting to

[178] *Re Kum Tong Restaurants (Dublin) Ltd; Byrne v Allied Irish Banks Ltd* [1978] IR 446.

sell its premises, its interest was not in the property but in the purchase money to be paid to it on completion.

[19.064] In *Re Interview Ltd*[179], an Irish company contracted with a German company to buy goods from the German company. The contract provided that the Irish company would assign to the German company any claims which it might have against persons to whom it sold the goods. Kenny J said:

> 'The first question is whether the clause ... created an absolute assignment (in which event it would not require registration) or was an assignment by way of security. I think it was an assignment by way of security. It was not an absolute assignment for if the purchaser had paid for the goods immediately, there would have been no assignment of the debt created by the sale to the purchaser. In addition the clause itself states that the assignment is 'by way of security' ... In my opinion, it follows that, as the terms for deliveries abroad were not registered under s 99 of the Act of 1963, they are void against any creditor in so far as they created an obligation to assign or gave a charge on the debts owing ...'[180]

Accordingly, because the assignment was found to be by way of security and not an absolute assignment, it was held to be a registrable charge on the Irish company's book debts[181].

[19.065] Other instruments which may be registrable as a book debt include *letters of hypothecation*[182]. This is a security by way of equitable charge which is used where it is impractical to give possession of the goods because they are not yet available. Letters of hypothecation have been described as a notification by a bank that the bank shall have a charge on personal property which comes into the bank's possession[183]. However, a bill of exchange or other negotiable instrument given to secure the payment of a book debt where the instrument is deposited to secure an advance to the company is not a registrable charge: s 99(6) of the CA 1963. A charge on cash which is on deposit at a bank is thought by some[184] perhaps not to be a charge which requires registration under s 99(2)(e) because standard accounting practice is to show cash on deposit under a separate heading in balance sheets; notwithstanding this, it is recommended that such charges are registered under s 99(2)(e)[185], unless they are exempted under the EC(FCA)R 2010.[186]

---

179 *Re Interview Ltd* [1975] IR 382.

180 *Re Interview Ltd* [1975] IR 382 at 396–397.

181 *Re Interview Ltd* [1975] IR 382 at 397 where Kenny J said: 'In my opinion, it follows that, as the terms for deliveries abroad were not registered under s 99 of the CA 1963, they are void against any creditor in so far as they created an obligation to assign or gave a charge on the debts owing to Interview and arising out of sales of goods delivered by AEG or Telefunken.'

182 See *Ladenburg & Co v Goodwin Ferreira Co Ltd & Garnett* [1912] KB 275.

183 See Hapgood, *Paget's Law of Banking* (11th edn, 1996), p 539.

184 See Lingard, *Bank Security Documents* (5th edn, 2011), para 3.19 and *Re Brightlife Ltd* [1986] 3 All ER 673 at 676.

185 See, Johnston, *Banking and Security Law in Ireland* (1998), para [17.21].

186 See para **[19.035]** *et seq.*

(f) Floating charges

[19.066] Floating charges have been considered in detail in the previous chapter[187]. All floating charges are registrable under s 99(2)(f) of the CA 1963 and in default will be void as against a liquidator or any creditor of the company. In the case of real property, a floating charge will also fall to be registered as being a charge on land under s 99(2)(d) of the CA 1963.

[19.067] Most floating charges are over personalty and are also registrable. Again the existence of a retention of title clause in a contract for the sale of goods may constitute a charge which requires registration as a floating charge under s 99(2)(f) of the CA 1963[188].

(g) Charges on calls of shares made but not paid

[19.068] Section 99(2)(g) of the CA 1963 provides that charges on calls of shares made but not paid are registrable. Although these are a sort of book debt, they are independently registrable under s 99(2)(g) of the CA 1963[189].

(h) Charges on – or any share in – a ship or aircraft

[19.069] Section 99(2)(h) of the CA 1963[190] provides that a charge on a ship or aircraft or any share in a ship or aircraft is registrable. In *Barber v Burke*[191], the Supreme Court held that a 'yacht' was not a 'ship' within the meaning of this subsection. Some doubt must be cast upon this decision by reason of the definition afforded to 'ship' in the Jurisdiction of Courts (Maritime Conventions) Act 1989 (the '1989 Act') which in s 13(2) provides that it includes 'every description of vessel used in navigation' and defines 'vessel' to include 'any ship or boat, or any other description of vessel used in navigation'. It should also be noted that in *Targe Towing Ltd v The Owners and all Persons Claiming an interest in the Vessel 'Von Rocks'*[192] the Supreme Court (*per* Keane J) held that a 'dredger' was a 'ship' for the purposes of the 1989 Act[193]. Whilst

187 Ch 18, *Corporate Borrowing: Debentures and Security*, para **[18.068]** *et seq.*

188 See the *dictum* of Templeman LJ in *Borden (UK) Ltd v Scottish Timber Products Ltd* [1981] Ch 35 at 44 where he said: '… if the buyers created a charge on chipboard, such a charge is void against the liquidator and creditors of the buyer under [s 99 of the CA 1963] which makes void against the company or its creditors an unregistered charge created or evidenced by an instrument which if executed by an individual, would require registration as a Bill of Sale. If the interest floated from the chipboard to proceeds of sale and onwards, so floated the charge, and [the equivalent to s 99(2) of the CA 1963] makes void any unregistered floating charge on the undertaking or property of the company.'

189 See Schmitthoff (ed), *Palmer's Company Law* (24th edn, 1987), para 46–06.

190 As amended by s 122 of the CA 1990.

191 *Barber v Burke* [1980] ILRM 186.

192 *Targe Towing Ltd v The Owners and all Persons Claiming an interest in the Vessel 'Von Rocks'* [1998] 1 ILRM 481.

193 Keane J said ([1998] 1 ILRM 481 at 491–492): 'The preponderance of judicial opinion would support the view that, provided the craft was built to do something on water and, for the purpose of carrying out that work, was so designed and constructed as to be capable of traversing significant water surfaces and did in fact regularly traverse them, it is capable of being classified as a "ship", despite the absence of any form of self-propulsion or steering mechanism, such as a rudder.'

specific to the 1989 Act, it is thought that some considerable doubt must be cast upon the earlier decision in *Barber v Burke* and that it is now prudent to register a charge over a yacht or any other 'vessel' pursuant to s 99(2)(h) of the CA 1963.

(i) Charges on goodwill and other intellectual property

[19.070] Section 99(2)(i) of the CA 1963 requires that any charge on goodwill, patents or licences under patents, trademarks, copyrights or licences under copyright created by a company must be registered. These may also be registrable under the relevant statutes on such intellectual property rights[194].

Disguised registrable charges: retention of title clauses

[19.071] Certain retention of title clauses have been held by the courts of both Ireland and other common law countries to give rise to a charge on the property of a company[195], which will be void unless registered with the CRO. In the late-1970s and 1980s, such clauses were of grave concern to unsecured creditors of insolvent companies, who often found that assets which they thought were available to them and other unsecured creditors, were in fact still owned by the person who supplied them to the company[196]. The immediate relevance of retention of title clauses to company law is that the courts have been repeatedly asked to determine whether the vendor of goods actually retained ownership in them, or whether title in the goods passed to the purchaser company which *then* created a charge over the goods. Where the purchaser company creates a registrable charge over goods, the charging retention of title clause must be registered pursuant to s 99(1) of the CA 1963. Where such charges are not registered, they will be void as against the company's liquidator and creditors[197]. The assets which are the subject of the retention of title clause will then be available to meet the claims of the Revenue Commissioners and the company's unsecured creditors.

[19.072] A retention of title clause[198] is a provision in a contract for the sale of goods which purports to reserve the title in the goods to the vendor until a future time when

194 See Hackett, 'Taking Security Over Intellectual Property Rights in Ireland' (1994) CLP 50.

195 See generally, Law Reform Commission, *Debt Collection: (2) Retention of Title* (LRC 28–1989); Dickson, 'Reservation of Title Clauses' (1978) SLS Legal Publications; Parris, *Effective Retention of Title Clauses* (1987, Collins); Hanley, 'Reservation of Title' (1989) Gazette ILSI 213; Thomas, 'Retention of Title Clauses in Business Contracts' (1989) Dli (Western Law Gazette) Autumn 28; Phillips & Schuster, 'Reservation of Title in the Commercial Laws of England and Ireland' (1979–80) DULJ 1; Maguire, 'Romalpa Misinterpreted' (1989) DULJ 40; Bradgate, 'Reservation of Title Ten Years On' (1987) Conv 434; McCormack, 'Reservation of Title – The House of Lords Speaks With A Scottish Accent' [1991] LMCLQ 154, the foregoing being a mere taste of the academic literature written on this most intriguing of topics.

196 *The Irish Independent* reported on 23 October 1987 that 'A significant number of suppliers to the H Williams chain are finding that the legal arrangements they had made to protect their title to goods supplied by them to the troubled supermarket firm are proving anything but watertight. "'There is around £7m worth of stock in the hands of the H Williams receiver. We assumed it was ours … [but] … we are now finding that recovery of around £3m worth of stock is in serious doubt".'

197 See para **[19.006]**.

198 Also referred to as a 'reservation of title', or a '*Romalpa*' clause, the latter after the first modern decision to consider such clauses, *Aluminium Industrie Vaasen BV v Romalpa Aluminium Ltd* [1976] 2 All ER 552.

certain conditions have been fulfilled. The statutory basis of a retention of title clause is s 17 of the Sale of Goods Act 1893 ('SGA 1893') which provides that property in goods in sale shall pass when the parties stipulate that it should. Since there are a variety of types of retention of title clauses in existence, it is proposed to systematically consider the four main generic forms which retention of title clauses may take.

(a) Simple retention of title clause

[19.073] A simple retention of title clause provides that property or title in specific goods shall not pass to the purchaser until the full purchase price of those goods has been paid to the vendor. It may be taken as established law that such clauses will, where properly drafted, be effective to retain title in the vendor, and that furthermore, for present purposes, will *not* constitute the creation of a registrable charge. So, in *Re Charles Dougherty*[199], animal feed was supplied to the purchaser company subject to a simple retention of title clause[200] and when the company went into receivership the food was still identifiable. The vendor sought its return, but the receiver to the company argued, *inter alia*, that the clause created a charge, which in the case of an individual should have been registered under the Bills of Sale (Ireland) Act 1879, and so ought to have been registered by the company by virtue of s 99(2)(c) of the CA 1963[201]. Carroll J rejected this saying that:

> 'If the goods are delivered to the buyer who has not paid for them, on terms that title remains with the seller until he is paid, the buyer's creditors cannot seize the goods. Even though the goods are in the apparent possession of the buyer, he is *not the maker or giver* of the Bill of Sale. He is the holder or grantee under the Bill ...
>
> However, if a contract deals with the future title of the buyer in the goods to be manufactured from the goods supplied, then, as regards that future title, the contract would be a Bill of Sale in which the buyer is the maker or giver and the seller is grantee ...
>
> In this case the clause in question is *not complex enough to create a charge* over future manufactured goods, the title to which cannot exist at the date of the contract. The contract deals only with the present title to the goods sold and not with future title of goods to be manufactured[202].'

As seen above, s 17 of the SGA 1893 allows the parties to decide amongst themselves when property is to pass, and so a simple title retention is permissible. This judgment makes it clear that a 'simple' retention of title clause will not create a charge registrable under s 99(1) of the CA 1963. It also demonstrates the fundamental principle that the creation of a charge is essentially *a matter of contract*, between the parties themselves. If the buyer never has title in the goods, then he cannot grant a proprietary right in those goods to someone else[203].

---

199 *Re Interview Ltd* [1984] ILRM 437.

200 It provided: 'The transfer of title to you of the goods as detailed in this contract shall not occur until the invoice covering same has been paid in full, and accordingly, the goods wherever situated shall be thereupon at your risk.'

201 See para **[19.046]**.

202 *Re Interview Ltd* [1984] ILRM 437 at 441, 442. Emphasis added.

203 See Jones, 'Retention of Title Clauses 10 Years from Romalpa' (1986) Co Lawyer 235. However contrast an alternative view put forward by McWilliams J in *Frigioscandia (Contracting) Ltd v Continental Irish Meat Ltd* [1982] ILRM 396 at 398 where he said: (contd.../)

[19.074] An entirely different situation arises where, in a simple retention of title clause, the vendor reserves the 'equitable and beneficial ownership' in the goods. It has been held in *Re Bond Worth Ltd*[204] that such a clause allows the legal title to pass to the purchaser, meaning that the net substance of the transaction is that the purchaser grants back the equitable title to the vendor[205]. This will create a charge, and where such a charge is of a kind described in s 99(2) of the CA 1963, will constitute a registrable charge.

[19.075] A supplier of goods sold on foot of a retention of title clause will have his claim defeated by a subsequent delivery of those goods to a *bona fide* third party without actual notice of the supplier's title. It has been held, however, that in order for a supplier's claim to be defeated, there must be an actual sale and that delivery under a mere agreement to sell is not sufficient[206]. Another issue to have been addressed by the courts is the effect of a retention of title clause, where the original goods are subsequently processed. The macabre question considered in *Chaigley Farms Ltd v Crawford, Kaye & Greyshire Ltd*[207] was whether the slaughtering and cutting into meat products of cattle, originally sold 'on the hoof' and subject to a retention of title clause, was sufficient to transfer title to the purchaser. It was held that there was an inescapable difference between a live animal and a dead one and that the effect of such processing was to transfer title to the purchaser[208]. Equally, where goods the subject of a retention of title clause become fixtures to real property, the title to them will pass with the title to the land, thereby defeating the supplier's *in rem* claim to them[209]. Where a supplier's *in*

---

203 (\...contd) 'A difficulty which arises with regard to clauses of this nature is that they are included in the contracts to secure the payment to the vendor of the price of the goods and therefore it may be said as has been argued that the goods once delivered, are intended to be held by the purchaser as security for such payment and that the transaction is in the category of a mortgage in that the vendor, although retaining ownership or an interest in the goods, cannot take possession of them provided that the specified instalments are paid, and that this leads to the conclusion that such a clause must be treated as creating a mortgage or a charge over the goods. In my opinion such a conclusion can have no general application to these clauses and each must depend on its own facts.'

204 *Re Bond Worth Ltd* [1979] 3 All ER 919.

205 Note that a clause which retained the equitable and beneficial ownership in goods was upheld in *Re Stokes & McKiernan* [1978] ILRM 240, by McWilliams J but the same judge accepted that there was a difference between a simple retention of title clause which retains *legal* ownership and one which retains *equitable* ownership in *Frigoscandia (Contracting) Ltd v Continental Irish Meats Ltd* [1982] ILRM 396.

206 *Re Highway Foods Ltd* (1994) Times, 1 November; Palmer's In Company, Issue 1/95, 18 January 1995.

207 *Chaigley Farms Ltd v Crawford, Kaye & Greyshire Ltd* [1996] BCC 957. See de Lacy, 'Processed Goods and Retention of Title Clauses' (1995) *Palmer's In Company*, Issue 10/97, 20 November 1997.

208 Cf *Re Weddel (NZ) Ltd* (1996) 5 NZBLC 104 and *Pongakawa Sawmill Ltd v New Zealand Forest Products Ltd* [1992] 3 NZLR 304.

209 *Aircool Installations v British Telecommunications* (1995) Current Law Week, 19 May 1995; (1995) Palmer's In Company, Issue 7/95, 19 July 1995. In this case, the supplier of air conditioning equipment delivered on foot of a retention of title clause had its claim to the equipment defeated after it became a fixture to real property.

rem claim to goods is defeated, he may still have an *in personam* claim against the purchaser, or a person acting on the purchaser's behalf, such as its liquidator[210].

(b) An aggregation retention of title clause

[19.076] An aggregation retention of title clause typically provides that until such time as the goods in sale have been paid for, not only will the title in those goods not pass, but the title in goods manufactured from the goods supplied, even where mixed with other goods not subject to the retention of title clause, will rest with the vendor[211]. This type of clause has almost invariably been held to be a charge over the assets of the purchaser company[212]. However, a distinction must be made between situations where the goods sold are irreversibly mixed with other goods as opposed to where they remain readily identifiable[213]. Where goods are still identifiable, although mixed with other goods, a simple retention of title clause has been held to retain the title in those goods, without necessarily being deemed to create a charge: *Hendy Lennox Ltd v Grahame Puttick Ltd*[214].

[19.077] Where goods supplied are irreversibly mixed it has been held by Bridge LJ in *Borden (UK) Ltd v Scottish Timber Products Ltd*[215] that the title in those goods is extinguished. There, resin (being the glue that makes the woodchips in chipboard adhere together) was supplied to the purchaser company and the terms of sale provided that property would not pass until full payment had been received and further provided that chipboard manufactured from the resin would be charged to the extent that it consisted of the resin. When the purchaser company went into liquidation, the vendors sought to rely on this clause, but Bridge LJ held that as soon as the resin was used in the manufacturing process, 'it ceased to exist as resin and accordingly, the title to the resin simply disappeared'.

[19.078] While this case did not consider an actual aggregation clause, Bridge LJ in *Borden* envisaged such a clause saying:

> '... if a seller of goods to a manufacturer who knows that his goods are to be used in the manufacturing process before they are paid for, wishes to reserve to himself an effective security for the payment of the price, he cannot rely on a simple reservation of title clause

---

210 In *Vale Sewing Machines v Robb* [1997] SCLR 797, Palmer's In Company, Issue 1/98, 28 January 1998, it was held by a Scottish Sheriff Court that a liquidator who disposed of goods that were held subject to a title retention clause might be personally liable to an unpaid supplier where there were reasonable grounds for believing that the goods were not the company's property.

211 See, generally, Webb, 'Title and Transformation: Who Owns Manufactured Goods?' [2000] JBL 513.

212 See *Re Andrabell Ltd* [1984] 3 All ER 407; *Pfeifer Weinkellerei v Arbuthnot Factors Ltd* [1988] 1 WLR 150; *Re Weldtech Ltd* [1991] BCC 16; and *Compaq Computers Ltd v Abercorn Group Ltd* [1991] BCC 484.

213 These different scenarios have been said to be to be analogous to the Roman concepts of '*accessio*'/'*confusio*' and '*commixtio*', respectively: see Parris, *Effective Retention of Title Clauses* (1987, Collins), p 88.

214 *Hendy Lennox Ltd v Grahame Puttick Ltd* [1984] 1 WLR 485.

215 *Borden (UK) Ltd v Scottish Timber Products Ltd* [1979] 3 All ER 961.

> such as that relied on by the sellers. If he wishes to acquire rights over the manufactured product, he can only do so by express contractual stipulation[216].'

However, while one can draft such a clause, it seems inescapable that it will be deemed to constitute a charge which requires registration under s 99(1) of the CA 1963. So in *Peachdart Ltd*[217], where leather was supplied to a company which was intended to be used to make handbags, Vinelott J refused to interpret such a clause as anything other than a charge. The Irish courts have also taken such a view. Hence, in *Kruppstahl AG v Quitmann Products Ltd*[218], while a simple reservation of title clause was upheld, an aggregation-type clause over processed steel was found to be a charge. Again, in *Re Charles Dougherty Ltd*[219] Carroll J said of the *Quitmann* case that it:

> '... therefore illustrates that a seller can make an effective reservation of title clause to goods prior to manufacture, but if he requires security over the manufactured goods the buyer will have to grant him this and this would require registration as a Bill of Sale[220].'

Essentially, while it is arguable that careful drafting[221] can prevent the purchaser company from ever acquiring full title in the goods, it is clear that the courts have turned their face against this and have held that in such circumstances, the purchaser *creates a charge* in favour of the vendor[222]. For an alternative view, however, see *Associated Alloys Pty Ltd v Metropolitan Engineering & Fabrication Ltd*[223], considered below[224], where a combined aggregation-proceeds of sale clause was found to be capable of being construed as a trust that is not required to be registered in order to be effective.

(c) Proceeds of sale clause

[19.079] This form of a retention of title clause purports to acknowledge that a purchaser company can sell the goods in sale, but provides that the proceeds are to be held *in trust* for the vendor. Genuine trusts are not registrable. So in *Fitzpatrick v Criminal Assets Bureau*[225] it had been held by the High Court that a Mercedes motor car which was in the legal ownership of a company was, in fact, beneficially owned by a director of the company. The Supreme Court held that there was no merit in a submission that the beneficial interest was void for want of registration because 'a trust is not a charge'[226]. One of the earlier cases, *Sugar Distributors Ltd v Monaghan Cash &*

216 *Borden (UK) Ltd v Scottish Timber Products Ltd* [1979] 3 All ER 961 at 971.

217 *Peachdart Ltd* [1984] 1 Ch 131, [1983] All ER 204.

218 *Kruppstahl AG v Quitmann Products Ltd* [1982] ILRM 551.

219 *Re Charles Dougherty Ltd* [1984] ILRM 437.

220 *Re Charles Dougherty Ltd* [1984] ILRM 437 at 441.

221 *Cf Aircool Installations vBritish Telecommunications* (1995) Current Law Week, 19 May 1995; Palmer's In Company, Issue 7/95, 19 July 1995 where the supplier of air conditioning equipment supplied on foot of a retention of title clause had its claim defeated by the application of the rule that if goods become fixtures to land their title passes with the land.

222 *Ian Chisholm Textiles Ltd v Griffiths* [1994] BCC 96.

223 *Associated Alloys Pty Ltd v Metropolitan Engineering & Fabrication Ltd* [1998] NSWSC 442 of 21 September 1998 (Supreme Court of New South Wales); [2000] HCA 25 of 11 May 2000 (High Court of Australia).

224 See para **[19.081]**.

225 *Fitzpatrick v Criminal Assets Bureau* [2000] 1 ILRM 299.

226 *Fitzpatrick v Criminal Assets Bureau* [2000] 1 ILRM 299 at 305.

Carry Ltd[227], went so far as to imply a proceeds of sale clause into a simple retention of title clause. This enabled the vendor to demand that the purchaser company account for the proceeds of sale. More recently, in *Re WJ Hickey Ltd*[228], electrical goods were sold to a company subject to a proceeds of sale clause. The clause provided:

> '(a) No property in any of the goods ... shall pass until full payment for all goods supplied hereunder has been received by the seller and until such payment has been received by the seller the buyer shall hold the goods in trust for the seller in a manner which enables them to be identified as the goods of the seller and the buyer shall immediately return the goods to the seller, should the seller so request.
>
> (b) Notwithstanding paragraph (a) hereof the buyer shall be permitted to sell the goods to third parties in the normal course of business, but the proceeds of any such sale shall whenever any sum whatsoever is due from the buyer to the seller be held in trust for the seller in a manner which enables such proceeds to be identified as such.'

There, Barron J held that for a charge to be created, all the property in the goods must pass to the purchaser company so that there could in fact be an assignment back to the chargee:

> 'I can find no ground for construing the clause in such a way that all the property must have passed to the company and that it assigned back an equitable interest in the goods by way of charge. The existence of such an assignment is essential to the applicant's case. Where charges have been found to exist ... there was a clear assignment of such an interest. There can be none since the entire property never passed. The words 'no property in any goods shall pass' must be given their literal interpretation[229].'

Of particular importance was the fact that the vendor had stipulated that the goods be held *in trust* for him, thus giving rise to a *fiduciary relationship* between vendor and purchaser. Furthermore, it was significant for the learned judge that the purchaser company was bound to keep a separate account.

[19.080] While the *Hickey* case suggested that proceeds of sale clauses will not amount to the creation of a charge by the purchaser company, *Carroll Group Distributors Ltd v G&JF Bourke Ltd*[230] found to the contrary. In that case, the court scorned the requirement that a separate account was to be kept. The vendor sold tobacco worth £54,000, subject to a clause which provided that property would not pass until all sums due were paid. Again, the clause allowed the purchaser a right to resell the goods in the normal course of business. In so doing, the purchaser company acted on its own behalf. Proceeds of sale were to be held in trust for the vendor, and the purchaser was obliged to keep a separate account[231] and provide details to the vendor on request. Murphy J took a very different view to that taken by Barron J and held that the substance of the

[227] *Sugar Distributors Ltd v Monaghan Cash & Carry Ltd* [1982] ILRM 399.

[228] *Re WJ Hickey Ltd* [1988] IR 126.

[229] *Re WJ Hickey Ltd* [1988] IR 126 at 131.

[230] *Carroll Group Distributors Ltd v G&JF Bourke Ltd* [1990] ILRM 285.

[231] *Carroll Group Distributors Ltd v G&JF Bourke Ltd* [1990] ILRM 285 at 289, where Murphy J said that no account was opened, and that the vendor was probably aware of this.

transaction was to create a charge, and he endorsed the views of McWilliam J in *Frigoscandia (Contracting) Ltd v Continental Irish Meat Ltd*[232]. He said:

> 'If one ... analyses the bargain made between the parties it is clear that such arrangements properly implemented would result in a bank account with sums of money credited thereto which would probably be in excess of the amounts due by Bourkes to Carrolls. This would arise partly from the fact that the goods would be resold at a marked up price and partly from the fact that the proceeds of sale would include some goods the cost price of which had been discharged and some had not. In other words the bank account would be a fund to which Carrolls could have recourse to ensure the discharge of the moneys due to them even though they would not be entitled to the entire of that fund. Accordingly the fund agreed to be credited would possess all the characteristics of a mortgage or charge ...'

Murphy J deemed the transaction to constitute a charge in substance, which was void for want of registration under s 99(1) of the CA 1963. It is thought that the views of Murphy J will ultimately prevail, and that such contractual stipulations will be held to constitute the creation of a charge by the parties[233]. Indeed, in Ireland, it was this decision which sounded the death-knell for proceeds of sale clauses.

[19.081] The High Court of Australia has, however, in *Associated Alloys Pty Ltd v Metropolitan Engineering & Fabrication Ltd*[234] breathed life into the proceeds of sale clause. In that case the plaintiff supplier sold steel to the defendant purchaser on foot of a clause which provided as follows:

> '... in the event that the purchaser uses the goods/product in some manufacturing or construction process of its own or some third party, then the purchaser shall hold such part of the proceeds of such manufacturing or construction process as relates to the goods/product in trust for the vendor. Such part shall be deemed to equal in dollar terms the amount owing by the purchaser to the vendor at the time of the receipt of such proceeds'.

This is a form of hybrid clause, which amounted to a combined aggregation-proceeds of sale clause. When the defendant purchaser went into liquidation the plaintiff supplier sought a declaration that its liquidator held over US$197,000 due in respect of steel supplied on trust for it. At trial it was held that the clause amounted to a registrable charge which was void for want of registration. On appeal the Supreme Court of New South Wales upheld the trial judge's decision that the clause created a charge which was void for want of registration. It went on to hold that the charge which the clause gave rise to was, on proper construction, a charge on book debts and not a floating charge. In arriving at this conclusion Sheller JA considered the decision in *Borden (UK) Ltd v Scottish Timber*[235], where Templeman LJ had stated that if a supplier's 'interest floated from the chipboard to proceeds of sale and onwards, so floated the charge and s 95 [of the Companies Act 1948 (UK)] makes void any unregistered floating charge on the undertaking or property of the company'. Sheller JA took a contrary view:

---

232 *Frigoscandia (Contracting) Ltd v Continental Irish Meat Ltd* [1982] ILRM 396.

233 See also *Compaq Computer Ltd v Abercorn Group Ltd* [1993] BCLC 602 and *Modelboard Ltd v Outer Box Ltd* [1993] BCLC 623.

234 *Associated Alloys Pty Ltd v Metropolitan Engineering & Fabrication Ltd* [1998] NSWSC 442 of 21 September 1998 (Supreme Court of New South Wales), [2000] HCA 25 of 11 May 2000 (High Court of Australia).

235 *Borden (UK) Ltd v Scottish Timber* [1981] Ch 25.

'What Templeman LJ said accords with the general concept of a floating charge as one 'intended by the parties to cover *a class of property* but not to attach to specific items within the class until some future event occurs' with the consequence that until that event occurs the chargor is free to dispose of items within the class in the ordinary course of business so that the taker from the chargor acquires the property free of the charge … But the [subclause in question] of the [plaintiff's] standard clause provided for the part of the proceeds charged to be held in trust for [the plaintiff] which inhibited [the defendant] from dealing with that part of the proceeds in any way contrary to the terms of the trust, that is to say, in any way other than for the benefit of [the plaintiff]. Moreover … a person in whose favour property is charged has only a security interest in the property and has not the equitable ownership in the same way as a beneficiary under a trust. I agree with [the trial judge] that any charge on the proceeds was not a floating charge'.

Shellar JA went on to hold that the retention of title clause went on to create a charge on book debts and that it was void for want of registration.

[19.082] Against all odds, the High Court of Australia held that the clause did not have to be construed as a registrable charge and that, if there was sufficient supporting evidence, it could be found to be a trust[236]. On the meaning of the phrase, 'the proceeds' as used in the clause, the majority decision rejected the contention that it included book debts. On this point it was said:

'The phrase has the meaning employed by Sir George Jessel MR in his ex tempore judgment in *Re Hallett's Estate; Knatchbull v Hallett*[237] where the Master of the Rolls eloquently states the principles of tracing in equity. The phrase 'the proceeds' is to be construed as referring to moneys received by the Buyer and not debts which may be set out in the Buyer's books (or computer records) from time to time[238]. The concluding sentence of the Proceeds Subclause would be strained if the phrase 'the proceeds' were to include book debts … In contrast, limiting the phrase 'the proceeds' to refer to payments made to the Buyer results in this equation operating with certainty[239].'

Having determined what was meant by the phrase 'the proceeds' the majority went on to consider whether it was possible for the parties to have intended to create a trust over the proceeds. After examining the language used and the requirements for a trust, the majority held that 'there was an agreement effective in equity to bind, from time to time, the relevant 'proceeds'[240]. The majority decision concluded that:

'The Proceeds Subclause is an agreement to constitute a trust of future acquired-property. It is therefore not a "charge" … and the detailed provisions of the law governing charges

[236] As it happened, it was held that there was insufficient evidence to support the finding that there was in fact a trust and despite the sea change in judicial attitude, the appeal was disallowed.

[237] *Re Hallett's Estate; Knatchbull v Hallett* (1880) 13 Ch D 696 at 798–709.

[238] The court's footnote reads: 'Questions as to the application of moneys received, which it is unnecessary now to answer, may arise where a running account exists between a supplier (eg the seller) and purchaser (eg the buyer).'

[239] *Associated Alloys Pty Ltd v Metropolitan Engineering & Fabrication Ltd* [2000] HCA 25 of 11 May 2000 (High Court of Australia) at para 25.

[240] *Associated Alloys Pty Ltd v Metropolitan Engineering & Fabrication Ltd* [2000] HCA 25 of 11 May 2000 (High Court of Australia) at para 42.

> thus do not apply to it. The Proceeds Subclause is not a 'registrable charge' … In turn, the Proceeds Subclause is not void as against the administrators or liquidator of the Buyer[241].'

The Australian High Court recognised that the lack of any statutory obligation to register the proceeds subclause created commercial incentives to incorporate such clauses into purchase agreements. They went on to comment on the lacunae they had identified in the following terms:

> 'In the law, the legislature has chosen to select as the criterion of operation of the registration provisions that which it defines as a 'charge'. The contractual and trust arrangement with which this appeal is concerned did not involve the creation of such a charge or an agreement to create one. To treat the Proceeds Subclause as an agreement which falls foul of the law is to rewrite the statute. It is not for the courts to destroy or impair property rights, such as those arising under trusts, by supplementing the list of those rights which the legislature has selected for such treatment[242].'

In the final analysis, however, the appeal was dismissed because there was a 'critical gap in the evidence' required to prove the receipt of 'the proceeds'. The decision of the majority[243] is certainly more in accord with the High Court decision in *Re WJ Hickey Ltd*[244] than in *Carroll Group Distributors Ltd v G&JF Bourke Ltd*[245]. There is an attractiveness to the decision of the Australian High Court, giving effect as it does to the clear words used by the parties.

(d) Current account clause

[19.083] Current account clauses are often appended to simple retention of title clauses and provide that title in the goods in sale shall not pass until such time as *all sums due* to the vendor have been paid. Often, sums due on foot of other contracts will also be included[246]. While these have been upheld in both Ireland[247] and England it was thought that they would ultimately be found to constitute a charge over the company's book debts or alternatively a floating charge over the company's assets. This is because the essence of the transaction is that the title in goods which are 'sold' to the purchaser company are contractually retained by the vendor, *as security*, until other moneys are paid by the purchaser company.

[19.084] Notwithstanding the foregoing reservations, the House of Lords has upheld the validity of a current account clause (which had not been registered) in *Armour v Thyssen Edelstahlwerke AG*[248]. There, it was held that the ownership of the goods in question did not pass to the purchaser company. Lord Keith said that a charge or right in security would only arise where:

---

241 *Associated Alloys Pty Ltd v Metropolitan Engineering & Fabrication Ltd* [2000] HCA 25 of 11 May 2000 (High Court of Australia) at para 48.

242 *Associated Alloys Pty Ltd v Metropolitan Engineering & Fabrication Ltd* [2000] HCA 25 of 11 May 2000 (High Court of Australia) at para 51.

243 The decision of the court was by a four (Gaudron, McHugh, Gummow and Hayne JJ) to one (Kirby J) majority.

244 *Re WJ Hickey Ltd* [1988] IR 126.

245 *Carroll Group Distributors Ltd v G&JF Bourke Ltd* [1990] ILRM 285.

246 See *Clough Mill Ltd v Martin* [1984] 3 All ER 982 at 987h.

247 See *Re Stokes & McKiernan* [1978] ILRM 240.

248 *Armour v Thyssen Edelstahlwerke AG* [1990] 3 WLR 810.

'... the contract of sale gave it the property in the goods, but the contract of sale said that the property in the goods was not to pass until all debts due to the appellants had been paid. We are here very far removed from the situation where a party in possession of corporeal movable is seeking to create a subordinate right in favour of a creditor while retaining the ultimate right to himself[249].'

It remains to be seen whether the Irish courts will accept this reasoning and hold that a current account retention of title clause does not constitute a charge that requires to be registered pursuant to s 99 of the CA 1963 if it is to be valid.

Judgment mortgages

[19.085] A judgment mortgage[250] is a peculiar form of security from a company because the company does not *create* the judgment mortgage; it cannot, therefore, be described as 'consensual security'. A judgment mortgage is created by a person ('a judgment creditor') who obtains a court judgment against another person ('a judgment debtor') and who then registers that judgment against real property owned by the judgment debtor. Section 102(1) of the CA 1963 provides that where a judgment is recovered against a company and is subsequently converted into a judgment mortgage affecting the property of the company, then:

'... the judgment creditor shall cause 2 copies (certified by the Land Registry or the Registry of Deeds, as the case may be, to be correct copies) of the affidavit required for the purpose of registering the judgment as a mortgage to be delivered to the company within twenty-one days of such registration, and the company shall within 3 days of receipt of such copies deliver one of such copies to the Registrar of Companies for registration in manner required by this Act. By way of further precaution, the Land Registry or Registry of Deeds, shall as soon as may be deliver a copy of the said affidavit to the Registrar of Companies.'

The sanction for contravention of this section is contained in s 102(2) of the CA 1963 which provides that a judgment creditor who acts in default shall be liable to a class C fine[251]. Although it has been suggested[252] that non-registration should make a judgment mortgage invalid, it is submitted that this should not be the case because such a mortgage is *not created by a company*, and moreover, for a mortgage or charge to be void if unregistered such must be expressly provided for by the legislature.

Charges over property outside of the State

[19.086] Section 99(3), (4) and (5) of the CA 1963 concern situations in which Irish formed and registered companies create charges over foreign property (ie, property situate outside the State). These subsections do not create any additional head of charge; they are intended to make provision for procedural matters which arise when either a charge is created outside the State or the subject matter of the charge is situate outside the State.

249 *Armour v Thyssen Edelstahlwerke AG* [1990] 3 WLR 810 at 815.
250 See Wylie, *Irish Land Law* (4th edn, Bloomsbury Professional, 2010), para 13.179 *et seq.*
251 As increased by s 15 of the C(A)A 1982 and modified by s 6 of the FA 2010.
252 Keane, *Company Law* (4th edn, Bloomsbury Professional, 2007), para [21.38].

[19.087] Section 99(3) of the CA 1963 deals with the situation where a charge is created *outside* of the State in respect of property that is situate *outside* of the State. It provides that where a charge is created out of the State then particulars must be delivered to the CRO:

> '... 21 days after the date on which the prescribed particulars could, in due course of post, and if despatched with due diligence, have been received in the State.'

By default[253], this requirement applies only to companies to which the Companies Acts apply.

[19.088] Section 99(4) of the CA 1963 is concerned with cases where a charge is created *within* the State over property that is situate *outside* of the State. This provides that, in such cases:

> '... the prescribed particulars *may* be sent for registration [ie, to the Irish CRO] under this section, notwithstanding that further proceedings may be necessary to make the charge valid or effectual according to the law of the country in which the property is situate.' [Emphasis added.]

It is notable that by the use of the word 'may', this provision is facilitatory and not mandatory in nature. Accordingly, any obligation to deliver particulars of a charge to the CRO in the circumstances envisaged by s 99(4) will arise elsewhere.

[19.089] Section 99(5) of the CA 1963 is concerned with where a charge comprises property situate *outside* the State, whether or not the charge is created inside or outside the State. Again, it is intended to provide for procedural matters associated with the registration of a charge over foreign property. It provides:

> 'Where a charge comprises property situate outside the State and registration in the country where the property is situate is necessary to make the charge valid or effectual according to the law of that country, a certificate in the prescribed form stating that the charge was presented for registration in the country where the property is situate on the date on which it was so presented shall be delivered to the Registrar of Companies for registration.'

This subsection might apply in the circumstances considered in either sub-s (3) or (4) last considered as an additional consideration, since both envisage circumstances where charges are created over foreign property over property within the State. The necessity and desirability of such a provision in Irish companies' legislation has been questioned[254], but unless and until the law is changed on this point, practitioners should be cautious. It is doubted whether non-compliance with s 99(5) of the CA 1963 will render a charge void. It is thought that provided there is compliance with s 99(1) of the CA 1963 – ie, that particulars of the charge have been delivered within the prescribed 21 days from creation – the failure to deliver a certificate that the charge was presented for registration in the foreign country should not render the charge void as against a

253 Section 111 of the CA 1963 which, by specifying to what charges Pt IV (ss 99 to 112) of the CA 1963 applies, implicitly means that s 99(3) must be taken as referring only to charges on foreign property created by companies formed and registered within the State, ie, within the meaning of s 2 of the CA 1963: see Ch 1, *The Private Company in Context*, at para **[1.056]**

254 See Nolan, 'Registration of Company Charges Over Foreign Property – Who Needs s 99(5) of the Companies Act 1963?' (1995) ILT 9.

liquidator or creditor. It would remain the case, of course, that an offence would have been committed[255].

Late registration of registrable charges[256]

[19.090] Failure to deliver particulars of a registrable charge to the CRO within the prescribed 21 days results in what was a secured charge becoming void against a liquidator and any creditor of the company. An attempt, of dubious value to a secured creditor so affected, is made to lessen the severity of this by s 106(1) of the CA 1963 which facilitates court-approved late registration. It states:

> 'The court, on being satisfied that the omission to register a charge within the time required by the Act or that the omission or mis-statement of any particular with respect to any such charge or in a memorandum of satisfaction was accidental, or due to inadvertence or to some other sufficient cause, or is not of a nature to prejudice the position of creditors or shareholders of the company, or that on other grounds it is just and equitable to grant relief, may, on the application of the company or any person interested, and on such terms and conditions as seem to the court just and expedient, order that the time for registration shall be extended, or, as the case may be, that the omission or mis-statement shall be rectified.'

Relief under s 106 is discretionary. The section makes reference to five separate grounds on foot of which the court may grant relief. There are many examples of cases where the courts have granted relief using each of the five grounds as a basis:

- accident[257];
- inadvertence[258];
- some other sufficient cause[259];
- not of a nature to prejudice the position of creditors or shareholders[260]; and
- it is just and equitable to grant relief on other grounds[261].

(a) The discretionary nature of s 106 of the CA 1963

[19.091] Section 106 of the CA 1963 is a discretionary relief[262]. Accordingly, the court will not grant relief where to do so would be futile. One example here of an Irish case

255 Section 100 of the CA 1963.

256 See generally, Gough, *Company Charges* (2nd edn, 1996), pp 762–807. See also Johnston, *Banking and Security Law in Ireland* (1998), pp 600–605.

257 In *Re Chantry House Developments plc* [1990] BCLC 813, the mortgagee's solicitor's failure to deliver particulars was found to be accidental.

258 In *Re Resinoid and Mica Products Ltd* [1983] Ch 132, the mortgagee's and mortgagor's solicitors each thought that the other was attending to the registration, when neither was, in fact. See also *Re RM Arnold & Co Ltd* [1984] BCLC 535.

259 The failure to recognise that a particular charge was registrable, through ignorance of the law: *Re s Abrahams & Sons* [1902] 1 Ch 695. Illness too has been accepted as an excuse for non-registration within time: *Re Joplin Brewery Co Ltd* [1902] 1 Ch 79.

260 In *Re Braemar Investments Ltd* [1989] Ch 54, it was observed that the company's solvency meant that the likelihood of prejudice to unsecured creditors was remote.

261 See *Re Chantry House Developments plc* [1990] BCLC 813 and *Re Braemar Investments Ltd* [1989] Ch 54.

262 *Re Kris Cruisers Ltd* [1949] Ch 138.

where late registration was refused is *Re Farm Fresh Frozen Foods Ltd*[263]. There, Keane J said that late registration would not be granted because:

> 'It is acknowledged that no useful purpose would be served by making such an order if it included the usual saver for the rights of parties acquired prior to the date of actual registration. I have no doubt that there would be no justification for making such an order in the present case[264].'

Where a creditor who is making an application for late registration of a charge is aware of matters that would influence the court's discretion, he should disclose these matters to the court. In *Re Telomatic Ltd*[265], a creditor's conduct was said to be 'deplorable' where it did not disclose to the court that at the time of making the application the company had been dissolved[266]. It should also be noted that it is unwise for an applicant to delay in making application under s 106 as in *Victoria Housing Estates Ltd v Aspurton Estates Ltd*[267] the English Court of Appeal refused an application for late registration on the ground that, fearing the application might precipitate the company's liquidation, the applicant had deliberately deferred his application 'to see which way the wind [was] going to blow'.

(b) Distinguishing a complete failure to register from a mere misstatement or omission

[19.092] The error sought to be rectified by s 106 of the CA 1963 can be one of two kinds. In the first place, there may have been a complete failure to register the charge within the prescribed time, ie, 21 days. In the second place, a charge may have been registered, but may have omitted or misstated one of the particulars required to be stated, eg, to misstate the total amount secured by stating that a charge which in reality secured €100,000, only secured €80,000. On the authority of Costello J in *Re Shannonside Holdings Ltd*[268] such an error will not affect the validity of the charge, nor preclude the chargee from having security up to the amount actually specified in the debenture[269]. Since the effect of an order under s 106(1) is that the charge becomes a valid charge *ab initio* from the date of registration but subject to such other conditions as the court may impose[270], on the authority of the decision of Costello J, it was suggested in the previous edition of this work[271] that a chargee who discovers that particulars of the charge were misstated in the Form C1 might be better served not to make an application for

263 *Re Farm Fresh Frozen Foods Ltd* [1980] ILRM 131.

264 *Re Farm Fresh Frozen Foods Ltd* [1980] ILRM 131 at 136.

265 *Re Telomatic Ltd* [1994] 1 BCLC 90.

266 *Re Telomatic Ltd* [1994] 1 BCLC 90 at 94, *per* Judge Micklem. As to the requirement for full disclosure of all material facts in *ex parte* applications, albeit from the perspective of *Mareva* applications, see Courtney, *Mareva Injunctions and Related Interlocutory Orders* (1998), pp 305–316.

267 *Victoria Housing Estates Ltd v Aspurton Estates Ltd* [1982] 3 All ER 665.

268 *Re Shannonside Holdings Ltd* (20 May 1993, unreported) HC.

269 See also *Re Valley Ice Cream (Ireland) Ltd* (22 July 1998, unreported) HC, McCracken J and generally para **[19.036]**.

270 See *Re Clarets Ltd; Spain v McCann* [1978] ILRM 215 at 217.

271 Courtney, *The Law of Private Companies* (2nd edn, 2002) at para [21.090].

rectification under s 106[272], but in the light of the decision of Laffoy J in *Re Investment Options and Solutions Ltd; Bank of Scotland (Ireland) Ltd v Investment Options and Solutions Ltd,* [273] it is thought that chargees should apply under s 106 as they will not be made the subject of the usual conditions that apply to a late registration. The suggestion made in the second edition was noted in MacCann & Courtney, *Companies Acts 1963–2006,* which Laffoy J cited as being a useful summary of the effect of s 106:

> 'An error in the particulars delivered to the Registrar will not affect the validity of the charge, once a certificate of registration has been issued pursuant to [the Act of 1963], s 104. Courtney, [*The Law of Private Companies* ... para 21.090] argues therefore that an application for rectification may be superfluous, particularly if the court were to impose the same conditions as are applied in the case of an order extending time. In any event, the jurisdiction conferred on the court by s 106 only allows it to correct an omission or mis-statement in the delivered particulars and does not allow for the deletion of an entire entry. Furthermore, the court's jurisdiction is confined to rectifying errors in the particulars which are required by law to be delivered to the Registrar of Companies: there is no jurisdiction to order the rectification of factual errors in particulars the delivery of which is not required by law.'

In the case before Laffoy J, the facts were that the form delivering particulars of a charge mistakenly referred to its date of creation as being 3 July 2001 instead of 22 June 2001. Referring to the suggestion that the application for rectification might be superfluous as suggested above in the light of the conclusiveness of the certificate of charge, Laffoy J said:

> 'Counsel for the applicant answered that question on the basis that the receiver, in reliance on his powers under, *inter alia*, the deed of mortgage and charge dated 22 June 2001, intends selling assets of the notice party and queries may arise as to his authority to do so and as to title derived therefrom, because of the misstatement of the date thereof. It seems to be reasonable, in order to obviate such potential difficulties, to apply to have the mis-statement of the date of the deed of mortgage and charge in the particulars filed in the CRO rectified[274].'

Laffoy J went on to address the concern that an applicant for rectification might be prejudiced by holding that it would not be appropriate in a case such as the one before the court to impose conditions to protect the rights of any other secured creditors acquired between the expiry of the 21-day period and the registration on foot of a s 106 order. The justification for not imposing conditions was clearly stated by Laffoy J in the following terms:

> 'The position here is that the charge was created on 22 June, 2001. The Form No 47[275] was received in the CRO on the 6 July, 2007, albeit with a mis-statement of the date of creation of the charge. However, the Form No 47 was received within twenty one days after the

---

[272] Other misstatements may well be 'protected' by reason of the conclusiveness of the register: see para **[19.011]–[19.020]**.

[273] *Re Investment Options and Solutions Ltd; Bank of Scotland (Ireland) Ltd v Investment Options and Solutions Ltd* [2010] IEHC 107 at para 6, quoting from p 225 of MacCann & Courtney, *Companies Acts 1963–2006* (Bloomsbury Professional, 2007).

[274] *Re Investment Options and Solutions Ltd; Bank of Scotland (Ireland) Ltd v Investment Options and Solutions Ltd* [2010] IEHC 107 at para 7.

[275] The *Form 47* was the predecessor to the *Form C1*.

date of the creation of the charge, as required by s 99. Aside from the conclusiveness of the certificate of registration under s 104, I am satisfied that s 99(1), which provides that failure to deliver the prescribed particulars within twenty one days after creation of a charge '*shall, so far as any security on the company's property or undertaking is conferred thereby, be void against the liquidator and any creditor of the company*' could not be applied in this case so as to render the deed of mortgage and charge dated 22 June, 2001 void as against Mr McNabb.

9. On the evidence before the Court, I think it is reasonable to infer that the mis-statement of the date on the Form No 47 was accidental. I am satisfied that an order should be made under s 106. That the order will direct the Registrar of Companies to rectify the mis-statement of the date of the instrument creating the charge by substituting 22 June, 2001 for 3 July, 2001 in the registered particulars and the certificate of registration.'

The decision not to impose conditions on a s 106 application where particulars (albeit incorrect particulars) are delivered to the registrar of companies within the 21-day period is considered to be wholly justified and in accordance with the policy behind the requirement that certain charges are registered.

[19.093] It has been held in the UK that the power of rectification is limited to correcting mistakes of omission or commission in the entry of any particular but did not confer jurisdiction to remove matters that were not required to have been delivered to the registrar. In *igroup Ltd v Ocwen and ors*[276], a debenture creating security over the company's interest in mortgages was created by a large number of its customers and, although not required by law to do so, a solicitor on behalf of one of the parties lodged forms with Companies House which included a schedule of the customers concerned, including their names, addresses, prices paid for their properties, the original loan amount, monthly payments and the interest rates charged. On it becoming apprehended that this might constitute a breach of the data protection laws and customer confidentiality, an application was brought to amend the forms by redacting this information. Lightman J held that the court had no jurisdiction to rectify the register or amend the forms as being either (a) 'a mis-statement of any particular' or (b) under the court's inherent jurisdiction. He held that the meaning of 'a mis-statement of any particular' referred only to any particular that the registrar was required to enter in the register and not to information supplied to the register which was not required to be entered in the register. Lightman J also distinguished the cases of *Exeter Trust Ltd v Screenways Ltd*[277] and *Re Calmex Ltd; Calmex Ltd v C Lila Ltd*[278] which were advanced as authorities for the proposition that the court had an inherent jurisdiction to order the rectification of the registers. It is thought that the decision in *igroup* is excessively legalistic and contrary to common sense and justice and that even if the proper construction of 'a mis-statement of any particular' compels an interpretation that refers to particulars required to be delivered, a redaction to protect privacy which was unnecessarily breached was not inconsistent with the policy behind registration of company charges and within the court's inherent jurisdiction. It is thought this decision should not be followed in Ireland.

276 *igroup Ltd v Ocwen and others* [2003] 4 All ER 1063.

277 *Exeter Trust Ltd v Screenways Ltd* [1991] BCLC 888.

278 *Re Calmex Ltd; Calmex Ltd v C Lila Ltd* [1989] 1 All ER 485.

(c) The Joplin proviso[279]

[19.094] Where a court exercises its discretion and allows a charge to be registered out of time, it is usual for the court to insist that late registration is to be without prejudice to rights acquired by others. Accordingly, the courts usually insert a proviso that the order for late registration under s 106 of the CA 1963 is '... without prejudice to the rights of parties acquired prior to the actual time of such registration and a copy of this Order to be left with the Registrar of Companies'[280]. A revised form of proviso also used is '... this order is without prejudice to the rights of the parties acquired during the period between the date of creation of the said charge and the date of its actual registration'[281]. Only rights of third parties which can be established are protected[282].

The first proviso (still inserted by Irish courts[283]) is said to provide an immune period, ie, a charge created after an unregistered charge, but before the expiration of 21 days from the creation of the unregistered charge (eg, created later the same day) will rank after an unregistered charge which is subsequently registered out of time[284]. The revised proviso will, however, protect rights acquired after the creation of the unregistered charge, the late registration of which is subsequently permitted[285].

[19.095] Those most clearly saved are other secured creditors who will be assisted by the insertion of this proviso. The proviso will not invariably be inserted into an order and was, for example, omitted in the case of *Re Fablehill Ltd*[286] where in an application for late registration of a prior unregistered charge it was heard that the company had, subsequent to the creation of that charge, created a later charge in favour of its own directors.

[19.096] The position of unsecured creditors will clearly be prejudiced where relief is granted pursuant to s 106 of the CA 1963 and the proviso to an order for late registration will not save them. In *Re Ehrmann Bros Ltd*[287], Romer J said:

> '... the true effect of that condition is that it was only intended to protect rights acquired against or affecting the property charged by debentures. In my opinion that condition did not mean that after registration the registration was to be of no effect whatever as a charge against all creditors then existing ... I think that they were intended to be treated as valid

[279] After *Re Joplin Brewery Co* [1902] 1 Ch 79.

[280] See *Re Clarets Ltd; Spain v McCann* [1978] ILRM 215 at 217.

[281] A variant of the form of proviso noted in *Watson v Duff Morgan and Vermont (Holdings) Ltd* [1974] 1 All ER 794, [1974] 1 WLR 450, namely: 'That the time for registering the charge be extended until the ... day of ... and this order is to be without prejudice to the rights of parties acquired during the period between the creation of the said charge and the datc of its actual registration.' Note also that this latter proviso is quoted in Keane, *Company Law* (4th edn, 2007), para [21.50].

[282] *Re Peleton Ltd* [2011] IEHC 479, Laffoy J at para 5.4.

[283] In *Re Manning Furniture Ltd (in receivership)* [1996] 1 ILRM 13, where the wording of the proviso inserted by Keane J is quoted as being '... without prejudice to the rights (if any) of parties acquired prior to the time when the said particulars shall actually be registered.'

[284] See, for example, *Watson v Duff Morgan & Vermont (Holdings) Ltd* [1974] 1 All ER 794.

[285] See Gough, *Company Charges* (2nd edn, 1996), p 799–801.

[286] *Re Fablehill Ltd* [1991] BCLC 830.

[287] *Re Ehrmann Bros Ltd* [1906] 2 Ch 697 at 707.

> charges subject only … to rights acquired which could have been enforced in some way against the property had not the extension of time been granted'.

Unsecured creditors may have relied upon the fact that there were no registered charges before giving the company credit, but it may not be said that they acquired any 'rights' in the company's assets, unless the company is being wound up[288].

[19.097] In Ireland, the position of preferential creditors may be different. In *Re Manning Furniture Ltd (in receivership)*[289], it was held that the effect of the proviso was to mean that the late registration of a charge was without prejudice to the rights of preferential creditors of a company which was in receivership. The background facts were that a receiver had been appointed pursuant to the provisions of a mortgage debenture and various other security documents which had been given in favour of ICC Bank plc. However, the company had earlier granted a prior first legal mortgage and charge over certain premises in favour of, what was then, First National Building Society. When it transpired that First National's charge had not been registered, and subsequent to the appointment by ICC of the receiver, application was made by First National for late registration under s 106 of the CA 1963. An order was made under that section by Keane J in the High Court containing a proviso which stated 'But this Order to be without prejudice to the rights (if any) of parties acquired prior to the time when the said particulars shall actually be registered'. After the receiver realised the chattels and contracted for the sale of the premises he sought directions under s 316 of the CA 1963 as to whether he was obliged to discharge the preferential creditors out of the surplus (after payment of ICC) before paying the balance to First National. McCracken J, in reliance upon *Re Eisc Teoranta*[290], held that the receiver was bound to discharge the preferential creditors. As to the priority between the preferential creditors and First National, a mortgagee permitted late registration under s 106, he said:

> 'If the judgment of Mr Justice Lardner in the *Eisc Teoranta* case is correct, then the liability to discharge the preferential creditors arose on the appointment of the receiver, and was an existing liability of the Company with a preferential status at the time of the Order extending time. It was sought to be argued that, while they may have been preferential creditors, they were simply ordinary creditors who were given some form of preferential treatment, but I do not think I can accept that argument. On the appointment of the receiver, the preferential creditors were given a priority under s 98, and that priority was a right acquired prior to the time of the registration of the particulars of the mortgage of the First National Building Society[291].'

In this case, the proviso was construed so as to afford protection to preferential creditors on the basis that the proviso protected those who had rights, and because the preferential creditors had rights upon the appointment of the receiver they had protection. If a receiver had not been appointed then, of course, the preferential creditors would not

---

[288] See Ussher, *Company Law in Ireland* (1986), p 465, *Re Spiral Globe Co Ltd* [1902] 1 Ch 396 and *Re Ehrmann Bros Ltd* [1906] 2 Ch 697. But see *Re Telford Motors Ltd* (27 January 1978, unreported) HC, *per* Hamilton J, where it was said that creditors acquire 'rights' once a winding-up order is made.

[289] *Re Manning Furniture Ltd (in receivership)* [1996] 1 ILRM 13.

[290] *Eisc Teoranta* [1991] ILRM 760. See Ch 20, *Corporate Borrowing: Receivers*, para **[20.068]**.

[291] *Re Manning Furniture Ltd (in receivership)* [1996] 1 ILRM 13 at 16.

have had s 98 'rights' and would not be entitled to priority ahead of any late registered floating charge.

In making an order under s 106 it is open to the court to modify[292] the traditional wording of the *Joplin* proviso to expressly exclude any possible reference to preferential creditors. Indeed, it is thought that justice will not, ordinarily, be served by allowing the Revenue Commissioners priority to a late registered prior fixed charge since the only reason why one would allow priority – the absence of informed consent through notice to dealing with the encumbered company – is not relevant to the Revenue Commissioners' relationship with the company. It is submitted that, in principle and save where a winding up has commenced[293], the only 'rights' which ought to be protected by a *Joplin* proviso are such rights as are consensually acquired for value without notice of the existence of a prior right which would affect the right acquired. The protection of rights acquired otherwise, for example, by statute, are not within the contemplation of the registration of charges provisions.

(d) Application for late registration where company being wound up

[19.098] A contentious question concerns the situation where the winding up of a company has commenced. In *Re International Retail Ltd*[294], Kenny J said that court practice was to insist upon evidence that no winding-up order had been made, pending or contemplated and that there were no judgments against the company which were unpaid before the granting of an extension of the time in which to register[295]. Upon a company going into liquidation, its existing unsecured creditors become interested in all the assets of the company; it has even been said that the creditors are in effect cestui que trust with beneficial interests in the company's property[296]. It has been said by Keane[297] that:

> 'Unsecured creditors are not protected by the proviso: it only applies to creditors who have acquired some form of proprietary interest in the property the subject of the charge. But once the company is wound up, the position is different: all the creditors of the company have an interest at that stage in the property, whether secured or not. The proviso would in such circumstances have to extend to all the creditors and this would render the making of the order a futile exercise. It has accordingly been held in England ... that an order extending the time cannot be made once the company has been wound up, save in the most exceptional circumstances.'

Once an actual order to wind up has been made, no extension of time in which to register can be granted[298]. Where no order to wind up has been granted, then evidence of

---

292 *Re s Abrahams & Sons* [1902] 1 Ch 695; *Re IC Johnson & Co Ltd* [1902] 2 Ch 101.

293 See para **[19.098]**.

294 *Re International Retail Ltd* (26 July 1974, unreported) HC, Kenny J.

295 Following *Re LH Charles and Co Ltd* [1935] WN 15.

296 See *Re Ashpurton Estates Ltd* [1983] Ch 110; *Re Anglo-Oriental Carpet Manufacturing Co* [1903] 1 Ch 914 and *R v Registrar of Companies, ex p Central Bank of India* [1986] 1 All ER 105.

297 Keane, *Company Law* (4th edn, 2007), para [21.45].

298 *Re Resinoid & Mica Products Ltd* [1983] Ch 132 and *Victoria Housing Estates Ltd v Ashpurton Estates Ltd* [1983] Ch 110.

the kind spoken of by Kenny J will be required[299]. However, in *Re Telford Motors Ltd*[300] a registrable charge was taken by a lender, but was not registered. When the lender received a notice that it was proposed to wind up the company, an extension of time in which to register was applied for. Hamilton J, as he then was, granted the order and particulars were delivered to the registrar of companies. When the company was being wound up, the liquidator again applied to Hamilton J, this time to have the extended registration set aside. This was granted because the unsecured creditors had then acquired rights in the winding up. While it has been held that the imminence of a winding-up order ought to preclude the court from extending time[301], it was held in *Re Ashpurton Estates Ltd*[302] and *Re Braemar Investments Ltd*[303] that the imminence of winding up is not an absolute bar to relief. The imminence of winding up is, rather, a ground for refusal to be considered with all other matters in deciding whether or not to exercise the court's discretion. In *Exeter Trust Ltd v Screenways Ltd*[304], the English Court of Appeal, *per* Nourse LJ, held that where leave is granted to register a charge out of time and where the registrar of companies acts on foot of this order and issues a certificate of registration this will be conclusive evidence that the charge was validly registered. Where a court order is subsequently made for the removal of the charge from the register this will not affect the validity of the original registration.

[19.099] One of the means which a court may employ to safeguard unsecured creditors' interests, where application is made for late registration of a charge created by a company which is insolvent and teetering on the brink of liquidation, is to make a so-called '*Charles form order*'[305]. The *Charles* form order permits extension of time for registration but gives liberty to the company, usually through its liquidator or unsecured creditors, to apply to discharge the order for late registration where a winding up occurs within a specified number of days of the order for late registration. Accordingly, the applicant for late registration may effect registration on foot of the order but submits himself to the court's jurisdiction for review of that order in the event of application being made consequent to a winding up. The *Charles* form order recognises that most applications for late registration are made *ex parte*, without creditors having an opportunity to be heard, and so justice requires that, should circumstances change (eg, a winding up occur) they ought to have a right to be heard. Most instructive on this form of order is the decision of Hoffmann J in *Re Braemar Investments Ltd*[306] where he said:

---

299 See *Re RM Arnold & Co Ltd* [1984] BCLC 535 where Harman J held that the imminence of liquidation was a relevant factor to be considered in deciding whether or not to exercise judicial discretion.

300 *Re Telford Motors Ltd* (27 January 1978, unreported) HC, Hamilton J.

301 The granting of an order for extension here would seem to follow the case of *Re MIG Trust Ltd* [1933] Ch 542. However, Keane, *Company Law* (4th edn, Bloomsbury Professional, 2007), para [21.46] notes a different view was taken in *Re LH Charles & Co Ltd* [1935] WN 15. See also *Re Resinoid and Victoria Housing Estates* [1983] Ch 132.

302 *Re Ashpurton Estates Ltd* [1983] Ch 54.

303 *Re Braemar Investments Ltd* [1988] BCLC 556.

304 *Exeter Trust Ltd v Screenways Ltd* [1991] BCLC 888.

305 So called after the case of *Re LH Charles & Co Ltd* [1935] WN 15. See Gough, *Company Charges* (2nd edn, 1996), p 782 *et seq.*

306 *Re Braemar Investments Ltd* [1989] Ch 54.

'The type of order made in this case appears to have been invented by Clauson J in *Re LH Charles & Co Ltd* [1935] WN 15. It was intended to meet a difficulty caused by two special features of applications to extend time for registration. The first is that they are essentially ex parte in character. The creditors who may be affected are not respondents to the summons and the company will not necessarily have an interest in protecting the position. Indeed, in cases such as the present, in which the company's directors have guaranteed the debt, their interests will be opposed to those of unsecured creditors. In a case in which the evidence shows that the company is solvent, the likelihood of prejudice to unsecured creditors is remote and the court is, therefore, not particularly concerned about their lack of representation. But this case is different when liquidation appears to be imminent. However – and this is the second special feature of these applications – the court cannot deal with this problem by adjourning the application to see whether a petition is presented or a resolution for winding up is passed. Once the resolution has been passed, the rights of the unsecured creditor crystallise and an order to extend time can no longer be made. An adjournment may, therefore, cause injustice to an applicant who turns out to have been entitled to an order at the time when the application first came before the court. An order in *Re LH Charles & Co Ltd* form enables the whole matter to be reconsidered without pre-empting the question by postponing registration until after the liquidation has supervened.'

To a court faced with an otherwise meritorious application for relief under s 106 of the CA 1963 against a company of dubious solvency, or even certain insolvency, the *Charles* form order will sometimes help it strike the appropriate balance between competing interests[307].

(e) Agreement to late registered charge taking priority over prior registered charge

[19.100] Normally the existence of the proviso as to the safeguarding of rights will mean that the registered secured creditor will have priority over the late registered charge, even if it was aware of the unregistered charge when its charge was created. However, where a prior registered chargee *agrees to take after* the late registered chargee, the court will give effect to this and the prior registered chargee will be estopped from arguing to the contrary. So in *Spain v McCann*[308] a charge which was allowed to be registered late had priority over a charge which had been registered in time. Costello J held that:

'... it was expressly agreed between the company and the bank that the bank's mortgage debenture was subject to the plaintiff's mortgage [ie, the one which was allowed to be registered late]. Thus, the bank's rights were at all times subject to those of the prior [then, unregistered] encumbrancer and therefore, the right to appoint a receiver, enforce their security by sale of the company's premises were expressly made subject to the defendant's rights under his prior mortgage. The effect of the court's order ... was that the defendant's security became a valid one when registration was effected without prejudice to the bank's

307 See *Barclays Bank plc v Stuart Landon Ltd and another* [2001] 2 BCLC 316 where the English Court of Appeal said that since it had not been shown that an application to set aside an extension order was bound to succeed, the proper course was to make an order with the *proviso* which protected the bank and unsecured creditors. See also, *Re Chantry House Developments plc* [1990] BCLC 813 which also shows how the respective periods within a *Charles* form order can be shortened where justified by the circumstances.

308 *Spain v McCann* [1978] ILRM 215 at 218.

> rights under their mortgage debenture. What were those rights? They were clearly limited and qualified ones – they were subject at all times to those of the first mortgagee. The bank, it seems to me, are bound by the words of their agreement and they cannot now obtain a priority which they expressly agree they would not have.'

Where parties agree to a particular arrangement the courts will, generally, be reluctant to upset such consensually agreed arrangements.

Registration

[19.101] Section 100(1) of the CA 1963 provides that it is the duty of the company which creates the charge to send details of the particulars to the CRO. However, it goes on to provide that registration 'may be effected on the application of any person interested therein'. This allows the solicitor for the chargee to apply for registration. In practice, this represents the norm, as it would indeed be unusual for a chargee to entrust this most important task to the company creating the charge[309]. Failure to deliver particulars of a registrable charge is punishable by a class C fine, although the threat of this is probably the last reason why compliance with Part IV of the CA 1963 tends to be so high[310].

Particulars required to be registered

[19.102] Section 103(1) of the CA 1963 details the particulars which are required to be delivered to the CRO. These details are:

> In the case of a charge to the benefit of which the holders of a *series of debentures*[311] are entitled, such particulars as are specified in s 99(8), namely:
>
> – the total amount secured by the whole series;
>
> – the dates and resolutions authorising the issue, the date of the covering deed by which the security is created or defined;
>
> – a general description of the property charged; and
>
> – the names of the trustees (if any).

In the case of any *other charge*:

– the date it was created by the company;

– if the charge exists on property acquired by the company, the date of the acquisition of the property;

– for a judgment mortgage, the date of creation;

– the amount secured by the charge;

– short particulars of the property charged;

– the persons entitled to the charge.

309 The cost of registration is, in practice, usually recovered from the company which creates the charge. At present the cost of registration is €40.

310 Increased by s 15 of the C(A)A 1982. See s 100(3) and (4) of the CA 1963 which allow the registrar of companies to bring and prosecute proceedings in relation to an offence under this section.

311 See para **[19.044]**.

In practice, the most commonly filed particulars are those in relation to 'other charges'. In private companies, charges over a 'series of debentures' were rarely created although such may now be more likely due to the changes to s 33 of the CA 1963[312].

[19.103] The orderly registration of charges is achieved through the use of official forms used to record the details specified above. Of these, the most common is the *Form C1* which is used to register particulars of a charge created by a company incorporated in the State[313]. An officer of the company which creates the charge should sign the form, by way of application for registration, and it is usual for the solicitor of the chargee to arrange for this to be done at the same time as the charge itself is executed, prior to draw down of the facilities. Once signed by an officer of the company, the particulars of the charge are *verified*, usually by the solicitor for the chargee. Alternatively, a certified copy of the instrument which creates or evidences the charge can be delivered with the Form C1 in which application for registration should be made by the solicitor for the chargee. In practice, some solicitors' firms create their own Form C1s on computer. Such are acceptable to the CRO although prior approval should be sought before using such a form.

[19.104] There are several other forms as follows:

- A *Form C2* is a certificate that a charge over property outside the State has been presented for registration in the country where the property is situate, pursuant to s 99(5) of the CA 1963.
- A *Form C3* is used to register particulars of a charge where a company acquires property which is already subject to a charge or mortgage.
- A *Form C4* is used to register particulars relating to a series of debentures giving any charge to the debenture holders.
- A *Form C5* is used to register particulars of a further issue of debentures.

The prescribed form for registration of particulars of a charge created by a foreign company over property within the State is a *Form 8E*. This is also used to deliver particulars of a charge created by a foreign company over property in the State where that company has not registered on the external register, ie, for filing on the *Slavenburg* file.

Satisfaction of charges

[19.105] When a charge created by a company is paid off, or satisfied, the register of charges should be brought up to date and this fact recorded. This is achieved by the delivery of a memorandum of satisfaction of charge to the CRO in a *Form C6 (the successor of the old Form 49)*. The registrar of companies is empowered to enter on the register a memorandum of satisfaction *in whole* or *in part* by virtue of s 105 of the CA 1963. Before entering a satisfaction she should have evidence that:

- the debt has been paid or satisfied in whole or in part; or
- part of the property or undertaking charged has been released from the charge or has ceased to form part of the company's property or undertaking.

312 See Ch 18, *Corporate Borrowing: Debentures and Security*, at para **[18.021]**.

313 The *Form C1* replaced the *Form 47*, which had been introduced by SI 45/1964. The *Form C1* became the prescribed form by SI 466/2001 with effect from 23 October 2001.

Unlike the application to have a charge registered, a *Form C6* must be under the seal of the chargor company, and particulars of the satisfaction must be verified by a director and the secretary of the company, and sworn before a commissioner for oaths. Upon the registrar receiving a completed *Form C6*, before entering a satisfaction on the register of charges she will write to the holder of the charge giving it notice. It is thought that it would be better were s 105 to provide that the charge holder should execute the *Form C6* to avoid the possibility that the notice might be overlooked.

[19.106] Where a *Form C6* is filed and there is an omission or misstatement of any particular in a memorandum of satisfaction (for example, it is stated that there has been an entire, instead of a partial, discharge of a charge) application can be made to the High Court under s 106(1) of the CA 1963. Where the court is satisfied that the omission or misstatement was accidental or due to inadvertence or to some other sufficient cause or is not of a nature to prejudice the position of creditors or shareholders of the company or that on other grounds it is just and equitable to grant relief, it may on the application of the company or any person interested and on such terms as it considers just and expedient, order that the omission or misstatement shall be rectified[314]. There has been little or no jurisprudence on this aspect of s 106(1) and applications brought under that provision appear to invariably involve omissions or misstatements in charges, rather than memoranda of satisfaction of charges. It is thought that where a charge is erroneously stated to have been discharged in full and another third party creditor relies on what it believes will be a charge that will rank ahead of the charge which was erroneously stated to have been discharged in full, the court would be unlikely to allow such an misstatement to be corrected by ordering that the memorandum of satisfaction be changed to record a partial discharge. Conversely, where no intervening charge, whether or not it is registrable, has been created over the assets in question, the court may be inclined to order the rectification of the omission or misstatement.

The chargor company's obligations

[19.107] In accordance with s 109 of the CA 1963 every instrument that creates a charge which requires registration must be kept at the registered office of the chargor company, or in the case of foreign companies, at its principal place of business[315]. Section 110(1) of the CA 1963 provides that copies of the instruments must be open for inspection by any creditor or member of the company, subject to reasonable restrictions which the company in general meeting may impose, provided that inspection is allowed for not less than two hours per day. Failure to allow inspection is punishable by a class C fine[316] and a court may order immediate inspection upon an application being made[317]. On a practical note, it is rare for a creditor or member to invoke this right, more rare for a company to be aware of this obligation, and bordering on fantasy for the average Irish private company to have a strategy which would roll into action should a knock come to the door seeking inspection of the company's register of charges.

---

314 See para **[19.090]** *ante*.

315 Section 111 of the CA 1963.

316 Section 110(2) of the CA 1963.

317 Section 110(3) of the CA 1963.

[illegible] charge registered [illegible] the charge or company [illegible] the particulars of the [illegible] the registrar of the company [illegible] charge [illegible] to the holder of the charge [illegible] would be better [illegible] that the charge holder should [illegible] to avoid the possibility that the matter might be overlooked.

110.1976 Where [illegible] there is an omission or misstatement of any particular [illegible] for example [illegible] the court [illegible] inadvertence or to some other sufficient cause [illegible] position of creditors or shareholders of the company [illegible] and equitable to grant relief [illegible] omission or misstatement shall be rectified [illegible] application [illegible] under the provision [illegible] charge is erroneously [illegible] third party [illegible] with the [illegible] registration [illegible] rectification of the [illegible].

The duty of company to register [illegible]

110.1977 In accordance with [illegible] charge, which requires [illegible] company [illegible] at the [illegible] of the company [illegible] to the inspection of any creditor or member of the company [illegible] to the inspection of the company's register of charges.

[illegible] See para [illegible]
[illegible] Section [illegible] of the CA 1985.
[illegible] Section [illegible] of the CA 1985.
[illegible] Section [illegible] of the CA 1985.

Chapter 20

Corporate Borrowing: Receivers

Introduction

[20.001] Where a company defaults on a financial obligation secured by a debenture that creates a legal mortgage or charge over land, it is open to the secured creditor to seek possession of the property (either voluntarily or by court order) and then to sell the property (either with or without the help of the court)[1]. More often than not, however, a secured creditor whose debenture so allows will seek to appoint a receiver: the appointment of a receiver is one of the most popular remedies availed of by secured creditors against defaulting companies[2]. In this chapter the following issues are considered:

1. Receiver defined.
2. Considerations on the appointment of a receiver under a debenture.
3. Qualifications of receivers.
4. Appointment of a receiver.
5. The effect of the appointment of a receiver.
6. The status of a receiver.
7. The remuneration of a receiver
8. Duties of receivers.
9. Liabilities of receivers.
10. Powers of receivers.
11. Applications for directions.
12. Multiple receivers to the same company.
13. Resignation and removal of receivers.

Receiver defined

[20.002] The appointment of a receiver is one of the oldest remedies known to equity[3]: 'the term deriv[ing] from the Latin *recipere* (re-capere, to take)'[4]. Howsoever receivers are appointed, they are persons whose function it is to '*receive*' a debtor's assets and

---

1 See Wylie, *Irish Land Law* (4th edn, Bloomsbury Professional, 2010), para [13.013] *et seq.*

2 See Lynch-Fannon & Murphy, *Corporate Insolvency and Rescue* (2nd edn, Bloomsbury Professional, 2012), pp 211–270 and Breslin, *Banking Law in the Republic of Ireland* (2nd edn, 2007), pp 589–610.

3 *Hoplins v Worcester and Birmingham Canal Proprietors* (1868) LR 6 Eq 437 at 446–447, *per* Giffard VC and, generally, in the context of court appointed pre-judgment and post-judgment receivers, Courtney, *Mareva Injunctions and Related Interlocutory Orders* (1998), pp 422–432.

4 *Per* Murphy J in *Re Bula Ltd* (20 June 2002, unreported) HC.

property for and on behalf of a creditor who is entitled to take them in satisfaction of the debtor's obligations. In the case of a court appointed receiver, the receiver is appointed by order of the court to gather-up and take into his possession the assets of another. In the case of a receiver appointed on foot of a deed (eg, a debenture) the purpose is the same: the receiver is appointed by the creditor to gather-up and take into his possession the debtor's assets for the purpose of selling them and applying the proceeds in satisfaction of the sums due to the creditor. This chapter is generally concerned with receivers appointed on foot of debentures.

[20.003] The term 'receiver' was defined in *Re Manchester and Milford Railway Co*[5], where Sir George Jessell MR said:

> 'A 'receiver' is a term which was well known in the Court of Chancery, as meaning a person who receives rents or other income paying ascertained outgoings, but who does not, if I may say so, manage the property in the sense of buying or selling or anything of that kind. We were most familiar with the distinction in the case of a partnership. If a receiver was appointed of partnership assets, the trade stopped immediately. He collected debts, sold the stock-in-trade and other assets, and then under the order of the court the debts of the concern were liquidated and the balance divided. If it was desired to continue the trade at all it was necessary to appoint a manager, or a receiver and manager as it was generally called. He could buy and sell and carry on the trade.'

This *dictum* clearly shows the distinction between two different types of receivers: the first type having the function of essentially 'collecting' property with a view to its sale (a 'receiver simpliciter'); the second of 'managing' the property, running it as a going concern and being more properly termed a 'receiver-manager'.

[20.004] A receiver is very different from either a liquidator or an examiner. A *liquidator* has the task of winding up a company, realising its assets and distributing those assets in accordance with law[6]. An *examiner* is appointed under the Companies (Amendment) Act 1990 ('C(A)A 1990') for the purpose of examining 'the situation, affairs and prospects of the company' and then reporting to the court on the company's prospects for survival[7]. A *receiver*, appointed on foot of a debenture, has the principal task of securing the assets of a company which have been mortgaged or charged in favour of the debenture holder which appointed him. A company which is *in liquidation* is in the process of being wound up. A company which is *in examinership* is being scrutinised by an examiner so that he may report back to the court with proposals for the company's survival. A company which is *in receivership* has had a receiver appointed, who is realising and receiving its assets and, or in the alternative, managing its affairs in the hope that the debts outstanding to the debenture holder which appointed him can be met.

Considerations on the appointment of a receiver under a debenture

[20.005] It is not unusual for companies to become gradually insolvent. Pleas for forbearance from insolvent companies' directors are common. The financial institutions

5 *Re Manchester and Milford Railway Co* (1880) 14 Ch D 645 at 653.

6 See generally Ch 25, *Realisation and Distribution of Assets in a Winding Up*.

7 *Re Atlantic Magnetics Ltd* [1993] 2 IR 561 at 572, *per* Finlay CJ. See generally Ch 23, *Examinerships*.

which have advanced facilities to such companies will often be faced with the hard financial (and human) decision of when to call in the facilities by seeking repayment.

(a) Default: the basis for the appointment of a receiver

[20.006] Before a receiver can be appointed on foot of a debenture there must usually have occurred an *act or event of default* by the borrower company. So-called 'events of default' will usually be set out in the debenture creating the mortgage or charge, although some may also be listed in the initial facility letter. While not exhaustive, the following[8] are a sample of the typical events of default which will be contained in either a facility letter or debenture (or a combination of both):

- if any of the money (principal and interest and all other sums) owing by the chargor company is not paid or discharged when due; or
- if there is a breach by the chargor company of any of the terms and conditions of the debenture or of any loan agreement with the chargee or of any offer letter or letter of sanction issued by the chargee to the chargor company or of any facility from the chargee or any representation or warranty or undertaking from time to time made to the chargee by the chargor company is or becomes incorrect or misleading in any material respect; or
- if (save for the purpose of and followed by an amalgamation or reconstruction which shall have first been approved in writing by the chargee) a petition is presented, or an order is made, or a resolution is passed, or a notice is issued convening a meeting for the purpose of considering a resolution, or analogous proceedings or action are taken, to wind up the chargor company or to place the chargor company under the protection of the court or to appoint an examiner, interim examiner, administrator, trustee or similar official to the chargor company or to a related company (within the meaning of the C(A)A 1990) or the chargee has reason to believe that any of the foregoing may be about to happen; or
- if an encumbrancer takes possession or exercises or attempts to exercise any power of sale or a receiver or similar official is appointed over the whole or any part of the undertaking, property, assets or revenues of the chargor company; or
- if any judgment or order made against the chargor company is not complied with within seven days or an execution, distress, sequestration or other process is levied or enforced upon or sued out against any part of the undertaking, property, assets or revenues of the chargor company; or
- if the chargor company without the prior consent in writing of the chargee ceases or threatens to cease to carry on its business or any material part thereof in the normal course or changes the nature or mode of conduct of its trading in any material respect or ceases to be a going concern; or
- if any indebtedness of the chargor company is not paid when due or becomes or is capable of being declared payable prior to its stated maturity or any encumbrance from time to time created by the chargor company becomes enforceable; or

---

8 See Parsons, *Lingard's Bank Security Documents* (5th edn, 2011) at p 249–267; Picarda, *The Law Relating to Receivers, Managers and Administrators* (2nd edn, 1990).

- if the chargor company commences negotiations to reschedule the whole or any part of its indebtedness which it would or might otherwise be unable to pay when due or is unable to pay its debts as they fall due within the meaning of s 214 of the CA 1963[9] or stops or threatens to stop payment or is deemed to be unable to pay its debts for the purpose of any law of any jurisdiction to which it is subject or enters into any compromise or arrangement for the benefit of its creditors generally; or
- if the debenture or any guarantee, indemnity or other security for any of the money (principal and interest and all other sums) owing fails or ceases in any respect to have full force and effect or to be continuing or is terminated or is disrupted or becomes in jeopardy, invalid or unenforceable; or
- if any licence, authorisation, consent or registration at any time necessary or desirable to enable the chargor company to comply with its obligations to the chargee or to carry on its business in the normal course shall be revoked, withheld or materially modified or shall fail to be granted or perfected or shall cease to remain in full force and effect; or
- if any material adverse change occurs in the affairs of the chargor company which in the opinion of the chargee gives ground for belief that the chargor company may not or may be unable to perform its obligations hereunder or under any facility from the chargee; or
- if there shall occur any event of default howsoever described under any document governing, regulating, securing, guaranteeing or supporting the obligations of the chargor company to the chargee; or
- if any event analogous to any of the foregoing events occurs without the prior consent in writing of the chargee in relation to (a) any third party which now or hereafter has guaranteed or provided security for or given an indemnity in respect of the money (principal and interest and all other sums) owing or (b) any subsidiary or holding company (as defined by s 155 of the CA 1963)[10] of the chargor company or of any such third party or any subsidiary of any such holding company; or if any individual now or hereafter liable as such third party shall commit an act of bankruptcy, die or become of unsound mind; or
- if the chargor company shall (without the prior written consent of the chargee) redeem or purchase any of its share capital or declare, make or pay any dividend or other distribution (in cash or in kind) in respect of any of its share capital.

[20.007] Upon the occurrence of one or more of the foregoing *an event of default* is said to occur. The effect of the occurrence of an event of default will depend upon the actual terms of a given debenture. The effect, in practice, will be that the loan to the company may be called in and if it is not repaid, steps can be taken to enforce any security given by the company. Some or all of the events listed in the preceding paragraph are often found in most debentures' 'default clauses', which provide that if any of these events occur, the chargor can forthwith demand repayment. Whilst, sometimes, default clauses

---

9 See generally, Ch 23, *Winding Up Companies*, at para **[23.074]**. See also *Re Creation Printing Company Ltd* [1981] IR 353 and *Byblos Bank SAC v AL Khudhairy* [1987] BCLC 232.

10 See Ch 12, *Groups of Companies*, at para **[12.008]**.

are stated to operate automatically, it is nevertheless common not to take any steps against a borrower until notice (coupled with a formal demand for repayment, where appropriate) is given in the manner prescribed by the debenture.

[20.008] It is incumbent upon a creditor to comply with the terms of his security document before taking action on foot of it in the form of, for example, appointing a receiver. Where provisions governing the service of notice or provisions as to who can serve notice are not strictly complied with, creditors will leave their subsequent appointment of a receiver open to challenge. Such was in issue in the Australian High Court case of *Pan Foods Company Importers & Distributors Pty Ltd v Australia and New Zealand Banking Group Ltd*[11]. There, however, in upholding the receiver's appointment in circumstances where the creditor's entitlement to declare monies owing to be due and payable, the service of notice to that effect and the status of the person serving the notice were called into question, the importance of construing commercial agreements practically was stressed. In the course of his judgment Kirby J said of commercial documents:

> 'In my view, such documents should be construed practically, so as to give effect to their presumed commercial purposes and so as not to defeat the achievement of such purposes by an excessively narrow and artificially restricted construction. The law facilitates and upholds commercial contractual obligations and the expectations that derive from them. Statute and equity may sometimes come to the aid of parties where various forms of unfairness or inequity can be shown. None was invoked in this appeal. But as between a commercial enterprise and a finance provider, such as a bank, the law should be the upholder of agreements. It should eschew artificialities and excessive technicalities for these will not be imputed to the ordinary businessperson. Business is entitled to look to the law to keep people to their commercial promises. In a world of global finances and trans-border capital markets, those jurisdictions flourish which do so. Those jurisdictions which do not soon become known. They pay a price in terms of the availability and costs of capital necessary as a consequence of the uncertainties of the enforcement of agreements in their courts[12].'

In the instant case, Kirby J found that one could not doubt that a reasonably informed businessperson 'looking at the notice in this case, and by whom it was handed to the company, would conclude that it was 'a notice from the Bank to the Customer … given by an Authorised Representative, in writing'. He concluded that in the absence of substantial, persuasive and practical reasons (of which there were none) the law could not come to a contrary conclusion.

(b) *Appointment following default in repaying money repayable on demand*

[20.009] Perhaps the most common event to cause a chargee to appoint a receiver to a company is where money owed to the chargee becomes due. It is common for debentures to provide that the repayment of all money (principal and interest and all

---

11 *Pan Foods Company Importers & Distributors Pty Ltd v Australia and New Zealand Banking Group Ltd* [2000] HCA 20.

12 *Pan Foods Company Importers & Distributors Pty Ltd v Australia and New Zealand Banking Group Ltd* (13 April 2000) High Court of Australia, at para 24.

other sums) owing by the chargee company is repayable '*on demand*'[13]. It has been held that where money is repayable on demand the amount need not be specified in any written demand[14]. Moreover, the debtor must have it ready and is not entitled to further time in order to look for the money[15], and a receiver can be appointed at any time thereafter[16]. The preferred test in England is the so-called 'mechanics of payment test'. In *Bank of Baroda v Panessar*[17], Walton J said:

> 'Money payable 'on demand' is repayable immediately on demand being made ... Nevertheless, it is physically impossible in most cases for a person to keep the money required to discharge the debt about his person. He may in a simple case keep it in a box under his bed; it may be at the bank or with a bailee. The debtor is therefore not in default in making the payment demanded unless and until he has had a *reasonable opportunity* of implementing whatever reasonable mechanics of payment he may need to employ to discharge the debt. Of course, this is limited to the time necessary for the mechanics of payment. It does not extend to any time to raise the money if it is not there to be paid.'

It is thought that the mechanics of payment test is correct and that no other reasonable interpretation can be placed on a document which provides that money is to be repayable 'on demand' as that term is understood in Ireland and the United Kingdom[18]. In *Sheppard & Cooper Ltd v TSB Bank plc*[19], the question which arose was the validity of an administrative receivership, the answer to which turned on whether the bank had allowed sufficient time to pass between making its demand of the plaintiff and its purported appointment of receivers, which happened not more than 60 minutes later. The facts were that the plaintiff owed over £618,000 which was secured on foot of a debenture incorporating a fixed and floating charge and the defendant was the bank then

---

13 See Hapgood, *Paget's Law of Banking* (11th edn, 1996), pp 179–181.

14 *Bunbury Foods Pty Ltd v National Bank of Australasia Ltd* (1984) 51 ALR 609; *Bank of Baroda v Panessar* [1986] 3 All ER 751.

15 *Brighty v Norton* (1862) 122 ER 116.

16 *Bank of Baroda v Panessar* [1986] 3 All ER 751 where a receiver was found to have been validly appointed one hour after the making of the demand. See also *Lloyds Bank plc v Lampert* [1999] BCC 507 where this was followed by Kennedy LJ in the English Court of Appeal.

17 *Bank of Baroda v Panessar* [1986] 3 All ER 751 at 759–760, emphasis added.

18 *Cf* the reasonable notice test applied in some Commonwealth countries such as Canada. So in *Lister (RE) Ltd v Dunlop Canada Ltd* [1982] 1 SCR 726 it was held that a bank was required to give a debtor reasonable notice of its intention to enforce the security and a reasonable time to pay following such notice of intention. In *Mister Broadloom Corp (1968) Ltd v Bank of Montreal* (1979) 25 OR (2d) 198 (HC) at 208, the following criteria were established in determining the length of time amounting to reasonable notice: (1) the amount of the loan; (2) the risk to the creditor of losing his money or the security; (3) the length of the relationship between the debtor and the creditor; (4) the character and reputation of the debtor; (5) the potential ability to raise the money required in a short period; (6) the circumstances surrounding the demand for payment; and (7) any other relevant factors. In *Royal Bank of Canada v W Got & Associates Electric Ltd* (15 October 1999) Supreme Court of Canada, the court upheld an earlier finding that a bank was, *inter alia*, in breach of contract for failing to give sufficient notice and that damages were payable for the wrongful appointment of a receiver in such circumstances.

19 *Sheppard & Cooper Ltd v TSB Bank plc* [1996] 2 All ER 654.

entitled to the loan and security, having acquired it from the original lender. The defendant's representatives met with the plaintiff's directors and at that meeting gave the directors a written demand requiring repayment of the plaintiff's indebtedness. During the course of the meeting one of the plaintiff's directors stated that the plaintiff was not in a position to meet the demand and that the best that he could hope for would be to pay half the excess on the company's overdraft over the following seven days. Within 60 minutes of the meeting ending, the defendant appointed administrative receivers. It was held by Blackburne J that whilst the mechanics of payment test required a creditor to give a debtor a reasonable opportunity to pay the amount demanded:

> 'If, however, he has made it clear to the creditor that the necessary moneys are not available, then, provided a proper demand has been made, I cannot see that the creditor need allow any time to elapse before being at liberty to treat the debtor as in default[20].'

It must always be remembered, however, that a receiver can only be validly appointed on foot of a debenture *in accordance with the provisions of that debenture*. Accordingly, the contractual circumstances that permit the appointment of a receiver (eg, the happening of an event of default) must have occurred. Where a receiver is wrongly appointed, the chargor company will have a cause of action against the secured creditor for breach of contract and possibly conversion occasioned by a wrongfully appointed receiver taking possession of the chargor company's assets[21]. Interlocutory relief, in the form of an injunction to restrain a receiver from purporting to act as a receiver of the company's assets, may be sought by a company which asserts that there is no entitlement to appoint a receiver[22].

(c) No additional duty of care over and above contract

[20.010] Subject to strict contractual compliance in the appointment of a receiver, case law indicates that a creditor owes no special duty to a company in deciding whether or not to appoint a receiver. The fundamental issue for the debenture holder is whether the appointment of a receiver will further the debenture holder's interests. However, where the appointment will not advance the debenture holder's interests, the appointment may be said to have been made in bad faith. So, in *Re Potters Oils Ltd (No 2)*[23] Hoffmann J said that:

> 'The debenture-holder is under no duty to refrain from exercising his rights merely because doing so may cause loss to the company or its unsecured creditors. He owes a duty of care to the company but this duty is subordinated to the protection of his own interests[24].'

A similar statement can be found in *Shamji v Johnson Matthey Bankers Ltd*[25] where again Hoffmann J said:

---

20 *Sheppard & Cooper Ltd v TSB Bank plc* [1996] 2 All ER 654 at 660b. See also *Massey v Sladen* (1868) LR 4 Exch 13 at 17, *per* Kelly CB.

21 Eg, see *Royal Bank of Canada v W Got & Associates Electric Ltd* (15 October 1999) Supreme Court of Canada.

22 See, eg, *Ferris v Ward; Ward's Wholesale Meats Ltd v Ferris* [1998] 2 IR 194.

23 *Re Potters Oils Ltd (No 2)* [1986] BCLC 98.

24 *Re Potters Oils Ltd (No 2)* [1986] BCLC 98 at 103a–g.

25 *Shamji v Johnson Matthey Bankers Ltd* [1986] BCLC 278.

> 'The appointment of a receiver seems to me to involve an inherent conflict of interest. The purpose of the power is to enable the mortgagee to take the management of the company's property out of the hands of the directors and entrust it to a person of the mortgagee's choice. That power is granted to the mortgagee by the security documents in completely unqualified terms. It seems to me that a decision by the mortgagee to exercise the power cannot be challenged except perhaps on grounds of bad faith. There is no room for the implication of a term that the mortgagee shall be under a duty to the mortgagor to 'consider all relevant matters' before exercising the power. If no such qualification can be read into the security documents, I do not think that a wider duty can exist in tort: see *Tai Hing Cotton Mill Ltd v Liu Chong Hing Bank Ltd* [1985] 2 All ER 947 at 959 ... I might add that Harman J once remarked that the analogous power of the mortgagee to enter into possession may be exercised 'before the ink is dry on the mortgage'. Certainly there has never been any suggestion that the right to exercise the power, as opposed to the way in which the mortgagee deals with the mortgaged property once he is in possession, is qualified by a duty of care to the mortgagor ... a mortgagee who acts in what he considers to be in good faith to be his own interests may exercise his contractual right to appoint a receiver without regard to the effect upon the mortgagor or a guarantor of the obligations of the mortgagor[26].'

It is thought to be right and proper that a debenture holder's duties to a company are exhausted upon compliance with the underlying contract which facilitates and makes provision for the appointment of a receiver.

Qualifications of receivers

[20.011] Although the law relating to receivers was revamped by the Companies Act 1990, it remains the case that the only qualifications that the law requires of receivers are negative, ie, certain persons are barred from becoming receivers. In the first place, a body corporate is not qualified for appointment as receiver to the property of a company, a prohibition that carries with it a class C fine by s 314 of the CA 1963[27]. Furthermore, s 315 of the CA 1963[28] provides that none of the following persons qualify for appointment as receiver:

- an undischarged bankrupt;
- a person who is, or has been within 12 months of the commencement of the receivership, an officer or servant of the company[29];
- a parent, spouse, brother, sister or child of an officer of the company;
- a person who is a partner of or in the employment of an officer or servant of the company;
- a person who is not qualified by virtue of s 315 of the CA 1963 for appointment as receiver of the property of any other body corporate which is that company's

26 *Shamji v Johnson Matthey Bankers Ltd* [1986] BCLC 278 at 284.

27 As increased by s 15 of the C(A)A 1982.

28 As amended by s 170 of the CA 1990.

29 References to officer or servant are deemed to include references to an auditor: s 315 of the CA 1963. See *The Wise Finance Company Ltd v O'Regan* (26 June 1998, unreported) HC, Laffoy J, where a person who was the company secretary of a chargee company was found to be ineligible for appointment as receiver.

subsidiary or holding company or a subsidiary of that company's holding company, or would be so disqualified if the body corporate were a company.

Where, after his initial appointment, a receiver becomes disqualified by virtue of the application of any of the foregoing, he must vacate the office and give notice in writing of this within 14 days to the company, the registrar of companies, and either the debenture holder or the court, depending upon which appointed the receiver[30]. Contravention of this section is an offence and liable on summary conviction to a class C fine, and for a continued contravention a daily default class E fine, and on indictment to a fine not exceeding €11,110.21, and for continued contravention, to a daily fine of €555.50[31].

Appointment of a receiver

[20.012] A receiver can be appointed in either of two ways: on foot of the powers contained in a debenture, or on foot of a court order. Of these, by far the most common is an appointment pursuant to the express power of appointment by the debenture holder which is contained in the debenture.

(a) Appointment on foot of a debenture

[20.013] Today, almost every debenture created by a company in favour of an institutional lender will provide that the debenture holder can appoint a receiver, at any time after the principal money secured shall become payable. Such moneys will generally become payable upon the occurrence of an event of default, considered above[32]. A typical provision found in a debenture for the appointment of a receiver will read:

> 'At any time after the security hereby constituted has become enforceable [ie, upon the occurrence of an event of default] or at any time after the Company so requests the Bank may from time to time appoint under seal or under hand of a duly authorised officer or employee of the Bank any person or persons to be receiver and manager or receivers and managers (herein called "Receiver" which expression shall where the context so admits include the plural and any substituted receiver and manager or receivers and managers) of the Secured Assets [this term will be defined elsewhere in the debenture] or any part or parts thereof and from time to time under seal or under hand of a duly authorised officer or employee of the Bank remove any Receiver so appointed and may so appoint another or others in his stead. If the Bank appoints more than one person as Receiver of any of the Secured Assets, each such person shall be entitled (unless the contrary shall be stated in the appointment) to exercise all the powers and discretions hereby or by statute conferred on Receivers individually and to the exclusion of the other or others of them.'

It has been held that the appointment of a receiver will be valid even if the debenture takes effect under hand as opposed to under seal[33]. However, this will mean that the debenture will not create a valid mortgage over real property, since such deeds of mortgage are required to be under seal[34]. Since the enactment of s 15(2) of the Powers of

30 Section 315(2) of the CA 1963.

31 Section 315(5) of the CA 1963, as modified by ss 6, 8 and 9 of the FA 2010.

32 See para **[20.006]**.

33 See *Byblos Bank SAL v Al–Khudhairy* [1987] BCLC 232.

34 See Ch 7, *Corporate Contracts, Capacity and Authority*, para **[7.014]**.

Attorney Act 1996, it has not been necessary to create a power of attorney under seal; accordingly, a receiver appointed on foot of a debenture executed under hand can validly be constituted the company's attorney[35].

Sometimes mortgage debentures do not contain an express power to appoint a receiver and instead rely on the statutory power to appoint a receiver. Such a statutory power was contained in s 19 of the Conveyancing Act 1881, now repealed by s 8 of the Land and Conveyancing Law Reform Act 2009. In *McEnery v Sheahan*[36] it was held that the effect of s 27(1)(c) of the Interpretation Act 2005 – which provides that where an enactment is repealed, that repeal does not prejudice or affect any right, privilege, obligation or liability acquired, accrued or incurred – was to mean the bank could continue to rely on s 19(1) of the Conveyancing Act 1881 to appoint a receiver.

[20.014] One bar to the appointment of a receiver to a company is where an examiner has been appointed. Section 5(2)(b) of the C(A)A 1990 provides that where a company has been placed under the protection of the court no receiver over any part of the property or undertaking of the company shall be appointed, or if appointed before the presentation of the petition to place the company under the protection of the court shall be unable to act. An examiner can apply to have a receiver removed[37].

[20.015] It is also thought that a receiver cannot be appointed to a company which has been dissolved; and that where a receiver is appointed to a company which is subsequently dissolved, the receiver's authority will cease[38]. By reason of s 20 of the Powers of Attorney Act 1996 where a receiver is appointed attorney and the power is expressed to be irrevocable and given to secure either a proprietary interest of the donee of the power or the performance of an obligation owed to the donee then the company's winding up or dissolution will not revoke the power of attorney[39]. In such a situation a debenture holder may seek to have the company reinstated onto the register of companies[40].

[20.016] It is not a bar to the appointment of a receiver that a winding-up order has been made or that a provisional liquidator has been appointed. It had been argued in *Re Motor Racing Circuits Ltd*[41] that upon a winding-up order being made or a provisional liquidator appointed, s 222 of the CA 1963 barred a secured creditor from appointing a receiver over the assets of the company. It was held by the Supreme Court that the

---

35 Section 15(3) of the POAA 1996 provides that: 'This section is without prejudice to any requirement in or under any other enactment as to the witnessing of powers of attorney or as to the execution of instruments by bodies corporate.' It is thought that there is no obstacle to a company appointing an attorney by deed under hand. Indeed, reg 81 of Table A provides: 'The directors may … by power of attorney appoint any company, firm or person or body of persons … to be the attorney or attorneys of the company …'

36 *McEnery v Sheahan* [2012] IEHC 331, Feeney J.

37 See para **[20.094]**. See also Ch 22, *Examinerships*, para **[22.070]** *et seq*.

38 In *Salton v New Boston Cycle Co* [1900] 1 Ch 43, the dissolution of a company had the effect of terminating the company's solicitors' authority.

39 Care would need to be taken in drafting the debenture since s 20 of the POAA 1996 refers to a proprietary interest or obligation *owed to the donee* it would seem to require the power to be drawn in favour of the chargee, not the receiver.

40 See Ch 26, *Strike Off and Restoration*, para **[26.025]**.

41 *Re Motor Racing Circuits Ltd* (31 January 1997, unreported) SC.

appointment of a receiver under a power contained in a debenture does not come within the meaning of an 'action or proceeding' as used in s 222 of the CA 1963 and, accordingly, there was no bar to the receiver's appointment.

[20.017] The distinction between a receiver simpliciter and a receiver-manager is important, and the appointment of either will be dependent upon the nature of the debenture under which the receiver was appointed. Where the primary property mortgaged or charged is a specific asset, or series of assets, the appropriate appointment is of a simple 'receiver'. However, where the debenture created charges over the entire undertaking and business of the company, the debenture holder may appoint a 'receiver-manager'[42].

[20.018] The validity of the appointment of a receiver is dependent upon compliance with the terms contained in the debenture and the capacity of the company and authority of its officers to create the debenture *ab initio*[43]; if the debenture is invalid, so too will the purported appointment of any receiver on foot thereof[44]. Where a company initially co-operates with a receiver but subsequently chooses to deny the validity of that receiver's appointment, such a company may be estopped from such a course[45].

From the viewpoint of the receiver, it is important that he receives an indemnity from the debenture holder who appoints him against any claims or other proceedings which may be brought against him. This is particularly true where the circumstances of the receivership indicate that it may be problematic[46]. However, it is commonplace for lending institutions which appoint receivers to resist the giving of such an indemnity, a stance which often prevails through market forces.

[20.019] Chapter 3 of Part 10 of the Land and Conveyancing Law Reform Act 2009 ('LCLRA 2009') provides in s 97(1) that 'a mortgagee shall not take possession of the mortgaged property without a court order granted under this section, unless the mortgagor consents in writing to such taking not more than 7 days prior to such taking'. In *ACC Bank plc v Kelly & Kelly*[47], a lay-litigant sought to argue that a receiver was precluded from seeking to go into possession of property by reason of s 97 of the LCLRA 2009. Clarke J in the High Court dismissed the argument in that case because the mortgage in question giving the power to appoint the receiver pre-dated the commencement of the relevant chapter of the LCLRA 2009 and s 96 of the LCLRA

42 See *Re Irish Oil and Cake Mills Ltd* (27 March 1983, unreported) HC, Costello J.

43 See generally Ch 7, *Corporate Contracts, Capacity and Authority*, para **[7.099]** *et seq.*

44 See, however, *Madden v Anglo Irish Bank plc* [1998] IESC 6, O'Flaherty J, where an appeal against a refusal to grant an injunction to restrain a receiver from completing a contract for the sale of charged assets was upheld. In that case the applicant had claimed that the debenture was illegal because it secured a loan made for the purpose of purchasing the company's own shares and was thus in breach of s 60 of the CA 1963. O'Flaherty J noted the claim that the proceedings were vexatious and that interest was running at £12,000 per month. Refusing the injunction he found that the applicant had been aware all along of what was happening and held that if there was anything in the applicant's points on the validity of the debenture they sounded in damages.

45 *Bank of Baroda v Panessar* [1986] 3 All ER 751.

46 See generally, Hayes & Moran, *Receiverships* (1988, Incorporated Law Society Continuing Legal Education Seminar Material), 13 June 1988 at p 17.

47 *ACC Bank plc v Kelly & Kelly* [2011] IEHC 7.

2009 provides that the powers and rights of a mortgagee under, inter alia, s 97 'apply to any mortgage created by deed after the commencment of the Chapter'. The learned judge did, however, say in relation to mortgages created post 1 December 2009, that:

> '... there is no doubt but that s 97, which is part of that Chapter, precludes a mortgagee from taking possession without a court order save in the case of consent. There may well be a question as to whether s 97 precludes a receiver from going into possession assuming the receiver to have been validly appointed[48].'

It is thought that should this issue come before the High Court again it will be found that s 97 has no application to the taking of possession of charged property by a receiver. To equate a receiver with a mortgagee would be to ignore the established law on the relationship between a receiver, a mortgagor and a mortgagee. For one thing, the receiver will invariably be constituted the *agent* of the mortgagor by the deed and not the agent of the mortgagee. For the LCLRA 2009 to prevent receivers taking possession of secured property without a court order in direct interference with the contractual rights and established practice and commercial expectations would, it is thought, require s 97 to have been made expressly applicable to receivers.

(b) Appointment on foot of a court order

[20.020] In an unusual case where a debenture does not empower the holder to appoint a receiver (or, indeed, where there is no debenture), recourse may be had to the courts. The High Court has an inherent equitable jurisdiction to appoint a receiver, upon application being made[49]. In addition the High Court has the power to appoint a receiver pursuant to s 28(8) of the Supreme Court of Judicature (Ireland) Act 1877, to which effect is given by Ord 50, r 6(1) of the Rules of the Superior Courts 1986. Although unusual, application for an order of confirmation may be made even in the case of a receiver appointed under the terms of a debenture[50]. It is beyond the scope of this work to consider pre- and post-judgment court appointed receivers.[51]

(c) Appointment to income under the Land and Conveyancing Law Reform Act 2009

[20.021] Where property is subject to a mortgage a receiver may, where certain conditions are met, be appointed by the mortgagee *over the income* of the mortgaged property under s 108(1) of the LCLRA 2009. This power exists whether the mortgagor is a company or a natural person. The conditions which must be met before a receiver can be appointed to the income of mortgaged property are that:

– following service of notice on the mortgagor requiring payment of the mortgage debt, default has been made in payment of that debt or part of it for three months after such notice; or

48 *ACC Bank plc v Kelly & Kelly* [2011] IEHC 7 at para 9.2.

49 See *Angelis v Algemene Bank Nederland (Ireland) Ltd* (4 June 1974, unreported) HC, *per* Kenny J at p 2. See also *Maclaine Watson & Co Ltd v International Tin Council* [1987] BCLC 653.

50 See *Re 'Slogger' Automatic Feeder Co* [1915] 1 Ch 478. See generally Keane, *Equity and the Law of Trusts in the Republic of Ireland* (2nd edn, Bloomsbury Professional, 2011), Ch 21.

51 See further, Courtney, *Mareva Injunctions and Related Interlocutory Orders* (1998), pp 422–432.

– some interest under the mortgage or, in the case of a mortgage debt payable by instalments, some instalment representing interest or part interest and part capital is in arrears and unpaid for two months after becoming due; or
– there has been a breach of some other provision in the mortgage or any statutory provision, other than a covenant for payment of the mortgage debt or interest.

Such a receiver will be the agent of the mortgagor who is solely responsible for the receiver's acts or defaults unless the mortgage provides otherwise: s 108(2). The application of money received by such a receiver must be applied in accordance with s 109(1).

(d) Statutory receivers

[20.022] The National Asset Management Agency Act 2009 ('NAMAA 2009') created the enforcement remedy of *statutory receiver*[52]. Only the National Asset Management Agency ('NAMA') can appoint a statutory receiver; NAMA's power to appoint a statutory receiver arises under s 147(1) of the NAMAA 2009 where, under the terms of an acquired bank asset (eg, the right to receive repayments on a loan made to a company by a bank which NAMA acquired from that bank) *either*:

– a power of sale becomes exercisable; *or*
– a power to appoint a receiver becomes exercisable.

Where those conditions are met, NAMA may appoint any person, including an officer of NAMA, as a statutory receiver of the property the subject of the bank asset (eg, property given as security for the loan which has been acquired by NAMA). NAMA will not invariably appoint statutory receivers; where NAMA has acquired a loan and the security for that loan includes a well-drafted debenture, NAMA may elect to rely upon the powers in that debenture to appoint a receiver.

[20.023] Section 148(1) of the NAMAA 2009 provides that a statutory receiver has the powers, rights and obligations that a receiver has under the Companies Acts, and the powers, rights and obligations specified in Schedule 1 of the NAMAA 2009[53]. Moreover, s 148(3) provides:

> Where a charge provides for a receiver appointed under it to have any power in addition to those referred to in subsection (1), a statutory receiver appointed in relation to the property subject to the charge also has that additional power. However, a statutory receiver exercising any such additional power is taken to do so by virtue of his or her appointment under this Chapter and is not bound by any restriction on its exercise specified in the charge.

---

52 NAMAA 2009, Part 9, Ch 3, ss 147–151 and Schedule 1. See generally, Kennedy, Whelan & O'Raghallaigh, *The National Asset Management Agency Act 2009: A Reference Guide* (2011, Gill & Macmillan) at pp 628–638 and Byrne & McEntagart, *The National Asset Management Agency Act 2009: Annotations and Commentary* (2010, Bloomsbury Professional) at pp 287–297.

53 Schedule 1 of the NAMAA 2009 confers 41 separate powers on a statutory receiver.

A statutory receiver is not subject to the restrictions on the powers of a receiver and the enforcement of a security in the Conveyancing Act 1881 or the LCLRA 2009[54].

[20.024] A statutory receiver shall be taken to be the agent of the chargor for all purposes, and the chargor is solely responsible for the remuneration, contracts, engagements, acts, omissions, defaults and losses of a statutory receiver and for liabilities incurred by a statutory receiver. NAMA does not incur any liability (either to the chargor or to any other person) by reason of the appointment of a statutory receiver or for the actions or inactions of a statutory receiver. A statutory receiver shall be taken to have been irrevocably appointed as an attorney of the chargor (with full powers of substitution and delegation) and to have the authority in the chargor's name, on the chargor's behalf to do a variety of things[55].

[20.025] Statutory receivers appointed by NAMA have extraordinary powers, not shared with privately appointed receivers. Section 150(1) of the NAMAA 2009 provides that the appointment of an examiner to a company whose assets or any part of them are under the control of a statutory receiver does not:

- displace the statutory receiver or affect his or her powers, authority or agency;
- prevent the statutory receiver from enforcing any security held by NAMA or a NAMA group entity; or
- cause the de-crystallisation of any charge created as a floating charge over assets that are under the control of the statutory receiver.

By s 150(2), the appointment of a liquidator to a company whose assets or any part of them are under the control of a statutory receiver does not displace the statutory receiver and does not affect his or her powers, authority and agency.

(e) Notice of appointment

[20.026] Section 107(1) of the CA 1963 provides that where an order is obtained for the appointment of a receiver, or a receiver is appointed pursuant to the terms of an instrument, the person appointing the receiver shall, within seven days after the date of the order or appointment, publish a notice of this in the Companies Registration Office Gazette. The notice must also be published in one daily newspaper, circulating in the district where the registered office of the company is situated. Notice of a receiver's appointment must also be given to the registrar of companies who, in turn, is obliged to notify the Director of Corporate Enforcement[56]. Similarly, notice must be given where a receiver resigns[57]. Default can result in a class C fine[58] but will not, however, invalidate a receiver's appointment[59]. A notice of appointment of a receiver will not, on its own and without satisfactory evidence of the power and authority of the person purporting to make the appointment, be sufficient proof of the valid appointment of a receiver[60].

---

54 Section 148(4) and (5) of the NAMAA 2009. Moreover, s 100(2) of the LCLRA 2009 does not apply to the exercise of a power of sale by NAMA or a statutory receiver.

55 Section 149 of the NAMAA 2009.

56 Section 319(7) of the CA 1963.

57 Section 107(2) of the CA 1963. See also duties to supply information to the registrar and the Director considered at para **[20.071]** *et seq.*

58 Section 107(3) of the CA 1963.

59 *Re Motor Racing Circuits Ltd* (31 January 1997, unreported) SC.

60 *The Wise Finance Company Ltd v O'Regan* (26 June 1998, unreported) HC, Laffoy J at p 9.

[20.027] Section 319 of the CA 1963 provides that where a receiver of the whole, or substantially the whole, of the property of a company is appointed on behalf of the holders of any debentures of the company secured by a floating charge, then certain steps must be taken:

- the receiver must send notice of his appointment to the company;
- within 14 days after receipt of the notice, or such longer period allowed by court or by the receiver, the company must make a statement in accordance with s 320 of the CA 1963 as to the affairs of the company;
- within two months of his appointment, the receiver must send to the registrar of companies, the court, any trustees for debenture holders and to the company, a copy of the said statement, together with a note of whatever comments the receiver sees fit.

[20.028] The desire to put the public on notice that a receiver has been appointed is also borne out by s 317 of the CA 1963, which provides that after such appointment, every invoice, order for goods or business letter issued by or on behalf of the company or the receiver, being a document in which the name of the company appears, shall contain a statement that a receiver has been appointed[61].

The effect of the appointment of a receiver

[20.029] Where a receiver is appointed in respect of the assets of a company, certain consequences follow. Keane has described these, succinctly, as follows:

(1) Any floating charges crystallise, and become fixed charges on the assets/undertaking over which they were created;

(2) The powers of the company and the directors' authority are suspended in relation to the assets affected by the receivership, and can only be exercised with the consent of the receiver;

(3) Where the receiver is appointed as manager, then he is entitled to carry on the business of the company;

(4) The receiver may, if he considers that the interests of the debenture holder so require, dispose of any asset of the company affected by the debenture, including the entire of its undertaking[62].

The appointment of a receiver will not, however, automatically terminate contracts[63] unless, of course, individual contracts are expressed to terminate upon the appointment of a receiver.

(a) Effect on management

[20.030] The appointment of a receiver to a company does not operate to automatically displace its board of directors. The directors' powers will continue save to the extent that

61 Default is visitable by a class C fine: s 317(2) of the CA 1963.

62 See Keane, *Company Law* (4th edn, Bloomsbury Professional, 2007), para 22.04.

63 In *Triffit Nurseries v Salads Etcetera Ltd* [2000] BCC 98, it was held by the English Court of Appeal that an agency relationship did not automatically terminate upon the appointment of a receiver to one of the parties.

they are ousted[64] or otherwise superseded by the powers granted to a receiver in the debenture on foot of which his appointment is made. In the New South Wales decision in *Hawkesbury Development Co Ltd v Landmark Finance Pty Ltd*[65], Street J said:

> 'Receivership and management may well dominate exclusively a company's affairs in its dealings and relations with the outside world. But it does not permeate the company's internal structure. That structure continues to exist notwithstanding that the directors no longer have authority to exercise their ordinary business-management functions. A valid receivership and management will ordinarily supersede, but not destroy, the company's own organs through which it conducts its affairs. The capacity of those organs to function bears a direct inverse relationship to the validity and scope of the receivership and management.'

[20.031] In *Lascomme Ltd v United Dominions Trust (Ireland) Ltd and James Gilligan*[66], Keane J held that company directors' powers to maintain proceedings, commenced against a debenture holder, were unaffected by the subsequent appointment of a receiver by the debenture holder. In that case, a company had commenced proceedings against a debenture holder. The debenture holder subsequently appointed a receiver to the company, and the receiver applied to court to stay the proceedings commenced by the company. Keane J held that the directors' powers to maintain proceedings were not terminated by the appointment of the receiver. He also held, however, that the debenture holder's position must also be considered and that the directors were not permitted to interfere with the receiver dealing with the company's property which had been charged to the bank or otherwise imperiling the company's assets which were the subject of the debenture. Keane J said:

> 'It is clear that when a receiver is appointed by a debenture holder under the powers in that behalf in the debenture, the powers vested by law in the directors of the company are not thereby terminated. They may not, however, be exercised in such a manner as to inhibit the receiver in dealing with and disposing of the assets charged by the debenture or in a manner which would adversely affect the position of the debenture holder by threatening or imperilling the assets which are subject to the charge. Subject to that important qualification, the powers vested in law in the directors remain exercisable by them and include the power to maintain and institute proceedings in the name of the company where, so to do, would be in the interests of the company or its creditors.'

In so holding, Keane J struck a balance between the rights of the company and the rights of the debenture holder[67]. This finding was in line with that of the New South Wales court in *Hawkesbury Development Co Ltd v Landmark Finance Pty Ltd*[68]. In the Federal

---

64 In *Village Cay Marine Ltd v Acland et al* [1998] BCC 417, it was noted that there the receiver had replaced the board of directors as the person having authority to exercise the company's powers, and by virtue of that position validly authorised the company's seal to be affixed to various under-leases.

65 *Hawkesbury Development Co Ltd v Landmark Finance Pty Ltd* (1969) 92 WN (NSW) 199 at 209.

66 *Lascomme Ltd v United Dominions Trust (Ireland) Ltd and James Gilligan* [1994] 1 ILRM 227.

67 See also *Wymes v Crowley* (27 February 1987, unreported) HC; *Newhart Developments Ltd v Cooperative Commercial Bank Ltd* [1978] 2 All ER 896; and *Grange Holdings Ltd v Citibank NA* [1991] 4 All ER 1.

68 *Hawkesbury Development Co Ltd v Landmark Finance Pty Ltd* (1969) 92 WN (NSW) 199 at 209.

Court of Australia, in *Deangrove Pty Ltd v Commonwealth Bank of Australia*[69], Sackville J stated the applicable principle to be:

> 'Where a company in receivership has a claim against the debenture holder and the receiver declines to pursue the claim, the directors are entitled to initiate and maintain proceedings in the name of the company, provided the directors offer the company a satisfactory indemnity against costs. The latter requirement is designed to ensure that the interests of the debenture holder, qua debenture holder, are not prejudiced.'

It should be noted that that decision has not received universal support, and in England in *Tudor Grange Holdings Ltd v Citibank NA*[70], Browne-Wilkinson VC distinguished it from the case in hand on the ground that the proceedings had been instituted in *Tudor Grange* on behalf of the companies in receivership which directly impinged on the companies' property in that no indemnity against costs had been offered by the directors[71].

[20.032] In *Re Cognotec Ltd*[72], McGovern J applied the decision of Keane J in *Lascomme Ltd v United Dominions Trust (Ireland) Ltd and James Gilligan*[73] to find that the directors of a company which had provided financial assistance in connection with the purchase of its own shares could not convene a board meeting to cause the company to void the security it had given on the grounds of a failure to file the statutory declaration required (where reliance had been placed upon the validation procedure).

(*b*) *Effect on employees*

[20.033] Contracts of employment between the company and its employees are not necessarily terminated by the appointment of a receiver out of court by a debenture holder[74]. This is, however, qualified by the fact that contracts of employment which are inconsistent with the appointment of a receiver, such as that of a managing director or chief executive officer can be terminated, where a receiver-manager takes over the management of the business. A receiver can, of course, terminate contracts of employment at his own discretion and his obligations will be thereby determined[75]. Where a receiver does not terminate contracts of employment, and allows employees to continue in employment, he does not himself become personally liable for their wages

69 *Deangrove Pty Ltd v Commonwealth Bank of Australia* (2001) 108 FCR 77 and [2002] FCA 1545 (11 December 2002). See also *Gartner v Ernst & Young* [2003] FCA 152.

70 *Tudor Grange Holdings Ltd v Citibank NA* [1992] Ch 53.

71 See *Deangrove Pty Ltd (Rec & Mgrs Aptd) v Commonwealth Bank of Australia* [2001] Federal Court of Australia 173, 6 March 2001.

72 *Re Cognotec Ltd* [2010] IEHC 309.

73 *Lascomme Ltd v United Dominions Trust (Ireland) Ltd and James Gilligan* [1994] 1 ILRM 227.

74 See *Griffiths v Secretary of State for Social Services* [1974] QB 468. At common law, the appointment of a receiver pursuant to a court order did terminate contracts of employment: *Reid v Explosives Co Ltd* [1887] 19 QBD 264.

75 Receivers will be obliged to comply with employment legislation such as the Minimum Notice (Terms of Employment) Act 1973: see *Bolands Ltd (in receivership) v Ward et al* [1988] ILRM 382.

from the date of his appointment because there is no new contract, and any contract which subsists does so between the company and the employees[76].

[20.034] Whilst it has been established that the European Communities (Safeguarding of Employees' Rights on Transfer of Undertakings) Regulations 1980[77] (which make provision for the continuity of contracts of employment of employees on the transfer of an undertaking) do not apply in liquidations[78], the position regarding receiverships in Ireland[79] remains unclear. In *Mythen v The Employment Appeals Tribunal*[80], Barrington J held that just because the European Court of Justice has held[81] that the Directive[82] on which the Irish regulations are based does not apply to a particular form of Dutch liquidation procedure, one could not assume '... that it would also hold that the Directive would not apply to a sale by a receiver appointed by a debenture holder'. In *Brett v Niall Collins Ltd (in receivership) and Oyster Investments Ltd*[83], a receiver sought to sell a business (premises, equipment and goodwill) as a going concern but purported to dismiss the staff by paying redundancy with the intention that the undertaking could be sold without employees. It was held by the Employment Appeals Tribunal ('EAT') that there had been a transfer of an undertaking and that the receipt and retention of the redundancy payments by the employees did not break their service for the purposes of s 15 of the Unfair Dismissals (Amendment) Act 1993. In the course of its determination, the EAT said:

> 'It should be pointed out that where a company is put into liquidation or an employer is declared a bankrupt the selling on of the assets of the insolvent person, natural or legal, is not a transfer of undertaking for the purposes of the Directive. A receivership is however, because the appointment of a receiver does not indicate in law that the company is insolvent although it operates to that effect for the purposes of the Protection of Employees (Employers' Insolvency) Act 1984[84].'

---

76 See *Nicoll v Cutts* [1985] BCLC 322.

77 SI 306/1980. See Lynch-Fannon & Murphy, *Corporate Insolvency and Rescue* (2nd edn, 2012), paras 7.61–7.64 and Redmond, *Dismissal Law in Ireland* (1999), p 403. For a very thorough review of the Directive from a general employment law perspective, see Byrne, 'Business Sales and Transfers, The Contracting out of Services and Employee Rights' (1996) 3 CLP 139.

78 *HBM Abels v Administrative Board of Bedrijfsvereniging Voor De Metaal – Industrie en de Electrotechnische Industrie* 2 ELC 434, [1987] 2 CMLR 406. See also *Re Castle Brand Ltd (In liquidation)* (25 March 1985, unreported) HC, per Hamilton J. In *Sanders v Europieces* Case C 399/96 (12/11/98), it was held by the European Court of Justice that the Directive also applies to voluntary liquidations.

79 It has been held in England in several cases, such as *Angus Jowett & Co v Taylors and Garment Workers Union* [1985] IRLR 326 (see also *Secretary of State for Employment v Spence* [1986] IRLR 248) that equivalent English regulations apply to receiverships and impose obligations on receivers, eg, to consult with employees.

80 *Mythen v The Employment Appeals Tribunal* [1989] ILRM 844.

81 In *HBM Abels v Administrative Board of Bedrijfsvereniging Voor De Metaal – Industrie en de Electrotechnische Industrie* 2 ELC 434, [1987] 2 CMLR 406.

82 European Council Directive 77/187/EEC.

83 *Brett v Niall Collins Ltd (in receivership) and Oyster Investments Ltd* [1995] ELR 69.

84 *Brett v Niall Collins Ltd (in receivership) and Oyster Investments Ltd* [1995] ELR 69 at 73.

Notwithstanding convincing argument to the contrary[85], it is thought, on balance, that it is unlikely that the Irish superior courts will exclude receiverships from the ambit of the regulations.

The status of a receiver

[20.035] As has been noted above[86], a receiver can be appointed to a company in either of two ways: by court appointment or by a debenture holder. The *status* of a receiver will depend initially upon how he has been appointed.

(a) Receivers appointed by the court[87]

[20.036] A receiver appointed by the court has the status of an officer of the court[88]. The significance of this is that such a receiver cannot concern himself exclusively with the interests of the creditor who procured his appointment. Rather, his concern ought to be the interests of all creditors of the company. It follows that, unlike the position considered next, the receiver will not be deemed to be the agent of any particular person.

(b) Receivers appointed by a debenture holder

[20.037] A receiver appointed pursuant to a debenture is essentially a creature of contract whose status will be determined by the debenture. Unless the contrary is stated in the debenture, the receiver will be the *agent* of the debenture holder, and will only be the agent of the company through necessity[89]. However, it would be a most unusual debenture which did not provide to the contrary, namely that any receiver appointed will be the agent of the company. The effect of this will be to make the company responsible not only for the receiver's acts or defaults but even for his remuneration. So, in *Irish Oil and Cake Mills Ltd v Donnelly*[90] Costello J said:

> 'The receiver derives his appointment and his authority from the contract entered into between the parties. In that case, as is usual, the parties agreed that he is to be treated as the agent of the mortgagors, the plaintiff herein. This provision protects the debenture holders from the liability as mortgagees in possession and establishes the relationship between the receiver and the company[91].'

(c) The receiver as agent of the company

[20.038] Most debenture instruments will contain a provision that on the appointment of a receiver, the receiver will have a *power of attorney* to do all acts necessary to enforce the security. The authority of a company to execute a power of attorney to do acts on its

---

85 The so-called ETO (economic, technical and organisational) defence. Note, though, that this defence was unsuccessfully invoked by a receiver in *Brett v Niall Collins Ltd (in receivership) and Oyster Investments Ltd* [1995] ELR 69.

86 See para **[20.012]** *et seq.*

87 See Picarda, *The Law Relating to Receivers, Managers and Administrators* (2nd edn, 1990), p 339 *et seq.*

88 See the *dictum* of Viscount Haldane LC in *Parsons v Sovereign Bank of Canada* [1913] AC 160.

89 See *Robinson Printing Co Ltd v Chic Ltd* [1905] 2 Ch 123.

90 *Irish Oil and Cake Mills Ltd v Donnelly* (27 March 1984, unreported) HC, *per* Costello J.

91 *Irish Oil and Cake Mills Ltd v Donnelly* (27 March 1984, unreported) HC at p 6. See also *W & L Crowe Ltd v Electricity Supply Board* (9 May 1984, unreported) HC, *per* Costello J.

behalf inside the country was recognised in *Industrial Development Authority v Moran*[92].

[20.039] Until recently, it had been questioned whether or not a company could be said to continue to be bound by a power of attorney after a winding up has commenced, in that at common law any agency created by the company would be terminated. One solution for the debenture holder is to include in the debenture a provision to the effect that the power of attorney granted to the donee is irrevocable although such a provision was, prior to the enactment of the Powers of Attorney Act 1996 ('POAA 1996'), questioned[93]. Since the enactment of that Act, the matter has been put beyond all doubt, s 20(1) of the POAA 1996 providing:

> 'Where a power of attorney is expressed to be irrevocable and is given to secure—
>
> (a) a proprietary interest of the donee of the power, or
>
> (b) the performance of an obligation owed to the donee,
>
> then, so long as the donee has that interest[94] or the obligation remains undischarged, the power shall not be revoked—
>
> (i) by the donor without the consent of the donee, or
>
> (ii) by the death, incapacity or bankruptcy of the donor or, *if the donor is a body corporate, by its winding-up or dissolution*[95].'

In order to rely upon s 20(1) of the POAA 1996, the power of attorney must be expressed to be '*irrevocable*'; moreover, it must be given to *secure* either *a proprietary interest* of the donee or *the performance of an obligation* owed to the donee. Subject to these requirements, s 20(3) of the POAA 1996 provides that the section applies to powers of attorney 'whenever created'. As the receiver will not have a proprietary interest nor will the company's obligations be owed to the receiver, consideration may be given to constituting the chargee the donee of the power and to giving the donee power to appoint somebody (the receiver) to act on the donee's behalf as a substitute.

[20.040] It is accepted that the relationship of agency created by a debenture between a receiver and a company is an unusual one[96]. As Costello J said in *Irish Oil and Cake Mills Ltd v Donnelly*[97]:

> 'The agency here is of course very different from the ordinary agency arising every day in commercial transactions. Here the receiver has been appointed by the owner in equity of

---

92 *Industrial Development Authority v Moran* [1978] IR 159. See Ch 7, *Corporate Contracts, Capacity and Authority*, para **[7.031]**.

93 See Keane, *Equity and the Law of Trusts in the Republic of Ireland* (1988), at para 24.04 and Schmitthoff (ed), *Palmer's Company Law* (24th edn, 1987), para 86.04.

94 Section 20(2) of the POAA1996 provides: 'A power of attorney given to secure a proprietary interest may be given, and shall be deemed to have been capable always of being given, to the person entitled to the interest and persons deriving title under that person to that interest, and those persons shall be duly constituted donees of the power for all purposes of the power but without prejudice to any right to appoint substitutes given by the power.'

95 Emphasis added.

96 See *Bula Ltd v Crowley* [2002] IEHC 4, Barr J and also *Gomba Holdings UK Ltd v Minories Finance Ltd* [1989] BCLC 115 at 117.

97 *Irish Oil and Cake Mills Ltd v Donnelly* (27 March 1984, unreported) HC, *per* Costello J.

these companies' assets with the object of realising their security and for this purpose to carry on the companies' business. The exceptional nature of his status is to be seen from the fact that notwithstanding his appointment as agent he is to be personally liable under contracts entered into by him …'

This is an agency that has some peculiar incidents[98]. The reasons why receivership is an unusual agency can be said to be threefold: while the receiver is an agent of the company, he is personally liable on contracts entered into on behalf of the company[99]; the company (principal) is unable to dismiss this particular agent; and this relationship of agency is, to use the expression employed by Maitland to describe a mortgage, founded on an underlying *falsio assumpit*, since the primary duty of the receiver is to realise the security held by the person who appoints him, and often not to manage the company to any other end. One consequence of the unusual nature of the agency between receivers and the companies to which they are appointed is that the law imposes certain *duties* on receivers[100].

[20.041] It is important to recognise that receiverships involve two distinct relationships. The nature of a receivership was considered by Barr J in *Bula Ltd v Crowley*[101], where he made the following observations:

'The relationship between a receiver, the mortgagee who appoints him and the debtor company which owns the secured assets is exceptional, if not unique. The appointment of a receiver is one of the remedies open to a debenture holder in respect of a defaulting company whose assets are secured by the debenture. There are two distinct relationships involved. As between the mortgagee and the debtor company, the duty of the receiver is to take control of the latter with a view to realising its assets in discharge of debt owing by the company to the mortgagee. This is the fundamental objective of the receivership. The appointment of the receiver entails taking possession of the company lands and in practical terms vis-à-vis the Banks and Bula in the instant case it amounts to possession by the mortgagees. In short, the Banks' purpose for the appointment of the receiver is to put him into control and effective possession of the company assets so as to realise the mortgagees' security by sale of the lands. The fact that under the terms of the debentures the receiver is stated to be the agent of the company does not detract from the foregoing relationship as between the receiver, the Banks and Bula. The agency as stated in the debentures is one which is relevant to the third party claims on the company. It is a long-standing practice in financial and commercial life that debenture holders (commonly banks or other such institutions) generally prefer not to become directly involved in the conduct of receiverships with consequent risk of liability to third parties, and so, in the context of dealings between a receiver on behalf of a company and third parties who make claims upon it, the debenture normally provides that the former is agent of the company. In short, a receivership, such as that in the instant case, involves two distinct relationships.

First, that between the appointing mortgagee and the receiver which relates to the fundamental objective of the receivership, being entry into possession of the company's

98 *Kerr on Receivers* (16th edn), p 304 states: '… the principal may not dismiss the agent, and his possession of his principal's assets is really that of the mortgagee who appointed him. He owes no prior duty to the principal other than that of a mortgagee in possession.' This was cited with approval in *Bula Ltd v Crowley* [2002] IEHC 4, Barr J.

99 See para **[20.074]** *et seq.*

100 See para **[20.045]** *et seq.*

101 *Bula Ltd v Crowley* [2002] IEHC 4, Barr J.

> assets for the purpose of sale in the interest of the mortgagee. In practical terms vis-à-vis mortgagee and mortgagor the control over the company's assets exercised by the receiver amounts to possession of the debtor's secured assets by him which in turn in practical terms is possession by the mortgagee who appointed him.
>
> The second relationship is that between the receiver and third parties arising out of the receivership. Debentures normally provide, as in the instant case, that such dealings are conducted by the receiver as agent of the company in receivership. The mortgagees have no right to interfere in the receivership in that regard. In my view there is no inconsistency between the foregoing relationships which represent long established commercial good sense.'

The facts in that case were that the plaintiff had created a mortgage and debenture, as security for monies loaned to it by a number of banks. After it encountered major financial difficulties, the lending banks appointed the first defendant as receiver over its property, issued proceedings seeking the recovery of the principal and interest and also sought a well-charging order. The first plaintiff contended that the banks' title to its land had been extinguished by ss 33[102] and 38[103] of the Statute of Limitations 1957 ('SL 1957'). The essence of the plaintiff's claim was that it had established adverse possession against the banks. It was submitted that the appointment of a receiver had placed the plaintiff company under the receiver's managerial control and had dis-empowered the directors but had not dislodged the plaintiff's possession of the lands and did not bring about possession of the lands by the receiver to the plaintiff's exclusion. The plaintiff's case was that the title of the banks to its lands had become, after 12 years, extinguished, as had the banks' right to principal and interest; in short, it was contended that the banks were statute barred. This was strongly disputed by the defendants who contended that the receiver, having been lawfully appointed under the debentures and having taken effective possession and control of the plaintiff, was outside the scope of the SL 1957. Barr J held that the activation of rights under the debentures (eg, appointing a receiver) did not create a situation of adverse possession within the meaning of s 18(1) of the SL 1957. This was because, having analysed[104] the relationship between the plaintiff, the receiver and the banks, there was no possession (eg, by the plaintiff) without right or authority which, it was said, is the essence of adverse possession within the meaning of the SL 1957.

[20.042] The company's appeal against the decision of the High Court was unsuccessful: *Bula Ltd v Crowley (No 3)*[105]. Denham J confirmed the law that on the

---

102 This provides: 'At the expiration of the period fixed by this Act for a mortgagee to bring an action claiming sale of the mortgaged land, the title of the mortgagee to the land shall be extinguished.'

103 This provides: 'At the expiration of the period fixed by this Act for a mortgagee of land to bring an action to recover the land or for a person claiming as mortgagee or chargeant to bring an action claiming sale of the land, the right of the mortgagee or such person to the principal sum and interest secured by the mortgage or charge shall be extinguished.'

104 Barr J cited and quoted with approval from: *Gomba Holdings v Homan* [1986] BCLC 331 at 334; *Gomba Holdings v Minories Finance* [1989] BCLC 115 at 117; *Rottenberg v Monjack* [1993] BCLC 374; *Irish Oil and Cake Mills v Donnelly* [ICLR (1963–1990) 564]; *Lascomme Ltd v UDT Bank* [1993] 3 IR 412 at 416; *Re Johnson and Co* [1955] 1 Ch 634 and *Ardmore Studies (Ireland) Ltd v Lynch et al* [1965] IR 1.

105 *Bula Ltd v Crowley (No 3)* [2003] 1 IR 396.

appointment of a receiver, two special relationships were established which were founded on the agreements entered into between the parties. These were between the company and the receiver on the one hand and the banks and the receiver on the other. Denham J adopted the following passage from the decision of Fox LJ in *Gomba Holdings Ltd v Minories Finance Ltd*[106] as a correct statement of the law:

> 'The agency of a receiver is not an ordinary agency. It is primarily a device to protect the mortgagee or debenture holder. Thus, the receiver acts as agent for the mortgagor in that he has power to affect the mortgagor's position by acts which, though done for the benefit of the debenture holder, are treated as if they were the acts of the mortgagor. The relationship set up by the debenture and the appointment of the receiver, however, is not simply between the mortgagor and the receiver. It is tripartite and involves the mortgagor, the receiver and the debenture holder. The receiver is appointed by the debenture holder, upon the happening of specified events, and becomes the mortgagor's agent whether the mortgagor likes it or not. And, as a matter of contract between the mortgagor and the debenture holder, the mortgagor will have to pay the receiver's fees. Further, the mortgagor cannot dismiss the receiver since that power is reserved to the debenture holder as another of the contractual terms of the loan. It is to be noted also that the mortgagor cannot instruct the receiver how to act in the conduct of the receivership[107].
>
> All this is far removed from the ordinary principal and agent situation so far as the mortgagor and the receiver are concerned. Whilst the receiver is the agent of the mortgagor he is the appointee of the debenture holder and, in practical terms, has a close association with him. Moreover he owes fiduciary duties to the debenture holder who has a right, as against the receiver, to be put in possession of all the information concerning the receivership available to the receiver: see *In re Magadi Soda Co Ltd* (1925) 41 TLR 297. The result is that the receiver, in the course of the receivership, performs duties on behalf of the debenture holder as well as the mortgagor. And these duties may relate closely to the affairs of the entity which is the subject of the receivership. It is, therefore, not satisfactory to approach the problem of the ownership of documents which come into existence in the course of the receivership on the basis that ownership depends upon whether the documents relate to the affairs of (in this case) the companies.'

Denham J also endorsed the passage from the decision of Costello J in *Irish Oil and Cake Mills Ltd v Donnelly*[108] quoted above[109]. Rejecting the appeal, the Supreme Court confirmed that on his appointment, the receiver went into possession and control of the company's assets for the benefit of the banks and there was no possession contrary to the bank's interests and no possession that could come within the concept of adverse possession so that the SL 1957 had no application[110].

---

106 *Gomba Holdings Ltd v Minories Finance Ltd* [1988] 1 WLR 1231 at 1233.

107 This passage was said by Laffoy J in *Lowe v Burns and Burns* [2012] IEHC 162 to 'reflect the law in this jurisdiction'.

108 *Irish Oil and Cake Mills Ltd v Donnelly* (27 March 1984, unreported) HC, *per* Costello J.

109 See para **[20.040]** *ante*.

110 The litigation of Bula Limited was described by Barr J in *Bula Ltd v Crowley* [1997] IEHC 72, as 'a vast panoply of litigation which is unique in Irish legal history as to duration, complexity, range and multiplicity of issues'. Eventually, the High Court made an *Isaac Wunder* order restraining the appellants from instituting any further proceedings against various parties without the prior leave of the High Court, which order was confirmed by the Supreme Court: see *Bula Ltd v Crowley* [2009] IESC 35.

[20.043] In *Moorview Developments Ltd et al v First Active plc et al*[111], it was held by Clarke J that it was not appropriate to register a *lis pendens* against a receiver or his appointing bank. As Clarke J said, a *lis pendens* is designed to give notice of the fact that proceedings relating to land are pending before the court and that its purpose must be to bring to the attention of any interested party, the fact that there are proceedings in being against the person concerned 'which relate to the ownership of property or an interest in property'. Clarke J said that the fundamental proposition is that 'the issue between the parties must relate to the ownership of some interest in land' and went on to hold that:

> ... it does not seem to me that the position of a receiver or agent is captured. A receiver does not own any interest in lands which are properly described as being owned by the company to which the receiver has been appointed. The lands remain owned by the company (in receivership). The fact that the receiver may well be entitled, provided that all necessary formalities are complied with, to execute a deed of transfer of a relevant interest in property in the name of the company does not alter that fact. It is the company which transfers the property. The receiver is simply entitled by virtue of the debentue in favour of the relevant lender, and his appointment, to cause the company to effect the transfer. There is a real sense in which the receiver's position in this regard is no different than that of the directors of a solvent company who are, of course, entitled to act on behalf of the company, to sell its property, and, within the articles of association and the law generally, to fix the company seal to any relevant deed of assurance. The fact that, in different circumstances, it may be the receiver rather than the directors who can cause the company to execute a deed of assurance, does not make the receiver any more a person with an interest in the land owned by the company than the directors were persons with an interest in the land owned by the company.
>
> 4.4 Therefore, it seems to me that, insofar as a plaintiff may wish to contest the ownership of land held by a company in receivership, then it is that company in receivership who is the proper defendant to that aspect of any relevant proceedings rather than the receiver himself. If a party wishes to obtain injunctive or similar relief against the receiver then that is, of course, possible, but such a claim is not a claim relating to an interest in land but rather is a claim to an injunction[112].'

The remuneration of a receiver

[20.044] Most debentures will provide that the receiver's remuneration, costs, charges and expenses will be discharged, by the company to which he is appointed, out of its assets. Many debentures will expressly provide that the statutory provisions dealing with the remuneration of receivers of income shall apply to a receiver manager of all of the property and assets of a company, a practice which is considered to be settled in law[113]. Whereas debentures before the advent of the Land and Conveyancing Law Reform Act 2009 ('LCLRA 2009') would have referred to s 24(6) of the Conveyancing Act 1881, the appropriate statutory reference now is to s 108(7) of the LCLRA 2009:

> 'The receiver may retain out of any money received, for remuneration and in satisfaction of all costs incurred as receiver, a commission at the prescribed rate[114].'

[111] *Moorview Developments Ltd et al v First Active plc et al* [2010] IEHC 35.

[112] At para 4.3 and 4.4 of the judgment.

[113] See *Re City Car Sales Ltd* [1995] ILRM 221 and *Re Red Sail Frozen Foods Ltd* [2006] IEHC 328, Laffoy J.

[114] 'Prescribed' is defined by s 3 as meaning prescribed by regulations made under s 5 of the LCLRA 2009.

In *Re Red Sail Frozen Foods Ltd*[115], Laffoy J held, as Geoghegan J had previously held in *Re City Car Sales Ltd*[116], that the court has jurisdiction to fix a higher rate of remuneration than, what would now be termed, the prescribed rate. Laffoy J also noted that the question as to whether the secured creditor's own costs (eg, legal expenses) would be covered would depend upon the terms of the security documents creating the charge and empowering the appointment of a receiver.

Duties of receivers

[20.045] Receivers owe an ever-increasing number of common law and statutory duties to the companies to which they are appointed. These duties include:

(a) The duty to provide information to the company.
(b) Duties of receiver-managers.
(c) Duties arising on the disposal of assets.
(d) Duties to guarantors.
(e) Duties in applying the proceeds of sale of assets.
(f) Duties to supply information to the registrar of companies and the Director of Corporate Enforcement.

(a) The duty to provide information to the company

[20.046] Although s 319 of the CA 1963[117] requires receivers to provide certain information to the registrar of companies, the law is somewhat unsettled upon whether or not a company is entitled to obtain further information from a receiver. On balance, the authorities indicate that a company, while owed a certain duty of care by a receiver, is not generally owed a duty to be provided with information. In *McGowan v Gannon*[118], Carroll J said, *obiter*, that under the ordinary law of contract where a company is deemed to be a principal it is entitled to obtain information from a receiver where he is the agent of the company. This was later distinguished in *Irish Oil and Cake Mills (Manufacturing) Ltd v Donnelly*[119] by Costello J who said:

> 'Whilst in that case the receiver had vouchsafed information about a sale to the directors there is nothing to suggest that he gave them details of his trading accounts and the court was in no way concerned with the point raised in that case, namely, the existence of a receiver's duty to account to the board of directors whilst managing the company's business[120].'

---

[115] *Re Red Sail Frozen Foods Ltd* [2006] IEHC 328, Laffoy J.

[116] *Re City Car Sales Ltd* [1995] ILRM 221.

[117] Within seven months of his appointment and every six months subsequently, a receiver has to send to the registrar of companies an abstract showing the assets of the company of which he has taken possession since his appointment, the estimated value of the assets, the proceeds of sale of any such assets since his appointment, his receipts and payments during that period of six months or, where he ceases to act, the aggregated amounts of his receipts and payments during all the preceding period since his appointment.

[118] *McGowan v Gannon* [1983] ILRM 516.

[119] *Irish Oil and Cake Mills (Manufacturing) Ltd v Donnelly* (27 March 1984, unreported) HC.

[120] *Irish Oil and Cake Mills (Manufacturing) Ltd v Donnelly* (27 March 1984, unreported) HC at p 7.

While accepting that the receiver does owe a certain duty of care to the company[121], Costello J held:

> 'It is said that apart from the special facts of this case the general duty on a receiver and manager to take reasonable steps to secure the best possible price for the companies' assets includes a duty 'to keep the company apprised of how the business of the company is going'. This is a very far-reaching proposition and I must reject it. There may well be special circumstances in which, to ensure that the best price possible is obtained for the assets, trading information since the appointment of the receiver should be given to the company's directors. But in the absence of special circumstances which might favourably affect the price, a receiver/manager is not under any duty of care which involves him in reporting as suggested to the directors on his management and business. It cannot be said that a receiver/manager is under *no* duty to account to the company whose affairs he is managing nor did the defendant so urge in that case. The extent and nature of the duty and the extent and nature of the accounts he must furnish will depend on the facts of each individual case[122].'

An example of such 'special circumstances' is seen in *Smiths Ltd v Middleton*[123] where it was held that a receiver as agent was under an equitable obligation to account.

[20.047] In *Kinsella v Somers*[124], the applicant was a director and shareholder in the Dublin Gas Company, which had been in receivership since a debenture holder had appointed a receiver pursuant to a mortgage debenture some 15 years' previously. The matter came before the High Court by way of a motion for directions under s 316 of the CA 1963. The applicant's motivation was information. Specifically he sought information about the nature of the assets of the company since the inception of the receivership, the changing nature of such assets, their estimated value and the basis for such evaluation, the manner of sale of such assets as were sold and the presale method of advertisement, the proceeds of sale realised and an account of offers received for the sale of each asset. The applicant also sought accounts in respect of the receiver's fees, the receivership on a yearly basis and an opportunity to inspect the documents relating to the receivership. The receiver contended, *inter alia*, that he had already furnished appropriate information to the company in October 1993. The receiver maintained that the applicant neither as a director nor as a shareholder had an entitlement to the type of information sought and in any event the lapse of time and the company's insolvency were such that it would no longer be just or equitable for him to have to furnish such information, particularly since the applicant and the other directors had, in 1993, failed to take up his then invitation to give more information. On the receiver's duty to disclose information Budd J took as the law on a receiver's duty to provide information, to be that as stated by Costello J in *Irish Oil and Cake Mills (Manufacturing) Ltd v Donnelly*[125]. He went on to find that while there may be some room for debate as to the extent of a receiver's duty towards the company to which he is appointed receiver, no authority

---

[121] To obtain the best price reasonably obtainable on a sale of the charged assets, considered at para **[20.051]** *et seq*.

[122] *Irish Oil and Cake Mills Ltd v Donnelly* (27 March 1984, unreported) HC, at pp 12–13.

[123] *Smiths Ltd v Middleton* [1979] 3 All ER 842.

[124] *Kinsella v Somers* (22 November 1999, unreported) HC, Budd J.

[125] *Irish Oil and Cake Mills (Manufacturing) Ltd v Donnelly* (27 March 1984, unreported) HC, considered at para **[20.046]**.

could be found to support the applicant's proposition that he was entitled as a director or shareholder to be furnished with accounts and documents.

[20.048] A related, although essentially distinct, issue concerns the right of a company to documents in the possession of a receiver. It has been held in the UK that such a claim will only succeed where it is based on a proprietary claim to ownership of those documents. So, in *Gomba Holdings UK Ltd v Minories Finance Ltd*[126] the defendant company had appointed receivers and managers over the plaintiff companies pursuant to debentures. When the receiverships were discharged, the receivers, pursuant to a court order, handed back certain documents to the plaintiff companies which belonged to them. However, other documents were retained on the basis that they never belonged to the plaintiff companies. The plaintiff companies argued that even documents which were actually created by the receivers belonged to them because the receivers were their agents and so the plaintiff companies, as principals, were entitled to those documents. This was rejected by Hoffmann J[127] and also by Fox LJ in the Court of Appeal. Fox LJ said that the agency relationship between a receiver and a company was very far removed from the ordinary principal and agent situation[128]:

> 'The result is that the receiver, in the course of the receivership, performs duties on behalf of the debenture holder as well as the mortgagor. And these duties may relate closely to the affairs of the entity which is the subject of the receivership. It is, therefore, not satisfactory to approach the problem of the ownership of the documents which come into existence in the course of the receivership on the basis that ownership depends on whether the documents relate to the affairs of ... the companies[129].'

The correct test to be adopted here is to ask whether or not the documents were brought into existence in discharge of the receiver's duties to the company, the debenture holder or neither. This approach envisages three categories of document. As Hoffmann J said at first instance[130]:

> 'The ownership of the documents depends in my judgment on whether they were created or received in discharge of the receivers' duties to the companies, or to the debenture holder, or neither. In the first category would fall documents generated or received by the receivers pursuant to their duty to manage the businesses of the companies or dispose of their assets. These documents belong to the companies. In the second category come documents containing advice and information about the receivership or the companies, brought into existence by the receivers for the purpose of being communicated to [the defendant company] or sent to the receivers to enable them to advise [the defendant company]. These documents belong to [the defendant company]. The third category will include notes, calculations and memoranda prepared by the receivers, their agents or employees not pursuant to any duty to prepare those specific documents but for the purpose of enabling them to discharge their professional duties to [the defendant company] ... These belong to the receivers themselves ...[131]'

---

[126] *Gomba Holdings UK Ltd v Minorities Finance Ltd* [1989] BCLC 115. This case was described as 'helpful' by Barr J in *Kinsella v Somers* (23 November 1999, unreported) HC.

[127] *Gomba Holdings UK Ltd v Minorities Finance Ltd* [1988] BCLC 60.

[128] *Gomba Holdings UK Ltd v Minorities Finance Ltd* [1989] BCLC 115 at 117.

[129] *Gomba Holdings UK Ltd v Minorities Finance Ltd* [1989] BCLC 115 at 117.

[130] *Gomba Holdings UK Ltd v Minorities Finance Ltd* [1988] BCLC 60 at 62.

[131] See also *Chantery Martin & Co v Martin* [1953] 2 All ER 691, [1953] 2 QB 286.

A company will, on this analysis, only be entitled to certain documents created by the receiver while managing the business of the company or selling its assets. It is submitted that such a stance makes eminent sense and places the agency relationship between the receiver and the company in perspective[132].

(b) Duties of receiver-managers

[20.049] The difference between managing a company for the benefit of a debenture holder and managing a company for the benefit of shareholders is clearly distinguished in case law. In *Downside Nominees Ltd v First City Corporation Ltd*[133], Lord Templeman said the remedy for a dissatisfied debenture holder was to revoke the receiver's appointment and the remedy for a dissatisfied shareholder was to either pay off the debenture holder or else place the company into liquidation. He went on to say:

> 'But if a receiver and manager decides at his discretion to manage and is allowed to manage and does manage in good faith with the object of preserving and realising the assets for the benefit of the debenture holder, he is subject to no further or greater liability.'

The breach of a duty of good faith requires some dishonest or improper motive or element of bad faith to be established[134]. The following passage (quoted with apparent approval by Barr J in *Kinsella v Somers*[135]) from the judgment of Jenkins LJ in *Re B Johnson & Co (Builders) Ltd*[136] is instructive as to the duties of receiver-managers:

> 'In a word, in the absence of fraud or mala fides ... the company cannot complain of any act or omission of the receiver and manager, provided that he does nothing that he is not empowered to do, and omits nothing that he is enjoined to do by the terms of his appointment. If the company conceives that it has a claim against the receiver and manager for breach of some duty owed by him to the company, the issue is not whether the receiver and manager has done or omitted to do anything which it would be wrongful in a manager of a company to do or omit, but whether he has exercised or abused or wrongfully omitted to use the special powers and discretions vested in him pursuant to the contract of loan constituted by the debenture for the special purpose of enabling the assets comprised in the debenture holders' security to be preserved and realised[137].'

In Medforth v Blake[138], the English Court of Appeal held that in failing to negotiate discounts on pig-feed whilst running the plaintiff mortgagor's pig-farming business, receiver-managers were liable for breach of a so-called 'equitable duty of care'. It was alleged that the farmer had reminded the receivers that it was normal commercial practice to give such discounts. It was accepted, though, that the receivers' failure to

---

[132] See also *Casson Beckman & Partners v Papi* [1991] BCLC 299 where the Court of Appeal held that the company was only entitled to those documents which were created or received by the receiver in pursuance of his duties as receiver or liquidator, the receivers were owners of any working papers.

[133] *Downside Nominees Ltd v First City Corporation Ltd* [1993] BCC 46.

[134] *Medforth v Blake* [1999] BCC 771 at 785.

[135] *Kinsella v Somers* (22 November 1999, unreported) HC, Budd J.

[136] *Re B Johnson & Co (Builders) Ltd* [1955] 1 Ch 634.

[137] *Re B Johnson & Co (Builders) Ltd* [1955] 1 Ch 634 at 663.

[138] *Medforth v Blake* [1999] BCC 771.

seek such discounts was not the result of any conscious or deliberate impropriety. Sir Richard Scott VC said of a receiver's duties:

> 'In my judgment, in principle and on the authorities, the following propositions can be stated:
>
> (1) A receiver managing mortgaged property owes duties to the mortgagor and anyone else with an interest in the equity of redemption.
>
> (2) The duties include, but are not necessarily confined to, a duty of good faith.
>
> (3) The extent and scope of any duty additional to that of good faith will depend on the facts and circumstances of the particular case.
>
> (4) In exercising his powers of management the primary duty of the receiver is to try and bring about a situation in which interest on the secured debt can be paid and the debt itself re-paid.
>
> (5) Subject to that primary duty, the receiver owes a duty to manage the property with due diligence.
>
> (6) Due diligence does not oblige the receiver to continue to carry on a business on the mortgaged premises previously carried on by the mortgagor.
>
> (7) If the receiver does carry on a business on the mortgaged premises, due diligence *requires reasonable steps to be taken in order to try to do so profitably*[139].'

On the substantive point of the extent of a receiver's duty Sir Richard Scott VC said:

> 'The proposition that, in managing and carrying on the mortgaged business, the receiver owes the mortgagor no duty other than that of good faith offends, in my opinion, commercial sense. The receiver is not obliged to carry on the business. He can decide not to do so. He can decide to close it down. In taking these decisions he is entitled, and perhaps bound, to have regard to the interests of the mortgagee in obtaining repayment of the secured debt. Provided he acts in good faith, he is entitled to sacrifice the interests of the mortgagor in pursuit of that end. But if he does decide to carry on the business why should he not be expected to do so with reasonable competence? The present case, if the pleaded facts are established, involves the failure of the receivers to obtain discounts that were freely available. Other glaring examples of managerial incompetence can be imagined. Suppose the receivers had decided to carry on the business but had not decided, through incompetence and not for any dishonest reason, that the pigs need not be fed or watered more than once a week, and, as a result a number of pigs had died. The receivers would, I suppose, be in trouble with the RSPCA but, if Mr Smith is right, although they might be liable to the mortgagee they would have no liability to the mortgagor. Or suppose, that, as may well be the case, it is common practice to inoculate weaners against disease to which pigs are prone but the receivers decide to save money by dispensing with inoculations, with the result that a number of the weaners contracted disease and died and that the rest had to be slaughtered. If Mr Smith is right, the receivers would have no liability to the mortgagor whose business they had, by incompetence, ruined. It is accepted that, if the mortgagee had gone into possession and carried on the business similarly incompetently, the mortgagee would have been accountable to the mortgagor for the loss caused to the mortgagor by the incompetence. But, it is submitted, not so the receivers[140].'

---

139 *Medforth v Blake* [1999] BCC 771 at 784–785.

140 *Medforth v Blake* [1999] BCC 771 at 777.

The distinction between the equitable duty of good faith and an equitable duty of care has been roundly criticised[141]. The Court of Appeal went on to hold that a receiver has duties in equity to manage a business with due diligence. The difficulty with this finding is that, for good reason, it has always been accepted that a receiver's duty in managing a business is best confined to a duty of good faith. How else can a receiver be judged on the peculiarities in the management of a particular business? Is a mortgagee to be fettered in his appointment of receivers by confining his choice to those with particular speciality business acumen? Certainly, receiver-managers must be bound to comply with the law of the land (eg, health and safety legislation, licensing laws, etc) in managing a business and to that extent owe duties over and above that of good faith. But to extend their duties to nebulous, perhaps even discretionary, matters is thought to go too far. A receiver cannot be expected to manage a business with the same care and dedication as a mortgagor; he might not, for example, be obliged to work 14 hours a day as a mortgagor, striving for his own benefit, might voluntarily work. This decision is likely to encourage frivolous and vexatious litigation by disgruntled mortgagors who believe that nobody but themselves has managed their business as well as they could manage it. It is thought that a receiver-manager's duty is best confined to that of good faith and, if necessary, mortgagees will seek, in their security documents, to confine it thus[142].

(c) Duties arising on the disposal of assets

[20.050] Prior to the passing of the CA 1990 it had been established by a number of Irish and Commonwealth cases that receivers owed a duty to take reasonable care to try to obtain the best possible price on the disposal of charged assets. In this respect the law always distinguished between duties owed on the disposal of assets and duties owed on the management of charged assets[143]. Receivers' duties on the disposal of assets were accepted in a number of Irish cases[144], most notably, *McGowan v Gannon*[145], and in England this continues to be known as 'the Cuckmere duty of care'[146].

(i) The statutory duty to obtain the best price reasonably obtainable

[20.051] This position is now enshrined in statute and s 316A(1) of the CA 1963[147] provides that:

---

141 See Anderson, 'Receivers' Duties to Mortgagors – Court of Appeal makes a Pig's Ear of it' *CCH's Company Law Newsletter*, Issue 37, 13 August 1999.

142 Although the decision in *Medforth* was cited by Laffoy J in *Lowe v Burns and Burns* [2012] IEHC 162, and although the learned judge noted that counsel for the receiver said it was not disputed that a duty of care was owed, the decision (and in particular the finding of a so-called duty of 'due diligence') was neither approved not rejected.

143 See para **[20.051]**.

144 See also, *Irish Oil and Cake Mills Ltd v Donnelly* (27 March 1984, unreported) HC, *per* Costello J; *Holohan v Friends Provident and Century Life Office* [1966] IR 1; *Casey v Intercontinental Bank* [1979] IR 364; *Standard Chartered Bank v Walker* [1982] 3 All ER 938 (extending this duty to guarantors: see para **[20.060]** *et seq*). See generally *Re Bula Ltd* (20 June 2002, unreported) HC, Murphy J, where the basis of receivers' duties is reviewed.

145 *McGowan v Gannon* [1983] ILRM 516.

146 See *Cuckmere Brick Co Ltd v Mutual Finance Ltd* [1971] Ch 949 where it was held that a mortgagee was obliged to obtain 'the true market value' of the property in sale.

147 As inserted by s 172 of the CA 1990.

> 'A receiver, in selling property of a company, shall exercise all reasonable care to obtain the best price reasonably obtainable for the property as at the time of sale[148].'

It has been observed by McCracken J in *Ruby Property Company Ltd v Kilty*[149] that 'this is simply a statutory acknowledgement of the position at common law'. The legislature contemplated that such a provision, if left to stand alone, would be avoided through the employment of counteracting contractual provisions in debentures, and so by s 316A(2)(a) of the CA 1963, notwithstanding the provisions of any debenture, it is *not* a defence to proceedings brought against a receiver that he was acting as the agent of the company or under a power of attorney given by the company. Section 316A(2)(b) of the CA 1963 provides that a receiver who breaches his duty in this regard is not entitled to be compensated or indemnified by the company for any liability which he may incur. The meaning of 'best price reasonably obtainable' was considered by Murphy J in *Re Bula Ltd*[150]. There he said that 'best price':

> '... begs the question as to the norm by which 'best' is measured. There is no statutory requirement for an independent valuation nor, indeed, a necessity to have more than one buyer. In the absence of a professional valuation or open market competition to establish a price how can a court approve of a sale as rendering a 'best price'? The requirement is not simply to get the best price reasonably obtainable'.

In that case, a receiver sought approval pursuant to s 326A of the CA 1963 for the sale of an ore body (a mine) to the company's adjoining landowner (and long time fellow litigant) Tara Mines Ltd. The company opposed the application. After examining the receiver's duties under s 316A(1), Murphy J held that:

> 'Section 316A refers not to value nor cost but to price. The receiver in selling the property of the company, which he is clearly entitled to do, must exercise all reasonable care to obtain the best price reasonably obtainable for the property at the time of sale ... What the court has to do is to ascertain that, given that a receiver has exercised all reasonable care, that the ultimate price is the best reasonably obtainable. That is the market 'best price'.'

Murphy J concluded that the receiver had exercised all reasonable care necessary to obtain the best price and allowed his application to complete the sale of the mine to Tara. The company's appeal to the Supreme Court was dismissed. There[151], Denham J, giving the decision of the court, held that the receiver had taken all reasonable care in the timing of the sale, that the receiver's first duty was to the secured creditor and that he was not obliged to wait for the market to rise[152]. On the question of his first duty being to

---

148 Section 142(7) of the NAMAA 2009 provides in virtually identical terms that a 'statutory receiver, in selling property the subject of a charge in favour of NAMA, shall exercise all reasonable care to obtain the best price reasonably obtainable for the property at the time of sale'.

149 *Ruby Property Company Ltd v Kilty* (1 December 1999, unreported) HC, McCracken J.

150 *Re Bula Ltd* (20 June 2002, unreported) HC.

151 *Re Bula Ltd* [2003] 2 IR 431.

152 Denham J cited *Re Edenfell Holdings Ltd* [1999] 1 IR 443 at 464 and Keane, *Company Law* (3rd edn, 2001) at para 22.20, which paragraph was adopted by Denham J as the law: '... while every case should be judged on its own facts, there is no general obligation on a receiver to wait for the market to rise. If he makes a reasonably prudent assessment of the market at the relevant time, he will not be held liable simply because it appears subsequently that by waiting he might have got a better price.'

the secured creditor, Denham J adopted the following passage from the decision of Millett J in *Re Charnley Davies Ltd (No 2)*[153]:

> 'A mortgagee is bound to have regard to the interests of the mortgagor, but he is entitled to give priority to his own interests, and may insist on an immediate sale whether or not that is calculated to realise the best price; he must 'take appropriate care' to obtain the true value of the property at the moment he chooses to sell it, see Cuckmere *Brick Co Ltd v Mutual Finance Ltd* [1971] Ch 949. An administrator, by contrast, like a liquidator, has no interest of his own to which he may give priority, and must take reasonable care in choosing the time at which to sell the property.'

[20.052] The requirement that a receiver should exercise all reasonable care in the sale of property entails a higher standard than merely acting in *good faith*. Where it is apprehended that a receiver is not endeavouring to obtain the best price reasonably possible, an injunction can be applied for to prevent the sale of the mortgaged or charged property. Such was successfully sought by a mortgagor in *Holohan v Friends Provident and Century Life Office*[154] against a mortgagee exercising his power of sale. There, the mortgagee had entered into a contract to sell the mortgaged property without vacant possession (ie, it was subject to existing tenancies) and had refused to consider an alternative. It was successfully argued by the mortgagor that if the mortgaged property was sold with vacant possession, a higher price could be obtained. A contrasting case is *Casey v Irish Intercontinental Bank Ltd*[155] where the Supreme Court again addressed this matter. There, an offer of £111,000 had been accepted by mortgagees who at the time of acceptance had considered that to be the best offer available. Later, an offer of £190,000 was received but rejected because of the prior contract. An application to order the mortgagee to rescind the first contract was rejected by Kenny J who said:

> 'The subsequent offer of £190,000 did not in any way invalidate that contract which, in my opinion, Intercontinental were bound to carry out. A mortgagee who enters into a contract for sale at a price which all the circumstances and valuations show is, *at the date of the contract*, the best price available is not discharged if a higher price is offered after the contract is made.' [Emphasis added.]

From this it is clear that at common law, the operative time to see whether or not the best price was obtained is the date of the contract. This is now further supported by s 316A(1) of the CA 1963 which specifically refers to 'as at the time of sale', which is the contract date not the completion date (of a conveyance).

[20.053] The safest course of action which a receiver can take when selling an asset of a company is to take expert advice on the most efficient and valuable method of disposal[156]. Expert or professional advice, however, will often not resolve a matter outright, since an equally reputable opinion may be obtained from another professional advising to the contrary. In such a situation, where there is conflicting professional

---

153 *Re Charnley Davies Ltd (No 2)* [1990] BCLC 760 at 775.

154 *Holohan v Friends Provident and Century Life Office* [1966] IR 1. See Wylie, *Irish Land Law* (3rd edn, 1997), para 13.036, and Wylie, *A Casebook on Irish Land Law* (1984), p 447.

155 *Casey v Irish Intercontinental Bank Ltd* [1979] IR 364.

156 In *American Express International Banking v Hurley* [1986] BCLC 52, it was held that a receiver was negligent in not seeking specialist advice in relation to the market value of specialist equipment.

advice, it is open to the receiver to make a commercial decision between the two. This was the case in *Lambert Jones Estates Ltd v Donnelly*[157]. There, one opinion on the disposal of the property charged would have involved the delay and expense of planning applications at a time when interest on the principal sum charged was running at over £3,000 per day. The receiver was entitled to follow another expert opinion which would mean the property would realise less, but would be sold more quickly. There, the receiver indicated that in any event he would be seeking court approval for the sale, a matter considered below[158]. In *Ruby Property Company Ltd and ors v Kilty and Superquinn (No 2)*[159], the question before the High Court was whether a receiver who had sold a company's property had acted in accordance with his duties under s 172 of the CA 1990, the basis of the plaintiff's' claim being that the property has been sold at an undervalue. Dismissing the plaintiffs' case, McKechnie J said:

> '... I cannot see how on the evidence adduced, which has been evaluated and analysed above, there is any scope for making a finding of negligence against the receiver. From the outset he put in place a team of professionals whose expertise has not and could not be challenged. All of the relevant areas of interest were covered by these individuals ... In my view it was reasonable on his part in consultation with Messrs Jones Lang and Wootton to identify the existence of special purchasers or persons with a special interest in the property and to have this group as the primary focus of their initial attention.'

[20.054] In *Re Edenfell Holdings Ltd*[160], the Supreme Court heard an appeal from a decision of Laffoy J in respect of an application for directions brought under s 316(1) of the CA 1963. The matter in dispute was whether a receiver had exercised all reasonable care to obtain the best price reasonably obtainable for the property as at the time of sale as required by s 316A of the CA 1963. Laffoy J had held that the receiver had not exercised all reasonable care and she had directed that the receiver should not complete the contract of sale that had been signed. The facts of this case were that a receiver was appointed by a debenture holder to a company after it had been placed into liquidation. Subsequently, a company called Stormdust Ltd ('Stormdust') issued proceedings claiming specific performance of an alleged contract to sell the charged lands to it. In the High Court it was held that Stormdust did not have an enforceable agreement but Stormdust appealed. Subsequently, a company called Astra Construction Services Ltd ('Astra') made an offer of £1.5 million for the charged lands and agreed to pay Stormdust £100,000 to withdraw the appeal. The receiver was advised by the auctioneers to accept this. The receiver refused to sign contracts until all interested parties were invited to better that offer; the liquidator was advised of this and the fact that the receiver would not sign until Astra had procured the withdrawal of Stormdust's appeal to the Supreme Court. The liquidator was told that after the bank was discharged and costs paid in respect of the proceedings against Stormdust, £45,000 would be made available to the liquidator; the liquidator said he had insufficient information as to

157 *Lambert Jones Estates Ltd v Donnelly* [1982] IEHC 25, O'Hanlon J.

158 See para **[20.085]**. See also Ussher, *Company Law in Ireland* (1986), p 442, where he agrees that a receiver when faced with such difficult choices should be able to have recourse to court to seek its '*imprimatur*'.

159 *Ruby Property Company Ltd v Kilty and Superquinn (No 2)* (31 January 2003, unreported) HC, McKechnie J.

160 *Re Edenfell Holdings Ltd* [1999] 1 IR 458 (SC).

whether the proposed transaction would discharge the receiver's duty under s 316A of the CA 1963 and he sought certain information. In all, 15 parties who had expressed an interest in the property were notified and invited to submit a better offer than Astra's. Only two responses were received. One simply expressed an interest; the other was from another company ('Anglo Eire') which confirmed that their previous offer of £1.6 million stood but was expressed to be subject to being furnished with copies of all relevant legal documentation in respect of the appeal and subject to its being satisfied with the contents and opinions therein.

The receiver decided to accept the Astra offer and he signed the contracts with Astra and £100,000 was thereupon paid by Astra to Stormdust in full and final settlement of all actions, etc, against the company and in particular the appeal to the Supreme Court. Stormdust then withdrew the appeal. The receiver then applied for directions in relation to the contract of sale and, if necessary, an order directing him to complete the sale and an order directing the liquidator to join in the contract to convey such interest as he may have had in an unregistered strip of land adjoining the secured property. Another application was also made by a director and shareholder in the company, seeking an order that the receiver should not complete the contract, directing the manner and method of marketing or reselling the secured property and directions as to whether the receiver was entitled to deduct the sum of £105,000 representing the costs of the proceedings involving Stormdust from the proceeds of sale. It was against this background that Laffoy J had held[161] that that the receiver could not be regarded as being unreasonable in concluding that the offer from Astra was the more attractive. However, the learned judge went on to find that, on the evidence, she was not satisfied that the receiver had exercised all reasonable care to free the lands of the encumbrance (which the appeal constituted) and to obtain for the company the best price reasonably obtainable for the lands and she directed the receiver not to complete the contract and to return the deposit paid thereunder.

[20.055] The Supreme Court reversed this decision. In giving the judgment of the court, Keane J held that the receiver had exercised all reasonable care. Adopting a very commercial approach, Keane J stated:

> 'It is not the function of the court in a case such as this to decide, with the benefit of hindsight, whether it might have been better for the creditors and anyone else interested in the property had the receiver rejected the Astra offer and continued to deal with Anglo Eire or anyone else who might be interested. The court was dealing with the matter with the advantage of hindsight: the receiver had to deal with the matter then and there and in the light of the expert evidence available to him from a valuer. Having tested the market again, without any response in the form of an unconditional offer, he was entitled, in all the circumstances, to take the view he did, that accepting the Astra proposal was the more prudent course[162].'

This case clearly demonstrates the highly subjective nature of a receiver's decision as to whether or not a particular price is the best price reasonably obtainable. Receivers would do well to heed the advice of Laffoy J when she suggested that an application under s 316 of the CA 1963 should be considered before committing oneself to a contract[163].

---

161 *Re Edenfell Holdings Ltd* [1999] 1 IR 443 (HC).

162 *Re Edenfell Holdings Ltd* [1999] 1 IR 458 (SC).

163 *Re Edenfell Holdings Ltd* [1999] 1 IR 443 (HC).

[20.056] In *Ruby Property Company Ltd v Kilty*[164], McCracken J said that where a receiver is appointed to a company that is not insolvent and where the sale of the charged asset will produce a surplus that will be repaid to the company:

> '... it is open for consideration by the court as to whether in those circumstances the receiver has some form of obligation at least to consider representations made to him by the company as to how to conduct the sale, provided he is satisfied it will, in any event, realise enough to discharge the debenture holder in full.'

In that case a receiver had been appointed to the plaintiff company. The receiver had taken possession of the company's premises and set about selling it. Despite a number of requests in correspondence from the company the receiver had refused to advertise the premises for sale. Initially, the receiver's estate agents had advised him to advertise but this advice had changed, subsequently. The premises was eventually sold by tender to Superquinn for £102,500. In an unsuccessful application to have the plaintiff's proceedings against the receiver struck out, it was heard that some four months' later there was evidence that the property was worth over £160,000. McCracken J's suggestion that a receiver is obliged to have a greater regard for a plaintiff company's wishes where the sale of assets is likely to produce a surplus over for the plaintiff company is superficially attractive. It must be remembered, however, that there is a clear duty on receivers to obtain the best price reasonably obtainable and, to this extent, a company's interests are already fully protected. It is thought that it would be an unnecessary fetter on the exercise of a receiver's powers to compel consultation with a company and that the statutory duty in s 316A of the CA 1963 is more than sufficient protection.

(ii) The extent of the duty to obtain the best price reasonable obtainable

[20.057] A receiver is not obliged to await an upturn in the market before selling, and his duty is merely to obtain the best price reasonably obtainable in any given economic climate[165]. Since the enactment in Ireland of s 316A of the CA 1963, English case law must be read with care. However, it has been held in a number of English cases – cited with apparent approval by Budd J in *Kinsella v Somers*[166] – that the scope of the so-called '*Cuckmere* duty of care' is to be interpreted narrowly. In particular, there is authority for the rule that any duty of care (whether arising at common law or by statute) only arises *after* 'the creditor has decided what and when to sell'[167]. So, in *Downside Nominees Ltd v First City Corporation Ltd*[168] Lord Templeman said:

---

[164] *Ruby Property Company Ltd v Kilty* (1 December 1999, unreported) HC, McCracken J.

[165] See *Re Bula Ltd* (20 June 2002, unreported) HC, Murphy J. See also *Bank of Cyprus (London) Ltd v Gill* [1980] 2 Lloyds' Rep 51 where it was held that a mortgagee was not obliged to await an upswing in the market; in *McGowan v Gannon* [1983] ILRM 516, Carroll J raised the question but left it unanswered.

[166] *Kinsella v Somers* (22 November 1999, unreported) HC, Budd J.

[167] See Judge Raymond Jack in *Huis v Ellis* [1995] BCC 462 at 466, citing *Re B Johnson & Co (Builders) Ltd* [1955] Ch 634 and *Downside Nominees Ltd v First City Corporation Ltd* [1993] BCC 46.

[168] *Downside Nominees Ltd v First City Corporation Ltd* [1993] BCC 46. For comment see Milman, 'Receiverships Reviewed' (21 October 1998) *Palmer's In Company*, Issue 9/98.

'The general duty of care said to be owed by a mortgagee to subsequent encumbrancers and the mortgagor in negligence is inconsistent with the right of the mortgagee and the duties which the courts applying equitable principles have imposed on the mortgagee ... If a mortgagee exercises his power of sale in good faith for the purpose of protecting his security, he is not liable to the mortgagor even though he might have obtained a higher price and even though the terms might be regarded as disadvantageous to the mortgagor. *Cuckmere Brick Co Ltd v Mutual Finance Ltd* [1971] Ch 949 is Court of Appeal authority for the proposition that, if the mortgagee decides to sell, he must take reasonable care to obtain a proper price *but is no authority for any wider proposition* ... The duties imposed by equity on a mortgagee and on a receiver and manager would be quite unnecessary if there existed a general duty in negligence to take reasonable care in the exercise of powers and to take reasonable care in dealing with the assets of the mortgagor company[169].'

It is thought that the foregoing passage applies equally to where the duty to obtain the best price reasonably obtainable 'at the time of sale' arises by statute as it does in Ireland. This principle has been followed in subsequent cases, such as *Routestone Ltd v Minorities Finance Ltd*[170], where Jacob J held that once a power of sale arises, a receiver cannot be found to be negligent in exercising it. So he said:

'Alleging that a decision to exercise a power is negligent is itself tantamount to saying that the mortgagee or receiver is a trustee of the power of sale which he is admittedly not. *No duty of care is owed by the mortgagee or receiver in relation to the actual decision to sell*[171].'

(iii) Sale of non-cash assets to past and present officers

[20.058] An additional feature of a receiver's duty to take reasonable care to obtain the best possible price obtainable in a sale is the negative duty contained in s 316A(3)(a) of the CA 1963 which provides:

'A receiver shall not sell by private contract a *non-cash asset* of the *requisite value* to a person who is, or who, within three years prior to the date of appointment of the receiver, has been, an officer of the company unless he has given at least 14 days' notice of his intention to do so to all the creditors of the company who are known to him or who have been intimated to him.' [Emphasis added.]

The expressions *non-cash asset* and *requisite value* have the meanings assigned to them by s 29 of the CA 1990[172]. The expression 'officer' includes a person connected to a director or shadow director within the meaning of s 26 of the CA 1990[173]. The consequences of a receiver contravening this provision are not spelt out in the legislation. Is such a sale void, voidable at the instance of the creditors of the company or at the instance of thc company itsclf or is the validity of thc sale unaffected by a contravention, the consequences being personal to the receiver? It is thought that the validity of the sale is unaffected as the legislature has not expressly provided that a sale

---

169 *Downside Nominees Ltd v First City Corporation Ltd* [1993] BCC 46 at 55–56, emphasis added.

170 *Routestone Ltd v Minorities Finance Ltd* [1997] BCC 180.

171 *Routestone Ltd v Minorities Finance Ltd* [1997] BCC 180 at 191, emphasis added.

172 Section 316A(3)(b)(I) of the CA 1963 and, see generally, Ch 16, *Statutory Regulation of Directors' Transactions*, paras **[16.028]** and **[16.029]**, respectively.

173 Section 316A(3)(b)(ii) of the CA 1963. For a consideration of shadow directors, see Ch 13, *Corporate Governance: Management by the Directors*, para **[13.055]**.

in breach of s 316A(3)(a) of the CA 1963 is void or voidable and such should not be implied. Notwithstanding this view, until such time as there has been a judicial consideration of this provision, it is thought that extreme care ought to be taken as it may well be found that where this provision is contravened, a subsequent purchaser might be affected.

[20.059] It has been decided in England and Wales that receivers are bound to comply with the English equivalent of s 29 of the CA 1990[174]. In *Demite Ltd v Protec Health Ltd*[175], it was held by Park J that a receiver, who had been appointed by a debenture holder, could not dispose of a company's property to a director or person connected with a director of that company without first obtaining the company's members' approval under s 320 of the Companies Act 1985 (UK). For a number of reasons it is thought that s 29 of the CA 1990 should not be so construed and that *Demite* should not be followed by the Irish courts. First, it is necessary to distinguish the differences in the statutory duties of receivers appointed under Irish and English legislation. Regard must be had to the fact that in Ireland a receiver has a statutory obligation to exercise all reasonable care to obtain the best price reasonably obtainable for property as at the time of sale: s 316A(1) of the CA 1963. The only legitimate statutory purpose of s 29 of the CA 1990 is to protect against possible distortions which may arise when directors self-deal; the obligation to exercise all reasonable care to obtain the best price reasonably obtainable for property as at the time of sale must surely be sufficient. Second, it is thought to be outside the spirit of s 29 of the CA 1990 to apply it to sales of company assets by receivers when it was clearly intended to regulate self-dealing by directors[176]. Third, in a receivership (particularly where the company is insolvent) it is the interests of the company's creditors and not the company's members which must come first. So s 316A(3) of the CA 1963 regulates the sale of non-cash assets to past and present officers by ensuring that creditors have notice of any such proposed transactions. Fourth, it can be convincingly argued that upon the appointment of a receiver to an insolvent company, the company has just a bare legal interest in its assets with the result that a sale of those assets might not be of the requisite value in order to trigger the application of s 29 of the CA 1990. Where the market for a particular asset over which it is proposed to take security is particularly small and there is a possibility that a receiver might find that only the company's directors are interested in acquiring the assets, a creditor might consider insisting that a validating resolution to any future sale to a director or other relevant person by the company acting by any receiver, be passed *prior* to draw down of credit facilities[177].

---

174 Section 320 of the Companies Act 1985 (UK). See generally Ch 16, *Statutory Regulation of Directors' Transactions*, para **[16.039]**.

175 *Demite Ltd v Protec Health Ltd* [1998] BCC 638. See generally, Courtney, 'Receiverships in Ireland in the Wake of *Demite Ltd v Protec Health Ltd*' (1998) 5 CLP 255.

176 On the purpose of s 20 of the CA 1990 see the decision of Carnwath J in *British Racing Drivers' Club Ltd v Hextall Erskine & Co (a firm)* [1996] 3 All ER 667 at 681j–682a and generally, Ch 16 *Statutory Regulation of Directors' Transactions*, para **[16.022]**.

177 See Courtney, 'Receiverships in Ireland in the Wake of *Demite Ltd v Protec Health Ltd*' (1998) 5 CLP 255 at 261. It may be noted that the *Company Law Review Group* in its *First Report* (February 2002) recommended that s 29(7) of the CA 1990 be amended by the addition of a third exception regarding the disposal of a company's assets by a receiver. See recommendation at 6.11.4.

(d) Duties to guarantors

[20.060] A receiver has also been held to owe a duty of care to persons who have guaranteed the debts of a company which has been placed into receivership. The exposure of such guarantors is possible, where, for example, after the receiver sells off assets charged there is a shortfall in the amount owed to the debenture holder[178]. In such a case, the guarantor would be secondarily liable to pay the secured debt and so has an interest to ensure that the highest price possible is obtained for the charged assets.

[20.061] It had been held that a receiver does not owe a duty to provide any information to a guarantor of the company's debts, nor indeed to any other creditors of the company: *McGowan v Gannon*[179].

[20.062] At common law, it was established in the case of *Standard Chartered Bank v Walker*[180] that a receiver owes a duty of care to guarantors in disposing of mortgaged or charged assets. The following passage of Lord Denning MR was cited by Carroll J in the Irish High Court in *McGowan v Gannon*[181]:

> 'If it should appear that the mortgagee or receiver have not used reasonable care to realise the assets to the best advantage, then the mortgagor, the company *and the guarantor* are entitled in equity to an allowance. They should be given credit for the amount which the sale should have realised if reasonable care had been used[182].'

Earlier, Carroll J had said that this case had held:

> '... that a guarantor could sue a receiver for negligence in disposing of the assets of a company whose debts were guaranteed as there was sufficient proximity between receiver and guarantor for the receiver to owe a duty of care to the guarantor[183].'

Where a receiver does not exercise reasonable care to obtain the best price reasonably possible, with the result that a property realises less than it ought to have realised, the amount for which the guarantor of the loan, secured by the instrument which permitted the appointment of the receiver is liable, will be reduced *pro tanto*[184].

[20.063] In *Ruby Property Company and ors v Kilty and Superquinn*[185], McKechnie J indicated that the notion that receivers owed duties to guarantors may not be considered to be settled law in Ireland:

---

178 See generally, *Ashley Guarantee plc v Zacaria* [1993] 1 All ER 254.

179 *McGowan v Gannon* [1983] ILRM 516. On the duty to provide information, see para **[20.071]**. However, note that the receiver does owe a duty of care in selling mortgaged or charged property, to any guarantor: see para **[20.060]**.

180 *Standard Chartered Bank v Walker* [1982] 3 All ER 938. See also, *Shamji v Johnson Matthey Bankers Ltd* [1986] BCLC 278 and *American Express International Banking Corp v Hurley* [1986] BCLC 52.

181 *McGowan v Gannon* [1983] ILRM 516.

182 *Standard Chartered Bank v Walker* [1982] 3 All ER 938 at 942, emphasis added.

183 *McGowan v Gannon* [1983] ILRM 516 at 518.

184 *Skipton Building Society v Bratley and another* [2000] TLR 15.

185 *Ruby Property Company and ors v Kilty and Superquinn* (31 January 2003, unreported) HC, McKechnie J.

'This duty of care in the case of a receiver is not only owed to the company but also to the guarantors of the company's liability. In addition, a mortgagee likewise owes a duty of care to the mortgagor and to the guarantor of the mortgagor's debts. In *Standard Chartered Bank Ltd v Walker* [1982] 3 All ER 938 at 942 Denning MR said 'If it should appear that the mortgagee or receiver have not used reasonable care to realise the assets to the best advantage, then the mortgagor, the company and the guarantor are entitled in equity to an allowance. They should be given credit for the amount which the sale should have realised if reasonable care had been used.' See also *American Express International Banking Corporation v Hurley* [1985] 3 All ER 564. This passage from *Standard Chartered Bank* was quoted with apparent approval by Carroll J in *McGowan*, *supra*, but in view of the later English decision on *Downsview Nominees Ltd v First Cty Corporation Ltd* [1993] AC 295 it remains to be seen whether in this jurisdiction the analysis of Denning MR requires to be reviewed or reconsidered.'

[20.064] Subject to McKechnie J's caveat, it would appear that the general duty of receivers to realise the best price reasonably obtainable on the sale of mortgaged or charged assets, as set out in s 316A(1) of the CA 1963, is also of relevance to guarantors. Since this section does not say to whom that duty is owed, one can infer that it is owed to all who suffer direct loss as a result of a receiver contravening it. The duty can, however, only be owed to persons with an interest in the equity of redemption in the sold property. This was confirmed in *Burgess v Auger; Burgess v Vansstock Ltd*[186] where Lightman J said:

'The fiduciary duties of the mortgagee and receiver relate only to the equity of redemption and are owed only to those interested in the equity of redemption; and all the duties owed by a mortgagee or receiver are historically merely developments or expanded forms of the duty of good faith arising from the existence of the fiduciary relationship[187].'

Those with an interest in the equity of redemption will be the mortgagor, and subsequent mortgagee and, by operation of the doctrine of subrogation, any guarantor of the primary debt. In the *Burgess* case, the claim of a director, shareholder, employee and guarantor were struck out. Furthermore, leave to amend the guarantor's claim was also refused because the guarantor had not then made any payment to the appointing mortgagee under the guarantee which would give rise to his having an interest in the equity of redemption.

[20.065] In *Ruby Property Company and ors v Kilty and Superquinn*[188], McKechnie J noted that the duty of receivers does not extend to unsecured creditors, citing *Lathia v Dronsfield Brothers Ltd*[189].

(e) Duties in applying the proceeds of sale of assets

[20.066] Ordinarily, the onus of discharging the general debts owed by the company is not the concern of a receiver since this is the primary function of a liquidator. However, to the general principle there is an exception. It is settled law that where a receiver realises assets which are the subject of a *fixed charge* or a *legal mortgage* his only

[186] *Burgess v Auger; Burgess v Vansstock Ltd* [1998] 2 BCLC 478.

[187] *Burgess v Auger; Burgess v Vansstock Ltd* [1998] 2 BCLC 478 at 482.

[188] *Ruby Property Company and ors v Kilty and Superquinn* (31 January 2003, unreported) HC, McKechnie J.

[189] *Lathia v Dronsfield Brothers Ltd* [1987] BCLC 321.

obligation is to apply the proceeds of these in discharge of the amount due and owing to the debenture holder. Any surplus over from the realisation can be paid back to the company, and is not to be applied in discharge of any debts owed to preferential creditors. However, in respect of a *floating charge*, s 98 of the CA 1963 provides that before a receiver can apply the proceeds realised in discharge of the debts owed to the debenture holder, he is obliged to first pay the company's preferential creditors[190].

[20.067] In *United Bars Ltd v Revenue Commissioners*[191], s 98 of the CA 1963 and its application to assets subject to a fixed and floating charge was considered. Section 98(1) of the CA 1963 provides that:

> 'Where either a receiver is appointed on behalf of the holders of any debenture of a company secured by a floating charge, or possession is taken by or on behalf of those debenture holders of any property comprised in or subject to the charge, then, if the company is not at the time, in course of being wound up, the debts which in every winding up are, under the provisions of Part VI relating to preferential payments to be paid in priority to all other debts, shall be paid out of any assets coming to the hands of the receiver or other person taking possession as aforesaid in priority to any claim for principal or interest in respect of the debentures.'

In that case, certain companies had created debentures which charged certain assets by both fixed and floating charges. The receiver successfully realised two properties, and having paid the debenture holder what was due and owing, was left with a surplus of £85,417. The issue to be decided by the court was whether the receiver was obliged to pay this money to the company, or to the Revenue Commissioners in discharge of sums due to them as a preferential creditor.[192] In his judgment, Murphy J referred to *Re GL Saunders Ltd*[193], where Nourse J had held that where a company created both a fixed and floating charge over its assets, and the receiver was left with a surplus of £444,000 from the sale of assets subject to the fixed charge, that this money should be repaid to the company and not applied in payment of the preferential creditors. There, Nourse J had relied on *Re Lewis Marlty Consolidated Collieries*[194], where Tomlin J had held that a similar section applied only in respect of accounts coming to a receiver which were the subject of a floating charge and not to the sale of assets the subject of a fixed charge. Counsel for the Revenue Commissioners argued against this on two main grounds. First of all, it was argued that on a true construction of the debenture in hand, the charge was primarily a floating charge and so s 98 of the CA 1963 applied. Secondly, it was 'courageously' argued that the authorities cited were wrong in law and ought not to be followed. Both arguments were rejected by Murphy J who held that the established authorities should prevail, one reason being that:

---

190 On *preferential creditors*, see Ch 25, *Realisation and Distribution of Assets in a Winding Up*, para **[25.183]**.

191 *United Bars Ltd v Revenue Commissioners* [1991] 1 IR 396.

192 In *Re Red Sail Frozen Foods Ltd* [2006] IEHC 328, Laffoy J, it was held that a receiver was entitled to pay the preferential claims of the Department of Enterprise Trade and Employment and by employees where there was a pre-receivership practice of making payments to employees without deduction of PAYE and PRSI.

193 *Re GL Saunders Ltd* [1986] BCLC 40, [1986] WLR 215.

194 *Re Lewis Marlty Consolidated Collieries* [1939] 1 Ch D 498.

'... it seems to me of the utmost importance in dealing with commercial matters to maintain some measure of consistency, and to proceed on the footing that parties to commercial transactions have organised their affairs on the basis of the law as they understand and believe it to be for many years, and any change to that law should be made preferably by the Oireachtas or at any rate by the final court of appeal in this country ...'[195]

[20.068] A receiver's duty under s 98 of the CA 1963 survives the making of a winding-up order and compels a receiver to pay the Revenue Commissioners in discharge of preferential debts ahead of any liquidator. In *Re Eisc Teo*[196], a company created both a fixed charge over certain assets and a floating charge over other assets. When the company defaulted on the loan, the chargee caused a receiver to be appointed and the charged assets were realised. The receiver paid off the chargee in full out of the fixed charge and was left in possession of the proceeds of sale of the assets the subject of the floating charge. A liquidator was later appointed and sought to compel the receiver to deliver up those proceeds, less his expenses. The receiver refused, believing he was under a statutory duty to apply the proceeds of a floating charge in discharge of preferential creditors pursuant to s 98 of the CA 1963. The liquidator argued that this had no application once a winding-up order had been made and that in any event, the liquidator would be under a duty to apply that money to the preferential creditors[197]. It was held by Lardner J that the receiver *was under a statutory duty* to pay the preferential creditors, saying:

'... in my judgment, in the present case the receiver was at the time of his appointment, the company at that time being in the course of being wound up, obliged by s 98 to make the preferential payments. This duty having once been imposed in unqualified terms by the section, was not terminated or affected by the circumstance either that a winding up order was made three months after the appointment of the receiver or that the receiver did not in fact require to make any payment out of the assets the subject of the floating charge. The section refers not to the payment out of the assets but to claims for principal or interest. I think such a claim clearly exists at the time of the receiver's appointment and that the duty was then imposed upon the receiver by the section[198].'

In *Re Manning Furniture Ltd (in receivership)*[199], it was sought to draw a distinction between a liquidator and a mortgagee. The facts in this case were that a receiver had been appointed to a company on foot of a mortgage debenture (incorporating a floating charge) and several chattel mortgages in favour of ICC Bank plc. It transpired that, some years' previously, the company had created a mortgage in favour of what was then First National Building Society ('FNSB') but that mortgage had not been registered pursuant to s 99 of the CA 1963 and application was made for late registration under s 106 of the CA 1963[200]. The receiver sold the chattels and at the time of seeking directions had contracted to sell the premises and held a surplus of £150,000. The direction sought by the receiver was whether he was obliged to discharge the preferential creditors of the company before paying the balance to FNBS. After considering the finding in *Re Eisc*

[195] *United Bars Ltd v Revenue Commissioners* [1991] 1 IR 396 at 401.

[196] *Re Eisc Teo* [1991] ILRM 760.

[197] Under s 285 of the CA 1963.

[198] *Re Eisc Teo* [1991] ILRM 760 at 763–764.

[199] *Re Manning Furniture Ltd (in receivership)* [1996] 1 ILRM 13.

[200] In this respect, see Ch 19, *Corporate Borrowing: Registration of Charges*, para **[19.090]**.

Teoranta[201], McCracken J noted that counsel for FNBS had sought to distinguish that case on that basis that there the question was whether the receiver should pay the revenue or the liquidator, whereas in the instant case the question was whether the receiver should pay the Revenue Commissioners or a mortgagee. McCracken J refused to distinguish the two cases and went on to find that the *Joplin proviso*[202] in the order for late registration meant that FNBS's mortgage took priority *after* the Revenue Commissioners who had, under s 98 of the CA 1963, 'a right acquired prior to the time of the registration of the particulars of the mortgage'[203].

[20.069] The Revenue Commissioners can make a preferential claim in a receivership and also in a subsequent liquidation of the same company. In *H Williams (Tallaght) Ltd (in receivership and liquidation)*[204], a receiver had been appointed to a company and, pursuant to s 98 of the CA 1963, treated the Revenue Commissioners as preferential creditors in relation to certain debts of the company in respect of PAYE and PRSI. Thereafter he discharged the entire debt of the debenture holders and had no further function to perform. Subsequently, the company went into liquidation and the Revenue Commissioners then claimed to be a preferential creditor under s 285 of the CA 1963 this time in respect of corporation tax due by the company. The liquidator was unsuccessful in arguing that the Revenue Commissioners could not claim to be a preferential creditor for a second time[205].

[20.070] It has been decided in a number of English and Australian cases that a receiver's duty to pay preferential creditors survives the satisfaction of his appointing debenture holder's claims. So in *Re Pearl Maintenance Services Ltd*[206] Carnwath J said of receivers' duties under s 40 of the Insolvency Act 1986 (UK):

> 'The cases show that s 40 creates a positive duty (not merely a restriction) in favour of the preferential creditors, and that it is a duty enforceable by action in tort for damages … Thus it is a duty which creates statutory private rights, enforceable as such by the preferential creditors. This being so, it would be very odd if those rights disappeared, merely because the debenture holder … had been paid off ...'[207]

In *Lumsden v Long*[208], it was held by the Federal Court of Australia that a receiver was under a personal obligation to discharge the preferential creditors. Whilst this obligation survived his resignation as receiver, it was held that whether the realised assets of the company are passed to a debenture holder[209] or to a liquidator, they are impressed with a constructive trust.

---

201 *Re Eisc Teoranta* [1991] ILRM 760.

202 See Ch 19, *Corporate Borrowing: Registration of Charges*, para **[19.094]**.

203 *Re Manning Furniture Ltd (in receivership)* [1996] 1 ILRM 13.

204 *H Williams (Tallaght) Ltd (in receivership and liquidation)* [1996] 3 IR 531.

205 The liquidator was, however, successful in arguing that the Revenue Commissioners' claim was out of time and so statute barred.

206 *Re Pearl Maintenance Services Ltd* [1995] 1 BCLC 449.

207 *Re Pearl Maintenance Services Ltd* [1995] 1 BCLC 449 at 457.

208 *Lumsden v Long* [1998] 1304 Federal Court of Australia (16 October 1998). See also *Stein v Saywell* (1969) 121 CLR 529 and *Chief Commissioner of Stamp Duties v Buckle* (1998) 151 ALR 1.

209 *Inland Revenue Commissioners v Goldblatt* [1972] 2 All ER 202.

(f) Duties to supply information to the registrar of companies and the Director of Corporate Enforcement

[20.071] In addition to the requirement that a receiver notify his appointment to the registrar of companies[210], a receiver is also obliged to furnish within one month of his appointment and, thereafter, at six-monthly intervals, an abstract in the prescribed form[211] to the registrar. The abstract must show the assets of the company of which he has taken possession since his appointment, their estimated value, the proceeds of sale of any such assets since his appointment, his receipts and payments during that period of six months or, where he ceases to act, during that period to the end of the period to which the last preceding abstract related up to the date of his ceasing and also the aggregate amounts of his receipts and of his payments during all preceding periods since his appointment.

[20.072] Section 319(2A) of the CA 1963 provides:

> 'Where a receiver ceases to act as receiver of the property of the company, the abstract under subsection (2) shall be accompanied by a statement from the receiver of his opinion as to whether or not the company is solvent and the registrar shall, on receiving the statement, forward a copy of it to the Director.'

Although this duty is owed by receivers to the registrar, the Director of Corporate Enforcement is also a beneficiary of the information. The purpose of this provision is to alert the Director as to whether or not a company that has been through a receivership is solvent. If the company is insolvent and it transpires that the company is not wound up, the Director has the opportunity to consider whether the case is an appropriate one in which to exercise his powers under s 251 of the CA 1990.

[20.073] In addition to the foregoing duties to supply information routinely, receivers can also be made amenable to provide specific information to the Director of Corporate Enforcement on a particular receivership or in relation to all receiverships undertaken by him. Section 323A(1) of the CA 1963 provides:

> 'The Director may, where he considers it necessary or appropriate, request (specifying the reason why the request is being made) the production of a receiver's books for examination, either in regard to a particular receivership or to all receiverships undertaken by the receiver.'

Receivers are obliged[212] to furnish their books to the Director, answer any questions concerning their content and the conduct of a particular receivership or receiverships and 'to give to the Director all assistance in the matter as the receiver is reasonably able to give'. The failure to comply is an offence[213]. It is notable that the Director must specify 'the reason why the request is made'; if the Director fails to provide a reason it is thought that a receiver is not obliged to comply. Moreover, requests may not be made in respect of books relating to a receivership that has concluded more than six years prior to the request[214].

---

210 Section 107(1) of the CA 1963.

211 Section 319(2) of the CA 1963.

212 By s 323A(2) of the CA 1963.

213 Section 323A(4) of the CA 1963.

214 Section 323A(3) of the CA 1963.

Liabilities of receivers

[20.074] The liability of a receiver arises primarily[215] in respect of contracts entered into by him on behalf of the company. Section 316(2) of the CA 1963 provides:

> 'A receiver of the property of a company shall be personally liable on any contract entered into by him in the performance of his functions (whether such contract is entered into by him in the name of such company or in his own name as receiver or otherwise) unless the contract provides that he is not to be personally liable on such contract, and he shall be entitled in respect of that liability to indemnity out of the assets; but nothing in this subsection shall be taken as limiting any right to indemnity which he would have apart from this subsection, or as limiting his liability on contracts entered into without authority or as conferring any right to indemnity in respect of that liability.'

From this it is clear that, unless personal liability is disclaimed *ab initio*, a receiver will be liable on any contract entered into by him in, for example, the sale of a business, or in respect of contracts entered into by him as manager while he is running the business. It seems to be commercial practice for receivers not to exclude their personal liability in contracts as a general rule. Even so, it should be noted that a person dealing with a company may insist upon the company/receiver paying sums owed prior to the receiver's appointment before agreeing to continue to contract with him or the company[216]. Where a receiver chooses not to fulfil a contract which has been entered into by a company, persons thereby affected may bring proceedings against the company for breach of contract. Where a receiver is appointed under an invalid debenture, it is open to the court to relieve him from incurring personal liability. Where such relief is granted, what was his liability will be juxtaposed onto those who appointed him, ie, the debenture holder[217]. As to a receiver's liability under s 98 of the CA 1963, see above[218].

[20.075] A receiver will not as a general rule, in the absence of bad faith, while acting within his authority be liable for a breach of a contract by the company, nor will he be guilty of inducing breach of contract[219]. This is illustrated by *Lathia v Dronsfield Bros Ltd*[220]. There, the first defendant company contracted to supply the plaintiff with certain goods, and when the company failed to do so the plaintiff began to sue them, and joined the second and third defendants who were managers and receivers to the first defendant company, alleging inducement to breach of contract. The receivers were successful in having the proceedings against them struck out for showing no reasonable cause of action. Sir Neil Lawson said:

> 'The receivers can adopt or decline to adopt a contract which the company has entered into and which is unexecuted. It follows from this, and the agency clause, that the agent is

215 Apart, that is, from those circumstances considered above, where a receiver acts in breach of a duty owed.

216 See *W & L Crowe Ltd et al v ESB* (9 May 1984, unreported) HC, Costello J.

217 Section 316(3) of the CA 1963.

218 At para **[20.066]**.

219 This sentence as it appeared in the second edition of this work (*The Law of Private Companies*, (2nd edn, 2002) at para [22.063]) was cited with apparent approval by Laffoy J in *Moylist Construction Ltd v Doheny et al* [2010] IEHC 162 and reference was made to the decision in *Lathia v Dronsfield Bros Ltd* [1987] BCLC 321.

220 *Lathia v Dronsfield Bros Ltd* [1987] BCLC 321.

> personally immune from claims for damages for breach of contract or procurement of breach of contract. The agent has an immunity from a claim for inducing breach of contract unless he has not acted *bona fide* or acted outside the scope of his authority, *ie* had not acted as agent. In my judgment, a mere assertion in a pleading of lack of *bona fides* is not enough. Particulars must be given, and one must look at the particulars in that case. So far as the authority is concerned, the authority of the receivers is to be found in cl 8 of the debenture[221]. Furthermore their authority resides on a general obligation to act so as to effect the best realisation of the company's assets for the debenture holders. On authority, one must look at the context to determine to whom the duties are owed. Primarily, they owe a duty to the debenture holders, and also as agents to the company. In my judgment, they do not owe a duty to the general creditors, to contributories, to officers of the company, and members[222].'

This case relied on *Re B Johnson & Co (Builders) Ltd*[223] and *Airlines Airspace Ltd v Handley Page Ltd*[224], both of which support the proposition that a receiver is not bound by contracts entered into by the company prior to his appointment.

[20.076] A receiver will not be liable in respect of a contract or agreement entered into by the company prior to his appointment. This is seen in the Irish case of *Ardmore Studios (Ireland) Ltd v Lynch*[225]. In that case, it was held that an agreement entered into between a trade union and a company would not bind the receiver to that company. McLoughlin J said:

> 'As agent for the company, the company is made responsible for his acts but it is not a corollary to this that he [the receiver] is bound by all company contracts entered into by the company before the date of his appointment[226].'

In that case, the receiver was found not to be bound by a collective agreement which had been entered into by the company. This position has, in that particular context, however, been altered by reg 4 of the European Communities (Safeguarding of Employees' Rights on the Transfer of Undertakings) Regulations 1980[227].

[20.077] In *Moylist Construction Ltd v Doheny et al*[228], Laffoy J also considered a receiver's liability on foot of a contract that had been entered into by a person to whom a receiver had been appointed. Laffoy J referred to the judgment of Vinelott J in *Astor*

221 Clause 8 of the debenture provided: 'At any time after the security shall have become enforceable the Bank may by writing under the hand of any area manager or manager of the Bank appoint any person (or persons) to be a Receiver of the property hereby charged and may similarly remove any Receiver and appoint another in his stead. Any Receiver so appointed shall be the agent of the Company and the Company shall be solely responsible for his acts or defaults and for his remuneration and any Receiver so appointed shall have power ...'

222 *Lathia v Dronsfield Bros Ltd* [1987] BCLC 321 at 324.

223 *Re B Johnson & Co (Builders) Ltd* [1955] 2 All ER 775.

224 *Airlines Airspace Ltd v Handley Page Ltd* [1970] 1 All ER 29 (where it was held that a receiver was entitled to adopt or decline to adopt any unexecuted contract).

225 *Ardmore Studios (Ireland) Ltd v Lynch* [1965] IR 1.

226 *Ardmore Studios (Ireland) Ltd v Lynch* [1965] IR 1 at 40.

227 SI 306/1980. See Lynch-Fannon & Murphy, *Corporate Insolvency and Rescue* (2nd edn, Bloomsbury Professional, 2012), paras 7.61–7.64 and 8.101–8.109.

228 *Moylist Construction Ltd v Doheny et al* [2010] IEHC 162.

Chemicals v Synthetic Technology[229] where he referred with approval to the following four principles as set out in Lightman & Moss, *Law of Receivers of Companies*:

> '(1) If a person is granted a charge on property with actual knowledge of a contractual obligation in favour of another person inconsistent either with the grant or enforcement of the charge, the grant or enforcement will constitute a tort and an injunction may be granted to restrain its commission.
>
> (2) In the absence of such knowledge, the chargee (and the receiver as his agent) is free (*vis-à-vis* the third parties) to cause the company to repudiate or ignore its outstanding contractual obligations to third parties, though this course may give rise to a claim in respect of the loss occasioned by the company if involving an unnecessary and unreasonable exercise of their powers.
>
> (3) The receiver as agent for the company is equally free of liability to third parties for causing the company to breach its contracts with them, for no person can be liable for the tort of interference with contractual relations if he acts as agent for one of the contracting parties …
>
> (4) Neither the receiver nor the debenture holder can interfere with existing equitable rights of third parties over property of the company having priority to the charge. A threat of such action may be restrained by injunction …'

Laffoy J noted that in the case under consideration it was alleged by a person who had a contract with the individual over whose lands a receiver was appointed that the bank which appointed the receiver was aware of the agreement and so did have the '*actual knowledge*' referred to in point (1) above. Laffoy J rejected the contractor's submissions for two reasons. First, she found that it was 'actual knowledge' that was required and that there was no evidence that the bank had such notice; second, Laffoy J pointed out that it purported to preserve a contractual obligation which is inconsistent with the grant of the enforcement of the charge, eg, a contract to sell the property as opposed to a contract to develop the property, the latter, which would not be inconsistent.'

[20.078] A receiver will, where appointed an agent of the company by the debenture, be bound to comply with court orders made against the company such as, for example, *Mareva* injunctions. So, in *Creatanor Maritime Co Ltd v Irish Marine Management Ltd*[230], the English Court of Appeal held that, having been appointed agent, a receiver to a company was not entitled to apply for the discharge of a *Mareva* injunction which bound the company. In that case, however, it was held that the debenture holder was entitled to apply to have the *Mareva* injunction discharged on the basis that his security took precedence over any *Mareva* plaintiff's rights as *Mareva* injunctions act *in personam* and not *in rem* against a *Mareva* defendant's assets.

Powers of receivers

[20.079] A court appointed receiver's powers are dependent upon the terms of the order of the court appointing him. These will usually be to collect, get assets in and receive

---

[229] *Astor Chemicals v Synthetic Technology* [1990] BCLC 1 at 9.

[230] *Creatanor Maritime Co Ltd v Irish Marine Management Ltd* [1978] 3 All ER 164. See generally, Courtney, *Mareva Injunctions and Related Interlocutory Orders* (1998), paras [9.40]–[9.41].

those assets. This express power is supported by the implicit power to do all acts which are incidental and consequential upon the exercise of the express power.

[20.080] Where a receiver is appointed out of court on foot of a debenture, his powers will generally be found in the debenture instrument itself[231] coupled with certain statutory powers[232]. The extent of the powers enjoyed by a receiver appointed under a standard form of debenture will vary according to whether or not the receiver is a receiver simpliciter, or a receiver-manager. The powers of a receiver simpliciter include:

- the power to take possession of charged assets;
- the power to collect, get in and receive the charged assets;
- the power to sell the charged assets.

[20.081] Although not divorced from the foregoing situation, a receiver-manager will often have the following express powers:

- the power to compromise debts of the company;
- the power to carry on the business of the company;
- the power to insure and repair property;
- the power to borrow money for the business;
- the power to employ and dismiss employees.

In addition, all receivers will have ancillary powers, which are incidental to or consequential upon the exercise of the foregoing powers[233]. One such implied power is the power to sue in the company's name[234], and this implied power survives the appointment of a liquidator[235].

[20.082] The power to sue in the company's name gives a receiver *locus standi* to make application for a so-called 'proprietary injunction'[236] to preserve the charged property[237]. Such an injunction should be distinguished from a *Mareva* injunction. So whereas a

[231] See generally, Picarda, *The Law Relating to Receivers, Managers and Administrators* (2nd edn, 1990), p 93.

[232] As found in, say, the Conveyancing Act 1881.

[233] In *Medforth v Blake et al* [1999] BCC 771 at 785, Sir Richard Scott VC said that a receiver's power to manage a business was not ancillary to the power of sale, but was independent.

[234] *M Wheeler & Co Ltd v Warren* [1928] Ch 840.

[235] *Gough's Garages Ltd v Pugsley* [1930] 1 KB 615. *Cf Re Henry Pound, Son and Hutchins* (1889) 42 Ch D 402.

[236] Proprietary injunctions must be distinguished from *Mareva* injunctions. Proprietary injunctions are available where the applicant can establish that he has a proprietary interest in a defendant's assets; *Mareva* injunctions can be granted where the applicant has no legal or equitable interest in a respondent's assets but where other criteria are met. See, generally, Courtney, *Mareva Injunctions and Related Interlocutory Orders* (1998), paras [1.16]–[1.29]. This distinction was accepted in *OBA Enterprises Ltd v TMC Trading International Ltd* (27 November 1998, unreported) HC, Laffoy J; on the evidence, however, the applicants did not establish that their claim was in the nature of a proprietary claim to the defendant's assets. This case is considered in Courtney, 'The Continuing Development of the Mareva Injunction in Ireland' (1999) 6 CLP 39.

[237] The mortgagee will, in any event, have sufficient *locus standi* for an injunction to preserve secured property.

Mareva injunction will operate to prevent a person from dealing with his own assets, an injunction sought by a receiver (as agent of his principal company) will be to prevent dealing with the company's own assets (by, say, its directors or indeed third parties) and so is in the nature of a proprietary injunction. An example of an application for a proprietary injunction restraining the disposal of assets is seen in *Rex Pet Foods Ltd and Murphy v Lamb Brothers (Dublin) Ltd*[238]. In that case, the plaintiff company and its receiver sought an injunction restraining the defendants from disposing of certain goods which had been produced by the plaintiff company and were at the time of the application in the possession of one or other of the defendants. In the alternative, the plaintiffs sought an injunction preventing such goods being disposed of until trial otherwise than on terms that the proceeds of sale would be held in a suspense or trust account pending resolution of the substantive question. Finlay P granted the injunction in that case, accepting that there was a 'serious question to be tried' and that the 'balance of convenience' favoured the granting of the injunction. This case also serves to demonstrate the inherent dangers of obtaining injunctions on an undertaking as to damages, in that there, it was ultimately held that the plaintiffs had no title in the goods and liberty was granted to apply in respect of the undertaking as to damages[239].

[20.083] In particular circumstances, a receiver may, on a company's behalf, make application for a *Mareva* injunction. Such might arise where a receiver believes that money or property is owed to a company by a third party and there is a risk that the third party will remove his assets from the jurisdiction or otherwise dissipate his assets with the intention of evading his obligations to the plaintiff and frustrating the anticipated order of the court. In such an event, the standard proofs for a *Mareva* injunction must be met before such an injunction will issue[240].

[20.084] The foregoing power to apply for an injunction to preserve the charged property has now been supplemented by statute. Section 55 of the CLEA 2001 confers *locus standi* on receivers to apply for an order directing a director or other officer not to remove his assets from the State or to reduce them within or without the State below a specified amount in certain circumstances. In addition to the requirement that the court must be satisfied as to the existence of a nefarious intention on the part of the respondent[241], the court must also be satisfied that an applicant receiver has a substantive civil cause of action against the respondent. The only circumstances in which it is thought that the court will make an order under this section is where a receiver seeks to recover charged property from a director or other officer which has been misappropriated or otherwise diverted away from the company (and so out of the receiver's grasp). In the light of the requirement to show a nefarious intention on the part

238 *Rex Pet Foods Ltd and Murphy v Lamb Brothers (Dublin) Ltd* (26 August 1982) HC, Finlay P, Irish Company Law Reports (1963–1993) 549.

239 *Rex Pet Foods Ltd and Murphy v Lamb Brothers (Dublin) Ltd (No 2)* (5 December 1985, unreported) HC, Costello J, Irish Company Law Reports (1963–1993) 585.

240 See generally, Courtney, *Mareva Injunctions and Related Interlocutory Orders* (1998), para [8.31].

241 Section 55(b) of the CLEA 2001: see Ch 25, *Realisation and Distribution of Assets in a Winding Up*, para **[25.050]**.

of a respondent, receivers might, in such cases, be better served by seeking a proprietary injunction to preserve the company's assets.

Applications for directions

[20.085] A receiver who finds that he is uncertain about the exercise of any powers or purported powers, which he has been granted in a debenture instrument, may apply to court for directions in 'relation to any matter in connection with the performance or otherwise ... of his functions': s 316(1) of the CA 1963. Furthermore, so also may officers, members, employees (at least half in number of full-time employees), creditors of the company[242], a liquidator, or contributories apply to the court for directions as to the exercise of a receiver's powers. On such an application the court may give such directions or make such an order declaring the rights of persons before the court or otherwise as the court thinks just.

[20.086] Where an application is made by a person other than a receiver, it must be supported by such evidence as the court may require that the applicant is being unfairly prejudiced by any actual or proposed action or omission of the receiver[243]. In *Kinsella v Somers*[244], the facts of which have been considered above[245], a director brought an application for directions under s 316 of the CA 1963. Budd J held, on the question of jurisdiction, that the court's discretion to make any order it thinks just in response to an application under s 316 was limited by s 316(1A) of the CA 1963. Budd J said:

> 'Unless the receiver is the applicant, the application must be supported by such evidence that the applicant is being unfairly prejudiced by any actual or proposed action or omission of the receiver as the Court may require. Accordingly, the right to apply for directions is rather limited and would seem not to cover an application for clarification of the receiver's powers or other general application for directions. If the application is being made by a director or shareholder then it would appear that a prerequisite is that proof is adduced that the applicant is being unfairly prejudiced by some action or omission on the part of the receiver.'

Accordingly, unless it is the receiver who brings the application, the application must be supported by evidence that the applicant is being 'unfairly prejudiced' by any actual or proposed action or omission of the receiver as the court may require. In that case, Budd J found that the applicant had not satisfied the court that it should make an order and it had not been shown that the receiver had been acting unreasonably in refusing to give further information to the applicant *qua* director and shareholder. He also found that the refusal was not actuated by bad faith on the receiver's part.

In *Re HSS*[246], Clarke J said of the requirement to show 'unfair prejudice':

> '... it seems to me that the prejudice that is spoken of in s 316(1A) is prejudice to the actual rights of individuals. In other words, a creditor applying under s 316 needs to show that that creditor's rights might be unfairly prejudiced by an action (or, indeed, inaction) of

[242] Defined as meaning one or more creditors to whom the company is indebted by more in aggregate than €12,697.38: s 316(1A) of the CA 1963, as inserted by s 171 of the CA 1990.

[243] Section 316(1B) of the CA 1963.

[244] *Kinsella v Somers* (22 November 1999, unreported) HC, Budd J.

[245] See para **[20.047]**.

[246] *Re HSS* [2011] IEHC 497.

a receiver. It does not give the Court some general jurisdiction to consider whether things are fair or unfair.'

Multiple receivers to the same company

[20.087] At any one time a company may have more than one receiver appointed to it. Indeed, where a company has created two debentures in favour of different lending institutions the appointment of a receiver under one of these debentures will invariably be an *event of default*[247], which will precipitate the appointment of a second receiver by the other debenture holder. Where two receivers have been appointed to the same company their respective functions and powers may be reduced to a question of priorities between the debenture holders who appointed them. A receiver may not have any greater priority to a company's assets than has his appointing debenture holder. Accordingly, where a receiver is appointed by the holder of a fixed mortgage or charge over specific land or property, it may well make sense for another debenture holder who holds a fixed mortgage or charge over different land or property to appoint another receiver. When it comes to receiving property which is subject to a floating charge the first validly created and registered floating charge to crystallise will generally have priority[248]. It follows that the receiver appointed by the holder of that floating charge should have priority to the company's assets which were within the class of asset subject to that floating charge. Where a conflict arises it will usually be open to one of the receivers to apply to court for directions under s 316(1) of the CA 1963[249].

Resignation and removal of receivers

(a) Resignation

[20.088] Section 322C of the CA 1963 alters the common law position which was that where a receiver resigned without the consent of the debenture holder which appointed him, he would be guilty of breach of contract, and thus liable in damages[250]. It is now the case that a receiver appointed by a debenture holder can resign upon giving one month's notice to holders of fixed and floating charges over the company's property, and to the company and (if applicable) to its liquidator. A receiver appointed by the court can only resign with the consent of the court: s 322C(3) of the CA 1963. A failure to comply with these requirements is liable to be visited by a class C fine[251].

[20.089] A receiver appointed by a debenture holder may be dismissed by that debenture holder pursuant to the terms of the receiver's appointment. The matter is essentially one of contract.

---

247 See para **[20.006]**.

248 See Ch 18, *Corporate Borrowing: Debentures and Security*, para **[18.093]**.

249 See para **[20.085]**.

250 See Picarda, *The Law Relating to Receivers, Managers and Administrators* (2nd edn, 1990), pp 250–251.

251 Section 322C(3) of the CA 1963.

(b) Removal by the court

[20.090] Section 322A(1) of the CA 1963[252] empowers the court, upon cause being shown, to remove a receiver and appoint another in his place[253].

[20.091] The power of the court under s 322A of the CA 1963 to remove a receiver is couched in wide and general terms. Clearly, misconduct on the part of the receiver will justify his removal and amount to the showing of sufficient cause[254]. However, misconduct on the part of the receiver is not necessary, and where it is shown that the interests of the general creditors are best served by removing the receiver, as it was in *Re Keypak Homecare Ltd*[255], the receiver will be removed.

[20.092] While the power to remove a receiver seems to be directed at a court appointed receiver, a number of cases suggest that a receiver appointed by a debenture holder can be similarly ousted[256].

(c) Removal of receiver at the instigation of a liquidator

[20.093] The appointment of a liquidator does not *per se* affect the appointment of a receiver to a company. Section 322B of the CA 1963 introduced a new measure providing that a liquidator can apply to court to have a receivership which began either before or after the commencement of the winding up, to be determined or limited. Thus, the court may order that the receiver shall cease to act as such and order that no further receiver be appointed, or may order that the receiver shall from a certain time act only in respect of certain assets specified by the court[257]. It is noticeable that s 322B(4) of the CA 1963 provides that no order made under this section shall affect any security or charge over the undertaking or property of the company. Even so, this subsection radically changes the law, particularly in so far as privately appointed receivers are concerned[258], as contrasted with court appointed receivers[259]. One remedy available to liquidators against receivers that stops short of removal is an injunction to prevent a receiver from acting.

(d) Removal of receiver at the instigation of an examiner

[20.094] A company cannot be placed under the protection of the court, and *ergo*, an examiner cannot be appointed to a company, where a receiver stands appointed for a

---

252 Section 175 of the CA 1990.

253 Notice that application is being made to have a receiver removed must be served on the receiver and on the person who appointed him, not less than seven days before the hearing of such proceedings, and at the hearing both can appear and be heard: s 322A(2) of the CA 1963.

254 See *Re St George's Estate* (1887) 19 LR Ir 556, where dereliction of duty by the receiver was shown.

255 *Re Keypak Homecare Ltd* [1987] BCLC 409.

256 See *Re Maskelyne British Typewriter Ltd* [1898] 1 Ch 133; *Re 'Slogger' Automatic Feeder Company Ltd* [1915] 1 Ch 478; and McCormack, *The New Companies Legislation* (1991), pp 174–175.

257 Section 176(3) of the CA 1990 provides that a receiver must get seven days' notice of such an application. The order of the court is not written in stone, and can be rescinded or amended on application of the liquidator or receiver: s 322B(2) of the CA 1963.

258 See *Re Potters Oil Ltd (No 2)* [1986] BCLC 98.

259 See *Re Joshua Stubbs Ltd* [1891] 1 Ch 475.

continuous period of at least three days, prior to the presentation of the petition to have the examiner appointed[260]. However, where an examiner is appointed within three days of the receiver's appointment the examiner may apply to court for an order under s 6(1) of the C(A)A 1990. The orders which may be made by the court under this provision are considered in Ch 22[261].

[260] Section 3(6) of the C(A)A 1990.

[261] See Ch 22, *Examinerships*, para **[22.071]**.

Chapter 21

Schemes of Arrangement and Reconstructions

Introduction

[21.001] Schemes of arrangement and compromises were a feature of Irish company law long before the passing of the Companies (Amendment) Act 1990 ('C(A)A 1990'), which gave birth to the examinership process. Section 201 of the CA 1963 contains a procedure whereby claims against a company can be compromised or arrangements made by the company with its members or creditors. These schemes of arrangement are the concern of Section A[1]. Another option, available only to a company that is in, or proposes to be in, voluntary liquidation[2], is a reconstruction pursuant to s 260 of the CA 1963. Reconstructions are treated in Section B.

[21.002] The end result of both an examinership under the C(A)A 1990 and the procedure envisaged by ss 201–203 of the CA 1963, can be similar: a scheme of arrangement that is sanctioned by the court and is binding. There are, however, a great many differences. First, each procedure is initiated in a very different way. In the case of an examinership, an independent officer of the court, an examiner, must be appointed by the court to put together proposals for a scheme of arrangement. In the case of a scheme put together under ss 201–203 of the CA 1963, the scheme is largely formulated in advance of court involvement and by the company itself (with, of course, professional advice and assistance). Second, the requirement for a majority in number of at least 75% in value of members and creditors to approve of a scheme of arrangement under ss 201–203 of the CA 1963 affords all parties with greater protection than in an examinership. Third, under s 201(2) the court is empowered to stay all proceedings and restrain further proceedings against a company in respect of which application is made 'for such period as to the court seems fit'.

[A] Schemes of Arrangement

[21.003] In this section the following issues are considered:

1. Key criteria in a s 201 application.
2. Limitations to schemes of arrangement.

---

1 See, generally, Lynch-Fannon & Murphy, *Corporate Insolvency and Rescue* (2nd edn, 2012) at p 620–637; Clarke, *Takeovers and Mergers Law in Ireland* (1999), p 250; Morse et al (eds), *Palmer's Company Law* (25th edn, 1992; loose leaf), p 12009; Sealy et al (eds), *British Company Law and Practice* (1983; loose leaf) at 68,001; and Lingard, *Corporate Rescues and Insolvencies* (2nd edn, 1989), Ch 5.

2 As to which, see Ch 23, *Winding Up Companies*, para **[21.002]** *ff*.

3. Initiating a scheme of arrangement: meetings of members and creditors.
4. Staying proceedings where application made under s 210(1).
5. Court sanction of scheme of arrangement.
6. Solvent schemes of arrangement.
7. Judicial powers to assist schemes in contemplation of reconstruction.
8. Setting aside a scheme for fraud.

Key criteria in a s 201 application

[21.004] The Companies Acts confer a wide array of statutory rights on companies' members and creditors. Where it is proposed to compromise the rights of either members or creditors or enter into an arrangement, the effect of which will be to vary their strict rights, ss 201–203 of the CA 1963, may be used to formalise the proposals even where there is not unanimous consent by either members or creditors. These provisions provide a structure for negotiation of a scheme for either or both the rearrangement of a company's capital structure amongst its members and the rearrangement (including compromise) of a company's obligations and liabilities to its creditors. Upon application being made to the court, s 201 of the CA 1963 empowers it to order the convening and holding of meetings of creditors or members and, where a majority representing 75% in value at those meetings approves of the scheme, to subsequently order that the scheme be binding – even on dissenting, absent or untraceable members or creditors. The court will be alert, however, to attempts to abuse the statutory mechanism contained in ss 201–203 of the CA 1963 by, for example, attempting to compulsorily acquire the shareholding of dissenting shareholders in circumstances where there is not an 80% majority since such cases are properly brought under s 204 of the CA 1963[3].

[21.005] Statutory schemes of arrangement can be utilised in many other circumstances too: the merger of two or more companies, the sub-division of a company into two or more companies, certain takeovers and other amalgamations[4]. Indeed, absent legislation that would facilitate the merger of companies in the way that the European Communities (Cross-Border Merger) Regulations 2008 apply to mergers involving non-Irish companies, s 201 of the CA 1963 is the only effective way to achieve a merger of private companies under Irish law.

[21.006] Section 201(1) of CA 1963 provides:

> 'Where a compromise or arrangement is proposed between a company and its creditors or any class of them or between the company and its members or any class of them, the court may, on the application of the company or of any creditor or member of the company, or, in the case of a company being wound up, of the liquidator, order a meeting of the

---

3 *Re National Bank* [1966] 1 WLR 819 and *Re Hellenic & General Trust Ltd* [1976] 1 WLR 123. *Cf Re TDG plc* [2009] 1 BCLC 445 where a more relaxed approach was taken to a scheme of arrangement involving an expropriation of shares. On compulsory purchase of dissenting shareholders' shares, see further Ch 9, *Share Transfer*, para **[9.087]**.

4 See generally, Morse et al (eds), *Palmer's Company Law* (25th edn, 1992; loose leaf), pp 12009–12013. On takeovers and mergers, see further Clarke, *Takeovers and Mergers Law in Ireland* (1999), p 248.

creditors or class of creditors, or of the members of the company or class of members, as the case may be, to be summoned in such manner as the court directs.'

Here, the following key terms used in s 201 are considered:

(a) Compromise or arrangement must be proposed by a 'company';
(b) Meaning of 'members';
(c) Creditors can be ordinary, secured and preferential;
(d) The meaning of 'arrangement', 'compromise' and 'between'.

(a) Compromise or arrangement must be proposed by a 'company'

[21.007] Section 201 of the CA 1963 is expressly concerned with compromises or arrangements between a *company* and its *creditors* or between a *company* and its *members*. As far as the reference to 'company' is concerned, this is defined by s 201(7) of the CA 1963, to mean 'any company liable to be wound up under this Act'. Since a foreign company can in certain circumstances be wound up by the High Court, this is a wider definition of 'company' to that contained in s 2 of the CA 1963[5]. In order for a foreign company to be liable to be wound up by the High Court it should have a sufficient connection with Ireland[6].

(b) Meaning of members

[21.008] The reference to 'members' means to persons who were either an original subscriber to the memorandum of association or persons who have agreed to become members and whose names have been entered on the register of members[7]. An option holder is not a 'member' for these purposes. Until such time as a person, even one who has paid valuable consideration for shares in a company, has been registered as a member, he or she cannot be included as a member in a scheme of arrangement pursuant to ss 201–203 of the CA 1963.

(c) Creditors: ordinary, secured and preferential

[21.009] All classes of creditor may be affected (and bound) by a court sanctioned scheme of arrangement. It has been held that the reference to 'creditors' ought to be widely construed[8], but it has been held too that a person who has relied upon a letter of comfort from a company is not a 'creditor' for the purposes of a scheme of arrangement[9]. A 'creditor' is any person with a pecuniary claim against the company, whether actual or contingent. A person with an unliquidated claim in tort against a company has been considered also to be a creditor[10]. It has been said that the only

5 See Ch 23, *Winding Up Companies*, para **[21.035]**.

6 See *Re Drax Holdings Ltd* [2003] EWHC 2743.

7 See Ch 8, *Shares and Membership*, para **[8.017]**.

8 See *Re Midland Coal, Coke and Iron Co* [1895] 1 Ch 267.

9 *Re Atlantic Computers plc (in admin); National Australia Bank Ltd v Soden* [1995] BCC 696.

10 *Re Millstream Recycling Ltd* [2009] IEHC 571, Laffoy J. See also Sealy et al (eds), *British Company Law and Practice* (1983; loose leaf) at 68,152 where the Australian case of *Re RL Child & Co Pty Ltd* is cited as authority on this point and *Trocko v Renlita Products Pty Ltd* (1973) 5 SASR 207 is distinguished.

workable test of who is a creditor, is any person who has the right to prove in a winding up[11].

[21.010] Whereas secured creditors may not be bound unless as a class they vote in favour of the scheme, dissenting secured creditors within a class can be bound by a scheme: *Re Alabama, New Orleans, Texas and Pacific Junction Railway Co*[12]. Lingard astutely observes, however:

> 'Secured creditors cannot usually be lumped together in one class because each will have different security which differently affects his judgment. Some secured creditors may be acutely conscious that their security is of little value; others may know that they are fully secured. Some secured creditors may have security which is readily saleable; others may know that it will be some time before they can realise their security[13].'

[21.011] It was held in *Re Pye (Ireland) Ltd; Hogan*[14] that the Revenue Commissioners' claims against a company ought not to be compromised. Costello J said:

> 'The court should not regard the Collector-General as just another creditor similar to other creditors; he is charged with the collection of monies due to the State. In this case I do not think that the Collector-General should be required to surrender for the benefit of other creditors contingently money owed to the public. The debt owed to the State in respect of VAT, PRSI, PAYE and Customs and Excise is at least £522,000. In those circumstances if the Collector General has decided that this scheme is not in the public interest I should be very slow indeed to order these meetings given the opposition of the Collector General. I see no reason to order this scheme to proceed[15].'

The Revenue Commissioners had taken the view that they were legally prevented from compromising taxes due to the State. It should be noted that any doubts as to the Revenue Commissioners' powers to compromise debts owed by companies in an examinership under the C(A)A 1990 have been dispelled by statute[16]. It is thought that a similar declaratory provision could usefully be introduced in respect of s 201 of the CA 1963 schemes of arrangement and compromises.

(d) The meaning of 'arrangement', 'compromise' and 'between'

[21.012] Not every proposal between a company and its creditors or its members, can be sanctioned by the court under ss 201–203 of the CA 1963. The legislation refers specifically only to an 'arrangement' and a 'compromise' 'between' a company and its members or creditors. The legislation itself gives little guidance as to the definition of these terms, although s 201(7) of the CA 1963 does provide that 'arrangement' 'includes a reorganisation of shares of different classes or by the division of shares into shares of different classes or by both those methods.'

---

11 *Re North Bucks Furniture Depositories Ltd* [1939] 2 All ER 549–551. See also *National Australia Bank Ltd v Market Holdings Pty Ltd* (26 October 2000) Supreme Court of New South Wales.

12 *New Orleans, Texas and Pacific Junction Railway Co* [1981] 1 Ch 213.

13 Lingard, *Corporate Rescues and Insolvencies* (2nd edn, 1989), para 5.30.

14 *Re Pye (Ireland) Ltd; Hogan* (12 November 1984, unreported) HC, Irish Company Law Reports 320.

15 Irish Company Law Reports 320 at 322.

16 See Ch 22, *Examinerships*, para **[22.131]**.

This is not an exhaustive definition of 'arrangement' which merely 'includes' the foregoing. One can approach the definition of 'arrangement' and 'compromise' from the perspective of their ordinary meaning and conclude that 'a "compromise" is an adjustment of conflicting interests by a modification of each and an "arrangement" is a putting into order or a settlement of a dispute'[17]. Case law on the definition of 'compromise' shows that in order for there to be a compromise, there must first be a dispute[18]. Although it was held in *Mercantile Investment and General Trust Co v International Co of Mexico*[19] that the giving up of a secured debenture in exchange for a preference share 'in the absence of all disputes as to the rights of the creditor, of all difficulty in enforcing those rights, and of any suggestion that the full fruits of these rights could not be obtained'[20] was not a compromise, Fry LJ found such to be capable of being described as an arrangement.

[21.013] Section 201 of the CA 1963 can be invoked where a company proposes to enter into an amicable arrangement by way of reconstruction. It is not necessary for the company to propose to compromise claims against it. This was made clear in *Re Guardian Assurance Company*[21]. At first instance, Younger J had held that, although the scheme was advantageous to the interests of the company, he would refuse to sanction it because the section necessarily involved some kind of dispute or difficulty to be resolved by a compromise or arrangement and that this was absent in the case in hand. The Court of Appeal reversed this finding. Lord Cozens-Hardy MR held that the arrangement proposed between the company and its members was in good faith, that a dispute was not necessary and that the section applied to any compromise or arrangement.

[21.014] An example of a proposal that was found not to be an arrangement or compromise is seen in *Re NFU Development Trust Ltd*[22]. In that case, the company concerned was a guarantee company with the main object of encouraging and assisting the production of fatstock and other livestock. The costs in administering the company, which had 94,000 members, were considered to be prohibitive: the cost of maintaining the register, posting accounts and other related administrative matters was in excess of £11,000 in the early 1970s. A scheme of arrangement was proposed whereby the only members would be a company which represented the farmers, and six other nominees would represent the interests of various English farmers' unions. In consequence it was proposed that all other members would forfeit all membership rights and cease to be members. Although nearly 85% of the members approved of the scheme, the court refused to sanction it because it was held that the proposal was neither an 'arrangement' nor a 'compromise'. Brightman J held:

> 'The word 'compromise' implies some element of accommodation on each side. It is not apt to describe total surrender. A claimant who abandons his claim is not compromising it.

---

17 Sealy et al (eds), *British Company Law and Practice* (1983, loose leaf) at 68,003.

18 *Snead v Valley Gold Ltd* [1893] 1 Ch 477.

19 *Mercantile Investment and General Trust Co v International Co of Mexico* [1893] 1 Ch 484.

20 *Mercantile Investment and General Trust Co v International Co of Mexico* [1893] 1 Ch 484 at 491.

21 *Re Guardian Assurance Company* [1917] 1 Ch 431.

22 *Re NFU Development Trust Ltd* [1972] 1 WLR 1548.

> Similarly, I think that the word 'arrangement' in this section implies some element of give and take. Confiscation is not my idea of an arrangement'.

The requirement of 'give and take' is also seen in the case of *Re Alabama, New Orleans, Texas and Pacific Junction Railway Co*[23], which additionally stressed the need for schemes of arrangement to be reasonable[24]. Indeed, Nourse J said[25] of *Re NFU Development Trust Ltd* that 'all that that case shows is that there must be some element of give and take. Beyond that it is neither necessary nor desirable to attempt a definition of "arrangement"'.

In *Commissioners of Inland Revenue v Adam & Partners Ltd*[26], the English Court of Appeal held that, having the requisite element of give and take, a moratorium on the prosecution of claims by creditors qualified as a 'scheme of arrangement'.

[21.015] The necessity for arrangements to be 'between' a company and its members was considered in *Re Savoy Hotel Ltd*[27]. In that case, a company's share capital was divided into 'A' shares and 'B' shares which ranked *pari passu* in all respects save that the 'B' shares carried 40 times as many votes as the 'A' shares. In consequence, the 'A' shareholders were entitled to 51.45% of the votes whilst the 'B' shareholders were entitled to 48.55% of the votes notwithstanding that the 'A' shareholders held 97.7% of the equity in the company, the 'B' shareholders holding the remaining 2.3%. Furthermore, 65.26% of the 'B' shares, which carried 31.68% of the votes, were held either beneficially or in trust *by* the members of the board. The applicant, an 'A' shareholder who held 88,000 shares, wished to gain control of the company by means of a scheme of arrangement. Among the issues decided by Nourse J was whether the rights and obligations existing between the company and its members would be sufficiently affected by the proposed scheme for it to constitute an arrangement 'between' the company and its members. The company, which opposed the proposed scheme, had submitted that the scheme was outside the statutory provisions because it was not one 'between' the company and its members or any class of them since it did not propose to materially affect the rights and obligations existing between the company and its members. Nourse J rejected this contention and found that it was not necessary that the rights and obligations existing between the company and its members should be 'materially affected, if by that is meant that there should be something more material or more substantial than there is in the present case'[28].

In so finding Nourse J relied upon the decision in *Singer Manufacturing Co v Robinow*[29], where the same point had been made on a transfer scheme of the same general nature. To the argument that the scheme was not one between the company and its members but a sale between two members Lord Clyde said:

> 'This contention is unwarranted ... the company had a very direct interest in the arrangement. If the arrangement was sanctioned by the court, they came under obligation

---

23 *Re Alabama, New Orleans, Texas and Pacific Junction Railway Co* [1891] 1 Ch 213.

24 See para **[21.055]**.

25 In *Re Savoy Hotel Ltd* [1981] 1 Ch 351 at 359.

26 *Commissioners of Inland Revenue v Adam & Partners Ltd* [2001] 1 BCLC 222.

27 *Re Savoy Hotel Ltd* [1981] 1 Ch 351, [1981] 3 All ER 646.

28 *Re Savoy Hotel Ltd* [1981] 1 Ch 351 at 361h.

29 *Singer Manufacturing Co v Robinow* (1971) SC 11.

> … on being satisfied that the consideration … had been paid … forthwith to register … the shares in respect of which the consideration has been so paid. The courts have always interpreted section 206 [of the Companies Act 1948 (UK)] and its statutory predecessors broadly, so as to enable a wide variety of different types of arrangements to be put forward, and it seems to us clear that the present scheme falls within what is competent to achieve under that section. The arrangement is an arrangement between the petitioning company and 'its members or any class of them' within the meaning of section 206[30].'

Support for the decision also appears in *Re Guardian Assurance Co*[31]. So too is there authority for this position in *Re Odhams Press Ltd*[32], where Eve J said that a scheme between classes of shareholders was a scheme inter socios but, for that, was none the less a scheme within the contemplation of the legislation.

Limitations to schemes of arrangement

[21.016] In order to avail of the provisions in ss 201–203 of the CA 1963, applicants must meet certain requirements:

(a) The applicant must have *locus standi*.
(b) The company must support the application.
(c) Schemes must not be contrary to law or *ultra vires*.
(d) Where capital is reduced the normal rules apply.
(e) Where relevant, there must be compliance with the rules of the Irish Takeover Panel.

(a) The applicant must have locus standi

[21.017] As shall be considered below[33], the statutory procedure involves application being made to the court under s 201(1) of the CA 1963 for the purpose of ordering a meeting or meetings of creditors or members to be summoned as directed. Section 201(1) of the CA 1963 provides that application may be brought by:

– the company;
– any creditor of the company;
– any member of the company; or, in the case of a company being wound up, by
– the liquidator of a company.

(b) The company must support the application

[21.018] Although ss 201–203 of the CA 1963 are silent on the point, it has been decided that the court cannot sanction an arrangement that does not have the approval of the company concerned. This was decided in *Re Savoy Hotel Ltd*[34], the facts of which have been given above[35]. In that case, the company's board of directors did not favour the proposed scheme of arrangement and withheld the company's consent to it. Nourse J held:

30 *Singer Manufacturing Co v Robinow* (1971) SC 11 at 13–14.
31 *Re Guardian Assurance Co* [1917] 1 Ch 431.
32 *Re Odhams Press Ltd* [1924] WN 10.
33 See para **[21.026]**.
34 *Re Savoy Hotel Ltd* [1981] 1 Ch 351, [1981] 3 All ER 646.
35 See para **[21.015]**.

> '… the court has no jurisdiction to sanction an arrangement under section 206 [of the Companies Act 1948 (UK)] which does not have the approval of the company either through the board or, if appropriate, by means of a simple majority of the members in general meeting[36].'

Although the statutory provisions clearly require the consent of at least 75% in value of a company's members and creditors, because the company is itself a separate legal entity with its own rights (which can be adversely affected by a scheme), the requirement that it is agreeable to a scheme of arrangement is implied.

[21.019] Where a company is in liquidation, its liquidator must also approve of the scheme of arrangement[37].

(c) Schemes must not be contrary to law or ultra vires

[21.020] A proposed scheme of arrangement or compromise must not be contrary to law or *ultra vires* the company concerned. So in *Re Oceanic Steam Navigation Co Ltd*[38] Simonds J said:

> 'The question then is whether, under [the statutory provision], the company can make and the court sanction an arrangement which is in excess of the corporate powers as defined by the memorandum. There is nothing in the language of [the statutory provision] which even remotely suggests such a conclusion. It contemplates a compromise or arrangement between a company and its creditors or any class of them or its members or any class of them, and provides machinery whereby such a compromise or arrangement may be made binding on dissenting persons by an order of the court. I find nothing here which would indicate that the company can effect an arrangement which would be otherwise *ultra vires* …'[39]

[21.021] There have been exceptions made to this general rule[40]. It is thought that where an arrangement is approved which is *ultra vires* it will generally be the result of an oversight, occasioned by a general consensus amongst the company and its members and creditors that the scheme of arrangement is desirable. It is very hard to see how, if met with an objection on the grounds of *ultra vires*, a court could sanction such a scheme, particularly since a member or secured creditor has *locus standi* to apply for an injunction to restrain the commission of an *ultra vires* act[41].

(d) Where capital is reduced the normal rules apply

[21.022] Where a scheme of arrangement involves the reduction of a company's capital, the requirements in s 72 of the CA 1963 must be complied with[42] as demonstrated by the

36 *Re Savoy Hotel Ltd* [1981] 1 Ch 351 at 366. Nourse J relied, *inter alia*, upon *Re International Contract Co (Hankey's Case)* (1872) 26 LT 358, 20 WR 506.

37 *Re International Contract Co (Hankey's Case)* (1872) 26 LT 358, 20 WR 506 and *Re Savoy Hotel Ltd* [1981] 1 Ch 351, [1981] 3 All ER 646.

38 *Re Oceanic Steam Navigation Co Ltd* [1939] Ch 41.

39 *Re Oceanic Steam Navigation Co Ltd* [1939] Ch 41 at 47. See also *Re Skinner* [1958] 3 All ER 273.

40 Eg, see *Barclays Bank plc v British & Commonwealth Holdings plc* [1996] 1 WLR 1, [1995] BCC 1059 where the Court of Appeal held that an arrangement which was possibly *ultra vires* was not open to challenge once approved by the court.

41 Section 8(2) of the CA 1963.

42 See Ch 3, *Constitutional Documentation*, para **[3.033]**.

application in *Re Readymix plc*[43] where the applicant under s 201 of the CA 1963 sought an order reducing the company's share capital in the event the former application was successful. In *Re Cooper, Cooper & Johnson Ltd*[44], Byrne J held that where a scheme of arrangement involved a reduction of capital, the reduction should be carried out in accordance with the statute specifically dealing with the reduction of capital[45]. Where a proposal will involve a reduction in capital, the applications may be brought in double-harness, under s 201 and under s 73 of the CA 1963, as happened in the case of *Re Readymix plc*[46]. In exceptional circumstances, it may even be permissible to reduce a company's share capital below the authorised minimum for a public limited company[47]. In such circumstances, however, the order under s 73 cannot be registered by the registrar of companies unless the company re-registers as a different type of company or *the court otherwise directs*[48].

(e) Where relevant, there must be compliance with the rules of the Irish Takeover Panel

[21.023] Section 201(6A) of the CA 1963[49] provides that ss 201–203 of the CA 1963 are without prejudice to the jurisdiction of the Irish Takeover Panel under the Irish Takeover Panel Act 1997 in relation to a compromise or scheme of arrangement that is proposed between a relevant company (as defined by the 1997 Act) and its members or any class of them and which constitutes a takeover. Specifically, the Irish Takeover Panel has the same power to make rules under s 8 of the Irish Takeover Panel Act 1997 in relation to such takeovers as it has in relation to any other kind of takeover. The Irish Takeover Panel is, however, statutorily obliged to have due regard to the High Court's exercise of its powers under the 1997 Act[50].

Initiating a scheme of arrangement: meetings of members and creditors

[21.024] The first procedural step is that application should be made to the court under s 201(1) of the CA 1963 to order a meeting of the creditors, or a class of creditors or members, or a class of members[51]. Where the court gives directions as to the advertisements notifying parties of the application, it does *not* have a discretion under s 201(1) to make orders regarding the submission and evaluation of claims. So in *Re Millstream Recycling Ltd (No 2)*[52], although notices were placed in several newspapers, a contingent creditor of the company overlooked the notices and did not notify the company of its proposed claim until after the date by which all creditors who wished to

43 *Re Readymix plc* [2012] IEHC 170.

44 *Re Cooper, Cooper & Johnson Ltd* [1902] WN 119.

45 See also *Re St James' Court Estate Ltd* [1944] Ch 6.

46 *Re Readymix plc* [2012] IEHC 194.

47 *Re Allied Domecq plc* [2000] 1 BCLC 134.

48 Section 17(3) of the C(A)A 1983.

49 As inserted by s 92 of the CLEA 2001.

50 Section 201(6B) of the CA 1963.

51 See *Re John Clarke & Co Ltd* [1912] IR 24.

52 *Re Millstream Recycling Ltd* [2010] IEHC 106, Laffoy J.

make a claim were required to have made it. The creditor applied for an order extending the time within which the claim could be made but was unsuccessful as Laffoy J held that the court had no jurisdiction to so order under either s 210 of the CA 1963 or Ord 122, r 7 of the RSC 1986 because the time for submitting a claim was laid down by the terms of the scheme, not by the court. Laffoy J did, however, say that the ramifications of the implementation of the process leading to the creditors' meetings and the approval of the scheme by the creditors, if that was achieved, and the relevant considerations on the application to the court under s 201(3) were 'matters for another day', implying that the applicant creditor could raise the issue of its exclusion at any future hearing to approve the scheme.

[21.025] Whilst a company, its members, its creditors and its liquidator all have *locus standi* to initiate the summoning of meetings, as has been considered above[53], it is a prerequisite to the court sanctioning a scheme of arrangement that the company agrees to it and, if in liquidation, that the liquidator agrees to it. Here, the following matters are considered:

(a) The responsibility for constituting proper classes.
(b) Constituting proper classes.
(c) Classes of members: shareholders' rights and interests.
(d) Providing information to members and creditors.
(e) Voting at meetings.
(f) Repeat applications under s 201 where first scheme proposed unacceptable.

(a) The responsibility for constituting proper classes

[21.026] At a hearing under s 201(1) of the CA 1963 the court may order such meeting or meetings to be summoned in such manner as it directs[54]. Traditionally, the position has been that the court will not at this time decide what classes of creditors or members should be made parties to the scheme, such being a matter for the applicant to decide. Different interests must be recognised and separate groups must be treated as separate classes for the purpose of the scheme. A separate class will be a group of persons whose rights are not so dissimilar as to make it impossible for them to consult together with a view to arriving at a common consensus of their position[55]. Where a class of members or a class of creditors will *not* be affected by a proposed compromise or arrangement, there is no requirement for a meeting of that class to be convened[56]. The traditional position, which places full responsibility on the applicant and excludes the court from expressing a view on the appropriateness of classes, needs to be reconsidered, however, following the decision in *Re Millstream Recycling Ltd*[57], but before considering it, the traditional authorities on the applicant's responsibilities in constituting classes will be reviewed.

53 See para **[21.017]**.

54 In *Re RMCA Reinsurance Ltd* [1994] BCC 378, the court directed that a meeting of a class of member could be held abroad.

55 See *Re Hawk Insurance Co Ltd* [2001] BCC 57.

56 *Re Tea Corporation* [1904] 1 Ch 12; *Re Mortgage Insurance Corporation* [1896] WN 4.

57 *Re Millstream Recycling Ltd* [2009] IEHC 571 and *Re Hawk Insurance Company Ltd* [2002] BCC 300.

[21.027] 'Great care must be taken in considering what for the purpose of the scheme constitutes a class. If meetings of the proper classes have not been held, the court may not sanction the scheme[58].' In *Nordic Bank plc v International Harvester Australia Ltd*[59], Lush J said:

> 'The application … for an order for meetings is a preliminary step, the applicant taking the risk that the classes which are fixed by the judge, usually on the applicant's request, are sufficient for the ultimate purpose of the section, the risk being that if in the result, and we emphasise the words 'in the result', they reveal inadequacies, the scheme will not be approved.'

The warning that applicants should, in forming appropriate classes, proceed with due diligence has been given by the courts on a large number of occasions. In *Re Hellenic Trust Ltd*[60], Templeman J said:

> 'Although s 206 [of the Companies Act 1948 (UK)] provides that the court may order meetings, it is the responsibility of the petitioners to see that the class meetings are properly constituted, and if they fail then the necessary agreement is not obtained and the court has no jurisdiction to sanction the arrangement. Thus in *In Re United Provident Assurance Co Ltd* [1910] 2 Ch 477 the court held that the holders of partly paid shares formed a different class from holders of fully paid shares. The objection was taken that there should have been separate meetings of the two classes, and Swinfen Eady J upheld the objection, saying at page 481: "… the objection that there has not been proper class meetings is fatal, and I cannot sanction the scheme".'

Similarly, Eve J issued a practice direction[61] in which he reminded UK practitioners, in dealing with the predecessor of s 206, that the responsibility for determining what creditors are to be summoned to any meeting as constituting a class rests with the petitioner, and if the meetings are incorrectly convened or constituted, or an objection is taken to the presence of any particular creditors as having interests competing with the others, the objection must be taken on the hearing of the petition to sanction and the petitioner must take the risk of having the petition dismissed[62].'

[21.028] It was thought that this is also the position in Ireland as in one of the few Irish cases on schemes of arrangement where a written judgment was delivered, *Re Pye (Ireland) Ltd*[63], the facts of which are given below, Costello J cited the quotation from

58 *Palmer's Company Law* (23rd edn), para 79-10, cited with approval by Costello J in *Re Pye (Ireland) Ltd* (11 March 1985, unreported) HC. Costello J also quoted with approval the following passage from *Palmer*: 'The court does not itself consider at this point [ie, when an application to convene meetings is brought] what classes of creditors or members should be made parties to scheme. This is for the company to decide … If there are different groups within a class the interests of which are different from the rest of the class, or which are to be treated differently under the scheme, such groups must be treated as separate classes for the purpose of the scheme.'

59 *Nordic Bank plc v International Harvester Australia Ltd* [1983] 2 VR 298 at 303 also cited by Morse et al (eds), *Palmer's Company Law* (25th edn, 1992; loose leaf), p 12016.

60 *Re Hellenic Trust Ltd* [1976] 1 WLR 123.

61 *Practice Note* (1934) WN 142.

62 *Re Hellenic Trust Ltd* [1976] 1 WLR 123 at 125.

63 *Re Pye (Ireland) Ltd* (11 March 1985, unreported) HC, Irish Company Law Reports 323.

Palmer set out above[64] and the dictum of Templeman J last quoted. A rethink is required, however, following the decision of Laffoy J in *Re Millstream Recycling Ltd*[65]. In that case, Laffoy J noted that the law on schemes of arrangement had been usefully reviewed by the English Court of Appeal by Chadwick LJ in *Re Hawk Insurance Company Ltd*[66]. Laffoy J noted that Chadwick LJ had recommended that existing practice in the UK should be re-examined and the learned judge went on to say:

> '… the first stage of the exercise of the useful and beneficial discretion which the entirety of s 201 confers on this Court to sanction a scheme of arrangement may be rendered useless and a waste of money if the Court postpones consideration of whether separate classes of meetings are required until the third stage. Subsection (1) of s 201 gives a very broad discretion to the Court in directing the creditors' meeting or meetings. Obviously, the discretion can only be exercised if the parties who are likely to be affected by the Court's determination have an opportunity to be heard on the issue, which necessitates the court being satisfied that they are on notice of the application under s 201 either by having been served or by advertisement. In this case, compliance with the notice and advertising requirements of the order of 16 November 2009 have been proven. Therefore, in my view, the court has jurisdiction to determine whether separate class meetings are required and, having regard to the procedure adopted on this application, can properly exercise the jurisdiction.'

Laffoy J was very definite in her determination that the court has no jurisdiction to embark on a general assessment as to whether the scheme is fair and equitable. The learned judge said:

> '… given that the express jurisdiction of the Court on this application under subsection (1) is to "order a meeting of the … class of creditors" to be summoned, it obviously is the case that whether the Court may pronounce at this stage on the constitution of the class or classes is a jurisdictional issue.'

In consequence, it now appears that whereas previously the Irish courts would, if inclined to make an order under s 201(1), order the convening of meetings without any regard to the classes of creditors or members, it is now the case that the court will have some regard to the constitution of classes. It is thought that the role of the court in this regard remains to be developed as a number of matters remain unclear. For example, in exercising its jurisdiction to determine that separate classes are required, is this a *prima facie* determination which will not preclude further examination of the appropriateness of the classification upon the application to confirm the scheme?

(b) Constituting proper classes

[21.029] There are few hard and fast rules as to what constitutes proper classes of members and creditors: in each situation the position and proposed fates of a company's creditors and members must be considered and their division into classes determined by their common interests. In relation to the test to be applied when determining whether separate meetings are required, in *Re Millstream Recycling Ltd*[67] Laffoy J relied upon the

64 See para **[21.027]** at fn 59.

65 *Re Millstream Recycling Ltd* [2009] IEHC 571.

66 *Re Hawk Insurance Company Ltd* [2002] BCC 300.

67 *Re Millstream Recycling Ltd* [2009] IEHC 571.

following passage from the judgment of Bowen LJ in *Soverign Life Assurance Co v Dodd*[68]:

> 'The word "class" is vague, and to find out what is meant by it we must look at the scope of the section, which is a section enabling the Court to order a meeting of a class of creditors to be called. It seems plain that we must give such a meaning to the term 'class' as will prevent the section being so worked as to result in confiscation and injustice, and that it must be confined to those persons whose rights are not so dissimilar as to make it impossible for them to consult together with a view to their common interest.'

In *Millstream Recycling*, the facts were that the company which was proposing the scheme of arrangement was beset with claims for compensation arising out of the contamination of certain of the company's feed products for pigs which contained dioxins and other contaminants. This had resulted in the slaughter of pigs and some cattle on farms in both Ireland and Northern Ireland, and the withdrawal of pork products from shop-shelves. While governments in both jurisdictions paid compensation, the company faced other claims for material and consequential loss and third-party claims from the use of contaminated feed products. An estimate of some €40m was put on the claims against the company which would render it insolvent. A scheme was proposed to make provision for 'scheme creditors' or 'contamination creditors', being parties entitled to compensation arising from a contamination event but not for ordinary creditors. The scheme was to be funded by the company's insurance policy and also the proceeds of an action pending against another company alleged to be responsible for the contamination. Some contamination creditors objected to the company's application, some supported it reluctantly or conditionally and some were in favour of it. The company had sought to include all contamination creditors in one class. Ultimately, Laffoy J held that there was only one exception to the requirement for one class meeting. That exception related to contamination creditors (referred to, somewhat ironically, as the Hogg companies), which were connected to the company being subsidiaries of a company, the shareholders of which owned the entire share capital in the applicant company. Laffoy J found that all other contamination creditors had a sufficient common interest including creditors who had obtained dates for the hearing of their claims against the company.

[21.030] The decision in *Re Pye (Ireland) Ltd*[69] is also instructive on the constitution of proper classes. The facts in this case were that in July 1984 it was ordered pursuant to s 201(1) of the CA 1963 that meetings of certain classes of creditors and members of the company concerned should be convened to consider a proposed scheme of arrangement. At the subsequent meetings, the Revenue Commissioners opposed the scheme and the statutory majority of 75% was not obtained. Subsequently, a second application was made under s 201(1) to discuss a new scheme of arrangement but this was refused when the High Court upheld the objections of the Revenue Commissioners who had been served as a notice party. On appeal the Supreme Court made an order summoning the convening of meetings upon the applicants' undertaking to pay a preferential debt to the Revenue Commissioners of over £52,000. In consequence, three meetings of creditors were convened: secured creditors; preferential creditors; and unsecured trade and sundry

---

68 *Soverign Life Assurance Co v Dodd* [1892] 2 QB 573.

69 *Re Pye (Ireland) Ltd* (11 March 1985, unreported) HC, Irish Company Law Reports 323.

creditors. The three meetings were held and the scheme of arrangement was approved by the 75% majority. The applicants then applied to the court to sanction the arrangement under s 201(3) of the CA 1963 but the Revenue Commissioners opposed their application. The Revenue Commissioners' had three objections to the applicants' classifications of creditors' meetings. Before addressing the specific classifications in that case, Costello J also quoted the following from the *dictum* of Bowen LJ in *Sovereign Life Assurance Co v Dodd*[70] cited by Laffoy j in Re *Millstream Recycling Ltd*[71]. Costello J then went on to address the three points of objection to the classification of creditors.

[21.031] Costello J agreed in principle with the first objection raised by the Revenue Commissioners, which was that those unsecured creditors whom it was proposed would be paid in full ought to have been constituted as a distinctive class from other unsecured creditors who would not fare so well. On this point he said:

> 'As they are to be paid in full within one month of its sanction it is impossible to see how they would vote against it and obviously their interests are different to the less favoured body of unsecured creditors amongst whom is the Collector General[72].'

Whilst accepting the point in principle, however, Costello J did not consider that, in the instant case, there was justification to refuse to sanction because he was not satisfied that if a separate class for the favoured creditors had been created this would have meant that the scheme would have been defeated.

[21.032] The Revenue Commissioners' second objection was that one of the applicants was a director in a firm which was an unsecured creditor and which it was intended by the proposal would be paid in full. On this point Costello J found that the firm of the unsecured creditor ought to have been in a class with the other 'favoured' unsecured creditors but he found that the connection between the firm and one of the applicants did not necessitate the creation of a further class of creditors.

[21.033] Finally, the Revenue Commissioners pointed out that one of the unsecured creditors was a company which owned a significant and substantial portion of the entire issued share capital of Pye (Ireland) Ltd. On this point Costello J held:

> 'Without its vote the statutory majority would not have been obtained. There is no doubt that if the scheme is successful that the prospect for the ordinary shareholders is very much better than in a liquidation (which is the alternative if the scheme is not adopted) in which it would appear the ordinary shareholders are likely to do very badly. So it seems to me that the interests of a substantial unsecured creditor who is also a substantial shareholder are very different to those of the general body of unsecured non-shareholding creditors and that there is in reality no common interest between them – the creditor/shareholder is almost certain to support the scheme, whilst the ordinary unsecured shareholder may have (as happened in the case of the Collector General [of the Revenue Commissioners]) what is considered as valid reasons for opposing it. I think therefore that there should have been a separate class created comprising unsecured creditors who are also shareholders in the company[73].'

---

70 *Sovereign Life Assurance Co v Dodd* (1892) 2 QB 573.

71 *Re Millstream Recycling Ltd* [2009] IEHC 571, Laffoy J.

72 *Irish Company Law Reports* 320 at 326.

73 *Irish Company Law Reports* 320 at 327.

Costello J declined to order the summoning of fresh meetings of the correct classes of unsecured creditors on the grounds that such 'would be an otiose exercise'[74]. This was because, had the proper classes been constituted, the views of a major creditor, the Revenue Commissioners, would not have been defeated and the requisite majority of 75% would not have been obtained.

[21.034] There are many other cases that are helpful, but not conclusive, as to when separate class meetings should be held. An example is *Sovereign Life Assurance Company v Dodd*[75] where it was held that in the reorganisation of an insurance company, the insured persons whose policies had matured formed a distinct class of creditors from those whose policies had not matured. This case was distinguished in *Re Osiris Insurance Ltd*[76] where another insurance company proposing a scheme had only constituted one class of creditors, notwithstanding that those summoned had different types of insurance. On this issue Neuberger J said:

> '… while it is true that those who were summoned to attend the meeting might be said to have been in different "classes", in the sense that they had different types of insurance, it does not seem to me that, bearing in mind the nature of the proposed scheme, their interests could be said to be different, let alone positively to conflict with each other, as was held to be the case in *Sovereign Life*. Whatever the nature of the policies which they held with the company, all actual or potential scheme creditors had policies which had expired some time ago, and were all "claims made" policies or "short tail" policies. Accordingly, claims under any of the policies issued by the company should, by the time of the meeting, at least in the absence of very unusual circumstances, have been the subject matter of notification to the company. The nature of the proposals embodied in the scheme apply equally to all former policyholders, to all scheme creditors. Furthermore, as Mr Snowden pointed out, once one starts dividing up former policyholders into different classes, it is not immediately obvious where one stops: one could argue that policyholders are in different classes not merely if their policies are of different types, if they were insured over different periods, or even through different brokers; even within a particular type of policy in a given year, there may be other differences which could similarly be invoked to justify sub-dividing into yet further classes[77].'

Of course the sense in this passage is patent; as is the fine balance which must be struck between ensuring that a particular class is not composed of persons without a common interest on the one hand and, on the other, sub-dividing into such small classes as to effectively guarantee that one meeting of a disgruntled minority can scupper a scheme acceptable to a majority.

(c) Classes of members: shareholders' rights and interests

[21.035] In *Re Hellenic Trust Ltd*[78], where one company was proposing to take over another company, Templeman J held that a particular shareholder in the target company formed a separate class to other shareholders in the target company because it was a subsidiary of the bidder company. It is thought that there is considerable force in

74 *Re Pye (Ireland) Ltd* (11 March 1985, unreported) HC at p 6.

75 *Sovereign Life Assurance Company v Dodd* (1892) 2 QB 573.

76 *Re Osiris Insurance Ltd* [1999] 1 BCLC 182.

77 *Re Osiris Insurance Ltd* [1999] 1 BCLC 182 at 188c–f.

78 *Re Hellenic Trust Ltd* [1976] 1 WLR 123.

criticism of this decision on the basis that members or creditors should not be split into classes for reasons that are purely personal to them[79]. It is also thought that this decision is distinguishable from that of Costello J in *Re Pye (Ireland) Ltd*[80] where one creditor happened to also be a shareholder, as there the shareholder had two clearly discernible interests and rights in two separate capacities.

[21.036] The usual guide for constituting classes is 'conflicting interests'. In the context of shareholding members, it is thought that the correct approach is one based on *conflicting rights*. In *Re Industrial Equity (Pacific) Ltd*[81], Nazareth J in the High Court of Hong Kong said:

> 'Is every different interest to constitute a different class? Clearly not, but where then is the line to be drawn? The difficulties in identifying shareholders with such interests, as in the present case, could raise in terms of practicality virtually insuperable difficulties. It is determination by reference to *rights* of shareholders that meets such difficulties, while leaving any conflict of interest which may result to a minority being overborne or coerced to be dealt with by the courts when their sanction is sought[82].'

Nazareth J also suggested that the genesis for constituting classes ought to be *interests based on rights*[83]. In *Re BTR plc*[84], the scheme of arrangement involved the cancellation of the company's ordinary shares and the allotment to the holders of these shares of other shares in a company with which it was being merged. A meeting of all the ordinary shareholders was convened and held. It was argued that such shareholders had diverse interests and that a single meeting was inappropriate. In particular, the hypothetical situation of an ordinary shareholder in BTR plc who also held shares in the company with which it was proposed to merge was posed and it was contended that such shareholders might well have very different interests in deciding whether or not to vote in favour of the scheme. This was rejected by Jonathan Parker J who, in so doing, distinguished the decision in *Re Hellenic Trust Ltd* and confined the ratio of that case to the point that the shareholder which was a subsidiary of the bidder company ought to have been in a separate class because the scheme only affected the other shareholders in the target company. Jonathan Parker J was not convinced by Nazareth J's analysis of 'interests based on rights' and found that the relevant test is that of 'differing rights

---

79 This decision has been criticised. Sealy et al (eds), *British Company Law and Practice* (1983; loose leaf) at 68301 say: 'There is, however, room for doubt whether this ruling was correct, for if the shareholders or creditors are split into separate "classes" for reasons which are personal to them rather than for reasons which apply to the group as a whole, the chances that one sub-group having adverse interests may block the entire scheme are significantly enhanced. It is surely the better approach for the court to allow the group to vote at a single meeting and to review their decision on the grounds of bona fides and fairness.'

80 *Re Pye (Ireland) Ltd* (11 March 1985, unreported) HC, Irish Company Law Reports 323.

81 *Re Industrial Equity (Pacific) Ltd* [1991] 2 HKLR 614.

82 *Re Industrial Equity (Pacific) Ltd* [1991] 2 HKLR 614 at 625.

83 In *Re Industrial Equity (Pacific) Ltd* [1991] 2 HKLR 614 at 624 he said: 'Moreover, in the *Sovereign* case, upon which he primarily relied, although Lord Esher did refer to interests in the passage Templeman J quotes, as I have said, that reference in my view must be construed as a reference to *interests arising out of rights in the company*' (emphasis added).

84 *Re BTR plc* [1999] 2 BCLC 675.

rather than differing interests', and he also found that 'interest' was not synonymous with 'right'. He held:

> 'Shareholders with the same rights in respect of the shares which they hold may be subject to an infinite number of different interests and may therefore, assessing their own personal interests (as they are perfectly entitled to do), vote their shares in the light of those interests. But that in itself, in my judgment, is simply a fact of life: it does not lead to the conclusion that shareholders who propose to vote differently are in some way a separate class of shareholders entitled to a separate class meeting. Indeed a journey down that road would in my judgment lead to impracticability and unworkability[85].'

In that case, it was held that there was no call to convene more than one meeting of the holders of the ordinary shares[86].

[21.037] In *Re Depfa Bank plc*[87], where the scheme proposed that the shareholders would swap their shares for a mixture of cash and shares in a German company, all of the shareholders had been comprised in a single class. The question arose as to whether the directors – who also held shares – might be regarded as a separate class on account of their having given undertakings to vote in favour of the scheme. Kelly J held that the decision to have a single meeting of a single class of members was correct, the learned judge's rationale being that identified in *Buckley*[88]:

> A company may enter into voting agreements with some of the members of a class, whereby those members bind themselves to vote in favour of the scheme. Such agreements can save the loss of time and expenditure which would otherwise arise where members of that class have expressed support for the scheme and subsequently changed their minds. Guidance on the execution of such an agreement in connection with a scheme of arrangement was given in *Re Telewest Communications plc (No 1)* [2004] EWHC 924 (Ch). Such an agreement is not open to objection if the member in question would not reasonably have voted differently in the absence of such an agreement, as, for example, where he can withdraw from the agreement in the event that reasonable grounds exist for a change of mind. The existence of such an agreement does not make the member signing it a separate class for the purpose of section 425(1) save where in consideration of entering into the agreement, a party obtains benefits not available to other members of the class. The existence of such an agreement is, however, relevant to the exercise of the discretion to sanction the scheme.

Kelly J considered that the same reasoning applied in *Depfa* saying the only basis upon which there would be a need to call a separate meeting is where a party obtained a benefit not available to other members of the class in consideration of the undertaking, something which clearly did not arise in that case.

[21.038] In *Re Millstream Recycling Ltd*[89], Laffoy J held that certain contamination creditors, referred to as the Hogg companies, were required to be in a separate class because they were connected to the company being subsidiaries of a company, the shareholders of which owned the entire share capital in the applicant company. Laffoy J

---

85 *Re BTR plc* [1999] 2 BCLC 675 at 682–683.

86 See further Morse et al (eds), *Palmer's Company Law* (25th edn, 1992; loose leaf), p 12024.

87 *Re Depfa Bank plc* [2007] IEHC 463, Kelly J.

88 Buckley, *The Companies Acts* (15th edn; LexisNexis Butterworths loose leaf issue 12, November 2006) at para 425.49A.

89 *Re Millstream Recycling Ltd* [2009] IEHC 571, Laffoy J.

found that 'it would not be possible for the other non-connected contamination creditors to consult with the Hogg companies with a view to their common interest'.

(d) Providing information to members and creditors

[21.039] Section 202(1) of the CA 1963 provides that where a meeting of creditors or members or any class of either is summoned certain information must[90] be given to the invitees. Section 202(1) provides that there shall:

> '(a) with every notice summoning the meeting which is sent to a creditor or member, be sent also a statement explaining the effect of the compromise or arrangement and in particular stating any material interests of the directors of the company, whether as directors[91] or as members or as creditors of the company or otherwise, and the effect thereon of the compromise or arrangement, in so far as it is different from the effect on the like interests of other persons; and
>
> (b) in every notice summoning the meeting which is given by advertisement, be included either such a statement as aforesaid or a notification of the place at which and the manner in which creditors or members entitled to attend the meeting may obtain copies of such statement as aforesaid[92].'

Special regard is had to the rights of debenture holders, and s 202(2) of the CA 1963, provides:

> 'Where the compromise or arrangement affects the rights of debenture holders of a company, the said statement shall give the like explanation in relation to the trustees of any deed for securing the issue of debentures as it is required to give in relation to the company's directors.'

[21.040] The duty to provide information in the form of a statement explaining the effect of the compromise or arrangement (and in particular stating any material interests of the directors of the company) to members and creditors has been considered in a number of cases. In *Re National Bank Ltd*[93], the facts were that, although the company had its head office in London, 72% of its shareholders had addresses in Ireland. This gave rise to difficulties and disadvantages because the large Irish business had been subject to the policies of successive English chancellors of the exchequer, which differed, sometimes, from those of Ireland, for example, in regard to liquidity ratios and interest rates. The board of directors eventually came to the conclusion that it was desirable to promote a scheme which involved the division of the bank's business into two parts. Its assets and liabilities attributable to the Irish business were to be transferred to a new Irish company (The National Bank of Ireland Ltd) and those of the English business were to remain with National Bank Ltd. The National Bank of Ireland Ltd was then to be acquired by the Governor and Company of the Bank of Ireland; National

90 On pain of criminal sanction: s 202(4) of the CA 1963; *cf* the defence in s 202(5) of the CA 1963.

91 It is the duty of directors (and trustees for debenture holders) to give notice to the company of such matters relating to themselves as may be necessary for the purposes of the section: s 202(6) of the CA 1963.

92 Members and creditors entitled to attend are required to be furnished with a copy of the statement explaining the effect of a compromise or arrangement, free of charge: s 202(3) of the CA 1963.

93 *Re National Bank Ltd* [1966] 1 WLR 819.

Bank Ltd was to become a wholly-owned subsidiary of the National Commercial Bank of Scotland Ltd. Shareholding-members of the company were sent a circular explaining the scheme. However, it did not disclose the value of the company's assets and liabilities. The reason for this, deliberate, non-disclosure was on account of the fact that banks were exempt from disclosing, in their accounts, certain information[94]. On this basis, just over 5% of the company's shareholders opposed the scheme. It was held that the court had the widest discretion to approve any sort of scheme between a company and its members. Since the Companies Act 1948 (UK) exempted the disclosure, in companies' accounts, of such information, the court felt it was appropriate to approve of the scheme in question.

[21.041] In *Re John Power & Son Ltd*[95], a scheme was proposed whereby the share capital of the famous whiskey manufacturer was to be restructured. The background to the scheme was that the company's profits had been in steady decline, attributable to increases in the excise duty on proof spirit. The company's share capital was divided into 400,000 preference shares of £1 each and 400,000 ordinary shares of £1 each. The preference shareholders were entitled to a fixed cumulative preference dividend of 8% and, after the ordinary shareholders received 8%, to a further distribution of dividend *pari passu* with the ordinary shareholders up to a maximum of 10%. The proposed scheme involved the reduction of the ordinary share capital to £200,000 by the write down of the value of the ordinary shares from £1 to 10 shillings each. As regards the preference shares, it was proposed that £400,000 redeemable debenture stock bearing interest at 5% would be created, that the preference share capital would be extinguished and that the preferential shareholders would be issued with £1 of the debenture stock in satisfaction of each £1 preference share held by them. All shareholders were circulated with the proposals. Subsequently, on application being made, the court summoned separate meetings of the ordinary and preference shareholders. The ordinary shareholders voted unanimously in favour of the proposed scheme. The preference shareholders by more than six to one, in value, were in favour of the scheme. It was subsequently argued in the High Court, *inter alia*, that the circular letter sent by the directors had been misleading. The High Court declined to approve the proposals. In reversing the High Court decision of Meredith J the Supreme Court held, *inter alia* (*per* Fitzgibbon J):

> 'I can find nothing misleading in the circular, and the proposals seem to me quite intelligible to any person of ordinary intelligence. The only omission which has occurred to me is one which was not stressed, or even mentioned during argument, of a statement as to the probable market value of the new debenture stock, but as any expression of opinion on this point would be purely speculative, and might be challenged as misleading, I am satisfied that it was properly omitted, and that it was not unfair to leave the shareholders to form their own estimate of the merits of the exchange which the learned judge considered might "reasonably be regarded as a more attractive investment"[96].'

[21.042] A specific disclosure to members and creditors, required by s 202(1) of the CA 1963, is any material interests of the directors of the company, whether as directors or as

94 Part 3 of Sch 8 of the CA 1948 (UK).

95 *Re John Power & Son Ltd* [1934] IR 412.

96 *Re John Power & Son Ltd* [1934] IR 412 at 419.

members or as creditors of the company or otherwise, and the effect thereon of the compromise or arrangement, in so far as it is different from the effect on the like interests of other persons[97]. By reason of the manifest potential for a conflict of interests, inherent in such a proposal, it is not hard to see why the legislation contains such a specific requirement. Where material changes arise between the issue of the explanatory statement and the voting on the proposals, such material changes must be disclosed to the members and creditors[98].

(e) Voting at meetings

[21.043] The statutory majority, required by s 201(3) of the CA 1963, is 'a majority in number representing three-fourths in value of the creditors or class of creditors or members or class of members' who are present and voting in person or by proxy. There is, therefore, a two-fold test so that 75% in *value* and >50% in *number* must support the scheme. To take two examples: where there are 10 creditors, nine of whom are owed €10,000 and one of whom is owed €200,000, were the one owed €200,000 to vote 'against' and the other nine to vote 'for', the test would not be met; equally, were the one owed €200,000 and three of those owed €10,000 to vote 'for' and the other six to vote 'against', the test would not be met.

[21.044] One issue that can arise is where a registered member holds shares in trust for more than one person; where some of the beneficial owners direct the registered member to vote their shares 'for' and some direct the member to vote 'against', is that member to be taken as having voted 'for' or 'against'? This question will arise more and more often for PLCs by reason of the proliferation of public companies' shares being held by nominee companies which list the underlying interest in those shares (ie, beneficial interests in the shares) as opposed to the shares. This issue arose in connection with a solvent scheme of arrangement in relation to Depfa Bank plc which was ultimately confirmed by Kelly J in *Re Depfa Bank plc*[99] although this issue did not feature in the judgment. It has been noted[100], however, that in that case although 353,019,660 shares were registered in the name of Clearstream Banking AG there were only seven shareholders, Clearstream being one and the other six being nominees who each held 10 shares in order to meet the requirement that a PLC have seven shareholders. It has been noted[101] that the Irish High court was satisfied, on the authority of the English decision in *Re Equitable Life Assurance Society*[102], that the appropriate action was to treat Clearstream as having voted both 'for' *and* 'against' (for the purposes of the >50% in number test) and in those circumstances the scheme was approved. In that case, Lloyd J had accepted the submission that a particular shareholder could be taken to vote both 'for' and 'against':

---

97 See, eg, *Re Pye (Ireland) Ltd* (11 March 1985, unreported) HC, Irish Company Law Reports 323 considered at para **[21.030]**.

98 *Re MB Group plc* [1989] BCLC 672 and *Re Minister Assets plc* [1985] BCLC 200.

99 *Re Depfa Bank plc* [2007] IEHC 463, Kelly J.

100 See Byers, King & Sustmann, 'The Takeover of Depfa Bank: A complex Exercise' (2007) PLC Magazine, December 2007.

101 Byers, King & Sustmann, 'The Takeover of Depfa Bank: A complex Exercise' (2007) PLC Magazine, December 2007.

102 *Re Equitable Life Assurance Society* [2002] BCC 319.

'The wording of [s 425(2) of the Companies Act 1985][103] is general. It is certainly true that if one were reading it at a first reading, it might not occur to one that, of the however many numbers of creditors there might be in the particular class according to a headcount, you could find one of those, or any given number of those, voting different ways in respect of different parts of his claim.

However, reviewing the section in the context of the widespread practice of nomineeship and trusteeship, both for debt, for example bonds, and rights under policies, many of which are held by trustees, for example under group pension schemes and, likewise in respect of shares, especially in an increasingly paperless securities world, it seems to me that it would be inappropriate to construe these general words as not permitting a particular member or creditor to cast different parts of the value of his claim or his membership rights in different ways[104].'

[21.045] Provided the statutory majority approves of a scheme at a meeting, it matters not that those present were only a fraction of those persons who were entitled to attend and vote provided that all who were entitled to attend were duly summoned under s 201(1)[105]. The meaning of 'three-fourths in value of the … members or class of members' was considered by Brightman J in *Re NFU Development Trust*[106]. There, the company in question was limited by guarantee. It had been contended that since the company had no share capital, and the right of membership was non-transferable and ceased on death, it was impossible to ascertain whether a particular majority did or did not represent three-fourths in value of the members present and voting. This was rejected by Brightman J, who held:

'It appears to me that section 206(2) of the Companies Act 1948 [(UK)] in referring to "three-fourths in value of the … members or class of members" is directing attention to the size of the stake which each member has in the company. The purpose is to prevent a numerical majority with a small stake outvoting a minority with a large stake, *eg* to prevent 51 members with one share each outvoting 49 members with 10 shares each. In a case such as the present where each member has precisely the same financial stake in the company, namely, a right if he survives the liquidation of the company to be considered for a payment at the discretion of the board, and a right to an aliquot share of any assets not distributed pursuant to such discretion, every member has in law an identical stake. The position therefore is the same as if each member owned a single share in the company, with the result that a three-quarter majority of votes satisfies the statutory requirements[107].'

[21.046] Where a resolution is passed at any adjourned meeting held under s 201, s 201(4) of the CA 1963 provides that s 144 of the CA 1963 shall apply to any such resolution[108] and the resolution shall be treated as having been passed on the date on which it was in fact passed, and not at any earlier date.

[21.047] Where a company has creditors with unliquidated claims, the scheme must provide for a mechanism for valuing unliquidated claims because the 75% majority

---

103 Which is materially identical to s 201(3) of the CA 1963.

104 *Re Equitable Life Assurance Society* [2002] BCC 319 at 327B–C.

105 *Re Osiris Insurance Ltd* [1999] 1 BCLC 182.

106 *Re NFU Development Trust* [1972] 1 WLR 1548.

107 *Re NFU Development Trust* [1972] 1 WLR 1548 at 1553F–H.

108 See Ch 14, *Corporate Governance: Meetings*, para **[14.117]**.

required by s 201(3) is based on claim value. In *Re Millstream Recycling Ltd*[109], Laffoy J said that:

> 'The responsibility for preparing the scheme and explaining it lies on the company and its advisers. It is not the function of the Court, at this stage of the s 201 process, to give its *imprimatur* to the content of the scheme.'

On that basis, Laffoy J refused to give ancillary directions in relation to the submission and valuation of the claims.

(f) Repeat applications under s 201 where first scheme proposed unacceptable

[21.048] There is authority that, where an applicant applies to court under s 201(1) of the CA 1963 to summon meetings of creditors and members and subsequently realises or is told that meetings of differently constituted classes ought to have been summoned, only in very exceptional circumstances will a second application under s 201(1) be entertained. In *Re Pye (Ireland) Ltd; Hogan*[110], Costello J held:

> 'In my view the section as interpreted in normal circumstances is that a second application should not be entertained unless very exceptional circumstances arise, as to do so would be to allow the section to be used as a means of improving a bid, which had failed under the first scheme, in favour of dissenting creditors, and it would be undesirable if the section was to be so used. The consequences of defeat therefore should flow; I would depart from this view only in exceptional cases. I cannot find that exceptional circumstances exist in the present case and therefore I must decline to exercise my discretion in this case[111].'

The applicants successfully appealed this decision to the Supreme Court which summoned meetings of certain classes of creditors and members on the applicants' undertaking to pay a sum to the Revenue Commissioners[112]. Unfortunately, there is no judgment in the appeal available and it is not clear whether Costello J's test was disapproved or whether the instant case was found to be 'very exceptional'. It is thought that repeated applications under s 201(1) for the purposes of improving bids is indeed undesirable; however, it must be questioned whether principle requires a general policy of refusing subsequent applications where a genuine mistake is made initially in constituting the meetings of appropriate classes.

Staying proceedings where application made under s 201(1)

[21.049] Section 201(2) of the CA 1963 provides that the court is empowered to stay all proceedings and restrain further proceedings against a company in respect of which application is made 'for such period as to the court seems fit'. This jurisdiction was considered by Laffoy J in *Re Millstream Recycling Ltd*[113] the facts of which have been

109 *Re Millstream Recycling Ltd* [2009] IEHC 571, Laffoy J.

110 *Re Pye (Ireland) Ltd v Hogan* (12 November 1984, unreported) HC, Irish Company Law Reports 320.

111 *Irish Company Law Reports* 320 at 321–322.

112 See '*Reporter's Note*' at 322.

113 *Re Millstream Recycling Ltd* [2009] IEHC 571, Laffoy J.

considered above[114]. There, a stay was put on the contamination creditors pursuing proceedings against the company:

> 'I consider that it is a proper exercise of the jurisdiction of the Court under s 201(2) to grant a stay in the terms sought by the company, primarily, because I am satisfied that it is essential to achieving one of the underlying objectives of the proposal, which is to limit the cost of the determination of the contamination creditors' claims against the company and thus provide a greater fund for distribution by way of dividend.'

Laffoy J rejected the suggestion that it was unfair or unjust because it affected all contamination creditors in the same way.

Court sanction of scheme of arrangement

[21.050] Even where a majority in number representing 75% in value of the creditors or class or creditors and members or class of members support a scheme of arrangement it is not automatically binding. In order for a scheme of arrangement or compromise to become binding, it must first receive the sanction of the court under s 201(3) of the CA 1963, which provides:

> 'If a majority in number representing three-fourths in value of the creditors or class of creditors or members or class of members, as the case may be, present and voting either in person or by proxy at the meeting, vote in favour of a resolution agreeing to any compromise or arrangement, the compromise or arrangement shall, if sanctioned by the court, be binding on all the creditors or the class of creditors, or on the members or class of members, as the case may be, and also on the company or, in the case of a company in the course of being wound up, on the liquidator and contributories of the company[115].'

In *Re John Power & Son Ltd*[116], the former Supreme Court, per Fitzgibbon J, quoted[117] with approval the following passage from the judgment of Lindley LJ in *Re Alabama, New Orleans, Texas and Pacific Junction Railway Company*[118]:

> 'What the court has to do is to see, first of all, that the provisions of that statute have been complied with; and secondly, that the majority have been acting *bona fide*. The court *also* has to see that the minority is not being overridden by a majority having interests of its own clashing with those of the minority whom they seek to coerce. *Further than that*, the court has to look at the scheme, and see whether it is one as to which persons acting honestly, and viewing the scheme laid before them in the interests of those whom they represent, take a view which can be reasonably taken by business men. The court must look at the scheme, and see whether the Act has been complied with, whether the majority are acting *bona fide*, and whether they are coercing the minority in order to promote interests adverse to those of the class they purport to represent; *and then* see whether the

---

[114] See para **[21.029]** *ante*.

[115] Section 201(5) of the CA 1963 provides, *inter alia*, that an order made under sub-s (3) shall have no effect until an office copy of the order has been delivered to the registrar of companies. A copy of every such order must be annexed to every copy of the company's memorandum of association issued after the order is made.

[116] *Re John Power & Son Ltd* [1934] IR 412.

[117] *Re John Power & Son Ltd* [1934] IR 412 at 424. See also *Re English, Scottish and Australian Chartered Bank* [1893] 3 Ch 385.

[118] *Re Alabama, New Orleans, Texas and Pacific Junction Railway Company* [1891] 1 Ch 213.

> scheme is a reasonable one *or* whether there is *any reasonable objection* to it, *or such an objection* to it as that *any reasonable man* might say that he could not approve of it.'

Greater succinctness is perhaps seen in the judgment of Astbury J in *Re Anglo-Continental Supply Co Ltd*[119], upon which the passage in *Buckley on the Companies Acts*[120], cited with approval in a number of recent English cases[121], is largely based. There, Astbury J said:

> 'In exercising its power of sanction under s 120 the court will see: First, that the provisions of the statute have been complied with. Secondly, that the class was fairly represented by those who attended the meeting and that the statutory majority are acting bona fide and are not coercing the minority in order to promote interests adverse to those of the class whom they purport to represent, and, thirdly, that the arrangement is such as a man of business would reasonably approve …'[122]

Buckley on the Companies Acts[123] says:

> 'The court does not sit merely to see that the majority are acting bona fide and thereupon to register the decision of the meeting, but, at the same time, the court will be slow to differ from the meeting, unless either the class has not been properly consulted, or the meeting has not considered the matter with a view to the interests of the class which it is empowered to bind, or some blot is found in the scheme.'

(a) Sufficient steps to identify and notify all interested parties

[21.051] As considered above, all members and creditors must be identified as must any other interested persons, such as regulators of the company.

(b) Compliance with statute and court directions

[21.052] The need for statutory compliance – with the provisions of s 201 of the CA 1963 – has already been considered. So all requirements concerning the summoning of meetings of members and creditors (and classes thereof) must have been complied with. In *Readymix plc*[124], one of the objections raised, which Kelly J had to consider, was whether there had been a defect in the online arrangements to deal with proxy voting. It was alleged that there was a conflict between the provisions in the company's articles of association and in the circular sent to shareholders in relation to proxies. Kelly J rejected this contention saying he was not satisfied that any point of substance had been made out and that there was no evidence of any confusion, less still any wrongful allowal or disallowal of proxy votes. Kelly J also determined that electronic voting was permitted by the company's articles of association.

[21.053] Moreover, members and creditors must have been provided with a statement of the proposal which must have made full and proper disclosure[125]; and the requisite

---

119 *Re Anglo-Continental Supply Co Ltd* [1922] 2 Ch 723.

120 *Buckley on the Companies Acts* (14th edn, 1981), Vol 1, pp 473–474.

121 *Re Osiris Insurance Ltd* [1999] 1 BCLC 182 at 188 and *Re BTR plc* [1999] 2 BCLC 675 at 680. See also *Re National Bank Ltd* [1966] 1 All ER 1006 at 1012.

122 *Re Anglo-Continental Supply Co Ltd* [1922] 2 Ch 723 at 736.

123 *Buckley on the Companies Acts* (14th edn, 1981), Vol 1, pp 473–474.

124 *Re Readymix plc* [2012] IEHC 170.

statutory majority of three-fourths (75%) in value must have approved of the scheme or compromise[126]. These are pre-requisites and the court should not sanction a scheme or compromise where there is non-compliance with these matters. It should be noted that it will not only be the Companies Acts which must be complied with: where a company is engaged in regulated activities, such as banking, or there are competition law issues, those must be complied with also: *Re Depfa Bank plc*[127].

(b) Class fairly represented and majority act bona fide

[21.054] The requirement that classes are fairly represented has been considered above[128]. Any inducement given to a creditor or member to vote in favour of a proposal can operate to negative the required *bona fides*. Whilst a member can vote selfishly in furtherance of his own interests, it has been held that he must do so *bona fide* and in the interests of the class as a whole[129].

(c) A man of business would reasonable approve

[21.055] The scheme must appear to the court to be reasonable in the eyes of an intelligent, honest man of business. Generally, the court will have regard to the views of those members and creditors who have approved the scheme. As Lord Lindley said in *Re English, Scottish and Australian Chartered Bank*[130]:

> 'If the creditors are acting on sufficient information and with time to consider what they are about, and are acting honestly, they are, I apprehend, much better judges of what is to their commercial advantages than the court can be.'

In *Re Depfa Bank plc*[131], Kelly J echoed this saying that 'the court will be slow to differ from experienced persons in the industry who are familiar with the subject matter of the scheme'. That said, the court will not simply 'rubber stamp' a scheme of arrangement, simply because a majority in value of creditors (or members) approves it[132]. The reasonableness or otherwise of each scheme will often turn on the facts of a particular scheme. In *Re Alabama, New Orleans, Texas and Pacific Junction Railway Company*[133], Bowen LJ set out the grounds upon which a court should exercise its discretion to confirm a scheme. He said:

> 'I do not think myself that the point of jurisdiction is worth discussing at much length, because everybody will agree that a compromise or agreement which has to be sanctioned by the court must be reasonable, and that no arrangement or compromise can be said to be reasonable in which you can get nothing and give up everything. A reasonable compromise must be a compromise which can, by reasonable people conversant with the

---

125 See para **[21.039]**.

126 See para **[21.043]**.

127 *Re Depfa Bank plc* [2007] IEHC 463, Kelly J.

128 See para **[21.029]**.

129 *British America Nickel Corporation Ltd v MJ O'Brien Ltd* [1927] AC 369 at 371. See also *Re Wedgewood Coal and Iron Co* (1877) 6 Ch D 627 at 637.

130 *Re English, Scottish and Australian Chartered Bank* [1893] 3 Ch 385 at 409.

131 *Re Depfa Bank plc* [2007] IEHC 463, Kelly J.

132 *Re Colonia Reinsurance (Ireland) Ltd* [2005] IEHC 115 and *Re Osiris Insurance Ltd* [1999] 1 BCLC 182 at 191 (*per* Neuberger J).

133 *Re Alabama, New Orleans, Texas and Pacific Junction Railway Company* [1891] 1 Ch 213.

> subject, be regarded as beneficial to those on both sides who are making it. Now, I have no doubt at all that it would be improper for the court to allow an arrangement to be forced on any class of creditors, if the arrangement cannot reasonably be supposed by sensible business people to be for the benefit of that class as such, otherwise the sanction of the court would be a sanction to what would be a scheme of confiscation. The object of this section is not confiscation … Its object is to enable compromises to be made which are for the common benefit of the creditors as creditors, or for the common benefit of some class of creditors as such[134].'

In *Re Dorman Long and Company Ltd*[135], Maugham J said that the court's duty is to see whether the proposal is such that an intelligent and honest man, a member of the class concerned and acting in respect of his interests, might reasonably approve[136]. In *Re John Power & Son Ltd*[137], the Supreme Court, per Murnaghan J, said of the proposed scheme in that case, and generally:

> 'The compromise or arrangement which can only be made binding against the wishes of the dissentient shareholders … requires the sanction of the court. In my opinion the court under this section can give all due weight to the opinion of the majority of the shareholders but the court is in no way bound merely to register the opinion of this majority. The sanction to be given by the court must be a real sanction, and to my mind the meaning of the section clearly is that no majority under the section can carry an arrangement which a fair and impartial mind would not sanction[138].'

Fairness, reasonableness and impartiality are prerequisites of any scheme that may be sanctioned by the court.

[21.056] Where the court is broadly satisfied with a proposed scheme, but has one or two reservations, it is open to the court to sanction the scheme subject to receiving certain undertakings. This was the approach adopted by Neuberger J in *Re Osiris Insurance Ltd*[139] where two undertakings in relation to relatively minor matters were required before he sanctioned the scheme.

[21.057] In the case of compromises and schemes of arrangement proposed between a relevant company (for the purposes of the Irish Takeover Panel Act 1997) and its members or any class of them and which constitutes a takeover (within the meaning of that Act), the High Court is statutorily obliged in exercising its powers under ss 201, 203 and 204 of the CA 1963 to have due regard to the exercise by the Irish Takeover Panel of its powers under the Irish Takeover Panel Act 1997. Mutual regard is required and a similar obligation is imposed on the Irish Takeover Panel[140].

---

134 *Re Alabama, New Orleans, Texas and Pacific Junction Railway Company* [1891] 1 Ch 213 at 243.

135 *Re Dorman Long and Company Ltd* [1934] 1 Ch 635.

136 See also *Re English, Scottish and Australian Chartered Bank* [1893] 3 Ch 385 where it was held that since there was nothing unreasonable or unfair about the proposed scheme, the court would defer to the expressed opinion of the great majority of creditors.

137 *Re John Power & Son Ltd* [1934] IR 412.

138 *Re John Power & Son Ltd* [1934] IR 412 at 432.

139 *Re Osiris Insurance Ltd* [1999] 1 BCLC 182.

140 See para **[21.023]**.

Solvent schemes of arrangement

[21.058] The first Irish case to consider a *solvent* scheme of arrangement was *Re Colonia Reinsurance (Ireland) Ltd*[141]. Kelly J accepted that there was jurisdiction to approve a scheme of arrangement in respect of a solvent company. Kelly J said that when approving a scheme of arrangement in respect of a solvent company, five conditions require to be fulfilled, which he repeated in *Re Depfa Bank plc*[142] in the following terms:

> '(i) The court must be satisfied that sufficient steps have been taken to identify and notify all interested parties;
>
> (ii) the court must be satisfied that the statutory requirements and all directions of the court have been complied with;
>
> (iii) the court must be satisfied that the classes of creditors were properly constituted;
>
> (iv) the issue of coercion must not arise; and
>
> (v) the scheme of arrangement must be such that an intelligent and honest man, a member of the class concerned, acting in respect of his interest might reasonably approve of it.

The scheme in the *Colonia* case concerned a non-life insurance company that had ceased to write new policies of insurance; the scheme was necessary so as to shorten the time for qualifying and paying-off so called 'run-off-liabilities' that were considered likely to arise on foot of the policies written by the company. Having considered the advantages of a scheme, Kelly J noted the disadvantages were that if a scheme creditor failed to return a claim form by the end date, such a creditor's claim would be valued at nil and that it was likely a number of claims would be estimated and in circumstances some creditors might receive less (or more) than if the claims were allowed to mature normally. Kelly J found that the disadvantages there were similar to those identified in the English decision in *Re Osiris Insurance Ltd*[143] where Neuberger J had said:

> 'There is, indeed, a risk that any scheme creditor will receive less under the scheme than he would receive in the normal way. However, the concern that one has about that aspect appears to me to be outweighed by the following factors. First, as already indicated, this risk is greatest for the London market policy holders, who will either be the sort of people who will have been able to take an informed view on the scheme and/or will have had access to brokers who would have been able to give them appropriate advice; they either voted in favour of the scheme or abstained, none voted against. Secondly, scheme creditors are just as likely, pursuant to the scheme, to receive a larger sum, as opposed to a smaller sum, than they would have received if they had pursued their claims in the run off in the normal way. Thirdly, their claims are to be determined by independent and properly qualified persons. Fourthly, their claims will be settled more quickly, and they are likely to be paid significantly more promptly, pursuant to the scheme, than in the normal way. Fifthly, a scheme creditor will almost certainly save on the costs of pursuing a claim under the scheme than in the normal way.'

Kelly J held that he was satisfied that the proposed scheme was such as an intelligent and honest man, a member of the class concerned and acting in respect of his interests,

141 *Colonia Reinsurance (Ireland) Ltd* [2005] IEHC 115, Kelly J.

142 *Re Depfa Bank plc* [2007] IEHC 463, Kelly J.

143 *Re Orisis Insurance Ltd* [1999] 1 BCLC 182.

might reasonably approve and so made an order under s 201(3) sanctioning the scheme and directed that the creditors be written to and notified of the making of the order which should be filed with the registrar of companies within 21 days of the date of its perfection.

[21.059] In *Re Depfa Bank plc*[144], the company was a licensed bank and the scheme there proposed that a German bank, Hypo Real Estate Holdings AG would acquire all of Depfa's issued share capital in payment of a consideration to its shareholders made up in cash and shares in Hypo. Kelly J applied the test formulated in *Colonia* and approved the scheme.

[21.060] *Readymix plc*[145] involved another solvent scheme of arrangement. In that case, Kelly J rejected the objections made by two shareholders representing a miniscule percentage of the shares in a company. Allegations that the company had made inappropriate payments to another company and that the company had engaged in below cost selling were not made out and Kelly J rejected their objections to the scheme.

Judicial powers to assist schemes in contemplation of reconstruction

[21.061] Section 203 of the CA 1963 contains provisions which can facilitate a compromise or arrangement proposed for the purposes of a scheme for the reconstruction of any company or companies or the amalgamation of any two or more companies. Where it is envisaged that the whole or any part of the undertaking or property of any company concerned in the scheme is to be transferred to another company, s 203(1) of the CA 1963 provides that the court may either by order sanction in the compromise or arrangement or, by subsequent order, make provision for all or any of the following matters:

- the transfer to the transferee company of the whole or any part of the undertaking and of the property or liabilities of any transferor company;
- the allotting or appropriation by the transferee company of any shares, debentures, policies or other like interests in that company which under the compromise or arrangement are to be allotted or appropriated by that company to or for any person;
- the continuation by or against the transferee company of any legal proceedings pending by or against any transferor company;
- the dissolution, without winding up, of any transferor company;
- the provision to be made for any persons who, within such time and in such manner as the court directs, dissent from the compromise or arrangement;
- such incidental, consequential and supplemental matters as are necessary to secure that the reconstruction or amalgamation shall be fully and effectively carried out.

144 *Re Depfa Bank plc* [2007] IEHC 463, Kelly J.

145 *Re Readymix plc* [2012] IEHC 170 and 194 (it appears two neutral citation numbers were assigned to this judgment).

[21.062] The power of the court is considerable. Section 203(2) of the CA 1963 provides:

> 'Where an order under this section provides for the transfer of property or liabilities, that property shall, by virtue of the order, be transferred to and become the liabilities of the transferee company, and in the case of any property, if the order so directs, freed from any charge which is, by virtue of the compromise or arrangement, to cease to have effect.'

Setting aside a scheme for fraud

[21.063] It is possible for a scheme of arrangement that has been sanctioned by the court to be subsequently set aside on grounds of fraud. So in *Fletcher v Royal Automobile Club Ltd* (the '*RAC* case')[146] Neuberger J said that:

> 'In the absence of authority, I would reject the suggestion that a court order sanctioning a scheme cannot be set aside for fraud, and if this resulted in the scheme having to be unravelled, the court and the parties would have to face that and deal with it as the justice of the case demanded and the law permitted[147].'

He went on to say:

> 'I would have thought that if parliament had intended an order under s 425 to have the special characteristic of not being liable to be set aside for fraud, and its effect unravelled, it would have said so. Many statutes state that something can only be done with a court order, or provide for the effect of a court order. It does not seem to me that this would take it outside the power of the court to set aside the court order and, in effect, to reverse the effect of that order. Indeed, I would regard it as remarkable if a court, which had been clearly, deliberately and systematically misled by a litigant so as to get a particular order, was not able to set aside the order and its effect simply because Parliament had said what the effect of the order was. In my judgment, when Parliament states the effect of a court order, it does not mean that the order cannot be set aside where it has been obtained by fraud'[148].

Neuberger J made it clear that the fact that an innocent third party may be affected by the setting aside of an order goes to the court's discretion, but not jurisdiction, in deciding whether or not to set aside an order that sanctioned a scheme of arrangement.

[21.064] The facts in the *RAC* case were that the rules of the club divided members into three classes: life members, full members and overseas members who resided outside of the UK. The life and full members were members of the company which effectively owned the RAC roadside service business. In 1996, it was decided by committee to amend the rules to redefine the classes of members: it was proposed that persons living in the EU would become full members and those living outside would remain overseas members. By an apparent oversight, the rule change was not put to the general meeting and by a further oversight, this went unnoticed. The effect was that the committee's decision did change the rules but only for a period: when the change was not put to the general meeting, it lapsed and the rules reverted to their original state, before the committee's decision to change them. On renewal of memberships in 1998, the proposal was implemented and EU members were renewed as full members. However, because,

[146] *Fletcher v Royal Automobile Club Ltd* [2000] 1 BCLC 331.

[147] *Fletcher v Royal Automobile Club Ltd* [2000] 1 BCLC 331 at 344c–d.

[148] *Fletcher v Royal Automobile Club Ltd* [2000] 1 BCLC 331 at 344g–i.

independently, any revision in subscription rates was not to affect overseas members aged over 65 years, such persons, though resident in the EU, continued to be treated as overseas members. When it was proposed to sell the roadside business, a scheme of arrangement was proposed under which life and full members would each receive circa £30,000. At least one EU resident member aged over 65 claimed he would be unfairly treated if he did not benefit from the change. Counsel on instructions told the court that there was no rule change and the court proceeded on that basis to sanction the scheme of arrangement. It subsequently became clear that there had been a rule change from the time of the committee's decision to change the rules to the lapsing of that change for want of subsequent approval in general meeting. The plaintiffs applied to set aside the order sanctioning the scheme of arrangement on the basis that it had been procured by misleading information.

[21.065] Neuberger J found that as a general rule the court would not set aside a judgment obtained by fraud if satisfied that the result would have been the same even if the fraud had not been perpetrated. On this point he said:

> 'If it is satisfied that some sort of fraud occurred, or may well have occurred, the court's powers are quite wide enough to ensure that appropriate sanctions are applied without having to incur the pointless cost, effort and court time in re-running a case whose result is a foregone conclusion[149].'

On the facts of the *RAC* case, Neuberger J found that there was insufficient evidence of any fraud, which he said must be shown to be actual dishonesty or recklessness – mere negligence or inadvertence was plainly not enough. Accordingly, the plaintiffs' application to set aside the earlier sanctioned scheme of arrangement was refused.

[B] RECONSTRUCTIONS[150]

[21.066] Section 260 of the CA 1963 provides for a procedure whereby a liquidator of a company being voluntarily wound up can transfer the assets of the company to a new company in circumstances where the members of the old company will be given shares in the new company. One of the primary differences between a reconstruction pursuant to s 260 and a scheme of arrangement under s 201 of the CA 1963 is that s 260 makes no provision for the compromise of creditors' claims. Accordingly, the s 260 machinery makes no provision for meetings of creditors. Whilst a reconstruction under s 260 may affect creditors, it is essentially an internal procedure which facilitates the adjustment of shareholders' rights. Moreover, although there is no requirement for the court to sanction a reconstruction under s 260, neither can dissenting shareholders be bound and they can insist upon being paid their entitlements as contributories[151].

---

149 *Fletcher v Royal Automobile Club Ltd* [2000] 1 BCLC 331 at 340i.

150 See, generally, Clarke, *Takeovers and Mergers Law in Ireland* (1999), p 248; Morse et al (eds), *Palmer's Company Law* (25th edn, 1992, loose leaf), p 12045; and Sealy et al (eds), *British Company Law and Practice*, (1983; loose leaf) at 68200.

151 As to the rights of contributories, see Ch 25, *The Realisation and Distribution of Assets in a Winding Up*, para **[25.130]**.

The s 260 machinery

[21.067] Section 260(1) of the CA 1963 provides:

> 'Where a company is proposed to be, or is in course of being, wound up voluntarily, and the whole or part of its business or property is proposed to be transferred or sold to another company, whether a company within the meaning of this Act or not (in this section referred to as "the transferee company"), the liquidator of the first-mentioned company (in this section referred to as "the transferor company") may, with the sanction of a special resolution of that company, conferring either a general authority on the liquidator or an authority in respect of any particular arrangement, receive in compensation or part compensation for the transfer or sale, shares, policies or other like interests in the transferee company for distribution among the members of the transferor company, or may enter into any other arrangement whereby the members of the transferor company may, in lieu of receiving cash, shares, policies or other like interests, or in addition thereto, participate in the profits of or receive any other benefit from the transferee company.'

It can be seen that the primary person vested with power under s 260 is the voluntary liquidator. Before any liquidator would even consider invoking his powers under s 260 he would, in practice, first need to have proposals from a company's shareholders whereby they are agreeable in principle to such a proposal. A number of points arise for consideration.

(a) Only available in a voluntary winding up

[21.068] It will be seen that the procedure is only available where a company proposes to be or is in the course of being wound up voluntarily; s 260 of the CA 1963 does not apply where a company goes into official, compulsory liquidation. Indeed, if an order is made converting a voluntary winding up to a compulsory winding up within a year of the special resolution being passed, it shall not be valid unless sanctioned by the court[152]. Accordingly, within what has been described as this 'year of uncertainty'[153], it is open to both creditors and members to seek to convert to a compulsory winding up where they feel their interests are prejudiced[154]. If a company is in creditors' voluntary liquidation, s 271 of the CA 1963 provides that s 260 of the CA 1963 will apply '... with the modification that the powers of the liquidator under that section shall not be exercised except with the sanction either of the court or the committee of inspection'.

In such cases the requirement that the liquidator obtains the sanction of the court or committee of inspection is in addition to obtaining the sanction of a special resolution of the company.

(b) The proposal

[21.069] The purpose of s 260 of the CA 1963 is to give effect to a proposal whereby the whole or part of a company's business or property is proposed to be transferred or sold to another company. The transferee need not be a company within the meaning of s 2 of the CA 1963[155] and so can be a foreign company. Often times the transferee company

---

[152] *Re Callao Bis Co* (1889) 42 Ch D 169.

[153] Ussher, *Company Law in Ireland* (1986), p 289.

[154] See, eg, *Re Consolidated South Rand Mines Deep Ltd* [1909] 1 Ch 491.

[155] Section 260(1) of the CA 1963.

will be specially formed, but this is not a prerequisite and an existing company can be a transferee company. Section 260 empowers a liquidator to:

– receive in compensation or part compensation shares, policies or other like interests in the transferee company for distribution among the members of the transferor company or
– enter into any other arrangement whereby the members of the transferor company participate in the profits of or receive any other benefit from the transferee company, in lieu of cash, shares or policies or other like interests.

(c) The requirement for sanction by special resolution of members

[21.070] Section 260 of the CA 1963 confers certain powers upon a liquidator where he has the sanction of a special resolution of the company[156]. The special resolution put to the members must propose to confer upon the liquidator a general authority or an authority in respect of a particular arrangement. It is advisable for the resolution to sanction the proposal to be accompanied by a resolution to wind up the company[157]. The usual notice provisions for special resolutions apply[158] and there is nothing to suggest that, where so permitted by a company's articles of association, the written resolution procedure provided for by s 141(8) of the CA 1963 cannot be availed of[159].

[21.071] Section 260(2) of the CA 1963 provides that any sale or arrangement in pursuance of sub-s (1) shall be binding on the members of the transferor company. This is, however, subject to s 260(3), which drives a horse and four through s 260(2). Section 260(3) of the CA 1963 provides that a member[160] who has not voted in favour of the special resolution may dissent from it in writing within seven days after the passing of the resolution and require the liquidator to abstain from effecting the proposal or, alternatively, to purchase that member's interest at a price to be determined by arbitration[161], in the absence of agreement. Where a liquidator elects to purchase the member's interest, s 260(4) of the CA 1963 provides:

> '… the purchase money must be paid before the company is dissolved and, unless otherwise provided for, shall be deemed to be and shall be paid as part of the costs, charges and expenses of the winding up.'

It has been held that a company's articles of association cannot dilute dissenting members' statutory rights[162]. It has also been held that a member who does not dissent pursuant to s 260(3) cannot be compelled or bound to accept new 'shares, policies or

156 See Ch 24, *Liquidators*, para **[24.048]**.

157 *Cleve v Financial Corporation* (1873) LR 16 Eq 363.

158 *Imperial Bank of China, India and Japan v Bank of Hindustan, China and Japan* (1868) LR 6 Eq 91.

159 As to which, see Ch 14, *Corporate Governance: Meetings*, para **[14.090]** *ff*.

160 This has been held to include a deceased member's personal representatives: *Llewellyn v Kasintoe Rubber Estates* [1914] 2 Ch 670.

161 As to which, see s 260(6) of the CA 1963.

162 *Payne v Cork Co Ltd* [1900] 1 Ch 308 and *Henderson's Transvaal Estates Ltd* [1908] 1 Ch 743.

other like interests' in the transferee company[163], an option that may prove attractive where the proposed interest to be given to the member is encumbered by contingent liabilities.

(d) Distribution of shares, policies or other interests

[21.072] A liquidator is obliged to distribute any shares, policies or other interests in accordance with the entitlements of the company's members. Where there are different classes of members, the respective rights of the various classes must be respected and distribution made in accordance therewith[164].

[163] *Re Bank of Hindustan, China and Japan; Higg's Case* (1865) 2 H & M 657. There Wood VC said (at 665) that a member who does not dissent within time '… may have lost all his rights over his own shares by his delay; but he may nevertheless decline to take this consideration for his shares if he thinks that that consideration would prove burdensome rather than beneficial.'

[164] See further Morse et al (eds), *Palmer's Company Law* (25th edn, 1992; loose leaf), p 12057.

Chapter 22

Examinerships

Introduction

[22.001] This chapter considers the law relating to examinerships[1]. An examinership is where the court places a company under its protection to enable a court appointed examiner to investigate the company's affairs and to report to the court on its prospects of survival. Where survival can be achieved, the court may sanction a scheme of arrangement which often involves the part-payment of the company's creditors and which enables the company to continue in business.

(a) The background to the Companies (Amendment) Act 1990

[22.002] The law relating to examinerships[2] has its origins in the Companies (Amendment) Act 1990 ('C(A)A 1990') which was passed in unusual circumstances. It initially began life as a part of the Companies Bill 1987. However, before that Bill could be passed into law, international events overtook the legislature. As a direct result of those events, the C(A)A 1990 was passed quickly into force[3]. When Iraq invaded Kuwait in 1990, one international response was a United Nations' trade embargo. This had potentially disastrous consequences for the Irish economy since an Irish company, Goodman International, exported most of the Irish beef produced to Iraq. Goodman International, which had borrowings on 17 August 1990 of £460 million, found itself in very serious difficulties[4]. Upon the viability of Goodman International coming into question, the government of the day decided to introduce as a stand-alone piece of legislation[5] what had been Part IX of the Companies (No 2) Bill 1987. This became the C(A)A 1990. Subsequently, on 22 December 1990, the Companies Act 1990 ('CA 1990') was passed and made minor amendments to the C(A)A 1990[6].

---

1 See generally, O'Donnell, *Examinerships* (1994) and Keane, *Company Law* (3rd edn, 2000), Ch 37.

2 Although the expression used in the C(A)A 1990 is 'court protection', the C(A)(No 2)A 1999 uses the term 'examinership'.

3 See McCormack, *The New Companies Legislation* (1991), p 185 *et seq*. See also the background analysis in (1990) Irish Times, 1 September.

4 See 126 *Seanad Debates* 1065 where the Minister for Industry and Commerce quoted a letter to him from IBI Corporate Finance Ltd. See also 401 *Dáil Debates* 2055–2291.

5 126 *Seanad Debates* 1059, *per* Mr Desmond O'Malley, the then Minister for Industry and Commerce.

6 Sections 180 and 181 of the CA 1990.

(b) The Gallagher Company Law Review Group

[22.003] There were many calls for a more far-reaching overhaul of the C(A)A 1990 throughout the 1990s[7] than that effected by the CA 1990. In April 1994, the then Minister for Enterprise and Employment established an ad hoc Company Law Review Group under the chairmanship of James Gallagher. This Group reported in November 1994 and its report included 29 recommendations and conclusions on the area of examinerships. The basis of its recommendations and conclusions is alluded to in the report:

> 'It is essential, however, while allowing for consideration of the individual merits of each case, to set limits to the availability of examinership, to set parameters for the operation of the legislation and to provide checks and balances. It is these parameters which can focus on viability and limit the impairment of the interests of individual creditors and competitors. Many of the submissions made to us criticised the existing legislation arguing, in particular, that it does not give sufficient focus to viable companies and that it does not give sufficient protection to the interests of creditors. We accept the thrust of these particular criticisms and many of our recommendations relate to these issues[8].'

Notwithstanding the speed with which the Group reported, it was not until late 1999 and the passing of the Companies (Amendment) (No 2) Act 1999 ('C(A)(No2)A 1999') that legislative effect was given to the Group's recommendations.

(c) The Companies (Amendment) (No 2) Act 1999

[22.004] The C(A)(No 2)A 1999 made very substantial and significant changes to the examinership regime[9]. Three changes stand to the fore. First, the C(A)(No 2)A 1999 introduced a stricter test for the appointment of an examiner: s 2(1) of the C(A)A 1990, as amended, now requires that an examiner shall not be appointed by the court unless it is satisfied that there is a reasonable *prospect of the survival of the company and the whole or any part of its undertaking as a going concern*[10]. It was previously the case that only '*some prospect*' of survival was required[11]. Second, the old requirement that an examiner make an initial report before his final report has been abolished and replaced with the requirement that a *pre-petition report* prepared by an independent accountant[12] be presented with the petition. Third, in an attempt to mitigate the prejudice suffered by creditors secured by fixed security, expenses (such as 'borrowings') incurred by examiners no longer rank ahead of such creditors[13]. The C(A)(No 2)A 1999's provisions on examinerships, contained in Part II of that Act, were brought into operation on 1 February 2000[14].

---

7 See Donnelly, 'Is There A Case For Corporate Rescue?' (1994) CLP 8.

8 *Report of the Company Law Review Group*, December 1994 at para 2.12.

9 Specifically repealed were ss 3(3)(b), (c), 14, 15, 16 and 17 of the C(A)A 1990.

10 As replaced by s 5(b) of the C(A)(No 2)A 1999. See para **[22.020]**.

11 *Re Atlantic Magnetics Ltd* [1993] 2 IR 561 at 572, 573. There Finlay CJ adopted the following test: 'It seems to me that the standard is this: does the evidence lead to the conclusion that in all the circumstances it appears worthwhile to order an investigation by the examiner into the company's affairs and see can it survive, there being some prospect of survival?'

12 See para **[22.036]**.

13 Section 29(3A) of the C(A)A 1990. See para **[22.085]**.

14 Companies (Amendment) (No 2) Act 1999 (Commencement) Order 1999 (SI 406/1999).

The purpose of the legislation

[22.005] The intention of the C(A)A 1990 is to provide a procedure for the rescue and return to financial health of ailing but potentially viable companies[15]. Section 2(2) of the C(A)A 1990[16] provides the key to the appointment of an examiner. It provides, unambiguously, that the court 'shall not make an order under this section unless it is satisfied that there is a reasonable prospect of the survival of the company and the whole or any part of its undertaking as a going concern'. In *Re Atlantic Magnetics Ltd*[17], McCarthy J stated the purpose of the Act in the following passage:

> 'It is, I believe, of great importance to bear in mind in the application of the Act that its purpose is protection – protection of the company and consequently of its shareholders, workforce and creditors. It is clear that parliament intended that the fate of the company and those who depend on it should not lie solely in the hands of one or more large creditors who can by appointing a receiver pursuant to a debenture effectively terminate its operation and secure as best they may the discharge of the monies due to them to the inevitable disadvantage of those less protected. The Act is to provide a breathing space albeit at the expense of some creditor or creditors[18].'

It is salutary to remember that Finlay CJ in the Supreme Court held that it is appropriate to approach the construction of any sections in the C(A)A 1990 on the basis that the two objectives of the legislature were to provide a period of protection for a company and that a company should be continued as a going concern[19].

[22.006] Upon the appointment of an examiner, the company is placed under the protection of the court. During the period of protection, s 5 of the C(A)A 1990 provides, *inter alia*, that no proceedings may be instituted against the company, whether against the company's assets or to wind up the company. Court protection lasts for an initial period of 70 days but this can be extended by the court for an additional 30 days. The examiner's main function is to propose a scheme of arrangement to the court, which if approved by the court, and supported by a majority of creditors, becomes binding.

[22.007] In this chapter, examiners and court protection are considered under the following headings:

[A] The appointment of an examiner: presenting the petition.

[B] The effects of court protection.

[C] The position of creditors.

[D] The powers of examiners.

[E] The examiner's report and schemes of arrangement.

[F] The examiner's remuneration, costs and expenses.

---

15 See the comments of the then Minister for Industry and Commerce, Desmond O'Malley at 126 *Seanad Debates* 1060.

16 As amended by s 5(b) of the C(A)(No 2)A 1999.

17 *Re Atlantic Magnetics Ltd* [1993] 2 IR 561.

18 *Re Atlantic Magnetics Ltd* [1993] 2 IR 561 at 578.

19 *Re Holidair Ltd* [1994] 1 ILRM 481 at 487.

[A] The Appointment of an Examiner: Presenting the Petition

[22.008] Here, the following matters associated with the appointment of an examiner are considered:

1. The jurisdiction to appoint an examiner: presenting the petition.
2. *Locus standi* to petition the court and be heard on the petition.
3. The grounds for appointing an examiner.
4. The petition and grounding affidavit.
5. The pre-petition report from an independent accountant.
6. Interim protection pending the submission of a pre-petition report.
7. Presenting the petition.
8. The hearing of the petition.
9. Related companies.
10. Formalities in the appointment of an examiner.
11. The commencement of protection.

The jurisdiction to appoint an examiner: presenting the petition

[22.009] Although all petitions to have an examiner appointed must be presented to the High Court[20], the High Court may remit the matter to the Circuit Court under s 3(9) of the C(A)A 1990 where it appears that the total liabilities of the company, including contingent and prospective liabilities, do not exceed €317,434. The appropriate circuit will be the circuit in which the company has its registered office. Where such an order is made, the Circuit Court has full jurisdiction to exercise all the powers of the court conferred by the Act in relation to the company[21]. If, on being remitted to the Circuit Court, it subsequently appears that the total liabilities of the company exceed €317,434, the Circuit Court is obliged to remit the matter back to the High Court after making such interim orders as it thinks fit[22].

[22.010] The C(A)A 1990 is silent as to what companies may be placed under the protection of the court. Because the Companies Acts are to be construed together, regard must be had to s 2 of the CA 1963 and its definition of a 'company'. Accordingly, all companies formed and registered under the Companies Acts and former Acts may be the subject of an application to have an examiner appointed. As shall be considered later, application can be made under s 4 of the C(A)A 1990 to have a *related company* placed under the protection of the court. The scope of this jurisdiction is wider than that contained in s 2 of the CA 1963 and for the purposes of s 4 of the C(A)A 1990,

20 RSC (SI 147/1991), Ord 75A, r 2 provides that all applications and proceedings in relation to examiners must be assigned to such judge or judges as the President of the High Court shall from time to time nominate to hear such. Where a nominated judge is unavailable, any judge may dispose of any such application.

21 Section 3(9)(b) of the C(A)A 1990.

22 Section 3(9)(c) of the C(A)A 1990.

'company' includes any body which is liable to be wound up under the Companies Acts[23].

Section 36(1) of the C(A)A 1990 provides that any order made by a court of any country recognised for the purposes of that section[24], and made for or in the course of the reorganisation or reconstruction of a company[25], may be enforced by the High Court in all respects as if the order had been made by the High Court. Where an application is made under s 36(1) to the High Court, an office copy of any order sought to be enforced is deemed to be sufficient evidence of the order[26].

Locus standi to petition the court and be heard on the petition

[22.011] Just as in the case of the presentation of a petition to have a company wound up, s 3 of the C(A)A 1990 sets out a list of those persons who may present a petition to have an examiner appointed and a company placed under the protection of the court. The *company* itself can present a petition to have an examiner appointed[27]. An ordinary resolution of the members will suffice, although support permitting, in view of the far-reaching effects, a special resolution of the members should be procured where possible. The resolution of the members may be exhibited with their verifying affidavit to have the company placed under the protection of the court.

[22.012] The *directors* of the company can also present a petition to have an examiner appointed[28]. To date, company directors have proven to be the most usual petitioners. Because the directors are given *locus standi* to present a petition, those who may petition to have a company placed under the protection of the court differ from those who may petition to have it wound up compulsorily[29]. It has been held in *Re Don Bluth Entertainment Ltd (No 1)*[30] that once there is a valid resolution of the directors of a company in favour of the presentation of a petition, one or all of them can present the

23 Section 4(6) of the C(A)A 1990. See para **[22.052]**. *Cf Re Tuskar Resources plc* [2001] 1 IR 668 (McCracken J) where it was held that a 'related company' in s 4(5) of the C(A)A 1990 did not include a company registered outside the State.

24 A 'recognised' country is one recognised by order made by the Minister for Jobs, Enterprise and Innovation: s 36(3) of the C(A)A 1990. See D*allhold Estates (UK) Pty Ltd* [1992] BCLC 621 where the High Court in the UK held that it had jurisdiction to make an order against an overseas company.

25 A 'company', in this context, means a body corporate incorporated outside the State: s 36(3) of the C(A)A 1990.

26 Section 36(2) of the C(A)A 1990. On foreign proceedings against a company under administration by virtue of the UK Insolvency Act 1986, see *Barclays Bank plc v Homan* [1993] BCLC 680.

27 Section 3(1)(a) of the C(A)A 1990.

28 Section 3(1)(b) of the C(A)A 1990. See, for example, *Re Maxwell Communication Corporation* [1992] BCLC 465.

29 See Ch 23, *Winding up Companies*, para **[23.037]** *et seq* and *Re Galway and Salthill Tramways Co* [1918] 1 IR 62.

30 *Re Don Bluth Entertainment Ltd (No 1)* (27 August 1992, unreported) HC *per* Murphy J. See also *Don Bluth Entertainment Ltd (No 2)* [1994] 3 IR 141.

petition[31]. Here too, the resolution of the directors can be exhibited with their verifying affidavit. The directors' resolution to petition the court must take place at a properly convened board meeting. In *Re Cavan Crystal Glass Ltd*[32], Kelly J noted the submission that a directors' petition was required to be presented by all of a company's directors, but expressed no view one way or the other. It is thought that a majority of the directors will suffice.

[22.013] In *Re Aston Colour Print Ltd*[33], a petition was presented which represented that a board resolution had been passed unanimously. Kelly J found that not only had no resolution, formal or informal, been passed by the board but neither had the meeting referred to been a board meeting. In this case, management meetings had been informal affairs attended by directors and non-directors alike; at these meetings no formal vote was usually taken, the participants preferring to see a consensus reached. As a result of his finding, Kelly J concluded that the petition had been improperly presented to the court and must be struck out, the interim examiner being discharged[34]. Where irregularity is of a technical nature, it is open to the court to cure it, and where it transpires that a person was not a director of a company at a particular time it is open to the court to allow him proceed in his own name and as a shareholder of the company[35].

[22.014] The *creditors* of the company are also given *locus standi* to present a petition[36]. The C(A)A 1990 specifies that contingent or prospective creditors[37], including employees of the company, can also present a petition. A contingent or prospective creditor's petition shall not be heard by the court until such security for costs has been given as the court thinks reasonable[38]. In practice, creditors have been very slow to petition the court to have an examiner appointed to a company.

[22.015] The *members* of the company may also petition to have the company placed under the protection of the court[39]. This right to petition is granted to members *qua* member, where such members hold, at the date of the presentation of the petition, not less than one-tenth of the paid-up capital of the company as carries, at that date, the right to vote at general meetings. In many private companies there will be a duplication between the categories of petitioner. In particular, the categories of company, directors and members will often overlap. Furthermore, a petition may be presented by any of the foregoing parties, either together or separately. In *Re Cavan Crystal Glass Ltd*[40], the original petitioners purported to be its directors but, on account of an irregularity, it was impossible for the petition to proceed on such a basis. One of the directors then sought

---

31 See *Re Equiticorp International plc* [1989] BCLC 597. *Cf Re Instrumentation Electrical Services Ltd* [1988] BCLC 550, although it should be noted that there a petition to have a company wound up was presented without any formal resolution of the board of directors.

32 *Re Cavan Crystal Glass Ltd* [1998] 3 IR 570.

33 *Aston Colour Print Ltd* (21 February 1997, unreported) HC, Kelly J.

34 See further Ch 14, *Corporate Governance: Meetings*, at **[14.109]**.

35 *Re Cavan Crystal Glass Ltd* [1998] 3 IR 591 at 593 (O'Flaherty J).

36 Section 3(1)(c) of the C(A)A 1990.

37 See Ch 23, *Winding up Companies*, para **[23.040]** *et seq*.

38 Section 3(5) of the C(A)A 1990.

39 Section 3(1)(d) of the C(A)A 1990.

40 *Re Cavan Crystal Glass Ltd* [1998] 3 IR 570.

for his name to be substituted for those of the initial petitioners and the petition presented by him as a members' petition by reason of the fact that he held in excess of 10% of the share capital of the company. This was objected to but Kelly J found that the petitioner could rely upon Ord 28, r 12 of the Rules of the Superior Courts 1986[41] and s 3(7) of the C(A)A 1990, and the court would cure the irregularity. On this point Kelly J said:

> 'There is no evidence to controvert the assertion made by [the petitioning member] to the effect that the failure to present this petition as a shareholder holding in excess of 10% of the capital of the company was a bona fide one. It is clear that this petition had to be prepared and presented as a matter of considerable urgency. I accept that the error made was a genuine one. In such circumstances it would be strange indeed if the court did not have the power to put right such an error. I am of the view that it does have such power under the provisions of Order 28, Rule 12 and s 3(7) of the Act.
>
> Needless to say, the Court must always be astute to ensure that its process is not abused. This is particularly so in petitions presented under the Act. The mere presentation of a petition in the Central Office of this court provides statutory protection to the company. No judicial determination is required for that protection to be afforded. Given that such protection brings about a drastic abridgement to the rights of creditors, the court must make certain that this procedure is not abused … Great care should therefore be given to the presentation of petitions under the Act. In the present case, however, I am satisfied that a genuine mistake was made and I therefore propose to allow the amendments sought[42].'

In that case, Kelly J went on to say that the amendment did not involve the substitution of new petitioners for the existing ones and merely changed the description applicable to one of the initial petitioners as petitioner.

[22.016] Special provisions apply to certain types of financial companies. In the case of an insurance company, only the Minister for Jobs, Enterprise and Innovation can present a petition to have an examiner appointed[43]. Only the Central Bank of Ireland has standing to present a petition in respect of certain companies such as banks[44]. In the case of a company referred to in Sch 2 of the C(A)(No 2)A 1999[45], certain other provisions apply[46]. First, those with *locus standi* are the company, its directors, creditors or members[47], the Central Bank or one or more of such persons and the Central Bank of Ireland acting together. Second, if the Central Bank does not present such a petition,

---

[41] Order 28, r 12 of the RSC 1986 provides: 'The court may at any time, and on such terms as to costs or otherwise as the court may think just, amend any defect or error in any proceedings, and all necessary amendments shall be made for the purpose of determining the real question or issue raised by or depending on the proceedings.'

[42] *Re Cavan Crystal Glass Ltd* [1998] 3 IR 570 at 581–582.

[43] Section 3(2)(a) of the C(A)A 1990.

[44] Section 3(2)(b) of the C(A)A 1990 provides that a petition can only be presented by the Central Bank of Ireland in the case of certain companies, such as the holder of a licence under the s 9 of the Central Bank Act 1971 and a company which was a building society.

[45] Excepting companies referred to in Sch 2, paras 18–20 of the C(A)(No 2)A 1999 or to which s 3(2)(b) of the C(A)A 1990 applies. The Second Schedule is reproduced in the Appendix to this work.

[46] Section 3(2)(c) of the C(A)A 1990.

[47] See para **[22.011]** *et seq, ante.*

prior to presenting the petition, the petitioner must give prior written notice to the Central Bank of his intention to present the petition and must, subsequent to presenting the petition, serve a copy thereof on the Central Bank. Moreover, the Central Bank shall be entitled to appear and be heard at any hearing relating to the petition.

[22.017] Section 3B(1) of the C(A)A 1990[48] provides that the court shall not make an order dismissing a petition presented under s 2 or an order appointing an examiner to a company without having afforded each creditor of the company who has indicated to the court his desire to be heard in the matter an opportunity to be so heard. This is without prejudice to the court's power under s 3(7) to make an interim order[49].

The grounds for appointing an examiner

(a) The test for the appointment of an examiner

[22.018] Section 2(1) of the C(A)A 1990[50] provides that:

> 'Subject to subsection (2), where it appears to the court that—
>
> (a) a company is or is likely to be unable to pay its debts, and
>
> (b) no resolution subsists for the winding-up of the company, and
>
> (c) no order has been made for the winding-up of the company,
>
> it may, on application by petition presented, appoint an examiner to the company for the purpose of examining the state of the company's affairs and performing such duties in relation to the company as may be imposed by or under this Act.'

This subsection sets out the general prerequisites which must exist before the court can appoint an examiner to a failing company. It is a prerequisite that the company in respect of which an application is made is neither perfectly solvent nor in the course of being wound up. Accordingly, the company must be ailing but not to the extent that it has been resolved to wind up the company. If an order has been made to wind up the company, it will be too late for the court to accede to an application to have the company placed under its protection. It will not, however, be fatal to an application that a petition has been presented to have a company wound up.

A company is deemed to be unable to pay its debts if: it is unable to pay its debts as they fall due; the value of its assets is less than the amount of its liabilities, taking into account both contingent and prospective liabilities; or where s 214(a) or (b) of the CA 1963 apply to the company[51]. It is not necessary that the company must be unable to pay its debts at the time of presentation of the petition to have an examiner appointed. Rather, it is sufficient that it is likely to be unable to pay its debts in the future. This permits the court to accede to an application where the petitioner can point to some future circumstance which is likely to result in the company's insolvency. Further guidance to the court is provided by s 2(4) of the C(A)A 1990 which says that in deciding whether or not to make an order, the court may also have regard to whether the company has sought from its creditors significant extensions of time for the payment of

48 Inserted by s 10 of the C(A)(No 2)A 1999.

49 Section 3B(2) of the C(A)A 1990.

50 As amended by s 5 of the C(A)(No 2)A 1999.

51 Section 2(3) of the C(A)A 1990. As to s 214 of the CA 1963, see Ch 23, *Winding up Companies*, para **[23.073]** *et seq*.

its debts, from which it could reasonably be inferred that the company was likely to be unable to pay its debts.

[22.019] Section 2(1) of the C(A)A 1990 is a general power and does not, of itself, give much guidance to either petitioners or to the court. Prior to its amendment[52] s 2(2) of the C(A)A 1990 provided that the court may make an order if it considered that such would be likely to facilitate the survival of the company and the whole or any part of its undertaking as a going concern. What was previously intended as guidance is now mandatory and this has 'raised the bar' for petitioners. The revised s 2(2) of the C(A)A 1990 now provides:

> 'The court shall not make an order under this section unless it is satisfied that there is a reasonable prospect of the survival of the company and the whole or any part of its undertaking as a going concern[53].'

This is a stricter test. Now, the court cannot appoint an examiner *unless* there is a *reasonable* prospect of the survival of the company itself *and* the whole or any part of its undertaking. This revision was made because of the fact that the appointment of an examiner to an insolvent company, even for a short period of time, is likely to result in the incurring of considerable cost and expense to the company. If the company cannot be salvaged, the already ill-fated creditors are likely to have their losses compounded.

(b) The need to show a 'reasonable prospect of survival of the company'

[22.020] Prior to the revision of s 2(2) of the C(A)A 1990, the leading authority on the test for the appointment of an examiner was the Supreme Court decision in *Re Atlantic Magnetics Ltd*[54]. The statutory revision of s 2(2) has effectively reversed that decision. There, Finlay CJ had said:

> 'The basic purpose of the appointment of an examiner is to do precisely what the word involves, *examine* the situation, affairs and prospects of the company.
>
> Having regard to these considerations, it is quite clear that there cannot be on a petitioner seeking an order for the appointment of an examiner an onus of proof to establish as a matter of probability that the company is capable of survival as a going concern[55].'

He therefore rejected that a petitioner must establish to the satisfaction of a court that there is 'a real prospect of survival of the company', saying:

> 'I accept that for a court to consider that there was a likelihood that an order would facilitate the survival of the company involves it in some evaluation as to the chances of the company surviving. The real importance of such an evaluation at the stage of the petition for the appointment of an examiner goes no further than that a court should be

---

52 The former s 2(2) of the C(A)A 1990 provided: 'Without prejudice to the general power of the court under sub-section (1), it may, in particular, make an order under this section if it considers that such order would be likely to facilitate the survival of the company, and the whole or any part of its undertaking, as a going concern.'

53 As replaced by s 5(b) of the C(A)(No2)A 1999.

54 *Re Atlantic Magnetics Ltd* [1993] 2 IR 561.

55 *Re Atlantic Magnetics Ltd* [1993] 2 IR 561 at 572.

> very slow indeed to make an order pursuant to either of the subsections of s 2, where it considers that there is no identifiable prospect of the survival of a company[56].'

The test adopted by Finlay CJ is now obsolete[57]. The Supreme Court's concern that it would have sufficient information upon which to decide whether there was a prospect of survival has been met by the requirement for a pre-petition report, also introduced by the C(A)(No 2)A 1999. Now, as a matter of law, a petitioner must show some justification for the appointment of an examiner.

[22.021] The foregoing views are supported by the decision of the High Court in *Re Tuskar Resources plc*[58], which was the first written decision on the appointment of an examiner since the changes effected by the C(A)(No 2)A 1999 were commenced. In this case, McCracken J analysed the changes effected to the test for the appointment of an examiner. He said that the new test in s 2(2) of the C(A)A 1990 was more in keeping with the decision of Lardner J in *Atlantic Magnetics* than with the decision of the Supreme Court. He also noted that the legislature did not accept the view of McCarthy J that no real decision could be reached on the question of survival until an examiner had been in place for some weeks and it was now clear that a decision must be made at the initial stages. Comparing the new test with the old test McCracken J said:

> 'In the *Atlantic Magnetics* case Finlay CJ also stated that there cannot be an onus of proof on a petitioner to establish as a matter of probability that the company is capable of surviving as a going concern. It seems to me that this is no longer the position under the 1999 Act by reason of the wording of the new subsection 2(2). Under [the C(A)A 1990] as originally enacted there would appear to be a wide discretion given to the Court. However, the new subsection prohibits the court from making an order unless it is satisfied there is a reasonable prospect of survival. If the court is to be "*satisfied*", it must be satisfied on the evidence before it, which is in the first instance the evidence of the petitioner. If that evidence does not satisfy the court, the order cannot be made, and in my view this is tantamount to saying that there is an onus of proof on the petitioner at the initial stage to satisfy the court that there is a reasonable prospect of survival. For this reason, the court has to view the evidence in a different manner to that applicable prior to the [C(A)(No 2)A 1999][59].'

After reviewing the evidence McCracken J declined to appoint an examiner because he was not satisfied that there was a reasonable prospect of the survival of the company and

---

56 *Re Atlantic Magnetics Ltd* [1993] 2 IR 561 at 572.

57 The test he had adopted was a modification of that put forward by Lardner J in the High Court. It provided: 'In some cases the evidence may make it clear that survival of the company is not a practical possibility and the order is likely to be refused. In other cases the evidence may give a strong possibility of requisite adjustment. With requisite adjustment the company will survive and prosper therein. Here, it may be clearly possible to make an order appointing the examiner. In other cases, such as the present, the evidence may not lead to a clear cut conclusion.There may, as here, be a conflict of evidence on matters concerning the company's affairs – in such a case by what standards should the court make its decision? It seems to me that the standard is this: does the evidence lead to the conclusion that in all the circumstances it appears worthwhile to order an investigation by the examiner into the company's affairs and see can it survive, there being some prospect of survival?'

58 *Re Tuskar Resources plc* [2001] 1 IR 668.

59 *Re Tuskar Resources plc* [2001] 1 IR 668 at 676.

the whole and or any part of its undertaking as a going concern. Several reasons were given, which included, that the company was purely a holding company that he held did not have an undertaking[60].

[22.022] The most authoritative pronouncement by the Supreme Court on the new test following the changes effected by the C(A)(No 2)A 1999 is in *Re Vantive Holdings and Ors*[61]. There, Murray CJ said:

> '... for the purpose of deciding whether a petitioner has satisfied the Court as to the first step in the test it is not sufficient for a petitioner to simply demonstrate that the assets of the company could be disposed of in a more orderly fashion to the benefit of its creditors since the provisions of subsection (2) preclude that as a sufficient test at that stage. Equally the fact that liquidation might be a far less attractive option from the point of view of the members of the company or its creditors is not sufficient to meet the test laid down in subsection (2) nor is the fact that the chances of the company surviving being simply better than an inevitable collapse following liquidation sufficient to meet the test. In order to be satisfied that a company has a reasonable prospect of survival as a going concern the Court must have before it sufficient evidence or material which will permit it to arrive at such a conclusion on the basis of an objective appraisal of that evidence or material. Mere assertions on behalf of a petitioner that a company has a reasonable prospect of survival as a going concern cannot be given significant weight unless it is supported by an objective appraisal of the circumstances of the company concerned and an objective rationale as to the manner in which the company can be reasonably expected to overcome the insolvency in which it finds itself and survive as a going concern.
>
> The opinion of the independent accountant as set out in the report which a petitioner is required to provide to the Court under the provisions of the Act, must be given due weight. Again, the weight to be attached to the accountant's opinion will depend on the degree and extent to which he supports that opinion by his or her own objective reasoning and the appraisal of material or factors relied upon for reaching his or her conclusions.
>
> Since, the court may not make an order appointing an examiner unless it is satisfied that there is a reasonable prospect of the survival of the company as a going concern, it follows that there is an onus on the appellant to satisfy the court that such a reasonable prospect exists. The applicant must provide objective evidence to satisfy the court of this fact. Examinership is a process designed to facilitate the rescue or survival of companies in financial difficulties. Whether the appointment of an examiner is supported by creditors of the company and the extent and reasons for that support is a relevant consideration but not determinative in considering whether there is a reasonable prospect of survival.'

It is not necessary to show that the company will *probably* survive. This was made clear by Fennelly J in the Supreme Court in *Re Gallium Ltd*[62] and also in *Re Vantive Holdings and Ors*[63], where Murray CJ said:

> 'It is not necessary, at the stage of application for the appointment of the examiner to show that the company will probably survive. The period of protection is designed to provide a "breathing space," during which the company will be protected from actions by its creditors, particularly a petition for winding up. The period of protection is short. It is

[60] See para **[22.027]**.

[61] *Re Vantive Holdings and Ors* [2009] IESC 68.

[62] *Re Gallium Ltd* [2009] IESC 8. See also *Re Slyne Properties Ltd* [2010] IEHC 37, McGovern J.

[63] *Re Vantive Holdings and Ors* [2009] IESC 68.

intended to enable the examiner, if appointed, to look into the financial state of the company.'

[22.023] Just because it has been established that there is a reasonable prospect of survival, does not mean that a petition will invariably succeed. The court retains a broad discretion as Murray CJ said in *Re Vantive Holdings and Ors*[64]:

> 'The fact, if established, that there is a reasonable prospect of survival of the company does not lead automatically to the appointment of the examiner. It merely triggers the power. The court retains a broad discretion. The court may consider whether one or more creditors will suffer prejudice as a result of the appointment of an examiner. The interests of the employees of the company and of employment generally may also be relevant. The independent accountant is required by section 3B(g) of the Act as amended to express his opinion as to whether "an attempt to continue the whole or any part of the undertaking would be likely to be more advantageous to the members as a whole and the creditors as a whole than a winding-up of the company." Thus it must be relevant to the exercise of the court's discretion to consider the effects of the alternatives of an examinership and of a winding-up. It is not possible to envisage every circumstance which may bear on the exercise of the court's discretion. The above are but a number of examples.'

In *Re Gallium Ltd*[65], this same point was made by Fennelly J:

> 'A petitioner does not, by getting over that threshold, acquire a right to have an order made. I think it is fair to say that the section confers a "wide discretion" on the court, or alternatively, that the court should take account of all the circumstances. The establishment of a reasonable prospect of the survival of the power merely triggers the power, which remains discretionary.'

In *Re Missford Ltd t/a Residence Members Club*[66], Kelly J reluctantly accepted that the only evidence proffered indicated a reasonable prospect of survival and so he accepted that this threshold proof had been met. Referring to his discretion, as seen in the passage of the decision of Fennelly J quoted above, Kelly J noted that in exercising that discretion he was entitled to take all of the circumstances into account, and he exercised his discretion against appointing an examiner. Among the reasons given for refusing to appoint an examiner was that the business of the company from its inception had been carried on with scant regard for its obligations under company law and to the Revenue Commissioners such that an enquiry into whether there was evidence of reckless or fraudulent trading would be justified although in reality this could not be possible in an examinership. Kelly J also said the effect of appointing an examiner would not be that the company would continue to trade profitably but that it would *commence* trading profitably! Kelly J was singularly unimpressed with the conduct of the company's directors and said:

> 'There must come a time when companies that have flouted the obligations of company law, revenue and their obligations to employees should not be allowed to call in aid the very legislation that they have ignored so as to save the enterprise. Still less should it be allowed when it has or is likely to have the beneficial effect for delinquent directors that I have referred to earlier in this part of the judgment. This is such a case.'

---

64 *Re Vantive Holdings and Ors* [2009] IESC 68.

65 *Re Gallium Ltd* [2009] IESC 8.

66 *Re Missford Ltd t/a Residence Members Club* [2010] IEHC 11.

In *Re Eircom Ltd*[67], proposals to restructure had already been the subject of intense discussions and had been voted on by various classes of creditors. Evidence was heard that an examinership would give a better outcome for creditors than either a receivership or a winding up. Kelly J stressed the fact that the order under s 2 of the C(A)A 1990 was a *discretionary* order, before going on to make the order giving court protection.

[22.024] In *Re Tivway Ltd*[68], Denham J said that the foundation upon which all orders may be made is that there is a firm policy by the Oireachtas that a court does not have jurisdiction to make an order appointing an examiner unless satisfied that there is a reasonable prospect of the survival of the company and the whole or any part of its undertaking as a going concern. In that case, the Supreme Court allowed an appeal against the High Court order approving a scheme of arrangement because it was found that it did not provide for the survival of each of the companies *as a going concern* as required by s 2(2) of the C(A)A 1990. There, Denham J found that central to the scheme was the survival of the companies – selling off the productive part of one company and keeping the sites in a land bank for 10 years in the hope of a recovery in the property market – but not *as a going concern*. Denham J gave a colourful description of what was proposed to be done in the following terms:

> 'The schemes of arrangement are analogous to a planned holding pattern for three airplanes ordered by the control tower of an airport, where it is ordered that three planes maintain a holding pattern over a specified area, at a specific height, until, say, the weather improves, at which time they will be permitted to land. By analogy, the three schemes of arrangement envisage a holding situation hovering over the property market, then if the property market improves, *and* if they have the support of the banks, they will be permitted to continue business. Failing an improved property market, or support of the banks, they will land in 10 years and the scrappage will be divided. This is not a plan for survival of the three companies as a going concern.'

[22.025] The support of a company's bank for the appointment of an examiner may indicate a belief by the bank that the company has a reasonable prospect of survival. However, as Clarke J said in *Re Vantive Holdings (No 2) Ltd*[69] and repeated in *Re McInerney Homes Ltd*[70] it does not necessarily follow from the fact that a bank may support an examinership that the bank truly believes that the company has a reasonable prospect of survival. As Clarke J said, distinguishing a bank from an investor:

> 'Rather the bank may simply take the view that a restructuring in examinership might lead it to having to suffer a reduced hit when the company ultimately succumbs. However, the same equation does not seem to me to apply in respect of an investor. While there can be circumstances in which an investor may take over a company with a view, not to its long term survival but rather in order that its more profitable parts be broken up and sold, it nonetheless logically follows that an investor can only make a profit if some elements of the company concerned are found to be capable of surviving on an on-going basis, unless, of course, there are sufficient saleable assets within the company which could be realised so as to leave the company with a surplus at the end of the day.'

---

67 *Re Eircom Ltd* [2012] IEHC 158.

68 *Re Tivway Ltd* [2010] IESC 11.

69 *Re Vantive Holdings (No 2) Ltd* [2009] IEHC 409.

70 *Re McInerney Homes Ltd* [2010] IEHC 340.

In that case, Clarke J went on to infer that the fact that the investor was willing to put a substantial investment into a company shows that it viewed the component parts of the company as being likely to be viable into the future.

(c) The need to show a 'reasonable prospect of survival of the whole or any part of its undertaking as a going concern'

[22.026] Not only must there be a reasonable prospect of the survival of the company, but so too must there also be a reasonable prospect of the survival of the whole or any *part of its undertaking* as a going concern. In the context of the old s 2(2), in *Re Clare Textiles Ltd*[71] Costello J said that the examiner in that case could only have come to the conclusion that the company alone was capable of survival: the undertaking of the company was not since the examiner proposed to sell the company's business and assets[72]. In *Re Fergus Haynes (Developments) Ltd*[73], Laffoy J held that the fact that a company had not traded for the four months preceding the petition to appoint an examiner did not mean that it was not operating as a going concern and in such circumstances the court did have jurisdiction to make an order under s 2 of the C(A)A 1990.

[22.027] In *Re Tuskar Resources plc*[74], McCracken J expressed the view that an examiner cannot be appointed to a company that is purely a holding company because such a company has no undertaking to continue as a going concern. He said of the company under scrutiny:

> 'Its only undertaking is the holding of shares in the Nigerian company, and I do not think that under any circumstances that could be called "a going concern". It seems to me that the wording of the Act precludes the court from making an order appointing an examiner to a holding company simpliciter, and that indeed to do so, particularly in the circumstances of this case, would be totally contrary to the objects of the Act. The Act is intended to give a breathing space to try to get the affairs of an insolvent company put in order. This is frequently to the detriment of some creditors, particularly secured creditors, but the legislature has considered that their interest may sometimes have to suffer if there would be a general benefit to other creditors, to the shareholders, and to the employees of the company. However, these considerations are unlikely to apply to a pure holding company[75].'

McCracken J went on to make it clear that the foregoing did not mean that a holding company could never have an examiner appointed and that under s 4 of the C(A)A 1990 a holding company (as a related company) could have an examiner appointed where an examiner had been appointed to one of its subsidiaries.

---

71 *Re Clare Textiles Ltd* [1993] 2 IR 213.

72 *Re Edenpark Construction Ltd* [1994] 3 IR 126, where Murphy J commented that it was important that some entity or business should be preserved. On the Insolvency Act 1986 (UK), see *Re Harris Simons Construction Ltd* [1989] BCLC 202 and *Re Primlaks (UK) Ltd* [1989] BCLC 734.

73 *Re Fergus Haynes (Developments) Ltd* [2008] IEHC 327.

74 *Re Tuskar Resources plc* [2001] 1 IR 668.

75 *Re Tuskar Resources plc* [2001] 1 IR 668 at 679.

(d) Companies with obligations to NAMA

[22.028] Section 2(5) of the C(A)A 1990, which was inserted by s 234 of the National Asset Management Agency Act 2009 ('NAMAA 2009')[76], provides:

> The court shall not make an order under this section unless—
>
> (a) the court is satisfied that the company has no obligations in relation to a bank asset that has been transferred to the National Asset Management Agency or a NAMA group entity, or
>
> (b) if the company has any such obligation—
>
> (i) a copy of the petition has been served on that Agency, and
>
> (ii) the court has heard that Agency in relation to the making of the order.

'NAMA group entity' and 'bank asset' have the same meanings as they have in the NAMAA 2009[77]. The effect is where NAMA has acquired an interest in a loan that was held by banks which are participating institutions under the NAMAA 2009, a company which is a borrower under that loan (or under security, such as a guarantee or surety mortgage, for that loan) cannot have an examiner appointed to it unless NAMA has been served with the petition to appoint an examiner *and* NAMA has been heard in relation to the making of the order. This does not preclude such companies from going into examinership; rather, it affords NAMA with a say in the application and allows it to voice its position.

The petition and grounding affidavit

[22.029] The petition to have an examiner appointed should be accompanied by a grounding affidavit from the petitioner[78]. Typically, the petition will be extensive, making detailed disclosures of all relevant matters to the court. Having averred to the petitioner's *locus standi*, the affidavit should give as full and detailed a history of the company as is possible. The company's difficulties and insolvency and the causes of insolvency should also be set out. Furthermore, a full and detailed list of the company's creditors, both secured and unsecured, and preferential debtors should be disclosed. Where proposals for a compromise or scheme of arrangement in relation to the company's affairs have been prepared for submission to interested parties for their approval, a copy of these proposals should accompany the petition[79]. Such proposals, if any, should now be referred to in the accompanying pre-petition report[80].

[22.030] The petition should also nominate a person to be appointed as examiner[81]. Furthermore, the proposed examiner must consent to his or her appointment[82]. In practice, an affidavit of fitness for the nominee to act as examiner will accompany the petition. Often, this will be sworn by another insolvency practitioner, such as an accountant or a solicitor.

---

76 Part 4 of Schedule 3 of the NAMAA 2009.

77 Section 2(6) of the C(A)A 1990.

78 See Ord 75A, r 3 of the RSC, as inserted by SI 27/1990.

79 Section 3(4)(b) of the C(A)A 1990.

80 See para **[22.036]**.

81 Section 3(3)(a) of the C(A)A 1990.

82 Section 3(4)(a) of the C(A)A 1990.

[22.031] As to who is qualified to act as an examiner, McCracken J held in *Re Tuskar Resources plc*[83] that there was no bar on the person who provides the independent person's report from acting as examiner. Whilst the learned judge said he had considerable sympathy with the contention that on the general basis that justice must be seen to be done, there can be a question mark over how independent an accountant can be if the purpose of his report is to determine whether he personally should or should not be appointed examiner. McCracken J said:

> 'It should be noted that in *Re Wogans (Drogheda) Ltd (No 3)*[84] Costello J held that the court would be very slow to appoint an accountant previously associated with the company as examiner, as his impartiality could be questioned. However, on the other side it can be argued that there would be considerable additional expense involved if two accountants had separately to investigate the prospects of the company, and there is also merit in that argument. In view of the fact that the legislature did not take on itself to prohibit the independent accountant from acting as examiner, I do not think that there is any statutory restriction on the court in so appointing him, although I can see there may be cases where it would be undesirable to do so[85].'

Whilst it would be preferable to have the examiner separate from the independent person, it is thought that the additional cost is too great a price, particularly since the company must be insolvent to qualify to have an examiner appointed.

[22.032] Where a petition is presented by either the company itself or its directors, it must include a statement of the assets and liabilities of the company, in so far as these are known, as they stand on a date not earlier than seven days before the presentation of the petition[86]. This requirement is confined to the directors and the company, presumably because it would be unfair to expect those not involved in the management of the company to have access to such details.

[22.033] Section 3(3)(b) of the C(A)A 1990 provides that a petition to have an examiner appointed shall:

> '... be supported by such evidence as the court may require for the purpose of showing that the petitioner has good reason for requiring the appointment of an examiner.'

Accordingly, a petitioner must both show that the company is in immediate danger of failing and also identify how the appointment of an examiner may be able to reverse this process. To show that a receiver has been appointed, that secured creditors are about to take other steps to enforce their security or that any creditor is threatening to place the company into liquidation are examples of dangers facing the company. Where a company is placed under the protection of the court, these and other immediate dangers will be temporarily stopped. Essentially, the matters which a petitioner must show will depend upon the circumstances of each case[87].

---

83 *Re Tuskar Resources plc* [2001] 1 IR 668.

84 *Re Wogans (Drogheda) Ltd (No 3)* [1993] 1 IR 157.

85 *Re Wogans (Drogheda) Ltd (No 3)* [1993] 1 IR 157.

86 Section 3(3)(c) of the C(A)A 1990.

87 See O'Donnell, *Examinerships* (1994), p 4.

The petition must be made in the utmost of good faith

[22.034] The petition to have an examiner appointed and the grounding affidavit must be made *uberrimae fides*, that is, in the utmost of good faith. What was first decided by Costello J in *Re Wogans (Drogheda) Ltd (No 2)*[88] has now been given statutory force. Section 4A of the C(A)A 1990[89] provides:

> 'The court may decline to hear a petition presented under section 2 or, as the case may be, may decline to continue hearing such a petition if it appears to the court that, in the preparation or presentation of the petition or in the preparation of the report of the independent accountant, the petitioner or independent accountant —
>
> (a) has failed to disclose any information available to him which is material to the exercise by the court of its powers under this Act, or
>
> (b) has in any other way failed to exercise utmost good faith.'

Where it is discovered that the court has been misled, the entire application will be tainted. If this is discovered early in the proceedings, the examiner will be discharged where the lack of good faith is sufficiently serious[90]. Furthermore, the court will not hesitate to refuse to confirm any subsequent proposals made by the examiner where this is justified in the circumstances[91]. However, a lack of candour and good faith will not always result in a refusal to confirm an examiner's proposals. In *Re Selukwe Ltd*[92], Costello J found there was a considerable lack of good faith but was swayed by the fact that there were 30 jobs at stake and confirmed the examiner's proposals. Notwithstanding this, petitioners should exercise the same caution as is required in the case of an *ex parte* interlocutory injunction[93]. Similarly, in *Re Tuskar Resources plc*[94] McCracken J said that he did 'not think that over-optimism is sufficient to show bad faith, and in any event there is clearly a wide discretion in the court under the

---

88 *Re Wogans (Drogheda) Ltd (No 2)* (7 May 1992, unreported) HC, *per* Costello J. There he said (at pp 5–6 of the transcript): 'When an application is made by a company for a protection order under the C(A)A 1990, it seems to me that the directors and all those associated with the application (including their professional advisers) are obliged to exercise the utmost good faith and that such a duty exists not just on an *ex parte* application to appoint an interim examiner but also on the application itself. This is because (a) of necessity, the court must depend to a considerable extent on the truth of what it is told by the company and (b) because of the potential injustice involved in the making of a protection order when the proper course is to wind up the company. This duty involves an obligation to disclose all relevant facts material to the exercise by the court of its discretion. *A fortiori*, it involves a duty not to deliberately mislead the court by false evidence.'

89 Inserted by s 13 of the C(A)(No 2)A 1999.

90 See the Court of Appeal decision in *Cornhill Insurance plc v Cornhill Financial Services Ltd* [1993] BCLC 914 where it was held that there was jurisdiction to discharge an administration order where full disclosure was not made to the court on the initial application. On the facts of this case, it was held that there was no non-disclosure as the court had been told all it needed to know.

91 *Re Wogans (Drogheda) Ltd (No 2)* (7 May 1992, unreported) HC, *per* Costello J.

92 *Re Selukwe Ltd* (20 December 1991, unreported) HC, *per* Costello J.

93 See generally Courtney, *Mareva Injunctions and Related Interlocutory Orders* (1998), paras [8.32]–[8.44].

94 *Re Tuskar Resources plc* [2001] 1 IR 668.

subsection, as it uses the word "*may*" rather than "*shall*".' In that case, he exercised his discretion in favour of hearing the petition, notwithstanding that it was claimed that the original grounding affidavit was misleading and had failed to disclose material matters.

[22.035] In *Re Vantive Holdings*[95], the Supreme Court considered an appeal by a secured creditor – ACC Bank plc – to a High Court decision which gave leave to the petitioner to proceed with a second petition for examinership in relation to a property company controlled by Liam Carroll. The circumstances were that the first petition was dismissed because of a lack of evidence about the likely future development of the property market. Kelly J dismissed the petition because although he was told that valuations existed, they had not been placed in evidence. Cooke J subsequently heard a second petition. In the second petition, it was admitted that the reasons for not putting the valuations in evidence before Kelly J was a deliberate strategic decision, taken against legal advice, which was acknowledged to be mistaken. The reason was an alleged apprehension that the public disclosure of valuations attributable to specific properties would jeopardise the future prospect of realising their best prices in the future. Cooke J decided that the C(A)A 1990 did not preclude the presentation of the second petition. The Supreme Court, while holding that the C(A)A 1990 does not preclude the presentation of a second petition, disagreed with Cooke J's assessment in exercising his discretion that the 'overriding consideration' must be the legislative objective of securing, if feasible, the interests of the creditors, employees and those doing business with companies and of the economy as a whole by investigating any reasonable prospect of survival of the enterprise in whole or in part. Denham J said:

> 'To take a deliberate strategic decision to withhold evidence from the court (contrary to legal and financial advice) when moving the first petition for the protection of the companies by the appointment of an examiner, and, having lost, to seek then to go again with fundamentally the same petition but this time with the previously withheld evidence, is an abuse of the court's process. In the circumstances, the explanation by the petitioner is not such as to ground an exception to fundamental principles of the administration of justice.'

The pre-petition report from an independent accountant

[22.036] In addition to the introduction of a stricter test, the C(A)(No 2)A 1999 also introduced the new requirement that a *pre-petition report* prepared by an 'independent accountant' must accompany the petition. Section 3(3A) of the C(A)A 1990[96] requires that the independent accountant must be either the company's auditor or a person who is qualified to be appointed as an examiner of the company. Section 3(3B) of the C(A)A 1990 requires that the report of the independent accountant must comprise the following:

> '(a) the names and permanent addresses of the officers of the company and, in so far as the independent accountant can establish, any person in accordance with whose directions or instructions the directors of the company are accustomed to act,
>
> (b) the names of any other bodies corporate of which the directors of the company are also directors,

---

95 *Re Vantive Holdings* [2009] IESC 69.

96 Inserted by s 7 of the C(A)(No 2)A 1999.

(c) a statement as to the affairs of the company, showing in so far as it is reasonably possible to do so, particulars of the company's assets and liabilities (including contingent and prospective liabilities) as at the latest practicable date, the names and addresses of its creditors, the securities held by them respectively and the dates when the securities were respectively given,

(d) whether in the opinion of the independent accountant any deficiency between the assets and liabilities of the company has been satisfactorily accounted for or, if not, whether there is evidence of a substantial disappearance of property that is not adequately accounted for,

(e) his opinion as to whether the company, and the whole or any part of its undertaking, would have a reasonable prospect of survival as a going concern and a statement of the conditions which he considers are essential to ensure such survival, whether as regards the internal management and controls of the company or otherwise,

(f) his opinion as to whether the formulation, acceptance and confirmation of proposals for a compromise or scheme of arrangement would offer a reasonable prospect of survival of the company, and the whole or any part of its undertaking, as a going concern,

(g) his opinion as to whether an attempt to continue the whole or any part of the undertaking would be likely to be more advantageous to the members as a whole and the creditors as a whole than a winding-up of the company,

(h) recommendations as to the course he thinks should be taken in relation to the company including, if warranted, draft proposals for a compromise or scheme of arrangement,

(i) his opinion as to whether the facts disclosed would warrant further inquiries with a view to proceedings under section 297 or 297A of the 1963 Act,

(j) details of the extent of the funding required to enable the company to continue trading during the period of protection and the sources of that funding,

(k) his recommendations as to which liabilities incurred before the presentation of the petition should be paid,

(l) his opinion as to whether the work of the examiner would be assisted by a direction of the court in relation to the role or membership of any creditor's committee referred to in section 21, and

(m) such other matters as he thinks relevant.'

Although it had been the practice for some time for the court to require certain of this information to be brought to its attention on the presentation of a petition, that was an informal practice without force of law. It is now the case that, save in the exceptional circumstances next considered where interim protection may be granted, such information *must* be provided to the court on the hearing of a petition. As to the content of the report, in *Re Tuskar Resources plc*[97] McCracken J said that s 3(3) of the C(A)A 1990 does not say that the independent accountant must set out *in detail* the evidence which leads him to the opinion that the company and the whole or any part of its undertaking would have a reasonable prospect of survival as a going concern. McCracken J acknowledged that it could only be a preliminary opinion and that if he is appointed, an examiner will usually find out a great deal more about the company and its prospects.

[97] *Re Tuskar Resources plc* [2001] 1 IR 668.

[22.037] The independent accountant must supply a copy of the pre-petition report to the company and to any interested party upon receiving written application[98]. On application being made to the court, the court may direct that in supplying copies of the report, such parts of the report as it directs may be omitted; in particular, any information which would be likely to prejudice the survival of the company or the whole or any part of its undertaking as a going concern may be omitted[99]. In *Re Vantive Holdings*[100], the Supreme Court said in relation to an opinion in an independent accountant's report:

> '... the weight to be attached to the accountant's opinion will depend on the degree and extent to which he supports that opinion with his or her own objective reasoning and appraisal of material or factors relied upon for reaching his or her conclusions.'

[22.038] The court will not accept without question the contents of the independent accountant's report. In *Re Missford Ltd t/a Residence Members Club*[101], Kelly J said:

> 'The court is entitled to look critically at the independent accountant's opinion and analysis. It is the unfortunate experience of the court that in an ever increasing number of cases, optimistic expressions of opinion by independent accountants at this stage of an examinership are, about 60–70 days into such examinership, shown to have been far too optimistic and the examinership collapses.'

In that case, Kelly J noted that the company had never traded profitably and that he was highly sceptical of the expression of opinion that revenue would increase as such would run counter to what was then actually happening in the hospitality sector of the Irish economy.

Interim protection pending the submission of a pre-petition report

[22.039] In exceptional circumstances the court may grant a company interim protection pending the presentation of a pre-petition report. Section 3A(1) of the C(A)A 1990[102] provides:

> 'If a petition presented under section 2 shows, and the court is satisfied—
>
> (a) that, by reason of exceptional circumstances outside the control of the petitioner, the report of the independent accountant is not available in time to accompany the petition, and
>
> (b) that the petitioner could not reasonably have anticipated the circumstances referred to in paragraph (a),
>
> and, accordingly, the court is unable to consider the making of an order under that section, the court may make an order under this section placing the company concerned under the

98 Section 3C(1) of the C(A)A 1990.

99 Section 3C(2) and (3) of the C(A)A 1990. Where the company is one referred to in s 3(2)(c) and the Central Bank has not and does not propose to present a petition under s 2 of the C(A)A 1990, the independent accountant must, as soon as may be after it is prepared, supply a copy of the report to the Central Bank and in such case subss (2) and (3) shall not apply to the copy sent to the Central Bank: s 3C(4) of the C(A)A 1990.

100 *Re Vantive Holdings* [2009] IESC 68.

101 *Re Missford Ltd t/a Residence Members Club* [2010] IEHC 11.

102 Inserted by s 9 of the C(A)(No 2)A 1999.

> protection of the court for such period as the court thinks appropriate in order to allow for the submission of the independent accountant's report.'

The first point to be noted here is that where a court grants interim protection, it does so under s 3A and not s 2 of the C(A)A 1990. Secondly, s 3A makes it very clear that there must exist *exceptional circumstances* that are *outside the petitioner's control* and which *could not have been reasonably anticipated*. It is thought that these requirements should be strictly construed as the clear thrust of the legislation is not to afford the exceptional remedy of interim protection to a petitioner who by reason of his own culpability cannot comply with the requirement to have a pre-petition report. Section 3A(3) provides that, for the avoidance of doubt, the fact that a receiver stands appointed to the whole or part of a company's property or undertaking at the time of the presentation of the petition shall not, in itself, constitute 'exceptional circumstances outside the control of the petitioner'. At the end of the interim protection period if an independent accountant's report is submitted to the court, the court shall then proceed to consider the petition and the report as if they were presented in accordance with s 2[103]; if the report is not submitted before the expiry of the interim protection period then the company shall cease to be under the protection of the court, but without prejudice to the presentation of a further petition under s 2[104].

[22.040] Section 3A of the C(A)A 1990 contains a number of very important additional safeguards to abuse of process. First, s 3A(2) provides that the period of interim protection shall expire not later than the tenth day after the date of the making of the order[105]. Second, s 3A(8) provides that any liabilities incurred by a company that has been granted interim protection may not be the subject of a certificate under s 10(2) of the C(A)A 1990.

[22.041] One difficulty, identified by the Gallagher Company Law Review Group[106], was that creditors or members who wish to present a petition may find it difficult or impossible to ascertain the information required by an independent accountant to produce a pre-petition report, unless they have the directors' co-operation. Section 3A(4) of the C(A)A 1990 provides that where a member or creditor has presented a petition and interim protection is granted, the directors of the company are obliged to co-operate in the preparation of the independent accountant's report[107].

[22.042] Although the legislation is silent on the point, it is thought that the only circumstances in which an *interim examiner* can be appointed is where interim relief is granted pursuant to s 3A. There is no specific reference to an interim examiner in the C(A)A 1990, although there is the general power in s 3(7) to make an interim order.

---

103 Section 3A(6) of the C(A)A 1990.

104 Section 3A(7) of the C(A)A 1990.

105 If the tenth day is a Saturday, Sunday or public holiday, then it will be the first following day that is not such a day.

106 *Report of the Gallagher Company Law Review Group*, December 1994 at para 2.19.

107 Under s 3A(5) of the C(A)A 1990 where the directors fail to comply with s 3A(4) of the C(A)A 1990, the petitioner or independent accountant can apply to court for an order requiring the directors to do specified things by way of compliance therewith and the court may, as it thinks fit, grant such an order accordingly.

Order 75A, r 5(2) of the RSC 1986 (as amended), however, refers to an interim examiner, providing:

> 'On the hearing of such *ex parte* application, the Court may, if it thinks fit, treat the application as the hearing of the petition and may make such order or any other order it thinks fit including adjourning the hearing and may appoint any proposed examiner on an interim basis until such adjourned hearing and an examiner so appointed over any company or any related company shall be referred to as the Interim Examiner and shall have the same powers and duties in relation to such company until the date of the adjourned hearing as if he were an examiner appointed other than on an interim basis.'

'Before an examiner can be appointed, whether interim or otherwise, the statutory conditions for such appointment must be met'[108]. One reason for this is because an interim examiner has the same powers of certification of expenses as has a full examiner[109] and so the court must be equally cautious in acceding to the appointment of an interim examiner. It has been suggested that where a petitioner seeks the appointment of an interim examiner, the justification for this should be set out in detail in the grounding affidavit[110]. In *Re Eircom Ltd*[111], Kelly J said most cases of examinership do not require the appointment of an interim examiner; in that case, an interim examiner was considered appropriate because there were advanced negotiations and it was considered that such an appointment would accelerate the process.

Presentation of the petition

[22.043] On the presentation[112] of a petition to place a company under the protection of the court, the petitioner is obliged to apply to the court for directions[113]. Although the court may treat this application as the full hearing of the petition, it rarely exercises this discretion[114]. The purpose of this requirement is principally to enable the court to direct the advertisement of the petition and to fix the date for the hearing of the petition. As in the presentation of the petition to have a company wound up, it is usual for the court to direct that the petition be advertised in two national daily newspapers, and to fix a Monday as the day for the hearing of the petition. The court will also normally direct the service of notice on certain parties at this point[115]. Depending upon who the petitioner is, the court will usually direct service on, *inter alios*, the following: the company; all secured creditors; a receiver, if one has been appointed; and where a receiver has been appointed, the creditor who appointed him; the Revenue Commissioners; and some or all of the unsecured creditors. Once served, the parties served will become 'notice parties' who from then on should be served with all further affidavits, notices and other relevant documentation. Because of the court's reluctance to appoint examiners in all but

---

108 *Per* Kelly J in *Re Advanced Technology College Ltd* (13 March 1997, unreported) HC at p 2.

109 See paras **[22.103]–[22.108]**. See, however, s 3A(8) considered at para **[22.108]**.

110 See O'Donnell, *Examinerships* (1994), p 11.

111 *Re Eircom Ltd* [2012] IEHC 158.

112 The petition is presented by lodging it with the Central Office of the High Court.

113 Order 75A, r 4(4) of the RSC now provides that: 'On the same day as the petition shall have been presented, the petitioner shall apply ex parte to the High Court for directions as to proceedings to be taken in relation thereto.'

114 Order 75A, r 5(2) of the RSC.

115 Order 75A, r 5(1) of the RSC.

the clearest of cases and the duty of petitioners to make full disclosure to the court, if in doubt as to what or who should be served, petitioners should serve everything conceivably relevant on everybody conceivably interested.

The hearing of the petition

[22.044] On the hearing of the petition, the C(A)A 1990 and the RSC 1986 try to ensure that all interested parties have an opportunity to hear and be heard. The rationale here is the same as in the hearing of a petition to have a company wound up and is evidenced by the advertisement of the hearing of the petition. For this reason the court has discretion to refuse to hear the petition until such time as such parties as the court directs have been notified[116].

[22.045] Section 3(6) of the C(A)A 1990 prohibits the court from hearing a petition for the appointment of an examiner where a receiver has been appointed to the company, and stands appointed for a continuous period of at least three days prior to the presentation of the petition. Secured creditors often try to take advantage of this provision by appointing a receiver on a Thursday or Friday[117]. The hope is that petitioners seeking to have an examiner appointed will not have ready access to the courts on a Saturday or Sunday. Determined petitioners, however, will succeed in locating a High Court judge on such days, at their home if necessary.

[22.046] In practice, s 3(6) of the C(A)A 1990 is tremendously important, even post-C(A)(No2)A 1999, because of the availability of interim protection under s 3A of the C(A)A 1990[118], pending the production of the report of an independent accountant. When a company is failing, the consequence of s 3(6) is often a game of cat-and-mouse between the directors of the company and its main secured creditor. The secured creditor's dilemma is whether the company has passed the point of no return, and if so should they rely upon their security and appoint a receiver under their security documentation? The 'point of no return' from a secured creditor's perspective may be very different to the court's perspective when it is asked to appoint an examiner to a company on the basis that there is a reasonable prospect for its survival.

The directors' dilemma will be different. The directors' concerns will often be based upon a reluctance to admit the company's insolvency and a fear of the consequences of corporate failure. To this will be added the expectation that the main secured creditor is likely to appoint a receiver coupled with a natural reluctance to precipitate failure by petitioning the court to appoint an examiner. The result is often a stand-off. When the secured creditor moves first and appoints a receiver, the race commences. The directors must not only present a petition to have the company placed under the protection of the court within three days of the receiver's appointment, but they must also present as full and persuasive a petition as possible. Unless the petition succeeds, the receivership is implicitly confirmed and, if the company's prospects are slim, its demise will be imminent. Directors of a company fearful that a receiver might be appointed should seek to procure the report of an independent accountant as early as possible or else their

---

116 Order 75A, r 5(3) of the RSC.

117 It is the case, however, that receivers have traditionally been appointed on Thursdays or Fridays.

118 Inserted by s 9 of the C(A)(No 2)A 1999. See para **[22.039]**.

petition will not be granted; indeed, even interim protection under s 3A will be refused unless there are 'exceptional circumstances' outside the control of the petitioner as to why this report is not available to accompany the petition. It is not sufficient to proffer the reason that the company is seeking to thwart the consequences arising from the appointment of a receiver[119].

The foregoing scenario represents a common pattern: the assumptions and expectations of the directors of an insolvent company do not necessarily accord with reality. It can be generally surmised that the directors of an insolvent company will sometimes either be procrastinating or seeking the implementation of a scheme of arrangement which would enable the company to wipe part of its slate clean. Unfortunately, where procrastination of the inevitable is the result of a successful application to have an examiner appointed, the directors themselves and the secured creditors are often among the losers. Where an examinership fails, often the only winners will be the lawyers and accountants for both sides who, usually, will be paid their fees in full.

[22.047] In *Cavan Crystal Glass Ltd*[120], Kelly J sanctioned an amendment to the name in which the petition had been brought so as to cure an irregularity. This was objected to by one secured creditor on the grounds that unless there was a valid petition before the court at midnight on the third day subsequent to the appointment of the receiver, an amendment was useless to avoid the provisions of s 3(6) of the C(A)A 1990. This point was rejected by Kelly J, who held:

> 'In my view, there was at all times a valid petition before the court albeit one which had a defect in form insofar as [the petitioning member] was concerned. At all times he could have presented the petition as a shareholder of the company holding in excess of 10% of its share capital but through what I have held to be a bona fide error, did so as a director of the company. The amendment which I am permitting merely puts that position right … I do not consider that by so doing and by regarding the petition as a valid one as of the date of its presentation, that I am in any way running counter to the provisions of s 3(6) of the Act. I cannot accept that it was ever the intention of the legislature that the making of a bona fide error, such as the one in suit, could have the drastic consequences for the company and its workforce as [the opposing creditor] suggests[121].'

[22.048] On the hearing of a petition to have an examiner appointed, the court has a wide discretion. It may hear the petition in full; it may adjourn the petition conditionally or unconditionally; or it may make any other order which the judge thinks fit[122]. It is also open for the petitioner to seek to have the application heard *in camera*. Section 31 of the C(A)A 1990 provides that the whole or any part of any proceedings under the Act may be heard otherwise than in public '... if the court, in the interests of justice, considers that the interests of the company concerned or of its creditors as a whole so require'.

In such circumstances, the court will follow the guidelines set out by the Supreme Court in *Re R Ltd*[123] and endorsed in *Irish Press plc v Ingersoll Irish Publications Ltd*[124].

---

119 Section 3A(3) of the C(A)A 1990.

120 *Cavan Crystal Glass Ltd* [1998] 3 IR 570.

121 *Cavan Crystal Glass Ltd* [1998] 3 IR 570 at 582.

122 See s 3(7) of the C(A)A 1990.

123 *Re R Ltd* [1989] IR 126; see Ch 11, *Shareholders' Remedies,* at para **[11.060]** *et seq.*

124 *Irish Press plc v Ingersoll Irish Publications Ltd* [1993] ILRM 747.

In *Re Chancery plc*[125], Harman J held that although ordinarily an administration petition under the Insolvency Act 1986 (UK) should rarely be heard *in camera*, this could be departed from in particular circumstances. The circumstances of that case were such that it was held that the petition should be heard *in camera* because of the commercially damaging nature of the evidence to be presented.

[22.049] After hearing the petition and reading of the grounding affidavit and replying affidavit (if any), the court will then address the central question of whether there is a reasonable prospect of survival for the company and, if so, whether the court should exercise its discretion to appoint an examiner in accordance with s 2[126]. It is also open to the court to dismiss the petition, which it will do where there is no reasonable prospect of survival. Where this occurs, a receiver who has been appointed can continue to secure the best position to protect the secured creditor who appointed him. It is open to the court to award costs against the unsuccessful petitioner(s)[127].

[22.050] Where, at first instance, a petition for the appointment of an examiner is refused, it is open to the petitioner to appeal that decision. It was said by the Supreme Court in *Re Cavan Crystal Glass Ltd*[128] that on appeal a fresh discretion must be brought to bear on the case.

Related companies

[22.051] Upon the appointment of an examiner to a company (the primary company), it is open to the court to accede to an application to extend the examinership to a related company or companies. This power has been exercised by the High Court on numerous occasions since the passing of the C(A)A 1990. Section 4(1) of the C(A)A 1990[129] provides that subject to sub-s (2), the court may make an order appointing the examiner of the primary company to be examiner to a related company and conferring on the examiner all or any of the powers or duties conferred upon him in relation to the primary company. In deciding whether or not to make such an order, guidance is given to the court by s 4(2), which provides that:

> '... the court shall have regard to whether the making of the order would be likely to facilitate the survival of the company, or of the related companies, or both, and the whole or any part of its or their undertaking, as a going concern and shall not, in any case, make such an order unless it is satisfied that there is a reasonable prospect of the survival of the related company, and the whole or any part of its undertaking, as a going concern[130].'

In consequence, no order can be made appointing an examiner to a related company unless the court is satisfied that the survival of it and the whole or any part of its undertaking as a going concern, is also a reasonable prospect[131]. It is not a prerequisite

---

125 *Re Chancery plc* [1991] BCLC 712.

126 See para **[22.018]** *et seq*.

127 In *Re Land and Property Trust Co (No 3)* [1991] BCLC 856 costs were awarded against the petitioners where they had acted irresponsibly.

128 *Re Cavan Crystal Glass Ltd* [1998] 3 IR 591 at 597 (O'Flaherty J).

129 As amended by s 12(a) of the C(A)(No 2)A 1999.

130 As amended by s 12(b) of the C(A)(No 2)A 1999.

131 In *Re Tuskar Resources plc* [2001] 1 IR 668, it was held that there was not sufficient evidence to show a reasonable prospect of survival of a Nigerian company; earlier, McCracken J had held that a foreign company could not be a related company: see para **[22.052]**.

that the related company is also unable to pay its debts, or insolvent. Sometimes the related company's financial health will be inter-dependent upon that of the primary company. This is particularly true where the related company has guaranteed some or all of the debts of the primary company. The fact that a related company has an examiner appointed to it has no bearing upon the question of either that company's separate legal existence being disregarded or its being directed to contribute to the assets of the primary company or the pooling of their assets on a winding up. These are separate questions that must be addressed in the context of a particular set of circumstances.

[22.052] Not every company, however, can have an examiner appointed to it on the grounds that it is a related company. Although a company may be owned by the same persons as the primary company, that by itself may be an insufficient connection. 'Related company' is very specifically defined by s 4(5) of the C(A)A 1990. This provides:

> 'For the purposes of this Act, a company is related to another company if—
>
> (a) that other company is its holding company or subsidiary; or
>
> (b) more than half in nominal value of its equity share capital (as defined in s 155(5) of the 1963 Act) is held by the other company and companies related to that other company (whether directly or indirectly, but other than in a fiduciary capacity); or
>
> (c) more than half in nominal value of the equity share capital (as defined in s 155(5) of the 1963 Act) of each of them is held by members of the other (whether directly or indirectly, but other than in a fiduciary capacity); or
>
> (d) that other company or a company or companies related to that other company or that other company together with a company or companies related to it are entitled to exercise or control the exercise of more than one half of the voting power at any general meeting of the company; or
>
> (e) the businesses of the companies have been so carried on that the separate business of each company, or a substantial part thereof, is not readily identifiable; or
>
> (f) there is another body corporate to which both companies are related;
>
> and "related company" has a corresponding meaning.'

Section 4(6) further provides that for the purposes of s 4, 'company' includes any body which is liable to be wound up under the Companies Acts[132]. Although a non-Irish formed and registered company cannot be placed under the protection of the court, such a company may be deemed to be a related company, and may have an examiner appointed to it[133]. A related body which has obligations to NAMA cannot be the subject of an order under s 4 unless a copy of the petition has been served on NAMA and NAMA has been heard on the application[134].

---

132 See Ch 23, *Winding Up Companies*, at para **[23.035]**.

133 In this regard it is thought that McCracken J in *Re Tuskar Resources plc* [2001] 1 IR 668 was mistaken. There he said '… in my view the definition of a related company in s 4(5) does not include a company registered outside this jurisdiction, as it sets out the conditions in which "a company is related to another company", and the word "*company*" as defined in the Companies Act 1963 means a company formed and registered under that Act, or an existing company'. This was, however, apparently without reference to s 4(6) of the C(A)A 1990.

134 Section 4(7) of the C(A)A 1990 as inserted by s 234 of the NAMAA 2009. See para **[22.028]** *ante*.

[22.053] In *Re Edenpark Construction Ltd and Edenpark Homes Ltd*[135], Edenpark Homes Ltd ('Homes') had an examiner appointed on the basis that it was a related company to Edenpark Construction Ltd ('Construction'). Murphy J said of Homes that it was 'a company which was related to Construction to the extent that Construction owned 25% of the shareholding in Homes and two directors were common to both companies'[136]. Such, by itself, was not sufficient for Homes to be a related company to Construction. Although it does not appear in Murphy J's judgment, it is surmised that the businesses of both companies must have been carried on in a manner so that they were not readily identifiable.

[22.054] Where an examiner is appointed to a related company the protection extended to the related company dates from the appointment of an examiner to the related company and *not* to the appointment of the examiner to the primary company[137]. The obvious difficulty which may arise is that a receiver is appointed to the related company for a period in excess of three days or that an order is made to wind up the related company. An interim examiner may also be appointed to a related company. It is suggested that petitioners who believe that the protection of a related company may be required for the survival of the primary company ought, in their petition for the appointment of an examiner to the primary company, seek the appointment of an interim examiner to the related company.

Formalities in the appointment of an examiner

[22.055] A number of provisions exist relating to the publicity of an examiner's appointment and the fact that a company has been placed under the protection of the court[138]. Within three days from the presentation of a petition, notice of the petition must be delivered to the registrar of companies as must the order appointing the examiner[139]. The appointment of the examiner, together with the date, if any, set for the hearing of his first report, must also be advertised. Advertisements must be placed in two daily newspapers circulating in the district where the company has its registered office within three days of the appointment and in *Iris Oifigiúil* within 21 days of the appointment[140]. In *Re Advanced Technology College Ltd*[141], Kelly J adjourned the hearing of a petition and directed re-advertisement of it because of defects in the proofs put before him, the principal one concerning omissions advertising the petition. This order was appealed to the Supreme Court where Barrington J (with whom Keane and Murphy JJ agreed) said:

> 'One must ask what is the purpose of such advertisements. It is to give notice to members of the public and included amongst them may be persons with no legal representation and

135 *Re Edenpark Construction Ltd and Edenpark Homes Ltd* [1994] 3 IR 126.

136 *Re Edenpark Construction Ltd and Edenpark Homes Ltd* [1994] 3 IR 126.

137 Section 4(3) of the C(A)A 1990.

138 Persons in default of these provisions are liable to a class C fine on summary conviction and a fine of up to €22,220.42 on conviction on indictment: s 12(5) of the C(A)A 1990.

139 See s 12(1) and (3) of the C(A)A 1990, respectively.

140 Section 12(2)(a) and (b) of the C(A)A 1990. Although s 72 of the IFCMPA 2005 substituted 'the Companies Registration Office Gazette' for '*Iris Oifigiúil*' that section has never been commenced.

141 *Re Advanced Technology College Ltd* (13 March 1997, unreported) HC at pp 7–8.

> persons who have never been in court. They should be informed where and when the application is to be made and its fundamental purpose. To be valid the advertisement must state the time, date and place where the application is to be heard. If it can, it should name the court in the Four Courts where the application will be heard. The learned trial judge was perfectly correct in the decision which he made which is unimpeachable[142].'

[22.056] Section 13(1) of the C(A)A 1990 provides that an examiner may resign, or on cause shown, be removed by the court[143]. In either eventuality, the court has power to fill the vacancy[144]. Any committee of creditors established under s 21 of the C(A)A 1990, the company or any interested party have *locus standi* to seek a court order to fill the vacancy[145].

[22.057] Where an examiner is appointed he must be described as 'the examiner' of the particular company in respect of which he is appointed and not by his individual name[146].

The commencement of protection

[22.058] Court protection of a failing company commences upon the presentation of a petition for the appointment of an examiner under the C(A)A 1990. As with the winding up of a company, the date upon which a company is deemed to be under the protection of the court is not the date of the court order, but the date upon which the petition is presented.

[B] The Effects of Court Protection

[22.059] Section 5(1) of the the C(A)A 1990[147] provides:

> 'Subject to section 3A, during the period beginning with the date of the presentation of a petition under section 2 and (subject to subsections (3) and (4) of section 18) ending on the expiry of 70 days from that date or on the withdrawal or refusal of the petition, whichever first happens, the company shall be deemed to be under the protection of the court.'

The most immediate and dramatic effect of a company being placed under the protection of the court is that creditors of the company are prevented from taking any action to enforce their security. The protected company is given a respite. Section 5(2) of the C(A)A 1990 sets out in detail the effect of court protection. Accordingly, for so long as a company is under the protection of the court:

---

142 Quoted in Kelly J's judgment of 13 March 1997 (at pp 7–8) on a subsequent application to, *inter alia*, reverse himself and the Supreme Court by dispensing with the need to further advertise the petition at all, which he described as 'wholly misconceived'.

143 On the removal of an administrator appointed under the Insolvency Act 1986 (UK), see *Re Exchange Travel (Holdings) Ltd* [1993] BCLC 887 where the peculiarities of the UK legislation were considered.

144 Section 13(2) of the C(A)A 1990.

145 Section 13(3) of the C(A)A 1990.

146 Section 13(4) of the C(A)A 1990.

147 As amended by s 14(a) of the C(A)(No 2)A 1999, the effect of such amendment being to shorten the period of examination from three months to 70 days from the date of presentation of a petition.

'(a) no proceedings for the winding-up of the company may be commenced, or resolution for winding-up passed, in relation to that company and any resolution so passed shall be of no effect[148];

(b) no receiver over any part of the property or undertaking of the company shall be appointed, or, if so appointed before the presentation of a petition under s 2, shall, subject to s 6, be unable to act;

(c) no attachment, sequestration, distress or execution shall be put into force against the company, except with the consent of the examiner;

(d) where any claim against the company is secured by a mortgage, charge, lien or other encumbrance or a pledge of, on or affecting the whole or any part of the property, effects or income of the company, no action may be taken to realise the whole or any part of that security, except with the consent of the examiner[149];

(e) no steps may be taken to repossess goods in the company's possession under any hire-purchase agreement (within the meaning of s 11(8)), except with the consent of the examiner[150];

(f) where under any enactment, rule of law or otherwise, any person other than the company ie a surety, is liable to pay all or any part of the debts of the company—

(i) no attachment, sequestration, distress or execution shall be put into force against the property or effects of such person in respect of the debts of the company, and

(ii) no proceedings of any sort may be commenced against such person in respect of the debts of the company;

(g) no order for relief shall be made under s 205 of the 1963 Act against the company in respect of complaints as to the conduct of the affairs of the company or the exercise of the powers of the directors prior to the presentation of the petition[151].'

[22.060] Section 5 of the C(A)A 1990 is so wide that, with minor exceptions, it may be considered to place a total embargo on creditors or other aggrieved persons taking any steps which would affect the protected company's assets. Although shareholders are prevented from taking proceedings under s 205 of the CA 1963[152], it is primarily the company's creditors who are affected by the appointment of an examiner.

[22.061] Section 5(3) of the C(A)A 1990 prohibits (subject to sub-s (2)) the issuing of all 'other proceedings' against a company that is under the protection of the court, except with leave of the court[153] and subject to such terms as the court may impose.

---

[148] See *Re a Company (No 001992 of 1988)* [1989] BCLC 9.

[149] As inserted by s 14(b)(i) of the C(A)(No 2)A 1999, to remedy the lacunae in the original s 5(2)(d) of the C(A)A 1990 which was capable of being interpreted as not preventing the enforcement of a mortgage.

[150] Section 11(8) of the C(A)A 1990 provides: 'References in this section to a hire-purchase agreement include a conditional sale agreement, a retention of title agreement and an agreement for the bailment of goods which is capable of subsisting for more than 3 months.' On hire-purchase agreements in UK administrations, see *Barclays Mercantile Business Finance Ltd v Sibec Development Ltd* [1993] BCLC 1077.

[151] Section 5(2)(h) of the C(A)A 1990 was deleted by s 14(b)(ii) of the C(A)(No 2)A 1999. See **[22.068]**.

[152] Section 5(4) of the C(A)A 1990 also provides that complaints concerning the conduct of the affairs of the company while it is under the protection of the court, shall not constitute the basis of the making of an order for relief under s 205 of the CA 1963.

[153] As to the court's discretion to give leave to institute proceedings under the Insolvency Act 1986 (UK), see *Royal Trust Bank v Buchler* [1989] BCLC 130.

Moreover, on the application of the examiner, the court may make such order as it thinks proper in relation to any existing proceedings, including an order to stay such proceedings. The prohibition on the commencement of 'other proceedings' other than with the leave of the court has been interpreted by the courts of England and Wales in the context of their, on this point, similarly-worded administration legislation[154] and found to encompass criminal proceedings[155]. The English courts have also held that there is no basis upon which to restrict the prohibition on the commencement of 'other proceedings' to actions brought by creditors, and in one case the court dismissed an application for a declaration that leave of the court was not required in order to bring proceedings for the infringement of a patent[156].

[22.062] Because proceedings cannot be issued, interlocutory injunctive proceedings cannot be commenced without the leave of the court. In the first proceedings under the C(A)A 1990, *Re Goodman International*, a *Mareva* injunction was refused by Hamilton P in an application brought by Banque Paribas of London[157]. Hamilton P is reported as having refused leave to issue proceedings against a number of subsidiary companies of the Goodman Group of companies and refused to grant the *Mareva* injunction sought to freeze the companies' assets. Although the plaintiff may have a substantive cause of action, the effect of s 5(3) of the C(A)A 1990 is that proceedings cannot be instituted without the leave of the court, and accordingly no ancillary *Mareva* (or other interlocutory) relief can be granted[158].

[22.063] An interesting issue arises where a *Mareva* injunction is granted against a company before an examiner has been appointed. In *Capital Cameras Ltd v Harold Lines Ltd*[159], Harman J held that in certain circumstances an administrative receiver appointed in England could apply for the discharge of a *Mareva* injunction which was granted before his appointment. The reasoning of the court was that the basis upon which the *Mareva* injunction was granted had changed substantially. The difference was that after the appointment of an administrative receiver, a licensed insolvency practitioner was in control of the company. In Ireland, it is thought that the appointment of an examiner cannot automatically result in the successful application to have a pre-protection period *Mareva* injunction discharged. Only where the directors' powers have

---

154 Section 11(3)(d) of the Insolvency Act 1986 (UK).

155 In *Re Rhondda Waste Disposal Company Ltd (in administration)* [1999] TLR 605, it was held that the English Environmental Agency could not bring criminal proceedings against a company in administration without the leave of the court. See also *A Straume (UK) Ltd v Bradlor Developments Ltd* [1999] TLR 478 where it was held that an adjudication procedure under the English Housing Grants, Construction and Regeneration Act 1986 constituted 'other proceedings'.

156 *Biosource Technologies Inc v Axis Genetics plc (in administration)* [1999] TLR 814. See also *Re Paramount Airways Ltd* [1990] BCC 130 and *Carr v British International Helicopters Ltd* [1994] 2 BCLC 474 where it was found that the word 'other' could not be construed *eiusdem generis* with what had gone before so as to confine 'other proceedings' to those relating to a debt. *Cf Air Ecossee Ltd v Civil Aviation Authority* [1987] 3 BCC 492.

157 An application reported in (1990) Irish Times, 20 October.

158 See generally, Courtney, *Mareva Injunctions and Related Interlocutory Orders* (1998), paras [4.10]–[4.13].

159 *Capital Cameras Ltd v Harold Lines Ltd* [1991] BCLC 884.

been transferred to the examiner under s 9 of the C(A)A 1990 can the court be assured that the company's affairs are being controlled by an officer of the court. In such a case it is thought that there will be a very clear case to have the injunction discharged since the risk of removal of assets from the jurisdiction or their dissipation with the *intention* of avoiding judgment or frustrating an order of the court must surely be remote.

[22.064] Where a company is, by virtue of s 5 of the C(A)A 1990, deemed to be under the protection of the court, every invoice, order for goods or business letter issued by or on behalf of the company, being a document on or in which the name of the company appears, must immediately after the mention of that name include the words 'in examination (under the Companies (Amendment) Act 1990)'[160].

[C] THE POSITION OF CREDITORS

[22.065] In *Re Butlers Engineering Ltd*[161], Keane J said of the consequences for creditors of the appointment of an examiner:

> 'It is almost superfluous to point out that while the purpose of the Act is the protection of the company and, as a result, its shareholders, employees and creditors, the court must never lose sight of the drastic abridgement that the giving of protection effects to the rights of the last mentioned category and I do not think that the judgments to which I have referred would lend any support to the view that the court must disregard those consequences in deciding whether an examiner should be appointed. In particular, it should be borne in mind that even the comparatively short breathing space … given by the appointment may have serious consequences for the creditors, given the fact that their nominal remedies remain in abeyance, while the control of the company remains in the hands of those who, in some cases at least, have contributed to its insolvency.'

The creditors of a company are those who are most directly and severely affected by the appointment of an examiner. It is proposed to consider here the effects of s 5 of the C(A)A 1990 on the company's creditors. It will also be necessary to consider some other relevant sections in the Act. The issues considered here are:

1. Ordinary and preferential creditors.
2. Provisional liquidators.
3. Receivers.
4. Secured creditors: general.
5. Negative pledge clauses in debentures.
6. De-crystallisation of floating charges.
7. Sureties and guarantors.
8. Priority of secured creditors and liquidators' costs, charges and expenses.

---

[160] Section 12(4) of the C(A)A 1990 as substituted by s 20(4) of the C(A)(No 2)A 1999. Previously, the required words were 'under the protection of the court'; the use of 'examinership' in the revised wording evidences a change in thinking as to the most appropriate description of the whole process.

[161] *Re Butlers Engineering Ltd* (1 March 1996, unreported) HC, Keane J at p 10 of the transcript. See O'Donnell, 'Appointing and Examiner: Learning to Live with the Culture of Corporate Rescue' (1997) Bar Review 246.

Ordinary and preferential creditors

[22.066] The main remedies ordinarily available to unsecured creditors are either to petition to have the company wound up on the basis that it is unable to pay its debts or to institute proceedings in order to obtain judgment against the company. Section 5(2)(a) of the C(A)A 1990 prohibits the commencement of proceedings for the winding up of a company in examinership. As considered above[162], no proceedings against a company under the protection of the court can be commenced without the leave of the court. As such, the ordinary creditor is deprived of his principal remedies against a debtor company. It is only fair that, upon the hearing of a petition to have an examiner appointed, ordinary creditors are afforded every opportunity possible to voice their concerns[163]. This is particularly true since even if the examinership is successful, the creditors will almost certainly be asked to write off part of the debts owing to them.

It should also be noted that not only is a creditor restricted in the enforcement of a liability owed by a company to which an examiner has been appointed, but so too is there a general restriction on the discharge of pre-petition liabilities by such a company[164].

[22.067] The courts frequently tend to pay particular attention to the Revenue Commissioners' position on an application for the appointment of an examiner. The Revenue Commissioners and secured creditors will frequently find themselves allies in opposing petitions for the appointment of examiners, both fearing that they will share the same fate: the writing-down of what they would otherwise be entitled to on the presumed inevitable liquidation. Where the Revenue Commissioners are neutral, this has been interpreted as being a 'sign of hope' for the ailing company[165].

[22.068] One substantial change arising from the C(A)(No 2)A 1999 is the deletion[166] of s 5(2)(h) of the C(A)A 1990[167]. That paragraph provided that no set-off between bank accounts of a company that had been placed under the court's protection could be effected, except with the consent of the examiner. The effect of this was to discriminate between banks and other creditors, ie, only set-off between bank accounts was prohibited. As a result of the recommendation of the Gallagher Company Law Review Group, this paragraph was repealed so that set-off between bank accounts is now permitted, despite the fact that a company is under the protection of the court.

Provisional liquidators

[22.069] Where at the date of the presentation of a petition to appoint an examiner to a company, a provisional liquidator stands appointed to that company, s 6(2) of the C(A)A 1990[168] provides that the court may make such order as it thinks fit, including an order as to any of the following matters:

---

162 See paras **[22.059]–[22.064]**.

163 As now provided for by s 3A of the C(A)A 1990.

164 Section 5A(1) of the C(A)A 1990.

165 *Per* O'Flaherty J in *Re Cavan Crystal Glass Ltd* [1998] 3 IR 591 at 594.

166 By s 14(b)(ii) of the C(A)(No 2)A 1999.

167 Itself inserted by s 181(1)(c) of the CA 1990.

168 As amended by s 16 of the C(A)(No 2)A 1999.

'(a) that the provisional liquidator be appointed as examiner of the company,

(b) appointing some other person as examiner of the company,

(c) that the provisional liquidator shall cease to act as such from the date specified by the court,

(d) directing the provisional liquidator to deliver all books, papers and other records, which relate to the property or undertaking of the company or any part thereof and are in his possession or control, to the examiner within a period to be specified by the court,

(e) directing the provisional liquidator to give the examiner full particulars of all dealings with the property or undertaking of the company.'

The court is also empowered to include such conditions in the order and make such ancillary or other orders as it deems fit for the purpose of giving full effect to an order under s 6(2)[169]. In deciding to make an order under s 6(2)(c) the court is obliged to have regard to whether the making of the order would be likely to facilitate the survival of the company, and the whole or any part of its undertaking, as a going concern[170]. Where a petition is presented to have an examiner appointed subsequent to the presentation of a petition for the winding up of a company but before a provisional liquidator is appointed, s 6(5) of the C(A)A 1990 requires both petitions to be heard together.

Receivers

[22.070] As has been considered above[171], the presentation of a petition to have an examiner appointed cannot be heard where a receiver has been appointed, and stands appointed for a period of at least three days prior to the presentation of the petition. Furthermore, after the presentation of a petition and for as long as the company is under the protection of the court, s 5(2)(b) of the C(A)A 1990 provides that no receiver shall be appointed over any part of the property or undertaking of the company.

[22.071] Where a receiver has been appointed for a lesser period of time than three days and the company is successfully placed under the protection of the court, the position of the receiver is affected greatly. Section 6(1) of the C(A)A 1990[172] provides, *inter alia*, that a receiver shall cease to act where, at the date of the presentation of a petition to appoint an examiner, he stands appointed to all or any part of the property or undertaking of the company. This section provides that the court may make such order as it thinks fit including an order as to any or all of the following matters:

'(a) that the receiver shall cease to act as such from a date specified by the court[173],

(b) that the receiver shall, from a date specified by the court, act as such only in respect of certain assets specified by the court,

(c) directing the receiver to deliver all books, papers and other records, which relate to the property or undertaking of the company (or any part thereof) and are in his possession or control, to the examiner within a period to be specified by the court,

169 Section 6(4) of the C(A)A 1990.

170 Section 6(3) of the C(A)A 1990, as amended by s 16 of the C(A)(No 2)A 1999.

171 Section 3(6) of the C(A)A 1990. See para **[22.045]**.

172 As amended by s 16 of the C(A)(No 2)A 1999.

173 This was what happened in *Re Holidair Ltd* [1994] 1 ILRM 481.

(d) directing the receiver to give the examiner full particulars of all his dealings with the property or undertaking of the company.'

This is a remarkable provision which displaces, without regard to both of the original parties' interests, a freely negotiated contract. The court is also empowered to include such conditions in the order and make such ancillary or other orders as it deems fit for the purpose of giving full effect to an order under s 6(3)[174]. Section 6(3)[175] provides that the court shall not make an order under paras (a) or (b) unless the court is satisfied that there is a reasonable prospect of the survival of the company, and the whole or any part of its undertaking, as a going concern. Whatever the merits or demerits, it seems irreconcilable with the rationale of examinerships to permit a receiver to enforce the appointing debenture holder's security. In all but the most exceptional of cases, the receiver will be held powerless during the period of the examinership.

[22.072] Upon his appointment a receiver owes duties, under s 98 of the CA 1963, to a company's preferential creditors[176]. Where an examiner has been appointed to a company or where in the opinion of the court such is likely, upon application being made, the court may, in relation to a receiver who stands appointed to the whole or any part of the property or undertaking of a company, make an order providing that s 98 shall not apply as respects payments made by the receiver out of assets coming into his hands[177]. The court must be of the opinion that the making of the order would be likely to facilitate the survival of the company and the whole or any part of its undertaking as a going concern[178]. Moreover, such an order cannot be made without the company's preferential creditors being afforded an opportunity to be heard[179].

Secured creditors: general

[22.073] Section 5(2)(d) of the C(A)A 1990[180] provides that while a company is under the protection of the court:

> '... where any claim against the company is secured by a mortgage, charge, lien or other encumbrance or a pledge of, on or affecting the whole or any part of the property, effects or income of the company, no action may be taken to realise the whole or any part of that security, except with the consent of the examiner.'

This provision has been substantially extended by the C(A)(No 2)A 1999 so that it is no longer possible to argue that only 'charges' of property (as distinct from 'mortgages') cannot be enforced during the period of protection. It is now the case that the enforcement of all forms of consensual security that can be created by a company is not permissible without the consent of an examiner. It is also clear that security which does not require to be registered pursuant to s 99 of the CA 1963 is also caught by the revised wording.

---

174 Section 6(4) of the C(A)A 1990.

175 As amended by s 16 of the C(A)(No 2)A 1999.

176 See Ch 20, *Corporate Borrowing: Receivers*, para **[20.066]** *et seq*.

177 Section 6A(1)(a) of the C(A)A 1990.

178 Section 6A(1)(b) of the C(A)A 1990.

179 Section 6A(2) of the C(A)A 1990.

180 As amended by s 14(b)(i) of the C(A)(No 2)A 1999.

[22.074] In *Re Holidair Ltd*[181], the question before the court was whether a bank's direction to a borrower company, which was under the protection of the court, to lodge the proceeds of the company's book debts to a designated account was in breach of s 5(2)(d) of the C(A)A 1990. Finlay CJ held that the action of the bank in directing for the first time, the payment of moneys collected from the company's debtors, into a nominated account in the name of a trustee, was in breach of the originally worded s 5(2)(d). Reversing the decision of Costello J in the High Court, he said:

> 'It is clear that this sub-section does not merely prohibit the realisation of the whole or any part of a security but prohibits the taking of any action to realise the whole or part of any security. It is in my view clear that to attempt to provide for the lodgment of the proceeds of book debts into a bank account in the name of the trustee of the debenture which could not be operated by the companies except with the consent of the trustee is an action taken to realise the security consisting of the book debts making them immediately available on the conclusion of the period provided for in s 5(1) as a set-off in respect of part of the debt of the banks. It is in my view irrelevant that the banks had reserved to themselves in the debenture a right to take this step once they did not take it and took it for the first time after the appointment of the examiner[182].'

Negative pledge clauses in debentures

[22.075] Most modern debentures contain a negative pledge clause. The purpose of this is to prevent the borrowing company from creating any other charge over its property without the prior consent in writing of the debenture holder[183]. Notwithstanding that the C(A)A 1990 does not authorise the court to give an examiner any power which is not exercisable by the directors, the Supreme Court has held that an examiner is *not* bound by a negative pledge clause. In *Re Holidair Ltd*[184], Finlay CJ held:

> 'I am however satisfied that he has got a power to dispense with the necessity to obtain such consent which is provided by s 7, sub-s 5 of the Act of 1990 ... The words in this sub-section "actual or proposed" when attached to the word "contract" of necessity means that the sub-section applies to contracts already in existence and must therefore include the contract of debenture entered into before the examiner was appointed. There can be no doubt that the portion of the contract of debenture providing for the necessity of the companies to apply for the consent of the debenture holders to borrowing and the stated intention of the debenture holders not to agree to the borrowing which is in issue in this case clearly constitutes a contract and conduct in pursuance of the contract which is likely to be to the detriment of the company and the examiner, I am satisfied, is therefore entitled to take such steps as are necessary to rectify, halt and prevent such effects. This must, it seems to me, include a power provided the sanction of the court for borrowing has been granted to carry out that borrowing without seeking or obtaining the consent of the debenture holders'[185].

Such an interpretation was not inevitable. This interpretation has, however, now been enshrined in statute. Whilst s 7(5A) of the C(A)A 1990[186] restricts examiners' powers to

181 *Re Holidair Ltd* [1994] 1 ILRM 481.

182 *Re Holidair Ltd* [1994] 1 ILRM 481 at 489.

183 See Ch 18, *Corporate Borrowing: Debentures and Security*, at para **[18.079]** *et seq*.

184 *Re Holidair Ltd* [1994] 1 ILRM 481.

185 *Re Holidair Ltd* [1994] 1 ILRM 481 at 488.

186 Inserted by s 18 of the C(A)(No 2)A 1999.

repudiate contracts entered into by the company prior to its being placed under the protection of the court, s 7(5B) specifically excludes negative pledge clauses from this restriction. Section 7(5B) provides:

> 'A provision referred to in subsection (5C) shall not be binding on the company at any time after the service of the notice under this subsection and before the expiration of the period during which the company concerned is under the protection of the court if the examiner is of the opinion that the provision, were it to be enforced, would be likely to prejudice the survival of the company or the whole or any part of its undertaking as a going concern and he serves a notice on the other party or parties to the agreement in which the provision is contained informing him or them of that opinion.'

Subsection (5C) provides:

> 'The provision referred to in subsection (5B) is a provision of an agreement entered into by the company concerned and any other person or persons at any time (including a time that is prior to the period during which the company is under the protection of the court) that provides that the company shall not, or shall not otherwise than in specified circumstances—
>
> (a) borrow moneys or otherwise obtain credit from any person other than the said person or persons, or
>
> (b) create or permit to subsist any mortgage, charge, lien or other encumbrance or any pledge over the whole or any part of the property or undertaking of the company.'

[22.076] Not only can an examiner, with the sanction of the court, ignore a negative pledge clause, but he can also borrow money[187]. Where such borrowing is 'certified' by the examiner under s 10 of the C(A)A 1990 it will have priority to all other claims (including a claim secured by a floating charge) but *after* 'any claim secured by a mortgage, charge, lien or other encumbrance *of a fixed nature* or a pledge': s 29(3A) of the C(A)A 1990[188]. This important concession to the holders of fixed security was introduced by the C(A)(No 2)A 1999; it remains the case, however, that the holders of floating charges – for whose protection negative pledge clauses are primarily intended – may still be prejudiced where subsequent borrowing is certified by an examiner[189]. An examiner's power to borrow is considered further below[190].

De-crystallisation of floating charges

[22.077] Floating charges will crystallise upon the happening of certain events[191]. One such event is the appointment of a receiver to a company. It has been held by the Supreme Court that notwithstanding the crystallisation of a floating charge occasioned by the appointment of a receiver, upon the appointment of an examiner the crystallised floating charge will *de-crystallise*. The effect of this is that the assets which were once the subject of a quasi-fixed charge become once more available for use by the company in the course of its business. De-crystallisation was introduced into Irish law by the

187 Section 9 of the C(A)A 1990.

188 As inserted by s 28 of the C(A)(No 2)A 1999.

189 On 'certification' of expenses, see para **[22.103]**.

190 See para **[22.098]**.

191 See Ch 18, *Corporate Borrowing: Debentures and Security*, para **[18.093]** *et seq*.

Supreme Court in *Re Holidair Ltd*[192]. In his concurring judgment, Blayney J accepted the submission on behalf of the companies under the protection of the court that a floating charge, which crystallised on the appointment of a receiver, de-crystallised on the appointment of an examiner. He said:

> 'Once the examiner was appointed, the receiver could no longer act (s 5 subs (2)(b) of the 1990 Amendment Act). It would accordingly have been pointless to keep the book debts frozen. The receiver would have had no right to collect them. Apart from this, since the purpose of the 1990 Amendment Act, as emphasised by the Chief Justice in his judgment, is the protection of the company and consequently of its shareholders workforce and creditors, it would be wholly inconsistent with that purpose that the company would be deprived of the use of its book debts particularly as it appears that they are absolutely essential for its survival during the protection period. Furthermore, it is no injustice to the debenture holders who appointed the receiver since the companies are continuing to trade and so continuing to create new book debts to replace those that may be paid and the proceeds of which may be used by the companies. Finally, it seems to me that if the receiver were to insist upon the charge on the book debts remaining crystallised, he would be in breach of s 5 subs (2)(d) of the 1990 Amendment Act ...[193]'

The writer finds the reasoning of Blayney J unconvincing[194]. It is clear from s 5(2)(d) of the C(A)A 1990 that the receiver could not realise the book debts (or their proceeds) which were the subject of a quasi-fixed charge, but he would not have been in breach of the section were he to sit out the examinership and enforce the fixed charge later.

[22.078] In particular, it must be asked whether it was necessary to go so far as to say that the floating charge had de-crystallised? It is submitted not. It would not have been pointless to have kept the book debts frozen: the debenture holder would at least have the certainty that he had a fixed charge over a quantifiable sum. The view that the debenture holders suffer no injustice because new book debts will be created is open to question on the same basis: on the crystallisation of the floating charge the debenture holder had certainty. It is certain that a company in examinership would not replace book debts as quickly as it would dispose of them. To use one of the purposes of the C(A)A 1990 (to protect creditors) as a justification for de-crystallisation seems most misplaced. Whatever about creditors generally, it is certainly not in the interests of the secured creditor in question to de-crystallise his fixed charge. Finally, to introduce the concept of de-crystallisation in the context of a freely negotiated debenture is at best an attack on the freedom on contract, and without specific legislative authority, amounts to judicial law-making. Where a debenture specifically provides that the crystallisation of a floating charge is irrevocable, a court should not, in the absence of express legislation, disregard such a freely contracted condition. The notion that a crystallised charge may de-crystallise has, until 1994, been a concept foreign to Irish law[195]. Without wishing to appear jingoistic, it is submitted that this concept ought to have remained foreign.

---

192 *Re Holidair Ltd* [1994] 1 ILRM 481.

193 *Re Holidair Ltd* [1994] 1 ILRM 481.

194 For a critique of this decision, see Johnston, *Banking and Security Law in Ireland* (1998), para 13.17.

195 The concept is recognised in Scotland by s 478(6) of the Companies Act 1985 (UK). See Parsons, *Lingard's Bank Security Documents* (5th edn, 2011), para 9.31.

Sureties and guarantors

[22.079] During the period of protection, not only is the company itself cocooned from creditors, but so also are persons who guarantee the company's debts. Section 5(2)(f) of the C(A)A 1990 provides:

> '... where, under any enactment, rule of law or otherwise, any person other than the company is liable to pay all or any part of the debts of the company;
>
> (i) no attachment, sequestration, distress or execution shall be put into force against the property or effects of such person in respect of the debts of the company, and
>
> (ii) no proceedings of any sort may be commenced against such person in respect of the debts of the company.'

It should be noted, though, that s 5(2)(f) does not prohibit the making of a demand on foot of a guarantee. Although the guarantor may be safeguarded from proceedings being instituted, in practice he may think it politically expedient to pay the sum demanded[196].

[22.080] When a scheme of arrangement is put to the court for approval, it may be sought to have the personal guarantees of the company's directors set aside. In *Re Selukwe*[197], Costello J refused to sanction that part of the scheme which purported to release the directors from their personal guarantees because there was no justification for depriving the bank of its security. The reason given for seeking the release of the guarantees was that the new investors did not wish the directors to face possible bankruptcy. In modifying the scheme to leave the personal guarantees in place, Costello J held that such a proposal was not fair and equitable as far as the bank was concerned.

Re Presswell Ltd[198] demonstrates that in certain circumstances the court may confirm the setting aside of directors' personal guarantees as part of a scheme of arrangement. There, one creditor, the Ulster Bank, objected to the examiner's proposed scheme of arrangement because the arrangement involved the bank abandoning, foregoing or losing the benefit of the directors' personal guarantees in respect of the company's indebtedness. For the learned Murphy J the real issue was:

> '... whether these guarantees are of significant value to the Ulster Bank so that the loss thereof would prejudice the Bank unfairly. Undoubtedly this is the very real type of objection which creates a particular problem. It does so where not merely is the liability of the primary debtor reduced or limited to the amount agreed by the creditors and approved by the court but where the carrying of the arrangement would necessarily release those guaranteeing the primary liability. That is one matter to be borne in mind[199].'

Murphy J recognised that an examiner is not usually in a position to evaluate personal guarantees, because he will only have access to the company's books and records. In *Re Presswell,* however, the directors had filed affidavits swearing to the extent of their assets. Although the Ulster Bank filed affidavits setting out its opinion, Murphy J found that in the event of the guarantees being called in, the guarantors would be liable to be adjudicated bankrupt. Murphy J held that the proposals were not unfairly prejudicial to

---

196 This is especially true of institutional guarantors who may find it embarrassing to resist a creditor's demand on foot of a guarantee entered by them.

197 *Re Selukwe* (20 December 1991, unreported) HC.

198 *Re Presswell Ltd* (4 November 1991, unreported) HC, *per* Murphy J.

199 *Re Presswell Ltd* (4 November 1991, unreported) HC at p 9.

Ulster Bank under s 25(1)(d) of the C(A)A 1990[200]. He noted that the directors' evidence as to their assets was uncontradicted and that it seemed to him that Ulster Bank would recover only a modest dividend from the guarantors, perhaps only after protracted proceedings. Even so, one might have thought that the beneficiary of the guarantee was the person best placed to say whether or not the guarantee had a value.

[22.081] Section 25A of the C(A)A 1990[201] specifically addresses guarantees. In a nutshell, s 25A(1) provides that third parties' guarantees[202] are enforceable notwithstanding that a scheme of arrangement compromises the creditor's recourse to the company, which is the primary debtor[203]. As Finlay Geoghegan J said in *Re Eylewood Ltd*[204]:

> 'The entire section appears intended, first, to protect the right of a creditor to enforce a guarantee of debts of a company which is the subject of a write-down in a scheme of arrangement, secondly, to limit the right of guarantors to enforce a guarantee and, thirdly, to make express provision in certain circumstances for payment by a company to the guarantor rather than to the creditor in accordance with the scheme.'

The one exception to the general rule is that it does not apply if the guarantor is a company to which an examiner has been appointed[205]. This is, however, without prejudice to s 5(2)(f), namely, that guarantees, etc, still cannot be enforced during the protection period[206].

[22.082] Section 25A(1)(d) has received judicial attention. This provides:

> 'if the third person [eg, guarantor] makes a payment to the creditor in respect of the liability after the period of protection has expired, then any amount that would, but for that payment, be payable to the creditor in respect of the debt under a compromise or scheme of arrangement that has taken effect under section 24(9) in relation to the company shall become and be payable to the third person upon and subject to the same terms and conditions as the compromise or scheme of arrangement provided that it was to be payable to the creditor.'

---

200 See para **[22.153]**.

201 Inserted by s 25 of the C(A)(No 2)A 1999.

202 Section 25A of the C(A)A 1990 is cast wider than just guarantees and applies 'in relation to the liability of any person ("the third person") whether under a guarantee or otherwise, in respect of a debt ("the debt") of a company to which an examiner has been appointed …'. Here, references to 'the guarantor' are intended as a shorthand.

203 Section 25A(1)(a) of the C(A)A 1990 provides that: 'subject to paragraph (b) and save where the contrary is provided in an agreement entered into by the third person and the person to whom he is liable in respect of the debt ("the creditor"), the liability shall, notwithstanding section 24(6), not be affected by the fact that the debt is the subject of a compromise or scheme of arrangement that has taken effect under section 24(9).'

204 *Re Eylewood Ltd* [2010] IEHC 57.

205 Section 25A(1)(b) of the C(A)A 1990.

206 Section 25A(2)(a) of the C(A)A 1990. Moreover, it is without prejudice to any rule of law whereby any act done by the creditor referred to in s 25A(1) of the C(A)A 1990 results in the guarantor being released from his obligations in respect of the liability concerned.

In *Re Eylewood Ltd*[207], the question arose as to whether s 25A(1)(d) of the C(A)A 1990 limits the indemnity and, or in the alternative, the subrogation rights of a company's existing guarantors upon payment pursuant to the guarantees after confirmation of the scheme of arrangement. The guarantors claimed that their right to look to the company in respect of any payments made by them under the guarantees constituted them contingent creditors and, as the rights of contingent creditors to subrogation and indemnity cannot be written down in a scheme, they were permitted to retain those rights as against the company. Finlay Geoghegan J held that the liability of a principal debtor to a guarantor of its debts where demand has not yet been made on the guarantor and payment has not been made pursuant to the guarantee is a contingent liability. The learned judge also held that it was permissible for the court to write-down guarantors' contingent liabilities and that this would bind the guarantors and prevent them from seeking future recourse to the company. In the instant case and the nature of the guarantees that had been given, Finlay Geoghegan J considered that it would be unfairly prejudicial to the guarantors to reduce their contingent right to an indemnity from the companies to the amount provided for in s 25A(1)(d).

[22.083] Where a creditor opts to enforce a guarantee, any rights he has in the examinership arising from his debt can pass to the guarantor. Where a creditor proposes to enforce, by legal proceedings or otherwise, the obligation of a guarantor he must serve a notice on the guarantor. The notice should contain a written offer to transfer to the guarantor any rights the creditor has, so far as they relate to the debt, to vote in respect of proposals for a compromise or scheme of arrangement in relation to the company: s 25A(1)(c) of the C(A)A 1990. Strict time limits apply to the sending of such a notice[208]. The usual legal requirements for a valid assignment of a chose in action appear to have been displaced. Where the guarantor accepts the creditor's offer, he should furnish it to the examiner at the meeting concerned and the offer will 'operate without the necessity for any assignment or the execution of any other instrument, to entitle the [guarantor] to exercise the said rights'[209]. The transfer of the voting rights (or the voting by the guarantor) is, however, without prejudice to the creditor's right to object to the proposals under s 25 of the C(A)A 1990. Where a creditor fails to make an offer, as described, to a guarantor he cannot enforce by legal proceedings or otherwise the obligation of the guarantor in respect of the liability[210] unless a compromise or scheme of arrangement is not entered into or does not take effect under s 24(9) of the C(A)A 1990 and the creditor has obtained the leave of the court to enforce the guarantor's obligation[211]. It should also be noted that where a guarantor makes a payment to a creditor in respect of the liability after the period of protection has expired, then any amount that would, but for that payment, be payable to the creditor in respect of the debt under a compromise or scheme of arrangement that has taken effect, shall

[207] *Re Eylewood Ltd* [2010] IEHC 57, Finlay Geoghegan J.

[208] If 14 days' notice or more is given of such meeting, at least 14 days before the day on which the meeting concerned under s 23 to consider the proposals is held (s 25A(1)(c)(i)(I) of the C(A)A 1990); or if less than 14 days' notice is given of such meeting, not more than 48 hours after he has received notice of such meeting (s 25A(1)(c)(i)(II) of the C(A)A 1990).

[209] Section 25A(1)(c)(ii) of the C(A)A 1990.

[210] Section 25A(1)(c)(iii) of the C(A)A 1990.

[211] Section 25A(1)(c)(iv) of the C(A)A 1990.

become payable to the guarantor on the same terms and conditions as it would otherwise be payable to the creditor[212].

Priority of secured creditors and liquidators' costs, charges and expenses

(a) Secured creditors

[22.084] Prior to the commencement of the C(A)A 1990, creditors whose debts were secured by a mortgage or charge over a company's property enjoyed priority over all other creditors where the company became insolvent. As shall be considered below, a scheme of arrangement, which involves the reduction of a secured creditor's claim, can be sanctioned by the court.

In addition, it was held in *Re Atlantic Magnetics Ltd*[213] that notwithstanding that a bank or other lender may have a first fixed charge over the company's property, the examiner could, with the sanction of the court, borrow against the company's fixed assets.

[22.085] The priority of secured creditors to look to the company's assets in satisfaction of their claims was also changed by s 29(3) of the C(A)A 1990. The costs, remuneration and expenses of an examiner now have, in the words of Murphy J, 'an extraordinary priority'[214] over all other debts of the company. Section 29(3)[215] provides:

> 'The remuneration, costs and expenses of an examiner which have been sanctioned by order of the court (other than the expenses referred to in subsection (3A)) shall be paid in full and shall be paid before any other claim, secured or unsecured, under any compromise or scheme of arrangement or in any receivership or winding-up of the company to which he has been appointed.'

The 'carve-out', contained in s 29(3A) of the C(A)A 1990[216], provides:

> 'Liabilities incurred by the company to which an examiner has been appointed that, by virtue of section 10(1), are treated as expenses properly incurred by the examiner shall be paid in full and shall be paid before any other claim (including a claim secured by a floating charge), but after any claim secured by a mortgage, charge, lien or other encumbrance of a fixed nature or a pledge, under any compromise or scheme of arrangement or in any receivership or winding-up of the company to which he has been appointed.'

The original s 29(3) was interpreted by the Supreme Court on a number of occasions. For creditors secured by a floating security, the result is exacerbated by virtue of the fact that virtually any expenditure, including further borrowings, can be deemed 'expenses' where so certified by the examiner under s 10 of the C(A)A 1990.

[22.086] In *Re Atlantic Magnetics Ltd*[217], Finlay CJ held that the remuneration, costs and expenses of an examiner which are sanctioned by the court, have priority even over a

---

212 Section 25A(1)(d) of the C(A)A 1990.

213 *Re Atlantic Magnetics Ltd* [1993] 2 IR 561.

214 In *Re Edenpark Construction Ltd* [1994] 3 IR 126 at 133.

215 As substituted by s 28 of the C(A)(No 2)A 1999.

216 Inserted by s 28 of the C(A)(No 2)A 1999.

217 *Re Atlantic Magnetics Ltd* [1993] 2 IR 561.

creditor whose debts are secured by a fixed charge. He rejected the submission that s 29(3) of the C(A)A 1990 affected all security other than a fixed charge. The Chief Justice repeated this view in *Re Holidair Ltd*[218]. There he said:

> '... the true interpretation of s 29(3) is that the remuneration, costs and expenses as defined in that section of an examiner which had been sanctioned by order of the court shall be paid in actual priority to the claims of any secured or unsecured creditor and that under the provisions of s 29(2) the court may if necessary and must if it has sanctioned such remuneration, costs and expenses in a case where unsecured assets are insufficient to pay the total of the amounts involved direct their payment out of secured assets[219].'

It is for this reason that secured creditors have been particularly vociferous in their opposition to petitions to have examiners appointed.

(b) Liquidators' costs, charges and expenses

[22.087] Section 29(3B) of the C(A)A 1990[220] provides:

> 'In subsections (3) and (3A) references to a claim shall be deemed to include references to any payment in a winding-up of the company in respect of the costs, charges and expenses of that winding-up (including the remuneration of any liquidator).'

This subsection gives statutory effect to the decision of the Supreme Court in *Re Springline*[221] which had reversed the earlier High Court decision of Shanley J[222]. There, it had been successfully argued by the official liquidator of a company that had been under the protection of the court that the examiner's costs, expenses and remuneration did not have priority to those of the official liquidator[223]. In Keane J's judgment for the Supreme Court it was held that the word 'claim' in s 29(3) had to be given its ordinary meaning which it was held included the liquidator's remuneration costs and expenses and so these ranked after those of the examiner. For better or for worse, the matter has been put beyond all doubt by s 29(3B). In *Re Sharmane Ltd*[224], it was argued that the weekly operating expenses of companies (eg, payments to employees, suppliers and a company engaged by the receiver to manage pubs owned by the companies) which were in receivership were not a claim in the receivership within the meaning of s 29(3). This was rejected by Finlay Geoghegan J who held that they were claims in the receivership ahead of which the examiner had priority.

---

218 *Re Holidair Ltd* [1994] 1 ILRM 481.

219 *Re Holidair Ltd* [1994] 1 ILRM 481 at 490.

220 *Re Holidair Ltd* [1994] 1 ILRM 481 at 490.

221 *Re Springline* [1999] 1 IR 478, [1999] 1 ILRM 15. See O'Donnell, 'Examinerships After Springline – Another Line in the Sand' (1998) 5 CLP 279.

222 *Re Springline* [1999] 1 IR 467, [1998] 1 ILRM 301.

223 Shanley J had held that while the examiner was given a priority by s 29(3) of the C(A)A 1990 it was 'not a priority in respect of anything other than all other claims against the company whether secured or unsecured'. He had found that the references to a future 'claim' or a future 'debt' could not be argued to refer in any way to the costs, expenses, remuneration or charges of an official liquidator (at p 476 of the report).

224 *Re Sharmane Ltd* [2009] IEHC 377.

[D] THE POWERS OF EXAMINERS

[22.088] A wide range of statutory powers are conferred upon examiners. It is important to note that the acts of an examiner, and so the exercise of his powers, shall be valid, notwithstanding any defects that may afterwards be discovered in his appointment or qualification[225]. Some powers can be exercised unilaterally by an examiner. Other powers can be exercised only with the approval of the court. The following are some of the powers which an examiner may have:

1. To seek a transfer of the directors' powers.
2. To obtain information.
3. To seek directions from the court.
4. To discharge pre-petition debts.
5. To borrow.
6. To deal with charged property.
7. To certify expenses.
8. To regularise improper transactions.

To seek a transfer of the directors' powers

[22.089] An examiner does not *per se* have an executive role in the company to which he is appointed and does not have functions akin to a receiver or liquidator. In the words of Murphy J in *Re Edenpark Construction Ltd*[226]:

> 'In the absence of some particular order of the High Court, he may not usurp the functions of the board of directors of the company over which he is appointed and it is the board or its officials who will continue to manage the business of the company during the period of protection and the continuance of the examinership.'

Usually, the directors of a company under the protection of the court will not be asked to relinquish their authority and where the directors have been delegated the power to manage the company's business (as invariably they will where model reg 80[227] has been adopted) they will continue to be the company's managers. However, it is open to an examiner to seek to have the directors' powers transferred to him by order of the High Court as alluded to by Murphy J in the foregoing passage. Where an examiner believes that it is necessary to take over the management of the company, he, and he alone, may apply to the court under s 9 of the C(A)A 1990:

> 'Contrary to some views, [an examiner] does not take over the running of the company or displace the directors. If he is to do so, then he must apply to the court for such powers under section 9 of the Act. That section makes it quite clear that only the examiner may make such an application[228].'

---

[225] Section 13(5) of the C(A)A 1990. In the context of the appointment of directors, s 178 of the CA 1963 makes a similar provision. It has been held in *Morris v Kanssen* [1946] AC 459 that the section only applies where there are procedural errors in the appointment and will not save substantive defects in an appointment.

[226] *Re Edenpark Construction Ltd* [1994] 3 IR 126 at 136.

[227] Regulation 80 of Table A in the model articles of association by which the members of a company delegate the power to manage the business of the company to its directors: see Ch 13, *Corporate Governance: Management by the Directors*, para **[13.127]**.

[228] *Per* Kelly J in *Re Advanced Technology College Ltd* (13 March 1997, unreported) HC at p 6.

[22.090] Section 9 of the C(A)A 1990 provides that an examiner may apply to court to seek the transfer to him of some, or all, of the powers exercised by the directors. Section 9(1) of the C(A)A 1990 states:

> 'Where it appears to the court, on the application of the examiner, that, having regard to the matters referred to in subsection (2), it is just and equitable to do so, it may make an order that all or any of the functions or powers which are vested in or exercisable by the directors (whether by virtue of the memorandum or articles of association of the company or by law or otherwise) shall be performable or exercisable only by the examiner.'

The matters to which the court must have regard are set out in s 9(2) of the C(A)A 1990:

> '(a) that the affairs of the company are being conducted, or are likely to be conducted, in a manner which is calculated or likely to prejudice the interests of the company or of its employees or of its creditors as a whole, or
>
> (b) that it is expedient for the purpose of preserving the assets of the company or of safeguarding the interests of the company or of its employees or of its creditors as a whole, that the carrying on of the business of the company by, or the exercise of the powers of, its directors or management should be curtailed or regulated in any particular respect, or
>
> (c) that the company, or its directors, have resolved that such an order should be sought, or
>
> (d) any other matter in relation to the company which the court thinks relevant.'

Where the court grants the order sought by the examiner, it may include such conditions in the order for the transfer of powers as it sees fit[229]. Any powers exercised by an examiner must not be *ultra vires* the company's capacity[230]. The court may also confer upon an examiner all or any of the powers that a liquidator appointed by the court would have: s 9(4) of the C(A)A 1990. In *Re Fate Park Ltd*[231], an examiner sought to argue that s 9(4) conferred a separate and distinct jurisdiction that was not dependent upon the court making an order under s 9(1). This was rejected by Finlay Geoghegan J who said:

> 'Construing subs 9(4) in accordance with the ordinary meaning of the words used by the Oireachtas in the context of s 9, it appears only capable of meaning that where an order is made under subs 9(1) that some or all of the functions or powers of the directors be performable or exercisable only by the Examiner, the court, in addition to including an order under subs (3) (limited in accordance with the decision of the Supreme Court in *Re Holidair*, *ie* that it may not include powers not exercisable by the directors), may also provide pursuant to subs (4) that an Examiner have all or any of the powers that he would have if he were a liquidator appointed by the court. Such powers may, of course, be additional to powers exercisable by directors.'

In that case, the examiner wanted the power of an official liquidator under s 290 of the CA 1963 to disclaim an alleged onerous contract between the company and one of its directors. No evidence was put before the court that any of the conditions in s 9(2) had been met and so the court declined to make an order under s 9(1), and in the absence of such an order, held that there was no jurisdiction to make an order granting the examiner the powers of an official liquidator.

---

229 Section 9(3) of the C(A)A 1990.

230 See *Re Home Treat Ltd* [1991] BCLC 705.

231 *Re Fate Park Ltd* [2009] IEHC 375.

[22.091] Even where an examiner does not seek the transfer of powers to him, he will still be entitled to supervise the management of the company under the protection of the court. Accordingly, an examiner has power to convene, set the agenda for and preside over meetings of the board of directors and general meetings of the members of the company, and he can propose motions or resolutions or give reports to such meetings[232]. In relation to meetings of the members and directors, the examiner is entitled to reasonable notice of, to attend and be heard at such meetings[233]. Reasonable notice in this context is deemed to include a description of the business to be transacted at any such meeting[234].

[22.092] Where an examiner assumes an executive role under s 9 of the C(A)A 1990 he may enter into contracts which purport to be on behalf of the company. Even where the directors' powers are not transferred to him, he may enter into contracts with third parties. Section 13(6) of the C(A)A 1990 provides:

> 'An examiner shall be personally liable on any contract entered into by him in the performance of his functions (whether such contract is entered into by him in the name of the company or in his own name as examiner or otherwise) unless the contract provides that he is not to be personally liable on such contract, and he shall be entitled in respect of that liability to indemnity out of the assets; but nothing in this subsection shall be taken as limiting any right to indemnify which he would have apart from this subsection, or as limiting his liability on contracts entered into without authority or as conferring any right to indemnity in respect of that liability.'

This provision should always be borne in mind by an examiner, but it should also be read in conjunction with s 29 of the C(A)A 1990, which deals with an examiner's remuneration, costs and expenses, considered below. As a general principle, an examiner must always be cautious not to exceed his power and authority[235].

To obtain information

[22.093] It is essential to the operation of the C(A)A 1990 that the examiner is given all of the information he requires. Section 7(1) of the C(A)A 1990 provides that any provision in the Companies Acts relating to the rights and powers of an auditor of a company and the supplying of information to and co-operation with such auditor shall with the necessary modifications apply to an examiner[236].

[22.094] Section 8(1) of the C(A)A 1990 imposes a duty on the officers and agents[237] of the company or of related companies to produce to the examiner all books and documents of, or relating to, such companies. This duty applies where such documents are in their custody or power. This section also provides that such officers and agents

232 Section 7(2) of the C(A)A 1990.

233 Section 7(3) of the C(A)A 1990.

234 Section 7(4) of the C(A)A 1990.

235 *Re Charnley Davies Ltd* [1988] BCLC 243.

236 See, generally, Ch 17, *Financial Statements, Audit and Annual Return*.

237 Subsection (6) provides that any reference to officers or to agents shall include past as well as present officers or agents and that 'agents' in relation to a company shall include the bankers and solicitors of the company and any person employed by the company as auditors whether those persons are or are not officers of the company.

must attend before the examiner when required to do so and otherwise give him all assistance in connection with his functions which they are reasonably able to give. An examiner may also require a person who is not an officer or agent of the company to attend before him and produce to him any books or documents in his custody or power[238]. An examiner also has powers to require directors to produce documents relating to bank accounts[239].

[22.095] Where an examiner finds that officers and agents of the company or related company are uncooperative, he may examine them in relation to the company's affairs on oath, either orally or on written interrogatories[240]. In such a case, the examiner may administer an oath accordingly and reduce the answers of such person to writing and require the person to sign them. A refusal by any officer or agent of the company or other person to produce any book or document as required or to attend before the examiner or to answer any question put to him in respect of the affairs of the company can be so certified by the examiner under his hand to the court; thereupon, the court may enquire into the case and, after hearing any witnesses who may be produced or any statement which may be offered in defence, make any order or direction it thinks fit[241]. Without prejudice to the foregoing, the court may, after such a hearing, make a direction to the person concerned to attend or re-attend before the examiner or produce particular books or documents or answer particular questions put to him by the examiner, or, that the person concerned need not do all or any of the foregoing[242].

To seek directions from the court

[22.096] Section 7(6) of the C(A)A 1990 provides that an examiner may apply to court to determine any question arising in the course of his office. Such a power is, in practice, very important as an examiner would be unwise to embark upon any drastic action without first obtaining court approval. It is also important to note that a company to which an examiner has been appointed, or any interested party, may apply to the court for the determination of any question arising out of the performance or otherwise by the examiner of his functions: s 13(7) of the C(A)A 1990.

To discharge pre-petition debts

[22.097] The C(A)(No 2)A 1999 introduced a general restriction on the discharge of pre-petition debts. So, s 5A(1) of the C(A)A 1990[243] now provides:

> 'Subject to subsection (2), no payment may be made by a company, during the period it is under the protection of the court, by way of satisfaction or discharge of the whole or a part of a liability incurred by the company before the date of the presentation under section 2 of the petition in relation to it unless the report of the independent accountant contains a

---

238 Section 8(2) of the C(A)A 1990.

239 Section 8(3) of the C(A)A 1990. See generally *British and Commonwealth Holdings plc v Spicer & Oppenheim* [1993] BCLC 168 and *Re Polly Peck International plc* [1992] BCLC 1025.

240 Section 8(4) of the C(A)A 1990.

241 Section 8(5) of the C(A)A 1990.

242 Section 8(5A) of the C(A)A 1990.

243 Inserted by s 15 of the C(A)(No 2)A 1999.

> recommendation that the whole or, as the case may be, the part of that liability should be discharged or satisfied.'

Where the independent accountant's report does not contain such a recommendation, pre-petition debts cannot be discharged. However, an examiner may apply to the court for an order authorising the discharge or satisfaction, in whole or in part, or a pre petition liability; the court can only make such an order where it is satisfied that a failure to discharge or satisfy such liability would 'considerably reduce the prospects of the company or the whole or any part of its undertaking surviving as a going concern'[244].

To borrow

[22.098] An examiner has power to borrow monies on behalf of the company under the protection of the court where he has the prior sanction of the court. The basis of an examiner's power to borrow money on behalf of the company is grounded in s 9 of the C(A)A 1990. This permits the court, on the examiner's application, to transfer any power enjoyed by the directors of the company to the examiner[245]. The court exercised its discretion to transfer the directors' borrowing powers to the examiner in *Re Holidair Ltd*. In that case, the judgment of Costello J in the High Court[246] explained that the reason for the examiner's application to exercise the directors' borrowing powers was:

> '... his belief that the formulation and acceptance of a scheme of arrangement under the Act depended on securing a substantial equity investor and that the continued survival of the group in the short term was dependent upon the ability of the companies to fund their current operations for the following 6 to 8 weeks by raising loans[247].'

Clearly, the court has discretion under s 9 to transfer such a power to an examiner. In the circumstances of *Re Holidair* the foregoing reasons were sufficient to justify the exercise of the court's discretion and the Supreme Court permitted the examiner to borrow.

[22.099] Few but the most altruistic of lending institutions would lend money to a company which is under the protection of the court without a special security. The fact that an examiner has been appointed to the company implies that it has been proved to the satisfaction of the court that the company is unable to pay its debts. Were the examiner with the sanction of the court to offer security to a lending institution, this would still be unsatisfactory because all securities can be set aside either in a subsequent scheme of arrangement or in the discharge of the examiner's costs, expenses and remuneration. For this reason, upon sanctioning an examiner to exercise the directors' borrowing powers, the court will often order that the examiner may certify, under s 10 of the C(A)A 1990, that the sums borrowed are 'expenses' of the examinership. As shall be considered below, the effect of such certification is to give the lending bank priority even ahead of a previously secured creditor[248], subject to the provision in s 29(3A) that certified borrowings will now only rank ahead of a creditor secured by a floating security[249].

---

244 Section 5A(2) of the C(A)A 1990.

245 See paras **[22.089]**.

246 *Re Holidair Ltd* [1994] 1 IR 416.

247 *Re Holidair Ltd* [1994] 1 IR 416 at 425.

248 *Re Holidair Ltd* [1994] 1 IR 416 at 425.

249 See para **[22.085]**.

In *Re Don Bluth Entertainment (No 2)*[250], Blayney J, giving the unanimous decision of the Supreme Court, held that a loan in US dollars, which was certified as an expense of the examinership, should be converted to Irish pounds on the date it was repaid. He held that were the conversion made on the termination of the examinership, the lender would not have the loan repaid in full, as required by s 29(3) of the C(A)A 1990, because the Irish pound had lost value against the dollar since the termination of the examinership.

To deal with charged property

[22.100] Section 11 of the C(A)A 1990 enables an examiner, with the sanction of the court, to deal with certain corporate property although it is charged in someone else's favour. It is crucial to distinguish between assets which are the subject of a fixed charge or mortgage and those which are the subject of a floating charge. Although the legislation is not so clear cut as to explicitly draw a distinction between fixed and floating charges, this classification shall be employed here in the consideration of s 11.

(a) Floating charges

[22.101] Section 11(1) of the C(A)A 1990 provides:

> 'Where, on an application by the examiner, the court is satisfied that the disposal (with or without other assets) of any property of the company which is subject to a security which, as created[251], was a floating charge or the exercise of his powers in relation to such property would be likely to facilitate the survival of the whole or any part of the company as a going concern, the court may by order authorise the examiner to dispose of the property, or exercise his powers in relation to it, as the case may be, as if it were not subject to the security.'

The effect of this is to enable an examiner to sell assets which are the subject of a floating charge. It is a pre-requisite that the court sanctions the exercise of this power and in deciding whether or not to sanction, the court must be satisfied that to do so would be likely to facilitate the survival of the whole or any part of the company as a going concern. It is important, though, to note that the interests of the holder of a floating charge are not totally foresaken.

Section 11(3) of the C(A)A 1990 provides:

> 'Where property is disposed of under sub-section (1), the holder of the security shall have the same priority in respect of any property of the company directly or indirectly representing the property disposed of as he would have had in respect of the property subject to the security.'

Whether this means that the holder of a floating charge is to be in exactly the same position as he was in before the power in s 11(1) is exercised is not clear from s 11(2)[252]. Upon the conversion of the property subject to a floating charge to another form of property, it is possible that its value may be less than the value which the debenture holder would have realised had crystallisation happened as envisaged by the debenture.

---

250 *Re Don Bluth Entertainment (No 2)* [1994] 3 IR 155.

251 The reference to 'as created' implies that a debenture holder may not argue that although the debenture created a floating charge, the charge had crystallised and is now a fixed charge.

252 See para **[22.101]**.

The use of the expression floating *charge* is significant and, it is thought, a floating *chattel mortgage* would not fall within s 11(1).

(b) Fixed charges and mortgages, etc

[22.102] The holder of a fixed charge or mortgage fares better than the holder of a floating charge. However, the examiner may also, with the sanction of the court, dispose of or otherwise deal with property which is subject to a fixed charge. Section 11(2) of the C(A)A 1990 states:

> 'Where, on the application by the examiner, the court is satisfied that the disposal (with or without other assets) of—
>
> (a) any property of the company subject to a security other than a security to which sub-section (1) applies, or
>
> (b) any goods in the possession of the company under a hire-purchase agreement,
>
> would be likely to facilitate the survival of the whole or any part of the company as a going concern, the court may by order authorise the examiner to dispose of the property as if it were not subject to the security or to dispose of the goods as if all rights of the owner under the hire-purchase agreement were vested in the company.'

The wording of s 11(1) and (2) of the C(A)A 1990 are not dramatically different. However, what is different is the protection afforded to persons with a security other than a floating charge.

Section 11(4) of the C(A)A 1990 provides:

> 'It shall be a condition of an order under subsection (2) that—
>
> (a) the net proceeds of the disposal, and
>
> (b) where those proceeds are less than such amount as may be determined by the court to be the net amount which would be realised on a sale of the property or goods in the open market by a willing vendor, such sums as may be required to make good the deficiency,
>
> shall be applied towards discharging the sums secured by the security or payable under the hire-purchase agreement.'

The essential difference is that the fixed charge holder or mortgagee is safeguarded to the extent that the court is empowered to determine the open market value of the property sold, and to order the company to make good the deficiency to the fixed charge holder[253]. In *Re Atlantic Magnetics Ltd*[254], McCarthy J said:

> 'In the case of a fixed charge, the court may authorise the examiner to dispose of the property as if it were not the subject of the security but requires as a condition of an order that the net proceeds shall be applied towards discharging the sum secured by the security with a provision for its shortfall.'

However, McCarthy J held, as did Finlay CJ, that s 11 does not qualify or restrict s 20 of the C(A)A 1990 and accordingly, an examiner's costs, expenses and remuneration will have priority over all other claims against the company. This includes a creditor's claim,

---

[253] See *Re ARV Aviation Ltd* [1989] BCLC 664.

[254] *Re Atlantic Magnetics Ltd* [1993] 2 IR 561 at 579.

even where secured by a fixed charge or mortgage[255], save examiner's expenses in the nature of certified borrowings.

To certify expenses[256]

[22.103] One of the most far-reaching and controversial powers of an examiner is to certify expenditure incurred during the period of court protection as *expenses* of the examination. The statutory basis of certification lies in s 20 of the C(A)A 1990 which provides that:

> '(1) Any liabilities incurred by the company during the protection period which are referred to in sub-section (2) shall be treated as expenses properly incurred, for the purpose of section 29, by the examiner.
>
> (2) The liabilities referred to in sub-section (1) are those certified by the examiner at the time they are incurred, to have been incurred in circumstances where, in the opinion of the examiner, the survival of the company as a going concern during the protection period would otherwise be seriously prejudiced.
>
> (3) In this section "protection period" means the period, beginning with the appointment of an examiner, during which the company is under the protection of the court.'

Even without any judicial interpretation it can immediately be seen that s 10 has the potential for drastic effects. This is seen to be the case when read in conjunction with s 29 of the C(A)A 1990. For the purposes of understanding the significance of an examiner's power of certification it is sufficient to realise that all expenses, so certified by an examiner, have priority over all other claims against a company, including sums secured by a fixed charge or mortgage and even a liquidator's fees, costs and expenses. In *Re Edenpark Construction Ltd*[257], Murphy J said that to elevate liabilities of the company to the status of expenses, the following must occur:

> '(1) The liabilities must be certified by the examiner to have been incurred in circumstances where the survival of the company as a going concern would otherwise be seriously prejudiced.
>
> (2) That the prejudice must be foreseen as occurring in the period which commenced with the appointment of an examiner and terminating with the cessation of the protection.
>
> (3) That the certification by the examiner must take place at the time when the liabilities are incurred[258].'

A number of points contained in s 10 require further consideration.

[22.104] In the first place, not all liabilitics of the company can be certified by an examiner. Section 10(1) of the C(A)A 1990 is quite explicit in specifying that only liabilities incurred *during the protection period* may be certified as expenses of the examination. Corporate liabilities, such as the cost of the presentation of a petition to have an examiner or interim examiner appointed, are *not* certifiable expenses. This is

255 See para **[22.102]** *et seq*.

256 See generally, O'Donnell, 'Nursing the Corporate Patient – Examinership and Certification Under the Companies (Amendment) Act 1990' (1994) CLP 83.

257 *Re Edenpark Construction Ltd* [1994] 3 IR 126.

258 *Re Edenpark Construction Ltd* [1994] 3 IR 126 at 134.

clear from the decision of Murphy J in *Re Don Bluth Entertainment Ltd*[259] where the fees of the firm of solicitors who presented the petition to have the examiner appointed were held not to be a certifiable expense of the examinership. In the words of Murphy J:

> 'The 1990 Amendment Act does not confer any priority on the costs of persons petitioning for the appointment of an examiner ... Furthermore, the general scheme of the Act could not have envisaged the Petitioner procuring a priority for his costs by means of certification under s 10 as ordinarily the examiner would not be appointed until after the expense of the petition had been incurred. It would seem to me to be inappropriate to alter the scheme of the Act by the fortuitous event that a provisional or interim examiner might be appointed and that his certificate would give to the petitioner a priority which the legislation had withheld. In so far as the examiner purported to certify liabilities already incurred, it is clear that the certificate has no statutory effect. In so far as the liabilities related ... to contemporaneous liabilities in respect of proceedings for the appointment of an examiner, it seems to me that the certificate is likewise invalid for the reason ... that the protection period during which the survival of the company falls to be considered is a period which commences with and postulates the existence of an examiner so that the appointment of an examiner or proceedings for that purpose can have no bearing on the survival of the company during the relevant period[260].'

It should be noted also that, generally, the costs of presenting a petition to have an examiner appointed to a *related* company will not be liabilities capable of being certified as expenses of the company already under the protection of the court. As Murphy J noted in *Re Edenpark Construction Ltd*[261], during the protection period the company is safeguarded by s 5 of the C(A)A 1990. Accordingly it could not be said that the failure to appoint an examiner over a related company would prejudice the primary company during the protection period.

[22.105] In the second place, the opinion of an examiner is not sacrosanct. It is subject to review by the courts[262]. The act of certification can be questioned by the court. This is clear from s 29 which, by using the word 'may', indicates that the court has a discretion. In *Re Don Bluth Entertainment Ltd,* Murphy J said that an examiner should:

> '... exercise great care and professional expertise in issuing certificates under s 10. I would anticipate that an examiner from whom a certificate is sought would require the directors managing the business of the company to submit to him their proposals in relation to any particular liabilities which they proposed to incur and to satisfy him as to how the services or goods to be obtained would benefit the company and in particular how they would contribute to the survival of the company "during the protection period".'

Where an examiner has successfully applied to have the directors' powers transferred to him, he ought to exercise even greater care in certifying liabilities as expenses of the examination.

[22.106] In the third place, even within the protection period itself, the court may refuse, *ab initio*, to sanction all but certain expenses certified by the examiner. Such an order

[259] *Re Don Bluth Entertainment Ltd* [1994] 3 IR 141.

[260] *Re Don Bluth Entertainment Ltd* [1994] 3 IR 141 at 151–152.

[261] *Re Edenpark Construction Ltd* [1994] 3 IR 126 at 138.

[262] See *Re Don Bluth Entertainment Ltd* [1994] 3 IR 141 and in particular the passage quoted in the preceding paragraph.

was made by Murphy J in *Re Don Bluth Entertainment Ltd*[263] which prevented the examiner certifying liabilities other than those of certain creditors. This was felt necessary in the circumstances, due to the concern of those who opposed the petition that the motive behind the presentation of the petition was to achieve a position in which the examiner would prefer certain creditors by issuing s 10 certificates.

[22.107] In the fourth place, the manner of certification is important. Although oral certification would appear to have been sanctioned by the courts[264], written certification is to be preferred, from an evidential standpoint if nothing else. In *Re Edenpark Construction Ltd*[265], Murphy J held that:

> '... I would accept that ordinarily the word "certify" does not necessarily connote a document in writing. Where such is required a draftsman would be expected to include the words "in writing". However even accepting that a certificate in writing is not a legislative requirement, one would have thought that it was an obvious and inescapable administrative necessity. Even where written documentation exists in the present case, it is by no means clear that the examiner directed his mind to the essential ingredients of a certificate for the purposes of s 10 aforesaid. In the absence of such documentation it is difficult to ask those creditors whose rights are postponed to accept that the parol certification was correct in its terms and in its content[266].'

Murphy J went on to hold that the examiner in that case erred in the manner in which he purported to certify the liabilities of the company under s 10 of the C(A)A 1990. He said that it was significant that:

> '... the examiner states that the liabilities were certified by him "at the time they were incurred" and goes on to say that he did so as he considered they were necessary to ensure the survival of the companies but he does not say that it was his opinion that the survival of the companies would be seriously prejudiced "during the protection period". It seems to me there is a vast difference between these two situations[267].'

The difference referred to by Murphy J is between forming an opinion that a company's survival might be seriously prejudiced during a period limited to six or seven weeks, and during a wholly indefinite period. Another point, which was also made by Murphy J in *Edenpark*, is the importance of an examiner maintaining a clear distinction between expenses which he himself incurred and those which were incurred by the corporate entity, whether or not those are certified by him.

[22.108] Fifthly, and finally, it should be noted that any liabilities incurred by a company during a period of interim protection, granted under s 3A(1) of the C(A)A 1990 (ie, where exceptional circumstances exist as to why the report of an independent accountant is not available) may not be the subject of a certificate under s 10(2) of the C(A)A 1990[268].

---

[263] *Re Don Bluth Entertainment Ltd* [1994] 3 IR 141.

[264] See O'Donnell, *Examinerships* (1994), who notes that oral certification was given to some creditors in the *United Meat Packers* examinership.

[265] *Re Edenpark Construction Ltd* [1994] 3 IR 126.

[266] *Re Edenpark Construction Ltd* [1994] 3 IR 126 at 134–135.

[267] *Re Edenpark Construction Ltd* [1994] 3 IR 126 at 135.

[268] Section 3A(8) of the C(A)A 1990.

To regularise improper transactions

[22.109] Once appointed, an examiner has certain duties to the court to ensure that any improprieties in the company's affairs are regularised. One example of this is an examiner's *locus standi* to make application under s 297A of the CA 1963, as amended, in respect of fraudulent and reckless trading[269].

[22.110] Section 139 of the CA 1990[270] provides that on the application, *inter alios,* of an examiner, if it can be shown to the satisfaction of the court that:

> '(a) any property of the company of any kind whatsoever was disposed of in anyway whatsoever, whether by act or omission, direct or indirect, and
>
> (b) the effect of such disposal was to perpetrate a fraud on the company, its creditors or members,
>
> the court can, if it deems it just and equitable so to do, order any person who appears to have the use, control or possession of such property or the proceeds of sale or development of such property to deliver it, or a sum in respect of it, to the examiner on such terms as the court sees fit.'

Section 139(2) of the CA 1990 provides that sub-s (1) has no application to fraudulent preferences which are governed by s 286 of the CA 1963. In deciding whether it is just and equitable to make such an order the court is obliged to have regard to the rights of persons who have *bona fide* and for value acquired an interest in the property concerned[271].

[E] THE EXAMINER'S REPORT AND SCHEMES OF ARRANGEMENT

[22.111] Once appointed, the examiner's primary duty is to conduct an examination into the company's affairs with a view to preparing his report under s 18 of the C(A)A 1990.

1. Examiners' duties.
2. Hearing regarding irregularities.
3. The formulation of proposals.
4. Restriction on compromise of leasing claims.
5. Meetings of creditors and members to consider the proposals.
6. The examiner's report under s 18 of the C(A)A 1990.
7. Hearing the proposals: court confirmation or rejection.
8. Matters arising after court confirmation of the proposals.

Examiners' duties

[22.112] An examiner's primary duty is to conduct an examination of the company's affairs and to report with the results to the court. Where he feels he cannot comply with his statutory duties within the prescribed time limit of 70 days, the examiner may apply *ex parte*[272] to the court for an extension of up to 30 days under s 18(3) of the C(A)A

[269] See Ch 15, *Duties of Directors and Other Officers*, para **[15.095]** *et seq.*

[270] See Ch 25, *Realisation and Distribution of Assets in a Winding Up*, para **[25.103]**.

[271] Section s 139(3) of the CA 1990.

[272] Order 75A, r 16 of the RSC 1986.

1990[273]. The court will be cautious to grant an extension to the prescribed time limit, particularly when met with the objections of creditors[274].

[22.113] An examiner also owes ancillary duties. In general terms, an examiner must act honestly, reasonably, and with the fullest candour to the court in respect of all matters which on objective criteria could be material. Some of the duties owed by examiners were considered by Costello J in *Re Wogans (Drogheda) Ltd (No 3)*[275]. There, he found that the examiner was in breach of his duties to the court and/or behaved improperly, *inter alia*, for the following reasons: failing to take reasonable steps to ensure that the court was not misled; failing to inform the company's solicitors of under-the-counter payments to employees, the effect of which meant that the company's liabilities were greater than previously thought by reason of outstanding taxes; failing to bring to the court's notice that the company's statement of affairs was incorrect; failing to enquire into the extent of the under-the-counter payments; failing to disclose to the court that he, the examiner, had acted as an informal interim examiner; failing to disclose that fees had been paid to him for his work as an informal interim examiner; failing to report adequately to the court on legal problems raised by directors' guarantees and the manner in which he dealt with them; failing to inform the Revenue Commissioners of the proposed investor's proposals for a tax write-down; and failing to disclose to the court the prospect that not all of the company's employees were proposed to be retained by the proposed investor[276]. The effects of the examiners' breaches of duties disentitled him to any remuneration, costs or expenses for his work as an examiner[277].

[22.114] It should also be noted that the examiner, or such other person as the court may direct, is obliged within 24 days after the delivery to the registrar of companies of every order made under ss 13A, 24 or 27 of the C(A)A 1990 to cause to be published, in *Iris Oifigiúil*, notice of such delivery[278].

Hearing regarding irregularities

[22.115] Where it appears to the court that there is evidence of a substantial disappearance of property of a company that is inadequately accounted for or of other serious irregularities in relation to the company's affairs, it may hold a hearing to consider that evidence[279]. Such may arise out of the presentation of the independent accountant's report or, indeed, otherwise. To assist the investigative process, the court may direct the examiner to prepare a report setting out such matters as he considers will assist it in considering the evidence concerned on a hearing[280]. A copy of any such

---

273 On extensions of time under the Insolvency Act 1986 (UK), see: *Re Newport County Association Football Club Ltd* [1987] BCLC 582.

274 Cf *Re NS Distribution Ltd* [1990] BCLC 169.

275 *Re Wogans (Drogheda) Ltd (No 3)* [1993] 1 IR 157.

276 See *Re Hartlebury Printers Ltd (in liq)* [1993] BCLC 902 for a consideration of a UK administrator's duty to employees of the company concerned.

277 Remuneration, costs and expenses are considered further at para **[22.163]**.

278 Section 30(1) of the C(A)A 1990. Although s 72 of IFCMPA 2005 substituted 'the Companies Registration Office Gazette' for '*Iris Oifigiúil*' that section has never been commenced.

279 Section 13A(1) of the C(A)A 1990.

280 Section 13A(2) of the C(A)A 1990.

examiner's report must be supplied to the company on the same day as he causes it to be delivered to the court[281]. Copies must also be given to persons mentioned in his report and, on written application, to any interested party[282]; on application being made to it, the court may direct that such parts of the report as it specifies may be omitted in any copy of the report supplied to such persons[283]. Guidance is given, in respect of such omissions, by s 13A(6) of the C(A)A 1990 which provides that the court may in particular direct the omission of such information as would be likely to prejudice the survival of the company or the whole or any part of its undertaking as a going concern. Section 13A(8) of the C(A)A 1990 lists those who have standing to appear and be heard at a hearing[284]. Arising from any such hearing the court may make such order or orders as it deems fit, including, where appropriate, an order for the trial of any issue relating to the matter concerned[285] and may direct that an office copy of any such order must be delivered to the registrar of companies by the examiner or such other person as it may specify[286].

The formulation of proposals

[22.116] The formulation of proposals is the most fundamental aspect of the examinership provisions. The examiner's report made pursuant to s 18 of the C(A)A 1990[287] is mandatory in nature. Section 18(1) provides that:

> 'An examiner shall—
>
> (a) as soon as practicable after he is appointed, formulate proposals for a compromise or scheme of arrangement in relation to the company concerned,
>
> (b) without prejudice to any other provision of this Act, carry out such other duties as the court may direct him to carry out.'

In *Re Clare Textiles Ltd*[288], Costello J said:

> 'In my opinion, it is quite clear that the only proposals he is permitted to formulate are those which make it likely that (a) the company and (b) the whole or part of its undertaking will survive as a going concern. The examiner has no authority to prepare proposals involving the sale of the company's assets and its business or its liquidation and in my opinion the court has no power to confirm proposals under s 24 which do not

281 Section 13A(3) of the C(A)A 1990. Where the company is a company referred to in s 3(2)(a) of the C(A)A 1990, a copy of the report must also be supplied to the Minister and where the company is a company referred to in s 3(2)(b) or (c) of the C(A)A 1990 a copy of the report must also be supplied to the Central Bank and in either case s 3(5) and (6) of the C(A)A 1990 (considered next) shall not apply to such copy: s 13A(7) of the C(A)A 1990.

282 Section 13A(4) of the C(A)A 1990.

283 Section 13A(5) of the C(A)A 1990.

284 Namely, the examiner, an independent accountant where the court decided to hold a hearing by reason of matters contained in his report, the company concerned, any interested party, any person referred to in the report, and in the case of a company referred to in s 3(2)(a) of the C(A)A 1990, the Minister, and in the case of a company referred to in s 3(2)(b) or (c) of the C(A)A 1990, the Central Bank.

285 Section 13A(9) of the C(A)A 1990.

286 Section 13A(10) of the C(A)A 1990.

287 As amended by s 22(a) of the C(A)(No 2)A 1999.

288 *Re Clare Textiles Ltd* [1993] 2 IR 213.

provide for the survival of the company and at least part of its undertaking as a going concern ...'

As has already been seen, an examiner who proceeds otherwise will be in breach of his statutory duty.

[22.117] Where an examiner is unable to reach agreement with interested parties or formulate proposals he may apply to the court for directions. Thus s 18(9) of the C(A)A 1990[289] provides:

'If the examiner is not able to enter into an agreement with the interested parties and any other persons concerned in the matter or formulate proposals for a compromise or scheme of arrangement in relation to the company concerned, he may apply to the court for the grant of directions in the matter and the court may, on such application, give such directions or make such order as it deems fit, including, if it considers it just and equitable to do so, an order for the winding up of the company.'

[22.118] Section 22(1) of the C(A)A 1990 specifies a number of matters which an examiner's proposals for a compromise or scheme of arrangement must address. Accordingly, the proposal must:

'(a) specify each class of members and creditors of the company,

(b) specify any class of members and creditors whose interests or claims will not be impaired by the proposals,

(c) specify any class of members and creditors whose interests or claims will be impaired by the proposals[290],

(d) provide equal treatment for each claim or interest of a particular class unless the holder of a particular claim or interest agrees to less favourable treatment,

(e) provide for the implementation of the proposals,

(f) if the examiner considers it necessary or desirable to do so to facilitate the survival of the company, and the whole or any part of its undertaking, as a going concern, specify whatever changes should be made in relation to the management or direction of the company,

(g) if the examiner considers it necessary or desirable as aforesaid, specify any changes he considers should be made in the memorandum or articles of the company, whether as regards the management or direction of the company or otherwise,

(h) include such other matters as the examiner deems appropriate.'

---

289 As inserted by s 22(d) of the C(A)(No 2)A 1999.

290 Section 22(6) of the C(A)A 1990 provides what is meant by the interests of members being impaired. It provides: 'For the purposes of this section and sections 24 and 25, the interest of a member of a company in a company is *impaired* if— (a) the nominal value of his shareholding in the company is reduced, (b) where he is entitled to a fixed dividend in respect of his shareholding in the company, the amount of that dividend is reduced, (c) he is deprived of all or any part of the rights accruing to him by virtue of his shareholding in the company, (d) his percentage interest in the total issued share capital of the company in reduced, or (e) he is deprived of his shareholding in the company.' As to the impairment of the interests of *creditors*, see para **[22.154]**.

[22.119] It has been noted[291] that the notion of proposals for a compromise is not a new concept in company law and has a parallel in the context of 'arrangements' under s 201 of the CA 1963, as was considered in Chapter 21.

[22.120] In addition to the matters detailed in s 22(1) of the C(A)A 1990, the examiner's proposals must be accompanied by a number of other documents. Section 22(2) provides that a statement of the assets and liabilities (including contingent and prospective liabilities) of the company as at the date of the proposals must be attached to each copy of the proposals to be submitted to meetings of members and creditors. Furthermore, s 22(3) provides that there shall also be attached to each such copy of the proposals, a description of the estimated financial outcome of a winding up of the company for each class of members and creditors.

[22.121] In reality, while the foregoing matters will be relevant to any proposals for a compromise or scheme of arrangement, they do not touch upon what is often one of the most important issues: the availability and willingness of an outside investor and the willingness of the company's creditors to compromise their claims. The availability and willingness of an outside investor will be a matter of fact in the context of any particular company. Sometimes investors will be found, but their agreement to become involved in the company will depend upon the inducements offered to them. Potential investors in an ailing company will be even more cautious than they would be if approached to become involved in a new company or a joint venture. The fact that a company is in examinership means, by definition, that the company is unable to pay its debts, ie, it is insolvent. Consequently, the probability of an investor coming on board is often slim. Nonetheless, investors are sometimes found and companies which were placed under the protection of the court have been saved.

[22.122] As to the terms that are permissible in a scheme, in *Re Eylewood Ltd*[292] it was held by Finlay Geoghegan J that an examiner could include a provision that a member transfer all of its shares in the company, propose amendments to the articles of association to give effect to such provisions and request the court to make appropriate orders under s 24(8) if it confirmed the scheme. Whether or not a scheme which contains such proposals will be confirmed, however, will depend upon whether the court is satisfied that the proposal is fair and reasonable to the member and not unfairly prejudicial to the member's interests.

[22.123] In *Michael McLoughlin (Pharmacy) Ltd*[293], it was noted that a practice had developed whereby indemnities in favour of examiners were 'creeping-in' to schemes of arrangement. In that case the indemnity provided:

> 'The examiner shall have no personal liability in relation to these proposals or his actions as examiner or the conduct of the examinership, (save in the case of wilful default, gross negligence, or fraud on the part of the examiner or his staff). Without prejudice to that exclusion of personal liability, if the examiner has, in the performance of his functions under the Act, assumed, or if in future during the protection period he were to assume, personal liability on any contracts as provided for in Section 13(6) of the Act, the examiner shall have a right to an indemnity out of the assets of the company in respect of

291 See O'Donnell, *Examinerships* (1994), p 55.

292 *Re Eylewood Ltd* [2010] IEHC 57.

293 *Re Michael McLoughlin (Pharmacy) Ltd* [2011] IEHC 28.

such personal liability. The examiner's right to be paid on foot of any such indemnity or indemnities in respect of any obligation entered into by him in the performance of his functions shall rank in priority to the payment of any part of the debt due to the creditors, and shall continue, notwithstanding the ending of the protection period.'

In that case, one of the company's creditor banks objected to the inclusion of this indemnity in principle. Clarke J noted that s 22 of the C(A)A 1990 did not expressly allow for an indemnity to be included in a scheme and further held that there was no implied power to include such an indemnity. Clarke J concluded:

'3.12 All in all it seemed to me that if it had been the intention of the Oireachtas that examiners could be immune from suit in negligence arising out of the exercise of their functions, the Oireachtas would have said so in the 1990 Act. There is no doubt that the 1990 Act does not expressly so provide. On a proper construction of the 1990 Act it did not seem to me that the court was conferred with a discretion to include such an immunity by the backdoor of an appropriate clause being included in a scheme of arrangement. The fact that the scheme proposed in this case proposed to preserve liability for fraud, gross negligence and the like did not, in those circumstances, seem to me to be of any relevance.

3.13 For all those reasons I was satisfied that the court does not have a jurisdiction to approve such a clause. I was further satisfied that, even if the court had a jurisdiction to include such a clause, there was no legitimate basis for the inclusion of such a clause on the facts of this case. If any jurisdiction existed, it would seem to me that it could only be exercised in a wholly exceptional case for to do otherwise would be to introduce, by the backdoor, an immunity measure into the 1990 Act.'

Restriction on compromise of leasing claims

[22.124] Section 25B(1)(a) of the C(A)A 1990[294] prohibits the compromise or scheme of arrangement from providing for the extinguishment or reduction in the amount of rent or other payment due in respect of a lease of land after the scheme is approved. Furthermore, s 25B(1)(b) addresses a failure to pay an amount of rent or other periodical payment reserved under a lease of land or to comply with any other covenant or obligation of such a lease that falls to be paid or complied with after a compromise or scheme of arrangement takes effect. This prohibits a compromise or scheme of arrangement from containing a requirement that restricts the exercise by a lessor of any right whether under the lease or otherwise to recover possession of the land, effect a forfeiture of the lease or otherwise enter on the land or to recover the amount of such rent or other payment or to claim damages or other reliefs in respect of the failure to comply with any covenant or obligation in such a lease. In both respects, a compromise or scheme of arrangement cannot be modified by the court under s 24 if the result would be as outlined. Again, in both cases, a compromise or scheme of arrangement can only contain such provisions where a lessor or owner of the property concerned has consented in writing to such provisions[295].

[22.125] The application of the foregoing prohibitions is confined to leases of land. However, s 25B(2) of the C(A)A 1990 provides that:

294 Inserted by s 26 of the C(A)(No 2)A 1999.

295 Section 25B(3) of the C(A)A 1990.

'... proposals for a compromise or scheme of arrangement in relation to a company shall not be held by the court to satisfy the condition specified in paragraph (c)(ii) of section 24(4) if the proposals contain a provision relating to a lease of, or any hiring agreement in relation to, property other than land and, in the opinion of the court—

(a) the value of that property is substantial, and

(b) the said provision is of like effect to a provision referred to in paragraph (a) or (b) of subsection (1).'

Some guidance is given to the court in deciding whether the value of property is substantial, and s 25B(4) provides that it shall have regard to the length of the unexpired term of the lease or the hiring agreement concerned.

[22.126] Section 25B of the C(A)A 1990 is only concerned with the extinguishment of the rights of the lessor landlord to the payment of any rent while the lessee tenant continues to have the benefit of the property which is the subject of the lease. This was made clear by the decision of the Supreme Court in *Re Linen Supply of Ireland Ltd*[296] which held that there was jurisdiction under s 20(1) of the C(A)A 1990 to repudiate a lease by the mutual release of both lessor and lessee from all rights and obligations and that such a repudiation was an entirely different matter to that contemplated by s 25B. Previously, it had been held by Ryan J in *Re O'Brien's Sandwich Bars Ltd*[297] that the jurisdiction under s 20(1) to repudiate 'contracts' did not include contracts that were leases. In that case, it was proposed to repudiate some 40 leases of premises which the company had leased from landlords and then sub-let to tenant franchisees of the O'Brien's Sandwich Bar brand. In the High Court decision in *Re Linen Supply of Ireland Ltd*, McGovern J had followed the decision of Ryan J and held:

'It seems to me that the thrust of s 25B of the Act is to the effect that a scheme of arrangement cannot provide for a reduction in rent or an extinguishment of the right of the lessor to the payment of rent that falls to be paid after the compromise or scheme of arrangement would take effect, unless the lessor or owner of the property concerned has consented in writing to the inclusion of such a provision in the proposals for the compromise or scheme of arrangement. If s 20 of the Act was to permit the repudiation of a lease, it would be completely at variance with s 25B. Since s 25B specifically refers to leases, as does s 290 of the Principal Act, I have come to the conclusion that s 20 of the Act does not permit the court to make an order entitling the company to repudiate the leases in this case.'

By a majority decision, the Supreme Court overruled the High Court and found that the jurisdiction in s 20(1) of the C(A)A 1990 to repudiate any contract included a lease because leases are, as a matter of law, contracts and if the Oireachtas had intended to exclude leases from s 20(1), it would have said so. Section 20(1) of the C(A)A 1990 provides:

Where proposals for a compromise or scheme of arrangement are to be formulated in relation to a company, the company may, subject to the approval of the court, affirm or

[296] *Re Linen Supply of Ireland Ltd* (10 December 2009, ex tempore) SC on appeal from the decision of the High Court reported at [2009] IEHC 544, McGovern J; noted by Feeney, 'Landlords and Examinership' (2010) 17(3) CLP 47 which is an excellent review of the law relating to repudiating leases in an examinership.

[297] *Re O'Brien's Sandwich Bars Ltd* [2009] IEHC 465, Ryan J.

> repudiate any contract under which some element of performance other than payment remains to be rendered both by the company and the other contracting party or parties.

The majority also found that to the extend that s 20(1) required a contract to involve '*some element of performance other than payment*' which remains to be rendered by the parties, a lease did involve the performance of obligations by both the lessor and lessee other than payment of money, eg, the right to quiet enjoyment and to insure.

[22.127] It is one thing to say that there is jurisdiction to repudiate leases, it is quite another to find that particular leases should be repudiated and that such repudiation does not constitute treating lessor landlords in an unfairly prejudicial manner. In the first place, for a contract to be repudiated under s 20(1) it has to be in the context of where proposals for a compromise or scheme of arrangement are to be formulated. When the matter was returned to the High Court in *Re Linen Supplies of Ireland Ltd*, McGovern J exercised his discretion to approve the repudiation of the lease in that case, but did so conditional upon the ultimate confirmation of the scheme of arrangement.

[22.128] In *Re Bestseller Retail Ltd*[298], orders were sought under s 20(1) and (3) of the C(A)A 1990 in respect of a number of leases where repudiation was sought, agreement not having been reached with the landlords. The company operated from 36 stores under 30 leases some of which had been guaranteed by the company's Danish holding company. McGovern J heard objection from some of the landlords who claimed that of those leases being repudiated, none of them had been guaranteed by the parent and so the repudiation would not result in any claim against the parent. Moreover, some of the leases which it was sought to repudiate related to profitable stores whereas some of those being retained which were guaranteed by the parent were unprofitable. Of this McGovern J said:

> 'No repudiation of a lease has been sought where there is a guarantee by the parent company. Objectively, this appears to be unfair. No reasonable explanation has been given for this difference in treatment of those premises. Counsel for the Company accepts that the holding company, which is a shareholder, does have a benefit in the repudiation sought because of the guarantee, but he argues that this has to be balanced against the benefits of an examinership. He argues that the court should weigh and balance the rights of other creditors and the other landlords who have entered into agreements to compromise their leases and the court should also consider the possible loss of 150 jobs if the examinership does not proceed. The purpose of the 1990 Act is the survival of the enterprise. It is difficult to escape the conclusion that the company is seeking to repudiate these leases because a guarantee has been given by the holding company. In the case of in *Re Traffic Group Ltd* [2008] 3 IR 253 at 260, Clarke J set out the principal focus of the legislation on examinership. He pointed out that, "It is not designed to help shareholders whose investment has proved to be unsuccessful. It is to seek to save enterprise and the jobs". The owners of the Dundalk store complain that although Dundalk is not on a list of underperforming stores in the independent accountant's report, it is sought, by the company, to repudiate that lease. There appears to be no satisfactory explanation for this. They argue that it is difficult to understand how a financial burden arises to the group if, in fact, the Dundalk store provides a net contribution. In any event, this situation would not warrant such a drastic step as a repudiation. The Company, for its part, argues that, in fact, the examiner has carried out a review of the Dundalk lease and is satisfied that,

298 *Re Bestseller Retail Ltd* [2010] IEHC 155.

having regard to the turnover of the unit and the rent, and forecasting further turnover, it is likely to reflect a loss.'

In that case, McGovern J held it was a material consideration in the exercise of the court's discretion that it was not sought to disclaim any lease which had been guaranteed by the parent and that it seemed that the sole or predominant basis for selection of leases to be redeemed was on the basis of the absence of guarantees given by the parent. Finding that the dominant motive was to help the shareholders, the learned judge rejected the application to repudiate certain leases.

[22.129] One thorny question which was addressed by McGovern J in *Re Linen Supplies of Ireland Ltd*[299], the decision which confirmed the scheme of arrangement proposed by the examiner, was whether a lessor landlord claim for damages under s 20(2) following the repudiation of a lease can be the subject of a write-down in the examination. The lessor landlord in that case claimed that the damages assessed in its favour was a post-petition liability and should be paid in full; moreover, it was claimed that the effect of s 22(5) of the C(A)A 1990 which provides that 'a creditor's claim against a company is impaired if he receives less than the full amount due in respect of the claim at the date of presentation of the petition for the appointment of the examiner' meant that the scheme could only write down debts in existence at the date of the petition. McGovern J rejected this on the basis that the Act applied to different types of creditors, and he held that prospective creditors at the date of the petition, which is what the landlords would be in relation to damages assessed under s 20(2), could have their debts written-down in a scheme[300].

Meetings of creditors and members to consider the proposals

[22.130] Upon an examiner formulating proposals for a compromise or scheme of arrangement, he is obliged to convene a meeting of the creditors and members of the company for the purpose of considering such proposals. Section 18(2) of the C(A)A 1990[301] provides for the convening and holding of meeting by examiners. This now provides:

> 'Notwithstanding any provision of the Companies Acts relating to notice of general meetings, (but subject to notice of not less than 3 days in any case) the examiner shall convene and preside at such meetings of members and creditors as he thinks proper, for the purpose of section 23 and shall report on those proposals to the court, within 35 days of his appointment or such longer period as the court may allow, in accordance with s 19.'

Order 75A, r 18 of the RSC 1986 details the appointed procedure for the convening and holding of members' and creditors' meetings. The essence of the procedure detailed in

299 *Re Linen Supplies of Ireland Ltd* [2010] IEHC 28.

300 Feeney, 'Landlords and Examinership' (2010) 17(3) CLP 47 argues that it is far from clear that the Oireachtas intended landlords whose leases were repudiated and had damages assessed being included in those unsecured creditors whose claims are liable to be written-down in a scheme and that while McGovern J relied on the fact that those creditors entitled to present a petition expressly include prospective creditors, whereas those whose debts could be written-down are only referred to as 'creditors', supports the view that prospective creditors are not liable to have their debts written-down.

301 As amended by s 22(b) of the C(A)(No 2)A 1999.

r 18 is that members and creditors should receive proper notice of their respective meetings. With each notice summoning a meeting of the members or creditors the examiner must send a statement explaining the effect of the compromise or scheme of arrangement.

[22.131] Formalities and procedure aside, the usual situation is that at meetings of the creditors of the typical private company placed under the protection of the court, the creditors will be asked to compromise their claims against the company and to accept that what is owed to them will be reduced. Section 23(1) of the C(A)A 1990[302] provides:

> 'This section applies to a meeting of members or creditors or any class of members or creditors summoned to consider proposals for a compromise or scheme of arrangement; save where expressly provided otherwise in this section, this section shall not authorise, at such a meeting, anything to be done in relation to such proposals by any member or creditor.'

The purpose of such a meeting is to enable members and creditors to consider the examiner's proposals. Every notice summoning a meeting of creditors or members must be accompanied by a statement explaining the effect of the compromise or scheme of arrangement and, in particular, must state any material interest of the directors of the company, whether as directors or as members or as creditors or otherwise and the effect thereon of the compromise or arrangement, insofar as it is different from the effect on the like interest of other persons[303]. Proposals shall be deemed to have been accepted by a meeting of creditors where a majority in number representing a majority in value of the claims represented at that meeting have voted, in person or by proxy, in favour of the resolution for the proposals[304]. Section 144 of the CA 1963 is deemed to apply to any resolution to which s 23(4) of the C(A)A 1990 relates if passed at any adjourned meeting. A creditor's abstention or other failure to cast a vote in respect of such proposals is not to be construed as a casting of a vote against the proposals[305].

For unsecured creditors, the prospect is often bleak. By agreeing to a compromise they will not recover in full what is due and owing to them. However, where the company concerned is their major or even a prominent customer, the alternative may well be that the company will no longer purchase their goods or services with the result that their interests will be harmed, in any event. The unsecured creditors may, for commercial reasons, vote for a scheme of arrangement. The unsecured creditor may decide to accept a compromise and thereby compromise financial recompense for goods or services rendered, in the anticipation of future business.

Prior to the C(A)A 1990, State authorities[306] that were creditors could not compromisc claims which were due and owing to them under statute. To do so would be

---

302 As amended by s 23(a) of the C(A)(No 2)A 1999.

303 Section 23(8) of the C(A)A 1990. In the case of companies referred to in s 3(2)(b) and (c) of the C(A)A 1990, without prejudice to s 23(1)(8), the examiner is obliged to also afford the Central Bank an opportunity to consider the proposals for a compromise or scheme of arrangement and for that purpose must furnish the Central Bank with a statement containing like information as that referred to in sub-s (8): s 23(9) of the C(A)A 1990.

304 Section 23(4) of the C(A)A 1990.

305 Section 23(4A) of the C(A)A 1990.

306 Section 23(5) of the C(A)A 1990. 'State authority' is defined to mean the State, a Minister of the Government, a local authority or the Revenue Commissioners.

ultra vires their statutory function and power. This has now been changed by s 23(5) of the C(A)A 1990. Often it will be the Revenue Commissioners who will be asked to bear the brunt of the compromise, the State being the creditor with the deepest pocket. The Revenue Commissioners tend to take a strong line in such cases and unreasonable proposals for a compromise of their claims will be rejected, both by them and by the court.

Secured creditors who have a fixed mortgage or fixed charge are also likely to suffer in a compromise or scheme of arrangement. As has been considered previously, secured creditors can have their previously unassailable security ignored and the proceeds used to discharge claims other than theirs. However, in the circumstances of a particular case a secured creditor may well be of the opinion that it is in its long-term interests to agree to a form of compromise.

[22.132] The company's creditors may not accept all of the examiner's proposals for a compromise or scheme of arrangement. Any modification of the proposals must be agreed by the examiner[307]. It has been, quite sensibly, suggested that where modifications are suggested at the last meeting, the examiner should reconvene previously held meetings to put the modified proposals to those meetings also[308].

The examiner's report under s 18 of the C(A)A 1990

[22.0133] The contents of the examiner's report must conform to s 19 of the C(A)A 1990. This provides that his report must include:

- the proposals placed before the required meetings;
- any modifications of those proposals adopted at any of those meetings;
- the outcome of each of the required meetings;
- the recommendation of the committee of creditors, if any;
- a statement of the assets and liabilities (including contingent and prospective liabilities) of the company as at the date of his report;
- a list of the creditors of the company, the amount owing to each such creditor, the nature and value of any security held by any such creditor, and the priority status of any such creditor under s 285 of the CA 1963 or any other statutory provision or rule of law;
- a list of the officers of the company;
- his recommendations;
- such other matters as the examiner deems appropriate or the court directs.

The examiner's report is designed to inform the court of his proposals for a compromise or scheme of arrangement and then to show whether the proposals have been accepted by the company's creditors. Where the proposals are acceptable to the company's creditors, the court's task will be made considerably easier than where the examiner's proposals are rejected by them.

---

307 Section 23(2) of the C(A)A 1990.

308 See O'Donnell, *Examinerships* (1994), p 62.

[22.134] The examiner must on the same day as he delivers the report to court, also deliver a copy of it to the company and to any interested party who applies in writing[309]. On the examiner's *ex parte* application[310], the court will, in an administrative action[311], receive the s 18 report without approving or rejecting it and set a date for the hearing of the examiner's proposals. The examiner should confirm in his application that the petitioner has complied with s 12(1) of the C(A)A 1990[312], and that he has complied with subss 12(2)[313] and (3)[314].

[22.135] On application being made, the court may direct that there may be an omission of such parts of the report as it specifies in any copy of the report supplied to any interested party who has made written application to the examiner for a copy of the report[315]. Guidance is given, in respect of such omissions, by s 18(8) of the C(A)A 1990, which provides that the court may, in particular, direct the omission of such information as would be likely to prejudice the survival of the company or the whole or any part of its undertaking as a going concern.

[22.136] Where the 70 days of protection specified in s 5 of the C(A)A 1990 and any extended period conferred by s 18(3), would expire, the court may under s 18(4) extend the protection period until it has heard the examiner's proposals under s 24. This is to ensure that after the examiner has delivered his report, but before the court has heard the proposals, the company will continue to be protected until the court has the opportunity to either confirm the proposals or abandon the attempt to save the company.

---

309 Section 18(5) of the C(A)A 1990. Where the company concerned is one referred to in s 3(2)(a) or s 3(2)(b) or (c) of the C(A)A 1990, the examiner must supply a copy of the report to the Minister and Central Bank, respectively: s 18(6) of the C(A)A 1990.

310 This application should be grounded upon a verifying affidavit, the contents of which are detailed in Ord 75A, r 17 of the RSC 1986.

311 In receiving the examiner's report the court will not be approving or disapproving the report. This was made clear by Costello J in *Re Clare Textiles Ltd* [1993] 2 IR 213 in the context of what was the examiner's 'first report' under s 15 of the C(A)A 1990 (now repealed). There he said (at 219) of the action of receiving the examiner's report that: 'The examiner has advanced the argument in support of his present application [for the sanction of the examiner's remuneration, costs and expenses] that the court had "approved" his s 15 report, that it had "approved" the course of action proposed in his s 15 report, and that the remuneration and costs which he now claims were incurred with the court's approval. But this is a misconception of the section. The court neither approves nor disapproves of the s 15 report when liberty to deliver it is given. It has no statutory function or power to express an opinion on the proposals (if any) for the company's survival contained in it. The order giving liberty to deliver the report has no relevance on the present application.'

312 Namely, that the petitioner has delivered notice of the examiner's appointment to the registrar of companies.

313 As substituted by s 20(1) of the C(A)(No2)A 1999, ie, whether the examiner has advertised a notice of his appointment and the date thereof in the Companies Registration Office Gazette and in at least two daily newspapers.

314 An examiner shall within three days after his appointment, deliver a copy of the order appointing him to the registrar of companies.

315 Section 18(7) of the C(A)A 1990.

Hearing the proposals: court confirmation or rejection

[22.137] All proposals for a compromise or scheme of arrangement must be sanctioned by the court before they become binding. Even where proposals are accepted by a majority of the company's creditors they cannot become binding without court approval. As soon as the examiner delivers his s 18 report, the C(A)A 1990 provides that it shall be set down for hearing as soon as may be after receipt of it by the court[316]. After hearing the proposals and any objections which may be raised against them, the court is empowered by s 24(3) of the C(A)A 1990 to confirm the proposals. This provides:

> 'At a hearing under sub-section (1) the court may, as it thinks proper, subject to the provisions of this section and section 25, confirm, confirm subject to modifications, or refuse to confirm the proposals[317].'

Where either the court refuses to confirm proposals under s 24, or, the examiner's s 18 report concludes that following the required meeting of creditors of a company it has not been possible to reach agreement on a compromise or scheme of arrangement, the court may, if it considers it just and equitable to do so, make an order for the winding up of the company, or any other order as it deems fit[318].

[22.138] The effect of the court confirming the examiner's proposals are most far-reaching. As far as the company and its members are concerned, s 24(5) of the C(A)A 1990 provides that upon the court confirming the proposals, with or without modification, the proposals shall be binding on all the members or class of members affected by the proposals and also on the company. In the vast majority of examinerships, the fate of the company's creditors is more important. Section 24(6) of the C(A)A 1990 provides:

> 'Where the court confirms proposals (with or without modification), the proposals shall, notwithstanding any other enactment, be binding on all the creditors or the class or classes of creditors, as the case may be, affected by the proposals in respect of any claim or claims against the company and any person other than the company who, under any statute, enactment, rule of law or otherwise, is liable for all or any part of the debts of the company.'

This is explicit as to the consequences of the confirmation of proposals for a number of reasons. One central reason is that, previously, the Revenue Commissioners felt they were prevented by statute from acceding to requests from companies to write-off or write-down revenue debts. It is also explicit because the court can, in confirming proposals, deprive a secured creditor of part of its claim against a company and prevent it from realising any security granted by the company over the reduced amount of the claim.

[22.139] Section 20(1) of the C(A)A 1990 provides that where proposals for a compromise or scheme of arrangement are to be formulated, the company concerned

---

[316] Section 24(1) of the C(A)A 1990.

[317] Section 18(8) of the C(A)A 1990 provides that where the court confirms proposals under s 24 of the C(A)A 1990, it may make such orders for the implementation of its decision as it deems fit. It should also be noted that s 18(9) of the C(A)A 1990 provides that a court-confirmed compromise or scheme of arrangement shall come into effect from a date fixed by the court provided this shall not be later than 21 days from the date of their confirmation.

[318] Section 24(11) of the C(A)A 1990.

can, with the approval of the court, affirm or repudiate any contract under which some element of performance, other than payment, remains to be rendered both by the company and the other contracting party or parties. One effect of this is to enable a company to renege on an onerous contractual obligation[319]. An application under this provision may be made by the company unilaterally, but where this is the case the examiner must be served with notice by the company and the examiner is entitled to appear and be heard on any such application[320]. In approving the affirmation or repudiation of a contract under this section the court may make such orders as it thinks fit for the purposes of giving full effect to its approval, including orders as to notice to, or declaring the rights of, any party affected by such affirmation or confirmation[321]. It has been held by the Supreme Court in *Re Linen Supply of Ireland Ltd*[322] that s 20(1) includes leases, overruling two earlier decisions of the High Court which held it did not apply to leases.

[22.140] The effects of s 20(1) of the C(A)A 1990 have the potential to cause great loss to other parties. Persons who suffer loss or damage as a result of the repudiation of any contract shall stand as unsecured creditors of the company for the amount of such loss or damage[323]. Unlike the compromise of a financial claim against a company, the loss suffered by a person may not be readily quantifiable. In this regard sub-s (3) empowers the court, in order to facilitate the formulation, consideration or confirmation of a compromise or scheme of arrangement, to hold a *hearing* and to make an order determining the amount of any such loss or damage. The amount so determined shall be due by the company to the creditor as a judgment debt.

[22.0141] Section 24(2) of the C(A)A 1990 sets out those parties who have *locus standi* to appear and be heard at a hearing of the proposals. They are:

- the company;
- the examiner;
- any creditor or member whose claim or interest would be impaired if the proposals were implemented;
- the Central Bank (in the case of a company referred to in s 3(2)(b) or (c))[324].

These are the only specified persons who have an entitlement to he heard by the court at the hearing of the examiner's proposals although the court has a general discretion to hear any person where the dictates of equity and justice require that person's presence[325].

---

319 Note, however, that s 25B(1) of the C(A)A 1990 restricts the compromise of leasing claims. See para **[22.124]**.

320 Section 20(4) of the C(A)A 1990.

321 Section 20(5) of the C(A)A 1990.

322 *Re Linen Supply of Ireland Ltd* (10 December 2009, ex tempore) SC. See further para **[22.126]** *post*.

323 Section 20(2) of the C(A)A 1990.

324 As inserted by s 24(a) of the C(A)(No 2)A 1999.

325 O'Donnell, *Examinerships* (1994), p 71 notes that in *Re 3V Multimedia Group* (20 August 1992, ex tempore) HC, Costello J allowed a proposed investor to address the court on the extent of a modification which the court had made to a proposed scheme.

(a) Substantive objections to court confirmation

[22.142] The hearing of the proposals will become contentious where the examiner's proposals are opposed by the company's creditors[326]. Creditors' objections are likely to be based on the factors set out in ss 24 and 25 of the C(A)A 1990 to guide the court's exercise of its discretion. Whereas s 25 may be said to contain procedural objections, s 24(4) contains substantive objections which prevent the court from confirming proposals. Section 24(4) of the C(A)A 1990 provides:

> 'The court shall not confirm any proposals—
>
> (a) unless at least one class of creditors whose interests or claims would be impaired by implementation of the proposals has accepted the proposals, or[327]
>
> (b) if the sole or primary purpose of the proposals is the avoidance of payment of tax due, or
>
> (c) unless the court is satisfied that—
>
> (i) the proposals are fair and equitable in relation to any class of members or creditors that has not accepted the proposals and whose interests or claims would be impaired by implementation, and
>
> (ii) the proposals are not unfairly prejudicial to the interests of any interested party.'

This section makes it very clear that the court's discretion is fettered. The court *cannot* confirm proposals where any of the matters set out in (a), (b), or (c) apply. The guiding principle for the court will be that the scheme should be fair and reasonable[328]. Moreover, the C(A)(No 2)A 1999 introduced the following further safeguard to the interests of creditors in s 24(4A) of the C(A)A 1990, which provides:

> 'Without prejudice to subsection (4), the court shall not confirm any proposals in respect of a company to which an examiner has been appointed under section 4 if the proposals would have the effect of impairing the interests of the creditors of the company in such a manner as to favour the interests of the creditors or members of any company to which it is related, being a company to which that examiner has been appointed examiner under section 2 or, as the case may be, 4.'

Notwithstanding sub-s (4) or any other provision of the C(A)A 1990, nothing therein shall prevent the examiner from including in a report under s 18, proposals which will not involve the impairment of the interests or members or creditors of the company, nor the court from confirming any such proposals[329].

[22.143] Many of the criteria contained in s 24(2) of the C(A)A 1990 were considered in *Re Wogan's (Drogheda) Ltd (No 2)*[330]. The judgment of Costello J commences by setting out the broad proposals made by the examiner. The background to the proposed scheme of arrangement is instructive and worth quoting in full:

---

326 It is conceivable that the company's members will oppose the examiner's proposals for a compromise or scheme of arrangement.

327 As amended by s 24(b) of the C(A)(No 2)A 1999.

328 See *Re John Power & Son Ltd* [1934] IR 412.

329 Section 24(12) of the C(A)A 1990.

330 *Re Wogan's (Drogheda) Ltd (No 2)* (7 May 1992, unreported) HC, *per* Costello J.

> 'The scheme involves the investment in the company of a Dublin firm (Dublin Providers Limited) which has successfully traded in the hardware trade in different parts of Ireland. The scheme will involve the purchase by the new investor of the issued share capital and the appointment of new directors (although one former director will be retained as an employee). The scheme will materially affect the interests of the company's two major creditors, one of which is Hill Samuel (Ireland) Limited, which is owed approximately £462,300 which is secured by a mortgage and a fixed and floating charge. The scheme proposed will result in the debts being written down to £235,000 and the revised amount being restructured as a 7-year term loan with a moratorium on repayment of principal for one year, thereafter payments to be made by equal quarterly amounts with interest as specified on the reducing balance. The other major creditor is the Revenue Commissioners. The total due to the Revenue Commissioners on 13th January 1992 was £293,402.71p, of which only a portion was a preferential debt. Under the proposed scheme the preferential amount was to be £82,598. The scheme involved a total payment to the Revenue Commissioners (over a period of years) of £73,467, that is about 25 per cent of the total taxes due. Both the Bank and the Revenue Commissioners voted against the scheme and object to its confirmation. The total debt due to the unsecured creditors is £857,800 approximately. Most of these creditors are small creditors and they are to be paid 10 per cent of the sums due to them. A majority in number and value of the unsecured creditors voted to accept the scheme[331].'

Costello J refused to confirm the examiner's proposals and he exercised his discretion by rejecting the suggested scheme and refusing to make any modifications[332]. In his judgment he said:

> 'Having carefully considered the scheme (and the suggested amendments to it during the proposed hearing) and the submissions made, I have come to the conclusion that I should not confirm it (a) because the evidence discloses that there was an abuse of the processes of the court at the time of the original application for protection on 13th January 1992; (b) because confirmation is conditional on orders being made relating to certain taxation issues which I do not think I should make; (c) because there are defects in the scheme which the examiner negotiated with the new investor of such a nature which preclude its confirmation[333].'

The exercise of Costello J's discretion was largely based on s 24(3) (general discretion) and s 24(4) (specific substantive objections).

[22.144] The first reason given by Costello J for refusing to confirm the scheme was because there had been an abuse of the court's process. He found that the details of the company's indebtedness which accompanied the petition to have the company placed under the protection of the court had been understated. He also found that at least two of the company's directors were aware of the deliberate untruth relating to the debt due to the Revenue Commissioners; and that had the court been informed of the true deficit and that the directors had for some time been consistently defrauding the Revenue Commissioners, it would not have made an order to place the company under the protection of the court. He found that two of the directors who had given personal

331 *Re Wogan's (Drogheda) Ltd (No 2)* (7 May 1992, unreported) HC at pp 1, 2.

332 It is worthy of note that were it not the case that a majority in number and value of the unsecured creditors voted to accept the scheme, further consideration would have been precluded on the basis of s 24(4)(a) of the C(A)A 1990.

333 *Re Wogan's (Drogheda) Ltd (No 2)* (7 May 1992, unreported) HC, at p 3.

guarantees had sought the protection order to obtain personal advantage and, in so doing, had abused the court's process. On the jurisdictional basis for his refusal to confirm the scheme, Costello J said:

> '... the court's discretion under s 24(3) to confirm, or to confirm subject to modifications, or to refuse to confirm the scheme proposed is not limited by the grounds set out in s 23. If an abuse of the court's processes has been established, I do not think that the court should ignore it and consider on its merits a scheme which had subsequently been prepared. To do so would be to condone the abusive behaviour and encourage similar conduct in the future.
>
> In my view the abuse of the processes of the court in this case is such as to require the court to refuse to make an order sanctioning the scheme of arrangement prepared consequent on an order of the court improperly obtained[334].'

Only some companies deserve to be placed under the protection of the court. Where a company is not worthy, the directors cannot mislead the court at the petition stage as to the company's worthiness. Where this is done, it is clear that the remainder of the examinership will be tainted.

[22.145] The second reason for refusing to confirm the proposals was because Costello J felt he should not make certain orders sought in relation to taxation matters. The new investor had sought a tax clearance certificate from the Revenue Commissioners, who had duly refused to provide him with one. Costello J found the revenue's attitude to be reasonable and refused to order them to do so. The new investor had also sought two specific orders in relation to corporation tax and value added tax. Costello J again refused to make the orders sought because such would be unfair to the Revenue Commissioners and to their further detriment and because the proposed order sought in relation to VAT had not been made clear to him. Because the new investor's involvement was dependant upon the court making the orders sought, Costello J said it followed that the scheme could not be confirmed.

[22.146] Finally, Costello J identified seven defects in the proposed scheme of arrangement, only some of which were capable of remedy:

- The heads of agreement with the investor were not legally binding. This could be remedied because the investor had accepted that they were binding.
- The heads of agreement were not made part of the scheme of arrangement and were not produced to the principal creditors until late in the proceedings. This precluded the confirmation of the scheme.
- The investor's obligations were ambiguous and imprecise. However, they were clarified by the investor and so the scheme could be confirmed.
- The scheme ignored the existence of the directors' two personal guarantees. Such are relevant matters for the court to consider; unless guarantees are extinguished by the court, a contingent liability exists against the company after the scheme is confirmed as the guarantor may enforce his subrogation rights against the company; and the directors voted in favour of the scheme on an erroneous understanding of the law, namely that their guarantees would be extinguished by confirmation of the scheme.

---

334 *Re Wogan's (Drogheda) Ltd (No 2)* (7 May 1992, unreported) HC, at p 7.

- It was unacceptable that the proposed new investor could unilaterally withdraw from the scheme or amend the proposed scheme. This was because it is unacceptable to incur the costs of a hearing where the proposed investor may decide not to proceed with the scheme and the court cannot confirm a scheme since it cannot conclude that the scheme as amended is likely to facilitate the survival of the company.
- One particular creditor's claim against the company was not adequately dealt with by the examiner and it was possible that the creditor could upset the proposed scheme of arrangement.
- A particularly serious defect was that the investor wished to compel the company's staff to accept a list of wage rates by providing that if they did not agree, their employment with the company would be terminated. Costello J said on this point that the C(A)A 1990 was not intended to provide investors with investment opportunities.

Notwithstanding that the foregoing list of defects in the proposed scheme were *obiter dicta*, they provide a very useful guide as to what to avoid for an examiner who is formulating proposals for a scheme of arrangement.

[22.147] The court will not confirm a scheme which involves the reduction of a company's share capital unless that reduction is expressly authorised by the Companies Acts. In *Re McEnaney Construction Ltd*[335], Finlay Geoghegan J said that the absence of an express provision allowing a company to which an examiner is appointed to reduce its share capital as part of a scheme was to be contrasted with other provisions (eg, repudiation of contracts under s 20 of the C(A)A 1990 and alteration of memorandum and articles of association under s 24(7)) to do matters which it would not otherwise be entitled to do. The learned judge said:

> '... the provision in the scheme of arrangement that the Company cancel its issued shares on the Effective Date, in effect, requires the Company to do something which appears to be unlawful having regard to s 72(1) of the Act of 1963.
>
> Section 24(5) of the Act provides that where the Court confirms proposals for a scheme of arrangement, such proposals are binding inter alia on all the members affected by the proposal and also on the company. If the Court were to confirm proposals containing a provision that the Company cancel its issued shares (and thereby reduce its share capital), it would be purporting to impose an obligation on the Company to do something which is unlawful having regard to s 72(1). The Court cannot make an order which has such an effect. Even if the proposals for the scheme of arrangement were drafted in such a way that the obligation to cancel the shares was not expressly imposed on the Company, it does not appear to me that the Court has jurisdiction under s 24(8) of the Act to make an order that issued shares credited as fully paid up in the capital of a company limited by shares be cancelled. If it did so, the Court would be assuming a jurisdiction to order that a step be taken, ie the shares be cancelled, which the Company itself has no power to do and is expressly prohibited by s 72(1). Notwithstanding the apparently wide discretion given to the Court under s 24(8), it does not appear to me to include the doing of an act which, if done by the Company, would be unlawful. Further, any such order of the Court would have to direct that some person or body cancel the shares. The obvious person to do this is the Company, which, again, comes back to the situation of the Court imposing on the

[335] *McEnaney Construction Ltd* [2008] IEHC 43, Finlay Geoghegan J.

> Company an obligation to do something which is unlawful pursuant to s 72(1) of the Act of 1963.'

Finlay Geoghegan J said it was fortunate that the issued share capital was very small (€126.97) and so it was possible to achieve the desired 75% investor: 25% existing shareholder split without cancelling the existing 100 ordinary shares but instead issuing 300 shares to the investor and modifying the scheme to so provide. In this decision, Finlay Geoghegan J went on to say that where a scheme involves the alteration of a company's memorandum or articles of association, the intended alterations must be specified in the scheme and, where the scheme is confirmed, a copy of the amended memorandum and articles should be filed in the CRO within 21 days so as to give the public notice of the changes[336].

[22.148] It was made clear in the first case in which the court was asked to confirm a scheme of arrangement that it was open to the court to confirm a scheme which the court itself had modified. In *Re Goodman International*[337], Hamilton P said of s 24(3) of the C(A)A 1990 that:

> 'This section appears to me to give absolute discretion to the court in this regard. It is of course a discretion that must be exercised judicially and if the modifications suggested were to fundamentally alter the proposals which had been considered by the members and creditors of the companies, then a court would be slow to modify the scheme in a fundamental manner without having the modifications considered by the members and creditors[338].'

Often, the court will modify a scheme to provide that it is fairer to the interests of the company's creditors. An example of this is found in *Re Selukwe Ltd*[339]. In that case, the company's two major creditors, AIB and the Revenue Commissioners objected to the examiner's proposals for a scheme of arrangement.

AIB objected to the scheme because the scheme proposed would require the bank to revoke its personal guarantees so that the directors would be freed from any liability on foot of them and the security obtained from the two directors would be nullified. The bank objected to the scheme on the basis that there was no justification for releasing the directors' personal guarantees. This objection found favour with Costello J who held that for so long as the proposals contained that provision they were not fair and equitable as far as the bank was concerned. In this regard, Costello J seems to have refused to confirm the scheme on the basis of s 24(4)(c)(i). Rather than simply refuse to confirm the scheme, Costello J exercised his jurisdiction to modify the proposal to read that 'nothing herein will affect the liability of the directors on foot of the personal guarantees to Allied Irish Bank'. He also limited the directors' subrogation rights against the company in the event that their guarantees were called in by the bank. Costello J did not accept that the proposals were invalid because they affected contracts entered into before the C(A)A 1990 came into operation.

---

336 On amendment of the memorandum and articles of association, see also *Re Cisti Gugan Barra Teoranta* [2008] IEHC 251.

337 *Re Goodman International* (28 January 1991, unreported) HC, Hamilton P.

338 *Re Goodman International* (28 January 1991, unreported) HC, at p 14.

339 *Re Selukwe Ltd* (20 December 1991, unreported) HC, Costello J.

The Revenue Commissioners objected to the proposals on a number of grounds. These included the following: the directors managed the business without causing the company to keep proper books and records; the directors totally disregarded their obligations to the Revenue Commissioners; they acknowledged the company's true indebtedness to them before presenting the petition; they failed to pay current taxes after presentation of the petition until ordered to do so by the court and they held a creditors' meeting without informing the revenue. Although Costello J held those objections were well founded, he decided that they did not constitute grounds for non-confirmation of the proposals under s 24(4) or s 25. They did, however, constitute grounds for *modification* of the proposals under s 24(3). Accordingly, Costello J modified the proposals to provide that the directors of the company would cease to act as directors as soon as new directors were appointed.

[22.149] Costello J's explanation for exercising his discretion is instructive. Having set out the reasons for his concern he said:

> '... the position in this case is such that these considerations to which I have referred are outweighed by what I consider to be the main consideration in this case, namely the fact that there are 30 jobs at stake. I do not think the court should turn down the proposals if there is any prospect of saving those jobs. So notwithstanding the doubts which I have expressed I have decided to confirm the proposals subject to the modifications to which I have referred[340].'

What is interesting is the prominence of social policy in the exercise of the court's discretion under s 24(3) of the C(A)A 1990. It is suggested that the survival of the company and some or all of its undertaking, and not the fate of its employees, are the paramount matters which should influence judicial discretion.

(b) Other substantive grounds for not confirming a scheme

[22.150] An equally substantive objection is that a scheme does not provide for the survival of a company as a going concern as required by s 2 of the C(A)A 1990. In effect, this ground for refusing to approve a scheme is tantamount to saying that an examiner ought never to have been appointed and was successfully invoked in *Re Tivway Ltd*[341], where the Supreme Court held that a scheme which proposed to hold the company's land bank in suspense pending an upturn in the property market, would protect the survival of the companies in question, but not as a going concern and refused to confirm the scheme.

[22.151] In *Re McInerney Homes Ltd (No 5)*[342], Clarke J characterised the increase in an offer by a potential investor to a prejudiced creditor after the court has decided to refuse to confirm a proposed scheme of arrangement as an abuse of process. Following the initial decision to appoint an examiner[343], Clarke J had, in a previous judgment[344], refused to confirm a scheme of arrangement on the grounds that it was unfairly

340 *Re Goodman International* (20 December 1991, unreported) HC, at p 8.

341 *Re Tivway Ltd* [2010] IESC 11. See para **[22.024]** *ante*.

342 *Re McInerney Homes Ltd (No 5)* [2011] IEHC 63. The number '5' is not an official number and is applied here to distinguish the other four judgments of Clarke J in this matter.

343 *Re McInerney Homes Ltd* [2010] IEHC 340.

344 *Re McInerney Homes Ltd (No 2)* [2011] IEHC 4.

prejudicial to certain secured creditors of the company who constituted a banking syndicate. Subsequently, the company filed further affidavit evidence, asking that the confirmation refusal be revisited. Clarke J then delivered a further judgment[345] setting out reasons why he was prepared to allow the matter to be revisited. Thereafter, significant additional evidence was filed, a further hearing occurred and judgment was delivered[346] again refusing to confirm the scheme of arrangement, but this time because it was held that one of the three secured creditors which constituted a banking syndicate – KBC Bank plc – had been unfairly prejudiced. After that judgment was delivered, the potential investor put in a new offer under which it proposed to pay a significant sum to KBC Bank plc. Clarke J determined that the potential investor was guilty of abuse of process and refused to consider the new offer. Clarke J observed that the effect of the Supreme Court's decision in *Re Vantive Holdings Ltd*[347] was that finality of litigation was a matter of fundamental importance and not just simply a matter of procedure. Clarke J went on to find that although the investor was not a party entitled to be heard in the petition, it was nonetheless an interested party who was subject to an obligation analagous to that identified by the Supreme Court in *Vantive* to put forward its best case at the confirmation or accept the consequences. Clarke J said that it seemed to him that the investor, '*Oaktree sought to have the issue run on one basis, and that, having lost that basis, Oaktree now wants to run it again on a different basis; the course of action is an abuse of process*'. Clarke J determined that on account of that abuse, it would be fundamentally inconsistent with basic principles of law to allow the matter to be now reopened.

(c) Procedural and other objections to court confirmation

[22.152] Section 25(1) of the C(A)A 1990 provides that dissenting members and creditors can object to court confirmation of the examiner's proposals on procedural and other grounds. These are:

'(a) that there was some material irregularity at or in relation to a meeting to which section 23 applies,

(b) that acceptance of the proposals by the meeting was obtained by improper means,

(c) that the proposals were put forward for an improper purpose,

(d) that the proposals unfairly prejudice the interests of the objector.'

Irregularity in a s 23 meeting must be material: not every deviation from the correct procedure will justify the court refusing to confirm the examiner's proposals. Examples of irregularity might include not notifying some creditors of the meeting or excluding certain creditors from voting. The ground of objection based on the fact that the acceptance of the proposals was obtained by improper means is wide. This could be invoked where, for example, creditors vote in favour of proposals on the basis of a misunderstanding of their position, encouraged by the examiner. It is thought that the ground stated in s 25(1)(c) relates to where the *examiner* puts forward proposals for an improper purpose, such as to favour the interests of the company's directors.

---

[345] *Re McInerney Homes Ltd (No 3)* [2011] IEHC 25.

[346] *Re McInerney Homes Ltd (No 4)* [2011] IEHC 61, Clarke J.

[347] *Re Vantive Holdings Ltd* [2009] IESC 69. See para **[22.022]** *ante*.

(d) Unfairly prejudicial proposals

[22.153] Section 25(1)(d) of the C(A)A 1990 and the objector's view that proposals are unfairly prejudicial has been considered in a number of cases. In *Re Presswell Ltd*[348], AIB Leasing claimed that particular proposals were unfairly prejudicial to them because as a matter of principle the cost or price of future services should not be waived or reduced; the commercial analysis of what they would recover on a liquidation; and doubts cast upon the availability of a substantial investor.

As to the first ground, Murphy J held that in principle there was nothing special about leasing creditors which would put them outside the scope of the C(A)A 1990. However they should constitute a separate class from either ordinary or secured creditors. Further, the fact that their rights extend into the future must always be taken into consideration. The second ground was based on the discrepancy between the value ascribed to the leased equipment by AIB Leasing and the value ascribed by the examiner. On the evidence presented, Murphy J favoured the examiner's judgment. He said:

> 'I approach this matter on the footing that the examiner is an experienced and competent accountant appointed by the court to report on the affairs of this company, as he has done. In that way he is distinguished from an arranging debtor who might bring proposals before his own creditor in ease of himself. The examiner expresses an opinion for the benefit of the court and carries out research to enable the court to impose, where appropriate, a solution on the parties; so I think that an opinion of the examiner is entitled to particular respect[349].'

In all the circumstances, Murphy J held that the proposals were not unfairly prejudicial to this leasing creditor[350].

[22.154] The impairment of the interests or claims of creditors has been considered in *Re Jetmara Teo*[351]. In that case, an examiner claimed that the interests of a secured creditor who would be repaid in full, but by instalments and without interest, were not 'impaired'. Costello J, in interpreting s 22(5) of the C(A)A 1990, held that the secured creditor's interests were impaired[352]. Section 22(5) of the C(A)A 1990 provides:

> 'For the purposes of this section and section 24 and 25, a creditor's claim against a company is impaired if he receives less in payment of his claim than the full amount due in respect of the claim at the date of presentation of the petition for the appointment of the examiner.'

The same question arose in *Re Antigen Holdings Ltd*[353] and McCracken J held as Costello J did, that a bank-creditor's interests would be impaired where asked to accept what was due to it immediately, instead, by way of instalments. The judgment in that case arose from an application to approve a scheme of arrangement arising from a

---

348 *Re Presswell Ltd* (4 November 1991, unreported) HC, Murphy J.

349 *Re Presswell Ltd* (4 November 1991, unreported) HC, at p 7.

350 On the question of whether the foregoing of directors' personal guarantees was unfairly prejudicial to another creditor, see para **[22.080]**.

351 *Re Jetmara Teo* [1992] 1 IR 147.

352 See also *Re British and Commonwealth Holdings plc (No 3)* [1992] BCLC 322, *per* Vinelott J.

353 *Re Antigen Holdings Ltd* (8 November 2001, unreported) HC, McCracken J.

company having been placed under the protection of the court. Certain bank-creditors had abstained from voting on the proposals and then had sought to have the scheme modified on the grounds that the scheme was *unfairly prejudicial* to them. The basis of the objection was that although it was proposed to pay off the preferential creditors in 16 months and the ordinary creditors in 18 months, the bank-creditors would be paid off over 30 months. The bank-creditors also objected to the fact that the company's shareholders would be bought-out by an incoming investor ahead of the company's liabilities to the bank being discharged. McCracken J said:

> 'I have to consider whether the banks have been unfairly prejudiced. It is beyond doubt that if the company has to go into liquidation then the banks will receive considerably less than they would receive under the scheme and this is a consideration to be taken into account. But it is not the only one. It has to be said no creditors are getting paid interest. The banks' debt of course is by far the largest proportion of the creditors and they undoubtedly are not being treated in the same way as the ordinary creditors. They are being paid off over a longer period and there is some validity in their point that interest to a bank is the equivalent to the profit made by an ordinary trade creditor on selling his goods and the trade creditors are in fact getting paid that profit. However the question is; is this unfair?
>
> The purpose of the scheme is to ensure the viability of the company, This can only be done if there is a reasonable time span in which to discharge the debt and that there is an amount being paid which is within the capacity of the company to pay. Now the vast bulk of remaining creditors are trade creditors who are presumably going to continue trading with the company. I don't think it is unfair that should get some priority because they are going to keep the company going.'

McCracken J held that the scheme of arrangement should be approved and that bank-creditors' interests would not be impaired or unfairly prejudiced. The judge did not accept that the payment to the shareholders for their shares in the company was prejudicial to the interests to the bank-creditors. It was said that such would only be prejudicial if the consideration would go to the creditors if it were not paid to the shareholders. It was held by McCracken J that the investor would not acquire the shares unless the shareholders gave the investor warranties and because the court could not insist that the shareholders gave warranties, the sale would not proceed were the warranties not given. Accordingly, it was not within the court's power to ensure that the sale would proceed without the shareholders' assent. It was also accepted that there was a serious danger that the scheme would collapse without the implementation of the agreement between the shareholders and the investors. McCracken J was also influenced by the fact that the company employed over 300 people whose jobs were at risk and the fact that he found as a probability that all of the creditors would eventually be paid – even if there was a delay. Notwithstanding that the bank-creditors might stand to lose £700,000 in interest, the court did not think that they were unfairly prejudiced in the light of the benefits of this scheme if the scheme proceeded. On the question of what is 'unfair', McCracken J followed the approach taken by Costello J in *Re Holidair (No 2)*[354] where he said:

> 'My first task is to consider whether I should confirm the proposals. I have come to the conclusion the court should confirm them. I do not think I can come to the view the

[354] *Re Holidair (No 2)* (6 May 1994, unreported) HC, Costello J.

> proposals are not fair and are in some way inequitable to the revenue and that the revenue are being unfairly prejudiced in some way by them. As I have already said this is a complex commercial situation. The revenue have got some benefits from the scheme of arrangement which they would not otherwise have got in that they are getting paid as preferential creditors some of their debt. Under the proposals a substantial dividend will be paid. In all the circumstances of the case including the substantial debt which the banks had to forgo and the costs which they are going to have to bear, I do not think it can be said that the scheme of arrangement is unfair to the revenue because they are disproportionately disadvantaged in comparison with the secured creditors. I agree that the revenue will have to wait for payment but this is not unreasonable in the difficult situation presented to those preparing this scheme of arrangement. Again I agree that they will not obtain any interest in their debt but I do not think that they are unfairly prejudiced. The undoubted fact which is not denied by anybody is not only would all the creditors be worse off but the 750 employees would be very severely prejudiced if the company goes into liquidation. The court should be very slow to turn down the scheme of arrangement once there is a chance of maintaining the positions of the employees.'

[22.155] Section 25(2) of the C(A)A 1990 limits those who may object under sub-s (1). Accordingly, any person who voted to accept the proposals may not object to their confirmation by the court except on the grounds that their acceptance was obtained by improper means or that after voting they become aware that the proposals were put forward for an improper purpose. Where the court upholds an objection under s 25(1), the court may make such an order as it deems fit, including an order that the decision of any meeting be set aside and an order that any meeting be reconvened[355].

[22.156] In *Re Cisti Gugan Barra Teoranta*[356], Finlay Geoghegan J refused to confirm a scheme of arrangement where the company and the investor had only 'conditionally' agreed to make the investment available by way of equity or loan capital, at the investor's discretion for the reason that to do so would be unfairly prejudicial to the company's creditors. The conditionality was subject to a number of conditions over and above the normal condition, that the court confirms the scheme, and included a condition that there would be no material adverse change in the company's trading position. Finlay Geoghegan J said that it was not appropriate to confirm proposals which had the effect of reducing the liability of the company to its creditors unless there are binding arrangements in place of the investment to enable the company to meet its obligations under the scheme on the grounds such would be unfairly prejudicial to the creditors. Ultimately, the court confirmed the scheme when the investor agreed to the removal of the conditionality.

[22.157] As Clarke J said in *Re Traffic Group Ltd*[357], the examinership legislation is not designed to immunise the principals or shareholders of a company from the consequences of the company getting into financial difficulties. It will generally, but not invariably, be the case that the shareholders in a company will have their equity stake reduced by the introduction of new equity share capital. An exception is seen in the case of *Re Tony Gray & Sons Ltd*[358] where because there was no new share capital being

---

355 Section 25(3) of the C(A)A 1990.

356 *Re Cisti Gugan Barra Teoranta* [2008] IEHC 251.

357 *Re Traffic Group Ltd* [2008] 3 IR 253.

358 *Re Tony Gray & Sons Ltd* [2009] IEHC 557.

introduced through the scheme, the company's shareholders' interest was being left undiluted. Clarke J noted that whereas the unsecured creditors were moving from a position of receiving nothing in a liquidation to receiving 5% under the scheme, the shareholders were moving from a position of receiving nothing in a liquidation to having the benefit of the full value of the company if the scheme was approved. Clarke J went on to determine that the shareholder value to be obtained by the scheme was limited and such that it would not be unfairly prejudicial to allow them to continue to have the benefit of their shareholding without the injection of new capital. The learned judge did say, however:

> 'I would comment that it is only in those unusual circumstances, however, that I am satisfied that what must be an untypical arrangement, whereby shareholders are permitted to retain their shareholdings in full without the introduction of any new capital, meets the test of lack of unfair prejudice as specified in the Act.'

In *Re McSweeney Dispensers 1 Ltd*[359], the only objection to the appointment of an examiner came from one of its creditors, AIB Bank plc, which was concerned because of the perceived intention of one of the shareholders and directors to use the process to significantly write down secured debt while avoiding making a very significant further capital contribution. Clarke J observed that he had in a number of other applications emphasised the importance of scrutinising schemes where the only additional capital being introduced comes from the existing shareholders or persons connected with them. Of this, the learned judge said:

> 'In such cases it is important for the court to analyse with some care the extent to which the scheme as a whole is fair not only as and between the various categories of creditors but also between the creditors on the one hand and shareholders on the other. Such a scheme may well be unfair if the shareholders get to keep their company (and frequently retain additional financial benefits such as contracts of employment or director's fees which go with it) and the introduction of very limited additional capital in circumstances where the creditors are expected to take huge write downs. If the examiner in this case was to ultimately come up with a scheme of arrangement which was unfair on that basis then there can be little doubt but that the scheme would not be confirmed.'

In that case, Clarke J granted the petition appointing the examiner on the grounds that there was a reasonable prospect of survival of the company as a going concern and the issues raised by AIB were questions which could more properly be addressed if a scheme of arrangement was put forward.

[22.158] Where a scheme of arrangement purports to affect parties who are outside the jurisdiction of the Irish courts, application may be brought in foreign courts for assistance by order of the foreign court that a scheme of arrangement and composition be made binding. Where the foreign jurisdiction is England and Wales, application can be brought pursuant to s 426 of the Insolvency Act 1986. In *Re Business City Express Ltd*[360], Rattee J held that assistance ought to be granted by an English court unless it was satisfied that there was some good reason not to do so. In that case, he granted an order which applied Irish law to certain English creditors as to the binding effect on creditors

[359] *Re McSweeney Dispensers 1 Ltd* [2011] IEHC 494.

[360] *Re Business City Express Ltd* [1997] BCC 826.

of a scheme approved by the Irish High Court. It should also be noted that the EU's Council Regulation on Insolvency Proceedings[361] can also be invoked by examiners[362].

Evidence of wrongdoing

[22.159] Where an examiner's report contains evidence of wrongdoing having occurred, the court has discretion to refuse to confirm the scheme[363]. Clarke J said in *Re Traffic Group Ltd*[364] that in the absence of particularly serious misconduct, the court should lean in favour of approving a scheme which was otherwise appropriate having regard to the saving of jobs and enterprise that might be secured. In *Re Irish Car Rentals Ltd*[365], Clarke J said that matters of potential wrongdoing by directors give rise to an obligation on the part of the court to consider what action to take. In that case, the appropriate action was considered to be to direct that the examiner's report be transmitted through his solicitors to the Director of Corporate Enforcement.

Matters arising after court confirmation of the proposals

[22.160] After the court confirms the examiner's proposals, the protection period will come to an end on the coming into effect of a compromise or scheme of arrangement[366]. If the proposals are not confirmed or the examinership aborts at any earlier time, the period of protection will cease on such earlier date as the court may direct[367]. Where the company ceases to be under the protection of the court, the appointment of the examiner terminates on the date of such cessation[368].

[22.161] Section 27(1) of the C(A)A 1990[369] provides that the company or any interested party may apply to the court within 180 days after an examiner's proposals have been confirmed, for the revocation of the court's confirmation on the grounds that it was procured by fraud. Where, upon such application being made, the court is satisfied that this was the case, it may revoke the confirmation on such terms and conditions as it thinks fit. The court must in particular have regard to the rights of parties acquiring interests or property in good faith and for value in reliance on that confirmation. This section has not, to date, been relied upon by any interested party or any company. It is thought that this jurisdiction represents a final safeguard for the rights of all those affected by the confirmation of proposals and is unlikely to be exercised, save in the most extraordinary of circumstances. In view of the fact that there will be many court hearings in an examinership, it is thought that only the most exceptional of cases will disclose, up to 180 days later, that the court was misled.

---

361 Council Regulation (EC) No 1346/2000 of 29 May 2000; see, also, SI 333/2002, which inserted the new s 1A in the C(A)A 1990.

362 See, further, Ch 24, *Liquidators*, para **[24.059]** *et seq.*

363 See *Re Traffic Group Ltd* [2008] 3 IR 253; *Re Wogans Drogheda Ltd* (7 May 1992) HC, Costello J; and *Re Selukwe Ltd* (20 December 1991) HC, Costello J.

364 *Re Traffic Group Ltd* [2008] 3 IR 253.

365 *Re Irish Car Rentals Ltd* [2010] IEHC 235.

366 Section 26(1)(a) of the C(A)A 1990.

367 Section 26(1)(b) of the C(A)A 1990.

368 Section 26(1)(2) of the C(A)A 1990.

369 Formerly s 27 of the C(A)A 1990 but renamed as s 27(1) by s 27(a) of the C(A)(No 2)A 1999.

[22.162] Section 27(2) of the C(A)A 1990[370] provides that as soon as practicable after the revocation under s 27(1) of such a confirmation, a copy of the order made by the court shall be delivered to the registrar of companies and to the Minister (in the case of a company referred to in s 3(2)(a) of the C(A)A 1990) and to the Central Bank (in the case of a company referred to in s 3(2)(b) or (c)) by such person as the court may direct.

[F] THE EXAMINER'S REMUNERATION, COSTS AND EXPENSES

[22.163] The extraordinary priority[371] conferred upon the payment of an examiner's costs, remuneration and expenses by s 29 of the C(A)A 1990 has been already considered in the context of his certifications of expenses[372]. What remains to be considered is an examiner's remuneration and costs. It is fundamental to realise that the examiner's costs, remuneration and expenses will normally have priority unless the court provides to the contrary. Section 29(2) of the C(A)A 1990 provides:

> 'Unless the court otherwise orders, the remuneration, costs and expenses of an examiner shall be paid and the examiner shall be entitled to be indemnified in respect thereof out of the revenue of the business of the company to which he has been appointed, or the proceeds of realisation of the assets (including investments).'

An examiner will ordinarily be entitled to such, unless he acts in breach of his duties[373] or acts outside of his statutory remit.

[22.164] In *Re Sharmane Ltd*[374], Finlay Geoghegan J held that where an examiner was appointed to a company and a number of related companies, the examiner was not entitled to an order under s 29(1) of the C(A)A 1990 that all companies be jointly and severally liable for the aggregate remuneration, costs and expenses of the examiner. The basis for this finding was that s 29(2) provides that the remuneration, etc, of an examiner is to be paid out of the revenue of the business '*of the company to which he has been appointed*'. Given the extraordinary priority afforded such remuneration, etc, Finlay Geoghegan J considered that a strict interpretation to the provisions of s 29(2) was required.

Examiner's remuneration

[22.00165] In *Re Sharmane Ltd*[375], Finlay Geoghegan J held that the entitlement to be paid out of *the revenue of the business of the company* to which he has been appointed, or *the proceeds of realisation of the assets* was to be read in the alternative rather than as 'either-or' so that there is an option to look to either.

[22.166] Again, an examiner's reasonable remuneration for work performed will ordinarily be accorded the priority bestowed by s 29 of the C(A)A 1990. Even where an examiner acts fully in accordance with his duties, the court may disallow his claimed

370 Inserted by s 27(b) of the C(A)(No 2)A 1999.

371 See Murphy J in *Re Edenpark Construction Ltd* [1994] 3 IR 126 at 133.

372 See para **[22.103]** *et seq*.

373 See para **[22.113]**.

374 *Re Sharmane Ltd* [2009] IEHC 377.

375 *Re Sharmane Ltd* [2009] IEHC 377.

remuneration where such is seen to be excessive. In *Re Coombe Importers Ltd*[376], Hamilton CJ said:

> 'There is no doubt that the court has jurisdiction to review and disallow the remuneration, costs and expenses of the examiner and in view of the priority given to such remuneration, costs and expenses there is an obligation on the court to be vigilant in scrutinising an examiner's application for sanction of payment[377].'

In that case, the court allowed reasonable remuneration, legal costs and most but not all expenses. What is considered excessive remuneration will depend upon the circumstances of each case. In *Re Don Bluth Entertainment Ltd*[378], Murphy J commented (in 1993) that the figure of £145 per hour was probably the highest hourly charge proposed by an accountant for services of that nature at that time. In the circumstances of that case, and in view of the fact that it was an important case involving enormous sums and an exceptional business with a large and highly-qualified labour force, Murphy J held that the examiner's fees were justified, especially in view of the fact that one of the company's major creditors did not object to the level of the examiner's fees[379]. Where the examiner ought to have concluded the examinership at a time when it was apparent that the company was not capable of surviving as a going concern, it has been held that the examiner will only be entitled to his remuneration (and costs) up to the time when he ought to have ceased acting as examiner[380].

[22.167] Indicative of the inflation in professional fees since 1993, in *Re Missford Ltd*[381] an interim examiner applied to the court to fix his remuneration based on a senior partner's hourly rate of €425. Kelly J observed that in exercising its powers under s 29, the court was 'not a cipher to rubber stamp claims made by an examiner' and that it would only make orders which it thinks proper[382]. Examiners are obliged under Ord 75A, r 22 of the RSC 1986 to place affidavit evidence before the court setting out a full account of the work carried out, of the costs and expenses and of the use made of the services of the staff or facilities of the company. Kelly J warned that the court must always be mindful of an examiner's limited functions and said that examiners would not be remunerated for work outside of their statutory remit. Additionally, he noted that the court will scrutinise the actual remuneration sought to be recovered and in this respect Kelly J considered the appropriateness of €425 per hour. Kelly J noted with approval the views of Finlay Geoghegan J, in *Re Sharmane Ltd*[383], who said hourly rates are but one element in determining reasonable remuneration and that the court must also have regard to the nature of the work carried out, the complexity of the work and the importance or value of the work to the client. In relation to the hourly rate of €425,

---

376 *Coombe Importers Ltd* (22 June 1995, unreported) SC, Hamilton CJ.

377 *Coombe Importers Ltd* (22 June 1995, unreported) SC, at p 6.

378 *Re Don Bluth Entertainment Ltd* [1994] 3 IR 141.

379 *Re Don Bluth Entertainment Ltd* [1994] 3 IR 141. See also *Re Irish Press Newspapers Ltd*, an application reported in (1995) Irish Times, 27 October, wherein Murphy J questioned an examiner's fees and sought an analysis of the hours worked.

380 *Re Clare Textiles Ltd* [1993] 2 IR 213.

381 *Re Missford Ltd* [2010] IEHC 240.

382 Citing *Re Coombe Importers Ltd* (22 June 1995) SC, Hamilton CJ.

383 *Re Sharmane Ltd* [2009] IEHC 377, Finlay Geoghegan J.

Kelly J was unhappy not to take account of the economic climate and noted that there was anecdotal evidence that professional fees have been reduced by the order of one third from what they were in 2007 (the year the examiner's hourly rate was set at €425). Accepting that anecdotal evidence was not good enough, Kelly J decided to use a comparator and determined that an acceptable comparator was fees paid by the State in respect of prosecution and defence work; noting that this had reduced by 16%, Kelly J discounted the examiner's hourly rate by that amount, resulting in an hourly rate of €357.

Kelly J criticised the examiner's decision to carry out a monitoring operation of the company's day-to-day operations because of the belief that there were inadequate financial controls in place. This was considered to amount to an executive act which the examiner was not empowered to do without an order under s 9 of the C(A)A 1990[384], and Kelly J applied a further reduction to the remuneration allowed by 15%. In *Re Marino Ltd*[385], Clarke J held that it was not appropriate to apply a uniform rate to all examiners and in that case determined that the appropriate hourly remuneration rate for the examiner was €375. In most all other respects, Clarke J followed the approach taken by Kelly J[386].

Examiner's costs

[22.168] Ordinarily, an examiner's full costs will be borne by the company under protection in priority to all other creditors' claims. Where the examiner acts in breach of his duties[387], he may be disentitled to his costs: *Re Wogans Drogheda Ltd (No 3)*[388]. Costello J held that the court did not have power to order the examiner to pay the creditors' costs under s 29 of the C(A)A 1990. However, he considered Ord 99, r 1(1) of the RSC 1986 sufficiently wide as to give the court jurisdiction to make orders relating to the costs incurred by parties, including creditors, who appeared in proceedings under the C(A)A 1990. In the circumstances of that case, Costello J held that the interests of justice did not require him to order the examiner to pay the costs of the aggrieved creditors. He did, however, think that such an order might be made in very exceptional circumstances.

Examiner's expenses

[22.169] An examiner's expenses and the certification of such expenses has been considered above[389].

---

384 See para **[22.103]** *ante*.

385 *Re Marino Ltd* [2010] IEHC 394, Clarke J.

386 In *Re ESG Reinsurance Ireland Ltd* [2010] IEHC 365, Kelly J said, in the context of an application to fix the remuneration of an administrator appointed under the provisions of the Insurance (No 2) Act 1983, that there was no good reason why a legal advisor to an administrator should be permitted to charge fees at a rate in excess of that applicable to the administrator and he reduced the solicitor's hourly rate to €375.

387 *Re Edenpark Construction Ltd* [1994] 3 IR 126.

388 *Re Wogans Drogheda Ltd (No 3)* [1993] 1 IR 157.

389 See para **[22.103]** *et seq*.

Chapter 23

Winding Up Companies

Introduction

[23.001] This chapter is concerned with the winding up of companies[1]. The first two methods of ending corporate existence are by means of a *members' voluntary winding up* and a *creditors' voluntary winding up*. These have in common the fact that court involvement is minimal, and a majority of the members of the company precipitate the winding up by voting in favour of it in a general meeting. The essential difference between these two forms of voluntary winding up is that in a members' voluntary winding up the company must be *solvent,* while this will not be the case in a creditors' voluntary winding up. The third method of winding up is that of a compulsory court winding up, also referred to as an *official liquidation*. In addition, the circumstances in which one mode of winding up can be converted to a different mode, the effect of a winding-up order and the special rules applicable to private companies that are licensed banks are also considered. In this chapter winding up is considered in the following sections:

- [A] Members' voluntary winding up.
- [B] Creditors' voluntary winding up.
- [C] Compulsory court winding up.
- [D] Conversion of windings up.
- [E] The winding-up order.
- [F] Winding up licensed banks and other authorised credit institutions.

The topic of *liquidators* (voluntary, official and provisional) is considered separately in Chapter 24. The principal tasks of liquidators, the *realisation and distribution of assets* in a winding up, are also considered separately, in Chapter 25.

[A] Members' Voluntary Winding Up

[23.002] The essential feature of a *members' voluntary winding up* is that the company must be *solvent*, and, for whatever reason, the members of that company decide to end its existence. Section 251(1) of the CA 1963 governs both members' *and* creditors' voluntary windings up, by stating three separate circumstances in which a company may be wound up voluntarily. Two of these grounds concern members' voluntary windings

1 See generally, Ussher, *Company Law in Ireland* (1986), p 472–535; Keane, *Company Law* (4th edn, 2007), Chs 36 and 38; Lynch-Fanon & Murphy, *Corporate Insolvency and Rescue* (2nd edn, 2012); Schmitthoff (ed), *Palmer's Company Law* (24th edn, 1987), pp 1353–1524.

up[2]. Of these two grounds, it is s 251(1)(b) that envisages the most common basis for a members' winding up, namely 'if the company resolves by special resolution that the company be wound up voluntarily'.

In addition to this, the event envisaged by s 251(1)(a) can also form the basis of a members' voluntary winding up, namely:

> 'when the period, if any, fixed for the duration of the company by the articles expires, or the event, if any, occurs, on the occurrence of which the articles provide that the company is to be dissolved, and the company in general meeting has passed a resolution that the company be wound up voluntarily ...'

The main difference between s 251(1)(a) and s 251(1)(b) is that where the circumstances envisaged by ground (1)(a) apply, an *ordinary resolution* will suffice; where ground (1)(b) is relied upon, a *special resolution* must be passed. As might be imagined, the scenario envisaged in sub-s (1)(a) above is a relatively rare occurrence, it being most unusual for a company's articles of association to provide that it should only last for a limited period of time. The most common catalyst for a members' voluntary winding up is, therefore, the passing of a special resolution by the members to wind up the company, as envisaged by s 251(1)(b). One reason why a solvent company may be wound up is where the members wish to legally take the assets out of the company by means of a *distribution in specie*, ie, in the form of the assets as opposed to their cash proceeds[3].

[23.003] In this section the following issues in members' voluntary windings up of companies are considered:

1. Declaration of solvency.
2. Report of an independent person.
3. Personal liability of the directors.
4. Resolution to wind up.
5. Commencement of a members' voluntary winding up.
6. Termination of a members' voluntary liquidation.

Declaration of solvency

[23.004] The essential feature of a members' voluntary winding up is that there is a *declaration of solvency* which must be sworn by the directors of a company, or a majority of them, at a meeting of the directors. This is required by s 256(1) of the CA 1963, as amended[4], which provides that the directors must make a statutory declaration to the effect that:

> '... they have made a full inquiry into the affairs of the company, and having done so, they have formed the opinion that the company will be able to pay its debts in full within such period not exceeding 12 months from the commencement of the winding up as may be specified in the declaration.'

Such a statutory declaration was required under the original s 256 of the CA 1963. The effect of the 1990 amendment lies in the consequences which ensue if the appropriate

2 The third circumstance in which a company can be wound up voluntarily is under s 251(1)(c) of the CA 1963 and this relates to a creditors' winding up: see para **[23.017]**.

3 The distribution of assets *in specie* is considered in detail in Ch 25, *Realisation and Distribution of Assets in a Winding Up*, para **[25.196]**.

4 As amended by s 128 of the CA 1990.

procedure is not followed and, more seriously, if the company is unable to pay its debts within 12 months from the commencement of the winding up: in such situations, the directors can be made personally liable for the company's debts[5].

[23.005] Section 256(2) of the CA 1963 provides that a declaration of solvency will have no effect unless[6]:

- it is made within the 28 days immediately preceding the date of the passing of the resolution to wind the company up;
- it is delivered to the registrar of companies not later than 15 days of the delivery of a copy of the resolution to wind the company up;
- it embodies a statement of the company's assets and liabilities as at the latest practicable date before the making of it, and not more than three months before the making of the declaration;
- a report by an independent person is attached to the declaration of solvency;
- a statement from the independent person is embodied which gives his unrevoked consent to the issue of the declaration with the report attached; and
- a copy of the declaration is attached to the notice issued by the company of the general meeting at which it is intended to propose a resolution for voluntary winding up.

Where these provisions are not, or cannot be, complied with, the winding up cannot be a members' voluntary winding up.

[23.006] The consequences which follow where the declaration of solvency is not delivered, within 15 days of the special resolution being delivered, to the registrar of companies was considered by Laffoy J in *Re Birchwell Developments Ltd*[7]. It was sought to regularise this oversight by making application to the court under s 131(5) of the CA 1990 which provides that:

> 'If default is made –
>
> (a) by the company in complying with subsection (1) or (2) of section 266 of the [Act of 1963], or
>
> (b) by the directors in complying with subsection (3) of the said section,
>
> the liquidator shall, within 7 days of the relevant day, apply to the court for directions as to the manner in which that default is to be remedied.'

Laffoy J began by noting that it is provided by s 256(11) of the CA 1963 that where a statutory declaration is made and delivered to the registrar of companies, it is a *members' voluntary winding up* and that where such has not been made and delivered, that it is a *creditors' voluntary winding up*. The learned judge stated that she was assuming that s 131 of the CA 1990 had application to a deemed creditors' voluntary winding up by virtue of s 256(11) of the CA 1963. Laffoy J also noted that s 280 of the CA 1963 confers the power on liquidators to apply to court to determine any question

5 See para **[23.010]**.

6 Section 256(2)(a)–(e) of the CA 1963. As to the qualifications of auditors, see Ch 17, *Financial Statements, Audit and Annual Return*, para **[17.296]**.

7 *Re Birchwell Developments Ltd* [2010] IEHC 319.

arising in a winding up. Laffoy J declined to make an order under s 131(5) of the CA 1990 giving the liquidator directions as to how to remedy the default. On this point the learned judge said:

> 'In my view, to accede to the suggested preferred relief indicated by the applicant would be, as the saying goes, to "*drive a coach-and-four*" through the companies legislation, which is designed to protect creditors and contributories of companies. Assuming that s 131 applies to a creditors' voluntary winding up which is deemed to exist by virtue of s 256(11), if the Court were to make an order at this juncture deeming the procedures adopted to date to be valid notwithstanding the failure to comply with s 256, the outcome would be to wholly defeat the purpose of s 131, which is to ensure that, until the members' nominee as liquidator is validly appointed at a creditors' meeting in accordance with the requirements of s 267, the liquidator, subject to the exceptions stipulated in subs (3) of s 131, may only exercise powers with the sanction of the Court ... if the Court were to ignore the failure to give notice to the public at large of a members' voluntary winding up and, in particular, the solvency of the company, the protection which s 256 is designed to give creditors of a company would be set at nought[8].'

Laffoy J indicated a strong preference for annulling the winding-up order so that the members would start the process *de novo* and, having indicated her inclination to do this, adjourned the matter to facilitate the parties' consideration of the issues and, in particular, whether the annulment of the winding-up order would have unforeseen consequences.

The report of an independent person

[23.007] The requirement that an independent person become involved in the procedure for a members' voluntary winding up was introduced by the CA 1990[9]. An 'independent person' is 'a person qualified at the time of the report to be appointed, or to continue to be, auditor of the company'[10].

[23.008] The report of the independent person must, in accordance with s 256(4) of the CA 1963, state whether in his opinion, and to the best of his information and according to the explanations given to him, the following are both reasonable:

- the opinion of the directors in the declaration of solvency; and
- the statement of the company's assets and liabilities embodied in the said declaration.

In this way, the legislature has sought to protect creditors. The point is, that by requiring an independent person to report on these matters, the veracity and accuracy of the declaration of solvency are inextricably connected to the skill, integrity and potential liability of the independent person who will be a professional. As noted above, the failure to comply fully with the provisions of s 256 of the CA 1963 concerning the statutory declaration of solvency will result in the ensuing liquidation being deemed *a creditors' voluntary winding up*[11]. In *Re Favon Investments Co Ltd*[12], the directors failed

8 *Re Birchwell Developments Ltd* [2010] IEHC 319 at para 5.1.

9 By s 128 of the CA 1990, which amended s 256 of the CA 1963.

10 Section 256(3) of the CA 1963.

11 See para **[23.006]** *ante* and the decision of Laffoy J in *Re Birchwell Developments Ltd* [2010] IEHC 319.

12 *Re Favon Investments Co Ltd* [1993] 1 IR 87 at 90.

to annex the report of an independent person to their declaration of solvency and it was held by Costello J that the court has no jurisdiction under s 280 of the CA 1963 to extend the time for making and filing the report and so the winding up would become a creditors' voluntary winding up. Where the company is out of time for holding a creditors' meeting in accordance with s 266 of the CA 1963, the court may annul the resolution that the company be wound up where nobody is prejudiced.

[23.009] The report of the independent person should be made *after* the directors have sworn their declaration of solvency. This appears to be the case because s 256(4) of the CA 1963 provides that this report should make reference to the opinion of the directors in the statutory declaration and this presupposes the prior existence of the directors' statutory declaration of solvency.

Personal liability of the directors

[23.010] Where, contrary to the statutory declaration sworn by the directors, a company is in fact insolvent, s 256(8) of the CA 1963 provides for the imposition of personal liability for the debts of the company, on the directors[13]. This states:

> 'Where a statutory declaration is made under this section and it is subsequently proved to the satisfaction of the court that the company is *unable to pay its debts*, the court on the application of the liquidator, or any creditor or contributory of the company may, if it thinks it proper to do so, declare that any director who was a party to the declaration without having reasonable grounds for the opinion that the company would be able to pay its debts in full within the period specified in the declaration *shall be personally responsible*, without any limitation of liability, *for all or any of the debts or other liabilities of the company as the court may direct*.' [Emphasis added.]

Subsection (9) provides that where a company's debts are not paid or provided for in full within the 12-month period after the commencement of the winding up, there is a presumption that the director did not have reasonable grounds for his opinion. Since the independent person must state whether or not in his view the opinion of the directors was reasonable, it would seem that a court would, in the absence of collusion, be loath to impose personal responsibility on the directors where their opinion is stated in the independent person's report to be reasonable. It would thus seem that the crucial statutory control will be getting the independent person's favourable report.

[23.011] The Supreme Court indicated in *Fay v Tegral Pipes Ltd and ors*[14] that it is questionable whether, in the absence of fraud, any action for negligence can lie against a director for his part in signing a declaration of solvency. There, McCracken J said:

> '... I would question whether, in the absence of fraud, any action for negligence can lie against a director for his part in signing a declaration of solvency. Section 256 embodies safeguards to ensure that a director will not act carelessly or recklessly. It requires an independent report by a person who is qualified to be an auditor of a company and it allows any creditor to apply to the Court within 28 days after the resolution of a winding up has been advertised if the creditor wishes to contest the solvency of the company. Where it transpires that in fact the declaration of solvency was incorrect, and the company is not able to pay its debts in full, then and only then is there a provision for personal

[13] See Ch 5, *Disregarding Separate Legal Personality*, para **[5.088]** *et seq*.

[14] *Fay v Tegral Pipes Ltd and ors* [2005] IESC 34.

liability of the directors, but in the present case I am quite satisfied that the company did pay its debts in full within the relevant period, and accordingly the directors do not have any liability under the statutory provisions of the section.'

In that case, the plaintiff was a former employee of a company which was wound up in members' voluntary winding up and its business and name taken over by a new company. The plaintiff's grievance was that he contracted asbestos scaring in his lungs due to handling asbestos and he had issued proceedings against the new company and six named directors, *inter alia*, for swearing a declaration of solvency without any reasonable belief in the truth of the declaration. As McCracken J said, the only suggestion that can be made was that the liquidation did not make any provision for contingent creditors in the event of potential future claims for asbestos related injury. McCracken J emphasised, however, that no such claim had been made against the company prior to or during its winding up and then neither the independent person not the liquidator saw fit to make any such provision. McCracken J found there was no direct evidence of wrongdoing by the directors in signing the declaration and did not think that the court could reasonably draw the inference from the facts that there had been wrongdoing. McCracken J concluded:

'In any event, this claim appears to be based on the fact that the defendants knew or ought to have known that the plaintiff, and possibly other employees, had a contingent claim against the company in the event of their contracting an illness due to contact with asbestos. In my view this totally misunderstands the nature of a contingent debt. For a contingent debt to exist, there must be a relationship between the company and a specific creditor in relation to a specific debt which may or may not become due depending upon the happening of some event. I do not think that some vague prospect in the future of some unidentified and unknown person making a claim could be construed as a contingent debt. Were it otherwise, it could lead to absurdities, particularly in relation to the winding up of a company. To my mind there must be certainty in the winding up of a company, and it would be ridiculous to suppose that a company in liquidation must make provision, and presumably retain monies, in case at some time, perhaps ten or twenty years in the future, a claim might be made against it by one or more of a class of claimants. In this regard it is relevant to note that the declaration required by s 256 must state that all debts will be paid in full within twelve months. Thus it is clear that the policy of the legislation is that where a solvent company is being wound up, its debts should be paid and the winding-up completed, within this period. Where, as in this case, the company can pay all its present debts within the twelve month period, there could be no question of negligence or breach of duty on the part of the directors in not making provision for possible unknown and unquantifiable claims which might arise after that period.'

The resolution to wind up

[23.012] After the directors of a company have made their declaration of solvency, and the independent person has given his report, the directors should then call an extraordinary general meeting ('EGM') of the company. This should be held within 28 days of the date of the declaration of solvency and the notice provisions specified for such in the company's articles of association must be adhered to[15].

[15] On notice periods for *general meetings*, see Ch 14, *Corporate Governance: Meetings*, para **[14.033]**.

[23.013] At the EGM, the members must pass a special resolution to wind up the company. Where a meeting is held, as opposed to the written resolution procedure being followed[16], the normal rules associated with the convening and holding of meetings, the giving of notice, the passing of special resolutions and the holding of polls must be followed[17]. Within 14 days from the passing of the winding-up resolution, notice of the resolution must be published in *Iris Oifigiúil*[18].

Commencement of a members' voluntary winding up

[23.014] Section 253 of the CA 1963 provides that a voluntary winding up 'shall be deemed to commence' at the time of the passing of the resolution for voluntary winding up. It does not lie within the gift of the members or anyone else to alter this statutory date of commencement[19]. In *Re Norditrack (UK) Ltd*[20], it was held that the resolution for voluntary winding up could not be passed conditionally on another event as it took effect, as statute provided, at the time when it was actually passed.

Termination of a members' voluntary liquidation

[23.015] Where a members' voluntary winding up continues for a period in excess of one year, the voluntary liquidator must within three months of the end of that year and in each succeeding year, summon a general meeting of the company. The purpose of this meeting is to lay before it an account of his acts and dealings and of the conduct of the winding up during the preceding year. Furthermore, the liquidator must send a copy of that account to the registrar of companies[21]. Non-compliance with this provision will render the liquidator liable to a class C fine[22].

[23.016] In a members' voluntary winding up, when the affairs of the company are fully wound up, the liquidator must, by s 263(1) of the CA 1963, make an account of the winding up. This account must show how the winding up was conducted and how the company's property was disposed of. The liquidator must then call a general meeting[23] and lay his account before the meeting, giving whatever explanations are required by the members. The meeting must be advertised in two daily newspapers, 28 days before it is held[24]. Within one week of the meeting the liquidator must send the account and make a

16 There is, however, no reason why the resolution cannot be passed pursuant to s 141(8) of the CA 1963 as a written resolution, where the articles of a company so permit.

17 See, generally, Ch 14, *Corporate Governance: Meetings*. So, for example, those present can demand a poll: *Re Hockerill Athletic Club Ltd* [1990] BCLC 921.

18 Section 252(1) of the CA 1963. Although s 72 of the IFCMPA 2005 substituted 'the Companies Registration Office Gazette' for '*Iris Oifigiúil*' it has not been commenced. A failure to do so by a company and every officer (including a liquidator) in default is an offence: s 252(2) of the CA 1963.

19 *Re West Cumberland Iron and Steel Company* (1889) 40 Ch D 361.

20 *Re Norditrack (UK) Ltd* [1999] TLR 782.

21 Section 262(1) of the CA 1963.

22 Section 262(2) of the CA 1963.

23 Failure to call the meeting renders the liquidator liable to a class C fine: s 263(7) of the CA 1963.

24 Section 263(2) of the CA 1963.

return to the registrar of companies who will register them[25]. Three months later, the company is deemed to be dissolved[26]. It should be noted that application can be made to court to have the dissolution of the company deferred[27]. Where such an order is granted it is the duty of the applicant to inform the registrar of companies, and to send her an office copy of the order for registration[28]. The distribution of assets to members, including distributions *in specie*, are considered in Chapter 25[29].

[B] Creditors' Voluntary Winding Up

[23.017] A *creditors' voluntary winding up* will arise either on the conversion of a members' voluntary winding up[30], or, *ab initio*, pursuant to s 251(1)(c) of the CA 1963. Section 251(1)(c) provides that the members in general meeting can resolve that the company cannot by reason of its liabilities continue its business, and that it be wound up voluntarily. The essential features of a creditors' voluntary winding up are the absence of a declaration of solvency and also the fact that the winding up is precipitated by the members themselves, usually on the advice of the directors. In this section the following issues in creditors' voluntary windings up are considered:

1. Statement of the position of the company's affairs.
2. The members' general meeting.
3. The creditors' meeting.
4. The committee of inspection.
5. Termination of a creditors' voluntary liquidation.

Statement of the position of the company's affairs

[23.018] The winding up of an insolvent company is not invariably the result of its creditors' actions. The directors (and in small companies, the members) will often be the first to realise that a company is insolvent. Indeed, the directors have *a duty* to take the necessary steps to initiate the winding up of an insolvent company. In *Re Shannonside Holdings Ltd*[31], the members' resolution to wind up the company was challenged by secured creditors who claimed that the decision was not *bona fide* and was intended to defeat their judgment mortgage. The resolution to wind up the company had been passed two-and-a-half months after the judgment mortgage had been registered and, accordingly, the judgment mortgage was invalid where the company was wound up within three months of its creation[32]. Costello J held on this question of fact that he found no evidence to suggest that there was an improper motive in adopting a resolution to wind up the company. Moreover, he held:

---

25 Section 263(3) of the CA 1963.

26 Section 263(4) of the CA 1963.

27 Section 263(5) of the CA 1963.

28 Section 263(6) of the CA 1963. Failure to do this can result in a person being liable on summary conviction to a class C fine.

29 See Ch 25, *Realisation and Distribution of Assets in a Winding Up*, at para **[25.196]**

30 See para **[23.113]**.

31 *Re Shannonside Holdings Ltd* (20 May 1993, unreported) HC.

32 Section 284(2) of the CA 1963.

> '... it is not denied that the company was insolvent and unable to pay its debts. The *directors had a duty* to wind up the company and the members of the company acceded to the request that a resolution to wind up be passed. Even though it may be advantageous to directors to pass a winding-up resolution, it seems to me that the resolution to wind up cannot be challenged on this ground once insolvency has been established and the *duty to wind up* shown to exist[33].'

The duty of directors to resolve to wind up a company that is insolvent is consistent with their general duties to creditors when a company becomes insolvent, as established by the Supreme Court in *Re Frederick Inns Ltd*[34].

[23.019] Where there is an internal decision to wind up a company on the grounds that it is insolvent the directors of the company should meet and resolve to convene two meetings: one of the members of the company, and one of the creditors. The next step, set out by s 266(3)(a) of the CA 1963, requires the directors to address the state of the company's affairs and to:

> '... cause a full statement of the position of the company's affairs, together with a list of the creditors of the company and the estimated amount of their claims to be laid before the meeting of the creditors ...'

The exact position of the company's affairs should be ascertained by the directors in conjunction with the company's financial advisors. The creditors will usually be divided into the categories of secured, preferential and unsecured. In addition, the directors must appoint one of their number to preside at the meeting of creditors, considered below[35].

The members' general meeting

[23.020] At this time, the directors will cause a general meeting of the members to be convened. The purpose of the general meeting is to pass an ordinary resolution, pursuant to s 251(1)(c) of the CA 1963, that the company cannot, by reason of its liabilities, continue its business and that it be wound up voluntarily. The directors must, subject to the company's own articles of association providing for longer[36] notice, give seven days' notice in writing to the members of the proposed EGM[37]. Again, this resolution must be advertised within 14 days of its passing in *Iris Oifigiúil*[38]. From the date of this resolution, the voluntary winding up of the company is deemed to commence[39]. The company should cease to carry on its business, save as may be required for the beneficial winding up of the company, but its corporate status and powers continue until its dissolution[40].

---

33 *Re Shannonside Holdings Ltd* (20 May 1993, unreported) HC at p 10 (emphasis added).

34 *Re Frederick Inns Ltd* [1994] 1 ILRM 387. See Ch 15, *Duties of Directors and Other Officers*, para **[15.013]**.

35 See para **[23.023]**.

36 See s 133(1) of the CA 1963. See also Ch 14, *Corporate Governance: Meetings*, para **[14.040]**.

37 Section 133(2)(b) of the CA 1963.

38 Under s 252(2) of the CA 1963 a class C fine is the penalty for default. Although s 72 of the IFCMPA 2005 substituted 'the Companies Registration Office Gazette' for '*Iris Oifigiúil*' it has not been commenced.

39 Section 253 of the CA 1963.

40 Section 254 of the CA 1963.

[23.021] At this meeting the members may nominate a liquidator under s 267(1) of the CA 1963 for the purpose of winding up the affairs and distributing the assets of the company. However, if the creditors nominate a different liquidator, as they are entitled to do, their nominee will prevail as the company's liquidator. This is subject to the application by any directors, members or creditors to court for an order that the liquidator nominated by the members shall be the liquidator or the joint liquidator with the liquidator nominated by the creditors[41].

[23.022] Where the general meeting of the members is adjourned for whatever reason, s 266(5) of the CA 1963 provides that any resolution passed at the creditors' meeting held on the same or the following day as the original members' meeting shall take effect as if it had been passed immediately after the passing of the resolution to wind up.

The creditors' meeting

[23.023] Section 266(1) of the CA 1963 imposes an obligation on the company to summon a meeting of its creditors[42], providing:

> 'The company shall cause a meeting of the creditors of the company to be summoned for the day, or the day next following the day, on which there is to be held the meeting at which the resolution for voluntary winding up is to be proposed, and shall cause the notices of the said meeting of creditors to be sent by post to the creditors at least 10 days before the date of the said meeting of the company.'

The first point to note here is the timing of the creditors' meeting, which must be held on the same day, or the day next following, the members' general meeting. The second point is that notices of the creditors' meeting must be sent by post to the creditors at least 10 days before the date of the meeting[43] together with two proxy forms[44] giving the creditors the right to appoint the chairman of the meeting or someone else as his proxy[45]. Thirdly, an advertisement should be placed at least 10 days before the creditors' meeting, once at least, in two daily newspapers circulating in the district where the company has its registered office or principal place of business[46].

[23.024] In order for a proxy to be entitled to participate in a vote on a resolution to appoint a liquidator, even where the creditor's debt has been proved or admitted, there must be compliance with Ord 74, r 81(1) of the Rules of the Superior Courts ('RSC')[47].

---

41 Section 267(2) of the CA 1963.

42 See generally, Comyn, 'The Calling and Conduct of a Creditors Meeting in a Voluntary Winding up' (1982) Gazette ILSI January/February and Comyn, 'Creditors' Meetings – Revisited' (1994) CLP 191.

43 Section 266(1) of the CA 1963.

44 RSC, Ord 74, r 76 provides that a general and special form of proxy shall be sent to each of the creditors with the notice summoning the meeting.

45 RSC, Ord 74, r 77.

46 Section 266(2) of the CA 1963.

47 In *Re CED Construction Ltd; Winthrop Engineering and Contracting Ltd v CED Construction Ltd* [2011] IEHC 420, Laffoy J noted that s 312 of the CA 1963 extended the power conferred by s 68 of the Courts of Justice Act 1936 in the Rules Committee of the Superior Courts to the making of rules in respect of the winding up of companies, whether by the court or voluntarily.

In *Re Hayes Homes Ltd*[48], a proxy appointed by a creditor whose debt owed by the company represented some 90% of its overall indebtedness was found to have been rightly excluded from the creditors' meeting where the instrument of proxy did not arrive at the company's registered office within the time prescribed by Ord 74, r 82(1). Strict compliance is required and in *Re CED Construction Ltd, Winthrop Engineering and Contracting Ltd v CED Construction Ltd*[49] it was held that a company's only creditor was not properly represented where the creditor had neither properly appointed a proxy nor appointed a representative under s 139 of the CA 1963. In that case, the company scored a Pyrrhic victory in disallowing the creditor's representative's votes because Laffoy J went on to find that the consequence was that the meeting was inquorate meaning that the meeting would have to be reconvened and the creditor presented with an opportunity to properly appoint a representative. Care should also be taken in completing the proxy: in *Re Stainless Pipeline Supplies (IRL) Ltd; Tyner v Lafferty and another*[50], a company purported to appoint a proxy to vote at a creditors' meeting pursuant to Ord 74, r 75 of the RSC. The notes to Form 21 and Form 22 require the form of proxy, in the case of a corporation, to be, *inter alia*, 'under its common seal ...'. Although the appointor company's articles of association were in the form of reg 115 of Table A, only one of its directors signed the proxy to which the common seal had been affixed. Laffoy J held that the proxy was not executed in accordance with Ord 74, r 75, *inter alia*, because the purported signing of the proxy was not in conformity with the company's own articles of association.

Re Michael Madden Quality Meats Ltd; Ballon Meats Ltd v Leahy and another[51] involved s 267 of the CA 1963 and a contest between two nominees of the creditors for the office of liquidator. Section 267 provides that the matter is to be put to a vote and that the resolution may be voted on by the creditors present personally or by proxy and the outcome determined by value, not numerically. In that case, the issue concerned the rules on Ord 74 governing a corporate creditor's right to vote on the nomination of a liquidator. Order 74, r 74 provides that where a person is authorised by s 139 of the CA 1963 to represent a corporation at a meeting of creditors, such person shall produce to the chairman of the meeting a copy of the resolution so authorising him which shall be either under the seal of the corporation or certified to be a true copy by the secretary or director of the company. Order 74, r 75 provides that every instrument of proxy shall be in the prescribed form and those forms provide that if the appointor is a company, the form of proxy must be under its common seal or the hand of a duly authorised officer, stating he is duly authorised. Order 74, r 82(3) provides that where a company is a creditor, anyone authorised under the seal to act generally on its behalf at meetings of creditors may fill in and sign the instrument of proxy and appoint himself to be the proxy.

In that case, a general and special proxy were sent to Ballon Meats Ltd and both were returned completed. In each case '*David Salter of Ballon Meats*' appointed '*John*

48 *Re Hayes Homes Ltd* [2004] IEHC 124, O'Neill J.

49 *Re CED Construction Ltd; Winthrop Engineering and Contracting Ltd v CED Construction Ltd* [2011] IEHC 420.

50 *Re Stainless Pipeline Supplies (IRL) Ltd; Tyner v Lafferty and another* [2010] IEHC 318.

51 *Re Michael Madden Quality Meats Ltd; Ballon Meats Ltd v Leahy and another* [2012] IEHC 122.

Salter of Ballon Meats' as proxy. The forms were signed by David Salter, a director of Ballon Meats Ltd ('Ballon'), but the form did not comply with the requirement that the fact the officer was authorised to make the appointment should be stated thereon as required by Ord 74, r 75. John Salter attended the meeting; Ballon was the largest creditor, representing 56% of the company's debts. The company's directors were also creditors and sought to appoint a particular individual as liquidator; Ballon wished to propose a different person. After taking legal advice, the chairperson, who was one of the creditor directors, rejected Ballon's proxy (and others) for being invalid for not complying with Ord 74, r 75. Accordingly, despite Ballon being owed circa €297,476, because of the proxies being invalid, the director creditors' nominee was appointed after receiving votes to the value of €29,698, as against only €3,917 for Ballon's proposed liquidator.

Laffoy J held that the chairperson had correctly declared Ballon's proxies invalid. The failure to comply with Ord 74 was fatal and despite the value of votes disallowed, and the fact that the chairperson may have known that David Salter was an officer of Ballon, to disregard Ord 74 would be to render it and its requirements nugatory or superfluous.

[23.025] The purposes of the creditors' meeting are generally accepted as being threefold:

- to consider the statement of affairs prepared by the directors;
- to consider the appointment of the liquidator appointed by the members and replace him if desired; and
- to appoint a committee of inspection.

Where, however, a liquidator has been appointed, his report must be presented to the meeting and the meeting advised as to whether or not he has exercised any powers since he was appointed by the members[52]. The creditors' meeting will be addressed by a director nominated by the board, who will usually give short reasons for the failure of the company, and answer any questions, usually through his solicitor. This is the reading of the statement of affairs which also includes providing a list of the company's creditors and an estimate of the amount of their claims[53].

[23.026] The procedures to be followed at creditors' meetings are largely determined by the RSC 1986. Order 74, r 66 provides that the quorum is three creditors, provided that if there are less than three creditors present, those present must represent all of the company's creditors. Unless a quorum is present, a meeting may not act for any purpose except for the election of a chairman and the adjournment of the meeting.

[23.027] To be entitled to vote, a creditor must have an ascertained debt, and a creditor shall not vote in respect of any unliquidated or contingent debt, the value of which is not ascertained[54]. A secured creditor can vote at the creditors' meeting. However, to do so he must provide certain details as to his security, namely the date of its creation and the

[52] Section 131 of the CA 1990. On liquidators' powers, see Ch 24, *Liquidations*, para **[24.027]** *et seq* and, especially, para **[24.046]** for the restrictions on the powers of liquidators appointed by members at the initiation of a creditors' voluntary winding up.

[53] Section 266(3)(a) of the CA 1963.

[54] RSC, Ord 74, r 68.

value at which he assesses it. He can then only vote in respect of the balance (if any) due to him after deducting the value of the security. If he votes in respect of the whole debt he shall be deemed to have *surrendered his security* unless the court, on application being made, is satisfied that this omission to value the security has arisen from inadvertence[55]. Where a secured creditor votes in respect of the value of his claim after deducting the value of his security the liquidator of the company may, within 28 days after the meeting, require the creditor to give up the security for the benefit of the creditors generally on payment of the value so estimated, but provided that the creditor may correct the valuation by a new proof, prior to giving up his security[56]. It is most unusual for secured creditors to surrender their security. Typically, secured creditors stand back from the liquidation and rely on their security.

[23.028] There are two different tests for the passing of a resolution at a creditors' meeting. In the case of a resolution to appoint the creditors' nominee as liquidator, as permitted by s 267(3) of the CA 1963, such a resolution:

> '… shall be deemed to be passed when *a majority, in value only*, of the creditors present personally or by proxy and voting on the resolution have voted in favour of the resolution.'

This represents a change to the law brought about by s 47 of the CLEA 2001, which inserted s 267(3) of the CA 1963[57]. For all other resolutions, they will be deemed to be passed when a *majority in number and value* of those present personally or by proxy vote in their favour[58]. The effect of this change in law is to make it easier to displace any liquidator ensconced by the members[59]. It should also be noted that s 131 of the CA 1990 restricted the powers that a members' liquidator can exercise prior to the holding of a creditors' meeting, the purpose of this provision being to prevent the practice of '*Centrebinding*' in Ireland[60].

[23.029] The chairman of the meeting can admit or reject a proof for the purpose of voting, subject to appeal to court[61]. Where there is doubt, the chairman should mark the proof as objected to and allow the creditor to vote subject to the vote being declared invalid in the event of the objection being sustained[62], and the court has held that application must be brought within two weeks[63]. Creditors may attend and vote in person or by proxy[64] and companies may send a 'representative'[65]. In *Jim Murnane Ltd*[66], the

55 RSC, Ord 74, r 69 which provides: '… if he votes in respect of his whole debt he shall be deemed to surrender his security unless the court on application is satisfied that the omission to value the security has arisen from inadvertence.'

56 RSC, Ord 74, r 70.

57 This provision commenced with effect from 1 October 2001: SI 438/2001.

58 RSC, Ord 74, r 62.

59 See Lynch-Fannon & Murphy, *Corporate Insolvency and Rescue* (2nd edn, 2012), para 3.22.

60 *Re Centrebind Ltd* [1966] 3 All ER 889. See Ch 24, *Liquidators*, para **[24.046]**.

61 See *Re Jim Murnane Ltd* [2009] IEHC 412, Laffoy J, and *Re Centrum Products Ltd* [2009] IEHC 592, Laffoy J; considered at **[23.030]** *post*.

62 RSC, Ord 74, r 71.

63 *Re Titan Transport Logistics Ltd* (19 February 2003, unreported) HC, Kelly J.

64 Proxies are dealt with in RSC, Ord 74, rr 74–83. Proxies must be lodged with the company not later than 4 pm on the day before the meeting: RSC, Ord 74, r 82(1).

65 Section 139 of the CA 1963.

66 *Re Jim Murnane Ltd* [2009] IEHC 412.

members of a company voted to put the company into voluntary liquidation and at the creditors' meeting there was a dispute as to the amount which one creditor claimed he was owed. The chairman disallowed the creditor's objection to the sum in the statement of affairs which the directors had prepared and would not allow him vote the higher amount. In the end, there was a contest between the members' nominee for liquidator and a nominee put forward by the creditor. The members' nominee was appointed as he was declared by the chairman to have votes to the value of €654,465, whereas the creditor's nominee was declared to have votes to the value to €410,812. The matter came before Laffoy J pursuant to Ord 74, r 71 which provides for an appeal against the chairman's determination. Laffoy J began by noting the change in law introduced by s 47 of the CLEA 2001, which inserted s 267(3) of the CA 1963, and that Ord 74, r 71 predated that amendment. The learned judge also noted that in admitting the amount stated in the proofs for voting purposes, the chairman had appeared to act in accordance with guidance given by the Institute of Chartered Accountants[67]. On the court's jurisdiction under Ord 74, r 71, Laffoy J said that it was concerned solely with the admission or rejection of a proof of debt 'for the purpose of voting' and that:

> 'Rule 71 as it exists seems to envisage admission or rejection of the proof of debt in whole. Unlike the UK provision considered in *Re a Company* [1995] 1 BCLC 459, it does not appear to address the difficulty which arose in this case – that the company's estimate of the debt represented only part of the amount claimed by the applicant creditor. It may be that there is a *casus omissus* in the legislative scheme constituted by s 267 and the Rules since the insertion of subs (3) in s 267. As it exists, in my view, the rule requires the chairman to give the creditor the benefit of the doubt, subject to the possibility of his decision being set aside on appeal. In the situation which arose in this case, there the amount of the applicant's claimed debt exceeded the company's estimate of the debt, it must be assumed that there was a doubt. On the rule as it exists, the decision of the chairman should have been to allow the applicant to vote on the basis that the value of its claim was the value asserted ... As a matter of law, I see no basis for applying para 31 of guidance document S8B in a situation to which r 71 applies.'

The learned judge said that on an appeal the court 'was concerned with much more than whether the chairman acted properly procedurally' and that the court is required to make some sort of determination on the substance of the dispute. Acknowledging that it was probably easier to determine whether someone was a creditor than to determine the value of their debt, Laffoy J said she thought that in many cases the court would be unable to determine the amount of the debt. In the instant case, Laffoy J held that the chairman should have allowed the proof in whole and treated the debt as the amount claimed by the applicant creditor and, on that basis, declared that the vote in favour of the liquidator who was the members' nominee was invalid, and to obviate the expense of calling another creditors' meeting purported to make an order under s 267(2) of the CA 1963 and appointed the liquidator nominated by the creditor.

---

67 Document S8B – *Planning and Administration of Creditors' Meetings* states at para 31: 'The amount for which the chairman admits the proof for voting purposes should normally be the lower of: (a) the amount stated in the proofs; and (b) the amount considered by the company to be due to the creditor. The amount for which the proof is admitted for voting purposes should be endorsed on it, and in most instances, it is expected that prior to the meeting, the chairman will do this.'

[23.030] In *Re Centrum Products Ltd*[68], Laffoy J elaborated on the court's jurisdiction on an appeal under Ord 74, r 71 and on reflection suggested that s 267(2) had no application. Laffoy J said that it was relatively narrow and fundamentally different to its broad jurisdiction on the hearing of a winding-up petition. The learned judge quoted with approval the following passage from the decision of Blackburne J in *Re a Company*[69]:

> 'In my view, the task of the court, on an appeal under rule 4.70(4) ... is simply to examine the evidence placed before it on the matter and come to a conclusion whether, on balance, the claim against the company is established and, if so, in what amount. I would only add that, in considering the matter, the court is not confined to the evidence that was before the chairman at the time that he made his decision but is entitled to consider whatever admissible evidence on the issue the parties to the appeal chose to place before the court.'

In a r 71 appeal, the court's function was said to be to determine whether the decision of the chairman on the admission or rejection of a proof for the purpose of voting was correct.

> 'Although it is not spelt out in the rule, the Court must have jurisdiction to deal with the consequences of the decision having been incorrect, if that is the case, where the Court considers that the correct decision would have impacted on the appointment of the liquidator. How the consequences are dealt with will depend on the particular circumstances in the case ...
>
> Adopting the approach adumbrated by Blackburne J in the passage quoted earlier, I consider that the only jurisdiction which the Court has on this application is to determine, by reference to the evidence before the Court, whether Mr Reynolds, as chairman of the creditors' meeting, was correct in admitting the proofs of the claims of himself and his wife for the purposes of voting the appointment of a liquidator. I do not think it is open to the Court in making such determination, where the question is whether a debt was properly admitted, to have regard to any factors other than whether the evidence shows that, on balance, the debt in issue is due by the company to the creditor in issue. In particular, I do not think that it is open to the Court to take into account the broader issues, such as the conduct of the creditor in issue in another capacity, whether as a director or a member of the company, which may give rise to a claim for reckless trading or fraudulent preference in the winding up. What the appeal is about is whether a particular proof was properly admitted or rejected and no more.'

In that case, the members of a company resolved that it be wound up voluntarily and its creditors resolved to appoint X, who was the members' nominee, as liquidator. It was claimed that the value attributed to the valid creditors' votes cast in favour of the resolution to appoint X was overstated and in fact the majority in value of the creditors did not support X but instead supported the appointment of Y as liquidator. The applicant, a creditor, sought, *inter alia*, declarations that the appointment of X was void, and that the majority in value of creditors supported Y and also sought orders that X be removed and Y be appointed liquidator. Laffoy J held that on the evidence, the company was indebted to the director and chairman of the meeting and his wife and another person in a sum which exceeded the debt due to the applicant and confirmed that X had been properly appointed.

---

68 *Re Centrum Products Ltd* [2009] IEHC 592.

69 *Re a Company* [1995] 1 BCLC 459.

The committee of inspection

[23.031] The creditors of a company have the power to appoint a committee of inspection under s 268(1) of the CA 1963. The creditors' committee will consist of not more than five persons nominated by the creditors. Where such a committee is appointed, the company, acting through its members, may appoint three persons to act as members of the committee. The committee members nominated by the members in general meeting can be objected to by the creditors and, subject to appeal to court, can be disqualified from so acting[70].

[23.032] The proceedings of the committee of inspection are the same as a committee of inspection appointed in a compulsory or official winding up[71]. These are enumerated in s 233(2)(9) of the CA 1963, which provides that:

- the committee can meet as it thinks fit;
- the liquidator can convene a meeting of the committee;
- a committee member can convene a meeting;
- the committee acts by majority, provided a majority is present;
- resignation is effected by notice in writing to the liquidator;
- a member is deemed to have vacated office on becoming bankrupt or by making an arrangement with his creditors or by being absent from five consecutive meetings without leave;
- a member of the committee can be removed by a majority of those who appointed him (members or creditors);
- on a vacancy arising the liquidator must convene a meeting of those who appointed the former member, save where he obtains a court order that this is unnecessary;
- on a vacancy, those left can continue if they number at least two.

In relation to liquidators, the committee of inspection has three other powers:

- to fix the remuneration of the liquidator[72];
- to determine whether the liquidator should continue the business of the company;
- to determine whether the powers of the directors should continue[73].

Termination of a creditors' voluntary liquidation

[23.033] In a creditors' voluntary winding up, when the affairs of a company are fully wound up the liquidator must make an account of the winding up, showing how it was conducted and how the property of the company has been disposed of, and then call a general meeting of the members and a meeting of the creditors and lay his account before them, giving whatever explanations are necessary[74]. This meeting is convened by advertisement in two daily newspapers circulating in the district where the registered office of the company is located specifying the place, time and object of the meeting and

70 Section 268(2) of the CA 1963.

71 See Ch 24, *Liquidators*, para **[24.023]**.

72 Section 269(1) of the CA 1963.

73 Section 269(3) of the CA 1963.

74 Section 273(1) of the CA 1963.

published at least 28 days before the meeting[75]. After the meeting, the liquidator must report to the registrar of companies who will register the report. On the expiration of three months the company shall be deemed to have been dissolved[76].

[C] Compulsory Court Winding Up

[23.034] A compulsory, or official, liquidation will arise where the High Court is petitioned to have a company compulsorily wound up[77]. Of the three processes by which a company can be wound up, compulsory winding up has given rise to the most case law as the petition will often be resisted strongly by the company. In this section the following issues are considered:

1. Jurisdiction to compulsorily wind up companies.
2. *Locus standi* to petition the court.
3. Procedural issues in compulsory windings up.
4. Grounds for ordering a company to be wound up.

Jurisdiction to compulsorily wind up companies

[23.035] Section 212 of the CA 1963 provides that: 'The High Court shall have jurisdiction to wind up any company.' 'Company' is defined by s 2 of the CA 1963 as a 'company formed and registered under this Act, or an existing company'. An 'existing company' is defined, also by s 2 of the CA 1963, as a company formed and registered under the Joint Stock Companies Acts, the Companies Act 1862 or the Companies (Consolidation) Act 1908. Moreover, s 344 of the CA 1963 applies Part X of the CA 1963 to 'unregistered companies' which are defined as:

> '... any trustee savings bank certified under the Trustee Savings Banks Acts 1863 to 1958, any partnership, whether limited or not, any association and any company with the following exceptions—
>
> (a) a company as defined by section 2;
>
> (b) a partnership, association or company which consists of less than eight members and is not formed outside the State.'

The companies which the High Court has *jurisdiction* to wind up, therefore, are those which are formed or registered under the Companies Acts, former Companies Acts[78] and unregistered companies[79]. In certain circumstances the Irish courts also have jurisdiction to wind up *foreign companies*, formed or registered abroad[80].

75 Section 273(2) of the CA 1963.

76 Section 273(4) of the CA 1963. The liquidator or another person may apply for an order deferring the date of the dissolution of the company (s 273(5) of the CA 1963).

77 See generally, Keane, *Company Law* (4th edn, 2007) at Ch 36; Ussher, *Company Law in Ireland* (1986), p 478 *ff*; Lynch-Fannon & Murphy, *Corporate Insolvency and Rescue* (2nd edn, 2012).

78 Sections 324 and 325 of the CA 1963.

79 See s 345 of the CA 1963. In *Western Counties Construction Ltd v Whitney Town Football and Social Club* (1993) Times, 19 November, it was held that a *club* was not an unregistered company and could not be wound up under the Insolvency Act 1986 (UK). For an example of where an unregistered company was wound up, see *Re Welsh Highland Railway Light Railway Co* [1993] BCLC 338.

80 See s 345 of the CA 1963. See also *International Westminster Bank plc v Okeanos Maritime Corp* [1987] BCLC 450. See generally Binchy, *Irish Conflicts of Law* (1988), pp 485–486.

[23.036] Section 345(1) of the CA 1963 provides that all 'unregistered companies' may be wound up under the Companies Acts, the provisions of which shall apply to such companies. It must be noted, however, that unregistered companies may *not* be wound up voluntarily, ie, they can only be wound up by court[81]. Section 345(4) enumerates three circumstances in which an unregistered company may be wound up:

- if the company is dissolved, or has ceased to carry on business, or is carrying on business only for the purpose of winding up its affairs;
- if the company is unable to pay its debts[82];
- if the court is of opinion that it is just and equitable that the company should be wound up.

Moreover, where a company incorporated outside the State, which has been carrying on business in the State, ceases to carry on business in the State, it may be wound up as an unregistered company notwithstanding that it has been dissolved or otherwise ceased to exist as a company under the laws of the country where it was incorporated[83]. It is not necessary that an unregistered company have assets within the State. In *Stocznia Gdanska SA v Latreefers Inc (No 2)*[84], the English Court of Appeal endorsed the finding of Lloyd J that, as the law has evolved[85], there are three core requirements before a court will exercise its discretion to order the winding up of an unregistered company:

> '(1) There must be a sufficient connection with England and Wales which may, but does not necessarily have to, consist of assets within the jurisdiction.
>
> (2) There must be a reasonable possibility, if a winding-up order is made, of benefit to those applying for the winding-up order.
>
> (3) One or more persons interested in the distribution of assets of the company must be persons over whom the court can exercise a jurisdiction.'

There, the Court of Appeal rejected the contention that it was a requirement that an unregistered company must have assets within the jurisdiction. In that case, it was held that potential claims for misfeasance and wrongful and fraudulent trading provided a reasonable possibility of benefit to those applying for a winding-up order and that this satisfied the second core requirement. In *Atlantic & General Investment Trust Ltd v Richbell Information Services Inc*[86], it was held that the first core requirement –

---

81 Section 345(3) of the CA 1963.

82 Section 345(5) of the CA 1963 lists four circumstances in which an unregistered company shall be 'deemed' to be unable to pay its debts.

83 Section 345(7) of the CA 1963.

84 *Stocznia Gdanska SA v Latreefers Inc (No 2)* [2000] TLR 182.

85 Lloyd J referred to the decisions of Megarry J in *Re Compania Merabello San Nicolas SA* [1972] 3 All ER 448, [1973] Ch 75; Nourse J in *Re Eloc Electro-Optiek and Communicatie BV* [1981] 2 All ER 111, [1982] Ch 43; and Peter Gibson J in *Re A Company (No 00359 of 1987)* [1987] Ch 210 (which he noted was also known, less enigmatically, *as International Westminster Bank plc v Okeanos Maritime Corp* [1987] BCLC 450, [1987] 2 All ER 137). Lloyd J also said that the statement of the relevant principles has evolved to the point at which they were summarised, most recently, by Knox J in *Real Estate Development Co* [1991] BCLC 210 at 217.

86 *Atlantic & General Investment Trust Ltd v Richbell Information Services Inc* [2000] BCC 111.

sufficient connection – was satisfied where a company's directors were resident in England at the relevant time, it was a member of a group of companies that consisted of English companies, a particular transaction had taken place in England and that it had assets in England and conducted correspondence from the London address of the group of companies.

Locus standi to petition the court

[23.037] Only certain persons have *locus standi* to petition to have a company wound up by the court, and those who can bring a petition are only permitted to do so on certain grounds[87]. Those who are entitled to petition the court to have a company wound up are: the company itself; a creditor of the company; a contributory; a member; the Director of Corporate Enforcement; and the registrar of companies.

(a) The company

[23.038] The grounds on which a company can petition for its own winding up are set out in s 213(c)(f) of the CA 1963.[88] Although a company can petition for its own winding up, such is rare. For the members of most companies it is preferable to resolve in favour of a members' or creditors' voluntary winding up because these are cheaper and less public.

[23.039] The general power of the directors of a company to manage the business of the company in reg 80 of Table A would appear to be insufficient authority for them to present a petition to wind up the company[89]. In *Re Galway & Salthill Tramways Co*[90], the petition to have the company wound up was presented by its directors, without the express authority of the shareholders in general meeting. Certain dissenting shareholders claimed that such an action exceeded the powers of the directors. The directors contended that they had power to present the petition, such being part of their general power to manage the company and to exercise all of the company's powers[91]. This contention was rejected by O'Connor MR who said:

> 'In my opinion that part of the section which gives the directors all the powers of the company ... must be read along with the opening words giving powers of management, and is merely in aid of the proper and effective exercise of such powers ... the powers of the directors are only powers of managing, and if the argument relied on is sound, a winding up of the company must come within the scope of its management. But the object of management is the working of the company's undertaking, while the object of a winding up is its stoppage. On this ground alone I would hold that the directors had no power to present the petition in the present case …'[92]

Of course, such an outcome is dependent upon the provisions of a particular company's articles of association, and it is possible for a company to give its directors express

---

87 Section 215 of the CA 1963.

88 See para **[23.067]**. In the case of a private company limited by shares or by guarantee, reg 11 of the EC(SMPLC)R 1994 (SI 275/1994) has provided that s 213(d) of the CA 1963 shall not apply; see para **[23.070]**.

89 See Ch 13, *Corporate Governance: Management by the Directors*, para **[13.127]**.

90 *Re Galway & Salthill Tramways Co* [1918] 1 IR 62.

91 Under s 90 of the Companies Clauses Act 1845, which was similar to reg 80 of Table A.

92 *Re Galway & Salthill Tramways Co* [1918] 1 IR 62 at 65.

power to present a petition. Similarly, a receiver appointed out of court may have power as agent for a company to present a petition where he is expressly authorised to do so in the debenture instrument where this appears necessary to secure the assets charged[93].

(b) Creditors

[23.040] The grounds upon which a creditor can petition for the winding up of a company are those set out in s 213(c)(f)[94] of the CA 1963. Section 215 provides that a creditor or creditors, including contingent or prospective creditors, have *locus standi* to petition the court to have a company wound up[95]. A contingent creditor is one who may, at some future time, be owed money where, for example, money becomes payable under a contract of indemnity or of guarantee; a prospective creditor is one who will be owed money at a future date, for example, to be repaid on, but not before, the maturity of a bond or a post-dated cheque[96].

[23.041] To be able to present a petition, however, a creditor must have a present[97] liquidated debt due and owing to him, and so a bare claim in tort would not be sufficient[98]. Similarly, the debt owed must be to the creditor himself, and so where the company has given a guarantee to the creditor this will not entitle that creditor to petition until the primary debtor has defaulted and the company has failed to pay on foot of the guarantee[99]. A liquidator of a company which is owed money by another company can petition the court to have the debtor company wound up[100]. In *Re Dollar Land Holdings plc*[101], Sir Donaldson Nicholls VC said of a 'prospective creditor' that: '... a person with an undisputed claim for unliquidated damages for more than a nominal amount qualifies as a prospective creditor[102].' In that case, the petitioner had guaranteed a bank loan to a company in return for a 25% stake in property being acquired by the company. When the property was not purchased he sought the release of his guarantee. When that was not done he simultaneously commenced proceedings for a mandatory order that the guarantee be released, an order for damages and he presented a petition to

93 See *Re Emmadart Ltd* [1979] 1 All ER 599; and Pennington, *Corporate Insolvency Law* (1991), pp 13–15.

94 See para **[23.067]**. In the case of private company limited by shares or by guarantee, reg 11 of the EC(SMPLC)R 1994 (SI 275/1994) has provided that s 213(d) of the CA 1963 shall not apply; see para **[23.070]**.

95 On a dispute as to a person's status as a *creditor*, see *Re Bank of Credit and Commerce International SA (No 5)* [1994] 1 BCLC 429.

96 See, generally, Coonan, 'Taking Contingent and Prospective Liabilities into Account in Assessing Corporate Insolvency' (2011) CLP 71 where the decision of the English Court of Appeal in *BNY Corporate Trustee Services Ltd v Eurosail-UK 2007 3BL plc and others* [2011] EWCA 227 is considered.

97 Where a judgment creditor's debt has been satisfied by a sheriff's successful execution, he ceases to be a creditor and has no standing to petition: *Debtor v Goacher* [1979] 1 All ER 870.

98 Note though that s 214(c) of the CA 1963 provides that in determining whether a company is unable to pay its debts, 'the court shall take into account the contingent and prospective liabilities of the company'.

99 See *Re Fitness Centre (South East) Ltd* [1986] BCLC 518.

100 *Re Shrinkpak Ltd* (20 December 1989, unreported) HC, (*unapproved*) *per* Barron J.

101 *Re Dollar Land Holdings plc* [1994] 1 BCLC 404.

102 *Re Dollar Land Holdings plc* [1994] 1 BCLC 404 at 407.

have the company wound up. It was held that the petitioner was entitled to present the petition as he was a contingent or prospective creditor of the company with respect to any unliquidated damages that he might suffer arising from the company's failure to obtain the release of the guarantee.

[23.042] Section 215(c) of the CA 1963 provides that a court shall not hear a winding-up petition presented by a contingent or prospective creditor unless such security for costs has been given as the court thinks reasonable and a *prima facie* case for winding up has been established[103]. In *Truck and Machinery Sales Ltd v Marubeni Komatsu Ltd*[104], Keane J held, in the context of applications to restrain the presentation of petitions by creditors, that:

> 'It is also clear that, where the would-be petitioner is a contingent or prospective creditor, the court which is asked to restrain the petition is not concerned with whether the creditor will be able to meet the requirements of the proviso in s 215, under which such a creditor must give security for costs and satisfy the court that a *prima facie* case for winding up has been established. I agree entirely with the view expressed by Goulding J in *Hold Southy v Catnic Components Ltd*[105], that, where it is shown that the would-be petitioner is a prospective or contingent creditor, it is for the court which hears the petition to determine whether the statutory requirements for the granting of the reliefs sought in the petition have been met[106].'

Re La Plagne Ltd[107] concerned a petition brought by a 50% shareholder in a company to have it wound up on the grounds that it was insolvent having an excess of liabilities over assets and was unable to meet its liabilities as they fell due for repayment. The petition was resisted by the other 50% shareholder in the company (Mr Rowan) on the grounds that the petitioner did not have standing as either a contingent or prospective creditor or as a contributory and, that in any event, the company was not insolvent. In relation to whether the petitioner was a contingent or prospective creditor, Laffoy J noted that he had, as required by s 215(c), undertaken to give security for costs in the form of a bond. Turning to the other pre-condition, that the court shall not give the petitioner a hearing until a *prima facie* case for winding up has been established to the court's satisfaction, Laffoy J noted that the question as to whether the court should hold a preliminary hearing had not been considered up to then in Ireland. Laffoy J noted that in *Re Fitness Centre (South East) Ltd*[108] Hoffmann J had said it was in order to hold a preliminary hearing but that the court could go on immediately to consider the petition; in the instant case, however, because the petitioner was also a contributory, Laffoy J expressed no view on this point.

The basis for the petitioner's claim to be a contingent or prospective creditor was that he had guaranteed the company's indebtedness to a bank. Laffoy J rejected the contention that this made the petitioner a contingent or prospective creditor. He was a

---

103 On security for costs generally, see Ch 6, *Corporate Civil Litigation*, para **[6.014]** *et seq*.

104 *Truck and Machinery Sales Ltd v Marubeni Komatsu Ltd* [1996] 1 IR 12. For comment, see Canniffe, 'Restraining a Creditor's Winding-up petition – The Position Since *Truck and Machinery Sales Ltd v Marubeni Komatsu Ltd*' (1997) 4 CLP 30.

105 *Hold Southy v Catnic Components Ltd* [1978] 2 All ER 276.

106 *Re Shrinkpak Ltd* (20 December 1989, unreported) HC, at p 21.

107 *Re La Plagne Ltd* [2011] IEHC 91.

108 *Re Fitness Centre (South East) Ltd* [1986] BCLC 518.

surety for a sum of up to €500,000 but until he had discharged the whole of the company's indebtedness to its bank, he was debarred by the rule against double proof from making any claim.

[23.043] A creditor who is owed a debt is said to be entitled *ex debito justiciae* to a winding-up order[109]. To this general rule there are a number of exceptions, and in *Re Burren Springs Ltd*[110] Laffoy J referred with apparent approval to the statement that the court 'still retains an overriding and unfettered discretion to refuse to order to wind up the company, albeit that it will only exercise this discretion sparingly and where good cause is shown'[111]. It has been held that a court will have regard to the wishes of other creditors where they are a majority in number and value. In *Re RW Sharman Ltd*[112], the court exercised its discretion and refused an order to wind up a company, where a majority of creditors opposed the petition by a judgment creditor[113].

[23.044] Another exception to the rule that a creditor is entitled *ex debito justiciae* to a winding-up order is that the petition presented must not be seen as an abuse of the court's process: *Re Bula Ltd*[114]. In *Re Bula Ltd,* the company owed money to various banks, its only asset being zinc and lead deposits in the ground. One of the creditors who had a judgment against the company, tried to become a secured creditor by way of registering a judgment mortgage, and this prompted the banks to petition for the winding up of the company. The purpose of this was, *inter alia*, to prevent the judgment mortgage from ranking with the banks[115]. The High Court order to wind up the company was discharged by the Supreme Court. McCarthy J said that, since there was nothing to be gained by the winding up:

> '... in my judgment, in this case of special facts, where a petition is brought by secured creditors whose security attaches to the entire assets of the debtor company and who have appointed a receiver whose power of sale is, effectively, at least as great as that of a liquidator, the court should refuse its aid[116].'

---

[109] See *Re Camburn Petroleum Products Ltd* [1979] 3 All ER 297. There, Slade J said (at 303) where a contributory challenged the petition of a creditor: 'While I recognise that it would have the right ... to pay regard to the wishes of contributories, in deciding whether or not to make a winding-up order on a creditors' petition, or to adjourn the hearing, in my judgment it can, and should, ordinarily attach little weight to the wishes of contributories, in comparison with the weight it attaches to the wishes of any creditor, who proves both that he is unpaid and that the company is "unable to pay its debts".' See also *Re JD Swain Ltd* [1965] 1 WLR 909 at 915.

[110] *Re Burren Springs Ltd* [2011] IEHC 480.

[111] MacCann & Courtney, *Companies Acts 1963–2009* (2010 edn) at p 446.

[112] *Re RW Sharman Ltd* [1957] 1 All ER 737.

[113] See also *Re Belfast Tailors' Co-partnership Ltd* [1909] 1 IR 49 and *Re Fitness Centre (South East) Ltd* [1986] BCLC 518. See, however, *Re George Downs & Co Ltd* [1943] IR 420 which shows that where the interests of a creditor will be prejudiced by *not* winding up the company, the court will grant the petition notwithstanding that there is opposition from other creditors. For the significance of creditors' views, see para **[23.069]**.

[114] *Re Bula Ltd* [1990] 1 IR 440.

[115] *Re Bula Ltd* [1990] 1 IR 440 at 447. On the invalidity of judgment mortgages, see s 284(2) of the CA 1963 and generally Ch 25, *Realisation and Distribution of Assets in a Winding Up*, para **[25.052]** *et seq*.

[116] *Re Bula Ltd* [1990] 1 IR 440 at 451.

Accepting that a creditor was prima facie entitled to a winding-up order[117], McCarthy J held that this had the effect of shifting the initial burden faced by those who present a petition to those who oppose a petition to have a company wound up.

(c) Contributories and members

[23.045] Contributories and members may petition for the winding up of a company upon the grounds set out in s 213(a)(g)[118] of the CA 1963. A *contributory* is defined by s 208 of the CA 1963 as:

> '... every person liable to contribute to the assets of a company in the event of its being wound up, and for the purposes of all proceedings for determining, and all proceedings prior to final determination of, the persons who are to be deemed contributories, includes any person alleged to be a contributory.'

Although all past and present members are *prima facie* entitled to present a petition, if the contributory is the holder of fully paid up shares, the court will be reluctant to accede to the application, unless it can be shown that the company is solvent and that a substantial surplus of assets will be available to the members, as otherwise the member will have no tangible interest in the winding up[119]. There is authority for the proposition that any member who has a potential liability to contribute to the assets of a company is a possible petitioner, even where he has no actual liability, ie, where his shares have been fully paid up[120]. This must, however, be considered as not being settled law in Ireland by reason of the decision in *Re La Plagne Ltd*[121], the facts of which were considered above[122]. There, it was contended that a fully paid-up shareholder does not have locus standi to bring a petition on the authority of a number of English decisions[123]. The petitioner sought to rely upon the statement of law in MacCann & Courtney, *Companies Acts 1963–2006* (2008 edn) where it was stated:

> 'Whilst the English courts have been reluctant to allow the holder of a fully paid share to petition to wind up a company unless it can be shown that the member will have a tangible interest in the liquidation, as where there would be a substantial surplus of assets available for members, the Irish courts have been prepared to make a winding-up order on a creditor's petition even where there is no prospect of a dividend in the liquidation.'

---

117 *Re Bula Ltd* [1990] 1 IR 440 at 448.

118 See para **[23.067]**. In the case of a private company limited by shares or by guarantee, reg 11 of the EC(SMPLC)R 1994 (SI 275/1994) has provided that s 213(d) of the CA 1963 shall not apply.

119 See Schmitthoff (ed), *Palmer's Company Law* (24th edn, 1987), para 88-16, citing, among other cases, *Re Expanded Plugs Ltd* [1966] 1 WLR 514 and *Re WR Willcocks & Co Ltd* [1973] 3 WLR 669. See also *Re Instrumentation Electrical Services Ltd* [1988] BCLC 550.

120 *Re Anglesea Colliery Co* [1866] 1 Ch App 555 at 559, *per* Turner LJ.

121 *Re La Plagne Ltd* [2011] IEHC 91.

122 See para **[23.042]** *ante*.

123 See *Re Rica Gold Washing Company* (1879) 11 CH D 36; *Re Othery Construction Ltd* [1966] 1 All ER 145; *Re Expanded Plugs Ltd* [1966] 1 All ER 877; *Re Chesterfield Catering Co Ltd* [1976] 3 All ER 294; and the Privy Council decision in *CVC/Opportunity Equity Partners Ltd and another v Almeida* [2002] UK PC 16.

Laffoy J noted that the authority cited for the foregoing was *Re Irish Tourist Promotions Ltd*[124] but found that not especially helpful in determining whether the petitioner was a contributory since in that case the petitioner had invoked the just and equitable ground whereas in the instant case the petitioner solely relied on what he asserted was the company's insolvency. Laffoy J concluded that she had some residual doubts as to whether the petitioner had *locus standi* to maintain the petition solely on s 231(e) but left the question as to whether he was a contributory open since on the evidence she found that the company was not insolvent.

[23.046] A contributory is restricted in his right to bring a petition by virtue of s 215(a) of the CA 1963 which prevents him from bringing a petition unless:

- the number of members is reduced, in the case of an unlimited private company[125] to one member; or
- his shares or some of them were either allotted to him, or have been held by him and registered in his name, for at least six months during the 18 months before the commencement of the winding up or have devolved on him through the death of the former holder.

The rationale for these restrictions is motivated by the desire to prevent past or present disgruntled members from petitioning unless they have good and substantial reason to do so[126].

[23.047] The question as to whether or not a person is a contributory or member will often be apparent without judicial scrutiny. Where a petitioner's standing is not clear cut, it has been held by the English Court of Appeal that it will not automatically be the case that this will be deferred to the hearing of the petition and that, on occasion, this question will be answered as a preliminary question, particularly where to do so would leave a petitioner without an effective remedy were the petition to be struck out[127].

(d) The Director of Corporate Enforcement

[23.048] The Director of Corporate Enforcement ('the Director') can petition for the winding up of a company on the grounds set out in s 12 of the CA 1990[128]. The Minister for Jobs, Enterprise and Innovation's *locus standi* was, in this respect, transferred to the Director by s 14 of the CLEA 2001. The Director's *locus standi* arises where the affairs of a company have been investigated by an inspector and it appears from the report or information obtained by the Director that the company should be wound up in the public

124 *Re Irish Tourist Promotions* (1963–1993) ICLR 383.

125 Regulation 11 of the EC(SMPLC)R 1994 (SI 275/1994) dis-applies s 215(a)(i) of the CA 1963 to private companies limited by shares or by guarantee; see para **[23.070]**.

126 See Schmitthoff (ed), *Palmer's Company Law* (24th edn, 1987), para 88-15 where it is said that this is to 'prevent a person buying shares in order to qualify himself to wreck the company'.

127 *Re UOC Corp; Alipour v Ary* [1997] BCC 377.

128 Surprisingly, s 215(d) of the CA 1963, which provides that the Minister can petition for a winding up in a case falling within s 170(3) of the CA 1963 – a section repealed by s 6(1) of the CA 1990 – was not also repealed by the CA 1990. The result is that s 215 of the CA 1963 now contains a superfluous and redundant provision, albeit one which will not affect the Director's right to petition for a winding up.

interest[129]. The Director's power is, however, dependent upon the court finding that it is just and equitable for the company to be wound up[130].

(e) The registrar of companies

[23.049] The registrar of companies can petition the court to have a company wound up on the grounds set out in s 213(h) and (i) of the CA 1963. It is rare for the registrar to petition to have a company wound up because of the registrar's power to strike a company off the register[131].

(f) Trustees of investment companies

[23.050] Section 215(g) of the CA 1963[132] provides that the only person with *locus standi* to petition for the winding up of an investment company on the grounds that such is just and equitable (pursuant to s 213(fa) of the CA 1963)[133] is the trustee of an investment company, ie, the person nominated by the Central Bank under s 257(4)(c) of the CA 1990.

Procedural issues in compulsory windings up

[23.051] Much of the law relating to the compulsory winding up of companies is procedural in nature[134]. At this point it is proposed to review the procedural steps in compulsorily winding up a company.

(a) The petition

[23.052] When it is sought to have a company wound up compulsorily the applicant must proceed by petition. A petition is an application to court, whereby the petitioner *prays* the court for a specified relief. The RSC 1986 set out the procedural rules applicable to a winding up, and the Appendix to the Rules sets out three precedent forms of petition. Among the details which will have to be included are:

- the date on which the company was incorporated;
- the registered office of the company;
- the nominal and issued share capital of the company;
- the principal objects of the company; and
- the ground or grounds upon which the petition is based, these being one of those listed in s 213 of the CA 1963.

The purpose of requiring these details is to provide the court with a certain amount of basic information on the company. In addition, the petitioner must swear a verifying affidavit as to the truthfulness of the contents of the petition[135].

---

129 See generally Ch 27, *Investigations and Inspectors*.

130 See para **[23.091]**.

131 See generally Ch 26, *Strike Off and Restoration*, para **[26.004]** *et seq*.

132 As inserted by s 94(c) of the CLEA 2001.

133 See para **[23.067]**.

134 See generally, the now dated but excellent account given by Marshall & MacDermott, 'Liquidations' (1991) Incorporated Law Society Continuing Legal Education Seminar of 27 June 1991.

135 In the case of a body corporate petitioner, an authorised officer should swear the verifying affidavit.

[23.053] Having prepared the petition, the petitioner then causes it to be *issued* by going to the Central Office of the High Court, where the Central Office will give it a hearing date, stamp and keep the original and a copy and endorse the date of hearing on a further copy of the petition. The Central Office will then direct the newspapers in which the petition is to be advertised. The verifying affidavit referred to must be filed within four days after the presentation of the petition.

[23.054] At this point, the petitioner must *serve* a copy of the petition on the company by ordinary post to the registered office of the company, or if there is none, at the principal or last known principal place of business of the company, or with a member, employee or officer of the company or some other place where the court, on application, directs[136]. While there is no prohibition on the petition being served *after* the advertisement of the petition, it makes common sense to serve the company first so as to give it an opportunity to settle the demand before the other creditors become aware of the proceedings. An affidavit of service is also required to be sworn, stating that the petition was served on the company.

(b) Advertisement of the petition

[23.055] Next, the petitioner must cause the petition to be *advertised* in those newspapers which the Registrar of the High Court directs. Usually this will be in *Iris Oifigiúil*, and two national newspapers. Order 74, r 10 of the RSC 1986 provides that the advertisements must appear at least seven clear days prior to the date on which the petition is to be heard[137]. These advertisements must be then *vouched* in the Central Office of the High Court, before the hearing of the petition. Advertisements must be accurate and any errors will invalidate them[138]. Where the winding up of a company commences within one year after the company has changed its name, s 23(6) of the CA 1963 provides that the former name as well as the existing name of the company must appear on all notices and advertisements in relation to the winding up.

(c) Options for a respondent company

[23.056] Upon being served with a petition to have it wound up, a company has a number of options open to it. It may *defend* the proceedings on all grounds open to it. This may involve the sometimes obstructive step of seeking security for costs against a corporate petitioner. Alternatively, it can *compromise* the claim against it. In such a case the petition can be struck out, although where the petition is advertised, another creditor can continue the process begun by the petitioner. Other creditors must notify the petitioner of their intention to appear at the hearing of the petition[139] and thc petitioner

136 See RSC, Ord 74, r 11. In *Re Corbenstoke Ltd* [1989] BCLC 496, an application to have a petition struck out was refused where it had been served at the wrong address because of the registrar of companies' failure to register a change of the company's registered office in the Companies House.

137 On the matter of notifying persons, it is necessary to decide upon a liquidator and obtain from him a *letter of consent* to act as such, and prepare an *affidavit of suitability* to act as such, usually prepared by a solicitor. Also, the area's sheriff should be notified as this compels him to hold goods seized from the company for proper distribution by the liquidator.

138 See *Re London and Provincial Pure Ice Manufacturing Company* (1904) WN 136.

139 See RSC, Ord 74, r 15.

must give a list of these persons to the Registrar of the High Court prior to the hearing of the petition. Similarly, affidavits of opposition to the petition must be filed within seven days after the publication of the last advertisement, and notice must be given to the petitioner[140].

[23.057] Where a company elects to pay off the petitioner who presented the petition, whether or not the petitioner will be entitled to his costs of the petition will depend upon the facts of the case and, in particular, whether the petitioner has behaved reasonably. In *Re MCR Personnel Ltd*[141], the petitioner was the company's former landlord who was owed €18,000 in respect of a settlement for arrears of rent. When it was not paid, the petitioner served a s 214(a) demand and after 21 days, the petitioner presented the petition and served it on the company. Within six days of service, the company transferred the sum of €18,000 to the petitioner's solicitors and subsequently wrote seeking the petitioner's consent to the petition being struck out with no order as to costs. The petitioner said it would be seeking costs but, the debt having been discharged, did not advertise the petition. Laffoy J noted that there was authority from the UK that where a debt is paid before the hearing of the petition the company will be ordered to pay the petitioner's costs *provided that the petition was advertised*[142]. Laffoy J noted that the rationale for requiring advertisement was because such was required by the RSC and because the petitioner should be in material compliance with all requirements of the RSC before becoming entitled to his costs and to dissuade petitioners from using the courts as a debt collecting agency. Laffoy J said that whether the court's jurisdiction arose under s 216(1) of the CA 1963 or its inherent jurisdiction, the primary consideration was the proper application of Ord 99 of the RSC which provides that the costs of and incidental to every proceeding are at the discretion of the court and the normal rule was that costs follow the event. The learned judge concluded:

> '4.3 I do not think it would be appropriate for the Court to lay down a strict rule that a petitioner whose debt has been satisfied before the petition comes before the Court, where the petition has not been advertised, should not be entitled to the costs of presenting the petition. While I am acutely conscious of the importance of the factor which motivated Nourse J in following the "modern practice" in *Re Shusella Ltd* only where the petition has been advertised, that the Court should be astute in ensuring that creditors do not use the winding up process as a debt collection process, nonetheless, there are other factors to which the Court should have regard in considering an application by a petitioner for his costs. One is that, if the debtor company is not at risk of having to discharge the costs of the petition where it discharges the debt after the petition is presented but before it is advertised, there will be little incentive for the debtor company to comply with the s 214 demand prior to the presentation of a petition. Another factor is that, if the petitioner has to bear the costs of the presentation of the petition to recover a debt to which he is clearly entitled, the defaulting debtor company gets off "scot-free", whereas the wronged petitioning creditor is penalised in costs. Further, in my view, it is contrary to common sense that there should be a practice whereby the petitioning creditor whose debt is discharged after presentation of the petition but before it is advertised will only have an

140 RSC, Ord 74, r 17.

141 *Re MCR Personnel Ltd* [2011] IEHC 319.

142 Reliance was placed on French, *Applications to Wind Up Companies* (2nd edn) at para 4.6.2.3 and the decision in *Re Shusella Ltd* [1983] BCLC 505; and *Re Nowmost Company Ltd* [1996] 2 BCLC 492.

entitlement to costs of presenting the petition in circumstances where the overall costs are unnecessarily ratcheted up by requiring him to advertise for no other reason than to comply with the Rules.

4.4 In the light of the factors outlined above, it seems to me that every case must be decided on its own facts, both in relation to the period before and the period after the presentation of the petition.'

In the case before the court, it was found that the petitioner ought to be awarded costs, despite the petition not having been advertised, because its actions were at all times reasonable.

(d) Substitution of petitioner

[23.058] The legal basis for substituting one creditor for the original petitioner is to be found in Ord 74, r 18 of the RSC 1986, which provides:

'When a petitioner consents to withdraw his petition, or to allow it to be dismissed, or the hearing adjourned or fails to appear in support of his petition when it is called in court on the day originally fixed for the hearing thereof, or on any day to which the hearing has been adjourned, or if appearing, does not apply for an order in the terms of the prayer of his petition, the Court may, if, and upon such terms as it shall deem just, substitute as petitioner any person who would have a right to present a petition, and who desires to prosecute the petition.'

In *Re Lycatel (Ireland) Ltd*[143], the ability of a creditor, who did not initiate a petition, to continue the process and be substituted as petitioner was considered. In that case, the initial petitioner had served a statutory notice under s 214(1) of the CA 1963 which had not been complied with; however, on the return date for the petition, its counsel advised that the petition had not been advertised and that the petitioner wanted to withdraw the petition. At this point another creditor applied to be substituted as the petitioner. Following an adjournment it was claimed that the company owed this creditor money and that it had served a statutory notice also which had not been complied with. The basis of the company's objection to the other creditor being substituted was that the petition had not been advertised in breach of Ord 74, r 10 of the RSC 1986. After considering a number of authorities[144], Laffoy J rejected the contention that the failure to advertise precluded the other creditor from being substituted:

'The purpose of the power of substitution of a petitioner conferred by r 18 is succinctly explained in the following passage from French on *Applications to Wind Up Companies* (Oxford University Press, 2nd ed, 2008) at p 245: "Without provision for substitution, an insolvent company could delay being wound up by paying off petitioning creditors one by one, forcing other creditors to present and advertise new petitions, then waiting until the petition by each creditor was at or neat hearing before paying that creditor off too. In order to counter these tactics, several creditors would have to present petitions simultaneously. AS Needham J said in *DMK Building Materials Pty Ltd v CB Baker Timbers Pty Ltd* (1985) 10 ACLR 16 at p 19: 'The purpose of substitution, in my opinion, is to ensure that once a prima facie right to the winding up of a company has arisen, the company should

143 *Re Lycatel (Ireland) Ltd* [2009] IEHC 264; Laffoy J. For a case note see Kirwan, 'Substituting a Petitioner in a Winding-Up Petition' (2009) CLP 220.

144 *Re United Stock Exchange Ltd; ex p Philip & Kidd* (1884) 28 CD D 183 and *Re Creative Handbook Ltd* [1985] BCLC 1.

> not escape from that position except upon the basis of fair dealing with all its creditors, not merely by paying off the particular [applicant].'"
>
> I reject the argument advanced by counsel for [the company] that r 18 is predicated on the petition having been advertised. On the contrary, each of the circumstances outlined in r 18 as giving rise to the discretion to substitute may arise even if the petition has not been advertised[145].'

[23.059] Where a petition has been issued on the grounds, say, that a company is unable to pay its debts and has been advertised, it is open to the company's controllers to accept, albeit belatedly, that the company is insolvent and suggest that it be wound up in a creditors' voluntary winding up. This was the position in *Re Jer Ryan Electrical Contractors Ltd*[146] and just before the petition was to be heard, counsel for the company sought an adjournment to facilitate the convening of a creditors' meeting. The petition was adjourned and when it was next before the court it was learned that the creditors' voluntary winding up had commenced and a liquidator appointed. The petitioner was agreeable to the petition being struck out but sought two orders; first, that the petitioner be awarded its costs of the petition and, second, that the petitioner's costs should rank pari passu with the costs of the liquidator. Laffoy J granted the petitioner the order for costs and in so doing distinguished the case in hand from that in *Re Balbradagh*[147] on the grounds that in the other case the matter had evolved into a contest as to whether the creditors' voluntary liquidation should continue as a compulsory winding up by the court, with the petitioner's nominee as liquidator rather than the liquidator chosen by the creditors. In so ordering, Laffoy J gave credit to the petitioner for adopting the sensible position that the company be wound up outside of the court. The learned judge was, however, not inclined to make the order that the petitioner's costs rank pari passu with those of the liquidator, at least not at that juncture. Noting that it could affect other parties' interests (eg, the liquidator's own remuneration, the committee of inspection's expenses and the unsecured creditors), Laffoy J said the court had no information on a range of relevant matters but said that this was not to prevent the petitioner from bringing an application under s 280 of the CA 1963 in accordance with r 138 of Ord 74 of the RSC 1986.

[23.060] Of course, where before a petition is heard a company is put into creditors' voluntary liquidation, the petitioner may not be disposed to allow this and may proceed to insist that the winding up be converted to an official liquidation. The conversion of windings up is considered below[148].

(e) Hearing the petition

[23.061] On the designated day, the petitioner's legal advisors will attend at the High Court in the Four Courts. The company may, or may not be represented. On the hearing of a winding-up petition, s 216(1) of the CA 1963 provides:

> '... the court may dismiss it, or adjourn the hearing conditionally or unconditionally, or make any interim order, or any other order that it thinks fit, but the court shall not refuse

145 *Re Lycatel (Ireland) Ltd* [2009] IEHC 264 at p 8, 9 of the judgment.

146 *Re Jer Ryan Electrical Contractors Ltd* [2011] IEHC 424, Laffoy J.

147 *Re Balbradagh* [2009] 1 IR 597.

148 See para **[23.113]** *post*.

> to make a winding-up order on the ground only that the assets of the company have been mortgaged to an amount equal to or in excess of those assets, or that the company has no assets.'

Section 216(2) of the CA 1963[149] provides that the court shall not make a winding-up order unless it is satisfied that the company has no obligations in relation to a bank asset that has been transferred to NAMA or a NAMA group entity or, if it has such an obligation, that a copy of the petition has been served on NAMA and NAMA has been heard on the application. A 'bank asset' has the same meaning as in the NAMAA 2009 and includes loans and security for loans. The most clear situation where this will be relevant is where a company had a commercial loan from, say, AIB – which is a participating institution under the NAMAA 2009 – and that loan and the security for it is acquired by NAMA. In those circumstances, NAMA has been substituted for AIB as the lender under the loan to the company and an order to wind up that company cannot be made unless NAMA has been served with a copy of the petition *and* NAMA has been heard on the application.

[23.062] Section 216(2) of the CA 1963 was considered by Laffoy J in *Re Albion Enterprises Ltd*[150]. In that case, Laffoy J found that the company in respect of which the petition had been brought had not paid on foot of a demand made in accordance with s 214 of the CA 1963 and that, accordingly, the company was deemed to be insolvent and unable to pay its debts. When the petition came on for hearing, NAMA intervened on the basis that NAMA had acquired a loan and the security for that loan made by Bank of Ireland to the company and had appointed joint-statutory receivers over assets charged for that loan[151]; moreover, NAMA claimed that it had acquired loans and security from Irish Nationwide Building Society and that NAMA had made a demand on foot of a guarantee and had appointed statutory receivers over certain other assets. Laffoy J noted that the reality of the situation was that NAMA had security over all the assets of the company and was in the course of enforcing that security and that it seemed highly unlikely that there were any assets that had escaped NAMA's wide net. Laffoy J went on, however, to make the winding-up order. The learned judge considered that having heard NAMA on the petition, it had not demonstrated that the winding-up order should be refused; an example given by Laffoy J of where a winding-up order might be refused was if the petitioner had an ulterior motive in bringing the petition. Laffoy J considered that the petitioner's right to a winding-up order *ex debito justitiae* should prevail:

> 'Accordingly, as a matter of law, as the petitioning creditor has proved that the company is insolvent and is unable to pay its debts as they fall due, in my view, it is entitled to a winding-up order *ex debito justitiae*. Notwithstanding the evidence put before the Court by NAMA, I consider that the Court must make a winding-up order.'

Given that any liquidator would not displace NAMA's statutory receivers and the extent of the company's indebtedness to NAMA (which was nearly €60m) it is difficult to see, as Laffoy J herself observed, how the company's liquidation would achieve the petitioner's objective of having its debt discharged.

---

149 Section 216(2) and (3) were inserted by s 233 (Schedule 3; Part 3) of the NAMAA 2009.

150 *Re Albion Enterprises Ltd* [2012] IEHC 115.

151 See Ch 20, *Corporate Borrowing: Receivers*, a para **[20.022]**.

[23.063] The courts will accede to a request to have the hearing of a petition *adjourned* in exceptional circumstances only[152]. *Re Coolfadda Developers Ltd*[153] is the leading Irish authority on the circumstances in which a winding-up petition will be adjourned on a petition for provisional liquidation of a company. In that case, a company had a provisional liquidator appointed and sought to have this extended to facilitate the completion of certain houses and their sale. This was an unusual application since the provision liquidator was in a sense performing a role more akin to an examiner than one who realises and distributes corporate assets. In the High Court, Laffoy J had conducted a thorough review of the authorities on the jurisdiction to adjourn a petition[154] and had held it was not appropriate to adjourn the petition to allow the provisional liquidator to continue in situ with the result that the company would most likely be wound up. The learned judge said:

> 'Winding up, or liquidation, as both terms suggest, is the process whereby assets of the company are got in, realised and distributed among the persons entitled thereto by law and eventually the company is dissolved. Pending the making of a winding-up order, s 226 empowers the Court to appoint a liquidator provisionally at any time after the presentation of the petition. The primary function of the provisional liquidator is to ensure the preservation of the company's assets until the winding-up order is made.
>
> What is proposed in this case by the company, the petitioner, is an extension of the appointment of the provisional liquidator and the continuation of his powers in a manner which is clearly not envisaged by the Act of 1963. Indeed, I would go so far as to say that the proposal goes against the spirit and intendment of the Act of 1963. The appointment of the provisional liquidator is a stopgap measure pending the making of the winding-up order and the appointment of the official liquidator, whose function is to liquidate the company in accordance with law. The official liquidator is given powers by virtue of s 231 of the Act of 1963 to achieve that objective, including, power "to carry on the business of the company so far as may be necessary for the beneficial winding up thereof" (s 231(1)(b)). As a matter of principle, I do not think it would be a proper exercise of the Court's discretion under s 216 to postpone the making of a winding-up order so as to enable the provisional liquidator, who was appointed after the presentation of the petition, to continue conducting most aspects of the business of the company with a view to maximising the assets of the company. To do so would be contrary to the scheme of the provisions in the Act of 1963 in relation to compulsory winding up.'

The decision of Laffoy J in the High Court not to adjourn the petition was upheld by the Supreme Court, which affirmed the order of the High Court.

[23.064] The Supreme Court decision of Denham J did, however, depart in one important respect from the decision of the High Court. It was held that the jurisdiction to adjourn a winding-up petition and permit the continuation of a provisional liquidation was a jurisdiction that: '... exists in rare cases, upon which a judge might then exercise a

---

152 In *Re Kanwell Developments Ltd and Salthill Properties Ltd* [2008] IEHC 3, Clarke J adjourned a petition to have a company wound up where it was established that there was a competing garnishee application in respect of the same debt, finding that the logical approach was that they be determined on the basis of the times when the respective procedures were initiated.

153 *Re Coolfadda Developers Ltd* [2009] IEHC 263 and [2009] IESC 54.

154 *Re Bula Ltd* [1990] 1 IR 440; *Re Demaglass Holdings Ltd* [2001] 2 BCLC 633; *Re Minrealm Ltd* [2008] 2 BCLC 141; *Re Rafidain Bank* (2000) LTL 23/3/2000.

discretion' as an exception to the underlying principle that 'the winding up of the company should proceed and that a provisional liquidator should not remain in place for an indefinite period.' Denham J cited the facts in *MHMH Ltd and ors v Carwood Barker Holdings Ltd*[155] as an example of where the exercise of such a jurisdiction might be justified. There, the court made an exception to the rule that a winding-up petition ought not to be left outstanding for a substantial period of time for the credible reason of realising substantial monies for the benefit of creditors in circumstances where there was no other asset but these monies as the companies involved were shells.

[23.065] In *Re Burren Springs Ltd*[156], Laffoy J noted the reluctance to grant lengthy adjournments of a winding-up petition was for good reason[157] and in that case refused to adjourn a petition presented by the Revenue Commissioners particularly having had regard to the fact that there were outstanding fiduciary taxes (VAT and PAYE/PRSI) which had been paid by customers or deducted from employees and ought to have been remitted to the Revenue Commissioners. In *Re Demaglass Holdings Ltd*[158], a petition was presented to wind up a company but the receivers who stood appointed sought to have the petition hearing adjourned so as to enable them to dispose of certain stock more advantageously. There, Neuberger J granted the adjournment sought for a period of 10 weeks. The court made clear that where some creditors were in favour and some were against the making of a winding-up order, an order would be made where the majority supported the petition. A bare majority of creditors against the making of a winding-up order would not be sufficient to dissuade the court from granting a dissenting minority of creditors their *prima facie* right to a winding-up order. Neuberger J went on to hold that there was an onus on those creditors who opposed the making of a winding-up order to satisfy the court that there was good reason for refusing to order a winding up. Where the majority and minority had both established their respective cases, the court accepted that it would be forced to carry out a balancing exercise.

[23.066] Although the general rule is that in the absence of statutory exception a limited company cannot be represented in court proceedings by its directors[159], in practice, where a director or member of a company appears in court without legal representation in response to a petition, the court will listen to their representations 'to ensure that no injustice would be perpetrated'[160].

Grounds for ordering a company to be wound up

[23.067] The circumstances, or causes, which will ground a petition to wind up a company are set out in s 213 of the CA 1963. This section provides that a company *may* be wound up by the court if:

(a) the company has by special resolution resolved that the company be wound up by the court[161];

---

155 *MHMH Ltd and ors v Carwood Barker Holdings Ltd* [2006] 1 BCLC 279.

156 *Re Burren Springs Ltd* [2011] IEHC 480.

157 Laffoy J quoted from MacCann & Courtney, *Companies Acts 1963–2009* (2010 edn) at p 452.

158 *Re Demaglass Holdings Ltd* [2001] 2 BCLC 633.

159 *Battle v Irish Art Promotion Centre Ltd* [1968] IR 252.

160 *Re Marble and Granite Tiles Ltd* [2009] IEHC 455 at p 9.

161 Section 213(b) of the CA 1963 was repealed by Sch 3 of the C(A)A 1983.

(c) the company does not commence its business within a year from its incorporation or suspends its business for a whole year;

(d) the number of members is reduced, in the case of a private company, below two, or, in the case of any other company, below seven[162];

(e) the company is unable to pay its debts;

(f) the court is of the opinion that it is just and equitable that the company, other than an investment company within the meaning of Part XIII of the Companies Act 1990, or the European Communities (Undertakings for Collective Investments in Transferable Securities) Regulations 1989 (SI 1989/78), should be wound up[163];

(fa) the court is of opinion that it is just and equitable that the company, being an investment company within the meaning aforesaid, should be wound up and the following conditions are complied with—

- (i) in the case of an investment company within the meaning of Part XIII of the Companies Act 1990
  - (I) the petition for such winding up has been presented by the trustee of the company, that is to say, the person nominated by the Central Bank of Ireland under section 257(4)(c) of the Companies Act 1990, in respect of that company;
  - (II) the said trustee has notified the investment company of its intention to resign as such trustee and six or more months have elapsed since the giving of that notification without a trustee having been appointed to replace it;
  - (III) the court, in considering the said petition, has regard to—
    - (A) any conditions imposed under section 257 of the Companies Act 1990, in relation to the resignation from office of such a trustee and the replacement of it by another trustee; and
    - (B) whether a winding up would best serve the interests of shareholders in the company;

    and
  - (IV) the petition for such winding up has been served on the company (if any) discharging, in relation to the first-mentioned company, functions of a company referred to in conditions imposed under section 257 of the Companies Act 1990, as a 'management company';

  and
- (ii) in the case of an investment company within the meaning of the European Communities (Undertakings for Collective Investment in Transferable Securities) Regulations 1989, such conditions as the Minister may prescribe by regulations[164];

(g) the court is satisfied that the company's affairs are being conducted, or the powers of the directors are being exercised, in a manner oppressive to any

162 Note that this is no longer a ground under which the court can be petitioned by single-member private companies: reg 11 of the EC(SMPLC)R 1994 (SI 275/1994). See para **[23.070]**.

163 As amended by s 93(a) of the CLEA 2001.

164 As inserted by s 93(b) of the CLEA 2001.

member or in disregard of his interests as a member and that, despite the existence of an alternative remedy, winding up would be justified in the general circumstances of the case so, however, that the court may dismiss a petition to wind up under this paragraph if it is of opinion that proceedings under s 205 would, in all the circumstances, be more appropriate;

(h) after the end of the general transitional period, within the meaning of the Companies (Amendment) Act 1983, the company is an old public limited company within the meaning of that Act;

(i) after the end of the transitional period for share capital, within the meaning of the Companies (Amendment) Act 1983, the company has not complied with the conditions specified in s 12(9) of 1983 Act.

The main grounds are now considered in some detail.

(a) The company has resolved by special resolution to wind up the company

[23.068] For the members of a company to pass a special resolution to have the company wound up, and proceed to petition the court to have the company wound up is a rare occurrence. If the members can combine to pass a special resolution, they will, in all probability, opt to have their company wound up voluntarily, this being the most economical and discreet route to take.

(b) The company does not commence its business within a year from its incorporation or suspends its business for a whole year

[23.069] Again, this ground is rarely relied upon since only contributories, the company itself and creditors may rely on it. Such parties will often find other, more appropriate grounds, on which to petition to have a company wound up.

(c) The number of members is reduced, in the case of a private company, below two, or, in the case of any other company, below seven

[23.070] In the case of private companies limited by shares or by guarantee this is no longer a ground to petition the court to have such a company wound up. Regulation 11 of the EC(SMPLC)R 1994[165] provides:

> 'Sections 213(d) and 215(a)(i) of the 1963 Act shall not apply to a private company limited by shares or by guarantee.'

It may be noted, however, that this ground continues to apply with full force and effect in the case of an *unlimited private company.* Of course, its application to public companies also continues.

(d) The company is unable to pay its debts

[23.071] It is upon this ground that most petitions of creditors are based for the understandable reason that they believe the company to be *insolvent* with the consequence that their debts may not be paid. This ground is considered here under the following headings:

(i) A discretionary ground.

(ii) Deeming companies to be unable to pay their debts.

---

[165] SI 275/1994.

(iii) The '21-day letter'.
(iv) Service of the demand.
(v) The *bona fides* of the debt.
(vi) The existence of a valid cross-claim.
(vii) The test for injuncting a petition based on s 213(e) of the CA 1963.
(viii) Liability for improperly presenting petitions.

(i) A discretionary ground

[23.072] Section 213 of the CA 1963 is a discretionary provision and even though a person may prove conclusively that a company is unable to pay its debts, there is no automatic right to a winding-up order. So, for example, a petitioner may be estopped from presenting a petition on equitable grounds[166]. The discretionary nature of s 213 was stressed by McCracken J in *Re Genport Ltd*[167]. In that case, the petitioner was one of several defendants in proceedings that had been taken by the respondent company and others. The action against the petitioner had been dismissed and the petitioner was awarded two-thirds of her costs against the plaintiffs. After taxation of her costs the petitioner served a demand under s 214(1) of the CA 1963 for her costs plus interest, and when these were not paid, issued the petition to wind up the respondent company. McCracken J noted that the proceedings that gave rise to the order for costs were part of a long-running series of disputes between the respondent company and other parties, including a landlord and tenant dispute concerning the respondent company's lease of Sachs Hotel in Dublin. McCracken J stated that s 213 sets out a list of circumstances in which a company *'may'* be wound up by the court. As to the instant case he said that there was no doubt but that the petitioner had proved (by reason of s 214[168]) that the company had been unable to pay its debts. McCracken J went on to say 'however, it is quite clear that s 213 is not mandatory, and there remains a discretion in the court'. McCracken J stated that the correct approach in such cases was that set out by McCarthy J in *Re Bula Ltd*[169], where he said:

> 'I would hold that a creditor is prima facie entitled to his order so as to shift the initial burden to those who oppose the winding up; the petitioner does not have to demonstrate positively that an order for winding up is for the benefit of the class of creditors to which he belongs, but, if issue is joined on the matter, and a case made that the petition is not for that purpose but for an ulterior, though not in itself improper object, then the burden shifts back to the petitioner.'

Applying that reasoning to the facts of *Re Genport Ltd,* McCracken J said of the claim that the petitioner had an ulterior motive (ie, to prevent further litigation) but that he did not think that that alone was sufficient to persuade him to exercise his discretion against the petitioner because the motive was not necessarily improper. What swayed the judge

166 An estoppel from presenting a petition was claimed by a respondent company but rejected by the English Court of Appeal in *Re Selectmove Ltd* [1995] 2 All ER 531 on the application of the decision in *Foakes v Beer* (1888) 9 App Cas 605 and the rule in *Pinnel's Case* (1605) 5 Co Rep 117a. The Court of Appeal's decision in *Selectmove Ltd* was applied by Keane J in *Truck and Machinery Sales Lt v Marubeni Komatsu Ltd* [1996] 1 IR 12.

167 *Re Genport Ltd* [1996] IEHC 34, McCracken J.

168 See para **[23.074]**.

169 *Re Bula Ltd* [1990] 1 IR 440 at 448.

in deciding to refuse to allow the petition to proceed, however, was the fact that the respondent's lease to Sachs Hotel would be forfeited were it wound up with the result that there would be little left by way of assets for the remaining creditors. McCracken J also considered it significant that four trade creditors, who were the only trade creditors to appear on the petition, were opposed to the company being wound up. He was also influenced by the fact that there was substantial litigation in being which a liquidator would have difficulty in taking over. In these circumstances McCracken J held that the combination of the ulterior (although not necessarily improper) motive and the fact that a winding up might not be of any real benefit to ordinary creditors were sufficient to persuade him to exercise his discretion to refuse to make a winding-up order[170].

The wishes of other creditors can, as seen in *Re Genport Ltd*, influence the court's discretion. Indeed, in that case McCracken J relied upon s 309(1) of the CA 1963, as authority for the proposition that the court 'may, as to all matters relating to the winding up of a company, have regard to the wishes of the creditors or contributories'[171]. Where there is a divergence of opinion and some creditors favour winding up and others do not, the court will ordinarily be inclined towards the wishes of those with the most money owed to them (s 309(2) of the 1963 Act) but where the opposing creditors are not independent, being persons associated with the company or its directors, their views will, at the judge's discretion, be discounted[172].

[23.073] In *Re Forrest Lennon Business Support Services Ltd*[173], a company had two 50:50 shareholders who were its only directors. One of the shareholding directors brought a petition seeking to have the company wound up on the basis that it was insolvent and unable to pay its debts within the meaning of s 214 of the CA 1963 having failed to pay him the sum of €46,585. The other shareholding director resisted the petition and the first question to be decided by Laffoy J was whether it was open to a shareholder, rather than the company, to dispute a debt allegedly due by the company to the petitioner.

---

170 The petition was, however, stayed with liberty to re-enter, pending the outcome of the litigation.

171 In *Re Genport Ltd (No 2)* [2001] IEHC 156, McCracken J, five years later, to the month, McCracken J again adjourned the petition generally with liberty to re-enter. There, McCracken J held that it appeared 'beyond doubt that if a winding-up order is made, the benefit to the petitioner will be negligible, and the probability is that neither she nor any of the ordinary creditors will recover anything at all'. Again, McCracken J identified the company's landlord (which would recover vacant possession of the property leased to the company) as thc principal beneficiary. On this point he said: 'This seems to me to be the motive of seeking a winding-up order at this state. It may well be said, as was in the *Bula* case, that the motive is not in itself improper, as the petitioner is an officer of Crofter Properties Ltd, and indeed Crofter Properties Ltd is almost certainly the largest creditor of the company. There is no doubt in my mind that this application is not being brought to benefit the ordinary creditors of the company, as such, but to benefit Crofter Properties in its position as lessor of the property to the company and as one particular general creditor. In those circumstances, while I am not taking the drastic remedy of dismissing the petition as was done in the *Bula Ltd* case, nevertheless I would propose to adjourn the petition generally, with liberty to re-enter.'

172 *Re Lummus Agricultural Services Ltd* [1999] BCC 953.

173 *Re Forrest Lennon Business Support Services Ltd* [2011] IEHC 523.

> 'Where, as here, two 50% shareholders of the company, who are the only directors of the company, have expressed and sworn to diametrically opposed views as to whether the debt, which forms the basis of the petition to wind up, is due by the company to the petitioner, in my view, the court has a discretion to consider the evidence put before it by the shareholder who opposes the petition on the ground that the debt is not owed by the company. Indeed, I would go so far as to say that in order to act in a principled manner that is fair and just, it is incumbent on the court to consider that evidence on hearing of the creditor's petition, without putting the onus on the opposing shareholder to establish the solvency of the company. At this juncture, in my view, whether the company is solvent or not, does not have to be addressed, because the issue for the court is whether the petitioning creditor has the status of creditor and has locus standi to present the petition seeking a winding-up order[174].'

Laffoy J went on to find that the petitioner did not have standing as a creditor to bring the petition because the debt was disputed on *bona fide* grounds[175].

The discretionary nature of the court's powers and the desire to act in the interests of members and creditors can also be seen in *Re WMG (Toughening) Ltd*[176]. In that case, the petitioner claimed that the respondent company owed a company in which he owned all of the issued shares some £138,000 on foot of a loan. The respondent company was owned as to 21% by another company called WMG Group Ltd, of which the petitioner was chairman. The petitioner demanded repayment of the loan and when this did not happen presented a petition to have the company wound up; the respondent company resisted the petition. The respondent company had been capitalised by a Forbairt grant of £125,000, the loan of £138,000 by the petitioners company and by two tranches of Business Expansion Scheme (BES) funds of £55,000 and £157,000. Murphy J said that it was clear that the respondent company had been set up for the purpose of financing (by grant aid and BES funding) an operation that was entirely dependent on another subsidiary of the group as its sole customer. It was also said that the respondent company did not have its own premises or, at all material times, a separate bank account. On the question of the respondent company's solvency, Murphy J said that this had to be considered in the context of what appeared to have been an artificial relationship between the group and the respondent company. Murphy J held that the petitioner had been party to a letter which envisaged that certain financial parameters would remain in place and despite the admitted vagueness, held that a court of equity must endeavour to give effect and efficacy to the parties intentions. Murphy J also held that the respondent company had grounds to dispute its liability and went on to say that given the dominance of the group with regard to the company it seemed to him that the chairman and director of the group owed a duty of care to a subsidiary company, especially where there was an allegation that the insolvency had been caused or contributed to by the group of which the petitioner was a director. Murphy J exercised his discretion by restraining the presentation of the petition on the grounds that he was not satisfied that it was being presented for the benefit of all of the members and creditors.

174 *Re Forrest Lennon Business Support Services Ltd* [2011] IEHC 523 at para 4.7 of the judgment, citing *Re Camburn Products Ltd* [1980] 1 WLR 86; *Bowes v Hope Life Insurance and Guarantee Co* (1865) 11 HL 389; *Re Rodencroft Ltd* [2004] 1 WLR 1566; *La Plagne Ltd* [2011] IEHC 91; and *Re Bula Ltd* [1990] 1 IR 440.

175 See para **[23.078]** *post*.

176 *Re WMG (Toughening) Ltd* (6 April 2001, unreported) HC, Roderick Murphy J.

(ii) Deeming companies to be unable to pay their debts

[23.074] Section 214 of the CA 1963 offers assistance to creditors in proving that a company is unable to pay its debts by *deeming* that a company is unable to pay its debts in certain circumstances. So, petitions based on s 213(e) of the CA 1963 are often expressed as being on the ground that the company is unable to pay its debts or should be deemed to be unable to pay its debts by reason of one of the events in s 214. The three circumstances in which a company will be *deemed* to be unable to pay its debts are:

> '(a) if a creditor, by assignment or otherwise, to whom the company is indebted in a sum exceeding €1,269.74 then due, has served on the company, by leaving it at the registered office of the company, a demand in writing requiring the company to pay the sum so due, and the company has for 3 weeks thereafter neglected to pay the sum or to secure or compound for it to the reasonable satisfaction of the creditor; or
>
> (b) if execution or other process issued on a judgment, decree or order of any court in favour of a creditor of the company is returned unsatisfied in whole or in part; or
>
> (c) if it is proved to the satisfaction of the court that the company is unable to pay its debts, and in determining whether a company is unable to pay its debts, the court shall take into account the contingent and prospective liabilities of the company.'

Where a creditor can rely on grounds (a) and (b) there is a presumption that the company is unable to pay its debts, and the court ought to grant the petition. While ground (c) does not contain any short cut on the question of proof, it can be most useful where a creditor has evidence of insolvency. Accordingly, ground (c) may be a faster method of proving the company's inability to pay its debts. Indeed, unlike ground (a), there is no three-week delay. Accordingly, ground (c) can be a convenient means by which to get standing to present a petition, and is exemplified by, say, an unexecuted *fi fa* marked '*nulla bona*' by a sheriff or perhaps a dishonoured cheque.

(iii) The '21-day letter'

[23.075] The '21-day letter', as it is called[177], is the most common way in which a creditor will prove that a company is unable to pay its debts. The section merely requires that the demand is made in writing, and so a letter to the company demanding payment has become the accepted means of meeting this requirement. The amount owed to the creditor must be at least €1,269.74[178] and should be undisputed. It has been held by the English Court of Appeal in *Taylors Industrial Flooring Ltd v M & H Plant Hire (Manchester) Ltd*[179] that where a debt owed by a company is not disputed, proof that the company has failed to pay is evidence of the company's 'inability to pay'. Dillon LJ held that there was no need to serve a statutory 21-day letter in order to prove an inability to pay debts, and noted that in England it was becoming common not to employ that method of proof, because three weeks had to elapse before a petition could be presented. Because the winding up of a company dates only from the date of the presentation of the petition, the demand procedure gives a company 'an extra three weeks' grace in which such assets as the company may have may be dissipated in attempting to keep an insolvent business afloat. While failure to pay on demand will be evidence of an

177 Notwithstanding that the CA 1963 refers to a period of '3 weeks'.

178 By s 214(a) of the CA 1963 as amended by s 123 of the CA 1990.

179 *Taylors Industrial Flooring Ltd v M & H Plant Hire (Manchester) Ltd* [1990] BCLC 216.

inability to pay, Dillon LJ noted that the reason for non-payment has to be substantial[180]. In *Re a Debtor (No 340 of 1992)*[181], Aldous J held that for execution to be returned unsatisfied it was necessary to show the manner in which it had been executed. A failure by a sheriff to obtain access to the debtor's premises was merely the reason why the writ was returned unsatisfied.

(iv) Service of the demand

[23.076] The requirement that the demand must be served by 'leaving it at the registered office of the company', has been interpreted as requiring that it should be delivered by hand. In *Re WMG (Toughening) Ltd*[182], Roderick Murphy J held that the faxing of a demand to the respondent company's registered office was defective service. Holding that the service of a formal document was 'required to be done with exactitude'[183], Murphy J expressly adopted the reasons given by Nourse J in *Re a Company*[184] for taking this position on the requirements for valid service of a petition. In that case, a petitioner had telexed the company claiming that it was owed a particular sum of money under a contract and giving notice of its intention to terminate the contract. The petitioner subsequently, without further notice, presented a petition to have the company wound up and claimed that the telex was a statutory demand. This was rejected by Nourse J who, in a passage quoted by Murphy J, said:

> 'Although I understand that it is sometimes the practice of the Companies Court to act on the basis of a statutory demand which has been sent through the post, it seems to me that once the point taken by counsel for the company has been taken, it seems to be a good one. Section 437(1)[185] [of the Companies Act 1948 (UK)] is in these terms: "A document may be served on a company by leaving it at or sending it by post to the registered office of the company". That shows clearly that sending it by post is not leaving it at the registered office within s 223(a). It may be that the provisions of the Companies Acts have not yet fully caught up with modern conditions and that there would be a case for allowing a statutory demand to be sent through the post, or indeed to be sent by telex. On the other hand a statutory demand is a solemn document with potentially serious consequences. I can well understand that the legislature might have consciously intended that the service of a document of that character should be carried out in much the same way as the service of a winding-up petition, which cannot be sent through the post and certainly cannot be sent on the telex machine[186].'

This case is also authority for the proposition that the written demand made must be unequivocal, of a peremptory character and unconditional: in that case Nourse J held that the demand made did not meet these criteria.

[23.077] It is thought that the only basis for finding that registered post or indeed ordinary mail is insufficient compliance with s 214(a) of the CA 1963 is because it appears from s 379(1) of the CA 1963 that leaving something at an address is an

---

180 Citing *Re Welsh Brick Industries Ltd* [1946] 2 All ER 197.

181 *Re a Debtor (No 340 of 1992)* [1994] 2 BCLC 171.

182 *Re WMG (Toughening) Ltd* (6 April 2001, unreported) HC, Murphy J.

183 *Re WMG (Toughening) Ltd* (6 April 2001, unreported) HC, at p 14.

184 *Re a Company* [1985] BCLC 37.

185 See s 379(1) of the CA 1963 considered in Ch 6, *Corporate Civil Litigation*, para **[6.011]**.

186 *Re a Company* [1985] BCLC 37 at 42.

alternative to sending it by post. Otherwise, surely, s 214(a) would be met where anybody left something at an address, whether it is a company, its officers or an employee of An Post! In *Re Riviera Leisure Ltd*[187], this question arose for consideration before Laffoy J. After considering the decision of Murphy J in *Re WMG (Toughening) Ltd* and Nourse J in *Re a Company* the learned judge went on to consider the decision of Morritt J in *Re a Company*[188] (a different case of the same name) where she noted that Morritt J stated:

> '... I cannot see any sense in a distinction which says that if it is proved that the document was left at the registered office that is should not be deemed or treated as adequate service because it was left by the postman rather than by a creditor, his employee or some perhaps independent third party. It seems to me that the alternatives posed by s 725 [of the English Companies Act 1985, which was similar to s 379 of the CA 1963] are alternative facts which have to be established to prove service. The draftsman of s 123 [of the English Companies Act 1985 which was materially identical to s 214 of the CA 1963], for the reasons indicated by Nourse J, namely the potentially serious consequences of service of a statutory demand, has required the creditor seeking to rely on it to prove that it was left at the office, not merely that he put it in the post box. But, once it is accepted as having been left at the office, although transmitted by means of the Royal Mail, it seems to me that it is served within s 123 perfectly properly.'

Laffoy J preferred this construction and shared Morritt J's view that the distinction as to the manner of service by reference to the person who physically left the demand at the registered office makes no sense. This decision has not, however, changed practice which is to continue to deliver demands by hand for one simple reason: evidence. By getting someone to deliver it by hand you can have them swear a statutory declaration as to service, providing evidence that s 214 of the CA 1963 was complied with; this evidence will not be possible where delivered by a postman who will have no idea what he delivered other than that he put possibly unconnected envelopes through the letterbox. As Laffoy J said, 'prudence dictates that a demand under s 214(1) should be delivered by a person from whom the petitioner will be able to obtain an affidavit of service'. The dangers for petitioners of seeking to rely on postal service – even by registered post – owing to the absence of evidence of delivery was borne out in *Re BCON Communications Ltd*[189] where Laffoy J held that such a petitioner could not rely upon 'deemed insolvency' under s 214(a) of the CA 1963 and was required to establish actual insolvency.

(v) The bona fides *of the debt*

[23.078] In order for a demand to be valid, it must be *bona fide*. Pennington[190] puts it thus:

> 'If the company contends that it is not liable to the creditor for the whole or the unpaid part of his claim, and can satisfy the court that it has a substantial and reasonable defence

187 *Re Riviera Leisure Ltd* [2009] IEHC 183, Laffoy J. For comment, see Kelliher, 'Service of the section 214 demand letter' (2011) CLP 62.

188 *Re a Company* [1991] BCLC 561.

189 *Re BCON Communications Ltd* [2012] IEHC 362, Laffoy J.

190 In Pennington, *Corporate Insolvency Law* (1991), p 39.

to plead, the court will hold that it is not in default, and will refuse to make a winding-up order.'

Where a creditor attempts to use the petition for inappropriate purposes, the court has discretion to refuse to make the order to wind up the company[191]. To seek to have a company wound up for failure to pay a debt that is disputed on *bona fide* grounds is an abuse of process[192]. In *Re Pageboy Couriers Ltd*[193], a creditor instituted a petition seeking the winding up of a company and relied upon s 214(a) of the CA 1963 to prove insolvency. The petition was 'hotly contested' by the company which disputed the debt. The petitioner had also instituted proceedings against the company for the sum and although the company had sought particulars of the claim from the plaintiff, such were not forthcoming. The proceedings against the company were then allowed to lie dormant, the petitioner instead seeking to have the company wound up. The company claimed that it was well established that a creditor should not proceed by petition where he is well aware that the company has a substantial and reasonable defence, and in this regard relied on *Stonegate Securities Ltd v Gregory*[194]. The following extract from the judgment of Buckley J in that case was cited with approval by O'Hanlon J:

> 'If a company in good faith and on substantial grounds disputes any liability in respect of the alleged debt, the petition will be dismissed, or if the matter is brought before a court before a petition is issued, its presentation will in normal circumstances be restrained. That is because a winding-up petition is not a legitimate means of seeking to enforce payment of a debt which is *bona fide* disputed. Ungood-Thomas J, put the matter thus in *Mann v Goldstein* [1968] 2 All ER 769 at 775: "For my part, I would prefer to rest the jurisdiction directly on the comparatively simple proposition that a 'creditor's petition can only be presented by a creditor, that the winding-up jurisdiction is not for the purpose of deciding a disputed debt (that is, disputed on substantial and not insubstantial grounds) since, until a creditor is established as a creditor he is not entitled to present the petition and has no locus standi in the companies' court: and that, therefore, to invoke the winding-up jurisdiction when the debt is disputed (that is on substantial grounds) or after it has become clear that it is so disputed is an abuse of the process of the court"[195].'

O'Hanlon J accepted 'the principles there enunciated as being applicable also when considering the propriety of proceeding by way of petition for the winding up of a company under the provisions of our own Companies Acts'. Accordingly, it was held that the petition was not well founded, and it was dismissed. Where there is a disputed fact, the court is likely to conclude that the dispute will require to be determined in plenary proceedings with appropriate cross-examination of both sides and not on a

---

191 See para **[23.069]** *ante*.

192 *Re Bula Ltd* [1990] 1 IR 440; *Ringinfo Ltd* [2002] 1 BCLC 210.

193 *Re Pageboy Couriers Ltd* [1983] ILRM 510.

194 *Stonegate Securities Ltd v Gregory* [1980] 1 All ER 241. See Keirse, 'Winding-up Petitions – Practical Application of the *Stonegate* test' (2005) CLP 91.

195 The passage from the decision of Buckley LJ in *Stonegate Securities* has been described by McCracken J in the Supreme Court in *Re WMG (Toughening) Ltd (No 2)* [2003] 1 IR 389 as 'the proper test to be applied by the court in the circumstances' See also *Re Silverhold Ltd* [2010] IEHC 111, Laffoy J.

petition to wind up[196]. Whether or not there is a genuine dispute will be a matter of fact in each case[197]. Evidence of a *bona fide* dispute pre-dating the service of the s 214 demand has on a number of occasions swayed the court towards finding that the dispute is *bona fide* and not a contrived response to the demand[198].

(vi) The existence of a valid cross-claim

[23.079] It has been established that even if the debt claimed by the petitioner is *bona fide*, a petition might be dismissed where the company has a legitimate cross-claim against the petitioner which would negate the amount owed to the petitioner[199]. In *Re WMG (Toughening) Ltd*[200], Murphy J quoted with approval the following passage from *Malayan Plant (PT) Ltd v Moscow Narodny Bank Ltd*[201]:

> 'There is no serious distinction in principle between a cross-claim of substance and the serious dispute regarding the indebtedness imputed against a company, which has long been held to constitute a proper ground upon which to reject a winding-up petition.'

The existence of a valid cross-claim will not, however, invariably cause the court to exercise its discretion to dismiss a winding-up petition[202]. Of course, it is also necessary

---

[196] In *Re Millhouse Taverns Ltd* [2000] IEHC 55, Finnegan J, the Revenue Commissioners' petition to wind up the respondent company was disputed. It was held by Finnegan J that the affidavits filed on behalf of the respondent company fell 'far short of showing that the company has a substantial and reasonable defence to the petitioner's claim which would enable it to defeat the entire of the claim brought against it'. See also *Re Amadeus Trading Ltd* [1997] TLR 184.

[197] In *McDonald's Restaurants Ltd v Urbandivide Co Ltd* [1994] 1 BCLC 306, it was held that the debtor company had an arguable defence by way of equitable set-off to the petitioner's claim. In *Re As Fresh As It Gets Ltd* [2011] IEHC 195, following a careful review of the facts, Laffoy J held that the company had not satisfied the court that there was a *bona fide* dispute in relation to the debt claimed by the petitioner on substantial grounds. In *Re Abbey Trinity Retail Ltd* [2010] IEHC 5, Laffoy J found there were not substantial grounds for the company disputing the petitioner's debt and was not satisfied that the challenge was *bona fide* as 'opposed to being an attempt, as the saying goes, "to put off the evil day"' and made the winding-up order.

[198] In *Re Mares Associates Ltd* [2006] IEHC 73, Laffoy J held that the company did establish that there was a *bona fide* dispute on the substantial grounds in relation to the claim embodied in the s 214 demand, the company's *bona fides* being supported by the fact that it had already initiated proceedings against the petitioner before the s 214 demand was served. In *Cotton Box Design Group Ltd v Earls Construction Company Ltd* [2009] IEHC 312, the company's claim that the debt was *bona fide* disputed was accepted and of significance was the fact that there was an email suggesting a way forward which had been sent five or six weeks before the statutory demand. Laffoy J found '... it is impossible to conclude, on the basis of the evidence, other than that the company is acting in good faith and on substantial grounds in disputing the petitioner's claim to be entitled to the sum in question'.

[199] *Re Bayoil SA* [1999] 1 All ER 374, where the English Court of Appeal relied upon the earlier authorities for this proposition in *Re Portman Provincial Cinemas Ltd* (1964) 108 Sol J 581 and *Re LHF Woods Ltd* [1970] Ch 27. See also *Montgomery v Wanda Modes Ltd* [2002] 1 BCLC 289.

[200] *Re WMG (Toughening) Ltd* (6 April 2001, unreported) HC, Roderick Murphy J.

[201] *Malayan Plant (PT) Ltd v Moscow Narodny Bank Ltd* (1980) MLJ 53 at 55.

[202] See *Re Richbell Information Services Inc* [1999] TLR 49 where it was held by Judge Weeks QC that the interests of the company and its creditors during the litigation of the cross-claim would be better protected by the appointment of a liquidator.

for the respondent company to establish that its cross-claim is 'genuine, serious and has substance'[203] and is for an amount in excess of that claimed by the petitioner[204]. In *Greenacre Publishing Group v The Manson Group*[205], the respondent company had refused to pay for printing services for a monthly magazine that had been delayed for seven days, because it claimed that it had lost revenue and advertising contracts. It argued that the petitioner's claim would be met with a substantial cross-claim and applied to have the petition struck out. Lloyd J held that where there was an undisputed debt but a disputed cross-claim, the court had to be satisfied that the evidence was such that the court would dismiss the petition because the case was so strong. In the instant case, Lloyd J held that the evidence for the cross-claim was unsatisfactory and the court could not conclude that the cross-claim would be sufficient to extinguish or reduce below the limit the petitioner's undisputed debt.

[23.080] In *Re Emerald Portable Building Systems Ltd*[206], the company in respect of which a petition had been made both disputed the debt and contended that it has a cross-claim against the petitioner. Clarke J cited the following passage from the decision of Nourse LJ in *Re Bayoil SA*[207] as to the reasoning behind allowing cross-claims as a defence to a petition to have a company wound up in appropriate cases:

> 'The ability of a petitioning creditor to levy execution against a company does not entitle him to have it wound up. Moreover an order that a company be wound up, unlike a bankruptcy order, is often a death knell. Nor can it be certain that a liquidator, even with security behind him, will prosecute the company's claims with the diligence and efficiency of its directors. These I believe are considerations which go to justify the practice in cross claim cases. I emphasise that the cross claim must be genuine and serious or if you prefer one of substance, that it must be one which the company has been unable to litigate and it must be in an amount exceeding the amount of the petitioner's debt.'

Clarke J accepted that it was the law that a cross-claim can be an appropriate defence to a winding-up petition and commented on the requisite quality and substance of the cross-claim in the following terms:

> 'It is clear, therefore, that a cross-claim can afford a company an answer to a winding-up petition even in circumstances where that cross-claim would not amount to a set off in equity so as to afford a defence to a claim for a liquidated sum. It follows that there may be cases where a plaintiff creditor might be entitled to obtain judgment against a company but where the same debt might, by virtue of a substantial cross-claim, be insufficient to lead to a winding up.'

In the case before him, Clarke J found that the company had a bona fide cross-claim of sufficient substance to justify dismissing the petition. The company had purchased a number of portable buildings from the petitioner for which it part paid €60,000. The portakabins required modification and it was claimed by the company that they were

---

203 See Laddie J in the English High Court in *Orion Media Marketing Ltd v Media Brook Ltd and another* [2002] 1 BCLC 184.

204 *Re Latreefers Inc* [1999] TLR 37. There, Lloyd J also commented that the respondent company was required to show that it had been unable to litigate the cross-claim.

205 *Greenacre Publishing Group v The Manson Group* [2000] BCC 11.

206 *Re Emerald Portable Building Systems Ltd* [2005] IEHC 301.

207 *Re Bayoil SA* [1991] 1 WLR 147.

defective and that it had suffered loss. The cheque for €60,000 was countermanded and was the specific debt relied upon by the petitioner. Clarke J noted that there was evidence of contemporary documentation evidencing the issues concerning the adequacy of the portakabins and also accepted that there was a valid reason why the petitioner had not issued proceedings in respect of the alleged defects, due to failures on the part of its solicitors. In *Re Silverhold Ltd*[208], Laffoy J applied the principles in the decision of Clarke J and, despite some reluctance, concluded that the cross-claim there was serious and genuine and that although there was no evidential basis for finding that the company had been unable to litigate the cross-claim, the existence of specific performance proceedings which pre-dated the petition were found to be a sufficient reason to dismiss the petition.

(vii) The test for injuncting a petition based on s 213(e) of the CA 1963

[23.081] It is one thing to successfully dispute the *bona fides* of a debt at the hearing of a petition; however, even where successful, the company is exposed to a glare of adverse publicity, wherein its solvency is questioned. Upon being served with a petition in respect of a genuinely disputed debt, therefore, a company might wish to restrain the advertisement of the petition and have the dispute out in interlocutory proceedings rather than on an advertised petition. Where the ground relied upon to present the petition is the inability of the company to pay its debts, the court may grant an injunction to prevent the advertisement of the petition as an abuse of process where the company disputes the claim of the petitioner on *bona fide* and substantial grounds[209]. At the outset, it should be noted that the courts will be slow to restrain a petitioner from advertising or presenting a petition.

The first Irish case to consider an application for an injunction to restrain the advertisement of a petition which had been lodged was *Clandown Ltd v Davis*[210]. In that case, the defendant had presented a petition to have the plaintiff company wound up. She had been a shareholder, director and employee of the company but had been removed as a director at the company's annual general meeting (AGM). The defendant claimed that the company owed her £56,889.69. Having demanded this and upon its not being paid, she sought to have the company wound up on the basis that it was unable to pay its debts. The plaintiff company claimed that this was an abuse of the courts process as there was a serious and genuine dispute as to the veracity of the defendants assertion that the plaintiff was indebted to the defendant in the amount claimed or in any amount. Indeed, the plaintiff company had counterclaimed that the defendant was indebted to it. Morris J said that the law was well settled on this point: where a company in good faith and on substantial grounds disputes any liability in respect of the alleged debt, the

208 *Re Silverhold Ltd* [2010] IEHC 111.

209 See *Mann v Goldstein* [1968] 2 All ER 769. In *Re a Company* [1986] BCLC 127, Hoffmann J held that the court has jurisdiction to restrain a petitioner not only from advertising the petition, but also from otherwise publicising it. In *Re a Company (No 001448 of 1989)* [1989] BCLC 715, Millett J held that an advertisement could be restrained where an undertaking to make application to put the company into administration (examination in Ireland) had been given by the company. See also *Re Garton (Western) Ltd* [1989] BCLC 304 and *Re a Company (No 00962 of 1991), ex p Electrical Engineering Contracts (London) Ltd* [1992] BCLC 248.

210 *Clandown Ltd v Davis* [1994] 2 ILRM 536.

petition will be dismissed. However[211], he commented that this was the first Irish case to his knowledge where the question concerned an injunction to restrain the advertisement of a petition which had been lodged. Citing the judgments of Hoffmann J in *Re a Company (No 008725 of 1991)*[212] and *Re a Company (No 0012209 of 1991)*[213] Morris J concluded that the law required that he consider the following:

> 'Is the defendant a "creditor" which would entitle her to present a petition to the court or put another way, is the plaintiff, the company, disputing this claim on bona fide and substantial grounds[214]?'

Applying this test to the facts of the case, Morris J considered the affidavits which had been filed. The defendant said that her claim in her letter was allegedly uncontradicted by the plaintiff company; that it was again uncontradicted in a minute presented to the directors' meeting of the plaintiff company; that the company's auditors checked off various amounts in the company's accounts and had passed them as accurate; that there were inaccuracies in the plaintiff company's accounting and that even taking the plaintiff company's figures there was a credit due to the defendant. Of this Morris J said:

> '... I am left with a very clear feeling that the plaintiffs have sought high and low to produce figures to challenge the defendant in her claim that there is money due to her. I am far from satisfied that the defendant's allegations of inaccurate accounting and improper bookkeeping have been made out to anything like the level necessary to satisfy a court trying the issues between the parties. However, that is not the test that I have to apply. I am satisfied that on the law I would have to be satisfied that the amount of the defendant's claim is clear and incapable of dispute. I am not satisfied of this. I am not satisfied how much of the matter contained in the defendant's affidavits will eventually be found to be accurate. I am unable to be satisfied that the defendant can be deemed to be a creditor of the plaintiff-company. In a matter of this complexity, in my view it would be inappropriate for a court at this stage to form a clear cut view on affidavits filed as to the parties' indebtedness to one another and accordingly, adopting the test of Thomas J in *Mann v Goldstein*, I am not prepared to say that the defendant in this case is "a creditor" entitled to present a petition and who would have locus standi in the Companies Court[215].'

Accordingly, the learned judge granted the injunction to restrain the publication of the petition to have the company wound up. One result of this decision is to reinforce the principle that the courts will not permit s 213 of the CA 1963 to be used as a method of debt collection.

[23.082] It should be noted, however, that the correctness of restraining a winding up even where only part of the debt was disputed was doubted by Keane J in what must now be considered to be the leading Irish case, *Truck and Machinery Sales Ltd v Marubeni*

---

211 Here, Morris J cited, and quoted from, *Re Pageboy Couriers Ltd* [1983] ILRM 510 and *Stonegate Securities Ltd v Gregory* [1980] 1 All ER 241. See para **[23.078]**.

212 *Re a Company (No 008725 of 1991)* [1992] BCLC 633. Here, Hoffmann J said (at 634): 'It is agreed that in order to restrain advertisement, I must be satisfied on the evidence before me that it would appear on the hearing of the petition that the debt is disputed in good faith and on substantial grounds.'

213 *Re a Company (No 0012209 of 1991)* [1992] BCLC 865.

214 *Clandown Ltd v Davis* [1994] 2 ILRM 536 at 540.

215 *Clandown Ltd v Davis* [1994] 2 ILRM 536 at 540–541.

Komatsu Ltd[216]. The facts there were that the defendant sought to have the plaintiff wound up for non-payment of moneys allegedly due. The plaintiff had purchased second-hand machinery from the defendant for approximately £2.9 million; the consideration was not payable until a particular date. The machinery was shipped to the United Arab Emirates but the plaintiff was prevented from distributing the machinery there because a third party claimed it had an exclusive distribution agreement with the defendant, which prevented the sale of the machinery there. The defendant had known that the plaintiff proposed to sell the machinery in the United Arab Emirates but considered that the distribution agreement was irrelevant, since it only concerned new machinery. Both parties attempted unsuccessfully to negotiate the distribution of the machinery. By this time the plaintiff had paid the defendant some £600,000 but it was claimed that in excess of £2.3 million remained outstanding. The defendant advised the plaintiff that if the balance was not forthcoming, it would bring a winding-up petition against the plaintiff. The plaintiffs claim that the defendant had agreed in a facsimile to waive the balance of the debt until the outcome of legal proceedings in the United Arab Emirates, was denied by the defendant. The plaintiff then sought an injunction to restrain both the advertisement of the petition and the bringing of the petition.

[23.083] In the High Court, Keane J began by distinguishing situations where a respondent company disputes that it has *any* liability in respect of an alleged debt from those where a company admits an indebtedness in a sum exceeding €1,269.74. In relation to the former situation, he said:

> 'It is clear that, where the company in good faith and on substantial grounds, disputes *any* liability in respect of the alleged debt, the petition will be dismissed, or if the matter is brought before the court before the petition is issued, its presentation will in normal circumstances be restrained. This is on the ground that a winding-up petition is not a legitimate means of seeking to enforce payment of a debt which is *bona fide* disputed[217].'

Where, however, a respondent company admits to an indebtedness in a sum exceeding €1,269.74 different considerations apply. Keane J held that where the company 'disputes the balance, even on substantial grounds, the creditor should not normally be restrained from presenting a petition'[218]. In this respect, Keane J preferred the authority of the decisions in *Re Tweeds Garage Ltd*[219] and *Taylor's Industrial Flooring Ltd v M&H Plant Hire (Manchester) Ltd*[220] to that in *Clandown v Davis*[221]. Keane J went on to acknowledge that even where a company is insolvent, the court could restrain the

---

216 *Truck and Machinery Sales Ltd v Marubeni Komatsu Ltd* [1996] 1 IR 12. For comment, see Canniffe, 'Restraining a Creditor's Winding-up Petition – The Position Since *Truck and Machinery Sales Ltd v Marubeni Komatsu Ltd*' (1997) 4 CLP 30.

217 *Truck and Machinery Sales Ltd v Marubeni Komatsu Ltd* [1996] 1 IR 12 at 16, citing *Mann v Goldstein* [1968] 2 All ER 769 and *Stongate Securities Ltd v Gregory* [1980] 1 All ER 241 as authorities.

218 In *Re Silverhold Ltd* [2010] IEHC 111, Laffoy J applied the principle that a company must dispute *any liability* in respect of the alleged debt in good faith and on substantial grounds to have a petition dismissed or its presentation restrained to where the court is satisfied that the company has an undischarged liability to the petitioner in excess of €1,269.74 on foot of a s 214 demand.

219 *Re Tweeds Garage Ltd* [1962] 1 All ER 121.

220 *Taylor's Industrial Flooring Ltd v M&H Plant Hire (Manchester) Ltd* [1990] BCLC 21.

presentation of a petition where presented for an ulterior or collateral purpose and not in good faith.

[23.084] Citing *Bryanston Finance Ltd v De Vries (No 2)*[222], Keane J went on to state that the jurisdiction to restrain the presentation of a petition to wind up is one to be exercised with great caution. Keane J held that the normal test for an interlocutory injunction, laid down by the Supreme Court in *Campus Oil Ltd v Minister for Industry and Energy (No 2)*[223], was not applicable to an injunction to restrain the presentation of a winding-up petition. Keane J's reason for so holding was:

> '… the object of the application is to prevent the respondent from exercising his right of access to the courts, whether by way of ordinary process or a winding-up petition. In such a case, the factors which the court should take into account were also identified in *Bryanston Finance*. Thus, Buckley LJ said that:- "The plaintiff-company cannot assert such a right in respect of any particular anticipated litigation without demonstrating that, at least *prima facie*, that litigation would be an abuse".'

Keane J noted that in the English Court of Appeal in *Coulson Sanderson & Ward v Ward*[224] Slade LJ had said of the former case that:

> 'This decision, therefore, is clear authority for the proposition that the court should not, on the hearing of an interlocutory motion, interfere with what would otherwise appear to be the legitimate presentation of a winding-up petition by someone qualified to present it unless the evidence before it is sufficient to establish prima facie that the plaintiff-company will succeed in establishing that the proceedings sought to be restrained would constitute an abuse'.

Accepting this, Keane J thereby disapplied the *Campus Oil/American Cyanamid* test to injunctions to restrain the presentation of a winding-up petition. He said:

---

221 Keane J noted that he had applied the principle in *Re Tweeds Garage Ltd in Patrick Butterly and Sons Ltd v Top Security Ltd* (27 September 1995, unreported) HC (*ex tempore*).

222 *Bryanston Finance Ltd v De Vries (No 2)* [1976] 1 Ch 63. Keane J quoted the following passage from the judgment of Buckley LJ: 'It has long been recognised that the jurisdiction of the court to stay an action *in limine* as an abuse of process is a jurisdiction to be exercised with great circumspection and exactly the same considerations must apply to a *quia timet* injunction to restrain commencement of proceedings. These principles are, in my opinion, just as applicable to a winding-up petition as to an action. The right to petition the court for a winding-up order in appropriate circumstances is a right conferred by statute. A would-be petitioner should not be restrained from exercising it except on clear and persuasive grounds. I recognise that the presentation of a petition may do great damage to a company's business and reputation, though I think that the potential damage in the present case may have been rather exaggerated. The restraint of a petition may also gravely affect the would-be petitioner and not only him but also others, whether creditors or contributories. If the presentation of the petition is prevented the commencement of the winding up will be postponed until such time as the petition is presented or a winding-up resolution is passed. This is capable of far reaching effects.'

223 *Campus Oil Ltd v Minister for Industry and Energy (No 2)* [1983] IR 88. See, generally, the discussion of this test in Courtney, *Mareva Injunctions and Related Interlocutory Orders* (1998), pp 173–179.

224 *Coulson Sanderson & Ward v Ward* [1986] BCLC 99.

> 'I am satisfied that this is the approach which should also be adopted in this jurisdiction. The constitutional right of recourse to the courts should not be inhibited, save in exceptional circumstances, and this applies as much to the presentation of a petition for the winding up of a company by a person with the appropriate locus standi as it does to any other form of proceedings. The undoubted power of the courts to restrain proceedings which are an abuse of process is one which should not be lightly exercised. *In the context of winding-up petitions, I have no doubt that it should be exercised only where the plaintiff-company has established at least a prima facie case that its presentation would constitute an abuse of process.* In many cases, a *prima facie* case will be established where the plaintiff-company adduced evidence which satisfies the court that the petition is bound to fail or, at the least, that there is a suitable alternative remedy.' [Emphasis added.]

Keane J went on to state that in considering an application for an injunction to restrain the presentation of a petition, the court must approach the matter with the interests of the creditors in mind[225]. Applying the law thus enunciated to the facts of the case in hand, Keane J held that the defendant could not be restrained from presenting a petition. To the argument that it had agreed not to proceed against the plaintiff, Keane J held that it was settled law that a promise to pay part of a debt was not good consideration and he rejected that there was any enforceable agreement[226] or any estoppel that bound the defendant. The result of these findings was that Keane J had not been satisfied that the company had established a *prima facie* case that the presentation of the petition would be an abuse of process[227].

[23.085] In *Meridian Communications Ltd v Eircell Ltd*[228], the Supreme Court applied the same principles but this time held that the defendant should be enjoined from presenting a petition to wind up the plaintiff. The background facts were that the plaintiff had rented certain telephone lines from the defendant and had leased them to its own subscribers of whom there were about 20,000. The agreement to supply these lines was due to be terminated and it was argued that this would cause the plaintiffs customer base to evaporate. The defendant claimed to be owed money from the plaintiff and had served a 21-day letter. The plaintiff asked to be allowed to try to sell its subscriber base before its arrangements with the defendants was terminated, ie, while it still had a valuable asset to sell, and claimed that a sale could generate £10 million, which would meet any indebtedness it had to the defendant and any other creditors. The defendant argued that the plaintiff had cancelled certain direct debits and appeared to be insolvent. Its argument was that it was both logical and reasonable to move to terminate the service it provided the plaintiff and to bring a petition under s 213 of the CA 1963 on the grounds of inability to pay the plaintiff's debts.

---

225 In reliance upon the decision of Street CJ in *Kinsella v Russell Kinsella Property Ltd* [1986) 4 NSWLR 722, which Keane J noted had been expressly approved of by the Supreme Court in *Re Frederick Inns Ltd* [1994] 1 ILRM 387.

226 Applying *Foakes v Beer* (1888) App Cas 605.

227 In *Re J McLaughlin and Co Ltd*, an application reported in (1996) Irish Times, 9 July (Barron J), it was reportedly held that it would be an abuse of process to issue a petition in that case when there was a dispute about the debt in question; in *D and F Partnership Ltd v Horan Keogan Ryan Ltd* [2011] IEHC 333, Ryan J, an injunction was refused on the basis that the debt could not be disputed on *bona fide* grounds.

228 *Meridian Communications Ltd v Eircell Ltd* [2001] IESC 42, McGuinness J, *nem diss*.

[23.086] McGuinness J held that the principles applicable to such injunctions had been fully and clearly set out by Keane J in *Truck and Machinery Sales Ltd v Marubei Komatsu Ltd*[229] and she quoted the head note from the reported decision which she said the Supreme Court accepted set out in principle the correct standards to be applied:

> '(a) Since a winding-up petition was not a legitimate means of enforcing payment of a debt which was *bona fide* disputed, the presentation of a petition would in normal circumstances be restrained if the company, in good faith and on substantial grounds disputed all liability in respect of the debt claimed.
>
> (b) Where a company admitted its indebtedness to the creditor in a sum exceeding £1,000 [€1,269.74] but disputed the balance, even on substantial grounds, the creditor should not normally be restrained from presenting a winding-up petition.
>
> (c) Even where the company appeared to be insolvent the court might in the exercise of its equitable jurisdiction, restrain the presentation of the petition where it was satisfied that the petition was being presented for an ulterior or collateral purpose and not in good faith; but that the court must approach the position of such a company with the interests of the creditors particularly in mind.
>
> (d) The jurisdiction to restrain the presentation of the petition should be exercised only with great caution.
>
> (e) Since an application to restrain the presentation of a winding-up petition involved not the restraint of an alleged violation of a plaintiff's right but of the exercise by a creditor of his right of access to the courts, the normal considerations of a fair question to be tried, the adequacy of damages as a remedy and the balance of convenience did not arise; instead, it was for the plaintiff to establish at least a prima facie case, which would in many instances be established by evidence that the petition was bound to fail or, at the least that there was a suitable alternative remedy.'

The Supreme Court held that it was extremely unlikely that the plaintiff's alleged debt to the defendant could be reduced below the sum of £1,000 and McGuinness J said:

> 'if the proposed sale and settlement of indebtedness does not proceed in the near future, there would seem to be no proper grounds for restraining [the defendant] from bringing the proposed petition'.

The Supreme Court, however, granted the injunction to restrain the presentation of the petition to wind up the plaintiff until the expiry of the other injunction which prevented the defendant from terminating the service agreement – a period of a few weeks.

[23.087] The possibility that the company may come into funds will not result in an injunction being granted to restrain a petition where the debt is undisputed. In *Troon Developments Ltd v Harrahill*[230], the company sought to injunct the Revenue Commissioners from presenting a petition in respect of arrears of tax which the company acknowledged was due; the basis of the company's injunction was that it was unable to pay the revenue because its former solicitor had remitted the net proceeds of the sale of units in a development to First Active plc including sums in respect of VAT and that this dispute was before the commercial court. Laffoy J noted that by virtue of ss 213 and 214 of the CA 1963, the defendant would be entitled to a winding-up order *ex debito justitiae* subject only to the court's discretion. In the circumstances, the learned

229 *Truck and Machinery Sales Ltd v Marubei Komatsu Ltd* [1996] 1 IR 12.

230 *Troon Developments Ltd v Harrahill* [2009] IEHC 590.

judge found that there was nothing in the circumstance of the case which would make it unjust or inequitable to adjourn the petition pending the outcome of the commercial court proceedings. Refusing the injunction, Laffoy J said that it would in fact be unfair and unjust to the defendant to grant it.

[23.088] In *Coalport Building Company Ltd v Castle Contracts (Ireland) Ltd*[231], Laffoy J applied the principles set out by Keane J in *Truck and Machinery Sales Ltd* and restrained the petitioner from advertising the petition. Interestingly, the learned judge made the injunction conditional upon the company lodging the sum of €108,137 in court to the credit of the proceedings as security for the alleged debt.

(viii) Liability for improperly presenting petitions

[23.089] Where a petition is wrongly presented, the company which it was sought to have wound up may have a civil remedy against the petitioner. So, it has been held that a solicitor, who swore an affidavit in support of a petition when no debt was in fact owed, had acted unreasonably as there were no grounds upon which a competent solicitor could have formed that view, and the solicitor was ordered to pay personally the company's wasted costs[232]. Petitioners are well advised to consider carefully the option of proceeding by winding-up petition instead of by ordinary action. Where a respondent company is forced to make application to restrain the advertisement of a petition that has been presented and (on being furnished with evidence of solvency) the petitioner undertakes not to advertise the petition, the petitioner might only be able to halt the process by undertaking and submitting to an order that they pay the costs incurred by the respondent company[233].

[23.090] It may also be noted that the tort of *malicious presentation of petition* was acknowledged by the English Court of Appeal in *Radivojevic v LR Industries Ltd*[234]. There it was said that in order to establish the tort, it is necessary to show three things:

- that the petition terminated in favour of the respondent company;
- that there was an absence of reasonable or probable cause for presenting the petition; and
- that there was malice or improper motive on the part of the petitioner in presenting the petition[235].

(e) The court is of the opinion that it is just and equitable that the company should be wound up

[23.091] This is the most dynamic ground for petitioning to have a company wound up. Previously, it was thought that the use of the words 'just and equitable', ought to be construed *ejusdem generis* to the preceding grounds in s 213 of the CA 1963[236]. However, this restrictive interpretation has now been abandoned, as seen in *Ebrahimi v*

231 *Coalport Building Company Ltd v Castle Contracts (Ireland) Ltd* [2004] IEHC 6.

232 See *Re A Company (No 006798 of 1995)* [1996] 1 WLR 491.

233 See *Re a Company (No 007356/98) (ITC Infotech Ltd)* [2000] BCC 214.

234 *Radivojevic v LR Industries Ltd* (22 November 1984, unreported) CA (Eng).

235 This test was applied, but found not to have been met, in *Partizan Ltd v OJ Kilkenny & Co Ltd* [1998] BCC 912.

236 See *Ex p Spackman* (1849) 1 Mac & G 170–174, *per* Lord Cottenham LC.

Westbourne Galleries Ltd[237]. Lord Wilberforce's judgment in that case was cited with approval by Gannon J in *Re Murph's Restaurants*[238]. Consequently, one can petition for the winding up of a company in a situation which is unrelated to any of the other grounds listed in s 213. An early Irish case which applied the liberal interpretation was *Re Newbridge Sanitary Steam Laundry Ltd*[239] where a company was ordered to be wound up on just and equitable grounds by Sir Ignatius O'Brien LC, because the controller of a company refused to account for money received by him for and on behalf of the company, notwithstanding that this action by the controller had been ratified by the members in general meeting. Despite the more recent restrictive interpretation in *Re Guidezone Ltd*[240] that the winding-up jurisdiction may be no wider than the jurisdiction in s 459 of the former Companies Act 1985 (UK) – namely to wind up where it has been shown that a company's affairs have been conducted in a manner unfairly prejudicial to a petitioner – it is thought that the 'just and equitable' test is not so confined and is, rather, available in any of the circumstances referred in the paragraph next following[241].

[23.092] The decided cases can be grouped into certain categories and it is proposed to adopt the following structure notwithstanding the danger of fettering the perceived latitude of this ground[242]:

(i) The 'quasi-partnership' cases.

(ii) Deadlock in corporate management.

(iii) Failure of substratum.

(iv) Illegal objects.

(v) Corporate instruments of fraud.

(vi) Public interest.

A jurisdiction that is driven by what is 'just and equitable' is the very essence of what is dynamic. The practice of law has an uncanny tendency to present factual situations which differ from established authorities, and so other situations which do not fit neatly into the foregoing categories may still merit the winding up of a company on just and equitable grounds.

---

237 *Ebrahimi v Westbourne Galleries Ltd* [1972] 2 All ER 492, [1973] AC 360.

238 *Re Murph's Restaurants* [1979] ILRM 141.

239 *Re Newbridge Sanitary Steam Laundry Ltd* [1917] 1 IR 237.

240 *Re Guidezone Ltd* [2000] 2 CLC 321. For notation of this case, see *CCH's Company Law Update* (2001) 5 September 2001. For further commentary, see Acton, 'Just and Equitable Winding Up – The Strange Case of the Disappearing Jurisdiction' (2001) 22 *Company Lawyer* 134.

241 It is relevant that s 125(2) of the Companies Act 1985 (UK) provides that an order for the winding up of a company should not be made on just and equitable grounds where 'some other remedy is available to the petitioners and that they are acting unreasonably in seeking to have the company wound up instead of pursuing that other remedy'. See *Re Murray Consultants and Nocrumb Ltd; Horgan v Murray and Milton* (9 July 1999, unreported) SC, at p 19. See, also, *Re Copeland & Craddock Ltd* [1997] BCC 294 where the English Court of Appeal refused to strike out a petition for winding up on the just and equitable ground, notwithstanding s 125(2) on the grounds that, *inter alia*, it was reasonable for the petitioner to pursue the winding-up remedy. See, further, *CCH's Company Law News* (1997) Issue 7/1997; 23 April 1997.

242 See *Ebrahimi v Westbourne Galleries Ltd* [1972] 2 All ER 492.

(i) The 'quasi-partnership' cases

[23.093] While certainly not always the case[243], the relations between the shareholders in many private companies can be tantamount to a partnership. So, of the three members of the company in *Re Murph's Restaurant Ltd*[244], Gannon J observed that it was clear from the evidence that the members were:

> '... equal partners in a joint venture, and that the company was no more than a vehicle to secure a limited liability for possible losses and to provide a means of earning and distributing profits to their best advantage with minimum disclosure[245].'

Such companies have more in common with partnerships than they have with companies formed and registered under the Companies Acts. Where the member partners of such companies 'fall out' and the stronger member partners banish the weaker from the company by inappropriate reliance on provisions in the Companies Acts, the court may be inclined to grant a petition to have the company wound up on 'just and equitable' grounds.

[23.094] The facts in *Re Murph's Restaurant Ltd* are instructive. Three men – two brothers and a friend – began a snack bar business. One brother and the friend advanced £800 each and a further £400 each on behalf of the second, then unemployed, brother so as to create an equal partnership. In time, the friend left his well-paid employment and began to work full-time in the company. The business was successful and the company acquired a delicatessen and a restaurant in Dublin and Cork, the latter being run by the friend.

The finances and affairs of the company were conducted in a most irregular manner, company meetings of sorts being held on Monday nights on the business premises over meals. Neither dividends nor directors' fees were paid. Instead, regular drawings were taken and the appropriate share equalised annually. In addition, up to £200 per month was taken in cash, no record being kept, referred to in the proceedings as 'slush money'. Regular sums were also taken in cash and lodged into building society accounts. According to Gannon J, at all times, great care was taken to ensure 'equality was maintained as between the three of them'. The Cork premises, being run by the friend, was regularly visited by the brothers. The Midas touch of the trio prevailed, and the Cork restaurant flourished. Around this time, the brothers acquired an hotel called 'The Strawberry Hill' which was part-financed through loans from the company. They set about developing this into three houses for use by the brothers for themselves and their families. The friend was unaware of this loan. To emphasise the equality of the relationship, it was noted that the time off used by the brothers in their private ventures was allowed to the friend who took similar time off to purchase a house.

In time, the brothers decided that they did not want the friend working in the company any longer and sent him notice of a meeting to be held where it was intended to remove him from office. This action was found by Gannon J to be entirely irregular and:

---

243 See Lord Wilberforce's observations in *Ebrahimi v Westbourne Galleries Ltd* [1972] 2 All ER 492 at 500d–h.

244 *Re Murph's Restaurant Ltd* [1979] ILRM 141.

245 *Re Murph's Restaurant Ltd* [1979] ILRM 141 at 150.

'... a deliberate and calculated repudiation by both of them [the brothers] of that relationship of equality, mutuality, trust and confidence between the three of them which constituted the very essence of the company[246].'

Gannon J rejected that there was any merit in the claim that they were getting rid of the friend because of alleged unsatisfactory work, because their complaint could:

'... not relate to the talents or qualifications which he had shown, and must have been known to them to have had, at the time he was induced to join with them in a venture of strictly drawn equality.'

The friend petitioned to have the company wound up on the basis of *oppression* under s 205 of the CA 1963[247] and also on the just and equitable ground. Gannon J found that it would be inappropriate to make an order under s 205 of the CA 1963 in view of the fundamental breakdown in the relationship. On the question of 'just and equitable' as a ground for winding up, Gannon J relied heavily on the judgment of Lord Wilberforce in *Ebrahimi v Westbourne Galleries Ltd*[248] and made the order sought to wind up the company. Several quotations of Lord Wilberforce and Lord Cross, cited with approval by Gannon J, are relevant. One particularly salient paragraph considers the quasi-partnership nature of certain private companies, namely that:

'People do not become partners unless they have confidence in one another and it is of the essence of the relationship that mutual confidence is maintained. If neither has any longer confidence in the other so that they cannot work together in the way originally contemplated then the relationship should be ended – unless, indeed, the party who wishes to end it has been solely responsible for the situation which has arisen. The relationship between the [parties there] was, of course, in form that of partners; they were equal shareholders in a limited company. But the court considered that it would be unduly fettered by matters of form if it did not deal with the situation as it would have dealt with it had the parties been partners in form as well as in substance.'

[23.095] The judgment of Lord Wilberforce extensively reviewed a number of relevant English and Commonwealth authorities which touched upon quasi-partnership companies and the availability of the just and equitable ground in their winding up[249]. In his opinion:

'... these authorities represent a sound and rational development of the law which should be endorsed. The foundation of it all lies in the words "just and equitable" and, if there is any respect in which some of the cases may be open to criticism, it is that the courts may sometimes have been too timorous in giving them full force. The words are a recognition

246 *Re Murph's Restaurant Ltd* [1979] ILRM 141 at 151.

247 See Ch 11, *Shareholders' Remedies*, para **[11.006]** *et seq*.

248 *Ebrahimi v Westbourne Galleries Ltd* [1972] 2 All ER 492, [1973] AC 360.

249 Eg, *Re Yenidje Tobacco Co Ltd* [1916] 2 Ch 426, [1916–1917] All ER Rep 1050 (a 'deadlock' case, which Lord Wilberforce held was not so confined); *Re Wondoflex Textiles Pty Ltd* [1951] VLR 458 (an 'expulsion' case where a quarter owner was removed and the company was held to resemble a partnership); *Lewis v Haas* (1970) SLT 67 (where 'exclusion' was accepted as a possible ground for having a company wound up, though on the facts there was insufficient evidence to justify this remedy); and *Re Lundie Brothers Ltd* [1965] 2 All ER 692 (where a director shareholder, who was 'excluded' from the management of the company, obtained an order that the company be wound up on 'just and equitable' grounds when Plowman J applied partnership principles).

of the fact that a limited company is more than a mere judicial entity, with a personality in law of its own: that there is room in company law for recognition of the fact that behind it, or amongst it, there are individuals, with rights, expectations and obligations inter se which are not necessarily submerged in the company structure. That structure is defined by the Companies Act 1948 and by the articles of association by which the shareholders agree to be bound. In most companies and in most contexts, this definition is sufficient and exhaustive, equally so whether the company is large or small. The "just and equitable" provision does not, as the respondents suggest, entitle one party to disregard the obligation he assumes by entering a company, nor the court to dispense him from it. It does, as equity always does, enable the court to subject the exercise of legal rights to equitable considerations; considerations, that is, of a personal character arising between one individual and another, which may make it unjust, or inequitable, to insist on legal rights, or to exercise them in a particular way.'

Some of the factors which Lord Wilberforce identified as being salient in deciding whether or not a company was of the quasi-partnership kind included, whether it was an association formed or continued on the basis of a personal relationship involving mutual confidence, an agreement or understanding that all of the members will participate in the management of the business and which had restrictions on the transfer of shares. In *Re Fildes Bros Ltd*[250], Megarry J said that the question is dependent upon both the contractual rights of the parties and the settled and accepted course of conduct between them. In that case, no order was made where the controlling director refused to permit another director to become involved in the day-to-day management of the company, because there was no such course of conduct in existence between the parties. It is important to note that Lord Wilberforce did warn against any automatic assumption that all private companies amounted to quasi-partnerships.

[23.096] Having established that a company may possess sufficient characteristics to amount to a quasi-partnership, and thus be liable to be wound up on just and equitable grounds, Lord Wilberforce then addressed the question of how the legal rights to expel a quasi-partner could be set aside. In a passage cited with approval by Gannon J in *Re Murph's Restaurants* he said:

'The question is, as always, whether it is equitable to allow one (or two) to make use of his legal rights to the prejudice of his associate(s). The law of companies recognises the right, in many ways, to remove a director from the board. Section 184 of the Companies Act 1948 confers this right upon the company in general meeting whatever the articles may say. Some articles may prescribe other methods: for example, a governing director may have the power to remove (compare in *Re Wondoflex Textiles Pty Ltd* [1951] VLR 458). And quite apart from removal powers, there are normally provisions for retirement of directors by rotation so that their re-election can be opposed and defeated by a majority, or even by a casting vote. In all these ways a particular director-member may find himself no longer a director, through removal, or non-re-election: this situation he must normally accept, unless he undertakes the burden of proving fraud or mala fides. The just and equitable provision nevertheless comes to his assistance if he can point to, and prove, some special underlying obligation of his fellow member(s) in good faith or confidence, that so long as the business continues he shall be entitled to management participation, an obligation so basic that, if broken, the conclusion must be that the association be

250 *Re Fildes Bros Ltd* [1970] 1 All ER 923.

dissolved. And the principles on which he may do so are those worked out by the courts in partnership cases where there has been exclusion from management …'

It is clear that in appropriate circumstances, a court will grant an order to have a company wound up on just and equitable grounds where there was a relationship of confidence, partnership and mutuality between the members of that company which has been sundered.

[23.097] Case law provides a number of examples of situations where a company will be wound up on the basis that it is just and equitable. In *Re Zinotty Properties Ltd*[251], a company was ordered to be wound up where the majority shareholders refused to elect one particular individual to the board of directors although he had purchased shares in the company on the understanding that he would be elected. Similarly, in *Tay Bok Choon v Tahansan Sdn Bhd*[252] a person subscribed for shares in a company on its formation and became a director at the same time. He not only incurred personal liability on foot of guarantees in respect of the company's debts, but lent other directors money so that they could increase their shareholdings. To exclude such a person from the management of the company in such circumstances was held to be a breach of the principles of equity, and justified the winding up of the company.

(ii) Deadlock in corporate management

[23.098] Another instance of companies being wound up on just and equitable grounds is where there is deadlock in the management of the company. This may arise where the voting power in the company is evenly divided between two diametrically opposed camps. In such cases to wind up the company may be the only way to resolve the deadlock. In *Bluzwed Metals Ltd v Transworld Metals SA*[253], the High Court held that where a company's activities are 'effectively paralysed to the detriment of both the members and creditors' such clearly indicates 'that the company may be wound up on the "just and equitable ground"', Lavan J citing as the leading case, that of *Re Yenidje Tobacco Company*[254] and noting that that principle was applied by Murphy J in *Re Vehicle Buildings and Insulations Ltd*[255] and by Kenny J in *Re Irish Tourist* Promotions[256].

[23.099] One of the first cases to establish this principle was *Re Yenidje Tobacco Company Ltd*[257]. There, a company was formed by two manufacturers of tobacco: Rothman and Weinberg, being equal shareholders and the only directors. Differences arose and they ceased to converse directly, only doing so through the company secretary. They also became engaged in costly litigation in respect of their differences. Although the company was profitable, the Court of Appeal granted an order to have the company wound up on the ground that it was just and equitable. The judgment of Lord Cozens-

[251] *Re Zinotty Properties Ltd* [1984] 3 All ER 754.

[252] *Tay Bok Choon v Tahansan Sdn Bhd* [1987] BCLC 472.

[253] *Bluzwed Metals Ltd v Transworld Metals SA* [2001] IEHC 89, Lavan J.

[254] *Re Yenidje Tobacco Company* [1916] 2 Ch 426.

[255] *Re Vehicle Buildings and Insulations Ltd* [1986] ILRM 239.

[256] *Re Irish Tourist Promotions* (22 April 1974, unreported) HC, Kenny J.

[257] *Re Yenidje Tobacco Company Ltd* [1916] 2 Ch 426.

Hardy MR was formulated on the quasi-partnership nature of the relations between the two shareholders. During the course of his judgment, he said of the shareholders:

> 'They assumed, and it is the foundation of the whole agreement that was made, that the two would act as reasonable men with reasonable courtesy and reasonable conduct in every way towards each other, and arbitration was only to be resorted to with regard to some particular dispute between the directors which could not be determined in any other way. Certainly, having regard to the fact that the only two directors will not speak to each other, and no business which deserves the name of business in the affairs of the company can be carried on, I think the company should not be allowed to continue. I have treated it as a partnership, and under the Partnership Act of course the application for a dissolution would take the form of an action; but this is not a partnership strictly, it is not a case in which it can be dissolved by action. But ought not precisely the same principles to apply to a case like this where in substance it is a partnership in the form of the guise of a private company? It is a private company, and there is no way to put an end to the state of things which now exists except by means of a compulsory order.'

While Lord Cozens-Hardy MR viewed this case as not being one of complete deadlock[258] he held that it was within the just and equitable jurisdiction of the court to grant the winding-up order.

[23.100] The leading Irish case is, as noted, *Re Vehicle Buildings and Insulations Ltd*[259]. In that case, a company was formed for the purpose of repairing and dealing in motor vehicles. The petitioner was an equal shareholder in the company, and alleged that a state of deadlock existed in the management of the company and that it would be just and equitable for the company to be wound up, just as it would be in the case of a partnership. It was also alleged that the company would become insolvent if tax assessments which were raised against the company were not successfully challenged on account of the deadlock in the company's management. As against the other shareholder, it was alleged that he ran the business in an inefficient manner and harassed the petitioner. The other shareholder replied that the petitioner was not harassed, that he was not incompetent and that the rift between the parties was because of the 'highly dubious manner' in which the petitioner managed the company's financial affairs. In this regard, he alleged that the garda fraud squad and the Revenue Commissioners were investigating the affairs of the company. While accepting there was a rift between the shareholders, he alleged that the petitioner was responsible for this. He also alleged that the petitioner seeking equitable relief was not coming to court with clean hands.

Murphy J ordered that the company be wound up and in doing so endorsed the principles established in *Re Yenidje Tobacco Company Ltd*. Although the onus of proving deadlock rested with the petitioner, Murphy J said that:

> '... in a case such as the present where the petitioner establishes equality of shareholding and equality of management and a complete unwillingness of each party to co-operate with each other it seems to me that to put it at its lowest that the onus shifts to the respondent or the company to show some means by which this apparently insoluble problem may be resolved[260].'

[258] There was a written agreement between the shareholder directors to submit disputes to arbitration.

[259] *Re Vehicle Buildings and Insulations Ltd* [1986] ILRM 239.

[260] *Re Vehicle Buildings and Insulations Ltd* [1986] ILRM 239 at 242.

In addressing the question of the 'clean hands' of a petitioner Murphy J said that a hearing on affidavit was not the appropriate place to establish the guilt of either party. So, he held that:

> '... the objective fact is that the shareholders/directors cannot legally or practically administer the company without the co-operation of each other and that in practice neither party would be able or willing at this stage to co-operate with the other.
>
> In these circumstances whilst I am not by any means prepared to exculpate the petitioner from any wrong doing I do not feel that I would be justified either in concluding that she was guilty of such misconduct as would dis-entitle her in the particular circumstances of this case to have an order made which seems to be required not only in her interest but in the interests of the creditors of the company[261].'

Expressing regret that a solvent business was going to be wound up, Murphy J nevertheless granted the order sought[262].

[23.101] Several other cases have consistently accepted that deadlock in corporate management can lead to the making of a winding-up order. In *Re Irish Tourist Promotions Ltd*[263], Kenny J ordered that a company be wound up on the basis that relations between the parties had become so bad that the business of the company had almost ceased[264].

(iii) Failure of substratum

[23.102] Failure of substratum is where the purpose for which a company was formed is no longer pursued, or where the company pursues a different venture to that originally envisaged. Frequently a company's substratum will equate with its main objects[265]. The intentions of the parties who come together to form the company are of crucial importance in determining a company's substratum. Where the substratum of a company disappears, it is open to bring a petition for the winding up of that company on just and equitable grounds[266]. Since the advent of the ability to alter a company's objects clause and, as Laffoy J noted in *Re Metafile Ltd*[267] where the objects clause has been drafted in the broadest possible terms, this ground has become somewhat anachronistic, although it probably can be invoked still to prevent a majority of shareholders from relying upon their strict legal rights to alter the objects clause.

---

261 *Re Vehicle Buildings and Insulations Ltd* [1986] ILRM 239 at 243.

262 Note that in an *ex tempore* judgment of 10 March 1986, an appeal was dismissed and the decision of Murphy J was affirmed.

263 *Re Irish Tourist Promotions Ltd* (22 April 1974, unreported) HC, Kenny J.

264 See *Re A & BC Chewing Gum Ltd* [1975] 1 All ER 1017 (where the relationship between the parties in the company was so destroyed that effective management could not be regained, thus justifying the winding up of the company); *Re Davis Investments (East Ham) Ltd* [1961] 3 All ER 926 (petitioner must show that deadlock is likely to remain); *Re American Pioneer Leather Co* [1918] 1 Ch 556 (the voting power of the parties at loggerheads need not be divided equally); and see also *Re Dublin and Eastern Regional Tourism Organisation Ltd* [1990] 1 IR 579.

265 See *Re German Date Coffee Co* [1882] 20 Ch D 169.

266 See also *Re Anglo-Continental Produce Ltd* [1939] All ER 99 and *Re Perfectair Holdings Ltd* [1990] BCLC 423.

267 *Re Metafile Ltd; Garvey v Metafile Ltd* [2006] IEHC 407.

[23.103] To wind up a company on the basis of failure of substratum, it is necessary to show that the real purpose for which the company was formed has been lost. Accordingly, in *Re Kitson & Co Ltd*[268] a company was formed to acquire a business which engaged in general engineering. Forty-six years later a petition was presented to have the company wound up when it was proposed to sell this business. While the members had passed a resolution to discontinue the business of engineering, this was subsequently withdrawn. There, Lord Green MR rationalised the substratum ground in the following terms:

> 'It must be remembered in these substratum cases that there is every difference between a company which on the true construction of its memorandum is formed for the paramount purpose of dealing with some specific subject-matter and a company which is formed with wider and more comprehensive objects. I would explain what I mean. With regard to a company which is formed to acquire and exploit a mine, and, accordingly, if the mine cannot be acquired or if the mine turns out to be no mine at all, the object of the company is frustrated, because the subject matter which the company was formed to exploit has ceased to exist. It is exactly the same way with a patent, as, in the well known *German Date Coffee* case. A patent is a defined subject matter, and, if the main object of a company is to acquire and work a patent and if it fails to acquire that patent, to compel the shareholders to remain bound together in order to work some other patent or make some unpatented article is to force them into a different adventure to that which they contracted to engage in together; but, when you come to subject matter of a totally different kind like the carrying on of a type of business, then so long as the company can carry on that type of business, it seems to me that *prima facie* at any rate, it is impossible to say that the substratum has gone.'

The Court of Appeal reversed an earlier order that the company be wound up on the basis that there remained an intention to carry on the business of general engineering. Accordingly, the abandonment of the main objects of the company must be total, if an application for such an order to wind up is to be granted.

[23.104] In *Re Metafile Ltd*[269], a petition was brought under s 213 of the CA 1963 on the grounds that there was a failure of substratum. In that case, a company was incorporated with an expansive objects clause eg, '... manufacturers, designers, importers, exporters, buyers, sellers (whether by wholesale or retail) ..." etc. As Laffoy J said, whilst it did not include candlestick maker, it did include butcher and baker! It even had an independent objects clause[270]. There was also a shareholders' agreement under which the company's business was to be the manufacturing and production of steel products. In fact, Laffoy J found the company never carried on any of the businesses in its objects clause or in the shareholders' agreement; rather what the learned judge referred to as 'an associated company (using that term in a non-technical sense)' carried on the engineering business and the company was the owner of the premises from which the other company carried on business. The shareholders and the proportion of shares in the company and the associated company were identical. The petitioner fell out with the other shareholders and threatened ss 205 and 213 of the CA 1963 proceedings; those proceedings were compromised on terms that (a) the petitioner get €30,000 from the associated company

---

[268] *Re Kitson & Co Ltd* [1946] All ER 435.

[269] *Re Metafile Ltd; Garvey v Metafile Ltd* [2006] IEHC 407; Laffoy J.

[270] See Ch 3, *Constitutional Documents*, at para **[3.028]**.

for loss of employment; (b) the petitioner would transfer his shares in both companies for €126,000; (c) and the petitioner would resign as director and secretary of both companies. However, the compromise was conditional upon the closing of the sale of the company's premises by a particular date and when this did not go ahead, the compromise became defunct save that the associated company was obliged to pay the petitioner €30,000 for loss of employment.

When that payment was not made, the petitioner succeeded in petitioning for an order to have the associated company wound up. The company eventually sold its premises, and at the hearing of this petition its only asset was the proceeds of sale; it being solvent and without creditors. The petitioner tried unsuccessfully to have the company wound up voluntarily but held only 42.9% of the votes and could only muster the support of 61.5% including his own votes and so failed to pass a special resolution. The petition for failure of substratum was brought thereafter. The company's managing director resisted the petition claiming that the company wished to continue in business, intended to sue the petitioner for alleged breach of fiduciary duties and had not decided how to proceed with the benefit of the proceeds of sale.

[23.105] After noting the passage from the judgment of Lord Greene MR in *Re Kitson & Co Ltd*[271], quoted above, where the decision was to dismiss the petition to wind up, Laffoy J noted the decision of the English High Court in *Re Perfectair Holdings Ltd*[272] where *Kitson* was distinguished and a petition granted to wind up for failure of substratum. Laffoy J noted that there were similarities between *Perfectair* and the case in hand: the company there was also a holding company; it also held property; the business was carried on through a subsidiary; it was agreed that to resolve a dispute between the shareholders the property would be sold and the company wound up; when the property was sold one faction sought to have the company wound up whereas the other resisted it on the basis that it had a pending action for damages against the subsidiary. In *Perfectair*, Scott J said that the majority of the shareholders wanted to get in the assets and wind up the companies and in relation to the litigation said:

> 'Counsel for the respondents said, and correctly said, that the sale of property and the bringing of actions is part of the normal business of an incorporated company. So it is. The sale of property and the prosecution of actions is for all companies, I would think, a legitimate ancillary purpose, ancillary to its principal objects. A trading company litigates to get in debts. It litigates for a variety of other reasons for the purpose of enhancing or protecting its principal object, its trading activity. A holding company does likewise for the purpose of protecting its assets that it holds for profit. The distinction between cases like that and the present case is that it is not for the purpose of any trading object that the assets of Holdings were being realised, that the action against Perfectair is being prosecuted. All of this has taken place and is taking place for the purpose of liquidation.'

Laffoy J, however, rejected the contention that the position was the same in the case before her:

> 'When the Settlement was entered into, while the only asset of the Company was already in the course of being sold, it was clearly envisaged that the petitioner's stake in both Carrig [ie, the associated company] and the Company would be bought out. Taking the Settlement at face value, it was not envisaged that either Carrig or the Company would be

271 *Re Kitson & Co Ltd* [1946] 1 All ER 435.

272 *Re Perfectair Holdings Ltd* [1990] BCLC 423.

wound up. Subsequently, Carrig was wound up at the instigation of the petitioner with a view to recovering the debt owed by it to him. Here the sale of the Company's asset and the winding up of Carrig were not part of an arrangement under which the Company was ultimately to be wound up. Accordingly, in my view, the position here is not analogous to the situation with which Scott J was dealing and there is no basis for adopting the approach he adopted on the facts of this case.'

The learned judge concluded that the substratum had not failed:

'The resolution of the core issue turns on the construction of the shareholders' contract with the Company and inter se. As a matter of construction of the memorandum of association of the Company, whether standing alone, or read by reference to clause 4.02 of the Shareholders' Agreement, the paramount purpose for which the Company was incorporated was to carry on a manufacturing business of a general kind. The fact that the members carried on a mechanical engineering contractor's business through the medium of Carrig does not take from the fact that the Company can carry on the type of manufacturing business envisaged in its memorandum. That being the case, in my view, it cannot be said that the substratum has gone. Indeed the Shareholders' Agreement expressly provided for the Company carrying on such other activities as should be agreed between them from time to time and all other business which the Company was empowered to carry out under its Memorandum of association. On the basis of that conclusion, the petition must be dismissed. I must come to that decision, notwithstanding a strong sense that there is no element of common sense or commercial reality behind the stance which the Company has adopted.'

(iv) Illegal objects

[23.106] The objects of a company must be legal. In *R v Registrar of Joint Stock Companies*[273], a company had as an object the sale of tickets in the Irish Sweepstakes lottery; lotteries were, however, illegal in England. The English registrar of companies refused to register the company, and his decision was upheld in court on the basis that a company could not be formed where its object included an offence against the law. Where a company slips through the registrar's net, it is open to petition for its winding up on just and equitable grounds where its objects are explicitly or implicitly illegal[274].

(v) Corporate instruments of fraud

[23.107] Where it is proved that a company is being used as an instrument of fraud the court will order that the company be wound up on the just and equitable ground. An example of such is seen in the decision in *Re Shrinkpak Ltd*[275] where Barron J granted the petition of the liquidator of Contract Packaging Ltd ('CPL') to have another company, Shrinkpak Ltd, wound up. The liquidator gave evidence that the winding up of CPL had been engineered to defraud the creditors of CPL by the diversion of CPL's

[273] *R v Registrar of Joint Stock Companies* [1931] 2 KB 197. See also *Bowman v Secular Society Ltd* [1917] AC 406 and *McEllistrim v Ballymacelligott Co-operative and Dairy Society Ltd* [1919] AC 549.

[274] See *Re Thomas Edward Brinsmead & Sons Ltd* [1897] 1 Ch 45, where the promoters deceived the subscribers into buying into the company.

[275] *Re Shrinkpak Ltd* (20 December 1989, unreported) HC (unapproved), *per* Barron J. The author acknowledges with gratitude the help of Mr Michael McInerney, Solicitor, for locating this unreported decision.

funds and business to Shrinkpak Ltd in blatant disregard of the duties owed by the directors to CPL. Although a separate legal entity, Shrinkpak Ltd was financed solely out of the assets of CPL. Whilst liabilities of Shrinkpak Ltd were attributed to CPL, assets of CPL were claimed to belong to Shrinkpak Ltd. On the evidence presented before him, Barron J was inclined to grant the petition to have the company wound up. He also rejected the contention that the liquidator of CPL was not a creditor and had no *locus standi*. On the question of the petition being presented on the just and equitable ground, Barron J appears to have held that if the company was being used as an instrument of fraud, it was preferable to have the company wound up than to have the claims litigated by way of plenary summons. Since he found on the evidence that the whole financial status of Shrinkpak Ltd was based on fraud, he granted the petition sought and ordered that Shrinkpak Ltd be wound up.

[23.108] Since the passing of s 141 of the CA 1990 it is thought that a similar result could be achieved by means of a *pooling order* which will allow two or more companies to be wound up together and their assets pooled[276]. Notwithstanding this statutory power, it is thought that the equitable jurisdiction exercised by Barron J may still be of use, particularly where a petitioner cannot bring his case within the terms of s 141 of the CA 1990.

(vi) Public interest

[23.109] By virtue of s 12 of the CA 1990, the Director of Corporate Enforcement can, following any report made under s 11 of the CA 1990 or by inspectors appointed under the CA 1990 or any information obtained by the Director under Part II of the CA 1990, bring a petition to have a company wound up on the grounds that such is just and equitable. This right of the Director is not confined to 'companies' within the meaning of s 2 of the CA 1963 and extends to all companies that are capable of being wound up under the Companies Acts[277]. In England and Wales, this right to petition the courts has come to be known as applications to wind up *in the public interest*. Although the English Secretary of State for Trade and Industry has had the power to petition the English courts since s 124A of the Insolvency Act 1986 (UK) was inserted by the Companies Act 1989 (UK), only in the last number of years have applications become commonplace[278]. Examples of when the English Secretary of State has sought to exercise his power to petition is where it is suspected that a company is being used to promote an illegal lottery[279] and where savings companies have sought to apply excessive charges that were allegedly concealed[280].

[23.110] The Irish High Court ordered a company to be wound up on just and equitable grounds on foot of Part II of the CA 1990 in *Re Rayhill Property Ltd, Home Affairs Ltd*

276 See Ch 25, *Realisation and Distribution of Assets in a Winding Up*, para **[25.125]** *et seq.*

277 Section 12(2) of the CA 1990 refers to a 'body corporate liable to be wound up under the Companies Acts'. See para **[23.035]**. As to the winding up of foreign companies in England, see *Re Normandy Marketing Ltd* [1993] BCC 879.

278 See, generally, Milman, 'Winding Up in the Public Interest' (1999) *Palmer's In Company*, (1999) Issue 3/99, 9 March 1999.

279 *Re Senator Hanseatische Verwaltungsgessellschaft mbh* [1996] 2 BCLC 562.

280 *Re North West Holdings plc; Secretary of State for Trade and Industry v Blackhouse* [2001] BCLC 468.

and Hilltop Catering Ltd[281], an order which has only been reported in the newspapers. There, the companies in question were involved in the running of the ill-fated Clonmannon retirement village in Co Wicklow. The elderly residents had complained for some time previously that the nursing service and food they had allegedly paid for was not satisfactory and that the estate had not been properly managed. The newspaper report of the petition reported that in October 1994 an accountant and employee of the Department of Enterprise, Trade and Employment had been appointed to examine the companies' books and to report to the Minister. In the light of the fact that the basis for such a Ministerial petition (which would, today, be brought instead by the Director of Corporate Enforcement) is rooted in the just and equitable ground, it is instructive to note that the newspaper reported that counsel for the Minister claimed that there had been a:

> 'failure of the substratum upon which the company was to be based and upon which it held itself out to the public as trading; that the company's affairs had been mismanaged; and that assets of the company had been improperly misappropriated.'

It was reported that Costello P ordered the winding up of the three companies.

[23.111] One of the issues that has arisen when the similar legislation has been considered by the English courts is whether the same practices regarding the advertisement of petitions apply to petitions brought on this basis. It would seem that the general rule remains, although the English Court of Appeal was sympathetic to the State-backed petitioner in *Secretary of State for Trade and Industry v North West Holdings plc*[282]. In that case, it was concluded that the public was entitled to know that the Secretary for State had taken the view that it was expedient and in the public interest to present a petition – especially where a court had been satisfied to appoint a provisional liquidator. Moreover, in *Re Applied Database Ltd*[283] it was held that the fact that exceptional damage might be caused a company would not justify a restraint on advertisement where the petition was not an abuse of process.

(f) Oppression

[23.112] Section 205 of the CA 1963 allows disgruntled members of a company to petition the court where the company is being run in a manner oppressive to them. One of the remedies available to the court in such circumstances is to order that the company be wound up[284]. Often, such a petition will be taken in tandem with a winding-up petition on just and equitable grounds[285]. Section 205 is considered in detail in Chapter 11[286].

---

281 An application reported in (1995) Irish Times, 17 October (Costello P).

282 *Secretary of State for Trade and Industry v North West Holdings plc* [1998] BCC 997.

283 *Re Applied Database Ltd* (17 February 1995, unreported) HC (Eng).

284 See *Re Commercial and Industrial Insulations Ltd* [1986] BCLC 191.

285 *Re Murph's Restaurants Ltd* [1979] ILRM 141.

286 See Ch 11, *Shareholders' Remedies*, para **[11.006]** *et seq*.

[D] Conversion of Windings Up

Converting a members' winding up to a creditors' winding up

[23.113] There are two ways in which a members' voluntary winding up can be converted to a creditors' voluntary winding up. Both of these methods of conversion have in common the fact that, notwithstanding the declaration of solvency, the company will not be able to pay its debts within 12 months of the commencement of the winding up. Where this occurs the company's creditors will usually wish to have a more active part in the liquidation.

[23.114] The first means of conversion is provided for in s 256(5) of the CA 1963 which provides that the court may convert the members' voluntary winding up into a creditors' voluntary winding up where certain conditions are met. Section 256(5) provides:

> 'If within 28 days after the resolution for voluntary winding up, has been advertised under subs (1) of s 252, a creditor applies to the court for an order under this subsection, and the court is satisfied that such creditor together with any creditors supporting him in his application represents one-fifth at least in number or value of the creditors of the company, and the court is of opinion that it is unlikely that the company will be able to pay its debts within the period specified in the declaration, the court may order that all the provisions of this Act relating to a creditors' voluntary winding up shall apply to the winding up.'

Where the court makes an order for the conversion of the winding up, any liquidator appointed by the members prior to this, or if none has been appointed, the company itself, shall deliver a copy of the court's order to the registrar of companies. s 256(6) of the CA 1963[287].

[23.115] The second means of conversion is provided by s 261 of the CA 1963[288] which imposes a duty on a liquidator appointed by the members to call a meeting of the creditors where he is of the opinion that the company will not be able to pay its debts in full within the time specified in the declaration of solvency. Where this happens, a liquidator must:

- call a meeting of the creditors within 14 days from the day he formed his opinion;
- mail notices of the meeting to the creditors not less than seven days before the day of the meeting;
- advertise in *Iris Oifigiúil* and in two daily newspapers at least 10 days before the meeting;
- furnish reasonable information to any interested creditor who requests such information;
- state in the notice of the meeting that he was under a duty to call the meeting having formed the opinion that the company was unable to pay its debts on time[289].

---

[287] Default in this regard is liable to be visited with a class C fine: s 256(7) of the CA 1963.

[288] As replaced by s 129 of the CA 1990.

[289] See s 261(1) of the CA 1963. Although s 72 of the IFCMPA 2005 substituted 'the *Companies Registration Office Gazette*' for '*Iris Oifigiúil*' it has not been commenced.

In addition, where an inadequate declaration of solvency is made by the directors because they do not annex the report of an independent person, a liquidator will have seven days in which to apply to court for directions[290]. Costello J held in *Re Favon Investments Co Ltd*[291] that where the liquidation is out of time the court has no jurisdiction in which to extend the time for making and filing the report. In such circumstances, there will be an automatic conversion from a members' voluntary winding up to a creditors' voluntary winding up. Where the company is out of time for holding a creditors' meeting in accordance with s 266 of the CA 1963, the court may annul the resolution of the members to have the company wound up where to do so would not prejudice anybody.

[23.116] At the creditors' meeting the liquidator must present a statement of affairs of the company (including its assets, liabilities, a list of outstanding creditors and an estimate of their claims). He must also attend and preside at the meeting of the creditors[292]. From this time onwards, the winding up becomes a creditors' voluntary winding up[293]. The creditors can then replace the liquidator and appoint their own, and where there is a dispute over the costs, charges or expenses of the members' liquidator, application can be made to court[294]. The validity of any acts which were previously done by the members' liquidator is not affected[295].

Converting a voluntary winding up to a compulsory winding up

[23.117] The mere fact that a company is in voluntary liquidation is not an absolute bar to its being wound up by the court and although there are many reasons for believing that a voluntary liquidator will be vigorous, there may be cause for converting[296]. As Laffoy J said in *Re Marcon Developments*[297]:

> '... although, in the majority of cases the safeguards which are now in place which ensure that a liquidator in a winding up outside the Court fulfils his role properly (the supervisory role of the Director of Corporate Enforcement, the existence of a committee of inspection, and the statutory entitlement of a creditor to apply to Court to have an issue determined under s 280 of the Act of 1963) afford ample protection for the interests of creditors in a winding up outside the Court, there are cases, such as this case, where in balancing all of the relevant factors it is clearly preferable that the winding up be under the supervision of the court from the outset[298].'

On application being made either by a company's members or creditors, prior to completion of a voluntary winding up, the court may order a conversion. Section 282 of the CA 1963 provides, however, that in the case of an application being made by a

290 Section 131(5) of the CA 1990.

291 *Re Favon Investments Co Ltd* [1993] 1 IR 87 and *Re Birchwell Developments Ltd* [2010] IEHC 319. See para **[23.008]**.

292 Section 131(2) of the CA 1990.

293 Section 131(3) of the CA 1990.

294 Section 131(5) of the CA 1990.

295 Section 131(4) of the CA 1990.

296 See Kirwan, 'Replacing a Creditors' Liquidator: No Sugar Coating the Bitter Pill' (2011) CLP 51.

297 *Re Marcon Developments* [2010] IEHC 373, Laffoy J.

298 *Re Marcon Developments* [2010] IEHC 373, Laffoy J, at para 9.12.

contributory[299], the court must be satisfied that the rights of the contributories will be prejudiced by a voluntary winding up, were it allowed to continue.

[23.118] In order to petition the court to wind up any company, the petitioner must come within one of the grounds set out in s 213 of the CA 1963. This is also the case where it is sought to have a company in voluntary liquidation wound up by the court. In addition, however, some ground must be advanced by the petitioner as to why the court ought to grant an order to have the company wound up compulsorily as opposed to allowing the company to continue to be wound up voluntarily[300]. In *Re Oakthorpe Holdings Ltd*[301], Carroll J advanced the view, *obiter*, that where the members of a trading company commenced a voluntary winding up by passing a resolution but did not deliver a statutory declaration of solvency or call a creditors' meeting, thereby creating an impasse, the creditors of the company could petition the court for a winding-up order[302].

[23.119] In *Re Fencore Services Ltd*[303], Laffoy J quoted with approval from the decision of Diplock LJ in *JD Swaine Ltd*[304] which the learned judge said gets to the core of how the court should exercise its descretion in determining whether to make a winding-up order where the company is already being voluntarily wound up. There, Diplock LJ distinguished opposition to a winding-up petition with a view to ensuring that there would be no winding-up order and the circumstances in which the court is asked to substitute a compulsory winding up for a voluntary winding up, stating as follows:

> 'In the case of a petition for compulsory winding up, if the only circumstances which are available are that the petitioner seeks a compulsory winding up and the majority of the creditors seek that there should be no winding up at all, then prima facie the petitioning creditor is entitled to a winding up unless there are some additional reasons for deciding to the contrary. If, on the other hand, the petitioner seeks a compulsory winding up and the majority of the creditors seek a voluntary winding up, then for the wishes of the petitioner to overrule those of the majority of the creditors there must be some special reason why the wishes of the majority should be overridden. The difference or distinction seems to me to be an obvious one, namely, in the former case, what is being resisted is any winding up at all, so that the petitioning creditor, if he fails, will be denied the class remedy which he would otherwise have if the winding up took place; whereas in the latter case he will get the class remedy anyway under the voluntary winding up, and the matter then turns on his being able to show some reason why the remedy under the voluntary winding up is not an adequate remedy for him.'

In determining whether a petitioner has established that a voluntary winding up will be inadequate for him. Laffoy J observed that it was established that the court has a discretion and that it must weigh up all the relevant factors, and that in *Re Hayes Homes*

299 Defined by s 208 of the CA 1963, and considered at para **[23.045]**.

300 See generally, Pennington, *Corporate Insolvency Law* (1991), pp 84–87.

301 *Re Oakthorpe Holdings Ltd* [1988] ILRM 62.

302 Alternatively, in such a situation, Carroll J recognised (at 64) that an order could be granted extending the time in which a creditors' meeting could be called, thus allowing the 'half-dead' company, to proceed to an orderly death, by a creditors' voluntary winding up.

303 *Re Fencore Services Ltd* [2010] IEHC 358, Laffoy J.

304 *Re JD Swaine Ltd* [1965] 2 All ER 762, which was relied on in *Re Southard & Co Ltd* [1979] 1 WLR 546.

Ltd[305] O'Neill J gave the following example of circumstances in which the court should intervene:

> 'In my view this court should be disposed to intervene if the circumstances deposed to on affidavit show that the assets of the company, such as the goodwill of its business, have gone to an associated company without any payment and the liquidation is in the hands of the nominee of the person or persons who had control over the company and the connected or associated companies, and where the nominee of the majority of the creditors who stand to lose substantial monies has been rejected.'

In the *Fencore* case, the company was in creditors' voluntary liquidation but the petitioner, Danske Bank, wished it to be converted to an official liquidation. Although the petitioner was a secured creditor, its security was over a ship which was within the jurisdiction of the French courts and the petitioner was concerned that any receiver it appointed would not be recognised, whereas a liquidator would be recognised in all countries of the European Union. After the petition was advertised but before it was heard, the company was placed into creditors' voluntary winding up; the petitioner, however, wished to proceed with the petition. One concern raised by the petitioner was in relation to a company called Green Star Shipping Company Limited, a significant creditor of the company, and the interest which it had in the ship which was the subject of the ship mortgage in favour of the petitioner, which mortgage prevented the company from being anything other than sole beneficial owner of the ship. It appeared that a bill of sale in favour of Green Star had been entered in the register maintained under the Mercantile Marine Act 1955. There was evidence that a director of the company was the owner of Green Star and one of its two directors. There was also evidence that, contrary to the terms of the mortgage in favour of the petitioner, the ship had been renamed and re-registered and had not received charter receipts resulting from the charter with Green Star. The petitioner considered that the responses it received to questions put to the company's directors at the creditors' meeting concerning the transaction with Green Star were inadequate and required to be investigated by an official liquidator under the supervision of the court. Laffoy J noted that the company had provided further explanations but concluded that they did not obviate the necessity for the liquidator to investigate fully the transaction with Green Star. Laffoy J ordered that the winding up be converted to an official winding up. Among the reasons for this were: the fact the directors only initiated the creditors' voluntary winding up after the petition had been presented, despite the company being seriously insolvent[306]; the fact it was impossible to form a view on what the majority in value of the creditors wished; the director's failure to allay the petitioner's concerns; the fact that another creditor, Bank of Scotland Ireland, which was owed significant sums, supported the petition; and, most significantly, the evidence concerning the transaction between the company and Green Star. On this point Laffoy J said:

> 'In my view, the petitioner has established that an investigation by the nominee of members of the company who entered into the transaction with Green Star, which is wholly owned by Mr Hanley, would not, and would not be seen to, afford the petitioner an adequate remedy even with the safeguards which are now in place to ensure that a

305 *Re Hayes Homes Ltd* [2004] IEHC 253.

306 This was also given as a reason for ordering the conversion to an official liquidation in *Re Marcon Developments* [2010] IEHC 373, Laffoy J.

> liquidator in a voluntary liquidation investigates matters properly, which I have outlined in my judgment in the *Balbradagh* case at para 15. In this case, the complexity of the issues, both factual and legal, to which the transaction between the company and Green Star gives rise, would almost inevitably lead to Court involvement, even if the creditors' voluntary winding up were to continue. Therefore, saving of costs and expedition are not in this case relevant factors which, in other circumstances, might induce the Court not to interfere.'

The need to investigate matters was also cited as a reason for ordering conversion in *Re Marcon Developments*[307], where Laffoy J said the liquidator faced a formidable investigative task which meant it was probable that he would require directions from the court throughout the liquidation and that in the circumstances it seemed sensible that the liquidation come under the supervision of the court.

[23.120] Other situations where such a conversion might be sought include the case of a liquidator refusing to investigate the alleged wrongs of the directors[308], or where the shareholders of a company appeared not to be required to pay all that was owing on partly paid-up shares[309]. Where a creditor petitions for a conversion, the court may refuse where a majority in number and value of other creditors are opposed to conversion to an official liquidation[310]. In *Re JD Swain Ltd*[311], Diplock LJ said that it was permissible to take cognisance of the objections of other creditors in an application to have a company wound up. This situation was distinguished from where there was no winding up at all in existence. In a petition for a conversion the creditor already has his remedy of winding up, and so must show cause as to why that is not adequate. By contrast, where there is no winding up in progress the views of creditors who oppose the petition will be disregarded in the absence of *mala fides* on the part of the petitioner as a creditor owed a debt is entitled to a winding-up order *ex debito justiciae*.

[23.121] One factor which the court will always consider is the cost of liquidation. Where a company is insolvent, ensuring that its creditors receive the highest dividend is manifestly in their interests. All things being equal, the Irish courts will be more inclined towards the cheaper creditors' voluntary winding up than the usually more expensive official liquidation. So, for example, in *Re Permanent Formwork Systems Ltd*[312] Laffoy J decided to dismiss the petition saying:

> 'The primary consideration which informed that decision is that it is in the interests of the general body of creditors that the liquidation of the company be effected as cheaply and as expeditiously as possible. In all probability, a winding up under the supervision of the court would be more costly and would be of longer duration than a creditors' voluntary winding up.'

---

307 *Re Marcon Developments* [2010] IEHC 373.

308 *Re Gutta Percha Corpn* [1900] 2 Ch 665; *Re United Service Co* (1868) LR 7 Eq 76; and *Re Gold Co* (1879) 11 Ch D 701.

309 *Re Northumberland and Durham District Banking Co* (1858) 2 De G & J 357.

310 *Re Wicklow Textiles Ltd* (1953) 87 ILTR 72. See also *Re Lowerstoft Traffic Services Ltd* [1986] BCLC 81; *Re Palmer Marine Surveys Ltd* [1986] BCLC 106; and *Re HJ Tomkins & Son Ltd* [1990] BCLC 76.

311 *Re JD Swain Ltd* [1965] 1 WLR 909 at 915.

312 *Re Permanent Formwork Systems Ltd* [2007] IEHC 268.

[23.122] In *Re Gilt Construction Ltd*[313], O'Hanlon J was asked to convert a creditors' voluntary winding up to an official winding up. The company concerned had only two shareholders whom the learned judge said could be loosely referred to as partners. On account of its insolvency, they resolved to wind the company up and agreed to appoint a named liquidator. Subsequently, at the creditors' meeting, one of the men had a change of heart and supported the appointment of another liquidator; this liquidator was appointed with the support of all creditors voting personally or by proxy, other than the petitioning shareholder and the company's solicitor who was also a creditor. The other shareholder's change of heart led to the petitioner bringing the petition and he also claimed that the other shareholder had been manipulating the assets of the company for his own benefit. The remedy claimed was to have the winding up converted to an official liquidation under the supervision of a court appointed liquidator. O'Hanlon J first noted that the court 'must be slow to dislodge a voluntary liquidator who has apparently been appointed to wind up the company with the concurrence of a majority, numerically and in value, of the creditors of the company'[314]. The learned judge next held that he did not consider that the credentials of the creditors' liquidator:

> '... either from the point of view of his professional qualifications and competence to carry out the task assigned to him, or in respect of his integrity and reliability in holding the scales evenly between the two partners when carrying out the winding up, have been impugned in any manner which would justify the court in taking the serious course of converting the voluntary liquidation into a liquidation under the direction of the court, and appointing a new liquidator ...[315]'

In refusing the order sought by the petitioner, O'Hanlon J noted that the authorities to which he had been referred[316] had stressed that the amount of assets to be administered in the winding up was of great importance. Of these authorities, the learned judge said:

> 'The general approach taken in these cases is to have due regard to the costs involved in winding up by the court and the delays which will be incurred; to the over-all value of the assets to be administered and the complexity or simplicity of the task facing the liquidator, as well as to other relevant factors, such as those raised by the petitioner in the present case, having to do with questions of *mala fides* on the part of a person or persons involved in the dispute. In the present case the value of the assets is small by comparison with the general run of cases where winding up by the court is deemed appropriate. I have had the experience of seeing substantial sums raised by sale of assets in court liquidations, only to be told that the entire of the sum is only sufficient to pay the legal costs and the liquidator's charges and that nothing remains for distribution to the creditors. The winding-up process in the present case appears to be comparatively straightforward and simple, and if any unexpected problems should arise where the guidance of the court is needed by the voluntary liquidator or any contributor or creditor, access to the court is provided by s 280 of the Companies Act 1963[317].'

---

313 *Re Gilt Construction Ltd* (3 June 1994, unreported) HC.

314 *Re Gilt Construction Ltd* (3 June 1994, unreported) HC at p 3.

315 *Re Gilt Construction Ltd* (3 June 1994, unreported) HC at pp 3–4.

316 *Re Belfast Tailors' Co-Partnership Ltd* [1909] 1 IR 49; *Re JD Swain Ltd* [1965] 2 All ER 761; *Re Lowerstoft Traffic Services Ltd* [1986] BCLC 81; *Re Palmer Marine Surveys Ltd* [1986] 1 WLR 573; and *Re Falcon RJ Development* [1987] BCLC 437.

317 *Re Gilt Construction Ltd* (3 June 1994, unreported) HC at pp 4–5.

The judgment of O'Hanlon J shows clearly that in the absence of a valid, compelling reason as to why it is inappropriate to continue the voluntary winding up of the company, the court will refuse to order a conversion.

[23.123] In two subsequent cases, the Irish High Court was asked to convert a creditors' voluntary winding up into an official winding up. In *Re Naiad Ltd*[318], a company was in the process of being wound up in a creditors' voluntary liquidation when one of its creditors petitioned the court to have it converted to a compulsory liquidation. The petitioning creditor sought the conversion on five stated grounds. First, notices convening creditors' meetings had not been received by him until the day before it was due to be held. Second, no notice of the meeting had been given to employee creditors. Third, it was alleged that the chairman of the meeting had refused to adjourn it when requested to do so by SIPTU, a creditor of the company. Fourth, it was alleged that the company had been trading insolvently and the directors might be found to be personally liable and that a voluntary liquidator would not prosecute such actions as diligently as an official liquidator. And fifth, whilst a majority in number of creditors attending the meeting voted in favour of one liquidator, a different liquidator was proposed by the petitioner who was by far the largest ordinary creditor and so was supported by a majority in value. McCracken J held that it was hard to think that the petitioner's sense of grievance was justifiable and rejected each of the five grounds. To the individual grounds, in order, McCracken J held: (1) the creditors' meeting had been properly convened in accordance with s 266 of the CA 1963; (2) at the date of the meeting the company's employees were not creditors and had no entitlement to notice of the meeting; (3) the petitioner had not requested an adjournment and SIPTU did not support the petition; (4) there was no specific allegation against the independence of the liquidator who had been appointed; and (5) the chairman was correct in abiding by the decision of the majority in number[319]. As to the general approach of the court in such applications, McCracken J cited with approval the first sentence of the second passage quoted above from the decision of O'Hanlon J in *Re Gilt Construction* Ltd[320].

[23.124] Again, in *Re Eurochick (Ireland) Ltd*[321] McCracken J was asked to displace a voluntary liquidator and appoint a court liquidator. In that case the liquidator's appointment was approved by 10 votes to three, the petitioner being one of the objectors. The petitioner did not criticise the liquidator's ability or impartiality and instead merely asserted a 'legitimate sense of grievance'. In that case, the judge found that the company (in liquidation) had been set up at the instigation of the management of the petitioner to process chickens sold to it by the petitioner. McCracken J said that it was clear it had been intended that the petitioner would beneficially own all or a substantial part of the company and he said that the petitioner's solicitor and a brother of one of the managers in the petitioner were the company's only shareholders and that the company operated from the same premises as the petitioner. After the company collapsed those connected

318 *Re Naiad Ltd* (13 February 1995, unreported) HC, McCracken J.

319 This was prior to the enactment of s 47 of the CLEA 2001 which inserted s 267(3) of the CA 1963 whereby now the majority in value will prevail on a resolution as to the creditors' nominee as liquidator. See para **[23.028]**.

320 *Re Gilt Construction Ltd* (3 June 1994, unreported) HC. See para **[23.122]**.

321 *Re Eurochick (Ireland) Ltd* [1988] IEHC 51, McCracken J.

with the company severed their connection with the petitioner. The judge noted the petitioner's claims, which suggested that it had been funding the company in various ways, the result of which was that the company could owe the petitioner more than shown in its books. McCracken J noted that in English cases such as *Re Magnus Consultants Ltd*[322] and *Re Falcon RJ Development Ltd*[323] the courts were inclined to order the conversion to a compulsory liquidation where there was some wrongdoing in the company which needed to be investigated. McCracken J was satisfied that there was no such wrongdoing alleged in the instant case and that the petitioner's complaint related to the conduct of its own affairs by its own management! The judge said of the petitioner's management that:

> 'they may have used funds of the petitioner to support the company, but there is no suggestion that they benefited personally in any way, or that they were guilty of any act which would reduce the assets of the company or increase its liability to its creditors, other than to the petitioner.'

McCracken J again cited the same passage from the decision of O'Hanlon J in *Re Gilt Construction Ltd*[324] and concluded:

> 'I can only repeat that it appears to me that the mala fides alleged in this case are the mala fides of the management of the petitioner itself, and it is not for the liquidator to investigate that matter. The assets in this case are very small compared with the liabilities, and I do not think there is any sense of grievance among the creditors generally which would justify the application of the principles in the English cases.'

In a number of English cases, a compulsory winding up has been ordered where it has been held that the creditors would otherwise have a 'genuine sense of grievance'. A totally unsatisfactory creditors' meeting was cited as sufficient reason in one case[325]. Generally, however, it would seem that the English courts are more inclined to accede to a creditor's petition than are the Irish courts[326], and in *Re Larkin Partnership Ltd*[327] an order was refused to convert a creditors' voluntary liquidation to an official liquidation even though Laffoy J acknowledged that the petitioner had a 'justifiable sense of grievance' and although the liquidator had demonstrated a lack of vigour to investigate the circumstances surrounding the company's ceasing to trade, because the learned judge was satisfied that the issues could be adequately addressed in the creditors' voluntary winding-up process.

[E] The Winding-up Order

[23.125] Upon the granting of an order for the winding up of a company the law treats the company as being analogous to a trustee of its own assets. The order to wind up the

---

322 *Re Magnus Consultants Ltd* [1995] 1 BCLC 203.

323 *Re Falcon RJ Development Ltd* [1987] BCLC 437.

324 *Re Gilt Construction Ltd* (3 June 1994, unreported) HC. See para **[23.122]**.

325 *Re Inside Sports Ltd* [2000] BCC 40.

326 In *Re Zirceram Ltd; Brodie & So v Zirceram Ltd* [2000] BCC 1048, it was said that a compulsory liquidation could be ordered so that there could be an investigation which was not only independent, but was seen to be independent.

327 *Re Larkin Partnership Ltd* [2010] IEHC 163, Laffoy J.

company dates back to the date of the presentation of the petition[328]. By s 222 of the CA 1963, another consequence of a winding-up order being granted is that no proceedings may be instituted against the company without the consent of the court. Once an order is made, the company's separate legal personality does not disappear until such time as it is actually *dissolved* by the court. In *Re Swedex Windows & Doors Ltd*[329], Finlay Geoghegan J held that, in general and subject to any special contractual provision or special circumstances which might require an audit to be completed, the effect of making a winding-up order and the appointment of an official liquidator is to discharge an auditor from the office then held.

[23.126] On the granting of the order to wind up a company, the company must deliver to the registrar of companies a copy of the winding-up order under s 221 of the CA 1963. In addition, a statement of the company's affairs must be prepared by the directors or others ordered to do so by the court, which must be filed in court unless the court orders otherwise[330]. To put the public on notice that the company is being wound up, every invoice, order for goods or business letter issued by or on behalf of the company or liquidator, or receiver which bears the name of the company, must, by s 303 of the CA 1963, contain a statement that the company is being wound up. From this point onwards, the liquidator assumes, and the directors usually lose, the functions and the authority which the directors previously held[331].

[23.127] By s 234(1) of the CA 1963 the court has power on its own or on the liquidator's application, to annul the order to wind the company up, on satisfactory proof. In addition, by s 234(2) it has jurisdiction to make an order to stay the winding-up proceedings

Annulling a members' winding up

[23.128] The court's power to annul an order to wind a company up in a compulsory liquidation has a parallel in a voluntary winding up. In *Re Oakthorpe Holdings Ltd*[332], Carroll J held that the reference in s 280(3) of the CA 1963 to an order annulling the resolution to wind up means that, by analogy with the power in s 234 of the CA 1963, 'the court can in a voluntary winding up annul the resolution to wind up in an appropriate case, just as it can stay proceedings[333]'. In that case, the company was not a

---

328 Section 220(2) of the CA 1963 . See *Burton v Deakin* [1977] 1 All ER 631. It may be noted that in *Emo Oil Ltd v Sun Alliance and London Insurance plc* [2009] IESC 2, the Supreme Court held that where an insurance policy insured against the plaintiff's customers' insolvency, a customer would not be considered as having '*gone into liquidation*' where a petition has been presented, only where an order was made. The High Court ([2005] IEHC 474, Gilligan J) had applied the relation back rule to find the opposite, *viz*, that the company would be said to have gone into liquidation at the date of the presentation of the petition. In reversing the High Court the consequence was that the plaintiff's losses were not insured as the policy had terminated at the point in time when the winding-up order had been made.

329 *Re Swedex Windows & Doors Ltd* [2010] IEHC 237.

330 Section 224 of the CA 1963.

331 See *Re Union Accident Insurance Co Ltd* [1972] 1 All ER 1105.

332 *Re Oakthorpe Holdings Ltd* [1988] ILRM 62.

333 See also, *Re Birchwell Developments Ltd* [2010] IEHC 319 where Laffoy J considered exercising the court's jurisdiction to annul a winding-up order.

trading company, and had no creditors and thus it was deemed appropriate to exercise the power of the court. Carroll J noted, however, that had there been creditors, an alternative remedy might have been the bringing of a petition to wind up the company by the court, so as to remedy the impasse[334].

Rescission of a compulsory winding-up order

[23.129] There would seem to be some uncertainty as to whether a compulsory winding-up order can be rescinded in Ireland. Prior to the coming into force of the Insolvency Rules 1986[335], the position in England and Wales seemed to be that a winding-up order could only be rescinded if application was made before the order was drawn up, ie, within a few days of the making of the order. As a result of the Insolvency Rules 1986, every court in England and Wales 'having jurisdiction ... to wind up companies may review, rescind or vary an order made by it in the exercise of that jurisdiction'. It would seem that the position in Ireland is that which prevailed in England before r 7.47. As to who has *locus standi* to apply for rescission of a winding-up order, further to the issue of a practice direction on 26 April 1971[336], the position in England and Wales is that only a creditor, a contributory or the company jointly with a creditor or contributory may apply to rescind an order[337].

Voiding dissolution following the making of a winding-up order

[23.130] Section 310 of the CA 1963 confers a statutory power on the courts to declare a dissolution of a company void. This is a different jurisdiction to that contained in s 311A of the CA 1963 or s 12C of the C(A)A 1982[338] because the dissolution envisaged by s 310 follows the making of a winding-up order, whether voluntary or compulsory, as opposed to dissolution following strike-off by the registrar of companies. As O'Neill J said in *Re Amantiss Enterprises Ltd; Framus Ltd v CRH* plc[339], s 310 is in contra-distinction to the other sections. Section 310(1) of the CA 1963 provides:

> 'Where a company has been dissolved, the court may at any time within 2 years of the date of the dissolution, on an application being made for the purpose by the liquidator of the company or by any other person who appears to the court to be interested, make an order, upon such terms as the court thinks fit, declaring the dissolution to have been void, and thereupon such proceedings may be taken as might have been taken if the company had not been dissolved.'

Where an applicant is successful in applying for an order to void a dissolution, he has a statutory duty to deliver an office copy of the court's order to the registrar of companies, on pain of fine[340]. It will be noted that once a dissolution has been declared void, 'thereupon such proceedings may be taken as might have been taken if the company had

---

334 Under s 282 of the CA 1963, considered at para **[23.117]** *ante*.

335 Insolvency Rules 1986, r 7.47.

336 *Practice Direction* [1971] 2 All ER 200.

337 See *Re Mid East Trading Ltd; Lehman Bros Inc v Phillips et al* [1997] 3 All ER 481.

338 As to which see Ch 26, *Strike Off and Restoration*, at para **[26.056]**.

339 *Re Amantiss Enterprises Ltd; Framus Ltd v CRH plc* [2000] 2 ILRM 177.

340 Section 310(2) of the CA 1963.

not been dissolved'. As to the meaning of this expression, in *Re Amantiss Enterprises Ltd; Framus Ltd v CRH plc*[341] O'Neill J said:

> '… s 310 of the Companies Act 1963 … deals with the situation where a dissolution occurs following a winding up in a voluntary or a court liquidation. Necessarily in these circumstances there will be no question of the company having, since dissolution, conducted trading or business operations. If acts were done in the name of the company following dissolution in these circumstances it is hard to imagine how they could have a lawful character and hence, as a matter of principle, retroactive validation could not ensue automatically on a declaration under s 310, that the dissolution was void. The use of the phrase in s 310: "*and thereupon such proceedings may be taken as might have been taken if the company had not been dissolved*" would seem intended to have the effect of enabling from that point, namely when the declaration is made, the company to sue or be sued.'

O'Neill J went on to note that s 310 of the 1963 Act was identical to s 223 of the Companies Act 1908 and that that section was so construed by the English House of Lords in *Morris v Harris*[342].

[23.131] In *Morris v Harris*[343], Mr Harris had a claim against a company which had gone to arbitration before the company was dissolved; after the dissolution the arbitrator purported to make an award against the company in favour of Mr Harris. In the House of Lords, Lord Sumner said of the English provision, which was materially identical to s 310(1) of the CA 1963, in a passage quoted with approval by Laffoy J in *Re Walsh Maguire & O'Shea Ltd*[344]:

> 'The object of the provision was, I think, to give a fresh start to proceedings, which owing to the dissolution had been impossible and had not been taken and thereupon it was to be open to those concerned to take them in the future as if the dissolution had not happened. In my opinion most of the proceedings in the arbitration in this case, and, above all, the award itself, are null, for they were taken and made against a company which did not exist, and no subsequent validity has been or could be given to them. The respondent must therefore prove his claim afresh in proceedings, to which [the company] will be a party[345].'

[23.132] The former English provision (identical to s 310 of the CA 1963) is s 651 of the Companies Act 1985 (UK). That section was interpreted in *Smith v White Knight Laundry Ltd*[346] as meaning that where a dissolved company is restored, a cause of action

---

341 *Re Amantiss Enterprises Ltd; Framus Ltd v CRH plc* [2000] 2 ILRM 177.

342 *Morris v Harris* [1927] AC 252.

343 *Morris v Harris* [1927] AC 252.

344 *Re Walsh Maguire & O'Shea Ltd* [2011] IEHC 457.

345 *Morris v Harris* [1927] AC 252 at 259. In *Foster Yates & Thom Ltd v HW Edgehill Equipment Ltd* (1978) 122 SJ 60, Megaw LJ said: 'Apart from authority, I should have taken the view that when a corporate body is dissolved as a result of a voluntary winding up, any action which is pending at the date of dissolution ceases, not temporarily and provisionally, but absolutely and for all time. If the company is brought to life under s 352 the cause of action is still there. It can, subject to any question of limitation, be pursued by fresh proceedings. If both parties to the abortive action consent, no doubt the pleadings, discovery, etc which had taken place in the abortive action before the dissolution could be treated as having been steps taken in the new action. But that would be a matter of consent.'

346 *Smith v White Knight Laundry Ltd* [2001] EWCA Civ 660, [2001] 3 All ER 862.

against the company accrued on the date on which it would otherwise have accrued but for the dissolution. The purported acts of a dissolved company were not validated by the operation of the section but that did not mean that a cause of action could not accrue on the date it would otherwise have accrued. As Jonathan Parker LJ said:

> '... a crucial distinction is made between on the one hand the corporate existence of the company, which is restored as from the date of the dissolution, and on the other hand proceedings which had taken place during the period of dissolution (referred by Lord Blanesburgh as "corporate activity"). In *Morris v Harris* the House of Lords decided that purported acts of a dissolved, and hence non-existent, company were not validated by the subsequent avoidance of the dissolution. But that is not the instant case. In the instant case, all that is needed for the accrual of a cause of action against the company is corporate existence, no question of 'corporate activity', in the sense in which Lord Blanesburgh used that expression, arises[347].'

It can be concluded that the period during which a company is dissolved will be counted in reckoning whether or not a particular cause of action is statute barred. It should be noted, however, that proceedings initiated against a company before its dissolution, which remained pending at the time of dissolution, or which were commenced during the period of dissolution, are a nullity and are not validated by a subsequent restoration[348].

[23.133] *Re Walsh Maguire & O'Shea Ltd*[349] concerned an application by an alleged contingent creditor of a former company under s 310(1) of the CA 1963 to void the dissolution of the company following a members' voluntary winding up and the distribution of over €1 million to its members. The petitioner sought initially to rely on a single ground as justifying the avoiding of the dissolution, namely, that substantial damages had been claimed against the company in plenary proceedings initiated before the company was put into members' voluntary winding up which were pending when the company was dissolved where no allowance had been made by the company for the debt and so the voiding of the dissolution was to enable him to pursue his claim in the existing plenary proceedings. The court noted that the petitioner subsequently added an alternative ground, namely to have the company restored to enable him to pursue his claim against the company in fresh proceedings in proving in the liquidation.

The key issue to be decided in this case was whether the effect of voiding a dissolution could revive proceedings initiated before the dissolution but not finalised and now statute barred. This was the first case in which the Irish High Court had to look at the decision in *Morris v Harris*[350] and the other English authorities on the point.

[23.134] Laffoy J rejected the petitioner's claim that she should not follow the English authorities. After reviewing the authorities, the learned judge said:

> '10.5 ... as a matter of construction of the Act of 1963, it is not possible to ignore the difference in effect of an order made under s 310(1) and an order under s 311(8). In contradistinction to the wording of s 310(1) ... it was expressly stated in s 311(8) in its

347 *Smith v White Knight Laundry Ltd* [2001] EWCA Civ 660, [2001] 3 All ER 862 at 876.

348 *Morris v Harris* [1927] AC 252; *Re Philip Powis Ltd* [1997] 2 BCLC 481. See, generally, Keay, 'The Pursuit of Legal Proceedings Against Dissolved Companies' [2000] JBL 405.

349 *Re Walsh Maguire & O'Shea Ltd* [2011] IEHC 457.

350 *Morris v Harris* [1927] AC 252.

> original unamended form (ie before it was amended by the Companies (Amendment) No 2 Act 1999) that when an order is made that the name of the company be restored to the register under that provision – "... the company shall be deemed to have continued in existence as if its name had not been struck off; and the court may, by the order give such directions and make such provisions as seem just for placing the company and all other persons in the same position as nearly as may be as if the name of the company had not been struck off". Since the amendment of s 311(8) in 1999 the discretion of the Court has been broadened to empower it to make "*such other order as seems just*", including an order of the type set out in subs (8A).
>
> 10.6 When one compares s 310(1) with s 311(8), in my view, the intention of the Oireachtas as to the scope of the exercise of the Court's discretion under s 310 in the context of the effect of an order under that section becomes quite clear. In particular, I do not think that the words "*upon such terms as the court thinks fit*" in s 310 give the Court discretion to give ancillary directions or make ancillary provisions of the type envisaged in s 311(8). What the Oireachtas intended I believe was that, in an order under s 310(1), terms might be imposed, for example, as to bringing the winding up to a conclusion in a situation where the purpose of voiding the dissolution was to enable the liquidator to deal with some unfinished business, or to deal fairly with the liability for costs of the application.
>
> 10.7 In my view, if the declaration sought by the petitioner is made, it will have the effect stated in s 310(1), which I believe is the effect which was outlined in *Morris v Harris* and the English authorities in which it was followed, and also by O'Neill J in *Re Amantiss Enterprises Ltd*, albeit obiter. Accordingly, the Court's decision cannot be based on a proposition that the petitioner will be entitled to continue the plenary proceedings against the company if the dissolution is voided.'

The law in Ireland and England on the effect of voiding a dissolution following the winding up of a company on legal proceedings is, therefore, the same.

[23.135] The decision in *Re Walsh Maguire & O'Shea Ltd*[351] is also instructive in relation to the court's approach to applications to void dissolutions under s 310(1) of the CA 1963. In that case, Laffoy J made an order voiding the dissolution on the grounds that: the application was brought within the two-year period, the petitioner had standing to present the petition, and, on balance, the petitioner had established that he had a legitimate purpose in seeking to have the dissolution made void. While Laffoy J held that the existing proceedings against the company could not be continued on the company's reinstatement, the learned judge felt that it was not appropriate for her to determine on the evidence before the court whether or not new proceedings could be instituted or whether these would be statute barred. Granting the order to void the dissolution, Laffoy J refused, however, to allow the petitioner's nominee to be liquidator (that function falling to the original liquidator) and made it a condition of the order that if the petitioner was unsuccessful in his claim against the company, the director who defended the petition would be entitled to his costs of the application.

---

[351] *Re Walsh Maguire & O'Shea Ltd* [2011] IEHC 457.

[F] Winding Up Licensed Banks and Other Authorised Credit Institutions

[23.136] In Ireland, many licensed banks are private companies limited by shares. Indeed, of the few hundred banks licensed in Ireland, only a small number are or are required to be public limited companies whose equity securities are listed on a stock exchange. Most, especially those in the IFSC, are subsidiaries of international banks and the only securities they list are bonds which can be done through a private company[352].

[23.137] Where a licensed bank becomes insolvent the public interest can dictate that the rights of the bank's creditors lose their position of importance. Winding up a bank can precipitate financial turmoil, uncertainty and, if the bank is big enough – as Lehman Brothers was – international recession. Ordinarily, the legal entity that is a company is subjugated to the interests of its creditors – if it becomes insolvent, it is wound up and its assets distributed in accordance with the priority ordained by law. In the case of a licensed bank, sometimes, it will be too big or too systemically important to a nation to be allowed to fail. In these circumstances, the options are to either to *bail-out* (eg, the State pumps money into the bank by way of share capital) or *bail-in* (ie, force the bank's creditors to convert their debt to equity by taking shares in lieu of their debt) or, in an exceptional case, by the writing-down or writing-off of debt[353]. Either a bail-out or a bail-in can be accompanied by *nationalisation*, whereby the shares (usually worthless) in the bank are expropriated by the State on the understanding that if they have any worth the shareholders will be compensated[354]. Conceptually, the most difficult nettle to grasp is that the survival of an insolvent bank should be placed ahead of its creditors.

[23.138] While there have always been some special rules for the liquidation of licensed banks, the regime has been revised and updated by Part 7 of the Central Bank and Credit Institutions (Resolution) Act 2011 ('CBCIRA 2011'). The general rule is that the Companies Acts apply to the winding up of authorised credit institutions[355] subject to the provisions of Part 7 of the CBCIRA 2011[356]. The differences in the law applicable to the winding up of private companies which are banks compared with ordinary private companies are considered under the following headings:

1. Rights enjoyed by the Central Bank.
2. Rules applicable to liquidators of authorised credit institutions.
3. The liquidation committee.

---

[352] This is not to say that all banks are either PLCs or private companies limited by shares; a number of licensed banks in Ireland are public unlimited companies (eg, Bank of Ireland Mortgage Bank, AIB Mortgage Bank and IRBC Mortgage Bank)

[353] This has come to be known colloquially as 'burning' creditors, especially bondholders. A limited statutory power to write-down debt owed to subordinated bondholders was provided for in Part 4 of the Credit Institutions (Stabilisation) Act 2010.

[354] As happened in the case of Anglo Irish Bank Corporation Plc (now, Irish Bank Resolution Corporation Limited) by operation of the Anglo Irish Bank Corporation Act 2009.

[355] Authorised credit institution means: a bank licensed under s 9 of the Central Bank Act 1971 (which can be a company, including a private company), a building society and a credit union: s 2(1) of the CBCIRA 2011. Section 90 of the CBCIRA 2011 provides that Part 7 also has application to bodies incorporated outside the State.

[356] Section 76 of the CBCIRA 2011. Section 89 of the CBCIRA 2011 sets out a table of modifications to the Companies Acts that apply to the winding up of authorised credit institutions.

Rights enjoyed by the Central Bank

[23.139] In addition to those with *locus standi* to petition to have a company wound up, the Central Bank has, pursuant to s 77 of the CBCIRA 2011, a statutory right to present a petition to court for the winding up of an authorised credit institution on any of the following grounds:

> '(a) that in the opinion of the Bank, the winding-up of that credit institution would be in the public interest;
>
> (b) that that credit institution is, or in the opinion of the Bank may be, unable to meet its obligations to its creditors;
>
> (c) that that credit institution has failed to comply with a direction of the Bank—
>
> (i) in the case of the holder of a licence under section 9 of the Act of 1971, under section 21 of that Act, or
>
> (ii) in the case of a building society, under section 40(2) of the Building Societies Act 1989, or
>
> (iii) in the case of a credit union, under section 87 of the Credit Union Act 1997;
>
> (d) that that credit institution's licence or authorisation (as applicable) has been revoked and (in the case of the holder of a licence under section 9 of the Act of 1971) that it has ceased to carry on banking business;
>
> (e) that the Bank considers that it is in the interest of persons having deposits (including deposits on current accounts) with that credit institution that it be wound up.

Another difference in the law applicable to petitioning to wind up a company that is a licensed bank is that no person other than the Central Bank may present a petition to the Central Office of the High Court, advertise such a petition or take any other step or make any other publication concerning that person's intention to cause an authorised credit institution to be wound up unless the putative petitioner has given 10 days' written notice to the Bank of his intention to do so *and* the Bank has confirmed in writing that it has no objection to the person so doing[357].

[23.140] Other rights of the Central Bank are: to apply to convert a voluntary liquidation to a court liquidation[358]; to receive all notices and documents that creditors receive even if the Central Bank is not a creditor[359]; and where it is not the petitioner, to be a notice party in all applications brought during the course of a winding up and to make representations to the court[360].

Rules applicable to liquidators of authorised credit institutions

[23.141] Although the law relating to liquidators is considered in the next chapter, it is convenient to treat all differences in the law applicable to authorised credit institutions here and so the rules relating to liquidators are considered here. First, only a liquidator approved by the Central Bank may be appointed to an authorised credit institution[361]. Once appointed, the essential difference is that the liquidator of an authorised credit institution is given two statutory objectives by s 80(1) of the CBCIRA 2011:

---

357 Section 78(1) of the CBCIRA 2011.
358 Section 78(2) of the CBCIRA 2011.
359 Section 78(3) of the CBCIRA 2011.
360 Section 78(4) of the CBCIRA 2011.
361 Section 79(1) of the CBCIRA 2011.

'(a) Objective 1—

(i) to facilitate the Bank in ensuring that each eligible depositor receives the prescribed amount payable under Regulation 4 of the Regulations of 1995 from the deposit protection account, or

(ii) to facilitate the Bank in transferring that amount from the deposit protection account to another authorised credit institution or to a credit institution approved by the Bank, to hold that amount on behalf of each such eligible depositor;

(b) Objective 2, to wind up the affairs of the authorised credit institution so as to achieve the best results for that credit institution's creditors as a whole.

It is provided that in the event of a conflict between Objective 1 and Objective 2, Objective 1 takes precedence and that the liquidator shall begin working towards both objectives immediately upon his or her appointment and that the liquidator and the Central Bank shall cooperate in the pursuit of those objectives[362]. The duties of a liquidator under Part 7 are expressed to be in addition to the other duties of a liquidator and one of those additional duties is to comply with a request of the Central Bank for information in relation to the liquidation, and the liquidator is authorised to provide the Central Bank with any other information that the liquidator thinks might be useful for the purpose of cooperating in the pursuit of Objective[363].

The liquidation committee

[23.142] The optional committee of inspection under s 232 of the CA 1963 in an ordinary winding up is replaced in the winding up of an authorised credit institution by a mandatory *liquidation committee*: s 83(1) of the CBCIRA 2011. As soon as practicable after the court makes a winding-up order in respect of an authorised credit institution, the Central Bank must nominate two individuals and the Minister for Finance one individual who will comprise the liquidation committee, with the function of ensuring that the liquidator properly carries out his or her functions under Part 7 and for the duration of the liquidation committee's existence, s 232 of the CA 1963 shall not apply. The liquidation committee's procedures are governed by the CBCIRA 2011[364]. The liquidation committee is also required to make recommendations to the liquidator concerning the achievement of Objective 1[365]. The liquidator must report to the liquidation committee on request and is required to keep it informed of progress towards achieving Objective 1 and shall notify it when it has been achieved entirely or so far as is reasonably practicable. Where the liquidation committee is satisfied that Objective 1 has been so achieved, it can pass a so-called 'full payment resolution' whereupon it shall cease to exist. Where it is not satisfied that Objective 1 has been so achieved, it can apply to court under s 280 of the CA 1963 for directions[366]. Where the liquidation committee ceases to exist and a committee of inspection is constituted, the Central Bank is empowered to attend its meetings, receive copies of documents and make representations to it[367].

362 Section 80(2) and (3) of the CBCIRA 2011.

363 Section 80(4) and (5) of the CBCIRA 2011.

364 Section 85 of the CBCIRA 2011.

365 Section 87 of the CBCIRA 2011.

366 Section 84(3) of the CBCIRA 2011.

367 Section 86 of the CBCIRA 2011.

Chapter 24

Liquidators

Introduction

[24.001] This chapter considers the persons who are charged by law with the winding up of companies and the realisation and distribution of their assets in accordance with law, namely, liquidators[1]. The law relating to liquidators is considered under the following headings:

1. The four types of liquidator.
2. Liquidators' qualifications.
3. The appointment and removal of liquidators.
4. Liquidators' duties.
5. Liquidators' powers.
6. The remuneration of liquidators.
7. Foreign liquidators and the EU Council Regulation on Insolvency Proceedings.
8. The Director of Corporate Enforcement's power to supervise liquidators.

The issues arising under these headings shall be considered, with appropriate distinctions being made between the various types of liquidator and winding up.

The four types of liquidator

[24.002] There are four distinct types of liquidator: members' voluntary liquidators; creditors' voluntary liquidators; official liquidators; and provisional liquidators. All liquidators stand in a fiduciary relationship to the company to which they are appointed.[2]

(a) Voluntary liquidators appointed by members and creditors

[24.003] In both members' voluntary liquidations and creditors' voluntary liquidations the person charged with the winding up of a company is called a *voluntary liquidator.* Although both types of liquidation are distinguished by the fact that in one the company is solvent, whereas in the other it is not, the commonality is that in both, the winding up is done privately and is not the subject of direct court supervision. Unlike an official liquidator, a voluntary liquidator is not, *ex officio*[3], an officer of the court and he is best

1 See, generally, Lynch-Fannon & Murphy, *Corporate Insolvency and Rescue* (2nd edn, 2012, Bloomsbury Professional) at Ch 5; and Bailey, Grove & Smith, *Corporate Insolvency: Law and Practice* (2nd edn, 2001), ch 10.

2 *Re Gertzenstein Ltd* [1937] Ch 115 and *Re Dr Developments (Youghal) Ltd* [2011] IEHC 307. See para **[24.004]** *post*.

3 A liquidator who is, by profession, a solicitor would be an 'officer of the court', but would be such by virtue of being a solicitor, not because of his position as a liquidator.

considered as a simple *agent* of the company[4]. The general rule is that a voluntary liquidator contracts with others as agent of the company and does not have a personal liability[5].

(b) Official liquidators

[24.004] Liquidators appointed by the court in a compulsory winding up are termed *official liquidators*[6]. In *Re Dr Developments (Youghal) Ltd*[7], Finlay Geoghegan J said:

> 'The official liquidator is an agent of the company with fiduciary obligations arising from his office and with statutory obligations imposed on him by the Companies Acts.'

An official liquidator is simultaneously an officer of the court and an agent of the company, owing fiduciary and statutory obligations to both. However, a liquidator is not a trustee for the shareholders or creditors[8].

(c) Provisional liquidators

[24.005] The final type of liquidator is termed a *provisional liquidator*. Such liquidators are appointed where a petition has been presented to have a company wound up compulsorily, but before a winding-up order is made where it is apprehended that a company's assets are required to be preserved immediately[9]. The position of a provisional liquidator is, by definition, provisional and an official liquidator will normally be appointed immediately upon the actual making of the winding-up order.

Liquidators' qualifications

[24.006] Notwithstanding that Irish company law does not impose any positive qualification requirement on liquidators, the vast majority of appointees are members of a recognised accountancy body[10]. Unless a person is specifically disqualified from becoming a liquidator, in theory, anybody can. Considering that liquidators are fiduciary agents who administer other people's money, it is thought that this is a most unsatisfactory state of affairs[11]. Section 300 of the CA 1963 merely says that a body corporate is not qualified to be a liquidator and any body corporate acting as a liquidator shall be liable to a fine, and the appointment will be void, *ab initio*.

[24.007] Persons who are specifically stated *not* to be qualified for appointment as liquidator of a company are dealt with in s 300A of the CA 1963[12], which lists:

---

4 See *Re Tailteann Freight Services Ltd* [1975] IR 376.

5 *Stewart v Engel* [2000] BCC 741, [1999] TLR 804.

6 Section 228(b) of the CA 1963.

7 *Re Dr Developments (Youghal) Ltd* [2011] IEHC 307, at para 11.

8 *Re Belfast Empire Theatre of Varieties Ltd* [1963] IR 41.

9 See para **[24.016]** *post*.

10 Solicitors will sometimes act as liquidator especially in a solvent members' voluntary winding up where the assets of a company are being distributed *in specie*: see Ch 25, *The Realisation and Distribution of Assets in a Winding Up*, para **[25.196]**.

11 See the *Company Law Review Group's First Report* (31 December 2001), ch 13, 'The Regulation of Insolvency Practitioners' and para 13.3.

12 Inserted by s 146 of the CA 1990.

- a person who was an officer[13] or employee of the company in liquidation within 12 months prior to the commencement of the winding up;
- a parent, spouse, brother, sister or child of an officer of the company, save with leave of the court;
- a partner or employee of an officer or employee of the company;
- a person disqualified on the basis of the foregoing grounds for appointment as liquidator of any other body corporate which is that company's subsidiary or holding company, or a subsidiary of the company's holding company, or would be disqualified if the body corporate were a company.

Where a liquidator becomes disqualified by reason of the foregoing, he must vacate office and give notice to the company or the company and the creditors, depending on the type of winding up[14]. To act as a liquidator while disqualified is an offence[15]. The Minister for Jobs, Enterprise and Innovation may, by regulations, add to the list of persons set out in s 300A of the CA 1963 who shall not be qualified for appointment as a liquidator: s 237 of the CA 1990.

[24.008] In *Re Swedex Windows & Doors Ltd*[16], the official liquidator to a company sought a declaration that he was not a person who was disqualified by ss 300 or 300A of the CA 1963 from being a liquidator and that he was entitled to continue to act as such. The circumstances were that the liquidator, Mr Michael McAteer, had been appointed provisional liquidator on 23 March 2007 and official liquidator on 16 April 2007. Subsequently, Mr McAteer became a partner in the firm of Grant Thornton on 1 November 2008. Prior to that, in July 2007, the former auditor (and, therefore, *officer*) of the company, Mr Colin Feely, had also joined Grant Thornton as a partner. Finlay Geoghegan J accepted the liquidator's submission that s 300A(1)(c) of the CA 1963 is couched in the present tense and should be construed as disqualifying a person who, at the relevant time, *is* a partner of a person who *is then* an officer of the company. The learned judge found that Mr Feely was not an auditor of the company in November 2008 and so not an officer for the purposes of s 300A(1) at that time because the effect of the winding-up order of 16 April 2017 was to discharge him from the office of auditor.

The appointment and removal of liquidators

(a) Members' voluntary liquidators

[24.009] Section 258(1) of the CA 1963 provides that in a members' voluntary winding up, the members in general meeting shall appoint a liquidator for the purpose of winding up the affairs of the company. The steps leading up to that appointment are considered in the previous chapter[17]. All voluntary liquidators appointed in either a members'[18], or creditors'[19], winding up must give their prior written consent to the proposed

[13] References to 'officer' or 'servant' are deemed to include references to 'auditor'.

[14] Or to the court in a compulsory winding up.

[15] Section 300A(4) of the CA 1963. Note that s 300A is not retrospective: s 300A(5).

[16] *Re Swedex Windows & Doors Ltd* [2010] IEHC 237.

[17] See, generally, Ch 23, *Winding Up Companies*.

[18] Section 276A(1) of the CA 1963.

[19] Section 274 of the CA 1963.

appointment[20]. Section 276A(1) of the CA 1963 provides that a liquidator's appointment is of no effect unless he gives his prior consent in writing. If the liquidator appointed by the members dies or resigns, the company in general meeting may fill the vacancy[21]. The court can appoint a voluntary liquidator where no liquidator is acting, or can remove one and appoint another where cause is shown[22].

(b) Creditors' voluntary liquidators

[24.010] In the case of a creditors' voluntary winding up, where a liquidator or his representative is not present at the meeting at which he is appointed, the chairman of the meeting is responsible for notifying him within seven days of his appointment to enable him to give his consent. The failure to comply can lead to a fine on conviction.

[24.011] Section 301A of the CA 1963[23] provides that any creditor who has a connection with a liquidator proposed by the other creditors must make this known to the chairman, who must in turn inform the creditors' meeting. The chairman himself must inform the meeting of any connection which he may have with the proposed liquidator. 'Connection' in this regard means being the parent, spouse, brother, sister, child, partner or employee of the proposed liquidator[24]. The failure to disclose a connection can result in a fine on conviction and the court can take such non-disclosure into consideration on an application for the appointment or removal of a liquidator[25].

[24.012] Where the liquidator appointed by the company's creditors dies, resigns or otherwise vacates office, the creditors may appoint another in his stead unless the deceased liquidator was appointed by or at the direction of the court[26]. Again, it should also be noted that the court can appoint a voluntary liquidator where no liquidator is acting, or can remove one and appoint another where cause is shown[27]. Alternatively, a creditors' liquidator can be displaced by an official liquidator where, on application being made to court, it is ordered that a creditors' voluntary winding up be converted to an official liquidation[28].

(c) Official liquidators

[24.013] Section 225 of the CA 1963 provides that for the purpose of conducting the proceedings in winding up a company and performing such duties in reference thereto as the court may impose, 'the court may appoint a liquidator or liquidators'[29]. It follows that a liquidator can only be appointed by the court where the court has ordered that a

20 As inserted by s 133 of the CA 1990.

21 Section 259(1) of the CA 1963. Such meeting can be convened by any contributory, or the other liquidators if there are more than one.

22 Section 277(1) and (2) of the CA 1963. As to 'cause shown' see para **[24.014]**.

23 As inserted by s 147 of the CA 1990.

24 Section 301A(4) of the CA 1963.

25 Section 301A(5) and (6) respectively of the CA 1963.

26 Section 270 of the CA 1963.

27 Section 277(1) and (2) of the CA 1963. As to 'cause shown' see para **[24.014]**.

28 See Ch 23, *Winding Up Companies*, para **[23.113]**.

29 Where the court appoints more than one liquidator, it is required, by s 228(f) of the CA 1963, to 'declare whether any act by this Act required or authorised to be done by the liquidator is to be done by all or any one of the persons appointed'.

company be wound up, upon its being satisfied as to the application of one of the grounds listed in s 213 of the CA 1963[30]. Section 228(a) of the CA 1963 empowers the court to require an official liquidator to enter into a bond by way of security for the performance of his functions[31]. An appointment is of no effect unless the person nominated has prior to his appointment signified his written consent to the appointment: s 276A(1) of the CA 1963. Once appointed by order of the court, the liquidator must within 21 days of his appointment publish, in *Iris Oifigiúil*, a notice of his appointment and deliver to the registrar of companies an office copy of the order appointing him[32]. The court can fill any vacancy in the office of official liquidator[33].

[24.014] A liquidator appointed by the court can resign or be removed by the court. Section 228(c) of the CA 1963 provides that a liquidator appointed by the court 'may resign or, on cause shown, be removed by the court'[34]. In *Re Doherty Advertising Ltd*[35], McGovern J found that a person who owed money to the company (ie, a debtor of the company) did not have *locus standi* to have a liquidator removed, saying:

> 'From the authorities opened to the court and the articles referred to I am satisfied that the applicant is not a person qualified to make the application for the removal of the liquidator in this case. While it could be said that the applicant may become a creditor if he repays the monies alleged to have been improperly obtained by him he is, at the time of this application, and for the purposes of this application, challenging the liquidator in a manner which puts his interests adverse to those of the creditors in the liquidation. I therefore hold that the applicant is not a person entitled to bring this application.
>
> But in any event the applicant has not shown sufficient cause for the removal of the liquidator in this case. The burden of proof is on the applicant to have a liquidator removed. I am not satisfied that the applicant has discharged this burden by showing unfitness of the liquidator to act in this matter.'

It has been held by the common law judicial equivalent of the universal-wrench – the Privy Council – in *Deloitte & Touche AG v Johnson*[36], a decision referred to by McGovern J, that the proper persons to make application are those who have an interest in the outcome of the liquidation. It was observed there that a contributory who was not a creditor could not apply to have a liquidator removed. In that case, the applicants were a firm of accountants who had acted as auditors to a company in liquidation and who were being sued for negligence. Following various mergers of accountancy practices, the applicants alleged that the liquidators had a conflict of interest by reason of the fact that

30 See Ch 23, *Winding Up Companies*, para **[23.068]** *et seq.*

31 This provides: 'the court may determine whether any and what security is to be given by a liquidator on his appointment.'

32 Section 227(1) of the CA 1963. Although s 72 of the IFCMPA 2005 substituted 'the Companies Registration Office Gazette' for '*Iris Oifigiúil*' it has not been commenced. Failure to do so is punishable by a class C fine: s 227(2) of the CA 1963.

33 Section 228(e) of the CA 1963.

34 A conflict of interest (see *Re P Turner (Wilsden) Ltd* [1987] BCLC 149 and *Re Corbenstoke Ltd (No 2)* [1990] BCLC 60) and a preference of shareholders (*Re Rubber and Produce Investment Trust* [1915] 1 Ch 382) have both been found to be 'causes' where it was appropriate to remove a liquidator.

35 *Re Doherty Advertising Ltd* [2006] IEHC 198.

36 *Deloitte & Touche AG v Johnson* [1999] BCC 992.

a firm of accountants, whom the applicants claimed had failed to provide them with material information, had now merged with the liquidators' firm. The Lords upheld the Cayman Islands' Court of Appeal decision that the applicants' application be struck-out. If there was a conflict, that was a matter for those who would be affected, namely, the company's creditors. This case was cited by McGovern J in an application brought by a debtor (or alleged debtor) of a company to remove a liquidator. The question before the court was whether such a debtor could apply under s 228(c) of the CA 1963 for the removal of a liquidator (in whom the creditors and contributories of a company appeared to have confidence) on the ground of a conflict of interest.

[24.015] In the decision of the Federal Court of Australia in *City & Suburban Pty Ltd v Smith*[37], it was stated of the court's entitlement to remove a liquidator 'on cause shown' that:

> 'It has long been accepted that the section and its predecessors were not confined to situations where it is established that there is personal unfitness, impropriety or breach of duty on the part of the liquidator. Cause is shown for removal whenever the court is satisfied that it is for the better conduct of the liquidation or, put another way, it is for the general advantage of those interested in the assets of the company that a liquidator be removed[38].'

Fair play to a liquidator is secondary to the expediency of the liquidation. In *Re Adam Eyton Ltd*; *ex p Charlesworth*[39], Bowen LJ said:

> 'Of course, fair play to the liquidator himself is not to be left out of sight, but the measure of due cause is the substantial and real interest of the liquidation.'

In the Australian case of *City & Suburban Pty Ltd v Smith*[40] it was held that cause had been shown to justify the removal of the liquidator where it had been established that:

– the liquidator had failed to conduct a proper investigation into allegations that the directors of the company had been in breach of their fiduciary duties;
– there were allegations that the liquidator had himself been in breach of his fiduciary duties to the company;
– there were allegations of over-delegation by the liquidator of his functions to his employees giving rise to his having an allegedly insufficient grasp of the issues involved in the liquidation; and
– the liquidator's insensitivity to the committee of inspection.

In *Re Trinity Products (Limerick) Ltd*[41], it was reported in The Irish Times that Finlay Geoghegan J removed an official liquidator on the grounds that the fact that he was

37 *City & Suburban Pty Ltd v Smith* [1998] Federal Court of Australia of 9 July 1998.

38 Authorities cited included: *Re Adam Eyton Ltd; ex p Charlesworth* (1887) 36 Ch D 299 at 306; *Re The Mutual Life Stock Financial and Agency Company Ltd* (1886) 12 VLR 777; and *Dallinger v Halcha Holdings Pty Ltd* (1995) 134 ALR 178 at 183–184.

39 *Re Adam Eyton Ltd; ex p Charlesworth* (1887) 36 Ch D 299 at 306.

40 *City & Suburban Pty Ltd v Smith* [1998] Federal Court of Australia of 9 July 1998.

41 *Re Trinity Products Ltd*, an application reported in (2005) Irish Times, of 26 April (Finlay Geoghegan J).

restricted as a director under s 150 of the CA 1990 and had been censured by the Institute of Chartered Accountants in Ireland had not been disclosed to the court. The learned judge was reported to have said that those facts alone did not automatically disqualify the person from being a liquidator, and it might well have been that on a full examination of all relevant facts the court would have appointed him, these were relevant facts that should have been considered by the court when deciding whether or not he was a fit and proper person to be appointed official liquidator.

(d) Provisional liquidators

[24.016] After a petition to have a company wound up has been presented, and before the making of an order for the winding up of the company, the court may, on application being made, order the appointment of a provisional liquidator under s 226(1) of the CA 1963. Such an application will usually be made by the petitioning creditor[42] who is concerned that, unless the assets of the company are immediately preserved[43], they are likely to be spirited away by the controllers of the company, or other anxious creditors, in disregard of the law of distribution on an insolvency[44]. However, where a provisional liquidator is appointed on foot of the petitioning creditor's application, he will not represent that creditor alone and must act in the interests of all of the company's creditors[45]. The appointment of a provisional liquidator is intrinsically detrimental[46] to a company and is a jurisdiction that will be exercised by the courts in the clearest of cases only.

The fears of the applicant must be supported by affidavit, showing 'sufficient ground'[47]. It has been held that the appointment of a provisional liquidator has the effect of terminating automatically the authority of agents who had been appointed to act on the company's behalf by its directors[48]. In this regard, the application for the appointment of a provisional liquidator may be seen as analogous to the application for a *Mareva* injunction by a plaintiff fearful that his litigation, if successful, could result in a

42 RSC, Ord 74, r 14(1) permits application to be made by either a creditor, contributory or the company itself. In *Re a company (No 002180 of 1996)* [1996] 2 BCLC 409, it was said by Knox J that applicants for the appointment of a provisional liquidator should, as a general rule, establish their standing to present a petition.

43 Note, though, that by s 229(2) of the CA 1963 for as long as there is no liquidator, all property of the company shall be deemed to be in the custody of the court.

44 In *Re EAEL*, an application reported in (1998) Irish Times, 12 February, it was reported that a provisional liquidator was appointed on the application of the Revenue Commissioners in circumstances where it was claimed that the company proposed to sell (at fair value) its assets to another company ahead of its inevitable liquidation. The newspaper report stated that the Revenue Commissioners were unhappy with the proposed approach to the sale of the company's assets and alleged that there was a connection with the company to which it was proposed to sell the assets.

45 *Bank of Credit and Commerce International SA (No 2)* [1992] BCLC 579.

46 *Re a Company (No 002180 of 1996)* [1996] 2 BCLC 409.

47 *Bank of Credit and Commerce International SA (No 2)* [1992] BCLC 579.

48 *Pacific and General Insurance Co Ltd v Hazell* [1997] BCC 400.

Pyrrhic victory[49]. Indeed, such an injunction may also be sought in a winding up so as to hold the threat of contempt of court over anyone who chooses to disregard the order[50].

[24.017] The primary purpose of the appointment of a provisional liquidator is to ensure the *preservation* of corporate assets, and thus to enable the official liquidator to effect an orderly *realisation* and subsequent *distribution* of those assets[51]. This is the purpose of the winding-up order itself, and the appointment of the provisional liquidator is merely to ensure that no assets are spirited away. Thus, s 229(1) of the CA 1963 provides that on either the making of the winding-up order *or* the appointment of a provisional liquidator, either the official or provisional liquidator 'shall take into his custody or under his control all the property and things in action to which the company is or appears to be entitled'.

The order of appointment must, by the Rules of the Superior Courts 1986 ('RSC'), Ord 74, r 14(2), describe the property which the provisional liquidator is ordered to take into his possession.

[24.018] A provisional liquidator is displaced by the appointment of an official liquidator, or he can be removed by order of the court where it refuses the petition to have the company wound up. In *Re Kingscroft Insurance Co Ltd*[52], it was held that upon the discharge of a provisional liquidator and the dismissal of the winding-up petition, any orders made against persons during the proceedings will also be discharged because the purpose behind the making of such ancillary orders no longer exists. The powers of provisional liquidators are considered below[53].

[24.019] *Re Coolfadda Developers Ltd*[54] involved a novel application by a company to which a provisional liquidator had been appointed, to adjourn a winding-up petition and allow the continuation of the provisional liquidator to enable the company to complete building contracts. In the High Court, Laffoy J refused the application to adjourn the winding-up petition even though it had been claimed that the company would do better in an extended provisional liquidation than were it to go into official liquidation. The basis for this assertion was that returns to the company (and therefore, ultimately, its creditors) would be maximised were the employers on construction contracts with the company not in a position to terminate those contracts, as they would be able to do if a winding-up order was made. The refusal of the High Court to adjourn the winding-up petition was upheld by Denham J in the Supreme Court who held that although there

---

49 In *Cope v Destination Education Pty Ltd* [1999] (12 January 1999, unreported) Supreme Court, New South Wales, an application for a *Mareva* injunction was declined on the grounds that the proofs had not been made out, but in the circumstances of that case, the judge said that the plaintiff should give consideration to applying for the appointment of a provisional liquidator.

50 See, eg, *Re Mark Synnott (Life and Pensions) Brokers Ltd* (1991) Irish Times, 2 July where after the making of a winding-up order, *Mareva* injunctions were applied for, as was a *Bayer* order to prevent the directors from leaving the country. This latter order was agreed on consent.

51 The importance of the preservation of corporate property in a provisional liquidator's function was stressed in *Re Bank of Credit and Commerce International SA* [1992] BCC 83.

52 *Re Kingscroft Insurance Co Ltd* [1994] 2 BCLC 80.

53 See para **[24.041]**.

54 *Re Coolfadda Developers Ltd* [2009] IEHC 263, [2009] IESC 54. See Ch 23, *Winding Up Companies*, para **[23.063]**.

was jurisdiction in an exceptional case to adjourn, from time to time, a winding-up petition, such a jurisdiction would rarely arise[55].

Liquidators' duties

[24.020] All liquidators, whether appointed by the members[56], the creditors[57] or the court[58] are appointed for the purpose of winding up the affairs of the company, which involves the realisation and distribution of a company's assets in accordance with law. The myriad issues arising in the discharge of liquidators' primary duties of *realisation* and *distribution* of assets on liquidation are considered comprehensively in Chapter 25.

(a) Fiduciary duties

[24.021] As recently noted by Finlay Geoghegan J in *Re Dr Developments (Youghal) Ltd*[59], in the discharge of their statutory obligations and duties, liquidators owe fiduciary duties to the company, as opposed to the individual creditors[60]. Liquidators may not make a secret profit as a result of their office[61] and are liable to account to the company where they do so.

(b) Statutory duties to members

[24.022] Liquidators owe many duties to members and these are referred to throughout this chapter. One particular duty owed by the liquidator in a members' voluntary winding up is that contained in s 261 of the CA 1963, which obliges a members' liquidator to call a meeting of the company's creditors where he is of the opinion that the company will not be able to meet its debts in full within the time specified in the directors' declaration of solvency[62]. This is probably the most important duty of voluntary liquidators in a members' voluntary winding up.

(c) Statutory duties to creditors

[24.023] Liquidators also owe many duties to creditors. In a creditors' voluntary winding up, the creditors can appoint a committee of inspection, pursuant to s 268(1) of the CA 1963[63]. In addition to such meetings as the committee of inspection holds, the liquidator is under a duty to call a meeting of the creditors and of the company at the end of the first year of the winding up, and within three months from the end of each succeeding year. The liquidator is obliged to lay before these meetings an account of his acts and dealings and of the conduct of the winding up during the preceding year and within seven days to send a copy of such account to the registrar of companies.

---

55 *MHMH Ltd and ors v Carwood Barker Holdings Ltd* [2006] 1 BCLC 279 cited as an example of where such an exceptional jurisdiction might arise: see, further, Ch 23, *Winding Up Companies*, para **[23.063]** *et seq*.

56 Section 258(1) of the CA 1963.

57 Section 267(1) of the CA 1963.

58 Section 225 of the CA 1963.

59 *Re Dr Developments (Youghal) Ltd* [2011] IEHC 307.

60 *Knowles v Scott* [1891] 1 Ch 717. A liquidator can, however, assume direct duties to creditors: *A&J Fabrications (Batley) Ltd v Grant Thornton* [1998] 2 BCLC 227, [1999] BCC 807.

61 *Re Gertzenstein Ltd* [1936] 3 All ER 341.

62 See, further, Ch 23, *Winding Up Companies*, at para **[23.004]**.

63 See, further, Ch 23, *Winding Up Companies*, at para **[23.031]**.

[24.024] In an official or compulsory winding up, the court may direct the liquidator to summon a meeting of the creditors of the company, or separate meetings of the creditors and contributories, for the purpose of determining whether or not an application is to be made to court for the appointment of a committee of inspection[64]. Where a committee of inspection is appointed, it will act in conjunction with the liquidator. It has been said of a committee of inspection that:

> 'Their task is to superintend and assist the liquidator in the performance of his duties and to watch over the interests of particular groups of creditors or contributories whom they are appointed to represent[65].'

When a company is insolvent, its creditors are the beneficiaries of whatever assets it has. Just as it has been held that directors of insolvent companies owe duties to creditors[66], it follows that where the directors are displaced, the person with supervening authority – the liquidator – should be amenable to creditor supervision. In an official liquidation, the court will determine who are to be the members of the committee. In respect of disputes that arise between the meetings of creditors and contributories, the court has jurisdiction to make any order[67]. The mechanics for the conduct of committees' of inspection are set out in s 223 of the CA 1963. Liquidators of private companies that are licensed banks have additional duties under the Central Bank and Credit Institutions Resolution Act 2011[68].

(d) The statutory duty to report to the Director of Corporate Enforcement

[24.025] Finally, it may be noted that by s 56 of the CLEA 2001 the liquidators of all insolvent companies are obliged to make a report to the Director of Corporate Enforcement on the conduct of the insolvent company's directors and, unless advised otherwise, must make application to have the directors restricted pursuant to s 150 of the CA 1990[69].

[24.026] Section 56(1) of the CLEA 2001 provides that the form of the liquidator's report will be prescribed by statutory instrument. A statutory instrument[70] has prescribed the form of the liquidator's report, which is a 10-page document, divided into seven sections:

- Liquidator's details.
- Company details.
- Company directors.
- Statement of affairs, accounts and report to creditors.
- Proceedings.

---

64 Section 232(1) of the CA 1963.

65 See the decision of the Federal Court of Australia in *City & Suburban Pty Ltd et al v Smith* [1998] Federal Court of Australia, 9 July 1998 where this passage was quoted from McPerson, *Law of Company Liquidation* (3rd edn, 1997, O'Donovan (ed)) at p 236.

66 *Re Frederick Inns Ltd* [1994] 1 ILRM 387.

67 Section 232(2) of the CA 1963.

68 See Ch 23, *Winding Up Companies*, at para **[23.141]**.

69 See Ch 28, *Compliance and Enforcement*, para **[28.062]**.

70 Company Law Enforcement Act 2001 (Section 56) Regulations 2002 (SI No 324 of 2002).

- Final report.
- Liquidator's statement.

Liquidators' powers

[24.027] The far-reaching extent of liquidators' duties is underscored by the fact that, on their appointment, liquidators will, generally, displace companies' directors. On the appointment of a members' voluntary liquidator[71], the powers of a company's directors cease, except so far as the company in general meeting or the liquidator sanctions their continuance. On the appointment of a creditors' voluntary liquidator[72], the powers of a company's directors shall cease except so far as the committee of inspection or if there is no committee, the creditors, sanction their continuance. Similarly, the appointment of a provisional liquidator[73] and an official liquidator will displace the powers of the directors to manage the company. The powers of liquidators are considered here as follows:

(a) Powers of official liquidators.
(b) Powers of provisional liquidators.
(c) Powers of voluntary liquidators.
(d) Restrictions on the exercise of powers by members' voluntary liquidators and other restrictions.
(e) Seeking directions from the court.

(a) Powers of official liquidators

[24.028] The statutory powers of official liquidators[74] are detailed in s 231 of the CA 1963. A twofold distinction can be made between official liquidators' powers that are exercisable with the sanction of the court or of the committee of inspection and those that are exercisable without prior sanction but subject to the control of the court. In addition, it should be noted that the creditors and contributories of a company that is in official or compulsory court liquidation have a statutory right to make application in relation to the exercise or proposed exercise of an official liquidator's powers under s 231.

(i) Powers exercisable with the sanction of the court or committee of inspection

[24.029] Section 231(1) of the CA 1963 provides that an official liquidator shall have power, with the sanction of the court or of the committee of inspection, to do the following:

> '(a) to bring or defend any action or other legal proceedings in the name and on behalf of the company;
>
> (b) to carry on the business of the company so far as may be necessary for the beneficial winding up thereof;

71 Section 258(2) of the CA 1963.

72 Section 269(3) of the CA 1963. On where no liquidator is appointed, see *Re A Company (No 006341 of 1992)* [1994] 1 BCLC 225.

73 *Re Mawcon Ltd* [1969] 1 WLR 78.

74 See Milman, 'Liquidators: Powers and Constraints' (1997) *Palmer's In Company,* Issue 7/97, 17 July 1997.

(c) to appoint a solicitor to assist him in the performance of his duties;

(d) to pay any classes of creditors in full;

(e) to make any compromise or arrangement with creditors or persons claiming to be creditors, or having or alleging themselves to have any claim present or future, certain or contingent, ascertained or unascertained or sounding only in damages against the company, or whereby the company may be rendered liable;

(f) to compromise all calls and liabilities to calls, debts and liabilities capable of resulting in debts, and all claims, present or future, certain or contingent, ascertained or sounding only in damages, subsisting or supposed to subsist between the company and a contributory or alleged contributory or other debtor or persons apprehending liability to the company, and all questions in any way relating to or affecting the assets or winding up of the company, on such terms as may be agreed, and take any security for the discharge of any such call, debt, liability or claim, and give a complete discharge in respect thereof.'

Some of the more significant powers conferred but subject to the sanction of the court or a committee of inspection are considered in the paragraphs that follow.

[24.030] Legal proceedings cannot be brought or defended in the name and on behalf of a company in liquidation without the sanction of the court or committee of inspection[75]. In *Re Greendale Developments Ltd*[76], the official liquidator of a company that was being wound up by the court applied for an order pursuant to s 231(1)(a) of the CA 1963 granting him liberty to continue two plenary actions. In the course of her judgment (see below[77]) Laffoy J said:

> 'The decision of the court on a contested application to continue proceedings under s 231 is qualitatively different from the decision of a board of directors of a solvent company in relation to prosecuting litigation. The decision of the board of directors should be informed by the interests of the company, not by the sectional interests of individual shareholders or creditors. Once a winding-up order is made, the company is doomed to extinction. The winding up process is the process of the administration of the assets of the company: their collection, realisation and distribution in discharge of the liabilities of the company to the creditors and of the entitlement of its contributories in accordance with the scheme of priorities in the Companies Acts. Insofar as the Companies Acts give an entitlement to a creditor or a contributory to be heard by the Court in relation to a matter arising in the winding up, in my view, the Court is required to have regard to the sectional interest of that creditor or contributory and, in particular, to the protection of his legal entitlement to a distribution from the assets of the company as defined by the Companies Acts[78].'

Accordingly, when it comes to an application for liberty to bring or defend legal proceedings, the court will have regard to whether the interests of the ultimate beneficiaries of the fruits of that litigation will be furthered[79]. In *Cork County Council v*

75 Section 231(1)(a) of the CA 1963.

76 *Re Greendale Developments Ltd* [1997] 3 IR 540 (Laffoy J).

77 At para **[24.004]**.

78 *Re Greendale Developments Ltd* [1997] 3 IR 540 at 547.

79 In *Re Greenhaven Motors Ltd* [1997] BCC 547, a contributory's challenge to a liquidator's right to settle legal proceedings against a third party was rejected on the grounds that it had not been shown that there would be a sufficient surplus after debts, to which he would be entitled.

CB Readymix Ltd[80], the Supreme Court held that only the liquidator who had been appointed to a company that was in the course of being wound up had *locus standi* to bring an appeal against a court judgment on behalf of the company.

[24.031] Another power that requires the sanction of the court or of a committee of inspection is the carrying on of the business of the company, so far as may be necessary for the beneficial winding up of the company[81]. This power recognises that sometimes, to realise assets for their true value, it will be necessary to continue in business, eg, to convert relatively worthless work in progress into valuable finished products. One of the reasons why the court will be loath to allow business be carried on for any length of time is because debts and other liabilities incurred by the company in the course of such post-liquidation trading in the *bona fide* belief that they were necessary for the beneficial winding up of the company will have priority to pre-liquidation debts[82].

[24.032] Where there is no committee of inspection, the court may provide in any order that the liquidator may exercise the powers detailed in s 231(1)(a) of the CA 1963 (bringing or defending legal proceedings) or (b) (carrying on the company's business) *without the sanction* or intervention of the court: s 231(4) of the CA 1963[83].

(ii) Powers exercisable without prior sanction but subject to the control of the court

[24.033] Certain other powers are exercisable by liquidators *without* the need to obtain the sanction of the court or of any committee of inspection. Section 231(2) of the CA 1963 provides that official liquidators have the following powers:

'(a) to sell the real and personal property and things in action of the company by public auction or private contract, with power to transfer the whole thereof to any person or company or to sell the same in lots and for the purpose of selling the company's land or any part thereof to carry out such sales by fee farm grant, sub fee farm grant, lease, sublease, or otherwise, and to sell any rent reserved on any such grant or any reversion expectant upon the determination of any such lease;

(b) to do all acts and to execute, in the name and on behalf of the company, all deeds, receipts and other documents, and for that purpose to use, when necessary, the company's seal;

(c) where any contributory has been adjudged bankrupt or has presented a petition for arrangement with his creditors in pursuance of the Bankruptcy Acts, to prove, rank and claim in the bankruptcy or arrangement for any balance against his estate, and to receive dividends in the bankruptcy or arrangement in respect of that balance, as a separate debt due from the bankrupt or arranging debtor, and rateably with the other separate creditors;

(d) to draw, accept, make and endorse any bill of exchange or promissory note in the name and on behalf of the company, with the same effect with respect to the liability of the company as if the bill or note had been drawn, accepted, made or endorsed by or on behalf of the company in the course of its business;

---

80 *Cork County Council v CB Readymix Ltd* (12 December 1997, unreported) SC; noted in (1999) 17 ILT 2.

81 Section 231(1)(b) of the CA 1963.

82 *Re Great Eastern Electric Co Ltd* [1941] 1 All ER 409; *Re Davis & Co Ltd* [1945] Ch 402.

83 *Re The 19th Ltd* [1989] ILRM 652.

(e) to raise on the security of the assets of the company any money requisite;

(f) to take out in his official name letters of administration to any deceased contributory and to do in his official name any other act necessary for obtaining payment of any money due from a contributory or his estate which cannot be conveniently done in the name of the company, and in all such cases the money due shall, for the purpose of enabling the liquidator to take out the letters of administration or recover the money, be deemed to be due to the liquidator himself;

(g) to give security for costs in any proceedings commenced by the company or by him in the name of the company;

(h) to appoint an agent to do any business which the liquidator is unable to do himself;

(i) to do all such other things as may be necessary for winding up the affairs of the company and distributing its assets.'

The foregoing powers are largely self-explanatory. In *Re Dr Developments (Youghal) Ltd*[84], Finlay Geoghegan J said:

> '13. An official liquidator may sell property of the company pursuant to s 231(2)(a) of the Act of 1963, without sanction of the court. However, in practice, by reason of the fact that the exercise of such powers are made expressly subject "to the control of the court" and the right of application given to creditors and contributories in s 231(3) and the general obligations in relation to achieving the best price court approval is often sought for significant sales.'

In that case, it was noted that where a liquidator disposed of assets, he is obliged to lodge the proceeds of sale into the liquidation account under rr 44 and 117 of Ord 74 of the RSC 1986. Finlay Geoghegan J held that this remained the case even where the proceeds related to an asset that was charged to a bank where the proceeds would not produce a surplus for the benefit of the general creditors. Accordingly, where a secured creditor comes to an arrangement with an official liquidator whereby the liquidator disposes of a charged asset, unless the sanction of the court is obtained prior to the sale, the proceeds must be paid into the liquidation account.

[24.034] One of the most important and frequently exercised powers is the power to sell corporate property. This power, like all of those in s 231(2) of the CA 1963, is subject to the right of creditors and contributories to apply to court for a determination in relation to the exercise or proposed exercise of the power. As Laffoy J said in *Re Greendale Developments Ltd; McQuaid v Malone and Fagan*[85], the powers of official liquidators to deal with corporate assets other than with the sanction of the court or the committee of inspection are 'extremely circumscribed'[86].

[24.035] Section 231(1A) of the CA 1963[87] imposes a restriction on the power of liquidators to sell corporate property to officers of the company and persons that are connected to officers. This provides:

---

84 *Re Dr Developments (Youghal) Ltd* [2011] IEHC 307, at para 13.

85 *Re Greendale Developments Ltd; McQuaid v Malone and Fagan* (2 July 1997, unreported) HC, Laffoy J.

86 *Re Greendale Developments Ltd; McQuaid v Malone and Fagan* (2 July 1997, unreported) HC, Laffoy J at p 6.

87 Introduced by s 124 of the CA 1990.

> 'The liquidator of a company shall not sell by private contract a non-cash asset of the requisite value to a person who is, or who, within three years prior to the date of the commencement of the winding-up, has been, an officer of the company unless the liquidator has given at least 14 days' notice of his intention to do so to all creditors of the company who are known to him or who have been intimated to him.'

On its face, s 231(1A) does not apply where a non-cash asset is sold to officers where the sale is at a public auction, ie, it only applies to sales by *private contract*. The key words are defined[88]: 'Non-cash asset' and 'requisite value' have the meaning assigned to them by s 29 of the CA 1990[89] and 'officer' is deemed to include a person connected with a director within the meaning of s 26 of the CA 1990 and a shadow director[90].

[24.036] One question which arises from a liquidator's statutory power to sell the 'real and personal property *and things in action*' is the extent to which a liquidator can enter into an arrangement that might be considered, in other circumstances, to be champertous. 'Champerty' has been described by the Irish House of Lords in *Kenny v Browne*[91], a case decided in 1796, to be '… maintaining a suit in consideration of having some part of the thing in dispute'.

In the Supreme Court decision of *Fraser v Buckle*[92], it was held that the laws of maintenance (champerty has been described as an 'aggravated form of maintenance'[93]) and champerty in Ireland have not undergone any change since the nineteenth century. The question that arises here is whether the laws on maintenance and champerty curtail a liquidator's power to dispose of corporate assets in the nature of causes of action[94]. The assignment of a right or cause of action closely associated with a debt is not considered to be champertous, and a liquidator may legitimately dispose of a debt in circumstances where the ownership of that debt confers an immediate right to litigate. This must, however, be distinguished from a purported sale of a 'bare' cause of action which is *prima facie* champertous. It has, however, been held consistently by the English courts that there is an exemption from the law of champerty for liquidators and trustees in bankruptcy. In *Grovewood Holdings plc v James Capel & Co Ltd*[95], it was explained that because a liquidator and a trustee in bankruptcy have a statutory power to dispose of all corporate property (and, specifically, things in action), these powers necessarily preclude any challenge to the sale of a cause of action (on terms that the assignees, by way of consideration, would pay over a share of the recoveries) on the grounds of maintenance and champerty. In that case, Lightman J traced the history of the exception:

> 'The Court of Appeal in *Seear v Lawson* (1880) 15 Ch D 426 held that a bare right to sue was included within the term "property" for the purpose of both provisions and

[88] Section 231(1A)(b)(i) and (ii) of the CA 1963.

[89] See Ch 16, *Statutory Regulation of Directors' Transactions*, para **[16.028]**.

[90] Ch 16, *Statutory Regulation of Directors' Transactions*, para **[16.003]**.

[91] *Kenny v Browne* (1796) 3 Ridg PC 462.

[92] *Fraser v Buckle* [1996] 2 ILRM 34. See also *O'Keeffe and O'Keeffe v Scales* [1998] 1 ILRM 393.

[93] See *Guy v Churchill* (1888) 40 Ch D 481 at 489.

[94] See, generally, Bailey, Grove & Smith *Corporate Insolvency: Law and Practice* (2nd edn, 2001), paras 20.27–20.33.

[95] *Grovewood Holdings plc v James Capel & Co Ltd* [1994] 4 All ER 417.

> accordingly (by way of statutory exception to the rules against maintenance) the trustee [in bankruptcy] could sell a bare right of action. Jessel MR remarked (at 433):
>
> "The proper office of the trustee is to realise the property for the sake of distributing the proceeds amongst the creditors. Why should we hold as a matter of policy that it is necessary for him to sue in his own name? He may have no funds, or he may be disinclined to run the risk of having to pay costs, or he may consider it undesirable to delay the winding up of the bankruptcy till the end of the litigation."
>
> The following year in *Re Park Gate Wagon Works Co* (1881) 17 Ch D 234 the Court of Appeal held that s 95 of the Companies Act 1862 (the ancestor of modern company legislation), which authorised a liquidator to sell the property (similarly defined) of the company, likewise permitted the liquidator to sell causes of action, notwithstanding the rule against maintenance[96].'

Lightman J went on to hold, however, that the exemption for liquidators in relation to the sale of bare causes of action would *not* be extended to sales of the fruits of litigation. In *Grovewood Holdings plc*, the plaintiff company had instituted proceedings for negligence and misrepresentation against the defendant. After the plaintiff company went into liquidation, the liquidator sought to continue the action, but when the plaintiff company's shareholders and creditors refused to provide financial support for the proceedings, the liquidator purported to enter into an arrangement with secret backers who agreed to finance the litigation in return for half of the recoveries in the action. Lightman J held that this was champertous. It is submitted that it is difficult to accept the rationale of the distinction made in this decision and it has been criticised in later cases[97]. It is also important to recognise that it is, in essence, an exception to an exception and it remains the case that a liquidator can sell a cause of action, something which a person other than a liquidator or official assignee in bankruptcy cannot do. So, in *Re Edennote Ltd (No 2)*[98] Lightman J held that where a liquidator was not in funds to pursue a particular cause of action that was in being, the interests of the creditors required that he either compromise or sell the action. In that case, the liquidator had sought (and was granted) the court's sanction to compromise the cause of action.

[24.037] In *Re Oasis Merchandising Services Ltd*[99], it was held that claims that arise in the course of a liquidation, eg, claims for fraudulent or reckless trading against an insolvent company's directors, cannot be assigned as these have been held not to be the 'property' of the company. There, Peter Gibson LJ held that the property, the sale of which came within the exemption to champerty, was the property of the company at the commencement of a winding up and not post-liquidation property.

[24.038] The attitude of the Irish courts to these questions very much remains to be seen. Although the decision in *Grovewood Holdings plc* was mentioned by the Supreme Court in *O'Keeffe and O'Keeffe v Scales*[100], no reference was made to the statements concerning the well-recognised exception for liquidators and trustees in bankruptcy. It is

96 *Grovewood Holdings plc v James Capel & Co Ltd* [1994] 4 All ER 417 at 421e–h.

97 *Re Oasis Merchandising Services Ltd* [1997] 1 BCLC 689 and *Abraham v Thompson* [1997] 4 All ER 362.

98 *Re Edennote Ltd (No 2)* [1997] 2 BCLC 89.

99 *Re Oasis Merchandising Services Ltd* [1997] 1 BCLC 689.

100 *O'Keeffe and O'Keeffe v Scales* [1998] 2 ILRM 393.

thought, however, that the Irish courts will follow the old authorities such as *Re Park Gate Waggon Works Co*[101], which accept that liquidators can dispose of causes of action being 'things in property'. Support for this view is derived from the judgment of Lynch J in *O'Keeffe and O'Keeffe v Scales*, where he said:

> 'While the law relating to maintenance and champerty therefore undoubtedly still subsists in this jurisdiction it must not be extended in such a way as to deprive people of their constitutional right of access to the courts to litigate reasonably statable claims[102].'

Equally, it is thought to be very much within the public interest to facilitate the maximum realisation of the assets of an insolvent company to enable the greatest number of creditors to recoup the debts owed to them.

(iii) Applications by creditors or contributories regarding the exercise of powers under s 231 of the CA 1963

[24.039] Section 231(3) of the CA 1963 provides that the exercise by an official liquidator of the powers in s 231(1):

> '... shall be subject to the control of the court, and any creditor or contributory may apply to the court in relation to any exercise or proposed exercise of any of those powers.'

It will be noted that only creditors or contributories have *locus standi* to apply to court under this provision[103].

[24.040] Any application made pursuant to s 231(3) of the CA 1963 by a creditor or contributory must be heard in public. In *Re Greendale Developments Ltd*[104], the official liquidator to a company that was being wound up by the court applied for directions in connection with the liquidation and in particular for an order pursuant to s 231(1)(a), granting him liberty to continue two plenary actions. Both actions had been commenced by the company prior to the commencement of its winding up, one being against a bank and a firm of chartered accountants, and the other being an action against a firm of solicitors. One creditor did not object to leave to continue but another creditor strenuously objected. The particular matter that arose for decision in that case was whether or not the court had the power to hear the application for directions otherwise than in public. After noting that it was well settled that the effect of Article 34.1 of the Constitution was that justice must be administered in public, in the absence of an exempting statutory provision, Laffoy J said the essential question was whether the making of the decision in hand was 'an administration of justice'. Applying the fivefold test advanced in *McDonald v Bord na gCon*[105], Laffoy J held that a decision under s 231 did involve the administration of justice and that the court had no discretion to hear the application otherwise than in public. The reasoning was as follows:

> 'In my view, when an application by a liquidator under s 231 involves either of the following situations—

[101] *Re Park Gate Waggon Works Co* (1881) 17 Ch D 234.

[102] *O'Keeffe and O'Keeffe v Scales* [1998] 2 ILRM 393 at 397.

[103] See *Mahomed v Morris* [2000] 2 BCLC 536.

[104] *Re Greendale Developments Ltd* [1997] 3 IR 540.

[105] *McDonald v Bord na gCon* [1965] IR 217.

> (i) the liquidator advocating that the relief sought to be granted in the interests of the general body of creditors and of the contributories as a whole and one creditor or contributor disputing the appropriateness of granting such relief, or
>
> (ii) the liquidator, as it were, "throwing in the ball" and individuals or factions proposing opposite points of view as to whether the relief sought by the liquidator should be granted,
>
> there is a contest between the parties. Moreover, in my view the consequences of the resolution of the contest cannot be defined with certainty at the time of resolution or, in certain circumstances, at any time, because there is inherent in the resolution a prediction as to the outcome of the proceedings sought to be continued, which outcome will only be known in the future if at all, nonetheless, the resolution does involve "the infliction of some form of liability or penalty on one of the parties". This can be illustrated by reference to the second scenario suggested above. If the proponent of the continuation of the proceedings loses the contest, he is deprived of the possibility of the assets of the company being augmented by an award of damages to his advantage. If the proponent of abandoning the proceedings loses the contest, he has foisted on him the possibility of assets which would have been available for distributing to him and the other creditors being favoured by an award of costs if the action is unsuccessful[106].'

In so deciding, Laffoy J distinguished the decision of Murphy J in *Re Countyglen plc*[107] where he had held that an application for directions by an inspector, appointed under Part II of the CA 1990, did not involve the administration of justice. The basis for that distinction was that, in that context, 'there was no contest between parties whereas in the instant case s 231(2) provides the machinery for the initiation of a contest. When a contest is initiated, its resolution must be a justiciable issue[108].'

(b) Powers of provisional liquidators

[24.041] The powers of a provisional liquidator are closely delimited by the order appointing him, the essence of the appointment being to preserve the status quo[109]. He will always be a creature of the order which appoints him and by s 226(2) of the CA 1963 the court 'may limit and restrict his powers by the order appointing him'. While often his powers will simply be to preserve assets, in suitable circumstances, he may be allowed to go further. So, while his power to carry on the business of the company will usually be only as far as is necessary for the beneficial winding up of the company, this may involve the actual continuance of the business, for instance, of a restaurant, as happened in *Re Gourmet Restaurants Ltd* where the goodwill of the restaurant was the company's main asset[110]. Just as the court is reluctant to allow the provisional liquidator to continue the business of the company, so too is it reluctant to allow him to close down the business. However, here too, in appropriate circumstances, such as where the business or a part of the business is making huge losses, the court may allow a provisional liquidator to close a business, as happened in *Re Union Accident Insurance*

106 *Re Greendale Developments Ltd* [1997] 3 IR 540 at 546–547.

107 *Re Countyglen plc* [1995] 1 IR 220.

108 *Re Greendale Developments Ltd* [1997] 3 IR 540 at 548.

109 See Ussher, *Company Law in Ireland* (1986), p 487.

110 See (1984) Irish Times, 3 August, *per* Egan J, considered by Ussher, *Company Law in Ireland* (1986), p 487.

Co Ltd[111]. Powers in aid of gathering information, more normally associated with an official liquidator[112], such as to apply for an examination under s 245 of the CA 1963 or for the arrest of an absconding contributory under s 247 of the CA 1963 or to get the statement of company affairs under s 224 of the CA 1963 or Ord 74, r 19 of the RSC 1986, are also available to a provisional liquidator. Where a winding-up order is made or a provisional liquidator is appointed, no action can be commenced without the sanction of the court: s 222 of the CA 1963.

[24.042] On the application for the appointment of a provisional liquidator, it is common to list the powers that he seeks from the court. Powers frequently sought by a provisional liquidator include to take possession of the assets in danger, to open a bank account, to retain a solicitor's services, to insure assets and hire security, to retain or dismiss employees and to continue trading. To minimise the number of occasions when application must be made to the court, the order might contain a proviso that the provisional liquidator has power to sell assets up to a certain *de minimis* amount but above that, the sanction of the court is required[113].

(c) Powers of voluntary liquidators

[24.043] The powers enjoyed by a voluntary liquidator are set out in s 276(1) of the CA 1963. This provides that a voluntary liquidator may:

> '(a) in the case of a members' voluntary winding up, with the sanction of a special resolution of the company, and, in the case of a creditors' voluntary winding up, with the sanction of the court or the committee of inspection or (if there is no such committee) a meeting of the creditors, exercise any of the powers given by paragraphs (d), (e) and (f) of subsection (1) of section 231 to a liquidator in a winding up by the court;
>
> (b) without sanction, exercise any of the other powers by this Act given to the liquidator in a winding up by the court;
>
> (c) exercise the power of the court under this Act of settling a list of contributories, and the list of contributories shall be prima facie evidence of the liability of the persons named therein to be contributories;
>
> (d) exercise the power of the court of making calls;
>
> (e) summon general meetings of the company for the purpose of obtaining the sanction of the company by resolution or for any other purpose he may think fit.'

Section 276(3) of the CA 1963 provides that when several liquidators are appointed, 'any power given by this Act may be exercised by such one or more of them as may be determined at the time of their appointment, or, in default of such determination, by any number not less than two'.

[24.044] It will be noted that a members' voluntary liquidator can only exercise the following powers with the sanction of a special resolution of the company:

---

111 *Re Union Accident Insurance Co Ltd* [1972] 1 All ER 1105. Here a provisional liquidator was permitted to close down a branch of the company's business and dismiss employees.

112 See generally, Ch 25, *Realisation and Distribution of Assets in a Winding Up*, para **[25.018]** *et seq.*

113 See *Re Goodwill Merchant Financial Services Ltd* [2001] 1 BCLC 259.

- to pay any class of creditor in full[114];
- to make any compromise or arrangement with creditors or persons claiming to be creditors[115];
- to compromise all calls and liabilities to calls, between the company and a contributory[116].

A creditors' voluntary liquidator can only exercise these three powers with the sanction of the court or the committee of inspection or (if there is no such committee) a meeting of the creditors.

[24.045] Without the sanction of the committee of inspection or a meeting of the creditors[117] or of the members by special resolution, a voluntary liquidator has the following powers, namely to:

- bring or defend any action or other legal proceeding in the name and on behalf of the company[118];
- carry on the business of the company so far as may be necessary for its beneficial winding up[119];
- appoint a solicitor to assist him in the performance of his duties[120];
- sell the real and personal property of the company and things in action by auction or private contract[121];
- do all acts and to execute in the name and on behalf of the company all deeds, receipts and documents and to use the company seal[122];
- prove, rank and claim in the bankruptcy of any contributory[123];
- draw, accept, make or endorse any bill of exchange or promissory note in the name and on behalf of the company[124];
- borrow money and give corporate assets as security[125];
- take out letters of administration for any contributory of the company[126];
- give security for costs in any proceedings commenced by the company or by him in the name of the company[127];
- appoint an agent to assist him[128];

114 Section 231(1)(d) of the CA 1963.
115 Section 231(1)(e) of the CA 1963.
116 Section 231(1)(f) of the CA 1963.
117 By virtue of s 276(1)(b) of the CA 1963.
118 Section 231(1)(a) of the CA 1963.
119 Section 231(1)(b) of the CA 1963.
120 Section 231(1)(c) of the CA 1963.
121 Section 231(2)(a) of the CA 1963.
122 Section 231(2)(b) of the CA 1963.
123 Section 231(2)(c) of the CA 1963.
124 Section 231(2)(d) of the CA 1963.
125 Section 231(2)(e) of the CA 1963.
126 Section 231(2)(f) of the CA 1963.
127 Section 231(2)(g) of the CA 1963.
128 Section 231(2)(h) of the CA 1963.

- do all such other things as may be necessary for winding up the affairs of the company and distributing its assets[129];
- exercise the power of the court to settle a list of contributories, such list being *prima facie* evidence of the liability of the persons named therein as contributories[130];
- exercise the power of the court in making calls[131];
- summon general meetings of the company for the purpose of obtaining the sanction of the company by resolution or for any other purpose he may think fit[132].

It can be seen from the foregoing list of powers that voluntary liquidators enjoy considerable freedom to get on with the job of realising and distributing the assets of the company to which they are appointed. This is in keeping with the essential private nature of a voluntary winding up.

(d) Restrictions on the exercise of powers by members' voluntary liquidators and other restrictions

[24.046] By virtue of s 131(2) of the CA 1990, a liquidator who is appointed by the members at the initiation of a creditors' voluntary winding up cannot exercise the powers granted to him by s 276 of the CA 1963 *before* the creditors' meeting is held. An exception is provided by s 131(3) of the CA 1990 and the foregoing ban does *not* apply in relation to the liquidator's powers:

> '(a) to take into his custody or under his control all the property to which the company is or appears to be entitled;
>
> (b) to dispose of perishable goods and other goods the value of which is likely to diminish if they are not immediately disposed of;
>
> (c) to do all such things as may be necessary for the protection of the company's assets.'

This section was inserted to prevent the practice which came to be known in England as 'centre-binding', after the case of *Re Centrebind Ltd*[133]. In that case, the members of an insolvent company put the company into voluntary liquidation and appointed a liquidator. Prior to the creditors' meeting, the liquidator prevented the English Revenue Commissioners from proceeding against the company's assets. Later, this was held to have been a valid exercise of his powers which were held to be unfettered until the creditors' meeting was held. While the actions of the liquidator in that case were *bona fide*, other, less scrupulous companies caused a members' meeting to be held with the sole purpose of appointing a liquidator with whom they could collude so as to have the assets of the company acquired by another company controlled by them. Section 131(4) of the CA 1990 provides that at the creditors' meeting the liquidator appointed by the members shall report any exercise of his powers under s 131 of the CA 1990 or ss 276 or 280 of the CA 1963 to the creditors' meeting.

---

129 Section 231(2)(i) of the CA 1963.

130 Section 276(1)(c) of the CA 1963.

131 Section 276(1)(d) of the CA 1963.

132 Section 276(1)(e) of the CA 1963.

133 *Re Centrebind Ltd* [1966] 3 All ER 889.

[24.047] Furthermore, if default is made by the company in complying with s 266(1) or (2) of the CA 1963 or by the directors in complying with sub-s (3), the liquidator shall, within seven days of the day he was nominated by the company or the day he becomes aware of the default (whichever is the later), apply to the court for directions as to the manner in which that default is to be remedied[134]. Failure to do this will make the liquidator liable to be convicted of an offence[135].

[24.048] The liquidator in a members' voluntary winding up has the power, subject to certain safeguards, to accept shares in another company as consideration for the sale of the property of the company being wound up[136]. Before a liquidator can accept shares in another company he must obtain the sanction of the company's members by means of a special resolution. The sale or arrangement is expressed to be binding on the members of the transferor company[137]. This reorganisation is also permitted in a creditors' voluntary winding up, with the necessary modification that the powers of the liquidator may not be exercised except with the sanction of either the court or the committee of inspection[138]. Reorganisations under s 260 of the CA 1963 have been considered in Chapter 21[139].

[24.049] While on his appointment a liquidator will generally assume the management of a company, any arrangement entered into between a company about to be wound up and its creditors is binding on the company where sanctioned by a special resolution in a members' meeting or three-quarters of the creditors in a creditors' meeting[140]. This is subject to a right of appeal to court by any creditor or contributory within three weeks from the completion of the arrangement[141].

[24.050] All liquidators' powers will be suspended where he is appointed to a company in respect of which an interim or interlocutory order or a disposal order has been made under the Proceeds of Crime Act 1996[142]. Section 13(1) of the 1996 Act provides:

> 'Where property the subject of an interim order, an interlocutory order or a disposal order made before the relevant time is in the possession or control of a company and an order for the winding up of the company has been made or a resolution has been passed by the company for a voluntary winding up, the functions of the liquidator (or any provisional liquidator) shall not be exercisable in relation to the property.'

Where a winding-up order has been made or a resolution passed to have a company wound up, an interim or interlocutory freezing order shall not be made in relation to any property held by the company in relation to which the functions of the liquidator are exercisable:

---

134 Section 131(5) and (6) of the CA 1990.

135 Section 131(7) of the CA 1990.

136 Section 260 of the CA 1963.

137 Section 260(2) of the CA 1963.

138 Section 271 of the CA 1963.

139 See Ch 21, *Schemes of Arrangement and Reconstructions*, para **[21.066]**.

140 Section 279(1) of the CA 1963.

141 Section 279(2) of the CA 1963.

142 See, generally, Courtney, *Mareva Injunctions and Related Interlocutory Orders* (1998), Ch 3, 'Statutory Jurisdictions to Freeze Assets'.

'(a) so as to inhibit him or her from exercising those functions for the purpose of distributing any property held by the company to the company's creditors, or

(b) so as to prevent the payment out of any property of expenses (including the remuneration of the liquidator or any provisional liquidator) properly incurred in the winding up in respect of the property[143].'

In that section, 'company' is defined to mean any company which may be wound up under the Companies Acts[144].

(e) Seeking directions from court

[24.051] Section 280(1) of the CA 1963, which applies to voluntary liquidators, provides:

> 'The liquidator or any contributory or creditor may apply to the court to determine any question arising in the winding up of a company, or to exercise in relation to the enforcing of calls or any other matter, all or any of the powers which the court might exercise if the company were being wound up by the court.'

An official liquidator is an officer of the court and, as seen above[145], he is subject to the control of the court in the exercise of his powers by s 231(3) of the CA 1963. Official liquidators too can apply for court directions. It is always advisable for a liquidator who is in doubt to make such an application for directions[146]. In *Re William Pickles plc*[147], it was held that a liquidator of more than one company could bring a single application for directions where there was an issue that required resolution and which was common to all of the companies in liquidation.

Remuneration of liquidators

[24.052] The members in general meeting set the remuneration of a members' voluntary liquidator[148]. The committee of inspection – or if there is no such committee, the creditors – fix the remuneration of a creditors' voluntary liquidator[149].

[24.053] The remuneration of an official liquidator is a matter for the court[150], whose direction in this regard will turn upon what it considers fair. Keane[151] has noted the practice whereby one creditor (usually the Revenue Commissioners) is appointed to

---

143 Section 13(2) of the Proceeds of Crime Act 1996.

144 Section 13(2) of the Proceeds of Crime Act 1996. 'Relevant time' is also defined in that section to mean: '(a) where no order for the winding up of the company has been made, the time of the passing of the resolution for voluntary winding up, (b) where such an order has been made and, before the presentation of the petition for the winding up of the company by the court, such a resolution had been passed by the company, the time of the passing of the resolution, and (c) in any other case where such an order has been made, the time of the making of the order.'

145 See para **[24.004]**.

146 *Roper v Ward* [1981] ILRM 408.

147 *Re William Pickles plc* [1996] 1 BCLC 681.

148 Section 258(1) of the CA 1963. Where remuneration is not fixed, it can be fixed by the court on application: *Re Amalgamated Syndicates Ltd* [1901] 2 Ch 181.

149 Section 269(1) of the CA 1963.

150 Section 228(d) of the CA 1963.

151 See Keane, *Company Law* (4th edn, 2007), para 36.89.

represent the other creditors before the examiner of the High Court at an inquiry into a liquidator's remuneration. In such cases, the report of the examiner as to the amount of such remuneration will be furnished to the High Court[152]. Notwithstanding the court's wide discretion under s 228(d) of the CA 1963, in *Re Car Replacements Ltd*[153] Murphy J noted that the practice of the courts has been for many years to determine the remuneration of an official liquidator on the basis of the hours worked by him and his staff. In that case, the company in the title of the matter was one of 39 companies being wound up by the same official liquidator, it being one of 10 companies that would have surplus assets available for distribution amongst its shareholders. All of the companies were directly or indirectly subsidiaries of the failed PMPA group of companies and were connected to each other. The official liquidator's fees were disputed, not on grounds of time worked or rate charged, but on the basis that 'the hours involved in such work had been allocated to the various companies by reference to their gross realisations'. The liquidator's justification was that such course of charging had been adopted by him on previous occasions with the consent of the interested parties and the approval of the court. In both his seventh and eighth status reports, the official liquidator had stated that certain hours worked were not attributable to a specific company and covered all companies involved and that he had allocated those hours by reference to gross realisations to date. As a general point of principle Murphy J stated that he had no doubt that it was correct to contend that an official liquidator of a group of companies was not entitled to deem or attribute hours worked by him in relation to the affairs of the group to different companies on the basis of the amount of the assets realised by them respectively, or indeed on any basis other than the hours actually worked in respect of the particular companies. In all of the circumstances of the case in hand, however, Murphy J accepted that it was appropriate to calculate the liquidator's remuneration on the basis proposed by the liquidator[154]. Ordinarily, provisional liquidators will go on to become official liquidators and will be remunerated in accordance with the foregoing rules[155].

[24.054] In *Re Dr Developments (Youghal) Ltd*[156], an official liquidator sought the sanction of the court to sell property that was the subject of a fixed charge in favour of AIB. Finlay Geoghegan J found that in disposing of the company's property for below

[152] See *Re Merchant Banking Ltd* [1987] ILRM 163 where McCarthy J said that this inquiry was 'one of amount and not of nature or kind'.

[153] *Re Car Replacements Ltd* (15 December 1999, unreported) HC, Murphy J.

[154] *Inter alia*, it was noted that there were no records available by reference to which the hours worked in respect of the affairs of each individual company could be ascertained and that to create them retrospectively would involve a very subjective element and would involve further delay and very considerable expense. Murphy J also noted that solicitors for parties substantially interested in the distributions in respect of the other 37 companies had submitted that the liquidator's means of calculation was the most practical and had been approved by the companies' creditors and contributories.

[155] In *Re UOC Corporation; Alipour v UOC Corporation* [1998] BCC 191, an unusual situation arose whereby a provisional liquidator was discharged before a petition was presented to wind up the company. Carnwath J held that the court had power under the English Insolvency Rules (r 4.31(2)) to direct that a provisional liquidator be discharged before the hearing of the petition, subject to the control of the court.

[156] *Re Dr Developments (Youghal) Ltd* [2011] IEHC 307, at para 11.

what was owed to AIB in circumstances where AIB would receive all of the proceeds of the sale, the liquidator would be doing significant work for the exclusive financial benefit of AIB. In finding that the liquidator should not be remunerated for that work, the learned judge said:

> '19. In such circumstances where an official liquidator is doing significant work for the exclusive financial benefit of a charge holder such as AIB, it would not appear appropriate that he be remunerated for such work out of any assets coming into the liquidation which might otherwise be available for distribution to the preferential and general unsecured creditors. Hence, it would appear to follow that where an official liquidator agrees to do work exclusively for the benefit of a secured creditor (including selling for the benefit of the holder of a fixed charge) that he should not include the work done as work for which he would claim remuneration in the winding-up. Insofar as he reaches agreement with the secured creditor for the discharge of remuneration to him, this requires sanction of the court for the reasons next set out. The position becomes more complex where an official liquidator does work which is in part for the benefit of a secured creditor and in part for the winding-up but similar principles apply. This is unlikely to arise on the facts herein.'

Finlay Geoghegan J went on to note that Ord 74, r 38 of the RSC 1986 expressly prohibits a liquidator from accepting remuneration from any solicitor, auctioneer or any other person connected with the company, consistent with a liquidator's fiduciary obligations. The learned judge pointed out that the liquidator was, therefore, not entitled to be paid by AIB without first obtaining the sanction of the court and cautioned against the practice that had developed whereby the Revenue Commissioners would agree to underwrite liquidators' remuneration but not obtain the sanction of the court.

[24.055] As regards the priority of voluntary liquidators' remuneration, s 281 of the CA 1963 provides that such is payable out of the assets of the company in priority to all other claims. Section 244 of the CA 1963 applies to official liquidations and provides that where assets are insufficient to meet liabilities, the court may make an order as to payment as it thinks fit. In this regard, guidance is provided by Ord 74, r 128(1) of the RSC 1986. The priority of the costs and expenses in liquidations (including the remuneration of liquidators) is considered in Chapter 25[157] but it may be noted that it has been held that where there is more than one liquidator and there are insufficient assets available to discharge their remuneration in full then their remuneration will rank equally[158].

Foreign liquidators and the EU Council Regulation on Insolvency Proceedings

(a) Assistance to foreign liquidators in Ireland

[24.056] A foreign liquidator (ie, one who is appointed by a foreign court or is appointed under the laws of another country to a body corporate incorporated there) may apply to the Irish High Court for assistance under s 250(1) of the CA 1963 which provides:

---

[157] Ch 25, *The Realisation and Distribution of Assets in a Winding Up*, para **[25.182]**.

[158] See *Re Salters Hall School Ltd; Merrygold v Horton* [1998] 1 BCLC 401.

'Any order made by a court of any country recognised for the purposes of this section and made for or in the course of winding up a company may be enforced by the High Court in the same manner in all respects as if the order had been made by the High Court.'

For the purposes of this section, 'company' means a body corporate incorporated outside the State, and 'recognised' means recognised by order made by the Minister[159]. To date, one such order has been made by the Minister, and Great Britain and Northern Ireland have been recognised[160]. Section 250(2) provides that an office copy of any order sought to be enforced shall be sufficient evidence of the order. It should be noted that this section has now been confined to applications by liquidators appointed by the courts of non-EU countries (except the State and Denmark)[161].

[24.057] In *Re Mount Capital Fund Ltd (in liquidation)*[162], Laffoy J said that although only Great Britain and Northern Ireland were recognised under s 250(1) of the CA 1963, this did not preclude the court from affording assistance to other common law jurisdictions. The learned judge said:

'I do not think that this Court could be regarded as usurping the powers of the relevant secondary legislator by making an order giving recognition in this case. As is clear from the judgment of Dunne J in the *Drumm* case, as long ago as 1920, in *In Re Bolton* [1920] 2 IR 324 the King's Bench Division of the Irish High Court acted in aid of the Supreme Court of South Africa in relation to a bankruptcy in that jurisdiction. Therefore, prior to the conferring of power by s 250(1) there appears to have been recognised an inherent common law jurisdiction to provide assistance to a foreign court in relation to insolvency proceedings. Section 250(1), in my view, did not eliminate that jurisdiction.'

In that case, the liquidators of two companies, registered in the British Virgin Islands, applied to the court for recognition of the liquidation orders and sought an order from the court to exercise the powers afforded to an official liquidator for examination under s 245 of the CA 1963. Laffoy J held there was an inherent jurisdiction to recognise orders of non-EU courts for the winding up of companies and the appointment of liquidators and that, in the instant case, the court was satisfied that the order was being sought for a legitimate purpose.

[24.058] A possible alternative to foreign liquidators is s 345 of the CA 1963. This has already been considered in the preceding chapter[163]. Of particular significance, however, is s 345(7) of the CA 1963 which provides:

'Where a company incorporated outside the State which has been carrying on business in the State ceases to carry on business in the State, it may be wound up as an unregistered company under this Part, notwithstanding that it has been dissolved or otherwise ceased to exist as a company under or by virtue of the laws of the country under which it was incorporated.'

159 Section 250(3) of the CA 1963.

160 SI 42/1964.

161 Section 250(4) of the CA 1963 as inserted by reg 3(d) of SI 333/2002.

162 *Re Mount Capital Fund Ltd (in liquidation)* [2012] IEHC 97.

163 See Ch 23, *Winding Up Companies*, para **[23.036]** *et seq.*

(b) The European Council Regulation on Insolvency Proceedings

[24.059] The most recent and far-reaching development in this area is the EU's Council Regulation on Insolvency Proceedings[164] (the 'Insolvency Regulation'). Although EU Council Regulations have direct effect in the State, the implementation of this Council Regulation has been assisted by regulations[165] which have amended the CA 1963. The purpose of the Insolvency Regulation is to improve the efficiency and effectiveness of insolvency proceedings having cross-EU border effects by harmonising the provisions in each Member State concerning jurisdiction, recognition and applicable law. The Insolvency Regulation is, by definition, concerned with insolvent liquidations, not members' voluntary windings up[166].

[24.060] The Insolvency Regulation provides in Article 3(1) that the courts of the Member State where the debtor's *main interests are situated* 'shall have jurisdiction to open insolvency proceedings' and in the case of a company this is presumed to be the place where its registered office is situate. The Insolvency Regulation goes on to recognise that *secondary proceedings*[167] may be opened up in a different Member State. However, Article 3(2) provides that the courts of a Member State, other than the state in which a debtor has his main interests, will only have jurisdiction to open insolvency proceedings against a debtor if he has an establishment there. And further, secondary proceedings can generally[168] only be opened after the main proceedings have been opened. From this it can be seen that the Insolvency Regulation introduces nothing new in principle to Irish law, bearing as it does a remarkable similarity in effect to s 345(7) of the CA 1963, which facilitates the Irish courts opening 'secondary' proceedings. The law applicable to insolvency proceedings is deemed to be the law of the Member State where the proceedings are opened[169]. That law determines the conditions for the opening of those proceedings, their conduct and closure[170]. Articles 5–15 of the Insolvency Regulation make provision for specific matters such as rights *in rem*, set-off, reservation of title, etc.

---

164 Council Regulation (EC) No 1346/2000 of 29 May 2000.

165 The European Communities (Corporate Insolvency) Regulations 2002 (SI 333/2002) ('EC(CI)R 2002').

166 Whilst it is the case that the Insolvency Regulation is not confined to companies, and extends to insolvent individuals and partnerships, it is only companies that are the subject of this work.

167 Article 3(3) of the Insolvency Regulation.

168 See, however, the exceptions to this generality in Article 3(4)(a) and (b) of the Insolvency Regulation.

169 Article 4(1) of the Insolvency Regulation.

170 Article 4(2) of the Insolvency Regulation provides that it shall determine, in particular: '(a) against which debtors insolvency proceedings may be brought on account of their capacity; (b) the assets which form part of the estate and the treatment of assets acquired by or devolving on the debtor after the opening of the insolvency proceedings; (c) the respective powers of the debtor and the liquidator; (d) the conditions under which set-offs may be invoked; (e) the effects of insolvency proceedings on current contracts to which the debtor is party; (f) the effects of the insolvency proceedings brought by individual creditors, with the exception of lawsuits pending; (g) the claims which are to be lodged against the debtor's estate and the treatment of claims arising after the opening of insolvency proceedings; (h) the rules governing the lodging, verification and admission of claims; (contd.../)

[24.061] Article 16(1) of the Insolvency Regulation is similar in effect to s 250 of the CA 1963. It provides:

> 'Any judgment opening insolvency proceedings handed down by a court of a Member State which has jurisdiction pursuant to Article 3 shall be recognised in all the other Member States from the time that it becomes effective in the State of the opening of proceedings.'

[24.062] The leading Irish case on the Insolvency Regulation is *Re Eurofood IFSC Ltd*[171]. In this case, Eurofood IFSC Ltd was the wholly-owned Irish registered subsidiary of the Italian company Parmalat SpA. After an administrator was appointed to Parmalat SpA in Italy, a creditor of the Irish company petitioned to have Eurofood wound up and a provisional liquidator was appointed. Subsequently, the Italian court appointed an administrator under Italian law to Eurofood, the Irish company. In the High Court, Kelly J held that the appointment of the provisional liquidator constituted a judgment opening insolvency proceedings in Ireland and that that fact precluded the Italian courts from appointing an administrator to the Irish company. On appeal to the Supreme Court, the matter was referred to the European Court of Justice ('ECJ') which determined, as Kelly J had determined, that the Italian court was wrong to appoint an administrator to the Irish company after Irish proceedings had been opened, the ECJ rejecting that the centre of main interests should be determined as Italy. The ECJ's conclusion was:

> '1. Where a debtor is a subsidiary company whose registered office and that of its parent company are situated in two different Member States, the presumption laid down in the second sentence of Article 3(1) of Council Regulation (EC) No 1346/2000 of 29 May 2000 on insolvency proceedings, whereby the centre of main interests of that subsidiary is situated in the Member State where its registered office is situated, can be rebutted only if factors which are both objective and ascertainable by third parties enable it to be established that an actual situation exists which is different from that which location at that registered office is deemed to reflect. That could be so in particular in the case of a company not carrying out any business in the territory of the Member State in which its registered office is situated. By contrast, where a company carries on its business in the territory of the Member State where its registered office is situated, the mere fact that its economic choices are or can be controlled by a parent company in another Member State is not enough to rebut the presumption laid down by that Regulation.
>
> 2. On a proper interpretation of the first subparagraph of Article 16(1) of Regulation No 1346/2000, the main insolvency proceedings opened by a court of a Member

---

170 (\...contd) (i) the rules governing the distribution of proceeds from the realisation of assets, the ranking of claims and the rights of creditors who have obtained partial satisfaction after the opening of insolvency proceedings by virtue of a right in rem or through a set-off; (j) the conditions for and the effects of closure of insolvency proceedings, in particular by composition; (k) creditors' rights after the closure of insolvency proceedings; (l) who is to bear the costs and expenses incurred in the insolvency proceedings; (m) the rules relating to voidness, voidability or unenforceability of legal acts detrimental to all the creditors.'

171 *Re Eurofood IFSC* Ltd [2004] 4 IR 370 (HC); [2006] IESC 41 (SC) and [2006] Ch 508; ECJ Case C-341/04 (European Court of Justice). See Gobbons & O'Riordan, 'Eurofood IFSC Limited: Judicial Clarification of Insolvency Regulation 1346/2000' (2006) Bar Review 111.

State must be recognised by the courts of the other Member States, without the latter being able to review the jurisdiction of the court of the opening State.

3. On a proper interpretation of the first subparagraph of Article 16(1) of the Regulation, a decision to open insolvency proceedings for the purposes of that provision is a decision handed down by a court of a Member State to which application for such a decision has been made, based on the debtor's insolvency and seeking the opening of proceedings referred to in Annex A to the Regulation, where that decision involves the divestment of the debtor and the appointment of a liquidator referred to in Annex C to the Regulation. Such divestment implies that the debtor loses the powers of management that he has over his assets.

4. On a proper interpretation of Article 26 of the Regulation, a Member State may refuse to recognise insolvency proceedings opened in another Member State where the decision to open the proceedings was taken in flagrant breach of the fundamental right to be heard, which a person concerned by such proceedings enjoys.'

[24.063] Perhaps the most significant development is the extra-judicial powers afforded to all EU liquidators of insolvent companies. Article 18(1) of the Insolvency Regulations provides that the liquidator appointed by the courts of the Member State where the debtor's main interests are situate (under Article 3(1)):

> '… may exercise all the powers conferred on him by the law of the State of the opening of proceedings *in another Member State*, so long as no other insolvency proceedings have been opened there nor any preservation measure to the contrary has been taken there further to a request for the opening of insolvency proceedings in that State. He may in particular remove the debtor's assets from the territory of the Member State in which they are situated, subject to Articles 5 and 7[172].'

So, a liquidator appointed by the Irish High Court to, say, an insolvent Irish company with assets in England can travel to England and will have authority to collect in any assets belonging to the insolvent company and expatriate them. Of course the liquidator will have to comply with the laws of England and Wales regarding the procedures on the realisation of assets, and coercive measures are specifically excluded[173]. A liquidator appointed by a court in secondary proceedings (under Article 3(2)) may in any other Member State claim through the courts or out of court that moveable property was removed from the jurisdiction of the state of the opening of the proceedings and may bring any action to set aside which is in the interests of the creditors[174].

[24.064] Article 19 of the Insolvency Regulations provides that a liquidator's appointment shall be evidenced by a certified copy of the original decision appointing him or by any other certificate issued by the court which has jurisdiction and, whilst individual Member States may, in their own laws, require it to be translated into one of its official languages, 'no legislation or other similar formality shall be required'. Individual Member States are also allowed to require the publication of notification of a liquidator's appointment by a court opening insolvency proceedings in another Member

172 Emphasis added. Article 5 of the Insolvency Regulation preserves third parties' *in rem* rights and Article 7 preserves the rights of sellers of goods under reservation of title clauses.

173 Article 18(3) of the Insolvency Regulation.

174 Article 18(2) of the Insolvency Regulation.

State in respect of companies that have an establishment there[175]. Section 227B(2) of the CA 1963[176] provides that liquidators must publish in the Companies Registration Office Gazette and once at least in two morning newspapers circulating in the State the following:

> '(a) notice of the judgment opening the insolvency proceedings concerned,
> (b) where appropriate, the decision appointing the liquidator in those proceedings,
> (c) the name and business address of the liquidator, and
> (d) the provision (either paragraph 1 or paragraph 2) of Article 3 of the Insolvency Regulation giving jurisdiction to open the proceedings[177].'

Publication must be as soon as practicable after the opening of an insolvency proceeding, where the debtor company has an establishment in the State[178]. Individual Member States may also require foreign liquidators to notify a central registry – such as the CRO in Ireland – of their appointment[179]. Judgments handed down by a court whose judgment concerning the opening of proceedings is recognised in accordance with Article 16 and which concern the court and closure of insolvency proceedings and compositions approved by that court must also be recognised with no further formalities[180]. Section 227A(1) of the CA 1963[181] provides that, without prejudice to Article 16(1) of the Insolvency Regulation, a liquidator appointed in insolvency proceedings who intends:

> '(a) to request under Article 21 of the Regulation that notice of the judgment opens the proceedings and, where appropriate, the decision appointing him or her be published in the state, or
> (b) to take any other action in the State under the Regulation,
>
> shall deliver to the Registrar of Companies for registration a duly certified copy of the judgment and, where appropriate, of the decision appointing the liquidator.'

Application can also be made by a liquidator who does not intend to take any action in the State, and the registrar may also cause such an application to be registered[182]. The certified copy judgment and, where appropriate, decision mentioned in s 227A(1) must be accompanied by a certified translation into the English or Irish language, a prescribed form and the appropriate fee[183]. It is also provided that the registrar shall issue a certificate of registration to the liquidator[184]. Although likely to arise infrequently, it is important to note the public policy exception contained in Article 26. This provides:

> 'Any Member State may refuse to recognise insolvency proceedings opened in another Member State or to enforce a judgment handed down in the context of such proceedings where the effects of such recognition or enforcement would be manifestly contrary to that

175 Article 21 of the Insolvency Regulation.

176 As inserted by reg 3(c) of the EC(CI)R 2002.

177 Section 227B of the CA 1963.

178 Section 227B(3) of the CA 1963.

179 Article 22 of the Insolvency Regulation.

180 Article 25 of the Insolvency Regulation.

181 As inserted by reg 3(8) of the EC(CI)R 2002.

182 Section 227(A) of the CA 1963.

183 Section 227A(3) of the CA 1963.

184 Section 227A(4) of the CA 1963.

> State's public policy, in particular its fundamental principles or the constitutional rights and liberties of the individual.'

[24.065] Articles 27–38 of the Insolvency Regulations deal with secondary insolvency proceedings. Those with standing to apply for the opening of secondary proceedings are the liquidator in the main proceedings and anybody else who has jurisdiction under the laws of the Member State whose courts are being asked to open secondary proceedings[185]. The liquidator in the main proceedings and the liquidators in the secondary proceedings are, by Article 31, 'duty bound to' communicate information and cooperate with each other.

[24.066] Regulation 6 of the EC(CI)R 2002 expressly provides that an insolvency judgment within the meaning of Article 25 of the Insolvency Regulation (read in accordance with Articles 38–58 of the Brussels Regulation on jurisdiction and the recognition and enforcement of judgments in civil and commercial matters[186]) can be declared enforceable immediately on completion of the formalities in Article 53 of the Brussels Regulation by the Master of the High Court. The Master is required to grant any preservation measures as are applied for where the High Court has jurisdiction to grant such relief[187]. It should be noted, however, that a request under Article 38 of the Brussels Regulations to secure and preserve any of a debtor's assets in the State must be made to the High Court[188].

[24.067] The Insolvency Regulation has also overturned for EU tax authorities the old common law rule that judgments by foreign revenue authorities are not enforceable, and in *Re Cedarlease Ltd*[189] Laffoy J held that the Commissioners of Customs & Excise for the United Kingdom had standing to present a petition to have an Irish company wound up. The learned judge concluded that:

> 'The grounds on which this court may wind up a company and the standing of a person or body to initiate the winding-up proceedings are governed by Irish law – the Act of 1963, as amended. In the instant case it has been established that the Company has failed to comply with a demand under s 214 of the Act of 1963, so that the Company is deemed to be unable to pay its debts. Therefore, a ground on which the Company may be wound up by the court exists (s 213(e)). While the Insolvency Regulation does not expressly provide that a creditor located in another Member State shall have the right to initiate insolvency proceedings, in my view, as the instant case illustrates, it would defeat the purpose of the Insolvency Regulation if that were not the case.'

As such, Laffoy J concluded that the Insolvency Regulation confers jurisdiction on the court to wind up the company on the petition of the petitioner and that, in effect, the common law principle was rendered inapplicable by the Insolvency Regulation.

[24.068] The foregoing is but a sample of the 47 articles contained in the Insolvency Regulation. As has been noted in the preceding paragraphs, there is nothing especially

185 Article 29 of the Insolvency Regulation.

186 Council Regulation (EC) No 44/2001 of 22 December 2000(2).

187 Regulation 6(7) and (8) of the EC(CI)R 2002.

188 Regulation 9(1) of the EC(CI)R 2002.

189 *Re Cedarlease Ltd* [2005] IEHC 67. See Black & Mangan, 'The Rule Against the Enforcement of Foreign Revenue Debts – Has Cedarlease Finished it for Good?' (2005) 23 ILT 189.

novel about secondary windings up or enforcing the orders of foreign courts. What is, however, significant is the effects of EU-wide regulations which force a degree of harmony in the insolvency laws of individual Member States.

(c) Assistance to Irish liquidators abroad

[24.069] Prior to the commencement of the Insolvency Regulation, the ability of Irish liquidators to bring application in the courts of other EU jurisdictions depended upon the legislative regime applicable in those jurisdictions. In *Re Business City Express Ltd*[190], an examiner who had been appointed to a company that had been placed under the protection of the Irish High Court successfully applied under s 426 of the Insolvency Act 1986 (UK) to the English Chancery Division for cooperation with the Irish High Court's decision. Specifically, the examiner required assistance in the form of an order that would bind English creditors. Rattee J said '… since the Irish court has requested assistance of this court, while I am not bound to give it, I should do so unless satisfied that there is some good reason not to do so[191]'.

Generally speaking the comity of the courts will prevail and courts will assist the enforcement of orders made by courts in other jurisdictions. Not only can Irish official liquidators avail of the Insolvency Regulation, so too can creditors' voluntary liquidators, who may obtain 'certification' of their status as such from the Master of the High Court. This is provided for by s 267A of the CA 1963[192] which allows application to be brought to the Master after a creditors' voluntary liquidator has been appointed provided that 'the centre of the company's main interests is situate in the State'.

The Director of Corporate Enforcement's power to supervise liquidators

[24.070] The CA 1963 provides that the court can make such order for inspection of the books and papers of a company by its creditors and contributories as it thinks fit[193]. The advent of the office of the Director of Corporate Enforcement has made liquidators amenable to supervision and inspection. Section 57(1) of the CLEA 2001 provides that the Director can on his own motion or where complaint is made to him by a member, contributory or creditor of the company, request, specifying the reason why the request is being made, the liquidator of a company to produce to the Director the liquidator's books for examination, and the liquidator is obliged to comply with such request. Failure

---

190 *Re Business City Express Ltd* [1997] BCC 826.

191 Citing *Re Dallhold Estates (UK) Pty Ltd* [1992] BCC 394; *Re Focus Insurance Co Ltd* [1996] BCC 659; and *Re Bank of Credit and Commerce International SA* [1993] BCC 787.

192 As inserted by reg 3(e) of the EC(CI)R 2002.

193 Section 243(1) of the CA 1963. Note that by s 234(1A), inserted by s 43 of the CLEA 2001, the court can on the application of the Director of Corporate Enforcement: '… make an order for the inspection by the Director of any books and papers in the possession of a company the subject of a winding-up order and the company, every officer of the company and the liquidator shall give to the Director such access to and facilities as are necessary for inspecting and taking copies of those books and papers as the Director may require.' It may also be noted that s 282A(1) and (2) of the CA 1963, inserted by s 49 of the CLEA 2001, expressly extend the provisions of s 243 of the CA 1963 (which primarily applies in official liquidations) to voluntary liquidations.

to comply is an offence[194]. Requests in respect of liquidations concluded more than six years prior to the request are prohibited[195]. It is particularly significant that the books which the director can seek can be *either* 'in relation to a particular liquidation process or to all liquidations undertaken by the liquidator'. Liquidators are obliged to answer the Director's questions concerning the content of the books requested to be produced and the conduct of a particular liquidation or all liquidations and is further obliged to give the Director such assistance in the matter as he is reasonably able to do[196].

[24.071] Section 58 of the CLEA 2001 imposes a statutory duty on liquidators' professional bodies to report misconduct to the Director. It provides:

> 'Where a disciplinary committee or tribunal (however called) of a prescribed professional body finds that a member conducting a liquidation or receivership has not maintained appropriate records, or it has reasonable grounds for believing that a member has committed an indictable offence under the Companies Acts during the course of a liquidation or receivership, the body shall report the matter, giving details of the finding or, as the case may be, of the alleged offence, to the Director forthwith and if the body fails to comply with this section it, and every officer of the body to whom the failure is attributable, is guilty of an offence.'

Ironically, by definition, liquidators who are not members of any profession, and so entirely unregulated, are not affected by this provision.

194 Section 57(4) of the CLEA 2001.
195 Section 57(3) of the CLEA 2001.
196 Section 57(2) of the CLEA 2001.

Chapter 25

Realisation and Distribution of Assets in a Winding Up

Introduction

[25.001] To use the term 'liquidation' in the context of the winding up of a company is to tell but half the story. As Laffoy J acknowledged in *Re Greendale Developments Ltd*[1]:

> 'Once a winding-up order is made, a company is doomed to extinction. The winding up process is the process of the administration of the assets of the company: their *collection, realisation and distribution* in discharge of the liabilities of the company to the creditors and of the entitlement of its contributories in accordance with the scheme of priorities prescribed in the Companies Acts.'

The essential nature of the winding up of a company entails two distinct concepts: the realisation of all assets belonging to the company following a full investigation into the company's assets, and the subsequent distribution of the proceeds of that realisation in the priority determined by law.

[25.002] The investigation into a company's affairs is an integral part of the realisation of a company's assets because the primary purpose of an investigation is invariably to bolster or swell the assets of the company. At the outset, it should be noted that the Company Law Enforcement Act 2001 ('CLEA 2001'), which created the office of the Director of Corporate Enforcement, has allowed the Director to piggyback on many of the powers of investigation afforded to liquidators. This is notwithstanding the fact that the Director has a very different purpose in mind to that of liquidators, namely, investigation with a view to prosecution or other sanction[2].

[25.003] The realisation and distribution of assets must be the theme of any treatment of the winding up of a company, whether of the voluntary or compulsory variety. Whilst often, the law of the consequences of a winding-up order are treated under the heading of 'the powers of a liquidator' or the 'incidents of a winding-up order', the reality is that the point under discussion is the realisation of corporate assets. In this regard, the word realisation is used in its wider meaning and includes the gathering-in of assets by whatever means. On this analysis, issues such as fraudulent preference, invalid floating charges and pooling and contribution orders are all examples of the principle that all corporate assets must be realised so as to be available for their subsequent distribution in accordance with the scheme of priorities in the Companies Acts. Consequently, this chapter treats the law in two sections:

1 *Re Greendale Developments Ltd* [1997] 3 IR 540 (emphasis added).

2 See Ch 28, *Compliance and Enforcement*, para **[28.020]** *et seq.*

[A] The realisation of corporate assets.
[B] The distribution of corporate assets.

[A] The Realisation of Corporate Assets

[25.004] In this section, the following matters are considered:

1. The liquidator's duty to realise corporate assets.
2. Officers' duties to assist liquidators.
3. The liquidator's starting point: gathering in assets.
4. The liquidator's starting point: gathering information.
5. Restraining the disposal or removal of corporate assets in a liquidation.
6. No litigation, execution, attachment or new judgment mortgages.
7. Disclaiming onerous property.
8. Post-commencement dispositions.
9. Fraudulent preference of creditors.
10. Fraudulent dispositions of property.
11. Invalidating certain floating charges.
12. Contribution by related companies to the assets.
13. Pooling the assets of related companies.
14. Claims against contributories.
15. Voidable transactions.
16. Litigating to swell corporate assets.

The liquidator's duty to realise corporate assets

[25.005] Liquidators, whether official or voluntary, are entrusted with the task of realising the company's assets. The term 'realise' does not have a specific statutory meaning and is used here in its dictionary sense. In *Re Private Motorists Provident Society Ltd; Horgan v Minister for Justice*[3], Murphy J said of the role of the official liquidator in the realisation of assets:

> 'An official liquidator is appointed under s 225 of the Companies Act 1963 to perform, *inter alia*, the statutory duty imposed in the court by s 235 of that Act which provides that the court shall cause "the assets of the company to be collected and applied in discharge of its liabilities". How assets will be "collected" will depend upon the nature of the particular assets and the circumstances of the case. The task may include litigation, sale or simply the reduction into possession by the official liquidator of "cash in hand". It seems to me that all or any of such procedures would be appropriate to make the assets of the company available for the discharge of its liabilities and indeed the payment of the costs and expenses of the litigation. All such procedures which make the assets of the company available for that purpose in my view constitute a "*realisation*" whether or not a sale of the assets is required[4].'

---

3 *Re Private Motorists Provident Society Ltd; Horgan v Minister for Justice* (23 June 1995, unreported) HC, Murphy J.

4 *Re Private Motorists Provident Society Ltd; Horgan v Minister for Justice* (23 June 1995, unreported) HC, at pp 7, 8. See *also Re Chipboard Products Ltd* (27 February 1997, unreported) HC, Laffoy J.

In the context of the realisation of corporate assets, the duties of liquidators may be seen to include:

- taking possession of all corporate assets, and protecting them, pending the distribution of the proceeds in accordance with law;
- pursuing all assets which in law or in equity belong to the company, but which may be in the possession of others;
- realising claims for compensation and damages against wrong-doing corporate officers and others who owe the company money; and,
- realising and liquidating all assets so as to have the proceeds available for distribution in accordance with law.

The foregoing duties of liquidators and the way in which they are governed by the Companies Acts, shall be considered in detail in this chapter.

Officers' duties to assist liquidators

[25.006] Directors and other officers[5] have statutory duties to assist and cooperate with liquidators. It should be noted that by s 293(1) of the CA 1963, if any person being a past or present officer of a company that is being wound up (whether officially or voluntarily) does not, *inter alia*, cooperate with a liquidator he shall, subject to s 293(2)[6], be guilty of an offence. The 16 offences set out there are:

'(a) does not to the best of his knowledge and belief fully and truly disclose to the liquidator when he requests such disclosure all the property, real and personal, of the company and how and to whom and for what consideration and when the company disposed of any part thereof, except such part as has been disposed of in the ordinary way of the business of the company; or

(b) does not deliver up to the liquidator, or as he directs, all such part of the real and personal property of the company as is in his custody or under his control, and which he is required by law to deliver up; or

(c) does not deliver up to the liquidator, or as he directs, all books and papers in his custody or under his control belonging to the company and which he is required by law to deliver up; or

(d) within 12 months next before the commencement of the winding up or at any time thereafter conceals any part of the property of the company to the value of €12.69 or upwards, or conceals any debt due to or from the company; or

(e) within 12 months next before the commencement of the winding up or at any time thereafter fraudulently removes any part of the property of the company to the value of €12.69 or upwards; or

(f) makes any material omission in any statement relating to the affairs of the company; or

---

5 For the purposes of s 293 of the CA 1963; s 293(4) provides that '"officer" shall include any person in accordance with whose directions or instructions the directors of a company have been accustomed to act'.

6 Section 293(2) of the CA 1963 provides: 'It shall be a good defence to a charge under any of paragraphs (a), (b), (c), (d), (f), (n) and (o) of subsection (1), if the accused proves that he had no intent to defraud and to a charge under any of paragraphs (h), (i) and (j) of subsection (1), if he proves that he had no intent to conceal the state of affairs of the company or to defeat the law.'

(g) knowing or believing that a false debt has been proved by any person under the winding up, fails for the period of a month to inform the liquidator thereof; or

(h) after the commencement of the winding up prevents the production of any book or paper affecting or relating to the property or affairs of the company; or

(i) within 12 months next before the commencement of the winding up or at any time thereafter conceals, destroys, mutilates or falsifies or is privy to the concealment, destruction, mutilation or falsification of any book or paper affecting or relating to the property or affairs of the company; or

(j) within 12 months next before the commencement of the winding up or at any time thereafter makes or is privy to the making of any false entry in any book or paper affecting or relating to the property or affairs of the company; or

(k) within 12 months next before the commencement of the winding up or at any time thereafter fraudulently parts with, alters or makes any omission in, or is privy to the fraudulent parting with, altering or making any omission in, any document affecting or relating to the property or affairs of the company; or

(l) after the commencement of the winding up or at any meeting of the creditors of the company within 12 months next before the commencement of the winding up attempts to account for any part of the property of the company by fictitious losses or expenses; or

(m) has within 12 months next before the commencement of the winding up or at any time thereafter, by any false representation or other fraud, obtained any property for or on behalf of the company on credit which the company does not subsequently pay for; or

(n) within 12 months next before the commencement of the winding up or at any time thereafter, under the false pretence that the company is carrying on its business, obtains on credit for or on behalf of the company, any property which the company does not subsequently pay for; or

(o) within 12 months next before the commencement of the winding up or at any time thereafter pawns, pledges or disposes of any property of the company which has been obtained on credit and has not been paid for, unless such pawning, pledging or disposing is in the ordinary way of business of the company; or

(p) is guilty of any false representation or other fraud for the purpose of obtaining the consent of the creditors of the company or any of them to an agreement with reference to the affairs of the company or to the winding up.'

In *R v McCredie*[7], the Court of Appeal heard an appeal against a conviction of two directors for failing to deliver up company books contrary to the English equivalent to our s 293(1)(c)[8]. The Court of Appeal quoted the English provision and said:

> 'We quote that section in full, to make the obvious but sometimes overlooked point that company officers in a winding up owe a duty to the company to comply with that section. The immediate relevance here depends on two points. First, these subsections require officers of the company to be pro-active, and not merely reactive. They must co-operate with the liquidator actively in "discovering" (ie disclosing) company property unknown to the liquidator, and the delivery up requirements significantly are not dependent on a prior request from the liquidator. It is clear that the delivery up requirement in s 208 is covered

7 *R v McCredie* [2000] BCC 617.

8 Section 208(1) of the Insolvency Act 1986 (UK).

> by s 12(1) of the Interpretation Act 1978[9]: "Where an Act … imposes a duty it is implied, unless the contrary intention appears, that … the duty is to be performed from time to time as occasion requires". This was a continuing duty, and not a once for all time duty. It did not have to be triggered by a request from the liquidator.'

In that case, the company's liquidator's agents had taken away the company's filing cabinets after emptying them of computer disks and documents. The directors had removed the disks and documents, compiled from them a list of the company's customers and had sold the list as part of the company's goodwill to another company. The directors' defence to the liquidator's demand for the return of the information was that the disks and documents had been 'abandoned' by the liquidator, acting through his agents. The Court of Appeal held that the liquidator had not abandoned the property as this could not be done without knowledge of its existence. Moreover, the directors had a statutory duty to make full discovery of the company's property to its liquidator[10]. That directors owe duties to liquidators to cooperate is, no doubt, a fact that liquidators should not be shy to point out to recalcitrant officers.

The liquidator's starting point: gathering in assets

[25.007] Upon his appointment, the liquidator should immediately set about ascertaining, securing and gathering in the company's assets. Official and provisional liquidators have very specific duties and express powers to gather in assets.

(a) The duty to gather-in assets

[25.008] Official and provisional liquidators have a statutory obligation to take a company's property under their control. Section 229(1) of the CA 1963 provides that where a winding-up order has been made or where a provisional liquidator has been appointed, an official or provisional liquidator:

> '... shall take into his custody or under his control all the property and things in action to which the company is or appears to be entitled.'

The reason why court appointed liquidators have such an express duty is because they are the agents of the court and the court is expressly charged with causing 'the assets of the company to be collected and applied in discharge of its liabilities'[11]. Indeed, in a compulsory winding up, where no liquidator has been appointed, s 229(2) provides that all the property of the company shall be deemed to be in the custody of the court.

---

9 Section 23 of our Interpretation Act 2005 also provides: '(1) A duty imposed by an enactment shall be performed from time to time as occasion requires. (2) A duty imposed by an enactment on the holder of an office as that holder shall be deemed to be imposed on, and shall accordingly be performed by, the holder for the time being of that office.'

10 The Court of Appeal's warning on the difficulties in a jury trial of explaining the defence of 'abandonment' should be noted. In that case, at trial, a nine-page paper had been prepared to assist the jury but had not been agreed by counsel. There, no issue had been taken with the document circulated to the jury but the Court of Appeal warned that such an omission might court disaster in another case.

11 Section 235(1) of the CA 1963; acknowledged in *Re Private Motorists Provident Society Ltd; Horgan v Minister for Justice* (23 June 1995, unreported) HC, Murphy J. See para **[25.005]**.

[25.009] By s 239(1) of the CA 1963 the court can order any person who owes money to the company to pay it into a bank account of the liquidator:

> 'The court may order any contributory, purchaser or other person from whom money is due to the company to pay the amount due into such bank as the court may appoint to the account of the liquidator instead of to the liquidator, and any such order may be enforced in like manner as if it had directed payment to the liquidator.'

Pending their distribution, the only person who is entitled to control the assets of a company that is in liquidation is its liquidator.

[25.010] In a members' voluntary liquidation the liquidator's powers derive from the members' resolution appointing him as liquidator which must appoint him 'for the purpose of winding up the affairs and distributing the assets of the company'[12]. A liquidator appointed in a creditors' voluntary liquidation has an identical statutory purpose[13]. In order to discharge these requirements, voluntary liquidators will be obliged to begin to gather-in the company's assets, something that voluntary liquidators have power to do without the sanction of either the members (in a members' voluntary) or the creditors (in a creditors' voluntary), by virtue of ss 276(1)(b) and 231(2)(i) of the CA 1963[14].

[25.011] By s 230 of the CA 1963, on the application of the liquidator, the court may:

> '... direct that all or any part of the property of whatsoever description belonging to the company or held by trustees on its behalf shall vest in the liquidator by his official name, and thereupon the property to which the order relates shall vest accordingly, and the liquidator may, after giving such indemnity, if any, as the court may direct, bring or defend in his official name any action or other legal proceedings which relates to that property or which it is necessary to bring or defend for the purpose of effectually winding up the company and recovering its property.'

It is relatively unusual for the court to order that the title to a company's assets vest in the liquidator. In *Re Private Motorists Provident Society Ltd; Horgan v Minister for Justice*[15], Murphy J held that it was not necessary for an order to have been made under s 230 in order for stamp duty on monies 'received by the liquidator in realisation of the assets of the company' to become due. There, it had been argued that monies realised by the society, itself, were not subject to duty and that monies could only be said to have been received by a liquidator where an order under s 230 has been made. Murphy J rejected this, saying:

> 'Clearly the realisation was brought about by the liquidator and he was the proper party to give a receipt for the proceeds of sale thereof even though the ownership rcmained vested in the Society[16].'

---

12 Section 258(1) of the CA 1963.

13 Section 267(1) of the CA 1963.

14 Section 231(2)(i) of the CA 1963 provides that the liquidator has power to 'do all such other things as may be necessary for winding up the affairs of the company and distributing its assets'.

15 *Re Private Motorists Provident Society Ltd; Horgan v Minister for Justice* (23 June 1995, unreported) HC, Murphy J.

16 *Re Private Motorists Provident Society Ltd; Horgan v Minister for Justice* (23 June 1995, unreported) HC, at p 5.

Whilst this decision accords with common sense, it is thought that the liquidator's contention was pedantically correct since monies received by a liquidator in the absence of an order being made under s 230 are received as agent of and on behalf of the company.

(b) The assets to be gathered in: the meaning of 'property and things in action'

[25.012] An official liquidator's statutory obligation to gather-in, contained in s 229(1) of the CA 1963, relates to all 'property and things in action'. Tangible personalty, such as chattels, is the most easily recognisable property that the liquidator must gather up for later distribution in accordance with the priority determined by law. Choses in action can be very varied in form and include, for example, shares, insurance rights, cheques, goodwill, debts and causes of action. Choses in action cannot be grasped or held and whilst they will invariably have some physical title document (eg, an insurance policy, share certificate or piece of paper acknowledging a debt, etc) the chose itself does not have a tangible manifestation. The courts in England have held that a milk quota is 'property' in a winding up and that the liquidators could direct its sale or other realisation[17]. So too was a waste management licence found to be 'property', only, this time, worthless property that could be disclaimed by the liquidator[18]. It has been held, also, that the fruits of a company's property are themselves the company's property[19]. It has been questioned, however, whether the proceeds of a successful action against company directors for breach of duty or, say, fraudulent trading, is 'company' property[20].

(c) No lien on company books and records

[25.013] The title to real property, evidenced by title deeds, may be in the possession of advisors or former advisors to the company. Similarly, files and other documents relating to company property may be held by third parties. Prior to the commencement of the Companies Act 1990 advisors to companies could retain possession of certain files and other documents until they had been paid for their services by exercising a lien. Now, by s 244A of the CA 1963[21], no person can withhold possession of deeds, instruments, or other documents, books of account, receipts, bills, invoices or other papers of a like nature relating to the accounts or trade, dealings or business of the company from the liquidator by claiming possession or lien. This is, however, without prejudice to the rights of the persons in whose possession such documents are, and the section is intended to assist the gathering of information by the liquidator, which will go to aid the orderly realisation of the company's assets. Section 244A does not apply

---

17 *Swift v Dairywise Farms Ltd* [2000] BCC 642.

18 *Official Receiver as Liquidator of Celtic Extraction Ltd & Bluestone Chemicals Ltd v Environment Agency* [2000] BCC 487.

19 *R v McCredie* [2000] BCC 617.

20 See *Re Floor Fourteen Ltd; Lewis v Inland Revenue Commissioners* [2001] 2 BCLC 392, considered at para **[25.139]**.

21 As inserted by s 125 of the CA 1990.

where the circumstances giving rise to the lien claimed arose prior to the enactment of the CA 1990: *Kelly v Scales*[22].

(d) Assets not beneficially owned by the company

[25.014] Certain assets in the company's possession may not in fact belong to the company. Examples include goods that are subject to a valid and effective retention of title clause, leased property and property that is held by the company in trust. The issues arising in relation to such property are considered in the context of the distribution of corporate assets, below[23]. Alternatively, certain property that belongs in law and in equity to a company may be more of a liability than a benefit to the company, and the liquidator may wish to *disclaim* it, something that is permitted by statute in certain circumstances[24].

[25.015] It is sometimes said that when a company is wound up it holds its property on trust for its creditors[25]. It is submitted that this is not in fact a helpful legal analysis of the ownership of property by a company in liquidation and that until such time as a liquidator pays over monies in the form of a dividend in a winding up to, say, a creditor, the company is the legal and beneficial owner of those monies. Whilst referring to the property of an insolvent company as being held 'in trust' for its creditors might be an apt analogy, it neither helpful nor, it is thought, legally correct to characterise the company's ownership of money or other property in its possession as being held, technically, in trust. This issue was considered in some detail by the Federal Court of Australia in *Commissioner of Taxation v Linter Textiles Australia Ltd*[26] where it was stated:

> '... we do not agree that a trust in the strict sense of that expression is imposed upon a company in liquidation, although we accept that some principles of trust law will be relevant.'

(e) Disputed assets

[25.016] Most problems for liquidators tend to arise in respect of assets that are not legally owned by the company but to which the company is nevertheless beneficially entitled. Often, the liquidator will have reason to believe that the total worth of the company's assets far exceeds those assets that he can readily lay his hands on. So, in a wide variety of situations, the liquidator will have to set about realising assets to which the company is beneficially entitled, thereby swelling the assets available for distribution in accordance with insolvency law. Particularly where wrongdoing by the controllers of the company is suspected, the liquidator may find that he requires more information on the affairs of the company and the whereabouts and ownership of assets than that being offered by the controllers. He may in such situations seek an order for examination, an

---

22 *Kelly v Scales* [1994] 1 IR 42.

23 See para **[25.149]** *et seq.*

24 See para **[25.058]**.

25 In *Re Frederick Inns Ltd* [1994] 1 ILRM 387, Blayney J said in the Supreme Court in reference to *Re Oriental Inland Steam Co* (1874) 9 Ch App 557 that 'It is clear from this case that as soon as a winding-up order has been made the company ceases to be the beneficial owner of its assets'. See Ch 15, *Duties of Directors and Other Officers*, at para **[15.013]**.

26 *Commissioner of Taxation v Linter Textiles Australia Ltd* [2003] FCAFC 63 (14 April 2003).

asset freezing order or even an arrest order against directors and others to enable him obtain the information he requires[27].

(f) Swelling assets through transaction avoidance and litigation

[25.017] In realising a company's assets a liquidator may find that some or all of the company's assets have been siphoned off through unlawful dispositions, either before or after the commencement of the winding up. He may indeed find that certain creditors have been *preferred* over the vast majority of other creditors[28]. He may find that certain persons have recently been granted floating charges as security for sums owed to them by the company, thus allowing them 'leap frog' the orderly queue which the liquidator will attempt to create on distribution[29]. Additionally, realisable assets may be increased by applying to have related companies contribute to the assets of the company which is being wound up by means of a contribution order[30]. Where the affairs of two companies have been intermingled, the liquidator may apply to have both companies wound up together, and their assets pooled[31]. He may find that the company has suffered loss through breaches of duty by its officers, or is owed money in contract, and he may decide to litigate to satisfy such claims. Other methods of swelling assets involve making a call on the contributories in limited companies in respect of outstanding payments on shares; and in the case of unlimited companies, on all the shareholders to make good any deficit between assets and liabilities. It is evident therefore that not only is the liquidator concerned with the gathering in of assets, but also with their lawful distribution since what he takes from one creditor he will ultimately pay to another creditor who is entitled in law to be paid in priority[32].

The liquidator's starting point: gathering information

[25.018] Commonly, liquidators will commence the liquidation of a company by gathering information to facilitate the gathering in of assets. These powers are considered under the following headings:

(a) Powers to obtain basic information.
(b) Power to obtain books and papers.
(c) Examination.
(d) Post-examination transfer and search and seizure orders.
(e) Powers of civil arrest.

(a) Powers to obtain basic information

[25.019] Information will often be the key to an effective realisation of corporate assets. Where it is suspected that assets were, or are, in the process of being spirited away their very whereabouts and the circumstances of their removal from the company may be unknown. Similarly, where delinquent behaviour on the part of the company's controllers is suspected, the best way of obtaining evidence is often by calling upon

27 See paras **[25.024]**, **[25.047]** and **[25.038]**, respectively.
28 See para **[25.081]**.
29 See para **[25.110]**.
30 See para **[25.119]**.
31 See para **[25.125]**.
32 See para **[25.140]**.

those suspected to give an account of their behaviour. Sometimes, a liquidator will be given full cooperation. Other times, a liquidator will be starved of cooperation in general and of information in particular[33], and in such circumstances may need to rely on certain statutory powers to extract the required information[34].

[25.020] The least draconian statutory measure designed to assist the liquidator to obtain information is contained in s 224 of the CA 1963[35]. Where a compulsory winding up has been ordered or a provisional liquidator has been appointed, the law prescribes that there shall, unless the court says otherwise:

> '... be made out and filed in the court a statement as to the affairs of the company in the prescribed form, verified by affidavit, and showing the particulars of its assets, debts and liabilities, the names, residences and occupations of its creditors, the securities held by them respectively, the dates when the securities were respectively given, and such further or other information as may be prescribed or as the court may require[36].'

The statement of affairs must be filed within 21 days of the order being made to wind up the company or from the date of the appointment of a provisional liquidator[37]. The statement of affairs may be inspected, and a copy or extract taken, by any person who states in writing that he is a creditor or contributory of the company on payment of the prescribed fee[38]. Where a person untruthfully states that he is a creditor or contributory he is guilty of contempt of court[39]. The costs incurred by any person making or concurring in making the statement and affidavit will be allowed and will be paid out of the assets of the company as the court may allow[40].

[25.021] The persons who must file and verify the statement of affairs are those who at the making of an order to wind up the company, or on the appointment of a provisional liquidator, are the company's directors, secretary, or others who are so ordered by the court to file and verify the statement[41]. These other persons include past officers and promoters and employees within the previous year. Order 74, r 24(2) of the Rules of the Superior Courts ('RSC') 1986 provides, in addition to s 224 of the CA 1963 that the court may require that these persons attend before the court at a set time.

[25.022] The directors in a members' voluntary winding up are required to embody in their declaration of solvency a statement of the company's assets and liabilities[42]. In a

---

33 Ussher, *Company Law in Ireland* (1986), p 491 aptly comments that 'Often the item of which the liquidator of an insolvent company is most short, apart from funds, is information'.

34 See also para **[25.022]** where officers' duties to cooperate with liquidators are considered.

35 See also RSC, Ord 24, rr 24–28.

36 See *Re Tipperary Self-Drive Ltd* reported in (1992) Irish Times, 21 January, where Costello J ordered the preparation of a statement of affairs by two directors of companies which had been ordered to be wound up. So too in *Re Eurokabin Ltd* reported in (1991) Irish Times, 19 September, one of the directors, in a company where fraudulent and reckless trading were suspected of having occurred, was ordered by Lynch J to make a statement of the affairs of the company.

37 Section 224(3) and (8) of the CA 1963.

38 Section 224(6) of the CA 1963.

39 Section 224(7) of the CA 1963.

40 Section 224(4) of the CA 1963.

41 Section 224(2) of the CA 1963.

42 Section 256(2)(b) of the CA 1963.

creditors' voluntary winding up the directors are required to cause a full statement of the position of the company's affairs together with a list of the creditors and the estimated amount of their claims to be laid before the creditors' meeting[43]. It is arguable that where they do not receive cooperation, voluntary liquidators can by virtue of s 280(1) of the CA 1963 apply to court for an order under s 224(1) of the CA 1963. Threatening to report non-compliant directors to the Office of the Director of Corporate Enforcement for breach of s 293(1) of the CA 1963 may also induce cooperation[44].

(b) Power to obtain books and papers

[25.023] Where liquidators experience difficulty in obtaining possession and control of corporate property, books or papers, recourse may be had to the court for an order under s 236 of the CA 1963 which provides:

> 'The court may, at any time after making a winding-up order, require any contributory for the time being on the list of contributories and any trustee, receiver, banker, agent or officer of the company to pay, deliver, convey, surrender or transfer forthwith, or within such time as the court directs, to the liquidator any money, property or books and papers in his hands to which the company is *prima facie* entitled.'

Both official and voluntary liquidators can apply to court for such an order[45]. It was held in *Re Industrial Services Company (Dublin) Ltd (No 2)*[46] that where a disposition from a company's bank account had been declared void under s 218 of the CA 1963[47], although s 218 did not permit the making of an order that the moneys disposed of should be repaid, it was open to the court to make an order under s 236 of the CA 1963 requiring the bank as banker to the company to pay the amount to the company 'being moneys which are prima facie an asset of the company'.

(c) Examination

[25.024] In addition to the power to require officers to attend meetings of the creditors, contributories or committee of inspection[48], application can be made to court to summon an officer and certain other persons and examine him and them on oath (whether by word of mouth or in writing). The power of the court to order an examination is found in s 245(1) of the CA 1963[49] which provides that:

> 'The court may, of its own motion or on the application of the Director, at any time after the appointment of a provisional liquidator or the making of a winding-up order, summon before it any officer of the company or person known or suspected to have in his possession any property of the company or supposed to be indebted to the company, or any person whom the court deems capable of giving information relating to the promotion, formation, trade, dealings, affairs or property of the company.'

---

43 Section 266(3)(a) of the CA 1963.

44 See para **[25.006]**.

45 Section 280(1) of the CA 1963.

46 *Re Industrial Services Company (Dublin) Ltd* (No 2) [2002] IEHC 57, McCracken J.

47 See para **[25.065]**.

48 Section 246 of the CA 1963; voluntary liquidators could apply for an order under this section by virtue of s 280(1) of the CA 1963.

49 As amended by s 126 of the CA 1990, and s 44(a) of the CLEA 2001.

The actual information extraction mechanism is to be found in s 245(2), which provides:

> 'The court may examine such person on oath concerning the matters aforesaid, either by word of mouth or on written interrogatories, and may reduce his answers to writing and require him to sign them.'

Examination is an investigative tool. The court may require an examinee to produce any 'accounting records, deed, instrument, or other document or paper relating to the company that are in his custody'[50]. Prior to being examined, the court may order that an examinee place before it 'a statement, in such form as the court may direct, of any transactions between him and the company of a type or class which the court may specify'[51].

[25.025] Sometimes, the examination will both bolster existing information and suspicions and also provide new information on wrongdoing or, indeed, simply indicate why a company failed[52]. Failure to attend an examination, without reasonable excuse, is treated as contempt of court[53]. The court also has power to order the civil arrest of a person who without reasonable excuse has failed to attend or a person in respect of whom there are reasonable grounds for believing that he has or is about to abscond[54].

(i) Locus standi in official liquidations

[25.026] An application to court to order an examination of a person under s 245(1) of the CA 1963 will usually be made by an official liquidator in pursuit of information to assist him in piecing together what went wrong, who caused things to go wrong, and where the company's assets might now be. Provisional liquidators also can apply under s 245(1).

[25.027] While usually it will be the official liquidator who will apply for an examination order, it is open to others to make application, although the circumstances in which a court will accede to such a request will be rare. In *Re Embassy Art Products Ltd*[55], an application was made by contributories of a company which, on the direction of its financing bank, caused, *inter alia*, the appointment of a non-executive chairman, the granting of fixed and floating charges over its assets and the retention of a firm of management consultants. When the company failed to adhere to other terms of the facility, receivers were appointed. On the application of another creditor, the company was wound up. The application for the examination of the bank-nominated chairman was refused. Acknowledging the draconian nature of such an order, Hoffmann J said:

> 'Any application to use the section, which is *prima facie* an invasion of the rights of privacy of the persons whom it is sought to examine, is subject to the overriding requirement that the examination must be necessary in the interests of the winding up and not oppressive or unfair on the respondent. It is clear, however, that in applying these principles there are significant differences in the court's approach to applications by liquidators, on the one hand, and contributories, on the other[56].'

---

[50] Section 245(3) of the CA 1963.

[51] Section 245(4) of the CA 1963.

[52] As in *Irish Commercial Society Ltd v Plunkett* [1987] ILRM 504 at 506, *per* Henchy J.

[53] Section 245(7) of the CA 1963.

[54] The court's powers of civil arrest in winding up are considered at para **[25.038]** *et seq.*

[55] *Re Embassy Art Products Ltd* [1988] BCLC 1.

[56] *Re Embassy Art Products Ltd* [1988] BCLC 1 at 6–7.

Hoffmann J gave four reasons for a different approach by the court to an application for an examination by a person other than a liquidator. First, an official liquidator is an officer of the court and has by virtue of that office *locus standi* to make application. A contributory or creditor on the other hand must show a probability of some benefit accruing to him, ie, he must show a special interest in the outcome of the winding up. Second, courts tend to attach more weight to the application of a liquidator because he is an independent professional person. Third, where a contributory is suing his company there is a presumption that he seeks to advance his personal interests unlike an application by a liquidator who is presumed to have no ulterior motive. Fourth, while a contributory may feel he needs information, the main purpose of the order is 'to assist the liquidator to discover the facts concerning transactions of which he will have had no personal knowledge'[57]. Clearly, although it is possible for a person, other than a liquidator, to obtain an order for examination, other persons will have to discharge a much higher evidential burden.

(ii) Locus standi in voluntary liquidations

[25.028] In the case of either a members' or creditors' voluntary winding up, the voluntary liquidator or any contributory or creditor may apply to court for an order under s 245(1)[58] or s 282B[59] of the CA 1963. In *Re Comet Food Machinery Company Ltd*[60], a creditor in a creditors' voluntary winding up successfully applied for an order for the examination of two of the company's directors. The facts in that case were that the company had been engaged in the supply of cooking machinery and the applicant creditors had purchased machinery from the company which, they claimed, was defective. The applicant creditors had been awarded £255,000 plus costs in uncontested proceedings. Subsequent to this, the company was placed into voluntary liquidation and in the absence of a declaration of solvency, it proceeded as a creditors' voluntary winding up. The applicant creditors learned that a new company owned by the same two directors had been formed, which occupied the same premises as the original company, and which appeared to employ the original company's employees. The company was insolvent and the Supreme Court stated that the conclusion, that all trade creditors other than the applicant creditors, had been paid prior to the litigation, seemed inescapable. In the High Court, Costello P granted the applicant creditors' application for an order under s 245(1) of the CA 1963; the applicant creditors had contended that the company had been liquidated and the new company formed with a view to carrying on effectively the same business and that the company's assets had been disposed of with a view to frustrating the applicant creditors' claim for damages. On the appeal to the Supreme Court, Keane J began his interpretation of the law by stating that it was clear that the

---

57 *Re Embassy Art Products Ltd* [1988] BCLC 1 at 7.

58 Section 280(1) of the CA 1963, which applies to voluntary windings up, provides that 'the liquidator or any contributory or creditor may apply to the court to determine any question arising in the winding up of a company, or to exercise in relation to the enforcing of calls or any other matter, *all or any of the powers which the court might exercise if the company were being wound up by the court*'.

59 It should be noted that this section mirrors the provisions of s 245 of the CA 1963. In the light of s 280(1) of the CA 1963, it is thought that it was unnecessary to state a separate power for voluntary liquidators.

60 *Re Comet Food Machinery Company Ltd* [1999] 1 IR 485.

High Court's power under s 245(1) was a discretionary one and also that it was clear that in the case of a voluntary winding up a creditor had, by virtue of s 280(1) of the CA 1963, the *locus standi* to make application. Keane J went on to state that the considerations stated by Hoffmann J in *Re Embassy Art Products Ltd*[61] – namely, that creditor applicants for an examination order need to demonstrate that the examination would probably result in some benefit accruing to them and also that their belief in the necessity of an examination would not carry the same weight as that of a liquidator – were 'undoubtedly applicable where, as here, the application is made in the course of a voluntary winding up'[62]. Noting that the applicant creditors' reason for wanting an order under s 245(1) was because of their suspicion that the company's assets had been diverted with a view to avoiding the payment of the judgment they had recovered might or might not have been well founded but that if it was, the ground might be laid for an application under s 139 of the CA 1990[63]. Keane J held:

> 'It cannot be said that, in these circumstances, the application is one which is manifestly brought by the applicants without any hope of recovering any benefit but simply in order to initiate an unnecessarily intrusive inquiry because of pique arising from the fact that their proceedings against [the company] have so far proved fruitless[64].'

It was concluded that the High Court was entitled to exercise its discretion in favour of the applicant creditors by making the order sought and that the court should not interfere with the exercise by Costello P of his discretion.

(iii) Locus standi of the Director of Corporate Enforcement

[25.029] It should also be noted that an order for examination under s 282B of the CA 1963 can be sought by the Director of Corporate Enforcement (for example, to assist in deciding whether or not to make an application under s 150 or 160 of the CA 1990 against the director of an insolvent company)[65]. Moreover, an order under s 245(1) can be sought where a company is not being wound up where the conditions set out in s 251 of the CA 1990 are satisfied, ie, where a company is unable to pay its debts and the reason that it is not being wound up is the insufficiency of its assets[66]. In *Alba Radio Ltd v Haltone (Cork) Ltd*[67], it was held by Barron J that to order the examination of a director of a company that was not being wound up in respect of circumstances that took place prior to the commencement of the CA 1990 was not the application of a retrospective penalty. Although the circumstances in which such an order might be made were changed by the CA 1990, no new liability would be imposed by the making of the order[68].

---

61 *Re Embassy Art Products Ltd* [1988] BCLC 1.

62 *Re Embassy Art Products Ltd* [1988] BCLC 1 at 7.

63 See para **[25.103]**.

64 *Re Embassy Art Products Ltd* [1988] BCLC 1 at 8.

65 See *Re Pantmaenog Timber Co Ltd* [2003] 4 ALL ER 18 where the UK's House of Lords considered the use of a similar provision by their Official Receiver to obtain evidence for use in proceedings under the English Disqualification Act.

66 See Ch 15, *Duties of Directors and Other Officers*, para **[15.141]** *et seq.*

67 *Alba Radio Ltd v Haltone (Cork) Ltd* [1995] 2 IR 170, [1995] 2 ILRM 466.

68 It must be questioned whether, if an order was disobeyed thereby giving rise to a contempt of court, would it still be considered that no new liability was being imposed.

(iv) The courts' attitude to making examination orders

[25.030] When application is made for an examination, the court will scrutinise the circumstances before exercising its discretion. Although Irish judicial pronouncement on the topic is scarce, it has been held in the UK that the order must not be oppressive. Accordingly, in *Re Adlards Motor Group Holding Ltd*[69] Harman J refused to make an order for an examination against a receiver because this would be oppressive in view of the amount of time which had elapsed since the receiver had been appointed.

[25.031] Common reasons for the ordering of an examination are that the person is suspected of having corporate property in his possession, is indebted to the company, or may generally be able to throw light on the affairs of the company. In *Re Mark Synnott (Life and Pension Brokers) Ltd*[70], an insurance company originally in voluntary liquidation was later placed into official liquidation. The provisional liquidator who was appointed to the company is reported as having told the court that, since he was appointed provisional liquidator by the court three weeks previously, he had not identified any mitigating factor which would not warrant a conclusion that the affairs of the company had been conducted in a fraudulent and reckless manner, to the extreme detriment of the company's clients[71]. Later, an application for the examination of certain directors was granted and these examinations were reported in the press[72]. Again, in *Re Aluminium Fabricators Ltd*[73], arising from an examination under s 245 of the CA 1963, it was learnt that two sets of accounts were kept by the directors of the company concerned.

(v) The holding of and procedure in examinations

[25.032] An examination is usually heard before the Master of the High Court and is held in public. While it was stated by the former Supreme Court in *Re Redbreast Preserving Co (Ireland) Ltd*[74] that examination could be held in private because it was not an 'administration of justice' and so was outside Article 34.1 of Bunreacht na hÉireann, this may now be said to be overruled in the light of the comments of Walsh J in *Re R Ltd*[75]. Walsh J said:

> 'If the dictum of the former Supreme Court in *Re Redbreast Preserving Co Ltd* means that the constitutional requirement that justice is to be administered in public is satisfied by the public pronouncement of a decision based on evidence taken other than in public, then where that is not expressly authorised by a post-constitutional statute it is clearly incorrect and ought not to be followed[76].'

---

69 *Re Adlards Motor Group Holding Ltd* [1990] BCLC 68.

70 An application reported in (1991) Irish Times, 15, 18, 19, 27, 29 June, 2, 3, 4, 6, 9, July and 6, 7, 8, 9 November.

71 See (1991) Irish Times, 2 July.

72 See (1991) Irish Times, 6, 7, 8 and 9 November.

73 *Re Aluminium Fabricators Ltd* [1984] ILRM 399.

74 *Re Redbreast Preserving Co Ltd* 91 ILTR 12, [1958] IR 234.

75 *Re R Ltd* [1988] ILRM 126.

76 On *in camera* applications under s 205(7) of the CA 1963, see Ch 11, *Shareholders' Remedies*, para **[11.060]**.

As Keane has commented[77], since s 245 of the CA 1963 contains no such express authorisation it would 'clearly be unsafe to hold the examination in private'. However, Keane seems to recognise that where it is anticipated that evidence obtained will not be required in court proceedings and will be solely for the benefit of the liquidator, examination in private may be allowed. Clearly, great care must be exercised by the courts in acceding to a request for a private examination because in all but the most clear-cut of cases, *other* evidence may well arise at the examination.

[25.033] During the examination the person being examined may be examined on oath, either orally or in writing, and he may be required to sign his written answers to the questions put to him[78]. The court may also require that he produce any accounting records, deed, instrument or other document or paper relating to the company that are in his custody or under his control or power[79]. Before an examination takes place the court may order the person to be examined to place before the court a statement, as directed by the court, of any transactions between him and the company of a type or class specified by the court[80]. Such a statement may provide the liquidator with evidence of voidable transactions which will enable him to swell the company's assets available for distribution[81]. Where it is the opinion of the court that it is just and equitable to do so, the court may order the person being examined to pay the costs of the examination[82].

(vi) Failure to cooperate

[25.034] The cooperation of the person being examined is required[83], and failure to answer questions can render the person liable for contempt of court[84].

(vii) Admissibility of evidence obtained in an examination

[25.035] Section 245(6) of the CA 1963[85] prohibits the person being examined from refusing to answer any questions put to him on the ground that his answer might incriminate him, and any answer by him to such a question may be used in evidence against him in any proceedings whatsoever (save proceedings for an offence (other than

77 Keane, *Company Law* (4th edn, Bloomsbury Professional, 2007), para 36.180.

78 Section 245(2) of the CA 1963.

79 Section 245(3) of the CA 1963.

80 Section 245(4) of the CA 1963.

81 This may occur where evidence is obtained of the contravention of s 60 of the CA 1963: see Ch 10, *The Maintenance of Capital*, para **[10.046]** *et seq* or; or in contravention of ss 29 or 31 of the CA 1990: see Ch 16, *Statutory Regulation of Directors' Transactions, at para* **[16.022]** *et seq and para* **[16.055]** *et seq, respectively.*

82 Section 245(5) of the CA 1963. Presumably, just as although a misfeasance suit may be successfully defended, if the examinee's conduct prompted the instigation of the application he may be directed to bear the costs of the examination: *Re David Ireland & Co Ltd* [1905] IR 133.

83 See the warning given by the Master of the High Court to a company director in *Re Europa Forklift Ltd,* an application reported in (1991) Irish Times, 22 November.

84 Section 245(7) of the CA 1963.

85 As substituted by s 44(b) of the CLEA 2001.

perjury) in respect of such an answer)[86]. It was held in *Re Aluminium Fabricators Ltd*[87] that evidence obtained from an examination was not admissible in other proceedings arising from the same winding up, such as under s 297 of the CA 1963[88]. Admissions of liability are somewhat rare, but are occasionally seen[89]. The position with regard to the use of such evidence against third parties is different though. Accordingly, in the case of *Irish Commercial Society Ltd v Plunkett*[90] Costello J held that evidence given by a person being examined does not preclude its use in proceedings against a third party, thus construing the subsection literally[91].

(d) Post-examination transfer and search and seizure orders

[25.036] If it appears to the court from an examination under s 245 of the CA 1963 that any person being examined is indebted to the company, or has in his possession or control any money, property, books or papers of the company, then by s 245A(1) of the CA 1963[92] the court may, of its own motion or on the application of the Director of Corporate Enforcement, order such person:

> '(a) to pay to the liquidator the amount or any part of the debt, or
>
> (b) to pay, deliver, convey, surrender or transfer to the liquidator such money, property or books and papers or any part thereof,
>
> at such time and in such manner and on such terms as it may direct.'

This order can be utilised to enable a liquidator to realise the assets of a company, since, on proof of misappropriation, the court is empowered to direct an immediate transfer of assets to the liquidator. Whilst s 245A(1)(6) of the CA 1963 applies to official liquidations, s 282C(1)–(6) of the CA 1963 applies to voluntary liquidations and gives the Director of Corporate Enforcement *locus standi* to make application for such an order. The two sections are in all material respects identical.[93] Official liquidators will continue to apply directly under s 245A for an order under that section. It is thought that voluntary liquidators should apply for a s 245A order in reliance upon s 280(1) and that only the Director should apply for an order under s 282C.

[25.037] Section 45(c) of the CLEA 2001 extended s 245A of the CA 1963 by the addition of five new subsections. Although thought to be intended primarily for the benefit of the Director of Corporate Enforcement, the new subsections are also of benefit to liquidators. So, the court is empowered to make an order in the nature of an *Anton Piller* – search and seizure – order[94]. Section 245A(2) provides:

---

86 For an English perspective, see *Re Mirror Group Newspapers* reported in (1992) Irish Times, 30 January. See also *Re Jeffrey s Levitt Ltd* [1992] All ER 509.

87 *Re Aluminium Fabricators Ltd* [1984] ILRM 399.

88 See Ch 15, *Duties of Directors and Other Officers*, para **[15.116]** *et seq.*

89 See the newspaper report of an examination in *Re Mark Synnott (Life and Pensions) Brokers Ltd* (1991) Irish Times, 8 November.

90 *Irish Commercial Society Ltd v Plunkett* [1986] ILRM 624.

91 See also *Re Jeffrey s Levitt Ltd* [1992] 2 All ER 509.

92 As inserted by s 127 of the CA 1990 and amended by s 45 of the CLEA 2001.

93 Again, in the light of s 280(1) of the CA 1963, the necessity for separate powers for voluntary liquidators is not obvious.

94 On *Anton Piller* orders, see generally, Courtney, *Mareva Injunctions and Related Interlocutory Orders* (1998), para [10.38] *et seq.*

> 'Where the court has made an order under subsection (1), it may, on the application of the Director or the liquidator, make a further order permitting the applicant, accompanied by such persons as the applicant thinks appropriate, to enter at any time or times within one month from the date of issue of the order, any premises (including a dwelling) owned or occupied by the person the subject of the order under subsection (1) (using such force as is reasonably necessary for the purpose), to search the premises and to seize any money, property or books and papers of the company found on the premises.'

It is important to note that only money, property, books or papers *of the company* may be seized. The obstruction of a right of entry, search and seizure is an offence[95] but proceedings on foot of this offence will not prejudice the power of the court to issue proceedings for contempt of court for failure to comply with an order under s 245A[96]. This order has the potential to be draconian and it is thought that the courts will exercise their jurisdiction very sparingly, especially when the property which it is sought to search is a person's dwelling house. Some safeguards are evident. So, s 245A(3) requires a successful applicant of a search and seizure order to report back to the court 'as soon as may be on the outcome of any action on foot of the court's order and the court shall direct the applicant as to the disposition of anything seized on foot of the order'[97].

(e) Powers of civil arrest

[25.038] Civil arrest[98] is an extraordinary and potentially draconian remedy which is available to a liquidator. The effect of civil arrest is that a person is deprived of his liberty or prevented from leaving the State where such is necessary to assist the civil process. An application for the civil arrest of a person in winding-up proceedings can be made in three circumstances:

(i) By statute to facilitate an examination.
(ii) In equity to facilitate an examination.
(iii) By statute to arrest an absconding officer or contributory.

(i) By statute to facilitate an examination

[25.039] Under s 245(8) of the CA 1963, where a person without reasonable excuse:

- fails at any time to attend his examination under s 245 of the CA 1963, or
- there are reasonable grounds for believing that a person has absconded, or is about to abscond,
- with a view to avoiding or delaying his examination under s 245 of the CA 1963,

then the court may cause that person to be arrested and his books and property seized and both to be detained until such time as the court may order. This subsection was

---

95 Section 245A(5) of the CA 1963.

96 Section 245A(6) of the CA 1963.

97 Section 245A(4) of the CA 1963 provides, somewhat cryptically, 'A direction under subsection (3) shall not be made in favour of the Director except in respect of the Director's costs and reasonable expenses'. By this it is thought that the court is precluded from ordering that any property seized be retained by the Director but that the court may order that the Director's costs are paid.

98 See generally, Courtney, *Mareva Injunctions and Related Interlocutory Orders* (1998), Ch 11, *'Restraining Defendants from Leaving the State'*.

inserted by s 126 of the CA 1990. Notwithstanding the provisions of s 280(1) of the CA 1963 which allow the court in a voluntary liquidation to make any order it has power to make in an official liquidation, s 282B(8) confers a separate statutory power to order the arrest of a person examined under s 282B(1), ie, in a voluntary liquidation[99]. It is thought that a voluntary liquidator seeking an arrest order should proceed on foot of s 280(1) for an order under s 245(8) but that an application by the Director of Corporate Enforcement should proceed under s 282B(8).

[25.040] Previously, it was the case that no order for arrest could be made until after an order for examination had been made, and the person who had been summoned to attend failed to do so. It is now the case that an order for the arrest of a person in connection with a s 245 of the CA 1963 examination is *not* dependant upon an actual order for examination having being made. Rather, where there is evidence that a person is about to abscond, with a view to avoiding or delaying an examination then, even though no order for examination exists, an order for arrest can be made. The old position led to the anomaly seen in the English case of *Re Oriental Credit Ltd*[100] and the Irish case of Re *J Ellis Pharmaceuticals Ltd*[101] where the court had no statutory power to order the arrest of a person in respect of an examination unless the person had been summoned to attend an examination and refused without excuse to come before the court. In *Re Oriental Credit Ltd,* an order for the defendant's examination had been made and there was a likelihood that the defendant would abscond. However, the court could not invoke its statutory power of arrest until after the time for the performance of the examination had passed. In *Re J Ellis Pharmaceuticals Ltd*, no order for examination had been made but the liquidator apprehended that the defendant might abscond before he had been examined. In both cases, the Irish and English courts in the absence of a statutory power of arrest, invoked their inherent equitable jurisdiction to grant an injunction to prevent the persons concerned from leaving the jurisdiction. While equitable intervention is no longer necessary in cases of absconding examinees, it remains a useful jurisdiction.

(ii) In equity to facilitate an examination

[25.041] There is an equitable jurisdiction to enjoin a person from leaving the State[102]. This may be either on foot of an ordinary injunction, or by the writ of *ne exeat regno*[103].

---

99 Section 49 of the CLEA 2001.

100 *Re Oriental Credit Ltd* [1988] 1 All ER 892.

101 *J Ellis Pharmaceuticals Ltd* reported in (1988) Irish Times, 13 August.

102 *O'Neill and Chiswick Ltd v O'Keeffe et al* (19 February 2002, unreported) HC, Kearns J. See para **[25.042]**.

103 The writ of *ne exeat regno* (meaning do not leave the realm) is an order whereby a person is directed not to leave the State. The best statement of the law relating to this writ is seen in *Felton v Callis* [1968] 3 All ER 673. The writ gives such relief in respect of 'equitable plaintiffs', whereas s 7 of the Debtors (Ireland) Act 1872 provides relief to 'legal plaintiffs'. The conditions before the writ will issue are fourfold: first, there is an equitable or legal action which prior to the passing of the 1872 Act would have entitled the plaintiff to seek the arrest of the defendant; second, that the plaintiff has a good cause of action over £20 or has sustained damage to that amount; third, that there is probable cause for believing that the defendant is about to quit Ireland; fourth, the defendant's absence would materially prejudice the plaintiff in the prosecution of his action. See generally, Courtney, *Mareva Injunctions and Related Interlocutory Orders* (1998), paras [11.02]–[11.21].

The injunction is an ever-adaptable and flexible remedy. The courts' power in s 28(8) of the Supreme Court of Judicature (Ireland) Act 1877 to grant an injunction is regulated by Ord 50, r 6 of the RSC 1986 which provides that the High Court 'may grant ... an injunction ... by an interlocutory order in all cases in which it appears to the court to be just or convenient so to do'. The novelty with this injunction concerns what the court is being asked to do, namely to prevent a person from leaving the State. It should be noted that the RSC do envisage such injunctions issuing; Ord 40, r 21 provides: 'where an injunction or order not to leave the jurisdiction has been granted' the person so enjoined is entitled to copies of the affidavit upon which the injunction was granted. English authorities have struggled to assert jurisdiction to prevent a person from leaving the country. In *Bayer AG v Winter*[104], such an injunction was sought to restrain a defendant in a counterfeit-pharmaceutical suit from leaving England. The Court of Appeal overturned the earlier High Court decision and granted the injunction sought, Fox LJ referring to the power to grant such injunctions said:

> 'Bearing in mind we are exercising a jurisdiction which is statutory, and which is expressed in terms of considerable width, it seems to me that the court should not shrink, if it is of the opinion that an injunction is necessary for the proper protection of a party to an action, from granting relief, notwithstanding it may, in its terms, be of novel character[105].'

The Court of Appeal granted the injunction after applying the 'balance of convenience' test and finding that it favoured the making of the injunction. The court also ordered the defendant to deliver up his passport. Other English cases have also recognised this jurisdiction[106] and several such orders have been granted also by the Irish courts on the application of liquidators, in apprehension that persons necessary to the orderly winding up of a company will absent themselves from the State[107].

[25.042] In *O'Neill and Chiswick Ltd v O'Keeffe and another*[108], Kearns J adopted the following criteria for granting a *Bayer* injunction, as suggested by Courtney[109]:

---

104 *Bayer AG v Winter* [1986] 1 All ER 733.

105 *Bayer AG v Winter* [1986] 1 All ER 733 at 737F–G after citing *Smith v Peters* (1875) LR 20 Eq 511.

106 See *Allied Arab Bank Ltd v Hajjar* [1987] 3 All ER 39.

107 In *Re J Ellis Pharmaceuticals Ltd*, reported in (1988) Irish Times, 13 August, a liquidator was reported in *The Irish Times* as stating on affidavit that his investigations of the defendant's pharmacy business made him desire to examine the respondent on oath in respect of several aspects of the company's property and that he believed that the director was about to leave the State. There, Blayney J granted the injunction sought, subject to the usual undertakings. In *Re Mark Synnott (Life and Pensions) Brokers Ltd*, reported in (1991) Irish Times, 3 July, a liquidator was given leave by Carroll J to make an application to require one of the directors of the company to surrender his passport, thus preventing him from leaving the State and going to Spain as the liquidator feared that the director would not return. In the end no order was made because the director agreed not to leave the country (see (1991) Irish Times, 4 July). Again, in *Re Tipperary Self-Drive Ltd et al*, reported in (1992) Irish Times, 4 February, a liquidator sought an injunction to prevent two directors from leaving the State. He claimed that his preliminary investigations suggested that the companies were involved in obtaining finance in respect of non-existent vehicles. It was reported that Murphy J granted the orders sought.

108 *O'Neill and Chiswick Ltd v O'Keeffe* (19 February 2002, unreported) HC, Kearns J.

109 Courtney, *Mareva Injunctions and Related Interlocutory Orders* (1998), pp 457–458.

> '(1) The court is satisfied that there is a probable cause for believing that the defendant is about to absent himself from the jurisdiction with the intention of frustrating the administration of justice and/or an order of the court.
>
> (2) The jurisdiction should not be exercised for punitive reasons; a defendant's presence should be required to prevent a court hearing or process or existing order from being rendered nugatory.
>
> (3) The injunction ought not to be granted where a lesser remedy would suffice.
>
> (4) The injunction should be interim in nature and limited to the shortest possible period of time.
>
> (5) The defendant's right to travel should be out-balanced by those of the plaintiff and the proper and effective administration of justice.
>
> (6) The grant of the injunction should not be futile.'

The facts in that case were that the plaintiffs (a US national and his investment vehicle) alleged that the first defendant had offered himself to the plaintiffs as a personal investment manager with particular expertise in trading foreign debt instruments through Swiss banks. Allegedly relying on his representations, the plaintiffs paid US$5 million into a Swiss bank account. This was to serve as a guarantee against any investment losses; the idea was that the first defendant and a company with which he was involved, Manro Group International, would suggest investment ideas. The monies were lodged in a joint account with the plaintiff as 'participant' and the first defendant as 'asset manager'. The plan was initially to last just one year but the first defendant advised the plaintiffs that he had unilaterally extended the period. On seeking a statement from the bank, the plaintiffs were instead given a fax from the first and second defendants stating that the value of the investment was then US$9.8 million. When, subsequently, the plaintiffs demanded the return of the monies they were met with a variety of excuses following which the plaintiffs initiated inquiries to be made in Dublin. Those inquiries revealed that the Dublin address was a private residence and that there was no evidence of 'Manro Group International' being there; a title search did not disclose the first defendant to be the owner of a farm in Cork as he had claimed. All requests for information and cooperation were unsuccessful and Kearns J noted that in the circumstances the plaintiff 'is apprehensive that his investment monies either have been or may be in the process of being dissipated or perhaps misappropriated altogether'. A *Mareva* injunction, proprietary injunction, *Anton Piller* order and an asset disclosure order were obtained by the plaintiffs and were faxed to the first defendant's Swiss and Dublin addresses. Entry to the first defendant's address in Ballsbridge could not be effected. A voice message from a man identifying himself as the first defendant was left on the plaintiffs' solicitor's telephone which, *inter alia*, claimed that the Ballsbridge address belonged to his daughter and not to him or Manro Group International. In these circumstances the plaintiffs applied for a *Bayer* injunction.

Kearns J quoted from *Bayer AG v Winter* with approval and also *House of Spring Gardens Ltd v Waite*[110] and concluded that 'it is clear from the foregoing that the jurisdiction to make such an order derives from the requirement to make court orders effective and is analogous to disclosure orders in aid of Mareva relief.' Kearns J also

[110] *House of Spring Gardens Ltd v Waite* [1985] 11 FSR 173.

noted s 28(8) of the Supreme Court of Judicature (Ireland) Act 1877, and went on to say that such relief would only be granted in exceptional and compelling circumstances because such an order 'is prima facie in breach of the constitutional right to travel, placing that right in abeyance for the specified period'. Acknowledging that in *Lennon v Ganley & Fitzgerald*[111] O'Hanlon J had recognised that the defendants there 'should only be restrained from exercising such right [to travel] if it was in some way unlawful for them to act in the manner in which they seek to act', Kearns J went on to point out that s 124 of the Bankruptcy Act 1988 criminalised the leaving of the State with the intention to defraud one's creditors[112]. After adopting the criteria set out in Courtney, Kearns J went on to conclude that it was appropriate that a *Bayer* injunction be made against the first defendant. Kearns J held:

> 'I am satisfied that the instant case requires the making of the orders sought, both in relation to the restriction on the defendant leaving the country and in requiring him to hand over his passport. A very substantial sum of money is unaccounted for in circumstances which give rise to considerable suspicion. The fact that two different solicitors consulted by Mr O'Keeffe within several days were denied instructions to enter an Appearance does nothing to allay one's concerns. The Court has a very real apprehension that the first-named defendant may be about to absent himself from the jurisdiction with the intention of frustrating the orders of the Court. Indeed, one concern is that he may already have done so, which brings into play the "futility" consideration last mentioned by Mr Courtney. However, this will often be a possibility in this sort of case and there is no positive evidence to this effect. Any order made cannot only be described as futile. It may prove quite effective. There is no punitive aspect to the order which I will qualify further by ordering that he shall not leave the jurisdiction before 4 March 2002 without leave of the court. From everything I have said I hope I have made it clear I have decided (at this point only) that the defendant's right to travel is out-balanced both by those of the plaintiff and the requirement to secure the proper and effective administration of justice.'

A *Bayer* injunction is an exceptional remedy and will be granted only in exceptional and compelling circumstances.

(iii) By statute to arrest an absconding officer or contributory

[25.043] The originally enacted s 247 of the CA 1963[113] provided that the court could make an order for the civil arrest of contributories. The purpose of this provision seemed intended to prevent contributories (ie, past or present members) from absconding to avoid calls on them in respect of outstanding liabilities on shares or guarantees or examination about the affairs of the company. The greatest handicap to the use of the

[111] *Lennon v Ganley & Fitzgerald* [1981] ILRM 84.

[112] See Courtney, *Mareva Injunctions and Related Interlocutory Orders* (1998), para [11.28].

[113] This provided: 'The court, at any time either before or after making a winding-up order, on proof of probable cause for believing that a contributory is about to quit the State or otherwise to abscond or to remove or conceal any of his property for the purpose of evading payment of calls or of avoiding examination about the affairs of the company, may cause the contributory to be arrested, and his books and papers to be seized and him and them to be detained until such time as the court may order.' See generally, Courtney, *Mareva Injunctions and Related Interlocutory Orders* (1998), paras [11.42]–[11.47].

originally enacted s 247 was that it could be invoked only in respect of *contributories*. The arrest of directors was entirely dependent upon their also happening to be contributories. Reform was effected on foot of the recommendations contained in the McDowell Report, and s 46 of the CLEA 2001 repealed and substituted a new section for the old s 247. The new s 247 provides:

> 'The court, at any time either before or after making a winding-up order, on proof of probable cause for believing that a contributory, director, shadow director or secretary or other officer is about to quit the State or otherwise to abscond or to remove or conceal any of his property for the purpose of evading payment of calls or of avoiding examination about the affairs of the company, may, of its own motion or on the application of the Director, a creditor of the company or any other interested person, cause the contributory, director, shadow director, secretary or other officer to be arrested, and his books and papers and movable personal property to be seized and him and them to be detained until such time as the court may order.'

Moreover, although it is thought that it was always the case that an arrest order could be made in a voluntary liquidation[114], s 282D of the CA 1963[115], which is couched in materially identical terms, is expressly available in a voluntary winding up. Those who have *locus standi* to apply for an arrest order are official and voluntary liquidators, the Director of Corporate Enforcement, a creditor of the company or any other interested person. Those who can be arrested are contributories, directors, shadow directors, secretaries and other officers. The application should be made by motion and may be made *ex parte*[116].

[25.044] The proofs required to obtain an order for arrest under s 247 of the CA 1963 were, and continue to be, onerous. Accordingly, *probable cause* for belief that a person is about to leave the State is required, the high evidential standard being required in view of the draconian effects of civil arrest[117]. In *Re Imperial Mercantile Credit Company*[118], the official liquidators of the company sought an order for the arrest of a contributory under s 118 of the Companies Act 1862, which was similar in most material respects to the originally enacted s 247 of the CA 1963. It was heard that a letter had been received by one of the liquidators from a solicitor, which stated that the contributory had advertised his property for sale and that it was 'well known in the neighbourhood that he was about to proceed to Lisbon'. This hearsay evidence did not impress Sir W Page Wood VC who said:

> 'I am not disposed to take the very strong step of arresting this gentleman without some more definite information upon oath as to his being about to abscond; but I think there is enough to induce me to stop the sale of his property until further notice'[119].

---

114 By reason of s 280(1) of the CA 1963.

115 Inserted by s 19 of the CLEA 2001.

116 RSC, Ord 74, r 135(2).

117 See *Felton v Callis* [1968] 3 All ER 673; *Re Underwood* (1903) 51 WR 335; *Re Imperial Mercantile Credit Company* (1867) LR 5 Eq 264; and *Sichel v Raphael* (1861) 4 LT 114, all in the context of the writ of *ne exeat regno*.

118 *Re Imperial Mercantile Credit Company* (1867) LR 5 Eq 264.

119 *Re Imperial Mercantile Credit Company* (1867) LR 5 Eq 264 at 265.

The official liquidators' subsequent application (grounded upon the actual affidavit of the solicitor referred to in the previous affidavit) to have the contributory arrested was also unsuccessful, although an order was made to seize his books, papers, moneys, securities for moneys, goods and chattels; in so ordering Sir W Page Wood VC thought it had been sufficiently proved that the contributory was about to remove his goods from the jurisdiction and held that whilst the section contemplates arrest at the same time as seizure of goods, one can be ordered without ordering the other[120].

[25.045] Not only is probable cause for absconding required, it must be shown also that there is, so to speak, a *mens rea*, namely that the person does so for the purpose of evading payment of calls or examination. Cases where such probable cause was shown include *Re The Ulster Land, Building and Investment Company Ltd*[121] where, after a winding-up order had been made, a liquidator sought the arrest of two contributories and the seizure of their property. One had sent his furniture to auction, given up his house, was generally disposing of his interests in property and was negotiating his passage to America. The other acted in a similar fashion and had actually taken his passage to San Francisco. An *ex parte* order for arrest was made, although on *inter partes* hearing this was discharged on security being given by recognizance that the remaining contributory would not leave Ireland without the consent of the court.

[25.046] A more recent Irish example is *Re Central Trust Investment Society*[122] where Murphy J ordered the arrest of a director (who was, presumably, also a contributory) where the liquidator sought to have him examined about the affairs of the company. In *Re O'Sheas (Dublin) Ltd*[123], an order for arrest was granted where there was evidence that the person concerned had sold his Irish home, had accommodation in Spain and had recently been abroad. The liquidator had made many unsuccessful attempts to contact the person concerned. The order for arrest was directed by Keane J to the Garda Commissioner and it directed him to bring the director before the court at the earliest opportunity. In both of the last two cases the court ordered the defendants to hand their passports over to the court[124].

Restraining the disposal or removal of corporate assets in a liquidation

[25.047] Where a liquidator suspects that a director or other person is likely to remove corporate assets from the jurisdiction or to dissipate those assets within the jurisdiction,

120 The requirement that there be 'probable cause' was also considered in the context of s 7 of the Debtors Act (Ireland) 1872; the similarities between civil arrest under s 118 of the Companies Act 1862 and the writ of *ne exeat* resulted in the remedies being referred to interchangeably in *Re Cotton Plantation Company of Natal* [1868] WN 79.

121 *Re The Ulster Land, Building and Investment Company Ltd* (1887) 17 LR Ir 591.

122 *Re Central Trust Investment Society* (1982) Irish Times, 31 August.

123 *Re O'Sheas (Dublin) Ltd* (1984) Irish Times, 6 July and (1987) Irish Times, 5 May.

124 For court orders on passports, see also *Re Mark Synnott (Life and Pension) Brokers Ltd and Re Bishopsgate Investment Management* (1991) Irish Times, 10 December, where Kevin and Ian Maxwell were ordered by the English High Court to surrender their passports.

he can apply for a *Mareva* injunction[125]. A *Mareva* injunction may be defined as a (pre-judgment or post-judgment) court order which restrains a defendant from removing from the State, or otherwise disposing of his own assets, whether generally, or up to a specified amount, until further order of the court or until the trial of the matter. Before a *Mareva* injunction will be granted, the following matters must be shown to exist to the satisfaction of the court:

- a substantive cause of action[126];
- a good arguable case[127];
- 'an intention on the part of the defendant to dispose of his assets with a view to evading his obligation to the plaintiff and to frustrate the anticipated order of the court'[128];
- the defendant's beneficial ownership of assets, situate whether inside[129] or outside[130] the jurisdiction; and
- a favourable balance of convenience[131].

Like all injunctions, a *Mareva* injunction cannot be demanded as of right, and its grant or refusal is dependent upon the discretion of the court[132]. The purpose of a *Mareva* injunction is not to confer security on the plaintiff but is, rather, to prevent the defendant

---

[125] After *Mareva Compania Naviera SA v International Bulk Carriers* [1980] 1 All ER 213. See generally, Courtney, *Mareva Injunctions and Related Interlocutory Orders* (1998); Capper, *Mareva Injunctions* (1988); and Ough & Flenley, *The Mareva Injunction and Anton Piller Order* (2nd edn, 1993).

[126] See *Caudron v Air Zaire* [1986] ILRM 10; *The Siskina* [1977] 3 All ER 803; and *Fourie v Le Roux and others* [2007] 1 All ER 1087.

[127] *Fleming v Ranks* [1983] ILRM 541; *The Tatiangela* [1980] 2 Lloyd's Reports 193; *Derby v Weldon* [1989] WLR 276; and *The Niedersachsen* [1984] 1 All ER 398.

[128] *Per* Hamilton CJ in the seminal Supreme Court decision in *Re John Horgan Livestock Ltd; O'Mahony v Horgan* [1995] 2 IR 411 at 419. See also *Fleming v Ranks* [1983] ILRM 541; *Larkin v NUM* [1985] IR 671; *Powerscourt Estates v Gallagher* [1984] ILRM 123; and *Moloney v Laurib Investments Ltd* (20 July 1993, unreported) HC, *per* Lynch J. *Cf Hughes v Hitachi Koki Imaging Solutions Europe* [2006] IEHC 233, where Clarke J said the need to prove the requisite intent had been relaxed, relying on his own decisions in *Tracey v Bowen* [2005] IEHC 138 and *McCourt v Tiernan* [2005] IEHC 268 and that of O'Sullivan J in *O'Mahony v Bennet Enterprises Inc* [1999] 2 IR 221.

[129] *Ashtiani v Kashi* [1986] 2 All ER 970 considered by Gill, (1986) ILT 18 and *Phelan v Master Meats Ltd* an application reported in (1989) Irish Times, 1 August, where Blayney J is reported as saying that the presence of assets within the jurisdiction was an issue in such an application.

[130] *Deutsche Bank Aktiengesellschaft v Murtagh & Murtagh* [1995] 2 IR 122; *Babanaft International Co SA v Bassatne* [1989] WLR 232; *Republic of Haiti v Duvallier* [1989] WLR 261 and *Derby v Weldon* [1989] WLR 276, which suggest that a *Mareva* can issue in respect of assets abroad by virtue of the court's powers in respect of those within its jurisdiction and the fact that an injunction acts *in personam*: *Lett v Lett* [1906] IR 618, *per* Porter MR.

[131] Such a consideration applies to all injunctions: *American Cyanamid Co v Ethicon Ltd* [1975] 1 All ER 504, accepted in principle in Ireland in *Campus Oil Ltd v Minister for Industry and Energy (No 2)* [1983] IR 88.

[132] *Countyglen plc v Carway* [1995] 1 IR 208; *Fleming v Ranks* [1983] ILRM 541 at 546.

from acting improperly so as to place his funds outside the control or jurisdiction of the court so as to frustrate execution of any judgment which might ultimately be obtained[133].

[25.048] In *Hughes v Hitachi Koki Imaging Solutions Europe*[134], Clarke J suggested that the normal *Mareva* principles may not apply in an insolvent company:

> 'While *O'Mahony v Horgan* is clear authority for the proposition that the payment of lawful debts in the course of an ongoing business should not give rise to any interference sufficient to justify the grant of a Mareva injunction, it seems to me that there is, at least in principle, a necessity to give different consideration to a corporate entity which maybe insolvent. In *Re Frederick Inns Ltd* [1994] ILRM 387 the Supreme Court had to consider the question of the duties of the directors in a situation where a company was being wound up or where any creditor could have it wound up on the ground of insolvency. Blayney J in giving the judgment of the court, found that in such circumstances the directors owed a duty to the creditors to preserve the assets so as to enable them to be applied in *pro tanto* discharge of the company's liabilities.'

Clarke J went on to find[135]:

> 'I am, therefore, satisfied that, in principle, it is open to a plaintiff to seek a Mareva type injunction in circumstances where it can be shown that an insolvent corporate entity intends to deal with its assets in a manner which would be in breach of the obligations on the company and its directors to ensure that those assets are maintained in a fashion which would enable them to be applied in accordance with corporate insolvency law. This situation may arise even where the company proposes to pay its lawful debts. It should, however, be emphasised that the primary means available in law for the enforcement of any such entitlement is to seek to place the company in liquidation so that the assets would, then, be dealt with by the liquidator in accordance with corporate insolvency law. However where, for whatever reason, it may not be possible for the plaintiff to seek to have the company put into liquidation or where, for whatever reason, liquidation may not be appropriate at that stage, it seems to me that it is open to a plaintiff, in such circumstances, to seek a Mareva type injunction.'

In that case, a company which owed the plaintiff a sum of money arising from disability payments due to her was winding down its Irish business and did not appear to be

---

133 See *Dowley & Dowley v O'Brien* [2009] IEHC 566, Clarke J.

134 *Hughes v Hitachi Koki Imaging Solutions Europe* [2006] IEHC 233 at para 3.7.

135 *Hughes v Hitachi Koki Imaging Solutions Europe* [2006] IEHC 233 at para 3.10, having said, at para 3.9: 'It is, therefore, clear that the directors of any company are under a fiduciary obligation (which arises in circumstances where the company does not have sufficient assets to meet its liabilities) to have regard to the insolvency provisions of the Companies Acts in the way in which the assets are managed. While an inappropriate disposition of the company's assets in such circumstances might not act for the benefit of the company itself, it seems to me that, nonetheless, in an appropriate case, it may be open to a plaintiff to seek *mareva* relief where it can be shown that an insolvent company intends to deal with its assets in a manner which would prevent those assets being dealt with in accordance with the provisions of the Companies Acts. In the ordinary way such a company must be taken, at least *prima facie*, to intend the natural consequences of its acts. Where it can be demonstrated that the company concerned intends to deal with its assets in such a manner as would be in breach of the obligations of the company and its directors under *Frederick Inns* and where such action would be likely to affect the position of the plaintiff, it seems to me that "requisite intention" required to justify the grant of a *mareva* type injunction would be established.'

making provision for her contingent claim. Clarke J held, however, that the directors had good reason to believe that adequate funds would exist to meet the plaintiff's claim if successful and declined to grant the plaintiff a *Mareva* injunction. The finding in this case is similar to the statutory remedy in s 55 of the CLEA 2001 which requires an applicant for a freezing order to establish that there are 'grounds for believing that the respondent may remove or dispose of his, her or the company's assets with a view to evading his, her or the company's obligations and frustrating an order of the court'. Given that the legislature has spoken on this point, it is thought that the equitable remedy of the *Mareva* injunction should not go beyond the remedy provided by s 55 of the CLEA 2001, which is considered below[136].

[25.049] There are many instances[137] where liquidators have availed of *Mareva* injunctions to preserve corporate assets in their efforts to make them amenable to realisation and distribution. Where it is apprehended that claims owed to a company being wound up are likely to be frustrated by its debtors, the person best placed to apply for a *Mareva* injunction will almost always be the liquidator. An extremely unusual application was made by the creditor who petitioned to have the company wound up in the case of *Revenue and Customs Commissioners v Egleton and others*[138]. There, a petitioner in a winding-up petition successfully obtained a *Mareva* injunction against debtors of the company (who were not debtors of the petitioner) whose only alleged liabilities were to the company or its liquidator under statutory claims arising in the event of liquidation. This was thought by Briggs J to be the first such application of its kind.

The obvious objection to the application for a *Mareva* injunction was that the petitioner, Her Majesty's Revenue & Customs, had no cause of action against the respondents, which is a key proof in an application for a *Mareva* injunction. Briggs J held that there was jurisdiction to grant a *Mareva* injunction as ancillary relief to a petition to have a company wound up, ie, that the petition was a satisfactory cause of action. The second objection was that a number of the respondents were not alleged to hold or have custody over any assets belonging to the company that was sufficient to justify their being joined in the injunction as third parties within the established principles for joining third-parties in *Mareva* injunctions as set out in *TSB Private Bank International SA v Chabra*[139]. Briggs J also rejected this point and held that there was jurisdiction to make a *Mareva* injunction against third parties where:

> '... some process, ultimately enforceable by the Courts, is or may be available to the judgment creditor as a consequence of a judgment against that actual or potential judgment debtor, pursuant to which, whether by appointment of a liquidator, trustee in bankruptcy, receiver or otherwise, the third party may be obliged to disgorge property or

---

136 See para **[25.005]** *post*.

137 See, eg, *Re Mark Synnott (Life and Pensions) Brokers Ltd* an application reported in (1991) Irish Times, 15 June; *Re Tipperary Self-Drive Ltd* an application reported in (1992) Irish Times, 4 February; and *Re Holbern Investments Ltd* an application reported in (1991) Irish Times, 9 October (obtained by creditors).

138 *Revenue and Customs Commissioners v Egleton and others* [2007] 1 All ER 606.

139 *TSB Private Bank International SA v Chabra* [1992] 2 All ER 245.

> otherwise contribute to the funds or property of the judgment debtor to help satisfy the judgment against the judgment debtor[140].'

Although Briggs J did acknowledge that where a petition has been presented the proper applicant for *Mareva* relief against the company's debtors will be a provisional liquidator in the absence of 'exceptional circumstances', which he clearly thought applied in the case in hand. There, HM Customs had petitioned as creditors to have a company wound up alleging that it had been engaged in a VAT fraud and that the respondents were implicated in that fraud.

It is thought that the Irish courts should be slow to follow the decision in *Egleton*. As the Supreme Court made clear in *Caudron v Air Zaire*[141], there must be a substantive cause of action against the primary person against whom relief is claimed. Where the applicant does not have a substantive cause of action against the primary person against whom the *Mareva* injunction is sought, it is thought that such persons may only be enjoined from disposing or dissipating their assets where the assets in their possession are beneficially owned by the applicant.

[25.050] There is also a statutory jurisdiction to restrain certain persons from disposing of their assets[142]. Section 55 of the CLEA 2001 provides:

> 'The court may, on the application of a company, director, member, liquidator, receiver, creditor or the Director, order a director or other officer of a company not to remove his or her assets from the State or to reduce his or her assets within or outside the State below an amount to be specified by the court, where the court is satisfied that—
>
> (a) the applicant has a substantive civil cause of action or right to seek a declaration of personal liability or claim for damages against the director, other officer or the company, and
>
> (b) there are grounds for believing that the respondent may remove or dispose of his, her or the company's assets with a view to evading his, her or the company's obligations and frustrating an order of the court.'

This is an unusual jurisdiction, borne out of the desire to provide the Director of Corporate Enforcement and all other persons battling against delinquent company law players with the means necessary to ensure justice is done. A wide variety of persons can apply for a s 55 freezing order: companies, directors, members, liquidators, receivers, creditors and the Director of Corporate Enforcement. Those who can have their assets frozen are a company's directors or other officers. This statutory jurisdiction is very closely aligned to the existing common law *Mareva* jurisdiction, particularly as it has developed in Ireland. Accordingly, an applicant under s 55 of the CLEA 2001 must have an independent substantive civil cause of action (eg, a claim for breach of duty, etc) or the right to seek a declaration of personal liability or claim for damages (eg, for fraudulent or reckless trading or failure to keep proper books of account, etc). Just as a *Mareva* injunction will not be granted where the applicant does not have a legal or

---

140 This passage is a quotation from the decision of the Australian High Court in *Cardile v LED Builders Pty Ltd* (1999) 162 ALR 294.

141 See *Caudron v Air Zaire* [1986] ILRM 10; *The Siskina* [1977] 3 All ER 803; and *Fourie v Le Roux and others* [2007] 1 All ER 1087.

142 See O'Reilly, 'Freezing Orders Under Section 55 of the Company Law Enforcement Act 2001' (2002) 9 CLP 109.

equitable right, neither will an order under s 55. Although s 55(a) is silent as against whom the applicant must have this substantive civil cause of action, it is submitted that such must subsist against the person against whom the order is sought. For example, if a creditor sought an order to freeze a director's assets, it would not be sufficient to show that he has a cause of action against the director's company: he must show he has a cause of action against the director. Any other construction would be draconian and, most likely, unconstitutional. The second similarity, which is also a curb on excesses, is s 55(b), which requires the proof of grounds for believing that the respondent may remove or dispose of his assets 'with a view to evading his, her or the company's obligations and frustrating an order of the court'. Just as applies in the case of *Mareva* injunctions, it is not sufficient to establish that the assets are likely to be dissipated in the ordinary course of business or in the payment of lawful debts. It is thought that, so powerful is this relief, in exercising its undoubted discretion (ie, 'the court may') the courts will give short shrift to unworthy applicants and be mindful that, just as the *Mareva* jurisdiction, s 55, 'if improperly invoked will bring about an injustice, something that it was designed to prevent'[143].

[25.051] *Mareva* injunctions and s 55 of the CLEA 2001 asset freezing orders must, however, be distinguished from injunctions in defence of a proprietary interest[144]. Where a liquidator believes that assets properly belonging to the company are in the hands of a third party and he has commenced proceedings for their return (eg, tracing)[145], where he seeks to preserve those assets and prevent the third party from disposing of them his proper remedy is to apply for an 'ordinary' interlocutory injunction[146]. Proprietary injunctions are distinguishable from *Mareva* injunctions or s 55 asset freezing orders because in both of these cases the respondent will have his personal assets frozen in anticipation that the applicant will be found to have an enforceable claim against the respondent; at the time of the order, however, the applicant does not need to have a proprietary (or *in rem*) claim in order to obtain a Mareva injunction or a s 55 order. Applicants for injunctions in defence of proprietary claims will be more readily afforded a remedy than *Mareva* applicants[147]. In such circumstances, the basis of the test to be applied for the grant of the injunction is that established in *Campus Oil Ltd v Minister for Industry and Energy*[148]. This is, is there a fair or serious question to be tried, does the balance of convenience favour the injunction and has the applicant established

143 *Re John Horgan Livestock Ltd; O'Mahony v Horgan* [1995] 2 IR 411 at 422 *per* O'Flaherty J. See also the caution sounded by McCracken J in *Production Association Minsk Tractor Works and Belarus Equipment (Ireland) Ltd v Saenko* (25 February 1998, unreported) HC, McCracken J.

144 See, Courtney, *Mareva Injunctions and Related Interlocutory Orders* (1998), paras [1.16]–[1.29]. The distinction between proprietary injunctions and *Mareva* injunctions was accepted in *OBA Enterprises Ltd (& Others) v TMC Trading International Ltd* [1998] IEHC 169, Laffoy J, noted in Courtney, 'The Continuing Development of the Mareva Injunction in Ireland' (1999) 6 CLP 39.

145 *Polly Peck International plc v Nadir (No 2)* [1992] 4 All ER 769.

146 RSC, Ord 50, r 4.

147 *Republic of Haiti v Duvalier* [1989] 1 All ER 456 at 464g.

148 *Campus Oil Ltd v Minister for Industry and Energy* [1983] IR 88.

reasonable grounds for claiming a proprietary interest in the property that is the subject matter of substantive proceedings?

No litigation, execution, attachment or new judgment mortgages

[25.052] In addition to gathering assets, liquidators must also preserve the existing assets of the company and, if necessary, take steps to prevent creditors jumping the queue of priorities ordained by the Companies Acts, by executing judgments and attaching company property after a winding up has commenced. Section 219 of the CA 1963 provides:

> 'Where any company is being wound up by the court, any attachment, sequestration, distress or execution put in force against the property or effects of the company after the commencement of the winding up shall be void to all intents.'

The attachment, sequestration and execution against corporate assets generally has been considered in Chapter 6[149]. Once a winding up has commenced, judgment creditors must take their chances with the other creditors of an insolvent company and rely on the liquidator to pay them their lawful dividend from the assets that he has realised[150].

[25.053] Moreover, no new action can be commenced against a company that is being wound up. Section 222 of the CA 1963 provides:

> 'When a winding-up order has been made or a provisional liquidator has been appointed no action or proceeding shall be proceeded with or commenced against a company except by leave of the court and subject to such terms as the court may impose.'

In *Re Motor Racing Circuits Ltd*[151], lay-litigants sought to argue that a receiver could not be appointed on foot of a debenture after the making of a winding-up order or, indeed, after the appointment of a provisional liquidator. The Supreme Court rejected this point, Blayney J holding:

> 'For the appointment of the receiver to be excluded his appointment by the bank would have had to constitute an action or proceeding and in my view it is quite clear that the appointment of a receiver is not an action or proceeding. An action or proceeding is something which is commenced by way of a court action, in other words by a summons being issued or some proceedings being issued before the court. But the appointment of a receiver does not come into that category, it is simply an appointment under a power contained in a debenture. It does not come within the definition of an action or a proceeding ...'[152].

Of course the appointment of a receiver other than by contractual right, eg, a receiver by way of equitable execution would, by s 222, be prohibited without the leave of the court. Also prohibited would be any action in any court of law, howsoever initiated, whether by process, bill, summons or originating notice of motion.

---

149 Ch 6, *Corporate Civil Litigation*, para **[6.071]** *et seq.*

150 *Re United English and Scottish Life Insurance Co* (1868) Lr 5 Eq 300; *Re Tumacacori Mining Co* (1874) LR 17 Eq 534.

151 *Re Motor Racing Circuits Ltd* (31 January 1997, unreported) SC.

152 *Re Motor Racing Circuits Ltd* (31 January 1997, unreported) SC, at p 3.

[25.054] In addition to the foregoing provision, the rights of creditors as to execution or attachment are further restricted by s 291 of the CA 1963 where a company is being wound up. Section 291(1) provides:

> 'Subject to subsections (2) to (4), where a creditor has issued execution against the goods[153] or lands of a company or has attached any debt due to the company, and the company is subsequently wound up, he shall not be entitled to retain the benefit of the execution or attachment against the liquidator in the winding up of the company unless he has completed the execution or attachment before the commencement of the winding up.'

The thrust of this section is that a creditor must hand back any goods or land unless the execution or attachment has been completed[154] before the commencement of the winding up[155]. Subsection (2) provides that where a creditor has notice of a meeting called for the voluntary winding up of the company, the date he had this notice is substituted for the date of the commencement of the winding up. Subsection (3) provides that a person who purchases in good faith under a sale by the sheriff any goods of a company on which an execution has been levied shall *in all cases* acquire good title to them against the company's liquidator. By sub-s (4) the court may set aside the rights conferred on a liquidator by subs (1) 'in favour of the creditor to such extent and subject to such terms as the court thinks fit'. In *Caribbean Producers (Yam Importers) Ltd*[156], Russell LJ said that weighty reasons would be required before the court would exercise its validating jurisdiction under this subsection as the purpose of s 291-type provisions is to further the principle that unsecured creditors of an insolvent company are to be paid *pari passu*. Subsection (5) provides:

> 'For the purposes of this section, an execution against goods shall be taken to be completed by seizure and sale, and an attachment of the debt shall be deemed to be completed by receipt of the debt, and an execution against land shall be deemed to be completed by seizure and, in the case of an equitable interest, by the appointment of a receiver.'

By sub-s (6), nothing in s 291 is expressed to give any validity to any payment which constitutes a fraudulent preference[157].

[25.055] One question that arises is whether 'execution' of a judgment is complete once a judgment mortgage is obtained or whether it is necessary to have taken steps to realise the property in order for it to be enforceable as against a liquidator. The decision in *Re Overseas Aviation Engineering (GB) Ltd*[158] is authority for the proposition that a judgment mortgage is not enforceable as against a liquidator unless it has been completed by, for example, the appointment of a receiver. Lord Denning MR said:

> 'there is nothing in section 325 [of the Companies Act 1948 (UK)] to suggest that the word "execution" is not used there in its ordinary sense. That section draws a distinction

153 'Goods' are defined by sub-s (7) to include all chattels personal.

154 On 'completion' see *Caribbean Products (Yam Importers) Ltd* [1966] Ch 331 where Russell LJ said an attachment is only complete where there has been an actual receipt of money by the creditor. See also s 291(5) of the CA 1963 considered below.

155 *Re Andrew* [1937] Ch 122.

156 *Caribbean Producers (Yam Importers) Ltd* [1966] Ch 331.

157 On 'fraudulent preference', see para **[25.081]** *et seq.*

158 *Re Overseas Aviation Engineering (GB) Ltd* [1963] 1 Ch 24.

> between an execution which the creditor "has completed" in fact; and an execution which is "taken to be completed" or "deemed to be completed," although it has not in fact been completed. It is completed in fact when the creditor gets his money. It is deemed to be completed "by seizure" or by "the appointment of a receiver" ...
>
> That the judgment charge is a form of "execution" it follows that the judgment creditor is not entitled to retain "the benefit" of the charge unless he has completed the execution before the commencement of the winding up.'

It is thought that, in Ireland at least, this is far from settled law. Indeed, in that case Russell LJ dissented, albeit on grounds related to the English law concerning the execution of judgments. It is thought that a strong case can be made out for the proposition that the registration of a judgment mortgage operates to create an *in rem* security interest in the judgment creditor over the property which is enforceable as against a liquidator. Given that a judgment mortgage which is registered within three months of the commencement of a company's winding up will be void[159] why should there be any other basis for finding a judgment mortgage to be void? Indeed, can it not be said that the registration of a judgment as a judgment mortgage is the *execution* of that judgment? Moreover, s 117 of the Land and Conveyancing Law Reform Act 2009 provides that the registration of a judgment mortgage under s 116 of that Act operates to charge the judgment debtor's estate or interest in the land with the judgment debt and entitles the judgment mortgagee to apply to the court for certain orders. The existence of such a recent enactment specifically providing for the creation, effect and discharge of judgment mortgages must create a presumption that a judgment mortgage created outside of three months of the commencement of a winding up will not be void against a liquidator under s 291 of the CA 1963, whether or not steps have been taken to enforce it. Nevertheless, the matter remains unclear and should be clarified by the legislature.

[25.056] Section 292 of the CA 1963 reinforces the effects of s 291 by providing that a sheriff is obliged to deliver goods and money seized from a company to its liquidator where he has been served with notice that a provisional liquidator has been appointed or that either a winding-up order has been made or a resolution passed to have a company wound up voluntarily. Again, the sheriff is only obliged to deliver goods or money to a liquidator before their sale or before the completion of the execution by the receipt or recovery of the full amount of the levy[160]. The rights of the liquidator conferred by subs (1) may again be set aside by the court in favour of the creditor to such extent and subject to such terms as the court thinks fit[161].

---

159 Section 284(2) of the CA 1963 incorporates s 51(1) of the Bankruptcy Act 1988 which provides: 'A judgment creditor who registers an affidavit of his judgment in accordance with sections 6 and 7 of the Judgment Mortgage (Ireland) Act, 1850, shall not, by reason of such registration, be entitled to any priority or preference over simple contract creditors in the event of the person against whom such affidavit is registered being adjudicated bankrupt, *unless the affidavit is registered at least three months before the date of the adjudication*.' See para **[25.057]** *post*.

160 Subsection (2) provides a partial saver for the sheriff's costs: see *Bluston and Bramley Ltd v Leigh* [1950] 2 KB 548; *Re Walkden Sheet Metal Co Ltd* [1960] Ch 170.

161 Section 292(3) of the CA 1963.

[25.057] As noted above, one effect[162] of s 284(2) of the CA 1963 applying the Bankruptcy Act 1988 to the winding up of companies is that judgment mortgages registered against a company's property within three months of the commencement of a winding up are invalid[163].

Disclaiming onerous property

[25.058] In a discussion of the means employed by a liquidator in realising corporate assets, it may seem strange to consider a measure whereby a liquidator can disclaim, or disown, 'assets' to which the company is entitled. However, certain assets may in fact be more of a liability than a benefit to the company. In such circumstances, a liquidator might decide that the company is better off without them and may make an application to disclaim them pursuant to s 290 of the CA 1963.

[25.059] Section 290(1) of the CA 1963 provides that:

> '... where any part of the property of a company which is being wound up consists of land of any tenure burdened with onerous covenants, of shares or stock in companies, of unprofitable contracts, or of any other property which is unsaleable by reason of its binding the possessor thereof to the performance of any onerous act or to the payment of any sum of money, the liquidator of the company, notwithstanding that he has endeavoured to sell or has taken possession of the property or exercised any act of ownership in relation thereto, may, with the leave of the court and subject to the provisions of this section, by writing signed by him, at any time within 12 months after the commencement of the winding up or such extended period as may be allowed by the court, disclaim the property.'

When one thinks of a company holding property, this tends to imply that it holds something having a value. However, sometimes owning property entails being subject to obligations. Where such obligations are burdened by onerous covenants, the legislature provides that a liquidator may disclaim such property. The purpose of s 290 is to streamline the realisation and distribution of a company's assets.

[25.060] In *Re Irish ISPAT Ltd*[164], Carroll J said of s 290(1):

> 'In my opinion, s 290(1) cannot be construed so that property described as unsaleable does not have any further qualification. In my view the section must be read so that property is either unsaleable by reason of having to perform onerous acts or the payment of money, or not readily saleable for the same reasons. The purpose of the section is to allow disclaimed of onerous property. If the property is not subject to the performance of onerous acts or the payment of money there is no valid reason why a liquidator should seek or be allowed to disclaim.'

In that case, Carroll J held that a pollution licence was 'property' which had onerous conditions attaching and which was amenable to being disclaimed under s 290 of the CA 1963 and rejected the contention that the Companies Acts were subjudicated to the Waste Management Act 1996. Accordingly, the company's creditors were to receive

---

162 For the effects of the bankruptcy legislation on the distribution of corporate assets on liquidation, see para **[25.141]**.

163 Section 51 of the Bankruptcy Act 1988, formerly s 311 of the the Irish Bankrupt and Insolvent Act 1857.

164 *Re Irish ISPAT Ltd; Minister for Environment v Irish ISPAT Ltd* [2005] 2 IR 338.

what was due to them in the liquidation and its available assets would not be diverted to meet financial conditions imposed under a licence granted by the Environment Protection Agency.

[25.061] In *Re Ballymitty Supplies Stores Ltd*[165], the liquidator of a company sought to disclaim two properties, one registered freehold land and the other unregistered freehold land; the company had also entered into a covenant with adjoining owners to contribute towards the maintenance of sewerage pipes and a septic tank but Laffoy J held there was nothing onerous or burdensome about its obligations. The reason why the liquidator sought to disclaim the properties was because whilst worth €180,000, Bank of Ireland, which held security over them, was owed in excess of €183,000, a financial contribution of over €31,000 was due to Wexford Co Co, commercial rates and water rates were outstanding and the cost of insuring the properties was ongoing. Laffoy J held that the property did not constitute 'land of any tenure burdened with onerous covenants' and so could not be disclaimed.

[25.062] The effect of a legal disclaimer is set out in s 290(3) of the CA 1963 which provides that:

> 'The disclaimer shall operate to determine, as from the date of disclaimer, the rights, interests and liabilities of the company, and the property of the company, in or in respect of the property disclaimed, but shall not, except so far as is necessary for the purpose of releasing the company and the property of the company from liability, affect the rights or liabilities of any other person.'

This provision was interpreted by Keane J in *Tempany v Royal Liver Trustees Ltd*[166] as meaning that the obligations of persons other than the company are not affected by the disclaimer. Consequently, the obligations of a guarantor of a lease taken by a company are not affected by a liquidator's disclaimer of that lease: the right of a landlord to recover rent from a guarantor, or the original lessee in the case where a company is a sub-lessee, is not affected by a disclaimer[167]. In the *Tempany* case, a liquidator sought to disclaim a lease held by a company. The lease represented a liability of £1.5 million because the rent paid by the company was greatly in excess of the market value; a schedule of dilapidations had been served; and there was no prospect of assigning the lessee's interest for value. The defendant was the guarantor of the company's obligations under the lease and opposed the application for disclaimer by the liquidator. Keane J allowed the liquidator to disclaim the lease: the exclusive concern of the court was the interests of the company, although the court would have some regard to the parties affected by the disclaimer. However, the release of the guarantor was not necessary in order to release the company from its liabilities. As one writer has observed:

> 'The only practical consequence of a disclaimer allowed in such circumstances is that the company's proprietary [*in rem*] right, an untidy item of undisposable property, disappears. The company's *in personam* liabilities in respect of the lease simply reappear in other guises as provable debts in the liquidation[168].'

---

165 *Re Ballymitty Supplies Stores Ltd* [2011] IEHC 471.

166 *Tempany v Royal Liver Trustees Ltd* [1984] ILRM 273.

167 See Keane, *Company Law* (4th edn, Bloomsbury Professional, 2007), para 36.106.

168 Ussher, *Company Law in Ireland* (1986), p 497.

That the rights and liabilities of persons other than the company being wound up remain intact, is seen in other subsections of s 290 of the CA 1963. The courts will seek to construe the statutory provision in such a way as to remove a company's onerous obligations whilst seeking to interfere with other parties' rights as little as possible[169]. The decision of Keane J in *Tempany v Royal Liver Trustees Ltd* previously distinguished the effects of a disclaimer of a lease on guarantors in Ireland from the prevailing position in England. In England, a series of cases had held that the effect of a lease being disclaimed is to discharge any surety or guarantor from their liabilities[170]. These cases have, however, been overturned by the House of Lords in *Hindcastle Ltd v Barbara Attenborough Associates Ltd*[171], where Keane J's decision was cited and followed in the Lords' decision that a liquidator's disclaimer does not affect the obligations of an original tenant or guarantor.

[25.063] The legislature goes on to protect the rights of persons other than the company in various subsections of s 290 of the CA 1963. Subsection (4) provides that the court, either before or upon allowing disclaimer, must require that notice be given to persons interested. Subsection (5) expressly prohibits a liquidator from disclaiming where any interested persons make application in writing requiring him to decide whether or not to disclaim, and he has not within 28 days thereafter given the interested person notice that he intends to apply to court for leave to disclaim. Subsection (6) provides that where a person is entitled to the benefit or subject to the burden under a contract, the court may rescind the contract on such terms as it thinks just, and any order for damages made against the company shall be a debt due on distribution by the liquidator. In *Re Ranks Ireland Ltd*[172], Murphy J restated the principle that all those who had contracted with the company, and whose rights were affected by a disclaimer, could prove in a winding up. There, Irish Telephone Rentals Ltd agreed to install and lease certain telephone equipment for 14 years. The liquidator of Ranks Ireland Ltd sought to disclaim these agreements and this disclaimer was permitted by Murphy J who said the appropriate measure of damages was not that provided for in the contract disclaimed, but simply 'the difference between the rent which would have been paid by the company under the lease and the rent which the lessor is likely to obtain during the unexpired residue'[173].

[25.064] In an attempt to tidy up loose ends, s 290(7) of the CA 1963 permits the court, on application by any person who either claims any interest in any disclaimed property or is under any liability not discharged by the Act, to make an order for the vesting of the property disclaimed. The vesting can take place without the need for a conveyance or assignment, to any person entitled thereto, or to whom it appears just. However, by sub-s (8):

> 'Where the property disclaimed is of a leasehold nature, the court shall not make a vesting order in favour of any person claiming under the company, whether as under-lessee or as mortgagee by demise, except upon the terms of making that person—

[169] See, eg, *Capital Prime Properties plc v Worthgate Ltd* [2000] BCC 525.

[170] See *Stacey v Hill* [1901] 1 KB 660; *Murphy v Sawyer-Hoare* [1994] 2 BCLC 59.

[171] *Hindcastle Ltd v Barbara Attenborough Associates Ltd* [1996] 2 BCLC 234.

[172] *Re Ranks Ireland Ltd* [1988] ILRM 751.

[173] Citing Keane, *Company Law in the Republic of Ireland* (1st edn, 1985) at p 321.

(a) subject to the same liabilities and obligations as those to which the company was subject under the lease in respect of the property at the commencement of the winding up; or

(b) if the court thinks fit, subject only to the same liabilities and obligations as if the lease had been assigned to that person at that date;

and in either event (if the case so requires), as if the lease had comprised only the property comprised in the vesting order, and any mortgagee or under-lessee declining to accept a vesting order upon such terms shall be excluded from all interest in and security upon the property, and, if there is no person claiming under the company who is willing to accept an order upon such terms, the court shall have power to vest the estate and interest of the company in the property in any person liable either personally or in a representative character, and either alone or jointly with the company, to perform the lessee's covenants in the lease, freed and discharged from all estates, encumbrances and interests created therein by the company.'

The fact that, on application, the court has power by sub-s (7) to make an order for the vesting of the property has been held by Carroll J in *Re Erris Investments Ltd*[174] to make it unsafe for the Registrar of Titles to cancel the leasehold burden on a freehold folio where the leasehold has been disclaimed by a company lessee. Furthermore, the learned judge also held that s 7 of Deasy's Act 1860[175], concerning the surrender of a lease, does not operate because it is based on an agreement between the lessor and lessee: such agreement did not exist in a disclaimer since this was a unilateral act of the liquidator and the court[176].

Post-commencement dispositions

[25.065] At the heart of the principles behind the realisation of corporate assets on a liquidation is the notion that *all* assets which belong to the company at the *commencement* of the winding up should be applied and distributed in accordance with the priority determined by law. Section 275(1) of the CA 1963 states the central principle that 'the property of a company on its winding up … shall … be applied in satisfaction of its liabilities *pari passu*'. The commencement of a winding up is deemed to occur, in an official or compulsory liquidation[177], at the time of the presentation of the petition to have the company wound up[178]. Section 218 of the CA 1963 provides:

'In a winding up by the court, any disposition of the property, including things in action, and any transfer of shares or alteration in the status of the members of the company, made after the commencement of the winding-up, shall, unless the court otherwise orders, be void[179].'

174 *Re Erris Investments Ltd* [1991] ILRM 377.

175 Landlord and Tenant Law Amendment (Ireland) Act 1860 (23 & 24 Vict c 154).

176 Cf Ussher, *Company Law in Ireland* (1986), p 498 whose interpretation of the judgment of Keane J in *Tempany v Royal Liver Trustees Ltd* [1984] ILRM 273 at 289 was not followed.

177 In the case of a voluntary winding up, commencement of the winding up occurs when the resolution is passed to this effect: s 253(1) of the CA 1963. See Ch 23, *Winding Up Companies, para* **[23.014]**.

178 Section 220(2) of the CA 1963.

179 On the transfer of shares and the alteration in the status of the members made after the commencement of the winding up, see para **[25.132]**.

This gives further statutory force to the *pari passu* principle in s 275 which requires that all creditors should be placed on an equal footing and that none should 'leap frog' the creditors' statutory queue. The basic point is clear, *all* dispositions are *void* after the commencement of a winding up. However, the court may in its discretion, *validate* a disposition. One judicial statement of the rationale[180] behind the jurisdiction to validate a disposition is provided by Cairns LJ in *Re Wiltshire Iron Co*[181] who said:

> 'This is a wholesome and necessary provision, to prevent, during the period which must elapse before a petition can be heard, the improper alienation and dissipation of the property of a company *in extremis*. But where a company actually trading, which it is in the interests of everyone to preserve, and ultimately to sell, as a going concern, is made the object of the winding-up petition which may fail or succeed, if it were to be supposed that transactions in the ordinary course of its current trade, *bona fide* entered into and completed, would be avoided, and would not in the discretion of the court, be maintained, the result would be that the presentation of a petition, groundless or well-founded, would *ipso facto*, paralyse the trade of the company, and great injury, without any counter-balance of advantage, would be done to those interested in the assets of the company.'

In *Re Worldport Ireland Ltd*[182], Clarke J said:

> 'It seems to me that the primary purpose of the section is to ensure, insofar as it may be possible, that the company is "frozen" as of the date of the presentation of the winding-up petition. Where it is sought to wind-up a company on the basis of insolvency it will, save in the most exceptional cases, be the case that the company will end up being unable to pay all of its debts. There may be unusual circumstances where either the amounts which the company ultimately has to pay out in the liquidation or the amounts which are recovered by the liquidator are significantly different from those anticipated in advance to the extent that they render the company able to meet all its debts (including the cost of the liquidation). There may also be rare cases where a company, though unable to meet its debts as they fall due, has an excess of assets over liabilities. Such cases are rare. It is, therefore, inevitable that, in virtually all cases where a company is liquidated on the basis of insolvency, some creditors will not be paid in full. The Companies Acts provide an elaborate code for determining where the burden of not being paid should lie. The primary purpose of the section, it seems to me, is to ensure that the court has ample power to prevent any adjustment occurring subsequent to the presentation of the petition, which would disturb that elaborate balance. In seeking to achieve that end there can, of course, be a series of subsidiary rights and obligations which necessarily arise. However, the precise extent to which any such principle might affect the ultimate distribution of the assets of the company is, of course, dependent, at least in part, on any view the court might take as to validation."

The ethos of these *dicta* ought to be continually borne in mind when considering the case law concerning whether there has been a disposition and the exercise of the jurisdiction to validate dispositions. Here, the following issues are considered:

(a) The concept of disposition.

(b) Post-commencement banking transactions.

(c) The jurisdiction to validate dispositions.

---

[180] See also the judgment of Mummery LJ in *Hollicourt (Contracts) Ltd v Bank of Ireland* [2001] 1 BCLC 233 at 238–239.

[181] *Re Wiltshire Iron Co* (1868) 3 Ch App 443 at 446–447.

[182] *Re Worldport Ireland Ltd* [2005] IEHC 189. See, generally, Keirse, 'Post-commencement Dispositions – An Analysis of Recent Case Law' (2005) CLP 317.

(a) The concept of disposition

[25.066] The ordinary meaning of disposition is the passing of an interest in something, or the giving away of something. Clearly, sales with or without consideration, gifts, payments for goods or services received, etc, are all dispositions. Where a company has entered into an unconditional contract before the presentation of a petition to wind up, the fact that it completes that contract after the petition has been presented has been held not to be a disposition[183].

[25.067] An interesting argument as to what constituted a disposition was advanced in *Re Motor Racing Circuits Ltd*[184]. In that case lay-litigants advanced the novel argument that the appointment of a receiver after the commencement of a winding up falls within s 218 of the CA 1963 because it entitled the receiver to take possession of the assets of a company. The Supreme Court rejected this. Giving the judgment of the court, Blayney J said:

> 'The position here is that there was no alteration in any way in the property of the company effected by the appointment of the receiver. The alteration in regard to the assets of the company was effected when the debenture was executed. As a result of the debenture being executed the bank had a charge on the particular property which was the subject of the debenture. So the bank from the date of the execution of the debenture was the mortgagee of the property in question. The property in question had been vested in the bank as security for the monies owing to the bank. The appointment of a receiver simply amounted to the normal way for a bank to recover what is due to it on foot of its charge. But there was no change whatsoever in regard to the ownership of the asset that had already been vested in the company under the debenture when the debenture was executed. The position is that the appointment of a receiver does not in any way come within s 218. It does not in any way represent any disposition of the property of the company; this disposition had taken place when the debenture was executed[185].'

Accordingly, any action taken subsequent to the commencement of a winding up on foot of security granted prior to a company being wound up, will not amount to a disposition within the meaning of s 218 of the CA 1963.

(b) Post-commencement banking transactions

[25.068] In the case of the drawing of a cheque, it is now established that there will be no disposition until the cheque is honoured: drawing a cheque in itself is not a disposition. In *Re Ashmark Ltd (No 2)*[186], Blayney J said the fact that a cheque was drawn before the commencement of a winding up was immaterial: the fact was that it was paid after the commencement, and so it was void, unless the court decided to validate it[187].

---

183 See *Re French's (Wine Bar) Ltd* [1987] BCLC 499.

184 *Re Motor Racing Circuits Ltd* (31 January 1997, unreported) SC.

185 *Re Motor Racing Circuits Ltd* (31 January 1997, unreported) SC at pp 10–11.

186 *Re Ashmark Ltd (No 2)* [1990] ILRM 455.

187 A contention supported by ss 3(1) and 73 of the Bills of Exchange Act 1882. In the words of Blayney J (at 457): 'The cheque was no more than an unconditional order by the company to its bankers to pay [the creditor] the sum named in it. Until [the bank] made the payment in accordance with the order there was no disposition.'

(i) Lodgments into an overdrawn account

[25.069] Lodgments by a company into its own overdrawn bank account are dispositions of that company's property in favour of the bank. In the English case of *Re Gray's Inn Construction Co Ltd*[188], after the commencement of its winding up, a company paid certain sums into its overdrawn bank account, thereby reducing its overdraft. At first hearing, Templeman J said these were not dispositions but this was rejected by Buckley LJ in the Court of Appeal who held:

> 'When a customer's account with his banker is overdrawn he is a debtor to his banker for the amount of the overdraft. When he pays a sum of money into the account, whether in cash or by payment in of a third party cheque, he discharges his indebtedness to the bank *pro tanto*. There is clearly in these circumstances, in my judgment, a disposition by the company to the bank of the amount of the cash or of the cheque[189].'

There is sometimes a temptation for companies to pay money into an overdrawn bank account, after the commencement of a winding up, where company directors have given personal guarantees in respect of the company's overdraft. Therefore, the lower the overdraft, the less the directors may be called upon to pay on foot of their personal guarantees to the bank.

(ii) Payments out of a company's account

[25.070] Clearly, payments out of a company's bank account will amount to dispositions within the meaning of s 218 of the CA 1963[190]. But where the disposition is effected by means of a cheque, drawn on the company's account, is the disposition in favour of the bank that honours the cheque or the third party in whose favour it is drawn? This question has recently received attention from both the Irish and English courts. In *Hollicourt (Contracts) Ltd v Bank of Ireland*[191], the English Court of Appeal reversed the decision of Blackburne J that the defendant bank was liable to reimburse a company for payments made in these circumstances. Blackburne J had held that the effect of the materially identical English provision[192] was to operate not only against third party recipients of cheques drawn by companies but also against the bank that made the payments. The Court of Appeal found that the provision was not intended by the legislature to impose a restitutionary liability on a bank. It was also held that the purpose – namely, to prevent directors from dissipating assets to the detriment of creditors – was accomplished without impinging upon the validity of the intermediate steps in a disposition by cheque. Mummery LJ rejected that there had been any disposition by the company to the bank, saying:

---

188 *Re Gray's Inn Construction Co Ltd* [1980] 1 All ER 814.

189 *Re Gray's Inn Construction Co Ltd* [1980] 1 All ER 814 at 818e–f.

190 See Costello J in *Re Pat Ruth Ltd* [1981] ILRM 51 at 52.

191 *Hollicourt (Contracts) Ltd v Bank of Ireland* [2001] 1 BCLC 233. See Sealy, 'Company Liquidations: When Should Post-Petition Banking Transactions be Avoided?' (2000) CCH's Company Law Newsletter, Issue 57, 11 July 2000 and Moore, 'Payments Received by Cheque Drawn on Bank Account of Company Following Presentation of Winding-up Petition' (2001) 8 CLP 10.

192 Section 127 of the Insolvency Act 1986 (UK).

> 'Consistent with that legislative policy the only dispositions of the company's property affected by the section in this case are the payments to the payees of the cheques drawn, after the presentation of the petition, on the company's bank account. What is needed for the section to operate is a disposition amounting to an alienation of the company's property (see *Mersey Steel & Iron Co Ltd v Naylor, Benzon & Co* (1884) 9 App Cas 434 at 440 per Earl of Selborne LC). The bank in honouring the company's cheque obeys as agent the order of its principal to pay out of the principal's money in the agent's hands the amount of the cheque to the payee (see *Westminster Bank Ltd v Hilton* (1926) 136 LT 315 at 317 per Lord Atkinson). The beneficial ownership of the property represented by the cheque was never transferred to the bank, to which no alienation of the company's property was made.'

It is thought that the final sentence is compelling. Where a bank effects a payment on foot of a company's mandate there is no disposition to the bank as the bank is not a 'disponee' – merely an intermediary, acting as agent of the company. Mummery LJ went on to quote with approval the following passage from the decision of Street CJ in *Re Mal Bower's Macquarie Electrical Centre Pty Ltd*[193] where he said there was 'great force' in the argument that:

> '… the paying by a bank of a company's cheque, presented by a stranger, does not involve the bank in a disposition of the property of the company so as to disentitle the bank to debit the amount of the cheque to the company's account. The word 'disposition' connotes in my view both a disponor and a disponee. The section operates to render the disposition void so far as concerns the disponee. It does not operate to affect the agencies interposing between the company, as disponor, and the recipient of the property, as disponee … The intermediary functions fulfilled by the bank in respect of paying cheques drawn by a company in favour of and presented on behalf of a third party do not implicate the bank in the consequences of the statutory avoidance prescribed by [the similar Australian provision] … I consider that the legislative intention … is such as to require an investigation of what happened to the property, that is to say, what was the disposition, and then to enable the liquidator to recover it upon the basis that the disposition was void. It is recovery from the disponee that forms the basic legislative purpose …[194]'

The Court of Appeal acknowledged that the decision of Buckley LJ in *Re Gray's Inn Construction Co Ltd*[195] did contain certain passages which, if read out of context supported the view that all post-presentation cheques drawn on a bank account were dispositions in favour of the bank and also that a bank had a liability to a liquidator to the extent that dispositions were irrecoverable from the third parties who cashed such cheques. It was held, however, that that judgment was not binding authority for either proposition because it concerned an overdrawn account. The Court of Appeal also favoured the interpretation given by Lightman J in *Coutts & Co v Stock*[196] where it was held that although the statute in question invalidated a disposition as between a company and a payee, it did not do so as against the company's bank where the bank merely fulfilled an agency or intermediary role between the company and the payee. It is thought that the decision of the Court of Appeal was correct in law and common sense.

---

[193] *Re Mal Bower's Macquarie Electrical Centre Pty Ltd* [1974] 1 NSWLR 245.

[194] *Re Mal Bower's Macquarie Electrical Centre Pty Ltd* [1974] 1 NSWLR 245 at 258.

[195] *Re Gray's Inn Construction Co Ltd* [1980] 1 All ER 814.

[196] *Coutts & Co v Stock* [2000] 1 BCLC 183.

[25.071] The current law in Ireland is the reverse. Shortly after the decision of the English Court of Appeal, the issue arose for consideration by the High Court. In *Re Industrial Services Company (Dublin) Ltd*[197], the official liquidator of the subject company objected to certain payments into and out of the company's bank account, after the presentation of a petition to wind up the company because the bank had failed to notice the advertisement. In finding for the liquidator, Kearns J began his exposition of the law by stating that in *Re Pat Ruth Ltd*[198] Costello J was in no doubt that 'such payments were "dispositions" within the meaning of s 218 of the CA 1963 be they lodgments into a company's bank account or payments out'[199]. It is thought that no such inference – that Costello J believed anything of the sort – can be drawn: in that case, the account in question was overdrawn whereas in the instant case the account had been in credit for much of the relevant time. Likewise, any reliance on the decision in *Re Gray's Inn Construction Co Ltd*[200] to find in favour of the liquidator is weakened by the fact that, in that case, the bank account under consideration was overdrawn, thereby rendering any postulation on accounts that are 'in credit', clearly *obiter dictum*. Although Kearns J went on to quote from the decision of Mummery LJ in *Hollicourt (Contracts) Ltd v Bank of Ireland*[201] and the passage from the judgment of Street CJ in *Re Mal Bower's Macquarie Electrical Centre Pty Ltd*[202], cited in the preceding paragraph, he went on to reject their conclusion[203]. Kearns J said:

> 'I feel that notwithstanding the passage just referred to, something more than a commercial desideratum as considered from the Bank's viewpoint would be required to persuade me to take a different view from that expressed by Costello J in *Re Pat Ruth Ltd*. I am not convinced that the reasoning by the Court of Appeal in *Hollicourt* is preferable to the different view taken by the same court in *Gray's Inn Construction Ltd*. I do not see that some commercial interpretation advantageous to the Bank must be given to s 218 when its meaning on the fact of it, is plain and straightforward. Had the legislature intended that some sort of derogation or qualification would apply in the case of banks, it would have been easy to frame this section appropriately.
>
> … banks discharge a dual function in their relationship with their customer. In one sense they act as agents, but, given that property in money passes to them, the true relationship is that of borrower and lender. Thus the bank can be both agent, creditor and debtor. They thus have a very special role of responsibility in winding up situations. Not the least part of that role is one of vigilance in respect of their client customers which, because of their assets and expertise, they are well placed to perform. Where they do exercise that role and

[197] *Re Industrial Services Company (Dublin) Ltd* [2001] 2 IR 118. See Moore, 'Section 218 of the Companies Act, 1963 Banks and Hollicourt: the Irish Perspective' (2001) 8 CLP 108.

[198] *Re Pat Ruth Ltd* [1981] ILRM 51.

[199] *Re Industrial Services Company (Dublin) Ltd* [2001] 2 IR 118 at 121.

[200] *Re Gray's Inn Construction Co Ltd* [1980] 1 All ER 814.

[201] *Hollicourt (Contracts) Ltd v Bank of Ireland* [2001] 1 BCLC 233. See Sealy, 'Company Liquidations: When Should Post-Petition Banking Transactions be Avoided?' (2000) CCH's Company Law Newsletter, Issue 57, 11 July 2000 and Moore, 'Payments Received by Cheque Drawn on Bank Account of Company Following Presentation of Winding-up Petition' (2001) 8 CLP 10.

[202] *Re Mal Bower's Macquarie Electrical Centre Pty Ltd* [1974] 1 NSWLR 245.

[203] Kearns J was also not swayed by the views in Breslin, *Banking Law in the Republic of Ireland* (1998), p 386.

function it seems to me at least they serve a wider commercial interest so the narrow commercial contention of the Bank's interest is not the issue. If the Bank in exercising its functions responsibly ensures greater protection for the general body of creditors, that surely is consistent with the policy of the section[204].'

[25.072] To the extent that Kearns J's conclusions are based on judicial precedent, it is thought that they are based on a *falsio assumpit*. Once it becomes clear that neither *Re Pat Ruth Ltd* nor the *Re Grey's Inn Construction* case are authorities for the conclusion reached by Kearns J, the legal basis for the decision collapses. It is thought that to find as the Court of Appeal did in *Hollicourt* or as the Supreme Court of New South Wales did in *Mal Bower's Macquarie Electrical Centre* is not to put 'some commercial interpretation advantageous to the Bank … to s 218 when its meaning on the fact of it, is plain and straightforward'. It is submitted that, given the extent of judicial disagreement, the meaning of s 218 of the CA 1963 can hardly be said to be 'plain' or 'straightforward'[205]. As for the interpretation being commercially advantageous to banks, if it is correct there is nothing to recoil from in that suggestion. It is submitted that the interpretation afforded to the term 'disposition' was incorrect and operates to perpetrate an injustice to a person who has not benefited from the transaction. Indeed, to the extent that the effect of that interpretation is to force the redistribution of property rights (ie, afford to certain creditors additional monies that never formed part of the company's assets) it is possibly an unconstitutional intrusion upon property rights. It is thought that a payment into a bank account is only a disposition within the meaning of s 218 where that account is overdrawn, as the effect of such a payment is to reduce the company's indebtedness to the bank, ie, the position of the bank in that situation is that of creditor. Payments into an account in credit should not, however, be treated as dispositions because the payment is not in reduction of any indebtedness. Payments out are a different matter but again, the bank in acting as an agent of the company should not be made to pick up the tab: the payment out should be voidable and returnable by the recipient, subject only to the court deciding whether or not to validate the payment. The disposition should be void only as against the actual beneficiary of the payment out.

[25.073] The decision in *Re Industrial Services Ltd* was followed by Clarke J in *Re Worldport Ireland Ltd*[206] but with an important twist, as it was found that the bank and the ultimate payee were *both* disponees which built upon the observations of Kearns J in *Re Industrial Services Company (Dublin) Ltd*[207] that it did not necessarily follow from his conclusions that liquidators could set their sights against banks alone or that they could ignore the ultimate recipients of the payments made[208]. In the *Worldport* case, the official liquidator of a company sought a declaration that a payment of over €256,000 was void under s 218. There, the company's winding up had commenced on 15 April 2002. On 22 April 2002, a transfer was made of funds from the company's bank account

[204] *Re Industrial Services Company (Dublin) Ltd* [2001] 2 IR 118 at 129.

[205] Indeed, in *Coutts & Co v Stock* [2000] 1 BCLC 183 at 185, Lightman J said that 'the authorities are in disarray and the state of the law is uncertain'.

[206] *Re Worldport Ireland Ltd* [2005] IEHC 189. See, generally, Keirse, 'Post-commencement Dispositions – An Analysis of Recent Case Law' (2005) CLP 317.

[207] *Re Industrial Services Company (Dublin) Ltd* [2001] 2 IR 118. See Moore, 'Section 218 of the Companies Act, 1963 Banks and Hollicourt: the Irish Perspective' (2001) 8 CLP 108.

[208] See para **[25.070]**.

in favour of the company's holding company. The issue which the High Court was asked to decide was whether s 218 had been breached and if so, to whom the disposition had been made. Analysing the transaction, Clarke J said:

> '... each of the three parties involved has two separate effects on its financial position which are equal and opposite. The customer has reduced the value of its asset in the form of the debt which the Bank owed to it by virtue of it having a credit account but also has reduced its indebtedness to the third party by the same amount. The Bank has reduced its obligation to the customer but also is out an equivalent amount of cash by virtue of having transferred that sum to the third party. The third party has received the relevant sum in cash from the Bank but has correspondingly reduced its entitlement to recover that sum (either in part or in its entirety) from the customer.
>
> It is necessary to consider that series of interlocking relationships in order to ascertain whom it might be said can properly be regarded as a disponee for the purposes of a disposition which is caught by s 218.'

Although Clarke J noted that many of the authorities related to bank accounts in debit and not in credit as was the case in *Industrial Services* and the case in hand, the learned judge felt that it would be inappropriate on the basis of judicial comity to revisit such a recently decided issue and therefore followed the *ratio* in *Industrial Services* and held that the bank was within the ambit of s 218 and was a disponee. The twist, referred to above, was that the holding company was also found to be a disponee. Referring to Kearns J's characterisation of the dualistic role of banks, Clarke J said:

> 'The very fact that the Bank has a dual role and that a transaction of the type which occurred in this case cannot be readily severed into its constituent parts leads to the inescapable conclusion that the entirety of the transaction needs to be looked at as a whole. It would not be possible for the Bank to make the payment of funds properly to the third party without the instruction from its client customer. It is not possible to look at one part of such a transaction without the other. Taking the transaction as a whole it is manifestly clear that the Company has caused money to be paid to its parent out of its bank account. As a result of the transaction which was, after all, carried out on the instructions of the Company, the Company had its assets in the form of its entitlement to receive money from the Bank reduced by the Sum and also had its obligations to its parent reduced by an equivalent amount. To say in those circumstances that the parent was not a disponee would, in my view, be to give a wholly unreal and unrealistic meaning to the transaction. If, as Kearns J pointed out, the Bank has a dual role, then, following *Industrial Services,* it seems to me that I must regard this case as being one where there are dual disponees. In those circumstances it seems to me that I should also regard Inc as a disponee.'

It should be noted that in *Re Industrial Services Company (Dublin) Ltd*[209] and *Re Worldport Ireland Ltd* both Kearns J and Clarke J acknowledged that the court did retain the important power of validation and that Kearns J said that any problem with 'double accounting' can be dealt with on application to the court by the bank to validate dispositions made[210]. The question of validation of dispositions is considered below[211].

[209] *Re Industrial Services Company (Dublin) Ltd* [2001] 2 IR 118. See Moore, 'Section 218 of the Companies Act, 1963 Banks and Hollicourt: the Irish Perspective' (2001) 8 CLP 108.

[210] *Re Industrial Services Company (Dublin) Ltd* [2001] 2 IR 118 at 130.

[211] See para **[25.075]**.

(iii) Debiting of interest post-commencement

[25.074] In *Re Ashmark Ltd: Ashmark Ltd v Allied Irish Bank plc*[212], the question of interest payable to a bank in respect of a company's overdraft account was considered by Lardner J. In this application, the company had an overdraft account with AIB, and on the date upon which the company's winding up commenced this account stood in credit. However, interest on the account, which had accrued on a day-to-day basis, was debited from the account after the commencement of the winding up. Lardner J held that the debiting of this interest was not a disposition within the meaning of s 218 of the CA 1963. Relying on the authority of Buckley LJ in *Halesowen Presswork and Assemblies Ltd v Westminster Bank Ltd*[213] Lardner J said:

> '... the company had incurred over a period a liability to pay interest to the bank on its overdraft. This liability accrued from day-to-day and constituted a debt due by the company to the bank over and above the amount of the overdraft. Then the company paid money into the account so that the account was in substantial credit. The overdraft debt was repaid by the company which became entitled to a credit in the computation of the account. The amount of the credit was not itself the property of the company but of the bank. The bank became a debtor to the company. At any time the amount of each party's liability to the other could only be ascertained by discovering the ultimate balance of their mutual dealings. Where interest has been accruing on a daily basis as in the present case which is a liability of the company to the bank and at the same time, the bank owes a debt in respect of the company's current account credit balance to the company, it is not in my judgment correct to treat the ascertainment of the ultimate balance as a disposition of property by the company on that date (or a disposition of a thing in action) within s 218 of the Companies Act. It seems to me properly considered as an account situation in which the existence and amount of the bank's liability in respect of the current account to the company can only be ascertained by discovering the ultimate balance of their mutual dealings[214].'

Where interest accrues after the commencement of a winding up it cannot be debited but remains due to the bank. In such cases, the bank can either prove for the debt in the subsequent liquidation or, where it is secured, it can stand outside the liquidation and recover principal and interest from the proceeds of sale of the secured property.

(c) The jurisdiction to validate dispositions

[25.075] There is some doubt as to the precise principles which a court should employ in exercising its jurisdiction to validate certain post-commencement dispositions. In *Re*

212 *Re Ashmark Ltd: Ashmark Ltd v Allied Irish Bank plc* [1994] 1 ILRM 223.

213 *Halesowen Presswork and Assemblies Ltd v Westminster Bank Ltd* [1971] 1 QB 1, where (at 46) Buckley LJ had said: 'Where the relationship of the banker and customer is a single relationship such as I have already mentioned, albeit embodied in a number of accounts, the situation is not in my judgment a situation of lien at all. A lien postulates property of the debtor in the possession or under the control of the creditor. Nor is it a set off situation which postulates mutual but independent obligations between the two parties. It is an accounting situation in which the existence and amount of the parties' liability to the other can only be ascertained by discovering the ultimate balance of their mutual dealings.'

214 *Re Ashmark Ltd: Ashmark Ltd v Allied Irish Bank plc* [1994] ILRM 223 at 226.

Lynch, Monaghan & O'Brien Ltd[215], Costello J said that the discretionary validation jurisdiction conferred on the courts is intended primarily for dispositions to creditors whose debts arise after the presentation of the petition to have the company wound up. In *Re Ashmark Ltd (No 1)*[216], certain payments were made after the commencement of the winding up and all were dispositions within the meaning of s 218 of the CA 1963. The first disposition was by cheque in respect of legal fees before the commencement of the winding up but which, due to the company's inability to provide funds, was not cashed until after the commencement. The second disposition was also in respect of services to the company prior to the commencement of the winding up. In respect of both of these dispositions, it was argued:

- that the solicitor disponee was unaware that the payment disposition in his favour was made after the commencement of the winding up; and
- that in so far as the payments were made to the solicitor who had an intimate knowledge of the affairs of the company, the dispositions in his favour were made in the best interests of the company and were beneficial to the creditors.

O'Hanlon J accepted that both of the foregoing were grounds which a court would consider in deciding whether or not to validate a disposition. However, on the facts of the case, he held that the evidence did not justify reliance on either of these grounds to validate the dispositions. He held that the disponee solicitor had constructive notice that the petition had been presented. On the validation of dispositions by a company after the commencement of its winding up, O'Hanlon J said:

> '... while transactions taking place after the commencement of the winding up have been validated under the provisions of s 218 of the Companies Act 1963, and under the comparable provisions found in the English statutes, where no dissipation of the company's assets have resulted therefrom, I find it hard to envisage a situation where the court would validate a payment in full made after the commencement of a winding up, in respect of services rendered, or goods sold, or other obligations incurred by the company *prior* to the winding up, and when similar treatment could not be accorded to the general body of unsecured creditors[217].'

This raises an important point. The primary rationale of the validation mechanism in s 218 of the CA 1963 is to protect creditors. Creditors who, in return for money, advance goods or services to a company after the commencement of its winding up may do so for either of two reasons. First, they may be unaware of the fact that a petition has been presented. Second, they may know that a petition has been presented but nevertheless continue to give the company credit thereby enabling the company to continue in business and not go-under merely because a petition is presented to which the company may have a defence[218].

---

[215] *Re Lynch, Monaghan & O'Brien Ltd* (9 June 1989, unreported) HC, the facts of which are considered by MacCann, 'Liquidation: *Pari Passu* Distribution and Section 218 of the Companies Act 1963' (1990) ILT 6 at pp 8, 9.

[216] *Re Ashmark Ltd (No 1)* [1990] ILRM 330.

[217] *Re Ashmark Ltd (No 1)* [1990] ILRM 330 at 333, 334.

[218] See MacCann, 'Liquidation: *Pari Passu* Distribution and Section 218 of the Companies Act 1963' (1990) ILT 6, where the recent case law in both Ireland and England is perceptively analysed.

[25.076] In *Re McBirney and Co Ltd*[219], Murphy J said that:

> '... the entire burden of the authorities is to the effect that the making of the payment (as opposed to the incurring of the expense) must be shown to be for the benefit of the company or at least desirable in the interests of the unsecured creditors as a body[220].'

However, having stated the general principle Murphy J departed from it saying, 'I do not think that the court should confine itself rigidly to particular propositions isolated from the very special features of the present case'[221]. The special features to which he referred were that the dispositions were made by an administrator and receiver-manager (acting in his capacity of receiver-manager) who was appointed under the Insurance (No 2) Act 1983 to PMPA Insurance plc. The payments made were disputed by the company's liquidator. Although it was rejected that s 218 of the CA 1963 had no application to a company to which a receiver-manager is appointed under the Insurance (No 2) Act 1983, the fact that the payments had been made by a receiver-manager was recognised as being a special feature. As Murphy J said:

> 'In my view it is important to recognise, therefore, that the public were dealing with the receiver in the belief, as was the case, that he was an officer appointed by the court to control and carry on the business of the company[222].'

The learned judge went on to exercise his jurisdiction and validated a number of payments made by the receiver-manager. Amongst the justifications given were the fact that some suppliers believed that they were supplying goods to a person whom they inferred was acting on the general authority of the court[223], and payments to employees did not prejudice the rights of unsecured creditors as the employees already had a preferential status[224]. Murphy J also distinguished payments which were made to *connected companies* from those which were made to *unconnected companies* and maintained this distinction in the subsequent decision of *Re McBirney and Company Ltd (No 2)*[225]. In this latter case, he said of the decision in the earlier case that:

> 'Certainly it is difficult to justify the decision on the basis of any benefit accruing on the unsecured creditors as a body by reason of the payment. However the justification for my earlier judgment may be found in the fact that the non-connected companies were perhaps unaware of the presentation of the petitions for the winding up of the companies and certainly less well informed concerning their affairs than the connected companies and the persons by whom they were controlled[226].'

With regard to the connected companies Murphy J ordered that they were obliged to repay the company in full all payments which had been made to them, notwithstanding that they were in liquidation.

---

219 *Re McBirney and Co Ltd* (2 July 1992, unreported) HC.

220 *Re McBirney and Co Ltd* (2 July 1992, unreported) HC at p 8.

221 *Re McBirney and Co Ltd* (2 July 1992, unreported) HC.

222 *Re McBirney and Co Ltd* (2 July 1992, unreported) HC at p 10.

223 *Re McBirney and Co Ltd* (2 July 1992, unreported) HC at p 11.

224 *Re McBirney and Co Ltd* (2 July 1992, unreported) HC at p 12.

225 *Re McBirney and Company Ltd* (No 2) (15 June 1993, unreported) HC.

226 *Re McBirney and Company Ltd (No 2)* (15 June 1993, unreported) HC at p 7.

[25.077] A clear example of a disposition which was for the benefit of the creditors is provided by *Re Al Levy (Holdings) Ltd*[227]. In that case, a disposition was validated where, after the presentation of a petition to wind the company up, it sold its leasehold interest in a property because the lease was liable to be forfeited if it, as the tenant, was wound up. By reason of this, the company sold the lease at market value before this happened. A further disposition was the payment of arrears of rent to the landlord, this being a condition to the landlord's consent to an assignment of the lease. Such dispositions were clearly to the benefit of the creditors of the company in that the company was put in funds arising from the sale of the lease, whereas had the company not disposed of its interest, it would have had neither funds nor a leasehold interest available for distribution amongst the creditors[228].

[25.078] Other cases are less easy to reconcile with the foregoing principles. In *Re Pat Ruth Ltd*[229], while all dispositions by the company into its overdrawn account were held to be void and would not be validated by the court, the other side of these same dispositions which were payments out of the bank account in favour of other creditors of the company were validated. So while the payment by cheque of creditors was validated, the honouring of those cheques by the bank was void: in effect, the bank paid the creditors from its own resources, and not from the company's account, which remained to the same extent in overdraft as it had been at the presentation of the petition. The reason why the dispositions to other creditors were validated was said by Costello J to be because:

> '... being persons whose debts were paid by means of the dispositions to which I have referred in good faith and in the ordinary course of business, come within the principle to which I have referred[230].'

The principle earlier referred to by Costello J in his judgment was that stated by Buckley LJ in *Re Gray's Inn Construction Co Ltd*[231] namely, that:

> 'A disposition carried out in good faith in the ordinary course of business at a time when the parties are unaware that a petition has been presented may, it seems, normally be validated by the court ...'

There are few truer examples of 'ordinary course of business' than a bank acting on foot of a customer's instruction to pay a cheque. This case has been criticised on several grounds. One critic[232] has said that it seems irreconcilable to distinguish between the

---

[227] *Re Al Levy (Holdings) Ltd* [1963] 2 All ER 85. See also *re Tain Construction Ltd; Rose v ABI Group (UK) plc and another* [2003] 2 BCLC 374.

[228] Where a disposition does not benefit the creditors, but at the same time does not deplete the assets of the company available for distribution, this fact will be a material consideration for the court: *Re Tramway Building and Construction Co Ltd* [1987] BCLC 632.

[229] *Re Pat Ruth Ltd* [1981] ILRM 51.

[230] *Re Pat Ruth Ltd* [1981] ILRM 51 at 52, 53.

[231] *Re Gray's Inn Construction Co Ltd* [1980] 1 All ER 814.

[232] Ussher, *Company Law in Ireland* (1986), p 483.

bank and the other creditors in this fashion, and in particular to deny that the dispositions to the bank were not made in the ordinary course of business[233].

[25.079] In *Re Industrial Services Company (Dublin) Ltd (No 2)*[234], the bank that had effected withdrawals from an account in credit after the commencement of the company's winding up, which withdrawals has been held by Kearns J to be voidable, applied to have them validated. The validation application was heard by McCracken J, who noted that the following payments were in issue:

- lodgments of £4,961.77 and withdrawals of £8,022.27 in the period from the presentation of the petition and the advertising of the petition; and
- lodgments of £11,041.76 and withdrawals of £8,761.97 in the period from the advertising of the petition and the making of the winding-up order.

As to the principles applicable to validating payments, the following passage from the decision of McCracken J is instructive:

> 'The view I take is that I should validate any payments made in the ordinary course of business which were in respect of current debts, whether these were before or after the advertisement, as these were payments which the liquidator would probably have to have made in any event. To that degree, they are payments which could be said to be made for the benefit of the general body of creditors. However, I do not think that I should validate any payments made which were not made in the ordinary course of business, and I note that many of these payments were in fact made to directors of the company or persons who were connected with directors ...'

McCracken J applied this and validated payments that had been made in the ordinary course of business but not payments made to directors or persons connected with directors. In all, payments totalling £2,125.57 were validated. McCracken J went on to consider the question of payments into and out of the bank accounts:

> 'There is an argument to be made that I should declare all payments into the bank account to be void dispositions, and only validate the sums that I have mentioned above in relation to the payments out of the bank account. However, to do so would lead to a windfall for the liquidator of the sum of £2,125.57, and would really be a form of double accounting. Accordingly, I would also validate the payment into the bank account of the sum of £2,125.57 by the company. All other payments into and out of the account are accordingly void, but again I would like to prevent any form of double benefit to the liquidator, which would result if he were able to recover the moneys paid in from the Bank and the moneys

233 As to the meaning of 'ordinary course of business', in *Countrywide Banking Corporation Ltd v Dean* [1998] 2 WLR 441 the Privy Council said at 451 (in the context of whether a transaction was a preferential one in the context of s 266 of the Companies Act 1955 (NZ)): 'Plainly the transaction must be examined in the actual setting in which it took place. That defines the circumstances in which it is to be determined whether it was in the ordinary course of business. The determination then is to be made objectively by reference to the standard of what amounts to the ordinary course of business ... the transaction must be such that it would be viewed by an objective observer as having taken place in the ordinary course of business. While there is to be reference to business practices in the commercial world in general, the focus must still be the ordinary operational activities of businesses as going concerns, not responses to abnormal financial difficulties.'

234 *Re Industrial Services Company (Dublin) Ltd (No 2)* (15 May 2002, unreported) HC, McCracken J.

> paid out from the recipients of the payments. What I would propose to do to try to meet this situation is that, while I am not validating any of these payments, I will direct that if the liquidator recovers the moneys from the Bank, he shall not seek to recover them from the recipients, and shall not in any way hinder the Bank from making such recovery should they be entitled to do so. It is then up to the Bank whether they wish to pursue the recipients themselves.'

This, it is thought, was a reasonable attempt by the court to do justice arising from the finding that payments into an in-credit bank account were 'dispositions'. Of course, the only reason why the possibility of 'windfalls' and 'double accounting' arose in the first place was because the payments by the company to its bank were treated as dispositions within the meaning of s 218 of the CA 1963[235].

[25.080] The High Court has confirmed that there is jurisdiction to prospectively validate a disposition by a company where, after a petition has been presented but before an order made winding up the company, it wishes to dispose of property freed from the concern that such a disposition might be set aside under s 218 should the petition be successful. In *Re Wellingford Construction Ltd; Joyce v Wellingford Construction Ltd and others*[236], a s 205 petition had been presented which, *inter alia*, sought relief in the nature of a winding-up order. As noted by Clarke J, by reason of the operation of ss 218 and 220 of the CA 1963 should a winding-up order have been made it would have been deemed to have commenced at the time of the presentation of the s 205 petition. In consequence, any disposal of property by the company was liable to be declared void. Clarke J accepted that there was jurisdiction to authorise the sale of property notwithstanding that a winding-up order had not been made and in this respect relied upon the authority of Buckley J in *Re AI Levy (Holdings) Ltd*[237]. Clarke J held, however, that he was not persuaded to make an order at that point in time and adjourned the matter with liberty to re-enter. The learned judge said that he would be prepared to validate a sale of the company's property (lands, berths and ancillary structures to Derg Marina) which was achieved having complied with certain conditions which included that the property was offered for sale on the open market, through an independent auctioneer and on instructions from the company to obtain the most commercially advantageous contract obtainable.

Fraudulent preference of creditors

[25.081] The corporate law of fraudulent preference has its origins in the laws of bankruptcy, applicable to insolvent individuals[238]. In the words of Lord Ellenborough in *De Tastet v Carroll*[239], the *raison d'être* of such legislation arose because:

---

235 For a criticism of the earlier decision of the High Court, see para **[25.072]**.

236 *Re Wellingford Construction Ltd, Joyce v Wellingford Construction Ltd and others* [2005] IEHC 392, Clarke J. For a short case note see Maher, 'In Whose Interest?' (2006) Law Society Gazette, December 2006 at p 30.

237 *Re AI Levy (Holdings) Ltd* [1963] 2 All ER 556.

238 For the law of fraudulent preference applicable to individual bankrupts as contained in the s 57 of the Bankruptcy Act 1988, see generally, Sanfey & Holohan, *Bankruptcy Law and Practice* (2nd edn, 2012), Ch 8.

239 *De Tastet v Carroll* (1813) 1 Stark 88.

'... it occurred to those who presided in the courts that it was unjust to permit a party on the eve of bankruptcy to make a voluntary disposition of his property in favour of a particular creditor, leaving the mere husk to the rest; and therefore that a transfer made at such a period, and under such circumstances, as evidently showed that it was made in contemplation of bankruptcy, and in order to favour a particular creditor, should be void.'

To allow an insolvent company on the verge of being wound up to freely dispose of its property would create an unacceptable loophole in the law of corporate insolvency. Fraudulent preference is addressed by s 286(1) of the CA 1963[240], which provides:

'Subject to the provisions of this section, any conveyance, mortgage, delivery of goods, payment, execution or other act relating to property made or done by or against a company which is *unable to pay its debts as they become due* in favour of any creditor, or of any person on trust for any creditor, *with a view* to giving such creditor, or any surety or guarantor for the debt due to such creditor, *a preference over the other creditors*, shall, if a winding-up of the company commences within *six months* of the making or doing the same and the company is *at the time of the commencement of the winding-up unable to pay its debts* (taking into account the contingent and prospective liabilities), be deemed a fraudulent preference of its creditors and be invalid accordingly.'

Although a number of points arise for consideration here, two points in particular must be stressed. In the first place, in order for s 286(1) to become operative the company making the preference must be *unable to pay its debts as they become due* at the time the disposition was made and on the commencement of the winding up of the company. The circumstances in which a company will be found to be unable to pay debts is considered below[241] in connection with the invalidity of certain floating charges on a winding up. Many cases stress the insolvency of the company at the time of the making of the preference[242] but it is clear that it is only where a company is insolvent on its winding up also, that an application under s 286 of the CA 1963 can be made.

[25.082] The following points arise for consideration in the treatment of the law of corporate fraudulent preference:

(a) The disposition of corporate property.
(b) The operative time for making a preference.
(c) The effect of a fraudulent preference.
(d) The onus of proof.
(e) The intention to prefer.
(f) The beneficiary of the disposition.

(a) The disposition of corporate property

[25.083] There must be a preferential disposition of the company's property before s 286 of the CA 1963 can be invoked. While this may seem obvious, an application to have a transaction set aside as being invalid failed in *Re Welding Plant Ltd; Cooney v Dargan*[243] because the transaction under scrutiny was held not to amount to a disposition of corporate property. There, it was intended that in consideration of the company

240 As amended by s 135 of the CA 1990 (emphasis added).

241 See para **[25.111]**.

242 Eg, see *Parkes & Sons Ltd v Hong Kong and Shanghai Banking Corp* [1990] ILRM 341 at 345.

243 *Re Welding Plant Ltd; Cooney v Dargan* (27 June 1984, unreported) HC, *per* McWilliam J.

transferring certain corporate property to the controllers of the company, the controllers would take two loans in their personal names. It was held that this transaction had not in fact or in law happened because nothing had been executed by the company which would give effect to this intention. The company continued to own the property and, therefore, there was no disposition.

[25.084] In order for there to be a fraudulent preference, the property disposed of by the company must be beneficially owned by the company. In *Re Gerry Bredin Hardware Ltd*[244], a liquidator of an insolvent company disputed the payment by the company to its directors of the proceeds of an insurance claim arising from the destruction by fire of the company's premises. The directors were also the company's landlords and owned the freehold in the premises. Whereas the liquidator claimed that the payment was a fraudulent preference of company property, the directors claimed that they were in fact beneficially entitled to the money so that there was no disposition which could be a fraudulent preference. Ryan J acknowledged that 'if the court was satisfied that the directors were presonally entitled to all of the insurance settlement money, the decision on the issue would be obvious', ie, it would not be a fraudulent preference since the company's creditors were not being denied anything as the proceeds would not be available for distribution amongst the creditors. In fact, Ryan J found that the company was the owner of the insurance money, subject to any legitimate claims which others may have had in respect of it.

[25.085] It should be noted also that the type of transaction or disposition which may be impugned by s 286(1) of the CA 1963 is any conveyance, mortgage, delivery of goods, payment, execution or other act relating to property made or done by or against a company.

(b) The operative time for making the preference

[25.086] Section 286(1) of the CA 1963 provides that the crucial time limit for the making of fraudulent preferences is six months before the commencement of the winding up, except in the case of fraudulent preferences in favour of connected persons, where s 286(3) of the CA 1963 provides such will be invalid where made within two years of the commencement of the winding up. Furthermore, a disposition is deemed to have been made with a view to giving such a person a preference over other creditors and to be a fraudulent preference, unless the contrary is shown. A connected person is defined by s 286(5) as a person who at the time of the transaction was:

- a director or shadow director of the company,
- a director's spouse, civil partner within the meaning of the Civil Partnership and Certain Rights and Obligations of Cohabitants Act 2010, parent, sibling or child,
- a related company within the meaning of s 140(5) of the CA 1990, considered below[245],
- any trustee of, or surety or guarantor for the debt due to any person referred to above.

---

244 *Re Gerry Bredin Hardware Ltd* [2011] IEHC 442, Ryan J.

245 See para **[25.120]**.

In this way the legislature has broadened the scope of the provision by targeting persons who are perceived to be in a special position of trust to the company. In *Elite Logistics Ltd v McNamara*[246], Laffoy J relied on the presumption of preference in s 286(3). In that case, the learned judge found that a transaction whereby the plaintiff company transferred to one of its directors, its principal asset being a 40% interest in a property, fell to be a fraudulent preference because it was made when the plaintiff company was unable to pay its debts, at the commencement of its winding up 10 days later; it was unable to pay its debts, the defendant was a director and there was a presumption that the transaction was made with a view to giving him a preference and the defendant had not adduced evidence sufficient to rebut that presumption.

(c) The effect of a fraudulent preference

[25.087] Where a fraudulent preference is deemed or found to have been made, then it is invalid. Elsewhere[247], it has been suggested that this must equate with 'void' as provided for in the Bankruptcy Act 1988. In spite of the legislature not reconciling this difference in its most recent review[248] of the law of fraudulent preference, it is thought that the consequence is indeed that the transaction is void in the case of a company[249].

[25.088] Section 286(2) of the CA 1963 provides that any conveyance or assignment by a company of all of its property to trustees for the benefit of all of its creditors shall be void to all intents. This provision clearly rejects the view that a company can come to a voluntary arrangement with its creditors which benefits them all, and implicitly insists that the liquidator of a company is the proper person to distribute the assets of an insolvent company[250].

[25.089] The familiar saver for the rights of that most favoured person, the *bona fide* purchaser for value, applies to fraudulent preferences. Section 286(4) of the CA 1963 provides that the rights of any person taking title in good faith and for valuable consideration through or under a creditor of the company shall not be affected[251]. This saver is not directed at the preferred creditor, but rather at a person taking under him who will not suffer by an avoidance of a disposition to a creditor unless he acquires property fraudulently preferred to his successor in title without valuable consideration or has notice of the fraudulent preference[252].

[25.090] Section 287(1) of the CA 1963 provides that where a company is being wound up and anything made or done on or after the operative date is void under s 286 of the

---

246 *Elite Logistics Ltd v McNamara* [2012] IEHC 246.

247 See Ussher, *Company Law in Ireland* (1986), p 505.

248 In drafting s 135 of the CA 1990, and s 57 of the the Bankruptcy Act 1988.

249 Support for this interpretation can be determined from s 287(1)(b) which makes reference to the situation where something is 'void under section 286 as a fraudulent preference'.

250 Contrast s 57 of the Bankruptcy Act 1988, following the recommendation of the *Bankruptcy Law Committee Report* (Budd Committee) 1972. See generally Sanfey & Holohan, *Bankruptcy Law and Practice* (2nd edn, 2012), para 8.3.

251 See *Butcher v Stead* (1875) LR 7 HL 839.

252 See *Ex p Tate* (1876) 35 LT 531.

CA 1963 as a fraudulent preference of a person interested in property mortgaged or charged to secure the company's debt, then:

> '... the person preferred shall be subject to the same liabilities and shall have the same rights as if he had undertaken to be personally liable as surety for the debt to the extent of the charge on the property or the value of his interest, whichever is the less.'

The effect of this section is that where a person who is preferred has a mortgage or a charge on company property to secure a debt due by the company he will become personally liable as a surety for the debt to the extent of the security on the property or the value of his interest (whichever is the lesser). The value of a person's interest is determined at the date of the fraudulent preference, and in determining the value of the interest the interest is taken to be free from encumbrances other than those to which the charge for the company's debt was then subject[253].

(d) The onus of proof

[25.091] Before a disposition of corporate property will be deemed to be a fraudulent preference, it must be shown that it was made with a view to giving a creditor a preference over the other creditors. As with other cases where an intention is sought to be attributed to a company, the law will look to the dominant intentions of the controllers of the company, usually its directors[254], but occasionally its members[255].

[25.092] The general rule is that the task of proving an intention to prefer falls on the liquidator, as seen in *Corran Construction Company v Bank of Ireland Finance Ltd*[256] and other Irish cases[257]. In a case where a disposition within the meaning of s 286(1) of the CA 1963 is made in favour of a connected person as defined above, then there is a presumption that the disposition was made with a view to giving that person a preference over other creditors and thus a fraudulent preference. This amendment introduced by the Companies Act 1990 is helpful to liquidators who, upon adducing evidence of a disposition in favour of a connected person, will see the evidential burden shift to the disponee to prove that the disposition was not a fraudulent preference.

---

253 Section 287(2) of the CA 1963.

254 Note though that in *Kelleher v Continental Irish Meat Ltd* (9 May 1978, unreported) HC, Costello J held that the intention of an employee to prefer was sufficient where he acted within his actual or ostensible authority.

255 See *Corran Construction Company v Bank of Ireland Finance Ltd* [1976–7] ILRM 175 at 178, where McWilliam J held that: '... I am bound to consider the matter on the basis of the intentions of the member of the company who was at that time in sole control of the affairs of the company.' There, the individual concerned was also a director.

256 *Corran Construction Company v Bank of Ireland Finance Ltd* [1976–7] ILRM 175, where *Peat v Gresham Trust Ltd* [1934] AC 252 and *Re FLE Holdings Ltd* [1967] 1 WLR 1409 were cited.

257 See also *Re Welding Plant Ltd; Cooney v Dargan* (27 June 1984, unreported) HC, *per* McWilliam J, in MacCann, *A Casebook on Company Law* (1991), para 20.47. See also *Re Station Motors Ltd v Allied Irish Banks Ltd* [1985] IR 756 and *Re O'Connors Nenagh Shopping Centre Ltd; Fitzpatrick v O'Connor and others* [2011] IEHC 508.

(e) The intention to prefer

[25.093] There is a presumption that transactions entered into in favour of connected persons within the statutory time limit were entered into with the intention of being a fraudulent preference[258]. Section 286(3) of the CA 1963 provides:

> 'A transaction to which subsection (1) applies in favour of a connected person which was made within two years before the commencement of the winding up of the company shall, unless the contrary is shown, be deemed in the event of the company being wound up —
>
> (a) to have been made with a view to giving such person a preference over the other creditors, and
>
> (b) to be a fraudulent preference,
>
> and be invalid accordingly.'

The power of such a presumption is evident from the decision of the English High Court in *Re Shapland Inc*[259]. In that case, a liquidator was successful in applying to have a charge set aside on the grounds of being a preference in circumstances where a company had entered into the charge in favour of its holding company within two years of its being wound up. It was held that the statutory presumption had not been displaced by the holding company[260].

[25.094] Other than in the case of connected persons, a liquidator must prove the intention of the company was to prefer one creditor over another. While the difficult burden of proving fraud[261] is not required there is an equally difficult proof, namely that the act of preference arose from the free volition of the company to prefer a particular creditor. It is well accepted that where a creditor exerts such pressure on the debtor company so as to overbear the free volition of the company, there will be no fraudulent preference. In *Re Daly & Co*[262], Porter MR said:

> 'Where pressure exists so as to overbear the volition of the debtor a payment is not made with a view to prefer the creditor exerting it, but because the debtor cannot help it. The view to prefer is absent; or at least is not the real view, or motive or reason actuating the debtor ...'

This has been said to be 'absurdly at odds with the aim of achieving an equitable distribution of the assets of an insolvent' company[263]. However, this is the established law and there are many cases where, upon proof that the company's will was overborne, the disposition was held not to be a fraudulent preference. Therefore, a fear of losing clients[264] or a fear that failure to make the preference would bring about the demise of

258 The requirement that there must be an intention to prefer has been criticised: see, for example, Keirse, 'Object and Effect: The Vexed Question of Intent in Fraudulent Preference Cases' (2005) 12(7) CLP 182.

259 *Re Shapland Inc* [2000] BCC 106.

260 The statutory presumption is contained in s 239(6) of the Insolvency Act 1986 (UK).

261 See Carroll J in *Re Station Motors Ltd* [1985] IR 756 and Porter MR in *Re Boyd* [1885–1886] 15 LR Ir 521.

262 *Re Daly & Co* [1887–8] 19 LR Ir 83 at 93.

263 See Ussher, *Company Law in Ireland* (1986), p 508.

264 See *Assignees of Taylor v Thompson* (1869–70) IRCL 129.

another company owned by the controller were both held to be sufficient to overbear the will of company controllers.

[25.095] In *Parkes & Sons Ltd v Hong Kong and Shanghai Banking Corporation*[265], a company's controller caused the company to enter into a guarantee and provide a mortgage in respect of the debts of another company. The controller was said to have been pressed by the bank for information, had many meetings with the bank, had the appointment of a receiver threatened, and had his affairs monitored closely by the bank. Blayney J held:

> 'It seems to me that the correct inference to draw from these facts is that [the controller] was concerned to save the claimant company and that this was his dominant motive in giving the mortgage. In view of the threat by the bank to put in a receiver, he had no alternative but to comply with their demand for further security. And while the giving of the mortgage may have taken some pressure off [his] personal guarantees, it did not relieve him from it or reduce his liability on it. In my opinion it has not been established that the facts are such that I should infer that [the controller's] dominant motive was to reduce his liability on the guarantees[266].'

This case shows that personal gain to the person responsible for the company taking the decision to make a preference is not the decisive factor in the court's decision. Nevertheless, it is thought that evidence that the dominant intention for making the preference was in furtherance of the controller's personal interest ought to be a particularly strong reason in finding that a transaction was a fraudulent preference.

[25.096] In *Corran Construction Company v Bank of Ireland Finance Ltd*[267], the plaintiff company deposited certain title deeds with the defendant bank by way of an equitable deposit as security for a loan. The mortgage was not registered under s 99(1) of the CA 1963[268]. Later, the bank became aware that the mortgage had not been registered and became concerned about the company's account. The bank persuaded the company to give a fresh equitable mortgage by deposit of title deeds which was then registered under s 99. Within six months of giving the fresh equitable mortgage the company was wound up. During the course of the winding up, the liquidator of the company sought to have the equitable mortgage set aside on the ground that it was a fraudulent preference. McWilliam J held that the liquidator had not established that there was an intention to make a fraudulent preference:

> 'I am satisfied that [the member director] was anxious to keep the company going notwithstanding the advice of the accountant and his knowledge of the unfortunate state of the company's affairs ... Although the defendant was not using pressure in the ordinary sense, I got the impression from the evidence that [the member director] was trying to avoid their representatives because they had been continually trying to get back the money due to the defendant and that, when they finally caught up with him when he was ill in bed, it was something of a relief to find they would be satisfied if he would remedy some defect in the mortgage. Although he undoubtedly appreciated that this would give the

---

265 *Parkes & Sons Ltd v Hong Kong and Shanghai Banking Corporation* [1990] ILRM 341.

266 *Parkes & Sons Ltd v Hong Kong and Shanghai Banking Corporation* [1990] ILRM 341 at 347–348.

267 *Corran Construction Company v Bank of Ireland Finance Ltd* [1976–7] ILRM 175.

268 See, generally, Ch 19, *Corporate Borrowing: Registration of Charges*.

> defendants security in case the company would not be able to pay the money back and should have appreciated that there was no real likelihood of the company being able to pay it back, this falls a long way short of making the deposit with the dominant intention of preferring the defendant over the other creditors.'

On this evidence it was held that there was not a fraudulent preference of the bank. The member director's will had been overborne by the pressure applied by the bank to give a fresh mortgage and keeping the company going was the dominant intention.

[25.097] A case said by Gilligan J to be similar to *Corran*, is *O'Connor's Nenagh Shopping Centre Ltd*[269]. In this case, a company created a mortgage in favour of Bank of Ireland at a time when the company, its directors and the bank all knew that it was insolvent. The company went into liquidation within six months of the mortgage being created and it was accepted by all parties that the *effect* of the mortgage was to prefer the bank over other creditors. Gilligan J approached the question as to whether the bank had been given a fraudulent preference by focusing upon the dominant intention of the company at the time of the mortgage, ie, was the dominant intention to prefer the bank over the other creditors? After quoting from the decision of Carroll J in *Station Motors Ltd v AIB Ltd*[270], Gilligan J said:

> '15. It is clear from the relevant legal authority that in order to prove that a transaction is a preference it is not sufficient to show that the effect of the transaction was to give a preference, as is the situation in this case. The transaction has to be entered into with the dominant intention to prefer, and that intention must have existed at the time of the transaction. Where there is no direct evidence of intention the court can draw an inference of an intention to prefer in a case where some other possible explanation is open. That is not the situation in this case because repeatedly the directors of the Company state that they were not under pressure from the bank and they believed that allowing the bank to register the charge was the only way to enable the Company to hold on and continue to trade, and it was much to their dismay that they did not succeed in achieving this objective ...
>
> 18. In my view there is direct evidence of intention which I accept that the charge, the subject matter of this application, was entered into by the directors of the Company in order to keep the business going and hopefully succeed with a restructuring plan.
>
> 19. I do not consider that there was any taint of dishonesty on the part of the directors and there is no evidence that their dominant intention in signing up to the charge which they had previously in any event agreed to do, was for the purpose of giving a preference to the Bank of Ireland.'

Establishing that the dominant intention was to prefer the creditor can be difficult, and in *Le Chatelaine Thudichum Ltd v Conway*[271] Murphy J refused to infer that the plaintiff-company's managing director's dominant intention was to prefer the respondent. In that case, the managing director had claimed that he had intended that the respondent would disperse certain sums paid to the respondent amongst other creditors.

---

269 *Re O'Connor's Nenagh Shopping Centre Ltd; Fitzpatrick v O'Connor and others* [2011] IEHC 508, Gilligan J.

270 *Station Motors Ltd v AIB Ltd* [1985] 756 at 760.

271 *Le Chatelaine Thudichum Ltd v Conway* [2008] IEHC 349. See para **[25.106]** *post*.

A parallel claim of fraudulent disposition under s 139 of the CA 1990 was, however, successful[272].

[25.098] In *Station Motors Ltd v Allied Irish Bank Ltd*[273], Carroll J followed the decision in *Re M Kushler Ltd*[274] and held that:

> '... where there is no direct evidence of intention [to prefer] there is no rule of law which precludes a court from drawing an inference of an intention to prefer, in a case where some other possible explanation is open.'

There, a husband and wife were the controllers of a company which had a large overdraft with the defendant bank. Furthermore, they had personally guaranteed the company's overdraft with the bank. When the company became insolvent, the husband and wife passed a resolution to put the company into creditors' voluntary liquidation. Before this happened they caused certain payments to be made into the company's overdrawn account so as to reduce the company's indebtedness to the bank, this having the indirect effect of reducing their personal exposure under the guarantees. Carroll J held that these payments were a fraudulent preference as they were made with the intention of preferring both the bank as a direct creditor and the directors themselves as guarantors of the company's overdraft. Among the facts which supported this conclusion were that:

- where the disposition has the effect of reducing personal exposure on guarantees, the court will find this to be a significant issue of fact in view of the strong element of private advantage;
- since the dispositions were made after they had resolved to call an EGM and creditors' meeting to put the company into creditors' voluntary winding up, they were aware that the company was insolvent; and
- of the cheques presented to the bank, only those which were to pay off the company's overdraft were honoured by the bank.

As a result, Carroll J held that the overwhelming evidence was that the lodgments were made to prefer the bank directly and the guarantors indirectly and this was the dominant purpose of the payments into the overdrawn account. In the course of her judgement, the learned judge said:

> 'Since this is a Company managed and run by Mr Murphy, it is Mr Murphy's intention which falls to be considered. There is no direct evidence here by Mr Murphy as to what his intention was. Nevertheless the court is not precluded from drawing an inference of an intent to prefer. *Re M Kushler Ltd* [1943] 2 All ER 22 deals with the following points:—
>
> 1. The phrase "with a view to giving such creditor a preference" means that the intention to prefer must be the dominant intention which actuates the payment (per Lord Greene MR at page 24).
> 2. It is not enough to prove that there was actual preferment from which an intention to prefer can, with hindsight, be inferred. The liquidator must prove an intention to prefer at the time the payment is made (per Goddard LJ at page 28).

---

272 See para **[25.103]** *post*.

273 *Station Motors Ltd v Allied Irish Bank Ltd* [1985] ILRM 756.

274 *Re M Kushler Ltd* [1943] 2 All ER 22, per Lord Greene MR.

3. Where there is no direct evidence of intention, there is no rule of law which precludes a court from drawing an inference of an intention to prefer, in a case where some other possible explanation is open (per Lord Greene MR at page 26).

   Also in relation to the absence of direct evidence as to intention, Lord Greene MR says at p 27:— "... it does not seem to me that he (ie Lord Tomlin in *Peat v Gresham Trust Ltd* [1934] AC 252) could have meant that in every case where there is no direct evidence you are bound to say the onus is not discharged on the grounds that there may have been another explanation. Of course, there may have been other explanations. One can scarcely imagine a case of circumstantial evidence where it would not be possible to say that there might be another explanation of the fact."

4. The method of ascertaining the state of mind of the payer is the ordinary method of evidence and inference, to be dealt with on the same principles which are commonly employed in drawing inferences of fact (per Lord Greene MR at page 26). He goes on to say that the inference to be drawn in a case of fraudulent preference is an inference of something which has about it, at the very least, the taint of dishonesty, and, in extreme cases, very much more than a mere taint of dishonesty, and that being so, the court, on ordinary principles, is not in the habit of drawing inferences which involve dishonesty or something approaching dishonesty, unless there are solid grounds for drawing them.'

[25.099] The *Station Motors* case is a paradigm for the so-called 'guarantee-cases', whereby the controllers of a company cause the company to pay from its few assets a liability to a bank where the controllers have given personal guarantees in respect of the company's indebtedness. Clearly, their act is self-serving, and will often be found to be a fraudulent preference. However, where the dominant intention is not to reduce one's personal liability, but is for another purpose, such as a fear that failure to make the disposition will result in another company having the financial rug pulled from under it, as in *Parkes & Sons Ltd v Hong Kong and Shanghai Banking Corp*[275], the preference will not necessarily be a fraudulent preference.

(f) The beneficiary of the disposition

[25.100] It is crucial to distinguish between a situation whereby a disposition is a *fraudulent preference* of one creditor over another, from where it is a *fraudulent disposition*[276]. Section 286 of the CA 1963 is only concerned with fraudulent preferences. Thus, s 286 is concerned with transactions which are:

> '... in favour of any creditor, or of any person on trust for any creditor, with a view of giving such creditor, or any surety or guarantor for the debt due to such creditor, a preference over the other creditors ...'

Thus, a disposition in favour of a person who is not a creditor (or a trustee of a creditor) of the company cannot be a fraudulent preference.

[25.101] This point is neatly illustrated by the decision of Blayney J in *Parkes & Sons Ltd v Hong Kong and Shanghai Banking Corporation*[277]. In that case, a company entered into a guarantee and provided a mortgage in favour of the defendant bank within six

275 *Parkes & Sons Ltd v Hong Kong and Shanghai Banking Corp* [1990] ILRM 341.

276 See para **[25.103]**.

277 *Parkes & Sons Ltd v Hong Kong and Shanghai Banking Corp* [1990] ILRM 341.

months of the commencement of its winding up. The facts were that a company (Walshe Kavanagh) was acquired by a Mr Collier who was the controller of the plaintiff company. After he acquired control, the plaintiff company's premises were destroyed by fire, and its business transferred to the premises of Walshe Kavanagh. Walshe Kavanagh was indebted in the amount of £200,000 to the defendant bank and its indebtedness was personally guaranteed by Collier. Subsequently, Walshe Kavanagh ceased trading and the plaintiff company purchased its entire stock. When the bank pressed for repayment, Collier agreed to cause Walshe Kavanagh to give an equitable mortgage by way of deposit of the title deeds to its premises. It was also agreed that the plaintiff company would guarantee the loan to Walshe Kavanagh. The proceeds of sale of the plaintiff company's former premises were to be used to discharge the indebtedness, and the companies' solicitors confirmed that following the release of the charge on the premises they would hold the monies on trust for the bank. Because of a problem with title, the defendant bank began to press the controller for repayment and said it would not continue its support unless the plaintiff company gave a mortgage of its property and its guarantee of the other company's indebtedness. This was eventually given at a time when both of the companies were insolvent. The bank agreed not to call in its security for a period of time. When both companies went into liquidation, it was argued, *inter alia*, that the guarantee and mortgage were fraudulent preferences.

It was held by Blayney J that these dispositions could not be fraudulent preferences because the bank was not a creditor of the plaintiff company: the plaintiff company did not in its own right owe the bank money. Construing the wording of s 286 of the CA 1963, Blayney J said:

> 'In my opinion the references in this section to a creditor or creditors in phrases "in favour of any creditor", and "with a view to giving such creditor ... a preference over the other creditors" must be construed as being references to a creditor or creditors of the person unable to pay his debts. What the section is concerned with is the bankrupt giving one of his creditors a preference over his other creditors. It is not concerned with someone other than the bankrupt paying off one of the bankrupt's creditors because such a person would have no obligation towards the other creditors, and so neither they nor the trustees in bankruptcy on their behalf, could have any ground for setting aside such a payment[278].'

The liquidator had attempted to split the giving of the guarantee and the giving of the mortgage into two separate transactions. By so arguing the liquidator had hoped that the court would find that the plaintiff company was a creditor on foot of its guarantee to the bank and that it had then made a fraudulent preference in the form of the mortgage. This argument was rejected by Blayney J who found that the guarantee and the mortgage constituted a single security, and that the plaintiff company was not a debtor of the plaintiff bank at the time the mortgage was created.

[25.102] In England, it has been held that it is immaterial that the disposition by way of fraudulent preference is far in excess of the amount owed, provided that it is in made in favour of a creditor. Accordingly, in *Re Clasper Group Services Ltd*[279], although the beneficiary of the disposition was owed approximately £60 in respect of damages for

[278] *Re M Kushler Ltd* [1990] ILRM 341 at 345.

[279] *Re Clasper Group Services Ltd* [1989] BCLC 143.

being dismissed from the company[280], he was paid £2,000. Warner J held this was a fraudulent preference in spite of the vastly different payment made, and refused to find that the disposition was a fraudulent disposition, as distinguished in *Expo International Proprietary Ltd v Torma*[281]. Helpful to Warner J was the argument of the liquidator that had a small creditor been given a motor car in satisfaction of his claim, the liquidator would be entitled to the return of the car, and would not be confined to recovering a sum equal to the amount of his claim. It is thought that the decision in *Clasper* is not persuasive, and that while the sum ought to be recoverable by the liquidator, fraudulent disposition, as opposed to fraudulent preference, would have been the appropriate remedy.

Fraudulent dispositions of property

[25.103] A fraudulent disposition of corporate property is liable to be subject to a court order that the property so disposed of be returned to the company. Section 139 of the CA 1990 provides that a liquidator (voluntary or official), creditor or contributory of a company being wound up[282] can in certain circumstances apply to court for the return of property. To be successful in applying for such an order, it must be shown to the satisfaction of the court that:

> '(a) any property of the company of any kind whatsoever was disposed of either by way of conveyance, transfer, mortgage, security, loan, or in any way whatsoever whether by act or omission, direct or indirect, and,
>
> (b) the effect of such disposal was to perpetrate a fraud on the company, its creditors or members …'

Where this is proved to the satisfaction of the court then the court may:

> '... if it deems it just and equitable to do so, order any person who appears to have the use, control or possession of such property or the proceeds of the sale or development thereof to deliver it or pay a sum in respect of it to the liquidator on such terms or conditions as the court sees fit.'

A 'return' of property, if ordered, is made to the liquidator making it clear that the purpose of this provision is to 'swell the assets of the insolvent company'.

[25.104] There is an important distinction between fraudulent preferences and fraudulent dispositions, as Warner J observed in *Clasper Group Services Ltd*[283] when he said:

> '... there is a distinction between a payment to a creditor as such and a payment which, albeit made to a person who is a creditor, is a sheer misapplication of the company's money.'

Section 139 of the CA 1990 does not apply to fraudulent preferences, which are addressed by s 286 of the CA 1963. Section 139 can be analysed by counter reference to the limits of s 286 of the 1963 Act. Accordingly, it is irrelevant for the purposes of s 139 that the company was insolvent at the time of the disposition or that it was made to a

---

280 The beneficiary was the 16-year-old son of the controller of the company when he was dismissed.

281 *Expo International Proprietary Ltd v Torma* [1985] 3 NSWLR 225.

282 Or, receivers, by s 178 of the CA 1990 and examiners, by s 180(2) of the CA 1990.

283 *Clasper Group Services Ltd* [1989] BCLC 143 at 148.

creditor, or that the disposition was made within a certain time frame. There needs only to be a disposal where the effect is to perpetrate a fraud on the company, its creditors or its members[284].

[25.105] In *Re Devey Enterprises Ltd*[285], the liquidator of a company sought declarations that certain payments identified by reference to a so-called 'directors' loan account' constituted a fraudulent preference and certain others constituted fraudulent dispositions. The company was in the business of plastering contractor until it ceased trading on account of being insolvent and placed into creditors' voluntary winding up. The liquidator's investigation revealed an apparent failure to maintain proper books and records and that certain personal expenditure of the directors had been recorded as business expenditure of the company. The total amount claimed by the liquidator was ultimately over €1.2m: over €686,000 due to fraudulent preferences and nearly €1.07m due to fraudulent dispositions. In relation to the fraudulent dispositions, Laffoy J noted that the liquidator's case was:

> '... that the company's money was misapplied in that it was gifted to or used to discharge the personal debts of the respondents, who were the directors of the company ... it is not that, in relation to the money in issue, the respondents, as creditors, had an entitlement to the money and they were preferred over other creditors of the company at a time when the company was insolvent. In other words, the liquidator's case is that the respondents had no entitlement whatsoever [to] the money in issue, being sums either paid to them or to third parties at their direction. In the circumstances, it seems to me that s 286 has no application.'

Turning to s 130 of the CA 1990, Laffoy J noted that despite having been enacted for over 20 years, it had received very little judicial consideration. The learned judge accepted that the respondents had procured a gratuitous disposition of the company's money in their own favour and held that she was satisfied that the effect was 'to perpetrate a fraud on the company and its creditors'. The respondents were ordered to pay the liquidator over €1.2m.

[25.106] It should be noted that an applicant under s 139 of the CA 1990 is not required to prove an intention to defraud, a difficult and problematic proof at the best of times. Rather, what is required to be shown is that the *effect* of the disposal *was to perpetrate a fraud* on the company, its creditors or members. It matters not what the *object* or *intention* was if the effect is to perpetrate a fraud: evidence of a subjective intent to defraud on the part of the company's controllers is *not* required. It must, however, be shown that the effect of the disposal was to perpetrate a fraud. In *Le Chatelaine Thudichum Ltd v Conway*[286], the proposition that by 'fraud' is meant the diversion of property from the entity or person who is lawfully entitled to it was accepted by Murphy J as a correct statement of the law. An example would be where a company was owed money for goods or services rendered by a third party and that third party's payment was diverted away from the rightful recipient, the company, to another person

---

284 See para **[25.106]** and *Le Chatelaine Thudichum Ltd v Conway* [2008] IEHC 349.

285 *Re Devey Enterprises Ltd; Stafford v Devey and Devey* [2011] IEHC 340.

286 In *Le Chatelaine Thudichum Ltd v Conway* [2008] IEHC 349, Murphy J adopted as a correct statement of the law this proposition as enunciated in the second edition of this work, *The Law of Private Companies*, at para [27.093].

or entity. Equally, a gratuitous disposition of company property in favour of, say, its controllers would have the effect of perpetrating a fraud on the company. Because company property is just that, 'company' property, the circumstances in which the effect of a disposal will be to perpetrate a fraud on members and creditors will be more rare than where the effect is to perpetrate a fraud on the company. In the case of members, the diversion of a dividend, properly declared before it was paid, would be to perpetrate a fraud on members. As to creditors, an example of what is envisaged under this section might be where a creditor has acquired an equitable or beneficial interest in property belonging to a company and that property is disposed of to another person.

[25.107] *Le Chatelaine Thudichum Ltd v Conway*[287] was one of the first decisions of the Irish High Court to consider the operation of s 139 of the CA 1990. In this case, the liquidator of the plaintiff company sought a declaration that a transfer of goods and cash to the respondent by the company constituted either a fraudulent preference or a fraudulent disposition. The facts of this case were that the respondent owned a Spar outlet in Ratoath Co Meath and arranged for Mr Thudichum to run it for him. Subsequently, an agreement was reached between the two that Mr Thudichum would form a company and take a lease of the shop and this was put into effect. Rent was payable by the plaintiff company to the respondent based on a percentage of certain turnover. Due to competition, the plaintiff company experienced trading losses and eventually control of the shop was returned to the respondent. At that point the plaintiff company was heavily indebted to the respondent and to other creditors and was unable to pay its debts. The indebtedness to the respondent was in respect of rent owing and four weeks unpaid invoices for goods ordered on behalf of the plaintiff company. On the date control was handed back, the respondent took possession of cash sums of €9,500 together with stock valued at €112,080. Thereafter, the plaintiff company was wound up and the liquidator appointed and it was the aforementioned transaction which was alleged to be a fraudulent preference or in the alternative a fraudulent disposition. As noted above, the fraudulent preference claim failed for want of establishing that Mr Thudichum's dominant intention was to prefer the respondent[288].

In his analysis of s 139 of the CA 1990, Murphy J observed that the term 'disposition' is apt to encompass almost any kind of transaction and that the giving possession of stock and cash appeared to be sufficient to come within the ambit of the section. The court went on to determine that the plaintiff company owned the stock which was claimed to have been the subject of a retention of title clause in favour of Spar and rejected that the respondent landlord only took what he was entitled to take by way of distress. Murphy J said:

> 'I am satisfied that the disposition in favour of the respondent had the effect of perpetrating a fraud on the applicant in depriving it of its assets, and on the creditors in diminishing the pool of assets available for distribution upon liquidation. The creditors were thus denied the possibility of having a portion of the debts owed to them repaid, and were accordingly deprived of a benefit to which they were lawfully entitled.'

Section 139(3) of the CA 1990 also provides that in exercising its just and equitable discretion, the court shall have regard to the rights of persons who have *bona fide* and

---

287 *Le Chatelaine Thudichum Ltd v Conway* [2008] IEHC 349.

288 See para **[25.097]** *ante*.

for value acquired an interest in the property that is the subject matter of the application. This is not limited to persons who take from creditors, and extends to those who are the direct recipients of the disposition. In the instant case, Murphy J held:

> 'Since the respondent acquired the cash and the proceeds of sale of stock he appears to have had the use, control or possession of such monies and is accordingly a person to whom the section applies. Since he acquired the stock and cash knowing that the company could not fully discharge its debts to its other creditors, he cannot be said to have acquired the property *bona fide*, and accordingly s 139(3) has no application to the present proceedings.'

Murphy J noted that s 139(1)(b) allows the court to order any person who appears to have the use, control or possession of such property or the proceeds of the sale or development thereof, to deliver it *or* to pay a sum in respect of it to the liquidator on such terms and conditions as the court sees fit. In this regard, the court allowed certain allowances in relation to mistaken payments to the plaintiff company by the respondent and exercised its discretion to order the respondent to pay the liquidator €121,580.

[25.108] Payments to secured or preferential creditors could never be considered to have the effect of perpetrating a fraud on unsecured creditors since on a liquidation they would not be lawfully entitled to participate in distributions ahead of the secured or preferential creditors. Every otherwise lawful payment made by an insolvent company to a legitimate unsecured creditor when it is insolvent should not fall automatically to be a fraudulent disposition on the grounds that it means there is less for distribution *pari passu* amongst the other unsecured creditors. Disposition of the entirety of an insolvent company's assets (as was the case in *Le Chatelaine Thudichum Ltd v Conway*[289]) or payments to shareholders or directors (as was the case in *Re Devey Enterprises Ltd*[290]) are perhaps more likely than other payments by an insolvent company to have the effect of perpetrating a fraud on the company or its creditors.

[25.109] It should also be remembered that a fraudulent conveyance or mortgage may be avoided under the Conveyances (Ireland) Act 1634[291]. That statute was successfully invoked by a liquidator in *Re Kill Inn Motel Ltd*[292] to set aside a mortgage in favour of a company's controller. Murphy J noted that it was the first time that that statute had been applied to a body corporate but said he saw no reason why it would not so apply.

Invalidating certain floating charges

[25.110] As seen in Chapter 18, *Corporate Borrowing: Debentures and Security*[293], the essential nature of a floating charge is that it allows a company to continue to deal with its assets notwithstanding that they have been charged. It has been recognised by the legislature that the granting of a floating charge over the assets of a company exposes other creditors to the risk of continuing to give credit to the company for goods supplied, notwithstanding that those goods become the subject of a floating charge held by

---

289 *Le Chatelaine Thudichum Ltd v Conway* [2008] IEHC 349.

290 *Re Devey Enterprises Ltd; Stafford v Devey and Devey* [2011] IEHC 340.

291 10 Charles 1. See generally Wylie, *Irish Conveyancing Statutes* (1994), pp 14–21.

292 *Re Kill Inn Motel Ltd* [1978–1987] Vol 3 ITR 706 (16 September 1987, unreported) HC, *per* Murphy J.

293 See Ch 18, *Corporate Borrowing: Debentures and Security*, para **[18.068]** *et seq.*

another creditor. For this reason the legislature has imposed certain statutory restrictions on the operation of floating charges. One such restriction[294] is that contained in s 288(1) of the CA 1963[295] which provides:

> 'Where a company is being wound up, a floating charge on the undertaking or property of the company created within 12 months before the commencement of the winding up shall, unless it is proved that the company immediately after the creation of the charge was solvent, be invalid, except as to money actually advanced or paid, or the actual price or value of goods or services sold or supplied, to the company at the time of or subsequently to the creation of, and in consideration for the charge, together with interest on that amount at a rate of 5 per cent per annum.'

The effect of this provision is that once the conditions contained in s 288 are satisfied, the security provided by the floating charge becomes invalid. However, it is vital to note that even though a floating charge may be found to be invalid, the validity of the debt that it secured is unaffected and continues to remain valid. Rather than be invalidated, the debt becomes unsecured and the holder of the charge is relegated to the ranks of the unsecured creditors. The law applicable to invalid floating charges is considered under the following headings:

(a) Proof of insolvency.
(b) The operative time limits.
(c) Invalid only where security unrealised on winding up.
(d) Valid to extent of money actually advanced or paid.
(e) Other circumstances in which a floating charge is invalid.

(a) Proof of solvency

[25.111] In respect of floating charges created within the operative time limits, the onus is on the holder of the floating charge to prove that the company was solvent at the time of its creation[296] or that money or goods or services were advanced contemporaneously with the creation of the floating charge[297]. The onus is on the holder of the floating charge to uphold its validity since s 288(1) of the CA 1963 creates a presumption of invalidity where a floating charge is created within the operative time limits. The concept of solvency has been considered by the Supreme Court in *Re Creation Printing Company Ltd*[298] where the proposition that 'solvency equals assets exceeding liabilities' was rejected. Holding that the rejection of that proposition was established by the decided cases[299], Kenny J said:

---

294 Another restriction is that contained in s 285(7)(b) of the CA 1963 which provides that the preferential debts of a company: 'so far as the assets of the company available for payment of general creditors are insufficient to meet them, have priority over the claims of holders of debentures under any floating charge created by the company, and be paid accordingly out of any property comprised in or subject to that charge.' See para **[25.185]**.

295 As amended by s 136 of the CA 1990.

296 See *Re Creation Printing Company Ltd; Crowley v Northern Bank Finance Co* [1981] IR 353 at 358, per Kenny J.

297 See para **[25.115]** *et seq.*

298 *Re Creation Printing Company Ltd* [1981] IR 353, [1978] ILRM 219.

299 See *Ex p Russell* [1882] 19 Ch D 588; *Re Patrick and Lyon Ltd* [1933] Ch 786 and *Re Panama, New Zealand, and Australian Royal Mail Co* [1870] 5 Ch App 318.

> '... the test to be applied in determining this question is whether immediately after the debenture was given, the company was able to pay its debts as they became due. The question is not whether its assets exceed the estimated value its liabilities, or whether a business man would have regarded it as solvent ... The question whether a company was solvent on a specified date is one of fact and it involves many difficult inferences. If there is, or is likely to be, a large deficiency of assets when the liquidation starts, the temptation to hold that the company was not solvent is strong. But the deficiency may have been caused by some change in economic or market conditions happening after the charge was given. So an examination of the financial history of the company, both before and after the charges were given, is necessary.'

This approach to determining solvency has been described as a 'cash flow test' rather than a 'balance sheet test'[300]. In *Re Creation Printing Company Ltd*, the company which went into liquidation had granted a floating charge on the undertaking of the company to secure money advanced by a bank to its parent company. The Supreme Court held that it was wrong to include the value of the company's fixed assets in considering the company's solvency because such were required for the purpose of generating income and would not, in the normal course of things, be sold by a company which intended to stay in business. Although the total assets of the company exceeded its liabilities, the company was held to be insolvent because its assets consisted mainly of fixed plant and machinery.

(b) The operative time limits

[25.112] In the case of a floating charge held by a person who is at arm's length to the company creating the floating charge, the operative time limit is 12 months from the date of the commencement of the winding up. Where however, the holder of the floating charge is a connected person, as defined above in relation to the law of fraudulent preference[301], the operative time limit is two years from the commencement of the winding up[302].

(c) Invalid only where security unrealised on winding up

[25.113] Section 288(1) of the CA 1963 is directed at a situation where the floating charge has not crystallised at the commencement of the winding up. Consequently, where a floating charge is created within 12 months of the commencement of the winding up, but crystallises three months from the commencement, then that floating charge is not liable to be deemed invalid under s 288(1) although in the appropriate circumstances, it could be a fraudulent preference[303]. The rationale behind this principle is that once the floating charge crystallises, previously inchoate rights become choate and the floating charge becomes a quasi-fixed charge. This principle is supported by the Court of Appeal case of *Mace Builders (Glasgow) Ltd v Lunn*[304] where the holder of a floating charge caused the charge to crystallise by appointing himself receiver under the

---

300 See *Melbase Corporation Pty Ltd v Segenhoe Ltd* (1995) 17 ACSR 187. See also *Cuthbertson & Richards Pty Ltd v Thomas* [1999] Federal Court of Australia of 30 March 1999.

301 See para **[25.086]** *ante*.

302 By s 288(3) of the CA 1963.

303 See para **[25.081]** *et seq, ante*.

304 *Mace Builders (Glasgow) Ltd v Lunn* [1987] Ch 191, [1987] BCLC 55. The trial judgment of Scott J is reported at [1985] BCLC 154.

debenture. He then sold the charged assets and repaid himself. It was accepted that the company was insolvent at the date of the creation of the floating charge. The Court of Appeal, *per* Glidewell LJ, concluded that the holder of the charge was not obliged to repay the money to the company although it was created within 12 months from the commencement of the winding up. The reasoning was based on a literal interpretation of the wording of the then corresponding English section:

> 'The opening words are "Where a company is being wound up..." The section thus has no application unless and until the company is being wound up. It would follow that if, for example, the company had mortgaged any part of its assets, otherwise than by a floating charge ... after the creation of the floating charge and before the winding up, the defendant could have claimed, and would have been granted, a declaration that his rights had priority over those of a subsequent mortgagee ... The application of [the section] at that time would have been entirely speculative. Yet if counsel's argument for the plaintiff is accepted, the result would be that ... immediately following the commencement of the winding up, the same court would have to declare that, contrary to what it had previously declared, the defendant had no such priority and, retrospectively, had never had any such priority. I am loath to accept, in the absence of much clearer words, that Parliament intended so Gilbertian a situation, ie order, counter-order, disorder[305].'

The court was further supported in its view by considering that no protection was given to a *bona fide* purchaser for value of the company's assets.

[25.114] Although uncertain, a distinction has been drawn between a situation where assets subject to a floating charge have been realised and paid over to the charge holder by the receiver and where the receiver still has possession of the realised proceeds of sale. In the New Zealand case of *Re Port Supermarket Ltd*[306], it was held that where a receiver had not completed the realisation of assets subject to a floating charge when a liquidator was appointed, the receiver was obliged to pay what he had over to the liquidator, and that the liquidator could set the floating charge aside. Perhaps the distinction lies in the fact that while the courts are disinclined to upset a charge holder's rights where he is in possession of realised proceeds, where a receiver has not paid the proceeds over, his status as agent for the company has significance. Such a distinction is hard to justify, and is motivated by a judicial attitude, set against floating charges. It is arguable that courts are obliged to accept the priority of the charge holder for as long as the Irish legislature has not taken the step taken in England[307], of defining 'floating charge' as including all charges which were '*originally created*' as floating charges.[308]

(d) Valid to extent of money actually advanced or paid

[25.115] Section 288(1) of the CA 1963 provides that a floating charge shall not be invalid as to money actually advanced or paid, or to the actual price or value of goods or services sold or supplied to the company at the time of or subsequent to the creation of and in consideration for the charge. However, the interest rate permitted in such

305 *Mace Builders (Glasgow) Ltd v Lunn* [1987] BCLC 55 at 58–59.

306 *Re Port Supermarket Ltd* [1978] NZLR 330, noted by *Milman* [1980] NILQ 255.

307 See s 251 of the Insolvency Act 1986 (UK).

308 Cf *Re JD Brian Ltd* [2011] IEHC 113, Finlay Geoghegan, at para 22. See also Ch 18, *Corporate Borrowing: Debentures and Security* at para **[18.094]** *et seq*.

circumstances is not that provided for in the debenture, but rather, is determined by s 288(1) as 5% per annum.

[25.116] This important saver for a floating charge operates on the rationale that there is a distinction between a situation where a previously unsecured creditor takes a floating charge to secure advances made in the past, and a situation where the floating charge holder advances *fresh* money to the company at the time of the creation of the charge. Although the company creates a floating charge over its assets, it also receives consideration. An example of the operation of this saver is provided by *Re Lakeglen Construction Ltd*[309] where a floating charge, created in favour of theretofore unsecured creditors in consideration for their *past advances* of money to the company, was held to be invalid.

[25.117] Money advanced between the time it was agreed to create the floating charge and its actual creation has been held to be a fresh advance. In the Irish case of *Re Daniel Murphy Ltd*[310], it was said that the delay between the agreement to give the floating charge and the creation of the floating charge must not have been with a view to deceive creditors. The delay there of 55 days was held not to have been unreasonable because the solicitors acting for both parties acted as fast as they would have done in any other transaction. The court also held that the requirement that the fresh advance be made, in consideration for the charge, does not mean that the advance must be given simultaneously with the charge. It has been accepted by the High Court in *Smurfit Paribas Bank Ltd v AAB Export Finance Ltd (No 2)*[311] that there is no one firm test to be applied in determining how long a time may elapse between the first payment and the execution of the charge for the proviso in s 288(1) of the CA 1963 to be excluded[312]. However, Barron J did give guidance as to what might validate a floating charge which was created within the operative time limit:

> 'In order to treat payments made to the company before the execution of the charge as payments made at the time of the charge, the necessary elements to be established are:- an honest transaction; advances made before the execution of the charge and reasonable expedition in and about the preparation and execution of the charge. Whether or not these particular elements have been established will depend upon the circumstances of each case[313].'

Barron J held that the security could not be validated in that case because, *inter alia*, of the unreasonable delay in putting the floating charge in place: two years and three months. There, two lenders had proposed entering into a deed of postponement whereby the second lender's debt would be postponed to the first lender's debt. However, this was never actually executed due to delay on the part of the first lender. In the circumstances, Barron J held that it would not be unconscionable for the second lender to insist on a

309 *Re Lakeglen Construction Ltd* [1980] IR 347.

310 *Re Daniel Murphy Ltd* [1964] IR 1.

311 *Smurfit Paribas Bank Ltd v AAB Export Finance Ltd (No 2)* [1991] 2 IR 19.

312 *Smurfit Paribas Bank Ltd v AAB Export Finance Ltd (No 2)* [1991] 2 IR 19 at 29, where Barron J cited Farwell LJ in *Re Columbian Fireproofing Co Ltd* [1910] 2 Ch 120 at 123; Powell J in *Re Olderfleet Shipbuilding & Engineering Co* [1922] 1 IR 26 at 41 and Maugham J in *Re F and E Stanton Ltd* [1929] 1 Ch 180 at 193–194.

313 *Smurfit Paribas Bank Ltd v AAB Export Finance Ltd (No 2)* [1991] 2 IR 19 at 30.

strict construction of the contract, and so was entitled to priority in the company's subsequent liquidation. Forbearance to sue has been held not to constitute 'cash paid': *Re Lakeglen Construction Ltd*[314].

(e) Other circumstances in which a floating charge is invalid

[25.118] Section 289(1) of the CA 1963 provides that where:

- a company is being wound up, and
- within 12 months of the commencement, the company was indebted to an officer of the company[315], and
- the indebtedness was discharged wholly or partly by the company or any other person, and
- the company created a floating charge on any of its assets or property within 12 months before the commencement of the winding up, in favour of the officer to whom the company was indebted,

then without prejudice to rights or liabilities arising apart from this section:

> '... such charge shall be invalid to the extent of the repayment referred to ... unless it is proved that the company immediately after the creation of the charge was solvent.'

Subsection (3) provides that in this section 'officer' includes the spouse, child or nominee of an officer.

Contribution by related companies to the assets

[25.119] Section 140 of the CA 1990 introduced a new means by which a liquidator can bolster or swell the assets of the company being wound up: by applying to court for an order directing that a related company contribute to its assets. Section 140(1) provides:

> 'On the application of the liquidator or any creditor or contributory of any company that is being wound up, the court, if it is satisfied that it is *just and equitable* to do so, may order that any company that is or has been related to the company being wound up shall pay to the liquidator of that company an amount equivalent to the whole or part of all or any of the debts provable in the winding up. Any order under this section may be made on such terms and conditions as the court thinks fit.'

This far reaching provision, which strikes at the root of group trading and the principle in *Salomon v Salomon & Co*[316], is designed to prevent companies creating a number of subsidiaries, using them to make profit, and then casting them (and their creditors) aside when they become insolvent[317]. Now, the court is empowered to order companies which are, or were, related, to contribute to the assets of the subsidiary which is being wound up[318]. The following issues raised by contribution orders are next considered:

---

314 *Re Lakeglen Construction Ltd* [1980] IR 347.

315 Defined by sub-s (3) as including 'the spouse, child or nominee of an officer'.

316 *Salomon v Salomon & Co* [1897] AC 22. See Ch 4, *Incorporation and its Consequences*, para **[4.026]** *et seq.*

317 A practice noted in *Re Southard & Co Ltd* [1979] 1 WLR 1198, *per* Templeman LJ.

318 See Templeman LJ's analogy and acknowledged mixed metaphor, *Re Southard & Co Ltd* [1979] 1 WLR 1198.

(a) The concept of related company.
(b) Retrospectivity of application.
(c) Jurisdiction to grant a contribution order.

(a) The concept of related company

[25.120] A company is *related* to another company under s 140(5) of the CA 1990 if:

- the other is its holding or subsidiary company; or
- more than half in nominal value of the equity share capital[319] is held of the other company, and companies related to that company, directly or indirectly, but not in a fiduciary capacity; or
- more than half in nominal value of the equity share capital[320] of each of them is held by members of the other company, directly or indirectly, but not in a fiduciary capacity; or
- that other company or a company or companies related to that company or that other company together with a company or companies related to it are entitled to exercise or control the exercise of more than one half of the voting power at any general meeting of the company; or
- the businesses of the companies have been so carried on that the separate business of each company, or a substantial part thereof, is not readily identifiable; or
- there is another company to which both companies are related.

'Related company' is deemed to have a corresponding meaning. Subsection (7) defines 'company' as a company which is liable to be wound up under the Companies Acts[321], and defines 'creditor' as one or more creditors to whom the company being wound up is indebted by more, in aggregate, than €12,697.38.

[25.121] By any standards, the scope of s 140 of the CA 1990 is very wide. Not only will a company be deemed to be related where (within the meaning of s 155 of the CA 1963) the company is part of a group of companies, but the reference in (e) means that companies which are members of a *de facto* group of companies may also be related companies. This could, for example, arise where two or more companies are owned and controlled by the same person or persons[322].

(b) Retrospectivity of application

[25.122] Although s 140 of the CA 1990 provides that an order to contribute can be made where a company is or was related, where the company was related *before* the coming into force of s 140, an order should not be made where the companies have not been related after the coming into operation of the Act. Such a view may be supported by the decisions in *Re Hefferon Kearns Ltd*[323] and *Re Chestvale Properties Ltd*[324] and the extreme implications for property rights resulting from a contribution order being made.

---

[319] As defined by s 155 of the CA 1963.

[320] Section 155 of the CA 1963.

[321] See Ch 23, *Winding Up Companies*, para **[23.035]**.

[322] On groups of companies see Ch 12, *Groups of Companies*, at para **[12.008]**.

[323] *Re Hefferon Kearns Ltd* [1992] ILRM 51.

[324] *Re Chestvale Properties Ltd* [1992] ILRM 221.

(c) Jurisdiction to grant a contribution order

[25.123] Section 140(2) of the CA 1990 provides that in deciding whether or not it is just and equitable to make a contribution order against a related company, the court shall have regard to the following matters:

- the extent to which the related company took part in the management of the company being wound up;
- the conduct of the related company towards the creditors of the company being wound up;
- the effect which such order would be likely to have on the creditors of the related company concerned.

The first two guidelines for judicial discretion aim at establishing a causal link between the conduct of the related company and the misfortune of the company being wound up. The third guideline recognises that the creditors of the company which the order is made against stand to be prejudiced by the contribution order. In this regard, a court must surely be loath to make an order where innocent creditors will be prejudiced. To deem creditors to have constructive notice[325] of charges created by a company may be harsh; to have the debts of another company paid by the company with which they traded is draconian. Subsection (4) provides that it shall *not* be just and equitable if the *only* ground which would justify the order is either:

(a) the fact that a company is related to another company, or,

(b) that the creditors of the company being wound up have relied on the fact that another company is or has been related to the first mentioned company.

Notably, a court cannot make an order based on the mere fact that the company being wound up is related to another company. Being a related company grounds the jurisdiction to hear an application, but unless there is more, a court cannot exercise its discretion to make a contribution order.

[25.124] Although the court's jurisdiction to make a contribution order is broad, it is vital to recognise that some culpability on the part of the company which is sought to be made the subject of a contribution order is required. By s 140(3) of the CA 1990, the court is expressly prohibited from making a contribution order, *unless*:

> '... the court is satisfied that the circumstances that gave rise to the winding up of the company are attributable to the actions or omissions of the related company.'

From this it is clear that an applicant must prove that the related company was the cause of the other being wound up. Surprisingly, there have been no reported instances of this section being successfully invoked by a liquidator.

Pooling the assets of related companies

[25.125] Another weapon in a liquidator's armoury is s 141 of the CA 1990 which goes further than merely ordering another company to contribute to the assets of a company being wound up. Section 141 allows a court to order that the assets of a related company

[325] See Ch 18, *Corporate Borrowing: Debentures and Security*, para **[18.081]**.

which is also being wound up should be pooled between the creditors of both companies. The empowering provision is s 141(1), which provides that:

> Where two or more related companies are being wound up and the court, on the application of the liquidator of any of the companies, is satisfied that it is *just and equitable* to make an order under this section, the court may order that, subject to such *terms and conditions* as the court may impose and to the extent that the court orders, the companies shall be wound up together as if they were one company, and, subject to the provisions of this section, the order shall have effect and all the provisions of this Part and Part VI of the Principal Act shall apply accordingly. (Emphasis added.)

The net effect of this provision is that upon application to have a related company wound up, the assets of two or more companies can be realised together, and then distributed amongst the creditors of all the companies. Clearly, this will be of benefit to the creditors of the insolvent company, only where the related company is sufficiently solvent to pay the creditors of both companies. Because the rights and interests of related companies will be affected by the making of such an order, s 141(6) provides that notice of an application for such an order must be served on every company specified in the application and on such other persons as the court may direct not later than the eighth day before the day on which the application is heard. Here the following issues which arise in the context of pooling orders are considered:

(a) The court's terms and conditions.
(b) The jurisdiction to make a pooling order.
(c) The consequences of a pooling order.

(a) The court's terms and conditions

[25.126] Section 141(2) of the CA 1990 provides that the court, in deciding upon what terms and conditions it should make a pooling order, should have particular regard to the interests of those persons who are members of some, but not all, of the companies which are the subject matter of the order. In this we see the recognition that in exercising its just and equitable discretion, the court may have regard to a wide number of factors.

(b) The jurisdiction to make a pooling order

[25.127] The jurisdiction to make a pooling order only applies to companies which are related within the meaning of s 140(5) of the CA 1990, considered above[326]. The discretion of the court is again based on a determination of what is just and equitable in the circumstances. Here, the factors which a court must consider in exercising its equitable discretion are:

- the extent to which any of the companies took part in the management of any of the other companies;
- the conduct of any of the companies towards the creditors of any of the other companies;
- the extent to which the circumstances that gave rise to the winding up of any of the companies are attributable to the actions or omissions of any of the other companies;
- the extent to which the businesses of the companies have been intermingled.

[326] See para **[25.120]**.

The first three factors are also relevant where the court is asked to make a contribution order, although the third is a basic prerequisite to the court making a contribution order whereas in the context of a pooling order it is but a factor in deciding what is just and equitable. The fourth factor, the concept of intermingling, is, even 22 years after the enactment of the CA 1990, a new and strange concept to practitioners and academics alike. Just how broad or narrow this will prove to be remains in the realm of speculation pending judicial analysis. Again, s 141(5) provides that certain factors shall not alone warrant the remedy, namely that a company is, without more, related to another company, or that the creditors of a company being wound up have relied on the fact that another company is or has been related to the first mentioned company.

(c) The consequences of a pooling order

[25.128] Where the court makes a pooling order, s 141(3) of the CA 1990 provides that the court is empowered to remove any liquidator of any of the companies and appoint any person to act as liquidator of any one or more of the companies. The wide control and supervision which the court has after an order is made is seen in the fact that it may give such directions as it thinks fit for the purpose of giving effect to the order[327].

[25.129] Section 141(3)(c) of the CA 1990 provides that nothing in the section or any court order shall affect the rights of any secured creditor of any of the companies. This implies that the security of both fixed and floating charge holders will remain unaffected. In particular, holders of floating charges will not have their charges placed after the claims of preferential creditors in companies other than their own debtor company: s 141(3)(d). As to the claims of unsecured creditors of the companies whose assets are pooled, unless the court orders otherwise their claims shall rank equally among themselves.

Claims against contributories

[25.130] One of the first duties of a liquidator is to settle a list of contributories of the company being wound up[328]. A contributory is a person who is liable under s 207 of the CA 1963 to contribute to the assets of a company that is being wound up[329]. Moreover, for the purposes of all proceedings for determining, and all proceedings prior to final determination of, the persons who are to be deemed contributories include any person alleged to be a contributory[330]. Section 207(1) of the CA 1963 provides:

> 'In the event of a company being wound up, every present and past member shall be liable to contribute to the assets of the company to an amount sufficient for payment of its debts and liabilities, and the costs, charges and expenses of the winding up, and for the adjustment of the rights of the contributories among themselves, subject to subsection (2) and the following qualifications:
>
> (a) a part member shall not be liable to contribute if he has ceased to be a member for one year or more before the commencement of the winding up;

327 On the question of liquidator's conflict of interest where appointed to two companies, see: *Re P Turner (Wilsden) Ltd* [1987] BCLC 149.

328 RSC, Ord 74, rr 86–89.

329 Section 208 of the CA 1963. See Ch 23, *Winding Up Companies*, para **[23.045]**.

330 Section 208 of the CA 1963.

(b) a past member shall not be liable to contribute in respect of any debt or liability of the company contracted after he ceased to be a member;

(c) a past member shall not be liable to contribute unless it appears to the court that the existing members are unable to satisfy the contributions required to be made by them in pursuance of this Act;

(d) in the case of a company limited by shares, no contribution shall be required from any member exceeding the amount, if any, unpaid on the shares in respect of which he is liable as a present or past member;

(e) in the case of a company limited by guarantee, no contribution shall, subject to subsection (3), be required from any member exceeding the amount undertaken to be contributed by him to the assets of the company in the event of its being wound up;

(f) nothing in this Act shall invalidate any provision contained in any policy of insurance or other contract whereby the liability of individual members on the policy or contract is restricted, or whereby the funds of the company are alone made liable in respect of the policy or contract;

(g) a sum due to any member of the company, in his character of a member, by way of dividends, profits or otherwise, shall not be deemed to be a debt of the company, payable to that member in a case of competition between himself and any other creditor not a member of the company, but any such sum may be taken into account for the purpose of the final adjustment of the rights of the contributories among themselves.'

The liability of a contributory creates a debt accruing due from him at the time when his liability commenced, but payable at the times when calls are made for enforcing the liability[331]. An action to recover a debt from a contributory must be brought within 12 years from the date on which the cause of action accrued[332]. The personal representatives of a deceased contributory are liable to contribute to the assets of the company and are themselves deemed to be contributories[333]. Bankrupt contributories are represented by the official assignee in bankruptcy who is also deemed to be a contributory[334].

[25.131] It is s 207(1)(d) of the CA 1963 which means that the liability of members of private companies limited by shares is limited to the amount, if any, 'unpaid on the shares'; and s 207(1)(e) which limits the liability of members of private companies limited by guarantee to the amount undertaken to be contributed by them. Therefore, in the vast majority of private companies, liquidators will not realise much, if any, money from the contributories of insolvent companies. This is because: first, the vast majority of companies are limited companies which have a nominal paid up share capital; and second, very few trading companies are unlimited companies. For many Irish private companies, this means that where a company has two €1 shares, the holders' liability is limited to €1 each, unless they have already paid this. Other persons liable to contribute are those rarest of creatures, directors with unlimited liability[335].

331 Section 209(1) of the CA 1963.

332 Section 209(2) of the CA 1963.

333 Section 210(1) of the CA 1963.

334 Section 211(a) of the CA 1963.

335 By s 197 of the CA 1963 the directors of a limited liability company may themselves have unlimited liability where this is provided for in the company's memorandum of association. See also s 207(2) of the CA 1963.

[25.132] Where contributories do, however, have a liability to contribute towards a company's debts, there may be a temptation to evade their liabilities. One means of preventing contributories from attempting to evade their liabilities is s 218 of the CA 1963, considered already in the context of post-commencement dispositions of property[336], which provides also that:

> 'In a winding up by the court ... any transfer of shares or alteration in the status of the members of the company, made after the commencement of the winding up, shall, unless the court otherwise orders, be void.'

Section 255 of the CA 1963 provides that any transfer of shares, *other than with the liquidator's sanction*, or any alteration in the status of members after the commencement of a voluntary winding up is also void. As in the case of any dispositions of property by a company, this aspect to s 218 does not become operational until the company is being wound up, *ie,* in an official liquidation, from the date of the presentation of the petition to have the company wound up[337]. In a voluntary winding up, the operative time for s 255 is the time of the passing of the resolution to wind up the company.

[25.133] By s 238 of the CA 1963, the court is only empowered to make calls on any of the contributories to the extent of their liability:

> '... for payment of any money which the court considers necessary to satisfy the debts and liabilities of the company, and the costs, charges and expenses of winding up, and for the adjustment of the rights of the contributories amongst themselves, and make an order for payment of any calls so made.'

The court may make such calls even though it has not ascertained the sufficiency of the assets of the company. 'Calls' on contributories are governed by the RSC 1986[338]. This is, however, subject to a number of major qualifications contained in s 207 of the CA 1963.

[25.134] Section 209 of the CA 1963 provides that the liability of a contributory creates a debt due from him at the time when his liability commenced, but payable at the times when calls are made by a liquidator for enforcing his liability. Calls against contributories survive their demise, and are payable out of their estate: s 210 of the CA 1963. Where a contributory becomes bankrupt, the Official Assignee shall represent him: s 211 of the CA 1963. Section 236 of the CA 1963 empowers the court to require a contributory on the list of contributories to pay, deliver, convey, surrender or transfer forthwith, or within such time as the court directs, any money, property or books and papers in his hands to which the company is *prima facie* entitled. Section 237 of the CA 1963 empowers the court to order a contributory to pay any money due by him to the company.

Voidable transactions

[25.135] Most transactions entered into by companies in contravention of the provisions of the Companies Acts are avoided when the company is in liquidation. Frequently, the

336 See para **[25.065]**.

337 See *Re Tumacacori Mining Co* (1874) LR 17 Eq 534; *Caratti Holding Co Party Ltd v Zampatti* [1975] WAR 183.

338 RSC, Ord 74, rr 92–94.

instigator of such avoidance will be the liquidator. His motivation for seeking to invalidate transactions will be his desire to swell the assets of the company which is in liquidation to facilitate the distribution of those assets in accordance with law.

[25.136] In examining the affairs of a company which is being wound up, liquidators will often scrutinise transactions for evidence that they are *ultra vires* the company[339]; an abuse of the directors' powers or outside of the directors' authority[340]; or, in contravention of provisions such as s 60 of the CA 1963[341] or s 29 or 31 of the CA 1990[342]. Where evidence of such abuses is found, the liquidator may succeed in avoiding guarantees entered into by the company, mortgages or charges of the company's property or other dispositions of the company's property.

Litigating to swell corporate assets

[25.137] Closely related to where a liquidator will seek to invalidate transactions is where he institutes proceedings against individuals or companies who appear to have *wronged* the company that is in liquidation. A liquidator may continue or initiate such proceedings with the leave of the court[343]. In such proceedings, he will have no greater rights than those enjoyed by the company.

[25.138] Often the liquidator may have reason to believe that those behind the company, whether directors, shadow directors or others, are responsible for causing the company loss. In such circumstances, he may issue proceedings against those persons under specific statutory provisions such as those on reckless trading or fraudulent trading and for other breaches of duty or trust in misfeasance proceedings under s 298 of the CA 1963[344]. In an appropriate case, a liquidator may seek an order for interrogatories under Ord 31, r 2 of the RSC 1986[345]. Where a liquidator is successful in such proceedings, any claims that a director might have against the company cannot be set-off against what he is ordered to pay the company[346].

[25.139] Certain causes of action open to liquidators may not, however, fall properly to be classified as 'property' of the company. So in *Re Floor Fourteen Ltd; Lewis v Inland Revenue Commissioners*[347] Peter Gibson LJ accepted the following statement of law:

> '*In Re Oasis Merchandising Services Ltd* [1997] 1 BCLC 689 this court drew a distinction between the property of the company existing at the commencement of the liquidation and assets which arise only after the liquidation of the company and are recoverable only by the liquidator pursuant to the statutory powers conferred on him. The right of action of a liquidator for preferences or wrongful trading and the fruits of such an action were said by this court not to be the property of the company but to be held on the statutory trust for

---

339 See Ch 7, *Corporate Contracts, Capacity and Authority*, para **[7.045]** *et seq.*

340 See Ch 7, *Corporate Contracts, Capacity and Authority*, para **[7.099]** *et seq.*

341 See Ch 10, *The Maintenance of Capital*, para **[10.046]** *et seq.*

342 See Ch 16, *Statutory Regulation of Directors' Transactions*, para **[16.022]** *et seq.*

343 Section 231(1)(a) of the CA 1963. See, generally, Ch 24, *Liquidators*, para **[24.029]** *et seq.*

344 See generally Ch 15, *Duties of Directors and Other Officers*.

345 See *Money Markets International Stock Brokers Ltd v Fanning* [2000] 3 IR 437. See, generally, Courtney, *Mareva Injunctions and Related Interlocutory Orders* (1998), para [10.36].

346 *Re Greendale Developments Ltd* [1998] 1 IR 8.

347 *Re Floor Fourteen Ltd; Lewis v Inland Revenue Commissioners* [2001] 2 BCLC 392.

distribution by the liquidator, and that distinction was said to be supported by a number of authorities including *Re MC Bacon Ltd (No 2)* [1990] BCLC 607[348].'

The distinction between property of the company and property held on a statutory trust by a liquidator for distribution holds good here in the context of, say, fraudulent trading, reckless trading, failure to keep proper books of account or indeed any statutory provision which allows application be made to impose personal liability 'for all, or such part as may be specified by the court, of the debts and other liabilities of the company'. In the case of other claims – claims that properly belong to the company – such as claims for breach of directors' duties, trust, negligence or other actionable wrong, including misfeasance under s 298 of the CA 1963, it is thought that such actions are properly classified as 'company property'. This is because at the commencement of the winding up the company had a right to sue the defendants. That right to sue is a chose in action that was the company's property and all that happens to it is that it is 'realised' by the liquidator.

[B] THE DISTRIBUTION OF CORPORATE ASSETS

Distribution of assets: basic principles

[25.140] Having realised all corporate assets, the task which next falls to the liquidator is the distribution of those assets amongst the creditors of the company in accordance with the Companies Acts. In *Re Lines Bros Ltd*[349], Brightman LJ said:

> '... the making of a winding-up order brings into operation a statutory scheme for dealing with the assets of a company which is being wound up. It matters not whether the winding up is by order or pursuant to a resolution. The assets of the company when realised provide a fund which the liquidator administers in many respects, but not in all, as if he were managing a trust fund. Creditors' contractual rights to be paid by the company become under the statutory scheme a statutory right to a share in the trust fund.'

The previous section having considered the realisation of assets, this section now considers the following issues in the distribution of assets:

1. The statutory basis for distribution.
2. Assets not available for distribution by liquidators.
3. The costs and expenses of winding up.
4. Proof of debts by the company's creditors.
5. Priorities in distribution.
6. Distributions *in specie*.

The statutory basis for distribution

[25.141] The process of distribution and the task of the liquidator is somewhat similar to that of the administrator of the estate of a deceased person, in that the latter must distribute the estate of the deceased in accordance with the Succession Act 1965. A more analogous situation is where the Official Assignee, after realising the assets of the

[348] *Re Floor Fourteen Ltd; Lewis v Inland Revenue Commissioners* [2001] 2 BCLC 392 at 404.

[349] *Re Lines Bros Ltd* [1983] Ch 1 at 14.

bankrupt, must distribute them amongst the bankrupt's creditors[350]. Indeed, it is this process of the distribution of a bankrupt's estate[351] upon which the laws of corporate insolvent distribution are based. This is because s 284(1) of the CA 1963 provides:

> 'In the winding up of an insolvent company the same rules shall prevail and be observed relating to the prospective rights of the secured and unsecured creditors and to debts provable and to the valuation of annuities and future and contingent liabilities as are in force for the time being under the law of bankruptcy relating to the estates of persons adjudged bankrupt, and all persons who in any such case would be entitled to prove for and receive dividends out of the assets of the company may come in under the winding up and make such claims against the company as they respectively are entitled to by virtue of this section.'

The effect of this provision is that the laws of distribution of a bankrupt's estate embodied in the Bankruptcy Act 1988 (which replaced the ancient Irish Bankrupt and Insolvent Act 1857) apply in a corporate insolvency[352]. However, before considering distribution amongst the creditors of the insolvent company, it is necessary to consider those assets that are in the ostensible ownership of a company but which are beneficially owned by someone else.

Assets not available for distribution by liquidators

[25.142] Not all assets that a liquidator realises or which appear to be in the apparent ownership of a company in liquidation may be available, in fact, for distribution to its creditors and contributories. Certain assets are *not available* for distribution. Five classes of assets that are unavailable for distribution can be identified:

- (a) Assets subject to a fixed mortgage or charge.
- (b) Assets that are held in trust.
- (c) Monies that must be set-off.
- (d) Super-preferential debts that are trust monies.
- (e) Stamp duty on monies received in realisation of company assets.

(a) Assets subject to a fixed mortgage or charge

[25.143] By reason of s 284(1) of the CA 1963 'the same rules shall prevail and be observed relating to the respective rights of secured and unsecured creditors' in an insolvent winding up as are in force under the law of bankruptcy[353]. In the law of bankruptcy, the general rule of creditors' rights is set out in s 136(1) of the Bankruptcy Act 1988. This provides:

---

[350] In *Oakes v Turquand* (1867) LR 2 HL 325, Lord Cranworth said (at 363): 'The winding up is but a mode of enforcing payment. It closely resembles a bankruptcy, and a bankruptcy has been called, not improperly, a statutable execution for the benefit of all creditors. The same description may be given to a winding up.'

[351] See, generally, Sanfey & Holohan, *Bankruptcy Law and Practice* (2nd edn, 2012).

[352] Many cases have applied the laws of bankruptcy to corporate insolvent distribution, for example, *Re McCairns (PMPA) Plc* [1990] ILRM 501, noted by Woulfe, (1989) DULJ 113; and *Re Hibernian Transport Company Ltd* [1990] ILRM 42 where different interpretations were given to the applicable laws of bankruptcy, discussed below. *Cf* the judgment of Nourse J in *Barclays Bank Ltd et al v TOSG Trust Fund Ltd et al* [1984] BCLC 1 at 25g–h.

[353] For the full text of s 284(1) of the CA 1963, see para **[25.141]**.

'On the making of an order of adjudication, a creditor to whom the bankrupt is indebted for any debt provable in bankruptcy shall not have any remedy against the property or person of the bankrupt in respect of the debt apart from his rights under this Act, and he shall not commence any proceedings in respect of such debts unless with the leave of the court and on such terms as the court may impose.'

However, there is an exception to this general rule in favour of secured creditors. Section 136(2) of the Bankruptcy Act 1988 provides:

'This section shall not affect the power of a secured creditor to realise or otherwise deal with his security in the same manner as he would have been entitled to realise or deal with it if this section had not been enacted.'

Accordingly, the power of a secured creditor[354] to realise or otherwise deal with his security is unaffected by the general rule. Secured creditors can proceed against their security and can remain outside the winding-up process.

[25.144] It may be noted that not all secured creditors are entitled to realise their securities in priority to all other creditors or to stand outside the winding up. Holders of floating charges are subordinated to the claims of preferential creditors[355]; holders of fixed charges over book debts may also be postponed and rank after the Revenue Commissioners[356]. Notwithstanding these legislative claw-backs, the holder of a fixed charge or fixed mortgage is entitled to remain outside a winding up and to rely on his own security to discharge the debt owed to him[357].

[25.145] Although a secured creditor can remain outside of a winding up, he is not obliged to do so[358]. Where a company is wound up insolvent, a secured creditor is afforded a number of options by virtue of the operation of para 24 of Schedule 1 to the Bankruptcy Act 1988. These options are:

- Realise the security and prove for the shortfall.
- Value the security and prove for the shortfall.
- Surrender the security and prove for the whole debt.

Where a secured creditor opts to realise his security and prove for the shortfall, para 24(1) provides that any dividends he receives from the general creditors' fund cannot disturb any dividend which is then already declared. The second option is to value the security and prove for the shortfall. Where this option is chosen, para 24(2) provides that, before ranking for dividend, the creditor must state in his proof the particulars of his security, the date on which it was given and the value at which he assesses it. He shall then be entitled to receive a dividend only in respect of the balance due to him after

---

354 *Secured creditor* is defined by s 3 of the Bankruptcy Act 1988 as meaning: 'any creditor holding any mortgage, charge or lien on the debtor's estate or any part thereof as security for a debt due to him.'

355 See para **[25.183]**.

356 See Ch 18, *Corporate Borrowing: Debentures and Security*, para **[18.057]**.

357 On the question of the payment of court fees incurred in a court sale of charged property, see *Re McCairns (PMPA) plc* [1992] ILRM 19 where the Supreme Court reversed Costello J, reported at [1989] ILRM 501. See also *Re Michael Orr (Kilternan) Ltd* [1986] IR 273.

358 See Sanfey & Holohan, *Bankruptcy Law and Practice* (2nd edn, 2012), at 12–27; and Pennington, *Corporate Insolvency Law* (1991), p 294 *et seq.*

deducting the assessed value of his security. Secured creditors will be slow to underestimate the value of their security in the hope of a windfall. A number of deterrents exist: the liquidator may redeem it on payment of the assessed value or require that the property be put up for sale[359]; the creditor will only be able to amend the valuation where he shows to the court that the valuation and proof were made *bona fide* on a mistaken belief[360]; and where a valuation is amended, any excess dividend received must be repaid[361]. The third option open to a secured creditor is to surrender the security and prove for the whole debt. It can readily be imagined that this option will very rarely be taken. Only where the value of the security is virtually worthless will a secured creditor surrender his security and take his chances with the company's unsecured creditors.

[25.146] Often a secured creditor will choose to remain outside of the winding up and to realise his security. Obviously, he will not have to prove for the shortfall where there is none. Where there is a surplus over after his debt is paid from the realisation of the security, he will be obliged to repay this either to the liquidator or the preferential creditors[362].

[25.147] The validity of a secured creditor's mortgage or charge will depend upon a number of factors: the capacity of the company and the authority of the directors to create the charge[363]; the legality of the charge[364]; and whether it has been registered pursuant to s 99(1) of the CA 1963[365]. Where a registrable charge has not been registered, the security will be void against the liquidator and any other creditors of the company. The consequence is that although the money secured becomes immediately repayable, the creditor of the money ceases to be a secured creditor and so must prove with the other unsecured creditors.

[25.148] Finally, it should be noted that where there are a number of secured creditors whose security extends to the same assets, the entitlement of each creditor will be determined by the law of priorities and the registration of security interests. This will be the case whether the secured assets comprise of real property[366] or personal property[367].

(b) Assets that are held in trust

[25.149] Property that is not beneficially owned by a company is not available for distribution by the liquidator. The equitable or beneficial owner of property held in trust by a company that is in liquidation does not have to prove for his property in the winding

359 Paragraph 24(4)(a) of Schedule 1 to the Bankruptcy Act 1988.

360 Paragraph 24(5) of Schedule 1 to the Bankruptcy Act 1988.

361 Paragraph 24(6) of Schedule 1 to the Bankruptcy Act 1988.

362 See Ch 20, *Corporate Borrowing: Receivers*, para **[20.066]**.

363 See Ch 7, *Corporate Contracts: Capacity and Authority*, para **[7.099]**.

364 See generally s 31 of the CA 1990 and s 60 of the CA 1963.

365 Note, however, that the security held by a creditor may on application by the liquidator be found to be a fraudulent preference or fraudulent disposition: see paras **[25.081]** and **[25.103]**, respectively.

366 See Keane, *Equity and the Law of Trusts in the Republic of Ireland* (1988), p 49 *et seq.*

367 See Bell, *Modern Law of Personal Property in England and Ireland* (1989), p 516 *et seq.*

up. Accordingly, when property is held by the company in trust, the beneficial owner is entitled to the property and does not have to prove with other creditors. In *Re Shanahans Stamp Auctions Ltd*[368], it was found that where a company held postage stamps in trust for investors, the investors were entitled to the stamps as of right and did not have to prove in the winding up of the company[369]. The principles discussed in that case were applied by Laffoy J in *Re Money Markets International Stockbrokers Ltd (No 1)*[370] and it was held that a particular client of a failed stockbroking firm was entitled to the return of monies that were in the liquidator's hands, in circumstances where they had been transferred to the company to complete a purchase of shares that had never completed. The applicant's claim was unusual because monies had been transferred to purchase the shares in advance of the settlement date and were identifiable in the client account of the company. Laffoy J considered whether, as between competing claimants to a client account, the rule in *Clayton's Case* (ie, last in first out – as seen in *Re Shanahans Stamp Auctions Ltd*[371]) or the so-called '*pari passu ex post facto* solution' (*pari passu* distribution – as seen in *Barlow Clowes International Ltd v Vaughan*[372]) applied. Laffoy J applied the rule in *Clayton's Case* to the benefit of the applicant. Similarly, where goods are purchased by a company subject to a valid retention of title clause the liquidator must hand back such goods to the vendor creditor[373]. On the other hand, in another application brought arising from the collapse of the same firm, *Re Money Markets International Stockbrokers Ltd (No 3)*[374], another client's claim to be entitled to a trust over monies in the client account was rejected. There, Carroll J rejected that the monies in question were subject to a trust, constructive or otherwise, and found that the applicant did not have a proprietary claim, or a right *in rem*, against the company's client account[375].

(c) Monies that must be set off

[25.150] A further consequence of the incorporation of the laws of bankruptcy into liquidations[376] is the application of the rules dealing with set-off in bankruptcy[377]. Paragraph 17(1) of Schedule 1 to the Bankruptcy Act 1988 provides:

---

368 *Re Shanahans Stamp Auctions Ltd* [1962] IR 38. See also *Re Ellis Sons & Vidler Ltd* [1994] BCC 532.

369 *Cf Re Goldcorp Exchange Ltd* [1994] 2 All ER 806. See Collins, 'Tracing into a Vanishing Asset: High Expectations and Equitable Remedies' (1994) CLP 211 where this case and the principles of tracing are perceptively analysed.

370 *Re Money Markets International Stockbrokers Ltd (No 1)* [1999] 4 IR 267.

371 *Re Shanahans Stamp Auctions Ltd* [1962] IR 38. See, generally, O'Dell, 'The Use and Abuse of Clayton's Case' (2000) 7(1) DULJ 161.

372 *Barlow Clowes International Ltd v Vaughan* [1992] BCLC 1910.

373 *Re WJ Hickey Ltd* [1988] IR 126.

374 *Re Money Markets International Stockbrokers Ltd (No 3)* [2001] 2 IR 17.

375 See also *Re Money Markets International Stockbrokers Ltd; Thomson and Thomson v Kavanagh* [2006] IEHC 349 where Laffoy J rejected that the applicants had a trust interest in a company's bank account where their funds and those of other clients were intermingled.

376 Section 284(1) of the CA 1963. See para **[25.141]**.

377 See, O'Callaghan, 'Set-off on Insolvency' (1998) 5 CLP 20.

> 'Where there are mutual debts or credits between the bankrupt and any person claiming as creditor, one debt or demand may be set off against the other and only the balance found owing is to be recoverable on one side or the other.'

Where set-off applies, its effect is to disapply the normal principle of pari passu distribution of assets. A creditor who is owed money by the company can avoid proving for that debt where he owes the company money. Unlike England and Wales[378], in Ireland set-off in a winding up is not mandatory[379].

[25.151] In order for debts to be capable of being set off in a liquidation, there must be *mutuality* of debits and credits between the creditor and the company. Accordingly, set-off can operate only where the obligations to be set off arise between the same parties and in the same right[380]. The Australian High Court has held that there are three aspects to mutuality: in *Gye v McIntyre*[381], it was said:

> 'The first is that the credits, the debits, or the claims arising from other dealings be between the same persons. The second is that the benefit or burden of them lie in the same interests. In determining whether credits, debits or claims arising from other dealings are between the same persons and in the same interests, it is the equitable or beneficial interests of the parties which must be considered … The third requirement of mutuality is that the credits, debits or claims arising in other dealings must be commensurable for the purposes of set-off under the section. That means that they must ultimately sound in money.'

Set-off was considered by the House of Lords in *Re Bank of Credit and Commerce International SA (No 8)*[382]. The facts were that BCCI had loaned money to a borrower on the security of a deposit, made by a surety. The surety was a controlling shareholder in the borrower company. Importantly, the security document signed by the surety did not contain an obligation on the surety to discharge the borrower's indebtedness, merely providing that BCCI had a lien or charge over the deposit which it could utilise to reduce the borrower's liabilities and providing that the surety could not withdraw the deposit until the borrower's liability to BCCI had been discharged. When BCCI went into

---

378 See *Re Bank of Credit and Commerce International SA (No 8)* [1997] 4 All ER 568; *Stein v Blake* [1995] 2 All ER 961; and *MS Fashions v BCCI SA* [1993] BCC 360.

379 In *Deering v Hyndman* (1886) LR (Ir) 18 QBD 323.

380 See *McKinnon v Armstrong* (1877) 2 App Cas 531 where a trustee could not set off a debt owed to him personally against a debt owed to him in his capacity as trustee, and *Re Irish Shipping* [1986] ILRM 518 where a bank could not set off money paid to it by mistake against a debt owed, since it held the money as constructive trustee. By way of contrast, in *MS Fashions Ltd v Bank of Credit and Commerce International* (1993) Independent, 6 January, a depositor with a bank was permitted to set off a claim against him on foot of a guarantee to another bank against his deposit with his own, now insolvent, bank, since his bank was the debtor of the other bank and the contract of guarantee expressly stated him to be 'principal debtor'.

381 *Gye v McIntyre* (1990-1991) 171 CLR 609 at 623. See O'Callaghan, 'Set-off on Insolvency' (1998) 5 CLP 20 at 24.

382 *Re Bank of Credit and Commerce International SA (No 8)* [1997] 4 All ER 568. See Hutchinson, 'Taking Security over Cash Deposits: The House of Lords Confirms the Conceptual Possibility of Charge-Backs' (1998) 5 CLP 3; Bannister, 'Liquidation Set-off and Security over Bank Deposits – The Uncertainties Removed' (1997) *CCH's Company Law Newsletter*, 15 December 1997.

liquidation, the liquidators applied for directions as to whether BCCI could claim repayment from the borrower *without resorting to the deposit* that had been given as security and thereby leaving the surety to prove with the other creditors. In essence, the liquidators wanted to know whether they were obliged to set-off the deposit against the borrower's indebtedness. At trial, in the Court of Appeal and in the House of Lords the basic answer was the same: the liquidators were not required to set-off the deposit account against the borrower's loan with the result that the liquidators could pursue the borrower for the monies loaned whilst at the same time forcing the surety who had made the deposit to prove in the liquidation along with all other creditors for the monies owed to him. In the House of Lords, Lord Hoffmann said that set-off was 'strictly limited to mutual claims' and that there 'can be no set-off of claims by third parties, even with their consent' as 'to do so would be to allow parties by agreement to subvert the fundamental principle of *pari passu* distribution of the insolvent company's assets'[383].

[25.152] The effect of a creditor being allowed to set off a debt which the company owes him against a debt which he owes the company is that the creditor does not have to prove with the other creditors in the winding up of the company for the debt the company owes him. The advantage of set-off to a creditor is seen in *Re Money Markets International Stockbrokers Ltd*[384]. There, Laffoy J described the operation of para 17(1) of Schedule 1 to the Bankruptcy Act 1988 by reference to one of the insolvent company's (MMI's) creditors, a Mr Murtagh:

> 'Mr Murtagh's position vis-à-vis MMI post-liquidation is that the credit balance on his ledger account with MMI is £288,291. However, by letter dated the 1st of March 1998 Mr Murtagh instructed MMI to use funds from that account to clear debts on certain other accounts, on two of which, according to the relevant ledger accounts, there were at the commencement of the winding-up debit balances which aggregate £231,061. Mr Murtagh, as a beneficiary of client funds has a trust or property claim, a right *in rem*, against the client funds and he also has a right *in personam* or a money claim, against the trustee, MMI (in liquidation). MMI has a claim in debt, a claim *in personam*, against Mr Murtagh under the letter of set-off in respect of the indebtedness to MMI on the two connected accounts. The mutuality required by paragraph 17(1) will only apply if Mr Murtagh decides not to pursue his trust claim, in which case by operation of paragraph 17(1) Mr Murtagh could prove for £57,320 in the liquidation of MMI. That illustration shows that a party who has a dual money/property claim against an insolvent company in liquidation may by pursuing one claim or cause of action, bring about a situation in which the parties are claiming in the same right and the mutuality requirement of paragraph 17(1) is fulfilled. It is not so much a question of the party with dual claim electing for set-off: it is a question of the claim or cause of action pursued by that party giving rise to a situation in which paragraph 17(1) comes into play.'

A creditor must, of course, pay any balance owing to the company after the set-off to the liquidator[385] or, where the company still owes him, he will have to prove with the

383 *Re Bank of Credit and Commerce International SA (No 8)* [1997] 4 All ER 568 at 573g, relying on the authority of *British Eagle International Airlines Ltd v Cie Nationale Air France* [1975] 2 All ER 390.

384 *Re Money Markets International Stockbrokers Ltd* [2000] 3 IR 437.

385 A secured creditor is not obliged to set off his claim against a debt owed to him: *Re Norman Holding Co Ltd* [1990] 3 All ER 757.

company's other creditors for the balance. The debt owed by the company may be set off in full. This gives the creditor the advantage of making full use of that debt to offset his liability to the company. If he does not exercise the set-off, he faces the prospect of having to pay his debt to the company in full and whilst perhaps receiving only a percentage of the debt owed by the company to him.

[25.153] Any debt, which is capable of being proved in bankruptcy or a winding up, can be the subject of a set-off in bankruptcy or a winding up[386]. The relevant date for set-off is the date on which a resolution is passed, or a court order made, to have the company wound up[387], and there must be mutual debts and credits in existence at that date[388]. Whether it is permissible to set off a debt which was a mere contingency or possibility at the relevant date is the subject of some doubt. In *Re a Debtor*[389], a guarantor, who was not called upon to pay under the guarantee until after the relevant date, was held not to be entitled to set off sums owed to him against his payment obligation, since, at the relevant date, his obligation to pay under the guarantee was a mere contingency. However, in *Re Charge Card Services Ltd*[390], Millet J said that it is sufficient merely that mutual dealings exist at the date of the winding up which involve rights and obligations, whether absolute or contingent, of such a nature that have developed into pecuniary demands capable of set off at the time the claim to set off is made[391]. This has been affirmed by the House of Lords in *Re Bank of Credit and Commerce International SA (No 8)*[392] where Lord Hoffmann said set-off under the English rules[393] 'requires at least the existence of a right to make a pecuniary demand'. Whatever about contingent debts, it is well settled that debts which are unliquidated or unquantified at the relevant date may be set off. Thus, for example, a claim for damages in contract or tort may be set off even though the amount of damages to be awarded has not been settled at the relevant date. To this end, s 61 of the Civil Liability Act 1961 provides:

> '(1) Notwithstanding any other enactment or any rule of law, a claim for damages or contribution in respect of a wrong shall be provable in bankruptcy where the wrong out of which the liability to damages or the right to contribution arose was committed before the time of the bankruptcy.

386 *Re DH Curtiss* [1978] 1 Ch 162.

387 Sections 220 and 253 of the CA 1963.

388 *Re Casey* (21 July 1986, unreported) HC, Hamilton P; See *Re Bank of Credit and Commerce International SA (No 8)* [1997] 4 All ER 568; and *MS Fashions v BCCI SA* [1993] BCC 360.

389 *Re a Debtor* [1956] 3 All ER 225. See also *Re Fenton* [1931] 1 Ch 85. Both cases feature in the judgment of the Supreme Court in *Dempsey v Bank of Ireland* (12 December 1985, unreported) SC.

390 *Re Charge Card Services Ltd* [1987] BCLC 17.

391 *Re Charge Card Services Ltd* [1987] BCLC 17 at 42–43. For authority on this point Millett J cited *Hiley v Peoples Prudential Assurance Co Ltd* (1938) 60 CLR 468 at 496.

392 *Re Bank of Credit and Commerce International SA (No 8)* [1997] 4 All ER 568. See Hutchinson, 'Taking Security over Cash Deposits: The House of Lords Confirms the Conceptual Possibility of Charge-Backs' (1998) 5 CLP 3; Bannister, 'Liquidation Set-off and Security over Bank Deposits – The Uncertainties Removed' (1997) CCH's Company Law Newsletter, 15 December 1997.

393 Insolvency Rules 1986, r 490 (UK).

(2) Where the damages or contribution have not been and cannot be otherwise liquidated or ascertained, the court may make such order as to it seems fit for the assessment of the damages or contribution, and the amount when so assessed shall be provable as if it were a debt due at the time of the bankruptcy.'

[25.154] Where a liquidator recovers damages against a director in respect of misfeasance or breach of trust or duty, a director or other officer of the company is not entitled to set off any debts owed to him by the company. In the Supreme Court decision of *Re Greendale Developments Ltd*[394], Keane J stated that this has been treated as settled law in England since the decision of the Court of Appeal in *Re Anglo French Co-Operative Society; ex p Pelly*[395], where it was held that:

'… an officer of a company who has been found liable to pay money to the company in misfeasance proceedings is not entitled to set off a debt owing by the company to him against that liability. It appears from the judgments in that and subsequent cases that the reason for the rule was that the right of set off only arose in the case of actions between parties. However, it was also pointed out by Hall VC in another case referred to in a footnote in *Pelly's* case that no right of set off would in any event arise unless the debts could be said to be mutual[396].'

In that case, Keane J held that there was no mutuality between the sums sought to be recovered by the liquidator as having been misapplied in breach of the director's fiduciary duties and the sums claimed by the director against the company. In such a case the director can prove for any sums owed to him as an unsecured creditor in the company's winding up.

[25.155] Section 237(1) of the CA 1963 addresses the extent to which a contributory's right of set-off can be overridden:

'The court may, at any time after making a winding-up order, make an order on any contributory for the time being on the list of contributories, to pay in manner directed by the order, any money due from him or from the estate of the person whom he represents to the company, exclusive of any money payable by him or the estate by virtue of any call in pursuance of this Act.'

Section 237(2) provides that in making such an order the court may:

'(a) in the case of an unlimited company, allow to the contributory by way of set-off any money due to him or to the estate which he represents from the company on any independent dealing or contract with the company, but not any money due to him as a member of the company in respect of any dividend or profit; and

(b) in the case of a limited company, make to any director whose liability is unlimited or to his estate a like allowance.'

Notwithstanding the foregoing, in any company, limited or unlimited, 'when all the creditors are paid in full, any money due on any account whatever to a contributory from the company may be allowed to him by way of set-off against any subsequent call'[397].

[394] *Re Greendale Developments Ltd* [1998] 1 IR 8.

[395] *Re Anglo French Co-Operative Society; ex p Pelly* [1882] 21 Ch D 492.

[396] *Re Greendale Developments Ltd* [1998] 1 IR 8 at 28.

[397] Section 237(3) of the CA 1963.

[25.156] In addition to set off in bankruptcy, a creditor may, in appropriate circumstances, exercise a contractual right of set off so as to set off his liabilities to the company against debts owed to him by the company[398]. In *Dempsey v Bank of Ireland*[399], the Supreme Court upheld the validity of a bank's contractual right to appropriate accounts (ie, to set off debit accounts against credit accounts) *after* the commencement of the account holders' winding up. The liquidator in that case argued that such a right ceased on the relevant date because on that date the assets of the company, including money kept in bank accounts, vested in him so that he might distribute them *pari passu* to the ordinary creditors. Henchy J, dismissing that argument, said:

> 'To say that when the liquidator takes over, the assets of his company vest in him is a less than complete statement of the legal position. The general rule is that because he acquires only such title to the assets as the company had – no more, no less. He cannot take any better title to any part of the assets than the company had. This means that he takes the assets subject to any pre-existing enforceable right of a third party in or over them. If that were not so, equities, liabilities and contractual rights validly and enforceably created while the assets were in the hands of the company would be unfairly swept aside and an unjust distribution of the assets would result[400].'

The debts in that case were contractually subject to the possible exercise of a right of set off when they first arose. Consequently, when they came into the hands of the liquidator, they remained subject to that contractual right.

[25.157] No mutuality of obligations need exist in cases of contractual set-off – consequently, a creditor may contractually set off the obligations of another of the company's creditors against his own. In *British Eagle International Airlines Ltd v Compagnie Nationale Air France*[401], the English House of Lords opposed the exercise of a contractual set-off in a liquidation where no mutuality existed, on the basis that the exercise contravened the requirement that the property of the company (in that case the debts owed to it) be distributed by the liquidator amongst the ordinary creditors *pari passu* in satisfaction of all its liabilities[402]. However, in *Glow Heating v Eastern Health Board*[403] Costello J held that the *pari passu* requirement did not render void every contract by which a creditor obtained rights over the company's assets superior to those given to the ordinary creditors, and that the liquidator took the subject matter of the set off subject to any liabilities which affected it in the company's hands. As a result, it would appear that non-mutual contractual set-off will be permitted in Irish liquidations.

[25.158] As was observed in Chapter 18[404], set-off can operate against debts which are the subject of a floating charge up until the moment of crystallisation[405]. Since

---

398 See generally, Shannon, 'Contractual Set-Off as a Form of Bank Security from an Irish Incorporated Company', a lecture delivered at the Irish Centre for Commercial Studies, University College, Dublin, 22 June 1992.

399 *Dempsey v Bank of Ireland* (6 December 1985, unreported) SC.

400 *Dempsey v Bank of Ireland* (6 December 1985, unreported), SC at pp 8–9.

401 *British Eagle International Airlines Ltd v Compagnie Nationale Air France* [1975] 2 All ER 390.

402 See s 275 of the CA 1963.

403 *Glow Heating v Eastern Health Board* [1988] IR 110.

404 See Ch 18, *Corporate Borrowing: Debentures and Security*, para **[18.090]**.

405 *Re Russell Murphy* [1976] IR 15.

crystallisation operates as an equitable assignment of the subject matter of the charge to the charge holder, once crystallisation occurs the mutuality of the debts secured by the charge is destroyed. Consequently, set-off in bankruptcy, under para 17(1) of Schedule 1 to the Bankruptcy Act 1988, will be precluded for want of mutuality in such circumstances[406].

(d) Super-preferential debts that are trust monies

[25.159] The Revenue Commissioners' claims in respect of employment contributions (PAYE and PRSI) that have actually been deducted from employees' remuneration but which have not been paid over to them, have what is referred to as a '*super-preferential*' status. Section 19(2) of the Social Welfare (Consolidation) Act 2005 ('SW(C)A 2005') provides:

> 'The assets of a limited company in a winding up under the Companies Acts 1963–2005 *shall not include*—
>
> (a) any sum deducted by an employer from such remuneration of an employee of the employer paid before the winding-up in respect of an employment contribution due and unpaid by the employer in respect of such contribution, or
>
> (b) any sum which would have been deducted from the remuneration of the employee in respect of an employment contribution for a period of employment before a winding-up had that remuneration been paid before the winding up
>
> and in such a winding up a sum equal in amount to the sum so deducted and payable shall notwithstanding anything in those Acts, be paid to the Social Insurance Fund in priority to the debt specified in section 285(2) of the Companies Act 1963. (Emphasis added.)

The effect of this provision is to impress a statutory trust on certain monies in a company's possession and to deem the Revenue Commissioners as beneficial owners. The result of this provision is the same as if the company held such monies on an express trust: they are not included in the company's assets and so are unavailable to preferential creditors, creditors secured by a floating charge and unsecured creditors.

[25.160] In *Re Coombe Importers Ltd*[407], Shanley J considered what sums, precisely, fell within the meaning of s 16(2)(a) and (b) of the Social Welfare (Consolidation) Act 1993, the similar predecessor to s 19(2) of the SW(C)A 2005. As to s 16(2)(a), he said that it is:

> '... a condition precedent to the super-preferential status of any sum is that it be a sum *deducted* by the employer in respect of the employment contribution of the employee which remains due and owing by the employer ... [It does not permit] a construction that super-preferential status can be afforded to sums which *ought* to have been deducted in respect of the employment contributions of an employee, but were not so deducted[408].'

As to s 16(2)(b), Shanley J said:

> '... it appears to me that that section deals with and is restricted to situations where employees were due remuneration prior to a winding up but did not receive such

406 *Lynch et al v Ardmore Studios (Ireland) Ltd* [1966] IR 133.

407 *Re Coombe Importers Ltd* [1999] 1 IR 492.

408 *Re Coombe Importers Ltd* [1999] 1 IR 492 at 500.

remuneration from their employer. It has no application … where employees did receive remuneration from their employer without deductions being made.'

In that case, neither provision could be invoked to confer super-preferential status on particular sums claimed. The facts there were that monies had been paid to the company's employees prior to its winding up without the deduction of any PAYE or PRSI. In those circumstances, neither s 16 nor its predecessor[409] applied and the monies due to the revenue did not have super-preferential status under s 16(2)(a) – because the taxes were not in fact actually deducted – or under s 16(2)(b) – because it only applies where employees are owed wages that are not in fact paid[410].

(e) *Stamp duty on monies received in realisation of company assets*

[25.161] Stamp duty is payable on 'the monies received by the liquidator in realisation of the assets of the company'[411]. The current rate of duty is 4%. This tax is only applicable in official or compulsory liquidations. Where it is payable, it must be paid before any other distribution, ie, ahead of the preferential creditors, floating charge holders and ordinary creditors. In *Re Private Motorists Provident Society Ltd; Horgan v Minister for Justice*[412], it was held that monies would be 'received by the liquidator in realisation of the assets' even in the absence of an order under s 230 of the CA 1963 vesting a company's assets in the liquidator[413]. There, the liquidator had claimed that monies received by a company were not liable to duty. The argument was, in effect, that in order for duty to be payable monies had to be received by the liquidator in his own capacity (where a s 230 order was made) and not in his capacity as agent of the company. This argument was rejected by Murphy J who held that the liquidator in that case had brought about the realisation and he was the proper party to give a receipt for the proceeds of sale, even if the ownership of the assets was not vested in him.

[25.162] In *Re Private Motorists Provident Society Ltd; Horgan v Minister for Justice*[414], the court also held that duty would not be payable on all monies received by a liquidator, but only those received in realisation of the company's assets. Murphy J rejected that the word 'realisation' necessarily involved a sale of assets and neither was a sale of assets necessarily a 'realisation'[415]. Murphy J held that, logically, assets could only be 'realised' once in the course of any liquidation:

---

409 Section 120 of the Social Welfare (Consolidation) Act 1981.

410 In that case it should also be noted that s 16(2)(b) of the Social Welfare (Consolidation) Act 1993 was disregarded on the grounds that it was not in force at the relevant time (it not having a counterpart in s 120 of the Social Welfare (Consolidation) Act 1981) and could not be invoked retrospectively.

411 Item 24 of Part 3 of Schedule 1 to the Supreme Court and High Court (Fees) Order 2012 (SI 110/2012) being the prescribed fees envisaged by s 65 of the Courts of Justice Act 1936.

412 *Re Private Motorists Provident Society Ltd; Horgan v Minister for Justice* (23 June 1995, unreported) HC, Murphy J.

413 See **[25.011]**.

414 *Re Private Motorists Provident Society Ltd; Horgan v Minister for Justice* (23 June 1995, unreported) HC, Murphy J.

415 See para **[25.005]** where Murphy J is quoted.

> 'To constitute a realisation the particular asset or property must be got in by the liquidator in such a fashion as to be available to meet the liabilities of the company (subject to the expenses of the liquidation). Once that has been achieved – and ordinarily its achievement can be verified by the lodgment of the proceeds into the Bank of Ireland to the account of the official liquidator – the realisation is complete and any further activities by the liquidator in relation to such proceeds may augment the available funds by an accrual of interest or otherwise but would not constitute a realisation of the assets of the company[416].'

Applying that reasoning, Murphy J held, *inter alia*, that the following receipts of monies were not liable to stamp duty: repayments of VAT representing the reversal of a liability created during the course of the winding up; a rebate from the Department of Labour in respect of statutory redundancy resulting from the liquidator's retention of certain employees for upwards of two years after the commencement of the winding up; a sum refunded by the company's bank that had been deducted in error and which arose solely from the liquidator's activities, not being an asset of the company; the costs of litigation initiated by the liquidator; the repayment of a dividend mistakenly paid; monies refunded by creditors whose claims were withdrawn – because this 'was merely the restoration or regularisation of the status quo above and not the realisation of an asset'; and interest received by the liquidator on the proceeds of realisation.

[25.163] The following receipts of money were, however, held by Murphy J to be liable to stamp duty: the repayment of corporation tax that had been overpaid prior to the liquidation; and sums received from associated companies, also in liquidation, that belonged to the company being wound up, even though duty had already been paid on those monies by those companies. Murphy J also held that monies received by the official liquidator from a previously appointed receiver constituted assets of the company and were liable to stamp duty. This matter again arose for consideration in *Re Chipboard Products Ltd*[417]. There, a liquidator sought directions as to whether stamp duty was payable on cash paid over to him by a receiver appointed over the company's assets. It was sought to distinguish Murphy J's decision on the grounds that, in the instant case, there had been a mere transfer of monies by the receiver to the official liquidator. Laffoy J rejected the liquidator's contentions and held that although the receiver had realised the proceeds and although the liquidator had to do no more than receive and lodge the cheques drawn by the receiver 'nonetheless, in my view, the monies represented by those cheques were received by the official liquidator "in realisation of the assets of the company"'[418].

The costs and expenses of winding up

[25.164] Liquidating a company is a costly business. Were the Companies Acts to provide that liquidators' expenses and remuneration were to be merely provable along with the claims of the general body of creditors there would, in the absence of the conscription of liquidators, be few insolvent windings up. For this reason, the Companies Acts provide for the disbursement of the costs and expenses of the winding up, *in priority* to the claims of the general creditors.

---

416 *Re Private Motorists Provident Society Ltd; Horgan v Minister for Justice* (23 June 1995, unreported) HC at pp 8–9.

417 *Re Chipboard Products Ltd* (27 February 1997, unreported) HC, Laffoy J.

418 *Re Chipboard Products Ltd* (27 February 1997, unreported) HCat p 8.

(a) *Liquidators' versus examiners' remuneration, costs and expenses*

[25.165] As shall be considered next, the payment of liquidators' remuneration, costs and expenses is afforded a high priority by Ord 74, r 128(1) of the RSC and, being part of the costs and expenses of a winding up, will rank ahead of preferential creditors, creditors secured by floating charges and unsecured creditors. Of course liquidators' remuneration costs and expenses cannot be paid out of assets that do not belong to the company and for that reason are not liable to be paid out of assets that are the subject of a fixed mortgage or a fixed charge. However, in the event of a deficiency in assets an examiner's remuneration, costs and expenses will have priority to those of a liquidator. In *Re Springline Ltd*[419], the Supreme Court, reversing the High Court decision of Shanley J[420], held that s 29(3) of the C(A)A 1990[421] gave an examiner's remuneration, costs and expenses priority over those of a liquidator. The finding in this decision was given statutory effect by s 29(3B) of the C(A)A 1990[422].

(b) *Official liquidations*

[25.166] In the context of official liquidations, s 244 of the CA 1963 provides:

> 'The court may, in the event of the assets being insufficient to satisfy the liabilities, make an order as to the payment out of the assets of the costs, charges and expenses incurred in the winding up in such order of priority as the court thinks just.'

Guidance is provided by Ord 74, r 128(1) of the RSC, which provides:

> 'The assets of a company in a winding up by the court remaining after payment of the fees and expenses properly incurred in preserving, realising or getting in the assets, including where the company has previously commenced to be wound up voluntarily such remuneration, costs and expenses as the court may allow to a Liquidator appointed in such voluntary winding up, shall, subject to any order of the court, be liable to the following payments which shall be made in the following order of priority, namely:

First	The costs of the petition, including the costs of any person appearing on the petition whose costs are allowed by the court.
Next	The costs and expenses of any person who makes or concurs in making the company's statement of affairs.
Next	The necessary disbursements of the Official Liquidator, other than expenses properly incurred in preserving, realising or getting in the assets hereinbefore provided for.
Next	The costs payable to the solicitor for the Official Liquidator.

419 *Re Springline Ltd* [1999] 1 ILRM 15.

420 *Re Springline Ltd* [1998] 1 ILRM 301.

421 See Ch 22, *Examinerships*, para **[22.087]** and para **[22.165]**.

422 Inserted by s 28 of the C(A)(No 2)A 1999. Section 29(3B) of the C(A)A 1990 provides: 'In subsections (3) and (3A) references to a claim shall be deemed to include references to any payment in a winding-up of the company in respect of the costs, charges and expenses of that winding-up (including the remuneration of any liquidator).'

Next	The remuneration of the Official Liquidator.
Next	The out-of-pocket expenses necessarily incurred by the committee of inspection (if any).'

As to the interaction between s 244 of the CA 1963 and Ord 74, r 128, in *Re CHA Ltd*[423] Laffoy J held that s 244 overrides the order of priority stipulated in the RSC, which provision by its terms is 'subject to any order of the court'[424].

(c) Voluntary liquidations

[25.167] Section 281 of the CA 1963, which applies in the case of voluntary liquidations, provides that:

> 'All costs, charges and expenses properly incurred in the winding up, including the remuneration of the liquidator, shall be payable out of the assets of the company in priority to all other claims[425].'

Both provisions have been the subject of considerable litigation, which has focused, in particular, upon whether or not certain taxes are payable in priority to all other claims. The case of *Re Compustore Ltd*[426] is a salutory warning to legal advisors and accountants who might be asked to advise the directors of a company on the cusp of a winding up to ensure that they get their fees paid up front lest they are forced to rank *pari passu* with other unsecured creditors. In that case, a firm of solicitors was consulted by the directors of the company for advice regarding the convening and holding of a creditors' meeting. Notwithstanding the decision of Hoffmann J in *Re AV Sorge & Company Ltd*[427], which the applicant solicitors' firm had relied on, Laffoy J held that the reference in s 281 to costs, etc, 'incurred in the winding up' was clear and unambiguous and that the intention of the legislature was plain. Laffoy J went on to determine that s 281 means only costs, etc, 'incurred while the winding up is in being, that is to say, after the resolution to wind up the company has been passed'.

(d) The meaning of 'necessary disbursement'

[25.168] Corporation tax payable to the Revenue Commissioners after the commencement of the winding up was held by the courts not to be an 'expense' or a 'necessary disbursement' within the meaning of Ord 74, r 128, although this has been reversed by s 56 of the Finance Act 1983 (now s 571 of the Taxes Consolidation Act 1997). In *Re Van Hool McArdle Ltd*[428], Carroll J said that corporation tax was merely a possible consequence of a sale where a profit was made by the company. In the Supreme

423 *Re CHA Ltd* (25 January 1999, unreported) HC, Laffoy J.

424 In *Secretary of State for Trade and Industry v Aurum Marketing Ltd* [2000] TLR 615, the English Court of Appeal held that it had the discretion to order a non-party – in that case the sole director and shareholder – to pay the costs of the winding up and that the company's costs should not be paid out of company assets until after the unsecured creditors had been paid.

425 Note that *Re Redbreast Preserving Co (Ireland) Ltd* [1958] IR 234 held that the priorities provided for in Ord 74, r 129(1) of the RSC also apply to voluntary liquidations with appropriate modification.

426 *Re Compustore Ltd* [2006] IEHC 52.

427 *Re AV Sorge & Company Ltd* [1986] BCLC 490.

428 *Re Van Hool McArdle Ltd* [1982] ILRM 340.

Court[429], the meaning of 'necessary disbursements' was given some consideration. O'Higgins CJ said that by necessary disbursement was meant 'expenses such as necessary maintenance of buildings or wages for caretaking or for other purposes'[430]. Somewhat strangely, in *Re A Noyek & Sons Ltd; Burns v Hearne*[431] s 281 of the CA 1963, which applies to companies in voluntary liquidation, was interpreted by the Supreme Court as meaning that corporation tax was a cost within the meaning of 'costs, charges and expenses properly incurred in the winding up', as is tax on deposit interest. The basis for the distinction from the *Van Hool McArdle* case was the reference to charges in s 281 and the absence of that word in Ord 74, r 129(1) of the RSC.

[25.169] Items which have been held to constitute 'necessary disbursements' include post-liquidation rent paid by a liquidator in respect of property the continual use of which is necessary to the winding up of the company[432]. An interesting dispute concerning the payment of post-liquidation rent arose in *Re CHA Ltd*[433]. In that case, the official liquidator of a company continued on in occupation of the company's premises and on failing to pay rent to the landlord, the landlord was given leave to institute proceedings against the company and successfully recovered judgment against the company for £5,000 plus costs. The landlord immediately recovered the sum of £2,000, which had been lodged by the liquidator. As to the balance, the landlord claimed in the High Court[434] that the balance of £3,000 was costs, charges and expenses incurred in the winding up, within the meaning of s 244 of the CA 1963. The landlord also claimed that it was entitled to be paid the taxed costs (a further £2,644.34) in priority to all other claims in the liquidation. On the question of taxed costs, Laffoy J held, on the authority of the Supreme Court in *Comhlucht Páipear Ríomhaireachto Teo v Údarás na Gaeltachta*, that the landlord was entitled to be paid in full the taxed costs of the rent recovery proceedings in priority to all other claims of the liquidation. In relation to the award of £3,000 by way of rent, it was conceded by the liquidator that that sum fell to be regarded as a debt contracted for the purpose of the winding up of the company and to be paid in full like any other debt or expense properly incurred by the liquidator.[435] Accordingly, Laffoy J declared that that sum represented 'costs, charges and expenses incurred in the winding up' within the meaning of s 244. As to the priority between the

[429] Reported as *Revenue Commissioners v Donnelly* [1983] ILRM 329.

[430] Note that in *Re Hibernian Transport Companies Ltd* [1984] ILRM 583, Costello J held that tax claimed in respect of post-liquidation deposit interest was not a 'necessary disbursement' and further could not be proved for by the Revenue Commissioners who were, in this regard, a *post*-liquidation creditor, meaning no tax was payable at all. It would appear that this position remains unchanged in spite of s 571 of the TCA 1997 (formerly s 56 of the Finance Act 1983).

[431] *Re A Noyek & Sons Ltd; Burns v Hearne* [1989] ILRM 155 (SC), [1987] ILRM 508 (HC).

[432] *Re Oak Pits Colliery Co* [1882] 21 Ch D 322.

[433] *Re CHA Ltd* [1997] 1 IR 437, Laffoy J.

[434] *Comhlucht Páipear Ríomhaireachto Teo v Údarás na Gaeltachta* [1991] IR 320. Laffoy J also cited with approval *Halsbury's Laws of England* (4th edn) Vol 7(2), para 1803: 'Similarly, where leave is given to bring an action against the company and to the liquidator to defend it, the successful plaintiff is entitled to have his costs in full out of the assets, including his costs of obtaining leave.' It was also noted that authority for that statement was stated to be *Bailey and Leetham's Case* (1869) LR 8 Eq 94 and *Re Wenborn & Company* (1905) 1 Ch 413.

[435] On the authority of *Re GWI Ltd* (16 November 1987, unreported) HC, Murphy J.

sum owing to the landlord and the liquidator's own legal expenses and remuneration, Laffoy J deferred ruling until the liquidator's application was brought.

[25.170] The costs of necessary litigation have also been considered to be 'necessary disbursements'[436]. Not all litigation will, however, be necessary and therefore automatically held to be payable out of the company's assets as an expense of the liquidation. So in *Re Floor Fourteen Ltd; Lewis v Inland Revenue Commissioners*[437] a liquidator of a company that was hopelessly insolvent proposed to institute proceedings against its directors for wrongful trading and preference. The realised monies meant that preferential creditors would receive only 44 pence in the pound whereas unsecured creditors would receive nothing. The liquidator was authorised by the unsecured creditors to institute proceedings but the preferential creditors, obviously wishing to cut their losses, wanted the proposed 44 pence in the pound. The liquidator applied successfully to the English High Court for a direction authorising the use of the realised assets to fund the litigation and contending that the costs would be 'expenses properly incurred in the winding up' payable out of the company's assets in priority to all other claims. The Deputy Judge held in favour of the liquidator. That decision was reversed by the Court of Appeal, which held that the similar English provision[438] to s 244 of the CA 1963 did not provide that all expenses properly incurred in the winding up were automatically payable out of the company's assets in priority to all other claims. Moreover, it was stated that liquidators did not have a right to recoup the costs of proposed litigation against directors automatically[439]. Of particular interest was the Court of Appeal's distinction between litigation to recover a company's assets and litigation to recover damages from directors, and its consequent finding that costs incurred in the latter were not costs of the proceedings and could not receive priority under the English equivalent to Ord 74, r 128(1)[440]. The Court of Appeal did, however, appear to accept that the court had an inherent discretion to recover the costs of proposed litigation from the company's assets but declined to exercise the court's discretion in that case by reason of insufficient information.

(e) Costs payable to the liquidator's solicitor

[25.171] Where legal expenses have been incurred in preserving or realising assets these will have priority to all claims. The costs of a legal cost accountant, retained by the liquidator's solicitor to tax their costs, have been held not to be a cost properly incurred by a liquidator. It would seem that the only way that such costs will receive priority is where the court exercises its discretion under Ord 74, r 129(2)[441].

---

436 *Re National Building and Land Co* (1885–86) 15 LR Ir 47.

437 *Re Floor Fourteen Ltd; Lewis v Inland Revenue Commissioners* [2001] 2 BCLC 392.

438 Section 115 of the Insolvency Act 1986 (UK).

439 Relying upon *Re MC Bacon Ltd (No 2)* [1990] BCLC 607.

440 *Re Oasis Merchandising Services Ltd* [1997] 1 BCLC 689.

441 See the judgment of Carroll J in *Re Castle Brand Ltd* [1990] ILRM 97.

Proof of debts by the company's creditors

[25.172] Life would indeed be wonderfully easy for liquidators if they could simply accept what a creditor claimed was owing to him and pay it out! In practice, however, before this can be done, all unsecured creditors must first *prove* what sums are due and owing to them. Those debts which may be proved are enumerated in s 283(1) of the CA 1963 which provides:

> '... all debts payable on a contingency, and all claims against the company, present or future, certain or contingent, ascertained or sounding only in damages, shall be admissible to proof against the company, a just estimate being made, so far as possible, of the value of such debts or claims which may be subject to any contingency or which sound only in damages, or for some other reason do not bear a certain value.'

A number of issues arise here, particularly in respect of contentious claims by creditors. The matters considered here are:

(a) Proving claims by creditors.
(b) Discounting claims.
(c) Contingent and periodical liabilities.
(d) Creditors' claims for interest.

(a) Proving claims by creditors

[25.173] The liquidator of a company must advertise to the creditors of the company, at a time directed by the court, advising them of where they should send their claims. Section 241 of the CA 1963 empowers the court to:

> '... fix a time or times within which creditors are to prove their debts or claims or to be excluded from the benefit of any distribution made before those debts are proved.'

Creditors are asked to give their names and addresses, particulars of their debts and claims and the names and addresses of their solicitors[442]. Creditors will not be obliged to attend before the liquidator to prove their debts unless the liquidator so requires[443]. Section 241 of the CA 1963 was considered by Laffoy J in *Re Unidare plc*[444]. There, the liquidator of a company in members' voluntary liquidation sought an order fixing the time within which creditors were to prove their debts. Laffoy J said that while there was a view that a voluntary liquidator can fix a time for proof on penalty of exclusion, because of the nature of the claims arising (asbestos related) the learned judge considered it was appropriate for the liquidator to make application under s 241 of the CA 1963. Laffoy J noted that while the fixing of a time limit is aimed at ensuring that the liquidator can make distributions to those creditors who submit claims in a timely manner, in the case of solvent liquidation, it also ensures that the liquidator can make a distribution to members in a timely manner.

[25.174] The task then falls to the liquidator to investigate the claims sent to him, and to 'ascertain in so far as he is able which of such debts or claims are legally due from the company'. In *Re Unidare plc*[445], Laffoy J noted the duty of liquidators to ascertain a

---

442 RSC, Ord 74, r 95.

443 RSC, Ord 74, r 96.

444 *Re Unidare plc* [2012] IEHC 114.

445 *Re Unidare plc* [2012] IEHC 114.

company's creditors which was ancillary to the duty to discharge the company's debts *pari passu*[446], and quoted with approval the following passage from the decision of Lord Denning MR in *Austin Securities v Northgate*[447]:

> 'It is the duty of a liquidator to inquire into all claims to see whether they are well founded or not, to pay the good claim, to reject the bad, to settle the doubtful, or, if need be to contest them. It is only in this way that a liquidator can fulfil his duty ... of seeing that the property of the company is applied in satisfaction of its liabilities *pari passu*.'

In certain circumstances, that duty can extend to writing to creditors of whose existence the liquidator knows.

In an official liquidation, the liquidator should notify the claims, identifying those which he considers valid, to the court Examiner, usually a court registrar or the Master of the High Court[448]. Claims which are illegal or contrary to public policy should be disallowed by the liquidator. Claims may also be statute barred under s 11(1)(a) of the Statute of Limitations 1957[449]. At the time appointed, the Examiner will adjudicate upon the claims allowing them or requiring them to be proved further as the case may be. The liquidator must then notify those creditors whose claims were allowed and those whose claims require to be proved further within certain time limits[450]. The result of the adjudication process must be certified by the Examiner[451].

[25.175] Save in cases where the official liquidator or the court Examiner requires claims to be proven on affidavit[452], claims ought to be made in writing and sent by post to the liquidator[453]. Unless the liquidator requires a creditor to attend and prove his claim further, the costs of proving the claim shall be borne by the creditor[454]. Those required to prove their debts are entitled to their costs where the claim is proved[455].

(b) Discounting claims

[25.176] Where a creditor has agreed to give the debtor company a discount in respect of, for example, the sale of goods, then the creditor must deduct from his claim any such trade discount to which the company would have been entitled if it had not gone into liquidation and any interest in excess of 2.5%[456].

---

446 Citing *Pulsford v Devenish* [1903] 2 Ch 625, *Re Armstrong Whitworth Securities Company Ltd* [1947] 1 Ch 673 and *Austin Securities v Northgate* [1969] 1 WLR 529.

447 *Austin Securities v Northgate* [1969] 1 WLR 529 at 532.

448 RSC, Ord 74, r 97.

449 See *Re Money Markets International Stockbrokers* [2012] IEHC 214 where McGovern J found a claim to be statute barred after reviewing the decisions in *Re General Rolling Stock Co Ltd* [1872] LR 7 Ch App 646 and *Financial Services Compensation Scheme v Larnell (Insurances) Ltd* [2006] QB 808.

450 RSC, Ord 74, r 98.

451 RSC, Ord 74, r 101.

452 As to the form and content, see RSC, Ord 74, r 103.

453 RSC, Ord 74, r 102.

454 RSC, Ord 74, r 104.

455 RSC, Ord 74, r 99.

456 RSC, Ord 74, r 105.

(c) Contingent and periodical liabilities

[25.177] Although a claim may be unascertained, it may still be proved by a creditor. An example is provided by Macfarlane's Claim[457] where a person had taken out a fire insurance policy with the company concerned. Even though no claim had arisen under the policy, it was held the person's claim in respect of the premium paid should be admitted[458]. Such is a contingent claim and is provable[459].

[25.178] A person who is entitled to recurring or periodical payments from a company may also prove against the company[460]. The creditor may prove for a proportionate part of a periodic payment only up to the date of the commencement of the winding up, save in the case of rent due to a landlord under a lease of land or property where the liquidator remains in possession. In such a case, the creditor landlord is entitled to further rent[461]. Even if the liquidator does not remain in possession, the creditor may claim for damages arising from the breach of, for example, a lease[462].

(d) Creditors' claims for interest[463]

[25.179] By reason of the application of the rules of bankruptcy to insolvent liquidations, the general rule is that creditors of a company may prove for interest. The sorts of interest for which a creditor may prove can be contractual interest[464], statutory interest on a judgment or interest under Ord 74, r 107 of the RSC[465]. The entitlement of a creditor to claim for interest in a winding up depends upon his status. In an insolvent liquidation, unsecured creditors and preferential creditors are entitled to prove for interest up to the date of the resolution to wind up in a voluntary winding up and to the date of the presentation of the petition in an insolvent official winding up[466].

[25.180] The general rule is that a secured creditor is entitled to claim for interest up to the date of repayment of the debt secured. By virtue of the incorporation of the laws of bankruptcy into the law of corporate insolvency, it has been held that interest is payable *after* the commencement of the winding up in priority to the claims of other creditors and of shareholders to the residue. In *Re McCairns (PMPA) plc*[467], the Supreme Court, reversing the judgment of Costello J, held that a bank was entitled to claim against its security for post-liquidation interest out of the proceeds of sale of a site after the liquidation. There, a chargee bank consented to the sale of a site by the liquidator of the

---

457 *Macfarlane's Claim* (1880) 17 Ch D 337.

458 See also *Butler v Broadhead* [1974] 2 All ER 401.

459 See RSC, Ord 74, r 108.

460 RSC, Ord 74, r 106.

461 *Re CHA Ltd* [1997] 1 IR 437, Laffoy J. See para **[25.169]**.

462 See *Re House Property and Investment Co Ltd* [1953] 2 All ER 1525.

463 See Marshall, 'Interested in Interest? A Perspective on Liquidations' (1994) 1 CLP 35.

464 See *Trustee Savings Bank Dublin v Maughan* [1992] 1 IR 488.

465 *Re Car Replacements Ltd* (11 May 1992, unreported) HC, *per* Murphy J.

466 *Re Amalgamated Investment and Property Company Ltd* [1984] 3 All ER 272; *Re Lines Bros Ltd (No 4)* [1982] 2 All ER 183.

467 *Re McCairns (PMPA) plc* [1989] ILRM 19. See [1989] ILRM 501 for the judgment of Costello J considered by Woolfe, (1989) DULJ 113.

company over which it held three charges. On the sale of the site, difficulties arose as to who was entitled to what monies. In the Supreme Court, McCarthy J held[468]:

> 'In my judgment, not having brought the property the subject of the charge into the winding up and not having sought to prove any claim in the winding up, the bank is entitled to be paid interest up to the date of redemption, in accordance with the terms of the charging documents.'

It should be noted that the decision of the Supreme Court only applies to situations where a secured creditor stays outside the winding up[469].

[25.181] A different situation arises where a *solvent* company is wound up and a dispute arises between the creditors' claims for interest after the commencement of the winding up and the shareholders' claims to the company's surplus assets. In *Re Hibernian Transport Company Ltd*[470], it was held by the Supreme Court that where a company was wound up solvent, s 284 of the CA 1963 did not apply and, accordingly, the normal bankruptcy rules did not apply. In that case, it was held that creditors who were entitled to contractual interest could claim interest up to the date on which their debts were discharged. The company's shareholders were entitled to any balance remaining after the payment of contractual interest to creditors, all outstanding debts and liabilities, and all fees, costs and expenses of the liquidator pursuant to s 242 of the CA 1963[471].

Priorities in a distribution

[25.182] After the debts due to the holders of fixed mortgages and charges have been satisfied, trust property has been excluded, set-off has happened, super-preferential debts have been discharged, stamp duty paid on the proceeds of realisation and provision made for the costs and expenses of the winding up, the liquidator will be left with a sum available for distribution. Distribution of the realised assets must be carried out in accordance with the priorities dictated by law. The priority of distribution is as follows:

(a) Preferential creditors.

(b) Floating charges.

(c) Unsecured creditors.

(d) Members and contributories of the company.

---

468 *Re McCairns (PMPA) plc* [1989] ILRM 19 at 25, reversing *Re Egan Electric Ltd* [1987] IR 398.

469 See para **[25.145]**.

470 *Re Hibernian Transport Company Ltd* [1994] 1 ILRM 48.

471 See generally *Re Lines Bros Ltd* [1984] BCLC 215; *Re Fine Industrial Commodities Ltd* [1956] Ch 256; *Re Rolls Royce Ltd* [1974] 1 WLR 1584; *Re Oldham Tradesmens' Insurance Company Ltd* (19 December 1980) HC (UK), Vinelott J; *Re Humber Ironworks and Shipbuilders Co* [1869] 41 Ch App 643; *Re Contract Corporation* [1871] LR 5 Ch App 112; *Re Imperial Land Company of Marseilles* [1871] LR 11 Eq 478; *Re Joint Stock Discount Company* [1869] LR 5 Ch App 86; *Re Alfred O'Dwyer & Co Ltd* (11 November 1988, unreported) HC, *per* Costello J; *Re Thomas Burgess* [1988] 23 LR Ir 5; *Re Michael Orr (Kilternan) Ltd* [1986] IR 273; and *Re Egan Electric Co Ltd* [1987] IR 398 which was reversed by the Supreme Court in *Re McCairns (PMPA) plc* [1992] ILRM 19.

(a) Preferential creditors

[25.183] Section 275(1)(a) of the CA 1963 provides that subject to the provisions of the Act as to preferential payments, the property of a company on its winding up shall be applied in satisfaction of its liabilities *pari passu*[472]. That principle is ousted, however, by s 285(2) of the CA 1963 in favour of preferential creditors which provides that in a winding up 'there shall be paid in priority to all other debts' certain preferential debts. Persons who are deemed by law to be preferential creditors enjoy an enviable position of priority. Without legislative demarcation, they would otherwise be mere unsecured creditors who would be entitled *pari passu* to share in the distribution of those assets available after the payment of the holders of floating charges. The Oireachtas has deemed certain persons and institutions to come within this select class of creditors, on grounds entirely based on public policy. To the fore in this favoured class are the Revenue Commissioners. Many will agree with the revenue's priority: we want to see others pay their taxes in much the same way as we all want to go to heaven. However, injustice is often perpetrated by this loaded ranking, and small creditors who have advanced credit to the company concerned and who rank *after* the preferred few may themselves face bankruptcy or liquidation as a result of the revenue's claims being *preferred* to theirs. However, other creditors who are members of this preferred club, such as employees who are owed wages, are more deserving of their membership. From this it must be recognised that the categorisation of certain persons as preferential creditors is based on purely normative factors.

[25.184] The claims of preferential creditors do not arise in liquidations alone and, as noted in a previous chapter, a receiver is obliged by s 98 of the CA 1963 to discharge the claims of preferential creditors out of the proceeds of his realisation[473]. In *Re H William (Tallaght) Ltd*[474], a company had been in receivership and the receiver had discharged the preferential creditors' claims. The company subsequently went into liquidation and the liquidator resisted a further preferential claim by the Revenue Commissioners on the grounds that it was never intended that ss 98 and 285 of the CA 1963 should enable the same creditor to make a preferential claim in a receivership and claim preference again in a subsequent liquidation. Geoghegan J rejected the liquidator's contention, finding the proposition unsustainable in the light of the clear wording in s 285(2) of the CA 1963. As considered below[475], however, there it was found that the revenue's claim was statute barred.

---

472 This is, however, subject to s 275(2) of the CA 1963 which provides that nothing in s 275(1) of the CA 1963: 'shall in any way affect any rights or obligations of the company or any other person arising as a result of any agreement entered into (whether before or after the commencement of section 132 of the Companies Act, 1990) by any person under which any particular liability of the company to any general creditor is postponed in favour or subordinated to the rights or claims of any other person to whom the company may be in any way liable.' The effect is to allow creditors to agree to subordinate liabilities and, therefore, contract out of the *pari passu* principle.

473 See Ch 20, *Corporate Borrowing: Receivers*, para **[20.066]**.

474 *Re H William (Tallaght) Ltd* [1996] 3 IR 531.

475 See para **[25.185]**.

[25.185] Those claims which the law deems to be preferred are contained in s 285 of the CA 1963 and various revenue and employee based statutes. These claims are:

- Rates levied by local authorities[476];
- Capital and income taxes levied by the revenue[477];
- The wages and salaries of employees[478];
- Holiday payments owed to employees[479];
- Social welfare contributions[480];
- Compensation and damages for uninsured accidents to employees[481];
- Sickness and superannuation payments[482];
- Claims for unfair dismissal[483];
- Claims for minimum notice payments[484];
- Redundancy payments to employees[485].

Although these are the 'preferred few' whose claims against the company rank only after the payment of the costs and expenses incurred in the winding up, this order of priority shall apply only to those debts which are notified, or 'have become known' to the liquidator within six months of his advertisement for claims in at least two daily newspapers[486]. In *Re H William (Tallaght) Ltd*[487], Geoghegan J held that the six-month time limit could not be extended. In that case, the Revenue Commissioners did not notify the liquidator of its claim to corporation tax within the six-month period. The learned judge rejected the argument that the company's corporation tax liability must 'have become known' to the liquidator on the grounds that the liquidator's affidavit makes it clear that he was not aware of the tax liability within the six-month period. Moreover, it was held that there had to be either actual notification or actual knowledge: constructive knowledge would not suffice.

[25.186] Where the assets are insufficient to go around amongst the preferential creditors, then all preferential creditors rank *pari passu* and will each receive so many cent for every euro owed[488].

---

476 Section 285(2)(a)(i) of the CA 1963.

477 Section 285(2)(a)(ii) of the CA 1963; Income Tax Act 1967; Capital Gains Tax Act 1975; Corporation Tax Act 1976; Value Added Tax Act 1972; and Finance Act 1972.

478 Section 285(2) of the CA 1963; s 10 of the C(A)A 1982; see *Re Castlemahon Poultry Products Ltd* [1987] ILRM 222.

479 Section 285(2) of the CA 1963.

480 Section 295(2) of the CA 1963.

481 Section 285(2) of the CA 1963. In *Re Irish ISPAT Ltd* [2004] IEHC 604, Carroll J refused to find that hearing loss claims incurred by employees in the course of their employment resulted from an accident or series of accidents so as to come within the category of preferential creditors.

482 Section 285(2) of the CA 1963.

483 Section 12 of the Unfair Dismissals Act 1977.

484 Minimum Notice and Terms of Employment Act 1973.

485 Redundancy Payments Acts 1967–1979.

486 Section 285(14) of the CA 1963.

487 *Re H William (Tallaght) Ltd* [1996] 3 IR 531.

488 Section 285(7)(a) of the CA 1963.

[25.187] It has been held that directors who have valid contracts of employment with the company will be deemed to be employees for the purposes of bringing them within the category of preferential creditor. In *Re Dairy Lee Ltd*[489], a director who was held to be an employee under an oral contract of employment had his claim admitted as a preferential debt[490]. Even where a director does not have an express contract of employment, it may be proved on the facts that where he works full-time for the company and draws a salary, he may be an employee under an implied contract of employment[491].

[25.188] Section 285(6) provides that where a payment has been made, *inter alia*, to an employee on account of salary, etc, out of money advanced by some person for that purpose, the person who advanced the money shall in a winding up have a right or priority in respect of the money advanced and paid to the amount by which the sum in respect of which the employee 'would have been entitled to priority in the winding up has been diminished by reason of the payment having been made'. In *Re Bell Lines Ltd and others*[492], the Supreme Court held that the English Insolvency Service and the Department of Employment and Learning in Northern Ireland, which had made payments to the employees of an insolvent Irish company in respect of wages, holiday pay and pension, had such a priority.

(b) Floating charges

[25.189] Although the holder of a floating charge is a secured creditor, his security is very much less than that enjoyed by the holder of a fixed charge or mortgage. What the legislature has given to secured creditors generally, the legislature has taken away from creditors secured by a floating charge. Section 285(7)(b) of the CA 1963 provides that the preferential claims, listed above[493], shall:

> '... so far as the assets of the company available for payment of general creditors are insufficient to meet them, have priority over the claims of holders of debentures under any floating charge created by the company, and be paid accordingly out of any property comprised in or subject to that charge.'

Accordingly, the effect of s 285(7)(b) is to oust the operation of s 136(2) of the Bankruptcy Act 1988, considered above[494]. For this reason, claims secured by a floating charge take subsequent to preferential claims.

[25.190] Before crystallisation, assets which are the subject of a floating charge can be whittled away through set-off, execution of process, and subsequent fixed charges where the holder of the fixed charge does not have notice of the existence of the prior floating

---

489 *Re H William (Tallaght) Ltd* [1976] IR 314.

490 See *Re Beeton & Co Ltd* [1913] 2 Ch 279 and *Lee v Lee's Air Farming Ltd* [1961] AC 12.

491 In this respect the court will apply a similar test to that applied in deciding whether or not a person is employed under a contract of service or contract for services, the latter making them an independent contractor; see *Re Sunday Tribune Ltd* [1985] ILRM 698.

492 *Re Bell Lines Ltd and others* [2010] IESC 15; High Court decision of Dunne J reported at [2006] IEHC 188.

493 See para **[25.185]**.

494 See para **[25.143]**.

charge[495]. After crystallisation, the assets subject to the floating charge become subject to a quasi-fixed charge.

[25.191] If a surplus remains after the preferential creditors have been paid, the holder of a floating charge is next in line. Where there are insufficient assets to satisfy the claims of all those whose claims are secured by floating charges the priority of payment will usually be based on the priority of the creation of their security.

(c) Unsecured creditors

[25.192] Next in line in an insolvent liquidation are those unfortunates who have advanced money, goods or services to the company without taking any security, or those whose security has been set aside. Their position is most vulnerable and in an insolvent liquidation, by definition, there will not be sufficient assets left to satisfy their claims. Where there are some but not enough assets to pay all of the claims of the unsecured creditors, the unsecured creditors will rank *pari passu* amongst themselves.

(d) Members and contributories of the company

[25.193] In a *solvent* liquidation, there may be a surplus remaining after all other creditors have been paid, and if there is that surplus will be available for distribution amongst the members of the company: s 275 of the CA 1963[496]. Members who are owed dividends by the company when it goes into liquidation do not lose their claims, although they will not rank as creditors of the company[497]. Rather, they will only be paid after all other creditors have been paid, whereupon, any sum so due to a member shall be taken into account for the purpose of finally adjusting the rights of the contributories of the company: s 207(1)(g) of the CA 1963[498]. The basic rule here is that sums due to a member 'in his character of a member' will only be paid after all creditors have been paid. The equivalent English provision[499] was considered in *Soden v British and Commonwealth Holdings plc*[500]. In that case, British and Commonwealth Holdings plc ('B&C') had acquired the entire issued share capital in Atlantic Computers plc ('A'). The acquisition proved to be disastrous for both companies and both were ultimately placed into administration. B&C instituted proceedings against A for alleged negligent misrepresentations in connection with its purchase of A's shares. A's liabilities greatly exceeded its assets – an arrangement was eventually approved by the court whereby all creditors would rank *pari passu* in the distribution of the company's assets. The administrators sought a declaration that, were B&C to be successful in its action for damages for negligent misrepresentation, it would not be entitled to share in that distribution. The basis for seeking the declaration was s 74(2)(f) of the Insolvency Act 1986 (UK) which, like s 207(1)(g) of the CA 1963, subordinates sums due to a member 'in his character of a member'. In the High Court, Court of Appeal and eventually the

495 See Ch 18, *Corporate Borrowing: Debentures and Security*, para **[18.090]** *et seq.*

496 See *Re Consolidated Gold Fields of New Zealand Ltd* [1953] All ER 791; *Re LB Holliday & Co Ltd* [1986] BCLC 227; and *Re Belfast Empire Theatre of Varieties Ltd* [1963] IR 41.

497 See *Wilson (Inspector of Taxes) v Dunnes Stores (Cork) Ltd* (22 January 1976, unreported) HC, *per* Kenny J.

498 See Ch 8, *Shares and Membership*, para **[8.077]**.

499 Section 74(2)(f) of the Insolvency Act 1986 (UK).

500 *Soden and another v British and Commonwealth Holdings plc* [1997] 4 All ER 353.

House of Lords it was consistently held that B&C *would* be entitled to share *pari passu* with other creditors in the distribution of A's assets because if B&C were awarded damages, those damages would be owed to B&C as a creditor, and not in its capacity as a member. In the House of Lords, Lord Browne-Wilkinson held:

> 'Section 74(2)(f) requires a distinction to be drawn between, on the one hand, sums due to a member in his character of a member by way of dividends, profits or otherwise and, on the other hand, sums due to a member otherwise than in his character as a member. In the absence of any other indication to the contrary, sums due in the character of a member must be sums falling due under and by virtue of the statutory contract between the members and the company and the members inter se constituted by s 14(1) of the Companies Act 1985 [ie, s 25 of the CA 1963] … In my judgment, in the absence of any contrary indication sums due to a member "in his character of a member" are only those sums the right to which is based by way of cause of action on the statutory contract'[501].

In the circumstances, the House of Lords held that any damages payable were not due in the capacity of a member and that the claim against A stood on exactly the same footing as any other claim by other creditors.

[25.194] In an official or compulsory liquidation, it is the duty of the court to settle a list of contributories[502] and to cause the assets of the company to be collected and applied in discharge of its liabilities: s 235(1) of the CA 1963. Moreover, by s 242 of the CA 1963 it is provided that:

> 'The court shall adjust the rights of the contributories among themselves and distribute any surplus among the persons entitled thereto.'

Accordingly, in an official winding up it is the duty of the court to determine which member contributories are entitled to which assets. By contrast, in a members' or creditors' voluntary winding up, it is the duty and function of the liquidator, after paying the debts of the company, to adjust the rights of the member contributories, distributing any surplus among them by virtue of s 276(2) of the CA 1963.

[25.195] Section 275(1)(b) of the CA 1963[503] provides that on every winding up[504] the property of a company shall, unless the articles of association provide otherwise, be distributed among the members according to their rights and interests in the company. The rights of all members cannot, however, be assumed to be equal. Individual shareholders may have different rights by virtue of the class of shares held by them, the rights accorded to such shares by the company's memorandum or articles of association and any shareholders' agreements that subsist between the shareholding members. In particular, conflicts may arise between the holders of ordinary shares and the holders of preferential shares to participate in a surplus of assets after the payment of a preferential dividend[505].

---

501 *Soden and another v British and Commonwealth Holdings plc* [1997] 4 All ER 353 at 357.

502 Only if necessary to make calls on or adjust the rights of contributories, otherwise the court may dispense with the settlement of a list of contributories: s 235(2) of the CA 1963.

503 See s 132 of the CA 1990.

504 Section 274 of the CA 1963 provides that ss 275–282 of the CA 1963 shall apply to every voluntary winding up, whether a members' or a creditors' winding up.

505 See generally, Ch 8, *Shares and Membership*, para **[8.109]** *et seq*; and *Re Cork Electric Supply Co Ltd* [1931] IR 314.

Distributions *in specie*

[25.196] One reason why a solvent company may be wound up is where the members wish to legally take the assets out of the company by means of a *distribution in specie*, ie, in the form of the assets and not in their equivalent in, say, cash. As Laffoy has commented:

> '... in the case of a private company, for example, a property holding company, it is frequently more desirable to vest the company's lands and premises in the members in specie on a members' voluntary winding up than to realise the assets and distribute the proceeds of realisation[506].'

[25.197] The first prerequisite to distributing a company's assets amongst its members, *in specie*, is that the company must be placed into members' voluntary liquidation. All of the formalities attendant upon this process and considered in Chapter 23[507] must be complied with in all respects[508]. In addition, it is necessary that the company's articles of association expressly provide for a distribution *in specie*. Regulation 137 of Table A provides:

> If the company is wound up, the liquidator may, with the sanction of a special resolution of the company and any other sanction required by the Act, divide among the members in specie or kind the whole or any part of the assets of the company (whether they shall consist of property of the same kind or not) and may, for such purpose, set such value as he deems fair upon any property to be divided as aforesaid and may determine how such division shall be carried out as between the members or different classes of members. The liquidator may, with the like sanction, vest the whole or any part of such assets in trustees upon such trusts for the benefit of the contributories as the liquidator, with the like sanction, shall think fit, but so that no member shall be compelled to accept any shares or other securities whereon there is any liability.

Care should be taken to ensure that such a provision is contained in a company's articles of association (or memorandum of association) before proceeding with a distribution *in specie*[509]. Since a liquidator is only entitled to make a distribution *in specie* where there are surplus assets, it is good practice to prepare a statutory declaration from the liquidator, for the members' benefit, confirming this fact[510]. It should be noted that where the effect of a distribution *in specie* is that a member director is to acquire a non-cash asset of the requisite amount (within the meaning of s 29(1)(a) of the CA 1990) such a substantial property transaction is expressly exempted by s 29(8) where the arrangement is made with a person 'in his character as such member', as would be the case in a distribution *in specie*[511].

---

506 Laffoy, *Irish Conveyancing Precedents* (looseleaf, Bloomsbury Professional), E264.

507 See Ch 23, *Winding Up Companies,* at paras **[23.002]** to **[23.009]**.

508 See *Re Strathblaine Estates Ltd* [1948] Ch 228, noted in Ch 4, *Incorporation and its Consequences*, para **[4.038]**.

509 Laffoy, *Irish Conveyancing Precedents* (Bloomsbury Professional), E264: 'in the absence of an express provision in either the memorandum or the articles of association, it is doubtful whether the liquidator has power to distribute the company's assets in specie on a winding-up.'

510 See Laffoy, *Irish Conveyancing Precedents* (looseleaf, Bloomsbury Professional), E264.

511 See Ch 16, *Statutory Regulation of Directors' Transactions*, para **[16.041]**.

[25.198] The great attraction with distributions *in specie* is that the company's real property can be conveyed or otherwise transferred to the company's members without the payment of *ad valorem* stamp duty. This is because *ad valorem* duty is not chargeable where a conveyance is from a trustee to a beneficiary[512]. In a distribution *in specie*, a liquidator will be a trustee for the members[513]. Even though money may not pass from the member to the company, the Revenue Commissioners must be satisfied that the distribution to members is being carried out in proportion to their entitlement as members to participate. Members' entitlement to participate will turn on their shareholding as at the date of the resolution to wind up the company, and it should be noted that shareholdings are *prima facie* immutable after the commencement of a winding up on account of s 255 of the CA 1963 which provides that 'any transfer of shares, not being a transfer made to or with the sanction of the liquidator, and any alteration in the status of the members of the company' made after the commencement of a voluntary winding up, is void.

---

512 Section 30(5) of the Stamp Duties Consolidation Act 1999.

513 Cf *Wigan Coal and Iron Co Ltd v Inland Revenue Commissioners* [1945] 1 All ER 392 where it was held that a company could not be the trustee of its own assets for its members and that any disposition to them operated as an *inter vivos* disposition that attracted *ad valorem* stamp duty.

Chapter 26

Strike-Off and Restoration

[26.001] Perhaps the most ignominious fate to befall a company is where it is struck off the register of companies. Being struck off the register is usually 'courted' by the company's controllers or advisors in their failure to file annual returns, contrary to ss 125 and 126 of the CA 1963[1]. While striking off may be regarded as being almost the 'just deserts'[2] of dormant companies, often it befalls the careless company, whose controllers may be more interested in conducting business than observing the Companies Acts. While certainly not intended to mitigate the omissions of such companies, it does explain why legislation also provides for the reinstatement of such companies.

[26.002] Strike-off is the registrar of companies' most powerful weapon in the war of attrition against non-compliance with filing and other requirements. In the 1990s and 2000s there was a dramatic increase in the numbers of companies that had been struck off the register, primarily for failure to file annual returns[3]. The increase followed the registrar's commencement of an extensive strike-off regime in September 1998 whereby companies that were in default with their obligation to file annual returns were selected at random for the initiation of the strike-off procedure. During 1999, over 28,000 companies were involuntarily struck off, the majority being private companies limited by shares. Involuntary strike-off almost invariably results from the company's failure to file its annual returns for two consecutive years. In consequence of the changes effected by the C(A)(No 2)A 1999, the registrar now has power to strike off where annual returns have not been filed for just one year[4].

[26.003] Where a company has been struck off the register and dissolved, subject to certain conditions being satisfied, it can for a period of up to one year be restored and reinstated to the register by the administrative act of the registrar and, for a period of up to 20 years be restored and reinstated by order of the court. In this Chapter, the law relating to striking off the register and restoration to the register is considered.

---

1. See Ch 17, *Financial Statements, Audit and Annual Return*, at para **[17.250]** *et seq*.
2. See McCormack, *The New Companies Legislation* (1991, Round Hall Press) at p 11.
3. See *Companies Report, 1999*, at pp 47, 48.
4. See para **[26.006]** *post*.

[A] STRIKING OFF THE REGISTER[5]

[26.004] The power of the registrar of companies to strike a company off the register is found in s 12 of the C(A)A 1982[6] and s 311 of the CA 1963[7]. Both of these sections have been heavily amended by the C(A)(No 2)A 1999. Here, the law on strike-off is considered under the following headings:

1. The grounds for strike-off.
2. The effect of strike-off on the liability of directors, officers and members.
3. The effect of strike-off on corporate property.
4. Trading whilst struck-off.
5. The winding up of dissolved companies.

The grounds for strike-off[8]

[26.005] There are five distinct circumstances in which the registrar of companies can cause a company to be struck off the register. These are:

(a) Failure to make an annual return;
(b) Failure to deliver required particulars to the revenue;
(c) Ceasing to carry on business;
(d) Having no recorded directors;
(e) Failure to have at least one EEA resident director.

It should be remembered that strike-off will not always be involuntary. Where a company ceases to trade and has no outstanding creditors, it is open to such a company to voluntarily initiate the strike-off procedure by requesting that the registrar strikes off the company under s 311 of the CA 1963. This is facilitated by ground (c) above, ie, *ceasing to carry on business*[9].

(a) Failure to make an annual return

[26.006] By far the most common ground for the involuntary striking-off of companies is where they fail to make their annual return. Section 12(1) of the C(A)A 1982[10] provides:

> 'Without prejudice to the generality of section 311 of the CA 1963, where a company does not, for one or more years, make an annual return required by section 125 or 126 of the CA 1963, the Registrar of Companies may send to the company by post a registered letter stating that, unless all annual returns which are outstanding are delivered to him within 1 month of the date of the letter, a notice will be published in *Iris Oifigiúil*

5 See, generally, Cahill, *Company Law Compliance and Enforcement* (2008, Bloomsbury Professional) at pp 713–735.

6 See generally, MacCann, 'Striking off the Register and Section 12 of the Companies (Amendment) Act 1982' (1990) Gazette ILSI 125.

7 As amended by s 11 of the C(A)A 1982 and s 8(2) and (3) of the C(A)A 1983.

8 For the practice and procedure of strike-off, see McGowan-Smyth & Daly, *Irish Company Secretary's Handbook* (2011, Bloomsbury Professional) at p 1201.

9 See para **[26.009]** *post*.

10 As replaced by s 46 of the C(A)(No 2)A 1999 and amended by s 72 of the IFCMPA 2005.

[the Companies Registration Office Gazette][11] with a view to striking the name of the company off the register.'

Where the registrar either (a) receives an answer to the effect that the company is not carrying on business or (b) does not within one month of the initial notice receive all outstanding annual returns, the registrar may then publish a notice in *Iris Oifigiúil* stating that after one month from the date of the notice, the name of the company shall be struck off the register, unless all annual returns are delivered to the Companies Registration Office ('CRO')[12]. Subject to the foregoing, at the expiration of the time in the notice and unless cause to the contrary is shown, the registrar then has statutory power to strike off a company's name from the register whereupon the registrar must publish a further notice in *Iris Oifigiúil* and on publication of that notice, the company is dissolved[13].

(b) Failure to deliver required particulars to the revenue

[26.007] Section 882(1) of the Taxes Consolidation Act (as inserted by s 83 of the Finance Act 1999) requires that every company, incorporated in the State or which commences to carry on a trade, profession or business within the State, shall within 30 days either of certain stated events[14], deliver a written statement to the Revenue Commissioners[15]. This statement must state: (i) the name of the company; (ii) the company's registered office; (iii) the address of its principal place of business; (iv) the name and address of the secretary; (v) the date of commencement of the trade, profession or business; (vi) the nature of such trade, profession or business; (vii) the date to which accounts relating to such trade, profession or business will be made up; (viii) such other information as the Revenue Commissioners may consider necessary. In addition, in the case of companies that are incorporated, but not resident in the State, and companies that are neither incorporated nor resident in the State, certain additional information is required[16]. This measure, which along with s 23A of the Taxes Consolidation Act 1997 (as inserted by s 82 of the Finance Act 1999) was intended to combat the problem posed by non-resident Irish companies[17], is considerably strengthened by s 12A of the C(A)A 1982. Section 882(3) of the Finance Act 1999 provides:

---

11 Although s 12(1), (2) and (3) of the C(A)A 1982 were amended by s 72 of the IFCMPA 2005, by the substitution for '*Iris Oifigiúil*', of 'the Companies Registration Office Gazette', s 72 has not as at the date of writing been commenced.

12 Section 12(2) of the C(A)A 1982.

13 Section 12(3) of the C(A)A 1982.

14 The stated events are: (a) the date it commences to carry on a trade, profession or business, wherever carried on, (b) the date at which there is a material change in information previously delivered by the company under that section; and (c) the giving of a notice to the company by an inspector requiring a statement under that section: s 882(2) of the Taxes Consolidation Act 1997.

15 This section applies: (a) in the case of companies that are incorporated on or after 11 February 1999, as on and from that date; and (b) in the case of companies that are incorporated before 11 February 1999, as on and from 1 October 1999: s 83(2) of the Finance Act 1999.

16 Section 83(2)(i) and (iii) of the Finance Act 1999.

17 See Ch 2, *Incorporation by Registration*, at para **[2.045]**.

> 'Where a company fails to deliver a statement which it is required to deliver under this section then, notwithstanding any obligations as to secrecy or other restriction upon disclosure of information imposed by or under any statute or otherwise, the Revenue Commissioners may give a notice in writing to the Registrar of Companies (within the meaning of the Companies Act, 1963) stating that the company has so failed to deliver a statement under this section.'

Enter s 12A of the C(A)A 1982. Section 12A(1) provides:

> 'Where the Revenue Commissioners give a notice in writing under subsection (3) of section 882 (inserted by the Finance Act, 1999) of the Taxes Consolidation Act, 1997, to the Registrar of Companies stating that a company has failed to deliver a statement which it is required to deliver under that section, then, without prejudice to section 311 of the CA 1963 or section 12 of this Act, the registrar may send to the company by post a registered letter stating that, unless the company delivers to the Revenue Commissioners the said statement within 1 month of the date of the letter, a notice will be published in *Iris Oifigiúil* [the Companies Registration Office Gazette][18] with a view to striking the name of the company off the register.'

Where the company does not deliver the required statement to the Revenue Commissioners within one month of the date of the registrar's warning letter, the registrar may publish a notice in *Iris Oifigiúil* stating that one month after the published notice, the name of the company will, unless the statement is delivered to the revenue, be struck off the register and the company dissolved[19]. Subject to the foregoing, at the expiration of the time in the published notice and unless cause to the contrary is shown, the registrar then has statutory power to strike off a company's name from the register whereupon she must publish a further notice in *Iris Oifigiúil* and, on publication of that notice, the company is dissolved[20].

[26.008] Protection against any action for breach of confidentiality against the revenue is afforded by s 12D of the C(A)A 1982. This provides that the revenue may disclose to the registrar any information in its possession required by the registrar for the purposes of that determination.

(c) Ceasing to carry on business

[26.009] It will be noticed that both of the two grounds, last considered, are expressed to be 'without prejudice to' s 311 of the CA 1963, which contains the generic ground for striking companies off the register, namely that a company is not 'carrying on business'. Section 311(1) of the CA 1963 provides:

> 'Where the Registrar of Companies has reasonable cause to believe that a company is not carrying on business, he may send to the company by post a registered letter inquiring whether the company is carrying on business and stating that, if an answer is not received within one month from the date of that letter, a notice will be published in *Iris Oifigiúil*

---

18 Although s 12A(1), (2) and (3) of the C(A)A 1982 was amended by s 72 of the IFCMPA 2005, by the substitution for '*Iris Oifigiúil*', of 'the Companies Registration Office Gazette', s 72 has not as at the date of writing been commenced.

19 Section 12A(2) of the C(A)A 1982.

20 Section 12A(3) of the C(A)A 1982.

[the Companies Registration Office Gazette][21] with a view to striking the name of the company off the register.'

The consequences that follow from this warning are similar to those that flow where a warning is issued under both ss 12 and 12A of the C(A)A 1982. So, if the registrar either receives an answer to the effect that the company is not carrying on business or, does not receive any answer within one month after sending the letter, the registrar may publish a notice in *Iris Oifigiúil* and send to the company a notice by registered post, stating that after one month from the date of the notice, the company will be struck off the register unless cause is shown to the contrary[22]. At the expiration of the time mentioned in the notice, the registrar is again empowered, unless cause to the contrary is previously shown, to strike the company's name off the register, in which case the registrar must publish notice thereof in *Iris Oifigiúil* and, upon such publication, the company is dissolved.

[26.010] Section 311(1) of the CA 1963 is the legal basis for the registrar of companies' *voluntary strike-off process*, which facilitates corporate euthanasia. This process acknowledges that companies can take the initiative to be struck off and that the registrar can be approached to exercise her powers under s 311(1) by being tendered 'reasonable cause to believe that a company is not carrying on business'. In March 2011, the registrar by administrative notice set out the following conditions which a private limited company must meet in order to avail of the voluntary strike-off regime:

(a) The company must have ceased trading or never have traded and must not re-commence or commence trading in the period from application to its being struck off;

(b) As at the date of the application for strike off:

  (i) The amount of the assets of the company must not exceed €150;

  (ii) The amount of the liabilities of the company (including contingent and prospective liabilities) does not exceed €150;

  (iii) The company does not have and did not have in the previous three years an issued share capital in excess of €150;

(c) All of the company's filing obligations under the Companies Acts must be fully up to date; and

(d) The company's tax affairs must be in order.

While condition (b)(iii) – the requirement for the company not to have had an issued share capital in excess of €150 in the previous three years – is new and will exclude many companies from applying for voluntary strike off, the procedure is, nevertheless, a very useful and pragmatic method of culling moribund and unwanted companies.

[26.011] Although the administrative procedure does not require the express consent of shareholders, it is thought that the directors of a company do not have express authority under Table A articles of association to make such an application. While reg 80

---

[21] Although s 311(1) and (2) of the CA 1963 was amended by s 72 of the IFCMPA 2005, by the substitution for '*Iris Oifigiúil*', of 'the Companies Registration Office Gazette', s 72 has not as at the date of writing been commenced.

[22] Section 311(2) of the CA 1963.

delegates the very wide power to manage the business of the company, applying to have the company struck off is, it is certainly arguable, not so authorised, strike-off being the very antithesis of carrying on business. To avoid any claims by a minority under s 205 of the CA 1963, it is thought that while the registrar may not require evidence of the shareholders' consent, the directors should obtain the assent of the company's shareholders before proceeding to apply for strike-off. Alternatively, the articles may by special resolution be amended to authorise the director to so apply on such conditions as may be provided for in the articles.

[26.012] A particular application of the cessation of business ground is where a company is 'half-wound-up'; this is provided by s 311(3) of the CA 1963. This provides that where a company is being wound up and the registrar has reasonable cause to believe either (a) that no liquidator is acting or (b) that the affairs of the company are fully wound up and the returns required to be made by the liquidator have not been made for a period of six consecutive months, the registrar may publish in *Iris Oifigiúil* and send to the company (or liquidator, if any)[23] a like notice as is provided for in s 311(2). In such circumstances, a company is clearly not carrying on business and this power permits the registrar to put the company out of its misery, and tidy up the register, by striking it off the register.

(d) Having no recorded directors

[26.013] This is a sub-set of the ground last considered in s 311(1) of the CA 1963. The essential prerequisite for the registrar's exercise of her power to strike off a company under s 311 is the registrar having 'reasonable cause to believe that a company is not carrying on business'. In addition to companies failing to make their annual returns, the other compliance offence that causes the CRO most concern is the failure to keep the registrar notified of changes in the particulars in directors as required by s 195 of the CA 1963[24]. Apart from the desire to have the register of companies completely up-to-date and a mirror image of the *de facto* particulars of companies, another reason why this is considered so important is that it facilitates the prosecution of defaulting companies' officers. Section 48 of the C(A)(No 2)A 1999 enables the registrar to exercise her statutory power of strike-off where it appears that a company has no directors. This is achieved by providing that where a copy of a notice of resignation or other documentary proof of a person's having ceased to be a director is forwarded to the registrar pursuant to s 195(11A) and (11B) of the CA 1963 and the result is that there are no persons recorded as being officers in the CRO, then this fact affords the registrar 'good grounds for believing that the company is not carrying on business' and provides the requisite cause for the registrar to exercise the powers of strike-off, conferred by s 311(1) of the CA 1963.

---

23 Section 311(9) provides that a notice under that section to a liquidator may be addressed to him at his last known place of business and a letter or notice to a company may be addressed to the company at its registered office or, if no office has been registered, to the care of some officer of the company, or if there is no officer of the company whose name is known to the register, to each of the persons who subscribed the memorandum at the addresses given therein.

24 See Ch 13, *Corporate Governance: Management by the Directors*, at para **[13.096]**.

(e) *Failure to have at least one EEA resident director*

[26.014] The requirement that, subject to certain exceptions, every Irish company must have at least one EEA resident director has been considered in a previous chapter[25]. It is indicative of the seriousness with which the agencies of the State treated the problems caused by the proliferation of Irish registered non-resident companies that the failure to comply with the requirements in s 43(1) and (2) of the C(A)(No 2)A 1999 will cause the registrar's power to strike off to arise. In a curious drafting style, s 43(15) of the C(A)(No 2)A 1999 provides that the provisions of s 311 of the CA 1963 shall apply for the purposes of s 43 of the C(A)(No 2)A 1999 'as they apply for the purposes of that s 311', subject to certain modifications. Those modifications are to s 311(1), (2) and (8) of the CA 1963. The modified s 311(1) provides:

> 'Where the Registrar of Companies has reasonable cause to believe that subsection (1) or, as the case may be, subsection (2) of section 43 of the Companies (Amendment) (No 2) Act, 1999, is not being complied with in relation to a company, he may send to the company by post a registered letter requesting the company to furnish to him evidence that the provision concerned is being complied with and stating that, if that request is not complied with within 1 month from the date of that letter, a notice will be published in the *Iris Oifigiúil* [the Companies Registration Office Gazette][26] with a view to striking the name of the company off the register.'

In the style of the other grounds which allow the registrar to exercise her powers of strike-off, the modified s 311(1), provides that if the register does not, within one month after sending the warning letter, receive satisfactory evidence that s 43(1) and (2) of the C(A)(No 2)A 1999 are being complied with, she may publish notice in *Iris Oifigiúil*. Thereafter, the registrar can send written notice to the company by registered post, to the effect that at the expiration of one month from the date of such notice, the company's name will be struck off the register and the company dissolved unless cause is shown to the contrary.

The effect of strike-off on the liability of directors, officers and members

[26.015] Both s 12B(1) of the C(A)A 1982 and s 311(6) of the CA 1963 (which taken together govern all five grounds for strike-off) provide that the dissolution of a company shall not affect the liability of directors, officers or members of that company 'which shall continue and may be enforced as if the company had not been dissolved'. Members who have an outstanding liability in respect of unpaid shares can also be called upon to honour them. Directors who are guilty of breaches of their duties to the company or contravention of the laws on fraudulent or reckless trading can be similarly pursued.

The effect of strike-off on corporate property

[26.016] Where a company is struck off, many potentially drastic consequences befall it, or more particularly, its assets[27]. Once the company is struck off, it ceases to have any

25 See Ch 13, *Corporate Governance: Management by the Directors*, at para **[13.012]**.

26 Although s 311(1) of the CA 1963 was amended by s 72 of the IFCMPA 2005, by the substitution for '*Iris Oifigiúil*', of 'the Companies Registration Office Gazette', s 72 has not as at the date of writing been commenced.

27 See, MacCann, 'Striking off the Register and Section 12 of the Companies (Amendment) Act 1982' (1990) Gazette ILSI 125.

legal existence. The fate of its assets is not found in the Companies Acts, but rather in the State Property Act 1954 (the 'SPA 1954'). Section 28 of the SPA 1954 provides that where a company is dissolved all of its property, both realty and personalty, including choses in action, automatically vests in the State and is held by the Minister of Finance on behalf of the State[28]. Section 28(2) of the SPA 1954 provides:

> 'Where a body corporate[29] is dissolved, either before, on or after the operative date, the following provisions shall apply and have effect and, in the case of a body corporate dissolved before the operative date, be deemed to have applied and to have had effect as from such dissolution, that is to say—
>
> (a) all land which was vested in or held in trust for such body corporate immediately before its dissolution (other than land held by such body corporate upon trust for another person) shall, immediately upon such dissolution, become and be the property of the State, subject however to any incumbrances or charges affecting the land immediately before such dissolution,
>
> (b) all personal property (excluding chattels real but including choses-in-action) which is vested in or held in trust for such body corporate immediately before its dissolution (other than personal property held by such body corporate upon trust for another person) shall, immediately upon such dissolution become and be State property.'

[26.017] Very often, the directors of companies that have been dissolved are unaware of that fact for some time. Often, it is only when the company wishes to dispose of property or avail of credit facilities that the enormity of strike-off become apparent. Many solicitors attempting to convey lands and buildings on behalf of companies are, on learning of their dissolution from a companies search, obliged to inform their clients that the transaction cannot be completed by reason of the fact that title to the properties has vested in the Minister for Finance! Other companies, however, do not become aware of the fact that they have been dissolved because they or third parties on their behalf have no occasion to conduct a companies office search. Such companies continue to trade whilst struck-off[30] and may even continue to operate banking facilities for industry practice is to search against a company only when it embarks upon a particularly significant transaction – such searches are not routinely conducted. It is not either usual or practical to obtain such a search before effecting a debit or credit to or from a company's account with a lending institution. Indeed, the world of commerce would grind to a slow halt were it to be suggested that in every case of every corporate transaction, a lending institution was to cause a companies office search to be conducted. Where it is discovered that a company has been dissolved, its directors will usually set about the process of seeking to have companies restored to the register[31].

---

28 Far from it being seen as a windfall to the State, the fact that the property of dissolved companies vests in the State ought to cause the State to ponder its liability. The most obvious example would be where a business premises becomes vested in the State; in the event of third party injury whilst on such premises, there must be at least a potential liability for the State in tort.

29 Body corporate is defined so as *not* to include 'a body corporate dissolved by an enactment wherein it is provided that the property of that body corporate shall, on such dissolution, vest in some other person': s 28(1) of the SPA 1954.

30 See para **[26.022]** *post*.

31 See para **[26.025]** *et seq*, *post*.

(a) Application of s 28 of the SPA 1954 to bodies corporate

[26.018] In *Re Clarkes of Ranelagh Ltd and Parmer Products Ltd*[32], the liquidators of two companies sought directions as to whether dividends payable in the windings up to creditors that were due to foreign bodies corporate that had been dissolved had vested in the Minister for Finance. The answer turned upon whether a foreign incorporated body corporate was a 'body corporate' within the meaning of s 28 of the SPA 1954. Finlay Geoghegan J held that s 28 applied to a foreign body corporate and that the dividends in question had become vested in the State.

(b) Mortgaged property: the distinction between real and personal property

[26.019] Real property held by a company which is dissolved and which is subject to a mortgage or charge, vests with the State subject to the interest of the mortgagee or chargee by virtue of s 28(2)(a) of the SPA 1954. It will be noted, however, that there is no such explicit saver for creditors secured by a mortgage or charge over *personalty*, such as a floating or specific chattel mortgage or a floating charge over tangible or intangible personalty. In the case of personal property, s 28(2)(b) provides that such property shall vest in the State and makes no express provision for where a third party has a security interest over such personal property. It is thought, however, that the holder of a security interest in personal property will have a *beneficial interest* in such property and to that extent it does not, unconditionally, vest in the State. Rather, such property is properly excluded from vesting in the State because it is 'held by such body corporate upon trust for another person'. Any other interpretation would be an unconstitutional deprivation of the property interests of the holders of security interests in personal property. Such a provision would be especially likely to be found unconstitutional because there is no justification for distinguishing between real and personal property and that would be a clear arbitrary attack on property rights. Where a third party such as a secured creditor is prejudiced by the operation of s 28(2)(b) it is open to him to petition the court to have the company reinstated to the register of companies, and where such an order is granted, it seems most likely that the court would make the order subject to the rights of that creditor being restored. In practice, it is opined that it is highly unlikely that the Minister for Finance would oppose a third party's security interest to the personal property of a dissolved company.

(c) Property held in trust

[26.020] Property that is held in trust *by* the company is expressly stated not to vest in the State, because the company is not the beneficial owner of that property. An alternative to applying for restoration of a company that was the trustee of property before it was dissolved is to apply for the appointment of a new trustee under s 25 or for a vesting order under s 26 of the Trustee Act 1893. As Laffoy J said in *Re Church*[33]:

> 'Before making an order under either s 25 or s 26 of the Act of 1893 the Court must be satisfied that the property to which the application relates is held in trust. An obvious example is where a company, which was a bare trustee of property having contracted to

32 *Re Clarkes of Ranelagh Ltd and Parmer Products Ltd* [2004] IEHC 320.

33 *Re Church* [2010] IEHC 113.

sell it and having been paid the purchase money, has been dissolved without conveying the property and it is necessary to get in the outstanding legal estate.'

The operation of this principle is seen in *Re Kavanagh & Cantwell*[34] where Costello J held, and the Attorney General conceded, that property which was held in trust by a company which was dissolved did not vest in the State. In that case, the court went on to hold that trust property is beneficially owned by the *cestui que trust*, or beneficial owner, and the legal title to such property could be vested in the beneficiary by the court under s 26 of the Trustee Act 1893 on the grounds that the trustees could not be found. In this respect, Costello J followed the English line of authority in *Re General Accident Assurance Corporation Ltd*[35] and *Re Richard Mills & Co (Brierly Hill)*[36] in preference to the line of authority in *Re No 9 Bomore Road*[37] and *Re Queenstown Dry Dock Ship Building Company*[38] where the court appointed a new trustee under s 25 of the 1893 Act with a consequential vesting order under s 26 of the 1893 Act. Costello J said:

'This Court, whenever it is expedient to appoint a new trustee, and if it is found impracticable to do so without its assistance, may make an order for the appointment of a new trustee under s 25 of the Trustee Act 1893 …

But the court has additional powers under s 26 of the Act. Where a trustee entitled to any land "cannot be found" (sub-section (ii)(c)) the Court may make a vesting order vesting the land in "any such person in any such manner and for any estate as the Court may direct".'

[26.021] In *Re Heidelstone Company Ltd et al*[39], a vendor company and a management company of an apartment complex were both struck off for failure to file annual returns and were dissolved before the scheme of disposal of common areas had been fully implemented. In consequence, the title of the apartment owners (and a townhouse owner) remained incomplete. The solution identified by the applicant apartment and townhouse owners was to apply for an order under s 26 of the Trustee Act 1893 vesting the interest of the vendor company and or in the alternative the management company in a new management company which the applicants had incorporated. Laffoy J adopted a similar approach to resolve the problem to that adopted by Costello J in *Re Kavanagh & Cantwell*[40], and made a vesting order under s 26 of the 1893 Act vesting the estate in the new management company for all the estate, right, title and interest as the dissolved companies had, subject to the leases and the easements that had been created. Of interest is Laffoy J's observation that the existence of a remedy under the Companies Acts did not preclude an order under the 1893 Act:

'It is not inconceivable that prior to 26th October 2010[41] an application might be brought under s 12B(3) of the Companies (Amendment) Act 1982 to have the First Company restored to the Register of Companies. If such an application were successful, the First

---

34 *Re Kavanagh & Cantwell* (23 November 1984, unreported) HC, Costello J.

35 *Re General Accident Assurance Corporation Ltd* [1904] 1 Ch 147.

36 *Re Richard Mills & Co (Brierly Hill)* [1905] WN 36.

37 *Re No 9 Bomore Road* [1906] 1 Ch 359.

38 *Re Queenstown Dry Dock Ship Building Company* [1918] 1 IR 356.

39 *Re Heidelstone Company Ltd et al* [2006] IEHC 408.

40 *Re Kavanagh & Cantwell* (23 November 1984, unreported) HC, Costello J.

41 That date being 20 years after one of the companies was struck off the register and dissolved.

> Company would be deemed to have continued in existence as if its name had not been struck off. However, in my view, that possibility does not in any way militate against the making of the vesting order I have made, because the restored First Company's interest in the Varied Estate would be subject to the trusts which have been clearly established in evidence, even if the vesting order were not made and the restored First Company could be compelled to execute a conveyance which would have the same effect as the vesting order. Finally, I am satisfied that, having regard to the circumstances of this case, it was probably more cost effective and it is certainly a more clear cut solution to the title problem to procure the incorporation of the New Management Company rather than seek to have the Second Company restored to the register of companies.'

Trading whilst struck off

[26.022] The McDowell Group did not favour the creation of a new offence of trading after having been struck off[42]. It did recognise, however, that the then existing offence under s 381 of the CA 1963, which prohibited the improper use of the words 'limited' or 'teoranta', was insufficient to address the phenomenon of trading whilst struck-off, especially as the maximum fine was then limited to £500. The CLEA 2001 did, however, take the opportunity to revamp s 381 of the CA 1963. It continues to be the case that if any person or persons trade or carry on business under a name or title of which 'limited' or 'teoranta' or any contraction or imitation of either is the last word, he or they will, unless duly incorporated, be guilty of an offence. It will be noted, however, that the maximum fine has been removed and the penalties for the offence now fall to be determined by s 240 of the CA 1990. Moreover, the Director and the registrar of companies now have power to serve a discontinuance notice on persons in contravention of the prohibition and if, within 14 days thereafter they fail to comply, the Director or the registrar may apply for a court order requiring the cessation of the contravention[43]. Where such an order is made, it may provide that all costs incidental to the application shall be borne by the persons against whom it is made[44].

[26.023] It has already been stated that where a company has been struck off and dissolved, its controllers have no authority to deal with the assets to which it was entitled prior to its dissolution since by operation of law the company is no longer the legal owner of these assets. It follows that to the extent that 'trading' involves the disposal of a dissolved company's 'assets', this is unlawful and technically exposes such controllers to civil and criminal liability. To the extent that 'trading' after strike-off involves the controllers of a dissolved company contracting with third parties, on first principles they will be contracting (and therefore liable) on their own behalf unless and until such time as (a) the company is restored to the register and (b) the court makes an order which deems such post-dissolution contracts to have been made with the company.

The winding up of dissolved companies

[26.024] Both s 12B(2) of the C(A)A 1982 and s 311(7) of the CA 1963 expressly provide that the fact a company has been dissolved, *shall not affect* the power of the court to wind up that company. However, in order for a winding up to have meaning the

---

42 See *The Working Group on Company Law Compliance and Enforcement* (1998) at para 3.31.

43 Section 381(2) of the CA 1963.

44 Section 381(3) of the CA 1963.

company must be reinstated to the register of companies[45]. The reason why it is necessary to reinstate a company is because until reinstated the title to its assets remains vested in the State[46].

[B] RESTORATION TO THE REGISTER[47]

[26.025] Where a company has been struck off the register and dissolved, it ceases to exist in law: its corporate personality is no more, and as an artificial legal person, a dissolved company is, as far as the law is concerned, 'dead'. This is, however, where the analogy with natural persons ends: dissolved companies can be restored to life because what the law takes away, the law may give back where certain conditions are met within certain time periods. Here, the two methods of restoring a company to the register of companies, restoration by administrative action and restoration by judicial order, are considered.

Restoration by administrative action

[26.026] Two different statutory provisions permit application to the registrar of companies to restore a company to the register. Application will be brought under either provision, depending upon the ground upon which the registrar struck off the company that is the subject of the application. Both regimes have in common the requirement that application can only be made to the registrar (as opposed to court) before the expiration of 12 months[48] from the publication in *Iris Oifigiúil* of the notice striking the company's name off the register.

[26.027] First, s 12C(1) of the C(A)A 1982 applies to applications for restoration where the company was struck off pursuant to s 12A(3) of the C(A)A 1982, ie, for a *failure to deliver the required particulars to the Revenue Commissioners*. Section 12C(1) provides:

> '... if a member or officer of a company is aggrieved by the fact of the company's having been struck off the register under s 12A(3) of this Act, the Registrar of Companies, on application made in the prescribed form by the member of officer before the expiration of 12 months from the publication in *Iris Oifigiúil* [the Companies Registration Office Gazette][49] of the notice striking the company name from the register, and provided he has received confirmation from the Revenue Commissioners that all outstanding, if any, statements required by s 882 of the Taxes Consolidation Act, 1997, have been delivered to the Revenue Commissioners, may restore the name of the company to the register.'

Upon the registration of an application under this subsection and on payment of the appropriate fee, 'the company shall be deemed to have continued in existence as if its

---

45 See, for example, *Re Lindsay Bowman Ltd* [1969] 1 WLR 1443.

46 The dissolved company has standing by s 12(6) of the C(A)A 1982 and s 311(8) of the CA 1963 to apply for its own restoration.

47 See Grier, 'Companies Arising from the Dead' (2006) 13 CLP 129.

48 Administrative restoration of an owners' management company can be made up to six years following the dissolution of such a company: see Ch 30, *Guarantee Companies*, at para **[30.072]**.

49 Although s 12C(1) of the C(A)A 1982 was amended by s 72 of the IFCMPA 2005, by the substitution for '*Iris Oifigiúil*', of 'the Companies Registration Office Gazette', s 72 has not as at the date of writing been commenced.

name had not been struck off': s 12C(2) of the C(A)A 1982. Moreover, subject to any court order to the contrary, the restoration shall not affect the rights or liabilities of the company in respect of any debt or obligation incurred or any contract entered into by, to, with or on behalf of the company between the date of its dissolution and its subsequent restoration[50].

[26.028] The use of the expression 'is aggrieved' is not without significance and it was held in *Re Contiv Uebersee Bank AG*[51] that a director who had initially agreed with the board's decision that a company should be dissolved but who later changed his mind, was not 'aggrieved' for the purposes of an application for restoration. In an Australian case, *Re Waldcourt Investment Co Pty Ltd*[52], it was said by Olney J that:

> 'I do not think that either a shareholder or a director as such must necessarily be aggrieved by the cancellation of the registration of a company. An applicant must, in my opinion, show that his interests have been or are likely to be prejudicially affected by the cancellation of registration.'

In *Casali v Crisp*[53], it was said that prejudice might be proved where a shareholder shows that he was also a creditor of the company or, alternatively, that there might well be a surplus of assets if the company were reinstated and certain events occurred.

[26.029] The registrar's statutory power to restore a company on such application being made is made expressly subject to a number of other statutory provisions: (a) a member's or creditor's right to apply to court for judicial restoration under s 311(8) of the CA 1963; (b) a company's right to apply itself to the registrar for restoration by administrative action under s 311A of the CA 1963; (c) a member's, officer's or creditor's right to apply to court for judicial restoration under s 12B(3) of the C(A)A 1982; and (d) the right of the registrar to apply to court for judicial restoration under s 12B(7) of the C(A)A 1982.

[26.030] It is important to note a number of points in relation to a s 12C(1) application for restoration by the registrar. First, only members or officers may apply – in particular, creditors and the company itself have no standing to apply. It is not readily apparent as to why the company itself should not be permitted to apply under this provision. Second, unless the Revenue Commissioners have been supplied with all outstanding statements and the registrar has received confirmation of this fact, it is pointless to make application as it will be refused outright. Finally, it is again important to stress the 12-month time period within which application must be made – if in excess of 12 months from the publication in *Iris Oifigiúil* of the notice striking the company name from the register, application will have to be made to the courts for restoration by judicial order.

[26.031] The second method of restoration by administrative action is provided for by s 311A(1) of the CA 1963. This applies to applications for restoration to the registrar where strike-off resulted from any of the other four grounds. Section 311A(1) provides that:

---

50 Section 12C(3) of the C(A)A 1982.

51 *Re Contiv Uebersee Bank AG* (1998) The Times Scots Law Report, 12 October.

52 *Re Waldcourt Investment Co Pty Ltd* (1986) 11 ACLR 12.

53 *Casali v Crisp* (3 October 2001) Supreme Court of New South Wales 860.

> '... if a company feels aggrieved by having been struck off the register, the Registrar of Companies on an application made in the prescribed form by the company before the expiration of twelve months after the publication in *Iris Oifigiúil* [the Companies Registration Office Gazette][54] of the notice striking the company name from the register, and provided he has received all annual returns outstanding, if any, from the company, may restore the name of the company to the register.'

The registrar's power to restore is again expressed to be without prejudice to s 311(8) of the CA 1963 and ss 12B(3), 12B(7) and 12C(1) of the C(A)A 1982. Again it is provided that, upon the registration of an application under this subsection and on payment of the appropriate fee, 'the company shall be deemed to have continued in existence as if its name had not been struck off': s 311A(2) of the CA 1963. Moreover, subject to any court order to the contrary, the restoration shall not affect the rights or liabilities of the company in respect of any debt or obligation incurred or any contract entered into by, to, with or on behalf of the company between the date of its dissolution and its subsequent restoration[55].

[26.032] The important points to remember here are, first, that only companies can make application to the registrar under s 311A(1). Second, it is imperative that all outstanding annual returns are filed. And third, application to the registrar must be brought within 12 months of dissolution.

Restoration by judicial order[56]

[26.033] In all cases where a company has been struck off for a period in excess of 12 months, application for restoration must be made to court. An example of such an application is seen in *Re Eden Quay Investments Ltd*[57]. In that application before Keane J, the directors of a company, which had been dissolved 18 years previously, successfully applied to have the company restored to the register. It had only been discovered that the company's 514,256 shares in Hibernian Transport Companies Ltd were not worthless, as previously had been thought. In May of 1993, the Supreme Court held that the shareholders in the company were entitled to benefit from a surplus of £2.5 million arising from the liquidation of the Hibernian companies, which also included Palgrave Murphy Ltd[58]. The company had been struck off the register in 1976 for failing to file its annual returns. Keane J is reported as having granted the application having heard that if the company were not restored to the register it would not be able to prove its claim in the winding up of Hibernian Transport Companies Ltd.

[26.034] There are three separate provisions under which application can be made to court for judicial restoration:

---

54 Although s 311A(1) of the CA 1963 was amended by s 72 of the IFCMPA 2005, by the substitution for '*Iris Oifigiúil*', of 'the Companies Registration Office Gazette', s 72 has not as at the date of writing been commenced.

55 Section 311A(3) of the CA 1963.

56 See Grier, 'Companies Arising from the Dead' (2006) 13 CLP 129.

57 *Re Eden Quay Investments Ltd*, an ex tempore order of the High Court reported in (1994) Irish Times, 12 April. See also *Stanhope Pension Trust Ltd v Registrar of Companies* [1994] 1 BCLC 628.

58 *In Re Hibernian Transport Companies Ltd* [1994] 1 ILRM 48.

(a) Section 12B of the C(A)A 1982 – application for restoration following a strike-off for failure to file annual returns or failure to deliver required particulars to the revenue;

(b) Section 12B(7) of the C(A)A 1982 – application following a strike-off for failure to file annual returns or failure to deliver required particulars to the revenue; and

(c) Section 311(8) of the CA 1963 – application following a strike-off on the grounds of ceasing to carry on business, having no recorded directors and having no resident director.

(a) Section 12B of the C(A)A 1982 – application for restoration following a strike-off for failure to file annual returns or failure to deliver required particulars to the revenue

[26.035] Section 12B(3) of the C(A)A 1982 provides that any member, officer or creditor of a company 'aggrieved'[59] by the fact that the company has been struck off for failure to file annual returns (s 12(3) of the C(A)A 1982) or for failure to deliver the required particulars to the revenue (s 12A(3) of the C(A)A 1982) may apply to court for restoration. Such application must be made on notice to the registrar of companies, the Revenue Commissioners and the Minister for Finance. In practice, the Chief State Solicitor, who represents the registrar of companies and the Minister for Finance, is served. Application must be brought before the expiration of 20 years after the company's dissolution. Provided that the foregoing conditions are met, s 12B(3) goes on to provide that the court may:

> '… if satisfied that it is just that the company be restored to the register, and, subject to subsection (4) of this section, upon an office copy of the order being delivered to the registrar for registration, the company shall be deemed to have continued in existence as if its name had not been struck off; and the court may by the order give such directions and make such provisions as seem just for placing the company and all other persons in the same position as nearly as may be as if the name of the company had not been struck off or make such other order as seems just (and such other order is referred to in subsection (4) of this section as an "alternative order").'

With the exception of the possibility that an alternative order may be made by the court, the effect of judicial restoration is identical to the effect of administrative restoration.

(i) Locus standi

[26.036] In order to have *locus standi* to petition for restoration under s 12B(3) of the C(A)A 1982, the petitioner must be a member, officer or creditor of the dissolved company. 'Members' are defined by s 31 of the CA 1963 as a company's subscribers and every other person who agrees to become a member and whose name is entered in its register of members. Beneficial owners of shares are not 'members' and will not have standing to petition to have a company reinstated: *Re Allied Metropole Hotel Ltd*[60]. Although it was held by Buckley J in the English case of *Re Bayswater Trading Co Ltd*[61]

---

[59] The authorities cited at para **[26.028]** *ante* that consider the significance of 'aggrieved' are equally relevant here.

[60] *Re Allied Metropole Hotel Ltd* (19 December 1998, unreported) HC, Gannon J.

[61] *Re Bayswater Trading Co Ltd* [1970] 1 WLR 343.

that a personal representative of a deceased shareholder had standing to petition to have a dissolved company reinstated, unlike s 205(6) of the CA 1963 which gives personal representatives *locus standi* to petition for minority oppression, s 12B(3) makes no such provision and it is thought that there is no jurisdiction for the courts to fill what might be thought to be a lacuna in the legislation since 'member' has a clear and unequivocal meaning under the Companies Acts.

[26.037] In addition to members, 'officers' of the dissolved company also have *locus standi*. 'Officer' is not clearly defined in the Companies Acts save by way of an inclusive definition in s 2(1) of the CA 1963 to include directors and secretaries. It is thought that the working definition of officer for the purposes of the Companies Acts, considered in Chapter 13[62], applies, ie, a person who is a director, secretary, auditor or who holds any other office that has been created by a company's memorandum or articles of association has *locus standi* to petition the court pursuant to s 12B(3). It is thought that for one to be an officer of a company one must have been an officer at the time the company was dissolved; a person cannot, in fact or in law, be appointed a director of dissolved company[63]. It was held, however, in *Re Witherdale*[64] that there was an exception to the rule that a person had standing if an officer at the date of dissolution. In that case, a person who had been a director of a dissolved company as at the date of its dissolution was subsequently made bankrupt. Evans-Lombe J held that since the dissolved company's articles provided that bankruptcy automatically terminated the office of director, the director lost the standing to apply for restoration.

[26.038] The other category of persons with *locus standi* under s 12B(3) is 'creditors'. 'Creditor' has been given a broad interpretation, and in *Re Deauville Communications Worldwide Ltd*[65] the Supreme Court held that 'creditor' in s 12B(3) of the C(A)(A) 1982 should be read as extending to contingent and prospective creditors. As the learned Keane CJ said:

> 'It would seem unjust that the question whether a person is entitled to have the company restored to the register for the purpose of recovering a judgment against them should be determined by whether this claim against the company is for a liquidated sum – in which case they would unarguably be a "creditor" – or takes the form of a claim for unliquidated damages[66].'

Keane CJ went on to note that in *Re Nelson Car Hire Ltd*[67] Kenny J had made reference to the creditors, the Revenue Commissioners, in that case having established that they had a reasonable prospect of success. On the authority of Laffoy J in *Re Nalto Construction*

62 See Ch 13, *Corporate Governance: Management by the Directors*, at para **[13.003]** *et seq*.

63 That the relevant time at which one must have been a member or creditor is the date of dissolution was held to be the law in *Re New Timbiqui Gold Mines* [1961] Ch 319 and *Re AGA Estate Agencies Ltd* [1986] BCC 99. See also *City of Westminister Assurance Company Ltd v Registrar of Companies* (28 June 1996, unreported) HC, Eng.

64 *Re Witherdale* [2006] BCC 412.

65 *Re Deauville Communications Worldwide Ltd* [2002] 2 IR 32.

66 Keane CJ noted that there was authority for the view he had taken in *Re Harvest Lane Motor Bodies Ltd* [1969] 1 Ch 457.

67 *Re Nelson Car Hire Ltd* (1973) 107 ILTR 97.

Ltd[68], however, it is inappropriate for the court to express a view on the likelihood of success, for example where a criminal prosecution is pending, it is sufficient to establish that the petitioner is pursuing the claim *bona fide* and not in a frivolous or vexatious manner[69].

(ii) The jurisdiction to hear the application

[26.039] Where application is brought by a creditor, the court to which application is made is the Circuit Court, a provision inserted by the C(A)(No 2)A 1999 to reduce the costs involved in applications for restoration which were previously brought in the High Court[70]. It was held by the Supreme Court in *Re Deauville Communication Worldwide Ltd*[71] that although the language used in s 12B of the C(A)A 1982 was capable of being construed so as to make it obligatory that application for restoration be brought in the Circuit Court as opposed to the High Court, a creditor was permitted still to bring an application for restoration in the High Court. Keane CJ held he was satisfied that '… when the subsection is placed in the appropriate context, it becomes clear that the intention of the Oireachtas was more likely to have been to enable the application to be brought either in the High Court or the Circuit Court'. It is very notable, however, that where application for restoration is brought by either members or officers, application must be brought in the High Court.

(iii) Establishing that the petitioner is 'aggrieved'

[26.040] Just as it is necessary for an applicant to the registrar for administrative restoration under s 12C(1) of the C(A)A 1982 to show that he or she is aggrieved, so too must a petitioner to the court under s 12B[72].

(iv) The weight attached to objections by third parties

[26.041] Deciding whether or not to grant an application for restoration is a matter for judicial discretion[73], and what will be considered to be 'just' will vary from case to case[74]. In deciding what is just, the court may have regard to the views of third parties, and the English Court of Appeal has held that there is a wide discretion to allow third parties to be joined in restoration applications[75].

[26.042] There is, however, a strong bias in favour of making a restoration order where strike-off was occasioned by a failure to file annual returns. Some of the factors that

---

68 *Re Nalto Construction Ltd* [2011] IEHC 251.

69 See para **[26.053]** *post* where the decision in *Re Nalto Construction Ltd* [2011] IEHC 251 is considered in the context of s 311(8) of the CA 1963, the provision under which it arose.

70 Section 12B(9), 12B(10) and 12B(11) of the C(A)A 1982 deal with the appropriate circuit in which to bring application.

71 *Re Deauville Communications Worldwide Ltd* [2002] 2 IR 32.

72 See para **[26.028]** *ante*.

73 See as to the court's jurisdiction, see *Re Portrafram Ltd* [1986] BCLC 533.

74 See *Re Workvale Ltd* [1991] BCLC 528 at 531 in regard to persons with a claim for unliquidated damages against a company which was dissolved; in *Re Forte's Manufacturing Ltd* [1994] BCC 84, the Court of Appeal restored a company to the register in order to reopen its liquidation and thereby admit new claims.

75 See *Re Blenheim Leisure (Restaurants) Ltd* [1999] TLR 603.

have been held to justify a court in exercising its discretion against ordering restoration were identified by the English High Court in *Re Priceland Ltd*[76] and include:

- the objector to restoration should demonstrate a substantial amount of prejudice[77];
- that such prejudice could be attributed to restoration; and
- that the objector changed its position on account of the strike-off.

In the English case of *Re Blenheim Leisure (Restaurants) Ltd (No 2)*[78], Neuberger J held that once the stated proofs – or gateways – in restoration provisions were satisfied, absent special circumstances, restoration should follow and exercising the court's discretion against restoration should be the exception and not the rule. In *Re Blue Note Enterprises Ltd*[79], the company, the subject of an application for restoration, had been struck off the register following its failure to file annual returns. The subject company had been retained to run three clubs in London for another company, Mean Fiddler Holdings Ltd, but, subsequently, had been dropped. The subject company had initiated proceedings for breach of contract but these had languished due to insufficient funds. Mean Fiddler Holdings Ltd was joined in the application for restoration, which it opposed, on the basis that the subject company had no prospect of taking the contract claim to judgment because it could not fund the litigation. It was again stated that the approach to applications for restoration following strike-off for failure to file annual returns was that 'exercising the discretion against restoration should be the exception not the rule'[80] and restoration was ordered.

[26.043] A different approach to third party objections to restoration is apparent from the Irish Supreme Court decision in *Re Bloomberg Developments Ltd; Good v Philips Electrical (Ireland) Ltd*[81]. There, it was said by the Supreme Court (Murphy J) that:

> '... restoration is primarily a matter between the petitioner on the one part and the regulatory authority – who has a duty to ensure compliance with the relevant provisions of the Companies Acts – and the Minister for Finance – in whom would vest the assets of the company as *bona vacantia* – of the other part[82].'

In that case, however, it was held that an opposing third party (which was being sued by the dissolved company) had properly been allowed to appear on the petition for restoration. This was because an application was made by the petitioner to extend a stay that had been put on the order it had obtained to have the proceedings against it struck out because the plaintiff company had been dissolved. Moreover, the Supreme Court accepted that the third party objector had been in a position to bring before the High Court evidence as to the petitioner's conduct, to which the High Court attached

---

76 *Re Priceland Ltd* [1997] 1 BCLC 467.

77 For an example of prejudice, see *City of Edinburge Council* [2010] CSOH 20.

78 *Re Blenheim Leisure (Restaurants) Ltd (No 2)* [2000] BCC 821.

79 *Re Blue Note Enterprises Ltd* [2001] 2 BCLC 427.

80 *Re Blue Note Enterprises Ltd* [2001] 2 BCLC 427 at 432e, citing *Re Priceland Ltd* [1997] 1 BCLC 467 at 476 and *Re Blenheim Leisure (Restaurants) Ltd (No 2)* [2000] BCC 821 at 829.

81 *Re Bloomberg Developments Ltd; Good v Philips Electrical (Ireland) Ltd* [2002] 2 IR 613. See a note of the judgment in O'Hanlon, 'Barrowland and Bloomberg – the new enfants terrible of restoration applications' (2003) CLP 256.

82 Citing *Conrad Hall & Co Ltd* [1916] WN 275 as authority.

considerable significance. Therefore, it was found that the High Court had discretion to allow the third party to be a notice party to the proceedings. The High Court had ordered the restored company to pay the third party's costs not only in relation to the application for restoration but also in relation to the underlying action that was being litigated between them. In this respect the Supreme Court held, however, that the High Court was not empowered to impose a penalty on a restored company by the making of an award of costs. Murphy J said:

> 'The order as to costs in respect of the underlying action was imposed, as I see it, by way of a sanction or penalty on Bloomberg for what the learned judge perceived as being some abuse of process by them. It may be that Phillips will be entitled to recover their costs against Bloomberg or obtain security for costs of those proceedings but any such order must be made in the underlying action itself ... I am satisfied that the law in this jurisdiction does confer power on the High Court to ensure that the power to restore a company to the register is used for the purpose for which it was intended but does not extend to the imposition of a penalty, such as was imposed in the present case, by an award of costs – whether taxed or otherwise – in proceedings which fall to be dealt with on their own merits independently of the application for restoration.'

(v) The requirement that outstanding annual returns are filed

[26.044] The legislature was quite prescriptive in detailing the conditions which the court should impose on making a restoration order. So, s 12B(5) provides that 'unless cause is shown to the contrary' the court shall include in a restoration order where application is brought by a *member or officer* a provision that the order shall not have effect unless within one month of the date of the order, all outstanding annual returns are delivered to the registrar (where dissolved on foot of s 12(3)) or that all outstanding statements are delivered to the Revenue Commissioners (where dissolved on foot of s 12A(3)).

[26.045] The law requires all outstanding annual returns to be filed as the *quid pro quo* to a company being restored to the register. Section 12B(5) provides that:

> 'The court shall, unless cause is shown to the contrary, include in an order under subsection (3) of this section, being an order made on the application of a member or officer of the company, a provision that the order shall not have effect unless, within 1 month from the date of the court's order—
>
> (a) if the order relates to a company that has been struck off the register under s 12(3) of this Act, all outstanding returns required by s 125 or 126 of the CA 1963 are delivered to the Registrar of Companies,
>
> (b) if the order relates to a company that has been struck off the register under section 12A(3) of this Act, all outstanding statements required by section 882 of the Taxes Consolidation Act 1997, are delivered to the Revenue Commissioners.'

Similarly, where application is brought by a creditor for the restoration of a company, s 12B(6) provides that the court shall direct that one or more specified members or officers shall, within a specified period, deliver all outstanding annual returns to the registrar or all outstanding statements to the revenue, as appropriate.

[26.046] Where application is brought by a creditor for the restoration of a company, s 12B(6) provides that the court shall direct that one or more specified members or officers shall, within a specified period, deliver all outstanding annual returns to the registrar or all outstanding statements to the revenue, as appropriate. The change to the law on restoration, effected by the C(A)(No 2)A 1999, will obviate the lacuna, identified (but circumvented) by O'Hanlon J in *Re Haltone (Cork) Ltd*[83]. In that case, the petitioner applied for the restoration of the above named company pursuant to the 'old' s 311(8) of the CA 1963 in circumstances where the petitioner claimed to have large unsatisfied debts against the company and had obtained judgment in England for over £40,000 plus costs. The petitioner said it wished to enforce the judgment against the company and also against its officers in reliance upon statutory personal liability provisions. The company in question had been struck off for failure to file annual returns and O'Hanlon J said that where application is made on behalf of the company itself it was normally granted upon condition that all outstanding annual returns would be filed. He noted, however:

> 'In the present case, however, the application is made, not by or on behalf of the company itself, but by a creditor who feels that there is greater scope for invoking the provisions of the Companies Acts against the officers of the company when the company has been restored to the register and is no longer to be regarded as a company which has been dissolved.
>
> Obviously, the petitioner is not in a position to file annual returns on behalf of the company to make good the default which has taken place in the past and is unlikely to secure the co-operation of the company or its officers in carrying out this procedure[84].'

In the event, O'Hanlon J acceded to the petitioner's application and restored the company to allow the petitioner a reasonable opportunity to pursue whatever remedy was available to it under the Companies Acts. O'Hanlon J went on to direct that the petitioner should be responsible for the payment of any fees payable to the registrar and suggested (but did not direct) that the registrar should give notice to the petitioner of any further attempt to strike the company off the register. Section 12B(6) of the C(A)A 1982 alleviates the burden on creditors seeking to have a company restored where the reason for its strike-off was failure to file annual returns, a default that is almost invariably beyond the ability of a creditor to remedy.

[26.047] The court has a very limited discretion to dispense with the requirement that outstanding returns be delivered to the registrar of companies. In *Re New Ad Advertising Ltd*[85], the company in question had been struck off the register for failure to file annual returns. The petitioner sought an order under s 12B of the C(A)A 1982 to restore the company to the register, the petition being made in his capacity as both a member and creditor. A person, who was a director of the company at the time it was struck off, objected to the restoration and, in the alternative, also submitted that if the court was mindful to make an order under s 12B(3), it should regard the application as having been made by a member or officer rather than by a creditor so that s 12B(5) rather than s 12B(6) would apply. Laffoy J said:

> 'In my view, a very limited discretion is given to the court in subs (5). The court is mandated to make the effect of the restoration order conditional on the outstanding returns being delivered "unless cause is shown to the contrary". The obvious situation in which

[83] *Re Haltone (Cork) Ltd* (7 February 1995, unreported) HC, O'Hanlon J.

[84] *Re Haltone (Cork) Ltd* (7 February 1995, unreported) HC, O'Hanlon J at p 2 of the judgment.

[85] *Re New Ad Advertising Ltd* [2006] IEHC 19.

cause is shown to the contrary is where, before the matter is heard in court, the outstanding returns have been delivered and there is confirmation from the relevant State authority that such is the case. In my view, it would be erroneous to assume that subs (6) is more rigorous than subs (5). The contrary, is, in fact, the case because under subs (5) the effect of the order is postponed until delivery of the outstanding returns within the period of one month, whereas in the case of subs (6) the order takes effect immediately, although there is an ancillary direction to the members or officers of the company to deliver the outstanding returns within a time period stipulated by the court. The reason for the different approach in the two sub-sections is because almost invariably a creditor petitioner will not be in a position to deliver returns on behalf of the company. In relation to both sub-sections, the legislative intent is clear. It is to ensure that the striking-off mechanism as a deterrent against breach of company law and tax law is not devalued. It would be devalued if a company could be restored to the Register without the breach which gave rise to its striking-off being remedied.

Here, the petitioner is both a creditor and a member of the Company. On the evidence, it would appear that, as a member, he is not in a position to file annual returns on behalf of the Company. In the circumstances, I propose treating this as the application of a creditor, which is what the Registrar has sought. I propose making an order under subs (6) that Mr McNulty deliver the outstanding returns to the Registrar of Companies within three months from the date of this judgment.'

Accordingly, despite the former director's protestations and claims that it was impossible to file outstanding returns due to lack of records, Laffoy J restored the company and ordered its directors to file its outstanding annual returns.

[26.048] *Re Zota Manufacturing Ltd; Application of Topping*[86] is authority for the proposition that in exceptional circumstances, restoration might be ordered pursuant to s 12B(3) of the C(A)A 1982 *without* requiring all outstanding annual returns to be filed in the CRO. In that case, the petitioner had been one of five directors of Zota Manufacturing Ltd ('Zota') which had been struck off and dissolved in December 2003 for failure to file annual returns. The petitioner sought to have Zota restored pursuant to s 12B of the C(A)A 1982 for the purposes of realising an insurance policy which had been put in place to secure the payment of royalties to two persons who had allowed Zota to use patents owned by companies controlled by them. The beneficiaries of that policy were a widow and a retired pharmacist, neither of whom had any responsibility for Zota's compliance with the Companies Acts. The court heard that owing to the death of one of the directors, who had been the managing director and in sole possession of all company records, it had become impossible because of the absence of relevant material to produce accounts and to make annual returns. In those circumstances Laffoy J said:

'The only persons who will benefit from the restoration of the company are persons who had no responsibility whatsoever for compliance with the provisions of the Companies Act 1963 in relation to making annual returns. On the basis of the facts averred to in Mr Geraghty's affidavit, and, in particular, the fact that Mr O'Flynn has died and that the relevant records of the company cannot be traced, I am satisfied that it is not feasible to deliver the outstanding returns at this remove. Therefore, I am satisfied that, in the very unusual circumstances of this case, cause has been shown contrary to requiring the outstanding annual returns to be delivered. I am also satisfied that it is just that the company should be restored to the register.'

86 *Re Zota Manufacturing Ltd; Application of Topping* [2010] IEHC 114.

The restoration was ordered dispensing with the requirement in s 12B(5)(a) but was made on the undertaking of the petitioner to apply to the registrar of companies to have the company dissolved once the proceeds of the policy were obtained and disbursed to the beneficiaries.

(vi) Alternative orders

[26.049] The ability to make an 'alternative order' was introduced by the C(A)(No 2)A 1999. Section 12B(4) of the C(A)A 1982 provides:

> 'An alternative order may, if the court considers it appropriate that it should do so, include a provision that, as respects a debt or liability incurred by, or on behalf or, the company during the period when it stood struck off the register, the officers of the company or such one or more of them as is or are specified in the order shall be liable for the whole or a part (as the court thinks just) of the debt or liability.'

Accordingly, officers who cause a company to trade and incur liabilities whilst it is dissolved may be rendered personally responsible for such liabilities. It is thought, however, that save in the most exceptional of circumstances (eg, where the company is insolvent) the courts will be loath to make an alternative order. It is not clear as to whether the alternative order can be made *in addition* to a restoration order or whether such is only permitted *in lieu* of a restoration order. The use of the word 'alternative' suggests such an order would not be made where a restoration order is made. In such a case the effect is that where the court declines to restore a company it can, in that event, pacify its creditors by making its officers personally responsible for the debts incurred whilst the company was dissolved[87].

(b) Section 12B(7) of the C(A)A 1982 – application following a strike-off for failure to file annual returns or failure to deliver required particulars to the revenue

[26.050] Section 12B(7) of the C(A)A 1982 gives *locus standi* to the registrar of companies to apply to court for a restoration order where a company has been struck off for either failure to file annual returns or failure to deliver required particulars to the revenue. Again, application must be brought within 20 years of dissolution and the application must be on notice to each person who, to the registrar's knowledge, is an officer of the company. The consequences for the company of the court acceding to the registrar's application are the same as where application is brought by members, officers or creditors under s 12B(3). Of significance is the fact that on such application being brought the court is again empowered to make an 'alternative order'. Again, it would seem to be open to the court to make such an order instead of making a restoration order. It would seem that this might indeed be the primary motivation behind this provision, namely, to allow the registrar to apply for an alternative order to make officers personally responsible for post-dissolution debts. It is thought that it would only be in rare cases that the registrar (who, after all, caused the company to be struck off) would want to bring application to have it restored.

---

87 It has been noted by Grier, 'Companies Arising from the Dead' (2006) CLP 129, that the Revenue Commissioners commonly seek to reserve their right in restoration applications to apply at a later date for an order that all or any of the officers are made liable for a debt incurred by or on behalf of the company during the period in which it was struck off.

(c) Section 311(8) of the CA 1963 – application following a strike-off on the grounds of ceasing to carry on business, having no recorded directors and having no resident director

[26.051] Section 311(8) of the CA 1963 is the applicable section where a judicial restoration order is sought in circumstances where the reason for the company being struck off was because it ceased to carry on business (s 311(2) of the CA 1963), had no recorded directors, or had no resident director (s 43(15) of the C(A)(No 2)A 1999). Those with *locus standi* to apply under this section are the company, any member and any creditor. Again, application must be brought within 20 years of the company's dissolution. The only notice party expressly mentioned in s 311(8) is the registrar of companies, and it has been noted[88] that the absence of an express requirement to join the Minister for Finance and Revenue Commissioners is a lacuna which should be filled by common sense and both parties served regardless.

[26.052] Where application is brought under s 311(8) of the CA 1963, the High Court may:

> '… if satisfied that the company was at the time of the striking off carrying on business or otherwise that it is just that the company be restored to the register, order that the name of the company be restored to the register, and upon an office copy of the order being delivered to the registrar for registration, the company shall be deemed to have continued in existence as if its name had not been struck off; and the court may by the order give such directions and make such provisions as seem just for placing the company and all other persons in the same position as nearly as may be as if the name of the company had not been struck off or make such other order as seems just (and such other order is referred to in subsection (8A) as an "alternative order").'

Again, an alternative order may include a provision that as respects a debt or liability incurred by or on behalf of the company during the period when it was dissolved, the officers of the company or any one or more of them shall be personally responsible for the whole or part, as the court thinks just, of the debt or liability. It will be noted that there is no provision for application to be brought under this provision to the Circuit Court and all applications have to go to the High Court.

[26.053] Under s 311(8), there are two independent reasons for the court to order the restoration of a company: if satisfied that the company was at the time of the striking-off carrying on business *or* otherwise 'that it is just' that the company be restored to the register. The second of these grounds was the basis of the court's jurisdiction to order restoration in the High Court decision of *Re Nalto Construction Ltd*[89]. In that case, the Revenue Commissioners accidentally provided a letter of no objection to the striking off of a company which had ceased to carry on business. The petitioner for the company's restoration was the Collector General of the Revenue Commissioners who claimed to be a contingent creditor of the company on the basis that it had an undischarged liability to the revenue arising from what it claimed had been the fraudulent claiming of a repayment of corporation tax to which it was not entitled. The restoration petition was resisted by a former director of the company who averred that although criminal

---

[88] See Grier, 'Companies Arising from the Dead' (2006) 13 CLP 129.

[89] *Re Nalto Construction Ltd* [2011] IEHC 251.

proceedings had been taken against the company relating to the delivery of incorrect accounts and wrongly claiming a repayment of corporation tax, no notice of assessment had been raised against the company or claim made of the alleged outstanding tax prior to his request for a voluntary strike-off. The former director argued that the Revenue Commissioners were not creditors because, on the authority of Kenny J in *Re Nelson Car Hire Ltd*[90], 'there is no liability for income tax or corporation profits tax until the assessment becomes final and that the Revenue are not, therefore, creditors' and because it was claimed that Keane CJ in *Re Deauville Communications Worldwide Ltd*[91] appeared to endorse the notion that a contingent or prospective creditor had to establish 'a reasonable prospect of success' in the action against the company. Laffoy J rejected that the latter interpretation of the decision of Keane CJ was correct, saying:

> 'In circumstances such as the circumstances which prevail on this application, where the DPP proposes to pursue criminal proceedings against the company if it is restored, it would be clearly inappropriate to express a view on the prospect of the Revenue Commissioners being successful in recovering the amount claimed if an assessment was raised on the basis of the same factual foundation as underlies the proposed criminal prosecution. On the other hand, where a petitioner who is a creditor invokes the Court's discretionary statutory jurisdiction to make a restoration order on the ground that "it is just" to do so (which is the ground relied on in this application, because there is no suggestion that the company was carrying on business at the time of strike off), clearly the court must be satisfied that the petitioner is pursuing the claim against the company bona fide and not in a frivolous or vexatious manner.'

Laffoy J held that she was satisfied that the Revenue Commissioners were acting *bona fide* in seeking to pursue a claim for the tax alleged to be due and considered it just to restore the company to the register to facilitate the revenue to pursue the claim and so that the DPP could prosecute the criminal proceedings which had been adjourned pending the determination of the application.

[26.054] Where the reason why the company was dissolved was on the ground of failure to have an EU or EEA resident director, s 311(8) of the CA 1963 is modified by s 43(15)(b) of the C(A)(No 2)A 1999. The effect is to provide that upon an application for restoration of such a company, the court should be 'satisfied that subsection (1) or, as the case may be, subsection (2) of section 43 of the Companies (Amendment) (No 2) Act, 1999, was at the time of the striking off being complied with in relation to the company'. It will be noted that even if the dissolved company was not complying with s 43(1) or (2) at the time of dissolution, the court may – where it considers it to be just – order its restoration. Presumably this would only be granted where the company in question had at the time of the application a resident director or where there was an undertaking from a resident to act as a director.

The timing of restoration

[26.055] On the restoration of a company to the register, it is deemed to have continued in existence, notwithstanding that it had been dissolved. Thus, s 12B(3) and 12B(7) of the C(A)A 1982 and s 311(8) of the CA 1963 all provide that the court may make an order that the name of the company be restored to the register:

90 *Re Nelson Car Hire Ltd* (1973) 107 ILTR 97.

91 *Re Deauville Communications Worldwide Ltd* [2002] 2 IR 32.

> '... and ... upon an office copy of the order being delivered to the registrar for registration, the company shall be deemed to have continued in existence as if its name had not been struck off.'

The court order does not itself effect the restoration; rather it is the first of a two-step process, that second step being the delivery of the order to the registrar of companies. Where a restoration order is made, it must be lodged with the registrar of companies forthwith and, in any event, not longer than three months following the making of the order. It was held in *Re Barrowland Ltd*[92] that the conjunctive 'and ... upon an office copy of the order being delivered to the registrar for registration':

> '... are a clear indication by the Oireachtas that it was not sufficient merely for the Court to make the pronouncement and make its order but that an office copy of the order should be delivered to the Registrar and it is upon the completion of both the making of the Court order and its delivery to the Registrar that the company is deemed to have continued in existence.'

In that case, the company failed to deliver a copy of the court order that its name be restored to the register for over five and a half years! Smyth J found that since the effect of an order is to validate retrospectively all acts done in the name and on behalf of the company during the period between its dissolution and the restoration of its name to the register, 'it follows that it is imperative that a copy of the Order of the Court be lodged as soon as ever possible with the Registrar of Companies'. Moreover, he stated that the registrar ought not to be bound to register restoration orders which are not lodged with the registrar forthwith:

> 'If the Registrar were to have a margin of appreciation in for example an Order pronounced at the end of a legal term which was not available in perfected form until the beginning of the following legal term then at its widest, his discretion could and should not exceed three months from the date of the pronouncement of the Order. Orders not lodged forthwith and at the very outside within three months should and do automatically lapse.'

The effect of restoration

[26.056] It is important to distinguish between restoration following strike-off for failure to comply with the Companies Acts and restoration following dissolution after the winding up of the company[93]. This distinction is significant in the context of the effect of a restoration order, particularly in relation to the consequence for proceedings by or against the company. The different effects of restoration, depending upon why a company was dissolved, were noted by O'Neill J in *Re Amantiss Enterprises Ltd; Framus Ltd et al v CRH plc et al*[94], considered below[95]. The potential for confusion was recognised by the English Court of Appeal in *Top Creative Ltd and another v St Albans*

---

92 *Re Barrowland Ltd* [2004] 3 IR 27: see note in O'Hanlon, 'Barrowland and Bloomberg – the new enfants terrible of restoration applications' (2003) CLP 256.

93 Dissolution following a winding up is governed by s 310 of the CA 1963. See Ch 23, *Winding Up Companies*, at para **[23.130]** *et seq*.

94 *Re Amantiss Enterprises Ltd; Framus Ltd et al v CRH plc et al* [1999] IEHC 74, O'Neill J.

95 See para **[26.059]** *post*.

District Council[96]. There, a county court judge had refused an application by the shareholders in a company that had been struck off the register, to remove an action from the 'warned list' and adjourn it pending the hearing of an application to restore the company. The Court of Appeal allowed the appeal and held that the judge had misdirected himself in two respects. The first misdirection was that the action involving the company was automatically and irrevocable at an end once the company was struck off and that the judge had no jurisdiction to grant the application sought by the dissolved company. The second misdirection was the judge's view that the company had no existence of any kind, once its name was removed from the register. In the Court of Appeal, Roch LJ accepted the appellant's contention that:

> 'Whereas the appellants accept that if a company is wound up by a liquidator that company ceases to have any existence, and existing actions by or against such a company when the winding up is complete and the company dissolved, cease to exist, the position is not the same when all that has occurred is that the company's name has been removed from the register by the administrative act of the registrar[97].'

Dissolution following a winding-up order has been considered in Chapter 23[98]. In *Top Creative Ltd*, the Court of Appeal went on to apply the decision in *Tyman's Ltd v Craven*[99], a case which O'Neill J also relied upon in *Re Amantiss Enterprises Ltd*.

[26.057] The effect of ss 12B(3), 12B(7) and 311(8) are very far-reaching, as seen in the case of *Re Dunleckney Ltd*[100]. In that case, a company that had been struck off and dissolved on 6 November 1990 was subsequently restored to the register on 21 October 1991. On 6 January 1992, an office copy of the restoration order was sent to the registrar for registration. Immediately thereafter, the company was wound up. The liquidator of the company had cause to believe that the directors had not acted honestly or responsibly and sought to have them restricted under s 150 of the CA 1990. The respondent directors argued that s 150 of the CA 1990 had only been commenced on 1 August 1991 and despite the fact that the company had been restored on 21 October 1991, no entitlement to pursue the directors under s 150 existed as it was not retrospective. Carroll J gave this argument short shrift:

> 'Under s 311(8) of the Companies Act, 1963 where a company is struck off and the name is restored to the register upon an office copy of the order being delivered, the company is deemed to have continued in existence as if its name had not been struck off.
>
> Therefore when the office copy was lodged on 6 January[101] 1992, the company was deemed to have continued in existence. If follows since the company is deemed to have continued in existence, Part VII [of the CA 1990, containing s 150] applies to the company because that Part came into operation on the 1 August 1991 and the company was not wound up until 21 October 1991. It was therefore a company in existence at the time Part VII came into operation. Since it is a company which at the date of the commencement of the winding-up order was unable to pay its debts, s 149 applies.'

---

96 *Top Creative Ltd and another v St Albans District Council* [1999] BCC 999.

97 *Top Creative Ltd and another v St Albans District Council* [1999] BCC 999 at 1003.

98 See Ch 23, *Winding up Companies*, at para **[23.130]**.

99 *Tyman's Ltd v Craven* [1952] 2 QB 100.

100 *Re Dunleckney Ltd* [1999] IEHC 109, Carroll J.

101 The judgment says 'December' but it is thought this was a typographical error.

Although this judgment concerned the interpretation of the 'old' s 311(8) of the CA 1963, the wording under consideration is identical to that used in both the 'new' s 311(8) of the CA 1963 and s 12B(3) and (7) of the C(A)A 1982.

The effect of restoration on legal proceedings involving the dissolved company

[26.058] All three[102] restoration provisions applicable where a company has been dissolved other than following the winding up of a company provide that 'the court may by order give such directions and make such provision as seem just for placing the company and all other persons in the same position as nearly may be as if the name of the company had not been struck off'. A truly miraculous judicial act indeed[103]. The consequences of this effect of restoration can be most contentious where the dissolved company was involved in legal proceedings[104]. The position in the case of restoration following dissolution where a company has been wound up has been considered in Chapter 23[105].

[26.059] The leading Irish decision on the effect of restoration is *Re Amantiss Enterprises Ltd; Framus Ltd et al v CRH plc et al*[106]. The facts there were that the petitioner company had ceased trading in March 1991 and had been placed into voluntary liquidation on 1 April 1994. On 4 December 1996, it (and other companies) commenced proceedings against the seven defendant companies, alleging that they had engaged in anti-competitive practices. One of the defendant companies motioned the court seeking, *inter alia*, to have the petitioner's name struck-out from the proceedings when it learned that the petitioner had been dissolved for failure to file annual returns with effect from 19 May 1993! To enable it to continue and validate the proceedings it had commenced, the petitioner petitioned the court, *inter alia*, to be restored to the register pursuant to s 12(6) of the C(A)A 1982. The petitioner also sought such directions as might seem just for placing the company and all persons in the same position as nearly as might be as if the name of the company had not been struck off. The court was asked to construe the proper meaning of the words in s 12(6) of the C(A)A 1982, namely:

> 'and upon an office copy of the order being delivered to the Registrar for registration the company shall be deemed to have continued in existence as if its name had not been struck-off; and the Court may by order give such directions and make such provisions as seem just for placing the company and all other persons in the same position as nearly as may be as if the name of the company had not been struck-off.'

The petitioner claimed that the effect of s 12(6) was to validate all acts done by the company between its dissolution and its restoration. The defendants rejected this,

---

102 Section 311(8) of the CA 1963 and s 12B(3) and (7) of the C(A)A 1982.

103 See *Re Boxco Ltd* [1970] Ch 442 where particulars of a charge created after the dissolution were delivered to the English Companies Registration Office, it was held that the charge had been properly registered by reason of the company's subsequent restoration.

104 See Keay, 'The Pursuit of Legal Proceedings Against Dissolved Companies' (2000) JBL 405.

105 See Ch 23, *Winding Up Companies,* at para **[23.130]** *post*.

106 *Re Amantiss Enterprises Ltd; Framus Ltd et al v CRH plc et al* [1999] IEHC 74, O'Neill J.

contending that the effect of the words 'the company shall be deemed to have continued in existence as if its name had not been struck off':

> 'have the effect merely of restoring the status of incorporation of the company and its identity but do not have the effect of validating retrospectively any acts done between dissolution and restoration to the register[107].'

The defendants also contended that the remainder of the subsection had 'the effect of giving to the Court the power by specific order to validate retrospectively acts that may have been done during dissolution'[108], the defendant's point being that retrospective validation was not automatic but subject to the court's discretion.

[26.060] O'Neill J rejected the defendant's arguments and held that s 12(6) operated to confer '*automatic retrospective validation*'. In so holding, O'Neill J followed the majority judgments of the English Court of Appeal in *Tymans Ltd v Craven*[109], which interpreted the materially identical s 353(6) of the English Companies Act 1948. On this point he said:

> '… I find the reasoning of the majority judgments in the *Tyman* case preferable, and hold that the words "the company shall be deemed to have continued in existence as if its name had not been struck off" have the effect of validating retrospectively all acts done in the name or on behalf of the company during the period between its dissolution and the restoration of its name to the register, and that the words "and the court may by order give such directions and make such provisions as seems just for placing the company and all other persons in the same position as nearly as may be as if the name of the company had not been struck off" are not expository qualifying the scope of the proceeding general word but are complementary only to those general words so as to enable the court to achieve to the fullest extent consistent with justice the "*as you were*" position of the company[110].'

As to the justification for this finding, O'Neill J said:

> 'In my view the plain and very reasonable and sensible intendment of s 12(6) is to preserve the validity of transactions entered into during a period of dissolution where frequently that dissolution is unknown to either the company and its officers or third parties dealing with it, and who conduct their business with each other and enter into engagements with each other on the basis that the company enjoys lawful existence. To remove legal validity from all of these transactions in circumstances where the parties to them at the time of their making intended them to have legal validity would in a great many instances work injustices and would provide the unscrupulous with much opportunity for mischief. I have no doubt that the legislature, in selecting the very clear language used in s 12(6), intended that such unfortunate consequences would not occur by

[107] *Re Amantiss Enterprises Ltd; Framus Ltd et al v CRH plc et al* (21 December 1999, unreported) HC, O'Neill J at p 16 of the judgment.

[108] *Re Amantiss Enterprises Ltd; Framus Ltd et al v CRH plc et al* (21 December 1999, unreported) HC, O'Neill J at p 17 of the judgment.

[109] *Tymans Ltd v Craven* [1952] 1 All ER 613.

[110] *Re Amantiss Enterprises Ltd; Framus Ltd et al v CRH plc et al* (21 December 1999, unreported) HC, O'Neill J at p 21 of the judgment. O'Neill J declined to follow *Re Townreach Ltd* [1995] Ch 8 and *Natural Nectar Products Canada Ltd v Michael Theodor* (6 June 1990) Court of Appeal of British Columbia.

> reason of an unintended dissolution where no orderly process of winding up had taken place[111].'

Overly forgiving of corporate non-compliance? Possibly. Realistic and practical? Most certainly so. O'Neill J himself pointed to the fact (noted by Evershed MR in *Tymans*) that to hold to thc contrary could give rise to a multiplicity of proceedings concerning the validation of all the multifarious engagements into which a dissolved company might have entered. O'Neill J went on to find that it was proper to order that the petitioner be restored to the register of companies. He also held that he did not accept that the institution of proceedings against the defendants at the time the company had been dissolved was a specific prejudice having regard to his conclusions as to the meaning and effect of s 12(6) of the C(A)A 1982. O'Neill J went on to say that he was impressed by the fact that counsel for the registrar of companies had no objection to the relief being sought in the petition being granted having regard to the uniqueness of the registrar's position in assessing compliance with the relevant statutory requirement.

[26.061] Where a company is dissolved following its winding up, a different regime applies to its restoration. Section 310(1) of the CA 1963 provides:

> 'Where a company has been dissolved, the court may at any time within 2 years of the date of the dissolution, on an application being made for the purpose by the liquidator of the company or by any other person who appears to the court to be interested, make an order, upon such terms as the court thinks fit, declaring the dissolution to have been void, and thereupon such proceedings may be taken as might have been taken if the company had not been dissolved.'

It has been observed[112] that the similar former provision in the English Companies Act[113] operated so that 'proceedings which either were initiated against the company before the advent of dissolution and remained pending at the time of dissolution or commenced during the period of dissolution, are null for they were against a company that did not exist, and the making of an order avoiding the dissolution is not sufficient to retrospectively validate the proceedings'. Whether or not proceedings are retrospectively validated will depend upon whether the court expressly so provides under its jurisdiction to make the order on such terms as it thinks fit[114].

Effect of restoration on claims against directors

[26.062] Where a company has been struck off the register and dissolved, contracts purportedly entered into by the dissolved company's directors become enforceable against those directors. Where such a company is restored to the register, it has been held in *Re Richmond Building Products Ltd v Soundgables Ltd et al*[115] that the claims against its directors fell and did not survive the restoration. In that case, the plaintiff sought judgment against the defendants for a sum in respect of goods sold during a time

[111] *Re Amantiss Enterprises Ltd; Framus Ltd et al v CRH plc et al* (21 December 1999, unreported) HC, O'Neill J at pp 22, 23 of the judgment.

[112] Keay, 'The Pursuit of Legal Proceedings Against Dissolved Companies' (2000) JBL 405.

[113] Section 651 of the Companies Act 1985.

[114] See *Re Mixhurst Ltd* [1994] 2 BCLC 19 and *Re Philip Powis Ltd* [1997] 2 BCLC 481. See further Ch 23, *Winding Up Companies*, at para **[23.130]**.

[115] *Re Richmond Building Products Ltd v Soundgables Ltd et al* [2005] 3 IR 321.

when the first defendant company had been dissolved following strike-off and was successful in its action against the company and third defendant, the action against the other defendants being sent for plenary hearing. The second and fourth defendants successfully argued before the High Court that because the legislation provides that on restoration the company is deemed to have continued in existence as if the name had not been struck off the register, the claim against them did not survive. The plaintiff had in argument relied upon the decision of Buckley J in *Re Brown Bayley's Steel Works Ltd*[116] where the provisions under consideration, s 7(5) of the Companies Act 1880, provided that where a company had been struck off for not carrying on business, it could be restored on application to the court. Buckley J had said:

> 'From the time when the company was struck off there was no corporation and its officers were personally liable for the engagements made as its agents. By simply making an order to restore the name to the register his Lordship would not relieve them – the personal liability would still remain. The Court could make an order under s 7(5) giving such directions that the officers would be relieved from this liability. His Lordship would not make that order, but would make an order which would not relieve them, by simply ordering the name of the company to be restored on the terms of its making the proper returns and paying the costs of the Board of Trade.'

The plaintiff also pointed out that s 12C(3) of the C(A)A 1982 referred to the rights or liabilities of the company and not those of the directors, but Finnegan P rejected this point on the ground that it has nothing to do with the position of those purporting to act on the company's behalf. As to the decision of Buckley J, Finnegan P noted that an opposite view has been taken in a series of cases beginning with *Morris v Harris*[117] and that the current position in the United Kingdom is that on a company being restored, its directors do not remain personally liable.

[26.063] Finnegan P went on to note the decision of Megarry J in *Re Lindsay Bowman Ltd*[118]. In that case, application was made to restore a company and, because the company was insolvent, for an order for its winding up. A creditor who had debts incurred both before and after the dissolution supported the petition but asked the court to make a so-called '*Rugby Auto Electrics*' order[119], which provided that the restoration order was to be 'without prejudice to any remedy which any creditor who became such on or after the date of dissolution might otherwise have against any person prior to the date of this order taking effect'. Megarry J distinguished the *Rugby Auto Electrics* case from *Re Donald Kenyon Ltd*[120] where creditors who were not statute barred at the date of dissolution were statute barred on restoration and a provision was included in the order that the period between dissolution and restoration was not to be counted for the

---

116 *Re Brown Bayley's Steel Works Ltd* [1904–05] 21 TLR 374.

117 *Morris v Harris* [1927] AC 252. Finnegan P also cited *Tyman's Ltd v Craven* [1952] 2 QB 100; *Re Rugby Auto Electric Services Ltd* (14 December 1959, unreported) HC Eng, Roxburgh J; *Re Huntington Poultry Ltd* [1969] 1 WLR 204; *Re Lindsay Bowman Ltd* [1969] 1 WLR 1443; *Re Pricelans Ltd* [1997] 1 BCLC 467.

118 *Re Lindsay Bowman Ltd* [1969] 1 WLR 1443.

119 So called, after the decision in *Re Rugby Auto Electric Services Ltd* (14 December 1959, unreported) HC Eng, Roxburgh J.

120 *Re Donald Kenyon Ltd* [1956] 1 WLR 1397.

purposes of the Statute of Limitations. In relation to the '*Rugby Auto Electrics*' clause, Megarry J said:

> 'In the present case, the position seems to me to be very different. What is sought is a provision that will preserve to the creditor the rights that he acquired while the company was defunct. The statutory fiction that results from an order under the subsection is that the company continued in existence throughout; and this, with all that flows from it, is the necessary consequence of the order. One of the consequences is that any liabilities properly incurred by a director in the name of the company would be liabilities of the company and not the director. What the concluding limb of the subsection empowers me to do is to give directions or make provisions for placing the company and others in the same position as nearly as may be as if the name of the company had *not* been struck off. What Mr Hamilton [the creditor seeking the *Rugby Auto Electrics* clause] seeks is a direction or provision putting him in the same position as if the company *had* been struck off, as in fact it was. In other words, he seeks a direction or provision which will negative the statutory fiction, whereas all that the subsection empowers me to do is to give a direction or make a provision which supports and carries out the statutory fiction as nearly as may be. I do not see what power I have to include such a direction or provision in the order.'

As Finnegan P concluded, there is no power to make the directors of a company, which was dissolved and is being restored, personally liable for debts incurred during the period when the company was dissolved.

Options where restoration is impossible

[26.064] Sometimes, however, it will prove virtually impossible to restore a dissolved company to the register, eg, where all its directors and shareholders are long since dead, or where the company has been struck off for a period in excess of 20 years[121]. What is to be done where it transpires that a conveyance by a company, long since dissolved, is defective, eg, where inoperative words of limitation mean that there is a resulting trust in favour of the defunct company? In such cases any interest previously held by the company now stands in the name of the Minister for Finance by reason of s 28 of the SPA 1954. In those circumstances, there are two avenues open to the conveyancer seeking to regularise the matter. In the first place, application can be made for the appointment of a trustee (usually a solicitor) under the Trustee Act 1893, as was done in the case of *Re Kavanagh & Cantwell*[122]. This will be appropriate where the company is a bare trustee of the property (as it would be in the example given where full consideration passed to the company but title to the purchaser failed for technical reasons). Such an application to correct a defect on title should be made on notice to the Minister for Finance, and the support of the Chief State Solicitor's office should be obtained. In practice, this procedure tends to be used where the property in issue is being sold. A different, possibly more time consuming but equally effective, route can also be pursued, usually where it is sought to simply remedy a defect in title and there is no immediacy about having to show good marketable title. In such a case, application can be made to

---

121 In all cases where the court is empowered to restore a company to the register, there is a maximum time limit within which the company must have been dissolved of 20 years. See para **[26.035]** *et seq*, *post*.

122 *Re Kavanagh & Cantwell* (23 November 1984, unreported) HC, *per* Costello J. See para **[26.020]**.

the Minister for Finance, through the Chief State Solicitor's office, under s 30 of the SPA 1954 for the Minister to execute a waiver of the property in question. Section 30 provides:

> 'Whenever, either before, on or after the operative date, any property of whatsoever nature or kind devolves upon the State by way of escheat or becomes the property of the State as bona vacantia or by virtue of section 28, the Minister may, if he thinks proper so to do, waive, in whole or in part and in favour of such person and upon such terms (whether including or not including the payment of money) as he thinks proper having regard to all the circumstances of the case, the right of the State to such property.'

In practice, neither of these options will, generally, be consented to by the Chief State Solicitor's office where it is reasonably possible for an applicant to apply to have a company restored to the register.

Chapter 27

Investigations and Inspectors

Introduction

[27.001] Part II of the Companies Act 1990[1] ('CA 1990') provides a number of means whereby the ownership, control or affairs of a company can be investigated. Such investigations fall into two broad categories. The first category includes the Director of Corporate Enforcement's powers to require a person to give information with regard to the ownership of shares or to require the production of books and documents relating to a company. That category of investigation may (though need not necessarily) be a precursor to the second and more invasive category of investigation which involves the appointment of an inspector or inspectors to conduct a detailed investigation and to report on their findings.

[27.002] The investigatory regime exists to ensure compliance with company law – 'to ensure that companies incorporated under the Acts do not abuse the privileges which incorporation confers on them to the detriment of their members, their creditors or indeed the public in general[2]'. Though the legislation is broadly worded, it seems unlikely that an investigation can be commenced in the absence of suspected abuse of the privilege of incorporation[3]. Moreover, the investigation must be warranted; the essential function of the investigation being to discover whether there are facts which are not already known and which may result in others taking action[4]. The information gathered in an investigation may be applied to various purposes. In particular, an inspector's report may be used as evidence in subsequent criminal or civil proceedings[5], and a company may be wound up on foot of information contained in an inspector's report. The information can also be released to other regulatory authorities (such as the Competition Authority or the Revenue Commissioners) who may decide to act upon it accordingly. The process will not be warranted, however, where the information in question is already available to the authorities and where the sole purpose is to put the applicant at a procedural or evidential advantage in other proceedings[6].

§ *This chapter has been contributed by G Brian Hutchinson.*

1 As amended by Part 3 of the CLEA 2001 and s 3 of the C(MP)A 2009.

2 *Per* Keane CJ in *Dunnes Stores Ireland Company v Ryan* [2002] IR 60, at 77 (SC).

3 The powers of the Director may be invoked to assist an investigation by a foreign company law authority: s 23A of the CA 1990, as amended.

4 *Director of Corporate Enforcement v DCC plc* [2009] 1 IR 464.

5 Indeed, an inspector's report will carry presumptive weight in civil proceedings, defying the hearsay rule: see para **[27.058]** *post.* It would appear to remain subject to the normal exclusionary rules of evidence in criminal proceedings: see para **[27.044]** *post.*

6 *Director of Corporate Enforcement v DCC plc* [2009] 1 IR 464.

Background

[27.003] The basic concept of appointing competent inspectors to investigate the books and affairs of a company is of venerable origin[7]. The power of the Board of Trade to appoint one or more competent inspectors was to be found in the Companies Act 1862[8]. The power does not appear to have been invoked with any great frequency, though it was continued in the Companies (Consolidation) Act 1908[9] and in a more extended form in the CA 1963[10], by which time the powers of the board had become vested in the Minister.

In theory, these powers should have proved useful in checking abuse by directors of their duties, and in controlling company fraud generally. By the 1980s, however, and probably for a long time before then, it was apparent that the investigation procedures as they then existed were not serving any useful purpose[11]. The principal problem seems to have been that no detailed procedures were outlined in the legislation and that, as a consequence, most investigations suffered from legal objections grounded on the requirements of natural justice[12]. Moreover, investigations tended to occur in private, and their findings were rarely published[13].

[27.004] The CA 1990 introduced new and more detailed procedures to make investigations more meaningful. The principal innovation was that the High Court, rather than the Minister, was conferred with the power to appoint inspectors to investigate 'the affairs of a company'. This transfer of function, it was hoped, would enable the procedures to be determined in a more efficient manner. Additionally, two new and distinct powers were conferred on the Minister. The first was the power to appoint an inspector or inspectors to investigate and report on 'the membership of any company and otherwise with respect to the company for the purpose of determining the true persons who are or have been financially interested in the success or failure (real or apparent) of the company or able to control or materially to influence the policy of the company,'[14] or to investigate and report share dealings[15]. The second was to require the

7 See *Chestvale Properties Ltd v Glackin* [1993] 3 IR 35; also generally McGrath, 'Investigations under the Companies Act 1990' (1993) ILT 264; Fraser, 'Administrative Powers of Investigations into Companies' (1971) 24 MLR 260; and McCormack, *The New Companies Legislation* (1991, Round Hall Press).

8 Section 56 of the Companies Act 1862.

9 Sections 109 to 111 of the Companies (Consolidation) Act 1908.

10 Sections 165 to 173 of the CA 1963.

11 See especially McCormack, *The New Companies Legislation* (1991, Round Hall Press) at p 37 where the author, writing in 1991, points out that the investigation procedures contained in ss 165–166 of the CA 1963 were employed only five times since their introduction in 1963, and with little success. It is apparent from the annual companies reports of the time that further applications were made for the appointment of inspectors during that time, but the outcome of those applications is not known.

12 See McCormack, *The New Companies Legislation* (1991, Round Hall Press).

13 An exception is the *Report of the Enquiry into Irish Estates Ltd* (Stationery Office, 23 October 1963), which enquiry was held under the provisions of the Companies (Consolidation) 1908.

14 Section 14 of the CA 1990.

15 Section 66 of the CA 1990.

production of books or documents. The CA 1990 gave inspectors more extensive powers, and the statutory effect of the inspector's report was extended.

[27.005] The CA 1990's reforms had substantially the desired effect. A little over a month after Part II of the CA 1990 came into force, the Minister appointed an inspector to investigate the ownership and control of a number of companies involved in the purchase of shares in Sugar Distributors (Holdings) Ltd and the subsequent resale of those shares to Siúicre Éireann cpt at a substantial profit (the so-called 'Greencore Affair'). Four days later the High Court, on the application of the Minister, appointed two more inspectors to investigate the affairs of Siúicre Éireann cpt. Less than a month later the Minister, acting on the recommendations of a committee of inquiry appointed by the Minister for Tourism, Transport and Communications, appointed an inspector to investigate the membership and control of Chestvale Properties Ltd and Hoddle Investments Ltd, two companies connected with the sale of a site in Ballsbridge, Dublin, to the state-owned telecommunications company Telecom Éireann at a price more than twice that which had been paid for it less than a year previously (the 'Telecom Affair'). Both investigations produced a number of judicial decisions interpreting the new procedures, and, in general, upholding the new investigatory scheme.

The investigation procedures have been deployed on at least 21 occasions since the commencement of the CA 1990[16]. The majority of these have been investigations requiring the production of books and documents, but inspections have been ordered on seven occasions in total – four by the High Court on the application of the Minister[17], and the remaining three by the Minister directly[18]. Most of the activity preceded the transfer of functions to the Director of Corporate Enforcement under the Company Law Enforcement Act 2001 ('CLEA 2001').

[27.006] The CLEA 2001 revised the detail of the investigatory regime while retaining its general structure. The principal innovation was the transfer of the Minister's investigatory functions to the Director of Corporate Enforcement ('the Director'). This transfer has the advantage of placing the investigation powers in the hands of a full-time, independent, less political, specialist office. The Act further enhanced the investigatory regime by, *inter alia,* strengthening the powers of inspectors to examine the affairs of companies not named in the warrant of appointment; by increasing the powers of the Director with regard to the examination of books in respect of the production of books and documents; by introducing new offences in connection with the destruction of books and documents; by increasing the grounds on which a search warrant can be obtained where books and documents have not been produced; and by extending the categories of persons to whom information gathered in the process can be revealed.

---

16 *Companies Report, 2006*, Appendix 4.

17 *Companies Report, 2006*, Appendix 4. In addition to the companies involved in the 'Telecom Affair', the High Court has appointed inspectors to CountyGlen plc (1994); National Irish Bank Ltd and NIB Financial Services Ltd (1998); to Ansbacher (Cayman) Ltd (1999); and to DCC plc, S&L Investments Ltd and Lotus Green Ltd (2008).

18 *Companies Report, 2006*, Appendix 4. In addition to the companies involved in the Telecom and Greencore affairs, the Minister appointed an inspector to Bula Resources (Holdings) plc in 1997.

Future

[27.007] Constitutional doubts about the inspection and investigation process have gradually been settled in the courts, and there is now a general acceptance that submission to its more Orwellian features must be seen as the price which is to be paid for the benefits of incorporation. Nonetheless, investigations are costly and complex affairs which it seems, as a practical matter, can only be justified where substantial wrongdoing is suspected and where a high profile is attached. Even then, such a sledgehammer may not crack every nut.

Should any pitfalls in the investigation procedure become apparent in the future, the Minister has purported power in s 24 of the CA 1990 to introduce regulations 'to do anything which appears to him to be necessary or expedient' to remove any difficulty, to bring provisions of Part II into operation, or secure or facilitate the operation of any provision in Part II, and any such regulations may modify the provisions of Part II insofar as may be necessary for the carrying into effect of the new regulations. That provision smacks of unconstitutionality, however, as an over-broad delegation of the law-making function reserved exclusively to the Oireachtas by Article 15 of *Bunreacht na hÉireann*[19]. Not surprisingly the section appears never to have been utilised.

Architecture of the investigatory regime

[27.008] The following table details generally the various types of investigation possible under the Companies Acts:

Statutory provision	Type of investigation	Scope	Persons who may initiate	Outcome
Section 7 of the CA 1990	Court-appointed inspector	Affairs of the company	The company; a director; a creditor; or the requisite number of members	Report to High Court
Section 8 of the CA 1990	Court-appointed inspector	Affairs of the company	Director of Corporate Enforcement	Report to High Court
Section 14 of the CA 1990	Inspector appointed by Director of Corporate Enforcement	True persons involved or interested in membership or control	Director of Corporate Enforcement	Report to Director
Section 15 of the CA 1990	Inquiry by Director of Corporate Enforcement	Interests in shares or debentures	Director of Corporate Enforcement	Information

19 *City View Press v An Comhairle Oiliúna* [1980] IR 381; *Cooke v Walsh* [1984] IR 710.

Statutory provision	Type of investigation	Scope	Persons who may initiate	Outcome
Section 19 of the CA 1990	Inquiry by Director of Corporate Enforcement	Books or documents	Director of Corporate Enforcement	Information
Section 66 of the CA 1990	Inspector appointed by Director of Corporate Enforcement	Share or debenture dealings	Director of Corporate Enforcement	Report to Director

[27.009] As was noted above[20], and as can be seen from the above table, investigations fall into either of two broad categories – those which involve the appointment of an inspector; and those which do not. We turn, now, to consider each of these categories in further detail under the following headings:

[A] Inspections.

[B] Other Investigations and Inquiries.

[A] INSPECTIONS

[27.010] Part II of the CA 1990 envisages two types of inspections. The first, which is ordered by the High Court, involves the appointment of an inspector or inspectors to investigate and report on the 'affairs' of a company. The second, which is ordered by the Director, involves the appointment of an inspector or inspectors to investigate and report on the narrower question of the true ownership or control of a company or its shares.

Although there are some differences between court-ordered inspections on the one hand and those ordered by the Director on the other, the powers and status of inspectors appointed by either means are the same, and the provisions of Part II of the CA 1990 dealing with inspectors' powers apply to both kinds of inspector. Accordingly we deal here with the law relating to both kinds of inspections under the following headings, distinguishing between the two types as necessary:

1. Appointment of inspectors;
2. The scope of the inspection;
3. The conduct of the inspection;
4. The powers of the inspectors;
5. The inspector's report;
6. The costs of the inspection;
7. Concurrent investigations

Appointment of inspectors

[27.011] An inspector may be appointed in one of two ways: (a) by the court, or (b) by the Director. Each of these methods will now be considered in turn.

[20] At para **[27.001]** *ante*.

(a) Appointment of inspectors by the court

[27.012] Sections 7 and 8 of the CA 1990 empower the court to appoint one or more competent inspectors to investigate *the affairs of a company* and to report thereon in such a manner as the court directs. The court's power of appointment is exercisable notwithstanding that the company or body corporate to which it relates is in the throes of being wound up[21]. Under s 7(1), the court's power of appointment is exercisable:

(a) in the case of a company having a share capital, on the application either of not less than 100 members or of a member or members holding not less than one-tenth of the paid up share capital of the company;

(b) in the case of a company not having a share capital, on the application of not less than one-fifth in number of the persons on the company's register of members;

(c) in any case, on the application of the company;

(d) in any case, on the application of a director of the company;

(e) in any case, on the application of a creditor of the company.

Notably, the court is not given a power to appoint an inspector of its own motion. Since private companies must restrict their membership to 99 and must have a share capital[22], neither (b) nor the first limb of (a) applies to private companies. All of s 7(1) of the CA 1990 relates only to companies formed and registered under the Companies Acts[23].

[27.013] These provisions have never been invoked, and the question arises as to whether they are redundant. Persons who are in a position to seek the appointment of an inspector under s 7 of the CA 1990 already have a more direct remedy against the company or the officers in default, such as an action under s 205 of the CA 1963[24] or a petition to have the company wound up under s 213 of the CA 1963[25]. Also, the risks involved in applying to the court for an investigation may be too great to warrant invocation of the court's powers, since the court may require the applicant to put up security for the costs of the investigation[26].

[27.014] An application under s 7(1) must be made by originating notice of motion[27] and must be supported 'by such evidence as the court may require, including such evidence as may be prescribed[28]'. *Prescribed* in this context means prescribed *by regulations*[29], but since no such regulations have been made, the grounds upon which the court may make an order under s 7(1) are at present a matter for the court alone. In

21 Section 8(2)(a) of the CA 1990.

22 Section 33(1) of the CA 1963. See Ch 1, *The Private Company in Context*, at para **[1.134]**.

23 Section 2(1) of the CA 1963. See Ch 1, *The Private Company in Context*, at para **[1.156]**.

24 See generally Ch 11, *Shareholders' Remedies*.

25 See Ch 23, *Winding Up Companies*.

26 See para **[27.014]** *post*.

27 Order 75B, r 3(a) of the RSC. If the application is brought by a member or creditor, the notice must be served on the company and all its directors; where brought by the company, the notice must be served on the directors; and where brought by a director, the notice must be served on the company and all other directors.

28 Section 7(2) of the CA 1990.

29 Section 3(1) of the CA 1990.

Director of Corporate Enforcement v DCC plc[30], Kelly J observed that 'The court is at large to exercise its discretion in determining whether there are circumstances which warrant investigation[31]'. Presumably, the court would wish to be satisfied that there was at least *prima facie* evidence of some irregularity in relation to the company's affairs[32]. Indeed, the court might have regard to the grounds for appointment enumerated in s 8(1), which apply where the Director is the applicant[33], but 'it is clear that the jurisdiction conferred on the court by s 7 is wider than that which is given under s 8[34]'. It seems unlikely that the court would order an investigation where it is clear that no useful result is likely to be achieved, but no doubt it would be difficult for the court to determine at the application stage whether a useful result is likely or not. To this end, s 7(3) seeks to deter vexatious applications by empowering the court, if it so chooses, to require applicants to put up security for the costs of the investigation[35]. The net effect of s 7(3) may be to deter all but the most assured of potential applicants from seeking the appointment of an inspector, an effect which rather militates against the purpose of having an investigation procedure in the first place.

[27.015] The Director may apply to the court for the appointment of an inspector, but in his case the grounds for the application are expressly limited by statute. Section 8(1) of the CA 1990, as amended[36], provides:

> 'Without prejudice to its powers under section 7, the court may on the application of the Director appoint one or more competent inspectors (who may be or include an officer or officers of the Director) to investigate the affairs of a company and to report thereon in such manner as the court shall direct, if the court is satisfied that there are circumstances suggesting
>
> (a) that its affairs are being or have been conducted with intent to defraud its creditors or the creditors of any other person or otherwise for a fraudulent or unlawful purpose or in an unlawful manner or in a manner which is unfairly prejudicial to some part of its members, or that any actual or proposed act or omission of the company (including an act or omission on its behalf) is or would be so prejudicial, or that it was formed for any fraudulent or unlawful purpose; or
>
> (b) that persons connected with its formation or the management of its affairs have in connection therewith been guilty of fraud, misfeasance or other misconduct towards it or towards its members; or
>
> (c) that its members have not been given all the information relating to its affairs which they might reasonably expect.'

30 *Director of Corporate Enforcement v DCC plc* [2009] 1 IR 464.

31 *Director of Corporate Enforcement v DCC plc* [2009] 1 IR 464 at 475.

32 *Re Miles Aircraft Ltd (No 2)* [1948] WN 178; *Sage Holdings Ltd v The Unisec Group Ltd* (1982) 1 SA 337.

33 *Sage Holdings v The Unisec Group* (1982) 1 SA 337. On s 8(1) of the CA 1990, see para **[27.015]** *post*.

34 *Per* Kelly J in *Director of Corporate Enforcement v DCC plc* [2009] 1 IR 464 at 475.

35 Section 7(3) of the CA 1990, as amended by s 3(b) of the C(MP)A 2009, which removed the monetary limits that the security must not exceed €317,435, but may not be less than €6,359. On security for costs generally see Ch 6, *Corporate Civil Litigation*, at para **[6.014]** *et seq*.

36 By s 21 of the CLEA 2001.

Section 8(1) relates not only to companies formed and registered under the Companies Acts, but also to all bodies corporate incorporated outside the State which are carrying on, or have carried on, business in the State[37].

[27.016] Taking each of the grounds contained in s 8(1) in turn, it should first be observed that the reference to 'members' in s 8(1)(a) includes persons to whom shares have been transferred or transmitted by operation of law though not registered as members[38]. For example, the interests of transferees of shares whom the directors wrongfully refuse to register as members may be taken into account[39]. It has been observed[40] euphemistically that the reference to 'unfairly prejudicial' in s 8(1)(a) is 'surprising,' since the concept of unfair prejudice, whilst familiar to English company law[41], is novel to Irish company law. The similarity of s 8(1) to the corresponding UK section[42] may provide a clue to this incursion; how the Irish courts will construe it in this context remains to be seen. The scope of s 8(1)(a) is broad, though the interests of members are better protected than those of creditors. Notably, past, present *or future* conduct which was, is, *or will be* unfairly prejudicial to the members may ground the Director's application, whereas only past or present conduct may be taken into account where the interests of creditors (of the company or otherwise) are concerned. Note also that evidence that the company was formed for a fraudulent or unlawful purpose may ground an application by the Director[43].

Secondly, s 8(1)(b) is clearly directed at situations where the promoters, directors, or other officers connected with the management of the company *have* breached their duties to the company[44]. Although less clear, it would also seem to encompass breaches by shadow directors. Significantly, the fraud, misfeasance or other misconduct may be towards the company *or* 'towards its members'. Perhaps, then, breach of a shareholders' agreement between the directors and some or all of the members could ground an application by the Director.

Thirdly, s 8(1)(c) refers to information relating to the affairs of the company which the members 'might reasonably expect'. Such information could include the annual accounts of the company and any group accounts[45], and also the information contained in the registers of the company which the members are entitled to inspect[46].

---

37 Section 17 of the CA 1990.

38 Section 8(2)(b) of the CA 1990.

39 See generally Ch 9, *Share Transfer*, at para **[9.042]** *et seq*.

40 MacCann and Courtney, *Companies Acts 1963–2009* (2010, Bloomsbury Professional) at p 542. In *Horgan v Murray* [1997] 3 IR 23, however, Murray J appears to have taken the view that there is little distinction in substance between the concepts of 'oppression / disregard of interests' and 'unfair prejudice'.

41 The concept was introduced by ss 459–461 of the Companies Act 1985 (UK) to replace the concepts of 'oppression' and 'disregard of interests,' both of which live on Ireland: see Ch 11, *Shareholders' Remedies*, at para **[11.006]** *et seq*.

42 Section 432 of the Companies Act 1985 (UK).

43 As to the remedies of creditors and members where the company is formed for an unlawful purpose, see principally Ch 23, *Winding Up Companies*, at para **[23.106]**.

44 See Ch 15, *Duties of Directors and Other Officers*, at para **[15.161]**.

45 See Ch 17, *Financial Statements, Audit and Annual Return*.

46 See Ch 8, *Shares and Membership*, at para **[8.086]** *et seq*. One might have thought that these situations are already covered by s 8(1)(b).

In order to justify an appointment under s 8 the court must thus be satisfied that there are circumstances suggesting the affairs of the companies are being or have been conducted in an unlawful manner. But the mere existence of such circumstances alone will not guarantee appointment; in *Director of Corporate Enforcement v DCC plc*[47], Kelly J observed as follows:

> 'before the court appoints an inspector it must be satisfied that there are circumstances suggesting that the affairs of the companies are being or have been conducted in an unlawful manner. In the absence of such circumstances no question of an appointment can arise at all. But the presence of such evidence does not give rise to an automatic entitlement to have inspectors appointed. That is because the section is framed in such a way as to confer a discretion on the court. The court "may" appoint inspectors; it is not bound to do so. Regardless of what evidence of wrongdoing might be adduced the court would not be justified in appointing inspectors unless the purpose of such appointment had a reasonable prospect of being achieved.'

In that case, the respondents argued that the Director's purpose in seeking the appointment of an inspector was not a legitimate one born of an insufficiency of knowledge, but rather was with a view to converting information already known into a form which (by virtue of s 22 of the CA 1990) makes it admissible in evidence in any proceedings including those taken with a view to obtaining disqualification orders against persons associated with the respondents. Kelly J observed that if the sole motivation of the Director in seeking the appointment of inspectors was to obtain the s 22 advantages then he would have no hesitation in dismissing the application. In the event, however, he was satisfied that that was not the sole motivation, and moreover, that the public interest and the interests of proportionality both justified the appointment.

(b) Appointment of inspectors by the Director

[27.017] Section 14 of the CA 1990, as amended[48], empowers the Director to appoint an inspector to investigate a company for the purposes of determining the identity of the true persons who are financially interested in it or who are able to shape its policy. Section 14(1)–(3) provide:

> '(1) The Director may, subject to subsection (2), appoint one or more competent inspectors to investigate and report on the membership of any company and otherwise with respect to the company for the purpose of determining the true persons who are or have been financially interested in the success or failure (real or apparent) of the company or able to control or materially to influence the policy of the company.
>
> (2) An appointment may be made by the Director if he is of the opinion that there are circumstances suggesting that it is necessary—
>
> (a) for the effective administration of the law relating to companies;
>
> (b) for the effective discharge by the Director of his functions under any enactment; or
>
> (c) in the public interest.
>
> (3) The appointment of an inspector under this section may define the scope of his investigation, whether as respects the matters or the period to which it is to extend or

[47] *Director of Corporate Enforcement v DCC plc* [2009] 1 IR 464.

[48] By ss 14 and 26 of the CLEA 2001.

otherwise, and in particular may limit the investigation to matters connected with particular shares or debentures.'

It will be noted that the Director must be satisfied as to at least one of the conditions contained in s 14(2) before making an appointment.

[27.018] Section 66 of the CA 1990, as amended, also confers on the Director the power to appoint an inspector to investigate and report on dealings in shares or debentures where there are circumstances suggesting a contravention of ss 30, 53, or 64(3)–(5) of the CA 1990. Those sections place limitations or prohibitions on certain types of share dealings involving directors and connected persons, and which impose an obligation on such persons to register their interests in shares and debentures.

[27.019] In reaching a decision in any case as to whether an inspector ought to be appointed, the Director must act *bona fide*. In *Desmond v Glackin (No 2)*[49], a case arising out of the Telecom affair, O'Hanlon J observed of the above provisions:

> 'These provisions appear to me to confer a discretion on the Minister when making such an appointment and expressing it to be made in the public interest, to spell out the matters to which the investigation is to extend, if he thinks fit to do so. I do not interpret the statute as imposing an obligation on the Minister to define in express terms the nature of the public interest upon which he relies as justifying the appointment.
>
> Following the decision of the Supreme Court in *The State (Lynch) v Cooney* [1982] IR 337 at 361, it appears that an appointment made under the section might be open to challenge if it could be shown that any opinion formed by the Minister and relied upon as justifying the appointment was not *bona fide* held, or not factually sustainable, or unreasonable.'

In that case, the applicant, Dermot Desmond, a stockbroker, was instrumental in negotiating the purchase of a site in Ballsbridge, Dublin, for £4 million, by United Property holdings Ltd (UPH). After the purchase, the property became vested in Chestvale Properties Ltd, a wholly owned subsidiary of UPH. UPH subsequently sold its subsidiary, Chestvale, to Delion Investment Dealings Ltd, a Cyprus registered company, for apparently £2.75 million. Delion immediately sold on to Hoddle Investments Ltd for £9.3 million, and Hoddle sold on to Telecom Éireann for £9.4 million, a transaction which Mr Desmond was, again, instrumental in negotiating. Public disquiet was aroused when it became apparent that Telecom Éireann, a semi-State company, had paid over twice what the property had sold for less than a year previously, and a good deal of speculation arose as to the identity of the parties who had benefited from this financial coup. A committee of inspection was appointed by the Minister for Transport and Communications, which, though it succeeded in establishing much background information, was stonewalled by a number of parties. The committee recommended to the Minister that he appoint an inspector under the CA 1990, and the Minister did so. The warrant of appointment of the inspector recited that the Minister was 'of the opinion that there are circumstances suggesting that it is necessary in the public interest' and that:

> 'the investigation shall extend to the investigation of any circumstances suggesting the existence of an arrangement or understanding which, though not legally binding, is likely to be observed in practice and which is relevant to the purposes of the investigation.'

49 *Desmond v Glackin (No 2)* [1993] 3 IR 67.

Mr Desmond, who was subjected to close scrutiny by the inspector, applied for judicial review of the warrant of appointment on the basis that it did not state the nature of the public interest relied upon by the Minister in making the appointment. O'Hanlon J observed that the appointment of the inspector followed the recommendation of a committee of inspection which had published an interim report making the nature of the public interest involved very clear, and that the applicant had at no stage of the investigation requested information as to the public interest involved. Additionally, wide publicity had already been given to the matters of public interest leading up to the appointment of the inspector. The learned judge concluded that the validity of the appointment under s 14 was not dependent on the recital in the warrant of the nature of the public interest influencing the Minister to make the appointment[50].

Thus the Director is not required to state in the warrant of appointment the reasons for the appointment[51]. The latter statement should be approached cautiously, not only in the light of the observations of O'Hanlon J that the appointment must be *bona fide*, factually sustainable, and reasonable, but also in the light of the High Court and Supreme Court decisions in *Dunnes Stores Ireland Company v Ryan*[52], which hold that the Director's decision to appoint an authorised officer under s 19 of the CA 1990 can be judicially reviewed where the reasons for the appointment make it clear that it is being done for a purpose not contemplated by the Oireachtas, or where the Director has exercised the power in a patently irrational fashion.

The scope of the inspection

[27.020] In *Chestvale Properties Ltd v Glackin*[53], Murphy J held that Part II of the CA 1990 had retrospective effect so that an inspector appointed under that Part could investigate the affairs, membership or control of a company for periods prior to the enactment of the CA 1990, and unless the investigation amounted to more than a limited intrusion on the contractual rights of persons it could not be seen as an unjust attack on the constitutional property rights of citizens. The scope of a court-ordered inspection differs from that of an inspection ordered by the Director. The scope of each will now be considered in turn.

(a) The scope of a court-ordered inspection

[27.021] The CA 1990 states that an investigation by a court-appointed inspector is into the affairs of the company in order to enquire into matters specified by the court, but does not elaborate further as to what is meant by the 'affairs' of the company. In the absence of an Irish authority, English precedent may prove useful here. In *R v Board of Trade ex parte St Martins Preserving Co Ltd*[54], a creditor of a company to which an inspector had been appointed under s 165(a)(1) of the Companies Act 1948 (UK) sought an order of *mandamus* compelling the inspector to investigate the conduct of a receiver-manager as agent of the company in disposing of its assets. The Board of Trade

50 The learned judge repeated his observations in *Probets v Glackin* [1993] 3 IR 134 at 139.

51 *Desmond v Glackin (No 2)* [1993] 3 IR 67; *R v Secretary of State for Trade, ex parte Perestrello* [1981] QB 19.

52 *Dunnes Stores Ireland Company v Ryan* [2002] 2 IR 60.

53 *Chestvale Properties Ltd v Glackin* [1993] 3 IR 35.

54 *R v Board of Trade ex parte St Martins Preserving Co Ltd* [1965] 1 QB 603.

contested the application on the basis that the actions of a receiver-manager for a debenture holder were not the 'affairs' of the company. Rejecting the latter contention, Phillimore J granted the order sought, saying:

> 'What are "its affairs" when the company is in full control? They must surely include its goodwill, its profits or losses, its contracts and assets including its shareholding in and ability to control the affairs of a subsidiary, or perhaps in the latter regard a sub-subsidiary ... How were "its affairs" changed on the appointment of a receiver and manager of the property of the applicant company by the debentureholders? Did its affairs cease to be its affairs and become solely the affairs of the receiver and manager or of the debentureholders? I think not. Could the debentureholder and/or its receiver and manager play "ducks and drakes" with "its affairs" without regard to any interests of the shareholders of the applicant company? ... In short what the receiver and manager does may in a narrow sense be his affair, but it is also the affair of the company in the broad and natural meaning of the phrase "its affairs". He acts in the name of the company – what he does may ruin its shareholders or leave them with some prospect of future recovery. The fact that an action of the receiver and manager may be primarily designed to serve the interests of the debentureholder and to that extent be his affair does not in my judgment prevent it being an affair of the company, whose future may depend upon such action carried out in its name. If he is the agent as provided for in the debenture, why should he not be answerable for his conduct of "its affairs"?'

'Affairs', therefore, has a broad meaning: it extends to the conduct of receiver-managers appointed by creditors to the company; and may include the affairs of subsidiary companies under the company's control. Of course, the order appointing the inspector will state specific matters to be enquired into.

Where there is doubt, the inspector may from time to time apply to the court under s 7(4) of the CA 1990 for such directions or otherwise as it thinks fit with a view to ensuring that the investigation is carried out as quickly and inexpensively as possible. Such applications may be heard otherwise than in public if there is a danger that disclosure of the application would prejudice sensitive enquiries. In *Re Countyglen plc*[55], Murphy J considered that the majority of such applications were administrative applications rather than administrations of justice and that, accordingly, the Constitution did not require them to be heard in public.

[27.022] As was observed in the preceding paragraph, the 'affairs' of a company may include the affairs of *subsidiaries* under its control. Whether the scope of a court-ordered investigation extends *without more* to the investigation of the broader category of *related* companies (within the meaning of s 140(5) of the CA 1990)[56] and rclated bodies corporate is unclear, but would seem to depend upon whether the related company is under the control of the company under investigation, since the investigation must relate to the 'affairs' of the company under investigation.

[27.023] In this regard, s 9 of the CA 1990, as amended[57], comes to the assistance of the inspector who thinks it is necessary to investigate a related company. Section 9 provides:

---

55 *Re Countyglen plc* [1995] 1 IR 220.

56 Section 3(1) of the CA 1990. See Ch 25, *The Realisation and Distribution of Assets in a Winding Up*, at para **[25.120]** *et seq*.

57 By s 22 of the CLEA 2001.

> 'If an inspector appointed under section 7 or 8 to investigate the affairs of a company thinks it necessary for the purposes of his investigation to investigate also the affairs of any other body corporate which is related to such company, he shall, with the approval of the court, have power so to do, and shall report on the affairs of the other body corporate so far as he thinks the results of his investigation thereof are relevant to the investigation of the affairs of the first-mentioned company.
>
> For the purposes of this section, a body corporate which is related to a company includes a body corporate with which the company has a commercial relationship, and a commercial relationship exists where goods or services are sold or given by one party to another.'

Thus, with the approval of the court, the investigation can be extended to the affairs of related companies. Section 9, however, applies only to related companies and bodies corporate which are formed and registered within the State or which have been incorporated outside the State and are carrying on, or have carried on, business within the State[58]. Where the court grants approval under s 9, the inspector must also report on the related company's or body corporate's affairs so far as he thinks the results of his investigation are relevant to his principal investigation[59].

(b) The scope of an inspection ordered by the Director

[27.024] Section 14(1) of the CA 1990 states that an inspection ordered by the Director is to be into 'the *membership* of any company and otherwise with respect to the company *for the purpose of determining the true persons* who are or have been financially interested in the success or failure (real or apparent) of the company or able to control or materially to influence the policy of the company'. The purpose of such an investigation is to look behind the separate legal personality of the company, as McCarthy J observed in *Desmond v Glackin (No 2)*[60]:

> 'Since the decision in *Salomon v Salomon & Co Ltd* [1897] AC 22, efforts at lifting the corporate veil have largely come from the legislature rather than the courts. Section 14, in my judgment, clearly entitled the Minister through his inspector to tear the veil of secrecy of ownership from the company and identify those financially interested in the success or failure of the company, whatever *personae* any such person may have.'

Such an investigation may prove useful in establishing whether directors or other officers of a company have hidden behind another company when acting in breach of their duties to the company. Section 14(4) further provides:

> Subject to the terms of an inspector's appointment his powers shall extend to the investigation of any circumstances suggesting the existence of an arrangement or understanding which, though not legally binding, is or was observed or likely to be observed in practice and which is relevant to the purposes of his investigation.

Clearly, then, the scope of an investigation ordered by the Director extends to the identification not only of the persons legally interested in the success or failure of a company, or in its control, but to those who *in practice* are so interested. Investigations

---

58 Section 17 of the CA 1990; See also *Desmond v Glackin (No 2)* [1993] 3 IR 67, *per* McCarthy J at 125, and *Minister for Justice v Siúicre Éireann, Greencore et al* [1992] 2 IR 215, which is discussed at para **[27.061]** *post*.

59 Section 9 of the CA 1990.

60 *Desmond v Glackin (No 2)* [1993] 3 IR 67 at 128–129.

under s 14 are not restricted to Irish companies; s 17 of the CA 1990 extends the scope of such investigations to all bodies corporate incorporated outside the State which are carrying on, or have carried on, business within the State, or have at any time carried on business therein as if they were companies registered under the CA 1963, subject to any necessary modification[61].

[27.025] The special purpose of an investigation under s 14 has the effect of extending the scope of the investigation beyond the examination of the companies named or identified in the inspector's warrant of appointment. This is because the expression 'true persons' in sub-s (1) refers to natural persons. In *Lyons, Keleghan and Murphy v Curran*[62], Blayney J explained:

> 'In my opinion the correct construction of this subsection is that an inspector appointed under it to investigate a particular company has the duty and power to investigate the membership of the company for the purpose of determining who are or have been financially interested in the success or failure of the company. And investigating the membership is not simply for the purpose of ascertaining who are the members. It is for the purpose of determining who are the true persons financially interested in the success or failure of the company. That would clearly cover ascertaining the identity of the beneficiary, where shares are held by a person or persons as trustees, or by a corporate trustee, but in my opinion it also covers ascertaining the identity of the persons entitled to the shares of a corporate member. Otherwise it would be necessary to conclude that where an inspector had ascertained that some or all of the shares in the company he was investigating belonged to another company, he had finished his investigation; he had determined the true persons financially interested in the success or failure of the company. In my opinion that could not be so. I am satisfied that the phrase "the true persons" means the real individuals who are financially interested, and cannot refer to a company. So, where an inspector finds a company as shareholder in the company he is investigating, he must go further and seek to determine the persons who are the beneficial owners of that company.'

Accordingly, an inspector appointed to investigate the membership of a company named in the warrant of appointment may, *without further approval of the Director*, investigate the membership of a company *not* named in the warrant, if such investigation is necessary for the purpose of enquiring into the identity of the natural persons interested in the success or failure, or involved in the control, of the company under investigation. Indeed, the inspector may, if needs be, extend his investigation to the personal business affairs of natural persons. In *Desmond v Glackin (No 2)*[63], O'Hanlon J found that the inspector was 'fully justified', having regard to the scope of his duty, in investigating the personal business affairs of the applicant. All the evidence made available to the inspector led him to believe that the applicant had master-minded all the relevant transactions in the Telecom Affair.

[27.026] These extended investigative powers create a curious inter-relationship between ss 14(1) and 9[64] of the CA 1990 as applied to investigations under s 14 by

61 As to 'carry on business' see the observations of Lynch J in *Minister for Justice v Siúicre Éireann, Greencore et al* [1992] 2 IR 215, discussed at para **[27.061]** *post*.

62 *Lyons, Keleghan and Murphy v Curran* [1993] ILRM 375. Blayney J's views were endorsed by McCarthy J in the Supreme Court in *Desmond v Glackin (No 2)* [1993] 3 IR 67, at 127–128.

63 *Desmond v Glackin (No 2)* [1993] 3 IR 67.

64 See para **[27.023]** *ante*.

s 14(5). That inter-relationship was considered by Blayney J in *Lyons, Keleghan and Murphy v Curran*[65]. The respondent in that case, Mr Maurice Curran, was appointed by the Minister for Industry and Commerce under s 14 of the CA 1990 to investigate and report on the activities of a number of companies involved in the 'Greencore Affair', including a company called Gladebrook. That affair concerned the purchase of shares in Sugar Distributor Holdings Ltd by Gladebrook, and the subsequent resale of those shares to Siúicre Éireann cpt (Irish Sugar plc) at a substantial profit to Gladebrook. Gladebrook was part owned by Talmino, a foreign company, which was not named in the warrant of appointment. Mr Curran investigated Talmino – without obtaining prior approval under s 9 of the CA 1990 – and concluded in his report that Mr Chris Comerford, a director of Siúicre Éireann, was beneficial owner of Talmino. The applicants sought an order of *certiorari* quashing Mr Curran's report, on the grounds that Mr Curran had not been appointed to investigate Talmino nor had he obtained approval under s 9. They argued that if the inspector could proceed without the necessity to have regard to s 9, then that section was superfluous.

Blayney J held that the inspector had both the power and a duty to investigate Talmino under the terms of his appointment, and he rejected the argument that s 9 was superfluous. He said:

> 'In finding that the respondent was entitled to report on Talmino as he has done, I am necessarily rejecting the applicants' submission that if the respondent was entitled to investigate Talmino it meant that s 9 was unnecessary. I will give briefly my reasons for taking this view. In my opinion s 9 applies to a situation different from that in which the respondent found himself in regard to Talmino. The respondent had to investigate Talmino in order to fulfil the purpose for which he was appointed. That is very different from the position of an inspector availing of s 9. Such an inspector simply "*thinks* it necessary for the purposes of his investigation to investigate also the membership" of another body corporate. He does not *know* that it is necessary, which was the respondent's position. An inspector seeking to investigate another body corporate under s 9 might not be correct in his view that it was necessary, and because of this further authority in the form of the approval of the minister is required. So there is a clear category of cases for which s 9 is needed, and an illustration of this is the respondent's application in the present case to the minister for his approval to investigate Siúicre Éireann CPT.' [Emphasis added.]

Accordingly, where an inspector *knows* that the investigation of a related company not named in the order of appointment is necessary for the performance of his function, he may proceed to investigate it without obtaining prior approval under s 9, but where he merely *thinks, but does not know,* that such an investigation is necessary, he must obtain approval. In practice, of course, it may well be nigh on impossible for anyone challenging the inspector's acts to prove that the inspector does not 'know' that investigation of the related company is not necessary for the purposes of his investigation[66], so s 9 may, in reality, be redundant after all.

---

65 *Lyons, Keleghan and Murphy v Curran* [1993] ILRM 375.

66 See McGrath, 'Investigations under the Companies Act 1990' (1993) ILT 264 at p 265.

Where the inspector does obtain approval under s 9, the section requires him to report on his findings as regards the related company 'so far as he *thinks*[67] the results' of his investigation are relevant.

[27.027] The advantage of regarding s 9 in this way is that an inspector may extend his investigation to the membership of other companies which are *not* related *in any way* to the companies named in the warrant of appointment. In this respect, investigations under s 14 of the CA 1990 may be said to differ from court-ordered investigations, since a court-appointed inspector may only investigate the 'affairs' (in the broadly construed meaning of that word)[68] of the company to which he is appointed, and, with the approval of the court, related companies which he thinks necessary for the purposes of his investigation. It remains to be seen whether the subtleties of Blayney J's distinction between 'knowing' and 'thinking' will be applied to court-ordered investigations.

The conduct of the inspection

[27.028] Is an inspector required to conduct his investigation in the same manner as a judicial inquiry in a court? Must he adhere strictly to the rules of natural justice during the conduct of the investigation? It would appear that the answer is no – at least until the investigation reaches a stage where adverse conclusions are to be drawn against a person or body. Thereafter, the person in respect of whom such conclusions are to be drawn must be afforded an opportunity to review and test the evidence against them, and to give evidence themselves.

The general issue came before the Supreme Court in the 1970s in *Re Haughey*[69] in connection with the rights of a witness appearing before the Dáil Public Accounts Committee. The court concluded that the applicant in that case, Mr Padraic Haughey, was entitled to such representation where the proceedings had reached the stage where[70]:

> '... Mr Haughey is more than a mere witness. The true analogy, in terms of High Court procedure, is not that of a witness but of a party. Mr Haughey's conduct is the very subject matter of the committee's examination and is to be the subject matter of the Committee's report.'

In those circumstances, the court held, the applicant was entitled not only to legal representation, but also to cross-examine witnesses, to introduce rebutting evidence, and to address the Committee in his own defence. While this approach represents the view of the Supreme Court, the case was not concerned with the duties of inspectors appointed under the Companies Acts. As shall be seen, however, it has had a significant influence on the courts' approach to investigations under the Companies Acts.

[27.029] In *Re Pergamon Press Ltd*[71], the English Court of Appeal was asked to consider whether the directors of Pergamon Press Ltd, which was under investigation by an

---

67 If one were to maintain Blayney J's distinction between 'knows' and 'thinks', one might conclude that the inspector is under no obligation to report on his findings *vis-à-vis* the related company where he knows that the results are relevant to the investigation of the companies named in the warrant of appointment.

68 See para **[27.021]** *ante*.

69 *Re Haughey* [1971] IR 217. See also *Chestvale Properties Ltd v Glackin* [1993] 3 IR 35 at 50.

70 *Re Haughey* [1971] IR 217 at 263, *per* Ó Dálaigh CJ.

71 *Re Pergamon Press Ltd* [1970] 3 All ER 589.

inspector appointed by the Board of Trade, were entitled to assurances that the investigation would be conducted in the same manner as a judicial inquiry in a court of law, so that the directors could see the transcripts of the evidence of witnesses adverse to them and could cross-examine those witnesses. Counsel for the inspector submitted that the rules of natural justice did not apply to an investigation. Lord Denning rejected that argument, saying:

> 'I cannot accept counsel for the inspector's submission. It is true, of course, that the inspectors are not a court of law. Their proceedings are not judicial proceedings: see *Re Grosvenor and West End Railway Terminus Hotel Co Ltd* (1897) 76 LT 337. They are not even quasi-judicial for they decide nothing; they determine nothing. They only investigate and report. They sit in private and are not entitled to admit the public to their meetings: see *Hearts of Oak Assurance Co Ltd v AG* [1932] AC 392. They do not even decide whether there is a *prima facie* case ... But this should not lead us to minimise the significance of their task. They have to make out a report which may have wide repercussions. They may, if they think fit, make findings of fact which are very damaging to those whom they name. They may accuse some; they may condemn others; they may ruin reputations or careers. Their report may lead to judicial proceedings. It may expose persons to criminal prosecutions or to civil actions. It may bring about the winding up of the company and be used itself as material for the winding up: see *Re SRA Properties Ltd* [1967] 2 All ER 615 ... When they do make their report the board are bound to send a copy of it to the company and the board may, in their discretion publish it, if they think fit, to the public at large. Seeing that their work and their report may lead to such consequences I am clearly of opinion that the inspectors must act fairly. This is a duty which rests on them, as on many other bodies, although they are not judicial nor quasi-judicial, but only administrative ... The inspectors can obtain information in any way which they think best, but before they condemn or criticise a man they must give him a fair opportunity for correcting or contradicting what is said against him. They need not quote chapter and verse. An outline of the charge will usually suffice.'

In *Maxwell v Department of Trade & Industry*[72], a further case arising out of the Pergamon Press affair, Lord Denning explained that a 'fair opportunity' meant *not* that the inspector must prepare a tentative report and circulate it to the persons to be criticised or condemned, *nor* did it mean that every relevant statement of other witnesses must be put to that person so as to give him an opportunity of answering them. Rather, the inspector is under a duty to do what is fair *to the best of his ability.* Consequently, where the inspector *bona fide* overlooks something of substance and fails to put it to the person to be criticised in the report, he has not failed in his duty to give a fair opportunity.

[27.030] A somewhat similar approach to the level of compliance with the rules of natural justice required of an inspector was taken by Murphy J in *Chestvale Properties Ltd v Glackin*[73]. In that case, the applicant contended that the inspector, a solicitor by profession, was disqualified from acting as inspector because his firm had previously acted as solicitors for a Mr Doherty, one of the persons who claimed to be interested in

72 *Maxwell v Department of Trade & Industry* [1974] QB 523; [1974] 2 All ER 122. See Pennington, 'Investigations under the Companies Acts and the Pergamon Affair' (1974) 118 Sol J 507.

73 *Chestvale Properties Ltd v Glackin* [1993] 3 IR 35.

one of the companies under investigation. Murphy J referred[74] to the Court of Appeal's decision in *Re Pergamon Press*, which he thought 'helpful', and to the decisions of the High Court in *The State (Shannon Atlantic Fisheries) v McPolin*[75] and the Supreme Court in *Re Haughey*[76]. He then continued:

> 'I think it would be correct to say that in every one of those cases the court concluded that the investigating authority was bound to exercise an appropriate measure of natural justice. On the other hand it is, I believe, equally clear that *the findings in that regard were directed and relevant only to certain issues* within the various investigations and were not intended to be applied and could not in fact be applied to each and every inquiry or communication emanating from the investigating authority.'

The learned judge concluded that the claim in the case before him was premature, since it was commenced when the investigation was only at a very preliminary and exploratory stage, at which stage it was too early to say whether the inspector had to 'enter any verdict' on any issue concerning Mr Doherty in the report. He said:

> 'In these circumstances it must be presumed that the respondent (unlike Inspector McPolin in *The State (Shannon Atlantic Fisheries Ltd) v McPolin* [1976] IR 93) will not have to "enter a verdict" on any issue between claimants to the shares in question. Even if the presumption were otherwise and that one should anticipate a stage being reached at which the respondent would find it necessary to make a choice as between conflicting claims, it is clear that that stage has not yet been reached. Accordingly the present application is premature insofar as it is based upon the contention that the inspector is engaged in a task which at present involves him in a quasi-judicial function. The respondents also contend that the applicants have no locus standi to challenge the impartiality of the respondent *vis-à-vis* Mr Doherty. In my view this point too is well founded. The case based on bias is constructed solely by reference to the injustice which Mr Doherty foresees he would suffer if and when the respondent is called upon to adjudicate on a contentious issue between him and some other party as yet unidentified. Whilst I have accepted that circumstances could exist in which bias would be perceived, it is only the parties whose rights would be affected by the adverse decision who could challenge the procedure in which it was reached.'

Notably, in contrast to Lord Denning's view in *Re Pergamon Press*, above, the learned judge was of the opinion that the inspector's role could become quasi-judicial at some stage in the proceedings.

[27.031] In *Re National Irish Bank Ltd (No 1)*[77], Shanley J adopted the approach employed by Murphy J in *Chestvale Properties Ltd v Glackin*, though this time in the context of inspectors appointed by the High Court rather than by the Minister (or now by the Director). The inspectors in this case had expressly proposed a two-stage process in their investigation: the first, being an information gathering exercise, would occur in private; the second, arising only when the first stage indicated the possibility that adverse conclusions might be drawn against any persons, would afford the individuals at risk an opportunity to attend, hear evidence, cross-examine witnesses, and give evidence themselves. Shanley J considered that the procedures adopted by the inspectors

74 *Chestvale Properties Ltd v Glackin* [1993] 3 IR 35 at 49.

75 *The State (Shannon Atlantic Fisheries) v McPolin* [1976] IR 93.

76 *Re Haughey* [1971] IR 217.

77 *Re National Irish Bank Ltd (No 1)* [1999] 3 IR 145.

accorded with the requirements of natural and constitutional justice and fair procedures. One of the employees of National Irish Bank Ltd disputed, however, that the investigation could maintain its character as a mere information gathering exercise when the media had already levelled a wide range of criminal accusations against the bank and its employees. Shanley J noted, however, that such anonymous accusations had not arisen in the course of the investigation, nor were they accepted as evidence in the investigation. Accordingly the challenge on procedural grounds was unfounded.

[27.032] That approach was subsequently endorsed by Kelly J in further proceedings arising out of the same investigation. In *Re National Irish Bank Ltd (No 2)*[78], the companies contended that the investigations could not be considered to be a mere information gathering exercise given that the Oireachtas had passed the Comptroller and Auditor General and Committees of the Houses of the Oireachtas (Special Provisions) Act 1998 which provided for a special investigation by the Comptroller and Auditor General and the Revenue Commissioners into the evasion of deposit interest retention tax ('DIRT') by certain financial institutions, including the National Irish Bank companies.

By this stage the inspectors had produced their second interim report to the court, in which they noted that some of the evidence of employees pointed to the willing opening and maintenance of fictitious non-resident bank accounts for Irish resident customers of the bank, and the facilitation of offshore bank accounts for customers in associated companies of the bank outside the State. Of particular significance is the fact that in their report the inspectors expressly emphasised that they had 'not yet formed any concluded view on these matters' and that they could not do so until they had had the opportunity of interviewing the relevant employees of the bank. Until such time, they said, 'it is not possible even to commence the process of considering whether the evidence should be accepted or not'.

Kelly J concluded that the companies' objections were unfounded. He quoted from Lord Denning's judgment in *Maxwell v Department of Trade & Industry*[79] as follows:

> 'Remember what it is not. It is not a trial of anyone, nor anything like it. There is no accused person. There is no prosecutor. There is no charge. It is not like a disciplinary proceeding before a professional body. Nor is it like an application to expel a man from a trade union or a club, or anything of that kind. It is not even like a committee which considers there is a *prima facie* case against a person. It is simply an investigation, without anyone being accused[80].'

Kelly J continued as follows[81]:

> 'Insofar as this jurisdiction is concerned, that, in my view, is a correct summary of the position which obtains at lest insofar as the investigatory stage of the Inspectors' task is concerned. Once one moves into the second stage then, whilst the investigation is not transformed into an adversarial hearing, nonetheless fair procedures have to be observed insofar as any adverse conclusions may be drawn in relation to individuals. The procedure which the Inspectors have outlined as one which they will follow if such a stage is reached is in compete compliance with their obligations to observe fair procedures under the relevant jurisprudence. It follows therefore, that I take precisely the same view as

78 *Re National Irish Bank Ltd (No 2)* [1999] 3 IR 190.

79 *Maxwell v Department of Trade & Industry* [1974] 2 All ER 122.

80 *Maxwell v Department of Trade & Industry* [1974] 2 All ER 122 at 127.

81 *Re National Irish Bank Ltd (No 2)* [1999] 3 IR 190 at 215.

Shanley J that there is no entitlement to invoke the rights established in *Re Haughey* at the information gathering stage of the Inspectors' work.'

As the investigation had not entered the second stage, the companies' objections were, at best, premature. Moreover, the challenge that the investigation had in fact entered the second stage was held to be unfounded. Kelly J observed[82] that the mere making of an allegation under oath does not carry the investigation into the second stage:

> 'It is not the mere fact of making an allegation under oath which elevates the status of an accusation to one which calls for a response. What brings that about is a determination by the Inspectors (a) that they will admit such an allegation as evidence and (b) that the admission of it may give rise to adverse conclusions being drawn against the party accused.'

[27.033] There are good reasons for this approach. Were an inspector bound to give every witness an opportunity of cross-examining the other witnesses, his ability to get to the heart of the matter efficiently would be substantially impaired. As one commentator[83] has observed, a requirement to proceed in accordance with the full rules of natural justice in the same manner as the court would be:

> 'a very impractical one, because when you are conducting one of these investigations, you don't know when you are getting evidence from the witnesses whether anybody has done anything wrong or whether it is just bad luck and it may not be until you have examined the fifty-fourth witness that you suddenly get the information which enables you to discover that the second, third or fourth witness has told you a pack of lies and that, in fact, he is the man who has stolen all the company's funds.
>
> Of course, I am not suggesting that a fair investigator would not, in those circumstances, seek to recall the man whom he examined second, third or fourth. Of course, he would ...'

Powers of inspectors

[27.034] Section 10 of the CA 1990 confers three wide powers on inspectors appointed either by the court or by the Director, namely:

- (a) to require the production of books, documents and information relating to the company;
- (b) to examine persons on oath;
- (c) to certify refusal to comply with requests for the production of books, documents and information or attendance before the inspector.

A fourth power, ie, to require the production of books and documents relating to directors' bank accounts, is given only to court-appointed inspectors. Each of these powers will now be considered in turn.

(a) Books, documents and information relating to the company

[27.035] Section 10(1) of the CA 1990[84] places a duty on officers and agents of the company to produce books and documents, to attend before the inspector, and otherwise to assist with the investigation. It provides:

---

82 *Re National Irish Bank Ltd (No 2)* [1999] 3 IR 190 at 216.

83 Judge Sir Richard Eggleston, Chairman of the Australian Company Law Reform Committee. See [1971] 45 ALJ 513 at 520.

84 By s 23 of the CLEA 2001.

> It shall be the duty of all officers and agents of the company and of all officers and agents of any other body corporate whose affairs are investigated by virtue of section 9 to produce to the inspectors all books and documents of or relating to the company, or, as the case may be, the other body corporate which are in their custody or power, to attend before the inspectors when required so to do and otherwise to give to the inspectors all assistance in connection with the investigation which they are reasonably able to give; but where any such person claims a lien on books or documents produced by the person, the production shall be without prejudice to the lien.

Section 10(7) provides that the reference in sub-s (1) to 'officers and agents' includes past, as well as present, officers and agents, and that 'agents' includes the company's bankers, solicitors and persons employed as auditors, accountants, book-keepers or taxation advisors, whether they are officers of the company or not.

[27.036] The obligations imposed by sub-s (1) are two-fold[85]. First of all, there is an obligation to produce books and documents, and secondly, there is an obligation to attend and give *viva voce* evidence. When giving oral evidence, the obligation is to provide all assistance in relation to the investigation.

Of course, the inspector and the officer or agent may have differing views as to what information may be of 'assistance in connection with the investigation'. In this regard, it seems that the officer or agent must produce all information which in his *honest opinion* may be of assistance to the inspector[86]. While this test might at first appear to favour the ignorant or the naive, it would seem to be the case that the officer or agent must have regard to the information stipulated in the inspector's request when forming his opinion[87]. There is something to be said for the latter approach: where the inspector makes a broad request, the officer or agent must not withhold any such information which he honestly believes may be of assistance; but where, however, the inspector identifies particular books or documents, or a particular class of books or documents, the officer or agent must comply with the request – since it would be impossible for him to form an honest belief that the specified information *may* not be of assistance.

[27.037] Section 10(2) extends these duties to persons, who are *not* officers or agents, whom the inspector considers to be in possession of relevant information, books or documents. It provides:

> If the inspectors consider that a person other than an officer or agent of the company or other body corporate is or may be in possession of any information concerning its affairs, they may require that person to produce to them any books or documents in his custody or power relating to the company or other body corporate, to attend before them and otherwise to give them all assistance in connection with the investigation which he is reasonably able to give; and it shall be the duty of that person to comply with the requirement; but where any such person claims a lien on books or documents produced by the person, the production shall be without prejudice to the lien.

---

85 See McGrath, 'Investigations under the Companies Act 1990' (1993) ILT 264 at p 264, where the author discusses the views of Murphy J in *Chestvale Properties Ltd v Glackin (No 2)* (10 March 1992) HC. Murphy J's construction of s 10(1) met with the approval of Costello J in *Glackin v Trustee Savings Bank* [1993] 3 IR 55.

86 See McGrath, 'Investigations under the Companies Act 1990' (1993) ILT 264 at 264.

87 McGrath, 'Investigations under the Companies Act 1990' (1993) ILT 264. McGrath here relies on the words of Murphy J in *Probets v Glackin* (25 May 1992) HC.

[27.038] *Any* books and documents may be required by the inspector under s 10(1) and (2) of the CA 1990, regardless of whether they are the property of the company. As Murphy J observed in *Chestvale Properties Ltd v Glackin*[88]:

> '... the fact that particular books and documents may be properly identified as being the property of or relating to one company does not necessarily preclude them from relating also to another company.'

That said, however, s 23(1) of the CA 1990 expressly provides that nothing in Part II of the Act is to be taken as compelling any person to divulge information which, in the opinion of the court, he would be entitled to refuse to produce on the grounds of legal professional privilege.

[27.039] Other duties of confidentiality are not so closely protected. In *Glackin v Trustee Savings Bank*[89], Costello J held that a bank may not refuse to cooperate on the basis that to do so would breach a duty of confidentiality which it owes a customer. In that case, the plaintiff inspector formed the opinion that part of the proceeds of one of the transactions in the 'Telecom Affair' had been credited to accounts in a branch of the defendant bank. In a wide-ranging request to the bank pursuant to s 10(2), he sought details of those accounts, including the name of the account holder and the mandate under which the accounts had been opened. The bank, on the advice of its solicitors, failed to respond to the requests. In an application by Mr Glackin to have the failure enquired into, Costello J said[90]:

> 'It seems to me that the bank has misunderstood its statutory duty. Its statutory duty has been made perfectly clear in the judgment of Murphy J in *Chestvale Properties Ltd v Glackin (No 2)* ... It is a duty to give assistance if requested to do so under s 10, sub-s 2 of the Act of 1990. It is not permitted to refuse assistance, because of a contractual arrangement with a customer which may have involved a term of confidentiality.
>
> The Oireachtas has made perfectly clear, to my mind, what people, statutory organisations such as the Trustee Savings Bank, are required to do. They are required to assist the inspector, who has been appointed by the Minister [or the court, as the case may be]. They are not entitled to obstruct him and they must observe his requests. They have a statutory obligation to do so. They are not entitled to ask their customer whether or not the customer objects. Whatever contractual arrangement there has been between the bank and the customer has been clearly over-ridden by the provisions put into this section by the Oireachtas and the manner in which it should comply with the request has been made clear by Mr Justice Murphy. They are to give assistance to the inspector when requested to do so ... What the bank has to do, and other persons who are subject to a request by an inspector under the section, is to comply with the request and to assist the inspector in the work which he has to perform and which is clearly set out in the section.'

Accordingly, only that privilege which is expressly mentioned in the Act, namely, legal professional privilege, may be relied upon in refusing an inspector's request[91] – and even then only if the court is of the opinion that it is so privileged.

---

88 *Chestvale Properties Ltd v Glackin* [1993] 3 IR 35 at 53.

89 *Glackin v Trustee Savings Bank* [1993] 3 IR 55.

90 *Glackin v Trustee Savings Bank* [1993] 3 IR 55 at 62–63.

91 See also *Re an Inquiry under the Company Securities (Insider Dealing) Act 1985* [1988] AC 660 where it was held in England that a journalist could not rely on a wish not to disclose his sources as a ground for refusal to comply with a request from an inspector appointed under the Company Securities (Insider Dealing) Act 1985 (UK).

[27.040] Where a person fails or refuses to produce books, documents or information in accordance with either s 10(1) or (2) of the CA 1990, the inspector may certify the refusal and apply to court for an order directing the production of the books, etc[92].

[27.041] A demand by the inspector under s 10(1) or (2) of the CA 1990 will not amount to an abuse of his statutory powers if the demand follows closely the terms of the CA 1990. In *Chestvale Properties Ltd v Glackin*[93], the applicants contended that the demand made by the inspector for books and documents was expressed in such general terms and imposed such time limits as to amount to an abuse of the inspector's statutory powers. Murphy J rejected that contention on the facts before him, saying:

> 'Whatever argument might be constructed on the basis of any such analysis, the reality is that both the bankers and the solicitors were able to comply with the demand and within the time limits prescribed by the inspector. Neither the bankers nor the solicitors raised any objection based upon administrative difficulties. Their only concern was to ensure that in performing the obligations which appeared to be imposed upon them by statute that they did not neglect the duty which they had to their clients or former clients as the case may be.
>
> In the circumstances it seems to me that there is no substance in this particular ground. Furthermore it would be difficult to sustain a challenge to the validity of the exercise of a statutory power which follows so closely the terms of the section by which it was conferred[94].'

In so saying, however, it seems that the learned judge implicitly recognised the possibility that a substantial demand by the inspector might amount to an abuse of power in appropriate circumstances.

(b) Examination of persons on oath

[27.042] Section 10(4) of the CA 1990 provides:

> An inspector may examine on oath, either by word of mouth or on written interrogatories, the officers and agents of the company or other body corporate and such person as is mentioned in subsection (2) in relation to its affairs and may—
>
> (a) administer an oath accordingly,
>
> (b) reduce the answers of such person to writing and require him to sign them.

There is old authority in *Re Redbreast Preserving Co (Ireland) Ltd*[95] for the proposition that the examination does not have to be held in public; however, the constitutional propriety of that decision was doubted by Walsh J in *Re R Ltd*[96] in the light of the constitutional requirement that justice, where possible, must be administered in public. It is hardly the case, however, that an inspector could be regarded as administering justice – even though he may have quasi-judicial functions[97].

---

92 See para **[27.046]** *post*.

93 *Chestvale Properties Ltd v Glackin* [1993] 3 IR 35.

94 *Chestvale Properties Ltd v Glackin* [1993] 3 IR 35 at 54.

95 *Re Redbreast Preserving Co (Ireland) Ltd* (1956) 91 ILTR 12. See also *Hearts of Oak Assurance Co v AG* [1932] AC 392.

96 *Re R Ltd* [1988] IR 126.

97 See, eg, *McDonald v Bord na gCon (No 2)* [1965] IR 217.

[27.043] In *Probets v Glackin*[98], another case arising out of the 'Telecom Affair', the applicant sought an order prohibiting the inspector from investigating the membership and control of Freezone Investments Ltd by taking evidence on oath on the basis that he had earlier voluntarily signed and submitted to the inspector a statutory declaration detailing the information in his possession. O'Hanlon J accepted that such a declaration *might* be sufficient for the inspector's purposes in the course of his investigation, but it could *not* be relied upon in judicial review proceedings such as this to prevent the inspector from seeking subsequent evidence on oath. He said:

> 'The applicants appear to take the view that the first respondent should accept at face value, and without further investigation, matters which have been deposed to by statutory declaration, or at least that there is some onus on him to show a *prima facie* case for disbelieving the averments made before continuing to seek further evidence to confirm or disprove the accuracy of what he has been told. In my opinion, this is not a correct interpretation of an inspector's functions when conducting an investigation.'

Accordingly, an examination under oath cannot be avoided by simply swearing a declaration or affidavit as to the facts in issue.

[27.044] The privilege against self-incrimination *cannot* be invoked by a witness as a valid basis for a refusal to answer a question put to him by the inspector. This is of particular importance, since s 18 of the CA 1990 provides that any answer given by a person to a question put to him in exercise of the powers under s 10 may be used in evidence against him.

In *Re National Irish Bank Ltd (No 1)*[99], the Supreme Court held that the privilege against self-incrimination is a judge-made rule which can be abrogated by the legislature, and that ss 10 and 18 of the CA 1990 have the effect of so abrogating the privilege. Accordingly, an individual cannot refuse to answer a question put by an inspector – unless it is covered by legal professional privilege which is expressly and separately protected by s 23 of the CA 1990. The Supreme Court added the *caveat*, however, that a confession given involuntarily cannot be admitted in subsequent *criminal* proceedings. Barrington J, with whom the other members of the court concurred, said[100]:

> '... a confession of a Bank official obtained by the Inspectors as a result of the exercise by them of their powers under section 10 of the Companies Act, 1990 would not, in general, be admissible at a subsequent criminal trial unless, in any particular case, the trial Judge was satisfied that the confession was voluntary.'

This saver provides cold comfort for those obliged to answer incriminating questions. The problem is how does one show that an answer given was done so involuntarily? It has been suggested that the only certain means of displaying involuntariness is to refuse to answer, whereupon the court may be called upon to compel an answer to be given[101].

---

98 *Probets v Glackin* [1993] 3 IR 134.

99 *Re National Irish Bank Ltd (No 1)* [1999] 3 IR 145. See Dillon-Malone, 'Voluntariness, The Whole Truth, and Self-Incrimination after *In Re National Irish Bank*' (1999) Bar Review 237.

100 *Re National Irish Bank Ltd (No 1)* [1999] 3 IR 145 at 189.

101 Dillon-Malone, 'Voluntariness, The Whole Truth, and Self-Incrimination after *In Re National Irish Bank*' (1999) Bar Review 237.

Such tactics, however, will inevitably result in sanctions of another kind for refusal to cooperate with the inspector[102].

[27.045] A similar approach is required from the perspective of European human rights. In *Saunders v United Kingdom*[103], the European Court of Human Rights found that the reliancc by prosecuting authorities on transcripts of interviews between Saunders, a former chief executive of Guinness plc, and inspectors appointed by the English Department of Trade and Industry was a violation of Article 6.1 of the European Convention on Human Rights. Under English law, Saunders could not refuse to answer questions put to him by inspectors relating to his involvement in an illegal share support scheme[104], and he was effectively compelled to incriminate himself. Both the European Commission on Human Rights and the European Court of Human Rights considered this aspect of the criminal trial to have been in breach of the entitlement to a fair hearing by an impartial and independent tribunal. It should be noted, however, that the decision relates only to the use of transcripts of answers in subsequent criminal proceedings, and provides no real grounds for a refusal to answer an inspector's question. Nor would it seem to prohibit reliance in criminal proceedings on other information obtained as a consequence of a self-incriminatory answer.

(c) Certification of refusal

[27.046] The inspector's powers would be worthless if he were unable to see that they were enforced. Section 10(5) and (6) of the CA 1990, as amended[105], enable the inspector to call upon the courts for assistance by certifying a refusal to cooperate with him. The court is then empowered to conduct a hearing into the refusal and hear any witnesses that may be produced against or on behalf of the person who refused, and to make any order which it thinks fit, including an order that the person concerned re-attend before the inspector, or produce the information sought. Alternatively, the court may direct that the person concerned need not produce the information sought.

[27.047] As enacted, s 10(5) of the CA 1990 gave the court the power to punish the person certified by the inspector 'in like manner as if he had been guilty of contempt of court'. However, in *Desmond v Glackin (No 2)*[106] O'Hanlon J, and on appeal, the Supreme Court, found that power to be unconstitutional since it enabled a person to be tried on a non-minor charge of contempt *without a jury.* The Supreme Court found that part of sub-s (5) bore a direct similarity to s 3(4) of the Dáil Éireann (Privilege and Procedure) Act 1970, which had been struck down as unconstitutional by the Supreme Court in *Re Haughey*[107] in 1971. Applying the 'severability' test laid down in *Maher v Attorney General*[108], the court was able to sever the unoffending words in sub-s (5) from the unconstitutional words. Section 10(6) was likewise doctored, since it contained a passage referring to s 10(5). The court seemed disappointed that the Oireachtas had

---

102 See para **[27.046]** *post*.

103 *Saunders v United Kingdom* [1997] BCC 872 (Case 43/1994/490/572).

104 *R v Harris* [1970] 3 All ER 746; *Bishopsgate v Maxwell* [1992] 2 All ER 856.

105 By s 23 of the CLEA 2001.

106 *Desmond v Glackin (No 2)* [1993] 3 IR 67.

107 *Re Haughey* [1971] IR 217.

108 *Maher v Attorney General* [1973] IR 140.

allowed this situation to arise; s 10(5) of the CA 1990 was modelled on s 168(3) of the CA 1963, which had, since the decision in *Re Haughey*, been amended by s 7 of the C(A)A 1982 in a manner which made it constitutional. Had the Oireachtas modelled the new subsections on the amended section the constitutional problem would not have arisen.

[27.048] Section 10(5) and (6) of the CA 1990 have been repealed and replaced by s 23 of the CLEA 2001 to give effect to the decision in *Desmond v Glackin (No 2)*. The new provisions are as follows:

> '(5) If an officer or agent of the company or other body corporate, or any such person as is mentioned in subsection (2), refuses or fails within a reasonable time to—
>
> (a) produce to the inspectors any book or document which it is his duty under this section so to produce,
>
> (b) attend before the inspectors when required so to do, or
>
> (c) answer a question put to him by the inspectors with respect to the affairs of the company or other body corporate as the case may be,
>
> the inspectors may certify the refusal or failure under their hand to the court, and the court may thereupon enquire into the case and, after hearing any witnesses who may be produced against or on behalf of the person alleged to have so refused or failed and any statement which may be offered in defence, make any order or direction it thinks fit.
>
> (6) Without prejudice to the generality of subsection (5), the court may, after a hearing under that subsection, direct—
>
> (a) the person concerned to attend or re-attend before the inspectors or produce particular books or documents or answer particular questions put to him by the inspectors, or
>
> (b) that the person concerned need not produce a particular book or document or answer a particular question put to him by the inspectors.'

(d) Books and documents relating to bank accounts

[27.049] Subsection (3) of s 10 of the CA 1990 contains a power which it seems is exercisable only by court-appointed inspectors (since it refers to an investigation into the 'affairs' of a company), and then only against *a director* – which, for the purposes of the subsection, includes past or present directors, past or present *connected persons*[109], and past or present shadow directors. In this respect, the power is supplemental to those contained in sub-ss (1) and (2). Essentially, the power enables the inspector to require a director to give details of his or her *private* bank accounts, whether held solely or jointly, within or outside the State, where the inspector *reasonably believes* that accounts exist containing amounts which have not been disclosed to the company or which are connected with misconduct. Subsection (3) provides:

> If an inspector has reasonable grounds for believing that a director of the company or other body corporate whose affairs the inspector is investigating maintains or has maintained a bank account of any description, whether alone or jointly with another person and whether in the State or elsewhere, into or out of which there has been paid—

---

109 As defined by s 26 of the CA 1990. See further Ch 16, *Statutory Regulation of Directors' Transactions,* at para **[16.003]** *et seq*.

(a) any money which has resulted from or been used in the financing of any transaction, arrangement or agreement—

(i) particulars of which have not been disclosed in a note to the accounts of any company for any financial year as required by section 41; or

(ii) in respect of which any amount outstanding was not included in the aggregate amounts outstanding in respect of certain transactions, arrangements or agreements as required by section 43 to be disclosed in a note to the accounts of any company for any financial year; or

(iii) particulars of which were not included in any register of certain transactions, arrangements and agreements as required by section 44; or

(b) any amount which has been in any way connected with any act or omission, or series of acts or omissions, which on the part of that director constituted misconduct (whether fraudulent or not) towards that company or body corporate or its members,

the inspector may require the director to produce to him all documents in the director's possession, or under his control, relating to that bank account ...'

'Bank account' is given an extended meaning by the section. The term relates not only to accounts held with licensed banks, but also to bodies exempt from the requirement in s 9 of the Central Bank Act 1972 to hold a banking licence.

[27.050] Though the power is wide, it is not without its limitations. First, the inspector must have *reasonable grounds* for his belief. The absence of such grounds may lead to the inspector's exercise of the power being overturned by judicial review. Second, it has been argued that the words '... relating to that bank account ...' require the inspector to *specify* a particular bank account, a requirement which, if true, is particularly difficult to meet without a corresponding power to require the director to disclose accounts maintained by him generally[110]. It is submitted that the latter power is to be found in sub-ss (1) and (2). Third, sub-s (3) appears not to relate to pension schemes and other investment funds; but, again, details of such funds may be obtained under sub-ss (1) and (2). Indeed, on the whole it is difficult to see how sub-s (3) adds anything to the powers given to inspectors by sub-ss (1) and (2): directors may be required under sub-s (1) to give the information referred to in sub-s (3), and shadow directors and connected persons may be required under sub-s (2) to give such information[111]. It could not be argued that sub-s (3), unlike sub-ss (1) and (2), entitles the inspector to investigate matters other than those which may relate to the affairs of the company under investigation – for in such circumstances the investigator would be exceeding the scope his brief under ss 7 and 8 of the CA 1990[112]. In the light of s 10(1) and (2) it is submitted that s 10(3) is redundant. Indeed, the Oireachtas thought it unnecessary to extend the powers in s 10(3) to inspectors appointed by the Director under s 14 of the CA 1990.

The inspector's report

[27.051] An inspector, no matter how appointed, must make a report at the end of the investigation[113]. Indeed, where the inspector investigates the affairs, membership or

[110] See Chaikin, (1982) 3 Co Law 115.

[111] *Desmond v Glackin (No 2)* [1993] 3 IR 67.

[112] See para **[27.020]** *ante*.

[113] Sections 7, 8 and 14 of the CA 1990.

control of a related company or body corporate with the approval of the court or the Director as the case may be, he is *obliged* by s 9 of the CA 1990 to report on the findings which he thinks relevant to his investigation of the company or companies to which he was appointed[114]. In *Lyons, Keleghan and Murphy v Curran*[115], Blayney J held that an inspector who, within the scope of his investigation, investigates the membership or control of a company or body corporate *not* specified in the warrant of appointment, is *entitled* to report his findings. The inspector may also give a recommendation in the report as to who he thinks ought to bear the costs of the investigation[116].

Section 11(1) of the CA 1990 also empowers the inspector to make an interim report, and, indeed, obliges him to make an interim report where so ordered by the court or the Director as the case may be. He may also inform the court, without having to make a report, of any matters coming to his attention which tend to show that an offence has been committed[117].

Publication of the report

[27.052] The extent to which the report of a court-appointed inspector is to be published or circulated is a matter for the court, with the rider that *all* inspectors' reports must be furnished to the Director[118]. Section 11(3) of the CA 1990, as amended[119], empowers the court, if it thinks fit, to:

'(a) forward any copy of the report made by the inspectors to the company's registered office;

(b) furnish a copy on request and payment of the prescribed fee to

(i) any member of the company or other body corporate which is the subject of the report;

(ii) any person whose conduct is referred to in the report;

(iii) the auditors of that company or body corporate;

(iv) the applicants for the investigation;

(v) any other person (including an employee) whose financial interests appear to the court to be affected by the matters dealt with in the report whether as a creditor of the company or body corporate or otherwise;

(vi) the Central Bank, in any case in which the report of the inspector relates, wholly or partly, to the affairs of the holder of a licence under *section 9 of the Central Bank Act 1971*;

(ba) furnish a copy to—

(i) an appropriate authority in relation to any of the matters referred to in section 21(1)(a) to (fb); or

(ii) a competent authority as defined in section 21(3)(a) to (i); and

(c) cause any such report to be printed and published.'

114 See para **[27.023]** *ante*.

115 *Lyons, Keleghan and Murphy v Curran* [1993] ILRM 375.

116 Section 13(3) of the CA 1990.

117 Section 11(2) of the CA 1990.

118 Section 11(3) of the CA 1990.

119 By s 24 of the CLEA 2001.

The power to decide whether or not to publish the report is discretionary, but the court will be inclined to exercise its discretion in favour of publication if that is the approach favoured by the inspectors, the company and any relevant regulatory authority[120].

[27.053] Where the court thinks it proper, it may direct that a particular part of a report be omitted from a copy of the report sent or published in the above manner[121]. The means by which the court may be approached in this regard gives rise to a procedural conundrum, however.

In *Re Ansbacher (Cayman) Ltd*[122], the High Court was approached by solicitors for two unnamed persons, apparently clients of the bank, who had been informed by the inspectors that their names were soon to be published in the forthcoming inspectors' report. Plainly, these persons intended to obtain a direction from the court that their names be omitted from published copies of the report. Their difficulty, however, was that if the application for such a direction had to be made in open court, their anonymity would be destroyed. McCracken J considered, as a preliminary matter, whether the application could be made *in camera,* but held that it could not be so heard given that it involved an administration of justice which the Constitution required to be conducted in public, and given the countervailing necessity that justice must not only be done but must be seen to be done.

[27.054] The manner and extent of publication of a report produced by an inspector who has been appointed by the Director is a matter for the Director. Section 14 of the CA 1990 confers the same powers on the Director as the court has under s 11(3) above. A *bona fide* decision by the Director *not* to publish the report or any part thereof will survive challenge by way of judicial review[123], and the Director is empowered to cause a copy of the report or part thereof to be kept by the registrar of companies[124].

[27.055] The publication of the report is privileged[125], so that persons affected by the report have no recourse by way of an action for defamation against those responsible for its publication.

Proceedings on foot of the inspector's report

[27.056] Section 12(1) of the CA 1990 confers wide powers on the court to make 'such order as it deems fit' on foot of a court-appointed inspector's report, including:

> '(a) an order of its own motion for the winding up of a body corporate, or
>
> (b) an order for the purpose of remedying any disability suffered by any person whose interests were adversely affected by the conduct of the affairs of the

[120] *Re National Irish Bank Ltd (No 3)* [2004] 4 IR 186. In that case, copies of the report were ordered to be furnished to a wide range of parties including regulatory and revenue authorities in Ireland, Australia, the United States and the Isle of Man, as well as affected creditors, the Revenue Commissioners, the Director of Public Prosecutions. The report was also ordered to be published on the Director of Corporate Enforcement's website.

[121] Section 11(4) of the CA 1990.

[122] *Re Ansbacher (Cayman) Ltd* [2002] 2 IR 517.

[123] Section 14(2) of the CA 1990; *Lonrho plc v Secretary of State for Trade and Industry* [1989] 2 All ER 609.

[124] Section 14(5)(b) of the CA 1990.

[125] Section 23(3) of the CA 1990.

> company, provided that, in making any such order, the court shall have regard to the interests of any other person who may be adversely affected by the order.'

In *Re National Irish Bank (No 3)*[126], Kelly J noted that the subsection 'confers an extraordinarily wide jurisdiction on the court. The court may make such order as it deems fit in relation to matters arising out of its consideration of a report made by inspectors pursuant to s 11 of the CA 1990. The court appears to be at large as to what order it can make under this provision.' The powers conferred on the court by s 12(1)(b) appear very wide indeed, and seem to envisage that the court could order the restoration of property or the setting aside of transactions. The court might even award damages to persons affected by the conduct of the company's affairs. Presumably, where granting relief to members of the company, the court would have to have regard to the rule in *Foss v Harbottle*[127] so as not to provide individual members with redress for a wrong which was done to the company itself.

The court's power to impose the corporate 'death penalty' of its own motion by ordering the winding-up of the company seems draconian. It is hard to imagine the circumstances in which the court might feel justified in making such an order, though presumably it would apply the established principles applicable to winding-up petitions, including, perhaps, the 'just and equitable' criterion[128]. It seems plain at any rate that the court would have to give full opportunity to be heard to all persons likely to be affected by such an order before proceeding. In *Re National Irish Bank (No 3)*[129], Kelly J balanced the gravity of the wrongs committed by the bank against the attitude and approach of the bank and the consequences of a winding up order on the bank, its customers and staff, before finding that it was not in the public interest that the court exercise its power of its own motion to wind up the bank.

The courts have held that the wide discretion conferred by s 12 includes the power to order the release of documents secured in the investigation to third party agencies. Thus, in *Re Ansbacher (Cayman) Ltd*[130], Finnegan P ordered under s 12 that certain classes of documents that had come into the possession of the inspectors during the course of the investigation be disclosed to the Revenue Commissioners so as to facilitate the recovery of taxes, on the basis that they had suffered a disability in that they had not been paid taxes which were lawfully due – despite the fact that some of that information might have been supplied in circumstances of confidentiality. And in *Re National Irish Bank (No 3)*[131], Kelly J ordered that the papers be retained by the firm of PricewaterhouseCoopers for a period of three years, and destroyed thereafter in the absence of any application being made prior to that date for further directions from the court. He further directed that any party seeking access to the documents should apply to the court on notice the bank, the company and the inspectors. In *Re National Irish*

---

126 *Re National Irish Bank (No 3)* [2004] 4 IR 186.

127 *Foss v Harbottle* (1843) 2 Hare 461. See Ch 11, *Shareholders' Remedies*, at para **[11.092]** *et seq*. See also *Minister for Justice v Siúicre Éireann cpt, Greencore plc et al* [1992] 2 IR 215, discussed at para **[27.061]** *post*.

128 As regards windings up on the 'just and equitable' ground see Ch 23, *Winding Up Companies*, at para **[23.091]** *et seq*.

129 *Re National Irish Bank (No 3)* [2004] 4 IR 186.

130 *Re Ansbacher (Cayman) Ltd* [2004] IEHC 222.

131 *Re National Irish Bank (No 3)* [2004] 4 IR 186.

Bank (No 4)[132], however, Kelly J refused to exercise the court's power under s 12 to order the inspectors to disclose the identities of the members of the audit committee of the bank to the Director of Corporate Enforcement in connection with disqualification proceedings in circumstances where that information was already in the Director's possession and no advantage would be gained by making the order. And again, in *Re National Irish Bank (No 6)*[133], Kelly J refused to exercise the court's discretion under s 12 to give the Director access to the documents retained by PriceWaterhouseCoopers so as to gain an advantage in disqualification proceedings, pointing to the need for finality in investigations and the danger of almost endless applications against inspectors for further and better access giving rise to endless obligations being placed on inspectors to revisit their reports. He further refused to make an order of non-party discovery against the firm, on the same basis.

[27.057] The Director is given the right by s 12(2) of the CA 1990 to petition the court for the winding up of any body corporate to which the winding up provisions of the Companies Acts apply, unless that body is already being wound up. The court may order the winding up if it thinks it 'just and equitable to do so[134]'. The Director's right to petition may *only* be exercised where it appears to him, from:

(a) any report of a court-appointed inspector who was appointed *on the application of the Director*[135]; or

(b) any report of an inspector appointed by the Director; or

(c) any information or document obtained by the Director on foot of the other investigatory procedures contained in Part II of the CA 1990[136],

that a petition should be presented for the winding up of the body. Accordingly, the Director may not petition the court on foot of information contained in a report of a court-appointed inspector who was appointed on the application of someone else.

It appears that the Director must keep the public interest in mind when deciding whether or not to petition the court for a winding-up order on foot of an inspector's report[137], and his decision may be overturned on judicial review if he has not acted *bona fide* in reaching his decision[138].

Admissibility and presumptive evidentiary effect of the report in civil proceedings

[27.058] The inspector's report is admissible in evidence in *any* civil proceedings as proof of the facts set out therein, despite the hearsay rule which would ordinarily prevent it being put to such use. Section 22 of the CA 1990 provides:

> 'A document purporting to be a copy of a report of an inspector appointed under this Part shall be admissible in any civil proceedings as evidence—

[132] *Re National Irish Bank (No 4)* [2005] 3 IR 90.

[133] *Re National Irish Bank (No 6)* [2007] 4 IR 451.

[134] *Re National Irish Bank (No 6)* [2007] 4 IR 451.

[135] See para **[27.015]** *ante*.

[136] See para **[27.067]** *et seq, post*.

[137] *Re Lubin, Rosen & Associates Ltd* [1975] 1 WLR 122.

[138] *Re Walter L Jacob & Co Ltd* [1989] BCLC 345.

(a) of the facts set out therein without further proof unless the contrary is shown, and

(b) of the opinion of the inspector in relation to any matter contained in the report.'

The civil proceedings in which the report is to be relied upon may be brought by any party. In *Countyglen plc v Carway*[139], for example, the report was relied upon by the company under investigation to ground an application for a *Mareva*-type injunction against a number of persons alleged to have defrauded it.

Section 22 does not purport to extend to criminal proceedings. That is not to say, however, that an inspector's report can have no evidentiary value in such proceedings. It would, however, have to be subjected to the normal exclusionary rules of evidence in criminal trials, and confessions or self-incriminatory statements which are sought to be relied upon would at least have to satisfy the voluntariness requirement[140]. The better approach, given the views of the European Court of Human Rights[141], might yet be to refrain from reliance on self-inculpatory statements in the report in criminal trials.

[27.059] It will be noted that the section does more than oust the hearsay rule – it further gives the report a presumptive evidentiary effect. In subsequent proceedings also entitled *Countyglen plc v Carway*[142], Laffoy J held that s 22 rendered the report of an inspector admissible in all civil actions to give all findings of primary fact clearly expressed as such in the report the status of proven fact unless disproved. The learned judge further held that the word 'facts' in s 22 did not extend to deductions of fact from the contents of the report, and that the word 'report' included the entire report, regardless of whether some of the report had been ordered not to be disclosed. She continued[143]:

> 'Section 22 does not prescribe that the facts thereby given the status of proven facts have any special probative value or that any particular weight should be attached thereto. Accordingly, the ordinary rules apply in determining whether an application for a direction should be acceded to at the end of the plaintiff's case and in determining the issues of fact when all the evidence is in.'

The point is, thus, that while the facts stated in the report are presumed to have been proved until the contrary is shown, the presumption can be rebutted by ordinary evidence.

[27.060] In *Countyglen v Carway*[144], Laffoy J raised the issue of whether s 22 might be constitutionally flawed; but since none of the parties had raised a constitutional challenge the section had to be presumed constitutional until some later occasion. The learned judge did not, however, elaborate on the reasons for her concerns about the constitutionality of the section. Presumably, they relate to the fact that the exclusionary rules of evidence are intimately bound up with the requirements of fair procedures.

It is submitted, in addition, that s 22 cannot have the effect of rendering admissible evidence in a report which was unconstitutionally obtained, for to allow it to be so used would be a failure to vindicate the constitutional rights of citizens.

---

139 *Countyglen plc v Carway* [1995] 1 IR 208.

140 See para **[27.044]** *ante.*

141 See para **[27.045]** *ante.*

142 *Countyglen plc v Carway* [1998] 2 IR 514.

143 *Countyglen plc v Carway* [1998] 2 IR 514 at 551.

144 *Countyglen plc v Carway* [1998] 2 IR 514 at 551.

The attendance of the inspector responsible for the report is not required in court. The copy of the inspector's report need only 'purport' to be such, so that the inspector is not needed in court to show that it is a true copy. Neither is he required at court to give further evidence as to the opinions stated in the report.

The costs of the inspection

(a) The costs of court-ordered inspections

[27.061] The costs, expenses and incidentals of a court-ordered inspection are, under s 13(1) of the CA 1990, as amended[145], to be defrayed initially by the Minister (or, in the case of inspectors appointed under s 7 of the CA 1990, by the Minister for Justice, Equality and Law Reform). The court, however, may direct that any body corporate dealt with in the report, or the applicants for the investigation, should be liable to reimburse the relevant Minister. In *Re National Irish Bank (No 4)*[146], for example, Kelly J ordered that the bank should pay the costs of the inspection *and* the legal costs of the inspectors on a solicitor and client basis, since the bank had expressed the view that the taxpayer should not be liable for such costs and expenses.

In *Minister for Justice v Siúicre Éireann, Greencore Plc et al*[147], Lynch J observed that only persons 'dealt with in the report' may be made liable under sub-s (1). He concluded that this meant that the only bodies corporate who could be made liable under the subsection were those which had been both under investigation and dealt with in the report, otherwise companies simply named in the report could be made liable to bear the costs of the investigation without being given the opportunity of putting their case to the inspector.

[27.062] In addition, under s 13(2) of the CA 1990, any person who is:

'(a) convicted on indictment of an offence on a prosecution instituted as a result of an investigation,

(b) ordered to pay damages or restore any property in proceedings brought as a result of an investigation, or

(c) awarded damages or to whom property is restored in proceedings brought as a result of an investigation,'

may, in the same proceedings, be ordered to repay all or part of the expenses of the investigation to the relevant Minister or to any person who has already been ordered to pay such expenses under s 13(1). A person awarded damages or to whom property is restored may not be ordered to pay in excess of one-tenth of the amount of the damages awarded or the value of the property restored, and the order may not be executed until such time as the person has received his damages or property.

[27.063] In *Minister for Justice v Siúicre Éireann, Greencore Plc et al*[148], an application was brought by the Minister for Justice under s 13(1)(a) of the CA 1990 to be reimbursed by the respondents. The expenses, totalling approximately £1,150,000 (€1,460,199), were incurred in a court-ordered investigation into the affairs of Siúicre

145 By s 25 of the CLEA 2001.

146 *Re National Irish Bank (No 4)* [2005] 3 IR 90.

147 *Minister for Justice v Siúicre Éireann, Greencore Plc et al* [1992] 2 IR 215.

148 *Minister for Justice v Siúicre Éireann, Greencore Plc et al* [1992] 2 IR 215.

Éireann, which was commenced by an application by the Minister for Industry and Commerce to the court under s 8 of the CA 1990[149]. Lynch J accepted that as a general rule, and subject to the facts in each case, the Minister for Justice should *prima facie* be reimbursed the expenses of an investigation by the company or companies dealt with in the report, whether adversely or not, who could, in turn, seek reimbursement from others under s 13(2). He found, however, that in the case before him the alleged wrongdoings which gave rise to the investigation had all taken place at a time when the Minister for Finance owned and controlled Greencore plc, of which Siúcre Éireann was a wholly-owned subsidiary. He had since sold 70% of his shares in Greencore to the public to facilitate a privatisation. The learned judge concluded that if the Minister were to be reimbursed by Greencore and Siúcre Éireann it would place an unjust liability on those who had purchased the shares in the meantime, the vast majority of whom had nothing to do with the companies under investigation at the time of the alleged wrongdoings and had been unaware of them at the time they purchased the shares. Furthermore, the State, through the Minister for Finance, had already benefited from the sale of the shares in Greencore at a time when the tax liabilities referred to in the report did not arise, and if the applicant were to get his order, the State would benefit doubly.

Moreover, the learned judge considered it just and equitable to take into account the factor of who was in ultimate control of the enterprise at the time of the wrongdoing, and he concluded that the rule in *Foss v Harbottle*[150] did not prevent him in this regard. He said[151]:

> 'Apart altogether from the fact that innocent shareholder owners of the enterprise would now be damnified by an order in favour of the State, there is the factor of who was in ultimate control of the enterprise at the material time. As between the body having ultimate control of the enterprise at the time of the alleged wrongdoing, and successors to that ultimate control, especially insofar as they are without any notice of the wrongdoing, it seems to me that it is more equitable that those in ultimate control at the time of the wrongdoing (even though unaware of it at that time) should bear the costs of the investigation rather than their successors especially to the extent that such successors were wholly unaware of any such wrongdoing. On this basis it might be suggested that the enterprise should pay 45% or 30% of the expenses seeing that the State retained ownership of those percentages as above but I do not think that that follows because the wholly innocent present shareholder owners will still be penalised to the benefit of the State.'

Accordingly, the controllers of the company at the time of the wrongdoings are more likely to be fixed with the expenses of the investigation if it is possible so to make them liablc. In this regard it must be remembered that the controllers, whoever they may be, may only be fixed with the costs of the investigation if they fall into one of the categories of persons identified in s 13(1)–(2) of the CA 1990. Only bodies corporate incorporated in the State, or which, incorporated outside the State, carry on business within the State, fall into these categories. In the *Siúcre Éireann* case, Lynch J agreed

149 On the Director's power to apply to the court for the appointment of an inspector, see para **[27.015]** *ante*.

150 *Foss v Harbottle* (1843) 2 Hare 461. See Ch 11, *Shareholder's Remedies,* at para **[11.092]** *et seq*.

151 *Minister for Justice v Siúcre Éireann, Greencore Plc et al* [1992] 2 IR 215 at 228.

that this was the conclusion to be drawn from s 17 of the CA 1990, and he added that the words 'carry on business' presupposed a sort of continuum of activity as opposed to one or two isolated transactions. Accordingly, Talmino, a company registered in Jersey, whose only transaction in the State was the purchase of 2,425 shares in a company in 1989 and the sale and transfer of those shares in 1990, could not be ordered to reimburse the Minister for Justice.

(b) The expenses of an inspection ordered by the Director

[27.064] Section 14 of the CA 1990 was added to by the CLEA 2001 to enable the Director to recoup the costs of an inspection ordered by the Director from the parties involved. The new provisions are similar in effect to those of s 13 relating to court-appointed inspections, and presumably the principles developed in relation to s 13 of the CA 1990, above, will be applied to the new provisions *mutatis mutandis*.

Section 14(6)–(8) provides:

> '(6) The court may, on the application of the Director, direct that a company the subject of an investigation under this section shall be liable, to such extent as the court may direct, to repay the Director the expenses of and incidental to the investigation.
>
> (7) Without prejudice to subsection (6) but subject to subsection (8), a person—
>
> (a) convicted on indictment of an offence on a prosecution instituted,
>
> (b) ordered to pay damages or restore any property in proceedings brought, or
>
> (c) awarded damages or to whom property is restored in proceedings brought,
>
> as a result of an investigation under this section may, in the same proceedings, be ordered to repay the Director all or part of the expenses referred to in subsection (6).
>
> (8) The court shall not order a person to whom subsection (7)(c) relates to make payment in excess of one-tenth of the amount of the damages awarded or of the value of the property restored, as the case may be, and any such order shall not be executed until the person concerned has received his damages or the property has been restored.'

Concurrent investigations

[27.065] The circumstances giving rise to the ordering of an inspection may also give rise to some other form of investigation being ordered by other authorities in the State. What is the effect of a concurrent investigation on an inspection under the Companies Acts? In *Re National Irish Bank Ltd (No 2)*[152], the applicants sought to limit the inspectors in their investigations into the compliance by the bank of its obligations concerning deposit interest retention tax ('DIRT'). They contended that the concurrent investigation by the Comptroller and Auditor General into the evasion of DIRT by a number of financial institutions including the applicants involved a duplication of process which opened them to double jeopardy and which placed them in an unfair position whereby the body reporting second was not bound by the findings of the body reporting first. Moreover, they claimed, the duplication of investigation was slowing up the work of the inspectors, and the court was bound, under s 7(4) of the CA 1990, to give directions 'with a view to ensuring that the investigation is carried out as quickly and as inexpensively as possible'.

---

[152] *Re National Irish Bank Ltd (No 2)* (19 March 1999) HC, Kelly J.

Kelly J dismissed the application, holding that the inspectors' focus was narrower than that of the Controller and Auditor General, who was concerned not merely with the applicants but with a number of other financial institutions. The learned judge further held that the question of double jeopardy did not arise as the investigations were only fact-finding exercises, not criminal trials in themselves. Likewise, the applicants' argument on the *res judicata* issue held force only in respect of criminal proceedings.

While the decision in *Re National Irish Bank Ltd (No 2)* may reveal a certain reluctance on the part of the court to interfere with the terms of reference of appointed inspectors, it does seem clear from the judgment that where the focus of a concurrent investigation is the same, there is some leeway for such interference.

[27.066] The issue may fall to be determined at some stage in the future should an inspector ever be appointed on the application of the members, directors, or creditors of a company under s 7 of the CA 1990. The legislation would not appear to forbid such an appointment even where an inspector has already been appointed by, or on the application of, the Director under ss 7 and 14 of the CA 1990 – or *vice versa*.

[B] OTHER INVESTIGATIONS AND INQUIRIES

[27.067] The CA 1990, as amended, places two further investigatory processes – which do *not* involve the appointment of an inspector – at the Director's disposal.

First, he is given the power in ss 19–20 of the CA 1990 to require the production of books and documents in circumstances where he thinks it may be necessary to make a decision as to whether an inspector ought to be appointed to investigate a company or body corporate, and in other specified circumstances.

Second, where the Director is of the opinion that a company ought to be investigated but it appears to him that the appointment of an inspector is unnecessary, he may, under s 15 of the CA 1990, conduct an inquiry himself.

The investigatory (and related) powers of the Director are considered here as follows:

1. Production of books and documents;
2. Inquiries by the Director;
3. The Director's power to impose restrictions on shares and debentures.

Production of books and documents

[27.068] Section 19(1) of the CA 1990, as amended[153], gives the Director the power to direct the production of specified books and documents of a company or other body[154] at such time and place as may be specified in the direction. The Director may take copies of the books and documents so produced, *and* may require the person producing them, or any past or present officer or employee (including professional or consultant) of the body at the relevant time, to provide any explanation of any of them, and of any omission.

153 By s 29 of the CLEA 2001.

154 The bodies which may be the subject of such a direction are listed in s 19(1) of the CA 1990 and include unincorporated bodies which appear to be insurance undertakings.

[27.069] The constitutionality of the section was considered and upheld in *Dunnes Stores Ireland Company v Ryan*[155]. In that case, the applicants argued that s 19 breached the constitutional rights to confidentiality and privacy, and also failed to have due regard to the privilege against self-incrimination. Kearns J held the general obligation under 19(5) to produce documents, copies thereof, and explanations relating thereto, and provide all reasonable assistance was found to be constitutional and that the obligations imposed thereby were necessary concomitant duties of those who enjoy the benefits of incorporation.

The learned judge did, however, find that the *old* s 19(6) (which had since been amended by s 29 of the CLEA 2001) *was* unconstitutional in that it failed to immunise answers given under compulsion from later use in criminal proceedings – it provided simply that: 'A statement made by a person in compliance with a requirement imposed by virtue of this section may be used in evidence against him.' Applying the proportionality test used by Supreme Court in *Re National Irish Bank (No 1)*[156], Kearns J found the old subsection unconstitutional, but noted that the 2001 revision corrected the problem, stating[157]:

> 'I find that s 19(6), by not immunising answers given from later use in criminal proceedings, (and to that extent only) infringes the "minimum invasion" test enunciated by Costello J in *Heaney v Ireland* [1994] 3 IR 593. I am somewhat fortified in reaching this conclusion by the knowledge that the new amending legislation has provided for just such an "immunisation" clause, although I could not and have not allowed that determine my own views on the matter which I have arrived at for the reasons stated.'

In a roundabout way he thus upheld the constitutionality of the new section.

(a) Grounds for investigation of books and documents

[27.070] The Director may exercise these powers where he is of the opinion that there are circumstances suggesting that:

> '(a) it is necessary[158] to examine the books and documents of the body with a view to determining whether an inspector should be appointed to conduct an investigation of the body under the Companies Acts; or
>
> (b) the affairs of the body are being or have been conducted with intent to defraud—
>
> (i) its creditors,
>
> (ii) the creditors of any other person[159], or
>
> (iii) its members;
>
> (c) the affairs of the body are being or have been conducted for a fraudulent purpose other than described in paragraph (b);

155 *Dunnes Stores Ireland Company v Ryan* [2002] 2 IR 60.

156 *Re National Irish Bank (No 1)* [1993] 3 IR 145

157 *Dunnes Stores Ireland Company v Ryan* [2002] 2 IR 60 at 123.

158 'Necessary' does not entail any extreme or compelling need, but could be equated to 'reasonably required': *per* Herbert J in the Supreme Court in *Dunnes Stores Ireland Company v Ryan* [2002] 2 IR 60.

159 The Revenue Commissioners might be regarded as creditors for these purposes: *Dunnes Stores Ireland Company v Ryan* [2002] 2 IR 60.

(d) the affairs of the body are being or have been conducted in a manner which is unfairly prejudicial to some part of its members[160];

(e) any actual or proposed act or omission or series of acts or omissions of the body or on behalf of the body are or would be unfairly prejudicial to some part of its member;

(f) that any actual or proposed act or omission or series of acts or omissions of the body or on behalf of the body are or are likely to be unlawful[161];

(g) that the body was formed for any fraudulent purpose;

(h) that the body was formed for any unlawful purpose; or

(i) the body may be in possession of books or documents containing information relating to the books or documents of a body which comes within the terms of one or more of paragraphs (a) to (h)[162].'

Whether such circumstances exist is a matter of subjective opinion for the Director. The Director is not required to give a person or body prior notice of his intention to make a direction[163].

[27.071] Such directions may be given to any person who appears to the Director to be in possession of the books or documents, or copies thereof, or books or documents relating thereto; but where that person claims a lien over the books, the production is not to prejudice their rights under the lien[164].

The power to require the production of books and documents relating to books and documents seems to be aimed at book-keeping professionals and the like who may have second-hand information. Where the Director requires the production of such books or documents, however, the Director must be of the opinion that there are reasonable grounds for believing that the two sets of books or documents are related; he must notify the person in possession of the reasons for his belief; and he must allow them 21 days in which to controvert his opinion. Moreover, the production of such books or documents can be refused on the basis that it is privileged – whether by virtue of legal professional privilege or otherwise[165].

[27.072] The Director may have to provide reasons for his decision to require the production of books and documents. In *Dunnes Stores Ireland Company v Maloney*[166], Laffoy J held that the decision of the Minister (as predecessor to the Director) under s 19 of the CA 1990 was one which was capable of being judicially reviewed. Accordingly, the person directed by the Minister was entitled to know the reasons for the decision to enable them to assess whether they should seek such review. Laffoy J said[167]:

---

160 The Director may proceed on this ground even though none of the members complains of unfairly prejudicial treatment and opposes the direction: *Dunnes Stores Ireland Company v Ryan* [2002] 2 IR 60.

161 The focus on present or future wrongdoing precludes the grounding of a decision solely on past unlawful conduct: *Dunnes Stores Ireland Company v Ryan* [2002] 2 IR 60.

162 Section 19(2) of the CA 1990.

163 *Dunnes Stores Ireland Company v Ryan* [2002] 2 IR 60.

164 Section 19(3) of the CA 1990.

165 Section 19(4) of the CA 1990.

166 *Dunnes Stores Ireland Company v Maloney* [1999] 3 IR 542.

167 *Dunnes Stores Ireland Company v Maloney* [1999] 3 IR 542 at 563.

> '... they are entitled to have the decision reviewed on the lines indicated above and, in my view, they are utterly stymied in the exercise of that right by reason of the refusal to give reasons for the decision. In my view, this is a case in which procedural fairness requires that the Minister give reasons for her decision. The Applicants have demonstrated that they bona fide believe that the Minister has misused her power in appointing an authorised officer. Whether that belief is well founded or not, they are entitled to explore the possibility of obtaining redress by way of judicial review. They have made a bona fide request for reasons. In the absence of reasons, they cannot explore the possibility of or pursue redress by way of judicial review. Consequently, they are suffering a significant detriment. I consider that the Minister is obliged to give reasons.'

[27.073] Notably, however, Laffoy J did not quash the investigation on foot of the failure to give reasons; instead the learned judge granted declaratory relief so that the Minister was given an opportunity to provide reasons. Moreover, the case was one in which reasons were sought by the recipient of the direction. It is unclear whether reasons are required in every case even if no such request is made.

Another important element in the decision is the finding that the direction was excessive and unreasonable in the context of a lack of reasons. Without reasons, the applicants were unable to determine from the very broad demand precisely what books and documents were being sought. Laffoy J said[168]:

> 'In my view, the applicants' criticisms of the demand are well founded. Without knowing the reasons why the Minister thought it appropriate to appoint an authorised officer, it is impossible to form any view as to whether even the categories of documents sought which are specific fall within the ambit of the entitlement to seek documents under s 19. The inclusion of the categories which are of a general nature gives the demand as a whole the hallmark of a trawl. That being the case, the only reasonable inference is that the demand was excessive in content.'

On balance, therefore, it would seem sensible that the Director should give reasons along with every direction under s 19.

[27.074] The reasons so given must, of course, coincide with the statutory purposes listed in s 19; moreover, they must not be patently irrational. In *Dunnes Stores Ireland Company v Ryan*[169], a case which followed when the applicants took issue with the reasons which ultimately were supplied in support of the appointment under s 19, the Supreme Court held that s 19(2) required simply that the Minister (and by implication, now, the Director)[170] should have reasonable grounds for the opinion, which could be subjectively held. However, in exercising her powers under s 19, the Minister had to do so for a purpose contemplated by the CA 1990 and within the terms of the section; she was required to give reasons for her decision, and the decision had to be rational and neither arbitrary nor disproportionate. The court held that these purposes could include investigation of breaches of corporate governance standards laid down by the Companies Acts, but should be something more than just a general expression of concern about corporate governance standards in general.

---

168 *Dunnes Stores Ireland Company v Maloney* [1999] 3 IR 542 at 564.

169 *Dunnes Stores Ireland Company v Ryan* [2002] 2 IR 60.

170 As to the transfer of functions to the Director in the context of s 19 and s 14 of the CA 1990 see *Dunnes Stores Ireland Company v Houlihan* (9 May 2003) HC, O'Neill J.

(b) *Limits of the procedure*

[27.075] A practical limitation on these powers is that the Director is required to *specify* the books and documents required. It may well be that the Director will be unaware of some relevant books and documents which, consequently, may slip through the net. In this regard it may be observed, however, that since the enactment of the CLEA 2001, a person directed to produce the books or documents under s 19 is now expressly obliged to give 'all assistance' in the same way as he or she would be were the direction to come from an inspector[171].

A second limitation is to be found in s 23(2) of the CA 1990 which prohibits the Director from requiring a bank to disclose a document relating to the business of its customer unless it appears to the Director that it is necessary to do so for the purpose of investigating the affairs of the bank or the customer – whether as a former or current customer. As was observed above, an inspector is not so prohibited[172].

Legal professional privilege may be relied upon to justify a refusal to cooperate with a direction made under s 19[173].

(c) *Consequences of failure to comply*

[27.076] If the books or documents are not produced, the person who was required to produce them may be asked to state, to the best of his knowledge, where they are[174]. A statement made by a person in compliance with these requirements may be used in evidence against him, save in proceedings for an offence other than an offence under s 19 of the CA 1990[175]. Moreover, the making of a false statement is now itself an offence[176]. Persons making statements in response to a direction should, thus, do so advisedly.

[27.077] Failure to comply with any direction made under s 19 of the CA 1990 is an offence[177]. The person charged with such an offence has a good defence, however, if he can prove that the books or documents in question were not in his possession or control and that it was not reasonably practical for him to comply with the requirement.

[27.078] The destruction, mutilation, falsification or concealment of any book or document which is the subject of a direction is also an offence if done by a person having notice of the direction[178], or if done by a person who knows or suspects that an investigation by the Director is being or is likely to be carried out. In the latter case the presumption of innocence is reversed so that the person is presumed to have known or suspected until reasonable doubt is established[179].

[27.079] A search warrant may issue under s 20 of the CA 1990 from a District Judge authorising a member designated officer of the Director and such other persons as the

171 See para **[27.035]** *ante*.

172 See para **[27.039]** *ante*.

173 Section 23(1) of the CA 1990.

174 Section 19(5) of the CA 1990.

175 Section 19(7) of the CA 1990.

176 Section 19(8) of the CA 1990 as inserted by the CLEA 2001.

177 Section 19(6) of the CA 1990.

178 Section 19(9) of the CA 1990.

179 Section 19A of the CA 1990.

officer thinks necessary to enter premises specified in the warrant, using force if necessary; to search the premises; to require persons found on the premises to give details of their name, home address and occupation and to produce material in their custody or possession; to seize and retain any material or information so found; and to take any other steps considered necessary to preserve the material or to prevent interference therewith. The warrant retains its force for one month from its issue, and the books or documents obtained under it may be kept for a period of six months or for such further time as a District Judge may permit as being necessary for the conclusion of any criminal proceedings initiated during the six-month period.

Computer-based information may be searched and seized in this process, and disclosure of passwords and other technical assistance can be required of persons identified as having that knowledge[180].

Obstruction of an entry and search under s 20 is also an offence.

(d) Publication or disclosure of information, books and documents

[27.080] Under s 21(1) of the CA 1990, as amended[181], no information, book or document which has been obtained in accordance with ss 19 and 20 of the CA 1990 may be disclosed or published without the prior written consent of the body to which it relates unless the publication or disclosure is to a 'competent authority' *or* is required:

'(a) with a view to the investigation or prosecution of any offence, being an offence—

- (i) under—
  - (I) the Companies Acts;
  - (II) the Central Bank Acts, 1942 to 1998;
  - (III) the Exchange Control Acts, 1954 to 1986;
  - (IV) the Insurance Acts, 1909 to 1990;
  - (V) the Taxes Consolidation Act, 1997 or an offence under an enactment referred to in section 1078(1) of that Act;
  - (VI) regulations relating to insurance made under the European Communities Act, 1972;

  or
- (ii) entailing misconduct in connection with the management of the body's affairs or misapplication or wrongful retainer of its property;

(b) for the purpose of assessing the liability of a person in respect of a tax or duty or other payment owed or payable to the State, a local authority (within the meaning of the Local Government Act, 1941) or a health board or for the purpose of collecting an amount due in respect of such a tax or duty or other payment;

(c) for the purpose of the performance by a tribunal (to which the Tribunals of Inquiry (Evidence) Acts, 1921 to 1998, apply) of any of its functions;

(d) for the purpose of assisting or facilitating the performance by any Minister of the Government of any of his functions;

(e) for the purpose of assisting or facilitating any accountancy or other professional organisation in the performance of its disciplinary functions with respect to any of its members;

---

180 Section 20(4) of the CA 1990.

181 By s 53 of the C(A)(No 2)A 1999 and s 31 of the CLEA 2001.

(f) for the purpose of the performance by the Irish Takeover Panel or any stock exchange established in the State of any of its functions in relation to the body or any other person who, in its opinion, is connected with the body;

(fa) for the purpose of the performance by the Competition Authority of any of its functions;

(fb) for the purpose of the performance by a committee (being a committee within the meaning of the Committees of the Houses of the Oireachtas (Compellability, Privileges and Immunities of Witnesses) Act, 1997, to which sections 3 to 14 and16 of that Act apply) of any of its functions;

(g) for the purposes of complying with the requirements of procedural fairness, to be made to—

(i) any company in relation to which an inspector has been appointed under section 14 or any person required by the Director to give any information under section 15, or

(ii) any body to which the Director has given a Direction under section 19 or any person named in a report relating to an examination under that section;

(h) for the purpose of complying with any requirement, or exercising any power, imposed or conferred by Part II of the CA 1990 with respect to reports made by inspectors appointed thereunder by the court or the Director;

(i) with a view to the institution by the Director of proceedings for the winding-up under CA 1963 of the body or otherwise for the purposes of proceedings instituted by him for that purpose;

for the purposes of proceedings under section 20 or 160[182].'

A person who publishes or discloses any information, book or document in contravention of these provisions will be guilty of an offence.

[27.081] For these purposes, 'competent authority' includes[183] the Minister; a person authorised by the Minister; an inspector appointed under the CA 1990; the Minister for Finance; an officer authorised by the Minister for Finance; any court of competent jurisdiction; the Central Bank; and any authority established outside the State in which there are vested (i) functions of investigating or prosecuting an offence similar to an offence referred to in s 21(1)(a) of the CA 1990 above, or (ii) functions of assessing the liability of a person in respect of a tax or duty or other payment owed or payable to the state in which it is established or any other authority established in that state or of collecting an amount due in respect of such a tax or duty or other payment, or (iii) functions which are similar to the functions referred to in s 21(1)(c), (d), (e) or (f).

Costs of the investigation

[27.082] The Director's costs and expenses incurred in an investigation under s 19 of the CA 1990 may be recouped by order of the court upon application by the Director from any person convicted on indictment as a result of a direction, or ordered to pay damages as a result of a direction, or awarded damages or restored property as a result of a

182 Section 21(1) of the CA 1990.

183 Section 21(2) of the CA 1990.

direction; but in the latter case the payment shall not exceed 10% of the amount of damages awarded or the value of the property restored[184].

Inquiries by the Director

[27.083] Section 15 of the CA 1990 permits an inquiry into the ownership of shares and debentures in a company without the need for the appointment of an inspector. In any case where it appears to the Director that it is necessary to investigate the ownership of any shares or debentures in a company on the grounds contained in s 14, he may, under s 15(1) of the CA 1990, if he thinks it unnecessary to appoint an investigator, require instead:

> ... any person whom he has reasonable cause to believe to have or to be able to obtain any information as to the present and past interests in those shares or debentures and the names and addresses of the persons interested and of any persons who act or have acted on their behalf in relation to the shares or debentures, to give any such information.

The subsection seems to require the Director to have reasonable cause to believe quite a number of things: first, that persons have, or are able to obtain, the information; second, that those persons also have, or are able to obtain, the names *and* addresses of interested persons; and third, that those persons also have the names and addresses of any persons who have acted on behalf of interested persons. Surely, the categories of persons who may be expected to have such information must be few in number.

[27.084] For the purposes of s 15(1) of the CA 1990 a person is deemed to have an interest in a share or debenture: if he has any right to acquire or dispose of the share or debenture or any interest therein; if he has a right to vote in respect of the shares or debentures; if his consent is necessary for the exercise of any of the rights of other persons interested in the shares or debentures; if the other persons interested in the shares or debentures can be required or are accustomed to exercise their rights in accordance with his instruction[185]. Any person who fails to give the required information, or who knowingly or recklessly gives materially false information, will be guilty of an offence.

Director's power to impose restrictions on shares and debentures

[27.085] Finally, it should be noted that s 16 of the CA 1990 gives the Director additional powers exercisable in connection with an investigation. Where, in connection with an inspection under s 14 or an inquiry under s 15 of the CA 1990, it appears to the Director that there is difficulty in finding out the relevant facts about any shares or debentures (whether issued or to be issued), the Director may direct, by notice in writing, that the shares or debentures shall, until further notice, be subject to the following restrictions under s 16(2):

> '(a) any transfer of those shares, or in the case of unissued shares any transfer of the right to be issued therewith and any issue thereof, shall be void;
>
> (b) no voting rights shall be exercisable in respect of those shares;
>
> (c) no further shares shall be issued in right of those shares or in pursuance of any offer made to the holder thereof; and

---

184 Section 19(10)–(12) of the CA 1990.

185 Section 15(2) of the CA 1990.

(d) no payment shall be made of any sums due from the company on those shares, whether in respect of capital or otherwise[186].'

In addition, any *agreement* to transfer the shares, debentures, or rights restricted by (a), (c) or (d) is deemed to be void[187]. The Director must, as soon as may be after the making of the direction, send notice of it to the company at its registered office and to the registrar of companies; notice must also be published in the Companies Registration Office Gazette and at least two daily newspapers[188].

[27.086] Under s 16(14), any person who:

'(a) exercises or purports to exercise any right to dispose of any shares which, to his knowledge, are for the time being subject to the said restrictions or of any right to be issued with any such shares; or

(b) votes in respect of any such shares, whether as holder or proxy, or appoints a proxy to vote in respect thereof; or

(c) being the holder of any such shares, fails to notify of their being subject to the said restrictions any person whom he does not know to be aware of that fact but does know to be entitled, apart from the said restrictions, to vote in respect of those shares whether as holder or proxy; or

(d) being the holder of any such shares, or being entitled to any such right as is mentioned in subsection (4) enters into an agreement which is void by virtue of [s 16],'

will be guilty of an offence. In addition, where shares or debentures are issued in contravention of the said restrictions, the company and every officer in default will be guilty of an offence. Summary proceedings may not be instituted under s 16 except by or with the consent of the Director.

[27.087] Where the Director directs that shares or debentures are to be subject to these restrictions, or refuses to direct that shares or debentures shall cease to be subject to such restrictions, any aggrieved person may apply to the court for an order that the shares or debentures shall cease to be subject to the restrictions[189]. However, neither the court nor the Director can order the restrictions to cease unless satisfied that the relevant facts about the shares or debentures have been disclosed to the company or the Director as appropriate, *or* the shares or debentures are to be sold and the court or the Director approves the sale[190]. In the English case of *Re Westminster Property Group plc*[191], it was held that the words 'to be sold' in this context should be construed as meaning transferred for a money consideration. Thus, it would appear that neither the court nor the Director has the authority to approve non-cash transfers of restricted shares or debentures, such as a share-for-share exchange.

---

186 Section 16(17) of the CA 1990 applies the provisions of the section to debentures.

187 Section 16(3)–(4) of the CA 1990.

188 Section 16(18) of the CA 1990.

189 Section 16(5) of the CA 1990.

190 Section 16(6) of the CA 1990. In *Re Greers Gross plc* [1987] 1 WLR 1649, the English Court of Appeal held that mere demonstration that the restricted shares were to be sold was of itself insufficient to justify the court in removing the restrictions, especially where the applicants had failed to disclose the identity of the owners of the shares. See McCormack, *The New Companies Legislation* (1991, Round Hall Press) pp 33–34.

191 *Re Westminster Property Group plc* [1985] 1 WLR 676.

[27.088] The company or the Director may apply to court for an order directing the restricted shares or debentures to be sold, subject to court approval[192]. The court, in granting the order, may decide to release the shares or debentures from all of the restrictions, or may continue the restrictions on issue of further shares or debentures or on payments on those shares or debentures[193].

Once a court-sanctioned sale takes place, the Director, the company, the person appointed to sell the shares or debentures, or any person interested in them may apply to the court for any further order relating to the sale or transfer of shares or debentures[194]. The proceeds of sale of the shares or debentures less the costs of the sale must be paid into court for the benefit of the persons who were beneficially interested in the shares or debentures, and any such person may apply to the court for the whole amount of those proceeds to be paid to him[195]. The court will order the payment to the applicant of that proportion of the proceeds of sale to which he is beneficially entitled, but may also order that the costs of the application by the Director or company for the sale be paid out of the proceeds of sale before any other sums are paid out[196].

---

192 Section 16(7) of the CA 1990.

193 Section 16(7) and (12) of the CA 1990.

194 Section 16(8) of the CA 1990.

195 Section 16(9) of the CA 1990.

196 Section 16(10) and (11) of the CA 1990.

Chapter 28

Compliance and Enforcement

Introduction

[28.001] It is accepted by most commentators that transgressions of the Companies Acts became a ubiquitous feature of Irish commercial life in the closing decades of the twentieth, and first decade of the twenty-first, centuries. Little more than lip-service had been paid to non-compliance with company law until the mid to late 1990s when, in the shadow of various tribunals of enquiry, the government took the decision to adopt what has come to be known as a 'zero-tolerance' stance on corporate transgressions. The impetus for the sea change was the announcement[1], on 7 August 1998, of the establishment of the *Working Group on Company Law Compliance and Enforcement*, chaired by Michael McDowell SC, which came to be known as the McDowell Group[2]. In establishing the working group the Tánaiste said that:

> '... the Government decision to set up the Group was influenced by the recent emergence of strong indications of abuses of company law which pose a particular problem for the integrity of the system of company regulation. The consequential public concerns must be allayed if the social consensus and Ireland's standing as a reputable place to do business which underlies our present economic success are to be maintained in the future.'

The McDowell Group first met in September 1998 and produced its report on 30 November of the same year[3], a remarkable achievement by any standard. Even more extraordinary, by Irish legislative standards, was the speed with which the recommendations of the McDowell Group were adopted by the Oireachtas and passed into law in July 2001, in the form of the Company Law Enforcement Act 2001 ('the CLEA 2001')[4]. While the financial crisis of 2008 has brought to light more suspected transgressions of the Companies Acts, despite some calls for tougher company law, it seems generally accepted that the company law was not the problem, rather it was its enforcement and the difficulties associated with proving contraventions[5].

[28.002] The most visible metric of abuse and disregard for company law is non-compliance with the registration requirements for companies formed and registered

1 By the then Tánaiste and Minister for Jobs, Enterprise and Innovation, Ms Mary Harney TD and Mr Noel Tracy TD, the then Minister for Science, Technology and Commerce.

2 The *McDowell Group* was an *ad hoc* group drawn from amongst the social partners, interested bodies and those whom it was perceived might add value to its deliberations.

3 See *The Report of the Working Group on Company Law Compliance and Enforcement*, 30 November 1998 (Pn 6697).

4 The CLEA 2001 was commenced in a piecemeal manner by various statutory instruments.

5 Some legislative tweaking to Part III of the CA 1990 was effected by the C(A)A 2009.

under, and therefore regulated by, the Companies Acts. The McDowell Group labelled these transgressions as *registration-type* cases; and concluded that:

> 'Irish company law has been characterised by a culture of non-compliance and a failure by companies and their officers to meet their obligations in respect of the filing of annual returns on time. For example, in 1997 only 13% of companies complied with their obligations to file annual returns on time[6].'

The McDowell Group made a number of recommendations designed to strengthen *registration-type* compliance with the Companies Acts.

[28.003] The McDowell Group distinguished these objectively less serious transgressions, which are policed by the registrar of companies, from what the Group termed *non-registration type* cases, the enforcement of which was primarily vested in the Director of Public Prosecutions and the Minister for Jobs, Enterprise and Innovation. It was recognised that culpability for *non-registration type* offences is not as cut and dry as in the case of registration-type offences. In addition to accepting that a strict three-year time limitation[7] on the prosecution of company law offences hampered prosecution, since many offences only came to light outside of the time limit, the McDowell Group recognised that the successful prosecution of such offences would require significant investment in staffing resources. In respect to *non-registration type* offences, and in reference to the unprecedented number of appointments of inspectors to investigate alleged malpractice, the Group said:

> 'Many of these investigations are the subject of intense public interest, and where they reveal possible breaches of the Companies Acts appropriate enforcement action will have to be taken if the framework of company law is not to be brought into disrepute. There has been limited enforcement of company law offences in the past, and in the circumstances, the Group has considered what form of response should be forthcoming from Government to allay public concern in the area of corporate affairs[8].'

What must be remembered is that, notwithstanding the McDowell Group's twin-fold classification, the second category identified – that is, *non-registration* offences – does not necessarily mean more serious offences. As shall be considered below[9], non-registration offences can be further broken down into (a) potentially serious offences involving acts or omissions contrary to the Companies Acts; (b) offences involving a failure to supply documents or provide information by and to various parties; and (c) offences in relation to the failure to maintain various statutory registers. The most far-reaching solution to the absence of an adequate State infrastructure for the detection and prosecution of serious company law offences, proposed by the McDowell Group, and accepted by the government in the CLEA 2001 was the establishment of the office of Director of Corporate Enforcement[10] ('ODCE').

---

6 At page ii, point 9.

7 It is very significant that s 240 of the CA 1990 was amended by the insertion of a new sub-s (5) to provide, *inter alia*, that the three-year time limit is now subject to discoverability: s 41 of the C(A)(No 2)A 1999: see para **[28.037]** *post*.

8 At pp 39, 40 at para 4.4.

9 See para **[28.055]** *post*.

10 See para **[28.009]** *et seq*, *post*.

[28.004] In this chapter the law relating to the compliance with and enforcement of company law will be considered in the following sections:

[A] The Agencies of Enforcement and Compliance.
[B] Enforcement and Compliance – Criminal Sanctions.
[C] Registration-Type Offences.
[D] Non-Registration Offences.
[E] Restriction of Directors.
[F] Disqualification of Directors and Other Officers.
[G] Injunctions to Compel Compliance with the Companies Acts.

[A] THE AGENCIES OF ENFORCEMENT AND COMPLIANCE

[28.005] Until the enactment of the CLEA 2001, the registrar of companies, the Minister for Jobs, Enterprise and Innovation and the Director of Public Prosecutions were the three agencies which shared the prosecution of offences under the Companies Acts. Since the CLEA 2001, the prosecution of company law offences and the enforcement of the Companies Acts are now shared by the following:

1. The registrar of companies;
2. The Director of Corporate Enforcement;
3. The Director of Public Prosecutions;
4. Private parties with *locus standi*.

The registrar of companies

[28.006] The office of the registrar of companies dates back to the Joint Stock Companies Act 1844, which first permitted incorporation *by registration*. Necessarily incidental to that momentous legislative decision to permit incorporation by registration was the creation of the office of the registrar of joint stock companies: the keeper of the register[11]. In *Business Communications Ltd v Baxter and Parsons*[12], Murphy J observed:

> 'Since the introduction of legislation permitting people to incorporate with limited liability, it has been recognised that the protection which this conferred on those taking advantage of the privilege has to be counterbalanced by statutory provisions to protect and safeguard the interests of those dealing with them. The original and essential protection to those dealing with companies incorporated under the Companies Acts from time to time was the creation of a registration office in which would be filed the essential information in relation to companies incorporated under the legislation so that outsiders would have an opportunity to ascertain the persons constituting the corporation and be in a position to form some estimate as to the assets which would be available to meet its liabilities[13].'

One of the original functions of the registrar of joint stock companies – now called the *registrar of companies* – the importance of which survives to today, is the receipt, evaluation and (if in order) the acceptance for registration of the documents lodged by persons desirous of incorporating a company. The registrar's primary function can thus

[11] See Ch 1, *The Private Company in Context*, at para **[1.080]**.

[12] *Business Communications Ltd v Baxter and Parsons* (21 July 1995, unreported) HC, Murphy J.

[13] *Business Communications Ltd v Baxter and Parsons* (21 July 1995, unreported) HC, Murphy J at p 15 of the judgment.

be seen as the statutory procreator of the artificial legal entity that is the registered company. The registrar's grant of a certificate of incorporation signals the birth of a company; s 18 of the CA 1963 providing that on the registration of the memorandum of association, the registrar 'shall certify under his hand that the company is incorporated'. The other three core functions of the registrar are: the receipt and registration of post incorporation documents; the enforcement of the Companies Acts in relation to the filing obligations of companies; and the making of information available to the public[14]. Notwithstanding the establishment of the office of Director of Corporate Enforcement, the registrar retains these four core functions.

[28.007] The Minister for Jobs, Enterprise and Innovation is responsible for the maintenance and administration of the Companies Registration Office ('CRO')[15] and for the appointment of the registrar and assistant registrars[16]. Section 368(4) of the CA 1963 provided that whenever any act is, by the CA 1963, or other statute, directed to be done to or by the registrar, 'it shall, until the Minister otherwise directs, be done to or by the existing Registrar of joint stock companies or, in his absence, to or by such person as the Minister may for the time being authorise'. It would appear that some doubt existed as to the validity of acts done to or by assistant registrars and others employed in the registrar's office. Section 52(1) of the C(A)(No 2)A 1999 provides that any act referred to in s 368(4) which, before the commencement of the C(A)(No 2)A 1999, was done to or by such persons:

> '… shall be valid and be deemed always to have been valid as if the Minister had directed under that subsection (4) that such an act was to be done to or by such an assistant Registrar or other such person (including in cases where the existing Registrar of joint stock companies (or his or her successor) was not absent).'

To put matters beyond all doubt, s 52(2) provides:

> 'On and from the commencement of this section, any act required or authorised by the Companies Acts 1963 to 1999, the Registration of Business Names Act, 1963 or the Limited Partnership Act, 1907 to be done to or by the Registrar of Companies, the Registrar of joint stock companies or, as the case may be, a person referred to in the enactment concerned as "the Registrar" may be done to or by a Registrar or assistant Registrar appointed under s 368(2) of the CA 1963 or any other person authorised in that behalf by the Minister.'

[28.008] The registrar is the person charged with securing compliance with the filing and registration requirements under the Companies Acts. The means of enforcement available to the registrar to ensure compliance (and to punish non-compliance) are: (a) the prosecution of companies and their officers for registration-type offences; (b) the imposition of on-the-spot fines[17]; and (c) strike-off of non-compliant companies[18].

---

[14] See the CRO website at www.cro.ie.

[15] Section 368(1) of the CA 1963.

[16] Section 368(2) of the CA 1963.

[17] See para **[28.041]** *post*.

[18] See, generally, Ch 26, *Strike-Off and Restoration*.

The Director of Corporate Enforcement

[28.009] The central recommendation of the McDowell Group was the establishment of a dedicated company law enforcement office, located within the Department of Jobs, Enterprise and Innovation, headed by a Director of Corporate Enforcement (the 'Director')[19]. In the light of its findings on the then existing enforcement regime, the McDowell Group recommended:

> 'An independent statutory officer – to be known as the Director of Corporate Enforcement – who would have general – but not exclusive – responsibility for the enforcement of company law should be appointed. The Director should have a similar role to that of the Director of Consumer Affairs, who has specific responsibility in law for the prosecution of offences under consumer legislation, and should be independent in the discharge of his functions[20].'

Part 2 of the CLEA 2001 gives legislative effect to the McDowell Group's recommendations. Here the following are considered: (a) the appointment, status and independence of the Director; and (b) the functions and powers of the Director.

(a) The appointment, status and independence of the Director

[28.010] Section 7(1) of the CLEA 2001 establishes the office of the Director, who is appointed by the Minister for Jobs, Enterprise and Innovation[21] after his election (following competition) by the Civil Service Commissioners[22]. Section 7(3) provides that:

> 'The Director shall be a corporation sole and, notwithstanding any casual vacancy in the office from time to time, shall have perpetual succession and shall be capable in his or her corporate name of holding and disposing of real or personal property and of suing and being sued.'

Section 11 of the CLEA 2001 facilitates the Ministerial appointment of an acting Director to perform the Director's functions during periods when the Director is absent from duty, out of the State, unable to perform the Director's functions, suspended from office or where there is a vacancy in the office[23].

[28.011] Although the Director is expressed to be 'independent in the performance of his or her functions'[24] and is expressly prohibited from holding any other office or

19 See *Report of the Working Group on Company Law Compliance and Enforcement* (1998) at para 4.7 *et seq*. A less radical recommendation was made by the *ad hoc*, Company Law Review Group (chaired by James Gallagher), which reported to Government in February 1995 and recommended the establishment of an 'executive unit' within the Department of Jobs, Enterprise and Innovation (at para 7.14) to pursue delinquent directors of insolvent companies. See Courtney, *Company Law Review 1995* (1996, Round Hall Sweet & Maxwell) at p 11.

20 See *Report of the Working Group on Company Law Compliance and Enforcement* (1998) at ii (Summary).

21 Section 7(2) of the CLEA 2001.

22 Section 7(3) of the CLEA 2001.

23 Section 11(2) and (3) of the CLEA 2001 provide, respectively, that a person may not be appointed as acting Director for a continuous period of more than six months during a vacancy in the office of the Director and that the Minister may, at any time, terminate the appointment of acting Director.

24 Section 12(5) of the CLEA 2001.

employment in respect of which emoluments are paid[25], the Director is politically accountable in a number of ways[26]. In the first place, the Director is expressed to be a 'civil servant'[27]. Secondly, the Director's term of office is for a maximum period of five years[28] but he can be removed by the Minister at any time for stated reasons, whereupon the Minister must cause a statement of the reasons for the removal to be laid before each house of the Oireachtas[29]; moreover, the Director will cease to be Director where he or she enters politics[30]. Thirdly, the Director is required to submit annual reports to the Minister for Jobs, Enterprise and Innovation concerning the performance of his functions and other activities[31]. Although the Director's report under s 16(1) of the CLEA 2001 shall include information in such form and about such matters as the Minister may direct, s 16(2) provides that nothing in either subsection 'shall be construed as requiring the Director to include in such report information the inclusion of which would, in the opinion of the Director, be likely to prejudice the performance by him or her of any of his or her functions'. Likewise, although the Director is obliged to furnish from time to time information as requested by the Minister and to account to an appropriately established committee of either House of the Oireachtas, he is not obliged to furnish any information or answer any question which would, in his opinion, be likely to prejudice the performance of his functions[32].

[28.012] It was envisaged by the McDowell Group and accepted by the Government that in addition to clerical staff, the enforcement office would be staffed by a number of solicitors and accountants and that a number of members of An Garda Síochána would be seconded to the enforcement office[33]. The Office of the Director of Corporate Enforcement is, at the time of writing, facing its biggest challenge under the glare of the media and public interest, in the investigation of a number of company law matters relating to the former Anglo Irish Bank Corporation.

---

25 Section 8(3) of the CLEA 2001.

26 Information obtained by the Director by virtue of the performance of his functions which has not otherwise come to the public's attention cannot be disclosed, save in accordance with law: see generally, s 17 of the CLEA 2001.

27 It is not clear as to whether the Director is a civil servant 'in the service of the Government' or 'in the service of the State', the latter importing a greater degree of independence: see Osborne, *The Company Law Enforcement Bill 2000 Seminar* (2002, Dublin Solicitors Bar Association) paper at p 4 and Hogan & Morgan, *Administrative Law in Ireland* (3rd edn, 1998) at pp 79–81.

28 Section 8(1) of the CLEA 2001.

29 Section 10(1) and (2) of the CLEA 2001.

30 Section 10(3) provides that a person shall cease to be Director if he is nominated as a member of Seanad Éireann, nominated as a candidate for election to either House of the Oireachtas, the European Parliament or becomes a member of a local authority, or is regarded under Part XIII of the Second Schedule to the European Parliament Elections Act 1997 as having been elected to the European Parliament; and sub-s (4) provides that a person who is entitled to sit in the Houses of the Oireachtas, or is a member of the European Parliament or is a member of a local authority is disqualified from being Director.

31 Section 16(1) of the CLEA 2001.

32 Section 16(3) and (4) of the CLEA 2001.

33 Gardaí seconded continue to be under the general direction and control of the Commissioner of An Garda Síochána: s 12(3) of the CLEA 2001.

(b) The functions and powers of the Director

[28.013] Section 12(1) of the CLEA 2001 states the Director's functions to be:

'(a) to enforce the Companies Acts, including by the prosecution of offences by way of summary proceedings,

(b) to encourage compliance with the Companies Acts,

(c) to investigate instances of suspected offences under the Companies Acts,

(d) at his or her discretion, to refer cases to the Director of Public Prosecutions where the Director of Corporate Enforcement has reasonable grounds for believing that an indictable offence under the Companies Acts has been committed,

(e) to exercise, insofar as the Director feels it necessary or appropriate, a supervisory role over the activity of liquidators and receivers in the discharge of their functions under the Companies Acts,

(f) for the purpose of ensuring effective application and enforcement of obligations, standards and procedures to which companies and their officers are subject, to perform such other functions in respect of any matters to which the Companies Acts relate as the Minister considers appropriate and may by order confer on the Director, and

(g) to perform such other functions for a purpose referred to in paragraph (f) as may be assigned to him or her by or under the Companies Acts or any other Act.'

Just as a company has 'objects' and 'powers', so too does the Director have power to 'do all such acts or things as are necessary or expedient for the purpose of the performance of his or her functions' under the CLEA 2001 or any other statute[34]. The Director's functions (and the statutory powers he is given to achieve them) can be classified as involving (i) supervision; (ii) investigation though the appointment of inspectors; (iii) criminal investigation, prosecution and on-the-spot fines; and (iv) civil enforcement and sanction.

[28.014] The statutory role of the Director is not always understood by political and media commentators. The Director is not generally empowered to supervise companies' *activities* or to investigate breaches of law committed by companies. The Director's remit is concentrated on the Companies Acts and while some banks, charities and owners' management companies will be companies formed and registered under the Companies Acts, the activities of 'banking', 'charitable activity' and 'property management' are not the responsibility of the Director. Indeed, not only are these not the responsibility of the Director, but it is thought that in the absence of amending legislation, that it would be *ultra vires* the Director's powers to meddle in such matters.

(i) Supervision

[28.015] The Director's supervisory function is expressly envisaged by s 12(1)(e) of the CLEA 2001 in the context of the activity of liquidators and receivers[35]. So s 323A of the CA 1963[36] provides that the Director may direct the production of a receiver's books

34 Section 12(2) of the CLEA 2001.

35 By s 319(2A) of the CA 1963, as inserted by s 52 of the CLEA 2001, the registrar must provide a copy of a retiring receiver's statement to the Director; the registrar must also notify the Director of the appointment of a receiver.

36 As inserted by s 53 of the CLEA 2001.

and, by s 57 of the CLEA 2001, the Director may direct the production of a liquidator's books. Section 58 of the CLEA 2001 provides:

> 'Where a disciplinary committee or tribunal (however called) of a prescribed professional body finds that a member conducting a liquidation or receivership has not maintained appropriate records, or it has reasonable grounds for believing that a member has committed an indictable offence under the Companies Acts during the course of a liquidation or receivership, the body shall report the matter, giving details of the finding or, as the case may be, of the alleged offence, to the Director forthwith and if the body fails to comply with this section it, and every officer of the body to whom the failure is attributable, is guilty of an offence.'

Although not expressly stated in s 12 of the CLEA 2001, the activity of examiners and auditors will also fall to be supervised by the Director to the extent at least that the Companies Acts impose particular requirements on such persons. So by s 192(6) of the CA 1990[37] there is a similar obligation to that in s 58 (last quoted) placed on bodies of accountants. By s 187(12) of the CA 1990[38] the Director is empowered to demand of a person acting as an auditor of a company or as a public auditor or purporting to be qualified to so act, the production of evidence of his qualifications. The Director may also require auditors – who pursuant to s 194 advise the registrar of companies and the Director that, in their opinion, proper books of account have not been kept – to furnish information, including an explanation of their reasons for forming their opinion and to give the Director access to documents, etc: s 194(3A) of the CA 1990[39]. Finally, s 194(5) of the CA 1990[40] provides:

> 'Where, in the course of, and by virtue of, their carrying out an audit of the accounts of the company, information comes into the possession of the auditors of a company that leads them to form the opinion that there are reasonable grounds for believing that the company or an officer or agent of it has committed an indictable offence under the Companies Acts, the auditors shall, forthwith and after having formed it, notify that opinion to the Director and provide the Director with details of the grounds on which they have formed that opinion.'

Where auditors comply with this provision, there is express protection against any claim for breach of professional or legal duty owed as auditor to the company, its shareholders, creditors or other interested parties[41].

[28.016] Also relevant here is the Director's function to 'encourage' compliance with the Companies Acts, as stated in s 12(1)(b) of the CLEA 2001. The use of the word 'encourage' is notable, since it connotes an almost educational role for the Director, which can only be meaningfully exercised following the ongoing supervision of the activities of all corporate players and the subsequent identification of deficiencies in compliance.

---

37 Inserted by s 73 of the CLEA 2001.

38 As inserted by s 72 of the CLEA 2001.

39 As inserted by s 74 of the CLEA 2001.

40 As inserted by s 74 of the CLEA 2001.

41 Section 194(6) of the CA 1990. On auditors' responsibilities to report offences, see Ch 17, *Financial Statements, Audit and Annual Return*, at para **[17.320]** *et seq*.

(ii) Investigation through inspectors

[28.017] The Director's investigative function arises in a number of contexts. In the first place, the Director has taken over the functions of the Minister for Jobs, Enterprise and Innovation in regard to the investigation of potential company law offences under Part II of the CA 1990. Although this was not one of the McDowell Group's recommendations, it was considered by the Government 'to be more cost-effective, more efficient and less politicised if the decision on whether to initiate a company law investigation or a criminal investigation in any particular case was centralised with the Director'[42]. The investigation of companies and the appointment of inspectors are considered in Chapter 27, *Investigations and Inspectors*.

[28.018] Section 12(1)(c) of the CLEA 2001 specifically details as a function of the Director, the investigation of suspected offences under the Companies Acts. The Director's investigative powers are also implicit in s 12(1)(a) (the enforcement of the Companies Acts and prosecution of summary offences) and s 12(1)(d) (the reference of cases to the Director of Public Prosecutions ('DPP') where the Director has reasonable grounds for believing an indictable offence has been committed) as in either case, an investigation would be required. To aid the investigation of offences, it is expressly provided that information relating to offences under the Companies Acts, held by the Competition Authority, gardaí or Revenue Commissioners may be disclosed to the Director or an officer of the Director[43].

[28.019] In investigating suspected breaches of the Companies Acts, the Director has certain powers to obtain information and preserve assets and secure the presence of persons to make them available for examination. This has been achieved by giving the Director all of the investigative powers enjoyed by official liquidators, and then some. In an official liquidation, the Director can seek an order for the civil arrest of absconding contributories and officers: s 247 of the CA 1963[44]; an order for the delivery-up of records in a winding up: s 245A of the CA 1963[45]; and an order for examination in a winding up: s 245 of the CA 1963[46]. Section 49 of the CLEA 2001 extends certain powers that were previously only held by official liquidators to voluntary liquidators. Accordingly, the Director can also apply for an order under s 282A of the CA 1963 for the inspection of books in a voluntary winding up and for an order under s 282B of the CA 1963 to summon persons for examination in a voluntary winding up or for an order under s 282C of the CA 1963 for the payment or delivery of property against a person examined in a voluntary winding up or for an order under s 282D of the CA 1963 to arrest an absconding contributory or director in a voluntary winding up. These provisions are considered in Chapter 25[47].

---

42 See 'Explanatory and Financial Memorandum' published with the Company Law Enforcement Bill 2000 at p 1.

43 Section 18 of the CLEA 2001.

44 See Ch 25, *Realisation and Distribution of Assets in a Winding Up*, at para **[25.038]**.

45 See Ch 25, *Realisation and Distribution of Assets in a Winding Up*, at para **[25.036]**.

46 See Ch 25, *Realisation and Distribution of Assets in a Winding Up*, at para **[25.026]**.

47 See Ch 25, *Realisation and Distribution of Assets in a Winding Up*, at para **[25.029]**.

(iii) Criminal investigation, prosecution and on-the-spot fines

[28.020] The Director is specifically empowered to enforce the Companies Acts by the prosecution of offences by way of summary proceedings: s 12(1)(a) of the CLEA 2001. As to the meaning of 'summary proceedings', s 240(3) of the CA 1990 provides:

> 'Every offence under the Companies Acts made punishable by a fine not exceeding £1,500 or by imprisonment for a term not exceeding 12 months, or by both, may be prosecuted summarily[48].'

In this respect the Director has taken over this power from the Minister and, in line with the McDowell Group's recommendations[49], the Minister has been divested of all power to prosecute summary offences under the Companies Acts in favour of the Director[50]. The prosecution of both summary and indictable offences is considered below[51]. The Director also has the power to impose on-the-spot fines, as an alternative to prosecuting for a summary offence; this too is considered below[52]. The standardisation of fines applicable to summary offences under the Companies Acts by the Fines Act 2010 is considered below[53].

[28.021] Central to the success of the Director's investigations will be the role played by the members of An Garda Síochána who have been seconded to the Director's office. Being trained investigators, it is to be expected that the quality of evidence collected by the gardaí, that will support referrals under s 12(1)(d) to the DPP, will facilitate the initiation of more prosecutions on indictment. The McDowell Group noted that they had been 'assured that any decision by the DPP not to commence criminal proceedings for breaches of the Companies Acts is due entirely to the quality of the evidential material available at the time of decision'[54].

[28.022] It should also be noted that the powers of investigation of breaches of the Companies Acts that constitute indictable offences have been greatly bolstered by the CLEA 2001. As has been alluded to already, one intentional[55] effect of increasing the maximum term of imprisonment for indictable offences under the Companies Acts to five years, is to cause the provisions of s 4 of the Criminal Justice Act 1984 ('CJA 1984') to apply to such offences. Heretofore, with certain limited exceptions, a person suspected of committing an indictable offence under the Companies Acts could – upon being approached by the gardaí – refuse to cooperate and 'refer' them to deal with his or her solicitor. Where the conditions of s 4 of the CJA 1984 are met, the gardaí in the

48 As amended by s 104(a) of the CLEA 2001.

49 See *The Report of the Working Group on Company Law Compliance and Enforcement* (1998) at para 4.24.

50 Section 14 of the CLEA 2001.

51 See para **[28.032]** *post*.

52 See para **[28.041]** *post*.

53 See para **[28.036]** *post*.

54 See *The Report of the Working Group on Company Law Compliance and Enforcement* (1998) at para 4.28.

55 The application of s 4 of the CJA 1984 to all indictable offences under the Companies Acts upon the increase in the maximum term of imprisonment to five years was noted by the McDowell Group: see *The Report of the Working Group on Company Law Compliance and Enforcement* (1998) at para 4.30.

Director's office will have the power to arrest a suspect without warrant and detain him for up to 12 hours where such is necessary for the proper investigation of the offence. Although it is thought that the persons who will make arrests without warrant will be the seconded gardaí, it is notable that civilian staff within the enforcement office also have, in certain circumstances, a similar power of arrest under s 4 of the Criminal Law Act 1997. The circumstances in which a civilian has a power to arrest a person suspected of committing an offence that carries a maximum term of imprisonment of five years, are where that person with reasonable cause suspects that the person to be arrested 'would otherwise attempt to avoid, or is avoiding, arrest by a member of the Garda Síochána'[56].

(iv) Civil enforcement and sanction

[28.023] The Director's statutory function to enforce the Companies Acts under s 12(1)(a) of the CLEA 2001 is considerably wider than the prosecution of summary offences and encompasses civil enforcement and sanction. As considered below[57], the Director has standing to apply under s 371 of the CA 1963 for an injunction to require a company or an officer in default to make good that default. The default can involve the commission of either a summary or indictable offence and the Director's lack of standing to prosecute indictable offences is no bar to his seeking a s 371 injunction. Moreover, the Director has express power to apply to court for an injunction to freeze the assets of companies, directors and others (s 55 of the CLEA 2001[58]) and other extensive powers of inspection and preservation, as noted above[59]. The Director can also apply for an order under s 298(2) of the CA 1963 that officers and others repay or restore, etc, money or property in cases of misfeasance. Also, as considered below[60], the Director has power to apply to court to have a person disqualified under s 160 of the CA 1990 or restricted under s 150 of the CA 1990. The Director's powers to apply for certain orders under s 251 of the CA 1990 in cases where companies have not been wound up by reason of the insufficiency of their assets are considered in Chapter 15[61].

The Director of Public Prosecutions

[28.024] The Director of Public Prosecutions ('DPP') is the only person who may prosecute, through to the end, proceedings in respect of an indictable offence. The office of the DPP was established by the Prosecution of Offences Act 1974. That Act also transferred most of the State's prosecution function from the Attorney General to the DPP[62]. It may be noted, in passing, that the CLEA 2001 took the opportunity to remove references in the CA 1963 to the 'Attorney General' and to replace them with references to the DPP[63].

---

56 Section 4(4) of the Criminal Law Act 1997; where such an arrest is effected, the arrested person must be transferred into the custody of the Garda Síochána as soon as practicable.

57 See para **[28.211]** *post*.

58 See Ch 25, *The Realisation and Distribution of Assets in a Winding Up*, at para **[25.050]**.

59 See para **[28.019]** *ante*.

60 See para **[28.148]** *post*.

61 See Ch 15, *Duties of Directors and Other Officers,* at para **[15.141]** *et seq*.

62 See generally, Hogan & Whyte, *The Irish Constitution* (4th edn, Bloomsbury Professional, 2003).

63 See s 51 of the CLEA 2001, which amends s 299 of the CA 1963, which was, of course, enacted prior to the passage of the Prosecution of Offences Act 1974.

[28.025] Prior to the enactment of the CLEA 2001, the authority to prosecute indictable offences vested with the DPP; and because the McDowell Group accepted this was the correct way to proceed, this remains the case. On the assumption that the reason for the dearth of prosecutions for indictable offences under the Companies Acts was on account of the quality of evidential material available at the time of the DPP's decision, the McDowell Group Report said:

> This leads us to recommend that the Director of Corporate Enforcement should play an active role in assisting the preparation of cases for possible criminal proceedings for breaches of the Companies Acts. We envisage that the Director and his staff will work closely with An Garda Síochána in identifying the indictable offences in any particular case and in supporting Garda enquiries (see paragraph 4.62). Such support would, we believe, be useful prior to the Gardaí submitting a case for possible criminal proceedings to the DPP[64].'

Accordingly, the role of the DPP in prosecuting indictable offences under the Companies Acts remains.

[28.026] One of the functions that the DPP did lose as a result of the CLEA 2001 was the right to apply for the disqualification of directors and other persons. Here, the McDowell Group recommended:

> 'The Group similarly found that although section 160 of the Companies Act, 1990, gives the Director of Public Prosecutions power to apply to the court to disqualify persons from acting as directors, auditors, officers, receivers, liquidators, examiners or being involved directly or indirectly in the promotion, formation or management of any company, the Office of the Director of Public Prosecutions is not equipped or organised to investigate and institute civil proceedings for disqualification in the manner envisaged by the Act. The Group concluded that there was an anomaly in providing a civil role in the monitoring of company directors for the Director of Public Prosecutions in matters which may not amount to or disclose the commission of a criminal offence[65].'

The McDowell Group's Report went on to say that the responsibility for the making of disqualification applications was 'generally inconsistent with the primary functions of the Director of Public Prosecutions in prosecuting criminal offences'[66]. The Group went on to recommend that it would be more appropriate for such functions to be carried out by either the registrar of companies or the Director and that the DPP should 'prosecute indictable offences under the Companies Acts on foot of completed investigations either by the Gardaí or by' the Director, or both[67].

Private parties with *locus standi*

[28.027] As regard the prosecution of criminal offences, it has long been recognised that, at common law, a so-called 'common informer', or private party, has *locus standi* to

64 See *The Report of the Working Group on Company Law Compliance and Enforcement* (1998) at para 4.29.

65 See *The Report of the Working Group on Company Law Compliance and Enforcement* (1998) at para 2.15.

66 *The Report of the Working Group on Company Law Compliance and Enforcement* (1998) at para 2.16.

67 *The Report of the Working Group on Company Law Compliance and Enforcement* (1998) at para 2.17.

institute proceedings[68]. It has been held, however, that at common law, a corporation has no power to prosecute as a common informer[69]. For human individuals, however, the right of private prosecution remains[70] although it will ordinarily be only an altruistic or fool-hardy individual who will embark upon such a course. For most people, it will be the civil law that provides the attraction.

[28.028] There are a number of statutory provisions that specifically *empower* third parties to institute proceedings to prevent acts or omissions that are contrary to the Companies Acts. The primary statutory provision is s 371 of the CA 1963[71], considered in detail below[72], which empowers any member, creditor, the registrar or the Director to apply to the High Court for an order to direct a company and any officer to make good a default in complying with any provision of the Companies Acts. This very important remedy is generally considered as having been 're-discovered' by the McDowell Group.

[28.029] Other, more specific, civil remedies are also contained in the Companies Acts. One such remedy is seen in s 8(2) of the CA 1963[73] which empowers a member or 'holder of debentures' of a company to apply to the High Court to restrain a company 'from doing any act or thing which the company has no power to do'. Where a creditor, secured by a debenture, or any member has reason to believe that a company is engaged in *ultra vires* activities, s 8(2) of the CA 1963 may be invoked and appropriate application made to the High Court.

[B] Enforcement and Compliance – Criminal Sanctions

[28.030] Compliance with the statutory obligations of the Companies Acts was for 50 years considered by many companies and their directors as if it was optional; the CLEA 2001 has put paid to that interpretation. It is fast becoming established that the statutory *quid pro quo* for being permitted to conduct business with the shelter provided by the registered limited liability company, is comprehensive and timely compliance with all statutory requirements imposed by the Companies Acts.

[28.031] In this section, the following criminal sanctions and remedies against both companies and defaulting officers are considered:

1. Criminal prosecution of companies and 'officers in default'.
2. On-the-spot fines.

The criminal sanctions for breaches of the Companies Acts can operate to deprive wrongdoers of their liberty and impose fines on them.

---

68 See, generally, Hogan & Whyte, *The Irish Constitution* (4th edn, Bloomsbury Professional, 2003) at paras 5.4.25–5.4.28.

69 *Cumann Luthchlas Gael Teo v Windle* (1993, unreported) SC, Finlay CJ.

70 *The State (Ennis) v Farrell* [1966] IR 107.

71 As amended by s 96 of the CLEA 2001.

72 See para **[28.210]** *post*.

73 See Ch 7, *Corporate Contracts, Capacity and Authority*, at para **[7.047]**.

Criminal prosecution of companies and 'officers in default'

[28.032] In Section [C] and Section [D] the many summary and indictable offences created by the Companies Acts are outlined. Here, it is proposed to review the mechanics of prosecution and other ancillary matters in respect of the offences created by the Companies Acts under the following headings:

(a) Prosecution of 'officers in default';
(b) The penalties specified by the Companies Acts;
(c) The effect of the Fines Act 2010 on summary offences;
(d) The statutory limitation period for prosecution of company law offences;
(e) The venue for prosecution;
(f) Evidence to juries in trials of indictable offences.

(a) Prosecution of 'officers in default'

[28.033] There are over 90 offences under the Companies Acts that are expressed to apply to the company *and* 'to every officer who is in default'[74]. The instance of prosecution of officers in default has been very rare[75], largely due to the high evidential hurdle set by the original s 383 of the CA 1963, which defined an officer in default as:

> '... any officer of the company who *knowingly and wilfully* authorises or permits the default, refusal or contravention ...[76]'

The use of the words 'knowingly and wilfully' in the definition of the phrase 'officer in default' created a very high evidential burden for the prosecution that necessitated proof of a defendant's subjective state of mind[77]. The McDowell Group recommended a revised definition of the concept of 'officer in default'[78] and this was effected by s 100 of the CLEA 2001, which replaced s 383 with the following provision:

> '(1) For the purpose of any provision of the Companies Acts which provides that an officer of a company who is in default shall be liable to a fine or penalty, an officer who is in default is *any officer who authorises or who, in breach of his duty as such officer, permits, the default mentioned in the provision.* [Emphasis added.]

---

74 As to the meaning of 'officer', see: Ch 13, *Corporate Governance: Management by the Directors*, at para **[13.003]**.

75 Although rare, the prosecution of officers in default was not unheard of. So in *Minister for Enterprise Trade and Employment v The Muckross Park Hotel Ltd et al* (20 February 2001) DC, reported in (2001) Irish Times, 21 February, two directors of the defendant company were fined for failing to hold the company's AGM in 1999, despite having been notified on a number of occasions by the Department. Section 131(6) of the CA 1963 criminalises the failure to hold an AGM where committed by a company and every officer who is in default. See further, the *Companies Report 1999*, Department of Jobs, Enterprise and Innovation at pp 44, 45 for examples of successful prosecutions of directors under ss 202 of the CA 1990, s 131 of the CA 1963, and s 116–124 of the CA 1963.

76 Emphasis added.

77 The meaning of 'wilful' is considered in Ch 6, *Corporate Civil Litigation*, at para **[6.080]** and the meaning of 'knowingly' is considered in Ch 15, *Duties of Directors and Other Officers*, at para **[15.101]**.

78 See *The Report of the Working Group on Company Law Compliance and Enforcement* (1998) at para 7.30.

(2) For the purposes of this section, an officer shall be presumed to have permitted a default by the company unless the officer can establish that he took all reasonable steps to prevent it or that, by reason of circumstances beyond his control, was unable to do so.

(3) It is the duty of each director and secretary of a company to ensure that the requirements of the Companies Acts are complied with by the company.

(4) In this section "default" includes a refusal or contravention.'

This is a very far-reaching provision. In the first place, the relevant test is now whether the officer *authorised* or, in breach of his duty as officer, *permitted* the default; this is substantially easier to prove than that old formulation of knowingly and wilfully. In the second place, there is an evidential presumption in favour of the prosecution, since an officer is *presumed* to have permitted a default, and the onus of proof is firmly on a defendant officer to prove that he took all reasonable steps to prevent the default or was unable to prevent it by reason of circumstances outside of his control. The prosecution is also assisted in proving that a defendant officer permitted a default *in breach of his duty as such officer* by sub-s (3) which categorically imposes a positive duty on each director and secretary to ensure that their companies comply with the requirements of the Companies Acts[79]. It is thought that this subsection will prove to be very far-reaching, because it imposes for the first time a positive and unqualified duty on directors and secretaries to comply with the Companies Acts[80].

The new definition of officer in default is expressed to apply for the purposes of any provision of the Companies Acts that provides that an officer of a company who is in default 'shall be liable to a fine or penalty'. When formulating charges against a person, care should be taken to ensure that the offence alleged is sufficiently described[81].

(b) The penalties specified by the Companies Acts

[28.034] Section 240(1) of the CA 1990[82] sets out the penalties for offences 'for which no punishment is specified'. It provides:

'A person guilty under any provision of the Companies Acts of an offence for which no punishment is specifically provided shall be liable—

(a) on summary conviction, to a [class C fine][83] or, at the discretion of the court, to imprisonment for a term not exceeding 12 months or to both, or

---

79 In *R v McCredie and Re v French* [1999] TLR 671, it was held by the English Court of Appeal that the officers of a company that was being would up owed a positive duty to comply with the provisions of s 208(1) of the English Insolvency Act 1986 which required them to cooperate proactively (and not merely reactively) with the company's liquidator.

80 As to the delegation of responsibility by directors, see Ch 15, *Duties of Directors and Other Officers*, at para **[15.051]**.

81 See *Lillyman and Pinkerton* (23 December 1982) Federal Court of Australia.

82 As amended by s 104(a) and (b) of the CLEA 2001.

83 £1,500 was substituted for £1,000 by s 104(a) of the CLEA 2001; £1,500 converted to €1,904.61; and a reference to such a fine in legislation between 1 January 1997 and 4 January 2011 is now a reference to a 'class C fine' defined as a fine not exceeding €2,500 by s 6(2) of the Fines Act 2010 ('FA 2010').

(b) on conviction on indictment, to a fine not exceeding €22,220.42[84] or, at the discretion of the court, to imprisonment for a term not exceeding 5 years[85] or to both.'

In addition, s 240(2) of the CA 1990[86], which is concerned with offences punishable by 'a fine or an unspecified amount', provides:

> 'A person guilty under any provision of the Companies Acts of an offence made punishable by a fine or an unspecified amount shall be liable—
>
> (c) on summary conviction, to a [class C fine][87] or
>
> (d) on conviction on indictment, to a fine not exceeding €22,220.42[88].'

In addition, the Companies Acts are littered with references to specific monetary fines and to specific maximum terms of imprisonment. Prior to the enactment of the CLEA 2001 this gave rise to an anomalous position: where particular sections of the CA 1963 specified particular monetary amounts, they tended to be lower in terms of the maximum fine or term of imprisonment than those applicable to offences for which no punishment was specified and those expressed to be punishable by fine or an unspecified amount. This anomaly was removed by s 104(c) of the CLEA 2001, which introduced new sub-ss (7) and (8) into s 240 of the CA 1990. These provide for an equalisation of penalties under the Companies Acts. Section 240(7) provides:

> 'In any provision of the Companies Acts for which a fine of any amount of less than [€1,904.61][89] is provided in respect of a summary conviction, the maximum amount of that fine shall be taken to be [€1,904.61][90].'

Moreover, the effect of s 6 of the Fines Act 2010 is considered below.

Section 240(8) of the CA 1990 now provides:

> 'In any provision of the Companies Acts for which a term of imprisonment of less than 5 years is provided in respect of a conviction on indictment, the maximum term of imprisonment shall be taken to be 5 years.'

---

84 '£10,000' converted to '€12,697.38' by Council Regulations (EC) No 1103/97, No 974/98 and No 2866/98 and s 6 of the Economic and Monetary Union Act 1998 and subjected to a multiplier of 1.75 by s 9 of the FA 2010.

85 Section 104(b) of the CLEA 2001 amends s 240(1)(b) of the CA 1990 by the substitution for '3 years' of '5 years'.

86 As amended by s 104(a) of the CLEA 2001.

87 £1,500 was substituted for £1,000 by s 104(a) of the CLEA 2001; £1,500 converted to €1,904.61; and a reference to such a fine in legislation between 1 January 1997 and 4 January 2011 is now a reference to a 'class C fine' defined as a fine not exceeding €2,500 by s 6(2) of the FA 2010.

88 '£10,000' converted to '€12,697.38' by Council Regulations (EC) No 1103/97, No 974/98 and No 2866/98 and s 6 of the Economic and Monetary Union Act 1998 and subjected to a multiplier of 1.75 by s 9 of the FA 2010.

89 Section 104(a) of the CLEA 2001 amends s 240 of the CA 1990 by the substitution for '£1,000' wherever occurring of '£1,500'. '£1,500' converted to '€1,904.61' by Council Regulations (EC) No 1103/97, No 974/98 and No 2866/98 and s 6 of the Economic and Monetary Union Act 1998.

90 Section 104(a) of the CLEA 2001 amends s 240 of the CA 1990 by the substitution for '£1,000' wherever occurring of '£1,500'. '£1,500' converted to '€1,904.61' by Council Regulations (EC) No 1103/97, No 974/98 and No 2866/98 and s 6 of the Economic and Monetary Union Act 1998.

In consequences of these measures, the maximum fine in the case of all summary offences is a class C fine and the maximum term of imprisonment is 12 months. These changes in the Companies Acts must, however, also be read in conjunction with the Fines Act 2010[91] which has replaced fines of particular monetary amounts with references to class A to class E fines.

[28.035] In respect of indictable offences, the maximum fine where none is set was, prior to the Fines Act 2010, €12,697.38 (but this can be more in relation to specified offences). Since the commencement of s 9 of the Fines Act 2010, the revised maximum, following the application of a multiplier of 1.75, is €22,220.42. Also in respect of indictable offences, the maximum term of imprisonment is five years (save in relation to a number of specified offences which provided for a greater maximum term)[92]. As noted earlier[93], one of the most tangible effects of increasing the maximum term of imprisonment for indictable offences to five years is that persons suspected of having committed such an offence may be arrested without warrant and detained in a garda station for up to 12 hours: s 4 of the CJA 1984[94].

(c) The effect of the Fines Act 2010 on summary offences

[28.036] Prior to the Fines Act 2010 ('FA 2010'), when the legislature created statutory offences and assigned maximum monetary fines, the amounts were rarely ever reviewed in line with inflation and amended. In consequence, many of the maximum fines on our statute book (and not just under the Companies Acts) were ridiculously low and provided no deterrent value to persons who, following conviction, had such fines imposed. This has now been redressed by the FA 2010[95]. In the first place, going forward, the maximum fine for summary offences will no longer generally be a fixed monetary amount. Instead, the maximum fine will be expressed as being one of five possible classes of fine: classes A to E. Section 3 of the FA 2010 has initially set maximum fines applicable to each class as follows:

> '"class A fine" means a fine not exceeding €5,000;
>
> "class B fine" means a fine not exceeding €4,000;
>
> "class C fine" means a fine not exceeding €2,500;
>
> "class D fine" means a fine not exceeding €1,000;
>
> "class E fine" means a fine not exceeding €500.'

For all new offences where the fines have been so classified, it will be a relatively simple matter to ensure that the amount of the fine is maintained in line with inflation by simply amending s 3 of the FA 2010.

---

91 Commenced in relation to Parts 1 and 2 and ss 12 and 14 by the Fines Act 2010 (Commencement) Order 2010 (SI 662/2010) with effect from 4 January 2011.

92 See para **[28.057]** *post*.

93 See para **[28.022]** *ante*.

94 See Charleton, McDermott & Bolger, *Criminal Law* (1999, Butterworths) at p 143;

95 Parts 1 and 2 of the FA 2010 were commenced with effect from 4 January 2011: Fines Act 2010 (Commencement) Order 2010 (SI 662/2010).

[28.037] The FA 2010 also applies to all existing offences which purport to have maximum fines applicable on summary conviction. In a very clever piece of statutory drafting, ss 4 to 8 of the FA 2010 index all summary offence fines so as to bring them up to date in line with inflation. The effect has been to make multiple 'virtual' amendments to the Companies Acts[96]. Technically, the existing provision specifying the old monetary amount is not expressly amended; rather, the approach taken is to say, almost, *notwithstanding* that the existing provision may say that the maximum fine is, say, €2,000, a person convicted of that offence shall 'not be liable to that fine but shall instead be liable to a class C fine'.

While clever, the formula used is intricate and requires some thought in order to determine what class of fine applies to a particular offence by reference to the monetary amount of the fine *and* to the date on which the fine was last set at that particular monetary amount (ie, the last time the provision was amended, not the first time the provision was enacted). The task of ascertaining the applicable class is not made any easier by the decimalisation of our currency on 15 February 1971 and its subsequent conversion to euro on 1 January 2002.

Most of the maximum fines applicable to summary offences created by the Companies Acts are *class C fines*, governed by s 6 of the FA 2010, and so s 6 will be used as the example as to how the indexing formula works. Section 6(1) concerns new offences which are expressed to be subject to a class C fine and simply provides that such shall be construed as a reference to a class C fine within the meaning of Part 2 of the FA 2010. Section 6(2) deals with existing offences where the amount of the fine was never amended, and provides:

> 'Subject to subsection (3), where an enactment enacted during a period specified in column (2) of the Table opposite a particular reference number specified in column (1) of the Table provides that a person who commits an offence under the enactment shall be liable, upon summary conviction, to a fine not exceeding an amount that falls within the range of amounts specified in column (3) of the Table opposite the same reference number, a person who commits that offence after the commencement date shall, upon summary conviction, not be liable to that fine, but shall instead be liable to a class C fine.'

Section 6(3) of the FA 2010 addresses existing summary offences where the maximum fine has been amended subsequent to its original enactment, and provides:

> 'Where an enactment enacted before the commencement date provides that a person who commits an offence under the enactment shall be liable, upon summary conviction, to a fine not exceeding an amount that—
>
> (a) was provided for by virtue of a subsequent enactment enacted during a period specified in column (2) of the Table opposite a particular reference number specified in column (1) of the Table, and
>
> (b) falls within the range of amounts specified in column (3) of the Table opposite the same reference number,
>
> a person who commits that offence after the commencement date shall, upon summary conviction, not be liable to that fine but shall instead be liable to a class C fine.'

---

[96] The forthcoming edition of MacCann & Courtney, *Companies Acts 1963–2012*, to be published in late 2012 by Bloomsbury Professional shows the amendments of every offence created by the Companies Acts in line with the FA 2010.

The Table referred to in s 6 of the FA 2010 provides:

Ref No (1)	Period (2)	Range of Amounts (3)
1.	1 January 1997 to day immediately before commencement date	Not greater than €2,500 but greater than €1,000
2.	1 January 1990 to 31 December 1996	Not greater than €1,731 but greater than €692
3.	1 January 1980 to 31 December 1989	Not greater than €1,455 but greater than €582
4.	1 January 1975 to 31 December 1979	Not greater than €606 but greater than €242
5.	1 January 1965 to 31 December 1974	Not greater than €307 but greater than €123
6.	1 January 1945 to 31 December 1964	Not greater than €147 but greater than €59
7.	1 January 1915 to 31 December 1944	Not greater than €79 but greater than €32
8.	Period ending on 31 December 1914	Not greater than €50 but greater than €25

The other sections (ss 4, 5, 7 and 8) dealing with classes A, B, D and E apply the same approach to determining the applicable classification.

The explanatory memorandum to the FA 2010 explains that the base year of 100 is 1914 because '(money values were relatively stable in the preceding century)' and that all fines that can be imposed on summary conviction since then are now updated in line with increases in the Consumer Price Index. It continues:

> 'Instead of attempting to update each fine separately, which would not be practicable, eight time periods and five classes of fine maxima have been created and placed in tables. Finding the current value of a fine is best illustrated by an example. Section 6 of the Prohibition of Incitement to Hatred Act 1989 provides maximum penalties for certain offences under that Act. The maximum financial penalty, on summary conviction, is a fine of £1,000 or €1,265. By examining the tables in sections 4 to 8 it will be seen that, in section 6, any maximum fine not greater than €1,455 but greater than €582 provided for in legislation between 1 January 1980 and 31 December 1989 will be a class C fine. The new maximum summary fine for an offence under section 6 of the Prohibition of Incitement to Hatred Act 1989 is, therefore, €2,500. This is not a real increase in the amount of the original fine. The Fines Act maintains the value of the fine and ensures that the intentions of the Oireachtas when passing the legislation are respected.'

It may be noted that this approach has been taken to another level in the draft Companies Bill which proposed that every offence in the Companies Act will be classified as being either a class A, B, C or D *offence* to which certain specified penalties (including, in the case of summary offences, class A–E fines) will apply.

(d) The statutory limitation period for prosecution of company law offences

[28.038] Prior to s 41 of the C(A)(No 2)A 1999 the limitation period within which a *summary prosecution* could be initiated under the Companies Acts was three years from the date of commission. The standard three-year limitation period has been retained: s 240(5)(a) of the CA 1990. This is, however, subject to two extensions. First, under s 240(5)(b) proceedings may be commenced if, at the expiry of the three-year period, the person against whom the proceedings are to be brought is outside the State, within six months from the date on which he next enters the State. More far reaching is s 240(5)(c), which provides that proceedings can be commenced:

> 'at any time within 3 years from the date on which evidence that, in the opinion of the person by whom the proceedings are brought, is sufficient to justify the bringing of the proceedings comes to that person's knowledge.'

Frequently, the suspected commission of offences under the Companies Acts will only come to light long after their commission following an independent investigation by a liquidator during the course of a winding up. Prosecutors are further assisted by s 240(5A) of the CA 1990, which provides that a certificate signed by or on behalf of the prosecutor as to the date on which the evidence referred to in s 240(5)(c) came to his knowledge, 'shall be *prima facie* evidence thereof'[97].

There is no statutory limitation period on the prosecution of indictable offences under the Companies Acts[98]. It has been noted[99], however, that Irish law has always recognised that inherent in the rights conferred on a person being investigated in respect of a crime is the right to reasonable dispatch; in *Hogan v The President of the Circuit Court*[100] the Supreme Court prohibited a prosecution for fraud where there had been a delay in excess of 10 years. Each case will, however, turn on its own facts. In *R v Thames Magistrates' Court; ex p Hogan*[101], it was held by Pill LJ (Garland J concurring) that the time limit in s 731(2) of the Companies Act 1985 (UK), for prosecuting offences that were capable of being tried summarily or on indictment, applied only to those that were *solely* summary offences; in respect of those capable of being prosecuted on indictment, no time limits applied.

(e) The venue for prosecution

[28.039] One of the difficulties previously encountered in the bringing of summary proceedings under the Companies Acts was that under the District Court Rules, proceedings have to be brought either in the court area where the accused resides or in the court area where the alleged offence was committed. The difficulties became manifest where it was not possible to identify the place where an act or omission

97 This subsection goes on to provide that 'in any legal proceedings a document purporting to be a certificate issued for the purpose of this subsection and to be so signed shall be deemed to be so signed and shall be admitted as evidence without proof of the signature of the person purporting to sign the certificate'.

98 *B v DPP* [1997] 2 ILRM 118.

99 See Charleton, McDermott & Bolger, *Criminal Law* (1999, Butterworths) at p 666.

100 *Hogan v The President of the Circuit Court* (21 June 1994, unreported) SC.

101 *R v Thames Magistrates' Court; ex p Hogan* [1997] TLR 633.

occurred and practice was to issue proceedings against directors in the court area of their home addresses and in the court area of a company's registered office, leading to unnecessary duplication of work and a waste of court time[102]. This anomaly is cured by s 240A of the CA 1990[103]. This provides:

> 'For the purposes of any provision of the Companies Acts which provides that the company and every officer of the company is guilty of an offence, summary proceedings against the company or an officer of the company may be brought, heard and determined either—
>
> (a) in the court area in which the offence charged or, if more than one offence is stated to have been committed, any one of the offences charged, is stated to have been committed,
>
> (b) in the court area in which the accused has been arrested,
>
> (c) in the court area in which the accused resides,
>
> (d) in the court area specified by order made pursuant to section 15 of the Courts Act, 1971, or
>
> (e) in the court area in which the registered office of the company is situated.'

It remains to be seen how this will operate in practice. If it is decided to centralise the hearing of summary prosecutions under the Companies Acts in one district, one side-effect that might be expected would be the building-up of company law enforcement expertise in that court.

(f) Evidence to juries in trials of indictable offences

[28.040] Section 110(1) of the CLEA 2001 provides that in a trial on indictment of an offence under the Companies Acts, the trial judge may order that copies of any or all of the following documents may be given to the jury 'in any form that the judge considers appropriate':

> '(a) any document admitted in evidence at the trial,
>
> (b) the transcript of the opening speeches of counsel,
>
> (c) any charts, diagrams, graphics, schedules or summaries of evidence produced at the trial,
>
> (d) the transcript of the whole or any part of the evidence given at the trial,
>
> (e) the transcript of the trial judge's charge to the jury,
>
> (f) any other document that in the opinion of the trial judge would be of assistance to the jury in its deliberations including, where appropriate, an affidavit by an accountant summarising, in a form which is likely to be comprehended by the jury, any transactions by the accused or other persons relevant to the offence.'

This extremely practical provision is intended to facilitate the comprehension of evidence of possibly complex and intricate commercial dealings by a jury composed of ordinary members of the public with no particular expertise in law, accounting or finance. To safeguard the rights of an accused, s 110(2) provides that if the prosecutor proposes to apply to the trial judge for an order that a document mentioned in s 110(1)(f) should be given to the jury, the prosecutor must give a copy of the document to the

---

102 See the 'Explanatory and Financial Memorandum to the Company Law Enforcement Bill' (2000) at p 28, 29.

103 As inserted by s 105 of the CLEA 2001.

accused in advance of the trial and, on the hearing of the application, the trial judge shall take into account any representations made by or on behalf of the accused in relation to it. Moreover, where the trial judge has made an order that an affidavit by an accountant pursuant to s 110(1)(f) is provided to a jury, the judge may 'with a view to further assisting the jury in its deliberations, require the accountant who prepared the affidavit to explain to the jury any relevant accounting procedures or principles'.

On-the-spot fines

[28.041] The McDowell Group recommended the introduction of on-the-spot fines for a select number of registration-type offences, such as the failure to file an annual return and the failure to file a liquidator's return[104]. Effect was given to this recommendation by s 66(1) of the CLEA 2001, which introduced to company law the on-the-spot fine, whereby the registrar can serve notice on a company or person in default requiring the payment of a particular sum in order to avoid the institution of proceedings. Section 66 goes further than seems to have been intended by the McDowell Group since it can be invoked by the registrar in the case of *all* returns or documents required to be delivered, filed or made to the registrar under the Companies Acts, and not the 'select number' as recommended. This notice will state that the person has failed to deliver, file or make a specified return or similar document to be registered under a specified section of the Companies Acts and that the person may, within 21 days, remedy the default and make a prescribed payment to the registrar. The notice must also specify that, where the person complies with the notice:

> 'a prosecution in respect of the person to whom the notice is delivered will not be instituted during the period specified in the notice, or, if the default is remedied and the payment specified in the notice is made during that period, at all[105].'

The hope is that this will avoid the institution of costly proceedings. Where a default has been remedied before the hearing of a prosecution in respect of the default, there must be a tendency to be lenient to the defaulter. Section 66(1) of the CLEA 2001 is, therefore, a welcome addition to the registrar of companies' armoury since it is designed to achieve compliance, without recourse to the courts.

[28.042] The Director of Corporate Enforcement also has the power to impose on-the-spot fines, as an alternative to prosecuting for a summary offence. This power – which is virtually identical to that of the registrar – is contained in s 109(1) of the CLEA 2001. This provides:

> 'Where the Director has reasonable grounds for believing that a person has committed an offence under the Companies Acts which is subject to summary prosecution, the Director may deliver to the person or, where the person believed to have committed the offence is a company, to an officer of the company, a notice in the prescribed form stating—
>
> (a) that the person or company is alleged to have committed that offence,
>
> (b) that the person to whom the notice is delivered may during a period of 21 days beginning on the date of the notice—

---

[104] See *The Report of the Working Group on Company Law Compliance and Enforcement* (1998) at para 3.21.

[105] Legal effect to the 'promise' not to prosecute contained in the s 66(1) notice is given effect by s 66(2)(c) of the CLEA 2001.

(i) remedy as far as practicable to the satisfaction of the Director any default that constitutes the offence, and

(ii) make to the Director a payment of a prescribed amount which shall be accompanied by the notice,

and

(c) that a prosecution of the person to whom the notice is delivered in respect of the alleged offence will not be instituted during the period satisfied in the notice or, if the default is remedied to the satisfaction of the Director and the payment specified in the notice is made during that period, at all.'

Section 109(2) provides that when such a notice is given and the person makes the specified payment during the specified period, the Director may receive and receipt the payment (which shall not be recoverable by the person who made it) and, in such a case:

> 'A prosecution in respect of the alleged offence shall not be instituted in the period specified in the notice and, if the default is remedied to the satisfaction of the Director and the payment specified in the notice is made during that period, no prosecution in respect of the alleged offence shall be instituted at all.'

Again, as in the case of the registrar's power to issue on-the-spot fines, the hope is that this will prove to be an effective and efficient means of ensuring compliance with the Companies Acts, without having to have recourse to the courts.

[C] Registration-type Offences

[28.043] The Companies Acts contain numerous requirements for companies (and their officers) to deliver various notices and documents to the registrar of companies (the 'registrar') at the Companies Registration Office (the 'CRO'). Section 368(1) of the CA 1963 requires the Minister for Jobs, Enterprise and Innovation to maintain and administer an office or offices (the CRO) for the purposes of the registration of companies and sub-s (2) provides that the Minister may appoint such registrars and assistant registrars as he thinks necessary[106]. Two of the primary functions of the registrar are the registration of new companies and the registration of a myriad of post-registration documents from, or in relation to, registered companies[107].

The purpose of registration

[28.044] The statutory purpose in requiring companies and others to file, deliver or register certain documents in relation to companies is to effect public disclosure, which is, in this respect, the *quid pro quo* for registration of companies. Public disclosure of the register is provided for by s 370(1)(a) of the CA 1963, which provides that any person may, on payment of a fee, 'inspect the documents kept by the Registrar of Companies'[108]. Being an artificial legal person, it is considered proper for the public at large to be able to consult with a central registry (the CRO) in order to elicit certain

106 The current registrar of companies is Ms Helen Dixon.

107 See para **[28.006]** *ante* where the registrar's enforcement functions are considered.

108 Section 370(1)(b) allows any person to require a certificate of incorporation of any company or a copy or extract of any other document or any part thereof to be certified by the registrar in return for a fee.

organisational, constitutional and financial information about a registered company[109]. It should be remembered, however, that public documents can be a twin-edged sword: whilst they make available information on companies, the public at large will be deemed to have *constructive notice* of their existence and contents[110].

Summary and indictable registration offences

[28.045] Of the *circa* 283 specified criminal offences identified in Appendix 2 to the McDowell Group's report[111] (which enumerate the criminal offences created by the Companies Acts 1963–1990 only), some 73 odd related to failures to file, deliver or lodge with the registrar, certain specified documents by companies and specified individuals. Of those 73 offences, only 14 can be prosecuted on indictment, the remainder being summary offences. Not only that, but only *one* of the indictable offences relating to registration relates to an offence committed by a company: s 226 of the CA 1990, which makes it an indictable offence to fail to deliver to the registrar, within 28 days, a return relating to a company's own-purchase of shares. The other registration offences that are indictable relate to failures by liquidators[112], receivers[113], petitioners for orders for court protection[114], examiners[115], auditors[116] and recognised bodies of accountants[117].

Failure to file annual return and notify changes in officers

[28.046] Ironically, the most common non-registration offence in respect of which the registrar has in recent years taken action – namely the failure by a company to file its *annual return* with the registrar within the set periods[118] – is merely a summary offence. The requirement for all Irish registered companies to file an annual return is considered in Chapter 17[119]. Even more ironic is the fact that non-compliance with this particular case of *non-registration* attracts the registrar's 'nuclear remedy' for defaulting companies: the much feared, *strike-off*. Strangely, no public justification, apart from statutory right, has ever been advanced for the invocation of the remedy of strike-off against companies, which fail to file an annual return. One can only surmise that it is considered to be a fundamental *quid pro quo* for corporate registration. The remedy of strike-off is comprehensively considered in Chapter 26[120].

---

[109] See, for example, the rationale behind the registration of charges created by companies given by Sargant J in *Esberg & Son Ltd v Capital Counties Bank* [1913] 2 Ch 366 at 374; Ch 19, *Corporate Borrowing: Registration of Charges*, at para **[19.003]**.

[110] For the relevance of this in the context of outsiders being bound by constitutional restrictions on corporate authority, see Ch 7, *Corporate Contracts, Capacity and Authority*, at para **[7.119]**.

[111] Appendix 2 was reproduced in the McDowell Group's Report from McGahon, *Irish Company Law Index* (1991, Gill & Macmillan).

[112] Section 306(1) of the CA 1963; ss 145, 151 of the CA 1990.

[113] Sections 319(2), 321(1) of the CA 1963.

[114] Section 12(5) of the C(A)A 1990.

[115] Section 12(5) of the C(A)A 1990.

[116] Sections 185, 186 and 194 of the CA 1990.

[117] Sections 199 and 200 of the CA 1990.

[118] Sections 125, 126 and 127 of the CA 1963, as replaced by ss 59 and 60 of the CLEA 2001.

[119] See Ch 17, *Financial Statements, Audit and Annual Return,* para **[17.250]** *et seq*.

[120] See Ch 26, *Strike-Off and Restoration,* at para **[26.004]** *et seq*.

[28.047] Perhaps the second most commonly spoken of non-registration offence is the failure by companies to notify the registrar of changes in their officers, particularly the *retirement* of company directors. Again, this is a summary offence: s 195 of the CA 1963[121]. Here, the reason for the registrar's concern lies in her remedies against the directors of defaulting companies and other 'officers in default':[122] without having identifiable officers to prosecute, the registrar's powers of enforcement are rendered impotent. This is exacerbated by the fact that as a matter of company law, a director's status as such is dependent upon whether or not *in fact* he continues to be a director *vis-à-vis* his company: the fact he is or is not registered in the CRO as a director does not determine his status as a director[123]. It is for that reason that statutory obstacles have been placed in the path of directors' attempts to self-notify the registrar of their resignations[124], since if companies notify the registrar of resignations they are duty bound to notify her of replacement directors of a sufficient number to satisfy the statutory minimum of two: s 174 of the CA 1963[125].

Other registration offences

[28.048] Many of the registration offences comprise of relatively innocuous transgressions of the Companies Acts; others – insofar as the failure to comply means that the public is unaware of serious matters affecting a company – have the potential to be very serious. Registration offences can be committed by companies, liquidators, receivers, petitioners for orders for court protection, examiners, auditors and recognised bodies of accountants.

(a) Registration offences by companies

[28.049] Most of the registration offences are directed at defaulting companies. In most cases, not only will the company be guilty of the offence, but so too will 'every officer in default'[126]. These *include* the failure to deliver/notify/file to or with the registrar the following:

- The altered memorandum where objects clause amended: s 10(9) of the CA 1963;
- A notice of an increase in members of an unlimited company: s 12(3) of the CA 1963;
- An endorsed copy prospectus before issue: s 47(1) of the CA 1963;
- A statement *in lieu* of prospectus: s 53(1) of the CA 1963;
- Return of allotment of shares: s 58(1) of the CA 1963;
- Details of authorised commissions on allotment: s 59(1) of the CA 1963;
- Notice of consolidation, etc, of shares: s 69(1) of the CA 1963;
- Notice of increase in authorised or nominal share capital: s 70(1) of the CA 1963;
- Court order for cancellation of variation of shareholders' rights: s 78(5) of the CA 1963;

---

121 See Ch 13, *Corporate Governance: Management by the Directors*, at para **[13.074]** *et seq*.

122 See para **[28.033]** *ante*.

123 *POW Services Ltd and another v Clare et al* [1995] 2 BCLC 435: see Ch 13, *Corporate Governance: Management by the Directors*, at para **[13.083]**.

124 See Ch 13, *Corporate Governance: Management by the Directors*, at para **[13.084]**.

125 See Ch 13, *Corporate Governance: Management by the Directors*, at para **[13.011]**.

126 'Every officer in default' is considered at para **[28.033]** *ante*.

- Particulars of a charge[127], acquisition of property subject to existing charges[128], and a copy of the affidavit of judgment mortgage[129];
- Notice of change in registered office: s 113(3) of the CA 1963;
- Notice of place/change in place where register of members is kept: s 116(7) of the CA 1963;
- Annual return: ss 125 and 127 of the CA 1963[130];
- Copy court order extending time in which annual return may be delivered: s 127(4) of the CA 1963[131];
- Annex balance sheet (and auditors' report, if applicable) to annual return: s 128(1) of the CA 1963;
- Copy resolution treating a meeting as AGM: s 131(5) of the CA 1963;
- Copy of special and certain other resolutions: s 143(2) of the CA 1963;
- Notice of removal of an auditor: s 160(5A)(a)(ii) of the CA 1963[132];
- List of persons consenting to be directors in prospectuses, etc: s 179(1) of the CA 1963;
- Consents of new directors or secretary: s 195 of the CA 1963;
- Copy of court order regarding compromises/arrangements: ss 201(1) and 203(3) of the CA 1963;
- Copy of court order in remedy for oppression: s 205(5) of the CA 1963;
- Copy winding-up order: s 221(1) of the CA 1963;
- Copy of court order annulling or staying winding up: s 234(4) of the CA 1963;
- Copy order annulling or staying the resolution to wind up: s 280(3) of the CA 1963;
- Register particulars required of foreign companies: s 358 of the CA 1963;
- Documents required of new unregistered companies: s 377(6) of the CA 1963;
- Notice of court application to cancel special resolution for re-registration of a PLC as a private company: s 15(5) of the C(A)A 1983;
- Copy court order cancelling/confirming special resolution to re-register as a private company: s 15(5) of the C(A)A 1983;
- Copy ordinary resolution and report in respect of payment of non-cash consideration (PLCs only): s 33(2) of the C(A)A 1983;
- Statement of rights attaching to shares, where not stated in memorandum or articles: s 39(1) of the C(A)A 1983;
- Statement of allotment of shares containing particulars of variation: s 39(3) of the C(A)A 1983;
- Notice of the assignment of name or designation to any class of shares: s 39(4) of the C(A)A 1983;
- Notice of petition to appoint an examiner (where presented by company itself): s 12(5) of the 1990 Amendment Act;
- Copy of statement by auditor to members: s 186 of the CA 1990;
- Return relating to purchase of own shares: s 226 of the CA 1990;
- Notice of cessation of last remaining State resident director: s 43(9) of the C(A)(No 2)A 1999.

---

127 Section 100(1) of the CA 1963.

128 Section 101(1) of the CA 1963.

129 Section 102(1) of the CA 1963. It was also an offence not to register a charge created before the coming into operation of the CA 1963, ie, 1 April 1964: s 112(1) of the CA 1963.

130 As inserted by ss 59 and 60 of the CLEA 2001.

131 As inserted by s 60 of the CLEA 2001.

132 Note, notice of the arising of the Minister's power to appoint an auditor must be given to the Minister: s 160(5A)(a)(i).

Offences that are obsolete in the sense that they concerned notifications after the commencement of particular Companies Acts are excluded from the foregoing list as they can no longer be prosecuted. Not all of the foregoing offences are also offences by 'officers in default' and each particular section should be consulted individually. As indicated, the requirement in each case varies from 'deliver to' or 'file with' or 'give notice to' the registrar and the precise requirement should, in each case, be scrutinised. It should also be remembered that in many of the above registration requirements, an offence will be committed even if delivery, etc, is effected, but is outside of particular *statutory time limits*. Where Ministerial regulations require the use of any symbol of classification on documents required to be delivered to the registrar, it is an offence not to comply[133].

(*b*) *Registration offences by liquidators, receivers and examiners*

[28.050] Most of the remaining registration offences are directed at defaulting insolvency practitioners. These *include* the failure to deliver/notify/file to or with the registrar the following:

- Notice of appointment (by a receiver): s 107(1) of the CA 1963;
- Notice of cessation to act (by a receiver): s 107(2) of the CA 1963;
- Statement of affairs (by a receiver): s 319(1) of the CA 1963;
- Abstract of receipts and payments every six months and statement as to whether the company is solvent (by a receiver): s 319(2) and (2A) of the CA 1963[134];
- Returns (by a receiver or liquidator): s 145 of the CA 1990;
- Notify directors that they are persons to whom ss 149–158 of the CA 1990 apply (by a liquidator): s 151 of the CA 1990;
- Copy of court order for dissolution of company (by a liquidator): s 249(2) of the CA 1963;
- Deliver office copy of order applying provisions ordinarily only applicable to a creditors' winding up to a members' winding up (by a liquidator): s 256(6) of the CA 1963;
- Copy final report of final general meeting in both members' and creditors' windings up (by a liquidator): ss 263(3) and 273(3) of the CA 1963;
- Notice of appointment (by a liquidator): s 278(3) of the CA 1963;
- Copy court order annulling or staying a winding up (by a liquidator): s 280(3) of the CA 1963;
- Particulars on the progress of a liquidation (by a liquidator): s 306(1) of the CA 1963;
- Office copy order permitting disposal of charged property (by an examiner): s 11(7) of the 1990 Amendment Act;
- Notice of appointment (by an examiner): s 12(5) of the 1990 Amendment Act;
- Copy court order s 24 of the 1990 Amendment Act (by an examiner): s 30(2) of the 1990 Amendment Act.

Again, many of the foregoing registration requirements must be effected within particular *statutory time limits*. There is anecdotal evidence that the registrar of companies has been less than pleased with the compliance by insolvency practitioners

133 Section 247(4) of the CA 1990.

134 Section 319(2A) of the CA 1963 was inserted by s 53(a) of the CLEA 2001.

with their statutory obligations to register, but that the situation has greatly improved in recent years.

(c) Registration offences by auditors and auditors' representative bodies

[28.051] Auditors and accountancy bodies are also required to make particular returns and deliver particular documents to the registrar. These offences *include* failure to deliver/notify/file:

- Notice of resignation of auditor (by an auditor): s 185 of the CA 1990;
- Opinion that company is contravening or has contravened its requirement to maintain proper books of account (by an auditor): s 194 of the CA 1990;
- Notice and (if applicable statement) of resignation (by an auditor): s 186 of the CA 1990;
- List of members qualified for appointment as auditors (by recognised body of accountants): s 199 of the CA 1990;
- List of members qualified for appointment as auditors, within one month of their qualification (by recognised body of accountants): s 200 of the CA 1990.

None of the foregoing is a particularly onerous or controversial obligation. The most significant reporting duty imposed upon auditors is pursuant to s 194(5) of the CA 1963, inserted by s 74 of the CLEA 2001. This obliges auditors to report to the Director of Corporate Enforcement, *inter alia*, the auditor's suspicion that a company or its officer or agent has committed an indictable offence under the Companies Acts[135].

(d) Registration offences by others

[28.052] The remaining registration offences can be committed by applicants to court who secure a court order deferring the date of dissolution of a company and who fail to file a copy thereof with the registrar[136]; and a petitioner for the appointment of an examiner who fails to deliver notice of the petition with the registrar[137].

The form of documents filed, returned or delivered

[28.053] In addition to the various registration requirements under the Companies Acts, there are also qualitative provisions regarding what is filed. Documents (which include any periodic account, abstract, statement or return)[138] required to be delivered must, by s 248(2) of the CA 1990:

> '(a) state in a prominent position the registered number of the company to which it relates,
>
> (b) satisfy any requirements prescribed for the purposes of this section as to the form and content of the document, and
>
> (c) conform to such requirements as may be prescribed for the purpose of enabling the Registrar to copy the document.'

---

135 See O'Reilly, 'Auditors' Responsibilities: Changed Responsibilities' (2002) 9 CLP 79.

136 Sections 263(6), 273(6) and 310(2) of the CA 1963.

137 Section 12(5) of the C(A)A 1990.

138 Section 248(8) of the CA 1990.

The 'public person' consent provisions in the Electronic Commerce Act 2000, which allow public bodies to specify their requirements if information is to be delivered electronically, had a forerunner in s 249 of the CA 1990. Section 249(2) facilitates the delivery of documents in any non-legible form prescribed for the purposes. As in the case of legible documents, non-legible documents must meet similar qualitative requirements.

[28.054] Section 249A of the CA 1990[139] amended both s 248 and s 249 of the CA 1990[140] and applies the 'rectify your return error' in s 66 of the CLEA 2001 (which applies to a complete failure to deliver) to qualitative errors in documents that have been delivered. This provides that the registrar can serve, on defaulting persons, a notice indicating the deficiency, where a document is delivered which does not comply with the requirements of s 248 or 249, any other requirement in the Companies Acts (particularly those requiring delivery of a document) and any requirements imposed by other legislation relating to the completion of a document and its delivery to the registrar[141]. Where the registrar serves such a notice, unless a replacement document is delivered to her within 14 days thereafter and it complies with the specified requirements, the original document shall be deemed not to have been delivered to the registrar[142]. Again, this deeming provision will assist the registrar in prosecuting a default. Where the failure to deliver the document gives rise to the imposition of a penalty for continued contravention, or a step-up-fee for late delivery, the 14-day notice period is discounted provided the document is delivered to the registrar within the 14-day period[143].

[D] NON-REGISTRATION OFFENCES

[28.055] Three categories of other offences, termed here *non-registration offences*, can be identified:

1. Indictable offences.
2. Failure to keep and maintain registers and records.
3. Miscellaneous offences

Indictable offences

[28.056] Although over 100 of the offences created by the Companies Acts are expressed to be *indictable* offences, some are more serious than others. By reason of s 104 of the CLEA 2001, all indictable offences punishable by imprisonment, now carry a maximum term of imprisonment of five years on conviction, the maximum having been raised from three years[144]. The significance of this is to make very many indictable

139 Inserted by s 107 of the CLEA 2001.

140 By the deletion of s 248(3)–(5) and s 249(5)–(7) of the CA 1990.

141 Section 249A(1) of the CA 1990.

142 Section 249A(2) of the CA 1990.

143 Section 249A(3) of the CA 1990.

144 Section 104 of the CLEA 2001 inserted a new sub-s (8) in s 240 of the CA 1990. See para **[28.034]** *ante*.

offences under the Companies Acts, *arrestable (without warrant) offences* under s 4 of the CJA 1984. The consequences of this are considered above[145].

[28.057] The most serious indictable offences, which carry maximum prison terms in excess of five years, are fraudulent trading[146], three specific offences in relation to insider dealing in shares, and furnishing false information. Fraudulent trading carries a maximum term of imprisonment of seven years. Market abuse carries a possible sentence of 10 years on conviction on indictment[147]. An often overlooked, but very serious, offence is the offence of furnishing false information in purported compliance with the Companies Acts contrary to s 242(1) of the CA 1990; in certain circumstances[148], a person convicted of this offence can be liable to be visited with a term of imprisonment not exceeding seven years.

[28.058] The offences set out hereunder are all indictable offences that attract, on conviction, a maximum term of imprisonment of five years. The seriousness with which the legislature is now taking these offences is borne out by the fact that persons suspected of their contravention are liable to arrest without warrant. Such indictable offences *include*:

- Delivering a statement in lieu of prospectus to the registrar containing any untrue statement: ss 35 and 54(5) of the CA 1963;
- Wrongly giving financial assistance in connection with the purchase of a company's own shares: s 60(15) of the CA 1963;
- False and deceitful impersonation of a shareholder, etc: s 90 of the CA 1963;
- Failure to ensure proper books of account are maintained on a continuous and consistent basis: s 202 of the CA 1990;
- Failure to keep proper books of account where this contributes to company's insolvency: s 203 of the CA 1990;
- Acting as an officer, liquidator or examiner or being involved in the promotion, formation or management of a company whilst an undischarged bankrupt: s 183 of the CA 1963;
- The several offences listed in s 293(1) of the CA 1963 that can be committed whilst a company is in liquidation;
- Destruction, mutilation, alteration or falsification of books, papers or securities by an officer or contributory: s 294 of the CA 1963;
- Fraud by an officer of a company that is ordered or resolves to be wound up: s 295 of the CA 1963;
- Failure by a receiver to submit a statement of affairs within two months of appointment: s 320A of the CA 1963;
- Issuing, circulating or distributing a prospectus of a foreign company knowingly in contravention of ss 361 to 364 of the CA 1963: s 365 of the CA 1963;

145 See para **[28.022]** *ante*.

146 Section 297(2)(b) of the CA 1963.

147 Section 32 of the IFCMPA 2005.

148 Where the court is of the opinion that any act, omission or conduct which constituted that offence has (a) substantially contributed to a company being unable to pay its debts, (b) prevented or seriously impeded the orderly winding up of the company, or (c) substantially facilitated the defrauding of the creditors of the company or creditors of any other person: s 242(2) of the CA 1990.

- Knowingly or recklessly permitting the inclusion of misleading, false or deceptive material in a directors' statement circulated with a special resolution to propose the allotment of shares without applying pre-emption rights: s 24(6) of the C(A)A 1983;
- Knowingly or recklessly making a misleading, false or deceptive statement to an expert carrying out a valuation or reporting on the consideration of a non-cash asset: s 31(3) of the C(A)A 1983;
- Failure of directors to convene an EGM upon becoming aware that the company has suffered a serious capital loss: s 40(1) of the C(A)A 1983;
- Knowingly and wilfully making a false statement in any return, report, balance sheet, etc required by the 1986 Act: s 22 of the 1986 Act;
- Failing to give information or knowingly or recklessly providing false information in relation to the ownership of shares/debentures in the context of an investigation: s 15 of the CA 1990;
- Disposing, etc, of shares contrary to the Director's[149] restriction order in an investigation: s 16 of the CA 1990;
- Issuing shares in contravention of the Director's restrictions in an investigation: s 16 of the CA 1990;
- Failing to comply with the Director's direction to produce books or provide explanations: s 19 of the CA 1990;
- Unauthorised publication of information, etc: s 21 of the CA 1990;
- Directors' dealing in right to call for or to make delivery at specified price, etc, of relevant shares and debentures: s 28 of the CA 1990;
- Failure by director to repay surplus business expenses: s 36 of the CA 1990;
- Making a prohibited loan, quasi-loan, credit transaction, guarantee or provision of security in connection with a loan, quasi-loan or credit transaction in favour of a director or person connected with a director contrary to s 31 of the CA 1990: s 40(1) of the CA 1990;
- Procuring the contravention of s 31 of the CA 1990: s 40(2) of the CA 1990;
- Failure of licensed bank to maintain (and allow inspection of) register of substantial contracts with directors: s 44 of the CA 1990;
- Failure by director, shadow director or secretary to notify interest in shares or notification by agent of acquisitions or disposals: ss 53 and 58 of the CA 1990;
- Failure by director, etc, to notify spouse's or minor children's grant of right to subscribe for shares/debentures or exercise of such right: s 64 of the CA 1990;
- Failure by listed company (PLC) to notify stock exchange of acquisitions or disposals by directors, etc: s 65 of the CA 1990;
- Failure to disclose acquisition of relevant own share capital exceeding notifiable level by a PLC: s 79 of the CA 1990;
- Failure by persons acting together to acquire interests in PLC to keep each other informed and for purchaser to ensure notification by agent of acquisitions/disposals: s 79 of the CA 1990;
- Acting as a director whilst disqualified: s 161 of the CA 1990;
- Failure to comply with court order to give information in relation to a restriction order under s 16 of the CA 1990: s 85 of the CA 1990;
- Failure to observe professional secrecy in the context of insider dealing: s 118 of the CA 1990;

[149] Formerly the Minister for Jobs, Enterprise and Innovation, but replaced with the Director by the CLEA 2001.

- Failure by liquidators to comply with provisions of s 131 of the CA 1990 in relation to creditors' meetings: s 131 of the CA 1990;
- Directors, etc, acting in accordance with the instructions of a disqualified person: s 164 of the CA 1990;
- Failure by director or shadow director charged with fraud to give court written notice of required particulars of directorships: s 166 of the CA 1990;
- Auditors' failure to notify registrar of his resignation and to include specified material in notice of resignation: s 185 of the CA 1990;
- Failure to give notice pursuant to s 159(1) of the CA 1963 of auditors' resignation: s 185 of the CA 1990;
- Auditor's failure to notify registrar of opinion that company is not keeping proper books of account and failure to comply with Director's requests for information: s 194 of the CA 1990[150];
- Failure to convene a general meeting within 14 days of auditors' notice: s 186 of the CA 1990;
- Failure to send persons entitled further statements by a retiring auditor: s 186 of the CA 1990;
- Failure to notify auditor or to permit auditor to attend a general meeting: s 186 of the CA 1990;
- Becoming or remaining as a partner in a firm of auditors when disqualified: s 195 of the CA 1990;
- Failure by subsidiary/auditor to give holding company's auditors information and explanations: s 196 of the CA 1990;
- Holding company's failure to obtain audit information from subsidiary: s 196 of the CA 1990;
- Knowingly or recklessly making a misleading, false or deceptive statement to the auditor by an officer or employee: s 197 of the CA 1990;
- Failure to provide an auditor with required information or explanations within two days: s 197 of the CA 1990;
- Failure by recognised body of accountants to deliver list of members qualified to be auditors within one month of renewal/recognition: s 199 of the CA 1990;
- Failure by recognised accountancy body to supply list of new members qualified to be auditors: s 200 of the CA 1990;
- Failure to retain and permit inspection of contracts for the purchase of own shares: s 222 of the CA 1990;
- Failure to comply with Ministerial direction relating to own share purchase: s 228 of the CA 1990;
- Failure by listed company to notify stock exchange of own share purchase: s 229 of the CA 1990;
- Contravention of procedures on own share purchase: s 234 of the CA 1990;
- Destroying, mutilating or falsifying books or documents: s 243 of the CA 1990;
- Fraudulently parting with, altering or making an omission in any book or document: s 243 of the CA 1990;
- Improper use of word 'limited': s 381 of the CA 1963[151];
- Disclosure of information other than that in the public domain by the ODCE: s 17(4) of the CLEA 2001;

[150] As amended by s 74 of the CLEA 2001.

[151] As replaced by s 98 of the CLEA 2001.

- Failure by liquidator of insolvent company to provide report to the Director: s 56(3) of the CLEA 2001;
- Failure by liquidator to produce books to the Director for examination, etc: s 57(4) of the CLEA 2001;
- Failure by professional body to report to Director a finding by disciplinary committee that a member conducting a receivership or liquidation failed to maintain appropriate records: s 58 of the CLEA 2001.

The foregoing is undoubtedly an onerous list of serious offences. It should be noted that only a short indicative description of each offence is given above and, as in all criminal proceedings, a careful analysis of each individual provision is required in order to establish contravention. Similarly, many of the foregoing offences are subject to time provisos and will only be committed where default arises after a particular period specified in the provision; again, careful scrutiny of the actual provision is required. Where fraud is a constituent element in the offence it should be remembered that the prosecution faces a high onus of proof[152].

[28.059] In addition to the foregoing indictable offences that carry a maximum term of imprisonment of five years, there are also a number of indictable offences that are only punishable by a fine. These offences *include*:

- Failure of directors and secretaries to provide information required to maintain register of directors and secretary, etc: s 195 of the CA 1963;
- Failure by voluntary liquidator to convene creditors' meeting when of the opinion that company is insolvent: s 261 of the CA 1963;
- Failure by liquidator to summon general meeting at end of first year of winding up and lay accounts: ss 262(1) and 272(1) of the CA 1963;
- Acting as liquidator whilst disqualified: s 300A of the CA 1963;
- Failure by liquidator to send particulars to registrar of progress of liquidation when not completed in two years: s 306 of the CA 1963;
- Acting as a receiver whilst an undischarged bankrupt: s 315 of the CA 1963;
- Failure by receiver to send abstract to registrar every six months: s 319(2) of the CA 1963;
- Failure to submit statement of affairs by receiver within two months: s 320A of the CA 1963;
- Failure by receiver to deliver abstract of receipts and payments made up every six months: s 321(1) of the CA 1963;
- Allotment of shares by directors without authority: s 201(1) of the C(A)A 1983;
- Failure to observe the consideration provisions on allotment of shares in s 36 of the C(A)A 1983;
- Failure by petitioner for an examiner to deliver notice of petition to registrar: s 12(5) of the 1990 Amendment Act;
- Failure by examiner to publish notice of appointment in *Iris Oifigiúil*: s 12(5) of the 1990 Amendment Act;
- Failure by examiner to publish notice of appointment in two daily newspapers: s 12(5) of the 1990 Amendment Act;

---

152 See, generally the position in England: Scanlan, 'Dishonesty in Corporate Offences A Need for Reform?' (2002) 23 Co Law 114.

- Failure by examiner to deliver notice of appointment to registrar: s 12(5) of the 1990 Amendment Act;
- Failure to publish statement 'in examination under the Companies (Amendment) Act 1990' on invoices, etc: s 12(4) of the 1990 Amendment Act;
- Failure by directors to make, verify by affidavit and submit to examiner statement as to company's affairs: s 14(3) of the 1990 Amendment Act;
- Acting as an examiner whilst not qualified: s 28(2) of the 1990 Amendment Act;
- Failure to amend share index following removal of entry: s 60 of the CA 1990;
- Improper deletion of register entry: s 62 of the CA 1990;
- Failure to restore an improper deletion: s 62 of the CA 1990;
- Failure to prepare report of investigation requisitioned by members: s 84 of the CA 1990.

Failure to keep and maintain registers and records

[28.060] There are a number of offences that involve the failure to keep and maintain registers and records created by the Companies Acts. Offences here *include* a failure by companies to:

- Keep and maintain a register of debenture holders: s 91 of the CA 1963;
- Maintain a register of members: s 116 of the CA 1963;
- Index the register of members: s 117(1) of the CA 1963;
- Prepare minutes of general meetings and directors' meetings: s 145(1) of the CA 1963;
- Ensure proper books of account are kept: s 202 of the CA 1990;
- Maintain register of directors' and secretary's shareholdings, and in chronological order, and to record new information within three days, and maintain index, and to amend index: s 60 of the CA 1990;
- Enter interests in contracts in book: s 194(5) of the CA 1963;
- Maintain register of directors and secretary: s 195 of the CA 1963;
- Keep proper books of account where company is wound up insolvent: s 203 of the CA 1990;
- Keep registers in the required manner: s 378 of the CA 1963;
- Maintain register of substantial contracts with directors (by a licensed bank): s 44 of the CA 1990;
- Keep copies of directors' service contracts: s 50 of the CA 1990;
- Maintain register of interests in shares: s 80 of the CA 1990.

Miscellaneous offences

[28.061] There are numerous other company law offences which do not fall neatly within one or other of the foregoing categories[153]. Many of these can be classified as involving the failure to supply information or documents to persons other than the

153 The offences concerning prospectuses only relate to public companies: ss 35, 44, 46, 54, 56, 57 and 115 of the CA 1963; ss 6, 21, 43, 47, 57 of the C(A)A 1983, etc. See, generally, Ch 29, *Public Limited Companies and SEs*.

registrar of companies[154]; the failure by persons such as liquidators, receivers or examiners to advertise their appointment, etc[155]; the failure to comply with directions[156]; the failure to meet requirements of the Companies Acts[157]; and the making of untrue statements, etc[158].

---

[154] For example, failure to supply copies of memorandum and articles when requested by a member: s 29(1) of the CA 1963; failure to ensure memorandum and articles reflect all changes made: s 30(2) of the CA 1963; wilful concealment of creditors entitled to object to capital reductions: s 77 of the CA 1963; failure to permit inspection of the register of debenture holders: s 92 of the CA 1963; failure to provide share certificates: s 86 of the CA 1963; failure to permit inspection of security instruments: s 110 of the CA 1963; failure to permit inspection of members' register: s 119 of the CA 1963; failure to include proxy notice when convening members' meetings and to only issue to some members: s 136 of the CA 1963; failure to issue, etc, resolution with copy of articles it changes and to supply a copy to members on request: s 143 of the CA 1963; failure to permit inspection of members' meetings minutes book: s 146 of the CA 1963; failure to supply copy of subsidiary accounts to requesting members: ss 150 and 154 of the CA 1963; failure to have same parent and subsidiary financial years: s 153 of the CA 1963; failure to provide information on subsidiary in accounts: s 22 of the 1986 Act; issuing accounts in the wrong format, etc, and not issuing in advance of AGM: ss 157, 158 and 159 of the CA 1963; failure to disclose payments to directors in connection with transfer of shares: s 188 of the CA 1963; failure to produce registers at AGM: s 190 of the CA 1963; failure of directors to provide various information: ss 193, 194 of the CA 1963; failure to permit inspection of register of directors and secretary: s 195 of the CA 1963; failure to state directors' names in business letters: s 196 of the CA 1963; failure of directors to advise their liability is unlimited: s 197 of the CA 1963; failure to attach court order of scheme of arrangement: s 201 of the CA 1963; failure to supply notices of creditors' meeting, etc: s 202 of the CA 1963; failure to file statement of affairs on a winding up or on receivership: ss 224 and 320 of the CA 1963; failure to publish notice of resolution to voluntarily wind up: s 252 of the CA 1963; non-disclosure by creditors' representative and voting for connected person: s 301A of the CA 1963; failure to include statement that company is in liquidation or receivership: ss 303 and 317 of the CA 1963; failure to maintain accounting principles and requirements in 1986 Act: s 22 of the 1986 Act; etc.

[155] Failure to publish notice of appointment in the Companies Registration Office Gazette by liquidator: s 227 of the CA 1963; failure by liquidator to hold final general meeting: ss 263 and 273 of the CA 1963; failure by liquidator to summon meeting of creditors: s 266 of the CA 1963; failure by liquidator to dispose of books, etc, in accordance with law: s 305 of the CA 1963; liquidator's failure to report that a disqualified person is a director: s 161 of the CA 1990; receiver's failure to notify appointment to company: s 319 of the CA 1963; receiver's failure to notify resignation, etc.

[156] For example, failure to change company's name when directed: ss 23(2) and 24(8) of the CA 1963; failure to re-register as a public company when ceasing to be a private company: s 35(2) of the CA 1963; acting as a director or auditor or liquidator whilst disqualified: ss 180, 162 and 300A of the CA 1963, etc.

[157] For example: failing to have a registered office in the State: s 113 of the CA 1963; failure to have name outside company's place of business, or use seal which does not have company's name: s 114 of the CA 1963; failure to hold an AGM: s 131 of the CA 1963; body corporate acting as liquidator or receiver: ss 300 and 314 of the CA 1963, etc.

[158] For example: making an unreasonable statutory declaration of solvency in the context of the s 60 validation procedure: s 60(5) of the CA 1963; inducing appointment of liquidator: s 301 of the CA 1963, etc.

[E] RESTRICTION OF DIRECTORS

[28.062] One of the most effective ways of punishing dishonest or irresponsible directors of insolvent companies and of protecting the public from their future wrongdoing is to have them *restricted* in future directorships under s 150 of the CA 1990. The chief effect of a restriction order is that any companies in which a 'restricted director' becomes involved must be capitalised to a particular amount. *Restriction* was introduced into Irish law by Chapter 1 of Part VII of the CA 1990[159] as a new means of combating the so-called 'phoenix syndrome', ie, the situation where the controllers of a company, which becomes insolvent by reason of their acts or omissions, walk away from their failed company (and especially its debts) and immediately re-establish themselves in a new company doing the same business, again availing of all the advantages of limited liability[160]. As Murphy J said in *Business Communications Ltd v Baxter and Parsons*[161], Chapter 1, Part VII of the CA 1990 (restriction provisions):

> '… contains provisions of the utmost importance to the commercial community generally and in particular to those who have undertaken or propose to undertake the duties of a director of a company[162].'

In *Re La Moselle Clothing Ltd and Rosegem Ltd*[163], Shanley J described the 'primary purpose' of s 150 as being:

> '… the protection of the public from persons who, by their conduct, have shown themselves unfit to hold the office of, and discharge the duties of, a director of a company and, in consequence, represent a danger to potential investors and traders dealing with such companies[164].'

In this can be seen the real purpose of Chapter 1 of Part VII of the CA 1990, albeit that it is the protection of *traders*, as opposed to *investors*, with which the law is most concerned.

[28.063] The original Companies (No 2) Bill 1987 proposed a drastic solution to the problem of the phoenix syndrome, namely, the *automatic* restriction of all directors of all insolvent companies, without any limitation on the period of restriction unless the new company met certain requirements. As noted by the McDowell Group Report[165], the 'outrage over those engaged in the practice of the phoenix syndrome was, ultimately tempered by the realistic recognition that it is unjust to penalise "honest" business failure' and the automatic restrictions were ultimately dropped from the 1987 Bill. As enacted, s 150 of the CA 1990 requires an application to be brought to the High Court in order to have a director restricted and also excuses directors from thc restriction regime

159 See generally, Cahill, *Company Law Compliance and* Enforcement (2008, Bloomsbury Professional) at chs 16–19.

160 See *Report of the Working Group on Company Law Compliance and Enforcement* (1998) Government Publications (Pn 6697) at pp 71–82.

161 *Business Communications Ltd v Baxter and Parsons* (21 July 1995, unreported) HC, Murphy J.

162 *Business Communications Ltd v Baxter and Parsons* (21 July 1995, unreported) HC, Murphy J at pp 4, 5 of the judgment.

163 *La Moselle Clothing Ltd and Rosegem Ltd v Soualhi* [1998] 2 ILRM 345.

164 *La Moselle Clothing Ltd and Rosegem Ltd v Soualhi* [1998] 2 ILRM 345 at 350, 351.

165 See the McDowell Report at para 6.4.

where the court is satisfied, *inter alia*, that they have acted *honestly and responsibly*. Where application was brought, the remedy was effective, but in the period 1991 to 1995 there was a complete absence of applications being brought. The problem was that, as initially drafted, s 150 did not specifically require any person to bring application to have a director restricted; it was, in effect, left up to individual liquidators of insolvent companies to decide whether or not to bother to bring application. Although following a practice direction made by Murphy J in 1994 which required all *official liquidators* of insolvent companies to make application under s 150, it was not until the CLEA 2001 that the lacuna, identified in *Business Communications Ltd v Baxter and Parsons*[166], was finally filled. The CLEA 2001 also gave the Director of Corporate Enforcement a central role in the bringing of applications to have directors of insolvent companies restricted. The law governing the restriction of directors in their directorships is treated here under the following headings:

1. The purpose of restriction orders.
2. The mandatory nature of s 150.
3. The consequences of a s 150 order.
4. The company must be insolvent.
5. Persons liable to be restricted.
6. The duties of liquidators of insolvent companies and the Director's role.
7. The *locus standi* of liquidators, receivers, creditors and the Director.
8. The costs of the application for restriction orders.
9. The burden of proof.
10. The defence of acting 'honestly and responsibly'.
11. The defences of being a financial institution's or a venture capital company's nominee and the non-statutory defences of delay and estoppel.
12. Post-order relief on just and equitable grounds.
13. The enforcement of restriction orders.

The purpose of restriction orders

[28.064] Section 150(1) of the CA 1990 provides:

> 'The court shall, unless it is satisfied as to any of the matters specified in subsection (2), declare that a person to whom this Chapter applies shall not, for a period of five years, be appointed or act in any way, whether directly or indirectly, as a director or secretary or be concerned or take part in the promotion or formation of any company unless it meets the requirements set out in subsection (3)…'

In the pages that follow, consideration shall be given to those persons who are liable to be restricted[167], the defences specified in s 150(2)[168], and to the requirements which a company must meet, where a restricted person becomes 'involved' with it[169].

[28.065] The purpose of the jurisdiction to make restriction orders is to protect the public. This was made clear by Finlay Geoghegan J in *Re Colm O'Neill Engineering*

[166] *Business Communications Ltd v Baxter and Parsons* (21 July 1995, unreported) HC, Murphy J.

[167] See para **[28.074]** *post*.

[168] See para **[28.087]** *et seq*, **[28.131]** *et seq*, and **[28.132]** *et seq, post*.

[169] See para **[28.068]** *post*.

Services Ltd[170], where the learned judge said of the legal framework provided by s 150 that:

> '... it is well established the purpose of the section is to protect the public against the future supervision and management of companies by persons whose past record as directors of insolvent companies have shown them to be a danger to creditors and others. It is also established that it is not the purpose of the section to punish the individuals concerned[171].'

Although the purpose may not be to punish individuals, this is almost invariably the effect, as the restriction of a person is a significant stigma, especially when reported with prominence in *The Irish Times*, *The Irish Independent* or *The Examiner*.

[28.066] It is settled law that the making of a restriction order for a five-year period is mandatory where application is brought against the directors of an insolvent company and where the defences in s 150(2) are found not to apply[172]. In the seminal decision of *Business Communications Ltd v Baxter and Parsons*[173], Murphy J observed:

> 'It is clear that Chapter 1 [of Part VII] of the Companies Act, 1990 contains provisions of the utmost importance to the commercial community generally and in particular to those who have undertaken or propose to undertake the duties of a director of a company. In appropriate circumstances the Chapter applies to every insolvent company which is being wound up, whether compulsorily or voluntarily, and – in consequence of s 154 aforesaid – to companies not being wound up but over which a receiver has been appointed. The next significant feature of the code created by Chapter 1 aforesaid is that the introductory words to s 150, that is to say, the phrase "the court shall" are clearly mandatory and leave the Court with no discretion in those cases to which the Chapter applies unless the persons concerned establish that the case falls within one or other of the three exceptions set out in sub-section (2) of s 150. Again it is notable that the period of the restriction is a fixed period of five years and that, in the first instance at any rate[174], the court has no discretion to impose a lesser restriction[175].'

Again in *Re Cavan Crystal Group Ltd*[176] Murphy J said that it was well accepted that 'this section is mandatory and that the court must impose the full statutory restriction unless the directors concerned discharge the onus of proof squarely imposed upon them as to any of the matters specified in subsection (2)'[177].

---

170 Re *Colm O'Neill Engineering Services Ltd* [2004] IEHC 83.

171 See also *Re Verit Hotel and Leisure (Ireland) Ltd* [2001] IESC 74 where the public interest is cited by Fennelly J.

172 See *Re James Murphy & Sons Sales (Dundalk) Ltd; Stafford v Murphy* [2010] IEHC 115 *per* Finlay Geoghegan J at para 9.

173 *Business Communications Ltd v Baxter and Parsons* (21 July 1995, unreported) HC, Murphy J.

174 This is a reference to s 152 of the CA 1990 which permits applications for relief to be brought subsequent to the making of a restriction order: see para **[28.136]** *post*.

175 *Business Communications Ltd v Baxter and Parsons* (21 July 1995, unreported) HC, Murphy J at pp 4, 5 of the judgment.

176 *Re Cavan Crystal Group Ltd* (26 April 1996, unreported) HC, Murphy J.

177 *Re Cavan Crystal Group Ltd* (26 April 1996, unreported) HC, Murphy J at pp 7, 8 of the judgment. See also *Mehigan v Duignan* [1997] 1 ILRM 171 at 194 where Shanley J accepted that he had no discretion but to impose the five-year restriction since the respondent did not bring himself within any of the three exceptions in s 150(2).

[28.067] The mandatory nature of s 150 is in contrast to disqualification orders which are made at the discretion of the court[178] (and excepting, therefore, deemed disqualification orders)[179]. In *Business Communications Ltd v Baxter and Parsons*[180], Murphy J recognised the justification for the distinction between these two sanctions for misfeasance, saying:

> 'Clearly, it is the comprehensive nature of a disqualification order which is seen as constituting an appropriately severe sentence for conduct which is manifestly more blameworthy than merely failing to exercise an appropriate degree of responsibility in relation to an insolvent company in liquidation of which the person was a director. Financially and commercially this is clearly a well-founded distinction. It is hardly unreasonable to require a person who was a director of a failed company in respect of which he committed no misconduct but for which he neglected to exercise an appropriate degree of responsibility from resuming such an office in another company, again with the privilege of limited liability except on condition that a stipulated and not excessive sum was provided for the paid-up capital thereof. The figure of £20,000[181] must represent a very modest sum as the capital for any commercial enterprise and a very limited obstacle to anyone wishing to engage in trade through the medium of a limited liability company. Indeed, it might not be unreasonable to suggest that every limited liability company should be required to have paid-up capital of at least that amount. It would seem, that the more serious penalty which the restraining order imposes is the stigma which attaches as a result of the making of the order and its filing in the Companies Office. In any event I would regard it as a far lesser penalty than that which may be imposed under s 160 of the CA 1990 and certainly would not elevate it to the status of s 33 of the 1990 Amendment Act – the reckless and fraudulent trading provisions – under which a director may be held personally responsible without limitation of liability for all the debts or other liabilities of the company and which Mr Justice Lynch in *Re Hefferon Kearns (No 2)* Ltd [1993] 3 IR 191 described as a "draconian measure"[182].'

Murphy J went on to quote with approval a passage from the decision of Henry LJ in the case of *Grayan Building Services Ltd*[183]. Although that case concerned disqualification of directors under English law, Murphy J said that the general thrust of the passage he

[178] See para **[28.148]** *et seq, post.*

[179] See para **[28.151]** *post.*

[180] *Business Communications Ltd v Baxter and Parsons* (21 July 1995, unreported) HC, Murphy J.

[181] Now €63,486.90 following the amendment effected by s 41(1) of the CLEA 2001.

[182] *Business Communications Ltd v Baxter and Parsons* (21 July 1995, unreported) HC, Murphy J at pp 13–15 of the judgment.

[183] *Grayan Building Services Ltd* [1995] 2 WLR 1 where Henry LJ said (at 15): 'The concept of limited liability and the sophistication of our corporate law offers great privileges and great opportunities for those who wish to trade under that regime. But the corporate environment carries with it the discipline that those who avail themselves of those privileges must accept the standards laid down and abide by the regulatory rules and disciplines in place to protect creditors and shareholders. And, while some significant corporate failures will occur despite the directors exercising best managerial practice, in many, too many, cases there have been serious breaches of those rules and disciplines, in situations where the observance of them would or at least might have prevented or reduced the scale of the failure and consequent loss to creditors and investors. Reliable figures are hard to come by, but it seems that losses from corporate fraud and mismanagement have never been higher. (contd../)

quoted was equally applicable to the restriction provisions under s 150 of the CA 1990 and to the standards of commercial practice demanded by our legislature.

[28.068] Restriction orders have consequences for two distinct legal entities: restricted persons and restricted companies. As far as the restricted person is concerned, the effect of a s 150 order is a simple injunction – he is restrained, for a period of five years, from being appointed or from acting in any way, whether directly or indirectly, as a director or secretary and from being concerned or taking part in the promotion or formation of any company unless that company meets certain requirements. The five-year period of restriction commences whenever the court says it commences. This was established by O'Donovan J in *Duignan v Carway et al*[184], rejecting the respondent directors' claims that the five-year period should commence from the date of the proceedings. It was recognised that to interpret s 150(1) in this manner would be to encourage respondent directors to employ delaying tactics.

[28.069] The consequences for a restricted company are more complicated. The requirements that must be met by any company with which a restricted person becomes involved are specified in s 150(3) of the CA 1990. This provides:

> '(a) the nominal value of the allotted share capital of the company shall—
>
> (i) in the case of a public limited company, be at least €317,434.52,
>
> (ii) in the case of any other company, be at least €63,486.90,
>
> (b) each allotted share to an aggregate amount not less than the amount referred to in subparagraph (i) or (ii) of paragraph (a), as the case may be, shall be fully paid up, including the whole or any premium thereon, and
>
> (c) each such allotted share and the whole of any premium thereon shall be paid for in cash[185].'

Where a restricted person becomes involved in another company (referred to here as a 'restricted company'), and the restricted company allots a share which *is not fully paid*

---

183 (\...contd) At the same time the regulatory regime has never been more stringent – on paper even if not in practice. The parliamentary intention to improve managerial safeguard and standards for the long term good of employees, creditors and investors is clear. Those who fail to reach those standards and whose failure contributes to others losing money will often both be plausible and capable of inspiring initial trust, often later regretted. Those attributes may make them attractive witnesses. But as s 6 [of the English Disqualification of Directors Act 1986] makes clear, the Court's focus should be on their conduct, on the offence rather than the offender, the statutory corporate climate is stricter than it has ever been, and those enforcing it should reflect the fact that parliament has seen the need for higher standards. Where serious breaches have been shown, tribunals when deciding the question of fitness should give clear reasons why they reached the decision they did on that question. I could not find such reasons here.'

184 *Duignan v Carway et al* [2001] 4 IR 550, O'Donovan J.

185 As amended by s 41(1)(a) and (b) of the CLEA 2001 which increased the monetary amounts from £100,000 to £250,000 and from £20,000 to £50,000, respectively. Note, however, that by virtue of s 41(2) of the CLEA 2001, these revised monetary amounts do not apply to companies which are 'restricted companies' by reason of a declaration made under s 150(1) *prior* to the commencement of s 41 of the CLEA 2001. It may be noted that primary legislation was not required to effect these changes since by s 158 of the CA 1990 the Minister has power to vary the amounts mentioned in s 150(3)(a).

up, with certain exceptions[186], the share shall be treated as if its nominal value together with the whole of any premium had been received, but the allottee shall be liable to pay the company in cash the full amount that should have been received plus interest, less the consideration actually paid[187]. Also, where a restricted company allots a share that is not fully paid for *in cash*, the allottee is liable to pay the company in cash an amount equal to its nominal value plus the whole of any premium and interest[188]. By reason of the application of s 26(4) of the C(A)A 1983 to s 156 of the CA 1990[189], any person – other than a *bona fide* purchaser for value without actual notice[190] of the requirements – who acquires shares that have not been fully paid up in the prescribed manner becomes jointly and severally liable with the original allottee to pay the foregoing amounts.

[28.070] Notwithstanding that a restricted company is a separate legal entity, the sins of its directors (who were directors of some insolvent company) will be visited upon it. This is in recognition of the fact that in most cases, the directors of failed companies will attempt to re-establish themselves in a new company; in these circumstances, no injustice is considered to be done to the restricted company. Not only is it subject to the capital restrictions seen above, but by s 155 of the CA 1990 there are additional fetters imposed on the restricted company. Accordingly, a restricted company cannot avail of: (a) the exceptions to the prohibition in s 60 of the CA 1963 on a company providing financial assistance in connection with the purchase of shares, contained in s 60(2)–(11) of the CA 1963[191]; and (b) the exceptions to the prohibition in s 31 of the CA 1990 on a company making loans, quasi-loans and entering into credit transactions, etc, in favour of directors and persons connected with a director, contained in ss 32 and 37 of the CA 1990[192]. Moreover, the restrictions that apply to allotments of shares in PLCs, other than in cash, contained in ss 32 to 36 of the C(A)A 1983, also apply to the restricted company even if it is not a PLC[193]. Finally, a restricted person is required not to accept appointment to a position or act directly or indirectly as a director or secretary or be concerned in or take part in the promotion or formation of a company unless he has, within 14 days immediately preceding such appointment or so acting, sent to the company's registered office a notice that he is a restricted person[194]. Although in many cases inappropriate, this protection for restricted companies is a necessary safeguard to prevent the sins of what may be a mere employee, being visited on a company, the

186 The exceptions relate (a) to the allotment of a bonus share which is not fully paid up unless the allottee knew or ought to have known that the share was so allotted (s 156(3)) and (b) to shares allotted in pursuance of an employees' share scheme within the meaning of s 2 of the C(A)A 1983.

187 Section 156(1) of the CA 1990. 'Interest' is payable at the appropriate rate within the meaning of s 2 of the C(A)A 1983.

188 Section 156(2) of the CA 1990.

189 Section 156(6) of the CA 1990.

190 As to the meaning of which, see Ch 16, *Statutory Regulation of Directors' Transactions*, at para **[16.105]** *et seq*.

191 Section 155(2) of the CA 1990: see Ch 10, *The Maintenance of Capital*, at para **[10.066]** *et seq*.

192 Section 155(4) of the CA 1990: see Ch 16, *Statutory Regulation of Directors' Transactions*, at para **[16.073]** *et seq*.

193 Section 155(3) of the CA 1990.

194 Section 155(5) of the CA 1990.

management of which may have a pristine compliance record. Although by virtue of s 157(1) of the CA 1990, the High Court can, if it deems it just and equitable to do so, grant relief to a restricted company in respect of any act or omission which contravenes the Companies Acts, but which would not have but for the provisions of s 155, eg, providing financial assistance in connection with an own share purchase in reliance upon the exceptions contained in s 60(2)–(11) of the CA 1963. The court's ability to grant relief is, however, confined to cases where the company has *not* been put on notice by the restricted person that they are so restricted as required by s 155(5) of the CA 1990[195].

[28.071] It should also be noted that by s 153 of the CA 1990 the registrar of companies is obliged to keep a register of restricted persons who are notified by the court Registrars and Examiner, who were prescribed as the persons responsible for informing the Registrar of Companies[196]. Section 150(4) obliges such prescribed officers of court to cause the registrar to be furnished with the prescribed particulars to enable her keep the register.

[28.072] The certificate of a liquidator or receiver that a company is unable to pay its debts (within the meaning of s 214 of the CA 1963)[197] is capable of being challenged and does not give rise to an irrebuttable presumption of insolvency. This was established in *Carway v The Attorney General*[198] where the plaintiff (who was a respondent in a s 150 application) claimed that s 149(1)(b) was unconstitutional on the basis that it precluded him from disproving the liquidator's certificate as to insolvency[199]. Carroll J held:

> 'In this case, there is no provision that the certificate is to be conclusive. It seems to me that the purpose of s 149 is to identify companies and persons to which Chapter 1 of Part VII applies. Section 149(1) applies to any company in liquidation that is unable to pay its debts within the meaning of s 214 of the Companies Act 1963. There are two categories, those which at the date of the commencement of the winding-up are proved to the Court to be unable to pay their debts and, secondly, those which during the course of the winding-up are certified by the liquidator to be unable to pay their debts or this fact is otherwise proved to the Court. It seems to me there is no basis for accepting the plaintiff's argument that the section must be construed as if the words "which certificate shall be irrebuttable" or words to that effect, were added after the word "certifies". It is straining the language of the section to do so. The section merely requires the certificate by the liquidator in order to trigger off the application of Chapter 1 of Part VII and the necessity for the court to be satisfied under s 150 that the directors concerned acted honestly and responsibly. I consider that the principle enunciated in *Re Haughey* [1971] IR 217 applies. In that case the Supreme Court held the certificate of the committee of Public Accounts of Dáil Éireann was a preliminary step to the commencement of a full trial of a criminal offence in the High Court. Since the certificate is a preliminary step, there is nothing in the section which would prevent a director from raising any issue in relation to the

195 Section 157(2) of the CA 1990.

196 SI 209/1991.

197 See Ch 23, *Winding Up Companies*, at para **[23.074]**.

198 *Carway v The Attorney General* (3 July 1996, unreported) HC, Carroll J.

199 Relying on *Maher v The Attorney General* [1973] IR 140 and *The State (McEldowney) v Kelleher* [1983] IR 289.

> insolvency of the company or adducing any evidence in order to satisfy the Court that he/she acted "honestly and responsibly in relation to the conduct of the affairs of the company". In my opinion, there is nothing in the section which warrants the interpretation that the certificate is to be conclusive evidence of insolvency[200].'

Accordingly, although s 149(1)(b) of the CA 1990 permits an application to go forward to the High Court, it is open to a director respondent who believes that the company is not insolvent to challenge the liquidator's certificate. In such a case, the effect of s 149(1)(b) is to put an onus on a director to disprove the company's insolvency. It is thought that such a challenge may be more likely where a receiver purports to certify insolvency than where a liquidator does so.

[28.073] Although the vast majority of applications will be brought by the liquidators of companies in the course of being wound up, provided a company is insolvent, it need not be in liquidation in order for a director to be restricted. Where a company is not being wound up but is insolvent, s 251(2A) of the CA 1990 (as amended by s 54 of the CLEA 2001) can be invoked by the Director to bring application for the restriction of a director of such an insolvent company. As to the conditions when s 251 can be invoked, see Chapter 15[201]. The first order made on the application of the Director of Corporate Enforcement was in *Re At Hand Cleaning Services Ltd; ODCE v Hutton*[202] where a director of the company which was found to be insolvent was restricted. The usual reason why insolvent companies are not wound up is insufficiency of assets to fund the liquidation process. This decision shows that the ODCE has the ability, notwithstanding the absence of a liquidator, to fill the lacunae caused by the absence of a liquidator.

[28.074] Section 149 of the CA 1990 provides that Chapter 1 of Part VII applies to any person who was either a director[203] or a shadow director[204] of an insolvent company at the date of, or within 12 months prior to, the commencement of its winding up. Section 149 is rather tortuously drafted, and instead of referring to an 'insolvent company', reference is made to a company to which Chapter 1 applies. By s 149(1), Chapter 1 is expressed to apply to any company[205] if:

- at the date of the commencement of its winding up (or receivership) it is proved to the court, or,
- during the course of the winding up the liquidator of the company certifies, or it is otherwise proved to the court,
- that the company is *unable to pay its debts*, ie, that the company is insolvent[206].

---

200 *Carway v The Attorney General* (3 July 1996, unreported) HC, Carroll J at p 5, 6 of the judgment.

201 See Ch 15, *Duties of Directors and Other Officers,* at para **[15.141]** *et seq.*

202 *Re At Hand Cleaning Services Ltd; ODCE v Hutton* (8 March 2004, unreported) HC, Finlay Geoghegan J.

203 Section 149(2) of the CA 1990.

204 Section 149(5) of the CA 1990.

205 'Company' in this context has a wider meaning than the definition in s 2(1) of the CA 1963, and by s 149(4) of the CA 1990 is deemed to include a company within the meaning of s 351 of the CA 1963, ie, foreign or overseas companies that establish a place of business in Ireland.

206 A company is unable to pay its debts when the provisions of s 214 of the CA 1963 are met: s 149(1) of the CA 1990.

Only the directors of insolvent companies in existence at the time of the commencement of s 150 (ie, 1 August 1991) can be restricted as the legislation is not retrospective. However, in *Re Dunleckney Ltd*[207] it was held that the directors of a company that had been struck off and dissolved, but was subsequently reinstated after the commencement of s 150, were susceptible to being made the subject of a restriction order.

(a) Persons who have been directors on or within 12 months of the winding up

[28.075] All persons who are directors at the date of the commencement of a company's winding up (or receivership)[208] may be restricted, but it is important to remember that not every past director is liable to be restricted. Only persons who were directors within the 12 months prior to the commencement of the winding up can be restricted. This point was noted in *Re Cavan Crystal Group Ltd*[209] where Murphy J held that one of the respondents in that case was not liable to be restricted because he had resigned as a director more than 12 months prior to the commencement of the receivership. It may also be noted that the fact that the director's resignation had not been notified to the CRO was found to be irrelevant[210]. In *Re Gasco Ltd*[211], McCracken J said that he thought it was:

> '... quite significant that no restrictions can attach to somebody who ceased to be a director of the company more than twelve months before the winding up. This seems to me to indicate that the primary aim of s 150 is to deal with directors who have behaved irresponsibly or dishonestly during the last twelve months of the life of the company, and that the actions of a director who is subject to s 150 are to be looked at primarily in the light of his actions during that period[212].'

Moreover, the obligation on liquidators under s 56(2) of the CLEA 2001 extends to bringing application against all such persons, despite its literal wording making no reference to past directors in the context of the obligation imposed on liquidators[213].

(b) Directors: de jure, de facto and shadow

[28.076] Directors and shadow directors are expressly mentioned as possible respondents. 'Persons occupying the position of director by whatever name called' or *de facto* directors are also liable to be restricted, since such persons are, by s 2(1) of the CA 1963, included in the definition of 'director'. The meanings of 'director' (both *de facto* and *de jure*) and 'shadow director' have been considered in Chapter 13[214]. Both

207 *Re Dunleckney Ltd* [1999] IEHC 109, Carroll J.

208 Section 154 of the CA 1990 also applies s 150 to receiverships, 'with the necessary modifications': see para **[28.089]** *post*.

209 *Re Cavan Crystal Group Ltd* (26 April 1996, unreported) HC, Murphy J.

210 In *Re Outdoor Advertising Services Ltd* (28 January 1997, unreported) HC, Costello J, it was held that the court was not required to make an order against a person who had ceased to act as a *de facto* director about nine months before the liquidation; to the extent that this suggests that a *de facto* director cannot be restricted it is thought to be incorrect.

211 *Re Gasco Ltd* (5 February 2001, unreported) HC, McCracken J.

212 *Re Gasco Ltd* (5 February 2001, unreported) HC, McCracken J at p 7 of the judgment.

213 See *USIT Ireland Ltd* [2003] 2 IR 635, considered in para **[28.084]** *post*.

214 See Ch 13, *Corporate Governance: Management by the Directors*, at paras **[13.025]** *et seq* and **[13.045]** *et seq*, respectively.

executive and non-executive directors are capable of being the subject of a s 150 order, but their status as either may go towards establishing whether they have acted responsibly[215].

[28.077] Persons who have been found to be shadow directors have been restricted on a number of occasions. In *Re Vehicle Imports Ltd*[216], Roderick Murphy J made an order restricting a person who it was claimed was a shadow director in circumstances where *prima facie* evidence as to his status as such had not been rebutted. So too in *Re Gasco Ltd*[217] McCracken J held that a person was liable to be restricted where there was evidence that he controlled the management of the company, was signatory to the company's cheques and when the only two directors of the company resigned, he had chosen not to appoint new directors but instead employed two persons to run the company. McCracken J held that there was 'no doubt' but that this person effectively ran the company on his own and 'in these circumstances, he was clearly a shadow director and therefore his position falls to be considered under s 150'[218]. But, is it that clear? It is thought that in circumstances where there are no directors and a person who is not a formally appointed director directs the operations of a company, he is not and cannot be a shadow director and is instead a *de facto* director[219]. Persons who have been found to be *de facto* directors have, however, been restricted in a number of cases, each of which necessarily turned on its own facts[220].

[28.078] In *Re Kelly Technical Services (Ireland) Ltd; Kavanagh v Kelly et al*[221], a person who had signed a B10 (the form used to notify the appointment of a *de jure*, properly appointed person as a director) was found by MacMenamin J not in fact to be a director at all! In that case, the person in question, who was a brother of two other respondents and who was a director of a related UK company, claimed he had not given an informed consent to becoming a director, that prior to the liquidation he was unaware that he was a director and therefore could not have acted dishonestly or irresponsibly. MacMenamin J accepted the respondent was not a director, saying:

> 'While I accept that a person's signature on the appropriate statutory form to act as a director is strong *prima facie* evidence that he consented to become a director, this is not conclusive[222] …
>
> In this regard the court considers that the burden of establishing that the respondent is "a person to whom s 150 applies" lies with the applicant accordingly that burden as distinct from the burden which arises once the application of the Act is established remains upon

215 See para **[28.118]** *post*.

216 *Re Vehicle Imports Ltd* (23 November 2000, unreported) HC, Murphy J.

217 *Re Gasco Ltd* (5 February 2001, unreported) HC, McCracken J.

218 *Re Gasco Ltd* (5 February 2001, unreported) HC, McCracken J at p 4 of the judgment.

219 See, generally, Ch 13, *Corporate Governance: Management by the Directors*, at para **[13.045]** *et seq*.

220 See *Re First Class Toy Traders Ltd; Gray v McLoughlin* [2004] IEHC 289 where Finlay Geoghegan J gave seven reasons for deciding that one of the respondents was a *de facto* director of the company.

221 *Re Kelly Technical Services (Ireland) Ltd; Kavanagh v Kelly et al* [2005] IEHC 421 (MacMenamin J).

222 Citing *Re CEM Connections* [2000] BCC 917.

> the liquidator. In the absence of cross-examination I am not satisfied that the burden has been discharged by the liquidator … I do not think that there has been any admissible or satisfactory evidence to demonstrate that the third named respondent was a person to whom s 150 applies.'

[28.079] It has been held by the Supreme Court that a body corporate cannot be a shadow director for the purposes of s 150 of the CA 1990. In *Re Worldport Ireland Ltd; Hughes v Worldport Communications Inc*[223], the liquidator of an Irish company applied to the High Court for a declaration that a US incorporated company was a shadow director of the company and sought a restriction order. The High Court had held that a body corporate could be a shadow director for the purposes of a restriction order, rejecting the contention that because s 176(1) of the CA 1963 prohibited bodies corporate from being directors, a body corporate could not be a shadow director, on the grounds that 'shadow directors' were a 'separate entity' to 'directors'. It was also held that there was no distinction between an Irish incorporated body corporate and a foreign incorporated body corporate.

The Supreme Court on appeal reversed the findings of the High Court. Although it was confirmed that a body corporate could be a shadow director for the purposes of s 27 of the CA 1990 by construing the word 'person' as importing a company by virtue of s 11(c) of the Interpretation Act 1937[224] and that any shadow director who was a natural person was subject to s 150 of the CA 1990, it was held that s 150 did not accommodate the extension of the meaning of 'person' to include a body corporate. The basis for this finding was that s 150(1) required that 'The court shall, unless it is satisfied as to any of the matters specified in subsection (2), declare that a person … shall not … be appointed … as a director'. Fennelly J noted that such an order would on its face imply that a body corporate, being restricted, would nonetheless be free to become a director of a company which met the capital requirements in s 150(3), would conflict with s 176 of the CA 1963 and the order would, at least to that extent, be 'meaningless and, arguably, absurd'. Fennelly J went on to say:

> '36. In the present case, the key problem is the form of order envisaged by the section. In the *Briggs* case, the Northern Ireland court was satisfied that a penalty (a fine) could be imposed on the company, even if other penalties (imprisonment or disqualification) could not. Some parts of the section could be applied. Others could not. Thus "person" could include the company. In the case of *Law Society v United Service Bureau Ltd*, on the other hand, the fact that a company could never have held a practicing certificate was decisive. I find that decision persuasive in considering the present case.
>
> 37. In the present case, the court would, if "person" includes a corporate shadow director, be required to make orders in a form which would be directly inconsistent with an express statutory provision which prohibits corporate bodies from being directors. The order would be made in a form which implied that a body corporate could hold the position of director contrary to section 176. It is not possible to make the section compatible with that legal provision without interpolating words into section 150(1), enabling the court to make orders in relation to some only of the acts mentioned. In a case such as the present, acting as a director would have to be excluded from the order. As the section stands, and without appropriate amendment, it does not accommodate the extension of the meaning of

223 *Re Worldport Ireland Ltd; Hughes v Worldport Communications Inc* [2009] 1 IR 398.

224 Now, s 18(c) of the Interpretation Act 2005 provides that 'person': 'shall be read as importing a body corporate (whether a corporation aggregate of a corporation sole) …'

"person" to include a body corporate. The reason is simple. The draftsman did not advert to the complication. I think the section evinces an intention contrary to the normal rule including a body corporate within the meaning of person.'

So, while the general rule is that a body corporate can be a shadow director within the meaning of s 27 of the CA 1990, a body corporate cannot be restricted pursuant to s 150 of the CA 1990 on the basis that it was a shadow director.

[28.080] In Chapter 13, the definition of 'shadow director' was considered[225] as was the decision of McKechnie in *Re Hocroft Developments Ltd; Dowall v Cullen et al*[226]. In applying the test for defining a shadow director to the facts concerning one of the directors, a Mr David Cullen, McKechnie J said:

'77. Apart perhaps from his attendance at meetings in respect of the hotel project, there is no evidence of any express type of direction or instruction given by David Cullen to the directors of Hocroft. The case therefore being made is that from his involvement in the transactions and events above outlined, together with the benefits accruing to him, this Court should conclude that he was in a position of and in fact exercised real influence over the affairs of the company. Accordingly, he should be regarded as a shadow director.

78. Having considered the evidence adduced on this issue, I have come to the conclusion that on the balance of probabilities, he was not so. I accept that taken at face value there were a number of facts which, had they been left uncontested, may well have lead me to the conclusion that he was in fact such a director; these include, *inter alia*, the land transactions, the fact that he was for many years an authorised signatory to the company accounts, the fact that he was heavily involved in the hotel project, and the allegation that this project was the only one ever undertaken by the Company. However, I find that the explanations forthcoming from the respondents have satisfied me that he should not in fact be regarded as a shadow director of the company.

79. The details of the land transactions are extensively set out at paras 22 and 33 *supra* and in light of the explanations given I could not conclude that in agreeing to enter into them the Company must be taken to have been directed by David Cullen to so do. The mere involvement of Mr Cullen in these transactions, even as purchaser, is not evidence of Company Acts impropriety on his part …

82. Furthermore, even if the explanations given, which I have accepted, fall short of fully satisfying the applicant's concern, the circumstances are at least equally explicable by his role as a property owner and developer as they are by his being a shadow director. Applying what O'Neill J said in *Lynrowan* (see para 59 supra) it must follow that Mr Cullen be given the benefit of such explanation and therefore no adverse finding should be made in that regard. In addition his ongoing participation in this project, even if intense, may not of itself be sufficient to render him a shadow director. A more expansive and broad-based involvement may be necessary: see that aspect of the decision of Laffoy J in *Fyffes*, where having found that Mr JF totally controlled the actions of the board of Lotus Green in the specific transactions in issue, the learned judge nevertheless held that the evidence did not establish ongoing reliance by the board on the instructions or directions of Mr JF. He was not therefore a shadow director of that company. For the above reasons I would likewise reach a similar conclusion regarding Mr Cullen.'

---

225 At para **[13.055]** *et seq*.

226 *Re Hocroft Developments Ltd; Dowall v Cullen et al* [2009] IEHC 580.

(c) Non-resident directors

[28.081] Persons who are, or were within 12 months of its being wound up, the directors of an insolvent company are liable to be restricted under s 150 notwithstanding that they are non-residents of Ireland. This was established by Finlay Geoghegan J in *Euroking Miracle (Ireland) Ltd; Fennell v Frost et al*[227]. In that case, the first four respondents were resident in England and it was noted that the Rules of the Superior Courts 1986 ('RSC 1986') did not make express provision for the service out of the jurisdiction of an originating notice of motion seeking a declaration under s 150. Finlay Geoghegan J said:

> 'I have concluded that the clear intent of the Oireachtas was to confer jurisdiction on the court to make declarations in respect of all persons who were directors of companies to whom s 150 applies (or who have acted as shadow directors in respect of such companies), irrespective of whether such persons were resident within or without the State.
>
> It is envisaged that persons of nationalities other than Irish and resident outside of the jurisdiction may become directors of companies incorporated in Ireland or registered in Ireland pursuant to s 351 of the Act of 1963 …
>
> It is presumed in Irish law that the operation of a statute is to be confined to the territory of the State unless a contrary intention is evident: *Chemical Bank v McCormack* [1983] ILRM 350. It appears to me that the use of the term "any person who was a director" in s 149(2) coupled with the purpose and nature of the provisions included in Chapter 1 of Part VII of the Companies Act 1990, including s 150, is evidence of such a contrary intent …
>
> Having regard to the frequency with which persons resident outside the State are appointed directors of Irish companies, it would clearly be absurd to suggest that the Oireachtas, in enacting these provisions in the public interest, intended to restrict only directors of insolvent companies who happened to be resident within the State and leave dishonest or irresponsible non-resident directors with unrestricted freedom to be directors of any Irish companies in the future. The use of the phrase "*any person*" in s 149(2) underlines what appears to be the obvious intent of the Oireachtas that restrictions provided for in s 150 should apply to all persons who agree to act as directors of Irish companies, irrespective of where they happen to be resident[228].'

Finlay Geoghegan J went on to hold that while there was no rule of court expressly governing service of the originating notice of motion on a director outside of the jurisdiction, the service effected by registered post to their residential addresses in England, as had been recorded in the CRO, was sufficient discharge of the court's obligation to ensure that applications under s 150 were heard and determined in accordance with the principles of constitutional justice.

The duties of liquidators of insolvent companies and the Director's role

[28.082] By virtue of s 56 of the CLEA 2001, the liquidators of all *insolvent companies* are obliged to bring application under s 150(1) of the CA 1990 unless directed otherwise by the Director of Corporate Enforcement. This measure was necessary to address the

---

227 *Euroking Miracle (Ireland) Ltd; Fennell v Frost et al* [2003] 3 IR 80. See also *360Atlantic (Ireland) Ltd; O'Ferral v Coughlan et al* [2004] 4 IR 266.

228 *Re Paramount Airways Ltd* [1993] Ch 233, noted.

deficiencies in the CA 1990, as identified by Murphy J in *Business Communications Ltd v Baxter and Parsons*[229]. The basic problem with the CA 1990 was that it did not expressly require anyone (whether liquidator, receiver or other) to bring an application under s 150(1) to have a director restricted. The dearth in applications under s 150(1) from its commencement in 1991 to 1994[230] was clearly influential in the Gallagher Company Law Review Group's implicit conclusion that s 150 was simply not working and that Group's consequent focus on bolstering disqualification provisions. During the course of 1994, Mr Justice Francis Murphy issued a practice direction to official liquidators (the only liquidators under the supervision of the court), the effect of which was to direct them to bring application under s 150(1) of the CA 1990 against the directors of the companies they were winding up. In *Business Communications Ltd v Baxter and Parsons*[231], Murphy J said of the original provisions on restriction:

> 'A particularly surprising feature of the novel provisions is that neither the legislation nor any rules made thereto imposes a duty on any party or person to bring a case before the court so that it can exercise the mandatory duty imposed upon it. In windings-up by the court this lacuna has been overcome by the court on further consideration of the order for liquidation directing the official liquidator to bring the appropriate application on notice to persons appearing to be directors thereof. In the case of voluntary liquidations the court does not have either the responsibility or the machinery for giving comparable directions. It may be that voluntary liquidators and receivers are not sufficiently conscious of the provisions of Chapter 1 of Part VII of the CA 1990 or else they do not see it as their function to bring relevant cases before the Court. Perhaps it will be necessary for the legislature to consider the provision of a particular sanction to ensure that the many cases which have obviously arisen since August 1991 are duly pursued. If not, there would be an apparent injustice to the directors of insolvent companies wound up by the court as against those wound up voluntarily[232].'

Subsequently, Shanley J observed in *La Moselle Clothing Ltd and Rosegem Ltd v Soualhi*[233] that the court's direction in official windings up resulted in applications being brought in almost all such cases[234]. However, Shanley J went on to note that the injustice, envisaged by Murphy J, still remained unredressed and that only a handful of cases of insolvent companies in receivership or creditors' voluntary liquidation had came before the courts. On the recommendations of the McDowell Group, the CLEA 2001 redressed the injustice, concluding that 'insolvency, and not the legal route by which a company is wound-up, should determine whether the directors should be the subject of sanctions[235]'.

229 *Business Communications Ltd v Baxter and Parsons* (21 July 1995, unreported) HC, Murphy J.

230 An inspection of the register would have disclosed that only 11 persons had been restricted: see *Report of the Working Group on Company Law Compliance and Enforcement* (1998) Government Publications (Pn 6697) at para 6.13.

231 *Business Communications Ltd v Baxter and Parsons* (21 July 1995, unreported) HC, Murphy J.

232 *Business Communications Ltd v Baxter and Parsons* (21 July 1995, unreported) HC, Murphy J at pp 5, 6 of the judgment.

233 *La Moselle Clothing Ltd and Rosegem Ltd v Soualhi* [1998] 2 ILRM 345.

234 As at 31 December 1997 there were 108 persons restricted: *Companies Report, 1997* at p 41; and as at 31 December 2011 there were 546 persons on the restricted persons' register: *Companies Report, 2011* at p 33.

235 At para 6.22.

[28.083] Section 56 of the CLEA 2001 provides:

> '(1) A liquidator of an insolvent company shall, within 6 months after his or her appointment or the commencement of this section, whichever is the later, and at intervals as required by the Director thereafter, provide to the Director a report in the prescribed form.
>
> (2) A liquidator of an insolvent company shall, not earlier than 3 months nor later than 5 months (or such later time as the court may allow and advises the Director) after the date on which he or she has provided to the Director a report under *subsection (1)*, apply to the court for the restriction under s 150 of the Act of 1990 of each of the directors of the company, unless the Director has relieved the liquidator of the obligation to make such an application.
>
> (3) A liquidator who fails to comply with *subsection (1)* or *(2)* is guilty of an offence.'

The consequence of s 56 is that there is now an express statutory duty on liquidators of *insolvent companies* (whether in official liquidation or in creditors' voluntary liquidation): (a) to report to the Director of Corporate Enforcement (the 'Director') in the prescribed form within six months of their appointment[236]; (b) not to bring a s 150 application within the three months immediately following their report; and (c) to bring application after the expiry of that three-month period but before the expiry of five months following his initial report, *unless the Director relieves him of the obligation to bring application under s 150*. The effect is to impose a positive obligation on liquidators of insolvent companies to make application under s 150 whilst simultaneously giving the Director a 'dead-man's brake'. The reasoning behind this section is that the 'private' (ie, not publicly sponsored) applications by official liquidators, was perceived to operate very effectively and efficiently and it was sought not to interfere with something that was working. The reason for allowing the Director to relieve liquidators from the obligation to bring a s 150 application is (a) to avoid inappropriate applications being forced into court (eg, worker directors; aged relations, persuaded to assume the role of director; celebrity non-executive directors who accepted the office for charitable or altruistic reasons)[237] and (b) to facilitate the Director making a decision as to whether application for a disqualification order is more appropriate.

[28.084] In *Re Usit Ireland Ltd*[238], it was held by Finlay Geoghegan J that the obligation on a liquidator to apply for the restriction under s 150 of the Act of 1990 'of each of the directors of the company,' was not confined to each of the directors at the time the obligation to bring the application arises, or the date of the winding up, but extended to every person who was a director within 12 months of the company being wound up. In so finding, Finlay Geoghegan J said:

> 'It is undisputed that the legislature in imposing the obligation in respect of "each of the directors of the company" did not expressly specify the point in time at which a person must be or have been a director … If one was to apply a very literal approach and consider that the section only referred to persons who were directors of the company at the date the obligation arose this would lead to an absurd result. Persons who potentially may have been the subject of a mandatory application could simply resign after the commencement

---

236 Or the commencement of the CLEA 2001, so that it affects then *existing* liquidators.

237 See para 6.23 of the McDowell Group's Report.

238 *Re USIT Ireland Ltd et al* [2003] 2 IR 635.

of the winding up and in advance of the relevant date and avoid the potential impact of the section. This could not have been the intention of the Oireachtas.

… Having regard to the power granted to a liquidator to bring an application under s 150(4A) of the Act of 1990 and the provisions of s 149(2) and the absence of any indication that the obligation under s 56(2) of the Act of 2001 is not to apply to all directors to whom s 150 applies, it appears that the intention of the Oireachtas was that, at minimum, the obligation of the liquidator under s 56(2) is to bring an application under s 150 in respect of persons who were directors of the company at the date of commencement of the winding up or within twelve months prior to that date.'

One would have thought that the wording of s 56(2) of the CLEA 2001 could not have been clearer, and it is significant for other areas of company law that the High Court applied such a purposive interpretation, effectively choosing to remedy a gap in the legislation.

[28.085] One of the consequences that flows from s 150 being mandatory in nature is that a liquidator would not have the authority to agree to refrain from bringing an application under s 150 of the CA 1990 for any reason, but particularly in return for a director's undertaking to act as if an order had been made. Authority for the proposition that liquidators cannot agree to refrain from bringing s 150 applications is *Re Verit Hotel and Leisure (Ireland) Ltd; Duignan v Carway et al*[239]. In that case, it was claimed that the liquidator was *estopped* from bringing the s 150 application because it was closely interrelated to other proceedings that had been settled. Rejecting this contention, McCracken J held:

'… there can be no estoppel in the present case because of the nature of the s 150 proceedings … the proceedings are mandatory, and the section provides that the court must be satisfied as to certain matters. That being so, there can be no question of such proceedings being settled, and there would have been no power in the liquidator to undertake as part of an overall settlement not to pursue the s 150 proceedings … There can be no question of the liquidator being estopped, as s 150 raises an issue between the directors and the courts and not between the directors and the liquidator.'

Although liquidators have no authority to agree not to make a s 150 application, it should be noted that s 56 of the CLEA 2001 confers statutory power on the Director to relieve liquidators from bringing application. It is thought that there would be no statutory bar to the Director accepting an undertaking from a director of an insolvent company to act or refrain from acting in a particular manner as a condition for the Director relieving a liquidator from bringing application under s 150.

[28.086] Section 151(1) of the CA 1990 imposes a duty on the liquidator of an insolvent company to inform the court of his opinion that the interests of any other company or its creditors may be placed in jeopardy by reason of the fact that a restricted person is 'involved'[240] in it. This duty also applies to receivers: s 154 of the CA 1990. Breach of

239 *Re Verit Hotel and Leisure (Ireland) Ltd; Duignan v Carway et al* (23 January 2002, unreported) HC, McCracken J.

240 By 'involved' is meant: 'is appointed or is acting in any way, whether directly or indirectly, as a director or is concerned or is taking part in the promotion or formation of such other company': s 151(2).

this duty is an offence, liable to fine[241]. Upon receipt of a liquidator's or receiver's report to this effect, the court is empowered to make whatever order it sees fit.

[28.087] Where a restricted person is or becomes a director of a company which commences to be wound up within five years of the commencement of the winding up of the originally insolvent company, and it appears to the liquidator that it is insolvent, the liquidator is obliged[242] to report those matters to the court and on receiving the liquidator's report, the court can, if it considers proper to do so, make a disqualification order against that person for such period as it thinks fit[243]. Disqualification orders are considered below[244].

The *locus standi* of liquidators, receivers, creditors and the Director

[28.088] Whereas the liquidators of insolvent companies have a legal duty (unless relieved by the Director) to bring application under s 150(1) of the CA 1990, other persons have *locus standi* to bring application without having an obligation to do so. In the first place, Chapter 1 of Part VII of the CA 1990 envisages that applications may be brought by receivers of insolvent companies. Section 154 of the CA 1990 provides:

> Where a receiver of the property of the company is appointed, the provisions of this Chapter shall, with the necessary modifications, apply as if the reference therein to the liquidator and to winding up were construed as references to the receiver and to the receivership.

As Murphy J said in *Re Cavan Crystal Group Ltd*[245], 'there is no doubt but that Chapter 1 of Part VII of the Companies Act 1990 … applies or may apply to a company over which a receiver has been appointed'[246]. It should be noted, however, that unlike liquidators, receivers are not subject to any obligation to report to the Director of Corporate Enforcement.

[28.089] By virtue of s 150(4A) of the CA 1990[247] there is now express authority for liquidators, receivers and the Director to make application for a restriction order, thereby remedying the deficiency in the original CA 1990, highlighted by Shanley J in *Re Steamline Ltd*[248]. In that case, in holding that the creditors of an insolvent company could bring application under s 150(1), he said:

> 'All enactments should be given a purposive construction: that is, a construction which promotes the remedy the Oireachtas has provided to cure a particular mischief. Armed with such a canon of construction, this Court approaches Part VII of the CA 1990 noting that the legislature has expressly provided a particular restriction for particular types of conduct; it is a restriction to be imposed by the Court, but which cannot realistically be imposed in the absence of a procedure whereby applications for such a

---

241 Section 151(3) of the CA 1990.

242 On pain of fine: s 161(6) of the CA 1990.

243 Section 161(5) of the CA 1990.

244 See para **[28.148]** *post*.

245 *Re Cavan Crystal Group Ltd* (26 April 1996, unreported) HC, Murphy J.

246 *Re Cavan Crystal Group Ltd* (26 April 1996, unreported) HC, Murphy J at p 2 of the judgment.

247 As inserted by s 41(1)(c) of the CLEA 2001.

248 *Re Steamline Ltd* (24 June 1998, unreported) HC, Shanley J. See, generally, Walker, 'Creditors' Rights to have Directors Restricted – A New Development' (1998) CLP 159.

restriction are made to the Court by parties with an interest in making such an application. I believe that the Court ought to construe s 150(1) in such a way as to promote, rather than restrict, the remedy provided for in that subsection: while the grounds for the disqualification of a director and other officers of a company differ from the grounds warranting restriction of a director, nonetheless, it does appear to me that the persons authorised by s 160(4)(b) to bring an application for a disqualification order are, broadly, the same category of persons who would have an interest in seeking an order for the restriction of a director. In promoting, rather than restricting, the remedy provided for in s 150(1), this court ought, in my view, construe the mandatory power provided therein as exercisable on the application of any one of the class of persons identified in s 160(4)(b) of the CA 1990 being persons identified by the legislature as having an interest in moving an application for a disqualification order and whom the legislature would have intended to have a like interest in relation to applications to restrict directors. Accordingly, in my view, Musgrave Ltd, as a creditor of Steamline Ltd are entitled to maintain this application[249].'

Since the reasoning of Shanley J no longer holds true – ie, the legislature *has now* specified who can bring application under s 150 – it is thought most probable that the effect of s 150(4A) is to reverse *Re Steamline* with the effect that creditors no longer have standing to bring application under s 150. This is borne out by the decision in *Re Document Imaging Systems Ltd*[250]. In that case, a liquidator of an insolvent company had applied to have four persons restricted. The court held that one of those persons was not a director within 12 months of the date of the commencement of the winding up and dismissed the application against him. That person applied under Ord 15, r 13 of the RSC 1986 to be jointed as a party to the official liquidator's application against the remaining three respondents; the liquidator applied for permission to be able to rely on that person's affidavit, in the event that he was not joined. Finlay Geoghegan J refused the application to join the person but permitted the liquidator to rely on his affidavits. The learned judge said that where a person sought to be joined voluntarily to proceedings, the court should consider whether he himself had *locus standi* to pursue the application. In that regard it was held:

'The Oireachtas has specifically, by the 2001 amendment, provided that the jurisdiction conferred on the High Court under s 150 should be exercised on the application of one of the persons named in sub-s (4A). They have done so in circumstances where they have in s 160(4) of the Act of 1990 specified a different class of persons who may bring applications under s 160(2) of the Act of 1990. Applying the well established principle of construction that the intention of the Oireachtas should be construed from the words used when given their ordinary meaning, I must conclude that the Oireachtas intend (since the passing of the Act of 2001) that applications under s 150 be brought by the persons named in s 150(4A) and not by any other person. If it were intended that other persons could bring such an application then the Oireachtas would have specified such additional categories as it has done in s 160(4) of the Act of 1990. Accordingly I have concluded that the court has no jurisdiction to permit a person who is not the Director of Corporate Enforcement, a liquidator or a receiver to be an applicant in proceedings under s 150(1) of the Act of 1990.'

---

249 *Re Steamline Ltd* (24 June 1998, unreported) HC, Shanley J at p 3 of the judgment.

250 *Re Document Imaging Systems Ltd* [2005] 3 IR 103.

Procedural aspects of restriction applications[251]

[28.090] The early practice has been to bring s 150 applications by way of notice of motion. In *Re Verit Hotel and Leisure (Ireland) Ltd; Duignan v Carway et al*[252], it was acknowledged by McCracken J that the RSC 1986 do not provide for bringing application under s 150 by way of notice of motion. Although in that matter it was contended that the liquidator's application ought, instead, to have been brought by way of a plenary summons, this was rejected on the grounds that, in that case, the respondent directors had up until then accepted the procedures followed by the liquidator and could not subsequently raise a procedural objection.

[28.091] In 2003, the President of the High Court issued a practice direction (HC28) in relation to the procedures to be followed on a s 150 application brought by the liquidator in a creditors' voluntary winding up. The practice direction provides:

> '1. An application for a declaration that a director of a company in voluntary liquidation be restricted under section 150(1) of the Companies Act 1990 shall be commenced by originating Notice of Motion (Form 1) and grounded upon the affidavit of the applicant (Form 2). Applications in respect of several directors of one company shall be made on one Notice of Motion except where the circumstances otherwise require.
>
> 2. Where necessary an application to the Court under section 56(2) of the Company Law Enforcement Act 2001 to extend the time for the making of the application under section 150(1) of the Companies Act 1990 shall be made on the same Notice of Motion.
>
> 3. The affidavit grounding the application for restriction shall set out all the facts the applicant considers should be brought to the attention of the court for the purpose of determining:
>
> i. whether each of the respondents has acted honestly in relation to the conduct of the affairs of the company;
>
> ii. whether each of the respondents has acted responsibly in relation to the conduct of the affairs of the company;
>
> iii. whether there is any other reason for which it would be just and equitable to restrict any of the respondents;
>
> iv. if appropriate whether any of the circumstances set out in s 150(2)(b) apply.
>
> 4. Motions shall be issued in the Central Office and made returnable for a date not less than 28 days from the date of issue and shall be served with the grounding affidavit and a copy of this practice direction (excluding forms 1 & 2) on the respondent(s) not less than 21 clear days prior to the return date.
>
> 5. An appearance to the Notice of Motion (Form 3) shall be entered in the Central Office and served on the applicant or where on record his/her solicitor within 10 days of the date of service of the Notice of Motion.
>
> 6. Where an application is opposed a respondent shall file and serve an affidavit setting out the facts upon which the application is opposed and shall file the affidavit in the Central Office and serve it on the applicant or where on record his/her solicitor not less

251 See, generally, Cahill, *Company Law Compliance and Enforcement* (2008, Bloomsbury Professional) at Ch 18, 'Procedure of Restriction Proceedings'.

252 *Re Verit Hotel and Leisure (Ireland) Ltd; Duignan v Carway et al* (23 January 2002, unreported) HC, McCracken J.

than 4 clear days before the return date or such further time as the court may exceptionally allow.

7. Where no appearance is entered by or on behalf of a respondent the applicant shall file an affidavit of service in the Central Office not less than 2 clear days prior to the return date.

8. Applications for the extension of time for the filing of affidavits by any party shall not be granted save exceptionally where the Court is satisfied that the extension of time is required for good reason.

9. Applications which are duly served may be determined by the court on the return date.'

Other procedural questions have been answered by the High Court. It was held in *Re Euroking Miracle (Ireland) Ltd; Fennell v Frost*[253] that service of restriction proceedings on a respondent director should be by means of personal service in accordance with Ord 9, r 2 of the RSC. In the same case, however, it was held that in relation to a respondent who was resident in the UK, service by registered pre-paid post was a sufficient discharge of the court's obligation to ensure that the application was heard and determined in accordance with constitutional justice. In *Silken Construction Ltd; Kavanagh v O'Donoghue*[254], it was held by Finlay Geoghegan J that discovery could be ordered of the liquidator's report to the Director of Corporate Enforcement under s 56 of the CLEA 2001.

The costs of the application for a restriction order[255]

[28.092] A considerable amount of jurisprudence has developed in relation to the costs of an application for a restriction order. Here, we consider the following matters that arise in connection with the costs of the application for a restriction order:

(a) The costs of a successful application;
(b) The costs of an unsuccessful application.

(a) The costs of a successful application

[28.093] Prior to the enactment of the CLEA 2001, s 150 of the CA 1990 was silent as regards liability for costs. Even before the CLEA 2001, the court exercised its discretion under Ord 99, r 1 of the RSC 1986 in this regard: so in *Re Cavan Crystal Group Ltd*[256], although Murphy J held that the directors there had acted honestly and responsibly, he ordered that each party was to bear his own costs[257]. Section 41(c) of the CLEA 2001

[253] *Re Euroking Miracle (Ireland) Ltd; Fennell v Frost* [2003] 3 IR 80.

[254] *Silken Construction Ltd; Kavanagh v O'Donoghue* [2003] 4 IR 443.

[255] See, generally, Cahill, *Company Law Compliance and Enforcement* (2008, Bloomsbury Professional) at pp 916–930.

[256] *Re Cavan Crystal Group Ltd* (26 April 1996, unreported) HC, Murphy J.

[257] In *Re Century Communications Ltd* (an application reported in (1996) Irish Times, 12 October), Carroll J found that nine directors – who included a number of celebrities like Terry Wogan and Chris de Burgh – had acted honestly and responsibly in relation to the collapse of Century Radio, but according to the newspaper report said the it was the liquidator's duty to bring application under s 150 and that each of the directors present should contribute £250 plus VAT to the liquidator's costs. At a later hearing (reported in (1997) Irish Times, 15 January, Carroll J) necessitated by Mr Wogan's failure to file an affidavit at the earlier hearing, Carroll J found that he too had acted honestly and responsibly; (contd.../)

inserted a new s 150(4B)[258] which was substituted by s 11(1) of the IFCMPA 2006 with the following provision:

> 'The court, on the hearing of an application for a declaration under subsection (1) by the Director, a liquidator or a receiver (in this subsection referred to as "the applicant"), may order that the directors against whom the declaration is made shall bear—
>
> (a) the costs of the application, and
>
> (b) the whole (or such portion of them as the court specifies) of the costs and expenses incurred by the applicant—
>
> (i) in investigating the matters the subject of the application, and
>
> (ii) in so far as they do not fall within paragraph (a), in collecting evidence in respect of those matters,
>
> including so much of the remuneration and expenses of the applicant as are attributable to such investigation and collection.'

Whereas it was held by Finlay Geoghegan J in *Re Tipperary Fresh Foods Ltd*[259] that s 150(4B) as inserted by the CLEA 2001 had retrospective effect, the substituted s 150(4B) only applies to liquidations which commenced after the date of its commencement, which was 29 January 2007[260].

[28.094] A prerequisite to the exercise of the court's discretion under s 150(4B) to award costs, etc, against directors is that the court must have made an order against those directors. The novelty of s 150(4B) is not that the costs of the application can be awarded against the respondent directors, for this was always part of the court's discretion[261], but that the applicant's costs and expenses of investigating the matters and of collecting evidence, including the applicant's remuneration and expenses, can be awarded against the respondent directors[262]. The test to be applied in deciding whether costs of investigative work are to be allowed is whether the costs are 'necessary or proper' and can include legal costs for investigative work conducted at the applicant's request[263].

(b) The costs of an unsuccessful application

[28.095] As noted earlier, s 150(4B) only allows the court make an order for costs, etc, against a director where the court makes a declaration restricting the director. Although Ord 99, r 1 of the RSC would permit the awarding of costs against respondent directors who successfully defended the application, it has been held by Finlay Geoghegan J in *Re*

---

257 (\...contd) however, because of the delay in producing the affidavit, Carroll J is reported as having ordered that he should pay more than the other directors towards the liquidator's costs and he was ordered to pay £500 plus VAT.

258 The original s 150(4B) provided: 'The court, in hearing an application for a declaration under subsection (1) from the Director, a liquidator or a receiver, may order that the directors against whom the declaration is made shall bear the costs of the application and any costs incurred by the applicant in investigating the matter.'

259 *Re Tipperary Fresh Foods Ltd* [2005] IEHC 96.

260 See *Sallyview Estates Ltd; Farrell v Balzarini and Balzarini* [2007] IEHC 424.

261 Order 99, r 1. See *Re GMT Engineering Services Ltd* [2003] 4 IR 133.

262 *Re Tipperary Fresh Foods Ltd* [2005] IEHC 96.

263 *Re Moypool Ltd; Gannon v O'Hora and O'Hora* [2007] 3 IR 563.

Visual Impact and Display Ltd; Murphy v Murphy[264] that the effect of s 150(4B) of the CA 1990 was to preclude the reliance by the court on Ord 99, r 1 since such an interpretation was necessary to give meaning to the words 'directors against whom the declaration of restriction is made'. As such, costs may not be awarded against a successful respondent director.

[28.096] In *Re Visual Impact and Displays Ltd; Murphy v Murphy*[265], it was held that the court had the power under Ord 99, r 1 to award costs against a liquidator in respect of a successful respondent's costs where the liquidator had included the respondent in his s 56 report without having sufficient evidence for the proposition that the respondent had been a director within 12 months of the commencement of the liquidation. Moreover, it was held that it was the liquidator, and not the company, who was liable to pay the costs. This decision was distinguished by O'Leary J, in *Re Doherty Advertising Ltd; Stafford v Beggs*[266], who questioned whether the rule that costs follow the event with the 'successful' party getting their costs against the 'unsuccessful' party should apply since a liquidator was in a special position in restriction proceedings, merely presenting an application without being a claimant or having an interest in the outcome. This decision does not, however, preclude costs being awarded against liquidators but highlights that the court will not exercise its discretion lightly to award costs against liquidators[267]. As Finlay Geoghegan J said in the later decision in *Re Kranks Korner Ltd; McCarthy v Gibbons and Gibbons*:[268]

> '… having regard to the highly unusual manner in which such applications come before the Court ie an involuntary applicant who is legally bound to bring the application (on some occasions against views expressed by him), following submission of a report to the Director under s 56(1) of the Act of 2001, that the Court should not start from a position where there exists a normal rule which applies to applications, but rather exercise its discretion in each case, having regard to the relevant facts and the statutory scheme.'

The defence of acting 'honestly and responsibly'

[28.097] Much of the case law on s 150 of the CA 1990 concerns the only real defence open to respondents, that they have acted 'honestly and responsibly'. The basis of this defence is s 150(2)(a) which provides that one of the matters which the court can take into consideration in deciding whether or not to impose the otherwise mandatory order is:

> 'that the director acted honestly and responsibly in relation to the conduct of the affairs of the company and there is no reason why it is just and equitable for restrictions to apply.'

This defence is obviously intended to save honest and responsible directors from being 'restricted' where, through no fault of theirs, a company goes into insolvent liquidation.

264 *Re Visual Impact and Display Ltd; Murphy v Murphy* [2003] IEHC 91; see also *Re GMT Engineering Services Ltd; Luby v McMahon* [2003] 4 IR 133.

265 *Re Visual Impact and Displays Ltd; Murphy v Murphy* [2003] IEHC 91.

266 *Re Doherty Advertising Ltd; Stafford v Beggs* [2006] IEHC 258; see Mitchell, 'Section 150 – Costs Follow the Event, but which One?' (2007) CLP 51.

267 See Cahill, *Company Law Compliance and Enforcement* (2008, Bloomsbury Professional) at p 927.

268 *Re Kranks Korner Ltd; McCarthy v Gibbons and Gibbons* [2008] IEHC 423.

It has long been established that the onus is on the respondents to establish that they acted honestly and responsibly. As Murphy J said in *Business Communications Ltd v Baxter and Parsons*:[269]

> '... it does seem that the most important feature of the legislature is that it effectively imposes a burden on the directors to establish that the insolvency occurred in circumstances in which no blame attaches to them as a result of either dishonesty or irresponsibility. In this respect the legislation differs from the very numerous other provisions contained in the Companies Acts which create various criminal and civil wrongs or remedies. These other provisions generally entail the expenditure of considerable sums of money in relation to matters on which the moving party rarely has direct or adequate evidence and the proceedings are, in the nature of things, brought against persons who being associated with an insolvent company may well be impecunious themselves. Commercial history in this country shows that this wide range of remedies, whether criminal or civil, are rarely invoked and even less frequently successful[270].'

[28.098] The considerable case law of the High and Supreme Court demonstrate that a number of distinct, but obviously related, matters consistently arise in the honest and responsible defence. In *La Moselle Clothing Ltd and Rosegem Ltd v Soualhi*[271], Shanley J said, in interpreting s 150(2)(a) of the CA 1990, that it was clear that there are three hurdles that a director, seeking to be exonerated, has to surmount:

> '(a) He must establish that he has acted honestly in relation to the affairs of the company.
>
> (a) He must establish that he has acted responsibly in relation to the affairs of the company.
>
> (b) He must satisfy the Court that there is no other reason why it would be just and equitable that he should be subject to the restrictions imposed by the section[272].'

(*a*) *Acting honestly in relation to the affairs of the company*

[28.099] As shall be considered next, judicial comment on whether respondent directors of insolvent companies have acted honestly and responsibly has tended to focus, almost exclusively, on whether they acted responsibly. Whether this is because in cases involving blatant dishonesty by directors the courts have not considered it necessary to examine, in a written judgment, their actions or because liquidators' prefer to allege *irresponsibility* rather than *dishonesty* remains to be seen. One case in which it was found that the directors had acted dishonestly was *Re Outdoor Advertising Services Ltd*[273]. There, Costello J held that two of the respondent directors had not acted honestly as they had consciously and deliberately sought to benefit themselves personally and two companies owned by them, at the expense of the insolvent company's creditors[274].

---

[269] *Business Communications Ltd v Baxter and Parsons* (21 July 1995, unreported) HC, Murphy J.

[270] *Business Communications Ltd v Baxter and Parsons* (21 July 1995, unreported) HC, Murphy J at p 18 of the judgment.

[271] *La Moselle Clothing Ltd v Soualhi* [1998] 2 ILRM 345.

[272] *Business Communications Ltd v Baxter and Parsons* (21 July 1995, unreported) HC, Murphy J at pp 7, 8 of the judgment.

[273] *Re Outdoor Advertising Services Ltd* (28 January 1997, unreported) HC, Costello J.

[274] *Re Outdoor Advertising Services Ltd* (28 January 1997, unreported) HC, Costello J at p 11 of the judgment.

[28.100] In *USIT World plc*[275], Peart J made the following *obiter dicta* observations on acting 'honestly' and what distinguished it from 'responsibly':

> 'Where honesty is at issue and the Court has not been satisfied that the director has acted honestly, that dishonesty is more fundamental and goes to the core of a person's integrity. I say that even though the section draws no distinction between honesty and responsibility. But it is significant that both words have been used in the section.
>
> Dishonesty implies something akin to improper dealing with money or other assets belonging to the company, or some form of fraudulent trading. In an extreme case this would involve a director depleting the assets of the company directly for his own benefit, rather than settling his creditors, thereby leading to the collapse of the company; or obtaining funds from others with a fraudulent intent. Clearly such a director who is prepared to steal or deal with the company's or another's assets in such a fashion, or behave in any other way in which dishonesty is manifest will have demonstrated that the trust invested in him in exchange for the privileges attaching to limited liability through the mechanism of a limited liability company has been abused to the extent that he should be restricted within the terms of the section from being a director. Such dishonesty will of course also amount to irresponsibility.
>
> But irresponsibility is a different concept. While dishonesty will always amount to irresponsibility the converse is not true. 
>
> In the present case no dishonesty has even been alleged by the liquidator against any director, and the Court is satisfied that none of the respondents has acted dishonestly.'

It remains the case that there have been few applications brought which turned upon whether a respondent had acted honestly, in almost all applications it is accepted that the respondent acted honestly but disputed that they acted 'responsibly'.

(*b*) *Acting responsibly in relation to the conduct of the affairs of the company*

[28.101] In *Re Squash (Ireland) Ltd*,[276] McGuinness J confirmed that the court should look at the entire tenure of the director and not merely the months in the run up to the liquidation.  In the earlier judgment of *Re Gasco Ltd*[277], McCracken J had said that there should be particular focus on the actions of the directors during the final months before winding up. His reasons were:

> 'I think it is quite significant that no restrictions can attach to somebody who ceased to be a director of the company more than twelve months before the winding up. This seems to me to indicate that the primary aim of s 150 is to deal with directors who have behaved irresponsibly or dishonestly during the last twelve months of the life of the company, and that the actions of a director who is subject to s 150 are to be looked at primarily in the light of his actions during that period. This indeed has a considerable practical logic, as it is presumably intended to focus attention on the behaviour of directors in the period leading up to the winding-up, and to try to ensure that they deal responsibly with creditors when a company is in difficulties. In my view, therefore, there should be particular scrutiny on the actions of directors during the final months before winding up[278].'

---

275 *USIT World plc* [2005] IEHC 285.

276 *Re Squash (Ireland) Ltd* [2001] 3 IR 35.

277 *Re Gasco Ltd* (5 February 2001, unreported) HC, McCracken J.

278 *Re Gasco Ltd* (5 February 2001, unreported) HC, McCracken J at p 7 of the judgment.

Are these two views compatible? To the extent that McGuinness J is saying that the court cannot ignore the totality of a director's tenure and should consider all aspects of his relationship with the company and to the extent that McCracken J is saying that, in practice, such dishonesty and irresponsibility as exists will be more visible and cause more significant damage in the final 12 months, it is thought that the findings are not mutually exclusive. What is clear, however, is that the entirety of a director's tenure is liable to be scrutinised.

[28.102] A director's conduct *after* a company has been wound up cannot be taken into consideration in determining whether that director has acted honestly and responsibly in relation to the conduct of the affairs of the company, although it can be taken into consideration in deciding whether there is another reason for which it would be just and equitable to make a restriction order[279].

[28.103] Respondent directors must also establish that they acted responsibly in relation to the company to which the liquidator has been appointed. That a director's conduct in relation to the affairs of another company was exemplary is irrelevant. This is a particularly important point to remember for directors of companies that constitute a group involving a holding company and its subsidiaries. Acting in the interests of the group may be permissible in certain circumstances relating to the discharge of directors' duties but a legal entity specific focus remains key in the context of the examination of a director's conduct in relation to defending restriction proceedings. In *Re 360Atlantic (Ireland) Ltd; O'Ferral v Coughlan et al*[280], Finlay Geoghegan J said:

> 'An issue raised by the above facts is whether and to what extent the Court should have regard to the fact that the Company is a wholly owned subsidiary within a worldwide group of companies and to what extent if any that fact alters the matters to which the Court should have regard when determining whether the respondents acted responsibly as a director of the subsidiary company.
>
> Section 150(2)(a) of the Act of 1990 requires the respondent director to satisfy the court that he/she 'has acted . . . responsibly in relation to the conduct of the affairs of the Company…'. It has previously been held and determined that this confines the Court to considering the respondent's conduct as a director in relation to the affairs of the Company in liquidation in the sense that the court may not take into account when considering whether or not it must make a declaration of restriction the fact, for example, that the respondent is acting or has acted responsibly as a director of other companies.'

(*c*) *Acting responsibly – the factors which the courts consider relevant*

[28.104] There has been considerable case law which interprets the meaning of acting responsibly. Here, the defence of acting responsibly is considered under the following headings:

(i) The test in *La Moselle*;
(ii) An objective standard;
(iii) Compliance with the Companies Acts and other duties;
(iv) Evidence of incompetence;

[279] *Re CMC (Ireland) Ltd; Fennell v Carolan* [2005] IEHC 59; see para **[28.130]** *post*.

[280] *Re 360Atlantic (Ireland) Ltd; O'Ferral v Coughlan et al* [2004] 4 IR 266 at 275.

(v) Responsibility for insolvency and net deficiency of assets;
(vi) The lack of commercial probity.

(i) The test in La Moselle

[28.105] It is very important to remember that corporate insolvency does not *per se* mean that directors have acted either dishonestly or irresponsibly. In *Business Communications Ltd v Baxter and Parsons*[281], Murphy J said:

> 'Of course one must be careful not to be wise after the event. There must be no "witch hunt" because a business failed as businesses will[282].'

Again, in *Re La Moselle Clothing Ltd and Rosegem Ltd*[283], Shanley J said 'the simple fact that a business fails is not evidence of a lack of responsibility nor indeed is it evidence of dishonesty'[284]. In that case, Shanley J quoted with approval from *Re Lo-Line Motors Ltd*[285]. Shanley J added that a director broadly complying with his obligations under the provisions of the Companies Acts 'and acting with a degree of commercial probity during his tenure as a director of the company will not be restricted on the grounds that he has acted irresponsibly'[286].

[28.106] The seminal test for determining whether a director has acted 'responsibly' was first promulgated by Shanley J in *Re La Moselle Clothing Ltd and Rosegem Ltd*[287] when he set out a five-fold test:

> 'It seems to me that in determining the "responsibility" of a director for the purposes of s 150(2)(a) the court should have regard to:-
>
> (a) The extent to which the director has or has not complied with any obligation imposed on him by the Companies Acts.
>
> (b) The extent to which his conduct could be regarded as so incompetent as to amount to irresponsibility.
>
> (c) The extent of the director's responsibility for the insolvency of the company.
>
> (d) The extent of the director's responsibility for the net deficiency in the assets of the company disclosed at the date of the winding up or thereafter.
>
> (e) The extent to which the director, in his conduct of the affairs of the company, has displayed a lack of commercial probity or want of proper standards[288].'

[28.107] Shanley J's criteria for deciding 'responsibility' were found to be of 'considerable assistance' and generally adopted by the Supreme Court in *Re Squash (Ireland) Ltd*[289]. As to the criteria, Shanley J himself acknowledged that they overlap:

---

[281] *Business Communications Ltd v Baxter and Parsons* (21 July 1995, unreported) HC, Murphy J.

[282] *Business Communications Ltd v Baxter and Parsons* (21 July 1995, unreported) HC, Murphy J at p 17 of the judgment.

[283] *La Moselle Clothing Ltd and Rosegem Ltd v Soualhi* [1998] 2 ILRM 345.

[284] *La Moselle Clothing Ltd and Rosegem Ltd v Soualhi* [1998] 2 ILRM 345 at 351. See also *Re Colm O'Neill Engineering Services Ltd* (13 February 2004, ex tempore) HC, Finlay Geoghegan J.

[285] *Re Lo-Line Motors Ltd* [1988] BCLC 698 at 703. See para **[28.155]** *post*.

[286] *La Moselle Clothing Ltd and Rosegem Ltd v Soualhi* [1998] 2 ILRM 345 at 352.

[287] *La Moselle Clothing Ltd and Rosegem Ltd v Soualhi* [1998] 2 ILRM 345.

[288] *La Moselle Clothing Ltd and Rosegem Ltd v Soualhi* [1998] 2 ILRM 345 at 352.

[289] *Re Squash (Ireland) Ltd* [2001] 3 IR 35.

'These criteria necessarily overlap: for example a failure to keep proper books of account may directly contribute to the company becoming insolvent and may be caused by the incompetence of a director. But not all situations of a want of responsibility will result from a breach of obligations imposed by the Companies Acts: for example, a director's inability to see the 'writing on the wall' (*eg* an inability to see from a perusal of the company's management accounts that the company was trading while insolvent) may result from sheer incompetence and justify a restriction (see *Re Continental Assurance Co of London plc; Secretary of State for Industry v Burrows* [1997] 1 BCLC 48 where an inability to read and understand the statutory accounts of a company was considered a ground for disqualification of a director). Equally, a director who takes excessive sums from the company by way of drawings for salary without regard to the financial state of health of the company may be said to have acted without commercial probity although he did not necessarily fail to comply with his obligations under the Companies Acts[290].'

[28.108] In *Re Squash (Ireland) Ltd*[291], McGuinness J went on to apply the criteria identified by Shanley J to the conduct of the directors of Squash (Ireland). It is useful to quote the learned judge's application of the criteria *in extenso*:

'It appears from the history of the company that [the directors] have always acted responsibly and honestly and have put the interests of the company in the forefront of their minds, even insofar as losing their own money in an effort to assist the continuation of the company. With regard to:

(a) *The extent to which the director has or has not complied with the Companies Acts.* There is no suggestion that there has been a failure to comply with the Companies Acts and indeed it is clear that the company held many board meetings to deal with the problems that faced them. These board meetings were well documented by proper minutes and the company was run in a correct fashion[292].

(b) *The extent to which his conduct could be regarded as so incompetent as to amount to irresponsibility.* Perhaps the plan put forward by the directors in this company was overly optimistic but, had their position in regard to the business lease on the Clontarf premises been correct, it was a sensible enough plan in view of the shrinkage of their business over the years. It is unfortunate that they did not identify the problem with regard to the lease at any earlier stage but it has to be said that at the time they had professional and legal advice which they took. They did not act contrary to the advice that was given to them. I do not feel that they could be described as incompetent to such a degree as would amount to irresponsibility.

(c) [*The extent of the director's responsibility for the insolvency of the company.*] The directors were not responsible in themselves for the insolvency of the company. This basically arose from the reduction in business.

(d) [The extent of the director's responsibility for the net deficiency in the assets of the company disclosed at the date of the winding up or thereafter.] They certainly

290 *La Moselle Clothing Ltd and Rosegem Ltd v Soualhi* [1998] 2 ILRM 345 at 353.

291 *Re Squash (Ireland) Ltd* [2001] 3 IR 35.

292 With respect to McGuinness J, the holding of board meetings is but one aspect of compliance with the Companies Acts; however, it may be that the fact that the company was 'run in a correct fashion' implies that all other aspects were also complied with. That board meetings were held regularly and minuted was also considered significant by Murphy J in *Re Cavan Crystal Group Ltd* (26 April 1996, unreported) HC, Murphy J at p 13 of the judgment.

> were not responsible for the net deficiency. I would expect this to include some degree of dishonesty or something very near dishonesty if a director is to be held responsible for the net deficiency in the assets of the company.
>
> (e) [The extent to which the director, in his conduct of the affairs of the company, has displayed a lack of commercial probity or want of proper standards.] This is the factor that [the liquidator] lays most emphasis on in his argument to the court in regard to lack of commercial probity and indeed this is the heading under which the matter of the subscriptions would arise. [The liquidator] stresses that the directors should have told the members at an early stage the financial position of the company. It is clear as I have said that this was also the main and indeed the sole matter of concern to the learned President of the High Court[293].'

In these circumstances, the Supreme Court allowed the appeal and reversed the order of the High Court, McGuinness J finding that 'what they did was open to criticism but I do not feel that it was sufficient to be categorised as irresponsible'[294]. Less than perfect behaviour will not automatically attract a restriction order[295].

(ii) An objective standard

[28.109] In *Re Squash (Ireland) Ltd*[296], McGuinness J said in the Supreme Court that respondent directors:

> '… must be judged by an objective standard. In the case of all companies which have become insolvent it is likely that some criticisms of the directors may be made. Commercial errors may have occurred; misjudgments may well have been made; but to categorise conduct as irresponsible I feel that one must go further than this[297].'

In this case, the High Court had previously found that the two directors of Squash (Ireland) had acted irresponsibly and, accordingly, they had been restricted under s 150(1). The respondent directors appealed to the Supreme Court. The facts were that the company had been in existence since the early 1970s, providing services of a sporting and leisure nature, especially squash; the two respondents had been directors for some 18 years. Members paid annual or other subscriptions. After successful beginnings it was noted that due to fashions in sporting and leisure activities changing, interest in membership declined and the company was forced to close some premises; by the late 1990s it was clearly in financial difficulties. In an attempt to assist the company, the respondent directors had made loans themselves, through a trust company, to the company. At a later stage one of the respondents did not draw his salary for a period of up to one year. One premises in Clontarf from which the company had operated was held on foot of a lease from the Department of Education and the directors believed that the company was entitled to a valuable interest in the property. The company contracted to sell this lease to a building firm for some £700,000. Upon enquiring as to the

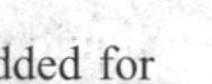

[293] *Re Squash (Ireland) Ltd* [2001] 3 IR 35 at 41. Criteria detailed in square brackets added for completeness; italics also added.

[294] *Re Squash (Ireland) Ltd* [2001] 3 IR 35 at 42.

[295] See also *Re Steamline Ltd* (24 June 1998, unreported) HC, Shanley J at p 11 of the judgment, where he found that the directors had acted honestly and responsibly even though a better explanation could have been tendered than that which was in the statement of affairs.

[296] *Re Squash (Ireland) Ltd* [2001] 3 IR 35.

[297] *Re Squash (Ireland) Ltd* [2001] 3 IR 35 at 39.

purchase of the freehold interest, it transpired, however, on 1 December 1997 that the Department of Education was not bound by the Landlord and Tenant (Amendment) Act 1980. The directors procured counsel's opinion, which, when obtained on 10 December 1997, confirmed this was the case. It seems that the sole ground for alleging that the directors were irresponsible was that in late November/early December 1997 they allowed the company's staff to issue reminders for subscriptions to its members. The directors had believed that the members would have been able to use the premises until the contract was completed and that, upon its being sold, the company would be able to refund subscriptions. It is significant that upon receiving counsel's opinion that the company did not have a valuable asset, the directors immediately ceased to seek subscriptions from members. Not only did the directors not act dishonestly, but they had actually lost considerable sums of their own money.

(iii) Compliance with the Companies Acts and other duties

[28.110] To facilitate the orderly consideration of the many issues that have arisen under this the first of the *La Moselle* criteria, the case law is considered under the following headings:

I. Maintenance of proper books and records;
II. Duties owed at common law;
III. Compliance with obligations and duties in the case of groups;
IV. Compliance with obligations and duties in the case of non-executive directors.

I. Maintenance of proper books and records

[28.111] One key feature of acting responsibly has been held to be compliance with the Companies Acts and the maintenance of proper books and records. In *Business Communications Ltd v Baxter and Parsons*[298], Murphy J said:

> 'Ordinarily "responsibility" will entail compliance with the principal features of the Companies Acts and the maintenance of the records required by those Acts. The records may be basic in form and modest in appearance. But they must exist in such a form as to enable the directors to make reasonable commercial decisions and auditors (or liquidators) to understand and follow the transactions in which the company was engaged[299].'

The absence of books and records was one of the factors which persuaded the court to make restriction orders against some of the directors in *Re Vehicle Imports Ltd*[300]. In *Re Gasco Ltd*[301], the liquidator of the company gave evidence that he found virtually no books and records, no monthly accounts for a particular two-year period and that this contributed to the difficulties in collecting the company's debts both before and after its liquidation. McCracken J said that 'the fact that no such records exist may make me suspect many things, but certainly is clear evidence of serious irresponsibility by [the

298 *Business Communications Ltd v Baxter and Parsons* (21 July 1995, unreported) HC, Murphy J.

299 *Business Communications Ltd v Baxter and Parsons* (21 July 1995, unreported) HC, Murphy J at p 18 of the judgment.

300 *Re Vehicle Imports Ltd* (23 November 2000, unreported) HC, Roderick Murphy J.

301 *Re Gasco Ltd* (5 February 2001, unreported) HC, McCracken J.

director] during the last few months of the trading life of the company'[302]. Putting the same proposition in a positive way, Murphy J said in *Re Costello Doors Ltd*:[303]

> 'On the face of it, the maintenance of proper books and accounts and the employment of appropriate experts in relation to them would go a long way to discharge the onus of showing that the directors behaved responsibly[304].'

Re Costello Doors Ltd[305] was the second written judgment on s 150 of the CA 1990 and was handed down by Murphy J on the same day as his decision in *Business Communications Ltd v Baxter and Parsons*. In *Costello Doors*, the evidence showed that appropriate books and records were kept up to September or October 1992, the time when the company ran into trading difficulties. However, from then until January 1993, when the company was placed into official liquidation, the books were not written up but the primary records were retained. On this point Murphy J said:

> 'I accept the contention made on behalf of the official liquidator that the preservation of basic records is not an adequate compliance with the requirements of the Companies Acts nor does it provide information in a suitable fashion so as to enable the management to make appropriate decisions or auditors to certify accounts but it does not seem to me that it is irresponsible to fail to write up the appropriate books for a particular period in the circumstances which existed in the present case. The fact was that the employment of the persons whose task it was to write up the records had been terminated in October 1992 …[306]'

It is thought to be significant that, in that case, it seemed clear that whilst the failure to maintain the company's books might have impeded the liquidation, it was not claimed that it contributed to the company's insolvency. Murphy J declined to make an order under s 150(1) against the company's directors.

[28.112] It should also be noted that the general rule is that the obligation to keep proper books and records is not limited to a period in which a fellow director has reputed responsibility for keeping the books and, as noted by Roderick Murphy J in *Re Vehicle Imports Ltd*[307] 'the responsibility is a joint and separate liability on each of the directors'. It is not sufficient for a director to say that the maintenance of books was the responsibility of his co-director and that he presumed that all was being attended to. As Peart J said in *Re Capital Auto Group Ltd; Foster v Swords and Chambers*[308]:

> 'Each director as part of acting responsibly has a duty to inform himself without any doubt, as to whether books and records are being kept. Sometimes this is achieved by the employment of suitable staff. Other times it is achieved by each director himself or herself making sure that all matters of that kind are looked after and being attended to as required.'

---

302 *Re Gasco Ltd* (5 February 2001, unreported) HC, McCracken J at p 6 of the judgment.

303 *Re Costello Doors Ltd* (21 July 1995, unreported) HC, Murphy J.

304 *Re Costello Doors Ltd* (21 July 1995, unreported) HC, Murphy J at p 5 of the judgment.

305 *Re Costello Doors Ltd* (21 July 1995, unreported) HC, Murphy J.

306 *Re Costello Doors Ltd* (21 July 1995, unreported) HC, Murphy J at p 7 of the judgment.

307 *Re Vehicle Imports Ltd* (23 November 2000, unreported) HC, Roderick Murphy J at p 14 of the judgment.

308 *Re Capital Auto Group Ltd; Foster v Swords and Chambers* [2005] IEHC 434.

In that case, Peart J said he was not satisfied that this was the case and made a restriction order against the respondent.

[28.113] In *Re AMS IT Consultants Ltd; Keane v Kalsi and Kalsi*[309], Clarke J held that where the reason why a company had failed to produce audited accounts was because of a difference in opinion with their auditors as to the proper accounting treatment of expenditure incurred on the development of a product (the directors seeking its treatment as an asset), he was not satisfied that they were guilty of irresponsible refusal to take professional advice on board. Clarke J was at pains to stress, however, that the fact of such difficulties does not absolve directors from an obligation to resolve such issues and produce audited accounts although it does provide a partial explanation for a delay, provided it is not excessive.

[28.114] Where directors are made personally responsible for a company's debts under s 204 of the CA 1990 on the basis that they were responsible for the company not keeping proper books of account, it will almost certainly follow that they will be also restricted under s 150[310]. In *Re Greenmount Holdings Ltd; Stafford v O'Connor et al*[311], McGovern J found that although the respondents had failed to maintain proper books of account and had failed to file audited accounts, there were not sufficient grounds to make a restriction order with regard to two of the respondent directors because there was evidence to establish that they were making some attempts to regularise the situation, which attempts were impeded by inter-shareholder disputes which led to s 205 litigation.

II. Duties owed at common law

[28.115] Directors owe duties outside of the Companies Acts, and in *Kavanagh v Delaney*[312] Finlay Geoghegan J held that the first limb of Shanley J's test in *La Moselle* extended to requiring the court to have regard to the duties imposed on directors at common law and agreed with the general formulation of the duty of an individual director as set out by Jonathan Parker J in *Re Barings plc (No 5)*[313]: 'each individual director owes duties to the company to inform himself about its affairs and to join with his co-directors in supervising and controlling them'. Finlay Geoghegan J also agreed with the following three propositions also stated by Jonathan Parker J:

'(i) Directors had, both collectively and individually, a continuing duty to acquire and maintain a sufficient knowledge and understanding of the company's business to enable them properly to discharge their duties as directors.

(ii) Whilst directors were entitled (subject to the articles of association of the company) to delegate particular functions to those below them in the management chain, and to trust their competence and integrity to a reasonable extent, the exercise of the power of delegation did not absolve a director from the duty to supervise the discharge of the delegated functions.

(iii) No rule of universal application can be formulated as to the duty referred to in (ii) above. The extent of the duty, and the question whether it has been discharged,

309 *Re AMS IT Consultants Ltd; Keane v Kalsi and Kalsi* [2006] IEHC 12.

310 See *Re Ashclad Ltd and Forrest v Harrington and Culleton* [2000] IEHC 174, Geoghegan J; and *Mehigan v Duignan* [1997] 1 ILRM 171.

311 *Re Greenmount Holdings Ltd; Stafford v O'Connor et al* [2007] IEHC 246.

312 *Kavanagh v Delaney* [2004] IEHC 283.

313 *Re Barings plc (No 5)* [1999] 1 BCLC 433.

depended on the facts of each particular case, including the director's role in the management of the company.'

What has been referred to as the 'amplification' of the *La Moselle* criteria to encompass common law duties owed by directors has been accepted by the Supreme Court in *Re Tralee Beef & Lamb Ltd*[314] where Hardiman J said he was in agreement with the propositions of law enunciated by Finlay Geoghegan J concerning common law duties, endorsed by Keane[315].

[28.116] In *Mitek Ltd; Grace v Kachkar*[316], Fennelly J accepted that directors' common law duty to exercise skill and diligence in the discharge of their functions and the decision in *City Equitable Fire Insurance Ltd*[317] were of assistance in considering the scope of the duties of a director but also said 'but section 150 is not concerned with the breach of duties to the company alone. It is broader.' Fennelly J's reference to the decision in *City Equitable* as 'reflecting the more relaxed standards of business in another age' indicates that a respondent in a s 150 application can expect to be judged by a higher standard. Fennelly J went on to endorse the following passage from the decision of Clarke J in *Re Swanpool Ltd; McLoughlin v Lannen*[318]:

> 'One of the most important obligations of any director is to ensure that when a company is facing an insolvency situation, its assets are dealt with in accordance with law. For the reasons identified by McCracken J in *Gasco* the actions taken at such a time must be subject to particular scrutiny. While understanding the pressures, which may have been on the directors it does have to be noted that all directors in insolvent circumstances are likely to be subjected to significant pressure. It is their job to resist such pressure and to ensure that the company's assets are properly dealt with. Any significant failure in that regard has to be taken as demonstrating a level of irresponsibility sufficient to warrant making an order under the section.'

Fennelly J referred to the following classification of the principal settings for consideration of the responsibility of directors in a modern business as being 'particularly useful':

> '1. Issues involving compliance by the company with its formal obligations under the Companies Acts including keeping books and records, making returns, holding meetings and the like;
>
> 2. The commercial management of the company most particularly at the period when the company was insolvent or heading in that direction; and
>
> 3. Compliance by the directors with the obligations identified in *Frederick Inns* [reported at [1994] 1 ILRM 387] to ensure that once the company was facing

314 *Re Tralee Beef & Lamb Ltd* [2008] 3 IR 347. Although there, Hardiman J allowed an appeal from the making of a restriction order because 'having regard to the need to respect the [appellant's] Constitutional rights, not only to fair procedures to his good name and the associated right to earn a living by the practice of his profession, I do not consider that it was appropriate to "amplify" the criteria for restricting a director *after the hearing* [emphasis added]. Furthermore, I do not consider that the findings against the [appellant] which were in fact made could have been made without such amplification.'

315 Keane, *Company Law* (3rd edn, 2000).

316 *Mitek Ltd; Grace v Kachkar* [2010] IESC 31.

317 *City Equitable Fire Insurance Ltd* [1925] Ch 407.

318 *Re Swanpool Ltd; McLoughlin v Lannen* [2006] 2 ILRM 217 at 244.

> insolvency its assets were dealt with in a manner designed to ensure the proper distribution of those assets in accordance with insolvency law.'

As such, not only has the Supreme Court endorsed the amplification of the first *La Moselle* criterion of complying with the Companies Acts to directors' traditional common law duties, but also to directors' newer duty to have regard to the interests of creditors where a company is insolvent. Not only that, but Fennelly J went further[319], saying that the criteria for determining responsibility should not be limited:

> 'I would not be disposed to limit the matters to which regard should be had or to substitute standardised judicial criteria for the general words of the statute. The judgments of Murphy J, Shanley J, McGuinness and Clarke J show that compliance with statutory requirements may be relevant. On the other hand, whether in that respect or in respect of common law duties, it is not every criticism that enables one, in the words of McGuinness J, "*to categorise conduct as irresponsible.*" In one sense, it is obvious that a director must behave responsibly. In order to discharge his duties, he must, in the first instance, inform himself about the business and affairs of the company and about his own duties as a director. Circumstances will inform the nature and extent of these duties. Even non-executive directors of companies must be increasingly conscious in the times we live in that they cannot be mere ciphers or purveyors of votes at the whim of management. There was a time when even such a distinguished text as Gower (*The Principles of Modern Company Law* 3rd Ed. Stevens, London 1969 page 549) could state: "public opinion has come to recognise that directorships are little more than sinecures, requiring, at the most, attendance at occasional board meetings." The Act of 1990 itself evinces public concern that directorships involve real responsibility and that persons who do not conform at least to some generally acceptable minimum standards either should not, in the public interest, be permitted or should be restricted in regard to future holding of directorships.'

In *Careca Investments Ltd; Ferris v Farrell and Coady*[320], the failure by a director to take adequate steps to ensure the winding up of the company within a reasonable period of it ceasing to trade and in circumstances where he knew or ought to have known that it was insolvent, was found to be a sufficient reason to restrict a director. In this regard, the duty of a director of an insolvent company to wind up the company referred to by Costello J in *Re Shannonside Holdings*[321] was relied upon by Clarke J in making the order.

III. Compliance with obligations and duties in the case of groups

[28.117] The importance of complying with the Companies Acts and directors' common law duties means that the directors of a company must have regard to that company's interests, even if it is a wholly-owned subsidiary in a large group. Those were the circumstances considered in *Re 360Atlantic (Ireland) Ltd; O'Ferral v Coughlan et al*[322]. In that case, the insolvent company was a wholly-owned subsidiary in a worldwide group of companies. The operations of the company were financed, managed and controlled as part of the worldwide group and the applicant liquidator contended that the company was treated as a division of the group rather than a separate legal entity and that the directors had abdicated their responsibilities. Finlay Geoghegan J held that

319 *Mitek Ltd; Grace v Kachkar* [2010] IESC 31 at para 79.

320 *Careca Investments Ltd; Ferris v Farrell and Coady* [2005] IEHC 62.

321 *Re Shannonside Holdings* (20 May 1993, unreported) HC, Costello J.

322 *Re 360Atlantic (Ireland) Ltd; O'Ferral v Coughlan et al* [2004] 4 IR 266.

whilst directors can have regard to the wider group and that it is a proper exercise of their duties to have such regard, a line will be crossed where they effectively abdicate all decision-making in relation to the affairs of the company. The following passage from the learned judge's judgment is worth quoting *in extenso*:

> 'The fact that the Company is a wholly owned subsidiary within a worldwide group does not appear to alter the legal principles applicable to the duties of directors but rather to create a particular factual scenario which must be taken into account when considering the discharge of those duties.
>
> The Company was at all material times effectively in a start up situation. It appears to have been dependent entirely for the financing of the operation in which it participated on other companies within the group. Its operation was also closely intertwined with operations being carried out by other companies within the group. The business which it was intended to conduct does not appear to have had any real separate identity or potential from the overall business of the Atlantic division of the group.
>
> However, the Company had its separate corporate and legal identity. It had its individual employees and had its separate and distinct creditors. The employees and creditors do not appear to have had any rights against or access to other companies within the group. Each respondent agreed to act as a director of that separate corporate entity.
>
> In such a factual scenario it would appear totally permissible and indeed a proper exercise of the duties of directors in the interests of the Company for the directors to fully take into account and indeed even to follow the policies adopted for the entire group when managing the business of the Irish Company. However, notwithstanding such a factual scenario and indeed the almost total dependence of the Company on other companies within the group it does not seem permissible for directors of the Company to effectively abdicate all decision-making in relation to the affairs of the Company. They must be considered to remain under a duty to inform themselves about the affairs of the Company as distinct from any other corporate part of the group and to join with each other in supervising and controlling the affairs of the Company. Otherwise their position as directors is meaningless. In real terms the directors may have a very small margin of discretion in the decisions to be taken but this cannot absolve them of the obligation to take the decisions.
>
> Accordingly it appears to me that where a group corporate structure exists, such as in the present case, and the issue under s 150 of the Act of 1990 is whether a director of the wholly owned Irish subsidiary company acted responsibly in the sense of discharging the minimum common law duties, he must be able to establish at a minimum that he did inform himself about the affairs of the Irish subsidiary company as distinct from any other company within the group and together with his fellow directors that he did take real steps to consider and take decisions upon at least significant transactions to be entered into or projects undertaken by the Irish subsidiary company. There must be evidence of a real consideration by the directors of whether significant transactions or operations to be undertaken were desirable in the interest of the Irish subsidiary company or could be said to be for the benefit of the Irish subsidiary company. I readily recognise that in many instances the interests of the Irish subsidiary company may be so intertwined with the affairs of the group as a whole that the answer may be obvious. However, the fact that the answer is obvious does not appear to absolve the directors from at least addressing the question[323].'

---

323 *Re 360Atlantic (Ireland) Ltd; O'Ferral v Coughlan et al* [2004] 4 IR 266 at 276.

This approach was followed in the later case of *Re Mitek Ltd; Grace v Kachkar*[324] where the High Court restricted two directors of an Irish subsidiary in circumstances where Finlay Geoghegan J found that they did not, *inter alia*, take steps to supervise and control the subsidiary's financial affairs concerning the transfers of monies from it to other group companies or give proper consideration to the creation of security over the subsidiary's assets. The restriction order imposed by the High Court was upheld on appeal to the Supreme Court[325], where Fennelly J said:

> '89. The appellants have provided no evidence of independent consideration of the rights and property interests of the Irish company. It may indeed be normal and permissible, within a group of companies, to take account of group policy. That does not mean that the property of one company can simply be transferred, at the behest of the parent, to another company in the group. That would be to ignore entirely the separate existence of each company. The expression "inter-company and corporate overhead allocations and/or transfers" used by the appellants is meaningless in the absence of some form of objective and lawful justification. Even if there were proper documented and quantified justification, a large question would arise as to whether the Irish companies were in a position to make corporate group contributions when they were unable to meet their basic obligations to normal creditors under the scheme of arrangement …
>
> 90. I am satisfied that the learned trial judge was quite correct to hold that the appellants had not acted responsibly in this respect.
>
> 91. I am also satisfied that she was correct to hold that they had not acted responsibly in the granting of security in September 2002 to CCL Industries.'

IV. Compliance with obligations and duties in the case of non-executive directors

[28.118] The Companies Acts do not distinguish executive directors from non-executive directors[326]. The traditional position at common law is that there is no distinction between the duties owed by a non-executive director and those owed by a director. That approach can be seen in the following passage from the decision of Peart J in the High Court decision in *Re Dublin Sports Cafe Ltd; Fennell v Long and Wright*[327] where, commenting on the fact that one of the respondents was a non-executive director, he said:

> '… the fact that he was a non-executive director is neither here nor there. He was a director and as such shares the responsibility to ensure that all is in order, and I venture to suggest that in a company where there are but two directors, the obligation on the non-executive director is even higher than a non-executive director of a much larger company who may have certain identifiable and particular responsibilities within the company, but who may rely on other directors to carry out their particular functions, even though he would be remiss not to be concerned and satisfied as a member of the Board of directors that all the affairs of the company were being properly attended to.'

324 *Re Mitek Ltd; Grace v Kachkar* [2005] IEHC 63 and [2010] IESC 31.

325 *Re Mitek Ltd; Grace v Kachkar* [2010] IESC 31.

326 See Ch 13, *Corporate Governance: Management by the Directors*, at para **[13.038]**

327 *Re Dublin Sports Cafe Ltd; Fennell v Long and Wright* [2005] IEHC 458.

On the other hand, in *Re RMF (Ireland) Ltd; Kavanagh v Riedler*[328] Finlay Geoghegan J recognised the realities of commercial life when she said:

> 'The distinction between executive and non-executive directors is well established in commercial life, if not expressly recognised in the relevant company's legislation. In considering whether a person has acted responsibly whilst a director of the company, it appears to me that this court must recognise the distinction between executive and non-executive directors. A person may, from time to time, be appointed as a non-executive director to bring a particular expertise to a board of directors. Where this is done it appears appropriate to consider such person's conduct as a director *inter alia* in relation to any such particular agreement or purpose. However, every person who agrees to become a director of a company, whether executive or non-executive or for the purpose of bringing a particular skill to the board of directors, must discharge the general duty of a director which has been summarised by Jonathan Parker KJ in *Re Barings plc and others Secretary of State for Trade and Industry v Baker and others* (No 5) [1999] 1 BCLC 433 at p 435 and cited with approval in *Re Vehicle Imports Ltd* (Unreported, High Court, Murphy J, 23 November 2000) as follows: "Each individual director owed duties to the company to inform himself about its affairs and to join with his co-directors in supervising and controlling them."
>
> In relation to the obligation of a director to supervise and control the affairs of the company, it is well established that directors may collectively delegate to executives or management certain functions but that such delegation does not absolve the directors from their obligation of ultimate supervision. In considering whether a non-executive director has acted responsibly for the purposes of s 150 of the Act of 1990, it appears to me that the courts should also recognise that, in general, a non-executive director is entitled both to rely upon the executive directors carrying out what might be considered to be normal or management functions. There may be factual circumstances which will put a non-executive director on notice that he should not continue to rely upon information provided or upon executive duties being properly performed and require further action from him or her[329].'

[28.119] It is thought to be safe to say that the traditional position has been abandoned by the Irish courts in the context of s 150 applications. In the Supreme Court appeal to that decision, Finnegan J acknowledged that: 'the duties of directors *inter se* may differ and in particular the duties of a non-executive director may not be co-extensive with those of an executive director. Each case will turn upon its own circumstances: *Re Tralee Beef & Lamb Ltd; Kavanagh v Delaney et al* [2008] 3 IR 347.'

[28.120] In *Re Tralee Beef & Lamb Ltd; Kavanagh v Delaney et al*[330], the Supreme Court overturned a restriction order that had been made in relation to a non-executive director of a company who had been appointed to the board as a nominee of a company which managed funds invested in a business expansion scheme. On this point, Hardiman J said that 'there is a yet unmet need to make authoritative findings after full debate, as to the respective duties of an executive and a non-executive director and, perhaps, a non-executive director appointed … for a particular and specific purpose. But this has yet to occur.' Hardiman J went on to say that he was not prepared simply to

[328] *Re RMF (Ireland) Ltd; Kavanagh v Riedler* [2004] 3 IR 498.

[329] *Re RMF (Ireland) Ltd; Kavanagh v Riedler* [2004] 3 IR 498 at 503, 504.

[330] *Re Tralee Beef & Lamb Ltd; Kavanagh v Delaney et al* [2008] 3 IR 347.

apply the criteria in *Re Barings plc*[331] to all these classes of director or to assume that their common law duties are identical, and:

> 'I am slightly uneasy that, in this case, there may have been an assimilation in particular of the position of a non-executive director to that of an executive one. Such an approach might derive some support from the judgment of Roderick Murphy J in *Vehicle Imports Ltd (in liquidation)* (Unreported, High Court, 23rd November 2000), but it is not explicit and in any event there does not appear to have been argument on the topic of the duties of the different classes of director, mentioned above.
>
> I do not consider that this case, or that of *Vehicle Imports*, mandates the assimilation of the position of a non-executive director to that of an executive in terms of their common law duties. The position of a highly paid executive director of a vast Bank may be of limited use in considering the common law duties of a non-executive director, appointed to keep BES investors informed, of a small company.
>
> Clearly, in applying words of general application from a decision relating to so vast a corporation, care must be taken to avoid being unrealistic in relation to a small meat company in rural Ireland run effectively, so the evidence in this case goes, by one man …'

[28.121] The most recent Supreme Court decision to note the difference between executive and non-executive directors is *Re Mitek Ltd; Grace v Kachkar*[332], where Fennelly J said:

> '80. There will usually be a real difference between the duties of executive and non-executive directors. The latter will usually be dependant on the former for information about the affairs and of the finances of the company, a fact which will impose correspondingly larger duties on the former. *Tralee Beef and Lamb* was a notable example of a non-executive director with little role or influence in the company.'

(iv) Evidence of incompetence

[28.122] Whilst it remains the case that directors are not required to have formal qualifications, in the context of s 150 of the CA 1990, proof of incompetence can amount to irresponsible behaviour. As MacMenamin J said in *Re Cooke's Events Co Limited; Kavanagh v Cooke and Byrne*[333], after describing some of the company's business affairs:

> 'Regrettably the court can only conclude that having regard to the foregoing matters, the first named respondent's conduct was such as can only be regarded as being so incompetent as to amount to irresponsibility.
>
> … The first named respondent had a continuing duty to acquire and maintain a sufficient knowledge and understanding of the company's business to enable him properly to discharge his duty as a director.'

Whilst incompetent behaviour can result in a finding of irresponsibility, this will not always be so and the court retains a discretion as to when incompetence crosses the line and becomes irresponsibility[334]. As McGuinness J said in the Supreme Court in *Re*

---

331 *Re Barings plc* [1999] 1 BCLC 433.

332 *Re Mitek Ltd; Grace v Kachkar* [2010] IESC 31.

333 *Re Cooke's Events Co Ltd; Kavanagh v Cooke and Byrne* [2006] 1 ILRM 191.

334 *Re Colm O'Neill Engineering Services Ltd* (13 February 2004, ex tempore) HC, Finlay Geoghegan J; *Re Club Tivoli Ltd; Foster v Davis and May* [2005] IEHC 468.

Squash Ireland[335], 'commercial errors may have occurred; misjudgments may well have been made; but to categorise conduct as irresponsible I feel that one must go further than this'[336].

(v) Responsibility for insolvency and net deficiency of assets

[28.123] The decision in *La Moselle Clothing Ltd and Rosegem Ltd v Soualhi*[337] is itself instructive in considering whether respondents were responsible for the company's insolvency and the net deficiency of assets. In that case, the facts were that La Moselle and Rosegem were incorporated in 1984 and 1987, respectively, and Mr Soualhi owned 99% of the issued shares in La Moselle and was beneficial owner of Rosegem, also being a director of both. La Moselle was a wholesaler of ladies' and children's clothing and some 65% of its sales were to retail companies owned and controlled by Mr Soualhi. Rosegem was one such company, which operated a retail shop in Dublin that it rented from An Post. La Moselle financed the purchase of stock by entering into an agreement with a finance house called Cambridge Confirming Ltd ('CCL') which, in consideration for a fee/interest, discharged La Moselle's monthly liabilities on the understanding that all La Moselle's liabilities to CCL were discharged at each year end. This facilitated La Moselle's cash flow in the two seasons in the clothing industry. Initially, in 1989, the facility was £250,000 *per* season, but in 1993 this was reduced to £165,000 *per* season. As a result Mr Soualhi claimed that he had to close two retail shops in Galway and Limerick. Upon the facility being reduced, in June 1993 it was also agreed that La Moselle would clear all of its liabilities to CCL by 15 October 1993; CCL would issue a cheque for £20,000 to La Moselle on 1 August 1993 and it in turn would issue a cheque payable to CCL for £50,000 on 31 July 1993. Mr Soualhi stopped the La Moselle cheque, claiming this was because CCL had refused to honour its agreement to pay La Moselle £20,000. A further La Moselle cheque dated 31 August 1993 was also stopped and La Moselle did not clear its indebtedness to CCL by 15 October as *per* the agreement. A further agreement was entered into but the indebtedness was still not discharged and in November 1994 CCL presented a petition in respect of some £219,000 owed to it and, consequent upon that, a winding-up order was made in March 1995. La Moselle had ceased trading in November 1994 and Rosegem ceased in September 1994. Ms Soualhi's statement of affairs for La Moselle disclosed gross assets (including a claim for £650,000 against CCL) of £695,075 and gross liabilities of £487,891. Rosegem had no assets and had liabilities of over £48,000. The liquidator of La Moselle and Rosegem claimed that La Moselle continued to trade and to supply Rosegem when Mr Soualhi knew both were insolvent and the liquidator sought to establish that Mr Soualhi had acted 'irresponsibly, if not dishonestly'[338]. The liquidator pointed to the following matters in support of this: no effort had been made to stop trading or wind up Rosegem when it was clearly insolvent; the unsecured creditors of La Moselle did not include any trade suppliers and it was argued Mr Soualhi had organised his affairs so that he could secure payment of suppliers at the expense of the revenue and

335 *Re Squash Ireland* [2001] 3 IR 35.

336 See also *Re Money Markets International Stockbrokers Ltd* [2006] IEHC 350 (MacMenamin J).

337 *La Moselle Clothing Ltd and Rosegem Ltd v Soualhi* [1998] 2 ILRM 345.

338 *La Moselle Clothing Ltd and Rosegem Ltd v Soualhi* [1998] 2 ILRM 345 at 355.

other creditors such as his landlords and Dublin Corporation; La Moselle wrote off debts to other companies owned by Mr Soualhi in the sum of over £476,000; the liquidator had extreme difficulty in obtaining the books and records of both companies and that Mr Soualhi had a cavalier attitude to the books and records of Rosegem; credit card statements disclosed payments of just under £100,000 of which over £35,000 were in respect of payments to restaurants and night clubs which had been described as 'motor and travel expenses'; substantial sums had been drawn from Rosegem and La Moselle without provision for tax being made; in a period when an analysis of cash flow disclosed a deficit of £21,000 Mr Soualhi had paid himself a salary of some £106,800; and an analysis of La Moselle's current account and deposit accounts indicated that the reason why its cheque for £50,000 to CCL had been stopped was because there were no funds to meet it. Mr Soualhi disputed these matters[339] but Shanley J found his evidence unconvincing. Shanley J did not accept that Mr Soualhi was a reliable witness; he did not accept the reasons given for La Moselle stopping the cheque to CCL. Shanley J also found him to be less than frank in his explanation of Rosegem's relationship with its landlord in relation to rent outstanding and did not accept the statement of affairs to be reliable. Other conclusions drawn were: that La Moselle had traded when Mr Soualhi knew both companies to be insolvent; that La Moselle forgave debts owed by associated companies without any apparent reason or justification; that Mr Soualhi maintained a very busy and expensive lifestyle whilst the companies were insolvent and there was no evidence – other than oral – that any of the many exotic foreign trips made were business related and that even if they were the travel and associated costs showed a 'want of commercial probity on Mr Soualhi's part, having regard to the overall parlous financial state of La Moselle and Rosegem'[340]. Shanley J also found that the drawing made at a time when the companies were in very poor financial health were not the 'actions of a responsible director'[341]. In making an order under s 150(1), Shanley J said:

> 'In conclusion, I have no doubt whatsoever that Mr Soualhi traded at a time when he knew that Rosegem and La Moselle were insolvent. I am quite satisfied that he used monies due to the Collector-General and CCL to finance his trading activities and his travel. I have little doubt that he was aware that Rosegem and La Moselle could not trade and at the same time discharge their liabilities to the Collector-General and CCL. Such conduct was, in my view, improper conduct and if it was not to be described as actual dishonesty it was certainly irresponsible[342].'

Gratuitous or otherwise improper payments to persons were said to be a ground for making a restriction order in *Re Outdoor Advertising Services Ltd*[343].

[28.124] In *Re Verit Hotel and Leisure (Ireland) Ltd; Duignan v Carway et al*[344], McCracken J held that the use of monies deducted from employees' wages as PAYE and PRSI contributions to keep a company going where it is short of funds is totally irresponsible and is sufficient, in itself, to justify the making of a restriction order.

339 *La Moselle Clothing Ltd and Rosegem Ltd v Soualhi* [1998] 2 ILRM 345 at 356.

340 *La Moselle Clothing Ltd and Rosegem Ltd v Soualhi* [1998] 2 ILRM 345 at 359.

341 *La Moselle Clothing Ltd and Rosegem Ltd v Soualhi* [1998] 2 ILRM 345 at 359.

342 *La Moselle Clothing Ltd and Rosegem Ltd v Soualhi* [1998] 2 ILRM 345 at 359.

343 *Re Outdoor Advertising Services Ltd* (28 January 1997, unreported) HC, Costello J.

344 *Re Verit Hotel and Leisure (Ireland) Ltd; Duignan v Carway et al* (23 January 2002, unreported) HC, McCracken J.

[28.125] In *DCS Ltd; Henley and Henley*[345], MacMenamin J found that the fact that certain creditors had been preferred in the period between the cessation of trading and the decision to wind up the company was a ground for making a restriction order, noting that 'the effect of the actions of the first named respondent has been to reduce the assets of the company, thereby preventing them being applied *pro tanto* in discharge of the company's liabilities'.

(*vi*) *The lack of commercial probity*

[28.126] It is thought that the ground of 'lack of commercial probity or want of proper standards' involves a finding of dishonourable conduct which falls short of criminality. Undoubtedly, this is a nebulous ground which in the absence of any assistance or guidance as to the type of standards in question has been described as meaningless and, in truth, a test developed by the courts of the UK in the context of disqualification of directors[346]. Where the activities of a particular company are governed by a voluntary code of practice, the contravention of such a code could constitute the 'proper standards' which the directors ought to have met.

[28.127] Failing to recognise that a company is hopelessly insolvent and unlikely to be able to trade out of its difficulties can show a lack of commercial probity. In *Re James Murphy & Sons Sales (Dundalk) Ltd; Stafford v Murphy and Murphy*[347], Finlay Geoghegan J said:

> 'Regrettably, it appears to me that the respondent directors failed, at latest, in early 2008 to face up to their responsibilities as directors of a then insolvent company. Even when the twenty-one day notice of demand was served by the Landlord in April 2008, they did not take steps themselves to cease trading and wind up the company, at latest in early 2008 when they knew or ought to have known that the Company had no reasonable prospect of discharging debts, is indicative of a lack of commercial probity and precludes me from being satisfied that the respondents acted responsibly as directors in the conduct of the affairs of the company[348].'

[28.128] It is thought, however, that although this ground implies the absence of criminality, it can include breach of legal obligations arising under enactments other than the Companies Acts since such conduct has its own ground under the *La Moselle* criteria. So while not paying taxes can be a criminal offence, in *Re James Murphy & Sons Sales (Dundalk) Ltd; Stafford v Murphy and Murphy*[349] Finlay Geoghegan J said 'a Court should consider in relation to the facts of each case whether the failure to make tax returns or pay the taxes displays a lack of commercial probity or want of proper standards, as identified by Shanley J at para (e) in *La Moselle*'. Earlier, in *Re Digital Channel Partners Ltd*[350] Finlay Geoghegan J had said:

---

[345] *DCS Ltd; Henley and Henley* [2006] IEHC 179.

[346] Cahill, *Company Law Compliance and Governance* (2008, Bloomsbury Professional) at p 850.

[347] *Re James Murphy & Sons Sales (Dundalk) Ltd; Stafford v Murphy and Murphy* [2010] IEHC 115.

[348] *Re James Murphy & Sons Sales (Dundalk) Ltd; Stafford v Murphy and Murphy* [2010] IEHC 115, at para 27 of the judgment.

[349] *Re James Murphy & Sons Sales (Dundalk) Ltd; Stafford v Murphy and Murphy* [2010] IEHC 115.

[350] *Re Digital Channel Partners Ltd* [2004] 2 ILRM 35 at 40.

'There are, I think, two ways of looking at the failures to make tax returns. The failures to make tax returns are clearly in breach of the relevant Taxes Acts. Similarly, the failure to make the payments is in breach of the Taxes Acts. The mere fact that a company is in breach for, as in this case, a relatively limited period will not of itself, it seems to me, indicate that the directors of the company have acted either dishonestly or irresponsibly in such a way as to preclude my concluding that overall they acted responsibly and honestly in relation to the conduct of the affairs of this company. Unfortunately and inevitably where companies are under significant financial pressure, this may occur.

It appears to me that in relation to tax liabilities there must be something more than a limited failure over a period to indicate that the directors have acted irresponsibly. This has been put in a number of different ways and certainly insofar as there may be evidence that there either has been selective distribution or selective payment of liabilities of a company or indeed a total disregard of obligations to the Revenue, or even a decision to effectively seek to use taxation liabilities for the purpose of financing a company, that of itself will normally be indicative of the fact that directors have been acting at least irresponsibly.'

While it will not be every instance of failure to file or pay taxes that will justify the making of a restriction order,[351] evidence that directors deliberately withheld taxes to finance trading is a very serious matter. To deduct PAYE or PRSI from employees' salaries or VAT from customers (ie, so-called fiduciary taxes) and not pay it over to the Revenue Commissioners must surely be considered a more serious breach of the law than not paying the company's own taxes[352].

(*d*) *Otherwise just or equitable to make restriction order*

[28.129] There has been little focus on this particular issue in the reported judgments, largely because the evidence of dishonesty or irresponsibility (or lack of same) has usually determined the matter. As to the interaction of this ground with 'honesty' and 'responsibility', the following passage from the judgment of Shanley J in *Re La Moselle Clothing Ltd and Rosegem Ltd*[353] is instructive:

'Apart from satisfying the court that he as a director acted honestly and responsibly, the director must also satisfy the court that there are no other reasons why it would be just and equitable to restrict him from acting as a director of a company. It is to be noted that acting honestly and responsibly relates to "the conduct of the affairs of the company" and arguably such bears no relation to any period after the commencement of a winding-up or receivership of the particular company where the person may not be involved any further in the conduct of the affairs of the company. That the director must satisfy the court that there is no other reason why it would be just and equitable to restrict the director, allows the court to take into account, in my view, any relevant conduct of the director after the commencement of the winding-up or the receivership (for example failure to co-operate with the liquidator or receiver) in deciding whether or not to make an order under s 150(1) of the CA 1990[354].'

351 In *Re Derbar Developments Ltd; McGuinness v Dobbin and Lavelle* [2012] IEHC 144, Finlay Geoghegan J did not restrict two directors, although the company had failed to discharge in full its capital gains tax liability, some three years prior to the company being wound up.

352 *Re Verit Hotel and Leisure (Ireland) Ltd* [2002] IEHC 1 (McCracken J); *Re SPH Ltd* [2005] IEHC 152; *Re Newcastle Timber Ltd* [2001] 4 IR 586; and *Re Pineroad Distribution Ltd Stafford v Fleming and Fleming* [2007] IEHC 55.

353 *La Moselle Clothing Ltd and Rosegem Ltd v Soualhi* [1998] 2 ILRM 345.

354 *La Moselle Clothing Ltd and Rosegem Ltd v Soualhi* [1998] 2 ILRM 345 at 353.

This catch-all provision provides the court with maximum latitude in deciding to make a restriction order, notwithstanding that a director has established that he has acted both honestly and responsibly in relation to the conduct of the company's affairs. 

[28.130] In *Re CMC (Ireland) Ltd; Fennell v Carolan*[355], the question which fell to be considered was whether, having regard to the respondent directors' conduct *after* the commencement of the winding up, it was just and equitable to restrict them. There was evidence that the directors had not returned a forklift truck, belonging to the company, to the liquidator; had failed to cooperate generally with the liquidator, declining to meet with him for a considerable period of time; and that they had filed witness claims in litigation taken by the liquidator on behalf of the company that were at variance with the company's records. On those bases it was found that the directors had departed from the reasonable standards that can be expected of a director or former director during a winding up and that it was just and equitable that they be restricted.

The defence of being a nominee

[28.131] There are two other statutory defences that may be invoked by a director whom it is sought to restrict. These are contained in s 150(2) of the CA 1990, namely:

> '(b) Subject to paragraph (a), that the person concerned was a director of the company solely by reason of his nomination as such by a financial institution in connection with the giving of credit facilities to the company by such institution, provided that the institution in question has not obtained from any director of the company a personal or individual guarantee of repayment to it of the loan or other forms of credit advanced to the company, or
>
> (c) Subject to paragraph (a), that the person concerned was a director of the company solely by reason of his nomination as such by a venture capital company in connection with the purchase of, or subscription for, shares by it, in the first mentioned company.'

These are intended to save banks and other financial institutions from having their *bona fide* nominees being made restricted persons, and venture capital companies from being treated similarly. They are, on their face, self-explanatory. The question that does arise, however, is whether a director seeking to rely upon either defence in (b) and (c) must *also* satisfy the court that they acted *honestly and responsibly*? This was addressed in *Re Cavan Crystal Group Ltd*[356]. In that case, it was argued early in the application that one of the directors could rely upon (b) and another could rely upon (c). The director seeking to rely upon (c) could not do so, however, because the venture capital company concerned had not been prescribed as such as required by s 150(5) in order to come with the meaning of 'venture capital company' as used in s 150(2)(c). It appeared that the director seeking to rely upon the defence in (b) – Mr Lynch – had in fact been appointed by a 'financial institution'[357]. On the question of whether a nominee director was also required to establish that he acted 'honestly and responsibly', Murphy J said, *obiter*:

---

355 *Re CMC (Ireland) Ltd; Fennell v Carolan* [2005] IEHC 59.

356 *Re Cavan Crystal Group Ltd* (26 April 1996, unreported) HC, Murphy J.

357 Defined by s 150(5) of the CA 1990 as meaning: (a) a licensed bank, within the meaning of s 25 of the CA 1990, or, (b) a company the ordinary business of which includes the making of loans or the giving of guarantees in connection with loans.

> 'On the face of it one would expect to find three independent bases on which the applicant might escape the statutory sanction. In practice to date every director has sought to rely on paragraph (a) by proving that he acted "honestly and responsibly in relation to the conduct of the affairs of the company". Can a person in the position of Mr Lynch rely on paragraph (b) on the basis that he is that type of nominee director described therein? Counsel has pointed to the fact that paragraph (b) is expressed to be "subject to paragraph (a)" so that in any event it would appear that whatever the status of the particular director he must always prove that he acted both honestly and responsibly. So construed it would seem to me that articles (b) and (c) are entirely meaningless. If a director has satisfied the court under paragraph (a) he does not have to rely on paragraph (b) and if notwithstanding the circumstances to which he became a director he must comply with the provisions of paragraph (a) there is no purpose served by relying on his special status. If it were necessary for me to resolve this conflict I would prefer to conclude that the legislature intended that where a person concerned established that he fell within the particular category of director designated in paragraphs (b) or (c) and it was not necessary for him to establish that he acted honestly or responsibly[358].'

In the end it was unnecessary for Murphy J to base his decision 'on any such dubious interpretation of the section' because he found that the directors had both acted honestly and responsibly and so neither was restricted[359]. In this respect, s 150(2) is unhappily drafted; it is hard to see how the legislature could possibly have intended the interpretation that Murphy J would have placed upon the subsection, if forced to do so. Nevertheless, if paras (b) and (c) are to have any meaning, Murphy J's interpretation should prevail. Ideally, all persons – regardless of whether they were nominees or otherwise – ought to have acted 'honestly' in relation to a company's affairs; a case can, however, be made for relieving nominees from the requirement to act 'responsibly' in relation to a company's affairs to the extent that this recognises the commercial reality that their primary duty is to their appointor[360].

The defence of delay and estoppel

[28.132] Before leaving defences that may be invoked by directors when an application is brought against them, the non-statutory defence of *delay* may be noted. Section 56(2) of the CLEA 2001 provides that a liquidator must, not later than five months or such other time as the court may allow, after making a report to the ODCE, apply to the court to have the directors of an insolvent company restricted. Where a liquidator does not bring an application within that timeframe, it has been held that he will not be precluded from bringing an application although he may have committed an offence under s 56(3)[361].

[28.133] It was recognised by O'Donovan J in *Re Verit Hotel and Leisure (Ireland) Ltd; Duignan v Carway et al*[362] that an inordinate and inexcusable delay in proceeding with

[358] *Re Cavan Crystal Group Ltd* (26 April 1996, unreported) HC, Murphy J at pp 8, 9 of the judgment.

[359] Another director conceded that s 150(1) applied to him and did not seek to argue that the statutory defences in s 150(2)(a)–(c) applied to him.

[360] On the duties of nominee directors, see Ch 15, *The Duties of Directors and Other Officers*, at para **[15.046]** *et seq*.

[361] *E Host Europe Ltd; Coyle v O'Brien et al* [2003] 2 IR 627.

[362] *Re Verit Hotel and Leisure (Ireland) Ltd; Duignan v Carway et al* (27 July 2000, unreported) HC, O'Donovan J.

an application may require its dismissal where to allow it to proceed would be against the balance of justice. In that case, application was first brought on 6 December 1994 but not proceeded with until some five years later. It was noted that in that period there had been constitutional proceedings in being brought by the directors and a claim for damages brought by the liquidator. O'Donovan J found, in the circumstances of the case, that whilst there had been some unreasonable delays, overall the delay was both inordinate and inexcusable. The learned judge noted, however, that that was not the end of the matter and that the Supreme Court had held in *Primor plc v Stokes Kennedy Crowley*[363] that 'even where the delay has been both inordinate and inexcusable the court must exercise a judgment on whether, in its discretion, on the facts the balance of justice was in favour of or against the case proceeding'. O'Donovan J held that there was no reason why the decision in that case should not apply to applications brought under s 150(1) of the CA 1990[364]. O'Donovan J noted that the respondent directors did not claim to have suffered specific prejudice but went on to note that it was claimed that they had suffered a general prejudice arising from the fact that the motion brought against them implied that they were not honest or responsible people, but he also rejected this. In exercising his discretion, O'Donovan J held:

> 'As to the balance of convenience, I am also influenced by the fact that the public interest requires that unsuitable persons should not be directors. In that context I think that the public interest would overcome any delay in this case. I accept, as [counsel for the respondent-directors] said, that perhaps a conscientious liquidator might have been more diligent in bringing these proceedings. However, as I have said, I do not think that the delay, however reprehensible it might be, is going to affect the respondents' capacity to get a fair trial if the motion proceeds. In my view public interest demands it.'

O'Donovan J dismissed the respondent directors' motion to dismiss the application on the grounds of delay. This decision was upheld on appeal to the Supreme Court[365], where Fennelly J said that 'prejudice' would not be presumed and held that O'Donovan J had correctly exercised his discretion. Only in the most exceptional of cases involving specific prejudice will delay in prosecuting a s 150 application justify dismissal.

[28.134] The defence of delay has, however, been successful in a number of subsequent cases[366]. In *Re Supreme Oil Company Ltd; Hughes v Duffy & Hanratty*[367], it was held by Finlay Geoghegan J that the respondents had a right to a fair and speedy trial of the issue as to whether their normal rights to become directors and take part in the formation of companies should be restricted or taken away. In relation to deciding where the balance of justice lay, the learned judge suggested that in *Duignan v Carway*[368] Fennelly J had:

---

363 *Primor plc v Stokes Kennedy Crowley* [1996] 2 IR 459.

364 In *Re Manlon Trading Ltd* [1995] 4 All ER 14 the English Court of Appeal held that the 'inordinate and inexcusable delay giving rise to serious prejudice' test applied to proceedings for disqualification under the English Company Directors Disqualification Act 1986 subject to its modification by an additional consideration, namely the need to protect the public. Interestingly, O'Donovan J also stressed the public interest.

365 *Re Verit Hotel and Leisure (Ireland) Ltd; Duignan v Carway et al* [2001] IESC 74, [2001] 4 IR 550.

366 *Re Knocklofty House Hotel Ltd; Kelly v O'Keeffe and O'Keeffe* [2005] 4 IR 497 and *Re Supreme Oil Company Ltd; Hughes v Duffy & Hanratty* [2005] 1 IR 571.

367 *Re Supreme Oil Company Ltd; Hughes v Duffy & Hanratty* [2005] 1 IR 571.

368 *Duignan v Carway* [2001] 4 IR 550 at 561.

'… envisaged two separate circumstances in which the court might determine the balance of justice was against proceeding with an application under s 150 of the Act of 1990:-

(i) where the delay is such as to put a just hearing at risk; and

(ii) where the delay would render it unjust to permit the application to proceed by reason of being in breach of the respondents' constitutional right to fair procedures including the right to have determined whether their normal rights to become directors and promote and take part in the formation of companies should be limited, restricted or taken away by reason of their prior involvement as directors of an insolvent company[369].'

[28.135] Another non-statutory defence is that of *estoppel*. Having unsuccessfully sought to rely upon the defence of delay, the respondent directors of Re Verit Hotel and Leisure (Ireland) Ltd contended in different proceedings, *Re Verit Hotel and Leisure (Ireland) Ltd; Duignan v Carway et al*[370], that the liquidator was *estopped* from bringing the s 150 application because it was closely interrelated to other proceedings that had been settled. As noted above[371], this defence was also rejected by McCracken J who said that an estoppel could not arise because a s 150 application was a matter between the court and the directors, not between the directors and the liquidator.

Post-order relief on just and equitable grounds

[28.136] Where application is brought against a director of an insolvent company and the director is unsuccessful in seeking to invoke the defences contained in s 150(2), and an order is made against him, he has a right of appeal to the Supreme Court[372]. If the Supreme Court confirms the restriction order, or where the High Court's order is not appealed, a restricted director may apply for relief under s 152(1) of the CA 1990. This provides:

'A person to whom section 150 applies may, within not more than one year after a declaration has been made in respect of him under that section, apply to the court for relief, either in whole or in part, from the restrictions referred to in that section or from any order made in relation to him under section 151 and the court may, if it deems it just and equitable to do so, grant such relief on whatever terms and conditions it sees fit.'

An applicant under this section is required to give not less than 14 days' notice of his intention to seek relief to the liquidator of all companies, the insolvency of which caused him to be restricted[373]. Upon receiving such notification, the liquidator is obliged to notify forthwith such creditors and contributories of the company as have been notified to him or known to him[374]. Where a liquidator fails to notify such persons, the application is likely to be adjourned to permit notification[375]. On the hearing of an

---

369 *Re Supreme Oil Company Ltd; Hughes v Duffy & Hanratty* [2005] 1 IR 571 at 575.

370 *Re Verit Hotel and Leisure (Ireland) Ltd; Duignan v Carway et al* (23 January 2002, unreported) HC, McCracken J.

371 See para **[28.085]** *ante*.

372 As occurred in *Re Squash (Ireland) Ltd* [2001] 3 IR 35.

373 Section 152(2) of the CA 1990.

374 Section 152(3) of the CA 1990. Failure to comply by the liquidator is an offence, which renders him liable to fine: sub-s (5).

375 See *Re Ferngara Associates Ltd; Robinson v Forrest* (11 February 1999, unreported) HC, Laffoy J at pp 4, 5 of the judgment.

application for relief, the liquidator and any relevant creditor or contributory has a right to appear and give evidence[376].

[28.137] The first application made under s 152 was in the matter of *Re Ferngara Associates Ltd; Robinson v Forrest*[377]. In that case, the High Court (Shanley J) had made an order pursuant to s 150(1) that the applicant should be restricted on the basis that it was not satisfied that he had acted responsibly in relation to the conduct of the affairs of the insolvent company of which he had been a director. Two separate applications brought by the liquidator under s 297A (reckless trading) and s 298 (misfeasance) were compromised by the liquidator with the leave of the court. Five months after the order had been made (although its operation had been stayed by Shanley J), the applicant brought an application under s 152. On the preliminary questions of procedure, Laffoy J said that on a s 152 application, the liquidator in discharge of his obligations under s 152(3) should personally swear an affidavit that he has notified all creditors and contributories. Laffoy J went on to compare the court's powers under s 152 with those under s 150(1) and noted that, unlike the mandatory provisions of s 150(1), s 152 gives the court a very broad discretion, allowing it to wholly negative the effect of a s 150 order, the only criterion being that such should be 'just and equitable'.

The applicant for relief contended that to grant relief was just and equitable on the following grounds. First, he bore a lesser level of culpability for the company's failure than his co-director. It was pointed out that Shanley J had found he had acted honestly and he claimed he had only acted irresponsibly because he was overborne by his co-director who had taken most management decisions. Second, he had personally contributed over £200,000 to meet the claims of the company's creditors and that this indicated that he had acted responsibly after the company was wound up. Third, he was, since the winding up, trading through another company of which he was a director and that this company's liabilities to the Revenue Commissioners were up to date. Fourth, his sole means of livelihood was derived from the business carried on by the new company, which had five employees and that if the restrictions were imposed, his livelihood and those of his employees would be seriously jeopardised.

The Revenue Commissioners opposed the applicant being granted relief, taking issue with the applicant on the facts as stated by him. It was first contended that although the applicant had ultimately acknowledged that he acted irresponsibly he had, initially, not cooperated with the liquidator; Laffoy J would not take this into consideration in the absence of evidence from the liquidator or the Revenue Commissioners. Second, it was contended that the applicant deserved no credit for discharging the company's debts as his motive was to assuage certain creditors with whom he wished to continue to deal. Third, it was pointed out that the company had been run as a fraudulent company, to which the applicant responded that he was less culpable than his co-director. Fourth, the revenue could not – in the absence of a revenue audit – verify that all taxes owed by the new company had been paid up to date. Finally, it was said that although Shanley J had indicated that the applicant could later apply under s 152, he had not indicated that the restriction would be removed.

[376] Section 152(4) of the CA 1990.

[377] *Re Ferngara Associates Ltd; Robinson v Forrest* (11 February 1999, unreported) HC, Laffoy J.

[28.138] Laffoy J did not accept the Revenue Commissioners' contention that, in principle, the sanction in s 150 would be devalued if a restricted director was relieved from the restriction imposed after six months. The revenue indicated that the policy it proposed adopting would be not to support a s 152 application unless the restriction was in place for at least two and a half years *and* that all of the company's debts had been fully discharged. Laffoy J said:

> 'This case, in my view, is an exceptional case, which falls to be determined on its own peculiar facts. It weighs heavily with me that the late Shanley J who dealt with the respondent's application for leave to compromise the substantive proceedings was aware of the issues of law and fact in the substantive proceedings and approved the compromise and who determined the applications under s 150 against both [directors] considered it appropriate to stay the order against the applicant for six months and to entertain the applicant's application for relief under s 152, which came before the court within the six month period, to the extent that he adjourned the matter to enable the liquidator to deal with the procedural shortcoming and, that, significantly, he extended the stay on the operation of the order. In the light of that factor and having regard to the facts as established on this application, for my part, I consider that it would be just and equitable to give the applicant relief in whole against the restriction contained in the order of 22 January 1998. In particular, it seems to me that the deterrent value of the restriction order highlighted in the passage from the judgment of Murphy J quoted above and such protection as it affords to current and prospective creditors of enterprises in which the applicant is or may become involved will not be undermined if the restriction is lifted now because, on the evidence, I am satisfied that the applicant has learned an expensive lesson from his involvement in the company[378].'

It is opined that it was indeed an exceptional case. The applicant's apparent ability to pursue his livelihood as a sole trader would seem to be very significant, especially when taken with Murphy J's comments in *Business Communications Ltd v Baxter and Parsons*[379], that the amount to which a new company must be capitalised – then £20,000 – must represent a very modest sum. The general rule must be that the courts will be loath, in the absence of compelling reasons (perhaps even to the extent of requiring new evidence as to the restricted director's behaviour or the fate of the employees of a business that *must* operate through the medium of a limited liability company) to set at nought a restriction order.

[28.139] Since the decision in *Re Ferngara Associates Ltd; Robinson v Forrest*, the courts have, on the occasions where s 152 of the CA 1990 has been considered, continued to accept that it confers a very wide discretion on the court[380]. In *Re Xnet Information Systems Ltd; Higgins v Stafford*[381], a director who had been restricted sought relief under s 152. He argued that he was impecunious but had nevertheless entered into an agreement with the liquidator to repay certain sums of money; that he had endured hardship as a result of the restriction; that he had not been found to have acted dishonestly; that he had endured a stigma; and that having regard to his conduct

[378] *Re Ferngara Associates Ltd; Robinson v Forrest* (11 February 1999, unreported) HC, Laffoy J at pp 12, 13 of the judgment.

[379] *Business Communications Ltd v Baxter and Parsons* (21 July 1995, unreported) HC, Murphy J.

[380] *Re CMC (Ireland) Ltd; Carolan and Cosgrave v Fennell* [2005] IEHC 340. See Conroy, 'Recent Developments on the Restriction of Directors' (2006) BLR 63 at 68.

[381] *Re Xnet Information Systems Ltd; Higgins v Stafford* [2006] IEHC 289.

since the making of the restriction order which was over two years previous, the value of the restriction order would not be undermined if the restriction was lifted. The Director of Corporate Enforcement had been added as a notice party and he opposed the granting of relief and argued that if it was granted, limited relief should be granted only and subject to certain conditions. By any standard, the proposed conditions[382] were so onerous that any relief granted under s 152 that was so subject would surely be a Pyrrhic victory for the applicant[383]. O'Neill J granted partial relief to the applicant, accepting his impecuniosity and inability to acquire capital, and reducing the capitalisation requirement to €7,500. The learned judge also ordered that the applicant notify the Director of the name of any company of which he becomes a director or secretary or takes up a position and gave the Director liberty to apply to vary any conditions. In arriving at his decision, the factors that O'Neill J had regard to in exercising his discretion were:

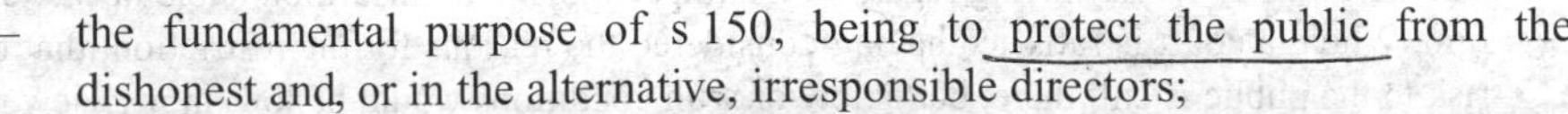

- the fundamental purpose of s 150, being to protect the public from the dishonest and, or in the alternative, irresponsible directors;
- the recognition by the Oireachtas that an application for relief could be brought after just one year following the making of a restriction order which evinced it was 'intent on the relatively speedy rehabilitation of directors';
- the fact that the statutory provision cannot be applied in such a way as to work an invidious discrimination against impecunious persons;
- the reasons which led to the restriction: the court must be satisfied that the risk to third parties is of such a low order as to safely lift in whole or in part the order;
- where an applicant's dishonest or irresponsible conduct was of an appalling nature, it may not be safe to remove the restriction early;
- the overriding principle is that the court must be satisfied that the public will not be harmed by the total removal or partial removal with conditions of the order;
- the court should have regard to the deterrent effect of the order;
- the court should have regard to the applicant's conduct since the winding up;
- the court should have regard to the hardship suffered by the applicant; and
- the court should have regard to the 'need' or 'interest' that the applicant has for having the restriction removed.

---

[382] The conditions included: that he be permitted to be a director of one private company limited be shares only; that the company be identified to the ODCE; that the company be capitalised to €40,000 instead of €63,487; that he continue to be in the s 153 register; that s 155 continue to apply to the company; that the company had a majority of directors independent to him or his wife or any relative and that no business be conducted at any meeting where the independent directors were not in the majority; that the company's cheques have two signatures at least one of whom was an independent director; that the applicant could not be an approved signatory on the bank account; and that the notice party have liberty to apply to vary the conditions.

[383] Of the conditions relating to independent directors and voting restrictions, O'Neill J said that these in his view 'would in the circumstances of the applicant be of such an embarrassing and burdensome nature as to probably defeat any prospect of launching a successful company' (at p 26 of the judgment).

In relation to the 'need' or 'interest' that an applicant must show, O'Neill J said:

> 'In this regard there cannot be any particular prescriptive test. This is for two reasons. Firstly, there is the very broad discretion given in s 152(1) which ought not to be cut down by judicial interpretation. Secondly, one has to have regard to the fact that a restricted director with ample funds is not in any way subject to any such requirement, to demonstrate a need for or interest in the removal of the restriction. An applicant must demonstrate some "need" or "interest" which requires the removal of the restriction in whole or in part. It would not be sufficient for an applicant, to seek the remedy simply to restore his reputation, where he had no plan or intention to re-engage in trade through the medium of a limited company. Hence in my view whilst the court should have regard to the "need" and/or "interest" these, on their own, should not be decisive factors in the determination of the application.
>
> In this context it is clear that an applicant must satisfy the court that the capitalisation threshold in s 150(3) is having regard to his impecuniosity an insurmountable obstacle to him. Where a court is satisfied having considered the reasons for the restriction, that the risk to the public is still there, but is low or with conditions would be low, in my view the appropriate course to follow is to reduce the capitalisation threshold to a level which is attainable to the applicant in question.'

[28.140] The court will allow the Director of Corporate Enforcement to be joined as a notice party in s 152 applications. In *Re CMC (Ireland) Ltd; Carolan and Cosgrave v Fennell*[384], Finlay Geoghegan J considered that there was jurisdiction to join the Director of Corporate Enforcement despite the fact that s 152(4) of the CA 1990 did not give the Director an express right to be heard, unlike the liquidator, creditors or contributories. In so finding, Finlay Geoghegan J distinguished her own decision in *Re Document Imaging Systems Ltd*[385], which concerned s 150(4A) of the CA 1990, and held that s 152(4) did not preclude the court from joining the Director as a notice party if it considers it necessary or desirable in the interests of justice to do so on the facts of the application.

[28.141] In *Re MDN Rochford Construction Ltd; Fennell v Rochford and Rochford*[386], MacMenamin J gave the following indication of the factors that a court might consider in an application under s 152:

> 'An application under this section must of course be made on notice, and there being satisfactory evidence before a court that it would be just and equitable to make such an order having regard to the interests of the public and other creditors. One factor, to which a court might have regard, may be as to whether there has been other evidence of want of duty on the part of the respondents. A further factor might be whether the respondents have taken steps to educate themselves as to the financial realities of running a company and their duties as directors. In the light of the evidence as to the respondents' honesty, and if there were sufficient proof of the respondents' ability competently to conduct the affairs of a company under the Act, a court might be prepared to entertain such application brought under section 152.'

As such, evidence of rehabilitation, through the appreciation of finance and company law on the part of restricted directors, might influence the court in granting relief under s 152 of the CA 1990.

---

384 *Re CMC (Ireland) Ltd; Carolan and Cosgrave v Fennell* [2005] IEHC 340.

385 *Re Document Imaging Systems Ltd* [2005] 3 IR 103.

386 *Re MDN Rochford Construction Ltd; Fennell v Rochford and Rochford* [2009] IEHC 397.

The enforcement of restriction orders

[28.142] The enforcement of the provisions on restricted directors is achieved in two ways, namely: against the director (civilly and criminally); and against those persons in the restricted company who become involved with a restricted director.

(*a*) *Breach of a s 150 order by restricted directors – criminal sanction*

[28.143] The penalty for acting contrary to the provisions of Chapter 1 is contained in s 161(1) of the CA 1990, the relevant part of which provides:

> 'Any person who, in relation to any company, acts in a manner or capacity which, by virtue of being a person to whom section 150 applies … he is prohibited from doing shall be guilty of an offence.'

This offence is punishable in accordance with s 240 of the CA 1990. Where convicted of such an offence, the person is also subject to automatic disqualification[387].

(*b*) *Breach of a s 150 order by restricted directors – civil sanctions*

[28.144] Where a restricted director acts contrary to the restrictions imposed upon him, he may well feel the disapproval in his pocket, since the *restricted company* can recover any consideration paid to him for services rendered: s 163(2) of the CA 1990. Furthermore, by s 163(3), if a restricted director becomes involved in a company which does not meet the requirements set out in s 150(3) and that company goes into insolvent liquidation, then on the application of a liquidator or creditor, the court can make the restricted director *personally liable* without limitation for the debts of the company incurred in the period in which he was acting in such manner or capacity[388]. In relation to proceedings brought under either s 163(2) or (3) the court may, having regard to the circumstances of the case and if it considers it just and equitable to do so, grant relief in whole or in part from the liability which would otherwise attach, subject to such conditions as it sees fit[389]. However, a director who has been restricted ought to ponder long and hard before acting contrary to the declaration made against him.

(*c*) *Criminal sanctions for officers of companies who act in accordance with the directions or instructions of restricted directors*

[28.145] Section 164(1) of the CA 1990 makes it an offence for officers[390] to act in accordance with the directions or instructions of a restricted director, knowing that such person is restricted. A person convicted of an offence under this section shall be deemed to be subject to a disqualification order from the date of conviction[391].

---

387 Section 161(2) of the CA 1990.

388 See Ch 5, *Disregarding Separate Legal Personality*, at para **[5.086]**.

389 Section 163(5) of the CA 1990.

390 Section 164(1) applies to 'a director or other officer or a member of a committee of management or trustee of any company'.

391 Section 164(2) of the CA 1990.

(*d*) *Civil sanctions for officers of companies with which restricted directors become involved which fail to comply with the requirements in s 150(3)*

[28.146] The officers of a company with which a restricted director becomes involved and does not comply with the requirements in s 150(3) of the CA 1990 can in certain circumstances be made personally liable for that company's debts. This is provided for in s 163(4). Before such officers can be made personally liable, it must be established that (a) the company received a notification under s 155(5); (b) the officer in question knew or ought to have known that the company had been so notified; (c) the requirements in s 155(3) were not fulfilled within a reasonable period; and (d) the company is subsequently wound up and at the commencement of such winding up is unable to pay its debts. Upon such being proved, s 163(4) provides that the court may:

> '... on the application of the liquidator or any creditor or contributory of the company, declare that any person who was an officer of the company while the company so carried on business ... shall be personally responsible, without any limitation of liability, for all or any part of the debts or other liabilities of the company as the court may direct.'

As in the case of liability imposed under s 163(2) and (3), the court may grant relief where in the circumstances of the case it considers it just and equitable to do so[392].

[28.147] Furthermore, a conviction under s 164 will also render a convicted person liable be held to be personally responsible under s 165 of the CA 1990 for the debts of the company incurred while they were acting, subject to their right to apply for just and equitable relief[393].

[F] Disqualification of Directors and Other Officers[394]

[28.148] A disqualification order is an altogether more severe remedy than a restriction order. A disqualification order is defined by s 159 of the CA 1990 as being:

> 'an order under this Part [ie, Part VII of the CA 1990] that the person against whom the order is made shall not be appointed or act as an auditor, director or other officer[395], receiver, liquidator or examiner or be in any way, whether directly or indirectly, concerned or take part in the promotion, formation or management of any company, or any society registered under the Industrial and Provident Societies Acts, 1893 to 1978.'

Accordingly, irrespective of how much another company is capitalised, a person against whom a disqualification order is made can have no involvement, whatsoever, in the promotion, formation or management of any company for the duration of the disqualification period. Discretionary disqualification (ie, upon application being made to court and the court being satisfied as to the proof of certain matters, making a disqualification order) existed before the CA 1990 in s 184 of the CA 1963[396]. The

---

392 Section 163(5) of the CA 1990.

393 Section 165(2) of the CA 1990.

394 For a comprehensive review of the law on disqualification, see, generally, Cahill, *Company Law Compliance and Enforcement* (2008, Bloomsbury Professional) chs 20–23.

395 'Officer' is defined by s 159 of the CA 1990 as including 'any director, shadow director or secretary'.

396 Such an order was made in *Re Kelly's Carpetdrome Ltd* (1 July 1983, unreported) HC, Costello J.

grounds for disqualification were greatly extended by Chapter 2 of Part VII of the CA 1990 and a considerable increase in the numbers of applications to have persons disqualified was expected by most commentators. The expected increase never materialised, and the numbers of persons against whom a disqualification order had been made in 1994 was in single figures, a fact noted by the *Gallagher Company Law Review Group* which reported in November 1998. The Gallagher Group made 10 recommendations on the area of disqualification and restriction, the thrust being that disqualification was a more appropriate sanction for the *phoenix syndrome* than was restriction[397]. The principal recommendations were for the establishment of an executive unit in the Department of Jobs, Enterprise and Innovation to apply, in appropriate cases, for the disqualification of directors of insolvent companies and that liquidators and receivers should be obliged to report appropriate cases to the executive unit. Following the McDowell Group's Report, the CLEA 2001 has made a number of changes not only to the law on the restriction of directors, but also to disqualification. In particular, the office of the Director of Corporate Enforcement can be seen as meeting the need identified by the Gallagher Group, although the powers, responsibilities and functions of the Director are far more comprehensive than were ever envisaged for the considerably more low key 'executive office'.

[28.149] Whereas at 31 December 1999 the total number of persons who stood disqualified under s 160 was two[398] as at 31 December 2011, 3,651 people were recorded as having been disqualified[399]. 

[28.150] Here, the following issues are considered in disqualification:

1. Deemed disqualification following conviction for fraud or dishonesty;
2. The persons who may be disqualified and the meaning of company;
3. The *locus standi* to apply for a disqualification order and the role of the Director of Corporate Enforcement
4. Notice to persons where application is to be made to disqualify;
5. The grounds for discretionary disqualification;
6. The nature of the disqualification order and the period of disqualification;
7. Relief for the disqualified;
8. The enforcement of disqualification orders.

Deemed disqualification following conviction for fraud or dishonesty[400]

[28.151] Where a person is convicted on indictment of any indictable offence in relation to a company, or involving fraud or dishonesty, then during the period of five years from the date of conviction[401] he shall be *deemed* to be subject to a disqualification order for

397 See Courtney, *Company Law Review, 1995* (1996, Round Hall Sweet & Maxwell) at p 4.

398 *Companies Report 1999*, at p 45.

399 See *Companies Registration Office Report 2011* at p 33.

400 See generally, Cahill, *Company Law Compliance and Enforcement* (2008, Bloomsbury Professional) at Ch 20.

401 Or such other period as the court, on the application of the prosecutor and having regard to all of the circumstances of the case, may order.

that period and shall not, for that period, be appointed or act as auditor, director or other officer, receiver, liquidator or examiner or be in any way, directly or indirectly, concerned or take part in the promotion, formation or management of any company[402]. This is provided for by s 160(1) of the CA 1990 and it will be noted that conviction of a relevant indictable offence will alone, and without the need for any judicial intervention, result in such a person's disqualification. The English Court of Appeal held in *Re Cedarwood Productions Ltd*[403] that the making of a disqualification order against a director on conviction for a relevant indictable offence did not bar discretionary disqualification proceedings being brought against the same director. The basis for this decision was that the court held that a deemed disqualification is a penal sanction against the director in person for proven misconduct whereas a discretionary disqualification order was aimed at protecting the public.

[28.152] The basis for deemed or automatic disqualification is that a person 'is convicted on indictment of any indictable offence in relation to a company, or involving fraud or dishonesty'. This potentially involves hundreds of offences, not only the 150 plus indictable offences under the Companies Acts but also indictable offences arising under other enactments which are 'in relation to a company' or which, having no relationship to a company, involve fraud or dishonesty. This is arguably so broad as to open the possibility that automatic disqualification following a conviction for a particular indictable offence would be a disproportionate and unconstitutional consequence. Indeed, the implication in s 167 of the CA 1990 that a prescribed officer of the court will be able readily to determine whether a person has been convicted of an offence 'which has the effect of his being deemed to be subject to a disqualification order' so as to be able to notify the registrar of companies, may be questioned[404]. Section 166 of the CA 1990 empowers the court to require directors charged with certain offences or civil proceedings to disclose details of their directorships and other details[405].

[28.153] Section 160(1A) of the CA 1990[406] also provides for the deemed disqualification of a person who either:

(a) fails to state in the statement to the registrar of companies (on incorporation) or notification on change in directors that he is disqualified in another jurisdiction and to provide the other details as required by s 3A of the C(A)A 1982[407] and s 195(8) of the CA 1963[408]; or

(b) in purported compliance with the foregoing provisions, permits either statement or notification to be accompanied by a statement signed by him which is false or misleading in a material respect.

---

402 Or any society registered under the Industrial and Provident Societies Acts 1893 to 1978.

403 *Re Cedarwood Productions Ltd* [2001] TLR 450.

404 The Companies Act 1990 (Parts IV and VII) Regulations 1991 (SI 209/1991) designate the appropriate Registrar or clerk of the court as prescribed officers for this purpose.

405 See Cahill, *Company Law Compliance and Enforcement* (2008, Bloomsbury Professional) at pp 940–942.

406 As inserted by s 42 of the CLEA 2001.

407 As inserted by s 101 of the CLEA 2001.

408 As inserted by s 91 of the CLEA 2001.

These sections require disclosure of any disqualification orders made by a foreign state. In such a case the person is deemed to be disqualified from the delivery of such to the registrar of companies. The period of the person's disqualification in such circumstances will equate with the outstanding period of the foreign disqualification and, if disqualified in more than one foreign state, the greater period outstanding.

Discretionary disqualification: the persons who may be disqualified and the meaning of 'company'

[28.154] Any 'person' who involves themselves in the affairs of a company and whose behaviour comes within one of the grounds enumerated in s 160(2)(a)–(i) of the CA 1990 is liable to be disqualified. That said, a number of *primary* respondents may be identified, namely: promoters, officers (which includes any director, shadow director[409] or secretary of a company[410]), receivers, liquidators, and examiners[411].

[28.155] Although the 'fraud' ground, the 'breach of duty' ground and the 'unfitness' ground only give jurisdiction to make a disqualification order against these named persons where such arises from their conduct *as* such, it is not necessary that a person should have been formally and properly appointed a director, liquidator, etc. In *Re CB Readymix Ltd; Cahill v Grimes*[412], it was held that there was jurisdiction to disqualify a *de facto* liquidator. In so holding the Supreme Court relied upon the decision of Sir Nicholas Browne-Wilkinson VC in *Re Lo-Line Electric Motors Ltd*[413] where it was held that in England there was jurisdiction to disqualify a *de facto* director:

> 'As a matter of construction, I would hold that the word "director" in s 300 does include a person who is *de facto* acting as a director even though not appointed as such. [It was] submitted that as the disqualification of a director is a penal process the words should be strictly construed. But, as I have said, the paramount purpose of disqualification is the protection of the public not punishment. I therefore approach the question of construction on the normal basis. Section 300 requires the court to have regard to "conduct as a director". I can see no reason why Parliament should have intended that the decision to disqualify should turn on the validity of his appointment. The conduct relevant to future suitability to act as a director depends upon a man's past record as a director irrespective of the circumstances in which he came to act as such.'

In the Supreme Court, Murphy J said of the foregoing passage that it was 'fully vindicated by a purposive reading of the relevant English and Irish legislation and it is, in my view, as applicable to a *de facto* liquidator as it is to a *de facto* director'[414]. On this basis, there is no reason to distinguish receivers, examiners, promoters or company secretaries. It remains the case, however, that in order to be disqualified a person must at least have *de facto* acted in such a capacity and, in England, this enquiry has given rise to

---

409 On the application of the provisions concerning disqualification of directors in the UK to *shadow directors*, see *Official Receiver v Nixon* (1992) Financial Times Law Reports, 6 March (Court of Appeal).

410 Section 159 of the CA 1990.

411 On the jurisdiction in England and Wales to make a disqualification order in respect of persons outside of the jurisdiction, see *Re Seagull Manufacturing Co Ltd (No 2)* [1994] 1 BCLC 273.

412 *Re CB Readymix Ltd; Cahill v Grimes* [2002] 1 IR 372.

413 *Re Lo-Line Electric Motors Ltd* [1988] BCLC 698, [1988] 2 All ER 692.

414 *Re CB Readymix Ltd; Cahill v Grimes* [2002] 1 IR 372 at 380.

a considerable number of judgments on who is or is not a director[415]. It may be noted, however, that since a non-officer or other person directly involved in a company can be made the subject of a declaration of personal responsibility under s 297A of the CA 1963, for fraudulent trading, such persons can also be disqualified where an order has been made against them under s 297A[416].

[28.156] It is important to note the extended meaning assigned to the term 'company' as it is used in Chapter 2 of Part VII of the CA 1990. Section 159 provides that, except where the context otherwise requires:

> 'company' includes every company and every body, whether corporate or unincorporated, which may be wound up under Part X of the CA 1963 and, without prejudice to the generality of the foregoing, includes a friendly society within the meaning of the Friendly Societies Acts, 1896 to 1977.

Those companies that can be wound up under Part X of the CA 1963 are considered in Chapter 23[417].

The *locus standi* to apply for a disqualification order and the role of the Director of Corporate Enforcement

[28.157] There are nine separate grounds that if proved will permit the court to exercise its discretion and make a disqualification order and there are four persons or classes of persons who have *locus standi* to make an application. However, the effect of s 160(4), (5)[418], (6) and (6A)[419] is to provide that not all persons can make application under all nine grounds. The result is best expressed in tabular form:

Applicant under s 160(2)	Permissible grounds
Director of Corporate Enforcement	All nine grounds
Director of Public Prosecutions	(a), (b), (c), (d), (e), (f) and (g)
Members, contributories, officers, employees and creditors	(a), (b), (c) and (d)
Registrar of companies	(f)

415 See, for example, *Re Moorgate Metals Ltd* [1995] 1 BCLC 503; *Re Richborough Furniture Ltd* [1996] 1 BCLC 507; *Re H Laing Demolition Building Contractors Ltd* [1998] BCC 561; *Re Sykes (Butchers) Ltd; Secretary of State v Richardson and another* [1998] 1 BCLC 110; *Secretary of State v Tjolle et al* [1998] BCC 282; *Secretary of State v Jones et al* [1999] BCC 336; *Re Kaytech International plc* [1999] BCC 390; *Re Red Label Fashions Ltd* [1999] BCC 308; *Re CEM Connections Ltd* [2000] BCC 917; and *Secretary of State v Deverell and another* [2000] BCC 1057. See, generally, Ch 13, *Corporate Governance: Management by the Directors*, at para **[13.045]** *et seq* and **[13.055]** *et seq* where these cases are considered in the context of the meaning of *de facto* director and shadow director, respectively.

416 Section 160(2)(c) of the CA 1990. See also grounds (e) and (f) which provided for the disqualification of 'persons' in certain specific situations.

417 See Ch 23, *Winding Up Companies*, at para **[23.035]**.

418 As inserted by s 42(d) of the CLEA 2001.

419 As inserted by s 42(e) of the CLEA 2001.

Of course, the court can act on its own initiative in respect of any of these grounds during the course of proceedings and no application is actually required before the court can make a disqualification order[420]. In the case of an application made by members, contributories, employees or creditors, the court may require such applicants to provide security for all or some of the costs of the application[421]. Whilst unusual, it is not unheard of for creditors to bring applications[422].

[28.158] In the years immediately following the passing of the CA 1990, applications to have persons disqualified were few and far between. The reason for the early dearth in the numbers of disqualification orders was primarily attributable to the fact that there was little motivation on the part of private parties and liquidators to bring proceedings. This was understandable to the extent that an applicant for a disqualification order will, if successful in his application, have little more to show for his efforts than the satisfaction of knowing that he has made life somewhat more difficult for the respondent. In commercial life, the desire for retribution of this nature rarely influences behaviour and the efforts in making application would be seen to be throwing good money after bad; equally, it is unreasonable to expect altruism from private parties who can justly believe that it is the State's role to pursue disqualification orders on grounds of public policy. Those state agencies which had, prior to the CLEA 2001, *locus standi* to make application may have had the right but it is arguable that they did not have the responsibility, resources or investigative powers to make applications for disqualification orders. It is in recognition of these matters that the McDowell Group recommended that the Director of Corporate Enforcement should have the responsibility for bringing disqualification applications in appropriate cases. The establishment of the ODCE has undoubtedly resulted in a dramatic increase in the numbers of applications to have persons disqualified.

[28.159] As alluded to in the reasons for the dearth of applications, the absence of investigative powers and information generally contributed to the reluctance on the part of the registrar of companies and the DPP to seek disqualification orders. The Director of Corporate Enforcement should not be impeded by a lack of information, since in all cases where a company goes into insolvent liquidation he is entitled to receive a report from the company's liquidator on the conduct of the directors under s 56(1) of the CLEA 2001[423]. It is this report which should provide the Director with sufficient information to: (a) relieve the liquidator from the obligation to make an application for a restriction order under s 150(1); (b) issue no direction in which case the liquidator must make an application for a restriction order; or (c) relieve the liquidator from the obligation to make application for a restriction order and, instead, for the Director himself to make application for a disqualification order, where he believes such to be more appropriate in the circumstances of the case.

---

420 On the striking out of proceedings for want of prosecution, see *Official Receiver v B Ltd* [1994] 2 BCLC 1.

421 Section 160(4) of the CA 1990.

422 See, for example, *Re Panabridge Company Ltd* (12 October 2007) HC, McGovern J; although the disqualification application was unsuccessful, the court ordered two persons to be restricted pursuant to s 150.

423 See para **[28.082]** *ante*.

[28.160] An example of the Director's powers to procure information with a view to making an application for a disqualification order is seen in s 183A of the CA 1963[424]. Section 183A(1) provides that where the Director has reason to believe that a company director is an undischarged bankrupt, he can require[425] him to produce by a specified date a sworn statement of all relevant facts pertaining to his financial position within and without the State and to any matter pertaining to bankruptcy as at a particular date. Thereafter, the court can on the Director's application require the company director to appear before it to answer on oath any question in relation to the statement[426]. By s 183A(3), the Director can apply to court for a disqualification order against such a company director and the court has jurisdiction to make such an order on the grounds that the company director is an undischarged bankrupt[427].

[28.161] Where an application is successful and the respondent is either disqualified or restricted[428], the court is empowered under s 160(9B) to order that the persons disqualified or restricted shall bear the costs of the application and, where the applicant is the Director of Corporate Enforcement, the DPP, a liquidator, or an examiner, any costs incurred in investigating the matter.

Notice to persons where application is to be made to disqualify

[28.162] In all cases involving an application under s 160(2) (ie, other than where the court acts on its own initiative during the course of proceedings) notice must be given to the person whom it is sought to disqualify. Section 160(7) of the CA 1990 provides that where it is intended to make an application under the section, the applicant must give not less than 10 days' notice to the proposed respondent. The similarly worded English section has been interpreted in *Re Jaymar Management Ltd*[429] to mean that the period of 10 days begins to run from the date on which proceedings are issued for an application to the court and not when the applicant addresses the court so as to obtain an order. Clearly, notice is required to protect the respondent's right to a fair trial. That the ordinary rules of natural justice apply in the case of making a disqualification order was stated in *Re Churchill Hotel Ltd*[430]. However, in *Secretary of State for Trade and Industry v Langridge*[431] the Court of Appeal said that the 10-day notice requirement is *directory as opposed to mandatory* in character. Thus, a failure to give the requisite 10 days' notice was merely a procedural irregularity, and did not render an application for a disqualification order void.

---

424 Inserted by s 40 of the 2001 Act.

425 Failure to comply is an offence: s 183A(4) of the CA 1963.

426 Section 183A(2) of the CA 1963.

427 In *Re Westminster Property Management Ltd* [2000] TLR 28, it was held by Sir Richard Scott VC that disqualification proceedings are 'regulatory civil proceedings' and that European law did not bar the use of statements given under compulsion.

428 As to the option to restrict respondents: see para **[28.172]** *post*.

429 *Re Jaymar Management Ltd* [1990] BCLC 617, which arose under s 16(1) of the Company Directors Disqualification Act 1986 (UK).

430 *Re Churchill Hotel Ltd* [1988] BCLC 341 at 344d–e.

431 *Secretary of State for Trade and Industry v Langridge* [1991] 3 All ER 591.

The grounds for discretionary disqualification

[28.163] Section 160(2) of the CA 1990, as amended by s 42 of the CLEA 2001, provides that the High Court[432] may of its own motion in any proceedings, or as a result of an application, make a disqualification order against a person for such period as it sees fit, on the following grounds:

> '(a) a person has been guilty, while a promoter, officer, auditor, receiver, liquidator or examiner of a company of any fraud in relation to the company, its members or creditors; or
>
> (b) a person has been guilty, while a promoter, officer, auditor, receiver, liquidator or examiner of a company, of any breach of his duty as such promoter, officer, auditor, receiver, liquidator or examiner; or
>
> (c) a declaration has been granted under section 297A of the CA 1963 (inserted by section 138 of this Act) in respect of a person; or
>
> (d) the conduct of any person as promoter, officer, auditor, receiver, liquidator or examiner of a company, makes him unfit to be concerned in the management of a company; or
>
> (e) in consequence of a report of inspectors appointed by the court or the Minister [now Director] under the Companies Acts, the conduct of any person makes him unfit to be concerned in the management of a company; or
>
> (f) a person has been persistently in default in relation to the relevant requirements; or
>
> (g) a person has been guilty of 2 or more offences under section 202(10)[433]; or
>
> (h) a person was a director or a company at the time of the sending, after the commencement of section 42 of the Company Law Enforcement Act, 2001, of a letter under subsection (1) of section 12 of the Companies (Amendment) Act, 1982, to the company and the name of which, following the taking of the other steps under that section consequent on the sending of that letter, was struck off the register under subsection (3) of that section[434]; or
>
> (i) a person is disqualified under the law of another state (whether pursuant to an order of a judge or a tribunal or otherwise) from being appointed or acting as a director or secretary of a body corporate or an undertaking and the court is satisfied that, if the conduct of the person or the circumstances otherwise affecting him that gave rise to the said order being made against him had occurred or arisen in the State, it would have been proper to make a disqualification order otherwise under this subsection against him[435].'

Of the three grounds added by the CLEA 2001, (g) adds the ground of having been guilty of two offences for failing to keep proper books or account; (h) adds the ground of being a director of a company that is struck off the register[436]; and (i) adds the ground of having been disqualified in another jurisdiction. The addition of these grounds –

[432] Section 159 provides that 'the court' means the High Court except in relation to a disqualification order made by a court of its own motion under s 160(2)(a), (b), (c), (d) or (f), in which case it includes any court.

[433] Inserted by s 42(b)(ii) of the CLEA 2001.

[434] Inserted by s 42(b)(ii) of the CLEA 2001.

[435] Inserted by s 42(b)(ii) of the CLEA 2001.

[436] See para **[28.194]** *post*.

although possibly unnecessary by reason of the breadth of the 'unfitness' criterion in s 160(2)(d) which would seem to encompass any of the additional matters – is indicative of the get-tough policy on non-compliance with the Companies Acts.

(a) Preliminary issues

[28.164] Before considering each of the nine grounds for discretionary disqualification, the following preliminary issues are considered:

(i) The discretionary nature of the order;
(ii) The purpose of disqualification and the 'proper approach';
(iii) The onus of proof;
(iv) The grounding affidavit;
(v) Delay;
(vi) Restriction as an alternative to disqualification.

(i) The discretionary nature of the order

[28.165] Section 160(2) of the CA 1990 confers a discretionary jurisdiction on the High Court to make a disqualification order, after a court has been satisfied as to the existence of any of the foregoing grounds. Unlike s 150(1), which concerns restriction orders, s 160(2) is not mandatory. This was made clear by Murphy J, in *Business Communications Ltd v Baxter and Parsons*[437], who said:

> 'The Chapter 2 disqualifications are not mandatory. Section 160 confers a discretion on the Court by the use of the word "may" (rather than the word shall which is used in s 150) with regard to the imposition of a disqualification order[438].'

Neither is the period of disqualification prescribed and it is a matter for the court to determine the duration of a disqualification order[439].

(ii) The purpose of disqualification and the 'proper approach'

[28.166] In *Re CB Readymix Ltd; Cahill v Grimes*[440], the Supreme Court said that the following passage from the decision of Browne-Wilkinson VC in *Re Lo-Line Motors Ltd*[441] was 'a correct statement of the law and represents a proper approach to the application and interpretation of s 160' of the CA 1990:

> 'What is the proper approach to deciding whether someone is unfit to be a director? The approach adopted in all the cases to which I have been referred is broadly the same. The primary purpose of the section is not to punish the individual but to protect the public against the future conduct of companies by persons whose past record as directors of insolvent companies have shown them to be a danger to creditors and others … Ordinary misjudgment is in itself not sufficient to justify disqualification. In the normal case, the

437 *Business Communications Ltd v Baxter and Parsons* (21 July 1995, unreported) HC, Murphy J.

438 *Business Communications Ltd v Baxter and Parsons* (21 July 1995, unreported) HC, Murphy J at p 12 of the judgment.

439 See para **[28.198]** *post*.

440 *Re CB Readymix Ltd; Cahill v Grimes* [2002] 1 IR 372, The same passage was quoted with approval in *La Moselle Clothing Ltd and Rosegem Ltd v Soualhi* [1998] 2 ILRM 345 and *Re Squash (Ireland) Ltd* [2001] 3 IR 35.

441 *Re Lo-Line Motors Ltd* [1988] BCLC 698.

> conduct complained of must display a lack of commercial probity, although I have no doubt that in an extreme case of gross negligence or total incompetence, disqualification could be appropriate[442].'

It is very important to note, however, that while the primary purpose of the section is not to punish the individual, it does *not* follow that the only purpose is to protect the public. This was made clear by the Supreme Court in *Kentford Securities Ltd; Director of Corporate Enforcement v McCann*[443]. In that case, despite finding against the respondent in respect of all the matters about which the ODCE had complained, the High Court[444] had refused to make a disqualification order on the grounds, *inter alia*, that the purpose of an order under s 160 was '*not punitive in nature, but rather protective of the community*'. O'Donnell J, who gave the decision of the Supreme Court, held:

> 'It seems clear that the complexity and variety of s 160 cannot be reduced to a single touchstone whether identified as the "*primary purpose*" or the "*only function*" of the Act. Instead, the Act ranges from very serious matters requiring mandatory disqualification to matters which might, in certain circumstances, be regarded as regulatory, posing no immediate or obvious threat to the public. It is also significant in my view that the deemed disqualification under s 160(1) is mandatory. The consequence of mandatory disqualification follows upon the conviction irrespective of the nature of the matters giving rise to the conviction, their age or any prediction as to the future risk to the public from the individual concerned.
>
> It is clear, therefore, that the section contains a number of different elements. Reducing this section to a single function excludes a number of factors which are plainly intended objectives of the Act and renders the consequent application of the Act likely to be unbalanced and one-dimensional.'

The Supreme Court, accordingly, reversed the decision of the High Court, finding that the judgment contained three interrelated errors of principle.

[28.167] O'Donnell J went on to criticise the approach in the High Court of applying the disqualification regime by reference to a 'single gloss on the provisions of the Act, whether phrased as "primary purpose" or "only function"'. Citing Fennelly J's decision of the Supreme Court in *Re Wood Products (Longford) Ltd; Director of Corporate Enforcement v McGowan and McGowan*[445], O'Donnell J said:

> 'The Act requires a two-stage inquiry. First, the court must consider whether one or more of the subparagraphs of s 160(2) have been established. These in the words of Fennelly J, are "*jurisdictional triggers*" or as counsel in this case put it "*gateways*", to the second stage of the inquiry which is a consideration of the court's discretion. In that case, there had in fact been no finding of unfitness, and as Fennelly J pointed out at para 32 of his judgment "*in the absence of a finding on fitness, the judge has not established jurisdiction to make a disqualification order. It was not logical for her to proceed to consider the exercise of her discretion*".

---

442 *Re Lo-Line Motors Ltd* [1988] BCLC 698 at 703.

443 See *Kentford Securities Ltd; Director of Corporate Enforcement v McCann* [2010] IESC 59.

444 *Kentford Securities Ltd; Director of Corporate Enforcement v McCann* [2007] IEHC 1 (Peart J).

445 *Re Wood Products (Longford) Ltd; Director of Corporate Enforcement v McGowan and McGowan* [2008] 4 IR 598.

The Act of 1990, as Fennelly J observed, requires a two-stage inquiry. First, the court must determine as a matter of objective forensic inquiry, whether one or more of the criteria under the subparagraphs of s 160(2) has been established to the degree and level required. These are the "*gateways*" to the second stage, which is the exercise of the court's discretion.

It is, I think, important to follow the decision-making structure thus implied in the Act, particularly when the inquiry involves such broad and general concepts as future unfitness to be concerned in the management of the company. Such an approach highlights the important fact that this case does not concern a single issue of unfitness under s 160(2)(d) but also a more focussed issue of breach of duty under s 160(2)(b)[446].'

The Supreme Court went on to stress the importance of looking at the respondent's past behaviour, saying it should not be a forward-looking only test. On this point O'Donnell J said:

'If the Court adopts a single, forward-looking test derived from a gloss upon the observations of Browne-Wilkinson VC in *Lo-Line*, then in my view it is almost inevitable that the inquiry will be focussed almost exclusively on the future conduct of the respondent. Such an inquiry is something a court will almost always consider to be somewhat speculative. At the same time, if the matter is approached on the assumption that the Act of 1990 has no penal consequence or deterrent function, then almost of necessity the past conduct of the respondent becomes much less relevant. However, the consideration of the behaviour of the respondent in the past and whether or not it can be established as a matter of fact, and if so the assessment of the gravity of such conduct, are all matters which fall more naturally within the powers and experience of the court. In my view, it is clear from an analysis of the Act, that the Act directs attention to that past conduct as certainly the best, if not the only, guide to the necessity for disqualification. It will be apparent therefore, that a test of future unfitness either detached from, or at least considerably distant from, an assessment of the gravity of past conduct, is a test which is skewed in favour of potential respondents. It has also been observed, that given the penal consequences of a disqualification order for any director or other officer, that a court must feel a high degree of confidence before making any such disqualification order. In such circumstances, it becomes increasingly likely that a court adopting the approach of a single, forward-looking test of future unfitness, and properly requiring a high degree of proof, will come to a conclusion which will not achieve the statutory objectives.

It seems clear to me that the Act of 1990 considers that past conduct is the key to disqualification, and which conduct, in itself, demonstrates either the breaches of duty or general unfitness which can justify disqualification unless the court, in the exercise of discretion, considers that such an order should not be made. This is a more focussed inquiry, and one which is rooted in the Act. It is an approach which has been repeatedly invoked in judgments of the courts both in this country and in the United Kingdom. Thus for example, the well known passage in *Lo-Line* identified the primary purpose of the

[446] Later in his judgment O'Donnell J said: 'The true test is contained in the words of the section. The section poses a two-stage test. First, whether conduct falling within any of the sub-categories of s 160(2) has been established as a matter of fact. Second, whether the court in the exercise of its discretion should proceed to disqualify. Had this approach been taken in this case, it would, in my view, have revealed that the conclusion to which the trial judge came was unduly indulgent. Indeed I think it can be fairly said that it was the framing of the question as one of proof of future dangerous behaviour which led the Court to the conclusion to which it came.'

section as protecting the public against "*the future conduct of companies by persons whose past records as directors ... have shown them to be a danger to creditors and others*" [emphasis added]. In the judgment in *Secretary of State for Trade and Industry v Langridge* [1991] Ch 402, already referred to above, Balcombe LJ stated, at p 414, that the purpose of the Act was to "*protect the public and its scope is the prevention of persons who have previously misconducted themselves in relation to companies, or have otherwise shown themselves as unfit to be concerned in the management of a company from being so concerned*" [emphasis added]. In the judgment of Finlay Geoghegan J in *Re Ansbacher (Cayman) Ltd Director of Corporate Enforcement v Collery* [2006] IEHC 67, a number of principles were set out for the determination of an appropriate disqualification period, one of which was expressed as follows at para 31:-

"The period of disqualification should reflect ... the gravity of the conduct as found by the inspectors which makes the respondent unfit to be concerned in the management of a company." [Emphasis added.]

This aptly encapsulates the close link which the Act, in my view effects between the past conduct inquired into, and the unfitness or other default justifying disqualification.'

(*iii*) *The onus of proof*

[28.168] Disqualification orders will not be made lightly, and in *Business Communications Ltd v Baxter and Parsons*[447] Murphy J said:

'... in relation to a disqualification order it is clear that there is a substantial burden to be discharged before the court has jurisdiction to make the appropriate order[448].' 

[28.169] The decision of McCracken J in *Re Newcastle Timber Ltd*[449] shows that the courts will not make a disqualification order lightly and that the onus of proof rests firmly with the applicant. In that case, an application to have two directors of a company that was wound up insolvent disqualified failed, and the court contented itself with making a restriction order under s 150 of the CA 1990. The liquidator identified five matters that he claimed showed that the directors had not acted honestly and responsibly. In respect of three of those claims McCracken J held that the liquidator had discharged the onus on him in relation to the s 160 disqualification proceedings. These were: first, that the company had failed to make CRO returns (it had at one point been struck off); second, that the company had traded whilst insolvent for some four years; and third, that after the company ceased to trade its directors had caused it to discharge trade creditors in priority to the Revenue Commissioners[450]. After quoting from the passage in the decision of Browne-Wilkinson VC in *Re Lo-Line Motors Ltd*[451] as to the 'proper

[447] *Business Communications Ltd v Baxter and Parsons* (21 July 1995, unreported) HC, Murphy J.

[448] *Business Communications Ltd v Baxter and Parsons* (21 July 1995, unreported) HC, Murphy J at p 13 of the judgment.

[449] *Re Newcastle Timber Ltd* [2001] 4 IR 586.

[450] The other two grounds were not upheld. First, it was not established that the company had not kept proper books and records because owing to a fire caused by vandalism, it was impossible to say what books and records did exist. Second, it was found that any irregularities in the acquisition by one of the directors of a property from the company had not prejudiced the company's creditors and could even have been said to have benefited them.

[451] *Re Lo-Line Motors Ltd* [1988] BCLC 698.

approach' to deciding whether someone is unfit to be a director[452], McCracken J declined to exercise his discretion in favour of making a disqualification order. Taking into account one of the director's involvement in another company – something that has been also done in England in *Re Bath Glass Ltd*[453] – McCracken J said of the respondent directors:

> 'I have no doubt that they acted incompetently, and, particularly in relation to insolvent trading and preference of trade creditors, I think they behaved irresponsibly. However, the liquidator has not satisfied me that the directors were so much in breach of their duties, that they are unfit to be concerned in the management of a company, particularly in view of the undoubted discretion which I have in this regard. The liquidator did rely to a considerable degree on the fact that the revenue debts remained unpaid, and cited a number of authorities as to the importance of this aspect of the case, but taking the overall behaviour of the directors I do not think it could be said that a disqualification order is necessary to protect the public against their future conduct. I say this particularly as it is now some six years since Newcastle ceased trading, during which time [one of the respondent directors] has been intimately concerned in the management of another company, which appears to be trading successfully and is complying with its obligations to the Revenue. Accordingly, I will refuse an order under s 160[454].'

In that case, a restriction order was, however, made against both of the directors. The making of a restriction order was virtually automatic following the finding that the respondent directors had acted 'irresponsibly'. From this decision it would appear that the Irish courts have a higher tolerance for incompetence and irresponsibility than do the English courts. Were it not for the Supreme Court's acceptance in *Re CB Readymix Ltd* that there is jurisdiction to disqualify *conditionally*, McCracken J's decision was likely to have dissuaded liquidators from bringing disqualification proceedings because of the tolerance for incompetence and irresponsibility seen in the exercise of the court's discretion. The effect of the Supreme Court's decision, however, is likely to be that conditional disqualification orders will be made where perhaps no disqualification order might otherwise be made.

[28.170] The approach of McCracken J in the High Court in *Re Newcastle Timber Ltd*[455] to the onus of proof was approved by the Supreme Court in *Cahill v Grimes*[456], where Murphy J said:

> 'The onus does fall on the applicant to establish the allegations on which he relies and, even where a case is made out, the use of the word "may" in s 160(2) confers a discretion on the court whether or not to make the order as was pointed out in *Re Newcastle Timber Ltd.*'

The Director of Corporate Enforcement has, on a number of occasions, accepted that the onus is on him to satisfy the court that the necessary conditions prescribed in s 160(2) are established[457].

---

452 See para **[28.166]** *ante*.

453 *Re Bath Glass Ltd* [1988] BCLC 329.

454 *Re Newcastle Timber Ltd* [2001] 4 IR 586 at 592.

455 *Re Newcastle Timber Ltd* [2001] 4 IR 586.

456 *Re CB Readymix Ltd; Cahill v Grimes* [2002] 1 IR 372.

457 See, for example, *National Irish Bank Ltd and National Irish Bank Financial Services; ODCE v D'Arcy* [2006] 2 IR 163 at 171.

(*iv*) *The grounding affidavit*

[28.171] The High Court set out a number of important procedural requirements concerning the bringing of disqualification applications in *Re Bovale Developments Ltd; Director of Corporate Enforcement v Bailey and Bailey*[458]. Irvine J said that in an application brought under s 160(2), the affidavit filed should contain the totality of evidence against the respondents. It was also noted that it would be a breach of fair procedures and natural justice to permit an applicant to swear an affidavit containing serious allegations of wrongdoing based on the opinion of third parties or relating to matters outside of the deponent's own personal knowledge. In *Re National Irish Bank Ltd; Director of Corporate Enforcement v Seymour*[459], O'Donovan J held that a deponent to an affidavit, in that case, a respondent, could be ordered to be cross-examined on his affidavits.

(*vi*) *Restriction as a alternative to disqualification*

[28.172] Section 160(9A) of the CA 1990[460] provides that in considering the penalty to be imposed the court may, as an alternative where it adjudicates that disqualification is not justified, make a declaration under s 150[461]. While very broad, it should be remembered that the heads of disqualification in s 160(2) are exhaustive. In *Reynard v Secretary of State for Trade and Industry*[462], it was held by Blackburne J that a respondent director's deceitful performance in the witness box did not constitute a separate head of misconduct, but could be highly relevant as to whether an allegation of misconduct was or was not established.

[28.173] Where made, a disqualification order can be a comprehensive order. In *Business Communications Ltd v Baxter and Parsons*[463], Murphy J said:

> 'Clearly, it is the comprehensive nature of a disqualification order which is seen as constituting an appropriately severe sentence for conduct which is manifestly more blameworthy than merely failing to exercise an appropriate degree of responsibility in relation to an insolvent company in liquidation of which the person is a director[464].'

A disqualification order may be made on grounds, which include matters other than criminal convictions even though the respondent may be criminally liable for those matters[465]. Each of the nine separate grounds, the proof of which will entitle the court to exercise its discretionary jurisdiction to make a disqualification order, shall next be considered.

---

458 *Re Bovale Developments Ltd; Director of Corporate Enforcement v Bailey and Bailey* [2008] 2 ILRM 13.

459 *Re National Irish Bank Ltd; Director of Corporate Enforcement v Seymour* [2006] IEHC 369.

460 Inserted by s 42 of the CLEA 2001.

461 In *Re Panabridge Company Ltd* (12 October 2007) HC, McGovern J, although a creditor's application for a disqualification order was unsuccessful, the court ordered two persons to be restricted pursuant to s 150.

462 *Reynard v Secretary of State for Trade and Industry* [2001] TLR 441.

463 *Business Communications Ltd v Baxter and Parsons* (21 July 1995, unreported) HC, Murphy J.

464 *Business Communications Ltd v Baxter and Parsons* (21 July 1995, unreported) HC, Murphy J at pp 13, 14 of the judgment.

465 Section 160(9) of the CA 1990.

(b) Guilty of any fraud: s 160(2)(a)

[28.174] '(a) a person has been guilty, while a promoter, officer, auditor, receiver, liquidator or examiner of a company of any fraud in relation to the company, its members or creditors.' The first ground is that the person whom it is sought to disqualify must be proved to have been guilty of any fraud in relation to the company, its members or directors, whilst that person was a promoter, officer, auditor, receiver, liquidator or examiner. The provisions on disqualification are not directed at directors alone and are primarily intended to provide a remedy against all persons who owe ex officio duties to a company. The use of the word 'guilty' implies that there should be a court conviction and, unlike s 160(1), that conviction may follow a summary prosecution as well as one on indictment, although proof of the latter is more likely to induce the court to exercise its discretion and make a disqualification order than the former. In England, it has been held that where no disqualification order was sought during a criminal trial, it was not an abuse of process to commence, subsequently, civil proceedings for disqualification[466].

(c) Guilty of breach of duty: s 160(2)(b)

[28.175] '(b) a person has been guilty, while a promoter, officer, auditor, receiver, liquidator or examiner of a company, of any breach of his duty as such promoter, officer, auditor, receiver, liquidator or examiner.' This is similar to the 'fraud' ground, but wider. Guilty of a breach of duty would imply that a criminal conviction is again a prerequisite to the exercise of the jurisdiction here.

(d) Proof of a declaration of liability for fraudulent trading: s 160(2)(c)

[28.176] '(c) a declaration has been granted under section 297A of the CA 1963 (inserted by section 138 of this Act) in respect of a person.' Where a declaration is made, under s 297A of the CA 1963, that a person has been party to the carrying on of the business of a company with intent to defraud its creditors, this too is a basis for the court making a disqualification order[467].

(e) Unfit to be concerned in the management of a company: s 160(2)(d)

[28.177] '(d) the conduct of any person as promoter, officer, auditor, receiver, liquidator or examiner of a company, makes him unfit to be concerned in the management of a company.' In the first edition of this book it was opined that of all the grounds enumerated in s 160(2) of the CA 1990, the ground which will be most litigated will be s 160(2)(d)[468]. Indeed, in *Business Communications Ltd v Baxter and Parsons*[469]

---

466 *Re Dennis Hilton Ltd* [2001] TLR 431.

467 On fraudulent trading, see Ch 15, *Duties of Directors and Others*, at para **[15.116]** *et seq*.

468 There have been very few disqualification orders made in Ireland. One, which is noted by MacCann, *Butterworth Ireland Companies Acts 1963–1990* (1993, Butterworths) at p 1014, is *Re Christy Kenneally Communications Ltd* (July 1992, unreported) HC, where Costello J disqualified two directors who refused to comply with a court order to prepare annual accounts and hold an AGM. An example of a disqualification order by consent is noted by Courtney, 'Company Law Update' (1994) CLP 56. In neither case was a judgment delivered.

469 *Business Communications Ltd v Baxter and Parsons* (21 July 1995, unreported) HC, Murphy J.

Murphy J said that of all the grounds, it was s 160(2)(h) which 'typifies the grounds for disqualification'[470]. Here, s 169(2)(d) is considered under the following three headings:

(i) Potential respondents under s 160(2)(d);

(ii) Unfitness, commercial probity and commercial morality;

(iii) Failing to maintain books and records.

(i) Potential respondents under s 160(2)(d)

[28.178] In order for a person to be disqualified under s 160(2)(d), one must have been either a promoter, officer, auditor, receiver, liquidator or examiner of a company. In *National Irish Bank Ltd and National Irish Bank Financial Services; ODCE v D'Arcy*[471], Kelly J was asked to make a disqualification order against a person who was a senior manager, but *not* a director. The learned judge noted that because 'officer' is defined by s 159 of the CA 1990 as including an director, shadow director or secretary, 'it is arguable that the respondent does not fall within it'. The ODCE argued that a manager was an officer and Kelly J concluded that 'I think that the applicant is probably correct in his submissions but I do not propose to make a finding on the issue since it is not necessary'. As has been considered in detail in Chapter 13[472], it is submitted that Mr D'Arcy was not an 'officer' and could not have been the subject of an order under s 160(2)(d) since 'officer' means a person within a company who holds an office as described by the Supreme Court in *Glover v BLN Ltd*[473].

(ii) Unfitness, commercial probity and commercial morality

[28.179] The 'unfitness' ground relates to where the person, whom it is sought to have disqualified, has behaved in a manner from which an inference can be drawn that such makes him unfit to be concerned in the management of a company. Among the salient factors that go to determine this question in the English courts is whether there has been a lack of probity in the conduct of the person concerned, or a lack of 'commercial morality'. The power to make a disqualification order is firmly rooted in policy:

> 'It is a power to be exercised to protect the public against those who display lack of commercial probity, "rip-off" the public in colloquial terms, or otherwise shelter a totally rash and unjustified venture behind the shield of limited liability so that they themselves do not suffer when their rash venture fails, as was predictable, but leave the creditors at large to suffer[474].'

In *Re Dawson Print Group Ltd*[475], Hoffmann J said:

> 'There must, I think, be something about the case, some conduct which if not dishonest is at any rate in breach of standards of commercial morality, or some really gross incompetence which persuades the court that it would be a danger to the public if he were

470 *Business Communications Ltd v Baxter and Parsons* (21 July 1995, unreported) HC, Murphy J at p 13 of the judgment.

471 *National Irish Bank Ltd and National Irish Bank Financial Services; ODCE v D'Arcy* [2006] 2 IR 163.

472 See Ch 13, *Corporate Governance: Management by the Directors,* at para **[13.003]**.

473 *Glover v BLN Ltd* [1973] IR 388 at 414, *per* Kenny J.

474 *Re Cladrose Ltd* [1990] BCLC 204 at 213, *per* Harman J.

475 *Re Dawson Print Group Ltd* [1987] BCLC 601.

to be allowed to continue to be involved in the management of companies, before a disqualification order is made. Obviously every case must turn on its own facts[476].'

In that case, the respondent was a director of two companies. The history of one company was that it suffered a setback in its first year of trading when one of its major creditors defaulted, and although it expanded it was finally wound up insolvent. The other company was wound up also being insolvent, both companies owing debts to the revenue. After the winding up, the director set up another business which seemed to be trading profitably. It was held by Hoffmann J that on the facts there was no evidence that the director had behaved recklessly or in a manner that was commercially immoral, and in all the circumstances it was inappropriate to make a disqualification order. Similarly, in *Re CU Fittings Ltd*[477] it was held that no disqualification order ought to be made, as there was no lack of probity. Hoffmann J stated:

> 'It may be that … a dispassionate mind would have reached the conclusion that the company was doomed. But the directors immersed in the day-to-day task of trying to keep their business afloat cannot be expected to have wholly dispassionate minds. They tend to cling to hope. Obviously there comes a point at which an honest businessman recognises that he is only gambling at the expense of his creditors on the possibility that something may turn up. But this is not such a case[478].'

[28.180] In *Re CB Readymix Ltd; Cahill v Grimes*[479], the Supreme Court said that the passage from the decision of Browne-Wilkinson VC in *Re Lo-Line Motors Ltd*[480] cited above[481] was 'a correct statement of the law and represents a proper approach to the application and interpretation' of s 160 of the CA 1990. As noted above, however, whilst the primary purpose of the section is not to punish the individual, it does not follow that the only purpose is to protect the public[482]. An enquiry into whether a respondent displayed commercial probity or morality is therefore a key feature in any application to have a person disqualified under s 160(2)(d) of the CA 1990[483].

---

476 *Re Dawson Print Group Ltd* [1987] BCLC 601 at 604e–f.

477 *Re CU Fittings Ltd* [1989] BCLC 556.

478 *Re CU Fittings Ltd* [1989] BCLC 556 at 559. See also *Re McNulty's Interchange Ltd* [1989] BCLC 709 where Browne-Wilkinson VC said: 'The Official Receiver says that although Mr McNulty was not aware that the company was insolvent when it was continuing to trade, he says that he ought to have been aware it was. I reject that allegation on the evidence before me. The evidence is that he was throughout advised by professional financial advisers. To suggest that somebody in those circumstances, who relies on his advisers, is in some way acting improperly, because he does not appreciate that his advisers' advise is wrong, seems to me untenable.'

479 *Re CB Readymix Ltd; Cahill v Grimes* [2002] 1 IR 372. The same passage was quoted with approval in *La Moselle Clothing Ltd and Rosegem Ltd v Soulahi* [1998] 2 ILRM 345 and *Re Squash (Ireland) Ltd* [2001] 3 IR 35.

480 *Re Lo-Line Motors Ltd* [1988] BCLC 698.

481 See para **[28.155]** *ante*.

482 See *Kenford Securities Ltd; Director of Corporate Enforcement v McCann* [2010] IESE 59.

483 Referring to the passage quoted above from the decision of Browne-Wilkinson VC in *Re Lo-Line Ltd* [1988] Ch 477, Finlay Geoghegan J disqualified two directors on the grounds of s 160(2)(d) of the CA 1990 where one of them was found to have been in breach of s 297A of the CA 1963 in *Re PSK Construction Ltd; Kavanagh v Killeen and Higgins* [2009] IEHC 538.

[28.181] In *Re Nationwide Transport Ltd; Forrest v Whelan et al*[484], it was found by O'Leary J that in preparation for the liquidation of the company the first and second respondents had transferred the goodwill and trade name of the company to a third party. Although stating at the creditors' meeting that nothing else had been transferred, it later appeared that certain of the company's debtors and invoices had also been transferred to a company in which one of the directors had an involvement, despite statements to the contrary at the creditors' meeting. The creditors' meeting was also misled as to the amount of collectable debtors. After quoting the passage from *Re Lo-Line Electric Motors Ltd* quoted by the Supreme Court in *Re Readymix Ltd; Cahill v Grimes*, O'Leary J held:

> '1. The replies by the second named respondent at the creditors' meeting to the representative of the Revenue were untruthful and showed a lack of commercial probity.
>
> 2. The silence of the first named respondent at the directors' meeting relating to the misinformation given by the second named respondent showed a lack of commercial probity.
>
> 3. The reply given that the creditors' meeting by the second named respondent (and the silence of the first named respondent) on the director's involvement in the new company was untrue. This reply and the silence were evidence of a lack of commercial probity.
>
> 4. The diverting of €155,000 [of invoices] from the old company to the new company without legal authority was at least tortious and at worst criminal. In participating in this matter the first and second named respondents displayed a gross lack of commercial probity.
>
> 5. If and to the extent that any of the company's trade creditors were paid by the money so taken (a fact not proved to the satisfaction of the court) then such creditors were improperly preferred contrary to the provisions of the Companies Acts. Any such action was a serious breach of the first and second named directors' company law duties.
>
> 6. The list of debtors produced by the directors at the creditors' meeting was overstated by at least the €155,000 diverted. The signing of a Statement of Affairs with incorrect realisable assets by the second named respondent and the support given to that breach of duty by the first named respondent was a serious breach of these directors' company law duty and showed a lack of commercial probity.
>
> 7. The first two respondents failed to co-operate with the applicant in the conduct of the liquidation. In so far as they appeared to cooperate in the collection of debts for the company post liquidation it is clear that this was motivated by the necessity to keep hidden from the liquidator the diversion of funds through the improper assigning of sales/debtors to the new company. The only positive action of these two directors in relation to the liquidation was the payment of €60,000 allegedly from their own resources (in fact probably from the new company) when the extent of their deceitful action on debtors was discovered. This was inadequate and motivated by self interest.
>
> The foregoing evidence of a lack of commercial probity, leads this court to a conclusion in each case that the respondent engaged in conduct which rendered him unfit to be concerned in the management of a company.'

---

[484] *Re Nationwide Transport Ltd; Forrest v Whelan et al* [2006] IEHC 87.

The first and second respondents were each disqualified for a period of five years and costs were awarded against them.

[28.182] The English courts have taken into account a number of factors in finding that persons have acted with a lack of commercial morality or probity. These include: acquiring the assets of a company which was insolvent for another company which the same directors were involved with[485]; failing to keep proper books of account or to make annual returns even if there was no personal gain to the directors responsible[486]; gross incompetence[487]; and trading when there is no prospect of the company surviving, ie, recklessly[488]. It is thought that proof of dishonesty will also justify a finding of 'unfitness' but that 'irresponsibility' as that term has been defined in the context of s 150(1) restriction orders will not alone justify a finding of 'unfitness' in the context of an application for a disqualification order. Another factor which has been held by the English courts to be very important in deciding whether or not to make a disqualification order is where a person was responsible for the company avoiding the payment of debts to the revenue. Thus in *Re Cladrose*[489] it was held that non-payment of 'Crown' debts was to be treated as a more serious matter than the failure to pay ordinary debts[490]. This was also stated to be the case in *Re Stanford Services Ltd*[491] by Vinelott J who saw an onus on the directors of a company not to use moneys collected on behalf of the Crown for the financing of the company. More recently the Court of Appeal in *Re Sevenoaks Stationers (Retail) Ltd*[492] has stated that the non-payment of 'Crown debts' is not to be treated as an automatic ground for disqualification. Rather, it is but a factor to be taken into consideration in determining whether a director is unfit. In the words of Dillon LJ:

> '[the director] made a deliberate decision to pay only those creditors who pressed for payment. The obvious result was that the two companies traded, when in fact insolvent, and known to be in difficulties, at the expense of those creditors who, like the Crown, happened not to be pressing for payment. Such conduct on the part of a director can well, in my judgment, be relied on as a ground for saying that he is unfit to be concerned in the management of a company. But what is relevant in the Crown's position is not that the debt was a debt which arose from a compulsory deduction … but that the Crown was not pressing for payment, and the director was taking unfair advantage of that forbearance on the part of the Crown [and] … was trading at the Crown's expense while the companies

485 See *Re Keypak Homecare Ltd* [1990] BCLC 440.

486 See Re Sevenoaks Stationers (Retail) Ltd [1990] BCLC 668 and *Re Chartmore Ltd* [1990] BCLC 673. On the duty to keep accounts, see MacCann 'Duty to Keep Proper Books of Account' (1991) ILT 177. Note that regarding s 160(2)(f) of the CA 1990, in respect of which only the registrar of companies or the DPP can make application, s 160(3)(a) provides that persistent default can be proved conclusively where it is shown that in the five years ending with the date of the application, the person has been adjudged guilty of three or more defaults.

487 *Re Churchill Hotel (Plymouth) Ltd* [1988] BCLC 341.

488 *Re J & B Lynch (Builders) Ltd* [1988] BCLC 376 at 379.

489 *Re Cladrose* [1990] BCLC 204.

490 See *Re J & B Lynch (Builders) Ltd* [1988] BCLC 376; *Re Lo-Line Electric Motors Ltd* [1988] BCLC 698. *Cf Re CU Fittings Ltd* [1989] BCLC 556.

491 *Re Stanford Services Ltd* [1987] BCLC 607 at 616.

492 *Re Sevenoaks Stationers (Retail) Ltd* [1991] 3 All ER 578, [1991] BCLC 325, [1990] 3 WLR 1165.

> were in jeopardy. It would be equally unfair to trade in that way and in such circumstances at the expense of creditors other than the Crown[493].'

Accordingly, in England and Wales, for a company to trade, owing debts to the revenue is not any more heinous than to behave in that way to creditors generally. In the Irish High Court, Smyth J said in *Re CB Readymix Ltd; Cahill v Grimes*[494] that whilst he did not consider it necessary to pronounce on the special nature of revenue debts, he contented himself to note that the legislature had laid down those debts, the payment of which is to have priority in a winding up and that, for the present, was 'sufficient indication of their special nature'.

[28.183] It has been held that the court can have regard to the fact that a director whom it is sought to disqualify has a professional qualification, as this will increase the standard of care expected of him. In *Re Cladrose Ltd*[495], where one of the directors was a chartered accountant, it was held that the other director without a professional qualification could reasonably rely on the accountant director to comply with the requirements governing the filing of accounts and annual returns[496]. This case is also authority for the fact that where a director has personal problems, such as the break up of his marriage, such will not be sufficient to exonerate him from the responsibilities attendant on being a director.

(*iii*) *Failing to maintain books and records*

[28.184] Whether or not a respondent maintained proper books and records is as important in an application for a disqualification order as it is in an application for a restriction order[497]. In *Re CB Readymix Ltd; Cahill v Grimes*[498], the 'dumping' of the company's records was the basis of the official liquidator's grievance with the respondent voluntary liquidator. The facts were that the respondent, Dr Grimes, had acted as voluntary liquidator in a company when he had, in fact, not been validly appointed liquidator. Subsequently, the applicant was appointed official liquidator. There was evidence from the directors that all books had been handed over to Dr Grimes and evidence that Dr Grimes had perused the books. Meetings were held and correspondence exchanged but the company's books and records were not handed over to the official liquidator. At one meeting the official liquidator claimed he was told that the 'books could have an accident'. Subsequently, Dr Grimes claimed he had sought a meeting with the official liquidator to hand over the books but that the official liquidator had declined to meet with him. For this reason, by his own admission, Dr Grimes said he reasoned that only the company's officers were responsible for the books, that he had not been involved in running the company and was not even liquidator so he had no duty to keep the records. For these reasons Dr Grimes 'dumped' the records by filling two and a half refuse sacks and putting them out for collection with the garbage. The Supreme

493 *Re Sevenoaks Stationers (Retail) Ltd* [1991] 3 All ER 578 at 589, 590. See also *Re Tansoft Ltd* [1991] BCLC 339, where the decision in the Court of Appeal was applied by Warner J.

494 *Re CB Readymix Ltd; Cahill v Grimes* (20 July 2001, unreported) HC at p 18 of the judgment.

495 *Re Cladrose Ltd* [1990] BCLC 204.

496 *Cf Re Majestic Recording Studios Ltd* [1989] BCLC 1 where it was held that a director cannot turn a blind eye to the affairs of the company to the neglect of his duties.

497 See para **[28.111]** *ante*.

498 *Re CB Readymix Ltd; Cahill v Grimes* [2002] 1 IR 372.

Court noted that Dr Grimes admitted to a feud with the Revenue Commissioners and that certain extreme statements had been attributed to him in the High Court[499]. Murphy J said:

> 'It is common case that Dr Grimes destroyed – or dumped with a view to their destruction – documents relating to the financial affairs of Readymix. In my view the inescapable conclusion is that those documents included the books and records of that company and that this was done with a view to depriving the official liquidator of access thereto. An experienced liquidator – and Dr Grimes rightly claims to be such – would immediately appreciate the importance of the records to which Dr Grimes admits he had access[500].'

It would seem that Dr Grimes had been motivated by the desire to save the jobs of those employed by the company. The Supreme Court, however, upheld the decision of Smyth , *inter alia*, to disqualify Dr Grimes for a period of seven years. Murphy J said:

> 'His apparent belief that the commendable motive of saving employment would justify the destruction of documents and the frustration of the liquidation of a company shows a completely mistaken view as to the duties of a liquidator and would undoubtedly raise concern as to the propriety of his being involved in the management of companies which are subject to detailed regulations for the protection of the public whether as shareholders, creditors or employees[501].'

Upholding the decision of the High Court, Murphy J justified the making of a disqualification order arising from one incident in the following terms:

> 'Adequate records are necessary to enable a liquidator to perform his statutory functions properly and some records are necessary to enable him to perform his functions at all. Whilst I accept that Dr Grimes did not act maliciously, his decision to destroy or permit the destruction of the books and records of Readymix was a very serious wrong indeed. Dr Grimes did argue that a liquidator or director should not be severely penalised for one error in relation to a particular company in a context where no allegations of inappropriate conduct are made against him in respect of many other such offices held by him. That argument has considerable force. However, a significant feature of the judgment of Mr Justice Smyth was his statement that he allowed time to Dr Grimes to reconsider the argument which he made to the court and notwithstanding the opportunity given to him he, Dr Grimes, "continued in a vein as to betoken a total disregard in his conduct complained of". It was the fact that Dr Grimes could not then – and does not now – appreciate the gravity of his misconduct that justifies the conclusion that he is unfit to hold the office of liquidator and casts serious doubt upon his suitability to participate in the management of any company[502].'

(f) Unfitness appearing from an inspector's report: s 160(2)(e)

[28.185] '(e) in consequence of a report of inspectors appointed by the court or the Director under the Companies Acts, the conduct of any person makes him unfit to be

[499] *Re CB Readymix Ltd; Cahill v Grimes* (20 July 2001, unreported) HC, Smyth J at p 12 of the judgment. The statements attributed to Dr Grimes were: 'I was determined to screw the revenue no matter what it took'; 'I was prepared to blow up anyone who got in my way'; 'I was going to make an example of Mr Cahill'; 'I would not obstruct the liquidator but I would not help'; and 'Whatever tactics it took I was going to bring the revenue to book'.

[500] *Re CB Readymix Ltd; Cahill v Grimes* [2002] 1 IR 372 at 376, 377.

[501] *Re CB Readymix Ltd; Cahill v Grimes* [2002] 1 IR 372 at 381.

[502] *Re CB Readymix Ltd; Cahill v Grimes* [2002] 1 IR 372 at 381, 382.

concerned in the management of a company.' Where an inspector has been appointed to a company and it appears from his report, as all inspectors are required to produce at the end of their investigation[503], that the conduct of any person makes him unfit to be concerned in the management of a company, this will give jurisdiction to the court to make a disqualification order against such person.

[28.186] In *National Irish Bank Ltd and National Irish Bank Financial Services; ODCE v D'Arcy*[504], the Director of Corporate Enforcement sought to have the respondent disqualified following the report of court appointed inspectors to NIB and its subsidiary NIBFS. The inspectors' report concluded that bogus non-resident accounts and fictitious accounts had been opened and maintained in NIB to evades tax; that Clerical Medical Insurance (CMI) policies were promoted as a secure investment for funds not disclosed to the Revenue Commissioners; that special savings accounts had a reduced rate of deposit investment retention tax applied notwithstanding that they did not meet the required statutory conditions; and that there was improper charging of both interest and fees to customers. The inspectors concluded that responsibility for these improper practices rested with senior management of NIB; they also noted that the financial advice and services division of the bank (FASD) was headed up by the respondent, Mr D'Arcy. The inspectors' findings in relation to Mr D'Arcy were that he was aware that monies which were undisclosed to the revenue, including funds in bogus non-resident and fictitious accounts, were being targeted by bank staff for investment in CMI policies; that he failed to stop that practice; that he was aware that the FASD managers were promoting CMI policies as a secure investment for undisclosed funds which served to facilitate tax evasion and that he was aware that prospective investors were being given an assurance by FASD managers that their investment would be kept confidential from the revenue and if made the subject of a trust would pass to their beneficiaries without obtaining probate.

[28.187] In considering the law, Kelly J focused on s 160(2)(e) which is not confined to 'officers' or other named persons and applies where, in consequence of a report of inspectors appointed by the court or the ODCE, the conduct of any person makes him unfit to be concerned in the management of a company. As Kelly J observed, the respondent 'was clearly a person who was animadverted upon by the inspectors appointed by this court. Was his conduct such as to make him unfit to be concerned in the management of a company?' Kelly J noted that the ODCE relied exclusively on the inspectors' report and that s 22 of the CA 1990 provides that such a report is admissible in civil proceedings as evidence of the facts set out without further proof unless the contrary is shown and of the opinion of the inspector. Turning to the question of the respondent's fitness, Kelly J quoted the 'proper approach' *dictum* from the decision in *Re Lo-Line Ltd* and went on to find that approach was not only confined to insolvencies, saying:

> 'Whilst the observations of Browne-Wilkinson VC were related to the unfitness of a director and dealt with an insolvent company, a similar line of reasoning is applicable to the question of the disqualification of a person whose conduct is alleged to have made him

503 Sections 7, 8 and 9 of the CA 1990.

504 *National Irish Bank Ltd and National Irish Bank Financial Services; ODCE v D'Arcy* [2006] 2 IR 163.

> unfit to be concerned in the management of a company. His conduct must show a lack of commercial probity or gross negligence or total incompetence before disqualification can be ordered[505].'

In considering the respondent's conduct Kelly J concluded that it was demonstrative of a lack of commercial probity such as made him unfit to be concerned in the management of a company and he disqualified him for 10 years.

[28.188] Following the report of inspectors appointed to inquire into the affairs of Ansbacher (Cayman) Limited, the decision in *Re Ansbacher (Cayman) Ltd; Director of Corporate Enforcement v Collery*[506] arose from the application by the Director of Corporate Enforcement pursuant to s 160(2)(e) to have a senior official in Guinness and Mahon Bank disqualified for having knowingly assisted Ansbacher to conduct its affairs in such a manner as to defraud the Revenue Commissioners of taxation due. Finlay Geoghegan J made the order disqualifying the respondent for a period of nine years and in so doing endorsed the approach taken by Kelly J in the *D'Arcy* case that a similar line of reasoning applies in an application under s 160(2)(e) to where a company is insolvent. Finlay Geoghegan J raised the question as to whether it was permissible to consider a respondent's conduct as found in an inspector's report before the commencement of s 160 of the CA 1990 but found it was not necessary to answer that as the applicant did not seek to rely on any adverse commentary in the inspectors' reports prior to the commencement of the section. In the event, it was held that the respondent's conduct was such as to make him unfit to be concerned in the management of a company[507].

[28.189] In considering whether a person is fit to be involved in management, it has been held in relation to the senior management of banks that the nature and degree of trust owed to customers, shareholders and creditors is relevant[508]. As Murphy J said in *Re National Irish Bank; Director of Corporate Enforcement v Boner*[509]: 'The conduct of a respondent will, accordingly, be judged more seriously where the business in question is founded on fiduciary relationships or trust where the protection of the public is paramount.'

(g) *Persistently in default in relation to 'relevant requirements': s 160(2)(f)*

[28.190] '(f) a person has been persistently in default in relation to the relevant requirements.' The meaning of 'relevant requirements' is defined by s 159 of the CA 1990 to mean:

---

505 *National Irish Bank Ltd and National Irish Bank Financial Services; ODCE v D'Arcy* [2006] 2 IR 163 at 175.

506 *Re Ansbacher (Cayman) Ltd; Director of Corporate Enforcement v Collery* [2007] 1 IR 580.

507 The fate of the various respondents in the National Irish Bank litigation has been diverse. Some, as in *D'Arcy* have been disqualified whereas others have not: eg, *Re National Irish Bank; Director of Corporate Enforcement v Boner* [2008] IEHC 151; *Re National Irish Bank; Director of Corporate Enforcement v Curran* [2007] IEHC 181; and *Re National Irish Bank Ltd; Director of Corporate Enforcement v Byrne* [2009] 2 ILRM 328 (on appeal to the Supreme Court)

508 *National Irish Bank Ltd and National Irish Bank Financial Services; ODCE v D'Arcy* [2006] 2 IR 163.

509 *Re National Irish Bank; Director of Corporate Enforcement v Boner* [2008] IEHC 151.

'any provision of the Companies Acts (including a provision repealed by this Act) which requires or required any return, account or other document to be filed with, delivered or sent to, or notice of any matter to be given to, the Registrar of Companies.'

The civil remedy of a disqualification order may be invoked in addition to a prosecution for a failure to file offence. It will be noted that this is the only ground for disqualification that the registrar of companies has *locus standi* to prosecute[510].

[28.191] The term 'persistently' is ambiguous: what is consistent to one might be occasional to another. Fortunately, guidance is given by s 160(3)(a) which provides:

'For the purposes of subsection (2)(f) the fact that a person has been persistently in default in relation to the relevant requirements may (without prejudice to its proof in any other manner) be conclusively proved by showing that in the five years ending with the date of the application he has been adjudicated guilty (whether or not on the same occasion) of three or more defaults in relation to those requirements.'

Moreover, the interpretation of 'default' is assisted by s 160(3)(b):

'A person shall be treated as being adjudged guilty of a default in relation to a relevant requirement for the purposes of this subsection if he is convicted of any offence consisting or a contravention of a relevant requirement or a default order is made against him.'

By 'default order' is meant an order or injunction made pursuant to s 371 of the CA 1963[511], by virtue of any contravention of or failure to comply with any relevant requirement (whether on his own part or on the part of any company)[512].

[28.192] Before making application on this ground, it would be prudent for the applicant to be able to prove that in the preceding five years, the respondent has been: (a) convicted of three offences relating to filing requirements or (b) has been enjoined under s 371 of the CA 1963 on three occasions to comply with a relevant requirement. It is thought that two convictions and one s 371 injunction, or vice versa, will suffice. It is important to note that a s 371 injunction can issue in respect of matters other than filing requirements, but that it seems only such an injunction compelling compliance with a filing requirement is cognisable. In *Re Wood Products (Longford) Ltd* [513], Laffoy J said:

'For s 160(2)(f) to apply, the Director must satisfy the court that the respondents have been persistently in default in relation to compliance with provisions of the Companies Acts, in relation to making returns to the CRO. Paragraph (f) does not extend to a company's failure to comply with statutory requirements to make returns to other bodies, for example, to the Revenue Commissioners.

The Director cannot avail of the evidential provisions contained in sub-s (3) because there is no evidence that the respondents were prosecuted, let alone convicted, of an offence under s 125 of the Act of 1963, as amended, for failure to make annual returns, nor is there any evidence that s 371 of the Act of 1963, as amended, was invoked, let alone successfully invoked, against the Company or the respondents.

---

510 See para **[28.157]** *ante*.

511 See para **[28.210]** *post*.

512 Section 159 of the CA 1990.

513 *Re Wood Products (Longford) Ltd* [2005] IEHC 41.

> Therefore, the question which falls to be considered is whether the Director has proved in any other manner that the respondents have been persistently in default in relation to making annual returns.
>
> In summary, the facts are that when these proceedings commenced, there had been default for thirteen consecutive years by the Company in making its annual return to the CRO as required by s 125 [of the CA 1963]. On the evidence, the only action taken by the CRO was to strike off the Company leading to its dissolution after nine years of default. When a third party brought an application to have the Company restored to the register, the court, presumably on the application of the Registrar of Companies, made an order directing the respondents to file the outstanding returns the respondents default continued and they failed to comply with the order of the court. The ordinary meaning of the verb "persist" in its primary sense is "to continue firmly or obstinately in a state, opinion, purpose, or course of action *esp* against opposition" (*Shorter Oxford English Dictionary*, 3rd ed). What might be called the "three strikes" philosophy which underlies sub-s (3) suggests that, on the proper construction of paragraph (f), persistent default is not merely default which has continued over a long period of time but is default which has continued in the teeth of intervention on the part of the courts more than once. Although the default by the Company in relation to its obligations under s 125 over such a long period and the failure of the respondents to comply with the order of 14th May, 2001 is to be deprecated, I am not satisfied that it has been established on the evidence that the respondents have been "persistently in default" in relation to their obligations under s 125 in the sense in which that expression is used in para (f).'

(h) Guilty of two or more offences for failing to keep proper books of account: s 160(2)(g)

[28.193] '(g) a person has been guilty of 2 or more offences under section 202(10).' The requirement in s 202 is considered in Chapter 17[514]. The requirement in s 202 of the CA 1990 that companies cause proper books of account to be kept is considered to be a fundamental aspect of corporate compliance and for this reason the CLEA 2001 took the opportunity of specifically providing that two convictions will ground an application for disqualification.

(i) Directorship of a company that has been struck off: s 160(2)(h)

[28.194] '(h) a person was a director of a company at the time of the sending, after the commencement of section 42 of the Company Law Enforcement Act, 2001, of a letter under subsection (1) of section 12 of the Companies (Amendment) Act, 1982, to the company and the name of which, following the taking of the other steps under that section consequent on the sending of that letter, was struck off the register under subsection (3) of that section.' This ground too was added by s 42 of the CLEA 2001 as an aid to bolster the remedy of strike-off[515]. Although strike-off will be a commercial disaster for the honest procrastinator, it can represent an opportunity for the delinquent director of an insolvent company to pursue a 'scorched earth'[516] policy and wrong-foot pursuing creditors. Being a director of a company that has been struck-off pursuant to s 12 of the C(A)A 1982 will ground an application for disqualification but the court is

---

514 See Ch 17, *Financial Statements, Audit and Annual Return,* at para **[17.005]**.

515 On strike-off, see Ch 26, *Strike-Off and Restoration* at para **[26.004]**.

516 As that term is used in the *Report of the Working Group on Compliance and Enforcement* (1998) at para 4.42.

not permitted to make an order in all cases. Section 160(3A) ensures, however, that those who avail of the voluntary (solvent) strike-off procedure[517] will not be thereby rendered liable to being disqualified. It provides:

> 'The court shall not make a disqualification order under paragraph (h) of subsection (2) against a person who shows to the court that the company referred to in that paragraph had no liabilities (whether actual, contingent or prospective) at the time its name was struck off the register or that any such liabilities that existed at that time were discharged before the date of the making of the application for the disqualification order.'

Accordingly, the legislature wisely employed a rapier as opposed to a cutlass by restricting this ground to directors of companies whose liabilities have not been discharged at the time it was struck off the register. This means that s 12 of the C(A)A 1982 can continue to facilitate persons who wish a swift end for a solvent company which has outlived its usefulness, without their exposure to a disqualification order.

[28.195] One of the first cases to consider this ground was *Re Clawhammer Ltd; Director of Corporate Enforcement v McDonnell and Endicott*[518]. In that case, Finlay Geoghegan J said it was important that the failure to file annual returns resulting in the dissolution of a company was considered to be a deliberate act more than a mere technical breach of the companies Acts. It was also held that whilst s 160(3A) provided a defence to directors, it did not require the Director of Corporate Enforcement to ascertain or assess the extent of the company's liabilities before applying for a disqualification order. It was also held that a successful application only required proof that a letter was sent subject to s 12 of the C(A)A 1982, that the company was struck off following the taking of the steps envisaged by s 12 and that the respondents were directors at that time. Finlay Geoghegan J also said that where the grounds for making an order were met, the respondent could provide exculpatory evidence which the court could consider in deciding the period of disqualification or whether to impose a restriction order in lieu of a disqualification order.

[28.196] Section 160(2)(h) was also considered by the High Court in *Re Anderson Kershaw Ltd and Anderson Conforming Ltd; Director of Corporate Enforcement v Collins and O'Connell*[519]. In that case, five-year disqualification orders were made against two persons who had been directors of a company which had been struck off the register for failure to file annual returns. Peart J held:

> 'It is important to state that officers, including directors, of a company must be taken to be aware of the statutory obligation to file annual returns for the company of which they are officers. Similarly they cannot contend successfully that they were unaware that if those returns are not filed for one or more years, as required, the company was at least at risk of being struck off the register. The privilege of being able to trade under the cloak of limited liability where certain protections are afforded to the company and those who own its shares is balanced in the interests of the creditors of the company by a corresponding obligation on the part of the company and its officers to comply with the statutory

[517] See Ch 26, *Strike-Off and Restoration* at para **[26.010]** *et seq*.

[518] *Re Clawhammer Ltd; Director of Corporate Enforcement v McDonnell and Endicott* [2005] 1 IR 503.

[519] *Re Anderson Kershaw Ltd and Anderson Conforming Ltd; Director of Corporate Enforcement v Collins and O'Connell* [2008] IEHC 456.

requirements of the Companies Acts. These are not requirements devoid of real purpose. They exist for the protection of creditors so that they can be aware, inter alia, of the financial status of a company with which they have or are considering having dealings. The requirement to file annual returns and to update when appropriate the other information required to be filed, such as the situation of the registered office, the names and addresses of the officers of the company, and details of any share transactions which have taken place during the previous twelve months, are all important pieces of information which must be publicly available at all relevant times as required by statute.

In the present case it is not disputed that the companies failed to comply with these requirements and it is insufficient for directors of the company to state, as they have, that they appointed accountants to take care of all these matters for them. The appointment of accountants who will have the expertise to look after these matters does not remove from the directors the primary obligation upon them as officers of the company to ensure that the necessary forms are filed in a timely fashion. The delegation of that task does not absolve the officers from ensuring that these matters are attended to. The responsibility remains with the officers concerned.'

In so finding, Peart J rejected that there was any obligation on the plaintiff's solicitor to seek out another address at which the directors of a company may reside where a strike-off warning letter is returned marked 'gone away'.

(j) The subject of a disqualification order made in a foreign state: s 160(2)(i)

[28.197] '(i) a person is disqualified under the law of another state (whether pursuant to an order of a judge or a tribunal or otherwise) from being appointed or acting as a director or secretary of a body corporate or an undertaking and the court is satisfied that, if the conduct of the person or the circumstances otherwise affecting him that gave rise to the said order being made against him had occurred or arisen in the State, it would have been proper to make a disqualification order otherwise under this subsection against him.' The final ground was also introduced by s 42 of the CLEA 2001. Section 160(3B) of the CA 1990 provides that a disqualification order based on this ground may be made notwithstanding that at the time of the order, the person is deemed by virtue of s 160(1A) to be subject to a disqualification order.

The nature of the disqualification order and the period of disqualification

[28.198] In *Re CB Readymix Ltd; Cahill v Grimes*[520], thc IIigh Court had made a twofold order against the respondent. First, the respondent was disqualified from 'being concerned in the management of a company as a liquidator, receiver or examiner for a period of seven years'. Second, the respondent was restricted in his acting as auditor, director or secretary to the extent that (i) he had such professional qualifications as are necessary or required by law so to do; and (ii) at no time was he to have in his possession, custody or control companies' seals, books or records provided always that he was to have access to them to discharge his legal obligations[521]. On appeal to the Supreme Court it was claimed that there was no jurisdiction to make such an order and

---

[520] *Re CB Readymix Ltd; Cahill v Grimes* [2002] 1 IR 372.

[521] *Re CB Readymix Ltd; Cahill v Grimes* (20 July 2001, unreported) HC, Smyth J.

that s 160 was in the nature of 'an all or nothing section'. The Supreme Court rejected that contention and upheld the form of order made by Smyth J in the High Court. Murphy J said:

> 'In my view this argument is refuted by the provisions of sub-s (8) of s 160 … The express power of the court to grant relief to a person who is subject or deemed subject to a disqualification order "either in whole or in part" and to "grant such relief on whatever terms and conditions it sees fit" would enable the court to review a disqualification order in the days immediately following the making thereof by imposing precisely those terms which Mr Justice Smyth had required in the first instance. In my view it would be unthinkable that the court could have a power to revise its own order in that way and in that time frame and not have the same powers in the first instance. I am fully satisfied that the learned trial judge did have the powers which he purported to exercise so humanely in disqualifying the respondent from filling certain offices and yet permitting him to fill others subject to stipulated conditions[522].'

It was also rejected by the Supreme Court that the restrictions on the respondent acting as auditor, director or secretary were either an impermissible intrusion into the affairs of a company or otherwise inappropriate.

[28.199] The periods of disqualification imposed by the English courts have varied greatly. An attempt was made to standardise disqualification periods by the English Court of Appeal in the case of *Re Sevenoaks Stationers (Retail) Ltd*[523]. There, the Court of Appeal introduced the following classification:

> '(i) The top bracket of disqualification for periods over ten years should be reserved for particularly serious cases. These may include cases where a director who has already had one period of disqualification imposed on him falls to be disqualified yet again. (ii) The minimum bracket of two to five years' disqualification should be applied where, though disqualification is mandatory, the case is, relatively, not very serious. (iii) The middle bracket of disqualification for from six to ten years should apply for serious cases which do not merit the top bracket[524].'

This scale continues to be applied in England[525] and was applied in Ireland by Smyth J in *Re CB Readymix Ltd; Cahill v Grimes*[526]. The maximum period of disqualification has, however, been found to be in excess of 10 years, and 15-year periods of disqualification are not unknown. An extreme example is seen in *Official Receiver v Vass and another*[527] where two directors were disqualified, one for 15 years and the other for 12 years in circumstances where the first had been acting as a director whilst disqualified and the second, a resident of the island of Sark, was nominee director of 1,313 UK companies and secretary of 513 UK companies, even after having resigned 282 directorships and 113 secretarial appointments! The court took a particularly dim view of acting as a director whilst already disqualified and such was the seriousness of this that a 15-year disqualification period was deemed appropriate. The second director's conduct in holding himself out as director for so many companies on a token basis and totally

---

522 *Re CB Readymix Ltd; Cahill v Grimes* [2002] 1 IR 372.

523 *Re Sevenoaks Stationers (Retail) Ltd* [1991] BCLC 325.

524 *Re Sevenoaks Stationers (Retail) Ltd* [1991] BCLC 325 at 328d–e.

525 See, for example, *Re Saver Ltd* [1999] BCC 221.

526 *Re CB Readymix Ltd; Cahill v Grimes* (20 July 2001, unreported) HC at p 18 of the judgment.

527 *Official Receiver v Vass and another* [1999] BCC 516.

abrogating responsibility was also considered to be an extremely serious matter and deserving of a substantial period of disqualification, ie 12 years.

[28.200] In *National Irish Bank Ltd and National Irish Bank Financial Services; ODCE v D'Arcy*[528], Kelly J considered the starting point for consideration of the length of the period of disqualification to be the decision in *Re Sevenoaks Stationers (Retail) Ltd* and this approach was followed in *Re Ansbacher (Cayman) Ltd; Director of Corporate Enforcement v Collery*[529] by Finlay Geoghegan J. Although recognising the English position as useful, the differences in the law were also noted, eg, the absence of minimum and maximum periods, that disqualification is not mandatory and the availability of an alternative, in the form of restriction. Both Kelly and Finlay Geoghegan JJ found the following observations of Lord Woolf to be helpful:

> '… other factors come into play in the wider interests of protecting the public ie a deterrent element in relation to the director himself and a deterrent element as far as other directors are concerned. Despite the fact that the courts have said that disqualification is not a "punishment" in truth the exercise that is being engaged in is little different from any sentencing exercise. The period of disqualification must reflect the gravity of the offence. It must contain deterrent elements. That is what sentencing is all about, and that is what fixing the appropriate period of the disqualification is all about. What Vinelott J (in *Re Pamstock Ltd* [1994] 1 BCLC 716 at p 737) called "tunnel vision" ie concentrating on the facts of the offence, is necessary when considering whether a director is unfit. In relation to the period of disqualification the facts of the offence are still obviously important but many other factors ought (and in reality do) come into play …
>
> We do not consider that it would send out a wrong message to fix the period of disqualification by starting with an assessment of the correct period to fit the gravity of the conduct, and then allowing for the mitigating factors, in much the same way as a sentencing court would do.'

Acknowledging the assistance she gleaned from the foregoing passages, in *Re Ansbacher (Cayman) Ltd; Director of Corporate Enforcement v Collery*[530] Finlay Geoghegan J set out the following helpful principles in determining the appropriate period, although she did say 'in this case' since it is accepted that each case must be looked at on its own facts[531]:

> '(1) the primary purpose of an order of disqualification is not to punish the individual but to protect the public against future conduct of companies by persons whose past record has shown them to be a danger to creditors and others.
>
> (2) The period of disqualification should reflect (in relation to an order under s 160(2)(e)) the gravity of the conduct as found by the inspectors which makes the respondent unfit to be concerned in the management of a company.
>
> (3) The period of disqualification should contain deterrent elements.

[528] *National Irish Bank Ltd and National Irish Bank Financial Services; ODCE v D'Arcy* [2006] 2 IR 163.

[529] *Re Ansbacher (Cayman) Ltd; Director of Corporate Enforcement v Collery* [2007] 1 IR 580.

[530] *Re Ansbacher (Cayman) Ltd; Director of Corporate Enforcement v Collery* [2007] 1 IR 580.

[531] Indeed, Finlay Geoghegan J considered it 'unnecessary and inappropriate' to be taken through the facts of other cases by means of comparison, citing Nourse J in *Re Civica Investments Ltd* [1983] BCLC 456 at 457–458.

(4) A period of disqualification in excess of ten years should be reserved for particularly serious cases.

(5) The court should firstly assess the correct period in accordance with the foregoing and then taken into account mitigating factors prior to fixing the actual period of disqualification[532].'

Applying those principles, the learned judge considered that a period of 12 years was justified, but mitigated by three years to nine years on account of the director's assistance to the inspectors 'with promptness and courtesy in difficult circumstances'.

[28.201] Although the principles enunciated by Finlay Geoghegan J in *Re Ansbacher (Cayman) Ltd; Director of Corporate Enforcement v Collery*[533] were in the context of an application brought under s 160(2)(e) of the CA 1990, the learned judge held in *Re FAI Finance Corporation Ltd; O'Riordan and Granger v Harvey*[534] that the principles apply equally in an application under s 160(2)(d) save that it is either the gravity of the conduct as found by the court or acknowledged by the respondent rather than as found by the inspectors that is to be considered.

Relief for the disqualified

[28.202] Section 160(8) of the CA 1990 provides:

> 'Any person who is subject or deemed subject to a disqualification order by virtue of this Part may apply to the court for relief, either in whole or in part, from that disqualification and the court may, if it deems it just and equitable to do so, grant such relief on whatever terms and conditions it sees fit.'

There is English authority that although a person's conduct justifies them being disqualified, the existence of certain mitigating factors may make it just in the circumstances for them to be disqualified generally but permitted to continue to act as the director of a particular company[535]. This is clearly within the inherent competence and jurisdiction of the Irish courts where the circumstances require such a partial dispensation to achieve justice and *conditional disqualification* has been upheld by the Supreme Court in *Re CB Ready Mix Ltd*[536]. There must, however, be a clear and convincing reason why a court that has determined that an individual is not fit to be a director and who disqualifies him from so acting, should do a volte-face and lift that order. Where a person is convicted of an offence under s 161(1) of the CA 1990, ie, acting contrary to a disqualification order or restriction order and his disqualification is

---

532 *Re Ansbacher (Cayman) Ltd; Director of Corporate Enforcement v Collery* [2007] 1 IR 580 at 589.

533 *Re Ansbacher (Cayman) Ltd; Director of Corporate Enforcement v Collery* [2007] 1 IR 580.

534 *Re FAI Finance Corporation Ltd; O'Riordan and Granger v Harvey* [2010] IEHC 225.

535 See *Re Chartmore Ltd* [1990] BCLC 673, where a person was disqualified for two years but was allowed to act as director of another particular company for one year with permission to apply for an extension. See also *Re Majestic Recording Studios Ltd* [1989] BCLC 1, where although disqualified generally, the person was allowed to continue to act as a director of another company with a co-director approved by the court where audited accounts were filed. Clearly, one of the overriding reasons for this was the fact that otherwise, the jobs of his employees would be jeopardised.

536 *Re CB Ready Mix Ltd* [2002] 1 IR 372.

extended by 10 years (in accordance with s 161(3)) recourse cannot be had to s 160(8) for relief.

[28.203] In *Re Barings plc; Secretary of State for Trade and Industry v Baker et al*[537], Sir Richard Scott VC cautioned against courts forgetting the original reasons for making a disqualification order in entertaining an application for relief. In that case, the applicant had been a director at the ill-fated Barings Bank Group and had been disqualified for four years in circumstances where there were no allegations of dishonest or fraudulent impropriety. He subsequently set up business as a management and advisory consultancy in partnership with his wife; he applied for leave to be allowed to act as director of four companies of which he had been a director before being disqualified. Although that case involved the interpretation of the use of the word 'need' in s 17 of the English Company Directors Disqualification Act 1986, it does provide guidance as to the court's general approach. Sir Richard Scott VC said:

> 'It seems to me that the importance of protecting the public from the conduct that led to the disqualification order and the need that the applicant should be able to act as director of a particular company must be kept in balance with one another. The court in considering whether or not to grant leave should, in particular, pay attention to the nature of the defects in company management that led to the disqualification order and ask itself whether, if leave were granted, a situation might arise in which there would be a risk of recurrence of those defects[538].'

On the facts of that case it was held that there was virtually no risk at all of such a recurrence and that it was appropriate to grant leave to the person to act as a director of the particular companies, subject to certain conditions[539].

The enforcement of disqualification orders

[28.204] Just as in the case of restriction orders, the enforcement of the provisions on disqualified directors is achieved in two ways, namely: against the director (civilly and criminally) and against those persons in the restricted company who become involved with him.

(a) Breach of disqualification order – criminal sanction

[28.205] The penalty for acting contrary to the provisions of Chapter 2 is contained in s 161(1) of the CA 1990, the relevant part of which provides:

> 'Any person who, in relation to any company, acts in a manner or capacity which, by virtue of being … subject or deemed to be subject to a disqualification order, he is prohibited from doing shall be guilty of an offence.'

This offence is punishable in accordance with s 240 of the CA 1990[540]. Where convicted of such an offence, the person is also subject to automatic disqualification[541]. Moreover,

---

537 *Re Barings plc; Secretary of State for Trade and Industry v Baker et al* [1999] BCC 960.

538 *Re Barings plc; Secretary of State for Trade and Industry v Baker et al* [1999] BCC 960 at 965.

539 See also *Shuttleworth v Secretary of State for Trade and Industry; Re Dawes and Henderson (Agencies) Ltd* [2000] BCC 204; *Re Amaron Ltd* [1998] BCC 264; and *Re TLL Realisations Ltd* [2000] BCC 998.

540 See para **[28.034]** *ante*.

541 Section 161(2) of the CA 1990.

where a person who is convicted of an offence under s 161(1) was subject or deemed to be subject to a disqualification order immediately prior to the date of such conviction, the period for which he was disqualified shall be extended for a further period of 10 years from such date or such further period as the court, on the application of the prosecutor and having regard to all of the circumstances, may order[542].

(b) Breach of disqualification order – civil sanctions

[28.206] Where a disqualified director acts contrary to the order imposed upon him, any company with which he becomes involved may recover any consideration paid to him for services rendered: s 163(2) of the CA 1990. Furthermore, by s 163(3), if a disqualified director becomes involved in a company and that company goes into insolvent liquidation, then on the application of a liquidator or creditor, the court can make the disqualified director *personally liable* without limitation for the debts of the company incurred in the period in which he was acting in such manner or capacity[543]. In relation to proceedings brought under either s 163(2) or (3) the court may, having regard to the circumstances of the case and if it considers it just and equitable to do so, grant relief in whole or in part from the liability which would otherwise attach, subject to such conditions as it sees fit[544].

(c) Criminal sanctions for officers of companies who act in accordance with the directions or instructions of disqualified directors

[28.207] Section 164(1) of the CA 1990 makes it an offence for officers[545] to act in accordance with the directions or instructions of a disqualified director where they know that he has been disqualified. A person convicted of an offence under this section shall be deemed to be subject to a disqualification order from the date of conviction[546].

(d) Civil sanctions for officers of companies with which disqualified directors become involved

[28.208] Section 165(1) of the CA 1990 provides that any person who is convicted of an offence under s 164 for acting in accordance with the directions or instructions of a disqualified person shall, subject to s 165(2), be personally liable for the debts of the company that were incurred in the period during which he was so acting. By virtue of s 165(2), the court may grant relief where in the circumstances of the case it considers it just and equitable to do so.

[28.209] Furthermore, a conviction under s 164 has the consequence that it will also render convicted persons liable be held to be personally responsible under s 165 of the CA 1990 for the debts of the company while they were acting, subject to their right to apply for just and equitable relief[547].

[542] Section 161(3) of the CA 1990.

[543] See Ch 5, *Disregarding Separate Legal Personality*, at para **[5.084]**.

[544] Section 163(5) of the CA 1990.

[545] Section 164(1) applies to 'a director or other officer or a member of a committee of management or trustee of any company'.

[546] Section 164(2) of the CA 1990.

[547] Section 165(2) of the CA 1990.

[G] INJUNCTIONS TO COMPEL COMPLIANCE WITH THE COMPANIES ACTS

[28.210] Section 371 of the CA 1963 seems never to have been used and, indeed, to have been practically forgotten about until 're-discovered' by the chair of the McDowell Group shortly after the Group's formation. In its report the Group said:

> 'The threat of fast track High Court civil proceedings and consequent costs would, in many cases, act as a major deterrent to non-compliance, not only in relation to the companies in question, but also in relation to individual officer defendants[548].'

The Group went on to recommend the expansion of the section in terms of breadth and in respect to those who can bring application[549]. Section 96 of the CLEA 2001 effected a number of changes to the originally drafted s 371 of the CA 1963, resulting in the following extended section:

> '(1) If a company or any officer of a company having made default in complying with any provision of this Act fails to make good the default within 14 days after the service of a notice on the company or officer requiring it or him to do so, the court may, on an application made to the court by any member or creditor of the company, by the Director or by the Registrar of Companies, make an order directing the company and any officer thereof to make good the default within such time as may be specified in the order.
>
> (2) Any such order may provide that all costs of and incidental to the application shall be borne by the company or by any officers of the company responsible for the default.
>
> (3) Nothing in this section shall be taken to prejudice the operation of any enactment imposing penalties (including restriction under section 150, or disqualification under section 160, of the Companies Act, 1990) on a company or its officers in respect of any such default as aforesaid.
>
> (4) In this section, "officer of a company" and cognate words include a director, shadow director, an officer, a promoter, a receiver, a liquidator or an auditor of a company.'

[28.211] The revamped s 371 of the CA 1963 provides company law enforcers (the Director of Corporate Enforcement and the registrar of companies) as well as disgruntled creditors or aggrieved members with the right to have recourse to the High Court for an injunction to compel compliance *by a company or any officer of a company* with *any default in complying with a provision of the Companies Acts*. Not everyone can apply for an order, however. In *Re Murray Browne Mulcahy Ltd; Murray v Mulcahy*[550], a *conditional* order was made under s 371(1) directing a director to make good his default in complying with s 202(8) of the CA 1990 and make available the books of account of the company to enable the preparation of statutory accounts for the years 2007 to 2009 because the applicants had not adduced evidence that they were *members*. The circumstances of the order were that the applicants and respondent were directors of a company which had been dissolved for failure to file annual returns and the applicants sought to have the company reinstated. Laffoy J held that in order to invoke s 371(1) the applicants had to establish that they were either *creditors or members* of the company;

---

548 At para 3.22 of the Report.

549 At para 4.33 of the Report.

550 *Re Murray Browne Mulcahy Ltd; Murray v Mulcahy* [2010] IEHC 112.

there was no evidence that they were either and so the order was conditional upon their establishing that they had standing to bring the application.

[28.212] Consequent upon s 371(4) – added to the section by s 96(c) of the CLEA 2001 – it can be seen that 'officer' of a company is very broadly defined, although why examiners were excluded, in view of the fact that there are serious duties imposed upon them, is unclear. The question as to whether *former officers* can be respondents was considered in *Brosnan and ors v Sommerville*[551]. This involved an application to, *inter alia*, compel the defendant to sign letters to facilitate the plaintiffs to obtain access to two companies' bank accounts pursuant to s 202 of the CA 1990 and, or in the alternative, s 371 of the CA 1963 and deliver up books and records in relation to those bank accounts. Smyth J noted that the defendant had been a director and company secretary but was no longer either and so was '*prima facie* not a person against whom an order under s 371 of the CA 1963 can be made'. However, Smyth J went on to note that in that case the defendant had been an officer at the time the request was made and he questioned whether that duty owed when the request was made could be terminated by resignation. Smyth J found that on a 'legalistic view of the facts' the plaintiffs were not entitled to an order under s 371(1) of the CA 1963; however, the Companies Acts had to be construed as a whole and the defendant's resignation did not prejudice s 202(1) of the CA 1990 and he found this supported by s 371(3) of the CA 1963, quoted above. Smyth J did not say that a former officer would be amenable to a s 371 order indefinitely, but seems to have concluded that where the request for compliance had been made before the resignation, there was jurisdiction to make an order under s 371(1) of the CA 1963 that the former director and secretary deliver up books and records to the applicants.

[28.213] It would seem to be a prerequisite to the invocation of s 371(1) of the CA 1963 that the default complained of is capable of being 'made good'. It is a remedial measure, designed to ensure compliance rather than to punish non-compliance; of course non-compliance with the High Court order is punishable as a contempt of court. In *Re Powertech Logistics Ltd; Airscape Ltd v Powertech Logistics Ltd, O'Reilly and McKee*[552], an order had been made under s 371(1) of the CA 1963 directing the respondents to make good the default of not filing annual returns and directed the respondents to submit all outstanding statutory annual returns and audited financial statements to the CRO for five years within 12 weeks of the making of the order. The applicant was a creditor of the company. Just over one week after the 12 weeks had passed, the applicant issued a motion seeking an order under Ord 42, r 31 of the RSC 1986 enforcing sequestration against the property of the three respondents and orders of attachment against the two natural respondents who were the first respondent's directors[553]. After that motion was issued, the annual returns were all filed. In these circumstances, Laffoy J refused to make an order of sequestration for three reasons. First, the purpose of an order under Ord 42, r 32 was coercive, not punitive, and given that the order under s 371 of the CA 1963 had then been complied with, an order of

---

551 *Brosnan and ors v Sommerville* [2006] IEHC 329.

552 *Re Powertech Logistics Ltd; Airscape Ltd v Powertech Logistics Ltd, O'Reilly and McKee* [2007] IEHC 43.

553 See Ch 6, *Corporate Civil Litigation,* at para **[6.078]** *et seq.*

sequestration would be merely punitive. Second, Laffoy J said, contrary to the orthodox view that a penal notice is only required in cases of attachment and committal, that even an order for sequestration should carry a penal notice[554]. Third, Laffoy J held that there was no evidence that the respondents had wilfully disobeyed the order.

[28.214] Where a person who is entitled to make complaint wishes to initiate the s 371 injunction, he should first serve a notice on the company or officer, requiring it or him to make good the default complained of within 14 days of the date of the notice. It would be prudent to head up the notice: 'Notice Pursuant to Section 371(1) of the Companies Act, 1963 Requiring a Default under the Companies Acts to be Made Good', or words to that effect, so that the addressee can be under do doubt but that the intention in serving the notice is to proceed to seek a court order should the default not be made good. Once this has been done the High Court has jurisdiction to make an order. On the authority of *Re Powertech Logistics Ltd; Airscape Ltd v Powertech Logistics Ltd, O'Reilly and McKee*[555] it may also be prudent to attach a penal notice where the applicant intends to proceed against the respondent company by way of sequestration if the order is not complied with.

[28.215] It is notable that there is no guidance provided to the court when it comes to the exercise of its discretion – not even that such an order should be made where the court considers it 'just' or 'just and equitable'. The order will operate in much the same way as an ordinary injunction and should require that the default is made good by a particular time. Section 371(2) expressly provides that the court, on making an order, can, at the court's discretion, provide that all costs of and incidental to the application shall be borne by the company or by any officers of the company responsible for the default. It is also significant that the making of an order under this section is expressed to be without prejudice to the operation of any enactment imposing penalties, including restriction and disqualification orders.

554 On the authority of *Prior v Johnston* 27 ILTR 108.

555 *Re Powertech Logistics Ltd; Airscape Ltd v Powertech Logistics Ltd, O'Reilly and McKee* [2007] IEHC 43.

Chapter 29

Public Limited Companies and SEs

[29.001] For very many people, the public limited company or 'PLC' epitomises company law. Indeed, most of the media coverage of company law tends to relate to issues that concern PLCs. Large annual general meetings involving hundreds or even thousands of shareholders venting their spleen to the board of directors, shareholder activism, debates over directors' remuneration, the Combined Code of Corporate Governance, what used to be called 'insider dealing' but is now termed 'market abuse', the Stock Exchange, uncertificated securities, etc, all very frequently make the news and when they do there is, perhaps, a tendency to believe these issues are at the centre of company law. The reality is very different as these issues are in fact relevant only to PLCs and, even then, only to a small cohort of PLCs which have their shares admitted to listing on a stock exchange. As at 31 December 2011, of the 185,181 registered companies a mere 1,799 were public limited companies accounting for just under 1% of all companies[1]. Of those a mere 70 to 100 PLCs list their shares on the Irish Stock Exchange. One particular type of PLC is an *investment company* which is used by the funds industry and regulated by the Central Bank and is considered separately from other PLCs.

The *Societas Europaea* or 'SE' is a European public limited company established in an EU Member State under Council Regulation EC 2157/2001 of 8 October 2001 on the Statute for a European Company (SE). SEs are considered along with PLCs because the law applicable to a PLC in the EU Member State in which the SE has its registered office supplements the SE-specific law contained in the Council Regulation.

In this chapter, we proceed to consider the PLC and SE sequentially and the chapter is divided into two sections:

[A] Public Limited Companies
[B] The Societas Europaea

[A] PUBLIC LIMITED COMPANIES

Public companies generally

[29.002] The term 'public company' does not connote a unique form of corporate construct but rather comprises a hetrogeneous grouping of disparate types of companies all sharing the following two features, namely – they are governed by the Companies Acts; and they are *not* private companies. Prior to the passing of the C(A)A 1983 every

---

§ *This chapter has been contributed by G Brian Hutchinson.*

1 See the *Companies Registration Office Report 2011* at p 10.

company was by implication a public company unless its articles of association contained the restrictions set out in s 33 of the CA 1963[2], though the term 'public company' does not appear in the Act. Section 2 of the C(A)A 1983 simplified matters somewhat by stating simply that for the purposes of that Act 'public company' means a company which is not a private company, and that interpretation has stuck.

[29.003] The range of different types of public company is limited therefore only by what is possible under the Companies Acts – though, naturally, some types are more common in practice than others. In principle, the list of types of public company possible today is as follows:

- the public limited company limited by shares;
- the public limited company limited by guarantee and having a share capital;
- the public limited company with a variable share capital;
- the public company limited by guarantee that does not have a share capital;
- the public unlimited company having a share capital; and
- the public unlimited company not having a share capital.

All public companies are multi-member companies – it is not permissible to have a single-member company that is not a private company. In practice, public companies can be grouped into three generic categories:

(a) Public limited companies;
(b) Companies limited by guarantee not having a share capital;
(c) Public unlimited companies.

The public company at (b) – the guarantee company – is considered in Chapter 30 and the public company at (c) – the public unlimited company – is considered in Chapter 31[3]. The focus of this chapter is, therefore, that described at (a) – the public limited company or 'PLC'.

Public limited companies defined

[29.004] Public limited company ('PLC') is defined by s 2 of the C(A)A 1983 as being:

> '... a public company limited by shares or a public company limited by guarantee and having a share capital, being a company—
>
> (a) the memorandum of which states that the company is to be a public limited company; and
>
> (b) in relation to which the provisions of the Companies Acts as to the registration or re-registration of a company as a public limited company have been complied with on or after the appointed day[4].'

The section envisages that a PLC can be either limited by shares *or* limited by guarantee, but in either case it *must* have a share capital – even where limited by guarantee.

2 See Ch 1, *The Private Company in Context*, at para **[1.133]**.

3 See, generally, Ch 31, *Unlimited Companies*.

4 The 'appointed day' means the day appointed by the Minister under s 1(3) of the C(A)A 1983 for the coming into operation of the Act: s 2(1) of the C(A)A 1983. The C(A)A 1983 was brought into operation on 13 October 1983: Companies (Amendment) Act 1983 (Commencement) Order 1983 (SI 288/1983).

However, entry to the club of PLCs which are limited by guarantee and which have a share capital is now closed, for s 7 of the C(A)A 1983 provides that:

> 'On or after the appointed day, no company shall be formed as, or become, a public company limited by guarantee and having a share capital.'

Thus, the only public companies in existence which are limited by guarantee *and which* have a share capital are those that were incorporated as such before 13 October 1983.

[29.005] In practice, the PLC limited by shares is by far the more common of the two possible forms of PLC envisaged by s 2 of the C(A)A 1983, particularly since it is the favoured corporate form for companies wishing to trade shares on the stock exchanges[5]. Indeed, as shall be seen, much of the law relating to PLCs nowadays stems from European measures concerned with the trade in securities on various markets across the European Union.

Approach adopted to treatment of the law of PLCs

[29.006] In this chapter we examine the public limited company following the structure which has been employed thus far in our examination of the private company, under headings corresponding to the titles of Chapters 2–28. It may be recalled[6] that until 1983 the Companies Acts were geared towards public companies as the default form of company, with exceptions being made for private companies[7]. Much of the law governing PLCs is therefore the same law that governs private companies, and accordingly we focus here on the main differences that apply in the case of plcs. The following areas are considered:

1. Formation and registration.
2. Constitutional documentation.
3. Incorporation and its consequences.
4. Corporate contracts, capacity and authority.
5. Shares and membership.
6. Share transfer.
7. The maintenance of capital.
8. Corporate governance: management by the directors.
9. Corporate governance: meetings.
10. Financial statements, audit and annual return.
11. Corporate borrowing.
12. Strike off and restoration.
13. Investigations and inspectors.
14. Compliance and enforcement.

---

5 See, generally, Ch 32, *Prospectus, Market Abuse & Transparency Law.*

6 See para **[29.002]** *ante*.

7 The Company Law Review Group ('CLRG') has noted the irony of the public company being the main focus in the legislation when over 90% of companies on the Irish register are in fact private – CLRG, *Report on General Scheme of Companies Consolidation and Reform Bill* (2007); the new legislation will reverse this trend by making the private company the primary focus before identifying the special rules applicable to PLCs and other types of company.

The law relating to disregarding separate legal personality, civil litigation, shareholders' remedies, groups, directors' duties, the statutory regulation of directors' transactions, schemes of arrangement, reconstructions and examiners, and winding up is broadly the same as that applicable to the private company.

After reviewing the 14 matters listed above, we will then turn to consider one particular type of PLC, namely *investment companies*[8].

Formation and registration[9]

[29.007] PLCs can be formed afresh or can be formed by the conversion of a private company. It is less usual to form a PLC afresh to act as a trading company; typically such companies begin life as a private company and convert to a PLC once the constraints of s 33 of the CA 1963 start to conflict with the company's operational requirements, and typically to enable the company to offer its shares for sale to the public and thereby to receive an injection of capital to finance its activities further without over-borrowing.

[29.008] The formation and registration of PLCs is considered here in the following manner:

(a) Formation of PLCs.
(b) Registration of PLCs and commencement of business.
(c) Converting from a private company to a PLC.
(d) Migration of companies into Ireland.

The related topics of prospectuses and stock exchange listing are considered separately in Chapter 32, below.

(a) Formation of PLCs

[29.009] A PLC may be formed in much the same way as a private company. The following documents must be filed in the Companies Registration Office ('CRO'):

– the memorandum and articles of association,
– the Form No A1.

Those features of the memorandum and articles of association which are peculiar to PLCs are set out later[10]. The details required to be completed in the Form No A1 have been set out in Chapter 2[11].

(b) Registration of PLCs and commencement of business

[29.010] The C(A)A 1983 places a number of restrictions on the registration of PLCs and the commencement of business – most significantly in the form of:

(i) minimum capital requirements;
(ii) minimum membership requirements;
(iii) certification requirements;

8 See para **[29.131]** *post*.
9 See generally Ch 2, *Incorporation by Registration*.
10 See para **[29.028]**.
11 See, Ch 2, *Incorporation by Registration*, at para **[2.024]**.

(iv) publication requirements;

(v) valuation requirements.

(i) Minimum capital requirements

[29.011] First, as far as registration is concerned, s 5(2) of the C(A)A 1983 prohibits the registrar of companies from registering the memorandum of a PLC unless the *authorised* capital set out therein is not less than the 'authorised minimum', which is set by s 19 of the C(A)A 1983 at €38,092.14[12].

Second, the restrictions on commencement of business contained in s 115 of the CA 1963 do not apply to PLCs[13], but s 6(1) of the C(A)A 1983 provides that a company registered as a PLC on its original incorporation *shall not do business or exercise any borrowing powers* unless the registrar of companies has issued it with a certificate under that section or the company has been re-registered as another form of company. Section 6(2) provides that the registrar may only issue a certificate if:

> 'he is satisfied that the nominal value of the company's allotted share capital is not less than the authorised minimum, and there is delivered to him a statutory declaration complying with subsection (3).'

Note that the section requires that the PLC has *allotted* shares to the value of at least the authorised minimum. In that regard, s 28(1) of the C(A)A 1983 imposes a further requirement in respect of the payment for allotted shares in a PLC: 'a public limited company shall not allot a share except as paid up to at least one-quarter of the nominal value of the share and the whole of any premium on it.' The upshot is that a PLC shall not commence business until it has a paid up share capital amounting to at least €9,523.04, ie, 25% of €38,092.14.

(ii) Minimum membership requirements

[29.012] Section 5(1) of the C(A)A 1983 further prohibits the registrar from registering a PLC unless the requirements of the Companies Acts in respect of registration and of matters precedent and incidental thereto have been complied with. A significant difference between private companies and PLCs in this regard is the requirement that a PLC, as with any company which is not a private company, must have a minimum of seven members[14]. The model memorandum for a PLC contained in Schedule II of the C(A)A 1983 thus provides for seven subscribers to the memorandum.

[29.013] Any shares taken by a subscriber to the memorandum of a PLC in pursuance of an undertaking of his in the memorandum and any premium on the shares shall be paid up in cash[15].

---

[12] £30,000 converted to €38,092.14 by Council Regulations (EC) No 1103/97, No 974/98 and No 2866/98 and s 6 of the Economic and Monetary Union Act 1998. This may be altered by the Minister by statutory instrument: s 19(2) of the C(A)A 1983. No such regulations have been made.

[13] Section 116(7) of the CA 1963.

[14] See ss 5 and 36 of the CA 1963.

[15] Section 35 of the C(A)A 1983. Note, however, that 'cash' includes many things other than just paper money or cash in the vernacular sense: see Ch 8, *Shares and Membership*, at para **[8.061]**.

(iii) Certification requirements

[29.014] The appropriate form to be filed with the registrar of companies is a *Form A4 (previously Form 70)*. This sets out the following matters which are enumerated in s 6(3) of the C(A)A 1983:

- that the nominal value of the company's allotted share capital is not less than the authorised minimum;
- the amount paid up, at the time of the application, on the allotted share capital of the company;
- the amount, or estimated amount, of the preliminary expenses of the company and the persons by whom any of those expenses have been paid or are payable; and
- any amount or benefit paid or given or intended to be paid or given to any promoter of the company, and the consideration for the payment or benefit.

Where a statutory declaration is made in accordance with s 6(2) of the C(A)A 1983, it is deemed to be sufficient evidence of the matters stated therein[16].

Where the registrar of companies issues a certificate under this section, it is conclusive evidence that the company is entitled to do business and exercise any borrowing powers[17]. While s 6(7) of the C(A)A 1983 makes contravention of the section a criminal offence, the general provisions of the section are without prejudice to the actual validity of any transaction. However, where a company does enter into a contravening transaction and fails to comply with the section within 21 days from being called upon to do so, s 6(8) of the C(A)A 1983 provides that the directors of the company shall be jointly and severally liable to indemnify the other party to the transaction in respect of any loss or damage suffered by the other party, by reason of the failure of the company to comply with the obligations contained in s 6 of the C(A)A 1983.

[29.015] A PLC, registered as such, which does not obtain a requisite '*s 6 certificate*' within one year from its original incorporation can be struck-off the register of companies by the registrar in accordance with s 311(5) of the CA 1963.

(iv) Publication requirements

[29.016] In addition to the usual statutory obligations incidental to incorporations, PLCs are further required by s 55 of the C(A)A 1983[18] to publish in *Iris Oifigiúil* a notice of delivery of the following documents to the registrar of companies:

> '(a) a statutory declaration under section 6(2);
>
> (b) a copy of a resolution which gives, varies, revokes or renews an authority for the purposes of section 20;
>
> (c) a copy of a special resolution under section 24(1), (2) or (3);
>
> (d) any expert's valuation report on a non-cash consideration under section 31(2);
>
> (e) any expert's valuation report on a non-cash asset acquired from a subscriber under section 33(2);

---

16 Section 6(5) of the C(A)A 1983.

17 Section 6(6) of the C(A)A 1983.

18 Although s 72 of the IFCMPA 2005 provides for the substitution of the 'Companies Registration Office Gazette' for *Iris Oifigiúil*, s 72 has not yet been commenced.

(f) any statement or notice under section 39(1), (3) or (4);

(g) any return of allotments under section 58(1) of the Principal Act;

(h) any notification of the redemption of preference shares under section 69(1) of the Principal Act;

(i) a copy of a special resolution to reduce its share capital under section 72(2) of the Principal Act;

(j) a copy of any resolution or agreement to which section 143 of the Principal Act applies and which—

  (i) states the rights attached to any shares in the company, other than shares which are, in all respects, uniform (for the purposes of section 39(1)) with shares previously allotted;

  (ii) varies rights attached to any shares in the company; or

  (iii) assigns a name or other designation, or a new name or other designation, to any class of shares in the company.'

Failure to comply with these requirements is an offence rendering the company and every officer in default liable to a class C fine[19].

(v) Valuation requirements

[29.017] Section 32 of the C(A)A 1983 requires PLCs to obtain an independent valuation of any agreement which it proposes to enter into within the period of two years from the date of obtaining its s 6 certificate for the transfer to it or to any other person of any non-cash assets from any of its subscribers in circumstances where the value of consideration payable by the PLC equals or exceeds 10% of the nominal value of the issued share capital.

In the case of a company that has converted to a PLC, the valuation requirement is triggered where the company proposes within two years of its re-registration to enter into an agreement for the transfer of any non-cash assets to it or another person from any of the persons who were members at the date of re-registration and where the value of consideration payable by the PLC equals or exceeds 10% of the nominal value of the issued share capital[20].The valuation procedure in s 30 of the C(A)A 1983 is deemed to apply[21], and the independent person has similar powers to require from the officers of the company such information and explanation as he thinks necessary to enable him to carry out the valuation or make the report[22]. In order for the company to lawfully enter into the agreement to acquire the non-cash asset the following must first occur:

– the valuation must be duly carried out and the independent person must present his report which must be made up to a date not more than six months prior to the date of the proposed agreement[23];

---

19 Section 55(3) of the C(A)A 1983.

20 Section 32(1) and (2)(b) of the C(A)A 1983.

21 See para **[29.050]** *post*. The contents of the report largely mirror those of a s 30 report: see s 32(5) of the C(A)A 1983.

22 Section 33(1) of the C(A)A 1983.

23 Section 32(3)(a) and (b) of the C(A)A 1983.

- the report must be circulated to all members entitled to receive notice of general meetings together with a draft resolution to approve the proposed agreement[24];
- the proposed agreement must be duly approved by ordinary resolution of the members[25].

A copy of the report must be given to the contracting party, and a copy of the resolution approving the acquisition together with a copy of the report must be delivered to the registrar of companies within 15 days of the actual passing of the resolution. Failure to do so is a criminal offence[26]. Notice of the delivery of the report must also be published in *Iris Oifigiúil*[27].

[29.018] If the PLC enters into an agreement to take a transfer of the type described above from its subscribers without first providing the contracting party with a copy of the independent person's report, or, if the agreement is otherwise entered into in circumstances where there has been some breach of s 32 of the C(A)A 1983 of which the other contracting party knew or ought to have known, then the agreement will be *void* in so far as not already carried out[28]. Moreover, to the extent that the agreement has already been performed, the company will be entitled to recover any consideration which has actually been paid by it[29] notwithstanding the fact that the non-cash asset may already have been transferred by the other party. In appropriate circumstances, however, relief against such potential liability may be obtained by applying to the court[30]. It should also be noted that if and to the extent that the consideration payable by the company would have involved the allotment of shares, the civil consequences are those stipulated by s 30[31].

(c) Converting from a private company to a PLC

[29.019] As was noted above, it is unusual nowadays for PLCs to be formed afresh except where they are intended for use as investment companies in capital markets activities. Rather, it is more common for trading PLCs to have begun life as a private company, converting to public status as the business grows. The conversion procedure is governed by ss 9 and 10 of the C(A)A 1983.

24 Section 32(3)(d) of the C(A)A 1983. If the other party to the proposed agreement is not a member entitled to receive notice of general meetings (as where he has since ceased to be a member or holds shares which do not entitle him to such notice), a copy of the report and draft resolution must also be circulated to him.

25 Section 32(3)(c) of the C(A)A 1983.

26 Section 33(2)(b) of the C(A)A 1983.

27 Section 55(1)(e) of the C(A)A 1983. Although s 72 of the IFCMPA 2005 provides for the substitution of the 'Companies Registration Office Gazette' for *Iris Oifigiúil*, s 72 has not yet been commenced.

28 Section 32(7)(b) of the C(A)A 1983.

29 Section 32(7)(a) of the C(A)A 1983.

30 Section 34(6) of the C(A)A 1983. See para **[29.055]** *post*.

31 Section 32(8) of the C(A)A 1983. See para **[29.050]** *post*.

[29.020] The first requirement is that a special resolution authorising the conversion is passed by the members in general meeting[32]. Section 9(1) provides that a private company may be registered as a public limited company, if:

- it passes a special resolution, which complies with s 9(2), to the effect that it should be so re-registered;
- it files in the CRO the requisite Forms 71 and 72 signed by a director and the secretary of the company;
- all other statutory requirements are complied with[33].

The resolution must not only approve the company's conversion but it must also make all the necessary amendments to the constitutional documentation to ensure that it complies with the statutory requirements applicable to PLCs. Section 9(2) requires it to address the following matters; it must:

- alter the company's memorandum so that it states that the company is to be a PLC;
- make such other alterations in the memorandum as are necessary to bring it in substance and in form into conformity with the requirements of the C(A)A 1983 with respect to the memorandum of a PLC; and
- make such alterations in the company's articles of association as are requisite in the circumstances.

These would include, amongst other things, replacing the word 'limited' or the abbreviation 'ltd' at the end of the company's name with 'public limited company' or 'plc'[3] and making any necessary changes to the capital clause so as to ensure that its *nominal* share capital is not less than the authorised minimum[34].

[29.021] In addition, certain documents must be lodged with the registrar of companies. These are set out in s 9(3) of the C(A)A 1983, as follows:

'(a) a printed copy of the memorandum and articles as altered in pursuance of the resolution;

(b) a copy of a written statement by the auditors of the company that in their opinion the relevant balance sheet shows that at the balance sheet date the amount of the company's net assets was not less than the aggregate of its called-up share capital and undistributable reserves;

(c) a copy of the relevant balance sheet, together with a copy of an unqualified report by the company's auditors in relation to that balance sheet;

(d) a copy of any report prepared under subsection (5)(b); and

(e) a statutory declaration in the prescribed form by a director or secretary of the company—

---

[32] It is possible, however, that the constitutional documentation or any shareholder agreement may confer a entrenched power of veto that might be used to prevent the resolution being passed; see, for example, *Growth Management and Hillside Apex Fund Ltd v Mutavchiev & Minev* [2007] 1 BCLC 645 where a permanent injunction was granted to prevent the company from being converted in contravention of the power of veto in a shareholders' agreement.

[33] Section 5(a) and (b) of the C(A)A 1983, where applicable, and s 10(1)(a)–(d) of the C(A)A 1983.

[34] On the constitutional documentation of PLCs, see para **[29.027]**.

(i) that the special resolution mentioned in subsection (1)(a) has been passed and that the conditions specified in subsection (1)(c) have been satisfied; and

(ii) that, between the balance sheet date and the application of the company for re-registration, there has been no change in the financial position of the company that has resulted in the amount of the company's net assets becoming less than the aggregate of its called-up share capital and undistributable reserves.

The statutory declaration required by s 9(3)(e) may be accepted by the registrar of companies as being sufficient evidence that the special resolution has been passed and that the said conditions have been satisfied[35].

[29.022] Special provisions apply where shares are allotted by the company either wholly or partly for non-cash consideration between the balance sheet date and the passing of the special resolution. Section 9(5) of the C(A)A 1983 provides that the company shall not make an application for re-registration under s 9 unless, before making the application, the consideration has been valued in accordance with ss 30 and 31 of the C(A)A 1983, and a report regarding the value has been made by the company.

[29.023] Section 9(6) of the C(A)A 1983 empowers the registrar of companies to issue a certificate of incorporation to the effect that the company is a PLC. The certificate is conclusive evidence[36] that the company is a PLC and that all requirements in the C(A)A 1983 in respect of re-registration and all matters precedent and incidental thereto have been complied with[37]. By s 9(7) of the C(A)A 1983, such a certificate shall not issue where it appears to the registrar that the court has made an order confirming a reduction of the company's capital where this reduces the nominal value of the company's allotted share capital below the authorised minimum.

[29.024] Although re-registration converts the company into a PLC, it retains its original corporate *persona* – thus all pre-existing rights and obligations of the company remain unaffected, including any legal proceedings commenced by or against it. Section 9(10) of the C(A)A 1983 provides that a conversion of a company to a PLC shall not affect any rights or obligations of the company, or render defective any legal proceedings by or against the company.

[29.025] Section 10 of the C(A)A 1983 deals with requirements as to share capital of a private company applying to re-register as a public company. In short, the minimum capital requirements of PLCs must be met by the company intending to convert. Section 10(1) provides:

> 'a private company shall not be re-registered under section 9 as a public limited company unless, at the time the special resolution referred to in that section is passed—
>
> (a) the nominal value of the company's allotted share capital is not less than the authorised minimum;
>
> (b) each of its allotted shares is paid up at least as to one-quarter of the nominal value of that share and the whole of any premium on it;

---

35 Section 9(4) of the C(A)A 1983.

36 On conclusive evidence see Ch 4, *Incorporation and its Consequences*, para **[4.018]**.

37 Section 9(9) of the C(A)A 1983.

(c) where any share in the company or any premium payable on it has been fully or partly paid up by an undertaking given by any person that he or another should do work or perform services for the company or another, the undertaking has been performed or otherwise discharged; and

(d) where shares have been allotted as fully or partly paid up as to their nominal value or any premium payable on them otherwise than in cash and the consideration for the allotment consists of or includes an undertaking (other than one to which paragraph (c) applies) to the company, either—

(i) that undertaking has been performed or otherwise discharged; or

(ii) there is a contract between the company and any person pursuant to which that undertaking must be performed within five years from that time.'

(d) Migration of PLCs

[29.026] The migration procedure provided in s 256F of the CA 1990 is *only* available to collective investment undertakings and is not available to other companies who wish to relocate in Ireland[38]. Nonetheless, recent years have witnessed some significant corporate migration into Ireland by major internationally recognised corporations, largely to benefit from the favourable corporation tax regime. This has typically been achieved by incorporating an Irish registered PLC which then replaces the existing foreign parent by means of a share-for-share swap under a court-sanctioned scheme of arrangement[39]. For public companies registered elsewhere in the EU it can also be achieved by converting to a *Societas Europaea* or SE[40] and then moving its registration to Ireland, or by merging with an Irish PLC under the cross-border merger regulations[41].

Constitutional documentation

[29.027] Shareholders' agreements are uncommon in public companies, and in a PLC the constitutional documents will invariably be limited to the memorandum and the articles of association; accordingly there will usually be no 'hidden constitution', and all constitutional documentation will be of public record[42].

(a) Memorandum of association

[29.028] The memorandum of association of a PLC limited by shares and of a PLC limited by guarantee must be in the form prescribed by Parts I and II, respectively, of Schedule 2 of the C(A)A 1983. The essential differences when compared to the memorandum of association of a private company are in the name clause, the incorporation clause, and the capital clause. The name clause must provide that the words 'public limited company' or 'plc' (or the Irish variants thereof)[43] are included in

---

38 See para **[29.137]** *post*.

39 On schemes of arrangement generally, see Ch 21, *Schemes of Arrangement and Reconstructions*.

40 On SEs, see further para **[29.150]** *post*.

41 European Communities (Cross Border Mergers) Regulations 2008 (SI 157/2008) implementing Directive 2005/56/EC on Cross Border Mergers.

42 See generally Ch 3, *Constitutional Documentation*.

43 'Cuideachta phoiblí theoranta' which may be abbreviated to 'cpt'. See s 4(1) of the C(A)A 1983.

the name of the company[44]. The incorporation clause must state that the company is a PLC[45]. No licence may be given under s 24 of the CA 1963 dispensing with the word 'limited' in the name of a PLC[46]. The capital clause must state that the minimum authorised share capital of the company is at least €38,092.14[47].

[29.029] As was noted earlier[48], a further difference is that in the case of a public company s 5 of the CA 1963 requires that there must be at least seven members. In most other respects the memorandum of association of a public company will be similar to that of a private company.

(b) Articles of association

[29.030] The model articles of association of a PLC limited by shares are to be found in Part I of Table A. Again, there are only a few differences between Part I and Part II. Naturally, PLCs listed on the stock exchanges will often adopt articles of association which are much more elaborate; for example, listed PLCs will usually have provisions in their articles of association dealing with the issue of uncertificated shares[49], and will have special provisions with regard to corporate governance covering non-executive directors, directors' remuneration, etc[50].

[29.031] PLCs that wish to avail of the CREST uncertificated share transfer system must also make provision for such transactions; this is discussed in greater detail below[51].

(c) Alteration of constitutional documentation

[29.032] The law applicable to the alteration of both constitutional documents is the same for private companies and PLCs. In practice, however, the constitutional documentation of a PLC will rarely be altered informally, though it remains possible in principle.

Incorporation and its consequences

[29.033] The incidents of corporate existence considered in Chapter 4 do not vary whether a company is private or a PLC. Accordingly, for example, the certificate of incorporation of a public company enjoys the same conclusiveness as that of a private company[52], and a PLC is no less a separate legal person from its members and management than a private company. A PLC does, of course, enjoy greater transferability of its interests since it is not obliged to place restrictions on the transfer of its shares or debentures in its constitutional documents.

---

44 It is an offence for any person that is not a plc to carry on any trade, profession or business under a name which includes, as its last part, the words 'public limited company', or 'cuideachta phoiblí theoranta' or abbreviations of those words: s 56 of the C(A)A 1983.

45 Section 2(1) of the C(A)A 1983.

46 Section 58 of the C(A)A 1983.

47 See para **[29.011]** *ante*.

48 See para **[29.012]** *ante*.

49 See para **[29.063]** *post*.

50 See para **[29.083]** *post*.

51 See para **[29.063]** *post*.

52 See Ch 4, *Incorporation and its Consequences*, para **[4.018]**.

Corporate contracts: capacity and authority

[29.034] The law concerning corporate contracts involving PLCs is substantially the same as that which applies to private companies[53]. There are no major differences as regards the *ultra vires* principle nor the law of authority of corporate agents; however, some minor distinctions may be made as regards the use of the corporate seal and as regards uncertificated securities.

(a) Securities seal

[29.035] Insofar as the corporate seal is concerned, the rules applicable to the use of a PLC's common seal are the same as those which have been considered in the context of the private company[54]. However, a PLC may, in practice, have an additional seal. Section 3 of the C(A)A 1977 provides that:

> 'A company other than a private company may have, for use for sealing securities issued by the company and for sealing documents creating or evidencing securities so issued, an official seal which is a facsimile of the common seal of the company with the addition on its face of the word "Securities" or the word "Urrúis".'

In all other respects, the law applicable to the sealing of documents by PLCs is the same as in a private company, considered in Chapter 7.

(b) Uncertificated securities

[29.036] In relation to uncertificated securities, reg 5 of the Companies Act 1990 (Uncertificated Securities) Regulations 1996[55] provides that s 6 of the Statute of Frauds Act (Ireland) 1695 and s 28(6) of the Supreme Court of Judicature (Ireland) Act 1877 and any other rule of law requiring the execution under hand or seal of a document in writing for the transfer of property, shall not apply (if they would otherwise do so) to any transfer of title to uncertificated units of a security through a relevant system[56].

(c) Validity of trading or borrowing carried out without an authorisation

[29.037] Furthermore, as was noted earlier[57], s 6 of the C(A)A 1983 places restrictions on PLCs which prohibit them from commencing business or exercising any borrowing powers pending the registrar of companies issuing a certificate under that section in connection with the minimum capital requirements. The fact that a company trades or borrows without such a certificate will not, however, prejudice the validity of any corporate contracts. Section 6(8) of the C(A)A 1983 provides that the validity of any activity conducted in breach of the provisions of the section is not to be prejudiced by the lack of a certificate. However, if such a company enters into a transaction in contravention therewith within 21 days from being called upon to comply with its obligations, the directors of the company shall be personally liable to indemnify the

---

53 See generally Ch 7, *Corporate Contracts: Capacity and Authority*.

54 See Ch 7, *Corporate Contracts: Capacity and Authority,* at para **[7.014]**.

55 SI 68/1996.

56 On uncertificated securities, see para **[29.063]**.

57 Note also that s 256F of the CA 1990 contains provisions preserving the integrity of corporate contracts affecting migrating investment companies – see para **[29.137]** *post*.

other party to the transaction in respect of any loss or damage suffered by the other party by reason of the failure of the company to comply with those obligations.

Shares and membership

[29.038] The *raison d'être* of the PLC is mainly to leverage the market for shares and securities in the company. It is not surprising, therefore, that there should be significant differences between PLCs and private companies as regards the law governing the issue and transfer of shares, and that there should be significant regulation to prevent market abuse. Much of this area has been the subject of substantial legislative effort at EU level, and this aspect is considered in detail in Chapter 32 below. However, there is much more in common between the two types of company when it comes to the law governing membership. Shares and membership in PLCs are considered further under the following headings:

(a) Membership of PLCs.

(b) Legal nature of shares in PLCs and the formalities which apply to them.

(c) Allotment of shares in PLCs, and consideration therefor.

(d) Disclosure of interests in shares in PLCs.

(e) Disclosure of stabilising activity during a stabilisation period.

(a) Membership of PLCs

[29.039] The law does not differentiate between PLCs and private companies when it comes to the question of who may become a member. Nor, for that matter, does it distinguish between them in the principles governing registration of members. In these respects the reader is referred to the discussion in Chapter 8. However, whereas the maximum number of members in a private company is 99[58], there is no upper limit to the number of members a PLC may have. It should also be recalled that the statutory *minimum* number of members for PLCs is seven[59], or two for a PLC which is an investment company[60].

[29.040] Special rules apply to any PLCs that require their directors to take up 'qualification' shares[61]. Regulation 77 of Table A, which applies to both private companies and PLCs, provides:

> 'The shareholding qualification for directors may be fixed by the company in general meeting and unless and until so fixed, no qualification shall be required.'

Section 179(1) of the CA 1963 provides that a person may not be capable of being appointed director of a public company – including a PLC[62] – by the articles of association, or be named as a director or proposed director in any prospectus or statement in lieu thereof, *unless* before the registration of the articles containing his

58 Section 33 of the CA 1963 as amended by s 7 of the IFCMPA 2006.

59 See para **[29.012]** *ante*.

60 See para **[29.135]** *post*.

61 On qualification shares, see Ch 13, *Corporate Governance: Management by the Directors*, at para **[13.019]**.

62 Section 179(5) of the CA 1963.

appointment, the publication of the prospectus, or the delivery of the statement, as the case may be, he has:

'(a) signed and delivered to the registrar of companies for registration a consent in writing to act as such director; and

(b) either—

(i) signed the memorandum for a number of shares not less than his qualification, if any; or

(ii) taken from the company and paid or agreed to pay for his qualification shares, if any; or

(iii) signed and delivered to the registrar for registration an undertaking in writing to take from the company and pay for his qualification shares, if any; or

(iv) made and delivered to the registrar for registration a statutory declaration to the effect that a number of shares, not less than his qualification, if any, are registered in his name.

Failure to comply does *not* render any subsequent transactions involving the director invalid[63], but it does render the person applying for registration of the articles liable to a class C fine[64]. Note that under reg 77 of the model articles, if a shareholding qualification is not fixed by the company in general meeting, then no such qualification shall apply, and neither, therefore, can the restrictions imposed by s 179(1)(b) of the CA 1963. If a director does not take up his qualification shareholding within two months of his appointment or such shorter time as may be fixed by the articles, his office will be vacated, and he may not be reappointed until such time as he meets the qualification[65].

(b) Legal nature of shares in PLCs and the formalities which apply to them

[29.041] A share in a PLC does not differ in its legal nature from a share in a private company and the reader is referred to Chapter 8 for a discussion of the legal nature of, and rights and obligations associated with, shares.

[29.042] The formalities associated with shares in private and public companies do not differ significantly. A public company, however, may issue a share warrant[66] instead of a share certificate, entitling the bearer of the warrant to the shares in question. Warrants may be transferred from bearer to bearer without the need for an appropriate instrument of transfer. They are not common in practice, however.

63 Section 178 of the CA 1963.

64 Section 179(4) of the CA 1963, as amended by s 240 of the CA 1990 and s 104 of the CLEA 2001.

65 Section 180 of the CA 1963. It is an offence to act as director whilst the qualification remains unmet.

66 Section 88 of the CA 1963. The company must be authorised by its articles to issue share warrants.

(c) Allotment of shares in PLCs, and consideration therefor

(i) Authorisation of allotment

[29.043] An allotment of shares by the directors of a PLC must be authorised in the same way as an allotment of shares in a private company[67]. The provisions of s 20 of the C(A)A 1983, which require the allotment to be authorised by the articles or by the company in general meeting, and which regulate the authority so conferred, apply to both. As a practical matter, allotments of shares in PLCs will normally involve more formal steps than those in private companies, and formal *letters of allotment*, including *renounceable letters of allotment*, are commonplace.

(ii) Statutory pre-emption rights

[29.044] The statutory pre-emption scheme introduced by ss 23–25 of the C(A)A 1983[68] applies to allotments of equity securities by both private companies and PLCs, except that PLCs do not enjoy the power to exclude generally the statutory pre-emption scheme by means of a provision to that effect in their memorandum or articles[69]. That said, all companies can exclude the statutory pre-emption scheme from applying to a *particular* allotment, either by providing for that exclusion in its articles or by passing a special resolution authorising the exclusion[70].

(iii) Minimum subscription requirements

[29.045] Under s 22 of the C(A)A 1983, no allotment is to be made of any share capital of a PLC offered for subscription unless:

> '(a) that capital is subscribed for in full; or
>
> (b) the offer states that, even if the capital is not subscribed for in full, the amount of that capital subscribed for may be allotted in any event or in the event of the conditions specified in the offer being satisfied.'

The idea behind this provision is to ensure that the company does not proceed with flotation until it has put in place the capital which it has represented as being required. A prospectus[71] will normally, therefore, state the minimum amount which, in the opinion of the directors, must be raised from an issue of shares.

[29.046] If the minimum subscription is not raised, whether in cash or in kind[72], on the expiration of 40 days after the first issue of the prospectus then all money received from applicants for shares must be forthwith repaid to them without interest. A failure to repay any such money within 48 days after the issue of the prospectus renders the directors of the company jointly and severally liable to repay that money with interest at the rate of 5% per annum, though relief may be obtained from the court if a director

67 See Ch 8, *Shares and Membership*, at para **[8.051]**.

68 See Ch 8, *Shares and Membership*, at para **[8.056]**.

69 Section 23(10) of the C(A)A 1983.

70 Section 24 of the C(A)A 1983.

71 On prospectuses see further Ch 32, *Prospectus, Market Abuse & Transparency Law*, below at para **[32.006]**.

72 See s 22(3) of the C(A)A 1983.

proves that the default in the repayment of the money was not due to any misconduct or negligence on his part[73].

(iv) Payment for allotted shares

[29.047] One of the most significant characteristics of PLCs is the requirement that all shares allotted be paid up to at least 25% of their nominal value and fully paid up as to any premium thereon[74]. This reflects the fact that the principal *raison d'etre* of the PLC corporate form is raising capital by issuing shares. Section 28(1) of the C(A)A 1983 provides:

> 'a public limited company shall not allot a share except as paid up at least as to one-quarter of the nominal value of the share and the whole of any premium on it.'

Section 28(4) of the C(A)A 1983 disapplies the requirement as regards shares allotted in pursuance of an employee share scheme.

[29.048] Where a PLC allots a share in contravention of s 28(1), the share is be treated by the company as though one-quarter of its nominal value together with the whole of any premium *had* been received, but the allottee becomes immediately liable to pay the company the balance owing to bring the amount paid up to the minimum amount which should have been received, together with interest at 5% per annum[75]. The subsection thus obviates the need for any call to be made on the shareholder by the company, and it overrides any deferred payment terms that might have been agreed to the contrary.

Allottees who are allotted bonus shares are relieved from liability under the subsection unless they knew or ought to have known that the shares were allotted in contravention of sub-s (1)[76].

[29.049] Where shares have been allotted in contravention of s 28(1) to someone *other than* the person who has agreed to pay for them, the allottee will also become similarly liable to pay any amounts due together with interest, and will be jointly and severally liable therefor with the person who agreed to pay for the shares[77]. Allottees who are purchasers for value without notice of the contravention at the time of purchase, or who derived title to the shares after the contravention, are not liable, however[78].

(v) Consideration for shares on allotment

[29.050] Shares in PLCs may be issued for non-cash consideration, but, unlike other companies, special restrictions apply. First, a PLC may not accept an undertaking to perform future services in consideration for an allotment[79]. If it does, the holder of the

---

73 Section 53(4) of the CA 1963 as applied by s 22(2) of the C(A)A 1983.

74 A share shall be taken as having been allotted in a company only when a person acquires an unconditional right to be included in the register of members in respect of that share: s 2(2) of the C(A)A 1983.

75 Section 28(2) of the C(A)A 1983. The interest rate, described as the 'appropriate rate' in the subsection, is set by C(A)A 1983 at 5% per annum or such other rate as the Minister may specify by order. Thus far, no Ministerial change has been made to the rate set in the Act.

76 Section 28(4) of the C(A)A 1983.

77 Section 28(5) of the C(A)A 1983 applying s 26(4) of the C(A)A 1983.

78 Section 28(5) of the C(A)A 1983 applying s 26(4) of the C(A)A 1983.

79 Section 23(2) of the C(A)A 1983.

shares is liable to pay the consideration in cash with interest. Second, a PLC may not accept as consideration for the allotment an undertaking (eg, to pay cash) which is to be performed more than five years after the allotment[80]. Third, non-cash consideration for the allotment of shares in a PLC must be independently valued in accordance with the provisions of s 30 of the C(A)A 1983.

[29.051] Section 30 of the C(A)A 1983 requires the allotment of shares in a PLC (except in a merger or share-for-share exchange) to be valued by an independent person who is qualified at the time to be appointed as auditor to the company[81]. The purpose of the report is to determine the adequacy of the non-cash consideration and to identify any deficiency in the value to be paid.

The independent person must report that the value of the non-cash consideration, together with any cash agreed to be paid, is not less than the amount that is being credited as having been paid up against the share[82]. If the non-cash consideration is inadequate in his view, he must state the amount of additional cash consideration required to put matters right[83]. The report must be supplied to the proposed allottees in advance of the allotment. Where this is not done, or where the valuation process has been contravened in some other way and the allottee knows or ought to have known that there was a contravention, he will be liable to the company for so much of the nominal capital as was treated as paid by the non-cash consideration together with interest at the rate of 5% per annum[84].

[29.052] Independent valuers are not expected to be experts in every aspect of valuation – they may accept the contents of another report made by any person who appears to them to have the requisite knowledge and experience necessary to value the consideration and who is not an officer of the company or an associated company, or a partner or employee of such an officer[85]. In carrying out his valuation the valuer is empowered to require from the officers of the company any information which he thinks necessary to enable him to carry out his duties[86].

[29.053] The report must be made within the six months preceding the allotment; must be sent to the proposed allottee; must be returned to the registrar of companies along with the return of allotments[87]; and (under s 30(6)) must state:

‘(a) the nominal value of the shares to be wholly or partly paid for by the consideration in question;

(b) the amount of any premium payable on those shares;

80 Section 29 of the C(A)A 1983.

81 On the qualifications of auditors, see ss 187–192 of the CA 1990 and discussion in Ch 17, *Financial Statements, Audit and Annual Return*, at para **[17.296]**.

82 Section 30(8)(d) of the C(A)A 1983.

83 Section s 30(6)(d) of the C(A)A 1983.

84 As to the rate of interest see note 70 above.

85 ‘Officer,’ in this context, excludes an auditor of the company: s 30(14)(c) of the C(A)A 1983.

86 Section 31(1) of the C(A)A 1983. Supplying the valuer with false or misleading information is an offence: s 31(3) of the C(A)A 1983.

87 Section 31(2) of the C(A)A 1983.

(c) the description of the consideration and, as respects so much of the consideration as he himself has valued, a description of that part of the consideration, the method used to value it and the date of the valuation; and

(d) the extent to which the nominal value of the shares and any premium are to be treated as paid up—

(i) by the consideration;

(ii) in cash.'

If any consideration is valued by a person other than the independent person, the report must state that fact and must also state the other person's name and what knowledge and experience he has to carry out the valuation, *and* describe so much of the consideration as was valued by that other person, the method used to value it and the date of valuation.

[29.054] The report must also contain, or be accompanied by, a note by the independent person stating (s 30(8)):

'(a) in the case of a valuation made by another person, that it appeared to the independent person reasonable to arrange for it to be so made, or to accept a valuation so made;

(b) whoever made the valuation, that the method of valuation was reasonable in all the circumstances;

(c) that it appears to the independent person that there has been no material change in the value of the consideration in question since the valuation; and

(d) that on the basis of the valuation the value of the consideration, together with any cash by which the nominal value of the shares or any premium payable on them is to be paid up, is not less than so much of the aggregate of the nominal value and the whole of any such premium as is treated as paid up by the consideration and any such cash.'

(vi) Relief for allottees, directors and others

[29.055] Where any person is liable to a company under either s 26 of the C(A)A 1983 (which prohibits PLCs from accepting undertakings to do work as consideration for shares), s 29 (which prohibits PLCs from accepting undertakings to performed in more than five years as consideration for shares), s 30 (which requires non-cash consideration for shares to be valued independently)[88] or s 32 (which requires transfers of non-cash assets to PLCs to be valued independently), they may apply to the court for relief, in whole or in part, from the statutory liability that has been imposed on them[89]. The court may grant relief where it considers it just and equitable to do so[90] and the 'overriding principle' for the court, according to the section, will be to ensure that the company has received money or money's worth at least equal to the aggregate of the nominal value of the shares and the whole premium payable in respect thereof[91]. In appropriate circumstances, however, it would seem that the court can grant relief even if the nominal value has not been achieved. In *Re Bradford Investments (No 2)*[92], Hoffmann J said:

---

88 See para **[29.051]** *ante*.

89 Section 34 of the C(A)A 1983.

90 Section 34(2) of the C(A)A 1983.

91 Section 34(4)(a) of the C(A)A 1983.

92 *Re Bradford Investments (No 2)* [1991] BCC 379.

> 'The designation of an "overriding principle" does not, I think, mean that the court would not have jurisdiction to grant exemption unless satisfied that the company had received assets worth at least the nominal value of the allotted shares and any premium. If that had been intended, it would have been framed as a rule. Instead, it is described as a "principle" and the court is required to "have regard" to it. That means, in my judgment, that very good reasons would be needed before the court could accept that it was just and equitable to exempt an applicant from liability notwithstanding that the company had not received sufficient value.'

The court may take into account the value of any other non-cash consideration paid or payable in respect of the shares by the allottee or any subsequent holder[93] and may also have regard to any other cash payments paid or payable in respect of the shares by the allottee or any subsequent holder[94]. Where the transaction does not involve the allotment of shares but merely involves the acquisition by the company of a non-cash asset in breach of s 32, the contracting party may similarly apply to the court for relief against his liability to reimburse any moneys paid by the company, as where he can show that he has already transferred the asset or assets to the company under the impugned agreement[95].

(vii) Allotments which are dependent on stock exchange listing

[29.056] Section 57 of the CA 1963 provides that where a prospectus provides that application has or will be made for permission to allow the shares to be dealt on any stock exchange, the allotment will be *void* unless the permission has been applied for or received within the requisite timeframes stated in the section. In such cases it must forthwith repay without interest any monies which were received by it from persons who had applied for the securities in question. If the money is not repaid within eight days, the directors become jointly and severally liable for the unreturned amounts together with interest thereon at 5% per annum. A director may, however, avoid personal liability by showing that the failure to repay was not due to any misconduct or negligence on his part[96]. Pending allotment of the securities or a return of moneys, as the case may be, the company must keep the sums in question in a separate bank account[97]. It has been held that these moneys are therefore held on trust in favour of the applicants and they will be entitled to trace the amounts paid by them into the account in the event of the company going into liquidation[98].

(d) *Disclosure of interests in shares in PLCs*

[29.057] Chapter 1 of Part IV of the CA 1990 imposes obligations on directors, secretaries and their families to disclose their shareholdings in a PLC. Chapter 2 of that Part imposes like obligations on groups and on individuals which acquire more than 5% of the issued share capital of a PLC. Every PLC is required to keep a register of disclosed interests[99].

---

93 Section 34(2) of the C(A)A 1983.

94 Section 34(3) of the C(A)A 1983.

95 Section 34(6) of the C(A)A 1983.

96 Section 57(2) of the CA 1963.

97 Section 57(3) of the CA 1963.

98 *Re Nanwa Gold Mines Ltd, Ballantyne v Nanwa Gold Mines Ltd* [1955] 3 All ER 219.

99 Section 80 of the CA 1990.

[29.058] An individual is obliged to make disclosure to a PLC whenever he acquires or disposes of an interest which brings his interest in it above or below 5% in nominal value of the 'relevant nominal capital' of the PLC – meaning the issued share capital of a class carrying voting rights at general meetings[100]. The interests of a spouse or child must be taken into account in determining the size of his interest, as must the interests of another company which is accustomed to act in accordance with his instructions, or if he holds more than one-third of the voting rights in that other company[101]. If he is unaware of those other interests at the time of the acquisition he must make disclosure when he becomes aware of them. Where he is part of a group among whom there is an agreement (whether legally enforceable or not) that the rights associated with shares in a PLC which are acquired by any of them will be exercised only according to the agreement, he will be treated as being interested in the interests of the other members of the group, including the interests of their spouses and minor children[102].

[29.059] The interests which must be disclosed are set out in detail in s 77 of the CA 1990 and include the interests of a beneficiary under a trust, a purchaser under a contract, or a person who is not a shareholder but who is authorised to exercise the rights of a shareholder or debenture holder. Certain interests are excluded, such as the interests of bare trustees, discretionary interests, the interest of the President of the High Court in an estate, interests of charities, interests arising through involvement in unit trusts, and 'exempt security interests' as defined in s 78 of the CA 1990. The latter include interests held by banks, insurance companies, trustee savings banks, post office savings banks, and stockbrokers carrying on business on a recognised stock exchange, which are held as security.

(e) Disclosure of stabilising activity during a stabilisation period

[29.060] The C(A)A 1999 introduced provisions to enable stabilising activities or measures to be undertaken in relation to the issue or sale of shares and securities. The Act permits official manipulation of the stock market in accordance with *stabilisation rules* which are set out in the Schedule to the Act, and for a limited time known as the *stabilisation period*. The immediate need for the Act stemmed from the sale by the State of its 50.1% stake in Bord Telecom Éireann PLC by way of initial public offering, in June 1999. The Act has been repealed by IFCMPA 2005 s 31 but with limited effect[103] – the Act continues to apply to Irish incorporated companies whose shares or other securities are admitted to trading on the Irish Stock Exchange.

---

[100] Section 67 of the CA 1990. A temporary suspension of voting rights is disregarded for these purposes.

[101] Section 72 of the CA 1990.

[102] Sections 73 and 74 of the CA 1990.

[103] The Investment Funds, Companies and Miscellaneous Provisions Act 2005 (Commencement) Order 2005 (SI 323/2005) art 5 provides: 'The 6th day of July 2005 is appointed as the day on which the following provisions of the Act come into operation, namely – (a) section 31 (but only for the purpose of repealing the enactments specified in that section in so far as they relate to a regulated market (within the meaning of Directive 2003/71/EC of the European Parliament and of the Council of 4 November 2003) operated by a recognised stock exchange within the meaning Part V of the Companies Act 1990 (No 33 of 1990)).'

[29.061] Section 3 of the C(A)A 1999 provides that acquisitions or disposals officially transacted during the stabilisation period for the purposes of stabilising the market and done in accordance with the stabilisation rules shall be disregarded for the purposes of the disclosure requirements of the CA 1990. Any interest in the relevant share capital acquired during the stabilising period is treated as having been acquired on the first day following the end of the stabilising period[104].

Share transfer

(a) Certificated and uncertificated securities

[29.062] Where shares in PLCs companies are 'certificated' (ie, their title is evidenced by a paper share certificate) the mechanics of share transfer do not differ greatly from the transfer of shares in private companies[105]. The transfer of shares in PLCs that are quoted on the Stock Exchange must be distinguished, however, from the transfer of shares in other types of public company, such as management-type public companies limited by guarantee without a share capital. In the case of listed PLCs that have opted to join CREST and have their shares in uncertificated format, the differences between the transfer of shares in public and private companies are most pronounced[106].

[29.063] CREST is an electronic system which settles the transfer of shares that are dealt on selected exchanges. It is operated by Euroclear UK and Ireland Ltd, previously known as CrestCo Limited. Euroclear UK and Ireland Ltd is a UK registered corporation, owned by Euroclear SA/NV incorporated in Belgium. Euroclear UK and Ireland Ltd is the authorised Central Securities Depository of the UK, Ireland, Guernsey, Jersey and the Isle of Man and it is the approved 'operator' of a 'relevant system' for the purposes of the Companies Act, 1990 (Uncertificated Securities) Regulations 1996 (the 'CA(US)R 1996').

CREST has been available to manage shares on the Dublin Stock Exchange since the end of 1996[107]. This was facilitated in Ireland by the passing of the CA(US)R 1996[108]. Regulation 4(1) and (2) of the CA(US)R 1996 provides:

> '(1) Notwithstanding section 79 or section 81 of the 1963 Act or section 2(1) of the Stock Transfer Act, 1963, title to securities may be evidenced and transferred without a written instrument provided that such title is evidenced and transferred in accordance with these regulations.
>
> (2) References in any enactment or rule of law to a proper instrument of transfer or to a transfer with respect to securities, or any expression having like meaning, shall be taken to

---

104 Section 3(2) of the C(A)A 1999.

105 Note, however, that where a stock transfer form is executed, common form model articles of association provide that in the case of a public company, the transfer must be executed by both the transferor and the transferee, and the instrument of transfer must be registered by the company: see CA 1963, Sch 1, Table A, Part I, reg 22.

106 See Ussher, *Company Law in Ireland* (1986), pp 198, 199; Doyle, *The Company Secretary* (1994), p 151; and Abrans, 'Talisman: A Legal Analysis' (1980) Co Law 17.

107 For an excellent overview of CREST, see McHugh, 'CREST in Ireland, The Uncertificated Securities Regulations, 1996' (1996) 3 CLP 219.

108 SI 68/1996.

include a reference to an operator-instruction to a participating issuer to register a transfer of title on the relevant register of securities in accordance with the operator-instruction[109].'

There are safeguards to the avoidance of stamp duty and reg 4 will not have effect in relation to an 'operator instruction' unless there is an agreement in place with the Revenue Commissioners in relation to the payment of any stamp duty chargeable[110].

[29.064] In order for a company to participate in CREST its articles of association must be consistent with the holding of shares in that class in uncertificated form; the transfer of title to shares in that class by means of a relevant system; and the CA(US)R 1996[111]. An alternative is that a company's directors must resolve that title to shares of a class issued or to be issued may be transferred electronically[112] and for as long as such resolution is in force, reg 8(3) of the CA(US)R 1996 provides:

> '… the articles of association in relation to the class of shares which were the subject of the directors' resolution, shall not apply to any uncertificated shares of that class to the extent that they are inconsistent with—
>
> (a) the holding of shares of that class in uncertificated form;
>
> (b) the transfer of title to shares of that class by means of a relevant system; and
>
> (c) any provision of these regulations.'

Where a directors' resolution is the means chosen to authorise the participation in CREST, notice must be given to all members, giving them 60 days' notice before the resolution becomes effective. It has been observed[113] that most Irish companies elected to change their articles of association to allow the transfer of shares in dematerialised form and that this has avoided any period of uncertainty that might otherwise arise if the decision were open to challenge by dissenting members. Participating issuers are debarred from issuing a certificate in relation to any uncertificated units of a participating security[114] and any document issued in breach of this, purportedly evidencing title to an uncertificated unit of a participating security, shall not be evidence of title to the unit of the security. In particular, s 87(1) of the CA 1963 is dis-applied to uncertificated securities[115].

[29.065] The main effect of CREST is that transfers of shares can be registered in a matter of hours, compared with the past when registration took a matter of days or even weeks. The supporting CREST documentation requires registrars to adhere to strict time limits in registering transfers, ie, two hours, and they are further required to advise

---

109 Regulation 5 of the Companies Act, 1990 (Uncertificated Securities) Regulations 1996 also disapplies s 6 of the Statute of Frauds Act (Ireland) 1695 and s 28(6) of the Supreme Court of Judicature (Ireland) Act 1877, and any other rule of law requiring the execution under hand or seal of a document in writing for the transfer of property shall not apply (if they would otherwise do so) to any transfer of title to uncertificated units of a security through a relevant system.

110 Regulation 4(3) of the CA(US)R 1996.

111 Regulation 7(1) of the Regulations.

112 Regulation 8(1) of the CA(US)R 1996.

113 McHugh, 'CREST in Ireland, The Uncertificated Securities Regulations, 1996' (1996) 3 CLP 219 at 220.

114 Regulation 19(1) of the CA(US)R 1996.

115 Regulation 19(2) of the CA(US)R 1996.

Euroclear electronically that a transaction has occurred. CREST is underpinned by an extensive framework including the CA(US)R 1996 and private contractual documentation and rules. This is a necessary support for the electronic system that connects investors with brokers, companies' registrars, the banks and of course Euroclear.

The essential features of the law of share transfers are, however, maintained subject to necessary modifications. Thus, listed PLCs (referred to as 'participating issuers') continue to be required to maintain a register of members. Regulation 10(1) of the CA(US)R 1996 provides:

> '... A participating issuer which is a company shall enter on its register of members, in respect of any class of shares which is a participating security, the number of shares each member holds in uncertificated form and certificated form respectively.'

Thus, the effect of registration of a share in uncertificated form is essentially the same as in the case of a 'certificated' share. Regulation 11 provides:

> (1) Subject to regulation 16(7), an entry on a register mentioned in paragraph (1) or (2) of regulation 10 which records a person as holding units of a security in uncertificated form shall be evidence of such title to the units as would be evidenced if the entry on the register related to units of that security held in certificated form.
>
> (2) Subject to regulation 16(7), an entry on a register maintained by virtue of paragraph (3) of regulation 10 shall be prima facie evidence that the person to whom the entry relates has such title to the units of the security which that person is recorded as holding in uncertificated form as if the units were held in certificated form.

The integrity of the register is protected by reg 12(1) which prevents participating issuers from rectifying a register of securities in relation to uncertificated units of a security held by a system member except (a) with the consent of the operator, or (b) by order of the High Court. Regulation 13 provides that notwithstanding s 121 of the CA 1963, a participating issuer shall not close a register of securities relating to a participating security without the consent of the operator.

[29.066] Regulation 16(1) of the CA(US)R 1996 imposes an obligation on participating issuers to register a transfer of title to uncertificated units of a security on a register of securities in accordance with an operator-instruction unless certain situations pertain[116]. Regulation 18 provides that at the time an operator-instruction is sent requiring a participating issuer to register on a register of securities a transfer of title to any uncertificated units of a security:

> '...the transferee shall acquire an *equitable interest* in the requisite number of uncertificated units of the security of the kind specified in the operator-instruction in which the transferor has an equitable interest by virtue of this regulation, or in relation to

[116] The excusing circumstances are: '(a) the transfer is prohibited—(i) by order of the High Court, provided both the participating issuer and the relevant operator shall both have had actual notice of the order before the operator-instruction is sent and the fact of such actual notice on the part of both such persons shall have been established to the satisfaction of the court by the person seeking to rely on the order, or (ii) by or under an enactment, or (b) the participating issuer has actual notice that the transfer is—(i) avoided by or under an enactment, or (ii) a transfer to a deceased person, or (c) the circumstances described in paragraph (2) apply, or (d) the participating issuer is entitled by virtue of paragraph (3) to refuse to register the transfer.'

which the transferor is recorded on the relevant register of securities as having title.'[Emphasis added.]

The equitable interest lasts until the transfer is registered.

The maintenance of capital

[29.067] The fundamental capital maintenance rules applicable to private companies apply equally to PLCs; but naturally the rules are more pronounced for PLCs whose corporate form is designed to allow them to exploit the market in their shares. In a PLC, the share capital is more genuinely a 'creditor's fund'.[117] Capital maintenance in PLCs is considered here as follows:

(a) Acquisition by PLCs of their own shares.

(b) Treatment of own shares acquired by PLCs.

(c) Financial assistance by PLCs in the purchase of their own shares.

(d) Distributions and the payment of dividends in PLCs.

(e) Restrictions on reduction of capital by PLCs.

(f) Power of creditors to object to a reduction of capital

(a) Acquisition by PLCs of their own shares

[29.068] PLCs will principally wish to engage in buybacks of their own shares for one of two reasons – either to reduce the number of shares available in the market and thereby to increase the value of the shares in circulation, or to reduce the number of shares available to those who wish to acquire a controlling stake in the company.

All companies are permitted by s 221 of the CA 1990 to buy back their own shares. But while private companies can only acquire their shares using the 'off-market purchase' procedure[118], PLCs can also use the 'market purchase' and 'overseas market purchase' procedures which can be effected more efficiently. PLCs must, however, exercise their authority to buy back within specified time limits, which do not apply to other companies, or else they must return to the general meeting for renewed authority[119].

[29.069] Section 212(1)(b) of the CA 1990, as amended by s 3(d)(i) of the Companies (Miscellaneous Provisions) Act 2009 (C(MP)A 2009), provides that a purchase by a company of its own shares is:

> '... a "market purchase" if the shares are purchased on a recognised stock exchange within the State and are subject to a marketing arrangement.'

Prior to the 2009 amendments a market purchase could only be effected if the shares were admitted to trading on the Irish Stock Exchange. Foreign buybacks had to follow the off-market purchase procedure. Section 212(1A) of the CA 1990, as inserted by s 3(d)(i) of the C(MP)A 2009, now provides that a purchase by a company of its own shares is:

---

117 *Guinness v Land Corporation of Ireland* (1882) 22 Ch D 349. See Ch 10, *The Maintenance of Capital,* at para **[10.003]**.

118 See Ch 10, *The Maintenance of Capital*, at para **[10.024]**.

119 Section 216 of the CA 1990. See para **[29.073]** *post*.

'... an "overseas market purchase" if the shares are purchased on a recognised stock exchange outside the State and are subject to a marketing arrangement.'

A major factor in the amendments was to facilitate international companies migrating to Ireland whose shares are listed on overseas stock exchanges to avail of the market purchase regime when undertaking share buyback programmes.

'Marketing arrangement' is defined in s 212(2), which provides that a company's shares are subject to a marketing arrangement on a recognised stock exchange if either they are listed on that stock exchange, or:

'... the company has been afforded facilities for dealing in those shares to take place on that stock exchange without prior permission for individual transactions from the authority governing that stock exchange and without limit as to the time during which those facilities are to be available.'

The essence of a market purchase is that the company purchases back its own shares on the open stock exchange, as opposed to by way of private treaty.

[29.070] The essential difference between the market purchase and off-market purchase procedures is that a general authorisation can be given for a market purchase (or overseas market purchase) whereas an off-market purchase requires the terms of the contract of purchase to be approved as well.

As with an off-market purchase[120], before a PLC can make a market purchase or overseas market purchase, certain approval must be obtained. Section 215 of the CA 1990 requires the general authority of the members of the company in general meeting to be obtained. In this regard, an ordinary resolution of the members is sufficient, although sub-s (2) provides that the provisions of s 143 of the CA 1963 shall apply to such a resolution. This provides that a copy of the resolution must within 15 days after its passing or making, be forwarded to the registrar of companies for registration. In this way the resolution becomes a public document, available for inspection by the public.

[29.071] The requisite authority may be varied, revoked or from time to time renewed by the company, in general meeting under s 215(1) of the CA 1990, which further provides that:

'This subsection shall not be construed as requiring any particular contract for the market purchase or overseas market purchase of shares to be authorised by the company in general meeting and for the purposes of this Part where a market purchase or overseas market purchase of shares has been authorised in accordance with this section any contract entered into pursuant to that authority in respect of such a purchase shall be deemed also to be so authorised.'

This emphasises the distinction between the market (and overseas market) and off market procedures.

Subsection (3) provides that in the case of a PLC, any authority granted under sub-s (1) shall specify the maximum number of shares authorised to be acquired and determine both the maximum and minimum prices which may be paid for the shares. In such a case, the authorising resolution may determine either or both the maximum and minimum prices by specifying a particular sum or providing a basis or formula for

---

120 See s 213 of the CA 1990 considered in Ch 10, *The Maintenance of Capital*, at para **[10.028]**.

calculating the prices in question without reference to any person's discretion or opinion[121].

[29.072] Section 216 of the CA 1990, which is addressed only to PLCs, provides that any authority granted for a purchase of own shares, whether using the market purchase (including overseas market) procedures or the off-market purchase procedures, must specify the date on which the authority is to expire which shall not be later than 18 months after the date on which the resolution granting the authority is passed[122].

However, where the contract to purchase was concluded before the authority expired and the terms of the authority permit the company to make a contract of purchase which might be executed wholly or partly after the authority expired, then a PLC may make a purchase after the expiry of any time limit imposed by s 216(1)[123].

[29.073] Copies of buyback contracts must be retained by PLCs for a period of 10 years and must be available for at least two hours each day at the registered office for inspection by any person[124].

(b) Treatment of own shares acquired by PLCs

[29.074] All companies can validly acquire their own fully paid shares otherwise than for valuable consideration (eg, by way of gift or bequest), or by any of the other methods described in s 41(4) of the C(A)A 1983[125]. However, if a PLC, or a company which re-registers as a PLC, has acquired any such shares beneficially and other than pursuant to one or other of the methods described in s 41(4)(1)(a)–(c) of the C(A)A 1983, then under s 43 it must either dispose of or cancel those shares within three years of the acquisition or re-registration, as the case may be, or within one year where the acquisition was by way of forfeiture or surrender in lieu of forfeiture[126].

[29.075] Should a PLC opt to cancel the shares rather than dispose of them, the company's capital must be reduced accordingly, despite the fact that this may be done without the directors having to obtain either the approval of the shareholders or the confirmation of the court for a reduction of capital under ss 72 and 73 of the CA 1963[127]. However, if the effect of the reduction of capital is to bring the PLC's allotted share capital below the authorised minimum of €38,092.14 it must take the necessary steps to re-register as some other form of company[128].

If in such circumstances the PLC fails to re-register within the relevant period of time it will be treated as a private company to the extent that it will be precluded from offering its shares or debentures to the public, but it will otherwise be regarded as a PLC

---

121 Section 215(4) of the CA 1990.

122 Section 216(1) of the CA 1990.

123 Section 216(2) of the CA 1990.

124 Section 222(2) of the CA 1990.

125 Section 41 of the C(A)A 1983. See Ch 10, *The Maintenance of Capital*, at para. **[10.015]**.

126 Section 43(1), (3), (12) and (14) of the C(A)A 1983.

127 Section 43(3) of the C(A)A 1983. On court sanctioned reductions of capital, see para **[10.020]**.

128 Section 43(3) and (5) of the C(A)A 1983.

unless and until formal re-registration is actually effected[129]. Meanwhile, the company itself and every officer in default will be guilty of a criminal offence where re-registration ought to have been effected but was not[130].

[29.076] Under reg 5(5) of the European Communities (Public Limited Companies Subsidiaries) Regulations 1997[131], where subsidiary of a PLC purchases, subscribes for or holds shares in the parent PLC and one of the following circumstances exists, namely:

- the shares were not fully paid when they were purchased; or
- the authorisation required from both holding company and subsidiary by s 224(3) of the CA 1990 has not been obtained; or
- the shares are held as treasury shares and their nominal value exceeds 10% of the nominal value of the issued share capital in the company contrary to s 209(2) of the CA 1990; or
- the purchase or subscription was effected with financial assistance in purported reliance on the whitewash procedure contained in s 60(2)–(11) of the CA 1963,

then the subsidiary must cancel or dispose of the shares as aforesaid under s 43(3) of the C(A)A 1983 with the modification that the shares in question must be disposed of or cancelled within a period of 12 months rather than three years[132].

(c) Financial assistance by PLCs in the purchase of their own shares

[29.077] Section 60 of the CA 1963 provides that it is unlawful for a company to give direct or indirect financial assistance for the purpose of or in connection with a purchase or subscription for the company's shares or the shares of its holding company[133]. The s 60 prohibition applies with equal force to PLCs. Significantly, however, the 'whitewash procedure' contained in s 60(2), whereby financial assistance can be approved by special resolution[134], cannot be availed of by a PLC[135] unless it was originally incorporated as another form of company and the special resolution was passed prior to the company's application for re-registration as a PLC.

[29.078] It will be recalled that s 60(12) of the CA 1963 exempts certain categories of transaction from the general prohibition against providing financial assistance, including where lending money is part of the ordinary business of the company, or where the company provides money or makes loans as part of a lawful employee share scheme[136]. Section 60(13)(a), as amended by s 56(1) of the IFCMPA 2005, provides that a PLC may only give financial assistance in those cases:

---

129 Section 43(7) of the C(A)A 1983.

130 Section 43(8) of the C(A)A 1983.

131 SI 67/1997.

132 Regulation 5(5) of the European Communities (Public Limited Liability Company) Regulations 2007 (SI 21/2007).

133 See generally, Ch 10, *The Maintenance of Capital*, at para **[10.046]**.

134 See para **[10.066]**.

135 Section 60(15A) of the CA 1963, as inserted by Sch 1, para 10 of the C(A)A 1983.

136 See Ch 10, *The Maintenance of Capital*, at para **[10.078]**.

> … if the company's net assets are not thereby reduced or, to the extent that those assets are thereby reduced, if the financial assistance is provided out of profits which are available for dividend[137].

(d) Distributions and the payment of dividends in PLCs

[29.079] In addition to the general restriction in s 45 of the C(A)A 1983 that companies may only make a distribution out of profits available for the purpose[138], a PLC is prohibited by s 46 of the C(A)A 1983 from making a distribution or paying a dividend unless its net assets are equal to, or in excess of, the aggregate of its called up share capital and undistributable reserves and the distribution does not reduce its net assets below such aggregate.

[29.080] Section 46(2) of the C(A)A 1983 provides that the 'undistributable reserves' for these purposes are:

> '(a) the share premium account;
>
> (b) the capital redemption reserve fund;
>
> (c) the amount by which the company's accumulated, unrealised profits, so far as not previously utilised by any capitalisation, exceed its accumulated, unrealised losses, so far as not previously written off in a reduction or reorganisation of capital duly made; and
>
> (d) any other reserve which the company is prohibited from distributing by any enactment, other than one contained in this Part, or by its memorandum or articles.'

PLCs are also prohibited from treating any part of their uncalled capital as an asset in determining the level of profits, if any, available for distribution[139].

(e) Restrictions on reduction of capital by PLCs

[29.081] Section 17 of the C(A)A 1983 provides that where a court confirms a reduction of capital in a PLC and the reduction has the effect of bringing the nominal value of the company's allotted share capital below the authorised minimum, the registrar shall not register the order (thereby preventing it from taking effect) unless the court otherwise directs or the company is first re-registered as another form of company. In practice, the court has ordered otherwise where the reduction of capital forms part of a restructuring of the company's capital and the company has given an undertaking to allot a sufficient number of new shares immediately after the reduction of capital has been implemented so as to bring the company's allotted share capital back above the authorised minimum. If the company opts to re-register as some other type of company, no special resolution is required for that purpose[140]. If the court orders the company to re-register then dissentient shareholders cannot invoke the objection provisions of s 15 of the C(A)A 1983[141].

---

137 Section 60(13)(b) of the CA 1963 provides that 'net assets' means the aggregate of the company's assets less the aggregate of its liabilities; and 'liabilities' includes any provision (within the meaning of the Schedule to the C(A)A 1986) except to the extent that provision is taken into account in calculating the value of any asset to the company.

138 See generally, Ch 10, *The Maintenance of Capital*, at para **[10.089]**.

139 Section 46(4) of the C(A)A 1983.

140 Section 17(4) of the C(A)A 1983.

141 Section 17(5) of the C(A)A 1983.

(f) Power of creditors to object to a reduction of capital

[29.082] Section 73 of the CA 1963 entitled creditors to object to a court approval of a reduction of capital under s 72 of the CA 1963[142]. The list of creditors so entitled differs however, in the case of PLCs. Section 73(2)(a) of the CA 1963 provides:

> 'in the case of a public limited company—
>
> (i) every creditor of the company who—
>
> (I) at the date fixed by the court, is entitled to a debt or claim that, if that date were the commencement of the winding up of the company, would be admissible in proof against the company, and
>
> (II) can credibly demonstrate that the proposed reduction in the share capital would be likely to put the satisfaction of that debt or claim at risk, and that no adequate safe-guards have been obtained from the company, is entitled to object to the reduction, and
>
> (ii) the court shall settle a list of creditors entitled to object, and for that purpose may publish notices fixing a day or days within which creditors are to claim to be entered on the list or are to be excluded from the right of objecting to the reduction of capital.'

In all other respects the procedure for objection remains the same as it is for private companies, save that the penalty imposed by s 73 of the CA 1963 on officers for concealment of certain information in a reduction does not apply to officers of a PLC[143].

Corporate governance: management by the directors

[29.083] The law relating to directors and other officers of private companies as considered in Chapter 13 below is of equal relevance to PLCs. Thus, for example, all PLCs must have at least two directors, one of whom is EEA resident (save where the law otherwise allows), none of whom may be a body corporate[144], and the law governing the appointment, removal, restriction and disqualification of directors, as well as the principles which govern shadow directors, non-executive directors, etc, remain the same for both types of company, with surprisingly few exceptions which are now considered here.

(a) Differences for PLCs

[29.084] First, as regards the restriction of directors under s 150 of the CA 1990, a restricted director may not act as director of a PLC unless the nominal value of its allotted share capital is at least €317,434.52[145] – a threshold which is higher than that for private companies.

Second, the limit, imposed by s 45 of the C(A)(No 2)A 1999, of 25 directorships that may be held by one person at one time does not apply to directorship of PLCs – indeed, directorships of PLCs need not even be counted in reckoning the number of directorships held by the director of a private company[146].

---

[142] See Ch 3, *Constitutional Documents*, at para **[3.035]**.

[143] Regulation 3(b) of the EC(PLC)R 2008.

[144] Section 176 of the CA 1963.

[145] Section 150(3) of the CA 1990 as amended by s 41(a) of the CLEA 2001.

[146] Section 45(3)(a) of the C(A)(No 2)A 1999.

Third, as has already been discussed above[147], directors of PLCs who are required to take up qualification shares must do so before they can be appointed director[148].

Fourth, the directors of PLCs have a statutory duty under s 236 of the CA 1990 to take all reasonable steps to ensure that the company secretary (or each joint secretary) is a person who appears to them to have the requisite knowledge and experience to discharge the functions of company secretary and who:

> '(a) on the commencement of s 236 of the CA 1990 held the office of secretary of the company, or,
>
> (b) held office in a company for at least three of the five years immediately preceding his appointment, or
>
> (c) is a member of a body for the time being recognised by the Minister for Enterprise, Trade and Employment, or
>
> (d) is a person who by reason of his holding or having held any other position or his being a member of any other body, appears to the directors to be capable of discharging those functions.'

This section recognises that the office of company secretary in a PLC is an onerous one and requires a certain basic knowledge and experience. However, insofar as the subjective opinion of the directors is the ultimate touchstone, the legislature stopped short of giving the Minister absolute control over the qualifications which such a company secretary must hold. There is no requirement that the secretary must be a natural person.

[29.085] Though it may appear otherwise from the short catalogue of statutory differences just listed, the roles of directors in listed PLCs and private companies are, in practice, worlds apart. The division of powers between the members and the directors is usually well defined in a PLC[149], and the office of director is usually more than merely a position of necessity (as it can often be in a private company where a person forms a company, beneficially owns all of its issued share capital and finds that he (together with at least one other person) must act as a director to fulfil a statutory requirement). Directors of PLCs will often have contracts of employment with the company. PLCs, especially, tend to appoint directors for their experience, expertise or business acumen, rather than because that person is a shareholder. Career directors may have a shareholding in the PLC[150], but this is usually secondary to their primary involvement which is that of professional director.

(b) Board committees

[29.086] Many PLCs, especially those where the board may have a heavy workload, establish board committees of directors to deal with particular matters in more detail. The chairman of each committee is normally required to report back to the board and the minutes of the committee meeting may be circulated to all the board members. Such committees are sometimes established to evaluate major proposals in relation to the corporate structure or the business activity. The creation of a committee does not relieve

---

[147] See para **[29.040]** *ante*.

[148] Section 179(1) of the CA 1963.

[149] See Ch 13, *Corporate Governance: Management by the Directors*, at para **[13.126]**.

[150] On qualification shares, para **[29.040]**.

the other board members of responsibility[151]. The three most common standing committees in PLCs are the remuneration committee, which makes decision on the level of directors' pay and conditions; the audit committee, which supervises the financial and operating reports of the company and ensures that the company has adequate financial controls in place; and the nomination committee, which identifies new board members and nominates directors for various positions on the board. The UK Corporate Governance Code, which applies to PLCs listed on the Irish and UK Stock Exchanges, requires that both the audit committee and the remuneration committee be comprised entirely of non-executive directors, and the nomination committee comprise a majority of non-executive directors. The only committee required by law, however, is the audit committee, and only then when the PLC is a 'public interest entity' within the meaning of reg 3(1) of the EC(SA)(D)R 2010, namely:

'(a) companies or other bodies corporate governed by the law of a Member State whose transferable securities are admitted to trading on a regulated market of any Member State within the meaning of point 14 of Article 4(1) of Directive 2004/39/EC,

(b) credit institutions as defined in point 1 of Article 1 of Directive 2000/12/EC of the European Parliament and of the Council of 20 March 2000 relating to the taking up and pursuit of the business of credit institutions, and

(c) insurance undertakings within the meaning of Article 2(1) of Directive 91/674/EEC.'

A public interest entity which comes within the exceptions in reg 91(9) does not, however, have to establish an audit committee.

While private companies can have debt admitted to trading on a regulated market, only PLCs can have shares admitted to trading on a regulated market. In the case of PLCs that are public interest entities, they are required by reg 91 of the EC(SA)(D)R 2010 to establish an audit committee. The members of the audit committee must included not less than two 'independent directors' of the PLC[152], one of whom must have competence in accounting or auditing[153].

The responsibilities of the audit committee are set out in reg 91(6) as being:

'(a) the monitoring of the financial reporting process;

(b) the monitoring of the effectiveness of the entity's systems of internal control, internal audit and risk management;

(c) the monitoring of the statutory audit of the annual and consolidated accounts; and

(d) the review and monitoring of the independence of the statutory auditor or audit firm, and in particular the provision of additional services to the audited entity.'

It is significant, however, that the foregoing responsibilities are expressed to be without prejudice to the responsibility of the board of directors. Any proposal of the board regarding the appointment of a statutory auditor or audit firm must be based on a recommendation made by the audit committee[154]. The statutory auditor or audit firm

---

151 See Ch 15, *Duties of Directors and Other Officers*, at para **[15.051]**.

152 Regulation 91(3) and (4) of the EC(SA)(D)R 2010. For the definition of 'independent director' see Ch 13, *Corporate Governance: Management by the Directors*, at para **[13.038]**.

153 Regulation 91(5) of the EC(SA)(D)R 2010.

154 Regulation 91(7) of the EC(SA)(D)R 2010.

must report to the audit committee on key matters arising from the statutory audit and in particular 'on material weaknesses in internal control in relation to the financial reporting process'[155]. Where such a report is made to an audit committee both it, and the board of directors, will have an onus on them to take steps to mitigate such weaknesses but, conversely, where no report is made, the directors may seek to rely on the absence of any such report as a defence to any claim that they ought to have taken action.

(c) Corporate governance regulation

[29.087] Not only is the distinction between ownership and control normally more pronounced in PLCs, but very often – especially in larger PLCs whose shares are traded on the stock exchanges – the membership is more diverse, diffuse and more widely dispersed[156]. This makes alignment of the interests of shareholders and directors, which is the main approach of the orthodox Anglo-American model[157] of corporate governance, more complex. In the wake of recent financial crises the need for better corporate governance has never been more pronounced.

Some jurisdictions have legislated for improved corporate governance. The US, for example, through the 2002 *Sarbanes-Oxley* Act, uses a mix of internal and external controls by prohibiting certain transactions involving directors and imposing mandatory structures for boards of directors, in particular requiring that they have established audit committees and by providing detailed instructions on when and how audit committees and boards shall report to the regulatory authorities. Significant fines can be imposed on US regulated companies that do not comply.

In the UK and Ireland, however, the majority of such matters are left to the self-regulatory requirements of the stock exchange. Companies listed on UK or Irish Stock Exchanges must adhere to the UK Corporate Governance Code, (formerly known as the 'combined code'), which dictates a catalogue of good governance principles, on a 'comply or explain' basis – ie, companies must report regularly on whether and how they have complied with the principles, or else they must explain why they have not. Though such explanations are commonplace in practice[158], Irish and UK listed companies have a good record of adhering to the code's comply or explain requirements.

---

155 Regulation 91(8) of the EC(SA)(D)R 2010.

156 See, generally, Clarke, 'Corporate Responsibility in Light of the Separation of Ownership and Control' [1997] 19 DULJ 50.

157 Ancillary multiple goals, favoured in some continental European jurisdictions, may include the protection of the interests of employees, the economy, or the environment. For an excellent overview of the various theories of corporate governance see Brennan, 'A Review of Corporate Governance Research: An Irish Perspective' in Hogan, Donnelly & O'Rourke (eds), '*Irish Business & Society. Governing, Participating & Transforming in the 21st Century* (2010, Oak Tree Press) Ch 7. See also generally Keane & O'Neill, *Corporate Governance: An Irish Perspective* (2009, RoundHall); and Kavanagh & O'Higgins, 'The development of corporate governance in Ireland' in Lopez-Iturriaga (ed), *Codes of Good Governance Around the World* (2009, Nova Press).

158 See *Report on Compliance with the Combined Code on Corporate Governance by Irish Listed Companies* (2010) commissioned by the Irish Stock Exchange and the Irish Association of Investment Managers. The report recommended a number of improvements which are now included in the Irish Annex to the UK Corporate Governance Code; see para **[29.112]** *post*.

(d) Failed intervention by the Companies Acts

[29.088] Apart from the general governance structures applicable to both PLCs and private companies discussed in Chapter 13, above, the Companies Acts have attempted to intervene in two ways to enhance corporate governance in all PLCs, whether listed on a stock exchange or otherwise – first, in s 205B of the CA 1990, by requiring the boards of all PLCs and large companies (whether listed or not) to have an audit committee[159]; and second, in s 205E of the CA 1990, by requiring directors to sign compliance statements certifying that the company has complied with relevant legal obligations, including tax law. Ironically, perhaps, neither provision was ever commenced[160], and it is not likely that they ever will in their current form since the provisions on audit committees have been superseded by the European Communities (Statutory Audits) (Directive 2006/43/EC) Regs 2010 ('EC(SA)(D)R 2010')[161], and the CLRG has recommended a modified version of the compliance statement[162].

(e) The UK Corporate Governance Code

[29.089] The UK Corporate Governance Code is published by the Financial Reporting Council in the UK, and it updated and replaced the so-called 'combined code'[163] in 2010. As was observed above, it sets out standards of governance for listed companies on a 'comply or explain' basis. The Code was adopted by the Irish Stock Exchange with effect from 30 September 2010. The Irish Stock Exchange further requires Irish listed companies to comply or explain against additional provisions set out in the Irish Corporate Governance Annex appended to the Irish Listing Rules.

[29.090] The key aspects of the Code are[164]:

'success of the company.

- Checks and balances including:
  - Separate Chairman and Chief Executive.

---

[159] See, however, para **[29.086]** *ante* for the new law on audit committees.

[160] Indeed the compliance statement envisaged in s 205E of the CA 1990 provoked significant opposition from stakeholders based on cost, potential damage to competitiveness of Irish companies, and the uncertainty associated with the section. In April 2005, the Minister referred the section and the related proposed s 205F to the CLRG chaired by Dr Thomas B Courtney, which published its report following its deliberations and consultations on the issue, in late 2005. This report proposed an amended version of the requirements of s 205E which subsequently received Cabinet endorsement. The amendments have been included in the draft Companies Bill published in 2011 and set to be introduced as a formal Bill in late 2012. See generally, Courtney, 'Directors' Compliance Statements: Attesting Corporate Compliance on a "Comply or Explain" Basis', in Keane & O'Neill, *Corporate Governance and Regulation: An Irish Perspective* (2009, Round Hall).

[161] SI 220/2010.

[162] See CLRG, *Report on Directors' Compliance Statements, 2005*, Ch 10.

[163] The UK Corporate Governance Code updates and replaces the 2008 edition of the combined code. The combined code was first published in 1999 bringing together and updating earlier reports on corporate governance, particularly the *Cadbury Report – The Financial Aspects of Corporate Governance* (1992) and the *Greenbury Report – Report of Study Group on Directors Remuneration* (1995), on remuneration of directors. The combined code was updated in 2006 and again in 2008.

[164] See Financial Reporting Council, *The UK Approach to Corporate Governance* (October 2010).

- A balance of executive and independent non-executive directors.
- Strong, independent audit and remuneration committees.
- Annual evaluation by the board of its performance.

Transparency on appointments and remuneration.

– Effective rights for shareholders, who are encouraged to engage with the companies in which they invest.'

The Code is regularly reviewed in consultation with companies and investors, and revisions are expected in late 2012. The proposed changes include:

– Requesting FTSE 350 companies to put the external audit contract out to tender at least every 10 years;
– Asking boards to explain why they believe their annual reports are fair and balanced;
– Encouraging more meaningful reporting by audit committees;
– Providing more guidance on explanations that should be provided to shareholders when a company chooses not to follow the Code.

Some of these changes have already been reflected in Ireland by the Irish Corporate Governance Annex[165]. The new Code is also expected to embody provisions previously announced requiring boards to report on their gender diversity policies.

(f) Main principles of the Code

[29.091] The Code comprises a list of main principles, followed by supporting principles and specific provisions. The main principles characterise the Code and are as follows:

'**Section A: Leadership**

A.1 The Role of the Board

Every company should be headed by an effective board which is collectively responsible for the long-term success of the company.

A.2 Division of Responsibilities

There should be a clear division of responsibilities at the head of the company between the running of the board and the executive responsibility for the running of the company's business. No one individual should have unfettered powers of decision.

A.3 The Chairman

The chairman is responsible for leadership of the board and ensuring its effectiveness on all aspects of its role.

A.4 Non-executive Directors

As part of their role as members of a unitary board, non-executive directors should constructively challenge and help develop proposals on strategy.

Section B: Effectiveness

B.1 The Composition of the Board

The board and its committees should have the appropriate balance of skills, experience, independence and knowledge of the company to enable them to discharge their respective duties and responsibilities effectively.

165 See para **[29.092]** *post*.

B.2 Appointments to the Board

There should be a formal, rigorous and transparent procedure for the appointment of new directors to the board.

B.3 Commitment

All directors should be able to allocate sufficient time to the company to discharge their responsibilities effectively.

B.4 Development

All directors should receive induction on joining the board and should regularly update and refresh their skills and knowledge.

B.5 Information and Support

The board should be supplied in a timely manner with information in a form and of a quality appropriate to enable it to discharge its duties.

B.6 Evaluation

The board should undertake a formal and rigorous annual evaluation of its own performance and that of its committees and individual directors.

B.7 Re-election

All directors should be submitted for re-election at regular intervals, subject to continued satisfactory performance.

Section C: Accountability

C.1 Financial and Business Reporting

The board should present a balanced and understandable assessment of the company's position and prospects.

C.2 Risk Management and Internal Control

The board is responsible for determining the nature and extent of the significant risks it is willing to take in achieving its strategic objectives. The board should maintain sound risk management and internal control systems.

C.3 Audit Committee and Auditors

The board should establish formal and transparent arrangements for considering how they should apply the corporate reporting and risk management and internal control principles and for maintaining an appropriate relationship with the company's auditor.

Section D: Remuneration

D.1 The Level and Components of Remuneration

Levels of remuneration should be sufficient to attract, retain and motivate directors of the quality required to run the company successfully, but a company should avoid paying more than is necessary for this purpose. A significant proportion of executive directors' remuneration should be structured so as to link rewards to corporate and individual performance.

D.2 Procedure

There should be a formal and transparent procedure for developing policy on executive remuneration and for fixing the remuneration packages of individual directors. No director should be involved in deciding his or her own remuneration.

Section E: Relations with Shareholders

> *E.1 Dialogue with Shareholders*
>
> There should be a dialogue with shareholders based on the mutual understanding of objectives. The board as a whole has responsibility for ensuring that a satisfactory dialogue with shareholders takes place.
>
> *E.2 Constructive Use of the AGM*
>
> The board should use the AGM to communicate with investors and to encourage their participation.'

(g) The Irish Corporate Governance Annex

[29.092] The listing rules of the Irish Stock Exchange further requires companies listed on the Main Securities Market of the Irish Stock Exchange to adhere to the principles of the Irish Corporate Governance Annex. A notable feature of the Annex is that it is designed to enhance the meaningfulness of the explanations given by companies of how they have applied the Code. The introduction to the Annex states in particular that:

> 'Companies should move away from the practice of recycling descriptions that replicate the wording of the UK Code or Irish Annex's provisions and provide informative disclosures that will provide shareholders with greater insight into the company and the environment in which it operates. Companies should also avoid the practice of copying wording contained in the corporate governance disclosures year on year as this practice does not reflect compliance with the spirit of the UK Code or the Irish Annex. This should not be interpreted as imposing an obligation on companies to change the wording of their corporate governance disclosures simply for the sake of change.
>
> However, companies should always have considered whether the circumstances have remained sufficiently constant that no wording changes are required.'

(h) Other corporate governance codes

[29.093] A plethora of other corporate governance codes exists, many of them voluntary, and most of them geared towards particular sectors of activity. Notable amongst this list are the Central Bank's *Corporate Governance Code for Credit Institutions and Insurance Undertakings*; the voluntary *Corporate Governance Code for Collective Investment Schemes and Management Companies* promulgated by the Irish Funds Industry Association; and the *Code of Practice for the Governance of State Bodies.* Many of the features of the UK Corporate Governance Code, especially in respect of the composition of the board of directors and committees, are shared by these and other codes; however, a detailed discussion of their provisions is beyond the scope of this work.

Corporate governance: meetings

[29.094] As was noted earlier[166], Irish company law relies heavily on the idea of corporate governance through democratic meetings, particularly through the shareholders in general meeting, who can exercise a measure of control over the directors by means of the special resolution procedure and who can control the appointment and removal of the directors. This model applies equally to PLCs, but in

[166] See generally Ch 14, *Corporate Governance: Meetings*.

practice the extent to which the general meeting can influence the governance of the company is reduced by a number of factors. First, for this model to work at all, effective participation and voting by shareholders must be both facilitated and protected. In this regard, the EU has been actively engaged in securing and protecting fully informed participation and voting rights for shareholders in listed companies, and a number of recent amendments have been made to Irish company law in consequence[167]. Likewise, the UK Corporate Governance Code[168] and the various guidelines and codes ancillary thereto, place a heavy emphasis on relations with shareholders and contain a number of provisions relating to meetings and participation therein[169].

[29.095] However, where the membership is large and dispersed, as it will often be in PLCs, and particularly in listed companies, ordinary private shareholders may often think it is not worth their while to bother engaging in meetings, given the relative size of their shareholding and the disproportionate investment of time involved. When they do become involved, rather than attend in person it is not uncommon for them to appoint a proxy, who will usually be one of the directors, and the board will normally have solicited proxy votes when it anticipates a contentious vote – thus the directors' position becomes entrenched. Only the institutional investors are left to exercise governance at meetings. Recent developments in the corporate governance codes are designed to make institutional investors recognise their responsibility in this regard and to encourage them to engage in an effective way[170].

[29.096] These factors become more pronounced as capital markets internationalise and shareholders become spread throughout the world. Internet technology is thought to offer some solution by improving accessibility to meetings, and recent amendments place a heavy emphasis on encouraging the use of such technology.

[29.097] The special features of the law governing meetings as it applies to PLCs is considered below as follows:

(a) Notice requirements generally;
(b) Additional rights conferred under the Shareholders' Rights Directive;
(c) The requirements of the UK Corporate Governance Code as regards meetings.

(a) Notice requirements generally

[29.098] Though most of the law relating to meetings discussed in Chapter 14 is equally applicable to PLCs, the notice period required for EGMs in PLCs and private companies differs. For a public company, s 133(1)(b) of the CA 1963 requires that at least 14 days' notice must be given of an EGM, whereas other companies need only give seven days' notice. For AGMs, the notice period remains the same for all companies at 21 days[171].

---

[167] See para **[29.099]** *post*.
[168] See para **[29.089]** *ante*.
[169] See para **[29.112]** *post*.
[170] See para **[29.0114** *post*.
[171] Section 133(1)(a) of the CA 1963.

(b) Additional rights conferred under the Shareholders' Rights Directive

[29.099] The Shareholders' Rights (Directive 2007/36/EC) Regulations 2009[172] (the 'SR(D)R 2009') implement the Shareholders' Rights Directive in Ireland. The Directive was introduced in order to provide common rules to improve corporate governance in listed companies across Europe by enabling shareholders to exercise their voting rights and rights to information across borders. The additional rights conferred apply therefore only to companies whose shares are traded on a regulated market in the EU. Accordingly, the provisions of the SR(D)R 2009 next considered do not apply to private companies with listed debt, nor to Irish PLCs whose shares (on interests therein) are traded on a stock exchange that is not in the EU, eg in America.

The preamble to the Directive states its aims as being that:

- shareholders should be able to cast informed votes at, or in advance of, the general meeting, no matter where they reside;
- the possibilities which modern technology offer to make information instantly accessible should be exploited;
- shareholders should, in principle, have the possibility to put items on the agenda of the general meeting and to table draft resolutions for items on the agenda. This right should be made subject to basic rules, namely that any threshold required for the exercise of those rights should not exceed 5% of the company's share capital and that all shareholders should in every case receive the final version of the agenda in sufficient time to prepare for the discussion and voting of each item on the agenda;
- every shareholder should, in principle, have the possibility to ask questions related to items on the agenda of the general meeting and to have them answered. The Directive proposes leaving the rules on how and when questions are to be asked and answered to be determined by Member States;
- companies should face no legal obstacles in offering to shareholders any means of electronic participation in the general meeting subject only to such constraints that are necessary for the verification of identity and the security of electronic communications;
- good corporate governance requires a smooth and effective process of proxy voting. The Directive therefore provides that proxy holders should be bound to observe any instruction received from shareholders and that shareholders have an unfettered right under this Directive to appoint proxy holders to attend and vote at general meetings in their name.

The additional rights conferred by the Directive are considered below under the following headings:

(i) Notice requirements;
(ii) Right to put items on the agenda of the general meeting and to table draft resolutions;
(iii) Requirements for participation in and voting at general meetings;
(iv) Right to participate in general meeting by electronic means;

[172] SI 316/2009.

(v) Right to ask questions at general meetings;
(vi) Right to equal treatment;
(vii) Proxies;
(viii) Voting by correspondence;
(ix) Posting of information on polls.

(i) Notice requirements

[29.100] The SR(D)R 2009 amend s 133 of the CA 1963 by introducing a new sub-s (1)(c) which restricts the circumstances in which companies whose shares are traded on a regulated market[173] can rely on a 14-day notice period for general meetings (other than AGMs or general meetings for the passing of a special resolution). Such companies can only employ a 14-day notice period if the company offers the facility to vote by electronic means, which is accessible to all members who hold shares that carry voting rights, and a special resolution reducing the period to 14 days has been passed at the immediately preceding AGM or at an EGM held since the AGM. If a company decides not to retain the 14-day notice period by facilitating members in the fashion described above, then it would appear from Article 5.1 of Directive 2007/36/EC that all general meetings must be held at 21 days' notice.

[29.101] Companies traded on a regulated market are further required to provide additional information to shareholders by s 133A of the CA 1963 as amended by the SR(D)R 2009.

Under s 133A(2), notice of a general meeting shall be issued, free of charge, in a manner ensuring fast access to the notice on a non-discriminatory basis, using such media as may reasonably be relied upon for the effective dissemination of information to the public throughout Member States. Subsection (3) requires that the notice shall set out the following:

> '(a) when and where the meeting is to take place and the proposed agenda for the meeting;
>
> (b) a clear and precise statement of any procedures a member must comply with in order to participate and vote in the meeting, including—
>
> (i) the right of a member to put items on the agenda of a general meeting and to table draft resolutions pursuant to section 133B and to ask questions relating to items on the agenda pursuant to section 134C, and the time limits applicable to the exercise of any of those rights,
>
> (ii) the right of a member entitled to attend, speak, ask questions and vote, to appoint a proxy pursuant to section 136 (including a proxy who is not a member) by electronic means or otherwise or, where allowed, one or more proxies, to attend, speak, ask questions and vote instead of the member,
>
> (iii) the procedure for voting by proxy pursuant to section 136, including the forms to be used and the means by which the company is prepared to accept electronic notification of the appointment of a proxy, and
>
> (iv) the procedure (where applicable) to be followed pursuant to sections 134B and 138 for voting electronically or by correspondence respectively;

[173] UCITS are expressly excluded – reg 3.

(c) the record date for eligibility for voting as defined in section 134A and state that only members registered on the record date shall have the right to participate and vote in the general meeting;

(d) where and how the full, unabridged text of the documents and draft resolutions referred to in subsection 4(c) and (d) may be obtained, and

(e) the internet site at which the information contained in subsection (4) shall be made available.'

In addition, under sub-s (4) a company shall make available to its members on its internet site, for a continuous period of at least 21 days before a general meeting (inclusive of the day of the meeting), the following:

'(a) a notice under section 133A(2),

(b) the total number of shares and voting rights at the date of the giving of the notice (including separate totals for each class of shares where the company's capital is divided into 2 or more classes of shares),

(c) the documents to be submitted to the meeting,

(d) a copy of any draft resolution or, where no such resolution is proposed to be adopted, a comment from the board of directors on each item of the proposed agenda of the meeting,

(e) a copy of forms to be used to vote by proxy and to vote by correspondence unless these forms are sent directly to each member.'

Where the forms referred to in sub-s (4)(e) cannot be made available on the company's internet site for technical reasons, the company must indicate on its internet site how the forms may be obtained in hard copy and the company must send the forms by post, free of charge, to every member who requests them[174]. The company must also make any draft resolutions tabled by members available on its internet site as soon as possible following their receipt[175].

(ii) Right to put items on the agenda of the general meeting and to table draft resolutions

[29.102] A significant new right is conferred by the SR(D)R 2009 on shareholders in a PLC traded on a regulated market. Members holding 3% of the issued share capital and representing at least 3% of the total voting rights of all members who have a right to vote at such meetings now have a statutory rights to put an item on the agenda of the AGM or a draft resolution to be adopted at the AGM, and to table a draft resolution for an item on the agenda of an EGM.

To facilitate members in exercising their rights in respect of the AGM, companies must ensure that the date of the next AGM is placed on its internet site by either the end of the previous financial year or not later than 70 days prior to the AGM, whichever is the earlier[176]. Where the exercise of the right in s 133(1)(a) involves a modification of the agenda for the AGM in circumstances where the AGM has already been communicated to members, the company must make available a revised agenda in the same manner as the previous agenda in advance of the applicable record date of share-ownership for purposes of entitlement to vote or, if no such record date applies,

---

174 Section 133A(6) of the CA 1963.

175 Section 133A(5) of the CA 1963.

176 Section 133B(4) of the CA 1963.

sufficiently in advance of the date of the AGM to enable the other members to appoint a proxy or vote by correspondence[177].

[29.103] There are a number of important conditions which must be met by shareholders who wish to exercise such rights.

First, the rights may be exercised by electronic or postal means, but in either case 'to an address specified by the company'[178], so a notice sent to any other address will almost certainly be ineffective.

Second, in the case of a request to put an item on the agenda of an AGM, the request must be accompanied by either stated grounds justifying the inclusion of the item or a draft resolution to be adopted at the AGM[179].

Third, a request to put an item on the agenda or to table a draft resolution at an AGM must be sent in sufficient time to ensure that it is received by the company in hard copy form or in electronic form at least 42 days before the meeting to which it relates[180].

(iii) Requirements for participation in and voting at general meetings

[29.104] The SR(D)R 2009 introduce a new s 134A to the CA 1963 which applies to traded companies and which stipulates that in order to be eligible to attend and vote at a meeting, the company can specify in the notice that a person must be entered on the register of securities for a period not more than 48 hours prior to the meeting – referred to as 'the record date'. The new provision largely restates the position that prevailed prior to 2009 under reg 14 of the Uncertificated Securities Regulations 1996.

Section 134A transposes Article 7.1(b) of the Shareholders' Rights Directive and operates against the practice of 'share-blocking' (a practice more common in some Member States but not practiced in Ireland) by ensuring that members can sell their shares between the record date and the date of the meeting[181]. Under s 134A(6) of the CA 1963, proof of qualification of a shareholder may only entail such requirements as are necessary to ensure the identification of shareholders and even then only to the extent that any such requirements are proportionate to achieving that objective.

(iv) Right to participate in general meeting by electronic means

[29.105] Another innovation brought about by the SR(D)R 2009 is introduced in s 134B of the CA 1963 which facilitates participation in a general meeting of a PLC traded on a regulated market by electronic means. Such companies are permitted to provide for the electronic casting of votes and transmission of the meeting and real-time, two-way, communication between members and the meeting.

Although the provisions are facilitative, where companies elect to provide for such participation, they become subject to certain requirements. In the first place, the use of electronic means may be made subject only to proportionate requirements and restrictions necessary to ensure the identification of participants and the security of the

177 Section 133B(3) of the CA 1963.

178 Section 133B(1) of the CA 1963.

179 Section 133B(1)(a) of the CA 1963.

180 Section 133B(2) of the CA 1963.

181 Section 134A(5) of the CA 1963.

electronic communications[182]. Secondly, members must also be informed of any requirements or restrictions and that companies that provide such facilities are secure[183].

(v) Right to ask questions at general meetings

[29.106] Prior to the coming into force of the SR(D)R 2009 there was no statutory right for members to ask questions at general meeting. That is now changed for PLCs whose shares are traded on a regulated market in the EU by s 134C(1) of the CA 1963 as inserted by reg 8 of the Regulations which provides:

> 'A member of a company traded on a regulated market has the right to ask questions related to items on the agenda of a general meeting and to have such questions answered by the company subject to any reasonable measures the company may take to ensure the identification of the member.'

An answer may be refused, however, where to give it would interfere unduly with the preparation for the meeting or the confidentiality and business interests of the company; or it has already been given on the company's internet site in a question and answer forum; or where it appears to the chairman of the meeting that it is undesirable in the interests of good order of the meeting that the question be answered[184].

(vi) Right to equal treatment

[29.107] A new s 132A is added to the CA 1963 by the SR(D)R 2009 for the purpose of ensuring equal treatment of members who are in the same position with regard to participation and the exercise of voting rights in the general meeting. The section applies to companies traded on a regulated market, and is concerned with shareholders 'who are in the same position' as regards voting rights.

(vii) Proxies

[29.108] Regulation 9 of the SR(D)R 2009 amends s 136 of the CA 1963 which provides that a member may appoint another person as proxy to attend and vote on their behalf at a meeting, by adding the words 'natural or legal' to 'another person' for clarification purposes. It is also provides that proxies do not need to be members of the company. The Irish legislation was already supportive of proxy voting and predates the Directive by not placing barriers or restrictions on the appointment of proxy shareholders[185]. Regulation 9 inserts a new sub-s (4A) into s 136 of the CA 1963 to prohibit any provision in a company's articles of association where such provision would have the effect of restricting the eligibility of a person to be appointed as a proxy. The only exception to this is the unremarkable requirement that a person appointed as a proxy must possess legal capacity. Though it is already implicit from contract law and the law governing fiduciaries, sub-s136(1A)(b) emphatically states, for the sake of certainty, that a proxy holder must act in accordance with shareholder instructions. Where instructions are unclear, Article 10(3)(b) of the Directive gives Member States the option of restricting proxy voting rights. However, the Irish practice of allowing the proxy himself, or in certain circumstances the chairman of the meeting, to vote on

---

182 Section 134B(2)(a) of the CA 1963.

183 Section 134B(2)(c) of the CA 1963.

184 Section 134C(2) of the CA 1963.

185 See Ch 14, *Corporate Governance: Meetings*, at para **[14.074]** *et seq.*

behalf of a shareholder where a clear 'for' or 'against' preference has not been expressed on the completed proxy form has been retained by not availing of the Article 10(3)(b) option; indeed, the new s 136(1A)(e) refers to 'voting instructions *if any*' (emphasis added).

[29.109] Proxies must be appointed in writing or electronically. In the case of electronic appointments, the appointment must be sent to an address specified by the company. Members also have a right to appoint a proxy electronically, rather than this being left to the company to decide. Identical provisions govern revocation of the appointment of a proxy[186].

The new provisions further provide that, notwithstanding anything in a company's articles, no limitation may be placed on the right to appoint more than one proxy to attend and vote at general meetings in respect of shares held in different securities accounts, provided that a member shall not be entitled to appoint more than one proxy to attend and vote on the same occasion unless the member is an intermediary acting on behalf of clients[187]. Members who are intermediaries cannot be prohibited from granting a proxy to each of their clients or their clients' nominees and also cannot be prevented from casting some votes differently to others[188].

(viii) Voting by correspondence

[29.110] The Shareholders' Rights Directive obliges Member States to offer shareholders of PLCs with shares traded on a regulated market in the EU the possibility to vote by correspondence without appointing a proxy in advance of the general meeting. Voting by correspondence can be differentiated from proxy voting in that the member casts his own vote in advance of the general meeting, rather than having a proxy to cast it for him at the meeting. The SR(D)R 2009 thus insert a revised s 138 of the CA 1963 which facilitates the taking of a poll by correspondence entered into prior to a meeting for companies traded on a regulated market. Companies wishing to avail of this option must make provision for voting by correspondence in their articles of association. This option is not mandatory, however, and companies may elect not to permit voting by correspondence.

Where companies elect to permit voting by correspondence, they may only insist on proportionate requirements and restrictions necessary to ensure identification of the member and are only obliged to count votes cast by correspondence where they are received before the date and time specified by the company provided such is no more than 24 hours before the time at which the vote is to be concluded[189].

(ix) Posting of information on polls

[29.111] Article 14 of the Shareholders' Rights Directive requires that companies should establish for each resolution at least the number of shares for which votes have been validly cast, the proportion of the share capital represented by those votes, the total number of votes validly cast as well as the number of votes cast in favour of and against each resolution and, where applicable, the number of abstentions. The SR(D)R 2009

186 Section 136(1A) and (1B) of the CA 1963.

187 Section 136(2A) of the CA 1963.

188 Section 136(2A) of the CA 1963.

189 Section 138(3) of the CA 1963.

thus insert a new s 145A of the CA 1963 obliging a company traded on a regulated market to establish such information and to publish it on its internet site within 15 days after the meeting at which the voting result was obtained. Section 145A(3) of the CA 1963 further provides, however, that where no shareholder requests a full account of the voting, it shall be sufficient to establish the voting results only to the extent needed to ensure the required majority is reached for each resolution.

(c) The requirements of the UK Corporate Governance Code as regards meetings

[29.112] The UK Corporate Governance Code, formerly known as the 'combined code,' was published in May 2010 and applies to financial years beginning on or after 29 June 2010. The Irish Stock Exchange requires Irish listed companies to comply with, or explain why they have not complied with, the UK Corporate Governance Code with effect from 30 September 2010[190].

[29.113] In so far as meetings are concerned, the UK Corporate Governance Code imposes a number of requirements, which go beyond the traditional notion of formal meetings, as follows:

> 'E.1 Dialogue with Shareholders
>
> *Main Principle*
>
> There should be a dialogue with shareholders based on the mutual understanding of objectives. The board as a whole has responsibility for ensuring that a satisfactory dialogue with shareholders takes place.
>
> *Supporting Principles*
>
> Whilst recognising that most shareholder contact is with the chief executive and finance director, the chairman should ensure that all directors are made aware of their major shareholders' issues and concerns. The board should keep in touch with shareholder opinion in whatever ways are most practical and efficient.
>
> *Code Provisions*
>
> E.1.1 The chairman should ensure that the views of shareholders are communicated to the board as a whole. The chairman should discuss governance and strategy with major shareholders. Non-executive directors should be offered the opportunity to attend scheduled meetings with major shareholders and should expect to attend meetings if requested by major shareholders. The senior independent director should attend sufficient meetings with a range of major shareholders to listen to their views in order to help develop a balanced understanding of the issues and concerns of major shareholders.
>
> E.1.2 The board should state in the annual report the steps they have taken to ensure that the members of the board, and, in particular, the non-executive directors, develop an understanding of the views of major shareholders about the company, for example through

[190] The Irish Stock Exchange also requires Irish listed companies to comply with, or explain why they have not complied with, the Irish Corporate Governance Annex which supplements the UK Corporate Governance Code. At the time of writing a number of revisions to the UK Code are expected, including enhanced explanations to shareholders as to why any provisions of the code have not been complied with.

direct face-to-face contact, analysts' or brokers' briefings and surveys of shareholder opinion.

E.2 Constructive Use of the AGM

Main Principle

The board should use the AGM to communicate with investors and to encourage their participation.

Code Provisions

E.2.1 At any general meeting, the company should propose a separate resolution on each substantially separate issue, and should, in particular, propose a resolution at the AGM relating to the report and accounts. For each resolution, proxy appointment forms should provide shareholders with the option to direct their proxy to vote either for or against the resolution or to withhold their vote. The proxy form and any announcement of the results of a vote should make it clear that a 'vote withheld' is not a vote in law and will not be counted in the calculation of the proportion of the votes for and against the resolution.

E.2.2 The company should ensure that all valid proxy appointments received for general meetings are properly recorded and counted. For each resolution, where a vote has been taken on a show of hands, the company should ensure that the following information is given at the meeting and made available as soon as reasonably practicable on a website which is maintained by or on behalf of the company:

- the number of shares in respect of which proxy appointments have been validly made;
- the number of votes for the resolution;
- the number of votes against the resolution; and
- the number of shares in respect of which the vote was directed to be withheld.

E.2.3 The chairman should arrange for the chairmen of the audit, remuneration and nomination committees to be available to answer questions at the AGM and for all directors to attend.

E.2.4 The company should arrange for the Notice of the AGM and related papers to be sent to shareholders at least 20 working days before the meeting.'

[29.114] Schedule C to the UK Corporate Governance Code introduces further principles to encourage effective engagement (often referred to as 'stewardship') from *institutional* shareholders. The three main principles in this regard are:

- institutional shareholders should enter into a dialogue with companies based on the mutual understanding of objectives;
- when evaluating companies' governance arrangements, particularly those relating to board structure and composition, institutional shareholders should give due weight to all relevant factors drawn to their attention; and
- institutional shareholders have a responsibility to make considered use of their votes.

Notably, institutional investors are advised to apply the principles set out in the Institutional Shareholders' Committee's 'Code on The Responsibilities of Institutional Investors'. Moreover, they are encouraged to consider carefully the explanations given for departure from the UK Corporate Governance Code and to make reasoned judgments in each case. The Schedule advises that they should give an explanation to the company, in writing where appropriate, and be prepared to enter a dialogue if they do not accept the company's position; they should avoid a box-ticking approach to assessing a company's corporate governance; and they should bear in mind, in particular, the size and complexity of the company and the nature of the risks and challenges it faces. Finally, the Schedule requires institutional shareholders to take steps to ensure that their voting intentions are being translated into practice. They should, on request, make available to their clients information on the proportion of resolutions on which votes were cast and non-discretionary proxies lodged. Major shareholders should attend AGMs where appropriate and practicable, and companies and registrars should facilitate this.

Financial statements, audit and annual return

[29.115] PLCs are required to keep proper books of accounts, and the same principles apply in this regard as apply in relation to private limited companies, as set out in Chapter 17[191].

[29.116] PLCs are also required to prepare accounts[192] in respect of each financial year[193], which will be either Companies Act individual accounts[194] or IFRS individual accounts[195]. In addition, where a PLC is a parent company[196] or a parent undertaking[197], that PLC will be required to prepare group accounts[198], which again will be either Companies Act group accounts[199] or IFRS group accounts[200].

[29.117] Where a PLC prepares such Companies Act or IFRS individual or group accounts, there are only very minor differences between the statutory provisions that apply in respect of the items to be disclosed in such accounts, or in the related directors' report, and in the corresponding accounts of private companies. For example, s 14 of the C(A)A 1986 requires disclosure in the directors' report of particular details[201] where shares in a company are:

(a) acquired by a nominee of the company from a third person without financial assistance, and the company has a beneficial interest in those shares, pursuant to s 43(1)(c) of the C(A)A 1983;

---

191 See Ch 17, *Financial Statements, Audit and Annual Return*, at paras **[17.005]** to **[17.015]**.

192 See Ch 17, *Financial Statements, Audit and Annual Return*, at paras **[17.017]** *et seq.*

193 See Ch 17, *Financial Statements, Audit and Annual Return*, at para **[17.016]**.

194 See Ch 17, *Financial Statements, Audit and Annual Return*, at paras **[17.025]** to **[17.130]**.

195 See Ch 17, *Financial Statements, Audit and Annual Return*, at paras **[17.131]** to **[17.143]**.

196 Within the meaning of s 2(1) of the CA 1963; see Ch 17, *Financial Statements, Audit and Annual Return*, at para **[17.154]**.

197 Within the meaning of reg 4(1) of the EC(C:GA) 1992; see Ch 17, *Financial Statements, Audit and Annual Return*, at para **[17.154]**.

198 See Ch 17, *Financial Statements, Audit and Annual Return*, at paras **[17.154]** to **[17.155]**.

199 See Ch 17, *Financial Statements, Audit and Annual Return*, at paras **[17.164]** to **[17.200]**.

200 See Ch 17, *Financial Statements, Audit and Annual Return*, at paras **[17.201]** to **[17.212]**.

201 In addition to the details set out in Ch 17, *Financial Statements, Audit and Annual Return*, at para **[17.215]** in respect of an acquisition of shares, the company must also set out the reasons for a liquidation or charge.

(b) acquired by a person (whether a nominee of the company or otherwise) with financial assistance given either directly or indirectly by the company, and the company has a beneficial interest in those shares, pursuant to s 43(1)(d) of the C(A)A 1983;

(c) made subject to a lien or other charge that is taken by the company and is permitted by paragraphs (a), (c) or (d) of s 44(2) of the C(A)A 1983.

As ss 43 and 44 only apply to shares in a PLC, the disclosure obligation will only apply to a PLC.

[29.118] An alternative accounting framework is available in respect of the preparation of accounts by a relevant parent undertaking within the meaning of s 1 of the C(MP)A 2009, whereby such an undertaking may give a true and fair view of its state of affairs and profit or loss in the preparation of Companies Act individual accounts, and if applicable that of itself and its subsidiary undertakings as a whole in the preparation of Companies Act group accounts, by the use of US generally accepted accounting principles ('US GAAP'), to the extent that that use does not contravene any provision of the Companies Acts or of any regulations made thereunder[202]. The notes to the financial statements must contain a note to this effect[203].

A 'relevant parent undertaking' is defined[204] as a parent undertaking:

'(a) which does not have securities admitted to trading on a regulated market (in general terms, the main markets of each EU State[205]);

(b) whose securities (or whose receipts in respect of those securities) are registered with the US Securities and Exchange Commission ('SEC'), or which is otherwise required under US law to report to the SEC; and

(c) which, either:

  (i) prior to 23 December 2009, did not make – and was not required to make – an annual return to the CRO to which accounts were required to have been annexed; or

  (ii) prior to 4 July 2012, did not make – and was not required to make – an annual return to the CRO to which accounts were required to have been annexed, other than accounts pursuant to this section.'

A relevant parent undertaking is allowed to use such an accounting framework for accounts prepared for such of its financial years after it is incorporated in Ireland as end or ends not later than 31 December 2020[206].

It is expected that this section will facilitate the migration to Ireland of certain US companies, in that it allows a transitional period for such companies during which they will not be required to rush into a change from US GAAP to either IFRS or Irish GAAP, as would previously have been the case.

---

202 Section 1(3) of the C(MP)A 2009.

203 Section 1(4) of the C(MP)A 2009.

204 Section 1(1) of the C(MP)A 2009, as amended by s 2(a) of the C(A)A 2012.

205 The list is published and updated by the European Commission in the *Official Journal* of the European Union, the current list being set out at 2010/C 348/09; in Ireland, the sole relevant market is currently the Main Securities Market of the Irish Stock Exchange.

206 Section 1(2) of the C(MP)A 2009, as amended by s 2(b) of the C(A)A 2012; prior to amendment, s 1 of the C(MP)A 2009 applied only to accounts for such of its first four financial years after incorporation in Ireland, ending not later than 31 December 2015.

[29.119] In addition, s 2 of the C(MP)A 2009 provides that the Minister[207] may make regulations providing for other categories of parent undertakings to use other specified accounting standards, as long as the preparation of such accounts shall not contravene any provision of the Companies Acts or any regulations made thereunder. No such regulations have yet been made.

[29.120] One key difference between PLCs and private limited companies is that the various exemptions available to private limited companies in respect of the preparation, auditing and disclosure of accounts are largely unavailable to PLCs.

First, PLCs are expressly excluded from availing of the exemptions and exclusions accorded to 'medium-sized' and 'small' private companies[208] in respect of the disclosure of accounts; nor may they avail of the exemption from filing individual accounts by virtue of being a subsidiary undertaking of an EU parent undertaking[209].

The exemption from the requirement to prepare group accounts related to size of the group[210] is also expressly limited to a parent undertaking that is a private company. In addition, while the other exemptions from preparing group accounts (for parent undertakings that are themselves subsidiary undertakings[211]) are not expressly stated as being limited to private companies, they are stated as not applying to a parent undertaking any of whose securities are admitted to trading on a regulated market[212] of an EEA State, which will greatly limit their application to public companies.

Finally, a PLC will also be precluded from availing of the exemption from having its accounts audited that applies to certain private limited companies[213].

Corporate borrowing

[29.121] The law relating to corporate borrowing, registration of charges, and receiverships in PLCs hardly differs from the principles discussed in Chapters 18–20. One difference, already considered above[214], is the prohibition in s 6(1) of the C(A)A 1983 against PLCs (other than investment companies) borrowing before they have fulfilled all requirements set out in that section.

[29.122] A further difference is that s 44(1) of the C(A)A 1983 invalidates a charge or lien taken (whether expressly or otherwise) by a PLC over its own shares. Section 44(2), however, excepts from this prohibition certain 'permitted charges', the following being the two main categories:

- charges on a PLC's own shares (not being fully paid) for any amount payable in respect of the shares;
- in the case of a PLC whose ordinary business includes the lending of money or the provision of credit or the bailment or hiring of goods under a hire-purchase

207 Currently, the Minister for Jobs, Enterprise and Innovation.

208 See Ch 17, *Financial Statements, Audit and Annual Return*, at paras [**17.267**] to [**17.284**].

209 See Ch 17, *Financial Statements, Audit and Annual Return*, at paras [**17.285**] to [**17.286**].

210 See Ch 17, *Financial Statements, Audit and Annual Return*, at paras [**17.157**] to [**17.158**].

211 See [**17.159**] to [**17.163**] *ante*.

212 See definition of 'regulated market' at [**29.099**] *ante* in the context of relevant parent undertakings.

213 See [**17.287**] *et seq ante*.

214 See para [**29.037**] *ante*.

agreement, a charge on the PLC's own shares, fully paid or not, which arises in connection with a transaction entered into by the company in the ordinary course of its business.

Strike off and restoration

[29.123] In addition to the circumstances in which a company may be struck off which were examined in Chapter 26, PLCs which fail to obtain a certificate under s 6 of the C(A)A 1983 within one year of incorporation can be struck off the register by the registrar of companies under s 8 of the C(A)A 1983.

The procedure is that the registrar shall send a warning letter stating that a notice will be published in *Iris Oifigiúil* with a view to having the company's name struck off the register of companies unless it obtains the certificate within a period of one month.[215] If the certificate has not been obtained within the prescribed one-month period the registrar may proceed to publish a further warning notice in *Iris Oifigiúil*. Thereafter, unless cause is shown to the contrary within a period of one month, she may proceed to dissolve the company and publish notice of that fact in *Iris Oifigiúil*.

A PLC which has been struck off the register under these provisions may be restored to the register following the procedure for restoration provided in s 311 of the CA 1963[216].

Investigations and inspectors

[29.124] The investigation procedures detailed in Chapter 27 also apply to PLCs, and the reader is referred to that chapter for detailed discussion of the generally applicable principles.

[29.125] The disclosure order procedure contained in ss 98–104 of the CA 1990, whereby the court can order persons to disclose their interest in shares, does not apply to PLCs. Instead, s 81 of the CA 1990 gives PLCs the additional power to conduct *their own* investigation into the ownership of shares in the company. Section 81(1) provides:

> 'A public limited company may by notice in writing require a person whom the company knows or has reasonable cause to believe to be or, at any time during the 3 years immediately preceding the date on which the notice is issued (but excluding any time before the commencement of this section), to have been interested in shares comprised in the company's relevant share capital—
>
> (a) to confirm that fact or (as the case may be) to indicate whether or not it is the case, and
>
> (b) where he holds or has during that time held an interest in shares so comprised, to give such further information as may be required in accordance with the following sub-section.'

The *relevant share capital* referred to in sub-s (1) is the company's issued share capital of a class carrying a right to vote in all circumstances at general meetings of the company, including shares in relation to which such rights have temporarily been

215 Although s 72 of the IFCMPA 2005 provides for the substitution of the 'Companies Registration Office Gazette' for *Iris Oifigiúil*, s 72 has not yet been commenced.

216 Section 8(3) of the C(A)A 1983. See Ch 26, *Strike off and Restoration*, at para **[26.051]**.

suspended[217]. The company may exercise these powers to see, *inter alia,* whether a takeover bid is imminent or possible[218].

[29.126] A notice under s 81(1) of the CA 1990 may require the person to whom it is addressed to provide the following information:

'(a) particulars of his own past or present interest in shares comprised in relevant share capital of the company (held by him at any time during the 3 year period mentioned in sub-s (1));

(b) where the interest is a present interest and any other interest in shares subsists or, in any case, where another interest in the shares subsisted during that 3 year period at any time when his own interest subsisted, to give (so far as lies within his knowledge) such particulars with respect to that other interest as may be required by the notice;

(c) where his interest is a past interest, to give (so far as lies within his knowledge) particulars of the identity of the person who held that interest immediately upon his ceasing to hold it.'

The particulars referred to in sub-ss (2)(a) and (2)(b) include particulars of the identity of persons interested in the shares in question and whether persons interested in the same shares are or were parties to any concerted agreement to which s 73 of the CA 1990 applies or to any agreement or arrangement relating to the exercise of any rights conferred by the holding of the shares. Interests of spouses, minor children and associated companies also come within the scope of such investigations. The section further applies in relation to a person who has or previously had, or is or was entitled to acquire, a right to subscribe for shares in a PLC which would, on issue, be comprised in the relevant share capital of that company. The notice must require any information given in response to the notice to be given in writing within such reasonable time as may be specified therein, and details of the information so obtained must be recorded in the register of interests. In *Re FH Lloyd Holdings plc*[219], it was held that a notice under the English equivalent of s 81 could be served on a person even though he was abroad.

[29.127] If any person fails to comply with the notice he will be guilty of an offence, and the court may, on the application of the company, impose restrictions of the kind envisaged by s 16 of the CA 1990 on those shares[220]. Moreover, the costs of the application will be borne by the party who failed to comply with the notice[221]. It will be a defence in any such criminal proceedings for the person to prove that the notice requiring him to give information was 'frivolous or vexatious[222]'. Where restrictions are imposed it is open to any person to apply to the court to have them lifted[223].

---

[217] Section 67(2) of the CA 1990.

[218] *Re TR Technology Investment PLC* [1988] BCLC 256.

[219] *Re FH Lloyd Holdings PLC* [1985] BCLC 293.

[220] See Ch 27, *Investigations and Inspectors,* at para **[27.085]**.

[221] *Re FH Lloyd Holdings PLC* [1988] BCLC 293.

[222] Section 85(4) of the CA 1990. See *Re FH Lloyd Holdings Ltd* [1985] BCLC 293, where the court refused to impose restrictions in such circumstances; also *Re Ricardo Group PLC (No 3)* [1989] BCLC 771, where it was held that restrictions would not be imposed since they would prejudice the rights of shareholders in a forthcoming takeover bid.

[223] Section 85(5) of the CA 1990.

[29.128] Under s 83 of the CA 1990 the company *must* conduct an investigation of this kind where requisitioned by the members holding not less than 10% of the company's paid up voting capital. The requisition must state that the requisitionists are requiring the exercise by the company of its investigative powers, the manner in which they require those powers to be exercised, and reasonable grounds as to why the investigation should be conducted in that manner. If the company defaults in holding a requisitioned investigation, the requisitionists or any one of them may apply to court for an order requiring the company to conduct an investigation. The court may grant the order where it seems reasonable so to order.

[29.129] The company is obliged to prepare a report to its members on the information received in a requisitioned investigation[224]. If the investigation is not concluded within three months of commencement, an interim report must be prepared. These reports must be made available at the company's registered office for a reasonable time after the conclusion of the investigation or the period to which they relate. Within 31 days of the making of a report, the company must notify the requisitionists of its having been made and its availability for inspection.

Compliance and enforcement

[29.130] The general body of law examined in the context of compliance and enforcement in Chapter 28 applies also to PLCs. Listed PLCs and PLCs which are investment companies are subject to considerable further regulation and supervision by the Stock Exchange and the Central Bank respectively. Those matters are considered elsewhere in this book[225]. Banks, insurance companies, and other financial services companies are also subjected to specific sectoral regulatory legislation which remains beyond the scope of this work.

Investment companies

[29.131] Many PLCs established in Ireland in recent times have been established as vehicles for investment whose main goal is the collective investment of their funds and property with the aim of spreading the investment risk. Ireland has seen a substantial growth in this important field of financial activity in the 25 years since the International Financial Services Centre, or IFSC, was first established in Dublin's docklands. The investment funds industry can be divided into two principal areas of activity – 'UCITS' and 'non-UCITS' (or 'alternative' funds). UCITS, or undertakings for collective investment in transferable securities, are creatures of European law[226], and the fundamental aim of Europe in this regard has been to achieve a system whereby UCITS established in one Member State can be marketed in the other Member States without need for further approval in those states. This single authorisation is commonly referred to as the *single European passport.* UCITS are retail investment products, and the range of investments into which UCITS can place their funds is limited. There has been a

224 Section 84 of the CA 1990.

225 See Ch 32, *Prospectus, Market Abuse and Transparency Law.*

226 UCITS established in Ireland are authorised under the European Communities (Undertakings for Collective Investment in Transferable Securities) Regulations 2011 (SI 352/2011). The Regulations, which transpose Council Directive 2009/65/EC, Commission Directive 2010/43/EC and Commission Directive 2010/44/EC into Irish law, are effective from 1 July 2011.

consequent growth in the non-UCITS or alternative investment funds market, where funds can be invested in a wider range of investments and which appeal to non-retail investors. Ireland has established itself as a highly-regarded international centre in both sectors, and as an international leader in the 'alternative' investments funds sector.

Both UCITS and non-UCITS can be constituted in a variety of legal forms. These include unit trusts[227], common contractual funds[228], and PLCs[229]. Non-UCITS may also be constituted as investment limited partnerships[230].

[29.132] Where a UCITS is constituted as a PLC, the company is governed by the European Communities (Undertakings for Collective Investment in Transferable Securities) Regulations 2011 ('the EC(UCITS)R 2011'), regs 39 and 40 of which disapply certain provisions of the Companies Acts, and reg 4 of which allows for the company to be established as an 'investment company' having fixed or variable capital. Regulation 4(3) provides:

> '... UCITS are undertakings—
>
> (a) the sole object of which is the collective investment in either or both—
>
> (i) transferable securities,
>
> (ii) other liquid financial assets referred to in Regulation 68, of capital raised from the public and which operate on the principle of risk-spreading, and
>
> (b) the units of which are, at the request of holders, repurchased or redeemed, directly or indirectly, out of those undertakings' assets.
>
> (4) Action taken by a UCITS to ensure that the stock exchange value of its units does not vary significantly from their net asset value shall be regarded as equivalent to repurchase or redemption referred to in paragraph (3)(b).
>
> (5) UCITS may consist of several sub-funds.
>
> (6) UCITS may be constituted as—
>
> (a) unit trusts,
>
> (b) investment companies with fixed capital that are registered as public limited companies,
>
> (c) investment companies with variable capital that are registered as public limited companies and the articles of which provide that—
>
> (i) the amount of the paid-up share capital of the investment company concerned shall at all times be equal to the net asset value of the company, and
>
> (ii) the shares of the investment company concerned shall have no par value,
>
> or
>
> (d) common contractual funds[231].

227 See the Unit Trusts Act 1990.

228 See the IFCMPA 2005.

229 See, eg, reg 4(6) of the EC(UCITS)R 2011 (SI 352/2011).

230 See the Investment Limited Partnerships Act 1994.

231 Regulation 4 of the EC(UCITS)R 2011. Regulation 4(9) excludes the Regulations from closed-ended type collective investments; investments in non-transferrable securities; investments conducted substantially through intermediaries; investments which are not offered to the public within the EU or which are only sold to the public outside the EU.

Where a non-UCITS investment fund is constituted as a PLC, the company is established as an 'investment company' governed by Part XIII of the CA 1990, as amended, which imposes particular requirements on the operation of such companies whilst relieving them of many of the restrictions in relation to share capital that apply to other companies. Section 253(2) of the CA 1990 disapplies the Part to companies to which the EC(UCITS)R 2011 apply. All investment companies are subject to authorisation and supervision by the Central Bank[232].

[29.133] Here, the following peculiarities in the law applicable to PLCs which are investment companies are considered:

(a) Formation and registration.
(b) Constitutional documentation.
(c) Incorporation and its consequences.
(d) Corporate contracts: capacity and authority.
(e) Shares and membership.
(f) The maintenance of capital.
(g) Financial Statements, audit and annual return.
(h) Winding up.

(a) Formation and registration

[29.134] A PLC will normally be formed afresh where the incorporators decide to establish a variable capital company to act as a vehicle for an investment fund.

(i) Share capital requirements

[29.135] The restriction in s 19 of the C(A)A 1983 on PLCs having an authorised minimum share capital does not apply to investment companies coming under Part XIII of the CA 1990[233]; their minimum capital requirements are imposed individually by the Central Bank[234]. Neither do the requirements in relation to the shares being paid up contained in s 28(1) of the C(A)A 1983 apply to investment companies[235]. The restrictions in s 5(1) of the C(A)A 1983 do not apply to investment companies within the meaning of Part XIII of the CA 1990, which can be formed with a minimum of two members[236]. Section 6 of the C(A)A 1983 does not apply to variable capital investment companies governed by the EC(UCITS)R 2011[237].

(ii) Authorisation requirements for investment companies

[29.136] PLCs which are incorporated as investment companies must obtain approval from the Central Bank which will continue to supervise their activities through their life. Section 256(1) of the CA 1990 provides that an investment company shall not carry on

232 Section 256 of the CA 1990. Authorisation does not constitute a warranty by the Bank as to the creditworthiness of the company nor does it render the Bank liable to any person save where it has acted in bad faith: s 259 of the CA 1990.

233 Section 260(3) of the CA 1990; reg 40(7)(a) of the EC(UCITS)R 2011.

234 Section 256(3) of the CA 1990.

235 Section 116(7) of the CA 1963.

236 Section 5 of the CA 1963.

237 Regulation 40(7) of the EC(UCITS)R 2011.

business in the State unless it has been authorised to do so by the Central Bank on the basis of criteria approved by the Minister. Foreign registered companies which would be classed as investment companies had they been registered in Ireland must likewise not advertise or market their shares in any way within the State without Central Bank approval[238].

(iii) Migration of companies into Ireland – investment companies

[29.137] Section 256F of the CA 1990[239] facilitates the migration to Ireland of bodies corporate which are established and registered under the laws of a 'relevant jurisdiction' and which are 'collective investment undertakings'. Relevant jurisdictions are jurisdictions so prescribed by the Minster for Jobs, Enterprise and Innovation[240].

Under s 256F(9) of the CA 1990, where the migration is successful, the body corporate will be deemed to be formed and registered under the Irish Companies Acts and will be de-registered in its jurisdiction of origin, all without affecting its corporate *persona* which remains intact; s 256F(9) expressly states that the provision does not operate to create a new legal entity and does not affect its previous identity, so that any contract made or resolution passed or other act or thing done in relation to the migrating company during the period that the migrating company was established and registered elsewhere remains unaffected.

[29.138] The migration procedure is detailed in s 256F of the CA 1990. An application must be made in the prescribed form to the registrar of companies detailing the prescribed details, supported by a statutory declaration. The registrar publishes a notice of the application in the Companies Registration Office Gazette. If the registrar decides to register the company, then she will issue a certificate of incorporation and enter any registrable charges against the company in the charges register[241]. The company must apply to be de-registered in its previous jurisdiction of incorporation. Where any material change occurs in the information supplied, the company must notify the registrar. If the company fails to meet any of the requirements of s 256F of the CA 1990, the registrar may strike the company off the register of incorporation by giving one month's notice, unless the matter is resolved.

(b) Constitutional documentation

[29.139] An investment company's sole object stated in the memorandum of association must be 'the collective investment of its funds in property with the aim of spreading investment risk and giving members of the company the benefit of the results of the management of its funds[242]'. Its capital clause may specify:

> "(a) that the share capital of the company shall be equal to the value for the time being of the issued share capital of the company,

238 Section 256(8) of the CA 1990.

239 Inserted by s 3(j) of the C(MP)A 2009.

240 The relevant jurisdictions are Bermuda, the British Virgin Islands, the Cayman Islands, Guernsey, Jersey and the Isle of Man.

241 On the registration of charges generally, see Ch 19, *Corporate Borrowing: Registration of Charges*.

242 Section 253 of the CA 1990.

(b) the division of that share capital into a specified number of shares without assigning any nominal value thereto, [and]

(c) that the issued share capital of the company for the time being shall not be less than a minimum amount nor more than a maximum amount specified in the memorandum[243].'

Otherwise, the memorandum of association of an investment company shall be in the normal statutory form prescribed by s 2 of the C(A)A 1983.

[29.140] The articles or memorandum of an investment company under Part XIII of the CA 1990 must provide:

'(i) that the actual value of the paid up share capital of the company shall be at all times equal to the value of the assets of any kind of the company after the deduction of its liabilities, and

(ii) that the shares of the company shall, at the request of any of the holders thereof, be purchased by the company directly or indirectly out of the company's assets[244].'

The memorandum or articles of a company shall be regarded as providing for the matters referred to in paras (a) and (b) of s 253(2) of the CA 1990 notwithstanding the inclusion in the memorandum or articles with respect thereto of incidental or supplementary provisions[245].

[29.141] Part XIII of the CA 1990 does not apply to PLCs which are incorporated as vehicles for UCITS[246], but the EC(UCITS)R 2011 require in any event that the memorandum and articles must contain sufficient provision so as to enable it to operate in accordance with the EC(UCITS)R 2011, and in accordance with any condition or requirement, or both, as the Central Bank may impose[247].

(c) Incorporation and its consequences

[29.142] Investment companies enjoy further significant privileges as regards limited liability. Section 256A of the CA 1990, inserted by s 25 of the IFCMPA 2005, allows an investment company to have segregated liability so far as each of its sub-funds is concerned. This amendment is the product of extensive consultation with the funds industry; the IFSC Funds Group having recommended the introduction of measures to government, France and Luxembourg having already introduced similar reforms.

Prior to the introduction of s 256A of the CA 1990, although investment companies were required to keep separate books, accounts and records for each sub-fund, and though the assets of each sub-fund remained attributable to that sub-fund, the company as a whole remained legally responsible to third parties for any liabilities in respect of each sub-fund. This was to be contrasted with the position of an 'umbrella' unit trust which in Irish law could segregate the assets and liabilities of each sub-fund from the other sub-funds. This had a particularly adverse impact on leveraged umbrella funds, or

243 Section 253(1) of the CA 1990.

244 Section 253 of the CA 1990.

245 Section 253(4) of the CA 1990.

246 Section 253(2) of the CA 1990.

247 Regulation 18(2)(b) of the EC(UCITS)R 2011.

on those which regularly used derivatives in the course of their trading, given their inherent exposure to liability.

Although these provisions allow for segregation of liability between sub-funds, s 256E(6) of the CA 1990 specifies that a sub-fund is not to be regarded as a separate legal person. Section 256E(1) of the CA 1990 further introduces a measure of creditor protection by requiring an umbrella fund with segregated liability to ensure that it includes the words 'An umbrella fund with segregated liability between sub-funds' in all its letterheads and in any agreement entered into in writing with a third party, and shall be obliged to disclose that it is a segregated liability umbrella fund to any third party with which it enters into an oral contract.

Umbrella investment companies established in Ireland after 30 June 2005 are automatically designated as segregated liability funds. Companies established before that date can apply to avail of segregated liability following the procedures set out in s 256A of the CA 1990.

(d) Corporate contracts: capacity and authority

[29.143] Section 256E of the CA 1990 implies a number of terms into every contract, agreement, arrangement or transaction entered into by an umbrella fund. It provides:

> 'There shall be implied in every contract, agreement, arrangement or transaction entered into by an umbrella fund to which section 256A applies the following terms, that—
>
> (a) the party or parties contracting with the umbrella fund shall not seek, whether in any proceedings or by any other means whatsoever or wheresoever, to have recourse to any assets of any sub-fund of the umbrella fund in the discharge of all or any part of a liability which was not incurred on behalf of that sub-fund,
>
> (b) if any party contracting with the umbrella fund shall succeed by any means whatsoever or wheresoever in having recourse to any assets of any sub-fund of the umbrella fund in the discharge of all or any part of a liability which was not incurred on behalf of that sub-fund, that party shall be liable to the umbrella fund to pay a sum equal to the value of the benefit thereby obtained by it, and
>
> (c) if any party contracting with the umbrella fund shall succeed in seizing or attaching by any means, or otherwise levying execution against, any assets of a sub-fund of an umbrella fund in respect of a liability which was not incurred on behalf of that sub-fund, that party shall hold those assets or the direct or indirect proceeds of the sale of such assets on trust for the umbrella fund and shall keep those assets or proceeds separate and identifiable as such trust property.

The goal of these provisions is to preserve the integrity of the sub-funds within the umbrella.

(e) Shares and membership

[29.144] An investment company within the meaning of Part XIII of the CA 1990 may have, in effect, *no par* shares[248]. An investment company is a PLC whose sole object is by definition 'the collective investment of its funds in property with the aim of spreading investment risk and giving the members of the company the benefit of the results of the management of its funds[249]'. Its memorandum or articles must also provide

---

[248] For a discussion of the par value of shares see Ch 8, *Shares and Membership*, at para **[8.045]**.

[249] Section 253(2) of the CA 1990.

that the actual value of the paid up share capital will at all times equal the value of its assets of any kind after the deduction of all liabilities, and that the shares of the company may be purchased at any time out of the company's assets.

Instead of stating the nominal value of its shares in the memorandum, an investment company is empowered to state in its memorandum that 'the share capital of the company shall be equal to the value for the time being of the issued share capital of the company' and to provide for 'the division of that share capital into a specified number of shares without assigning any nominal value thereto[250]'.

[29.145] The statutory pre-emption provisions in ss 23 to 25 of the C(A)A 1983 do not apply to investment companies[251]. The provisions of s 119 of the CA 1963, which allow for the inspection of the register and index of members, do not apply to investment companies[252].

(f) The maintenance of capital

[29.146] The provisions of s 72 of the CA 1963, which only allow for the reduction of share capital where sanctioned by the court, do not apply to investment companies[253].

Section 254 of the CA 1990 provides that the purchase by an *investment company* of its own shares shall be on such terms and in such manner as may be provided by its articles. The only limitation imposed is that where the shares are shares which give the holder the right to request that they be redeemed by the company, then they must be fully paid; but this does not prevent an umbrella fund from acquiring non-paid shares in a sub-fund.

The treatment of shares bought back by investment companies is governed separately by s 255 of the CA 1990 which provides in sub-s (1) that they shall be cancelled and the amount of the company's issued share capital shall be reduced by the amount of the consideration paid by the company for the purchase of the shares. Section 255(2) of the CA 1990 provides that the company may issue new shares at the same time and that stamp duty will only be chargeable if the amount raised exceeds the amount spent on the buyback. Subsection (3) allows umbrella funds to acquire sub-funds from the same umbrella fund provided that the acquisition complies with conditions laid down by the Central Bank, without the need to cancel the shares or reduce the issued share capital under sub-s (1).

A more liberal regime applies to PLCs which are investment companies as regards the making of distributions. By virtue of s 47 of the C(A)A 1983, as amended[254], in determining the amount of its distributable profits an investment a company need only have regard to its revenue profits and losses capital profits and losses may be ignored, subject to certain conditions stipulated in s 47(5). Were it otherwise, an investment

250 Section 253(1) of the CA 1990.

251 Section 260 of the CA 1990. Nor do they apply to UCITS which are incorporated as PLCs: regs 39 and 40 of the EC(UCITS)R 2011 (SI 352/2011).

252 Section 260(2) of the CA 1990.

253 Section 260 of the CA 1990.

254 By reg 8 of the European Communities (Adjustment of Non-Comparable Amounts in Accounts and Distributions by Certain Investment Companies) Regulations 2005 (SI 840/2005) and the European Communities (International Financial Reporting Standards and Miscellaneous Amendments) Regulations 2005 (SI 116/2005).

company might be prevented by s 46 of the C(A)A 1983 from declaring dividends because of temporary fluctuations in the value of its investments.

(g) Financial Statements, audit and annual return

[29.147] An investment company may opt to prepare its individual accounts in accordance with s 149A of the CA 1963 and an 'alternative body of accounting standards' as if references in s 149A of the CA 1963 to international financial reporting standards were references to that alternative body of accounting standards[255]. To date, the accounting standards of the United States of America, Canada and Japan have each been specified as being an alternative body of accounting standards for the purposes of this provision[256].

In addition, the obligations whereby a company must disclose specified details in respect of particular transactions involving its shares[257] are expressly stated as not applying to an investment company[258].

(h) Winding up

[29.148] The power of the court contained in s 213(f) of the CA 1963 to wind up a company on 'just and equitable' grounds does not apply to investment companies under Part XIII of the CA 1990 or to UCITS[259]. However, s 213(fa) of the CA 1963 separately empowers the court to wind up investment companies on just and equitable grounds provided the following conditions are fulfilled:

> '(I) the petition for such winding-up has been presented by the trustee of the company, that is to say, the person nominated by the Central Bank of Ireland under section 257(4)(c) of the Companies Act, 1990, in respect of that company;
>
> (II) the said trustee has notified the investment company of its intention to resign as such trustee and six or more months have elapsed since the giving of that notification without a trustee having been appointed to replace it;
>
> (III) the court, in considering the said petition, has regard to—
>
> (A) any conditions imposed under section 257 of the Companies Act, 1990, in relation to the resignation from office of such a trustee and the replacement of it by another trustee; and
>
> (B) whether a winding-up would best serve the interests of shareholders in the company; and
>
> (IV) the petition for such winding-up has been served on the company (if any) discharging, in relation to the first-mentioned company, functions of a company referred to in conditions imposed under section 257 of the Companies Act, 1990, as a 'management company'.

Section 213(fa)(ii) of the CA 1963 provides that if the company is a UCITS then the court must also have regard to any conditions that the Minister may by regulation introduce, but as yet the subsection has not been brought into force.

---

255 Section 260A(1) of the CA 1990.

256 Section 260A(4) of the CA 1990.

257 See **[17.215]**.

258 Section 260(4) of the CA 1990.

259 Section 213(f) of the CA 1963.

[29.149] As regards investment companies operating as umbrella funds with segregated liability[260], s 256E(8) of the CA 1990 provides that a sub-fund can be wound up as though it were a separate company. It provides:

> 'A sub-fund may be wound up in accordance with the provisions of section 213(e) and section 251(1)(c) of the Principal Act as if the sub-fund were a separate company, provided always that the appointment of the liquidator or any provisional liquidator and the powers, rights, duties and responsibilities of the liquidator or any provisional liquidator shall be confined to the sub-fund or sub-funds which is or are being wound up.'

For these purposes the relevant provisions of the Companies Acts are to be interpreted such that the word 'company' refers to the sub-fund or sub-funds that are being wound up; the word 'member' means a shareholder in that sub-fund; and 'creditor' means a creditor of that sub-fund[261]. The normal rules of law that would make the sub-fund liable for some or all of the liabilities of any other sub-fund, such as fraud or misrepresentation and, in particular, the application of the fraudulent preference principle under s 286 of the CA 1963 and the power of the court under s 139 of the CA 1990 to order the return of assets which have been improperly transferred, are dis-applied[262].

[B] Societas Europaea

Introduction and overview

[29.150] The *Societas Europaea*, or 'SE', is a European public limited company established in an EU Member State under Council Regulation EC 2157/2001 of 8 October 2001 on the Statute for a European Company (SE) and subject otherwise to the laws applicable to a public limited company in the EU Member State in which the SE has its registered office – regardless of where it operates. The essential idea behind the SE is the creation of a legal and corporate framework for companies which operate in more than one country within the European Economic Area ('EEA'), so that the need for such companies to comply with multiple regulatory requirements is obviated, and so that mergers between different types of company in two or more Member States are facilitated.

[29.151] The notion of a European public company as an autonomous legal entity governed by an EU statute is an old one – it was first proposed as early as the 1950s in the Council of Europe[263]. The first formal proposal, however, was made by the European Commission in 1970 when a draft Statute for a European Company was presented[264]. The model of corporation envisaged by the statute was truly supra-national, governed

---

260 See para **[29.142]** *ante*.

261 Section 256E(9) of the CA 1990.

262 Section 256E (8) of the CA 1990.

263 See Teichmann, 'The European Company – A Challenge to Academics, Legislatures and Practitioners' (2003) 4 German Law Journal 300; Lenoir, 'The Societas Europaea (SE) in Europe – A promising start and an option with good prospects' (2008) 4 Utrecht Law Review 13; Stolowy, 'Does the "Societas Europaea" or "European Company" make a significant contribution to construction of a European company law?' (2012) JBL 363.

264 Proposal for a Council Regulation Embodying a Statute for the European Company, [1970] OJ C 124/1.

only by European law, administration and taxation, but political disagreement ensued regarding the model of governance that should apply at board level and over the degree to which employees should be involved in board decisions. Taxation issues also became divisive. In the end it was to be some 31 years before the statute finally saw the light of day. The statute's delay reaching a consensus can be attributed in part to the social objective it was given by the European Commission, who considered that the SE should be a vehicle for promoting employees' participation on management and supervisory boards, along the lines of the German co-management or *mitbestimmung* model. The statute which finally emerged was in a greatly modified form which saw the text shrink from over 300 articles to just 70, and which saw a substantial increase in the role played by national company laws. It is recognised that the 2001 statute is effectively a compromise, and the European Commission has been actively engaged in reviewing the take-up and operation of the SE with a view to amending the statute in due course. Having set out to achieve a new entity with the same features across the EU, the problem with the SE is that it is not governed by the same laws in each Member State. It is, rather, a 'Heinz' with as many varieties as there are Member States with their own code of law governing PLCs.

[29.152] The following features of SEs may be of interest by way of overview. SEs can be formed in several different ways:

- by merger;
- as a holding company;
- as a subsidiary;
- an SE can form a subsidiary SE;
- by conversion from a PLC to an SE.

Upon registration, an SE has a separate legal personality. There is no EU-wide register of SEs, so SEs are registered on the national companies register of the Member State in which the SE has its registered office, and a notice of the registration is published in the *Official Journal* of the EU. The SE must have its registered office and head office in the same Member State where the SE has its true centre of operations.

The capital of the SE, and its securities, remain governed by national laws in the same way as they apply to public limited companies, and in most other respects Member States must treat an SE as though it is a public limited company formed in accordance with the law of the Member State in which it has its registered office, except that the authorised minimum capital of an SE is set at €120,000 and the share capital must be denominated in euro.

An SE can choose to have a one-tier or a two-tier governance structure, ie, a unitary or two-tier board of directors[265].

The essence of the SE is that it can transfer its seat and registered office from one Member State to another without having to wind up and re-register, and without having to encounter the events and complications consequent on a winding up[266].

The formation of an SE therefore offers certain advantages to companies with mobility ambitions within the EU. These include the confirmation of a true European

---

[265] See para **[29.154]** *post*. See also Ch 13, *Corporate Governance: Management by the Directors*, at para **[13.128]**.

[266] As to which see generally Ch 23, *Winding Up Companies*.

identify, in that the SE is the only form of company that enjoys complete freedom of establishment, both with regard to registered office and branches. Moreover, they also include the benefit of true intra-community mobility, since the SE has Community legal personality and enjoys complete freedom of movement[267]. In recent times, and for a variety of reasons (eg, more favourable tax treatment, or to meet capital or solvency requirements), the potential for companies to restructure by moving head office and other functions from one State and into another has become particularly attractive, and the SE can facilitate such migration without undue complexity.

Sources of the law applicable to SEs

[29.153] Two European legislative instruments in particular apply to SEs. The first, and obvious, one is Council Regulation EC 2157/2001 of 8 October 2001 on the Statute for a European Company (hereafter the 'SE Regulation'), which has direct effect in all Member States and does not require further implementation in any of the 27 Member States of the European Union, including Bulgaria and Romania. Most Member States have, however, implemented supporting measures to designate the appropriate registration authorities, etc – in Ireland the relevant measure is the European Communities (European Public Limited Liability Company) Regulations 2007[268] ('EC(EPLLC)R 2007').

[29.154] Second, under Article 12 of the SE Regulation, an SE cannot be registered unless an agreement on arrangements has been reached for employee involvement pursuant to Article 4 of Directive 2001/86/EC of 8 October 2001 supplementing the Statute for a European Company with regard to the Involvement of Employees. The Directive does not have direct effect and must be implemented nationally; the Irish measures in this regard are the European Communities (European Public Limited Liability Company) (Employee Involvement) Regulations 2006[269] ('EC(EPLC)(EI)R 2006').

[29.155] Third, wherever the SE Regulation is silent, the local law governing public limited companies in the Member State where the SE is registered applies by virtue of Article 10 of the SE Regulation. Indeed, in many instances in the SE Regulation such local law is expressly applied to the matters in question by the Regulation.

---

[267] The European Court of Justice has already extended this mobility to some degree to nationally incorporated companies in *Centros* Case C-208/00 [1999] ECR I-1459, where the court has admitted the possibility for a company to register in the state of its choice and to then carry out the entirety of its activities through a subsidiary based in another state; in *Überseering* Case C-167/01 [2002] ECR I-9919, where the court judged that a Member State could not deny a company of another state the ability to be a party to legal proceedings in order to defend their rights, in spite of the absence of a European Convention on mutual recognition of legal entities; in *Inspire* Art Case C-411/03 [2003] ECR I-10155, where the court decided that a Member State cannot impose specific obligations, even as 'a matter of form' on foreign companies incorporated in another Member State; and in *Sevic Systems* [2005] ECR I-10805 where the court found against a Member State that refused to register a company resulting from a cross-border merger, therefore requiring all Member States to acknowledge the validity of cross-border mergers.

[268] SI 21/2007.

[269] SI 622/2006.

Particular aspects of the law relating to SEs

[29.156] The law relating to SEs is now examined in further detail under the following headings:

(a) Formation and registration of SEs;
(b) Constitutional documentation in SEs;
(c) Governance structure of SEs;
(d) Requirements for employee involvement in SEs;
(e) Meetings in SEs;
(f) Financial reporting, audit and annual returns in SEs;
(g) Transfer of SEs between Member States;
(h) Conversion of SEs to PLCs;
(i) Winding up SEs.

(a) Formation and registration of SEs

[29.157] Article 2 of the SE Regulation lists the ways in which an SE may be formed, namely:

- by the *merger* of two or more *public* limited liability companies[270] who are registered under the laws of a Member State and having registered offices and head offices within the Community, provided that at least two of them are governed by the law of *different* Member States[271].
- By the formation of a *holding* SE by two or more *public or private* limited liability companies who are registered under the laws of a Member State and having registered offices and head offices within the Community, provided that at least two of them are governed by the laws of different Member States, or one has had a subsidiary company governed by the law of another Member State or a branch situated in another Member State for at least two years[272].
- By the formation of a *subsidiary* SE by companies and firms within the meaning of Article 48 of the Treaty and other legal bodies governed by public or private law, formed under the law of a Member State provided that at least two of them are governed by the laws of different Member States, or one has had a subsidiary company governed by the law of another Member State or a branch situated in another Member State for at least two years[273].
- By the *conversion* of a public limited liability company, formed under the law of a Member State, which has its registered office and head office within the Community, if for at least two years it has had a subsidiary company governed by the law of another Member State[274].

It will be noted that an SE cannot be formed except by conversion or restructuring of existing companies. Furthermore, an international dimension is required in the

[270] Annex II of the SE Regulation details the types of company in each Member State which can be categorised as public limited liability companies for the purposes of the Regulation.

[271] Article 2.1 of the SE Regulation.

[272] Article 2.2 of the SE Regulation.

[273] Article 2.3 of the SE Regulation.

[274] Article 2.4 of the SE Regulation.

formation either through engagement with a separate entity or a connected subsidiary in another Member State[275]. Note also that only public companies can form an SE by merger or conversion, whereas private and public companies can form a holding SE, and other legal bodies can form a subsidiary.

(i) Formation by merger

[29.158] The procedure for formation of an SE by merger is detailed in Articles 17 to 31 of the SE Regulation, and requires the obtaining of shareholder approval in general meeting and a confirmation order from the court. The process is based on that used in the Third Council Directive 78/855/EEC of 9 October 1978 based on Article 54(3)(g) of the Treaty concerning mergers of public limited liability companies, and Article 17 of the SE Regulation applies those merger provisions to the merger in which the SE is created. The procedures differ depending on whether the merger occurs *by acquisition* or whether the merger occurs *through formation of a new company.*

[29.159] In the case of a merger by acquisition, the acquiring company takes the form of an SE when the merger is completed[276]. In such cases, according to Article 3 of the Third Council Directive, the target company or companies shall thereafter be wound up without going into liquidation and automatically transfer to the acquirer all their assets and liabilities in exchange for the issue to its shareholders of shares in the acquiring company and a cash payment, if any, not exceeding 10% of the nominal value of the shares so issued or, where they have no nominal value, of their accounting par value. Where the merger is by the formation of a new company, the SE shall be the newly formed company[277], and the existing companies are wound up without going into liquidation and transfer all their assets and liabilities to a new company that they set up in exchange for the issue to their shareholders of shares in the new company and a cash payment, if any, not exceeding 10% of the nominal value of the shares so issued or, where they have no nominal value, of their accounting par value.

[29.160] In each case, draft terms for the merger detailing the matters listed in Article 20 of the SE Regulation must be drawn up by both companies and presented to general meetings of their shareholders for approval. The matters to be addressed are:

'(a) the name and registered office of each of the merging companies together with those proposed for the SE;

(b) the share-exchange ratio and the amount of any compensation;

(c) the terms for the allotment of shares in the SE;

(d) the date from which the holding of shares in the SE will entitle the holders to share in profits and any special conditions affecting that entitlement;

(e) the date from which the transactions of the merging companies will be treated for accounting purposes as being those of the SE;

---

275 Under Article 2.5, Member States may provide companies whose head office is outside the EU can participate in the formation of an SE provided that company is formed under the law of a Member State, has its registered office in that Member State and has a real and continuous link with a Member State's economy. In Ireland, this is achieved by reg 6 of the EC(EPLLC)R 2007.

276 Article 17.2 of the SE Regulation.

277 Article 17.2 of the SE Regulation.

(f) the rights conferred by the SE on the holders of shares to which special rights are attached and on the holders of securities other than shares, or the measures proposed concerning them;

(g) any special advantage granted to the experts who examine the draft terms of merger or to members of the administrative, management, supervisory or controlling organs of the merging companies;

(h) the statutes of the SE;

(i) information on the procedures by which arrangements for employee involvement are determined pursuant to Directive 2001/86/EC.'

The merging companies may include further items in the draft terms of the merger.

[29.161] The merger and the formation of the SE will be then scrutinised by the competent authority – in Ireland the High Court – which, if satisfied that all is in order, will confirm that the merger has been completed and that the SE has been formed.

[29.162] Under Article 19, the Director of Corporate Enforcement may, subject to judicial review, oppose a merger involving an Irish PLC on the grounds of public interest only[278].

[29.163] The merger has the following consequences *ipso jure* and simultaneously[279]:

– In a merger by acquisition:

(a) all the assets and liabilities of each company being acquired are transferred to the acquiring company;

(b) the shareholders of the company being acquired become shareholders of the acquiring company;

(c) the company being acquired ceases to exist;

(d) the acquiring company adopts the form of an SE.

– In a merger by formation of a new company:

(a) all the assets and liabilities of the merging companies are transferred to the SE;

(b) the shareholders of the merging companies become shareholders of the SE;

(c) the merging companies cease to exist.

(ii) Formation of a holding SE

[29.164] Formation of a holding SE is governed by Articles 32 to 34 of the SE Regulation. Article 32.1 confirms that a company promoting the formation of a holding SE shall continue to exist. Formation of a holding SE is achieved by a process of approval of draft terms of formation by the shareholders of each of the companies involved[280]. Regardless of where the holding SE will be registered, any Irish registered company involved in its formation must file the draft terms for its formation with the

278 The Director of Corporate Enforcement was designated for this function by reg 16 of the EC(EPLC)R 2007.

279 Article 29 of the SE Regulation.

280 Article 32.6 of the SE Regulation.

registrar of companies in Ireland at least one month before the company's general meeting[281].

The process is initiated by the management or administrative organs of the companies promoting the formation drawing up, in the same terms, draft terms for the formation of the holding SE. The draft terms must include an explanatory report explaining and justifying the legal and economic aspects of the formation and indicating the implications for the shareholders and for the employees of the adoption of the form of a holding SE. The draft terms must also set out the particulars required in Article 20(1)(a), (b), (c), (f), (g), (h) and (i), above, and must fix the minimum proportion of the shares in each of the companies promoting the operation which the shareholders must contribute to the formation of the holding SE[282]. The terms of formation must be examined by independent experts and a written report prepared by them for the shareholders[283], indicating any particular difficulties of valuation and stating whether the proposed share-exchange ratio is fair and reasonable, and also indicating the methods used to arrive at it and whether such methods are adequate in the case in question.

[29.165] Once the draft terms have been approved, shareholders have three months to notify the company as to whether they intend to contribute their shares to the formation of the holding SE. Only if the minimum proportions of shares (which, according to Article 32.2, shall be shares conferring more than 50% of the permanent voting rights) are assigned within that time can the SE be formed. Where those conditions are fulfilled, a notice to that effect must be publicised in the national registers – in Ireland, it must be delivered to the CRO[284]. Shareholders who have not previously indicated that they intend to make their shares available have a further month in which to indicate whether they intend to make their shares available for the purposes of forming the holding SE[285]. The holding SE may not be registered until it is shown that the formalities have been completed and any conditions fulfilled. Shareholders who have contributed their securities to the formation of the SE shall receive shares in the holding SE.

(iii) Formation of a subsidiary SE

[29.166] The rules governing the formation of a subsidiary SE are the same as those applicable to the formation of subsidiaries of public limited liability companies under local law[286]. An SE may itself set up one or more subsidiaries in the form of SEs[287].

(iv) Conversion of an existing PLC into an SE

[29.167] Conversion of existing PLCs into SEs is governed by Article 37 of the SE Regulation. The process is one involving shareholder approval following preparation, presentation and consideration of the draft terms of the conversion statute of the SE and

281 Article 32.3 of the SE Regulation. See also reg 21 of the EC(EPLLC)R 2007.

282 Article 32.2 of the SE Regulation.

283 Article 33.4 of the SE Regulation. The independent experts are persons who are eligible to act as such under Directive 78/855/EEC, implemented in Ireland by the European Communities (Mergers and Division of Companies) Regulations 1987 (SI 137/1987).

284 Article 33.3 of the SE Regulation. See reg 23 of the EC(EPLC)R 2007.

285 Article 33.3 of the SE Regulation.

286 Article 36 of the SE Regulation.

287 Article 3.2 of the SE Regulation.

independent experts' reports. It should be recalled that the PLC must have had a subsidiary incorporated in another Member State for at least two years prior to the conversion, so there can be no overnight incorporation from scratch of an SE using this method. Article 37.2 confirms for the avoidance of doubt that the conversion of a PLC into an SE 'shall *not* result in the winding of the company or in the creation of a new legal person'.

[29.168] The management or administrative organ of the PLC in question must draw up draft terms of conversion and a report explaining and justifying the legal and economic aspects of the conversion and indicating the implications for the shareholders and for the employees of the adoption of the form of an SE. The draft terms must be publicised in the manner laid down in each Member State (in Ireland by delivery to the registrar of companies and publication in the Companies Registration Office Gazette) at least one month before the general meeting called upon to decide on the conversion. An independent expert must report that the company has net assets at least equivalent to its capital plus those reserves which must not be distributed under the law or the statutes.

[29.169] The general meeting of the company in question must approve the draft terms of conversion and the statutes of the SE. Article 37.7 provides that the decision of the general meeting shall be passed as laid down in the provisions of national law adopted in implementation of Article 7 of Directive 78/855/EEC – which in Ireland means by special resolution[288]. Article 37.8 preserves terms and conditions of employment arising from national law, practice and individual employment contracts or employment relationships existing at the date of the registration, and transfers them to the SE.

(v) Registration of SEs

[29.170] As was noted earlier[289], there is no single European register for SEs, and Article 12 of the SE Regulation thus requires every SE to be registered in the Member State in which it has its registered office. In Ireland, a number of forms have been specified for these purposes by the European Communities (European Public Limited Company) (Forms) Regulations 2007[290]. Notice of the registration of an SE must also be published in the *Official Journal* of the EU under Articles 13 and 14 of the SE Regulation.

(b) Constitutional documentation in SEs

[29.171] Article 9 of the SE regulation contemplates that the SE shall have 'statutes', and as has been noted above, the draft statutes form an integral part in the formation process. No format is prescribed for the statutes, and accordingly they can be in the form of the memorandum and articles used in Ireland, subject to appropriate modification.

The SE Regulation makes particular mention that the name of the company shall contain the abbreviation 'SE'[291]. And, as was observed above, the capital of the SE must be denominated in euro.

---

288 Regulation 13.2 of the EC(MDC)R 1987.

289 See para **[29.152]** *ante*.

290 SI 222/2007.

291 Article 11.1. Only SEs may use this abbreviation (save for companies which had the abbreviation in their name before the coming into force of the Regulation).

[29.172] Article 59 of the SE Regulation makes specific provision for the amendment of the statutes of an SE. Amendment is possible and requires a decision by the majority at general meeting. Article 59.1 provides that the majority shall not be less than two-thirds of the votes cast:

> '*unless* the law applicable to public limited-liability companies in the Member State in which an SE's registered office is situated requires or permits a larger majority.'

It will be recalled that Irish law requires a 75% majority of the votes cast for most resolutions to alter the constitutional documentation[292]; accordingly, a similar majority will be required for most changes to the statutes of an SE, subject to a minimum of two-thirds where it is not[293].

Where there is a conflict between the arrangements made for employee involvement and the statutes of an SE, the statutes may be amended by the management or administrative organ without a decision of shareholders but only to the extent needed to resolve the conflict.

[29.173] Any amendments of the statutes must be publicised according to local law. In Ireland, the amendments must be notified to the registrar of companies who will cause a notice to be published in the Companies Registration Office Gazette[294].

(c) Governance structures of SEs

[29.174] SEs must choose and adopt one of two governance structures provided in Article 38 of the SE Regulation. It may have a 'one-tier system' (the system already common in most Irish private companies) where management is conducted by a single administrative organ (the board of directors) or it may have a two-tiered structure whereby a separate supervisory organ supervises the executive management and ensures efficient management and compliance with regulatory requirements (as is common in some continental jurisdictions, notably Germany, and as is increasingly required in PLCs by the stock exchange listing requirements and lately the EC(SA)(D)R 2010 as regards audit committees made up of non-executive directors[295]).

[29.175] The two-tier structure is legislated for in Articles 39–42 of the SE Regulation. In such systems the management organ shall be responsible for the executive management of the SE. A Member State may provide that a managing director or managing directors shall be responsible for the current management under the same conditions as for public limited liability companies that have registered offices within that Member State's territory.

Members of the management organ are to be appointed by the supervisory organ, and the supervisory organ cannot itself exercise powers to manage the SE. Member States may provide that the members of the management organ can be appointed directly by the general meeting; Ireland, in keeping with the tradition of the PLC, has opted to allow such appointments, and thus in an Irish SE, the statutes may permit the members of the management organ to be appointed and removed by the general meeting[296]. No

---

292 See Ch 3, *Constitutional Documentation*, at para **[3.056]**.

293 Member States may provide, however, that where at least half of an SE's subscribed capital is represented, a simple majority of the votes cast shall suffice: Article 59.2.

294 Regulation 24 of the EC(EPLLC)R 2007.

295 See para **[29.086]** *ante*.

person can be a member of both the management and supervisory organ at the same time except where a vacancy arises, at which point their role on the supervisory organ is suspended.

The members of the supervisory organ are appointed by the shareholders at the general meeting. The members of the supervisory organ can be appointed by the statutes for the first supervisory organ. The supervisory organ may elect a chairman. The management organ must report to the supervisory organ on a regular basis, or immediately where there are issues of appreciable importance, and the supervisory organ is given information and investigatory powers to enable it to carry out its functions.

[29.176] The one-tier structure is legislated for in Articles 43–45 of the SE Regulation. Under this structure an 'administrative organ,' the members of which are appointed by the general meeting, manages the SE, though managing directors may be appointed to conduct the day-to-day management. A chairman may be appointed to the administrative organ and it must meet at least once every three months. The number of members of the administrative organ, or the rules for determining it, must be laid down in the SE's statutes. The minimum number of members of the administrative organ of an SE is two[297].

[29.177] Rules common to both governance structures are set out in Articles 46–51 of the SE Regulation. Members of company organs shall be appointed for a period laid down in the statutes not exceeding six years, but may be reappointed if the statutes allow. Members of the organs may be bodies corporate, but in all cases members must meet the local requirements as regards qualification and eligibility for membership of such boards or committees in public limited companies. The local rules of liability for loss or damage sustained by the SE following any breach on their part of the legal, statutory or other obligations inherent in their duties, apply to members of organs of the SE[298]. Moreover, a duty of confidentiality is imposed on the members of the organs of SEs by Article 49 of the SE Regulation, which provides:

> 'The members of an SE's organs shall be under a duty, even after they have ceased to hold office, not to divulge any information which they have concerning the SE the disclosure of which might be prejudicial to the company's interests, except where such disclosure is required or permitted under national law provisions applicable to public limited-liability companies or is in the public interest.'

The statutes of the SE must list the categories of transaction which require authorisation from the management organ or the supervisory organ, or an express decision by the administrative organ in the one-tier system.

(d) Requirements for employee involvement in SEs

[29.178] Article 12.2 of the SE Regulation provides that no SE shall be registered unless arrangements for employee involvement pursuant to Article 4 of Directive 2001/86/EC (the 'Employee Involvement Directive') have been concluded, or a decision pursuant to Article 3(6) of the Directive has been taken, or the period for negotiations pursuant to

296 Regulation 17 of the EC(EPLLC)R 2007.

297 Regulation 19 of the EC(EPLLC)R 2007.

298 Article 51 of the SE Regulation.

Article 5 of the Directive has expired without an agreement having been concluded; and the statutes of the SE must not conflict with the arrangements so made.

[29.179] Employee involvement in the SE will thus be decided upon by negotiations between employees and management before the creation of the SE. The Employee Involvement Directive is implemented in Ireland by the European Communities (European Public Limited Liability Company) (Employee Involvement) Regulations 2006 ('EC(EPLLC)(EI)R 2006') which set out the rules of engagement in negotiating and agreeing such arrangements. If an agreement cannot be reached through the negotiations, the default provisions of the Directive will apply.

[29.180] Involvement is possible at three levels – *information, consultation* and *participation*. The Directive defines involvement of employees as:

> 'any mechanism, including information, consultation and participation, through which employees' representatives may exercise an influence on decisions to be taken within the company[299].'

Standard rules and procedures for each of the information, consultation and participation models are set out in the Schedule to the EC(EPLLC)(EI)R 2006, along the following lines:

- Participation model – where employees form part of the supervisory board or of the administrative board, as the case may be;
- Consultation model – in which the employees' representative body is entitled to be consulted;
- Information and consultation model – a stronger version of the second model, in which the employees are entitled to seek and receive information;
- Variations on the models can be agreed between the management or administrative boards of the founding companies of the SEs and their employees or their representatives, provided the level of information and consultation is the same.

[29.181] Of particular importance is the question: to what extent, if any, is employee involvement at board level required where an SE is formed by the merger of two existing companies or through the formation of a holding SE or subsidiary SE? Part 3 of the Annex to the Employee Involvement Directive confirms that participation is *not* required if there was no employee participation in the boards of the merging companies. It provides:

> 'If none of the participating companies was governed by participation rules before registration of the SE, the latter shall not be required to establish provisions for employee participation.'

However, where any of the founding companies has employee participation itself then proposals for employee participation in the SE must be put forward, and voting on such proposals shall be proportionate to the level of participation in the company with the highest amount of participation prior to the formation of the SE. Similar provisions apply where the proposals purport to reduce the level of employee participation. Where

[299] Article 2 of the Employee Involvement Directive.

an SE is formed by conversion then, unsurprisingly, in all respects the employee participation is to continue in the SE[300].

(c) Meetings in SEs

(i) General meetings

[29.182] General meetings are dealt with in Articles 52–60 of the SE Regulation, subject to the rider in Article 53 that the local rules governing the organisation and conduct of general meetings together with voting procedures applicable to public limited liability companies in the Member State in which the SE's registered office is situated shall otherwise apply. Thus, for example, the Director of Corporate Enforcement in Ireland may be called upon under Irish law by the members to convene a general meeting where the directors have failed to do so.

[29.183] General meetings may be convened at any time by the administrative organ, management organ or supervisory organ. Shareholders holding at least 10% of the SE's subscribed capital (or some lesser percentage, if this is set down in the statutes) may request the SE to convene a general meeting and draw up the agenda. The request will state the items to be placed on the agenda. Shareholders holding at least 10% of the SE's subscribed share capital may request that additional items be placed on the agenda of a general meeting.

The first general meeting of an SE must be held within 18 months of incorporation, and at least once each calendar year thereafter, within six months of the end of its financial year. So long as an SE holds its first annual general meeting within 18 months of its registration in the State, it need not hold such a meeting in the year of its registration or in the following year[301].

[29.184] As regards voting at meetings, Article 57 of the SE Regulation provides that most decisions can be passed by a majority voting in favour, and Article 58 excludes spoiled votes and votes attaching to shares in respect of which the shareholder has not taken part in the vote or has abstained, from the reckoning. Where an SE has two or more classes of shares, every decision by the general meeting shall be subject to a separate vote by each class of shareholders whose class rights are affected thereby[302].

(ii) Management meetings

[29.185] As regards management meetings, Article 50 of the SE Regulation deals with quorums in meetings of the management, administrative or supervisory organs. The Regulation imposes the following rules:

- quorum: at least half of the members must be present or represented;
- decision-taking: a majority of the members must be present or represented.

In a vote, the chairman of the organ is given a casting vote in the event of a tie, subject to exception where half the supervisory organ consists of employees' representatives. Where employee participation is provided for in accordance with Directive 2001/86/EC, a Member State may provide that the supervisory organ's quorum and decision-making shall be subject to the rules applicable, under the same conditions, to public limited liability companies governed by the law of the Member State concerned.

---

[300] Part 3(a) of the Annex to the Employee Involvement Directive.

[301] Regulation 20 of the EC(EPLLC)R 2007.

[302] Article 60 of the SE Regulation.

(f) Financial reporting, audit and annual returns in SEs

[29.186] SEs are subject to the same rules applicable to public limited liability companies under the law of the Member State in which its registered office is situated as regards the preparation of its annual and, where appropriate, consolidated accounts including the accompanying annual report and the auditing and publication of those accounts[303]. SEs which are credit or financial institutions, or which are insurance undertakings, must additionally comply with the rules laid down in the national law of the Member State implementing the special EU law requirements relating to their accounts[304].

(g) Transfer of an SE's registered office between Member States

[29.187] SEs may transfer their registered office from one Member State to another within the EU without having to wind up and re-register. An SE may not transfer its registered office if proceedings for winding up, liquidation, insolvency or suspension of payments or other similar proceedings have been brought against it[305].

The transfer procedures are provided in Article 8 of the SE Regulation. The management or administrative organ must draws up a *transfer proposal*. The proposal must state the current name, registered office and number of the SE and must cover[306]:

> '(a) the proposed registered office of the SE;
>
> (b) the proposed statutes of the SE including, where appropriate, its new name;
>
> (c) any implication the transfer may have on employees' involvement;
>
> (d) the proposed transfer timetable;
>
> (e) any rights provided for the protection of shareholders and/or creditors.'

The management or administrative organ shall then draw up a report explaining and justifying the legal and economic aspects of the transfer and explaining the implications of the transfer for shareholders, creditors and employees[307]. Shareholders and creditors are entitled, at least one month before the general meeting called upon to decide on the transfer, to examine the transfer proposal and the report at the SE's registered office, and, on request, to obtain copies of those documents free of charge[308].

No decision to transfer may be taken for two months after publication of the proposal[309].

In the Member State in which an SE has its registered office, the court, notary or other competent authority shall issue a certificate attesting to the completion of the acts and formalities to be accomplished before the transfer. The competent authority in Ireland is the registrar of companies. Before the competent authority issues the certificate, the SE shall satisfy it that, in respect of any liabilities arising prior to the publication of the transfer proposal, the interests of creditors and holders of other rights in respect of the SE (including those of public bodies) have been adequately protected in

303 Article 61 of the SE Regulation.

304 Article 62 of the SE Regulation.

305 Article 8.15 of the SE Regulation.

306 Article 8.2 of the SE Regulation.

307 Article 8.3 of the SE Regulation.

308 Article 8.4 of the SE Regulation.

309 Article 8.6 of the SE Regulation.

accordance with requirements laid down by the Member State where the SE has its registered office prior to the transfer[310].

Every invoice, order for goods or business letter, shall, at any time between the date on which the transfer proposal and the SE's registration transfers, contain a statement that the SE is proposing to transfer its registered office to another Member State under Article 8 and identifying that Member State[311].

[29.188] The Director of Corporate Enforcement may exercise the power to oppose the transfer of a registered office[312]. Such opposition may be based only on grounds of public interest. Where an SE is supervised by a national financial supervisory authority according to Community directives, the right to oppose the change of registered office applies to this authority as well. Review by a judicial authority is possible[313].

[29.189] Minorities are also protected in a transfer by reg 12 of the EC(EPLLC)R 2007 as follows. Where it is proposed to transfer the registered office of an SE from the State to another Member State, any member or members holding, in the aggregate, not less than 10% in nominal value of the issued share capital of the SE, being persons who did not consent to or vote in favour of the resolution for the transfer, may apply to the court:

'(a) to have the decision to transfer annulled,

(b) to require the SE to acquire for cash the securities of the shareholders opposed to the transfer, or

(c) for such other remedy as the Court considers just.'

On an application, the court may, as it considers appropriate, annul the decision to transfer, require the SE to acquire for cash the securities of the shareholders opposed to the transfer or grant such other remedy as it considers just.

[29.190] The new registration may not be effected until the certificate has been submitted, and evidence produced that the formalities required for registration in the country of the new registered office have been completed[314].

The transfer of an SE's registered office and the consequent amendment of its statutes shall take effect on the date on which the SE is registered in the register for its new registered office. When the SE's new registration has been effected, the registry for its new registration shall notify the registry for its old registration. Deletion of the old registration shall be effected on receipt of that notification, but not before[315].

[29.191] An SE which has transferred its registered office to another Member State shall be considered, in respect of any cause of action arising prior to the transfer, as having its registered office in the Member States where the SE was registered prior to the transfer, even if the SE is sued after the transfer[316]. In effect, therefore, it is to be regarded as a foreign company in subsequent proceedings even on a cause of action which accrued before the transfer.

---

310 Article 8.7 of the SE Regulation.

311 Regulation 11 of the EC(EPLLC)R 2007.

312 Regulation 14 of the EC(EPLLC)R 2007.

313 Article 8.14 of the SE Regulation.

314 Article 8.9 of the SE Regulation.

315 Articles 8.10 and 8.11 of the SE Regulation.

316 Article 8.16 of the SE Regulation.

(h) Conversion of SE to PLC

[29.192] An SE may be converted into a PLC governed by the law of the Member State in which its registered office is situated[317]. No decision on conversion may be taken before two years have elapsed since its registration or before the first two sets of annual accounts have been approved. The conversion of an SE into a public limited liability company shall not result in the winding up of the company or in the creation of a new legal person.

The procedure for conversion is set out in Article 66 of the SE Regulation and it requires a resolution of the members reached in accordance with the article. The management or administrative organ of the SE must draw up draft terms of conversion and a report explaining and justifying the legal and economic aspects of the conversion and indicating the implications of the adoption of the PLC form for the shareholders and for the employees. The draft terms of conversion shall be publicised in the manner laid down in each Member State's law at least one month before the general meeting called to decide thereon. Before the general meeting, an independent experts' report must certify that the company has assets at least equivalent to its capital. The general meeting of the SE must approve the draft terms of conversion together with the new memorandum and articles of association of the PLC[318].

(i) Winding up SEs

[29.193] SEs are governed by the same rules that govern the winding up, liquidation, insolvency, cessation of payments and similar procedures, which apply to PLCs in the Member State where the SE is registered, including provisions relating to decision-making by the general meeting[319].

[29.194] Article 64 of the SE Regulation contains a further provisions enabling an SE to be wound up where it has failed to meet the requirements in respect of having its registered office and head office in the same Member State. In such circumstances, the Member State in which the SE's registered office is situated shall take appropriate measures to oblige the SE to regularise its position within a specified period either:

> '(a) by re-establishing its head office in the Member State in which its registered office is situated, or
>
> (b) by transferring the registered office by means of the procedure laid down in Article 8.'

If an SE fails to regularise its position in either of these ways then measures can be taken to ensure that it is wound up. Member States must provide a judicial remedy with regard to any such procedures and they will have suspensory effect until the court renders its decision. Where it is established on the initiative of either the authorities or any interested party that an SE has its head office within the territory of another Member State, the authorities of that Member State must immediately inform the Member State in which the SE's registered office is situated.

---

317 Article 66 of the SE Regulation.

318 Article 66 of the SE Regulation. The decision of the general meeting shall be passed as laid down in the provisions of national law adopted in implementation of Article 7 of Directive 78/855/EEC.

319 Article 63 of the SE Regulation.

Chapter 30

Guarantee Companies

The guarantee company in context

[30.001] This chapter considers the law applicable to the public company, limited by guarantee, which does not have a share capital, referred to herein as a 'guarantee company'[1]. It may come as a surprise, but guarantee companies are the second most popular form of company formed and registered under the Irish Companies Acts and as at 31 December 2011 accounted for nearly 8.5% of all companies on the Irish register[2].

[30.002] In this chapter, the law relating to guarantee companies is considered under the following headings:

1. The primary uses of the guarantee company.
2. The key features of the guarantee company.
3. Formation and constitutional documentation of guarantee companies.
4. Disregarding separate legal personality.
5. Membership.
6. The maintenance of capital.
7. Corporate governance: management by the directors.
8. Corporate governance: meetings.
9. Financial statements, audit and annual return.
10. Winding up guarantee companies and realisation and distribution of assets.
11. Strike-off and restoration.
12. Compliance and enforcement.

The law relating to incorporation and its consequences, corporate civil litigation, corporate contracts, capacity and authority, members' remedies, groups of companies, duties of directors, statutory regulation of directors' transactions, corporate borrowing, schemes of arrangement, examinerships, investigations and inspectors is broadly similar for guarantee companies as it is for private companies as set out in Chapters 2 to 27 dealing with these issues.

The primary uses of the guarantee company

[30.003] Guarantee companies are most often utilised by people who require a company with a separate legal personality and limited liability for a purpose other than trading for

---

1. There is no specific Irish text on guarantee companies but one such English text is Mullen & Lewison, *Companies Ltd by Guarantee* (3rd edn, Jordans, 2011).
2. The *Companies Registration Office Report 2011* at p 10.

profit and while there is no prohibition on guarantee companies trading for profit, most guarantee companies are formed to operate as one of the following:

(a) charities;

(b) management companies; or

(c) sports or social clubs.

Citizens are more likely to find themselves a member or even a director of a guarantee company than any other company type and, indeed, in some cases not to appreciate that the entity is a company regulated by the Companies Acts.

(a) Charities

[30.004] The legal framework by which most charities in Ireland are organised is either as a guarantee company or as an unincorporated association[3]. Charities that organise themselves as guarantee companies protect their members from personal liability for the debts of the charity, operate a separate legal entity with perpetual succession, which can hold their own property without the need for trustees, and avail of a recognised corporate form which operates within a well-settled and developed company law regime. In order to be conferred with charitable tax exempt status, charities are required to meet certain requirements and the guarantee company is well placed to facilitate compliance with these requirements. Accordingly, the memorandum of association can facilitate charities having tightly-written objects clauses which contain a main object meeting a recognised charitable purpose[4]; a requirement that its income and property be applied solely towards promotion of its main objects and a prohibition on its income and property being distributed to members by way of dividend, profit, bonus or profit[5]; a prohibition on the remuneration of directors[6]; a requirement that in the event of the charity being wound up its net assets be transferred to another body having similar objects or failing that for some other charitable object[7]; and a requirement that the memorandum and articles are not amended without the consent of the Revenue Commissioners and that annual audited accounts are provided to the Revenue Commissioners[8]. Moreover, the Companies Acts can facilitate charities dispensing with the word 'limited' in their names where certain conditions are satisfied[9]. Most charities formed as guarantee companies will have a memorandum of association which contain all these features. In addition, the articles of association are a versatile document, which can be tailored to reflect current good practice in corporate structure and governance.

---

3 See Ch 1, *The Private Company in Context*, at para **[1.050]**. In relation to charities, there are a number of very interesting articles published in Practical Law for Companies on English law: Protani & Coen, 'Charitable Companies: Changes under the Companies Act 2006' (2008) PLC 43 and Protani & Coen, 'Dealing with Charities: Key Points for Businesses' (2007) PLC 37.

4 See para **[30.020]** *post*.

5 See para **[30.026]** *post*.

6 See para **[30.026]** *post*.

7 See para **[30.027]** *post*.

8 See para **[30.030]** *post*.

9 See para **[30.015]** *post*.

(b) Management companies

[30.005] In buildings, divided into apartments or retail units, there will always be common areas, for the shared use and enjoyment of the owners of the apartments or units. Such corridors, lifts, conduits, hallways, etc, need to be owned by a legal entity other than the owners but in which the owners can have an interest. Guarantee companies became the chosen legal entity used by developers when establishing both residential apartment developments and commercial developments for two main reasons. In the first place, the concept of membership without holding an economic interest in the nature of a share sits easily with the notion that the only reason why members are members of management companies is because of a common bond in being, say, an apartment owner in an apartment complex. The second, more practical reason, is that apartment and retail complexes can have a few hundred units and, until 2006, the maximum number of members of a private company was 50; even now, the maximum is only 99. There has been much debate about management companies[10] and whilst some have sought to characterise the problems as having a solution in company law, the reality was and is that the problems derive from the activities (ie, property management) in which guarantee companies engage and the absence of a regulator of these activities.

[30.006] A form of statutory regulation has come in the nature of the Multi-Unit Developments Act 2011 ('MUDA 2011') and its provisions that concern company law are considered throughout this chapter as they modify or override the otherwise applicable provisions of the Companies Acts. At this outset it may be noted that the MUDA 2011 applies to what are termed '*owners' management companies*'. An '*owners' management company*' is defined by s 1(1) of the MUDA 2011 as meaning:

> '... subject to subsection (3), a company established for the purposes of becoming the owner of the common areas of a multi-unit development and the management, maintenance and repair of such areas and which is a company registered under the Companies Acts.'

Accordingly, whilst it might be imagined that most owners' management companies will be guarantee companies, the definition would admit any type of company registered[11] under the Companies Acts, such as private companies limited by shares or even PLCs; moreover, when the definition in s 1(1) is read as extended by s 1(3) of the MUDA 2011[12], an 'owners' management company' could be virtually any body corporate or even an unincorporated association.

---

10 See the LRC's Consultation Paper on *Multi-Unit Developments* (LRC CP 42-2006).

11 'Registered' as opposed to 'formed and registered' means that a foreign company that establishes a place of business or branch and is registered under s 352 of the CA 1963 or the Branch Disclosure Regulations 1993 will also come within the definition because whilst not *formed* under the Companies Acts it will have *registered*. It would seem not to include a foreign company which should have registered (because it established a branch or place of business) but did not.

12 Section 1(3) provides that in the MUDA 2011: 'a reference to an owners' management company shall be construed, other than in the case of an owners' management company to which section 3 or section 14 applies, (contd.../)

Central to the definition of owners' management company are the concepts of 'multi-unit development'[13] and 'residential unit'[14] and the circumstances in which the provisions of the Act will apply depend upon the nature of the development[15].

(c) Sports or social clubs

[30.007] Guarantee companies are also used by those who form social clubs and associations. Again, the concept of membership existing by virtue of being a subscriber or of being admitted a member by the directors, in either case without being accompanied by an economic interest in the nature of a share, lends itself readily to the nature of a sports or social club or other association. Often social clubs will begin life as unincorporated associations because, being small, the costs of incorporation and its ongoing maintenance cannot be justified but, once they grow, they will then incorporate.

The key features of the guarantee company

[30.008] The key distinguishing features of guarantee companies are that they do not have any shares, are public, not private, companies, and are limited by the guarantee of their members. Each of these key traits is now considered:

(a) Guarantee companies have no shares

[30.009] Although it is possible for a company to be limited by guarantee and to have a share capital, such companies are not the concern of this chapter, being private companies to which the law in Chapters 1 to 28 is concerned. Guarantee companies the subject of this chapter, do not have shares or shareholders but instead have *members* whose membership arises otherwise than by holding a share in the company.

(b) Guarantee companies are public companies

[30.010] It is axiomatic that a company that does not have a share capital must be a public company, since it cannot be a private company[16]. This feature of the guarantee company can sometimes be overlooked since for many it is counterintuitive to consider a charity, a management company or a club as being a 'public' company. Some of the consequences of the fact that guarantee companies are public companies are that they must have at least seven members, cannot dispense with holding an AGM and cannot claim the exemption from having auditors.

(c) Guarantee companies are limited by their members' guarantee

[30.011] Like any limited company, in a guarantee company it is the liability of its members and not of the company itself which is limited. In a private company limited by

---

12 (\...contd) as including a reference to an industrial and provident society and to a partnership or unincorporated body or group of persons owning the common areas of a multi-unit development, and in the case where such ownership is held by a partnership or unincorporated body or group of persons any of the persons in such partnership, body or group shall be entitled to enforce the covenants and house rules concerned.'

13 Section 1(1) of the MUDA 2011.

14 Section 1(1) of the MUDA 2011.

15 See s 2 of the MUDA 2011 which specifies the application of the Act.

16 Section 33(1) of the CA 1963 provides that a private company 'means a company which has a share capital …'.

shares or a PLC, the liability of the shareholding members to contribute to the assets of the company in the event of an insolvent winding up is limited to the amount, if any, outstanding on their shares. In companies limited by shares it is very common for some if not all of the shareholding members' liability on their shares to be paid up so that in the event of a call being made by a liquidator, they will have no further liability. In a guarantee company, the members' liability will usually be for a nominal amount, eg, €1, but in all cases, nothing will have been paid up since the guarantee will not have been called upon. Of course, whether it is worth a liquidator's while to make a call and spend the price of a letter, envelope and stamp, where perhaps only €1 may be recouped, is another matter!

Formation and constitutional documentation of guarantee companies

(a) Formation of guarantee companies

[30.012] The only way of forming a guarantee company is by lodging all documentation on the 'ordinary list' with the Companies Registration Office ('CRO'). Unlike private companies, the 10-day list or CRODisk cannot be used to form a guarantee company. The documents required to be filed are:

- memorandum of association;
- articles of association;
- Form No A1 (incorporating a statutory declaration that an activity will be carried on in Ireland); and
- the appropriate fee.

In the case of charities and social clubs, the application to incorporate will often be accompanied by an application to dispense with the word 'limited' in the form of a statutory declaration for the purposes of s 24 of the CA 1963[17].

(b) Memorandum of association

[30.013] The memorandum of association of a guarantee company must comply with s 6 of the CA 1963. A form of model memorandum of association is provided in Table C of the First Schedule of the CA 1963.

(c) Memorandum of association: name clause

[30.014] The law relating to the names of guarantee companies is peculiar in two main respects. In the first place, charities and social clubs which incorporate as guarantee companies will typically seek to dispense with the obligation to have the word 'limited' in their name[18]. In the second place, companies to which s 14 of the MUDA 2011 applies are required to include the words 'owners' management company' or 'OMC' in their names. It might also be noted that many guarantee companies will, in their memorandum and articles of association, elect to refer to themselves (ie, the entity that is the company) other than as the 'company', choosing instead names such as the 'society', 'council' or 'association' or other nomenclature which does not have a commercial or business connotation.

---

17 See para **[30.016]** *post*.

18 Section 24 of the CA 1963.

(i) Dispensing with the word 'limited'

[30.015] Section 6(1)(b) of the CA 1963 requires the memorandum of association of a guarantee company to state the name of the company 'with "limited" or "teoranta" as the last word of the name'. Prior to the CLEA 2001, Ministerial permission could be sought by a limited company to dispense with the use of the word 'limited' in its name[19]. It is now the case that any company that satisfies the provisions of s 24 of the CA 1963 (the original wording of which was repealed and substituted by s 88 of the CLEA 2001) will be exempt, automatically, from having to use the word 'limited' in its name. It is extremely rare for any company other than a guarantee company to be exempted from having the word 'limited' in its name.

[30.016] The new regime operates by providing that a limited company will be exempt from the provisions of the Companies Acts relating to the use of the word 'limited' as part of its name and publishing of its name but shall enjoy all the privileges and be subject to all the obligations of limited companies provided it complies with the provisions of s 24(1) of the CA 1963, namely:

> '(a) its objects are the promotion of commerce, art, science, education, religion, charity or any other prescribed object, and
>
> (b) its memorandum or articles of association—
>
> (i) require its profits (if any) or other income to be applied to the promotion of its objects,
>
> (ii) prohibit the payment of dividends to its members, and
>
> (iii) require all the assets which would otherwise be available to its members to be transferred on its winding up to another company whose objects comply with paragraph (a) and which meets the requirements of this paragraph, and
>
> (c) a director or secretary of the company (or, in the case of an association about to be formed as a limited company, one of the persons who are to be the first directors or the person who is to be the first secretary of the company) has delivered to the registrar of companies a statutory declaration in the prescribed form that the company complies or, where applicable, will comply with the requirements of paragraphs (a) and (b).'

The form of declaration of compliance with the requirements of s 24(1)(a) and (b) of the CA 1963 has been prescribed by statutory instrument[20]. This procedure should also be followed where a company that is already incorporated wishes to omit 'limited' on a change of name application[21].

[30.017] The registrar of companies is empowered to refuse to register a limited company without the word 'limited' in its corporate name where the declaration referred to in s 24(1)(c) is not forthcoming[22]. Companies that are exempt cannot subsequently change their memoranda or articles of association so as to cease to comply with

19 Section 88(2) of the CLEA 2001 saves exemptions made by Ministerial direction under the 'old' s 24 of the CA 1963, notwithstanding its repeal by s 88(1).

20 See the Schedule to the Companies Act, 1963 (Section 24) Regulations 2001 (SI 571/2001).

21 Section 24(3) of the CA 1963.

22 Section 24(2) of the CA 1963.

s 24(1)(b)[23]. Where it appears to the registrar of companies that a company that has qualified for exemption has:

- carried on business in furtherance of an object other than those mentioned in s 24(1)(a); or
- has applied any of its profits or other income otherwise than in promoting such objects; or
- has paid a dividend to any shareholders;

the registrar may in writing direct the company to change its name[24] and such change must be effected in accordance with s 23 of the CA 1963. Providing incorrect, false or misleading information in the s 24(1)(c) statutory declaration, altering the articles so as not to comply with s 24(1)(b) and failing to comply with a direction from the registrar are all offences[25] that can be prosecuted summarily by the registrar[26].

(ii) The requirement to have 'Owners' Management Company' in company name

[30.018] Section 14 of the MUDA 2011 is said by s 14(4) to apply:

> '... to owners' management companies of multi-unit developments in respect of which no contract for the sale of a residential unit has been entered into prior to the enactment of this Act.'

Accordingly, this requirement applies to all management companies of multi-unit developments *except* those in respect of which a contract for the sale of a residential unit was entered into prior to 24 January 2011. Therefore, for pre-existing owners' management companies, they will not have to change their name to comply with s 14(3) of the MUDA 2011. In relation to owners' management companies that fall within s 14, s 14(3) provides that the words 'owners' management company' must be included in their name, which may be abbreviated to 'OMC'.

(d) Memorandum of association: objects clause

[30.019] The objects clauses in certain guarantee companies are in themselves no different to any other company; however, where they engage in particular activities the regulators or authorities of those activities may have particular requirements. The most obviously regulated activity commonly engaged in by guarantee companies is that of charity; in order to receive (and maintain) *charitable tax exempt status* from the Revenue Commissioners (for there is no such thing as 'registering' as a charity) such a company's objects clause must disclose charitable purposes. Most such companies' objects clauses will explicitly demarcate the company's main object from its ancillary objects and from its powers.

---

23 Section 24(4) of the CA 1963.

24 Section 24(5) of the CA 1963. Where a company receives a direction, it may not in future avail of the automatic exemption and must seek the registrar's approval: s 24(6).

25 Section 24(7) of the CA 1963.

26 Section 24(8) of the CA 1963.

(i) Main object

[30.020] The main object of a charity will set out the main purpose for which the company exists and that will be a recognised charitable purpose. So, s 3(1) of the Charities Act 2009 provides that the following, where of public benefit, are recognised charitable purposes:

- the prevention or relief of poverty or economic hardship;
- the advancement of education;
- the advancement of religion; and
- any other purpose that is of benefit to the community[27].

(ii) Subsidiary or ancillary objects

[30.021] Whereas most companies go to great efforts to avoid creating a hierarchy of objects, most trying to elevate all objects to main objects using an *independent objects clause*[28], charities' objects clauses will typically set out a series of objects which they intend to pursue exclusively in order to achieve their main object. Such ancillary objects are typically prefaced with words such as 'the following objects set out hereafter are exclusively subsidiary and ancillary to the main object set out above and these objects are to be used only for the attainment of that main object and any income generated therefrom is to be applied for the main object only…'.

(iii) Powers

[30.022] Here too, the objects clause of a charity will differ from that of other companies, which often try to elevate powers to objects by not distinguishing between objects and powers. In charities, pure powers (ie, matters which are the means to an end and not an end in themselves) are set out as things the company can do in order to achieve its main and subsidiary objects.

[30.023] In the case of guarantee companies which are not charities, their objects clauses will typically follow the same pattern as private or public limited companies and set out extensive objects and powers coupled with a *Bell Houses* clause and independent objects clause. Where such companies wish to dispense with the word 'limited' in their names, their objects must, however, be for the promotion of commerce, art, science, education, religion, charity or other prescribed object[29].

---

27 Section 3(11) of the Charities Act 2009 provides that purposes of benefit to the community *include*: (a) the advancement of community welfare including the relief of those in need by reason of youth, age, ill-health, or disability; (b) the advancement of community development, including rural or urban regeneration; (c) the promotion of civic responsibility or voluntary work; (d) the promotion of health, including the prevention or relief of sickness, disease or human suffering; (e) the advancement of conflict resolution or reconciliation; (f) the promotion of religious or racial harmony and harmonious community relations; (g) the protection of the natural environment; (h) the advancement of environmental sustainability; (i) the advancement of the efficient and effective use of the property of charitable organisations; (j) the prevention or relief of suffering of animals; (k) the advancement of the arts, culture, heritage or sciences; and (l) the integration of those who are disadvantaged, and the promotion of their full participation, in society.

28 See Ch 7, *Corporate Contracts, Capacity and Authority*, at para **[7.052]**.

29 Section 24(1)(a) of the CA 1963; see para **[30.016]** *ante*.

(e) Memorandum of association: guarantee clause

[30.024] In a guarantee company the liability of the members will be limited to the amount of their guarantee and this must be stated in the memorandum[30]. Moreover, the memorandum of a guarantee company must also state that each member undertakes to contribute to the assets of the company in the event of its being wound up while he is a member or within one year after he ceases to be a member for payment of the debts and liabilities of the company contracted before he ceases to be a member and of the costs, charges and expenses of winding up and for the adjustment of the rights of the contributories among themselves such amount as may be required not exceeding a specified amount[31]. Table C's model memorandum of association for a guarantee company without a share capital satisfies this requirement by providing:

> 'Every member of the company undertakes to contribute to the assets of the company in the event of its being wound up while he is a member, or within one year afterwards, for payment of the debts and liabilities of the company contracted before he ceases to be a member, and the costs, charges and expenses of winding up, and for the adjustment of the rights of the contributories among themselves, such amount as may be required not exceeding €1[32].'

This means that the liability of the members is limited to the amount of their guarantee to contribute to the company's assets in a winding up. Accordingly, if the members guarantee to contribute an amount not exceeding €1 to the company, their liability to the company is limited to €1. It should be noted that a company can only look to its guarantee fund *when it is being wound up* and cannot rely on the guarantees of its members to secure a loan, ie, the guarantee fund cannot be charged: *Re Irish Club Ltd*[33]. It would appear that there is no reason in law why different classes of members cannot provide different levels of guarantee[34] but it is hard to conceive of a reason for making such a distinction.

(f) Memorandum of association: distributions of income and property

[30.025] Guarantee companies that are charities or, not being charities, that wish to dispense with having the word 'limited' in their name must provide in their memoranda of association that they cannot distribute the company's income and property to its members. This prohibition must apply during the life of the company and also on its winding up; any surplus remaining after the payment of the company's debts cannot be distributed to members and must, instead, be applied to another company with either charitable objects (for a charity) or whose objects satisfy s 24(1)(a) of the CA 1963 (for any other company seeking to omit the word 'limited' in its name). In the case of charities, it is also standard to provide that directors shall not be entitled to fees or other remuneration, although occasionally the Revenue Commissioners make limited exceptions for a stipend to be paid to a chairperson with onerous duties.

---

30 Section 6(2) of the CA 1963.

31 Section 6(3) of the CA 1963.

32 £1 is replaced here by €1. It can be as little as 1 cent or as high as members wish to set it, although it would be very unusual to set the guarantee as a significant or material sum.

33 *Re Irish Club Ltd* (1906) WN 127; *Re Pyle Works* (1890) 44 Ch D 534, 59 LJ Ch 489, CA.

34 See West, *Companies Ltd by Guarantee* (2nd edn, 2004) at pp 47, 48.

[30.026] A reasonably common form of clause preventing distributions of income and property (capital) to members and preventing the payment of remuneration to directors is as follows:

> 'The income and property of the company shall be applied solely towards the promotion of its main objects as set forth in this Memorandum of Association. No portion of the company's income and property shall be paid or transferred directly or indirectly by way of dividend, bonus or otherwise howsoever by way of profit to members of the company. No director shall be appointed to any office of the company paid by salary or fees, or receive any remuneration or other benefit in money or money's worth from the company. Nothing, however, shall prevent any payment in good faith by the company of:
>
> (1) reasonable and proper remuneration to any employee or secretary of the company (not being a director) for any services rendered to the company;
>
> (2) interest at a rate not exceeding 5% per annum on money lent by directors or other members of the company to the company;
>
> (3) reasonable and proper rent for premises demised and let by any member or director of the company to the company;
>
> (4) reasonable and proper out of pocket expenses incurred by any director in connection with attendance to any matter affecting the company;
>
> (5) fees, remuneration or other benefit in money's worth to any company of which a director may be a member holding not more than one hundredth part of the issued capital of such company; and
>
> (6) insurance premia in respect of any directors' and officers' liability indemnity insurance policy or policies.'

This provision will operate to prevent members obtaining distributions of capital and income *qua* member. Such a provision would not ordinarily operate to prevent, for example, the payment by a charity of aid or grants or assistance to persons who happened to be members in their capacity as *bona fide* recipients of the charity's benevolence. The key here is '*bona fide*' and any evidence of abuse could result in the loss of the company's charitable tax exempt status. The existence of this provision in the memorandum of charities also explains why the salaried CEOs of charities are generally not appointed directors.

[30.027] Another reasonably standard form of clause dealing with the consequences for property on the winding up or dissolution of a company is as follows:

> 'If upon the winding up or dissolution of the company there remains after the satisfaction of all its debts and liabilities, any property whatsoever, the same shall not be paid to or distributed among the members of the company but shall be given or transferred to some other charitable institution or institutions having main objects similar to the main object of the company[35] and which shall prohibit the distribution of its or their income and property among its or their members to an extent at least as great as imposed on this company by the clause to that effect in this memorandum, such institution or institutions to be determined by the members of the company at or before the time of dissolution, and if and so far as effect cannot be given to such provision, then to some charitable object.'

---

35 This would be varied in the case of a company that is not a charity but seeks to dispense with 'Limited' in its name by substituting the reference to 'some other charitable institution or institutions having main objects similar to the main object of the company …' with 'some other company whose objects complies with section 24(1)(a) of the Companies Act 1963'.

[30.028] The provisions of s 26 of the CA 1963 are often overlooked. Section 26(1) provides that in the case of a guarantee company registered on or after 1 January 1901:

> '... every provision in the memorandum or articles, or in any resolution of the company, purporting to give any person a right to participate in the divisible profits of the company, otherwise than as a member, shall be void.'

Given that a company's memorandum and articles of association are generally considered to be enforceable by the company and its members (and even then in respect of rights enjoyed *qua* member)[36] and not third parties, this is a peculiar provision. On a literal interpretation this would appear to prohibit the issue by a guarantee company of debentures with an interest rate tied into the company's distributable profits[37].

[30.029] Section 26(2) of the CA 1963 operates to prevent guarantee companies from having a 'quasi-share capital' by deeming such to be share capital, by providing:

> 'For the purpose of the provisions of this Act relating to the memorandum of a company limited by guarantee and of this section, every provision in the memorandum or articles, or in any resolution, of a company limited by guarantee and registered on or after the date aforesaid, purporting to divide the undertaking of the company into shares or interests, shall be treated as a provision for a share capital, notwithstanding that the nominal amount or number of the shares or interests is not specified thereby.'

This provides that a provision of the memorandum or articles or resolution of a guarantee company registered on or after 1 January 1901 purporting to divide the undertaking of the company into shares or interests 'shall be treated as a provision for a share capital, notwithstanding that the nominal amount or number of the shares or interests is not specified thereby'. The effect would be to cause such a company to cease to be a guarantee company without a share capital and become a guarantee company with a share capital. Such a company could become a private company limited by guarantee having a share capital but it remains to be seen whether an existing guarantee company which introduced such a provision into its memorandum could become a public company limited by guarantee having a share capital, given the prohibition on the formation of such companies by s 7 of the C(A)A 1983. It is thought that since such a company was already *formed* the prohibition in s 7 might not, perhaps, prevent an existing company converting to a public company limited by guarantee and having a share capital.

(g) Memorandum of association: other clauses

[30.030] In guarantee companies that are charities it is also common to find non-compulsory clauses which require audited accounts to be made available to the Revenue Commissioners and which prevent amendments to the memorandum (and sometimes the articles of association) without the prior approval of the Revenue Commissioners. This latter clause can be used to give control over the amendment of memoranda of association in a series of contexts and is often used where Ministers of Government establish companies.

---

36 *Eley v The Positive Government Security Life Assurance Co Ltd* (1876) 1 Ex D 20; see further Ch 3, *Constitutional Documents*, at para **[3.099]** *et seq.*

37 See MacCann & Courtney, *Companies Acts 1963–2009* (Bloomsbury Professional, 2010) at p 95.

(h) Alterations and amendments to the memorandum of association

[30.031] Section 9 of the CA 1963 provides, rather starkly, that:

> 'a company may not alter the provisions contained in its memorandum except in the cases, in the mode and to the extent for which express provision is made in this Act.'

In making provision for the alteration of clauses in a memorandum of association, the Companies Acts distinguish between clauses which are required to be in the memorandum of association and clauses which are contained in the memorandum of association although they could lawfully be contained in the articles of association.

Only certain clauses are *required* to be contained in the memorandum of association of a guarantee company: the name clause[38], the objects clause[39], the liability clause[40], and the guarantee clause[41]. The provisions concerning the alteration of the first three of these clauses have been considered in Chapter 3[42].

[30.032] The guarantee clause[43], a clause required to be in the memorandum of association, cannot be amended or altered because there is no provision in the Companies Acts facilitating its alteration and because s 28(1) of the CA 1963, considered next, only permits the alteration of clauses 'which could lawfully have been contained in articles of association' whereas the guarantee clause must be contained in the memorandum of association[44]. Converting an original guarantee of £1 to €1.27 would not amount to an alteration of the guarantee clause; rounding it down to €1 would, however, not be permitted.

[30.033] In relation to clauses which are not required by law to be included in the memorandum of association, s 28 of the CA 1963 facilitates their removal subject to certain restrictions. Section 28(1) provides:

> 'Subject to subsection (2) and sections 27 and 205, any provision contained in a company's memorandum which could lawfully have been contained in articles of association instead of in the memorandum may, subject to the provisions of this section, be altered by the company by special resolution.'

Accordingly, a non-compulsory clause (eg, an income and property clause[45]) can be amended. Members' liabilities cannot, however, be increased as a result of the alteration of a non-compulsory clause since s 28(1) is subject to s 27 of the CA 1963[46]. Moreover, the alteration of non-compulsory clauses is subject to the effect not being to amount to oppression or disregard of interests since the power to alter such clauses is also subject to s 205 of the CA 1963[47]. Finally, it should be noted that the power in s 28(1) of the CA

---

38 Section 6(1)(a) of the CA 1963.

39 Section 6(1)(c) of the CA 1963.

40 Section 6(2) of the CA 1963.

41 Section 6(3) of the CA 1963.

42 See Ch 3, *Constitutional Documentation*, at para **[3.023]** *et seq*, para **[3.026]** *et seq* and para **[3.029]** *et seq*, respectively.

43 See para **[30.024]** *ante*.

44 See West, *Companies Ltd by Guarantee* (2nd edn, Jordans, 2004) at p 52.

45 See para **[30.025]** *ante*.

46 See para **[30.044]** *post*.

47 See Ch 11, *Shareholders' Remedies*, at para **[11.006]** *et seq*.

1963 to alter clauses in the memorandum is subject to the power of the holders of not less than 15% of the company's members or the holders of not less than 15% of the company's debentures to apply to court for the alteration to be cancelled, and where such application is made any alteration shall not have effect except in so far as it is confirmed by the court[48].

[30.034] The power to alter non-compulsory clauses is also subject to the caveat that the memorandum of association may contain a clause which provides that such non-compulsory clauses are unalterable. Section 28(3) of the CA 1963 provides that:

> 'This section shall not apply where the memorandum itself provides for or prohibits the alteration of all or any of the said provisions, and shall not authorise any variation or abrogation of the special rights of any class of members.'

This facilitates the *entrenchment* of rights and could be used, for example, to ensure that a director cannot be removed during his or her lifetime. Other entrenchment provisions might include requiring special majorities over and above the ordinary requirements of a special resolution (eg, 80% of members) to support an alteration[49]. The need for the prior written consent of the Revenue Commissioners to alter the memorandum and articles of association is also a requirement of a company which has been given charitable tax exempt status.

(i) Articles of association

[30.035] The model articles of association applicable to guarantee companies are those contained in Table C set out in the First Schedule to the CA 1963[50]. Guarantee companies (which do not have a share capital) are not required by law to register with their memorandum, any articles of association signed by the subscribers to the memorandum and prescribing regulations for the company[51]. Where a guarantee company does not register articles of association or if articles are registered in so far as they do not exclude or modify Table C, then Table C of the First Schedule to the CA 1963 will apply[52]. It would be very rare for the members of a guarantee company to rely upon the provisions contained in Table C, and the promoters of most guarantee companies will spend a considerable amount of time, cost and effort in drafting articles of association suitable to the sort of company they wish to have.

[30.036] The articles of association of a guarantee company must state the number of members with which the company proposes to be registered[53]. This requirement can only be construed as operating at the time a guarantee company is incorporated (ie, before it is registered) since the obligation is prospective and once a guarantee company is registered, this requirement no longer applies to, for example, the adoption of new articles of association in substitution for those with which the company is registered[54]. It

48 Section 28(2) of the CA 1963.

49 See West, *Companies Ltd by Guarantee* (2nd edn, Jordans, 2004) at p 52–53.

50 Section 13A(1) of the CA 1963.

51 Section 11 of the CA 1963.

52 Section 13A(2) of the CA 1963.

53 Section 12(2) of the CA 1963.

54 Regulation 2 of Table C satisfies this requirement by providing: 'The number of members with which the company proposes to be registered is 500, but the directors may from time to time register an increase of members.'

should also be noted that where a company limited by guarantee has increased the number of members beyond the registered number it must, within 15 days after the increase was resolved on or took place, give to the registrar notice of the increase, which the registrar shall record[55].

[30.037] The articles of association of guarantee companies should be considered carefully so that they are supportive of how the members and directors intend the company to operate in practice. Careful thought and drafting is needed in relation to membership in charities and social clubs: who is entitled to become a member, how are they to be admitted, who may remove them as members and what are their rights as members or, where there is more than one category of member, their rights vis-à-vis other members? Similarly, the provisions concerning directors require careful thought: may anyone become a director or only members or persons who meet certain criteria, who may nominate persons to become directors, how are directors to be appointed, are directors to retire by rotation and if so in what order, should there be a limit on the continuous time within which one can be a director? The Companies Acts are non-prescriptive in relation to these matters, which means it will fall to the promoters and subsequently the members and directors to ensure that their companies' articles of association are fit for purpose.

[30.038] In the case of certain companies that are owners' management companies, the MUDA 2011 has introduced a number of requirements concerning voting rights by members, and particular qualified majorities are required to effect certain decisions. These are considered further under the heading *corporate governance: meetings*, below[56].

Disregarding separate legal personality

[30.039] There are no particularly significant features of the law relating to the disregard of separate legal personality in the case of guarantee companies which are different from those already considered in relation to private companies. One difference which may be noted is that membership must be retained at seven members if the remaining members are to avoid becoming personally liable under s 36 of the CA 1963, which provides:

> 'If at any time the number of members of a company is reduced ... below seven, and it carries on business for more than 6 months while the number is so reduced, every person who is a member of the company during the time that it so carries on business after those 6 months and knows that it is carrying on business with fewer than ... seven members ... shall be severally liable for the payment of the whole debts of the company contracted during that time, and may be severally sued therefor.'

Membership

[30.040] Membership of a guarantee company can arise where a person is an initial subscriber to a guarantee company upon its formation or where subsequent to its formation, that person is admitted to membership whether by the directors (as is more

55 Section 12(3) of the CA 1963: default in complying with this subsection renders the company and every officer in default, found guilty, liable to a class C fine.

56 See para **[30.049]** *post*.

usual) or by the members. The key difference between a company limited by guarantee without a share capital and one with a share capital is that membership is not dependent upon the holding of a share in the company. The basic rule as to who a member is, is set out in s 31 of the CA 1963:

> '(1) The subscribers of the memorandum of a company shall be deemed to have agreed to become members of the company, and, on its registration, shall be entered as members in its register of members.
>
> (2) Every other person who agrees to become a member of a company, and whose names is entered in its register of members, shall be a member of the company.'

Charities, sports clubs and social clubs that are constituted as guarantee companies must provide in their articles of association who are to be their members. The most relaxed provision might say anyone who is admitted by the directors. Most companies will require the directors to determine who can be members although some will reserve the right to admit new members to the members themselves in general meeting, whether on foot of an ordinary or special resolution. More elaborate articles might specify *eligibility* criteria which go to establish that a person has sufficient interests or traits to mean that they have a common bond with the existing members, eg, that in a rabbit breeders' club, that would-be members satisfy the directors that they have bred rabbits of a particular kind, for a particular period and, perhaps, with particular success. Sometimes members are given a certificate to prove membership (although this is more common in an owners' management company); in every case, however, in order to comply with s 31 of the CA 1963, there must be evidence that the person has agreed to become a member and the best form of such evidence is an acknowledgement in writing, signed by the member, to this effect.

[30.041] In the case of a guarantee company that is an owners' management company within the meaning of the MUDA 2011, membership of the company will automatically transfer where the ownership of a unit in a multi-unit development changes *without the express agreement of the new member to become a member.* Section 8(1) of the MUDA 2011 provides:

> 'Where ownership of a unit in a multi-unit development is transferred, whether by conveyance, transfer, assignment, by operation of law or otherwise, membership of the unit shall, notwithstanding any provision to the contrary in the Companies Acts or any other enactment, on such transfer stand transferred to the person becoming entitled to the freehold or leasehold interest in the unit concerned without the need to execute a transfer or have it approved by the directors of the company, and such person shall—
>
> (a) be entitled to exercise the powers, rights and entitlement of a member in the company concerned, and
>
> (b) be obliged to perform all the obligations (including the payment of service charges) pertaining to the membership of such company concerned.'

Accordingly, s 31(2) of the CA 1963 may be seen as modified in the case of such companies since an express[57] agreement to become a member is not required. Section

57 Of course it may be argued that the agreement to acquire the unit is the essential 'agreement' and that by agreeing to acquire the unit (which would usually have a contractual obligation to become a member) one also agrees implicitly to become a member of the owners' management company.

8(2) of the MUDA 2011 makes clear that the intention is not to entirely oust the operation of the Companies Acts, as an owners' management company is required to take all steps necessary to ensure that the membership certificate (or share certificate in the case of an owners' management company having a share capital) is issued to the member following notification of the change of ownership of the unit, that the register of members is altered accordingly 'and that there is compliance with all other relevant requirements under the Companies Acts'. This is a very useful provision since it means that neither the OMC nor its directors are required to take action on a change of ownership of an apartment or unit and gives comfort to the purchaser of an apartment that they automatically and immediately become a member of the OMC with consequential membership rights, eg, they become immediately entitled to notice of meetings, etc.

The maintenance of capital

[30.042] Although a guarantee company will not have a *share* capital, it will still have capital from gifts or profitable trading. The prohibition on distributions otherwise than out of distributable profits contained in s 45 of the C(A)A 1983[58] applies equally to companies limited by guarantee, and as *public* companies, they are, in fact, subject to a tighter regime than private limited companies. In addition, however, as noted above[59], guarantee companies that wish to avail of the exemption from having 'Limited' in their name and guarantee companies that are charities will be required to *prohibit* the making of distributions to members.

[30.043] It has already been observed that a guarantee company cannot amend its guarantee clause; there is no statutory mechanism whereby the amount that members guarantee to pay can be decreased or increased. In *Hennessy et al v National Agricultural and Industrial Development Association et al*[60], Overend J characterised the proposed discharge of member guarantors as a reduction of capital saying:

> 'If, in a company limited by guarantee, the guarantors are discharged from liability to any appreciable extent, is not the effect upon the creditors of the company precisely the same as the effect of paying back capital to the shareholders, in a company limited by shares? Furthermore, is not the effect on guarantors who remain to increase their liability? Could the Association alter its memorandum so as to reduce the liability of guarantors from £1 to 6s 8d? I am of the opinion it could not[61].'

It is thought that the discharge of a guarantor's liability is very different to the effect upon the creditors of the company as the paying back of paid-up share capital to shareholders, in a company limited by shares. In the case of a company limited by shares, where the capital has been put into the company, this is very different to where a guarantor has a liability to contribute up to a particular amount in the case of a winding up. Even in a company limited by shares, in a case where the shares are not fully paid up

---

58 See Ch 10, *The Maintenance of Capital*, at para **[10.089]** *et seq*.

59 See para **[30.026]** *ante*.

60 *Hennessy et al v National Agricultural and Industrial Development Association et al* [1947] IR 159.

61 *Hennessy et al v National Agricultural and Industrial Development Association et al* [1947] IR 159 at 191.

the similarities are not as great as contended by Overend J. Given that a member can resign and after one year have no liability under his guarantee demonstrates that there is no comparison between a guarantee and share capital in the context of creditor protection. Moreover, a guarantee is only as good as its 'mark' and the financial strength of members will vary greatly. By comparison, in the case of a company limited by shares, where those shares are paid up it does not matter how financially strong or weak a member is since members have no further liability.

[30.044] While a member's guarantee cannot be decreased, neither can a member's liability be increased without his or her express written consent. Section 27(1) of the CA 1963 provides:

> 'Subject to subsection (2), and notwithstanding anything in the memorandum or articles of a company, no member of the company shall be bound by an alteration made in the memorandum or articles after the date on which he became a member, if and so far as the alteration requires him to take or subscribe for more shares than the number held by him at the date on which the alteration is made, or in any way increases his liability as at that date to contribute to the share capital of, or otherwise to pay money to, the company.'

While a guarantee company will not have a share capital, a liability could be imposed by purporting to increase a fixed subscription or annual members' fee. Guarantee companies will often require members to pay an annual fee. If a fixed amount is contained in the articles of association which does not provide a mechanism for its increase, that amount will be fossilised and cannot be increased to take account of inflation, etc, unless every member agrees in writing to be so bound[62]. Where there is a mechanism, even something as simple as 'the subscription fee shall be such sum as may from time to time be set by the directors' this will not offend s 27(1) or constitute the imposition of a fresh liability because the liability exists from the outset and its future increase is contemplated.

Corporate governance: management by the directors

[30.045] There are no particularly significant features of the law relating to corporate governance, management by the directors in the case of guarantee companies which are different from those already considered in relation to private companies. It may be observed, however, that many directors of guarantee companies are not 'professional directors' and can 'find themselves' occupying the position of director in consequence of wanting to do charitable work, be involved in their social or sports club or because they have purchased an apartment and became a member of an OMC.

[30.046] There are some differences in practice, if not law, in relation to corporate governance and management by the directors which may be noted. In the first place, many guarantee companies which are charities or social clubs will relatively frequently provide in their articles of association for positions of 'management' other than director. Accordingly, social clubs in particular will often create positions such as 'treasurer', 'honorary secretary', 'patron', etc. It should be noted that where a person occupies a position created by a company's memorandum (or more likely) articles of association, that person will hold an office in the company and be an '*officer*' for the purposes of the

---

62 *Ding v Sylvania Waterways Ltd* [1999] NSWSC 58; see Ch 3, *Constitutional Documentation*, at para **[3.061]**.

Companies Acts. Such persons, if not formally appointed directors, may also be found to be *de facto* directors[63].

[30.047] Most guarantee companies will follow reg 35 of Table C (which is identical to reg 80 of Table A) and provide in their articles of association that the business of the company is managed by the directors. In this way the members of guarantee companies will delegate the management of the company to the directors. Sometimes the members of guarantee companies (particularly charities and social clubs) will seek to propose and pass resolutions at the company's AGM, the effect of which is to encroach upon the powers of management which have been delegated to the directors. The complete delegation of power to the directors of, say, a social or sports club, may not always rest easy with the wishes of the members to take decisions affecting themselves at general meetings. One approach to avoid the members becoming *de facto* or even shadow directors is for the articles of association to provide that the effect of such resolutions is not to bind the board or the company but is intended to be indicative of the members' wishes to which the directors should have regard in their management of the company. The delegation to directors is an inevitable consequence of using the company form to organise charities, social or sports clubs, and necessary. Since company law imposes duties on directors and not on members, it would be anathema to corporate governance for members to be able to take decisions concerning the company's operations for which they would not be responsible while the directors would!

[30.048] In the case of an owners' management company within the meaning of the MUDA 2011, a person shall not be appointed as a director after the coming into operation of s 16 of that Act, if such appointment is (a) for life or (b) for a term greater than three years[64]. In the case of persons who, on the coming into operation of s 16, stood appointed as a director for life or for a term greater than three years, such persons shall be deemed to vacate office (i) in the case of an appointment for life, on the day which is three years after the coming into operation of s 16 and (ii) in the case of an appointment for a term in excess of three years, on the expiry of that term or on the day which is three years after the coming into operation of s 16, whichever is the earlier[65]. It is expressly provided, however, that nothing in s 16(2) shall prevent the appointment or election of a person as a director at an AGM of an OMC unless such is prohibited by the company's own articles of association.

Corporate governance: meetings

[30.049] Meetings in guarantee companies that are charities and social clubs can have more in common with listed PLCs than private limited companies. For many such companies, the AGM is a big event at which the members can meet the directors and voice their questions, concerns and perhaps criticism to the directors. The comments made above[66] concerning the practice in many guarantee companies of proposing resolutions the effect of which would be encroach on the directors' powers of management are also relevant here.

---

63 See Ch 13, *Corporate Governance: Management by the Directors*, at para **[13.045]** *et seq*.

64 Section 16(1) of the MUDA 2011.

65 Section 16(2) of the MUDA 2011.

66 See para **[30.047]** *ante*.

[30.050] Meetings and voting rights in certain guarantee companies that are owners' management companies have been significantly affected by the MUDA 2011. The new rules on voting at meetings may be summarised thus:

(a) Voting: one vote for each unit and fair and equitable voting rights;
(b) Meetings to consider annual report;
(c) Service charge must be considered in general meeting and can be disapproved;
(d) Service charges cannot include costs that are developers' responsibility unless approved of in general meeting;
(e) House rules must be considered and approved by general meeting.

Each of these topics is next considered.

(a) Voting: one vote for each unit and fair and equitable voting rights

[30.051] Section 14(1) of the MUDA 2011 provides that:

> 'The voting rights of members in an owners' management company to which this section applies shall be structured in such a matter that in the determination of any matter by the members of the company one vote shall attach to each residential unit in a multi-unit development to which the owners' management company relates, and that no other person has voting rights in respect of such determination.'

Section 14 applies to owners' management companies of multi-unit developments in respect of which no contract for the sale of a residential unit has been entered into prior to 24 January 2011. It does not apply, therefore, to a management company with existing residential units. Section 14(2) provides that each vote shall be 'of equal value' so that a *Bushel v Faith* type provision could not operate to load one unit owner's votes.

[30.052] Section 14 applies to the owners' management company of a mixed use multi-unit development, subject to s 2(4) of the MUDA 2011[67]. A 'mixed use multi-unit development' is defined in s 1(1) as meaning 'a multi-unit development of which a commercial unit (other than a childcare facility) forms part of the development'. Section 2(4) provides that in the case of a mixed use multi-unit development, instead of the requirement in s 14(1), if the voting rights of the members are apportioned in a manner which is fair and equitable, the obligations imposed in respect of such a company shall be regarded as having been complied with.

[30.053] One issue with s 14(1) of the MUDA 2011 concerns decision making in an owners' management company after its incorporation but before any residential units either come into existence *or* are sold. Section 14(1) does not contemplate the situation where there are no residential units or no occupied residential units. If an OMC is incorporated it cannot have been intended that there should be nobody able to take a decision in general meeting pending the sale of residential units.

Once residential units have been constructed, it is thought, on a literal interpretation, the developer (who is the owner of all the units until they are sold) is entitled to one vote for every residential unit in existence. On this analysis, the developer as a subscriber (*qua* subscriber) would have no votes but would have one vote for each residential unit owned by the developer, which would gradually reduce as the units were sold. Indeed, if

67 Section 14(5) of the MUDA 2011.

the developer were to hold back 20 of 50 units as an investment rental property, the developer would in law have those 20 votes so why should it be any different until the developer sells them?

And what of the situation before any residential units have been constructed? It is suggested that a purposive interpretation has to be applied so that *until* there are actually residential units in existence, the prohibition on others (eg, subscribers) having voting rights does not apply, ie, until there are residential units in existence, the company is not an OMC and so s 14(1) does not apply to it.

[30.054] Section 15 of the MUDA 2011 applies to owners' management companies to which s 14 does not apply and which are not mixed use-multi unit developments. In other words, s 15 applies to *existing* residential multi-unit developments. The requirements here, as provided for in s 15(2), are that:

> '... the voting rights of members in the owners' management company ... shall be structured in such a manner that in the determination of any matter by the members of the company, one vote shall attach to each residential unit in the multi-unit development to which the owners' management company relates, and that no other person has voting rights in respect of such determination.'

The foregoing is, however, subject to s 15(3) which provides that where voting rights are allocated on a basis other than that described in s 15(2) (eg, where the articles of association provide that, say, the developer has voting rights) the person with those rights may not exercise them without first obtaining an authorisation from the Circuit Court, following an application under s 24 of the MUDA 2011. This is designed to safeguard against a constitutional challenge by developers and other persons who already have voting rights under the articles of association of existing companies. The onus is placed on such persons to make an application to the Circuit Court before exercising those rights, and on that application, the court is, by s 15(4), required not to make an order authorising the exercise of such voting rights unless is it satisfied:

> '(a) that the person concerned has an essential economic interest in the development concerned or as a part of the development concerned (other than as the owner of a residential unit in the development) and that in order to adequately protect such interest it is necessary to authorise that person to exercise such voting rights, or
>
> (b) that, for any other reason, it is necessary in the interests of fairness and justice to authorise that person to exercise such voting rights.'

It remains to be seen how the Circuit Court will deal with applications from disenfranchised developers or nominee subscribers of owners' management companies.

(b) Meetings to consider annual report

[30.055] Section 17(1)(a) of the MUDA 2011 requires an owners' management company to prepare and furnish to each member an annual report which complies with s 17(2) and to hold a meeting at least once in each year for purposes which include the consideration of that report. The information required to be included in the report is:

> '(a) a statement of income and expenditure relating to the period covered by the report;
>
> (b) a statement of the assets and liabilities of the company;
>
> (c) where the owners' management company is required to establish and maintain a sinking fund, a statement of the funds standing to the credit of that fund and

details of the amount of the annual contribution to the fund and the basis on which such contribution is calculated;

(d) a statement of the amount of the annual service charge and the basis of such charge in respect of the period covered by the report;

(e) a statement of the projected or agreed annual service charge relating to the current period;

(f) a statement of any planned expenditure on the refurbishment, improvement or maintenance of a non-recurring nature which it is intended to carry out in the current period;

(g) a statement of the insured value of the multi-unit development, the amount of the premium charged, the name of the insurance company with which the policy of insurance is held and a summary of the principal risks covered;

(h) a statement setting out, in general terms, the fire safety equipment installed in the development and the arrangements in place for the maintenance of such equipment; and

(i) a statement fully disclosing any contracts entered into or in force between the owners' management company and a director or shadow director of the company or a person who is a connected person as respects that director or shadow director.'

Although it is not expressly stated, it would seem clear that a guarantee company can comply with s 17 by considering the s 17(1)(a) report at its AGM held as required by s 131 of the CA 1963. Although s 17(6) of the MUDA 2011 states that the obligations in s 15 are 'in addition to any other obligation or duty of such company whether arising under an Act, statutory instrument, by rule of law or otherwise' this does not mean that a separate meeting to a guarantee company's AGM is required. This is because of the fact that s 17(1)(b) states that the purposes of the meeting can 'include' the consideration of the s 17(1)(a) annual report, meaning that the meeting can have other purposes, such as, to comply with s 131 of the CA 1963.

[30.056] The requirement in s 17 to give 21 days' notice of the meeting is, however, in line with the notice which a guarantee company would be required to give to its members of an AGM[68]. Although the s 17(1)(a) report is only required to be furnished to members 10 days before the meeting[69], to avoid having to send out two communications it is thought likely that most such reports will issue with notice of the AGM, at least 21 days before the meeting. A requirement in relation to the meeting over and above that imposed by the Companies Acts is that the meeting must take place *within reasonable proximity to the multi-unit development* and *at a reasonable time* (unless otherwise agreed in writing by a qualified majority vote of 75% of the members). Neither 'reasonable proximity' nor 'reasonable time' are defined and it is unclear whether members could vote in writing or whether a resolution would have to be passed at a meeting properly convened and held in order to vote by a 75% majority to hold a meeting at either a distant location or (if somewhat bizarrely) at an unreasonable time!

[30.057] It should be noted that the qualified majority vote of 75% of members referred to in s 17(5) is *not* a special resolution. Accordingly, notice of the wording of that

---

68 Section 17(3) of the MUDA 2011.

69 Section 17(4) of the MUDA 2011.

resolution is not required under the Companies Acts to be given to members 21 days before the meeting, and provided 75% of the members vote in favour (and not 75% of those present and voting) such a resolution can be put to a meeting of members without any prior notice of the text of the resolution being given. Potentially, such a resolution might never be capable of being voted upon if fewer than 75% of those entitled to vote do not attend the meeting at which the resolution is to be considered. In those circumstances, however, it is thought that it would be permissible to secure the vote in writing of a sufficient number of members other than at a meeting since although it would be a written majority decision as opposed to the unanimous written resolution required under s 141(8) of the CA 1963, the vote would be on a matter not regulated by the Companies Acts. This might also be addressed in the owners' management company's articles of association.

(c) Service charge must be considered in general meeting and can be disapproved

[30.058] The setting of a service charge is normally the remit of the board of directors who have duties and responsibilities under the Companies Acts to ensure that a company has sufficient income to meet its expenditure and other outgoings. Since OMC have no trading income, the only way they can get income is by levying a service charge on their members. Owners' management companies are now required to establish and maintain a scheme in respect of annual service charges[70]. Section 18(2) of the MUDA 2011 provides that the annual service charge in respect of a multi-unit development shall not be levied unless it has been considered by a general meeting of the members concerned called for purposes which include the consideration of an estimate of the expenditure it is anticipated will be incurred by the company in that period. Moreover, it is provided that 'the meeting shall take place within reasonable proximity to the multi-unit development and at a reasonable time (unless otherwise agreed in writing by a 75% majority vote of the members)'[71]. Section 18(4)(a) of the MUDA 2011, however, goes on to provide that the proposal (put forward by the directors) in relation to the setting of an annual service charge 'may be amended at the meeting ... with the approval of 60% of those present and voting at the meeting'. Section 18(4)(b) provides that where the service charge proposed to the general meeting is disapproved by not less than 75% of the persons attending and entitled to vote, the proposed service charge shall not take effect. It would seem that this does not require a positive resolution to be put to the meeting that the service charge be approved but that any member could object and call for support from other members so that if 75% of those present and entitled to vote[72], vote against the service charge it can be blocked[73]. It is in effect a form of 'dead-man's brake'. This can give rise to a serious dilemma for the directors. If they believe that the company's solvency requires the service charge to be set at a particular level, will they

---

70 Section 18(1) of the MUDA 2011.

71 See para **[30.056]** *ante*.

72 As distinct from 75% of those entitled to attend and vote who are not present.

73 Where a service charge is not approved the previous charge shall continue to apply (s 18(4)(b)) although where no such charge was ever set the directors' powers will resurface and they can determine 'a scheme to operate for a period of 4 months from the date of the meeting' (s 18(5) of the MUDA 2011).

incur liability where their decision to levy that amount is overridden by the members? Moreover, might it be found that in not approving the service charge and usurping the directors' powers, the members are acting as either *de facto* directors or shadow directors? The MUDA 2011 does not preclude members from being found to be *de facto* or shadow directors of an OMC so care must be taken to avoid behaviour that would cause a member to be found to be such a director under normal company law rules.

(d) Service charges cannot include costs that are developers' responsibility unless approved of in general meeting

[30.059] Section 18(6) contains a further restriction on the ordinary powers of the directors of a guarantee company to set a service charge. This provides that a service charge levied under s 18:

> 'may not be used to defray expense on matters which are or were the responsibility of the developer or builder of the multi-unit development concerned unless such expenditure is approved by a general meeting of the owners' management company concerned where 75% of those attending and entitled to vote have voted in favour of such expenditure being incurred.'

Accordingly, if a developer was supposed to paint the common entrance hall of an apartment building but failed to do so, the service charge could not be used to paint the entrance hall without the authority of a resolution passed in general meeting supported by 75% of those attending and entitled to vote. Again, it should be noted that this is not a *special resolution* within the meaning of the Companies Acts, merely an ordinary resolution which requires a qualified majority to support its passing[74].

(e) House rules must be considered and approved by general meeting

[30.060] While an owners' management company's board of directors can commission and prepare 'house rules' for the running of an apartment, house rules cannot come into operation unless that have been considered and approved by a meeting of the unit owners in the development[75]. Any such meeting must be held on not less than 21 days' notice[76] and the notice of the meeting must be accompanied by a draft of the proposed rules[77]. Such rules may be amended in the same manner as that in which they may be made[78].

---

74 An approval under s 18(6) is, however, by reason of s 18(7) of no effect unless (a) at least 65% of the units in the development have been transferred to a person who is not a connected person as respects the person who was (i) the developer or builder or (ii) a director or shadow director of a company which was the developer or builder and (b) at least three years have elapsed since the transfer of the ownership of the relevant parts of the common areas of the development.

75 Section 23(4) of the MUDA 2011.

76 Section 23(5) of the MUDA 2011.

77 Section 23(6) of the MUDA 2011.

78 Section 23(8) of the MUDA 2011.

Financial statements, audit and annual return

(a) Books of account

[30.061] Guarantee companies are required to meet the same obligations in regard to keeping proper books of account as apply to companies limited by shares[79].

(b) Accounts of guarantee companies

[30.062] The majority of guarantee companies will fall into one of the following categories of company, which are required[80] to prepare Companies Act individual accounts, and will *not* be permitted to prepare IFRS individual accounts[81]:

- a company not trading for the acquisition for gain by the members;
- a company to which s 128 (4)(c) of the CA 1963 applies (ie, a guarantee company formed for a charitable object, and which is under the control of, and exercises its functions in accordance with, a religion 'recognised by the State under Article 44 of the Constitution'[82]); or
- a company formed for charitable purposes in respect of which the Commissioners of Charitable Donations and Bequests[83] make an order under s 128(5) of the CA 1963 exempting the company from the obligation that it annex its balance sheet (and any document required to be annexed thereto), directors' report and auditor's report to its annual return.

In addition, such companies do not fall within the scope of the C(A)A 1986[84], and so any accounts prepared by them will be required to comply with the provisions of the Sixth Schedule to the CA 1963[85]. This is in addition to any other disclosure obligation imposed by statute, such as the requirements to disclose:

---

79 See Ch 17, *Financial Statements, Audit and Annual Return*, at paras **[17.005]** to **[17.015]** *ante*.

80 Section 148(3) of the CA 1963.

81 See Ch 17, *Financial Statements, Audit and Annual Return*, at paras **[17.023]** to **[17.024]** in respect of the choice of accounting framework that would otherwise be allowed.

82 The provisions in Article 44 of the Constitution whereby the State recognised 'the special position of the Holy Catholic Apostolic and Roman Church', 'the Church of Ireland, the Presbyterian Church in Ireland, the Methodist Church in Ireland, the Religious Society of Friends in Ireland, as well as the Jewish Congregations and the other religious denominations existing in Ireland at [1 July 1937]' were deleted by the Fifth Amendment with effect from 5 January 1973. Accordingly, it is unclear whether a company formed for a religious charitable object will, as such, be required to prepare Companies Act accounts; however, it is likely in any case that such a company will be required to do so as a not-for-profit company.

83 Parts 2 and 6 of the Charities Act 2009 envisage that the Commissioners of Charitable Donations and Bequests will be dissolved, and the functions carried out by them pass to a new Charities Regulatory Authority; however, Minister for Justice Alan Shatter on 21 May 2012 cited a 2011 review of expenditure as having caused him to take the view that it was 'not possible to proceed with the full implementation of the Act at this time given the likely scale of the financial and staffing resources implied', and to date Parts 2 and 6 of the Charities Act 2009 have not been commenced.

84 Section 2(1) of the C(A)A 1986.

85 Section 149(3)(e) of the CA 1963.

- (in aggregate) directors' emoluments, pensions and compensation for loss of office[86];
- certain transactions entered into with directors or connected persons (such as loans and quasi-loans provided to them)[87];
- details of interests of a director or secretary in the company's debentures[88]; and
- details in respect of the remuneration of auditors[89].

The Sixth Schedule of the CA 1963 does not impose any material obligations additional to those set out in the C(A)A 1986. Unlike the C(A)A 1986, the Sixth Schedule does not prescribe a format for the balance sheet or profit and loss account, nor does it set out the same level of detail as does the C(A)A 1986 in relation to disclosures to be made in notes to the accounts. However it is significant that the statutory obligations are in addition to those required by Irish GAAP, and in addition that the overriding obligation applies under both frameworks that the accounts give a 'true and fair view'[90].

In the absence of express statutory provision, a company preparing accounts in accordance with the Sixth Schedule will therefore face uncertainty as to the level of detail required to meet this obligation; where this is the case – and bearing in mind that compliance with the requirements of the C(A)A 1986 and Irish GAAP is generally accepted as meeting the obligation to give a 'true and fair view' – one might expect that the company would meet the level of detail in the C(A)A 1986 as a means of reducing this uncertainty. Accordingly, in practice, accounts prepared in accordance with the Sixth Schedule of the CA 1963 would tend not to be significantly different from those prepared in accordance with the C(A)A 1986.

Similarly, while the Sixth Schedule does not specify a particular format for the balance sheet or profit and loss account, accountants, auditors and users of accounts generally are familiar with the format specified in the C(A)A 1986. To avoid raising unnecessary concerns among such parties, companies preparing accounts in accordance with the Sixth Schedule tend to follow one of the formats in the C(A)A 1986 save insofar as there is strong reason not to do so.

[30.063] A company of the type referred to above will continue to be subject to the obligation to prepare a directors' report[91], but will not be required to include the additional information required by ss 13 and 14 of the C(A)A 1986[92].

---

86 Section 191 of the CA 1963; see Ch 17, *Financial Statements, Audit and Annual Return*, at para **[17.112]**.

87 Section 41 of the CA 1990; see Ch 17, *Financial Statements, Audit and Annual Return*, at paras **[17.113]** to **[17.120]**.

88 Section 63 of the CA 1990; see Ch 17, *Financial Statements, Audit and Annual Return*, at paras **[17.121]**.

89 Section 161D of the CA 1963; see Ch 17, *Financial Statements, Audit and Annual Return*, at paras **[17.122]** to **[17.124]**.

90 In respect of Companies Act individual and group accounts under the Sixth Schedule to CA 1963, under ss 149(2) and 150A(2) of the CA 1963; and in respect of such accounts under the C(A)A 1986 and the EC(CGA)R 1992, under s 3 of the C(A)A 1986 and reg 14 of EC(CGA)R 1992.

91 Section 158 of the CA 1963; see Ch 17, *Financial Statements, Audit and Annual Return*, at para **[17.214]**.

92 As set out in Ch 17, *Financial Statements, Audit and Annual Return*, at para **[17.215]**.

[30.064] Similar to the requirement that a company falling into one of the three categories above prepare Companies Act rather than IFRS individual accounts, where such a company is a parent company, it is required to prepare Companies Act group accounts[93]. However there is no provision corresponding to s 2(1) of the C(A)A 1986[94] in respect of the preparation of group accounts, and therefore such a company is subject to the EC(C:GA)R 1992 just as is the case for a company limited by shares preparing Companies Act group accounts.

[30.065] A guarantee company which is not such an entity (which would be likely to include, for example, a property management company) will be permitted to prepare either Companies Act or IFRS individual accounts, and, where required to prepare group accounts, will be permitted to prepare either Companies Act or IFRS group accounts. Such a company will be subject to the same provisions in relation to the preparation of individual (and where applicable, group) accounts, as apply to a company limited by shares.

(c) Annual return of guarantee companies

[30.066] Guarantee companies are subject to the same requirement to file an annual return as applies to a company limited by shares[95].

Most guarantee companies will also be required to annex the same documents (eg, balance sheet, directors' and auditors' reports) to their annual returns[96]. The exceptions are as set out in paras (4)(c) and (5) of s 128 of the CA 1963, ie:

- a guarantee company formed for a charitable object, and which is under the control of, and exercises its functions in accordance with, a religion 'recognised by the State under Article 44 of the Constitution'[97]; or
- a company formed for charitable purposes in respect of which the Commissioners of Charitable Donations and Bequests[98] makes an order exempting the company (either altogether or for a limited period) from the obligation that it annex its balance sheet (and any document required to be annexed thereto), directors' report and auditor's report to its annual return.

Such a company is instead required[99] to have its auditors prepare a report to the directors confirming that they audited the accounts for the year and including within it their report to the members pursuant to s 193 of the CA 1990. The report made by the auditors to the directors must be certified by a director and the secretary as being a true copy of that report, and must be attached to the company's annual return[100].

---

93 Section 150(4) of the CA 1963.

94 See **[30.062]** *ante*.

95 Section 125(1) of the CA 1963; see Ch 17, *Financial Statements, Audit and Annual Return*, at para **[17.250]** *et seq*.

96 Section 128(1) of the CA 1963; see Ch 17, *Financial Statements, Audit and Annual Return*, at para **[17.262]** *et seq*.

97 See fn 83, *ante*.

98 See fn 84, *ante*.

99 Section 128(6B) of the CA 1963.

100 Section 128(6C) of the CA 1963.

It should be noted that this exemption – unlike the provisions above in respect of the preparation of the accounts – does not apply to not-for-profit companies generally but only to the two specific categories of companies identified above.

[30.067] Guarantee companies are not required to return the particulars of their members to the CRO when returning their annual return as such is not required by the statutory instrument prescribing the information required to be contained in a B1. Where the number of members with which a guarantee company is registered is increased beyond that number, however, that fact must be notified to the CRO at that time[101].

[30.068] It is proposed under s 52 of the Charities Act 2009 that a charitable organisation[102] that is a company and is not required to annex its accounts to the annual return made by it to the registrar of companies under the Companies Acts, shall attach a copy of the accounts prepared by it to an annual report to be submitted by it to the Charities Regulatory Authority. However, neither this section nor the sections of the Charities Act 2009 establishing the proposed Charities Regulatory Authority[103] have yet been commenced.

(d) Exemptions in relation to preparation, audit and disclosure of accounts

[30.069] As a guarantee company is a public company, it will be subject to similar restrictions as a public limited company in respect of the various exemptions which would be available to private limited companies in respect of the preparation, auditing and disclosure of accounts[104].

First, public companies are expressly excluded from availing of the exemptions and exclusions accorded to 'medium-sized' and 'small' private companies[105] in respect of the disclosure of accounts; nor may they avail of the exemption from filing individual accounts by virtue of being a subsidiary undertaking of an EU parent undertaking[106].

Second, the exemption from the requirement to prepare group accounts related to size of the group[107] is also expressly limited to a parent undertaking that is a private company. A guarantee company is, however, more likely than a public limited company to be able to avail of one of the other exemptions from preparing group accounts (for parent undertakings that are themselves subsidiary undertakings[108]), in that the provision whereby such exemptions are stated as not applying to a parent undertaking any of

---

101 Section 12(3) of the CA 1963: see para **[30.036]** *ante*.

102 As defined in s 2(1) of the Charities Act 2009, being a body that promotes a charitable purpose only, and that applies prescribed restrictions in respect of the application of its property.

103 In respect of the proposed establishment of the Charities Regulatory Authority, Minister for Justice Alan Shatter on 21 May 2012 cited a 2011 review of expenditure as having caused him to take the view that it was 'not possible to proceed with the full implementation of the Act at this time given the likely scale of the financial and staffing resources implied'.

104 As discussed in the context of public limited companies: see Ch 29, *Public Limited Companies and SEs*, at para **[29.119]**.

105 See Ch 17, *Financial Statements, Audit and Annual Return*, at paras **[17.267]** to **[17.284]**.

106 See Ch 17, *Financial Statements, Audit and Annual Return*, at paras **[17.285]** to **[17.286]**.

107 See Ch 17, *Financial Statements, Audit and Annual Return*, at paras **[17.157]** to **[17.158]**.

108 See Ch 17, *Financial Statements, Audit and Annual Return*, at paras **[17.159]** to **[17.163]**.

whose securities are admitted to trading on a regulated market[109] of an EEA State, is less likely to affect guarantee companies.

Finally, a public company will also be precluded from availing of the exemption from having its accounts audited that applies to certain private limited companies[110].

Winding up guarantee companies and realisation and distribution of assets

[30.070] As observed in Chapter 25, one of the first duties of a liquidator is to settle a list of contributories of the company being wound up[111]. Section 207(1)(e) of the CA 1963 provides:

> 'in the case of a company limited by guarantee, no contribution shall, subject to subsection (3), be required from any member exceeding the amount undertaken to be contributed by him to the assets of the company in the event of its being wound up.'

Where a guarantee company is wound up insolvent, for most members their liability will be nominal, eg, €1; so nominal, in fact, that it will not be worth a liquidator's time to ever seek its payment. In common with companies limited by shares, persons who are no longer members of a guarantee company but who were members within 12 months of the commencement of the winding up are also liable to contribute[112], but only in respect of debts contracted while they were members[113] and only then when it appears that the existing members are unable to pay[114].

[30.071] Where a guarantee company is wound up solvent, those that are charities and those that availed of the exception in s 24 of the CA 1963 and dispensed with having their name end in 'Limited', the normal rule – set out in s 275(1)(b) of the CA 1963[115] – concerning the distribution of surplus property to members will not apply by operation of the 'no-distribution-on-winding-up' clause contained in their memorandum of association[116]. Instead, the liquidator will distribute any surplus remaining after the discharge of all liabilities, to another company with similar objects to those of the guarantee company or to a charity, if so required by the memorandum of association[117].

Strike-off and restoration

[30.072] One of the perceived needs for new law on management companies was to provide a more expeditious remedy where such companies were struck off the register of companies for failing to file their annual returns. The consequences which can befall a

---

109 See the definition of 'regulated market' at para **[29.099]** in the context of relevant parent undertakings.

110 See Ch 17, *Financial Statements, Audit and Annual Return*, at para **[17.287]** *et seq.*

111 RSC, Ord 74, rr 86–89; see Ch 25, *Realisation and Distribution of Assets in a Winding Up*, at para **[25.130]**.

112 Section 207(1)(a) of the CA 1963.

113 Section 207(1)(b) of the CA 1963.

114 Section 207(1)(c) of the CA 1963.

115 See Ch 25, *Realisation and Distribution of Assets in a Winding Up*, at para **[25.195]**.

116 See para **[30.027]** *ante*.

117 See the sample clause adopted by many companies set out in para **[30.027]** *ante*.

company which does not file its annual returns have been described in Chapter 26[118]. Ordinarily, an application for administrative restoration must be brought to the registrar of companies within 12 months of a company being struck off, however, in the case of a company to which s 30 of the MUDA 2011 applies, this is extended to six years. Section 30(1) provides:

> 'Where a company to which this section applies has been struck off the register in accordance with—
>
> (a) section 311 of the Act of 1963, or
>
> (b) section 12 of the Act of 1982,
>
> then, without prejudice to the provisions of section 311(8) or 311A(1) of the Act of 1963 or subsection (3) or (7) of section 12B of the Act of 1982, if a member or officer of a company is aggrieved by the fact of the company having been struck off the register under section 311 of the Act of 1963 or section 12 of the Act of 1982 the registrar of companies, on an application made in the prescribed form by the member or officer before the expiration of 6 years from the publication in *Iris Oifigiúil* of the notice that the company was struck off the register, provided that the registrar has received all annual returns outstanding, if any, from the company, may restore the name of the company to the register.'

Upon the registration of such an application and the payment of the prescribed fees, the company will be deemed to have continued in existence as if its name had not been struck off[119]. This section applies to any company which is an owners' management company (and not just to guarantee companies) and which immediately prior to the name of the company being struck off pursuant to s 311 of the CA 1963 or s 12 of the C(A)A 1982 had vested in it ownership of the common areas or a part thereof of the multi-unit development in respect of which the company was incorporated[120]. The application under s 30(1) of the MUDA 2011 must be accompanied by a certificate from a solicitor or an accountant certifying that the company is an owners' management company operating as such[121].

Compliance and enforcement

[30.073] There are no particularly significant features of the law relating to company law compliance and enforcement in the case of guarantee companies which are different from those already considered in relation to private companies.

[30.074] In the case of a guarantee company that is an owners' management company an application can be brought under s 24 of the MUDA 2011 to the Circuit Court for an order to enforce any rights conferred or obligations imposed by the MUDA 2011 or any rule of law. It is thought that this provision and the reference to 'any rule of law' is not sufficient to facilitate the litigation of any provision of the Companies Acts relevant to such a company – since if that were the intention, the section could have made reference to the Companies Acts or even to 'under this Act *or any other enactment*' and that, as such, s 24 is confined to statutory rights and obligations arising under the MUDA 2011.

---

118 See Ch 26, *Strike-Off and Restoration*, at para **[26.026]**.

119 Section 30(2) of the MUDA 2011.

120 Section 30(3) of the MUDA 2011.

121 Section 30(4) of the MUDA 2011.

Chapter 31

Unlimited Companies

The unlimited company in context

[31.001] For reasons that are obvious, unlimited companies are not a particularly popular corporate form in Ireland and as at 31 December 2011 accounted for just 4,126 companies or nearly 2.23% of all companies on the Irish register[1]. This chapter considers the law applicable to unlimited companies insofar as it differs from the law applicable to other types of company. The Companies Acts permit three specific types of unlimited company:

(a) the private unlimited company with a share capital;
(b) the public unlimited company with a share capital;
(c) the public unlimited company without a share capital.

It has been proposed by the Company Law Review Group that all three types of unlimited company will be preserved and can be formed under the proposed new Companies Bill and the review group's report abbreviates the three types of unlimited company as ULCs, PUCs and PULCs. In fact, there are very few specific differences in the law applicable to unlimited companies. Whereas the private unlimited company will have much in common with the private company limited by shares, the public unlimited company with a share capital will have much in common with the PLC and the public unlimited company without a share capital will have much in common with guarantee companies, the one feature which unifies all three is that their members will have an unlimited secondary liability for the company's debts and liabilities. However, those differences that do exist are very significant and are the concern of this chapter.

[31.002] People choose to use unlimited companies for a number of reasons. One of the chief reasons why unlimited companies are used is that private unlimited companies that meet certain criteria are not required to file their accounts with the registrar of companies and so can keep their affairs confidential. Public unlimited companies with a share capital have been used by the main Irish banks as the chosen vehicle for their mortgage bank subsidiaries which have listed debt securities (ie, mortgage bonds).

[31.003] In this chapter, the law relating to unlimited companies is considered under the following headings:

1. Formation and constitutional documentation of unlimited companies.
2. Incorporation and its consequences.
3. Disregarding separate legal personality.

---

1 *The Companies Registration Office Report 2011* at p 10.

4. Corporate civil litigation.
5. Corporate contracts, capacity and authority.
6. Shares and membership.
7. Share transfer in unlimited companies.
8. The maintenance of capital.
9. Financial statements, audit and annual return.
10. Winding up, liquidators and realisation and distribution of assets

The law relating to members' and shareholders' remedies, groups of companies, corporate governance: management by the directors, corporate governance: meetings, duties of directors, statutory regulation of directors' transactions, corporate borrowing[2], schemes of arrangement, examinerships, investigations and inspectors, strike-off and restoration, and compliance and enforcement is broadly similar for unlimited companies as it is for private companies as set out in the chapters dealing with these issues.

Formation and constitutional documentation of unlimited companies

(a) Formation of unlimited companies

[31.004] The only way of forming either type of unlimited company is by lodging all documentation on the 'ordinary list' with the Companies Registration Office ('CRO'). Unlike private companies, the 10-day list or CRODisk cannot be used to form an unlimited company. The documents and other matters required to be lodged are:

– memorandum of association;
– articles of association;
– Form No A1 (incorporating a statutory declaration that an activity will be carried on in Ireland); and
– the appropriate fee.

(b) The memorandum of association of an unlimited company

[31.005] The memorandum of association of a private unlimited company must comply with s 6 of the CA 1963. In particular, it must state the objects of the company: s 6(1)(c) of the CA 1963. The objects clause in unlimited companies will typically follow the same pattern as private or public limited companies and set out extensive objects and powers coupled with a *Bell Houses* clause and independent objects clause.

[31.006] Although it is common practice for the memorandum of association of an unlimited company to state the company's name, this is not in fact a statutory requirement under s 6. It used to be the case under s 6(1) of the CA 1963 before it was substituted by the C(A)A 1983 but it seems the focus was on the PLC and not the unlimited company and the requirement, it would seem, was, inadvertently, dropped. The name of an unlimited company is not required to indicate that it is unlimited as is evidenced by the form of model memorandum of association provided in Part I of Table E of the First Schedule of the CA 1963. Neither is the name of an unlimited company required to indicate that it is a company at all, with the result that in theory an unlimited

2 A public unlimited company with a share capital may not exercise its borrowing without first obtaining a certificate to commence business under s 115(2) of the CA 1963: see para **[31.011]** *post*.

company could adopt a name that could make it appear to be a natural person; in practice, however, the registrar of companies does not permit unlimited companies to have names which would make them appear to be natural persons on the grounds that such is undesirable within the meaning of s 21 of the CA 1963.

[31.007] The objects clause of an unlimited company can be amended in accordance with s 10 of the CA 1963 and an unlimited company can amend its name in accordance with s 23 of the CA 1963. Other clauses in an unlimited company's memorandum of association that are not required by law to be included in the memorandum of association can be amended in accordance with s 28 of the CA 1963[3].

[31.008] A private unlimited company must have at least two members, the EC(SMPLC)R 1994 only applying to private companies that are limited; and both types of public unlimited company must have at least seven members: s 5(1) of the CA 1963.

(c) The articles of association of an unlimited company

[31.009] There are no statutorily prescribed articles of association applicable to unlimited companies. That said, Part II of Table E of the CA 1963 does provide for a form of articles of association for a public unlimited company and Part III of Table E provides a form of articles for a private unlimited company.

[31.010] The articles of association of an unlimited company, like those of a guarantee company[4], must state the number of members with which the company proposes to be registered and if that company has a share capital, the amount of share capital with which it proposes to be registered[5]. This requirement can only be construed as operating at the time an unlimited company is incorporated (ie, before it is registered) since the obligation is prospective and once an unlimited company is registered, this requirement no longer applies to, for example, the adoption of new articles of association in substitution for those with which the company is registered[6]. It should also be noted that where an unlimited company has increased the number of members beyond the registered number it shall, within 15 days after the increase was resolved on or took place, give to the registrar notice of the increase and she shall record the increase[7].

(d) Restrictions on the commencement of business

[31.011] There are no restrictions on the commencement of business for a private unlimited company[8] or a public unlimited company which does not have a share capital. A public unlimited company with a share capital, however, is subject to the restrictions contained in s 115(2) of the CA 1963 and may not commence business or exercise any

3 See Ch 30, *Guarantee Companies*, at para **[30.031]** *et seq*.

4 See Ch 30, *Guarantee Companies*, at para **[30.036]** *et seq*.

5 Section 12(1) of the CA 1963.

6 Regulation 1 of Part II of Table E satisfies s 12(1) of the CA 1963 in the case of a public unlimited company and regs 1 and 2 of Part III of Table E satisfy that provision in the case of a private unlimited company.

7 Section 12(3) of the CA 1963: default in complying with this subsection renders the company and every officer in default, found guilty, liable to a class C fine.

8 Section 115(7)(a) of the CA 1963.

borrowing powers before first obtaining a certificate to commence business from the registrar of companies. Section 115(2) of the CA 1963 provides:

> 'Where a company having a share capital has not issued a prospectus inviting the public to subscribe for its shares, the company shall not commence any business or exercise any borrowing powers unless—
>
> (a) there has been delivered to the registrar of companies for registration a statement in lieu of prospectus; and
>
> (b) every director of the company has paid to the company, on each of the shares taken or contracted to be taken by him and for which he is liable to pay in cash, a proportion equal to the proportion payable on application and allotment on the shares payable in cash; and
>
> (c) there has been delivered to the registrar of companies for registration a statutory declaration by the secretary or one of the directors, in the prescribed form, that paragraph (b) of this subsection has been complied with.'

It would be unthinkable for an unlimited company to invite the public to subscribe for its shares and so it will be s 115(2) and not s 115(1) of the CA 1963 that will apply to public unlimited companies with a share capital ('PUCs'). The failure to get a certificate to do business makes it impossible for a PUC to function since s 115(4) provides:

> 'Any contract made or ratified by a company before the date at which it is entitled to commence business shall be provisional only, and shall not be binding on the company until that date, and on that date it shall become binding.'

Upon receiving the requisite statutory declaration, the registrar of companies will issue a certificate which will be conclusive evidence that the PUC is entitled to do business[9]. The failure to obtain such a certificate before commencing business or exercising the PUC's borrowing powers renders every person responsible for the contravention liable to a class C fine[10].

[31.012] The archaic requirements of s 115 of the CA 1963 in relation to trading certificates for PUCs can be lawfully side-stepped by first incorporating as a PLC and then converting the PLC to a PUC because s 115(7)(d) provides that nothing in s 115 shall apply to a PLC registered as such on its original incorporation under the C(A)A 1983[11].

Incorporation and its consequences

[31.013] There are no particularly significant features of the law relating to the incorporation of unlimited companies and its consequences which are different from those already considered in relation to private limited companies. One important point is that an unlimited company is just as much a legal person that is separate and apart from its members and directors as is a limited company. The rule in *Salomon v A Salomon & Co Ltd*[12] applies to unlimited companies with the same force as limited companies. In consequence, the members of an unlimited company are not jointly and severally liable

9 Section 115(3) of the CA 1963.

10 Section 115(6) of the CA 1963.

11 On conversion from limited to unlimited, see Ch 33, *Conversion by Re-registration*, at para **[33.001]**.

12 *Salomon v A Salomon & Co Ltd* [1897] AC 22.

with the unlimited company on contracts; where the unlimited company commits a tort there is no *locus standi* to sue its members directly or even to join them in the action. The legal personality of the unlimited company remains separate and apart from that of its members unless and until it is wound up insolvent, whereupon, as is considered below[13], its existing and certain former members can be liable to *contribute* to any deficiency in the assets that are available to meet its liabilities.

Disregarding separate legal personality

[31.014] With the exception of the defining feature of unlimited companies, namely, that their members can be liable for the company's debts on its being wound up and which is treated in this chapter in the context of winding up, there are no particularly significant features of the law relating to the disregard of separate legal personality in the case of unlimited companies which are different from those already considered in relation to private limited companies.

Corporate civil litigation

[31.015] The primary difference in law between unlimited companies and the law relating to corporate civil litigation applicable to private limited companies is that an order for security for costs under s 390 of the CA 1963 may not be made against an unlimited company since the jurisdiction is expressly confined to cases where 'a limited company is plaintiff'. As Laffoy J observed in *ABM Construction v Habbingley Ltd*[14], 'the power to make an order for security for costs against a company has been confined to limited companies for over one hundred and fifty years. One must assume that the approach which has been adopted over such a long time span represents deliberative legislative policy.'

[31.016] It might be thought that different rules would apply where an unlimited company's members are all limited companies; it is clear, however, that in such circumstances s 390 of the CA 1963 still has no application. An application for security for costs cannot be brought under s 390 against an unlimited company even if its members are all limited liability companies[15]. In *Goode Concrete v CRH plc*[16] Cooke J refused to adopt a 'purposive approach' to override the 'clear and obviously deliberate terms' of s 390 and declined to lift the veil on the 'justice of the case' ground because, in that case, the unlimited company's members were limited foreign companies.

Moreover, in *ABM Construction v Habbingley*[17] Laffoy J rejected the suggestion that there was an inherent jurisdiction in the court to make an order for security for costs where an application did not come within with s 390 of the CA 1963 (because the plaintiff was not a limited company) or Ord 29 of the RSC 1986 (because the plaintiff was not resident outside of the jurisdiction). There, the learned judge said:

> 'As regards a corporation, such as an unlimited company, which does not come within the terms of the specific statutory provision which has expressly provided for the Court

13 See para **[31.036]** *post*.

14 *ABM Construction v Habbingley Ltd* [2012] IEHC 61.

15 See, further, Ch 6, *Corporate Civil Litigation,* at para **[6.025]** *et seq*.

16 *Goode Concrete v CRH plc* [2012] IEHC 116.

17 *ABM Construction v Habbingley Ltd* [2012] IEHC 61.

> making an order for security for costs against a company, but has confined the jurisdiction to a limited company, for at least one hundred and fifty years, currently s 390 of the Act of 1963, if the Court were to find that it has an inherent power to exercise a parallel jurisdiction to s 390 against such a corporation, in my view, it would be usurping the functions of the Oireachtas or the secondary legislature which is statutorily empowered to make rules for the administration of the business of the Superior Courts, the Superior Courts Rules Committee. Accordingly, I am satisfied that the Court has no inherent power to order security for costs against an unlimited company, such as the claimant[18].'

[31.017] In the case of a non-resident unlimited company, there would be jurisdiction under Ord 29 of the RSC 1986 to make an order for security for costs but such a jurisdiction is entirely independent of the Companies Acts. This issue was considered for the first time by an Irish court in *ABM Construction v Habbingley Ltd*[19]. In that case, the claimant unlimited Irish company had two shareholders, an Isle of Man limited company and an Isle of Man unlimited company; its registered office was in Swords, County Dublin and all its directors and its secretary resided in Ireland. It was in the construction business and there was evidence that it was involved in substantial construction projects in the State. After noting that s 390 of the CA 1963 had no application to unlimited companies, Laffoy J went on to consider whether an order could be made under Ord 29 of the RSC 1986, finding that although the language used in Ord 29 was suggestive of a natural person, 'nonetheless Ord 29 can be invoked against a plaintiff which is a body corporate, provided it "resides" outside the jurisdiction'[20]. Laffoy J noted that in *Re Little Olympian Each Ways Ltd*[21] Lindsay J had found that a plaintiff corporation was 'ordinarily resident' outside of the jurisdiction for the purpose of their analogous rule if the central control and management of the company actually abided and was exercised overseas. Although the respondent ignored that requirement in Ord 29 and did not attempt to show as a matter of fact and law that the claimant was resident outside the jurisdiction, it instead urged the court to substitute the test in s 390 of the CA 1963, namely, that there is reason to believe that the company will be unable to pay its costs if successful in its defence. On the facts, Laffoy J found that the claimant did not reside outside of the jurisdiction:

> 'Although the corporate structure is such that the shares in the claimant are held by two companies incorporated in the Isle of Man, the evidence indicates that the central control and management of the claimant takes place in this jurisdiction, where it is registered and has its registered office, where its directors reside, where its accounts are audited, where it pays its taxes, where it complies with its statutory obligation to file its annual return together with a copy of the auditor's report pursuant to s 128(6B) of the Act of 1963 attached, and where it is involved in substantial construction projects, in many cases under contract to public authorities in this jurisdiction[22].'

---

18 *ABM Construction v Habbingley Ltd* [2012] IEHC 61 at para 5.5.

19 *ABM Construction v Habbingley Ltd* [2012] IEHC 61.

20 *ABM Construction v Habbingley Ltd* [2012] IEHC 61 at para 4.3.

21 *Re Little Olympian Each Ways Ltd* [1994] 4 All ER 561.

22 *ABM Construction v Habbingley Ltd* [2012] IEHC 61 at para 4.6.

Corporate contracts, capacity and authority

[31.018] With one exception, there are no particularly significant features of the law relating to corporate contracts, capacity and authority in the case of unlimited companies which are different from those already considered in relation to private companies. The exception concerns reg 6 of the EC(C)R 1973[23], which has been considered in detail in Chapter 7[24], because the 1973 regulations have no application to unlimited companies[25].

Shares and membership

[31.019] A public unlimited company without a share capital may have members who are not shareholders. Membership of such companies can arise where a person is an initial subscriber to a guarantee company upon its formation or where subsequent to its formation, that person is admitted to membership whether by the directors (as is more usual) or by the members.

[31.020] A private unlimited company and a public unlimited company with a share capital will both have shareholders who are members and in this respect the law applicable to shareholder members of private limited companies and PLCs, in general, apply.

Share transfers in unlimited companies

[31.021] Although model reg 22 of Part I of Table A requires share transfers of shares in limited companies to be signed by both the transferor and the transferee, this regulation is invariably modified to dispense with the need for the transferee to sign the stock transfer form save where the shares have not been fully paid up. Unlimited companies are different and again, invariably, their articles of association will provide that the stock transfer form must be signed by both transferor and transferee. The simplified transfer of securities provided for in the Stock Transfer Act 1963 ('STA 1963') specifically excludes securities in unlimited companies from its application[26].

The maintenance of capital

[31.022] The need for capital maintenance rules in unlimited companies is less than in limited companies because of the fact that the members of an unlimited company are liable to contribute to its liabilities, should it be wound up insolvent. The primary prohibition on a company reducing its share capital does not extend to unlimited companies, s 72(1) of the CA 1963 providing:

---

23 SI 163/1973.

24 Ch 7, *Corporate Contracts, Capacity and Authority*, at paras **[7.087]–[7.127]**.

25 Regulation 3 of the EC(C)R 1973. The EC(C)R 1973 were not considered in the landmark Irish decision on corporate capacity, *Northern Bank Finance Company Ltd v Quinn and Achates Investment Co* [1979] ILRM 221, most likely because Achates Investment Co was an unlimited company with the result that Keane J's analysis of the law on the matter was confined to s 8(1) of the CA 1963.

26 Section 2(4) of the STA 1963.

> 'Except in so far as this Act permits, it shall not be lawful for *a company limited by shares or a company limited by guarantee* and having a share capital to reduce its share capital in any way.' (Emphasis added.)

Moreover, s 41(1) of the C(A)A 1983 provides:

> 'Subject to the following provisions of this section, no *company limited by shares or limited by guarantee and having a share capital* shall acquire its own shares (whether by purchase, subscription or otherwise).' (Emphasis added.)

Accordingly, the Companies Acts do not prevent public or private unlimited companies from reducing their share capital. This reflects the traditional common law position enunciated by Vaughan Williams J in *Re Borough Commercial and Building Society*[27] where he distinguished the application of the principles in *Trevor v Whitworth*[28] to unlimited companies. In *Trevor v Whitworth*, Lord Hershell had said:

> 'The Companies Act, 1862, requires (section 8) that in the case of a company where the liability of the shareholders is limited, the memorandum shall contain the amount of the capital with which the company proposes to be registered, divided into shares of a certain fixed amount; and provides (section 12) that such a company may increase its capital and divide it into shares of larger amount than the existing shares, or convert its paid-up shares into stock, but that, "save as aforesaid, no alteration shall be made by any company in the conditions contained in its memorandum of association." What is the meaning of the distinction thus drawn between a company without limit on the liability of its members and a company where the liability is limited, but, in the latter case, to assure to those dealing with the company that the whole of the subscribed capital, unless diminished by expenditure upon the objects defined by the memorandum, shall remain available for the discharge of its liabilities? The capital may, no doubt, be diminished by expenditure upon and reasonably incidental to all the objects specified. A part of its capital may be lost in carrying on the business operations authorised. Of this all persons trusting the company are aware, and take the risk. But I think that they have a right to rely, and were intended by the Legislature to have a right to rely, on the capital remaining undiminished by any expenditure outside these limits, or by the return of any part of it to the shareholders.'

Vaughan Williams J acknowledged the distinction drawn between limited and unlimited companies in the foregoing passage and went on to find:

> 'I am of opinion further, having carefully looked through the Companies Acts, 1862 and 1867, that there is nothing to prevent a company unlimited from providing by its memorandum or association and its articles for a return of capital to the members of the partnership, or for a withdrawal of members from the company.'

One of the reasons given by Vaughan Williams J as to why the creditors were not prejudiced by a withdrawal of capital was that in dealing with an unlimited company they know that there is no fixed capital and so have no right to complain. Of course, should the company be wound up insolvent, the creditors may also, through the liquidator, expect the members to contribute to the deficiency in assets.

[31.023] Because neither s 72 of the CA 1963 nor s 41 of the C(A)A 1983 applies to an unlimited company, it may therefore acquire its own shares from its members by buying them back. This will typically be authorised by the company's articles of association,

27 *Re Borough Commercial and Building Society* [1893] 2 Ch 242.

28 *Trevor v Whitworth* (1887) 12 App Cas 409.

and so reg 3(e) of Table E of the CA 1963 provides that an unlimited company can by special resolution '*reduce its share capital in any way*'. Shares can therefore be bought back without complying with the buyback procedure in s 211 of the CA 1990[29].

One anomaly concerns distributions and dividends. Despite the ability of an unlimited company to reduce its capital in any way, it is still required by s 45 of the C(A)A 1983 to pay dividends from distributable profits only.

Financial statements, audit and annual returns

(a) Annual return

[31.024] Every company is required to make an annual return to the registrar of companies[30]. However, while a public unlimited company has always been required to annex its balance sheet (and any document required by law to be annexed to the balance sheet), directors' report and auditor's report to its annual return, and a corresponding obligation is imposed on limited companies by s 7(1) of the C(A)A 1986, no such obligation applied pursuant to these enactments to a *private* unlimited company in respect of its individual accounts, as s 128 of the CA 1963 does not apply to a private company[31], and the C(A)A 1986 is expressed not to apply to unlimited companies[32].

Similarly, while reg 39 of the EC(CGA)R 1992 requires that where a company is a parent undertaking, it shall annex its group accounts, directors' report and auditor's report to its annual return, the requirement to present group accounts under the EC(CGA)R 1992 is expressed not to apply to unlimited companies[33].

Therefore, prior to 1993, private unlimited companies had no obligation to annex individual or group accounts to their annual returns.

[31.025] This was changed in respect of certain private unlimited companies, however, by the EC(A)R 1993. Regulation 7(1) of the EC(A)R 1993 provides that the C(A)A 1986 will apply to undertakings to which Part III of the EC(A)R 1993 applies, while reg 9(1) of EC(A)R 1992 provides that the EC(CGA)R 1992 will apply to an undertaking to which Part III of the EC(A)R 1993 applies that is a parent undertaking.

Regulation 6(1) of the EC(A)R 1993 states that Part III of the EC(A)R 1993 applies to *certain* types of private unlimited companies, namely:

> 'Unlimited companies ... where all the members thereof ... are[34]
>
> (a) companies limited by shares or by guarantee, or

---

29 See Ch 10, *The Maintenance of Capital*, at para **[10.024]** *et seq*.

30 See s 125(1) of the CA 1963, and Ch 17, *Financial Statements, Audit and Annual Return*, at para [**17.250**] *et seq*.

31 Section 128(4)(a) of the CA 1963.

32 Section 1(1) of the C(A)A 1986 defines 'company' as not including an unlimited company and also alters the general definition of 'private company' in s 33 of the CA 1963 as, for the purposes of the C(A)A 1986, not including an unlimited company.

33 Regulation 5(3) of the EC(CGA)R 1992 provides that the obligation to present group accounts under the EC(CGA)R 1992 shall only apply to a parent undertaking if it is limited by shares or by guarantee.

34 Regulation 6(1) also applies to partnerships and the text reads: 'unlimited companies and partnerships where all the members thereof who do not have a limit on their liability are ...'

(b) bodies not governed by the law of the State but equivalent to those in paragraph (a), or

(c) any combination of the types of bodies referred to in subparagraphs (a) and (b).'

Accordingly, where an unlimited company's members are themselves limited liability companies, the unlimited company will have to disclose its financial statements. It does not matter whether the members are Irish companies, EU companies or non-EU companies. Where a private unlimited company has a natural person as a member, it will not have to disclose its accounts.

[31.026] Regulation 6(1) could, however, have so easily been avoided were it to have been left at that, since it would mean that if an unlimited company had two members one of which was itself an unlimited company but with two limited liability members, such a company would not be required to disclose its accounts. The door on this 'out' was closed by reg 6(2) of the EC(A)R 1993 which provides:

'unlimited companies ...where all the members thereof ... are[35]

(a) (i) unlimited companies or partnerships of the type referred to in paragraph (1) that are governed by the laws of a Member State, or

(ii) bodies governed by the laws of a Member State that are of a legal form comparable to those referred to in paragraph (i), or

(b) any combination of the types of bodies referred to in subparagraph (a) and subparagraphs (a) and (b) of paragraph (1).'

Regulation 6(2) is important in that it requires that where a private unlimited company has a member which is an unlimited EU company, one must *look through* to the next layer of liability. Regulation 6(2) means, for example, that where the members of a private unlimited company are EU (including Irish) unlimited companies whose members are limited companies (thereby making them a company of the type referred to in reg 6(1)) it will be required to file its financial statements.

An unlimited private company with a member which is an unlimited company *from outside of the EU* will not, however, be required to disclose its financial statements since it falls outside of both reg 6(1) and (2) of the EC(A)R 1993.

Accordingly, the most common basis upon which an Irish private unlimited company is not required to disclose its accounts is where its members include either a natural person or a non-EU unlimited company. A private unlimited company which has such a member will not be required to annex its financial statements, directors' report or auditor's report to the annual return it delivers to the registrar of companies.

(b) Financial statements

[31.027] A private unlimited company is required under s 148 of the CA 1963 to prepare either Companies Act individual accounts or IFRS individual accounts, and if the company is a parent company, Companies Act group accounts or IFRS group accounts, just as is the case for a private limited company[36].

---

35 Regulation 6(2) also applies to partnerships and the text reads: 'unlimited companies and partnerships where all the members thereof who do not have a limit on their liability are ...'

36 See Ch 17, *Financial Statements, Audit and Annual Return*, at para **[17.017]**.

[31.028] The requirements in relation to the format of IFRS individual and (if applicable) group accounts will be the same for private unlimited companies as for private limited companies[37].

In the case of the format of Companies Act individual and (if applicable) group accounts by private unlimited companies which fall within the scope of reg 6 of the EC(A)R 1993, the requirements of the C(A)A 1986 and of the EC(CGA) 1992 shall apply as for private limited companies.

[31.029] In the case of the format of Companies Act individual and group accounts of unlimited companies which do not fall within the scope of reg 6 of the EC(A)R 1993, s 149(3)(e) of the CA 1963 provides that Companies Act individual accounts shall comply with the provisions of the Sixth Schedule to the CA 1963. Section 152 of the CA 1963 provides similarly that Companies Act group accounts shall comply with the requirements of the Sixth Schedule to the CA 1963 so far as applicable, or shall give the same or equivalent information.

This is in addition to any other disclosure obligation imposed by statute, such as the requirements to disclose:

(a) (in aggregate) directors' emoluments, pensions and compensation for loss of office[38];

(b) certain transactions entered into with directors or connected persons (such as loans and quasi-loans provided to them)[39];

(c) details of interests of a director or secretary in the company's debentures[40]; and

(d) details in respect of the remuneration of auditors[41].

[31.030] The Sixth Schedule of the CA 1963 does not impose any material obligations in relation to individual accounts additional to those set out in the C(A)A 1986. Unlike the C(A)A 1986, the Sixth Schedule does not prescribe a format for the balance sheet or profit and loss account, nor does it set out the same level of detail as does the C(A)A 1986 in relation to disclosures to be made in notes to the accounts. However, it is significant that the statutory obligations are in addition to those required by Irish GAAP, and further that the overriding obligation that applies under both frameworks is that the accounts give a 'true and fair view'[42].

[31.031] In the absence of express statutory provision, a company preparing accounts in accordance with the Sixth Schedule will therefore face uncertainty as to the level of

---

37 See Ch 17, *Financial Statements, Audit and Annual Return*, at paras **[17.121]** to **[17.143]**.

38 Section 191 of the CA 1963; see Ch 17, *Financial Statements, Audit and Annual Return*, at para **[17.112]**.

39 Section 41 of the CA 1990; see Ch 17, *Financial Statements, Audit and Annual Return*, at para **[17.113]** to **[17.120]**.

40 Section 63 of the CA 1990; see Ch 17, *Financial Statements, Audit and Annual Return*, at para **[17.121]**.

41 Section 161D of the CA 1963; see Ch 17, *Financial Statements, Audit and Annual Return*, at para **[17.122]** to **[17.124]**.

42 In respect of Companies Act individual and group accounts under the Sixth Schedule to CA 1963, under ss 149(2) and 150A(2) of the CA 1963; and in respect of such accounts under the C(A)A 1986 and the EC(CGA)R 1992, under s 3 of the C(A)A 1986 and reg 14 of the EC(CGA)R 1992.

detail required to meet this obligation; where this is the case – and bearing in mind that compliance with the requirements of the C(A)A 1986 and Irish GAAP is generally accepted as meeting the obligation to give a 'true and fair view' – one might expect that the company would meet the level of detail in the C(A)A 1986 as a means of reducing this uncertainty. Accordingly, in practice, accounts prepared in accordance with the Sixth Schedule of the CA 1963 tend not to be significantly different from those prepared in accordance with the C(A)A 1986.

Similarly, while the Sixth Schedule does not specify a particular format for the balance sheet or profit and loss account, accountants, auditors and users of accounts generally are familiar with the format specified in the C(A)A 1986. To avoid raising unnecessary concerns among such parties, one would therefore expect that a company preparing accounts in accordance with the Sixth Schedule would follow one of the formats in the C(A)A 1986 save insofar as there was strong reason not to do so.

[31.032] Similarly, the Sixth Schedule of the CA 1963 does not impose any material obligations in relation to group accounts additional to those set out in the EC(C:GA)R 1992, and while the Sixth Schedule does not prescribe a format for group accounts, nor does it set out the same level of detail in respect of disclosures as is required by the EC(C:GA)R 1992, the format, and level of disclosure, in group accounts prepared in accordance with the Sixth Schedule of the CA 1963 do not tend to be significantly different from those prepared in accordance with the EC(C:GA)R 1992.

[31.033] A private unlimited company will continue to be subject to the obligation to prepare a directors' report[43]; however, a private unlimited company which does not fall within the scope of reg 6 of the EC(A)R 1993 will not be required to include the additional information required by ss 13 and 14 of the C(A)A 1986[44].

(c) *Exemptions in relation to preparation, audit and disclosure of accounts*

[31.034] A private unlimited company that falls within the scope of reg 6 of the EC(A)R 1993 will, if it meets the necessary criteria, be able to avail of the same exemption from the obligation to have its accounts audited as applies to certain private limited companies[45]. A private unlimited company that does not fall within the scope of reg 6 will not be able to avail of the exemption.[46]

[31.035] A private unlimited company that falls within the scope of reg 6 of the EC(A)R 1993 will, if it meets the necessary criteria, be able to avail of the exemptions and exclusions accorded to 'medium-sized' and 'small' private companies[47] in respect of the disclosure of accounts, and the exemption from filing individual accounts by virtue of being a subsidiary undertaking of an EU parent undertaking[48].

---

43 Section 158 of the CA 1963; see Ch 17, *Financial Statements, Audit and Annual Return*, at para **[17.214]**.

44 As set out at Ch 17, *Financial Statements, Audit and Annual Return*, at para **[17.215]**.

45 See Ch 17, *Financial Statements, Audit and Annual Return*, at para **[17.287]** *et seq.*

46 Section 31 of C(A)(No 2)A 1999.

47 See Ch 17, *Financial Statements, Audit and Annual Return*, at paras **[17.267]** to **[17.284]**.

48 See Ch 17, *Financial Statements, Audit and Annual Return*, at paras **[17.285]** to **[17.286]**.

Such a private unlimited company that is a parent undertaking will also be permitted to avail of the exemptions from the requirement to prepare group accounts, whether related to the size of the group[49] or to the parent undertaking itself being a subsidiary undertaking[50].

[31.036] A private unlimited company that is a parent undertaking, but does not fall within the scope of reg 6 of the EC(A)R 1993, will not be able to avail of the exemptions from preparing group accounts, in that such exemptions only apply to companies to which the EC(C:GA)R 1992 apply[51].

A private unlimited company that does not fall within the scope of reg 6 of the EC(A)R 1993 will also not be permitted to avail of the exemptions and exclusions in respect of filing obligations accorded to 'medium-sized' and 'small' private companies, but this is of course immaterial in that such a private unlimited company will in any case not be required to file accounts.

Winding up, liquidators and realisation and distribution of assets

[31.037] Where an unlimited company is wound up solvent, its members will share in the surplus assets available after the discharge of all liabilities. Where, however, an unlimited company is wound up insolvent, its current members, and certain past members (ie, contributories), will be liable to make good any shortfall. It can be said that the liability of the members of an unlimited company is a *secondary liability* in the sense that while the company is a going concern, it is a separate legal entity and its debts are its debts, not its members' debts; its members cannot, for example, be sued for its debts. On the insolvent winding up of an unlimited company, however, everything changes and its members' secondary liability will activate upon the liquidator making a call on its contributories.

[31.038] As noted in Chapter 25, one of the first duties of a liquidator is to settle a list of contributories of the company being wound up[52]. A contributory is a person who is liable under s 207 of the CA 1963 to contribute to the assets of a company that is being wound up[53]. Moreover, for the purposes of all proceedings for determining, and all proceedings prior to final determination of, the persons who are to be deemed contributories, includes any person alleged to be a contributory[54].

[31.039] Section 207(1) of the CA 1963 provides:

> 'In the event of a company being wound up, every present and past member shall be liable to contribute to the assets of the company to an amount sufficient for payment of its debts and liabilities, and the costs, charges and expenses of the winding up, and for the adjustment of the rights of the contributories among themselves, subject to subsection (2) and the following qualifications:

49 See Ch 17, *Financial Statements, Audit and Annual Return*, at paras **[17.157]** to **[17.158]**.

50 See Ch 17, *Financial Statements, Audit and Annual Return*, at paras **[17.159]** to **[17.163]**.

51 Regulations 7, 8, 9 and 9A of the EC(C:GA)R 1992 and s 150(8) of the CA 1963.

52 RSC, Ord 74, rr 86–89.

53 Section 208 of the CA 1963. See Ch 23, *Winding Up Companies*, para **[23.045]**.

54 Section 208 of the CA 1963.

(a) a past member shall not be liable to contribute if he has ceased to be a member for one year or more before the commencement of the winding up;

(b) a past member shall not be liable to contribute in respect of any debt or liability of the company contracted after he ceased to be a member;

(c) a past member shall not be liable to contribute unless it appears to the court that the existing members are unable to satisfy the contributions required to be made by them in pursuance of this Act;

(d) in the case of a company limited by shares, no contribution shall be required from any member exceeding the amount, if any, unpaid on the shares in respect of which he is liable as a present or past member;

(e) in the case of a company limited by guarantee, no contribution shall, subject to subsection (3), be required from any member exceeding the amount undertaken to be contributed by him to the assets of the company in the event of its being wound up;

(f) nothing in this Act shall invalidate any provision contained in any policy of insurance or other contract whereby the liability of individual members on the policy or contract is restricted, or whereby the funds of the company are alone made liable in respect of the policy or contract;

(g) a sum due to any member of the company, in his character of a member, by way of dividends, profits or otherwise, shall not be deemed to be a debt of the company, payable to that member in a case of competition between himself and any other creditor not a member of the company, but any such sum may be taken into account for the purpose of the final adjustment of the rights of the contributories among themselves.'

The effect of the foregoing provision is that the present members of an unlimited company are liable to contribute to the assets of the company to an amount sufficient for payment of its debts and liabilities, and the costs, charges and expenses of the winding up, and for the adjustment of the rights of the contributories among themselves, without limitation, since none of the qualifications in paras (a) to (g) will apply.

A past member of an unlimited company is liable to contribute to any shortfall, unless:

- he ceased to be a member for one year or more before the commencement of the winding up[55];
- the debt or liability was contracted after he ceased to be a member[56]; or
- the court is satisfied that the existing members are able to satisfy the contributions required to be made[57].

[31.040] The liability of a contributory creates a debt accruing due from him at the time when his liability commenced, but payable at the times when calls are made for enforcing the liability[58]. An action to recover a debt from a contributory must be brought within 12 years from the date on which the cause of action accrued[59]. The personal representatives of a deceased contributory are liable to contribute to the assets of the

55 Section 207(1)(a) of the CA 1963.

56 Section 207(1)(b) of the CA 1963.

57 Section 207(1)(c) of the CA 1963.

58 Section 209(1) of the CA 1963.

59 Section 209(2) of the CA 1963.

company and are themselves deemed to be contributories[60]. Bankrupt contributories are represented by the official assignee in bankruptcy who is also deemed to be a contributory[61].

[31.041] By s 238 of the CA 1963 the court is only empowered to make calls on any of the contributories to the extent of their liability:

> '... for payment of any money which the court considers necessary to satisfy the debts and liabilities of the company, and the costs, charges and expenses of winding up, and for the adjustment of the rights of the contributories amongst themselves, and make an order for payment of any calls so made.'

The court may make such calls even though it has not ascertained the sufficiency of the assets of the company. 'Calls' on contributories by liquidators are governed by Ord 74, rr 92–94 of the RSC 1986. These provide:

> '92. Every application to the Court to make any call on the contributories or any of them for any purpose authorised by the Act shall be made by motion on notice in the Form No 28 stating the proposed amount of such call. Such motion which shall be grounded on an affidavit of the Official Liquidator in the Form No 29 shall be served six clear days at the least before the hearing of the application on every contributory proposed to be included in such call, or if the Court shall so direct, notice of such intended call may be given by advertisement in the Form No 30.
>
> 93. When an order for a call has been made, a copy thereof shall be forthwith served upon each of the contributories included in such call together with a notice in the Form No 31 from the Official Liquidator specifying the amount or balance due from such contributory (having regard to the provisions of the Act) in respect of such call but such order need not be advertised unless for any special reason the Court shall so direct.
>
> 94. At the time of making an order for a call the further proceedings relating thereto shall be adjourned to a time subsequent to the day appointed for the payment thereof, and afterwards from time to time, so long as may be necessary. At the time appointed by any such adjournment or upon a motion to enforce payment of a call duly served and upon proof of the service of the order and notice of the amount due and non-payment, an order may be made that such of the contributories who have made default or that such of them against whom it shall be thought proper to make such an order, do pay the sum which by such former order and notice they were respectively required to pay, or any less sum which may appear to be due from them respectively.'

---

60 Section 210(1) of the CA 1963.

61 Section 211(a) of the CA 1963.

Chapter 32

Prospectus, Market Abuse and Transparency Law

Introduction

[32.001] When companies require large amounts of capital to expand their operations it will usually be necessary for them to make an offering of shares or securities to the public and to have the shares publicly marketed and traded, or 'quoted,' on a stock exchange. Companies which reach this stage will normally already have a history of successful trading, having grown with the benefit of venture capital from a variety of sources[1]. Apart from the prospect of raising capital immediately, stock exchange listing improves the liquidity of the shares by providing a ready market for them; this should make them more attractive to buyers, with the consequence that subsequent offerings can be made by the company over time. Likewise, the potential for increased attractiveness of the company's shares means that the company can make share-for-share take-over bids to the shareholders of other companies, thus enabling the company to grow by acquisition.

Such access to potential riches comes at a price. Where a company's shares are traded on a stock exchange, market disciplines will apply – shareholdings will become widely held and dispersed, which carries with it the risk of hostile take-over bids, particularly if the company is seen to be performing worse than similar companies or competitors. The founding entrepreneurs may find their influence and control diminishes substantially as their controlling shareholding is diluted; power struggles and boardroom coups are not at all uncommon. Moreover, having one's shares traded on the stock exchange brings with it increased monitoring, by the exchange itself and by the financial press, and nowadays by the Central Bank, as well as 'comply or explain' adherence to the corporate governance code[2], and substantial disclosure and reporting obligations on a continued basis – with heavy sanctions for failure to comply[3].

[32.002] Much of the disclosure and monitoring regime associated with publicly quoted shares and securities exists because of the age old concern that investors should not be

§ *This chapter has been contributed by G Brian Hutchinson.*

1 Investment companies, by way of contrast, commonly come straight to market. Occasionally trading companies follow suit; a famous example is the Eurotunnel Group SA which raised substantial sums of money (£976m) in advance for the Channel Tunnel project by means of stock exchange flotations in London and Paris in the late 1980s.

2 See Ch 29, *Public Limited Companies and SEs*, at para **[29.087]**.

3 See, for example, the liability and sanctions that can arise for breach of the Prospectus Directive, at para **[32.044]** *post*.

misled or deceived[4]; and the corollary that shareholders will feel more confident investing in companies about which they have maximum information. In the latter regard, the EU has been of paramount influence in the last 10 years and most of the legislation on publication and disclosure, as well as the legislation protecting investors from market abuse, now emanates from Europe as the EU strides towards a common market in financial services. Between 1999 and 2005 the EU undertook a range of measures[5] to implement its *Financial Services Action Plan*[6] ('FSAP') to fill gaps and remove remaining barriers so as to provide a legal and regulatory environment supporting the integration of EU financial markets. The FSAP focuses on harmonising a number of areas, ranging from securities issuance and trading, to accounting, to insurance, to long term savings, and to money laundering, to name but a few. But in the context of public offerings of shares it is the reforms in the area of issuance and trading of securities which are of most concern to this chapter.

[32.003] The Irish Stock Exchange ('ISE') is Ireland's only stock exchange and has been in existence since 1793[7]. It is a private company limited by guarantee and owned by Irish stockbrokers. In the years between 1973 and 1999 it was merged with what is now the London Stock Exchange, but since 1999 it has operated independently. It is the recognised stock exchange for the purpose of Part V of the CA 1990[8]. The ISE operates three markets – the Main Securities Market (MSM), the Global Exchange Market (GEM) and the Enterprise Securities Market (ESM). The MSM is the principal market for both Irish and foreign companies, and it admits a range of securities, both equity and non-equity, to listing and trading. The GEM, launched in 2009 to replace the Alternative Securities Market, is a specialist market for debt and derivative securities and is aimed towards professional investors. The ESM, formerly known as the Irish Enterprise Exchange, is an equities market geared towards smaller and medium-sized companies which are aiming to grow.

---

4 For a succinct and lucid history see Horan, *Corporate Crime* (2011, Bloomsbury Professional) Ch 15.

5 A key feature of the EU reforms is the so-called 'Lamfalussy' process which was launched in 2001 for the purpose of strengthening the European regulatory and financial sector supervision framework. It consists of four levels of action, starting with the adoption of the framework legislation by means of directive (Level 1) and detailed implementing measures by means of regulation (Level 2). For the technical preparation of the implementing measures, the Commission is advised by committees, made up of representatives of national supervisory bodies, which exist in three sectors: banking; insurance and occupational pensions; and the securities markets. These committees then contribute to the consistent implementation of Community directives in the Member States, ensuring effective cooperation between the supervisory authorities and convergence of their practices (Level 3). Finally, the Commission enforces the timely and correct transposition of EU legislation into national law (Level 4). Since January 1 2011, the system of Level 3 committees has been replaced by a system of supervisory bodies, including ESMA – see para **[32.008]** *post*.

6 Full details of the Financial Services Action Plan (FSAP) are available on the Commission's website at ec.europa.eu/internal_market/finances/actionplan/index_en.htm. In June 2010, the Commission published a package of reforms in a communication entitled 'Regulating Financial Services for Sustainable Growth'.

7 See the Irish Stock Exchange website at www.ise.ie.

8 Companies (Stock Exchange) Regulations 1995 (SI 310/1995).

'Regulated market' defined

[32.004] The MSM is a 'regulated market' as defined in the Markets in Financial Instruments Directive (2004/39/EC) ('MIFID')[9] and as such it comes within the purview of the Prospectus, Market Abuse and Transparency Directives considered in further depth in this chapter. By way of contrast the GEM and ESM are not regulated markets but rather are designated Multilateral Trading Facilities (MTFs) and as such fall outside the provisions of the Directives insofar as they apply to regulated markets, but the ISE's '*Global Exchange Markets Listing and Admission to Trading Rules*' and the '*ESM Rules for Companies*' contain many requirements similar to those of the Directives, especially with regard to prospectuses. Moreover, there are proposals at EU level to extend the Market Abuse Directive to MTFs[10].

It is important to bear in mind that in the main the provisions of this chapter apply only to Irish companies that have securities traded on a regulated market within the EU/EEA. An Irish company with securities traded on a US exchange or other exchange outside of the EU/EEA will not be subject to the prospectus, market abuse or transparency regimes.

[32.005] Three aspects of the regulatory regime governing the issuance and trading of securities – relating to prospectuses, market abuse, and transparency law – are the focus of this chapter and are treated below as follows:

[A] Prospectuses;

[B] Market Abuse;

[C] Transparency Law.

[A] PROSPECTUSES

Introduction

[32.006] The advertising of shares to the public is commonly achieved by the issuing of a *prospectus*. Because of the potential for abuse of investors, both small and large, the legislature, the common law and the stock exchange, and more recently the EU, have all variously sought to regulate the issuing of shares to the investing public. Although it is possible for a public company to sell its shares directly to the investing public, it will rarely make sense to do so without selling its shares through the stock exchange and

9 The Prospectus Directive provides in art 2 that 'regulated market' shall have the meaning given to it in art 1(13) of Directive 93/22/EC, the Investment Services Directive. That directive was repealed by MIFID in 2004. Article 69 of MIFID provides that: 'References to terms defined in, or Articles of, Directive 93/22/EEC shall be construed as references to the equivalent term defined in, or Article of, this Directive.' Thus, 'regulated market' for the purposes of the Prospectus Directive (and the Market Abuse and Transparency Directives) is now defined by art 4(2)(14) of MIFID as '... a multilateral system operated and/or managed by a market operator, which brings together or facilitates the bringing together of multiple third-party buying and selling interests in financial instruments – in the system and in accordance with its nondiscretionary rules – in a way that results in a contract, in respect of the financial instruments admitted to trading under its rules and/or systems, and which is authorised and functions regularly and in accordance with the provisions of Title III'.

10 See para **[32.060]** *post*.

floating the company in this way. The flotation of a public company may be effected in, or in a combination of, any of the following ways[11]:

- *offer for sale* to the public, achieved by the sale of all shares to an 'issuing house', which will endeavour to sell on the shares to the investing public;
- *placing* the shares by offering them for sale to an issuing house, which will try to place them with an institutional investor;
- *sale by tender* where the shares are set at a minimum price and offered for sale;
- *rights issue*, where an existing public company raises additional capital through a fresh allotment of shares to existing members.

[32.007] A prospectus is a disclosure document, relating key financial and non-financial information about a company, which the company makes available to potential investors when it is offering securities (shares, bonds, derivative securities, etc) to the public to raise capital, or when it wants its securities admitted to trading on a regulated market. The regulation of prospectuses and the obligation to publish a prospectus was once a domestic affair; the Companies Act 1963 ('CA 1963'), for example, prescribed a range of requirements, now mostly repealed, with regard to the obligation to publish a prospectus when shares were offered to the public[12] and with regard to the information to be supplied in a prospectus[13]. Nowadays, the area is substantially influenced by EU legislation imposing common requirements across the EU and EEA Member States. With the adoption of the Prospectus Directive[14] there is now uniformity as to when a prospectus is required and what it must contain, namely:[15]

> 'all information which, according to the particular nature of the issuer and of the securities offered to the public or admitted to trading on a regulated market, is necessary to enable investors to make an informed assessment of the assets and liabilities, financial position, profit and losses, and prospects of the issuer and of any guarantor, and of the rights attaching to such securities. The information must be presented in an easily analysable and comprehensible form.'

That was generally already the case under domestic law in many Member States, but it remained open to Member States to require *other* information to be included in the prospectus with the consequence that mutual recognition of prospectuses, though expected by law, was very difficult in practice (and often subject to subjective interpretation by the authorities in some Member States). Nowadays, regional variations are avoided by the requirement that prospectuses adhere to a standard set of requirements as to content and form; and approval, once given in the home state, holds good across all Member States.

Sources of law on prospectuses

[32.008] The creation of a common regime regarding prospectuses was a cornerstone of the EU FSAP so far as it concerned the issuance and trading of securities. The

---

11 See Keane, *Company Law* (4th edn, Bloomsbury Professional, 2007), p 89.

12 Section 44(3) of the CA 1963.

13 Schedule 3 to the CA 1963.

14 See para **[32.008]** *post*.

15 Article 5(1) of the Prospectus Directive; see para **[32.029]** *post*.

prospectus regime, consequent to the Lamfalussy procedure, is achieved through a number of measures:

- The *Prospectus Directive*: the Level 1 Lamfalussy measure in this regard is the Prospectus Directive[16], which came into effect on 31 December 2003 and was required to be implemented in all Member States by 1 July 2005. It was recently amended by the Prospectus Directive Amending Directive which took effect across Member States on 1 July 2012[17]. The Prospectus Directive itself amended the Consolidated Admissions and Reporting Directive[18]. The Prospectus Directive is implemented in Ireland by the Prospectus (Directive 2003/71) Regulations 2005[19] ('P(D)R 2005') as amended by the Prospectus (Directive 2003/71/EC) (Amendment) Regulations 2012[20] ('P(D)(A)R 2012') and also by Part 5 of the IFCMPA 2005 which repeals[21] the provisions of the CA 1963 dealing with prospectuses and their contents and which confers powers on the Central Bank as the competent authority for scrutinising and approving prospectuses.
- The *Prospectus Regulation*: the Level 2 Lamfalussy measure which prescribes the detailed technical requirements in respect of prospectuses is the Prospectus Regulation[22]. The Prospectus Regulation became directly applicable in Member States on 1 July 2005. A detailed document, the English text being some 187 pages, people across Europe have literally made careers out of being expert in its requirements. It was amended on 30 March 2012 by Commission Delegated Regulation No 406/2012 (also having direct effect) which made changes as regards the format and the content of the prospectus, the base prospectus, the summary and the final terms, and as regards disclosure requirements. A second amending regulation, of 4 June 2012, has yet to take effect in Ireland and other Member States pending approval by the European Parliament and Council. It deals with information on the consent to use the prospectus, information on the underlying indexes, and the requirement for a report produced by independent accountants or auditors.
- *Guideline Measures*: ESMA, the European Securities and Markets Authority (formerly known as CESR – the Committee of European Securities Regulators), plays a pivotal role in advising the EU Commission on the shape of the prospectus amendments and the issuing public at large on the application of the Directive and Regulation. It has been involved in coordinating a range of Lamfalussy Level 3 guideline measures, including *Recommendations for the consistent implementation of the Prospectus Regulation*, and a catalogue of common questions and answers about prospectuses entitled *Frequently asked questions regarding Prospectuses: Common positions agreed by ESMA*

16 2003/71/EC.

17 2010/73/EU.

18 2001/34/EC.

19 SI 324/2005.

20 SI 239/2012.

21 Section 40 of the IFCMPA 2005 repeals ss 40–47, 49, 52, 54, 56, 59, 60(15B) and (15c), 61, and 361–367 and the Third and Fourth Schedules of the CA 1963.

22 Commission Regulation (EC) 809/2004 ([2004] OJ L149/1).

Members[23]. In a somewhat similar vein, the Central Bank of Ireland produced in 2011 a *Prospectus Handbook: A Guide to Prospectus Approval in Ireland* (2011) which incorporates the *Prospectus Rules* issued by the Bank under the IFCMPA 2005 and which improves the accessibility of the regime to those wishing to avail of it. The Central Bank also publishes approved prospectuses on its website.

Key features of the EU prospectus regime

[32.009] The key features of the Prospectus Directive regime may be considered briefly here by way of introduction. At the heart of the regime is an EEA-wide requirement to produce a prospectus whenever securities are offered to the public or admitted to trading on a regulated market. The Directive imposes a common definition of what is meant by 'offer to the public' and clarifies the situations in which a prospectus is either required or exempt.

A second key feature is the single regime governing content, format, approval and publication of prospectuses. Previous EU legislation relating to listing and public offers had provided for mutual recognition of prospectuses in different states but with limited success; now, the Prospectus Regulation strives to achieve a common format for prospectuses by heavily prescribing the form and content of the prospectus across Europe. Once drawn up, a prospectus has to be reviewed and approved by the competent authority (in Ireland, the Central Bank) of the issuer's 'home Member State' before the prospectus is issued. The home Member State is typically the state in which the issuer has its registered office, but there are different rules for certain non-equity securities and for issuers who are incorporated outside the EEA[24].

A third feature of the Prospectus Directive regime is the 'single-passport' procedure, whereby prospectuses approved in one Member State are automatically eligible to be issued or 'passported' into another Member State without having to be re-subjected to approval in the 'host Member State' (ie, the state in which the securities are offered or where admission to trading is sought)[25], so that issuers can in principle raise capital across Europe on the basis of a single prospectus.

Scope of the Prospectus Directive

[32.010] The Prospectus Directive imposes a general EEA-wide obligation to produce a prospectus in particular circumstances. Under Article 3 of the Prospectus Directive, a prospectus is required to be drawn up, approved and published whenever:

- securities are offered to the public;[26] or
- securities are admitted to trading on a regulated market[27].

The Directive overrides any local rules regarding prospectuses (or lack thereof) in the Member States in the above circumstances. The Directive does *not* apply to issues outside of the above circumstances, eg, where the offer is not being made to *the public*,

---

23 See the ESMA website at www.esma.europa.eu.

24 Article 2(1)(m) of the Prospectus Directive.

25 Article 2(1)(n) of the Prospectus Directive.

26 Article 3(1) of the Prospectus Directive.

27 Article 3(3) of the Prospectus Directive.

or where admission is not being sought on a *regulated market*, or where the instruments being offered for sale are not *securities* within the meaning of the Directive. In such circumstances, Member States may make or retain their own rules.

[32.011] As regards securities covered by the Prospectus Directive, the definition is taken from the definition of 'transferable securities' in the Investment Services Directive (93/22/EC), which provides as follows:

> '"Transferable securities" shall mean:
>
> (a) shares in companies and other securities equivalent to shares in companies,
>
> (b) bonds and other forms of securitised debt which are negotiable on the capital market and
>
> (c) any other securities normally dealt in giving the right to acquire any such transferable securities by subscription or exchange or giving rise to a cash settlement excluding instruments of payment.'

It is of note that the Investment Services Directive has since been superseded by the MIFID which gives a broader definition of transferable securities but which is not applicable to the Prospectus Directive; there is substantial overlap but potential room for divergence. In any event it may be noted that the Prospectus Directive applies both to equity and non-equity securities, but money market instruments with a maturity of less than 12 months are expressly excluded.

[32.012] Article 1.2 of Prospectus Directive, as amended, and Part 2 of the P(D)R 2005, as amended, implementing the Directive, list a number of types of securities that are specifically outside the scope of the Prospectus Directive. Securities issued or guaranteed by Member States or their local or regional governments, securities issued by certain non-profit making bodies are excluded, as are continuous or repeated issues of non-equity securities by credit institutions where the total consideration of the offer in the EU is less than €75 million.

[32.013] Of most significance to the general body of issuers is the exclusion of securities in an offer where the total consideration payable in respect of the offer across the EEA for those securities is less than €5 million calculated over a 12-month period[28] – so there is no need for a prospectus in EU law if the total issue is to raise less than €5 million by way of public offering[29]. This is above the thresholds for the Irish Revenue Commissioners' approved Business Expansion Schemes, or BES, which are thus outside the scope of the Prospectus Directive, though, of course, subject to their own publication requirements. Securities issued by open-ended collective investment funds are also expressly excluded, though again they are subject to their own special requirements. Section 49 of the IFCMPA 2005 requires the offer document to provide a series of specified warnings and the offer document must be filed with the CRO. Moreover, ESMA has expressed the opinion in *Guidance from the Committee of European*

---

28 Article 1(2)(h) of the Prospectus Directive as amended; reg 8(1)(h) of the P(D)R 2005 as amended.

29 According to ESMA, equity and debt securities should be considered separately for calculation of the limit. Also, offers made during a 12-month period which qualify for other exemptions (such as offers to qualified investors) or where a prospectus has already been registered should not be taken into account for the calculation of the limit.

Securities Regulators[30] that non-transferable employee share options do *not* constitute securities, and accordingly do not fall under the Prospectus Directive.

[32.014] Though the securities listed in the preceding paragraph are outside the scope of the Prospectus Directive, art 1(3) of the Directive clarifies that an issuer may still, should it so wish, issue a prospectus when making a public offer or when seeking admission to a regulated market.

[32.015] Having considered the circumstances in which the Prospectus Directive does not apply, we now turn to consider the circumstances in which it does apply, as follows:

1. Public offer of securities.
2. Offerings exempt from prospectus requirements.
3. Admission to trading on a regulated market.
4. Format and content of the prospectus.
5. Requirement for prospectus to contain a summary.
6. Approval and publication of a prospectus.
7. Passporting of prospectuses.
8. Languages used in prospectus.
9. Supplements to prospectuses.
10. Liability and sanctions for misstatements in prospectuses.

Public offer of securities

[32.016] Regulation 2(1) of the P(D)R 2005, implementing art 2.1(d) of the Prospectus Directive, provides:

> '"offer of securities to the public" or "public offer" means a communication to persons in any form and by any means, presenting sufficient information on the terms of the offer and the securities to be offered, so as to enable an investor to decide to purchase or subscribe for those securities or apply to purchase or subscribe for those securities and this definition shall be construed as—
>
> (a) being also applicable to the placing of securities through financial intermediaries, and
>
> (b) as not being applicable to trading on a regulated market or any other market operated by an approved stock exchange.'

Regulation 2(6) of the P(D)R 2005 adds:

> 'For the purpose of the definition of "offer of securities to the public" in this Regulation "communication" shall include an invitation to treat.'

The definition is very broad and encompasses most communications to more than one person providing sufficient details on the offer of securities to enable investors to make a decision as to whether to invest or not. It does not have to constitute an offer in the contractual sense, a mere invitation to treat will suffice. Note, however, that preliminary promotional material[31] which does not refer to the offer price or to the quantum of securities to be issued is unlikely to enable investors to decide whether to invest and

---

30 CESR, 18 July 2006, Ref CESR/06-296d.

31 Including so-called *red-herring* prospectuses common in the US – these are preliminary prospectuses labelled as such with a warning on their cover in red.

therefore would not in principle be governed by the Directive – though in due course it should be followed with a prospectus.

[32.017] A notable feature of the definition of public offer in the Directive is that it places no emphasis at all on the notion of whether the recipient is a member of the public, as opposed to someone of domestic concern or internal to the issuer. In this regard the Prospectus Directive eschews the old common law concern[32] with such matters, illustrated in *Shwernell v Combined Incandescent Mantles Syndicate*[33] where an invitation to a few friends of the directors was held not to be 'an issue to the public'. In *Nash v Lynde*[34], the directors of a private company prepared a document which was in the form of a general offer for shares. It was not advertised, but a copy was shown to one person with a view to his subscribing to the company and becoming a director. It was held by the House of Lords that the document was not issued to the public as a prospectus, Lord Sumner holding:

> '"The Public" in the definition section ... is of course a general word. No particular numbers are prescribed. Anything from two to infinity may serve; perhaps even one, if he is intended to be the first of a series of subscribers but makes further proceedings needless by himself subscribing the whole. The point is that the offer is such as to be open to anyone who brings his money and applies in due form, whether the prospectus was addressed to him on behalf of the company or not. A private communication is thus not open ... [to being deemed to be made to the public].'

By way of contrast, all that is required by the Prospectus Directive is that the offer is made to 'persons', plural, regardless of who they might be.

Offerings exempt from prospectus requirements

[32.018] Article 3 of the Prospectus Directive, as amended, exempts a number of public offerings from the requirement to produce a prospectus[35]:

- offers made exclusively to qualified investors[36];
- offers made to less than 150 persons per Member State (apart from qualified investors);
- offers where the minimum consideration payable per investor is at least €100,000;
- offers of securities having a denomination per-unit of at least €100,000;
- offers where the total consideration of securities offered within the territory of the Member State is less than €100,000, calculated over a 12-month period.
- subsequent onwards offers of sale to the public by financial intermediaries (known as 'retail cascade') where there has already been a valid prospectus and

[32] See also *Re South of England Natural Gas and Petroleum Co Ltd* [1911] 1 Ch 573 and generally Eaton, 'Implementing the Prospectus Directive' (2006) 1 CLP 8.

[33] *Shwernell v Combined Incandescent Mantles Syndicate* [1907] WN 110.

[34] *Nash v Lynde* [1929] AC 158.

[35] Article 3(2) of the Prospectus Directive as amended. Regulation 9(1) of the P(D)R 2005 as amended.

[36] See para **[32.020]** *post.*

the person originally responsible for drawing it up consents to its being used again.

However, any subsequent resale of securities which were previously the subject of one or more of the types of offer listed above is to be regarded as a separate offer and capable of constituting an offer of securities to the public. The placement of securities through financial intermediaries is also subject to publication of a prospectus if none of the conditions listed above is met for the final placement.

A company wishing to avail of these exemptions does not have to seek prior agreement of the Central Bank – the onus is on the company to satisfy itself of its entitlement to the exemption. It may be noted, however, that these exclusions relate to only public offers, not to admissions to trading on a regulated market or any other market operated by an approved stock exchange[37].

[32.019] In addition, art 4 of the Prospectus Directive exempts certain other offerings by reason of the nature of the security type, rather than by reason of the nature of the addressees of the offer. Next we consider:

(a) Offers to qualified investors; and
(b) Offers of exempted securities; and
(a) Offers to qualified investors.

(a) Offers to qualified investors

[32.020] A prospectus is not required where securities are offered in a public offering exclusively to qualified investors, who are essentially professionals or seasoned players. The Prospectus Directive Amendment Directive, implemented in Ireland by the P(D)(D)R 2012[38], amends the definition of qualified investor in the Prospectus Directive to align it with the professional client or eligible counterparty definition in the Markets in Financial Instruments Directive (2004/39/EC) ('MIFID'). This has the advantage that issuers will now have to have regard only to the MIFID when structuring offerings of securities. Accordingly 'qualified investor' now automatically includes[39]:

> '(1) Entities which are required to be authorised or regulated to operate in the financial markets. The list below should be understood as including all authorised entities carrying out the characteristic activities of the entities mentioned: entities authorised by a Member State under a Directive, entities authorise or regulated by a Member State without reference to a Directive, and entities authorised or regulated by a non-Member State:
>
> (a) Credit institutions
> (b) Investment firms
> (c) Other authorised or regulated financial institutions
> (d) Insurance companies
> (e) Collective investment schemes and management companies of such schemes
> (f) Pension funds and management companies of such funds
> (g) Commodity and commodity derivatives dealers

---

37 Regulation 2(1) of the P(D)R 2005. As to the (broadly similar) exemptions when admission is sought to a regulated market, etc, see para **[32.026]** *post*.

38 SI 317/2012.

39 Annexe I of the MIFID.

(h) Locals

(i) Other institutional investors.

(2) Large undertakings meeting two of the following size requirements on a company basis:

– balance sheet total: €20,000,000,

– net turnover: €40,000,000,

– own funds: €2,000,000.

(3) National and regional governments, public bodies that manage public debt, Central Banks, international and supranational institutions such as the World Bank, the IMF, the ECB, the EIB and other similar international organisations.

(4) Other institutional investors whose main activity is to invest in financial instruments, including entities dedicated to the securitisation of assets or other financing transactions.'

[32.021] 'Eligible counterparties' within the meaning of art 24 of the MIFID are also automatically included in the definition of qualified investor. These include investment firms, credit institutions, insurance companies, UCITS and their management companies, pension funds and their management companies, other financial institutions authorised or regulated under Community legislation or the national law of a Member State, MIFID exempted undertakings, national governments and their corresponding offices including public bodies that deal with public debt, central banks and supranational organisations.

[32.022] In addition to the above categories of entity which are automatically recognised as qualified investors, it is possible for individuals and legal entities to apply for recognition as a qualified investor and to join a qualified investor list maintained by the competent authorities. The Prospectus Directive Amendment Directive follows the MIFID by allowing Member States to recognise those who meet the requirements of professional investors within the meaning of Annexe II to the Schedule of the MIFID to apply to be recognised as qualified investors. The thresholds for recognition of individuals are broadly the same as those prescribed by the Prospectus Directive prior to amendment; two of the following three criteria must be satisfied:

– the investor has carried out transactions of a significant size on securities markets at an average frequency of, at least, 10 per quarter over the previous four quarters;

– the size of the investor's securities portfolio exceeds €500,000;

– the investor works or has worked for at least one year in the financial sector in a professional position which requires knowledge of securities investment.

(b) Offers of exempted securities

[32.023] Article 4 of the Prospectus Directive, as amended, further exempts public offerings of certain types of securities from the requirement of having to produce a prospectus. The list includes[40]:

---

40 Article 4(1) of the Prospectus Directive; reg 10 of the P(D)R 2005.

- securities offered in connection with a takeover by means of an exchange offer which is regarded by the Central Bank as being equivalent to that of a prospectus;
- bonus issues and scrip dividends;
- employee share schemes provided the shares are of the same class already listed on a regulated market or a market for which the Commission has adopted an equivalence decision.

[32.024] Rights issues are *not* excluded and so a rights issue will also require a prospectus unless it comes under some other exemption.

Admission to trading on a regulated market

[32.025] A prospectus will also be required where securities are admitted to trading on a regulated market[41]. Markets which are not 'regulated markets' fall outside the scope of the requirement and may make their own rules – see, for example, the *ESM Rules for Companies*[42]. Where the home Member State is Ireland the prospectus must be approved by the Central Bank[43]; where Ireland is a host state then no offer of the securities may be made to the public within the State without the publication of a prospectus pursuant to the applicable provisions of the EU prospectus law[44] that, in respect of the offer, has been approved by the home Member State.

[32.026] Though the exemptions discussed above in respect of public offerings do not apply to admissions to trading, art 4(2) of the Prospectus Directive sets out almost identical and additional exemptions which apply when seeking admission to trading on a regulated market. These include admissions of shares representing, over a period of 12 months, less than 10% of the number of shares of the same class already admitted to the same regulated market; securities already admitted to trading on another regulated market, subject to certain conditions; securities offered in connection with takeovers in certain circumstances; and securities offered, allotted or to be allotted in connection with a merger in certain circumstances[45]. Shares that are also the subject of a public offer will not benefit from exemption unless another exemption applies.

[32.027] The 'wholesale debt' exemption – ie, where debt securities are issued in denominations of greater than €100,000 each – which applies in the case of public offerings[46] does not apply similarly to admissions to trading on EU or EEA stock

---

41 Article 3(3) of the Prospectus Directive; reg 13 of the P(D)R 2005. As to the meaning of regulated market, see para **[32.004]** *ante*.

42 Available on the Irish Stock Exchange website at www.ise.ie.

43 Regulation 13 of the P(D)R 2005.

44 EU prospectus law is defined by s 38(1) of the IFCMPA 2005 as '(a) the measures adopted for the time being by a Member State (including the State) or a Member State of the EEA to implement the Prospectus Directive 2003 or (b) any measures directly applicable in consequence of the Prospectus Directive 2003 and, without prejudice to the generality of this paragraph, includes the Prospectus Regulation, and (c) any supplementary and consequential measures adopted for the time being by a Member State (including the State) or a Member State of the EEA in respect of the Prospectus Regulation.'

45 Regulation 11 of the P(D)R 2005.

46 See para **[32.018]** *ante*.

exchanges. Such issuers can, however, rely on the 'lighter' prospectus requirements in Annexes IX and XIII of the Prospectus Regulation.

Format and content of the prospectus

[32.028] The form and content of a prospectus must comply with the requirements of the Prospectus Directive and the Prospectus Regulation[47], the latter a detailed and lengthy instrument requiring interpretative guidance from the ESMA, the realm of professional specialists, of whom many excellent examples are to be found in Irish legal and regulatory practice. It is not feasible here to give any more than a brief summary of the requirements[48].

[32.029] As regards format, the Prospectus Directive, as amended, requires the prospectus to conform to one of the following formats:[49]

- a single standalone document; or
- a tri-partite document comprising a registration document, a securities note and, where the minimum denomination of the securities is less than €100,000, a summary; or
- a base prospectus and subsequent final terms; or
- a single standalone document which incorporates by reference all or part of a base prospectus (commonly known as a 'drawdown prospectus').

[32.030] The tri-partite document approach can be used to facilitate shelf-registration, since the registration document remains valid for a period of 12 months[50] and can be used with a new securities note and summary note for any new issues during that period. In practice, shelf-registration can be used for rights issues, and by keeping a registration document current and in place a company will be in a position to bring securities to market quickly.

[32.031] A *base prospectus* may be issued for non-equity securities issued under an offering programme (ie, a programme for the continuous or a repeated offering of non-equity securities of a broadly similar type or class over a specified period). The base prospectus must contain all relevant information about the issuer and the securities but can be supplemented by filing the final terms of particular issues with the competent authority without the need for any further approval[51]. Recital 7 of Commission Delegated Regulation 486/2012/EU states that:

> 'the final terms should not amend or replace any information contained in the base prospectus as any new information which may affect the investor's assessment of the issuer and of the securities is to be included in a supplement or a new base prospectus, which is subject to prior approval by the competent authority. Accordingly, the final terms

---

47 Commission Regulation EC No 809/2001 of 29 April 2004.

48 An authoritative and accessible guide is to be found in Section 1 of the Central Bank's *Prospectus Handbook: A Guide to Prospectus Approval in Ireland* which is available to download on the Bank's website at www.centralbank.ie.

49 Articles 5(3) and 5(4) of the Prospectus Directive; regs 21(4), 22(1) of the P(D)R 2005.

50 Article 9 of the Prospectus Directive; reg 30 of the P(D)R 2005.

51 Article 5(4) of the Prospectus Directive.

should not include any new description of any new payment conditions which was not included in the base prospectus.'

The Delegated Regulation introduces a new annex to the Prospectus Regulation which groups the information requirements set out in the existing annexes of the Prospectus Regulation into categories 'A', 'B' and 'C' to clarify and delimit exactly what type of information is eligible to be included in the final terms. ESMA has recently published guidance in relation to these changes which includes examples of final terms incorporating some of the changes.

Requirement for prospectus to contain a summary

[32.032] The prospectus must contain a *summary* which in a brief and non-technical manner conveys the essential characteristics and risks associated with the issuer and any guarantor, and the securities themselves. The requirements as to format and content of the summary have been changed by the Amending Directive and the P(D)(A)R 2012. The summary must contain 'key information' including:

- a short description of the risks associated with the essential characteristics of the issuer, guarantor and securities;
- the general terms of the offer;
- details of admission to trading; and
- reasons for the offer and use of proceeds.

[32.033] The amended requirements stipulate a standard format for summaries in order to facilitate comparability of the summaries of similar securities. Detailed requirements in relation to the format of the summary and key information are set out in Commission Delegated Regulation 486/2012/EU. In particular, the delegated regulation amends art 24 of the Prospectus Regulation, so that a summary must contain tables titled as follows:

A. Introduction and Warnings,
B. Issuer and any Guarantor,
C. Securities,
D. Risks, and
E. Offer.

Each table must list out 'elements' of such key information in a prescribed order, and irrelevant elements must be labelled 'non-applicable' rather than be omitted. The length of the summary is also rigidly prescribed by the Delegated Regulation, which states that it must not exceed 7% of the length of the prospectus, or 15 pages, whichever is longer[52]. The summary must be a standalone document and it must not contain cross-references to other parts of the prospectus.

The warnings on the face of the summary must state[53]:

- [this] summary should be read as introduction to the prospectus;
- any decision to invest in the securities should be based on consideration of the prospectus as a whole by the investor;

---

52 15 pages would be quite an achievement given that the blank summary in Commission Delegated Regulation 486/2012/EU runs to 7½ pages before any information is filled in.

53 Annex, Commission Delegated Regulation 486/2012/EU, adding a new Annex XXII to the Prospectus Regulation.

- where a claim relating to the information contained in [the] prospectus is brought before a court, the plaintiff investor might, under the national legislation of the Member States, have to bear the costs of translating the prospectus before the legal proceedings are initiated; and
- civil liability attaches only to those persons who have tabled the summary including any translation thereof, but only if the summary is misleading, inaccurate or inconsistent when read together with the other parts of the prospectus or it does not provide, when read together with the other parts of the prospectus, key information in order to aid investors when considering whether to invest in such securities.'

[32.034] Issuers of wholesale debt in denominations above €100,000 do not have to produce a summary unless requested to do so by a competent authority in a Member State[54].

[32.035] As regards content, the requirements are legion, but the fundamental requirement is that the prospectus should contain all the information which is necessary to enable an investor to make an informed assessment of the assets and liabilities, financial position, profit and losses and prospects of the issuer and the rights attached to the securities[55]. A list of the minimum information required is listed in art 7 of the Prospectus Directive. All issuers, EU and non-EU, must include in the prospectus IAS accounts or accounts reconciled, restated or equivalent to IAS.

Approval and publication of a prospectus

[32.036] Every prospectus is required to be approved in advance of publication by the competent authority of the home Member State of the issuer, which, in Ireland, is the Central Bank of Ireland. Article 13 of the Prospectus Directive provides for time limits of between 10 and 20 working days depending on the circumstances, within which the competent authority is to approve or reject the prospectus, as the case may be.

[32.037] Article 14 of the Prospectus Directive, as amended, provides issuers, offerors and persons seeking admission to trading with a choice of publication methods:

- insertion in one or more newspapers widely circulated in the Member States in which the offer or listing is made;
- in printed form at the offices of the market in which the securities are to be listed or at the registered office of the issuer and at the offices of the financial intermediaries placing or selling the securities including paying agents;
- in electronic form on the issuer's website (or, if applicable, on the website of the financial intermediaries placing or selling the securities);
- in electronic form on the website of the regulated market where the admission to trading is sought; or
- in electronic form on the website of the competent authority of the home Member State if the said authority has decided to offer this service.

Investors have the right to receive a hard copy of the prospectus free of charge where it has been made available in electronic form.

---

54 Article 5(2) of the Prospectus Directive.

55 Article 5(1) of the Prospectus Directive.

[32.038] Article 15 of the Prospectus Directive, as implemented by Part 12 of the P(D)R 2005, establishes principles in relation to advertising and promotional activity concerning public offers or admissions to trading. Advertisements must comply with the principles set out in Sch 2 of the P(D)R 2005. Advertisements must state that the prospectus has been or will be published, and must be clearly recognisable as advertisements and the information contained in them must not be inaccurate or misleading. All advertised information, including information disclosed orally, must be consistent with that contained in the prospectus. Any material information selectively disclosed to a selected group of investors must be included in the prospectus. Where, however, a prospectus is not required under the Prospectus Directive then the selective disclosure of material information to particular qualified investors or to special categories of investors is prohibited – any such information must be disclosed to all qualified investors or special categories of investors to whom the offer is addressed[56].

[32.039] The annual information requirement imposed by art 10 of the Prospectus Directive, whereby issuers had to prepare and file annual information documents with the competent authority, detailing all information made available by the issuer in the preceding 12 months, has been abolished by the Amending Directive.

Passporting of prospectuses

[32.040] Chapter IV of the Prospectus Directive, as implemented in Ireland by Part 9 of the P(D)R 2005, provides for the 'passporting' of prospectuses and sets out the procedures for cross-border offers and admissions to trading. A prospectus approved by the competent authority in the home Member State can be used as a prospectus in all of the Member States of the EU and the EEA without the requirement for further approvals or administrative procedures in other Member States. There is, however, a requirement to notify the competent authority in each Member State where the offer or admission is to be made.

The concept of home Member State is determined by the following principles set out in art 2(1)(m) of the Prospectus Directive:

- for EU and EEA incorporated bodies the home Member State is the Member State where that body has its registered office;
- for bodies incorporated outside the EU or the EEA the home Member State will be the Member State where the securities were or are offered to the public for the first time after 31 December 2003 or where the first application for admission to trading on a regulated market is made;
- separate rules determine the home Member State in respect of non-equity securities whose denomination per unit amounts to at least €1,000 and certain other kinds of non-equity securities.

Languages used in prospectuses

[32.041] Chapter V of the Prospectus Directive contains detailed rules governing the use of languages in which the prospectus is required to be drawn up and published. Generally speaking, the language of the home state must be used, and the host state can

56 Article 15(5) of the Prospectus Directive.

only require that the summary[57] – and not the entire document – shall be translated into the local official language.

Supplements to prospectuses

[32.042] Any significant new fact or mistake or inaccuracy relating to information in a prospectus and which is capable of influencing the assessment of the securities and which emerges between the time when the prospectus is approved and the closing of the offer or the commencement of trading on a regulated market must be set out in a supplement to the prospectus. This supplement must be approved and published in the same manner as the original prospectus. Investors who agree to purchase or subscribe for the securities before the supplement is published shall have the right to withdraw their acceptances within a time limit to be prescribed by national implementing legislation[58].

Liability and sanctions for misstatements in prospectuses

[32.043] The requirements surrounding prospectuses and their contents are designed to ensure that investors are properly informed of the nature of their investments and the risks attaching. It will, therefore, come as no surprise to learn that severe civil, criminal and administrative sanctions can apply to those responsible for misstatements in prospectuses. Here, the following matters are considered:

(a) civil sanctions for false particulars;
(b) criminal liability relating to prospectuses;
(c) administrative sanctions.

(a) Civil sanctions for false particulars

[32.044] There exist three ways in which a misstatement in a prospectus can give rise to civil liability, each of which is considered in turn:

(i) Statutory liability;
(ii) Liability and remedies in equity;
(iii) Liability at common law.

(i) Statutory liability

[32.045] Prior to the implementation of the Prospectus Directive in Ireland a statutory right to compensation for untrue statements in a prospectus was given by s 49(1) of the CA 1963. That has been repealed and replaced by s 41 of the IFCMPA 2005 in broadly similar terms, but with the difference that unlike the old s 49 where liability could arise only in favour of those who subscribed for securities, liability under the new provision can arise in favour of persons acquiring the securities in a secondary market transaction. Moreover, unlike the old provision where liability could arise only in respect of an untrue statement in the prospectus, s 41 of the IFCMPA 2005 provides that liability can arise in respect of omissions of information required under the new prospectus legislation. Furthermore, in respect of equity securities, s 41 of the IFCMPA 2005 adds the company itself; an offeror in the case of secondary market transactions; any person

---

57 See para **[32.032]** *ante*.

58 Article 16 of the Prospectus Directive.

applying to have the securities admitted to trading; and any guarantor of the issue, to the list of responsible persons. In the case of non-equity securities, however, the list of responsible persons is shorter. The Prospectus Directive requires that the persons responsible under national legislation are to be clearly identified in the prospectus by their names and functions and the prospectus is to include a declaration by them that to the best of their knowledge, the information contained in the prospectus is in accordance with the facts and that the prospectus makes no omission likely to affect its import[59].

[32.046] Section 41 of the IFCMPA 2005 provides as follows:

> '(1) Subject to sections 42 and 43, the following persons shall be liable to pay compensation to all persons who acquire any securities on the faith of a prospectus for the loss or damage they may have sustained by reason of—
>
> (a) any untrue statement included therein, or
>
> (b) any omission of information required by EU prospectus law to be contained in the prospectus, namely—
>
> (i) the issuer who has issued the prospectus or on whose behalf the prospectus has been issued,
>
> (ii) the offeror of securities to which the prospectus relates,
>
> (iii) every person who has sought the admission of the securities to which the prospectus relates to trading on a regulated market,
>
> (iv) the guarantor of the issue of securities to which the prospectus relates,
>
> (v) every person who is a director of the issuer at the time of the issue of the prospectus,
>
> (vi) every person who has authorised himself or herself to be named and is named in the prospectus as a director of the issuer or as having agreed to become such a director either immediately or after an interval of time,
>
> (vii) every person being a promoter of the issuer,
>
> (viii) every person who has authorised the issue of the prospectus (not being the competent authority designated under Irish prospectus law).
>
> (2) In addition to the persons specified in subsection (1) as being liable in the circumstances there set out, an expert who has given the consent required by section 45 to the inclusion in a prospectus of a statement purporting to be made by him or her shall, subject to sections 42 and 43, be liable to pay compensation to all persons who acquire any securities on the faith of the prospectus for the loss or damage they may have sustained by reason of an untrue statement in the prospectus purporting to be made by him or her as an expert.'

Persons are not liable under s 41 of the IFCMPA 2005 where:

- they withdrew their consent to become directors;
- they withdrew their consent to the issue of the prospectus and where it was issued without their authority and consent[60];
- the prospectus was issued without their knowledge or consent and they gave reasonable public notice that it was issued without their consent or knowledge upon their becoming aware of its issue[61];

---

59 Article 6 of the Prospectus Directive.

60 Section 42(3)(a) of the IFCMPA 2005.

61 Section 42(3)(b) of the IFCMPA 2005.

- after the issue of the prospectus but before any allotment thereunder they withdrew their consent on becoming aware of any untrue statement contained therein and gave reasonable public notice of the withdrawal and the reason therefor[62];
- in respect of non-expert statements, they had reasonable grounds to believe and did believe that the statement was true[63];
- in respect of expert statements, the statement fairly represented the statement or copies of extracts from reports that were correct and fair copies of the report and they had reasonable grounds to believe that the expert was competent to make the statement and had given their consent which was not revoked[64]; or
- in respect of untrue statements made by official persons or contained in what purports to be a copy of or extract from a public official document, that it was a correct and fair representation of the statement or copy of or extract from the document[65].

However, the foregoing savers shall not apply in respect of an expert who authorised the issue of the prospectus in respect of an untrue statement purporting to be made by him as an expert[66]. Further savers from liability are contained in s 43 of the IFCMPA 2005 in respect only of non-equity funds.

(ii) Liability and remedies in equity

[32.047] Rescission of the contract of allotment of shares is available to an investor where he has been induced by a misstatement in a prospectus to enter into a contract of allotment. It is crucial to realise that the contract of allotment will not be void *ab initio*, but voidable at the instance of the duped investor. In this respect, the misstatement has the same effect as does a misrepresentation which induces a person to enter into any contract. As with a misrepresentation, rescission will not be permitted where *restitutio in integrum* is impossible[67]. In *Components Tube Co v Naylor*[68], O'Brien LCJ said:

> 'It appears to me to be one of the most elementary obligations of law as well as of morality that a prospectus, upon which the public are invited to buy, should be an honest and a candid one. When an invitation is held out to the public to buy on the faith of a prospectus, candour, entire candour, becomes an essential element of honesty.'

An example of a situation which may give rise to the rescission of a contract of allotment is provided by *Aaron's Reefs v Twiss*[69]. There, the prospectus of the company described a gold mine, the intended venture which the flotation was to finance, as being rich in gold. The existence of a contract between the company and its promoters, whereby the company would purchase the mine from the promoters, was disclosed.

---

62 Section 42(3)(c) of the IFCMPA 2005.

63 Section 42(3) (d)(i) of the IFCMPA 2005.

64 Section 42(3)(d)(ii) of the IFCMPA 2005.

65 Section 42(3)(d)(iii) of the IFCMPA 2005.

66 Section 42(4) of the IFCMPA 2005.

67 Such as where the company concerned has gone into liquidation: *Oakes v Turquand and Harding* (1867) LR 2 HL 325.

68 *Components Tube Co v Naylor* [1900] 2 IR 1.

69 *Aaron's Reefs v Twiss* [1895] 2 IR 207 (CA) and [1896] AC 273 (HL).

What was not disclosed, however, was that the proposed consideration would expend three quarters of the proposed outside public investment, leaving the company with very little working capital with which to undertake the business of mining[70]. The defendant subscribed for 100 shares in the company and subsequently the company made a call of four shillings per share. The defendant refused to pay this because of the company's poor performance, whereupon he was sued by the company. His defence was that he was fraudulently induced to enter the contract of allotment, and this succeeded, the court allowing him to rescind the contract.

(iii) Liability at common law

[32.048] An action for breach of contract may also be available to a person who has suffered as a result of a misstatement in a prospectus. It has been held that it is not open to a person who remains a member of the company to sue for breach of contract and recover compensation[71]. In such a case the disgruntled member should repudiate the shares, distance himself from the company and then sue for compensation for breach of contract[72].

[32.049] An action for damages for the tort of deceit may be appropriate where a person suffers loss or damage on account of a fraudulent misrepresentation in a prospectus made to him which induces him to enter into a contract for the allotment of shares. This action is open to a person while he is still a member of the company, unlike an action for damages for breach of contract. One of the most celebrated cases of an action for deceit is *Derry v Peek*[73]. There, the directors of a company issued a prospectus which led investors to believe that the company was empowered by statute to employ the use of automotive power to run the company's tramways, as opposed to the use of horses. Such authority was in fact solely dependent upon the fiat of the Board of Trade, which had not been granted. The plaintiff subscriber sued when the Board of Trade subsequently refused permission. However, because the directors honestly believed the contents of the prospectus, they were not liable in the tort of deceit. Lord Herschell stated:

> 'First, in order to sustain an action of deceit, there must be proof of fraud, and nothing short of that will suffice. Secondly, fraud is proved when it is shown that a false representation has been made (1) knowingly, or (2) without belief in its truth, or (3) recklessly, careless whether it be true or false[74].'

That case may be contrasted with *Jury v Stoker & Jackson*[75] where the plaintiff successfully recovered damages for deceit where it was proved that the directors fraudulently misrepresented in the prospectus that a particular individual would invest £7,500 in the company[76].

---

70 The modern prospectus requirements in Sch 3 of the CA 1963 and the Listings Directive would now require the detailed disclosure of all material terms of such a contract.

71 *Houldsworth v City of Glasgow Bank* (1880) 5 App Cas 317.

72 *Re Addlestone Linoleum Co* (1887) 37 Ch D 191.

73 *Derry v Peek* (1889) 14 App Cas 337.

74 *Derry v Peek* (1889) 14 App Cas 337 at 374.

75 *Jury v Stoker & Jackson* (1882) 9 LR Ir 385.

76 Sullivan MR said: 'In my opinion, the prospectus was deliberately and fraudulently adopted to make the concern attractive. (contd.../)

[32.050] The final possible course of action for a person who is induced to enter into a contract for the allotment of shares is to sue for damages for the tort of negligent misstatement. The leading authority is *Hedley Byrne & Co v Heller & Partners*[77] which established that liability can arise in appropriate circumstances from negligent misstatement[78]. It is not necessary that the misstatement in the prospectus be the sole factor inducing the plaintiff to acquire the shares or securities[79].

(b) Criminal liability relating to prospectuses

[32.051] Criminal liability in connection with prospectuses arises in two contexts:

(i) first, in respect of offences for breach of the prospectus requirements under Irish prospectus law[80]; and

(ii) second, in respect of untrue statements and omissions in prospectuses.

Each of these contexts is now considered in further detail, in turn, below.

(i) Offences under Irish prospectus law

[32.052] Section 47 of the IFCMPA 2005 provides for penalties on conviction on indictment and defences in respect of offences created by Irish prospectus law. These offences are those prescribed by regs 14 and 15 of the P(D)R 2005 in connection with failure to draw up and file a prospectus in connection with a public offering or an admission to trading as required by the Regulations and the Prospectus Directive.

A number of presumptions widen the scope for criminal liability to be proved. Under s 38(3) of the IFCMPA 2005, a statement included in a prospectus is deemed to be untrue if it is misleading in the form and context in which it is included. Moreover, a statement is deemed to be included in a prospectus if it is included in any report or memorandum appearing on the face thereof or by reference incorporated therein. A statement includes a report or a valuation[81].

[32.053] Section 47 of the IFCMPA 2005 provides for fines of up to €1 million or imprisonment for up to five years, or both. Under sub-s (2), however, it is a defence for the defendant to prove:

---

76 (\...contd) The plaintiff acted on the prospectus and took the shares. I have a very strong opinion that the representation was false and fraudulent, to induce men to take shares in this company, and if loss has resulted from it, the person who made the false representation should be made to answer for the loss ... The representation was false, fraudulent and material, made to induce a man to take the shares and loss has resulted to the plaintiff.'

77 *Hedley Byrne & Co v Heller & Partners* [1964] AC 465.

78 See also *Securities Trust Ltd v Hugh Moore & Alexander Ltd* [1964] IR 417.

79 *Edington v Fitzmaurice* (1885) 29 ChD 459.

80 Section 38(1) of the IFCMPA 2005 defines Irish prospectus law as: '(a) the measures adopted for the time being by the State to implement the 2003 Prospectus Directive (whether an Act of the Oireachtas, regulations under s 3 of the European Communities Act 1972, regulations under section 46 or any other enactment (other than, save where the context otherwise admits, this Part)), (b) any measures directly applicable in the State in consequence of the 2003 Prospectus Directive and, without prejudice to the generality of this paragraph, includes the Prospectus Regulation, and (c) any supplementary and consequential measures adopted for the time being by the State in respect of the Prospectus Regulation.'

81 Section 38(A) of the IFCMPA 2005 as inserted by s 15(a) of the IFCMPA 2006.

'(a) as regards any matter not disclosed in the prospectus concerned, that he or she did not know it, or

(b) the contravention arose from an honest mistake of fact on his or her part, or

(c) the contravention was in respect of matters which, having regard to the circumstances of the case, was immaterial or as respects which, having regard to those circumstances, he or she ought otherwise reasonably to be excused.'

Regulation 107(3) of the P(D)R 2005 further provides that a person who is found guilty of an offence under the P(D)R 2005 is liable on summary conviction to a class A fine or imprisonment for a term not exceeding 12 months, or both. Moreover, where a contravention is continued after conviction, the person shall be guilty of a further offence for every day on which the contravention continues[82].

[32.054] Where an offence is committed by a body corporate but with the consent, connivance or approval of, or is attributable to the wilful neglect of, any director, manager, secretary or other officer, that individual as well as the body corporate is guilty of an offence[83].

(ii) Criminal liability for false statements and omissions in prospectuses

[32.055] Under s 48 of the IFCMPA 2005, where a prospectus is issued and includes any untrue statement or omits any information required by EU prospectus law[84] to be contained in it, any person who authorised the issue (not being the Central Bank) shall be guilty of an offence, unless he or she proves:

'(i) as regards an untrue statement, either that the statement was, having regard to the circumstances of the case, immaterial or that he or she honestly believed and did, up to the time of the issue of the prospectus, believe that the statement was true, or

(ii) as regards any information omitted, either that the omission was, having regard to the circumstances of the case, immaterial or that he or she did not know it, or

(iii) that the making of the statement or omission was otherwise such as, having regard to the circumstances of the case, ought reasonably to be excused.'

The penalties on conviction are in the same order as those for an offence of breaching Irish prospectus law discussed above[85].

If at a trial for an offence under this section or an offence created by Irish prospectus law, the judge or jury has to consider whether the defendant honestly believed a particular thing or was honestly mistaken in relation to a particular thing, the presence or absence of reasonable grounds for such a belief or for his or her having been so mistaken is a matter to which the judge or jury is to have regard, in conjunction with any other relevant matters, in considering whether the defendant so believed or was so mistaken[86].

---

82 Regulation 107(1) of the P(D)R 2005.

83 Regulation 107(2) of the P(D)R 2005.

84 See para **[32.025]** *ante*.

85 See para **[32.053]** *ante*.

86 Section 48(5) of the IFCMPA 2005.

(iii) Other offences

[32.056] It is possible in principle for further offences, both statutory and common law, to be committed in the context of prospectuses. In *R v Irish*[87], for example, two directors were convicted of conspiracy to defraud in connection with untrue statements in prospectuses – the prospectuses understated the promotion costs of flotation by a considerable degree.

(c) Administrative sanctions

[32.057] The Central Bank is generally empowered by ss 33AQ and 33AR of the Central Bank Act 1942, as amended[88], to impose administrative sanctions in respect of breaches of the administrative requirements over which is has supervisory responsibility. In the context of prospectuses, the Bank's powers extend to approving a prospectus, scrutinising a prospectus and requiring a person to include information or provide information, and to give directions and suspend or prohibit prospectuses or disclose information to the public[89]. The Bank may intervene even after publication of the prospectus, and may require further steps to be taken[90]. The Bank may impose administrative sanctions for any contravention, and these include caution or reprimand; direction to withhold money; a monetary penalty of up to €5 million in the case of a body corporate or €500,000 in the case of a natural person; disqualification of authorised persons; direction to cease continuance of a contravention; and direction to pay all or part of the inquiry[91]. Adverse assessments are enforceable in the High Court and may be publicised. The Bank also has sweeping powers of investigation and enforcement, including the appointment of authorised officers under regs 85 and 86 of the P(D)R 2005, with powers to enter premises with the consent of the occupier, search and inspect, secure premises for later inspection, require the production of relevant records and to copy or remove and retain them, and ask for explanations, either alone or in the company of a member of An Garda Síochána or another authorised officer. An authorised officer can apply directly to the District Court for a warrant against any person preventing him from entering any premises, and any person who impedes an authorised officer in the exercise of his or her functions is guilty of an offence[92]. None of the above, however, will override the privilege against self-incrimination which is expressly preserved by reg 91 of the P(D)R 2005.

[B] MARKET ABUSE

[32.058] The second element in the EU Financial Services Action Plan ('FSAP') which we focus upon in this chapter – though chronologically it was enacted first – is the Market Abuse Directive[93], which establishes a common EEA-wide anti-market abuse

87 *R v Irish* [2001] EWCA Crim 1393.

88 By s 10 of the Central Bank and Financial Services Authority of Ireland Act 2004. The Central Bank Reform Act 2010 also strengthens the Central Bank's powers in respect of regulation, investigation and enforcement,

89 Part 7 of the P(D)R 2005.

90 Regulation 83 of the P(D)R 2005.

91 See generally Horan, *Corporate Crime* (2011, Bloomsbury Professional) at paras 15.50 *et seq*.

92 Regulation 86(6) of the P(D)R 2005.

93 Directive 2003/6/EC of the European Parliament and of the Council of 28 January 2003 on insider dealing and market manipulation (market abuse).

regime and a framework for establishing a proper flow of information to the market. It is designed to improve confidence in the integrity of the integrated European market and greater crossborder cooperation. The objectives of the Directive are explained in its preamble as follows:

> 'An integrated and efficient financial market requires market integrity. The smooth functioning of securities markets and public confidence in markets are prerequisites for economic growth and wealth. Market abuse harms the integrity of financial markets and public confidence in securities and derivatives … Market abuse consists of insider dealing and market manipulation. The objective of legislation against insider dealing is the same as that of legislation against market manipulation: to ensure the integrity of Community financial markets and to enhance investor confidence in those markets. It is therefore advisable to adopt combined rules to combat both insider dealing and market manipulation …'

The Directive is aimed, therefore, at combating two principal types of market abuse:

- 'insider dealing' – ie, the misuse of price-sensitive information not generally available to the investing public[94]; and
- 'market manipulation' – ie, the making of statements or engaging in conduct which distorts the market by creating a false or misleading impression about the value, supply or demand for traded securities or financial products[95].

The Directive requires Member States to adopt combined rules to combat both insider dealing and market manipulation, and provides[96] for related matters, including requirements to draw up and maintain insiders' lists, to disclose manager's deals, to report suspicious transactions, and exempting share buybacks and stabilisation measures[97], and research disclosure.

[32.059] The legislative framework of the Market Abuse Directive regime is as follows:

- *Market Abuse Directive and Supplemental Directives and Regulation*: the framework (Level 1 Lamfalussy) legislative measure on market abuse is the Market Abuse Directive[98] of 28 January 2003. The Directive repeals and re-enacts provisions against insider dealing originally contained in the Insider Dealing Directive[99] of 13 November 1989. The Directive is supplemented by three (Level 2 Lamfalussy) Commission Directives[100] which deal with the

94 See further para **[32.068]** *post.*

95 See further para **[32.099]** *post.*

96 Particularly via the Supplemental Directives and Market Abuse Regulation.

97 Stabilisation is the repurchase of securities in order to smooth out the peaks and troughs in market prices which might otherwise follow when there has been an over-allotment of securities in a public issue.

98 See para **[32.008]** *ante.*

99 Directive 89/592/EEC of 13 November 1989 ([1989] OJ L334/30).

100 (a) 2003/124/EC ([2003] OJ L339/70) as regards the definition and public disclosure of inside information and the definition of market manipulation; (b) 2003/125/EC of 22 December 2003 ([2003] OJ L339/73) as regards the fair presentation of investment recommendations and the disclosure of conflicts of interest; and (c) 2004/72/EC of 29 April 2004 ([2004] OJ L162/70) as regards accepted market practices, the definition of inside information in relation to derivatives on commodities, the drawing up of lists of insiders, the notification of managers' transactions and the notification of suspicious transactions.

definition and public disclosure of inside information and the definition of market manipulation; the fair presentation of investment recommendations and the disclosure of conflicts of interest; and exemptions for buyback programmes and stabilisation of financial instruments. The Directive is also supplemented by a Level 2 Regulation, the Market Abuse Regulation[101], which concerns exemptions for buyback programmes and stabilisation of financial instruments.

– *Irish Market Abuse Regulations 2005*: in Ireland, the Market Abuse Directive and Supplemental Directives and Regulation are implemented by the Market Abuse (Directive 2003/6/EC) Regulations 2005[102] ('MA(D)R 2005') which came into operation on 6 July 2005. The Regulations are to be construed as one with the Companies Acts.
– *ESMA (CESR) and Central Bank Guidance*: CESR (now subsumed into ESMA, the European Securities and Markets Authority) published four Level 3 Lamfalussy measures – three sets of Level 3 guidelines[103] on the application of the Market Abuse Directive and ensuring a common approach by supervisors in the Member States: and a set of common questions and answers[104]. The Central Bank has followed with Market Abuse Rules[105] under IFCMPA 2005.

[32.060] Following a process of consultation and review that began in 2009, in October 2011 the Commission adopted proposals for the reform of the market abuse regime. There are two elements to the proposed reforms: first is the proposed new Regulation on Market Abuse[106] which is to replace the Market Abuse Directive, with some modifications and extensions. Second, the Commission has proposed a new Directive specifically dealing with criminal sanctions for insider dealing and market manipulation[107]. These proposals must be discussed by the European Parliament, following which possible amendments would have to be re-examined by the Commission and ultimately approved by the Council. In July 2012, the Commission

---

101 Commission Regulation (EC)2273/2003 of 22 December 2003 implementing Directive 2003/6/EC of the European Parliament and of the Council as regards exemptions for buy-back programmes and stabilisation of financial instruments.

102 SI 342/2005.

103 First set of CESR guidance and information on the common operation of the Directive (Ref CESR/04-505b; May 2005); second set of CESR guidance and information on the common operation of MAD (Ref CESR/06-562b; July 2007); third set of CESR guidance and information on the common operation of the Directive to the market (Ref CESR/09-219; 15 May 2009).

104 'Questions and Answers on the common operation of the Market Abuse Directive', 9 January 2012 (Ref ESMA/2012/9).

105 February 2012. See www.centralbank.ie.

106 Proposal for a Regulation of the European Parliament and of the Council on insider dealing and market manipulation (market abuse), COM (2011) 651 final of 20 October 2011.

107 Proposal for a Directive of the European Parliament and of the Council on criminal sanctions for insider dealing and market manipulation (market abuse), COM (2011) 654 final of 20 October 2011. Criminal sanctions could not be addressed in the draft regulation since the approximation of criminal laws is only permissible in EU law by way of directives. The draft directive requires Member States to treat intentional insider dealing and market manipulation as criminal offences and to provide for sanctions which are effective, proportionate and dissuasive.

amended its proposals to bring possible manipulation of the EURIBOR and LIBOR benchmarks for interbank lending rates within the scope of the reforms following revelations of possible manipulation of LIBOR by a number of banks[108]. Overall, the proposals aim to provide more effective and uniform enforcement of market abuse, with some degree of uniformity in the sanctions to be imposed[109]. Whether the proposed structure of the reforms – a Level 1 Regulation and a Level 2 Directive running counter to Lamfalussy – is such a good idea will remain to be seen; unlike the Directives, which are implemented in local legislation, Regulations are directly effective and require no local legislation; so regulators and lawyers will have to look both to the local legislation and the EU regulation for the law – perhaps not such a great challenge to the modern lawyer.

Application of the market abuse measures

[32.061] The Market Abuse Directive regime applies to insider dealing and market manipulation in respect of financial instruments admitted to trading – or for which an application to admit to trade has been made – on a regulated market[110] in the EEA[111]. In Ireland, thus, it applies to the MSM of the Irish Stock Exchange, which is a regulated market, but not to the GEM or ESM, which as MTFs are not regulated markets[112].

[32.062] As regards such secondary markets in Ireland, they continue to be covered by Part V of the CA 1990 which, though on the face of it was repealed by s 31 of the IFCMPA 2005, is in fact continued in force by reg 6 of the Investment Funds, Companies and Miscellaneous Provisions Act 2005 (Commencement) Order 2005[113], designating 6 July 2005 as the date for the commencement of s 31, but:

> 'only for the purpose of repealing the enactments specified in that section in so far as they relate to a regulated market (within the meaning of Directive 2003/71/EC of the European Parliament and of the Council of 4 November 2003) operated by a recognised stock exchange within the meaning Pt V of the Companies Act 1990 (No 33 of 1990).'

There is general approval in the ISE, however, that the Directive regime should be applied to the secondary markets, with some modification[114].

Moreover, instruments traded on markets which are not EEA regulated markets, eg, the secondary markets, or non-EEA markets, still come within the purview of the

---

108 Amended proposal for a Regulation of the European Parliament and of the Council on insider dealing and market manipulation (market abuse) (submitted in accordance with article 293(2) TFEU), 2011/0295 (COD); and Amended proposal for a Directive of the European Parliament and of the Council on criminal sanctions for insider dealing and market manipulation (submitted in accordance with Article 293(2) TFEU), 2011/0297 (COD).

109 See also Communication from the Commission to the European Parliament, the Council, the European Economic and Social Committee and the Committee of the Regions, Reinforcing sanctioning regimes in the financial sector, COM (2010) 716 of 8 December 2010.

110 As to the meaning of 'regulated market', see para **[32.004]** *ante*.

111 Article 1(3) of the Market Abuse Directive.

112 See para **[32.004]** *ante*.

113 SI 323/2005.

114 Irish Stock Exchange Response to the European Commission's Consultation on the Market Abuse Directive (MAD), 23 July 2010. IFCMPA 2005.

Directive if their value depends on a financial instrument which is traded – or for which an application to trade has been made – on an EEA regulated market.

[32.063] The Market Abuse Directive regime applies even though the abuse does not occur in the territory of the regulated market[115]. Under Article 10 of the Directive, in addition to prohibiting market abuse, both at home and abroad, in respect of their own regulated markets, Member States must apply the prohibitions to actions carried out in their territories on financial instruments that are traded on a regulated market in another Member State[116]. Thus, the Irish authorities must, for example, act against activities in Ireland which affect, say, shares traded on the London Stock Exchange; and the UK authorities have a similar obligation in respect of shares traded on the MSM of the Irish Stock Exchange; and the Irish authorities may also take action insofar as they can against any abuse occurring outside the State in respect of instruments traded on the Irish Stock Exchange.

[32.064] Under art 7 of the Market Abuse Directive, the Directive shall expressly not apply to transactions carried out in pursuit of monetary, exchange-rate or public debt-management policy by a Member State, by the European System of Central Banks, by a national central bank or by any other officially designated body, or by any person acting on their behalf (in Ireland the Central Bank, Minister for Finance, or National Treasury Management Agency)[117]. Member States may extend this exemption to their federated states or similar local authorities in respect of the management of their public debt.

Financial instruments to which the Market Abuse Directive applies

[32.065] The financial instruments to which the Market Abuse Directive applies are very broad. Article 1.3 the Market Abuse Directive provides:

> '"Financial instrument" shall mean:
>
> – transferable securities as defined in Council Directive 93/22/EEC of 10 May 1993 on investment services in the securities field[118],
> – units in collective investment undertakings,
> – money-market instruments,
> – financial-futures contracts, including equivalent cash-settled instruments,
> – forward interest-rate agreements,
> – interest-rate, currency and equity swaps,
> – options to acquire or dispose of any instrument falling into these categories, including equivalent cash-settled instruments. This category includes in particular options on currency and on interest rates,
> – derivatives on commodities,
> – any other instrument admitted to trading on a regulated market in a Member State or for which a request for admission to trading on such a market has been made.'

115 Article 9 of the Market Abuse Directive.

116 Regulation 4(2)(b) of the MA(D)R 2005.

117 Regulation 4(3) of the MA(D)R 2005.

118 See para **[32.011]** *ante*.

Central Bank as competent authority in Ireland

[32.066] As with the Prospectus Directive (and the Transparency Directive, which is discussed below)[119], the Central Bank of Ireland has been appointed[120] the competent authority in Ireland for the purposes of the Market Abuse Directive; however, certain duties have been delegated to the Irish Stock Exchange[121].

The elements of market abuse

[32.067] Regulation 2(1) of the MA(D)R 2005 provides that 'market abuse' means '(a) insider dealing, or (b) market manipulation'[122]. We now turn to consider each of the elements of market abuse in further detail, as follows:

- (a) Insider dealing;
- (b) Market manipulation;
- (c) Notification obligations under the Market Abuse Directive;
- (d) Criminal liability for breaches of the Market Abuse Directive;
- (e) Administrative sanctions for breaches of the Market Abuse Directive;
- (f) Civil liability for breaches of the Market Abuse Directive.

(a) Insider dealing[123]

[32.068] Regulation 2(1) of the MA(D)R 2005 provides that 'insider dealing' means any act which contravenes reg 5(1) or 5(2) of the MA(D)R 2005, the latter implementing arts 2–4 of the Market Abuse Directive, and provides as follows that, subject to certain exceptions[124]:

> '(1) … a person to whom this paragraph applies who possesses inside information shall not use that information by acquiring or disposing of, or by trying to acquire or dispose of, for the person's own account or for the account of a third party, directly or indirectly, financial instruments to which that information relates.
>
> (2) A person to whom paragraph (1) applies shall not—
>
> (a) disclose inside information to any other person unless such disclosure is made in the normal course of the exercise of the first-mentioned person's employment, profession or duties, or
>
> (b) recommend or induce another person, on the basis of inside information, to acquire or dispose of financial instruments to which that information relates.'

---

119 See para **[32.118]** *post*.

120 Under s 34 of the IFCMPA 2005.

121 Regulation 33 of the MA(D)R 2005.

122 See para **[32.058]** *ante*.

123 For a detailed look at the development of the law in this area see MacCann, 'Liability for Insider Dealing' (1999) ILT (ns) 130; Ashe, 'The Directive on Insider Dealing' (1992) Company Lawyer 15–19; and Ashe & Murphy, *Insider Dealing* (1992, Round Hall Press); and more recently Abrahamson, 'Another look at insider dealing' (2010) 5 CLP 92. For a wider review see Carlton & Fischel, 'The regulation of insider trading' (1983) Stanford Law Review 857; and for consideration of the broader need to combat insider dealing see Manne, 'In defense of insider trading' (1966) Harvard Business Review 113; and McVea, 'What's wrong with insider dealing?' (1995) Legal Studies 390.

124 As to the exceptions, see para **[32.083]** *post*.

There are thus three distinct limbs to the prohibition. First is a prohibition against using inside information to acquire or dispose, or to try to acquire or dispose, of financial instruments; second is a prohibition on disclosing inside information to anyone outside the ordinary course of professional duty; and third is a prohibition on recommending or inducing another to acquire or dispose of financial instruments on the basis of related inside information. Critical to all three limbs are:

- (i) The persons to whom reg 5 applies;
- (ii) The definition of 'inside information';
- (iii) Information of a precise nature;
- (iv) Information relating to financial instruments;
- (v) Price sensitivity;
- (vi) Information not available to the public;
- (vii) Innocent insider information;
- (viii) Exception to insider dealing;
- (ix) Public disclosure and selective disclosure;
- (x) Insider lists;
- (xi) Fair presentation of recommendations;
- (xii) Insider dealing under Part V of the CA 1990;
- (xiii) Liability for insider dealing at common law.

Each of these aspects is now considered in turn.

(i) The persons to whom reg 5 applies

[32.069] The obligation not to engage in insider dealing applies, according to reg 5(3) of the MA(D)R 2005, to:

> '(a) any person who possesses the inside information concerned—
>
> (i) by virtue of the person's membership of the administrative, management or supervisory bodies of the issuer of the financial instrument,
>
> (ii) by virtue of the person's holding in the capital of the issuer,
>
> (iii) by virtue of having access to the information through the exercise of the person's employment, profession or duties, or
>
> (iv) by virtue of the person's criminal activities,
>
> (b) if any person falling within subparagraph (a) is a legal person, and without prejudice to the generality of Regulation 52, any natural person who takes part in the decision to carry out, for the account of the legal person, any transaction in financial instruments, or
>
> (c) subject to regulation 8(3), any other person who possesses the inside information concerned while the person knows, or ought to have known, that it is inside information.'

The list is broad enough to include not merely directors, secretaries, managers and shareholders, but also potentially auditors, liquidators, receivers, examiners, and those who act 'for the account of the legal person' which might include lawyers, stockbrokers and other advisors, employees or agents. It also includes persons who have acquired information illegally from the company whether through bribery or corruption, fraud or theft. It also includes any person who knew or ought to have known that what they possessed was inside information[125].

---

[125] Regulation 5(3)(c) of the MA(D)R 2005.

[32.070] Shadow directors[126] are not expressly included in the list – an omission which is thought to be unusual but the consequences of which have yet to be explored in the context of the Market Abuse Directive[127]. In *Fyffes plc v DCC plc and S&L Investments Ltd and Others*[128], however, Laffoy J considered that DCC was in the circumstances a shadow director of the company Lotus Green and therefore an officer of the company under the Companies Acts in the context of the old Part V of the CA 1990. Having regard to the corporate governance structure of Lotus Green and in particular the role of one of its directors, Mr O'Dwyer, who was a director of Lotus Green with a veto over the decisions of the board of Lotus Green as well as being the chief financial officer of DCC, this was objective evidence that DCC could exercise influence over Lotus through Mr O'Dwyer. Laffoy J said:

> 'DCC chose to appoint the chief financial officer of DCC to the board of Lotus Green as a sole "A" director in circumstances where, under the provisions of the articles of association of Lotus Green, that director had effectively a veto over the actions of the board. That appointment in those circumstances enabled DCC, through Mr O'Dwyer, to exercise a level of real influence over the corporate affairs of Lotus Green on an ongoing basis. That state of affairs could have been avoided, and DCC could have ensured that the board of Lotus Green would be, and would be seen to be, independent of DCC had it appointed one or more persons to be "A" directors who were independent of DCC. By the course it chose, DCC rendered the making of an objective assessment as to whether Lotus Green was acting under the directions or influence of DCC, exerted through Mr O'Dwyer, or acting independently of DCC very difficult. If it was a live issue, I would incline to the view that DCC was a shadow director of Lotus Green.'

The learned judge found however that no offence was committed by DCC under Part V of the CA 1990 since it was not on the facts a 'tipee'. She further found that James Flavin, the principal director of DCC, though influential, was not a shadow director of Lotus Green for want of continued influence on an on-going basis.

(ii) The definition of 'inside information'

[32.071] The definition of 'inside information' is set out in art 1(1) of the Market Abuse Directive and is expanded upon in the Level 2 Commission Directive 2003/124/EC. Article 1(1) sets out three definitions of inside information, depending on the circumstances. First, it is generally:

> 'information of a precise nature which has not been made public, relating, directly or indirectly, to one or more issuers of financial instruments or to one or more financial instruments and which, if it were made public, would be likely to have a significant effect on the prices of those financial instruments or on the price of related derivative financial instruments.'

However, a second, specialised definition is provided for derivatives on commodities, where inside information means:

> 'information of a precise nature which has not been made public, relating, directly or indirectly, to one or more such derivatives and which users of markets on which such

126 See Ch 13, *Corporate Governance: Management by the Directors*, at para **[13.055]**

127 See Horan, *Corporate Crime* (2011, Bloomsbury Professional) para 15.222.

128 *Fyffes plc v DCC plc and S&L Investments Ltd and Others* [2005] IEHC 477.

derivatives are traded would expect to receive in accordance with accepted market practices on those markets.'

Thus, derivatives on commodities are subjected to an accepted market practices test rather than a price-sensitivity test.

A third definition appears for persons charged with the execution of orders concerning financial instruments:

> 'information conveyed by a client and related to the client's pending orders, which is of a precise nature, which relates directly or indirectly, to one or more issuers of financial instruments or to one or more financial instruments and which, if it were made public, would be likely have a significant effect on the prices of those financial instruments or on the price of related derivative financial instruments.'

The focus here is on information from clients relating to their pending orders.

[32.072] To constitute inside information, there are five prerequisites to be fulfilled:[129]

- The information must be of a 'precise nature'.
- The information must relate, directly or indirectly, to one or more issuers of financial instruments or to one or more financial instruments.
- In relation to derivatives on commodities, the information must be information which users of markets on which derivatives are traded would expect to receive in accordance with accepted market practices on those markets.
- The information must not have been 'made public'.
- The information must be information which, if it were made public, would be likely to have a significant effect on the prices of those financial instruments or on the price of related derivatives.

[32.073] CESR's level 3 second set of guidelines on the Market Abuse Directive[130] list the following as non-exhaustive and purely indicative examples of things that might constitute inside information:

- Information which directly concerns the issuer:
- Operating business performance;
- Changes in control and control agreements;
- Changes in management and supervisory boards;
- Changes in auditors or any other information related to the auditors' activity;
- Operations involving the capital or the issue of debt securities or warrants to buy or subscribe securities;
- Decisions to increase or decrease the share capital;
- Mergers, splits and spin-offs;
- Purchase or disposal of equity interests or other major assets or branches of corporate activity;

---

129 For an excellent and detailed analysis see Clarke, 'Inside Information and the European Market Abuse Directive 2003/6' in Ali & Gregoriu (eds), *Insider Trading: Global Developments and Analysis* (2009, CRC Press) ch 7.

130 Level 3 – second set of CESR guidance and information on the common operation of the Directive: CESR/06-562b.

- Restructurings or reorganisations that have an effect on the issuer's assets and liabilities, financial position or profits and losses;
- Decisions concerning buy-back programmes or transactions in other listed financial instruments;
- Changes in the class rights of the issuer's own listed shares;
- Filing of petitions in bankruptcy or the issuing of orders for bankruptcy
- proceedings;
- Legal disputes;
- Revocation or cancellation of credit lines by one or more banks;
- Dissolution or verification of a cause of dissolution;
- Changes in the assets' value;
- Insolvency of relevant debtors;
- Reduction of real properties' values;
- Physical destruction of uninsured goods;
- New licences, patents, registered trademarks;
- Decrease or increase in value of financial instruments in portfolio;
- Decrease in value of patents or rights or intangible assets due to market innovation;
- Receiving acquisition bids for relevant assets;
- Innovative products or processes;
- Product liability or environmental damages cases;
- Changes in expected earnings or losses;
- Orders received from customers, their cancellation or important changes;
- Withdrawal from or entry into new core business areas;
- Changes in the investment policy of the issuer;
- Ex-dividend date, changes in dividend payment date and amount of the dividend;
- Changes in dividend policy.

(iii) Information of a precise nature

[32.074] Ironically, perhaps, there is some confusion about what is meant by 'precise nature'[131], though art 1(1) of the Level 2 Directive 2003/124, as implemented in Ireland by reg 2 of the MA(D)R 2005, provides that information shall be deemed to be of a precise nature if it indicates a set of circumstances which exists or may reasonably be expected to come into existence or an event which has occurred or may reasonably be expected to do so and if it is specific enough to enable a conclusion to be drawn as to the possible effect of that set of circumstances or event on the prices of financial instruments or related derivative financial instruments. The guidance and information issued by CESR would suggest that the precise nature of the information must be assessed on a case-by-case basis and depends on what the information is, and the

[131] Rider, Alexander & Linklater, *Market Abuse and Insider Dealing* (2007, Bloomsbury Professional) p 6; Conceicao, 'Tackling Cross-Border Market Abuse' (2006) 14(1) Journal of Financial Regulation and Compliance 32; Clarke, 'Inside Information and the European Market Abuse Directive 2003/6' in Ali & Gregoriu (eds), *Insider Trading: Global Developments and Analysis* (2009, CRC Press) p 105.

surrounding context.[132] CESR has published a number of examples to suggest that information is precise when, from an objective standpoint, it is firm or exact and contains hard fact rather than mere rumour or speculation, though it need not be comprehensive to be precise[133], and it gives the example of information about an impending take-over bid where the price of the bid is not known.

(iv) Information relating to financial instruments

[32.075] As regards the information having to relate to financial instruments, derivatives on commodities, or pertaining to pending orders concerning financial instruments, the Court of Justice of the EU has noted in *Ipourgos Ikonomikon v Georgakis*[134] that the information must relate to the issuer (ie, the company) or to the transferable securities themselves. CESR suggests[135], by way of example, that information which directly concerns the issuer might include changes in control, changes in management and supervisory boards, changes in auditors or any other information related to the auditors' activity, new licenses, patents, registered trademarks, and decisions to increase or decrease the share capital. In addition, any kind of information that is relevant to the market position of an issuer can be regarded as relating to that issuer.

(v) Price sensitivity

[32.076] Price sensitivity is a major element in the definition. It is settled that *price sensitivity* must be assessed using the 'objective investor' test on the basis of the *ex-ante* position[136] – basically, would the reasonable investor have considered the information material to his or her investment decision at the time of the act? That approach is not expressly provided for in the Directive nor in the supporting instruments, save obliquely in the preamble to the Definition Directive[137] where the language is of 'reasonable investors' making investment decisions on the basis of *ex-ante* available information. However, the reasonable investor is evident in the guidelines of ESMA and the approach was cited without any criticism by the Court of Justice of the EU in *Spector Photo Group NV v Commisie voor het Bank, Financie en Assurantiewezen*[138]. In Ireland, the reasonable investor test was applied by Laffoy J in the High Court in *Fyffes plc v DCC plc and Others*[139] though on appeal the Supreme Court rejected the test on the basis that it had no origin in Part V of the CA 1990 upon which the insider dealing allegations were based; but that decision concerned the legislation since repealed by IFCMPA 2005

[132] CESR – second set of CESR guidance and information on the common operation of the Directive to the Market (CESR/02-089d), p 4.

[133] CESR – second set of CESR guidance and information on the common operation of the Directive to the Market (CESR/02-089d), p 5.

[134] *Ipourgos Ikonomikon v Georgakis* Case C-391/04 [2007] ECR I-3741.

[135] CESR – second set of CESR guidance and information on the common operation of the Directive to the Market (CESR/02-089d), para. 47.

[136] See Clarke, 'Inside Information and the European Market Abuse Directive 2003/6' in Ali & Gregoriu (eds), *Insider Trading: Global Developments and Analysis* (2009, CRC Press) p 116.

[137] 2003/124 EC.

[138] *Spector Photo Group NV v Commisie voor het Bank, Financie en Assurantiewezen* [2010] 2 CMLR 30.

[139] *Fyffes plc v DCC plc and Others* [2009] 2 IR 417.

to make way for the Market Abuse Directive. Following the implementation of the Market Abuse Directive, for example, the Central Bank, like its counterparts in other jurisdictions, has attempted to embrace the reasonable investor test by listing examples of information which is likely to be considered relevant to a reasonable investor's decision. This involves information which affects: the issuer's assets and liabilities; the performance or expectation of performance of the issuer's business; the issuer's financial condition; the course of the issuer's business; major new developments in the issuer's business; information previously disclosed to the market; and events that may significantly affect the issuer's ability to meet its commitments[140].

[32.077] Though the decision in *Fyffes* can be relegated somewhat to the annals of history insofar as the provisions with which it was concerned have been repealed[141], the case illustrates that price sensitivity can be one of the most complex and costly elements to establish in any insider dealing case and it particularly illuminates the nuances which are possible in interpreting and applying the reasonable investor approach. As was observed above, the High Court and, on appeal, the Supreme Court differed as regards the applicability of the reasonable investor test. The facts of the case have been considered in Chapter 5[142] and, as was noted there, the case concerned Fyffes Plc, an Irish company listed on both the London and Irish Stock Exchanges. At the heart of the case, a civil action for damages for insider dealing under Part V of the CA 1990, was an allegation that Mr Jim Flavin, a non-executive director of Fyffes, had procured DCC plc, the company he founded and of which he was chief executive, to dispose of its shareholding in Fyffes in the days shortly before the 2000 AGM at which an unexpected profit warning was announced. In the immediately preceding two announcements to market, Fyffes had reported a growth in operating profit of 3.8% and had posted an outlook for further growth. DCC sold the shares in three tranches at prices of €3.20, €3.60, and €3.90, respectively, grossing in excess of €106 million. By the close of trading on the day of the AGM the price fell to €2.70, and a month later the price had fallen further to €1.85.

In January 2002, Fyffes initiated an action against the defendants claiming that the share sales were unlawful because they were effected by Mr Flavin who at the time was in possession of price-sensitive information by reason of his directorship of Fyffes. The specific information alleged to constitute inside information was contained in the November and December 1999 trading reports which were made available to the Fyffes board in January 2000 and which inferred that Fyffes' own expectations and their analysts' expectations for the year would not be met. Interestingly, there was little dispute concerning the facts – all parties were agreed as to what had happened. The dispute was whether Fyffes had any cause of action against Mr Flavin and the defendant companies. In the event, the High Court action, though based on a single set of undisputed facts described by Fennelly J in the Supreme Court as 'comparatively simple facts ... the sort of facts upon which common-sense judgments and opinions can be formed without the input of an extraordinary degree of expertise', took 87 days and

140 Central Bank, Market Abuse Rules, Rule 5.3. See also the UK FSA Disclosure Rules and Transparency Rules 2.2.5 and 2.2.6.

141 At least as far as financial instruments traded on regulated markets are concerned. Part V of the CA 1990 still prevails for other markets.

142 See Ch 5, *Disregarding Separate Legal Personality*, at para **[5.063]**.

involved lengthy expert testimony yielding disparate conclusions from distinguished international academics and market experts.

[32.078] A central pillar of the defence was that the information in Mr Flavin's possession was not price sensitive information *vis-à-vis* the shares in Fyffes. Expert evidence was produced to show that the exceptional share price preceding the 2000 AGM was precipitated by market infatuation with Fyffe's website venture, World-of-Fruit.com The defence argued that the reasonable investor approach applied, relying on US, Singapore, and Malaysian case law[143] all of which the learned judge considered useful. The plaintiff argued that the reasonable investor was not to be found at the extremes of the market. Laffoy J, following a detailed review of the comparative authorities, found that the reasonable investor is the investor who is typically found in the market at the time of dealing and that actual stock price history could be used to determine whether the reasonable investor was, or was not, interested in investing in internet stock. Laffoy J found that the strength of the sentiment for Fyffes' internet venture at the time, as evidenced by what was happening to the share price, was such that the reasonable investor would have concluded that an adverse share price reaction was not likely in response to the profit warning.

[32.079] The Supreme Court roundly rejected the reasonable investor test as the appropriate test in the context of Part V of the CA 1990. The Supreme Court further suggested that Laffoy J had in some respects misinterpreted the reasonable investor test. Finnegan J in the Supreme Court cautioned against the 'averaging' effect of the reasonable investor test:

> 'The judge may be well fitted to identify the conduct to be expected of the reasonable man but may not be fitted by knowledge or experience to fulfil the same function in relation to the reasonable investor … The difficulty in using the reasonable investor as a test, and not just to categorise the test as objective, is compounded in that it is, to my mind, impossible to profile the reasonable investor. There are innumerable categories of investor from the small private investor who will check the value of his shares but now and then to the institutional investor who is in touch with the market throughout the trading day. Is it the dealer who trades within the account or the trustee whose shareholding dates back decades? One investor may concentrate on return, another on capital gain. An investor may be cautious or adventurous and to a greater or lesser degree.'

The Supreme Court rejected what it viewed as the use by the High Court of a modified version of the reasonable investor test. Fennelly J stated that Laffoy J:

> '... used the reasonable investor not as a representative of all investors in the market whose response to the information might or might not lead to a material effect on the share price, but rather as a test of opinion as to how the market would respond.'

The Supreme Court's approach to the reasonable investor test, thus, is that it should be used to determine whether the reasonable investor would rely on the information as part of his or her investment decision, and not, as in the High Court, to determine what market reaction would be to the information. It has been suggested that the Supreme Court's approach to the reasonable investor is in line with the Market Abuse Directive

143 *TSC Industries Inc v Northway Inc* 426 US 438 (US SCt); *Basic Inc v Levinson* 485 US 224 (US SCt); *Public Prosecutor v Allen Ng Poh Meng* [1990] 1 MLJ (Singapore); and *Public Prosecutor v Chua Seng Huat* ([1999] 3 MLJ 305) (Malaysia).

and ESMA's level 3 guidance[144]. Two other aspects of the Supreme Court decision with regard to price sensitivity may be noted. First, Denham and Fennelly JJ noted that it was erroneous to 'offset' the effect of the information against various factors – such as the timing, the market sentiment to the fruit industry, etc. Fennelly J noted that:

> 'The very notion of offset supposes that there something to "offset". It suggests a balancing of one influence against another. If the effect of the worldoffruit.com venture was to counteract or to cancel the effect of the "bad news", it would still have materially affected the price. The statutory test does not postulate a fall in price.'

Second, the Supreme Court endorsed to some degree the so-called 'proof of the pudding' approach rejected by Laffoy J in the High Court. The Supreme Court held that the 20 March announcement was relevant to the consideration of whether the information in the trading report was price sensitive. Fennelly J rejected the proposition that evidence of a comparator requires complete parity of information and market, viewing this as an 'extraordinarily rigid' approach which was not supported by the case law. Some consideration was thus given to the *ex post facto* market reaction to the information.

(vi) Information not available to the public

[32.080] It is axiomatic that inside information cannot be inside information if it is available to the public. The nuances of this notion were further explored by the High Court in *Fyffes*, Laffoy J noting that it must be presumed that published information is accessible by investors[145]. Moreover, users of markets on which derivatives on commodities are traded are deemed to expect to receive information relating, directly or indirectly, to one or more such derivatives, which is routinely made available to the users of those markets, or required to be disclosed in accordance with the legal or regulatory provisions, market rules, contracts or customs on the relevant underlying commodity market or commodity derivatives market[146].

(vii) Innocent insider dealing

[32.081] In *Spector Photo Group NV v Commisie voor het Bank, Financie en Assurantiewezen*[147], the Court of Justice of the EU considered the question of whether there was a necessity for an intent to use inside information before the prohibition and obligations arising under the Market Abuse Directive apply. In that case, the Belgian Banking, Finance and Insurance Commission decided in 2006 that a Belgian listed company, Spector Photo Group NV ('Spector'), and its management, had engaged in insider trading by continuing a routine share buyback programme to cover employee stock options in 2003 just before the company announced its intent to acquire the business of a competitor and approximately a month before it published its results for the first half of 2003. Spector appealed the decision to the Belgian courts who referred a question of interpretation of arts 2 and 14 of the Market Abuse Directive to the Court of Justice of the EU. Advocate General Kokott considered that, as a general rule,

144 Clarke, 'Insider Dealing: Getting under the skin of *Fyffes plc v DCC* plc' [2009] 1 JBL 68

145 *Fyffes plc v DCC plc* [2009] 2 IR 417 at 581.

146 Regulation 5(4) of the MA(D)R 2005.

147 *Spector Photo Group NV v Commisie voor het Bank, Financie en Assurantiewezen* [2010] 2 CMLR 30.

possessing inside information which a person knows or ought to know is inside information and acquiring or disposing of financial instruments to which the information relates, is sufficient to constitute insider dealing – without any requirement to show intent to use the information. However, at the same time the Advocate General acknowledged that certain exceptions exist to this general rule. The ECJ considered art 2 of the Market Abuse Directive and the requirement that each Member State should prohibit persons who possess inside information by virtue of specified circumstances from:

> 'using that information by acquiring or disposing of, or by trying to acquire or dispose of, for his own account or for the account of a third party, either directly or indirectly, financial instruments to which that information relates.'

The court considered that this provision defines insider dealing in an objective manner without the need to demonstrate that there was intent to use the inside information. As a general rule, possessing inside information and acquiring or disposing of financial instruments to which that information relates is sufficient to constitute insider dealing. In the court's view, however, the absence of any express requirement of intent to use the inside information does not mean that any insider in possession of inside information, who enters into a market transaction, automatically falls within the prohibition on insider dealing. Rather, the prohibition must be analysed in light of the objectives of the Directive, which is that market transactions, by persons who hold inside information, which do not infringe the integrity of financial markets and investor confidence, should not be prohibited.

[32.082] The court gave some examples of transactions that cannot be considered as prohibited insider dealing, such as transactions by market-makers and bodies which are authorised to act as counterparties pursuing their legitimate business and persons authorised to execute orders on behalf of third parties dutifully carrying out those orders; the operation whereby a company, after obtaining inside information concerning a specific target, subsequently launches a public take-over bid for the capital of that company at a rate higher than the market rate; and since the carrying out of a market transaction necessarily involves a prior decision on the part of its author, the carrying out of that transaction should not be deemed in itself to constitute the use of inside information. These examples do not, however, dispense with all doubt about the scope of the provisions and it is unclear whether some circumstances of 'innocent' insider may yet be caught by the prohibitions and requirements. In consequence, it is thought that persons in possession of inside information – even inadvertently – should refrain altogether from trading in the securities to which that information relates, even if they can demonstrate that they do not intend to use the inside information, for example by showing that they would have traded even if they did not have any inside information.

(viii) Exceptions to insider dealing

[32.083] The prohibition against insider dealing contained in arts 2 and 3 of the Market Abuse Directive does not apply to transactions conducted in the discharge of an obligation that has become due to acquire or dispose of financial instruments where that obligation results from an agreement concluded before the person concerned possessed inside information[148]. Likewise, where a takeover is conducted in accordance with the

[148] Article 2(3) of the Market Abuse Directive; reg 5(5) of the MA(D)R 2005.

Takeover Rules[149] the possession and use of information in the context of the takeover is not a contravention of the insider dealing prohibition, provided the requirements of the Takeover Rules and the Takeover Panel Act 1997 are complied with[150]. Moreover, where the information is obtained in accordance with accepted market practices (AMPs) identified in accordance with para 1.1 of Schedule 1 of the MA(D)R 2005 then there is no contravention. No such AMPs have been identified by the Central Bank to date. And, as was previously noted, buyback programmes with a view to market stabilisation do not attract the prohibition against market abuse or insider dealing provided they follow the scheme established in reg 9 and Schedule 5 of the MA(D)R 2005.

Schedule 5 of the MA(D)R 2005 sets out the provisions of the EU Market Abuse Regulation on programmes of stabilisation of financial instruments. Stabilisation is defined as:

> 'any purchase or offer means any purchase or offer to purchase relevant securities, or any transaction in associated instruments equivalent thereto, by investment firms or credit institutions, which is undertaken in the context of a significant distribution of such relevant securities exclusively for supporting the market price of these relevant securities for a predetermined period of time, due to a selling pressure in such securities.'

Buyback programmes must be fully disclosed to the public and trading in own shares may be carried out through derivative financial instruments.

[32.084] There exists also the possibility of a so-called *face to face* exception to the insider dealing prohibition. It is illustrated by *Ipourgos Ikonomikon v Georgakis*[151], a case under the old Insider Trading Directive arising in the context of a buyback programme, where the Court of Justice of the EU established that insider information is required to be of advantage before it becomes protected information. In that case, Mr Georgakis and certain members of his family were the main shareholders of Parnassos. At the same time, Parnassos and its subsidiary, Syrios AVEE, held the majority of shares in Atemke. Mr Georgakis and most of the members of his family were members of the board of directors of Parnassos and of Atemke, companies in which they performed managerial functions. In 1996, Parnassos shares started to come under downward pressure, and Mr Georgakis and members of his family decided, on the recommendation of their financial advisers, to support the price of shares in Parnassos. Later that year the Greek Capital Markets Commission found Mr Georgakis guilty of insider dealing in connection with these transactions and fined him GRD70 million and that was appealed to the Greek courts who sent a question of law to the European court as to whether what took place was insider dealing. The ECJ held that there was no insider dealing in the circumstances. The court held that the regulations on insider dealing must be interpreted as meaning that, when the main shareholders and members of the board of directors of a company agree to effect between themselves stock-market transactions in the transferable securities of that company in order to support artificially the price of those securities, they are in possession of inside information of which they do not take

[149] Made by the Irish Takeover Panel under the Irish Takeover Panel Act 1997. See www.irishtakeoverpanel.ie.

[150] Regulation 8(4) of the MA(D)R 2005.

[151] *Ipourgos Ikonomikon and Proistamenos DOY Amfissas v Charilaos Georgakis* Case C-391/04 [2007] CMLR 4.

advantage with full knowledge of the facts when they carry out those transactions. Knowledge of the existence of such a decision and of its content constitutes, for those who participated in its adoption, inside information. However, the court further held that where all of the contracting parties have the same information, they are on an equal footing and the information ceases to be inside information for them in the context of the implementation of the decision adopted within the group. Against this background, since none of them is in a position to derive an advantage over the others, the transactions effected between the members of the group on the basis of that information do not constitute taking advantage, with full knowledge of the facts, of inside information. The decision has echoes of the old Irish law on 'offers to the public'[152] and it has received mention by the Court of Justice of the EU in *Spector Photo Group NV*, above[153].

(ix) Public disclosure and selective disclosure

[32.085] An issuer of a financial instrument must disclose publicly, without delay, inside information, which directly concerns the issuer, and in a manner which enables fast access and complete, correct and timely assessment of the information by the public[154]. Without prejudice to any such measures, the issuer must, for a period of not less than six months, post on the issuer's internet site or sites any inside information that the issuer is required to publicly disclose. The issuer must not combine, in a manner likely to be misleading, the provision of inside information to the public with the marketing of the issuer's activities. The issuer is deemed to have complied with these requirements where, upon the coming into existence of a set of circumstances or the occurrence of an event, albeit not yet formalised, the issuer has without delay informed the public of those circumstances or that event, as the case may be. Where there is any significant change concerning already publicly disclosed inside information, the issuer must publicly and without delay disclose the change immediately after the change occurs, and through the same channel as the one used for public disclosure of the original information. The issuer must take reasonable care to ensure that the disclosure of inside information to the public is synchronised as closely as possible between all categories of investors in regulated markets in all Member States on which the issuer's financial instruments concerned are admitted to trading, or where the issuer has requested admission to trading of the financial instruments concerned.

[32.086] The issuer may selectively delay the public disclosure of inside information to avoid prejudicing the issuer's 'legitimate interests' provided that the failure to disclose the information would not be likely to mislead the public, and the issuer is able to ensure the confidentiality of the information. The Central Bank has indicated that this exemption will be narrowly construed[155]. The legitimate interests that will justify such selective disclosure are listed in reg 10(8) of the MA(D)R 2005 as including:

> '(a) negotiations in course, or related elements, where the outcome or normal pattern of those negotiations would be likely to be affected by public disclosure (in particular, in the event that the financial viability of the issuer is in grave and

---

[152] See para **[32.016]** *ante*.

[153] See para **[32.076]** *ante*.

[154] Regulation 10 of the MA(D)R 2005.

[155] Central Bank Market Abuse Rules 2012, para 5.0.5.

imminent danger, although not within the scope of the applicable insolvency law, public disclosure of information may be delayed for a limited period where such a public disclosure would seriously jeopardise the interest of existing and potential shareholders by undermining the conclusion of specific negotiations designed to ensure the long-term financial recovery of the issuer),

(b) decisions taken or contracts made by the management body of the issuer which need the approval of another body of the issuer in order to become effective, provided that—

(i) the organisation of the issuer requires separation between those bodies, and

(ii) a public disclosure of the information before such approval together with the simultaneous announcement that this approval is still pending would jeopardise the correct assessment of the information by the public.'

[32.087] The Central Bank has warned that several or any of these circumstances might not justify selective disclosure, and that circumstances not listed are unlikely to be viewed as justifying selective disclosure[156]. CESR, likewise, has stated that the ability to delay disclosure of inside information arises by way of derogation from the general rule rather than as the norm, and it remains the issuer's responsibility to determine whether the disclosure can be delayed having due regard to the conditions[157]. A meeting for the test to determine whether there is a legitimate interest in delaying the disclosure is not of itself sufficient reason to delay disclosure; other factors should be considered, such as whether the delay would mislead the public or whether the issuer can ensure confidentiality. Regulation 10(9) of the MA(D)R 2005 requires that:

'the issuer shall control access to the information and, in particular—

(a) take effective measures to deny access to the information to persons other than those who require it for the exercise of their functions within the issuer,

(b) take the measures necessary to ensure that a person with access to the information acknowledges the legal and regulatory duties entailed and is aware of the sanctions attaching to the misuse or improper circulation of the information, and

(c) without prejudice to paragraph (11), have in place measures which allow immediate public disclosure in case the issuer was not able to ensure the confidentiality of the information.'

Companies are recommended by CESR to record the reasons for the delay so as to provide a satisfactory audit trail should the competent authority intervene[158].

[32.088] Where the issuer, or a person acting on the issuer's behalf or for the issuer's account, discloses any inside information to any third party in the normal exercise of the issuer's or person's employment, profession or duties, the issuer or person, as the case may be, shall make complete and effective public disclosure of that information, simultaneously in the case of an intentional disclosure and without delay in the case of a non-intentional disclosure[159].

---

[156] Central Bank Market Abuse Rules 2012, para 5.0.5.

[157] CESR Level 3 – second set of CESR guidance and information on the common operation of the Directive to the Market (CESR/02-089d), para 9-10.

[158] CESR Level 3 – second set of CESR guidance and information on the common operation of the Directive to the Market (CESR/02-089d), para 9-10.

[159] Regulation 10(11) of the MA(D)R 2005.

(x) Insider lists

[32.089] Paragraph 1 of reg 11 of the MA(D)R 2005 requires that each relevant person[160] shall draw up a list of those persons working for the relevant person, under a contract of employment or otherwise, who have access to inside information relating directly or indirectly to the relevant person who is the issuer, and containing the information set out in Schedule 4 of the MA(D)R 2005. Each relevant person must regularly update the list, and the Central Bank may request from any relevant person any list drawn up by the relevant person pursuant to para 1 of reg 11 and the relevant person must comply[161].

[32.090] Schedule 4 of the MA(D)R 2005 provides that the list of insiders must state the identity of any person having access to inside information, the reason why any such person is on the list, and the date at which the list of insiders was created and updated. The lists must be updated promptly whenever there is a change in the reason why any person is already on the list, or whenever any new person has to be added to the list, and must mention whether and when any person already on the list has no longer access to inside information. In May 2010, the Financial Regulator entered into a settlement agreement with Allied Irish Banks, plc arising from AIB's acknowledged breach of an administrative requirement to regularly and promptly update an insider list in accordance with reg 11 of the MC(D)R 2005. The delay related to two individuals who saw a trading statement from the Central Bank before it was published in 2009[162].

[32.091] Lists of insiders must be kept for at least five years after being drawn up or updated. Persons required to draw up lists of insiders must take the necessary measures to ensure that any person on such a list that has access to inside information acknowledges the legal and regulatory duties entailed and is aware of the sanctions attaching to the misuse or improper circulation of such information[163].

(xi) Fair presentation of recommendations about financial instruments or their issuers.

[32.092] Article 6(5) of the Market Abuse Directive requires Member States to put appropriate regulation in place to ensure that persons who produce or disseminate research concerning financial instruments or issuers of financial instruments and persons who produce or disseminate other information recommending or suggesting investment strategy, intended for distribution channels or for the public, take reasonable care to ensure that such information is fairly presented. They are also required to disclose their interests or indicate conflicts of interest concerning the financial instruments to which that information relates. Part 3 of the MA(D)R 2005 fleshes out

---

160 Regulation 11(5) and (6) of the MA(D)R 2005 provides that 'relevant person' means the issuer, a person acting on behalf of the issuer, or a person acting for the account of the issuer. However, reg 11 does not apply to the issuer of the financial instrument concerned (or persons acting on behalf of, or for the account of, the issuer) where the issuer neither made a request for the financial instrument to be admitted to trading on a regulated market, nor approved the admission of the financial instrument to trading on a regulated market.

161 Regulation 11 of the MA(D)R 2005.

162 The settlement agreement is published on the Central Bank's website at www.centralbank.ie.

163 Regulation 11 of the MA(D)R 2005.

the requirements. 'Relevant person' means a person producing or disseminating recommendations in the exercise of the person's profession or the conduct of the person's business[164]. That can include journalists and the media; indeed the Central Bank has reached two settlement agreements with members of the print media, Penfield Enterprises Ltd, which publishes *The Phoenix* magazine, was fined €5,000 in October 2007; and *The Irish Times*'s owner was fined €10,000 in April 2008. Both were alleged to have breached reg 18 of the MA(D)R 2005 by failing to accurately identify a person who made a recommendation which was published in their publications. A 'recommendation' for these purposes is research or other information recommending or suggesting an investment strategy, explicitly or implicitly, concerning one or several financial instruments or the issuers of financial instruments, including any opinion as to the present or future value or price of such instruments, intended for distribution channels or for the public[165]. An exemption exists under reg 26 of the MA(D)R 2005 for journalists where they are regulated by 'appropriate equivalent legislation,' including self-regulation, approved by the Central Bank. No such equivalent has been designated by the Central Bank to date. Nonetheless, under reg 26(2) of the MA(D)R 2005 where a journalist acts in a journalist's professional capacity, the dissemination of information will be assessed, for the purposes of the definition of 'market manipulation', taking into account the code of conduct governing the journalist's profession, unless the journalist derives, directly or indirectly, an advantage or profit from the dissemination of the information concerned.

(xii) Insider dealing under Part V of the CA 1990

[32.093] As was previously observed[166], Part V of the CA 1990, though repealed in respect of financial instruments and market abuse activity to which the Market Abuse Directive applies, remains applicable to companies whose financial instruments are not traded on an EEA regulated market, including the ESM and GEM of the Irish Stock Exchange. Part V introduced criminal and civil penalties for insider dealing. The basic provision is to be found in s 107 of the CA 1990 which renders unlawful dealings in securities of a company within six months of a person 'connected with' that company coming into possession of information which, if it were generally available, would affect the price of those securities. 'Dealing' in this context includes acquiring, disposing, subscribing for, or underwriting securities, and agreeing or offering to make an agreement as to any of the foregoing. Certain dealings, such as the acquisition of securities under a will or intestacy, are exempted[167]. 'Securities' means shares and debentures for which dealing facilities are provided on a recognised stock exchange (thus, it does not include shares or debentures of a private company). The Minister for Jobs, Enterprise and Innovation may extend the category of shares and debentures covered by the term. 'Persons connected with' a company include its officers, officers of related companies, shareholders in the company and related companies, and persons who might reasonably be expected to have access to such information through

164 Regulation 16 of the MA(D)R 2005.

165 Regulation 16 of the MA(D)R 2005.

166 See para [**32.062**] *ante* (ICMPFA Commencement Order 2005).

167 Section 110 of the CA 1990.

professional relationships with the company or through their position as officers of companies which have a shareholding in the company concerned.

[32.094] The nuances of the concept of insider dealing provided in s 107 of the CA 1990 have been considered by the High Court and Supreme Court in the *Fyffes* decision, above[168]. It will be recalled that the Supreme Court held that the reasonable investor test as regards the effect which information might have was not applicable to the concept of insider dealing provided in Part V of the CA 1990.

[32.095] Section 109 of the CA 1990 renders a person guilty of insider dealing liable to compensate any other party who was not in possession of the relevant information for any difference between the price at which the securities were dealt and the price at which they would have been dealt if he had been in possession of the relevant information. Such a person is also liable to account to the company for any profit made on the deal. A two-year limitation period applies to actions under this section.

[32.096] Insider dealing is also a criminal offence, rendering the guilty party liable, on summary conviction, to a class C fine or imprisonment for up to 12 months, or both, and on indictment to a fine of up to €444,408.32 (when the multiplier in the FA 2010 is applied) or imprisonment for 10 years, or both[169]. A person convicted of insider dealing commits a further offence if he deals in any securities in the following 12 months.

The Stock Exchange is given the duty of reporting to the Director of Public Prosecutions wherever it is of the opinion that insider dealing has occurred[170]. It may also conduct an investigation to enable it to report to the Director of Corporate Enforcement, and it may cooperate with, or receive the cooperation of other EU stock exchanges in this regard[171].

[32.097] In *DPP v Byrne*[172], a company director was prosecuted in the Circuit Criminal Court for breach of s 111 of the CA 1990 for dealing in securities in a manner declared unlawful by s 108 of the CA 1990. In that case, the circuit judge held that the jury had to be satisfied beyond any reasonable doubt that the defendant had been in possession of price sensitive information at the time he sold the shares *and* that he *intended* to profit by using the inside information. This places a high onus on the prosecution and is to be contrasted with the Court of Justice of the EU's decision in *Spector Photo Group* above[173] which considers the prospect of 'innocent' insider dealing.

(xiii) Liability for insider dealing at common law

[32.098] At common law the directors of a company owe fiduciary duties to exercise their powers *bona fide* in the best interests of the company as a whole; and they are bound not to put themselves in a position in which their duties to the company and their personal interests may conflict[174]. Where the duty is breached, a constructive trust may potentially arise in favour of the company. In *Fyffes plc v DCC plc*[175], a claim was made

---

168 See para **[32.077]** *ante*.

169 Section 111 and 114 of the CA 1990.

170 Section 115 of the CA 1990 as amended by s 37 of the CLEA 2001.

171 Section 116 of the CA 1990.

172 (2002) Irish Times, 15, 16, 17, 18, 19, 22, 24, 25, 26, 29 and 30 January.

173 See para **[32.081]** *ante*.

174 See Ch 15, *Duties of Directors and other Officers,* at para **[15.071]**.

175 *Fyffes plc v DCC plc* [2009] 2 IR 417.

at common law that a constructive trust should be imposed on the defendants. Laffoy J, however, held that the profit sought to be attached in the instant case was not the result of exploitation by the insider director, in breach of his fiduciary duty, of confidential price-sensitive information for his own benefit. In principle, however, it has been argued that a constructive trust may arise in circumstances where liability for insider dealing is established[176]. More recently, in *Quinn & Ors v Irish Bank Resolution Corporation & Anor*[177] the High Court considered that the introduction of specific offences of insider dealing and market manipulation did not prevent the courts considering other complaints, such as illegality in contracts, where the events in question fell within the purview of the Market Abuse Directive.

(b) Market manipulation

[32.099] Article 5 of the Market Abuse Directive succinctly requires Member States to 'prohibit any person from engaging in market manipulation'. The concept of market manipulation is fleshed out somewhat in art 2 of the Market Abuse Directive. In general terms, whereas insider dealing is focused more on dealings in financial instruments, market manipulation is concerned with misleading transactions and information which undermine or distort the market. The definition in art 2 of the Market Abuse Directive is extremely broad in its scope, and it remains to be seen whether the definition enjoys the requisite specificity required for the definition of criminal offences; it has been commented that the criminal offences of market manipulation created by reg 2 of the MA(D)R 2005 most likely require *mens rea* to be shown given the serious nature of the sanctions that can be imposed[178].

(i) 'Market manipulation' defined

[32.100] Regulation 2 of the MA(D)R 2005 provides that 'market manipulation' means:

> '(a) transactions or orders to trade—
>
> (i) which give, or are likely to give, false or misleading signals as to the supply of, demand for or price of financial instruments, or
>
> (ii) which secure, by a person, or persons acting in collaboration, the price of one or several financial instruments at an abnormal or artificial level,
>
> unless the person who entered into the transactions or issued the orders to trade establishes that the person's reasons for so doing are legitimate and the transactions or orders to trade, as the case may be, conform to accepted market practices on the regulated market concerned,
>
> (b) transactions or orders to trade which employ fictitious devices or any other form of deception or contrivance, or
>
> (c) dissemination of information through the media, including the Internet, or by any other means, which gives, or is likely to give, false or misleading signals as to financial instruments, including the dissemination of rumours and false or misleading news, where the person who made the dissemination knew, or ought to have known, that the information was false or misleading.'

---

176 See Abrahamson, 'Another Look at Insider Dealing' (2010) CLP 99.

177 *Quinn & Ors v Irish Bank Resolution Corporation & Anor* [2012] IEHC 36.

178 Horan, *Corporate Crime* (2011, Bloomsbury Professional) para [15.180].

It may be noted that this definition of market manipulation comprises four broad categories of manipulating activity:

- giving false or misleading signals – reg 2(a)(i) above;
- securing price at abnormal or artificial levels – reg 2(a)(ii) above;
- employing fictitious devices or any other form of deception or contrivance – reg 2(b) above; and
- dissemination of information through the internet or by any other means, including dissemination of rumours and false or misleading news – reg 2(c) above.

[32.101] Schedule 2 to the MA(D)R 2005 provides further insight into the first two categories which should be considered by market participants or the Central Bank. Insofar as giving false or misleading signals and securing price are concerned, consideration must be given to:

- the extent to which orders to trade given or transactions undertaken represent a significant proportion of the daily volume of transactions in the relevant financial instrument on the regulated market concerned, in particular when these activities lead to a significant change in the price of the financial instrument;
- the extent to which orders to trade given or transactions undertaken by persons with a significant buying or selling position in a financial instrument lead to significant changes in the price of the financial instrument or related derivative or underlying asset admitted to trading on a regulated market;
- whether transactions undertaken lead to no change in beneficial ownership of financial instruments admitted to trading on a regulated market;
- the extent to which orders to trade given or transactions undertaken include position reversals in a short period and represent a significant proportion of the daily volume of transactions in the relevant financial instrument on the regulated market concerned, and might be associated with significant changes in the price of a financial instrument admitted to trading on a regulated market;
- the extent to which orders to trade given or transactions undertaken are concentrated within a short time span in the trading session and lead to a price change which is subsequently reversed;
- the extent to which orders to trade given change the representation of the best bid or offer prices in a financial instrument admitted to trading on a regulated market, or more generally the representation of the order book available to market participants, and are removed before they are executed; and
- the extent to which orders to trade are given or transactions are undertaken at or around a specific time when reference prices, settlement prices and valuations are calculated and lead to price changes which have an effect on such prices and valuations.

[32.102] Moreover, Schedule 3 to the MA(D)R 2005 provides further insight into the third categories which should be considered by market participants or the Central Bank. Insofar as transactions or orders to trade which employ fictitious devices or any other form of deception or contrivance are concerned, consideration should be given to the following non-exhaustive signals, which should not necessarily be deemed in themselves to constitute market manipulation:

- whether orders to trade given or transactions undertaken by persons are preceded or followed by dissemination of false or misleading information by the same persons or persons linked to them, and
- whether orders to trade are given or transactions are undertaken by persons before or after the same persons or persons linked to them produce or disseminate research or investment recommendations which are erroneous or biased or demonstrably influenced by material interest.

(ii) Exceptions to market manipulation – accepted market practices

[32.103] Where the person who entered into the transactions or issued the orders to trade establishes that the person's reasons for so doing are legitimate and the transactions or orders to trade, as the case may be, conform to accepted market practices on the regulated market concerned, the practice is expressly excluded from the definition of market manipulation[179]. 'Accepted market practices' or AMPs for these purposes are practices that are reasonably expected in one or more financial markets and are accepted by the Central Bank of Ireland in accordance with certain criteria as specified in Schedule 1 of the MA(D)R 2005. Thus far no AMPs have been issued in Ireland in connection with market manipulation.

(c) Notification obligations under the Market Abuse Directive

[32.104] In addition to prohibiting market abuse in the form of insider dealing and market manipulation, the Market Abuse Directive imposes certain notification requirements on managers and other persons in respect of managers' transactions and suspicions transaction.

(i) Notification of managers' transactions

[32.105] Regulation 12 of the MA(D)R 2005 requires 'persons discharging managerial responsibilities' within an issuer of financial instruments registered in the State, and 'persons closely associated' with them, to notify to the Central Bank in writing of transactions conducted on their own account relating to shares of the issuer, or to derivatives or other financial instruments linked to them. Managers, and persons associated with them, within an issuer of financial instruments *not* registered in the State, must likewise notify transactions conducted on their own account relating to shares of the issuer, or to derivatives on other instruments linked to them if the issuer is registered in another Member State, in accordance with the rules of notification relating thereto of that Member State, or if the issuer is not registered in another Member State, to the competent authority of the home Member State of the issuer within the terms of the Prospectus Directive. Notification is required to be made to the Bank within five working days of the day of the transaction. The Bank may provide for exemptions where the total amount of the transactions is less than €5,000 at the end of a calendar year, or notification may be delayed until 31 January of the following year[180].

---

179 Regulation 2(a) of the MA(D)R 2005.

180 Regulation 12(4) of the MA(D)R 2005. Under reg 12(5), the total amount of transactions shall be calculated by adding together the transactions conducted on the own account of a person discharging managerial responsibilities within an issuer, and the transactions conducted on the own account of persons closely associated with the person referred *ante*.

[32.106] 'Person discharging managerial responsibilities', in relation to an issuer of financial instruments, means a person who is a member of the administrative, management or supervisory bodies of the issuer[181], or a senior executive who is not a member of the administrative or supervisory bodies of the issuer and has regular access to inside information relating, directly or indirectly, to the issuer, and who has the power to make managerial decisions affecting the future developments and business prospects of the issuer[182]. 'Person closely associated', for these purposes, includes the spouse of the person discharging managerial responsibilities; dependent children of the person discharging managerial responsibilities; other relatives of the person discharging managerial responsibilities, who have shared the same household as that person for at least one year on the date of the transaction concerned; as well as others linked by economic interests.

[32.107] The notification by managers must contain:[183]

> '(a) the name of the person discharging managerial responsibilities within the issuer or, where applicable, the name of a person closely associated with such a person,
> (b) the reason for responsibility to notify,
> (c) the name of the relevant issuer,
> (d) a description of the financial instrument,
> (e) the nature of the transaction (for example, acquisition or disposal),
> (f) the date and place of the transaction, and
> (g) the price and volume of the transaction.'

The Central Bank must ensure that public access to information concerning the transactions notified to it is readily available, at least on an individual basis, without delay.

(ii) Notification of suspicious transactions

[32.108] Regulation 13(1) of the MA(D)R 2005 introduces a whistle-blowing requirement such that any 'prescribed person' must decide on a case-by-case basis whether there are reasonable grounds for suspecting that a transaction involves market abuse after taking into account the elements constituting market abuse. If he or she reasonably suspects that a transaction might constitute market abuse, they must notify the Central Bank without delay. A prescribed person is any person (including any investment firm, credit institution or market operator) professionally arranging transactions in financial instruments who is registered in the State, or consists of a branch operating in the State of any person including any investment firm, credit institution or market operator) professionally arranging transactions in financial instruments, and registered in another Member State.

[32.109] The notification may be by telephone call to a telephone number specified by the Bank (indeed the Bank has provided a form on its webpage) provided that a notification in writing to the same effect is made as soon as is practicable after that call,

---

181 As to administrative and advisory organs see the discussion of such bodies in respect of SEs, discussed in Ch 29, *Public Limited Companies and SEs*, at para **[29.174]**. In simple terms, the concepts relate to the board of directors of the company and any management committees.

182 Regulation 12 of the MA(D)R 2005.

183 Regulation 12(6) of the MA(D)R 2005.

and it must contain a description of the transactions concerned, including the type of order (such as limit order, market order or other characteristics of the order) and the type of trading market (such as block trade). It must also give the reason or reasons for suspecting that the transactions might constitute market abuse and the names, or means of identification, of the persons on behalf of whom the transactions have been carried out, and of other persons involved in the transactions, the capacity in which the prescribed person operates (such as for own account or on behalf of third parties), and any other information which may be significant in reviewing the transactions. If all of the above information is not available at the time of notification then the notification must at least contain the reason or reasons for the suspicion.

[32.110] On receipt, the Central Bank must transmit the notification immediately to the relevant competent authority of each regulated market on which the financial instrument concerned is admitted to trading, or is the subject of a request to be admitted to trading of which the Bank is aware.

[32.111] CESR has issued guidance and examples on the notification of suspicious transactions, indicating that blanket reporting is neither expected nor required[184]. CESR further recommends that firms should notify suspicious events subsequent to key events that retrospectively become suspicious.

[32.112] A prescribed person shall not be liable for any act done, or purporting to be done, in good faith by the person pursuant to these obligations[185]. Moreover, the Central Bank must not disclose the identity of the whistle-blower to any person if such disclosure would, or would be likely to, harm the notifier. Regulation 14(2) of the MA(D)R 2005 imposes a like obligation on the person making the notification not to inform any other person, in particular the persons on behalf of whom the transactions concerned have been carried out, or parties related to those persons.

(d) Criminal liability for breaches of the Market Abuse Directive

[32.113] Regulation 49 of the MA(D)R 2005 imposes criminal liability on any person who breaches the requirements of the Market Abuse Directive, with limited exception. Offences under reg 49 are triable summarily. The Central Bank may bring the prosecution, and a person convicted will be subject to a fine of up to €5,000 or imprisonment for up to 12 months, or both. A contravention of regs 5 and 6 of the MA(D)R 2005 (prohibiting insider dealing and market manipulation) may alternatively be prosecuted on indictment and persons convicted will be liable to a fine of up to €10 million or imprisonment for 10 years, or both[186]. Where contravention continues after conviction a further offence is committed for each day the contravention continues[187]. Where an offence is committed by a body corporate and is proved to have been committed with the consent, connivance or approval of or to have been attributable to the wilful neglect on the part of any person, being a director, manager, secretary or other officer of the body corporate or a person who was purporting to act in any such capacity,

---

184 CESR Level 3 – Third Set of CESR guidance and information on the common operation of the Directive to the market (CESR /09-219).

185 Regulation 13(6) of the MA(D)R 2005.

186 Regulation 49(2) of the MA(D)R 2005; s 32 of the IFCMPA 2005.

187 Regulation 49(3) of the MA(D)R 2005.

that person as well as the body corporate is guilty of an offence and is liable to be proceeded against and punished as if that person were guilty of the first-mentioned offence. A person may be charged with having committed an offence under the MA(D)R 2005 even if the body corporate concerned is not charged with having committed an offence under the Regulations in relation to the same matter[188].

(e) *Administrative sanctions for breaches of the Market Abuse Directive*

[32.114] Under Part 4 of the MA(D)R 2005, the Central Bank has extensive powers to appoint authorised officers who may, in turn, investigate and inspect those who operate in the financial market. The Central Bank may suspend the trading of any financial instrument, stop payments, block subscriptions, prevent a business from carrying on further, block a business from dealing with specified transactions or use the same power subject to specified conditions and may publish information. These powers do not include a measure allowing the Central Bank to invalidate any transaction that has taken place. The Central Bank is authorised to impose a penalty under reg 41 of the MA(D)R 2005 which can include a reprimand in private or in public, a penalty not exceeding €2.5 million and a disqualification order.

(f) *Civil liability for breaches of the Market Abuse Directive*

[32.115] If a person contravenes the prohibition against insider dealing then under s 33 of the IFCMPA 2005 that person shall further be liable:

> '(a) to compensate any other party to the transaction concerned who was not in possession of the relevant information for any loss sustained by that party by reason of any difference between the price at which the financial instruments concerned were acquired or disposed of and the price at which they would have been likely to have been acquired or disposed of in such a transaction at the time when the first-mentioned transaction took place if that information had been generally available, and
>
> (b) to account to the body corporate or other legal entity which issued the financial instruments concerned for any profit accruing to the first-mentioned person from acquiring or disposing of those instruments.'

[32.116] Likewise, where a person contravenes the market manipulation prohibition, that person shall be liable:

> '(a) to compensate any other party who acquired or disposed of financial instruments by reason of the contravention, and
>
> (b) to account to the body corporate or other legal entity which issued the financial instruments concerned for any profit accruing to the first-mentioned person from acquiring or disposing of those instruments.'

These provisions are expressed to be without prejudice to any other cause of action which may lie against the person for contravening the provision concerned. However, an action under these provisions shall not be commenced more than two years after the date of the contravention concerned.

---

188 Regulation 52 of the MA(D)R 2005.

[32.117] In *Quinn & Ors v Irish Bank Resolution Corporation & Anor*[189], the High Court considered that the introduction of specific offences of insider dealing and market manipulation did not prevent the courts considering other complaints, such as illegality in contracts, where the events in question fell within the purview of the Market Abuse Directive. Charleton J stated[190]:

> 'I cannot accept that this Act of 2005 is not a directive to the courts to respond under the illegality principle to contracts which flagrantly breach its provisions. Nor can I accept that the introduction of illegality into the context within which Anglo and Seán Quinn were said to have acted would introduce chaos into the marketplace and undermine the scheme of careful regulation which the legislation set up. On the contrary, weighing heavily on the balance against the success of this argument is the removal thereby of a proportionate remedy against the wrongdoers alleged in this case, namely Seán Quinn and Anglo, to ensure that there is no unjust and massive enrichment as a reward for market manipulation. It is difficult to comprehend a sensible view of what is right which would enable Anglo, as the defendant in this case, to gain from the financial manipulation of the Quinns and to plead that because new instruments were added on to what may, if proved, be Anglo deliberately causing egregious loss through illegality. It is possible that, in addition to what is pleaded, the Quinns as plaintiffs may be entitled to seek a remedy under section 33(2) of the Act of 2005. I cannot fairly assess the leaving open by the Oireachtas of other causes of action under section 33(3) as being anything other than deliberate. In that regard, I am not convinced that what is at issue here is what is condemned by Kirby J at p 244 of *Fitzgerald v Leonhardt* as the addition of random and unfair civil consequences. On the contrary, it seems to me that illegality as a plea is neither an arbitrary nor an unnecessary supplement to the remedies provided.'

[C] TRANSPARENCY

[32.118] The Transparency Directive[191], as amended[192], is the third piece of legislation under the EU's Financial Services Action Plan ('FSAP') which seeks to improve investor protection and market efficiency by enhancing transparency in EU capital markets. It introduces a common requirement across EU Member States requiring listed companies to prepare and publish periodic financial reports and other specific investor-relevant information. There are three principal elements to the Transparency Directive regime:

- a requirement that issuers issue periodic financial reports;
- a requirement that shareholders disclose major shareholdings;
- a requirement for issuers to disseminate regulated information.

The Directive further provides for centralised mechanisms for sharing regulated information to investors throughout the EU.

The Directive is implemented in Ireland through the IFCMPA 2006 and the Transparency (Directive 2004/109/EC) Regulations 2007 ('T(D)R 2007') with effect

189 *Quinn & Ors v Irish Bank Resolution Corporation & Anor* [2012] IEHC 36.

190 *Quinn & Ors v Irish Bank Resolution Corporation & Anor* [2012] IEHC 36 at para G9 of the transcript.

191 Directive 2004/109/EC of the European Parliament and of the Council of 15 December 2004.

192 By Directive 2010/73/EU of the European Parliament and of the Council of 24 November 2010.

from 13 June 2007, as amended by the Transparency (Directive 2004/109/EC) (Amendment) Regulations 2010 ('T(D)(A)R 2010')[193] and the Transparency Directive (Amendment) Regulations 2012[194] ('TD(A)R 2012') with effect from 1 July 2012.

[32.119] Regulation 36 of the T(D)R 2007 designates the Central Bank of Ireland as the competent authority in Ireland for all aspects of the Directive other than monitoring compliance by issuers with the relevant financial reporting framework; that role is given to the IAASA[195]. The Central Bank has chosen to exercise certain of its functions as central competent authority under the Regulations by delegating certain tasks to the Irish Stock Exchange Limited[196]. However, final responsibility for discharging the functions of the central competent authority under the Regulations remains with the Central Bank, and as such it and the IAASA are given extensive investigatory and disciplinary powers by art 34 of the Directive, and Parts 9–10 of the T(D)R 2007 flesh these out to include the issuing of directions, the appointment of authorised officers to investigate, and the imposition of administrative sanctions.

[32.120] The Central Bank has published[197] *Transparency Rules 2009* to assist issuers and shareholders in meeting their obligations under the Directive. The rules contain guidance, contact details, and, significantly, standard forms (to be used when making a notification or publication under the Directive). It also published, in 2009, a guidance note on the periodic publication obligations imposed by the Directive[198].

Scope of the Transparency Directive

[32.121] The Transparency Directive is addressed at issuers whose securities are already admitted to trading on a regulated market situated or operating within a Member State[199]. An issuer for these purposes is:

> 'a legal entity governed by private or public law, including a State, whose securities are admitted to trading on a regulated market, the issuer being, in the case of depository receipts representing securities, the issuer of the securities represented[200].'

And 'securities' for these purposes means:

> 'those classes of securities which are negotiable on the capital market, with the exception of instruments of payment, such as:
>
> (a) shares in companies and other securities equivalent to shares in companies, partnerships or other entities, and depositary receipts in respect of shares;
>
> (b) bonds or other forms of securitised debt, including depositary receipts in respect of such securities;

---

193 SI 102/2010.

194 SI 238/2012.

195 Regulation 36(2) of the T(D)R 2007. The Bank and IAASA (the Irish Auditing and Accounting Supervisory Authority) shall each be independent in the performance of its functions under these Regulations: reg 36(3).

196 Regulation 37 of the T(D)R 2007.

197 Under s 22 of the IFCMPA 2006.

198 Guidance Note No 1, 2009. See www.centralbank.ie.

199 Article 1 of the Transparency Directive.

200 Article 2(1)(d) of the Transparency Directive.

> (c) any other securities giving the right to acquire or sell any such transferable securities or giving rise to a cash settlement determined by reference to transferable securities, currencies, interest rates or yields, commodities or other indices or measures[201].'

The Directive therefore applies to issuers of shares, debt securities, derivative securities and closed-end investment funds admitted to listing and trading on the regulated markets. Open-end investment funds and UCITS are, however, specifically excluded from the scope of the Directive[202].

In the Irish context, it was noted above that the Transparency Directive does not apply to the GSM and ESM of the Irish Stock Exchange, since they are regarded as multilateral trading facilities and not regulated markets, though there are proposals to bring them within the purview of the Directive in the future[203].

(a) Periodic financial reports required by the Transparency Directive

[32.122] The Transparency Directive sets out requirements on both the content and the timing of annual and half-yearly financial reports, and introduces a further requirement for 'interim management statements' by issuers who do not produce quarterly reports.

[32.123] As regards the annual financial report, art 4 of the Transparency Directive, as implemented by reg 4 of the T(D)R 2007, requires an issuer whose securities are admitted to trading on a regulated market and whose home Member State is the State to make public its annual financial report at the latest four months after the end of each financial year and to ensure that it remains publicly available for at least five years. The annual financial report must include:[204]

- audited financial statements prepared in accordance with the applicable accounting standards;
- a management report; and
- responsibility statements.

Responsibility statements are statements made by the persons responsible within the issuer, and must state the name and function of the person or persons making the responsibility statement. Depending on the type of statement, the person making the responsibility statement must set out that, to the best of his or her knowledge:[205]

> '(i) the financial statements, prepared in accordance with the applicable set of accounting standards, give a true and fair view of the assets, liabilities, financial position and profit or loss of the issuer and the undertakings included in the consolidation taken as a whole; and
>
> (ii) the management report includes a fair review of the development and performance of the business and the position of the issuer and the undertakings included in the consolidation taken as a whole, together with a description of the principal risks and uncertainties that they face.'

---

201 Article 4(18) of Directive 2004/39 EC (the Markets in Financial Instruments Directive, or 'MIFID') as applied by art 2.1 of the Transparency Directive.

202 Article 1(2) of the Transparency Directive.

203 See para **[32.004]** *ante*.

204 Article 4(2) of the Transparency Directive; reg 4(3) of the T(D)R 2007.

205 Article 4.2 of the Transparency Directive; reg 5(4) of the T(D)R 2007.

If the issuer is required to produce consolidated group accounts then the audited financial statements must comprise consolidated accounts drawn up in line with Regulation (EC) No 1606/2002, and the financial statements must also include the annual accounts of the parent company, drawn up in line with the national law of the Member State where the parent company is incorporated. Where the issuer is not required to prepare consolidated accounts the audited financial statements must be prepared in accordance with the issuer's national law[206]. Moreover, the audit report must be disclosed along with the annual financial report[207].

[32.124] As regards the half-yearly financial report – previously known as 'interim results' – art 5 of the Transparency Directive requires issuers to make public a half-yearly financial report covering the first six months of the financial year as soon as possible after the end of the relevant period, but at the latest two months thereafter. Again, the issuer is required to ensure that the half-yearly financial report remains available to the public for at least five years.

The half-yearly report must contain[208]:

- a condensed set of financial statements prepared in accordance with the applicable accounting standards;
- an interim management report; and
- responsibility statements.

Where the issuer is required to produce consolidated accounts, the condensed set of financial statements must be prepared in line with Regulation No 1606/2002 (on the application of international accounting standards)[209]. Where the issuer is not required to prepare consolidated accounts, the condensed financial statements must at least include a condensed balance sheet, and a condensed profit and loss account and explanatory notes, prepared in line with the same principles applied to the annual financial accounts. If the half-yearly report has been audited or reviewed by an auditor then the auditors' report or review must also be published[210].

An important feature of the interim management report is that it must include an indication of important events that have occurred during the first six months of the financial year and their impact on the condensed set of financial statements, together with a description of the principal risks and uncertainties for the remaining six months of the financial year. For issuers of shares, a description of major related party transactions is also required[211].

A responsibility statement must also be included in the half-yearly report certifying that, to the best of the knowledge of the persons making the statement, the condensed set of financial statements have been prepared in accordance with the applicable accounting standards and give a true and fair view of the assets, liabilities, financial position and profit or loss of the issuer or the undertakings included in the consolidation and that the interim management statement includes a fair review of the information required[212]. In

206 Article 4.3 of the Transparency Directive; reg 5 of the T(D)R 2007.

207 Article 4.4 of the Transparency Directive; reg 5(2)(c) of the T(D)R 2007.

208 Article 5.2 of the Transparency Directive; reg 6(3) of the T(D)R 2007.

209 See Ch 17, *Financial Statements, Audit and Annual Return*, at para **[17.023]**.

210 Article 5.5 of the Transparency Directive; reg 8(4)(b) of the T(D)R 2007.

211 Article 5.4 of the Transparency Directive; reg 8(3) of the T(D)R 2007.

212 Article 5.2(c) of the Transparency Directive.

the Irish context, the T(D)R 2007 clarify what is expected as regards 'true and fair' in relation to the half-yearly reports; the standard is different to that required in respect of the annual reports. Regulation 8(5)(d) of the T(D)R 2007 provides that:

> 'A person making a responsibility statement shall be regarded as satisfying the requirement … by including a statement that the condensed set of financial statements have been prepared in accordance with:
>
> (i) the international accounting standard applicable to the interim financial reporting adopted pursuant to the procedure provided for under Article 6 of Regulation (EC) No 1606/2002 of the European Parliament and of the Council of 19 July 2002; or
>
> (ii) for Irish issuers not using IFRS, pronouncements on half-yearly reports issued by the Accounting Standards Board; or
>
> (iii) for all other issuers not using IFRS, a national accounting standard relating to interim reporting,
>
> provided always that a person making such a statement has reasonable grounds to be satisfied that the condensed set of financial statements prepared in accordance with such a standard is not misleading.'

This application of true and fair view has no effect on the interpretation of the true and fair view for annual accounts[213].

[32.125] Interim management statements are provided for in art 6 of the Transparency Directive. Issuers of shares are required to publish two interim management statements during a financial year, in a period between 10 weeks after the beginning and six weeks before the end of the relevant six-month period, containing:[214]

> 'an explanation of material events and transactions that have taken place during the relevant period and their impact on the financial position of the issuer and its controlled undertakings, and
>
> a general description of the financial position and performance of the issuer and its controlled undertakings during the relevant period.'

This requirement does not apply to companies that publish quarterly financial reports[215].

[32.126] Exemptions from the periodic financial reporting requirements of the Transparency Directive exist for certain types of issuers, notably issuers of debt securities with a minimum denomination of €100,000, and Member States[216].

(b) Civil liability for false or misleading information in the periodic reports

[32.127] Article 7 of the Transparency Directive requires Member States to ensure that responsibility for the information in the periodic reports and statements lies *at least* with the issuer. In the Irish context, reg 12 of the T(D)R 2007 provides that as regards securities traded on the Irish market, or traded by Irish companies in another Member

213 Regulation 8(5)(d) of the T(D)R 2007. Regulation 8(5)(f) confines 'Irish Issuers' in the context of 8(5)d(ii) to Irish registered PLCs.

214 Article 6.1 of the Transparency Directive.

215 Article 6.2 of the Transparency Directive.

216 Article 8 of the Transparency Directive, as amended by art 2.2 of Directive 2010/73/EU.

State, an issuer of securities is liable to pay compensation to a person who has acquired securities issued by it, and who has suffered loss in respect of them as a result of any untrue or misleading statement in the periodic reports or statements, or the omission from any such publication of any matter required to be included in it. Knowledge or recklessness by a person discharging managerial responsibilities in relation to the publication within the issuer is required to be proved; the issuer is liable only if such a person knew the statement to be untrue or misleading or was reckless as to whether it was untrue or misleading, or knew the omission to be a dishonest concealment of a material fact. Persons discharging managerial responsibility in relation to the reports include[217]:

> '(i) any director of the issuer (or person occupying the position of director, by whatever name called),
>
> (ii) in the case of an issuer whose affairs are managed by its members, any member of the issuer,
>
> (iii) in the case of an issuer that has no persons falling within clause (i) or (ii), any senior executive of the issuer having responsibilities in relation to the publication.'

Moreover, a loss is not regarded as suffered as a result of the statement or omission in the publication unless the person suffering it acquired the relevant securities in reliance on the information in the publication, and at a time when, and in circumstances in which, it was reasonable for him to rely on that information.

[32.128] Regulation 12(6) of the T(D)R 2007 expressly excludes any other type of liability (eg, liability at common law)[218] for issuers. Most significantly, personal liability of any other person, including, for example, directors, managers and officers, and responsible persons, is also expressly excluded. Regulation 12(6) provides:

> '(a) the issuer is not subject to any other liability than that provided for by this Regulation in respect of loss suffered as a result of reliance by any person on—
>
> > (i) an untrue or misleading statement in a publication to which this Regulation applies, or
> >
> > (ii) the omission from any such publication of any matter required to be included in it, and
>
> (b) a person other than the issuer is not subject to any liability, other than to the issuer, in respect of any such loss.'

The right of a third party to repudiate an agreement to acquire securities on the basis of false or misleading information is also subjected to the requirements of reg 12(6) of the T(D)R 2007. Regulation 12(7) of the T(D)R 2007 provides that any reference to a person being subject to a liability includes a reference to another person being entitled as against him or her to be granted any civil remedy or to rescind or repudiate an agreement. However, none of these exclusions extends to non-civil liability, most notably criminal liability[219].

---

[217] Regulation 12(9) of the T(D)R 2007.

[218] On liability at common law in respect of false or misleading statements, see para **[32.048]** *ante*.

[219] Regulation 12(8) of the T(D)R 2007.

(c) On-going information requirements

[32.129] Chapter III of the Transparency Directive deals with ongoing information requirements relating to major shareholdings or voting rights. The requirements vary according to whether the person is (i) a shareholder, directly or indirectly, or (ii) an issuer. Each of these situations is now examined below.

(i) Obligations on shareholders concerning major shareholdings

[32.130] Shareholders must notify issuers and the competent authority concerning acquisition or disposal of major shareholdings and voting rights. Article 9 requires Member States to ensure that shareholders notify an issuer when they acquire or dispose of a major shareholding having voting rights attached. In Ireland, this is implemented by regs 14 to 17 of the T(D)R 2007. The Regulations require a shareholder to notify the issuer of the percentage of voting rights he holds where the percentage of the voting rights he holds as shareholder, or through his direct or indirect holding of financial instruments, or a combination of such holdings, reaches, exceeds or falls below thresholds of 5%, 10%, 15%, 20%, 30%, 50% and 75%. The notification requirements apply equally to any person with a direct or indirect holding of financial instruments (including derivative securities) carrying an unconditional right to acquire securities to which voting rights attach[220]. Notably, a disposal will take place where proxies are used and accordingly notification is required in such circumstances when the thresholds are met[221].

One notable exception from the requirement to disclose interests in shares were interests in simple *contracts for difference* or CFDs, the build-up of which by Sean Quinn resulted in so much trouble for Anglo Irish Bank Corporation plc. A simple CFD is a form of derivative financial instrument whereby the holder has a right to payment (an economic interest) which is related to the price of shares but does not have any rights in relation to the shares themselves. Complex CFDs can, however, give the holder the right to call for the shares or be entitled to the voting rights attaching to the shares and such CFDs can give rise to an obligation to make disclosure to the company under the T(D)R 2007.

[32.131] The duty of disclosure by major shareholders does not remove the obligation of directors and secretaries to disclose their personal, family and corporate interests in shares or debentures of a company under s 53 of the CA 1990. Nor does it dispense with the need for 'persons discharging managerial responsibilities' to disclose their personal, family and corporate interests in shares of a company whose shares are admitted to trading on a regulated market, under reg 12 of the MA(D)R 2005. Likewise, the duty of shareholders in a company subject to the Irish Takeover Rules or the Substantial Acquisition Rules to notify certain dealings in shares in such a company remains. However, the disclosure provisions of Ch 2 of Part IV of the CA 1990 and the related provisions of that chapter do not apply to an acquisition or disposal of shares which must be notified under the T(D)R 2007 or an acquisition or disposal of shares which, but for an express exemption provided by or under the T(D)R 2007 (whether the word 'exempted' is used or not), would be required to be notified under the Regulations[222].

---

220 Regulation 17 of the T(D)R 2007.

221 Regulation 15 of the T(D)R 2007.

222 Regulation 18 of the T(D)R 2007.

[32.132] The procedure for notification is prescribed in regs 21 and 22 of the T(D)R 2007. Notification must simultaneously be made to the issuer and the competent authority in the Member State[223]. The time frame has a subjective element in that notification must be made within four trading days after the date on which the shareholder first learned of the acquisition, disposal, or possibility of exercising voting rights, regardless of when the event actually occurred[224]. The issuer is required to make the information public within three trading days of receipt[225].

The information required to be supplied is detailed in reg 21(1) and (2) of the T(D)R 2007 and includes:

'(a) the resulting situation in terms of voting rights;

(b) the chain of controlled undertakings through which voting rights are effectively held, if applicable;

(c) the date on which the threshold was reached or crossed; and

(d) the identity of the shareholder even if that shareholder is not entitled to exercise voting rights under the conditions specified in Regulation 15 and of the person entitled to exercise voting rights on behalf of that shareholder.'

In Ireland, the notification is to be made using a form TR-1 as specified in the Transparency Rules 2009. 'Market makers', ie, persons who hold themselves out on the financial markets on a continuous basis as being willing to deal on their own account by buying and selling financial instruments against their proprietary capital at prices defined by themselves, are required to make separate notifications using standard form TR-2.

(ii) Obligations on issuers concerning shareholdings and voting rights

[32.133] Under reg 19 of the T(D)R 2007 an issuer who acquires or disposes of its own shares, either itself or through a person acting on its behalf, must publicly disclose the percentage of voting rights attributable to those shares as soon as possible, but not later than four trading days following the acquisition or disposal, where the percentage reaches, exceeds or falls below a 5% or 10% threshold, based on voting rights.

In addition, issuers must publicly disclose the total number of voting rights and capital at the end of each calendar month during which an increase or decrease occurs[226].

(d) Continuing obligations and access to information

[32.134] Articles 16 to 18 of the Transparency Directive stipulate continuing obligations on issuers with regard to information and access to information. The requirements vary depending upon whether it is the issuer's shares or the issuer's debt securities which are traded on the regulated market. In either case there is an overriding obligation of pari passu treatment, and an ongoing obligation to publicise any proposed changes to the rights attaching to the shares or the securities, and there are detailed requirements as regards making available information concerning the meetings at which such decisions are to be made and the holders' rights to participate in such decisions. Regulations 25–29 of the T(D)R 2007 flesh out these requirements in the Irish context and, notably,

223 Regulation 22 of the T(D)R 2007.

224 Regulation 21(3)(a)(1) of the T(D)R 2007.

225 Regulation 21(9) of the T(D)R 2007.

226 Regulation 20 of the T(D)R 2007.

countenance the use of information technology in the publication of information and participation in decision making.

[32.135] Likewise, any proposed changes to the memorandum and articles of association of the issuer must be notified to the competent authority, accompanied by the draft amendment, at the latest on the date of calling the general meeting which is to vote on, or be informed of, the amendment[227].

(e) General obligations with regard to the dissemination of regulated information

[32.136] Under art 19 of the Transparency Directive, any time an issuer is required to disclose regulated information it must simultaneously notify that information to the competent authority in the home Member State. In Ireland, under the T(D)R 2007 and the Transparency Rules 2009 an issuer will typically disclose regulated information to the market using a regulatory information service or via the company announcements service of the Irish Stock Exchange. These mechanisms also ensure that the information is filed with the Central Bank as required by the Transparency Directive and reg 31 of the T(D)R 2007.

[32.137] Detailed requirements apply to the language in which disclosure is made. Consistent with the idea of home state control, the Transparency Directive requires regulated information to be supplied in a language acceptable to the competent authority in the home Member State[228]. Where the securities are also traded in other states, then the information must also be supplied in a language acceptable to the competent authorities of the other state, or in a language customary in the sphere of international finance[229]. There is an exemption for large denomination securities: if securities whose denomination per unit amounts to at least €100,000 (or an equivalent amount), regulated information shall be disclosed to the public in either a language accepted by the competent authorities of the home Member State and host Member States, or in a language customary in the sphere of international finance, at the election of the issuer or of the person who, without the issuer's consent, has requested such admission[230].

---

227 Article 19 of the Transparency Directive; reg 25(2)(a) of the T(D)R 2007.

228 Article 20.1 of the Transparency Directive; reg 32 of the T(D)R 2007.

229 Article 20.1 of the Transparency Directive; reg 32 of the T(D)R 2007.

230 Article 20(6) of the Transparency Directive, as amended by art 2(4) of Directive 2010/73/EU. Regulation 32(6) of the T(D)R 2007 as amended by reg 2 of the Transparency (Directive 2004/109/EC) (Amendment) Regulations 2012. The €100,000 threshold applies to securities issued after 31 December 2010. For earlier securities the threshold is €50,000 as originally prescribed in the Transparency Directive.

Chapter 33

Conversion by Re-registration

[33.001] When registered, a company will be of a specific type: eg, limited by shares, limited by guarantee or unlimited; it may be either public or private and in the case of a private company it may be single-member or multi-member. At any time subsequent to its original registration a company may convert to another type of company. Currently, not every type of company can convert to every other type of company but this will be addressed in the new Companies Bill which the Company Law Review Group recommended would facilitate every type of company having the capability to convert to every other type of company.

In this chapter, it is proposed to outline the legal regime applicable to the following types of conversion by re-registration that are currently permitted:

1. Unlimited to limited.
2. Limited to unlimited.
3. PLC to private.
4. Private to PLC[1].
5. Multi-member private company to single-member company.
6. Single-member private company to multi-member private company.

Unlimited to limited

[33.002] Both private unlimited companies and public unlimited companies can convert to limited companies[2]. Two separate regimes apply, however, depending upon whether the re-registration is to be a *private limited company* or a PLC.

(a) Unlimited company to private limited company

[33.003] A private unlimited company can be converted to a private limited company by re-registering in accordance with s 53 of the C(A)A 1983[3]. Section 53(1) provides:

> 'A company which, on the appointed day, is registered as unlimited or thereafter is so registered (otherwise than by virtue of section 52) may be re-registered under the Principal Act as limited if a special resolution that it should be so re-registered (complying with the requirements of subsection (2)) is passed and an application in that behalf, made in the prescribed form and signed by a director or by the secretary of the company, is delivered to the registrar, together with the documents mentioned in subsection (3) not earlier than

---

1 See also Ch 29, *Public Limited Companies and SEs*, at para **[29.019]** where the conversion from private company to PLC is considered because of the fact that many PLCs, especially those admitted to trading shares, will have begun life as private companies.

2 See, generally, Ch 31, *Unlimited Companies*.

3 Note that s 20 of the CA 1963 has been repealed by s 54 of the C(A)A 1983.

> the day on which the copy of the resolution forwarded to him in pursuance of section 143 of the Principal Act is received by him.'

The key trigger needed to effect re-registration as a limited company is that the members of the unlimited company must pass a *special resolution* that it should re-register as a company limited by shares or by guarantee. In addition, the special resolution should set out the necessary changes to its memorandum and articles of association so as to make them appropriate to a limited company[4].

The requirements that the special resolution must comply with are set out in s 53(2) of the C(A)A 1983:

> 'The said requirements are that the resolution must state whether the company is to be limited by shares or by guarantee and—
>
> (a) if it is to be limited by shares, must state what the share capital is to be and provide for the making of such alterations in the memorandum as are necessary to bring it, both in substance and in form, into conformity with the requirements of the Companies Acts with respect to the memorandum of a company so limited, and such alterations in the articles as are requisite in the circumstances;
>
> (b) if it is to be limited by guarantee, must provide for the making of such alterations in its memorandum and articles as are necessary to bring them, both in substance and in form, into conformity with the requirements of the Principal Act with respect to the memorandum and articles of a company so limited.'

Not every company can re-register as a private limited company. An unlimited company which was previously a limited company but converted pursuant to s 52 of the C(A)A 1983[5] may not again re-register as a limited company. This is because s 53(1) applies to any unlimited company wishing to re-register *other* than a company that was registered as an unlimited company by virtue of s 52.

[33.004] The mechanics of re-registration[6] involve the company lodging the following documents in the CRO:

(a) Form G1 containing the text of the special resolution referred to in s 53(1) and (2);

(b) Amended memorandum and articles of association as are applicable to a private limited company;

(c) Form D12/86 completed by a director and secretary.

Upon receiving the foregoing documents properly completed, the registrar of companies shall issue an appropriate certificate of incorporation[7].

[33.005] Upon its re-registration the private limited company will be given a new 'birth certificate', in the form of a certificate of incorporation on re-registration as s 53(5) of the C(A)A 1983 provides:

---

4 Section 53(3) of the C(A)A 1983.

5 See para **[33.009]** *post*.

6 See McGowan-Smyth & Daly, *Irish company Secretary's Handbook* (2011, Bloomsbury Professional) at pp 280–295.

7 Section 53(4) of the C(A)A 1983.

'A certificate of incorporation issued by virtue of this section shall be conclusive evidence that the requirements of this section with respect to re-registration and of matters precedent and incidental thereto have been complied with, and that the company was authorised to be re-registered under the Principal Act in pursuance of this section and was duly so re-registered.'

The resulting private limited company will be the same legal entity as the unlimited company and all rights and obligations of the company and all legal proceedings will not be affected by the re-registration, s 53(8) providing:

'The re-registration of an unlimited company as a limited company pursuant to this Act shall not affect any rights or obligations of the company, or render defective any legal proceedings by or against the company, and any legal proceedings which might have been continued or commenced against it in its former status may be continued or commenced against it in its new status.'

[33.006] Upon its re-registration as a limited company, the most significant change relates to the liability of its members upon the company's winding up[8]. Section 53(7) of the C(A)A 1983 sets out the consequences of the re-registration for members:

'In the event of the winding-up of a company re-registered in pursuance of this section, the following provisions shall have effect—

(a) notwithstanding paragraph (a) of subsection (1) of section 207 of the Principal Act, a past member of the company who was a member thereof at the time of re-registration shall, if the winding-up commences within the period of three years beginning with the day on which the company is re-registered, be liable to contribute to the assets of the company in respect of its debts and liabilities contracted before that time;

(b) where no persons who were members of the company at that time are existing members of the company, a person who, at that time, was a present or past member thereof shall, subject to paragraph (a) of the said subsection (1) and to paragraph (a) of this subsection, but notwithstanding paragraph (c) of the said subsection (1), be liable to contribute as aforesaid notwithstanding that the existing members have satisfied the contributions required to be made by them in pursuance of the Principal Act;

(c) notwithstanding paragraphs (d) and (e) of the said subsection (1), there shall be no limit on the amount which a person who, at that time, was a past or present member of the company is liable to contribute as aforesaid.'

Section 53(7) of the C(A)A 1983 is by any standards a convoluted provision but it is clear that limited liability does not immediately follow from the re-registration of an unlimited company as limited. The effect of its three paragraphs may be summarised as follows:

– the past members of the re-registered 'limited liability' company will, in fact, continue to have unlimited liability for a period of three years following the company's re-registration and only after these three years have elapsed will the past members not be liable for its debts[9];

---

8 As to the liability of the members of an unlimited company, see Ch 31, *Unlimited Companies*, at para **[31.036]** *et seq*.

9 Section 53(7)(a) of the C(A)A 1983.

- where a re-registered limited company is wound up, where none of its members at the time it is wound up were members at the time of its re-registration (ie, where *all* of its members at the time it is wound up became members subsequent to its re-registration) then the people who were members at the time of re-registration or who were at the time of registration past members (ie, they were members within the previous three years) will be liable to contribute to the company's liabilities[10]. This will be so even where the then current members have paid up the amount, if any, owed by them on their shares. In order for this provision to be triggered, however, *none* of the members at the time it is wound up can have been members at the time of its re-registration; if even one of the members at the time of the winding up was a member at the time of the re-registration, this provision will not apply;
- there will be no limit on the amount which a person, who, at the time of re-registration, was a past or present member, is liable to contribute.

To understand s 53(7) it is necessary to recognise that it sets out a series of modifications to the normal rule which limit present and past members' liability to contribute to a shortfall in assets in a limited liability company. The provision looks back to who the members were when the unlimited company was re-registered and, where certain conditions are fulfilled, visits liability on them despite the fact that the company is now a limited liability company.

[33.007] The re-registration of an unlimited company as a limited company should be undertaken in the knowledge that many consequences will follow the re-registration. From being able to reduce its share capital in any way it liked, it will become the subject of the capital maintenance rules and unable to reduce its share capital otherwise than as permitted by law[11]. Moreover, the company will become obliged to disclose its financial statements when filing its annual returns.

(b) Unlimited company to PLC

[33.008] Where an unlimited company wishes to convert directly[12] into a PLC it must comply with s 11 of the C(A)A 1983 which provides:

> '(1) An unlimited company may be re-registered as a public limited company and for the purposes of such re-registration sections 9 and 53(6) and (7) shall have effect subject to the modifications contained in this section.
>
> (2) The special resolution required by section 9(1) must, in addition to the matters mentioned in section 9(2)—
>
> (a) state that the liability of the members is to be limited by shares and what the share capital of the company is to be; and
>
> (b) make such alterations in the company's memorandum as are necessary to bring it in substance and in form into conformity with the requirements of the Companies Acts with respect to the memorandum of a company limited by shares.

10 Section 53(7)(b) of the C(A)A 1983.

11 See, generally, Ch 10, *The Maintenance of Capital*.

12 An unlimited company could convert to a private limited company as described at para **[33.003]** *ante* and the resulting private limited company could subsequently convert to a PLC as described in para **[33.015]** *post*.

(3) The certificate of incorporation issued under section 9(6) shall, in addition to containing the statement required by paragraph (b) of that subsection, state that the company has been incorporated as a company limited by shares and—

(a) the company shall by virtue of the issue of that certificate become a public limited company so limited; and

(b) the certificate shall be conclusive evidence of the fact that it is such a public limited company.

(4) Section 53(6) and (7) shall have effect as if any reference to the re-registration of a company in pursuance of that section included a reference to the re-registration of an unlimited company as a public limited company in accordance with subsection (1), but except as aforesaid the said section 53 shall not apply in relation to the re-registration of an unlimited company as a public limited company.'

Limited to unlimited

[33.009] A limited liability company can change its status to that of an unlimited company in accordance with s 52 of the C(A)A 1983. A more stringent statutory procedure exists on the conversion of a limited liability company to an unlimited company. It is a fundamental principle of company law that the liability of a member cannot be increased without his consent[13]. Accordingly, because all of the members will on conversion assume full personal liability for the debts of the company if it is subsequently wound up insolvent, their *unanimous* assent to the conversion is required. So, s 52(1) of the C(A)A 1983 provides:

'A company which, on the appointed day, is registered as limited or thereafter is so registered (otherwise than in pursuance of section 53) may be re-registered under the Principal Act as unlimited in pursuance of an application in that behalf complying with the requirements of subsection (2), made in the prescribed form and signed by a director or by the secretary of the company and delivered to the registrar together with the documents mentioned in subsection (3).'

It will be noted that, again, not every company can convert from limited to unlimited. By its very terms, s 52(1) precludes companies which converted from unlimited to limited from converting back to unlimited. The reason for this restriction is to prevent companies from registering and re-registering in order to avoid the restrictions on limited liability companies reducing their share capital and availing of the exemptions from having to file financial statements.

[33.010] The *requirements* referred to in s 52(1) are to those in s 52(2) of the C(A)A 1983, which provides that the application for re-registration as unlimited, must:

'(a) set out such alterations in the company's memorandum as—

(i) if it is to have a share capital, are requisite to bring it, both in substance and in form into conformity with the requirements imposed by the Principal Act with respect to the memorandum of a company to be formed under that Act as an unlimited company having a share capital; or

(ii) if it is not to have a share capital, are requisite in the circumstances; and

---

[13] Section 27 of the CA 1963.

(b) if articles have been registered, set out such alterations therein and additions thereto as—

(i) if it is to have a share capital, are requisite to bring them, both in substance and in form, into conformity with the requirements imposed by the Principal Act with respect to the articles of a company to be formed under that Act as an unlimited company having a share capital; or

(ii) if it is not to have a share capital, are requisite in the circumstances; and

(c) if articles have not been registered—

(i) have annexed thereto, and request the registration of, printed articles, bearing the same stamp as if they were contained in a deed, being, if the company is to have a share capital, articles complying with the said requirements; or

(ii) if it is not to have a share capital, articles appropriate to the circumstances.'

The purpose of these requirements is to ensure that the unlimited company's memorandum and articles of association are appropriate to an unlimited company following its re-registration as such. What is peculiar is that the requirements seem to suggest that a company limited by guarantee can re-register as an unlimited company with a share capital. It is understood that the registrar of companies takes the view that such a re-registration is not permitted because there is no mechanism provided in the legislation for a company without a share capital to acquire a share capital. Presumably, the basis for this position is the interpretation of the reference in s 52(2)(a) to the unlimited company not having a share capital as only being applicable where the limited company does not have a share capital before re-registration and the reference to having a share capital construed *mutatis mutandis*.

[33.011] In addition, the *documents* referred to in s 52(1) of the C(A)A 1983, which must be lodged with the application, are set out in s 52(3) which provides:

'The documents referred to in subsection (1) are—

(a) the prescribed form of assent to the company's being registered as unlimited subscribed by or on behalf of all members of the company;

(b) a statutory declaration made by the directors of the company that the persons by whom or on whose behalf the form of assent is subscribed constitute the whole membership of the company, and, if any of the members have not subscribed that form themselves, that the directors have taken all reasonable steps to satisfy themselves that each person who subscribed it on behalf of a member was lawfully empowered so to do;

(c) a printed copy of the memorandum incorporating the alterations therein set out in the application; and

(d) if articles have been registered, a printed copy thereof incorporating the alterations therein and additions thereto set out in the application.'

The procedure applicable to the making of the application for re-registration is considered in detail in McGowan-Smyth & Daly[14].

---

[14] McGowan-Smyth & Daly, *Irish Company Secretary's Handbook* (2011, Bloomsbury Professional) at pp 280–282.

[33.012] The unanimous consent of the members of a limited company wishing to re-register as unlimited is required. The consent is contained in the CRO's Form D6 which all members must sign. As to who can sign for a member, s 52(8) provides:

> 'For the purposes of this section—
>
> (a) subscription to a form of assent by the legal personal representative of a deceased member of a company shall be deemed to be subscription by him;
>
> (b) a trustee in bankruptcy of a person who is a member of a company shall, to the exclusion of that person, be deemed to be a member of the company.'

Important protection is, however, provided for persons who were members who left the company and who might be liable as contributories under s 207 of the CA 1963 to contribute to the debts of an unlimited company[15]. Thus, the new unlimited liability of the members does not extend to past members, who are only liable to contribute the amount which they would have had to contribute, had the conversion not taken place[16].

[33.013] Re-registration will result in the issue of a new certificate of incorporation on re-registration, s 52(6) of the C(A)A 1983 providing:

> 'A certificate of incorporation issued by virtue of this section shall be conclusive evidence that the requirements of this section with respect to re-registration and of matters precedent and incidental thereto have been complied with, and that the company was authorised to be re-registered under the Principal Act in pursuance of this section and was duly so re-registered.'

Again, the resulting unlimited liability company will be the same legal entity as was the limited company. Section 52(7) providing:

> 'The re-registration of a limited company as an unlimited company pursuant to this Act shall not affect any rights or obligations of the company, or render defective any legal proceedings by or against the company, and any legal proceedings which might have been continued or commenced against it in its former status may be continued or commenced against it in its new status.'

Converting from PLC to private

[33.014] PLCs may convert to private companies. In order to become re-registered as a private company, a PLC must change its memorandum and articles of association in order to comply with the requirements set out in s 33(1) of the CA 1963[17]. Alterations to a PLC's constitution must be effected by special resolution. Section 14 of the C(A)A 1983 provides that the PLC's memorandum of association must be changed by the deletion of the reference to the statement that the company is a PLC. Section 15 of the

---

[15] As to the liability of the members of an unlimited company, see Ch 31, *Unlimited Companies*, at para **[31.036]** *et seq*.

[16] Section 52(6) of the C(A)A 1983 provides: 'Where a company is re-registered in pursuance of this section a person who, at the time when the application for it to be re-registered was delivered to the registrar, was a past member of the company and did not thereafter again become a member thereof shall not, in the event of the company's being wound up, be liable to contribute to the assets of the company more than he would have been liable to contribute thereto had it not been so re-registered.'

[17] See Ch 1, *The Private Company in Context*, at para **[1.0133]**.

C(A)A 1983 affords protection to dissenting minority shareholders, unhappy with the re-registration as a private company.

Converting from private to PLC

[33.015] Of the relatively few public limited companies formed in Ireland many will have begun corporate life as private companies which were subsequently converted. A conversion of this nature requires a private company to amend its constitutional documentation and capital structure to accord with the requirements for a public limited company. The capital requirements for a public limited company include:

(a) the nominal share capital must be at least €38,092.14 (s 19 of the C(A)A 1983);

(b) the nominal share capital must be paid up in money or money's worth to at least 25% of the nominal value;

(c) the net assets of the company as *per* the balance sheet must at least equal the total of its called up share capital and undistributed reserves.

Sections 9 and 10 of the C(A)A 1983 set out the basic conditions which must be satisfied and have already been considered in Chapter 29[18]. It should be noted that before a public company can commence business, there exist additional statutory requirements under the Companies Acts[19].

Multi-member private company to single-member private company

[33.016] The circumstances in which a private company limited by shares or by guarantee can convert to being a single-member private company are set out in reg 5(1) of the EC(SMPLC)R 1994[20]. This provides:

> 'A private company limited by shares or by guarantee registered with two or more subscribers to its memorandum of association, in accordance with the Companies Acts, shall become a single-member company, on such date as the number of members is reduced to one and all the shares in the company are registered in the name of a sole member.'

It will be noted, immediately, that an unlimited private company may not convert to a single-member company; the regulations only apply to private companies limited by shares or by guarantee. It should also be noted that where the circumstances set out in reg 5(1) are met, the conversion of the company to a single-member company *is automatic*, occurring by operation of law. In this regard, such a conversion is the least encumbered by restrictions as it is not dependent upon the issue of a new certificate of incorporation or any action by the CRO. However, the company must cause the fact of conversion, the date upon which the conversion occurred and the identity of the single member to be notified in writing, in the prescribed form, to the registrar of companies within 28 days from the date of conversion[21].

---

18 See Ch 29, *Public Limited Companies and SEs*, at para **[29.019]**.

19 See Ch 29, *Public Limited Companies and SEs*, at para **[29.010]** *et seq*.

20 SI 275/1994.

21 Regulation 5(2). The prescribed form (M1) has been ordained by Part I of the European Communities (Single-Member Private Limited Companies) (Forms) Regulations 1994 (SI 306/1994). Failure to comply with reg 5(2) will mean that the company and every officer of the company, who is in default, is guilty of an offence: reg 5(3).

Single-Member Private Company to Multi-Member Private Company

[33.017] A single-member company will be deemed to have *automatically* converted to a multi-member private company limited by shares or by guarantee where the circumstances in reg 6(1) of the EC(SMPLC)R 1994 are satisfied. This provides:

> 'A company which is incorporated as, or becomes, a single-member company, in accordance with these regulations, shall cease to be a single-member company on such date as the number of members increases to more then one but shall continue to be a private company limited by shares or guarantee, as the case may be, while the number of members does not exceed 50.'

Here again, the company is obliged to cause the fact and date on which it ceased to be a single-member company to be notified in writing to the registrar of companies in the prescribed form within 28 days from the date of the conversion[22].

---

[22] Regulation 6(2). The prescribed form (M2) has been ordained by Part II of the European Communities (Single-Member Private Limited Companies) (Forms) Regulations 1994 (SI 306/1994). Failure to comply with reg 6(2) is an offence for both the company and every officer of the company who is in default: reg 6(3).

Chapter 34

External Companies and Branches

[34.001] While the primary focus of the Companies Acts is with companies that have been formed and registered in Ireland, that is not their exclusive concern and they can have application to external, or foreign, companies. Certain types of external companies – that is, bodies corporate which have been formed under the laws of another country – that establish a place of business in Ireland or establish a branch must comply with the Companies Acts. The rationale for asserting jurisdiction over foreign companies and seeking to regulate them is premised on the fact that, because they choose to come to Ireland and do business here, Ireland has a right to protect the creditors, customers and other stakeholders of such companies by requiring them to comply with certain basic requirements that are essentially rooted in disclosure. In the present internet age, there is a distinct disconnect between the law, technology and reality in this respect. A very significant number of consumer purchases are today concluded over the internet: Irish consumers buy (and sell) all manner of goods on internet sites such as amazon or ebay (whether .co.uk or .com) and in so doing contract with external or foreign companies which, through their websites, can be said to be doing business in Ireland. Despite this, the law on external companies and branches is concerned with external or foreign companies that *physically* locate in Ireland.

[34.002] There are currently two separate regimes applicable to foreign companies which overlap considerably, and these two regimes are the concern of this chapter:

[A] External Companies.

[B] Branches.

[A] External Companies[1]

[34.003] While Irish company law is mainly concerned with facilitating the formation and registration of Irish companies, in common with the company law in other jurisdictions, there are exceptions to that rule and the Companies Acts seek to regulate foreign or as they have traditionally been known, external companies, in certain circumstances. The rationale is simple: the public is entitled by law to find out who owns and who directs companies formed and registered in Ireland so if people choose to incorporate a foreign company and come to Ireland to do business, then the public is entitled to find out the same information about those companies and to do so without

[1] See, generally, McGowan-Smyth & Daly, *Irish Company Secretary's Handbook* (2011, Bloomsbury Professional) at p 296. See also Sealy (ed), *British Company Law and Practice* (2012, loose leaf, Sweet & Maxwell) Vol 1 at 85-600.

having to search their home registries[2]. In this section, the term 'external company' is used to describe companies to which Part XI of the CA 1963 applies[3].

[34.004] The following issues in the regulation of external companies are considered next:

1. Companies to which Part XI of the CA 1963 applies.
2. Establishing a place of business.
3. The obligation to register.
4. The ongoing obligation to file documents.
5. Other obligations of external companies.
6. Charges created by external companies.
7. Service of documents
8. Offences for breach of the requirements under Part XI of the CA 1963.

Companies to which Part XI of the CA 1963 applies

[34.005] Part XI of the Companies Act 1963 is expressed, by s 351 of the CA 1963, to apply to:

> '... all companies incorporated outside the State which, after the operative date, establish a place of business within the State, and to companies incorporated outside the State which have, before the operative date, established a place of business within the State and continue to have an established place of business within the State on the operative date.'

Part XI of the CA 1963 applies, therefore, to all foreign incorporated or external companies, which have an *established place of business* within the State. In order for an external company to be liable to register under Part XI, it must be an incorporated company, ie, it must be a body corporate with perpetual succession, be able to hold property and sue in its own name and be recognised by its home country as being a separate legal person. Unlike the EC(BD)R 1993 which apply only to limited companies, Part XI applies to all companies, limited or unlimited, that establish a place of business in Ireland. Regulation 14(1) of the EC(BD)R 1993 provides that where a foreign limited company establishes a branch, Part XI of the CA 1963 shall not apply to that company.

Establishing a place of business

[34.006] The key driver in the application of Part XI of the CA 1963 to external companies is that they *establish a place of business* in Ireland. The Companies Acts do not provide any test for when an external company will be said to have established a place of business in the State and the only guidance given is that a place of business

---

2 A recent development in this area is Directive 2012/17/EU which concerns interconnection of central, commercial and companies registries; at present, however, it is necessary to search in each Member State separately. See para **[34.027]** *post*.

3 'External companies' are sometimes referred to in the law of England and Wales as 'overseas companies' but such a description is inappropriate in Irish law because companies formed and registered in Northern Ireland – which are external companies – could not be referred to as overseas companies.

includes 'a share transfer or share registration office'[4]. The definition of 'established place of business' has not been the subject of discussion proper in the Irish courts. The decision in *Donovan v North German Lloyd Steamship Co*[5] is, however, instructive. In that case, it was held that service of proceedings on an external company were not satisfied by serving the summons on an address in Ireland, because although the defendant company did have an 'office' here, it did not have a *place of business* in the State. The defendant company's connection with Ireland was set out in the course of O'Byrne J's judgment:

> 'Apparently the defendant company is a foreign corporation, whose ships from time to time, make calls of port in this country, particularly at Cobh. At Cobh there is, and has been for some time, an office bearing the name of the defendant Company in large letters, and this fact and several others were relied upon for the purpose of showing that the defendant Company resided in this country in the sense in which a corporation can be said to reside in any country. Reliance was also placed on the fact that the name of the defendant Company appeared in the telephone directory, and on the fact, as alleged, that they were the rated occupiers of the premises in which the aforesaid office is situate.'

However, the lease of the premises used by the defendant company was held by another company, which acted as 'agent' not only for the defendant company, but also for other external companies[6]. There, it was held that the defendant company could not have proceedings served upon it in this manner. However, whether the facts of this case would today justify an Irish court to hold that it did not have an *established place of business* in the context under consideration here is considered to be debatable.

The following issues in the term 'established place of business' are next considered:

(a) The external company must conduct a business;
(b) Indicia in determining whether a place of business has been established;
(c) Business carried on may be incidental to a company's main business;
(d) Places of business and branches distinguished.

(a) The external company must conduct a business

[34.007] To establish a place of business in the State, the foreign company's activities here must as a matter of fact amount to the carrying on of a business. In *Rome v Punjab National Bank (No 2)*[7], a bank registered on the external register ceased to carry on business in the UK. A hiving-down operation began and while the company did no new business in the UK, two employees remained to finalise outstanding matters. These two persons were registered as persons upon whom proceedings could be served, satisfying the requirements of the English equivalent to Part XI of the CA 1963[8]. The company subsequently served notice on the registrar of companies that, after a certain date, the

4 Section 360 of the CA 1963.

5 *Donovan v North German Lloyd Steamship Co* [1933] IR 33.

6 In *Rakusens Ltd v Baser Ambalaj Plastik Sanayi Ticaret Asi* [2002] 1 BCLC 104, it was held that where it was sought to establish that a foreign company had established a place of business by the conduct of persons who were agents (as opposed to employees) it was insufficient to merely show that the 'agent' had established a place of business in the State.

7 *Rome v Punjab National Bank (No 2)* [1989] BCLC 328.

8 See para **[34.024]** *post*.

company would cease to have a place of business in the UK. The registrar responded by closing the company's file. Even though this had been done, proceedings were served on one of the employees, and this was held to be a valid service. Incidental to this it was also held that at the time of service of the writ, the company did not have an established place of business. As to the determination of this question, Hirst J said:

> 'In my judgment, the correct approach is that adopted in the *South India case*, namely to examine the actual activities which are revealed on the evidence in order to decide whether or not they qualify.
>
> Examining those described above, I have no hesitation whatsoever in concluding that all but the last are no more than loose ends which needed to be tied up after the cessation of business; and the last, which ... involves no more than maintaining a point of contact with English solicitors, does not in my judgment constitute a business activity at all. Consequently there was no business activity being carried out here by the defendants at the relevant date[9].'

From this it is suggested that an external company that is a charity or a social club and which establishes itself in Ireland may not be required to register under Part XI of the CA 1963 because being such an entity, it may not in fact carry on a 'business'. It may not, however be correct to assume that a not-for-profit company does not transact 'business' and it is thought that business does not mean, necessarily, the pursuit of commercial activities.

(b) Indicia in determining whether a place of business has been established

[34.008] The use of the word *established* connotes some ensconced or settled place of business: to have an established place of business, a place must have some degree of permanence. It must not be merely transitory or dependent upon, say, the chance presence of a representative of the external company in Ireland. In summary, some of the factors which will go towards the finding by a court that an external company has an established place of business include:

- having a specified or identifiable place at which it carries on business although the company does not necessarily have to own or lease a premises;
- having a visible sign or physical indication that the company is connected to a place;
- that the company's physical connections are more than merely fleeting or transitory;
- that there is a degree of permanence or ensconcement about the connection;
- a regularity of business being conducted there by the company.

Clearly, any precise definition of what is meant by established place of business is fraught with difficulty. Every case will turn on its own facts and the presence of the foregoing factors will merely influence the outcome[10].

---

9 *Rome v Punjab National Bank (No 2)* [1984] BCLC 328 at 338–339.

10 See, for example, *Matchnet plc v William Blair & Co LLC* [2003] 2 BCLC 195 where, after reviewing the facts it was found that the defendant did not have a place of business in London.

[34.009] In *Re Oriel Ltd*[11], a decision which considered the term in the context of whether particulars of a charge created by it ought to have been delivered to the Companies House in England for noting on the *Slavenberg* file[12], Oliver LJ said of the concept of 'established place of business' that it was to suggest[13]:

> '... that it is essential to an "established place of business" that there should be some visible sign or physical indication that the company has a connection with particular premises ...
>
> Speaking for myself, I think also that when the word "established" is used adjectivally, as it is in [s 111 of the CA 1963], it connotes not only the setting-up of a place of business at a specific location, but a degree of permanence or recognisability as being a location of the company's business. If, for instance, agents of an overseas company conduct business from time to time by meeting clients or potential customers in the public rooms of an hotel in London, they have, no doubt, "carried on business" in England, but I would for my part find it very difficult to persuade myself that the hotel lounge was "an established place of business". The concept, as it seems to me, is of some more or less permanent location, not necessarily owned or even leased by the company, but at least associated with the company and from which habitually or with some degree of regularity business is conducted[14].'

(c) Business carried on may be incidental to a company's main business

[34.010] It has also been decided that a company will be deemed to have an established place of business even if the business carried on in the State is only incidental to its main business. Authority for this is *South India Shipping Corp Ltd v Export-Import Bank of Korea*[15] where the English Court of Appeal, *per* Ackner LJ, said:

> 'The defendant bank are an export-import bank, not a high street bank. They have both premises and staff within the jurisdiction. They conduct external relations with other banks and financial institutions. They carry out preliminary work in relation to granting or obtaining loans. They seek to give publicity to the foreign bank and encourage trade between Korea and the United Kingdom, and they consult with other banks and financial institutions on the usual operating matters. They have therefore an established place of business within Great Britain and it matters not that they do not conclude within the jurisdiction any banking dealings with the general public as opposed to other banks or financial institutions.'

This was re-stated in *Rome v Punjab National Bank (No 2)*[16] where Hirst J noted with approval that the *South India Shipping Corp* case had held:

> '... that it was sufficient to show the establishment of an office in Great Britain where activities incidental to the main business of the company were carried on, and that it was

---

11 *Re Oriel Ltd* [1985] 3 All ER 216; [1985] BCLC 343.

12 See para **[34.020]** *post*.

13 On the authority of *Derverall v Grant Advertising Inc* [1954] 3 All ER 389.

14 *Re Oriel Ltd* [1985] BCLC 343 at 347.

15 *South India Shipping Corp Ltd v Export–Import Bank of Korea* [1985] 2 All ER 219; [1985] BCLC 163.

16 *Rome v Punjab National Bank (No 2)* [1989] BCLC 328.

unnecessary to show that a substantial part of its business was conducted within the jurisdiction.'

(d) Places of business and branches distinguished

[34.011] *Branches* of foreign companies are considered in Section [B]. A 'branch' is considered to refer to a presence that is bigger than a 'place of business' so that every branch will constitute a place of business but every place of business will not necessarily constitute a branch. It may be noted that reg 14(3) of the EC(BD)R 1993 provides that for the avoidance of doubt:

> '... references in Part XI of the Principal Act to the establishment of a place of business shall include the changing of a branch within the meaning of the 1989 Directive into a place of business that is not a branch within the meaning of the 1989 Directive and the date of establishment of that place of business shall, for the purposes of the said Part XI, be construed as the date on which such change occurs and from that date the exemption in paragraph (1) shall not apply.'

Regulation 14(1) provides that Part XI of the CA 1963 shall not apply to a company as a result of that company having established a branch, where, by virtue of having established that branch, the EC(BD)R 1993 apply.

[34.012] Regulation 16(1) of the EC(BD)R 1993 provides that where Part XI of the CA 1963 applies to a company by virtue of its having established a place of business and where prior to the establishment of that place of business, the company has, in complying with the EC(BD)R 1993, returned to the registrar documents which are the same in all respects as the documents required by s 352(1)(a) of the CA 1963, and it has no outstanding obligation to make a return to the registrar under the EC(BD)R 1993, so far as concerns any alterations to those documents, then the company may return, in lieu of the documents required by s 352(1)(a), a statement in the prescribed form, that this information has already been returned pursuant to the EC(BD)R 1993. Moreover, reg 16(2) provides that where Part XI of the CA 1963 applies to a company by virtue of its having established a place of business and where prior to the establishment of that place of business, the company has, in complying with the Regulations, returned to the registrar particulars which are the same in all respects as the particulars required by s 352(1)(b) and (2), and it has no outstanding obligation to make a return to the registrar, so far as concerns any alterations to those particulars, then the company may return, in lieu of the documents required by s 352(1)(b) and (2) of the CA 1963, a statement in the prescribed form, that this information has already been returned pursuant to the EC(BD)R 1993.

The obligation to register

[34.013] Section 352(1) of the CA 1963 details an external company's registration obligations where it establishes a place of business in the State, providing:

> 'Companies incorporated outside the State, which, after the operative date, establish a place of business within the State, shall, within one month of the establishment of the place of business, deliver to the registrar of companies for registration—
>
> (a) a certified copy of the charter, statutes or memorandum and articles of the company, or other instrument constituting or defining the constitution of the

company, and, if the instrument is not written in the English or Irish language, a certified translation thereof;

(b) a list of the directors and secretary of the company containing the particulars mentioned in subsection (2);

(c) the names and addresses of some one or more persons resident in the State authorised to accept on behalf of the company service of process and any notices required to be served on the company and also the address of the company's principal place of business in the State.'

The requirements are not particularly onerous and are designed to make accessible to the public in Ireland, the external company's constitution, the identity of its management[17] and the identity of a person in the State who is authorised to accept service of notices and proceedings. Registration is effected using a Form F1[18]. For the purposes of Part XI of the CA 1963, 'director' is stated to include any person in accordance with whose directions and instructions the directors of the company are accustomed to act[19], and so can be said to include what are elsewhere referred to in the Companies Acts as 'shadow directors'; 'secretary' is expressed to include any person occupying the position of secretary by whatever name called[20].

The ongoing obligation to file documents

[34.014] In addition to the initial obligation to register, there is an ongoing obligation to make returns to the registrar of companies where the external company's constitution (eg, memorandum and articles of association, whatsoever called) is altered or the identity of its directors or secretary or persons authorised to accept service of processes and notices changes[21].

[34.015] By virtue of s 354(1) of the CA 1963 an external company, with the exception of an external company with provisions in its constitution which would entitle it to rank as a private company if it has been registered in Ireland[22], is required to prepare, lay and deliver copies of its accounts to the registrar of companies. It is notable that the requirement is not just to file or deliver the accounts to the CRO but that external companies are required to *prepare* a balance sheet and profit and loss account and, if it is a holding company, group accounts, even if it is not required to do so under the law of its country of incorporation. It is somewhat peculiar that external companies are also required by s 354(1) to *lay* the accounts before their members in general meeting, without regard to what the law of their country of incorporation requires. The effect of the carve-out for external companies that would be classified as private companies in Ireland means that where, say, a UK registered private company establishes a place of business here but its presence does not constitute a 'branch' so as to come within the EC(BD)R 1993, it will not be required to prepare, lay or file accounts.

---

17 The requisite particulars of what must be registered in the case of directors and secretaries are detailed in s 352(2) of the CA 1963.

18 See, generally, McGowan-Smyth & Daly, *Irish Company Secretary's Handbook* (2011, Bloomsbury Professional) at pp 301, 302.

19 Section 360 of the CA 1963.

20 Section 360 of the CA 1963.

21 Section 353 of the CA 1963.

22 Section 354(4) of the CA 1963.

An external company that has unlimited liability and would by reason of its constitution be entitled to rank as a private company will never have to file accounts under Part XI of the CA 1963 nor under the EC(BD)R 1993 which do not apply to unlimited companies.

[34.016] Section 357 provides that where an external company ceases to have a place of business in the State it 'shall forthwith give notice of the fact to the registrar of companies'. From the date on which notice is so given, the obligation of the company to deliver any document shall cease.

Other obligations of external companies

[34.017] Although the primary obligations imposed by Part XI of the CA 1963 on external companies are to register, provide certain very basic information and keep that information as maintained on the register of external companies up to date, there are a small number of additional obligations. Section 355 of the CA 1963 obliges an external company to:

- (a) state its country of incorporation in every prospectus inviting subscriptions for its share or debentures that it issues;
- (b) exhibit conspicuously its name and country of incorporation on every place where it carries on business in the State;
- (c) cause its name and country of incorporation to be stated in legible characters on all billheads and letter-paper and in all notices and other official publications of the company; and
- (d) if the liability of its members is limited, cause notice of that fact to be stated in legible characters in every such prospectus and in all billheads, letter-paper, notices and other official publications in the State and to be affixed on every place where it carries on its business.

In addition, s 196(1) of the CA 1963, which requires companies to state the names and nationality of their directors on all business letters, is expressly applied to external companies: s 196(3)(a) of the CA 1963.

The obligation on external companies to register certain charges created by them is considered next.

Charges created by external companies[23]

[34.018] Charges created by external companies over foreign property are of no concern to Irish law. The validity of such charges will be determined by the *lex situs* and not by the Companies Acts. Charges created by external companies over property in the State are, however, required to be registered under Part IV of the CA 1963 where an external company has an established place of business in the State[24]. It has been held in a series of English decisions that where a foreign company establishes a place of business but by accident or design fails to register as an external company, it will still be required to deliver particulars of any charges created by it over property in the state and that where such particulars are not delivered, that charge will be void[25] against a liquidator or

---

23 See Courtney, 'Registration of Charges: Foreign Companies and the *Slavenburg* File' (1992) Gazette ILSI 151.

24 Gill, 'Foreign Companies and Establishing "A Place of Business"' (1989) ILT 264.

creditor of the company. Here, we will first consider foreign companies that establish a place of business in the State and register pursuant to Part XI as external companies, and then foreign companies which establish a place of business but do not register as external companies.

(a) External companies

[34.019] Section 111 of the CA 1963 provides:

> 'The provisions of [Part IV of the CA 1963] shall extend to charges on property in the State which are created ... and to charges on property in the State which is acquired ... by a company incorporated outside the State which has an established place of business within the State, and to judgment mortgages created ... and affecting property in the State of such a company and to receivers ... of property in the State of such a company, and for the purposes of those provisions, the principal place of business of such a company in the State shall be deemed to be its registered office.'

Where a foreign company establishes a place of business and registers as an external company and subsequently creates a registrable charge within the meaning of s 99(2) of the CA 1963[26] over a property in the State, then the requisite particulars must be delivered to the registrar of companies using a Form 8E. Such charges are then registered on the CRO register of charges, by reference to the number assigned to it on its registration as an external company.

(b) Unregistered external companies: the Slavenburg file

[34.020] An external company which *has* an established place of business in the State but which does *not register* as an external company as it is required to do under s 352(1) of the CA 1963 is, nevertheless, obliged to deliver particulars of a charge over property in Ireland to the CRO in the same way (by using a Form 8E) as a company which has registered under s 352 of the CA 1963. This was decided in the UK in *NV Slavenburg's Bank v Intercontinental Natural Resources Ltd*[27]. In that case, a company, which was incorporated in Bermuda, had an established place of business in England and created charges over assets which subsequently came to be reposited in England. The company was not registered in England nor were the particulars of the charges delivered to the English Companies House. The property in England was later sold, and the proceeds of sale paid into a joint account in the names of the parties' solicitors. Subsequently, a Bermudan court wound up the company. In subsequent proceedings before the English courts it was argued, *inter alia*, that the charges over the property situated in England were void for non-registration. It was held by Lloyd J that although there was no formal method for registering such charges because the external company did not have a company number which it would have had were it registered on the external register, particulars of such charges could still *be delivered* to the English Companies House. Where particulars were not delivered those charges would be void as against a liquidator or any creditor. The mere fact that such charges could not formally be registered was not

---

25 *NV Slavenburg's Bank v Intercontinental Natural Resources Ltd* [1980] 1 All ER 955.

26 As to the meaning of 'registered charge' see Ch 19, *Corporate Borrowing: Registration of Charges*, at para **[19.042]** *et seq*.

27 *NV Slavenburg's Bank v Intercontinental Natural Resources Ltd* [1980] 1 All ER 955.

a sufficient reason for failing to deliver particulars to the registrar of companies. In the words of Lloyd J:

> 'The fallacy in the argument lies in regarding registration of the charge under [Part IV of the CA 1963] as a condition precedent to its validity. It is clear both from the language of [s 99 of the CA 1963] ... that it is delivery of particulars of the charge, together with the instrument (if any) by which it is created or evidenced that saves that charge, and not its registration. In the *National Provincial Bank*[28] case Scrutton LJ said, after referring to the language of the section: "That makes the avoidance dependant on the neglect to send in the particulars. The neglect to register the charge will not make it void" ... So far as I am concerned, it seems to follow that the bank could have preserved the validity of its charges by delivering particulars within twenty-one days, despite the unwillingness of the registrar to register the charge without prior registration by the company under [Part XI of the CA 1963]. In those circumstances ... [t]here is nothing certainly in [s 111 of the CA 1963] to suggest that the operation of that section is dependant in any way on the company having registered under [Part XI of the CA 1963, ie, as an external company], and I am unwilling to imply any such limitation[29].'

Ironically, the decision in *Slavenburg* has now been reversed by the British Parliament enacting the Companies Act 2006[30]. It continues to be the law in Ireland that where an external company which has an established place of business in the State, but which has not registered as an external company under Part XI of the CA 1963 creates a charge over property, real or personal, situate in Ireland, the company, or the holder of that charge, must deliver particulars of that charge to the Irish registrar of companies. Failure to do so will render that charge invalid[31].

[34.021] In Ireland, charges created by unregistered foreign companies in such circumstances should be delivered to the CRO[32]. What is the registrar and her staff to do in such circumstances? The plight of the registrar was addressed in *Slavenburg*'s case where Lloyd J said:

> 'Before leaving the point, I should say that counsel for the defendants expressly disclaimed any criticism of the registrar's current practice. Nor would I, myself, wish to

---

28 *Re National Provincial Bank* [1924] 1 KB 431 at 447.

29 *NV Slavenburg's Bank v Intercontinental Natural Resources Ltd* [1980] 1 All ER 955 at 963–964. References to the CA 1963 have been added.

30 Change was mooted by the Companies Act 1989 (UK) Sch 15, which inserted new ss 703A to 703N into the Companies Act 1985 (UK) but these provisions were never brought into effect and have now been surpassed by the UK Companies Act 2006. See generally, Dine, 'Registration of Company Charges' (1991) BLR 31 and Ferran & Mayo, 'Registration of Company Charges – The New Regime' (1990) JBL 152.

31 It may be noted that this contrasts with the case of a judgment mortgage registered against a foreign company which has an established place of business in Ireland and which is not registered on the external register. It is submitted that the comments referred to above in the case of judgment mortgages against Irish registered companies apply here, and that the only sanction is a fine, the *charge* itself remaining valid.

32 See also *Re Oriel Ltd* [1985] BCLC 343 where the liquidator contended, and Oliver LJ accepted, at 346 that: '... although the company was a foreign company which had never filed any of the documents required to be filed by an overseas company under [Part XI of the CA 1963], it was nevertheless a company to which the provisions of [s 99] of the Act were applicable.' See also *Re Alton Corporation* [1985] BCLC 27.

> criticise it in any way. His reasons for insisting on the company first registering under [Part XI] are clear enough. But they cannot affect the outcome of this case[33].'

Following the lead set by the English registrar, the Irish registrar opened a so-called, '*Slavenburg* file', in which is noted the fact of having received delivery of the required particulars[34]. In due course the registrar will issue a letter to the person who delivered particulars of the charge to the effect that delivery of the particulars has been received, but because the company is not registered as an external company, *registration* of the charge cannot be effected. Such a letter is a sufficient safeguard for any lender who takes a charge in such circumstances, and this letter should be treated as if it were a certificate of registration[35]. Indeed, in that the common parlance of the Irish CRO is that delivery of such particulars has been noted on the *Slavenburg* file, the 'hibernisation' of the decision and its implications is clear.

(c) Established place of business in the context of creating charges

[34.022] Unless a foreign company has an established place of business[36] in the State, neither full registration on the ordinary register of charges nor informal 'notation' on the *Slavenburg* file is required. In *Re Oriel Ltd*[37], the issue of established place of business was considered where an external company delivered particulars of the charges it had created, where it had not registered under the English equivalent of Part XI of the CA 1963. The company in question had been incorporated and registered in the Isle of Man. Its objects were the acquisition, mortgaging and management of a company which was controlled by a husband and wife who lived in England. Subsequently, the company acquired three garage sites in England and upon entering a solus agreement charged them to a petrol supplier. Subsequently, three more sites were acquired, and charged. The management of the company was conducted by the husband director, who gave as an address the registered office of the company and his own personal address. When the company was wound up, the validity of the charges was questioned since they had never been registered nor particulars of them delivered to the English Companies House. Central to the argument of the liquidator was that the company had an established place of business in England, and as such the charges ought to have been registered, or at least particulars delivered since the company had never registered on the external register. Arising from this case, the Court of Appeal decided two particularly contentious issues. First, it was decided that the relevant date for determining whether or not a company had an established place of business was the date on which it executed a charge over its property in the state, while having an established place of business. Second, on the facts of the case it was held that in respect of the first three charges, particulars were not

---

33 *NV Slavenburg's Bank v Intercontinental Natural Resources Ltd* [1980] 1 All ER 955 at 964b.

34 The Irish *Slavenburg* file was assigned a number by the registrar and so all particulars for all companies which are delivered to the CRO were assigned the same number: 950000.

35 However, it may be noted that this letter is different from a certificate of registration by reason of the fact that it does not have the advantage of being *conclusive evidence* that the requirements of Part IV of the CA 1963 have been complied with.

36 See Courtney, 'Registration of Charges: Foreign Companies and the *Slavenburg* File' (1992) Gazette ILSI 151 and Gill, 'Foreign Companies and Establishing "A Place of Business"' (1989) ILT 264.

37 *Re Oriel Ltd* [1985] 3 All ER 216; [1985] BCLC 343.

required to be delivered to the Companies House because, on their creation, the company did not have an established place of business in England and Wales. However, in respect of the second three charges, particulars of these ought to have been delivered to the Companies House since on their creation, the company had an established place of business in England and Wales.

[34.023] A particular problem arises for the solicitor acting for a lending institution where an external company, without any property or established place of business in Ireland, borrows money for the express purpose of acquiring a business premises in Ireland. Is one to insist upon registration of the charge? Is the operative date, for determining whether a company has an established place of business, the date on which the charge is created? This point was considered in *Re Oriel Ltd*[38] where Oliver LJ said:

> '... it is difficult to see how, when premises are acquired for the first time and immediately charged, the established place of business which the company has can be the premises charged. There is, in fact, no evidence that the company had any connection with those premises prior to the charge beyond being designated, prior to its incorporation, as the intended owner.'

Where there is any doubt as to whether an established place of business has been created, the safest course for chargees is to insist that particulars of a charge are delivered to the CRO.

Service of documents

[34.024] The act of registration as an external company which involves providing the names and addresses of one or more persons resident in Ireland who are authorised to accept, on the external company's behalf, service of processes and notices constitutes a submission to the jurisdiction of the Irish courts[39]. Section 356(1) of the CA 1963 provides that subject to sub-s (2), any process or notice required to be served on an external company shall be sufficiently served if addressed to any person whose name has been delivered to the registrar of companies and left at or sent by post to the address which has been so delivered. Section 356(2) provides that a document may be served on an external company by leaving it at or sending it by post to any place of business established in the State where the company makes default in delivering to the registrar the name and address of a person resident in the State who is authorised to accept service or if such persons whose names and address have been so delivered are dead or have ceased to reside or refuse to accept service or for any reason cannot be served. Both sub-ss (1) and (2) of s 356 are expressly subject to the fact that they will cease to apply to a company on the expiration of two years after it has given notice that it has ceased to have a place of business.

[34.025] Where an external company fails to register pursuant to s 352(1) of the CA 1963 it might be claimed that service may still be effected in accordance with s 356. It is thought that it is open to a court to find that service on the unregistered external company, by leaving the legal process or other notice at its place of business, is permitted pursuant to s 356(2)(b) of the CA 1963 because the reason it cannot be served on a registered person is that no authorised person was ever registered.

---

38 *Re Oriel Ltd* [1985] 3 All ER 216 at 221.

39 *Employers' Liability Assurance Corporation v Sedgwick, Collins & Co* [1927] AC 95.

Offences for breach of the requirements under Part XI of the CA 1963

[34.026] If any company to which Part XI of the CA 1963 applies fails to comply with any of the provisions of that Part, the company and every officer or agent of the company who knowingly and wilfully authorises or permits the default shall be guilty of an offence and liable to a class C fine[40].

[B] BRANCHES

[34.027] The second regime applicable to foreign companies which come to Ireland is the European Communities (Branch Disclosures) Regulations 1993 ('EC(BD)R 1993')[41] which implement in Irish law the Eleventh Company Law Directive, Council Directive No 89/666/EEC of 21 December 1989 ('BD Directive'). The objective of the Directive is to facilitate the right to establishment contained in the Treaty of Rome by enabling companies to establish branches in other Member States. In this section, the following matters are considered:

1. Companies to which the EC(BD)R 1993 apply;
2. The meaning of 'branch';
3. Establishing a branch;
4. EU companies: the obligation to register and deliver documents;
5. Non-EU companies: the obligation to register and deliver documents;
6. Requirements in relation to letterheads;
7. Accounting documents to be delivered to the registrar of companies;
8. Miscellaneous obligations;
9. Service of process or notice;
10. Duty to secure compliance with Regulations;
11. Offences for breach of Regulations.

Directive 2012/17/EU of 13 June 2012 on the Interconnection of Central, Commercial and Companies Registers effects certain amendments to the BD Directive, one of which is the requirement that every branch will have a unique identifier allowing it to be unequivocally identified within the EU[42]. Moreover, it will require a clear connection between the register of companies and their branches to enable access to information on winding up and insolvency proceedings, strike-off, etc[43].

Companies to which the EC(BD)R 1993 apply

[34.028] The EC(BD)R 1993 apply to EU bodies corporate and non-EU bodies corporate that establish a 'branch' in Ireland. Unlike Part XI of the CA 1963, the EC(BD)R 1993 apply only to *limited* companies. The Regulations are structured so that Part II applies to companies to which art 1 of Council Directive 68/151/EEC of 9 March

---

40 Section 358 of the CA 1963 and s 6(3) of the Fines Act 2010.

41 SI 395/1993.

42 Article 1 amends art 1 of the BD Directive by inserting a new art 1.4 to require Member States to give branches a unique identifier.

43 Article 1 amends art 1 of the BD Directive by inserting a new art 5a.

1968 applies (ie, that are limited companies) which are incorporated in another EU Member State and which establish a branch in the State[44]. Part III applies to companies incorporated outside of the State other than companies to which Part II applies, which are of a legal form comparable with a company to which Article 1 of the 1968 Directive applies and which establish a branch in the State[45].

The meaning of 'branch'

[34.029] Neither the EC(BD)R 1993 nor the BD Directive define what is meant by a 'branch'. When a foreign company establishes a branch in Ireland, it establishes a physical location in Ireland where it can do business with third parties, such that it has people in Ireland authorised to bind the foreign company in contract. For the average person, the very term 'branch' is synonymous with a local retail outlet of a national licensed bank; however, a branch established by a foreign company within the meaning of the EC(BD)R 1993 is usually quite different in form and in substance. Generally, there can often be confusion as to the legal status of a branch registered under the EC(BD)R 1993. Perhaps it is because a branch or a foreign company is assigned a distinct registration number by the registrar of companies that it is sometimes asked whether a branch is a separate legal entity: in fact, and in law, it is not. A 'branch' is merely the Irish manifestation of a foreign company; it has no legal personality outside that of the foreign company; any restrictions on the capacity of the foreign company apply equally to the branch because, in this respect, a branch of a foreign company has the same lack of legal independence of the foreign company as the branch of a bank has of head office. Every contract concluded by the branch will be a contract concluded by the foreign company; every tort or civil wrong committed by managers or other personnel in the Irish branch will, in law, be torts committed by the foreign company. Employees of the branch will in law be employees of the legal entity that is the foreign company. Creditors of the branch will be creditors of the foreign company. Sometimes, the execution block of deeds and contracts executed by 'branches' mistakenly disguises the identity of the contracting party by referring to the 'Irish branch of' such-and-such company. In law, the execution block should reflect the fact that the contract is with the foreign company and any reference to branch should acknowledge that fact. To refer exclusively to the branch makes about as much sense as a lease of the Galway branch of AIB Bank plc containing an execution block in a contract providing: 'Signed for and on behalf of the Galway Branch of AIB Bank, plc.'

Establishing a branch

[34.030] In *Somafer SA v Saar-Ferngas AG*[46], the European Court of justice gave the following description of a 'branch' in the context of the meaning of 'branch, agency or other establishment' in art 5(5) of the Brussels Convention:

> 'The concept of branch, agency or other establishment implies a place of business which has the appearance of permanency, such as the extension of a parent body, has a management and is materially equipped to negotiate business with third parties so that the later, although knowing that there will if necessary be a legal link with the parent body, the

[44] Regulation 3 of the EC(BD)R 1993.

[45] Regulation 6 of the EC(BD)R 1993.

[46] *Somafer SA v Saar-Ferngas AG* Case 33/78 [1978] ECR 2183.

> head office of which is abroad, do not have to deal directly with such parent body but may transact business at the place of business constituting the extension.'

From this it is clear that for a foreign company to establish a branch it Ireland, the following facts must exist:

- the foreign company must establish a place of business here;
- the place of business must have the 'appearance of permanency';
- the place of business must have a person or persons to manage the place of business;
- the manager or management (or people reporting to him or them) must be materially equipped to negotiate business with third parties; and
- the manager or management (or people reporting to him or them) must have the authority to enter into contracts and otherwise transact business in Ireland, at least in relation to some matters, without having to defer to the foreign company.

It is evident that every 'branch' will constitute a place of business within the meaning of Part XI of the CA 1963 but not every place of business will constitute a branch. This is perhaps why the Companies Acts only provide that Part XI of the CA 1963 does not apply to a foreign company that registers a branch under the Branch Disclosures Regulations[47] whereas there is no similar disapplication for a foreign company that registers a place of business. A place of business where the employees or persons representing the foreign company cannot enter into any contracts with third parties but can only refer them to the foreign company is likely to be a place of business and not a branch.

[34.031] Regulation 14(2) provides, for the avoidance of doubt and subject to para (4), that references in the EC(BD)R 1993 to:

> 'the establishment of a branch shall include the changing of a place of business that is not a branch within the meaning of the 1989 Directive into such a branch and the date of establishment of the branch shall be construed as the date on which such change occurs.'

Regulation 14(4)(a) provides that, subject to subpara (b), where a company to which the EC(BD)R 1993 apply, established a branch in the State before the commencement of the EC(BD)R 1993 and where that branch has not closed, a reference in the EC(BD)R 1993 to the date of establishment of a branch shall in the case of that branch be construed as a reference to the date of the commencement of the EC(BD)R 1993, ie, 1 February 1994. Regulation 14(4)(b) provides that where a company to which subpara (a) applies has, in respect of a branch established in the State, complied with all the requirements of Part XI of the CA 1963 applicable following the establishment of that branch, the date of establishment of that branch for the purposes of applying the EC(BD)R 1993 shall be construed as the date which is three months after the date of commencement of the EC(BD)R 1993.

47 Regulation 14(1) of the EC(BD)R 1993.

EU companies: the obligation to register and deliver documents

[34.032] The law applicable to foreign companies that were formed and registered in another EU Member State is contained in Part II of the EC(BD)R 1993. Where such a company establishes a branch in Ireland, reg 4(1) provides that it:

> '... shall, within one month of the date of the establishment of a branch in the State, deliver to the registrar for registration a certified copy of the memorandum and articles of association or the charter, statutes or other instrument constituting or defining the constitution of the company.'

Moreover, a company is also required by reg 4(2) to notify the registrar in the prescribed form[48] of the following matters at the same time as delivering its constitution:

> '(a) the name and legal form of the company and the name of the branch if that is different from the name of the company;
>
> (b) a certificate of incorporation of the company;
>
> (c) the address of the branch;
>
> (d) the activities of the branch;
>
> (e) the place of registration of the company and the number with which it is registered;
>
> (f) a list of the persons who are authorised to represent the company in accordance with Article 2.1(e) of the 1989 Directive together with the specified personal details;
>
> (g) without prejudice to the generality of subparagraph (f), the name and addresses of some one or more persons resident in the State authorised to accept on behalf of the company service of process and any notices required to be served on the company;
>
> (h) without prejudice to the generality of subparagraph (f), the name and address of every person resident in the State authorised by the company to ensure compliance with the provisions of these Regulations together with a consent signed by each such person to act in this capacity;
>
> (i) copies of the latest accounting documents prepared in relation to a financial year of the company to have been publicly disclosed in accordance with the law of the State in which it is incorporated before the end of the period allowed for compliance with a paragraph (1) in respect of the branch, or if earlier, the date on which the company complies with paragraph (1) in respect of the branch.'

There is an ongoing obligation by reason of reg 4(3) on such companies that register a branch here to provide the following documents to the registrar of companies within 14 days of the occurrence of the event concerned:

> '(a) any document making or evidencing an alteration in its memorandum or articles of association;
>
> (b) every amended text of its memorandum or articles of association;
>
> (c) notice of a change among the persons referred to in paragraphs (2)(f), (g), or (h) or in any of the particulars relating to such persons specifying the date of the change;

[48] From F12. See McGowan-Smyth & Daly, *Irish Company Secretary's Handbook* (2011, Bloomsbury Professional) at p 298.

(d) notice of a change in the address referred to in paragraph (2)(c) together with the new address of the branch;

(e) notice of the winding-up of the company, the appointment of liquidators, particulars concerning them and their powers and the termination of the liquidation in accordance with disclosure by the company as provided for in Article 2 (1)(h), (i) and (j) of the 1968 Directive and particulars concerning insolvency proceedings, arrangements, compositions or any analogous proceedings to which the company is subject;

(f) the closure of the branch.'

Non-EU companies: the obligation to register and deliver documents

[34.033] The law applicable to foreign companies that are formed and registered outside of the State and outside of the EU is contained in Part III of the EC(BD)R 1993. Where such a company establishes a branch in Ireland, reg 7(1) provides that it:

> '... shall, within one month of the date of the establishment of a branch in the State, deliver to the registrar for registration a certified copy of the memorandum and articles of association or the charter, statutes or other instrument constituting or defining the constitution of the company.'

Moreover, a company is also required by reg 7(2) to notify the registrar in the prescribed form[49] of the following matters at the same time as delivering its constitution:

'(a) the name and legal form of the company, its principal place of business and its objects;

(b) a certificate of incorporation of the company;

(c) the address of the branch;

(d) the activities of the branch;

(e) the name of the branch if that is different from the name of the company;

(f) the State in which the company is incorporated and, where the law of that state so provides, the place of registration of the company and the number with which it is registered;

(g) a list of the persons who are authorised to represent the company in accordance with Article 8(h) of the 1989 Directive together with the specified personal details;

(h) without prejudice to the generality of subparagraph (g), the name and addresses of some one or more persons resident in the State authorised to accept on behalf of the company service of process and any notices required to be served on the company;

(i) without prejudice to the generality of subparagraph (g), the name and address of every person resident in the State authorised by the company to ensure compliance with the provisions of these Regulations together with a consent signed by each such person to act in this capacity;

(j) copies of the latest accounting documents prepared in relation to a financial year of the company to have been publicly disclosed in accordance with the law of the State in which it is incorporated before the end of the period allowed for

---

49 From F13. See McGowan-Smyth & Daly, *Irish Company Secretary's Handbook* (2011, Bloomsbury Professional) at p 298.

compliance with paragraph (1) in respect of the branch, or if earlier, the date on which the company complies with paragraph (1) in respect of the branch.'

There is an ongoing obligation by reg 7(3) on such companies that register a branch here to provide the following documents to the registrar of companies within 14 days of the occurrence of the event concerned:

'(a) any document making or evidencing an alteration in its memorandum or articles of association;

(b) every amended text of its memorandum or articles of association;

(c) notice of a change among the persons referred to in paragraphs (2)(g), (h), or (i) or in any of the particulars relating to such persons specifying the date of the change;

(d) notice of a change in the address referred to in paragraph (2)(c) together with the new address of the branch;

(e) notice of the winding-up of the company, the appointment of liquidators, particulars concerning them and their powers and the termination of the liquidation insolvency proceedings, arrangements, compositions or any analogous proceedings to which the company is subject;

(f) the closure of the branch.'

Requirements in relation to letterheads

[34.034] Every letter and order form used by the Irish branch of an EU company is required to bear the following particulars pursuant to reg 5(1) of the EC(BD)R 1993:

'(a) the place of registration of the company and the number with which it is registered;

(b) the legal form of the company and the address of its registered office;

(c) in the case of a company which is being wound up, the fact that that is so;

(d) the place of registration of the branch and the number with which it is registered.'

Moreover, if on any letters or order forms there is reference to the share capital of the company, the reference must be to the paid-up share capital[50].

[34.035] The requirements for the branch of a foreign company that has been formed and registered outside of the State and outside of the EU is somewhat different. Regulation 8(1) provides that the letterhead of such a branch shall bear the following particulars:

'(a) the place of registration of the branch and the number with which it is registered;

(b) if the law of the State in which the company is incorporated requires entry in a register, the place of registration of the company and the number with which it is registered.'

Moreover, if on any letters or order forms there is reference to the share capital of the company, the reference must be to the paid-up share capital[51].

50 Regulation 5(2) of the EC(BD)R 1993.

51 Regulation 8(2) of the EC(BD)R 1993.

Accounting documents to be delivered to the registrar of companies

[34.036] Both EU companies and non-EU companies that establish a branch in Ireland are required to deliver, each year, to the registrar of companies their accounting documents[52], as drawn up, audited and where required by the law of their place of incorporation, disclosed. Regulation 11(1) provides:

> 'Subject to paragraphs (2) to (6) every company within the meaning of Part II or Part III of these Regulations shall, once in every year, deliver to the registrar the accounting documents of the company as drawn up, audited and, where so required, disclosed in accordance with the law of the State in which it is incorporated and in the case of a company to which Part II applies in accordance with Council Directives 78/660/EEC (OJ No 222, 14.08.78, pp 11–31), 83/349/EEC [OJ No 193, 18.07.83, pp 1–17] and 84/253/EEC (OJ No 126, 12.05.84, pp 20–26).'

In the case of a non-EU company that is incorporated in some country that does not require its limited companies to draw up accounts and have them audited, this will not excuse the company from having to do this in Ireland if it establishes an Irish branch. Regulation 11(2) provides:

> 'A company to which Part III applies, shall, where there is no requirement in the law of the State in which it is incorporated to have accounting documents drawn up, deliver to the registrar accounting documents drawn up and audited in accordance with Council Directives 78/660/EEC and 83/349/EEC.'

Even where there is a requirement in the law of the place of its incorporation, a non-EU company that establishes a branch here has the option of filing accounts drawn up and audited in accordance with EU law instead of its own law[53]. It is thought that this is wishful thinking on the part of the EU in thinking that a foreign company would go to the trouble and expense of preparing separate accounts for its branch when it is already obliged to prepare accounts under its own law.

[34.037] With regard to the timing of when accounts are to be filed in the CRO, reg 11(4) of the EC(BD)R 1993 provides that in the case of accounts referred to in reg 11(1) and (3), the requisite period is 11 months from the end of the company's financial year *or* at the same time as the foreign company's local law requires them to be published, whichever is the earlier. In the case of foreign companies that elect to draw up accounts that comply with EU law, they have 11 months to file from the company's financial year end[54].

---

52 Regulation 12 provides that references to accounting documents, in relation to a financial year of a company, are to: (a) the accounts of the company for the period, including, if it has one or more subsidiaries, any consolidated accounts of the group, (b) any annual report of the directors for the period, (c) the report of the auditors on the accounts mentioned in subparagraph (a), and (d) any report of the auditors on the report mentioned in subparagraph (b).

53 Regulation 11(3) of the EC(BD)R 1993.

54 Regulation 11(5) of the EC(BD)R 1993.

Miscellaneous obligations

[34.038] Regulation 15(1) provides that where, prior to the date referred to in reg 4(1) or 7(1), as appropriate, a company, which has established a branch in the State, in complying with either Part XI of the CA 1963 or the EC(BD)R 1993 in respect of another branch established in the State, had returned to the registrar documents[55] which are the same in all respects as the documents required by reg 4(1) or 7(1), as appropriate, and it has no outstanding obligation to make a return to the registrar so far as concerns any alterations to those documents, then the company may return, in lieu of the documents required by reg 4(1) or 7(1), a statement in the prescribed form that this information has already been returned to the registrar.

Regulation 15(2) provides that where prior to the date referred to in reg 4(1) or 7(1), as appropriate, a company, which has established a branch in the State, in complying with either Part XI of the CA 1963 or the EC(BD)R 1993 in respect of another branch established in the State, had returned to the registrar particulars which are the same in all respects as the corresponding particulars required by reg 4(2)(f), (g) or (h) or reg 7(2)(g), (h) or (i), as appropriate, and it has no outstanding obligation to make a return to the registrar so far as concerns any alterations to those particulars, then the company may return, in lieu of the corresponding particulars required by reg 4(2)(f), (g), or (h), or reg 7(2)(g), (h) or (i), as appropriate, a statement in the prescribed form that this information has already been returned to the registrar.

Service of process or notice

[34.039] Regulation 17 of the EC(BD)R 1993 provides that subject to para (2):

> 'any process or notice required to be served on a company to which these regulations apply shall be sufficiently served if addressed to any person whose name has been delivered to the registrar under Regulation 4(2)(g) or 7(2)(h) (or any changes notified thereto) and left at or sent by post to the address which has been so delivered.'

Regulation 17(2) provides:

> 'A document may be served on any such company by leaving it at or sending it by post to any branch established by the company in the State—
>
> (a) where the company makes default in delivering to the registrar the name and address of a person resident in the State who is authorised to accept on behalf of the company service of process; or
>
> (b) if at any time all the persons whose names and addresses have been so delivered are dead or have ceased to so reside, or refuse to accept service on behalf of the company, or for any reason it cannot be served.'

Duty to secure compliance with Regulations

[34.040] Regulation 18 of the EC(BD)R 1993 provides that the duty of securing compliance by a company with the provisions of the EC(BD)R 1993 shall, without prejudice to the duty of the company concerned, also lie upon the persons appointed by

55 Regulation 15(3) provides that where para (1) applies: 'a reference to the delivery of the matter referred to in Regulation 4(1) or Regulation 7(1) shall be construed as a reference to the return of the statement referred to in paragraph (1).'

the company to ensure compliance with the EC(BD)R 1993. If the EC(BD)R 1993 are to be capable of being enforced, it is important that there should be someone in the State who can be directed to comply with the EC(BD)R 1993 and who can, in default, be prosecuted. Whereas the prospect of being responsible for a company's compliance with anything can have the effect of sending hard men running for cover, the extent of a company's obligations under the EC(BD)R 1993 are relatively modest being primarily in the nature of causing filings to be made upon the occurrence of specified events.

Offences for breach of Regulations

[34.041] Regulation 19(1) of the EC(BD)R 1993 provides that a person who contravenes any provision of these Regulations shall be guilty of an offence. Contravention includes a failure to comply[56]. The offence is a summary offence and a person guilty of an offence under para (1) shall be liable on summary conviction to a class C fine[57] or, at the discretion of the court in the case of an individual, to imprisonment for a term not exceeding 12 months or to both. Regulation 19(3) provides that a person shall not be liable to be sentenced to imprisonment for such an offence unless, in the opinion of the court, the offence was committed wilfully. Regulation 19(4) provides that where an offence committed by a body or by a person purporting to act on behalf of a body is proved to have been so committed with the consent or connivance of or to be attributable to, or to have been facilitated by, any neglect on the part of any officer or employee of that body, that person shall also be guilty of an offence.

---

56 Regulation 19(5).

57 Secton 6(2) of Fines Act 2010.

the company to assist cooperators with the BGDNR 1997 [illegible] whose [illegible] be capable of being [illegible] that there should be someone in the State who can be prosecuted [illegible] who are [illegible] be prosecuted, whereas [illegible] company [illegible] anyone can [illegible] company's obligations under the BGDNR 1997 are [illegible] failure of causing [illegible] specified events.

[illegible]

[illegible] Regulation 19 [illegible] of the BGDNR 1997 [illegible] provides that [illegible] offences [illegible] regulations [illegible] [illegible] the offender is [illegible] or [illegible] conviction to a [illegible] fine [illegible] or [illegible] imprisonment [illegible] Regulation 19(2) provides that a person shall not be [illegible] unless [illegible] the consent [illegible] provides that where an offence committed by a body corporate is proved to have been committed with the consent or connivance of, or to be attributable to any neglect on the part of, any director, manager, secretary or other similar officer of the body corporate [illegible] guilty of that offence.

[illegible]

[illegible] of the [illegible] Act 20[illegible]

Companies (Amendment) (No 2) Act 1999

Second Schedule

List of Companies for Purposes of Section 3(2)(c) of Act of 1990 and Sections 32 and 45

1. A company that is a member firm within the meaning of the Stock Exchange Act, 1995.
2. A company that is a stock exchange within the meaning of the Stock Exchange Act, 1995.
3. A company that is an associated undertaking or a related undertaking of a member firm or stock exchange within the meaning of the Stock Exchange Act, 1995.
4. A company that is an investment business firm within the meaning of the Investment Intermediaries Act, 1995.
5. A company that is an associated undertaking or a related undertaking of an investment business firm within the meaning of the Investment Intermediaries Act, 1995.
6. A company to which Chapter VII, VIII or IX of Part II of the Central Bank Act, 1989, applies.
7. A company that is engaged in the business of accepting deposits or other repayable funds or granting credit for its own account.
8. A company that is an associated body of a building society within the meaning of the Building Societies Act, 1989.
9. A company that is an associated enterprise of a credit institution within the meaning of the European Communities (Consolidated Supervision of Credit Institutions) Regulations, 1992 (S.I. No. 396 of 1992).
10. An investment company within the meaning of Part XIII of the Companies Act, 1990.
11. A company that is a management company or trustee within the meaning of Part XIII of the Companies Act, 1990.
12. A company that is an undertaking for collective investment in transferable securities within the meaning of the European Communities (Undertakings for Collective Investment in Transferable Securities) Regulations, 1989 (S.I. No. 78 of 1989).
13. A company that is a management company or trustee of an undertaking for collective investment in transferable securities within the meaning of the European Communities (Undertakings for Collective Investment in Transferable Securities) Regulations, 1989 (S.I. No. 78 of 1989).
14. A company that is a management company or trustee of a unit trust scheme within the meaning of the Unit Trusts Act, 1990.

15. A company that is a general partner or custodian of an investment limited partnership within the meaning of the Investment Limited Partnerships Act, 1994.
16. A company that is an undertaking with close links with a financial undertaking within the meaning of the Supervision of Credit Institutions, Stock Exchange Member Firms and Investment Business Firms Regulations, 1996 (S.I. No. 267 of 1996).
17. Any other company the carrying on of business by which is required, by virtue of any enactment or instrument thereunder, to be authorised by the Central Bank.
18. A company that is—
    (a) a holder of an authorisation within the meaning of—
        (i) Regulation 2 of the European Communities (Non-Life Insurance) Regulations, 1976 (S.I. No. 115 of 1976),
        (ii) Regulation 2 of the European Communities (Non-Life Insurance) Framework Regulations, 1994 (S.I. No. 359 of 1994),
        (iii) Regulation 2 of the European Communities (Life Assurance) Regulations, 1984 (S.I. No. 57 of 1984),
        or
        (iv) Regulation 2 of the European Communities (Life Assurance) Framework Regulations, 1994 (S.I. No. 360 of 1994),
        or
    (b) a holder of an authorisation granted under the European Communities (Non-Life Insurance) (Amendment) (No. 2) Regulations, 1991 (S.I. No. 142 of 1991).
19. A company that is an insurance intermediary within the meaning of the Insurance Act, 1989.
20. A company that is an excepted body within the meaning of the Trade Union Acts, 1871 to 1990.

Index

Note: references are to *paragraph* number

Abridged accounts
medium-sized companies
balance sheet, 17.270–17.272
directors' statement, 17.275
profit and loss account, 17.263–17.264
special auditor's report, 17.276
small companies
balance sheet, 17.279–17.280
directors' statement, 17.281
profit and loss account, 17.282
special auditor's report, 17.283–17.284
Absconding officers
realisation of assets, and, 25.043–25.046
Abuse
directors' duties, and, 15.054
Abuse of process
oppression, and, 11.053–11.056
Account and indemnity
directors' loans, and, 16.110–16.112
Account of profits
conflicts of interest, and, 15.067–15.068
Accounting framework
annual accounts, and, 17.023–17.024
Accounting policies
balance sheet, and, 17.071
profit and loss account, and, 17.099
Accounting principles
Companies Act individual accounts, and, 17.028–17.029
Accounts
accounting frameworks, 17.023–17.024
application of obligations, 17.021
approval, 17.213
balance sheet
accounting policies, 17.071
alternative valuation rules, 17.076–17.077
approval, 17.213
debentures, 17.092
debt owed by company exceeding consideration received, 17.086
development costs, 17.082
disaggregation of fixed assets, 17.073
distributable profits, 17.095
dividends, 17.096
fair valuation of assets and liabilities, 17.078–17.081
financial assets held as investments, 17.084
financial commitments, 17.097
formats 17.031–17.036
goodwill, 17.083
group undertakings, 17.072
guarantees, 17.097
historic cost valuation rules, 17.074–17.075
indebtedness, 17.087–17.089
introduction, 17.030
loans given as financial assistance, 17.085
medium-sized companies, and, 17.270–17.272
notes, 17.070–17.097
obligation to circulate, 17.243–17.245
reserves and provisions, 17.094
revaluation reserve treatment, 17.091
share capital, 17.092
signature, 17.213
small companies, and, 17.279–17.280
subsidiary undertaking shares, 17.093
taxation provision, 17.090
valuation rules, 17.037–17.058
branches, 34.036–34.037
building societies, 1.045
directors' liability, 17.018
EU law, and, 1.116
GAAP, 17.024
GAAP, 17.024
groups of companies
Companies Act, 17.164–17.200
exemptions from obligation, 17.156–17.163
IFRS, 17.201–17.212
introduction, 17.144–17.153

Accounts (contd)
obligation to circulate, 17.243–17.245
obligation to prepare, 17.154–17.155
groups of companies (Companies Act)
acquisition and merger accounting, 17.190–17.195
acquisitions, 17.177
associated undertakings, 17.197–17.200
auditors' remuneration, 17.189
contents, 17.171–17.175
directors' remuneration, 17.181
directors' report, and, 17.216
directors' transactions, 17.185
foreign currencies, 17.178
form, 17.165–17.169
format, 17.170
indebtedness, 17.179
introduction, 17.164
joint ventures, 17.196
name and office of undertakings, 17.186–17.187
notes, 17.176–17.189
qualifying capital interests, 17.186–17.187
staff numbers and remuneration, 17.180
transactions with connected persons, 17.185
valuation of assets, 17.182–17.184
groups of companies (IFRS)
debentures, 17.207
debentures held by subsidiaries, 17.211
directors' interests in shares, 17.204
directors' remuneration, 17.202
directors' report, and, 17.217
directors' transactions, 17.203
distributability of profits, 17.208–17.209
financial assistance for purchase of own shares, 17.210
group undertakings, 17.205
interests in shares, 17.204
introduction, 17.201
off balance sheet items, 17.212
share capital, 17.207
shares held by subsidiaries, 17.211
staff numbers, 17.206
staff remuneration, 17.206
transactions with connected persons, 17.203
guarantee companies, and, 30.062–30.065
IAS 1, and, 17.017
individual accounts
Companies Acts, 17.025–17.130
IFRS, 17.131–17.143
individual accounts (Companies Acts)
accounting principles, 17.028–17.029
auditors' remuneration, 17.122–17.124
balance sheet, 17.030–17.058
directors' interests in shares, 17.121
directors' remuneration, 17.112
directors' transactions, 17.113–17.120
group undertakings, and, 17.127–17.129
interests in shares, 17.121
introduction, 17.025
laying before company at general meeting, 17.249
notes, 17.069–17.130
off balance sheet items, 17.126
profit and loss account, 17.059–17.068
related party transactions, 17.125
subsidiary undertakings, and, 17.130
transactions with connected persons, 17.113–17.120
'true and fair view', 17.026–17.027
individual accounts (IFRS)
auditors' remuneration, 17.143
debentures, 17.136
debentures held by subsidiaries, 17.141
directors' interests in shares, 17.134
directors' remuneration, 17.132
directors' report, and, 17.217
directors' transactions, 17.133
distributability of profits, 17.137

Accounts (contd)
financial assistance for purchase of own shares, 17.139
group undertakings, 17.135
guarantees, 17.138
interests in shares, 17.134
introduction, 17.131
laying before company at general meeting, 17.249
off balance sheet items, 17.142
share capital, 17.136
shares held by subsidiaries, 17.141
staff numbers, 17.140
staff remuneration, 17.140
transactions with connected persons, 17.133
introduction, 17.017–17.022
medium-sized companies, and, 17.276
parent undertakings, and, 17.017
profit and loss account (Companies Acts)
accounting policies, 17.099
approval, 17.213
charges payable, 17.106
depreciation, 17.102–17.103
diminution in value of fixed assets, 17.102
directors' emoluments, 17.105
extraordinary income or charges, 17.108
foreign currencies, 17.109
formats, 17.060–17.068
generally, 17.059
improvements in value of written down fixed assets, 17.104
interest payable, 17.106
medium-sized companies, and, 17.273–17.274
movements, 17.110
notes, 17.098–17.110
obligation to circulate, 17.243–17.245
reconciliation of depreciation figures, 17.103
signature, 17.213
staff number and remuneration, 17.101
tax, 17.107
turnover, 17.100
public limited companies, and, 29.116–29.120
publication
demand for copies of accounts and reports, 17.246–17.247
general requirements, 17.248
laying before company at general meeting, 17.249
meaning, 17.248
obligation to circulate, 17.243–17.245
single-member private companies, and, 17.020
SSAPs, 17.023
unlimited companies, and, 31.026–31.032
Acquisition accounting
disclosures, 17.195
generally, 17.191
introduction, 17.190
Acquisition by company of own shares
authorised by articles, 10.027
common law prohibition, 10.014
contingent purchase contracts, 10.031
distributable profits, 10.026
exceptions to statutory prohibition
forfeiture, 10.022
fully paid shares for no consideration, 10.018
introduction, 10.017
redemption of shares, 10.019
reduction of capital, 10.020
remedial court orders, 10.021
foot of remedial court orders, on, 10.021
forfeiture of shares, and, 10.022
fully paid shares for no consideration, 10.018
introduction, 10.013
Ministerial regulations, 10.035
prohibitions
common law, at, 10.014
statute, under, 10.015–10.035
Pt.XI CA 1990, under
authorised by articles, 10.027

Acquisition by company of own shares (contd)
contingent purchase contracts, 10.031
distributable profits, 10.026
introduction, 10.023
Ministerial regulations, 10.035
own-share purchase, 10.024–10.025
repudiation by company, 10.033
safeguards, 10.032
special resolution, 10.028–10.030
winding up, 10.034
public limited companies, and
financial assistance, 29.077–29.078
generally, 29.068–29.073
marketing arrangement, 29.069
treatment, 29.074–29.076
'put' and 'call' contracts, 10.031
redemption of shares, and, 10.019
reduction of capital, and, 10.020
remedial court orders, and, 10.021
s 65 CA 1963, under, 10.019
s 72 CA 1963, under, 10.020
s 211 CA 1990, under, 10.024–10.025
special resolution, 10.028–10.030
statutory prohibition, 10.015–10.016
Tomlin orders, 10.30
winding up, 10.034
Acquisition of shares in holding company
generally, 10.036–10.040
Acquisition of corporate status
certificates of incorporation
constitutionality of conclusive effect, 4.018–4.019
effect, 4.004–4.005
EU nullity provisions, and, 4.008–4.010
generally, 4.002–4.007
introduction, 4.001
judicial review of decision to issue, 4.015–4.017
rationale for conclusive effect, 4.006–4.007
cesser, 4.020
failure to register, and, 4.003
impeachment of incorporation
constitutionality of effect of certificate, 4.018–4.019
introduction, 4.012
judicial review of decision to issue certificate, 4.015–4.017
trade unions registered as companies, 4.013–4.014
incorporation, and, 4.002
introduction, 4.001
mandamus, and, 4.003
nullity provisions
First EU Companies Directive, 4.008
Ireland, in, 4.009–4.010
refusal to register, and, 4.003
registration, 4.002–4.003
re-registration, 4.002
Acting in interests of company
directors' duties, and, 15.027–15.028
Actions in rem
recovery of money given by company ultra vires, and, 7.091–7.092
Actual authority
generally, 7.100
representor, 7.107
Adjournment
directors' meetings, and, 14.117
members' meetings, and, 14.058–14.060
'Affairs of the company'
investigations, and
And see **Investigations**
background, 27.003—27.006
introduction, 27.001
oppression, and, 11.033–11.034
Agency
implied agency, 5.023–5.027
introduction, 5.020–5.022
undisclosed agency, 5.028
Agents
auditors, and, 17.312
authority, and
actual authority, 7.100
constructive notice of public documents, 7.119–7.120
generally, 7.099
implied authority, 7.100

Agents (contd)
indoor management rule, 7.121–7.122
investment companies, 29.143
ostensible authority, 7.101–7.118
public limited companies, 29.034
reg 6 EC(C)R 1973, 7.129–7.135
reg 10 EC(C)R 1973, 7.128
rule in *Turquand's* case, 7.123–7.127
investment companies, and, 29.143
pre-incorporation contracts, and, 7.041–7.042
public limited companies, and
generally, 29.034
investment companies, 29.143
receivers, and, 20.038–20.044
Aggregation retention of title clause
registration of charges, and, 19.022
'Agree to become a member'
definition of 'member', and, 8.004
estoppel, 8.008
introduction, 8.006
membership agreements, 8.007
overview, 8.001
Aircraft
registration of charges, and, 19.069
All sums due debentures
generally, 18.038–18.039
Allotment of shares
consideration
'cash', 8.061
discount, at a, 8.064
introduction, 8.060
non-cash consideration, 8.062–8.063
premium, at a, 8.065–8.067
directors' authority, 8.051–8.053
introduction, 8.050
issue at a discount, 8.064
issue at a premium, 8.065–8.067
mechanics, 8.054–8.055
non-cash consideration, 8.062–8.063
pre-emption rights, 8.056–8.059
public limited companies, and
authorisation, 29.043
consideration, 29.050–29.054
minimum subscription requirements, 29.045–29.046
payment, 29.047–29.049
pre-emption rights, 29.044
relief for allottees, directors and others, 29.055
stock exchange listing, and, 29.056
rectification of defects, 8.068–8.070
Alterations
articles of association, and
additional liability imposed on members, where, 3.060–3.063
class rights, of, 3.064–3.066
contrary to law, where, 3.059
generally, 3.056–3.058
informal, 3.085–3.087
not bona fide and in interests of company as whole, where, 3.067–3.084
restrictions, 3.058–3.084
shareholders' agreement, by, 3.085–3.087
memorandum of association, and
capital clause, 3.031–3.036
generally, 3.022
liability clause, 3.029–3.030
name clause, 3.023–3.025
non-compulsory clauses, 3.037
objects clause, 3.026–3.028
oppression, and, 11.085
Alternate directors
generally, 13.042
Amalgamations
building societies, and, 1.047
Amendment
articles of association, and
directors, 3.050–3.052
introduction, 3.043–3.044
members' meetings, 3.047–3.049
shares, 3.045–3.046
voting rights, 3.053–3.055
Annual accounts
accounting frameworks, 17.023–17.024
application of obligations, 17.021
approval, 17.213
balance sheet
accounting policies, 17.071
alternative valuation rules, 17.076–17.077

Annual accounts (contd)
approval, 17.213
debentures, 17.092
debt owed by company exceeding consideration received, 17.086
development costs, 17.082
disaggregation of fixed assets, 17.073
distributable profits, 17.095
dividends, 17.096
fair valuation of assets and liabilities, 17.078–17.081
financial assets held as investments, 17.084
financial commitments, 17.097
formats 17.031–17.036
goodwill, 17.083
group undertakings, 17.072
guarantees, 170.97
historic cost valuation rules, 17.074–17.075
indebtedness, 17.087–17.089
introduction, 17.030
loans given as financial assistance, 17.085
medium-sized companies, and, 17.270–17.272
notes, 17.070–17.097
obligation to circulate, 17.243–17.245
reserves and provisions, 17.094
revaluation reserve treatment, 17.091
share capital, 17.092
signature, 17.213
small companies, and, 17.279–17.280
subsidiary undertaking shares, 17.093
taxation provision, 17.090
valuation rules, 17.037–17.058
directors' liability, 17.018
EU law, and, 1.116
GAAP, 17.024
GAAP, 17.024
group accounts
Companies Act, 17.164–17.200
exemptions from obligation, 17.156–17.163
IFRS, 17.201–17.212
introduction, 17.144–17.153
obligation to circulate, 17.243–17.245
obligation to prepare, 17.154–17.155
parent undertakings that are subsidiaries of EEA undertakings, 17.159–17.161
parent undertakings that are subsidiaries of non-EEA undertakings, 17.162–17.163
size of group, 17.157–17.158
group accounts (Companies Act)
acquisition and merger accounting, 17.190–17.195
acquisitions, 17.177
associated undertakings, 17.197–17.200
auditors' remuneration, 17.189
contents, 17.171–17.175
directors' remuneration, 17.181
directors' report, and, 17.216
directors' transactions, 17.185
foreign currencies, 17.178
form, 17.165–17.169
format, 17.170
indebtedness, 17.179
introduction, 17.164
joint ventures, 17.196
name and office of undertakings, 17.186–17.187
notes, 17.176–17.189
qualifying capital interests, 17.186–17.187
staff numbers and remuneration, 17.180
transactions with connected persons, 17.185
valuation of assets, 17.182–17.184
group accounts (IFRS)
debentures, 17.207
debentures held by subsidiaries, 17.211
directors' interests in shares, 17.204
directors' remuneration, 17.202
directors' report, and, 17.217
directors' transactions, 17.203
distributability of profits, 17.208–17.209

Annual accounts (contd)
financial assistance for purchase of own shares, 17.210
group undertakings, 17.205
interests in shares, 17.204
introduction, 17.201
off balance sheet items, 17.212
share capital, 17.207
shares held by subsidiaries, 17.211
staff numbers, 17.206
staff remuneration, 17.206
transactions with connected persons, 17.203
IAS 1, and, 17.017
individual accounts
Companies Acts, 17.025–17.130
IFRS, 17.131–17.143
individual accounts (Companies Acts)
accounting principles, 17.028–17.029
auditors' remuneration, 17.122–17.124
balance sheet, 17.030–17.058
directors' interests in shares, 17.121
directors' remuneration, 17.112
directors' transactions, 17.113–17.120
group undertakings, and, 17.127–17.129
interests in shares, 17.121
introduction, 17.025
laying before company at general meeting, 17.249
notes, 17.069–17.130
off balance sheet items, 17.126
profit and loss account, 17.059–17.068
related party transactions, 17.125
subsidiary undertakings, and, 17.130
transactions with connected persons, 17.113–17.120
'true and fair view', 17.026–17.027
individual accounts (IFRS)
auditors' remuneration, 17.143
debentures, 17.136
debentures held by subsidiaries, 17.141
directors' interests in shares, 17.134
directors' remuneration, 17.132
directors' report, and, 17.217
directors' transactions, 17.133
distributability of profits, 17.137
financial assistance for purchase of own shares, 17.139
group undertakings, 17.135
guarantees, 17.138
interests in shares, 17.134
introduction, 17.131
laying before company at general meeting, 17.249
off balance sheet items, 17.142
share capital, 17.136
shares held by subsidiaries, 17.141
staff numbers, 17.140
staff remuneration, 17.140
transactions with connected persons, 17.133
introduction, 17.017–17.22
medium-sized companies, and, 17.276
parent undertakings, and, 17.017
profit and loss account (Companies Acts)
accounting policies, 17.099
approval, 17.213
charges payable, 17.106
depreciation, 17.102–17.103
diminution in value of fixed assets, 17.102
directors' emoluments, 17.105
extraordinary income or charges, 17.108
foreign currencies, 17.109
formats, 17.060–17.068
generally, 17.059
improvements in value of written down fixed assets, 17.104
interest payable, 17.106
medium-sized companies, and, 17.273–17.274
movements, 17.110
notes, 17.98–17.110
obligation to circulate, 17.243–17.245
reconciliation of depreciation figures, 17.103

Annual accounts (contd)
signature, 17.213
staff number and remuneration, 17.101
tax, 17.107
turnover, 17.100
publication
demand for copies of accounts and reports, 17.246–17.247
general requirements, 17.248
laying before company at general meeting, 17.249
meaning, 17.248
obligation to circulate, 17.243–17.245
single-member private companies, and, 17.020
SSAPs, 17.023
Annual general meetings
consequences where not held, 14.012–14.013
financial statements, and, 17.002
frequency, 14.006
generally, 14.006–14.007
Ministerial direction to call, 14.011
minutes, 14.077–14.080
notice
business to be conducted, 14.050–14.054
introduction, 14.033
periods, 14.040–14.049
notice of business to be conducted
amendment of resolution, 14.054
basis for need for resolutions, 14.053
introduction, 14.050
other matters, 14.053–14.054
special business, 14.051
special resolutions, 14.052
notice periods
accidental omission, 14.048
extended, 14.044–14.047
short notice, 14.041–14.043
standard notice, 14.040
summary of provisions, 14.049
place, 14.010
purpose, 14.008–14.009
single-member private limited companies, 14.014
'special business', 14.009
venue, 14.010
Annual returns
accompanying documents
exemption, 17.264–17.266
generally, 17.262–17.263
consequences of incorporation, and, 4.092
contents, 17.257–17.259
documents to be annexed
exemption, 17.264–17.266
generally, 17.262–17.263
draft Companies Bill, and, 1.177
failure to file
generally, 17.255–17.256
restoration to register, 26.035–26.049
failure to file on time, 17.255–17.256
form, 17.260–17.261
guarantee companies, and, 30.066–30.068
introduction, 17.250–17.251
restoration to register, and
'aggrieved' petitioner, 26.040
alternative orders, 26.049
introduction, 26.035
jurisdiction to hear application, 26.039
locus standi, 26.036–26.038
requirement to file outstanding annual returns, 26.044–26.048
weight attached to third party objections, 26.041–26.043
Societas Europaea, and, 29.186
time for filing, 17.252–17.254
unlimited companies, and, 31.023–31.025
Anti-avoidance
directors' loans, and, 16.062–16.063
Anton Piller orders
realisation of assets, and, 25.037
Appearance in court
civil litigation, and, 6.066–6.070
Appointment
auditors, and
approval, 17.299–17.305

Appointment (contd)
audit requirement, and, 17.225
disqualified persons, 17.306–17.307
general requirement, 17.292–17.195
member of recognised accountancy body, 17.300
Member State auditor, 17.301
qualification, 17.296–17.298
third country auditor, 17.302
Director of Corporate Enforcement, and, 28.010
directors, and
first director, 13.028
generally, 13.025–13.027
subsequent directors, 13.029–13.032
examiners, and
affidavit in support, 22.029–22.033
formalities, 22.055–22.057
grounds, 22.018–22.028
jurisdiction, 22.009–22.010
locus standi, 22.011–22.017
petition, 22.029–22.033
test, 22.018–22.019
liquidators, and
creditors' voluntary liquidators, 24.010–24.012
members' voluntary liquidators, 24.009
official liquidators, 24.013–24.015
provisional liquidators, 24.016–24.019
receivers, and
acts of default, 20.006–20.008
basis, 20.006
considerations, 20.005–20.010
default in repayment on demand, 20.009
duty of care of creditor, 20.010
events of default, 20.006–20.008
effect, 20.029–20.034
events of default, 20.006–20.008
foot of court order, on, 20.020
foot of debenture, on, 20.013–20.019
generally, 20.012
income under LCLRA 2009, under, 20.021
NAMA, by, 20.022–20.024
notice, 20.026–20.028
qualifications, 20.011
statutory receiver, as, 20.022–20.024
secretary, and, 13.120

Arrest
realisation of assets, and
absconding officers, 25.043–25.046
contributories, 25.043–25.046
facilitate examination, by, 25.039–25.042
introduction, 25.038

Articles of association
additional liability imposed on members, and, 3.060–3.063
alteration
additional liability imposed on members, where, 3.060–3.063
class rights, of, 3.064–3.066
contrary to law, where, 3.059
generally, 3.056–3.058
informal, 3.085–3.087
not bona fide and in interests of company as whole, where, 3.067–3.084
restrictions, 3.058–3.084
shareholders' agreement, by, 3.085–3.087
shareholders' remedies, and, 11.003
alteration bona fide and in interests of company as whole
alternative approaches, 3.081–3.084
appropriate test, 3.073–3.075
'company as a whole', 3.070–3.072
divergent disputes, 3.076–3.080
introduction, 3.067
traditional test, 3.068–3.080
amendments to model articles
directors, 3.050–3.052
introduction, 3.043–3.044
members' meetings, 3.047–3.049
shares, 3.045–3.046
voting rights, 3.053–3.055
class rights, and, 3.064–3.066
construction of, 3.089–3.091
contrary to law, 3.059
directors, 3.050–3.052
generally, 3.038–3.091

Articles of association (contd)
guarantee companies, and
generally, 30.035–30.038
introduction, 3.039
importance, 3.002
introduction, 3.001
meaning, 3.038
members' meetings, 3.047–3.049
memorandum of association, and, 3.088
model form
amendments, 3.043–3.055
generally, 3.040–3.042
introduction, 3.039
nature, 3.038–3.039
public limited companies, and
alterations, 29.032
generally, 29.030–29.031
investment companies, 29.139–29.141
registration, 3.039
shareholders' agreements, and
generally, 3.107
informal alteration, 3.085–3.087
introduction, 3.038
shares, 3.045–3.046
Societas Europaea, and, 29.171
unlimited companies, and
generally, 31.009–31.010
introduction, 3.039
voting rights, 3.053–3.055
Assignee directors
generally, 13.043
Assisting purchase of company's own shares
'any transaction', 10.051–10.052
breadth of prohibition, 10.062–10.063
civil consequences
'any transaction', 10.051–10.052
introduction, 10.049
'notice', 10.053–10.057
voidability, 10.049–10.050
covenants, 10.064
criminal consequences, 10.048
dividends, 10.078–10.083
'financial assistance'
actual vs potential, 10.065
breadth of prohibition, 10.062–10.063
covenants, 10.064
express forms, 10.059–10.061
'in connection with', 10.063
introduction, 10.058
'otherwise', 10.062
warranties, 10.064
general prohibition, 10.047
'in connection with', 10.063
introduction, 10.046
lawful liabilities, 10.078–10.083
miscellaneous, 10.084
'notice', 10.053–10.057
'otherwise', 10.062
private companies, and, 10.047
s 60 CA 1963, under
application, 10.047
consequences of contravention, 10.048–10.057
'financial assistance', 10.058–10.065
general rule, 10.046
shareholders' remedies, and, 11.003
validation procedure
excluded companies, 10.069–10.070
introduction, 10.066
practice, in, 10.067–10.068
restrospectivity, 10.075–10.076
shareholder protection, 10.077
special resolution, 10.072
statutory declaration, 10.071
strict compliance, 10.073–10.074
voidability, 10.049–10.050
warranties and covenants, 10.064
'whitewash' procedure, 10.066–10.077
Associated undertakings
generally, 12.041
Associate directors
generally, 13.044
Association clause
memorandum of association, and, 3.020
Association concept
constitution of private companies, and, 3.002
Associations
formation, 4.090

Attachment
enforcement of judgments and orders, and, 6.095–6.099
Attestation
common seal, and
generally, 7.024
Reg 76 of Table A of Sch.1 to C(C)A 1908, 7.027–7.028
Reg 115 of Table A of Sch.1 to CA 1963, 7.025–7.026
Audit requirement
appointment of auditor, 17.225
auditor's report, 17.226–17.286
building societies, and, 1.045
draft Companies Bill, and, 1.177
exemption, 17.287–17.191
guarantee companies, and, 30.062–30.069
public limited companies, and
generally, 29.116–29.120
investment companies, 29.147
report on accounts by auditor, 17.226
Societas Europapaea, and, 29.186
unlimited companies, and, 31.026–31.035
Auditors
appointment
approval, 17.299–17.305
audit requirement, and, 17.225
disqualified persons, 17.306–17.307
general requirement, 17.292–17.195
member of recognised accountancy body, 17.300
Member State auditor, 17.301
qualification, 17.296–17.298
third country auditor, 17.302
approval as statutory audit firm, 17.303–17.305
approval as statutory auditor
introduction, 17.299
member of recognised accountancy body, 17.300
Member State auditor, 17.301
third country auditor, 17.302
civil liability
company, to, 17.329
exclusion, 17.336–17.337
others, to, 17.330–17.335
common law duties, 17.323–17.328
disclose directors' emoluments, 17.319
disqualified persons, 17.306–17.307
duties
common law, at, 17.323–17.328
disclose directors' emoluments, 17.319
exercise professional integrity, 17.315
introduction, 17.313–17.314
report failures to keep proper books of account, 17.316–17.318
report suspected indictable offences, 17.320–17.322
EU law, and, 1.119
exclusion of liability, 17.336–17.337
exercise professional integrity, 17.315
expenses, 17.308–17.309
liability to the company, 17.329
liability to third parties, 17.330–17.335
notification to supervisory authority of certain matters, 17.346–17.348
persons who may not act, 17.306–17.307
professional integrity, 17.315
registration-type offences, and, 28.051
removal, 17.338–17.342
remuneration, 17.308–17.309
replacement, 17.338–17.342
report failures to keep proper books of account, 17.316–17.318
report suspected indictable offences, 17.320–17.322
reports
adverse opinion, 17.236
auditors' duties, and, 17.314
content, 17.228–17.232
dating, 17.241
disclaimer of opinion, 17.237
emphasis of matter, 17.239–17.240
form, 17.233–17.240
general requirement, 17.227
introduction, 17.226
laying before company at general meeting, 17.249
'material' and 'pervasive' effects, 17.238

Auditors (contd)
obligation to circulate, 17.243–17.245
qualified opinion, 17.235
reading at the AGM, 17.242
signature, 17.241
small companies, and, 17.283–17.284
unqualified opinion, 17.234
resignation, 17.343–17.345
rights and powers, 17.310–17.311
status, 17.312
statutory duties, 17.313–17.322

Auditors' remuneration
generally, 17.308–17.309
groups of companies, 17.189
individual accounts, and
Companies Acts, 17.122–17.124
IFRS, 17.143

Auditor's report
adverse opinion, 17.236
auditors' duties, and, 17.314
contents, 17.228–17.232
dating, 17.241
disclaimer of opinion, 17.237
emphasis of matter, 17.239–17.240
form
adverse opinion, 17.236
disclaimer of opinion, 17.237
emphasis of matter, 17.239–17.240
introduction, 17.233
material' and 'pervasive' effects, 17.238
qualified opinion, 17.235
unqualified opinion, 17.234
general requirement, 17.227
introduction, 17.226
laying before company at general meeting, 17.249
'material' effects, 17.238
obligation to circulate, 17.243–17.245
'pervasive' effects, 17.238
qualified opinion, 17.235
reading at the AGM, 17.242
signature, 17.241
small companies, and, 17.283–17.284
unqualified opinion, 17.234

Audits
building societies, and, 1.045
draft Companies Bill, and, 1.177
guarantee companies, and, 30.062–30.069
public limited companies, and
generally, 29.116–29.120
investment companies, 29.147
Societas Europaea, and, 29.186
unlimited companies, and, 31.026–31.035

Authority
actual authority, 7.100
agents, of
actual authority, 7.100
constructive notice of public documents, 7.119–7.120
generally, 7.099
implied authority, 7.100
indoor management rule, 7.121–7.122
ostensible authority, 7.101–7.118
public limited companies, and, 29.034
reg 6 EC(C)R 1973, 7.129–7.135
reg 10 EC(C)R 1973, 7.128
rule in *Turquand's* case, 7.123–7.127
borrow, to, 18.011
capacity, and
borrow, to, 18.011
guarantee, to, 18.012–18.013
introduction, 18.010
secure, to, 18.011
civil litigation, and, 6.006–6.009
constructive notice of public documents, 7.119–7.120
generally, 7.099
guarantee companies, and, 30.002
guarantee, to, 18.012–18.013
implied authority, 7.100
indoor management rule, 7.121–7.122
ostensible authority
actual authority of representor, 7.107
board of directors, 7.112–7.113
chairman of the board, 7.115
company secretary, 7.117

Authority (contd)
contract within permitted capacity and authority of company, 7.109–7.110
corporate representations, 7.104–7.106
directors, 7.116
generally, 7.101–7.103
managing director, 7.114
particular corporate organs, of, 7.111–7.118
reliance on representation, 7.108
sole member of single-member private company, 7.118
partnerships, and, 1.022
reg 6 EC(C)R 1973, 7.129–7.135
reg 10 EC(C)R 1973, 7.128
rule in *Turquand's* case
generally, 7.123
irregularity is of public record, 7.124
outsider must act in good faith, 7.125–7.126
secure, to, 18.011
unlimited companies, and, 31.018

Authority of company
borrow, to, 18.011
guarantee, to, 18.012–18.013
introduction, 18.010
secure, to, 18.011

Balance sheet
accounting policies, 17.071
alternative valuation rules, 17.076–17.077
approval, 17.213
debentures, 17.092
debt owed by company exceeding consideration received, 17.086
development costs, 17.082
disaggregation of fixed assets, 17.073
distributable profits, 17.095
dividends, 17.096
fair valuation of assets and liabilities, 17.078–17.081
financial assets held as investments, 17.084
financial commitments, 17.097
formats 17.031–17.036
goodwill, 17.083
group undertakings, 17.072
guarantees, 17.097
historic cost valuation rules, 17.074–17.075
indebtedness, 17.087–17.089
introduction, 17.030
loans given as financial assistance, 17.085
medium-sized companies, and, 17.270–17.272
notes
accounting policies, 17.071
alternative valuation rules, 17.076–17.077
debentures, 17.092
debt owed by company exceeding consideration received, 17.086
development costs, 17.082
disaggregation of fixed assets, 17.073
distributable profits, 17.095
dividends, 17.096
fair valuation of assets and liabilities, 17.078–17.081
financial assets held as investments, 17.084
financial commitments, 17.097
goodwill, 17.083
group undertakings, 17.072
guarantees, 17.097
historic cost valuation rules, 17.074–17.075
indebtedness, 17.087–17.089
introduction, 17.070
loans given as financial assistance, 17.085
reserves and provisions, 17.094
revaluation reserve treatment, 17.091
share capital, 17.092
subsidiary undertaking shares, 17.093
taxation provision, 17.090
obligation to circulate, 17.243–17.245
reserves and provisions, 17.094
revaluation reserve treatment, 17.091
share capital, 17.92
signature, 17.213
small companies, and, 17.279–17.280

Balance sheet (contd)
subsidiary undertaking shares, 170.93
taxation provision, 17.090
valuation of assets
current assets, 17.050–17.058
fixed assets, 17.039–17.049
introduction, 17.037–17.038
valuation of current assets
alternative accounting rules, 17.055–17.057
fair value accounting, 17.058
historical cost rules, 17.050–17.054
valuation of fixed assets
alternative accounting rules, 17.042–17.045
fair value accounting, 17.046–17.049
historical cost rules, 17.040–17.041
introduction, 17.039
Bankruptcy
compulsory transfer of shares, and, 9.089
share transfers, and, 9.031
Bankers' liens
generally, 19.027
Banks
Central Bank's rights, 23.139–23.140
generally, 23.136–23.138
liquidation committee, 23.14223.
rules applicable to liquidators, 23.141
Beneficial interests
membership, and
generally, 8.025–8.030
limits, 8.032
protection, 8.031
pre-emption rights, and, 9.080–9.083
Bills of sale
registration of charges, and, 19.046–19.051
Binding effect
section 25 contracts, and
members and company, 3.095
members to members, 3.096–3.098
shareholders' agreements, and, 3.127–3.128
Board of directors
ostensible authority, and, 7.112–7.113
Bodies corporate
generally, 1.057
Bona fides
security for costs, and, 6.045–6.046
Bonus shares
See also **Shares**
distributions, and, 10.090
generally, 8.114
Book debts
fixed charges, and
curtailment of priority, 18.057–18.064
exercise of control by chargee as of legal right, 18.050
generally, 18.040–18.041
hybrid charges, 18.051–18.056
registration, 19.059–19.065
restrictions on chargor's use of debts, 18.044–18.049
validity, 18.042–18.043
registration of charges, and, 19.059–19.065
Booking deposits
liens, and, 19.030
Books and documents
investigations, and
consequences of failure to comply, 27.076–27.079
costs, 27.082
disclosure, 27.080–27.081
grounds for investigation, 27.070–27.074
introduction, 27.068–27.069
limits of procedure, 27.075
publication, 27.080–27.081
Books of account
approval, 17.213
civil liability, 17.013
concealment, 17.014–17.015
contents, 17.006
criminal liability, 17.011–17.012
destruction, 17.014–17.015
failure to keep proper books
discretion of court, 15.134–15.135
generally, 15.131
personal responsibility, 15.132–15.133

Books of account (contd)
proofs, 15.136–15.140
falsification, 17.014–17.015
form, 17.008
guarantee companies, and, 30.061
inspection, 17.009–17.010
introduction, 17.005
liability for failure to keep
civil liability, 17.013
criminal liability, 17.011–17.012
location, 17.007
public limited companies, and, 29.115
signature, 17.213

Borrowing
all sums due debentures, 18.038–18.039
authority
borrow, to, 18.011
guarantee, to, 18.012–18.013
introduction, 18.010
secure, to, 18.011
capacity
borrow, to, 18.005–18.006
guarantee, to, 18.007–18.008
introduction, 18.004
secure, to, 18.009
choses in action, 18.030
crystallisation of floating charges
appointment of receiver, 18.098
automatic clauses, 18.103–18.109
causes, 18.097–18.109
ceasing to carry on business, 18.100–18.102
express clauses, 18.103–18.109
introduction, 18.093–18.096
winding up of charger company, 18.099
debentures
all sums due, 18.038–18.039
debt securities, as, 18.021
definition, 18.018–18.020
facility letters, 18.016–18.017
fixed charges, 18.040–18.067
floating charges, 18.068–18.110
introduction, 18.014–18.015
mechanics, 18.014
security, 18.024–18.037
transfer, 18.022–18.023
equitable charges, 18.028–18.029
equitable mortgages
creation, 18.034
generally, 18.031
examiners' powers, and, 22.098–22.099
facility letters
generally, 18.016–18.017
introduction, 18.014
fixed charges
book debts, on, 18.040–18.064
deposit accounts, on, 18.065–18.067
identifiability, 18.035
fixed charges on book debts
curtailment of priority, 18.057–18.064
exercise of control by chargee as of legal right, 18.050
generally, 18.040–18.041
hybrid charges, 18.051–18.056
restrictions on chargor's use of debts, 18.044–18.049
validity, 18.042–18.043
floating charges
ability of charger to deal with property, 18.072–18.073
characteristics, 18.068–18.071
Coslett (Contractors) Ltd case, 18.074–18.077
creation, 18.078
crystallisation, 18.093–18.109
de-crystallisation, 18.110
events which affect assets, 18.087–18.092
execution of judgment, 18.092
generally, 18.068–18.078
liens, 18.091
nature, 18.069–18.071
negative pledge clauses, 18.079–18.086
set-off, 18.090
subsequent mortgages and charges, 18.089
guarantee companies, and, 30.002
introduction, 18.001–18.003
legal mortgages, 18.030
liens, 18.027
mortgages

Borrowing (contd)
creation, 18.033–18.034
definition, 18.032–18.037
equitable, 18.031
introduction, 18.030
legal, 18.030
types, 18.030–18.031
negative pledge clauses
competition law, and, 18.085–18.086
generally, 18.079
priority of accompanied charges, 18.080–18.084
pledges, 18.026
public limited companies, and, 29.121–29.122
purpose, 18.001–18.003
receivers
And see **Receivers**
appointment, 20.005–20.034
considerations on appointment, 20.005–20.010
definition, 20.002–20.004
directions, 20.085–20.086
duties, 20.045–20.073
effect of appointment, 20.029–20.034
introduction, 20.001
liabilities, 20.074–20.078
multiple appointments, 20.087
powers, 20.079–20.084
qualifications, 20.011
removal, 20.090–20.094
remuneration, 20.044
resignation, 20.088–20.089
status, 20.035–20.043
registration
And see **Registration of charges**
charger company's obligations, 19.107
conclusiveness of certificate, 19.011–19.020
consequences of non-registration, 19.006–19.010
disguised registrable charges, 19.071–19.084
introduction, 19.001
judgment mortgages, 19.085
late applications, 19.090–19.100
non-registrable security interests, 19.021–19.041
procedure, 19.101–19.107
property outside of the State, and, 19.086–19.089
register of charges, 19.002–19.005
registrable charges, 19.042–19.070
registrable particulars, 19.102–19.104
retention of title clauses, 19.071–19.084
satisfaction of charges, 19.105–19.106
security
equitable charges, 18.028–18.029
introduction, 18.024–18.025
liens, 18.027
mortgages, 18.030–18.037
pledges, 18.026
source of capital, as, 18.001–18.003
unlimited companies, and, 31.003
Branches
accounting documents, 34.036–34.037
'branch', 34.029
compliance, 34.040
definition, 34.029
delivery of documents
EU companies, 34.032
non-EU companies, 34.033
establishment, 34.030–34.031
EU companies, 34.032
EU law, and, 1.120
introduction, 34.027
legislative framework, 34.027
letterheads, 34.034–34.035
miscellaneous obligations, 34.038
non-EU companies, 34.033
obligations
accounting documents, 34.036–34.037
delivery of documents, 34.032–34.033
letterheads, 34.034–34.035
miscellaneous, 34.038
registration, 34.032–34.033
returns, 34.038
offences for breach, 34.041
registration

Branches (contd)
EU companies, 34.032
non-EU companies, 34.033
relevant companies, 34.028
service of process or notice, 34.039
Breach of restriction or disqualification orders
disregarding legal personality, and, 5.083–5.085
'Buchanan principle'
resolutions, and, 14.093
Building societies
accounts, 1.045
amalgamations, 1.047
audits, 1.045
conversion to companies, 1.046
directors, 1.043
formation, 1.037
generally, 1.036–1.047
governance, 1.043
management, 1.043
meetings, 1.044
membership, 1.041
NAMA, and, 1.036
powers, 1.038–1.040
supervision, 1.042
transfer of engagements, 1.047
Business letters
incorporation, and, 2.039–2.042
Business names
incorporation, and, 2.044
partnerships, and, 1.018
sole traders, and, 1.007–1.011
Business organisations
And see under individual headings
building societies, 1.036–1.047
credit unions, 1.048–1.049
friendly societies, 1.052–1.053
industrial and provident societies, 1.032–1.035
introduction, 1.004
partnerships, 1.014–1.031
sole traders, 1.005–1.013
unincorporated associations, 1.050–1.051
unregistered companies, 1.054–1.055
Business transactions
directors' loans, and, 16.095–16.097
Buyback of own shares
And see **Acquisition by company of own shares**
public limited companies, and, 29.068–29.073
Calls of shares
registration of charges, and, 19.068
Cancellation of transactions
oppression, and, 11.084
Capacity
ancillary powers
express, 7.057–7.067
generally, 7.055–7.056
implied powers, 7.068–7.069
borrow, to, 18.005–18.006
classification
ancillary powers, 7.055–7.059
existence of commercial benefit, 7.057–7.059
introduction, 7.054
substantive objects, 7.055–7.056
conditions on exercise of powers, 7.060–7.067
enforcement of ultra vires contracts, 7.088
existence of commercial benefit, 7.057–7.059
express ancillary powers
conditions on exercise, 7.060–7.067
generally, 7.057–7.059
generally, 7.048
gratuitous dispositions of corporate property
express object or power, 7.073–7.075
generally, 7.070
implicit power where reasonably incidental, 7.071–7.072
not in furtherance of company's interests, 7.076–7.079
guarantee companies, and, 30.002
guarantee, to, 18.007–18.008
implied ancillary powers, 7.068–7.069
judicial construction of objects clause, 7.049–7.053
objects clause, and

Capacity (contd)
generally, 3.012
judicial construction, 7.049–7.053
public limited companies, and
generally, 29.034
investment companies, 29.143
recovery of money given by company ultra vires
action in rem, 7.091–7.092
Belmont principle, 7.091–7.092
constructive trusts, 7.091–7.092
estoppel, 7.094–7.095
generally, 7.089
quasi-contract, 7.093
unenforceable, 7.090
reform of ultra vires doctrine, 7.096–7.098
reg 6 EC(C)R 1973, 7.087
s 8 CA 1963
actually aware, 7.086
generally, 7.080–7.081
in favour of any person, 7.085
lawfully and effectively done, 7.082–7.083
secure, to, 18.009
significance of conditions on exercise of powers, 7.060–7.067
substantive objects, 7.055–7.056
ultra vires, and, 7.045–7.047
unlimited companies, and, 31.018

Capital
maintenance
acquisition by company of own shares, 10.013–10.035
acquisition of shares in holding company, 10.036–10.040
assisting purchase of company's own shares, 10.046–10.084
capital reduction, 10.085–10.088
distributions, 10.089–10.104
dividend payments, 10.089–10.104
introduction, 10.001
miscellaneous rules, 10.105–10.112
overview of rules, 10.011–10.012
private companies, and, 10.004–10.010
rationale of rules, 10.002–10.003
redemption of shares, 10.041–10.045
preference shares, and, 8.108–8.109
public limited companies, and, 1.114
reduction
generally, 10.085
s 10(6) CA 1963, under, 10.086
s 205(3) CA 1963, under, 10.087
s 15 C(A)A 1983, under, 10.088
Societas Europaea, and, 29.152

Capital clause
alteration
generally, 3.031
increasing share capital, 3.032
reducing share capital, 3.033–3.036
generally, 3.017–3.019

Capital maintenance
acquisition by company of own shares
common law prohibition, 10.014
exceptions to statutory prohibition, 10.017–10.035
forfeiture of shares, and, 10.022
fully paid shares for no consideration, 10.018
introduction, 10.013
Pt.XI CA 1990, under, 10.023–10.035
redemption of shares, and, 10.019
reduction of capital, and, 10.020
remedial court orders, and, 10.021
statutory prohibition, 10.015–10.016
acquisition of shares in holding company, 10.036–10.040
assisting purchase of company's own shares
'any transaction', 10.051–10.052
civil consequences, 10.049–10.057
criminal consequences, 10.048
dividends, 10.078–10.083
financial assistance', 10.058–10.065
general prohibition, 10.047
introduction, 10.046
lawful liabilities, 10.078–10.083
miscellaneous, 10.084
'notice', 10.053–10.057
private companies, and, 10.047
validation procedure, 10.066–10.077
voidability, 10.049–10.050
warranties and covenants, 10.064

Capital maintenance (contd)
'whitewash' procedure, 10.066–10.077
capital reduction
generally, 10.085
s 10(6) CA 1963, under, 10.086
s 205(3) CA 1963, under, 10.087
s 15 C(A)A 1983, under, 10.088
consequences of incorporation, and, 4.092
distributions
determining availability of profits, 10.096–10.097
disguised distributions, 10.099–10.102
generally, 10.089
liability for unlawful payments, 10.103–10.104
meaning, 10.090–10.092
'member' qua member, to, 10.098
'profits available for distribution', 10.093–10.095
dividend payments, 10.089–10.104
forfeiture of unpaid or partly paid shares, 10.106–10.107
introduction, 10.001
issue of shares at a discount, 10.108–10.109
issue of shares at a premium, 10.111–10.112
liens on shares, 10.110
miscellaneous rules, 10.105–10.112
overview of rules, 10.011–10.012
private companies, and, 10.004–10.010
public limited companies
acquisition of their own shares, 29.068–29.078
buybacks, 29.068–29.073
distributions, 29.079–29.080
dividend payments, 29.079–29.080
financial assistance in purchase of their own shares, 29.077–29.078
introduction, 29.067
investment companies, 29.146
market purchase procedure, 29.068–29.069
off-market purchase procedure, 29.068–29.069
overseas purchase procedure, 29.068–29.069
purchase of their own shares, 29.068–29.078
reduction of capital, 29.081–29.082
rationale of rules, 10.002–10.003
redemption of shares
generally, 10.041–10.045
s 65 CA 1963, under, 10.019
'share capital', 10.001
subsidiaries, and, 12.042

Capital reduction
acquisition by company of own shares, and, 10.020
alteration of objects clause, 10.086
distributions, and, 10.090
generally, 10.085
memorandum of association, and, 3.033–3.036
minority shareholders' rights, 10.087
re-registration of PLC as private company, 10.088
s 10(6) CA 1963, under, 10.086
s 205(3) CA 1963, under, 10.087
s 15 C(A)A 1983, under, 10.088
schemes of arrangement, and, 21.022

Capital requirements
disregarding legal personality, and, 5.086

Care, skill and diligence
general principles, 15.075–15.077
introduction, 15.074
need, 15.081–15.084
qualifications, and, 15.078–15.080
reliance on others for advice, 15.085
tortious liability, 15.086–15.087

Caretaker directors
generally, 13.041

Carrying on activities within the State
consequences of incorporation, and, 4.092
incorporation, and, 2.030

Ceasing to carry on business
crystallisation of floating charges, and, 18.100–18.102
striking off, and, 26.009–26.012

Certificated securities
public limited companies, and
generally, 29.036
transfer, 29.062–29.066
Certificates of incorporation
constitutionality of conclusive effect, 4.018–4.019
effect, 4.004–4.005
EU nullity provisions, and
effect, 4.009–4.010
generally, 4.008
generally, 4.002–4.007
introduction, 4.001
judicial review of decision to issue, 4.015–4.017
rationale for conclusive effect, 4.006–4.007
Certificates of registration
errors in Form C1, 19.014–19.017
generally, 19.011–19.013
limits to *Amurec* decision, 19.018–19.020
Cessation of office
automatic removal, 13.076
compensation on loss of office
damages for breach of contract, 13.090–13.091
disclosure, 13.093
introduction, 13.086–13.087
pensions, 13.092
resolution, 13.093
s 186 CA 1963, and, 13.088–13.089
transfers of undertakings or property, 13.094
compulsory transfer of shares, and, 9.089
introduction, 13.072
notification to CRO, 13.083–13.085
removal
automatic, 13.075
directors, by, 13.076–13.082
resignation, 13.073
retirement by rotation, 13.074
Cesser
membership, and, 8.033
Chairman of the board
generally, 13.036
ostensible authority, and, 7.115
Change of control
compulsory transfer of shares, and, 9.089
Characterisation
culpability, 5.074
introduction, 5.068
licensing purposes, 5.075
mens rea, 5.074
residence, 5.069–5.073
Charges
draft Companies Bill, and, 1.178
external companies, and
established place of business, 34.022–34.023
generally, 34.019
introduction, 34.018
registration of charges, and, 19.001
Slavenburg file, 34.020
unregistered companies, 34.020–34.021
Charities
guarantee companies, and, 30.004
Choses in action
generally, 18.030
nature of shares, and, 8.038
Civil fraudulent trading
beneficiary of awards, 15.124–15.125
intention to defraud, 15.117–15.119
introduction, 15.116
personal responsibility imposed, 15.126–15.127
proof, 15.120–15.123
Civil litigation
appearance in court, 6.066–6.070
attachment, 6.095–6.099
authority to institute proceedings, 6.006–6.009
contractual liability, 4.043–4.048
discovery, 6.061–6.065
enforcement of judgments and orders
attachment, 6.095–6.099
beyond reasonable doubt, 6.083
breach of undertakings given in lieu of court orders, 6.087–6.094

Civil litigation (contd)
- fines, 6.104–6.105
- generally, 6.078–6.079
- introduction, 6.071
- money judgments, 6.072–6.077
- sequestration, 6.100–6.103
- standard of proof, 6.083
- wilful disobeyance by companies, 6.080–6.081
- wilful disobeyance due to employees' acts or omissions, 6.084–6.086

enforcement of money judgments
- introduction, 6.072
- judgment mortgages, 6.075
- sale of goods by sheriff, 6.073–6.074
- seizure of goods by sheriff, 6.073–6.074
- sequestration, 6.077
- winding up, 6.076

fines, 6.104–6.105
guarantee companies, and, 30.002
interrogatories, 6.061–6.065
introduction, 6.001
proper plaintiff where company is wronged, 6.002–6.005
res judicata, 6.004–6.005
rule in *Foss v Harbottle*, 6.002
sale of goods by sheriff, 6.073–6.074
Salomon's case, 6.002
security for costs
- 'action or other legal proceedings', 6.021–6.024
- amount, 6.057–6.060
- appellants, and, 6.030–6.031
- applicants, 6.032
- bona fides of defendants, 6.045–6.046
- companies, against, 6.016
- constitutionality, 6.017–6.018
- counterclaims by defendant, and, 6.030–6.031
- delay in applications, 6.055–6.056
- evidence of inability to pay costs, 6.033–6.037
- evidence of prima facie defence to substantive claim, 6.038–6.040
- generally, 6.014
- human rights, 6.017–6.018
- individuals, against, 6.016
- insolvency of plaintiff caused by defendant, 6.047–6.051
- judicial discretion, 6.041–6.056
- jurisdiction, 6.014
- lack of bona fides on part of defendant, 6.045–6.046
- non-residents, against, 6.015
- personal co-plaintiffs, 6.054
- plaintiff company with limited liability, and, 6.025–6.029
- 'special circumstances', 6.041–6.056
- statutory test, 6.019–6.060
- stay of proceedings, and, 6.014
- vindication of public interest, 6.052–6.053

seizure of goods by sheriff, 6.073–6.074
separate legal personality, and
- contracts, 4.043–4.048
- crime, 4.055–4.076
- introduction, 4.042
- torts, 4.049–4.053

sequestration
- enforcement of judgments and orders, 6.100–6.103
- enforcement of money judgments, 6.077

service of proceedings
- CRO, on, 6.011
- directors, on, 6.012
- generally, 6.010–6.013
- registered office, at, 6.013

tortious liability, 4.049–4.053
unlimited companies, and, 31.015–31.017
winding up, 6.076

Class rights
- articles of association, and, 3.064–3.066

Closely-held private companies
- generally, 1.150

Clubs
- guarantee companies, and, 30.007

Comfort letters
- disregarding legal personality, and, 5.017

Committees
directors' meetings, and, 14.122–14.123
Common seal
And see **Company seal**
generally, 4.087
Companies Act individual accounts
accounting principles, 17.028–17.029
auditors' remuneration, 17.122–17.124
balance sheet
accounting policies, 17.071
alternative valuation rules, 17.076–17.077
approval, 17.213
debentures, 17.092
debt owed by company exceeding consideration received, 17.086
development costs, 17.082
disaggregation of fixed assets, 17.073
distributable profits, 17.095
dividends, 17.096
fair valuation of assets and liabilities, 17.078–17.081
financial assets held as investments, 17.084
financial commitments, 17.097
formats 17.031–17.036
goodwill, 17.083
group undertakings, 17.072
guarantees, 17.097
historic cost valuation rules, 17.074–17.075
indebtedness, 17.087–17.089
introduction, 17.030
loans given as financial assistance, 17.085
medium-sized companies, and, 17.270–17.272
notes, 17.070–17.097
obligation to circulate, 17.243–17.245
reserves and provisions, 17.094
revaluation reserve treatment, 17.091
share capital, 17.092
signature, 17.213
small companies, and, 17.279–17.280
subsidiary undertaking shares, 17.093
taxation provision, 17.090
valuation rules, 17.037–17.058
directors' interests in shares, 17.121
directors' remuneration, 17.112
directors' transactions, 17.113–17.120
group undertakings, and, 17.127–17.129
interests in shares, 17.121
introduction, 17.25
laying before company at general meeting, 17.249
notes, 17.069–17.130
off balance sheet items, 17.126
profit and loss account, 17.059–17.068
related party transactions, 17.125
subsidiary undertakings, and, 17.130
transactions with connected persons, 17.113–17.120
'true and fair view', 17.026–17.027
Companies Acts
disregarding legal personality, and
breach of restriction or disqualification orders, 5.083–5.085
failure to keep proper records, 5.087
failure to meet capital requirements, 5.086
failure to state correctly company's name, 5.081–5.082
fraudulent trading, 5.091
introduction, 5.077–5.091
liquidation of related companies, 5.090
overview, 5.076
reckless trading, 5.091
reduction of number of members, 5.078–5.080
unreasonably inaccurate declaration of solvency, 5.088–5.089
generally, 1.163–1.164
Companies Bill (draft)
acquisitions, 1.180
annual returns, 1.177
audits, 1.177
charges, 1.178
compliance and enforcement, 1.185
corporate governance, 1.175
debentures, 1.178

Companies Bill (draft) (contd)
Director of Corporate Enforcement, 1.186
directors' duties, 1.176
divisions, 1.180
examinerships, 1.181
financial statements, 1.177
incorporation, 1.173
introduction, 1.171
investigations, 1.184
mergers, 1.180
officers' duties, 1.176
preliminary, 1.172
receivers, 1.179
registrar's functions, 1.186
registration, 1.173
regulatory bodies, 1.186
reorganisations, 1.180
restoration to register, 1.183
share capital, 1.174
shares, 1.174
striking off, 1.183
winding up, 1.182

Companies Registration Office (CRO)
compliance and enforcement, and, 28.043
generally, 1.056–1.059
service of proceedings, and, 6.011

Company
meaning, 1.156–1.162

Company books and records
realisation of assets, and, 25.013

Company Incorporation Scheme
incorporation, and, 2.019–2.021

Company Law Review Group (CLRG)
first report, 1.168–1.169
generally, 1.165–1.167
other reports, 1.170

Company name
disregarding legal personality, and, 5.081–5.082

Company seal
attestation
generally, 7.024
Reg 76 of Table A of Sch.1 to C(C)A 1908, 7.027–7.028
Reg 115 of Table A of Sch.1 to CA 1963, 7.025–7.026
general requirement, 7.022–7.023
public limited companies, and, 29.035

Company secretary
appointment, 13.120
cessation, 13.120
duties
common law, at, 15.155
generally, 15.152–15.153
introduction, 13.122–13.124
persons to whom owed, 15.154
statute, under, 15.156–15.160
functions, 13.122–13.124
general requirement, 13.119
disclosure obligations
generally, 13.125
interests in shares and debentures, 13.100–13.118
introduction, 13.095
register of secretaries, 13.096–13.099
incorporation, and, 2.038
indemnities, 15.091–15.093
insurance, 15.094
interests in shares and debentures
consequences of failure to comply, 13.114–13.115
disclosable interests, 13.108–13.113
disregarded interests, 13.112
family interests, 13.110–13.111
generally, 13.125
introduction, 13.100
investigation of suspected contravention, 13.118
notification procedure, 13.113
notification to stock exchange, 13.117
obligation during appointment, 13.103–13.107
obligation on appointment, 13.101–13.102
register, 13.116
introduction, 13.119
liability
indemnities, 15.091–15.093
insurance, 15.094
relief, 15.088–15.090

Company secretary (contd)
- public limited companies, and, 29.084
- register of interests, 13.116
- register of secretaries, 13.096–13.099
- remuneration, 13.121
- status, 13.121
- statutory duties, 15.156–15.160

Compensation on loss of office
- damages for breach of contract, 13.090–13.091
- disclosure, 13.093
- introduction, 13.086–13.087
- pensions, 13.092
- resolution, 13.093
- s 186 CA 1963, and, 13.088–13.089
- transfers of undertakings or property, 13.094

Compensatory damages
- oppression, and, 11.074–11.076

Competition law
- negative pledge clauses, and, 18.085–18.086

Competition with the company
- directors' duties, and, 15.070–15.073

Compliance and enforcement
- agencies
  - Director of Corporate Enforcement, 28.009–28.023
  - Director of Public Prosecutions, 28.024–28.026
  - introduction, 28.005
  - private individuals, 28.027–28.029
  - Registrar of Companies, 28.006–28.008
- Companies Registration Office, 28.043
- criminal sanctions
  - DCE, and, 28.020–28.022
  - introduction, 28.030–28.031
  - on-the-spot fines, 28.041–28.042
  - prosecution of companies and 'officers in default', 28.032–28.040
- Director of Corporate Enforcement
  - accountability, 28.011
  - annual reports, 28.011
  - appointment, 28.010
  - background, 28.009
  - criminal prosecution function, 28.020–28.022
  - establishment of office, 28.010
  - functions, 28.013–28.022
  - independence, 28.011
  - introduction, 28.009
  - investigation function, 28.017–28.019
  - on-the-spot fines, 29.020
  - powers, 28.013–28.022
  - staffing, 28.012
  - status, 28.010
  - supervision function, 28.015–28.016
- Director of Public Prosecutions, 28.024–28.026
- disqualification of directors
  - breach of duty, 28.175
  - breach orders, 28.205–28.206
  - declaration of liability for fraudulent trading, 28.176
  - deemed disqualification, 28.151–28.153
  - directorship of company struck-off, 28.193–28.197
  - discretionary disqualification, 28.154–28.156
  - dishonesty convictions, 28.151–28.153
  - enforcement of orders, 28.204–28.209
  - failure to keep proper books of account, 28.193
  - fraud, 28.174
  - fraud convictions, 28.151–28.153
  - fraudulent trading, 28.176
  - grounding affidavit, 28.171
  - grounds, 28.163–28.197
  - guilty of breach of duty, 28.175
  - guilty of fraud, 28.174
  - introduction, 28.148–28.150
  - locus standi of applicants, 28.157–28.161
  - nature of order, 28.198
  - notice of application, 28.162
  - onus of proof, 28.168–28.170
  - period, 28.198–28.201
  - persistently in default as to relevant requirements, 28.190–28.192

Compliance and enforcement (contd)
- persons liable, 28.154–28.156
- preliminary issues, 28.164–28.173
- purpose of disqualification, 28.166–28.167
- relief, 28.202–28.203
- restriction orders, and, 28.172–28.173
- subject of order made in a foreign state, 28.197
- unfit to manage company, 28.177–28.184
- unfitness appearing from inspector's report, 28.185–28.189

draft Companies Bill, and, 1.185
failure to file annual return, 28.046–28.048
failure to notify changes in officers, 28.046–28.048
failure to keep and maintain registers and records, 28.060
guarantee companies, and, 30.073–30.074
injunctions to compel compliance, 28.210–28.215
introduction, 28.001–28.004
non-registration offences
- failure to keep and maintain registers and records, 28.060
- indictable offences, 28.056–28.059
- introduction, 28.055
- miscellaneous offences, 28.061

private individuals with locus standi, 28.027–28.029
prosecution of companies and 'officers in default'
- effect of Fines Act 2010, 28.036–28.037
- evidence available to juries, 28.040
- generally, 28.033
- limitation period, 28.038
- specified penalties, 28.034–28.035
- venue, 28.039

public limited companies, and, 29.130
Registrar of Companies, 28.006–28.008
registration-type offences
- applicants to court, by, 28.052
- auditors, by, 28.051
- companies, by, 28.049
- examiners, by, 28.050
- failure to file annual return, 28.046–28.048
- failure to notify changes in officers, 28.046–28.048
- form of documents filed, returned or delivered, 28.053–28.054
- indictable offences, 28.045
- introduction, 28.043
- liquidators, by, 28.050
- other offences, 28.048–28.052
- purpose of registration, 28.044
- receivers, by, 28.050
- summary offences, 28.045

restriction of directors
- acting honestly and responsibly, 28.097–28.128
- applications, 28.090–28.091
- background, 28.062
- breach of orders, 28.143–28.144
- civil sanctions, 28.146–28.147
- consequences of orders, 28.068–28.071
- costs, 28.092–28.096
- criminal sanctions, 28.145
- defences, 28.097–28.132
- delay, and, 28.132–28.135
- directors, 28.076–28.080
- enforcement of orders, 28.142–28.147
- estoppel, and, 28.132–28.135
- generally, 28.062–28.063
- honestly and responsibly defence, 28.097–28.128
- insolvency requirement, 28.072–28.073
- just and equitable to make order, 28.129–28.130
- liquidators' duties, 28.082–28.087
- locus standi of applicants, 28.088–28.089
- mandatory nature of orders, 28.066–28.067
- nominee defence, 28.131–28.135
- non-resident directors, 28.081

Compliance and enforcement (contd)
persons liable to be restricted, 28.074–28.081
persons who have been directors on or within 12 months of winding up, 28.075
post-order relief, 28.136–28.141
procedure, 28.090–28.091
purpose of orders, 28.064–28.065
role of the DCE, 28.082–28.087
shadow directors, 28.076–28.080
unlimited companies, and, 31.003
Compromises
See also **Schemes of arrangement**
generally, 21.003–21.065
meaning, 21.012–21.015
overview, 21.001–21.002
Compulsory acquisition of shares
shareholders' remedies, and, 11.003
Compulsory transfer of shares
articles of association, under, 9.088–9.090
bankruptcy, on, 9.089
bona fides of transferee, 9.100–9.107
cessation of directorship, on, 9.089
change of control, on, 9.089
criminal conviction, on, 9.089
death, on, 9.089
disclosure of full particulars, 9.096
discretion of court
bona fides of transferee, 9.100–9.107
disclosure of full particulars, 9.096
introduction, 9.095
independence of transferee, 9.100–9.107
onus of proof, 9.097–9.099
independence of transferee, 9.100–9.107
introduction, 9.087
mental incapacity, on, 9.089
s 204 CA 1963, under
bona fides of transferee, 9.100–9.107
disclosure of full particulars, 9.096
discretion of court, 9.095–9.107
generally, 9.091–9.092
independence of transferee, 9.100–9.107
mandatory requirements, 9.093–9.094
onus of proof, 9.097–9.099
s 205 CA 1963, under, 9.087
valuation, and, 9.090
winding up, on, 9.089
Compulsory winding up
advertisement of petition
generally, 23.055
injunction to restrain, 23.081–23.088
annulment of members' winding up, 23.128
banks
Central Bank's rights, 23.139–23.140
generally, 23.136–23.138
liquidation committee, 23.14223.
rules applicable to liquidators, 23.141
company, by, 23.038–23.039
contributories, 23.045–23.047
conversion from members' to creditors', 23.113–23.116
conversion from voluntary winding up, 23.117–23.124
corporate instruments of fraud, 23.107–23.108
creditors, 23.040–23.044
deadlock in management, 23.098–23.101
Director of Corporate Enforcement, 23.048
failure of substratum, 23.102–23.105
failure to commence business within a year of incorporation, 23.069
financial institutions
Central Bank's rights, 23.139–23.140
generally, 23.136–23.138
liquidation committee, 23.14223.
rules applicable to liquidators, 23.141
grounds
failure to commence business within a year of incorporation, 23.069
inability of company to pay its debts, 23.071–23.090
introduction, 23.067
just and equitable, 23.091–23.111
number of members is reduced below minimum, 23.070

Compulsory winding up (contd)
oppression, 23.112
special resolution to wind up company, 23.068
hearing petition, 23.061–23.066
illegal objects, 23.106
improper presentation of petition, 23.089–23.090
inability of company to pay its debts
'21-day letter', 23.075
bona fides of the debt, 23.078
deeming companies, 23.074
discretion, 23.072–23.073
improper presentation of petition, and, 23.089–23.090
introduction, 23.071
restraint of advertisement of petition, 23.081–23.088
service of demand, 23.076–23.077
valid cross-claims, 23.079–23.080
introduction, 23.034
jurisdiction, 23.035–23.036
just and equitable
deadlock in management, 23.098–23.101
failure of substratum, 23.102–23.105
illegal objects, 23.106
instruments of fraud, 23.107–23.108
introduction, 23.091–23.092
public interest, 23.109–23.111
'quasi-partnership' cases, 23.093–23.097
locus standi to petition
company, 23.038–23.039
contributories, 23.045–23.047
creditors, 23.040–23.044
Director of Corporate Enforcement, 23.048
introduction, 23.037
members, 23.045–23.047
Registrar of Companies, 23.049
trustees of investment companies, 23.050
members, 23.045–23.047
number of members is reduced below minimum, 23.070
oppression, 23.112
orders, 23.125–23.135
petition
advertisement, 23.055
generally, 23.052–23.054
hearing, 23.061–23.066
procedure
advertisement of petition, 23.055
hearing petition, 23.061–23.066
introduction, 23.051
respondent company's options, 23.056–23.057
petition, 23.052–23.054
substitution of petitioner, 23.058–23.060
public interest, 23.109–23.111
'quasi-partnerships', 23.093–23.097
Registrar of Companies, 23.049
rescission, 23.129
respondent company's options, 23.056–23.057
special resolution to wind up company, 23.068
substitution of petitioner, 23.058–23.060
suspension of business for a year, 23.069
trustees of investment companies, 23.050
voiding dissolution following making of order, 23.130–23.135
Concealment of impropriety
disregarding legal personality, and, 5.032–5.036
Concession theory
generally, 1.060–1.062
non-state statutory corporations, 1.068
registered corporations, 1.069–1.070
royal charter corporations, 1.063–1.064
state corporations, 1.066–1.067
statutory corporations, 1.065–1.068
Conflicts of interest
account of profits, 15.067–15.068
general rule, 15.058–19.061
introduction, 15.055–15.057
profit, and, 15.058–19.061
rejected business opportunities, 15.062–15.066

Conflicts of interest (contd)
remedies for breach, 15.067–15.069
setting aside transactions, 15.069
Connected guarantees
directors' loans, and, 16.069
Connected persons
bodies corporate that are connected persons
body corporate controlled by body corporate controlled by a director, 16.019
'control', 16.011–16.013
generally, 16.010
'interested in', 16.014–16.018
subsidiary controlled by a director, 16.020
natural persons, 16.006–16.009
summary, 16.021
Connected security
directors' loans, and, 16.070
Consent to act
directors, and, 13.026–13.027
Consideration
allotment of shares, and
'cash', 8.061
discount, at a, 8.064
introduction, 8.060
non-cash consideration, 8.062–8.063
premium, at a, 8.065–8.067
share transfers, and
generally, 9.004
valuation, 9.117–9.134
Consolidated accounts
EU law, and, 1.118
Consolidation
shares, and, 8.117
Constitutional documentation
And see under individual headings
alteration
articles of association, 3.056–3.084
memorandum of association, 3.022–3.037
oppression, and, 11.085
articles of association
alteration, 3.056–3.084
amendments, 3.043–3.055
construction of, 3.089–3.091
directors, 3.050–3.052
generally, 3.038–3.091
importance, 3.002
introduction, 3.001
members' meetings, 3.047–3.049
memorandum of association, and, 3.088
model form, 3.040–3.042
nature, 3.038–3.039
shareholders' agreements, and, 3.085–3.087
shares, 3.045–3.046
voting rights, 3.053–3.055
association concept, and, 3.002
corporations aggregate, and, 3.002
guarantee companies, and
articles of association, 30.035–30.038
introduction, 30.012
memorandum of association, 30.013–30.034
introduction, 3.001–3.002
memorandum of association
additional clauses, 3.021
alteration, 3.022–3.037
articles of association, and, 3.088
association clause, 3.020
capital clause, 3.017–3.019
compulsory clauses, 3.004–3.020
construction of, 3.089–3.091
form, 3.004
generally, 3.003–3.037
importance, 3.002
introduction, 3.001
liability clause, 3.014–3.016
name clause, 3.006–3.011
non-compulsory clauses, 3.021
objects clause, 3.012–3.013
prescribed form, 3.004
reference document, 3.005
subscription clause, 3.020
Table B, 3.004
Table D, 3.004
oppression, and, 11.085
public limited companies, and
alterations, 29.032
articles of association, 29.030–29.031
introduction, 29.027

Constitutional documentation (contd)
investment companies, 29.139–29.141
memorandum of association, 29.028–29.029
section 25 contract
binding effect, 3.095–3.098
distinction from 'special contracts', 3.102–3.105
features, 3.094–3.101
generally, 3.092–3.105
introduction, 3.092–3.093
rights and obligations qua member, 3.099–3.101
shareholders' agreements
binding effect, 3.127–3.128
contrasted with articles of association, 3.107
directors fettering their fiduciary powers, 3.126
enforcement, 3.120–3.128
filing in the CRO, 3.108–3.111
generally, 3.106–3.128
injunctions, 3.123–3.125
introduction, 3.001
types, 3.117–3.119
uses, 3.112–3.116
single-member private limited companies, and, 3.002
Societas Europaea, and, 29.171–29.172
unlimited companies, and
articles of association, 31.009–31.010
introduction, 31.004
memorandum of association, 31.005–31.008
Constitutional rights and duties
separate legal personality, and, 4.068–4.075
Construction
articles of association, and, 3.089–3.091
memorandum of association, and, 3.089–3.091
Constructive notice
registration of charges, and, 19.004–19.005
Constructive trusts
recovery of money given by company ultra vires, and, 7.091–7.092
Contingent purchase contracts
acquisition by company of own shares, and, 10.031
Contractual liability
separate legal personality, and, 4.043–4.048
Contractual liens
generally, 19.031–19.032
Contractual rights and obligations
nature of shares, and, 8.039
Contracts
And see **Corporate contracts**
disregarding legal personality, and
comfort letters, 5.017
guarantees, 5.015
indemnities, 5.016
introduction, 5.012–5.014
personal guarantees, 5.015
receivers, and
employment, of, 20.033–20.034
generally, 20.029
Contracts under seal
attestation of the common seal
generally, 7.024
Reg 76 of Table A of Sch.1 to C(C)A 1908, 7.027–7.028
Reg 115 of Table A of Sch.1 to CA 1963, 7.025–7.026
delivery by company, 7.029
generally, 7.014–7.021
requirement to have a seal, 7.022–7.023
Controllers of the company
disregarding legal personality, and, 5.009
Conversion by re-registration
introduction, 33.001
limited company to unlimited company, 33.009–33.013
multi-member private company to single-member private company, 33.016
PLC to private limited company
generally, 33.014
reduction of capital, and, 10.088

Conversion by re-registration (contd)
PLC to Societas Europaea, 29.167–29.169
private limited company to PLC, 33.015
single-member private company to multi-member private company, 33.017
Societas Europaea to PLC, 29.192
unlimited company to private limited company, 33.002–33.007
unlimited company to PLC, 33.008
Conversion of shares
consolidation, 8.117
generally, 8.116
redeemable shares, into, 8.120
stock, into, 8.118
subdivision, 8.119
Conversion to companies
building societies, and, 1.046
Convictions
compulsory transfer of shares, and, 9.089
Corporate borrowing
And see **Borrowing**
all sums due debentures, 18.038–18.039
authority, 18.010–18.013
capacity, 18.004–18.009
debentures, 18.014–18.110
equitable charges, 18.028–18.029
facility letters, 18.016–18.017
fixed charges
book debts, on, 18.040–18.064
deposit accounts, on, 18.065–18.067
floating charges
crystallisation, 18.093–18.109
de-crystallisation, 18.110
events which affect assets, 18.087–18.092
generally, 18.068–18.078
negative pledge clauses, 18.079–18.086
introduction, 18.001–18.003
liens, 18.027
mortgages, 18.030–18.037
negative pledge clauses, 18.079–18.086
pledges, 18.026
public limited companies, and, 29.121–29.122
purpose, 18.001–18.003
receivers
And see **Receivers**
generally, 20.001–20.094
registration of charges
And see **Registration of charges**
generally, 19.001–19.107
security, 18.024–18.037
unlimited companies, and, 31.003
Corporate civil litigation
appearance in court, 6.066–6.070
attachment, 6.095–6.099
authority to institute proceedings, 6.006–6.009
contractual liability, 4.043–4.048
discovery, 6.061–6.065
enforcement of judgments and orders
attachment, 6.095–6.099
beyond reasonable doubt, 6.083
breach of undertakings given in lieu of court orders, 6.087–6.094
fines, 6.104–6.105
generally, 6.078–6.079
introduction, 6.071
money judgments, 6.072–6.077
sequestration, 6.100–6.103
standard of proof, 6.083
wilful disobeyance by companies, 6.080–6.081
wilful disobeyance due to employees' acts or omissions, 6.084–6.086
enforcement of money judgments
introduction, 6.072
judgment mortgages, 6.075
sale of goods by sheriff, 6.073–6.074
seizure of goods by sheriff, 6.073–6.074
sequestration, 6.077
winding up, 6.076
fines, 6.104–6.105
interrogatories, 6.061–6.065
introduction, 6.001
proper plaintiff where company is wronged, 6.002–6.005
res judicata, 6.004–6.005

Corporate civil litigation (contd)
rule in *Foss v Harbottle*, 6.002
sale of goods by sheriff, 6.073–6.074
Salomon's case, 6.002
security for costs
'action or other legal proceedings', 6.021–6.024
amount, 6.057–6.060
appellants, and, 6.030–6.031
applicants, 6.032
bona fides of defendants, 6.045–6.046
companies, against, 6.016
constitutionality, 6.017–6.018
counterclaims by defendant, and, 6.030–6.031
delay in applications, 6.055–6.056
evidence of inability to pay costs, 6.033–6.037
evidence of prima facie defence to substantive claim, 6.038–6.040
generally, 6.014
human rights, 6.017–6.018
individuals, against, 6.016
insolvency of plaintiff caused by defendant, 6.047–6.051
judicial discretion, 6.041–6.056
jurisdiction, 6.014
lack of bona fides on part of defendant, 6.045–6.046
non-residents, against, 6.015
personal co-plaintiffs, 6.054
plaintiff company with limited liability, and, 6.025–6.029
'special circumstances', 6.041–6.056
statutory test, 6.019–6.060
stay of proceedings, and, 6.014
vindication of public interest, 6.052–6.053
seizure of goods by sheriff, 6.073–6.074
separate legal personality, and
contracts, 4.043–4.048
crime, 4.055–4.076
introduction, 4.042
torts, 4.049–4.053
sequestration
enforcement of judgments and orders, 6.100–6.103
enforcement of money judgments, 6.077
service of proceedings
CRO, on, 6.011
directors, on, 6.012
generally, 6.010–6.013
registered office, at, 6.013
tortious liability, 4.049–4.053
unlimited companies, and, 31.015–31.017
winding up, 6.076
Corporate capacity
ancillary powers
express, 7.057–7.067
generally, 7.055–7.056
implied powers, 7.068–7.069
borrow, to, 18.005–18.006
classification
ancillary powers, 7.055–7.059
existence of commercial benefit, 7.057–7.059
introduction, 7.054
substantive objects, 7.055–7.056
conditions on exercise of powers, 7.060–7.067
enforcement of ultra vires contracts, 7.088
existence of commercial benefit, 7.057–7.059
express ancillary powers
conditions on exercise, 7.060–7.067
generally, 7.057–7.059
generally, 7.048
gratuitous dispositions of corporate property
express object or power, 7.073–7.075
generally, 7.070
implicit power where reasonably incidental, 7.071–7.072
not in furtherance of company's interests, 7.076–7.079
guarantee, to, 18.007–18.008
implied ancillary powers, 7.068–7.069
judicial construction of objects clause, 7.049–7.053

Corporate capacity (contd)
objects clause, and
generally, 3.012
judicial construction, 7.049–7.053
recovery of money given by company ultra vires
action in rem, 7.091–7.092
Belmont principle, 7.091–7.092
constructive trusts, 7.091–7.092
estoppel, 7.094–7.095
generally, 7.089
quasi-contract, 7.093
unenforceable, 7.090
reform of ultra vires doctrine, 7.096–7.098
reg 6 EC(C)R 1973, 7.087
s 8 CA 1963
actually aware, 7.086
generally, 7.080–7.081
in favour of any person, 7.085
lawfully and effectively done, 7.082–7.083
secure, to, 18.009
significance of conditions on exercise of powers, 7.060–7.067
substantive objects, 7.055–7.056
ultra vires, and, 7.045–7.047
Corporate contracts
actual authority, 7.100
attestation of the common seal
generally, 7.024
Reg 76 of Table A of Sch.1 to C(C)A 1908, 7.027–7.028
Reg 115 of Table A of Sch.1 to CA 1963, 7.025–7.026
authority of agents
actual authority, 7.100
constructive notice of public documents, 7.119–7.120
generally, 7.099
implied authority, 7.100
indoor management rule, 7.121–7.122
ostensible authority, 7.101–7.118
reg 6 EC(C)R 1973, 7.129–7.135
reg 10 EC(C)R 1973, 7.128
rule in *Turquand's* case, 7.123–7.127
capacity
classification, 7.054–7.059
enforcement of ultra vires contracts, 7.088
existence of commercial benefit, 7.057–7.059
express ancillary powers, 7.057–7.059
generally, 7.048
gratuitous dispositions of property, 7.070–7.079
implied ancillary powers, 7.068–7.069
judicial construction of objects clause, 7.049–7.053
recovery of money given by company ultra vires, 7.089–7.095
reform of ultra vires doctrine, 7.096–7.098
reg 6 EC(C)R 1973, 7.087
s 8 CA 1963, 7.080–7.086
significance of conditions on exercise of powers, 7.060–7.067
substantive objects, 7.055–7.056
ultra vires, and, 7,.045–7.047
comfort letters, 5.017
company seal
attestation, 7.024–7.028
general requirement, 7.022–7.023
contracts under seal
attestation of the common seal, 7.024–7.028
delivery by company, 7.029
execution by power of attorney, 7.030–7.034
generally, 7.014–7.021
requirement to have a seal, 7.022–7.023
deeds
attestation of the common seal, 7.024–7.028
delivery by company, 7.029
generally, 7.014–7.021
requirement to have a seal, 7.022–7.023
disregarding legal personality, and
comfort letters, 5.017

Corporate contracts (contd)
guarantees, 5.015
indemnities, 5.016
introduction, 5.012–5.014
personal guarantees, 5.015
execution by power of attorney, 7.030–7.034
form and formalities
contracts under seal, 7.014–7.028
deeds, 7.014–7.029
execution by power of attorney, 7.030–7.034
introduction, 7.003–7.004
oral contracts, 7.005–7.006
written contracts, 7.007–7.013
gratuitous dispositions of corporate property
express object or power, 7.073–7.075
generally, 7.070
implicit power where reasonably incidental, 7.071–7.072
not in furtherance of company's interests, 7.076–7.079
guarantee companies, and, 30.002
guarantees, 5.015
implied authority, 7.100
indemnities, 5.016
introduction, 7.001–7.002
objects clause
Bell Houses clause, 7.053
generally, 7.045–7.046
independent objects clause, 7.052
judicial construction, 7.049–7.053
main objects rule, 7.051
oral contracts, 7.005–7.006
ostensible authority
actual authority of representor, 7.107
board of directors, 7.112–7.113
chairman of the board, 7.115
company secretary, 7.117
contract within permitted capacity and authority of company, 7.109–7.110
corporate representations, 7.104–7.106
directors, 7.116
generally, 7.101–7.103
managing director, 7.114
particular corporate organs, of, 7.111–7.118
reliance on representation, 7.108
sole member of single-member private company, 7.118
personal guarantees, 5.015
pre-incorporation contracts
generally, 7.035–7.036
liability of agents, 7.041–7.042
s 37 CA 1963, 7.037–7.044
public limited companies, and
introduction, 29.034
investment companies, 29.143
securities seal, 29.035
uncertificated securities, 29.036
validity of trading or borrowing carried out without an authorisation, 29.037
recovery of money given by company ultra vires
action in rem, 7.091–7.092
Belmont principle, 7.091–7.092
constructive trusts, 7.091–7.092
estoppel, 7.094–7.095
generally, 7.089
quasi-contract, 7.093
unenforceable, 7.090
rule in *Turquand's* case
generally, 7.123
irregularity is of public record, 7.124
outsider must act in good faith, 7.125–7.126
s 8 CA 1963
actually aware, 7.086
generally, 7.080–7.081
in favour of any person, 7.085
lawfully and effectively done, 7.082–7.083
ultra vires
capacity, 7.048–7.087
enforcement of contracts, 7.088
objects clause, and, 7.045–7.046
recovery of money given by company, 7.089–7.095
reform of doctrine, 7.096–7.098
restraint of activities, 7.047

Corporate contracts (contd)
unlimited companies, and, 31.018
written contracts, 7.007–7.013
Corporate governance
building societies, and, 1.043
directors
alternate directors, 13.042
appointment, 13.025–13.032
assignee directors, 13.043
associate directors, 13.044
automatic removal, 13.076
caretaker directors, 13.041
cessation of role, 13.072–13.094
Chairmen, 13.036
compensation on loss of office, 13.086–13.094
consent to act, 13.026–13.027
de facto directors, 13.045–13.054
debarred persons, 13.018
delegation of managerial power, 13.126–13.143
disclosure obligations, 13.095–13.118
disqualification, 13.021
disqualified persons, 13.017
duties, 15.001–15.151
EEA-resident, 13.012–13.015
executive directors, 13.037
first appointment, 13.028
generally, 13.009–13.010
interests in shares and debentures, 13.100–13.118
managing directors, 13.034–13.035
minimum number, 13.011
natural persons, 13.016
nominee directors, 13.040
non-executive directors, 13.038–13.039
number of directorships, 13.022–13.024
persons debarred, 13.018
persons restricted, 13.020
qualification shareholding, 13.019
qualifications, 13.017
register of directors, 13.096–13.099
register of interests, 13.116
regulation of transactions, 16.001–16.135
removal, 13.075–13.082
remuneration, 13.070–13.071
resignation, 13.073
restriction orders, and, 13.020
retirement by rotation, 13.074
shadow directors, 13.055–13.069
subsequent appointment, 13.029–13.032
types, 13.033–13.069
directors' meetings
adjournment, 14.117
business to be conducted, 14.112
committees, 14.122–14.123
conduct, 14.109–14.111
convening, 14.105–14.108
introduction, 14.102–14.103
minutes, 14.118–14.121
notice, 14.105–14.108
quorum, 14.113–14.115
regulation, 14.104
resolutions, 14.124–14.128
voting, 14.124–14.128
draft Companies Bill, and, 1.175
guarantee companies, and
directors, 30.045–30.048
meetings, 30.049–30.060
introduction, 13.001–13.002
meetings
directors' meetings, 14.102–14.128
introduction, 14.001–14.003
members' meetings, 14.004–14.101
members' meetings
adjournment, 14.058–14.060
annual general meetings, 14.006–14.014
business to be conducted, 14.050–14.054
extraordinary general meetings, 14.015–14.032
introduction, 14.004–14.005
minutes, 14.077–14.080
notice, 14.033–14.049
postponement, 14.058–14.060
public companies, and, 14.002
quorum, 14.055–14.057

Corporate governance (contd)
resolutions, 14.081–14.101
voting, 14.061–14.076
officers
consequences, 13.006 13.008
disqualification, 13.007
generally, 13.003–13.005
public limited companies, and
corporate governance
audit committees, 29.088
Board committees, 29.086
codes, 29.089–29.093
company secretary, 29.084
compliance statements, 29.088
differences from private company regime, 29.084
directors, 29.083–29.085
generally, 29.083
introduction, 29.083
Irish Annex, 29.092
meetings, 29.094–29.0
regulation, 29.087
restrictions on directors, 29.084
UK Code, 29.089–29.091
secretaries
appointment, 13.120
cessation, 13.120
disclosure obligations, 13.095–13.118
duties, 15.152–15.160
functions, 13.122–13.124
general requirement, 13.119
interests in shares and debentures, 13.100–13.118
introduction, 13.119
register of interests, 13.116
register of secretary, 13.096–13.099
remuneration, 13.121
status, 13.121
Societas Europaea, and
employee involvement, 29.178–29.181
general structure, 29.174–29.177
meetings, 29.182–29.185
overview, 29.152
unlimited companies, and, 31.003
Corporate litigation
See also **Corporate civil litigation**
contractual liability, 4.043–4.048
criminal liability
attribution principles, 4.063–4.067
constitutional rights and duties, 4.068 4.075
corporations as prosecutors, 4.056
introduction, 4.055
justification, 4.057–4.061
legal rights and duties, 4.076
practical limitations, 4.062
separate legal personality, and
contracts, 4.043–4.048
crime, 4.055–4.076
introduction, 4.042
torts, 4.049–4.053
tortious liability, 4.049–4.053
Corporate manslaughter
generally, 4.059–4.060
Corporate personality
And see **Separate legal personality**
generally, 1.057
Corporate property
compensation, 4.040
generally, 4.032–4.037
insurable interests, 4.039
statutory tenancies, 4.041
transfer, 4.038
generally, 4.032–4.041
Corporations
generally, 1.057
Corporations aggregate
constitution of private companies, and, 3.002
generally, 1.057
Corporations sole
generally, 1.057
Costs
oppression, and, 11.087
Counterclaims
security for costs, and, 6.030–6.031
Court orders
disregarding legal personality, and, 5.065–5.067
receivers, and
appointment, 20.020
status, 20.036

Covenants
assisting purchase of company's own shares, and, 10.064
Credit transactions
directors' loans, and, 16.067–16.068
Credit unions
generally, 1.048–1.049
Creditors
directors' duties, and, 15.010–15.017
Creditors' meetings
creditors' voluntary winding up, and, 23.023–23.030
examinership, and, 22.130–22.132
reconstructions, and, 21.066
schemes of arrangement, and
classes of members, 21.035–21.038
constituting proper classes, 21.029–21.034
introduction, 21.024–21.025
provision of information, 21.039–21.042
repeat applications, 21.048
responsibility for constituting proper classes, 21.026–21.028
shareholders' rights and interests, 21.035–21.038
voting, 21.043–21.047
Creditors' voluntary winding up
committee of inspection, 23.031–23.032
creditors' meeting, 23.023–23.030
introduction, 23.017
liquidators
appointment, 24.010–24.012
generally, 24.003
powers, 24.043–24.045
members' general meeting, 23.020–23.022
statement of position of company's affairs, 23.018–23.019
termination, 23.033
CREST
public limited companies, and, 29.062–29.066
Criminal convictions
compulsory transfer of shares, and, 9.089
Criminal fraudulent trading
generally, 15.128–15.130
Criminal liability
attribution principles, 4.063–4.067
constitutional rights and duties, 4.068–4.075
corporations as prosecutors, 4.056
introduction, 4.055
justification, 4.057–4.061
legal rights and duties, 4.076
practical limitations, 4.062
Criminal offences
directors' loans, and, 16.118–16.120
Criminal sanctions
DCE, and, 28.020–28.022
disqualification of directors, and, 28.205
insider dealing, and, 32.115–32.117
common law, at, 32.098
competent authority, 32.066
criminal sanctions, 32.113
introduction, 28.030–28.031
market abuse, and, 32.115–32.117
on-the-spot fines, 28.041–28.042
prosecution of companies and 'officers in default', 28.032–28.040
restriction orders, and, 28.145
CRODisk Scheme
incorporation, and, 2.022
Cross-border mergers
EU law, and, 1.123
Crystallisation of floating charges
appointment of receiver, 18.098
automatic clauses, 18.103–18.109
causes, 18.097–18.109
ceasing to carry on business, 18.100–18.102
express clauses, 18.103–18.109
introduction, 18.093–18.096
winding up of charger company, 18.099
Culpability
disregarding legal personality, and, 5.074
Current assets
valuation, and
alternative accounting rules, 17.055–17.057

Current assets (contd)
fair value accounting, 17.058
historical cost rules, 17.050–17.054
Damages for breach of contract
compensation on loss of office, and, 13.090–13.091
De facto directors
English case law, 13.047–13.048
generally, 13.045–13.046
Irish case law, 13.049–13.054
De minimis exception
directors' loans, and, 16.075–16.079
Death
compulsory transfer of shares, and, 9.089
share transfers, and, 9.026–9.030
Debentures
all sums due, 18.038–18.039
balance sheet, and, 17.092
crystallisation of floating charges
appointment of receiver, 18.098
automatic clauses, 18.103–18.109
causes, 18.097–18.109
ceasing to carry on business, 18.100–18.102
express clauses, 18.103–18.109
introduction, 18.093–18.096
winding up of charger company, 18.099
debt securities, as, 18.021
definition, 18.018–18.020
draft Companies Bill, and, 1.178
facility letters
generally, 18.016–18.017
introduction, 18.014
fixed charges
book debts, on, 18.040–18.064
deposit accounts, on, 18.065–18.067
identifiability, 18.035
fixed charges on book debts
curtailment of priority, 18.057–18.064
exercise of control by chargee as of legal right, 18.050
generally, 18.040–18.041
hybrid charges, 18.051–18.056
restrictions on chargor's use of debts, 18.044–18.049
validity, 18.042–18.043
floating charges
ability of charger to deal with property, 18.072–18.073
characteristics, 18.068–18.071
Coslett (Contractors) Ltd case, 18.074–18.077
creation, 18.078
crystallisation, 18.093–18.109
de-crystallisation, 18.110
events which affect assets, 18.087–18.092
execution of judgment, 18.092
generally, 18.068–18.078
liens, 18.091
nature, 18.069–18.071
negative pledge clauses, 18.079–18.086
set-off, 18.090
subsequent mortgages and charges, 18.089
group accounts, and
generally, 17.207
held by subsidiaries, 17.211
individual accounts, and
generally 17.136
held by subsidiaries, 17.141
introduction, 18.014–18.015
investigations as to ownership, and
generally, 27.083–27.084
power of DCE to impose restrictions, 27.085–27.088
mechanics, 18.014
receivers
And see **Receivers**
appointment, 20.005–20.034
considerations on appointment, 20.005–20.010
definition, 20.002–20.004
directions, 20.085–20.086
duties, 20.045–20.073
effect of appointment, 20.029–20.034
introduction, 20.001
liabilities, 20.074–20.078
multiple appointments, 20.087

Debentures (contd)
powers, 20.079–20.084
qualifications, 20.011
removal, 20.090–20.094
remuneration, 20.044
resignation, 20.088–20.089
status, 20.035–20.043
registration
charger company's obligations, 19.107
conclusiveness of certificate, 19.011–19.020
consequences of non-registration, 19.006–19.010
disguised registrable charges, 19.071–19.084
introduction, 19.001
judgment mortgages, 19.085
late applications, 19.090–19.100
non-registrable security interests, 19.021–19.041
procedure, 19.101–19.107
property outside of the State, and, 19.086–19.089
register of charges, 19.002–19.005
registrable charges, 19.042–19.070
registrable particulars, 19.102–19.104
retention of title clauses, 19.071–19.084
satisfaction of charges, 19.105–19.106
security
equitable charges, 18.028–18.029
introduction, 18.024–18.025
liens, 18.027
mortgages, 18.030–18.037
pledges, 18.026
transfer, 18.022–18.023

Declaration of solvency
disregarding legal personality, and, 5.088–5.089
members' voluntary winding up, and, 23.004–23.006

De-crystallisation of floating charges
examinership, and, 22.077–22.078

Deed of settlement companies
generally, 1.077

Deeds
attestation of the common seal
generally, 7.024
Reg 76 of Table A of Sch.1 to C(C)A 1908, 7.027–7.028
Reg 115 of Table A of Sch.1 to CA 1963, 7.025–7.026
delivery by company, 7.029
generally, 7.014–7.021
requirement to have a seal, 7.022–7.023

Deferred shares
See also **Shares**
generally, 8.112

Delay
oppression, and, 11.053–11.056
security for costs, and, 6.055–6.056

Delegation of managerial power
directors act in breach of duties, 13.142–13.143
directors' duties, and, 15.051–15.053
directors exceed delegated authority, 13.141
express reservations to members
introduction, 13.130
subject to directions by members, 13.133–13.138
subject to other articles, 13.132
subject to the Companies Acts, 13.131
generally, 13.127–13.129
members' powers
directors act in breach of duties, 13.142–13.143
directors exceed delegated authority, 13.141
no directors capable of acting, 13.140
no directors capable of acting, 13.140
residual authority, 13.126
subject to directions by members, 13.133–13.138
subject to other articles, 13.132
subject to the Companies Acts, 13.131

Delivery of documents
branches, and
EU companies, 34.032
non-EU companies, 34.033

Delivery of particulars to Revenue Commissioners
consequences of incorporation, and, 4.092
incorporation, and, 2.034
Deposit accounts
fixed charges, and, 18.065–18.067
Depreciation
profit and loss account, and, 17.102–17.103
Derivative actions
generally, 11.110
indemnity for costs, 11.118–11.120
nature, 11.111–11.112
preliminary considerations, 11.108–11.109
test, 11.113–11.117
Designated activity companies (DACs)
generally, 1.171
Development costs
balance sheet, and, 17.082
Diminution in value of fixed assets
profit and loss account, and, 17.102
Directions
receivers, and, 20.085–20.086
Directions of disqualified person
disregarding legal personality, and, 5.085
Director of Corporate Enforcement (DCE)
accountability, 28.011
annual reports, 28.011
appointment, 28.010
background, 28.009
compulsory winding up, and, 23.048
creation of office, 25.002
criminal prosecution function, 28.020–28.022
draft Companies Bill, and, 1.186
establishment of office, 28.010
functions, 28.013–28.022
independence, 28.011
inquiries, 27.083–27.084
inspection as to ownership or control of company or its shares, and
appointment of inspectors, 27.017–27.019
conduct, 27.028–27.033
costs, 27.064
generally, 27.010
powers of inspectors, 27.034–27.048
scope, 27.024–27.027
introduction, 28.009
investigation function, 28.017–28.019
liquidators, and
duty to report, 24.025–24.026
supervision, 24.070–24.071
on-the-spot fines, 29.020
powers, 28.013–28.022
receivers' duties, and, 20.071–20.073
staffing, 28.012
status, 28.010
supervision function, 28.015–28.016
Director of Public Prosecutions
generally, 28.024–28.026
Directors
allotment of shares, and, 8.051–8.053
alternate directors, 13.042
appointment
first director, 13.028
generally, 13.025–13.027
subsequent directors, 13.029–13.032
articles of association, and, 3.050–3.052
assignee directors, 13.043
associate directors, 13.044
automatic removal, 13.076
building societies, and, 1.043
caretaker directors, 13.041
cessation of office
automatic removal, 13.076
compensation on loss of office, 13.086–13.094
compulsory transfer of shares, 9.089
introduction, 13.072
notification to CRO, 13.083–13.085
removal, 13.075–13.082
resignation, 13.073
retirement by rotation, 13.074
Chairmen, 13.036
compensation on loss of office
damages for breach of contract, 13.090–13.091
disclosure, 13.093
introduction, 13.086–13.087

Directors (contd)
pensions, 13.092
resolution, 13.093
s 186 CA 1963, and, 13.088–13.089
transfers of undertakings or property, 13.094
compulsory transfer of shares, 9.089
consent to act, 13.026–13.027
de facto directors
English case law, 13.047–13.048
generally, 13.045–13.046
Irish case law, 13.049–13.054
debarred persons, 13.018
delegation of managerial power, and
directors act in breach of duties, 13.142–13.143
directors exceed delegated authority, 13.141
express reservations to members, 13.130–13.138
generally, 13.127–13.129
members' powers, 13.139–13.143
no directors capable of acting, 13.140
residual authority, 13.126
subject to directions by members, 13.133–13.138
subject to other articles, 13.132
subject to the Companies Acts, 13.131
directors' report
additional obligations, 17.216–17.218
approval, 17.221
Companies Act group accounts, 17.216
criminal offences, 17.222–17.224
general obligation, 17.214–17.215
IFRS group accounts, 17.217
IFRS individual accounts, 17.217
laying before company at general meeting, 17.249
listed companies, 17.218–17.220
medium-sized companies, and, 17.275
obligation to circulate, 17.243–17.245
signature, 17.221
small companies, and, 17.281
directors' transactions
See also **Directors' transactions**
bodies corporate that are connected persons, 16.010
connected persons, 16.006–16.020
directors, 16.004–16.005
disclosure of interests in contracts, 16.121–16.135
holding company directors, 16.004–16.005
introduction, 16.001–16.002
loans etc to directors, 16.055–16.120
natural persons that are connected persons, 16.006–16.009
regulated persons, 16.003–16.021
shadow directors, 16.021
substantial property transactions, 16.022–16.054
disclosure obligations
interests in shares and debentures, 13.100–13.118
introduction, 13.095
register of directors, 13.096–13.099
disqualification orders
breach, 28.205–28.206
breach of duty, 28.175
declaration of liability for fraudulent trading, 28.176
deemed disqualification, 28.151–28.153
directorship of company struck-off, 28.193–28.197
discretionary disqualification, 28.154–28.156
dishonesty convictions, 28.151–28.153
enforcement, 28.204–28.209
failure to keep proper books of account, 28.193
fraud, 28.174
fraud convictions, 28.151–28.153
fraudulent trading, 28.176
generally, 28.148–28.150
grounding affidavit, 28.171
grounds, 28.163–28.197
guilty of breach of duty, 28.175
guilty of fraud, 28.174

Directors (contd)
introduction, 13.021
locus standi of applicants, 28.157–28.161
nature, 28.198
notice of application, 28.162
onus of proof, 28.168–28.170
period, 28.198–28.201
persistently in default as to relevant requirements, 28.190–28.192
persons liable, 28.154–28.156
preliminary issues, 28.164–28.173
purpose of disqualification, 28.166–28.167
relief, 28.202–28.203
restriction orders, and, 28.172–28.173
subject of order made in a foreign state, 28.197
unfit to manage company, 28.177–28.184
unfitness appearing from inspector's report, 28.185–28.189
disqualified persons, 13.017
duties
See also **Directors' duties**
care, skill and diligence, 15.074–15.087
common law, at, 15.024–15.
competition with the company, 15.070–15.073
conflicts of interest, 15.055–15.069
creditors, to, 15.010–15.017
employees, to, 15.018
exercise, 15.026–15.054
expansion of, 15.008–15.009
fiduciary, 15.055–15.073
general rule, 15.004–15.007
indemnities, 15.091–15.093
insolvency, and, 15.095–15.151
introduction, 15.001–15.003
judicial relief, 15.088–15.090
liability insurance, 15.094
members, to, 15.018
qualifications, and, 15.078–15.080
shareholders, to, 15.019–15.023
EEA-resident, 13.012–13.015
examinership, and, 22.089–22.092
executive directors, 13.037
fettering their fiduciary powers
shareholders' agreements, and, 3.126
first appointment, 13.028
generally, 13.009–13.010
holding-subsidiary relationship, and, 12.052
incorporation, and, 2.038
interests in shares and debentures
consequences of failure to comply, 13.114–13.115
disclosable interests, 13.108–13.113
disregarded interests, 13.112
family interests, 13.110–13.111
introduction, 13.100
investigation of suspected contravention, 13.118
notification procedure, 13.113
notification to stock exchange, 13.117
obligation during appointment, 13.103–13.107
obligation on appointment, 13.101–13.102
register, 13.116
managing directors, 13.034–13.035
meetings
See also **Directors' meetings**
adjournment, 14.117
business to be conducted, 14.112
committees, 14.122–14.123
conduct, 14.109–14.111
convening, 14.105–14.108
introduction, 14.102–14.103
minutes, 14.118–14.121
notice, 14.105–14.108
quorum, 14.113–14.115
regulation, 14.104
resolutions, 14.124–14.128
voting, 14.124–14.128
minimum number, 13.011
natural persons, 13.016
nominee directors, 13.040
non-executive directors, 13.038–13.039
number of directorships, 13.022–13.024
ostensible authority, and 7.116
persons debarred, 13.018

Directors (contd)
persons restricted, 13.020
'professional advice', and, 13.057
public limited companies, and, 29.083–29.085
qualification shareholding, 13.019
qualifications, 13.017
receivers, and, 20.030–20.032
refusal of registration of share transfers
bona fides of directors, 9.052–9.057
challenging, 9.066–9.068
consequences, 9.064–9.065
introduction, 9.042
lapsing of powers of directors, 9.058–9.061
model reg 3 restriction, 9.043–9.047
overview, 9.22
procedure for challenging, 9.066–9.068
quality of transferee, 9.050–9.051
s 205 CA 1963 relief, 9.062–9.063
status of transferee, 9.048–9.049
register of directors, 13.096–13.099
register of interests, 13.116
regulation of transactions
See also **Directors' transactions**
bodies corporate that are connected persons, 16.010
connected persons, 16.006–16.020
directors, 16.004–16.005
disclosure of interests in contracts, 16.121–16.135
holding company directors, 16.004–16.005
introduction, 16.001–16.002
loans etc to directors, 16.055–16.120
natural persons that are connected persons, 16.006–16.009
regulated persons, 16.003–16.021
shadow directors, 16.021
substantial property transactions, 16.022–16.054
removal
automatic, 13.075
directors, by, 13.076–13.082
remuneration, 13.070–13.071
resignation, 13.073
restriction orders, and
acting honestly and responsibly, 28.097–28.128
applications, 28.090–28.091
background, 28.062
breach of orders, 28.143–28.144
civil sanctions, 28.146–28.147
consequences of orders, 28.068–28.071
costs, 28.092–28.096
criminal sanctions, 28.145
defences, 28.097–28.132
delay, and, 28.132–28.135
directors, 28.076–28.080
enforcement of orders, 28.142–28.147
estoppel, and, 28.132–28.135
generally, 28.062–28.063
honestly and responsibly defence, 28.097–28.128
insolvency requirement, 28.072–28.073
introduction, 13.020
just and equitable to make order, 28.129–28.130
liquidators' duties, 28.082–28.087
locus standi of applicants, 28.088–28.089
mandatory nature of orders, 28.066–28.067
nominee defence, 28.131–28.135
non-resident directors, 28.081
persons liable to be restricted, 28.074–28.081
persons who have been directors on or within 12 months of winding up, 28.075
post-order relief, 28.136–28.141
procedure, 28.090–28.091
purpose of orders, 28.064–28.065
role of the DCE, 28.082–28.087
shadow directors, 28.076–28.080
retirement by rotation, 13.074
service of proceedings, and, 6.012

Directors (contd)
shadow directors
'acted in accordance with such directions or instructions', 13.063–13.064
bodies corporate, and, 13.066–13.069
'directed or instructed', 13.060–13.062
generally, 13.0565–13.056
'professional advice' exception, 13.057
proofs required, 13.058–13.059
restriction orders, 28.076–28.080
'were accustomed so to act', 13.065
shareholders' agreements, and, 3.126
subsequent appointment, 13.029–13.032
transactions
See also **Directors' transactions**
bodies corporate that are connected persons, 16.010
connected persons, 16.006–16.020
directors, 16.004–16.005
disclosure of interests in contracts, 16.121–16.135
holding company directors, 16.004–16.005
introduction, 16.001–16.002
loans etc to directors, 16.055–16.120
natural persons that are connected persons, 16.006–16.009
regulated persons, 16.003–16.021
shadow directors, 16.021
substantial property transactions, 16.022–16.054
types, 13.033–13.069
unlimited companies, and, 31.003

Directors' duties
abuse, and, 15.054
acting in interests of company, 15.027–15.028
care, skill and diligence
general principles, 15.075–15.077
introduction, 15.074
need, 15.081–15.084
qualifications, and, 15.078–15.080
reliance on others for advice, 15.085
tortious liability, 15.086–15.087
civil fraudulent trading, and
beneficiary of awards, 15.124–15.125
intention to defraud, 15.117–15.119
introduction, 15.116
personal responsibility imposed, 15.126–15.127
proof, 15.120–15.123
common law, at
nature, 15.024–15.025
sources, 15.024
company, to, 15.005–15.007
competition with the company, 15.070–15.073
conflicts of interest
account of profits, 15.067–15.068
general rule, 15.058–19.061
introduction, 15.055–15.057
profit, and, 15.058–19.061
rejected business opportunities, 15.062–15.066
remedies for breach, 15.067–15.069
setting aside transactions, 15.069
creditors, to, 15.010–15.017
criminal fraudulent trading, and, 15.128–15.130
delegation, 15.051–15.053
discretion, and, 15.035–15.041
draft Companies Bill, and, 1.176
employees, to, 15.018
examinership, and, 22.089–22.092
executive directors, and, 15.042–15.044
exercise
acting in interests of company, 15.027–15.028
consequences of abuse, 15.054
delegation, 15.051–15.053
executive directors, by, 15.042–15.044
family companies, in, 15.049–15.050
fettering discretion, and, 15.035–15.041
good faith, 15.029–15.034
independent discretion, 15.035–15.041
introduction, 15.026
nominee directors, by, 15.045–15.048

Directors' duties (contd)
non-executive directors, by, 15.042–15.044
'token' directors, by, 15.049–15.050
expansion of, 15.008–15.009
failure to keep proper books of account, and
discretion of court, 15.134–15.135
generally, 15.131
personal responsibility, 15.132–15.133
proofs, 15.136–15.140
family companies, in, 15.049–15.050
fettering discretion, and, 15.035–15.041
fiduciary duties
competition with the company, 15.070–15.073
conflicts of interest, 15.055–15.069
shareholders' rights, and, 8.091
fraudulent trading, and
civil, 15.116–15.127
criminal, 15.128–15.130
general rule, 15.004–15.007
good faith, 15.029–15.034
guarantee companies, and, 30.002
indemnities, 15.091–15.093
independent discretion, 15.035–15.041
insolvency, and
civil fraudulent trading, 15.128–15.130
criminal fraudulent trading, 15.116–15.127
failure to keep proper books of account,
fraudulent trading, 15.116–15.130
introduction, 15.095
misfeasance, 15.149–15.151
reckless trading, 15.096–15.115
s 251 CA 1990, 15.141–15.148
insurance, 15.094
introduction, 15.001–15.003
judicial relief, 15.088–15.090
liability
indemnities, 15.091–15.093
insurance, 15.094
relief, 15.088–15.090
members, to, 15.018
misfeasance, and, 15.149–15.151
nominee directors, and, 15.045–15.048
non-executive directors, and, 15.042–15.044
qualifications, and, 15.078–15.080
receivers, and, 20.030–20.032
reckless trading, and
'a party to', 15.106
applicant requirement, 15.108–15.109
'carrying on the business', 15.107
date of conduct complained of, 15.114
deemed, 15.103–15.104
defences, 15.112
examinership proceedings, and, 15.115
generally, 15.096–15.097
insolvency requirement, 15.105
'knowingly', 15.098–15.102
nominee directors, and, 15.111
officers, and, 15.110
'party to', 15.106
personal responsibility imposed, 15.126–15.127
'reckless', 15.098–15.102
respondents, 15.110–15.111
scope of court's order, 15.113
shadow directors, and, 15.110
reliance on others for advice, 15.085
s 251 CA 1990, and
generally, 15.141
insufficiency of assets condition, 15.145–15.146
locus standi, 15.142
operation of provisions, 15.147–15.148
orders available, 15.143–15.144
'sexually transmitted debt', 15.049–15.050
shareholders, to, 15.019–15.023
shareholders' rights, and, 8.091
'token' directors, by, 15.049–15.050
tortious liability, 15.086–15.087
unlimited companies, and, 31.003
Directors' emoluments
profit and loss account, and, 17.105

Directors' expenses
directors' loans, and, 16.093–16.094
Directors' interests in shares
consequences of failure to comply, 13.114–13.115
disclosable interests, 13.108–13.113
disregarded interests, 13.112
family interests, 13.110–13.111
group accounts, and, 17.204
individual accounts, and
Companies Acts, 17.121
IFRS, 17.134
introduction, 13.100
investigation of suspected contravention, 13.118
notification procedure, 13.113
notification to stock exchange, 13.117
obligation during appointment, 13.103–13.107
obligation on appointment, 13.101–13.102
register, 13.116
Directors' loans
account and indemnity, 16.110–16.112
anti-avoidance, 16.062–16.063
bodies corporate that are connected persons
body corporate controlled by body corporate controlled by a director, 16.019
'control', 16.011–16.013
generally, 16.010
'interested in', 16.014–16.018
subsidiary controlled by a director, 16.020
summary, 16.021
business transactions, 16.095–16.097
connected guarantees, 16.069
connected persons
bodies corporate, 16.010
natural persons, 16.006–16.009
summary, 16.021
connected security, 16.070
consequences of contravention
account and indemnity, 16.110–16.112
acquisition 'for value', 16.108
actual notice, 16.105–16.108
bona fide, 16.105–16.109
criminal offences, 16.118–16.120
generally, 16.100–16.102
indemnity, 16.104
personal liability, 16.113–16.117
restitutio in integrum, 16.103
credit transactions, 16.067–16.068
criminal offences, 16.118–16.120
de minimis exception, 16.075–16.079
directors
generally, 16.004–16.005
summary, 16.021
directors' expenses, 16.093–16.094
exceptions to general prohibition
applicability to prohibited transactions and arrangements, , 16.074
business transactions, 16.095–16.097
de minimis, 16.075–16.079
directors' expenses, 16.093–16.094
groups, 16.089–16.092
introduction, 16.073
validation procedure, 16.080–16.088
'for' a director etc, 16.071
general prohibition, 16.060–16.061
group exception, 16.089–16.092
guarantees, 16.069
holding company directors
generally, 16.004–16.005
summary, 16.021
indirect activity, 16.062–16.063
introduction, 16.055–16.059
loans, 16.065
natural persons that are connected persons
generally, 16.006–16.009
summary, 16.021
overview, 16.001–16.002
personal liability, 16.113–16.117
primary prohibition, 16.058
prohibited transactions and arrangements, 16.064–16.072
prohibition on indirect activity, 16.062–16.063
quasi-loans, 16.066

Directors' loans (contd)
regulated persons
connected persons, 16.006–16.020
directors, 16.004–16.005
holding company directors, 16.004–16.005
introduction, 16.003
summary, 16.021
restitutio in integrum, 16.103
security, 16.070
shadow directors, 16.021
validation procedure
consequences of swearing declaration based on unreasonable grounds, 16.088
generally, 16.080–16.081
independent person's report, 16.087
special resolution, 16.082–16.083
statutory declaration of solvency, 16.084–16.086
voidability, 16.100–16.109
Directors' meetings
adjournment, 14.117
business to be conducted, 14.112
committees, 14.122–14.123
conduct, 14.109–14.111
convening, 14.105–14.108
introduction, 14.102–14.103
minutes, 14.118–14.121
notice, 14.105–14.108
quorum, 14.113–14.115
regulation, 14.104
resolutions
formal resolutions, 14.125
introduction, 14.124
unanimous acts of directors, 14.128
written resolutions, 14.126–14.127
technology facilities, 14.110
voting, 14.124–14.128
Directors' powers
examinership, and, 22.089–22.092
receivers, and, 20.030–20.032
refusal of registration of shares, and
bona fides of directors, 9.052–9.057
challenging, 9.066–9.068
consequences, 9.064–9.065
introduction, 9.042
lapsing of powers of directors, 9.058–9.061
model reg 3 restriction, 9.043–9.047
overview, 9.22
procedure for challenging, 9.066–9.068
quality of transferee, 9.050–9.051
s 205 CA 1963 relief, 9.062–9.063
status of transferee, 9.048–9.049
Directors' remuneration
generally, 13.070–13.071
group accounts, and
Companies Act, 17.181
IFRS, 17.202
individual accounts, and
Companies Acts, 17.112
IFRS, 17.132
profit and loss account, and, 17.105
Directors' reports
additional obligations, 17.216–17.218
approval, 17.221
Companies Act group accounts, 17.216
criminal offences, 17.222–17.224
general obligation, 17.214–17.215
IFRS group accounts, 17.217
IFRS individual accounts, 17.217
laying before company at general meeting, 17.249
listed companies, 17.218–17.220
medium-sized companies, and, 17.275
obligation to circulate, 17.243–17.245
signature, 17.221
small companies, and, 17.281
Directors' transactions
bodies corporate that are connected persons
body corporate controlled by body corporate controlled by a director, 16.019
'control', 16.011–16.013
generally, 16.010
'interested in', 16.014–16.018
subsidiary controlled by a director, 16.020
summary, 16.021
connected persons
bodies corporate, 16.010

Directors' transactions (contd)
natural persons, 16.006–16.009
summary, 16.021
directors
generally, 16.004–16.005
summary, 16.021
disclosure of interests in contracts
application of provision, 16.123
consequences of breach of provision, 16.132–16.134
criminal offences, 16.135
'directly or indirectly, interested in a contract', 16.124–16.
generally, 16.121–16.122
methods, 16.127–16.130
overview, 16.001–16.002
register of directors' interests, 16.131
scope of provision, 16.123
transactions and arrangements with connected persons, 16.126
transactions which are not contracts, 16.125
transactions with shadow directors, 16.123
group accounts, and
Companies Act, 17.185
IFRS, 17.203
guarantee companies, and, 30.002
holding company directors
generally, 16.004–16.005
summary, 16.021
individual accounts, and
Companies Acts, 17.113–17.120
IFRS, 17.133
introduction, 16.001–16.002
loans etc to directors
account and indemnity, 16.110–16.112
anti-avoidance, 16.062–16.063
business transactions, 16.095–16.097
connected guarantees, 16.069
connected security, 16.070
consequences of contravention, 16.100–16.120
credit transactions, 16.067–16.068
criminal offences, 16.118–16.120
de minimis exception, 16.075–16.079
directors' expenses, 16.093–16.094
exceptions to general prohibition, 16.073–16.099
'for' a director etc, 16.071
general prohibition, 16.060–16.061
group exception, 16.089–16.092
guarantees, 16.069
indirect activity, 16.062–16.063
introduction, 16.055–16.059
loans, 16.065
overview, 16.001–16.002
personal liability, 16.113–16.117
primary prohibition, 16.058
prohibited transactions and arrangements, 16.064–16.072
prohibition on indirect activity, 16.062–16.063
quasi-loans, 16.066
regulated persons, 16.003–16.021
'relevant people', 16.072
restitutio in integrum, 16.103
security, 16.070
validation procedure, 16.080–16.088
voidability, 16.100–16.109
natural persons that are connected persons
generally, 16.006–16.009
summary, 16.021
regulated persons
connected persons, 16.006–16.020
directors, 16.004–16.005
holding company directors, 16.004–16.005
introduction, 16.003
summary, 16.021
shadow directors, 16.021
substantial property transactions
acquisitions by members acting 'qua member', 16.041
arrangements in insolvent winding up, 16.038–16.040
compliance by approving resolution, 16.042–16.045
consequences of breach of provision, 16.046–16.048
exceptions, 16.036–16.041
generally, 16.022–16.025

Directors' transactions (contd)
inter-group arrangements, 16.037
liability of directors etc for breach, 16.049–16.054
'non-cash asset', 16.028
overview, 16.001–16.002
regulated persons, 16.003–16.021
regulatory provisions, 16.026–16.027
'relevant assets', 16.029
'requisite value', 16.029–16.035
unlimited companies, and, 31.003
Disaggregation of fixed assets
balance sheet, and, 17.073
Disclaiming onerous property
realisation of assets, and, 25.058–25.065
Disclosure
company secretary, and
generally, 13.125
interests in shares and debentures, 13.100–13.118
introduction, 13.095
register of secretaries, 13.096–13.099
compensation on loss of office, and, 13.093
directors, and
interests in shares and debentures, 13.100–13.118
introduction, 13.095
register of directors, 13.096–13.099
interests in contracts, and
application of provision, 16.123
consequences of breach of provision, 16.132–16.134
criminal offences, 16.135
'directly or indirectly, interested in a contract', 16.124–16.
generally, 16.121–16.122
methods, 16.127–16.130
overview, 16.001–16.002
register of directors' interests, 16.131
scope of provision, 16.123
transactions and arrangements with connected persons, 16.126
transactions which are not contracts, 16.125
transactions with shadow directors, 16.123
interests in shares and debentures, and
consequences of failure to comply, 13.114–13.115
disclosable interests, 13.108–13.113
disregarded interests, 13.112
family interests, 13.110–13.111
introduction, 13.100
investigation of suspected contravention, 13.118
notification procedure, 13.113
notification to stock exchange, 13.117
obligation during appointment, 13.103–13.107
obligation on appointment, 13.101–13.102
register, 13.116
register of directors, 13.096–13.099
Disclosure of interests in contracts
application of provision, 16.123
consequences of breach of provision, 16.132–16.134
criminal offences, 16.135
'directly or indirectly, interested in a contract'
introduction, 16.124
transactions and arrangements with connected persons, 16.126
transactions which are not contracts, 16.125
generally, 16.121–16.122
methods, 16.127–16.130
overview, 16.001–16.002
register of directors' interests, 16.131
scope of provision, 16.123
transactions and arrangements with connected persons, 16.126
transactions which are not contracts, 16.125
transactions with shadow directors, 16.123
Disclosure of interests in shares
consequences of failure to comply, 13.114–13.115
disclosable interests, 13.108–13.113

Disclosure of interests in shares (contd)
disclosure orders
consequences of contravention, 8.134
generally, 8.127–8.128
powers of court, 8.132 8.133
scope, 8.129–8.131
disregarded interests, 13.112
family interests, 13.110–13.111
generally, 8.127
introduction, 13.100
investigation of suspected contravention, 13.118
notification procedure, 13.113
notification to stock exchange, 13.117
obligation during appointment, 13.103–13.107
obligation on appointment, 13.101–13.102
public limited companies, and,
generally, 29.057–29.059
investigations, and, 29.125–29.129
register, 13.116

Disclosure letters
share purchase agreements, and, 9.112

Disclosure orders
consequences of contravention, 8.134
generally, 8.127–8.128
powers of court, 8.132–8.133
scope, 8.129–8.131

Discount
allotment of shares, and, 8.064
maintenance of capital, and, 10.108–10.109
valuation of shares, and, 9.122–9.125

Discovery
civil litigation, and, 6.061–6.065

Discretion
compulsory transfer of shares, and
bona fides of transferee, 9.100–9.107
disclosure of full particulars, 9.096
introduction, 9.095
independence of transferee, 9.100–9.107
onus of proof, 9.097–9.099
directors' duties, and, 15.035–15.041
failure to keep proper books of account, and, 15.134–15.135

Disguised distributions
generally, 10.099–10.102

Display of information
consequences of incorporation, and, 4.092
incorporation, and, 2.039–2.042

Disposition of corporate property
beneficiary of disposition, 25.100–25.102
effect, 25.087–25.090
intention to prefer, 25.093–25.099
introduction, 25.083–25.085
onus of proof, 25.091–25.092
operative time, 25.086

Disqualification of directors
breach of duty, 28.175
breach of orders
civil sanctions, 28.206
criminal sanctions, 28.205
declaration of liability for fraudulent trading, 28.176
deemed disqualification, 28.151–28.153
directorship of company struck-off, 28.193–28.197
discretionary disqualification, 28.154–28.156
dishonesty convictions, 28.151–28.153
disregarding legal personality, and, 5.083–5.085
enforcement of orders, 28.204–28.209
failure to keep proper books of account, 28.193
failure to maintain books and records, 28.184
fraud, 28.174
fraud convictions, 28.151–28.153
fraudulent trading, 28.176
generally, 28.148–28.150
grounding affidavit, 28.171
grounds
directorship of company struck-off, 28.193–28.197
failure to keep proper books of account, 28.193
fraudulent trading, 28.176
guilty of breach of duty, 28.175

Disqualification of directors (contd)
guilty of fraud, 28.174
introduction, 28.163
persistently in default as to relevant requirements, 28.190–28.192
preliminary issues, 28.164–28.173
subject of order made in a foreign state, 28.197
unfit to manage company, 28.177–28.184
unfitness appearing from inspector's report, 28.185–28.189
guilty of breach of duty, 28.175
guilty of fraud, 28.174
introduction, 13.021
locus standi of applicants, 28.157–28.161
nature of order, 28.198
notice of application, 28.162
onus of proof, 28.168–28.170
period, 28.198–28.201
persistently in default as to relevant requirements, 28.190–28.192
persons liable, 28.154–28.156
preliminary issues
discretionary nature of order, 28.165
grounding affidavit, 28.171
introduction, 28.164
onus of proof, 28.168–28.170
purpose of disqualification, 28.166–28.167
restriction as alternative to disqualification, 28.172–28.173
purpose of disqualification, 28.166–28.167
relief, 28.202–28.203
restriction orders, and, 28.172 28.173
subject of order made in a foreign state, 28.197
unfit to manage company, 28.177–28.184
unfitness appearing from inspector's report, 28.185–28.189

Disqualification orders
And see **Disqualification of directors**
disregarding legal personality, and, 5.083–5.085

Disregard of interests
abuse of process, 11.053–11.056
'affairs of the company', 11.033–11.034
alteration of constitutional documents, 11.085
cancellation of transactions, 11.084
company's position, 11.057–11.059
compensatory damages, and, 11.074–11.076
contracting-out of provision, 11.091
contrast with unfairly prejudicial remedy, 11.088–11.090
costs, 11.087
delay in prosecution, 11.053–11.056
'disregarding member's interest', 11.029–11.032
ending matters complained of, 11.073–11.086
futile orders, and, 11.078
in camera applications, 11.060–11.066
introduction, 11.006–11.007
'legitimate expectations', 11.035–11.041
locus standi, 11.042–11.052
members of the company, 11.044–11.051
nature of remedy, 11.008–11.009
personal representatives of deceased members, 11.052
'powers of directors', 11.033–11.034
purchase of petitioner's shares, 11.080–11.081
purchase of respondent's shares, 11.082
purchase of shares by company, 11.083
quasi-partnership companies, 11.035–11.041
restraining removal of shareholder director, 11.067–11.072
variation of transactions, 11.084

Disregarding legal personality
acting on directions of disqualified person, 5.085
agency
implied agency, 5.023–5.027
introduction, 5.020–5.022
undisclosed agency, 5.028

Disregarding legal personality (contd)
avoidance of future legal obligations, 5.049–5.050
breach of restriction or disqualification orders, 5.083–5.085
characterisation
culpability, 5.074
introduction, 5.068
licensing purposes, 5.075
mens rea, 5.074
residence, 5.069–5.073
circumstances in which occur
agency, 5.020–5.028
contract, by, 5.012–5.017
injunctions, 5.065–5.067
introduction, 5.010
misuse of corporate form, 5.031–5.050
orders, 5.065–5.067
single economic entity, 5.051–5.064
torts, 5.018–5.019
trusts, 5.029–5.030
comfort letters, 5.017
Companies Acts provisions
breach of restriction or disqualification orders, 5.083–5.085
failure to keep proper records, 5.087
failure to meet capital requirements, 5.086
failure to state correctly company's name, 5.081–5.082
fraudulent trading, 5.091
introduction, 5.077–5.091
liquidation of related companies, 5.090
overview, 5.076
reckless trading, 5.091
reduction of number of members, 5.078–5.080
unreasonably inaccurate declaration of solvency, 5.088–5.089
concealment of impropriety, 5.032–5.036
contract, by
comfort letters, 5.017
guarantees, 5.015
indemnities, 5.016
introduction, 5.012–5.014
personal guarantees, 5.015
controllers of the company, and, 5.009
court orders, 5.065–5.067
culpability, 5.074
directions of disqualified person, 5.085
disqualification orders, 5.083–5.085
evasion of existing legal obligations, 5.039–5.048
failure to keep proper records, 5.087
failure to meet capital requirements, 5.086
failure to state correctly company's name, 5.081–5.082
fraudulent trading, 5.091
guarantees, 5.015
implied agency, 5.023–5.027
inaccurate declaration of solvency, 5.088–5.089
indemnities, 5.016
injunctions, 5.065–5.067
introduction, 5.001–5.007
licensing purposes, 5.075
'lifting the veil', 5.002
liquidation of related companies, 5.090
manner, 5.008
mens rea, 5.074
mismanagement, 5.037–5.038
misuse of corporate form
avoidance of future legal obligations, 5.049–5.050
concealment of impropriety, 5.032–5.036
evasion of existing legal obligations, 5.039–5.048
introduction, 5.031
mismanagement, 5.037–5.038
personal guarantees, 5.015
'piercing the veil', 5.002
reckless trading, 5.091
reduction of number of members, 5.078–5.080
residence, 5.069–5.073
restriction orders, 5.083–5.085
Salomon's case, and, 5.001–5.006
single economic entity, 5.051–5.064
statutory provisions

Disregarding legal personality (contd)
Companies Acts, 5.077–5.091
introduction, 5.076
other legislation,
tax legislation, 5.092
torts, 5.018–5.019
trusts, 5.029–5.030
undisclosed agency, 5.028
unreasonably inaccurate declaration of solvency, 5.088–5.089
vicarious liability of directors and employees, 5.093–5.096
Dissolution
partnerships, and, 1.025
Distributable profits
balance sheet, and, 17.095
Distribution of assets
basic principles, 25.140
claims by creditors
contingent liabilities, 25.177–25.178
creditors, by, 25.173–25.175
discounting claims, 25.176
interest, 25.179–25.181
introduction, 25.172
periodical liabilities, 25.177–25.178
contributories of the company, 25.193–25.195
costs and expenses of winding up
examiners, 25.165
introduction, 25.164
liquidators, 25.165
'necessary disbursement', 25.168–25.170
official liquidation, 25.166
payable to liquidator's solicitor, 25.171
voluntary liquidation, 25.167
fixed mortgage or charge, subject to, 25.143–25.148
floating charges, 25.189–25.191
guarantee companies, and, 30.070–30.071
held in trust, 25.149
in specie, 25.196–25.198
members of the company, 25.193–25.195
monies that must be set off, 25.150–25.158
not available
fixed mortgage or charge, 25.143–25.148
held in trust, 25.149
introduction, 25.142
monies that must be set off, 25.150–25.158
super-preferential debts that are trust monies, 25.159–25.160
preferential creditors, 25.183–25.188
priorities
contributories of the company, 25.193–25.195
floating charges, 25.189–25.191
introduction, 25.182
members of the company, 25.193–25.195
preferential creditors, 25.183–25.188
unsecured creditors, 25.192
proof of debts
contingent liabilities, 25.177–25.178
creditors, by, 25.173–25.175
discounting claims, 25.176
interest, 25.179–25.181
introduction, 25.172
periodical liabilities, 25.177–25.178
remuneration, costs and expenses, 25.165
specie, in, 25.196–25.198
stamp duty on monies received in realisation, 25.161–25.163
statutory basis, 25.141
super-preferential debts that are trust monies, 25.159–25.160
trust, in, 25.149
unlimited companies, and, 31.036–31.040
unsecured creditors, 25.192
Distributions
bonus shares, 10.090
determining availability of profits, 10.096–10.097
definition, 10.090–10.092
disguised distributions, 10.099–10.102
distribution of assets, 10.090

Distributions (contd)
dividends, 10.091
generally, 10.089
liability for unlawful payments, 10.103–10.104
maintenance of capital, and
determining availability of profits, 10.096–10.097
disguised distributions, 10.099–10.102
generally, 10.089
liability for unlawful payments, 10.103–10.104
meaning, 10.090–10.092
'member' qua member, to, 10.098
'profits available for distribution', 10.093–10.095
meaning, 10.090–10.092
'member' qua member, to, 10.098
'profits available for distribution', 10.093–10.095
'properly prepared' accounts, 10.097
public limited companies, and, 29.079–29.080
redemption of shares, 10.090
reduction of share capital, 10.090
'relevant accounts', 10.096–10.097
Dividends
assisting purchase of company's own shares, and, 10.078–10.083
balance sheet, and, 17.096
declaration, 8.078
distributions, and, 10.091
entitlement
company a going concern, 8.074–8.075
company being wound up, 8.077
forfeiture, 8.076
form, 8.079
generally, 8.073
maintenance of capital, and
determining availability of profits, 10.096–10.097
disguised distributions, 10.099–10.102
generally, 10.089
liability for unlawful payments, 10.103–10.104
meaning, 10.090–10.092
'member' qua member, to, 10.098
'profits available for distribution', 10.093–10.095
preference shares, and, 8.103–8.107
public limited companies, and, 29.079–29.080
shareholders' rights, and, 8.073–8.079
Divisions
draft Companies Bill, and, 1.180
public limited companies, and, 1.117
Dominant influence
groups of companies, and, 12.035–12.038
EEA residence
directors, and, 13.012–13.015
Electronic scheme
incorporation, and, 2.022
Employee involvement
Societas Europaea, and, 29.178–29.181
Employees
directors' duties, and, 15.018
Employees' shares
See also **Shares**
generally, 8.115
Employment contracts
receivers, and, 20.033–20.034
Enforcement
See also **Compliance and enforcement**
pre-emption rights, and, 9.084–9.086
public limited companies, and, 29.130
shareholders' agreements, and
binding effect, 3.127–3.128
directors fettering their fiduciary powers, 3.126
generally, 3.120–3.122
injunctions, 3.123–3.125
Enforcement of judgments and orders
attachment, 6.095–6.099
beyond reasonable doubt, 6.083
breach of undertakings given in lieu of court orders, 6.087–6.094
fines, 6.104–6.105
generally, 6.078–6.079
introduction, 6.071

Enforcement of judgments and orders (contd)
judgment mortgages, 6.07
money judgments
introduction, 6.072
judgment mortgages, 6.075
sale of goods, 6.073–6.074
seizure of goods, 6.073–6.074
sequestration, 6.077
winding up, 6.076
officers, against
attachment, 6.095–6.099
fines, 6.104–6.105
introduction, 6.071
sequestration, 6.100–6.103
sale of goods by sheriff, 6.073–6.074
seizure of goods by sheriff, 6.073–6.074
sequestration
companies' and officers' assets, 6.100–6.103
money judgments, 6.077
standard of proof, 6.083
wilful disobeyance
companies, by, 6.080–6.081
employees' acts or omissions, due to, 6.084–6.086
winding up, 6.076

Equitable charges
security of shares, and, 18.028–18.029

Equitable liens
generally, 19.029–19.030

Equitable mortgages
creation, 18.034
generally, 18.031
share transfers, and, 9.036–9.037

Estoppel
membership, and, 8.008
recovery of money given by company ultra vires, and, 7.094–7.095
restriction orders, and, 28.132–28.135

EU law
harmonisation Directives, 1.111–1.127

European Company (SE)
annual returns, 29.186
articles of association, 29.171
audits, 29.186
background, 29.150–29.151
capital, 29.152
constitutional documentation, 29.171–29.172
conversion from PLC, 29.167–29.169
conversion to PLC, 29.192
employee involvement, 29.178–29.181
EU law, and, 1.126
financial reporting, 29.186
formation
conversion of PLC, by, 29.167–29.169
holding SE, of, 29.164–29.165
introduction, 29.157
merger, by, 29.158–29.163
overview, 29.152
subsidiary SE, of, 29.166
general meetings, 29.182–29.184
governance
employee involvement, 29.178–29.181
general structure, 29.174–29.177
meetings, 29.182–29.185
overview, 29.152
holding SE, 29.164–29.165
introduction, 29.150–29.152
management meetings, 29.185
meetings
general meetings, 29.182–29.184
management meetings, 29.185
memorandum of association, 29.171
merger, 29.158–29.163
purpose, 29.150
registration, 29.170
separate legal personality, 29.152
sources of applicable law, 29.153–29.155
statutes
amendments, 29.172–29.173
generally, 29.171
subsidiary SE, 29.166
transfer of registered office, 29.187–29.191
winding up, 29.193–29.194

European economic interest groupings (EEIGs)
EU law, and, 1.125

Evasion of legal obligations
disregarding legal personality, and, 5.039–5.048
Examination
realisation of assets, and
admissibility of evidence obtained, 25.035
conduct, 25.032–25.033
courts' approach, 25.030–25.031
Director of Corporate Enforcement, 25.029
failure to cooperate, 25.034
introduction, 25.024–25.025
official liquidations, 25.026–25.027
procedure, 25.032–25.033
voluntary liquidations, 25.028
Examiners
appointment
affidavit in support, 22.029–22.033
formalities, 22.055–22.057
grounds, 22.018–22.028
jurisdiction, 22.009–22.010
locus standi, 22.011–22.017
petition, 22.029–22.033
test, 22.018–22.019
borrowing monies, 22.098–22.099
certifying expenses, 22.103–22.108
costs, 22.168
dealing with charged property
fixed charges, 22.102
floating charges, 22.101
introduction, 22.100
mortgages, 22.102
directions from the court, 22.096
discharging pre-petition debts, 22.097
expenses, 22.169
grounds for appointment
companies with obligations to NAMA, 22.028
introduction, 22.018–22.019
'reasonable prospect of survival', 22.020–22.027
obtaining information, 22.093–22.095
powers
borrow monies, 22.098–22.099
certify expenses, 22.103–22.108
deal with charged property, 22.100–22.102
directions from the court, 22.096
discharge pre-petition debts, 22.097
introduction, 22.088
obtain information, 22.093–22.095
regularise improper transactions, 22.109–22.110
transfer of directors' powers, 22.089–22.092
receivers, and, 20.004
registration-type offences, and, 28.050
regularising improper transactions, 22.109–22.110
remuneration
costs, 22.168
expenses, 22.169
generally, 22.165–22.167
introduction, 22.163–22.164
transfer of directors' powers, 22.089–22.092
Examinership
affidavit in support, 22.029–22.033
application for directions, 22.043
appointment of examiner
affidavit in support, 22.029–22.033
formalities, 22.055–22.057
grounds, 22.018–22.028
jurisdiction, 22.009–22.010
locus standi, 22.011–22.017
petition, 22.029–22.033
test, 22.018–22.019
background
Company Law Review Group, 22.003
generally, 22.002–22.004
borrowing monies, 22.098–22.099
certifying expenses, 22.103–22.108
charged property, 22.100–22.102
companies with obligations to NAMA, 22.028
compromise of leasing claims, 22.124–22.129
court's determination of proposals
evidence of wrongdoing, 22.159
generally, 22.137–22.141
matters arising after confirmation, 22.160–22.162

Examinership (contd)
other substantive grounds for not confirming a scheme, 22.150–22.151
procedural objections to court confirmation, 22.152
substantive objections to court confirmation, 22.142–22.149
unfairly prejudicial proposals, 22.153–22.158
creditors' meetings, 22.130–22.132
creditors' position
introduction, 22.065
ordinary creditors, 22.066–22.068
preferential creditors, 22.066–22.068
secured creditors, 22.073–22.074
dealing with charged property
fixed charges, 22.102
floating charges, 22.101
introduction, 22.100
mortgages, 22.102
de-crystallisation of floating charges, 22.077–22.078
directions from the court, 22.096
directors' powers, and, 22.089–22.092
discharging pre-petition debts, 22.097
draft Companies Bill, and, 1.181
effects
creditors, on, 22.065–22.068
floating charges, on, 22.077–22.078
generally, 22.059–22.064
guarantors, on, 22.079–22.083
negative pledge clauses, on, 22.075–22.076
ordinary creditors, on, 22.066–22.068
preferential creditors, on, 22.066–22.068
provisional liquidators, on, 22.069
receivers, on, 22.070–22.072
secured creditors, on, 22.073–22.074
sureties, on, 22.079–22.083
evidence of wrongdoing, 22.159
examination of company's affairs
compromise of leasing claims, 22.124–22.129
consideration of proposals, 22.130–22.132
court's determination of proposals, 22.137–22.141
examiners' duties, 22.112–22.114
examiner's report, 22.133–22.136
formulation of proposals, 22.116–22.123
hearing regarding irregularities, 22.115
introduction, 22.111
meetings of creditors and members, 22.130–22.132
examiners' duties, 22.112–22.114
examiner's report, 22.133–22.136
fixed charges, 22.102
floating charges
dealing with charged property, 22.101
generally, 22.077–22.078
formulation of proposals, 22.116–22.123
grounds for appointment of examiner
companies with obligations to NAMA, 22.028
introduction, 22.018–22.019
'reasonable prospect of survival', 22.020–22.027
guarantee companies, and, 30.002
guarantors, and, 22.079–22.083
hearing, 22.044–22.050
hearing regarding irregularities, 22.115
improper transactions, 22.109–22.110
interim protection, 22.039–22.042
introduction, 22.001
liquidators' costs, charges and expenses, 22.087
locus standi, 22.011–22.017
Mareva injunctions, and, 22.063
matters arising after confirmation, 22.160–22.162
meaning, 22.001
meetings of creditors and members, 22.130–22.132
National Asset Management Agency, and, 22.028
negative pledge clauses, and, 22.075–22.076
obtaining information, 22.093–22.095
ordinary creditors, and, 22.066–22.068

Examinership (contd)
petition
application for directions, 22.043
generally, 22.029–22.033
hearing, 22.044–22.050
locus standi, 22.011–22.017
presentation, 22.009–22.010
supporting evidence, 22.029–22.033
utmost good faith, 22.034–22.038
powers of examiners
borrow monies, 22.098–22.099
certify expenses, 22.103–22.108
deal with charged property, 22.100–22.102
directions from the court, 22.096
discharge pre-petition debts, 22.097
introduction, 22.088
obtain information, 22.093–22.095
regularise improper transactions, 22.109–22.110
transfer of directors' powers, 22.089–22.092
preferential creditors, and, 22.066–22.068
pre-petition debts, 22.097
priorities
liquidators' costs, charges and expenses, 22.087
secured creditors, 22.084–22.086
procedural objections to court confirmation, 22.152
provisional liquidators, and, 22.069
purpose of legislation, 22.005–22.006
reasonable prospect of survival
company, of, 22.020–22.025
whole or part of its undertaking as a gong concern, of, 22.026–22.027
receivers, and, 22.070–22.072
reckless trading, and, 15.115
regularising improper transactions, 22.109–22.110
related companies, 22.051–22.054
remuneration of examiner
costs, 22.168
expenses, 22.169
generally, 22.165–22.167
introduction, 22.163–22.164
schemes of arrangement, and, 21.002
secured creditors, and
effects, 22.073–22.074
priorities, 22.084–22.086
substantive objections to court confirmation, 22.142–22.149
supporting evidence, 22.029–22.033
sureties, and, 22.079–22.083
transfer of directors' powers, 22.089–22.092
unfairly prejudicial proposals, 22.153–22.158
utmost good faith, 22.034–22.038

Execution
instrument of share transfer, and, 9.011–9.012
power of attorney, and, 7.030–7.034

Executive directors
directors' duties, and, 15.042–15.044
generally, 13.037

External companies
creation of charges
established place of business, 34.022–34.023
generally, 34.019
introduction, 34.018
registration of charges, and, 19.001
Slavenburg file, 34.020
unregistered companies, 34.020–34.021
establishing place of business
conducting a business, 34.007
criteria in determining establishment, 34.008–34.009
distinguished from branch, 34.011–34.012
incidental to company's main business, 34.010
introduction, 34.006
filing documents, 34.014–34.016
introduction, 34.003–34.004
jurisdiction of Companies Acts, 34.001
obligations
filing documents, 34.014–34.016
other, 34.017
registration, 34.013

External companies (contd)
offences for breach of requirements, 34.026
overview, 34.001–34.002
Part XI of CA 1963 applies, to which, 34.005
registration obligation, 34.013
registration of charges, and, 19.001
service of documents, 34.024–34.025

Extraordinary general meetings
directors, 14.016-14.018
generally, 14.015
minutes, 14.077–14.080
notice
business to be conducted, 14.050–14.054
introduction, 14.033
periods, 14.040–14.049
notice of business to be conducted
amendment of resolution, 14.054
basis for need for resolutions, 14.053
introduction, 14.050
other matters, 14.053–14.054
special business, 14.051
special resolutions, 14.052
notice periods
accidental omission, 14.048
extended, 14.044–14.047
short notice, 14.041–14.043
standard notice, 14.040
summary of provisions, 14.049
order of the court, 14.024–14.031
requisition of qualified members, 14.019–14.023
retiring auditor, 14.032

Extraordinary income or charges
profit and loss account, and, 17.108

Facility letters
generally, 18.016–18.017
introduction, 18.014

Failure to file annual return
'aggrieved' petitioner, 26.040
alternative orders, 26.049
generally, 28.046–28.048
introduction, 26.035
jurisdiction to hear application, 26.039
locus standi, 26.036–26.038
requirement to file outstanding annual returns, 26.044–26.048
weight attached to third party objections, 26.041–26.043

Failure to keep proper books of account
discretion of court, 15.134–15.135
disqualification of directors, and, 28.193
generally, 15.131
personal responsibility, 15.132–15.133
proofs, 15.136–15.140

Failure to maintain books and records
disqualification of directors, and, 28.184
generally, 28.060

Failure to notify changes in officers
generally, 28.046–28.048

Fair valuation of assets and liabilities
balance sheet, and, 17.078–17.081

Fair value
valuation of assets, and
current assets, 17.058
fixed assets, 17.046–17.049
valuation of shares, and, 9.126–9.128

False information
shares, and, 8.048

Family companies
directors' duties, and, 15.049–15.050

Family owned private companies
generally, 1.149

Fé Phráinn
incorporation, and, 2.019–2.021

Fettering discretion
directors' duties, and, 15.035–15.041

Fiduciary duties
competition with the company, 15.070–15.073
conflicts of interest
account of profits, 15.067–15.068
general rule, 15.058–19.061
introduction, 15.055–15.057
profit, and, 15.058–19.061
rejected business opportunities, 15.062–15.066
remedies for breach, 15.067–15.069
setting aside transactions, 15.069
shareholders' rights, and, 8.091

Fiduciary relationship
partnerships, and, 1.024
Filing
resolutions, and, 14.100–14.101
shareholders' agreements, and
generally, 3.108–3.111
'resolutions or agreements', 3.109
Financial assistance for the purchase of company's own shares
'any transaction', 10.051–10.052
breadth of prohibition, 10.062–10.063
civil consequences
'any transaction', 10.051–10.052
introduction, 10.049
'notice', 10.053–10.057
voidability, 10.049–10.050
covenants, 10.064
criminal consequences, 10.048
dividends, 10.078–10.083
'financial assistance'
actual vs potential, 10.065
breadth of prohibition, 10.062–10.063
covenants, 10.064
express forms, 10.059–10.061
'in connection with', 10.063
introduction, 10.058
'otherwise', 10.062
warranties, 10.064
general prohibition, 10.047
group accounts, and, 17.210
'in connection with', 10.063
individual accounts, and, 17.139
introduction, 10.046
lawful liabilities, 10.078–10.083
miscellaneous, 10.084
'notice', 10.053–10.057
'otherwise', 10.062
private companies, and, 10.047
public limited companies, and, 29.077–29.078
s 60 CA 1963, under
application, 10.047
consequences of contravention, 10.048–10.057
'financial assistance', 10.058–10.065
general rule, 10.046
validation procedure
excluded companies, 10.069–10.070
introduction, 10.066
practice, in, 10.067–10.068
restrospectivity, 10.075–10.076
shareholder protection, 10.077
special resolution, 10.072
statutory declaration, 10.071
strict compliance, 10.073–10.074
voidability, 10.049–10.050
warranties and covenants, 10.064
'whitewash' procedure, 10.066–10.077
Financial collateral arrangements
registration of charges, and, 19.035–19.041
Financial commitments
balance sheet, and, 17.097
Financial institutions
winding up, and
Central Bank's rights, 23.139–23.140
generally, 23.136–23.138
liquidation committee, 23.14223.
rules applicable to liquidators, 23.141
Financial reporting
Societas Europaea, and, 29.186
Financial statements
abridged accounts
medium-sized companies, 17.270–17.276
small companies, 17.279–17.284
acquisition accounting
disclosures, 17.195
generally, 17.191
introduction, 17.190
annual accounts
accounting frameworks, 17.023–17.024
application of obligations, 17.021
approval, 17.213
Companies Acts group accounts, 17.164–17.200
Companies Acts individual accounts, 17.25–17.130
directors' liability, 17.018
GAAP, 17.024
group accounts, 17.144–17.212
IAS 1, and, 17.017

Financial statements (contd)
- IFRS group accounts, 17.201–17.212
- IFRS individual accounts, 17.131–17.143
- individual accounts, 17.25–17.143
- introduction, 17.17–17.22
- medium-sized companies, and, 17.276
- parent undertakings, and, 17.017
- single-member private companies, and, 17.020
- SSAPs, 17.023

annual general meeting, and, 17.002
annual return
- accompanying documents, 17.262–17.266
- contents, 17.257–17.259
- failure to file on time, 17.255–17.256
- form, 17.260–17.261
- introduction, 17.250–17.251
- time for filing, 17.252–17.254

appointment of auditors
- approval, 17.299–17.305
- audit requirement, and, 17.225
- disqualified persons, 17.306–17.307
- general requirement, 17.292–17.195
- member of recognised accountancy body, 17.300
- Member State auditor, 17.301
- qualification, 17.296–17.298
- third country auditor, 17.302

audit requirement
- appointment of auditor, 17.225
- auditor's report, 17.226–17.286
- exemption, 17.287–17.191
- report on accounts by auditor, 17.226

auditors
- appointment, 17.292–17.298
- approval as statutory audit firm, 17.303–17.305
- approval as statutory auditor, 17.299–17.302
- civil liability, 17.329–17.337
- common law duties, 17.323–17.328
- disclose directors' emoluments, 17.319
- disqualified persons, 17.306–17.307
- duties, 17.313–17.328
- exclusion of liability, 17.336–17.337
- exercise professional integrity, 17.315
- expenses, 17.308–17.309
- liability to the company, 17.329
- liability to third parties, 17.330–17.335
- notification to supervisory authority of certain matters, 17.346–17.348
- persons who may not act, 17.306–17.307
- professional integrity, 17.315
- removal, 17.338–17.342
- remuneration, 17.308–17.309
- replacement, 17.338–17.342
- report failures to keep proper books of account, 17.316–17.318
- report suspected indictable offences, 17.320–17.322
- report to members, 17.314
- reports, 17.226–17.242
- resignation, 17.343–17.345
- rights and powers, 17.310–17.311
- status, 17.312
- statutory duties, 17.313–17.322

auditor's report
- adverse opinion, 17.236
- content, 17.228–17.232
- dating, 17.241
- disclaimer of opinion, 17.237
- emphasis of matter, 17.239–17.240
- form, 17.233–17.240
- general requirement, 17.227
- introduction, 17.226
- laying before company at general meeting, 17.249
- 'material' and 'pervasive' effects, 17.238
- obligation to circulate, 17.243–17.245
- qualified opinion, 17.235
- reading at the AGM, 17.242
- signature, 17.241
- small companies, and, 17.283–17.284
- unqualified opinion, 17.234

balance sheet
- accounting policies, 17.71

Financial statements (contd)
- alternative valuation rules, 17.76–17.77
- approval, 17.213
- debentures, 17.092
- debt owed by company exceeding consideration received, 17.086
- development costs, 17.082
- disaggregation of fixed assets, 17.073
- distributable profits, 17.095
- dividends, 17.096
- fair valuation of assets and liabilities, 17.078–17.081
- financial assets held as investments, 17.084
- financial commitments, 17.097
- formats 17.031–17.036
- goodwill, 17.083
- group undertakings, 17.072
- guarantees, 17.097
- historic cost valuation rules, 17.074–17.075
- indebtedness, 17.087–17.809
- introduction, 17.030
- loans given as financial assistance, 17.085
- medium-sized companies, and, 17.270–17.272
- notes, 17.070–17.097
- obligation to circulate, 17.243–17.245
- reserves and provisions, 17.094
- revaluation reserve treatment, 17.091
- share capital, 17.092
- signature, 17.213
- small companies, and, 17.279–17.280
- subsidiary undertaking shares, 17.093
- taxation provision, 17.090
- valuation rules, 17.037–17.058

books of account
- approval, 17.213
- civil liability, 17.013
- concealment, 17.014–17.015
- contents, 17.006
- criminal liability, 17.011–17.012
- destruction, 17.014–17.015
- falsification, 17.014–17.015
- form, 17.008
- inspection, 17.009–17.010
- introduction, 17.005
- liability for failure to keep, 17.011–17.013
- location, 17.007
- signature, 17.213

directors' report
- additional obligations, 17.216–17.218
- approval, 17.221
- Companies Act group accounts, 17.216
- criminal offences, 17.222–17.224
- general obligation, 17.214–17.215
- IFRS group accounts, 17.217
- IFRS individual accounts, 17.217
- laying before company at general meeting, 17.249
- listed companies, 17.218–17.220
- medium-sized companies, and, 17.275
- obligation to circulate, 17.243–17.245
- signature, 17.221
- small companies, and, 17.281

disclosure, 17.002

draft Companies Bill, and, 1.177

'financial year', 17.16

GAAP, 17.024

group accounts
- Companies Act, 17.164–17.200
- exemptions from obligation, 17.156–17.163
- IFRS, 17.201–17.212
- introduction, 17.144–17.153
- obligation to circulate, 17.243–17.245
- obligation to prepare, 17.154–17.155
- parent undertakings that are subsidiaries of EEA undertakings, 17.159–17.161
- parent undertakings that are subsidiaries of non-EEA undertakings, 17.162–17.163
- size of group, 17.157–17.158

Financial statements (contd)
group accounts (Companies Act)
acquisition and merger accounting, 17.190–17.195
acquisitions, 17.177
associated undertakings, 17.197–17.200
auditors' remuneration, 17.189
contents, 17.171–17.175
directors' remuneration, 17.181
directors' report, and, 17.216
directors' transactions, 17.185
foreign currencies, 17.178
form, 17.165–17.169
format, 17.170
indebtedness, 17.179
introduction, 17.164
joint ventures, 17.196
name and office of undertakings, 17.186–17.187
notes, 17.176–17.189
qualifying capital interests, 17.186–17.187
staff numbers and remuneration, 17.180
transactions with connected persons, 17.185
valuation of assets, 17.182–17.184
group accounts (IFRS)
debentures, 17.207
debentures held by subsidiaries, 17.211
directors' interests in shares, 17.204
directors' remuneration, 17.202
directors' report, and, 17.217
directors' transactions, 17.203
distributability of profits, 17.208–17.209
financial assistance for purchase of own shares, 17.210
group undertakings, 17.205
interests in shares, 17.204
introduction, 17.201
off balance sheet items, 17.212
share capital, 17.207
shares held by subsidiaries, 17.211
staff numbers, 17.206
staff remuneration, 17.206
transactions with connected persons, 17.203
guarantee companies, and
accounts, 30.062–30.065
annual returns, 30.066–30.068
audits, 30.062–30.069
books of account, 30.061
exemptions, 30.069
individual accounts (Companies Acts)
accounting principles, 17.028–17.029
auditors' remuneration, 17.122–17.124
balance sheet, 17.030–17.058
directors' interests in shares, 17.121
directors' remuneration, 17.112
directors' transactions, 17.113–17.120
group undertakings, and, 17.127–17.129
interests in shares, 17.121
introduction, 17.025
laying before company at general meeting, 17.249
notes, 17.069–17.130
off balance sheet items, 17.126
profit and loss account, 17.059–17.068
related party transactions, 17.125
subsidiary undertakings, and, 17.130
transactions with connected persons, 17.113–17.120
'true and fair view', 17.026–17.027
individual accounts (IFRS)
auditors' remuneration, 17.143
debentures, 17.136
debentures held by subsidiaries, 17.141
directors' interests in shares, 17.134
directors' remuneration, 17.132
directors' report, and, 17.217
directors' transactions, 17.133
distributability of profits, 17.137
financial assistance for purchase of own shares, 17.139
group undertakings, 17.135
guarantees, 17.138

Financial statements (contd)
interests in shares, 17.134
introduction, 17.131
laying before company at general meeting, 17.249
off balance sheet items, 17.142
share capital, 17.136
shares held by subsidiaries, 17.141
staff numbers, 17.140
staff remuneration, 17.140
transactions with connected persons, 17.133
introduction, 17.001–17.004
medium-sized companies, and
abridged accounts, 17.270–17.276
auditor's reports, 17.276
balance sheet, 17.270–17.272
definition, 17.267–17.269
directors' statement, 17.275
profit and loss account, 17.273–17.274
merger accounting
disclosures, 17.195
generally, 17.192–17.194
introduction, 17.190
profit and loss account (Companies Acts)
accounting policies, 17.099
approval, 17.213
charges payable, 17.106
depreciation, 17.102–17.103
diminution in value of fixed assets, 17.102
directors' emoluments, 17.105
extraordinary income or charges, 17.108
foreign currencies, 17.109
formats, 17.60–17.68
generally, 17.059
improvements in value of written down fixed assets, 17.104
interest payable, 17.106
medium-sized companies, and, 17.273–17.274
movements, 17.110
notes, 17.098–17.110
obligation to circulate, 17.243–17.245
reconciliation of depreciation figures, 17.103
signature, 17.213
staff number and remuneration, 17.101
tax, 17.107
turnover, 17.100
public limited companies, and,
generally, 29.115–29.120
investment companies, 29.147
publication of accounts
demand for copies of accounts and reports, 17.246–17.247
general requirements, 17.248
laying before company at general meeting, 17.249
meaning, 17.248
obligation to circulate, 17.243–17.245
small companies, and
abridged accounts, 17.279–17.284
auditor's reports, 17.283–17.284
balance sheet, 17.279–17.280
definition, 17.277–17.278
directors' statement, 17.281
Societas Europaea, and, 29.186
Statements of Standard Accounting Practice (SSAPs), 17.023
statement of comprehensive income, 17.017
statement of financial position, 17.017
unlimited companies, and
accounts, 31.026–31.032
annual returns, 31.023–31.025
audits, 31.026–31.035
exemptions, 31.033–31.035
valuation of assets
current assets, 17.050–17.058
fixed assets, 17.039–17.049
introduction, 17.037–17.038
valuation of current assets
alternative accounting rules, 170.055–17.057
fair value accounting, 17.058
historical cost rules, 17.050–17.054

Financial statements (contd)
overview, 17.037–17.038
valuation of fixed assets
alternative accounting rules, 17.042–17.045
fair value accounting, 17.046–17.049
historical cost rules, 17.040–17.041
introduction, 17.039
overview, 17.037–17.038

Financial year
generally, 17.016

Fines
criminal sanctions, and, 28.041–28.042
Director of Corporate Enforcement, and, 29.020
enforcement of judgments and orders, and, 6.104–6.105
prosecution of companies and 'officers in default', and, 28.036–28.037

Firm name
partnerships, and, 1.018

First appointment
directors, and, 13.028

Fixed assets
valuation, and
alternative accounting rules, 17.042–17.045
fair value accounting, 17.046–17.049
historical cost rules, 17.040–17.041
introduction, 17.039

Fixed charges
book debts, on
curtailment of priority, 18.057–18.064
exercise of control by chargee as of legal right, 18.050
generally, 18.040–18.041
hybrid charges, 18.051–18.056
restrictions on chargor's use of debts, 18.044–18.049
validity, 18.042–18.043
deposit accounts, on, 18.065–18.067
identifiability, 18.035
registration
charger company's obligations, 19.107
conclusiveness of certificate, 19.011–19.020
consequences of non-registration, 19.006–19.010
disguised registrable charges, 19.071–19.084
introduction, 19.001
judgment mortgages, 19.085
late applications, 19.090–19.100
non-registrable security interests, 19.021–19.041
procedure, 19.101–19.107
property outside of the State, and, 19.086–19.089
register of charges, 19.002–19.005
registrable charges, 19.042–19.070
registrable particulars, 19.102–19.104
retention of title clauses, 19.071–19.084
satisfaction of charges, 19.105–19.106

Floating charges
ability of charger to deal with property, 18.072–18.073
characteristics, 18.068–18.071
Coslett (Contractors) Ltd case, 18.074–18.077
creation, 18.078
crystallisation
appointment of receiver, 18.098
automatic clauses, 18.103–18.109
causes, 18.097–18.109
ceasing to carry on business, 18.100–18.102
express clauses, 18.103–18.109
introduction, 18.093–18.096
winding up of charger company, 18.099
de-crystallisation, 18.110
events which affect assets, 18.087–18.092
examinership, and, 22.077–22.078
execution of judgment, 18.092
generally, 18.068–18.078
introduction, 4.088–4.089
invalidation of certain charges, and

Floating charges (contd)
extent of money actually advanced or paid, 25.115–25.117
introduction, 25.110
operative time limits, 25.112
other circumstances, 25.118
proof of solvency, 25.111
security unrealised on winding up, 25.113–25.114
liens, 18.091
nature, 18.069–18.071
negative pledge clauses
competition law, and, 18.085–18.086
generally, 18.079
priority of accompanied charges, 18.080–18.084
realisation of corporate assets, and
extent of money actually advanced or paid, 25.115–25.117
introduction, 25.110
operative time limits, 25.112
other circumstances, 25.118
proof of solvency, 25.111
security unrealised on winding up, 25.113–25.114
registration
charger company's obligations, 19.107
conclusiveness of certificate, 19.011–19.020
consequences of non-registration, 19.006–19.010
disguised registrable charges, 19.071–19.084
introduction, 19.001
judgment mortgages, 19.085
late applications, 19.090–19.100
non-registrable security interests, 19.021–19.041
procedure, 19.101–19.107
property outside of the State, and, 19.086–19.089
register of charges, 19.002–19.005
registrable charges, 19.042–19.070
registrable particulars, 19.102–19.104
retention of title clauses, 19.071–19.084
satisfaction of charges, 19.105–19.106
set-off, 18.090
subsequent mortgages and charges, 18.089

Foreign companies
registration of charges, and, 19.001

Foreign currencies
profit and loss account, and, 17.109

Foreign property
registration of charges, and, 19.086–19.088

Forfeiture
acquisition by company of own shares, and, 10.022
dividends, and, 8.076
partly paid shares, and, 10.106–10.107
shares, and, 8.123–8.125
unpaid paid shares, and, 10.106–10.107

Forgery
share certificates, and, 8.049

Formation agreements
And see **Shareholders' agreements**
generally, 3.117

Formation of associations
generally, 4.090

Formation of companies
guarantee companies, and
constitutional documentation, 30.013–30.038
generally, 30.012
introduction, 2.028
public limited companies, and,
generally, 29.007–29.009
investment companies, 29.134–29.138
Societas Europaea, and
conversion of PLC, by, 29.167–29.169
holding SE, of, 29.164–29.165
introduction, 29.157
merger, by, 29.158–29.163
overview, 29.152
subsidiary SE, of, 29.166
unlimited companies, and
constitutional documentation, 31.005–31.010

Formation of companies (contd)
generally, 31.004
introduction, 2.029
restrictions on commencement of business, 31.011–31.012

Forms of business organisation
And see under individual headings
building societies, 1.036–1.047
credit unions, 1.048–1.049
friendly societies, 1.052–1.053
industrial and provident societies, 1.032–1.035
introduction, 1.004
partnerships, 1.014–1.031
sole traders, 1.005–1.013
unincorporated associations, 1.050–1.051
unregistered companies, 1.054–1.055

Foss v Harbottle
civil litigation, and, 6.002
derivative actions, and, 11.110–11.120
distinguishing corporate rights from personal rights, 11.100–11.102
distinguishing personal rights from actions for reflective loss, 11.103–11.107
exceptions, 11.121–11.145
fraud on minority by those in control, 11.129–11.142
general principles, 11.093–11.094
generally, 11.095–11.096
illegal acts, and, 11.122–11.125
infringement of personal rights, and, 11.128
introduction, 11.092
justice requires derivative action to be brought, 11.143–11.145
summary, 11.097–11.099
transactions unratifiable by bare majority, and, 11.126–11.127
ultra vires acts, and, 11.122–11.125

Founders' shares
See also **Shares**
generally, 8.112

Fraud
disqualification of directors, and, 28.174
rule in *Foss v Harbottle*, and, 11.129–11.142
schemes of arrangement, and, 21.063–21.065

Fraudulent dispositions of property
generally, 25.103–25.109

Fraudulent preference of creditors
beneficiary of disposition, 25.100–25.102
disposition of corporate property, 25.083–25.085
effect, 25.087–25.090
intention to prefer, 25.093–25.099
introduction, 25.081–25.082
onus of proof, 25.091–25.092
operative time, 25.086

Fraudulent trading
civil
beneficiary of awards, 15.124–15.125
intention to defraud, 15.117–15.119
introduction, 15.116
personal responsibility imposed, 15.126–15.127
proof, 15.120–15.123
criminal, 15.128–15.130
disqualification of directors, and, 28.176
disregarding legal personality, and, 5.091

Fraudulent transactions
oppression, and, 11.017–11.019

Friendly societies
generally, 1.052–1.053

Futile orders
oppression, and, 11.078

GAAP
generally, 17.024

General meetings
Societas Europaea, and, 29.182–29.184

Golden share
groups of companies, and, 12.009–12.016

Good faith
directors' duties, and, 15.029–15.034

Goodwill
balance sheet, and, 17.083
registration of charges, and, 19.070

Governance
See also **Corporate governance**
building societies, and, 1.043
Societas Europaea, and
employee involvement, 29.178–29.181
general structure, 29.174–29.177
meetings, 29.182–29.185
overview, 29.152
Gratuitous dispositions of corporate property
express object or power, 7.073–7.075
generally, 7.070
implicit power where reasonably incidental, 7.071–7.072
not in furtherance of company's interests, 7.076–7.079
Group accounts
Companies Act
acquisition and merger accounting, 17.190–17.195
acquisitions, 17.177
associated undertakings, 17.197–17.200
auditors' remuneration, 17.189
contents, 17.171–17.175
directors' remuneration, 17.181
directors' report, and, 17.216
directors' transactions, 17.185
foreign currencies, 17.178
form, 17.165–17.169
format, 17.170
indebtedness, 17.179
introduction, 17.164
joint ventures, 17.196
name and office of undertakings, 17.186–17.187
notes, 17.176–17.189
qualifying capital interests, 17.186–17.187
staff numbers and remuneration, 17.180
transactions with connected persons, 17.185
valuation of assets, 17.182–17.184
exemptions from obligation
introduction, 17.156
parent undertakings, 17.159–17.163
size of group, 17.157–17.158
IFRS
debentures, 17.207
debentures held by subsidiaries, 17.211
directors' interests in shares, 17.204
directors' remuneration, 17.202
directors' report, and, 17.217
directors' transactions, 17.203
distributability of profits, 17.208–17.209
financial assistance for purchase of own shares, 17.210
group undertakings, 17.205
interests in shares, 17.204
introduction, 17.201
off balance sheet items, 17.212
share capital, 17.207
shares held by subsidiaries, 17.211
staff numbers, 17.206
staff remuneration, 17.206
transactions with connected persons, 17.203
introduction, 17.144–17.153
obligation to circulate, 17.243–17.245
obligation to prepare
exemptions, 17.156–17.163
generally, 17.154–17.155
parent undertakings
subsidiaries of EEA undertakings, 17.159–17.161
subsidiaries of non-EEA undertakings, 17.162–17.163
public limited companies, and, 29.116–29.117
size of group, 17.157–17.158
Group undertakings
balance sheet, and, 17.072
Groups of companies
accounts
Companies Act, 17.164–17.200
exemptions from obligation, 17.156–17.163
IFRS, 17.201–17.212
introduction, 17.144–17.153

Groups of companies (contd)
- obligation to circulate, 17.243–17.245
- obligation to prepare, 17.154–17.155

accounts (Companies Act)
- acquisition and merger accounting, 17.190–17.195
- acquisitions, 17.177
- associated undertakings, 17.197–17.200
- auditors' remuneration, 17.189
- contents, 17.171–17.175
- directors' remuneration, 17.181
- directors' report, and, 17.216
- directors' transactions, 17.185
- foreign currencies, 17.178
- form, 17.165–17.169
- format, 17.170
- indebtedness, 17.179
- introduction, 17.164
- joint ventures, 17.196
- name and office of undertakings, 17.186–17.187
- notes, 17.176–17.189
- qualifying capital interests, 17.186–17.187
- staff numbers and remuneration, 17.180
- transactions with connected persons, 17.185
- valuation of assets, 17.182–17.184

accounts (IFRS)
- debentures, 17.207
- debentures held by subsidiaries, 17.211
- directors' interests in shares, 17.204
- dirсctors' rcmuneration, 17.202
- directors' report, and, 17.217
- directors' transactions, 17.203
- distributability of profits, 17.208–17.209
- financial assistance for purchase of own shares, 17.210
- group undertakings, 17.205
- interests in shares, 17.204
- introduction, 17.201
- off balance sheet items, 17.212
- share capital, 17.207
- shares held by subsidiaries, 17.211
- staff numbers, 17.206
- staff remuneration, 17.206
- transactions with connected persons, 17.203

'associated undertaking', 12.041
directors' loans, and, 16.089–16.092
'dominant influence', 12.035–12.038
'golden share', 12.009–12.016
guarantee companies, and, 30.002
'holding company'
- company law purposes, for, 12.006–12.007
- corporation tax purposes, for, 12.043–12.045
- stamp duty purposes, for, 12.046

holding-subsidiary relationship
- directors' duties, 12.052
- issues, 12.047–12.052
- liability for negligence, 12.51
- separate legal personality, 12.048–12.050
- significance, 12.002–12.005

introduction, 12.001
liability for negligence, 12.51
'parent undertaking', 12.030–12.031
'participating influence', 12.039–12.040
separate legal personality, 12.048–12.050
'subsidiary'
- capital maintenance, and, 12.042
- control of composition of board by a member, 12.009–12.016
- corporation tax purposes, for, 12.043–12.045
- 'golden share', 12.009–12.016
- holding more than half in nominal value of share capital, 12.017–12.020
- introduction, 12.088
- shares held and powers exercisable in fiduciary capacity, as nominee or pursuant to debenture or trust, 12.021–12.027
- stamp duty purposes, for, 12.046

Groups of companies (contd)
subsidiary of a subsidiary, 12.028
wholly-owned subsidiaries, 12.029
subsidiary of a subsidiary, 12.028
'subsidiary undertaking'
'associated undertaking', 12.041
control of composition of board, 12.032
discounting of voting rights, 12.034
'dominant influence', 12.035–12.038
generally, 12.031
'participating influence', 12.039–12.040
shares held and powers exercisable by nominees, 12.033
'undertakings', 12.030
unlimited companies, and, 31.003
wholly-owned subsidiaries, 12.029
Group undertakings
group accounts, and, 17.205
individual accounts, and
Companies Acts, 17.127–17.129
IFRS, 17.135
Guarantee companies
accounts, 30.062–30.065
ancillary objects, 30.021
annual returns, 30.066–30.068
articles of association
generally, 30.035–30.038
introduction, 3.039
audits, 30.062–30.069
authority, 30.002
blocks of flats etc, 30.005–30.006
books of account, 30.061
borrowing, 30.002
capacity, 30.002
charities, and, 30.004
civil litigation, 30.002
clubs, and, 30.007
compliance and enforcement, 30.073–30.074
constitutional documentation
articles of association, 30.035–30.038
introduction, 30.012
memorandum of association, 30.013–30.034
context, in, 30.001
corporate contracts, 30.002
corporate governance
directors, 30.045–30.048
meetings, 30.049–30.060
directors' duties, 30.002
directors' transactions, 30.002
distribution of assets, 30.070–30.071
distributions of income and property, 30.025–30.029
examinership, 30.002
features
introduction, 30.008
limited by members' guarantee, 30.011
no shares, 30.009
public companies, 30.010
financial statements
accounts, 30.062–30.065
annual returns, 30.066–30.068
audits, 30.062–30.069
books of account, 30.061
exemptions, 30.069
formation
constitutional documentation, 30.013–30.038
generally, 30.012
introduction, 2.028
function, 2.010–2.012
groups of companies, 30.002
guarantee clause, 30.024
incorporation, and
formation, 2.028
function, 2.010–2.012
generally, 30.002
inspections, 30.002
introduction, 30.001–30.002
investigations, 30.002
legal personality, 30.003
liability of members, 30.011
main object, 30.020
maintenance of capital, 30.042–30.044
management companies, and
directors, 30.048
generally, 30.005–30.006
meetings
consider annual report, to, 30.055–30.057

Guarantee companies (contd)
consider house rules, to, 30.060
consider service charges, to, 30.058–30.059
fair and equitable voting rights, 30.051–30.054
generally, 30.049–30.050
voting rights, 30.051–30.054
membership, 30.040–30.041
memorandum of association
alterations, 30.031–30.034
distributions of income and property, 30.025–30.029
generally, 30.013
guarantee clause, 30.024
introduction, 3.004
name clause, 30.014–30.018
objects clause, 30.019–30.23
other clauses, 30.030
multi-unit developments, 30.005–30.006
name clause
dispensing with word 'limited', 30.015–30.017
introduction, 30.014
'owners' management company' requirement, 30.018
objects clause
ancillary objects, 30.021
generally, 30.019
main object, 30.020
powers, 30.022–30.023
subsidiary object, 30.021
powers, 30.022–30.023
public companies, as, 30.010
realisation of assets, 30.070–30.071
restoration, 30.072
schemes of arrangement, 30.002
separate legal personality, and
disregarding, 30.039
introduction, 30.003
shares, and, 30.009
social clubs, and, 30.007
sports clubs, and, 30.007
striking off, 30.072
subsidiary object, 30.021
uses, 30.003
voting rights, 30.051–30.054
winding up, 30.070–30.071
Guarantees
balance sheet, and, 17.097
directors' loans, and, 16.069
disregarding legal personality, and, 5.015
individual accounts, and, 17.138
Guarantors
examinership, and, 22.079–22.083
receivers' duties, and, 20.060–20.065
Historic cost valuation rules
balance sheet, and, 17.074–17.075
Holding companies
company law purposes, for, 12.006–12.007
corporation tax purposes, for, 12.043–12.045
directors' transactions, and
generally, 16.004–16.005
summary, 16.021
membership, and, 8.011
relationship with subsidiaries
directors' duties, 12.052
issues, 12.047–12.052
liability for negligence, 12.51
separate legal personality, 12.048–12.050
significance, 12.002–12.005
Societas Europaea, and, 29.164–29.165
stamp duty purposes, for, 12.046
Honestly and responsibly defence
affairs of the company, as to, 28.099–28.100
common law duties, 28.115–28.116
compliance with Companies Acts, 28.110–28.121
conduct of the affairs of the company, as to, 28.101–28.103
group obligations, 28.117
incompetence, 28.122
introduction, 28.097–28.128
La Mosselle test, 28.105–28.108
lack of commercial probity, 28.126–28.128
maintenance of proper records and books, 28.111–28.114

Honestly and responsibly defence (contd)
net deficiency of assets, 28.123–28.125
non-executive directors, 28.118–28.121
objective standard, 28.109
relevant factors, 28.104–28.128
responsibility for insolvency, 28.123–28.125
Human rights
security for costs, and, 6.017–6.018
IFRS
group accounts
debentures, 17.207
debentures held by subsidiaries, 17.211
directors' interests in shares, 17.204
directors' remuneration, 17.202
directors' report, and, 17.217
directors' transactions, 17.203
distributability of profits, 17.208–17.209
financial assistance for purchase of own shares, 17.210
group undertakings, 17.205
interests in shares, 17.204
introduction, 17.201
off balance sheet items, 17.212
share capital, 17.207
shares held by subsidiaries, 17.211
staff numbers, 17.206
staff remuneration, 17.206
transactions with connected persons, 17.203
individual accounts
auditors' remuneration, 17.143
debentures, 17.136
debentures held by subsidiaries, 17.141
directors' interests in shares, 17.134
directors' remuneration, 17.132
directors' report, and, 17.217
directors' transactions, 17.133
distributability of profits, 17.137
financial assistance for purchase of own shares, 17.139
group undertakings, 17.135
guarantees, 17.138
interests in shares, 17.134
introduction, 17.131
laying before company at general meeting, 17.249
off balance sheet items, 17.142
share capital, 17.136
shares held by subsidiaries, 17.141
staff numbers, 17.140
staff remuneration, 17.140
transactions with connected persons, 17.133
Impeachment
constitutionality of effect of certificate, 4.018–4.019
introduction, 4.012
judicial review of decision to issue certificate, 4.015–4.017
trade unions registered as companies, 4.013–4.014
Implied agency
disregarding legal personality, and, 5.023–5.027
Implied authority
corporate contracts, and, 7.100
Inability of company to pay its debts
'21-day letter', 23.075
bona fides of the debt, 23.078
deeming companies, 23.074
discretion, 23.072–23.073
improper presentation of petition, and, 23.089–23.090
introduction, 23.071
restraint of advertisement of petition, 23.081–23.088
service of demand, 23.076–23.077
valid cross-claims, 23.079–23.080
Inability to pay costs
security for costs, and, 6.033–6.037
Incorporation
business letters, 2.039–2.042
business name, 2.044
carrying on an 'activity' in the State, 2.030
certificates of incorporation
constitutionality of conclusive effect, 4.018–4.019
effect, 4.004–4.005

Incorporation (contd)
EU nullity provisions, and, 4.008–4.010
generally, 4.002–4.007
introduction, 4.001
judicial review of decision to issue, 4.015–4.017
rationale for conclusive effect, 4.006–4.007
cesser of corporate status, 4.020
common seal, 4.087
Company Incorporation Scheme, 2.019–2.021
company secretary, 2.038
consequences
common seal, 4.087
corporate property, 4.032–4.041
floating charges, 4.088–4.089
formation of associations, 4.090
generally, 4.021–4.022
introduction, 4.001
limited liability, 4.081–4.084
other, 4.092
perpetual succession, 4.086
privileges and obligations, 4.077–4.080
separate legal personality, 4.023–4.080
statutory requirements, 4.092
suing and being sued, 4.042–4.076
taxation, 4.091
transferability of interests, 4.085
constitutional documents, and
And see **Constitution of private companies**
articles of association, 3.038–3.091
generally, 2.024
introduction, 3.001–3.002
memorandum of association, 3.003–3.037
section 25 contract, 3.092–3.105
shareholders' agreements, 3.106–3.128
corporate litigation
contracts, 4.043–4.048
crime, 4.055–4.076
introduction, 4.042
torts, 4.049–4.053
corporate property, 4.032–4.041
CRODisk Scheme, 2.022
delivery of particulars to Revenue Commissioners, 2.034
determination by registrar, 2.031–2.033
directors, 2.038
display of information, 2.039–2.042
draft Companies Bill, and, 1.173
electronic scheme, 2.022
existing business, of, 2.004–2.007
Fé Phráinn, 2.019–2.021
floating charges, 4.088–4.089
formation of associations, 4.090
generally, 2.008–2.016
guarantee companies
formation, 2.028
function, 2.010–2.012
generally, 30.002
impeachment
constitutionality of effect of certificate, 4.018–4.019
introduction, 4.012
judicial review of decision to issue certificate, 4.015–4.017
trade unions registered as companies, 4.013–4.014
incidental obligations, 2.035–2.044
introduction, 2.001
Irish registered non-resident companies
carrying on an 'activity' in the State, and, 2.030
generally, 2.045–2.046
limited liability, 4.081–4.084
methods
Company Incorporation Scheme, 2.019–2.021
CRODisk Scheme, 2.022
introduction, 2.017
ordinary list, 2.018
shelf companies, 2.023
nullity provisions, and
effect, 4.009–4.010
generally, 4.008
ordinary list, in, 2.018
perpetual succession, 4.086

Incorporation (contd)
private company limited by guarantee, of
formation, 2.028
function, 2.010–2.012
private company limited by shares, of
formation, 2.024–2.026
function, 2.009
private unlimited company with share capital, of
formation, 2.029
function, 2.013–2.014
privileges and obligations, 4.077–4.080
public limited companies, and,
generally, 29.033
investment companies, 29.142
publication of notices, 2.043
purpose, 2.002–2.003
registered office, 2.036–2.037
registrar of companies, by, 2.031–2.033
secretary, 2.038
separate legal personality
artificial personality, 4.024–4.025
constitutional rights and duties, 4.068–4.075
contractual liability, 4.043–4.048
corporate manslaughter, 4.059–4.060
corporate property, 4.032–4.041
criminal liability, 4.055–4.076
disregarding, 5.001–5.096
fictional personality, 4.024–4.025
generally, 4.023
insurable interests, 4.039
legal rights and duties, 4.076
privileges and obligations, 4.077–4.080
regulatory relationships, 4.077
Salomon's case, 4.026–4.031
statutory tenancies, 4.041
suing and being sued, 4.042–4.076
tortious liability, 4.049–4.053
shelf companies, 2.023
single-member private limited company
formation, 2.027
function, 2.015–2.016
statutory requirements, 4.092
steps
guarantee companies, 2.028
private limited company, 2.024–2.026
single-member private limited company, 2.027
unlimited companies, 2.029
suing and being sued
contracts, 4.043–4.048
crime, 4.055–4.076
introduction, 4.042
torts, 4.049–4.053
taxation, 4.091
transferability of interests, 4.085
unlimited companies
formation, 2.029
function, 2.013–2.014
generally, 31.013
'veil of incorporation', and, 5.002
Increasing share capital
memorandum of association, and, 3.032
Indebtedness
balance sheet, and, 17.087–17.089
Indemnities
directors' duties, and, 15.091–15.093
disregarding legal personality, and, 5.016
share purchase agreements, and, 9.116
Individual accounts
Companies Acts
accounting principles, 17.028–17.029
auditors' remuneration, 17.122–17.124
balance sheet, 17.030–17.058
directors' interests in shares, 17.121
directors' remuneration, 17.112
directors' transactions, 17.113–17.120
group undertakings, and, 17.127–17.129
interests in shares, 17.121
introduction, 17.025
laying before company at general meeting, 17.249
notes, 17.069–17.130
off balance sheet items, 17.126
profit and loss account, 17.59–17.68
related party transactions, 17.125
subsidiary undertakings, and, 17.130

Individual accounts (contd)
transactions with connected persons, 17.113–17.120
'true and fair view', 17.026–17.027
IFRS
auditors' remuneration, 17.143
debentures, 17.136
debentures held by subsidiaries, 17.141
directors' interests in shares, 17.134
directors' remuneration, 17.132
directors' report, and, 17.217
directors' transactions, 17.133
distributability of profits, 17.137
financial assistance for purchase of own shares, 17.139
group undertakings, 17.135
guarantees, 17.138
interests in shares, 17.134
introduction, 17.131
laying before company at general meeting, 17.249
off balance sheet items, 17.142
share capital, 17.136
shares held by subsidiaries, 17.141
staff numbers, 17.140
staff remuneration, 17.140
transactions with connected persons, 17.133
public limited companies, and, 29.116
Industrial and provident societies
generally, 1.032–1.035
Injunctions
compliance with Companies Acts, and, 28.210–28.215
disregarding legal personality, and, 5.065–5.067
shareholders' agreements, and, 3.123–3.125
Insider dealing
administrative sanctions, 32.114
background, 32.058–32.060
CESR guidelines, 32.073
civil sanctions, 32.115–32.117
common law, at, 32.098
competent authority, 32.066
criminal sanctions, 32.113
disclosure obligations
introduction, 32.104
managers' transactions, of, 32.105–32.107
suspicious transactions, of, 32.108–32.112
EU law, and, 32.058
exceptions, 32.083–32.084
excluded transactions, 32.064
fair presentation of recommendations about instruments or issuers, 32.092
'financial instrument', 32.065
FSAP, and, 32.058
generally, 32.061–32.064
information not available to the public, 32.080
information of a 'precise nature', 32.074
information relating to financial instruments, 32.075
innocent insider dealing, 32.081–32.082
'inside information', 32.071–32.073
insider lists, 32.089–32.091
instruments admitted to trading, 32.062
legislative framework, 32.059–32.060
liability for breach
administrative sanctions, 32.114
civil sanctions, 32.115–32.117
criminal sanctions, 32.113
managers' transactions, 32.105–32.107
Market Abuse Directive, under
exceptions, 32.083–32.084
fair presentation of recommendations about instruments or issuers, 32.092
financial instruments, 32.075
information not available to the public, 32.080
information of a 'precise nature', 32.074
information relating to financial instruments, 32.075
innocent insider dealing, 32.081–32.082
'inside information', 32.071–32.073
insider lists, 32.089–32.091
introduction, 32.068

Insider dealing (contd)
persons to whom Reg 5 applies, 32.069–32.070
'precise nature', 32.074
prerequisites, 32.072
price sensitivity, 32.076–32.079
public disclosure, 32.085–32.088
selective disclosure, 32.085–32.088
notification obligations
introduction, 32.104
managers' transactions, of, 32.105–32.107
suspicious transactions, of, 32.108–32.112
Part V of CA 1990, under, 32.093–32.097
persons to whom Reg 5 applies, 32.069–32.070
'precise nature', 32.074
prerequisites, 32.072
price sensitivity, 32.076–32.079
public debt management, and, 32.064
public disclosure, 32.085–32.088
relevant financial instruments, 32.065
sanctions for breach
administrative sanctions, 32.114
civil sanctions, 32.115–32.117
criminal sanctions, 32.113
secondary markets, and, 32.062
selective disclosure, 32.085–32.088
shadow directors, 32.070
suspicious transactions, 32.108–32.112
territorial jurisdiction, 32.063
Insolvency
civil fraudulent trading
beneficiary of awards, 15.124–15.125
intention to defraud, 15.117–15.119
introduction, 15.116
personal responsibility imposed, 15.126–15.127
proof, 15.120–15.123
criminal fraudulent trading, 15.128–15.130
directors' duties, and
civil fraudulent trading, 15.128–15.130
criminal fraudulent trading, 15.116–15.127
failure to keep proper books of account,
fraudulent trading, 15.116 15.130
introduction, 15.095
misfeasance, 15.149–15.151
reckless trading, 15.096–15.115
s 251 CA 1990, 15.141–15.148
failure to keep proper books of account
discretion of court, 15.134–15.135
generally, 15.131
personal responsibility, 15.132–15.133
proofs, 15.136–15.140
fraudulent trading
civil, 15.116–15.127
criminal, 15.128–15.130
introduction, 15.095
misfeasance, 15.149–15.151
reckless trading
'a party to', 15.106
applicant requirement, 15.108–15.109
'carrying on the business', 15.107
date of conduct complained of, 15.114
deemed, 15.103–15.104
defences, 15.112
examinership proceedings, and, 15.115
generally, 15.096–15.097
insolvency requirement, 15.105
'knowingly', 15.098–15.102
nominee directors, and, 15.111
officers, and, 15.110
'party to', 15.106
personal responsibility imposed, 15.126–15.127
'reckless', 15.098–15.102
respondents, 15.110–15.111
scope of court's order, 15.113
shadow directors, and, 15.110
s 251 CA 1990
generally, 15.141
insufficiency of assets condition, 15.145–15.146

Insolvency (contd)
locus standi, 15.142
operation of provisions, 15.147–15.148
orders available, 15.143–15.144
security for costs, and, 6.047–6.051

Inspections
affairs of the company, as to
appointment of inspectors, 27.011–27.016
conduct, 27.028–27.033
costs, 27.061–27.063
generally, 27.010
powers of inspectors, 27.034–27.050
scope, 27.021–27.023
appointment of inspectors
court, by, 27.011–27.016
Director of Corporate Enforcement, by, 27.017–27.019
concurrent investigations, 27.065–327.066
conduct, 27.028–27.033
costs
court-ordered inspections, 27.061–27.063
DCE-ordered inspections, 27.064
court order, by
appointment of inspectors, 27.011–27.016
conduct, 27.028–27.033
costs, 27.061–27.063
generally, 27.010
powers of inspectors, 27.034–27.050
scope, 27.021–27.023
Director of Corporate Enforcement, by
appointment of inspectors, 27.017–27.019
conduct, 27.028–27.033
costs, 27.064
generally, 27.010
powers of inspectors, 27.034–27.048
scope, 27.024–27.027
guarantee companies, and, 30.002
introduction, 27.010
ownership or control of company or its shares, as to
appointment of inspectors, 27.017–27.019
conduct, 27.028–27.033
costs, 27.064
generally, 27.010
powers of inspectors, 27.034–27.048
scope, 27.024–27.027
powers of inspectors
certification of refusal of person to cooperate, 27.046–27.048
examination of persons on oath, 27.042–27.045
introduction, 27.034
production of books and documents as to bank accounts, 27.049–27.050
production of books, documents and information, 27.035–27.041
report by inspector
admissibility in proceedings, 27.058–27.060
introduction, 27.051
presumptive evidentiary effect in proceedings, 27.058–27.060
proceedings on foot of, 27.056–27.057
publication, 27.052–27.055
scope
court-ordered inspections, 27.021–27.023
DCE-ordered inspections, 27.024–27.027
introduction, 27.020
types, 27.010

Insurable interests
separate legal personality, and, 4.039

Insurance
directors' duties, and, 15.094

Intellectual property
registration of charges, and, 19.070

Interest payable
profit and loss account, and, 17.106

Interests in shares and debentures
consequences of failure to comply, 13.114–13.115
disclosable interests, 13.108–13.113
disregarded interests, 13.112
family interests, 13.110–13.111

Interests in shares and debentures (contd)
group accounts, and, 17.204
individual accounts, and
Companies Acts, 17.121
IFRS, 17.134
introduction, 13.100
investigation of suspected contravention, 13.118
notification procedure, 13.113
notification to stock exchange, 13.117
obligation during appointment, 13.103–13.107
obligation on appointment, 13.101–13.102
register, 13.116

Interrogatories
civil litigation, and, 6.061–6.065

Investigations
background, 27.003–27.006
draft Companies Bill, and, 1.184
future changes, 27.007
guarantee companies, and, 30.002
inquiries by the DCE, 27.083–27.084
inspections
And see **Inspections**
appointment of inspectors, 27.011–27.019
concurrent investigations, 27.065–327.066
conduct, 27.028–27.033
costs, 27.061–27.064
introduction, 27.010
powers of inspectors, 27.034–27.050
report by inspector, 27.051–27.060
scope, 27.020–27.027
introduction, 27.001–27.002
ownership of shares and debentures
generally, 27.083–27.084
power of DCE to impose restrictions, 27.085–27.088
production of books and documents
consequences of failure to comply, 27.076–27.079
costs, 27.082
disclosure, 27.080–27.081
grounds for investigation, 27.070–27.074
introduction, 27.068–27.069
limits of procedure, 27.075
publication, 27.080–27.081
public limited companies, and, 29.124–29.129
regime architecture, 27.008–27.009
types, 27.008

Investment companies
alternative funds, 29.131–29.132
annual returns, 29.147
articles of association, 29.139–29.141
audits, 29.147
authorisation requirement, 29.136
authority of agents, 29.143
capacity, 29.143
constitutional documentation, 29.139–29.141
contracts, 29.143
financial statements, 29.147
formation, 29.134–29.138
generally, 29.131–29.133
incorporation, 29.142
maintenance of capital, 29.146
membership, 29.144–29.145
memorandum of association, 29.139–29.141
migration, 29.137–29.138
pre-emption rights, 29.145
registration, 29.134–29.138
share capital requirements, 29.135
shares, 29.144–29.145
UCITS, 29.131–29.132
winding up, 29.148–29.149

Irish company law
Companies Acts, 1.090–1.110
European Community dimension, 1.111–1.127
historical developments, 1.056–1.087
introduction, 1.001–1.003
overview, 1.088–1.127

Irish registered non-resident companies
carrying on an 'activity' in the State, and, 2.030
generally, 2.045–2.046

Joint and several liability
partnerships, and, 1.021

Joint stock companies
generally, 1.072–1.083
Judicial discretion
security for costs, and, 6.041–6.056
Judgment mortgages
registration of charges, and, 19.085
Jurisdiction of Companies Acts
external companies, and, 34.001
Just and equitable winding up
deadlock in management, 23.098–23.101
failure of substratum, 23.102–23.105
illegal objects, 23.106
instruments of fraud, 23.107–23.108
introduction, 23.091–23.092
public interest, 23.109–23.111
'quasi-partnership' cases, 23.093–23.097
shareholders' remedies, and, 11.002
Land
registration of charges, and, 19.052–19.058
Late registration of charges
discretion, 19.091
introduction, 19.090
Joplin proviso, 19.094–19.097
mere misstatements, and, 19.092–19.093
omissions, and, 19.092–19.093
priority, 19.100
winding up of company, and, 19.098–19.099
Law reform
CLRG reports, 1.165–1.170
draft Companies Bill, 1.171–1.186
Laying accounts before company at general meeting
individual accounts, and
Companies Acts, 17.249
IFRS, 17.249
Legal mortgages
And see **Mortgages**
generally, 18.030
security of shares, and, 9.035
Legal personality
artificial personality, 4.024–4.025
constitutional rights and duties, 4.068–4.075
contractual liability, 4.043–4.048
corporate litigation, and
contracts, 4.043–4.048
crime, 4.055–4.076
introduction, 4.042
torts, 4.049–4.053
corporate manslaughter, 4.059–4.060
corporate property
compensation, 4.040
generally, 4.032–4.037
insurable interests, 4.039
statutory tenancies, 4.041
transfer, 4.038
criminal liability
attribution principles, 4.063–4.067
constitutional rights and duties, 4.068–4.075
corporations as prosecutors, 4.056
introduction, 4.055
justification, 4.057–4.061
legal rights and duties, 4.076
practical limitations, 4.062
disregarding
acting on directions of disqualified person, 5.085
agency, 5.020–5.028
avoidance of future legal obligations, 5.049–5.050
breach of restriction or disqualification orders, 5.083–5.085
characterisation, 5.068–5.075
circumstances, 5.010–5.095
comfort letters, 5.017
Companies Acts provisions, 5.077–5.091
concealment of impropriety, 5.032–5.036
contract, by, 5.012–5.017
controllers of the company, and, 5.009
court orders, 5.065–5.067
culpability, 5.074
disqualification orders, 5.083–5.085
evasion of existing legal obligations, 5.039–5.048
failure to keep proper records, 5.087

Legal personality (contd)
failure to meet capital requirements, 5.086
failure to state correctly company's name, 5.081–5.082
fraudulent trading, 5.091
implied agency, 5.023–5.027
indemnities, 5.016
injunctions, 5.065–5.067
introduction, 5.001–5.007
licensing purposes, 5.075
liquidation of related companies, 5.090
manner, 5.008
mens rea, 5.074
mismanagement, 5.037–5.038
misuse of corporate form, 5.031–5.050
personal guarantees, 5.015
reckless trading, 5.091
reduction of number of members, 5.078–5.080
residence, 5.069–5.073
restriction orders, 5.083–5.085
single economic entity, 5.051–5.064
statutory provisions, 5.076–5.096
tax legislation, 5.092
torts, 5.018–5.019
trusts, 5.029–5.030
undisclosed agency, 5.028
unreasonably inaccurate declaration of solvency, 5.088–5.089
vicarious liability of directors and employees, 5.093–5.096
fictional personality, 4.024–4.025
generally, 4.023
groups of companies, and, 12.048–12.050
guarantee companies, and
disregarding, 30.039
introduction, 30.003
insurable interests, 4.039
legal rights and duties, 4.076
'lifting the veil', and, 5.002
privileges and obligations, 4.077–4.080
regulatory relationships, 4.077
Salomon's case, 4.026–4.031
Societas Europaea, 29.152
statutory tenancies, 4.041
suing and being sued
contracts, 4.043–4.048
crime, 4.055–4.076
introduction, 4.042
torts, 4.049–4.053
tortious liability, 4.049–4.053
transfer of property, 4.038
unlimited companies, 31.014
'veil of incorporation', and, 5.002
Legitimate expectations
oppression, and, 11.035–11.041
Letterheads
branches, and, 34.034–34.035
Liabilities
receivers, and, 20.074–20.078
Liability clause
alteration, 3.029–3.030
generally, 3.014–3.016
Licensing
disregarding legal personality, and, 5.075
Liens
bankers' liens, 19.027
booking deposits, 19.030
borrowing, and, 18.027
common law liens, 19.025
contractual liens, 19.031–19.032
equitable liens, 19.029–19.030
floating charges, and, 18.091
general liens, 19.026–19.028
introduction, 19.024
maintenance of capital, and, 10.110
purchasers' liens, 19.029
registration of charges, and, 19.024
shares, and, 8.21–8.22
solicitors' liens, 19.028
unpaid vendors' liens, 19.029
'Lifting the veil'
disregarding legal personality, and, 5.002
Limited companies
See also **Private limited companies**
conversion by re-registration, and
limited company to unlimited company, 33.009–33.013

Limited companies (contd)
multi-member private company to single-member private company, 33.016
PLC to private limited company, 33.014
private limited company to PLC, 33.015
single-member private company to multi-member private company, 33.017
unlimited company to private limited company, 33.002–33.007
Limited liability
generally, 4.081–4.084
Limited partnerships
See also **Partnerships**
generally, 1.026–1.029
Limited shareholders' agreements
See also **Shareholders' agreements**
generally, 3.117
Liquidation
banks
Central Bank's rights, 23.139–23.140
generally, 23.136–23.138
liquidation committee, 23.14223.
rules applicable to liquidators, 23.141
compulsory transfer of shares, and, 9.089
compulsory winding up
advertisement of petition, 23.055
annulment, 23.128
company, by, 23.038–23.039
contributories, 23.045–23.047
conversion from members' to creditors', 23.113–23.116
conversion from voluntary winding up, 23.117–23.124
corporate instruments of fraud, 23.107–23.108
creditors, 23.040–23.044
deadlock in management, 23.098–23.101
Director of Corporate Enforcement, 23.048
failure to commence business within a year of incorporation, 23.069
grounds, 23.067–23.112
hearing petition, 23.061–23.066
illegal objects, 23.106
inability of company to pay its debts, 23.071–23.090
introduction, 23.034
jurisdiction, 23.035–23.036
just and equitable, 23.091–23.111
locus standi to petition, 23.037–23.0050
members, 23.045–23.047
number of members is reduced below minimum, 23.070
oppression, 23.112
orders, 23.125–23.135
petition, 23.052–23.054
procedure, 23.051–23.066
public interest, 23.109–23.111
Registrar of Companies, 23.049
rescission, 23.129
respondent company's options, 23.056–23.057
special resolution to wind up company, 23.068
substitution of petitioner, 23.058–23.060
suspension of business for a year, 23.069
trustees of investment companies, 23.050
voiding dissolution following making of order, 23.130–23.135
creditors' voluntary winding up
committee of inspection, 23.031–23.032
creditors' meeting, 23.023–23.030
introduction, 23.017
members' general meeting, 23.020–23.022
statement of position of company's affairs, 23.018–23.019
termination, 23.033
dissolved companies, of, 26.024
distribution of assets
And see **Distribution of assets**
basic principles, 25.140

Liquidation (contd)
costs and expenses of winding up, 25.164–25.171
fixed mortgage or charge, 25.143–25.148
held in trust, 25.149
in specie, 25.196–25.198
monies that must be set off, 25.150–25.158
not available, 25.142–25.163
priorities, 25.182–25.196
proof of debts, 25.172–25.181
remuneration, costs and expenses, 25.165
stamp duty on monies received in realisation, 25.161–25.163
statutory basis, 25.141
super-preferential debts that are trust monies, 25.159–25.160
draft Companies Bill, and, 1.182
enforcement of judgments and orders, and, 6.076
financial institutions
Central Bank's rights, 23.139–23.140
generally, 23.136–23.138
liquidation committee, 23.14223.
rules applicable to liquidators, 23.141
introduction, 23.001
liquidators
And see **Liquidators**
appointment, 24.009–24.020
assistance to Irish liquidation abroad, 24.069
Council Regulation on Insolvency Proceedings, 24.059–24.068
duties, 24.020–24.026
foreign appointments, 24.056–24.058
introduction, 24.001
powers, 24.027–24.051
qualifications, 24.006–24.008
remuneration, 24.052–24.055
supervision, 24.070–24.071
types, 24.002–24.005
members' voluntary winding up
commencement, 23.014
declaration of solvency, 23.004–23.006
directors' personal liability, 23.010–23.011
introduction, 23.002–23.003
report of independent person, 23.007–23.009
resolution, 23.012–23.013
termination, 23.015–23.016
realisation of assets
And see **Realisation of assets**
civil arrest powers, 25.038–25.046
claims against contributories, 25.130–25.134
company books and records, 25.013
contribution by related companies to assets, 25.119–25.124
disclaiming onerous property, 25.058–25.065
disputed assets, 25.016
examination, 25.024–25.035
fraudulent dispositions of property, 25.103–25.109
fraudulent preference of creditors, 25.081–25.102
gathering information, 25.018–25.046
gathering in assets, 25.007–25.017
introduction, 25.001–25.003
invalidating floating charges, 25.110–25.118
liquidator's duty, 25.005
litigating to swell asset pool, 25.137–25.139
not beneficially owned by company, 25.014–25.015
obtaining books and papers, 25.023
officers' duty to assist, 25.006
overview, 25.004
pooling assets of related companies, 25.125–25.129
post-commencement dispositions, 25.065–25.080
post-examination transfer, 25.036–25.037
prohibiting litigation, execution, attachment or judgment, 25.052–25.057
property, 25.012

Liquidation (contd)
restraining disposal or removal, 25.047–25.051
swelling assets, 24.017
things in action, 25.012
transaction avoidance, 25.017
voidable transactions, 25.135–25.136
shareholders' remedies, and, 11.002
shareholders' rights, and, 8.085
Societas Europaea, and, 29.193–29.194
substantial property transactions, and, 16.038–16.040
voluntary winding up
conversion to compulsory winding up, 23.117–23.124
creditors', 23.017–23.033
members', 23.002–23.016

Liquidators
appointment
creditors' voluntary liquidators, 24.010–24.012
members' voluntary liquidators, 24.009
official liquidators, 24.013–24.015
provisional liquidators, 24.016–24.019
assistance to liquidators abroad
foreign liquidations in Ireland, 24.056–24.058
Irish liquidations abroad, 24.069
Council Regulation on Insolvency Proceedings, 24.059–24.068
court appointment, 24.004
creditors' voluntary liquidators
appointment, 24.010–24.012
generally, 24.003
powers, 24.043–24.045
directions from court, 24.051
duties
fiduciary, 24.021
introduction, 24.020
statutory, 24.022–24.026
fiduciary duties, 24.021
foreign liquidators
assistance in Ireland, 24.056–24.058
Council Regulation on Insolvency Proceedings, 24.059–24.068
introduction, 24.001
members' voluntary liquidators
appointment, 24.009
generally, 24.003
powers, 24.043–24.050
official liquidators
appointment, 24.013–24.015
generally, 24.004
powers, 24.028–24.040
powers
directions from court, 24.051
introduction, 24.027
official liquidators, 24.028–24.040
provisional liquidators, 24.041–24.042
restrictions on exercise, 24.046–24.050
voluntary liquidators, 24.043–24.045
provisional liquidators
appointment, 24.016–24.019
generally, 24.005
powers, 24.041–24.042
qualifications, 24.006–24.008
receivers, and, 20.004
registration-type offences, and, 28.050
removal
creditors' voluntary liquidators, 24.010–24.012
members' voluntary liquidators, 24.009
official liquidators, 24.013–24.015
provisional liquidators, 24.016–24.019
remuneration, 24.052–24.055
report to the DCE, 24.025–24.026
seeking directions from court, 24.051
statutory duties
creditors, to, 24.023–24.024
members, to, 24.022
report to the DCE, 24.025–24.026
supervision by DCE, 24.070–24.071
types
introduction, 24.002
official liquidators, 24.004
provisional liquidators, 24.005
voluntary liquidators, 24.003

Liquidators (contd)
voluntary liquidators
appointment, 24.009–24.012
generally, 24.003
powers, 24.043–24.050
Loans etc to directors
account and indemnity, 16.110–16.112
anti-avoidance, 16.062–16.063
bodies corporate that are connected persons
body corporate controlled by body corporate controlled by a director, 16.019
'control', 16.011–16.013
generally, 16.010
'interested in', 16.014–16.018
subsidiary controlled by a director, 16.020
summary, 16.021
business transactions, 16.095–16.097
connected guarantees, 16.069
connected persons
bodies corporate, 16.010
natural persons, 16.006–16.009
summary, 16.021
connected security, 16.070
consequences of contravention
account and indemnity, 16.110–16.112
acquisition 'for value', 16.108
actual notice, 16.105–16.108
bona fide, 16.105–16.109
criminal offences, 16.118–16.120
generally, 16.100–16.102
indemnity, 16.104
personal liability, 16.113–16.117
restitutio in integrum, 16.103
credit transactions, 16.067–16.068
criminal offences, 16.118–16.120
de minimis exception, 16.075–16.079
directors
generally, 16.004–16.005
summary, 16.021
directors' expenses, 16.093–16.094
exceptions to general prohibition
applicability to prohibited transactions and arrangements, 16.074
business transactions, 16.095–16.097
de minimis, 16.075–16.079
directors' expenses, 16.093–16.094
groups, 16.089–16.092
introduction, 16.073
validation procedure, 16.080–16.088
'for' a director etc, 16.071
general prohibition, 16.060–16.061
group exception, 16.089–16.092
guarantees, 16.069
holding company directors
generally, 16.004–16.005
summary, 16.021
indirect activity, 16.062–16.063
introduction, 16.055–16.059
loans, 16.065
natural persons that are connected persons
generally, 16.006–16.009
summary, 16.021
overview, 16.001–16.002
personal liability, 16.113–16.117
primary prohibition, 16.058
prohibited transactions and arrangements, 16.064–16.072
prohibition on indirect activity, 16.062–16.063
quasi-loans, 16.066
regulated persons
connected persons, 16.006–16.020
directors, 16.004–16.005
holding company directors, 16.004–16.005
introduction, 16.003
summary, 16.021
restitutio in integrum, 16.103
security, 16.070
shadow directors, 16.021
validation procedure
consequences of swearing declaration based on unreasonable grounds, 16.088
generally, 16.080–16.081
independent person's report, 16.087

Loans etc to directors (contd)
special resolution, 16.082–16.083
statutory declaration of solvency, 16.084–16.086
voidability, 16.100–16.109
Locus standi
compulsory winding up, and
company, 23.038–23.039
contributories, 23.045–23.047
creditors, 23.040–23.044
Director of Corporate Enforcement, 23.048
introduction, 23.037
members, 23.045–23.047
Registrar of Companies, 23.049
trustees of investment companies, 23.050
examinership, and, 22.011–22.017
oppression, and, 11.042–11.052
restoration to register after failure to file annual return, and, 26.036–26.038
restriction orders, and, 28.088–28.089
s 251 CA 1990, and, 15.142
schemes of arrangement, and, 21.017
Maintenance of capital
acquisition by company of own shares
common law prohibition, 10.014
exceptions to statutory prohibition, 10.017–10.035
forfeiture of shares, and, 10.022
fully paid shares for no consideration, 10.018
introduction, 10.013
Pt.XI CA 1990, under, 10.023–10.035
redemption of shares, and, 10.019
reduction of capital, and, 10.020
remedial court orders, and, 10.021
statutory prohibition, 10.015–10.016
acquisition of shares in holding company, 10.036–10.040
assisting purchase of company's own shares
'any transaction', 10.051–10.052
civil consequences, 10.049–10.057
criminal consequences, 10.048
dividends, 10.078–10.083
financial assistance', 10.058–10.065
general prohibition, 10.047
introduction, 10.046
lawful liabilities, 10.078–10.083
miscellaneous, 10.084
'notice', 10.053–10.057
private companies, and, 10.047
validation procedure, 10.066–10.077
voidability, 10.049–10.050
warranties and covenants, 10.064
'whitewash' procedure, 10.066–10.077
capital reduction
generally, 10.085
s 10(6) CA 1963, under, 10.086
s 205(3) CA 1963, under, 10.087
s 15 C(A)A 1983, under, 10.088
consequences of incorporation, and, 4.092
distributions
determining availability of profits, 10.096–10.097
disguised distributions, 10.099–10.102
generally, 10.089
liability for unlawful payments, 10.103–10.104
meaning, 10.090–10.092
'member' qua member, to, 10.098
'profits available for distribution', 10.093–10.095
dividend payments, 10.089–10.104
forfeiture of unpaid or partly paid shares, 10.106–10.107
guarantee companies, and, 30.042–30.044
introduction, 10.001
issue of shares at a discount, 10.108–10.109
issue of shares at a premium, 10.111–10.112
liens on shares, 10.110
miscellaneous rules, 10.105–10.112
overview of rules, 10.011–10.012
private companies, and, 10.004–10.010
public limited companies
acquisition of their own shares, 29.068–29.078

Maintenance of capital (contd)
buybacks, 29.068–29.073
distributions, 29.079–29.080
dividend payments, 29.079–29.080
financial assistance in purchase of their own shares, 29.077–29.078
introduction, 29.067
investment companies, 29.146
market purchase procedure, 29.068–29.069
off-market purchase procedure, 29.068–29.069
overseas purchase procedure, 29.068–29.069
purchase of their own shares, 29.068–29.078
reduction of capital, 29.081–29.082
rationale of rules, 10.002–10.003
redemption of shares
generally, 10.041–10.045
s 65 CA 1963, under, 10.019
reduction of capital
generally, 10.085
s 10(6) CA 1963, under, 10.086
s 205(3) CA 1963, under, 10.087
s 15 C(A)A 1983, under, 10.088
'share capital', 10.001
subsidiaries, and, 12.042
unlimited companies, and, 31.021–31.022

Maintenance of registers
consequences of incorporation, and, 4.092

Management
building societies, and, 1.043

Management meetings
Societas Europaea, and, 29.185

Mandamus
failure or refusal to register companies, and, 4.003

Managing directors
generally, 13.034–13.035
ostensible authority, and, 7.114

Mareva injunctions
examinership, and, 22.063

Market abuse
administrative sanctions, 32.114
admission to trading, 32.062
background, 32.058–32.060
civil sanctions, 32.115–32.117
competent authority, 32.066
criminal sanctions, 32.113
disclosure obligations
introduction, 32.104
managers' transactions, of, 32.105–32.107
suspicious transactions, of, 32.108–32.112
elements
insider dealing, 32.068–32.098
introduction, 32.067
market manipulation, 32.100–32.103
EU law, and, 32.058
excluded transactions, 32.064
'financial instrument', 32.065
FSAP, and, 32.058
generally, 32.061–32.064
insider dealing
common law, at, 32.098
MAD, under, 32.068–32.092
Part V of CA 1990, under, 32.093–32.097
insider dealing under MAD
CESR guidelines, 32.073
exceptions, 32.083–32.084
fair presentation of recommendations about instruments or issuers, 32.092
financial instruments, 32.075
information not available to the public, 32.080
information of a 'precise nature', 32.074
information relating to financial instruments, 32.075
innocent insider dealing, 32.081–32.082
'inside information', 32.071–32.073
insider lists, 32.089–32.091
introduction, 32.068
liability for breach, 32.113–32.117
notification obligations, 32.104–32.112
persons to whom Reg 5 applies, 32.069–32.070

Market abuse (contd)
'precise nature', 32.074
prerequisites, 32.072
price sensitivity, 32.076–32.079
public disclosure, 32.085–32.088
selective disclosure, 32.085–32.088
shadow directors, 32.070
instruments admitted to trading, 32.062
introduction, 32.058–32.059
legislative framework, 32.059–32.060
liability for breach
administrative sanctions, 32.114
civil sanctions, 32.115–32.117
criminal sanctions, 32.113
managers' transactions, 32.105–32.107
Market Abuse Directive
application, 32.061–32.064
background, 32.058–32.060
competent authority, 32.066
elements, 32.067–32.103
insider dealing, 32.068–32.098
liability for breach, 32.113–32.117
market manipulation, 32.100–32.103
notification obligations, 32.104–32.112
relevant financial instruments, 32.065
sanctions for breach, 32.113–32.117
Market Abuse Regulation, 32.060
market manipulation
accepted market practices, 32.103
definition, 32.100–32.102
exceptions, 32.103
introduction, 32.099
liability for breach, 32.113–32.117
notification obligations, 32.104–32.112
monetary policy, and, 32.064
notification obligations
introduction, 32.104
managers' transactions, of, 32.105–32.107
suspicious transactions, of, 32.108–32.112
price sensitivity, 32.076–32.079
public debt management, and, 32.064
relevant financial instruments, 32.065
sanctions for breach
administrative sanctions, 32.114
civil sanctions, 32.115–32.117
criminal sanctions, 32.113
secondary markets, and, 32.062
suspicious transactions, 32.108–32.112
territorial jurisdiction, 32.063
Market manipulation
accepted market practices, 32.103
administrative sanctions, 32.114
background, 32.058–32.060
civil sanctions, 32.115–32.117
competent authority, 32.066
criminal sanctions, 32.113
definition, 32.100–32.102
disclosure obligations
introduction, 32.104
managers' transactions, of, 32.105–32.107
suspicious transactions, of, 32.108–32.112
EU law, and, 32.058
exceptions, 32.1039
excluded transactions, 32.064
'financial instrument', 32.065
FSAP, and, 32.058
generally, 32.061–32.064
instruments admitted to trading, 32.062
introduction, 32.09
legislative framework, 32.059–32.060
liability for breach
administrative sanctions, 32.114
civil sanctions, 32.115–32.117
criminal sanctions, 32.113
managers' transactions, 32.105–32.107
monetary policy, and, 32.064
notification obligations
introduction, 32.104
managers' transactions, of, 32.105–32.107
suspicious transactions, of, 32.108–32.112
price sensitivity, 32.076–32.079
public debt management, and, 32.064
relevant financial instruments, 32.065
sanctions for breach
administrative sanctions, 32.114
civil sanctions, 32.115–32.117

Market manipulation (contd)
criminal sanctions, 32.113
secondary markets, and, 32.062
suspicious transactions, 32.108–32.112
territorial jurisdiction, 32.063
Medium-sized companies
abridged accounts, 17.270–17.276
auditor's reports, 17.276
balance sheet, 17.270–17.272
definition, 17.267–17.269
directors' statement, 17.275
profit and loss account, 17.273–17.274
Meetings
articles of association, and, 3.047–3.049
building societies, and, 1.044
directors' meetings
adjournment, 14.117
business to be conducted, 14.112
committees, 14.122–14.123
conduct, 14.109–14.111
convening, 14.105–14.108
introduction, 14.102–14.103
minutes, 14.118–14.121
notice, 14.105–14.108
quorum, 14.113–14.115
regulation, 14.104
resolutions, 14.124–14.128
voting, 14.124–14.128
guarantee companies, and
consider annual report, to, 30.055–30.057
consider house rules, to, 30.060
consider service charges, to, 30.058–30.059
fair and equitable voting rights, 30.051–30.054
generally, 30.049–30.050
voting rights, 30.051–30.054
introduction, 14.001–14.003
members' meetings
adjournment, 14.058–14.060
annual general meetings, 14.006–14.014
business to be conducted, 14.050–14.054
extraordinary general meetings, 14.015–14.032
introduction, 14.004–14.005
minutes, 14.077–14.080
notice, 14.033–14.049
postponement, 14.058–14.060
public companies, and, 14.002
quorum, 14.055–14.057
resolutions, 14.081–14.101
voting, 14.061–14.076
public limited companies
agenda items, 29.102–29.103
electronic participation, 29.105
equal treatment right, 29.107
generally, 29.094–29.097
notice requirements, 29.098, 29.100–29.101
participation requirements, 29.104
poll information, 29.111
proxies, 29.108–29.109
questions, 29.106
resolutions, 29.102–29.103
Shareholders' Rights Directive, and, 29.099–29.111
UK Corporate Governance Code, and, 29.112–29.114
voting, 29.104
voting by correspondence, 29.110
schemes of arrangement, and
classes of members, 21.035–21.038
constituting proper classes, 21.029–21.034
introduction, 21.024–21.025
provision of information, 21.039–21.042
repeat applications, 21.048
responsibility for constituting proper classes, 21.026–21.028
shareholders' rights and interests, 21.035–21.038
voting, 21.043–21.047
Societas Europaea, and
general meetings, 29.182–29.184
management meetings, 29.185
unlimited companies, and, 31.003
Members
directors' duties, and, 15.018

Members' meetings
adjournment, 14.058–14.060
amendments to model articles, and, 3.047–3.049
annual general meetings
consequences where not held, 14.012–14.013
frequency, 14.006
generally, 14.006–14.007
Ministerial direction to call, 14.011
notice, 14.033–14.049
place, 14.010
purpose, 14.008–14.009
single-member private limited companies, 14.014
'special business', 14.009
articles of association, and, 3.047–3.049
business to be conducted
amendment of resolution, 14.054
basis for need for resolutions, 14.053
introduction, 14.050
other matters, 14.053–14.054
special business, 14.051
special resolutions, 14.052
creditors' voluntary winding up, and, 23.020–23.022
extraordinary general meetings
directors, 14.016-14.018
generally, 14.015
notice, 14.033–14.049
order of the court, 14.024–14.031
requisition of qualified members, 14.019–14.023
retiring auditor, 14.032
introduction, 14.004–14.005
minutes, 14.077–14.080
notice
business to be conducted, 14.050–14.054
introduction, 14.033
periods, 14.040–14.049
notice of business to be conducted
amendment of resolution, 14.054
basis for need for resolutions, 14.053
introduction, 14.050
other matters, 14.053–14.054
special business, 14.051
special resolutions, 14.052
notice periods
accidental omission, 14.048
extended, 14.044–14.047
short notice, 14.041–14.043
standard notice, 14.040
summary of provisions, 14.049
postponement, 14.058–14.060
public limited companies, and, 14.002
quorum, 14.055–14.057
resolutions
'Buchanan principle', 14.093
business to be conducted, and, 14.052–14.054
filing, 14.100–14.101
introduction, 14.081
ordinary resolutions, 14.082–14.083
single-member private companies, 14.088–14.089
special resolutions, 14.084–14.087
unanimous consent of members to course of action, 14.093–14.099
written resolutions, 14.090–14.092
schemes of arrangement, and
classes of members, 21.035–21.038
constituting proper classes, 21.029–21.034
introduction, 21.024–21.025
provision of information, 21.039–21.042
repeat applications, 21.048
responsibility for constituting proper classes, 21.026–21.028
shareholders' rights and interests, 21.035–21.038
voting, 21.043–21.047
short notice
generally, 14.041
special resolutions, 14.042–14.043
special business, 14.051
special resolutions, 14.052
standard notice, 14.040
voting
introduction, 14.061
'one member one vote', 14.062–14.066
one vote per share, 14.062–14.066

Members' meetings (contd)
poll, on, 14.067–14.071
proxy, by, 14.074–14.076
representation, by, 14.072–14.073
Members' voluntary winding up
commencement, 23.014
declaration of solvency, 23.004–23.006
directors' personal liability, 23.010–23.011
introduction, 23.002–23.003
liquidators
appointment, 24.009
generally, 24.003
powers, 24.043–24.050
report of independent person, 23.007–23.009
resolution, 23.012–23.013
termination, 23.015–23.016
Membership of private companies
'agree to become a member'
definition of 'member', and, 8.004
estoppel, 8.008
introduction, 8.006
membership agreements, 8.007
overview, 8.001
agreements, 8.007
beneficial interests
generally, 8.025–8.030
limits, 8.032
protection, 8.031
cesser, 8.033
companies
holding companies, 8.011
introduction, 8.010–8.016
s 32 CA 1963 restriction, 8.012–8.013
s 224 CA 1990 restriction, 8.014–8.016
subsidiary companies, 8.011
definition of 'member'
introduction, 8.004
other persons, 8.006
subscribers, 8.005
estoppel, 8.008
generally, 8.003
holding companies, 8.011
introduction, 8.001–8.002
meaning, 8.004–8.008
'member'
introduction, 8.004
other persons, 8.006
subscribers, 8.005
membership agreements, 8.007
natural persons, 8.009
persons entitled to
companies, 8.010–8.016
natural persons, 8.009
rectification of register
company, by, 8.022
court, by, 8.023–8.024
register of members
beneficial interests, 8.025–8.032
changes in particulars, 8.021
definition of 'member', and, 8.004
form, 8.017
inspection, 8.018
introduction, 8.006
legal significance of particulars, 8.020
location, 8.017
overview, 8.001
rectification, 8.022–8.024
registrable particulars, 8.019
subscribers of the memorandum
definition of 'member', and, 8.004
generally, 8.005
overview, 8.001
subsidiary companies, 8.011
Membership of public limited companies
generally, 29.039–29.040
introduction, 29.038
investment companies, 29.144–29.145
Memorandum of association
additional clauses, 3.021
alteration
capital clause, 3.031–3.036
generally, 3.022
liability clause, 3.029–3.030
name clause, 3.023–3.025
non-compulsory clauses, 3.037
objects clause, 3.026–3.028
articles of association, and, 3.088
association clause, 3.020

Memorandum of association (contd)
capital clause
alteration, 3.031–3.036
increasing share capital, 3.032
generally, 3.017–3.019
reducing share capital, 3.033–3.036
compulsory clauses
association clause, 3.020
capital clause, 3.017–3.019
introduction, 3.004–3.005
liability clause, 3.014–3.016
name clause, 3.006–3.011
objects clause, 3.012–3.013
subscription clause, 3.020
construction of, 3.089–3.091
form, 3.004
generally, 3.003–3.037
guarantee companies, and
alterations, 30.031–30.034
distributions of income and property, 30.025–30.029
generally, 30.013
guarantee clause, 30.024
introduction, 3.004
name clause, 30.014–30.018
objects clause, 30.019–30.23
other clauses, 30.030
importance, 3.002
increasing share capital, 3.032
introduction, 3.001
liability clause
alteration, 3.029–3.030
generally, 3.014–3.016
meaning, 3.003
name clause
alteration, 3.023–3.025
generally, 3.006–3.011
non-compulsory clauses
alteration, 3.037
generally, 3.021
objects clause
alteration, 3.026–3.028
generally, 3.012–3.013
prescribed form, 3.004
public limited companies
alterations, 29.032
generally, 29.028–29.029
investment companies, 29.139–29.141
reducing share capital, 3.033–3.036
reference document, 3.005
single-member private companies, and, 3.003
Societas Europaea, and, 29.171
subscription clause, 3.020
Table B, 3.004
Table D, 3.004
Table E, 3.004
unlimited companies, and
generally, 31.005–31.008
introduction, 3.004

Mens rea
disregarding legal personality, and, 5.074

Mental incapacity
compulsory transfer of shares, and, 9.089

Merger accounting
disclosures, 17.195
generally, 17.192–17.194
introduction, 17.190

Mergers
accounting
disclosures, 17.195
generally, 17.192–17.194
introduction, 17.190
draft Companies Bill, and, 1.180
share transfers, and
generally, 9.032–9.033
introduction, 9.001
Societas Europaea, and, 29.158–29.163

Migration procedure
public limited companies, and,
generally, 29.026
investment companies, 29.137–29.138

Ministerial direction to call
annual general meetings, and, 14.011

Minority shareholdings
reduction of capital, and, 10.087
shareholders' agreements, and, 3.114
valuation of shares, and, 9.122–9.125

Minutes
directors' meetings, and, 14.118–14.121
members' meetings, and, 14.077–14.080
Misfeasance
directors' duties, and, 15.149–15.151
generally, 15.149–15.151
Mismanagement
disregarding legal personality, and, 5.037–5.038
Mortgages
And see **Borrowing**
creation, 18.033–18.034
definition, 18.032–18.037
equitable, 18.031
introduction, 18.030
legal, 18.030
registration
charger company's obligations, 19.107
conclusiveness of certificate, 19.011–19.020
consequences of non-registration, 19.006–19.010
disguised registrable charges, 19.071–19.084
introduction, 19.001
judgment mortgages, 19.085
late applications, 19.090–19.100
non-registrable security interests, 19.021–19.041
procedure, 19.101–19.107
property outside of the State, and, 19.086–19.089
register of charges, 19.002–19.005
registrable charges, 19.042–19.070
registrable particulars, 19.102–19.104
retention of title clauses, 19.071–19.084
satisfaction of charges, 19.105–19.106
security of shares, and, 9.035
types, 18.030–18.031
Multi-unit developments
guarantee companies, and, 30.005–30.006
Name clause
alteration, 3.023–3.025
generally, 3.006–3.011
guarantee companies, and
dispensing with word 'limited', 30.015–30.017
introduction, 30.014
'owners' management company' requirement, 30.018
National Asset Management Agency (NAMA)
building societies, and, 1.036
examinership, and, 22.028
receivers, and
appointment, 20.022
generally, 20.022
powers, rights and obligations, 20.023
status, 20.024
Negative pledge clauses
competition law, and, 18.085–18.086
examinership, and, 22.075–22.076
generally, 18.079
priority of accompanied charges, 18.080–18.084
'No par'
shares, and, 8.045
'No partnership' clause
shareholders' agreements, and, 3.116
Nominal value
shares, and, 8.044–8.045
Nominee directors
directors' duties, and, 15.045–15.048
generally, 13.040
reckless trading, and, 15.111
Non-cash consideration
allotment of shares, and, 8.062–8.063
Non-executive directors
directors' duties, and, 15.042–15.044
generally, 13.038–13.039
Non-residents
security for costs, and, 6.015
Notice of directors' meetings
generally, 14.105–14.108
Notice of members' meetings
accidental omission, 14.048
business to be conducted
amendment of resolution, 14.054

Notice of members' meetings (contd)
basis for need for resolutions, 14.053
introduction, 14.050
other matters, 14.053–14.054
special business, 14.051
special resolutions, 14.052
extended notice, 14.044–14.047
introduction, 14.033
periods
accidental omission, 14.048
extended, 14.044–14.047
short notice, 14.041–14.043
standard notice, 14.040
summary of provisions, 14.049
short notice
generally, 14.041
special resolutions, 14.042–14.043
standard notice, 14.040
Objects clause
alteration
generally, 3.026–3.028
reduction of capital, and, 10.086
shareholders' remedies, and, 11.003
capacity, and
Bell Houses clause, 7.053
generally, 7.045–7.046
independent objects clause, 7.052
introduction, 3.012
judicial construction, 7.049–7.053
main objects rule, 7.051
generally, 3.012–3.013
guarantee companies, and
ancillary objects, 30.021
generally, 30.019
main object, 30.020
powers, 30.022–30.023
subsidiary object, 30.021
reduction of capital, and, 10.086
Off balance sheet items
group accounts, and, 17.212
individual accounts, and
Companies Acts, 17.126
IFRS, 17.142
Offences for breach
branches, and, 34.041
external companies, and, 34.026
Officers
consequences, 13.006–13.008
directors
alternate directors, 13.042
appointment, 13.025–13.032
assignee directors, 13.043
associate directors, 13.044
automatic removal, 13.076
caretaker directors, 13.041
cessation of role, 13.072–13.094
Chairmen, 13.036
compensation on loss of office, 13.086–13.094
consent to act, 13.026–13.027
de facto directors, 13.045–13.054
debarred persons, 13.018
delegation of managerial power, 13.126–13.143
disclosure obligations, 13.095–13.118
disqualification, 13.021
disqualified persons, 13.017
duties, 15.001–15.151
EEA-resident, 13.012–13.015
executive directors, 13.037
first appointment, 13.028
generally, 13.009–13.010
interests in shares and debentures, 13.100–13.118
managing directors, 13.034–13.035
minimum number, 13.011
natural persons, 13.016
nominee directors, 13.040
non-executive directors, 13.038–13.039
number of directorships, 13.022–13.024
persons debarred, 13.018
persons restricted, 13.020
qualification shareholding, 13.019
qualifications, 13.017
register of directors, 13.096–13.099
register of interests, 13.116
removal, 13.075–13.082
remuneration, 13.070–13.071
resignation, 13.073
restriction orders, and, 13.020

Officers (contd)
retirement by rotation, 13.074
shadow directors, 13.055–13.069
subsequent appointment, 13.029–13.032
types, 13.033–13.069
disqualification, 13.007
draft Companies Bill, and, 1.176
generally, 13.003–13.005
introduction, 13.001–13.002
reckless trading, and, 15.110
secretaries
appointment, 13.120
cessation, 13.120
disclosure obligations, 13.095–13.118
duties, 15.152–15.160
functions, 13.122–13.124
general requirement, 13.119
interests in shares and debentures, 13.100–13.118
introduction, 13.119
register of interests, 13.116
register of secretary, 13.096–13.099
remuneration, 13.121
status, 13.121

Official liquidators
appointment, 24.013–24.015
generally, 24.004
powers, 24.028–24.040

On-the-spot fines
Director of Corporate Enforcement, and, 29.020
generally, 28.041–28.042

'One member one vote'
members' meetings, and, 14.062–14.066

Operation of law
share transfers, and
bankruptcy, 9.031
death, 9.026–9.030
introduction, 9.025
overview, 9.001
merger, 9.032–9.033

Oppression
abuse of process, 11.053–11.056
'affairs of the company', 11.033–11.034
alteration of constitutional documents, 11.085
cancellation of transactions, 11.084
company's position, 11.057–11.059
compensatory damages, and, 11.074–11.076
contracting-out of provision, 11.091
contrast with unfairly prejudicial remedy, 11.088–11.090
costs, 11.087
delay in prosecution, 11.053–11.056
ending matters complained of, 11.073–11.086
exclusion from management, 11.025–11.026
fraudulent transactions, 11.017–11.019
futile orders, and, 11.078
in camera applications, 11.060–11.066
introduction, 11.006–11.007
isolated acts, 11.016
'legitimate expectations', 11.035–11.041
locus standi, 11.042–11.052
management, 11.020–11.024
members of the company, 11.044–11.051
nature of remedy, 11.008–11.009
need not be qua member, 11.014–11.015
non-consultation with shareholders, 11.027
'oppression', 11.010–11.028
personal representatives of deceased members, 11.052
'powers of directors', 11.033–11.034
purchase of petitioner's shares, 11.080–11.081
purchase of respondent's shares, 11.082
purchase of shares by company, 11.083
quasi-partnership companies, 11.035–11.041
restraining removal of shareholder director, 11.067–11.072
technical oppression, 11.028
test, 11.011–11.013

Oppression (contd)
unlawful transactions, 11.017–11.019
variation of transactions, 11.084
Oral contracts
And see **Corporate contracts**
generally, 7.005–7.006
Ordinary creditors
examinership, and, 22.066–22.068
Ordinary list
incorporation, and, 2.018
Ordinary resolutions
generally, 14.082–14.083
Ordinary shares
See also **Shares**
generally, 8.101
Ostensible authority
actual authority of representor, 7.107
board of directors, 7.112–7.113
chairman of the board, 7.115
company secretary, 7.117
contract within permitted capacity and authority of company, 7.109–7.110
corporate representations, 7.104–7.106
directors, 7.116
generally, 7.101–7.103
managing director, 7.114
particular corporate organs, of, 7.111–7.118
partnerships, and, 1.022
reliance on representation, 7.108
sole member of single-member private company, 7.118
Ownership of shares and debentures
investigations, and
generally, 27.083–27.084
power of DCE to impose restrictions, 27.085–27.088
Parent undertakings
annual accounts, and, 17.017
generally, 12.030–12.031
Participating influence
groups of companies, and, 12.039–12.040
Partnerships
actual authority, 1.022
advantages, 1.030
apparent authority, 1.022
dealings inter se, 1.023–1.024
dealings with outsiders, 1.021–1.022
definition, 1.015–1.020
disadvantages, 1.031
dissolution, 1.025
fiduciary relationship, 1.024
firm name, 1.018
generally, 1.014–1.031
joint and several liability, 1.021
legislative framework, 1.016
limited partnerships, 1.026–1.029
management, 1.020
membership, 1.015
nature, 1.015
number of partners, 1.017
ostensible authority, 1.022
partnership property, 1.019
profit sharing, 1.023
registration, and, 1.015
Pensions
compensation on loss of office, and, 13.092
Perpetual succession
generally, 4.086
Personal guarantees
disregarding legal personality, and, 5.015
Personal liability
directors' loans, and, 16.113–16.117
Personal representatives
oppression, and, 11.052
Personal responsibility
reckless trading, and, 15.126–15.127
Personal rights
directors' fiduciary duties, and, 8.091
generally, 8.087–8.088
s 25 contracts, and, 8.089–8.090
shareholders' remedies, and
distinguishing actions for reflective loss, 11.103–11.107
distinguishing corporate rights, 11.100–11.102
generally, 11.004
statute, under, 8.092
'Piercing the veil'
disregarding legal personality, and, 5.002

Place of business
external companies, and
conducting a business, 34.007
criteria in determining establishment, 34.008–34.009
distinguished from branch, 34.011–34.012
incidental to company's main business, 34.010
introduction, 34.006
Pledges
borrowing, and, 18.026
registration of charges, and, 19.033
Polls
members' meetings, and, 14.067–14.071
shareholders' rights, and, 8.083
'Pooling agreements'
shareholders' agreements, and, 3.114
Postponement
members' meetings, and, 14.058–14.060
Pre-emption rights
allotment of shares, and, 8.056–8.059
beneficial interests in shares, and, 9.080–9.083
enforceability, 9.084–9.086
generally, 9.069–9.072
judicial construction, 9.076–9.079
need, 9.073–9.075
public limited companies, and
generally, 29.044
investment companies, 29.145
sample clause, 9.070
Preference shares
See also **Shares**
capital, as to, 8.108–8.109
dividend, as to, 8.103–8.107
generally, 8.102
voting, as to, 8.110
Preferential creditors
examinership, and, 22.066–22.068
schemes of arrangement, and, 21.009–21.011
Pre-incorporation contracts
generally, 7.035–7.036
liability of agents, 7.041–7.042
s 37 CA 1963, 7.037–7.044
Premium
allotment of shares, and, 8.065–8.067
maintenance of capital, and, 10.111–10.112
valuation of shares, and, 9.121
Private companies
acquisition of corporate status
certificate of incorporation, 4.002–4.007
cesser, 4.020
impeachment of incorporation, 4.012–4.019
introduction, 4.001
nullity provisions, 4.008–4.010
registration, 4.002–4.003
closely-held private companies, 1.150
'Companies Acts', 1.163–1.164
'company', 1.156–1.162
concessions to, 1.132
constitutional documentation
And see **Constitution**
articles of association, 3.038–3.091
introduction, 3.001–3.002
memorandum of association, 3.003–3.037
section 25 contract, 3.092–3.105
shareholders' agreements, 3.106–3.128
context, in
forms of business organisation, 1.004–1.055
historical outline, 1.056–1.087
introduction, 1.001–1.003
overview of Irish company law, 1.088–1.127
definition, 1.133–1.142
family owned private companies, 1.149
incorporation
And see **Incorporation**
carrying on an 'activity' in the State, 2.030
consequences, 4.001–4.092
delivery of particulars to Revenue Commissioners, 2.034
determination by registrar, 2.031–2.033
directors, 2.038

Private companies (contd)
- disregarding separate legal personality, 5.001–5.096
- documentation, 3.001–3.128
- existing business, of, 2.004–2.007
- generally, 2.008–2.016
- incidental obligations, 2.035–2.044
- introduction, 2.001
- Irish registered non-resident companies, 2.045–2.046
- methods, 2.017–2.023
- purpose, 2.002–2.003
- secretary, 2.038
- steps, 2.024–2.029

introduction, 1.001–1.003
law reform
- CLRG reports, 1.165–1.170
- draft Companies Bill, 1.171–1.186

legislative concessions, 1.132
membership
- *And see* **Membership**
- cesser, 8.033
- generally, 8.003
- introduction, 8.001–8.002
- meaning, 8.004–8.008
- persons entitled to, 8.009–8.016
- register, 8.017–8.032

public companies, and, 1.128–1.131
quasi-partnership private companies, 1.151–1.154
separate legal personality
- artificial personality, 4.024–4.025
- constitutional rights and duties, 4.068–4.075
- contractual liability, 4.043–4.048
- corporate manslaughter, 4.059–4.060
- corporate property, 4.032–4.041
- criminal liability, 4.055–4.076
- disregarding, 5.001–5.096
- fictional personality, 4.024–4.025
- generally, 4.023
- insurable interests, 4.039
- legal rights and duties, 4.076
- privileges and obligations, 4.077–4.080
- regulatory relationships, 4.077
- Salomon's case, 4.026–4.031
- statutory tenancies, 4.041
- suing and being sued, 4.042–4.076
- tortious liability, 4.049–4.053

single-member private limited company, 1.143–1.148
unconnected membership, with, 1.155

Privileges and obligations
- separate legal personality, and, 4.077–4.080

Pro rata basis
- valuation of shares, and, 9.121

Production of books and documents
- investigations, and
  - consequences of failure to comply, 27.076–27.079
  - costs, 27.082
  - disclosure, 27.080–27.081
  - grounds for investigation, 27.070–27.074
  - introduction, 27.068–27.069
  - limits of procedure, 27.075
  - publication, 27.080–27.081

Professional advice
- directors, and, 13.057

Profit and loss account (Companies Acts)
- accounting policies, 17.099
- approval, 17.213
- charges payable, 17.106
- depreciation, 17.102–17.103
- diminution in value of fixed assets, 17.102
- directors' emoluments, 17.105
- extraordinary income or charges, 17.108
- foreign currencies, 17.109
- formats, 17.060–17.068
- generally, 17.059
- improvements in value of written down fixed assets, 17.104
- interest payable, 17.106
- medium-sized companies, and, 17.273–17.274
- movements, 17.110
- notes, 17.098–17.110
- obligation to circulate, 17.243–17.245

Profit and loss account (Companies Acts) (contd)
reconciliation of depreciation figures, 17.108
signature, 17.213
staff number and remuneration, 17.101
tax, 17.107
turnover, 17.100
Profits available for distribution
distributions, and, 10.093–10.095
Promoters
definition, 15.161
fiduciary duties
breach, 15.164–15.169
generally, 15.162–15.163
generally, 15.161
transactions with the company, 15.170
Property
partnerships, and, 1.019
Profit sharing
partnerships, and, 1.023
Prospectus
administrative sanctions, 32.057
admission to trading on a regulated market, 32.025–32.027
approval, 32.026
base format, 32.031
civil liability
common law, at, 32.048–32.050
equity, in, 32.047
introduction, 32.044
statute, under, 32.045–32.046
Central Bank sanctions, 32.057
content, 32.028–32.031
criminal liability
false statements and omissions, 32.055
introduction, 32.051
Irish prospectus law offences, 32.052–32.054
other offences, 32.056
drawdown format, 32.029
'eligible counterparties, 32.021
EU law, and
generally, 32.008
introduction, 23.002
excluded securities, 32.012–32.014
exempt offerings
generally, 32.018–32.019
offers of exempted securities, 32.023–32.024
offers to qualified investors, 32.020–32.022
false particulars
common law, at, 32.048–32.050
equity, in, 32.047
introduction, 32.044
statute, under, 32.045–32.046
false statements and omissions, 32.055–32.056
Financial Services Action Plan, 32.002
format
base, 32.031
drawdown, 32.029
generally, 32.028–32.031
standalone, 32.029
tri-partite, 32.030
generally, 32.008
Guideline Measures, 32.008
introduction, 32.006–32.007
Irish Stock Exchange, 32.003
key information, 32.032–32.033
language used, 32.041
liability for misstatements
administrative sanctions, 32.057
civil sanctions, 32.044–32.050
criminal liability, 32.051–32.056
introduction, 32.043
meaning, 32.007
methods of flotation of companies, 32.006
MiFID, and, 32.004
offences, 32.052–32.053
offers of exempted securities, 32.023–32.024
offers to qualified investors, 32.020–32.022
overview, 32.001–32.005
passporting, 32.040
Prospectus Directive
admission to trading on a regulated market, 32.025–32.027
approval, 32.026
content, 32.028–32.035

Prospectus (contd)
exempt offerings, 32.018–32.024
features, 32.009
format, 32.028–32.035
generally, 32.008
language used, 32.041
liability for misstatements, 32.043–32.057
passporting, 32.040
public offer of securities, 32.016–32.017
publication, 32.037–32.039
sanctions for misstatements, 32.043–32.057
scope, 32.010–32.015
supplements, 32.042
Prospectus Regulation, 32.008
public offer of securities, 32.016–32.017
publication, 32.037–32.039
'qualified investors', 32.30
'regulated market', 32.004
sanctions for misstatements, 32.043–32.057
scope, 32.010–32.015
securities outside the scope, 32.012–32.014
sources of law, 32.008
standalone format, 32.029
structure, 32.007
summary requirement, 32.032–32.035
supplements, 32.042
'transferable securities', 32.011
tri-partite format, 32.030
Provisional liquidators
appointment, 24.016–24.019
examinership, and, 22.069
generally, 24.005
powers, 24.041–24.042
Proxy voting
members' meetings, and, 14.074–14.076
shareholders' rights, and, 8.084
Public companies
And see **Public limited company**
generally, 1.128–1.131
Public documents
registration of charges, and, 19.004
shareholders' agreements, and, 3.107
Public limited companies (PLC)
accounts, 29.116–29.120
acquisition of their own shares
financial assistance, 29.077–29.078
generally, 29.068–29.073
marketing arrangement, 29.069
treatment, 29.074–29.076
allotment of shares
authorisation, 29.043
consideration, 29.050–29.054
minimum subscription requirements, 29.045–29.046
payment, 29.047–29.049
pre-emption rights, 29.044
relief for allottees, directors and others, 29.055
stock exchange listing, and, 29.056
articles of association
alterations, 29.032
generally, 29.030–29.031
investment companies, 29.139–29.141
audits
generally, 29.116–29.120
investment companies, 29.147
authority of agents
generally, 29.034
investment companies, 29.143
books of accounts, 29.115
borrowing, 29.121–29.122
buyback of own shares, 29.068–29.073
capacity
generally, 29.034
investment companies, 29.143
capital requirements, 1.114
certificated securities
generally, 29.036
transfer, 29.062–29.066
certification requirements, 29.014–29.015
commencement of business
certification, 29.014–29.015
introduction, 29.010
minimum capital, 29-011

Public limited companies (PLC) (contd)
minimum membership, 29.012–29.013
publication, 29.016
valuation, 29.017–29.018
common seal, 29.035
company secretary, 29.084
compliance and enforcement, 29.130
constitutional documentation
alterations, 29.032
articles of association, 29.030–29.031
introduction, 29.027
investment companies, 29.139–29.141
memorandum of association, 29.028–29.029
conversion by re-registration, and
generally, 29.019–29.025
PLC to private limited company, 33.014
PLC to Societas Europaea, 29.167–29.169
private limited company to PLC, 33.015
Societas Europaea to PLC, 29.192
unlimited company to PLC, 33.008
corporate borrowing, 29.121–29.122
corporate contracts
introduction, 29.034
investment companies, 29.143
securities seal, 29.035
uncertificated securities, 29.036
validity of trading or borrowing carried out without an authorisation, 29.037
corporate governance
audit committees, 29.088
Board committees, 29.086
codes, 29.089–29.093
company secretary, 29.084
compliance statements, 29.088
differences from private company regime, 29.084
directors, 29.083–29.085
generally, 29.083
introduction, 29.083
Irish Annex, 29.092
meetings, 29.094–29.0
regulation, 29.087
restrictions on directors, 29.084
UK Code, 29.089–29.091
CREST, 29.062–29.066
definition, 29.004–29.005
directors, 29.083–29.085
disclosure of interests in shares
generally, 29.057–29.059
investigations, and, 29.125–29.129
disclosure of stabilising activity during a stabilisation period, 29.060–29.061
distributions, 29.079–29.080
dividend payments, 29.079–29.080
division, 1.117
enforcement, 29.130
financial assistance in purchase of their own shares, 29.077–29.078
financial statements
generally, 29.115–29.120
investment companies, 29.147
formation
generally, 29.007–29.009
investment companies, 29.134–29.138
generally, 29.002–29.003
group accounts, 29.116–29.117
incorporation
generally, 29.033
investment companies, 29.142
individual accounts, 29.116
investigations and inspections, 29.124–29.129
investment companies
alternative funds, 29.131–29.132
annual returns, 29.147
articles of association, 29.139–29.141
audits, 29.147
authorisation requirement, 29.136
authority of agents, 29.143
capacity, 29.143
constitutional documentation, 29.139–29.141
contracts, 29.143
financial statements, 29.147
formation, 29.134–29.138
generally, 29.131–29.133

Public limited companies (PLC) (contd)
incorporation, 29.142
maintenance of capital, 29.146
membership, 29.144–29.145
memorandum of association, 29.139–29.141
migration, 29.137–29.138
pre-emption rights, 29.145
registration, 29.134–29.138
share capital requirements, 29.135
shares, 29.144–29.145
UCITS, 29.131–29.132
winding up, 29.148–29.149
maintenance of capital
acquisition of their own shares, 29.068–29.078
buybacks, 29.068–29.073
distributions, 29.079–29.080
dividend payments, 29.079–29.080
financial assistance in purchase of their own shares, 29.077–29.078
introduction, 29.067
investment companies, 29.146
market purchase procedure, 29.068–29.069
off-market purchase procedure, 29.068–29.069
overseas purchase procedure, 29.068–29.069
purchase of their own shares, 29.068–29.078
reduction of capital, 29.081–29.082
market purchase procedure, 29.068–29.069
meetings
agenda items, 29.102–29.103
electronic participation, 29.105
equal treatment right, 29.107
generally, 29.094–29.097
notice requirements, 29.098, 29.100–29.101
participation requirements, 29.104
poll information, 29.111
proxies, 29.108–29.109
questions, 29.106
resolutions, 29.102–29.103
Shareholders' Rights Directive, and, 29.099–29.111
UK Corporate Governance Code, and, 29.112–29.114
voting, 29.104
voting by correspondence, 29.110
members' meetings, and, 14.002
membership
generally, 29.039–29.040
introduction, 29.038
investment companies, 29.144–29.145
memorandum of association
alterations, 29.032
generally, 29.028–29.029
investment companies, 29.139–29.141
migration procedure
generally, 29.026
investment companies, 29.137–29.138
minimum capital requirements, 29-011
minimum membership requirements, 29.012–29.013
minimum subscription requirements, 29.045–29.046
national mergers, 1.115
off-market purchase procedure, 29.068–29.069
overseas purchase procedure, 29.068–29.069
overview, 29.001
pre-emption rights
generally, 29.044
investment companies, 29.145
publication requirements, 29.016
purchase of their own shares
financial assistance, 29.077–29.078
generally, 29.068–29.073
marketing arrangement, 29.069
treatment, 29.074–29.076
reduction of capital
general restrictions, 29.081
objections by creditors, 29.082
registration
certification, 29.014–29.015
introduction, 29.010

Public limited companies (PLC) (contd)
investment companies, 29.134–29.138
minimum capital, 29-011
minimum membership, 29.012–29.013
publication, 29.016
valuation, 29.017–29.018
restoration, 29.123
securities seal, 29.035
share buybacks, 29.068–29.073
share transfers
certificated securities, 29.062–29.066
uncertificated securities, 29.062–29.066
shares
allotment, 29.043–29.044
disclosure of interests, 29.057–29.059
disclosure of stabilising activity during a stabilisation period, 29.060–29.061
formalities, 29.041–29.042
introduction, 29.038
investment companies, 29.144–29.145
legal nature, 29.041–29.042
membership, 29.039–29.040
transfers, 29.062–29.066
striking off, 29.123
treatment, 29.006
UCITS, 29.131–29.132
UK Corporate Governance Code
generally, 29.089–29.090
meetings, 29.112–29.114
principles, 29.091
ultra vires, 29.034
uncertificated securities
generally, 29.036
transfer, 29.062–29.066
validity of trading or borrowing carried out without an authorisation, 29.037
valuation requirements, 29.017–29.018

Publication of accounts
demand for copies of accounts and reports, 17.246–17.247
general requirements, 17.248
laying before company at general meeting, 17.249
meaning, 17.248
obligation to circulate, 17.243–17.245

Publication of notices
incorporation, and, 2.043

Purchase by company of own shares
common law prohibition, 10.014
exceptions to statutory prohibition
forfeiture, 10.022
fully paid shares for no consideration, 10.018
introduction, 10.017
redemption of shares, 10.019
reduction of capital, 10.020
remedial court orders, 10.021
foot of remedial court orders, on, 10.021
forfeiture of shares, and, 10.022
fully paid shares for no consideration, 10.018
introduction, 10.013
prohibitions
common law, at, 10.014
statute, under, 10.015–10.035
Pt.XI CA 1990, under
authorised by articles, 10.027
contingent purchase contracts, 10.031
distributable profits, 10.026
introduction, 10.023
Ministerial regulations, 10.035
own-share purchase, 10.024–10.025
repudiation by company, 10.033
safeguards, 10.032
special resolution, 10.028–10.030
winding up, 10.034
public limited companies, and,
financial assistance, 29.077–29.078
generally, 29.068–29.073
marketing arrangement, 29.069
treatment, 29.074–29.076
redemption of shares, and, 10.019
reduction of capital, and, 10.020
remedial court orders, and, 10.021
s 65 CA 1963, under, 10.019
s 72 CA 1963, under, 10.020
s 211 CA 1990, under, 10.024–10.025
statutory prohibition, 10.015–10.016

Purchasers' liens
generally, 19.029

'Put' and 'call' contracts
acquisition by company of own shares, and, 10.031
Qualifications
directors, and, 13.017
duty of care, skill and diligence, and, 15.078–15.080
Quasi-loans
directors' loans, and, 16.066
Quasi-contracts
recovery of money given by company ultra vires, and, 7.093
Quasi-partnerships
compulsory winding up, and, 23.093–23.097
generally, 1.151–1.154
oppression, and, 11.035–11.041
Quorum
directors' meetings, and, 14.113–14.115
members' meetings, and, 14.055–14.057
Raising capital
consequences of incorporation, and, 4.092
Realisation of assets
absconding officers, 25.043–25.046
Anton Piller orders, 25.037
avoiding transactions, 25.017
civil arrest powers
absconding officers, 25.043–25.046
contributories, 25.043–25.046
facilitate examination, by, 25.039–25.042
introduction, 25.038
claims against contributories, 25.130–25.134
company books and records, 25.013
contribution by related companies to assets
introduction, 25.119
jurisdiction to grant order, 25.123–25.124
'related company', 25.120–25.121
retrospectivity of application, 25.122
contributories, 25.043–25.046
debiting of interest, 25.074
disclaiming onerous property, 25.058–25.065
disposition of corporate property
beneficiary of disposition, 25.100–25.102
effect, 25.087–25.090
intention to prefer, 25.093–25.099
introduction, 25.083–25.085
onus of proof, 25.091–25.092
operative time, 25.086
disputed assets, 25.016
examination
admissibility of evidence obtained, 25.035
conduct, 25.032–25.033
courts' approach, 25.030–25.031
Director of Corporate Enforcement, 25.029
failure to cooperate, 25.034
introduction, 25.024–25.025
official liquidations, 25.026–25.027
procedure, 25.032–25.033
voluntary liquidations, 25.028
facilitating examination
equity, in, 25.041–25.042
statute, by, 25.039–25.040
fraudulent dispositions of property, 25.103–25.109
fraudulent preference of creditors
beneficiary of disposition, 25.100–25.102
disposition of corporate property, 25.083–25.085
effect, 25.087–25.090
intention to prefer, 25.093–25.099
introduction, 25.081–25.082
onus of proof, 25.091–25.092
operative time, 25.086
gathering information
civil arrest powers, 25.038–25.046
examination, 25.024–25.035
introduction, 25.018
obtaining basic information, 25.019–25.022
obtaining books and papers, 25.023
post-examination transfer, 25.036
search and seizure orders, 25.037

Realisation of assets (contd)
- gathering in assets
  - company books and records, 25.013
  - disputed assets, 25.016
  - introduction, 25.007
  - liquidators' duty, 25.008–25.011
  - not beneficially owned by company, 25.014–25.015
  - property, 25.012
  - things in action, 25.012
  - transaction avoidance, 25.017
- guarantee companies, and, 30.070–30.071
- introduction, 25.001–25.003
- invalidating floating charges
  - extent of money actually advanced or paid, 25.115–25.117
  - introduction, 25.110
  - operative time limits, 25.112
  - other circumstances, 25.118
  - proof of solvency, 25.111
  - security unrealised on winding up, 25.113 25.114
- liquidator's duty, 25.005
- litigating to swell asset pool, 25.137–25.139
- lodgments into overdrawn account, 25.069
- not beneficially owned by company, 25.014–25.015
- obtaining books and papers, 25.023
- officers' duty to assist, 25.006
- overview, 25.004
- payments out of company's account, 25.070–25.073
- pooling assets of related companies
  - consequences, 25.128–25.129
  - court's terms and conditions, 25.126
  - introduction, 25.125
  - jurisdiction to make orders, 25.127
- post-commencement banking transactions
  - debiting of interest, 25.074
  - introduction, 25.068
  - lodgments into overdrawn account, 25.069
  - payments out of company's account, 25.070–25.073
- post-commencement dispositions
  - banking transactions, 25.068–25.074
  - 'disposition', 25.066–25.067
  - introduction, 25.065
  - jurisdiction to validate, 25.075–25.080
- post-examination transfer, 25.036
- prohibiting litigation, execution, attachment or judgment, 25.052–25.057
- property, 25.012
- restraining disposal or removal, 25.047–25.051
- search and seizure orders, 25.037
- swelling assets, 24.017
- things in action, 25.012
- transaction avoidance, 25.017
- unlimited companies, and, 31.036–31.040
- voidable transactions, 25.135–25.136

Receivers
- acts of default, 20.006–20.008
- agent of company, as, 20.038–20.044
- application of proceeds of sale, 20.066–20.079
- applications for directions, 20.085–20.086
- appointment
  - acts of default, 20.006–20.008
  - basis, 20.006
  - considerations, 20.005–20.010
  - default in repayment on demand, 20.009
  - duty of care of creditor, 20.010
  - events of default, 20.006–20.008
  - effect, 20.029–20.034
  - events of default, 20.006–20.008
  - foot of court order, on, 20.020
  - foot of debenture, on, 20.013–20.019
  - generally, 20.012
  - income under LCLRA 2009, under, 20.021
  - NAMA, by, 20.022–20.024
  - notice, 20.026–20.028
  - qualifications, 20.011

Receivers (contd)
statutory receiver, as, 20.022–20.024
considerations on appointment
acts of default, 20.006–20.008
default in repayment on demand, 20.009
duty of care of creditor, 20.010
events of default, 20.006–20.008
introduction, 20.005
contracts, and
employment, of, 20.033–20.034
generally, 20.029
court order, under
appointment, 20.020
status, 20.036
crystallisation of floating charges, and, 18.098
debenture, under
appointment, 20.013–20.019
status, 20.037
default in repayment on demand, 20.009
definition, 20.002–20.004
directions, 20.085–20.086
directors' powers, and, 20.030–20.032
disposal of assets
application of proceeds, 20.066–20.079
guarantors, and, 20.060–20.065
introduction, 20.050
obtain best price reasonably obtainable, 20.051–20.059
draft Companies Bill, and, 1.179
duties
application of proceeds of sale, in, 20.066–20.079
disposal of assets, on, 20.050–20.059
guarantors, to, 20.060–20.065
introduction, 20.045
provide information to company, 20.046–20.048
receiver-managers, of, 20.049
supply of information to registrar of companies and DCE, 20.071–20.073
duty of care of creditor, 20.010
effect of appointment
contracts, on, 20.029
directors, on, 20.030–20.032
employees, on, 20.033–20.034
introduction, 20.029
management, on, 20.030–20.032
employment contracts, and, 20.033–20.034
events of default, 20.006–20.008
examinership, and
generally, 22.070–22.072
introduction, 20.004
floating charges, and, 18.098
guarantors, and, 20.060–20.065
introduction, 20.001
liabilities, 20.074–20.078
liquidators, and, 20.004
management of business, and, 20.030–20.032
multiple appointments, 20.087
National Asset Management Agency, and
appointment, 20.022
generally, 20.022
powers, rights and obligations, 20.023
status, 20.024
obtaining best price reasonably obtainable
extent of duty, 20.057–20.059
general duty, 20.051–20.056
guarantors, and, 20.060–20.065
powers, 20.079–20.084
provision of information to company, 20.046–20.048
qualifications, 20.011
receiver-managers, 20.049
registration-type offences, and, 28.050
removal
court, by, 20.090–20.092
instigation of examiner, at, 20.094
instigation of liquidator, at, 20.093
remuneration, 20.044
resignation, 20.088–20.089
status
agent of company, as, 20.038–20.044
court appointees, 20.036
debenture holder appointees, 20.037
introduction, 20.035
statutory receivers

Receivers (contd)
appointment, 20.022
generally, 20.022
powers, rights and obligations, 20.023
status, 20.024
supply of information to registrar of companies and DCE, 20.071–20.073
termination of contracts, and, 20.029
Reckless trading
'a party to', 15.106
applicant requirement, 15.108–15.109
'carrying on the business', 15.107
date of conduct complained of, 15.114
deemed, 15.103–15.104
defences, 15.112
disregarding legal personality, and, 5.091
examinership proceedings, and, 15.115
generally, 15.096–15.097
insolvency requirement, 15.105
'knowingly', 15.098–15.102
nominee directors, and, 15.111
officers, and, 15.110
'party to', 15.106
personal responsibility imposed, 15.126–15.127
'reckless', 15.098–15.102
respondents, 15.110–15.111
scope of court's order, 15.113
separate legal personality, and, 5.091
shadow directors, and, 15.110
Reconstructions
approval by special resolution, 21.070–21.071
creditors' meetings, and, 21.066
criteria for proposal
approval, 21.070–21.071
distribution, 21.072
introduction, 21.067
proposals, 21.069
voluntary winding up, 21.068
distribution of shares, policies or other interests, 21.072
introduction, 21.066
meaning, 21.066
overview, 21.001
proposals
approval, 21.070–21.071
generally, 21.069
schemes of arrangement, and, 21.061–21.062
shareholders' remedies, and, 11.003
statutory basis, 21.067
voluntary winding up, 21.068
Records
disregarding legal personality, and, 5.087
Recovery of money given by company ultra vires
action in rem, 7.091–7.092
Belmont principle, 7.091–7.092
constructive trusts, 7.091–7.092
estoppel, 7.094–7.095
generally, 7.089
quasi-contract, 7.093
unenforceable, 7.090
Rectification of register of members
company, by, 8.022
court, by, 8.023–8.024
Redeemable shares
See also **Shares**
conversion into, 8.120
generally, 8.111
Redemption of shares
distributions, and, 10.090
generally, 10.041–10.045
s 65 CA 1963, under, 10.019
Reduction of capital
acquisition by company of own shares, and, 10.020
alteration of objects clause, 10.086
distributions, and, 10.090
generally, 10.085
memorandum of association, and, 3.033–3.036
minority shareholders' rights, 10.087
public limited companies, and,
general restrictions, 29.081
objections by creditors, 29.082
re-registration of PLC as private company, 10.088
s 10(6) CA 1963, under, 10.086
s 205(3) CA 1963, under, 10.087
s 15 C(A)A 1983, under, 10.088
schemes of arrangement, and, 21.022

Reduction of number of members
disregarding legal personality, and, 5.078–5.080
Reference document
memorandum of association, and, 3.005
Refusal of registration of shares
bona fides of directors, 9.052–9.057
challenge procedure, 9.066–9.068
consequences, 9.064–9.065
directors' power
generally, 9.042
lapse, 9.058–9.061
model restriction, 9.043–9.047
introduction, 9.042
lapse of powers of directors, 9.058–9.061
model reg 3 restriction, 9.043–9.047
procedure for challenging, 9.066–9.068
quality of transferee, 9.050–9.051
s 205 CA 1963 relief, 9.062–9.063
status of transferee, 9.048–9.049
Register of charges
generally, 19.002
notice, 19.004–19.005
rationale, 19.003
Register of companies
restoration
administrative action, by, 26.026–26.032
directors, and, 26.062–26.063
effect, 26.056–26.063
introduction, 26.025
judicial order, by, 26.033–26.054
legal proceedings involving dissolved company, and, 26.058–26.061
options where impossible, 26.064
timing, 26.055
striking off
corporate property, and, 26.016–26.021
directors' liability, 26.015
effect, 26.015–26.021
grounds, 26.005–26.014
introduction, 26.004
members' liability, 26.015
officers' liability, 26.015
Register of directors
generally, 13.096–13.099
Register of interests
generally, 13.116
Register of members
beneficial interests
generally, 8.025–8.030
limits, 8.032
protection, 8.031
changes in particulars, 8.021
definition of 'member', and, 8.004
form, 8.017
inspection, 8.018
introduction, 8.006
legal significance of particulars, 8.020
location, 8.017
overview, 8.001
rectification
company, by, 8.022
court, by, 8.023–8.024
registrable particulars, 8.019
Register of secretaries
generally, 13.096–13.099
Registered companies
concession theory, and, 1.069–1.070
generally, 1.056–1.059
Registered office
incorporation, and, 2.036–2.037
service of proceedings, and, 6.013
Societas Europaea, and, 29.187–29.191
Registers
consequences of incorporation, and, 4.092
Registrar of Companies
compulsory winding up, and, 23.049
creation of office, 28.006
draft Companies Bill, and, 1.186
functions, 28.006
generally, 28.006–28.008
incorporation, and, 2.031–2.033
responsibilities, 28.007
Registration
See also **Registration of charges**
articles of association, and, 3.039
branches, and
EU companies, 34.032
non-EU companies, 34.033

Registration (contd)
draft Companies Bill, and, 1.173
external companies, and 34.013
incorporation, and
And see **Incorporation**
carrying in an activity, 2.030
delivery of particulars, 2.034
existing business, 2.004–2.007
formation, 2.024–2.029
incidental statutory obligations, 2.035–2.044
introduction, 2.001
Irish registered non-resident companies, 2.045–2.046
methods, 2.017–2.023
private companies, 2.008–2.016
purpose, 2.002–2.003
registration by registrar, 2.031–2.033
partnerships, and, 1.015
public limited companies, and
certification, 29.014–29.015
introduction, 29.010
investment companies, 29.134–29.138
minimum capital, 29-011
minimum membership, 29.012–29.013
publication, 29.016
valuation, 29.017–29.018
Societas Europaea, and, 29.170

Registration of charges
aggregation retention of title clause, and, 19.022
aircraft, 19.069
bills of sale, 19.046–19.051
book debts of the company, 19.059–19.065
calls of shares made but not paid, 19.068
certificate of registration
errors in Form C1, 19.014–19.017
generally, 19.011–19.013
limits to *Amurec* decision, 19.018–19.020
charges not created by companies, and, 19.022
charges over proceeds of sale, and, 19.023
chargor company's obligations, 19.107
conclusiveness of certificate
errors in Form C1, 19.014–19.017
generally, 19.011–19.013
limits to *Amurec* decision, 19.018–19.020
consequences of non-registration, 19.006–19.010
constructive notice, and, 19.004–19.005
created by instrument amounting to a bill of sale, 19.046–19.051
disguised registrable charges, 19.071–19.084
external companies, and, 19.001
failure to register, 19.006–19.010
financial collateral arrangements, and, 19.035–19.041
floating charges, 19.066–19.067
foreign companies, and, 19.001
foreign property, and, 19.086–19.088
goodwill, 19.070
intellectual property, 19.070
introduction, 19.001
judgment mortgages, 19.085
land, 19.052–19.058
late applications
discretion, 19.091
introduction, 19.090
Joplin proviso, 19.094–19.097
mere misstatements, and, 19.092–19.093
omissions, and, 19.092–19.093
priority, 19.100
winding up of company, and, 19.098–19.099
liens, and
bankers' liens, 19.027
booking deposits, 19.030
common law liens, 19.025
contractual liens, 19.031–19.032
equitable liens, 19.029–19.030
general liens, 19.026–19.028
introduction, 19.024
purchasers' liens, 19.029
solicitors' liens, 19.028

Registration of charges (contd)
unpaid vendors' liens, 19.029
non-registrable security interests
aggregation retention of title clause, 19.022
charges not created by companies, 19.022
charges over proceeds of sale, 19.023
financial collateral arrangements, 19.035–19.041
introduction, 19.021
liens, 9.024–19.032
pledges, 19.033
trusts, 19.034
non-registration, 19.006–19.010
pledges, and, 19.033
procedure
introduction, 19.101
registrable particulars, 19.102–19.104
satisfaction of charges, 19.105–19.106
property outside of the State, and, 19.086–19.089
public documents, and, 19.004
purpose of securing issue of debentures, 19.044
register of charges
generally, 19.002
notice, 19.004–19.005
rationale, 19.003
registrable charges
aircraft, on, 19.069
book debts of the company, on, 19.059–19.065
calls of shares made but not paid, on, 19.068
created by instrument amounting to a bill of sale, 19.046–19.051
floating charges, on, 19.066–19.067
goodwill, on, 19.070
intellectual property, on, 19.070
introduction, 19.042–19.043
land, on, 19.052–19.058
purpose of securing issue of debentures, for, 19.044
ships, on, 19.069
uncalled share capital of the company, on, 19.045
registrable particulars, 19.102–19.104
retention of title clauses
aggregation clauses, 19.076–19.078
current account clause, 19.083–19.084
introduction, 19.071–19.072
proceeds of sale clause, 19.079–19.082
simple clauses, 19.073–19.075
satisfaction of charges, 19.105–19.106
ships, on, 19.069
trusts, and, 19.034
uncalled share capital of the company, 19.045

Registration-type offences
applicants to court, by, 28.052
auditors, by, 28.051
companies, by, 28.049
examiners, by, 28.050
failure to file annual return, 28.046–28.048
failure to notify changes in officers, 28.046–28.048
form of documents filed, returned or delivered, 28.053–28.054
indictable offences, 28.045
introduction, 28.043
liquidators, by, 28.050
other offences, 28.048–28.052
purpose of registration, 28.044
receivers, by, 28.050
summary offences, 28.045

Regulation of directors' transactions
See also **Directors' transactions**
bodies corporate that are connected persons, 16.010
connected persons, 16.006–16.020
directors, 16.004–16.005
disclosure of interests in contracts, 16.121–16.135
holding company directors, 16.004–16.005
introduction, 16.001–16.002
loans etc to directors, 16.055–16.120

Regulation of directors' transactions (contd)
natural persons that are connected persons, 16.006–16.009
regulated persons, 16.003–16.021
shadow directors, 16.021
substantial property transactions, 16.022–16.054
Regulatory relationships
separate legal personality, and, 4.077
Rejected business opportunities
conflicts of interest, and, 15.062–15.066
Related party transactions
individual accounts, and, 17.125
Remedial court orders
acquisition by company of own shares, and, 10.021
Removal of directors
automatic, 13.075
directors, by, 13.076–13.082
Remuneration
auditors, and
Companies Acts individual accounts, 17.122–17.124
generally, 17.308–17.309
groups of companies, 17.189
IFRS individual accounts, 17.143
directors, and, 13.070–13.071
examiners, and
costs, 22.168
expenses, 22.169
generally, 22.165–22.167
introduction, 22.163–22.164
liquidators, and, 24.052–24.055
receivers, and, 20.044
secretary, and, 13.121
Reorganisations
draft Companies Bill, and, 1.180
Representation
voting at members' meetings, and, 14.072–14.073
Representations
ostensible authority, and, 7.104–7.106
Re-registration
introduction, 33.001
limited company to unlimited company, 33.009–33.013
multi-member private company to single-member private company, 33.016
PLC to private limited company
generally, 33.014
reduction of capital, and, 10.088
PLC to Societas Europaea, 29.167–29.169
private limited company to PLC, 33.015
single-member private company to multi-member private company, 33.017
Societas Europaea to PLC, 29.192
unlimited company to private limited company, 33.002–33.007
unlimited company to PLC, 33.008
Res judicata
civil litigation, and, 6.004–6.005
Reserves and provisions
balance sheet, and, 17.094
Residence
disregarding legal personality, and, 5.069–5.073
Resignation
auditors, and, 17.343–17.345
directors, and, 13.073
receivers, and, 20.088–20.089
Resolutions
'Buchanan principle', 14.093
business to be conducted, and
amendment, 14.054
basis for need, 14.053
introduction, 14.050
other matters, 14.053–14.054
special business, 14.051
special resolutions, 14.052
compensation on loss of office, and, 13.093
directors' meetings, and
formal resolutions, 14.125
introduction, 14.124
unanimous acts of directors, 14.128
written resolutions, 14.126–14.127
filing, 14.100–14.101
introduction, 14.081
ordinary resolutions, 14.082–14.083

Resolutions (contd)
single-member private companies, 14.088–14.089
special resolutions
business to be conducted, 14.052
generally, 14.084–14.087
unanimous acts of directors, 14.128
unanimous consent of members to course of action, 14.093–14.099
written resolutions
directors' meetings, 14.126–14.127
members' meetings, 14.090–14.092
Restitutio in integrum
directors' loans, and, 16.103
Restoration to register
administrative action, by, 26.026–26.032
ceasing to carry on business, after, 26.051–26.054
directors, and, 26.062–26.063
draft Companies Bill, and, 1.183
effect
claims against directors, on, 26.062–26.063
generally, 26.056–26.057
legal proceedings involving dissolved company, on, 26.058–26.061
failure to file annual return, after
'aggrieved' petitioner, 26.040
alternative orders, 26.049
introduction, 26.035
jurisdiction to hear application, 26.039
locus standi, 26.036–26.038
requirement to file outstanding annual returns, 26.044–26.048
weight attached to third party objections, 26.041–26.043
guarantee companies, and, 30.072
having no EEA resident directors, after, 26.051–26.054
having no recorded directors, after, 26.051–26.054
introduction, 26.025
judicial order, by
introduction, 26.033–26.034
strike off for failure to deliver particulars to the revenue, for, 26.035
strike off for failure to file annual return, after, 26.035
legal proceedings involving dissolved company, and, 26.058–26.061
options where impossible, 26.064
public limited companies, and, 29.123
timing, 26.055
Restraining removal of shareholder director
oppression, and, 11.067–11.072
Restriction orders
acting honestly and responsibly, 28.097–28.128
applications, 28.090–28.091
background, 28.062
breach
civil sanctions, 28.144
criminal sanctions, 28.143
civil sanctions, 28.146–28.147
consequences, 28.068–28.071
costs
introduction, 28.092
successful applications, 28.093–28.094
unsuccessful applications, 28.095–28.096
criminal sanctions, 28.145
de jure directors, 28.076–28.080
defences
delay, 28.132–28.135
estoppel, 28.132–28.135
honestly and responsibly, 28.097–28.128
just and equitable, 28.129–28.130
nominees, 28.131
delay, and, 28.132–28.135
directors, 28.076–28.080
disregarding legal personality, and, 5.083–5.085
enforcement
breach, 28.143–28.144
civil sanctions, 28.146–28.147
criminal sanctions, 28.145
introduction, 28.142

Restriction orders (contd)
- estoppel, and, 28.132–28.135
- generally, 28.062–28.063
- honestly and responsibly defence
  - affairs of the company, as to, 28.099–28.100
  - common law duties, 28.115–28.116
  - compliance with Companies Acts, 28.110–28.121
  - conduct of the affairs of the company, as to, 28.101–28.103
  - group obligations, 28.117
  - incompetence, 28.122
  - introduction, 28.097–28.128
  - *La Mosselle* test, 28.105–28.108
  - lack of commercial probity, 28.126–28.128
  - maintenance of proper records and books, 28.111–28.114
  - net deficiency of assets, 28.123–28.125
  - non-executive directors, 28.118–28.121
  - objective standard, 28.109
  - relevant factors, 28.104–28.128
  - responsibility for insolvency, 28.123–28.125
- insolvency requirement, 28.072–28.073
- introduction, 13.020
- just and equitable to make order, 28.129–28.130
- liquidators' duties, 28.082–28.087
- locus standi of applicants, 28.088–28.089
- mandatory nature, 28.066–28.067
- nominee defence, 28.131
- non-resident directors, 28.081
- persons liable to be restricted
  - de jure directors, 28.076–28.080
  - directors on or within 12 months of winding up, 28.075
  - introduction, 28.074
  - non-resident directors, 28.081
  - shadow directors, 28.076–28.080
- persons who have been directors on or within 12 months of winding up, 28.075
- post-order relief, 28.136–28.141
- procedure, 28.090–28.091
- purpose, 28.064–28.065
- role of the DCE, 28.082–28.087
- shadow directors, 28.076–28.080

Retention of title clauses
- registration of charges, and
  - aggregation clauses, 19.076–19.078
  - current account clause, 19.083–19.084
  - introduction, 19.071–19.072
  - proceeds of sale clause, 19.079–19.082
  - simple clauses, 19.073–19.075

Retirement
- directors, and, 13.074

Revaluation reserve treatment
- balance sheet, and, 17.091

Rights of first refusal
- allotment of shares, and, 8.056–8.059
- beneficial interests in shares, and, 9.080–9.083
- enforceability, 9.084–9.086
- generally, 9.069–9.072
- judicial construction, 9.076–9.079
- need, 9.073–9.075
- sample clause, 9.070

Royal charter corporations
- generally, 1.063–1.064

Rule in *Foss v Harbottle*
- derivative actions, and, 11.110–11.120
- distinguishing corporate rights from personal rights, 11.100–11.102
- distinguishing personal rights from actions for reflective loss, 11.103–11.107
- exceptions, 11.121–11.145
- fraud on minority by those in control, 11.129–11.142
- general principles, 11.093–11.094
- generally, 11.095–11.096
- illegal acts, and, 11.122–11.125
- infringement of personal rights, and, 11.128
- introduction, 11.092
- justice requires derivative action to be brought, 11.143–11.145

Rule in Foss v Harbottle *(contd)*
- summary, 11.097–11.099
- transactions unratifiable by bare majority, and, 11.126–11.127
- ultra vires acts, and, 11.122–11.125

Rule in *Turquand's* case
- generally, 7.123
- irregularity is of public record, 7.124
- outsider must act in good faith, 7.125–7.126

s 60 CA 1963
- *See also* **Assisting purchase of company's own shares**
- application, 10.047
- consequences of contravention, 10.048–10.057
- 'financial assistance', 10.058–10.065
- general rule, 10.046

s 204 CA 1963
- bona fides of transferee, 9.100–9.107
- disclosure of full particulars, 9.096
- discretion of court, 9.095–9.107
- generally, 9.091–9.092
- independence of transferee, 9.100–9.107
- mandatory requirements, 9.093–9.094
- onus of proof, 9.097–9.099

s 205 CA 1963
- generally, 9.087

s 251 CA 1990
- generally, 15.141
- insufficiency of assets condition, 15.145–15.146
- locus standi, 15.142
- operation of provisions, 15.147–15.148
- orders available, 15.143–15.144

Sale of goods by sheriff
- enforcement of judgments and orders, and, 6.073–6.074

***Salomon's* case**
- civil litigation, and, 6.002
- disregarding legal personality, and, 5.001–5.006
- separate legal personality, and, 4.026–4.031

Schemes of arrangement
- 'arrangement', 21.012–21.015
- 'between', 21.012–21.015
- classes of members, 21.035–21.038
- commencement, 21.024
- compliance with court directions, 21.052–21.053
- compliance with statute, 21.052–21.053
- compliance with Takeover Panel rules, 21.023
- 'compromise', 21.012–21.015
- constituting proper classes
  - classes of members, 21.035–21.038
  - generally, 21.029–21.034
  - responsibility, 21.026–21.028
- contrary to law, and, 21.020
- court approval
  - compliance with court directions, 21.052–21.053
  - compliance with statute, 21.052–21.053
  - introduction, 21.050
  - 'man' of business would reasonably approve, 21.055–21.057
  - sufficient steps taken to contact all interested parties, 21.051
- criteria in application
  - 'arrangement', 21.012–21.015
  - 'between', 21.012–21.015
  - 'compromise', 21.012–21.015
  - creditors' status, 21.009–21.011
  - introduction, 21.004–21.006
  - 'members', 21.008
  - proposal for arrangement from a company, 21.007
- examinership, and, 21.002
- facilitation in contemplation of reconstruction, 21.061–21.062
- fraud, 21.063–21.065
- guarantee companies, and, 30.002
- introduction, 21.003
- judicial powers to facilitate, 21.061–21.062
- limitations
  - compliance with Takeover Panel rules, 21.023
  - introduction, 21.016
  - locus standi of applicant, 21.017

Schemes of arrangement (contd)
proposal must not be contrary to law or ultra vires, 21.020
reduction of capital, 21.022
support for application by company, 21.018–21.019
locus standi of applicant, 21.017
'man' of business would reasonably approve, 21.055–21.057
meetings of members and creditors
classes of members, 21.035–21.038
constituting proper classes, 21.029–21.034
introduction, 21.024–21.025
provision of information, 21.039–21.042
repeat applications, 21.048
responsibility for constituting proper classes, 21.026–21.028
shareholders' rights and interests, 21.035–21.038
voting, 21.043–21.047
ordinary creditors, 21.009–21.011
overview, 21.001–21.002
preferential creditors, 21.009–21.011
provision of information, 21.039–21.042
reconstructions, and, 21.061–21.062
reduction of capital, and, 21.022
repeat applications, 21.048
secured creditors, 21.009–21.011
setting aside, 21.063–21.065
shareholders' remedies, and, 11.033
shareholders' rights and interests, 21.035–21.038
solvent companies, for, 21.058–21.060
stay of proceedings, 21.049
sufficient steps taken to contact all interested parties, 21.051
support for application by company, 21.018–21.019
Takeover Panel rules, and, 21.023
ultra vires, and, 21.020
unlimited companies, and, 31.003
voting, 21.043–21.047
Secretaries
appointment, 13.120
cessation, 13.120
duties
common law, at, 15.155
generally, 15.152–15.153
introduction, 13.122–13.124
persons to whom owed, 15.154
statute, under, 15.156–15.160
functions, 13.122–13.124
general requirement, 13.119
disclosure obligations
generally, 13.125
interests in shares and debentures, 13.100–13.118
introduction, 13.095
register of secretaries, 13.096–13.099
incorporation, and, 2.038
indemnities, 15.091–15.093
insurance, 15.094
interests in shares and debentures
consequences of failure to comply, 13.114–13.115
disclosable interests, 13.108–13.113
disregarded interests, 13.112
family interests, 13.110–13.111
generally, 13.125
introduction, 13.100
investigation of suspected contravention, 13.118
notification procedure, 13.113
notification to stock exchange, 13.117
obligation during appointment, 13.103–13.107
obligation on appointment, 13.101–13.102
register, 13.116
introduction, 13.119
liability
indemnities, 15.091–15.093
insurance, 15.094
relief, 15.088–15.090
register of interests, 13.116
register of secretaries, 13.096–13.099
remuneration, 13.121
status, 13.121
statutory duties, 15.156–15.160

Section 25 contracts
binding effect
members and company, 3.095
members to members, 3.096–3.098
distinction from 'special contracts', 3.102–3.105
features
binding effect, 3.095–3.098
introduction, 3.094
rights and obligations qua member, 3.099–3.101
generally, 3.092–3.105
introduction, 3.092–3.093
rights and obligations qua member, 3.099–3.101
shareholders' rights, and, 8.089–8.090
single-member private companies, and, 3.092
'special contracts', and, 3.102–3.105
Secured creditors
examinership, and
effects, 22.073–22.074
priorities, 22.084–22.086
schemes of arrangement, and, 21.009–21.011
Secured debentures
equitable charges, 18.028–18.029
introduction, 18.024–18.025
liens, 18.027
mortgages, 18.030–18.037
pledges, 18.026
Security
directors' loans, and, 16.070
shares, and, 9.034–9.041
Security for costs
'action or other legal proceedings', 6.021–6.024
amount, 6.057–6.060
appellants, and, 6.030–6.031
applicants, 6.032
bona fides of defendants, 6.045–6.046
companies, against, 6.016
constitutionality, 6.017–6.018
counterclaims by defendant, and, 6.030–6.031
delay in applications, 6.055–6.056
evidence of inability to pay costs, 6.033–6.037
evidence of prima facie defence to substantive claim, 6.038–6.040
generally, 6.014
human rights, 6.017–6.018
individuals, against, 6.016
insolvency of plaintiff caused by defendant, 6.047–6.051
judicial discretion, 6.041–6.056
jurisdiction, 6.014
lack of bona fides on part of defendant, 6.045–6.046
non-residents, against, 6.015
notice party, 6.032
personal co-plaintiffs, 6.054
plaintiff company with limited liability, and, 6.025–6.029
public interest, 6.052–6.053
'special circumstances'
defendant's lack of bona fides, 6.045–6.046
delay in applications, 6.055–6.056
generally, 6.041–6.044
insolvency of plaintiff caused by defendant, 6.047–6.051
personal co-plaintiffs, 6.054
vindication of public interest, 6.052–6.053
statutory test
'action or other legal proceedings', 6.021–6.024
appellants, and, 6.030–6.031
applicants, 6.032
counterclaims by defendant, and, 6.030–6.031
evidence of inability to pay costs, 6.033–6.037
evidence of prima facie defence to substantive claim, 6.038–6.040
introduction, 6.019–6.020
judicial discretion, 6.041–6.056
plaintiff company with limited liability, 6.025–6.029
plaintiffs, 6.030–6.031
sequential test, 6.020
'special circumstances', 6.041–6.056

Security for costs (contd)
stay of proceedings, and, 6.014
vindication of public interest, 6.052–6.053
Seizure of goods by sheriff
civil litigation, and, 6.073–6.074
Separate legal personality
artificial personality, 4.024–4.025
constitutional rights and duties, 4.068–4.075
contractual liability, 4.043–4.048
corporate litigation, and
contracts, 4.043–4.048
crime, 4.055–4.076
introduction, 4.042
torts, 4.049–4.053
corporate manslaughter, 4.059–4.060
corporate property
compensation, 4.040
generally, 4.032–4.037
insurable interests, 4.039
statutory tenancies, 4.041
transfer, 4.038
criminal liability
attribution principles, 4.063–4.067
constitutional rights and duties, 4.068–4.075
corporations as prosecutors, 4.056
introduction, 4.055
justification, 4.057–4.061
legal rights and duties, 4.076
practical limitations, 4.062
disregarding
acting on directions of disqualified person, 5.085
agency, 5.020–5.028
avoidance of future legal obligations, 5.049–5.050
breach of restriction or disqualification orders, 5.083–5.085
characterisation, 5.068–5.075
circumstances, 5.010–5.095
comfort letters, 5.017
Companies Acts provisions, 5.077–5.091
concealment of impropriety, 5.032–5.036
contract, by, 5.012–5.017
controllers of the company, and, 5.009
court orders, 5.065–5.067
culpability, 5.074
disqualification orders, 5.083 5.085
evasion of existing legal obligations, 5.039–5.048
failure to keep proper records, 5.087
failure to meet capital requirements, 5.086
failure to state correctly company's name, 5.081–5.082
fraudulent trading, 5.091
implied agency, 5.023–5.027
indemnities, 5.016
injunctions, 5.065–5.067
introduction, 5.001–5.007
licensing purposes, 5.075
liquidation of related companies, 5.090
manner, 5.008
mens rea, 5.074
mismanagement, 5.037–5.038
misuse of corporate form, 5.031–5.050
personal guarantees, 5.015
reckless trading, 5.091
reduction of number of members, 5.078–5.080
residence, 5.069–5.073
restriction orders, 5.083–5.085
single economic entity, 5.051–5.064
statutory provisions, 5.076–5.096
tax legislation, 5.092
torts, 5.018–5.019
trusts, 5.029–5.030
undisclosed agency, 5.028
unreasonably inaccurate declaration of solvency, 5.088–5.089
vicarious liability of directors and employees, 5.093–5.096
fictional personality, 4.024–4.025
generally, 4.023
groups of companies, and, 12.048–12.050
guarantee companies, and
disregarding, 30.039

Separate legal personality (contd)
introduction, 30.003
insurable interests, 4.039
legal rights and duties, 4.076
'lifting the veil', and, 5.002
privileges and obligations, 4.077–4.080
regulatory relationships, 4.077
Salomon's case, 4.026–4.031
Societas Europaea, 29.152
statutory tenancies, 4.041
suing and being sued
contracts, 4.043–4.048
crime, 4.055–4.076
introduction, 4.042
torts, 4.049–4.053
tortious liability, 4.049–4.053
transfer of property, 4.038
unlimited companies, 31.014
'veil of incorporation', and, 5.002

Sequestration
general judgments and orders, 6.100–6.103
money judgments, 6.077

Service
branches, and, 34.039
external companies, and, 34.024–34.025

Service of proceedings
CRO, on, 6.011
directors, on, 6.012
generally, 6.010–6.013
registered office, at, 6.013

Set-off
floating charges, and, 18.090

Setting aside
schemes of arrangement, and, 21.063–21.065

Setting aside transactions
conflicts of interest, and, 15.069
'sexually transmitted debt', 15.049–15.050
shareholders, to, 15.019–15.023
shareholders' rights, and, 8.091
'token' directors, by, 15.049–15.050

'Sexually transmitted debt'
setting aside transactions, and, 15.049–15.050

Shadow directors
'acted in accordance with such directions or instructions', 13.063–13.064
bodies corporate, and, 13.066–13.069
'directed or instructed', 13.060–13.062
directors' transactions, and, 16.021
disclosure of interests in contracts, and, 16.123
generally, 13.0565–13.056
'professional advice' exception, 13.057
proofs required, 13.058–13.059
reckless trading, and, 15.110
'were accustomed so to act', 13.065

Share buybacks
public limited companies, and, 29.068–29.073

Share capital
balance sheet, and, 17.092
draft Companies Bill, and, 1.174
group accounts, and, 17.207
individual accounts, and, 17.136

Share certificates
forgery, 8.049
introduction, 8.047
liability for false information, 8.048

Share purchase agreements
contrast with asset purchases, 9.109–9.110
disclosure letters, 9.112
indemnities, 9.116
introduction, 9.108
nature, 9.111–9.116
warranties, 9.113–9.115

Share transfers
bankruptcy, on, 9.031
compulsory transfers
articles of association, under, 9.088–9.090
introduction, 9.087
s 204 CA 1963, under, 9.091–9.107
consideration
generally, 9.004
valuation, 9.117–9.134
death, on, 9.026–9.030
directors' powers to refuse registration
bona fides of directors, 9.052–9.057

Share transfers (contd)
challenging, 9.066–9.068
consequences, 9.064–9.065
introduction, 9.042
lapsing of powers of directors, 9.058–9.061
model reg 3 restriction, 9.043–9.047
overview, 9.22
procedure for challenging, 9.066–9.068
quality of transferee, 9.050–9.051
s 205 CA 1963 relief, 9.062–9.063
status of transferee, 9.048–9.049
equitable mortgages, by, 9.036–9.037
execution of instrument, 9.011–9.012
forms, 9.009
introduction, 9.001–9.005
legal mortgages, by, 9.035
meaning of 'transfer', 9.008
mechanics, 9.006–9.010
merger, on
generally, 9.032–9.033
introduction, 9.001
operation of law, by
bankruptcy, 9.031
death, 9.026–9.030
introduction, 9.025
overview, 9.001
merger, 9.032–9.033
pre-emption rights
beneficial interests in shares, and, 9.080–9.083
enforceability, 9.084–9.086
generally, 9.069–9.072
judicial construction, 9.076–9.079
need, 9.073–9.075
'proper instrument' requirement, 9.006–9.010
public limited companies, and
certificated securities, 29.062–29.066
uncertificated securities, 29.062–29.066
refusal of registration
bona fides of directors, 9.052–9.057
challenging, 9.066–9.068
consequences, 9.064–9.065
introduction, 9.042
lapsing of powers of directors, 9.058–9.061
model reg 3 restriction, 9.043–9.047
overview, 9.22
procedure for challenging, 9.066–9.068
quality of transferee, 9.050–9.051
s 205 CA 1963 relief, 9.062–9.063
status of transferee, 9.048–9.049
registration by directors, 9.022
restrictions
classification, 9.002
directors' powers to refuse registration, 9.042–9.068
generally, 9.017–9.019
introduction, 9.002
pre-emption rights, 9.069–9.086
rationale, 9.20–9.21
rights of first refusal, 9.002
security, and
equitable mortgage, 9.036–9.037
introduction, 9.034
legal mortgage, 9.035
stop notices, 9.038–9.041
share purchase agreements
contrast with asset purchases, 9.109–9.110
disclosure letters, 9.112
indemnities, 9.116
introduction, 9.108
nature, 9.111–9.116
warranties, 9.113–9.115
shareholders' agreements, and, 9.001
stock transfer forms, 9.009
stop notices, 9.038–9.041
'transfer', 9.008
transferability, 9.016–9.024
'transferee', 9.001
transferee's obligations, 9.013–9.015
transferee's position pending registration, 9.023–9.024
'transferor', 9.001
unlimited companies, and, 31.020
valuation
appropriate date, 9.129–9.134
assessment, 9.121

Share transfers (contd)
- determination of company's total worth, 9.119–9.120
- discounting for minority holding, 9.122–9.125
- fair value, 9.126–9.128
- introduction, 9.117
- premium, 9.121
- principles, 9.118–9.125
- pro rata basis, 9.121

Shareholders
- attendance at meetings, 8.080
- dividends, and
  - declaration, 8.078
  - entitlement where company a going concern, 8.074–8.075
  - entitlement where company being wound up, 8.077
  - forfeiture, 8.076
  - form, 8.079
  - generally, 8.073
- duties, 8.093–8.097
- participation in winding up, 8.085
- personal rights, 8.087–8.092
- remedies
  - *And see* **Shareholders' remedies**
  - derivative actions, 11.108–11.145
  - introduction, 11.001–11.005
  - oppression and disregard of interests, 11.006–11.091
  - personal rights, under, 11.004
  - rule in Foss v Harbottle, 11.092–11.107
  - statute, under, 11.003
  - winding up petitions, 11.002
- rights
  - attendance at meetings, 8.080
  - dividends, 8.073–8.079
  - generally, 8.071–8.072
  - participation in winding up, 8.085
  - personal rights, 8.087–8.092
  - statute, under, 8.086
  - voting at meetings, 8.081–8.084
- statutory rights, 8.086
- voting rights
  - generally, 8.081
  - poll, 8.083
  - proxy, 8.084
  - show of hands, 8.082

Shareholders' agreements
- articles of association, and
  - generally, 3.107
  - informal alteration, 3.085–3.087
  - introduction, 3.038
- binding effect, 3.127–3.128
- contrasted with articles of association, 3.107
- definition, 3.106
- directors fettering their fiduciary powers, 3.126
- enforcement
  - binding effect, 3.127–3.128
  - directors fettering their fiduciary powers, 3.126
  - generally, 3.120–3.122
  - injunctions, 3.123–3.125
- filing in the CRO
  - generally, 3.108–3.111
  - 'resolutions or agreements', 3.109
- formation agreements, 3.117
- generally, 3.106–3.128
- injunctions, 3.123–3.125
- introduction, 3.001
- limited shareholders' agreements, 3.117
- meaning, 3.106
- minority shareholders, 3.114
- 'no partnership' clause, 3.116
- 'pooling agreements', 3.114
- public documents, and, 3.107
- rights and obligations of parties, 3.113
- share transfers, and, 9.001
- types, 3.117–3.119
- uses, 3.112–3.116

Shareholders' duties
- generally, 8.093–8.097

Shareholders' remedies
- alteration of articles of association, 11.003
- alteration of objects clause, 11.003
- assisting purchase of company's own shares, 11.003
- compulsory acquisition of shares, 11.003

Shareholders' remedies (contd)
derivative actions
generally, 11.110
indemnity for costs, 11.118–11.120
nature, 11.111–11.112
preliminary considerations, 11.108–11.109
test, 11.113–11.117
disregard of interests
abuse of process, 11.053–11.056
'affairs of the company', 11.033–11.034
alteration of constitutional documents, 11.085
cancellation of transactions, 11.084
company's position, 11.057–11.059
compensatory damages, and, 11.074–11.076
contracting-out of provision, 11.091
contrast with unfairly prejudicial remedy, 11.088–11.090
costs, 11.087
delay in prosecution, 11.053–11.056
'disregarding member's interest', 11.029–11.032
ending matters complained of, 11.073–11.086
futile orders, and, 11.078
in camera applications, 11.060–11.066
introduction, 11.006–11.007
'legitimate expectations', 11.035–11.041
locus standi, 11.042–11.052
members of the company, 11.044–11.051
nature of remedy, 11.008–11.009
personal representatives of deceased members, 11.052
'powers of directors', 11.033–11.034
purchase of petitioner's shares, 11.080–11.081
purchase of respondent's shares, 11.082
purchase of shares by company, 11.083
quasi-partnership companies, 11.035–11.041
restraining removal of shareholder director, 11.067–11.072
variation of transactions, 11.084
introduction, 11.001–11.005
just and equitable winding up, 11.002
oppression
abuse of process, 11.053–11.056
'affairs of the company', 11.033–11.034
alteration of constitutional documents, 11.085
cancellation of transactions, 11.084
company's position, 11.057–11.059
compensatory damages, and, 11.074–11.076
contracting-out of provision, 11.091
contrast with unfairly prejudicial remedy, 11.088–11.090
costs, 11.087
delay in prosecution, 11.053–11.056
ending matters complained of, 11.073–11.086
exclusion from management, 11.025–11.026
fraudulent transactions, 11.017–11.019
futile orders, and, 11.078
in camera applications, 11.060–11.066
introduction, 11.006–11.007
isolated acts, 11.016
'legitimate expectations', 11.035–11.041
locus standi, 11.042–11.052
management, 11.020–11.024
members of the company, 11.044–11.051
nature of remedy, 11.008–11.009
need not be qua member, 11.014–11.015
non-consultation with shareholders, 11.027
'oppression', 11.010–11.028
personal representatives of deceased members, 11.052

Shareholders' remedies (contd)
'powers of directors', 11.033–11.034
purchase of petitioner's shares, 11.080–11.081
purchase of respondent's shares, 11.082
purchase of shares by company, 11.083
quasi-partnership companies, 11.035–11.041
restraining removal of shareholder director, 11.067–11.072
technical oppression, 11.028
test, 11.011–11.013
unlawful transactions, 11.017–11.019
variation of transactions, 11.084
personal rights, under
distinguishing actions for reflective loss, 11.103–11.107
distinguishing corporate rights, 11.100–11.102
generally, 11.004
reconstructions, 11.003
rule in *Foss v Harbottle*
derivative actions, and, 11.110–11.120
distinguishing corporate rights from personal rights, 11.100–11.102
distinguishing personal rights from actions for reflective loss, 11.103–11.107
exceptions, 11.121–11.145
fraud on minority by those in control, 11.129–11.142
general principles, 11.093–11.094
generally, 11.095–11.096
illegal acts, and, 11.122–11.125
infringement of personal rights, and, 11.128
introduction, 11.092
justice requires derivative action to be brought, 11.143–11.145
summary, 11.097–11.099
transactions unratifiable by bare majority, and, 11.126–11.127
ultra vires acts, and, 11.122–11.125
schemes of arrangement, 11.033
statute, under, 11.003
unlimited companies, and, 31.003
winding up petitions, 11.002
Shareholders' rights
attendance at meetings, 8.080
dividends, 8.073–8.079
EU law, and, 1.124
generally, 8.071–8.072
participation in winding up, 8.085
personal rights
directors' fiduciary duties, 8.091
generally, 8.087–8.088
s 25 contract, 8.089–8.090
statute, under, 8.092
statute, under
generally, 8.086
personal rights, and, 8.092
voting at meetings
generally, 8.081
poll, 8.083
proxy, 8.084
show of hands, 8.082
winding up, and, 8.085
Shares
allotment
consideration, 8.060–8.067
directors' authority, 8.051–8.053
introduction, 8.050
mechanics, 8.054–8.055
pre-emption rights, 8.056–8.059
rectification of defects, 8.068–8.070
articles of association, and, 3.045–3.046
bonus shares, 8.114
certificates
forgery, 8.049
introduction, 8.047
liability for false information, 8.048
choses in action, as, 8.038
classes
bonus shares, 8.114
categories, 8.100–8.115
deferred shares, 8.112
employees' shares, 8.115
founders' shares, 8.112
generally, 8.100
ordinary shares, 8.101
power to create, 8.099

Shares (contd)
- preference shares, 8.102–8.110
- presumptions, 8.098
- redeemable shares, 8.111
- Treasury shares, 8.113

compulsory transfers
- articles of association, under, 9.088–9.090
- introduction, 9.087
- s 204 CA 1963, under, 9.091–9.107

consideration on allotment
- 'cash', 8.061
- discount, at a, 8.064
- introduction, 8.060
- non-cash consideration, 8.062–8.063
- premium, at a, 8.065–8.067

consolidation, 8.117
contractual rights and obligations, 8.039
conversion
- consolidation, 8.117
- generally, 8.116
- redeemable shares, into, 8.120
- stock, into, 8.118
- subdivision, 8.119

deferred shares, 8.112
disclosure of interests
- disclosure orders, 8.128–8.134
- generally, 8.127

disclosure orders
- consequences of contravention, 8.134
- generally, 8.127–8.128
- powers of court, 8.132–8.133
- scope, 8.129–8.131

dividends, and
- declaration, 8.078
- entitlement where company a going concern, 8.074–8.075
- entitlement where company being wound up, 8.077
- forfeiture, 8.076
- form, 8.079
- generally, 8.073

draft Companies Bill, and, 1.174
employees' shares, 8.115
false information, 8.048
forfeiture, 8.123–8.125
forgery, 8.049
formal requirements
- certificates, 8.047–8.049
- introduction, 8.043
- nominal value, 8.044–8.045
- numbering, 8.046

founders' shares, 8.112
guarantee companies, and, 30.009
interest in company itself, 8.040
interest in nature of personalty, 8.037
interests and rights protected by the Constitution, 8.042
introduction, 8.034
investigations as to ownership, and
- generally, 27.083–27.084
- power of DCE to impose restrictions, 27.085–27.088

legal nature
- chose in action, 8.038
- contractual rights and obligations, 8.039
- interest in company itself, 8.040
- interest in nature of personalty, 8.037
- interests and rights protected by the Constitution, 8.042
- introduction, 8.035
- no interest in company's assets, 8.036
- statutory rights and obligations, 8.041

liability for false information, 8.048
liens, 8.21–8.22
no interest in company's assets, 8.036
'no par', 8.045
nominal value, 8.044–8.045
numbering, 8.046
ordinary shares, 8.101
power to create classes, 8.099
pre-emption rights
- beneficial interests in shares, and, 9.080–9.083
- enforceability, 9.084–9.086
- generally, 9.069–9.072
- judicial construction, 9.076–9.079
- need, 9.073–9.075

preference shares
- capital, as to, 8.108–8.109
- dividend, as to, 8.103–8.107
- generally, 8.102
- voting, as to, 8.110

Shares (contd)
presumptions, 8.098
public limited companies, and
allotment, 29.043–29.044
disclosure of interests, 29.057–29.059
disclosure of stabilising activity during a stabilisation period, 29.060–29.061
formalities, 29.041–29.042
introduction, 29.038
investment companies, 29.144–29.145
legal nature, 29.041–29.042
membership, 29.039–29.040
transfers, 29.062–29.066
redeemable shares
conversion into, 8.120
generally, 8.111
refusal of registration
bona fides of directors, 9.052–9.057
challenging, 9.066–9.068
consequences, 9.064–9.065
introduction, 9.042
lapsing of powers of directors, 9.058–9.061
model reg 3 restriction, 9.043–9.047
procedure for challenging, 9.066–9.068
quality of transferee, 9.050–9.051
s 205 CA 1963 relief, 9.062–9.063
status of transferee, 9.048–9.049
share purchase agreements
contrast with asset purchases, 9.109–9.110
disclosure letters, 9.112
indemnities, 9.116
introduction, 9.108
nature, 9.111–9.116
warranties, 9.113–9.115
shareholders' duties, 8.093–8.097
shareholders' rights
attendance at meetings, 8.080
dividends, 8.073–8.079
generally, 8.071–8.072
participation in winding up, 8.085
personal rights, 8.087–8.092
statute, under, 8.086
voting at meetings, 8.081–8.084
statutory rights and obligations, 8.041
subdivision, 8.119
surrender, 8.126
transfers
bankruptcy, on, 9.031
compulsory, 9.087–9.107
death, on, 9.026–9.030
directors' powers to refuse registration, 9.042–9.068
equitable mortgages, by, 9.036–9.037
execution of instrument, 9.011–9.012
introduction, 9.001–9.005
legal mortgages, by, 9.035
mechanics, 9.006–9.010
merger, on, 9.032–9.033
operation of law, by, 9.025–9.033
pre-emption rights, 9.069–9.086
'proper instrument' requirement, 9.006–9.010
registration by directors, 9.022
restrictions, 9.017–9.021
security, and, 9.034–9.041
share purchase agreements, 9.108–9.116
stop notices, 9.038–9.041
transferability, 9.016–9.024
transferee's obligations, 9.013–9.015
transferee's position pending registration, 9.023–9.024
valuation, 9.117–9.134
Treasury shares, 8.113
unlimited companies, and, 31.019
valuation
appropriate date, 9.129–9.134
assessment, 9.121
determination of company's total worth, 9.119–9.120
discounting for minority holding, 9.122–9.125
fair value, 9.126–9.128
introduction, 9.117
premium, 9.121
principles, 9.118–9.
pro rata basis, 9.121
voting rights
generally, 8.081

Shares (contd)
poll, 8.083
proxy, 8.084
show of hands, 8.082
Shelf companies
incorporation, and, 2.023
Ships
registration of charges, 19.069
Short notice
generally, 14.041
special resolutions, 14.042–14.043
Show of hands
voting, and, 8.082
Single economic entity
disregarding legal personality, and, 5.051–5.064
Single-member private limited companies
annual accounts, and, 17.20
annual general meetings, and, 14.014
constitution of private companies, and, 3.002
conversion by re-registration, and
multi-member company to single-member company, 33.016
single-member company to multi-member company, 33.017
EU law, and, 1.121
formation, 2.027
function, 2.015–2.016
generally, 1.143–1.148
memorandum of association, and, 3.003
ostensible authority, and, 7.118
resolutions, and, 14.088–14.089
statutory contracts, and, 3.092
Small companies
abridged accounts, 17.279–17.284
auditor's reports, 17.283–17.284
balance sheet, 17.279–17.280
definition, 17.277–17.278
directors' statement, 17.281
Social clubs
guarantee companies, and, 30.007
Societas Europaea (SE)
annual returns, 29.186
articles of association, 29.171
audits, 29.186
background, 29.150–29.151
capital, 29.152
constitutional documentation, 29.171–29.172
conversion from PLC, 29.167–29.169
conversion to PLC, 29.192
employee involvement, 29.178–29.181
EU law, and, 1.126
financial reporting, 29.186
formation
conversion of PLC, by, 29.167–29.169
holding SE, of, 29.164–29.165
introduction, 29.157
merger, by, 29.158–29.163
overview, 29.152
subsidiary SE, of, 29.166
general meetings, 29.182–29.184
governance
employee involvement, 29.178–29.181
general structure, 29.174–29.177
meetings, 29.182–29.185
overview, 29.152
holding SE, 29.164–29.165
introduction, 29.150–29.152
management meetings, 29.185
meetings
general meetings, 29.182–29.184
management meetings, 29.185
memorandum of association, 29.171
merger, 29.158–29.163
purpose, 29.150
registration, 29.170
separate legal personality, 29.152
sources of applicable law, 29.153–29.155
statutes
amendments, 29.172–29.173
generally, 29.171
subsidiary SE, 29.166
transfer of registered office, 29.187–29.191
winding up, 29.193–29.194
Sole traders
advantages, 1.012
business name, 1.007–1.011

Sole traders (contd)
definition, 1.005
disadvantages, 1.013
generally, 1.005–1.013
registration of name, 1.007–1.011
restrictions on acting, 1.006
Solicitors' liens
generally, 19.028
Special business
annual general meetings, and, 14.009
notice of business to be conducted, and, 14.051
Special contracts
memorandum of association, and, 3.102–3.105
Special resolutions
assisting purchase of company's own shares, and, 10.072
business to be conducted, 14.052
compulsory winding up, and, 23.068
generally, 14.084–14.087
reconstructions, and, 21.070–21.071
Sports clubs
guarantee companies, and, 30.007
Staff numbers and remuneration
group accounts, and
Companies Act, 17.180
IFRS, 17.206
individual accounts, and, 17.140
profit and loss account, and, 17.101
Stamp duty
holding companies, and, 12.046
subsidiaries, and, 12.046
Standard notice
generally, 14.040
State corporations
generally, 1.066–1.067
Statements of Standard Accounting Practice (SSAPs)
generally, 17.023
Statements of comprehensive income
generally, 17.017
Statements of financial position
generally, 17.017
Statutes
And see **Memorandum of association**
Societas Europaea, and
amendments, 29.172–29.173
generally, 29.171
Statutory contracts
binding effect
members and company, 3.095
members to members, 3.096–3.098
distinction from 'special contracts', 3.102–3.105
features
binding effect, 3.095–3.098
introduction, 3.094
rights and obligations qua member, 3.099–3.101
generally, 3.092–3.105
introduction, 3.092–3.093
rights and obligations qua member, 3.099–3.101
shareholders' personal rights, and, 8.087–8.088
single-member private companies, and, 3.092
'special contracts', and, 3.102–3.105
Statutory corporations
generally, 1.065–1.068
Statutory declarations
assisting purchase of company's own shares, and, 10.071
Statutory receivers
See also **Receivers**
appointment, 20.022
generally, 20.022
powers, rights and obligations, 20.023
status, 20.024
Statutory tenancies
separate legal personality, and, 4.041
Stay of proceedings
schemes of arrangement, and, 21.049
security for costs, and, 6.014
Stock transfer forms
generally, 9.009
Stop notices
security over shares, and, 9.038–9.041
Striking off
corporate property, and, 26.016–26.021
directors' liability, 26.015
draft Companies Bill, and, 1.183
effect

Striking off (contd)
corporate property, on, 26.016–26.021
liability of directors etc, on, 26.015
mortgaged property, on, 26.019
trust property, on, 26.020–26.021
grounds
ceasing to carry on business, 26.009–26.012
failure to deliver particulars to the revenue, 26.007–26.008
failure to have at least one EEA resident director, 26.014
failure to make annual return, 26.006
having no recorded directors, 26.013
introduction, 26.005
guarantee companies, and, 30.072
introduction, 26.004
members' liability, 26.015
mortgaged property, and, 26.019
officers' liability, 26.015
overview, 26.001–26.003
public limited companies, and, 29.123
trading whilst struck off, 26.022–26.023
trust property, and, 26.020–26.021
Subdivision
shares, and, 8.119
Subscribers of the memorandum
definition of 'member', and, 8.004
generally, 8.005
overview, 8.001
Subscription clause
memorandum of association, and, 3.020
Subsidiaries
capital maintenance, and, 12.042
control of composition of board by a member, 12.009–12.016
corporation tax purposes, for, 12.043–12.045
'golden share', 12.009–12.016
holding more than half in nominal value of share capital
introduction, 12.017
more than half in nominal value, 12.018
'of equity share capital', 12.019
'of shares carrying voting rights', 12.020
introduction, 12.088
membership, and, 8.011
shares held and powers exercisable in fiduciary capacity, as nominee or pursuant to debenture or trust, 12.021–12.027
Societas Europaea, and, 29.166
stamp duty purposes, for, 12.046
subsidiary of a subsidiary, 12.028
wholly-owned subsidiaries, 12.029
Subsidiary of a subsidiary
generally, 12.028
Subsidiary undertakings
'associated undertaking', 12.041
control of composition of board, 12.032
discounting of voting rights, 12.034
'dominant influence', 12.035–12.038
generally, 12.031
individual accounts, and, 17.130
'participating influence', 12.039–12.040
shares held and powers exercisable by nominees, 12.033
Substantial property transactions
acquisitions by members acting 'qua member', 16.041
arrangements in insolvent winding up, 16.038–16.040
bodies corporate that are connected persons
body corporate controlled by body corporate controlled by a director, 16.019
'control', 16.011–16.013
generally, 16.010
'interested in', 16.014–16.018
subsidiary controlled by a director, 16.020
summary, 16.021
breach of provision
consequences, 16.046–16.048
liability of directors, 16.049–16.054
compliance by approving resolution, 16.042–16.045

Substantial property transactions (contd)
connected persons
bodies corporate, 16.010
natural persons, 16.006–16.009
summary, 16.021
consequences of breach of provision, 16.046–16.048
directors
generally, 16.004–16.005
summary, 16.021
exceptions
acquisitions by members acting 'qua member', 16.041
arrangements in insolvent winding up, 16.038–16.040
inter-group arrangements, 16.037
introduction, 16.036
generally, 16.022–16.025
holding company directors
generally, 16.004–16.005
summary, 16.021
inter-group arrangements, 16.037
liability of directors etc for breach, 16.049–16.054
natural persons that are connected persons
generally, 16.006–16.009
summary, 16.021
'non-cash asset', 16.028
overview, 16.001–16.002
regulated persons
connected persons, 16.006–16.020
directors, 16.004–16.005
holding company directors, 16.004–16.005
introduction, 16.003
summary, 16.021
regulatory provisions, 16.026–16.027
'relevant assets', 16.029
'requisite value', 16.029–16.035
shadow directors, 16.021
winding up, and, 16.038–16.040
Suing and being sued
contractual liability, 4.043–4.048
criminal liability
attribution principles, 4.063–4.067
constitutional rights and duties, 4.068–4.075
corporations as prosecutors, 4.056
introduction, 4.055
justification, 4.057–4.061
legal rights and duties, 4.076
practical limitations, 4.062
separate legal personality, and
contracts, 4.043–4.048
crime, 4.055–4.076
introduction, 4.042
torts, 4.049–4.053
tortious liability, 4.049–4.053
Supervision
building societies, and, 1.042
Sureties
examinership, and, 22.079–22.083
Surrender
shares, and, 8.126
Takeover Panel rules
schemes of arrangement, and, 21.023
Takeovers
EU law, and, 1.122
Taxation
balance sheet, and, 17.090
disregarding legal personality, and 5.092
generally, 4.091
profit and loss account, and, 17.107
Technology facilities
directors' meetings, and, 14.110
'Token' directors
setting aside transactions, and, 15.049–15.050
Tomlin orders
acquisition by company of own shares, and, 10.030
Tortious liability
duty of care, skill and diligence, and, 15.086–15.087
separate legal personality, and, 4.049–4.053
Torts
disregarding legal personality, and, 5.018–5.019
Transfer of engagements
building societies, and, 1.047

Transfer of property
separate legal personality, and, 4.038
Transfer of shares
bankruptcy, on, 9.031
compulsory transfers
articles of association, under, 9.088–9.090
introduction, 9.087
s 204 CA 1963, under, 9.091–9.107
consideration
generally, 9.004
valuation, 9.117–9.134
death, on, 9.026–9.030
directors' powers to refuse registration
bona fides of directors, 9.052–9.057
challenging, 9.066–9.068
consequences, 9.064–9.065
introduction, 9.042
lapsing of powers of directors, 9.058–9.061
model reg 3 restriction, 9.043–9.047
overview, 9.22
procedure for challenging, 9.066–9.068
quality of transferee, 9.050–9.051
s 205 CA 1963 relief, 9.062–9.063
status of transferee, 9.048–9.049
equitable mortgages, by, 9.036–9.037
execution of instrument, 9.011–9.012
forms, 9.009
introduction, 9.001–9.005
legal mortgages, by, 9.035
meaning of 'transfer', 9.008
mechanics, 9.006–9.010
merger, on
generally, 9.032–9.033
introduction, 9.001
operation of law, by
bankruptcy, 9.031
death, 9.026–9.030
introduction, 9.025
overview, 9.001
merger, 9.032–9.033
pre-emption rights
beneficial interests in shares, and, 9.080–9.083
enforceability, 9.084–9.086
generally, 9.069–9.072
judicial construction, 9.076–9.079
need, 9.073–9.075
'proper instrument' requirement, 9.006–9.010
refusal of registration
bona fides of directors, 9.052–9.057
challenging, 9.066–9.068
consequences, 9.064–9.065
introduction, 9.042
lapsing of powers of directors, 9.058–9.061
model reg 3 restriction, 9.043–9.047
overview, 9.22
procedure for challenging, 9.066–9.068
quality of transferee, 9.050–9.051
s 205 CA 1963 relief, 9.062–9.063
status of transferee, 9.048–9.049
registration by directors, 9.022
restrictions
classification, 9.002
directors' powers to refuse registration, 9.042–9.068
generally, 9.017–9.019
introduction, 9.002
pre-emption rights, 9.069–9.086
rationale, 9.20–9.21
rights of first refusal, 9.002
security, and
equitable mortgage, 9.036–9.037
introduction, 9.034
legal mortgage, 9.035
stop notices, 9.038–9.041
share purchase agreements
contrast with asset purchases, 9.109–9.110
disclosure letters, 9.112
indemnities, 9.116
introduction, 9.108
nature, 9.111–9.116
warranties, 9.113–9.115
shareholders' agreements, and, 9.001
stock transfer forms, 9.009
stop notices, 9.038–9.041
'transfer', 9.008
transferability, 9.016–9.024

Transfer of shares (contd)
'transferee', 9.001
transferee's obligations, 9.013–9.015
transferee's position pending registration, 9.023–9.024
'transferor', 9.001
valuation
appropriate date, 9.129–9.134
assessment, 9.121
determination of company's total worth, 9.119–9.120
discounting for minority holding, 9.122–9.125
fair value, 9.126–9.128
introduction, 9.117
premium, 9.121
principles, 9.118–9.125
pro rata basis, 9.121

Transferability of interests
generally, 4.085

Transfers of undertakings or property
compensation on loss of office, and, 13.094

Transparency
access to information, 32.134–32.135
annual financial report, 32.123
background, 32.118
Central Bank Rules, 32.120
civil liability, 32.127
competent authority, 32.119
continuing information
access to information, and, 32.134–32.135
introduction, 32.129
issuers, 32.133
major shareholdings, 32.130–32.132
dissemination of regulated information, 32.136–32.137
false or misleading information, 32.127–32.128
FSAP, and, 32.118
generally, 32.121
half-yearly results, 32.124
interim management statements, 32.125
interim results, 32.124
introduction, 32.118–32.120
'issuer', 32.121
legislative framework, 32.118
major shareholdings, 32.130–32.132
misleading information, 32.127–32.128
ongoing information
access to information, and, 32.134–32.135
introduction, 32.129
issuers, 32.133
major shareholdings, 32.130–32.132
periodic financial reports
annual financial report, 32.123
exemptions, 32.126
false or misleading information, 32.127–32.128
generally, 32.122–32.125
half-yearly results, 32.124
interim management statements, 32.125
responsibility statements, 32.123
'securities', 32.121
Transparency Directive
background, 32.118–32.120
scope, 32.121–32.137

Treasury shares
See also **Shares**
generally, 8.113

'True and fair view'
individual accounts, and, 17.026–17.027

Trusts
disregarding legal personality, and, 5.029–5.030
registration of charges, and, 19.034

Turnover
profit and loss account, and, 17.100

***Turquand's* case**
generally, 7.123
irregularity is of public record, 7.124
outsider must act in good faith, 7.125–7.126

UCITS
public limited companies, and, 29.131–29.132

UK Corporate Governance Code
generally, 29.089–29.090
meetings, 29.112–29.114
principles, 29.091

Ultra vires
capacity
classification, 7.054–7.059
enforcement of ultra vires contracts, 7.088
existence of commercial benefit, 7.057–7.059
express ancillary powers, 7.057–7.059
generally, 7.048
gratuitous dispositions of property, 7.070–7.079
implied ancillary powers, 7.068–7.069
judicial construction of objects clause, 7.049–7.053
recovery of money given by company ultra vires, 7.089–7.095
reform of ultra vires doctrine, 7.096–7.098
reg 6 EC(C)R 1973, 7.087
s 8 CA 1963, 7.080–7.086
significance of conditions on exercise of powers, 7.060–7.067
substantive objects, 7.055–7.056
ultra vires, and, 7,.045–7.047
consequences of incorporation, and, 4.092
enforcement of contracts, 7.088
objects clause, and, 7.045–7.046
public limited companies, and, 29.034
recovery of money given by company
action in rem, 7.091–7.092
Belmont principle, 7.091–7.092
constructive trusts, 7.091–7.092
estoppel, 7.094–7.095
generally, 7.089
quasi-contract, 7.093
unenforceable, 7.090
reform of doctrine, 7.096–7.098
restraint of activities, 7.047
rule in *Foss v Harbottle*, and, 11.122–11.125
schemes of arrangement, and, 21.020
Unanimous acts
directors' meetings, and, 14.128
members' meetings, and, 14.093–14.099
Uncalled share capital of the company
registration of charges, 19.045
Uncertificated securities
generally, 29.036
transfer, 29.062–29.066
Unconnected membership, private company with
generally, 1.155
Undertakings
groups of companies, and, 12.030
Undisclosed agency
disregarding legal personality, and, 5.028
Unfairly prejudicial
examinership, and, 22.153–22.158
oppression, and, 11.088–11.090
Unincorporated associations
generally, 1.050–1.051
Unlimited companies
accounts, 31.026–31.032
annual returns, 31.023–31.025
articles of association, and
generally, 31.009–31.010
introduction, 3.039
audits, 31.026–31.035
authority to contract, 31.018
borrowing, 31.003
capacity, 31.018
civil litigation, 31.015–31.017
commencement of business, 31.011–31.012
compliance and enforcement, 31.003
constitutional documentation
articles of association, 31.009–31.010
introduction, 31.004
memorandum of association, 31.005–31.008
context, in, 31.001
conversion by re-registration, and
limited company to unlimited company, 33.009–33.013
unlimited company to private limited company, 33.002–33.007
unlimited company to PLC, 33.008
corporate contracts, 31.018

Unlimited companies (contd)
corporate governance, 31.003
directors, 31.003
directors' duties, 31.003
directors' transactions, 31.003
distribution of assets, 31.036–31.040
financial statements
accounts, 31.026–31.032
annual returns, 31.023–31.025
audits, 31.026–31.035
exemptions, 31.033–31.035
formation
constitutional documentation, 31.005–31.010
generally, 31.004
introduction, 2.029
restrictions on commencement of business, 31.011–31.012
function, 2.013–2.014
groups of companies, 31.003
incorporation, and
formation, 2.029
function, 2.013–2.014
generally, 31.013
introduction, 31.001–31.003
legal personality, and, 31.014
maintenance of capital, 31.021–31.022
meetings, 31.003
membership. 31.019
memorandum of association
generally, 31.005–31.008
introduction, 3.004
realisation of assets, 31.036–31.040
schemes of arrangement, 31.003
separate legal personality, and, 31.014
share transfers, 31.020
shareholders' remedies, 31.003
shares, 31.019
types, 31.001
winding up, 31.036–31.040
Unpaid vendors' liens
generally, 19.029
Unregistered companies
generally, 1.054–1.055
Utmost good faith
examinership, and, 22.034–22.038
Validation procedure
directors' transactions, and
consequences of swearing declaration based on unreasonable grounds, 16.088
generally, 16.080–16.081
independent person's report, 16.087
special resolution, 16.082–16.083
statutory declaration of solvency, 16.084–16.086
Valuation of assets
current assets
alternative accounting rules, 17.055–17.057
fair value accounting, 17.058
historical cost rules, 17.050–17.054
fixed assets
alternative accounting rules, 17.042–17.045
fair value accounting, 17.046–17.049
historical cost rules, 17.040–17.041
introduction, 17.039
introduction, 17.037–17.038
Valuation of shares
appropriate date, 9.129–9.134
assessment, 9.121
compulsory transfer of shares, and, 9.090
determination of company's total worth, 9.119–9.120
discounting for minority holding, 9.122–9.125
fair value, 9.126–9.128
introduction, 9.117
premium, 9.121
principles
assessment, 9.121
determination of company's total worth, 9.119–9.120
introduction, 9.118–9.125
pro rata basis, 9.121
Vicarious liability
disregarding legal personality, and, 5.093–5.096
Voidability
assisting purchase of company's own shares, and, 10.049–10.050
directors' loans, and, 16.100–16.109

Voluntary winding up
conversion to compulsory winding up, 23.117–23.124
creditors' voluntary winding up
committee of inspection, 23.031–23.032
creditors' meeting, 23.023–23.030
introduction, 23.017
members' general meeting, 23.020–23.022
statement of position of company's affairs, 23.018–23.019
termination, 23.033
liquidators
appointment, 24.009–24.012
generally, 24.003
powers, 24.043–24.050
members' voluntary winding up
commencement, 23.014
declaration of solvency, 23.004–23.006
directors' personal liability, 23.010–23.011
introduction, 23.002–23.003
report of independent person, 23.007–23.009
resolution, 23.012–23.013
termination, 23.015–23.016
reconstructions, and, 21.068

Voting
articles of association, and, 3.053–3.055
directors' meetings, and, 14.124–14.128
guarantee companies, and, 30.051–30.054
members' meetings, and
introduction, 14.061
'one member one vote', 14.062–14.066
one vote per share, 14.062–14.066
poll, on, 14.067–14.071
proxy, by, 14.074–14.076
representation, by, 14.072–14.073
'one member one vote', 14.062–14.066
one vote per share, 14.062–14.066
poll
generally, 14.067–14.071
shareholders' rights, and, 8.083
proxy
generally, 14.074–14.076
shareholders' rights, and, 8.084
representation, 14.072–14.073
schemes of arrangement, and, 21.043–21.047
shareholders' rights, and
generally, 8.081
poll, 8.083
proxy, 8.084
show of hands, 8.082
show of hands, 8.082

Warranties
assisting purchase of company's own shares, and, 10.064
share purchase agreements, and, 9.113–9.115

'Whitewash' procedure
assisting purchase of company's own shares, and, 10.066–10.077

Wholly-owned subsidiaries
generally, 12.029

Winding up
banks
Central Bank's rights, 23.139–23.140
generally, 23.136–23.138
liquidation committee, 23.14223.
rules applicable to liquidators, 23.141
compulsory transfer of shares, and, 9.089
compulsory winding up
advertisement of petition, 23.055
annulment, 23.128
company, by, 23.038–23.039
contributories, 23.045–23.047
conversion from members' to creditors', 23.113–23.116
conversion from voluntary winding up, 23.117–23.124
corporate instruments of fraud, 23.107–23.108
creditors, 23.040–23.044
deadlock in management, 23.098–23.101
Director of Corporate Enforcement, 23.048

Winding up (contd)
failure to commence business within a year of incorporation, 23.069
grounds, 23.067–23.112
hearing petition, 23.061–23.066
illegal objects, 23.106
inability of company to pay its debts, 23.071–23.090
introduction, 23.034
jurisdiction, 23.035–23.036
just and equitable, 23.091–23.111
locus standi to petition, 23.037–23.050
members, 23.045–23.047
number of members is reduced below minimum, 23.070
oppression, 23.112
orders, 23.125–23.135
petition, 23.052–23.054
procedure, 23.051–23.066
public interest, 23.109–23.111
Registrar of Companies, 23.049
rescission, 23.129
respondent company's options, 23.056–23.057
special resolution to wind up company, 23.068
substitution of petitioner, 23.058–23.060
suspension of business for a year, 23.069
trustees of investment companies, 23.050
voiding dissolution following making of order, 23.130–23.135
creditors' voluntary winding up
committee of inspection, 23.031–23.032
creditors' meeting, 23.023–23.030
introduction, 23.017
members' general meeting, 23.020–23.022
statement of position of company's affairs, 23.018–23.019
termination, 23.033
crystallisation of floating charges, and, 18.099
dissolved companies, of, 26.024
distribution of assets
And see **Distribution of assets**
basic principles, 25.140
costs and expenses of winding up, 25.164–25.171
fixed mortgage or charge, 25.143–25.148
held in trust, 25.149
in specie, 25.196–25.198
monies that must be set off, 25.150–25.158
not available, 25.142–25.163
priorities, 25.182–25.196
proof of debts, 25.172–25.181
remuneration, costs and expenses, 25.165
stamp duty on monies received in realisation, 25.161–25.163
statutory basis, 25.141
super-preferential debts that are trust monies, 25.159–25.160
draft Companies Bill, and, 1.182
enforcement of judgments and orders, and, 6.076
financial institutions
Central Bank's rights, 23.139–23.140
generally, 23.136–23.138
liquidation committee, 23.14223.
rules applicable to liquidators, 23.141
floating charges, and, 18.099
guarantee companies, and, 30.070–30.071
introduction, 23.001
liquidators
And see **Liquidators**
appointment, 24.009–24.020
assistance to Irish liquidation abroad, 24.069
Council Regulation on Insolvency Proceedings, 24.059–24.068
duties, 24.020–24.026
foreign appointments, 24.056–24.058
introduction, 24.001
powers, 24.027–24.051
qualifications, 24.006–24.008
remuneration, 24.052–24.055

Winding up (contd)
supervision, 24.070–24.071
types, 24.002–24.005
members' voluntary winding up
commencement, 23.014
declaration of solvency, 23.004–23.006
directors' personal liability, 23.010–23.011
introduction, 23.002–23.003
report of independent person, 23.007–23.009
resolution, 23.012–23.013
termination, 23.015–23.016
realisation of assets
And see **Realisation of assets**
civil arrest powers, 25.038–25.046
claims against contributories, 25.130–25.134
company books and records, 25.013
contribution by related companies to assets, 25.119–25.124
disclaiming onerous property, 25.058–25.065
disputed assets, 25.016
examination, 25.024–25.035
fraudulent dispositions of property, 25.103–25.109
fraudulent preference of creditors, 25.081–25.102
gathering information, 25.018–25.046
gathering in assets, 25.007–25.017
introduction, 25.001–25.003
invalidating floating charges, 25.110–25.118
liquidator's duty, 25.005
litigating to swell asset pool, 25.137–25.139
not beneficially owned by company, 25.014–25.015
obtaining books and papers, 25.023
officers' duty to assist, 25.006
overview, 25.004
pooling assets of related companies, 25.125–25.129
post-commencement dispositions, 25.065–25.080
post-examination transfer, 25.036–25.037
prohibiting litigation, execution, attachment or judgment, 25.052–25.057
property, 25.012
restraining disposal or removal, 25.047–25.051
swelling assets, 24.017
things in action, 25.012
transaction avoidance, 25.017
voidable transactions, 25.135–25.136
shareholders' remedies, and, 11.002
shareholders' rights, and, 8.085
Societas Europaea, and, 29.193–29.194
substantial property transactions, and, 16.038–16.040
unlimited companies, and, 31.036–31.040
voluntary winding up
conversion to compulsory winding up, 23.117–23.124
creditors', 23.017–23.033
members', 23.002–23.016
Written contracts
And see **Corporate contracts**
generally, 7.007–7.013
Written resolutions
directors' meetings, and, 14.126–14.127
members' meetings, and, 14.090–14.092